PREFACE

This book attempts to present Shakespeare as a unified and connected subject of study—his life, his work, his reactions to his age and upon it, his significance to our age, and the opinions of other times and nations. It attempts to enrich in various ways the study of Shakespeare in schools and colleges. The stress is laid, not on passages, characters, scene, and plays as independent units, but on these things as they are related to drama, to the development of Shakespeare's powers as a dramatist, and to Renaissance literature as a whole. Recent critical and textual work on Shakespeare is so important that it deserves to be explained and digested into its appropriate places in the scholarship of Shakespeare and to be made intelligible to students, who are sometimes obliged to study Shakespeare in disconnected single works and from points of view which, if not antiquated, are at least more restricted than they need to be.

In order to accomplish this purpose we have presented twenty-one of the best plays of Shakespeare with full introductions and notes, all the needed information about the omitted plays with a critical summary of each, and a full treatment not only of the usual topics, but of many topics not ordinarily presented, such as the history and principles of Shakespeare criticism, Shakespeare's English, his relation to the Middle Ages and the Renaissance and to the culture of his times. The result of this has been the production of a handbook of considerable dimensions, in which stand the principal plays in their proper positions. The general introduction, the plays, and the intercalary chapters form thus a connected work. Indeed, it has been attempted to embody in one book, insofar as such a thing is possible, all that a student needs to embody for the comprehension of Shakespeare.

A special effort was made necessary to render intelligible within the pages of the book, without too much reference, the knowledge of backgrounds demanded for complete comprehension. This has been done by the employment of the utmost simplicity and clarity at the author's command and by tying the parts of the book together by recurrent reference to the fundamental features of Elizabethan dramatic art and of Elizabethan culture and opinion. The book has been made, so far as possible, a self-contained unit, not only as a whole, but in the treatment of special parts and subjects. This has been achieved by the repetition of necessary explanations and references. There is thus in the treatment of each play and subject considerable independence even of other parts of the book, while at the same time the parts have been connected together by continual cross reference and by careful subject indexing. Even in the treatment of plays not included in the volume this principle has been observed. Such plays have been summarized and interpreted, so that they may contribute their part to the total effect aimed at, which is a picture of Shakespeare as detailed and complete as the limits of the book would permit.

The index is primarily a subject index and a list of characters, but it has been made also to supply a small amount of definite information explanatory of many literary and theatrical allusions. It is not glossarial but records only such materials from the plays and notes as bear on the subjects treated in the general introduction and the intercalary chapters on Shakespeare's life and work. It lists all references in the book to the following matters: characters in the plays; plays and other works by Shakespeare; matters pertaining to the drama, the stage, and the theater; authors, both English and foreign; the Renaissance, its culture, beliefs, and characteristics; all that pertains to England and native English ways in the age of Shakespeare; and the history of Shakespeare on the stage. From the index the student may collect fairly adequate information on these topics, together with bibliographical guidance, and find in the notes by means of the index illustrations in the work of Shakespeare of the matters discussed in the ancillary or auxiliary parts of the volume. This will supply in some measure the lack of a glossary of individual words, a lack which is further supplied by a list of the commonest Shakespearean words and their meanings (pp. 70-72). In order to render allusions more definite the index has been made to contain a small amount of biographical information about historical and literary persons who are no longer living.

The Globe text has been chosen and has been reprinted with the utmost possible exactitude. This text was chosen for two reasons: first, because the Globe is the model of all complete modern texts and is, by and large, as good as any modern text. The study of textual problems in recent years has, however, indicated some passages in which the Globe text is wrong in its readings. Although the Globe has been, in every case, allowed to stand, frank attention has been called in the notes to erroneous readings, and an extensive body of variant readings, including, so far as possible, all crucial cases, has also been prepared and published as an appendix to the volume (pp. 1143-1160). The second reason for reprinting the Globe text is that it has been made the principal basis for Shakespearean reference in the modern world. Not only is the line numbering of the Globe text the accepted means of reference, but the text itself has been used in Bartlett's *Concordance to Shakespeare*, the *Oxford English Dictionary*, all Shakespeare grammars and dictionaries, and in literary citation without limit.

Care has been taken to reproduce in the texts of the plays chosen the exact numbering of the Globe text. In prose passages, owing to slight differences in type and column width, the lines cannot always be made to count out exactly. This fact need

not, however, cause difficulty, since the words as they stand referred to in the notes have always the correct Globe numbering and since in setting up the text numerous additional line numbers, correctly placed according to the Globe text, have been introduced in order to facilitate reference and to render it exact.

The dagger (†) which occurs occasionally in the text was included in the Globe edition in cases of considerable doubt as to the original text, i.e., wherever the original had been corrupted so as to affect the sense, no admissible correction having been proposed, or wherever a gap occurred too great to be filled with certainty.

Few abbreviations have been employed, and most of them will be readily intelligible. F refers to the text of the first folio edition of 1623, F_2 to the second folio edition of 1632, and so on; Q_1, Q_2, etc., are used to designate the first, second, etc., quarto editions of various plays. Citations in the notes of various editors, commentators, and textual critics are usually by the name of the person concerned; sometimes by the name of the edition. The sources of such information will be readily traced through editions of Shakespeare or by reference to the index. In order to make clear the nature and extent of indebtedness and to facilitate the tracing of readings and interpretations it has seemed worth while to embody all such references in the index.

The author wishes to acknowledge his debt for assistance to a number of his former pupils—to Miss Marie Lyle of Keuka College, to Mr. David Patrick of Stanford University, and particularly to Miss Sina K. Spiker of the State Teachers College at Oshkosh, Wisconsin—and, last but not least, to his wife, Gertrude Craig. Other indebtednesses, although not here mentioned, are, nevertheless, not unappreciated.

STANFORD UNIVESITY
JUNE 15, 1931   H. C.

CONTENTS

[1]The following plays are discussed: *Love's Labour's Lost* (p. 89), *The Comedy of Errors* (p. 91), *The Two Gentlemen of Verona* (p. 94), and *A Midsummer-Night's Dream* (p. 96).

[2]The following plays are discussed: the three *Henry VI* plays (p. 100) and *Richard III* (p. 104).

[3]The following plays are discussed: *Titus Andronicus* (p. 107) and *Romeo and Juliet* (p. 109).

[4]The following plays are discussed: *The Merchant of Venice* (p. 291), *The Taming of the Shrew* (p. 296), *Much Ado about Nothing* (p. 298), *The Merry Wives of Windsor* (p. 301), *As You Like It* (p. 303), and *Twelfth Night* (p. 307).

[5]The following plays are discussed: *King John* (p. 310), *Richard II* (p. 312), *1* and *2 Henry IV* (p. 316), and *Henry V* (p. 319).

[6]*Julius Cæsar.*

CONTENTS

⁷The following plays are discussed: *All's Well That Ends Well* (p. 701), *Troilus and Cressida* (p. 702), and *Measure for Measure* (p. 705).

⁸The following plays are discussed: *Hamlet* (p. 707), *Othello* (p. 713), *King Lear* (p. 717), *Macbeth* (p. 720), *Antony and Cleopatra* (p. 724), *Coriolanus* (p. 727), and *Timon of Athens* (p. 731).

⁹The following plays are discussed: *Pericles Prince of Tyre* (p. 994), *Cymbeline* (p. 996), *The Winter's Tale* (p. 999), *The Tempest* (p. 1001), *Henry VIII* (p. 1004), and *The Two Noble Kinsmen* (p. 1006).

GENERAL INTRODUCTION

I. THE MIDDLE AGES AND THE RENAISSANCE

The Middle Ages Two terms of constant recurrence in the study of the history of literature are the Middle Ages and the Renaissance, and with both we are concerned in the study of Shakespeare. The terms cannot be clearly discriminated or accurately defined in narrow compass, but we must have some idea of their meanings; for Shakespeare, possibly the greatest product of the Renaissance, partook of the mediæval, and the Renaissance itself was but a vast transition from the mediæval to the modern world. The old and the new existed side by side in Shakespeare's age and are to be seen side by side in his works. It is ordinarily said that the period of the Middle Ages extended from 500 to 1500 A.D., yet the latter of these dates, as we shall see, has little enough validity when applied to the Renaissance in England. One must be content with recognizing certain rather general attitudes of the human mind during so long a period. The things which the Middle Ages created are for the most part institutional, having to do with the organizations and classes of society. Many of its social, religious, and political forms are still present in western civilization. The Church, the modern state, and the municipality received their constitutions. Schools, universities, and courts of law took on their characteristic forms. It was the period of feudalism, of the orders of chivalry, of the Crusades, of the friars, and of the revival of learning. In spirit there was a world-wide reverence for authority and precedent and an almost universal aim toward union and centralization. Europe sought, at least as an ideal, a united Christendom under Pope and Emperor, one or both.

The Renaissance The Renaissance as it affects England may be roughly located in the years from 1500 to 1642. As a period of transition it had naturally many varying lines of change. The movement ultimately affected all departments of life—religion, art, letters, philosophy, science, ethics, and politics; but, while one group or nation was proceeding along one particular path of change, it might be, and often was, fiercely conservative with reference to other matters, and the great mass of beliefs and principles of which civilized life was made up continued to be mediæval. Specifically, the conception of the cosmogony, or doctrine of the universe and man's relation to it, continued unchanged. The Renaissance produced great scientists like Galileo, Copernicus, Kepler, and Harvey, but left recognition of their value to succeeding less gifted ages. For the men of the Renaissance the material universe was still geocentric. Even the circumnavigation of the globe seemed to fit in with that conception. Around about the earth there still moved as hollow spheres the seven planets, the fixed stars, and the *primum mobile*. Beyond this spherical universe was Chaos organized at the top into the Empyrean, or dwelling-place of God, and at the bottom into Hell, where dwelt the fallen angels with their chieftain Lucifer. The Renaissance still believed in an order of beings made up, in ascending series and perfect subordination of powers and privileges, of inanimate objects, plants, animals, man (further divided into common men, nobles, and kings), the nine orders of the angels, and God himself. The doctrine of providence was still largely astrological, for the Renaissance thought that God communicated His will to man through the mysteriously varied regularity of the movements of heavenly bodies. As to man himself, he was regarded as a microcosm, made up of the four elements—earth, air, fire, and water—his nature being determined by the proportion in him of the four qualities of hot, dry, cold, and moist. As a

1

microcosm he corresponded in his parts to the outside world, or macrocosm. Such a system, it may be believed, leaves little room for individuality, and, though it was the function of the Renaissance to break this system up, it was a long process, and the Renaissance itself never realized the thing it was doing or had done.

The beginnings of the Renaissance were in Italy, and the leadership was always with that country. The Italians were the first to study and imitate the art and letters of ancient Greece and Rome. They may be said to have constructed the great bridge of neoclassicism which led to the modern world. When new things are to be done in the realm of the intellect, as in the material realm, new and adequate tools must be found or invented for doing them. These tools are ideas and discoveries. The Renaissance borrowed forms of thinking from the ancient world and by means of them thought its new thoughts. The results were widely different from those of the Middle Ages, since the greater body of mediæval literature had been theological or religious and in Latin. With the Renaissance came the use of the vernacular, and secular subjects, though not by any means displacing religious subjects, became the more common of the two. The art of printing, by the sixteenth century widespread and highly perfected, stimulated popular education and brought into being new groups of readers. The Renaissance was in progress in Italy for nearly three centuries. Petrarch and Boccaccio established the movement in Italy and in Europe in the fourteenth century, but Ariosto, Tasso, Castiglione, and others of the sixteenth century are its most characteristic literary manifestations. In Italy, and in most countries where the movement was felt, there was first a period of scholarship, later followed by a period of literary and artistic production. The early sixteenth century shows the Renaissance effective in France and Spain. Both had their group of scholars and later their group of poets, dramatists, and philosophers. In both France and Spain moral and religious elements entered more deeply into the movement than they had done in Italy. The next great region to seek (slightly later) the new learning and feel the new impulse to creativity was the region of ancient Burgundy—Holland, Belgium, and the valley of the Rhine; but here the movement was so deeply involved both in moral and religious issues and in the wars between Reformation and Counter-Reformation that this great region in spite of its promise yielded least of all. Meantime the Renaissance had manifested itself in painting, architecture, sculpture, and other arts as well as in literature. There had been a long line of great artists in Italy from Giotto, a contemporary of Dante, to the great trio of the earlier sixteenth century—Leonardo da Vinci, Raphael, and Michael Angelo—and other countries had not been without the artistic as well as the literary impulse. In art as in literature we find the same bold spirit, bold rather in the emulation of the ancients than in self-propelled originality, the same renewed interest in Greek and Roman history, and in the study of the works of Plato, Aristotle, Galen, Pliny, and the Roman poets and historians, with the consequent new attention to the problems of philosophy, science, and society. Cicero in particular was a favorite on account of his noble style, his wisdom and learning, and his spirit of enlightenment. The new literature differed widely not only from the logical and theological works of the Middle Ages, but also from native popular literature in the vernacular—ballads, romances, saints' lives, didactic poems, and mystery plays. The Renaissance, which was catholic in its tastes, did not reject mediæval subjects, but broke up their traditional forms and treated them according to new models and for different ends.

The English Renaissance The Renaissance came slowly to England and was long in making itself felt. Chaucer was one of the first, as he is certainly the greatest, of the followers of Petrarch and Boccaccio, but for nearly two centuries he stands almost alone. The fifteenth century in England was mediæval, and its mediævalism was not of the best. Englishmen, however, began to study in Italy during the fifteenth century, and at the beginning of the sixteenth a group of Renaissance scholars, called humanists, made their appearance. The important names in this group are those of Thomas Linacre, physician and teacher of Greek at Oxford; John Colet, Dean of St. Paul's Cathedral and founder of St. Paul's school; Sir Thomas More, author of the *Utopia;* and Thomas Lupset—all friends of Erasmus, the great Dutch scholar, who visited England more than once and studied and taught there. These men lighted the torch of the new learning in England, and the illumination was carried on in the next generation by such men as Sir John Cheke, Roger Ascham, and Sir Thomas Elyot. Literary manifestations in the new manner were for a long time few and imperfect; but *Tottel's Miscellany,* published in 1557, contained the poems of Sir Thomas Wyatt and of Henry Howard, Earl of Surrey, both of whom brought into English the contemporary Petrarchistic love poetry of Italy and France. After Edmund Spenser published *The Shepheardes Calender* in 1579, the progress of the literary Renaissance in England was almost incredibly rapid. This work appealed strongly to the England of Elizabeth, now grown prosperous after years of peace and gaining rapidly in academic culture. It was a poetry of ideas, possessed beauty of form, and presented the latest literary fashions of the continent. Lyly's *Euphues* was published in that year and a second part, *Euphues and his England,* in 1580. With those works there began to appear a reading public such as we know in our own times. Lyly's comedies *Campaspe* and *Sapho and Phao* were published in 1584 as having been acted by her Majesty's Children, that is, by the boys in the choir school of the Royal Chapel, and by the Children of St. Paul's School. Lyly's other comedies were written probably by 1589. They are genuine works of the Renaissance. *Campaspe,* for example, is the dramatization of an incident in the life of Alexander the Great as told by Pliny in his *Natural History* and by Plutarch in his Life of Alexander in *Lives of the Noble Grecians and Romans,* the story being filled out and amplified with simple detail about ancient philosophers and the ancient world, which had to Lyly and his age both freshness and delight. The same impulse which started Spenser had also started Sidney, who wrote his sonnet-cycle *Astrophel and Stella* in 1580 and the succeeding years, and began his pastoral romance *Arcadia* also in 1580. The drama until the appearance of Lyly had been incredibly crude, if we may judge by such plays as Bale's *Kynge Johan,* Preston's *Cambises,* Edwards's *Damon and Pithias;* but by 1590 Marlowe had written both parts of *Tamburlaine,* Kyd had written *The Spanish Tragedy,* Greene and Peele had both written plays, and probably Shakespeare himself had made a beginning. In that year Spenser published the first three books of *The Faerie Queene.* Three more decades gave us the best that the English Renaissance was to produce, if one excepts Milton's *Paradise Lost,* usually regarded as belonging to the Renaissance rather than the succeeding time. In the years from 1579 to 1626 England produced a body of literary work hardly equaled by any nation ancient or modern: it includes the drama of Shakespeare, Marlowe, Jonson, Dekker, Webster, Beaumont and Fletcher, Middleton, and Ford; Bacon's *Essays,* his *Advancement of Learning,* and his *New Atlantis;* the poetry of Spenser, Drayton, Daniel, and Campion; the prose of Richard Hooker and the Authorized Version of the Bible. The age grew quickly mature in literary skill and method.

In quality the literature of the reigns of Queen Elizabeth and King James I remains a Renaissance expression. The impulse, the forms, and largely the subject-matter came from abroad, and the English Renaissance is the reaction of the English race to a European movement; but one must not neglect those elements which are native or personal. Without a properly responsive spirit in the race and without favorable conditions in the country, particularly without the appearance of men of adequate quality in sufficient numbers, foreign influences are powerless. These prerequisites were provided by the England of Queen Elizabeth. They were not at hand in many other European countries, or appeared only sporadically; but the English Renaissance was as genuine as that of Italy itself. "What the word Renaissance really means," says John Addington Symonds, the historian of the Italian Renaissance, "is new birth to liberty—the spirit of mankind recovering consciousness, and the power of self-determination, recognizing the beauty of the outer world, and of the body through art, liberating the reason in science, and the conscience in religion, restoring culture to the intelligence, and establishing the principle of political freedom." Fortunately for the expression of these aspirations, England happened for a time to have peace, economic prosperity, and a condition of society in which men of talent and power might secure recognition relatively unhampered by barriers between social classes, so that a gifted individual might rise from a lower to a higher station; particularly, England happened to produce, along with many other gifted men and in rather unexpected surroundings, William Shakespeare, one of the world's greatest individuals, certainly the most masterly and typical product of the Renaissance. He expressed himself through one of the greatest of the arts, the art of the theater.

The study of Shakespeare presents a personal as well as a general aspect. He belonged to a family just establishing itself in the middle class of society. He was born and reared in a small town, with which he maintained constant connection during his active life and to which he returned after his retirement. His native town of Stratford-on-Avon and what it stood for culturally is therefore a factor in the complete understanding of Shakespeare.

Shakespeare and English life The England into which Shakespeare was born, although retaining many features of the Middle Ages, was very different from what it had recently been, and very different from what it was shortly to become; for England at the end of the sixteenth and the beginning of the seventeenth centuries was in a condition of rapid change. Religious, political, and social revolutions were gathering head; so that after the triumph of Puritanism under Oliver Cromwell, England was never the same in its religion, its social ethics, and its politics. Parliamentary government established itself at the expense of royal prerogative in the generation after Shakespeare. Social classes were shifting rapidly, and many ancient social barriers were already breaking down. Most important of all,

there began, while Shakespeare was still alive, the modern scientific movement, which produced in the lapse of time a new attitude on the part of man toward the universe into which he is born. The England of Shakespeare was a different land from the one we know, different in its physical aspect, its religion, its politics, its amusements, its social classes and social ideals, and, particularly, in the spirit of its individual men.

Shakespeare's known occupations, which were numerous, all show influences peculiar to his time. He was, besides being a citizen and business man in the town of Stratford, a poet, a playwright, an actor, a part-owner of a theater, and no doubt, therefore, a theatrical manager. As a poet he was affected by the now obsolete system of patronage, according to which poets wrote in the hope of favor and gain to be derived from persons of wealth and influence, to whom they dedicated their works. As an actor, he was a member of a sort of trade guild and was affected by the rules and customs of his association. As a playwright, his immediate activity in the writing of plays was controlled by the demands of the company of actors who hired his services and, consequently, by the dictates of fashion in the theater and the rivalry of other companies of players; and as a dramatic artist he was affected by the situation then present in the development of the drama. During the period of about twenty years (1590-1610) in which he was active, drama passed from a crude amalgam of folk-play, didactic interlude, and classical comedy and tragedy to the new form of romantic drama of which his own plays are the best examples.

It is to some extent an accident of the times that Shakespeare secured the great representative audience that he seems to have had. During the period of his activity the propriety of stage plays was being more and more called in question by religious persons, for religious and moral scruples bore heavily on the theater, and before Shakespeare ceased writing, the religious element of the community had definitely consigned the stage to the powers of evil and had withdrawn itself from the theater. Had the Puritans remained in the audience and won the battle against the more worldly-minded elements of society, they might have made of the drama a religious institution. We might in that case have had something as noble as the religious tragedies of Racine; but it would not have been the Elizabethan drama. Fortunately for Shakespeare and for us, the Puritans could not dominate the stage. It was protected by the favor of Queen Elizabeth and King James I and of the nobility, all of whom were turning away from Puritanism. But during most of Shakespeare's career as a dramatist ordinary Londoners were still in the theater, making their wishes and interests felt, so that Shakespeare, not perhaps of his own desire, wrote for all classes of society. At a later time, that of Shakespeare's immediate successors, dramatists wrote mainly to please the courtly classes.

Shakespeare and the Renaissance This man from a country town did not, however, write mainly about country matters; he made up his plays and poems from the newly imported culture of France and Italy, coloring it and making it real by his closeness to ordinary English life. We must think of Shakespeare's work, therefore, as part of the literary tradition and book-culture of the Renaissance. If we would know Shakespeare we must attend to this great basal fact. He does not yield his full message to those who approach him from the point of view of the uneducated. Most of the important things which Shakespeare has to tell us about life are, except for the special touch of his genius, merely the best that his age was able to discover about life. This expression of the culture of his age is a large part of what we mean by Shakespeare. Many of the ideas to which he gave artistic expression and embodiment are commonplaces in the learning of the age; it remained for him to make them vital and applicable.

Shakespeare through the ages Even when we have studied Shakespeare's life, his relation to his age, and his own artistic development, we are not yet done. Shakespeare has been a favorite topic in the world's thought for more than two hundred years, and because he has been so often read and played, so often interpreted and misinterpreted, he is not the same poet he would be had he lain obscure for three centuries to be re-discovered by the scholarship of our own day. Even in such a case his importance would have been quickly recognized, so that he would have been studied in somewhat the same way in which Chaucer has been studied during the last sixty or seventy years; but Shakespeare has been with us so long that his phrases and allusions, like "yeoman's service," "caviare to the general," and "a Daniel come to judgment," have become parts of our ordinary speech; situations in his plots are part of our folk-lore, and his characters exist in the popular mind almost independent of the dramas in which they appear. He has in a very real sense created his own world public. One does not approach Shakespeare as one approaches authors less well-known, authors to whom the track has been opened mainly by historical scholars. The road to Shakespeare is a well-traveled highway. Every modern person who has any pretense to culture knows something about Shakespeare and considers himself in some sense an authority in the interpretation of such characters as Hamlet and Shylock, and usually has a firmly rooted opinion that Shakespeare was a self-made man with a proclivity for deer-stealing. To ask a person if he knows anything about Shakespeare is to ask him if he belongs to a respectable family and has had any care in his upbringing. No author ingrained in popular thought as Shakespeare, no author whose words are proverbs for daily use, can be properly studied without some attention to such questions as how he got into print and how his fame grew and throve through the centuries. The materials gathered together in the following pages are intended to furnish grounds for a liberal and just comprehension of the greatest of all authors, and, in some measure, as a corrective of popular error.

REFERENCES

BESANT, SIR WALTER, *London.* 1903-1909. Made up of works on various periods.

BURCKHARDT, JACOB, *The Civilization of The Renaissance in Italy.* New ed. London, 1929.

BURR, GEORGE L., "Anent the Middle Ages," *American Historical Review, XVIII*, 710-726. Consideration of the limits of the Middle Ages and the Renaissance, with references.

Cambridge Medieval History, Vol. V, *et passim*.

Cambridge Modern History, Vol. I, chs. i, ii, vi, vii, xii, xiv, xv, xvi (The Classical Renaissance), xvii (The Christian Renaissance), xix; Vol. II, chs. iv, ix, xiii, xiv, xv, xvi, xix; Vol. III, chs. ii (French Humanism and Montaigne), ix, x (Last Years of Elizabeth), xi (The Elizabethan Age of English Literature), xix (The End of the Italian Renaissance). Each chapter is provided with a bibliography.

CHEYNEY, EDWARD P., *A History of England from the Defeat of the Armada to the Death of Elizabeth*. Two vols. London, 1914, 1926.

DAVIS, H. W. C., *Mediæval England*. New edition of Barnard's *Companion to English History*. Oxford, 1924.

HUIZINGA, J., *The Waning of The Middle Ages*. London, 1924.

INNES, ARTHUR D., *England Under the Tudors*. London, 1905.

JUSSERAND, J. J., *A Literary History of The English People*. Two vols. in 3. New York, 1895-1909. *English Wayfaring Life in The Middle Ages*. Third ed. London, 1890.

RAMSAY, SIR JAMES H., *Lancaster and York*. Two vols. Oxford, 1892.

TAYLOR, HENRY OSBORN, *The Mediæval Mind*. Two vols. New York, 1919. *Thought and Expression in the Sixteenth Century*. New York, 1920.

TRAILL, H. D. *Social England*, Vol. II: From the Accession of Edward I to the Death of Henry VII. Vol. III: From the Accession of Henry VIII to the Death of Elizabeth. New York, 1894.

SYMONDS, JOHN ADDINGTON, *Renaissance in Italy*. Eight vols. New York, 1887-1888; 1921-1923.

See also the references listed on page 18.

II. LIFE IN ENGLAND IN SHAKESPEARE'S TIME

England and its neighbors The reign of Queen Elizabeth (1558-1603) saw the end of the ancient English ambition for a continental empire, or at least for a port on the French coast. The continental possessions of the English crown were all gone, and the statement in the royal title that Elizabeth was queen of France as well as of England and Ireland had become a mere reminiscence. Elizabeth gained and held Havre for a little time, but had to abandon it; the English were then confined to their island home. In 1588 they gained an easy victory in the defeat of the Spanish Armada over the greatest power the modern world had seen, and found in it a becoming source of pride. Besides this, the English were enjoying the prospect of added power in the anticipated annexation of Scotland. Although this country was an independent kingdom, both peoples were looking forward with more or less expectancy to a union of the crowns under James VI of Scotland, Elizabeth's second cousin and the grandson of Margaret Tudor, daughter of Henry VII. The kingdoms were drawing closer together, and the Scotch were beginning, as schoolmasters and traders, their peaceful invasion of England. The common people of Scotland were now being educated, and were adapting themselves, for the profit of both parties, to the ways of English life. Ireland, loosely held and turbulent, was subjected at the end of the Queen's long reign, to the most terrible of its conquests. The main issue in foreign politics and the main source of political unrest during the Queen's reign arose from the fact that England stood as the champion of Protestantism against the mighty power of Catholic Spain.

The kingdom England was a land in which its people might well take pride; yet what a different aspect from that of the England of today it must then have presented! There were probably not more than five million people in the England ruled over by Elizabeth, not so many as there are now in London, or in the state of Ohio. By and large England was a rural land. Much of the kingdom was still wooded, though the timber was being destroyed to burn lime, smelt iron, and build ships. The greatest contrast to modern days would appear in the survey of a county like York or Lancaster. There were then in the landscape no heaps of slag and cinders as there are now, no blackened scanty vegetation; it was a region of great trees, green fields, and clear streams. The chief industry of the country was agriculture, which had been in a bad way for two generations when Elizabeth came to the throne, but was destined to improve during her reign. The growing of crops was giving way more and more to cattle-raising, which, compared to the old-fashioned agriculture, was a capitalized industry. Moreover, the seizure of common lands and the eviction of tenants from cultivated areas in order to increase pasturage were still, as they had been for generations past, sources of discontent and agrarian misery. It may be said in very general terms that England in the reign of Queen Elizabeth, like the United States during the last thirty years, was transforming itself at the cost of the tillers of the soil into a commercial and, to some extent, an industrial nation. Manufacture was at first slack or inconsiderable, commerce was undeveloped and crude in its methods, and social and economic legislation was of the poorest. All of these conditions improved during the Queen's reign. The English began to weave woolen cloth; the north country began to shake off its ancient backwardness and turbulence and to make beginnings in the great career of manufacture which has made it one of the greatest productive regions of the world.

Thus during the first thirty years of Elizabeth's reign the country, though still liable to outbreaks of lawlessness and rebellion, passed gradually from poverty, civil broil, and social injustice into a condition of fair stability, domestic prosperity, and national unity. The opportunity for this was the peace with the continent of Europe which Elizabeth, in spite of many temptations, insisted on maintaining. But these things were gradual growths to be recognized only by the eye of history.

London Sixteenth century London was at once more attractive and less attractive than twentieth century London.

It was full of trees and gardens; meadows and cultivated lands came in some places down to its very walls. The way in which it bordered clear streams and green fields might be imagined from a distant view of some uncommercial provincial city of modern times, like Lincoln, York, or Hereford. Most American cities are too smoky even to suggest it. Something like the narrowness and filth of the crooked streets of old London, used as places of trade, social intercourse, and congregation, may be found in southern Europe or the near east.

London was a walled city, or rather, a city just overflowing its walls. The fortification along the river Thames had disappeared, though its existence is still attested by such names as Billingsgate; but the wall was intact along the east, north, and west of the city. The gates of the city were closed with the ringing of the curfew at nine at night. The course of the walls is still easily traced in the midst of the modern city, for the old names of streets and gateways have been very largely retained. The ancient city was in the form of an irregular parallelogram on the north bank of the Thames, about a mile long east and west, and about a half mile wide north and south. If one begins with the Tower of London and follows the street called Minories northwesterly to Aldgate, then still more westerly along the streets, Camomile, Wormwood, and London Wall, one comes to the church of St. Giles, Cripplegate, roughly the northwest corner of the city wall. From St. Giles, Cripplegate, one goes south along Noble Street, west close to the site of Aldersgate, southwest between St. Bartholomew's Church and Christ's Hospital to Newgate, and thence to Ludgate Circus and the river. The area is roughly that known as the City, which now probably occupies not more than one-fortieth of the modern metropolis.

There were in Shakespeare's time perhaps one hundred thousand people within the walls, and as many more in the suburbs. London was for its time a marvel of rapid metropolitan growth. Southwark across the river, where one still sees Southwark Cathedral and other ancient monuments, was the largest of the suburbs; but the city had also extended westward along the Strand and the river toward Westminster, which was the capital of the kingdom, and northwestward to Clerkenwell. Houses were being built outside the wall in every direction, though Islington was still in the fields, and Camdentown, Hampstead, and Highgate were remote villages. Old St. Paul's dominated from its central hill the irregular and closely packed city with its many churches. All-told it was a fine city, though it had lost something of its glory with the ruin and pillage, in the reign of Henry VIII, of monastic establishments, which had been rich and magnificent institutions. From the point of view of social and economic importance, however, London was, in comparison with the rest of the kingdom, relatively greater even than London is today.

Travel Travel was still extremely painful and slow, because of the unimproved condition of the roads, and dangerous on account of highway robbers, although English inns seem to have been good, certainly much better than the inns of the continent. Travel on horseback was the most common method, and, one may believe, the most comfortable, for coach-building was a new and imperfect art. Coaches of state, some of which we see in prints and pictures, were lumbering affairs, no doubt handsome enough in processions, but springless, unwieldy, and hard to transport. Carts and wagons were used for carrying merchandise, but that too went most quickly, safely, and easily on the pack-saddle. Under such difficulties as these, no metropolitan area as great as London could possibly have subsisted from the interior; the river with its foreign commerce built London into a great city.

Commerce The most important foreign trade which England had when Elizabeth came to the throne was with Antwerp, Bruges, and other Belgian cities. When the Spanish king, Philip II, made his onslaught on his Protestant subjects in the Low Countries, Elizabeth's government held off for a long time from openly assisting them because a war with Spain would have broken down English commerce with Belgium; but through his short-sighted policy, King Philip managed, for the sake of punishing religious obduracy, to undo himself. In 1576 eight thousand citizens of Antwerp were put to the sword; and when the Duke of Parma in 1585 besieged the city and captured it, Antwerp, the commercial metropolis of northern Europe, was totally ruined. One-third of its merchants are said to have settled in London, bringing with them their expert knowledge of commerce. Two things are notable: England was becoming the home of the refugee; and, as the export trade of Flanders died away, London became the greatest market in the world. English ships took over the Mediterranean trade, formerly carried on mainly by the Venetians; also the trade of the Baltic, which formerly the free cities of the Hanseatic League had borne. Bristol throve on commerce with Ireland and subsequently on trade with the western hemisphere. Boston and Hull increased their business with Scandinavian ports. Archangel was discovered, and a new trade sprang up with Russia. Fisheries were developed in the North Sea, the waters north of Ireland, and the banks of Newfoundland. The greatness of Elizabeth and her ministers is seen in the fact that they encouraged this commerce. Nearly all other kings and rulers whom Europe had seen until that time regarded commerce with jealousy and preyed on it themselves like pirates; whereas Elizabeth and her ministers were so surprisingly intelligent and advanced in their views that they made definite efforts to foster it. Lord Burghley recommended the use of articles of home manufacture; in order to encourage the fisheries, he caused the publication of documents which might be translated in terms of current propaganda with the words, "Eat more fish!"

The Poor Laws The obvious and important result of this new prosperity under Queen Elizabeth was a decrease in unemployment; but there was room for vast improvement. The country had, particularly since the suppression of the monasteries (1536-1539), been more or less flooded with the unemployed, both with the vagabond class and with the helpless poor. The reign of Elizabeth brought about a betterment of conditions with reference to the burden of their support. In 1572 there was passed an act of Parliament which made the mayors and other officers of towns and cities, magistrates and county officials, responsible for the care of their local poor and for the enforcement of stern measures against vagabonds. Under this act vagabonds were arrested and sent back to their own parishes and there compelled to work. This localization of responsibility laid the basis for what has been known historically as the poor rate, or the local tax levied for the support of the poor, and for that sinister institution, the workhouse. The provisions of the act of 1572 were continued for centuries. We, from our more extensive knowledge, think of them as inadequate and liable to abuse; but, for their day, they were serviceable and progressive. This law, together with some improvement in agriculture and manufacture and much improvement in commerce, reduced unemployment and made prosperity general.

An age of opportunity Another result of this prosperity was a social readjustment which is sometimes spoken of as the passing of feudalism, but which might be better described as a condition in which society needed more men. England became what we should call an important world power with extended interests and a new dignity and efficiency; London became a world market and later a cultural center; and, as a result of these things, opportunity came more abundantly to the ordinary man. This opening up of opportunity, more perhaps than any other one thing, had brought about the Italian Renaissance. In the Italy of the fourteenth and fifteenth centuries there had been many little states and dukedoms, rather prosperous, but mutually jealous, the power shifting from leader to leader, each attended by a new flock of men. Any man who could use a sword had an opportunity to use it, and any man who could contribute by his purse, his pen, his brush, or his chisel to the glory of his princely master's little court was in demand. In the England of Elizabeth there was also a chance for new men, which arose from a sort of shuffling in the ranks of

society. This new freedom enabled Shakespeare himself and other literary men to rise to power and importance, although he and certain of the conservative thinkers of the age inveighed against it because they saw in it something inimical to the good old times. Many of Elizabeth's favorites were men whose families were of no importance. It was an age of self-made men. No American ought to have difficulty in understanding a situation in which, more perhaps than ever before, young men had a chance to make their fortunes and to rise in the social scale. Abraham Lincoln thought that free opportunity to rise in the social scale was the greatest of American national blessings.

The beggar on horseback Not only did the lovers of the old order see, as they always do in every social change, the disagreeable spectacle of the beggar on horseback; but, since the rise of all sorts and conditions of men was marked and advertised by the display of luxury, they saw also degeneracy and social decay. The Puritan, whether gentle or simple, saw an alarming increase of worldliness and sin. Immersed as they were in the changing order, writers were unable to comprehend the greatness of the time; and it may be said that never was satire more active and more bitter, and social pessimism more genuine. It cannot be said that Shakespeare voices the reaction more potently than he does the spirit of progress. Perhaps it is fair to see something of social conscience in his depiction of the wickedness of city life in *Measure for Measure*, or in his casual pictures of upstart courtiers and the paintings and patchings of court ladies; but in general one turns to Shakespeare's contemporaries for the recognition of social evils in the large. Shakespeare, being a man from the country, knew mainly two classes, the nobleman and the peasant. He does not distress himself about the aggressions of the new commercial magnate, or the impertinent ways of the city madam, his wife. It is Jonson, Chapman, and Beaumont and Fletcher who do this.

The rise in the scale of living Most of the best thinkers of the day saw ominous things in the increase of wealth and the improvement of the scale of living. Harrison, a brilliant man but a thoroughgoing reactionary, in his *Description of England* sees disaster in the fine new Elizabethan dwelling-houses, built of oak, with locked doors, glazed windows, and many chimneys. These things made men delicate, he thought, and he attributed the increase in rheums and catarrhs to the fact that householders no longer breathed in their own healthful smoke, but sent it up the new chimneys. So also conservative thinkers regarded the long-bow as the mainstay of the kingdom in war, although, in point of fact, guns and artillery had long ago superseded it. In the armory at the Tower of London there is a corselet shot through with a bullet at Bosworth field. It illustrates what had happened to the knightly style of warfare, though Elizabethan aristocrats, with their countless jousts and tourneys, refused to recognize it. The French rapier with a new style of fence had superseded the sword and buckler. Although this supersession was disgusting to Mercutio and many a stout gallant of the old order, the rapier was nevertheless a much more dangerous weapon because of its thrusting style of fence than the old broadsword with its "swashing blow."

Satirists and reactionaries saw the country beset with "flaming youth" and dangerous modernism. The introduction of Italian manners had been cried out against for two generations; but still the young men resorted to Italy and came back, as it was thought, godless in their manner of life and corrupted in the purity of their religion. French clothes were also an abomination. Never had Englishmen worn such wealth on their backs. There is a familiar story of a country nobleman who came to court in the reign of Henry VIII dressed rudely in country apparel, but with a hundred stout followers in his train. The king reproved him for his lack of propriety in his dress; he returned later in silk and velvet. When the king asked him about his hundred retainers, he threw down his cloak and his feathered hat and declared that he had put his retainers on his back. Plain gentlemen, citizens, and even yeomen dressed better than had the earls and barons of an earlier time. Nothing so offended the strictness of the Puritans as to behold this vanity in

dress; for, since Adam's fall was symbolized by his adoption of raiment in place of innocent nudity, fine clothes seemed to advertise man's submergence in sin and to flout God's will. Not only was raiment fine in Elizabeth's day, a thing which was of itself bad enough in the minds of Puritans, but clothes were slashed, trimmed, and ornamented as never before. Rouge and false hair became common, and also the great and growing pleated collar known as the ruff, its expansive stiffness made possible by the discovery of starch. Breeches were first narrow and then wide, for Dame Fashion had never been so busy in changing styles. Other causes for consternation and disgust were the new habit of "tobacco drinking," the use of many new sorts of wines with a new habit of drunkenness, and the general chameleon-like behavior of the Englishman, who, according to the texts of a hundred satires, derived his goods and his fashions from every quarter. "What say you, then, to Falconbridge, the young baron of England?" asks Nerissa of Portia, who in her reply declares, "How oddly he is suited! I think he bought his doublet in Italy, his round hose in France, his bonnet in Germany, and his behavior everywhere." (*Merchant of Venice*, I, ii, 71, 79-82.)

The contrasts between rich and poor were of course very great, and along with the youth seeking his fortune were innumerable masterless men, mercenary soldiers who had been engaged in continental wars, decayed serving-men, knaves in buckram, and the pitifully poor, whose condition was made worse than of old by the greedy quest for wealth, the desertion of the country by ancient landholders, the enclosure of common lands, and the enormous increase in rents. The era, like our own, was one of inflation; and although men were richer, there was something factitious in their prosperity. Perhaps the most hated man among those who preyed on society was the usurer or dealer in money, for no point was clearer in Elizabethan morals than the belief that interest-taking was a sin. Interest-taking is made the chief mark of discrimination between Shylock the Jew and Antonio the Christian in *The Merchant of Venice*. Burghley recognized the danger of having power in the hands of those who control money and used an almost modern style of propaganda in seeking to develop public morals and public conscience. He would have usurers and smugglers desist from their ill-gotten gains because of the evil results to the kingdom. He sought to prevent high prices by a similar moral suasion, and to foster industry by an appeal to patriotism.

Elizabethan houses   As England grew rich with its national and usually international peace, its wise and thrifty government, and its prosperous trade, the old-fashioned thatched and wattled houses of the peasantry, like the narrow cottage of Chaucer's poor widow in *The Nun's Priest's Tale*, gave place to houses of brick and stone. Chimneys were built for fireplaces, so that the smoke no longer wandered about the house searching for the hole in the roof by which to escape. Pewter dishes, or even silver dishes, took the place of the wooden spoon and trencher. Beds and even pillows became common. Carpets replaced rushes as covering for the floors; wainscoting, tapestries or hangings, and pictures appeared on the walls; and, most wonderful of all, glass began to be used extensively for windows. Let those who "viewed with alarm" say what they might, domestic comfort established itself in England. In witness of this fact there still stand, with their gardens and terraces, a good many of the lofty Tudor mansions. The battlement, the moat, the fortified gate, the narrow window for archery or firearms, were no longer necessary in a land at peace; nor was it any longer imperative for the peasant to bring his cows, his pigs, and his poultry into his house at night in order to protect them from thieves. The row of splendid houses of the Elizabethan nobility along the bank of the Thames in London was swept away by the fire of 1666, as were also the really fine houses of city merchants, bankers, and traders. A little bit of the old city was left by the fire along the eastern wall, in Holborn, and in the vicinity of Smithfield. Only a few of the old city houses still stand and but one of the churches, but there are many sixteenth century houses in provincial cities such as Chester and Coventry. They were often large and imposing structures, three or four stories in height, usually framed of strong oak with the walls filled in with brick and plaster. The frontage on the street in old London was usually narrow, but there were trees and gardens at the rear. With these finer houses, too, came features of privacy which we are accustomed to associate with culture. Most of the life of the household of the mediæval magnate had gone on in the great hall, which was often kitchen, dining-hall, and sitting-room for the whole body of family and retainers, the men drinking there in the evenings and sleeping there at night. In the new houses were withdrawing rooms into which, even if dinner were taken in the hall, the family and the chief guests might retire for privacy.

The Elizabethans did their building and improvements well. Not only do we still admire their houses, but from their oriel windows and the bits of their stained glass which have here and there remained, the broad staircases by which they approached their newly invented second stories, their jewels, and their costumes, we can see that they were children of the Renaissance indulging a characteristic love of beauty. Graphic and plastic arts did not thrive as in Italy, or even in France and the Low Countries, but literature, drama, and architecture became flourishing arts in the English Renaissance.

The Queen   The most dominant, versatile, and beneficent figure of the reign of Queen Elizabeth was the Queen herself. Her character and her brains, her tastes and opinions, produced greater results than any other single force. On one side of her nature she was a masculine woman possessed of some of the finest of masculine qualities. Her judgment was sound, her policy simple and firm, and her courage strong. She wished England to prosper, and therefore wished to keep it out of foreign wars and domestic disturbances. There were many occasions for both kinds of discord. Reformation and Counter-Reformation were fighting it out all over Europe, and England sided strongly with the Protestant cause. Within the kingdom religious quarrels were fierce and incessant, and the matter of the succession to the crown was unsure. Elizabeth's subjects had many invitations to rebel against her in behalf of one or another claimant to power. She was not in general a theorist in governmental matters, but had a few simple principles which were in line with the best political thinking of the Renaissance. She avoided partisanship, believed strongly in social gradation, in the supremacy of wise princes, and in governmental economy. She was imperious to a degree, headstrong in fact; but, when it came to the final issue, reason rose above passion, and she was able to take advice. Whatever her vanities of ostentation and display, or her mad quest for pleasure, she understood that business is business. It may even be said that she took to heart the most widely current maxim of the Renaissance, that self-knowledge is the *summum bonum*. She therefore indulged her vanities in her court and acted the statesman in her council. She could deny herself her dearest wish if, after having tried in vain to bully her advisers into agreement with her, she found that they still stood out against her proposal.

Tudor absolutism The crown had been the dominant force in English government since the time of Edward IV, and the last strongholds of baronial authority had been broken down under Henry VIII. There had been occasional revivals of oligarchical power among the greater nobles, such as that of Somerset in the reign of Edward VI; but, for the most part, the only rival of the crown was the authority of the House of Commons of Parliament. The Commons had been strengthened by the growth in wealth of the commercial classes and by a league with rural magnates. They were making themselves felt under Elizabeth and were to become the controlling element under Elizabeth's successors. One reason no doubt for Elizabeth's rigid economy in government was her desire to be independent of the Commons; but, as it was, she had conceded a good deal to the Parliament for the sake of harmony. She had convened Parliament several times to obtain grants to cover the expenses of her wars, and they had shown a disposition to demand redress of grievances and a desire to get power into their hands; but she had managed affairs so well that the burden of taxes was light and there was little reason to ask questions about the expenditures of the crown; whereas her successor, King James I, exhausted his exchequer, and Parliament secured its hold through the power of the purse. Elizabeth had little partisanship, but used men of all parties and played rivals off against each other; and therein lay probably her greatest ability. If one follows the history of her relations with her great minister, William Cecil, Baron of Burghley, one learns the story. Burghley was a Protestant and a partisan, not free from self-seeking, but, as a whole, honest and reliable. She knew she could get from him the truth even when it was against herself; and, when she had failed to make him abandon his position on any question, she knew that it was a statesman's opinion with which she had to do, and she usually heeded him in the end. He, too, desired the prosperity and peace of England, though for religious and political reasons he would often enough have been glad to go to war; here, however, the Queen controlled him and insisted on maintaining peace. Elizabeth had other able ministers like Walsingham and Sir Nicholas Bacon, father of the famous Lord Chancellor. Out of the Queen's opinions and her relation to Parliament and the people, and out of the political doctrines of France and Italy transplanted into England, there grew the characteristic political views which Shakespeare expresses; for example, that of the glory and inviolability of sovereignty, even of *de facto* sovereignty, that of the greatness of honesty in courtiers and of the wickedness of flatterers, and above all, that of the feeling for the glory and greatness of the commonwealth.

The Virgin Queen The Queen, being unmarried, made a cult of her virginity. Her vanity and her ridiculous affectation of youth and beauty, her greed of flattery and adulation, caused her to adopt favorite after favorite, often for no better reason than charm of person and manner. Of these the most famous is Robert Dudley, the Earl of Leicester, whom at one time the Queen may have been tempted to marry. Later in her reign, when Burghley was dead and the Queen was older and more foolish, the ill-starred Earl of Essex was a prime favorite. This was the time when Shakespeare may have come to court, and one has a feeling that there may have been a basis for Aubrey's statement about Shakespeare: "If he was invited to court, he was in pain." He had written *Richard II* about a king who listened to flatterers to his own ruin; Elizabeth resented being compared to this king, and Shakespeare, so far as we know, may have written as a partisan of Essex and his friend Southampton; for they believed that the Queen was beset by flatterers. He may have resented the overthrow of Essex and Southampton, for he wrote no commendatory verses when the Queen died.

The amusements of Elizabeth We have our picture of Good Queen Bess cuffing a disobedient lady - in - waiting, reproving a statesman, laughing at coarse jests and making them herself, witnessing the cruel sport of bear-baiting, delivering addresses in Latin or Greek, riding with great ceremony in her litter surrounded by lords and ladies, entering London, her great sword of state borne before her, or "going a progress" through the counties of England. She loved to travel about her kingdom visiting provincial cities and the country-seats of noblemen; and these things pleased her particularly well when, like an invading army, she could live off the country. The Queen loved plays and pageants and supported with some liberality the Office of the Revels under the Lord Chamberlain, in whose records we first find Shakespeare's name after his departure from Stratford. The Master of the Revels from 1578 to 1610, Edmund Tilney, called the players together before Christmas and selected from their repertory those plays which were to be presented before her Majesty, and for their service the actors received a reward generally amounting to £10. Many of Shakespeare's plays were so performed, and he may have had to do with we know not how much other dramatic activity at court. The masque, a form of drama combined with music and pageantry and introduced from the continent, was the rival of the play, and under King James, probably because his greater generosity provided its producers with more money, it grew, with Ben Jonson and the architect Inigo Jones, into something much more gorgeous than the drama. The masque was,

however, an established institution when Shakespeare wrote and long before that time. *Love's Labour's Lost, A Midsummer-Night's Dream, Much Ado about Nothing*, and other plays have features from the masque, and no doubt most of his comedies dared to be more poetical, more dainty, and more grotesque because of his knowledge of this form of entertainment.

Education, politics, the state Shakespeare was not interested in politics in the narrow sense in which we usually use the word, but in the broad Aristotelian sense of social welfare he was certainly not indifferent to political considerations. He saw politics and history, like Plutarch and the chroniclers, as always embodied in the persons of kings and leaders. Political issues thus embodied in persons seem to form the bases of his historical plays. The conflicts of the chief characters of these plays are to some extent conflicts of political and ethical ideas. It is clear that with Shakespeare the character of the government lies in the character of the prince. Anarchy and disunion were all too well known, and the questions at issue were not so much about ideals and general principles as those which arose out of the simple theory that, with a wise prince and an honest court, a country might secure prosperity at home and peace and safety abroad. The flatterer, a selfish man placed near the prince and often responsible for his actions, was thus the worst enemy of the state and the people. The educational theory of the day was also simple and perfectly understood. It moved in the same direction, calling for the liberal education of princes and rulers of the state in morals, intellect, and personality. The vulgar herd below made no difference; there must be virtue and power at the top in order to hold the bottom in order. Such were Shakespeare's views, and in this respect he aligns himself with the greatest thinkers of his time, particularly with conservatives like Hooker. Rank and grade in society were necessary and beneficent in a grand system of co-ordination and subordination extending from inanimate nature to heaven itself, through the degrees of vegetable and animal kingdoms, mankind, spirits, angels, archangels, dominions, principalities, powers, up to the godhead. It was the law of nature that each order should know and observe its sphere and its limitations, for it was by ambition that the angels in heaven fell. Likewise on earth there were grades in society which bore the sanction of God in every degree from beggar to king. On the contented discharge of function in each rank rested the condition of social order; witness the speech of Ulysses in *Troilus and Cressida:*

> Degree being vizarded,
> The unworthiest shows as fairly in the mask.
> The heavens themselves, the planets and this
>   centre
> Observe degree, priority and place,
> Insisture, course, proportion, season, form,
> Office and custom, in all line of order;
> And therefore is the glorious planet Sol
> *in* noble eminence enthroned and sphered
> Amidst the other; whose medicinable eye
> Corrects the ill aspects of planets evil,
> And posts, like the commandment of a king,
> Sans check to good and bad: but when the planets
> In evil mixture to disorder wander,
> What plagues and what portents! what mutiny!
> What raging of the sea! shaking of earth!
> Commotion in the winds! frights, changes, horrors,
> Divert and crack, rend and deracinate
> The unity and married calm of states
> Quite from their fixture! O, when degree is shaked,
> Which is the ladder to all high designs,
> The enterprise is sick! How could communities,
> Degrees in schools and brotherhoods in cities,
> Peaceful commerce from dividable shores,
> The primogenitive and due of birth,
> Prerogative of age, crowns, sceptres, laurels,
> But by degree, stand in authentic place?
> Take but degree away, untune that string,
> And, hark, what discord follows!   (I, iii, 83-110)

This is the approved mode of Renaissance thought about politics. Machiavelli's *Prince* lays down with cold-blooded calculation the rules by which a sovereign may govern securely and successfully. This book is not a document of oppression and tyranny, although lovers of human liberty have long considered it so. It is a calm discussion of the methods by which the conditions of social order recommended by Shakespeare's Ulysses and by Richard Hooker may be maintained. Shakespeare was on the side of the royal government; and, although he does not often expound the doctrines of Tudor absolutism, they are everywhere implicit in his treatment of society. They are

in his delineations of kings and, particularly, in his descriptions of mobs like those in *2 Henry VI, Julius Cæsar,* and *Coriolanus.* The reasons why this is not more apparent to the casual reader are that Shakespeare was not apparently anxious to expound this or any doctrine except dramatically, and because there is in Shakespeare always a quality of breadth and fairness. His common men have in them a dash of humanity and nobility, as his kings are made to have a kinship with common men; and both kings and common men have intelligible motives, as do even his worst villains. In his pictures of society there is always a coloring of elemental justice. But Shakespeare could have entertained no views except those described above, and it is absurd to hunt in his works for nineteenth century theories of social justice or to blame him for not expressing views possible only to later generations.

The religious question After Elizabeth came to the throne there was a bitter reaction against the Catholics. Those Protestants who had fled abroad to avoid persecution under Queen Mary brought back with them continental ideas of theology and a new and stiffer type of Protestantism. The Church of England assumed a middle position between this extreme Protestantism and Catholicism; this was the position of Burghley and the Queen. By the middle of her reign extreme Protestantism was expressing itself either in Presbyterianism or Independency, and the time came when it offered a violent attack on the middle position held by the Church of England. Shakespeare hardly shows himself aware of this powerful and pregnant force. His allusions to Puritanism are few and indefinite, but they have been thought to be scornful. His position on religious matters was probably that of the Queen. He is equally non-committal as regards the Church of Rome, although he shows a sympathetic understanding of the institutions of the Catholic church in *Hamlet, King John,* and elsewhere.

The moral question There was a great change in the temper of the public in moral matters in the early years of King James's reign. Elizabethan gayety gave place to satire and moral reflection, and grave men were thinking critically, though not always fruitfully, about the state of the church and the state of society. Human life was seen by such thinkers more and more against a background of responsibility to God, iniquity in man, and uncertainty of fate. This may be the temper which we see reflected in the tragedies of Shakespeare as well as in the bitter carelessness of his later contemporaries, their sensuality, and their adoption of the point of view of a class instead of the point of view of humanity at large. The later dramatists belonged to the court. There was something innocent in the frank love of finery, sport, and show in Elizabeth Tudor; for she loved books and art, as well as clothes and jewels, and she labored to make herself a mistress of languages and learning. Possibly her love affairs were silly rather than wicked. Certainly in her court decency usually prevailed, whereas in the court of King James I there was sordid intrigue. It is a very fortunate circumstance that Shakespeare was old enough to have felt with Marlowe and Spenser rather than young enough to have felt with Fletcher and Ford.

We have seen that Shakespeare's England, still largely rural and mediæval, but coming into possession of material wealth in the midst of a long peace, was much better governed and unified than it had ever been, and socially so constituted that the individual, of whatever rank and station, had a reasonable opportunity for recognition. Another circumstance which needs to be mentioned is the growth of the book-trade. Books had become cheap, and for the first time many classes of people had learned to read. But are these material circumstances sufficient to have produced such a blossoming of the human mind as the world saw between 1590 and 1610? If we look into the matter, we find that there are spiritual factors that need to be taken into consideration.

Renaissance learning Renaissance learning was largely a development and amplification of mediæval learning. It retained the old science, not only of the earlier Middle Ages, but all the additions to it made by the thirteenth and later centuries from their study of classical antiquity. It comprehended the doctrine of the microcosm and the macrocosm, or the belief that man was a little world whose parts, physical and spiritual, were analogous to the parts of the commonwealth, the solar system, and the kingdom of heaven. This embraced the doctrine of planetary and elemental correspondences; namely, that the temperament, fortunes, and physique of the human being are dependent upon the mixture within him of the four elements and on the influence of the stars and planets, which have in them corresponding parts. All things in heaven and earth had been created, according to this belief, to fit into proper places in a perfectly constructed system. This means that the man of science did not expect to find any new principle, but merely to fit things into their pre-established places. The science of the time was bad, not so much because things were crowded into the wrong pigeonhole, as because the pigeonhole itself was often an unwarranted restriction of the freedom and variety of nature. Compared to modern thought of the abstract kind, Renaissance thought was superficial and vague, often made up merely of comparison or the enunciation of old postulates under new forms. It was prone therefore to quackery and the too ready acceptance of analogy. It was not, however, lacking in variety and was so active in the observation of likeness and unlikeness that it lent itself readily to the uses of poetry.

Basal knowledge The following brief digest may indicate the material of Elizabethan thought: (1) Matter pertaining particularly to the Renaissance, such as the proverb or dictum and the habit of aphoristic thought, the belief in culture, the freedom of the will, and the adaptability of the individual; (2) matter from the classics, such as the intimate interest in mythology, ancient history and story, eloquence, and the sort of philosophic reflection which one associates with Cicero; (3) matters of current fashion, including the theme of the good old times versus modernity, clothes, fashions, and courtly life; (4) matters of domestic life, such as the management of the household, woman's sphere, the relations of parent and child, husband and wife, master and servant, courtship and betrothal, clownage, conviviality; (5) magic, the ways of the occult world, folklore, superstition, ghosts, witches, demons, signs, omens, old wives' tales, and childbed superstitions; (6) a body of popular natural history (which, erroneous as it is, no doubt helped men at least to understand themselves) about the ape, the cat, the bat, the hare, the hedgehog, the rat, the cock, the basilisk, the toad, the bee, and the spider, as well as a knowledge of various herbs and stones and their properties.

The lives of ordinary men must of course have been steeped in such lore as was in common circulation. In fact we have abundant testimony from the age of Queen Elizabeth that such was the case. Reginald Scot, whose book, *The Discovery of Witchcraft*, was published in 1584, gives the following description of the superstitious terrors against which he protested; for Scot was a skeptic with reference to witchcraft and superstition, in which, however, King James devoutly believed:

In our childhood our mothers' maids have so terrified us with an ugly devil having horns on his head, fire in his mouth, and a tail in his breech, eyes like a bason, fangs like a dog, claws like a bear, a skin like a nigger, and a roaring voice like a lion, whereby we start and are afraid when we hear one cry Boo: and they have so frayed us with bull-beggars, spirits, witches, urchins, elves, hags, fairies, satyrs, pans, fauns, sylens, Kit with the canstick, tritons, centaurs, dwarfs, giants, imps, calcars, conjurors, nymphs, changelings, incubus, Robin Goodfellow, the spoorne, the mare, the man in the oak, the hell wain, the firedrake, the puckle, Tom Thumb, hobgoblin, Tom Tumbler, boneless, and such other bugs, that we are afraid of our own shadows: in so much that some never fear the devil, but in a dark night; and then a polled sheep is a perilous beast, and many times is taken for our father's soul, specially in a church-yard, where a right hardy man heretofore scant durst pass by night, but his hair would stand upright. (Pp. 152-3.)

Joseph Hall in *Characters of Vertues and Vices* (1608) bears similar testimony:

Superstition is godless religion, devout impiety. . . . If but a hare cross him the way, he returns; or, if his journey began unawares on the dismal day; or, if he stumbled at the threshold. If he see a snake unkilled, he fears a mischief: if the salt falls towards him, he looks pale and red, and is not quiet, till one of the waiters have poured wine on his lap: and when he sneezeth, thinks them not his friends that uncover not. In the morning, he listens whether the crow crieth even or odd; and, by that token, presages of the weather. If he hear but a raven croak from the next roof, he makes his will; or, if a bittour fly over his head by night: but, if his troubled fancy shall second his thoughts with the dream of a fair garden, or green rushes, or the salutation of a dead friend, he takes leave of the world, and says he cannot live. . . . Old wives and stars are his counsellors: his nightspell is his guard; and charms, his physicians. He wears Paracelsian characters for the toothache: and a little hallowed wax is his antidote for all evils. This man is strangely credulous; and calls impossible things, miraculous. If he hear that some sacred block speaks, moves, weeps, smiles, his bare feet carry him thither with an offering; and, if a danger miss him in the way, his saint hath the thanks. Some ways he will not go; and some he dares not: either there are bugs, or he feigneth them: every lantern is a ghost, and every noise is of chains. He knows not why, but his custom is to go a little about, and to leave the cross still on the right hand. One event is enough to make a rule: out of these rules he concludes fashions, proper to himself; and nothing can turn him out of his own course. If he have done his task, he is safe; it matters not with what affection. Finally, if God would let him be the carver of his own obedience, he could not have a better subject: as he is, he cannot have a worse. (Seconde Booke, p. 87.)

In an age when superstitions of the kinds just described were so common, when there was so much ignorance and so much misinformation, how could the minds of men have been free? And yet they were relatively so. Man had acquired a new measure of freedom and responsibility. The Reformation had put his salvation into his own hands and made him responsible for it. The invention of printing, the cheapness of the printed book, and the extension of the ability to read had given him the wherewithal to learn. The spirit of the Englishman of the Renaissance rose with a noble aspiration, and he put out his hand to reach, not only the newly realized joys of salvation, but also the newly revealed promises of science. But the age of authority was by no means over, and the sciences, supported by the prestige of antiquity, had enormous authority back of their alluring promises.

What were the things offered by learning to this the first generation of modern times equipped to enjoy them?

What learning had to offer The main source of learning was of course the curriculum of schools and colleges, and this curriculum the Renaissance took over almost unchanged from the Middle Ages. It was made up of the Seven Liberal Arts: grammar, rhetoric, and logic, called the trivium and corresponding roughly to the work for a bachelor's degree; and arithmetic, geometry, astronomy, and music, called the quadrivium and corresponding roughly to the work for a master's degree. Since the thirteenth century there had been added to it what were known as the Three Philosophies, namely, natural philosophy, ethics, and metaphysics (made up mainly of psychology). This addition, consisting largely of the works of Aristotle, introduced into Europe from the Arabs, had served to enrich the curriculum of liberal studies and had been in the schools long enough to have made its way into the minds of educated persons, whether university bred or not. The Seven Liberal Arts went back to Aristotle and the Greeks by the long road of the Middle Ages; the Three Philosophies were a more recent importation from the same source.

Aristotelian logic offered, and still offers, much. It claims to be able to discover truth and detect error. Elizabethan writers on the subject said that they could unlock the Scriptures, avoid the snares of the Papacy, and reward their students with salvation. Dudley Fenner wrote a book of logic in which he taught how to solve all the problems of domestic life by means of logic, and Abraham Fraunce showed how it might straighten out all the wrinkles and kinks of the law. Aristotelian ethics also is a practical subject. It had been made more so when it came to Elizabethan England in the works of Italian Aristotelians. It was, and is, a science of behavior. There is no categorical imperative in it; no hortatory quality; no positivism; no Christian piety. It tells men how to live successfully and tells them to be good in order to be successful. It flatters man by supposing that there is no limit to the possibility of his attainment. Politics is but a continuation of ethics both in Aristotle and in the Renaissance. It teaches how to rule a state, how to gain power and hold it, how to educate a governor and a statesman, and how to conduct wars and negotiate the treaties which interrupt them. Its ideal is efficiency. Alchemy, astrology, and magic were practical as well as learned arts, and they had their claims and their followers.

The subjects mentioned in the preceding paragraph were old sciences which were for the first time advertised and rendered easily accessible; but there were some sciences which underwent important adaptations and, therefore, exercised special influences. Psychology, derived also from the writings of Aristotle, had always had implications of importance in man's life on earth. The psychology of Aristotle and his followers offers a shrewd and, for the most part, a satisfactory explanation of what takes place in the mental constitution of man. Its erroneous anatomy and physiology are largely compensated for by careful observation in the realm of human consciousness. The ancients themselves, Chaucer, and other later writers had made free use of psychology in their determination of motive and their description of the passions of the mind. There arose in the last quarter of the sixteenth century a far wider realization of the possibilities of psychology and a far greater faith in what it might accomplish. Timothy Bright and Robert Burton applied it to the diagnosis and cure of insanity. John Huarte offered it as a method by which men might be classified for trades and professions, through a determination of the proportions in them of the qualities of hot, cold, moist, and dry. Besides these there was a great group of writers, partly scientific and partly popular, who saw in psychological phenomena, often called "humors," a means of explaining and depicting the emotional life of man. The subject passed from the scientist to the literary men, just as we have seen pragmatism and psychoanalysis pass in our own day. Shakespeare and nearly all of the dramatists became psychologists and, according to their ability and genius, made use of psychology in their plays.

The new learning coming from Greece and Rome through France and Italy was, and is, serviceable to those who wish to know the world. It was conspicuous in the exorbitance of claims which in the nature of things could never be realized; but the act of faith, the belief in learning, brought the Elizabethan further in creative and imaginative insight than any modern age has ever been brought in the same length of time. It seems that learning offered a great intellectual bargain counter, and the men of the English Renaissance were foolish enough, or wise enough, to invest.

Summary We have thus passed in rapid review what Elizabethan men knew and believed and what they tried to learn. The things which we ordinarily associate with them, however, are not these things, although these things are fundamental to correct understanding. We normally and correctly enough think of the Elizabethan age as a time when there were many poets, many soldiers, and many explorers; as a time when the race was reaching out in every direction in response to its love of power and beauty. Perhaps never has the spirit of a race and an age been so active and so bold. It was also an age of versatility. Sir Philip Sidney was a gallant soldier; he was also a poet, a novelist, a critic, and no mean thinker about the affairs of state. Raleigh, the soldier, warrior, and courtier, was a world in himself, being also a skillful poet and spending his long years in prison in the writing of a learned history. Bacon was capable of almost anything practical, scientific, or literary. There was no man who showed quite the diversity of splendid talent which appeared in Leonardo da Vinci at the height of the Italian Renaissance, but the tendency to a full participation in all the available activities of life was present and widespread. Shakespeare we know only as a poet and dramatist, but his vast comprehension of the variety of life and its zest makes his the most significant voice of the age.

REFERENCES

BESANT, SIR WALTER, *London in the Times of the Tudors.* London, 1908.

CHAMBERS, E. K., *The Elizabethan Stage.* Four vols. Oxford, 1923.

CHEYNEY, EDWARD P., *A History of England from the Defeat of the Spanish Armada to the Death of Elizabeth.* London, 1914, 1926.

CREIGHTON, M., *The Age of Elizabeth.* New York, 1892.

CREIZENACH, W., *The English Drama in the Age of Shakespeare* (translation of Band IV, *Geschichte des neueren Dramas*). London, 1916.

HARRISON, G. B., *England in Shakespeare's Day.* London, 1928. *An Elizabethan Journal.* London, 1928.

HARRISON, WILLIAM, *Description of Britaine and England.* 1577 (in Holinshed's *Chronicle*; a number of reprints).

LEE, SIR SIDNEY, *Stratford-on-Avon from the Earliest Times to the Death of Shakespeare.* London, 1907.

MADDEN, D. H., *The Diary of Master William Silence: A Study of Shakespeare and of Elizabethan Sport.* Second ed. London, 1907.

NICHOLS, J., *The Progresses and Processions of Queen Elizabeth.* New ed. London, 1823. *The Progresses, Processions, and Festivities of King James I.* London, 1828.

READ, CONYERS, *Mr. Secretary Walsingham and the Policy of Queen Elizabeth.* Cambridge, 1925.

Shakespeare's England. Oxford, 1916.

STEPHENSON, H. T., *Shakespeare's London.* New York, 1905. *The Elizabethan People.* New York, 1910.

STOW, JOHN, *Survey of London.* Ed. C. L. Kingsford. Oxford, 1908.

STRACHEY, LYTTON, *Elizabeth and Essex.* London, 1928.

STRUTT, J., *Sports and Pastimes of the People of England.* New ed. London, 1903.

TRAILL, H. D., *Social England.* Second ed. London, 1909.

WEBB, SIDNEY AND BEATRICE, *English Poor Law History.* Part I. London, 1927.

WHEATLEY, H. B., *London, Past and Present.* London, 1891.

WILSON, J. D., *Life in Shakespeare's England.* Cambridge, 1911.

Bibliographies will be found in *Cambridge Modern History, Cambridge History of English Literature, Shakespeare's England,* and *A Shakespeare Bibliography* (Ebisch and Schücking, Oxford, 1931).

III. THE PRE-SHAKESPEAREAN DRAMA

The religious drama At some time between 1585 and 1592 William Shakespeare left Stratford-on-Avon and established himself, apparently in a position of relative importance, in the theater in London. The theater was even then an important institution and of such complexity that it is necessary for us to inquire into its origin and growth in order to understand the opportunity that it offered Shakespeare and the power, both personal and literary, that it enabled him to achieve. We must consider the origin of the Elizabethan drama as an artistic form, the gradual provision of an adequate physical equipment for the theater and the stage, and the assemblage and organization of the personnel, under proper leadership, into licensed companies of players with effective business management.

Mystery plays From very early times, certainly from the beginning of the fourteenth century, until Shakespeare's own day, there had existed in England what we should call a community drama acted mainly by amateurs. The most important variety of it had been made up of mystery plays presented usually by craft guilds and telling in varying forms, but with conventional patterns, the story of the Bible, or rather the story of man's creation, fall, redemption, and ultimate judgment as depicted in the church services of the liturgical year. This drama had begun in the ninth century with certain musical variations of the ritual called tropes, which in the course of a century and a half developed into dramatic "offices," special services presenting, still in song, scenes of the Resurrection and the Nativity in the services of Easter and Christmas. By 1300 these beginnings had grown with the addition of scene after scene into two great dramas, had been transferred, we do not know exactly how, from the hands of the clergy to the hands of the laity, and has been translated gradually from Latin into the modern languages. One of these treated the Passion and the Resurrection, and probably the patriarchs of the Old Testament; and the other, the Messianic

prophets, the Nativity, and probably the Last Judgment. Other church festivals had also developed dramatic offices, or as they are called, liturgical dramas, dealing with special subjects such as the Conversion of St. Paul, the life of St. Mary Magdalene, and the Miracles of the Blessed Virgin Mary. The festival of Corpus Christi was established in honor of the Sacrament by the church in 1264 and carried into complete observance in Europe by about 1320. Somewhere in Europe, possibly in England itself, there was invented a significant device for the celebration of the new festival. The Easter and the Christmas group of plays, and possibly plays from other festivals, were combined into a gigantic continuous story, the Corpus Christi play, and acted on Corpus Christi day. Its most important subjects were the Creation, the Fall of Man and his Expulsion from Paradise, Cain and Abel, Noah and the Flood, Abraham and Isaac, Moses, the Prophets, the Annunciation, the Visit of the Shepherds and the Magi, the Flight into Egypt with the Slaughter of the Innocents, Christ before the Doctors, the Entry into Jerusalem, the Betrayal, the Capture, the Trial, the Crucifixion, the Burial with the Setting of the Watch, the Resurrection with the Harrowing of Hell, the appearances to the disciples, the Ascension, Pentecost, the Assumption of the Blessed Virgin Mary, the Coming of Antichrist, and Doomsday.

The Corpus Christi play The festival of Corpus Christi seems from the beginning to have called for a procession, and the play was in most places made processional; that is, each scene or group of scenes was put on a movable stage, called a pageant, and was hauled through the streets of the city on Corpus Christi day. These pageants with their actors stopped at open places in the city, where a crowd might assemble, and acted their scenes, one after another in the order demanded by the story as a whole, the audience, which had witnessed the first scene, remaining at their station until the succeeding pageants were rolled into place. This practical device brought with it a significant change in staging. Previously the aggregated play had been performed on a stage of multiple places, where Rome and Jerusalem, Heaven and Hell, Calvary and the Temple, were ranged about the same open space and conventionally understood to be separated by various distances. By mounting only the one or two settings required for a particular scene on a float and conveying it from station to station, the mystery play no doubt achieved a superior degree of unity. The processional play was not, however, universal even in England. In places like Wakefield where the streets were very narrow, or Lincoln where they were very steep, the older multiple-place stage was probably retained. In the market-place at Wakefield and in the cathedral close at Lincoln, the pageants were ranged in order about the open space and the spectators themselves moved on from scene to scene. They certainly had the multiple-place stage in London and the south of England, and it was the regular form of the mystery play stage on the continent.

Each subject or group of subjects in the Corpus Christi play was assigned to a particular company of artisans or to certain associated companies, who had their own play-book and pageant, and even pageant-house in which to store the pageant. For example, at Coventry the shearmen and tailors acted for a long period of time the scenes of the Nativity, the Shepherds, the Visit of the Magi, the Flight into Egypt, and the Slaughter of the Innocents. The weavers acted the story of the Presentation of Jesus in the Temple and the Disputation of Jesus with the Jewish Doctors. The texts of both of these plays are preserved. In the former, the *Shearmen and Taylors Pageant*, Herod is a comic character who acts what Bottom in *A Midsummer-Night's Dream* calls "a part to tear a cat in." At the point where the Magi, warned by an angel to depart into their own country by another way, escape his clutches, a quaint stage direction in the play says, "Here Erode ragis in the pagond and in the strete also," a detail which indicates what Hamlet means when he says, "it out-herods Herod." The scenes dealing with the infancy of Jesus, though very crude, are full of sweetness and reverence. The rich mercers' com-

pany of Coventry, able to supply clothes and hangings galore, acted the magnificent pageant of the Assumption of the Blessed Virgin Mary. In some other places we find the goldsmiths' company presenting the play of the Magi, or "The Three Kings of Cologne," apparently because they were able to supply the necessary crowns and jewels. At Coventry the drapers' company presented the play of the Last Judgment and each year made provision for three "worlds" to be burnt. They had also an earthquake "with a barrel for the same." Among their characters were God, two demons, three white souls, three black souls, two spirits, four angels, three patriarchs, two worms of conscience, a prologue, two "clarks" for singing (one to sing bass), and a Pharisee. Unfortunately the text of this pageant, as well as that of the mercers, has been lost.

The annual Corpus Christi play was a source of municipal pride at Coventry and elsewhere, and of profit also, since it drew crowds of spectators. Royal persons and great noblemen frequently attended. It is recorded, for example, that King Richard III, being at Kenilworth in 1484, came to Coventry at Corpus Christi-tide to see the pageants, rejoicing perhaps in the Slaughter of the Innocents. There were possibly as many as twenty full scope plays, mostly of the Corpus Christi type, in the kingdom, though the full texts of only four have been preserved. We have the cycles from York and Chester and two others: the Towneley cycle, almost certainly acted at Wakefield, and *Ludus Coventriæ*, possibly acted at Lincoln. There are two pageants, fragments of the full Corpus Christi play, from Coventry, one each from Norwich and Newcastle-on-Tyne, and several other single scenes from places not located. There is also preserved an example of another type of religious drama, a great passion play, of the form common on the continent, in the now extinct Celtic language of Cornwall. The passion play, which seems also to have been the type acted at London and in the south of England, centers in the theme of man's redemption and does not include the scenes dealing with the Nativity. The Cornish drama includes Old Testament subjects, a circumstance not unusual in the continental passion plays. There was considerable variety of form and contents even within the mystery play itself. Small places seem, for example, to have had plays of narrower scope and on special subjects, as in the case of the lost Shipwrights' play of Noah at Hull.

Miracles and moralities The miracle play, also widely current in England, shows a different variety of religious drama, although mystery plays and miracle plays shade off gradually into each other, and are not different in origin. Miracle plays, as distinguished from mystery plays, are those which tell the stories of the lives and miracles of saints and martyrs. English records are preserved in considerable numbers of plays on St. Katharine, St. Laurence, St. Nicholas, and other saints; but the texts of only two or three have been preserved, and they are not representative. To know what went on dramatically in honor of the saints one must study the plays preserved in French. One finds there a variety of saints' plays as well as the great *Miracles de Notre Dame*. At Lincoln, York, and Beverley there was a long play known as the *Pater Noster Play*, which dealt somehow with the Seven Deadly Sins, the content and form of which are not now known. At York also there was a *Crede Play*, which seems to have presented the lives of the Apostles. Besides these there was a great group of dramatized allegories of varying lengths, known as moralities. A number of them, such as *The Castle of Perseverance*, *Mankind*, and *Everyman*, are still in existence. Moralities were less offensive to the taste of the Reformation than were mystery and miracle plays, so that they had a better chance to survive. There was, finally, in the late Middle Ages, much miscellaneous dramatic activity, often so casual and ephemeral as to escape record. This included Robin Hood plays, of which examples have been preserved, farces, and other forms of the drama, which have mainly been lost to posterity.

This popular drama, existing for many centuries and carried out over wide areas, must have affected very greatly the moral and religious instruction of the common people. It must have given them a command of a form of literary culture and trained them in dramatic ways of thinking.

Indeed the plays were so dear to the popular heart that they yielded slowly to the influences of the Reformation and the Renaissance. They had bred a sort of dramatizing habit which expressed itself in the heterogeneous drama of the first nine decades of the sixteenth century, in which we see the old forms of mystery play, morality, and farce undergoing transformation through the influence of tragedy and comedy reintroduced by the Renaissance from Greece and Rome. The old drama in its native sincerity, humor, and realism—all popular qualities—laid an excellent foundation for the Elizabethan drama.

Shakespeare knew the old drama That Shakespeare knew the mystery and morality plays in their old forms is evident from his references, always containing a suggestion of ridicule, to various episodes and characters in them. Herod, who was a blood-and-thunder tyrant in the mystery plays, and Termagant, who figured in a similar rôle in the play of St. Nicholas, appear together in Hamlet's advice to the players (*Hamlet*, III, ii, 14-16). Falstaff he compares (*1 Henry IV*, II, iv, 498) to the Manningtree ox, a reference which seems to show knowledge of the Manningtree fair, if not the Manningtree morals, and it is Falstaff himself who remarks contemptuously of Justice Shallow, "And now is this Vice's dagger become a squire" (*2 Henry IV*, III, ii, 343). The Vice, the principal clownish character in the moralities, was armed with a dagger of lath. Again Falstaff is reported to have likened a flea on Bardolph's nose to a black soul burning in hell-fire (*Henry V*, II, iii, 42-4), which is almost certainly an allusion to the play of the Last Judgment. Shakespeare had opportunity to see the old plays, for the Corpus Christi play was performed annually at Coventry, only fourteen miles from Stratford, until Shakespeare was sixteen years old, and it is no extravagant guess that he joined the throng of those who attended the play at the chief city in Warwickshire. In some places in England the Corpus Christi play continued to be performed until after the beginning of the seventeenth century in spite of the fact that such plays were obviously "blasted with antiquity." Shakespeare was a child of his time and therefore looked with amusement if not contempt on these old-fashioned folk practices. He and his colleagues in the theater were absorbed in the new art of the Renaissance. His picture of the play of "Pyramus and Thisbe" presented by the "rude mechanicals" in *A Midsummer-Night's Dream* furnishes an indication of his point of view.

Early Tudor drama If Shakespeare began his work as a playwright about 1590, the Tudor drama had come well into line with the standards of the Renaissance before he began, and several great Elizabethan dramatists had already made their appearance. These things had not, however, occurred very long before his time. Sixteenth century drama is in general a drama of transition and experiment. With the exception of certain definite imitations, or translations of imitations, of ancient comedy and tragedy, sixteenth century drama from the reign of Henry VII to the last twenty years of Elizabeth's reign consists of what are loosely and rather absurdly called interludes. These are plays made up in varying proportions of native elements from the moralities, from the dialogue or *débat*, from the farce, and even from the mystery and miracle plays, more or less imperfectly reshaped according to the models of classical tragedy and comedy.

Other countries in Europe were undergoing, or had undergone, in their drama, somewhat the same process of transformation, and a new drama had sprung up in imitation of classical comedy and tragedy. The English copied this and at the same time translated and imitated the classics themselves. Since both the originals and the new continental drama were equally available, it is not always easy to tell whether we have to do with direct imitations of the works of Plautus and Terence, the Latin comedy writers, and Seneca, the writer of Latin tragedy, or with continental adaptations and imitations of these authors. In any case, it was the inferior Latin drama which was imitated and not the superior drama of Greece. In spite of these influences, however, Elizabethan drama was not destined to follow closely in the path of the classics. Perfection of form, convention-

ality, and restraint—qualities which we call classical—did not commend themselves to the enterprising, ebullient, and sentimental Elizabethans. In building their drama, freedom of fancy in conception and treatment, variety, adventure, and vigor if not extravagance of sentiment pleased them better, and we call their drama romantic.

In the shaping of the English drama of the Renaissance the amateur element is relatively large. Schools and colleges, their masters and graduates, felt most strongly the new influence coming in from the continent and were the first to write and act the new drama. The Tudors themselves were proponents of Renaissance culture, and royal entertainment was a chief occasion for the composition and production of drama. *Ralph Roister Doister*, written by Nicholas Udall, headmaster of both Eton College and Westminster School, is a scholastic play imitative of Terence and intended probably to please the royal taste. *Gammer Gurton's Needle* originated at Cambridge at about the same time. *Gorboduc, or Ferrex and Porrex*, written by Sackville and Norton, two young law students of the Inner Temple, and acted before Queen Elizabeth on January 18, 1562, is Senecan and voices in every line the Senecan craze of Italy and all Europe. Seneca, the most romantic of the ancients, satisfied the taste of the Renaissance, since he was, in spite of his classical manner, cosmopolitan, sententious, passionate, and sensational. Such plays as the three just mentioned, and there were many of them, were written by educated men largely for royal and noble entertainment and were acted in royal palaces, the houses of noblemen, the dining halls of colleges, and, when they got into the hands of professional actors, in the courtyards of inns. The staging was thus to some extent impromptu. School boys had been acting plays for perhaps a century before Queen Elizabeth was crowned. The Children of the Royal Chapel are known to have presented plays as early as 1506. The boys of St. Paul's School acted before King Henry VIII in 1528. Boys of other schools also gave theatrical performances. The Children of the Royal Chapel and the Children of Paul's were later organized into professional companies and have a long dramatic history. Schoolmasters and choirmasters became the first professional playwrights. The interlude and the contemporary continental drama are colored by their scholastic origin.

For example, there is a collection of Latin plays called *Dramata Sacra*, published at Basle in 1547, which exercised great influence in England. The so-called "prodigal son" plays, *Nice Wanton*, *The Disobedient Child*, *Thersites*, and some others, are school plays of the same type as those in this collection. They show the same process of adapting native themes to Latin models, which had gone on more rapidly on the continent than in England; whether the English were in such cases borrowing plays from the Low Countries or making their own adaptations of Latin comedy is frequently a matter of doubt. *Godly Queen Hester*, *Jacob and Esau*, *King Darius*, and other plays on biblical subjects are certainly derived from the scholastic drama of the continent rather than from an English dramatic impulse. The same thing is probably also true of certain plays on heroic subjects, such as *Appius and Virginia*, *Damon and Pithias*, and *Calisto and Meliboea*.

Bishop John Bale wrote *Kynge Johan* and many dramas on religious themes quite according to the old technique of the mystery plays. One might think from its title that *Kynge Johan* was the first of the history plays; it is, in point of fact, an adaptation of the old play of *Antichrist* written to serve as a controversial document against Catholicism. The play is named from King John merely because tradition had misrepresented him as an antagonist of the pope. John Skelton's *Magnificence* is merely a morality play; Lewis Wager's *Life and Repentance of Mary Magdalene* is a most interesting combination of mystery and morality; and John Heywood, several of whose plays are French farces, wrote some plays which are merely dialogues. The mawkish and ridiculous *Cambises*, "a lamentable tragedie, mixed full of pleasant mirth," is poetically and dramatically as crude as the mystery play of Noah. When the Renaissance drama was once under way, it preferred to draw its themes from ancient writers, like Ovid, and from Italian stories, rather than from the Bible or from allegory.

Italy supplied a number of bright comedies after the Roman model. *The Supposes*, translated from the Italian poet Ariosto by George Gascoigne, supplied the minor plot both for *The Taming of a Shrew* and *The Taming of the Shrew*; *Bugbears* is a jolly play translated from Grazzini's *La spiritata*; and there are others directly out of the Italian.

The Tudor interlude is therefore indefinable. It is merely a name applied to a disconnected and varied body of survivals, borrowings, and sporadic beginnings. The only group of dramatists which had any cohesion is made up of Henry Medwall, John Rastell, and John Heywood; and even this cohesion was due not so much to similarity of dramatic work as to association with the circle of Sir Thomas More. We have recently had restored to us an early romantic drama *Fulgens and Lucrece* by Henry Medwall, which shows in faint foreshadowing the sentiment and humor which were to characterize the work of Lyly, Peele, and Shakespeare. Medwall was also the author of a morality called *Nature*, which is not without poetic interest. Both of his plays were printed by John Rastell, with whom he was associated, like More, in the service of Cardinal Morton. Rastell, who married More's sister, certainly was the author of the moral interlude of the *Four Elements* and probably of *Gentleness and Nobility*. It has been suggested that he adapted and compiled *Calisto and Meliboea* on the basis of the Spanish comedy *Celestina;* if so, he was carrying on the tradition of the romantic drama, that is, the secular, often poetic drama, which became the stock-in-trade of Shakespeare and his contemporaries. John Heywood, son-in-law of John Rastell, was the most important and versatile dramatist of the group. All of his plays, except *Witty and Witless*, which has been preserved in manuscript, were printed by John Rastell or his son William Rastell. These form a really delightful group of significant variety. There are among them three small comic interludes, scarcely more than dialogues in form: *The Play of Love*, *The Play of the Wether*, and *Witty and Witless*. In the second of these a gentleman, a merchant, a forest ranger, a water-miller, a wind-miller, a gentlewoman, a launderer, and a small boy ("the least that can play"), all in turn petition Jupiter to send them the kind of weather that each would like to have. Of course they do not agree, so that Jupiter has to send what he pleases. There are also three farces—*The Pardoner and the Friar; John, Tib, and Sir John;* and *The Four PP*—which are of a more robust nature; so that the latest commentator thinks they were done under the manly influence of Sir Thomas More.

Early comedy Among the really important achievements of the sixteenth century are two comedies, already casually mentioned, *Ralph Roister Doister* and *Gammer Gurton's Needle*. Both show the influence of Latin comedy, and both arose from the practice in the sixteenth century of schoolmasters' presenting the comedies of Plautus and Terence, or comedies imitated from them, on stages in their schools with their scholars as actors. *Ralph Roister Doister* is the work of Nicholas Udall, and was acted probably by the boys of Westminster School between 1552 and 1554. It is perhaps the first play in English in which there is a clearly constructed plot, a rapid dialogue, and a set of characters so conceived as to furnish a dramatic clash. To be sure, the characters are in large part borrowed from Plautus and Terence, but they are sufficiently adapted to their English situation to bring the comedy through satisfactorily. It is still amusing to see on the stage. Roister Doister is a conceited braggart who pays court to a virtuous lady, Dame Custance, not for herself but for her thousand pounds. He cannot imagine being refused by her. Her refusal, when it comes, is couched in a letter which the ingenuity of his rascally servant Matthew Merrygreek construes, by changing the punctuation of clauses, into an acceptance. Roister Doister advances upon his lady-love, but is routed in warlike fashion by the lady and her maids.

Gammer Gurton's Needle was shown by the late distinguished scholar Henry Bradley to be the work of William Stevenson, fellow of Christ's College, Cambridge, and to date probably from almost exactly the same time as *Ralph Roister Doister*. It is a secular comedy in English, the only one of its kind preserved, and has about it a roaring farcical quality which suggests the English village of the sixteenth century in all its naturalness. It is much slighter in plot than *Roister Doister;* it is, in fact, a farce and not a comedy, but was done by a man who knew the movement of Latin comedy, and is, as a piece of literature, far superior to Udall's piece. A needle in the sixteenth century was, we may believe, a precious possession. Gammer Gurton, while mending her servant's breeches, loses her needle and institutes a lively search for its recovery. She suspects various people in turn of stealing it. She carries on for five acts; in the fifth and last act Hodge, her servant, painfully finds the needle in the seat of his breeches when he receives a blow. The play contains a song, a feature which was to become characteristic of English comedy:

> I cannot eat but little meat;
> My stomach is not good;
> But sure I think that I could drink
> With him that wear'th an hood.
> Drink is my life; although my wife
> Some time do chide and scold,
> Yet spare I not to ply the pot
> Of jolly good ale and old.

> *Back and side go bare, go bare;*
> *Both hand and foot grow cold;*
> *But, belly, send thee good ale enough,*
> *Whether it be new or old.*

Early tragedy In the establishment of comedy on the English stage, even in its characteristic romantic form, there was no battle of the critics in behalf of classical principles. Plautus and Terence contributed their share of technique, in the matter of comic devices and scenes, in plot, and in the matter of characterization. They were the ultimate models of Jonson and his school in the comedy of manners; but, because comedy was a freer dramatic *genre* than tragedy, the comic dramatists, liberally and without reproach, added their sentiment to the Romans' wit. But there was an essential clash between classical tragedy and the native sort, and it was necessary to invent a new kind of tragedy. The most important of the differences between classical and romantic, or Eliza-

bethan, tragedy arises from the fact that the latter chose to tell a complete story while the former contented itself with merely the climax. This is, of course, only roughly true, but it may be said to hold by and large that the classical mode concerned itself mainly with what an Elizabethan tragedy would have embodied in the fifth act. The rest of the story, so far as it needed to be known, was presented in the form of narrative. It follows that in classical tragedy narrative interest is subordinated to dramatic or lyrical interest. Most of the plots of the tragedy of the Greeks and Romans were entirely familiar to the audiences for whom they were written; the stories were already well known in literature and mythology, which to Greeks and Romans was religion. A tragedy was thus exploitation of a great event. Oratory, poetry, music, and philosophic comment, the latter usually from the mouths of a chorus, all united to produce a single great effect. Unity was thus the most striking quality of classical tragedy, and, when the tragedy was revived and restudied in the Renaissance, was regarded as all-important. Unity, which had been more or less an inevitable characteristic of classical tragedy, was understood by the dramatic critics of the Renaissance to mean, not only unity of action, but unity of time and place, and even unity of sentiment; so that the element of comedy was theoretically excluded from tragedy, because it destroyed the perfection of tragic tone. These are the views, not of the ancients themselves, but of Renaissance commentators on Aristotle; and these commentators never understood that the three unities, as they conceived them, cannot be preserved if a sweep of epic material is presented, nor that there is a different and a broader type of unity possible even when complete narratives are treated.

Sir Philip Sidney There is a possibility that romantic tragedy would never have developed in England to so high a point or been accepted as the standard form of tragedy but for two things: in the first place, very few Elizabethan dramatists knew how to write classical tragedy; and, in the second, the Elizabethan audience, with a taste for native English drama, demanded new, varied, sensational plots accompanied with clownage and vaudeville in the shape of songs and special features. Such drama was condemned by well-informed persons for following popular taste rather than classical models, but to make it comply with classical rules would have meant changing its nature. In France, where in Shakespeare's time the drama came into the control of the court and the learned classes, tragedy was transformed according to classical rules into the drama of Corneille and Racine; but in England, fortunately for the world, Shakespeare and his fellows made a virtue of their necessities and created, no doubt against their better judgment, the new form of romantic tragedy. Neither they nor their critics knew exactly what the issues were. The most famous classical reformer was Sir Philip Sidney. He has given us his views in a very charming book called *The Defence of Poesie*, written in 1581 or slightly later. One can see from the following passage how he looked at the English drama of his day:

Our tragedies and comedies not without cause cried out against, observing rules neither of honest civility nor of skilful poetry, excepting Gorboduc —again I say of those that I have seen. Which not withstanding as it is full of stately speeches and well-sounding phrases, climbing to the height of Seneca's style, and as full of notable morality, which it doth most delightfully teach, and so obtain the very end of poesy; yet in truth it is very defectious in the circumstances, which grieveth me, because it might not remain as an exact model of all tragedies. For it is faulty both in place and time, the two necessary companions of all corporal actions. For where the stage should always represent but one place, and the uttermost time presupposed in it should be, both by Aristotle's precept and common reason, but one day; there is both many days and many places inartificially imagined.

But if it be so in Gorboduc, how much more in all the rest? where you shall have Asia of the one side and Afric of the other, and so many other under-kingdoms, that the player, when he cometh in, must ever begin with telling where he is, or else the tale will not be conceived. Now ye shall have three ladies walk to gather flowers, and then we must believe the stage to be a garden. By and by we hear news of shipwreck in the same place, and then we are to blame if we accept it not for a rock. Upon the back of that comes out a hideous monster with fire and smoke, and then the miserable beholders are bound to take it for

a cave. While in the meantime two armies fly in, represented with four swords and bucklers, and then what hard heart will not receive it for a pitched field?

Now of time they are much more liberal. For ordinary it is that two young princes fall in love; after many traverses she is got with child, delivered of a fair boy, he is lost, groweth a man, falleth in love, and is ready to get another child,— and all this in two hours space; which how absurd it is in sense even sense may imagine, and art hath taught, and all ancient examples justified, and at this day the ordinary players in Italy will not err in. . . .

Later he tells us that English plays are "neither right tragedies nor right comedies," but that they mingle clowns and kings with "neither decency nor discretion."

This merrily written criticism presents an excellent picture of the conditions prevailing upon the English stage when Sidney wrote, and, as criticism from a strictly classical point of view, it is perfectly just; but after all it is just as easy for an audience to imagine the lapse of a period of twenty years with its concomitant changes as it is to imagine the lapse of a period of two hours. And if an audience is willing so far to grant any author "that willing suspension of disbelief for the moment which constitutes poetic faith," as Coleridge puts it, that they will believe one scene in the theater is in Asia instead of London, they will be equally willing to believe in the same way that another scene following it is in Africa. Human emotion, moreover, is sufficiently mobile to switch itself quickly from a serious to a comic theme and back again. In human emotion the comic, the pathetic, the grotesque, and the tragic often blend and reinforce each other in the most inexplicable ways; so that Shakespeare and his fellows seem to have had nature as well as native bias on their side.

Early Senecan tragedy The tragedy of *Gorboduc*, praised by Sidney, is an interesting work in the history of the English drama. The play was written in the Senecan manner, the first three acts by Thomas Norton and the last two by Thomas Sackville, for performance before the Queen at Whitehall in 1562. It employs, for the first time in English tragedy, blank verse, a dignified and yet flexible measure. *Gorboduc* is also a forerunner of the chronicle play, since it deals with the mythical history of Britain as recorded by Geoffrey of Monmouth in the *Historia Britonum*. The authors wished to impress upon the Queen the necessity of immediate marriage, so that England might be saved from the disorder and confusion arising from a condition in which there were rival claimants for the crown. Not only, therefore, is *Gorboduc* a forerunner of *Tamburlaine*, the first great English tragedy, in the use of blank verse and in the maintenance of a serious tragic tone; but in its use of the chronicles and its pursuance of a patriotic purpose, it is also a forerunner of the history play. In 1587 eight gentlemen of Gray's Inn, led by Thomas Hughes and including Francis Bacon, presented before the Queen a drama similar in form to *Gorboduc*, namely, *The Misfortunes of Arthur*. It violates the unities, as does *Gorboduc*, but it differs from *Gorboduc* in borrowing from Seneca, not only chorus, messengers, and machinery, but ideas, sentiments, and words. *The Misfortunes of Arthur* again resorts to the chronicle history of Britain, which became one of the chief sources of the subject-matter of tragedy.

The other principal source of tragic themes was the Italian short story, which, because it was also impassioned and serious, offered to writers of tragedy many themes. *Gismond of Salerne* dramatizes a well-known Italian tale, and, like *Gorboduc* and *The Misfortunes of Arthur*, is Senecan in form and nature. It was acted before the Queen in 1568. In the same magazine of narrative Shakespeare was later to find his sources for *Romeo and Juliet* and *Othello* and for such tragi-comedies as *The Merchant of Venice* and *Measure for Measure*.

The Countess of Pembroke Seneca's tragedies were published in English in 1581, and there was at least one attempt to win the English stage to Seneca. It was made by Lady Mary Sidney, the Countess of Pembroke, sister of Sir Philip Sidney, whose *Defence of Poesie* we have already mentioned. She undertook, largely as a labor of love and loyalty to her great brother, we may believe, to introduce the Senecan form of tragedy to English readers. She was not in a position to have her tragedy

this earliest form of the prose romance reflects the adventurous life which they lived. Such romances, as written by Helio-dorus, Achilles Tatius, and others, are made up of a succession of strange and often im-probable adventures, chance meetings, pi-racies, children exposed in infancy and re-stored grown and beautiful to their parents, families separated and re-united, indistin-guishable twins, and many of the plot devices rendered familiar to us in the literature of the Renaissance; for the Renaissance in its thirst for antiquity did not distinguish between this kind of sensationalism and the real classics. From the Greek novel, and also no doubt from his own experience in life, Greene got the new conception of woman which the world has learned from Shakespeare. The society depicted by the Greek novel gave women great liberty, and like them Greene's heroines are independent, witty, resourceful, and boylike, though at the same time feminine. Greene's dramas are almost the first modern productions in which woman is in any degree represented as assuming her station as the friend and companion of man. The Greek novel itself had a large element of the pastoral, and here again we find a parallel with Greene. His plays, particularly *James IV* and *Friar Bacon and Friar Bungay*, give us that blend of the pastoral and the romantic which the world has enjoyed in *As You Like It* and *Love's Labour's Lost*. Greene must be regarded as the first great master of plot in the English drama. Toward the wretched end of his life he wrote many pamphlets, some about London roguery, some about his own hard usage at the hands of the world. In one of the latter, *A Groatsworth of Wit Bought with a Million of Repentance* (1592), he gave us our first personal reference to Shake-speare, a circumstance which must engage our attention later. One should point out that it is not Shakespeare only who felt the influence of Greene, but Munday, Dekker, and most of the popular dramatists of the next decade.

Thomas Kyd While romantic comedy was being shaped and developed in the hands of Lyly, Peele, and Greene, the Senecan tradition was finding its proponents on the popular stage, which had chosen just the parts of Senecan tragedy which suited its purpose. This appears from a large number of crude native dramas to which Seneca has added an element of intensity and sensationalism, while they still retain clownage and disorderly action. It remained for the genius of Thomas Kyd (1558-94) to seize upon the essentials of Senecan action and adapt them to conditions on the English stage. What he produced was *The Spanish Tragedy* (1583-4?), a stirring melodrama in blank verse and the pattern of subsequent revenge plays, acted perhaps a thousand times during the next fifteen years. Kyd caught the unabashed brutality and horror of Senecan story and revealed it openly. Instead of having the action re-ported as taking place off the stage, he presented it. For tales of Greek mythology he substituted a modern story of love, con-spiracy, murder, and political intrigue. He retained the Senecan ghost, the revenge motive, the spirit of stoicism, and a modified form of the chorus. He tells the tale of the revenge of Hieronimo whose son, Horatio, had been seized and hanged in the garden of his father's house by Balthazar and Lorenzo, his rival in love and his enemy in politics. Hieronimo feigns insanity and waits for his revenge. Ultimately in a masque which he had written for the enter-tainment of the court, Hieronimo plays a part and stabs in deadly earnest his enemies, who were also actors in the tragic masque. Kyd is also probably the author of the first dramatic version of the story of Hamlet, an important circumstance to be treated later.

Christopher Marlowe Kyd's work gave rise to a series of revenge plays not only in his own time, but later, in 1600 and the years following, when the revenge tragedy again became fashionable. Moreover, Kyd seems to have had a shaping influence on Greene and on Christopher Marlowe (1564-1593). *The Spanish Tragedy* probably preceded by three or four years Marlowe's *Tamburlaine*, which is conjecturally dated 1587, and which in turn became a pattern for Greene's earliest play, *Alphonsus, King of Aragon*. In blank verse style Kyd was therefore the forerunner of Marlowe, whose *Jew of Malta* (c. 1589) in its extravagance and sensational intrigue seems to follow *The Spanish Trag-edy*. Nevertheless, however much Kyd may have contributed in matters of style and form, the fact remains that Marlowe became the leader in the great romantic type of Elizabethan tragedy; he it is who shaped the *genre* subsequently perfected by Shakespeare. This he achieved by giving the English drama a hero more striking even than Hieronimo and by centering dramatic interest in personality and character; for the aspiring spirit of the Renaissance finds expression in Marlowe's heroes. Tamburlaine has a thirst for world conquest; Dr. Faustus would go to the utmost bounds of knowledge and the power which knowledge gives; and Barabas in *The Jew of Malta* sets no limit to his longing for wealth. Back of Marlowe lies the hero-worship of the times, which had expressed itself in a taste for ballads and romances and in plays from mediæval romance, a veritable worship of deeds. There is little idea of structure or tragic conflict in *Tamburlaine*. It was enough for the Elizabethan playgoer to behold the Scythian warrior proceeding from conquest to conquest and to hear him "threatening the world with high astounding terms." The plot is merely a series of episodes. The same is true of *Dr. Faustus* (c. 1588), so far as the theme itself would permit merely successive action; but Faustus sells his soul to the common enemy of mankind, and, when the day of payment comes, the situation of Faustus becomes tragic. In the last scene of the play, therefore, Marlowe reaches the first high point in the structural progress of English tragedy in the concrete representation of the struggle of a human soul. The play is thus a series of episodes enveloped by a tragic theme. In *The Jew of Malta* Marlowe treats a melodramatic plot, but makes no use of the tragic principle of the conflict of characters. Whether he makes use of this principle in *Edward II* (c. 1592) is a matter of doubt. In that play Marlowe does not center the interest in the psychology of one character only, as in the earlier plays, but introduces a succession of characters in opposition to his hero. The protagonist of tragedy Marlowe had re-invented, and he needed only to embody his adversative forces in one character to have the antagonist also. It is doubtful indeed whether the principle of the interplay of two characters,

one upon another, was hit upon by anybody before Shakespeare. In *Richard II* Shakespeare has, in the person of the king, a great central figure whom he exploits after the Marlowan fashion; but, possibly because his plot was so much like that which Marlowe had used in *Edward II*, he placed over against King Richard the contrasting figure of Bolingbroke and thus discovered that principle which he was later to use in *Othello* and *Iago* and in whole groups of contrasting characters as they appear in *Julius Cæsar*, *King Lear*, and other plays. *Richard III* and *Henry V* are dramas of Marlowan technique, and so even is *Hamlet*, though of course the epic quality which comes from Marlowe is much slighter in *Hamlet* than in the others.

Even if Marlowe himself never consciously employed the principle of dramatic conflict, he gave to English tragedy its realization of character and still more its dignity and seriousness. Marlowe was educated at Cambridge, was a good scholar and a born poet. He it was who gave to the English drama the aspiration of the Renaissance. Shakespeare was to be followed by a group of realists and satirists, but fortunately, be it said again, he was early enough in his appearance to catch the enthusiasm for beauty which Spenser and Marlowe had. Not the least among Marlowe's gifts to English drama is blank verse, which he wrote in a new and more flexible way. In this matter he was conscious of what he was doing. In the following familiar lines which constitute the prologue to *Tamburlaine the Great*, part one, it will be seen that Marlowe does not treat each blank verse line as a separate unit, but runs the sense on from line to line and produces what might be described as a blank verse paragraph, a thing most necessary to the drama if it was to represent widely varying emotions, thoughts, and characters:

From jigging veins of rhyming mother wits,
And such conceits as clownage keeps in pay,
We'll lead you to the stately tent of war,
Where you shall hear the Scythian Tamburlaine
Threat'ning the world with high astounding
　　terms,
And scourging kingdoms with his conquering
　　sword.

View but his picture in this tragic glass,
And then applaud his fortunes as you please.

This is not only the pronunciamento of
tragic seriousness; it is also, in spite of its
elevated style, one of the first examples in
English tragedy of vigorous, natural,
straightforward expression. Tamburlaine
in his utterances is a typical Renaissance
poet on the themes of both love and war;
and the following lines, almost as familiar
to students of the English drama as those
just quoted, will express the insatiable quality of Marlowe's aspiration:

If all the pens that ever poets held
Had fed the feeling of their masters' thoughts,
And every sweetness that inspir'd their hearts,
Their minds, and muses on admired themes;
If all the heavenly quintessence they still
From their immortal flowers of poesy,
Wherein, as in a mirror, we perceive
The highest reaches of a human wit;
If these had made one poem's period,
And all combin'd in beauty's worthiness,
Yet should there hover in their restless heads
One thought, one grace, one wonder, at the least,
Which into words no virtue can digest.
                    —*Tamburlaine*, Pt. I, V, ii, 98-110.

One feels that but for Marlowe Shakespeare
might not have talked so bravely about
"the young-eyed cherubim" or the "lights
that do mislead the morn."

Elements of tragedy and comedy in Shakespeare   Shakespearean tragedy is thus to be
described roughly as
a combination of
Marlowe and Kyd: poetry, character, and
style from Marlowe; motive, plot, and tragic
intensity from Kyd. It was for Shakespeare
himself in some of his great plays, such as
Richard II, *Julius Cæsar*, *Othello*, and *King
Lear*, to make tragic action spring from
tragic motive. One cannot say that Shakespeare was conscious of the thing he was
doing. He was "holding the mirror up to
nature," and showing "virtue her own feature, scorn her own image, and the very age
and body of the time his form and pressure."
He achieved the perfect union of action and
character in the first instance possibly because it resided in certain stories which he
chose to tell, such as that of Hamlet or of
Richard II. Great art does not need to be
conscious of its ways. All that one can say

of Shakespeare and Aristotelian tragedy is
that sometimes, when Shakespeare is telling
a story of universal human significance, he
does exemplify Aristotelian principles.
Greene and many others sought to imitate
Marlowe in tragedy with but indifferent success. Shakespeare was Marlowe's only
successful imitator, and he bettered Marlowe
by humanizing him and rendering him more
natural.

Likewise the elements of Shakespearean
comedy are in part derivative from Lyly,
Peele, and Greene. The contributions of
Lyly and Peele were those of style, setting, and movement. Greene, primarily a
writer of romance, an adapter of the Greek
novel, furnished the element of love and
adventure which makes so many Elizabethan plays delightful merely as stories;
and, although there are not many women
in comedy and tragedy who illustrate the
type, one acknowledges that it was Greene
who put upon the stage the witty, independ-
ent-minded woman, usually in boy's clothes,
who gives point and naturalness to love
intrigue whether in serious drama or in
comedy. Not only did Shakespeare, who
was a far greater genius than any of them,
combine the elements of the comedies of
these men and better the instruction, but
he realized on a broad scale, as his career
went on, the possibilities of the comic point
of view in the representation of human
life and character. Atmosphere in his
comedies reinforces plot, and plot gives
rise to character. Even the simple ep-
isodic clownage of his predecessors becomes
organic in his hands and contributes to
the total artistic effect he chooses to produce.

All in all, we find Shakespeare falling
heir to a form which through three centuries
of religious drama had become endeared
to the tastes of the popular mind, and which
had, in the early sixteenth century interlude,
undergone a process of development at the
hands of conscious creators. This traditional
pattern, enriched in material by the wide
interests of the Renaissance, and infused
with new spirit by his immediate predecessors, offered to Shakespeare an instrument
which under his touch became a transcendent artistic medium for the depiction
of human emotions and experiences.

REFERENCES

CHAMBERS, E. K., *The Elizabethan Stage.* Four vols. Oxford, 1923. This important work supplements and completes the same author's *The Mediæval Stage.* Two vols. Oxford, 1903. Both books have extensive bibliographies.

The following works may be more readily available and will often be more comprehensible:

ADAMS, J. Q., *Shakespearean Playhouses.* Boston, 1917.

BOAS, F. S., *Shakspere and his Predecessors.* London and New York, 1896.

BOND, R. W., *Early Plays from the Italian.* Oxford, 1911.

BROOKE, C. F. TUCKER, *The Tudor Drama.* Boston, 1912.

CREIZENACH, W., *The English Drama in the Age of Shakespeare.* London, 1916. This is translated from the fourth volume of the writer's comprehensive and important *Geschichte des neueren Dramas*, 1893-1916.

GREG, W. W., *A List of English Plays written before 1643 and printed before 1700.* Bibliographical Society, 1900. *A List of Masques, Pageants, etc.*, Bibliographical Society, 1902.

REED, A. W., *Early Tudor Drama.* London, 1926.

SCHELLING, F. E., *Elizabethan Drama.* Two vols. Boston, 1908. *The English Chronicle Play.* New York, 1902. *English Literature during the Lifetime of Shakespeare.* New York, 1910. Other works by the same important author.

STOPES, Mrs. C. C., *The Life of Henry, Third Earl of Southampton.* Cambridge, 1922. Other works by the same author.

Texts of the plays will be found in the following works:

ADAMS, J. Q., *Chief Pre-Shakespearean Dramas.* Boston, 1924.

BRANDL, ALOIS. *Quellen des weltlichen Dramas in England vor Shakespeare.* Strassburg, 1898.

DODSLEY, ROBERT, *A Collection of Old English Plays*, edited by W. C. Hazlitt, 1874-1876.

GAYLEY, C. M., *Representative English Comedies.* Three vols. New York, 1903-1914.

Malone Society Reprints, 1906 ff.

MANLY, J. M., *Specimens of the Pre-Shakespearean Drama.* Two vols. Boston, 1897.

Materialien zur Kunde des älteren englischen Dramas. Louvain, edited by W. Bang, 1902-1915; 1926 ff.

Mermaid Series, *The Best Plays of the Old Dramatists.*

POLLARD, A. W., *English Miracle Plays, Moralities and Interludes.* Seventh ed. London, 1923.

Student's Facsimile Edition, *Old English Plays*, 1909-1914, edited by J. S. Farmer.

Tudor Facsimile Texts, edited by J. S. Farmer, 1909-1913.

Most of the remains of the mystery and morality plays have been edited for the Early English Text Society: The Towneley plays, the Chester plays, the so-called Coventry plays and the two remaining fragments of the true Coventry plays, the non-cycle plays, the Digby plays, and the Macro morals. The York plays were edited for the Clarendon Press by Miss Lucy Toulmin Smith in 1884, and the ancient Cornish cycle was published with a translation by E. Norris in 1859.

Mention should also be made of the modern collected editions of Shakespeare's early contemporaries; as J. Churton Collins's *Greene*, F. S. Boas's *Kyd*, R. W. Bond's *Lyly*, R. H. Case's *Marlowe*, R. B. McKerrow's *Nashe*.

IV. LONDON THEATERS AND DRAMATIC COMPANIES

Religious and moral opposition to the stage The propriety of acting any plays at all was throughout Shakespeare's life a matter of bitter controversy. Indeed, when one considers the power and earnestness of the opposition, one is surprised that there could come into being such a wealth of dramatic excellence, and that Shakespeare's plays should reflect so little the bitterness of the controversy which was waged in his time. The Puritans objected to the plays because they thought them immoral. The Puritan city of London was naturally the headquarters of this opposition. By an order of the Common Council of London, dated December 6, 1574, the players were driven out of the city. The order cites the reasons. The players, it was charged, had been acting in the inn-yards of the city, which in consequence were haunted by great multitudes of people, especially youths. These gatherings had been the occasions of frays and quarrels, "evil practices of incontinency in great inns"; the players published "uncomely and immodest speeches and doings," withdrew the Queen's subjects from divine service on Sundays and holidays, wasted the money of "poor and fond persons," gave opportunity to pickpockets, uttered "busy and seditious matters," and injured and maimed people by engines, by the falling of their scaffolds, and by weapons and powder used in plays. The order goes on to state the Common Council's fear that if the plays, which had been forbidden on account of the plague, should be resumed, God's wrath would manifest itself by an increase of the infection. Therefore no inn-keeper, tavern-keeper, or other person, might cause or suffer to be openly played "any play, interlude, comedy, tragedy, matter, or show" which had not been first licensed by the mayor and the court of aldermen. The mayor and aldermen did not, in this order and elsewhere, always state their case plainly, because the Queen was a patron of the players, and because the players had friends and patrons in the Privy Council and among the nobility; sometimes, however, they did so quite boldly. One sees the case against plays stated syllogistically in the following words of Thomas White, a preacher at Paul's cross in 1577:

Looke but vppon the common playes of London, and see the multitude that flocketh to them and followeth them: beholde the sumptuous Theater houses, a continuall monument of London prodigalitie and folly. But I vnderstande they are now forbidden bycause of the plague. I like the pollicye well if it hold still, for a disease is but bodged or patched vp that is not cured in the cause, and the cause of plagues is sinne, if you looke to it well: and the cause of sinne are playes: therfore the cause of plagues are playes.[1]

Moved no doubt by the prohibition of the Common Council, James Burbage, with a company of actors under the patronage of the Earl of Leicester, leased a site in Shoreditch, a London suburb in Middlesex, beyond the immediate jurisdiction of the official enemies in the Common Council, whose authority extended only to the city limits. By 1576 he had completed the Theater. This building was in general patterned after the inn-yard, being open to the sky and having galleries round about like the porches and balconies of the inn-

yard, with a stage at one side and dressing rooms back of it. Because he expected that the same building would be used for bear-baiting and bull-baiting, he made it circular in form. The Theater thus became the model for all the public playhouses later constructed, such as the Curtain, the Swan, and the Globe.

Burbage had in this manner availed himself of that immunity from the enforcement of law which arises from indirect jurisdiction. The city fathers could not suppress plays nor control them with perfect success if they were performed in Middlesex or on the famous Bankside across the Thames in Surrey. In order to get at them in these suburban regions it was necessary to petition the Queen's Privy Council to give orders to the magistrates and officers of the law in these counties. The Queen's Privy Council, although always on the most polite terms with the Lord Mayor and his brethren of the city and always open to the argument that the assemblage of crowds caused the spread of the plague, were to a much less degree in sympathy with the moral scruples of the City. There were, moreover, current arguments for the plays, derived from the works of scholars, poets, and playwrights; namely, that there was precedent in antiquity for dramatic spectacles; that by drawing a true picture of both the bad and the good in life, plays enabled men to choose the good; that the people should have wholesome amusement; and that plays provided livelihood for loyal subjects of the Queen. Of these arguments the Privy Council made little use, resting the case for plays on what was no doubt an unanswerable argument—that, since the players were to appear before her Majesty, the players needed practice in order to prepare themselves to please the royal taste. There was a good deal of politic fencing over the whole matter, and, so far as orders, complaints, and denunciations are concerned, the Puritan opposition had much the better of it. The preachers thundered against plays. Pamphleteers denounced all matters pertaining to the stage: Stephen Gosson in *The Schoole of Abuse, Containing a pleasant invectiue against Poets, Pipers, plaiers, Iesters and such like Caterpillars of a Commonwealth* (1579) and other works;

[1] From *A Sermon preached at Paules Cross . . . in the time of the Plague.* By T. W. London, 1578.

Philip Stubbes in *The Anatomie of Abuses* (1583); and finally and most furiously of all, William Prynne in *Histrio-Mastix: the Players Scourge or Actors Tragedy* (1633). Gosson spoke of plays as "the inventions of the devil, the offerings of idolatry, the pomp of worldlings, the blossoms of vanity, the root of apostacy, food of iniquity, riot and adultery." "Detest them," he warns. "Players are masters of vice, teachers of wantonness, spurs to impurity, the sons of idleness." Since such extreme bitterness is hardly warranted by what we know of the Elizabethan drama or the men who created it, we look for an explanation of the Puritan opposition in the not unexpected quarter of political and religious partisanship. Though the subject-matter of plays had become somewhat less biblical and their connection with any branch of the church was broken, they were associated from their origin with the old religion; therefore to have the people cling to them was, in the minds of Puritan leaders, to have them cling to idolatry and adopt the fashions of the Catholic continent. Because of their banishment from the city and from the favor of the more godly classes of people, plays and players were thrown into bad company. Shoreditch and the Bankside were low and vicious regions. Plays were patronized by the idle and the ungodly. Fortunately they were also patronized by the Queen, the highest nobility, and by many cultivated and intelligent persons. In spite, however, of the strength and virulence of the opposition, the theater flourished. One does not know just how it managed to do so.

The public theaters A year or more after Burbage built the Theater, Philip Henslowe made his first venture as a theater-builder and put up near it the Curtain. About ten years later Henslowe built the Rose, the first playhouse on the Bankside. The Swan was built there in 1594, and in 1599 Richard and Cuthbert Burbage, sons of James Burbage, the former being the great actor of Shakespeare's heroes, tore down the Theater because of trouble about the lease of the land, and rebuilt it as the Globe on the Bankside. The Globe, a round structure, was burned June 29, 1613, from cannon wadding which set fire to the roof after the discharge of

ordnance during the acting of a play called *All is True*, thought to be identical with Shakespeare's *Henry VIII*. The Globe was quickly rebuilt in octagonal form. In 1614 Henslowe built the Fortune, specifications for which have been preserved at Dulwich College with the other invaluable papers of the old theater manager. This college, it may be said in passing, was founded by the munificence of the great actor Edward Alleyn, who had married Henslowe's step-daughter. Henslowe's Fortune Theater was apparently a counter-move to the activities of the Burbage group, who constituted a joint stock company for the support of the King's company, whereas Henslowe operated as theater proprietor. He managed the Lord Admiral's men and secured, we may be sure, a large part of the profits of their activities. The contract for building the Fortune was let to the same contractor who had built the new Globe, and, since it was specified that it should be like the Globe in all its main features, except that it was to be square instead of octagonal, we may gain from these specifications an idea of the Globe. There is also preserved a drawing of the Swan, a Bankside theater, which accompanies a description of the playhouse by Johannes De Witt, who visited London in 1596. The drawing, which was discovered in the University Library at Utrecht, is the work of one Van Buchell and may be based on drawings by De Witt himself. Besides these there are two or three little pictures of the Elizabethan public stage on the title-pages of published plays, the most important being that on the title-page of William Alabaster's *Roxana* (1630).

The public stage From these documents and pictures and from scattered references to the theaters, and also from extended studies of stage directions and scenic conditions in plays themselves, it has come about that we have a fairly clear idea of the public stage. Its features are these: a pit, usually circular and open to the sky; surrounding this, galleries in three tiers, where were the most expensive seats; a rectangular stage, longer than it was broad, sometimes on trestles, so that it could be removed if the house was also customarily used for bear-baiting and bull-baiting. Part of the stage was covered by a sort of wooden awning, which might constitute "the heavens." At the back of the stage was a partition wall with at least two doors opening out of the actors' dressing rooms. Between these two doors a third opening, probably wide and curtained off, led to the rear-stage, a recess ordinarily used for interior scenes, such as bed-chambers, grottoes, caves, and tombs. An arras, or curtain, was stretched along the back wall, just how far from it one cannot tell. Over the inner-room behind the stage was a gallery used for city walls, upper windows, and all sorts of high places. Above this in turn arose a turret from the top of which a flag was hung out when a play was about to begin, and from which, for further advertisement, a trumpeter blew three blasts to announce the opening of the performance.

One still encounters serious difficulties in understanding the staging of Elizabethan plays. For example, though some of the seats most prized by the spectators were those in the gallery behind the stage, it is hard to perceive how such persons could have seen and heard while the recess was in use or while action was going on under the canopy. One does, however, get an excellent idea of the general conditions and, particularly, of how the Elizabethan public stage got along with the same scenic conditions as those of the miracles and morality plays, namely, actors on a central platform and the audience around them on every side. From such a situation we can understand the close intimacy between the actor and the audience, some of whom possibly sat on the stage, and the consequent opportunities as well as difficulties which were before the dramatist.[1]

This public stage of the London theaters represents a development, through intermediate adaptations for inn-yard performances, from the early pageants of the religious drama. When the players of Tudor interludes resorted to inn-yards to act their plays in towns and cities, they carried with

them two general features from the mediæval stage: a stage of three dimensions, like the individual pageants of the Corpus Christi plays, and a central multiple stage like that shown in the famous drawing of *The Castle of Perseverance*, in which the play was performed in a central area with the spectators seated or standing round about it. This was originally an out-of-doors stage with a central playing "place" and various *loca* or *sedes* for particular minor actions. In other words, features from both the pageant stage and the multiple stage were used in the interlude as acted in inn-yards. Later the inn-yard stage was adopted by James Burbage for use in the Theater.

The court stage   Meanwhile, another type of stage, on which some, at least, of Shakespeare's plays were written to be performed, found favor in London; namely, the so-called court stage, one designed for indoor performance and set up in a hall or, in later times, in a roofed-in theater. Indirectly it was a development from the ancient classical theater, at least as regards a fixed structural background, which suggested, if it did not enforce, unity of place. This type of stage came to England from Italy, where there had been preserved, or rather regained, some knowledge of the ancient stage. Such changes of scene as the Italian drama allowed were provided for by the introduction of properties or possibly by labels over the fixed structures at the rear. These fixed structures provided background, essentially a classical element.

The problem which the European stage was engaged for centuries in solving was not, however, continuity of scenes, but change of scenes. France and most of the continent had during the Renaissance accepted the mediæval solution of the difficulty by adopting a multiple stage, like that of *The Castle of Perseverance* mentioned above, in which the audience was asked to believe for the purpose of the drama that a series of independent structures within a few feet of each other represented places as far apart as Rome and Jerusalem, or Heaven and Hell. We see this, for example, in the picture of the stage of the passion play at Valenciennes. This stage, as naïve as the games of children, had been used

---

[1] On the many perplexities connected with both the public and the court stages, see Schelling, *Eliz. Drama*, Vol. II, ch. iv, and the references there given; also Baker, *The Development of Sh. as a Dramatist*, pp. 75-6, *et passim*, and Chambers, *Eliz. Stage*, Bk. IV.

in all European countries in the Middle Ages. There are cases in the Corpus Christi play where two or more quite distant places were conceived of as being located on different parts of the same pageant wagon. Sidney and others who knew the classical drama felt deeply the absurdity of this convention; but the actual convention appears in Tudor drama and even in Shakespeare more than once. An instance occurs in the fifth act of *Richard III*, where the tents of the rival commanders, Richard and Richmond, are conventionally located on opposite sides of the same narrow stage. Although the convention is usually not so apparent as here, the principle continued in the wide use of the unlocated scene, which was simply a "general" scene descended from the *platea*, or unlocated middle area, of the mediæval stage. The stage managers, however, brought up trees through the trap, let down thrones or gallowses, and carried in tables, chairs, or even beds.

Such changes of scene as could be provided for in the background were possible only on the court stage. We know certainly that for the court stage "houses" made of lath and canvas were erected, analogous to the *case* of the Italian stages. Certain features of the public stage had, however, been borrowed from the court stage, such as the two side doors with a central aperture and the rear tapestry or arras sometimes painted in perspective with attempts at foreshortening to represent the houses of a city street. All such fixation of background indicates continental influence. Oxford, Cambridge, and London had many direct connections with Italy by which such influences could become effective. Italian plays were translated and Italian players visited England. There may also have been slighter Italian influences from France into which Italian elements had made their way.

The court stage, then, brought with it certain features of another set of theatrical conditions different from those of the native traditional stage. However, it did not bring them very perfectly into England. This deficiency is due, no doubt, to two factors. In the first place, the hall or court drama in its most primitive form was probably acted simply on the floor of a hall with the more noble guests looking down on it from a raised dais, the inferior guests moving aside to give it room. On the other hand, the public theaters, like the Globe, had pretty thoroughly established scenic conventions before the roofed-in theaters like Blackfriars were very much used. English tradition, as we have seen, followed the statuesque type of stage which was to be looked at from all sides like a group of statuary. The continental stage was more picture-like and to be looked at from the front only.

It must not be thought that the continental stage succeeded widely in England or played a large part in Shakespeare's staging; but it was known, advocated, and had a certain influence both on the form of the stage and on the drama. When Polonius speaks of "scene individible, or poem unlimited," he is recognizing the continuity of action in one place, which was admired in Shakespeare's time, and which Shakespeare himself respects up to a certain point, in most of his comedies. The great matter, to be sure, is that all these theatrical conditions affected Shakespeare; for no dramatist, whether Shakespeare, Sophocles, or Molière, can be entirely independent of stage conditions, and no dramatist can be properly appreciated unless one understands what parts and qualities of his work are there because of the necessities which conditioned him in the telling of his dramatic story.

London court theaters The important court theaters of Shakespeare's London were two in the precinct, or "liberty," of Blackfriars, an early one in Whitefriars about which little is known, a later one there, and a theater at Paul's, the exact location and nature of which is not well known. On the sloping ground between St. Paul's Cathedral and the river had been established in the thirteenth century, as the mother house of the Dominican friars, or Blackfriars, a great institution, which ultimately covered about five acres of ground. It stood on the very border of the city, and, after the custom of the time, was made a liberty; that is to say, it had its own local government and was removed from the immediate jurisdiction of the city of London. After the suppression of the friary and the confiscation of its lands, the jealousy existing between the Privy Council, representing the crown, and the mayor and aldermen, representing the city and probably also the rights of property-holders, prevented the district of the Blackfriars from losing its political independence of the municipality. It was still a liberty, and, therefore, offered a fair chance for the encroachments on the part of those who wanted plays upon those who regarded them as sinful abominations. No doubt also Blackfriars gathered into its precincts many persons whose activities were slightly beyond the pale of the law; but there were also aristocratic residents in the region who demanded protection, and the crown had certain rights still in its control.

From 1576 to 1584 the Children of the Queen's Chapel, one of the two most important companies of boy actors, had used a hall in the precinct of Blackfriars in which to act their plays, and here were acted some, at least, of Lyly's plays and also Peele's *Arraignment of Paris*. In 1596 James Burbage purchased property in this precinct and seems to have spent a good deal of money in its adaptation for use as an indoor theater. He probably appreciated its advantages over Cripplegate or the Bankside, particularly for use in winter. But the aristocratic residents of the Blackfriars by petition to the Privy Council prevented him from making use of his theater. Plays within the city proper had just been finally and successfully prohibited, and the petitioners no doubt objected to their intrusion into Blackfriars on the grounds that they and their crowds were a nuisance. Burbage's new indoor theater may have lain idle from the time of its preparation until 1600; but, in any case, in that year it became the scene of many plays. It was let by lease to a group of men for the use of the Children of the Chapel, who in 1604 became the Children of the Queen's Revels. These theater managers brought into their service a number of new dramatists, Jonson, Marston, Chapman, and later Webster; the vogue of the plays acted by the Children of the Chapel was so great as to damage the patronage of the established companies and to compel them to go on the road. Out of this rivalry between the children and the adult actors arose that "War of the Theaters"

alluded to in *Hamlet* (II, ii). In 1608 the Burbage interests secured the evacuation of the lease, so that the theater in Blackfriars became the winter playhouse of Shakespeare's company from that time forward.

The licensing of players In 1572 common players of interludes, along with minstrels, bearwards, and fencers, were included within the hard terms of the act for the punishment of vagabonds, provided that such common players were not enrolled as the servants of a baron of the realm or of some honorable person of greater degree. The result was the system of patronage of theatrical companies in Elizabethan and Jacobean times, according to which players became the "servants" of some nobleman or of some member of the royal family. There were in existence before Shakespeare came to London more than a dozen of these companies, some of them long antedating the passage of the act of 1572. In the provincial records of the visits of players to various towns and cities it is sometimes difficult, however, to tell whether we have to do with actors or with acrobats, since other public performers, as well as players, were similarly organized; but, at any rate, we may say that there were in London about the time that Shakespeare arrived there companies of players under the patronage of the Queen, the Earl of Worcester, the Earl of Leicester, the Earl of Oxford, the Earl of Sussex, the Lord Admiral, and Charles, Lord Howard of Effingham. The companies were gradually to be very greatly reduced in number, so that there were usually only three adult companies acting in London during Shakespeare's prime. In addition to these were the children's companies, privately controlled, acting intermittently, but at times very successfully. The most important of these were the Children of the Chapel and Queen's Revels and the Children of Paul's; but there were also boy players of Windsor, Eton College, The Merchant Taylors, Westminster, and other schools.

Shakespeare and the Lord Chamberlain's Company Since, in the first mention of Shakespeare as an actor and in all subsequent notices of him in that capacity, he is associated with the group of men originally under the patronage of the Earl of Leicester, the most probable supposition is that he joined that group when he first came to London and remained with them throughout his career. This is strengthened by the consideration that, if he served an apprenticeship as an actor, which along with his fellow-actors he may have done, there would have been no reason for mentioning him until he became a full-fledged member of a company. His obscurity during the period from about 1587 to 1594 would thus be accounted for. The first mention of Shakespeare indicates that he was a regular member of a company in 1594, and, if one subtracts the seven years' apprenticeship period from this, one accounts for the "seven dark years." If he began his work as a playwright before his apprenticeship was over, as he may well have done, his career would be normal and intelligible. It has been ordinarily thought that the Earl of Leicester's men formed the nucleus of a company, reconstructed under the patronage of Lord Strange about 1590-1, known after September 25, 1593, as Lord Derby's men. This in turn probably became the new company of the Lord Chamberlain in 1594 of which Shakespeare was a member when he was first mentioned. But the matter is somewhat complicated. In 1594 the theatrical companies had for four or five years been greatly disturbed in their membership, so that there is much likelihood that the Lord Chamberlain's company of 1594 was made up of various elements. Shakespeare's apprenticeship, if he served one, may, therefore, have been in some other company besides that successively under the patronage of the Earl of Leicester, Lord Strange, and the Earl of Derby, supposing that this company was in a true sense continuous. The important features of the alignment of 1594 are these: A company, with Edward Alleyn as its principal actor and the Lord Admiral as its patron, reconstructed itself to act in Henslowe's theaters; and a company, with Richard Burbage as its principal actor and the Lord Chamberlain and later the King as its patrons, reconstituted itself as an independent stock company to act at the Theater, the Globe, and the Blackfriars.

Thus were the two great rival companies formed, the first-mentioned already illuminated through the activities of its great tragedian, Edward Alleyn, acting in the plays of Marlowe and Greene, and henceforth to be served by the dramatists Dekker, Chettle, Drayton, Munday, and Middleton; and the second, then less popular, but subsequently to become far the more important, through the activities of the great tragic actor, Richard Burbage, and the plays of Shakespeare, Jonson, and Beaumont and Fletcher. This latter company had, besides Burbage, for whom Shakespeare wrote his great tragic parts, John Heminge, or Heminges, Augustine Phillips, Will Kemp, Henry Condell, and other competent actors.

Shakespeare possibly a member of Lord Pembroke's company We owe to Professor Adams and other recent writers on Shakespeare the interesting and, on some grounds, plausible argument that Shakespeare was first associated with Lord Pembroke's company. This theory is based on the belief that two of his plays, *Titus Andronicus* and *1 Henry VI*, as well as several other plays which he subsequently rewrote, were originally in the repertory of Lord Pembroke's company. The following piece of stage history also bears on this question: The Earl of Leicester's company is supposed to have passed in 1588 into the patronage of Ferdinand Stanley, Lord Strange, who in 1593 became the Earl of Derby, a circumstance which caused a change in the name of the company. It happens that for this company we have for the year 1592 particularly full records. During this year it was acting in one of the theaters—the Rose or Newington Butts—owned and operated by Philip Henslowe, who left behind him his famous *Diary*, found in the papers of his son-in-law, Edward Alleyn, at Dulwich College. This diary is a sort of journal or account-book in which Henslowe entered sums of money taken in at the plays and amounts paid for various manuscripts or lent on account to various actors and dramatists. Of the plays of Shakespeare which are believed to have been written before 1594, not one is certainly mentioned by Henslowe as acted by Lord Strange's players during their engagement with Henslowe in 1592; nor does Shakespeare's name appear in two different lists which have been elsewhere preserved of the members of Lord Strange's company. Henslowe, however, does mention a play of "harey the vi," which has sometimes been thought to indicate a connection with Shakespeare, and a play of "Tittus and Vespacia," thought without sufficient reason to be *Titus Andronicus*. And three plays associated with Shakespeare's name, *Titus Andronicus*, *The Taming of a Shrew*, and a *Hamlet* (probably an early play on the same subject as Shakespeare's masterpiece) were, according to the *Diary*, acted in Henslowe's theater during the brief period in 1594 in which the Lord Chamberlain's company was acting in conjunction with the Lord Admiral's men. All three were probably old plays, and although they were new to Henslowe's theater he does not mark them, according to his custom, as "ne." They had not appeared when Lord Strange's men were acting with Henslowe in 1592. Had Shakespeare brought them in from elsewhere into the newly formed Lord Chamberlain's company? This question remains unanswered.

Further detail about the Pembroke plays Although publishers were eager enough to issue them, plays did not ordinarily get into print unless the company found it no longer profitable to act them, or unless the owners disposed of them to the printers in some unusual circumstances. It happens that several plays which had evidently belonged to Lord Pembroke's company were printed in 1594, some of which are plays connected with Shakespeare's name. The company, which had started out prosperously about 1590 with Marlowe as chief dramatist and the Earl of Pembroke as generous patron, fell into adversity. All plays in London were, at the end of June, 1592, stopped by order of the Privy Council because of riots among London apprentices. Before the theaters could open again the plague made its appearance, and they were again interdicted for a period of nearly two years, except for a little while in December and January, 1592-3. We know from a letter from Henslowe to his son-in-law Alleyn, dated September 28, 1593, that the Earl of Pembroke's company, which like other companies had taken to the road, failed in their tour of the provinces and were obliged to pawn their property:

As for my Lord Pembroke's [men], which you desire to know where they be, they are all at home, and have been these five or six weeks, for they cannot save their charges with travel, as I hear, and were fain to pawn their apparel.

We hear of that company no more. Its players found new connections, and its repertory of plays was apparently sold. The Lord Chamberlain's men seem to have obtained some of them, for they are later played by this company; and the printers procured, probably in part at least by purchase from members of the disbanding company, also a number of plays, including *The First Part of the Contention betwixt the Two Famous Houses of York and Lancaster* and *The True Tragedy of Richard Duke of York*,[1] plays on the same subjects as *2* and *3 Henry VI*, respectively. It is stated on the title-page of *The Taming of a Shrew* (1594) and of *Titus Andronicus* (1594) that these plays had been acted by the Lord Pembroke's men, the latter being said also to have been acted by the servants of the Earl of Derby, the Earl of Sussex, and the Lord Chamberlain. The ownership of *Titus Andronicus* was probably in dispute, a circumstance which may account for its publication. There were then certain plays published as acted by Lord Pembroke's men with which Shakespeare is thought to have had some connection; but the more important plays which he had by this time written, such as *Love's Labour's Lost*, *The Two Gentlemen of Verona*, *Romeo and Juliet*, and *Richard III*, were not printed. They may have been taken over by the Lord Chamberlain's men (if Shakespeare

---

[1] P. Alexander, *Shakespeare's "Henry VI" and "Richard III*," Cambridge, 1929. These plays were long thought of as early versions of *2* and *3 Henry VI* and usually attributed to Marlowe. It has lately been argued, however, that these plays are too faulty to be attributed to any competent playwright and that they must have come into existence by being written down mainly from memory by actors who had played parts in *2* and *3 Henry VI*; and that the plays are, therefore, to be regarded as "reported" versions of Shakespeare's plays.

joined that company first in 1594), or to have continued in their possession (if he had already been associated with that company). Shakespeare's plays were thus pretty well protected from the publishers, and several of even the earliest ones did not see the light in printed form until the issue of the First Folio in 1623.

The Talbot play The only play now attributed to Shakespeare which appears in the repertory of Lord Strange's company, as given by Henslowe in 1592, seems to have been *1 Henry VI*, which may, however, have been a version of the story which Shakespeare had not yet touched. It seems probable to Professor Adams that the later parts of the story of King Henry VI which are treated in *2* and *3 Henry VI* were written or revamped by Shakespeare for Lord Pembroke's company in order to form a counter-attraction to this very play which Henslowe calls "harey vi" then enjoying enormous popularity at the Rose as acted by Lord Strange's men. As an indication of this popularity we have not only Henslowe's entries of numerous performances and good returns, but we have independent testimony. The play tells from a strongly patriotic point of view the story of the warfare, betrayal, and heroic death of the English general Talbot, who was fighting in France to save that kingdom from reconquest by the French king and Joan of Arc. The play in its old form is sometimes thought to have been the work of George Peele; at any rate, Peele's friend Thomas Nashe in *Pierce Penniless* (1592) has this to say:

How it would haue ioyed brave Talbot (the terror of the French) to thinke that after he had lyne two hundred yeares in his Tombe, hee should triumphe again on the Stage, and haue his bones newe embalmed with the teares of ten thousand spectators at least (at seuerall times), who, in the Tragedian that represents his person, imagine that they behold him fresh bleeding.

It is not contended that Shakespeare, if he belonged to Lord Pembroke's unfortunate company, went on the road with them; but rather that he stayed behind and occupied himself as a poet, writing, in the amatory manner then fashionable, *Venus and Adonis* and *The Rape of Lucrece*, as possibly also the *Sonnets*, or some considerable part of them. The case then for Shakespeare's membership in Lord Pembroke's company or Lord Strange's company is by no means clear, and some scholars have seen evidence for his affiliation with the Queen's players or those of the Earl of Sussex.

REFERENCES

ADAMS, J. Q., *Shakespearean Playhouses*. Boston, 1917.

ALBRIGHT, VICTOR, *The Shakespearian Stage*. New Edition. New York, 1926.

BALDWIN, T. W., as above, and article "Posting Henslowe's Accounts," *Journal of English and Germanic Philology*, XXVI, 42-90.

CAMPBELL, LILY B., *Scenes and Machines on the English Stage during the Renaissance*. Cambridge, 1923.

CHAMBERS, SIR E. K., *The Elizabethan Stage*, as above.

FEUILLERAT, A., *Documents relating to the Office of the Revels in the Time of Queen Elizabeth* (Materialien xxi), 1908. Other publications by the same author.

FLEAY, F. G., *A Chronicle History of the London Stage, 1559-1642*. London, 1890.

GRAVES, T. S., *The Court and the London Theaters during the Reign of Elizabeth*. Chicago, 1913; also, "Notes on Puritanism and the Stage," *Studies in Philology*, XVII, 141-169, and other magazine articles by the same author.

Henslowe's Diary, edited by W. W. Greg, London, 1904-8; *The Henslowe Papers*, by the same editor, London, 1907.

LAWRENCE, W. J., *The Elizabethan Playhouse and other Studies*. Stratford-upon-Avon, 1912, 1913. *The Physical Conditions of the Elizabethan Public Playhouse*. Cambridge, 1927.

MURRAY, J. T., *English Dramatic Companies, 1558-1642*. London, 1910.

ORDISH, T. F., *Early London Theaters*. London, 1894.

POEL, W., *Shakespeare in the Theater*. London, 1913.

REYNOLDS, G. F., "Some Principles of Elizabethan Staging," *Modern Philology*, II, 581-614; III, 609-907.

SCHELLING, F. E., *Elizabethan Drama*, as above.

THOMPSON, E. N. S., *The Controversy between the Puritans and the Stage*. New Haven, 1903.

THORNDIKE, A. H., *Shakespeare's Theater*. New York, 1916.

V. THE ORDER OF SHAKESPEARE'S PLAYS: HIS DRAMATIC DEVELOPMENT

The arrangement of the First Folio The plays of Shakespeare in the first collected edition (the First Folio, published in 1623) are arranged in three groups—Comedies, Histories, and Tragedies, there having been no attempt to arrange them in the order of their composition. The first comedy is *The Tempest,* which is known to be one of the very latest plays; the second is *The Two Gentlemen of Verona,* one of the very earliest. The Histories are arranged in order of the English kings whose reigns they treat, although it is obvious that Shakespeare did not write them in this order; nor is there any discoverable order in the arrangement of the tragedies. In order to understand Shakespeare one must view him as a whole, or, as we say, come to a knowledge of his development. Since this cannot be done if his work is studied as a conglomerate of isolated plays, we must see what scholars have discovered with reference to the order in which Shakespeare wrote his plays and the method they have followed in their investigations.

External evidence Eighteen of the thirty-six plays in the First Folio had been previously published singly at various dates in quarto form. The remaining eighteen saw light for the first time in the First Folio. *Pericles* was not included in the First Folio, but existed as a quarto only until its inclusion in the Third Folio of 1663-4. All of the quarto editions, except *Romeo and Juliet* and *Love's Labour's Lost,* appear in the Register of the Stationers' Company of London; and two, *As You Like It* (1600) and *Antony and Cleopatra* (1608), which were not printed in quarto, are entered there, this step having been taken, possibly, to forestall publication by printers who had no right to them. The date of entry of a play in the register indicates that by that date the play was at least in existence. The quarto editions have also certain information on their title-pages as regards date, author, and publisher, and sometimes tell what theatrical company had acted the play. Since we know something of the history of the companies, it not infrequently happens that we can infer something as to the date of the play from that knowledge. There have been found references to the performance of certain plays in diaries, journals, and accounts; as also quotations from various plays and allusions to them. There are a few complimentary references to Shakespeare as a dramatist and poet which allude to his plays, such as John Weever's sonnet *Ad Gulielmum Shakespeare* (1599), which refers to "Richard" and "Romeo." The most important of these is an enumeration, in a book called *Palladis Tamia, or Wit's Treasury,* by Francis Meres, of plays Shakespeare had written by 1598, the date at which the book was published.

As the soule of *Euphorbus* was thought to liue in *Pythagoras:* so the sweete wittie soule of *Ouid* liues in mellifluous & hony-tongued *Shakespeare,* witnes his *Venus* and *Adonis,* his *Lucrece,* his sugred Sonnets among his priuate friends, &c.

As *Plautus* and *Seneca* are accounted the best for Comedy and Tragedy among the Latines: so *Shakespeare* among ye English is the most excellent in both kinds for the stage; for Comedy, witnes his *Gentlemen of Verona,* his *Errors,* his *Loue labors lost,* his *Loue labours wonne,* his *Midsummers night dreame,* & his *Merchant of Venice:* for Tragedy his *Richard the 2.,* *Richard the 3.,* *Henry the 4.,* *King John,* *Titus Andronicus* and his *Romeo* and *Iuliet.*

As *Epius Stolo* said, that the Muses would speake with *Plautus* tongue, if they would speak Latin: so I say that the Muses would speak with *Shakespeares* fine filed phrase, if they would speake English. . . .

And as *Horace* saith of his; *Exegi monumentum ære perennius; Regalique; situ pyramidum altius; Quod non imber edax; Non Aquilo impotens possit diruere; aut innumerabilis annorum feries &c fuga temporum:* so say I seuerally of sir *Philip Sidneys, Spencers, Daniels, Draytons, Shakespeares,* and *Warners workes.*

Such references as this one, which shows that certain plays had been written by 1598, are usually described as external evidence for the dating of the plays.

Evidence partly internal and partly external So also there are in a few instances allusions in plays to contemporary events of known dates, as in the case of the prologue to the fifth act of *Henry V*, which alludes to the Earl of Essex as being in command of the Queen's army in Ireland in his campaign in the spring of 1599 against Tyrone's rebellion. The expedition turned out disastrously, and the allusion would not have been appropriate except during a few months. It is sometimes thought also that the Nurse's allusion to the earthquake eleven years before as a means of fixing Juliet's age in *Romeo and Juliet* (I, iii, 22-34) shows that the play was first written in 1591, since there was a famous earthquake in England in 1580. Likewise, when the Porter in *Macbeth* (II, iii, 4-5) speaks of the "farmer, that hanged himself on the expectation of plenty," it is thought that he alludes to the plentiful harvest and the consequent low price of corn in the year 1606. Evidence of this kind, although abundant, is often uncertain, since in most cases the allusions are by their very nature vague or capable of more than one interpretation; this is in spite of the fact that the Elizabethan drama has a constant habit of alluding to contemporary events and of making the time of its plays correspond to the current calendar. Such evidence is referred to as partly external and partly internal.

Evidence wholly internal It is possible to say from evidence of the kinds just described that certain plays are undoubtedly early, middle, or late in Shakespeare's career; and, by a consideration of the qualities of style which appear in them, to see that Shakespeare's manner of writing underwent certain known and predictable variations during the course of his work as a dramatist. By putting down, so to speak, certain plays as fixed points of departure one can arrange plays of like style together and make a list which is approximately sequential for the whole body of his work. Having determined such an order, one is able to make freer use of vague and casual allusions, to see how Shakespeare reflected the varying tastes of his time, and, above all, to observe his development as a dramatist. From this synoptic view comes a conception of Shakespeare as of one piece and, in the midst of varying and transitory qualities, the ability to achieve an understanding of his progressively developing attitude and style.

We are not concerned, however, with a development of style in Shakespeare only, but in other dramatists as well, his associates and contemporaries. English poetry was undergoing, particularly in the drama, a great growth in the direction of freedom and skill. Shakespeare and other dramatic poets were learning how to express themselves on the stage. Various forms of expression had been tried out in the drama before the Elizabethan mixture of blank verse and prose was hit upon. The writers of older chronicle plays and interludes had used a native measure, called doggerel, preserved for us in such nursery rhymes as

There was a man in our town, and he was won-
      drous wise;
He jumped into a bramble bush and scratched out
      both his eyes.

Lyly and Gascoigne had used prose; but Marlowe had established blank verse and taught it to his fellows. Shakespeare naturally began where the literary skill of the day then was, namely, with Marlowan blank verse, and we can see in him and others a progressive growth in the direction of freedom from the more awkward and constraining forms in the style employed on the stage when he began. In general, dramatic verse became better suited to dialogue.

Difficulties in the problem One is to understand, of course, that there was a whole body of characteristic changes in subject-matter as well as in style; but it has been found possible to isolate and tabulate particular changes in style as distinguished from subject-matter and other features. Since these changes in style are unconscious responses on Shakespeare's part to his own needs and to the fashion of the times, they form an independent record of his progress; and, if they are used cautiously, they are a means for the approximate dating of his plays. Such evidence is spoken of as wholly internal. The matter would be relatively simple if we could be sure that Shakespeare wrote each play at one time and in the form in which it has come down to us and had not revised his work at later times, or had not rewritten other men's work and left much of it standing, or in early work had not anticipated a late style, or in late work recurred to an earlier style, or, finally, had not during his career had various collaborators in his undertakings. Unfortunately we know that all of these puzzling things happened. Moreover, when we get beyond the consideration of the unconscious record and have to resort to our sympathetic interpretation of how Shakespeare would have felt at a certain time, how the circumstances of his private life might have been affecting him, or what the activities of other playwrights might have caused him to say or to refrain from saying, we are on very shaky ground. Although in this favorite exercise of amateur critics we may satisfy ourselves and make matters plausible to others, so great is the difference of taste, knowledge, and temperament among critics that we cannot claim to be dealing with facts.

Mixture of prose and blank verse Shakespeare's use of prose is slight in certain early plays, such as *Richard III*, produced under the influence of Marlowe. From the earliest times, however, in plays not of a Marlowan character, prose is freely employed for the speeches of clowns, servants, and rustics. Marlowe himself in *Dr. Faustus* and elsewhere had used it in this way. Later in his career, however, Shakespeare extended the use of prose to matter which we should call high comedy, as in *Much Ado about Nothing* and *The Merry Wives of Windsor*, and used it even in speeches of sententious importance or great formal dignity, as in the oration of Brutus in *Julius Cæsar* (III, ii, 13-52). Very little can be told as to the date of a play merely by the amount of prose it contains; it is at best only an indication. Similarly, the amount of blank verse is not definitive. The plays written under the influence of Marlowe early in Shakespeare's career tend, with the exception of *Richard II*, to be written throughout in blank verse; from the very beginning, and more and more as time goes on, the serious business of the plot and passages of dignity and poetic beauty appear in this measure.

Rhyme The amount of rhyme is more significant. In early plays, such as *A Midsummer - Night's Dream* and *Romeo and Juliet*, there is a great deal of rhyme, and in the latest plays there is practically none. The commonest form of rhyme is the pentameter measure rhymed in couplets; as when Phebe, quoting Marlowe's *Hero and Leander*, says in *As You Like It* (III, v, 81-2),

Dead shepherd, now I find thy saw of might,
'Who ever loved that loved not at first sight?'

But Shakespeare in his rhyming sometimes goes even further than the couplet. *Romeo and Juliet* and *Love's Labour's Lost* each contain a number of complete sonnets, as well as rhymed sequences made up of a quatrain followed by a couplet, and a good deal of alternate rhyme. Doggerel appears in some of the early plays. One quite formal use of the rhymed couplet, which should here be noted, interrupts the calculation as to the significance of the amount of rhyme: There was of course no dropping of a curtain at the close of a scene in the Elizabethan theater. The actors simply left the stage at the end of a scene, carrying with them sick, wounded, or slain persons, or other impedimenta, so that the stage might be left empty. In order to mark strongly the cue for the first actor in the succeeding scene, so it is thought, the dramatist composed a couplet to mark the close of the scene. Thus Hamlet leaves the stage at the end of the fifth scene of the first act crying,

The time is out of joint: O cursed spite,
That ever I was born to set it right!

The chief thing to remember about the use of rhyme is that it is always consciously employed. Shakespeare tends to use it for sentiment and the conversation of lovers and to mark other passages of lighter tone. When so used a large quantity is indicative of an early date.

Quality of the blank verse The way in which Shakespeare composed blank verse in his early plays and in his later ones forms the basis of a more significant test than the mere amount of blank verse or of rhyme. There is in Shakespeare's blank verse a gradual movement in the direction of freedom from formality, which is progressive and therefore safely calculable. Blank verse is five-foot iambic measure without rhyme, and if composed with perfect regularity, it is monotonous. If every line is made to contain five feet and each foot two syllables, the second accented and the first unaccented, one says that the verse is regular. If there is a pause, however slight, in the sense, and consequently also in the rhythm, at the end of the line, one says the verse is end-stopped. The single verse and not a group of verses is then the unit of composition. Blank verse before Marlowe's time was written very much in this formal manner, and what Marlowe did for it, and therefore for dramatic style, was to introduce variety. His verses are so constructed that they often flow into each other, there being no pauses in the sense at the ends of the lines. In other words, some of them were not end-stopped, but run-on lines. Marlowe also varied the measure by breaking up the regularity in the forms of the individual feet within the line, sometimes substituting for the regular iambic a trochaic foot. But the shifting of the medial pause, or cæsura, was the chief means of rendering the verse sufficiently flexible to be used in dialogue. Compared to Shakespeare in his later works, Marlowe is relatively stiff in manner; but it may be said of Shakespeare that in certain of his early works he out-Marlowes Marlowe in the rigidity of his style. Later, however, along with other dramatists, he varied his style with the greatest freedom. Fletcher carried this license so far that, if his lines were written as prose, one would have difficulty in rearranging them as verse. The relation in numbers of run-on lines to end-stopped lines at any one time in Shakespeare's career forms a convenient test for placing his plays roughly in the order in which he wrote them. If, for example, a play has many run-on lines, the pauses occurring not at the ends of lines, but within them, it would be judged late in date of composition.

The following passage from Clarence's description of his dream in *Richard III* (I, iv, 21-33) may be taken as an example of Shakespeare's earlier manner. Note that there is a pause at the end of every line except the ninth:

Lord, Lord! methought, what pain it was to
    drown!
What dreadful noise of waters in mine ears!
What ugly sights of death within mine eyes!
Methought I saw a thousand fearful wrecks;
Ten thousand men that fishes gnaw'd upon;
Wedges of gold, great anchors, heaps of pearl,
Inestimable stones, unvalued jewels,
All scatter'd in the bottom of the sea:
Some lay in dead men's skulls; and, in those holes
Where eyes did once inhabit, there were crept,
As 'twere in scorn of eyes, reflecting gems,
Which woo'd the slimy bottom of the deep,
And mock'd the dead bones that lay scatter'd by.

As an example of the latest manner, consider Prospero's description of his magic in *The Tempest* (V, i, 33-50) where only the first, fifth, eighth, and tenth lines are end-stopped:

Ye elves of hills, brooks, standing lakes and
    groves,
And ye that on the sands with printless foot
Do chase the ebbing Neptune and do fly him
When he comes back; you demi-puppets that
By moonshine do the green sour ringlets make,
Whereof the ewe not bites, and you whose pastime
Is to make midnight mushrooms, that rejoice
To hear the solemn curfew; by whose aid,
Weak masters though ye be, I have bedimm'd
The noontide sun, call'd forth the mutinous
    winds,
And 'twixt the green sea and the azured vault
Set roaring war: to the dread rattling thunder
Have I given fire and rifted Jove's stout oak
With his own bolt; the strong-based promontory
Have I made shake and by the spurs pluck'd up
The pine and cedar: graves at my command
Have waked their sleepers, oped, and let 'em forth
By my so potent art.

The speech-ending test A phenomenon somewhat akin to the principle of the end-stopped and run-on lines is the growing habit of dividing a line between two speakers, or even among several speakers. These speech endings which break lines increase steadily from *The Comedy of Errors*, where there are almost none, to *The Winter's Tale*, where eighty-seven per cent of the speeches end in this fashion. The speech-ending test would be one of the very best but for the fact that, in cases where the play has been cut for acting or otherwise tampered with, the way in which the speeches end has been modified after the play was first written.

Feminine endings Another variation in the way in which blank verse is written is in the kind of foot which stands at the end of the line. In the early type of dramatic blank verse the lines were usually end-stopped, the last syllable was accented, and the line closed abruptly; thus the line is emphasized as the unit of composition. In the passage from *Richard III* quoted above, it will be noticed that every line except the seventh ends in an accented syllable. As a means of breaking away from this regular and monotonous partition of the sense, Shakespeare introduces more and more frequently words of two syllables at the ends of lines, thus making the line consist of eleven instead of ten syllables. By those who discovered this stylistic peculiarity it was thought that the effect on the ear was sweeter and less abrupt, and they said fancifully that these lines having an extra syllable at the end had "feminine" endings, whereas those which ended in an accented syllable were said to have "masculine" endings. The relative number of masculine and feminine endings forms another test of the time of the composition, since feminine endings increase as Shakespeare's development progresses. A similar tendency also causes the introduction, more and more, of extra syllables before the pauses within the lines.

Light and weak endings One other among the various tests is of major importance. Early in his career, in fact until after 1600, Shakespeare almost never ended lines with conjunctions, prepositions, auxiliary verbs, possessive pronouns, and other lightly-stressed words. After that time, however, he uses such endings with increasing freedom. There are more than a hundred such lines each in *Coriolanus* and *Cymbeline*. In *The Comedy of Errors* and *The Two Gentlemen of Verona* there are none at all. We have, therefore, the light- and weak-ending test.

In order to show the results of all these tests, a table based on Fleay (as interpreted and corrected by Dr. Furnivall) and on König is given on page 46.

Dowden's grouping of Shakespeare's plays The late Professor Dowden, guided by the evidence described and by his sympathetic interpretation of Shakespeare's mind and art, made groupings of Shakespeare's plays which show the varying quality of his genius during four great periods of his dramatic life, and suggest somewhat fancifully the phases of experience through which he was passing. The first period (1590-1594) Dowden called "In the Workshop," and by this he meant Shakespeare's period of pupilage, while he was doing his first original plays and rewriting old ones, either alone or with some other, possibly more experienced, dramatist to assist him. Here belong the Henry VI plays, *Love's Labour's Lost*, *The Comedy of Errors*, *The Two Gentlemen of Verona*, and that crude and terrible play *Titus Andronicus*. We may suppose that the period closes with the two youthful masterpieces *Richard III* and *A Midsummer - Night's Dream*. There was probably in this period also an early version of *Romeo and Juliet*. The second period (1595-1601) Dowden called "In the World," for Shakespeare, having by that time learned his art, was rising on the tide of success as a dramatist. We may be pretty sure that *Richard II* and *The Merchant of Venice* belong at the very beginning of this period and that there was also a draft of the Henry IV plays very early in it. The final versions of these plays and *Henry V*, together with the brilliant romantic comedies, *Much Ado about Nothing*, *As You Like It*, and *Twelfth Night*, are the characteristic plays of the period. Dowden's third period, called "De Profundis," or "Out of the Depths," in which tragic or gloomy subjects engage Shakespeare's pen, occupied the years 1602-1608. He then wrote his great tragedies, beginning, let us say, with *Hamlet*. Here are *Othello*, *King Lear*, and *Macbeth*, and the bitter comedies *All's Well that Ends Well* and *Measure for Measure*. Finally Dowden provided a fourth period (1608-1612), "On the Heights," so called because the plays composed during the period reveal a quiet serenity and conscious reconciliation to life as "somehow good." The characteristic plays of the period are *Cymbeline*, *The Tempest*, and *The Winter's Tale*, which are rather reflective romances than comedies. Many writers, like George Brandes and Frank Harris, have seen in this succession of moods an immediate reflection of the stages of experience through which Shakespeare was passing in his life and have brought into connection with the plays various events of his life. It has, however, been shown that Shakespeare followed the fashion of the stage and that other dramatists were writing plays of the successive styles and kinds that he wrote; also that Shakespeare was influenced by current movements of literary thought. If this is true, one may say that, the more Shakespeare was reflecting current fashions, the less chance there is that he was expressing independently his personal feelings about life. One would not say that his art is less sincere, but one would be disposed to call in question the romance of the critics. It is none the less convenient as well as customary to divide his plays into four groups: first, those which were probably written by the beginning of 1595 when Shakespeare first emerged as a member of the Lord Chamberlain's company, second, those written between this date and 1600, except that certain comedies written soon after 1600 will be more conveniently treated with the second group; third, those written between 1600 and 1608; fourth, the latest plays, those written after 1608.

TABLE OF METRICAL TESTS APPLIED TO SHAKESPEARE'S PLAYS

NAME OF PLAY	NO. OF LINES	PROSE	BLANK VERSE	5-FOOT RHYMES	RUN-ON LINES %	DOUBLE ENDINGS	SPEECH ENDING %	NO. LIGHT & WEAK END.	PROBABLE DATES[1]
L. L. L.	2789	1086	579	1028	18.4	9	10.0	3	1589 (1597)
Com. Er.	1778	240	1150	380	12.9	137	0.6	0	1589, 1593
Two Gent.	2294	409	1510	116	12.4	203	5.8	0	1590, 1595(?)
Tit. And.	2523	43	2338	144	9.5	154	2.5	5	1592, 1594
1 Hen. VI	2677	0	2379	314	10.4	140	0.5	4	1591-2
2 Hen. VI	3162	448	2562	122	11.4	255	1.1	3	1591-2
3 Hen. VI	2904	0	2749	155	9.5	346	0.9	3	1591-2
Rich. III	3619	55(?)	3374	170	13.1	570	2.9	4	1593
R. & J.	3052	405	2111	486	14.2	118	14.9	7	1591 (1598)
Mids. Dream	2174	441	878	731	13.2	29	17.3	1	1590-1, 1594
K. John	2570	0	2403	150	17.7	54	12.7	7	1595
Rich. II	2756	0	2107	537	19.9	148	7.3	4	1595-6
Mer. Ven.	2660	673	1896	93	21.5	297	22.2	7	1596-7
Tam. Shrew	2649	516	1971	169	8.1	260	3.6	14(?)	1594, 1596
1 Hen. IV	3176	1464	1622	84	22.8	60	14.2	7	1596-7
2 Hen. IV	3446	1860	1417	74	21.4	203	16.8	1	1597-8
Much Ado	2826	2106	643	40	19.3	129	20.7	2	1598
Hen. V	3380	1531	1678	101	21.8	291	18.3	2	1599
Merry Wives	3018	2703	227	69	20.1	32	20.5	1	1599, 1603
J. C.	2478	165	2241	34	19.3	369	20.3	10	1599
A. Y. L. I.	2857	1681	925	71	17.1	211	21.6	2	1600
12th Night	2690	1741	763	120	14.7	152	36.3	4	1600-2
T. & C.	3496	1186	2025	196	27.4	441	31.3	6	1601-3
All's Well	2966	1453	1234	280	28.4	223	74.4	13	1602, 1607
Hamlet	3931	1208	2490	81	23.1	508	51.6	8	1601-2, 1593(?)
Meas. Meas.	2821	1134	1574	73	23.0	338	51.4	7	1603-4
Othello	3316	541	2672	86	19.5	646	41.4	2	1604
K. Lear	3334	903	2238	74	29.3	567	60.9	6	1605-6
Macbeth	2108	158	1588	118	36.6	399	77.2	23	1605-6
A. & C.	3063	255	2761	42	43.3	613	77.5	99	1606
Tim. of Ath.	2373	596	1560	184	32.5	257	62.8	30	1605, 1607
Coriolanus	3410	829	2521	42	45.9	708	79.0	104	1606, 1608
Pericles	2389	418	1436	225	18.2	120	71.0	82	1607
Cymbeline	3339	638	2585	107	46.0	726	85.0	130	1609-10
Wint. Tale	3075	844	1825	0	37.5	639	87.6	100	1610-11
Tempest	2064	458	1458	2	41.5	476	84.5	67	1611
Henry VIII	2822	67(?)	2613	16	46.3	1195	72.4	82	1612-13

[1]When there is a wide divergence of opinion among critics, two dates, separated by commas, are given. Dates in parentheses indicate early versions or late revisions.

REFERENCES

CHAMBERS, E. K., *William Shakespeare*. Two vols. Oxford, 1930. Appendix H, with bibliographical note.

DOWDEN, EDWARD, *Introduction to Shakspere*. New York and London, 1893. *Shakspere, his Mind and Art*. New York and London, 1874. *A Shakspere Primer*. New York, 1877.

FLEAY, F. G., *Shakespere Manual*. London, 1878.

FURNIVALL, F. J., *The Leopold Shakespeare*. London, 1876. The preface contains an explanation of the system of testing and dating plays.

FURNIVALL, F. J., AND MUNRO, JOHN, *Shakespeare, Life and Work*. London, 1908.

KÖNIG, G., "Der Vers in Shaksperes Dramen," *Quellen und Forschungen*, vol. lxi, 1888. Contains the most extensive presentation of the numerical results of verse tests.

LAMBERT, D. H., *Shakespeare Documents*. London, 1904.

MUNRO, JOHN, editor, *The Shakespeare Allusion Book: A Collection of Allusions to Shakespeare from 1591 to 1700*. Two vols. London and New York, 1909.

NEILSON, WILLIAM ALLAN, and THORNDIKE, ASHLEY H., *Facts about Shakespeare*. New York, 1913. Rev. ed., 1931.

New Shakespeare Society, *Publications*, 1874. Contains Fleay's original tests, Furnivall's discussion, and Ingram on weak endings. *Publications*, 1877-1879. Contains F. S. Pulling's work on the speech-ending test; this work is summarized in Fleay's *Shakspere Manual*.

Nearly all modern editions of Shakespeare contain discussions of the dating of his plays.

VI. SHAKESPEARE CRITICISM: HOW TO READ SHAKESPEARE

Seventeenth and eighteenth century critics The critics of the seventeenth century appreciated Shakespeare's genius although they found him crude and faulty when compared to the French dramatists whom they regarded as a standard; but since they were actually closer to Shakespeare in point of time and consequent ease of comprehension, and were not theory-ridden, they had certain advantages over later critics. Dryden in his essay *Of Dramatick Poesie* (1668) writes finely of Shakespeare as the man of all the moderns who "had the largest and most comprehensive soul," and yet he is careful to point out Shakespeare's irregularities and inconsistencies. Thomas Rymer in *A Short View of Tragedy* (1693) states the case of late seventeenth century England against Shakespeare, saying he was barbarous, irrational, and over-exuberant; and, though there was no lack of defenders, that is the gist of the dramatic criticism of the age. Yet it was practically always admitted that Shakespeare was possessed of a transcendent genius. It may even be said that such adaptations as Nahum Tate's version of *King Lear* (which has a happy ending),

Dryden's version of *Antony and Cleopatra*, entitled *All for Love*, and Colley Cibber's version of *Richard III* (still on the stage), are evidences that the classicists admired Shakespeare's genius. They were not disposed to err on the side of Shakespeare worship;[1] nor indeed were the critics of the eighteenth century. Dr. Samuel Johnson, an editor of Shakespeare, was in most respects an admirable Shakespeare critic. He had no metaphysical theory of Shakespeare's genius but looked at Shakespeare directly and sensibly. He it was who first paid serious attention to the conditions in which Shakespeare did his work.[2] The great Shakespeare scholar Edmund Malone (1741-1812) and his contemporaries late in the eighteenth century did Shakespeare the honor to study him and his age profoundly. They gave us our principal body of Elizabethan material for the study of Shakespeare.

[1] See *The Tempest, The Mock Tempest, and King Lear*, ed. Montague Summers, 1922; George C. D. Odell, *Shakespeare from Betterton to Irving*, New York, 1920; Hazelton Spencer, *Shakespeare Improved*, Cambridge, 1928.

[2] Karl Young, "Samuel Johnson on Shakespeare: One Aspect," *University of Wisconsin Studies in Language and Literature*, No. 18.

Shakespeare and the Romantic generation A powerful impulse came to the study and appreciation of Shakespeare with the generation who lived during the epoch of the French Revolution. A new Shakespeare criticism was part of that revival of art and letters which we ordinarily call the Romantic Movement. The thinkers of that day, being interested in a wider variety of ideas about life than were the pseudo-classicists, found in Shakespeare such a marvelously significant and consistent picture of life that they came to think of him as endowed with the insight of a seer and the power of a poet, as greater and more significant than life itself. Each of his plays became a microcosm capable of yielding to the student, if he came with love and admiration in his heart, finer truth than science could yield. Science, they argued, bounds itself by fact; poetry has no such limits, but is a mode of revelation of the philosophy of life, presenting in concrete and constructive form what life means and what life might be. Shakespeare, the poet, was thus metamorphosed into a philosopher and teacher, so that his works became a hunting-ground where one might find the greatest thoughts about existence. This his admirers did in the strength of the conviction that his had been a vision of life at its fullest, purest, and most significant stage. Since Coleridge's day the world has belonged to Shakespeare. The approach of Coleridge and his contemporaries to Shakespeare is still the prevailing one, as witnessed by our textbooks, which are made from this idealistic, if not mystical, point of view.

The new point of view Shakespeare, like every artist, has a right to be seen and understood as he desired to be seen and understood. There has sprung up, mainly in the twentieth century, a group of critics whose methods are more strictly historical and whose attitude toward the perfections of Shakespeare's work is more skeptical. They are as willing to recognize the limits placed upon Shakespeare by the time in which he lived, the conditions in which he practiced his art, and even the flaws in his workmanship, as were the critics of the seventeenth and eighteenth centuries. They consequently regard with distrust the great body of panegyrical criticism of the nineteenth century. Their object, in the words reported from the eminent American Shakespeare scholar, Professor G. L. Kittredge, is to ascertain what Shakespeare said and what he meant when he said it.[1]

The conditions under which Shakespeare worked Although the Shakespearean drama was not acted under such conditions as now prevail in dramatic production, it is at least so far one and the same with modern drama that it can be freely enacted on the modern stage and seen by the modern spectator with great enjoyment and fair comprehension. But it cannot be seen exactly as it was seen by the Elizabethan Londoners for whom it was written. Perhaps no art, literary or pictorial, can be brought back exactly as it was originally produced and enjoyed. Matthew Arnold points out, with reference to translation in his lectures "On Translating Homer," that we cannot know exactly the effect of a classic on the age for which it was written; we can only approximate such knowledge. All art of a bygone age has this limitation. Everyone would admit, however, that the more nearly we can see as Shakespeare meant us to see, the more adequate will be our vision and the keener our enjoyment. Neither the Elizabethan writer nor the Elizabethan audience had a body of ideas like ours, knew what we know or in the way we know it, wanted the same things from life that we want, or thought of drama or life as we think of them. Much water, so to speak, has flowed under the

[1] See G. L. Kittredge, *Shakespeare*, Cambridge, 1916; L. L. Schücking, *Character Problems in Shakespeare's Plays*, New York, 1922; Barrett Wendell, *William Shakespeare*, New York, 1894; *The Works of William Shakespeare*, ed. R. Bridges, Stratford, 1907 (Vol. X, pp. 321-324); C. M. Lewis, *The Genesis of "Hamlet,"* 1907; John Corbin, *The Elizabethan "Hamlet,"* 1895; J. M. Robertson, *The Problem of "Hamlet,"* 1919, and other works by the same author; G. B. Shaw, *Dramatic Opinions and Other Essays*, 1907, and various introductions and prefaces; E. E. Stoll, *Shakespeare Studies*, New York, 1927, and various articles in learned journals. This historical point of view is not wanting in Mr. A. C. Bradley's work, though his chief adherence is to philosophical considerations. See for a general statement of the position, Professor Karl Young's review of Schücking, *Phil. Quarterly*, I, 228-234, and "Shakespeare Skeptics," *No. Amer. Rev.*, CCXV, 382-393; also L. Abercrombie, *A Plea for the Liberty of Interpreting*, Oxford, 1930.

bridge since Bacon and Bruno were making their tentative beginnings in the scientific thought which has transformed the world. All of the magnification of the individual man and his immediate relation to God which came from Puritanism; all of the democracy or republicanism which came from Algernon Sidney, John Locke, and J. J. Rousseau; all that was done in the way of untying men's minds by the idealism of Berkeley and Kant, the rationalism of Hume and his followers, and by Hegelianism, transcendentalism, pessimism, socialism, Nietzcheism; all the social teachings of the nineteenth century, the doctrine of organic evolution, the development of experimental science and of public education, the extension of European civilization over the world—these things and a thousand more are influences in the enlightened mind of today which were unknown to the Englishman of the sixteenth century. Since Shakespeare did not and could not talk about such things, he should not be made to do so.

Shakespeare on the stage No doubt, however, if we know the meaning of the Elizabethan language used, the rudiments of the culture of Elizabethan times, so as to understand fashions and opinions then current, and know something of the dramatic practices of the day, we may proceed to the enjoyment of Shakespeare's drama without let or hindrance. Human nature has a way of remaining the same from age to age. Indeed we are the more likely to be entrapped into misreading Shakespeare because we do not see his plays on the stage very frequently; or, because when we do, they are acted on a very different stage from Shakespeare's and frequently deformed by false critical interpretations. In the physical conditions of dramatic art, there are two factors, a stage and an audience, and both of these have changed since Shakespeare's time; the audience, multifariously; the stage, definitely and specifically. Writers on the stage have called the modern stage two-dimensional and have likened it to a picture; and the Elizabethan stage, three-dimensional, and have likened it to a pageant, or a procession, or an athletic contest. In the modern theater we sit like privileged spies and behold what we are asked to accept as a section of actual life. Since we are not supposed to be present, we do not wish to be talked to in asides and soliloquy, because such practices spoil the illusion. In the Elizabethan theater the actors were literally surrounded by the audience, some of whom actually sat on the stage, and it was the allowed convention of that drama that the actors might talk to the audience much more intimately than they may now talk, and make them comprehend the story by actual explanation. The Elizabethan audience was too much a fact to be disregarded, and the dramatist made terms with it.

Piece out our imperfections with your thoughts,

cries Shakespeare in the prologue to *Henry V;* and he elsewhere shows us that he realizes his difficulties. He must have the co-operation of his audience if his play, presented on such a stage and relatively without costume or scenery, is to be understood. In *A Midsummer-Night's Dream* (V, i, 213-217) Theseus replies to Hippolyta's statement that the interlude of "Pyramus and Thisbe" is the silliest stuff she ever heard, with these words:

The best in this kind are but shadows; and the worst are no worse, if imagination amend them.

And she retorts,

It must be your imagination then, and not theirs.

They thus express the principle at the basis of all artistic appreciation, which Coleridge described as "that willing suspension of disbelief for the moment which constitutes poetic faith."

Elizabethan dramatic art conventional Elizabethan dramatic art was certainly more conventional than most modern dramatic art, and, as acted on our stage, Shakespeare's plays are made more naturalistic than they were on the Elizabethan stage. They are less declamatory and more conversational. The actors are costumed according to the time and place of the plot and do not appear merely in the ruff, the doublet, and the trunk hose of the Tudor stage, and only experimentally in the coat, waistcoat, and trousers of our own day. Women's parts are played by women; whereas, on Shakespeare's stage, they were played by boys. On our stage scenes are set with care and appropriateness; the stage is not bare, and it has a curtain. Actors take time to characterize by gesture and movement to a greater degree than they did at the time the plays were written. The prologue to *Romeo and Juliet* speaks of the play as "the two hours' traffic of our stage," thus indicating the approximate length of an Elizabethan play. The performance of a full text of a Shakespearean play acted with the slower modern methods becomes a horror from sheer length. Unfortunately most of us do not like to see Shakespeare done in the old way, for what we are used to seems to us natural if not inevitable. It requires a somewhat critical acquaintance with any contemporary art form to be able to perceive and identify the conventions which are being habitually observed. In the judgment of contemporary art it is difficult not to mistake mere novelty for originality. In the art of a past age, however, fashions and conventions betray themselves to us very quickly. Not infrequently, even when the art is good, we find ourselves repelled by its antique fashion. It is the essence of literary education to learn to look beyond these unaccustomed and sometimes absurd features to the mind of the artist, and if possible to see the work of earlier writers, like Shakespeare, Chaucer, and Dante, so sympathetically that the limits of their technique and their knowledge are accepted and endorsed as they were accepted and endorsed by the keenest and most appreciative of their contemporaries.

Shakespeare not devoid of naturalism Some careful study of nature is necessary in every great school of art. That Shakespeare sought naturalism we know from the character of his works and from his own words, as when Hamlet, using the voice of the dramatist, speaks of the art of playing, "whose end, both at the first and now, was and is, to hold, as 'twere, the mirror up to nature; to show virtue her own feature, scorn her own image, and the very age and body of the time his form and pressure." (*Hamlet*, III, ii, 18-39.) A swing

from conventionality to naturalism can be traced from Shakespeare's early plays to his late ones, and be followed with equal certainty in the works of his contemporaries. He himself, from his consistent character, achieved the most perfect balance between the objective and the subjective spirit, or, as we say, between naturalism and conventionality; but this belief in his naturalism can be easily exaggerated. He did not go the whole way in ridding himself of obvious conventionalities, such as the use of the aside and the soliloquy; for, after all, he could not change the habits of his audience or the form of his stage and theater. If we understand that Shakespeare's mind flourished in an earlier time than ours, as regards the history of thought, and that his task —the telling of a story by dramatic means— was primarily an artist's task, recognized by him in some such terms as those quoted above, we shall be better able to avoid the habit of reading into his plays things that he never meant to say, and to find out a method of approach which will lead to a fuller, more genuine enjoyment of his work.

The stuff of Shakespeare's ideas In considering the cultural and psychological background of Shakespeare and his audience we have to do, not only with tastes and temperaments in the age of Elizabeth, but with the actual fund of ideas of that age. His stock of ideals was relatively small, most of them coming from Aristotle and the Renaissance; and he utters his great simple truths, exalted commonplaces, and aphoristic wisdoms without calling them very consciously into question. He presents the insoluble problems of life, but he does not do so speculatively. It is fate or the stars which are to blame. Our trap is his suggestiveness. As a poet he calls up the backgrounds of our minds in instincts, sensations, motor impulses, emotions and thoughts; these we sublimate, carrying his suggestions further than he could have carried them, into the higher region of ideals and rational actions. There is little gain and much confusion in making this greatest of poets into an elucidator or even an illustrator of philosophic enigmas, many of which he never dreamed of. By taking him on his own terms we may often reinforce his greatness by perceiving his anticipations of the thought of a more advanced age. Still, if one should exaggerate the differences between Shakespeare's age and ours, one would make a greater mistake than if one should minimize them; for the essentials of social and domestic life remain, in most of their important aspects, relatively unchanged. In so far as the conduct of life is determined by elemental biological fact and by fundamental social institutions, Shakespeare deals with it for our world as for his own. Parental and filial love, courtship and marriage, youth and age, riches and poverty, sickness and health, peace and war; the social inter-relations which spring out of these conditions; most matters of law and civil polity; the qualities which come from the practice of trades and professions; the fundamental types of human character; the behavior of individual men arising from their instincts, emotions, and affections; man's essential relation to generation, death, God, and the hereafter—these things remain, so that Shakespeare's favorite world is the one in which we spend most of our lives. There is usually only a difference of emphasis to be known and noted. For example, Shakespeare had exalted ideals of loyalty and hospitality, so that when Macbeth murders Duncan, he is killing his king and his guest. Well may Macbeth speak of the "deep damnation of his taking off," for it is as horrible a sin as Shakespeare could imagine for his hero to commit.

Collective treatment of Shakespeare's sources The belief that Shakespeare was a careless worker, who put his plays hastily together largely out of other people's ideas, is erroneous. His genius was no doubt happy and rapid, but there is no positive evidence that he slighted his work or regarded it as a perfunctory means of making his livelihood. In most instances of apparent carelessness there are indications that the work was tampered with after it left his hand. The evidence indeed points rather to a studious person who was conscientious about his art. In order to understand this matter and to form a fair opinion on so important a question it is necessary that we should consider his relation to his sources. The discovery of a Shakespearean

source is an interesting fact no doubt in and for itself and because it tells us what materials the great poet made to serve his turn; but, after all, the knowledge that Shakespeare used such and such a work is of little importance compared to the knowledge of how he used it. Did he follow it slavishly? If so, was it worth following? How did he change it? What did it teach him or suggest to him? Did he content himself with one source only? Did he respect a serious historical source? These are a few of the really important questions about Shakespeare's sources.

The books Shakespeare knew were of two sorts: those he used in the making of plays and those he encountered apparently as a general reader and student. Of the former class the most striking are the old plays which we have reason to believe that he used. The number of these plays is surprising, and in order to understand how Shakespeare, a great original genius, could have used so much second-hand stuff, we have to recall to our minds the fact that stories were more or less common property and that their interest did not depend upon their novelty. We must likewise ask about the way in which Shakespeare used his borrowed plots. Only a general idea can be given here, since the specific cases are considered in the introductions to various plays further on in this volume. Among the comedies we have one play, George Whetstone's *Promos and Cassandra*, which Shakespeare certainly rewrote as *Measure for Measure*. *The Taming of a Shrew* is not Shakespeare's original for *The Taming of the Shrew*, but we have George Gascoigne's *The Supposes*, which is ultimately the source of Shakespeare's minor plot, and we have reason to believe that there was an old "shrew" play, now lost, back of the major plot. For *The Comedy of Errors* we have Plautus's *Menæchmi* and his *Amphitruo*. There was almost certainly an intermediary play (now lost) between Shakespeare and Plautus, possibly the *Historie of Error*, acted at Hampton Court by the Children of Paul's on New Year's Day 1577. It is believed on various grounds that earlier plays, now lost, existed on the subjects treated in *The Two Gentlemen of Verona*, *The Merchant of Venice*, *Much Ado about Nothing*, *The Merry Wives of Windsor,* and *Troilus and Cressida.* Not much then can be told from Shakespeare's comedies about his methods of work, though it is noteworthy that he did a thorough job on Whetstone's play, rewriting it completely and modifying it in such a manner as to change its significance as a whole, and that he knew Plautus at first hand and made direct use of *The Supposes.* It is in the history plays that one really sees how Shakespeare went to work. Probably every historical subject he treated, including *Henry VIII,* had been put on the stage before he used it. This may not be true in the case of *2* and *3 Henry VI,* though nearly all Shakespeare scholars believe that it was. There was certainly an old play, now lost, on the same subject as *1 Henry VI;* at least two plays on *Richard III;* probably several dramatic treatments of *Richard II;* and there is an extant play on *King John.* For *1* and *2 Henry IV* and *Henry V* we have in *The Famous Victories of Henry V,* a badly garbled version of Shakespeare's source. From *The Famous Victories,* or more probably from the play which it so inadequately represents, Shakespeare drew only scenes and suggestions for the comic and the biographic parts of his play. For the historical events of the three plays he went to the best book of English history of his time, namely, Raphael Holinshed's *Chronicles of England, Scotland, and Ireland,* which he used in the second edition of 1587. This he did for all of the historical plays. For *Richard II* and *1* and *2 Henry IV,* he used also Samuel Daniel's *History of the Civil Wars,* a compendious historical poem published in 1595. So many details in the history plays of Shakespeare seem to be drawn from Hall's *Chronicles* and from Stow's *Annals* that one is almost forced to conclude that Shakespeare knew also these sources. In *Henry VIII* we find not only Holinshed but John Foxe's *Acts and Monuments.* For *King John* there exists a full and meritorious dramatic source, *The Troublesome Raigne of John King of England,* published in two parts in 1591. Here it must be admitted that Shakespeare followed very closely his anonymous source, which in turn, however, had followed Holinshed with fidelity and dramatic skill. Shake-

speare does little violence anywhere to historical truth as he knew it. *Richard III,* as Shakespeare presents him, is the Richard III of Tudor history, as pictured originally by Sir Thomas More and by Polydore Vergil. Shakespeare's version is far more "historical" than is *The True Tragedy of Richard III,* from which he is wrongly supposed to have borrowed. In the tragedies again we have not much to go upon. Old plays on the subjects treated in *Titus Andronicus* and *Romeo and Juliet* probably existed. His handling of the former we cannot pass judgment upon, for we have no source; but the latter is written directly from Arthur Brooke's poem *Romeus and Juliet,* with such changes and artistic developments as we might expect. There were no doubt many plays on Julius Cæsar; but Shakespeare's play is a masterly and respectful dramatization of the best available source—Plutarch's lives of Cæsar, Brutus, and Antonius, with possible hints from Appian's *Chronicle of the Roman Wars.* About *Hamlet* we can tell little. There was an old play on the subject, possibly by Thomas Kyd, which is now lost. Other earlier sources are remote. It is *King Lear* from which we get our great lesson. There Shakespeare had an old play to work on, *The True Chronicle History of King Leir and his three daughters,* published in 1605. Shakespeare drew some features of his major plot from this play, but he cannot be said to have rewritten it; for before he composed his play he actually read up his story in practically every known version: Holinshed's *Chronicles,* *The Mirror for Magistrates,* Spenser's *The Faerie Queene,* William Warner's *Albion's England,* and even Geoffrey of Monmouth's *Historia Regum Britonum.* His minor plot he drew from Sidney's *Arcadia.* Here then at least is a clear case, clearer even than that of *Richard II,* where Shakespeare, having before him a literary task, underwent the labor and study of a literary man in order to accomplish his results. With reference to his sources Shakespeare seems to have followed a very simple plan. If the sources were good, he followed them closely; if they were not, he did not. Some of his later plays show this very clearly. *Antony and Cleopatra* and *Coriolanus* are based closely on Plutarch; the parallels are often striking. *Othello*, one of Shakespeare's finest pieces of workmanship, is based on a very crude tale in Giraldi Cinthio's *Heccatomithi*. From it he borrows nothing but the thread of the narrative. *The Winter's Tale* is likewise quite remote from its source in Greene's *Pandosto*.

Shakespeare's working library seems then to have been made up of Holinshed and the other chroniclers, Plutarch, old plays, and of collections of stories, most of these from the Italian. He enriched the themes he derived from these sources from his general reading. This in turn was made up of Ovid, Virgil, and other simple Latin authors; of English poets and prose writers, such as Chaucer, Gower, Spenser, Marlowe, Sidney, Daniel, Drayton, Lyly, Greene, and Lodge; of Arthurian romances, popular songs and ballads, proverbs, and fables; of Montaigne, whom he seems to have known well; and of the Bible (and the Prayer Book), of which his knowledge was extensive. He was acquainted with Rabelais, Ronsard, the Greek romances, Hakluyt and other voyagers, and with a good many current pamphlets. Probably his reading in classical criticism was slight or none at all. We do not, therefore, expect to find in him a high degree of theoretical dramatic art, though he was the greatest of all dramatists.

His purpose was to tell a story Shakespeare's purpose as a writer of plays was really very simple; it was to tell a story on the stage in accordance with the practice of the best Elizabethan dramatists; and this practice paid scant respect to Aristotle and theories of dramatic construction. As a story-teller his means were his scenes and characters; hence it is a mistake to think of the scenes as actual events and of the characters, not as symbols and dramatic puppets employed with the object of narration, but as actual people tied to history or to consistency as by the events of a life. Again, as a story-teller, Shakespeare was certainly not indifferent to the moral of his tales; but he did not, any more than other great story-tellers, tell the tale for the sake of the moral. He did not fail, of course, when opportunity offered, to bring in "wise saws and modern instances," which he no doubt, as well as his audience,

greatly enjoyed, even though "some necessary question of the play be then to be considered." Technically also he is conditioned, not only by the theater in which he worked and the kind of drama he had learned to write, but also apparently by his personal situation. In a few instances he shows signs of haste or carelessness, omitting or slurring over steps in a story; sometimes he writes with a rapidity and compression almost impossible to follow.

Dramatic situation and convention Many of the artistic conventions according to which Shakespeare worked arose out of the Elizabethan stage, such as his practice of using characters in certain situations, like the soliloquy, as his mouthpieces. We must believe what characters say seriously, especially in soliloquies, about themselves and their motives, and what other characters say seriously about them in dialogue. These seem to have been Shakespeare's ways of imparting to the audience his own conceptions. We should, therefore, usually accept at their face value explicitly stated motives; as, for example, that Hamlet is not mad but that he "puts an antic disposition on"; that Shylock hates Antonio not out of gratuitous malice, but because Antonio is a Christian and because "in low simplicity he lends out money gratis and brings down the rate of usance here with us in Venice"; and that Iago's grudge is in part at least a soldier's grudge, because in his case the principle of "old gradation" has been violated. We may acknowledge that, just as Shakespeare often mixes up his time schemes, because on his stage the inconsistency would not be noticed, so also, in the treatment of episodes, characters may run away with his imagination, violate consistency, and so strain the old ready-made plot by putting into it, like new wine in old bottles, utterance which is too vigorous, original, or poetic for the situation. Shakespeare may drag in bits of historical or fictional action which are not in harmony with his treatment of the plot, because presumably they please him or are parts of his source. He is certainly not averse to sententious and poetical speeches which are undramatic and for which the cue in character or plot is of doubtful appropriateness; as when Falstaff soliloquizes on honor,

Mercutio describes Queen Mab, or Romeo, having heard of Juliet's death, stops in his suicidal purpose to speculate on gold, "worse poison to men's souls . . . than these poor compounds that thou mayst not sell."

Shakespearean exuberance All of this repeats, from another point of view, an age-old criticism of Shakespeare; namely, that he is an exuberant artist, that he is not restrained and classical. This exuberance has been his chief source of power; we merely cite the facts in order to control, in the interest of a true and vivid appreciation of Shakespeare, idle and unintelligent speculation on the intepretation of Shakespearean characters and plots. We should learn to surrender ourselves so completely and so intelligently to Shakespeare's artistic appeal that we, as did the audiences for which he wrote, can enjoy his art in spite of its conventions. In doing this we shall not need commentators who insist forever on doing the work over with needless elaborations. We should put ourselves, if we can, into a sufficiently receptive mood to enjoy Shakespeare's appeal to simple emotions, though in so doing it may be necessary for us to suspend our demand for naturalism and philosophy. We should recognize that what we have is a story, told usually marvelously well, with the somewhat crude device of the Elizabethan stage; and that it is a story, moreover, which, however replete with originality, had, oftener than not, no novelty, since it was already familiar to the audience for which it was written.

REFERENCES

Seventeenth and Eighteenth Centuries

BABCOCK, R. W., *The Genesis of Shakespeare Idolatry, 1766-1799*. Chapel Hill, 1931.

DRYDEN, JOHN, *Essays*, edited by W. P. Ker. Oxford, 1900.

FARMER, RICHARD, *Essay on the Learning of Shakespeare*. London, 1767.

JOHNSON, SAMUEL, Preface to an edition of Shakespeare and current criticism within the edition, 1765.

LOUNSBURY, T. R., *Shakespearian Wars*. New Haven, 1901.

MORGANN, MAURICE, *Essay on the Dramatic Character of Sir John Falstaff*. London, 1777.

MUNRO, JOHN, *Shakespeare Allusion-Book*. London, 1909.

SMITH, D. NICHOL, editor, *Eighteenth Century Essays on Shakespeare*. Glasgow, 1903. *Shakespeare in the Eighteenth Century*. Oxford, 1928.

SPENCER, HAZELTON, *Shakespeare Improved*. Cambridge, 1928.

SPINGARN, J. E., editor, *Critical Essays of the Seventeenth Century*. Oxford, 1908.

Extensive quotations from the literary criticism of Shakespeare will be found in Furness's Variorum editions of the plays and in Moulton's *Library of Literary Criticism*.

Nineteenth Century

BOAS, F. S., *Shakspere and his Predecessors*. New York, 1910.

BRANDES, GEORGE, *William Shakespeare*. Engl. trans., New York, 1924.

BROOKE, S. A., *On Ten Plays of Shakespeare* and *On Ten More Plays of Shakespeare*. London, 1905, 1913.

COLERIDGE, S. T., *Notes and Lectures upon Shakespeare* (many reprints).

DOWDEN, EDWARD, *Shakspere, His Mind and Art*. London, 1875.

ELZE, KARL, *William Shakespeare*. Engl. trans., London, 1888.

EMERSON, R. W., "Shakespeare the Poet," in *Representative Men*.

HAZLITT, WILLIAM, *Characters of Shakespeare's Plays* (many reprints).

HUDSON, H. N., *Shakespeare, his Life, Art and Characters*. New ed. London, 1895.

JAMESON, ANNA, *Characteristics of Women*. Boston, 1898; reprinted as *Shakespeare's Women*.

LAMB, CHARLES, "On the Tragedies of Shakespeare," in *Miscellaneous Essays*.

MARTIN, LADY (HELEN FAUCIT), *On Some of Shakespeare's Female Characters*. Edinburgh, 1887.

MOULTON, R. G., *Shakespeare as a Dramatic Artist*. Oxford, 1906. *The Moral System of Shakespeare*. New York, 1903; reissued under the title *Shakespeare as a Dramatic Thinker*.

SCHLEGEL, A. W. VON, *Lectures on Dramatic Art and Literature*. Engl. trans., second edition, London, 1902.

SWINBURNE, A. C., *A Study of Shakespeare*. London, 1895.

WENDELL, BARRETT, *William Shakespeare*. New York, 1894.

WHITE, R. G., *Studies in Shakespeare*, Boston, 1885.

Twentieth Century

BAKER, GEORGE P., *The Development of Shakespeare as a Dramatist*. New York, 1907.

BRADLEY, A. C., *Shakespearean Tragedy*. London, 1904. *Oxford Lectures on Poetry*. London, 1908.

CHAMBERS, E. K., *William Shakespeare*. Oxford, 1930.

LAWRENCE, W. W., *Shakespeare's Problem Comedies*. New York, 1931.

LEE, SIR SIDNEY, *Shakespeare and the Modern Stage*. New York, 1906.

MacCALLUM, M. W., *Shakespeare's Roman Plays and their Background*. London, 1910.

MATTHEWS, BRANDER, *Shakespeare as a Playwright*. New York, 1913.

RALEIGH, SIR WALTER, *Shakespeare*. New York, 1907.

SCHELLING, F. E., *Elizabethan Drama*. Boston, 1908. Invaluable in its presentation of Shakespeare in his relation to Elizabethan drama as a whole.

SCHÜCKING, L. L., *Character Problems in Shakespeare's Plays*. New York, 1922.

STOLL, E. E., *Shakespeare Studies*. New York, 1927.

Drama as a Fine Art

BAKER, GEORGE P., *Dramatic Technique*. Boston, 1919.

BUTCHER, SAMUEL H., *Aristotle's Theory of Poetry and Fine Art*. Second edition. London, 1898.

COOPER, LANE, amplified edition of Aristotle's *Poetics*. Boston, 1913. *Aristotelian Theory of Comedy*. New York, 1922.

FREYTAG, G., *Technique of the Drama*. Engl. trans., Chicago, 1895.

MATTHEWS, BRANDER, *A Study of the Drama*. Boston, 1910.

WOODBRIDGE, ELISABETH, *The Drama, its Law and Technique*. Boston, 1900.

VII. EDITIONS, EDITORS, AND ACTORS OF SHAKESPEARE: HIS POSTHUMOUS REPUTATION

The First Folio During the period of Shakespeare's dramatic activity eighteen of his plays were printed separately in quarto editions. A nineteenth, *Othello*, appeared in quarto in 1622. Seven years after Shakespeare's death, in 1623, John Heminge and Henry Condell, two of his fellow-actors, collected for publication the texts of thirty-six plays, which were printed in a single folio volume bearing a title-page as follows:

MR. WILLIAM / SHAKESPEARES / COMEDIES, / HISTORIES, & / TRAGEDIES. / Published according to the True Originall Copies./ [Droeshout engraving here] / LONDON / Printed by Isaac Iaggard and Ed. Blount. 1623.

The book contains an epistle dedicatory to the Earl of Pembroke and the Earl of Montgomery, Shakespeare's patrons, and an address *To the Great Variety of Readers*, both signed by John Heminge and Henry Condell; also Ben Jonson's famous ode *To the memory of my beloued, The AVTHOR Mr. William Shakespeare: And what he hath left us*, and other commendatory verses signed variously by Hugh Holland, L. Digges, and I[ames] M[abbe]. Another important document in the book is a list of "The Names of the Principall Actors in all these Playes."

The plays in the volume are grouped as comedies, histories, and tragedies, each new group beginning with separate pagina-

tion—a circumstance which may indicate that the publishers had planned originally to make it a three-volume work. *Troilus and Cressida* is omitted from the table of contents, but is inserted with incomplete and erroneous pagination between the histories and the tragedies. *Pericles*, which had appeared in quarto in 1609 with Shakespeare's name on its title-page, is omitted altogether. The histories are arranged chronologically with respect to the kings they treat. Other than this, the collectors seem to have followed no scheme of arrangement excepting the three-fold grouping according to type.

The introductory material to the First Folio supplies us with considerable information. Ben Jonson's prophetic ode with its high evaluation of Shakespeare's talents offers an estimate by his most rigorous contemporary critic of his place as an artist among both his predecessors and his fellow-dramatists. Jonson hails him as

Soule of the Age!
The applause! delight! the wonder of our Stage!
My *Shakespeare*, rise; I will not lodge thee by
Chaucer, or *Spenser*, or bid *Beaumont* lye
A little further, to make thee a roome:
Thou art a Moniment, without a tombe,
And art aliue still, while thy Booke doth liue,
And we haue wit to read, and praise to giue.
That I not mixe thee so, my braine excuses;
I meane with great, but disproportion'd *Muses*.
For, if I thought my iudgement were of yeeres,
I should commit thee surely with thy peeres.

And tell, how farre thou didst our *Lyly* out-shine,
　Or sporting *Kid*, or *Marlowes* mighty line.
And though thou hadst small *Latine*, and lesse
　Greeke,
　From thence to honour thee, I would not seeke
For names; but call forth thund'ring *Æschilus*,
　Euripides, and *Sophocles* to vs,
Paccuuius, *Accius*, him of *Cordoua* dead,
　To life againe, to heare thy Buskin tread,
And shake a Stage: Or, when thy Sockes were on,
　Leaue thee alone, for the comparison
Of all, that insolent *Greece*, or haughtie *Rome*
　Sent forth, or since did from their ashes come.
Triumph, my *Britaine*, thou hast one to showe,
　To whom all Scenes of *Europe* homage owe.
He was not of an age, but for all time!

. . . .

Nature her selfe was proud of his designes,
　And ioy'd to weare the dressing of his lines!
Which were so richly spun, and wouen so fit,
　As, since, she will vouchsafe no other Wit.

. . . .

Yet must I not giue Nature all: Thy Art,
　My gentle *Shakespeare*, must enioy a part.
For though the *Poets* matter, Nature be,
　His art doth giue the fashion. . . .
. . . . Looke how the father's face
Liues in his issue, euen so, the race
Of *Shakespeare's* minde, and manners brightly
　shines,
　In his well torned, and true-filed lines:
In each of which, he seemes to shake a Lance,
　As brandish't at the eyes of Ignorance.
Sweet Swan of *Auon!* what a sight it were
　To see thee in our waters yet appeare,
And make those flights vpon the bankes of
　Thames,
　That so did take *Eliza*, and our *Iames!*
But stay, I see thee in the *Hemisphere*
　Aduanc'd, and made a Constellation there!
Shine forth, thou Starre of *Poets*. . . .

Heminge and Condell in the epistle
dedicatory seem to assume the responsibility for the publication of the Folio,
claiming that their act is purely a labor
of love:

We haue but collected them [the plays], and
done an office to the dead, to procure his Orphanes,
Guardians; vvithout ambition either of selfe-
profit, or fame: onely to keepe the memory of so
worthy a Friend, & Fellow aliue, as was our
Shakespeare. . . .

In the advertisement *To the Great Variety
of Readers*, they repeat this claim; they also
make assertions which, at the hands of
editors and critics, have been made to
yield a number of inferences concerning the

nature of the original materials which were
used in making up the printed text of the
Folio:

It had bene a thing, we confesse, worthie to
haue bene wished, that the Author himselfe had
liu'd to haue set forth, and ouerseen his owne
writings; But since it hath bin ordain'd otherwise, and he by death departed from that right,
we pray you do not envie his Friends, the office
of their care, and paine, to haue collected &
publish'd them; and so to haue publish'd them,
as where (before) you were abus'd with diuerse
stolne, and surreptitious copies, maimed, and
deformed by the frauds and stealthes of iniurious
impostors, that expos'd them: euen those, are
now offer'd to your view cur'd, and perfect of
their limbes; and all the rest, absolute in their
numbers, as he conceiued the*m*. Who, as he
was a happie imitator of Nature, was a most
gentle expresser of it. His mind and hand went
together: And what he thought, he vttered with
that easinesse, that wee haue scarse receiued from
him a blot in his papers. But it is not our
prouince, who onely gather his works, and giue
them you, to praise him. It is yours that reade
him.

In view of the fact that the quarto texts
in the majority of instances differ in varying degrees from those of the Folio, the
Shakespeare student often has two versions
of a play to consider. For many years after
the appearance of the First Folio, the editors
and critics accorded the greater authenticity
to it, basing their ascriptions of superiority
on the circumstances of its publication and
on the claims made by Heminge and Condell
in the prefatory matter. In its various addresses to the reader, in its commendatory
verses by Shakespeare's fellow-poets, and in
the very sanction of the two senior members
of the dramatic company which held
Shakespeare's plays in its possession, the
Folio has strong claims to authenticity.
The title-page of the book announces that
the plays are "Published according to the
True Originall Copies," as does the page
containing the list of actors, where it is
stated that the book contains "all his
comedies, histories, and tragedies: truely
set forth, according to their first originall."

**The copy for
the Folio** Although it is more or less
generally agreed that the
superlative quality of these
addresses is conventional eulogy, much
significance is to be attached to some of
the statements there made. Heminge and

Condell, regretting that Shakespeare did not live to "haue set forth, and ouerseen his owne writings," make no professions of having done it for him. They have merely "collected them, and done an office to the dead"; that is, they have brought together and turned over to the printer copies of the plays which they had at hand. Furthermore, the reference to the unblotted pages would imply that these copies were in Shakespeare's own autograph. This, however, is not always the case. Mr. J. Dover Wilson has pointed out[1] that eight of the Folio plays were printed from existing quartos: *Titus Andronicus, Much Ado about Nothing, Love's Labour's Lost, A Midsummer-Night's Dream, The Merchant of Venice, Richard II, 1 Henry IV*, and *Romeo and Juliet*. At least two of the plays, *The Two Gentlemen of Verona* and *The Merry Wives of Windsor*, he thinks, have been assembled "by piecing together the players' parts and arranging them in scenes with the aid of the 'plot.'" By "plot" is meant a skeleton of the play used in staging it and containing, scene by scene, the names of the characters and the actors in order of their entrance. A considerable number of the plays in the Folio, Mr. Wilson shows, were printed directly from the prompt books of the Globe Theater.

The good and bad quartos Most conspicuous among the assertions of Heminge and Condell is that concerning the "diuerse stolne, and surreptitious copies, maimed, and deformed by the frauds and stealthes of iniurious impostors." For a long time this statement was regarded by many as a condemnation of the quartos that had previously appeared. However, the fact that the quartos frequently offer as good texts as the Folio, occasionally even better, and that Shakespeare's fellows made use of eight of them in preparing the Folio copy, caused a group of recent scholars to subject all of the quartos to bibliographical examination. Mr. A. W. Pollard, a pioneer in this type of investigation,[2] offers as a result, a new classification of Shakespeare texts wherein the quartos fall into two distinct groups which he designates as "good"

and "bad." In arriving at this grouping, Mr. Pollard selects as good texts, first, those quartos which have been used as copy for the Folio, and, secondly, those which have been generally agreed upon by Shakespeare editors as being good texts. There are fourteen of them:

Titus Andronicus	1594
Richard II	1597
Richard III	1597
Love's Labour's Lost	1598
1 Henry IV	1598
Romeo and Juliet	1599
The Merchant of Venice	1600
Much Ado about Nothing	1600
2 Henry IV	1600
A Midsummer-Night's Dream	1600
Hamlet	1604–5
King Lear	1608
Troilus and Cressida	1609
Othello	1622

Of these fourteen "good" quartos, twelve, Mr. Pollard notes, were regularly entered in the Stationers' Register to the printers or publishers whose names appear on the title-pages. The two exceptions are *Love's Labour's Lost* and *Romeo and Juliet*. A very poor version of the latter play had been published in 1597, in allusion to which the "good" quarto of 1599 bore on its title-page the statement, "*Newly corrected, augmented, and amended.*" Since this good copy was a second edition, license for its publication was not required. The title-page of *Love's Labour's Lost* indicates that it too was intended to supersede a first quarto (now lost), and that license was not required for its reissue. Finding the absence of an entry in the Stationers' Register in the case of these two good quartos explainable by their both being possibly second editions, Mr. Pollard proposes, as another characteristic of the "good quarto," its authorized publication.

The converse of this situation is true in regard to the "bad" quartos. The texts which comprise this group are:

Romeo and Juliet	1597
Henry V	1600
The Merry Wives of Windsor	1602
Hamlet	1603
Pericles	1609

Of these quartos *Romeo and Juliet* and *Henry V* were printed without license

[1] "The Task of Heminge and Condell," in *Studies in the First Folio*, pp. 55-77.
[2] See his *Shakespeare's Folios and Quartos* and *Shakespeare's Fight with the Pirates*.

from the Stationers' Company, and *Hamlet* and *Pericles* were entered to other firms than those publishing them. *The Merry Wives of Windsor* presents the anomaly of having been transferred to a second publisher on the very day of its license. John Busby, the man to whom it was entered, and the printer, Thomas Creed, were also responsible for the bad version of *Henry V* in 1600—another circumstance which gives the quarto of *The Merry Wives* a questionable reputation. The actual publisher, Arthur Johnson, Mr. Pollard remarks, was probably cautious enough to insist on Busby's entering the book before he would buy it for publication. At any rate, all five of these quartos have suspicious records with respect to the regulations of the book trade. To this group should also be added *The First Part of the Contention betwixt the two famous Houses of York and Lancaster* (1594) and *The True Tragedy of Richard Duke of York* (1595) as imperfect versions of *2* and *3 Henry VI* respectively. The former was entered in the Stationers' Register; the latter was not.

These "bad" quartos, in addition to their not being regularly authorized for publication, present inferior texts; that is, they are abbreviated and badly garbled in comparison with the texts of corresponding plays in the Folio. Such a condition may be due to their having been pirated by stenography during a performance, or to a dishonest actor's patching up of a version from his own player's part and what he could remember of the parts of others. Such thefts may have been, and probably were, committed in order to get a version for acting rather than printing; and such stolen texts may later have fallen into the hands of the printers. The piracy explanation is in accord with Heminge and Condell's allusion to the "stolne and surreptitious copies." In whatever way these bad texts came into existence, there is every indication that they are some distance removed from the author's original. The final discrimination between good and bad texts must rest on the relation they bear to the manuscripts as the author prepared them. For some plays the Folio is the only authoritative source of text; for others, good quartos claim superiority to the Folio. However, in a few cases, such as *Richard III*, there is occasion for indecision between a quarto and the Folio, since each presents a text independent of the other, and both are in themselves good.

The playwright and his play   Such is the complex situation with regard to Shakespeare's printed texts. The problem of how Shakespeare got into print owes its complexity to the fact that the poet was in no way concerned with the printing of his plays; moreover, that he did not prepare his manuscripts with any expectation of their appearing in this way. Shakespeare wrote, apparently, with one idea in mind—that of producing plays which would act well on the stage, attract large numbers of spectators, and swell the receipts of the Globe Theater. The somewhat hostile reception in 1616 of the folio collection of Ben Jonson's plays indicates a lack of regard on the part of the Elizabethan public for stage plays as serious literary productions. The relation of the playwright to his play and to its actors explains one aspect of the problem. Playwriting was an occupation of the hour, an activity in which men engaged to supply an immediate demand. A dramatist was usually attached by contract to a specific company for which he was under bond to furnish a stipulated number of plays. He did not work out his play independently of the players. In fact, it was his duty to produce a piece which would provide parts for the several actors of the company. Shakespeare's skill in adapting rôles to actors is attested in the new type of clown which he introduced into his plays about 1599, when by a change in the Lord Chamberlain's company, Robert Armin took Will Kemp's place as chief comic actor. The poet may have chosen his own theme for a play, he may have been given a piece to revise, or he may have been instructed to write a new play to rival a popular one in another theater. At any rate, the company bought the completed play outright; and with the exception, possibly, of realizing a "benefit" for its first performances, or, in case he were also an actor, of assuming one of its rôles, or of subjecting it later to revision, the dramatist was severed by the sale from all connections with his drama.

If the play made its appearance in print, the text for it had to be acquired by the publisher through the company owning it, or through some means of piracy.

The printing of plays It was not to the interests of a dramatic company to have its plays printed. A popular play, available to the public only through a stage performance by its owners, was one of the greatest assets of a company. The agreement between the members of the Company of the Revels in 1608 attests the higher value which was placed on an unprinted play. Among other terms, they agree:

> That no man of the said company shall at any time put into print, any manner of play-book now in use, or that hereafter shall be sold unto them, upon the penalty and forfeiture of forty pounds sterling, or the loss of his place and share of all things amongst them.[1]

Many stage plays were nevertheless printed. The Stationers' Register shows that between 1590 and 1600 over 150 plays were authorized for publication. As Professor Adams observes,[2] it is difficult to believe that such a large number would have been so authorized without the consent of the owners. He also points out possible reasons for which acting companies may have released manuscripts for printing. In the first place, when a company disbanded, play manuscripts, along with their other mutual property, were divided among the shareholders, who, to realize some profit, might sell them either to other acting companies or to publishers. In the second place, some misfortune might necessitate the sale of play manuscripts. It is significant that at times when the theaters were closed for long periods on account of the plague, or were threatened by Puritan agitation, the number of plays licensed for printing increased greatly. Again, the publication of a play might follow upon some unusual circumstance. It is thought that *1 Henry IV* was printed soon after its composition and while it was still creating a great sensation, in order to placate the Cobham family, who had taken offense at the name of their ancestor Oldcastle's being applied to the fat knight whom Shakespeare subsequently rechristened Falstaff. Lastly, the company might give an author permission to have a play or a collection of plays printed. Instances of this are found in the publication of Heywood's *The Rape of Lucrece* and Ben Jonson's folio collection of 1616. Indeed, Shakespeare's First Folio itself is an instance in which the owners authorized the publication of plays.

The mode of procedure, when acting companies permitted the printing of their plays, would be for the publisher who bought the book from the company to take the manuscript to the warden of the Stationers' Company, to whom he paid sixpence for having it entered on the Register of the company. The man who acquired the copy for a book by dishonest means was not likely to apply for a license, but would run the risk of printing it without. Mr. Pollard observes that the presence in London of more printers than there was work for contributed to the prevalence of piracy of books. An unscrupulous printer, if he were in hard straits financially, would be willing to pay a few pence for a bad copy. But since the acting companies were likely to safeguard themselves against piracies as much as possible, the pirate must resort to surreptitious means of acquiring a text. A means of piracy frequently relied upon in explanation of a bad text is that of the shorthand reporter. That such men sat in the theater and took down plays by stenography is known. Thomas Heywood alludes to such a method when he makes the complaint that some of his plays had, without his knowledge or direction, "come into the Printers hands, and therefore so corrupt and mangled, (coppied only by the eare) that I have been as vnable to know them, as ashamed to challenge them. . . ."[3] Recent scholarship has also attempted to explain some of the bad texts by means of the theory of the dishonest actor. Some one of the cast, most likely not a shareholder of the company but a hired-man, would, they think, put together a garbled text, piecing it out from memory with the aid of his own lines and cues. Something of

---

[1] New Sh. Soc. *Trans.* 1887-1890 p. 276.
[2] *Life of William Shakespeare*, pp. 511 ff.

[3] From Heywood's preface to *The Rape of Lucrece*. Heywood repeats the complaint in *Pleasant Dialogues and Dramas*.

this sort must have been alluded to by Heminge and Condell when they decried the "stolne, and surreptitious copies, maimed, and deformed by iniurious impostors." Either method, it is obvious, would produce a bad text, and it may very well be true that the five so-called bad quartos, since they lack the endorsement of proper license, have come into existence in one of these ways. In some cases also a whole company, knowing a play but having no book, may have collaborated in the production of a necessarily imperfect text.

Plays "to be stayed" Some of the plays are entered in the Stationers' Register with special provisions which have been regarded as means of precaution against piracy. *The Merchant of Venice* was licensed on July 22, 1598, to James Roberts, "Prouided, that yt bee not prynted by the said James Robertes or anye other whatsoeuer without lycence first had from the Right honorable the lord Chamberlen." *Troilus and Cressida* was entered to Roberts in 1603 "to print when he hath gotten sufficient aucthority for yt." Evidently sufficient authority was not forthcoming, for in 1609 this play was printed after a second entry "by *G. Eld* for *R. Bonian* and *H. Walley*." *Henry V, As You Like It*, and *Much Ado about Nothing* are named "to be staied" on a fly-leaf of *Register C* on August 4, 1600, in a list of "My lord chamberlens mens plaies Entred." In commenting on this note Mr. Pollard says, "As there is no book-seller's name to the staying entries, it is clear that they were made directly at the instance of 'my lord chamberlens men.'"[1] Such notes and entries, Mr. Pollard thinks, indicate precaution on the part of the company to safeguard its property. That a staying entry was not altogether effective in preventing piracy is proved by the appearance in 1600 of the bad quarto of *Henry V*, just as the ordinary entry of *Hamlet* to Roberts in 1602 did not insure against its publication by Valentine Sims and Nicholas Ling in 1603. The stipulated terms here quoted, may, however, indicate an effort by Shakespeare's company to keep certain plays out of print.

The known facts and inferences with regard to original Shakespeare texts may be summed up as follows: In 1623, thirty-six of the plays were authoritatively published in the First Folio. Prior to this date nineteen had appeared in quarto, twelve of which present texts undoubtedly authentic; three have every indication of illegitimate origin; and two exist in both good and bad quartos. *The Contention* and *The True Tragedy*, distorted versions of *2* and *3 Henry VI*, are also to be regarded as "bad" quartos, though they may have originated, not from a definite act of piracy, but from the joint effort of a group of actors to record from memory plays to which they had a claim. Repeated editions of some of the quartos evince Shakespeare's immediate popularity. Two, *Richard III* and *1 Henry IV*, were each printed five times during Shakespeare's lifetime. Several other plays went through three or four editions before the printing of the Folio.

The collection of 1619 In 1619 an attempt was made to publish a collection of Shakespeare's plays. Thomas Pavier, a stationer of questionable standing in the brotherhood, undertook the project. He had the copyright to *Henry V*[2] and to three other plays which had some connection with Shakespeare's name. These plays are *A Yorkshire Tragedy*, printed in 1608 for Pavier with Shakespeare's name on the title-page; *The Whole Contention between the Famous Houses of Lancaster and York*, already published separately as *The Contention* and *The True Tragedy*; and *Sir John Oldcastle*, which is reminiscent of Shakespeare's Falstaff. With these four plays as a nucleus, he appropriated five other plays to which he had no right: *The Merchant of Venice, A Midsummer-Night's Dream, The Merry Wives of Windsor, King Lear*, and *Pericles*. It appears that his design was to publish these nine plays in a single quarto volume which William Jaggard was to print for him. For some reason Pavier abandoned his original plan, but, in order that he might not suffer too great financial loss, broke the volume up into separate quartos. Why he abandoned his

---

[1] *Shakespeare's Folios and Quartos*, p. 35.

[2] This play was assigned to Pavier, by whom it is not stated, on August 14, 1600, ten days after a staying entry.

scheme is a matter for conjecture. It may be that some of the rightful owners of the good quartos got wind of the venture and threatened to prosecute him. His unscrupulousness is thought to appear in his placing on some of the title-pages fictitious dates, and on all of them curtailed and abbreviated imprints;[1] but he may have intended to place a correctly dated title-page in front of the collected volume.

The Folio copyrights This abandoned attempt at a collected edition of Shakespeare may have furnished the suggestion for publishing the 1623 Folio. At any rate, the Folio followed hard upon the Pavier venture. Since William Jaggard was the printer in both enterprises, one is tempted to infer that he was the promoter of this second project. But if he did conceive the idea, he could not consummate it alone. In the first place, he possessed copyrights of only those plays which had been licensed to James Roberts, whose printing business he had acquired in 1608. The copyrights of the other quartos were distributed principally among William Aspley and John Smethwick. Matters were facilitated by bringing these men in as joint publishers. Edward Blount, who held the right to *Antony and Cleopatra* and to *Pericles*, also became a member of the partnership. By such a coalition the group had control of all the licensed quartos except *Troilus and Cressida*, which belonged to Henry Walley, *Richard II*, *Richard III*, and *1 Henry IV*, all belonging to Matthew Law, and the two pirated plays, *Henry V* and *The Merry Wives of Windsor*, belonging to Thomas Pavier and Arthur Johnson respectively. What negotiation took place between the Folio editors and these men is not known. The fact that *Troilus and Cressida* is inserted between the histories and the tragedies with incorrect pagination, and is omitted from the catalogue of plays at the head of the volume, has suggested that Walley for a long time refused to allow the inclusion of this play. Its inclusion was finally achieved. There remained then the eighteen plays as yet unprinted in any form

[1]For a full discussion see Pollard, *Shakespeare's Folios and Quartos*, ch. IV; W. J. Neidig, "The Shakespeare Quartos of 1619," in *Modern Philology*, VII (1910), pp. 145 ff.

to be supplied by the King's men. This copy one may believe, was not always in easily usable condition. For more than twenty years many of the manuscripts had been used as prompt books. In at least two cases, as has been mentioned, it is possible that texts for the Folio were made up from players' parts with the aid of the "plot." Heminge and Condell were, however, able to produce respectable texts of *2* and *3 Henry VI*, *Henry V*, and *The Merry Wives of Windsor*, which had been circulating for twenty years or more in only maimed and deformed state. On November 8, 1623, the entry for the First Folio was made in the Stationer's Register.

Mr. Blount: Isaak Jaggard. Entred for their Copie under the hands of Mr. Doctor Worrall and Mr. Cole, Warden, Mr. William Shakspeers Comedyes, Histories and Tragedyes, soe manie of the said Copies as are not formerly entred to other men vizt, Comedyes. The Tempest. The two gentlemen of Verona. Measure for Measure. The Comedy of Errors. As you Like it. All's well that ends well. Twelft Night. The winters tale. Histories. The thirde parte of Henry the sixt. Henry the eight. Tragedies. Coriolanus. Timon of Athens. Julius Caesar. Mackbeth. Anthonie and Cleopatra. Cymbeline.

It is impossible to know how many copies of the book were printed. Sir Sidney Lee has estimated that there were about 750. About 150 copies are now extant. The book sold in 1623 for twenty shillings. In 1922 the Burdett-Coutts copy was sold in London for 8600 pounds.

The later folios After nine years, the first edition of the First Folio being exhausted, a second was printed. In 1663 a third appeared. A second issue of the third edition came out in 1664 in which were included seven pseudo-Shakespearean plays not previously printed in folio: *Pericles, The London Prodigal, The History of Thomas Lord Cromwell, Sir John Oldcastle, The Puritan Widow, A Yorkshire Tragedy,* and *Locrine.* All of these have been rejected from the canon except *Pericles,* and its claim is questionable. These seven plays were also included in the Fourth Folio of 1685. Each of the three folios subsequent to the first is a reprint of the one next preceding it, each adding new errors and frequently unwarranted corrections.

Later editions   The conscious editing of Shakespeare began in 1709 with Nicholas Rowe's six-volume work, containing the plays as they are in the Fourth Folio. He made some corrections, some emendations, marked the exits and entrances of characters, divided the plays into acts and scenes where this had not been already done, and placed a list of *dramatis personæ* at the beginning of each play. His edition was re-issued in 1714. Alexander Pope next undertook the editing of Shakespeare. His edition, comprising six volumes, appeared in 1725. He excluded from his work the spurious plays which had been added to the Third Folio. His text is based substantially on that of Rowe, but he added to each scene the place of action, and made some changes in scene-division. Pope sometimes rewrote the text of Shakespeare, regularizing the blank verse and filling in passages with his own composition. The next editor was Lewis Theobald, a man of unusual critical skill, who made many brilliant conjectural emendations. He was the first to consult the original quartos and the First Folio. His text, first appearing in 1733, was reissued in 1740, 1752, 1772, and 1773. There followed successively editions by Sir Thomas Hanmer in 1744, by Bishop Warburton in 1747, by Dr. Samuel Johnson in 1765 (who made a beginning in the historical point of view in Shakespeare criticism), by Edward Capell in 1768, and by George Steevens in 1773 (a revision of the edition of Dr. Johnson). In 1790 Edmund Malone produced his ten-volume edition. He re-introduced *Pericles*, which had been excluded since the time of Pope. Malone was a man of great intellectual vigor and a careful scholar. Not content to work on Shakespeare's text in isolation, he read widely in the Elizabethan drama and collected numerous letters and documents of the time. He made use of Henslowe's *Diary*, the Stationers' Register, and the records of the Master of Revels. Malone began work on the first Variorum edition of Shakespeare, which was finished in 1821 by James Boswell, the son of Johnson's biographer.

Malone's work marks the close of the first period of Shakespeare scholarship. It is a period characterized by objective treatment, with no search for subtleties.

Shakespeare study was as yet not hampered by "problems" of character interpretation.

The nineteenth century produced many editions of Shakespeare, and the work of editing still goes on. The following are the more important: William Harness (1825, 8 vols.), S. W. Singer (1826, 1856, 10 vols.), J. Payne Collier (1841-4, 8 vols.), Charles Knight (1838-42, 8 vols.), Alexander Dyce (1857, 9 vols.), Howard Staunton (1868-70, 3 vols.), Nikolaus Delius (1854-61, 7 vols.), H. N. Hudson (1851-56, 11 vols.), J. O. Halliwell [-Phillipps] (1853-61, 15 vols.), William George Clark and Aldis Wright (Cambridge, 1863-6, 9 vols.; Globe, 1864, 1 vol.), Richard Grant White (1857-65, 12 vols.), W. J. Rolfe (1871-96, 40 vols.), Appleton Morgan (Bankside, 1888 ff.), F. A. Marshall and others (The Henry Irving Shakespeare, 1888-90, 8 vols.), C. H. Herford (Eversley, 1899, 10 vols.), F. J. Furnivall (Leopold with Delius' text, 1874, 1 vol.), Sir Israel Gollancz (Temple, 1894-5, 40 vols.), W. J. Craig (Oxford, 1894, 1 vol.), Helen Porter and Charlotte Clarke (First Folio, 1903), W. A. Neilson (Cambridge, 1906, 1 vol.). Besides these there are the recently completed annotated editions, one play to the volume, under the editorship of various scholars: Tudor (W. A. Neilson and A. H. Thorndike, general editors), Arden (W. J. Craig, general editor), and Yale (W. L. Cross, Tucker Brooke, and W. H. Durham, general editors). The new Variorum Edition, under the editorship of H. H. Furness, and later of H. H. Furness, jun., is still in progress; rather more than half of the total number of Shakespeare's plays have appeared. A facsimile of the First Folio with an introduction by Sir Sidney Lee was published by the Oxford University Press in 1902, and facsimiles of all four Folios by Methuen, 1904-10. Most of the early quartos were reproduced by photographic process by J. W. Griggs under the supervision of Dr. F. J. Furnivall, 1883-8, in 43 volumes. A good deal of the work of nineteenth century English scholars is included in the publications of the Shakespeare Society (1841-53) and of the New Shakespeare Society (1874-94), though Shakespeare material is scattered over a wide range.

Shakespeare on the Continent English players traveled widely in the later years of Queen Elizabeth and in the time of King James, in Scotland, Ireland, France, and the countries of northern Europe. They carried with them their plays, and in Germany particularly the English drama took root. The players had their patrons and their imitators on German soil. The days of the wanderings of the English actors extended from about 1586 until at least the time of the outbreak of the Thirty Years' War in 1618.

A number of their play-lists are in existence, and most of the plays can be recognized as those of the London stage. A few of the plays themselves have been preserved—translated into German, adapted to German tastes, and often rendered almost unrecognizable. There is no one of them of which it can be certainly said that it is based on a play of Shakespeare, although there are six or more which are somehow related to his plays. We seem in every case to have to do with pre-Shakespearean versions rather than with Shakespeare, a condition to be explained by the circumstance that the greater number of the English dramas imported by the players into Germany were carried there in the early nineties of the sixteenth century.

A volume of *Engelische Comedien und Tragedien* (1620) contains among others *Julio und Hyppolita* related to *The Two Gentlemen of Verona*, and *Titus Andronicus* related to Shakespeare's play of the same name. Jacob Ayrer of Nuremberg wrote about 1595, apparently under English influence, *Die schöne Sidea*, and *Die schöne Phænicia*, related in theme to *The Tempest* and *Much Ado about Nothing*, respectively. There is a German *Romeo and Juliet* from a seventeenth century Vienna manuscript; and the best known of all is *Der bestraffte Brudermord*, a play on the subject of *Hamlet*, derived from a manuscript now lost which bore the date 1710. There are also a few other puzzling relations between Shakespeare and the plays of this first period of English influence in Germany.[1]

The continent yielded slowly to Shakespeare's influence. After Lessing's *Hamburgische Dramaturgie* (1767) there began in Germany a profound interest in Shakespeare, which has increased rather than diminished in force as time has gone on. Germany has produced a great group of Shakespeare scholars. Goethe was much interested in Shakespeare, and Schiller was his imitator. Among the important German names in Shakespeare scholarship are A. W. von Schlegel and Ludwig Tieck, who together produced a famous translation of Shakespeare, which has itself taken rank as a classic; others are: Hermann Ulrici, G. G. Gervinus, Friedrich Kreyssig, Karl Elze, Nikolaus Delius, Bernhard ten Brink (a Hollander, most of whose work was in German), and Wilhelm Creizenach. The Germans have been in recent years effective students of staging, and indeed always have given Shakespeare the advantage of frequent presentation on the stage. Much of the work of German Shakespeareans is contained in the Shakespeare *Jahrbuch*, the sixty-sixth volume of which appeared in 1930. In France Shakespeare met with long opposition, though he won the favor of Victor Hugo, has been frequently seen on the French stage, and now has a relatively large following. In Italy likewise Shakespeare was little known before the nineteenth century, but there too he has been acted with great success and has attracted the attention of many scholars. In recent years Shakespeare has been eagerly studied in Slavic countries, in Japan, and in India.

Stage history It may be that the seventeenth and eighteenth centuries were inferior to the nineteenth in high appreciation of Shakespeare's genius and in their methods of studying his plays; but in another respect they were not inferior. They acted Shakespeare so well that the foundations of his posthumous reputation were laid by his career on the stage. The results of the work of scholars and critics is slow in coming, their appeal being to readers; interpretation by actors is, on the other hand, immediately addressed to the multitude, who have been deliberately prepared in their emotions both to understand and to feel.

[1]A. Cohn, *Shakespeare in Germany*, London, 1865; W. Creizenach, *Schauspiele der englischen Komödianten*, Berlin, 1903; Chambers, *The Elizabethan Stage*, I, 342-7; II, 272-92.

The actors for whom Shakespeare wrote his plays were evidently a great group. This appears not less in the case of Richard Burbage, for whom he created the parts of Richard III, Romeo, Brutus, Hamlet, Othello, Lear, Macbeth, Antony, Coriolanus, and Prospero, than in actors like Thomas Pope, for whom he may have written the part of Falstaff; John Heminge, who may have played the parts of Polonius and Kent; Will Kemp, who played Dogberry and may have played Bottom; Robert Armin, for whom Shakespeare wrote the parts of Touchstone, Feste, and the Fool in *King Lear;* and, finally, the boy actor, possibly Robert Goffe, who played Portia and Juliet, and the one, possibly John Edmans, to whom was confided the task of playing Lady Macbeth and Cleopatra. Burbage's immediate successor in the principal rôles was Joseph Taylor, who is known to have played the part of Iago and who played leading rôles in the dramas of Beaumont and Fletcher and of Massinger.

When the theaters were re-opened after the Restoration of Charles II, Shakespeare was frequently acted, and there appeared in Thomas Betterton (1635?-1710) a great Shakespeare actor. Betterton made some investigations as to Shakespeare's life, learned what he could about the stage tradition of the earlier age, and acted a large number of Shakespeare rôles, principally Hamlet, Othello, Brutus, Coriolanus, and Macbeth. He encouraged the appearance of women in women's parts on the stage, instead of boys in these parts as had been the Elizabethan and Jacobean custom, and his wife, who was first known on the stage as Mrs. Saunderson, played Ophelia to his Hamlet and Lady Macbeth to his Macbeth. Another actor of the time was Barton Booth (1681-1733), a man of great ability and charming disposition. The Irishman Robert Wilks (1635?-1732) was on the stage in time to be Betterton's rival. He was an actor of very great versatility and appeared in many plays. Charles Macklin (1697?-1797), also Irish, carried on the Betterton tradition and is illustrious because it was he who perceived the deeper human qualities in the character of Shylock, a part which had been played as a sort of comic villain until Macklin made of him a figure of dignity and pathos.

The great David Garrick (1717-1779) made his appearance on the stage in 1741 and for thirty-five years was a completely dominant figure. Garrick is the originator of the modern school of acting. Before his time acting was highly conventionalized and certainly declamatory. Garrick "held a mirror up to nature," and the consequent variety of passion and mood and versatility in impersonation gave the English stage its pre-eminence for a hundred years. He was a scholarly, intelligent man, who saw that Shakespeare was better than his adapters, and, although he did do a good deal of violence to Shakespeare in the texts he played, it may be said that his claim that he had restored the true Shakespeare to the stage is by and large valid. Mrs. Clive, Mrs. Cibber, and Mrs. Pritchard played leading women's parts in Garrick's performances. He had won his reputation with the part of Richard III and played that play as part of the repertory of his farewell appearance in 1776. With him on that occasion Sarah Siddons (1755-1831), the greatest of English tragic actresses, played the part of Lady Anne. Her career really began in 1782 and lasted until her retirement in 1812. During that time hers was a name to conjure with. She belonged to the famous stage family of the Kembles. Her brother Charles Kemble was a talented actor, and her elder brother John Philip Kemble (1757-1825) succeeded Garrick in the leadership of the English stage. John Philip Kemble was a man of such taste, learning, and power that his influence was long felt.

A few years before Kemble's death a new star of the first magnitude appeared. Edmund Kean (1787-1833), who is regarded as the greatest genius who has ever appeared on the English stage, played in London for the first time on February 26, 1814, at Drury Lane Theater in the part of Shylock. He was the greatest of Richards, Hamlets, Othellos, and his King Lear has set the pattern for all subsequent impersonations and has probably never been equaled. His wonderful career came to an end in 1833. After Kean, William Charles Macready (1793-1873) was the leading Shakespeare actor in England for more than forty years. With him were associated Mrs. Warner and Helen Faucit (Lady Martin). One of the most important ventures in the acting of Shakespeare during the nineteenth century was a series of excellent revivals of nearly all the plays under the leadership of Samuel Phelps (1804-1878) at Sadler's Wells Theater from 1844 to 1862. Nothing quite so good and so successful has been done in England since. Sir Henry Irving (1838-1905) was an actor of great distinction, who played in many roles and was noteworthy for the perfection of his staging and costumes. From 1878 until 1901 he was assisted by Miss Ellen Terry. The most important actor of Shakespeare since Sir Henry Irving is Sir Johnston Forbes-Robertson. Meantime in America there had sprung up a vigorous interest in the dramatic presentation of Shakespeare. Contemporary with Kean and Macready were Junius Brutus Booth (1796-1852) and Edwin Forrest (1806-1892). Then came John Edward McCullough (1837-1885), a follower of Forrest's in the more rhetorical style of acting. Edwin Booth (1833-1893) was the greatest of American actors of Shakespeare. Refined in his methods and not wanting in culture and scholarship, he was a highly gifted actor, and his fame was world-wide. Associated with him for a time in the acting of Shakespeare was Lawrence Barrett (1831-1891). Since Booth's time we have had the very excellent work of Mr. E. H. Sothern, who has carried on the Booth tradition. The greatest American Shakespeare actresses have been Charlotte Cushman (1816-1876), Mary Anderson, Ada Rehan, and Julia Marlowe. The four eminent actors of Shakespeare in Germany in the nineteenth century, as given by Sir Sidney Lee, were Friedrich Ulrich Ludwig Schroeder (1744-1816), Ludwig Devrient (1784-1832), and his nephew Gustav Emil Devrient (1803-1872), and Ludwig Barnay (b. 1842). In recent years work of the greatest distinction has been done by Max Reinhardt (b. 1873). From 1893 to 1903 he was an actor at Salzburg and at Berlin. Since 1903 he has produced at the Deutsches Theater and his own theaters in Berlin practically all of Shakespeare, as well as of Molière, Goethe, Ibsen, and other important dramatists. His method of staging, which employs the principle of artistic suggestion in form and color rather than accurate historical detail, has been followed all over the world. In England the new staging methods have appeared in the work of Edward Gordon Craig, Harley Granville-Barker, and Sir Barry Jackson. France has produced a few eminent Shakespeare actors including Mme. Bernhardt, and Italy has had Mme. Ristori, Salvini, and Rossi.

REFERENCES

ADAMS, J. Q., *Life of William Shakespeare*, Chapters XXVII, XXVIII, XXIX, XXX.

ALBRIGHT, EVELYN MAY, *Dramatic Publication in England, 1580-1640*. New York, 1927.

ALEXANDER, PETER, *Shakespeare's "Henry VI" and "Richard III."* Cambridge, 1929.

BALDWIN, T. W., *Organization and Personnel of the Shakespearean Company*. Princeton, 1927.

CHAMBERS, SIR E. K., *William Shakespeare*. Two vols. Oxford, 1930. *The Disintegration of Shakespeare*, Annual Shakespeare Lecture of the British Academy. Oxford, 1924.

CRAIG, HARDIN, "Recent Shakespeare Scholarship," in *The Shakespeare Association Bulletin*, V, 39-54.

GREG, W. W., "The Bibliographical History of the First Folio," in *The Library*, series ii, no. 15, Vol. IV (1903), pp. 258-286. *Principles of Emendation in Shakespeare*, Annual Shakespeare Lecture of the British Academy. London, 1928. *Two Elizabethan Stage Abridgements: The Battle of Alcazar & Orlando Furioso*. Oxford, 1923.

HERFORD, C. H., *A Sketch of the Recent Shakespeare Investigation*. London, 1923.

LEE, SIR SIDNEY, Introduction to the Oxford Facsimile of the First Folio, 1902.

McKERROW, RONALD B., *An Introduction to Bibliography*. Oxford, 1927.

NEIDIG, W. J., "The Shakespeare Quartos of 1619," in *Modern Philology*, Vol. VIII (1910), pp. 145 ff.

PLOMER, H. R., "The Printers of Shakespeare's Plays and Poems," in *The Library*, Vol. VII (1916), p. 149 ff.

POLLARD, A. W., *Foundations of Shakespeare's Text*. London, 1923. *Shakespeare's War with the Pirates*. Cambridge, 1920. *Shakespeare's Folios and Quartos*. London, 1909. Edition of *The Tragedy of King Richard II*. Introduction. London, 1916.

POLLARD, A. W., AND BARTLETT, H. C., *A Census of Shakespeare's Plays in Quarto, 1594-1709*. New Haven and London, 1916.

POLLARD, A. W. AND OTHERS, *Shakespeare's Hand in the Play of "Sir Thomas More."* Cambridge, 1923.

POLLARD, A. W., AND WILSON, J. DOVER, "The 'Stolne and Surreptitious' Copies," articles in the *Times Literary Supplement*, Jan. 9, 1919,

p. 18; Jan. 16, 1919, p. 20; Mar. 13, 1919, p. 134; Aug. 7, 1919, p. 420; Aug. 14, 1919, p. 434.

RHODES, RAYMOND CROMPTON, *Shakespeare's First Folio, A Study.* Oxford, 1923. "Shakespeare's Prompt Books," in the *Times Literary Supplement*, July 21, 1921, p. 467; July 28, 1921, p. 482. *Studies in the First Folio (1623-1923),* written for the Shakespeare Association. Oxford, 1924.

Bibliographies of Shakespeare on the Continent will be found in *The Cambridge History of English Literature*, Vol. V, pp. 456-472, Ebisch and Schücking, *A Shakespeare Bibliography*, pp. 129-130, and in Neilson and Thorndike, *The Facts about Shakespeare*, pp. 262-3. See also the following books on the subject:

BÖHTLINGK, A. R. A., *Goethe und Shakespeare.* Leipzig, 1909.

CROCE, BENEDETTO, *Ariosto, Shakespeare and Corneille.* New York, 1922.

GENÉE, R., *Geschichte der Shakespeareschen Dramen in Deutschland.* Leipzig, 1870.

GUNDOLF, FRIEDRICH, *Shakespeare und der deutsche Geist.* Berlin, 1922.

HAINES, C. M., *Shakespeare in France.* London, 1928.

HUGO, VICTOR, *William Shakespeare.* Paris, 1864.

JUSSERAND, J. J., *Shakespeare in France under the ancien régime.* London, 1899

KREYSSIG, F., *Vorlesungen über Shakespeare.* Two vols. Berlin, 1877.

LEE, SIR SIDNEY, "Shakespeare in France," in *Shakespeare and the Modern Stage.* London, 1907.

LOUNSBURY, T. R., *Shakespeare and Voltaire.* New York, 1902.

STENDHAL [MARIE HENRI BEYLE], *Racine et Shakespeare.* Paris, 1925.

TEN BRINK, BERNHARD, *Shakespeare.* Strassburg, 1893.

TOLSTOI, L. N., *Tolstoi on Shakespeare.* London and New York, 1907.

The lives and memoirs of actors and dramatic critics offer important information on the stage history of Shakespeare's plays; for example, those of Betterton, Booth, Cibber, Forbes-Robertson, Garrick, Irving, Kean, Kemble, Macready, Macklin, Phelps, Winter. See also the following list of books:

BAKER, HENRY BARTON, *Our Old Actors.* Two vols. London, 1878.

BROWN, J. S., *A History of the New York Stage, 1732-1901.* Three vols. New York, 1903.

DORAN, JOHN. *Annals of the English Stage from Thomas Betterton to Edmund Kean.* Edited and revised by Robert W. Lowe. London, 1888.

FITZGERALD, PERCY. *A New History of the English Stage.* Two vols. London, 1882.

GENEST, J., *Some Account of the English Stage, from the Restoration in 1660 to 1830.* Ten vols. Bath, 1832.

LEE, SIR SIDNEY, *Life of William Shakespeare,* pp. 342-371.

MURRAY, JOHN TUCKER. *English Dramatic Companies, 1558-1642.* Two vols. London, 1910.

ODELL, G. C. D., *Shakespeare from Betterton to Irving.* New York, 1926. *Annals of the New York Stage.* Four vols. New York, 1927-8.

SCOTT, CLEMENT, *The Drama of Yesterday and Today.* Two vols. London, 1899.

SEILHEIMER, G. O., *A History of the American Theater.* Philadelphia, 1891.

VIII. SHAKESPEARE'S ENGLISH

Pronunciation We should probably understand the spoken English of Shakespeare's time; but the speaker, even when his words were just such as we should use, would seem to us to be speaking a strange dialect. This is because spoken English, mainly in the pronunciation of vowel sounds, has undergone many striking changes. Some authorities have claimed that the original pronunciation adds something to the melody of Shakespeare's verse and to the vividness of his speech, so that the experiment of learning it may be worth trying. One can, however, indicate only approximately what the pronunciation was, because local dialects seem then to have been far more commonly used by educated persons than they are now and because several of the commonest vowel sounds were in a state of transition and are, therefore, difficult to fix definitely. We know that Sir Walter Raleigh spoke his native Devonshire dialect, and it may be that Shakespeare's oral utterance was colored by the Warwickshire dialect. A few Warwickshire words and expressions occur in his plays. The London dialect had become even more dominant than it was in Chaucer's time, but because of a wider national intercourse London speech had taken in a larger admixture of northern, eastern, and southern forms.

Consonants were in general pronounced as they are now. There were, however, a few differences. The *k* and *g* were pronounced in such words as *knife* and *gnaw*, and *l* was sounded in *should, would, folk*, etc. The *-tion* and *-sion* endings were usually made dissyllabic and were not yet given the sounds of *sh* and *zh*. The letter *r* was clearly pronounced, but was probably losing its trilled quality.

The short vowels *a, e*, and *i* were pronounced as at present, although short *a* was in transition from *a* in *Colorado* to *a* in *that*. Short *o* was probably more distinctly an *o*-sound than it is with us; that is, it was like the *o* in *folk* rather than the *o* in *hot*. A greater number of the short *u*'s had the genuine *u*-sound, rather than the lax vowel we now hear in many words; that is, *brush* rhymed exactly with *push*, and *dull* with *pull*. Long *a* in words like *state* was an open sound like the *a* in *hat* prolonged and diphthongized. Open and close long *e* were discriminated; that is *seam* and *seem* were not sounded alike, the former being somewhat like *same* only more open, and the latter pretty much as it is now. Long *i* was in a transitional state and was variously uttered. Bradley[1] expresses the opinion that it usually had the sound·of *i* in *pin* followed by the consonantal *y*. Long open *o* (like the *oa* in *broad*) still had its proper sound, so that a word like *old* was pronounced *auld*. Long close *o* had probably completed its change from the *o*-sound to the *oo*-sound. Long *u* was approximately short *i* followed by *w*, so that *tiwn* and *riwl* represent the pronunciation of *tune* and *rule*. The change which gave us our pronunciation of *blue, rue*, and *jury* did not occur until the eighteenth century. Perhaps *ai* and *ay* were usually pronounced like our long *i*; that is, *day* was like our word *die*. The diphthong *oi* (*oy*) may be represented by *ooi*. The sound of *ou* and *ow* varied, as it still does, according to descent. When the sound came from Old English long *u* or French *ou* it was like *oo* in *boot*; when it came from Old English *ag, ah, aw*, or *ow* with a long vowel, it was sounded like *au* in *autumn*; for example, *house* was pronounced *hoos*, and *soul*,

know, and *own*, as *saul, naw*, and *awn*, respectively.

A matter of more practical importance than phonetic changes is that of differences in Shakespeare's English and ours in the accentuation of syllables. There are many cases of variable stress in Shakespeare, in which he seems to have been at liberty to accent the word in two different ways; in other cases words were customarily accented on a different syllable from that in current speech. For example, the following accentuations are either usual or frequent: *aspect', charac'ter, com'mendable, com'plete, con'ceal'd, con'fessor, consort'* (n.), *contract'* (n.), *de'testable, dis'tinct, envy', for'lorn, hu'mane, instinct', ob'scure, persev'er, pi'oner, ple'beians, portents', pur'sue, record'* (n.), *se'cure, sinis'ter, welcome'*.

Not only are *-tion* and *-sion* regularly pronounced as two syllables, but the same situation causes other words in which *e* or *i* stand before vowels to be uttered in Shakespeare's language with one more syllable than in ours; for example, *oce-an, courti-er, marri-age*. We may even have *cre-ature, tre-asure*, and *venge-ance*. Nasals and liquids are frequently pronounced as if an extra vowel were introduced between them and a preceding letter. We accordingly have *wrest(e)ler, Eng(e)land, assemb(e)ly*, and *ent(e)rance*, as well as *de-ar, you(e)r*, and *mo-re*. Final *-er* often has a greater syllabic importance than it ever has in later poetry, as in the line: "And thére / upón, / gíve me / your daúgh / tér" (*Henry V*, V, ii, 375). Final *-(e)s* in the genitive singular and the plural of nouns not ending in an *s*-sound may constitute a separate syllable.

Differences in accentuation and lengthening of words have of course great importance in the reading and scanning of Shakespeare's verse, as do also the various ways by which words are shortened. Shortening of words by elision or by slurring is of course very common in Shakespeare, but in this matter the modern practice forms a very good guide. Syllables ending in vowels are not infrequently elided before words beginning with a vowel, as in "How cáme / we ashóre" (*The Tempest*, I, ii, 158) and "too hárd / a knót / for mé / to untie" (*Twelfth Night*, II, ii, 42). Syncopation often occurs in syllables with *r*, as "I wár-

[1]Article on "Shakespeare's English" in *Shakespeare's England*, II, 543.

rant / it will" (*Hamlet*, I, ii, 243); and in final *-er*, *-el*, and *-le*, as "Trável you / far ón" (*The Taming of the Shrew*, IV, ii, 73) and "I am / a géntle / mán of / a cóm / pané" (*Henry V*, IV, i, 39). The following words and other similar ones may be treated as monosyllabic in Shakespeare's verse: *whether, ever, hither, other, father, evil, having*. Almost any unaccented syllable of a polysyllabic word (especially if it contains an *i*) may be softened and almost ignored; this syncopation is especially frequent in polysyllabic proper names; as "Thoughts spécu / latíve" (*Macbeth*, V, iv, 19) and "Did sláy / this Fórtinbras; / who, bý / a seál'd / compáct" (*Hamlet*, I, i, 86). Other occasions for slurring, as listed by Abbott in his *Shakespearian Grammar*, are light vowels preceded by heavy vowels (as *pow*er, *dy*ing, etc.), plurals and possessives of nouns ending in an *s*-sound, final *-ed* following *d* or *t* (as "you háve / exceéded / all prómise," *As You Like It*, I, ii, 256), and the *-est* of superlatives (pronounced *-st*) after dentals and liquids (as "the stérn'st / good-níght," *Macbeth*, II, ii, 4, and "thy éld'st / son's són," *King John*, II, i, 177).

Grammar Shakespeare's grammar presents but few formal differences from the grammar of current modern English, though the functional differences are striking. The *-eth*-ending in the third person singular of the present tense, indicative mood, was very commonly used, especially in serious prose. Shakespeare frequently uses the older form, especially *hath, doth*, and *saith*, but seems to prefer the form in *-s* or *-es*. There are also a few cases in which he seems to use the old northern plural in *-s* or *-es* in the third person of the present indicative; as ". . . at those springs On chaliced flowers that *lies* (*Cymbeline*, II, iii, 24-5). He does not always agree with modern usage in the forms of the past tenses and the perfect participles of the verbs which he employs. He retains some lost forms of the strong verbs, sometimes confuses the past tense with the perfect participle, or *vice versa*, and treats some verbs as weak which are now strong. For example, he uses *arose* for *arisen, swam* for *swum, foughten* for *fought, gave* for *given, took* for *taken, sprung*

for *sprang, writ* for *wrote*. He has *blowed* for *blew, weaved* for *wove, shaked* for *shaken*. Forms like *degenerate* for *degenerated* and *exhaust* for *exhausted* are especially common. There are a few cases of the archaic *y-* with the past participle, as in *yclad*. The regular form of the possessive case of the neuter personal pronoun *it* was *his*. This is Shakespeare's usual form; but he has also a possessive form *it*, and in the First Folio, published seven years after Shakespeare's death, there are several occurrences of the new form *its*. Shakespeare uses the old form *moe* as the plural of *many*, and the form *enow* as the plural of *enough*. *Near* and *next* are employed, along with *nearer* and *nearest*, as the comparative and superlative of *nigh*. These are the most obvious of the formal differences between Shakespeare's grammar and our own.

The functional differences are more considerable. Elizabethan language exercised an extraordinary freedom, even for English, in the use of one part of speech for another. Shakespeare uses verbs, adjectives, adverbs, and pronouns as nouns. He makes verbs out of nouns and adjectives, and of course uses nouns as adjectives, for this is a distinguishing characteristic of English speech; but he uses also adverbs, verbs, and prepositional phrases as adjectives. Almost any adjective may be freely used as an adverb. He makes active words, both adjectives and adverbs, discharge a passive function; as "the sightless [invisible] couriers of the air" (*Macbeth*, I, vii, 23) and "this aspect of mine Hath fear'd the valiant" (*The Merchant of Venice*, II, i, 8-9). There is a wider use in Shakespeare of the infinitive as a verbal noun or as a gerundive participle than in our language; as "This to be true, I do engage my life" (*As You Like It*, V, iv, 171-2), "My operant powers their functions leave to do" (*Hamlet*, III, ii, 184), "Nor do I now make moan to be abridged" (*The Merchant of Venice*, I, i, 126), and "you might have saved me my pains, to have taken [by having taken] it away yourself" (*Twelfth Night*, II, ii, 6). The functions of prepositions in Elizabethan English were so various that one can only refer the student to the dictionary.

In certain other features, however, Shakespeare's language is as restricted and conventional as ours, or even more so. *Shall* is regularly used in Shakespeare to express something inevitable in future time, and is, therefore, the usual future tense for all persons. *Will*, which originally expressed intention, determination, or willingness, was, however, beginning to encroach on *shall* for the expression of futurity in the second and third persons; but in its use there is usually a consciousness of its original meaning. *Should* and *would* had their original senses of obligation and volition, respectively, and had other peculiarities, then as now, of considerable difficulty. The subjunctive mood was not only vital in Shakespeare but was used carefully. It expressed condition, doubt, concession, and command. It was used optatively and in dependent clauses. Note the following examples:

But if my father *had* not scanted me . . .
Yourself, renowned prince, then *stood* as fair.
　　　　(*The Merchant of Venice*, II, i, 17-20.)
　　　　　　Live a thousand years,
I shall not find myself so apt to die.
　　　　(*Julius Cæsar*, III, i, 159-160.)
Lest your retirement *do amaze* your friends.
　　　　(*1 Henry IV*, V, iv, 6.)
'Twere best he speak no harm of Brutus here.
　　　　(*Julius Cæsar*, III, ii, 73.)
Melt Egypt into Nile! and kindly creatures
Turn all to serpents!
　　　　(*Antony and Cleopatra*, II, v, 78-79.)
　　　　　　Yet were it true
To say this boy *were* like me.
　　　　(*The Winter's Tale*, I, ii, 134-135.)
And may direct his course as *please* himself.
　　　　(*Richard III*, II, ii, 129.)

The following minor features of Shakespeare's grammar deserve notice: He often omits the relative pronoun; often uses the nominative case of the pronoun for the accusative case, and *vice versa;* uses *him, her, me,* and *them* as true reflexives to mean *himself, herself, myself,* and *themselves;* employs double negatives and double comparatives and superlatives; shows a consciousness in the use of *thee* and *thou* of their application to intimates and inferiors; employs *which* to refer to both persons and things; does not discriminate closely between *ye*, nominative, and *you*, objective; and, finally, uses both the ethical dative and the dative of the agent (e.g., "give *me* your present to one Master Bassanio," *The*

Merchant of Venice, II, ii, 115, and "I am appointed *him* [by him] to murder you," *The Winter's Tale*, I, ii, 412).

Of the forms and figures of rhetoric there are in Shakespeare, as in other poets, innumerable instances. He is very fond, for example, of using the abstract for the concrete, as in the words addressed by Surrey to Cardinal Wolsey, "Thou scarlet sin" (*Henry VIII*, III, ii, 255). Transferred epithets are numerous, as are inversions, ellipses, and broken or confused constructions; as in the following examples:

　　　　That thing you speak of,
I took it for a man.　(*King Lear*, IV, vi, 77-78.)
Souls and bodies hath he divorced three.
　　　　(*Twelfth Night*, III, iv, 260.)
A happy gentleman in blood and lineaments.
　　　　(*Richard II*, III, i, 9.)
Your state of fortune and your due of birth.
　　　　(*Richard III*, III, vii, 120.)
She calls me proud, and that she could not love me.
　　　　(*As You Like It*, IV, iii, 16.)
Returning were as tedious as go o'er.
　　　　(*Macbeth*, III, iv, 138.)
They call him Doricles; and boasts himself
To have a worthy feeding.
　　　　(*The Winter's Tale*, IV, iv, 168-169.)
Of all men else I have avoided thee.
　　　　(*Macbeth*, V, viii, 4.)
The venom of such looks, we fairly hope,
Have lost their quality.
　　　　(*Henry V*, V, ii, 18-19.)
Rather proclaim it, Westmoreland, through my host,
That he which hath no stomach to this fight,
Let him depart.　　(*Henry V*, IV, iii, 34-6.)

The Shakespearean vocabulary　With reference to words and their meanings the spirit of the Renaissance manifested itself in England in very great hospitality to foreign importations. Large numbers of words were taken directly from Latin. In fact there was an inundation of classicism, for it was a fashion among writers to pillage the Latin language. Many of the words so introduced were naturalized and served to enrich the language, its power to express thought, and its rhythmical capabilities; many were discarded. The principal borrowings were in the realm of learning and culture, and they were usually employed with distinct recollection of their Latin sense. Sometimes such words have not replaced native words of the same meaning, so that we have such pairs of synonyms as *acknowledge* and *confess*; just as Shakespeare had *wonder* and *admiration*. It follows that even a slight knowledge of Latin is a great advantage in the correct understanding of Elizabethan writers, since many Latin borrowings have taken on since the sixteenth century a different shade of meaning from that in which they were borrowed. The Latin sense of *aggravate* still struggles for recognition; but *apparent* no longer means *visible* or *evident*, and *intention* does not convey the idea of *intentness*. Latin words were often taken over in their Latin forms, as *objectum* and *subjectum*, *statua* and *aristocratia*, and later were made to conform to English spelling and accentuation, though a few such as *decorum* still have a Latin form. French continued to be drawn upon and sometimes caused a new Latin borrowing to be adopted in a French form; just as, on the other hand, such words as *adventure* were supplied with a *d* to make them conform to Latin spelling. Spanish, Italian, and Dutch were made to supply many terms. Spanish gave words having to do with commerce, religion, and the New World; such as *mosquito*, *alligator*, *ambuscado*, and *grandee*. From Italian came terms of art, learning, and dueling: *bandetto*, *portico*, *canto*, *stoccato*. The Dutch contributed many nautical words and words from the Orient.

These foreign borrowings were a part of what might be called the linguistic ambition of the age, a desire for forcible expression. Language was in a plastic state, so that it had an unparalleled freedom in both vocabulary and form; and with this came a consequent confusion, since there were few efforts at clearness and precision. Such efforts were made by the age of Dryden and the Royal Society, who felt that English was too vague and irregular for use as a means of scientific expression. Indeed the task of rendering the language more precise has been the object of the learned part of the population ever since the sixteenth century, and yet it must be acknowledged that English could never have been as great a language as it is without its Renaissance expansion and its subsequent familiarity with Shakespeare

and the English Bible. It gained, for example, an increased facility in the making of compounds. Shakespeare, with his *cloud-capp'd towers* and his *home-keeping wits*, was a genius at this. Likewise from Shakespeare's time came the English power in the use of prefixes, such as *dis-*, *re-*, *en-*, and suffixes, such as *-ful*, *-less*, *-ness*, *-hood*.

Obsolete words, however, and words employed by Shakespeare in entirely different meanings give the student little trouble. The difficulty arises from the innumerable cases in which the student is able to get without effort an idea fairly close to Shakespeare's meaning, so that he constantly understands Shakespeare imperfectly. He is thus liable to miss the exact shade of meaning and consequently the tone of Shakespeare's feeling. In Othello's account to the Venetian senators of the circumstances of his courtship of Desdemona (*Othello*, I, iii, 158-166) he says:

My story being done,
She gave me for my pains a world of sighs: . . .
She wish'd she had not heard it, yet she wish'd
That heaven had made her such a man; she thank'd me,
And bade me, if I had a friend that lov'd her,
I should but teach him how to tell my story,
And that would woo her. Upon this *hint* I spake.

The word *hint* means *occasion* or *opportunity*; it does not mean *invitation* or *suggestion by covert allusion*. To understand the word in the contemporary sense changes subtly the meaning of the passage.

The following is a list of words, of very common occurrence, whose Shakespearean meanings often differ from their present meanings. Such words are not defined in the notes to the plays given in this volume unless there is special liability to misunderstanding:

A, he
Ability, means, wealth
Abuse, deceive; mistreat
Addition, title
Admiration, wonder
Admire, wonder at
After, afterwards
Against, by the time of
All as, quite as
An, if
An if, if
Annoy (v. and n.), hurt, sorrow
Anon, straightway, immediately

Apparent, evident, plain

Argument, theme, story

As, according as; as far as; as if; in the capacity of; that

Assay, make trial

At, on

At large, in detail, in full

Atone, reconcile

Atonement, reconciliation

Attach, arrest

Awful, full of awe; commanding reverence

Ay, yes

Band, bond

Bate, beat with the wings (as a hawk); abate, reduce

Battle, army

Beshrew, blame greatly

Bespeak, address

Bestow, lodge, house

Blood, emotion, passion

Bold, boldly

Brake, broke

Brave, fine, gallant, splendid

Brook, endure, tolerate

But, but that; than; otherwise; who, which, or that . . . not

By, concerning; of, by reason of

Come your ways, come on

Care, desire

Careful, anxious

Carry, manage

Case, encase

Character (n.), handwriting; (v.), inscribe

Check, reprove

Close, secret

Compare, comparison

Complexion, external appearance; temperament

Conceit, conception, idea

Condition, temperament

Confound, waste, destroy

Confusion, ruin, overthrow

Constant, steady, unmoved

Continent, that which contains or encloses

Contrive, plot

Conveniency, expediency

Convenient, suitable

Convert, change to, turn to

Corse, corpse

Cousin, any relative not belonging to one's immediate family

Cuckold, husband whose wife is unfaithful

Dear, costly, precious; affectionate; hard, grievous

Debate, discuss; fight

Defeat (v. and n.), destroy, destruction

Defend, forbid

Discover, reveal

Dispute, discuss

Doubt, fear, suspect

Eat, ate

Enlarge, set free

Enow, enough

Entertain, receive, employ

Envy, malice, hate

Ere, before

Even, just, exact; direct, straightforward; equally; fully

Every, everyone

Fall, let fall, cause to fall

Fancy, love

Fear (n.), danger; (v.), frighten

Fearful, fear-inspiring; full of fear

Fell, fierce, cruel

Fellow, equal

Fond, foolish

For, as; as for; in spite of; instead of

For that, because

For why, because

Forfend, forbid

From, away from; different from; of

Furnish, equip

Gear, matter, stuff, thing, business

Get, beget

Go to, reproachful exclamation

Gone about, endeavored

Habit, dress

Happily, haply, perchance

Having, estate, wealth, possessions

Head, armed force

High, highly

His, its

Honest, chaste; honorable

Horrid, horrible

Humour, moisture; one of the four fluids of the body (sanguis, cholera, melancholia, phlegma); temperament; whim, caprice

Idle, empty, foolish, trifling

Ill, bad

In, in the exercise of; into

Incivil, uncivil

Incertain, uncertain

Indifferent, impartial

Infinite, infinity

Ingrateful, ungrateful

Influence, power exerted by a heavenly body

Instance, motive; argument; illustration or example

Jade, worthless horse

Jealousy, suspicion

Kind, nature; sort

Late, lately

Lie, lodge

Learn, teach

Let, hinder

Liberal, free, unrestrained

Like, likely

Like, please

List, listen

Listen, listen to

Look, look for

Love, lover

Make, do

Marry, oath by the Virgin Mary

May, can

Mere, complete, simple, absolute; from which the adverb "merely"

Modern, common, ordinary

Modest, moderate

Moe, more

Mortal, fatal, deadly

Motion, impulse, prompting; motive, reason

Must, can

Naught, worthless, wicked

Nice, precise, particular; trivial, unimportant

Nothing, not at all

Occasion, necessitate

Of, concerning; for; from; in; on; with

Office, duty; proper function; officer

On, at; on the ground of; to; upon

Operation, effects

Opinion, credit, reputation

Opposite, opponent

Or . . . or, either . . . or

Orchard, garden

Other, others

Owe, own, possess

Paid, paid for

Part, party, side, faction

Passing, surpassing, or surpassingly

Peevish, foolish

Perforce, of necessity

Pitch, highest point of a falcon's flight; height

Pompous, ceremonial

Ports, gates

Possess, inform

Post, messenger

Practice (or practise) (v. and n.), plot, scheme; use stratagem

Pregnant, resourceful, apt, inclined

Present, immediate; from which adverb "presently"

Prevent, anticipate, hinder

Proof, experience

Proper, own, special

Purchase, acquire, obtain, procure

Put on, instigate

Quaint, skilled, pretty, ingeniously wrought

Qualify, moderate, appease

Quality, natural gift; accomplishment; profession; rank

Question, consideration; conversation

Quick, alive

Quit, acquit; repay

Reason, talk

Remember, remind

Remorse, pity, compassion

Render, give back; describe, make out to be

Respect, thought, consideration

Round, plain, direct; severe, peremptory

Sad, serious

Safe, sound, sane

Satisfy, inform fully

Season, qualify, mitigate, temper

Self, same

Sennet, set of notes played on a trumpet to announce processions

Sensible, possessing the power of physical feeling or perception

Sentence, maxim

Shall, will inevitably; will

Should, would; was likely to, might have

Show (v. and n.), appear, seem; appearance

Shrewd, accursed; sharp, shrewish

Silly, simple, innocent

Sirrah, form of address to an inferior

Skill, intelligence, ability

Society, companionship

Something, somewhat

Sometime, formerly

Sort, select

Sorts, ranks, classes

Speak, bespeak, proclaim

State, ceremony; station, kingship

Still, always, continually, ever

Stomach, inclination; courage, spirit

Straight, immediately

Stout, valiant, bold

Success, outcome

Sudden, impetuous, violent

Swear, swear by

Take, bewitch, charm

Take in, capture

Tall, valiant

Tell, count

That, such; he or she who(m); that which; in that; in order that

There, thereupon

Therefore, hence

Thorough, through

To, compared to; for; in addition to; with

Toys, trifles

Uncapable, incapable

Unhappy, unfortunate

Unjust, faithless, dishonest

Unkind, unnatural

Unpossible, impossible

Unthrift, unthrifty

Upon, on account of, on the side of; bent upon; at or just about; against; after

Vantage, advantage

Virtue, power

Want, lack

Ware, aware

Waste, consume, spend

Weeds, garments

What, why

Where, whereas

Which, who

Whiles, while

Who, which

Wit, mental faculty, intellectual power, wisdom

With, against; by, by reason of, owing to; from

Withal, with it; therewith

REFERENCES

ABBOTT, E. A., *A Shakespearian Grammar.* London, 1869; often reprinted.

ATKINS, J. W. H., "The Language from Chaucer to Shakespeare," in *Cambridge History of English Literature*, Vol. III, pp. 499-530; accompanied by a bibliography of sixteenth century English language.

BARTLETT, JOHN, *Concordance to Shakespeare.* New edition. London, 1922.

BRADLEY, HENRY, "Shakespeare's English," in *Shakespeare's England*, Vol. II, pp. 539-574. *The Making of English*, London, 1904.

CUNLIFFE, R. J., *New Shakespearean Dictionary.* London, 1910.

FRANZ, W., *Shakespeare-Grammatik.* Second edition. Heidelberg, 1909.

JESPERSEN, OTTO, *Growth and Structure of the English Language.* Third edition. Leipzig, 1919.

KAUFMAN, PAUL, *Outline Guide to Shakespeare.* New York, 1924.

KENNEDY, A. G., *A Bibliography of the Writings on the English Language.* Cambridge, 1927.

ONIONS, C. T., *A Shakespeare Glossary.* Oxford, 1911, 1919.

SCHMIDT, ALEXANDER, *Shakespeare-Lexicon.* Third edition. Berlin, 1902.

VIETOR, W., *A Shakespeare Phonology.* Marburg, 1906.

WYLD, H. C., *Short History of English.* London, 1914.

ZACHRISSEN, R. E., *Pronunciation of English Vowels*, 1400-1700. Göteborg, 1913.

IX. CHRONOLOGICAL OUTLINE[1]

YEAR	HISTORICAL AND BIOGRAPHICAL EVENTS	LITERARY WORKS
1557	Stationers' Company incorporated.	*Tottel's Miscellany.*
1558	Elizabeth crowned Queen.	
1559		Third part of *A Mirror for Magistrates.*
1561	Bacon born.	Hoby's translation of Castiglione's *Il Cortegiano.* Sackville and Norton's *Gorboduc* acted.
1563		John Foxe's *Acts and Monuments.*
1564	Marlowe, Shakespeare, and Galileo born. Shakespeare baptized April 26.	
1565		Golding's translation of Ovid's *Metamorphoses*, I-IV.
1566		Gascoigne's *Jocasta* and *Supposes* acted; printed 1573. Painter's *Palace of Pleasure*, Vol. I. Nicholas Udall's *Ralph Roister Doister.*
1567	Abdication of Mary Queen of Scots.	
1570		Roger Ascham's *Scholemaster.*
1572	Massacre of St. Bartholomew.	
1573	Donne and Ben Jonson(?) born.	
1574	James Burbage and others granted special license as the Earl of Leicester's men.	First part of *A Mirror for Magistrates.*

[1] The dates indicated for works listed in the right-hand column are, unless otherwise stated, those of publication.

CHRONOLOGICAL OUTLINE—*Continued*

YEAR	HISTORICAL AND BIOGRAPHICAL EVENTS	LITERARY WORKS
1575	The Earl of Leicester's festivities at Kenilworth in honor of the Queen.	
1576	The fall of Antwerp. The Theater and The Curtain built.	
1577	Drake's circumnavigation of the earth.	Holinshed's *Chronicles*.
1578	William Harvey born.	Harrison's *Description of England*. John Florio's *First Fruits*. Second part of *A Mirror for Magistrates*.
1579	John Fletcher born.	John Lyly's *Euphues, The Anatomy of Wit*. North's translation of Plutarch's *Lives*. Edmund Spenser's *The Shepheardes Calender*.
1580	Earthquake.	Lyly's *Euphues and his England*. Montaigne's *Essais* (first edition). Stow's *Chronicles of England*.
1581		Sir Philip Sidney's *Defence of Poesie* written. Newton and others' translation of Seneca's *Tenne Tragedies*.
1582	Edinburgh University founded.	Richard Hakluyt's *Divers Voyages touching the Discovery of America*.
1583	Philip Massinger born. The Queen's company formed.	
1584	Raleigh's charter of colonization for Virginia.	Lyly's *Campaspe* and *Sapho and Phao*. Peele's *Arraignment of Paris*. Reginald Scot's *Discovery of Witchcraft*.
1585	Shakespeare's twins Hamnet and Judith baptized.	
1586	Sir Philip Sidney killed at Zutphen. John Ford born.	Greene's *Orlando Furioso* acted.
1587	Mary Queen of Scots put to death. The Queen's players visit Stratford.	Marlowe's *Tamburlaine* acted?
1588	Defeat of the Spanish Armada.	Montaigne's *Essais*, Book III.
1589	Henry IV crowned king of France.	Greene's *Menaphon; James IV* acted. Hakluyt's *Principall Navigations;* final form 1598-1600. Marlowe's *Dr. Faustus* acted?
1590	Battle of Ivry.	Lodge's *Rosalynde*. Marlowe's *Tamburlaine* both parts. His *Massacre of Paris* acted. Sir Philip Sidney's *Arcadia* (written 1580-1583?). Spenser's *The Faerie Queene*, Books I-III.

CHRONOLOGICAL OUTLINE—*Continued*

YEAR	HISTORICAL AND BIOGRAPHICAL EVENTS	LITERARY WORKS
1592	Robert Greene and Montaigne died.	Greene's *A Groatsworth of Wit* written. Henry Chettle's *Kind-Harts Dreame.* Marlowe's *Edward II* acted? *Arden of Feversham* acted?
1593	Death of Marlowe.	Shakespeare's *Venus and Adonis.*
1594	The Lord Chamberlain's Company formed. Shakespeare mentioned (1595) as a member of the company in the accounts of the Treasurer of the Chamber. *The Comedy of Errors* acted at Gray's Inn.	Greene's *Friar Bacon and Friar Bungay* and *Orlando Furioso.* Richard Hooker's *The Laws of Ecclesiastical Polity.* Marlowe's *Edward II.* Shakespeare's *The Rape of Lucrece,* and *Titus Andronicus.*
1595	Execution of Robert Southwell, the Jesuit. Raleigh's first expedition to Guiana. Weever's sonnet in praise of Shakespeare.	Samuel Daniel's *The Civil Wars of Lancaster and York.* Peele's *The Old Wives Tale.* Sir Philip Sidney's *Defence of Poesie.* Spenser's *Colin Clout, Astrophel, Amoretti, Epithalamium.*
1596	Draft of arms to John Shakespeare. Shakespeare's only son Hamnet died.	Spenser's *The Faerie Queene,* Books IV-VI, *Four Hymns,* and *Prothalamium.*
1597	Shakespeare buys New Place for £60.	Bacon's *Essays* (first edition). King James VI's *Demonologie.* Shakespeare's *Romeo and Juliet,* first quarto; *Richard II, Richard III.*
1598	Edict of Nantes. Death of Lord Burghley.	Chapman's translation of Homer's *Iliad,* Books I, II, VII-XI. Jonson's *Every Man in his Humour* acted. Francis Meres's *Palladis Tamia.* Shakespeare's *Henry IV,* Part I, and *Love's Labour's Lost.* Joshua Sylvester's translation of Du Bartas's *Divine Weeks and Works.*
1599	Death of Spenser. Globe Theater built. Essex's expedition to Ireland.	Sir John Davies's *Nosce Teipsum.* Jonson's *Every Man out of his Humour* acted. Shakespeare's *Romeo and Juliet,* second quarto. *The Two Angry Women of Abingdon.*
1600	Foundation of the East India Company.	Dekker's *Old Fortunatus* and *The Shoemaker's Holiday.* Shakespeare's *Henry IV,* Part II, *Henry V,* quarto version, *A Midsummer-Night's Dream, The Merchant of Venice, Much Ado about Nothing.*
1601	Insurrection of the Earl of Essex.	Jonson's *The Poetaster* acted. *Phœnix and Turtle* printed in Chester's *Love's Martyr.*
1602	Sir Thomas Bodley's Library permanently founded at Oxford. Manningham's diary records his seeing of *Twelfth Night.*	Thomas Campion's *Observations in the Art of English Poesy.* Samuel Daniel's *Defence of Ryme?* Shakespeare's *The Merry Wives of Windsor,* first quarto. *Hamlet* and *Twelfth Night* acted.

CHRONOLOGICAL OUTLINE—*Continued*

YEAR	HISTORICAL AND BIOGRAPHICAL EVENTS	LITERARY WORKS
1603	King James VI of Scotland crowned as James I of England. Shakespeare's company licensed as the "King's Players."	John Florio's translation of Montaigne's *Essays.* Thomas Heywood's *A Woman Killed with Kindness.* Philemon Holland's translation of Plutarch's *Morals.* Shakespeare's *Hamlet,* first quarto.
1604	Treaty of peace with Spain. Hampton Court Conference.	Jonson, Chapman, and Marston's *Eastward Ho* acted. Marston's *Malcontent.* Shakespeare's *Hamlet,* second quarto. *Othello* acted?
1605	Gunpowder Plot. Sir Thomas Browne born.	Bacon's *Advancement of Learning.* Cervantes's *Don Quixote,* Part I. Jonson's *Volpone* acted. Jonson's *Sejanus.*
1607	Settlement of Jamestown. Shakespeare's daughter Susanna wedded to Dr. John Hall. Bacon became Solicitor-General.	Chapman's *Bussy d'Ambois.* Cyril Tourneur's *The Revenger's Tragedy.*
1608	John Milton born.	Shakespeare's *King Lear.*
1609	Galileo discovered the satellites of Jupiter.	Shakespeare's *Sonnets, Troilus and Cressida,* and *Pericles.*
1610		Jonson's *The Alchemist* acted. First complete edition of *A Mirror for Magistrates.*
1611	The first breach between the Parliament and the King.	Chapman's translation of *Iliad* completed. *The Authorized Version of the Bible.* Raleigh's *History of the World* entered in Stationers' Register; published 1614 or 1615. Beaumont and Fletcher's *The Maid's Tragedy* acted?
1612	Marriage of the Princess Elizabeth. Bacon became Attorney-General.	Bacon's *Essays,* second enlarged edition. Thomas Shelton's translation of Cervantes's *Don Quixote,* Part I. Webster's *The White Devil.*
1613	The Globe Theater burned.	Shakespeare's *Henry VIII* acted.
1616	Shakespeare, Francis Beaumont, and Cervantes died.	Webster's *The Duchess of Malfi* acted; printed 1623.
1618	Raleigh put to death. Beginning of the Thirty Years' War. Bacon became Lord Chancellor.	
1620	Settlement of Plymouth.	Bacon's *Novum Organum.*
1621	Impeachment of Bacon.	Robert Burton's *The Anatomy of Melancholy.*
1622		Shakespeare's *Othello.*
1623		*The First Folio.*

SHAKESPEARE'S EARLY PERIOD

I. SHAKESPEARE'S LIFE AND TIMES, 1564-1594

SHAKESPEARE DOCUMENTS

Sources of our knowledge of Shakespeare It is important, before we attempt to give a connected account of Shakespeare's life and work, to indicate how and where we gather the facts about him. There are two sources for the biography of Shakespeare—documents and traditions. Formal written records are impersonal, often official, and may usually be relied upon implicitly. No motive for falsification existed in the making of the legal and commercial records that concerned Shakespeare. Such records, because they often give us only the insignificant and routine features of his life, remain dead and dry. Tradition, on the other hand, is likely to be fanciful, even false, arising as it does, for the most part, from posterity's craving for personal detail and anecdote.

Documents Manuscripts of some of Shakespeare's plays and many documents containing personal information about him must have perished in the great fire of London in 1666. However, the records of Stratford, where he spent his first and his last years, still remain and give us about what we should expect. Dates for his birth and death are determined from the baptismal and burial registers of Stratford-on-Avon. The *Episcopal Register* of the Diocese of Worcester records the issue of his marriage license and of the marriage bond. At Somerset House in London, a British government building which contains a depository of legal documents, is to be found his will, dated March 25, 1616. Other records, as those of the land that he bought and sold, the lawsuits to which he was a party, and the tax returns which listed his property for taxation, indicate his financial resources and his activities as a man of the world. From these purely official documents one can usually learn where Shakespeare happened to be living at a particular time of his life, and often something about his activities at such times.

The accumulation of these documentary details about Shakespeare has been carried on with unparalleled zeal. Our own generation, even after more than two centuries of Shakespeare scholarship, has made very considerable additions to the formal records of Shakespeare's life. Such formal records often lead to important inferences. For example, in 1910 Professor C. W. Wallace published[1] his discovery, in the Public Record Office in London, of papers pertaining to a suit in Chancery in the year 1612, in which Shakespeare was called as a witness. Shakespeare's deposition in the case is signed with his own hand. Thus there was added a sixth authentic signature to those previously known. Shakespeare's testimony in this lawsuit shows that he had been, possibly for some years after 1602, a lodger in the house of a Huguenot wigmaker named Mountjoy, at the corner of Muggle and Silver streets, London. One infers from this document that, whether Shakespeare knew French or not, he was for a long time in contact with French-speaking people.

Of Shakespeare's correspondence only one short letter is known to exist; in it a Stratford neighbor, Richard Quyny, asked Shakespeare for the loan of thirty pounds. Shakespeare is mentioned, however, in several letters, mainly in connection with his activities as a citizen of Stratford. Notes on his plays and one or two personal anecdotes about him appear in diaries of the time. Because he acted with his company at court, the accounts of the Revels office, a sort of royal department of court amusements, often contain his name; and, being one of the principal members of his company, he is several times mentioned among those to whom payment is made.

[1] "Shakespeare and his London Associates," in *University Studies*, Lincoln, Nebraska, Vol. X, No. 4.

First publications of Shakespeare's works furnish a great deal of information about him. The famous First Folio of 1623 was edited by his fellow actors, John Heminge and Henry Condell, whose names are signed to a dedicatory epistle and to an epistle "To the great Variety of Readers." The book contains, besides other laudatory verses, a poetic eulogy of Shakespeare by his celebrated contemporary Ben Jonson. The title-pages and dedicatory epistles of the two poems *Venus and Adonis* (1593) and *The Rape of Lucrece* (1594), the title-pages of various plays issued singly before the collected edition of 1623, and the entries of plays in the register of the Stationers' Company of London furnish information as to Shakespeare's claims to courtly patronage, his association with printers and dramatic companies, and approximate dates of composition of some of his works.

The practice of quoting Shakespeare and alluding to his work began apparently as soon as his plays appeared on the stage; there is a wealth of such material. Some of it is contemporary, some late; sometimes it is definite, sometimes vague and uncertain. Where the quotations are unmistakable, they constitute a valuable kind of information. Outstanding among contemporary allusions is the estimate of Francis Meres, who published in 1598 an odd and formal little book on contemporary literature and art called *Palladis Tamia, or Wit's Treasury*, which gave an early and enthusiastic recognition of Shakespeare's greatness as a poet and dramatist.

Traditions Matters of this kind are matters of fact, all too scanty and bare, though very considerable in amount— more considerable indeed than about any other Elizabethan playwright except Ben Jonson. But posterity has craved personal details about Shakespeare as it always does about its heroes, and has made an attempt to collect them. Thus has arisen the body of what are called traditions. Such traditions, usually late in getting recorded, are often inconsistent with each other and with knowledge we have from more definite sources; hence one faces always the question of their validity. They are important because they may be true and because even our own day clings to them; and, however much scholars may do to discredit them, they continue to crop up. One has simply to record them and do one's best to discriminate amongst them.

The seventeenth century, from which come the best of the traditions, was not indifferent to Shakespeare, though we sometimes think that it was. It issued and consumed four full editions of his plays besides numerous reprints of single plays and of the poems. This century was also interested in Shakespeare's life and made numerous characteristic efforts to accumulate information about him. Fuller wrote a useless little life in his *Worthies* (1662). John Aubrey includes Shakespeare in his *Lives of Eminent Men* (compiled between 1669 and 1696, but not published until 1813), where he records matters derived from the actor and theater manager William Beeston, whose father had almost certainly been an associate of Shakespeare's. The Reverend John Ward, vicar of Stratford, the Reverend William Fulmam, and the Reverend Richard Davies, and some others collected local traditions and examined some records. All of these accounts, except Aubrey's, were gathered up and used by the first modern editor of Shakespeare, Nicholas Rowe, who prefixed a life of the dramatist to his edition of the plays in 1709, the first modern edition.

Not only was the science of biography in a bad state in the seventeenth century, but these investigators were too late in beginning. Too many generations had passed since Shakespeare lived, and the fire of London of 1666 had done its work. Most of the more important personal mementoes of the poet had perished, and his family was practically extinct. But there were traditions about Shakespeare floating about unrecorded even as late as the time of the great Shakespeare editors, Dr. Samuel Johnson and Edmund Malone, in the second half of the eighteenth century. A tradition is not necessarily negligible because it is late, but its lateness is at least an occasion of suspicion. Take, for example, two well-known traditions, the first of which seems improbable because it does not fit into what we know from other sources; the other probable because, though less well descended, it does. The *Lives of the Poets* (1753), attributed to Theophilus Cibber, states, on the basis of a tradition claimed to be handed down through William D'Avenant and Betterton, the Restoration theatrical manager and the Shakespearean actor, that Shakespeare's first employment in the theater after he came to London was as a holder of horses for the gentlemen who rode to the playhouse to see the plays; and further that Shakespeare organized the boys of the neighborhood into a company of horse-holders known as "Will's Boys." This is a well-descended tradition, but it simply does not fit in with anything we know about the conditions of entry into the craft of acting.

The other tradition comes through William Oldys, who, writing about 1750-1760, says that one of Shakespeare's younger brothers, "who lived to a good old age, even some years, as I compute, after the Restoration of King Charles the Second," came on more than one occasion to London to see his brother act in plays. When he was asked at a later time what parts his brother played, "he was so stricken in years, and possibly his memory so weakened with infirmities, which might make him the easier pass for a man of weak intellects, that he could give them but little light into their inquiries; and all that could be recollected from him of his brother Will in that station was the faint, general, and almost lost ideas he had of having once seen him act a part in one of his own comedies, wherein, being to personate a decrepit old man, he wore a long beard, and appeared so weak and drooping and unable to walk, that he was forced to be supported and carried by another person to a table, at which he was seated among some company who were eating, and one of them sung a song." Shakespeare, who died in 1616, outlived all of his brothers, and the tradition on its face is a bad one; and yet it bears the mark of being an authentic recollection, and its reference to the part of Adam in *As You Like It* is unmistakable. There was little to be gained by the fabrication of such a tradition, and we know that Shakespeare acted just such parts in plays.

We cannot be content with a bare documentary record of a person so interesting as Shakespeare; nor do we find it necessary to agree with a particular school of critics who insist that Shakespeare was so completely objective and stood so apart from his work that, even if we knew all about his life, it would have no significance in the interpretation of his work. On the other hand, one cannot give credence to a body of ignorant and inconsistent traditions, or agree with the practice of critics like Harris and Brandes, who manufacture a biography for Shakespeare out of the characters and situations of his plays. The scholarship of recent years has brought great gain in our ability to see the real Shakespeare, and we can but believe that with the further application of thought to the materials we now have, and with the possible discovery of other materials, greater progress will yet be made.

SHAKESPEARE'S CHILDHOOD AND YOUTH: HIS DEPARTURE FROM STRATFORD

Stratford-on-Avon — Some members of the group of modernists who have in recent years sought to rob Shakespeare of the authorship of the plays in favor of Francis or of Anthony Bacon, the Earl of Rutland, the Earl of Southampton, the Earl of Derby, the Earl of Oxford, Sir Walter Raleigh, the Earl of Devonshire, or others, have formed the habit of referring scornfully to William Shakespeare as "the man of Stratford." In this there is at least a recognition of the fact that Shakespeare from birth to death is very solidly connected with the town of Stratford-on-Avon. Some excellent critics also insist that Shakespeare, in spite of his mastery of Renaissance lore, was to the end a local genius, never losing the point of view of his native town. If so, it must be that in him we have exemplified Thoreau's doctrine that, if one knows his own neighborhood, one knows the world. At any rate, it is worth while to consider the Stratford of Shakespeare's day, which was a little market town of 1500 people, with narrow, crooked streets, and timbered houses, roofed with thatch—picturesque but insanitary. It had something to boast of in the way of beauty and antiquity, particularly the river Avon, sluggish but clear-watered, spanned by the noble bridge of fourteen arches, which had been built in 1496 by Sir Hugh Clopton, Lord Mayor of London. Beside the Avon stood Trinity Church built on the site of a Saxon monastery. The chapel of the Guild of the Holy Trinity dating from the thirteenth century and an old King Edward VI grammar school, no very pretentious affair, complete the list of the monuments of Shakespeare's day and of the present time. Stratford had maintained a grammar school at least since 1424 and probably long before that. It was a town without the domination of clergy, aristocracy, or great wealth, where simple, honest people plied their trades and occupied their own positions of honor in the local society.

Warwickshire Warwickshire, in which Stratford lies, is a midland county just south of the center of England and almost as far inland as one can get in that country. On the north side is Staffordshire, on the south Gloucestershire and Oxfordshire, on the east Leicestershire and Northampton, and on the west Worcestershire. It is an agricultural region broken by the rich valleys of the Avon, the Stour, and the Thames. The northern part of the county was once occupied by the Forest of Arden, but even in Shakespeare's day almost the whole county was under cultivation. In his time the famous industrial city of Birmingham was inconspicuous, and Coventry, which is now a manufacturing center, was a neat, clean, progressive borough devoted to varied industries of the old-fashioned sort and noted for its active community life. Warwick, the county seat, where the great Warwick Castle still stands, and Kenilworth, whose royal castle was destroyed by Oliver Cromwell, are on the road between Stratford and Coventry, the total distance between these places being about fourteen miles. Warwickshire in the reign of Queen Elizabeth was a rich county in which the standard of living was relatively high. Families and towns were more or less independent and self-supporting units, and agriculture was the basal occupation. Familiarity with the abundant fifteenth and sixteenth century records of Coventry convinces me that the ordinary people of Warwickshire were not only fundamentally sound and honest, but fundamentally open-minded and aspiring.

The Shakespeares The family which bore the suggestive name of Shakespeare was well-distributed throughout England, but was especially numerous in Warwickshire. A name "Saquespee" in various spellings, is found in Normandy at an early date. It means, according to Professor Adams, "to draw out the sword quickly." That name, in the form "Sakspee," with many variants, is found in England; also the name "Saksper," varying gradually to the form "Shakespeare." It may have been wrought into that form by the obvious military meaning of "one who shakes the spear." We have a substantial beginning of the line with Richard Shakespeare, who was in all probability Shakespeare's grandfather, a farmer living in the village of Snitterfield four miles from Stratford and a tenant on the property of Robert Arden of Wilmcote, a wealthy man with the social status of gentleman. Richard Shakespeare died about 1561 possessed of an estate valued at the very respectable sum of £38 17s.

John Shakespeare No doubt the prosperity of Richard laid the basis for the fortunes of John, the poet's father. John Shakespeare, who is the first of the family to become in any way conspicuous, was a man about whom it is possible to know a good deal. He made a great step forward in the world by his marriage with Mary Arden, daughter of his father's landlord. She became the mother of William Shakespeare. John Shakespeare, who had some property of his own and through his wife acquired a good deal more, moved from Snitterfield to Stratford at some date before 1552. He rose to great local importance in Stratford and bought several houses, among them in 1564 the one on Henley Street familiar to all the world as Shakespeare's birthplace. This house, though changed in various and unknown ways during the years which have intervened since Shakespeare's birth, still stands. It is of considerable size, having four rooms on the ground floor, and must, therefore, have been an important business house in the Stratford of those days. The business that John Shakespeare carried on seems to have been that of a glover; the records also indicate that he was a tanner and a dealer in wool, grain, malt, and other farm produce.

The long story, beginning in 1552, of John Shakespeare's successes and misfortunes in Stratford is attested by many borough records. He held various city offices. He was ale-taster (inspector of bread and malt), burgess (petty constable), affeeror (assessor of fines), city chamberlain (treasurer), and bailiff of the town, which last was a position of very considerable honor. These are his successes. When William was fourteen years old, John Shakespeare's misfortunes began. He got into debt, lost the fine farms of Asbies and Snitterfield, inherited by his wife from her father, was involved, as time went on, in much litigation, was finally dismissed from membership in the town council, and in 1586 was declared a bankrupt. About 1576, in the midst of his prosperity, John Shakespeare had applied to the Herald's office for the right to bear arms; namely, the right to have a coat-of-arms and to sign himself as a person belonging to the class of gentleman. This application was later to be renewed and carried through by his famous son. Through all of John Shakespeare's troubles and lawsuits, he seems from the evidence to have been respected and spared by his fellow townsmen. The impression he leaves is that of a hopeful, aspiring, unsuccessful man, more sinned against than sinning.

In 1904 a note in the Memoranda of Archdeacon Plume of Rochester, written about 1656, came to light, which gives us our only bit of personal detail about John Shakespeare. It means that the old man thought well of his own wit and was willing to match it at any time against that of his famous son in the current game of wit-combat:

He [Shakespeare] was a glover's son. Sir John Mennes saw once his old father in his shop— a merry cheekt old man that said, "Will was a good honest fellow, but he [himself] darest have crackt a jest with him at any time."

The family of Shakespeare's mother was of the best, and his father, in spite of his troubles, was a citizen of importance. John Shakespeare made his mark instead of writing his name, but so did other men of the time who we know could read and write; and his offices, particularly that of chamberlain, and the various public functions he discharged, incline us to believe that he must have had some education.

Shakespeare in school It is strange that one should have to argue that such a man as John Shakespeare in such a community as Stratford did actually send his son to school; but, as there are no records of the grammar school covering the period of Shakespeare's school years, such is the case. The principal reasons for believing that Shakespeare went to school are these: First, because, as the son of a member of the town council, he would have been entitled to attend the grammar school without charge; in any case the family during his boyhood was abundantly able to have had him attend. Secondly, Shakespeare shows in his works familiarity with the studies of just such a school as the King Edward VI Grammar School of Stratford. On this point Dr. F. J. Furnivall quotes J. H. Lupton, the editor of Colet, as follows:

I think you would be safe in concluding that at such a school as Stratford, about 1570, there would be taught—(1) an 'A B C book,' for which a pupil teacher, or 'A-B-C-darius,' is sometimes mentioned as having a salary; (2) a catechism in English and Latin, probably Nowell's; (3) the authorized Latin grammar, i.e., Lilly's, put out with a proclamation adapted to each king's reign; (4) some easy Latin construing book, such as Eramus's *Colloquies*, Corderius's *Colloquies*, or Baptista Mantuanus [an Italian poet of the Renaissance who wrote Latin eclogues; quoted by Shakespeare in *Love's Labor's Lost*]; and the familiar 'Cato,' or *Disticha de Moribus*, which is often prescribed in Statutes.

Dr. Furnivall adds: "From these easier Latin books the students proceeded to construe such Latin authors as Seneca, Terence, Plautus, Cicero, Ovid, and Vergil." Instruction in Greek, he says, was more rare, "but the quickest scholars were often given lessons in it." Thirdly, it was the period of the Renaissance, when all the world was eagerly interested in education, and, since we must recognize in Shakespeare a true child of the Renaissance, the probabilities of his having been properly schooled are still further increased. The conception of Shakespeare as an educated man, by the standards of his time, is of importance, since from it one gets a truer idea of the nature of his works;

namely, that they are not the output of un-tutored genius, but works whose texture is the culture of his time. Shakespeare did not build his plays out of what he saw in the streets of Stratford and London; their sub-stance is primarily the literary culture of the Renaissance.

Shakespeare's marriage   When Shakespeare was eighteen years old, his father being then in the depths of financial distress, he married. The bishop's register of Worcester, the central city of the diocese, shows for November 28, 1582, the issue of a bishop's license for the marriage of William Shake-speare and Anne Hathaway, who has been identified with all reasonable probability as Agnes (or Anne) Hathaway, daughter of the then recently deceased Richard Hath-away of the hamlet of Shottery a short dis-tance from Stratford. The custom of asking the banns on three separate Sundays or holy-days was regularly suspended during the period of about two months from Advent Sunday to the Octave of Epiphany, and the method of securing a license through the bishop enabled persons to be married without asking the banns and thus losing the time of the prohibited period. One does not know where the young couple were married. It would naturally have been in the parish of which the bride was a resident. It has been suggested with some probability that it was at Temple Grafton, where Anne Hathaway had relatives; but, in any case, Shakespeare and his wife became resident in Stratford, where on May 26, 1583, Susanna, daughter to William Shakespeare, was baptized. Also on February 2, 1585, Shakespeare's only other children, the twins Hamnet and Judith, were baptized in Stratford Church. The twins seem to have been named after Shakespeare's friends and neighbors, Hamnet Sadler, a baker of Stratford, and his wife Judith.

The seven dark years   With this entry of the bap-tism of his children the con-nection with the records of Stratford and vicinity for William Shake-speare in the period of his youth and obscurity comes to an end; and we are faced with a great blank of seven or nine years which history has failed to fill and conjecture has filled entirely too full. In

1592 Shakespeare is apparently alluded to by the poet Robert Greene as an actor and dramatist of growing importance. The next year his poem *Venus and Adonis* is entered for publication in the Stationers' Register and published in London; and in 1595 his name appears, for the first time, in the accounts of the Treasurer of the Royal Chamber as a member of the Lord Chamberlain's company of players, who had been summoned to present two comedies before the Queen at Greenwich in the Christmas season of 1594.

Shakespeare possibly taught school   The fascinating question of what Shakespeare did dur-ing the dark years may yet be answered. Meantime, one can only record traditions and guesses. One of the oldest accounts and one of the most probable and authentic has received the support of Professor Adams in his life of Shakespeare and is not ruled out by Sir Sidney Lee. It comes from John Aubrey, an antiquary and biographer of the period of the Restoration. In collecting information about actors and dramatists for his "Minutes of Lives" he resorted to William Beeston, whom Dryden character-ized as "the chronicle of the stage." Aubrey seems also to have had a high opinion of Beeston's knowledge, for he noted on his manuscript, "W. Shakespeare—quære (i.e., inquire of) Mr. Beeston, who knows most of him." Then, apparently in refutation of Ben Jonson's famous charge that Shake-speare knew "little Latin and less Greek," Aubrey says,

Though, as Ben Jonson says of him, that he knew but little Latin and less Greek, he under-stood Latin pretty well, for he had been in his younger years a schoolmaster in the country.

On the margin opposite this Aubrey writes "from Mr. Beeston." William Beeston had been a theatrical manager all his life, and was the son of an actor and theater manager who was unquestionably associated with Shakespeare during his career in Lon-don. The idea of Shakespeare's having taught school is not unattractive and explains much. School-teaching would in some measure have taken the place of a university in his education and would go far in accounting for his technical knowledge of schoolbooks and schoolmasters in his earliest plays, such as *Love's Labour's Lost* and *The Comedy of Errors*, and also for his familiarity with Ovid appearing in *Titus Andronicus*, *Venus and Adonis*, and *The Rape of Lucrece*. It would also change the conception of his early relation to the theater, putting it more in line with that of other dramatists of the time, since it would show him, like Marlowe and Greene, coming up to London, in order to fulfill his ambition as a poet and to try his fortune in the newly fashionable profession of playwright.

Possible apprenticeship In other traditions, the idea has prevailed of Shakespeare as an unlettered genius and self-made man, a notion always fascinating to the popular mind. One of these traditions was picked up by John Dowdall when traveling through Warwickshire in 1693, from an old parish clerk who was showing him about the town of Stratford. Shakespeare, he was told, was bound prentice to a butcher, but ran from his master to London, where he was received into the playhouse as a "serviture." Part of this Aubrey also records, namely, that "when he [Shakespeare] was a boy he exercised his father's trade," which Aubrey thought was that of butcher; and "when he killed a calf, he would doe it in a high style and make a speech." There is no other evidence that Shakespeare was a runaway apprentice. He was of age in 1585 and would have been free to go where he pleased. The allusion to "killing a calf" throws doubt on the whole thing. Canon Raine explained half a century ago that the words are an allusion to an ancient rural amusement which consisted in representing behind a curtain the slaughter of a calf, a sort of semi-dramatic game in which we may believe simple visitors at country fairs took great delight. From some casual recollection of Shakespeare's participation in this forgotten game, probably when he was a boy, may have come, absurdly enough, the tradition that he was a butcher's apprentice. "Killing a calf in a high style": butcher's apprentice—and the tradition is complete![1]

[1]See review of Joseph Quincy Adams, *A Life of William Shakespeare*, by Professor John M. Manly, *New Republic*, September 26, 1923.

Deer-stealing also a doubtful tradition Another tradition, that of the deer-stealing, has some plausibility about it and has been widely accepted. It appears as one of the gossipy interpolations made, after 1688 and before 1709, by the Reverend Richard Davies in the manuscripts of the Reverend William Fulman, who in his collections of antiquarian detail made notes on Shakespeare and Stratford. In 1709 the tradition was seized upon and augmented by Nicholas Rowe, the first editor of Shakespeare. Shakespeare introduced into *2 Henry IV* Justice Shallow as a butt for Falstaff's humor. Shallow was a popular character, and Shakespeare introduced him again into *The Merry Wives of Windsor*. He is a caricature of the rural magistrate and country squire. In the opening scene of the latter play there is a vulgar pun, a very old and easy joke, on Justice Shallow's coat of arms, which Shakespeare imagines as consisting of a dozen white luces. The luce is a fish frequently employed as an heraldic device. Parson Evans, desiring to flatter Shallow and misled by the similarity of sounds between the words "luce" and "louse," says,

The dozen white louses do become an old coat [of arms] well; it agrees well, passant; it is a familiar beast to man, and signifies love. (I, i, 19-21).

When Falstaff enters in the same scene, Justice Shallow thus accuses him: "Knight, you have beaten my men, killed my deer, and broke open my lodge." And the Justice is disposed to make a "star-chamber matter" of it. It happens that a family of gentry named Lucy, who lived at Charlecote Hall near Stratford, had by an easy pun on their own name adopted three white luces as a device; and, that in the end of the seventeenth century, though not in Shakespeare's youth, they owned a deer park. These local circumstances seem to have been used to explain the puns and allusions in the play, and these in turn to support a tradition arising out of such an explanation. Rowe gives the following flamboyant version:

He had, by a misfortune common enough to young fellows, fallen into ill company, and amongst them, some that made a frequent practice of deer-stealing engaged him more than once in robbing a park belonging to Sir Thomas Lucy, of Charlecote, near Stratford. For this he was prosecuted by that gentleman, as he thought, somewhat too severely; and in order to revenge that ill usage made a ballad upon him. And though this, probably the first essay of his poetry, be lost, yet it is said to have been so very bitter that it redoubled the prosecution against him to that degree that he was obliged to leave his business and family in Warwickshire for some time, and shelter himself in London.[1]

The ballad, however, is preserved and turns out to be manifestly a late production.

Shakespeare's social position Mr. D. H. Madden[2] argues that Shakespeare must have spent some time in Gloucestershire, since he betrays in more than one of his plays an intimate knowledge of that county and its people. One asks how he obtained this knowledge and still more how it is that even his earliest plays show so perfect a familiarity with the ways of good society; particularly, since social behavior is a kind of knowledge which must be acquired by social contacts. Indeed too much stress has been put upon Shakespeare's lowly origin. His family was of good position and, on the mother's side, well connected. There were gentle-folk in the neighborhood of Stratford with whom, when he retired to his native town, he is known to have had social relations. It is certainly no very wild conjecture to suppose that such associations were also open to Shakespeare in his youth, before he betook himself to London.

Shakespeare's arrival in London Betake himself to London he did, whether for refuge, as Rowe puts it, or not; and conjecture has busied itself with the way in which he made his start in the theatrical world. Malone made the unsupported statement in 1790 that "his first office in the theater was that as prompter's attendant," which Sir Sidney Lee explains as "call boy." There is of course no reason to think that Shakespeare, a young man from the country, would not have had to begin at the bottom; his intimate knowledge of stagecraft fits in well with the idea that he may have had experience in the prompter's end of the business.

In any case, as a young man of education and probably an aspiring poet, he would have come very early into the society of his fellows. He had in all probability at least one prosperous acquaintance in London; namely, Richard Field, formerly of Stratford and the son of an associate of Shakespeare's father. Field was a printer, and in 1593 and 1594 published for Shakespeare in very good style his two poems *Venus and Adonis* and *The Rape of Lucrece*.

"The only Shake-scene in a countrey" There comes into consideration at this time one of the best known but most puzzling references to Shakespeare in his whole life story, the first allusion to him after the Stratford days. It is the attack of an enemy, one who was himself disappointed, ruined, and dying in poverty. Robert Greene, to whom we owe the passage which follows, in a pamphlet entitled *A Groatsworth of Wit Bought with a Million of Repentance*, attacks the players who have deserted him and advises three other dramatists to quit writing plays, since, if they continue to do so, they too will suffer a like fate to his. The pamphlet was written in the summer of 1592 before Greene's death on the third of September following. He attacks particularly a fourth playwright, a man of the baser sort, who has, he thinks, superseded him in the favor of the actors. This is apparently Shakespeare. The three dramatists he addresses are his fellow University Wits, Christopher Marlowe, Thomas Nashe, and George Peele. "Gentlemen, his Quondam acquaintance, that spend their wits in making Plaies, R. G. wisheth a better exercise, and to preuent his extermities":

. . . Base minded men al three of you, if by my miserie ye be not warned: for vnto none of you (like me) sought those burres to cleaue: those Puppits (I meane) that spake from our mouths, those Anticks garnisht in our colours. Is it not strange that I, to whom they al haue beene beholding: is it not like that you, to whome they all haue beene beholding, shall (were yee in that case that I am now) bee both at once of them forsaken? Yes trust them not: for there is an vpstart Crow, beautified with our feathers, that with his Tygers heart wrapt in a Players hyde, supposes he is as well able to bombast out a blanke verse as the best of you: and beeing an absolute *Iohannes fac totum*, is in his owne conceit the onely Shake-scene in a countrey.

[1] For a different interpretation see below, p. 289.
[2] *The Diary of Master William Silence*, London, 1897, pp. 372-4.

The "burres" are the actors who have forsaken him in his poverty for the rival playwright, "Shakescene," or we must believe Shakespeare, who is also properly enough described as a "Johannes Factotum," or Jack-at-all-trades—actor, playwright, poet, and probably engaged in various ways about the management of the theater. To make the reference still more unmistakable, there is the burlesque line, "Tygers heart wrapt in a Players hyde," modeled after, "O tiger's heart wrapt in a woman's hide!" which occurs in *3 Henry VI* (I, iv, 137). The possible implication is that this highly rhetorical line is one of the "fine feathers" with which Shakespeare has "beautified" himself, though it may be merely a selected example of bombast.

Chettle's apology There is evidence that Shakespeare or his friends were with good reason offended at this attack, as apparently was Marlowe, since Greene states in his address that he had once been an atheist as Marlowe was, but now saw the folly and wickedness of atheism. As to reparations, Greene was dead and beyond reach; but Nashe, who was a bitter satirist, was suspected of having had a hand in the affair. Nashe denied this vigorously, and Henry Chettle, also a dramatist, was brought into the matter. Chettle, in his *Kind-Harts Dreame*, denied any responsibility except that which arose from his having prepared Greene's manuscript for the press:

. . . I had onely in the copy this share: it was il written, as sometime *Greenes* hand was none of the best; licensd it must be, ere it could bee printed, which could neuer be if it might not be read. To be breife, *I* writ it ouer; and as neare as *I* could, followed the copy; onely in that letter *I* put something out, but in the whole booke not a worde in; for I protest it was all *Greenes*, not mine nor Maister *Nashes*, as some vniustly haue affirmed.

With reference to Marlowe, whose reputation as an atheist was then at its height, he says:

With neither of them that take offence was *I* acquainted, and with one of them [Marlowe] *I* care not if *I* neuer be.

He then goes on more particularly about Shakespeare:

The other, whome at that time I did not so much spare, as since I wish I had, for that as *I* haue moderated the heate of liuing writers, and might haue vsde my owne discretion (especially in such a case) the Author beeing dead, that *I* did not, *I* am as sory as if the originall fault had beene my fault, because my selfe haue seene his demeanor no lesse ciuill, than he exelent in the qualitie he professes: Besides, diuers of worship haue reported his vprightnes of dealing, which argues his honesty, and his facetious grace in writting, that approoues his Art.

About this handsome apology one notes that Shakespeare, hitherto unknown to Chettle, has made a characteristic impression of personal civility upon him; and that Shakespeare is excellent in the "qualitie" he professes, that is, excellent as an actor. Shakespeare is also not without the favor of persons of importance, some of whom have borne witness to his uprightness in dealing. By "divers of worship" Chettle does not mean actors or theatrical people, but persons of gentle blood. This first rather rancorous allusion to Shakespeare serves then to bring out the fact that in 1592 Shakespeare was regarded as a man of pleasant demeanor, honest reputation, and acknowledged skill as an actor and writer; and that he was a popular dramatist of imitative tendencies.

Dramatic apprenticeship By the end of the year 1594, when after the long plague the theatrical companies were again permitted to act before London audiences and we find Shakespeare a member of the Lord Chamberlain's company, he had, it is believed on various grounds, written ten plays—comedies: *Love's Labour's Lost, The Comedy of Errors, The Two Gentlemen of Verona*, and *A Midsummer-Night's Dream*; histories: *1, 2*, and *3 Henry VI*, and *Richard III*; tragedies: *Titus Andronicus* and *Romeo and Juliet*. Many critics, to be sure, deny him the authorship of *Titus Andronicus* and any but a small part in the Henry VI plays; but nobody questions the facts that they are early plays and that in the general principles of grouping they belong here. Almost every one of the ten plays shows evidence of having been revised at a later time, so that we have before us the difficult task of dating plays from their earliest parts. Among these plays certain ones,

Love's Labour's Lost, The Comedy of Errors, The Two Gentlemen of Verona, the Henry VI plays, and *Titus Andronicus,* belong to the earliest period, while *A Midsummer-Night's Dream, Romeo and Juliet,* and *Richard III* might be associated with *King John, Richard II,* and *The Taming of the Shrew* to form an early, but not the earliest, group of Shakespeare's plays. It is possible that we do not possess all of the plays that Shakespeare wrote during the period of his apprenticeship, and no play can be accurately dated. A play, not otherwise known, called *Love's Labour's Won,* is mentioned by Francis Meres in *Palladis Tamia.* It is natural to believe from its title that such a play was a companion piece to *Love's Labour's Lost* and was, therefore, written at about the same time. These two plays may be his earliest dramatic efforts; if so, they may go back to 1588 or 1589.

Shakespeare's early development is hard to follow, not only because he seems to have later revised so many of his early plays presumably for stage revivals, so that one and the same play shows both earlier and later styles; but also because he, a learner making rapid progress in the skill of his art, was subjected to outside influences which can be only partly determined. One of these, we may be sure, was the dramatic style of the plays he revamped and of the plays of contemporary dramatists writing for his company and for the rival companies. If one could define these influences and form an idea of the kinds of plays acceptable on the stage during his early period, one could better understand the group of plays written by the year 1594. Fortunately we are not without material for doing this, since Henslowe's *Diary* records the daily performances of plays by the Lord Strange's men from the 19th of February to the 22nd of June, 1592. Many of their plays unfortunately are lost, but enough of them are preserved to indicate the taste of the time. They had Marlowe's *Jew of Malta,* Greene's *Orlando Furioso* and *Friar Bacon and Friar Bungay,* Lodge's *A Looking Glass for London,* Kyd's *The Spanish Tragedy,* the anonymous cutpurse comedy *A Knack to Know a Knave,* possibly Peele's *Battle of Alcazar,* and an early form of Shakespeare's *1 Henry VI.* There is thus

a tragedy with a villain hero, a heroic play, a play of a necromancer, a comedy of London life, a revenge tragedy, and two history plays, the one English, the other foreign in theme, besides other plays now lost whose titles are suggestive of rough clownage and wide romantic sweep. Probably few plays were written during the period when plays were forbidden on account of the long plague of 1592-4; for, when the Lord Chamberlain's men and the Lord Admiral's men acted together under Henslowe's management at the suburban theater of Newington Butts from the third to the 13th of June, 1594, their repertories seem to have consisted largely of old plays. In this brief period, before we lose sight of them, the Lord Chamberlain's men are thought to have acted *Titus Andronicus, Hamlet* (probably the pre-Shakespearean play), *The Taming of a Shrew,* and a lost play called *Hester and Ahasuerus.* The Lord Admiral's men probably moved at once to the Rose on the Bankside, across the river Thames from the city of London, where they continued to play under Henslowe's management until 1603. During the years 1594-7 Henslowe kept in his *Diary* a careful record of their plays and of the sums of money taken, a circumstance which enables us to know a great deal more about the repertory of Shakespeare's rival company than we can ever know about his own. When the Lord Admiral's men began again in 1594, they had five of Marlowe's plays. They seem also to have had Peele's *Edward I,* Kyd's *The Spanish Tragedy,* and a Henry V play. They may also have had plays by both Greene and Peele (Henslowe's illiteracy makes it hard to determine), although some of the principal dramas of these two authors having got into print ceased to be acted.

We do not know the repertory of the Lord Chamberlain's company as a whole as we do that of the Lord Admiral's; but we know enough of it to be sure that both companies were acting in 1594 the same sort of thing that had been on the boards in 1592. We have, therefore, ground for assuming that, in spite of the loss of many plays (some of which may have been very potent), the chief influences upon Shakespeare during his early period were those of

Marlowe, Greene, Peele, and Kyd. As an actor in Lord Strange's company he would have been familiar with their plays; if he belonged to Lord Pembroke's company, he would also have fallen under the same influences. He learned a great deal from Lyly, but how this came about is more puzzling. Lyly wrote mainly for the boys' company at St. Paul's, and, when their acting was suspended about 1591, a number of his plays were printed; so that one concludes that Shakespeare, although he may have seen Lyly's plays on the stage, is more likely to have read them in print than to have acted in them. In any case, Shakespeare's trend as a dramatist was determined by the powerful group who from about 1581 to 1591 created the Elizabethan drama. As will appear in the following account of the plays of Shakespeare's early period, there are from the first many original features which are not to be accounted for on any theory of imitation.

The early plays We see Shakespeare then writing tragedy with the revenge motive and all the attendant horrors of murder and cruelty, comedy with the Plautine theme of mistaken identity, and chronicle plays of a strongly patriotic nature. In these forms and with these underlying purposes he follows the great group of his early contemporaries in whose curiosity, energy, and aspirations he fully participates. From the influence of Lyly, Greene, and Peele he has begun in *Love's Labour's Lost*, *The Two Gentlemen of Verona*, and *A Midsummer-Night's Dream* his production of romantic comedy, the comedy of love and friendship, in which form he was to excel, producing later such plays as *The Merchant of Venice*, *As You Like It*, and *Twelfth Night*. What were, one asks, the powers that were specifically his in the writing of these early plays?

The most striking of his powers was that of construction. He was careful about it, ingenious, and detailed even to the point of formalism. Back of *The Comedy of Errors* lie two skillfully plotted plays of the great master Plautus. Shakespeare combines them, betters them, renders them more intricate but not less clear. In *Love's Labour's Lost* he selects a theme from the more fashionable culture of the day, arranges four

lovers over against their four lady-loves, and carries his formal plot to a triumphant denouement. This element of careful balance is obvious also in *The Two Gentlemen of Verona*. *A Midsummer-Night's Dream* is a still more brilliant piece of plotting, there being four parallel or contrasting themes woven together, each displaying its own special order of existence: Theseus and Hippolita of the blood royal, mature and regulative; the four young lovers from the court, most ingeniously shifted about in their attachments until a proper relation is achieved; the fairy king and queen, Oberon and Titania, themselves quite humanly at cross-purposes and manipulating human affairs with a combination of magic and chance; and finally Bottom and his associates burlesquing serious love interest in their play on Pyramus and Thisbe. *Titus Andronicus* is also a play of careful combination, and we may believe that the story of *Romeo and Juliet* was chosen in part at least because in that case Shakespeare found already shaped to his hand one of the most perfectly articulated of all plots. The greatest manifestation, however, of his early eminence in architectonic ability is to be seen in the history plays. The many events, the multitudinous characters, and the long expanse of time of the Wars of the Roses are condensed and unified. *Richard III* is made, quite according to the best historical authority, to bear the final and supreme burden of tragic guilt and to embody the rancors of a century. One of the best evidences for Shakespeare's authorship of *1, 2,* and *3 Henry VI* is the way in which they lead up, through the characters of Suffolk, York, Margaret, Henry VI, and Gloucester to the play of *Richard III*, and the extent to which they are mindful of the historic past in the dethronement of Richard II, and of the principle of loyalty to king and country.

Something has already been said about Shakespeare's early style. It is a style which bears the impress of youth, but of youth burning with enthusiasm and gifted with wonderful powers. His characters are still liable to be merely types who do not as yet speak as individuals words appropriate to them and to them only. Instead we have puns, conceits, and ingenious stylistic devices; such as oxymoron, stichomythia, clownish quibbling, and far-fetched allusions. The plays are examples of mental and verbal agility, but from the point of view of construction they are nevertheless great plays.

REFERENCES (SHAKESPEARE'S LIFE AND TIMES)

ADAMS, JOSEPH QUINCY, *A Life of William Shakespeare*. Boston, 1923.

BALDWIN, T. W., *The Organization and Personnel of the Shakespearean Company*. Princeton, 1927.

BARTON, SIR D. P., *Links between Shakespeare and the Law*. London, 1929.

BROOKE, C. F. TUCKER, *The Tudor Drama*. Boston, 1912. *Shakespeare of Stratford*. New Haven, 1926.

CHAMBERS, E. K., *William Shakespeare*. Oxford, 1930. *The Elizabethan Stage*. Oxford, 1923.

EBISCH, WALTHER, AND SCHÜCKING, L. L., *A Shakespeare Bibliography*. Oxford, 1931.

FRIPP, EDGAR I., AND SAVAGE, RICHARD, *Minutes and Accounts of the Corporation of Stratford-upon-Avon and other Records*. London, 1924, 1926.

FURNIVAL, F. J., AND MUNRO, JOHN. *Shakespeare, Life and Work*. London, 1908.

GRAY, J. W., *Shakespeare's Marriage*. London, 1905.

HALLIWELL-PHILLIPPS, J. O., *Outlines of the Life of Shakespeare*. Eleventh ed., London, 1907; the greatest collection of Shakespeare documents.

LAMBERT, D. H., *Shakespeare Documents*. London, 1904.

LEE, SIR SIDNEY, *A Life of William Shakespeare*. Fourth edition of the revised version, rewritten and enlarged. London, 1925.

NEILSON, WILLIAM ALLAN, AND THORNDIKE, ASHLEY H., *Facts about Shakespeare*. New York, 1913.

NICOLL, ALLARDYCE, *British Drama*. London and New York, 1925.

RALEIGH, SIR WALTER, *Shakespeare* (English Men of Letters). New York, 1907.

ROLFE, W. J., *Life of Shakespeare*. Boston, 1904. *Shakespeare the Boy*. 1897.

Shakespeare's England. Oxford, 1916.

STOPES, MRS. C. C., *Shakespeare's Family*. London, 1901. *Shakespeare's Warwickshire Contemporaries*. Stratford-upon-Avon, 1907. *Shakespeare's Environment*. London, 1914. Other works by the same author.

WALLACE, C. W., "New Shakespeare Discoveries," *Harper's Magazine*, March, 1910.

Additional references will be found in the General Introduction, pages 18, 54-55. The articles on Shakespeare in the ninth and the eleventh editions of the *Encyclopædia Britannica* are also worth the student's attention.

On Shakespeare's book-learning in school and out the following are important sources of information:

ANDERS, H. R. D., *Shakespeare's Books*. Berlin, 1904.

BAYNES, T. S., "What Shakespeare Learned at School," in *Shakespeare Studies*. London, 1894.

BOSWELL-STONE, W. G., *Shakespeare's Holinshed*. London, 1907.

COLLINS, J. C., "Shakespeare as a Classical Scholar," in *Studies in Shakespeare*. Westminster, 1904.

FARMER, R., *Essay on the Learning of Shakespeare*. Cambridge, 1767. This important work is not usually readily accessible.

GOLLANCZ, SIR ISRAEL, *The Shakespeare Classics*. A series in progress since 1907 which has reprinted the chief sources of Shakespeare's plays.

NICOLL, JOSEPHINE AND ALLARDYCE, *Holinshed's Chronicle as used in Shakespeare's Plays*. Everyman's Library, 1927.

SKEAT, W. W., *Shakespeare's Plutarch*. London, 1875; also in *The Shakespeare Classics*, there edited by C. F. Tucker Brooke.

Further bibliographical materials will be found in F. E. SCHELLING's *Elizabethan Drama*, Boston, 1908, in Rolfe's and Lee's lives of Shakespeare, in Ebisch and Schücking, *A Shakespeare Bibliography*, and in the voluminous *Shakespeare Bibliography* by W. Jaggard, Stratford-upon-Avon, 1911; also in many editions of the works of Shakespeare and of separate plays. Furness's Variorum edition of Shakespeare reprints many sources of plays and many citations from Shakespeare criticism. Sir E. K. Chambers's recently published *William Shakespeare* furnishes extensive bibliography, both general and special, and reprints practically the whole body of Shakespeare documents.

II. EARLY COMEDIES

LOVE'S LABOUR'S LOST

Publication Love's Labour's Lost, which is possibly Shakespeare's earliest play, was issued in 1598 in quarto form with the following title-page:

A PLEASANT Conceited Comedie CALLED, Loues labors lost. As it vvas presented before her Highnes this last Christmas. Newly corrected and augmented *By W. Shakespere.* Imprinted at London by *W. W.* for *Cutburt Burby.* 1598.

Noteworthy here is the information that the play was acted before Queen Elizabeth at Christmas 1597; and, in addition to this, that the text in hand purports to supplant an unauthorized and probably incorrect version of the play. A parallel inference from a similar statement on the title-page of the quarto of *Romeo and Juliet* printed in 1599 that the play was "newly corrected, augmented, and amended," is substantiated by the existence of a bad quarto of that play printed in 1597. Although no early and imperfect version of *Love's Labour's Lost* has been preserved, the probability of there having been, to use the words of the Folio editors, "a stolen and surreptitious copy," is further increased by the fact that the play was never entered in the Stationers' Register. If the play had already been published, even from a dishonestly acquired copy and without the consent of the Stationers' Company, it would not have been necessary to relicense it in order to issue another text. The text itself, moreover, shows evidence of revision in at least two places: Biron's speech in Act IV, scene iii, lines 289-365, shows parts of the old version and the new standing side by side. Lines 296-304, for example, are repeated in expanded form in lines 318-351. Again in Act V, scene ii, Rosaline's speech in lines 828-832 is apparently the first draft of her speech in lines 851-864. There is also a certain amount of confusion in the play in the assignment of speeches, which can often be explained on the assumption that the speech in question was part of the revised version and was wrongly labeled by the printer when he set up the copy. Cuthbert Burby was apparently a friend of the players and would not have stolen their play, which fact, taken with the appearance of Shakespeare's name on the title-page and the excellence of the text, points to this quarto as an authorized version. The text of the play in the First Folio is printed directly from the text of the quarto of 1598.

The date Love's Labour's Lost is mentioned by Francis Meres in *Palladis Tamia* and is alluded to by Robert Tofte in *Alba*, both in the year 1598. It must have been an old work by 1598, since it shows, even in what is evidently a revised state, all the characteristics of Shakespeare's earliest style. The play abounds in rhyme, both in couplets and quatrains, in doggerel verse, and in blank verse which is largely end-stopped and free from light and weak endings. Numerous sonnets are also introduced into the text. In these qualities it is on a par with *The Comedy of Errors*, so that no one can tell on purely internal evidence which is the older of these two plays. *Love's Labour's Lost*, like *The Comedy of Errors*, teems with puns and conceits and is artificial and highly elaborate in plot. The characters are balanced off oné against another—a princess and three ladies in waiting are wooed with mechanical ardor by a prince and three attendant lords. Of all of Shakespeare's plays *Love's Labour's Lost* is closest to John Lyly, the creator of the social comedy of the court. One sees in the play the Renaissance fashion of establishing academies for the pursuit of learning and the training of courtiers, the gossip of the court itself, and the language of euphuism; all so employed that it is difficult to say how far Shakespeare means to ridicule these things and how far he was working delightedly in an atmosphere and style whose extravagance he really enjoyed. Men and women never grow tired of having it demonstrated to them that they cannot live without each other. *Love's Labour's Lost* goes further and says what Tudor England found much to its liking; namely, that there is no true learning without true love. This play, featuring an ideal commonwealth of learning from which all women were to be excluded, recalls a vast array of courtly circles, learned coteries in Italy, France, and England, for the discussion of such Renaissance topics as the relation of men and women, education true and false, and the value of courtly culture. No wonder the play was popular at court. It is very like *The Comedy of Errors* also in its abundant use of school Latin authors and its numerous copy-book quotations from Latin and French.

It has been suggested that the play was written in the first instance to be performed before the Queen, and that the performance of 1597 was, therefore, a revival. Professor Baldwin dates the play in the winter of 1588. Professor Adams thinks it was one of the two plays presented before her majesty by Lord Pembroke's men in the Christmas season of 1592. If so, it must have been acquired by the Lord Chamberlain's company on the disbanding of the Earl of Pembroke's players and added permanently to their repertory.

Topical allusions in *Love's Labour's Lost* *Love's Labour's Lost* is one of the few plays of Shakespeare's for which no definite source is known; it introduces, nevertheless, in larger quantity than elsewhere references which seem to bear upon contemporary matters. Henry of Navarre was the popular figure of the day. The names Biron and Longaville belonged to two of his followers; Dumain seems also to have been a French nobleman of Henry's time. Some critics have seen in the play a reminiscence of a meeting between Ferdinand of Navarre and a French princess, an event from the earlier history of Navarre, at which meeting about 1425 certain territory was ceded by Navarre to France. Others have seen a poetical treatment of one of the progresses of Queen Elizabeth in which she was entertained with plays and masques. Armado and his page, Moth, are thought to burlesque, respectively, a certain "fantastical Spaniard," resident at the court of the Queen, and a French ambassador, De la Mothe, long popular in England. The disguising of the lovers as Russians seems to travesty a well-known incident of the year 1584 when Russian ambassadors came to England to seek among the nobility for a wife for the Czar, an event which was both

flattering and amusing to the Queen. Tubal Holofernes, tutor of Gargantua in *Rabelais*, seems to supply the name for the schoolmaster and also, of course, some of his pedantry, although pedants were stock characters in sixteenth century comedy in England, France, and Italy. We thus have Shakespeare writing a court comedy completely up-to-date both as regards current gossip and Renaissance fashion.

The French scholar M. Abel Lefranc, in his unsuccessful attempt to prove that the Earl of Derby was the author of Shakespeare's plays, discovered an important parallel to the events narrated in *Love's Labour's Lost*. Catharine de Medici and her daughter Marguerite, subsequently the wife of Henry of Navarre, made an expedition to the court of Navarre at Nérac in 1578 in order to effect a settlement of the question of sovereignty of Aquitaine and the matter of the payment of one hundred thousand crowns to Navarre by the king of France. The diplomatic matters being quickly turned over to specialists, the king and his court devoted themselves to festivities for the entertainment of their royal guests. This love episode in the life of the most popular prince in Europe, himself the pattern of Renaissance chivalry, would have been an appropriate subject for a comedy designed to entertain and flatter Queen Elizabeth on one of her many visits to her noblemen during some one of her progresses. It has been suggested that *Love's Labour's Lost* was devised at the instigation of Southampton for the entertainment of Queen Elizabeth on the occasion of her visit to Tichfield Park in 1591, since the plot seems to suit his desire at that time of postponing his marriage with Lady Elizabeth Vere. In any case there was abundant opportunity for Shakespeare to learn at second hand not only the historical purposes which prompted the visit of Queen Catharine and her daughter, but the atmosphere of the court of Navarre and the nature of the dramatic entertainments then fashionable in France.[1]

[1]See O. J. Campbell, "*Love's Labour's Lost* Restudied," in *Studies in Shakespeare, Milton, and Donne*, by Members of the English Department of the University of Michigan, Ann Arbor, 1925; and Austin K. Gray, "The Secret of *Love's Labour's Lost* and the Earl of Southampton," *Publications of the Modern Language Association*, XXXIX, 581-611.

The story of the play Ferdinand, king of Navarre, turns his court into an academy for the promotion of true learning. The partners of his enterprise are three courtiers, Biron, Dumain, and Longaville, who swear with him to study for three years, see no woman, fast one day a week and eat but one meal on other days. Biron's reluctant agreement warns us of the lack of common sense in the enterprise. The men have scarcely confirmed their oath when the Princess of France arrives bearing her father's offer to repay 100,000 crowns of the 200,000 disbursed by Navarre's father in the wars, together with a demand for the surrender of Navarre's claim to Aquitaine. She brings her three ladies-in-waiting, Rosaline, Maria, and Katharine, to match Navarre's three lords. In spite of vows to the contrary there is a general falling in love. The king leads off with the princess, and Biron, the first of Shakespeare's critical and intellectual heroes, falls in love with Rosaline, the first of Shakespeare's witty and self-possessed heroines. Each of the four men writes verses to the woman he loves. Each goes to the wood to sigh and read his verses aloud. Each in turn becomes aware by process of eavesdropping of the perfidy of his predecessors in the wood. Last of all, the cynical Biron stands revealed. He shows no shame but speaks in justification of them all: a lady's love is worth all the books in the world. The four men therefore frankly turn lovers and, dressing themselves as Russians, present a masque of the Nine Worthies. The ladies exchange their favors; each lover gets the wrong lady-love and is scorned for his inconstancy. The end of the play comes with the news of the death of the French king. The voice of worldly affairs demands an adjustment according to custom and common sense. Navarre goes to a hermitage for a year; Dumain and Longaville must wait for a like period, and Biron must spend his year tending the sick in a hospital as a cure for his jibing spirit. The moral is: Not only can men not do without women, but they must work hard to get them. The minor plot is filled with stock characters from the comedy of the time, particularly from French comedy and the Italian *commedia dell'arte* (a form of drama played extem-poraneously from an outline of the plot), such as the pedant, the braggart, the hedge-priest, the fool, the boy, and the stupid constable. Biron is the most highly individualized character of the play; a scourger of the follies of others, his own folly is hardest of all to eradicate. This type was to appear later in Jaques in *As You Like It*. Shakespeare is not free in this play from the artificiality he ridicules, although *Love's Labour's Lost* is witty and exuberant beyond anything else he ever wrote, unless it be *A Midsummer-Night's Dream*. It is youthful and pastoral, full of the Renaissance zest for learning and of the recollections of schoolbooks, school days, and of the Warwickshire countryside.

Stage history *Love's Labour's Lost* is said on the title-page of the 1598 quarto to have been "presented before her Highnes this last Christmas," which probably means the Christmas of 1597. It was also presented before King James I in 1604 and probably performed with fair frequency at the Globe and the Blackfriars. It was not heard of on the stage again until 1839, when it was presented by Charles James Mathews at Covent Garden. *Love's Labour's Lost* was acted by Phelps in 1857 and has been acted several times at the Shakespeare Memorial Theater at Stratford. It has also been presented on the public stage at least twice in America. It has not been a popular play but has been received with pleasure on the few occasions on which it has been presented.

THE COMEDY OF ERRORS

An example of an early play The first known edition of *The Comedy of Errors* is that of the First Folio in 1623. There are, however, a number of indications that the play was in existence at an early date. Mention is made of a performance of the play on Holy Innocents' Day (December 28), 1594. At this time the members of Gray's Inn, one of the four ancient societies of lawyers and law students in London, were celebrating an annual revel which had begun, according to custom, with the election of a Lord of Misrule on December 20. They had invited the members of the Inner Temple to be present with them on the night of the twenty-eighth, on which occasion they had arranged with Shakespeare's company for the performance of a play. So many outside guests had been asked, however, that when the Templars arrived, there were no seats for them, and such a hubbub ensued that the play could not proceed. Offended at this, the members of the Inner Temple left, after which the play was given. The *Gesta Grayorum*, a chronicle history of Gray's Inn by Henry Helmes (?), gives a facetious account of the night, describing the performance of the play in the following terms:

. . . after such sports, a Comedy of Errors (like to Plautus his *Menechmus*) was played by the players. So that the night was begun and continued to the end in nothing but confusion and errors; whereupon it was ever afterwards called *The Night of Errors*.

Certain features, moreover, within the play itself suggest that it was not at the date of this performance a new production. (1) There is an allusion to France in Act III, sc. ii, by Dromio of Syracuse as "armed and reverted, making war against her heir," which seems to refer to the fact that between August, 1589, and July, 1593, Henry of Navarre, later Henry IV of France, was at war with the Catholic League and had indeed been heir to the French crown and at war with France since 1585. In the same scene (line 140) Dromio represents Spain in the same vulgar fashion as sending "whole armadoes of caracks to be ballast at her nose," which seems to allude to the Invincible Armada and to indicate some reasonable nearness to its overthrow in 1588. (2) In no other play does Shakespeare show so much artificiality of style, as evidenced by an abundance of doggerel verses, speeches balanced between characters, alternate rhymes, puns and conceits—all indicative of an early period. The play has little prose, few run-on lines, and proportionally still fewer light and weak endings. (3) The plot-construction of *The Comedy of Errors* is bookish and obviously "careful." Almost nowhere else does Shakespeare take such pains in the elaboration of a plot and the knitting together of certain sources and structural ideas. (4) Finally, the text as it appears in the Folio shows evidence of the revision of the play in a later style.

What were the features of this revision? In the first two acts the Antipholi appear as "Antipholus Erotes" and "Antipholus Sereptus," as if these names had been their earlier designations and had been carelessly left standing at the time of the revision. So old-fashioned are the fourteen syllable doggerel verses of the Dromios that some critics have thought they come bodily from an early play on which Shakespeare originally worked. A *Historie of Error*, now lost, was acted before the Queen at Hampton Court by the children of St. Paul's School on New Year's night, 1577. Nothing is known about this play, but the title is so suggestive that many critics have believed it to be Shakespeare's original source. On the present basis of knowledge we have nothing but the likeness of the names. It is, however, possible to see that Shakespeare revised his own work, perhaps on the occasion when the play was revived for presentation at Gray's Inn.[1]

Sources   In the light of his use of known sources, about to be mentioned, one must admit that Shakespeare worked from the first with a good deal of originality. He would certainly have known the *Menæchmi* and the *Amphitruo*, the most popular of the plays of Plautus. On the *Menæchmi* rests the plot of the indistinguishable twins, and on the *Amphitruo* the incident of the exclusion of Antipholus of Ephesus and his servant from his own house. It was probably also the construction of the *Amphitruo* which caused Shakespeare to begin his play on a basis of error, whereas the *Menæchmi* begins on a basis of truth. That Shakespeare, even supposing there was in existence an old play on the same theme, went directly to Plautus is fairly evident. The chances are also that he used the Latin version and not an English translation; for, although a translation of Plautus was published in 1595 and may previously have been circulated in manuscript, there are few cases in which Shakespeare's words resemble those of the

[1]See the edition of the play by Sir Arthur Quiller-Couch and John Dover Wilson in the New Cambridge Shakespeare (Cambridge University Press, 1922); Allison Gaw, "The Evolution of *The Comedy of Errors*," *Publications of the Modern Language Association*, XLI, 620-666; T. W. Baldwin, Introduction to *The Comedy of Errors*, New York, 1928, pp. xvi-xix.

translator. Moreover, there are names in Shakespeare from the original which do not appear in the translation.

Shakespeare and Plautus Shakespeare has enveloped the two plots from Plautus with a romantic story of the separation and ultimate reunion of the members of one family. This theme was familiar in Greek romance, an example of which lived throughout the ages in the old story of Apollonius of Tyre. Shakespeare has, of course, preserved a good deal of the spirit of Roman comedy, and, working with the technique of that dramatic form, has given us something which in sheer confusions is superior to his original. It might be thought that in giving us two Dromios to Plautus's one he has violated probability, but it is as easy to believe in two sets of identical twins as in one, particularly since the whole comedy is played in an atmosphere of conventionality and make-believe, and since it preserves the Plautine atmosphere of the witch-haunted Ephesus. One would freely admit that but for the example of Plautus, a master in the management of intricate plot, Shakespeare could not have succeeded as he has. Since Plautine comedy had been on the English stage for many years, it was easier for the youthful Shakespeare to achieve mastery in that form than in the form of romantic comedy in which later he was to excel all dramatists ancient and modern. In this play itself, however, Shakespeare's most significant advance toward his own greatness was in his use of romantic material; for he thus adapted his Latin comedy to a public which craved variety of a deeper interest and a greater emotional appeal.

Detailed changes The Antipholi of Shakespeare correspond to the Menæchmi of Plautus; Dromio of Syracuse to Messenio; Adriana to Mulier; the Courtesan to Erotium; Pinch to Medicus. Plautus's parasite is discarded, probably because the type was unknown to Shakespeare's age and country. Another Dromio (of Ephesus), exactly like Dromio of Syracuse, is added. Plautus's cook and handmaiden are omitted as unimportant, and the rôle of the Courtesan is greatly reduced; perhaps Shakespeare found Roman libertinism out of place in London. Indeed in this play may be seen Shakespeare's characteristic quality of moral stability, as well as his justice and tenderness of heart.

Although the plot remains superficially the same in *The Comedy of Errors* as in the *Menæchmi*, Shakespeare's changes are significant. Senex, the father of Mulier who acts as her adviser, is replaced by Luciana, the charming sister of Adriana. Luciana becomes the counselor of her sister, serves as a lady-love for the unattached Antipholus of Syracuse, and prefigures the dutiful and obedient wife in contrast to her sister Adriana, who is a shrew. Adriana, who is losing the affection of her husband by her virago-like behavior, is thus made to see the error of her way. Shakespeare supplies outright Solinus, Ægeon, Æmilia, Luce, and the two merchants, new characters who produce a great change in the atmosphere of the play. The main plot goes on in its dry, unmoral, somewhat rascally and licentious fashion, but the romantic minor plot of Ægeon and Æmilia deepens the seriousness of the whole story. Shakespeare loved to play with edged tools. Somebody's life, or somebody's happiness must be at stake even in his comedies. Shakespearean comedy is not, therefore, pure comedy at all. It lacks the independent, carefree coolness of Plautus, Molière, and Sheridan, or even of Shakespeare's contemporary, Ben Jonson. After the introduction of the good Ægeon with his moving appeal to the magistrate to spare his life—an episode brilliantly conceived for making us understand the intricate plot which is to follow—we never get him out of our minds, and, in the midst of the fun and confusion, we continue to wonder if he will be saved. The love-affair between Luciana and Antipholus of Syracuse is a characteristic feature of romantic comedy which interrupts and modifies the comedy of errors, which with its wit and satire on Roman types was enough to satisfy Plautus, but not Shakespeare. Even the crudeness of the conventional comedy of women, Adriana representing the shrew and Luciana the obedient wife, is humanized by the fact that Æmilia the abbess advises her newly found daughter-in-law in a natural and affectionate way. Shakespeare's people are real people whose destinies matter. Finally, the element of surprise is made more emotionaliy gratifying by the completed family reunion in the fifth act. In spite of these changes the comedy is still Plautine: The masters beat the wrong slaves; the wife scolds the wrong husband; one slave is arrested for lunacy, the other for dishonesty; the servants quibble and lie in truly Plautine fashion. In the end all persons are by one means or another assembled in front of the priory, and everything is explained. No doubt from this exercise Shakespeare learned the device, brilliantly employed in such plays as *Twelfth Night* and *Cymbeline*, of keeping certain persons apart while the story was running and bringing them together for inevitable explanations when the fifth act had been reached. Comedies of mistaken identity were also no doubt already numerous on the London stage and continued long afterwards to be popular, as witnessed by Shakespeare's employment of that kind of plot again in his *Twelfth Night*.

Stage history The only recorded performance of *The Comedy of Errors* for more than one hundred and fifty years after the one described in the *Gesta Grayorum* was before King James I at Whitehall on Innocents' Night, 1604. An adaptation of the play called '*Tis all a Mistake* was played at Covent Garden in 1734. After that it was acted for the next hundred years, probably always in altered versions, with considerable frequency. Thomas Hull's version of the comedy held the boards until 1855, when Samuel Phelps presented Shakespeare's version at Sadler's Wells. Since then it has been staged in public theaters a few times. It has gone well as a farce, and its greatest successes have arisen from a happy casting of the Dromios.

An annotated edition of *The Comedy of Errors* is printed on pages 125-152 of this volume.

THE TWO GENTLEMEN OF VERONA

Date and publication *The Two Gentlemen of Verona* was first published in the folio of 1623 and is not mentioned in any way prior to that date except in the list of Shakespeare's comedies given by Francis Meres in *Palladis Tamia* in 1598. It has been assigned on internal evidence to the very earliest period, since it has the same stylistic qualities which distinguish

The Comedy of Errors and *Love's Labour's Lost*. One is inclined to think it later than these plays, however, because of its greater romantic interest. The text of *The Two Gentlemen of Verona* in the First Folio is a peculiar one; so much so, that the editors of the New Cambridge Shakespeare have suggested that the copy for the printers was made up in an unusual fashion. In the acting of an Elizabethan play there were three necessary documents: (1) a copy for the use of the prompter, frequently the author's manuscript, which bore on it the certification of license by the Master of the Revels; (2) the players' parts written out with cues for the use of actors; and (3) a single sheet called the plot or plat, which was hung up behind the scenes so that it might be consulted by the actors while the play was in progress. The prompter's copy contained entrances, exits, and stage directions, all at their appropriate places in the text. The separate parts contained no such information, but were probably from the point of view of intelligibility very accurate, since they presented the lines as spoken. The plat contained nothing but scene-divisions and the names of actors who were to play in the different scenes, the beginning of scenes being indicated by horizontal lines drawn across the sheet and beneath them the names of the actors in the order in which they were to appear in the scene. Since the 1623 folio text of *The Two Gentlemen of Verona* contains almost no stage directions, entrances, or exits, and since the names of actors are grouped together at the beginnings of scenes and not distributed throughout at the places where they enter, it is argued that we do not have in this case a prompter's copy. The hypothesis suggested is that, when the editors of the First Folio came to prepare the manuscript of this play for the printers, the prompt copy could not be found; they, therefore, sent the players' parts and the plat to a copyist who made up the play anew from these documents. It followed that he produced an intelligible text, but a text without stage directions. This is an ingenious and plausible hypothesis, but the peculiarities of the text may be merely due to the play's having been printed from a non-theatrical manuscript. The editors above referred to also advance the theory that the play has been shortened for some special stage presentation by the cutting out of about six hundred lines. As compared to the normal length of an Elizabethan play, about 3000 lines, *The Two Gentlemen of Verona* has but 2380, a fact which would indicate abridgment. Of this abridgment they also find indications in the curtailment of scenes and speeches, the disruption of the time-scheme of the play, confusion of names of places, and dramatic inferiority in several different parts, particularly in the last scene. In order to account for these inferiorities in the last scene, the editors assign a good many passages to an adapter, always a doubtful procedure.[1]

Sources At the basis of the plot lies the story of a lover Proteus, who, having left behind him in Verona his faithful sweetheart Julia, falls in love with Silvia, the sweetheart of his best friend. This act, which is a violation of the proper canons of friendship as well as of love, furnishes a typical Renaissance theme. It appears in all forms of amatory literature, serving always to give occasion for the courtly discriminations in which the Renaissance delighted. The fact that this theme is employed in *The Two Gentlemen of Verona*, with its numerous discussions of love and friendship, duty and honor, throws the play at once into the commonest current of Renaissance literature. In plot *The Two Gentlemen of Verona* is a typical Italian comedy, for dozens of Italian comedies, extant or on record, parallel the play either in the principal situation of friendship versus love or in the minor devices by which it is carried out. Nothing is so common as to have the heroine disguise herself as a page. Indeed an Italian dramatist could not plausibly present a respectable girl as walking abroad (since the stage was a general scene in the open) unless she were disguised. The only other device was to have her speak from a balcony. A like degree of conventionality belongs to the attack by robbers, the rescue, and other events, but particularly to the mixture of sincere emotion and mere ingenuity in the discussion of love, sometimes called Petrarchism, which permeated European literature during the

Renaissance. Nothing can be more absurd than to imagine that Shakespeare constructed this plot with the free hand of a modern author. His originality consisted in infusing into a plot, already developed in its most minute detail and fully supplied with stock figures, actual forms of life and authentic emotion.

It has long been thought that this particular version of a favorite Renaissance plot came from a pastoral romance *Diana Enamorada* by the Portuguese Jorge de Montemayor (1520-1561), in which Felismena is wooed by Don Felix, a courtship which resembles that of Julia by Proteus in the matter of the delivery of the letter by the lady's maid. The father of Don Felix disapproves of the match with Felismena and sends Don Felix away to court. Felismena, like Julia, disguises herself as a page and follows Don Felix. The host of the inn where Felismena stops takes her to a place to hear music. There she overhears a passionate serenade addressed by her false lover to the lady Celia, just as Julia listens to Proteus at the window of Silvia. Felismena enters the service of her false lover as a page and bears messages and gifts to Celia. Here the resemblance between Montemayor's story and *The Two Gentlemen of Verona* ceases. Celia falls in love with the disguised Felismena, as Olivia in *Twelfth Night* falls in love with the disguised Viola, and, finding her passion unreturned, dies of a broken heart. Felix disappears. Felismena becomes a shepherdess. One day she rescues by her skill in archery a knight beset by three foemen. This rescued knight turns out to be Don Felix; the two lovers recognize each others and are united. This novel might well have served as a primary source for Shakespeare's play. It was translated into French in 1578 and may have existed in English at least in manuscript form; but we are prevented from concluding that Shakespeare did use it by the interposition of another old play. A comedy, now lost, called *Felix and Philiomena* (certainly an error for *Filismena*) is known from the records of the Office of the Revels to have been acted before Queen Elizabeth on January 3, 1584.

Such plots as that of Montemayor existed not merely for dramatization, but for the sake of their sentimental material. There

---

[1] See Sir Arthur Quiller-Couch and John Dover Wilson, edition of *The Two Gentlemen of Verona*, in the New Cambridge Shakespeare, pp. xii-xvi, 72-82.

are many parallels in thought and sentiment between *The Two Gentlemen of Verona* and Sidney's *Arcadia*, Lyly's *Euphues*, the Elizabethan sonnet sequences, and numerous contemporary works all over Europe. The greatest critical crux of the play arises out of Renaissance sentiment. Valentine, the faithful hero, not only forgives his false friend Proteus, from whose ravishing clutches he has just rescued Silvia; but, when Proteus has repented and asked forgiveness, Valentine makes a fine speech and offers to renounce Silvia in favor of Proteus. For the modern critic this is simply too much; he cannot believe that Shakespeare would ever have put down in black and white such a ridiculous and unendurable piece of false sentiment. It is in vain to say that the form called for just such artificial heroics. Therefore, all editors, including the New Cambridge editors, have devoted themselves to proving that Shakespeare could not have been responsible for this particular conclusion to the comedy.

As a forerunner of other plays Shakespeare did not invent the type of comedy represented in *The Two Gentlemen of Verona*. It existed in all of its important features long before his day. What then is the significance of this play? Shakespeare took a slender and conventional dramatic form and attempted, with but mediocre success, to ingraft upon it a body of material in which he and his audiences were interested. Part of this is stock-in-trade Petrarchism; part of it is perhaps English life in an English atmosphere. The smallest part of all, and yet the most precious, is in those cases, all too few, where Shakespeare has rendered certain of his characters individual. Julia is a faint early sketch for Viola and Imogen; perhaps Silvia foreshadows Portia and Rosalind. The two women in *The Two Gentlemen of Verona* are at least conceived of in the Shakespearean way. Launce and Speed, themselves no doubt from Italian comedy, are forerunners of a long line of funny serving-men, the one a dull-witted rustic, the other a quick-witted rogue. The poetry of the play is also often memorable; as, for example,

O, how this spring of love resembleth
The uncertain glory of an April day!

Stage history *The Two Gentlemen of Verona* has not been a popular or successful stage play. It appeared in altered version three or four times in the eighteenth century and in the repertory of the Kembles. It was revived in the nineteenth century on special occasions which brought about the staging of the less well-known Shakespearean plays: by Phelps and Macready; at the Shakespeare Festival of 1890; and at the Court Theater in London in 1904. Whenever it has been staged, its runs have been very short.

A MIDSUMMER-NIGHT'S DREAM

Date and publication *A Midsummer-Night's Dream* is first mentioned by Francis Meres in 1598 as one of Shakespeare's excellent comedies. It is dated by pretty general agreement, for reasons to be stated below, in the winter of 1594-5. It was entered in the Stationers' Register on October 8, 1600, and issued that year as a quarto:

A Misommer nights dreame. As it hath beene sundry times pub*lickely acted, by the Right honour*able, the Lord Chamberlaine his *seruants. Written by William Shakespeare.* Imprinted at London, for *Thomas Fisher,* and are to be soulde at his shoppe, at the Signe of the White Hart, in *Fleete-streete.* 1600.

There exists also another quarto bearing the same date and the statement, "Printed by James Roberts." Critics were for a long time undecided as to which of these was the earlier. The recent investigations of Messrs. Neidig, Pollard, and Greg have, however, made it clear that Thomas Pavier, the publisher who was about to issue a collection of Shakespeare's plays in 1619 together with others attributed to Shakespeare, and who was somehow stopped in his venture, gave, to this quarto and others printed in 1619, fictitious dates. His text is a very good reproduction of the first quarto and was used by the folio editors, with the addition of more detailed stage directions and of the division into acts, as copy for the text of the First Folio.[1]

[1]W. J. Neidig, "The Shakespeare Quartos of 1619," *Modern Philology,* VII, 145; A. W. Pollard, *Shakespeare Folios and Quartos,* 1909, and *Shakespeare's Fight with the Pirates,* 1920.

Because of the appropriateness of the play to a wedding festival it has long been thought that it must have been prepared for the occasion of some wedding in courtly circles. The marriage of the Earl of Derby to Elizabeth Vere, daughter of the Earl of Oxford, on January 26, 1595, and that of Thomas, son of Lord Berkeley, to Elizabeth, daughter of Sir George Carey, on February 19, 1596, have both been suggested, as well as that of the third Earl of Bedford to Lucy Harrington, on December 12, 1594.[1]

Occasion Whatever may have been the immediate occasion for the presentation of *A Midsummer-Night's Dream*, or whether it was ever presented at all at court before it made its appearance in the public theaters, the play seems to show traces of political propaganda. The passage (II, i, 148 ff.) known as "Oberon's Vision" seems meant to recall to the Queen herself some occasion of festival and pageantry. A very probable event of this kind is the famous entertainment of the queen by her favorite Leicester at Kenilworth in 1575. Shakespeare may easily have had personal recollections of it. Kenilworth is only fifteen miles from Stratford, and Shakespeare at the time was eleven years old. The wooing of the queen by her mighty favorite may have become a tender memory by the time the play was written, and Shakespeare may have been recalling it to her mind. Scott seems to have this play in mind as he writes *Kenilworth*. Many scholars have also given assent to the theory. An American scholar has recently advanced a more attractive theory; namely, that the play is a reminiscence, not of the festivities at Kenilworth in 1575, but of those at Elvetham held in 1591 by Edward Seymour, Earl of Hertford.[2] The resemblances between the play and the description of the pageant at Elvetham are closer than those to the Kenilworth pageant, for a contemporary pamphlet shows a picture of a "promontory" at the north, the

Queen herself "throned by the west," and a mermaid on the deck of a ship (which may have been described figuratively as a "dolphin"). Since all these royal pageants were cast pretty much on the same lines from Kenilworth onwards, these resemblances need not of themselves be taken too seriously; but when one asks why the Earl of Hertford wished to compliment and propitiate the Queen, a whole series of connections comes into view. The Earl had married secretly in 1560 Lady Catherine Grey, who was descended from the Duchess of Suffolk, a sister of Henry VIII, by whose will any legitimate child of hers stood next in succession to the throne. A son was born to the Earl of Hertford and his countess. On her discovery of the marriage Queen Elizabeth, out of fear and jealousy, had the marriage declared illegal and the child illegitimate, and so the status had continued. Another son was born, and in 1568 Lady Catherine died of the harsh treatment she had received. Hertford's one ambition, of course, throughout the rest of his life was to have his sons and heirs rendered legitimate, and the entertainment at Elvetham was part of his long and repeated effort to win the favor of the Queen. This situation may have offered an occasion for the play. Since Hertford had continued to protest the findings of the court with reference to his marriage, matters were brought to a head in 1595 when his protests came to the knowledge of the Queen. He was put in the Tower in jeopardy of his life. Possibly in anticipation of this event Shakespeare, known to certain noblemen intimate with Hertford, was induced to prepare a play of more than courtly grace for the palate of the Queen. That this was in 1594-5 is borne out by the long familiar reference in "the lion among ladies" (III, i, 30 ff.) to the baptismal ceremony of the infant Prince Henry at Sterling, August 30, 1594, where a Moor, for reasons of prudence, was substituted for a lion to draw in the baptismal car; also by the weather passage (II, i, 82 ff.) which has long been taken to refer to the bad season extending from the spring of 1594 to the summer of 1595. According to this interpretation the votaress of Titania (that is of Elizabeth as the virgin queen), who had died, represents Lady

[1]Sir Sidney Lee, *A Life of William Shakespeare*, 165-6; E. K. Chambers, *The Elizabethan Stage*, II, 194; Sir Israel Gollancz, "The Occasion of *A Midsummer Night's Dream*," in *A Book of Homage to Shakespere*, 1916.

[2]Edith Rickert, "Political Propaganda and Satire in *A Midsummer Night's Dream*," *Modern Philology*, XXI, 53-87, 133-154. The reference to Elvetham instead of Kenilworth is also accepted by Chambers, *The Elizabethan Stage*, I, 122-4.

Catherine Grey; and her child, the "changeling boy," becomes the son whose legitimacy Queen Elizabeth had impugned. But since the Queen had been in her way gracious to this boy, he is a member of her train. He belongs, however, properly to the train of Oberon. Oberon stands in various works of the time for Henry VIII, whose will had designated this child as his next heir. This interpretation of the play would regard the lovers' plot as having been written several years before the Theseus-Hippolyta and the fairy plots and would give it no political significance. It would also demand a final revision of the play about 1598, at which time the more obvious traces of political propaganda were removed. It should be said that the interpretation just given has been vigorously opposed and almost universally rejected, but nevertheless it is at least sufficiently plausible to be worth repeating.

Plots and sources Whatever revisions may have been made, the fact remains that no play composed of such various elements achieves a more satisfactory blending into one than does *A Midsummer-Night's Dream*. No less than four plots are in progress throughout this play, each intersecting or tangent to the others at some point. Plot materials Shakespeare derives from such diversified sources as classical myth and legend, native English fairy lore, and his own intimate knowledge of amateur theatricals. A somewhat detailed consideration of the treatment of these various factors will illustrate Shakespeare's skill in plot manipulation.

Theseus-Hippolyta plot The Theseus-Hippolyta story with which the play opens announces the theme of love and marriage. We have in the approaching nuptials of the Duke and his Amazon bride the closing episode of their romance. Shakespeare had learned of Theseus from North's translation of Plutarch's *Lives of the Noble Grecians and Romans*. To him and his age Theseus was as historical as Julius Caesar. He knew also the gracious, authoritative, and noble Theseus from Chaucer's *Knight's Tale*. The season of the pre-nuptial festivities of Theseus and Hippolyta becomes here, as in *The Knight's Tale* and *The Two Noble Kinsmen*, the temporal setting for the various plots of the play proper.

The plot of the lovers The major plot, an Italianate story whose immediate source is not known, is also an affair of a proposed marriage. It interrupts, early in the scene, the tranquil anticipations of the older lovers with the discordant cry that "the course of true love never did run smooth." The theme here of the willful and disobedient daughter who would choose her own husband is a familiar one. Shakespeare probably did not deny the conventional right of fathers to arrange their daughters' marriages, yet he and his audiences, like all persons and all audiences, sympathized with true love. This major plot is in itself highly intricate. Before the play opened and before Demetrius deserted Helena, the situation was this:

> Demetrius loved Helena
> Lysander loved Hermia

When the play opens, however, matters stand as follows:

> Demetrius loves Hermia
> Lysander loves Hermia
> Helena is forsaken.

Demetrius' affections must be shunted back; but by magic and mistake the faithful Lysander is tampered with and we have:

> Demetrius loves Hermia
> Lysander loves Helena.

This is confusion worse confounded. Two more changes are necessary to swing the whole circle. First, it is brought about that

> Demetrius loves Helena
> Lysander loves Helena
> Hermia is forsaken.

Then comes the final corrective change which reproduces the first situation. In Puck's words,

> Jack shall have Jill;
> Nought shall go ill;
> The man shall have his mare again and all shall be well.

The fairy plot The transformations in the love plot are wrought by fairy magic. The materials used here were familiar to both Shakespeare and his audience. There were fairies on the stage, in

John Lyly's *Endymion*, for example, before *A Midsummer-Night's Dream*. Oberon, the fairy-king, appears as prologue in Greene's *James IV*, a play which Shakespeare knew well. Oberon has been identified with Alberich, king of the elves and guardian of the treasure of the Nibelungs. He also appears as a character in the romance *Huon of Bordeaux*, translated by Lord Berners and read by thousands of people in Shakespeare's time. The lore of fairies blended with that of nymphs, satyrs, and mermaids in the pageantry of the day. Spenser called his greatest work *The Faerie Queene*, and this heroine queen he names Gloriana to identify her with Queen Elizabeth. The Queen would have understood the compliment quite as well and been as greatly flattered had he called her Titania, a name which Ovid applies to Diana, the goddess of chastity. Although the fairies form an organic part of the plot structure in that they maneuver the events of the love story, they are at the same time engaged in difficulties of their own. Their story, independent in itself—sufficiently so that it has been allegorically construed—finds a point of contact not only with the main plot, but also with the ludicrous activities of the "rude mechanicals."

The "rude mechanicals" In the Pyramus and Thisbe episode, Shakespeare is making fun of the rustic drama, a form at one time strictly religious, which in the hands of the artisans was now branching out to the treatment of delicate romantic stories with the stiffness of technique which, in the traditional plays, had been in some sense venerable. This group, a sort of artisans' dramatic club, having heard of the royal desire for theatrical entertainments, meets at the home of the carpenter Peter Quince, their stage manager, to plan something worthy of the occasion. They have decided upon *The most lamentable comedy, and most cruel death of Pyramus and Thisby*, a pitiful tale in Ovid, and the worst of possible choices. This consideration does not deter Peter Quince and his crew. Others, their betters, had presented on the public stage, plays with names almost as absurd, as, for example, Preston's "lamentable tragedy, mixed full of pleasant mirth, containing the life of Cambises,

king of Persia." Much is to be learned from the rustic actors about the formal membership of a dramatic troupe, the nature of the current rustic drama, and the trials of a stage manager, about which last Shakespeare may have had special knowledge. Bottom expects to be cast in one of two parts, a lover or a tyrant. He prefers the rôle of tyrant; in fact he recites a few lines in "Ercles' vein." Hercules became with Seneca's play, *Hercules Furens*, in ancient times and in its revival in the Renaissance, a character famous for ranting on the stage. Flute is reluctant to play women's parts, because he has a beard coming; he would prefer to be a "wandering knight." One also learns about the use of masks and beards and other properties and something about the trials of rehearsal where amateur actors already showed a disposition to recite their parts, cues and all. The presentation of Lion, Moonshine, and Wall gives Shakespeare opportunity to display the literalness of the rustic mind, which insisted upon casting as actors' parts even the scenery and the stage-setting. Certain resemblances in the style of the verse have recently been pointed out between the Pyramus and Thisbe episode and Thomas Moffett's *The Silkworms and their Flies* (1599).[1]

The different groups of characters in the play are discriminated by the style which appears in their lines. The rustics, of course, speak in prose. The story of the young lovers is written largely in rhyme, a sign of Shakespeare's early period. Rhyme in this case is particularly appropriate, since it prevents us from taking the lovers' scenes too seriously. The kingly actions of Theseus come out in blank verse. The fairies speak in a bright meter of their own, always rhymed, usually in lyrical lines of four trochaic feet each, although sometimes Oberon, as a royal person, shifts to five-foot unrhymed iambics.

The tying together of the plots All of these varying interests have a meeting place in the Theseus episode, which, as has been said, provides the outer shell for the plot proper. Hermia's fate is to be decided on Theseus's and

---

[1] See Margaret L. Farrand, "An Additional Source for *A Midsummer-Night's Dream*," *Studies in Philology.* XXVII, 233-243.

Hippolyta's wedding day. The fairies have come hither "from the farthest steep of India" to give joy and prosperity to the nuptials, and the "hempen homespuns" will furnish merriment for the occasion. In the progress of events, however, the fairy magic controls the fortunes of the young lovers, and the rustic weaver, Bottom, becomes the punishment of Titania. Finally, when all has been righted, the young lovers join the celebrations of Theseus and Hippolyta, the rude mechanicals entertain them with a lamentable love comedy, and the fairies, having reconciled their differences, call down good fortune on the newly wedded pairs.

Stage history A Midsummer-Night's Dream evidently continued to be acted until the closing of the theaters in 1642, possibly sometimes in the form of a "droll," or clown-play. Such a piece, called The Merry Conceited Humors of Bottom the Weaver, was published in 1661. The comedy as Shakespeare wrote it was revived when plays began again after the Restoration of Charles II, but was soon subjected to revision and alteration and practically lost to the stage. A Midsummer-Night's Dream was specially liable to be revamped, Garrick himself probably having done violence to the play in The Fairies (published in 1755). False versions continued to hold the stage, for the play has always been popular, until well into the nineteenth century, when Charles Mathews (1840) and Samuel Phelps (1853) came to its rescue. Phelps was famous as Bottom the Weaver. Since the restoration of the true version A Midsummer-Night's Dream has been often played both professionally and by amateurs.

An annotated edition of A Midsummer-Night's Dream is printed on pages 153-183.

III. EARLY HISTORY PLAYS

THE HENRY VI PLAYS

Shakespeare as an adapter and reviser The accepted opinion with reference to the three plays known as 1, 2, and 3 Henry VI is that we have in them the hand of Shakespeare as a reviser of the work of other men. Some critics have been disposed to deny to Shakespeare any hand at all in these plays because of the inferiority of the workmanship. It has also been pointed out that the plays are not mentioned by Francis Meres in his list in Palladis Tamia; but, to take up the second point first, Meres sets six comedies over against six tragedies and probably did not intend to enumerate all of the plays which Shakespeare had written by 1598. He merely gave formal examples to prove Shakespeare's double superiority in both tragedy and comedy. It may also be said that Shakespeare's work is not of uniform and perfect excellence. We may fairly believe that as a beginner Shakespeare did not completely know his art either as a poet or a dramatist. The principal reasons for thinking the Henry VI plays are in large part his work are that they were included by his colleagues Heminge and Condell in the First Folio and must have been known in the repertory of the theater as Shakespeare's plays, that almost all critics have found in them evidences of Shakespeare's hand, and that Henry V and Richard III, which respectively precede and follow them in historical sequence, both show many evidences of the knitting together of all the plays as one great historical sequence.[1]

[1]Adams, Life of Shakespeare, passim; Boswell-Stone, Shakespeare's Holinshed; C. F. Tucker Brooke, The Authorship of the Second and Third Parts of "King Henry the Sixth," New Haven, 1912; the same author's edition of all three parts in The Yale Shakespeare; Fleay, Life and Work of Shakespeare; H. D. Gray, "The Purport of Shakespeare's Contributions to 1 Henry VI," Publ. Mod. Lang. Ass'n., XXXIII, 367-382; Halliwell-Phillipps, The First Sketches of the Second and Third Parts of "King Henry the Sixth," Shakespeare Society, London, 1843; J. B. Henneman, "The Episodes in 1 Henry VI," Pub. Mod. Lang. Ass'n., XV, 290-320; Sir A. W. Ward, Collected Papers, Vol. III, pp. 231-291, Cambridge, 1921; Madeleine Doran, "Henry VI," Parts II and III: Their Relation to the "Contention" and the "True Tragedy," Iowa City, 1928; Peter Alexander, Shakespeare's "Henry VI" and "Richard III," Cambridge, 1929; Gaw, Allison, The Origin and Development of "1 Henry VI" in relation to Shakespeare, Marlowe, Peele, and Greene, Los Angeles, 1926.

2 and 3 Henry VI To the second and third members of the Henry VI trilogy there exist parallel versions as follows:

THE First part of the Contention betwixt the two famous Houses of Yorke and Lancaster, with the death of the good Duke Humphrey: And the banishment and death of the Duke of *Suffolke*, and the Tragicall end of the proud Cardinall of *VVinchester*, vvith the notable Rebellion of *Iacke Cade: And the Duke of Yorkes first claime vnto the Crowne.* LONDON. Printed by Thomas Creed, for Thomas Millington, and are to be sold at his shop vnder Saint Peters Church in Cornwall. 1594.

and its sequel:

The true Tragedie of Richard *Duke of Yorke, and the death of* good King Henrie the Sixt, *with the whole contention betweene* the two Houses Lancaster and Yorke, as it was sundrie times acted by the Right Honourabie the Earle of Pembrooke his seruants. Printed at London by P. S. for Thomas Millin*gton, and are to be sold at his shoppe under Saint Peters Church in Cornwal.* 1595.

Two theories are offered to account for the existence of double versions of the two plays in question. According to one of these *2* and *3 Henry VI* are regarded as Shakespeare's revisions of the two chronicle plays whose elaborate title-pages have just been quoted, they themselves being the works of other dramatists; according to the other, which is to be preferred, *The Contention* and *The True Tragedy* are debased versions of *2* and *3 Henry VI* supplied to the printers by dishonest actors who stole them from the theater.[1] In conformity with either theory it may be believed that *The Contention* and *The True Tragedy* passed in somewhat corrupted versions into the hands of the printers on the breaking up of Lord Pembroke's company.

Professor Adams in his *Life of Shakespeare* (pp. 214-15) expresses the opinion that the two plays came into existence because of the popularity in Henslowe's theater in 1592 of an earlier form of the play now known as *1 Henry VI*, a play presenting the exploits of the brave English general Talbot in France. Shakespeare, then (according to Professor Adams) a member of Pembroke's company, wrote the plays to rival this popular success. His theory does not preclude the possibility that Shakespeare was even then revising the work of other men, a fact which seems to be indicated by Greene's attack on Shakespeare in *A Groatsworth of Wit* (1592) as "an upstart crow beautified with our feathers," and, particularly, by the allusion to the "tyger's heart wrapped in a player's hyde," which parodies a line occurring both in *The True Tragedy* and in *3 Henry VI*.

Meantime, those who believe that *2* and *3 Henry VI* are Shakespeare's revisions of *The Contention* and *The True Tragedy*, respectively, and that the latter plays are actually the work of other men, do so partly on the ground that Shakespeare has not always bettered his originals. The best current opinion of this school would assign *The Contention* and *The True Tragedy* to Marlowe, or would give to Peele or to Greene a share in the authorship. Almost all critics admit that these plays show Shakespeare's hand as they stand, and in that particular they are certainly right.

1 Henry VI It is probable that Shakespeare wrote *2* and *3 Henry VI* about 1591-2, and that he revised *1 Henry VI* about 1599. It is possible also that he had rewritten *1 Henry VI* at the earlier date. In the case of *1 Henry VI* we have a slightly different type of problem from that presented by its sequels. A play of "Harry the Sixth" makes its appearance in Henslowe's *Diary* in the spring of 1592 as acted by Lord Strange's men at the Rose Theater. We have reason to believe from Nashe's description in *Pierce Penniless* (see p. 40) that it treated the same subject which is treated in *1 Henry VI*. Professor Brooke finds some indications that *1 Henry VI* may have been revived about 1599 in order to take advantage of the interest in the theme re-awakened by the popularity of *Henry V* and thinks that the reference to Henry VI in the epilogue of *Henry V* is a hint of such a revival. He also finds indications of a revision at that time in the publication of Talbot's epitaph

[1]P. Alexander, "*II Henry VI* and the Copy for '*The Contention*' (1594)," Literary Supplement of the Times (London), Oct. 9, 1924, pp. 629-630, and "*III Henry VI and Richard, Duke of York*," ibid., Nov. 13, 1924, p. 730; see also Pollard, *The Quartos of "The Contention" and "Richard, Duke of York*," ibid., Nov. 27, 1924, p. 797; and the fuller treatment of the same theme in Mr. Alexander's book listed in the preceding note.

in Richard Crompton's *Mansion of Magnanimitie* (1599), for Shakespeare (IV, vii, 63-71) follows it almost word for word. The truth of the matter is that Shakespeare's plays were for a long time stock plays in the repertory of the theater and were likely to be revised and revived at almost any time up to 1623. Early and late work is inextricably mixed in many plays, and probably in *1 Henry VI*.

Authorship of
1 Henry VI
As to authorship, there has been a long debate. Almost nobody now believes that Shakespeare was the author of the original play; and, on the other hand, few people now believe that he had no share in revising it. The original "Harry the Sixth" has been attributed to Marlowe, Greene, and Peele severally or with collaboration among them. Peele's claim seems the best because of the frequent parallels between the play as we have it and the known work of Peele, and because the spirit of rampant patriotism, or chauvinism, which must have characterized the original version and is not absent from the present play, is characteristic of Peele. Shakespeare's revision is most clearly seen in those parts of the play which make it fit into a series with *2* and *3 Henry VI* and *Richard III*.

The story:
1 Henry VI
1 Henry VI begins with the funeral of the great king and conqueror Henry V, and ends with the loss of the French possessions he had conquered for the English crown. Very free use is made of history, and the play has many inconsistencies. Some of these we may believe are due to Shakespeare's revision, possibly of the work of Peele, and more of them to Peele's freedom in the handling of history. The first act tells of the rise to power of Joan of Arc in France. The not unsympathetic picture of her here is based on Shakespeare's favorite chronicle, the second edition of Holinshed, and may be Shakespeare's own. She relieves the besieged city of Orleans as the act closes. The second act tells of the recovery of the city by Talbot and contains a famous scene (II, iv) in which originate the symbols of the red and the white rose. In the Temple gardens certain young noblemen, probably Templars, quarrel about the respective claims of the reigning house of Lancaster and those of the Yorkist line displaced by Henry IV, son of John the Gaunt, fourth son of Edward III. The Yorkist line was descended from Lionel Duke of Clarence, third son of Edward III. Richard Plantagenet, who represents the elder claim in behalf of his uncle Edmund Mortimer, exclaims,

Let him that is a true-born gentleman
And stands upon the honour of his birth,
If he suppose that I have pleaded truth,
From off this brier pluck a white rose with me.

Somerset, an angry partisan of King Henry VI, cries out in turn,

Let him that is no coward nor no flatterer,
But dare maintain the party of the truth,
Pluck a red rose from off this thorn with me.

Thus begin "York and Lancaster's long jars." In the same act Mortimer dies a prisoner in the Tower, and the young Plantagenet, "dogged York" as he became, undertakes with much stubbornness and subtlety to gain for himself and his heirs the English crown. The third act continues the quarrel among the nobles and shows the triumph of Joan. The conception of her here seems to be that she is a patriot proceeding in her mission under God's special favor. In the fourth act the great brave Talbot battles for his life, and, because neither York nor Somerset, on account of their hatred for each other, will succor him, is overcome and slain, together with his gallant young son. The bases of these scenes must of course have been in the old play; but nowhere does the hand of Shakespeare appear more clearly than in the lines as they now stand. The fifth act shows evidence of revision to make it lead up to the second and third parts of the play. By the intercession of the Pope, the Emperor, and the Earl of Armagnac, a peace, to be secured by the marriage of King Henry and the daughter of the Earl of Armagnac, is brought about between the countries, and is favorable to the English. Perhaps this is the note of triumph with which the older play ended. The original playwright, and not in the first instance Shakespeare, is also probably responsible for the grossly unfair picture of Joan of Arc. She is here represented as a witch in league with the powers of evil and is burned at the stake. This is not Holinshed's view, and, therefore, probably not Shakespeare's, but comes from earlier chroniclers. What Shakespeare introduced seems to have been the features of the play which spoiled the effect of the victory but led up to the disasters to be recorded in the sequels. The Earl of Suffolk captures Margaret, daughter of Regnier Duke of Anjou. He falls in love with her and forms the wicked plot of having her marry his king, so that he may be her lover. He goes to England and persuades the weak young king to go back on his promise to marry Armagnac's daughter and take Margaret instead, take her without dower and surrendering at the same time vast provinces to secure the marriage.

The story:
2 Henry VI

This disgraceful pact helps to create the ills described in the next play. Humphrey Duke of Gloucester, the king's uncle, his best friend, long his protector, has opposed the king's marriage and is in consequence hated by the party of Margaret and Suffolk, as by Cardinal Winchester, his lifelong enemy, and by Plantagenet, now Duke of York, in whose way he stands. He thus becomes the object of general attack. Through the folly of his duchess he is overthrown. She, wishing to be queen herself, indulges in sorcery and witchcraft to bring about that end. She is betrayed and condemned to walk barefoot and sparsely clad through the street amid the hootings of the mob. In the third act Humphrey is murdered, since the king is too weak and inefficient to protect him. In this act also Suffolk, the queen's lover, is banished, and in the fourth he is killed by pirates into whose hands he has fallen. He dies a brave defiant death. Winchester also dies. Thus the way is cleared for York to gain the crown. He has already been joined by the powerful Earl of Warwick, the famous "Kingmaker." York goes to Ireland, ostensibly to fight against rebels, but really to create for himself an army. Before he leaves he stirs up to rebellion the famous Jack Cade. The account of the peasant revolt is a good place to learn what Shakespeare thought about the political activities of the lowest classes. When Cade rules England, "seven halfpenny loaves shall be sold for a penny; the three hooped pot shall have ten hoops," and he will make it a felony to drink small beer. Lord Say is beheaded, because he has "most traitorously corrupted the youth of this realm in erecting a grammar school," besides being known to talk of "a noun and a verb, and such abominable words as no Christian ear can endure to hear." The clerk of Chatham is hanged because he can write his name. York returns with an army from Ireland, defeats the king at the battle of St. Albans, and with this the play ends.

The story:
3 Henry VI

The next play in the series, *3 Henry VI*, is also a crude but powerful play. After the battle of St. Albans York proceeds to London and at a parliament at Westminster seats himself on the throne. In the wrangle that ensues Henry VI weakly agrees that, if he may rule quietly during his life, York and his heirs shall be his successors to the crown, thus disinheriting his own son. Queen Margaret, known as the "she-wolf of France," in furious rage flies to battle, beats the Yorkists at Wakefield, and gloats over the murder of York. York's three sons, Edward, later King Edward IV, George Duke of Clarence, and Richard Duke of Gloucester, later King Richard III, are all important characters in this play and in *Richard III*. They rally their forces and with the help of the great Warwick win the fierce battle of Towton. Henry escapes to Scotland, Margaret and the young prince to France. The Yorkists are completely triumphant at the end of the second act; but base personal motive interferes with their prosperity. In the third act Warwick is dispatched to France to offer the hand of the young king, Edward IV, to Bona, the French king's niece. Margaret is also there to seek assistance. Just at the moment when the French king has yielded to Warwick's attractive offer, messengers arrive with the surprising news that Edward IV, swayed by his own passions and forgetful of his honor, has married Lady Gray, a widow, at home. The French king is offended; Warwick is outraged and turns to the support of Margaret. With Warwick goes his son-in-law George Duke of Clarence, the "false, fleeting, perjured Clarence" of *Richard III*. The fourth act tells how Warwick reseated Henry VI on the throne, how Edward escaped from captivity to Flanders, returned with troops, and surprised and captured King Henry in London. Edward IV and Richard of Gloucester march on Warwick at Coventry, and there Clarence deserts Warwick for his brothers. Later at Barnet Warwick is overthrown and slain. Margaret, having landed from France, gives battle at Tewkesbury, but is also defeated. Her son, Prince Edward, the young Lancastrian heir, is murdered by the Yorkist brethren, and Richard Crookback posts off to London. In a scene in the Tower, used as the first scene in Colley Cibber's stage version of *Richard III*, Richard prowls like a wolf about the weak and saintly king and then murders him in cold blood. Throughout the play he has been muttering his ambitious villainies. He has fought for his brother, but only that he himself might draw nearer to the crown which he covets. He is a self-confessed villain, a Machiavellian, and even if Shakespeare drew the portrait, Richard has the deviltry of Barabas and is conceived in Marlowe's vein.

Stage history Evidence has been given to the effect that a play on King Henry VI celebrating the bravery of the English general Talbot was a popular play at the time when Shakespeare was probably beginning his career as a dramatist and that *1 Henry VI* was revived about 1599 in connection with the interest aroused in the history of the House of Lancaster by Shakespeare's *Henry V*. J. H. Merivale constructed a play called *Richard, Duke of York*, to be acted by Edmund Kean in 1817, out of *2 Henry VI* with slight additions from *1* and *3 Henry VI*, and Charles Kemble made an abridgment of all three parts, which was, however, probably never acted. *1 Henry VI* was revived in 1738 and was staged in recent times by Benson at the Stratford Memorial Theater in May, 1906, at which time the entire series from *Richard II* to *Richard III* was presented. Beyond this the play has almost no stage history.

John Crowne wrote Restoration versions of both *2* and *3 Henry VI* for the Bettertons at the Duke of York's Theater. Ambrose Philips wrote a play called *Humfrey Duke of Gloucester* which is based on *2 Henry VI* and is also the main source of the play, *Richard, Duke of York*, written by Merivale for Kean. The third part underwent adaptation by Crowne and contributed to J. H. Merivale's play, to Charles Kemble's condensation, and to Colley Cibber's stage version of *Richard III*. Like the other parts of the series it appeared in Benson's revival at Stratford in 1906.

RICHARD III

Editions The first edition of *Richard III* was issued in quarto form in 1597 with the following descriptive title-page:

THE TRAGEDY OF King Richard the third. Containing, His treacherous Plots against his brother Clarence: the pittiefull murther of his iunocent nephewes: his tyrannicall vsurpation: with the whole course of his detested life, and most deserued death. As it hath beene lately Acted by the Right honourable the Lord Chamberlaine his seruants. AT LONDON. Printed by Valentine Sims, for Andrew Wise, dwelling in Paules Church-yard, at the Signe of the Angell. 1597.

This is apparently an authentic version printed from a prompter's copy, which had possibly been sold to the printer along with *Richard II* in order to prevent the sort of piracy the players had suffered in the corrupt and unlicensed edition of *Romeo and Juliet*, and possibly *Love's Labour's Lost*, issued that year. The same version of the play was re-issued in 1598, 1602, 1605, 1612, 1622, 1629, 1634, all in quarto and all ultimately derived from the first quarto. The numerous printings of the play indicate its popularity. When the editors of the First Folio came to select their text for the collected edition, however, they chose to print an independent version, certainly authentic, containing a good many variations and expansions. We have, therefore, as had Heminge and Condell, a choice between two versions, both good. The folio version, though in part set up from the third and the sixth quartos, is, nevertheless, the original, and some irregularities in the text of the quartos suggest that that version may have been made up from oral delivery.

Date John Weever in his *Epigrams*, published in 1599, but according to him written two or three years earlier, refers in his epigram *Ad Gulielmum Shakespeare* to *Romeo, Richard*, more whose names I know not.

The statement on the title-page that the play was lately acted by the Lord Chamberlain's servants may indicate a date prior to July 23, 1596, after which Shakespeare's company was for a period of about eight months known as Lord Hunsdon's servants. But the strongest evidence of an early date is strictly internal. The high percentage of end-stopped lines in the blank verse, the scarcity of rhyme and prose, and the Senecan quality of the play both as to style and tone indicate the period when Marlowe was dominant in tragedy. Richard's soliloquies are like the choruses of Senecan tragedy, and like that form too are the abundant use of dramatic irony and the thread of nemesis, or the working out of fate, which run through the play. We have also ghosts, murders, and bloodshed, and a declamatory quality, all of which are unmistakable features of the tragedy of Marlowe and of his contemporary Kyd.[1] The very immediate connection both in style and subject with the Henry VI plays is another indication of early date. On the basis of internal evidence *Richard III* is assigned to 1593 or 1594.

The subject of the play Shakespeare's inspiration for *Richard III* is to be found in the three parts of *Henry VI*. In these plays he had no doubt acted a part, probably also he had written or rewritten them all, certainly the second and third parts; but the story of the Wars of the Roses was incomplete. The downfall of the house of York had no doubt been treated before; but it is easy to see that in the Henry VI plays a conception, which is Shakespeare's own, of the nature of that struggle is taking shape, and it is natural that Shakespeare should himself have written the final chapter of the story.

Richard and the chroniclers The house of York went down in defeat before Henry Tudor, the proponent of the house of Lancaster, who became Henry VII. There were, however, doubtful features in the claim of Henry VII, since his legitimate descent from John of Gaunt admitted of question, and since a son and daughter of the Duke of Clarence

still lived. It was thought also that one at least of the sons of Edward IV might have escaped being put to death; hence the importance in the eyes of Henry VII that his claim should be supported in every possible way. Out of the struggle for the crown during the Wars of the Roses had come the conception of Richard III as the evil genius of his own house and a monster in shape of man. Polydore Vergil in *Historia Angliæ* (1534) had so presented him. Polydore Vergil was an Italian and was, therefore, familiar with the Renaissance conception of absolute villainy. His making of Richard III the scapegoat for the crimes of his family and of his time was no doubt gratifying to Henry VII, who considered himself Lancastrian, since by making Richard a villain and a usurper beyond the pale of human sympathy his own claim was the more completely vindicated. Sir Thomas More, Lord Chancellor under Henry VIII, also wrote in the same unfair manner, *The Life of King Richard III*, which was adopted by the chroniclers Hall, Grafton (publisher of Hall), and Holinshed himself, so that the belief that Richard was a human fiend became universal. Richard was bad enough, and although he may not have been the chief instrument in the murder of Clarence, no doubt committed most of the terrible crimes imputed to him, and some others besides.[2] The things which probably most misrepresent him, however, are endowing him with superhuman subtlety and hypocrisy and putting him with his self-confessed accursedness before us as a living force. These features are literary and not historical.

In *3 Henry VI* Richard, Duke of Gloucester, is a fearful menace to all good and is the ultimate doom of the house of York. *Richard III*, the final play of the series, further develops this idea, and, going back to Polydore Vergil and Sir Thomas More, seizes upon another conception which does much to humanize and render terrible the picture of Richard's villainy; namely, the attribution to Richard of a conscience. Vergil invented Richard's horrible dream in which his victims return to reproach him for his crimes, and, in true Renaissance

---

[1] J. W. Cunliffe, *The Influence of Seneca on Elizabethan Tragedy*, London, 1893; Rudolf Fischer, *Zur Kunstentwicklung der englischen Tragödie*, Strassburg, 1893.

[2] G. B. Churchill, *Richard III up to Shakespeare.* Berlin, 1900.

spirit, traces out in his career the idea of fate or nemesis.

Richard III as a tragedy We have therefore not only the antique conception of tragedy as the story of one who stood high in the world's eyes and fell from his great estate; but also the conception, probably somewhat unconsciously developed on Shakespeare's part, of the working out of inscrutable providence. This conception is at once true to Aristotle and to the best knowledge and taste. The play also takes lessons from the English followers of Seneca, and proceeds through dreams, portents, superstitions, inspired and inescapable curses, bloodshed, broken oaths, and revenge. These darker forces express themselves very largely through the words of the dethroned queen Margaret. On the other hand, not only do we get a sense of the certainty of the downfall of the wicked, but of their torments in this world; our general sense of human insecurity is wrought upon by beholding an unnatural war on kindred, innocent bystanders, weak women, and defenseless children. A great national struggle over the subordination of public welfare to the ambitions of wicked men ends in the triumph of virtue. The righteous Henry Earl of Richmond is seated on the English throne, bringing with him a promise of peace and security for the kingdom. Henry VII, a selfish, rather mean ruler, hardly deserves to be presented as an unstained hero and leader, like Fortinbras in *Hamlet* and Malcolm in *Macbeth;* but in the light of beneficent Tudor rule and greatness it was a proper compliment to the Queen, his granddaughter, so to present him.

Richard as a stage villain Remembering then the effect that was to be produced, we may consider the manner in which it was done. Shakespeare takes up the story at the moment of complete Yorkist triumph. The kingdom is at peace. The king, Edward IV, is provided with a gallant young prince as his heir. His brother Clarence is trustworthy; his brothers-in-law are powerful nobles and devoted to his throne; most of the noblemen of his court are loyal and brave, though split by factions; he himself, as his death approaches, is moved by a desire to provide for the future by making peace among all jarring elements. Against this established virtue stands Richard, a deformed and malignant hunchback, hated by all the world. He is an example of the single dominant character about whom Marlowe had learned to unify his plays. The unnatural conventions of the Marlowan drama had made it proper for the villain hero to avow his villainy and explain it. Such was thought to be Machiavellian policy, for the great Florentine statesman had come to stand in the popular mind for open, complete, and unscrupulous malignity.[1] Perhaps the bareness of the stage and the crudity of the dramatic technique had made it almost necessary for the drama to proceed by soliloquy and open confession in order that the plot might be understood. The actor thus dominated the audience face to face and front to front. The villainy, from that of Marlowe's Barabas in *The Jew of Malta* on, is cynical as well as malignant. It is also opportunist; that is, it does not plot long ahead of the current time, but plots step by step and stands ready to profit by whatever may occur. This opportunism is in Marlowe, and is a feature which Shakespeare learned and developed in Iago, his greatest scoundrel.

If this single dominant character with his chorus-like soliloquy came from Marlowe, no small share of the clap-trap of blood, dreams, portents, revenge, vows, curses, and avenging nemesis came from Kyd; and in the style of *Richard III* both Marlowe and Kyd appear. *Richard III* is written in blank verse of a Marlowan type, and, like Marlowe's *Tamburlaine*, it has very little prose in it; that is to say very little comicality, for the expression of which it was customary to employ prose. Shakespeare probably meant the play to be somber. It has very little rhyme. Kyd had used a good deal of rhyme largely for the expression of sententious wisdom and for variety in the effects of speeches, but Marlowe had been opposed to the use of rhyme; so that in the use of blank verse the play is Marlowan. *Richard III* has in it also a great deal of artificiality in the form of repetitions, balanced utterances, and stichomythia, a device borrowed from Senecan tragedy in which

[1] E. S. Meyer, *Machiavelli and the Elizabethan Drama,* Weimar, 1897.

characters engaged in dialogue utter each a single complete line. The effects of these rhetorical peculiarities, frequently employed in the women's parts in the expression of grief and other passions, are far from the naturalness of style in the great tragedies that Shakespeare was yet to write.

The history of the play *Richard III* has lived as a popular play on the stage ever since its composition. It is evident, however, that it is the character of Richard, rather than Shakespeare's play as a whole, that has had the power to maintain itself from age to age without the prestige of artistic and learned approval. *Richard III* was evidently first made popular by the acting of Shakespeare's companion, Richard Burbage, and no other play is more frequently alluded to in the literature of the time. It disappeared with the closing of the theaters in 1642, but Richard III himself was presented in several dramas of the Restoration with something approaching the force of Shakespeare's conception. In the year 1700 the play was rewritten by the actor and dramatist Colley Cibber; his version to this day draws audiences in all sorts of theaters in all sorts of places. Cibber begins his play, as before said, with the scene of the murder of King Henry VI from *3 Henry VI,* shortens the play by dropping many scenes, omits the parts of Margaret and Clarence, invents a scene in which the fiendlike Richard chuckles with malign satisfaction as he overhears the murderers at their work of killing the little princes, and makes of the play the picture of a single dominant villain. Some familiar quotations, often thought to be from Shakespeare, such as, "So much for Buckingham," and "Richard's himself again," are really from Cibber. In this version have appeared the greatest actors of England and America—Garrick, Kean, Kemble, Edwin Forrest, and the Booths. Edwin Booth and Sir Henry Irving went back to Shakespeare's text, from which by abridgment they made their versions; but it can hardly be said that Cibber's version has ever been superseded. The fine breadth and careful articulation, therefore, of Shakespeare's work have been lost except to students.

An annotated edition of *Richard III* is printed on pages 184-241 of this volume.

IV. EARLY TRAGEDIES

TITUS ANDRONICUS

Authorship of *Titus Andronicus* There has been a disposition on the part of critics to deny to Shakespeare the authorship of *Titus Andronicus* because of its exaggerated expression of passion and its repulsive subject-matter. Everyone agrees that, if it is Shakespeare's play, it is certainly his first essay in tragedy, written when he was unskilled and inexperienced; or, rather, written before his naturally gentle tastes had had time to assert themselves.[1] Nobody doubts the power of the play, which beats even the writers of the tragedy of blood and revenge at their own game. It was not for nothing that, when Burns's schoolmaster Murdock was reading *Titus Andronicus* to the family at Mt. Oliphant, the sensitive boy should have begged him "in an agony of distress" to read no more.

The style too would have been, it is said, more "Shakespearean" had Shakespeare written the play. The style does, however, assume in places a very penetrating and impressive quality. Indeed it may be said that the level of the style is high, though the style is not of a free or original quality. The verse reminds one of that of *2 Henry VI,* to which play it has, as we shall see, some resemblance as regards its history. Shakespeare's work in *2 Henry VI* is not inspired, but labored and at times inferior, probably because of the fact that he was imitating Marlowe. In *Titus Andronicus* he was also taking leaves from Marlowe's book, for thence come such characterizations as Aaron and Tamora, as also the wildness and scope of event. But in *Titus Andronicus*

[1]H. Dugdale Sykes, *Sidelights on Shakespeare,* London, 1920; J. M. Robertson, *The Authorship of "Titus Andronicus": An Introduction to the Study of the Canon of Shakespeare,* London, 1924; E. K. Chambers, *William Shakespeare,* I, 312-322.

Shakespeare has a still more insistent model, that of the man who was most Senecan of Elizabethan dramatists, Thomas Kyd. We have only one original play which we are absolutely certain is by Kyd, namely, *The Spanish Tragedy*, a revenge play of the utmost influence on the history of the drama. Titus Andronicus himself is modeled after the hero of Kyd's play, Hieronimo, whose madness, tricks, delays, and passion for vengeance are repeated in Titus.

The history of the play Almost no early play of Shakespeare's has a clearer title on external evidence to be considered genuine. A play entitled *A Noble Roman Historye of Tytus Andronicus* was entered for publication in the Stationers' Register on January 23, 1594; in 1905 a copy of a first edition, not hitherto known, was discovered at Malmö in Sweden. It has this title-page:

The Most Lamentable Romaine Tragedie of Titus Andronicus: As it was Plaide by the Right Honourable the Earle of Darbie, Earle of Pembrooke, and Earle of Sussex their Seruants. London. Printed by Iohn Danter, and are to be sold by Edward White & Thomas Millington, at the little North doore of Paules at the signe of the Gunne. 1594.

A second quarto edition appeared in 1600, adding the Lord Chamberlain's company to those who had acted the play, and a third quarto in 1611. The text in the First Folio is printed from this third quarto, but adds a new scene, the second of the third act, a circumstance which indicates that the Folio editors had at their disposal some text of their own, independent of the printed versions. There is nothing to indicate that the new scene is by another than the original author. The play evidently belonged to the repertory of Shakespeare's company since Heminge and Condell regarded it as Shakespeare's work. Francis Meres in his list of 1598 mentions *Titus Andronicus* as one of Shakespeare's tragedies (see p. 41). Ravenscroft reported (1687) a stage tradition that the play was by a "private author" but had been touched up by Shakespeare.

Titus Andronicus in Henslowe's Diary The title-pages in the quartos and the entries in Henslowe's *Diary* enable one to make a plausible guess as to the origin of the play. On April 11,

1591, Henslowe enters a new play which he calls "Titus and Vespacia" as acted by Lord Strange's men, which with varying spellings he carries through the rest of the recorded engagements until January 29, 1593. That this may have been a play on the same theme as *Titus Andronicus* is indicated by one piece of confirmatory evidence: In a German version of *Titus Andronicus*, published in 1620, Lucius, a son of Titus, is called by the name Vespasian. Besides this German *Titus Andronicus* there is a Dutch play called *Aran and Titus* by Jan Vos. These two plays and another acted at Linz of which a program survives are all possibly based, not on Shakespeare's play, but on the play called by Henslowe "Titus and Vespacia," which was carried to the continent by traveling companies of English actors. Again Henslowe records as *ne* (by which he indicates revisions as well as new plays) a play under the illiterate title of "titus ond ondronicus" as acted by the Earl of Sussex's servants. Later still he records what is apparently the same play as acted by the Lord Admiral's and the Lord Chamberlain's men at Newington Butts on June 5, 1594. Sir E. K. Chambers and others think it possible that Shakespeare passed, on the breaking up of Lord Pembroke's company, into the Earl of Sussex's company and from that into the Lord Chamberlain's company, carrying with him in his migration some of the plays which are thought to show his workmanship, such as *Titus Andronicus*, *The Taming of a Shrew*, *2* and *3 Henry VI*, *Richard III*, and possibly *Hamlet*. He was able to keep his versions of the plays out of the hands of the printers in all cases except that of *Titus Andronicus*. This play possibly shows, they think, on its title-page Shakespeare's various dramatic affiliations. But one need not permit this circumstance or the theory that goes with it to determine Shakespeare's theatrical migrations, since the whole subject of the ownership of plays and the migrations of actors is obscurely known and uncertain.[1]

The story of the play *Titus Andronicus* is so inferior to Shakespeare's first successful tragedy, *Romeo and Juliet*, that it might be disregarded in estimating the value of his work. It is, how-

[1] E. K. Chambers, *The Elizabethan Stage*, II, 126, 129-30, 202.

ever, so much the sort of thing out of which *Hamlet* grew that it is worth our while to indicate the nature of the plot. It is a story, apparently without historical foundation, about a Roman emperor at war with the Goths. His chief military commander, Titus Andronicus, has just returned from a successful campaign against the enemy with the Gothic queen Tamora and her three sons as captives to grace his triumph. The emperor, however, has just died, and his two sons, Saturninus and Bassianus, are quarreling about the succession to the throne; they resolve to leave the issue to Titus Andronicus. Of Titus's five and twenty valiant sons all but four have met death in their country's cause. Titus appears before the family tomb where they lie and, being importuned by his living sons, sacrifices to the shades of the dead one of the three sons of Tamora. Titus decides that Saturninus shall be emperor and shall marry Titus's daughter Lavinia; but Saturninus, after his coronation, falls in love with Tamora. While Saturninus, the emperor, is thus engaged, Bassianus, with the aid of the sons of Titus, steals Lavinia away and marries her. In trying to prevent this elopement Titus slays his own son Mutius. The machinations of Tamora, outraged by the sacrifice of her son, then begin. By her promptings her two remaining sons seek out Bassianus and Lavinia in a wood; they slay Bassianus and throw his body into a pit; they ravish Lavinia, cut off her hands, and cut out her tongue. Two of Titus's sons are accused of the crime by Tamora and the emperor. Aaron, a Moor in the service of Tamora, tells Titus that if he will lop off his own hand and send it to the emperor as a propitiatory offering, his sons will be spared. This Titus does, but notwithstanding the sons are put to death, and their heads and Titus's hand are brought back to him. Lucius, the last remaining son of Titus, is banished and joins the Goths in order to bring war back to Rome. Tamora gives birth to a blackamoor child; Aaron, the father, murders the nurse and the midwife and gleefully carries off his cub. In a most pitiful scene Lavinia reveals the villainy of the sons of Tamora, partly, by directing attention to the story of Philomela in Ovid's *Metamorphoses* and, partly, by writing in the sand with a staff held be-

tween the stumps of her arms. Tamora and her sons go to Titus disguised, thinking to persuade him to recall Lucius, now threatening the city with an army of Goths. Titus, feigning madness, induces Tamora to leave her sons behind, whereupon he slays them, makes up a pie of their blood and bones, and invites in Tamora and the emperor to the feast. The Thyestean banquet becomes a scene of carnage. Titus slays Lavinia, as Virginius slew Virginia; he also slays Tamora, and is slain by Saturninus. Lucius, after having killed Saturninus, is proclaimed emperor. Since Lucrece, another figure from ancient story, is paralleled here, the play is a mixture of Ovidian and Senecan materials. It is indeed an abomination among plots, and one may judge from it the barbarous tastes of the Elizabethan audience. That Shakespeare wrote it is almost unthinkable, and yet much of our reluctance to attribute it to him may arise from our inability to understand the contemporary tastes for gross horrors on the stage.

Stage history   *Titus Andronicus* was popular in its day, and the play or some version of it was recorded fifteen times in Henslowe's *Diary*. Jonson, looking back at its vogue, speaks scornfully in *Bartholomew Fair* (1614) of those "who swear *Ieronimo* and *Andronicus* are the best plays yet." Ravenscroft made a Restoration version of it, acted in 1678, and it was revived at Drury Lane Theater in 1717. The only performance recorded in the nineteenth century was that of Ira Aldridge in London and Dublin in 1852-1856. It is said that Aldridge's company was reluctant to appear in it.

ROMEO AND JULIET

Publication   In 1597 a corrupt edition in quarto of *Romeo and Juliet* appeared with the following title-page:

AN EXCELLENT conceited Tragedie *OF* Romeo and Iuliet, As it hath been often (with great applause) plaid publiquely, by the right Honourable the L. of *Hunsdon* his Seruants. LONDON, Printed by Iohn Danter. 1597.

John Danter was an outlaw publisher, and the "great applause" referred to was probably the cause of his unlicensed venture.

Two years later, as if out of mortification at having so bad a version in circulation, or possibly to prevent its reissue, a second quarto was published:

THE MOST EXcellent and lamentable Tragedie, of Romeo and *Juliet*. *Newly corrected, augmented, and amended:* As it hath bene sundry times publiquely acted, by the right Honourable the Lord Chamberlaine his Seruants. LONDON. Printed by Thomas Creede, for Cuthbert Burby, and are to be sold at his shop neare the Exchange. 1599.

The version thus issued as "corrected, augmented, and amended" is in the main the same version as the earlier one, but is fuller and more correct. We have in these two publications the reflection of a situation more than once repeated in the printing of Shakespeare's plays. Possibly there was about the playhouse some dishonest person who was stealing bit by bit the plays and selling them to such unscrupulous printers as Danter. To defeat such dishonesty Shakespeare's company may have sent their copy, or prompt book, to Burby to have it issued in proper form, or to gain such profit as they could from a publication already achieved. Something similar seems to have happened, as we have seen, in the case of *Love's Labour's Lost*. Good versions of *Richard II* and *Richard III*, possibly issued to forestall the pirates, also appeared in 1597. It is also possible that the piracy in the case of the first quarto of *Romeo and Juliet* was for the sake of obtaining a copy to be acted, this stage version being later sold to Danter. That in issuing the second, "good" quarto of *Romeo and Juliet* the printers used a playhouse copy can be seen from the fact that we have at one place for the entry of the clown, not "Enter Peter," but "Enter Will Kempe." Will Kemp was one of the actors in Shakespeare's company, whose name the stage manager had apparently written on the copy instead of that of the character he was playing. The same fact seems also reflected in other stage directions of the second quarto, which are often just those brief hortatory notes a stage manager might make to direct the performance; such as, "Whistle, Boy," "Knock," and "Play, Music." A third quarto of *Romeo and Juliet* came out in 1609, and there were later quartos, all based on the second quarto. The text in the First Folio was set up from the third quarto.

The date of the play   The many allusions to the play in the years following 1597 indicate that it enjoyed great popularity. For certain reasons, however, it is impossible to conclude that the play was written so late as that. Professor Adams has suggested that it is a play which Shakespeare had written earlier and laid aside unfinished until about 1596. Its close kinship with the sonnets, which were probably being written in 1593-6, and to *Venus and Adonis* (1593) and *The Rape of Lucrece* (1594), its lyrical quality, its youthful zest, and the stiffness of much of its blank verse are certainly indications of an early date; and yet one need not for these reasons put it far in advance of *A Midsummer-Night's Dream*, or even *The Merchant of Venice*. The title-page of the first quarto refers to Shakespeare's company as "Lord Hunsdon's servants," by which name they were designated from July 22, 1596, to April 17, 1597. Weever refers to the play in his *Epigrams*, believed to have been written by 1596 and possibly before 1595. Finally, the Nurse reckons Juliet's age by an earthquake eleven years before. The Nurse is probably not to be taken too seriously as a chronologer; but, if she were taken literally, her words would refer to a famous earthquake in England in 1580 and would point to 1591 as the date of composition. If there is any virtue in the dating of Shakespeare's play by internal evidence, and we know that there is, we must conclude that at least a part of the play was written very early in his career. A great deal of rhyme appears in *Romeo and Juliet*, in couplets, quatrains, sestets, and even in sonnets. There are also a number of set lyrical pieces in blank verse (I, iv, 53 ff.; III, ii, 1 ff.); and here, more markedly than in his mature work, Shakespeare revels in puns and conceits, wit combats, and passages of elaborate social courtesy.

The sources of the play   In spite of these artificial and conventional features, however, there is something new to Shakespeare and to English drama in *Romeo and Juliet*. It is a tragedy, not Senecan or Marlowan, although there are certain tricks of the older form still retained, such as its declamatory speeches and poetical reminiscences of classical mythology. *Romeo and Juliet* is, nevertheless, more original and independent than much of the work Shakespeare was yet to do. The mystery is in part explained by the stuff of the play, which comes from the Italian *novella*, a form influential on Shakespeare's genius. These novels, or short stories, had been known in Italy for more than two hundred and fifty years, and had been very popular since the middle of the fourteenth century when Boccaccio wrote the *Decameron*. Many of them had been translated into French and from French into English. They were made up of materials from history, tradition, romance, fable, popular anecdote and narrative, and in some instances no doubt from invention. Among them is a story of more than usually broad appeal. It tells of a woman who, in order to escape a hated marriage about to be forced upon her, took a sleeping potion. This is earliest found in the *Ephesiaca*, a Greek romance of about the fifth century, A.D., attributed to Xenephon of Ephesus. The story appears also in a collection of *Novellini* in 1476 by Masuccio of Salerno. In this version Mariotto of Siena marries Gianozza privately by the good offices of a friar and is shortly afterwards compelled to fly the country for killing a fellow citizen in a street fight. He has an interview with his wife before he departs, and, after he is gone, she has a marriage urged upon her by her friends. She takes into her confidence the friar, who gives her a soporific powder by which she may be thrown into a trance. She swallows the powder, is laid away in a tomb, and on her awakening rescued, thus escaping the marriage. Before Mariotto, who has fled to Alexandria, receives a letter from the friar explaining the plot, the word reaches him that she is dead. Gianozza awakes and sets out to seek her husband at Alexandria. Mariotto, having returned to shed tears at his wife's grave, is arrested and put to death. Gianozza retires to a convent and soon dies. This is essentially Shakespeare's story; but it was yet to receive full localization and final form at the hands of Luigi da Porto, or, as some think, at the hands of the famous Cardinal Bembo, his patron. Luigi's work, called *Istoria novellamente ritrovata di due nobili amanti*, was published at Venice about 1530. The scene is now laid in Verona. The story grows out of a feud between the two noble families of Monteschi and Capelli; the lovers are called Romeo and Giulietta. The story was so popular that it was written down as part of the authentic history of Verona. It passed into the famous *Novelle* of Bandello (1554); thence into the French translation of Boaistuau (1559); thence in 1562 into an English poetical version by Arthur Brooke, *The Tragicall History of Romeus and Juliet*, a poem very well written in old-fashioned rhyming couplets of twelve and fourteen syllables alternately. Brooke followed Boaistuau very closely, and it cannot be shown that Shakespeare had any other source than Brooke. In Boaistuau and Brooke appears for the first time the feature of having Juliet awake to find Romeo dead and to slay herself with his dagger. Another English version is that in Painter's *Palace of Pleasure*, a collection of prose tales, mainly Italian, which appeared in 1567. Brooke, however, introduces another possibility as to Shakespeare's source, for he says in his preface,

Though I saw the same argument lately set forth on the stage with more commendation, then I can looke for: (being there much better set forth then I have or can dooe) yet the same matter penned as it is, may serve to lyke good effect.

This brings up the ever present possibility that Shakespeare was working over an old play. We have every reason to think, however, in the light of his known practice and of the detailed resemblances that he read Brooke and other sources in addition to the old play.[1]

The technique of Romeo and Juliet The general technique of tragedy at the time went hardly farther than the Senecan forms of Kyd and the Marlowan type of heroic play built about a single colossal figure. For the rest, it was merely the telling of a story on the stage in

[1]Dr. H. De W. Fuller (*Modern Philology*, IV, 75) has argued that the Dutch play *Romeo en Juliette* rests, not upon Shakespeare's, but upon a lost play, probably that referred to by Brooke.

the best way one could; so that it follows that the best chance of success would lie in having a good story to tell. Although the love story of Romeo and Juliet did not lend itself to either Kyd's or Marlowe's pattern, it was an extremely good story, set in the very heart of Italian domestic and civil life. The bringing of these moving realistic elements from the Italian *novelle* upon the English stage was the task of the dramatists, Shakespeare going further than any of his known predecessors. It must not be forgotten that Shakespeare followed his truly artistic source with great fidelity. Much, though by no means all, of the greatness of his masterpiece lies in this fact.

How Shakespeare tells the story Shakespeare's part in the story is, of course, his management of it, his realization of the interplay of human character and motive, his sense of the scene and background of the action, and, more than all, the poetic beauty of his style. The household of the Capulets is made over into an Elizabethan household with enough, however, of the original to preserve the comradeship of the Italian servant and master. The young gentlemen of the story become Elizabethans with tastes and occupations of current fashion. Note, for example, Mercutio's prejudice against new forms of swordplay, and also the wit combats in which he, Benvolio, and Romeo engage. In Shakespeare's version the story is begun by the henchmen of the jarring houses in a quarrel in the street, which catches the attention of the audience and reveals the atmosphere of the feud. In the same sensational fashion, Shakespeare introduces the furious Tybalt into the merry scene of the Capulets' ball. Shakespeare's is the visit of the County Paris to the tomb of Juliet. The part of Mercutio is greatly amplified in Shakespeare, and the Nurse of the original is transformed according to an earlier dramatic model into a garrulous serving-woman. These are Shakespeare's principal additions to the story; he also permeates it with his spirit. Aside from the cases mentioned, Shakespeare's characters and incidents are for the most part derived from the original.

Stage history The stage history of *Romeo and Juliet* is long and illustrious. Apparently popular in its own day, it was revived immediately after the opening of the theaters in 1660. Betterton played Romeo and Mrs. Sanderson Juliet. Before long, however, the Shakespearean version was displaced by Thomas Otway's famous adaptation *The History and Fall of Caius Marius*. It was in this degenerate form that Mrs. Barry and Mrs. Bracegirdle won applause. Garrick played the Shakespearean play (with modifications) with Mrs. Bellamy as Juliet at Drury Lane. It was at the time of Garrick's triumph that occurred the famous rivalry between him and the Irish actor Spranger Barry, who was also playing Romeo, with Mrs. Cibber as Juliet, at Covent Garden. "Had I been Juliet to Garrick's Romeo," said a lady who had witnessed both performances, "so ardent and impassioned was he, I should have expected that he would *come up* to me in the balcony; but had I been Juliet to Barry's Romeo, so tender, so eloquent, and so seductive was he, I should certainly have *gone down* to him." Since the return of Shakespeare's play to the stage it has been popular all over the world, and the greatest actors and actresses have played in it.

An annotated edition of *Romeo and Juliet* is printed on pages 242-286 of this volume.

V. SUMMARY

We have, then, reason to think that by the end of the year 1594 Shakespeare had written at least three great plays, *Richard III*, *A Midsummer-Night's Dream*, and *Romeo and Juliet*, as well as about eight others valuable in themselves and particularly interesting because of their establishment of trends in his workmanship toward the greatness which was to follow. As to themes, the historical group was well started. For interest in history pure and simple perhaps he was never to surpass *Richard III*. The Italian subject-matter had also been found, and as an Italian story not even *Othello* is greater than *Romeo and Juliet*; but in Italian comedy *The Two Gentlemen of Verona* is a poor indication of the greatness of *Much Ado about Nothing*, *Twelfth Night*, and *The Tempest*. He had learned skill of manipulation from Plautus and was to use it later in many places, particularly in *Twelfth Night* and *Cymbeline*. The great pictures of English common life, such as the plays of *1* and *2 Henry IV*, *Henry V*, and *Twelfth Night* were to furnish, are scarcely to be found even in outline. In the characterization of both women and men Shakespeare had already made astonishing advances even upon his greatest predecessors. His most striking creation up to this time is Richard III, a study in the psychology of evil, great even in comparison with Macbeth, Iago, and Edmund; but in human naturalness in all parts, minor characters as well as major characters, *Romeo and Juliet* is his greatest achievement in the early period. Fame as a writer for the stage was yet to come. The bases for it, however, were already laid in *A Midsummer-Night's Dream*, *Romeo and Juliet*, and *Richard III*, in which Richard Burbage and other great actors of his company were already gaining great applause. In the plays of the next period Shakespeare, not yet rivaled or eclipsed by Ben Jonson, Chapman, Beaumont and Fletcher, became for a time the most popular dramatist on the London stage.

VI. POEMS AND SONNETS

We should be neglecting an important and lasting aspect of Shakespeare's genius if we stopped in our treatment of the early period with a description of Shakespeare's dramatic works, for during this time Shakespeare established his reputation as a great lyric and descriptive poet. It will be remembered that the invaluable Francis Meres says in *Palladis Tamia*,

As the soul of Euphorbus was thought to live in Pythagoras: so the sweet witty soul of Ovid lives in mellifluous and honey-tongued Shakespeare, witness his Venus and Adonis, his Lucrece, his sugared Sonnets among his private friends, &c.

In saying this he is offering testimony that Shakespeare's reputation among his contemporaries arose quite as much from the poems as from the plays. This part of his work was no doubt more highly regarded by Shakespeare himself and by his contemporaries than were the plays, since plays were thought of as ephemeral if not mercenary. Most of the playwrights of the age, including Shakespeare, were singularly indifferent to the honor of successful dramatic composition, although John Webster, Thomas Heywood, and especially Ben Jonson show pride in dramatic works. The indifference is perfectly clear in Shakespeare's case. We have not the slightest evidence that he took any literary pride in his plays or thought of them as a basis on which his fame might be built. He was sensitive enough to the issues which arose, such as the offense given Lord Cobham over his portrait of Sir John Oldcastle, and had a workmanlike knowledge of how the thing ought to be done, as witnessed by his advice to the Players in *Hamlet*; but there are no boastful prologues from Shakespeare and no personal utterances about his dramas. On the contrary, there is evidence in the *Sonnets* that he regarded his connection with the theater as of doubtful respectability; whereas in the circumstances of the publication of *Venus and Adonis* and *Lucrece* and in the words of the *Sonnets* there is a definite bid for fame.

Venus and Adonis It has been said that the public playhouses of London and the suburbs were closed on account of plague, except for two brief periods, from June 1592 to May 1594. We know from Greene's attack on Shakespeare in *A Groatsworth of Wit* (1592) and from Chettle's apology to Shakespeare in *Kind-Harts Dreame* (December 1592) that Shakespeare was an actor and playwright of importance before the closing of the theaters. He would thus have had enforced leisure during the period when his services as a playwright were not required. There is reason to think that he used some portion of this leisure in the composition of poems in the hope that he might by their means gain the favor of a nobleman, who, as a patron of letters, would be of material assistance to him; for under the system of royal and noble patronage such was the hope of many poets and the good fortune of not a few. During the period Shakespeare may also have written and rewritten plays, for a good many of his works group themselves about the years 1594-5, just after the theaters had reopened. In any case we have the publication in 1593 from the press of Richard Field, a native of Stratford and at the time a successful London printer, of *Venus and Adonis*, carefully and correctly printed, and sold "at the signe of the white Greyhound," the bookshop of a respectable bookseller named John Harrison. The poem is dedicated in the following epistle to the third Earl of Southampton, then in his twentieth year and recognized at court as a most brilliant and promising youth:

Right Honourable,—I know not how I shall offend in dedicating my vnpolisht lines to your Lordship, nor how the worlde will censure mee for choosing so strong a proppe to support so weak a burthen, onelye if your Honour seeme but pleased, I account my selfe highly praised, and vowe to take aduantage of all idle houres, till I have honoured you with some grauer labour. But if the first heire of my inuention proue deformed, I shall be sorie it had so noble a godfather: and neuer after eare so barren a land, for feare it yeeld me still so bad a haruest, I leave it to your Honourable suruey, and your Honor to your hearts content which I wish may alwaies answere your owne wish, and the worlds hopefull expectation.—Your Honors in all dutie,

William Shakespeare.

Shakespeare calls the poem "the first heire of my inuention," by which he probably means, disregarding his plays, that it is his first publication or composition as a poet. The epistle is formal and diffident to such a degree that it seems to imply that the dedication was made without Southampton's definite permission.

In this poem Shakespeare is writing as a courtly poet and following the latest vogue in fashionable literature. Marlowe, who died in 1593, had written a gorgeously worded amatory poem on an Ovidian theme, *Hero and Leander*, left unfinished at his death. It was published in 1598, and supplied the same year with a continuation from the hand of George Chapman. This poem Shakespeare must have known in manuscript; for though some critics have thought that *Venus and Adonis* is the earlier poem, the fact is probably the other way. If so, Shakespeare may have drawn a suggestion for his poem from the following lines from Marlowe:

At Sestos Hero dwelt; Hero the fair,
Whom young Apollo courted for her hair,
And offer'd as a dower his burning throne,
Where she should sit for men to gaze upon.
The outside of her garments were of lawn,
The lining purple silk, with gilt stars drawn;
Her wide sleeves green, and bordered with a grove,
Where Venus in her naked glory strove
To please the careless and disdainful eyes
Of proud Adonis, that before her lies.

In 1589 Thomas Lodge's *Glaucus and Scilla* had appeared under the title *Scillaes Metamorphosis*, and from this poem Shakespeare drew more than a suggestion. In it an amorous nymph courts an indifferent swain much as Venus courts Adonis in Shakespeare's poem. The situations are the same, and there are a number of parallels in expression. Both poems are written in sestinas; that is, in five-foot iambic verses grouped in stanzas of six lines each, rhyming *ababcc*. There were a good many poems of the same *genre*, including Drayton's *Endim-*

ion and *Phoebe* and Daniel's *Complaint of Rosamond* (1592), in England, and many on the continent of Europe. Shakespeare made use of the *Metamorphoses* of Ovid for his main theme and for several minor parts; indeed it has been suggested that the story of the wooing of Adonis has been deepened in its passion by use of another tale in the same poem, that of Salmacis and Hermaphroditus.

Venus and Adonis is, as Shakespeare professed it to be, the poem of a beginner. So great is it in its promise that none but a Shakespeare could have realized it in his mature work. Coleridge saw this, and in his brief section on "Shakespeare, a Poet Generally" in *Notes and Lectures upon Shakespeare* he selects *Venus and Adonis* to show that Shakespeare possessed "the chief, if not every requisite of a poet—deep feeling and exquisite sense of beauty, both as exhibited to the eye in the combinations of form and to the ear in sweet and appropriate melody; that these feelings were under the command of his own will; that in his very first productions he projected his mind out of his own particular being, and felt, and made others feel, on subjects no way connected with himself, except by force of contemplation and that sublime faculty by which a great mind becomes that on which it meditates." "To this," he says later, "must be added that affectionate love of nature and natural objects, without which no man could have observed so steadily, or painted so truly and passionately, the very minutest beauties of the external world." He then quotes the following stanzas from *Venus and Adonis* (ll. 679-708):

And when thou hast on foot the purblind hare,
Mark the poor wretch, to overshoot his troubles
How he outruns the wind and with what care
He cranks and crosses with a thousand doubles:
  The many musets through the which he goes
  Are like a labyrinth to amaze his foes.

Sometime he runs among a flock of sheep,
To make the cunning hounds mistake their smell,
And sometime where earth-delving conies keep,
To stop the loud pursuers in their yell,
  And sometime sorteth with a herd of deer:
  Danger deviseth shifts; wit waits on fear;

For there his smell with others being mingled,
The hot scent-snuffing hounds are driven to doubt,
Ceasing their clamorous cry till they have singled
With much ado the cold fault cleanly out;
  Then do they spend their mouths: Echo replies,
  As if another chase were in the skies.

By this, poor Wat, far off upon a hill,
Stands on his hinder legs with listening ear,
To hearken if his foes pursue him still:
Anon their loud alarums he doth hear;
  And now his grief may be compared well
  To one sore sick that hears the passing-bell.

Then shalt thou see the dew-bedabbled wretch
Turn, and return, indenting with the way;
Each envious brier his weary legs doth scratch,
Each shadow makes him stop, each murmur stay:
  For misery is trodden on by many,
  And being low never reliev'd by any.

Coleridge says again, "In this beautiful poem there is an endless activity of thought in all the possible associations of thought with thought, thought with feeling, or with words, of feelings with feelings, and of words with words," quoting this stanza, the first in the poem:

Even as the sun with purple-colour'd face
Had ta'en his last leave of the weeping morn,
Rose-cheek'd Adonis hied him to the chase;
Hunting he lov'd, but love he laugh'd to scorn;
  Sick-thoughted Venus makes amain unto him,
  And like a bold-faced suitor 'gins to woo him.

Lucrece *Venus and Adonis* was very popular, running through five subsequent editions by the year 1602. It was, however, criticized from the first for its exploitation of sensuality; at least we may judge so from a number of references. Gabriel Harvey, for example, noted on the margin of his copy of Speght's Chaucer at some time between 1598 and 1601:

The younger sort takes much delight in Shakespeare's Venus and Adonis; but his Lucrece and his tragedy of Hamlet, Prince of Denmark, have it in them to please the wiser sort.

It may have been in response to this censure that Shakespeare set himself immediately to the writing of *Lucrece*, or it may have been in fulfillment of his promise to Southampton to honor him with "some graver labour." The poem is professedly written in celebration of the virtue of chastity and treats the story of the ravishment of the

Roman Lucretia by the Tyrant Tarquin. For his material he went to Ovid in the *Fasti*, Bk. II, ll. 721-852, and to the *Roman History* of Livy, Bk. I, chapters 57-9. He may also have known the story as told by Chaucer in *The Legend of Good Women*. Indeed he may have known many versions of the tale, which was extremely popular during the Renaissance. The poem was issued in 1594, like *Venus and Adonis*, from the press of Richard Field; but in this case the name of John Harrison appears as publisher. It is likewise addressed to the Earl of Southampton but in a very different tone and couched in language so intimate as to show without question that his attempt to gain not only the nobleman's favor but his friendship had been successful. There is no longer any doubt that his gifts will be received as the gifts of a devoted friend:

THE loue I dedicate to your Lordship is without end: whereof this Pamphlet without beginning is but a superfluous Moity. The warrant I haue of your Honourable disposition, not the worth of my vntutord Lines makes it assured of acceptance. VVhat I haue done is yours, what I haue to doe is yours, being part in all I haue, deuoted yours. VVere my worth greater, my duety would shew greater, meane time, as it is, it is bound to your Lordship; To whom I wish long life still lengthned with all happinesse.

> Your Lordships in all duety.
> William Shakespeare.

The substantial fact of these two dedications to the Earl of Southampton stands out in the midst of a world of conjecture.

Lucrece is a finished and elegant poem written in rhyme royal, a seven-line five-foot iambic stanza rhyming *ababbcc*. Rhyme royal had been employed by Chaucer, Sackville, Spenser, and was a long established English verse-form, having greater dignity and sweetness than the six-line stanza of *Venus and Adonis*. More immediately Shakespeare borrowed the stanza-form and certain important ideas of his poem from Daniel's *Complaint of Rosamond*, which treats with equal seriousness, though from a different point of view, the theme of chastity.

Lucrece is at once greater and less than *Venus and Adonis*. It is superior in care and elaboration of workmanship and in perfec-

tion of thought, but it lacks the naturalness and the brilliancy of the earlier poem. In spite of greater praises it was less popular and passed through only three editions subsequent to the first during the poet's life. *Venus and Adonis* is frankly amatory though saved by Shakespeare's coolness and objectivity from the excesses of the form to which it belonged. *Lucrece* is a formal vindication of chastity, carefully and sincerely wrought, but unrelieved and too long. Both poems are full of episodes and digressions, proceeding by images, conceits, and pictures. They are in this sense hardly to be regarded as narrative poems at all. The following lines are from *Lucrece* (ll. 1380-1442) and treat the "skilful painting, made for Priam's Troy":

There might you see the labouring pioner
Begrimed with sweat, and smeared all with dust;
And from the towers of Troy there would appear
The very eyes of men through loop-holes thrust,
Gazing upon the Greeks with little lust:
　Such sweet observance in this work was had,
　That one might see those far-off eyes look sad.

In great commanders grace and majesty
You might behold, triumphing in their faces;
In youth, quick bearing and dexterity;
And here and there the painter interlaces
Pale cowards, marching on with trembling paces;
　Which heartless peasants did so well resemble,
　That one would swear he saw them quake and
　　tremble. . . .

There pleading might you see grave Nestor stand,
As 'twere encouraging the Greeks to fight;
Making such sober action with his hand,
That it beguiled attention, charm'd the sight:
In speech, it seem'd, his beard, all silver white,
　Wagg'd up and down, and from his lips did fly
　Thin winding breath, which purl'd up to the
　　sky.

About him were a press of gaping faces,
Which seem'd to swallow up his sound advice;
All jointly listening, but with several graces,
As if some mermaid did their ears entice,
Some high, some low, the painter was so nice;
　The scalps of many, almost hid behind,
　To jump up higher seem'd, to mock the
　　mind. . . .

And from the walls of strong-besieged Troy
When their brave hope, bold Hector, march'd to
　field,
Stood many Trojan mothers, sharing joy

To see their youthful sons bright weapons wield;
And to their hope they such odd action yield,
  That through their light joy seemed to appear,
  Like bright things stain'd, a kind of heavy fear.

And from the strand of Dardan, where they
    fought,
To Simois' reedy banks the red blood ran,
Whose waves to imitate the battle sought
With swelling ridges; and their ranks began
To break upon the galled shore, and then
  Retire again, till, meeting greater ranks,
  They join and shoot their foam at Simois'
    banks.

These stanzas illustrate what has been said above with reference to the careful and elaborate workmanship of *Lucrece* as compared with *Venus and Adonis*, as also its more informational and discursive quality. Shakespeare lets one forget his story while he employs himself with the contemplation of ancient Troy and expresses his quiet joy in the beauties of Renaissance art.

The *Sonnets* In 1598 Francis Meres speaks admiringly of Shakespeare's "sugared sonnets among his private friends." The *Sonnets* were entered in the Stationers' Register by Thomas Thorpe on May 20, 1609, and published, together with *A Lover's Complaint*, by him that year. The volume has as a full page this puzzling dedication:

TO. THE. ONLIE. BEGETTER. OF. THESE. INSVING. SONNETS. Mr. W. H. ALL. HAPPINESSE. AND. THAT. ETERNITIE. PROMISED. BY. OVR. EVER-LIVING. POET. WISHETH. THE. WELL-WISHING. ADVENTURER. IN. SETTING. FORTH. T. T.

"T.T." obviously stands for Thomas Thorpe. There is, so far as known, no later quarto edition; but in 1640 John Benson re-issued 146 of the sonnets in a different order and with a poorer text. The text of the 1609 edition is a good one in spite of unusually numerous misprints and bad punctuation. Two of the sonnets (Nos. cxxxviii and clxiv) had been issued before in a volume printed by Jaggard in 1599, attributed to Shakespeare, and entitled *The Passionate Pilgrim*. This volume contains besides the two sonnets three poems from *Love's Labour's Lost*, and several poems attributed in other publications to Marlowe, Drayton, Barnfield, Griffin, and others.

It has been recognized by most scholars that the volume of the *Sonnets*, as published by Thorpe, falls into two divisions: Nos. i-cxxvi seems to be addressed to a young high-born patron and friend; Nos. cxxvii-clii are addressed to, or refer to, a dark woman of beauty and malign influence. This division is in conformity to the first four lines in one of the sonnets printed by Jaggard (No. cxliv):

Two loves I have of comfort and despair,
Which like two spirits do suggest me still:
The better angel is a man right fair,
The worser spirit a woman colour'd ill.

The history of the sonnet Before taking up the special problems connected with Shakespeare's *Sonnets*, it is desirable to make clear the main features of the sonnet as it came to Shakespeare's hand. The sonnet is to be regarded as a characteristic literary form of the Renaissance. It took shape in the thirteenth century in Italy in the hands of Dante and his contemporaries and secured its worldwide appeal in the two cycles of the poet Petrarch (1304-1374), who is the master sonneteer of the world and one of the greatest of poetical influences. He wrote 227 sonnets addressed to his mistress Laura during her lifetime and 90 after her death. With the sonnets are interspersed other lyrical forms, such as the ode, the sestina, the ballad, and the madrigal. Petrarch's sonnets are devoted to the celebration of love as an ethereal sentiment, and show the whole course of his amorous emotion. Love is the worship of beauty and virtue, and the *milieu* is the person of the beloved, which according to Plato was regarded as the outward expression of an eternal and beautiful soul within—her eyes, her smile, her lips, her tresses. With a conscious exercise of the imagination Petrarch depicts the hopes and despairs which fill his breast, and sees his love and its aspects reflected in the seasons of the year, the coming of day and night, the heavens and the earth. The variety of subjects for comparison is almost endless, though certain themes recur with greater frequency than others. A few sonnets treat other subjects besides love. Friendship is a kindred theme; politics enters now and then; and the second series has a large element of religious emotion. There is little sensuality in Petrarch and much metaphysical speculation. These matters are important, for as Petrarch wrote the sonnet, so it continued for the most part until the end. His followers of course made certain alterations and expansions. In their hands there was an infusion of classical mythology from Ovid and Catullus, pastoralism from the Sicilian idyllists, and in some instances the frankest of sensuality; still the Petrarchan doctrine of the ethereal nature of beauty manifesting itself in the actual world is strong even in the latest sonneteers, such as Sidney, Spenser, and Shakespeare. Petrarch's greatest group of followers came long after his own time; in Italy in the later fifteenth and the earlier sixteenth centuries in poets like Lodovico Ariosto, Torquato Tasso, Pietro Bembo, Lodovico Dolce, and Battista Guarini. French imitators appeared in the first half of the sixteenth century: Mellin de St.-Gelais and Clément Marot; then the great Pierre Ronsard and the group of poets known as *La Pléiade*. The sonnet was introduced into England by Sir Thomas Wyatt and by Henry Howard, Earl of Surrey, under both Italian and French influence. Wyatt wrote in the Italian form; that is, he wrote a fourteen-line iambic pentameter sonnet divided into two parts, the first eight lines constituting the octave always rhymed *abbaabba*, the last six lines constituting the sestet rhymed in a variety of ways, most often perhaps *cdcdee*. Surrey changed the rhyme-scheme and in so doing changed the effect of the poem as a whole. He wrote a fourteen-line poem made up of three quatrains and a final couplet, *ababcdcdefefgg*. The eight and the six of the Italian sonnet are in some measure parallel, sometimes expressing a thought in two different ways, sometimes devoting the sestet to commentary on the thought developed in the octave. Surrey's sonnet, which became the general Elizabethan form and was followed by Shakespeare, breaks often into three thoughts or phases of the same thought, each within the limit of a quatrain, and usually employs the couplet ending for a shift in point of view or for aphoristic commentary. These principles can be seen in the management of Shakespeare's sonnet No. lxxiii:

That time of year thou mayst in me behold
When yellow leaves, or none, or few, do hang
Upon those boughs which shake against the cold,
Bare ruin'd choirs, where late the sweet birds
   sang.
In me thou see'st the twilight of such day
As after sunset fadeth in the west,
Which by and by black night doth take away,
Death's second self, that seals up all in rest.
In me thou see'st the glowing of such fire
That on the ashes of his youth doth lie,
As the death-bed whereon it must expire
Consumed with that which it was nourish'd by.
  This thou perceivest, which makes thy love
   more strong,
  To love that well which thou must leave ere
   long.

Wyatt and Surrey wrote their sonnets in the reign of Henry VIII, but the real outburst of sonnet-writing came to England with the publication in 1591 of Sir Philip Sidney's beautiful cycle called *Astrophel and Stella* and lasted until about 1597. Sidney had died in 1586, and Thomas Nashe was responsible for the publication of Sidney's sonnets. In the same volume with *Astrophel and Stella* were sonnets by other men, notably twenty-eight sonnets by Samuel Daniel, who, more than any other, was Shakespeare's immediate master in the writing of the form. The next year Daniel issued his famous cycle called *Delia*. Henry Constable's *Diana* was published in 1592, Michael Drayton's *Idea's Mirror* and Edmund Spenser's *Amoretti* in 1595. All in all there were hundreds of sonnets published within a few years. They were mainly in cycle form. They occupied themselves with the superlative and ethereal quality of the beauty of the beloved, her cruelty or sweetness, the pangs of separation from her, the relief to be found in sleep, and the sympathetic or antipathetic aspects of the moon and other natural objects. They promised the mistress an immortality in their verse; they lamented a pretended old age on the part of the poet and apostrophized Venus, Cupid, and other deities. They at least succeeded in revealing the wit and ingenuity of the author, or his lack of them.

Problems of Shakespeare's Sonnets No Shakespearean subject has been fraught with such perplexity as that of the *Sonnets*, and no subject has in general yielded less to the research and ingenuity of the scholar. One asks, in the first place, whether or not the *Sonnets* are a true cycle, or only a series of sonnet-groups and individual poems; and, if it is granted that the *Sonnets* are one cycle, whether or not the arrangement in Thorpe's volume is the true one, or if a true one can be discovered. One asks, in the second place, whether or not the *Sonnets* are pure fiction, or in part fiction, or wholly devoted to the expression of Shakespeare's personal reactions to situations in his own life arising from his primary affection for a man and his secondary affection for a woman; and of course one asks who the man and the woman were.

The fact that the *Sonnets* have the somewhat unusual characteristic of being mainly addressed to a man instead of a woman and of treating friendship instead of love as the basal sentiment and applying to it the conventional passion of the sonnet, and the fact that, in spite of the difficulty, in writing sonnets, of following a thread of narrative, the same large themes recur and the groups hang together, make one conclude that the *Sonnets* constitute a cycle, not, however, a completed and unified whole. One of the most convincing of modern opinions is that the *Sonnets* were written as a series of poetical epistles and gathered up, at least the first one hundred twenty-six of them, roughly in the order in which they were composed. It was for Sir Sidney Lee to call stern attention to the circumstance that Shakespeare's *Sonnets* partake of the nature of Renaissance sonnets in general and have a full measure of the conventionality of that conventional form. He has demonstrated this by an overpowering body of parallels. The inference from his work, one in which he did not fully share, is that Shakespeare set himself the task of composing a sonnet-cycle of the ordinary mode and that that task was a literary exercise, only faintly, if at all, grounded in the circumstances of his own life. The view has found few adherents, mainly because the *Sonnets* seem too personal, too convincingly individual, to admit a merely fictitious basis.

Story of the *Sonnets* As a matter of general Shakespearean interest and in order that we may understand the various attempts which have been made to interpret the *Sonnets* in terms of Shakespeare's life, it is desirable to describe briefly the contents of the collection. It is made up of groups of sonnets, of varying length, tied together by continuity of theme but not usually joined group to group. The themes, however, frequently recur. Between these groups, and not infrequently imbedded within the groups, are some sonnets of a personal nature, whose interpretation is obscure, and others of an apparently formal or artificial character. In quality the sonnets vary greatly, from the conventional and sometimes intricately worded constructions of sonneteering commonplace to the finest and most original of all lyric verse. The collection begins with a group of twenty-six sonnets. The first seventeen are addressed (as indeed the first one hundred twenty-six) to a youth of nobility and beauty, who is urged to marry in order that his beauty may be perpetuated in his offspring; the next eight are on a variety of themes having to do with the poet's relation to the person addressed, and the last (No. xxvi) seems designed to accompany a gift, a "written ambassage":

Lord of my love, to whom in vassalage
Thy merit hath my duty strongly knit,
To thee I send this written ambassage,
To witness duty, not to show my wit:
Duty so great, which wit so poor as mine
May make seem bare, in wanting words to show it,
But that I hope some good conceit of thine
In thy soul's thought, all naked, will bestow it;
Till whatsoever star that guides my moving
Points on me graciously with fair aspect
And puts apparel on my tattered loving,
To show me worthy of thy sweet respect:
  Then may I dare to boast how I do love thee;
  Till then not show my head where thou mayst prove me.

This sonnet will serve to illustrate the poet's use of the language of love in addressing his patron, a practice seen elsewhere in Elizabethan literature. Nos. xxvii-xxviii and xliii-lii mark periods in which the poet is absent from his friend, and lvi-lviii a period when the friend was absent from the poet. No. xxix is the sonnet beginning, "When, in disgrace with fortune and men's eyes," and No. xxx the one beginning, "When to the sessions of sweet silent thought." Nos. xxxiii-xxxv foreshadow an estrangement caused by a fault in the friend. No. xxxiii is "Full many a glorious morning have I seen." Nos. xxxviii-xlii tell specifically what the fault mentioned in Nos. xxxiii-xxxv was: The fair youth has robbed the poet of his mistress. This subject recurs at length in Nos. cxxvii-clii, the so-called Dark Lady sonnets. There is no valid reason for thinking that the reference there is not to the episode presented in xxxviii-xlii. The sonnets from liii to lxxvii are on a variety of topics and resemble nothing so much as a series of personal letters in sonnet-form. They treat the power of love and beauty, the eternizing faculty of poetry (a theme of frequent recurrence), self-love as friend's love, the evil days of the present rescued by the perfections of the friend, a vision of the poet's death (Nos. lxxi-lxxiv), the bestowal of an album. The first lines of some of the more distinguished sonnets in this division are: No. lx: "Like as the waves make towards the pebbled shore," No. lxiv: "When I have seen by Time's fell hand defaced," No. lxxiii: "That time of year thou mayst in me behold." Next comes the famous series on the "Rival Poet," Nos. lxxviii-lxxxvii. The poet reproaches his patron for the favor which has been bestowed upon some other candidate, a poet. Nos. lxxxviii-xciii continue the theme of estrangement, now a personal matter, and the loss of loving confidence rather than mere patronage. Nos. xciv-xcvi dwell obscurely on some fault committed by the friend (a subject also touched upon in Nos. lxix-lxx), and Nos. xcvii-xcix recur to the theme of absence. Nos. c-civ are a sort of apology for long silence, No. civ being a sketch of the duration of the friendship, which is seen to have been three years:

To me, fair friend, you never can be old,
For as you were when first your eye I eyed,
Such seems your beauty still. Three winters cold
Have from the forests shook three summers'
    pride,
Three beauteous springs to yellow autumn turn'd
In process of the seasons I have seen,
Three April perfumes in three hot Junes burn'd,
Since first I saw you fresh, which yet are green.
Ah! yet doth beauty, like a dial-hand,
Steal from his figure and no pace perceived;
So your sweet hue, which methinks still doth
    stand,
Hath motion and mine eyes may be deceived:
    For fear of which, hear this, thou age unbred;
    Ere you were born was beauty's summer dead.

Nos. civ-cxxv are much variegated in the thoughts and emotions they express. In some cases the youth is addressed with all the lavish affection of the earlier sonnets. They celebrate his beauty and virtue and renew protests of eternal faithfulness, as if they arose from an attempt to restore a dying affection. Here occur: (No. cv) "Let not my love be called idolatry," (No. cvi) "When in the chronicle of wasted time," (No. cix) "O, never say that I was false of heart," (No. cx) "Alas, 'tis true I have gone here and there / And made myself a motley to the view," and (No. cxvi) "Let me not to the marriage of true minds." No. cxxvi is not a true sonnet but a twelve-line poem in couplets, often regarded as an envoy to the series. Its connection, however, is not apparent, since it seems to repeat as an affectionate warning the frequently recurrent thought that, although the youth is still beautiful, his beauty must perish. Perhaps it foreshadows some more immediate doom. Sonnets cxxvii-clii are mainly addressed to a woman, the Dark Lady. They perhaps introduce no new element into the story but appear in their present setting because they were so placed in the printer's manuscript. They apparently refer to the issue of love and rivalry elaborated in the first series. Mr. J. A. Fort, whose interpretation of the *Sonnets* is mentioned below, thinks that Nos. cxxvii, cxxviii, cxxx-cxxxii were written at a time when the mistress still favored the poet, and that Nos. cxxxv-clii represent an attempt on the poet's part to regain his mistress for himself, except, however, that Nos. cxxxviii, cxliv, and cxlvi were never intended for the mistress's eye. Nos. cliii and cliv are sonnets on Cupid, which seem superfluous, and were placed at the end no doubt by the printer's perplexity as to where they might belong.

Shakespeare and Southampton   It is natural that scholars in search of the fair youth of noble blood, Shakespeare's adored friend in the *Sonnets*, should have bethought them of Henry Wriothesley, third Earl of Southampton, since the dedications of both *Venus and Adonis* (1593) and *Lucrece* (1594) furnish evidence of acquaintanceship and probably special personal relations between Shakespeare and Southampton at the very time when sonnets were being written by most living English poets. Nathan Drake in *Shakespeare and his Times* (1817) not only suggested that Southampton was the patron and friend to whom Shakespeare addressed the *Sonnets*, but brought forward one of the best pieces of evidence yet discovered to prove that it was so, namely, that "the language of the *Dedication to the Rape of Lucrece*, and that part of the 26th sonnet, are almost precisely the same." Mr. Fort has put forward in this connection the attractive idea that the first twenty-six sonnets were sent to Southampton with the copy of *Lucrece*, which was thus the "written ambassage." The Southampton theory was advocated at great length by Gerald Massey in *The Secret Drama of Shakespeare's Sonnets* (1888) and has the support of the best contemporary opinion, notably, that of the late Sir Sidney Lee. An important recent study of the question is that of Mr. Fort, who has displayed great ingenuity in fitting the various groups of the sonnets into situations in the lives of Shakespeare and Southampton during a period from the spring of the year 1593 to January or February 1601. He assumes that Southampton was the person addressed in the *Sonnets*, sees in the Dark Lady sonnets (xxxviii-xlii, cxxvii-clii) and others reflections of special events which indicate that the fair youth was not an imaginary person. The Rival Poet group (lxxviii-lxxxviii) indicates, he thinks, that the sonnets were addressed to a single individual; and from the parallel between the dedication of *Lucrece* and sonnet No. xxvi he concludes that there was an actual connection between Shakespeare and Southampton. From sonnet No. civ he traces the chronology of the relationship. Shakespeare shows no personal acquaintance with Southampton in the dedication to *Venus and Adonis*, and the date of its entry in the Stationers' Register (April, 1593) would have been an inevitable time for such an acquaintance to have been made. Sonnet civ marks the end of the third year of their friendship. It follows then that, if Thorpe's arrangement reproduces the order in which the sonnets were written, the first one hundred four of them at least had been composed by the spring of 1596. Mr. Fort then proceeds by the study of the absence groups and other details to distribute the various sonnets through the years 1593-1596. Sonnet cvii he dates in November 1598 on the hypothesis that it celebrates Southampton's release from prison whither he had been consigned because of the Queen's anger at his marriage with Lady Elizabeth Vernon. The year 1599, after Southampton's return from Essex's Irish expedition, occasioned a brief renewal of the intimacy between Shakespeare and his patron during which time were written certain of the sonnets Nos. cvii-cxxv. Sonnet cxxvi he regards as the conclusion of the intimacy and as a warning to Southampton against his participation in the machinations of Essex. After 1601 Southampton was a close prisoner for the rest of the Queen's reign and under sentence of death for treason.

Pembroke—"Mr. W. H." The rival theory to that of Southampton is the one which makes William Herbert, third Earl of Pembroke, the person addressed in the *Sonnets*. He too was a brilliant youth at the court of Elizabeth in the last years of her reign. To him and his brother Philip, Earl of Montgomery, was dedicated the First Folio in 1623, and it is there stated that these noblemen had "prosecuted" both the plays and their author living with much favor. Thorpe's dedication of the volume of the *Sonnets* of 1609 is to "Mr. W. H.," described as "the onlie begetter of these insuing sonnets." "W. H.," it has been thought, may stand for "William Herbert," though it has also been pointed out that "W. H." may be the inverted initials of "Henry Wriothesley," and therefore refer quite as well to Southampton. Against both identifications is the objection that it would have been most unbecoming, if not actually punishable by law, for Thorpe to have addressed either of these great noblemen in such a fashion. Many explanations of Thorpe's puzzling words have been attempted. "Onlie begetter" seems to indicate the very source of the inspiration which caused the *Sonnets* to be written. The best of these theories, itself somewhat lame, is that which identifies "Mr. W. H." with one William Hall, a person known to have supplied manuscripts to publishers. This compels us to understand the words "onlie begetter of these insuing sonnets" as meaning the sole procurer of the manuscript from which they were printed. In any case one is inclined to believe that the manuscript came from Shakespeare or from Southampton (if Southampton was the sonneteer's friend), or was transcribed from a manuscript coming from one of them, since the collection as printed has hardly a trace of formal arrangement such as might have been expected had it been intended for publication or general circulation in manuscript. Against the Pembroke theory is Pembroke's youth. He was born in 1580 and was, therefore, between his thirteenth and his seventeenth years during the period of sonnet writing. With him comes the identification of Mary Fitton with the Dark Lady; with Southampton comes Mrs. Davenant in that capacity. For neither identification is there so far a shred of really convincing evidence.

This sketch will have served to suggest by quotation and description the literary nature of the sonnets and the chief controversies which have raged about them. With reference to the main question of personal significance we may take a moderate view and believe that, although the *Sonnets* do veritably belong to the Petrarchan tradition, employ its language and its situations, and resemble the sonnets of many other poets, they nevertheless are sincere personal utterances of Shakespeare as to events in his life and embody not only the results of his constructive imagination but the feelings of his heart.[1]

[1]From the large body of writings about the *Sonnets* may be selected, in addition to those referred to in the text, the following: Raymond M. Alden, *The Sonnets of Shakespeare*, Variorum edition, Boston, 1916; Sir Denys Bray, *The Original Order of Shakespeare's Sonnets*, London, 1925; Edward Dowden, *Shakespeare's Sonnets*, London, 1881; J. A. Fort, *The Two Dated Sonnets of Shakespeare*, London, 1924, "Further Notes on Shakespeare's Sonnets," in *The Library*, N. S. IX, 305-325, and *A Time Scheme for Shakespeare's Sonnets*, London, 1930; Sir Sidney Lee, *A Life of William Shakespeare*, new and rev. ed., pp. 87-164, 390-461, and *Elizabethan Sonnets*, two vols., Westminster, 1904, Introduction; C. Knox Pooler, *The Sonnets*, London, 1918, Introduction; Mrs. C. C. Stopes, *Shakespeare's Sonnets*, London, 1904; T. G. Tucker, *The Sonnets of Shakespeare*, London, 1924, Introduction and notes.

TEXT OF FOUR PLAYS
FROM THE EARLY PERIOD

The Comedy of Errors
A Midsummer-Night's Dream
Richard III
Romeo and Juliet

THE COMEDY OF ERRORS

DRAMATIS PERSONÆ

SOLINUS, duke of Ephesus.

ÆGEON, a merchant of Syracuse.

ANTIPHOLUS of Ephesus,
ANTIPHOLUS of Syracuse, } twin brothers, and sons to Ægeon and Æmilia.

DROMIO of Ephesus,
DROMIO of Syracuse, } twin brothers, and attendants on the two Antipholuses.

BALTHAZAR, a merchant.

ANGELO, a goldsmith.

First Merchant, friend to Antipholus of Syracuse.

Second Merchant, to whom Angelo is a debtor.

PINCH, a schoolmaster.

ÆMILIA, wife to Ægeon, an abbess at Ephesus.

ADRIANA, wife to Antipholus of Ephesus.

LUCIANA, her sister.

LUCE, servant to Adriana.

A Courtezan.

Gaoler, Officers, and other Attendants.

SCENE: *Ephesus.*

ACT I.

SCENE I. *A hall in the* DUKE'S *palace.*

Enter DUKE, ÆGEON, Gaoler, Officers, *and other* Attendants.

Æge. Proceed, Solinus, to procure my fall
And by the doom of death end woes and all.
Duke. Merchant of Syracusa, plead no
  more;
I am not partial to infringe our laws:
The enmity and discord which of late
Sprung from the rancorous outrage of your
  duke
To merchants, our well-dealing countrymen,
Who wanting guilders to redeem their lives
Have seal'd his rigorous statutes with their
  bloods,
Excludes all pity from our threatening looks.
For, since the mortal and intestine jars   11
'Twixt thy seditious countrymen and us,
It hath in solemn synods been decreed,
Both by the Syracusians and ourselves,
To admit no traffic to our adverse towns:
Nay, more,
If any born at Ephesus be seen
At any Syracusian marts and fairs;
Again: if any Syracusian born
Come to the bay of Ephesus, he dies,   20
His goods confiscate to the duke's dispose,
Unless a thousand marks be levied,
To quit the penalty and to ransom him.
Thy substance, valued at the highest rate,
Cannot amount unto a hundred marks;
Therefore by law thou art condemn'd to die.
  Æge. Yet this my comfort: when your
    words are done,
My woes end likewise with the evening sun.
  Duke. Well, Syracusian, say in brief the
    cause
Why thou departed'st from thy native
  home   30
And for what cause thou camest to Ephe-
  sus.

Stage Direction: **A hall in the Duke's palace.** The New Cambridge editors (*The Works of Shakespeare,* edited by Sir Arthur Quiller-Couch and John Dover Wilson, Cambridge University Press, *in progress*) limit the settings of the entire play to two. Considering the play as preserved to have been prepared for acting on the dais of a hall with three rear doors, they suggest two localities: (*a*) an open space before the house of Antipholus with a priory on one side and a street exit on the other; and (*b*) the Mart with Courtesan's house in the center and street exits on each side, one of them leading to the bay. The setting for the first scene is (*a*). **2. doom,** judgment. **4. partial,** sufficiently disposed to favor you. **8. guilders,** money; the guilder was a Dutch silver coin worth about 1s. 8d. English; also a gold coin used in the Netherlands, and parts of Germany.

11. mortal, deadly. **intestine.** The usual meaning is "civil" or "internal"; used with *mortal* it emphasizes the idea of "deadly civil war." **21. confiscate,** confiscated; accent on second syllable. **dispose,** disposal. **22. marks.** A mark was the sum of 13s. 4d. **23. quit,** pay or clear off.

Æge. A heavier task could not have been
   imposed
Than I to speak my griefs unspeakable:
Yet, that the world may witness that my end
Was wrought by nature, not by vile offence,
I'll utter what my sorrow gives me leave.
In Syracusa was I born, and wed
Unto a woman, happy but for me,
And by me, had not our hap been bad.
With her I lived in joy; our wealth in-
   creased   40
By prosperous voyages I often made
To Epidamnum; till my factor's death
And the great care of goods at random left
Drew me from kind embracements of my
   spouse:
From whom my absence was not six months
   old
Before herself, almost at fainting under
The pleasing punishment that women bear,
Had made provision for her following me
And soon and safe arrived where I was.
There had she not been long but she be-
   came   50
A joyful mother of two goodly sons;
And, which was strange, the one so like the
   other
As could not be distinguish'd but by names.
That very hour and in the self-same inn
A meaner woman was delivered
Of such a burden, male twins, both alike:
Those, for their parents were exceeding poor,
I bought and brought up to attend my sons.
My wife, not meanly proud of two such boys,
Made daily motions for our home return: 60
Unwilling I agreed; alas! too soon
We came aboard.
A league from Epidamnum had we sail'd,
Before the always wind-obeying deep
Gave any tragic instance of our harm:
But longer did we not retain much hope;
For what obscured light the heavens did
   grant
Did but convey unto our fearful minds
A doubtful warrant of immediate death;
Which though myself would gladly have em-
   braced,   70
Yet the incessant weepings of my wife,
Weeping before for what she saw must come,

And piteous plainings of the pretty babes,
That mourn'd for fashion, ignorant what to
   fear,
Forced me to seek delays for them and me.
And this it was, for other means was none:
The sailors sought for safety by our boat,
And left the ship, then sinking-ripe, to us:
My wife, more careful for the latter-born,
Had fasten'd him unto a small spare mast, 80
Such as seafaring men provide for storms;
To him one of the other twins was bound,
Whilst I had been like heedful of the other:
The children thus disposed, my wife and I,
Fixing our eyes on whom our care was fix'd,
Fasten'd ourselves at either end the mast;
And floating straight, obedient to the stream,
Was carried towards Corinth, as we thought.
At length the sun, gazing upon the earth,
Dispersed those vapours that offended us; 90
And, by the benefit of his wished light,
The seas wax'd calm, and we discovered
Two ships from far making amain to us,
Of Corinth that, of Epidaurus this:
But ere they came,—O, let me say no more!
Gather the sequel by that went before.
   Duke. Nay, forward, old man; do not
     break off so;
For we may pity, though not pardon thee.
   Æge. O, had the gods done so, I had not
     now
Worthily term'd them merciless to us! 100
For, ere the ships could meet by twice five
   leagues,
We were encounter'd by a mighty rock;
Which being violently borne upon,
Our helpful ship was splitted in the midst;
So that, in this unjust divorce of us,
Fortune had left to both of us alike
What to delight in, what to sorrow for.
Her part, poor soul! seeming as burdened
With lesser weight but not with lesser woe,
Was carried with more speed before the
   wind;   110
And in our sight they three were taken up
By fishermen of Corinth, as we thought.
At length, another ship had seized on us;
And, knowing whom it was their hap to save,

---

73. **plainings**, wailings. 78. **sinking-ripe**, ready to
sink. 79. **latter-born**. Cf. line 125, from which we
learn that the younger of the twins was saved with the
father. 84. **disposed**, stowed. 93. **amain**, with might
and main. 94. **Epidaurus**, a town in Argolis on the
Saronic Gulf. 96. **that**, that which. 104. **helpful**.
Rowe's conjecture *helpless* is unnecessary; the word may
refer to the masts after the wreck (lines 80-86) or to the
general quality of the ship while she held together.

---

35. **nature**, i.e., by natural affection, which prompted
him to seek his son at Ephesus. 42. **factor's**, agent's.
53. **As**, that they. 55. **meaner**, i.e., of lower rank.
59. **meanly**, in a slight degree. 60. **motions**, proposals. 65. **instance**, proof, sign. 69. **doubtful**, i.e.,
almost certain.

Gave healthful welcome to their shipwreck'd
 guests;
And would have reft the fishers of their prey,
Had not their bark been very slow of sail;
And therefore homeward did they bend their
 course.
Thus have you heard me sever'd from my
 bliss,
That by misfortunes was my life prolong'd,
To tell sad stories of my own mishaps. 121
 Duke. And, for the sake of them thou
 sorrowest for,
Do me the favour to dilate at full
What hath befall'n of them and thee till now.
 Æge. My youngest boy, and yet my
 eldest care,
At eighteen years became inquisitive
After his brother; and importuned me
That his attendant—so his case was like,
Reft of his brother, but retain'd his name—
Might bear him company in the quest of him:
Whom whilst I labour'd of a love to see, 131
I hazarded the loss of whom I loved.
Five summers have I spent in furthest Greece,
Roaming clean through the bounds of Asia,
And, coasting homeward, came to Ephesus;
Hopeless to find, yet loath to leave unsought
Or that or any place that harbours men.
But here must end the story of my life;
And happy were I in my timely death,
Could all my travels warrant me they live.
 Duke. Hapless Ægeon, whom the fates
 have mark'd 141
To bear the extremity of dire mishap!
Now, trust me, were it not against our laws,
Against my crown, my oath, my dignity,
Which princes, would they, may not disannul,
My soul should sue as advocate for thee.
But, though thou art adjudged to the death
And passed sentence may not be recall'd
But to our honour's great disparagement,
Yet I will favour thee in what I can. 150
Therefore, merchant, I'll limit thee this day
To seek thy life by beneficial help:
Try all the friends thou hast in Ephesus;

Beg thou, or borrow, to make up the sum,
And live; if no, then thou art doom'd to die.
Gaoler, take him to thy custody.
 Gaol. I will, my lord.
 Æge. Hopeless and helpless doth Ægeon
 wend,
But to procrastinate his lifeless end. [*Exeunt.*

Scene II. *The Mart.*

Enter Antipholus *of Syracuse*, Dromio *of
 Syracuse, and* First Merchant.

 First Mer. Therefore give out you are of
 Epidamnum,
Lest that your goods too soon be confis-
 cate.
This very day a Syracusian merchant
Is apprehended for arrival here;
And not being able to buy out his life
According to the statute of the town
Dies ere the weary sun set in the west.
There is your money that I had to keep.
 Ant. S. Go bear it to the Centaur, where
 we host,
And stay there, Dromio, till I come to thee.
Within this hour it will be dinner-time: 11
Till that, I'll view the manners of the town,
Peruse the traders, gaze upon the build-
 ings,
And then return and sleep within mine inn,
For with long travel I am stiff and weary.
Get thee away.
 Dro. S. Many a man would take you at
 your word,
And go indeed, having so good a mean.
 [*Exit.*
 Ant. S. A trusty villain, sir, that very oft,
When I am dull with care and melancholy, 20
Lightens my humour with his merry jests.
What, will you walk with me about the town,
And then go to my inn and dine with me?
 First. Mer. I am invited, sir, to certain
 merchants,
Of whom I hope to make much benefit;
I crave your pardon. Soon at five o'clock,
Please you, I'll meet with you upon the mart
And afterward consort you till bed-time:
My present business calls me from you now.

---

115. **healthful**, implying, perhaps, *recovery* from the
sufferings of shipwreck (Cuningham). 123. **dilate**,
relate. 128. **so his case was like.** In *Menæchmi* of
Plautus one twin takes the name of his stolen brother
Menæchmus; in a similar way in this play Shakespeare
has taken it for granted that the twin slave has taken
the name of his lost brother Dromio (cf. line 53). 131.
of, i.e., out of, impelled by. 134. **clean**, entirely. 137.
Or . . . or, either . . . or. 139. **timely**, early, speedy.
140. **travels**, *travails* as well as *travels*. **warrant**, assure. 145. **disannul**, annul. 147. **the death**, i.e.,
death by judicial sentence. 152. **life.** F: *helpe*, possibly
for *helthe* meaning "welfare."

Scene ii. 9. **host**, lodge, put up. 13. **Peruse**, observe. 18. **mean**, opportunity, money. 19. **villain**,
used good-humoredly, or as a term of endearment.
21. **humour**, a physiological term here used, as often
in Shakespeare's time, to mean a particular mood,
disposition, vagary. 26. **Soon at**, about. 28. **consort**,
attend.

Ant. S. Farewell till then: I will go lose
　　myself　　　　　　　　　　　　　　30
And wander up and down to view the city.
　　First Mer. Sir, I commend you to your
　　own content.　　　　　　　[*Exit.*
　　Ant. S. He that commends me to mine
　　own content
Commends me to the thing I cannot get.
I to the world am like a drop of water
That in the ocean seeks another drop,
Who, falling there to find his fellow forth,
Unseen, inquisitive, confounds himself:
So I, to find a mother and a brother,
In quest of them, unhappy, lose myself.　40

　　　　Enter Dromio *of Ephesus.*

Here comes the almanac of my true date.
What now? how chance thou art return'd so
　　soon?
　　Dro. E. Return'd so soon! rather ap-
　　proach'd too late:
The capon burns, the pig falls from the spit,
The clock hath strucken twelve upon the bell;
My mistress made it one upon my cheek:
She is so hot because the meat is cold;
The meat is cold because you come not home;
You come not home because you have no
　　stomach;
You have no stomach having broke your fast;
But we that know what 'tis to fast and pray
Are penitent for your default to-day.　　52
　　Ant. S. Stop in your wind, sir: tell me
　　this, I pray:
Where have you left the money that I gave
　　you?
　　Dro. E. O,—sixpence, that I had o'
　　Wednesday last
To pay the saddler for my mistress' crupper?
The saddler had it, sir; I kept it not.
　　Ant. S. I am not in a sportive humour now:

Tell me, and dally not, where is the money?
We being strangers here, how darest thou
　　trust　　　　　　　　　　　　　　60
So great a charge from thine own custody?
　　Dro. E. I pray you, jest, sir, as you sit at
　　dinner:
I from my mistress come to you in post;
If I return, I shall be post indeed,
For she will score your fault upon my pate.
Methinks your maw, like mine, should be
　　your clock
And strike you home without a messenger.
　　Ant. S. Come, Dromio, come, these jests
　　are out of season;
Reserve them till a merrier hour than this.
Where is the gold I gave in charge to thee? 70
　　Dro. E. To me, sir? why, you gave no
　　gold to me.
　　Ant. S. Come on, sir knave, have done
　　your foolishness
And tell me how thou hast disposed thy
　　charge.
　　Dro. E. My charge was but to fetch you
　　from the mart
Home to your house, the Phœnix, sir, to
　　dinner:
My mistress and her sister stays for you.
　　Ant. S. Now, as I am a Christian, answer
　　me
In what safe place you have bestow'd my
　　money,
Or I shall break that merry sconce of yours
That stands on tricks when I am undisposed:
Where is the thousand marks thou hadst of
　　me?　　　　　　　　　　　　　　81
　　Dro. E. I have some marks of yours upon
　　my pate,
Some of my mistress' marks upon my
　　shoulders,
But not a thousand marks between you both.
If I should pay your worship those again,
Perchance you will not bear them patiently.
　　Ant. S. Thy mistress' marks? what mis-
　　tress, slave, hast thou?
　　Dro. E. Your worship's wife, my mistress
　　at the Phœnix;
She that doth fast till you come home to
　　dinner
And prays that you will hie you home to
　　dinner.　　　　　　　　　　　　90

37. **forth**, out. 38. **confounds**, mingles indistin-
guishably. 40. *Stage Direction:* **Enter Dromio of Ephesus.** There are two Plautine plays which Shakespeare probably had in mind in the management of
the plot of *The Comedy of Errors*—*Menæchmi* and
Amphitruo, both of which treat the theme of mistaken
identity. It is noticeable that Shakespeare's technique
resembles that of *Amphitruo* rather than that of *Menæchmi,* which he definitely follows in his plot. *Menæchmi* begins with a true situation which is followed by
a false situation; *Amphitruo,* like *The Comedy of Errors,*
begins with a false situation to be followed by a
true situation. The confusion is therefore more bewildering and interesting because of this method. The
effect is further increased in Shakespeare by his quad-
rupling of the chances for confusion in the introduction of
identical servants as well as identical masters. 41. **almanac . . . date,** i.e., being born in the same hour,
Dromio serves as an almanac by which Antipholus can
see his age. 45. **twelve.** The usual dinner hour was
half after eleven. 49. **stomach,** appetite. 52. **penitent,**
undergoing punishment. 53. **wind,** words.

63. **post,** haste. 64. **post,** doorpost of a tavern used
for keeping reckonings. 73. **disposed,** put away, deposited. 75. **Phœnix,** the sign of his master's shop.
78. **bestow'd,** deposited. 79. **sconce,** head. 80.
stands on, concerns or troubles itself about.

Ant. S. What, wilt thou flout me thus
  unto my face,
Being forbid? There, take you that, sir
  knave.
   Dro. E. What mean you, sir? for God's
  sake, hold your hands!
Nay, an you will not, sir, I'll take my heels.
                            [*Exit.*
   Ant. S. Upon my life, by some device or
  other
The villain is o'er-raught of all my money.
They say this town is full of cozenage,
As, nimble jugglers that deceive the eye,
Dark-working sorcerers that change the
  mind,   99
Soul-killing witches that deform the body,
Disguised cheaters, prating mountebanks,
And many such-like liberties of sin:
If it prove so, I will be gone the sooner.
I'll to the Centaur, to go seek this slave:
I greatly fear my money is not safe. [*Exit.*

ACT II.

Scene I. *The house of* Antipholus *of*
           Ephesus.

Enter Adriana *and* Luciana.

   Adr. Neither my husband nor the slave
  return'd,
That in such haste I sent to seek his master!
Sure, Luciana, it is two o'clock.
   Luc. Perhaps some merchant hath invited
  him
And from the mart he's somewhere gone to
  dinner.
Good sister, let us dine and never fret:
A man is master of his liberty:
Time is their master, and when they see time
They'll go or come: if so, be patient, sister.
   Adr. Why should their liberty than ours
  be more?   10
   Luc. Because their business still lies out
  o' door.
   Adr. Look, when I serve him so, he takes
  it ill.
   Luc. O, know he is the bridle of your will.
   Adr. There's none but asses will be
  bridled so.

   Luc. Why, headstrong liberty is lash'd
  with woe.
There's nothing situate under heaven's eye
But hath his bound, in earth, in sea, in sky:
The beasts, the fishes and the winged fowls
Are their males' subjects and at their
  controls:
Men, more divine, the masters of all these,
Lords of the wide world and wild watery
  seas,   21
Indued with intellectual sense and souls,
Of more pre-eminence than fish and fowls,
Are masters to their females, and their
  lords:
Then let your will attend on their accords.
   Adr. This servitude makes you to keep
  unwed.
   Luc. Not this, but troubles of the
  marriage-bed.
   Adr. But, were you wedded, you would
  bear some sway.
   Luc. Ere I learn love, I'll practise to
  obey.
   Adr. How if your husband start some
  other where?   30
   Luc. Till he come home again, I would
  forbear.
   Adr. Patience unmoved! no marvel
  though she pause;
They can be meek that have no other cause.
A wretched soul, bruised with adversity,
We bid be quiet when we hear it cry;
But were we burden'd with like weight of
  pain,
As much or more we should ourselves
  complain:
So thou, that hast no unkind mate to grieve
  thee,
With urging helpless patience wouldst
  relieve me;
But, if thou live to see like right bereft, 40
This fool-begg'd patience in thee will be
  left.
   Luc. Well, I will marry one day, but
  to try.
Here comes your man; now is your husband
  nigh.

Enter Dromio *of Ephesus.*

   Adr. Say, is your tardy master now at
  hand?

---

96. **o'er-raught,** over-reached, cheated.   99-100.
Dark-working . . . Soul-killing. It was Johnson's idea
that these epithets should be interchanged. 102. **liberties of sin,** persons allowed improper freedom to sin.
Act II. Scene i. 7. **A man . . . liberty.** With this
line begins the formal issue between the two women. It
presents the theme of the shrew and the patient wife.

15. **lash'd,** scourged, castigated; possibly used for
leash'd. 30. **some other where,** somewhere else. 39.
helpless, unavailing, unprofitable. 41. **fool-begg'd,**
made foolish by asking (me to be patient).

Dro. E. Nay, he's at two hands with me,
and that my two ears can witness.

Adr. Say, didst thou speak with him?
know'st thou his mind?

Dro. E. Ay, ay, he told his mind upon
mine ear:
Beshrew his hand, I scarce could understand
it.

Luc. Spake he so doubtfully, thou couldst
not feel his meaning?   51

Dro. E. Nay, he struck so plainly, I
could too well feel his blows; and withal so
doubtfully that I could scarce understand
them.

Adr. But say, I prithee, is he coming
home? It seems he hath great care to please
his wife.

Dro. E. Why, mistress, sure my master
is horn-mad.

Adr. Horn-mad, thou villain!

Dro. E.   I mean not cuckold-mad;
But, sure, he is stark mad.
When I desired him to come home to dinner,   60
He ask'd me for a thousand marks in gold:
''Tis dinner-time,' quoth I; 'My gold!'
quoth he:
'Your meat doth burn,' quoth I; 'My gold!'
quoth he:
'Will you come home?' quoth I; 'My gold!'
quoth he,
'Where is the thousand marks I gave thee,
villain?'
'The pig,' quoth I, 'is burn'd'; 'My gold!'
quoth he:
'My mistress, sir,' quoth I; 'Hang up thy
mistress!
I know not thy mistress; out on thy mistress!'

Luc. Quoth who?

Dro. E. Quoth my master: 70
'I know,' quoth he, 'no house, no wife, no
mistress.'
So that my errand, due unto my tongue,
I thank him, I bare home upon my shoulders;
For, in conclusion, he did beat me there.

Adr. Go back again, thou slave, and
fetch him home.

Dro. E. Go back again, and be new beaten
home?
For God's sake, send some other messenger.

Adr. Back, slave, or I will break thy pate
across.

Dro. E. And he will bless that cross with
other beating:
Between you I shall have a holy head.   80

Adr. Hence, prating peasant! fetch thy
master home.

Dro. E. Am I so round with you as you
with me,
That like a football you do spurn me thus?
You spurn me hence, and he will spurn me
hither:
If I last in this service, you must case me in
leather.   [*Exit.*

Luc. Fie, how impatience loureth in
your face!

Adr. His company must do his minions grace,
Whilst I at home starve for a merry look.
Hath homely age the alluring beauty took
From my poor cheek? then he hath wasted
it: 90
Are my discourses dull? barren my wit?
If voluble and sharp discourse be marr'd,
Unkindness blunts it more than marble
hard:
Do their gay vestments his affections bait?
That's not my fault; he's master of my state:
What ruins are in me that can be found,
By him not ruin'd? then is he the ground
Of my defeatures. My decayed fair
A sunny look of his would soon repair:
But, too unruly deer, he breaks the pale   100
And feeds from home; poor I am but his
stale.

Luc. Self-harming jealousy! fie, beat it
hence!

Adr. Unfeeling fools can with such
wrongs dispense.
I know his eye doth homage otherwhere;
Or else what lets it but he would be here?
Sister, you know he promised me a chain;
Would that alone, alone he would detain,

49. **Beshrew**, bad luck to. **Understand**, stand under. 57. **horn-mad**, mad as a horned beast, with a quibble on the sense of "rage at being made a cuckold." 72. **due unto my tongue**, i.e., instead of committing to me a message that I might deliver (with my tongue), he gave me one to bear home on my shoulders (i.e., a beating).

79. **bless**, consecrate; also, beat. 80. **holy**, with quibble on the sense "full of holes." 82. **round**, spherical, with pun on the sense of "plain spoken." 87. **minions**, favorites, darlings. 94. **bait**, entice. 95. **state**, outward display, i.e., clothes. 97. **ground**, cause. 98. **defeatures**, disfigurements. **fair**, beauty. 101. **stale**. She is stale to him, he dear (deer) to her; a *stale* is a lover made into a dupe, or a laughing-stock. 103. **dispense**, pardon, condone by dispensation. 105. **lets**, hinders. 107. **detain**, withhold.

So he would keep fair quarter with his bed!
I see the jewel best enamelled
Will lose his beauty; yet the gold bides still,
That others touch, and often touching
    will   111
†Wear gold: and no man that hath a name,
By falsehood and corruption doth it shame.
Since that my beauty cannot please his eye,
I'll weep what's left away, and weeping die.
    Luc. How many fond fools serve mad
jealousy!   [*Exeunt.*

SCENE II.   *A public place.*

Enter ANTIPHOLUS *of Syracuse.*

Ant. S. The gold I gave to Dromio is
    laid up
Safe at the Centaur; and the heedful slave
Is wander'd forth, in care to seek me out
By computation and mine host's report.
I could not speak with Dromio since at first
I sent him from the mart. See, here he
    comes.

Enter DROMIO *of Syracuse.*

How now, sir! is your merry humour alter'd?
As you love strokes, so jest with me again.
You know no Centaur? you received no gold?
Your mistress sent to have me home to
    dinner?   10
My house was at the Phœnix? Wast thou
    mad,
That thus so madly thou didst answer me?
    Dro. S. What answer, sir? when spake I
    such a word?
    Ant. S. Even now, even here, not half an
    hour since.
    Dro. S. I did not see you since you sent
    me hence,
Home to the Centaur, with the gold you gave
    me.
    Ant. S. Villain, thou didst deny the gold's
    receipt
And told'st me of a mistress and a dinner;
For which, I hope, thou felt'st I was dis-
    pleased.

Dro. S. I am glad to see you in this merry
    vein: 20
What means this jest? I pray you, master,
    tell me.
    Ant. S. Yea, dost thou jeer and flout me
    in the teeth?
Think'st thou I jest? Hold, take thou that,
    and that.   [*Beating him.*
    Dro. S. Hold, sir, for God's sake! now
    your jest is earnest:
Upon what bargain do you give it me?
    Ant. S. Because that I familiarly some-
    times
Do use you for my fool and chat with you,
Your sauciness will jest upon my love
And make a common of my serious hours.
When the sun shines let foolish gnats make
    sport,   30
But creep in crannies when he hides his
    beams.
If you will jest with me, know my aspect
And fashion your demeanour to my looks,
Or I will beat this method in your sconce.
    Dro. S. Sconce call you it? so you would
leave battering, I had rather have it a head:
an you use these blows long, I must get a
sconce for my head and insconce it too; or
else I shall seek my wit in my shoulders.
But, I pray, sir, why am I beaten?   40
    Ant. S. Dost thou not know?
    Dro. S. Nothing, sir, but that I am
beaten.
    Ant. S. Shall I tell you why?
    Dro. S. Ay, sir, and wherefore; for they
say every why hath a wherefore.
    Ant. S. Why, first,—for flouting me; and
    then, wherefore,—
For urging it the second time to me.
    Dro. S. Was there ever any man thus
    beaten out of season,
When in the why and the wherefore is neither
    rhyme nor reason?
Well, sir, I thank you.   50
    Ant. S. Thank me, sir! for what?
    Dro. S. Marry, sir, for this something
that you gave me for nothing.
    Ant. S. I'll make you amends next, to

108. **keep fair quarter,** be on good terms. 109–113.
I see . . . shame. This is a difficult passage, possibly
corrupt. Herford explains: "The best enameled jewel
tarnishes, but the gold setting keeps its luster; however,
it may be worn by the touch. Similarly, a man of assured reputation can commit domestic infidelity without
blasting it." 116. **fond,** doting.
    Scene ii. Stage Direction: **A public place.** New
Cambridge: *The Mart of Ephesus.*

22. **in the teeth,** to my face. 24. **earnest,** money
paid as an installment to secure a bargain, with quibble
on the meaning "serious." 28. **jest upon,** trifle with.
29. **common,** public playground. 32. **aspect,** look,
expression; also, favor or disfavor of a heavenly body.
34. **sconce,** head; fort (l. 35); helmet (l. 38). 38. **insconce,** to shelter behind or within a *sconce,* or fortification. 39. **seek . . . shoulders,** run away, show my back
(Cuningham); but Dromio probably means that his
head will be beaten into his shoulders.

give you nothing for something. But say, sir, is it dinner-time?

Dro. S. No, sir: I think the meat wants that I have.

Ant. S. In good time, sir; what's that?

Dro. S. Basting.

Ant. S. Well, sir, then 'twill be dry.   60

Dro. S. If it be, sir, I pray you, eat none of it.

Ant. S. Your reason?

Dro. S. Lest it make you choleric and purchase me another dry basting.

Ant. S. Well, sir, learn to jest in good time: there's a time for all things.

Dro. S. I durst have denied that, before you were so choleric.

Ant. S. By what rule, sir?

Dro. S. Marry, sir, by a rule as plain as the plain bald pate of father Time himself.   71

Ant. S. Let's hear it.

Dro. S. There's no time for a man to recover his hair that grows bald by nature.

Ant. S. May he not do it by fine and recovery?

Dro. S. Yes, to pay a fine for a periwig and recover the lost hair of another man.

Ant. S. Why is Time such a niggard of hair, being, as it is, so plentiful an excrement?   79

Dro. S. Because it is a blessing that he bestows on beasts; and what he hath scanted men in hair he hath given them in wit.

Ant. S. Why, but there's many a man hath more hair than wit.

Dro. S. Not a man of those but he hath the wit to lose his hair.

Ant. S. Why, thou didst conclude hairy men plain dealers without wit.

Dro. S. The plainer dealer, the sooner lost: yet he loseth it in a kind of jollity.   90

Ant. S. For what reason?

Dro. S. For two; and sound ones too.

Ant. S. Nay, not sound, I pray you.

Dro. S. Sure ones then.

Ant. S. Nay, not sure, in a thing falsing.

Dro. S. Certain ones then.

Ant. S. Name them.

Dro. S. The one, to save the money that he spends in tiring; the other that at dinner they should not drop in his porridge.   100

Ant. S. You would all this time have proved there is no time for all things.

Dro. S. Marry, and did, sir; namely, no time to recover hair lost by nature.

Ant. S. But your reason was not substantial, why there is no time to recover.

Dro. S. Thus I mend it: Time himself is bald and therefore to the world's end will have bald followers.

Ant. S. I knew 'twould be a bald conclusion: But, soft! who wafts us yonder?   111

Enter ADRIANA *and* LUCIANA.

Adr. Ay, ay, Antipholus, look strange and frown:
Some other mistress hath thy sweet aspects;
I am not Adriana nor thy wife.
The time was once when thou unurged wouldst vow
That never words were music to thine ear,
That never object pleasing in thine eye,
That never touch well welcome to thy hand,
That never meat sweet-savour'd in thy taste,
Unless I spake, or look'd, or touch'd, or carved to thee.   120
How comes it now, my husband, O, how comes it,
That thou art thus estranged from thyself?
Thyself I call it, being strange to me,
That, undividable, incorporate,
Am better than thy dear self's better part.
Ah, do not tear away thyself from me!
For know, my love, as easy mayst thou fall
A drop of water in the breaking gulf
And take unmingled thence that drop again,
Without addition or diminishing,   130
As take from me thyself and not me too.
How dearly would it touch thee to the quick,
Shouldst thou but hear I were licentious
And that this body, consecrate to thee,
By ruffian lust should be contaminate!
Wouldst thou not spit at me and spurn at me
And hurl the name of husband in my face
And tear the stain'd skin off my harlot-brow
And from my false hand cut the wedding-ring
And break it with a deep-divorcing vow?   140

---

57. that, what. **58. In good time,** indeed. **63. choleric.** Hot or dry food would produce or aggravate the choleric humor. **64. dry basting,** hard beating. **70. Marry,** an oath by the Virgin Mary. **75. fine and recovery,** legal procedure; Schmidt: "finery and re-covery." **79. excrement,** outgrowth (of hair). **84. more . . . wit,** a proverbial phrase. **85-86. he . . . hair,** a reference to the diseases in which loss of hair was a symptom. **90. jollity.** This word and *sound* and *falsing* (lines 93, 95) continue the reference to disease. **95. falsing,** deceptive.

99. tiring, dressing the hair. **110. bald,** senseless. **111. wafts,** beckons. **113. aspects,** looks, glances. **125. better part,** i.e., soul, spirit. **127. fall,** i.e., let fall. **132. dearly,** seriously, grievously.

I know thou canst; and therefore see thou
  do it.
I am possess'd with an adulterate blot;
My blood is mingled with the crime of lust:
For if we two be one and thou play false,
I do digest the poison of thy flesh,
Being strumpeted by thy contagion.
Keep then fair league and truce with thy true
  bed;
I live unstain'd, thou undishonoured.
    Ant. S. Plead you to me, fair dame? I
  know you not:
In Ephesus I am but two hours old,   150
As strange unto your town as to your talk;
Who, every word by all my wit being
  scann'd,
Want wit in all one word to understand.
    Luc. Fie, brother! how the world is
  changed with you!
When were you wont to use my sister thus?
She sent for you by Dromio home to din-
  ner.
    Ant. S. By Dromio?
    Dro. S. By me?
    Adr. By thee; and this thou didst return
  from him,
That he did buffet thee and in his blows 160
Denied my house for his, me for his wife.
    Ant. S. Did you converse, sir, with this
  gentlewoman?
What is the course and drift of your compact?
    Dro. S. I, sir? I never saw her till this
  time.
    Ant. S. Villain, thou liest; for even her
  very words
Didst thou deliver to me on the mart.
    Dro. S. I never spake with her in all my
  life.
    Ant. S. How can she thus then call us by
  our names?
Unless it be by inspiration.   169
    Adr. How ill agrees it with your gravity
To counterfeit thus grossly with your slave,
Abetting him to thwart me in my mood!
Be it my wrong you are from me exempt,
But wrong not that wrong with a more
  contempt.
Come, I will fasten on this sleeve of thine:
Thou art an elm, my husband, I a vine,

Whose weakness married to thy stronger
  state
Makes me with thy strength to communi-
  cate:
If aught possess thee from me, it is dross,
Usurping ivy, brier, or idle moss;   180
Who, all for want of pruning, with intrusion
Infect thy sap and live on thy confusion.
    Ant. S. To me she speaks; she moves me
  for her theme:
What, was I married to her in my dream?
Or sleep I now and think I hear all this?
What error drives our eyes and ears amiss?
Until I know this sure uncertainty,
I'll entertain the offer'd fallacy.
    Luc. Dromio, go bid the servants spread
  for dinner.
    Dro. S. O, for my beads! I cross me for a
  sinner.   190
This is the fairy land: O spite of spites!
We talk with goblins, owls and sprites:
If we obey them not, this will ensue,
They'll suck our breath or pinch us black
  and blue.
    Luc. Why pratest thou to thyself and
  answer'st not?
Dromio, thou drone, thou snail, thou slug,
  thou sot!
    Dro. S. I am transformed, master, am I
  not?
    Ant. S. I think thou art in mind, and so
  am I.
    Dro. S. Nay, master, both in mind and
  in my shape.
    Ant. S. Thou hast thine own form.
    Dro. S.   No, I am an ape.
    Luc. If thou art changed to aught, 'tis
  to an ass.   201
    Dro. S. 'Tis true; she rides me and I long
  for grass.
'Tis so, I am an ass; else it could never be
But I should know her as well as she knows
  me.
    Adr. Come, come, no longer will I be a
  fool,
To put the finger in the eye and weep,
Whilst man and master laugh my woes to
  scorn.

180. **idle**, unprofitable. 182. **confusion**, overthrow,
ruin. 183. **moves**, appeals to. **theme**, subject, i.e.,
trouble. 186. **error.** Cf. I, ii, 97, *this town is full of
cozenage;* Antipholus and Dromio continue in their belief
in the witchery of Ephesus. 188. **fallacy**, delusive
notion, error. 190. **beads**, rosary. 194. **suck . . .
breath.** This piece of folk-lore was perhaps connected
with the old idea that the breath of man was his soul.
196. **sot**, fool.

146. **strumpeted**, made a strumpet. 148. **unstain'd.** The F reading *distain'd* Dyce interpreted as
"I, as a wife, receive the *stain* of your present conduct,
while you, as a husband, suffer no loss of honour."
163. **compact**, plot. 172. **mood**, anger, displeasure.
173. **exempt**, separated.

Come, sir, to dinner. Dromio, keep the gate.
Husband, I'll dine above with you to-day
And shrive you of a thousand idle pranks. 210
Sirrah, if any ask you for your master,
Say he dines forth and let no creature enter.
Come, sister. Dromio, play the porter well.

   Ant. S. Am I in earth, in heaven, or in
    hell?
Sleeping or waking? mad or well-advised?
Known unto these, and to myself disguised!
I'll say as they say and persever so
And in this mist at all adventures go.

   Dro. S. Master, shall I be porter at the
    gate?

   Adr. Ay; and let none enter, lest I break
    your pate.   220

   Luc. Come, come, Antipholus, we dine
    too late.   [*Exeunt.*

ACT III.

Scene I. *Before the house of* Antipholus *of*
Ephesus.

Enter Antipholus *of* Ephesus, Dromio
of Ephesus, Angelo, *and* Balthazar.

   Ant. E. Good Signior Angelo, you must
    excuse us all;
My wife is shrewish when I keep not hours;
Say that I linger'd with you at your shop
To see the making of her carcanet   4
And that to-morrow you will bring it home.
But here's a villain that would face me down
He met me on the mart and that I beat him
And charged him with a thousand marks in
    gold
And that I did deny my wife and house.
Thou drunkard, thou, what didst thou mean
    by this?   10

   Dro. E. Say what you will, sir, but I know
    what I know;
That you beat me at the mart, I have your
    hand to show:
If the skin were parchment and the blows
    you gave were ink,

Your own handwriting would tell you what
    I think.

   Ant. E. I think thou art an ass.

   Dro. E.   Marry, so it doth appear
By the wrongs I suffer and the blows I
    bear.
I should kick, being kick'd; and, being at
    that pass,
You would keep from my heels and beware
    of an ass.

   Ant. E. You're sad, Signior Balthazar:
    pray God our cheer
May answer my good will and your good
    welcome here.   20

   Bal. I hold your dainties cheap, sir, and
    your welcome dear.

   Ant. E. O, Signior Balthazar, either at
    flesh or fish,
A table full of welcome makes scarce one
    dainty dish.

   Bal. Good meat, sir, is common; that
    every churl affords.

   Ant. E. And welcome more common; for
    that's nothing but words.

   Bal. Small cheer and great welcome
    makes a merry feast.

   Ant. E. Ay to a niggardly host and more
    sparing guest:
But though my cates be mean, take them in
    good part;
Better cheer may you have, but not with
    better heart.
But, soft! my door is lock'd. Go bid them
    let us in.   30

   Dro. E. Maud, Bridget, Marian, Cicely,
    Gillian, Ginn!

   Dro. S. [*Within*] Mome, malt-horse,
    capon, coxcomb, idiot, patch!
Either get thee from the door or sit down
    at the hatch.
Dost thou conjure for wenches, that thou
    call'st for such store,
When one is one too many? Go get thee
    from the door.

   Dro. E. What patch is made our porter?
    My master stays in the street.

   Dro. S. [*Within*] Let him walk from whence
    he came, lest he catch cold on 's feet.

   Ant. E. Who talks within there? ho, open
    the door!

---

209. **dine above.** This indicates that the balcony is
used in the next scene. 210. **shrive,** to hear a person's
confession and give him absolution. 212. **forth,** out.
215. **well-advised,** in my right mind.

  Act III. Scene i. 4. **carcanet,** necklace of jewels.
6. **face me down,** maintain to my face that. 8 **with,**
i.e., with possession of. 11 ff. Note the appearance of
doggerel at this point and in the following lines. Balthazar appears here only; Luce is elsewhere known as
Nell; the conversation of the Dromios is probably from
the old play taken over as it stood. 12. **hand,** quibble
on *handwriting.*

24. **churl,** one of mean station. 28. **cates,** dainties.
31. **Gillian, Ginn,** Juliana, Jenny (?) 32. **Mome,**
dolt, blockhead. **malt-horse,** brewer's horse; stupid
person. **patch,** fool, clown. 33. **hatch,** a wicket or
half-door.

Dro. S. [*Within*] Right, sir; I'll tell you when, an you'll tell me wherefore.

Ant. E. Wherefore? for my dinner: I have not dined to-day.   40

Dro. S. [*Within*] Nor to-day here you must not; come again when you may.

Ant. E. What art thou that keepest me out from the house I owe?

Dro. S. [*Within*] The porter for this time, sir, and my name is Dromio.

Dro. E. O villain! thou hast stolen both mine office and my name.

The one ne'er got me credit, the other mickle blame.

If thou hadst been Dromio to-day in my place,

Thou wouldst have changed thy face for a name or thy name for an ass.

Luce. [*Within*] What a coil is there, Dromio? who are those at the gate?

Dro. E. Let my master in, Luce.

Luce. [*Within*] Faith, no; he comes too late;

And so tell your master.

Dro E.   O Lord, I must laugh!

Have at you with a proverb—Shall I set in my staff?   51

Luce. [*Within*] Have at you with another; that's—When? can you tell?

Dro. S. [*Within*] If thy name be call'd Luce,—Luce, thou hast answer'd him well.

Ant. E. Do you hear, you minion? you'll let us in, I hope?

Luce. [*Within*] I thought to have ask'd you.

Dro. S.   [*Within*] And you said no.

Dro. E. So, come, help: well struck! there was blow for blow.

Ant. E. Thou baggage, let me in.

Luce. [*Within*] Can you tell for whose sake?

Dro. E. Master, knock the door hard.

Luce. [*Within*] Let him knock till it ache.

Ant. E. You'll cry for this, minion, if I beat the door down.

Luce. [*Within*] What needs all that, and a pair of stocks in the town?   60

Adr. [*Within*] Who is that at the door that keeps all this noise?

Dro. S. [*Within*] By my troth, your town is troubled with unruly boys.

Ant. E. Are you there, wife? you might have come before.

Adr. [*Within*] Your wife, sir knave! go get you from the door.

Dro. E. If you went in pain, master, this 'knave' would go sore.

Ang. Here is neither cheer, sir, nor welcome: we would fain have either.

Bal. In debating which was best, we shall part with neither.

Dro. E. They stand at the door, master; bid them welcome hither.

Ant. E. There is something in the wind, that we cannot get in.

Dro. E. You would say so, master, if your garments were thin.   70

Your cake there is warm within; you stand here in the cold:

It would make a man mad as a buck, to be so bought and sold.

Ant. E. Go fetch me something: I'll break ope the gate.

Dro. S. [*Within*] Break any breaking here, and I'll break your knave's pate.

Dro. E. A man may break a word with you, sir, and words are but wind,

Ay, and break it in your face, so he break it not behind.

Dro. S. [*Within*] It seems thou want'st breaking: out upon thee, hind!

Dro. E. Here's too much 'out upon thee!' I pray thee, let me in.

Dro. S. [*Within*] Ay, when fowls have no feathers and fish have no fin.

Ant. E. Well, I'll break in: go borrow me a crow.   80

Dro. E. A crow without feather? Master, mean you so?

For a fish without a fin, there's a fowl without a feather:

If a crow help us in, sirrah, we'll pluck a crow together.

---

42. **owe**, own; frequent in Shakespeare. 45. **mickle**, much. 47. **face for a name**. New Cambridge editors suggest pun "face for an aim," when he was beaten by Antipholus and Adriana; otherwise unexplained. 48. **Luce [Within]**. New Cambridge editors suggest that Luce and Adriana in this scene are on the upper stage, not able to see Antipholus and Dromio of Ephesus at rear door under the balcony. **coil**, noise, disturbance. 51. **Shall I set in my staff**, i.e., take up my abode. 52. **When . . . tell**, a proverbial expression used to turn aside a question. 54. **minion**, saucy woman, hussy. **hope**. Theobald read *trow*, making a triple rhyme. Malone thought that a line had been dropped out; if so, it would account for the obscurity of the next two lines.

67. **part with**, depart with. 72. **buck**, i.e., in rutting time. **bought and sold**, imposed upon. 77. **hind**, slave. 83. **pluck a crow together**, to pick a bone together, settle accounts; suggested by *crow* meaning "crowbar."

Ant. E. Go get thee gone; fetch me an
  iron crow.
  Bal. Have patience, sir; O, let it not be
  so!
Herein you war against your reputation
And draw within the compass of suspect
The unviolated honour of your wife.
Once this,—your long experience of her
  wisdom,
Her sober virtue, years and modesty,   90
Plead on her part some cause to you un-
  known;
And doubt not, sir, but she will well ex-
  cuse
Why at this time the doors are made against
  you.
Be ruled by me: depart in patience,
And let us to the Tiger all to dinner,
And about evening come yourself alone
To know the reason of this strange restraint.
If by strong hand you offer to break in
Now in the stirring passage of the day,
A vulgar comment will be made of it,   100
And that supposed by the common rout
Against your yet ungalled estimation
That may with foul intrusion enter in
And dwell upon your grave when you are
  dead;
For slander lives upon succession,
For ever housed where it gets possession.
  Ant. E. You have prevail'd: I will depart
  in quiet,
And, in despite of mirth, mean to be merry.
I know a wench of excellent discourse,
Pretty and witty, wild and yet, too, gentle:
There will we dine. This woman that I
  mean,   111
My wife—but, I protest, without desert—
Hath oftentimes upbraided me withal:
To her will we to dinner. [*To Ang.*] Get you
  home
And fetch the chain; by this I know 'tis
  made:
Bring it, I pray you, to the Porpentine;
For there's the house: that chain will I
  bestow—
Be it for nothing but to spite my wife—

Upon mine hostess there: good sir, make
  haste.
Since mine own doors refuse to entertain
  me,   120
I'll knock elsewhere, to see if they'll disdain
  me.
  Ang. I'll meet you at that place some
  hour hence.
  Ant. E. Do so. This jest shall cost me
  some expense.   [*Exeunt.*

SCENE II. *The same.*

Enter LUCIANA *and* ANTIPHOLUS *of Syracuse.*

  Luc. And may it be that you have quite
  forgot
A husband's office? shall, Antipholus,
Even in the spring of love, thy love-springs
  rot?
  Shall love, in building, grow so ruinous?
If you did wed my sister for her wealth,
  Then for her wealth's sake use her with
  more kindness:
Or if you like elsewhere, do it by stealth;
  Muffle your false love with some show of
  blindness:
Let not my sister read it in your eye;
  Be not thy tongue thy own shame's orator;
Look sweet, speak fair, become disloyalty; 11
  Apparel vice like virtue's harbinger;
Bear a fair presence, though your heart be
  tainted;
  Teach sin the carriage of a holy saint;
Be secret-false: what need she be acquainted?
  What simple thief brags of his own attaint?
'Tis double wrong, to truant with your bed
  And let her read it in thy looks at board:
Shame hath a bastard fame, well managed;
  Ill deeds are doubled with an evil word. 20
Alas, poor women! make us but believe,
  Being compact of credit, that you love us;
Though others have the arm, show us the
  sleeve;
  We in your motion turn and you may
  move us.
Then, gentle brother, get you in again;
  Comfort my sister, cheer her, call her wife:
'Tis holy sport to be a little vain,
  When the sweet breath of flattery con-
  quers strife.

---

87. **draw . . . suspect,** bring under suspicion. 89.
Once this, to be brief, in short. 93. **made,** fastened.
99. **passage,** people passing by. 100. **vulgar,** public.
102. **ungalled,** uninjured. 105. **slander . . . succes-**
sion, i.e., one slander grows out of another. 108. **in**
. . . mirth, in despite of mirth, which has abandoned me.
Theobald suggested *wrath* for *mirth.* 112. **desert,** my
deserving it. 115. **this,** this time. 116. **Porpentine,**
name of an inn; the word means "porcupine."

Scene ii. 3. **love-springs,** tender "shoots" of love.
11. **become disloyalty,** carry falseness gracefully.
14. **carriage,** demeanor, behavior. 16. **attaint,** stain,
dishonor; or possibly, conviction of crime. 18. **board,**
table. 22. **compact of credit,** made up of credulity.
27. **vain,** false.

Ant. S. Sweet mistress,—what your name
is else, I know not,
Nor by what wonder you do hit of
mine,—   30
Less in your knowledge and your grace you
show not
Than our earth's wonder, more than earth
divine.
Teach me, dear creature, how to think and
speak;
Lay open to my earthy-gross conceit,
Smother'd in errors, feeble, shallow, weak,
The folded meaning of your words' deceit.
Against my soul's pure truth why labour
you
To make it wander in an unknown field?
Are you a god? would you create me new?
Transform me then, and to your power
I'll yield.   40
But if that I am I, then well I know
Your weeping sister is no wife of mine,
Nor to her bed no homage do I owe:
Far more, far more to you do I decline.
O, train me not, sweet mermaid, with thy
note,
To drown me in thy sister's flood of tears:
Sing, siren, for thyself and I will dote:
Spread o'er the silver waves thy golden
hairs,
And as a bed I'll take them and there lie,
And in that glorious supposition think   50
He gains by death that hath such means to
die:
Let Love, being light, be drowned if she
sink!
Luc. What, are you mad, that you do
reason so?
Ant. S. Not mad, but mated; how, I do
not know.
Luc. It is a fault that springeth from
your eye.
Ant. S. For gazing on your beams, fair
sun, being by.
Luc. Gaze where you should, and that
will clear your sight.
Ant. S. As good to wink, sweet love, as
look on night.

Luc. Why call you me love? call my
sister so.
Ant. S. Thy sister's sister.
Luc.   That's my sister.
Ant. S.   No;   60
It is thyself, mine own self's better part,
Mine eye's clear eye, my dear heart's dearer
heart,
My food, my fortune and my sweet hope's
aim,
My sole earth's heaven and my heaven's
claim.
Luc. All this my sister is, or else should
be.
Ant. S. Call thyself sister, sweet, for I
am thee.
Thee will I love and with thee lead my life:
Thou hast no husband yet nor I no wife.
Give me thy hand.
Luc.   O, soft, sir! hold you still:
I'll fetch my sister, to get her good will.   70
[*Exit.*

Enter Dromio of Syracuse.

Ant. S. Why, how now, Dromio! where
runn'st thou so fast?
Dro. S. Do you know me, sir? am I
Dromio? am I your man? am I myself?
Ant. S. Thou art Dromio, thou art my
man, thou art thyself.
Dro. S. I am an ass, I am a woman's man
and besides myself.
Ant. S. What woman's man? and how
besides thyself?   80
Dro. S. Marry, sir, besides myself, I am
due to a woman; one that claims me, one
that haunts me, one that will have me.
Ant. S. What claim lays she to thee?
Dro. S. Marry, sir, such claim as you
would lay to your horse; and she would have
me as a beast: not that, I being a beast, she
would have me; but that she, being a very
beastly creature, lays claim to me.
Ant. S. What is she?   90
Dro. S. A very reverent body; ay, such a
one as a man may not speak of without he say
'Sir-reverence.' I have but lean luck in the
match, and yet is she a wondrous fat marriage.
Ant. S. How dost thou mean a fat marriage?

30. **hit of,** hit upon, guess. 32. **earth's wonder.**
Douce sees in this a reference to Queen Elizabeth. 36.
folded, concealed. 44. **decline,** incline, lean toward.
45. **train,** entice, allure. 52. **light,** buoyant, with
quibble on the sense of "wanton." The idea is that
Love cannot possibly sink. 53. **reason,** talk. 54.
mated, amazed, confounded, with quibble on the sense
of "matched with a wife." 56. **being by,** i.e., being
near you. 58. **wink,** close the eyes in sleep.

64. **My . . . claim,** i.e., my heaven on earth and my
claim on heaven hereafter. 93. **'Sir-reverence,'** i.e.,
save your reverence, an expression used in apology for
the remark that follows it. **lean,** poor, meager.

Dro. S. Marry, sir, she's the kitchen wench and all grease; and I know not what use to put her to but to make a lamp of her and run from her by her own light. I warrant, her rags and the tallow in them will burn a Poland winter: if she lives till doomsday, she'll burn a week longer than the whole world.

Ant. S. What complexion is she of?

Dro. S. Swart, like my shoe, but her face nothing like so clean kept: for why, she sweats; a man may go over shoes in the grime of it.

Ant. S. That's a fault that water will mend.

Dro. S. No, sir, 'tis in grain; Noah's flood could not do it.

Ant. S. What's her name?   110

Dro. S. Nell, sir; but her name and three quarters, that's an ell and three quarters, will not measure her from hip to hip.

Ant. S. Then she bears some breadth?

Dro. S. No longer from head to foot than from hip to hip: she is spherical, like a globe; I could find out countries in her.

Ant. S. In what part of her body stands Ireland?

Dro. S. Marry, sir, in her buttocks: I found it out by the bogs.   121

Ant. S. Where Scotland?

Dro. S. I found it by the barrenness; hard in the palm of the hand.

Ant. S. Where France?

Dro. S. In her forehead; armed and reverted, making war against her heir.

Ant. S. Where England?

Dro. S. I looked for the chalky cliffs, but I could find no whiteness in them; but I guess it stood in her chin, by the salt rheum that ran between France and it.

Ant. S. Where Spain?

Dro. S. Faith, I saw it not; but I felt it hot in her breath.

Ant. S. Where America, the Indies?

Dro. S. Oh, sir, upon her nose, all o'er embellished with rubies, carbuncles, sapphires, declining their rich aspect to the hot breath of Spain; who sent whole armadoes of caracks to be ballast at her nose.   141

Ant. S. Where stood Belgia, the Netherlands?

Dro. S. Oh, sir, I did not look so low. To conclude, this drudge, or diviner, laid claim to me; called me Dromio; swore I was assured to her; told me what privy marks I had about me, as, the mark of my shoulder, the mole in my neck, the great wart on my left arm, that I amazed ran from her as a witch: And, I think, if my breast had not been made of faith and my heart of steel,   150 She had transform'd me to a curtal dog and made me turn i' the wheel.

Ant. S. Go hie thee presently, post to the road:
An if the wind blow any way from shore,
I will not harbour in this town to-night:
If any bark put forth, come to the mart,
Where I will walk till thou return to me.
If every one knows us and we know none,
'Tis time, I think, to trudge, pack and be gone.

Dro. S. As from a bear a man would run for life,
So fly I from her that would be my wife.
      [*Exit.*

Ant. S. There's none but witches do inhabit here;   161
And therefore 'tis high time that I were hence.
She that doth call me husband, even my soul
Doth for a wife abhor. But her fair sister,
Possess'd with such a gentle sovereign grace,
Of such enchanting presence and discourse,
Hath almost made me traitor to myself:
But, lest myself be guilty to self-wrong,
I'll stop mine ears against the mermaid's song.

Enter ANGELO *with the chain.*

Ang. Master Antipholus,—

Ant. S.   Ay, that's my name.   170

Ang. I know it well, sir: lo, here is the chain.
I thought to have ta'en you at the Porpentine:
The chain unfinish'd made me stay thus long.

Ant. S. What is your will that I shall do with this?

104. **Swart**, swarthy, dark. 108. **in grain**, indelible, ineradicable. 123. **barrenness.** New Cambridge editors print *barren-nesses*, indicating a pun on *ness*, a promontory. 126. **armed and reverted.** See *Introduction* for explanation of reference to the French war. 130. **them**; i.e., her teeth. 139. **declining**, bending. 140. **armadoes of caracks**, fleets of galleons. 141. **ballast**, loaded, freighted.

144. **diviner**, sorceress. 145. **assured**, affianced. 151. **curtal dog**, dog with docked tail, of no service in the chase. **turn . . . wheel.** Dogs, by running in a wheel, turned the spit. 152. **road**, harbor, roadstead. 168. **to**, of.

Ang. What please yourself, sir: I have
made it for you.

Ant. S. Made it for me, sir! I bespoke
it not.

Ang. Not once, nor twice, but twenty
times you have.

Go home with it and please your wife withal;

And soon at supper-time I'll visit you

And then receive my money for the chain. 180

Ant. S. I pray you, sir, receive the money
now,

For fear you ne'er see chain nor money
more.

Ang. You are a merry man, sir: fare you
well.   [*Exit.*

Ant. S. What I should think of this, I
cannot tell:

But this I think, there's no man is so vain

That would refuse so fair an offer'd chain.

I see a man here needs not live by shifts,

When in the streets he meets such golden
gifts.

I'll to the mart and there for Dromio
stay: 190

If any ship put out, then straight away.[*Exit.*

ACT IV.

Scene I. *A public place.*

Enter Second Merchant, Angelo, *and an*
Officer.

Sec. Mer. You know since Pentecost the
sum is due,

And since I have not much importuned you;

Nor now I had not, but that I am bound

To Persia and want guilders for my voyage:

Therefore make present satisfaction,

Or I'll attach you by this officer.

Ang. Even just the sum that I do owe
to you

Is growing to me by Antipholus,

And in the instant that I met with you

He had of me a chain: at five o'clock   10

I shall receive the money for the same.

Pleaseth you walk with me down to his
house,

I will discharge my bond and thank you too.

185. vain, oolish, silly.
Act IV. Scene i. Stage Direction: **A public place.**
New Cambridge: *Place in the Mart.* 6. **attach**, arrest,
seize. 8. **growing**, due, accruing.

Enter Antipholus *of Ephesus and* Dromio
of Ephesus *from the courtezan's.*

Off. That labour may you save: see where
he comes.

Ant. E. While I go to the goldsmith's
house, go thou

And buy a rope's end: that will I bestow

Among my wife and her confederates,

For locking me out of my doors by day.

But, soft! I see the goldsmith. Get thee
gone;

Buy thou a rope and bring it home to me. 20

Dro. E. I buy a thousand pound a year:
I buy a rope.   [*Exit.*

Ant. E. A man is well holp up that trusts
to you:

I promised your presence and the chain;

But neither chain nor goldsmith came to me.

Belike you thought our love would last too
long,

If it were chain'd together, and therefore
came not.

Ang. Saving your merry humour, here's
the note

How much your chain weighs to the utmost
carat,

The fineness of the gold and chargeful
fashion,

Which doth amount to three odd ducats
more   30

Than I stand debted to this gentleman:

I pray you, see him presently discharged,

For he is bound to sea and stays but for it.

Ant. E. I am not furnish'd with the
present money;

Besides, I have some business in the town.

Good signior, take the stranger to my house

And with you take the chain and bid my wife

Disburse the sum on the receipt thereof:

Perchance I will be there as soon as you.

Ang. Then you will bring the chain to her
yourself?   40

Ant. E. No; bear it with you, lest I come
not time enough.

Ang. Well, sir, I will. Have you the chain
about you?

Ant. E. An if I have not, sir, I hope you
have;

Or else you may return without your money.

16. **bestow**, employ. 21. **buy a thousand pound
a year**, doubtfully explained as "a thousand pounds
(blows) a year"; possibly, "I'll buy a rope as gladly as
I would buy," etc. 29. **chargeful**, expensive. 31.
debted, indebted.

Ang. Nay, come, I pray you, sir, give me the chain:
Both wind and tide stays for this gentleman,
And I, to blame, have held him here too long.
  Ant. E. Good Lord! you use this dalliance to excuse
Your breach of promise to the Porpentine.
I should have chid you for not bringing it, 50
But, like a shrew, you first begin to brawl.
  Sec. Mer. The hour steals on; I pray you, sir, dispatch.
  Ang. You hear how he importunes me;—the chain!
  Ant E. Why, give it to my wife and fetch your money.
  Ang. Come, come, you know I gave it you even now.
Either send the chain or send me by some token.
  Ant. E. Fie, now you run this humour out of breath,
Come, where's the chain? I pray you, let me see it.
  Sec. Mer. My business cannot brook this dalliance.
Good sir, say whether you'll answer me or no: 60
If not, I'll leave him to the officer.
  Ant. E. I answer you! what should I answer you?
  Ang. The money that you owe me for the chain.
  Ant. E. I owe you none till I receive the chain.
  Ang. You know I gave it you half an hour since.
  Ant. E. You gave me none: you wrong me much to say so.
  Ang. You wrong me more, sir, in denying it:
Consider how it stands upon my credit.
  Sec. Mer. Well, officer, arrest him at my suit.
  Off. I do; and charge you in the duke's name to obey me.   70
  Ang. This touches me in reputation.
Either consent to pay this sum for me
Or I attach you by this officer.

  Ant. E. Consent to pay thee that I never had!
Arrest me, foolish fellow, if thou darest.
  Ang. Here is thy fee; arrest him, officer.
I would not spare my brother in this case,
If he should scorn me so apparently.
  Off. I do arrest you, sir: you hear the suit.
  Ant. E. I do obey thee till I give thee bail.
But, sirrah, you shall buy this sport as dear   81
As all the metal in your shop will answer.
  Ang. Sir, sir, I shall have law in Ephesus,
To your notorious shame; I doubt it not.

Enter DROMIO *of Syracuse, from the bay.*

  Dro. S. Master, there is a bark of Epidamnum
That stays but till her owner comes aboard
And then, sir, she bears away. Our fraughtage, sir,
I have convey'd aboard and I have bought
The oil, the balsamum and aqua-vitæ.
The ship is in her trim: the merry wind   90
Blows fair from land: they stay for nought at all
But for their owner, master, and yourself.
  Ant. E. How now! a madman! Why, thou peevish sheep,
What ship of Epidamnum stays for me?
  Dro. S. A ship you sent me to, to hire waftage.
  Ant. E. Thou drunken slave, I sent thee for a rope
And told thee to what purpose and what end.
  Dro. S. You sent me for a rope's end as soon:
You sent me to the bay, sir, for a bark.
  Ant. E. I will debate this matter at more leisure   100
And teach your ears to list me with more heed.
To Adriana, villain, hie thee straight:
Give her this key, and tell her, in the desk
That's cover'd o'er with Turkish tapestry
There is a purse of ducats; let her send it:
Tell her I am arrested in the street

---

56. **send . . . token,** i.e., send me with some sign authorizing me to receive payment. 57. **humour,** whim. 60. **answer,** pay, discharge a debt. 68. **stands upon,** concerns.

87. **fraughtage,** freight. 89. **balsamum . . . aqua-vitæ,** balm . . . ardent spirits. 90. **in her trim,** rigged and ready to sail. 93. **peevish,** silly, senseless. **sheep,** a pun; pronounced much like "ship." 95. **waftage,** conveyance by ship. 98. **rope's end,** a hangman's noose. 101. **list,** listen to.

And that shall bail me: hie thee, slave, be
  gone!
On, officer, to prison till it come.
            [*Exeunt Sec. Merchant, Angelo,
                    Officer, and Ant. E.*
Dro. S. To Adriana! that is where we
  dined,
Where Dowsabel did claim me for her hus-
  band: 110
She is too big, I hope, for me to compass.
Thither I must, although against my will,
For servants must their masters' minds
  fulfil.   [*Exit.*

SCENE II. *The house of* ANTIPHOLUS *of*
              Ephesus.

         Enter ADRIANA *and* LUCIANA.

Adr. Ah, Luciana, did he tempt thee so?
Mightst thou perceive austerely in his eye
That he did plead in earnest? yea or no?
Look'd he or red or pale, or sad or merrily?
What observation madest thou in this case
Of his heart's meteors tilting in his face?
  Luc. First he denied you had in him no
right.
  Adr. He meant he did me none; the more
my spite.
  Luc. Then swore he that he was a
stranger here.
  Adr. And true he swore, though yet for-
sworn he were.   10
  Luc. Then pleaded I for you.
  Adr.   And what said he?
  Luc. That love I begg'd for you he begg'd
of me.
  Adr. With what persuasion did he tempt
thy love?
  Luc. With words that in an honest suit
might move.
First he did praise my beauty, then my
speech.
  Adr. Didst speak him fair?
  Luc.   Have patience, I beseech.
  Adr. I cannot, nor I will not, hold me
still;
My tongue, though not my heart, shall have
  his will.
He is deformed, crooked, old and sere,

Ill-faced, worse bodied, shapeless every-
  where;   20
Vicious, ungentle, foolish, blunt, unkind,
Stigmatical in making, worse in mind.
  Luc. Who would be jealous then of such
  a one?
No evil lost is wail'd when it is gone.
  Adr. Ah, but I think him better than I
  say,
And yet would herein others' eyes were
  worse.
Far from her nest the lapwing cries away:
My heart prays for him, though my tongue
  do curse.

         Enter DROMIO *of Syracuse.*

  Dro. S. Here! go; the desk, the purse!
  sweet, now, make haste.
  Luc. How hast thou lost thy breath?
  Dro. S.   By running fast.   30
  Adr. Where is thy master, Dromio? is
  he well?
  Dro. S. No, he's in Tartar limbo, worse
  than hell.
†A devil in an everlasting garment hath him;
One whose hard heart is button'd up with
  steel;
A fiend, a fury, pitiless and rough;
A wolf, nay, worse, a fellow all in buff;
A back-friend, a shoulder-clapper, one that
  countermands
The passages of alleys, creeks and narrow
  lands;
A hound that runs counter and yet draws
  dry-foot well;
One that before the judgement carries poor
  souls to hell.   40
  Adr. Why, man, what is the matter?
  Dro. S. I do not know the matter: he is
  'rested on the case.
  Adr. What, is he arrested? Tell me at
  whose suit.
  Dro. S. I know not at whose suit he is
  arrested well;

110. **Dowsabel**, used ironically for *Nell;* from *douce
et belle.*
  Scene ii. 2. **austerely**, i.e., not being affected by his
pleas. 6. **meteors**, changes of color and expression.
7 ff. Note the use of *stichomythia*, dialogue in which each
speech consists of a single line; much used in classical
drama. 8. **spite**, grief.

20. **shapeless**, misshapen. 22. **Stigmatical**, crooked,
or branded with deformity. **making**, form. 32. **Tartar
limbo**, Tartar or Mohammedan hell, worse than Christian hell. 33. **everlasting garment**, *buff*, leatner used
as the attire of police officers (l. 36). 37. **back-friend**,
a false friend; the police officer who comes up behind and
claps one on the back. **countermands**, prohibits, forbids. 38. **creeks**, narrow or winding passages. **narrow
lands**, not explained. 39. **runs counter**, follows a
trail in a direction opposite to that which the game
has taken, with quibble on *counter*, a prison. **draws
dry-foot**, follows game by mere scent of the foot.
40. **judgement**, quibble on "day of judgement" and
"legal decision." **hell**, debtor's prison. 42. **case**, form
of procedure, "action on the case," with quibble on
case meaning "the container of *matter.*"

But he's in a suit of buff which 'rested him,
    that can I tell.
Will you send him, mistress, redemption, the
    money in his desk?
   Adr. Go fetch it, sister. [*Exit Luciana.*]
    This I wonder at,
That he, unknown to me, should be in debt.
Tell me, was he arrested on a band?
   Dro. S. Not on a band, but on a stronger
    thing;   50
A chain, a chain! Do you not hear it ring?
   Adr. What, the chain?
   Dro. S. No, no, the bell: 'tis time that I
    were gone:
It was two ere I left him, and now the clock
    strikes one.
   Adr. The hours come back! that did I
    never hear.
   Dro. S. O, yes; if any hour meet a
    sergeant, a' turns back for very fear.
   Adr. As if Time were in debt! how fondly
    dost thou reason!
   Dro. S. Time is a very bankrupt and owes
    more than he's worth to season.
Nay, he's a thief too: have you not heard
    men say,
That Time comes stealing on by night and
    day?
If Time be in debt and theft, and a sergeant
    in the way,   61
Hath he not reason to turn back an hour in
    a day?

      Re-enter LUCIANA *with a purse.*

   Adr. Go, Dromio; there's the money,
    bear it straight,
And bring thy master home immediately.
Come, sister: I am press'd down with
    conceit—
Conceit, my comfort and my injury.
                          [*Exeunt.*

      SCENE III. *A public place.*

      Enter ANTIPHOLUS *of Syracuse.*

   Ant. S. There's not a man I meet but
    doth salute me
As if I were their well-acquainted friend;

And every one doth call me by my name.
Some tender money to me; some invite me;
Some other give me thanks for kindnesses;
Some offer me commodities to buy:
Even now a tailor call'd me in his shop
And show'd me silks that he had bought
    for me
And therewithal took measure of my body.
Sure, these are but imaginary wiles   10
And Lapland sorcerers inhabit here.

      Enter DROMIO *of Syracuse.*

   Dro. S. Master, here's the gold you sent
me for. What, have you got the picture of
old Adam new-apparelled?
   Ant. S. What gold is this? what Adam
    dost thou mean?
   Dro. S. Not that Adam that kept the
Paradise, but that Adam that keeps the
prison: he that goes in the calf's skin that
was killed for the Prodigal; he that came
behind you, sir, like an evil angel, and bid
you forsake your liberty.   20
   Ant. S. I understand thee not.
   Dro. S. No? why, 'tis a plain case: he that
went, like a bass-viol, in a case of leather;
the man, sir, that, when gentlemen are tired,
gives them a sob and 'rests them; he, sir,
that takes pity on decayed men and gives
them suits of durance; he that sets up his
rest to do more exploits with his mace than
a morris-pike.   28
   Ant. S. What, thou meanest an officer?
   Dro. S. Ay, sir, the sergeant of the band;
he that brings any man to answer it that
breaks his band; one that thinks a man always going to bed and says 'God give you
good rest!'
   Ant. S. Well, sir, there rest in your
foolery. Is there any ship puts forth to-
night? may we be gone?   36
   Dro. S. Why, sir, I brought you word an
hour since that the bark Expedition put
forth to-night; and then were you hindered
by the sergeant, to tarry for the hoy Delay.

---

46. **mistress, redemption.** New Cambridge editors
read *Mistress Redemption,* with F₄, as suggestive of
morality plays alluded to in *judgement,* etc., above.
49. **band,** bond: also, manacle, leash for a dog. 56. **a',**
he (it). 58. **season,** opportunity. 65, 66. **conceit,**
imagination, or apprehension.
   Scene iii. Stage Direction: **A public place.** New
Cambridge: *The Mart.*

11. **Lapland sorcerers.** Lapland was said to surpass
all nations in the practice of witchcraft and sorcery.
14. **old Adam.** This is taken to mean, "Have you got
rid of the picture of old Adam, namely, the sergeant
dressed in buff, as Adam was dressed in skins" (*Gen.* iii,
21). 18-19. **calf's . . . Prodigal.** Cf. *St. Luke* xv, 23.
25. **sob,** breathing space. 27. **durance,** a kind of long-
wearing cloth like buff, as well as prison. **sets . . . rest,**
stakes his all; metaphor from the game of primero.
28. **mace,** staff of office carried by a sergeant. **morris-
pike,** Moorish pike. 40. **hoy,** a small coasting vessel.

Here are the angels that you sent for to
deliver you.   41
  Ant. S. The fellow is distract, and so am
I;
And here we wander in illusions:
Some blessed power deliver us from hence!

Enter a Courtezan.

  Cour. Well met, well met, Master Antipholus.
I see, sir, you have found the goldsmith now:
Is that the chain you promised me to-day?
  Ant. S. Satan, avoid! I charge thee,
tempt me not.
  Dro. S. Master, is this Mistress Satan?
  Ant. S. It is the devil.   50
  Dro. S. Nay, she is worse, she is the devil's
dam; and here she comes in the habit of a
light wench: and thereof comes that the
wenches say 'God damn me;' that's as much
to say 'God make me a light wench.' It is
written, they appear to men like angels of
light: light is an effect of fire, and fire will
burn; ergo, light wenches will burn. Come
not near her.
  Cour. Your man and you are marvellous
merry, sir.
Will you go with me? We'll mend our
dinner here?   60
  Dro. S. Master, if you do, expect spoon-
meat; or bespeak a long spoon.
  Ant. S. Why, Dromio?
  Dro. S. Marry, he must have a long spoon
that must eat with the devil.
  Ant. S. Avoid then, fiend! what tell'st
thou me of supping?
Thou art, as you are all, a sorceress:
I conjure thee to leave me and be gone.
  Cour. Give me the ring of mine you had
at dinner,   69
Or, for my diamond, the chain you promised,
And I'll be gone, sir, and not trouble you.
  Dro. S. Some devils ask but the parings
of one's nail,   72
A rush, a hair, a drop of blood, a pin,

A nut, a cherry-stone;
But she, more covetous, would have a chain.
Master, be wise: and if you give it her,
The devil will shake her chain and fright us
with it.
  Cour. I pray you, sir, my ring, or else the
chain:
I hope you do not mean to cheat me so.
  Ant. S. Avaunt, thou witch! Come, Dro-
mio, let us go.   80
  Dro. S. 'Fly pride,' says the peacock:
mistress, that you know.
[*Exeunt Ant. S. and Dro. S.*
  Cour. Now, out of doubt Antipholus is
mad,
Else would he never so demean himself.
A ring he hath of mine worth forty ducats,
And for the same he promised me a chain:
Both one and other he denies me now.
The reason that I gather he is mad,
Besides this present instance of his rage,
Is a mad tale he told to-day at dinner,
Of his own doors being shut against his
entrance.   90
Belike his wife, acquainted with his fits,
On purpose shut the doors against his way.
My way is now to hie home to his house,
And tell his wife that, being lunatic,
He rush'd into my house and took perforce
My ring away. This course I fittest choose;
For forty ducats is too much to lose. [*Exit.*

SCENE IV. *A street.*

Enter ANTIPHOLUS *of Ephesus and the* Officer.

  Ant. E. Fear me not, man; I will not
break away:
I'll give thee, ere I leave thee, so much money,
To warrant thee, as I am 'rested for.
My wife is in a wayward mood to-day,
And will not lightly trust the messenger.
That I should be attach'd in Ephesus,
I tell you, 'twill sound harshly in her ears.

Enter DROMIO *of Ephesus with a rope's-end.*

Here comes my man; I think he brings the
money.
How now, sir! have you that I sent you for?
  Dro. E. Here's that, I warrant you, will
pay them all.   10

---

41. **angels,** gold coins worth about 10s.; "good angels
this time, sent by Mistress Redemption" (New Cambridge). 42. **distract,** distracted. 49. **Mistress Satan,**
"yet another character in Dromio's miracle play" (New
Cambridge). 53. **light,** wanton. 56. **angels of light.**
Cf. *2 Cor.* xi, 14. 58. **will burn,** i.e., are diseased.
60. **mend,** supplement, supply the deficiencies. 61.
spoon-meat, food for infants, hence, delicacies; but the
sense is obscure. 72-77. **Some . . . it.** F prints this as
prose, which fact, with the broken line at 74, suggests
revision or abridgment (New Cambridge).

81. **Fly . . . peacock.** The accusation of dishonesty
coming from this woman, whom Dromio takes to be
dishonest, seems to him as out of place as a warning
against pride given by the peacock. 83. **demean,**
conduct. 95. **perforce,** forcibly.

Ant. E. But where's the money?

Dro. E. Why, sir, I gave the money for the rope.

Ant. E. Five hundred ducats, villain, for a rope?

Dro. E. I'll serve you, sir, five hundred at the rate.

Ant. E. To what end did I bid thee hie thee home?

Dro. E. To a rope's-end, sir; and to that end am I returned.

Ant. E. And to that end, sir, I will welcome you.   [*Beating him.*

Off. Good sir, be patient.

Dro. E. Nay, 'tis for me to be patient; I am in adversity.   21

Off. Good now, hold thy tongue.

Dro. E. Nay, rather persuade him to hold his hands.

Ant. E. Thou whoreson, senseless villain!

Dro. E. I would I were senseless, sir, that I might not feel your blows.

Ant. E. Thou art sensible in nothing but blows, and so is an ass.   29

Dro. E. I am an ass, indeed; you may prove it by my long ears. I have served him from the hour of my nativity to this instant, and have nothing at his hands for my service but blows. When I am cold, he heats me with beating; when I am warm, he cools me with beating: I am waked with it when I sleep; raised with it when I sit; driven out of doors with it when I go from home; welcomed home with it when I return: nay, I bear it on my shoulders, as a beggar wont her brat; 40 and, I think, when he hath lamed me, I shall beg with it from door to door.

Ant. E. Come, go along; my wife is coming yonder.

Enter ADRIANA, LUCIANA, *the* Courtezan, *and* PINCH.

Dro. E. Mistress, 'respice finem,' respect your end; or rather, †the prophecy like the parrot, 'beware the rope's end.'   46

Ant. E. Wilt thou still talk? [*Beating him.*

Cour. How say you now? is not your husband mad?

Adr. His incivility confirms no less.

Good Doctor Pinch, you are a conjurer;   50
Establish him in his true sense again,
And I will please you what you will demand.

Luc. Alas, how fiery and how sharp he looks!

Cour. Mark how he trembles in his ecstasy!

Pinch. Give me your hand and let me feel your pulse.

Ant. E. There is my hand, and let it feel your ear.   [*Striking him.*

Pinch. I charge thee, Satan, housed within this man,
To yield possession to my holy prayers
And to thy state of darkness hie thee straight:
I conjure thee by all the saints in heaven! 60

Ant. E. Peace, doting wizard, peace! I am not mad.

Adr. O, that thou wert not, poor distressed soul!

Ant. E. You minion, you, are these your customers?
Did this companion with the saffron face
Revel and feast it at my house to-day,
Whilst upon me the guilty doors were shut
And I denied to enter in my house?

Adr. O husband, God doth know you dined at home;
Where would you had remain'd until this time,
Free from these slanders and this open shame!

Ant. E. Dined at home! Thou villain, what sayest thou?   71

Dro. E. Sir, sooth to say, you did not dine at home.

Ant. E. Were not my doors lock'd up and I shut out?

Dro. E. Perdie, your doors were lock'd and you shut out.

Ant. E. And did not she herself revile me there?

Dro. E. Sans fable, she herself reviled you there.

Ant. E. Did not her kitchen-maid rail, taunt and scorn me?

Dro. E. Certes, she did; the kitchen-vestal scorn'd you.

---

22. **Good now**, pray thee. 28, **sensible**, sensitive. 40. **wont**, i.e., is wont to carry. 44. **'respice finem.'** *Respice funem*, "consider the hangman's rope," was a jesting variant of this expression. 46. **'beware the rope's end,'** i.e., beware the halter; possibly a phrase taught by sailors to parrots.

50. **conjurer.** Being able to speak Latin, Pinch could conjure spirits. 52. **please**, pay. 54. **ecstasy**, madness. 63. **minion**, favorite (used contemptuously). **customers**, guests (in a bad sense). 64. **companion**, fellow. **saffron**, yellow. 74. **Perdie**, oath from *par Dieu*. 76. **Sans**, without. 78. **kitchen-vestal**, "her charge being, like that of the vestal virgins, to keep the fire burning" (Johnson).

Ant. E. And did not I in rage depart from thence?

Dro. E. In verity you did; my bones bear witness,   80

That since have felt the vigour of his rage.

Adr. Is 't good to soothe him in these contraries?

Pinch. It is no shame: the fellow finds his vein

And yielding to him humours well his frenzy.

Ant. E. Thou hast suborn'd the goldsmith to arrest me.

Adr. Alas, I sent you money to redeem you,

By Dromio here, who came in haste for it.

Dro. E. Money by me! heart and goodwill you might;

But surely, master, not a rag of money.

Ant. E. Went'st not thou to her for a purse of ducats?   90

Adr. He came to me and I deliver'd it.

Luc. And I am witness with her that she did.

Dro. E. God and the rope-maker bear me witness

That I was sent for nothing but a rope!

Pinch. Mistress, both man and master is possess'd;

I know it by their pale and deadly looks:

They must be bound and laid in some dark room.

Ant. E. Say, wherefore didst thou lock me forth to-day?

And why dost thou deny the bag of gold?

Adr. I did not, gentle husband, lock thee forth.   100

Dro. E. And, gentle master, I received no gold;

But I confess, sir, that we were lock'd out.

Adr. Dissembling villain, thou speak'st false in both.

Ant. E. Dissembling harlot, thou art false in all

And art confederate with a damned pack

To make a loathsome abject scorn of me:

But with these nails I'll pluck out these false eyes

That would behold in me this shameful sport.

Enter three or four, and offer to bind him. He strives.

Adr. O, bind him, bind him! let him not come near me.

Pinch. More company! The fiend is strong within him.   110

Luc. Ay me, poor man, how pale and wan he looks!

Ant. E. What, will you murder me? Thou gaoler, thou,

I am thy prisoner: wilt thou suffer them

To make a rescue?

Off.   Masters, let him go:

He is my prisoner, and you shall not have him.

Pinch. Go bind this man, for he is frantic too.   [*They offer to bind Dro. E.*

Adr. What wilt thou do, thou peevish officer?

Hast thou delight to see a wretched man

Do outrage and displeasure to himself?

Off. He is my prisoner: if I let him go,   120

The debt he owes will be required of me.

Adr. I will discharge thee ere I go from thee:

Bear me forthwith unto his creditor

And, knowing how the debt grows, I will pay it.

Good master doctor, see him safe convey'd

Home to my house. O most unhappy day!

Ant. E. O most unhappy strumpet!

Dro. E. Master, I am here enter'd in bond for you.

Ant. E. Out on thee, villain! wherefore dost thou mad me?

Dro. E. Will you be bound for nothing? be mad, good master: cry 'The devil!'   131

Luc. God help, poor souls, how idly do they talk!

Adr. Go bear him hence. Sister, go you with me. [*Exeunt all but Adriana, Luciana, Officer and Courtezan.*]

Say now, whose suit is he arrested at?

Off. One Angelo, a goldsmith: do you know him?

Adr. I know the man. What is the sum he owes?

Off. Two hundred ducats.

Adr.   Say, how grows it due?

Off. Due for a chain your husband had of him.

---

82. **soothe**, encourage, humor. 89. **rag**, scrap. 96. **deadly**, deathlike. 97. **bound . . . room**, the regular treatment for lunacy in Shakespeare's day.

117. **peevish**, foolish. 126, 127. **unhappy**, fatal . . . miserable.

Adr. He did bespeak a chain for me, but
　had it not.

Cour. When as your husband all in rage
　to-day　　　　　　　　　　　　　140
Came to my house and took away my ring—
The ring I saw upon his finger now—
Straight after did I meet him with a chain.

Adr. It may be so, but I did never see it.
Come, gaoler, bring me where the goldsmith
　is:
I long to know the truth hereof at large.

Enter ANTIPHOLUS *of Syracuse with his rapier
　drawn, and* DROMIO *of Syracuse.*

Luc. God, for thy mercy! they are loose
　again.

Adr. And come with naked swords.
Let's call more help to have them bound
　again.

Off. Away! they'll kill us.　　　　150
　　　[*Exeunt all but Ant. S. and Dro. S.*

Ant. S. I see these witches are afraid of
　swords.

Dro. S. She that would be your wife now
　ran from you.

Ant. S. Come to the Centaur; fetch our
　stuff from thence:
I long that we were safe and sound aboard.

Dro. S. Faith, stay here this night; they
will surely do us no harm: you saw they
speak us fair, give us gold: methinks they are
such a gentle nation that, but for the mountain of mad flesh that claims marriage of me,
I could find in my heart to stay here still
and turn witch.　　　　　　　　160

Ant. S. I will not stay to-night for all the
　town;
Therefore away, to get our stuff aboard.
　　　　　　　　　　　　　　[*Exeunt.*

ACT V.

SCENE I. *A street before a Priory.*

Enter Second Merchant *and* ANGELO.

Ang. I am sorry, sir, that I have hinder'd
　you;
But, I protest, he had the chain of me,
Though most dishonestly he doth deny it.

Sec. Mer. How is the man esteem'd here
　in the city?

Ang. Of very reverend reputation, sir,
Of credit infinite, highly beloved,
Second to none that lives here in the city:
His word might bear my wealth at any time.

Sec. Mer. Speak softly: yonder, as I
　think, he walks.

Enter ANTIPHOLUS *of Syracuse and* DROMIO
　of Syracuse.

Ang. 'Tis so; and that self chain about his
　neck　　　　　　　　　　　　　10
Which he forswore most monstrously to
　have.
Good sir, draw near to me, I'll speak to him.
Signior Antipholus, I wonder much
That you would put me to this shame and
　trouble;
And, not without some scandal to yourself,
With circumstance and oaths so to deny
This chain which now you wear so openly:
Beside the charge, the shame, imprisonment,
You have done wrong to this my honest
　friend,
Who, but for staying on our controversy,　20
Had hoisted sail and put to sea to-day:
This chain you had of me; can you deny it?

Ant. S. I think I had; I never did deny it.

Sec. Mer. Yes, that you did, sir, and for-
　swore it too.

Ant. S. Who heard me to deny it or for-
　swear it?

Sec. Mer. These ears of mine, thou
　know'st, did hear thee.
Fie on thee, wretch! 'tis pity that thou livest
To walk where any honest men resort.

Ant. S. Thou art a villain to impeach me
　thus:
I'll prove mine honour and mine honesty　30
Against thee presently, if thou darest stand.

Sec. Mer. I dare, and do defy thee for a
　villain.　　　　　　　　　　[*They draw.*

Enter ADRIANA, LUCIANA, *the* Courtezan, *and
　others.*

Adr. Hold, hurt him not, for God's sake!
　he is mad.
Some get within him, take his sword away:
Bind Dromio too, and bear them to my
　house.

---

139. **bespeak,** order. 140. **When as,** when. 150. *Stage
Direction:* **Exeunt all,** etc. F prints *Runne all out* after
line 149, and *Exeunt omnes as fast as may be, frighted,*
after line 150. *Exeunt omnes* was the original stage direction, the rest being written in the margin of the manuscript (New Cambridge). 153. **stuff,** goods, baggage.
　Act V. Scene i. Stage Direction: **A street before a
Priory.** New Cambridge: *The square before the house of
Antipholus.*

8. **bear,** carry off. 11. **forswore,** repudiated on oath
or with strong words. 16. **circumstance,** details,
particulars. 34. **within him,** under his guard.

Dro. S. Run, master, run; for God's sake, take a house!
This is some priory. In, or we are spoil'd!

[*Exeunt Ant. S. and Dro. S. to the Priory.*

Enter the Lady Abbess.

Abb. Be quiet, people. Wherefore throng you hither?

Adr. To fetch my poor distracted husband hence.
Let us come in, that we may bind him fast 40
And bear him home for his recovery.

Ang. I knew he was not in his perfect wits.

Sec. Mer. I am sorry now that I did draw on him.

Abb. How long hath this possession held the man?

Adr. This week he hath been heavy, sour, sad,
And much different from the man he was;
But till this afternoon his passion
Ne'er brake into extremity of rage.

Abb. Hath he not lost much wealth by wreck of sea?
Buried some dear friend? Hath not else his eye
Stray'd his affection in unlawful love? 51
A sin prevailing much in youthful men,
Who give their eyes the liberty of gazing.
Which of these sorrows is he subject to?

Adr. To none of these, except it be the last;
Namely, some love that drew him oft from home.

Abb. You should for that have reprehended him.

Adr. Why, so I did.

Abb.   Ay, but not rough enough.

Adr. As roughly as my modesty would let me.

Abb. Haply, in private.

Adr.   And in assemblies too.

Abb. Ay, but not enough. 61

Adr. It was the copy of our conference:
In bed he slept not for my urging it;
At board he fed not for my urging it;
Alone, it was the subject of my theme;
In company I often glanced it;
Still did I tell him it was vile and bad.

Abb. And thereof came it that the man was mad:
The venom clamours of a jealous woman
Poisons more deadly than a mad dog's tooth. 70
It seems his sleeps were hinder'd by thy railing,
And thereof comes it that his head is light.
Thou say'st his meat was sauced with thy upbraidings:
Unquiet meals make ill digestions;
Thereof the raging fire of fever bred;
And what's a fever but a fit of madness?
Thou say'st his sports were hinder'd by thy brawls:
Sweet recreation barr'd, what doth ensue
But moody and dull melancholy,
Kinsman to grim and comfortless despair, 80
And at her heels a huge infectious troop
Of pale distemperatures and foes to life?
In food, in sport and life-preserving rest
To be disturb'd, would mad or man or beast:
The consequence is then thy jealous fits
Have scared thy husband from the use of wits.

Luc. She never reprehended him but mildly,
When he demean'd himself rough, rude and wildly.
Why bear you these rebukes and answer not?

Adr. She did betray me to my own reproof. 90
Good people, enter and lay hold on him.

Abb. No, not a creature enters in my house.

Adr. Then let your servants bring my husband forth.

Abb. Neither: he took this place for sanctuary,
And it shall privilege him from your hands
Till I have brought him to his wits again,
Or lose my labour in assaying it.

Adr. I will attend my husband, be his nurse,
Diet his sickness, for it is my office,
And will have no attorney but myself; 100
And therefore let me have him home with me.

Abb. Be patient; for I will not let him stir
Till I have used the approved means I have,
With wholesome syrups, drugs and holy prayers,

---

36. **take,** repair to for refuge.   51. **Stray'd,** led astray.
57 ff. **reprehended him,** etc. Note the shrewdness of the Abbess in bringing out the true quality of Adriana's behavior, and the dramatic irony of the dialogue. 62. **copy,** minutes or memoranda. 66. **glanced,** alluded to.

82. **distemperatures,** physical disorders, illness. 100. **attorney,** agent, deputy.

To make of him a formal man again:
It is a branch and parcel of mine oath,
A charitable duty of my order.
Therefore depart and leave him here with
    me.
    Adr. I will not hence and leave my hus-
    band here:
And ill it doth beseem your holiness   110
To separate the husband and the wife.
    Abb. Be quiet and depart: thou shalt not
    have him.   [*Exit.*
    Luc. Complain unto the duke of this in-
    dignity.
    Adr. Come, go: I will fall prostrate at his
    feet
And never rise until my tears and prayers
Have won his grace to come in person
    hither
And take perforce my husband from the
    abbess.
    Sec. Mer. By this, I think, the dial points
    at five:
Anon, I'm sure, the duke himself in person
Comes this way to the melancholy vale,   120
The place of death and sorry execution,
Behind the ditches of the abbey here.
    Ang. Upon what cause?
    Sec. Mer. To see a reverend Syracusian
    merchant,
Who put unluckily into this bay
Against the laws and statutes of this town,
Beheaded publicly for his offence.
    Ang. See where they come: we will behold
    his death.
    Luc. Kneel to the duke before he pass the
    abbey.

Enter Duke, *attended;* Ægeon *bareheaded;*
    with the Headsman *and other* Officers.

    Duke. Yet once again proclaim it pub-
    licly,   130
If any friend will pay the sum for him,
He shall not die; so much we tender him.
    Adr. Justice, most sacred duke, against
    the abbess!
    Duke. She is a virtuous and a reverend
    lady:
It cannot be that she hath done thee wrong.
    Adr. May it please your grace, Antipholus
    my husband,
Whom I made lord of me and all I had,

At your important letters,—this ill day
A most outrageous fit of madness took him;
That desperately he hurried through the
    street,—   140
With him his bondman, all as mad as he,—
Doing displeasure to the citizens
By rushing in their houses, bearing thence
Rings, jewels, any thing his rage did like.
Once did I get him bound and sent him
    home,
Whilst to take order for the wrongs I went
That here and there his fury had committed.
Anon, I wot not by what strong escape,
He broke from those that had the guard of
    him;
And with his mad attendant and himself, 150
Each one with ireful passion, with drawn
    swords,
Met us again and madly bent on us
Chased us away, till raising of more aid
We came again to bind them. Then they fled
Into this abbey, whither we pursued them:
And here the abbess shuts the gates on us
And will not suffer us to fetch him out,
Nor send him forth that we may bear him
    hence.
Therefore, most gracious duke, with thy
    command
Let him be brought forth and borne hence
    for help.   160
    Duke. Long since thy husband served me
    in my wars,
And I to thee engaged a prince's word,
When thou didst make him master of thy
    bed,
To do him all the grace and good I could.
Go, some of you, knock at the abbey-gate
And bid the lady abbess come to me.
I will determine this before I stir.

Enter a Servant.

    Serv. O mistress, mistress, shift and save
    yourself!
My master and his man are both broke loose,
Beaten the maids a-row and bound the
    doctor,
Whose beard they have singed off with
    brands of fire;   171
And ever, as it blazed, they threw on him
Great pails of puddled mire to quench the
    hair:

105. **formal**, normal. 106. **parcel**, part, portion.
121. **sorry**, exciting sorrow, sad. 132. **so much**, i.e.,
so much consideration.

138. **important**, urgent, pressing. **letters**. Adriana
would seem to have been ward to the Duke. 146. **order
for**, measures for settling. 148. **strong**, violent. 170.
a-row, one after another.

My master preaches patience to him and the
    while
His man with scissors nicks him like a fool,
And sure, unless you send some present help,
Between them they will kill the conjurer.
    Adr. Peace, fool! thy master and his man
    are here.
And that is false thou dost report to us.   179
    Serv. Mistress, upon my life, I tell you
    true;
I have not breathed almost since I did see it.
He cries for you and vows, if he can take you,
To scorch your face and to disfigure you.
                          [*Cry within*.
Hark, hark! I hear him, mistress: fly, be
    gone!
    Duke. Come, stand by me; fear nothing.
    Guard with halberds!
    Adr. Ay me, it is my husband! Witness
    you,
That he is borne about invisible:
Even now we housed him in the abbey here;
And now he's there, past thought of human
    reason.

Enter Antipholus *of Ephesus and* Dromio
          of Ephesus.

    Ant. E. Justice, most gracious duke, O,
    grant me justice!   190
Even for the service that long since I did
    thee,
When I bestrid thee in the wars and took
Deep scars to save thy life; even for the blood
That then I lost for thee, now grant me
    justice.
    Æge. Unless the fear of death doth make
    me dote,
I see my son Antipholus and Dromio.
    Ant. E. Justice, sweet prince, against that
    woman there!
She whom thou gavest to me to be my wife,
That hath abused and dishonour'd me
Even in the strength and height of injury!
Beyond imagination is the wrong   201
That she this day hath shameless thrown on
    me.
    Duke. Discover how, and thou shalt find
    me just.
    Ant. E. This day, great duke, she shut
    the doors upon me,

While she with harlots feasted in my
    house.
    Duke. A grievous fault! Say, woman,
    didst thou so?
    Adr. No, my good lord: myself, he and my
    sister
To-day did dine together. So befall my soul
As this is false he burdens me withal!
    Luc. Ne'er may I look on day, nor sleep
    on night,   210
But she tells to your highness simple truth!
    Ang. O perjured woman! They are both
    forsworn:
In this the madman justly chargeth them.
    Ant. E. My liege, I am advised what I
    say,
Neither disturbed with the effect of wine,
Nor heady-rash, provoked with raging ire,
Albeit my wrongs might make one wiser
    mad.
This woman lock'd me out this day from
    dinner:
That goldsmith there, were he not pack'd
    with her,
Could witness it, for he was with me then; 220
Who parted with me to go fetch a chain,
Promising to bring it to the Porpentine,
Where Balthazar and I did dine together.
Our dinner done, and he not coming thither,
I went to seek him: in the street I met him
And in his company that gentleman.
There did this perjured goldsmith swear me
    down
That I this day of him received the chain,
Which, God he knows, I saw not: for the
    which
He did arrest me with an officer.   230
I did obey, and sent my peasant home
For certain ducats: he with none return'd.
Then fairly I bespoke the officer
To go in person with me to my house.
By the way we met
My wife, her sister, and a rabble more
Of vile confederates. Along with them
They brought one Pinch, a hungry lean-
    faced villain,
A mere anatomy, a mountebank,
A threadbare juggler and a fortune-teller,
A needy, hollow-eyed, sharp-looking wretch,
A living-dead man: this pernicious slave, 241

---

175. **nicks him like a fool.** Fools or professional
jesters were accustomed to cut their hair in fantastic
shapes. 192. **bestrid**, stood over to defend him when
fallen in battle.

205. **harlots**, probably, vagabonds, rascals. 209.
burdens, charges. 214. **am advised**, know very well.
219. **pack'd with**, in conspiracy with. 231. **peasant**,
servant. 238. **anatomy**, skeleton.

Forsooth, took on him as a conjurer,
And, gazing in mine eyes, feeling my pulse,
And with no face, as 'twere, outfacing me,
Cries out, I was possess'd. Then all together
They fell upon me, bound me, bore me
    thence
And in a dark and dankish vault at home
There left me and my man, both bound to-
    gether;
Till, gnawing with my teeth my bonds in
    sunder,
I gain'd my freedom and immediately   250
Ran hither to your grace; whom I beseech
To give me ample satisfaction
For these deep shames and great indignities.

Ang. My lord, in truth, thus far I
    witness with him,
That he dined not at home, but was lock'd
    out.

Duke. But had he such a chain of thee
    or no?

Ang. He had, my lord: and when he ran
    in here,
These people saw the chain about his neck.

Sec. Mer. Besides, I will be sworn these
    ears of mine
Heard you confess you had the chain of him
After you first forswore it on the mart: 261
And thereupon I drew my sword on you;
And then you fled into this abbey here,
From whence, I think, you are come by
    miracle.

Ant. E. I never came within these abbey-
    walls,
Nor ever didst thou draw thy sword on me:
I never saw the chain, so help me Heaven!
And this is false you burden me withal.

Duke. Why, what an intricate impeach is
    this!
I think you all have drunk of Circe's cup. 270
If here you housed him, here he would have
    been;
If he were mad, he would not plead so
    coldly:
You say he dined at home; the goldsmith
    here
Denies that saying. Sirrah, what say you?

Dro. E. Sir, he dined with her there, at
    the Porpentine.

Cour. He did, and from my finger
    snatch'd that ring.

Ant. E. 'Tis true, my liege; this ring I
    had of her.

Duke. Saw'st thou him enter at the abbey
    here?

Cour. As sure, my liege, as I do see your
    grace.

Duke. Why, this is strange. Go call the
    abbess hither.   280
I think you are all mated or stark mad.
             [Exit one to the Abbess.

Æge. Most mighty duke, vouchsafe me
    speak a word:
Haply I see a friend will save my life
And pay the sum that may deliver me.

Duke. Speak freely, Syracusian, what
    thou wilt.

Æge. Is not your name, sir, call'd Antiph-
    olus?
And is not that your bondman, Dromio?

Dro. E. Within this hour I was his bond-
    man, sir,
But he, I thank him, gnaw'd in two my cords:
Now am I Dromio and his man unbound. 290

Æge. I am sure you both of you remember
    me.

Dro. E. Ourselves we do remember, sir,
    by you;
For lately we were bound, as you are now.
You are not Pinch's patient, are you, sir?

Æge. Why look you strange on me? you
    know me well.

Ant. E. I never saw you in my life till
    now.

Æge. O, grief hath changed me since you
    saw me last,
And careful hours with time's deformed hand
Have written strange defeatures in my face:
But tell me yet, dost thou not know my
    voice?   300

Ant. E. Neither.

Æge. Dromio, nor thou?

Dro. E.   No, trust me, sir, nor I.

Æge. I am sure thou dost.

Dro. E. Ay, sir, but I am sure I do not;
and whatsoever a man denies, you are now
bound to believe him.

Æge. Not know my voice! O time's ex-
    tremity,

---

242. **took . . . as,** pretended to be. 269. **impeach,** charge, accusation. 270. **Circe's cup,** the poisoned cup, a draft of which turned men into beasts. 272. **coldly,** calmly.

281. **mated,** bewildered. 294. **Pinch's patient.** Dromio refers to the binding, evidently the feature of Pinch's treatment which most impressed him. 298. **deformed,** deforming. 299. **defeatures,** disfigurements. 307. **Not know my voice!** Genuine feeling comes out in the speech of Ægeon, a serious element in this play, which thus aligns it with Shakespeare's romantic comedies.

Hast thou so crack'd and splitted my poor
　　tongue　　　　　　　　　　　　　　308
In seven short years, that here my only son
Knows not my feeble key of untuned cares?
Though now this grained face of mine be hid
In sap-consuming winter's drizzled snow
And all the conduits of my blood froze up,
Yet hath my night of life some memory,
My wasting lamps some fading glimmer left,
My dull deaf ears a little use to hear:
All these old witnesses—I cannot err—
Tell me thou art my son Antipholus.

Ant. E. I never saw my father in my life.
Æge. But seven years since, in Syracusa,
　　boy,　　　　　　　　　　　　　　320
Thou know'st we parted: but perhaps, my
　　son,
Thou shamest to acknowledge me in misery.
Ant. E. The duke and all that know me in
　　the city
Can witness with me that it is not so:
I ne'er saw Syracusa in my life.
Duke. I tell thee, Syracusian, twenty
　　years
Have I been patron to Antipholus,
During which time he ne'er saw Syracusa:
I see thy age and dangers make thee dote.

Re-enter Abbess, *with* Antipholus *of Syra-*
　　cuse and Dromio *of Syracuse.*

Abb. Most mighty duke, behold a man
　　much wrong'd. 　[*All gather to see them.*
Adr. I see two husbands, or mine eyes
　　deceive me.　　　　　　　　　　331
Duke. One of these men is Genius to the
　　other;
And so of these. Which is the natural man,
And which the spirit? who deciphers them?
Dro. S. I, sir, am Dromio: command him
　　away.
Dro. E. I, sir, am Dromio: pray, let me
　　stay.
Ant. S. Ægeon art thou not? or else his
　　ghost?
Dro. S. O, my old master! who hath
　　bound him here?
Abb. Whoever bound him, I will loose his
　　bonds
And gain a husband by his liberty.　　340
Speak, old Ægeon, if thou be'st the man

That hadst a wife once call'd Æmilia
That bore thee at a burden two fair sons:
O, if thou be'st the same Ægeon, speak,
And speak unto the same Æmilia!
Æge. If I dream not, thou art Æmilia:
If thou art she, tell me where is that son
That floated with thee on the fatal raft?
Abb. By men of Epidamnum he and I
And the twin Dromio all were taken up; 　350
But by and by rude fishermen of Corinth
By force took Dromio and my son from
　　them
And me they left with those of Epidamnum.
What then became of them I cannot tell;
I to this fortune that you see me in.
Duke. Why, here begins his morning story
　　right:
These two Antipholuses, these two so like,
And these two Dromios, one in semblance,—
Besides her urging of her wreck at sea,—
These are the parents to these children, 　360
Which accidentally are met together.
Antipholus, thou camest from Corinth first?
Ant. S. No, sir, not I; I came from Syra-
　　cuse.
Duke. Stay, stand apart; I know not
　　which is which.
Ant. E. I came from Corinth, my most
　　gracious lord,—
Dro. E. And I with him.
Ant. E. Brought to this town by that
　　most famous warrior,
Duke Menaphon, your most renowned uncle.
Adr. Which of you two did dine with me
　　to-day?
Ant. S. I, gentle mistress.
Adr.　　And are not you my husband?
Ant. E. No; I say nay to that. 　　371
Ant. S. And so do I; yet did she call me
　　so:
And this fair gentlewoman, her sister here,
Did call me brother. [*To Luc.*] What I told
　　you then,
I hope I shall have leisure to make good;
If this be not a dream I see and hear.
Ang. That is the chain, sir, which you
　　had of me.
Ant. S. I think it be, sir; I deny it not.
Ant. E. And you, sir, for this chain arrest-
　　ed me.
Ang. I think I did, sir; I deny it not. 　380

---

310. **my . . . cares,** the whole tone of my voice which
is altered by sorrow.　311. **grained,** lined, furrowed.
315. **lamps.** Ægeon clearly means his eyes.　332.
Genius, attendant spirit.　334. **deciphers,** distinguishes.

343. **burden,** birth.　358. **semblance,** trisyllabic;
also *children* in line 360.　359. **Besides . . . sea.** Perhaps a line has dropped out following this.

Adr. I sent you money, sir, to be your
     bail,
By Dromio; but I think he brought it not.
Dro. E. No, none by me.
Ant. S. This purse of ducats I received
     from you
And Dromio my man did bring them me.
I see we still did meet each other's man,
And I was ta'en for him, and he for me,
And thereupon these ERRORS are arose.
Ant. E. These ducats pawn I for my
     father here.
Duke. It shall not need; thy father hath
     his life.   390
Cour. Sir, I must have that diamond from
     you.
Ant. E. There, take it; and much thanks
     for my good cheer.
Abb. Renowned duke, vouchsafe to take
     the pains
To go with us into the abbey here
And hear at large discoursed all our fortunes:
And all that are assembled in this place,
That by this sympathized one day's error
Have suffer'd wrong, go keep us company,
And we shall make full satisfaction.   399
Thirty-three years have I but gone in travail
Of you, my sons; and till this present hour
My heavy burthen ne'er delivered.
The duke, my husband and my children
     both,
And you the calendars of their nativity,
Go to a gossips' feast, and go with me;
After so long grief, such festivity!

Duke. With all my heart, I'll gossip at
     this feast. [*Exeunt all but Ant. S., Ant. E.,
                         Dro. S., and Dro. E.*
Dro. S. Master, shall I fetch your stuff
     from shipboard?
Ant. E. Dromio, what stuff of mine hast
     thou embark'd?
Dro. S. Your goods that lay at host, sir,
     in the Centaur.   410
Ant. S. He speaks to me. I am your
     master, Dromio:
Come, go with us; we'll look to that anon:
Embrace thy brother there; rejoice with him.
                    [*Exeunt Ant. S. and Ant. E.*
Dro. S. There is a fat friend at your
     master's house,
That kitchen'd me for you to-day at din-
     ner:
She now shall be my sister, not my wife.
Dro. E. Methinks you are my glass, and
     not my brother:
I see by you I am a sweet-faced youth.
Will you walk in to see their gossiping?
Dro. S. Not I, sir; you are my elder.   420
Dro. E. That's a question: how shall we
     try it?
Dro. S. We'll draw cuts for the senior:
     till then lead thou first.
Dro. E. Nay, then, thus:
We came into the world like brother and
     brother;
And now let's go hand in hand, not one
     before another.   [*Exeunt.*

---

397. **sympathized**, i.e., from which all have suffered.
404. **calendars . . . nativity**, the Dromios.   405.
gossips' feast. A gossip is the godparent to one's child.

407. **gossip**, i.e., be a gossip, in the sense of boon-
companion, familiar acquaintance.   410. **lay at host**,
were put up.   415. **kitchen'd**, entertained in the
kitchen.   419. **gossiping**, merry-making.

A MIDSUMMER-NIGHT'S DREAM

DRAMATIS PERSONÆ

THESEUS, Duke of Athens.
EGEUS, father to Hermia.
LYSANDER, } in love with Hermia.
DEMETRIUS,
PHILOSTRATE, master of the revels to Theseus.
QUINCE, a carpenter.
SNUG, a joiner.
BOTTOM, a weaver.
FLUTE, a bellows-mender.
SNOUT, a tinker.
STARVELING, a tailor.
HIPPOLYTA, queen of the Amazons, betrothed to Theseus.

HERMIA, daughter to Egeus, in love with Lysander.
HELENA, in love with Demetrius.
OBERON, king of the fairies.
TITANIA, queen of the fairies.
PUCK, or Robin Goodfellow.
PEASEBLOSSOM,
COBWEB,
MOTH, } fairies.
MUSTARDSEED,
Other fairies attending their King and Queen.
Attendants on Theseus and Hippolyta.
SCENE: *Athens, and a wood near it.*

ACT I.

SCENE I. *Athens. The palace of* THESEUS.

Enter THESEUS, HIPPOLYTA, PHILOSTRATE, *and* Attendants.

The. Now, fair Hippolyta, our nuptial hour
Draws on apace; four happy days bring in
Another moon: but, O, methinks, how slow
This old moon wanes! she lingers my desires,
Like to a step-dame or a dowager
Long withering out a young man's revenue.
Hip. Four days will quickly steep themselves in night;
Four nights will quickly dream away the time;
And then the moon, like to a silver bow
New-bent in heaven, shall behold the night
Of our solemnities.
The.   Go, Philostrate, 11
Stir up the Athenian youth to merriments;
Awake the pert and nimble spirit of mirth:

Turn melancholy forth to funerals;
The pale companion is not for our pomp.
                              [*Exit Philostrate.*
Hippolyta, I woo'd thee with my sword,
And won thy love, doing thee injuries;
But I will wed thee in another key,
With pomp, with triumph and with revelling.

Enter EGEUS, HERMIA, LYSANDER, *and* DEMETRIUS.

Ege. Happy be Theseus, our renowned duke!
The. Thanks, good Egeus: what's the news with thee? 21
Ege. Full of vexation come I, with complaint
Against my child, my daughter Hermia.
Stand forth, Demetrius. My noble lord,
This man hath my consent to marry her.
Stand forth, Lysander: and, my gracious duke,
This man hath bewitch'd the bosom of my child:

153

Thou, thou, Lysander, thou hast given her
  rhymes
And interchanged love-tokens with my child:
Thou hast by moonlight at her window sung
With feigning voice verses of feigning love,31
And stolen the impression of her fantasy
With bracelets of thy hair, rings, gawds,
  conceits,
Knacks, trifles, nosegays, sweetmeats, mes-
  sengers
Of strong prevailment in unharden'd youth:
With cunning hast thou filch'd my daugh-
  ter's heart,
Turn'd her obedience, which is due to me,
To stubborn harshness: and, my gracious
  duke,
Be it so she will not here before your grace
Consent to marry with Demetrius,   40
I beg the ancient privilege of Athens,
As she is mine, I may dispose of her:
Which shall be either to this gentleman
Or to her death, according to our law
Immediately provided in that case.
  The. What say you, Hermia? be advised,
    fair maid:
To you your father should be as a god;
One that composed your beauties, yea, and
  one
To whom you are but as a form in wax
By him imprinted and within his power   50
To leave the figure or disfigure it.
Demetrius is a worthy gentleman.
  Her. So is Lysander.
  The.   In himself he is;
But in this kind, wanting your father's voice,
The other must be held the worthier.
  Her. I would my father look'd but with
    my eyes.
  The. Rather your eyes must with his
    judgement look.
  Her. I do entreat your grace to pardon me.
I know not by what power I am made bold,
Nor how it may concern my modesty,   60
In such a presence here to plead my
  thoughts;
But I beseech your grace that I may know
The worst that may befall me in this case,
If I refuse to wed Demetrius.
  The. Either to die the death or to abjure

For ever the society of men.
Therefore, fair Hermia, question your
  desires;
Know of your youth, examine well your
  blood,
Whether, if you yield not to your father's
  choice,
You can endure the livery of a nun,   70
For aye to be in shady cloister mew'd,
To live a barren sister all your life,
Chanting faint hymns to the cold fruitless
  moon.
Thrice-blessed they that master so their
  blood,
To undergo such maiden pilgrimage;
But earthlier happy is the rose distill'd,
Than that which withering on the virgin
  thorn
Grows, lives and dies in single blessedness.
  Her. So will I grow, so live, so die, my
    lord,
Ere I will yield my virgin patent up   80
Unto his lordship, whose unwished yoke
My soul consents not to give sovereignty.
  The. Take time to pause; and, by the next
    new moon—
The sealing-day betwixt my love and me,
For everlasting bond of fellowship—
Upon that day either prepare to die
For disobedience to your father's will,
Or else to wed Demetrius, as he would;
Or on Diana's altar to protest
For aye austerity and single life.   90
  Dem. Relent, sweet Hermia: and, Ly-
    sander, yield
Thy crazed title to my certain right.
  Lys. You have her father's love, Deme-
    trius;
Let me have Hermia's: do you marry him.
  Ege. Scornful Lysander! true, he hath my
    love,
And what is mine my love shall render him.
And she is mine, and all my right of her
I do estate unto Demetrius.
  Lys. I am, my lord, as well derived as he,
As well possess'd; my love is more than
  his;
My fortunes every way as fairly rank'd, 101
If not with vantage, as Demetrius';

And, which is more than all these boasts can
    be,
I am beloved of beauteous Hermia:
Why should not I then prosecute my right?
Demetrius, I'll avouch it to his head,
Made love to Nedar's daughter, Helena,
And won her soul; and she, sweet lady, dotes,
Devoutly dotes, dotes in idolatry,
Upon this spotted and inconstant man.   110
    The. I must confess that I have heard so
    much,
And with Demetrius thought to have spoke
    thereof;
But, being over-full of self-affairs,
My mind did lose it. But, Demetrius, come;
And come, Egeus; you shall go with me,
I have some private schooling for you both.
For you, fair Hermia, look you arm yourself
To fit your fancies to your father's will;
Or else the law of Athens yields you up—
Which by no means we may extenuate—   120
To death, or to a vow of single life.
Come, my Hippolyta: what cheer, my love?
Demetrius and Egeus, go along:
I must employ you in some business
Against our nuptial and confer with you
Of something nearly that concerns your-
    selves.
    Ege. With duty and desire we follow you.
        [*Exeunt all but Lysander and Hermia.*
    Lys. How now, my love! why is your
    cheek so pale?
How chance the roses there do fade so
    fast?
    Her. Belike for want of rain, which I
    could well   130
Beteem them from the tempest of my eyes.
    Lys. Ay me! for aught that I could ever
    read,
Could ever hear by tale or history,
The course of true love never did run
    smooth;
But, either it was different in blood,—
    Her. O cross! too high to be enthrall'd to
    low.
    Lys. Or else misgraffed in respect of
    years,—
    Her. O spite! too old to be engaged to
    young.
    Lys. Or else it stood upon the choice of
    friends,—

    Her. O hell! to choose love by another's
    eyes.   140
    Lys. Or, if there were a sympathy in
    choice,
War, death, or sickness did lay siege to it,
Making it momentany as a sound,
Swift as a shadow, short as any dream;
Brief as the lightning in the collied night,
That, in a spleen, unfolds both heaven and
    earth,
And ere a man hath power to say 'Behold!'
The jaws of darkness do devour it up:
So quick bright things come to confusion.
    Her. If then true lovers have been ever
    cross'd,   150
It stands as an edict in destiny:
Then let us teach our trial patience,
Because it is a customary cross,
As due to love as thoughts and dreams and
    sighs,
Wishes and tears, poor fancy's followers.
    Lys. A good persuasion: therefore, hear
    me, Hermia.
I have a widow aunt, a dowager
Of great revenue, and she hath no child:
From Athens is her house remote seven
    leagues;
And she respects me as her only son.   160
There, gentle Hermia, may I marry thee;
And to that place the sharp Athenian law
Cannot pursue us. If thou lovest me then,
Steal forth thy father's house to-morrow
    night;
And in the wood, a league without the town,
Where I did meet thee once with Helena,
To do observance to a morn of May,
There will I stay for thee.
    Her.   My good Lysander!
I swear to thee, by Cupid's strongest bow,
By his best arrow with the golden head,   170
By the simplicity of Venus' doves,
By that which knitteth souls and prospers
    loves,
And by that fire which burn'd the Carthage
    queen,

---

143. **momentany,** lasting but a moment. 145.
collied, blackened, darkened. 146. **spleen,** violent
passion. 149. **confusion,** ruin, destruction. 155.
fancy's, amorous passion's. 160. **respects,** regards,
considers. 167. **do . . . May,** perform the ceremonies of
May-day. 171-251. **By the simplicity,** etc. The style
here shifts to the rhymed couplet. While Thesus was on
the scene and the business was serious, the play was in
blank verse. The transition indicates the lighter import
of the conversation of the lovers. 173-174. **Carthage
queen, false Troyan.** According to Virgil (*Æneid* iv.)
Dido, queen of Carthage, slew herself after desertion by
the Trojan hero Æneas.

---

106. **avouch . . . head,** declare it to his face. 120.
extenuate, mitigate. 125. **Against,** by the time of.
126. **nearly that,** that closely. 130. **Belike,** very likely.
131. **Beteem,** grant. 137. **misgraffed,** badly matched.

When the false Troyan under sail was seen,
By all the vows that ever men have broke,
In number more than ever women spoke,
In that same place thou hast appointed me,
To-morrow truly will I meet with thee.

Lys. Keep promise, love. Look, here
comes Helena. 179

Enter HELENA.

Her. God speed fair Helena! whither away?

Hel. Call you me fair? that fair again
unsay.
Demetrius loves your fair: O happy fair!
Your eyes are lode-stars; and your tongue's
sweet air
More tuneable than lark to shepherd's ear,
When wheat is green, when hawthorn buds
appear.
Sickness is catching: O, were favour so,
Yours would I catch, fair Hermia, ere I go;
My ear should catch your voice, my eye
your eye,
My tongue should catch your tongue's sweet
melody.
Were the world mine, Demetrius being bated,
The rest I'ld give to be to you translated.191
O, teach me how you look, and with what art
You sway the motion of Demetrius' heart.

Her. I frown upon him, yet he loves me
still.

Hel. O that your frowns would teach my
smiles such skill!

Her. I give him curses, yet he gives me
love.

Hel. O that my prayers could such affection move!

Her. The more I hate, the more he follows
me.

Hel. The more I love, the more he hateth
me.

Her. His folly, Helena, is no fault of mine.

Hel. None, but your beauty: would that
fault were mine! 201

Her. Take comfort: he no more shall see
my face;
Lysander and myself will fly this place.
Before the time I did Lysander see,
Seem'd Athens as a paradise to me:
O, then, what graces in my love do dwell,
That he hath turn'd a heaven unto a hell!

Lys. Helen, to you our minds we will un-
fold:
To-morrow night, when Phœbe doth behold
Her silver visage in the watery glass, 210
Decking with liquid pearl the bladed grass,
A time that lovers' flights doth still conceal,
Through Athens' gates have we devised to
steal.

Her. And in the wood, where often you
and I
Upon faint primrose-beds were wont to lie,
Emptying our bosoms of their counsel sweet,
There my Lysander and myself shall meet;
And thence from Athens turn away our eyes,
To seek new friends and stranger companies.
Farewell, sweet playfellow: pray thou for us;
And good luck grant thee thy Demetrius! 221
Keep word, Lysander: we must starve our
sight
From lovers' food till morrow deep midnight.

Lys. I will, my Hermia. [*Exit Herm.*
Helena, adieu:
As you on him, Demetrius dote on you! [*Exit.*

Hel. How happy some o'er other some
can be!
Through Athens I am thought as fair as she.
But what of that? Demetrius thinks not so;
He will not know what all but he do know:
And as he errs, doting on Hermia's eyes, 230
So I, admiring of his qualities:
Things base and vile, holding no quantity,
Love can transpose to form and dignity:
Love looks not with the eyes, but with the
mind;
And therefore is wing'd Cupid painted blind:
Nor hath Love's mind of any judgement
taste;
Wings and no eyes figure unheedy haste:
And therefore is Love said to be a child,
Because in choice he is so oft beguiled.
As waggish boys in game themselves forswear,
So the boy Love is perjured every where: 241
For ere Demetrius look'd on Hermia's eyne,
He hail'd down oaths that he was only mine;
And when this hail some heat from Hermia
felt,
So he dissolved, and showers of oaths did
melt.
I will go tell him of fair Hermia's flight:
Then to the wood will he to-morrow night
Pursue her; and for this intelligence

---

182. **fair**, beauty. 183. **lode-stars**, stars of guidance. 184. **tuneable**, tuneful. 190. **bated**, excepted. 194-201. **I frown . . . mine.** Each character speaks one line of the dialogue. This artificiality of style is called *stichomythia*; it is characteristic of classical drama.

209. **Phœbe**, Diana, the moon. 215. **faint**, pale. 237. **figure**, are a symbol of. 242. **eyne**, eyes; old form of plural.

If I have thanks, it is a dear expense:
But herein mean I to enrich my pain,   250
To have his sight thither and back again.
                                    [*Exit.*

Scene II. *Athens.* Quince's *house.*

Enter Quince, Snug, Bottom, Flute,
    Snout, *and* Starveling.

Quin. Is all our company here?

Bot. You were best to call them generally,
man by man, according to the scrip.

Quin. Here is the scroll of every man's
name, which is thought fit, through all Athens,
to play in our interlude before the duke and
the duchess, on his wedding-day at night.

Bot. First, good Peter Quince, say what
the play treats on, then read the names of the
actors, and so grow to a point.   10

Quin. Marry, our play is, The most lamentable comedy, and most cruel death of
Pyramus and Thisby.

Bot. A very good piece of work, I assure
you, and a merry. Now, good Peter Quince,
call forth your actors by the scroll. Masters,
spread yourselves.

Quin. Answer as I call you. Nick Bottom,
the weaver.

Bot. Ready. Name what part I am for,
and proceed.   21

Quin. You, Nick Bottom, are set down
for Pyramus.

Bot. What is Pyramus? a lover, or a tyrant?

Quin. A lover, that kills himself most
gallant for love.

Bot. That will ask some tears in the true
performing of it: if I do it, let the audience
look to their eyes; I will move storms, I will
condole in some measure. To the rest: 29
yet my chief humour is for a tyrant: I could
play Ercles rarely, or a part to tear a cat
in, to make all split.

> The raging rocks
>   And shivering shocks
> Shall break the locks
>   Of prison gates;

And Phibbus' car
    Shall shine from far
And make and mar
        The foolish Fates.   40

This was lofty! Now name the rest of the
players. This is Ercles' vein, a tyrant's vein;
a lover is more condoling.

Quin. Francis Flute, the bellows-mender.

Flu. Here, Peter Quince.

Quin. Flute, you must take Thisby on you.

Flu. What is Thisby? a wandering knight?

Quin. It is the lady that Pyramus must
love.

Flu. Nay, faith, let not me play a woman;
I have a beard coming.   50

Quin. That's all one: you shall play it in
a mask, and you may speak as small as you
will.

Bot. An I may hide my face, let me play
Thisby too, I'll speak in a monstrous little
voice, 'Thisne, Thisne;' 'Ah Pyramus, my
lover dear! thy Thisby dear, and lady dear!'

Quin. No, no; you must play Pyramus:
and, Flute, you Thisby.

Bot. Well, proceed.

Quin. Robin Starveling, the tailor.   60

Star. Here, Peter Quince.

Quin. Robin Starveling, you must play
Thisby's mother. Tom Snout, the tinker.

Snout. Here, Peter Quince.

Quin. You, Pyramus' father: myself,
Thisby's father. Snug, the joiner; you, the
lion's part: and, I hope, here is a play fitted.

Snug. Have you the lion's part written?
pray you, if it be, give it to me, for I am
slow of study.   70

Quin. You may do it extempore, for it is
nothing but roaring.

Bot. Let me play the lion too: I will roar,
that I will do any man's heart good to hear
me; I will roar, that I will make the duke
say 'Let him roar again, let him roar again.'

Quin. An you should do it too terribly,
you would fright the duchess and the ladies,
that they would shriek; and that were
enough to hang us all.

All. That would hang us, every mother's
son.   80

Bot. I grant you, friends, if that you should
fright the ladies out of their wits, they would
have no more discretion but to hang us: but

---

249. **a dear expense,** a thing for which I shall pay
dearly.
  Scene ii. 2. **generally,** Bottom's blunder for *severally.*
3. **scrip,** writing, written list. 10. **grow to,** come to.
29. **condole,** grieve; here in some blundering sense.
31. **Ercles,** Hercules, a popular character in Tudor
drama. From Seneca's *Hercules Furens* had come the
tradition of ranting in this part, as in the case of Herod
in the mystery plays. **tear a cat,** proverbial for "rant."
32. **make all split,** proverbial for "cause a commotion."

37. **Phibbus',** Phœbus'. 47. **wandering knight,**
knight-errant. 54. **An,** if.

I will aggravate my voice so that I will roar you as gently as any sucking dove; I will roar you as 'twere any nightingale.   86

Quin. Ycu can play no part but Pyramus; for Pyramus is a sweet-faced man; a proper man, as one shall see in a summer's day; a most lovely gentleman-like man: therefore you must needs play Pyramus.   91

Bot. Well, I will undertake it. What beard were I best to play it in?

Quin. Why, what you will.

Bot. I will discharge it in either your straw-colour beard, your orange-tawny beard, your purple-in-grain beard, or your French-crown-colour beard, your perfect yellow.   98

Quin. Some of your French crowns have no hair at all, and then you will play bare-faced. But, masters, here are your parts: and I am to entreat you, request you and desire you, to con them by to-morrow night; and meet me in the palace wood, a mile without the town, by moonlight; there will we re-hearse, for if we meet in the city, we shall be dogged with company, and our devices 107 known. In the meantime I will draw a bill of properties, such as our play wants. I pray you, fail me not.

Bot. We will meet; and there we may re-hearse most obscenely and courageously. Take pains; be perfect: adieu.   112

Quin. At the duke's oak we meet.

Bot. Enough; hold or cut bow-strings.
                                        [*Exeunt.*

ACT II.

SCENE I. *A wood near Athens.*

Enter, from opposite sides, a Fairy, *and* Puck.

Puck. How now, spirit! whither wander you?

Fai. Over hill, over dale,
          Thorough bush, thorough brier,
     Over park, over pale,
          Thorough flood, thorough fire,
I do wander every where,
Swifter than the moon's sphere;

And I serve the fairy queen,
To dew her orbs upon the green.
The cowslips tall her pensioners be: 10
In their gold coats spots you see;
Those be rubies, fairy favours,
In those freckles live their savours:
I must go seek some dewdrops here
And hang a pearl in every cowslip's ear.
Farewell, thou lob of spirits; I'll be gone:
Our queen and all her elves come here anon.

Puck. The king doth keep his revels here to-night:
Take heed the queen come not within his sight;
For Oberon is passing fell and wrath,   20
Because that she as her attendant hath
A lovely boy, stolen from an Indian king;
She never had so sweet a changeling;
And jealous Oberon would have the child
Knight of his train, to trace the forests wild;
But she perforce withholds the loved boy,
Crowns him with flowers and makes him all her joy:
And now they never meet in grove or green,
By fountain clear, or spangled starlight sheen,
But they do square, that all their elves for fear
Creep into acorn-cups and hide them there.31

Fai. Either I mistake your shape and making quite,
Or else you are that shrewd and knavish sprite
Call'd Robin Goodfellow: are not you he
That frights the maidens of the villagery;
Skim milk, and sometimes labour in the quern
And bootless make the breathless housewife churn;
And sometime make the drink to bear no barm;
Mislead night-wanderers, laughing at their harm?
Those that Hobgoblin call you and sweet Puck,
You do their work, and they shall have good luck: 41
Are not you he?

---

84. **aggravate**, Bottom's blunder for *diminish*. 88. **proper**, handsome. 95. **discharge**, perform. 97. **purple-in-grain**, very deep red. **French-crown-colour**, color of a French crown; a gold coin. 103. **con**, learn by heart. 107. **devices**, things devised for dramatic presentation. 111. **obscenely**, Bottom's blunder for *obscurely*(?) 114. **hold . . . bow-strings**, an archer's expression not definitely explained, but easy to understand; Chambers suggests, "keep your promises, or give up the play."

9. **orbs**, fairy rings. 10. **pensioners**, bodyguards of the sovereign; possible allusion to Queen Elizabeth's fifty gentlemen pensioners. 13. **savours**, sweet smells. 16. **lob**, country bumpkin. 20. **passing fell**, exceedingly angry. **wrath**, wrathful. 23. **changeling**, child left by fairies in exchange for one stolen; here, the stolen child. 30. **square**, quarrel. 33. **shrewd**, mischievous. 34. **Robin Goodfellow**, a mischievous household spirit of very ancient folklore; Shakespeare associates him with fairies. 35. **villagery**, villages or villagers collectively. 36. **quern**, handmill. 38. **barm**, yeast.

Puck.   Thou speak'st aright;
I am that merry wanderer of the night.
I jest to Oberon and make him smile
When I a fat and bean-fed horse beguile,
Neighing in likeness of a filly foal:
And sometime lurk I in a gossip's bowl,
In very likeness of a roasted crab,
And when she drinks, against her lips I bob
And on her wither'd dewlap pour the ale. 50
The wisest aunt, telling the saddest tale,
Sometime for three-foot stool mistaketh me;
Then slip I from her bum, down topples she,
And 'tailor' cries, and falls into a cough;
And then the whole quire hold their hips and
     laugh,
And waxen in their mirth and neeze and
     swear
A merrier hour was never wasted there.
But, room, fairy! here comes Oberon.
Fai. And here my mistress. Would that
     he were gone!

Enter, from one side, OBERON, *with his train;
from the other,* TITANIA, *with hers.*

Obe. Ill met by moonlight, proud Titania.
Tita. What, jealous Oberon! Fairies, skip
     hence: 61
I have forsworn his bed and company.
Obe. Tarry, rash wanton: am not I thy
     lord?
Tita. Then I must be thy lady: but I
     know
When thou hast stolen away from fairy land,
And in the shape of Corin sat all day,
Playing on pipes of corn and versing love
To amorous Phillida. Why art thou here,
Come from the farthest steppe of India?
But that, forsooth, the bouncing Amazon,
Your buskin'd mistress and your warrior
     love,   71
To Theseus must be wedded, and you come
To give their bed joy and prosperity.
Obe. How canst thou thus for shame,
     Titania,
Glance at my credit with Hippolyta,
Knowing I know thy love to Theseus?
Didst thou not lead him through the glim-
     mering night

From Perigenia, whom he ravished?
And make him with fair Ægle break his faith,
With Ariadne and Antiopa?   80
Tita. These are the forgeries of jealousy:
And never, since the middle summer's spring,
Met we on hill, in dale, forest or mead,
By paved fountain or by rushy brook,
Or in the beached margent of the sea,
To dance our ringlets to the whistling wind,
But with thy brawls thou hast disturb'd our
     sport.
Therefore the winds, piping to us in vain,
As in revenge, have suck'd up from the sea
Contagious fogs; which falling in the land 90
Have every pelting river made so proud
That they have overborne their continents:
The ox hath therefore stretch'd his yoke in
     vain,
The ploughman lost his sweat, and the green
     corn
Hath rotted ere his youth attain'd a beard;
The fold stands empty in the drowned field,
And crows are fatted with the murrion flock;
The nine men's morris is fill'd up with mud,
And the quaint mazes in the wanton green
For lack of tread are undistinguishable: 100
The human mortals want their winter here;
No night is now with hymn or carol blest:
Therefore the moon, the governess of floods,
Pale in her anger, washes all the air,
That rheumatic diseases do abound:
And thorough this distemperature we see
The seasons alter: hoary-headed frosts
Fall in the fresh lap of the crimson rose,
And on old Hiems' thin and icy crown 109
An odorous chaplet of sweet summer buds
Is, as in mockery, set: the spring, the sum-
     mer,
The childing autumn, angry winter, change
Their wonted liveries, and the mazed world,

78. **Perigenia**, Perigouna (Grant White), daughter of
the robber Sinnis; story from Plutarch. 79. **Ægle**, a
nymph beloved by Theseus, for whom he deserted
Ariadne; QF: *Eagles*, corrected by Rowe; form should be
Ægles as in Plutarch's *Life of Theseus*, from which
Shakespeare took the names in this passage. 80. **Ariadne**, daughter of Minos, king of Crete; by her aid
Theseus slew the Minotaur and escaped from the labyrinth. **Antiopa**, queen of the Amazons and wife of
Theseus, elsewhere called Hippolyta. 82. **middle
summer's spring**, beginning of midsummer. 85. **in**,
on. 86. **ringlets**. See *orbs* above, line 9. 91. **pelting**,
paltry. 92. **continents**, i.e., banks that contain them.
97. **murrion**, murrain (plague); here, diseased. 98.
nine men's morris, rustic game played on a board or
squares laid out on the village green with nine pebbles
or pegs. 99. **mazes**, figures marked out on the village
green for sports. **wanton**, luxuriant or sportive. 101.
want, lack. 106. **thorough**, through. **distemperature**, ill humor; also, bad weather. 109. **Hiems'**.
Hiems is the god of winter. 112. **childing**, fruitful.
113. **mazed**, bewildered.

47. **gossip's bowl**, drink of gossiping women. 48.
crab, crab apple. 50. **dewlap**, loose skin on neck. 51.
aunt, old woman. 54. **'tailor' cries**, allusion obscure;
N.E.D. suggests that *tailor* (corruption of *tailard*),
means "one with a tail." 56. **neeze**, sneeze. 66-68.
Corin . . . Phillida, names of pastoral lovers. 69.
steppe; so Q; better F: *steep*, mountain range. 71.
buskin'd, shod with half-boots. 75. **Glance at**, hit at,
reflect upon.

By their increase, now knows not which is
   which:
And this same progeny of evils comes
From our debate, from our dissension;
We are their parents and original.
  Obe. Do you amend it then; it lies in you:
Why should Titania cross her Oberon?
I do but beg a little changeling boy,   120
To be my henchman.
  Tita.   Set your heart at rest:
The fairy land buys not the child of me.
His mother was a votaress of my order:
And, in the spiced Indian air, by night,
Full often hath she gossip'd by my side,
And sat with me on Neptune's yellow sands,
Marking the embarked traders on the flood,
When we have laugh'd to see the sails con-
   ceive
And grow big-bellied with the wanton wind;
Which she, with pretty and with swimming
   gait   130
Following,—her womb then rich with my
   young squire,—
Would imitate, and sail upon the land,
To fetch me trifles, and return again,
As from a voyage, rich with merchandise.
But she, being mortal, of that boy did die;
And for her sake do I rear up her boy,
And for her sake I will not part with him.
  Obe. How long within this wood intend
   you stay?
  Tita. Perchance till after Theseus' wed-
   ding-day.
If you will patiently dance in our round 140
And see our moonlight revels, go with us;
If not, shun me, and I will spare your haunts.
  Obe. Give me that boy, and I will go with
   thee.
  Tita. Not for thy fairy kingdom. Fairies,
   away!
We shall chide downright, if I longer stay.
          [*Exit Titania with her train.*
  Obe. Well, go thy way: thou shalt not
   from this grove
Till I torment thee for this injury.
My gentle Puck, come hither. Thou re-
   memberest
Since once I sat upon a promontory,
And heard a mermaid on a dolphin's back 150

Uttering such dulcet and harmonious breath
That the rude sea grew civil at her song
And certain stars shot madly from their
   spheres,
To hear the sea-maid's music.
  Puck.   I remember.
  Obe. That very time I saw, but thou
   couldst not,
Flying between the cold moon and the earth,
Cupid all arm'd: a certain aim he took
At a fair vestal throned by the west,
And loosed his love-shaft smartly from his
   bow,
As it should pierce a hundred thousand
   hearts;   160
But I might see young Cupid's fiery shaft
Quench'd in the chaste beams of the watery
   moon,
And the imperial votaress passed on,
In maiden meditation, fancy-free.
Yet mark'd I where the bolt of Cupid fell:
It fell upon a little western flower,
Before milk-white, now purple with love's
   wound,
And maidens call it love-in-idleness.
Fetch me that flower; the herb I shew'd thee
   once:
The juice of it on sleeping eye-lids laid   170
Will make or man or woman madly dote
Upon the next live creature that it sees.
Fetch me this herb; and be thou here again
Ere the leviathan can swim a league.
  Puck. I'll put a girdle round about the
   earth
In forty minutes.   [*Exit.*
  Obe.   Having once this juice,
I'll watch Titania when she is asleep,
And drop the liquor of it in her eyes.
The next thing then she waking looks upon,
Be it on lion, bear, or wolf, or bull,   180
On meddling monkey, or on busy ape,
She shall pursue it with the soul of love:
And ere I take this charm from off her sight,
As I can take it with another herb,
I'll make her render up her page to me.
But who comes here? I am invisible;
And I will overhear their conference.

  Enter DEMETRIUS, HELENA *following him.*

  Dem. I love thee not, therefore pursue me
   not.

---

117. **original**, origin. 121. **henchman**, attendant,
page. 148-168. **Thou . . . love-in-idleness.** This
famous passage contains an allusion to Queen Elizabeth
and probably to some entertainment in her honor at
Kenilworth in 1575, or more probably at Elvetham in
1591; see *Introduction.*

151. **breath**, voice, notes. 157, **all**, fully. 168.
love-in-idleness, pansy, heartsease. 176. **forty**, used
indefinitely.

Where is Lysander and fair Hermia?
The one I'll slay, the other slayeth me. 190
Thou told'st me they were stolen unto this
    wood;
And here am I, and wode within this wood,
Because I cannot meet my Hermia.
Hence, get thee gone, and follow me no more.
    Hel. You draw me, you hard-hearted ada-
    mant;
But yet you draw not iron, for my heart
Is true as steel: leave you your power to
    draw,
And I shall have no power to follow you.
    Dem. Do I entice you? do I speak you
    fair?
Or, rather, do I not in plainest truth   200
Tell you, I do not, nor I cannot love you?
    Hel. And even for that do I love you the
    more.
I am your spaniel; and, Demetrius,
The more you beat me, I will fawn on you:
Use me but as your spaniel, spurn me, strike
    me,
Neglect me, lose me; only give me leave,
Unworthy as I am, to follow you.
What worser place can I beg in your love,—
And yet a place of high respect with me,—
Than to be used as you use your dog?   210
    Dem. Tempt not too much the hatred of
    my spirit,
For I am sick when I do look on thee.
    Hel. And I am sick when I look not on
    you.
    Dem. You do impeach your modesty too
    much,
To leave the city and commit yourself
Into the hands of one that loves you not;
To trust the opportunity of night
And the ill counsel of a desert place
With the rich worth of your virginity.
    Hel. Your virtue is my privilege: for that
It is not night when I do see your face, 221
Therefore I think I am not in the night;
Nor doth this wood lack worlds of company,
For you in my respect are all the world:
Then how can it be said I am alone,
When all the world is here to look on me?
    Dem. I'll run from thee and hide me in
    the brakes,
And leave thee to the mercy of wild beasts.

    Hel. The wildest hath not such a heart as
    you.
Run when you will, the story shall be
    changed: 230
Apollo flies, and Daphne holds the chase;
The dove pursues the griffin; the mild hind
Makes speed to catch the tiger; bootless
    speed,
When cowardice pursues and valour flies.
    Dem. I will not stay thy questions; let me
    go:
Or, if thou follow me, do not believe
But I shall do thee mischief in the wood.
    Hel. Ay, in the temple, in the town, the
    field,
You do me mischief. Fie, Demetrius!
Your wrongs do set a scandal on my sex:
We cannot fight for love, as men may do; 241
We should be woo'd and were not made to
    woo.   [*Exit Dem.*
I'll follow thee and make a heaven of hell,
To die upon the hand I love so well. [*Exit.*
    Obe. Fare thee well, nymph: ere he do
    leave this grove,
Thou shalt fly him and he shall seek thy love.

            Re-enter PUCK.

Hast thou the flower there? Welcome,
    wanderer.   247
    Puck. Ay, there it is.
    Obe.   I pray thee, give it me.
I know a bank where the wild thyme blows,
Where oxlips and the nodding violet grows,
†Quite over-canopied with luscious woodbine,
With sweet musk-roses and with eglantine:
There sleeps Titania sometime of the night,
Lull'd in these flowers with dances and de-
    light;
And there the snake throws her enamell'd
    skin,
Weed wide enough to wrap a fairy in:
And with the juice of this I'll streak her eyes,
And make her full of hateful fantasies.
Take thou some of it, and seek through this
    grove:
A sweet Athenian lady is in love   260
With a disdainful youth: anoint his eyes;

---

192. **wode**, mad; usual form, *wood.* 195. **ada-**
mant, very hard stone; here lode-stone. 197. **leave**,
give up. 220. **privilege**, safeguard. **for that**, because.
224. **in my respect**, as far as I am concerned.

231. **Apollo . . . chase**, allusion to the story of
Apollo's pursuit of Daphne; here Daphne *holds the*
chase, or pursues, instead of Apollo. 232. **griffin**,
a fabulous monster with the head of an eagle and the
body of a lion. **hind**, female of the red deer. 235.
questions, talk or argument. 244. **upon**, by. 250.
oxlips, flowers resembling cowslip and primrose. 251.
woodbine, honeysuckle. 252. **eglantine**, sweet-briar.
254. **dances and delight**, delightful dances. 256.
Weed, garment. 257. **streak**, stroke, touch softly.

But do it when the next thing he espies
May be the lady: thou shalt know the man
By the Athenian garments he hath on.   264
Effect it with some care that he may prove
More fond on her than she upon her love:
And look thou meet me ere the first cock
 crow.
 Puck. Fear not, my lord, your servant
shall do so.   [*Exeunt.*

SCENE II. *Another part of the wood.*

Enter TITANIA, *with her train.*

 Tita. Come, now a roundel and a fairy
 song;
Then, for the third part of a minute, hence;
Some to kill cankers in the musk-rose buds,
Some war with rere-mice for their leathern
 wings,
To make my small elves coats, and some
 keep back
The clamorous owl that nightly hoots and
 wonders
At our quaint spirits. Sing me now asleep;
Then to your offices and let me rest.

The Fairies sing.

You spotted snakes with double tongue,
 Thorny hedgehogs, be not seen;   10
Newts and blind-worms, do no wrong,
 Come not near our fairy queen.
Philomel, with melody
 Sing in our sweet lullaby;
Lulla, lulla, lullaby, lulla, lulla, lullaby:
 Never harm,
 Nor spell nor charm,
Come our lovely lady nigh;
So, good night, with lullaby.
Weaving spiders, come not here;   20

 Hence, you long-legg'd spinners, hence!
Beetles black, approach not near;
 Worm nor snail, do no offence.
 Philomel, with melody, &c.

A Fairy. Hence, away! now all is well:
 One aloof stand sentinel.
   [*Exeunt Fairies. Titania sleeps.*

Enter OBERON, *and squeezes the flower on
Titania's eyelids.*

 Obe. What thou seest when thou dost wake,
Do it for thy true-love take,
Love and languish for his sake:
Be it ounce, or cat, or bear,   30
Pard, or boar with bristled hair,
In thy eye that shall appear
When thou wakest, it is thy dear:
Wake when some vile thing is near.
      [*Exit.*

Enter LYSANDER *and* HERMIA.

 Lys. Fair love, you faint with wandering in
 the wood;
And to speak troth, I have forgot our way:
We'll rest us, Hermia, if you think it good,
And tarry for the comfort of the day.
 Her. Be it so, Lysander: find you out a bed;
For I upon this bank will rest my head.   40
 Lys. One turf shall serve as pillow for us
 both;
One heart, one bed, two bosoms and one
 troth.
 Her. Nay, good Lysander; for my sake,
 my dear,
Lie further off yet, do not lie so near.
 Lys. O, take the sense, sweet, of my in-
 nocence!
Love takes the meaning in love's conference.
I mean, that my heart unto yours is knit
So that but one heart we can make of it;
Two bosoms interchained with an oath;
So then two bosoms and a single troth.   50
Then by your side no bed-room me deny;
For lying so, Hermia, I do not lie.
 Her. Lysander riddles very prettily:
Now much beshrew my manners and my
 pride,
If Hermia meant to say Lysander lied.
But, gentle friend, for love and courtesy
Lie further off; in human modesty,
Such separation as may well be said
Becomes a virtuous bachelor and a maid,
So far be distant; and, good night, sweet
 friend: 60
Thy love ne'er alter till thy sweet life end!
 Lys. Amen, amen, to that fair prayer,
 say I;
And then end life when I end loyalty!
Here is my bed: sleep give thee all his rest!
 Her. With half that wish the wisher's eyes
 be press'd!   [*They sleep.*

Enter Puck.

Puck. Through the forest have I gone,
But Athenian found I none,
On whose eyes I might approve
This flower's force in stirring love.
Night and silence.—Who is here? 70
Weeds of Athens he doth wear:
This is he, my master said,
Despised the Athenian maid;
And here the maiden, sleeping sound,
On the dank and dirty ground.
Pretty soul! she durst not lie
Near this lack-love, this kill-
    courtesy.
Churl, upon thy eyes I throw
All the power this charm doth owe.
When thou wakest, let love forbid
Sleep his seat on thy eyelid: 81
So awake when I am gone;
For I must now to Oberon. [*Exit.*

Enter Demetrius *and* Helena, *running.*

Hel. Stay, though thou kill me, sweet De-
    metrius.
Dem. I charge thee, hence, and do not
    haunt me thus.
Hel. O, wilt thou darkling leave me? do
    not so.
Dem. Stay, on thy peril: I alone will go.
    [*Exit.*
Hel. O, I am out of breath in this fond
    chase!
The more my prayer, the lesser is my grace.
Happy is Hermia, wheresoe'er she lies; 90
For she hath blessed and attractive eyes.
How came her eyes so bright? Not with salt
    tears:
If so, my eyes are oftener wash'd than hers.
No, no, I am as ugly as a bear;
For beasts that meet me run away for fear:
Therefore no marvel though Demetrius
Do, as a monster, fly my presence thus. 97
What wicked and dissembling glass of mine
Made me compare with Hermia's sphery eyne?
But who is here? Lysander! on the ground!
Dead? or asleep? I see no blood, no wound.
Lysander, if you live, good sir, awake.
Lys. [*Awaking*] And run through fire I
    will for thy sweet sake.

Transparent Helena! Nature shows art,
That through thy bosom makes me see thy
    heart.
Where is Demetrius? O, how fit a word
Is that vile name to perish on my sword!
Hel. Do not say so, Lysander; say not
    so.
What though he love your Hermia? Lord,
    what though? 109
Yet Hermia still loves you: then be content.
Lys. Content with Hermia! No; I do
    repent
The tedious minutes I with her have spent.
Not Hermia but Helena I love:
Who will not change a raven for a dove?
The will of man is by his reason sway'd;
And reason says you are the worthier maid.
Things growing are not ripe until their sea-
    son:
So I, being young, till now ripe not to rea-
    son;
And touching now the point of human skill,
Reason becomes the marshal to my will 120
And leads me to your eyes, where I o'erlook
Love's stories written in love's richest book.
Hel. Wherefore was I to this keen mock-
    ery born?
When at your hands did I deserve this scorn?
Is 't not enough, is 't not enough, young man,
That I did never, no, nor never can,
Deserve a sweet look from Demetrius' eye,
But you must flout my insufficiency?
Good troth, you do me wrong, good sooth,
    you do,
In such disdainful manner me to woo. 130
But fare you well: perforce I must confess
I thought you lord of more true gentleness.
O, that a lady, of one man refused,
Should of another therefore be abused! [*Exit.*
Lys. She sees not Hermia. Hermia, sleep
    thou there:
And never mayst thou come Lysander near!
For as a surfeit of the sweetest things
The deepest loathing to the stomach brings,
Or as the heresies that men do leave
Are hated most of those they did deceive, 140
So thou, my surfeit and my heresy,
Of all be hated, but the most of me!
And, all my powers, address your love and
    might
To honour Helen and to be her knight!
    [*Exit.*

---

68. **approve**, prove. 71. **Weeds**, clothes. 79. **owe**,
own. 86. **darkling**, in the dark. 88. **fond**, foolish.
89. **grace**, favor I obtain. 99. **sphery eyne**, starlike
eyes. 103. **run through fire**, proverbial for any hard
task.

118. **ripe**, usually understood as a verb in this passage meaning "grow ripe."

Her. [*Awaking*] Help me, Lysander, help me! do thy best

To pluck this crawling serpent from my breast!

Ay me, for pity! what a dream was here!

Lysander, look how I do quake with fear:

Methought a serpent eat my heart away,

And you sat smiling at his cruel prey.   150

Lysander! what, removed? Lysander! lord!

What, out of hearing? gone? no sound, no word?

Alack, where are you? speak, an if you hear;

Speak, of all loves! I swoon almost with fear.

No? then I well perceive you are not nigh:

Either death or you I'll find immediately.

                   [*Exit.*

ACT III.

SCENE I. *The wood. Titania lying asleep.*

Enter QUINCE, SNUG, BOTTOM, FLUTE, SNOUT, *and* STARVELING.

Bot. Are we all met?

Quin. Pat, pat; and here's a marvellous convenient place for our rehearsal. This green plot shall be our stage, this hawthorn-brake our tiring-house; and we will do it in action as we will do it before the duke.   6

Bot. Peter Quince,—

Quin. What sayest thou, bully Bottom?

Bot. There are things in this comedy of Pyramus and Thisby that will never please. First, Pyramus must draw a sword to kill himself; which the ladies cannot abide. How answer you that?   13

Snout. By'r lakin, a parlous fear.

Star. I believe we must leave the killing out, when all is done.

Bot. Not a whit: I have a device to make all well. Write me a prologue; and let the prologue seem to say, we will do no harm with our swords and that Pyramus is not killed indeed; and, for the more better assurance, tell them that I Pyramus am not Pyramus, but Bottom the weaver: this will put them out of fear.

Quin. Well, we will have such a prologue; and it shall be written in eight and six.   25

Bot. No, make it two more; let it be written in eight and eight.

Snout. Will not the ladies be afeard of the lion?

Star. I fear it, I promise you.   29

Bot. Masters, you ought to consider with yourselves: to bring in—God shield us!—a lion among ladies, is a most dreadful thing; for there is not a more fearful wild-fowl than your lion living; and we ought to look to't.

Snout. Therefore another prologue must tell he is not a lion.   36

Bot. Nay, you must name his name, and half his face must be seen through the lion's neck: and he himself must speak through, saying thus, or to the same defect,—'Ladies,' —or 'Fair ladies,—I would wish you,'—or 'I would request you,'—or 'I would entreat you,—not to fear, not to tremble: my life for yours. If you think I come hither as a lion, it were pity of my life: no, I am no such thing; I am a man as other men are;' and there indeed let him name his name, and tell them plainly he is Snug the joiner.

Quin. Well, it shall be so. But there is two hard things; that is, to bring the moonlight into a chamber; for, you know, Pyramus and Thisby meet by moonlight.   51

Snout. Doth the moon shine that night we play our play?

Bot. A calendar, a calendar! look in the almanac; find out moonshine, find out moonshine.

Quin. Yes, it doth shine that night.

Bot. Why, then may you leave a casement of the great chamber window, where we play, open, and the moon may shine in at the casement.   59

Quin. Ay; or else one must come in with a bush of thorns and a lanthorn, and say he comes to disfigure, or to present, the person of Moonshine. Then, there is another thing: we must have a wall in the great chamber; for Pyramus and Thisby, says the story, did talk through the chink of a wall.

Snout. You can never bring in a wall. What say you, Bottom?   68

---

150. prey, act of preying upon. **154. of all loves,** for all love's sake.
Act III. Scene i. **5. tiring-house,** dressing room. **8. bully,** term of companionship. **14. By'r lakin,** by our ladykin, i.e., the Virgin. **parlous,** perilous. **25. eight and six,** alternate lines of eight and six syllables, ballad measure.

32. lion among ladies. Malone called attention to a pamphlet (*Somers' Tracts*, ii, 179) which tells how at the christening of Prince Henry, eldest son of King James I, then James VI of Scotland, a "blackmoor" instead of a lion drew the triumphal chariot, since the lion's presence might have "brought some fear to the nearest." This circumstance has been used in the interpretation of the allegory; see *Introduction.* **40. defect,** Bottom's blunder for *effect.* **44. pity of my life,** sad thing for me. **62. disfigure,** blunder for *prefigure.*

Bot. Some man or other must present Wall: and let him have some plaster, or some loam, or some rough-cast about 71 him, to signify wall; and let him hold his fingers thus, and through that cranny shall Pyramus and Thisby whisper.

Quin. If that may be, then all is well. Come, sit down, every mother's son, and rehearse your parts. Pyramus, you begin: when you have spoken your speech, enter into that brake: and so every one according to his cue.

Enter Puck *behind.*

Puck. What hempen home-spuns have we swaggering here,
So near the cradle of the fairy queen?   80
What, a play toward! I'll be an auditor;
An actor too perhaps, if I see cause.

Quin. Speak, Pyramus. Thisby, stand forth.

Bot. Thisby, the flowers of odious savours sweet,—

Quin. Odours, odours.

Bot. —— odours savours sweet:
So hath thy breath, my dearest Thisby dear.
But hark, a voice! stay thou but here awhile,
And by and by I will to thee appear. [*Exit.*

Puck. A stranger Pyramus than e'er played here.   [*Exit.*

Flu. Must I speak now?   91

Quin. Ay, marry, must you; for you must understand he goes but to see a noise that he heard, and is to come again.

Flu. Most radiant Pyramus, most lily-white of hue,
Of colour like the red rose on triumphant brier,
Most brisky juvenal and eke most lovely Jew,
As true as truest horse that yet would never tire.   98
I'll meet thee, Pyramus, at Ninny's tomb.

Quin. 'Ninus' tomb,' man: why, you must not speak that yet; that you answer to Pyramus: you speak all your part at once, cues and all. Pyramus enter: your cue is past; it is, 'never tire.'

Flu. O,—As true as truest horse, that yet would never tire.

Re-enter Puck, *and* Bottom *with an ass's head.*

Bot. If I were fair, Thisby, I were only thine.

Quin. O monstrous! O strange! we are haunted. Pray, masters! fly, masters! Help!
[*Exeunt Quince, Snug, Flute, Snout, and Starveling.*

Puck. I'll follow you, I'll lead you about a round,
Through bog, through bush, through brake, through brier: 110
Sometime a horse I'll be, sometime a hound,
A hog, a headless bear, sometime a fire;
And neigh, and bark, and grunt, and roar, and burn,
Like horse, hound, hog, bear, fire, at every turn.   [*Exit.*

Bot. Why do they run away? this is a knavery of them to make me afeard.

Re-enter Snout.

Snout. O Bottom, thou art changed! what do I see on thee?

Bot. What do you see? you see an ass-head of your own, do you?   [*Exit Snout.*

Re-enter Quince.

Quin. Bless thee, Bottom! bless thee! thou art translated.   [*Exit.* 122

Bot. I see their knavery: this is to make an ass of me; to fright me, if they could. But I will not stir from this place, do what they can: I will walk up and down here, and I will sing, that they shall hear I am not afraid.   [*Sings.*

The ousel cock so black of hue,
    With orange-tawny bill,
The throstle with his note so true,   130
    The wren with little quill,—

Tita. [*Awakening*] What angel wakes me from my flowery bed?

Bot. [*Sings.*]
The finch, the sparrow and the lark,
    The plain-song cuckoo gray,
Whose note full many a man doth mark,
    And dares not answer nay;—
for, indeed, who would set his wit to so foolish a bird? who would give a bird the lie, though he cry 'cuckoo' never so?

---

71. **rough-cast,** coarse plaster for the outside of buildings. 81. **toward,** about to take place. 97. **brisky juvenal,** brisk juvenile or youth. **Jew,** probably an absurd repetition of the first syllable of *juvenal.* 100. 'Ninus,' mythical founder of Babylon, at which place the scene of the story of Pyramus and Thisbe is laid.

106. *Stage Direction:* F has *Enter Pyramus with the Asse head,* a form of statement which indicates one particular stage property. 122. **translated,** transformed. 128. **ousel,** blackbird. 134. **plain-song,** melody without variations; adjective.

Tita. I pray thee, gentle mortal, sing
again: 140
Mine ear is much enamour'd of thy note;
So is mine eye enthralled to thy shape;
And thy fair virtue's force perforce doth
move me
On the first view to say, to swear, I love thee.
Bot. Methinks, mistress, you should have
little reason for that: and yet, to say the
truth, reason and love keep little company
together now-a-days; the more the pity
that some honest neighbours will not make
them friends. Nay, I can gleek upon
occasion. 150
Tita. Thou art as wise as thou art beautiful.
Bot. Not so, neither: but if I had wit
enough to get out of this wood, I have
enough to serve mine own turn.
Tita. Out of this wood do not desire to go:
Thou shalt remain here, whether thou wilt
or no.
I am a spirit of no common rate:
The summer still doth tend upon my state;
And I do love thee: therefore, go with me;
I'll give thee fairies to attend on thee, 160
And they shall fetch thee jewels from the
deep,
And sing while thou on pressed flowers dost
sleep:
And I will purge thy mortal grossness so
That thou shalt like an airy spirit go.
Peaseblossom! Cobweb! Moth! and Mus-
tardseed!

Enter Peaseblossom, Cobweb, Moth, *and*
Mustardseed.

Peas. Ready.
Cob. And I.
Moth. And I.
Mus. And I.
All. Where shall we go?
Tita. Be kind and courteous to this gen-
tleman;
Hop in his walks and gambol in his eyes;
Feed him with apricocks and dewberries,
With purple grapes, green figs, and mul-
berries; 170
The honey-bags steal from the humble-bees,
And for night-tapers crop their waxen thighs
And light them at the fiery glow-worm's
eyes,
To have my love to bed and to arise;

And pluck the wings from painted butterflies
To fan the moonbeams from his sleeping
eyes:
Nod to him, elves, and do him courtesies.
Peas. Hail, mortal!
Cob. Hail!
Moth. Hail! 180
Mus. Hail!
Bot. I cry your worships mercy, heartily:
I beseech your worship's name.
Cob. Cobweb.
Bot. I shall desire you of more acquaint-
ance, good Master Cobweb: if I cut my fin-
ger, I shall make bold with you. Your name,
honest gentleman?
Peas. Peaseblossom. 189
Bot. I pray you, commend me to Mistress
Squash, your mother, and to Master Peas-
cod, your father. Good Master Pease-
blossom, I shall desire you of more ac-
quaintance too. Your name, I beseech
you, sir?
Mus. Mustardseed. 195
Bot. Good Master Mustardseed, I know
your patience well: that same cowardly,
giant-like ox-beef hath devoured many a
gentleman of your house: I promise you
your kindred hath made my eyes water ere
now. I desire your more acquaintance, good
Master Mustardseed. 201
Tita. Come, wait upon him; lead him to
my bower.
The moon methinks looks with a watery
eye;
And when she weeps, weeps every little
flower,
Lamenting some enforced chastity.
Tie up my love's tongue, bring him
silently. [*Exeunt.*

Scene II. *Another part of the wood.*

Enter Oberon.

Obe. I wonder if Titania be awaked;
Then, what it was that next came in her eye,
Which she must dote on in extremity.

Enter Puck.

Here comes my messenger.
How now, mad spirit!

143. **thy fair virtue's force**, the power of thy beauty.
150. **gleek**, scoff, jest. 158. **still**, ever, always.

191. **Squash**, unripe pea pod. 197. **patience**, what
you have endured. 205. **enforced**, forced, violated.
Scene ii. 2. **next**, nearest, first. 3. **in extremity**,
to the utmost degree.

What night-rule now about this haunted
   grove?
  Puck. My mistress with a monster is in
   love.
Near to her close and consecrated bower,
While she was in her dull and sleeping hour,
A crew of patches, rude mechanicals,
That work for bread upon Athenian stalls, 10
Were met together to rehearse a play
Intended for great Theseus' nuptial-day.
The shallowest thick-skin of that barren
   sort,
Who Pyramus presented, in their sport
Forsook his scene and enter'd in a brake:
When I did him at this advantage take,
An ass's nole I fixed on his head:
Anon his Thisbe must be answered,
And forth my mimic comes. When they him
   spy,
As wild geese that the creeping fowler eye, 20
Or russet-pated choughs, many in sort,
Rising and cawing at the gun's report,
Sever themselves and madly sweep the sky,
So, at his sight, away his fellows fly;
And, at our stamp, here o'er and o'er one
   falls;
He murder cries and help from Athens calls.
Their sense thus weak, lost with their fears
   thus strong,
Made senseless things begin to do them
   wrong;
For briers and thorns at their apparel snatch;
Some sleeves, some hats, from yielders all
   things catch.   30
I led them on in this distracted fear,
And left sweet Pyramus translated there:
When in that moment, so it came to pass,
Titania waked and straightway loved an ass.
  Obe. This falls out better than I could
   devise.
But hast thou yet latch'd the Athenian's
   eyes
With the love-juice, as I did bid thee do?
  Puck. I took him sleeping,—that is fin-
   ish'd too,—
And the Athenian woman by his side;
That, when he waked, of force she must be
   eyed.   40

Enter HERMIA *and* DEMETRIUS.

  Obe. Stand close: this is the same Athen-
   ian.
  Puck. This is the woman, but not this
   the man.
  Dem. O, why rebuke you him that loves
   you so?
Lay breath so bitter on your bitter foe.
  Her. Now I but chide; but I should use
   thee worse,
For thou, I fear, hast given me cause to curse.
If thou hast slain Lysander in his sleep,
Being o'er shoes in blood, plunge in the deep,
And kill me too.
The sun was not so true unto the day   50
As he to me: would he have stolen away
From sleeping Hermia? I'll believe as soon
The whole earth may be bored and that the
   moon
May through the centre creep and so dis-
   please
Her brother's noontide with the Antipodes.
It cannot be but thou hast murder'd him;
So should a murderer look, so dead, so grim.
  Dem. So should the murder'd look, and
   so should I,
Pierced through the heart with your stern
   cruelty:
Yet you, the murderer, look as bright, as
   clear,   60
As yonder Venus in her glimmering sphere.
  Her. What's this to my Lysander? where
   is he?
Ah, good Demetrius, wilt thou give him me?
  Dem. I had rather give his carcass to my
   hounds.
  Her. Out, dog! out, cur! thou drivest me
   past the bounds
Of maiden's patience. Hast thou slain him,
   then?
Henceforth be never number'd among men!
O, once tell true, tell true, even for my sake!
Durst thou have look'd upon him being
   awake,
And hast thou kill'd him sleeping? O brave
   touch!   70
Could not a worm, an adder, do so much?
An adder did it; for with doubler tongue
Than thine, thou serpent, never adder stung.
  Dem. You spend your passion on a mis-
   prised mood:

---

5. **night-rule,** regular diversion for the night. 9.
patches, clowns, fools. **mechanicals,** artisans, work-
ingmen. 13. **barren sort,** stupid company or crew.
17. **nole,** head. 19. **mimic,** burlesque actor. 21.
choughs, probably, jackdaws; Cambridge reads *russet-
padded,* meaning "red-legged," to refer to the red-legged
Cornish chough. 36. **latch'd,** caught and held fast as
by a charm. 40. **of force,** perforce.

57. **dead,** deadly. 70. **brave touch,** noble exploit.
71. **worm,** serpent. 74. **misprised,** mistaken.

I am not guilty of Lysander's blood;
Nor is he dead, for aught that I can tell.

Her. I pray thee, tell me then that he is
well.

Dem. An if I could, what should I get
therefore?

Her. A privilege never to see me more.
And from thy hated presence part I so: 80
See me no more, whether he be dead or no.
                                        [*Exit.*

Dem. There is no following her in this
fierce vein:
Here therefore for a while I will remain.
So sorrow's heaviness doth heavier grow
For debt that bankrupt sleep doth sorrow
owe;
Which now in some slight measure it will
pay,
If for his tender here I make some stay.
                        [*Lies down and sleeps.*

Obe. What hast thou done? thou hast
mistaken quite
And laid the love-juice on some true-love's
sight:
Of thy misprision must perforce ensue   90
Some true love turn'd and not a false turn'd
true.

Puck. Then fate o'er-rules, that, one man
holding troth,
A million fail, confounding oath on oath.

Obe. About the wood go swifter than the
wind,
And Helena of Athens look thou find:
All fancy-sick she is and pale of cheer,
With sighs of love, that costs the fresh blood
dear:
By some illusion see thou bring her here:
I'll charm his eyes against she do appear.

Puck. I go, I go; look how I go,   100
Swifter than arrow from the Tartar's bow.
                                        [*Exit.*

Obe. Flower of this purple dye,
Hit with Cupid's archery,
Sink in apple of his eye.
When his love he doth espy,
Let her shine as gloriously
As the Venus of the sky.
When thou wakest, if she be by,
Beg of her for remedy.

Re-enter PUCK.

Puck. Captain of our fairy band,   110
Helena is here at hand;
And the youth, mistook by me,
Pleading for a lover's fee.
Shall we their fond pageant see?
Lord, what fools these mortals be!

Obe. Stand aside: the noise they make
Will cause Demetrius to awake.

Puck. Then will two at once woo one;
That must needs be sport alone;
And those things do best please me
That befal preposterously.   121

Enter LYSANDER *and* HELENA.

Lys. Why should you think that I should
woo in scorn?
Scorn and derision never come in tears:
Look, when I vow, I weep; and vows so
born,
In their nativity all truth appears.
How can these things in me seem scorn to
you,
Bearing the badge of faith, to prove them
true?

Hel. You do advance your cunning more
and more.
When truth kills truth, O devilish-holy
fray!
These vows are Hermia's: will you give her
o'er?   130
Weigh oath with oath, and you will
nothing weigh:
Your vows to her and me, put in two scales,
Will even weigh, and both as light as tales.

Lys. I had no judgement when to her I
swore.

Hel. Nor none, in my mind, now you give
her o'er.

Lys. Demetrius loves her, and he loves
not you.

Dem. [*Awaking*] O Helen, goddess, nymph,
perfect, divine!
To what, my love, shall I compare thine
eyne?
Crystal is muddy. O, how ripe in show
Thy lips, those kissing cherries, tempting
grow!   140
That pure congealed white, high **Taurus'**
snow,

86-87. **Which . . . stay,** i.e., if she waits until sleep
"tenders" itself, she will derive some consolation for her
sorrow. 90. **misprision,** mistake. 96. **fancy-sick,**
love-sick. **cheer,** face. 97. **sighs . . . blood,** allusion
to the physiological theory that each sigh cost the heart
a drop of blood. 101. **Tartar's bow.** Tartars were
famed for their skill with the bow.

114. **fond pageant,** foolish exhibition. 121. **preposterously,** in inverted order. 125. **In . . . appears,**
i.e., vows so born appear in their nativity to be wholly
true. 141. **Taurus',** a lofty mountain range in Asia
Minor.

Fann'd with the eastern wind, turns to a
crow
When thou hold'st up thy hand: O, let me
kiss
This princess of pure white, this seal of bliss!
  Hel. O spite! O hell! I see you all are bent
To set against me for your merriment:
If you were civil and knew courtesy,
You would not do me thus much injury.
Can you not hate me, as I know you do,
But you must join in souls to mock me too?
If you were men, as men you are in show, 151
You would not use a gentle lady so;
To vow, and swear, and superpraise my
parts,
When I am sure you hate me with your
hearts.
You both are rivals, and love Hermia;
And now both rivals, to mock Helena:
A trim exploit, a manly enterprise,
To conjure tears up in a poor maid's eyes
With your derision! none of noble sort
Would so offend a virgin and extort 160
A poor soul's patience, all to make you sport.
  Lys. You are unkind, Demetrius; be not
so;
For you love Hermia; this you know I know:
And here, with all good will, with all my
heart,
In Hermia's love I yield you up my part;
And yours of Helena to me bequeath,
Whom I do love and will do till my death.
  Hel. Never did mockers waste more idle
breath.
  Dem. Lysander, keep thy Hermia; I will
none:
If e'er I loved her, all that love is gone. 170
My heart to her but as guest-wise sojourn'd,
And now to Helen is it home return'd,
There to remain.
  Lys.   Helen, it is not so.
  Dem. Disparage not the faith thou dost
not know,
Lest, to thy peril, thou aby it dear.
Look, where thy love comes; yonder is thy
dear.

           Re-enter HERMIA.

  Her. Dark night, that from the eye his
function takes,
The ear more quick of apprehension makes;

Wherein it doth impair the seeing sense,
It pays the hearing double recompense. 180
Thou art not by mine eye, Lysander, found;
Mine ear, I thank it, brought me to thy
sound.
But why unkindly didst thou leave me so?
  Lys. Why should he stay, whom love
doth press to go?
  Her. What love could press Lysander
from my side?
  Lys. Lysander's love, that would not let
him bide,
Fair Helena, who more engilds the night
Than all yon fiery oes and eyes of light.
Why seek'st thou me? could not this make
thee know,
The hate I bear thee made me leave thee so?
  Her. You speak not as you think: it
cannot be. 191
  Hel. Lo, she is one of this confederacy!
Now I perceive they have conjoin'd all three
To fashion this false sport, in spite of me.
Injurious Hermia! most ungrateful maid!
Have you conspired, have you with these
contrived
To bait me with this foul derision?
Is all the counsel that we two have shared,
The sisters' vows, the hours that we have
spent,
When we have chid the hasty-footed time 200
For parting us,—O, is it all forgot?
All school-days' friendship, childhood inno-
cence?
We, Hermia, like two artificial gods,
Have with our needles created both one
flower,
Both on one sampler, sitting on one cushion,
Both warbling of one song, both in one key,
As if our hands, our sides, voices and minds,
Had been incorporate. So we grew together,
Like to a double cherry, seeming parted,
But yet an union in partition; 210
Two lovely berries moulded on one stem;
So, with two seeming bodies, but one heart;
Two of the first, like coats in heraldry,
Due but to one and crowned with one crest.
And will you rent our ancient love asunder,
To join with men in scorning your poor
friend?

---

144. seal, pledge, covenant. 153. superpraise, over-
praise. parts, qualities. 157. trim, pretty; used ironically. 169, will none, i.e., of her. 175. aby, pay for.
177. his, its.

188. oes, general word for *circles* and *orbs*. 195. Injurious, insulting. 203. artificial, skilled in art.
208. incorporate, united in one body. 213. Two of
the first, i.e., two bodies, referred to like colors in the
description of a coat-of-arms. "The first" is the color
first mentioned.

It is not friendly, 'tis not maidenly:
Our sex, as well as I, may chide you for it,
Though I alone do feel the injury.

   Her. I am amazed at your passionate
     words.   220
I scorn you not: it seems that you scorn me.

   Hel. Have you not set Lysander, as in
     scorn,
To follow me and praise my eyes and face?
And made your other love, Demetrius,
Who even but now did spurn me with his
     foot,
To call me goddess, nymph, divine and rare,
Precious, celestial? Wherefore speaks he
     this
To her he hates? and wherefore doth Ly-
     sander
Deny your love, so rich within his soul,
And tender me, forsooth, affection,   230
But by your setting on, by your consent?
What though I be not so in grace as you,
So hung upon with love, so fortunate,
But miserable most, to love unloved?
This you should pity rather than despise.

   Her. I understand not what you mean by
     this.

   Hel. Ay, do, persever, counterfeit sad
     looks,
Make mouths upon me when I turn my back;
Wink each at other; hold the sweet jest up:
This sport, well carried, shall be chronicled.
If you have any pity, grace, or manners,   241
You would not make me such an argument.
But fare ye well: 'tis partly my own fault;
Which death or absence soon shall remedy.

   Lys. Stay, gentle Helena; hear my excuse:
My love, my life, my soul, fair Helena!

   Hel. O excellent!

   Her.   Sweet, do not scorn her so.

   Dem. If she cannot entreat, I can compel.

   Lys. Thou canst compel no more than
     she entreat:
Thy threats have no more strength than her
     weak prayers.   250
Helen, I love thee; by my life, I do:
I swear by that which I will lose for thee,
To prove him false that says I love thee not.

   Dem. I say I love thee more than he can
     do.

   Lys. If thou say so, withdraw, and prove
     it too.

   Dem. Quick, come!

   Her.   Lysander, whereto tends al!
     this?

   Lys. Away, you Ethiope!

   Dem.   †No, no; he'll . . .
Seem to break loose; take on as you would
     follow,
But yet come not: you are a tame man, go!

   Lys. Hang off, thou cat, thou burr! vile
     thing, let loose,   260
Or I will shake thee from me like a serpent!

   Her. Why are you grown so rude? what
     change is this?
Sweet love,—

   Lys.   Thy love! out, tawny
     Tartar, out!
Out, loathed medicine! hated potion, hence!

   Her. Do you not jest?

   Hel.   Yes, sooth; and so do you.

   Lys. Demetrius, I will keep my word with
     thee.

   Dem. I would I had your bond, for I per-
     ceive
A weak bond holds you: I'll not trust your
     word.

   Lys. What, should I hurt her, strike her,
     kill her dead?
Although I hate her, I'll not harm her so.   270

   Her. What, can you do me greater harm
     than hate?
Hate me! wherefore? O me! what news, my
     love!
Am not I Hermia? are not you Lysander?
I am as fair now as I was erewhile.
Since night you loved me; yet since night
     you left me:
Why, then you left me—O, the gods forbid!—
In earnest, shall I say?

   Lys.   Ay, by my life;
And never did desire to see thee more.
Therefore be out of hope, of question, of
     doubt;
Be certain, nothing truer; 'tis no jest   280
That I do hate thee and love Helena.

   Her. O me! you juggler! you canker-
     blossom!
You thief of love! what, have you come by
     night
And stolen my love's heart from him?

   Hel.   Fine, i' faith!

---

237. **persever,** persevere; accented on the second
syllable. **sad,** grave, serious. 238. **Make mouths
upon,** make faces at. 242. **argument,** subject for
a story.

257. **No, no; he'll.** Q: *No, no: heele.* F: *No, Sir;* text
apparently corrupt. We may understand that Demetrius
first addresses Helena and breaks off, then turns to chide
Lysander. 260. **Hang off, let go.** 272. **what news?**
what is the matter? 274. **erewhile,** just now.

Have you no modesty, no maiden shame,
No touch of bashfulness? What, will you
    tear
Impatient answers from my gentle tongue?
Fie, fie! you counterfeit, you puppet, you!

  Her. Puppet? why so? ay, that way goes
    the game.
Now I perceive that she hath made compare
Between our statures; she hath urged her
    height;   291
And with her personage, her tall personage,
Her height, forsooth, she hath prevail'd with
    him.
And are you grown so high in his esteem,
Because I am so dwarfish and so low?
How low am I, thou painted maypole?
    speak;
How low am I? I am not yet so low
But that my nails can reach unto thine eyes.

  Hel. I pray you, though you mock me,
    gentlemen,
Let her not hurt me: I was never curst;   300
I have no gift at all in shrewishness;
I am a right maid for my cowardice:
Let her not strike me. You perhaps may
    think,
Because she is something lower than myself,
That I can match her.

  Her.   Lower! hark, again.

  Hel. Good Hermia, do not be so bitter
    with me.
I evermore did love you, Hermia,
Did ever keep your counsels, never wrong'd
    you;
Save that, in love unto Demetrius,
I told him of your stealth unto this wood. 310
He follow'd you; for love I follow'd him;
But he hath chid me hence and threaten'd me
To strike me, spurn me, nay, to kill me too:
And now, so you will let me quiet go,
To Athens will I bear my folly back
And follow you no further: let me go:
You see how simple and how fond I am.

  Her. Why, get you gone: who is 't that
    hinders you?

  Hel. A foolish heart, that I leave here
    behind.

  Her. What, with Lysander?

  Hel.   With Demetrius. 320

  Lys. Be not afraid; she shall not harm
    thee, Helena.

  Dem. No, sir, she shall not, though you
    take her part.

  Hel. O, when she's angry, she is keen and
    shrewd!
She was a vixen when she went to school;
And though she be but little, she is fierce.

  Her. 'Little' again! nothing but 'low' and
    'little'!
Why will you suffer her to flout me thus?
Let me come to her.

  Lys.   Get you gone, you dwarf;
You minimus, of hindering knot-grass made;
You bead, you acorn.

  Dem.   You are too officious   330
In her behalf that scorns your services.
Let her alone: speak not of Helena;
Take not her part; for, if thou dost intend
Never so little show of love to her,
Thou shalt aby it.

  Lys.   Now she holds me not;
Now follow, if thou darest, to try whose
    right,
Of thine or mine, is most in Helena.

  Dem. Follow! nay, I'll go with thee, cheek
    by jole.

    [*Exeunt Lysander and Demetrius.*

  Her. You, mistress, all this coil is 'long of
    you:
Nay, go not back.

  Hel.   I will not trust you, I,   340
Nor longer stay in your curst company.
Your hands than mine are quicker for a
    fray,
My legs are longer though, to run away.
    [*Exit.*

  Her. I am amazed, and know not what to
    say.   [*Exit.*

  Obe. This is thy negligence: still thou
    mistakest,
Or else committ'st thy knaveries wilfully.

  Puck. Believe me, king of shadows, I mis-
    took.
Did not you tell me I should know the man
By the Athenian garments he had on?
And so far blameless proves my enterprise,
That I have 'nointed an Athenian's eyes; 351
And so far am I glad it so did sort
As this their jangling I esteem a sport.

323. **shrewd**, sharp of tongue. 329. **minimus**, diminutive creature. **knot-grass**, a weed (*polygonum aviculare*), an infusion of which was thought to stunt the growth. 333. **intend**, offer, or incline to. 335. **aby**, pay the penalty for. 338. **cheek by jole**, cheek by jowl, side by side. 339. **coil**, turmoil. 341. **curst**, spiteful. 347. **king of shadows**. Note the suggestion in this and other passages of a larger aspect of Oberon's power. 352. **sort**, turn out.

288. **puppet**. This word, *Ethiope* (l. 257), and *dwarf-ish* (l. 295) indicate that Hermia is short and dark. 300. **curst**, shrewish. 302. **right**, true. 310. **stealth**, stealing away.

Obe. Thou see'st these lovers seek a place
    to fight:
Hie therefore, Robin, overcast the night;
The starry welkin cover thou anon
With drooping fog as black as Acheron,
And lead these testy rivals so astray
As one come not within another's way.
Like to Lysander sometime frame thy
    tongue,   360
Then stir Demetrius up with bitter wrong;
And sometime rail thou like Demetrius;
And from each other look thou lead them
    thus,
Till o'er their brows death-counterfeiting
    sleep
With leaden legs and batty wings doth creep:
Then crush this herb into Lysander's eye;
Whose liquor hath this virtuous property,
To take from thence all error with his might,
And make his eyeballs roll with wonted sight.
When they next wake, all this derision   370
Shall seem a dream and fruitless vision,
And back to Athens shall the lovers wend,
With league whose date till death shall never
    end.
Whiles I in this affair do thee employ,
I'll to my queen and beg her Indian boy:
And then I will her charmed eye release
From monster's view, and all things shall be
    peace.
Puck. My fairy lord, this must be done
    with haste,
For night's swift dragons cut the clouds full
    fast,
And yonder shines Aurora's harbinger;   380
At whose approach, ghosts, wandering here
    and there,
Troop home to churchyards: damned spirits
    all,
That in crossways and floods have burial,
Already to their wormy beds are gone;
For fear lest day should look their shames
    upon,
They wilfully themselves exile from light
And must for aye consort with black-brow'd
    night.
Obe. But we are spirits of another sort:

I with the morning's love have oft made
    sport,
And, like a forester, the groves may tread, 390
Even till the eastern gate, all fiery-red,
Opening on Neptune with fair blessed beams,
Turns into yellow gold his salt green streams.
But, notwithstanding, haste; make no delay:
We may effect this business yet ere day.
                    [*Exit.*
Puck. Up and down, up and down,
    I will lead them up and down:
    I am fear'd in field and town:
    Goblin, lead them up and down.
Here comes one.   400

            Re-enter LYSANDER.

Lys. Where art thou, proud Demetrius?
    speak thou now.
Puck. Here, villain; drawn and ready.
    Where art thou?
Lys. I will be with thee straight.
Puck.   Follow me, then,
To plainer ground.
    [*Exit Lysander, as following the voice.*

            Re-enter DEMETRIUS.

Dem.   Lysander! speak again:
Thou runaway, thou coward, art thou fled?
Speak! In some bush? Where dost thou
    hide thy head?
Puck. Thou coward, art thou bragging to
    the stars,
Telling the bushes that thou look'st for wars,
And wilt not come? Come, recreant; come,
    thou child,
I'll whip thee with a rod: he is defiled   410
That draws a sword on thee.
Dem.   Yea, art thou there?
Puck. Follow my voice: we'll try no man-
    hood here.   [*Exeunt.*

            Re-enter LYSANDER.

Lys. He goes before me and still dares me
    on:
When I come where he calls, then he is gone.
The villain is much lighter-heel'd than I:
I follow'd fast, but faster he did fly;
That fallen am I in dark uneven way,
And here will rest me. [*Lies down.*] Come,
    thou gentle day!

357. **Acheron**, river of hell, which Shakespeare seems
to have thought of as a pit or lake. 359. **As**, so that.
370. **derision**, four syllables. 379. **dragons**, supposed
by Shakespeare to be yoked to the car of the goddess of
night. 380. **Aurora's harbinger**, the morning star.
383. **crossways . . . burial.** Those who had committed
suicide were buried at crossways, with a stake driven
through them; those drowned, i.e., buried in floods or
great waters, would be condemned to wander disconsolate
for want of burial rites.

389. **morning's love**, Cephalus, a beautiful youth
beloved by Diana; sometimes taken to refer to the goddess herself. 402. **drawn**, with drawn sword.

For if but once thou show me thy grey light,
I'll find Demetrius and revenge this spite. 420
                                    [*Sleeps.*

Re-enter Puck *and* Demetrius.

Puck. Ho, ho, ho! Coward, why comest
  thou not?
Dem. Abide me, if thou darest; for well
  I wot
Thou runn'st before me, shifting every place,
And darest not stand, nor look me in the
  face.
Where art thou now?
Puck.   Come hither: I am here.
Dem. Nay, then, thou mock'st me. Thou
  shalt buy this dear,
If ever I thy face by daylight see:
Now, go thy way. Faintness constraineth
  me
To measure out my length on this cold bed.
By day's approach look to be visited.   430
                          [*Lies down and sleeps.*

Re-enter Helena.

Hel. O weary night, O long and tedious
  night,
  Abate thy hours! Shine comforts from the
    east,
That I may back to Athens by daylight,
  From these that my poor company detest:
And sleep, that sometimes shuts up sorrow's
  eye,
Steal me awhile from mine own company.
                          [*Lies down and sleeps.*
Puck. Yet but three? Come one more;
  Two of both kinds makes up four.
  Here she comes, curst and sad:
  Cupid is a knavish lad,   440
  Thus to make poor females mad.

Re-enter Hermia.

Her. Never so weary, never so in woe,
Bedabbled with the dew and torn with
  briers,
I can no further crawl, no further go;
  My legs can keep no pace with my desires.
Here will I rest me till the break of day.
Heavens shield Lysander, if they mean a
  fray!   [*Lies down and sleeps.*
Puck.   On the ground
          Sleep sound:
          I'll apply   450

To your eye,
  Gentle lover, remedy.
[*Squeezing the juice on Lysander's eyes.*
  When thou wakest,
  Thou takest
  True delight
  In the sight
Of thy former lady's eye:
  And the country proverb known,
  That every man should take his own,
  In your waking shall be shown: 460
          Jack shall have Jill;
          Nought shall go ill;
The man shall have his mare again, and all
  shall be well.   [*Exit.*

ACT IV.

Scene I. *The same.* Lysander, Demetrius,
  Helena, *and* Hermia *lying asleep.*

Enter Titania *and* Bottom; Peaseblossom,
  Cobweb, Moth, Mustardseed, *and other*
  Fairies attending; Oberon *behind unseen.*

Tita. Come, sit thee down upon this flowery
  bed,
  While I thy amiable cheeks do coy,
And stick musk-roses in thy sleek smooth
  head,
  And kiss thy fair large ears, my gentle joy.
Bot. Where's Peaseblossom?
Peas. Ready.
Bot. Scratch my head, Peaseblossom.
Where's Mounsieur Cobweb?
Cob. Ready.   9
Bot. Mounsieur Cobweb, good mounsieur,
get you your weapons in your hand, and kill
me a red-hipped humble-bee on the top of a
thistle; and, good mounsieur, bring me the
honey-bag. Do not fret yourself too much in
the action, mounsieur; and, good mounsieur,
have a care the honey-bag break not; I would
be loath to have you overflown with a honey-
bag, signior. Where's Mounsieur Mustardseed?
Mus. Ready.   19
Bot. Give me your neaf, Mounsieur Mustardseed. Pray you, leave your courtesy,
good mounsieur.
Mus. What's your will?
Bot. Nothing, good mounsieur, but to

---

422. wot, know.

Act IV. *Scene i.* 2. coy, caress. 20. neaf, fist.
21. leave your courtesy, put on your hat.

help Cavalery Cobweb to scratch. I must 25
to the barber's, mounsieur; for methinks I
am marvellous hairy about the face; and I
am such a tender ass, if my hair do but
tickle me, I must scratch.

Tita. What, wilt thou hear some music,
my sweet love?   29

Bot. I have a reasonable good ear in
music. Let's have the tongs and the bones.

Tita. Or say, sweet love, what thou desirest to eat.

Bot. Truly, a peck of provender: I could
munch your good dry oats. Methinks I
have a great desire to a bottle of hay: good
hay, sweet hay, hath no fellow.   36

Tita. I have a venturous fairy that shall
seek
The squirrel's hoard, and fetch thee new
nuts.

Bot. I had rather have a handful or two
of dried peas. But, I pray you, let none of
your people stir me: I have an exposition of
sleep come upon me.   42

Tita. Sleep thou, and I will wind thee in
my arms.
Fairies, be gone, and be all ways away.
    [*Exeunt fairies.*
So doth the woodbine the sweet honeysuckle
Gentle entwist; the female ivy so
Enrings the barky fingers of the elm.
O, how I love thee! how I dote on thee!
    [*They sleep.*

Enter Puck.

Obe. [*Advancing*] Welcome, good Robin.
See'st thou this sweet sight?
Her dotage now I do begin to pity: 50
For, meeting her of late behind the wood,
Seeking sweet favours for this hateful fool,
I did upbraid her and fall out with her;
For she his hairy temples then had rounded
With coronet of fresh and fragrant flowers;
And that same dew, which sometime on the
buds
Was wont to swell like round and orient
pearls,
Stood now within the pretty flowerets' eyes
Like tears that did their own disgrace bewail.

When I had at my pleasure taunted her   60
And she in mild terms begg'd my patience,
I then did ask of her changeling child;
Which straight she gave me, and her fairy
sent
To bear him to my bower in fairy land.
And now I have the boy, I will undo
This hateful imperfection of her eyes:
And, gentle Puck, take this transformed
scalp
From off the head of this Athenian swain;
That, he awaking when the other do,
May all to Athens back again repair   70
And think no more of this night's accidents
But as the fierce vexation of a dream.
But first I will release the fairy queen.
    Be as thou wast wont to be;
    See as thou wast wont to see:
    Dian's bud o'er Cupid's flower
    Hath such force and blessed power.
Now, my Titania; wake you, my sweet
queen.

Tita. My Oberon! what visions have I
seen!
Methought I was enamour'd of an ass.   80

Obe. There lies your love.

Tita.   How came these things to pass?
O, how mine eyes do loathe his visage
now!

Obe. Silence awhile. Robin, take off this
head.
Titania, music call; and strike more dead
Than common sleep of all these five the
sense.

Tita. Music, ho! music, such as charmeth
sleep!   [*Music, still.*

Puck. Now, when thou wakest, with thine
own fool's eyes peep.

Obe. Sound, music! Come, my queen, take
hands with me,
And rock the ground whereon these sleepers
be.   90
Now thou and I are new in amity
And will to-morrow midnight solemnly
Dance in Duke Theseus' house triumphantly
And bless it to all fair prosperity:
There shall the pair of faithful lovers be
Wedded, with Theseus, all in jollity.

Puck. Fairy king, attend, and mark:
    I do hear the morning lark.

---

25. **Cavalery**, cavalero, gentleman; form of address.
31. **tongs and bones**, instruments for rustic music,
the former described as an instrument played like the
triangle. 35. **bottle**, bundle (of hay). 36. **fellow**,
equal. 41. **exposition**, Bottom's word for *disposition*.
44. **all ways**, in all directions. 52. **favours**, i.e.,
nosegays of flowers. 57. **orient pearls**, i.e., the most
beautiful of all pearls, those coming from the orient.

69. **other**, others. 76. **Dian's bud**, sometimes defined as *agnus castus* or chaste-tree, which could preserve
chastity; perhaps simply invented by Shakespeare to
correspond to *Cupid's flower*. 85. **these five**, i.e.,
the four lovers and Bottom.

Obe. Then, my queen, in silence sad,
   Trip we after night's shade: 100
   We the globe can compass soon,
   Swifter than the wandering moon.
Tita. Come, my lord, and in our flight
   Tell me how it came this night
   That I sleeping here was found
   With these mortals on the ground.
                              [*Exeunt.*
                    [*Horns winded within.*

Enter THESEUS, HIPPOLYTA, EGEUS, *and
         train.*

The. Go, one of you, find out the forester;
For now our observation is perform'd;
And since we have the vaward of the day, 109
My love shall hear the music of my hounds.
Uncouple in the western valley; let them
   go:
Dispatch, I say, and find the forester.
                         [*Exit an Attendant.*
We will, fair queen, up to the mountain's top
And mark the musical confusion
Of hounds and echo in conjunction.
Hip. I was with Hercules and Cadmus
   once,
When in a wood of Crete they bay'd the bear
With hounds of Sparta: never did I hear
Such gallant chiding; for, besides the groves,
The skies, the fountains, every region near
Seem'd all one mutual cry: I never heard 121
So musical a discord, such sweet thunder.
The. My hounds are bred out of the
   Spartan kind,
So flew'd, so sanded, and their heads are hung
With ears that sweep away the morning dew;
Crook-knee'd, and dew-lapp'd like Thes-
   salian bulls;
Slow in pursuit, but match'd in mouth like
   bells,
Each under each. A cry more tuneable
Was never holla'd to, nor cheer'd with
   horn,
In Crete, in Sparta, nor in Thessaly: 130
Judge when you hear. But, soft! what
   nymphs are these?

Ege. My lord, this is my daughter here
   asleep;
And this, Lysander; this Demetrius is;
This Helena, old Nedar's Helena:
I wonder of their being here together.
The. No doubt they rose up early to
   observe
The rite of May, and, hearing our intent,
Came here in grace of our solemnity.
But speak, Egeus; is not this the day
That Hermia should give answer of her
   choice?
Ege. It is, my lord. 141
The. Go, bid the huntsmen wake them
   with their horns. [*Horns and shout
   within. Lys., Dem., Hel., and Her.,
   wake and start up.*
Good morrow, friends. Saint Valentine is
   past:
Begin these wood-birds but to couple now?
Lys. Pardon, my lord.
The.   I pray you all, stand up.
I know you two are rival enemies:
How comes this gentle concord in the world,
That hatred is so far from jealousy,
To sleep by hate, and fear no enmity?
Lys. My lord, I shall reply amazedly, 150
Half sleep, half waking: but as yet, I swear,
I cannot truly say how I came here;
But, as I think,—for truly would I speak,
And now I do bethink me, so it is,—
I came with Hermia hither: our intent
Was to be gone from Athens, where we
   might,
Without the peril of the Athenian law.
Ege. Enough, enough, my lord; you
   have enough:
I beg the law, the law, upon his head.
They would have stolen away; they would,
   Demetrius, 160
Thereby to have defeated you and me,
You of your wife and me of my consent,
Of my consent that she should be your
   wife.
Dem. My lord, fair Helen told me of
   their stealth,
Of this their purpose hither to this wood;
And I in fury hither follow'd them,
Fair Helena in fancy following me.

99. sad, grave, serious. 100. night's, dissyllable.
108. observation, i.e., *observance to a morn of May*
(I, i, 167). 109. vaward, vanguard. 116-122. I was
. . . thunder. This reminiscence, which brings such
unlikely huntsmen into the field together, is probably
of Shakespeare's invention. Hounds of Crete and of
Sparta were alike celebrated, the Spartan the more
famous. The whole passage is, of course, made up of
the talk of English huntsmen. 124. flew'd, with large
overhanging jaws. sanded, of sandy color. 127.
mouth, voice (of hounds). 128. Each under each,
with differing notes. cry, pack of hounds.

138. solemnity, i.e., solemnization of their marriage.
143. Saint Valentine. Birds were supposed to choose
their mates on St. Valentine's Day. 156 where,
wherever. 157. Without, outside of, beyond. 158.
Enough, i.e., evidence to convict him. 167. fancy,
love.

But, my good lord, I wot not by what
power,—
But by some power it is,—my love to
Hermia,
Melted as the snow, seems to me now   170
As the remembrance of an idle gawd
Which in my childhood I did dote upon;
And all the faith, the virtue of my heart,
The object and the pleasure of mine eye,
Is only Helena. To her, my lord,
Was I betroth'd ere I saw Hermia:
But, like in sickness, did I loathe this food;
But, as in health, come to my natural taste,
Now I do wish it, love it, long for it,
And will for evermore be true to it.   180
    The. Fair lovers, you are fortunately met:
Of this discourse we more will hear anon.
Egeus, I will overbear your will;
For in the temple, by and by, with us
These couples shall eternally be knit:
And, for the morning now is something
worn,
Our purposed hunting shall be set aside.
Away with us to Athens; three and three,
We'll hold a feast in great solemnity.
Come, Hippolyta.   190
[*Exeunt Theseus, Hippolyta, Egeus, and train.*
    Dem. These things seem small and un-
distinguishable,
Like far-off mountains turned into clouds.
    Her. Methinks I see these things with
parted eye,
When every thing seems double.
    Hel.   So methinks:
And I have found Demetrius like a jewel,
Mine own, and not mine own.
    Dem.   Are you sure
That we are awake? It seems to me
That yet we sleep, we dream. Do not you
think
The duke was here, and bid us follow him?
    Her. Yea; and my father.
    Hel.   And Hippolyta. 200
    Lys. And he did bid us follow to the
temple.
    Dem. Why, then, we are awake: let's
follow him;
And by the way let us recount our dreams.
[*Exeunt.*
    Bot. [*Awaking*] When my cue comes, call
me, and I will answer: my next is, 'Most fair
Pyramus.' Heigh-ho! Peter Quince! Flute,
the bellows-mender! Snout, the tinker!
Starveling! God's my life, stolen hence,
and left me asleep! I have had a most rare

vision. I have had a dream, past the wit
of man to say what dream it was: man is
but an ass, if he go about to expound   212
this dream. Methought I was—there is no
man can tell what. Methought I was,—
and methought I had,—but man is but a
patched fool, if he will offer to say what
methought I had. The eye of man hath not
heard, the ear of man hath not seen, man's
hand is not able to taste, his tongue to
conceive, nor his heart to report, what my
dream was. I will get Peter Quince to
write a ballad of this dream: it shall be
called Bottom's Dream, because it hath no
bottom; and I will sing it in the latter end
of a play, before the duke: peradventure, to
make it the more gracious, † I shall sing it
at her death.   [*Exit.*

SCENE II. *Athens.* QUINCE'S *house.*

Enter QUINCE, FLUTE, SNOUT, *and*
STARVELING.

    Quin. Have you sent to Bottom's house?
is he come home yet?
    Star. He cannot be heard of. Out of
doubt he is transported.   4
    Flu. If he come not, then the play is
marred: it goes not forward, doth it?
    Quin. It is not possible: you have not a
man in all Athens able to discharge Pyramus
but he.
    Flu. No, he hath simply the best wit of
any handicraft man in Athens.   10
    Quin. Yea, and the best person too; and
he is a very paramour for a sweet voice.
    Flu. You must say 'paragon:' a paramour
is, God bless us, a thing of naught.

Enter SNUG.

    Snug. Masters, the duke is coming from
the temple, and there is two or three lords
and ladies more married: if our sport had
gone forward, we had all been made men. 18
    Flu. O sweet bully Bottom! Thus hath
he lost sixpence a day during his life; he
could not have 'scaped sixpence a day: an
the duke had not given him sixpence a
day for playing Pyramus, I'll be hanged; he

212. **go about,** attempt.   216. **patched,** wearing
motley, i.e., a dress of various colors.
Scene ii. 4. **transported,** carried off, or possibly,
transformed.   20. **sixpence a day, i.e.,** as a royal
pension.

would have deserved it: sixpence a day in Pyramus, or nothing.

Enter Bottom.

Bot. Where are these lads? where are these hearts?   26

Quin. Bottom! O most courageous day! O most happy hour!

Bot. Masters, I am to discourse wonders: but ask me not what; for if I tell you, I am no true Athenian. I will tell you every thing, right as it fell out.

Quin. Let us hear, sweet Bottom.   33

Bot. Not a word of me. All that I will tell you is, that the duke hath dined. Get your apparel together, good strings to your beards, new ribbons to your pumps; meet presently at the palace; every man look o'er his part; for the short and the long is, our play is preferred. In any case, let Thisby have clean linen; and let not him that plays the lion pare his nails, for they shall hang out for the lion's claws. And, most dear actors, eat no onions nor garlic, for we are to utter sweet breath; and I do not doubt but to hear them say, it is a sweet comedy. No more words: away! go, away!   [*Exeunt.*

ACT V.

Scene I. *Athens. The palace of* Theseus.

Enter Theseus, Hippolyta, Philostrate, Lords, *and* Attendants.

Hip. 'Tis strange, my Theseus, that these lovers speak of.

The. More strange than true: I never may believe
These antique fables, nor these fairy toys.
Lovers and madmen have such seething brains,

Such shaping fantasies, that apprehend
More than cool reason ever comprehends.
The lunatic, the lover and the poet
Are of imagination all compact:
One sees more devils than vast hell can hold,
That is, the madman: the lover, all as frantic,
Sees Helen's beauty in a brow of Egypt: 11
The poet's eye, in a fine frenzy rolling,
Doth glance from heaven to earth, from earth to heaven;
And as imagination bodies forth
The forms of things unknown, the poet's pen
Turns them to shapes and gives to airy nothing
A local habitation and a name.
Such tricks hath strong imagination,
That, if it would but apprehend some joy,
It comprehends some bringer of that joy; 20
Or in the night, imagining some fear,
How easy is a bush supposed a bear!

Hip. But all the story of the night told over,
And all their minds transfigured so together,
More witnesseth than fancy's images
And grows to something of great constancy;
But, howsoever, strange and admirable.

The. Here come the lovers, full of joy and mirth.

Enter Lysander, Demetrius, Hermia, *and* Helena.

Joy, gentle friends! joy and fresh days of love
Accompany your hearts!

Lys.   More than to us   30
Wait in your royal walks, your board, your bed!

The. Come now; what masques, what dances shall we have,
To wear away this long age of three hours
Between our after-supper and bed-time?
Where is our usual manager of mirth?
What revels are in hand? Is there no play,
To ease the anguish of a torturing hour?
Call Philostrate.

Phil.   Here, mighty Theseus.

The. Say, what abridgement have you for this evening?

26. **hearts,** good fellows. 27. **courageous,** used blunderingly. 38. **presently,** immediately. 40. **preferred,** selected for consideration.

Act V. Scene i. 2. **may,** can. 3. **antique,** strange, grotesque. **toys,** trifles. 4-22. **Lovers . . . a bear.** These lines furnish a probable illustration of the discoveries of the bibliographical students of Shakespeare. If lines 4-6, 9-11, and 18-22 are read consecutively without paying attention to the lines omitted, it will be found that they make complete sense, and that they refer only to the madman and the lover. The other lines, which refer to the poet, are found in the earliest printed texts of the play to be slightly deranged in verse form. It is inferred that Shakespeare's first draft introduced only the figures of the lover and the madman, and that he subsequently expanded them in his happiest vein with the lines referring to the poet, writing the new lines on the margin. The printers, working from the original playbook, were unable to get them exactly correct in the alignment of the verse.

8. **compact,** formed, composed. 11. **Helen's,** i.e., Helen of Troy, pattern of beauty. **brow of Egypt,** i.e., the face of a gypsy. 26. **constancy,** certainty. 39. **abridgement,** pastime.

What masque? what music? How shall we
    beguile   40
The lazy time, if not with some delight?
  Phil. There is a brief how many sports
    are ripe:
Make choice of which your highness will see
    first.   *[Giving a paper.*
  The. [*Reads*] 'The battle with the Cen-
    taurs, to be sung
By an Athenian eunuch to the harp.'
We'll none of that: that have I told my love,
In glory of my kinsman Hercules.
[*Reads*] 'The riot of the tipsy Bacchanals,
Tearing the Thracian singer in their rage.'
That is an old device; and it was play'd   50
When I from Thebes came last a conqueror.
[*Reads*] 'The thrice three Muses mourning
    for the death
Of Learning, late deceased in beggary.'
That is some satire, keen and critical,
Not sorting with a nuptial ceremony.
[*Reads*] 'A tedious brief scene of young
    Pyramus
And his love Thisbe; very tragical mirth.'
Merry and tragical! tedious and brief!
  That is, hot ice and wondrous strange
    snow.
How shall we find the concord of this
    discord?   60
  Phil. A play there is, my lord, some ten
    words long,
Which is as brief as I have known a play;
But by ten words, my lord, it is too long,
Which makes it tedious; for in all the play
There is not one word apt, one player fitted:
And tragical, my noble lord, it is;
For Pyramus therein doth kill himself.
Which, when I saw rehearsed, I must
    confess,
Made mine eyes water; but more merry
    tears
The passion of loud laughter never shed. 70
  The. What are they that do play it?

  Phil. Hard-handed men that work in
    Athens here,
Which never labour'd in their minds till now,
And now have toil'd their unbreathed mem-
    ories
With this same play, against your nuptial.
  The. And we will hear it.
  Phil.   No, my noble lord;
It is not for you: I have heard it over,
And it is nothing, nothing in the world;
Unless you can find sport in their intents,
Extremely stretch'd and conn'd with cruel
    pain,   80
To do you service.
  The.   I will hear that play;
For never anything can be amiss,
When simpleness and duty tender it.
Go, bring them in: and take your places,
    ladies.   *[Exit Philostrate.*
  Hip. I love not to see wretchedness o'er-
    charged
And duty in his service perishing.
  The. Why, gentle sweet, you shall see no
    such thing.
  Hip. He says they can do nothing in this
    kind.
  The. The kinder we, to give them thanks
    for nothing.   89
Our sport shall be to take what they mistake:
And what poor duty cannot do, noble respect
†Takes it in might, not merit.
Where I have come, great clerks have pur-
    posed
To greet me with premeditated welcomes;
Where I have seen them shiver and look
    pale,
Make periods in the midst of sentences,
Throttle their practised accent in their
    fears
And in conclusion dumbly have broke off,
Not paying me a welcome. Trust me, sweet,
Out of this silence yet I pick'd a welcome;
And in the modesty of fearful duty   101
I read as much as from the rattling tongue
Of saucy and audacious eloquence.
Love, therefore, and tongue-tied simplic-
    ity
In least speak most, to my capacity.

42. brief, short written statement. **44. battle with
the Centaurs**, probably refers to the battle of the
Centaurs and the Lapithæ, as narrated in Ovid, *Metamorphoses*, Bk. xii. **47. kinsman.** Plutarch's *Life of
Theseus* states that Hercules and Theseus were near
kinsmen. **48-49. tipsy Bacchanals . . . Thracian
singer.** This is the story of the death of Orpheus, as
told in *Metamorphoses*, Bk. xi. **52-53. The thrice three
Muses . . . beggary.** These two lines were long thought
to have some reference to Spenser's *Teares of the Muses*
(1591) and were connected by Knight with the death in
poverty of the learned poet, Robert Greene. The editors
of the New Cambridge Shakespeare see in the lines following, which describe the piece as a satire, a mild retaliation on Shakespeare's part for Greene's attack on
Shakespeare as "an upstart crow"; see *Introduction*.
55. Not sorting with, not befitting.

74. unbreathed, unexercised. **80. stretch'd**, strained.
92. Takes . . . merit, values it for the effort made
rather than the excellence achieved (?). **93. clerks**,
learned men. **96. periods**, full stops. **100. I pick'd a
welcome.** In the kindly speech of Theseus we are
probably to see a tribute to the graciousness of Queen
Elizabeth. Attempts have been made to see in the
passage a reference to a particular occasion. **105. to my
capacity**, as far as I am able to understand.

Re-enter PHILOSTRATE.

Phil. So please your grace, the Prologue is
　address'd.　106
The. Let him approach.

　　　　　　　[*Flourish of trumpets.*

Enter QUINCE *for the* Prologue.

Pro. If we offend, it is with our good will.
That you should think, we come not to
　offend,
But with good will. To show our simple
　skill,　110
That is the true beginning of our end.
Consider then we come but in despite.
　We do not come as minding to content you,
Our true intent is. All for your delight
　We are not here. That you should here
　　repent you,
The actors are at hand and by their show
You shall know all that you are like to know.
The. This fellow doth not stand upon
　points.　118
Lys. He hath rid his prologue like a rough
colt; he knows not the stop. A good moral,
my lord: it is not enough to speak, but to
speak true.
Hip. Indeed he hath played on his pro-
logue like a child on a recorder; a sound, but
not in government.　124
The. His speech was like a tangled chain;
nothing impaired, but all disordered. Who is
next?

Enter PYRAMUS *and* THISBE, WALL,
MOONSHINE, *and* LION.

Pro. Gentles, perchance you wonder at
　this show;
But wonder on, till truth make all things
　plain.
This man is Pyramus, if you would know;
　This beauteous lady Thisby is certain.　131
This man, with lime and rough-cast, doth
　present
Wall, that vile Wall which did these lovers
　sunder;
And through Wall's chink, poor souls, they
　are content

To whisper. At the which let no man
　wonder.
This man, with lanthorn, dog, and bush of
　thorn,
　Presenteth Moonshine; for, if you will
　　know,
By moonshine did these lovers think no
　scorn
　To meet at Ninus' tomb, there, there to
　　woo.　139
This grisly beast, which Lion hight by name,
The trusty Thisby, coming first by night,
Did scare away, or rather did affright;
And, as she fled, her mantle she did fall,
　Which Lion vile with bloody mouth did
　　stain.
Anon comes Pyramus, sweet youth and tall,
　And finds his trusty Thisby's mantle slain:
Whereat, with blade, with bloody blameful
　blade,
　He bravely broach'd his boiling bloody
　　breast;
And Thisby, tarrying in mulberry shade,
　His dagger drew, and died. For all the
　　rest,　150
Let Lion, Moonshine, Wall, and lovers twain
At large discourse, while here they do remain.
[*Exeunt Prologue, Pyramus, Thisbe, Lion,
　　　　　　　and Moonshine.*

The. I wonder if the lion be to speak.
Dem. No wonder, my lord: one lion may,
when many asses do.
Wall. In this same interlude it doth be-
　fall
That I, one Snout by name, present a wall;
And such a wall, as I would have you
　think,
That had in it a crannied hole or chink,
Through which the lovers, Pyramus and
　Thisby,　160
Did whisper often very secretly.
This loam, this rough-cast and this stone
　doth show
That I am that same wall; the truth is so:
And this the cranny is, right and sinister,
Through which the fearful lovers are to
　whisper.
The. Would you desire lime and hair to
speak better?
Dem. It is the wittiest partition that ever
heard discourse, my lord.

106. **Prologue**, speaker of the Prologue. **address'd,**
ready. 108-117. **If we . . . to know.** The humor of the
passage is in the blunders of its punctuation. There is a
similar piece in *Ralph Roister Doister*, which is quoted in
Wilson's *Arte of Rhetoric*, a book which Shakespeare
knew. 118. **not stand upon points,** quibbling upon
the two meanings (1) "to be overscrupulous" and (2) "to
mind his stops in reading." 123. **recorder,** a wind instrument like a flute or flageolet. 124. **governme**
control.

140. **hight**, is called. 143. **fall**, let fall. 148.
broach'd, stabbed; used rantingly. 164. **sinister**,
left. 168. **partition**, wall, and section of a learned
book.

Re-enter PYRAMUS.

The. Pyramus draws near the wall: silence! 170
Pyr. O grim-look'd night! O night with hue so black!
O night, which ever art when day is not!
O night, O night! alack, alack, alack,
I fear my Thisby's promise is forgot!
And thou, O wall, O sweet, O lovely wall,
That stand'st between her father's ground and mine!
Thou wall, O wall, O sweet and lovely wall,
Show me thy chink, to blink through with mine eyne! [*Wall holds up his fingers.*
Thanks, courteous wall: Jove shield thee well for this!
But what see I? No Thisby do I see. 180
O wicked wall, through whom I see no bliss!
Cursed be thy stones for thus deceiving me!
The. The wall, methinks, being sensible, should curse again.
Pyr. No, in truth, sir, he should not. 'Deceiving me' is Thisby's cue: she is to enter now, and I am to spy her through the wall. You shall see, it will fall pat as I told you. Yonder she comes.

Re-enter THISBE.

This. O wall, full often hast thou heard my moans, 190
For parting my fair Pyramus and me!
My cherry lips have often kiss'd thy stones,
Thy stones with lime and hair knit up in thee.
Pyr. I see a voice: now will I to the chink,
To spy an I can hear my Thisby's face.
Thisby!
This. My love thou art, my love I think.
Pyr. Think what thou wilt, I am thy lover's grace;
And, like Limander, am I trusty still.
This. And I like Helen, till the Fates me kill. 199
Pyr. Not Shafalus to Procrus was so true.
This. As Shafalus to Procrus, I to you.
Pyr. O, kiss me through the hole of this vile wall!

This. I kiss the wall's hole, not your lips at all.
Pyr. Wilt thou at Ninny's tomb meet me straightway?
This. 'Tide life, 'tide death, I come without delay. [*Exeunt Pyramus and Thisbe.*
Wall. Thus have I, Wall, my part discharged so;
And, being done, thus Wall away doth go. [*Exit.*
The. Now is the mural down between the two neighbours.
Dem. No remedy, my lord, when walls are so wilful to hear without warning. 211
Hip. This is the silliest stuff that ever I heard.
The. The best in this kind are but shadows; and the worst are no worse, if imagination amend them.
Hip. It must be your imagination then, and not theirs.
The. If we imagine no worse of them than they of themselves, they may pass for excellent men. Here come two noble beasts in, a man and a lion. 221

Re-enter LION *and* MOONSHINE.

Lion. You, ladies, you, whose gentle hearts do fear
The smallest monstrous mouse that creeps on floor,
May now perchance both quake and tremble here,
When lion rough in wildest rage doth roar.
Then know that I, one Snug the joiner, am
A lion-fell, nor else no lion's dam;
For, if I should as lion come in strife
Into this place, 'twere pity on my life.
The. A very gentle beast, and of a good conscience. 231
Dem. The very best at a beast, my lord, that e'er I saw.
Lys. This lion is a very fox for his valour.
The. True; and a goose for his discretion.
Dem. Not so, my lord; for his valour cannot carry his discretion; and the fox carries the goose.
The. His discretion, I am sure, cannot carry his valour; for the goose carries not the

---

171. **grim-look'd**, grim-looking. 178. **eyne**, eyes. 183. **sensible**, capable of feeling. 198-199. **Limander . . . Helen**, blunders for *Leander* and *Hero*. 201. **Shafalus to Procrus**, blunder for *Cephalus to Procris*, also famous lovers.

205. **'Tide life, 'tide death**, whether life or death betide. 214. **if imagination amend them.** The idea in this passage is fundamental in art and recurs so frequently in Shakespeare as to be a recognizable article of his faith. 227. **lion-fell**, lion's skin; QF: *lion fell*, i.e., fierce lion.

fox. It is well: leave it to his discretion, and let us listen to the moon. 242

Moon. This lanthorn doth the horned moon present;—

Dem. He should have worn the horns on his head.

The. He is no crescent, and his horns are invisible within the circumference.

Moon. This lanthorn doth the horned moon present;

Myself the man i' the moon do seem to be.

The. This is the greatest error of all the rest: the man should be put into the lanthorn. How is it else the man i' the moon? 252

Dem. He dares not come there for the candle; for, you see, it is already in snuff.

Hip. I am aweary of this moon: would he would change!

The. It appears, by his small light of discretion, that he is in the wane; but yet, in courtesy, in all reason, we must stay the time.

Lys. Proceed, Moon. 260

Moon. All that I have to say, is, to tell you that the lanthorn is the moon; I, the man in the moon; this thorn-bush, my thorn-bush; and this dog, my dog.

Dem. Why, all these should be in the lanthorn; for all these are in the moon. But, silence! here comes Thisbe.

Re-enter Thisbe.

This. This is old Ninny's tomb. Where is my love?

Lion: [*Roaring*] Oh—— [*Thisbe runs off.*

Dem. Well roared, Lion. 270

The. Well run, Thisbe.

Hip. Well shone, Moon. Truly, the moon shines with a good grace.

[*The Lion shakes Thisbe's mantle, and exit.*

The. Well moused, Lion.

Lys. And so the lion vanished.

Dem. And then came Pyramus.

Re-enter Pyramus.

Pry. Sweet Moon, I thank thee for thy sunny beams;

I thank thee, Moon, for shining now so bright;

For, by thy gracious, golden, glittering gleams,

I trust to take of truest Thisby sight. 280

But stay, O spite!

But mark, poor knight,

What dreadful dole is here!

Eyes, do you see?

How can it be?

O dainty duck! O dear!

Thy mantle good,

What, stain'd with blood!

Approach, ye Furies fell!

O Fates, come, come, 290

Cut thread and thrum;

Quail, crush, conclude, and quell!

The. This passion, and the death of a dear friend, would go near to make a man look sad.

Hip. Beshrew my heart, but I pity the man.

Pyr. O wherefore, Nature, didst thou lions frame?

Since lion vile hath here deflower'd my dear:

Which is—no, no—which was the fairest dame

That lived, that loved, that liked, that look'd with cheer.

Come, tears, confound; 300

Out, sword, and wound

The pap of Pyramus;

Ay, that left pap,

Where heart doth hop: [*Stabs himself.*

Thus die I, thus, thus, thus.

Now am I dead,

Now am I fled;

My soul is in the sky:

Tongue, lose thy light;

Moon, take thy flight: 310

[*Exit Moonshine.*

Now die, die, die, die, die. [*Dies.*

Dem. No die, but an ace, for him; for he is but one.

Lys. Less than an ace, man; for he is dead; he is nothing.

The. With the help of a surgeon he might yet recover, and prove an ass.

Hip. How chance Moonshine is gone before Thisbe comes back and finds her lover?

The. She will find him by starlight. Here she comes; and her passion ends the play. 321

---

244. **horns on his head,** the customary jest about the horns of the cuckold. 253. **for,** because of. 254. **in snuff,** pun on the meanings "to be offended" and "to be in need of snuffing."

283. **dole,** grief. 291. **thread and thrum,** the warp in weaving and the loose end of the warp; Bottom was a weaver. 292. **Quail,** overpower. **quell,** kill, destroy. 299. **cheer,** face. 312. **ace,** the side of the die containing one pip, or spot.

Re-enter THISBE.

Hip. Methinks she should not use a long one for such a Pyramus: I hope she will be brief.

Dem. A mote will turn the balance, which Pyramus, which Thisbe, is the better; he for a man, God warrant us; she for a woman, God bless us.

Lys. She hath spied him already with those sweet eyes.

Dem. And thus she means, videlicet:—

This. Alseep, my love?   331
    What, dead, my dove?
O Pyramus, arise!
    Speak, speak. Quite dumb?
    Dead, dead? A tomb
Must cover thy sweet eyes.
    These lily lips,
    This cherry nose,
These yellow cowslip cheeks,
    Are gone, are gone: 340
    Lovers, make moan:
His eyes were green as leeks.
    O Sisters Three,
    Come, come to me,
With hands as pale as milk;
    Lay them in gore,
    Since you have shore
With shears his thread of silk.
    Tongue, not a word:
    Come, trusty sword;   350
Come, blade, my breast imbrue:
        [*Stabs herself.*
    And, farewell, friends;
    Thus Thisby ends:
    Adieu, adieu, adieu.   [*Dies.*

The. Moonshine and Lion are left to bury the dead.

Dem. Ay, and Wall too.

Bot. [*Starting up*] No, I assure you; the wall is down that parted their fathers. Will it please you to see the epilogue, or to hear a Bergomask dance between two of our company?   360

The. No epilogue, I pray you; for your play needs no excuse. Never excuse; for when the players are all dead, there need none to be blamed. Marry, if he that writ it

had played Pyramus and hanged himself in Thisbe's garter, it would have been a fine tragedy: and so it is, truly; and very notably discharged. But, come, your Bergomask; let your epilogue alone.   [*A dance.*
The iron tongue of midnight hath told
    twelve: 370
Lovers, to bed; 'tis almost fairy time.
I fear we shall out-sleep the coming morn
As much as we this night have overwatch'd.
This palpable-gross play hath well beguiled
The heavy gait of night. Sweet friends, to
    bed.
A fortnight hold we this solemnity,
In nightly revels and new jollity.   [*Exeunt.*

Enter PUCK.

Puck. Now the hungry lion roars,
    And the wolf behowls the moon;
Whilst the heavy ploughman snores,   380
    All with weary task fordone.
Now the wasted brands do glow,
    Whilst the screech-owl, screeching loud,
Puts the wretch that lies in woe
    In remembrance of a shroud.
Now it is the time of night
    That the graves all gaping wide,
Every one lets forth his sprite,
    In the church-way paths to glide:
And we fairies, that do run   390
    By the triple Hecate's team,
From the presence of the sun,
    Following darkness like a dream,
Now are frolic: not a mouse
Shall disturb this hallow'd house:
I am sent with broom before,
To sweep the dust behind the door.

Enter OBERON *and* TITANIA *with their train.*

    Obe. Through the house give glimmering
        light,
    By the dead and drowsy fire:
    Every elf and fairy sprite   400
        Hop as light as bird from brier;

374. **palpable-gross,** palpably gross. 381. **fordone,** exhausted. 391. **triple Hecate's.** Hecate ruled in three capacities: as Luna or Cynthia in heaven, as Diana on earth, and as Proserpina in hell. 394. **frolic,** merry. 397. **sweep the dust behind the door,** i.e., where it would not show. Robin Goodfellow was a household spirit and helped good housemaids and punished lazy ones. 398-407. **Through . . . place.** The editors of the New Cambridge Shakespeare find in this passage evidence that the play was written for performance in the great chamber of some private house on the occasion of the celebration of a marriage. Theseus and the court leave the stage; the lights are extinguished, all but one; the fairies enter, kindle their torches at the remaining flame, place them on their heads and exhibit their dance; then depart as if to bless the bridal chamber.

330. **means,** moans, laments. 343. **Sisters Three,** the Fates. 347. **shore,** shorn, 351. **imbrue,** stain with blood. 360. **Bergomask dance,** dance named from Bergamo, a province in the state of Venice, noted for the rusticity of its manners. The New Cambridge edition points out that this rustic dance is the anti-masque, or grotesque contrasting measure, to the dance of the fairies which is to follow.

And this ditty, after me,
Sing, and dance it trippingly.
Tita. First, rehearse your song by rote,
To each word a warbling note:
Hand in hand, with fairy grace,
Will we sing, and bless this place.

[*Song and dance.*

Obe. Now, until the break of day,
Through this house each fairy stray.
To the best bride-bed will we,   410
Which by us shall blessed be;
And the issue there create
Ever shall be fortunate.
So shall all the couples three
Ever true in loving be;
And the blots of Nature's hand
Shall not in their issue stand;
Never mole, hare lip, nor scar,
Nor mark prodigious, such as are
Despised in nativity,   420
Shall upon their children be.
With this field-dew consecrate,
Every fairy take his gait;

And each several chamber bless,
Through this palace, with sweet peace;
And the owner of it blest
Ever shall in safety rest.
Trip away; make no stay;
Meet me all by break of day.

[*Exeunt Oberon, Titania, and train.*

Puck. If we shadows have offended,   430
Think but this, and all is mended,
That you have but slumber'd here
While these visions did appear.
And this weak and idle theme,
No more yielding but a dream,
Gentles, do not reprehend:
If you pardon, we will mend:
And, as I am an honest Puck,
If we have unearned luck
Now to 'scape the serpent's tongue,   440
We will make amends ere long;
Else the Puck a liar call:
So, good night unto you all.
Give me your hands, if we be friends,
And Robin shall restore amends. [*Exit.*

412. **create**, created.   419. **prodigious**, monstrous, unnatural.   422. **consecrate**, consecrated.

432. **That . . . here**, i.e., that it is a "midsummer-night's dream."   440. **serpent's tongue**, hissing.   444. **Give . . . hands**, applaud by clapping.

THE TRAGEDY OF
KING RICHARD THE THIRD

DRAMATIS PERSONÆ

KING EDWARD the Fourth.

EDWARD, Prince of Wales, afterwards King Edward V.,
RICHARD, Duke of York, } sons to the King.

GEORGE, Duke of Clarence,
RICHARD, Duke of Gloucester, afterwards King Richard III., } brothers to the King.

A young son of Clarence.

HENRY, Earl of Richmond, afterwards King Henry VII.

CARDINAL BOURCHIER, Archbishop of Canterbury.

THOMAS ROTHERHAM, Archbishop of York.

JOHN MORTON, Bishop of Ely.

DUKE OF BUCKINGHAM.

DUKE OF NORFOLK.

EARL OF SURREY, his son.

EARL RIVERS, brother to Elizabeth.

MARQUIS OF DORSET and LORD GREY, sons to Elizabeth.

EARL OF OXFORD.

LORD HASTINGS.

LORD STANLEY, called also EARL OF DERBY.

LORD LOVEL.

SIR THOMAS VAUGHAN.

SIR RICHARD RATCLIFF.

SIR WILLIAM CATESBY.

SIR JAMES TYRREL.

SIR JAMES BLOUNT.

SIR WALTER HERBERT.

SIR ROBERT BRAKENBURY, Lieutenant of the Tower.

CHRISTOPHER URSWICK, a priest. Another Priest.

TRESSEL and BERKELEY, gentlemen attending on the Lady Anne.

Lord Mayor of London. Sheriff of Wiltshire.

ELIZABETH, queen to King Edward IV.

MARGARET, widow of King Henry VI.

DUCHESS OF YORK, mother to King Edward IV.

LADY ANNE, widow of Edward Prince of Wales, son to King Henry VI.; afterwards married to Richard.

A young daughter of Clarence (MARGARET PLANTAGENET).

Ghosts of those murdered by Richard III., Lords and other Attendants; a Pursuivant, Scrivener, Citizens, Murderers, Messengers, Soldiers, &c.

SCENE: *England.*

ACT I.

SCENE I. *London. A street.*

Enter RICHARD, DUKE OF GLOUCESTER, *solus.*

Glou. Now is the winter of our discontent
Made glorious summer by this sun of York;
And all the clouds that lour'd upon our house
In the deep bosom of the ocean buried.
Now are our brows bound with victorious
    wreaths;
Our bruised arms hung up for monuments;
Our stern alarums changed to merry meetings,
Our dreadful marches to delightful measures.
Grim-visaged war hath smooth'd his wrinkled front;
And now, instead of mounting barbed
    steeds   10
To fright the souls of fearful adversaries,
He capers nimbly in a lady's chamber
To the lascivious pleasing of a lute.
But I, that am not shaped for sportive tricks,

2. **sun of York.** Edward IV assumed a sun as his badge in memory of the three suns which appeared to him before the battle of Mortimer's Cross in 1461 (*3 Henry VI*, II, i, 26-40). As used here there is a play on the words *son* and *sun*, probably reflected in the readings of Ff *son* and Qq *sonne*.

6. **monuments**, probably, memorial trophies. 8. **measures**, stately dances. 9. **front**, forehead. 10. **barbed**, properly, *barded*, i.e., armored. 14. **sportive**, amorous.

Nor made to court an amorous looking-glass;
I, that am rudely stamp'd, and want love's
  majesty
To strut before a wanton ambling nymph;
I, that am curtail'd of this fair proportion,
Cheated of feature by dissembling nature,
Deform'd, unfinish'd, sent before my time 20
Into this breathing world, scarce half made
  up,
And that so lamely and unfashionable
That dogs bark at me as I halt by them;
Why, I, in this weak piping time of peace,
Have no delight to pass away the time,
Unless to spy my shadow in the sun
And descant on mine own deformity:
And therefore, since I cannot prove a lover,
To entertain these fair well-spoken days,
I am determined to prove a villain   30
And hate the idle pleasures of these days.
Plots have I laid, inductions dangerous,
By drunken prophecies, libels and dreams,
To set my brother Clarence and the king
In deadly hate the one against the other:
And if King Edward be as true and just
As I am subtle, false and treacherous,
This day should Clarence closely be mew'd
  up,
About a prophecy, which says that G
Of Edward's heirs the murderer shall be. 40
Dive, thoughts, down to my soul: here
  Clarence comes.

Enter Clarence, *guarded, and*
  Brakenbury.

Brother, good day: what means this armed
  guard
That waits upon your grace?
  Clar.   His majesty,

17. **ambling**, walking affectedly, i.e., wantonly. 18-23. **I, that . . . them.** From Sir Thomas More's life of Richard III comes the information that Richard was small of stature, ill-shapen in limbs, crookbacked, left shoulder higher than the right, ugly in visage. According to the theory of Plato beauty of person should go with beauty of soul, an idea which is reflected in this passage and elsewhere in the play. 19. **dissembling**, fraudulent, false. 22. **unfashionable**, without comeliness. 24. **piping time**; i.e., a time when the music heard is that of pipes and not fifes and drums. 27. **descant**, make varied comments on. 29. **entertain**, pass away pleasurably. 30. **I am. . . villain.** This frank announcement is characteristic of the Machiavellian villain of Marlowe and other early dramatists and is to be connected with the idea that Richard is born outside the pale of normal humanity, so that his trend is toward evil as that of normal men is toward good. 32. **inductions**, preparations, beginnings. 33. **drunken**, outrageously impossible and irresponsible. **libels**, defamatory bills or pamphlets. 38. **mew'd up**, confined; properly, of a hawk while mewing, or moulting its feathers. 39. **prophecy . . . G.** The prophecy is mentioned in Holinshed; the quibble is that *G* stands for Gloucester and not George, given name of the duke of Clarence.

Tendering my person's safety, hath ap-
  pointed
This conduct to convey me to the Tower.
  Glou. Upon what cause?
  Clar.   Because my name is George.
  Glou. Alack, my lord, that fault is none
    of yours;
He should, for that, commit your godfathers:
O, belike his majesty hath some intent   49
That you shall be new-christen'd in the
  Tower.
But what's the matter, Clarence? may I
  know?
  Clar. Yea, Richard, when I know; for I
    protest
As yet I do not: but, as I can learn,
He hearkens after prophecies and dreams;
And from the cross-row plucks the letter G,
And says a wizard told him that by G
His issue disinherited should be;
And, for my name of George begins with G,
It follows in his thought that I am he.   59
These, as I learn, and such like toys as these
Have moved his highness to commit me now.
  Glou. Why, this it is, when men are ruled
    by women:
'Tis not the king that sends you to the
  Tower;
My Lady Grey his wife, Clarence, 'tis she
That tempers him to this extremity.
Was it not she and that good man of wor-
  ship,
Anthony Woodville, her brother there,
That made him send Lord Hastings to the
  Tower,
From whence this present day he is deliver'd?
We are not safe, Clarence; we are not safe. 70
  Clar. By heaven, I think there's no man
    is secure
But the queen's kindred and night-walking
  heralds
That trudge betwixt the king and Mistress
  Shore.
Heard ye not what an humble suppliant
Lord Hastings was to her for his delivery?

48. **commit your godfathers,** an example of Richard's cynical humor. 54. **hearkens**, inquires. 55. **cross-row**, Christ-cross-row, or alphabet, so called from the cross printed before the alphabet in the hornbook. 61. **commit**, arrest. 64. **My Lady Grey**, a disrespectful reference to the queen, whose maiden name was Elizabeth Woodville and who, when the king married her, was the widow of Sir John Grey. 65. **tempers**, changes the normal mixture of the humors in him. 67. **Woodville**, three syllables; originally, *Wydeville.* 73. **Mistress Shore.** Jane Shore, the king's mistress, was the daughter of a Cheapside merchant and the wife of a goldsmith in Lombard Street.

Glou. Humbly complaining to her deity
Got my lord chamberlain his liberty.
I'll tell you what; I think it is our way,
If we will keep in favour with the king,
To be her men and wear her livery: 80
The jealous o'erworn widow and herself,
Since that our brother dubb'd them gentle-
        women,
Are mighty gossips in this monarchy.
    Brak. I beseech your graces both to par-
        don me;
His majesty hath straitly given in charge
That no man shall have private conference,
Of what degree soever, with his brother.
    Glou. Even so; an 't please your worship,
        Brakenbury,
You may partake of any thing we say:
We speak no treason, man: we say the king 90
Is wise and virtuous, and his noble queen
Well struck in years, fair, and not jealous;
We say that Shore's wife hath a pretty foot,
A cherry lip, a bonny eye, a passing pleasing
        tongue;
And that the queen's kindred are made
        gentlefolks:
How say you, sir? can you deny all this?
    Brak. With this, my lord, myself have
        nought to do.
    Glou. Naught to do with Mistress Shore!
        I tell thee, fellow,
He that doth naught with her, excepting
        one,
Were best he do it secretly, alone.   100
    Brak. What one, my lord?
    Glou. Her husband, knave: wouldst thou
        betray me?
    Brak. I beseech your grace to pardon me,
        and withal
Forbear your conference with the noble duke.
    Clar. We know thy charge, Brakenbury,
        and will obey.   105
    Glou. We are the queen's abjects, and
        must obey.
Brother, farewell: I will unto the king;
And whatsoever you will employ me in,
Were it to call King Edward's widow sister,
I will perform it to enfranchise you.   110

Meantime, this deep disgrace in brother-
        hood
Touches me deeper than you can imagine.
    Clar. I know it pleaseth neither of us
        well.
    Glou. Well, your imprisonment shall not
        be long;
I will deliver you, or else lie for you: 115
Meantime, have patience.
    Clar.   I must perforce. Farewell.
[*Exeunt Clarence, Brakenbury, and Guard.*
    Glou. Go, tread the path that thou shalt
        ne'er return,
Simple, plain Clarence! I do love thee so,
That I will shortly send thy soul to heaven,
If heaven will take the present at our hands.
But who comes here? the new-deliver'd
        Hastings?   121

Enter LORD HASTINGS.

    Hast. Good time of day unto my gracious
        lord!
    Glou. As much unto my good lord cham-
        berlain!
Well are you welcome to the open air.
How hath your lordship brook'd imprison-
        ment?
    Hast. With patience, noble lord, as prison-
        ers must:
But I shall live, my lord, to give them
        thanks
That were the cause of my imprisonment.
    Glou. No doubt, no doubt; and so shall
        Clarence too;
For they that were your enemies are his, 130
And have prevail'd as much on him as you.
    Hast. More pity that the eagle should be
        mew'd,
While kites and buzzards prey at liberty.
    Glou. What news abroad?
    Hast. No news so bad abroad as this at
        home;
The king is sickly, weak and melancholy,
And his physicians fear him mightily.
    Glou. Now, by Saint Paul, this news is
        bad indeed.
O, he hath kept an evil diet long,
And overmuch consumed his royal person:
'Tis very grievous to be thought upon.   141
What, is he in his bed?
    Hast. He is.

---

77. **chamberlain**, i.e., Hastings. 81. **jealous o'erworn widow**, i.e., the queen. **herself**, i.e., Jane Shore.
82. **gentlewomen**, a sneer at the queen's family, which
was gentle but not noble until after her marriage with
the king; Jane Shore was of course neither gentle nor
noble. 83. **gossips**, companions (conveying the idea
of vulgar familiarity). 106. **abjects**, abjectly servile
subjects. 109. **King Edward's widow**, i.e., the widow
whom he has made queen.

115. **lie**, quibble on "lying in prison" and "telling
lies." 127. **give them thanks**, ironical for "pay them
off." 133. **buzzards**, common species of hawk.

Glou. Go you before, and I will follow
  you.   [*Exit Hastings.*
He cannot live, I hope; and must not die
Till George be pack'd with post-horse up to
  heaven.   146
I'll in, to urge his hatred more to Clarence,
With lies well steel'd with weighty argu-
  ments;
And, if I fail not in my deep intent,
Clarence hath not another day to live: 150
Which done, God take King Edward to his
  mercy,
And leave the world for me to bustle in!
For then I'll marry Warwick's youngest
  daughter.
What though I kill'd her husband and her
  father?
The readiest way to make the wench amends
Is to become her husband and her father:
The which will I; not all so much for love
As for another secret close intent,
By marrying her which I must reach un-
  to.
But yet I run before my horse to market: 160
Clarence still breathes; Edward still lives and
  reigns:
When they are gone, then must I count my
  gains.   [*Exit.*

SCENE II. *The same. Another street.*

Enter the corpse of KING HENRY *the Sixth,
Gentlemen* with halberds to guard it; LADY
ANNE *being the mourner*

Anne. Set down, set down your honour-
  able load,
If honour may be shrouded in a hearse,
Whilst I awhile obsequiously lament
The untimely fall of virtuous Lancaster.
Poor key-cold figure of a holy king!   5
Pale ashes of the house of Lancaster!
Thou bloodless remnant of that royal blood!
Be it lawful that I invocate thy ghost,
To hear the lamentations of poor Anne,
Wife to thy Edward, to thy slaughter'd
  son,   10
Stabb'd by the selfsame hand that made
  these wounds!

Lo, in these windows that let forth thy life,
I pour the helpless balm of my poor eyes.
Cursed be the hand that made these fatal
  holes!
Cursed be the heart that had the heart to
  do it!
Cursed the blood that let this blood from
  hence!
More direful hap betide that hated wretch,
That makes us wretched by the death of thee,
Than I can wish to adders, spiders, toads,
Or any creeping venom'd thing that lives! 20
If ever he have child, abortive be it,
Prodigious, and untimely brought to light,
Whose ugly and unnatural aspect
May fright the hopeful mother at the view;
And that be heir to his unhappiness!
If ever he have wife, let her be made
As miserable by the death of him
As I am made by my poor lord and thee!
Come, now towards Chertsey with your holy
  load,
Taken from Paul's to be interred there; 30
And still, as you are weary of the weight,
Rest you, whiles I lament King Henry's
  corse.

Enter GLOUCESTER!

Glou. Stay, you that bear the corse, and
  set it down.
Anne. What black magician conjures up
  this fiend,
To stop devoted charitable deeds?
Glou. Villains, set down the corse; or, by
  Saint Paul,
I'll make a corse of him that disobeys.
Gent. My lord, stand back, and let the
  coffin pass.
Glou. Unmanner'd dog! stand thou, when
  I command:
Advance thy halberd higher than my
  breast,   40
Or, by Saint Paul, I'll strike thee to my foot,
And spurn upon thee, beggar, for thy bold-
  ness.
Anne. What, do you tremble? are you all
  afraid?
Alas, I blame you not; for you are mortal,

---

146. **with post-horse,** by post-horses, i.e., by swiftest possible means.   153. **Warwick's youngest daughter,** Lady Anne, widow of Edward Prince of Wales, son
of King Henry VI.
  Scene ii.   3. **obsequiously,** as befits the funeral,
mournfully.   5. **key-cold,** extremely cold; used proverbially.   8. **invocate,** invoke.

13. **helpless,** useless, unavailing.   17. **hap,** fortune.
22. **Prodigious,** monstrous, unnatural.   25. **that,** i.e.,
that creature.   **unhappiness,** prodigious nature.   29.
Chertsey, a town in Surrey, where King Henry's body
was buried.   30. **Paul's,** St. Paul's Church in London.
31. **still,** as often as.   34. **black magician,** one leagued
with the devil.   35. **devoted** pious, holy.

And mortal eyes cannot endure the devil.
Avaunt, thou dreadful minister of hell!
Thou hadst but power over his mortal body,
His soul thou canst not have; therefore, be
  gone.
  Glou. Sweet saint, for charity, be not so
  curst.
  Anne. Foul devil, for God's sake, hence,
  and trouble us not;   50
For thou hast made the happy earth thy
  hell,
Fill'd it with cursing cries and deep exclaims.
If thou delight to view thy heinous deeds,
Behold this pattern of thy butcheries.
O, gentlemen, see, see! dead Henry's wounds
Open their congeal'd mouths and bleed
  afresh!
Blush, blush, thou lump of foul deformity;
For 'tis thy presence that exhales this blood
From cold and empty veins, where no blood
  dwells;
Thy deed, inhuman and unnatural,   60
Provokes this deluge most unnatural.
O God, which this blood madest, revenge his
  death!
O earth, which this blood drink'st, revenge
  his death!
Either heaven with lightning strike the
  murderer dead,
Or earth, gape open wide and eat him quick,
As thou dost swallow up this good king's
  blood,
Which his hell-govern'd arm hath butchered!
  Glou. Lady, you know no rules of charity,
Which renders good for bad, blessings for
  curses.
  Anne. Villain, thou know'st no law of
  God nor man: 70
No beast so fierce but knows some touch of
  pity.
  Glou. But I know none, and therefore am
  no beast.
  Anne. O wonderful, when devils tell the
  truth!
  Glou. More wonderful, when angels are
  so angry.
Vouchsafe, divine perfection of a woman,
Of these supposed evils, to give me leave,
By circumstance, but to acquit myself.

  Anne. Vouchsafe, defused infection of a
  man,
For these known evils, but to give me
  leave,
By circumstance, to curse thy cursed self. 80
  Glou. Fairer than tongue can name thee,
  let me have
Some patient leisure to excuse myself.
  Anne. Fouler than heart can think thee,
  thou canst make
No excuse current, but to hang thyself.
  Glou. By such despair, I should accuse
  myself.
  Anne. And, by despairing, shouldst thou
  stand excused;
For doing worthy vengeance on thyself,
Which didst unworthy slaughter upon
  others.
  Glou. Say that I slew them not?
  Anne.   Why, then they are not dead:
But dead they are, and, devilish slave, by
  thee.   90
  Glou. I did not kill your husband.
  Anne.   Why, then he is alive.
  Glou. Nay, he is dead; and slain by
  Edward's hand.
  Anne. In thy foul throat thou liest: Queen
  Margaret saw
Thy murderous falchion smoking in his
  blood;
The which thou once didst bend against her
  breast,
But that thy brothers beat aside the point.
  Glou. I was provoked by her slanderous
  tongue,
Which laid their guilt upon my guiltless
  shoulders.
  Anne. Thou wast provoked by thy bloody
  mind,
Which never dreamt on aught but butcher-
  ies:
Didst thou not kill this king?
  Glou.   I grant ye. 101
  Anne. Dost grant me, hedgehog? then,
  God grant me too
Thou mayst be damned for that wicked
  deed!
O, he was gentle, mild, and virtuous!
  Glou. The fitter for the King of heaven,
  that hath him.

---

49. **curst**, spiteful, shrewish. 52. **exclaims**, exclamations. 54. **pattern**, example. 58. **thy presence**,
an allusion to the legend that dead bodies bleed in the
presence of their murderers. 76. **evils**. Some editors
follow the F reading, *crimes*, which preserves the par-
allelism of lines 75-77 and 78-80. 77. **circumstance**,
detailed argument.

78. **defused**, disordered, shapeless. 82. **patient**,
tranquil. 84. **current**, genuine. 94. **falchion**, a curved
sword. 95. **bend**, direct, aim. 102. **hedgehog**, a double
allusion to Richard's hump and to his heraldic emblem,
a boar.

Anne. He is in heaven, where thou shalt never come.

Glou. Let him thank me, that holp to send him thither;

For he was fitter for that place than earth.

Anne. And thou unfit for any place but hell.

Glou. Yes, one place else, if you will hear me name it.   110

Anne. Some dungeon.

Glou.   Your bed-chamber.

Anne. Ill rest betide the chamber where thou liest!

Glou. So will it, madam, till I lie with you.

Anne. I hope so.

Glou.   I know so. But, gentle Lady Anne,

To leave this keen encounter of our wits,

And fall somewhat into a slower method,

Is not the causer of the timeless deaths

Of these Plantagenets, Henry and Edward,

As blameful as the executioner?

Anne. Thou art the cause, and most accursed effect.   120

Glou. Your beauty was the cause of that effect;

Your beauty, which did haunt me in my sleep

To undertake the death of all the world,

So I might live one hour in your sweet bosom.

Anne. If I thought that, I tell thee, homicide,

These nails should rend that beauty from my cheeks.

Glou. These eyes could never endure sweet beauty's wreck;

You should not blemish it, if I stood by:

As all the world is cheered by the sun,

So I by that; it is my day, my life.   130

Anne. Black night o'ershade thy day, and death thy life!

Glou. Curse not thyself, fair creature; thou art both.

Anne. I would I were, to be revenged on thee.

Glou. It is a quarrel most unnatural,

To be revenged on him that loveth you.

Anne. It is a quarrel just and reasonable,

To be revenged on him that slew my husband.

Glou. He that bereft thee, lady, of thy husband,

Did it to help thee to a better husband.

Anne. His better doth not breathe upon the earth.   140

Glou. He lives that loves thee better than he could.

Anne. Name him.

Glou.   Plantagenet.

Anne.   Why, that was he.

Glou. The selfsame name, but one of better nature.

Anne. Where is he?

Glou.   Here. [*She spitteth at him.*] Why dost thou spit at me?

Anne. Would it were mortal poison, for thy sake!

Glou. Never came poison from so sweet a place.

Anne. Never hung poison on a fouler toad.

Out of my sight! thou dost infect my eyes.

Glou. Thine eyes, sweet lady, have infected mine.   150

Anne. Would they were basilisks, to strike thee dead!

Glou. I would they were, that I might die at once;

For now they kill me with a living death.

Those eyes of thine from mine have drawn salt tears,

Shamed their aspect with store of childish drops:

These eyes, which never shed remorseful tear,

No, when my father York and Edward wept,

To hear the piteous moan that Rutland made

When black-faced Clifford shook his sword at him;

Nor when thy warlike father, like a child, 160

Told the sad story of my father's death,

And twenty times made pause to sob and weep,

That all the standers-by had wet their cheeks,

Like trees bedash'd with rain: in that sad time

My manly eyes did scorn an humble tear;

And what these sorrows could not thence exhale,

Thy beauty hath, and made them blind with weeping.

---

117. **timeless**, untimely.   120. **effect**, agent.

151. **basilisks.** The basilisk of popular superstition was a creature with legs, wings, a serpentine and winding tail, and a crest or comb somewhat like a cock (Sir Thomas Browne). It was the offspring of a cock's egg hatched under a toad or serpent and had the power of killing by its glance.   158. **Rutland**, second son of Richard Duke of York.   163. **That**, so that.

I never sued to friend nor enemy;
My tongue could never learn sweet smooth-
　　ing words;
But, now thy beauty is proposed my fee, 170
My proud heart sues and prompts my tongue
　　to speak. [*She looks scornfully at him.*
Teach not thy lips such scorn, for they were
　　made
For kissing, lady, not for such contempt.
If thy revengeful heart cannot forgive,
Lo, here I lend thee this sharp-pointed
　　sword;
Which if thou please to hide in this true
　　bosom,
And let the soul forth that adoreth thee,
I lay it naked to the deadly stroke,
And humbly beg the death upon my knee.
　　[*He lays his breast open: she offers at it*
　　　　　　　　　　　　　with his sword.
Nay, do not pause; for I did kill King Henry,
But 'twas thy beauty that provoked me. 181
Nay, now dispatch; 'twas I that stabb'd
　　young Edward,
But 'twas thy heavenly face that set me on.
　　　　　　　　[*Here she lets fall the sword.*
Take up the sword again, or take up me.
　Anne. Arise, dissembler: though I wish
　　thy death,
I will not be the executioner.
　Glou. Then bid me kill myself, and I will
　　do it.
　Anne. I have already.
　Glou.　　Tush, that was in thy rage:
Speak it again, and, even with the word,
That hand, which, for thy love, did kill thy
　　love,　　　　　　　　　　　　　190
Shall, for thy love, kill a far truer love;
To both their deaths thou shalt be accessary.
　Anne. I would I knew thy heart.
　Glou. 'Tis figured in my tongue.
　Anne. I fear me both are false.
　Glou. Then never man was true.
　Anne. Well, well, put up your sword.
　Glou. Say, then, my peace is made.
　Anne. That shall you know hereafter.
　Glou. But shall I live in hope?　　200
　Anne. All men, I hope, live so.
　Glou. Vouchsafe to wear this ring.
　Anne. To take is not to give.
　Glou. Look, how this ring encompasseth
　　thy finger,
Even so thy breast encloseth my poor heart;

Wear both of them, for both of them are
　　thine.
And if thy poor devoted suppliant may
But beg one favour at thy gracious hand,
Thou dost confirm his happiness for ever.
　Anne. What is it?　　　　　　　210
　Glou. That it would please thee leave
　　these sad designs
To him that hath more cause to be a
　　mourner,
And presently repair to Crosby Place;
Where, after I have solemnly interr'd
At Chertsey monastery this noble king,
And wet his grave with my repentant tears,
I will with all expedient duty see you:
For divers unknown reasons, I beseech you,
Grant me this boon.
　Anne. With all my heart; and much it
　　joys me too,　　　　　　　　220
To see you are become so penitent.
Tressel and Berkeley, go along with me.
　Glou. Bid me farewell.
　Anne.　　'Tis more than you deserve;
But since you teach me how to flatter you,
Imagine I have said farewell already.
　　[*Exeunt Lady Anne, Tressel, and Berkeley.*
　Glou. Sirs, take up the corse.
　Gent.　　Towards Chertsey, noble lord?
　Glou. No, to White-Friars; there attend
　　my coming.　 [*Exeunt all but Gloucester.*
Was ever woman in this humour woo'd?
Was ever woman in this humour won?
I'll have her; but I will not keep her long. 230
What! I, that kill'd her husband and his
　　father,
To take her in her heart's extremest hate,
With curses in her mouth, tears in her eyes,
The bleeding witness of her hatred by;
Having God, her conscience, and these bars
　　against me,
And I nothing to back my suit at all,
But the plain devil and dissembling looks,
And yet to win her, all the world to nothing!
Ha!
Hath she forgot already that brave prince,
Edward, her lord, whom I, some three
　　months since,　　　　　　　241

213. **Crosby Place**, built by Sir John Crosby in 1456
and fronted on Bishop's-gate Street Within. Richard,
when lord Protector, was lodged in this house. 217. **expedient**, expeditious. 227. **White-Friars**, the Carme-
lite priory in ancient London; the chronicles, however,
state that the body was taken to Blackfriars. 228-229.
Was . . . won. Similar passages are found in *Titus Andronicus*, II, i, 82-3, and *1 Henry VI*, V, iii, 77-8. 234.
her hatred, i.e., Henry's wounds are a witness to the
justice of Anne's hatred.

169. **smoothing**, flattering.　179. **the death**, i.e.,
death after judicial sentence.　194. **figured**, portrayed.

Stabb'd in my angry mood at Tewksbury?
A sweeter and a lovelier gentleman,
Framed in the prodigality of nature,
Young, valiant, wise, and, no doubt, right royal,
The spacious world cannot again afford:
And will she yet debase her eyes on me,
That cropp'd the golden prime of this sweet prince,
And made her widow to a woful bed?
On me, whose all not equals Edward's moiety? 250
On me, that halt and am unshapen thus?
My dukedom to a beggarly denier,
I do mistake my person all this while:
Upon my life, she finds, although I cannot,
Myself to be a marvellous proper man.
I'll be at charges for a looking-glass,
And entertain some score or two of tailors,
To study fashions to adorn my body:
Since I am crept in favour with myself,
I will maintain it with some little cost. 260
But first I'll turn yon fellow in his grave;
And then return lamenting to my love.
Shine out, fair sun, till I have bought a glass,
That I may see my shadow as I pass. [*Exit.*

Scene III. *The palace.*

Enter Queen Elizabeth, Lord Rivers, *and* Lord Grey.

Riv. Have patience, madam: there's no doubt his majesty
Will soon recover his accustom'd health.
Grey. In that you brook it ill, it makes him worse:
Therefore, for God's sake, entertain good comfort,
And cheer his grace with quick and merry words.
Q. Eliz. If he were dead, what would betide of me?
Riv. No other harm but loss of such a lord.
Q. Eliz. The loss of such a lord includes all harm.
Grey. The heavens have bless'd you with a goodly son,
To be your comforter when he is gone. 10

Q. Eliz. Oh, he is young, and his minority
Is put unto the trust of Richard Gloucester,
A man that loves not me, nor none of you.
Riv. Is it concluded he shall be protector?
Q. Eliz. It is determined, not concluded yet:
But so it must be, if the king miscarry.

Enter Buckingham *and* Derby.

Grey. Here come the lords of Buckingham and Derby.
Buck. Good time of day unto your royal grace!
Der. God make your majesty joyful as you have been!
Q. Eliz. The Countess Richmond, good my Lord of Derby, 20
To your good prayers will scarcely say amen.
Yet, Derby, notwithstanding she's your wife,
And loves not me, be you, good lord, assured
I hate not you for her proud arrogance.
Der. I do beseech you, either not believe
The envious slanders of her false accusers;
Or, if she be accused in true report,
Bear with her weakness, which, I think, proceeds
From wayward sickness, and no grounded malice.
Riv. Saw you the king to-day, my Lord of Derby? 30
Der. But now the Duke of Buckingham and I
Are come from visiting his majesty.
Q. Eliz. What likelihood of his amendment, lords?
Buck. Madam, good hope; his grace speaks cheerfully.
Q. Eliz. God grant him health! Did you confer with him?
Buck. Madam, we did: he desires to make atonement
Betwixt the Duke of Gloucester and your brothers,
And betwixt them and my lord chamberlain;
And sent to warn them to his royal presence.
Q. Eliz. Would all were well! but that will never be: 40
I fear our happiness is at the highest.

---

244. the . . . nature, i.e., nature's most prodigal mood. 245. right royal. This compliment to the young prince is to be understood, not as characteristic justice in Richard, but as a conventional means of informing the audience through soliloquy. 250. moiety, part of (Edward's virtues). 252. denier, small copper coin, the twelfth part of a sou. 261. in, into.
Scene iii. 6. betide of, become of.

15. determined . . . concluded, i.e., decided though not performed. 16. miscarry, perish. 20. Countess Richmond, Margaret Beaufort (1443-1509), who married successively Edmund Tudor Earl of Richmond, Lord Henry Stafford, and Thomas Lord Stanley (here called also Earl of Derby). She was not friendly to Queen Elizabeth's faction.

Enter GLOUCESTER, HASTINGS, *and* DORSET.

Glou. They do me wrong, and I will not
  endure it:
Who are they that complain unto the king,
That I, forsooth, am stern and love them
  not?
By holy Paul, they love his grace but lightly
That fill his ears with such dissentious
  rumours.
Because I cannot flatter and speak fair,
Smile in men's faces, smooth, deceive and
  cog,
Duck with French nods and apish courtesy,
I must be held a rancorous enemy.   50
Cannot a plain man live and think no harm,
But thus his simple truth must be abused
By silken, sly, insinuating Jacks?
  Riv. To whom in all this presence speaks
  your grace?
  Glou. To thee, that hast nor honesty nor
  grace.
When have I injured thee? when done thee
  wrong?
Or thee? or thee? or any of your faction?
A plague upon you all! His royal person,—
Whom God preserve better than you would
  wish!—
Cannot be quiet scarce a breathing-while, 60
But you must trouble him with lewd com-
  plaints.
  Q. Eliz. Brother of Gloucester, you mis-
  take the matter.
The king, of his own royal disposition,
And not provoked by any suitor else;
Aiming, belike, at your interior hatred,
Which in your outward actions shows itself
Against my kindred, brothers, and myself,
Makes him to send; that thereby he may
  gather
The ground of your ill-will, and so remove it.
  Glou. I cannot tell: the world is grown so
  bad,   70
That wrens make prey where eagles dare not
  perch:
Since every Jack became a gentleman,
There's many a gentle person made a Jack.
  Q. Eliz. Come, come, we know your
  meaning, brother Gloucester;
You envy my advancement and my friends':
God grant we never may have need of you!

Glou. Meantime, God grants that we
  have need of you:
Our brother is imprison'd by your means,
Myself disgraced, and the nobility
Held in contempt; whilst many fair promo-
  tions   80
Are daily given to ennoble those
That scarce, some two days since, were
  worth a noble.
  Q. Eliz. By Him that raised me to this
  careful height
From that contented hap which I enjoy'd,
I never did incense his majesty
Against the Duke of Clarence, but have been
An earnest advocate to plead for him.
My lord, you do me shameful injury,
Falsely to draw me in these vile suspects.
  Glou. You may deny that you were not
  the cause   90
Of my Lord Hastings' late imprisonment.
  Riv. She may, my lord, for—
  Glou. She may, Lord Rivers! why, who
  knows not so?
She may do more, sir, than denying that:
She may help you to many fair preferments;
And then deny her aiding hand therein,
And lay those honours on your high deserts.
What may she not? She may, yea, marry,
  may she,—
  Riv. What, marry, may she?
  Glou. What, marry, may she! marry with
  a king,   100
A bachelor, a handsome stripling too:
I wis your grandam had a worser match.
  Q. Eliz. My Lord of Gloucester, I have
  too long borne
Your blunt upbraidings and your bitter
  scoffs:
By heaven, I will acquaint his majesty
With those gross taunts I often have en-
  dured.
I had rather be a country servant-maid
Than a great queen, with this condition,
To be thus taunted, scorn'd, and baited at:

Enter QUEEN MARGARET, *behind.*

Small joy have I in being England's queen.
  Q. Mar. And lessen'd be that small, God,
  I beseech thee!   111
Thy honour, state and seat is due to me.

---

48. **smooth,** flatter. **cog,** cheat. 53. **Jacks,** low-
bred persons. 60. **breathing-while,** moment of rest.
61. **lewd,** vile, base. 63. **disposition,** inclination.
72. **Jack,** peasant, with play on the meaning "base fellow" in the next line.

77. **need of you,** are in trouble on account of you.
82. **noble,** a coin, with quibble on the sense of "en-
noblement." 89. **suspects,** suspicions. 100. **marry
with.** In all preceding cases the word *marry* has been
used as an oath meaning "by the Virgin Mary." 112.
seat, throne.

Glou. What! threat you me with telling
    of the king?
Tell him, and spare not: look, what I have
    said
I will avouch in presence of the king:
I dare adventure to be sent to the Tower.
'Tis time to speak; my pains are quite forgot.
    Q. Mar. Out, devil! I remember them too
    well:
Thou slewest my husband Henry in the
    Tower,
And Edward, my poor son, at Tewksbury.
    Glou. Ere you were queen, yea, or your
    husband king,   121
I was a pack-horse in his great affairs;
A weeder-out of his proud adversaries,
A liberal rewarder of his friends:
To royalise his blood I spilt mine own.
    Q. Mar. Yea, and much better blood than
    his or thine.
    Glou. In all which time you and your
    husband Grey
Were factious for the house of Lancaster;
And, Rivers, so were you. Was not your
    husband
In Margaret's battle at Saint Alban's slain?
Let me put in your minds, if you forget, 131
What you have been ere now, and what you
    are;
Withal, what I have been, and what I am.
    Q. Mar. A murderous villain, and so still
    thou art.
    Glou. Poor Clarence did forsake his father,
    Warwick;
Yea, and forswore himself,—which Jesu par-
    don!—
    Q. Mar. Which God revenge!
    Glou. To fight on Edward's party for the
    crown;
And for his meed, poor lord, he is mew'd up.
I would to God my heart were flint, like
    Edward's;   140
Or Edward's soft and pitiful, like mine:
I am too childish-foolish for this world.
    Q. Mar. Hie thee to hell for shame, and
    leave the world,
Thou cacodemon! there thy kingdom is.
    Riv. My Lord of Gloucester, in those busy
    days
Which here you urge to prove us enemies,
We follow'd then our lord, our lawful king:

So should we you, if you should be our
    king.
    Glou. If I should be! I had rather be a
    pedlar:
Far be it from my heart, the thought of it! 150
    Q. Eliz. As little joy, my lord, as you
    suppose
You should enjoy, were you this country's
    king,
As little joy may you suppose in me,
That I enjoy, being the queen thereof.
    Q. Mar. A little joy enjoys the queen
    thereof;
For I am she, and altogether joyless.
I can no longer hold me patient. [*Advancing.*
Hear me, you wrangling pirates, that fall
    out
In sharing that which you have pill'd from
    me!
Which of you trembles not that looks on me?
If not, that, I being queen, you bow like
    subjects,   161
Yet that, by you deposed, you quake like
    rebels?
O gentle villain, do not turn away!
    Glou. Foul wrinkled witch, what makest
    thou in my sight?
    Q. Mar. But repetition of what thou hast
    marr'd;
That will I make before I let thee go.
    Glou. Wert thou not banished on pain of
    death?
    Q. Mar. I was; but I do find more pain in
    banishment
Than death can yield me here by my abode.
A husband and a son thou owest to me; 170
And thou a kingdom; all of you allegiance:
The sorrow that I have, by right is yours,
And all the pleasures you usurp are mine.
    Glou. The curse my noble father laid on
    thee,
When thou didst crown his warlike brows
    with paper
And with thy scorns drew'st rivers from his
    eyes,
And then, to dry them, gavest the duke a
    clout

---

116. **adventure to be**, risk being. 121-2. **Ere . . .
affairs.** Edward IV became king in 1460 when Richard
was eight years old. 130. **Margaret's battle**, probably, the battle of Bernard's Heath fought at St. Alban's
in 1461. 144. **cacodemon**, evil spirit.

159. **pill'd**, robbed, pillaged. 160-62. **Which . . .
rebels.** If you do not tremble before me, bowing in
awe because I am your queen, you quake as rebels who
have deposed me. 165. **But . . . marr'd**, I merely rehearse your crimes. 167. **banished.** Margaret was
banished in 1464, returned to England in 1471, and after
the battle of Tewksbury was confined in the Tower until
1476 when she returned to France, dying there in 1482,
one year before the historical time of this scene. 170.
thou, Richard. 171. **thou**, i.e., Elizabeth. 174. **curse.**
Cf. *3 Henry VI*, I, iv. 164-66. 177. **clout**, cloth.

Steep'd in the faultless blood of pretty Rut-
    land,—

His curses, then from bitterness of soul

Denounced against thee, are all fall'n upon
    thee;   180

And God, not we, hath plagued thy bloody
    deed.

  Q. Eliz. So just is God, to right the inno-
    cent.

  Hast. O, 'twas the foulest deed to slay
    that babe,

And the most merciless that e'er was heard
    of!

  Riv. Tyrants themselves wept when it was
    reported.

  Dor. No man but prophesied revenge for
    it.

  Buck. Northumberland, then present,
    wept to see it.

  Q. Mar. What! were you snarling all be-
    fore I came,

Ready to catch each other by the throat,

And turn you all your hatred now on me? 190

Did York's dread curse prevail so much with
    heaven

That Henry's death, my lovely Edward's
    death,

Their kingdom's loss, my woful banishment,

Could all but answer for that peevish brat?

Can curses pierce the clouds and enter
    heaven?

Why, then, give way, dull clouds, to my
    quick curses!

If not by war, by surfeit die your king,

As ours by murder, to make him a king!

Edward thy son, which now is Prince of
    Wales,

For Edward my son, which was Prince of
    Wales,   200

Die in his youth by like untimely violence!

Thyself a queen, for me that was a queen,

Outlive thy glory, like my wretched self!

Long mayst thou live to wail thy children's
    loss;

And see another, as I see thee now,

Deck'd in thy rights, as thou art stall'd in
    mine!

Long die thy happy days before thy death;

And, after many lengthen'd hours of grief,

Die neither mother, wife, nor England's
    queen!

Rivers and Dorset, you were standers by, 210

And so wast thou, Lord Hastings, when my
    son

Was stabb'd with bloody daggers: God, I
    pray him,

That none of you may live your natural age,

But by some unlook'd accident cut off!

  Glou. Have done thy charm, thou hateful
    wither'd hag!

  Q. Mar. And leave out thee? stay, dog,
    for thou shalt hear me.

If heaven have any grievous plague in store

Exceeding those that I can wish upon thee,

O, let them keep it till thy sins be ripe,

And then hurl down their indignation   220

On thee, the troubler of the poor world's
    peace!

The worm of conscience still begnaw thy
    soul!

Thy friends suspect for traitors while thou
    livest,

And take deep traitors for thy dearest
    friends!

No sleep close up that deadly eye of thine,

Unless it be whilst some tormenting dream

Affrights thee with a hell of ugly devils!

Thou elvish-mark'd, abortive, rooting hog!

Thou that wast seal'd in thy nativity

The slave of nature and the son of hell!   230

Thou slander of thy mother's heavy womb!

Thou loathed issue of thy father's loins!

Thou rag of honour! thou detested—

  Glou.   Margaret.

  Q. Mar.   Richard!

  Glou.   Ha!

  Q. Mar.   I call thee not.

  Glou. I cry thee mercy then, for I had
    thought

That thou hadst call'd me all these bitter
    names.

  Q. Mar. Why, so I did; but look'd for no
    reply.

O, let me make the period to my curse!

  Glou. 'Tis done by me, and ends in 'Mar-
    garet.'

  Q. Eliz. Thus have you breathed your
    curse against yourself.   240

---

187. **Northumberland**, Sir Henry Percy, third Earl
of Northumberland, killed at Towton in 1461. Cf. *3
Henry VI*, I, iv, 150-1, 169-174. 196. **quick**, sharp,
piercing. 197. **surfeit**, luxurious living.

214. **cut off**, elliptic, but co-ordinate with the preceding line, i.e., live until you are cut off. 228. **elvish-
mark'd**, marked by elves at birth. **rooting hog**, an allusion to Richard's badge, the wild boar. In 1484 William
Colyngborne, a Wiltshire gentleman, was executed for
publishing the lines: "The Cat, the Rat, and Louell our
dog | Rull all England vnder an hog." 229. **seal'd**,
stamped. 230. **slave of nature**, i.e., by the malignancy
of nature. 238. **period**, conclusion. 239. **by me**, i.e.,
in line 234 where he completes Margaret's sentence.

Q. Mar. Poor painted queen, vain flourish
  of my fortune!
Why strew'st thou sugar on that bottled
  spider,
Whose deadly web ensnareth thee about?
Fool, fool! thou whet'st a knife to kill thy-
  self.
The time will come when thou shalt wish for
  me
To help thee curse that poisonous bunch-
  back'd toad.
Hast. False-boding woman, end thy fran-
  tic curse,
Lest to thy harm thou move our patience.
  Q. Mar. Foul shame upon you! you have
  all moved mine.
  Riv. Were you well served, you would be
  taught your duty.   250
  Q. Mar. To serve me well, you all should
  do me duty,
Teach me to be your queen, and you my sub-
  jects:
O, serve me well, and teach yourselves that
  duty!
  Dor. Dispute not with her; she is lunatic.
  Q. Mar. Peace, master marquess, you are
  malapert:
Your fire-new stamp of honour is scarce cur-
  rent.
O, that your young nobility could judge
What 'twere to lose it, and be miserable!
They that stand high have many blasts to
  shake them;
And if they fall, they dash themselves to
  pieces.   260
  Glou. Good counsel, marry: learn it, learn
  it, marquess.
  Dor. It toucheth you, my lord, as much as
  me.
  Glou. Yea, and much more: but I was
  born so high,
Our aery buildeth in the cedar's top,
And dallies with the wind and scorns the
  sun.
  Q. Mar. And turns the sun to shade; alas!
  alas!
Witness my son, now in the shade of death;
Whose bright out-shining beams thy cloudy
  wrath

Hath in eternal darkness folded up.
Your aery buildeth in our aery's nest.   270
O God, that seest it, do not suffer it;
As it was won with blood, lost be it so!
  Buck. Have done! for shame, if not for
  charity.
  Q. Mar. Urge neither charity nor shame
  to me:
Uncharitably with me have you dealt,
And shamefully by you my hopes are butch-
  er'd.
My charity is outrage, life my shame;
And in that shame still live my sorrow's rage!
  Buck. Have done, have done.
  Q. Mar. O princely Buckingham, I'll kiss
  thy hand,   280
In sign of league and amity with thee:
Now fair befal thee and thy noble house!
Thy garments are not spotted with our
  blood,
Nor thou within the compass of my curse.
  Buck. Nor no one here; for curses never
  pass
The lips of those that breathe them in the air.
  Q. Mar. I'll not believe but they ascend
  the sky,
And there awake God's gentle-sleeping
  peace.
O Buckingham, take heed of yonder dog!
Look, when he fawns, he bites; and when he
  bites,   290
His venom tooth will rankle to the death:
Have not to do with him, beware of him;
Sin, death, and hell have set their marks on
  him,
And all their ministers attend on him.
  Glou. What doth she say, my Lord of
  Buckingham?
  Buck. Nothing that I respect, my gracious
  lord.
  Q. Mar. What, dost thou scorn me for my
  gentle counsel?
And soothe the devil that I warn thee from?
O, but remember this another day,
When he shall split thy very heart with
  sorrow,   300
And say poor Margaret was a prophetess!
Live each of you the subjects to his hate,
And he to yours, and all of you to God's!
                                        [*Exit.*

---

241. **painted**, counterfeit. **vain . . . fortune**, i.e.,
mere ornament of a position which is mine by right.
242. **bottled**, bottle-shaped, swollen. 250. **well served**,
i.e., if you had what you have deserved. Margaret takes
the word in its other sense in line 253. 255. **malapert**,
impudent. 256. **fire-new**, newly coined. **current**,
put into circulation. 264. **aery**, brood of an eagle.

277. **My . . . outrage**, i.e., instead of charity I receive outrage. 285-86. **curses . . . air.** Probably, curses
have no effect except on those who utter them. 291.
venom, envenomed. **rankle**, cause a festering wound.
298. **soothe**, flatter.

Hast. My hair doth stand on end to hear
  her curses.

Riv. And so doth mine: I muse why she's
  at liberty.

Glou. I cannot blame her: by God's holy
  mother,

She hath had too much wrong; and I repent

My part thereof that I have done to her.

Q. Eliz. I never did her any, to my knowledge.

Glou. But you have all the vantage of her
  wrong.   310

I was too hot to do somebody good,

That is too cold in thinking of it now.

Marry, as for Clarence, he is well repaid;

He is frank'd up to fatting for his pains:

God pardon them that are the cause of it!

Riv. A virtuous and a Christian-like conclusion,

To pray for them that have done scathe to
  us.

Glou. So do I ever: [*Aside*] being well advised.

For had I cursed now, I had cursed myself.

Enter CATESBY.

Cates. Madam, his majesty doth call for
  you;   320

And for your grace; and you, my noble lords.

Q. Eliz. Catesby, we come. Lords, will
  you go with us?

Riv. Madam, we will attend your grace.
                    [*Exeunt all but Gloucester.*

Glou. I do the wrong, and first begin to
  brawl.

The secret mischiefs that I set abroach

I lay unto the grievous charge of others.

Clarence, whom I, indeed, have laid in darkness,

I do beweep to many simple gulls;

Namely, to Hastings, Derby, Buckingham;

And say it is the queen and her allies   330

That stir the king against the duke my
  brother.

Now, they believe it; and withal whet me

To be revenged on Rivers, Vaughan, Grey:

But then I sigh; and, with a piece of scripture,

Tell them that God bids us do good for evil:

And thus I clothe my naked villany

---

311. **hot**, eager. 312. **cold**, ungrateful. 314. **frank'd
up**, shut up in a frank, or sty. 317. **scathe**, harm.
319. **cursed myself**, i.e., Richard himself is the *cause*
mentioned in line 315. 325. **set abroach**, begin, set on
foot.

With old odd ends stolen out of holy writ;

And seem a saint, when most I play the
  devil.

Enter two Murderers.

But, soft! here come my executioners.

How now, my hardy, stout resolved mates!

Are you now going to dispatch this deed? 341

First Murd. We are, my lord; and come to
  have the warrant,

That we may be admitted where he is.

Glou. Well thought upon; I have it here
  about me.   [*Gives the warrant.*

When you have done, repair to Crosby Place.

But, sirs, be sudden in the execution,

Withal obdurate, do not hear him plead;

For Clarence is well-spoken, and perhaps

May move your hearts to pity, if you mark
  him.

First Murd. Tush!   350

Fear not, my lord, we will not stand to prate;

Talkers are no good doers: be assured

We come to use our hands and not our
  tongues.

Glou. Your eyes drop millstones, when
  fools' eyes drop tears:

I like you, lads; about your business
  straight;

Go, go, dispatch.

First Murd. We will, my noble lord.
                                  [*Exeunt.*

Scene IV. *London. The Tower.*

Enter CLARENCE *and* BRAKENBURY.

Brak. Why looks your grace so heavily
  to-day?

Clar. O, I have pass'd a miserable night,

So full of ugly sights, of ghastly dreams,

That, as I am a Christian faithful man,

I would not spend another such a night,

Though 'twere to buy a world of happy days,

So full of dismal terror was the time!

Brak. What was your dream? I long to
  hear you tell it.

Clar. Methoughts that I had broken from
  the Tower,

And was embark'd to cross to Burgundy; 10

And, in my company, my brother Gloucester;

Who from my cabin tempted me to walk

Scene IV. 10. **Burgundy**, i.e., the Netherlands.
Clarence when a child had been under the Burgundian
protection at Utrecht.

Upon the hatches: thence we look'd toward
    England,
And cited up a thousand fearful times,
During the wars of York and Lancaster
That had befall'n us.   As we paced along
Upon the giddy footing of the hatches,
Methought that Gloucester stumbled; and,
    in falling,
Struck me, that thought to stay him, over-
    board,
Into the tumbling billows of the main.   20
Lord, Lord! methought, what pain it was to
    drown!
What dreadful noise of waters in mine ears!
What ugly sights of death within mine eyes!
Methought I saw a thousand fearful wrecks;
Ten thousand men that fishes gnaw'd upon;
Wedges of gold, great anchors, heaps of
    pearl,
Inestimable stones, unvalued jewels,
All scatter'd in the bottom of the sea:
Some lay in dead men's skulls; and, in those
    holes
Where eyes did once inhabit, there were
    crept,   30
As 'twere in scorn of eyes, reflecting gems,
Which woo'd the slimy bottom of the deep,
And mock'd the dead bones that lay scat-
    ter'd by.
    Brak. Had you such leisure in the time of
    death
To gaze upon the secrets of the deep?
    Clar. Methought I had; and often did I
    strive
To yield the ghost: but still the envious
    flood
Kept in my soul, and would not let it forth
To seek the empty, vast and wandering air;
But smother'd it within my panting bulk, 40
Which almost burst to belch it in the sea.
    Brak. Awaked you not with this sore
    agony?
    Clar. O, no, my dream was lengthen'd
    after life;
O, then began the tempest to my soul,
Who pass'd, methought, the melancholy
    flood,
With that grim ferryman which poets write
    of,
Unto the kingdom of perpetual night.

The first that there did greet my stranger
    soul,
Was my great father-in-law, renowned War-
    wick;
Who cried aloud, 'What scourge for perjury
Can this dark monarchy afford false Clar-
    ence?'   51
And so he vanish'd: then came wandering by
A shadow like an angel, with bright hair
Dabbled in blood; and he squeak'd out aloud,
'Clarence is come; false, fleeting, perjured
    Clarence,
That stabb'd me in the field by Tewksbury;
Seize on him, Furies, take him to your tor-
    ments!'
With that, methoughts, a legion of foul
    fiends
Environ'd me about, and howled in mine
    ears
Such hideous cries, that with the very noise
I trembling waked, and for a season after 61
Could not believe but that I was in hell,
Such terrible impression made the dream.
    Brak. No marvel, my lord, though it af-
    frighted you;
I promise you, I am afraid to hear you
    tell it.
    Clar. O Brakenbury, I have done those
    things,
Which now bear evidence against my soul,
For Edward's sake; and see how he requites
    me!
O God! if my deep prayers cannot appease
    thee,
But thou wilt be avenged on my misdeeds, 70
Yet execute thy wrath in me alone,
O, spare my guiltless wife and my poor
    children!
I pray thee, gentle keeper, stay by me;
My soul is heavy, and I fain would sleep.
    Brak. I will, my lord: God give your grace
    good rest!   [*Clarence sleeps.*
Sorrow breaks seasons and reposing hours,
Makes the night morning, and the noon-tide
    night.
Princes have but their titles for their glories,
An outward honour for an inward toil;
And, for unfelt imagination,   80
They often feel a world of restless cares:

---

37. envious, malicious.   **39. vast.** Malone suggests
that this word is a substantive.   **40. bulk,** body.   **45.
melancholy flood,** i.e., the river Styx.   **46. ferryman,**
i.e., Charon, who ferried souls to Hades, *the kingdom of
perpetual night* (l. 47).

49. father-in-law. Clarence's wife, Isabel Neville,
was the elder daughter of the Earl of Warwick.   **50.
scourge for perjury.** Cf. *3 Henry VI*, V, i, 106.   **53.
shadow,** i.e., ghost of Edward Prince of Wales, son of
Henry VI.   **55. fleeting,** fickle, deceitful.   **56. stabb'd
me.** Cf. *3 Henry VI*, V, v, 40.   **80. unfelt,** unrealized.

So that, betwixt their titles and low names,
There's nothing differs but the outward
fame.

Enter the two Murderers.

First Murd. Ho! who's here?

Brak. In God's name what are you, and
how came you hither?

First Murd. I would speak with Clarence,
and I came hither on my legs.

Brak. Yea, are you so brief?

Sec. Murd. O sir, it is better to be brief
than tedious. Show him our commission;
talk no more.   [*Brakenbury reads it.*

Brak. I am, in this, commanded to deliver
The noble Duke of Clarence to your hands:
I will not reason what is meant hereby,
Because I will be guiltless of the meaning.
Here are the keys, there sits the duke asleep:
I'll to the king; and signify to him
That thus I have resign'd my charge to you.

First Murd. Do so, it is a point of wisdom:
fare you well.   [*Exit Brakenbury.* 100

Sec. Murd. What, shall we stab him as he
sleeps?

First Murd. No; then he will say 'twas
done cowardly, when he wakes.

Sec. Murd. When he wakes! why, fool, he
shall never wake till the judgement-day.

First Murd. Why, then he will say we
stabbed him sleeping.

Sec. Murd. The urging of that word 'judgement' hath bred a kind of remorse in me. 110

First Murd. What, art thou afraid?

Sec. Murd. Not to kill him, having a warrant for it; but to be damned for killing him,
from which no warrant can defend us.

First Murd. I thought thou hadst been
resolute.

Sec. Murd. So I am, to let him live.

First Murd. Back to the Duke of Gloucester, tell him so.   119

Sec. Murd. I pray thee, stay a while: I
hope my holy humour will change; 'twas
wont to hold me but while one would tell
twenty.

First Murd. How dost thou feel thyself
now?

Sec. Murd. 'Faith, some certain dregs of
conscience are yet within me.

First Murd. Remember our reward, when
the deed is done.

122. **tell**, count.

Sec. Murd. 'Zounds, he dies: I had forgot
the reward.

First Murd. Where is thy conscience now?

Sec. Murd. In the Duke of Gloucester's
purse.   131

First Murd. So when he opens his purse
to give us our reward, thy conscience flies out.

Sec. Murd. Let it go; there's few or none
will entertain it.

First Murd. How if it come to thee again?

Sec. Murd. I'll not meddle with it: it is a
dangerous thing: it makes a man a coward: a
man cannot steal, but it accuseth him; he
cannot swear, but it checks him; he cannot
lie with his neighbour's wife, but it detects
him: 'tis a blushing shamefast spirit that
mutinies in a man's bosom; it fills one full of
obstacles: it made me once restore a purse of
gold that I found; it beggars any man that
keeps it: it is turned out of all towns and
cities for a dangerous thing; and every man
that means to live well endeavours to trust
to himself and to live without it.

First Murd. 'Zounds, it is even now at my
elbow, persuading me not to kill the duke. 150

Sec. Murd. Take the devil in thy mind,
and believe him not: he would insinuate with
thee but to make thee sigh.

First Murd. Tut, I am strong-framed, he
cannot prevail with me, I warrant thee.

Sec. Murd. Spoke like a tall fellow that
respects his reputation. Come, shall we to
this gear?

First Murd. Take him over the costard with
the hilts of thy sword, and then we will chop
him in the malmsey-butt in the next room. 161

Sec. Murd. O excellent device! make a
sop of him.

First Murd. Hark! he stirs: shall I strike?

Sec. Murd. No, first let's reason with him.

Clar. Where art thou, keeper? give me a
cup of wine.

Sec. Murd. You shall have wine enough,
my lord, anon.

Clar. In God's name, what art thou?

Sec. Murd. A man, as you are.   170

Clar. But not, as I am, royal.

Sec. Murd. Nor you, as we are, loyal.

Clar. Thy voice is thunder, but thy looks
are humble.

135. **entertain it**, follow the dictates of conscience.
142. **shamefast**, bashful. 152. **him**, conscience, which
he identifies with the devil. 159. **costard**, head; literally, a kind of large apple. 161. **malmsey-butt**,
wine barrel. 162. **sop**, bread dipped in wine.

Sec. Murd. My voice is now the king's,
   my looks mine own.
Clar. How darkly and how deadly dost
   thou speak!
Your eyes do menace me: why look you pale?
Who sent you hither? Wherefore do you
   come?
Both. To, to, to—
Clar. To murder me?
Both. Ay, ay.
Clar. You scarcely have the hearts to tell
   me so,   180
And therefore cannot have the hearts to do
   it.
Wherein, my friends, have I offended you?
First Murd. Offended us you have not,
   but the king.
Clar. I shall be reconciled to him again.
Sec. Murd. Never, my lord; therefore pre-
   pare to die.
Clar. Are you call'd forth from out a
   world of men
To slay the innocent? What is my offence?
Where are the evidence that do accuse me?
What lawful quest have given their verdict
   up   189
Unto the frowning judge? or who pronounced
The bitter sentence of poor Clarence' death?
Before I be convict by course of law,
To threaten me with death is most unlawful.
I charge you, as you hope to have redemp-
   tion
By Christ's dear blood shed for our grievous
   sins,
That you depart and lay no hands on me:
The deed you undertake is damnable.
First Murd. What we will do, we do upon
   command.
Sec. Murd. And he that hath commanded
   is the king.
Clar. Erroneous vassal! the great King of
   kings   200
Hath in the tables of his law commanded
That thou shalt do no murder: and wilt thou,
   then,
Spurn at his edict and fulfil a man's?
Take heed; for he holds vengeance in his
   hands,
To hurl upon their heads that break his law.
Sec. Murd. And that same vengeance
   doth he hurl on thee,

For false forswearing and for murder too:
Thou didst receive the holy sacrament,
To fight in quarrel of the house of Lancaster.
First Murd. And, like a traitor to the
   name of God,   210
Didst break that vow; and with thy treacher-
   ous blade
Unrip'dst the bowels of thy sovereign's son.
Sec. Murd. Whom thou wert sworn to
   cherish and defend.
First Murd. How canst thou urge God's
   dreadful law to us,
When thou hast broke it in so dear degree?
Clar. Alas! for whose sake did I that ill
   deed?
For Edward, for my brother, for his sake:
Why, sirs,
He sends ye not to murder me for this;
For in this sin he is as deep as I.   220
If God will be revenged for this deed,
O, know you yet, he doth it publicly:
Take not the quarrel from his powerful arm;
He needs no indirect nor lawless course
To cut off those that have offended him.
First Murd. Who made thee, then, a
   bloody minister,
When gallant-springing brave Plantagenet,
That princely novice, was struck dead by
   thee?
Clar. My brother's love, the devil, and
   my rage.
First Murd. Thy brother's love, our duty,
   and thy fault,   230
Provoke us hither now to slaughter thee.
Clar. Oh, if you love my brother, hate not
   me;
I am his brother, and I love him well.
If you be hired for meed, go back again,
And I will send you to my brother Glou-
   cester,
Who shall reward you better for my life
Than Edward will for tidings of my death.
Sec. Murd. You are deceived, your bro-
   ther Gloucester hates you.
Clar. O, no, he loves me, and he holds me
   dear:
Go you to him from me.
Both.   Ay, so we will.   240
Clar. Tell him, when that our princely
   father York
Bless'd his three sons with his victorious
   arm,

---

175. **darkly**, frowningly.   189. **quest**, inquest; possibly, jury.   192. **convict**, convicted.   200. **Erroneous**,
mistaken.

227. **gallant-springing**, blooming in the spring-
time of life.   228. **novice**, youth.

And charged us from his soul to love each other,

He little thought of this divided friend- ship:

Bid Gloucester think of this, and he will weep.

   First Murd. Ay, millstones; as he lesson'd us to weep.

   Clar. O, do not slander him, for he is kind.

   First Murd. Right,

As snow in harvest. Thou deceivest thyself:
'Tis he that sent us hither now to slaughter thee. 250

   Clar. It cannot be; for when I parted with him,

He hugg'd me in his arms, and swore, with sobs,

That he would labour my delivery.

   Sec. Murd. Why, so he doth, now he delivers thee

From this world's thraldom to the joys of heaven.

   First Murd. Make peace with God, for you must die, my lord.

   Clar. Hast thou that holy feeling in thy soul,

To counsel me to make my peace with God,
And art thou yet to thy own soul so blind,
That thou wilt war with God by murdering me? 260

Ah, sirs, consider, he that set you on
To do this deed will hate you for the deed.

   Sec. Murd. What shall we do?

   Clar.   Relent, and save your souls.

   First Murd. Relent! 'tis cowardly and wo- manish.

   Clar. Not to relent is beastly, savage, devilish.

Which of you, if you were a prince's son,
Being pent from liberty, as I am now,
If two such murderers as yourselves came to you,

Would not entreat for life?

My friend, I spy some pity in thy looks; 270
O, if thine eye be not a flatterer,
Come thou on my side, and entreat for me,
As you would beg, were you in my distress:
A begging prince what beggar pities not?

   Sec. Murd. Look behind you, my lord.

   First Murd. Take that, and that: if all this will not do,   [*Stabs him.*

I'll drown you in the malmsey-butt with- in.   [*Exit, with the body.*

   Sec. Murd. A bloody deed, and desper- ately dispatch'd!

How fain, like Pilate, would I wash my hands
Of this most grievous guilty murder done! 280

Re-enter First Murderer.

   First Murd. How now! what mean'st thou, that thou help'st me not?

By heavens, the duke shall know how slack thou art!

   Sec. Murd. I would he knew that I had saved his brother!

Take thou the fee, and tell him what I say;
For I repent me that the duke is slain. [*Exit.*

   First Murd. So do not I: go, coward as thou art.

Now must I hide his body in some hole,
Until the duke take order for his burial:
And when I have my meed, I must away;
For this will out, and here I must not stay. 290
                     [*Exit.*

ACT II.

SCENE I. *London. The palace.*

Flourish. Enter KING EDWARD *sick*, QUEEN ELIZABETH, DORSET, RIVERS, HASTINGS, BUCKINGHAM, GREY, *and others*.

   K. Edw. Why, so: now have I done a good day's work:

You peers, continue this united league:
I every day expect an embassage
From my Redeemer to redeem me hence;
And now in peace my soul shall part to heaven,

Since I have set my friends at peace on earth.

Rivers and Hastings, take each other's hand;
Dissemble not your hatred, swear your love.

   Riv. By heaven, my heart is purged from grudging hate;

And with my hand I seal my true heart's love.   10

   Hast. So thrive I, as I truly swear the like!

   K. Edw. Take heed you dally not before your king;

Lest he that is the supreme King of kings

249. **snow in harvest.** Cf. *Proverbs* xxvi, 1. 253. **labour my delivery,** i.e., work to procure my freedom. 267. **pent from,** shut up from.

277. **malmsey-butt.** Shakespeare here follows Holinshed. The scene up to this point has no historical basis.
Act II. *Scene* i. 8. **Dissemble . . . hatred,** i.e., do not conceal it merely. 12. **dally,** trifle.

Confound your hidden falsehood, and award
Either of you to be the other's end.

Hast. So prosper I, as I swear perfect love!

Riv. And I, as I love Hastings with my
heart!

K. Edw. Madam, yourself are not exempt
in this,
Nor your son Dorset, Buckingham, nor you;
You have been factious one against the
other.   20
Wife, love Lord Hastings, let him kiss your
hand;
And what you do, do it unfeignedly.

Q. Eliz. Here, Hastings; I will never more
remember
Our former hatred, so thrive I and mine!

K. Edw. Dorset, embrace him; Hastings,
love lord marquess.

Dor. This interchange of love, I here protest,
Upon my part shall be unviolable.

Hast. And so swear I, my lord.
                                    [*They embrace.*

K. Edw. Now, princely Buckingham, seal
thou this league
With thy embracements to my wife's allies,
And make me happy in your unity.   31

Buck. Whenever Buckingham doth turn
his hate
On you or yours [*to the Queen*], but with all
duteous love
Doth cherish you and yours, God punish me
With hate in those where I expect most love!
When I have most need to employ a friend,
And most assured that he is a friend,
Deep, hollow, treacherous, and full of guile,
Be he unto me! this do I beg of God,
When I am cold in zeal to you or yours. 40
                                    [*They embrace.*

K. Edw. A pleasing cordial, princely
Buckingham,
Is this thy vow unto my sickly heart.
There wanteth now our brother Gloucester
here,
To make the perfect period of this peace.

Buck. And, in good time, here comes the
noble duke.

Enter GLOUCESTER.

Glou. Good morrow to my sovereign king
and queen;
And, princely peers, a happy time of day!

K. Edw. Happy, indeed, as we have spent
the day.
Brother, we have done deeds of charity;
Made peace of enmity, fair love of hate, 50
Between these swelling wrong-incensed
peers.

Glou. A blessed labour, my most sovereign
liege:
Amongst this princely heap, if any here,
By false intelligence, or wrong surmise,
Hold me a foe;
If I unwittingly, or in my rage,
Have aught committed that is hardly borne
By any in this presence, I desire
To reconcile me to his friendly peace:
'Tis death to me to be at enmity;   60
I hate it, and desire all good men's love.
First, madam, I entreat true peace of you,
Which I will purchase with my duteous serv-
ice;
Of you, my noble cousin Buckingham,
If ever any grudge were lodged between us;
Of you, Lord Rivers, and, Lord Grey, of you;
That all without desert have frown'd on me;
Dukes, earls, lords, gentlemen; indeed, of all.
I do not know that Englishman alive
With whom my soul is any jot at odds   70
More than the infant that is born to-night:
I thank my God for my humility.

Q. Eliz. A holy day shall this be kept
hereafter:
I would to God all strifes were well compounded.
My sovereign liege, I do beseech your majesty
To take our brother Clarence to your grace.

Glou. Why, madam, have I offer'd love
for this,
To be so flouted in this royal presence?
Who knows not that the noble duke is dead?
                                    [*They all start.*
You do him injury to scorn his corse.   80

Riv. Who knows not he is dead! who
knows he is?

Q. Eliz. All-seeing heaven, what a world
is this!

Buck. Look I so pale, Lord Dorset, as the
rest?

---

15. **Either . . . end**, i.e., each of you to die at the hands of the other. 20. **factious**, i.e., guilty of factious conduct. 37. **most**, am most.

50. **of**, out of. 51. **swelling**, i.e., with anger or rivalry. 53. **heap**, assembly. 54. **false intelligence**, being misinformed. 57. **hardly borne**, taken amiss. 66. **Lord Rivers.** There is a difficult crux in this passage. After line 67 F adds *Of you Lord Wooduill and Lord Scales of you*. Woodville was Lord Rivers and, also, Lord Scales by right of his wife. Thus in F one person is given three names. 67. **without desert**, i.e., on my part. 74. **compounded**, settled.

Dor. Ay, my good lord; and no one in this presence
But his red colour hath forsook his cheeks.
K. Edw. Is Clarence dead? the order was reversed.
Glou. But he, poor soul, by your first order died,
And that a winged Mercury did bear;
Some tardy cripple bore the countermand,
That came too lag to see him buried.   90
God grant that some, less noble and less loyal,
Nearer in bloody thoughts, but not in blood,
Deserve not worse than wretched Clarence did,
And yet go current from suspicion!

Enter DERBY.

Der. A boon, my sovereign, for my service done!
K. Edw. I pray thee, peace: my soul is full of sorrow.
Der. I will not rise, unless your highness grant.
K. Edw. Then speak at once what is it thou demand'st.
Der. The forfeit, sovereign, of my servant's life;
Who slew to-day a riotous gentleman   100
Lately attendant on the Duke of Norfolk.
K. Edw. Have I a tongue to doom my brother's death,
And shall the same give pardon to a slave?
My brother slew no man; his fault was thought,
And yet his punishment was cruel death.
Who sued to me for him? who, in my rage,
Kneel'd at my feet, and bade me be advised?
Who spake of brotherhood? who spake of love?
Who told me how the poor soul did forsake
The mighty Warwick, and did fight for me?
Who told me, in the field by Tewksbury,   111
When Oxford had me down, he rescued me,
And said, 'Dear brother, live, and be a king'?
Who told me, when we both lay in the field
Frozen almost to death, how he did lap me
Even in his own garments, and gave himself,
All thin and naked, to the numb cold night?
All this from my remembrance brutish wrath

90. lag, late. 94. current . . . suspicion, free and
not attacked by suspicion. 99. forfeit, i.e., the remission of the forfeit. 107. advised, cautious. 112. Oxford. Cf. *3 Henry VI*, V, v, 2.

Sinfully pluck'd, and not a man of you
Had so much grace to put it in my mind. 120
But when your carters or your waiting-vassals
Have done a drunken slaughter, and defaced
The precious image of our dear Redeemer,
You straight are on your knees for pardon, pardon;
And I, unjustly too, must grant it you:
But for my brother not a man would speak,
Nor I, ungracious, speak unto myself
For him, poor soul. The proudest of you all
Have been beholding to him in his life;
Yet none of you would once plead for his life.
O God, I fear thy justice will take hold   131
On me, and you, and mine, and yours for this!
Come, Hastings, help me to my closet. Oh, poor Clarence!
            [*Exeunt some with King and Queen.*
Glou. This is the fruit of rashness! Mark'd you not
How that the guilty kindred of the queen
Look'd pale when they did hear of Clarence' death?
O, they did urge it still unto the king!
God will revenge it. But come, let us in,
To comfort Edward with our company.
Buck. We wait upon your grace. [*Exeunt.*

Scene II. *The palace.*

Enter the DUCHESS OF YORK, *with the two
children of* CLARENCE.

Boy. Tell me, good grandam, is our father dead?
Duch. No, boy.
Boy. Why do you wring your hands, and beat your breast,
And cry 'O Clarence, my unhappy son!'
Girl. Why do you look on us, and shake your head,   5
And call us wretches, orphans, castaways,
If that our noble father be alive?
Duch. My pretty cousins, you mistake me much;
I do lament the sickness of the king,
As loath to lose him, not your father's death;
It were lost sorrow to wail one that's lost. 11
Boy. Then, grandam, you conclude that he is dead.

The king my uncle is to blame for this:
God will revenge it; whom I will impor-
    tune
With daily prayers all to that effect.
  Girl. And so will I.
  Duch. Peace, children, peace! the king
doth love you well:
Incapable and shallow innocents,
You cannot guess who caused your father's
death.
  Boy. Grandam, we can; for my good uncle
Gloucester   20
Told me, the king, provoked by the queen,
Devised impeachments to imprison him:
And when my uncle told me so, he wept,
And hugg'd me in his arm, and kindly kiss'd
    my cheek;
Bade me rely on him as on my father,
And he would love me dearly as his child.
  Duch. Oh, that deceit should steal such
    gentle shapes,
And with a virtuous vizard hide foul guile!
He is my son; yea, and therein my shame;
Yet from my dugs he drew not this deceit. 30
  Boy. Think you my uncle did dissemble,
    grandam?
  Duch. Ay, boy.
  Boy. I cannot think it. Hark! what noise
is this?

Enter Queen Elizabeth, *with her hair about
her ears;* Rivers *and* Dorset *after her.*

  Q. Eliz. Oh, who shall hinder me to wail
    and weep,
To chide my fortune, and torment myself?
I'll join with black despair against my soul,
And to myself become an enemy.
  Duch. What means this scene of rude im-
    patience?
  Q. Eliz. To make an act of tragic vio-
    lence:
Edward, my lord, your son, our king, is
    dead.   40
Why grow the branches now the root is
    wither'd?
Why wither not the leaves the sap being
    gone?
If you will live, lament; if die, be brief,
That our swift-winged souls may catch the
    king's;

Or, like obedient subjects, follow him
To his new kingdom of perpetual rest.
  Duch. Ah, so much interest have I in thy
    sorrow
As I had title in thy noble husband!
I have bewept a worthy husband's death,
And lived by looking on his images: 50
But now two mirrors of his princely sem-
    blance
Are crack'd in pieces by malignant death,
And I for comfort have but one false
    glass,
Which grieves me when I see my shame in
    him.
Thou art a widow; yet thou art a mother,
And hast the comfort of thy children left
    thee:
But death hath snatch'd my husband from
    mine arms,
And pluck'd two crutches from my feeble
    limbs,
Edward and Clarence. O, what cause have I,
Thine being but a moiety of my grief,   60
To overgo thy plaints and drown thy cries!
  Boy. Good aunt, you wept not for our
    father's death;
How can we aid you with our kindred tears?
  Girl. Our fatherless distress was left un-
    moan'd;
Your widow-dolour likewise be unwept!
  Q. Eliz. Give me no help in lamentation;
I am not barren to bring forth complaints:
All springs reduce their currents to mine
    eyes,
That I, being govern'd by the watery moon,
May send forth plenteous tears to drown the
    world!   70
Oh for my husband, for my dear lord Ed-
    ward!
  Chil. Oh for our father, for our dear lord
    Clarence!
  Duch. Alas for both, both mine, Edward
    and Clarence!
  Q. Eliz. What stay had I but Edward?
    and he's gone.
  Chil. What stay had we but Clarence?
    and he's gone.
  Duch. What stays had I but they? and
    they are gone.
  Q. Eliz. Was never widow had so dear a
    loss!

18. **Incapable**, unable to understand. 22. **impeach-**
ments, accusations. 28. **vizard**, mask. 39. **make**,
make up, complete. 40. **Edward . . . dead.** Clarence's
death (February, 1478) and Edward IV's death (April,
1483) are treated as if they had occurred near together.

50. **images**, i.e., children. 53. **false glass**, i.e.,
Richard. 60. **moiety**, small part. 65. **widow-dolour**,
widow's grief. 67. **barren to**, unable to. 68. **reduce**,
bring back.

Chil. Were never orphans had so dear a
   loss!
Duch. Was never mother had so dear a
   loss!
Alas, I am the mother of these moans!   80
Their woes are parcell'd, mine are general.
She for an Edward weeps, and so do I;
I for a Clarence weep, so doth not she:
These babes for Clarence weep, and so do I;
I for an Edward weep, so do not they:
Alas, you three, on me, threefold distress'd,
Pour all your tears! I am your sorrow's nurse,
And I will pamper it with lamentations.
   Dor. Comfort, dear mother; God is much
   displeased
That you take with unthankfulness his
   doing: 90
In common worldly things, 'tis call'd un-
   grateful,
With dull unwillingness to repay a debt
Which with a bounteous hand was kindly
   lent;
Much more to be thus opposite with heaven,
For it requires the royal debt it lent you.
   Riv. Madam, bethink you, like a careful
   mother,
Of the young prince your son: send straight
   for him;
Let him be crown'd; in him your comfort
   lives:
Drown desperate sorrow in dead Edward's
   grave,
And plant your joys in living Edward's
   throne.   100

Enter GLOUCESTER, BUCKINGHAM, DERBY,
   HASTINGS, *and* RATCLIFF.

   Glou. Madam, have comfort: all of us
   have cause
To wail the dimming of our shining star;
But none can cure their harms by wailing
   them.
Madam, my mother, I do cry you mercy;
I did not see your grace: humbly on my knee
I crave your blessing.
   Duch. God bless thee; and put meekness
   in thy mind,
Love, charity, obedience, and true duty!
   Glou. [*Aside*] Amen; and make me die a
   good old man!
That is the butt-end of a mother's blessing:
I marvel why her grace did leave it out.   111

   Buck. You cloudy princes and heart-
   sorrowing peers,
That bear this mutual heavy load of moan,
Now cheer each other in each other's love:
Though we have spent our harvest of this
   king,
We are to reap the harvest of his son.
The broken rancour of your high-swoln
   hearts,
But lately splinter'd, knit, and join'd to-
   gether,
Must gently be preserved, cherish'd, and
   kept:
Me seemeth good, that, with some little
   train,   120
Forthwith from Ludlow the young prince be
   fetch'd
Hither to London, to be crown'd our king.
   Riv. Why with some little train, my Lord
   of Buckingham?
   Buck. Marry, my lord, lest, by a multi-
   tude,
The new-heal'd wound of malice should
   break out;
Which would be so much the more danger-
   ous,
By how much the estate is green and yet un-
   govern'd:
Where every horse bears his commanding
   rein,
And may direct his course as please him-
   self,
As well the fear of harm, as harm apparent,
In my opinion, ought to be prevented.   131
   Glou. I hope the king made peace with
   all of us;
And the compact is firm and true in me.
   Riv. And so in me; and so, I think, in all:
Yet, since it is but green, it should be put
To no apparent likelihood of breach,
Which haply by much company might be
   urged:
Therefore I say with noble Buckingham,
That it is meet so few should fetch the
   prince.
   Hast. And so say I.   140
   Glou. Then be it so; and go we to deter-
   mine

112. **cloudy**, clouded with grief. 117-19. **The
broken . . . kept**, i.e., the differences caused by the
inveterate bitterness of the rancor in your hearts toward
each other has recently been healed, and this peace
between you must be preserved. 118. **splinter'd**,
splinted, bound up with splints. 121. **Ludlow**, the
royal castle at Ludlow in Wales. 127. **estate**, state,
government. **green**, i.e., newly established. 137.
urged, encouraged.

94. **opposite with**, in opposition to.

Who they shall be that straight shall post to
  Ludlow.
Madam, and you, my mother, will you go
To give your censures in this weighty busi-
  ness?
  Q. Eliz.⎫
  Duch. ⎬With all our hearts.
[Exeunt all but Buckingham and Gloucester.
  Buck. My lord, whoever journeys to the
  prince,
For God's sake, let not us two be behind;
For, by the way, I'll sort occasion,
As index to the story we late talk'd of,
To part the queen's proud kindred from the
  king.   150
  Glou. My other self, my counsel's con-
  sistory,
My oracle, my prophet! My dear cousin,
I, like a child, will go by thy direction.
Towards Ludlow then, for we'll not stay
  behind.   [*Exeunt.*

SCENE III. *London. A street.*

Enter two Citizens, *meeting.*

  First Cit. Neighbour, well met: whither
  away so fast?
  Sec. Cit. I promise you, I scarcely know
  myself:
Hear you the news abroad?
  First Cit.   Ay, that the king is dead.
  Sec. Cit. Bad news, by 'r lady; seldom
  comes the better:
I fear, I fear 'twill prove a troublous world.

Enter another Citizen.

  Third Cit. Neighbours, God speed!
  First Cit.   Give you good morrow, sir.
  Third Cit. Doth this news hold of good
  King Edward's death?
  Sec. Cit. Ay, sir, it is too true; God help
  the while!
  Third Cit. Then, masters, look to see a
  troublous world.
  First Cit. No, no; by God's good grace his
  son shall reign.
  Third Cit. Woe to that land that's gov-
  ern'd by a child!
  Sec. Cit. In him there is a hope of govern-
  ment,
That in his nonage council under him,
And in his full and ripen'd years himself,

No doubt, shall then and till then govern
  well.
  First Cit. So stood the state when Henry
  the Sixth
Was crown'd in Paris but at nine months
  old.
  Third Cit. Stood the state so? No, no,
  good friends, God wot;
For then this land was famously enrich'd
With politic grave counsel; then the king 20
Had virtuous uncles to protect his grace.
  First Cit. Why, so hath this, both by the
  father and mother.
  Third Cit. Better it were they all came by
  the father,
Or by the father there were none at all;
For emulation now, who shall be nearest,
Will touch us all too near, if God prevent
  not.
O, full of danger is the Duke of Gloucester!
And the queen's sons and brothers haught
  and proud:
And were they to be ruled, and not to
  rule,
This sickly land might solace as before.   30
  First Cit. Come, come, we fear the
  worst; all shall be well.
  Third Cit. When clouds appear, wise men
  put on their cloaks;
When great leaves fall, the winter is at
  hand;
When the sun sets, who doth not look for
  night?
Untimely storms make men expect a dearth.
All may be well; but, if God sort it so,
'Tis more than we deserve, or I expect.
  Sec. Cit. Truly, the souls of men are full
  of dread:
Ye cannot reason almost with a man
That looks not heavily and full of fear.   40
  Third Cit. Before the times of change,
  still is it so:
By a divine instinct men's minds mistrust
Ensuing dangers; as, by proof, we see
The waters swell before a boisterous storm.
But leave it all to God. Whither away?
  Sec. Cit. Marry, we were sent for to the
  justices.
  Third Cit. And so was I: I'll bear you
  company.
                                  [*Exeunt.*

144. **censures**, judgments. 148. **sort occasion**,
contrive opportunity. 151. **consistory**, council-chamber.
Scene iii. 11. **Woe . . . child.** Cf. *Ecclesiastes* x, 16.
13. **nonage**, minority.

17. **nine months.** Henry VI, proclaimed king of
France, October, 1422, was then about a year old. He
was not crowned in Paris until December, 1430. 30.
solace, be happy, have comfort. 40. **heavily**, sad.

SCENE IV. *London. The palace.*

Enter the ARCHBISHOP OF YORK, *the young* DUKE OF YORK, QUEEN ELIZABETH, *and the* DUCHESS OF YORK.

Arch. Last night, I hear, they lay at
   Northampton;
At Stony-Stratford will they be to-night:
To-morrow, or next day, they will be here.
  Duch. I long with all my heart to see the
   prince:
I hope he is much grown since last I saw him.
  Q. Eliz. But I hear, no; they say my son
   of York
Hath almost overta'en him in his growth.
  York. Ay, mother; but I would not have
   it so.
  Duch. Why, my young cousin, it is good
   to grow.
  York. Grandam, one night, as we did sit
   at supper,   10
My uncle Rivers talk'd how I did grow
More than my brother: 'Ay,' quoth my uncle
   Gloucester,
'Small herbs have grace, great weeds do
   grow apace:'
And since, methinks, I would not grow so
   fast,
Because sweet flowers are slow and weeds
   make haste.
  Duch. Good faith, good faith, the saying
   did not hold
In him that did object the same to thee:
He was the wretched'st thing when he was
   young,
So long a-growing and so leisurely,
That, if this rule were true, he should be
   gracious.   20
  Arch. Why, madam, so, no doubt, he is.
  Duch. I hope he is; but yet let mothers
   doubt.
  York. Now, by my troth, if I had been
   remember'd,
I could have given my uncle's grace a flout,

To touch his growth nearer than he touch'd
   mine.
  Duch. How, my pretty York? I pray
   thee, let me hear it.
  York. Marry, they say my uncle grew so
   fast
That he could gnaw a crust at two hours old:
'Twas full two years ere I could get a tooth.
Grandam, this would have been a biting jest.
  Duch. I pray thee, pretty York, who told
   thee this?   31
  York. Grandam, his nurse.
  Duch. His nurse! why, she was dead ere
   thou wert born.
  York. If 'twere not she, I cannot tell who
   told me.
  Q. Eliz. A parlous boy: go to, you are too
   shrewd.
  Arch. Good madam, be not angry with the
   child.
  Q. Eliz. Pitchers have ears.

Enter a Messenger.

  Arch. Here comes a messenger. What
   news?
  Mess. Such news, my lord, as grieves me
   to unfold.
  Q. Eliz. How fares the prince?
  Mess.   Well, madam, and in health. 40
  Duch. What is thy news then?
  Mess. Lord Rivers and Lord Grey are
   sent to Pomfret,
With them Sir Thomas Vaughan, prisoners.
  Duch. Who hath committed them?
  Mess.   The mighty dukes
Gloucester and Buckingham.
  Q. Eliz.   For what offence?
  Mess. The sum of all I can, I have dis-
   closed;
Why or for what these nobles were com-
   mitted
Is all unknown to me, my gracious lady.
  Q. Eliz. Ay me, I see the downfall of our
   house!
The tiger now hath seized the gentle hind; 50
Insulting tyranny begins to jet
Upon the innocent and aweless throne:
Welcome, destruction, death, and massacre!
I see, as in a map, the end of all.

Stage Direction: **Enter . . . York.** The Archbishop of York was Thomas Rotherham; the Cardinal of III, i, was Thomas Bouchier, made Archbishop of Canterbury in 1454. The Qq stage direction, *Enter Cardinal,* indicates perhaps that one actor took both parts. 1-3. **Last . . . here.** Stony-Stratford is nearer London; the Prince was taken back to Northampton after the arrest of Rivers, Grey, and Vaughan. The F reading (which interchanges these two place names) is in accordance with the facts, but it is dramatically impossible, for if the Archbishop is to have news of Richard's movements he must know also of his actions. That he does not know is clear from his conduct in this scene. 24. **flout,** dig, insult.

28. **That . . . old.** The legend is mentioned by More; cf. also *3 Henry VI,* V, vi, 53-4. 35. **parlous,** terrible (exaggerated epithet). **shrewd,** malicious. 37. **Pitchers have ears.** Proverb: "Little pitchers have large ears." 50. **hind,** doe. 52. **aweless,** i.e., because of the youth of the king.

Duch. Accursed and unquiet wrangling
    days,
How many of you have mine eyes beheld!
My husband lost his life to get the crown;
And often up and down my sons were toss'd,
For me to joy and weep their gain and loss:
And being seated, and domestic broils   60
Clean over-blown, themselves, the con-
    querors,
Make war upon themselves; blood against
    blood,
Self against self: O, preposterous
And frantic outrage, end thy damned spleen;
Or let me die, to look on death no more!
    Q. Eliz. Come, come, my boy; we will to
    sanctuary.
Madam, farewell.
    Duch.   I'll go along with you.
    Q. Eliz. You have no cause.
    Arch.   My gracious lady, go;
And thither bear your treasure and your
    goods.
For my part, I'll resign unto your grace   70
The seal I keep: and so betide to me
As well I tender you and all of yours!
Come, I'll conduct you to the sanctuary.
                                    [*Exeunt.*

ACT III.

Scene I. *London. A street.*

The trumpets sound. Enter the young Prince,
    the Dukes of Gloucester *and* Bucking-
    ham, Cardinal Bourchier, Catesby,
    and others.

    Buck. Welcome, sweet prince, to London,
    to your chamber.
    Glou. Welcome, dear cousin, my thoughts'
    sovereign:
The weary way hath made you melancholy.
    Prince. No, uncle; but our crosses on the
    way
Have made it tedious, wearisome, and heavy:
I want more uncles here to welcome me.
    Glou. Sweet prince, the untainted virtue
    of your years
Hath not yet dived into the world's deceit:
Nor more can you distinguish of a man

Than of his outward show; which, God he
    knows,   10
Seldom or never jumpeth with the heart.
Those uncles which you want were danger-
    ous;
Your grace attended to their sugar'd words,
But look'd not on the poison of their hearts:
God keep you from them, and from such
    false friends!
    Prince. God keep me from false friends!
    but they were none.
    Glou. My lord, the mayor of London
    comes to greet you.

Enter the Lord Mayor, *and his train.*

    May. God bless your grace with health
    and happy days!
    Prince. I thank you, good my lord; and
    thank you all.   19
I thought my mother, and my brother York,
Would long ere this have met us on the way:
Fie, what a slug is Hastings, that he comes
    not
To tell us whether they will come or no!

Enter Lord Hastings.

    Buck. And, in good time, here comes the
    sweating lord.
    Prince. Welcome, my lord: what, will our
    mother come?
    Hast. On what occasion, God he knows,
    not I,
The queen your mother, and your brother
    York,
Have taken sanctuary: the tender prince
Would fain have come with me to meet your
    grace,
But by his mother was perforce withheld.   30
    Buck. Fie, what an indirect and peevish
    course
Is this of hers! Lord cardinal, will your
    grace
Persuade the queen to send the Duke of
    York
Unto his princely brother presently?
If she deny, Lord Hastings, go with him,
And from her jealous arms pluck him per-
    force.
    Card. My Lord of Buckingham, if my
    weak oratory
Can from his mother win the Duke of York,

---

64. **spleen,** anger. 66. **sanctuary.** Queen Elizabeth
lodged in the building which served as a legal refuge for
criminals and persons in danger of their lives. 71. **seal,**
i.e., the Great Seal. 71-72. **so . . . you,** may my fortunes be measured by the care I take of yours.
Act III. Scene i. 1. **chamber,** i.e., London, anciently called the *camera regis,* or king's chamber.

11. **jumpeth,** agrees. 22. **slug,** sluggard; it also
means "impediment to progress." 26. **On what occasion,** for what reason.

Anon expect him here; but if she be obdurate
To mild entreaties, God in heaven forbid 40
We should infringe the holy privilege
Of blessed sanctuary! not for all this land
Would I be guilty of so deep a sin.
  Buck. You are too senseless-obstinate,
      my lord,
Too ceremonious and traditional:
Weigh it but with the grossness of this age,
You break not sanctuary in seizing him.
The benefit thereof is always granted
To those whose dealings have deserved the
      place,
And those who have the wit to claim the
      place:
This prince hath neither claim'd it nor de-
      served it;   51
And therefore, in mine opinion, cannot have
      it:
Then, taking him from thence that is not
      there,
You break no privilege nor charter there.
Oft have I heard of sanctuary men;
But sanctuary children ne'er till now.
  Card. My lord, you shall o'er-rule my
      mind for once.
Come on, Lord Hastings, will you go with
      me?
  Hast. I go, my lord.
  Prince. Good lords, make all the speedy
      haste you may.   60
          [*Exeunt Cardinal and Hastings.*
Say, uncle Gloucester, if our brother come,
Where shall we sojourn till our coronation?
  Glou. Where it seems best unto your
      royal self.
If I may counsel you, some day or two
Your highness shall repose you at the Tower:
Then where you please, and shall be thought
      most fit
For your best health and recreation.
  Prince. I do not like the Tower, of any
      place.
Did Julius Cæsar build that place, my lord?
  Buck. He did, my gracious lord, begin
      that place;   70
Which, since, succeeding ages have re-
      edified.
  Prince. Is it upon record, or else reported
Successively from age to age, he built it?

  Buck. Upon record, my gracious lord.
  Prince. But say, my lord, it were not
      register'd,
Methinks the truth should live from age to
      age,
As 'twere retail'd to all posterity,
Even to the general all-ending day.
  Glou. [*Aside*] So wise so young, they say,
      do never live long.
  Prince. What say you, uncle?   80
  Glou. I say, without characters, fame lives
      long,
[*Aside*] Thus, like the formal vice, Iniquity,
I moralize two meanings in one word.
  Prince. That Julius Cæsar was a famous
      man;
With what his valour did enrich his wit,
His wit set down to make his valour live:
Death makes no conquest of this conqueror;
For now he lives in fame, though not in life.
I'll tell you what, my cousin Buckingham,—
  Buck. What, my gracious lord?   90
  Prince. An if I live until I be a man,
I'll win our ancient right in France again,
Or die a soldier, as I lived a king.
  Glou. [*Aside*] Short summers lightly have
      a forward spring.

        Enter young YORK, HASTINGS, *and the*
                  CARDINAL.

  Buck. Now, in good time, here comes the
      Duke of York.
  Prince. Richard of York! how fares our
      loving brother?
  York. Well, my dread lord; so must I call
      you now.
  Prince. Ay, brother, to our grief, as it is
      yours:
Too late he died that might have kept that
      title,
Which by his death hath lost much majesty.
  Glou. How fares our cousin, noble Lord of
      York?   101
  York. I thank you, gentle uncle. O, my
      lord,
You said that idle weeds are fast in growth:
The prince my brother hath outgrown me far.
  Glou. He hath, my lord.
  York.   And therefore is he idle?

---

44. **senseless-obstinate**, unreasonably obstinate. 46.
Weigh ... age, i.e., take into consideration the laxness
with which this age regards the right of sanctuary.
65. **Tower.** In the fifteenth century the Tower of
London was a royal palace. 68. **of any place**, I dislike
it most of all places. 71. **re-edified**, rebuilt.

77. **retail'd**, handed down from one to another. 81.
without characters, lack of written records, with
quibble on the sense, "having no moral character";
these are the *two meanings* referred to in line 83. 82.
vice, conventional comic villain of the morality plays.
85. **what**, that with which. 94. **lightly**, commonly,
often. 99. **Too ... died**, i.e., the loss is fresh in our
memories.

Glou. O, my fair cousin, I must not say so.

York. Then he is more beholding to you than I.

Glou. He may command me as my sovereign;

But you have power in me as in a kinsman.

York. I pray you, uncle, give me this dagger.

Glou. My dagger, little cousin? with all my heart.   111

Prince. A beggar, brother?

York. Of my kind uncle, that I know will give;

And being but a toy, which is no grief to give.

Glou. A greater gift than that I'll give my cousin.

York. A greater gift! O, that's the sword to it.

Glou. Ay, gentle cousin, were it light enough.

York. O, then, I see, you will part but with light gifts;

In weightier things you'll say a beggar nay.

Glou. It is too heavy for your grace to wear.   120

York. I weigh it lightly, were it heavier.

Glou. What, would you have my weapon, little lord?

York. I would, that I might thank you as you call me.

Glou. How?

York. Little.

Prince. My Lord of York will still be cross in talk:

Uncle, your grace knows how to bear with him.

York. You mean, to bear me, not to bear with me:

Uncle, my brother mocks both you and me;

Because that I am little, like an ape,   130

He thinks that you should bear me on your shoulders.

Buck. With what a sharp-provided wit he reasons!

To mitigate the scorn he gives his uncle,

He prettily and aptly taunts himself:

So cunning and so young is wonderful.

Glou. My lord, will't please you pass along?

Myself and my good cousin Buckingham

Will to your mother, to entreat of her

To meet you at the Tower and welcome you.

York. What, will you go unto the Tower, my lord?   140

Prince. My lord protector needs will have it so.

York. I shall not sleep in quiet at the Tower.

Glou. Why, what should you fear?

York. Marry, my uncle Clarence' angry ghost:

My grandam told me he was murder'd there.

Prince. I fear no uncles dead.

Glou. Nor none that live, I hope.

Prince. An if they live, I hope I need not fear.

But come, my lord; and with a heavy heart,

Thinking on them, go I unto the Tower. 150

[*A Sennet. Exeunt all but Gloucester, Buckingham and Catesby.*

Buck. Think you, my lord, this little prating York

Was not incensed by his subtle mother

To taunt and scorn you thus opprobriously?

Glou. No doubt, no doubt: O, 'tis a parlous boy;

Bold, quick, ingenious, forward, capable:

He is all the mother's, from the top to toe.

Buck. Well, let them rest. Come hither, Catesby.

Thou art sworn as deeply to effect what we intend

As closely to conceal what we impart:

Thou know'st our reasons urged upon the way;   160

What think'st thou? is it not an easy matter

To make William Lord Hastings of our mind,

For the instalment of this noble duke

In the seat royal of this famous isle?

Cate. He for his father's sake so loves the prince,

That he will not be won to aught against him.

Buck. What think'st thou, then, of Stanley? what will he?

Cate. He will do all in all as Hastings doth.

Buck. Well, then, no more but this: go, gentle Catesby,

---

109. **in me,** with me. 121. **were it heavier,** i.e., I should still consider it a trifling gift. 128-131. **bear . . . shoulders.** At fairs the bear commonly carried an ape on his back. The speech is doubtless an allusion to Richard's hump. 133. **scorn,** taunt, insult.

148. **fear,** i.e., fear for the uncles Richard has had arrested. 152. **incensed,** instigated. 155. **capable,** intelligent. 160. **the way,** the journey to London. 165. **his father's sake.** Hastings was particularly intimate with Edward IV.

And, as it were far off, sound thou Lord
Hastings,   170
How he doth stand affected to our pur-
pose;
And summon him to-morrow to the Tower,
To sit about the coronation.
If thou dost find him tractable to us,
Encourage him, and show him all our
reasons:
If he be leaden, icy-cold, unwilling,
Be thou so too; and so break off your talk,
And give us notice of his inclination:
For we to-morrow hold divided councils,
Wherein thyself shalt highly be employ'd. 180
   Glou. Commend me to Lord William:
tell him, Catesby,
His ancient knot of dangerous adversaries
To-morrow are let blood at Pomfret-castle;
And bid my friend, for joy of this good news,
Give Mistress Shore one gentle kiss the more.
   Buck. Good Catesby, go, effect this busi-
ness soundly.
   Cate. My good lords both, with all the
heed I may.
   Glou. Shall we hear from you, Catesby,
ere we sleep?
   Cate. You shall, my lord.
   Glou. At Crosby Place, there shall you
find us both.   [*Exit Catesby.*   190
   Buck. Now, my lord, what shall we do, if
we perceive
Lord Hastings will not yield to our complots?
   Glou. Chop off his head, man; somewhat
we will do:
And, look, when I am king, claim thou of me
The earldom of Hereford, and the moveables
Whereof the king my brother stood possess'd.
   Buck. I'll claim that promise at your
grace's hands.
   Glou. And look to have it yielded with all
willingness.
Come, let us sup betimes, that after-
wards
We may digest our complots in some form.200
                       [*Exeunt.*

---

170. **far off**, i.e., with great tact.   173. **sit**, sit in
council.   179. **divided councils**. Richard would be
plotting to seize the crown, while Hastings and others
friendly to the Prince were arranging for his coronation.
180. **highly**, i.e., on important errands.   183. **let blood**,
i.e., are executed.   185. **Mistress Shore**. Jane Shore had
become the mistress of Hastings after the death of
Edward IV.   192. **complots**, conspiracies.   195. **earldom of Hereford.** This is an important promise.
Buckingham claimed this earldom by right of his descent
from Thomas of Woodstock. The offer is therefore
peculiarly tempting to Buckingham.   200. **digest**, arrange, perfect.

SCENE II.   *Before Lord Hastings' house.*

Enter a MESSENGER.

   Mess. What, ho! my lord!
   Hast. [*Within*] Who knocks at the door?
   Mess. A messenger from the Lord Stan-
ley.

Enter LORD HASTINGS.

   Hast. What is 't o'clock?
   Mess. Upon the stroke of four.
   Hast. Cannot thy master sleep these
tedious nights?
   Mess. So it should seem by that I have to
say.
First, he commends him to your noble lord-
ship.
   Hast. And then?
   Mess. And then he sends you word   10
He dreamt to-night the boar had razed his
helm:
Besides, he says there are two councils held;
And that may be determined at the one
Which may make you and him to rue at the
other.
Therefore he sends to know your lordship's
pleasure,
If presently you will take horse with him,
And with all speed post with him toward the
north,
To shun the danger that his soul divines.
   Hast. Go, fellow, go, return unto thy
lord;
Bid him not fear the separated councils: 20
His honour and myself are at the one,
And at the other is my servant Catesby;
Where nothing can proceed that toucheth us
Whereof I shall not have intelligence.
Tell him his fears are shallow, wanting in-
stance:
And for his dreams, I wonder he is so fond
To trust the mockery of unquiet slumbers:
To fly the boar before the boar pursues,
Were to incense the boar to follow us
And make pursuit where he did mean no
chase.   30
Go, bid thy master rise and come to me;
And we will both together to the Tower,
Where, he shall see, the boar will use us kind-
ly.

---

11. **boar**, Richard. **razed**, cut, slashed.   33. **kindly**,
gently, courteously. The sense "according to his nature" is not intended by Hastings, but is present as
dramatic irony.

Mess. My gracious lord, I'll tell him what you say.　　　　　　　　　　　　　[*Exit.*

Enter Catesby.

Cate. Many good morrows to my noble lord!

Hast. Good morrow, Catesby; you are early stirring:
What news, what news, in this our tottering state?

Cate. It is a reeling world, indeed, my lord.
And I believe 'twill never stand upright
Till Richard wear the garland of the realm. 40

Hast. How! wear the garland! dost thou mean the crown?

Cate. Ay, my good lord.

Hast. I'll have this crown of mine cut from my shoulders
Ere I will see the crown so foul misplaced.
But canst thou guess that he doth aim at it?

Cate. Ay, on my life; and hopes to find you forward
Upon his party for the gain thereof:
And thereupon he sends you this good news,
That this same very day your enemies,
The kindred of the queen, must die at Pomfret.

Hast. Indeed, I am no mourner for that news,　　　　　　　　　　　　　　51
Because they have been still mine enemies:
But, that I'll give my voice on Richard's side,
To bar my master's heirs in true descent,
God knows I will not do it, to the death.

Cate. God keep your lordship in that gracious mind!

Hast. But I shall laugh at this a twelve-month hence,
That they who brought me in my master's hate,
I live to look upon their tragedy.
I tell thee, Catesby,—　　　　　　　　　60

Cate. What, my lord?

Hast. Ere a fortnight make me elder,
I'll send some packing that yet think not on it.

Cate. 'Tis a vile thing to die, my gracious lord,
When men are unprepared and look not for it.

Hast. O monstrous, monstrous! and so falls it out
With Rivers, Vaughan, Grey: and so 'twill do

With some men else, who think themselves as safe
As thou and I; who, as thou know'st, are dear
To princely Richard and to Buckingham. 70

Cate. The princes both make high account of you;
[*Aside*] For they account his head upon the bridge.

Hast. I know they do; and I have well deserved it.

Enter Lord Stanley.

Come on, come on; where is your boar-spear, man?
Fear you the boar, and go so unprovided?

Stan. My lord, good morrow; good morrow, Catesby:
You may jest on, but, by the holy rood,
I do not like these several councils, I.

Hast. My lord,
I hold my life as dear as you do yours; 80
And never in my life, I do protest,
Was it more precious to me than 'tis now:
Think you, but that I know our state secure,
I would be so triumphant as I am?

Stan. The lords at Pomfret, when they rode from London,
Were jocund, and supposed their state was sure,
And they indeed had no cause to mistrust;
But yet, you see, how soon the day o'ercast.
This sudden stab of rancour I misdoubt:
Pray God, I say, I prove a needless coward!
What, shall we toward the Tower? the day is spent.　　　　　　　　　　　　　91

Hast. Come, come, have with you. Wot you what, my lord?
To-day the lords you talk of are beheaded.

Stan. They, for their truth, might better wear their heads
Than some that have accused them wear their hats.
But come, my lord, let us away.

Enter a Pursuivant.

Hast. Go on before; I'll talk with this good fellow. [*Exeunt Stanley and Catesby.*

---

71. **high account**, great estimation; the quibble on *high* appears in the next line.　72. **the bridge**, London Bridge, on a tower of which the heads of traitors were exposed.　77. **holy rood**, the cross of Christ.　85. **London**. Ludlow seems to have been intended.　92. **have with you**, come along!　95. **wear their hats**, i.e., hold their offices.　96. *Stage Direction:* **Pursuivant.** According to More the pursuivant's name was also Hastings. A *pursuivant* is an attendant upon a herald.

---

47. **Upon his party**, on his side.　55. **to the death**, though I lose my life.

How now, sirrah! how goes the world with
 thee?
Purs. The better that your lordship please
 to ask.
Hast. I tell thee, man, 'tis better with me
 now   100
Than when I met thee last where now we
 meet:
Then was I going prisoner to the Tower,
By the suggestion of the queen's allies;
But now, I tell thee—keep it to thyself—
This day those enemies are put to death,
And I in better state than e'er I was.
Purs. God hold it, to your honour's good
 content!
Hast. Gramercy, fellow: there, drink that
 for me.   *[Throws him his purse.*
Purs. God save your lordship! *[Exit.*

Enter a Priest.

Priest. Well met, my lord; I am glad to
 see your honour.   110
Hast. I thank thee, good Sir John, with all
 my heart.
I am in your debt for your last exercise;
Come the next Sabbath, and I will content
 you.   *[He whispers in his ear.*

Enter Buckingham.

Buck. What, talking with a priest, lord
 chamberlain?
Your friends at Pomfret, they do need the
 priest;
Your honour hath no shriving work in
 hand.
Hast. Good faith, and when I met this
 holy man,
Those men you talk of came into my
 mind.
What, go you toward the Tower?
Buck. I do, my lord; but long I shall not
 stay: 120
I shall return before your lordship thence.
Hast. 'Tis like enough, for I stay dinner
 there.
Buck. [*Aside*] And supper too, although
 thou know'st it not.
Come, will you go?
Hast. I'll wait upon your lordship.
        [Exeunt.

Scene III. *Pomfret Castle.*

Enter Sir Richard Ratcliff, *with halberds,
carrying* Rivers, Grey, *and* Vaughan *to
death.*

Rat. Come, bring forth the prisoners.
Riv. Sir Richard Ratcliff, let me tell thee
 this:
To-day shalt thou behold a subject die
For truth, for duty, and for loyalty.
Grey. God keep the prince from all the
 pack of you!
A knot you are of damned blood-suckers.
Vaug. You live that shall cry woe for this
 hereafter.
Rat. Dispatch; the limit of your lives is
 out.
Riv. O Pomfret, Pomfret! O thou bloody
 prison,
Fatal and ominous to noble peers! 10
Within the guilty closure of thy walls
Richard the second here was hack'd to
 death;
And, for more slander to thy dismal seat,
We give thee up our guiltless blood to drink.
Grey. Now Margaret's curse is fall'n upon
 our heads,
For standing by when Richard stabb'd her
 son.
Riv. Then cursed she Hastings, then
 cursed she Buckingham,
Then cursed she Richard. O, remember,
 God,
To hear her prayers for them, as now for us!
And for my sister and her princely sons, 20
Be satisfied, dear God, with our true blood,
Which, as thou know'st, unjustly must be
 spilt.
Rat. Make haste; the hour of death is
 expiate.
Riv. Come, Grey, come, Vaughan, let us
 all embrace:
And take our leave, until we meet in heaven.
        [Exeunt.

Scene IV. *The Tower of London.*

Enter Buckingham, Derby, Hastings, *the*
Bishop of Ely, Ratcliff, Lovel, *with
others, and take their seats at a table.*

Hast. My lords, at once: the cause why
 we are met

Is, to determine of the coronation.
In God's name, speak: when is the royal day?
  Buck. Are all things fitting for that royal
    time?
  Der. It is, and wants but nomination.
  Ely. To-morrow, then, I judge a happy
    day.
  Buck. Who knows the lord protector's
    mind herein?
Who is most inward with the noble duke?
  Ely. Your grace, we think, should soonest
    know his mind.
  Buck. Who, I, my lord! we know each
    other's faces,   10
But for our hearts, he knows no more of
  mine,
Than I of yours;
Nor I no more of his, than you of mine.
Lord Hastings, you and he are near in love.
  Hast. I thank his grace, I know he loves
    me well;
But, for his purpose in the coronation,
I have not sounded him, nor he deliver'd
His gracious pleasure any way therein:
But you, my noble lords, may name the
  time;
And in the duke's behalf I'll give my voice, 20
Which, I presume, he'll take in gentle part.

     Enter GLOUCESTER.

  Ely. Now in good time, here comes the
    duke himself.
  Glou. My noble lords and cousins all, good
    morrow.
I have been long a sleeper; but, I hope,
My absence doth neglect no great designs,
Which by my presence might have been con-
  cluded.
  Buck. Had not you come upon your cue,
    my lord,
William Lord Hastings had pronounced your
  part,—
I mean, your voice,—for crowning of the
  king.
  Glou. Than my Lord Hastings no man
    might be bolder;   30
His lordship knows me well, and loves me
  well.
  Hast. I thank your grace.
  Glou.   My lord of Ely!
  Ely.   My lord?

  Glou. When I was last in Holborn,
I saw good strawberries in your garden there
I do beseech you send for some of them.
  Ely. Marry, and will, my lord, with all my
    heart.   [*Exit.*
  Glou. Cousin of Buckingham, a word with
    you.   [*Drawing him aside.*
Catesby hath sounded Hastings in our busi-
  ness,
And finds the testy gentleman so hot,
As he will lose his head ere give consent   40
His master's son, as worshipful he terms it,
Shall lose the royalty of England's throne.
  Buck. Withdraw you hence, my lord, I'll
    follow you.
  [*Exit Gloucester, Buckingham following.*
  Der. We have not yet set down this day of
    triumph.
To-morrow, in mine opinion, is too sudden;
For I myself am not so well provided
As else I would be, were the day prolong'd.

    Re-enter BISHOP OF ELY.

  Ely. Where is my lord protector? I have
sent for these strawberries.
  Hast. His grace looks cheerfully and
    smooth to-day;   50
There's some conceit or other likes him well,
When he doth bid good morrow with such
  a spirit.
I think there's never a man in Christendom
That can less hide his love or hate than he;
For by his face straight shall you know his
  heart.
  Der. What of his heart perceive you in his
    face
By any likelihood he show'd to-day?
  Hast. Marry, that with no man here he is
    offended;
For, were he, he had shown it in his looks.
  Der. I pray God he be not, I say.   60

  Re-enter GLOUCESTER *and* BUCKINGHAM.

  Glou. I pray you all, tell me what they
    deserve
That do conspire my death with devilish
  plots
Of damned witchcraft, and that have pre-
  vail'd
Upon my body with their hellish charms?

---

2. **determine of**, decide upon. 8. **inward with**,
i.e., acquainted with the mind of, intimate. 25. **designs**,
projects, enterprises.

   34. **strawberries**, apparently intended for the dinner
after the meeting of the council. Richard is engaged in
disarming suspicion. 47. **prolong'd**, postponed. 50.
smooth, mild, bland. 51. **conceit**, idea, fancy. **likes**,
pleases.

Hast. The tender love I bear your grace,
  my lord,
Makes me most forward in this noble pres-
  ence
To doom the offenders, whatsoever they be:
I say, my lord, they have deserved death.
   Glou. Then be your eyes the witness of
  this ill:
See how I am bewitch'd; behold mine arm 70
Is, like a blasted sapling, wither'd up:
And this is Edwards' wife, that monstrous
  witch,
Consorted with that harlot strumpet Shore,
That by their witchcraft thus have marked
  me.
   Hast. If they have done this thing, my
  gracious lord,—
   Glou. If! thou protector of this damned
  strumpet,
Tellest thou me of 'ifs'? Thou art a traitor:
Off with his head! Now, by Saint Paul I
  swear,
I will not dine until I see the same.
Lovel and Ratcliff, look that it be done: 80
The rest, that love me, rise and follow me.
[*Exeunt all but Hastings, Ratcliff, and Lovel*.
   Hast. Woe, woe for England! not a whit
  for me;
For I, too fond, might have prevented this.
Stanley did dream the boar did raze his
  helm;
But I disdain'd it, and did scorn to fly:
Three times to-day my foot-cloth horse did
  stumble,
And startled, when he look'd upon the
  Tower,
As loath to bear me to the slaughter-house.
O, now I want the priest that spake to me:
I now repent I told the pursuivant, 90
As 'twere triumphing at mine enemies,
How they at Pomfret bloodily were butch-
  er'd,
And I myself secure in grace and favour.
O Margaret, Margaret, now thy heavy curse
Is lighted on poor Hastings' wretched head!
   Rat. Dispatch, my lord; the duke would
  be at dinner:
Make a short shrift; he longs to see your
  head.
   Hast. O momentary grace of mortal men,

Which we more hunt for than the grace of
  God!
Who builds his hopes in air of your good
  looks, 100
Lives like a drunken sailor on a mast,
Ready, with every nod, to tumble down
Into the fatal bowels of the deep.
   Lov. Come, come, dispatch; 'tis bootless
  to exclaim.
   Hast. O bloody Richard! miserable Eng-
  land!
I prophesy the fearfull'st time to thee
That ever wretched age hath look'd upon.
Come, lead me to the block; bear him my
  head:
They smile at me that shortly shall be dead.
                      [*Exeunt*.

Scene V. *The Tower-walls*.

Enter Gloucester *and* Buckingham, *in
rotten armour, marvellous ill-favoured*.

   Glou. Come, cousin, canst thou quake,
  and change thy colour,
Murder thy breath in middle of a word,
And then begin again, and stop again,
As if thou wert distraught and mad with
  terror?
   Buck. Tut, I can counterfeit the deep
  tragedian;
Speak and look back, and pry on every side,
Tremble and start at wagging of a straw,
Intending deep suspicion: ghastly looks
Are at my service, like enforced smiles;
And both are ready in their offices, 10
At any time, to grace my stratagems.
But what, is Catesby gone?
   Glou. He is; and, see, he brings the mayor
  along.

Enter the Mayor *and* Catesby.

   Buck. Lord mayor,—
   Glou. Look to the drawbridge there!
   Buck. Hark! a drum.
   Glou. Catesby, o'erlook the walls.
   Buck. Lord mayor, the reason we have
  sent—
   Glou. Look back, defend thee, here are
  enemies.

---

86. **foot-cloth**, a large, richly ornamented cloth laid
over the back of a horse, and hanging down to the ground
on each side. **stumble**. The stumbling of one's horse
was an omen of misfortune.

100. **air**, outward appearance, manner.
Scene v. Stage Direction: **rotten**, rusty. 8. **Intending**, pretending. 10. **offices**, uses, functions.

Buck. God and our innocency defend and
guard us!   20
Glou. Be patient, they are friends, Ratcliff and Lovel.

Enter Lovel *and* Ratcliff, *with* Hastings'
head.

Lov. Here is the head of that ignoble
traitor,
The dangerous and unsuspected Hastings.
Glou. So dear I loved the man, that I must
weep.
I took him for the plainest harmless creature
That breathed upon this earth a Christian;
Made him my book, wherein my soul re-
corded
The history of all her secret thoughts:
So smooth he daub'd his vice with show of
virtue,
That, his apparent open guilt omitted,   30
I mean, his conversation with Shore's wife,
He lived from all attainder of suspect.
Buck. Well, well, he was the covert'st
shelter'd traitor
That ever lived.
Would you imagine, or almost believe,
Were't not that, by great preservation,
We live to tell it you, the subtle traitor
This day had plotted, in the council-house
To murder me and my good Lord of Glou-
cester?
May. What, had he so?   40
Glou. What, think you we are Turks or
infidels?
Or that we would, against the form of law,
Proceed thus rashly to the villain's death,
But that the extreme peril of the case,
The peace of England and our persons'
safety,
Enforced us to this execution?
May. Now, fair befall you! he deserved
his death;
And you my good lords, both have well pro-
ceeded,
To warn false traitors from the like at-
tempts.
I never look'd for better at his hands,   50
After he once fell in with Mistress Shore.
Glou. Yet had not we determined he
should die,
Until your lordship came to see his death;

Which now the loving haste of these our
friends,
Somewhat against our meaning, have pre-
vented:
Because, my lord, we would have had you
heard
The traitor speak, and timorously confess
The manner and the purpose of his treason;
That you might well have signified the same
Unto the citizens, who haply may   60
Misconstrue us in him and wail his death.
May. But, my good lord, your grace's
word shall serve,
As well as I had seen and heard him speak:
And doubt you not, right noble princes both,
But I'll acquaint our duteous citizens
With all your just proceedings in this cause.
Glou. And to that end we wish'd your
lordship here,
To avoid the carping censures of the world.
Buck. But since you come too late of our
intents,
Yet witness what you hear we did intend: 70
And so, my good lord mayor, we bid farewell.
                                    [*Exit Mayor.*
Glou. Go, after, after, cousin Bucking-
ham.
The mayor towards Guildhall hies him in all
post:
There, at your meet'st advantage of the
time,
Infer the bastardy of Edward's children:
Tell them how Edward put to death a citi-
zen,
Only for saying he would make his son
Heir to the crown; meaning indeed his house,
Which, by the sign thereof, was termed so.
Moreover, urge his hateful luxury,   80
And bestial appetite in change of lust;
Which stretched to their servants, daughters,
wives,
Even where his lustful eye or savage heart,
Without control, listed to make his prey.
Nay, for a need, thus far come near my
person:
Tell them, when that my mother went with
child
Of that unsatiate Edward, noble York

---

30. **omitted**, i.e., aside from that. 35. **almost**,
even.

55. **have**, has. 73. **post**, haste. 75. **Infer**, allege,
adduce. **bastardy**. It was said that Edward was contracted to one Elizabeth Lucy before his marriage to the
mother of his children, Lady Grey. 76. **a citizen**, a
grocer of Cheapside named Walker (or, according to
Hall, Burdet). 80. **luxury**, lechery. 81. **in change
of**, instead of (possibly, as being worse than).

My princely father then had wars in France;
And, by just computation of the time,
Found that the issue was not his begot;   90
Which well appeared in his lineaments,
Being nothing like the noble duke my father:
But touch this sparingly, as 'twere far off;
Because you know, my lord, my mother
     lives.
     Buck. Fear not, my lord, I'll play the
     orator
As if the golden fee for which I plead
Were for myself: and so, my lord, adieu.
     Glou. If you thrive well, bring them to
     Baynard's Castle;
Where you shall find me well accompanied
With reverend fathers and well-learned
     bishops.   100
     Buck. I go; and towards three or four
     o'clock
Look for the news that the Guildhall af-
     fords.   [*Exit.*
     Glou. Go, Lovel, with all speed to Doctor
     Shaw;
[*To Cate.*] Go thou to Friar Penker; bid them
     both
Meet me within this hour at Baynard's
     Castle.   [*Exeunt all but Gloucester.*
Now will I in, to take some privy order,
To draw the brats of Clarence out of sight;
And to give notice, that no manner of person
At any time have recourse unto the princes.
                       [*Exit.*

     Scene VI.   *The same. A street.*

Enter a Scrivener, *with a paper in his hand.*

     Scriv. This is the indictment of the good
     Lord Hastings;
Which in a set hand fairly is engross'd,
That it may be this day read o'er in Paul's.
And mark how well the sequel hangs to-
     gether:
Eleven hours I spent to write it over,
For yesternight by Catesby was it brought
     me;
The precedent was full as long a-doing:

And yet within these five hours lived Lord
     Hastings,
Untainted, unexamined, free, at liberty.
Here's a good world the while! Why who's
     so gross,   10
That seeth not this palpable device?
Yet who's so blind, but says he sees it not?
Bad is the world; and all will come to
     nought,
When such bad dealing must be seen in
     thought.   [*Exit.*

     Scene VII.   *Baynard's Castle.*

Enter Gloucester *and* Buckingham, *at
     several doors.*

     Glou. How now, my lord, what say the
     citizens?
     Buck. Now, by the holy mother of our
     Lord,
The citizens are mum and speak not a word.
     Glou. Touch'd you the bastardy of Ed-
     ward's children?
     Buck. I did; with his contract with Lady
     Lucy,
And his contract by deputy in France;
The insatiate greediness of his desires,
And his enforcement of the city wives;
His tyranny for trifles; his own bastardy,
As being got, your father then in France, 10
And his resemblance, being not like the
     duke:
Withal I did infer your lineaments,
Being the right idea of your father,
Both in your form and nobleness of mind:
Laid open all your victories in Scotland,
Your discipline in war, wisdom in peace,
Your bounty, virtue, fair humility,
Indeed, left nothing fitting for the purpose
Untouch'd, or slightly handled, in discourse:
And when mine oratory grew to an end,   20
I bid them that did love their country's good
Cry 'God save Richard, England's royal
     king!'
     Glou. Ah! and did they so?

---

98. **Baynard's Castle,** on the north bank of the
Thames, between Paul's-wharf and Blackfriars. It was
founded by Baynard, a nobleman of the time of the
Conquest, and belonged to Richard's father, Duke of
York. 103-4. **Doctor Shaw . . . Friar Penker.** These men
delivered sermons in Richard's favor. More describes
them as "John Shaa clerke brother to the Maier, and
freer Penker prouincial of the Augustine freers, both
doctors of diuinite, both gret prechars, both of more
learning then vertue, of more fame then lerning."
Scene vi. 4. **sequel,** what follows.

9. **Untainted,** unaccused. 10. **gross,** dull. 12. **blind,**
i.e., to the danger of speaking.
Scene vii. 6. **deputy.** Cf. *3 Henry VI,* III, iii, 49 ff.,
where Warwick, as deputy, contracts with Louis VI of
France for the marriage of King Edward to Lady Bona,
sister of the French queen. 9. **tyranny for trifles,**
cruelty on account of trifling matters. 13. **right idea,**
exact image. 15. **victories in Scotland.** Richard had
commanded the English forces in the Scottish expedition
of 1482. 17. **bounty,** liberality. **fair,** probably, open
to view, distinct.

Buck. No, so God help me, they spake
    not a word;
But, like dumb statuas or breathing stones,
Gazed each on other, and look'd deadly pale,
Which when I saw, I reprehended them;
And ask'd the mayor what meant this wilful
    silence:
His answer was, the people were not wont
To be spoke to but by the recorder.   30
Then he was urged to tell my tale again,
'Thus saith the duke, thus hath the duke in-
    ferr'd;'
But nothing spake in warrant from himself.
When he had done, some followers of mine
    own,
At the lower end of the hall, hurl'd up their
    caps,
And some ten voices cried 'God save King
    Richard!'
And thus I took the vantage of those few,
'Thanks, gentle citizens and friends,' quoth
    I;
'This general applause and loving shout
Argues your wisdoms and your love to Rich-
    ard:'   40
And even here brake off, and came away.
   Glou. What tongueless blocks were they!
    would they not speak?
   Buck. No, by my troth, my lord.
   Glou. Will not the mayor then and his
    brethren come?
   Buck. The mayor is here at hand: intend
    some fear;
Be not you spoke with, but by mighty
    suit:
And look you get a prayer-book in your
    hand,
And stand betwixt two churchmen, good my
    lord;
For on that ground I'll build a holy descant:
And be not easily won to our request: 50
Play the maid's part, still answer nay, and
    take it.
   Glou. I go; and if you plead as well for
    them
As I can say nay to thee for myself,
No doubt we'll bring it to a happy issue.
   Buck. Go, go, up to the leads; the lord
    mayor knocks.   [*Exit Gloucester.*

Enter the Mayor *and* Citizens.

Welcome, my lord: I dance attendance here;
I think the duke will not be spoke withal.

Enter CATESBY.

Here comes his servant: how now, Catesby,
What says he?
   Cate. My lord, he doth entreat your grace
To visit him to-morrow or next day: 60
He is within, with two right reverend fathers,
Divinely bent to meditation;
And in no worldly suit would he be moved,
To draw him from his holy exercise.
   Buck. Return, good Catesby, to thy lord
    again;
Tell him, myself, the mayor and citizens,
In deep designs and matters of great
    moment,
No less importing than our general good,
Are come to have some conference with his
    grace.
   Cate. I'll tell him what you say, my lord.
                                [*Exit.*
   Buck. Ah, ha, my lord, this prince is not
    an Edward!   71
He is not lolling on a lewd day-bed,
But on his knees at meditation;
Not dallying with a brace of courtezans,
But meditating with two deep divines;
Not sleeping, to engross his idle body,
But praying, to enrich his watchful soul:
Happy were England, would this gracious
    prince
Take on himself the sovereignty thereof:
But, sure, I fear, we shall ne'er win him to it.
   May. Marry, God forbid his grace should
    say us nay!   81
   Buck. I fear he will.

Re-enter CATESBY.

How now, Catesby, what says your lord?
   Cate.   My lord,
He wonders to what end you have assembled
Such troops of citizens to speak with him,
His grace not being warn'd thereof before:
My lord, he fears you mean no good to him.
   Buck. Sorry I am my noble cousin should
Suspect me, that I mean no good to him:
By heaven, I come in perfect love to him; 90
And so once more return and tell his grace.
                          [*Exit Catesby.*

---

    30. **recorder,** keeper of the city rolls; at this time
Thomas Fitzwilliam.   33. **in . . . himself,** on his own
responsibility.   49. **descant,** argument.   53. **thee,**
i.e., Buckingham, as spokesman for the citizens.   54. **it,**
i.e., the plan to make Richard king.   55. **leads,** roof.

    76. **engross,** fatten.

When holy and devout religious men
Are at their beads, 'tis hard to draw them
    thence,
So sweet is zealous contemplation.

Enter GLOUCESTER *aloft, between two* Bishops.
CATESBY *returns.*

  May. See, where he stands between two
    clergymen!
  Buck. Two props of virtue for a Christian
    prince,
To stay him from the fall of vanity:
And, see, a book of prayer in his hand,
True ornaments to know a holy man.
Famous Plantagenet, most gracious prince,
Lend favourable ears to our request;   101
And pardon us the interruption
Of thy devotion and right Christian zeal.
  Glou. My lord, there needs no such apol-
    ogy:
I rather do beseech you pardon me,
Who, earnest in the service of my God,
Neglect the visitation of my friends.
But, leaving this, what is your grace's pleas-
    ure?
  Buck. Even that, I hope, which pleaseth
    God above,
And all good men of this ungovern'd isle. 110
  Glou. I do suspect I have done some
    offence
That seems disgracious in the city's eyes,
And that you come to reprehend my igno-
    rance.
  Buck. You have, my lord: would it might
    please your grace,
At our entreaties, to amend that fault!
  Glou. Else wherefore breathe I in a Chris-
    tian land?
  Buck. Then know, it is your fault that
    you resign
The supreme seat, the throne majestical,
The scepter'd office of your ancestors,
Your state of fortune and your due of
    birth,   120
The lineal glory of your royal house,
To the corruption of a blemish'd stock:
Whilst, in the mildness of your sleepy
    thoughts,
Which here we waken to our country's good,

This noble isle doth want her proper limbs;
Her face defaced with scars of infamy,
Her royal stock graft with ignoble plants,
And almost shoulder'd in the swallowing gulf
Of blind forgetfulness and dark oblivion.
Which to recure, we heartily solicit   130
Your gracious self to take on you the charge
And kingly government of this your land,
Not as protector, steward, substitute,
Or lowly factor for another's gain;
But as successively from blood to blood,
Your right of birth, your empery, your own.
For this, consorted with the citizens,
Your very worshipful and loving friends,
And by their vehement instigation,
In this just suit come I to move your grace.
  Glou. I know not whether to depart in
    silence,   141
Or bitterly to speak in your reproof,
Best fitteth my degree or your condition:
If not to answer, you might haply think
Tongue-tied ambition, not replying, yielded
To bear the golden yoke of sovereignty,
Which fondly you would here impose on me;
If to reprove you for this suit of yours,
So season'd with your faithful love to me,
Then, on the other side, I check'd my
    friends.   150
Therefore, to speak, and to avoid the first,
And then, in speaking, not to incur the last,
Definitively thus I answer you.
Your love deserves my thanks; but my
    desert
Unmeritable shuns your high request.
First, if all obstacles were cut away,
And that my path were even to the crown,
As my ripe revenue and due by birth;
Yet so much is my poverty of spirit,
So mighty and so many my defects,   160
As I had rather hide me from my greatness,
Being a bark to brook no mighty sea,
Than in my greatness covet to be hid,
And in the vapour of my glory smother'd.
But, God be thanked, there's no need of me,
And much I need to help you, if need were;

94. *Stage Direction:* **aloft,** i.e., on the gallery above
the stage. 97. **stay,** sustain. **the . . . vanity,** i.e.,
falling into the sin of vanity. 99. **ornaments,** i.e., the
bishops as well as the prayer-book. 112. **disgracious,**
unbecoming. 116. **Else.** if not, otherwise.

128. **shoulder'd,** jostled; or it may mean "immersed
up to the shoulders." Johnson conjectured *smouldered,*
smothered; anonymous conjecture: *foundered.*   130.
recure, restore, make whole. 134. **factor,** agent. 136.
empery, empire. 137. **consorted,** associated, leagued.
143. **degree,** rank. **condition,** social status. 155.
Unmeritable, undeserving. 157. **even,** smooth. 158.
ripe revenue, a possession ready to be inherited.
161. **my greatness,** my claim to the throne. 163.
in my greatness, i.e., as king. **covet,** desire.
164. **vapour of my glory,** effluence of my kingship.
166. **need,** ought; perhaps, as Johnson suggested, lack
the ability requisite.

The royal tree hath left us royal fruit,
Which, mellow'd by the stealing hours of
　time,
Will well become the seat of majesty,
And make, no doubt, us happy by his reign.
On him I lay what you would lay on me, 171
The right and fortune of his happy stars;
Which God defend that I should wring from
　him!
　　Buck. My lord, this argues conscience in
　　your grace;
But the respects thereof are nice and trivial,
All circumstances well considered.
You say that Edward is your brother's son:
So say we too, but not by Edward's wife;
For first he was contract to Lady Lucy—
Your mother lives a witness to that vow— 180
And afterward by substitute betroth'd
To Bona, sister to the King of France.
These both put by, a poor petitioner,
A care-crazed mother of a many children,
A beauty-waning and distressed widow,
Even in the afternoon of her best days,
Made prize and purchase of his lustful eye,
Seduced the pitch and height of all his
　thoughts
To base declension and loathed bigamy:
By her, in his unlawful bed, he got　　190
This Edward, whom our manners term the
　prince.
More bitterly could I expostulate,
Save that, for reverence to some alive,
I give a sparing limit to my tongue.
Then, good my lord, take to your royal
　self
This proffer'd benefit of dignity;
If not to bless us and the land withal,
Yet to draw forth your noble ancestry
From the corruption of abusing times,
Unto a lineal true-derived course.　　200
　　May. Do, good my lord, your citizens en-
　　treat you.

　　Buck. Refuse not, mighty lord, this
　　proffer'd love.
　　Cate. O, make them joyful, grant their
　　lawful suit!
　　Glou. Alas, why would you heap these
　　cares on me?
I am unfit for state and majesty:
I do beseech you, take it not amiss;
I cannot nor I will not yield to you.
　　Buck. If you refuse it,—as, in love and
　　zeal,
Loath to depose the child, your brother's
　son;
As well we know your tenderness of heart 210
And gentle, kind, effeminate remorse,
Which we have noted in you to your kin,
And egally indeed to all estates,—
Yet whether you accept our suit or no,
Your brother's son shall never reign our
　king;
But we will plant some other in the throne,
To the disgrace and downfall of your house:
And in this resolution here we leave you.—
Come, citizens: 'zounds! I'll entreat no
　more.
　　Glou. O, do not swear, my lord of Buck-
　　ingham.　　220
　　　[*Exit Buckingham with the Citizens.*
　　Cate. Call them again, my lord, and ac-
　　cept their suit.
　　Another. Do, good my lord, lest all the
　　land do rue it.
　　Glou. Would you enforce me to a world of
　　care?
Well, call them again. I am not made of
　stones,
But penetrable to your kind entreats,
Albeit against my conscience and my soul.

　　Re-enter Buckingham *and the rest.*

Cousin of Buckingham, and you sage, grave
　men,
Since you will buckle fortune on my back,
To bear her burthen, whether I will or no,
I must have patience to endure the load: 230
But if black scandal or foul-faced reproach
Attend the sequel of your imposition,
Your mere enforcement shall acquittance me
From all the impure blots and stains thereof;
For God he knows, and you may partly see,
How far I am from the desire thereof.

---

175. **respects thereof,** considerations by which you support your argument. **nice,** insignificant. 179-82. **For . . . France.** In the petition of 1484, ratified by Parliament at Richard's accession, it was stated that before his marriage to Elizabeth Edward IV was engaged by troth-plight to Lady Eleanor Butler, daughter of the Earl of Shrewsbury. A later tradition which Shakespeare followed held that Richard's mother, in her opposition to Edward's intention of marrying Lady Grey, which was interfering with the negotiations for his marriage to Bona of Savoy, asserted that Lady Elizabeth Lucy was already Edward's troth-plight wife. Cf. III, v, 75, and vii. 6. 187. **purchase,** booty. 189. **declension,** falling away from a high standard. 192. **expostulate,** discourse, discuss. 193-94. **reverence . . . tongue.** The allusion is to the pretended illegitimacy of Edward and Clarence. By *some alive* he means their mother, the Duchess of York; cf. III, v, 93-94, where Richard says *my mother lives.*

213. **egally,** equally, evenly. 232. **your imposition,** the duty which you lay upon me.

May. God bless your grace! we see it, and
will say it.

Glou. In saying so, you shall but say the
truth.

Buck. Then I salute you with this kingly
title:

Long live Richard, England's royal king! 240

May. and Cit. Amen.

Buck. To-morrow will it please you to be
crown'd?

Glou. Even when you please, since you
will have it so.

Buck. To-morrow, then, we will attend
your grace:

And so most joyfully we take our leave.

Glou. Come, let us to our holy task again.

Farewell, good cousin; farewell, gentle
friends.   [*Exeunt.*

ACT IV.

SCENE I. *Before the Tower.*

Enter, on one side, QUEEN ELIZABETH,
DUCHESS OF YORK, *and* MARQUESS OF
DORSET; *on the other,* ANNE, DUCHESS OF
GLOUCESTER, *leading* LADY MARGARET
PLANTAGENET, CLARENCE'S *young Daughter.*

Duch. Who meets us here? my niece
Plantagenet

Led in the hand of her kind aunt of Gloucester?

Now, for my life, she's wandering to the
Tower,

On pure heart's love to greet the tender
princes.

Daughter, well met.

Anne.   God give your graces both
A happy and a joyful time of day!

Q. Eliz. As much to you, good sister!
Whither away?

Anne. No farther than the Tower; and, as
I guess,

Upon the like devotion as yourselves,

To gratulate the gentle princes there.   10

Q. Eliz. Kind sister, thanks: we'll enter
all together.

Enter BRAKENBURY.

And, in good time, here the lieutenant comes.

Master lieutenant, pray you, by your leave,

How doth the prince, and my young son of
York?

Brak. Right well, dear madam. By your
patience,

I may not suffer you to visit them;

The king hath straitly charged the contrary.

Q. Eliz. The king! why, who's that?

Brak. I cry you mercy: I mean the lord
protector.

Q. Eliz. The Lord protect him from that
kingly title!   20

Hath he set bounds betwixt their love and
me?

I am their mother; who should keep me from
them?

Duch. I am their father's mother; I will
see them.

Anne. Their aunt I am in law, in love their
mother:

Then bring me to their sights; I'll bear thy
blame

And take thy office from thee, on my peril.

Brak. No, madam, no; I may not leave
it so:

I am bound by oath, and therefore pardon
me.   [*Exit.*

Enter LORD STANLEY.

Stan. Let me but meet you, ladies, one
hour hence,

And I'll salute your grace of York as mother,

And reverend looker on, of two fair queens. 31

[*To Anne*] Come, madam, you must straight
to Westminster,

There to be crowned Richard's royal queen.

Q. Eliz. O, cut my lace in sunder, that my
pent heart

May have some scope to beat, or else I swoon

With this dead-killing news!

Anne. Despiteful tidings! O unpleasing
news!

Dor. Be of good cheer: mother, how fares
your grace?

Q. Eliz. O Dorset, speak not to me, get
thee hence!   39

Death and destruction dog thee at the heels;

Thy mother's name is ominous to children.

If thou wilt outstrip death, go cross the seas,

And live with Richmond, from the reach of
hell:

Act IV. *Scene* i. 1. **niece**, here, granddaughter.
9. **like devotion**, same devout errand. 10. **gratulate**,
greet, salute.

21. **bounds**, barriers. 31. **reverend looker on**, one
who esteems reverently. **two fair queens**, Elizabeth and Anne. 34. **pent heart**. According to Elizabethan psychology, the passion of sorrow would cause a
rush of spirits to the heart, thus making it swell. 43.
with Richmond, i. e., Henry Tudor, Earl of Richmond,
at this time in Brittany.

Go, hie thee, hie thee from this slaughter-
house,
Lest thou increase the number of the dead;
And make me die the thrall of Margaret's
curse,
Nor mother, wife, nor England's counted
queen.
  Stan. Full of wise care is this your counsel,
madam.
Take all the swift advantage of the hours;
You shall have letters from me to my son 50
To meet you on the way, and welcome you.
Be not ta'en tardy by unwise delay.
  Duch. O ill-dispersing wind of misery!
O my accursed womb, the bed of death!
A cockatrice hast thou hatch'd to the world,
Whose unavoided eye is murderous.
  Stan. Come, madam, come; I in all haste
was sent.
  Anne. And I in all unwillingness will go.
I would to God that the inclusive verge
Of golden metal that must round my brow 60
Were red-hot steel, to sear me to the brain!
Anointed let me be with deadly venom,
And die, ere men can say, God save the
queen!
  Q. Eliz. Go, go, poor soul, I envy not thy
glory;
To feed my humour, wish thyself no harm.
  Anne. No! why? When he that is my
husband now
Came to me, as I follow'd Henry's corse,
When scarce the blood was well wash'd from
his hands
Which issued from my other angel husband
And that dead saint which then I weeping
follow'd;   70
O, when, I say, I look'd on Richard's face,
This was my wish: 'Be thou,' quoth I, 'ac-
cursed,
For making me, so young, so old a widow!
And, when thou wed'st, let sorrow haunt thy
bed;
And be thy wife—if any be so mad—
As miserable by the life of thee
As thou hast made me by my dear lord's
death!'
Lo, ere I can repeat this curse again,
Even in so short a space, my woman's heart

Grossly grew captive to his honey words 80
And proved the subject of my own soul's
curse,
Which ever since hath kept my eyes from
rest;
For never yet one hour in his bed
Have I enjoy'd the golden dew of sleep,
But have been waked by his timorous
dreams.
Besides, he hates me for my father Warwick;
And will, no doubt, shortly be rid of me.
  Q. Eliz. Poor heart, adieu! I pity thy
complaining.
  Anne. No more than from my soul I
mourn for yours.
  Q. Eliz. Farewell, thou woful welcomer of
glory!   90
  Anne. Adieu, poor soul, that takest thy
leave of it!
  Duch. [*To Dorset*] Go thou to Richmond,
and good fortune guide thee!
[*To Anne*] Go thou to Richard, and good
angels guard thee!
[*To Queen Eliz.*] Go thou to sanctuary, and
good thoughts possess thee!
I to my grave, where peace and rest lie with
me!
Eighty odd years of sorrow have I seen,
And each hour's joy wreck'd with a week of
teen.
  Q. Eliz. Stay, yet look back with me unto
the Tower.
Pity, you ancient stones, those tender babes
Whom envy hath immured within your
walls!   100
Rough cradle for such little pretty ones!
Rude ragged nurse, old sullen playfellow
For tender princes, use my babies well!
So foolish sorrow bids your stones farewell.
                                    [*Exeunt.*

Scene II.   *London.   The palace.*

Sennet. Enter RICHARD, *in pomp, crowned;*
  BUCKINGHAM, CATESBY, *a* Page, *and others.*

  K. Rich. Stand all apart.   Cousin of
Buckingham!
  Buck. My gracious sovereign?
  K. Rich. Give me thy hand. [*Here he
ascendeth his throne.*] Thus high, by thy
advice
And thy assistance, is King Richard seated:

47. **counted**, accepted. 50. **son**, Richmond, whose mother Stanley had married. 61. **brain**. Anne is alluding to an ancient method of punishing regicides, or other criminals. 65. **To . . . humour**, to make me feel better. 69. **husband**, Edward, son of Henry VI, to whom she was betrothed, but never married. 70. **which**, whom. 73. **old**, i.e., old in sorrow.

80. **Grossly**, stupidly. 86. **Warwick**, Richard Neville, earl of Warwick. 97. **teen**, affliction, woe.

But shall we wear these honours for a
   day?
Or shall they last, and we rejoice in them?
  Buck. Still live they and for ever may they
   last!
  K. Rich. O Buckingham, now do I play
   the touch,
To try if thou be current gold indeed:
Young Edward lives: think now what I
   would say.   10
  Buck. Say on, my loving lord.
  K. Rich. Why, Buckingham, I say, I
   would be king.
  Buck. Why, so you are, my thrice re-
   nowned liege.
  K. Rich. Ha! am I king? 'tis so: but
   Edward lives.
  Buck. True, noble prince.
  K. Rich.   O bitter consequence,
That Edward still should live! 'True, noble
   prince!'
Cousin, thou wert not wont to be so dull:
Shall I be plain? I wish the bastards dead;
And I would have it suddenly perform'd.
What sayest thou? speak suddenly; be brief.
  Buck. Your grace may do your pleasure.21
  K. Rich. Tut, tut, thou art all ice, thy
   kindness freezeth:
Say, have I thy consent that they shall die?
  Buck. Give me some breath, some little
   pause, my lord,
Before I positively speak herein:
I will resolve your grace immediately. [*Exit.*
  Cate. [*Aside to a stander by*] The king is
   angry: see, he bites the lip.
  K. Rich. I will converse with iron-witted
   fools
And unrespective boys: none are for me
That look into me with considerate eyes: 30
High-reaching Buckingham grows circum-
   spect.
Boy!
  Page. My lord?
  K. Rich. Know'st thou not any whom
   corrupting gold
Would tempt unto a close exploit of death?
  Page. My lord, I know a discontented
   gentleman,   36
Whose humble means match not his haughty
   mind:

Gold were as good as twenty orators,
And will, no doubt, tempt him to any thing.
  K. Rich. What is his name?
  Page.   His name, my lord, is Tyrrel.
  K. Rich. I partly know the man: go, call
   him hither.   [*Exit Page.*
The deep-revolving witty Buckingham 42
No more shall be the neighbour to my
   counsel:
Hath he so long held out with me untired,
And stops he now for breath?

        Enter STANLEY.

     How now! what news with you?
  Stan. My lord, I hear the Marquis Dor-
   set's fled
To Richmond, in those parts beyond the sea
Where he abides.   [*Stands apart.*
  K. Rich. Catesby!
  Cate. My lord?   50
  K. Rich. Rumour it abroad
That Anne, my wife, is sick and like to die:
I will take order for her keeping close.
Inquire me out some mean-born gentleman,
Whom I will marry straight to Clarence'
   daughter:
The boy is foolish, and I fear not him.
Look, how thou dream'st! I say again, give
   out
That Anne my wife is sick and like to die:
About it; for it stands me much upon,
To stop all hopes whose growth may damage
   me.   [*Exit Catesby.* 60
I must be married to my brother's daughter,
Or else my kingdom stands on brittle glass.
Murder her brothers, and then marry her!
Uncertain way of gain! But I am in
So far in blood that sin will pluck on sin:
Tear-falling pity dwells not in this eye.

    Re-enter Page, *with* TYRREL.

Is thy name Tyrrel?
  Tyr. James Tyrrel, and your most obedi-
   ent subject.
  K. Rich. Art thou, indeed?
  Tyr.   Prove me, my gracious sovereign.
  K. Rich. Darest thou resolve to kill a
   friend of mine?   70
  Tyr. Ay, my lord;
But I had rather kill two enemies.

---

8. **play the touch,** play the part of a touchstone.
9. **current,** sterling, genuine. 14. **Edward,** i.e., Edward V. 15. **O bitter consequence,** an intolerable
answer to his words and an intolerable fact (Churchill).
28. **iron-witted,** harsh-minded, unfeeling. 29. **unrespective,** unobservant, heedless. 30. **considerate,**
considering, reflecting.

42. **deep-revolving,** deeply scheming. **witty,** cunning, clever. 53. **close,** imprisoned, confined. 54.
mean-born, of low degree. 59. **stands . . . upon,** is
a matter of the utmost importance to me. 61. **brother's
daughter,** i.e., Elizabeth of York, daughter to Edward
IV, who became the queen of Henry VII. 64-66. **But I
. . . eye.** Cf. *Macbeth,* III, iv, 136-38. 65. **pluck on,**
draw on.

K. Rich. Why, there thou hast it: two deep enemies,
Foes to my rest and my sweet sleep's disturbers
Are they that I would have thee deal upon:
Tyrrel, I mean those bastards in the Tower.
    Tyr. Let me have open means to come to them,
And soon I'll rid you from the fear of them.
    K. Rich. Thou sing'st sweet music. Hark, come hither, Tyrrel:
Go, by this token: rise, and lend thine ear: 80
                                        [*Whispers.*
There is no more but so: say it is done,
And I will love thee, and prefer thee too.
    Tyr. 'Tis done, my gracious lord.
    K. Rich. Shall we hear from thee, Tyrrel, ere we sleep?
    Tyr. Ye shall, my lord.   [*Exit.*

Re-enter BUCKINGHAM.

    Buck. My lord, I have consider'd in my mind
The late demand that you did sound me in.
    K. Rich. Well, let that pass. Dorset is fled to Richmond.
    Buck. I hear that news, my lord.
    K. Rich. Stanley, he is your wife's son: well, look to it.   90
    Buck. My lord, I claim your gift, my due by promise,
For which your honour and your faith is pawn'd;
The earldom of Hereford and the moveables
The which you promised I should possess.
    K. Rich. Stanley, look to your wife: if she convey
Letters to Richmond, you shall answer it.
    Buck. What says your highness to my just demand?
    K. Rich. As I remember, Henry the Sixth
Did prophesy that Richmond should be king,
When Richmond was a little peevish boy. 100
A king, perhaps, perhaps,—
    Buck. My lord!
    K. Rich. How chance the prophet could not at that time
Have told me, I being by, that I should kill him?
    Buck. My lord, your promise for the earldom,—

K. Rich. Richmond! When last I was at Exeter,
The mayor in courtesy show'd me the castle,
And call'd it Rougemont: at which name I started,
Because a bard of Ireland told me once,
I should not live long after I saw Richmond.
    Buck. My lord!   111
    K. Rich. Ay, what's o'clock?
    Buck. I am thus bold to put your grace in mind
Of what you promised me.
    K. Rich.   Well, but what's o'clock?
    Buck. Upon the stroke of ten.
    K. Rich.   Well, let it strike.
    Buck. Why let it strike?
    K. Rich. Because that, like a Jack, thou keep'st the stroke
Betwixt thy begging and my meditation.
I am not in the giving vein to-day.
    Buck. Why, then resolve me whether you will or no.   120
    K. Rich. Tut, tut,
Thou troublest me; I am not in the vein.
                    [*Exeunt all but Buckingham.*
    Buck. Is it even so? rewards he my true service
With such deep contempt? made I him king for this?
O, let me think on Hastings, and be gone
To Brecknock, while my fearful head is on!
                                        [*Exit.*

SCENE III.   *The same.*

Enter TYRREL.

    Tyr. The tyrannous and bloody deed is done,
The most arch act of piteous massacre
That ever yet this land was guilty of.
Dighton and Forrest, whom I did suborn
To do this ruthless piece of butchery,
Although they were flesh'd villains, bloody dogs,
Melting with tenderness and kind compassion

---

117. **Jack**, the figure of a man which strikes the bell on the outside of a clock. 117–18. **thou ... meditation**, i.e., regularly or mechanically as the striking of a clock you interrupt my meditation with your begging. 126. **Brecknock**, Brecknock Castle in Wales on Buckingham's estate.
    Scene iii. 2. **arch act**, i.e., chief or notorious act. 4. **Dighton and Forrest.** John Dighton, Tyrrel's horsekeeper, and Miles Forrest, one of the four appointed by Tyrrel to take charge of the princes. 6. **flesh'd**, trained, hardened (used of dogs who were broken in by suffering them to eat of the game pursued).

---

75. **deal upon**, set to work upon. 82. **prefer**, promote, advance. 90. **he**, i.e., Richmond. 96. **it**, i.e., for it.

Wept like two children in their deaths' sad
stories.
'Lo, thus,' quoth Dighton, 'lay those tender
babes:'
'Thus, thus,' quoth Forrest, 'girdling one an-
other   10
Within their innocent alabaster arms:
Their lips were four red roses on a stalk,
Which in their summer beauty kiss'd each
other.
A book of prayers on their pillow lay;
Which once,' quoth Forrest, 'almost changed
my mind;
But O! the devil'—there the villain stopp'd;
Whilst Dighton thus told on: 'We smothered
The most replenished sweet work of nature,
That from the prime creation e'er she
framed.'
Thus both are gone with conscience and re-
morse;   20
They could not speak; and so I left them
both,
To bring this tidings to the bloody king.
And here he comes.

Enter KING RICHARD.

　　　　　　　　All hail, my sovereign liege!
K. Rich. Kind Tyrrel, am I happy in thy
news?
Tyr. If to have done the thing you gave in
charge
Beget your happiness, be happy then,
For it is done, my lord.
K. Rich.　　　But didst thou see them dead?
Tyr. I did, my lord.
K. Rich.　　　And buried, gentle Tyrrel?
Tyr. The chaplain of the Tower hath
buried them;
But how or in what place I do not know. 30
K. Rich. Come to me, Tyrrel, soon at
after supper,
And thou shalt tell the process of their
death.
Meantime, but think how I may do thee
good,
And be inheritor of thy desire.

Farewell till soon.　　　　　　[*Exit Tyrrel.*
The son of Clarence have I pent up close;
His daughter meanly have I match'd in
marriage;
The sons of Edward sleep in Abraham's
bosom,
And Anne my wife hath bid the world good
night.
Now, for I know the Breton Richmond aims
At young Elizabeth, my brother's daughter,
And, by that knot, looks proudly o'er the
crown,   42
To her I go, a jolly thriving wooer.

Enter CATESBY.

Cate. My lord!
K. Rich. Good news or bad, that thou
comest in so bluntly?
Cate. Bad news, my lord: Ely is fled to
Richmond;
And Buckingham, back'd with the hardy
Welshmen,
Is in the field, and still his power increaseth.
K. Rich. Ely with Richmond troubles me
more near
Than Buckingham and his rash-levied army.
Come, I have heard that fearful commenting
Is leaden servitor to dull delay;   52
Delay leads impotent and snail-paced beg-
gary:
Then fiery expedition be my wing,
Jove's Mercury, and herald for a king!
Come, muster men: my counsel is my
shield;
We must be brief when traitors brave the
field.　　　　　　　　　　　[*Exeunt.*

SCENE IV.　*Before the palace.*

Enter QUEEN MARGARET.

Q. Mar. So, now prosperity begins to
mellow
And drop into the rotten mouth of death.
Here in these confines slily have I lurk'd,

18. **replenished**, complete, perfect.　19. **prime**,
first.　20. **gone with**, completely overcome by.　25.
gave in charge, ordered, commanded.　30. **I . . . know**.
More records that Tyrrel ordered the murderers to bury
the bodies "at the staire foot, meetlie deepe in the
ground vnder a great heape of stone." In 1674, during
some repairs at the White Tower, there was unearthed
a wooden chest containing bones which were pronounced
those of two boys of 13 and 11 years. By the order of
Charles II they were removed to Westminster Abbey.
31. **soon**, toward evening. **at after supper**, i.e.,
dessert after supper.　32. **process**. story.

36. **The . . . close**. Richard kept Clarence's son
prisoner at Sheriff Hutton Castle in Yorkshire. 37.
His . . . marriage. Margaret Plantagenet was about
twelve years old when Richard died. Shakespeare has
apparently confused her with Lady Cicely, her first cousin,
whom Richard, according to Holinshed, intended to
marry to "a man found in a cloud, and of an unknown
linge and familie." 38. **Abraham's bosom**. *See Luke*
xvi, 22. 41. **my brother's**, Edward's. 42. **by that
knot**, by virtue of that alliance. 46. **Ely**, John Morton,
Bishop of Ely, who had been kept prisoner at Brecknock
Castle. 51-52. **fearful . . . delay**, timorous thought
and cautious disquisition are dull attendants on delay
(Johnson). 54-55. **fiery . . . king**. Fiery expedition is
to be Richard's herald, as Mercury was Jove's herald.

To watch the waning of mine adversaries.
A dire induction am I witness to, 5
And will to France, hoping the consequence
Will prove as bitter, black, and tragical.
Withdraw thee, wretched Margaret: who
  comes here?

Enter Queen Elizabeth *and the* Duchess
    of York.

  Q. Eliz. Ah, my young princes! ah, my
  tender babes!
My unblown flowers, new-appearing sweets!
If yet your gentle souls fly in the air 11
And be not fix'd in doom perpetual,
Hover about me with your airy wings
And hear your mother's lamentation!
  Q. Mar. Hover about her; say, that right
  for right
Hath dimm'd your infant morn to aged
  night.
  Duch. So many miseries have crazed my
  voice,
That my woe-wearied tongue is mute and
  dumb;
Edward Plantagenet, why art thou dead?
  Q. Mar. Plantagenet doth quit Planta-
  genet. 20
Edward for Edward pays a dying debt.
  Q. Eliz. Wilt thou, O God, fly from such
  gentle lambs,
And throw them in the entrails of the wolf?
When didst thou sleep when such a deed
  was done?
  Q. Mar. When holy Harry died, and my
  sweet son.
  Duch. Blind sight, dead life, poor mortal
  living ghost,
Woe's scene, world's shame, grave's due by
  life usurp'd,
Brief abstract and record of tedious days,
Rest thy unrest on England's lawful earth,
                  [Sitting down.
Unlawfully made drunk with innocents'
  blood! 30
  Q. Eliz. O, that thou wouldst as well
  afford a grave
As thou canst yield a melancholy seat!

Then would I hide my bones, not rest them
  here.
O, who hath any cause to mourn but I?
                [Sitting down by her.
  Q. Mar. If ancient sorrow be most rev-
  erend,
Give mine the benefit of seniory,
And let my woes frown on the upper hand.
If sorrow can admit society,
             [Sitting down with them.
Tell o'er your woes again by viewing mine:
I had an Edward, till a Richard kill'd him; 40
I had a Harry, till a Richard kill'd him:
Thou hadst an Edward, till a Richard kill'd
  him;
Thou hadst a Richard, till a Richard kill'd
  him.
  Duch. I had a Richard too, and thou didst
  kill him;
I had a Rutland too, thou holp'st to kill
  him.
  Q. Mar. Thou hadst a Clarence too, and
  Richard kill'd him.
From forth the kennel of thy womb hath
  crept
A hell-hound that doth hunt us all to death:
That dog, that had his teeth before his
  eyes,
To worry lambs and lap their gentle blood, 50
That foul defacer of God's handiwork,
That excellent grand tyrant of the earth,
That reigns in galled eyes of weeping souls,
Thy womb let loose, to chase us to our
  graves.
O upright, just, and true-disposing God,
How do I thank thee, that this carnal cur
Preys on the issue of his mother's body,
And makes her pew-fellow with others'
  moan!
  Duch. O Harry's wife, triumph not in my
  woes!
God witness with me, I have wept for
  thine. 60
  Q. Mar. Bear with me; I am hungry for
  revenge,
And now I cloy me with beholding it.

---

5. **induction**, first step. 6. **the consequence**, what
follows, the sequel. 10. **unblown**, unopened. 15.
right for right, a just punishment for an offense against
justice (Wright). 16. **dimm'd . . . night**, i.e., brought
your recently acquired glory to eternal ruin. 20. **Plantagenet . . . Plantagenet**, Edward IV . . . Edward,
son of Henry VI and Margaret, former Prince of Wales,
killed by the Yorkists at Tewksbury. 25. **Harry**, i.e.,
Henry VI. 26-7. **Blind . . . usurp'd.** By these paradoxes the mother of Edward IV describes herself and expresses her sense of the disordered state of the land.

36. **seniory**, superiority of claim, priority. 37. **on . . .
hand**, i.e., in the place of precedence. 40 **Edward**, her
son, former Prince of Wales; cf. note, l. 20. 41. **Harry**,
her husband. 42. **Edward**, i.e. Edward IV. 43.
Richard, the young Duke of York, son of Edward IV
and Elizabeth Woodville. 44. **Richard**, Duke of York,
her husband and father of Richard III, killed by
Margaret's army at the battle of Wakefield in 1460.
45. **Rutland**, Edmund, son of the Duke of York, also
killed at Wakefield. 49. **teeth**, an allusion to the
legend that Richard was born with teeth. 53. **galled**,
sore with weeping. 56. **carnal**, flesh-eating. 58. **pew-
fellow**, intimate associate.

Thy Edward he is dead, that stabb'd my
    Edward;
Thy other Edward dead, to quit my Edward;
Young York he is but boot, because both
    they
Match not the high perfection of my loss:
Thy Clarence he is dead that kill'd my
    Edward;
And the beholders of this tragic play,
The adulterate Hastings, Rivers, Vaughan,
    Grey,
Untimely smother'd in their dusky graves. 70
Richard yet lives, hell's black intelligencer,
Only reserved their factor, to buy souls
And send them thither: but at hand, at
    hand,
Ensues his piteous and unpitied end:
Earth gapes, hell burns, fiends roar, saints
    pray,
To have him suddenly convey'd away.
Cancel his bond of life, dear God, I pray,
That I may live to say, The dog is dead!
    Q. Eliz. O, thou didst prophesy the time
      would come   79
That I should wish for thee to help me curse
That bottled spider, that foul bunch-back'd
    toad!
    Q. Mar. I call'd thee then vain flourish of
      my fortune;
I call'd thee then poor shadow, painted
    queen;
The presentation of but what I was;
The flattering index of a direful pageant;
One heaved a-high, to be hurl'd down below;
A mother only mock'd with two sweet babes;
A dream of what thou wert, a breath, a
    bubble,
A sign of dignity, a garish flag,
To be the aim of every dangerous shot; 90
A queen in jest, only to fill the scene.
Where is thy husband now? where be thy
    brothers?
Where are thy children? wherein dost thou
    joy?
Who sues to thee and cries 'God save the
    queen'?
Where be the bending peers that flatter'd
    thee?

Where be the thronging troops that follow'd
    thee?   96
Decline all this, and see what now thou art:
For happy wife, a most distressed widow;
For joyful mother, one that wails the name;
For queen, a very caitiff crown'd with
    care;
For one being sued to, one that humbly
    sues;   101
For one that scorn'd at me, now scorn'd of
    me;
For one being fear'd of all, now fearing one;
For one commanding all, obey'd of none.
Thus hath the course of justice wheel'd
    about,
And left thee but a very prey to time;
Having no more but thought of what thou
    wert,
To torture thee the more, being what thou
    art.
Thou didst usurp my place, and dost thou
    not
Usurp the just proportion of my sorrow? 110
Now thy proud neck bears half my burthen'd
    yoke;
From which even here I slip my weary neck,
And leave the burthen of it all on thee.
Farewell, York's wife, and queen of sad mis-
    chance:
These English woes will make me smile in
    France.
    Q. Eliz. O thou well skill'd in curses, stay
      awhile,
And teach me how to curse mine enemies!
    Q. Mar. Forbear to sleep the nights, and
      fast the days;
Compare dead happiness with living woe;
Think that thy babes were fairer than they
    were,   120
And he that slew them fouler than he is:
Bettering thy loss makes the bad causer
    worse:
Revolving this will teach thee how to curse.
    Q. Eliz. My words are dull; O, quicken
      them with thine!
    Q. Mar. Thy woes will make them sharp,
      and pierce like mine.   [*Exit.*
    Duch. Why should calamity be full of
      words?
    Q. Eliz. Windy attorneys to their client
      woes,

63. **Thy Edward**, Edward IV. **my Edward**, son of
Henry VI. 64. **other Edward**, Edward V. 65. **Young
York**, Richard, Duke of York, the younger of the
princes murdered in the Tower. **but boot**, merely that
which is "thrown in." 69. **adulterate**, adulterous. 71.
intelligencer, agent, go-between. 72. **factor**, agent
(of the powers of hell). 85. **index**, argument, preface,
prologue. 89. **sign**, mere sign.

97. **Decline**, go through from beginning to end. 100.
caitiff, miserable wretch. 102. **scorn'd at**, taunted.
scorn'd of, taunted by. 110. **Usurp**, here used for
"deserve." 122. **Bettering**, exaggerating.

Airy succeeders of intestate joys,
Poor breathing orators of miseries!
Let them have scope: though what they do
    impart   130
Help not at all, yet do they ease the heart.
    Duch. If so, then be not tongue-tied: go
    with me,
And in the breath of bitter words let's
    smother
My damned son, which thy two sweet sons
    smother'd.
I hear his drum: be copious in exclaims.

Enter King Richard, *marching, with drums
    and trumpets.*

    K. Rich. Who intercepts my expedition?
    Duch. O, she that might have intercepted
    thee,
By strangling thee in her accursed womb,
From all the slaughters, wretch, that thou
    hast done!
    Q. Eliz. Hidest thou that forehead with a
    golden crown,   140
Where should be graven, if that right were
    right,
The slaughter of the prince that owed that
    crown,
And the dire death of my two sons and
    brothers?
Tell me, thou villain slave, where are my
    children?
    Duch. Thou toad, thou toad, where is thy
    brother Clarence?
And little Ned Plantagenet, his son?
    Q. Eliz. Where is kind Hastings, Rivers,
    Vaughan, Grey?
    K. Rich. A flourish, trumpets! strike
    alarum, drums!
Let not the heavens hear these tell-tale
    women
Rail on the Lord's anointed: strike, I say! 150
    [*Flourish. Alarums.*
Either be patient, and entreat me fair,
Or with the clamorous report of war
Thus will I drown your exclamations.
    Duch. Art thou my son?
    K. Rich. Ay, I thank God, my father,
    and yourself.

    Duch. Then patiently hear my impa-
    tience.
    K. Rich. Madam, I have a touch of your
    condition,
Which cannot brook the accent of reproof.
    Duch. O, let me speak!
    K. Rich.   Do then; but I'll not hear.
    Duch. I will be mild and gentle in my
    speech.   160
    K. Rich. And brief, good mother; for I
    am in haste.
    Duch. Art thou so hasty? I have stay'd
    for thee,
God knows, in anguish, pain and agony.
    K. Rich. And came I not at last to com-
    fort you?
    Duch. No, by the holy rood, thou know'st
    it well,
Thou camest on earth to make the earth my
    hell.
A grievous burthen was thy birth to me;
Tetchy and wayward was thy infancy;
Thy school-days frightful, desperate, wild,
    and furious,
Thy prime of manhood daring, bold, and
    venturous,   170
Thy age confirm'd, proud, subtle, bloody,
    treacherous,
More mild, but yet more harmful, kind in
    hatred:
What comfortable hour canst thou name,
That ever graced me in thy company?
    K. Rich. Faith, none, but Humphrey
    Hour, that call'd your grace
To breakfast once forth of my company.
If I be so disgracious in your sight,
Let me march on, and not offend your grace.
Strike up the drum.
    Duch.   I prithee, hear me speak.
    K. Rich. You speak too bitterly.
    Duch.   Hear me a word;   180
For I shall never speak to thee again.
    K. Rich. So.
    Duch. Either thou wilt die, by God's just
    ordinance,
Ere from this war thou turn a conqueror,
Or I with grief and extreme age shall perish

128. **intestate**, apparently used in the sense "bequeathing nothing," the general notion being that words
are of no consequence. 129. **breathing**, speaking.
135. **exclaims**, exclamations. 141. **right were right**,
justice were done. 146. **Ned Plantagenet.** Cf. note,
IV, iii, 36. 148. **alarum**, the cry or signal "allarme"
(to arms). 149. **tell-tale**, tattling, gabbling.

157. **touch . . . condition**, a dash or your disposition. 162. **stay'd for**, waited the coming of. 168.
Tetchy, fretful, peevish. 170. **prime of**, first. 171.
age confirm'd, riper manhood. 172. **kind in hatred**,
concealing hatred under pretense of kindness. 175.
Humphrey Hour. To "dine with Duke Humphrey"
was to go hungry. The passage is obscure but seems to
mean that Richard's comfortable hour came when his
mother did not appear for breakfast.

And never look upon thy face again.
Therefore take with thee my most heavy
curse;
Which, in the day of battle, tire thee more
Than all the complete armour that thou
wear'st!
My prayers on the adverse party fight; 190
And there the little souls of Edward's
children
Whisper the spirits of thine enemies
And promise them success and victory.
Bloody thou art, bloody will be thy end;
Shame serves thy life and doth thy death
attend.   [*Exit*.
    Q. Eliz. Though far more cause, yet much
    less spirit to curse
Abides in me; I say amen to all.
    K. Rich. Stay, madam; I must speak a
    word with you.
    Q. Eliz. I have no moe sons of the royal
    blood
For thee to murder: for my daughters,
Richard,
They shall be praying nuns, not weeping
queens;   201
And therefore level not to hit their lives.
    K. Rich. You have a daughter call'd
    Elizabeth,
Virtuous and fair, royal and gracious.
    Q. Eliz. And must she die for this? O, let
    her live,
And I'll corrupt her manners, stain her
beauty;
Slander myself as false to Edward's bed;
Throw over her the veil of infamy:
So she may live unscarr'd of bleeding
slaughter,
I will confess she was not Edward's daugh-
ter.
    K. Rich. Wrong not her birth, she is of
    royal blood.   211
    Q. Eliz. To save her life, I'll say she is not
    so.
    K. Rich. Her life is only safest in her
    birth.
    Q. Eliz. And only in that safety died her
    brothers.
    K. Rich. Lo, at their births good stars
    were opposite.   215

    Q. Eliz. No, to their lives bad friends
    were contrary.
    K. Rich. All unavoided is the doom of
    destiny.
    Q. Eliz. True, when avoided grace makes
    destiny:
My babes were destined to a fairer death,
If grace had bless'd thee with a fairer life. 220
    K. Rich. You speak as if that I had slain
    my cousins.
    Q. Eliz. Cousins, indeed; and by their
    uncle cozen'd
Of comfort, kingdom, kindred, freedom, life.
Whose hand soever lanced their tender
hearts,
Thy head, all indirectly, gave direction:
No doubt the murderous knife was dull and
blunt
Till it was whetted on thy stone-hard heart,
To revel in the entrails of my lambs.
But that still use of grief makes wild grief
tame,
My tongue should to thy ears not name my
boys   230
Till that my nails were anchor'd in thine
eyes;
And I, in such a desperate bay of death,
Like a poor bark, of sails and tackling reft,
Rush all to pieces on thy rocky bosom.
    K. Rich. Madam, so thrive I in my enter-
    prise
And dangerous success of bloody wars,
As I intend more good to you and yours
Than ever you or yours were by me wrong'd!
    Q. Eliz. What good is cover'd with the
    face of heaven,
To be discover'd, that can do me good? 240
    K. Rich. The advancement of your child-
    ren, gentle lady.
    Q. Eliz. Up to some scaffold, there to lose
    their heads?
    K. Rich. No, to the dignity and height of
    honour,
The high imperial type of this earth's glory.
    Q. Eliz. Flatter my sorrows with report
    of it;
Tell me what state, what dignity, what
honour,

---

188. **tire**. This and the co-ordinate verbs *fight*
(l. 190), *Whisper* (l. 192), and *promise* (l. 193) are opta-
tive subjunctives. 190. **on . . . party**, with the enemy.
195. **serves**, accompanies. 202. **level**, aim. 206.
manners, morals. 214. **only in**, by reason of. 215.
opposite, hostile, antagonistic.

216. **contrary**, opposed. 217. **unavoided**, unavoidable. 218. **avoided grace**, i.e., Richard in whom grace
is void or lacking. 222. **cozen'd**, cheated; obvious pun.
229. **still**, constant. 232. **bay, a** body of water in
which the *poor bark* is floundering, and also a reference to the position of a hunted animal who has turned
to face the hounds. 236. **success**, sequel, result.

Canst thou demise to any child of mine?

  K. Rich. Even all I have; yea, and myself and all,

Will I withal endow a child of thine;

So in the Lethe of thy angry soul   250

Thou drown the sad remembrance of those wrongs

Which thou supposest I have done to thee.

  Q. Eliz. Be brief, lest that the process of thy kindness

Last longer telling than thy kindness' date.

  K. Rich. Then know, that from my soul I love thy daughter.

  Q. Eliz. My daughter's mother thinks it with her soul.

  K. Rich. What do you think?

  Q. Eliz. That thou dost love my daughter from thy soul:

So from thy soul's love didst thou love her brothers;

And from my heart's love I do thank thee for it.   260

  K. Rich. Be not so hasty to confound my meaning:

I mean, that with my soul I love thy daughter,

And mean to make her queen of England.

  Q. Eliz. Say then, who dost thou mean shall be her king?

  K. Rich. Even he that makes her queen: who should be else?

  Q. Eliz. What, thou?

  K. Rich. I, even I: what think you of it, madam?

  Q. Eliz. How canst thou woo her?

  K. Rich.   That would I learn of you,

As one that are best acquainted with her humour.

  Q. Eliz. And wilt thou learn of me?

  K. Rich. Madam, with all my heart. 270

  Q. Eliz. Send to her, by the man that slew her brothers,

A pair of bleeding hearts; thereon engrave

Edward and York; then haply she will weep:

Therefore present to her,—as sometime Margaret

Did to thy father, steep'd in Rutland's blood,—

A handkerchief; which, say to her, did drain

The purple sap from her sweet brother's body.

And bid her dry her weeping eyes therewith.

If this inducement force her not to love,

Send her a story of thy noble acts;   280

Tell her thou madest away her uncle Clarence,

Her uncle Rivers; yea, and, for her sake,

Madest quick conveyance with her good aunt Anne.

  K. Rich. Come, come, you mock me; this is not the way

To win your daughter.

  Q. Eliz.   There is no other way;

Unless thou couldst put on some other shape,

And not be Richard that hath done all this.

  K. Rich. Say that I did all this for love of her.

  Q. Eliz. Nay, then indeed she cannot choose but hate thee,

Having bought love with such a bloody spoil.

  K. Rich. Look, what is done cannot be now amended: 291

Men shall deal unadvisedly sometimes,

Which after hours give leisure to repent.

If I did take the kingdom from your sons,

To make amends, I'll give it to your daughter.

If I have kill'd the issue of your womb,

To quicken your increase, I will beget

Mine issue of your blood upon your daughter:

A grandam's name is little less in love

Than is the doting title of a mother;   300

They are as children but one step below,

Even of your mettle, of your very blood;

Of all one pain, save for a night of groans

Endured of her, for whom you bid like sorrow.

Your children were vexation to your youth,

But mine shall be a comfort to your age.

The loss you have is but a son being king,

And by that loss your daughter is made queen.

I cannot make you what amends I would,

Therefore accept such kindness as I can. 310

Dorset your son, that with a fearful soul

Leads discontented steps in foreign soil,

247. **demise**, convey, transmit, lease. 250. **Lethe**, the river Lethe, the waters of which produce forgetfulness. 253. **process**, story, narrative. 259. **from**, used sarcastically in the sense "apart from." 269. **wilt thou**, i.e., do you really wish to. 274. **Therefore**, for that reason. **sometime**, once.

283. **conveyance**, removal. 293. **Which**, i.e., from which dealing. 297. **quicken**, make pregnant. 302. **mettle**, temper, disposition. 304. **bid**, endured. 307. **son being king**, Edward, who was Edward V. 311-12. **Dorset . . . soil.** Dorset did not join Richmond abroad until after the failure of Buckingham's revolt.

This fair alliance quickly shall call home
To high promotions and great dignity:
The king, that calls your beauteous daughter
    wife,
Familiarly shall call thy Dorset brother;
Again shall you be mother to a king,
And all the ruins of distressful times
Repair'd with double riches of content.
What! we have many goodly days to see: 320
The liquid drops of tears that you have shed
Shall come again, transform'd to orient pearl,
Advantaging their loan with interest
Of ten times double gain of happiness.
Go, then, my mother, to thy daughter go;
Make bold her bashful years with your
    experience;
Prepare her ears to hear a wooer's tale;
Put in her tender heart the aspiring flame
Of golden sovereignty; acquaint the princess
With the sweet silent hours of marriage joys:
And when this arm of mine hath chastised 331
The petty rebel, dull-brain'd Buckingham,
Bound with triumphant garlands will I come
And lead thy daughter to a conqueror's bed;
To whom I will retail my conquest won,
And she shall be sole victress, Cæsar's Cæsar.
  Q. Eliz. What were I best to say? her
    father's brother
Would be her lord? or shall I say, her uncle?
Or, he that slew her brothers and her uncles?
Under what title shall I woo for thee,   340
That God, the law, my honour and her love,
Can make seem pleasing to her tender years?
  K. Rich. Infer fair England's peace by
    this alliance.
  Q. Eliz. Which she shall purchase with
    still lasting war.
  K. Rich. Say that the king, which may
    command, entreats.
  Q. Eliz. That at her hands which the
    king's King forbids.
  K. Rich. Say, she shall be a high and
    mighty queen.
  Q. Eliz. To wail the title, as her mother
    doth.
  K. Rich. Say, I will love her everlastingly.
  Q. Eliz. But how long shall that title
    'ever' last?   350
  K. Rich. Sweetly in force unto her fair
    life's end.

  Q. Eliz. But how long fairly shall her
    sweet life last?
  K. Rich. So long as heaven and nature
    lengthens it.
  Q. Eliz. So long as hell and Richard likes
    of it.
  K. Rich. Say, I, her sovereign, am her
    subject love.
  Q. Eliz. But she, your subject, loathes
    such sovereignty.
  K. Rich. Be eloquent in my behalf to her.
  Q. Eliz. An honest tale speeds best being
    plainly told.
  K. Rich. Then in plain terms tell her my
    loving tale.
  Q. Eliz. Plain and not honest is too harsh
    a style.   360
  K. Rich. Your reasons are too shallow and
    too quick.
  Q. Eliz. O no, my reasons are too deep and
    dead;
Too deep and dead, poor infants, in their
    grave.
  K. Rich. Harp not on that string, madam;
    that is past.
  Q. Eliz. Harp on it still shall I till heart-
    strings break.
  K. Rich. Now, by my George, my garter,
    and my crown,—
  Q. Eliz. Profaned, dishonour'd, and the
    third usurp'd.
  K. Rich. I swear—
  Q. Eliz.   By nothing; for this is no
    oath:
The George, profaned, hath lost his holy
    honour;
The garter, blemish'd, pawn'd his knightly
    virtue;   370
The crown, usurp'd, disgraced his kingly
    glory.
If something thou wilt swear to be believed,
Swear then by something that thou hast not
    wrong'd.
  K. Rich. Now, by the world—
  Q. Eliz.   'Tis full of thy foul wrongs.
  K. Rich. My father's death—
  Q. Eliz.   Thy life hath that dishonour'd.
  K. Rich. Then, by myself—
  Q. Eliz.   Thyself thyself misusest.

322. **orient**, bright, shining. 323. **Advantaging**,
augmenting. 343. **Infer**, possibly, bring about; or
adduce (as a reason). 351. **in force**, i.e., my love will
continue.

360. **too . . . style**, i.e., a discordant combination.
361. **reasons**, observations, remarks. **quick**, hasty,
shallow. 366. **George . . . garter**. The George, a
badge showing St. George slaying the dragon, was not
added to the insignia of the Order of the Garter until
the reign of Henry VII or Henry VIII.

K. Rich. Why then, by God—
Q. Eliz.   God's wrong is most of all.
If thou hadst fear'd to break an oath by
  Him,
The unity the king thy brother made
Had not been broken, nor my brother slain:
If thou hadst fear'd to break an oath by
  Him,   381
The imperial metal, circling now thy brow,
Had graced the tender temples of my child,
And both the princes had been breathing
  here,
Which now, two tender playfellows for dust,
Thy broken faith hath made a prey for
  worms.
What canst thou swear by now?
  K. Rich.   The time to come.
  Q. Eliz. That thou hast wronged in the
    time o'erpast;
For I myself have many tears to wash
Hereafter time, for time past wrong'd by
  thee.   390
The children live, whose parents thou hast
  slaughter'd,
Ungovern'd youth, to wail it in their age;
The parents live, whose children thou hast
  butcher'd,
Old wither'd plants, to wail it with their age.
Swear not by time to come; for that thou
  hast
Misused ere used, by time misused o'erpast.
  K. Rich. As I intend to prosper and re-
    pent,
So thrive I in my dangerous attempt
Of hostile arms! myself myself confound!
Heaven and fortune bar me happy hours! 400
Day, yield me not thy light; nor, night, thy
  rest!
Be opposite all planets of good luck
To my proceedings, if, with pure heart's love,
Immaculate devotion, holy thoughts,
I tender not thy beauteous princely daugh-
  ter!
In her consists my happiness and thine;
Without her, follows to this land and me,
To thee, herself, and many a Christian soul,
Death, desolation, ruin and decay:
It cannot be avoided but by this;   410
It will not be avoided but by this.

Therefore, good mother,—I must call you
  so—
Be the attorney of my love to her:
Plead what I will be, not what I have been;
Not my deserts, but what I will deserve:
Urge the necessity and state of times,   416
And be not peevish-fond in great designs.
  Q. Eliz. Shall I be tempted of the devil
    thus?
  K. Rich. Ay, if the devil tempt thee to do
    good.
  Q. Eliz. Shall I forget myself to be my-
    self?   420
  K. Rich. Ay, if yourself's remembrance
    wrong yourself.
  Q. Eliz. But thou didst kill my children.
  K. Rich. But in your daughter's womb I
    bury them:
Where in that nest of spicery they shall
  breed
Selves of themselves, to your recomforture.
  Q. Eliz. Shall I go win my daughter to
    thy will?
  K. Rich. And be a happy mother by the
    deed.
  Q. Eliz. I go. Write to me very shortly,
And you shall understand from me her mind.
  K. Rich. Bear her my true love's kiss;
    and so, farewell.   430
                    [*Exit Queen Elizabeth.*
Relenting fool, and shallow, changing
  woman!

Enter RATCLIFF; CATESBY *following.*

How now! what news?
  Rat. My gracious sovereign, on the
    western coast
Rideth a puissant navy; to the shore
Throng many doubtful hollow-hearted
  friends,
Unarm'd, and unresolved to beat them back:
'Tis thought that Richmond is their admiral;
And there they hull, expecting but the aid
Of Buckingham to welcome them ashore.
  K. Rich. Some light-foot friend post to
    the Duke of Norfolk: 440
Ratcliff, thyself, or Catesby; where is he?
  Cate. Here, my lord.

---

390. **Hereafter,** after this. 392. **Ungovern'd,** i.e., without a father's guidance or rule. 397-98. **As . . . I,** i.e., I swear that as I hope to thrive and intend to repent. 399. **myself . . . confound,** may I destroy myself. 405. **tender,** have a tender regard for. 406. **consists,** resides, inheres.

417. **peevish-fond,** childishly foolish. 420. **myself . . . myself,** i.e., that person wronged by Richard. 421. **wrong yourself,** i.e., interfere with what is to your advantage. 424. **nest of spicery,** a reference to the fabled phœnix which rose anew from the nest of spices, its funeral pyre. 425. **recomforture,** comfort, consolation. 438. **hull,** drift with the sails furled. 440. **light-foot,** swift-footed.

K. Rich. Fly to the duke: [*To Ratcliff*]
Post thou to Salisbury:
When thou comest thither,—[*To Catesby*]
Dull, unmindful villain,
Why stand'st thou still, and go'st not to the
duke?   445
Cate. First, mighty sovereign, let me know
your mind,
What from your grace I shall deliver to him.
K. Rich. O, true, good Catesby: bid him
levy straight
The greatest strength and power he can
make,
And meet me presently at Salisbury.   450
Cate. I go.   [*Exit.*
Rat. What is 't your highness' pleasure I
shall do
At Salisbury?
K. Rich. Why, what wouldst thou do
there before I go?
Rat. Your highness told me I should post
before.
K. Rich. My mind is changed, sir, my
mind is changed.

Enter Lord Stanley.

How now, what news with you?
Stan. None good, my lord, to please you
with the hearing;
Nor none so bad, but it may well be told.
K. Rich. Hoyday, a riddle! neither good
nor bad!   460
Why dost thou run so many mile about,
When thou mayst tell thy tale a nearer way?
Once more, what news?
Stan.   Richmond is on the seas.
K. Rich. There let him sink, and be the
seas on him!
White-liver'd runagate, what doth he there?
Stan. I know not, mighty sovereign, but
by guess.
K. Rich. Well, sir, as you guess, as you
guess?
Stan. Stirr'd up by Dorset, Buckingham,
and Ely,
He makes for England, there to claim the
crown.
K. Rich. Is the chair empty? is the sword
unsway'd?   470
Is the king dead? the empire unpossess'd?

What heir of York is there alive but we?
And who is England's king but great York's
heir?
Then, tell me, what doth he upon the sea?
Stan. Unless for that, my liege, I cannot
guess.
K. Rich. Unless for that he comes to be
your liege,
You cannot guess wherefore the Welshman
comes.
Thou wilt revolt, and fly to him, I fear.
Stan. No, mighty liege; therefore mistrust
me not.
K. Rich. Where is thy power, then, to
beat him back?   480
Where are thy tenants and thy followers?
Are they not now upon the western shore,
Safe-conducting the rebels from their ships?
Stan. No, my good lord, my friends are
in the north.
K. Rich. Cold friends to Richard: what
do they in the north,
When they should serve their sovereign in
the west?
Stan. They have not been commanded,
mighty sovereign:
Please it your majesty to give me leave,
I'll muster up my friends, and meet your
grace
Where and what time your majesty shall
please.   490
K. Rich. Ay, ay, thou wouldst be gone to
join with Richmond:
I will not trust you, sir.
Stan.   Most mighty sovereign,
You have no cause to hold my friendship
doubtful:
I never was nor never will be false.
K. Rich. Well,
Go muster men; but, hear you, leave behind
Your son, George Stanley: look your faith be
firm,
Or else his head's assurance is but frail.
Stan. So deal with him as I prove true to
you.   [*Exit.*
Enter a Messenger.
Mess. My gracious sovereign, now in
Devonshire,   500

446-47. **First . . . him.** Note this first evidence of
confusion in Richard's mind. 450. **at Salisbury,** where
Richard would be in a position to prevent the junction
of Buckingham and Richmond. 465. **white-liver'd,**
cowardly. **runagate,** renegade.

473. **great York's,** i.e., Richard, Duke of York, father
of Edward IV. 475. **that,** i.e., to claim the crown.
477. **Welshman.** Richmond was the grandson of Owen
Tudor, a Welshman of Anglesea, who had married
Catharine of France, widow of Henry V. Richmond's
claim was descent through the Beauforts from John of
Gaunt and Catharine Swynford. 479. **therefore,** on
that account.

As I by friends am well advertised,
Sir Edward Courtney, and the haughty
    prelate
Bishop of Exeter, his brother there,
With many moe confederates, are in arms.

Enter another Messenger.

Sec. Mess. My liege, in Kent the Guild-
    fords are in arms;
And every hour more competitors
Flock to their aid, and still their power in-
    creaseth.

Enter another Messenger.

Third Mess. My lord, the army of the
    Duke of Buckingham—
K. Rich. Out on you, owls! nothing but
    songs of death?   [*He striketh him.*
Take that, until thou bring me better news.
Third Mess. The news I have to tell your
    majesty   511
Is, that by sudden floods and fall of waters,
Buckingham's army is dispersed and scat-
    ter'd;
And he himself wander'd away alone,
No man knows whither.
K. Rich.   I cry thee mercy:
There is my purse to cure that blow of thine.
Hath any well-advised friend proclaim'd
Reward to him that brings the traitor in?
Third Mess. Such proclamation hath been
    made, my liege.

Enter another Messenger.

Fourth Mess. Sir Thomas Lovel and Lord
    Marquis Dorset,   520
'Tis said, my liege, in Yorkshire are in arms.
Yet this good comfort bring I to your grace,
The Breton navy is dispersed by tempest:
Richmond, in Dorsetshire, sent out a boat
Unto the shore, to ask those on the banks
If they were his assistants, yea or no;
Who answer'd him, they came from Bucking-
    ham
Upon his party: he, mistrusting them,
Hoised sail and made away for Brittany.

K. Rich. March on, march on, since we
    are up in arms;   530
If not to fight with foreign enemies,
Yet to beat down these rebels here at home.

Re-enter Catesby.

Cate. My liege, the Duke of Buckingham
    is taken;
That is the best news: that the Earl of
    Richmond
Is with a mighty power landed at Milford,
Is colder tidings, yet they must be told.
K. Rich. Away towards Salisbury! while
    we reason here,
A royal battle might be won and lost:
Some one take order Buckingham be brought
To Salisbury; the rest march on with me. 540
                    [*Flourish.   Exeunt.*

Scene V.   *Lord Derby's house.*

Enter Derby *and* Sir Christopher
    Urswick.

Der. Sir Christopher, tell Richmond this
    from me:
That in the sty of this most bloody boar
My son George Stanley is frank'd up in hold:
If I revolt, off goes young George's head;
The fear of that withholds my present aid.
But, tell me, where is princely Richmond
    now?
Chris. At Pembroke, or at Ha'rford-west,
    in Wales.
Der. What men of name resort to him?
Chris. Sir Walter Herbert, a renowned
    soldier;
Sir Gilbert Talbot, Sir William Stanley; 10
Oxford, redoubted Pembroke, Sir James
    Blunt,
And Rice ap Thomas, with a valiant crew;

---

501. advertised, informed.   502-3. Sir Edward
Courtney, i.e., of Haccombe, created Earl of Devon
on the accession of Henry VII. He was only distantly
related to Peter Courtenay, Bishop of Exeter.   505.
Guildfords, a family led by Sir Richard Guildford of
Hempstead in Kent.   506. competitors, confederates.
509. owls. It was thought that the cry of the owl
portended death.   515. I cry thee mercy, I beg your
pardon. 528. Upon his party, i.e., to fight on his side.
529. Hoised, hoisted.

535. Milford, Milford Haven on the coast of Wales
in the county of Pembroke.   A gap of two years is
here bridged. Richmond's first fruitless expedition was in
October, 1483; his landing at Milford was in August, 1485.
536. colder, more chilling, dampening.   538. royal
battle, battle on which a kingdom depends.
    Scene v. Stage Direction: Sir Christopher Urswick,
a priest, confessor to the Countess of Richmond, Henry
VII's mother. 3. frank'd up, shut up (in a sty). hold,
custody, prison. 7. Ha'rford-west, Haverfordwest,
near Milford Haven. 8. name, honorable repute. 9.
Sir Walter Herbert, a Welshman of old family and considerable influence. 10. Sir Gilbert Talbot, uncle to
the young Earl of Shrewsbury.   Sir William Stanley,
brother to Thomas, Lord Stanley. 11. Oxford, John
de Vere, Earl of Oxford.   Pembroke, Jasper Tudor,
Earl of Pembroke, uncle to Richmond.   Sir James
Blunt, son of Sir Walter Blunt, Baron Mountjoy; he
was lieutenant of Hammes Castle, 1476, where he was
custodian of the Earl of Oxford. 12. Rice ap Thomas,
an influential Welsh knight.

And many moe of noble fame and worth:
And towards London they do bend their
course,
If by the way they be not fought withal.

Der. Return unto thy lord; commend me
to him:
Tell him the queen hath heartily consented
He shall espouse Elizabeth her daughter. 18
These letters will resolve him of my mind.
Farewell. [*Exeunt.*

ACT V.

Scene I. *Salisbury. An open place.*

Enter the Sheriff, *and* Buckingham, *with
halberds, led to execution.*

Buck. Will not King Richard let me
speak with him?

Sher. No, my good lord; therefore be
patient.

Buck. Hastings, and Edward's children,
Rivers, Grey,
Holy King Henry, and thy fair son Edward,
Vaughan, and all that have miscarried
By underhand corrupted foul injustice,
If that your moody discontented souls
Do through the clouds behold this present
hour,
Even for revenge mock my destruction!
This is All-Souls' day, fellows, is it not? 10

Sher. It is, my lord.

Buck. Why, then All-Souls' day is my
body's doomsday.
This is the day that, in King Edward's time,
I wish'd might fall on me, when I was found
False to his children or his wife's allies;
This is the day wherein I wish'd to fall
By the false faith of him I trusted most;
This, this All-Souls' day to my fearful soul
Is the determined respite of my wrongs:
That high All-Seer that I dallied with   20
Hath turn'd my feigned prayer on my head
And given in earnest what I begg'd in jest.
Thus doth he force the swords of wicked men
To turn their own points on their masters'
bosoms:

Now Margaret's curse is fallen upon my
head;   25
'When he,' quoth she, 'shall split thy heart
with sorrow,
Remember Margaret was a prophetess.'
Come, sirs, convey me to the block of shame;
Wrong hath but wrong, and blame the due
of blame.   [*Exeunt.*

Scene II. *The camp near Tamworth.*

Enter Richmond, Oxford, Blunt, Herbert,
and others, with drum and colours.

Richm. Fellows in arms, and my most
loving friends,
Bruised underneath the yoke of tyranny,
Thus far into the bowels of the land
Have we march'd on without impediment;
And here receive we from our father Stanley
Lines of fair comfort and encouragement.
The wretched, bloody, and usurping boar,
That spoil'd your summer fields and fruitful
vines,
Swills your warm blood like wash, and makes
his trough
In your embowell'd bosoms, this foul swine 10
Lies now even in the centre of this isle,
Near to the town of Leicester, as we learn:
From Tamworth thither is but one day's
march.
In God's name, cheerly on, courageous
friends,
To reap the harvest of perpetual peace
By this one bloody trial of sharp war.

Oxf. Every man's conscience is a thousand
swords,
To fight against that bloody homicide.

Herb. I doubt not but his friends will fly
to us.

Blunt. He hath no friends but who are
friends for fear,   20
Which in his greatest need will shrink from
him.

Richm. All for our vantage. Then, in
God's name, march:
True hope is swift, and flies with swallow's
wings;
Kings it makes gods, and meaner creatures
kings.   [*Exeunt.*

---

19. resolve him of, inform him concerning.
Act V. *Scene* i. 4. thy, i.e., Henry's. 5. miscarried,
perished. 10. All-Souls' day, "Festa Animarum,"
Nov. 2, in commemoration of the dead, who on this
day may communicate with the living. 13. day. Cf.
II, i, 32 ff. 19. determined . . . wrongs, the time to
which the punishment of my evil practices was respited
(Johnson following Hanmer).

26. 'When he' . . . sorrow. Cf. I, iii, 300-1.
Scene ii. 5. Stanley, Sir William Stanley. 9. wash,
hog's wash, swill. 10. embowell'd, disembowelled.
20. for fear, i.e., because they fear him. 24. meaner,
of lower degree.

Scene III.   *Bosworth Field.*

Enter King Richard *in arms, with* Norfolk, *the* Earl of Surrey, *and others.*

K. Rich. Here pitch our tents, even here
  in Bosworth field.
My Lord of Surrey, why look you so sad?
  Sur. My heart is ten times lighter than
  my looks.
  K. Rich. My Lord of Norfolk,—
  Nor.   Here, most gracious liege.
  K. Rich. Norfolk, we must have knocks;
  ha! must we not?
  Nor. We must both give and take, my
  gracious lord.
  K. Rich. Up with my tent there! here will
  I lie to-night;
But where to-morrow? Well, all's one for
  that.
Who hath descried the number of the foe?
  Nor. Six or seven thousand is their ut-
  most power.   10
  K. Rich. Why, our battalion trebles that
  account:
Besides, the king's name is a tower of
  strength,
Which they upon the adverse party want.
Up with my tent there! Valiant gentlemen,
Let us survey the vantage of the field;
Call for some men of sound direction:
Let's want no discipline, make no delay;
For, lords, to-morrow is a busy day. [*Exeunt.*

Enter, on the other side of the field, Richmond,
Sir William Brandon, Oxford, *and
others. Some of the* Soldiers *pitch Richmond's tent.*

Richm. The weary sun hath made a
  golden set,
And, by the bright track of his fiery car, 20
Gives signal of a goodly day to-morrow.
Sir William Brandon, you shall bear my
  standard.
Give me some ink and paper in my tent:
I'll draw the form and model of our battle,
Limit each leader to his several charge,
And part in just proportion our small
  strength.
My Lord of Oxford, you, Sir William
  Brandon,

And you, Sir Walter Herbert, stay with me.
The Earl of Pembroke keeps his regiment:
Good Captain Blunt, bear my good-night to
  him,   30
And by the second hour in the morning
Desire the earl to see me in my tent:
Yet one thing more, good Blunt, before thou
  go'st,
Where is Lord Stanley quarter'd, dost thou
  know?
  Blunt. Unless I have mista'en his colours
  much,
Which well I am assured I have not done,
His regiment lies half a mile at least
South from the mighty power of the king.
  Richm. If without peril it be possible,
Good Captain Blunt, bear my good-night to
  him,   40
And give him from me this most needful
  scroll.
  Blunt. Upon my life, my lord, I'll under-
  take it;
And so, God give you quiet rest to-night!
  Richm. Good night, good Captain Blunt.
  Come, gentlemen,
Let us consult upon to-morrow's business:
In to our tent; the air is raw and cold.
                 [*They withdraw into the tent.*

Enter, to his tent, King Richard, Norfolk,
Ratcliff, Catesby, *and others.*

  K. Rich. What is't o'clock?
  Cate.   It's supper-time, my lord;
It's nine o'clock.
  K. Rich.   I will not sup to-night.
Give me some ink and paper.
What, is my beaver easier than it was?   50
And all my armour laid into my tent?
  Cate. It is, my liege; and all things are in
  readiness.
  K. Rich. Good Norfolk, hie thee to thy
  charge;
Use careful watch, choose trusty sentinels.
  Nor. I go, my lord.
  K. Rich. Stir with the lark to-morrow,
  gentle Norfolk.
  Nor. I warrant you, my lord.   [*Exit.*
  K. Rich. Catesby!
  Cate. My lord?
  K. Rich.   Send out a pursuivant at arms

8. **all's . . . that,** be that as it may. 11. **battalion,**
army. 16. **sound direction,** true judgment, sound
military skill. 20. **fiery car,** a reference to the car of
Phœbus.

29. **keeps,** i.e., is with. 50. **beaver,** helmet. **easier,**
more loosely fitting. 57. **warrant,** promise. 59.
pursuivant at arms, one of the junior officers
attendant on the heralds.

To Stanley's regiment; bid him bring his
    power   60
Before sunrising, lest his son George fall
Into the blind cave of eternal night.
                          [*Exit Catesby.*
Fill me a bowl of wine. Give me a watch.
Saddle white Surrey for the field to-morrow.
Look that my staves be sound, and not too
    heavy.
Ratcliff!
    Rat. My lord?
    K. Rich. Saw'st thou the melancholy
      Lord Northumberland?
    Rat. Thomas the Earl of Surrey, and him-
      self,
Much about cock-shut time, from troop to
    troop   70
Went through the army, cheering up the
    soldiers.
    K. Rich. So, I am satisfied. Give me a
      bowl of wine:
I have not that alacrity of spirit,
Nor cheer of mind, that I was wont to have.
Set it down. Is ink and paper ready?
    Rat. It is, my lord.
    K. Rich.   Bid my guard watch; leave
    me.
Ratcliff, about the mid of night come to my
    tent
And help to arm me. Leave me, I say.
    [*Exeunt Ratcliff and the other Attendants.*

Enter DERBY *to* RICHMOND *in his tent, Lords
and others attending.*

    Der. Fortune and victory sit on thy helm!
    Richm. All comfort that the dark night
      can afford   80
Be to thy person, noble father-in-law!
Tell me, how fares our loving mother?
    Der. I, by attorney, bless thee from thy
      mother,
Who prays continually for Richmond's good:
So much for that. The silent hours steal on,
And flaky darkness breaks within the east.
In brief,—for so the season bids us be,—
Prepare thy battle early in the morning,
And put thy fortune to the arbitrement

Of bloody strokes and mortal-staring war. 90
I, as I may—that which I would I cannot,—
With best advantage will deceive the time,
And aid thee in this doubtful shock of arms:
But on thy side I may not be too forward,
Lest, being seen, thy brother, tender George,
Be executed in his father's sight.
Farewell: the leisure and the fearful time
Cuts off the ceremonious vows of love
And ample interchange of sweet discourse,
Which so long sunder'd friends should dwell
    upon: 100
God give us leisure for these rites of love!
Once more, adieu: be valiant, and speed well!
    Richm. Good lords, conduct him to his
      regiment:
I'll strive, with troubled thoughts, to take a
    nap,
Lest leaden slumber peise me down to-mor-
    row,   105
When I should mount with wings of victory:
Once more, good night, kind lords and gentle-
    men.   [*Exeunt all but Richmond.*
O Thou, whose captain I account myself,
Look on my forces with a gracious eye;
Put in their hands thy bruising irons of
    wrath,   110
That they may crush down with a heavy fall
The usurping helmets of our adversaries!
Make us thy ministers of chastisement,
That we may praise thee in the victory!
To thee I do commend my watchful soul,
Ere I let fall the windows of mine eyes:
Sleeping and waking, O, defend me still!
                         [*Sleeps.*

Enter the Ghost of PRINCE EDWARD, *son to*
HENRY *the Sixth.*

    Ghost. [*To Richard*] Let me sit heavy on
      thy soul to-morrow!
Think, how thou stab'dst me in my prime of
    youth   119
At Tewksbury: despair, therefore, and die!
[*To Richmond*] Be cheerful, Richmond; for
    the wronged souls
Of butcher'd princes fight in thy behalf:
King Henry's issue, Richmond, comforts
    thee.

---

63. **watch**, watch-light, a candle marked into equal
divisions to show time; or perhaps, sentinel. 64. **white
Surrey.** The name seems to be Shakespeare's invention. Hall says that Richard was mounted on a
"great white courser." 65. **staves**, the staves or handles of his lances. 70. **cock-shut time**, evening twilight; possibly, the time at which poultry are shut up.
81. **father-in-law.** Stanley was step-father to Richmond. 86. **flaky**, broken into flakes of cloud. 87.
season, time of day. 88. **battle**, army, battle-array.

90. **mortal-staring**, fatal-visaged. 91. **that . . .
cannot**, i.e., sleep. 92. **With best advantage**, to the
best purpose. 94. **be too forward**, appear too openly.
95. **tender**, young, of tender years. In point of fact
George Stanley was a mature man. 97. **leisure**, i.e.,
lack of leisure. 105. **peise**, weigh. 110. **bruising
irons**, maces, weapons. 119. **prime**, early time. 123.
issue, son.

Enter the Ghost of Henry *the Sixth.*

Ghost. [*To Richard*] When I was mortal,
  my anointed body
By thee was punched full of deadly holes:
Think on the Tower and me: despair, and
  die!
Harry the Sixth bids thee despair and die!
[*To Richmond*] Virtuous and holy, be thou
  conqueror!
Harry, that prophesied thou shouldst be
  king,
Doth comfort thee in thy sleep: live, and
  flourish!   130

Enter the Ghost of Clarence.

Ghost [*To Richard*] Let me sit heavy on
  thy soul to-morrow!
I, that was wash'd to death with fulsome
  wine,
Poor Clarence, by thy guile betrayed to
  death!
To-morrow in the battle think on me,
And fall thy edgeless sword: despair, and
  die!—
[*To Richmond*] Thou offspring of the house of
  Lancaster,
The wronged heirs of York do pray for thee:
Good angels guard thy battle! live, and
  flourish!

Enter the Ghosts of Rivers, Grey, *and*
  Vaughan.

Ghost of R. [*To Richard*] Let me sit heavy
  on thy soul to-morrow,
Rivers, that died at Pomfret! despair, and
  die!   140
Ghost of G. [*To Richard*] Think upon Grey,
  and let thy soul despair!
Ghost of V. [*To Richard*] Think upon
  Vaughan, and, with guilty fear,
Let fall thy lance: despair, and die!
All. [*To Richmond*] Awake, and think our
  wrongs in Richard's bosom
Will conquer him! awake, and win the day!

Enter the Ghost of Hastings.

Ghost. [*To Richard*] Bloody and guilty,
  guiltily awake,
And in a bloody battle end thy days!
Think on Lord Hastings: despair, and die!

[*To Richmond*] Quiet untroubled soul, awake,
  awake!
Arm, fight, and conquer, for fair England's
  sake!   150

Enter the Ghosts of the two young Princes.

Ghosts. [*To Richard*] Dream on thy cousins
  smother'd in the Tower:
Let us be lead within thy bosom, Richard,
And weigh thee down to ruin, shame, and
  death!
Thy nephews' souls bid thee despair and die!
[*To Richmond*] Sleep, Richmond, sleep in
  peace, and wake in joy;
Good angels guard thee from the boar's
  annoy!   156
Live, and beget a happy race of kings!
Edward's unhappy sons do bid thee flourish.

Enter the Ghost of Lady Anne.

Ghost. [*To Richard*] Richard, thy wife,
  that wretched Anne thy wife,
That never slept a quiet hour with thee, 160
Now fills thy sleep with perturbations:
To-morrow in the battle think on me,
And fall thy edgeless sword: despair, and
  die!
[*To Richmond*] Thou quiet soul, sleep thou a
  quiet sleep;
Dream of success and happy victory!
Thy adversary's wife doth pray for thee.

Enter the Ghost of Buckingham.

Ghost. [*To Richard*] The first was I that
  help'd thee to the crown;
The last was I that felt thy tyranny:
O, in the battle think on Buckingham,
And die in terror of thy guiltiness!   170
Dream on, dream on, of bloody deeds and
  death:
Fainting, despair; despairing, yield thy
  breath!
[*To Richmond*] I died for hope ere I could
  lend thee aid:
But cheer thy heart, and be thou not dis-
  may'd:
God and good angels fight on Richmond's
  side;
And Richard falls in height of all his pride.

---

126. **Tower,** where Henry VI was supposed to have
been murdered.   132. **wash'd to death,** i.e., drowned
in the butt of malmsey. **fulsome,** cloying. 135. **fall,**
may it fall. **edgeless,** futile.

151. **cousins,** relations; here, nephews. 156. **the
boar's annoy,** i.e., Richard's attack. 173. **for hope,**
i.e., for want of hope; Steevens conjectured *for holpe,*
deserted, unhelped.

*[The Ghosts vanish. King Richard starts
                    out of his dream.*

K. Rich. Give me another horse: bind up
      my wounds.
Have mercy, Jesu!—Soft! I did but dream.
O coward conscience, how dost thou
      afflict me!
The lights burn blue. It is now dead mid-
      night.   180
Cold fearful drops stand on my trembling
      flesh.
What do I fear? myself? there's none else by:
Richard loves Richard; that is, I am I.
Is there a murderer here? No. Yes, I am:
Then fly. What, from myself? Great reason
      why:
Lest I revenge. What, myself upon myself?
Alack, I love myself. Wherefore? for any
      good
That I myself have done unto myself?
O, no! alas, I rather hate myself
For hateful deeds committed by myself! 190
I am a villain: yet I lie, I am not.
Fool, of thyself speak well: fool, do not
      flatter.
My conscience hath a thousand several
      tongues,
And every tongue brings in a several tale,
And every tale condemns me for a villain.
Perjury, perjury, in the high'st degree;
Murder, stern murder, in the direst degree;
All several sins, all used in each degree,
Throng to the bar, crying all, Guilty! guilty!
I shall despair. There is no creature loves
      me;   200
And if I die, no soul shall pity me:
Nay, wherefore should they, since that I my-
      self
Find in myself no pity to myself?
Methought the souls of all that I had mur-
      der'd
Came to my tent; and every one did threat
To-morrow's vengeance on the head of
      Richard.

Enter RATCLIFF.

Rat. My lord!
K. Rich. 'Zounds! who is there?
Rat. Ratcliff, my lord; 'tis I. The early
      village-cock

Hath twice done salutation to the morn; 210
Your friends are up, and buckle on their
      armour.
      K. Rich. O Ratcliff, I have dream'd a
      fearful dream!
What thinkest thou, will our friends prove
      all true?
Rat. No doubt, my lord.
K. Rich.   O Ratcliff, I fear, I fear, —
Rat. Nay, good my lord, be not afraid of
      shadows.
K. Rich. By the apostle Paul, shadows
      to-night
Have struck more terror to the soul of
      Richard
Than can the substance of ten thousand sol-
      diers
Armed in proof, and led by shallow Rich-
      mond.
It is not yet near day. Come, go with me; 220
Under our tents I'll play the eaves-dropper,
To see if any mean to shrink from me.
                                          [*Exeunt.*

Enter the Lords *to* RICHMOND, *sitting in his
                    tent.*

Lords. Good morrow, Richmond!
Richm. Cry mercy, lords and watchful
      gentlemen,
That you have ta'en a tardy sluggard here.
Lords. How have you slept, my lord?
Richm. The sweetest sleep, and fairest-
      boding dreams
That ever enter'd in a drowsy head,
Have I since your departure had, my lords.
Methought their souls, whose bodies Rich-
      ard murder'd,   230
Came to my tent, and cried on victory:
I promise you, my soul is very jocund
In the remembrance of so fair a dream.
How far into the morning is it, lords?
Lords. Upon the stroke of four.   235
Richm. Why, then 'tis time to arm and
      give direction.

His oration to his soldiers.

More than I have said, loving countrymen,
The leisure and enforcement of the time
Forbids to dwell upon: yet remember this,
God and our good cause fight upon our side;

---

180. lights burn blue, superstitiously regarded as
evidence of the presence of ghosts. **193, 194. several,**
different. **198. used,** committed. **199. bar,** i.e., bar
of justice.

218. substance, bodies; used in contrast to *shadows*
(l. 216). **219. in proof,** in armour which is proof against
weapons. **231. cried on,** uttered the cry of. **236. direction,** orders. **238. leisure,** i.e., lack of leisure.
enforcement, exigency.

The prayers of holy saints and wronged
  souls, 241
Like high-rear'd bulwarks, stand before our
  faces;
Richard except, those whom we fight against
Had rather have us win than him they
  follow:
For what is he they follow? truly, gentlemen,
A bloody tyrant and a homicide;
One raised in blood, and one in blood estab-
  lish'd;
One that made means to come by what he
  hath,
And slaughter'd those that were the means
  to help him;
A base foul stone, made precious by the foil
Of England's chair, where he is falsely set; 251
One that hath ever been God's enemy:
Then, if you fight against God's enemy,
God will in justice ward you as his soldiers;
If you do sweat to put a tyrant down,
You sleep in peace, the tyrant being slain;
If you do fight against your country's foes,
Your country's fat shall pay your pains the
  hire;
If you do fight in safeguard of your wives,
Your wives shall welcome home the con-
  querors; 260
If you do free your children from the sword,
Your children's children quit it in your age.
Then, in the name of God and all these rights,
Advance your standards, draw your willing
  swords.
For me, the ransom of my bold attempt
Shall be this cold corpse on the earth's cold
  face;
But if I thrive, the gain of my attempt
The least of you shall share his part thereof.
Sound drums and trumpets boldly and
  cheerfully;
God and Saint George! Richmond and vic-
  tory!   [*Exeunt.* 270

Re-enter KING RICHARD, RATCLIFF, *Attendants and Forces.*

K. Rich. What said Northumberland as
  touching Richmond?
Rat. That he was never trained up in
  arms.

K. Rich. He said the truth: and what said
  Surrey then?
Rat. He smiled and said 'The better for
  our purpose.'
K. Rich. He was in the right; and so in-
  deed it is.   [*Clock striketh.*
Tell the clock there. Give me a calendar.
Who saw the sun to-day?
Rat.   Not I, my lord.
K. Rich. Then he disdains to shine; for by
  the book
He should have braved the east an hour ago:
A black day will it be to somebody.   280
Ratcliff!
Rat. My lord?
K. Rich. The sun will not be seen to-day;
The sky doth frown and lour upon our army.
I would these dewy tears were from the
  ground.
Not shine to-day! Why, what is that to me
More than to Richmond? for the selfsame
  heaven
That frowns on me looks sadly upon him.

Enter NORFOLK.

Nor. Arm, arm, my lord; the foe vaunts in
  the field.
K. Rich. Come, bustle, bustle; caparison
  my horse.
Call up Lord Stanley, bid him bring his
  power: 290
I will lead forth my soldiers to the plain,
And thus my battle shall be ordered:
My foreward shall be drawn out all in
  length,
Consisting equally of horse and foot;
Our archers shall be placed in the midst:
John Duke of Norfolk, Thomas Earl of
  Surrey,
Shall have the leading of this foot and horse.
They thus directed, we will follow
In the main battle, whose puissance on
  either side
Shall be well winged with our chiefest horse.
This, and Saint George to boot! What
  think'st thou, Norfolk?   301
Nor. A good direction, warlike sovereign.
This found I on my tent this morning.
    [*He sheweth him a paper.*

---

247. **raised . . . establish'd**, i.e., in the kingship.
250. **foil**, a thin leaf of metal placed under a stone
to set it off to advantage. 254. **ward**, protect. 258.
fat, prosperity, wealth. 265. **ransom**, etc. If he fails,
there will be no question of ransom, but of death. 272.
up in, i.e., to.

278. **book**, i.e., the calendar. 279. **braved**, made
splendid. 288. **vaunts**, boasts. 289. **caparison**, put
on the trappings. 293. **foreward**, vanguard. 299. **main
battle**, main body of troops. 301. **to boot**, i.e., to give
us aid in addition.

K. Rich. [*Reads*] 'Jockey of Norfolk, be not too bold,
For Dickon thy master is bought and sold.'
A thing devised by the enemy.
Go, gentlemen, every man unto his charge:
Let not our babbling dreams affright our souls:
Conscience is but a word that cowards use,
Devised at first to keep the strong in awe: 310
Our strong arms be our conscience, swords our law.
March on, join bravely, let us to't pell-mell;
If not to heaven, then hand in hand to hell.

His oration to his Army.

What shall I say more than I have inferr'd?
Remember whom you are to cope withal;
A sort of vagabonds, rascals, and runaways,
A scum of Bretons, and base lackey peasants,
Whom their o'er-cloyed country vomits forth
To desperate ventures and assured destruction.
You sleeping safe, they bring to you unrest;
You having lands, and blest with beauteous wives, 321
They would restrain the one, distain the other.
And who doth lead them but a paltry fellow,
Long kept in Bretagne at our mother's cost?
A milk-sop, one that never in his life
Felt so much cold as over shoes in snow?
Let's whip these stragglers o'er the seas again;
Lash hence these overweening rags of France,
These famish'd beggars, weary of their lives;
Who, but for dreaming on this fond exploit,
For want of means, poor rats, had hang'd themselves: 331
If we be conquer'd, let men conquer us,
And not these bastard Bretons; whom our fathers

Have in their own land beaten, bobb'd, and thump'd,
And in record, left them the heirs of shame.
Shall these enjoy our lands? lie with our wives?
Ravish our daughters? [*Drum afar off.*]
Hark! I hear their drum.
Fight, gentlemen of England! fight, bold yeomen!
Draw, archers, draw your arrows to the head!
Spur your proud horses hard, and ride in blood; 340
Amaze the welkin with your broken staves!

Enter a Messenger.

What says Lord Stanley? will he bring his power?
Mess. My lord, he doth deny to come.
K. Rich. Off with his son George's head!
Nor. My lord, the enemy is past the marsh:
After the battle let George Stanley die.
K. Rich. A thousand hearts are great within my bosom:
Advance our standards, set upon our foes;
Our ancient word of courage, fair Saint George,
Inspire us with the spleen of fiery dragons!
Upon them! Victory sits on our helms. 351
[*Exeunt.*

SCENE IV. *Another part of the field.*

Alarum: excursions. Enter NORFOLK *and forces fighting; to him* CATESBY.

Cate. Rescue, my Lord of Norfolk, rescue, rescue!
The king enacts more wonders than a man,
Daring an opposite to every danger:
His horse is slain, and all on foot he fights,
Seeking for Richmond in the throat of death.
Rescue, fair lord, or else the day is lost!

Alarums. Enter KING RICHARD.

K. Rich. A horse! a horse! my kingdom for a horse!

304-5. 'Jockey . . . sold.' The rhyme occurs in the chronicles. 304. **Jockey,** familiar form of "Jack." 305. **Dickon,** i.e., Dick, Richard. **bought and sold,** betrayed for a bribe. 308. **babbling,** foolish. 314. **inferr'd,** stated. 317. **lackey,** a running footman; here, servile. 322. **restrain,** keep back, withhold. **distain,** defile, sully. 324. **our mother's.** Richmond's mother was not Richard's. This error occurs in the second edition of Holinshed's *Chronicles.* The first edition reads "brothers," the reference being to the fact that Richmond had been supported at the court of the Duke of Bretagne at the cost of the Duke of Burgundy, Richard's brother-in-law. 326. **as over shoes,** i.e., as one being over his shoe-tops. 331. **want of means,** poverty.

334. **bobb'd** banged. 335. **record,** history. 341. **Amaze . . . staves,** i.e., fright the skies with the shining of your lances (Johnson). 350. **spleen,** rage. *Scene iv.* 2. **than a man,** than seems possible for a human being. 3. **Daring . . . danger,** boldly facing every danger of battle.

Cate. Withdraw, my lord; I'll help you to a horse.

K. Rich. Slave, I have set my life upon a cast,

And I will stand the hazard of the die: 10
I think there be six Richmonds in the field;
Five have I slain to-day instead of him.
A horse! a horse! my kingdom for a horse!
     [*Exeunt*.

Scene V. *Another part of the field*.

Alarum. Enter Richard *and* Richmond; *they fight*. Richard *is slain. Retreat and flourish. Re-enter* Richmond, Derby *bearing the crown, with divers other Lords*.

Richm. God and your arms be praised, victorious friends;
The day is ours, the bloody dog is dead.

Der. Courageous Richmond, well hast thou acquit thee.

Lo, here, this long-usurped royalty
From the dead temples of this bloody wretch
Have I pluck'd off, to grace thy brows withal:
Wear it, enjoy it, and make much of it.

Richm. Great God of heaven, say Amen to all!

But, tell me, is young George Stanley living?

Der. He is, my lord, and safe in Leicester town;   10
Whither, if it please you, we may now withdraw us.

Richm. What men of name are slain on either side?

Der. John Duke of Norfolk, Walter Lord Ferrers,

Sir Robert Brakenbury, and Sir William Brandon.

---

10. **hazard . . . die**, i.e., the turn of the die.

Richm. Inter their bodies as becomes their births:
Proclaim a pardon to the soldiers fled
That in submission will return to us:
And then, as we have ta'en the sacrament,
We will unite the white rose and the red:
Smile heaven upon this fair conjunction,   20
That long have frown'd upon their enmity!
What traitor hears me, and says not amen?
England hath long been mad, and scarr'd herself;
The brother blindly shed the brother's blood,
The father rashly slaughter'd his own son,
The son, compell'd, been butcher to the sire:
All this divided York and Lancaster,
Divided in their dire division,
O, now, let Richmond and Elizabeth,
The true succeeders of each royal house,   30
By God's fair ordinance conjoin together!
And let their heirs, God, if thy will be so,
Enrich the time to come with smooth-faced peace,
With smiling plenty and fair prosperous days!
Abate the edge of traitors, gracious Lord,
That would reduce these bloody days again,
And make poor England weep in streams of blood!
Let them not live to taste this land's increase
That would with treason wound this fair land's peace!
Now civil wounds are stopp'd, peace lives again: 40
That she may long live here, God say amen!
     [*Exeunt*.

---

18. **as . . . sacrament**, as I am sworn to do. 19. **white . . . red**, house of York and house of Lancaster, i.e., by his marriage to Elizabeth, daughter of Edward IV. 28. **division**, estrangement. 33. **smooth-faced**, calm-visaged. 35. **Abate the edge**, i.e., render their opposition ineffective. 38. **increase**, i.e., new prosperity.

ROMEO AND JULIET

DRAMATIS PERSONÆ

ESCALUS, prince of Verona.
PARIS, a young nobleman, kinsman to the prince.
MONTAGUE,⎱ heads of two houses at
CAPULET, ⎰ variance with each other.
An old man, cousin to Capulet.
ROMEO, son to Montague.
MERCUTIO, kinsman to the prince, and friend to Romeo.
BENVOLIO, nephew to Montague, and friend to Romeo.
TYBALT, nephew to Lady Capulet.
FRIAR LAURENCE,⎫
FRIAR JOHN, ⎬ Franciscans.
BALTHASAR, servant to Romeo.
SAMPSON,⎱ servants to Capulet.
GREGORY,⎰

PETER, servant to Juliet's nurse.
ABRAHAM, servant to Montague.
An Apothecary.
Three Musicians.
Page to Paris; another Page; an Officer.

LADY MONTAGUE, wife to Montague.
LADY CAPULET, wife to Capulet.
JULIET, daughter to Capulet.
Nurse to Juliet.

Citizens of Verona; several Men and Women, relations to both houses; Maskers, Guards, Watchmen, and Attendants. Chorus.

SCENE: *Verona; Mantua.*

PROLOGUE.

Two households, both alike in dignity,
  In fair Verona, where we lay our scene,
From ancient grudge break to new mutiny,
  Where civil blood makes civil hands unclean.
From forth the fatal loins of these two foes
  A pair of star-cross'd lovers take their life;
Whose misadventured piteous overthrows
  Do with their death bury their parents' strife.
The fearful passage of their death-mark'd love,
  And the continuance of their parents' rage,
Which, but their children's end, nought could remove,   11
  Is now the two hours' traffic of our stage;

The which if you with patient ears attend,
What here shall miss, our toil shall strive to mend.

ACT I.

SCENE I. *Verona. A public place.*

Enter SAMPSON *and* GREGORY, *of the house of Capulet, armed with swords and bucklers.*

Sam. Gregory, o' my word, we'll not carry coals.
Gre. No, for then we should be colliers.
Sam. I mean, an we be in choler, we'll draw.
Gre. Ay, while you live, draw your neck out o' the collar.
Sam. I strike quickly, being moved.
Gre. But thou art not quickly moved to strike.
Sam. A dog of the house of Montague moves me.   10
Gre. To move is to stir; and to be valiant

---

3. **mutiny,** state of discord. 6. **star-cross'd,** thwarted by destiny. Shakespeare shows in this play particularly, and throughout his plays generally, the current belief in the power of the stars. The idea blends with that of divine providence. 9. **passage,** progress. 12. **two hours' traffic of our stage.** This line is one of a small number of references which enable us to tell the length of time occupied by a Shakespearean play. If the time was nearer two hours than three, the play must have been rapidly recited, with little loss of time between scenes. The bareness of the stage and the lack of a curtain would have contributed to the speed of presentation.

Act I, Scene i. This scene serves to give us the atmosphere of the whole play, an atmosphere of feud. Sampson is a stupid bully, Gregory a merry one. 1. **carry coals,** endure insults. 4. **choler,** one of the four humors, productive of anger.

is to stand: therefore, if thou art moved, thou runn'st away.

Sam. A dog of that house shall move me to stand: I will take the wall of any man or maid of Montague's.   16

Gre. That shows thee a weak slave; for the weakest goes to the wall.

Sam. True; and therefore women, being the weaker vessels, are ever thrust to the wall: therefore I will push Montague's men from the wall, and thrust his maids to the wall.

Gre. The quarrel is between our masters and us their men.

Sam. 'Tis all one, I will show myself a tyrant: when I have fought with the men, I will be cruel with the maids, and cut off their heads.

Gre. The heads of the maids?   29

Sam. Ay, the heads of the maids, or their maidenheads; take it in what sense thou wilt.

Gre. They must take it in sense that feel it.

Sam. Me they shall feel while I am able to stand: and 'tis known I am a pretty piece of flesh.   35

Gre. 'Tis well thou art not fish; if thou hadst, thou hadst been poor John. Draw thy tool; here comes two of the house of the Montagues.

Sam. My naked weapon is out: quarrel, I will back thee.   40

Gre. How! turn thy back and run?

Sam. Fear me not.

Gre. No, marry; I fear thee!

Sam. Let us take the law of our sides; let them begin.

Gre. I will frown as I pass by, and let them take it as they list.

Sam. Nay, as they dare. I will bite my thumb at them; which is a disgrace to them, if they bear it.   50

Enter ABRAHAM *and* BALTHASAR.

Abr. Do you bite your thumb at us, sir?

Sam. I do bite my thumb, sir.

Abr. Do you bite your thumb at us, sir?

Sam. [*Aside to Gre.*] Is the law of our side, if I say ay?

Gre. No.

Sam. No, sir, I do not bite my thumb at you sir, but I bite my thumb, sir.

Gre. Do you quarrel, sir?

Abr. Quarrel, sir! no, sir.   60

Sam. If you do, sir, I am for you: I serve as good a man as you.

Abr. No better.

Sam. Well, sir.

Gre. Say 'better:' here comes one of my master's kinsmen.

Sam. Yes, better, sir.

Abr. You lie.

Sam. Draw, if you be men. Gregory, remember thy swashing blow. [*They fight.* 70

Enter BENVOLIO.

Ben. Part, fools!
Put up your swords; you know not what
    you do.   [*Beats down their swords.*

Enter TYBALT.

Tyb. What, art thou drawn among these
    heartless hinds?   73
Turn thee, Benvolio, look upon thy death.

Ben. I do but keep the peace: put up thy
    sword,
Or manage it to part these men with me.

Tyb. What, drawn, and talk of peace! I
    hate the word,
As I hate hell, all Montagues, and thee:
Have at thee, coward!   [*They fight.*

*Enter several of both houses, who join the
    fray; then enter* Citizens, *with clubs.*

First Cit. Clubs, bills, and partisans!
    strike! beat them down!   80
Down with the Capulets! down with the
    Montagues!

Enter CAPULET *in his gown, and* LADY
    CAPULET.

Cap. What noise is this? Give me my long
    sword, ho!

La. Cap. A crutch, a crutch! why call you
    for a sword?

Cap. My sword, I say! Old Montague is
    come,
And flourishes his blade in spite of me.

Enter MONTAGUE *and* LADY MONTAGUE.

Mon. Thou villian Capulet,—Hold me
    not, let me go.

---

15. **take the wall**, take the side of the walk nearest the wall, an act of discourtesy. 37. **poor John**, hake salted and dried—a poor kind of food. 43. **marry**, a degenerate oath, originally *Mary!* 48. **bite my thumb**, an insulting gesture.

70. **swashing**, crushing. 73. **drawn**, with drawn sword. **heartless hinds**, cowardly menials. Tybalt's spirit is irreconcilable throughout. 80. **Clubs, bills, and partisans**, a rallying cry of London apprentices. *Bills* and *partisans* were long-handled spears with cutting blades.

La. Mon. Thou shalt not stir a foot to
seek a foe.

Enter PRINCE, *with* Attendants.

Prin. Rebellious subjects, enemies to
peace,
Profaners of this neighbour-stained steel,—
Will they not hear? What, ho! you men, you
beasts,   90
That quench the fire of your pernicious rage
With purple fountains issuing from your
veins,
On pain of torture, from those bloody hands
Throw your mistemper'd weapons to the
ground,
And hear the sentence of your moved prince.
Three civil brawls, bred of an airy word,
By thee, old Capulet, and Montague,
Have thrice disturb'd the quiet of our streets,
And made Verona's ancient citizens
Cast by their grave beseeming ornaments, 100
To wield old partisans, in hands as old,
Canker'd with peace, to part your canker'd
hate:
If ever you disturb our streets again,
Your lives shall pay the forfeit of the peace.
For this time, all the rest depart away:
You, Capulet, shall go along with me:
And, Montague, come you this afternoon,
To know our further pleasure in this case,
To old Free-town, our common judgement-
place.
Once more, on pain of death, all men depart.
   [*Exeunt all but Montague, Lady Mon-*
               tague, and Benvolio.
Mon. Who set this ancient quarrel new
abroach?   111
Speak, nephew, were you by when it began?
Ben. Here were the servants of your ad-
versary,
And yours, close fighting ere I did approach:
I drew to part them: in the instant came
The fiery Tybalt, with his sword prepared,
Which, as he breathed defiance to my ears,
He swung about his head and cut the winds,
Who nothing hurt withal hiss'd him in scorn:
While we were interchanging thrusts and
blows,
Came more and more and fought on part and
part,   121
Till the prince came, who parted either part.

La. Mon. O, where is Romeo? saw you
him to-day?
Right glad I am he was not at this fray.
   Ben. Madam, an hour before the wor-
shipp'd sun
Peer'd forth the golden window of the east,
A troubled mind drave me to walk abroad;
Where, underneath the grove of sycamore
That westward rooteth from the city's side,
So early walking did I see your son: 130
Towards him I made, but he was ware of me
And stole into the covert of the wood:
I, measuring his affections by my own,
That most are busied when they're most
alone,
Pursued my humour not pursuing his,
And gladly shunn'd who gladly fled from me.
   Mon. Many a morning hath he there been
seen,
With tears augmenting the fresh morning's
dew,
Adding to clouds more clouds with his deep
sighs;
But all so soon as the all-cheering sun   140
Should in the furthest east begin to draw
The shady curtains from Aurora's bed,
Away from light steals home my heavy son,
And private in his chamber pens himself,
Shuts up his windows, locks fair daylight out
And makes himself an artificial night:
Black and portentous must this humour
prove,
Unless good counsel may the cause remove.
   Ben. My noble uncle, do you know the
cause?
   Mon. I neither know it nor can learn of
him.   150
   Ben. Have you importuned him by any
means?
   Mon. Both by myself and many other
friends:
But he, his own affections' counsellor,
Is to himself—I will not say how true—
But to himself so secret and so close,
So far from sounding and discovery,
As is the bud bit with an envious worm,
Ere he can spread his sweet leaves to the air,
Or dedicate his beauty to the sun,
Could we but learn from whence his sorrows
grow,   160
We would as willingly give cure as know.

Enter ROMEO.

---

102. **Canker'd** . . . **canker'd**, corroded . . . malignant.
109. **Free-town**, Villa Franca in Brooke's poem
Romeus and Juliet. 111. **set** . . . **abroach**, reopened.

143. **heavy**, sad. 157. **envious**, malicious.

Ben. See, where he comes: so please you, step aside;
I'll know his grievance, or be much denied.
Mon. I would thou wert so happy by thy stay,
To hear true shrift. Come, madam, let's away. [*Exeunt Montague and Lady.* 165
Ben. Good morrow, cousin.
Rom.   Is the day so young?
Ben. But new struck nine.
Rom.   Ay me! sad hours seem long.
Was that my father that went hence so fast?
Ben. It was. What sadness lengthens Romeo's hours?
Rom. Not having that, which, having, makes them short.   170
Ben. In love?
Rom. Out—
Ben. Of love?
Rom. Out of her favour, where I am in love.
Ben. Alas, that love, so gentle in his view,
Should be so tyrannous and rough in proof!
Rom. Alas, that love, whose view is muffled still,
Should, without eyes, see pathways to his will!
Where shall we dine? O me! What fray was here?
Yet tell me not, for I have heard it all.   180
Here's much to do with hate, but more with love.
Why, then, O brawling love! O loving hate!
O any thing, of nothing first create!
O heavy lightness! serious vanity!
Mis-shapen chaos of well-seeming forms!
Feather of lead, bright smoke, cold fire, sick health!
Still-waking sleep, that is not what it is!
This love feel I, that feel no love in this.
Dost thou not laugh?
Ben.   No, coz, I rather weep.   189
Rom. Good heart, at what?
Ben.   At thy good heart's oppression.
Rom. Why, such is love's transgression.
Griefs of mine own lie heavy in my breast,
Which thou wilt propagate, to have it prest

With more of thine: this love that thou hast shown
Doth add more grief to too much of mine own.
Love is a smoke raised with the fume of sighs;
Being purged, a fire sparkling in lovers' eyes;
Being vex'd, a sea nourish'd with lovers' tears:
What is it else? a madness most discreet,
A choking gall and a preserving sweet.   200
Farewell, my coz.
Ben.   Soft! I will go along;
An if you leave me so, you do me wrong.
Rom. Tut, I have lost myself; I am not here;
This is not Romeo, he's some other where.
Ben. Tell me in sadness, who is that you love.
Rom. What, shall I groan and tell thee?
Ben.   Groan! why, no:
But sadly tell me who.
Rom. Bid a sick man in sadness make his will:
Ah, word ill urged to one that is so ill!
In sadness, cousin, I do love a woman.   210
Ben. I aim'd so near, when I supposed you loved.
Rom. A right good mark-man! And she's fair I love.
Ben. A right fair mark, fair coz, is soonest hit.
Rom. Well, in that hit you miss: she'll not be hit
With Cupid's arrow; she hath Dian's wit;
And, in strong proof of chastity well arm'd,
From love's weak childish bow she lives unharm'd.
She will not stay the siege of loving terms,
Nor bide the encounter of assailing eyes,
Nor ope her lap to saint-seducing gold: 220
O, she is rich in beauty, only poor,
That when she dies with beauty dies her store.
Ben. Then she hath sworn that she will still live chaste?
Rom. She hath, and in that sparing makes huge waste,
For beauty starved with her severity
Cuts beauty off from all posterity.
She is too fair, too wise, wisely too fair,

---

165. **shrift,** confession. 166. **morrow,** morning.
168. **Was . . . fast.** This line is matter of fact, not sentimental like Romeo's other utterances. See also line 179. 176. **proof,** experience. 181-188. **Here's . . . this.** These lines, abounding in paradoxical phrases called *oxymoron,* such as *loving hate, cold fire,* are characteristic of artificial love poetry. They indicate Romeo's sentimentality. 193. **propagate,** increase.

208. **sadness,** seriousness. 216. **proof,** impenetrable armor. 218. **stay,** withstand. 222. **store.** She will die without children and therefore her beauty will die with her. 225. **starved,** allowed to die.

To merit bliss by making me despair:
She hath forsworn to love, and in that vow
Do I live dead that live to tell it now.   230
   Ben. Be ruled by me, forget to think of
her.
   Rom. O, teach me how I should forget to
think.
   Ben. By giving liberty unto thine eyes;
Examine other beauties.
   Rom.   'Tis the way
To call hers exquisite, in question more:
These happy masks that kiss fair ladies'
brows
Being black put us in mind they hide the fair;
He that is strucken blind cannot forget
The precious treasure of his eyesight lost:
Show me a mistress that is passing fair,   240
What doth her beauty serve, but as a note
Where I may read who pass'd that passing
fair?
Farewell: thou canst not teach me to forget.
   Ben. I'll pay that doctrine, or else die in
debt.   [*Exeunt.*

SCENE II. *A street.*

Enter CAPULET, PARIS, *and* Servant.

   Cap. But Montague is bound as well as I,
In penalty alike; and 'tis not hard, I think,
For men so old as we to keep the peace.
   Par. Of honourable reckoning are you
both;
And pity 'tis you lived at odds so long.
But now, my lord, what say you to my suit?
   Cap. But saying o'er what I have said
before:
My child is yet a stranger in the world;
She hath not seen the change of fourteen
years;
Let two more summers wither in their pride,
Ere we may think her ripe to be a bride.   11
   Par. Younger than she are happy mothers
made.
   Cap. And too soon marr'd are those so
early made.
The earth hath swallow'd all my hopes but
she,
She is the hopeful lady of my earth:
But woo her, gentle Paris, get her heart,
My will to her consent is but a part;

An she agree, within her scope of choice
Lies my consent and fair according voice.
This night I hold an old accustom'd feast,   20
Whereto I have invited many a guest,
Such as I love; and you, among the store,
One more, most welcome, makes my number
more.
At my poor house look to behold this night
Earth-treading stars that make dark heaven
light:
Such comfort as do lusty young men feel
When well-apparell'd April on the heel
Of limping winter treads, even such delight
Among fresh female buds shall you this night
Inherit at my house; hear all, all see,   30
And like her most whose merit most shall be:
†Which on more view, of many mine being
one
May stand in number, though in reckoning
none.
Come, go with me. [*To Serv., giving a paper.*]
   Go, sirrah, trudge about
Through fair Verona; find those persons out
Whose names are written there, and to them
say,
My house and welcome on their pleasure
stay.   [*Exeunt Capulet and Paris.*   37
   Serv. Find them out whose names are
written here! It is written, that the shoemaker should meddle with his yard, and the
tailor with his last, the fisher with his pencil,
and the painter with his nets; but I am sent
to find those persons whose names are here
writ, and can never find what names the
writing person hath here writ. I must to
the learned.—In good time.   45

Enter BENVOLIO *and* ROMEO.

   Ben. Tut, man, one fire burns out an-
other's burning,
One pain is lessen'd by another's anguish;
Turn giddy, and be holp by backward turn-
ing;
One desperate grief cures with another's
languish:
Take thou some new infection to thy eye,   50
And the rank poison of the old will die.

---

235. **in question more**, into greater consideration.
240. **passing**, surpassingly. 244. **pay that doctrine**,
give that instruction.
  Scene ii. 4. **reckoning**, estimation, repute. 8.
stranger in the world. Capulet's reluctance is largely
a matter of manners. 17. **My will . . . part.** This is
also a conventional statement, since Capulet has no idea
of letting Juliet have her way.

29. **female**, so Q₁; Q₂ and Ff read *fennel*, which can
be justified by the circumstance that fennel was thought
to have the power of awakening passion. 32-33. **Which
. . . none.** Capulet may mean that his daughter will
lose her identity by being swallowed up in a number of
others. He is punning on the saying, "one is no number."
The Arden editor places a comma after *of* and dashes
after *many* and *one.* He explains *reckoning* to mean estimation (as in line 4, above), with word play, i.e., counting
heads. 48. **holp**, helped; obsolete form of past tense.

Rom. Your plaintain-leaf is excellent for that.

Ben. For what, I pray thee?

Rom. For your broken shin.

Ben. Why, Romeo, art thou mad?

Rom. Not mad, but bound more than a madman is; 55
Shut up in prison, kept without my food,
Whipp'd and tormented and—God-den, good fellow.

Serv. God gi' god-den. I pray, sir, can you read?

Rom. Ay, mine own fortune in my misery.

Serv. Perhaps you have learned it without book: but, I pray, can you read any thing you see?

Rom. Ay, if I know the letters and the language.

Serv. Ye say honestly: rest you merry!

Rom. Stay, fellow; I can read. [*Reads.*
'Signior Martino and his wife and daughters; County Anselme and his beauteous sisters; the lady widow of Vitruvio; Signior Placentio and his lovely nieces; Mercutio and his brother Valentine; mine uncle Capulet, his wife, and daughters; my fair niece Rosaline; Livia; Signior Valentio and his cousin Tybalt; Lucio and the lively Helena.'
A fair assembly: whither should they come?

Serv. Up.

Rom. Wither?

Serv. To supper; to our house.

Rom. Whose house?

Serv. My master's. 80

Rom. Indeed, I should have asked you that before.

Serv. Now I'll tell you without asking: my master is the great rich Capulet; and if you be not of the house of Montagues, I pray, come and crush a cup of wine. Rest you merry!
[*Exit.*

Ben. At this same ancient feast of Capulet's
Sups the fair Rosaline whom thou so lovest,
With all the admired beauties of Verona:
Go thither; and, with unattainted eye, 90
Compare her face with some that I shall show,
And I will make thee think thy swan a crow.

Rom. When the devout religion of mine eye

Maintains such falsehood, then turn tears to fires;
And these, who often drown'd could never die,
Transparent heretics, be burnt for liars!
One fairer than my love! the all-seeing sun
Ne'er saw her match since first the world begun.

Ben. Tut, you saw her fair, none else being by,
Herself poised with herself in either eye: 100
But in that crystal scales let there be weigh'd
Your lady's love against some other maid
That I will show you shining at this feast,
And she shall scant show well that now shows best.

Rom. I'll go along, no such sight to be shown,
But to rejoice in splendour of mine own.
[*Exeunt.*

SCENE III. *A room in Capulet's house.*

Enter Lady Capulet *and* Nurse.

La. Cap. Nurse, where's my daughter? call her forth to me.

Nurse. Now, by my maidenhead, at twelve year old,
I bade her come. What, lamb! what, lady-bird!
God forbid! Where's this girl? What, Juliet!

Enter Juliet.

Jul. How now! who calls?

Nurse. Your mother.

Jul. Madam, I am here.
What is your will?

La. Cap. This is the matter:—Nurse, give leave awhile,
We must talk in secret:—nurse, come back again;
I have remember'd me, thou 's hear our counsel.
Thou know'st my daughter's of a pretty age.

Nurse. Faith, I can tell her age unto an hour. 11

La. Cap. She's not fourteen.

Nurse. I'll lay fourteen of my teeth,—
And yet, to my teen be it spoken, I have but four,—

---

57. **God-den**, good evening. 86. **crush a cup of wine**, drink a cup of wine. Cf. "crack a bottle." 87. **ancient**, customary. 90. **unattainted**, impartial.

95. **these**, i.e., these eyes.
Scene iii. 7. **give leave**, leave us. 9. **thou's**, thou shalt. 14. **teen**, sorrow.

She is not fourteen. How long is it now
To Lammas-tide?
   La. Cap.   A fortnight and odd days.
   Nurse. Even or odd, of all days in the
     year,
Come Lammas-eve at night shall she be
     fourteen.
Susan and she—God rest all Christian souls!–
Were of an age: well, Susan is with God;
She was too good for me: but, as I said,   20
On Lammas-eve at night shall she be four-
     teen;
That shall she, marry; I remember it well.
'Tis since the earthquake now eleven years;
And she was wean'd,—I never shall forget
     it,—
Of all the days of the year, upon that day:
For I had then laid wormwood to my dug,
Sitting in the sun under the dove-house wall;
My lord and you were then at Mantua:—
Nay, I do bear a brain:—but, as I said,
When it did taste the wormwood on the
     nipple   30
Of my dug and felt it bitter, pretty fool,
To see it tetchy and fall out with the dug!
'Shake' quoth the dove-house: 'twas no
     need, I trow,
To bid me trudge:
And since that time it is eleven years;
For then she could stand alone; nay, by the
     rood,
She could have run and waddled all about;
For even the day before, she broke her brow:
And then my husband—God be with his soul!
A' was a merry man—took up the child: 40
'Yea,' quoth he, 'dost thou fall upon thy
     face?
Thou wilt fall backward when thou hast
     more wit;
Wilt thou not, Jule?' and, by my holidame,
The pretty wretch left crying and said 'Ay.'
To see, now, how a jest shall come about!
I warrant, an I should live a thousand years,
I never should forget it: 'Wilt thou not,
     Jule?' quoth he;
And, pretty fool, it stinted and said 'Ay.'
   La. Cap. Enough of this; I pray thee,
     hold thy peace.

   Nurse. Yes, madam: yet I cannot choose
     but laugh,   50
To think it should leave crying and say 'Ay.'
And yet, I warrant, it had upon its brow
A bump as big as a young cockerel's stone;
A parlous knock; and it cried bitterly:
'Yea,' quoth my husband, "fall'st upon thy
     face?
Thou wilt fall backward when thou comest to
     age;
Wilt thou not, Jule?' it stinted and said 'Ay.'
   Jul. And stint thou too, I pray thee,
     nurse, say I.
   Nurse. Peace, I have done. God mark
     thee to his grace!
Thou wast the prettiest babe that e'er I
     nursed: 60
An I might live to see thee married once,
I have my wish.
   La. Cap. Marry, that 'marry' is the very
     theme
I came to talk of. Tell me, daughter Juliet,
How stands your disposition to be married?
   Jul. It is an honour that I dream not of.
   Nurse. An honour! were not I thine only
     nurse,
I would say thou hadst suck'd wisdom from
     thy teat.
   La. Cap. Well, think of marriage now;
     younger than you,
Here in Verona, ladies of esteem,   70
Are made already mothers: by my count,
I was your mother much upon these years
That you are now a maid. Thus then in brief:
The valiant Paris seeks you for his love.
   Nurse. A man, young lady! lady, such a
     man
As all the world—why, he's a man of wax.
   La. Cap. Verona's summer hath not such
     a flower.
   Nurse. Nay, he's a flower; in faith, a very
     flower.
   La. Cap. What say you? can you love the
     gentleman?
This night you shall behold him at our feast;
Read o'er the volume of young Paris' face   81
And find delight writ there with beauty's
     pen;
Examine every married lineament
And see how one another lends content,
And what obscured in this fair volume lies

---

15. **Lammas-tide,** August 1. 23. **'Tis . . . years.** It
has been thought that Shakespeare was alluding in this
line to a famous earthquake in 1580 and was, therefore,
writing in 1591. 29. **bear a brain.** The nurse prides
herself on her memory. 32. **tetchy,** fretful. 40. **A',**
he; there is no need to use the apostrophe. 43. **holidame,** same as *halidom,* a relic or holy thing. 48.
stinted, ceased.

76. **a man of wax,** such as one would picture in wax,
i.e., handsome. 83. **married.** Hudson defines prettily,
"harmonized into mutual helpfulness."

Find written in the margent of his eyes.
This precious book of love, this unbound
  lover,
To beautify him, only lacks a cover:
The fish lives in the sea, and 'tis much pride
For fair without the fair within to hide: 90
That book in many's eyes doth share the
  glory,
That in gold clasps locks in the golden story;
So shall you share all that he doth possess,
By having him, making yourself no less.
  Nurse. No less! nay, bigger; women grow
  by men.
  La. Cap. Speak briefly, can you like of
  Paris' love?
  Jul. I'll look to like, if looking liking
  move:
But no more deep will I endart mine eye
Than your consent gives strength to make it
  fly.   99

Enter *a* Servant.

  Serv. Madam, the guests are come, supper served up, you called, my young lady
asked for, the nurse cursed in the pantry, and
every thing in extremity. I must hence to
wait; I beseech you, follow straight.
  La. Cap. We follow thee. [*Exit Servant.*]
Juliet, the county stays.   105
  Nurse. Go, girl, seek happy nights to
  happy days.   [*Exeunt.*

Scene IV. *A street.*

Enter Romeo, Mercutio, Benvolio, *with
five or six* Maskers, Torch-bearers, *and
others.*

  Rom. What, shall this speech be spoke for
  our excuse?
Or shall we on without apology?
  Ben. The date is out of such prolixity:
We'll have no Cupid hood wink'd with a
  scarf,
Bearing a Tartar's painted bow of lath,
Scaring the ladies like a crow-keeper;
Nor no without-book prologue, faintly spoke

After the prompter, for our entrance:
But let them measure us by what they will;
We'll measure them a measure, and be gone. 10
  Rom. Give me a torch: I am not for this
  ambling;
Being but heavy, I will bear the light.
  Mer. Nay, gentle Romeo, we must have
  you dance.
  Rom. Not I, believe me: you have dancing
  shoes
With nimble soles: I have a soul of lead
So stakes me to the ground I cannot move.
  Mer. You are a lover; borrow Cupid's
  wings,
And soar with them above a common bound.
  Rom. I am too sore enpierced with his
  shaft
To soar with his light feathers, and so bound,
I cannot bound a pitch above dull woe: 21
Under love's heavy burden do I sink.
  Mer. And, to sink in it, should you bur-
  den love;
Too great oppression for a tender thing.
  Rom. Is love a tender thing? it is too
  rough,
Too rude, too boisterous, and it pricks like
  thorn.
  Mer. If love be rough with you, be rough
  with love;
Prick love for pricking, and you beat love
  down.
Give me a case to put my visage in:
A visor for a visor! what care I   30
What curious eye doth quote deformities?
Here are the beetle brows shall blush for me.
  Ben. Come, knock and enter; and no
  sooner in,
But every man betake him to his legs.
  Rom. A torch for me: let wantons light of
  heart
Tickle the senseless rushes with their heels,
For I am proverb'd with a grandsire phrase;
I'll be a candle-holder, and look on.
The game was ne'er so fair, and I am done.
  Mer. Tut, dun's the mouse, the constable's
  own word: 40

---

86. **margent,** commentary or marginal gloss. 89.
fish lives in the sea. The figure of speech is of the
binding of a book; since fish-skins were used to cover
books, this "unbound lover" is yet to be made complete.
97-99. **I'll . . . fly.** Juliet's attitude is one of proper
obedience. 105. **county,** count. **stays,** waits.
  Scene iv. 1. **speech.** The older fashion was for
maskers to be preceded by a messenger with a set
speech, but "the date is out" for "such prolixity." 5.
Tartar's painted bow. Tartar's bows are said to have
resembled the old Roman bow with which Cupid was
pictured. 6. **crow-keeper,** scarecrow.

10. **measure . . . measure,** perform a dance. 11.
ambling, walking affectedly; used contemptuously of
dancing. 21. **pitch,** a term in falconry, the height to
which a hawk soars before striking at her prey. 30.
visor, a mask, for an ugly mask-like face. 31. **quote,**
take notice of. 36. **rushes.** Rushes were used for floor
coverings. 38. **candle-holder,** an allusion to the proverb "A good candle-holder (i.e., a mere onlooker) is a
good gamester." 40. **dun's the mouse,** a common
phrase usually taken to mean "keep still." *Dun* (l. 41)
alludes to a Christmas game, "Dun is in the mire,"
in which a heavy log was lifted by the players.

If thou art dun, we'll draw thee from the
    mire
Of this sir-reverence love, wherein thou
    stick'st
Up to the ears. Come, we burn daylight, ho!
    Rom. Nay, that's not so.
    Mer.   I mean, sir, in delay
We waste our lights in vain, like lamps by
    day.
Take our good meaning, for our judgement
    sits
Five times in that ere once in our five wits.
    Rom. And we mean well in going to this
    mask;
But 'tis no wit to go.
    Mer.   Why, may one ask?
    Rom. I dream'd a dream to-night.
    Mer.   And so did I.   50
    Rom. Well, what was yours?
    Mer.   That dreamers often lie.
    Rom. In bed asleep, while they do dream
    things true.
    Mer. O, then, I see Queen Mab hath been
    with you.
She is the fairies' midwife, and she comes
In shape no bigger than an agate-stone
On the fore-finger of an alderman,
Drawn with a team of little atomies
Athwart men's noses as they lie asleep;
Her waggon-spokes made of long spinners'
    legs,
The cover of the wings of grasshoppers,   60
The traces of the smallest spider's web,
The collars of the moonshine's watery
    beams,
Her whip of cricket's bone, the lash of film,
Her waggoner a small grey-coated gnat,
Not half so big as a round little worm
Prick'd from the lazy finger of a maid;
Her chariot is an empty hazel-nut
Made by the joiner squirrel or old grub,
Time out o' mind the fairies' coachmakers.
And in this state she gallops night by night 70
Through lovers' brains, and then they dream
    of love;
O'er courtiers' knees, that dream on court'-
    sies straight,

O'er lawyers' fingers, who straight dream on
    fees,
O'er ladies' lips, who straight on kisses dream,
Which oft the angry Mab with blisters
    plagues,
Because their breaths with sweetmeats
    tainted are:
Sometime she gallops o'er a courtier's nose,
And then dreams he of smelling out a suit;
And sometime comes she with a tithe-pig's tail
Tickling a parson's nose as a' lies asleep,   80
Then dreams he of another benefice:
Sometime she driveth o'er a soldier's neck,
And then dreams he of cutting foreign
    throats,
Of breaches, ambuscadoes, Spanish blades,
Of healths five-fathom deep; and then anon
Drums in his ear, at which he starts and
    wakes,
And being thus frighted swears a prayer or
    two
And sleeps again. This is that very Mab
That plats the manes of horses in the night,
And bakes the elf-locks in foul sluttish hairs, 90
Which once untangled much misfortune
    bodes:
This is the hag, when maids lie on their
    backs,
That presses them and learns them first to
    bear,
Making them women of good carriage:
This is she—
    Rom.   Peace, peace, Mercutio, peace!
Thou talk'st of nothing.
    Mer.   True, I talk of dreams,
Which are the children of an idle brain,
Begot of nothing but vain fantasy,
Which is as thin of substance as the air
And more inconstant than the wind, who
    wooes   100
Even now the frozen bosom of the north,
And, being anger'd, puffs away from thence,
Turning his face to the dew-dropping south.
    Ben. This wind, you talk of, blows us
    from ourselves;
Supper is done, and we shall come too late.
    Rom. I fear, too early: for my mind mis-
    gives   106
Some consequence yet hanging in the stars
Shall bitterly begin his fearful date

---

42. **sir-reverence**, corruption of *save-reverence* (*salve-
reverentia*), an apology for something improper. 47. **five
wits**, the five faculties, usually given as common wit,
imagination, fantasy, judgment, and reason. 53. **Queen
Mab**, a name of Celtic origin for the fairy queen. Mercutio's famous speech interested the audience, no doubt,
but has little connection with plot or character. 57.
atomies, tiny creatures. 63. **film**, gossamer thread.
64. **waggoner**, coachman. 65. **worm**. This alludes
to an ancient and no doubt useful superstition that
"worms breed in the fingers of the idle."

78. **suit**, a request or plea at court. 79. **tithe-pig's
tail**. This alludes to the tenth pig given the parson as a
church tax. 89. **plats the manes of horses**, an allusion
to the familiar superstition of "witches stirrups," tangles
in the manes of horses. 98. **vain**, empty, foolish. 108.
date, time.

With this night's revels and expire the term
Of a despised life closed in my breast   110
By some vile forfeit of untimely death.
But He, that hath the steerage of my course,
Direct my sail! On, lusty gentlemen.

Ben. Strike, drum.   [*Exeunt.*

Scene V. *A hall in Capulet's house.*

Musicians *waiting.* Enter Servingmen, *with napkins.*

First Serv. Where's Potpan, that he helps
not to take away? He shift a trencher? he
scrape a trencher!

Sec. Serv. When good manners shall lie
all in one or two men's hands and they, unwashed too, 'tis a foul thing.   6

First Serv. Away with the joint-stools, remove the court-cupboard, look to the plate.
Good thou, save me a piece of marchpane; and,
as thou lovest me, let the porter let in Susan
Grindstone and Nell. Antony, and Potpan! 11

Sec. Serv. Ay, boy, ready.

First Serv. You are looked for and called
for, asked for and sought for, in the great
chamber.

Sec. Serv. We cannot be here and there
too. Cheerly, boys; be brisk awhile, and the
longer liver take all.

Enter CAPULET, *with* JULIET *and others of his house, meeting the* Guests *and* Maskers.

Cap. Welcome, gentlemen! ladies that
have their toes
Unplagued with corns will have a bout with
you.
Ah ha, my mistresses! which of you all   20
Will now deny to dance? she that makes
dainty,
She, I'll swear, hath corns; am I come near
ye now?
Welcome, gentlemen! I have seen the day
That I have worn a visor and could tell
A whispering tale in a fair lady's ear,
Such as would please: 'tis gone, 'tis gone, 'tis
gone:
You are welcome, gentlemen! Come, musi-
cians, play.
A hall, a hall! give room! and foot it, girls.

[*Music plays, and they dance.*

More light, you knaves; and turn the tables
up,
And quench the fire, the room is grown too
hot.   30
Ah, sirrah, this unlook'd-for sport comes
well.
Nay, sit, nay, sit, good cousin Capulet;
For you and I are past our dancing days:
How long is 't now since last yourself and I
Were in a mask?

Sec. Cap.   By 'r lady, thirty years.

Cap. What, man! 'tis not so much, 'tis not
so much:
'Tis since the nuptial of Lucentio,
Come pentecost as quickly as it will,
Some five and twenty years; and then we
mask'd.

Sec. Cap. 'Tis more, 'tis more: his son is
elder, sir;   40
His son is thirty.

Cap.   Will you tell me that?
His son was but a ward two years ago.

Rom. [*To a Servingman*] What lady is that,
which doth enrich the hand
Of yonder knight?

Serv. I know not, sir.

Rom. O, she doth teach the torches to
burn bright!
It seems she hangs upon the cheek of night
Like a rich jewel in an Ethiope's ear;
Beauty too rich for use, for earth too dear!
So shows a snowy dove trooping with crows,
As yonder lady o'er her fellows shows.   51
The measure done, I'll watch her place of
stand,
And, touching hers, make blessed my rude
hand.
Did my heart love till now? forswear it,
sight!
For I ne'er saw true beauty till this night.

Tyb. This, by his voice, should be a
Montague.
Fetch me my rapier, boy. What dares the
slave
Come hither, cover'd with an antic face,
To fleer and scorn at our solemnity?
Now, by the stock and honour of my kin, 60
To strike him dead I hold it not a sin.

---

109. **expire** (transitive), bring to an end. *Scene v.* 2. **trencher,** wooden plate. 7. **joint-stools,** stools, properly those made by a joiner. 8. **court-cupboard,** sideboard. 9. **marchpane,** cake made from sugar and almonds. 21. **makes dainty,** hesitates from affectation to dance.

29. **turn the tables up.** Tables were probably made of hinged leaves and placed on trestles. They were put aside for dancing. 46-55. **O, she . . . night.** Romeo's love is love at first sight, a type of love provided for in Elizabethan psychological doctrine and no doubt in life. 57. **Fetch me my rapier.** This speech of Tybalt's is in immediate contrast to the happy sentiment of Romeo's speech. 58. **antic,** fantastic. 59. **fleer,** to look mockingly.

Cap. Why, how now, kinsman! wherefore storm you so?

Tyb. Uncle, this is a Montague, our foe,
A villain that is hither come in spite,
To scorn at our solemnity this night.   65

Cap. Young Romeo is it?

Tyb.   'Tis he, that villain Romeo.

Cap. Content thee, gentle coz, let him alone;
He bears him like a portly gentleman;
And, to say truth, Verona brags of him
To be a virtuous and well govern'd youth: 70
I would not for the wealth of all the town
Here in my house do him disparagement:
Therefore be patient, take no note of him:
It is my will, the which if thou respect,
Show a fair presence and put off these frowns,
An ill-beseeming semblance for a feast.

Tyb. It fits, when such a villain is a guest:
I'll not endure him.

Cap.   He shall be endured:
What, goodman boy! I say, he shall: go to;
Am I the master here, or you? go to.   80
You'll not endure him! God shall mend my soul!
You'll make a mutiny among my guests!
You will set cock-a-hoop! you'll be the man!

Tyb. Why, uncle, 'tis a shame.

Cap.   Go to, go to;
You are a saucy boy: is 't so, indeed?
This trick may chance to scathe you, I know what:
You must contrary me! marry, 'tis time.
Well said, my hearts! You are a princox; go:
Be quiet, or—More light, more light! For shame!
I'll make you quiet. What, cheerly, my hearts!   90

Tyb. Patience perforce with wilful choler meeting
Makes my flesh tremble in their different greeting.
I will withdraw: but this intrusion shall
Now seeming sweet convert to bitter gall.
                              [*Exit.*

Rom. [*To Juliet*] If I profane with my unworthiest hand
This holy shrine, the gentle fine is this:

My lips, two blushing pilgrims, ready stand
To smooth that rough touch with a tender kiss.

Jul. Good pilgrim, you do wrong your hand too much,
Which mannerly devotion shows in this;
For saints have hands that pilgrims' hands do touch,   101
And palm to palm is holy palmers' kiss.

Rom. Have not saints lips, and holy palmers too?

Jul. Ay, pilgrim, lips that they must use in prayer.

Rom. O, then, dear saint, let lips do what hands do;
They pray, grant thou, lest faith turn to despair.

Jul. Saints do not move, though grant for prayers' sake.

Rom. Then move not, while my prayer's effect I take.
Thus from my lips, by yours, my sin is purged.

Jul. Then have my lips the sin that they have took.   110

Rom. Sin from my lips? O trespass sweetly urged!
Give me my sin again.

Jul.   You kiss by the book.

Nurse. Madam, your mother craves a word with you.

Rom. What is her mother?

Nurse.   Marry, bachelor,
Her mother is the lady of the house,
And a good lady, and a wise and virtuous:
I nursed her daughter, that you talk'd withal;
I tell you, he that can lay hold of her
Shall have the chinks.

Rom.   Is she a Capulet?
O dear account! my life is my foe's debt.   120

Ben. Away, be gone; the sport is at the best.

Rom. Ay, so I fear; the more is my unrest.

Cap. Nay, gentlemen, prepare not to be gone;
We have a trifling foolish banquet towards.
Is it e'en so? why, then, I thank you all;
I thank you, honest gentlemen; good night.
More torches here! Come on then, let's to bed.

68. **portly,** of excellent bearing. 79. **goodman boy,** a belittling ironical epithet. Capulet has a spirit more reconcilable than that of Tybalt. 83. **cock-a-hoop,** complete disorder. 91. **Patience perforce,** patience upon compulsion; *patience* is a general word for *self-control.* 94. **convert,** change (to). 95-108. **If I . . . take.** These lines are in the form of a sonnet. They afford an example of Shakespeare's early exuberance in poetic style.

99. **pilgrim.** Romeo was masquerading as a pilgrim or palmer. 107. **move,** make a proposal to. 112. **by the book,** according to rule. 119. **chinks,** money. 120. **my foe's debt,** due to my foe, at his mercy. 124. **foolish,** insignificant. **banquet,** dessert. **towards,** in preparation.

Ah, sirrah, by my fay, it waxes late:
I'll to my rest.
            [*Exeunt all but Juliet and Nurse.*
Jul. Come hither, nurse. What is yond
    gentleman?   130
Nurse. The son and heir of old Tiberio.
Jul. What's he that now is going out of
    door?
Nurse. Marry, that, I think, be young
    Petrucio.
Jul. What's he that follows there, that
    would not dance?
Nurse. I know not.
Jul. Go, ask his name: if he be married,
My grave is like to be my wedding bed.
Nurse. His name is Romeo, and a Mon-
    tague;
The only son of your great enemy.
Jul. My only love sprung from my only
    hate!   140
Too early seen unknown, and known too
    late!
Prodigious birth of love it is to me,
That I must love a loathed enemy.
Nurse. What's this? what's this?
Jul.   A rhyme I learn'd even now
Of one I danced withal. [*One calls within*
                    'Juliet.'
Nurse.   Anon, anon!
Come, let's away; the strangers all are gone.
                  [*Exeunt.*

ACT II.

PROLOGUE.

Enter Chorus.

Chor. Now old desire doth in his death-
    bed lie,
And young affection gapes to be his heir;
That fair for which love groan'd for and
    would die,
    With tender Juliet match'd, is now not
    fair.
Now Romeo is beloved and loves again,
    Alike bewitched by the charm of looks,
But to his foe supposed he must complain,
    And she steal love's sweet bait from fearful
    hooks:
Being held a foe, he may not have access
    To breathe such vows as lovers use to
    swear;   10

And she as much in love, her means much
    less
    To meet her new-beloved any where:
But passion lends them power, time means,
    to meet,
Tempering extremities with extreme sweet.
                [*Exit.*

SCENE I. *A lane by the wall of Capulet's*
      orchard.

Enter ROMEO.

Rom. Can I go forward when my heart is
    here?
Turn back, dull earth, and find thy centre
    out.
[*He climbs the wall, and leaps down within it.*

Enter BENVOLIO *and* MERCUTIO.

Ben. Romeo! my cousin Romeo!
Mer.   He is wise;
And, on my life, hath stol'n him home to bed.
Ben. He ran this way, and leap'd this
    orchard wall: 5
Call, good Mercutio.
Mer.   Nay, I'll conjure too.
Romeo! humours! madman! passion! lover!
Appear thou in the likeness of a sigh:
Speak but one rhyme, and I am satisfied;
Cry but 'Ay me!' pronounce but 'love' and
    'dove;'   10
Speak to my gossip Venus one fair word,
One nick-name for her purblind son and heir,
Young Adam Cupid, he that shot so trim,
When King Cophetua loved the beggar-
    maid!
He heareth not, he stirreth not, he moveth
    not;
The ape is dead, and I must conjure him.
I conjure thee by Rosaline's bright eyes,
By her high forehead and her scarlet lip,
By her fine foot, straight leg and quivering
    thigh
And the demesnes that there adjacent lie, 20
That in thy likeness thou appear to us!
Ben. An if he hear thee, thou wilt anger
    him.

---

128. fay, faith.
Act II. Prologue. 10. use to swear, are in the habit
of swearing.

Scene i. 2. dull earth, Romeo himself. thy centre,
Juliet. The figure of speech is that of man as a microcosm or little world. 6. conjure, utter incantation.
12. purblind, completely blind. 13. Adam, Upton's
conjecture; Qq and F: *Abraham.* It is thought that
Adam may refer to Adam Bell, a famous archer in the
old ballads; *Abraham* is a form of "abram" or "auburn,"
which would refer to Cupid's flaxen hair. 14. Cophetua,
reference to the ballad *King Cophetua and the Beggar
Maid.* 16. ape, used as a term of endearment. 20.
demesnes, regions.

Mer. This cannot anger him: 'twould
   anger him
To raise a spirit in his mistress' circle
Of some strange nature, letting it there stand
Till she had laid it and conjured it down;
That were some spite: my invocation
Is fair and honest, and in his mistress' name
I conjure only but to raise up him.

Ben. Come, he hath hid himself among
   these trees,   30
To be consorted with the humorous night:
Blind is his love and best befits the dark.

Mer. If love be blind, love cannot hit the
   mark.
Now will he sit under a medlar tree,
And wish his mistress were that kind of fruit
As maids call medlars, when they laugh alone.
O, Romeo, that she were, O, that she were
An open et cætera, thou a poperin pear!
Romeo, good night: I'll to my truckle-bed;
This field-bed is too cold for me to sleep: 40
Come, shall we go?

Ben.   Go, then; for 'tis in vain
To seek him here that means not to be found.
                         [*Exeunt.*

SCENE II. *Capulet's orchard.*

Enter ROMEO.

Rom. He jests at scars that never felt a
   wound.
      [*Juliet appears above at a window.*
But, soft! what light through yonder window
   breaks?
It is the east, and Juliet is the sun.
Arise, fair sun, and kill the envious moon,
Who is already sick and pale with grief,
That thou her maid art far more fair than
   she:
Be not her maid, since she is envious;
Her vestal livery is but sick and green
And none but fools do wear it; cast it off.
It is my lady, O, it is my love!   10
O, that she knew she were!
She speaks, yet she says nothing: what of
   that?

27. **spite**, injury. 28. **honest**, chaste. 31. **con-**
sorted, associated. **humorous**, moist; also, influenced
by humor or mood. 34. **medlar**, the fruit of the *Mes-*
pilus germanica, edible only when partly decayed.
38. **poperin**, variety of pear; derived from the Flemish
town *Poperinghe* in Flanders. 39. **truckle-bed**, a bed
on casters to be shoved under a standing bed. 40. **field-**
bed, large bed; here, the ground.
   Scene ii. There is no break in the action. Romeo must
have been standing on the front stage behind some obstruction to represent the garden wall. He speaks at
once, then turns to observe Juliet.

Her eye discourses; I will answer it.
I am too bold, 'tis not to me she speaks:
Two of the fairest stars in all the heaven,
Having some business, do entreat her eyes
To twinkle in their spheres till they return.
What if her eyes were there, they in her
   head?
The brightness of her cheek would shame
   those stars,
As daylight doth a lamp; her eyes in heaven
Would through the airy region stream so
   bright   21
That birds would sing and think it were not
   night.
See, how she leans her cheek upon her hand!
O, that I were a glove upon that hand,
That I might touch that cheek!

Jul.   Ay me!

Rom.   She speaks:
O, speak again, bright angel! for thou art
As glorious to this night, being o'er my head,
As is a winged messenger of heaven
Unto the white-upturned wondering eyes
Of mortals that fall back to gaze on him   30
When he bestrides the lazy-pacing clouds
And sails upon the bosom of the air.

Jul. O Romeo, Romeo! wherefore art
   thou Romeo?
Deny thy father and refuse thy name;
Or, if thou wilt not, be but sworn my love,
And I'll no longer be a Capulet.

Rom. [*Aside*] Shall I hear more, or shall I
   speak at this?

Jul. 'Tis but thy name that is my enemy;
Thou art thyself, though not a Montague.
What's Montague? it is nor hand, nor foot,   40
Nor arm, nor face, nor any other part
Belonging to a man. O, be some other name!
What's in a name? that which we call a rose
By any other name would smell as sweet;   44
So Romeo would, were he not Romeo call'd,
Retain that dear perfection which he owes
Without that title. Romeo, doff thy name,
And for that name which is no part of thee
Take all myself.

Rom.   I take thee at thy word:
Call me but love, and I'll be new baptized;   50
Henceforth I never will be Romeo.

Jul. What man art thou that thus be-
   screen'd in night
So stumblest on my counsel?

17. **spheres**, transparent concentric shells supposed
to carry the heavenly bodies with them in their revolution
around the earth. 46. **owes**, owns. 53. **counsel**, secret
thought.

Rom.   By a name
I know not how to tell thee who I am:
My name, dear saint, is hateful to myself,
Because it is an enemy to thee;
Had I it written, I would tear the word.
   Jul. My ears have not yet drunk a hun-
     dred words
Of that tongue's utterance, yet I know the
     sound:
Art thou not Romeo and a Montague?   60
   Rom. Neither, fair saint, if either thee dis-
     like.
   Jul. How camest thou hither, tell me, and
     wherefore?
The orchard walls are high and hard to climb,
And the place death, considering who thou
     art,
If any of my kinsmen find thee here.
   Rom. With love's light wings did I o'er-
     perch these walls;
For stony limits cannot hold love out,
And what love can do that dares love at-
     tempt;
Therefore thy kinsmen are no let to me.
   Jul. If they do see thee, they will murder
     thee.   70
   Rom. Alack, there lies more peril in thine
     eye
Than twenty of their swords: look thou but
     sweet,
And I am proof against their enmity.
   Jul. I would not for the world they saw
     thee here.
   Rom. I have night's cloak to hide me from
     their sight;
And but thou love me, let them find me here:
My life were better ended by their hate,
Than death prorogued, wanting of thy love.
   Jul. By whose direction found'st thou
     out this place?
   Rom. By love, who first did prompt me to
     inquire;   80
He lent me counsel and I lent him eyes.
I am no pilot; yet, wert thou as far
As that vast shore wash'd with the farthest
     sea,
I would adventure for such merchandise.
   Jul. Thou know'st the mask of night is
     on my face,
Else would a maiden blush bepaint my cheek
For that which thou hast heard me speak to-
     night.

Fain would I dwell on form, fain, fain deny
What I have spoke: but farewell compliment!
Dost thou love me? I know thou wilt say
     'Ay,'   90
And I will take thy word: yet, if thou swear'st,
Thou mayst prove false; at lovers' perjuries,
They say, Jove laughs. O gentle Romeo,
If thou dost love, pronounce it faithfully:
Or if thou think'st I am too quickly won,
I'll frown and be perverse and say thee nay,
So thou wilt woo; but else, not for the world.
In truth, fair Montague, I am too fond,
And therefore thou mayst think my 'haviour
     light:
But trust me, gentleman, I'll prove more
     true   100
Than those that have more cunning to be
     strange.
I should have been more strange, I must
     confess,
But that thou overheard'st, ere I was ware,
My true love's passion; therefore pardon me,
And not impute this yielding to light love,
Which the dark night hath so discovered.
   Rom. Lady, by yonder blessed moon I
     swear
That tips with silver all these fruit-tree tops—
   Jul. O, swear not by the moon, the incon-
     stant moon,
That monthly changes in her circled orb,   110
Lest that thy love prove likewise variable.
   Rom. What shall I swear by?
   Jul.   Do not swear at all;
Or, if thou wilt, swear by thy gracious self,
Which is the god of my idolatry,
And I'll believe thee.
   Rom.   If my heart's dear love—
   Jul. Well, do not swear: although I joy in
     thee,
I have no joy of this contract to-night:
It is too rash, too unadvised, too sudden;
Too like the lightning, which doth cease to be
Ere one can say 'It lightens.' Sweet, good
     night!   120
This bud of love, by summer's ripening
     breath,
May prove a beauteous flower when next we
     meet.
Good night, good night! as sweet repose and
     rest
Come to thy heart as that within my breast!

---

61. **dislike,** displease. 66. **o'er-perch,** fly over and
perch beyond. 78. **prorogued,** postponed.

89. **compliment,** punctiliousness, ceremony. 101.
strange, reserved. 110. **orb,** equivalent to *sphere;* see
above, line 17.

Rom. O, wilt thou leave me so unsatisfied?

Jul. What satisfaction canst thou have
    to-night?

Rom. The exchange of thy love's faithful
    vow for mine.

Jul. I gave thee mine before thou didst
    request it:

And yet I would it were to give again.

Rom. Wouldst thou withdraw it? for
    what purpose, love?   130

Jul. But to be frank, and give it thee
    again.

And yet I wish but for the thing I have:

My bounty is as boundless as the sea,

My love as deep; the more I give to thee,

The more I have, for both are infinite.

        [Nurse calls within.

I hear some noise within; dear love, adieu!

Anon, good nurse! Sweet Montague, be true.

Stay but a little, I will come again.

        [Exit, above.

Rom. O blessed, blessed night! I am
    afeard,

Being in night, all this is but a dream,   140

Too flattering-sweet to be substantial.

      Re-enter JULIET, *above.*

Jul. Three words, dear Romeo, and good
    night indeed.

If that thy bent of love be honourable,

Thy purpose marriage, send me word to-
    morrow,   144

By one that I'll procure to come to thee,

Where and what time thou wilt perform the
    rite;

And all my fortunes at thy foot I'll lay

And follow thee my lord throughout the
    world.

Nurse. [*Within*] Madam!

Jul. I come, anon.—But if thou mean'st
    not well,   150

I do beseech thee—

Nurse. [*Within*] Madam!

Jul.   By and by, I come:—

To cease thy suit, and leave me to my grief:

To-morrow will I send.

Rom.   So thrive my soul—

Jul. A thousand times good night!

        [Exit, above.

Rom. A thousand times the worse, to
    want thy light.

Love goes toward love, as schoolboys from
    their books,

But love from love, toward school with heavy
    looks.   *[Retiring.*

      Re-enter JULIET, *above.*

Jul. Hist! Romeo, hist! O, for a falconer's
    voice,

To lure this tassel-gentle back again!   160

Bondage is hoarse, and may not speak aloud;

Else would I tear the cave where Echo lies,

And make her airy tongue more hoarse than
    mine,

With repetition of my Romeo's name.

Rom. It is my soul that calls upon my
    name:

How silver-sweet sound lovers' tongues by
    night,

Like softest music to attending ears!

Jul. Romeo!

Rom.   My dear?

Jul.   At what o'clock to-morrow

Shall I send to thee?

Rom.   At the hour of nine.

Jul. I will not fail: 'tis twenty years till
    then.   170

I have forgot why I did call thee back.

Rom. Let me stand here till thou remem-
    ber it.

Jul. I shall forget, to have thee still stand
    there,

Remembering how I love thy company.

Rom. And I'll still stay, to have thee still
    forget,

Forgetting any other home but this.

Jul. 'Tis almost morning; I would have
    thee gone:

And yet no further than a wanton's bird;

Who lets it hop a little from her hand,

Like a poor prisoner in his twisted gyves,   180

And with a silk thread plucks it back again,

So loving-jealous of his liberty.

Rom. I would I were thy bird.

Jul.   Sweet, so would I:

Yet I should kill thee with much cherishing.

Good night, good night! parting is such sweet
    sorrow,

That I shall say good night till it be morrow.

        [Exit, above.

Rom. Sleep dwell upon thine eyes, peace
    in thy breast!

---

131. **frank,** liberal, bounteous. 143. **bent,** purpose; from the idea of the tension of a bow. 145. **procure,** cause. 151. **By and by,** immediately.

160. **tassel-gentle,** *tercel-gentle,* the male of the goshawk. 180. **gyves,** fetters.

Would I were sleep and peace, so sweet to
   rest!
Hence will I to my ghostly father's cell,
His help to crave, and my dear hap to tell. 190
                            [*Exit.*

SCENE III. *Friar Laurence's cell.*

Enter FRIAR LAURENCE, *with a basket.*

Fri. L. The grey-eyed morn smiles on
   the frowning night,
Chequering the eastern clouds with streaks
   of light,
And flecked darkness like a drunkard reels
From forth day's path and Titan's fiery
   wheels:
Now, ere the sun advance his burning eye,
The day to cheer and night's dank dew to
   dry,
I must up-fill this osier cage of ours
With baleful weeds and precious-juiced
   flowers.
The earth that's nature's mother is her tomb;
What is her burying grave that is her womb,10
And from her womb children of divers kind
We sucking on her natural bosom find,
Many for many virtues excellent,
None but for some and yet all different.
O, mickle is the powerful grace that lies
In herbs, plants, stones, and their true quali-
   ties:
For nought so vile that on the earth doth live
But to the earth some special good doth give,
Nor aught so good but strain'd from that fair
   use
Revolts from true birth, stumbling on
   abuse: 20
Virtue itself turns vice, being misapplied;
And vice sometimes by action dignified.
Within the infant rind of this small flower
Poison hath residence and medicine power:
For this, being smelt, with that part cheers
   each part;
Being tasted, slays all senses with the heart.
Two such opposed kings encamp them still
In man as well as herbs, grace and rude will;
And where the worser is predominant,
Full soon the canker death eats up that
   plant.   30

Enter ROMEO.

Rom. Good morrow, father.
Fri. L.   Benedicite!
What early tongue so sweet saluteth me?
Young son, it argues a distemper'd head
So soon to bid good morrow to thy bed:
Care keeps his watch in every old man's
   eye,   35
And where care lodges, sleep will never lie;
But where unbruised youth with unstuff'd
   brain
Doth couch his limbs, there golden sleep doth
   reign:
Therefore thy earliness doth me assure
Thou art up-roused by some distempera-
   ture;
Or if not so, then here I hit it right,   41
Our Romeo hath not been in bed to-night.
  Rom. That last is true; the sweeter rest
   was mine.
  Fri. L. God pardon sin! wast thou with
   Rosaline?
  Rom. With Rosaline, my ghostly father?
   no;
I have forgot that name, and that name's
   woe.
  Fri. L. That's my good son: but where
   hast thou been, then?
  Rom. I'll tell thee, ere thou ask it me
   again.
I have been feasting with mine enemy,
Where on a sudden one hath wounded me, 50
That's by me wounded: both our remedies
Within thy help and holy physic lies:
I bear no hatred, blessed man, for, lo,
My intercession likewise steads my foe.
  Fri. L. Be plain, good son, and homely in
   thy drift;
Riddling confession finds but riddling shrift.
  Rom. Then plainly know my heart's dear
   love is set
On the fair daughter of rich Capulet:
As mine on hers, so hers is set on mine;
And all combined, save what thou must com-
   bine   60
By holy marriage: when and where and how
We met, we woo'd and made exchange of
   vow,
I'll tell thee as we pass; but this I pray,
That thou consent to marry us to-day.

---

189. **ghostly**, spiritual. 190. **dear hap**, good fortune.
  Scene iii. 3. **flecked**, dappled. 4. **Titan's.** Helios,
the sun-god, was a descendant of the race of Titans. 7.
osier cage, willow basket. 15. **mickle**, great. 30.
canker, cankerworm.

33. **distemper'd**, ill; a reference to a state of the humors in the body. 34. **morrow**, morning. 37. **unstuff'd**, not over-charged; another reference to the state
of the humors. 54. **steads**, helps. 56. **shrift**, absolution.

Fri. L. Holy Saint Francis, what a
change is here!
Is Rosaline, whom thou didst love so dear,
So soon forsaken? young men's love then lies
Not truly in their hearts, but in their eyes.
Jesu Maria, what a deal of brine   69
Hath wash'd thy sallow cheeks for Rosaline!
How much salt water thrown away in waste,
To season love, that of it doth not taste!
The sun not yet thy sighs from heaven clears,
Thy old groans ring yet in my ancient ears;
Lo, here upon thy cheek the stain doth sit
Of an old tear that is not wash'd off yet:
If e'er thou wast thyself and these woes thine,
Thou and these woes were all for Rosaline:
And art thou changed? pronounce this sen-
tence then,
Women may fall, when there's no strength in
men.   80
Rom. Thou chid'st me oft for loving Rosa-
line.
Fri. L. For doting, not for loving, pupil
mine.
Rom. And bad'st me bury love.
Fri. L.   Not in a grave,
To lay one in, another out to have.
Rom. I pray thee, chide not: she whom I
love now
Doth grace for grace and love for love allow;
The other did not so.
Fri. L.   O, she knew well
Thy love did read by rote and could not
spell.
But come, young waverer, come, go with me,
In one respect I'll thy assistant be;   90
For this alliance may so happy prove,
To turn your households' rancour to pure
love.
Rom. O, let us hence; I stand on sudden
haste.
Fri. L. Wisely and slow; they stumble
that run fast.   [*Exeunt.*

SCENE IV. *A street.*

Enter BENVOLIO *and* MERCUTIO.

Mer. Where the devil should this Romeo
be?
Came he not home to-night?

88. **did read by rote,** was merely a matter of repeating conventional expressions of love. 93. **stand on,**
am in a position calling for.

Ben. Not to his father's; I spoke with his
man.
Mer. Ah, that same pale hard-hearted
wench, that Rosaline,
Torments him so, that he will sure run
mad.
Ben. Tybalt, the kinsman of old Capulet,
Hath sent a letter to his father's house.
Mer. A challenge, on my life.
Ben. Romeo will answer it.
Mer. Any man that can write may answer
a letter.   10
Ben. Nay, he will answer the letter's
master, how he dares, being dared.
Mer. Alas, poor Romeo! he is already
dead; stabbed with a white wench's black
eye; shot thorough the ear with a love-song;
the very pin of his heart cleft with the blind
bow-boy's butt-shaft: and is he a man to encounter Tybalt?   17
Ben. Why, what is Tybalt?
Mer. More than prince of cats, I can tell
you. O, he is the courageous captain of complements. He fights as you sing prick-song,
keeps time, distance, and proportion; rests
me his minim rest, one, two, and the third in
your bosom: the very butcher of a silk
button, a duellist, a duellist; a gentleman of
the very first house, of the first and second
cause: ah, the immortal passado! the punto
reverso! the hai!   27
Ben. The what?
Mer. The pox of such antic, lisping, affecting fantasticoes; these new tuners of
accents! 'By Jesu, a very good blade! a very
tall man! a very good whore!' Why, is not
this a lamentable thing, grandsire, that we
should be thus afflicted with these strange
flies, these fashion-mongers, these perdona-
mi's, who stand so much on the new form,
that they cannot sit at ease on the old bench?
O, their bones, their bones!   37

15. **pin,** peg in the center of a target. 16. **butt-
shaft,** an unbarbed arrow. 19. **prince of cats.** The
name of the king of cats in *Reynard the Fox* was Tybalt. 20. **captain of complements,** master of ceremony and outward show. 21. **prick-song,** music
written out. 22. **proportion,** rhythm. 23. **minim,**
half measure in music. 24. **butcher of a silk button,**
one able to strike a button on his adversary's person.
26. **first house,** possibly one of the best school of fencing.
first and second cause, ready to quarrel for a trifle;
probably an allusion to the supposed code of quarreling.
27. **passado,** forward thrust. **punto reverso,** back-
handed stroke. **hai,** home thrust. 30. **fantasticoes,**
coxcombs. 31. **accents,** language. 35. **flies,** affected persons. **perdona-mi's,** Italian for *pardon me's;* a reference
to the affectation of using foreign phrases. 36-37. **form...
bench.** *Form* means both "fashion" and "bench." 37.
bones, French *bon* with play on English *bone.*

Enter Romeo.

Ben. Here comes Romeo, here comes Romeo.   38

Mer. Without his roe, like a dried herring: O flesh, flesh, how art thou fishified! Now is he for the numbers that Petrarch flowed in: Laura to his lady was but a kitchen-wench; marry, she had a better love to be-rhyme her; Dido a dowdy; Cleopatra a gipsy; Helen and Hero hildings and harlots; Thisbe a grey eye or so, but not to the purpose. Signior Romeo, bon jour! there's a French salutation to your French slop. You gave us the counterfeit fairly last night.

Rom. Good morrow to you both. What counterfeit did I give you?   50

Mer. The slip, sir, the slip; can you not conceive?

Rom. Pardon, good Mercutio, my business was great; and in such a case as mine a man may strain courtesy.

Mer. That's as much as to say, such a case as yours constrains a man to bow in the hams.

Rom. Meaning, to court'sy.

Mer. Thou hast most kindly hit it.

Rom. A most courteous exposition.   60

Mer. Nay, I am the very pink of courtesy.

Rom. Pink for flower.

Mer. Right.

Rom. Why, then is my pump well flowered.   64

Mer. Well said: follow me this jest now till thou hast worn out thy pump, that when the single sole of it is worn, the jest may remain after the wearing sole singular.

Rom. O single-soled jest, solely singular for the singleness!   70

Mer. Come between us, good Benvolio; my wits faint.

Rom. Switch and spurs, switch and spurs; or I'll cry a match.

Mer. Nay, if thy wits run the wild-goose chase, I have done, for thou hast more of the wild-goose in one of thy wits than, I am sure,

I have in my whole five: was I with you there for the goose?

Rom. Thou wast never with me for any thing when thou wast not there for the goose.

Mer. I will bite thee by the ear for that jest.

Rom. Nay, good goose, bite not.

Mer. Thy wit is a very bitter sweeting; it is a most sharp sauce.

Rom. And is it not well served in to a sweet goose?   86

Mer. O, here's a wit of cheveril, that stretches from an inch narrow to an ell broad!

Rom. I stretch it out for that word 'broad;' which added to the goose, proves thee far and wide a broad goose.   91

Mer. Why, is not this better now than groaning for love? now art thou sociable, now art thou Romeo; now art thou what thou art, by art as well as by nature; for this drivelling love is like a great natural, that runs lolling up and down to hide his bauble in a hole.

Ben. Stop there, stop there.

Mer. Thou desirest me to stop in my tale against the hair.   100

Ben. Thou wouldst else have made thy tale large.

Mer. O, thou art deceived; I would have made it short: for I was come to the whole depth of my tale; and meant, indeed, to occupy the argument no longer.

Rom. Here's goodly gear!

Enter Nurse *and* PETER.

Mer. A sail, a sail!

Ben. Two, two; a shirt and a smock.

Nurse. Peter!   110

Peter. Anon!

Nurse. My fan, Peter.

Mer. Good Peter, to hide her face; for her fan's the fairer face.

Nurse. God ye good morrow, gentlemen.

Mer. God ye good den, fair gentlewoman.

Nurse. Is it good den?

Mer. 'Tis no less, I tell you, for the bawdy hand of the dial is now upon the prick of noon.

Nurse. Out upon you! what a man are you!

39. **Without his roe**, sometimes explained as a pun on first syllable of Romeo's name, in which case the last syllables might be taken as an expression of woe.   41. **Petrarch**, Italian poet of the Renaissance who addressed his sonnets to Laura.   45. **hildings**, good-for-nothings.   48. **slop**, loose trousers of French fashion.   51. **slip**. Counterfeit coins were called *slips*.   56. **case**, mask. 59. **kindly**, naturally.   64. **is my pump well flowered**. The pump is pinked or perforated in ornamental figures. 69. **single-soled**, thin; contemptible, with pun on *soul*. 70. **singleness**, feebleness.   74. **cry a match**, claim a victory.   75. **wild-goose chase**, a horse-race in which the leading rider might force his competitors to follow him wherever he went.

Rom. One, gentlewoman, that God hath made for himself to mar.　122

Nurse. By my troth, it is well said; 'for himself to mar,' quoth a'? Gentlemen, can any of you tell me where I may find the young Romeo?

Rom. I can tell you; but young Romeo will be older when you have found him than he was when you sought him: I am the youngest of that name, for fault of a worse.

Nurse. You say well.　130

Mer. Yea, is the worst well? very well took, i' faith; wisely, wisely.

Nurse. If you be he, sir, I desire some confidence with you.

Ben. She will indite him to some supper.

Mer. A bawd, a bawd, a bawd! So ho!

Rom. What hast thou found?

Mer. No hare, sir; unless a hare, sir, in a lenten pie, that is something stale and hoar ere it be spent.　　　　　　　*[Sings.*

> An old hare hoar,　141
> And an old hare hoar,
> Is very good meat in lent:
> But a hare that is hoar
> Is too much for a score,
> When it hoars ere it be spent.

Romeo, will you come to your father's? we'll to dinner, thither.

Rom. I will follow you.

Mer. Farewell, ancient lady; farewell, [*singing*] 'lady, lady, lady.'　151

　　　　　　[Exeunt Mercutio and Benvolio.

Nurse. Marry, farewell! I pray you, sir, what saucy merchant was this, that was so full of his ropery?

Rom. A gentleman, nurse, that loves to hear himself talk, and will speak more in a minute than he will stand to in a month. 157

Nurse. An a' speak any thing against me, I'll take him down, an a' were lustier than he is, and twenty such Jacks; and if I cannot, I'll find those that shall. Scurvy knave! I am none of his flirt-gills; I am none of his skains-mates. And thou must stand by too, and suffer every knave to use me at his pleasure?　164

Peter. I saw no man use you at his pleasure; if I had, my weapon should quickly have been out, I warrant you: I dare draw as soon as another man, if I see occasion in a good quarrel, and the law on my side.　169

Nurse. Now, afore God, I am so vexed, that every part about me quivers. Scurvy knave! Pray you, sir, a word: and as I told you, my young lady bade me inquire you out; what she bade me say, I will keep to myself: but first let me tell ye, if ye should lead her into a fool's paradise, as they say, it were a very gross kind of behaviour, as they say: for the gentlewoman is young; and, therefore, if you should deal double with her, truly it were an ill thing to be offered to any gentlewoman, and very weak dealing.　181

Rom. Nurse, commend me to thy lady and mistress. I protest unto thee—

Nurse. Good heart, and, i' faith, I will tell her as much: Lord, Lord, she will be a joyful woman.

Rom. What wilt thou tell her, nurse? thou dost not mark me.

Nurse. I will tell her, sir, that you do protest; which, as I take it, is a gentlemanlike offer.

Rom. Bid her devise　191
Some means to come to shrift this afternoon;
And there she shall at Friar Laurence' cell
Be shrived and married. Here is for thy pains.

Nurse. No, truly, sir; not a penny.

Rom. Go to; I say you shall.

Nurse. This afternoon, sir? well, she shall be there.

Rom. And stay, good nurse, behind the abbey wall:　199
Within this hour my man shall be with thee,
And bring thee cords made like a tackled stair;
Which to the high top-gallant of my joy
Must be my convoy in the secret night.
Farewell; be trusty, and I'll quit thy pains:
Farewell; commend me to thy mistress.

Nurse. Now God in heaven bless thee!
　　Hark you sir.

Rom. What say'st thou, my dear nurse?

Nurse. Is your man secret? Did you ne'er hear say,
Two may keep counsel, putting one away?

---

134. **confidence,** the nurse's mistake for *conference.*
135. **indite,** Benvolio's malapropism for *invite.* 138. **hare,** used as a slang word for *courtesan.* 144. **hoar,** moldy. 151. 'lady, lady, lady,' refrain from the ballad *Chaste Susanna.* 153. **merchant,** fellow. 154. **ropery,** the nurse's mistake for *roguery.* 160. **Jacks,** used as a term of disparagement. 162. **flirt-gills,** loose women. 163. **skains-mates,** not well understood; sometimes connected with *skein* (of thread) or with *skain,* a dagger.

183. **protest,** vow. 188. **mark,** attend to. 201. **tackled stair,** rope ladder. 202. **top-gallant,** summit. 203. **convoy,** a thing that conducts. 204. **quit,** reward, requite. 208. **secret,** trustworthy.

Rom. I warrant thee, my man's as true
  as steel.   210
Nurse. Well, sir; my mistress is the sweetest lady—Lord, Lord! when 'twas a little
prating thing:—O, there is a nobleman in
town, one Paris, that would fain lay knife
aboard; but she, good soul, had as lief see a
toad, a very toad, as see him. I anger her
sometimes and tell her that Paris is the properer man; but, I'll warrant you, when I say
so, she looks as pale as any clout in the versal
world. Doth not rosemary and Romeo begin
both with a letter?   220
Rom. Ay, nurse; what of that? both with
an R.
Nurse. Ah, mocker! that's the dog's
name; R is for the— No; I know it begins
with some other letter:—and she hath the
prettiest sententious of it, of you and rosemary, that it would do you good to hear it.
Rom. Commend me to thy lady.
Nurse. Ay, a thousand times.
                             [*Exit Romeo.*]
Peter!   230
Pet. Anon!
Nurse. Peter, take my fan, and go before,
and apace.   [*Exeunt.*

Scene V. *Capulet's orchard.*

Enter Juliet.

Jul. The clock struck nine when I did
  send the nurse;
In half an hour she promised to return.
Perchance she cannot meet him: that's not
  so.
O, she is lame! love's heralds should be
  thoughts,
Which ten times faster glide than the sun's
  beams,
Driving back shadows over louring hills:
Therefore do nimble-pinion'd doves draw
  love,
And therefore hath the wind-swift Cupid
  wings.
Now is the sun upon the highmost hill
Of this day's journey, and from nine till
  twelve   10
Is three long hours, yet she is not come.

217. **properer**, handsomer. 219. **clout**, rag; a proverbial expression. **versal**, universal. 220. **a**, the same.
223. **the dog's name.** The letter R was thought to resemble the dog's growl. 226. **sententious.** The nurse
probably means *sentences*, pithy sayings.
  Scene v. 7. **love**, Venus, whose chariot was drawn by
doves.

Had she affections and warm youthful blood,
She would be as swift in motion as a ball;
My words would bandy her to my sweet love,
And his to me:
†But old folks, many feign as they were dead;
Unwieldy, slow, heavy and pale as lead.
O God, she comes!

Enter Nurse *and* Peter.

                        O honey nurse, what news?
Hast thou met with him? Send thy man
  away.
Nurse. Peter, stay at the gate. [*Exit Peter.*
Jul. Now, good sweet nurse,—O Lord,
  why look'st thou sad?   21
Though news be sad, yet tell them merrily;
If good, thou shamest the music of sweet
  news
By playing it to me with so sour a face.
Nurse. I am a-weary, give me leave
  awhile:
Fie, how my bones ache! what a jaunt have
  I had!
Jul. I would thou hadst my bones, and I
  thy news.
Nay, come, I pray thee, speak; good, good
  nurse, speak.
Nurse. Jesu, what haste? can you not
  stay awhile?
Do you not see that I am out of breath?   30
Jul. How art thou out of breath, when
  thou hast breath
To say to me that thou art out of breath?
The excuse that thou dost make in this delay
Is longer than the tale thou dost excuse.
Is thy news good, or bad? answer to that;
Say either, and I'll stay the circumstance:
Let me be satisfied, is 't good or bad?   37
Nurse. Well, you have made a simple
choice; you know not how to choose a man:
Romeo! no, not he; though his face be better
than any man's, yet his leg excels all men's;
and for a hand, and a foot, and a body,
though they be not to be talked on, yet they
are past compare: he is not the flower of
courtesy, but, I'll warrant him, as gentle as a
lamb. Go thy ways, wench; serve God.
What, have you dined at home?   46
Jul. No, no: but all this did I know before.
What says he of our marriage? what of that?

14. **bandy**, toss to and fro; term from tennis. 25.
give me leave, let me alone. 36. **stay the circumstance**, await details.

Nurse. Lord, how my head aches! what a head have I!
It beats as it would fall in twenty pieces. 50
My back o' t' other side,—O my back, my back!
Beshrew your heart for sending me about,
To catch my death with jaunting up and down!
Jul. I' faith, I am sorry that thou art not well.
Sweet, sweet, sweet nurse, tell me, what says my love?
Nurse. Your love says, like an honest gentleman, and a courteous, and a kind, and a handsome, and, I warrant, a virtuous,—
Where is your mother?
Jul. Where is my mother! why, she is within; 60
Where should she be? How oddly thou repliest!
'Your love says, like an honest gentleman,
Where is your mother?'
Nurse.   O God's lady dear!
Are you so hot? marry, come up, I trow;
Is this the poultice for my aching bones?
Henceforward do your messages yourself.
Jul. Here's such a coil! come, what says Romeo?
Nurse. Have you got leave to go to shrift to-day?
Jul. I have.
Nurse. Then hie you hence to Friar Laurence' cell; 70
There stays a husband to make you a wife:
Now comes the wanton blood up in your cheeks,
They'll be in scarlet straight at any news.
Hie you to church; I must another way,
To fetch a ladder, by the which your love
Must climb a bird's nest soon when it is dark:
I am the drudge and toil in your delight,
But you shall bear the burden soon at night.
Go; I'll to dinner; hie you to the cell. 79
Jul. Hie to high fortune! Honest nurse, farewell.   [*Exeunt.*

SCENE VI. *Friar Laurence's cell.*

Enter FRIAR LAURENCE *and* ROMEO.

Fri. L. So smile the heavens upon this holy act,
That after hours with sorrow chide us not!

Rom. Amen, amen! but come what sorrow can,
It cannot countervail the exchange of joy
That one short minute gives me in her sight:
Do thou but close our hands with holy words,
Then love-devouring death do what he dare;
It is enough I may but call her mine.
Fri. L. These violent delights have violent ends
And in their triumph die, like fire and powder, 10
Which as they kiss consume: the sweetest honey
Is loathsome in his own deliciousness
And in the taste confounds the appetite:
Therefore love moderately; long love doth so;
Too swift arrives as tardy as too slow.

Enter JULIET.

Here comes the lady: O, so light a foot
Will ne'er wear out the everlasting flint:
A lover may bestride the gossamer
That idles in the wanton summer air,
And yet not fall; so light is vanity. 20
Jul. Good even to my ghostly confessor.
Fri. L. Romeo shall thank thee, daughter, for us both.
Jul. As much to him, else is his thanks too much.
Rom. Ah, Juliet, if the measure of thy joy
Be heap'ed like mine and that thy skill be more
To blazon it, then sweeten with thy breath
This neighbour air, and let rich music's tongue
Unfold the imagined happiness that both
Receive in either by this dear encounter.
Jul. Conceit, more rich in matter than in words, 30
Brags of his substance, not of ornament:
They are but beggars that can count their worth;
But my true love is grown to such excess
I cannot sum up sum of half my wealth.
Fri. L. Come, come with me, and we will make short work;
For, by your leaves, you shall not stay alone
Till holy church incorporate two in one.   [*Exeunt.*

---

52. **Beshrew**, common objurgation meaning "ill-luck." 64. **come up**, expressive of impatience like "go to." 67. **coil**, turmoil, bustle.

4. **countervail**, equal. 9. **These violent delights**, etc., expresses a premonition of evil. 13. **confounds**, destroys. 18. **gossamer**, spider's thread. 26. **blazon**, heraldic term meaning "to describe" or "to set forth." 30. **Conceit**, imagination, thought.

ACT III.

Scene I. *A public place.*

Enter Mercutio, Benvolio, Page, *and*
Servants.

Ben. I pray thee, good Mercutio, let's
retire:
The day is hot, the Capulets abroad,
And, if we meet, we shall not scape a
brawl;
For now, these hot days, is the mad blood
stirring.　　　　　　　　　　　　　4
Mer. Thou art like one of those fellows
that when he enters the confines of a tavern
claps me his sword upon the table and says
'God send me no need of thee!' and by the
operation of the second cup draws it on the
drawer, when indeed there is no need.　　10
Ben. Am I like such a fellow?
Mer. Come, come, thou art as hot a Jack
in thy mood as any in Italy, and as soon
moved to be moody, and as soon moody to
be moved.
Ben. And what to?
Mer. Nay, an there were two such, we
should have none shortly, for one would kill
the other. Thou! why, thou wilt quarrel with
a man that hath a hair more, or a hair less, in
his beard, than thou hast: thou wilt quarrel
with a man for cracking nuts, having no
other reason but because thou hast hazel
eyes: what eye but such an eye would spy
out such a quarrel? Thy head is as full of
quarrels as an egg is full of meat, and yet thy
head hath been beaten as addle as an egg for
quarrelling: thou hast quarrelled with a man
for coughing in the street, because he hath
wakened thy dog that hath lain asleep in the
sun: didst thou not fall out with a tailor for
wearing his new doublet before Easter? with
another, for tying his new shoes with old
riband? and yet thou wilt tutor me from
quarrelling!　　　　　　　　　　　33
Ben. An I were so apt to quarrel as thou
art, any man should buy the fee-simple of my
life for an hour and a quarter.
Mer. The fee simple! O simple!
Ben. By my head, here come the Capulets.
Mer. By my heel, I care not.

Enter Tybalt *and others.*

Tyb. Follow me close, for I will speak to
them.　　　　　　　　　　　　　40
Gentlemen, good den: a word with one of
you.
Mer. And but one word with one of us?
couple it with something; make it a word and
a blow.
Tyb. You shall find me apt enough to
that, sir, an you will give me occasion.
Mer. Could you not take some occasion
without giving?
Tyb. Mercutio, thou consort'st with Ro-
meo,—　　　　　　　　　　　　　47
Mer. Consort! what, dost thou make us
minstrels? an thou make minstrels of us, look
to hear nothing but discords: here's my fid-
dlestick; here's that shall make you dance.
'Zounds, consort!　　　　　　　　52
Ben. We talk here in the public haunt of
men:
Either withdraw unto some private place,
And reason coldly of your grievances,
Or else depart; here all eyes gaze on us.
Mer. Men's eyes were made to look, and
let them gaze;
I will not budge for no man's pleasure, I.

Enter Romeo.

Tyb. Well, peace be with you, sir: here
comes my man.
Mer. But I'll be hang'd, sir, if he wear
your livery:　　　　　　　　　　60
Marry, go before to field, he'll be your
follower;
Your worship in that sense may call him
'man.'
Tyb. Romeo, the hate I bear thee can af-
ford
No better term than this,—thou art a villain.
Rom. Tybalt, the reason that I have to
love thee
Doth much excuse the appertaining rage
To such a greeting: villain am I none;
Therefore farewell; I see thou know'st me
not.
Tyb. Boy, this shall not excuse the in-
juries
That thou hast done me; therefore turn and
draw.
Rom. I do protest, I never injured thee,
But love thee better than thou canst devise,
Till thou shalt know the reason of my love:

---

2. **The day is hot.** This offers a little touch of
Italian atmosphere. 14. **moody,** angry.

47. **consort'st.** *To consort* meant "to accompany"
and also "to attend or wait upon." 52. **'Zounds,** a
modified form of the oath, "by God's wounds." 61.
field, field of encounter.

And so, good Capulet,—which name I
    tender
As dearly as my own,—be satisfied.
    Mer. O calm, dishonourable, vile sub-
        mission!
Alla stoccata carries it away.   [*Draws.*
Tybalt, you rat-catcher, will you walk?
    Tyb. What wouldst thou have with me? 79
    Mer. Good king of cats, nothing but one
of your nine lives; that I mean to make
bold withal, and, as you shall use me hereafter, dry-beat the rest of the eight. Will
you pluck your sword out of his pilcher by
the ears? make haste, lest mine be about
your ears ere it be out.
    Tyb. I am for you.   [*Drawing.*
    Rom. Gentle Mercutio, put thy rapier up.
    Mer. Come, sir, your passado. [*They fight.*
    Rom. Draw, Benvolio; beat down their
        weapons.   89
Gentlemen, for shame, forbear this outrage!
Tybalt, Mercutio, the prince expressly hath
Forbidden bandying in Verona streets:
Hold, Tybalt! good Mercutio!
    [*Tybalt under Romeo's arm stabs Mercutio,*
                and flies with his followers
    Mer.   I am hurt.   93
A plague o' both your houses! I am sped.
Is he gone, and hath nothing?
    Ben.   What, art thou hurt?
    Mer. Ay, ay, a scratch, a scratch; marry,
        'tis enough.
Where is my page? Go, villain, fetch a
    surgeon.   [*Exit Page.*
    Rom. Courage, man; the hurt cannot be
        much.   98
    Mer. No, 'tis not so deep as a well, nor so
wide as a church-door; but 'tis enough, 'twill
serve: ask for me to-morrow, and you shall
find me a grave man. I am peppered, I warrant, for this world. A plague o' both your
houses! 'Zounds, a dog, a rat, a mouse, a cat,
to scratch a man to death! a braggart, a
rogue, a villain, that fights by the book of
arithmetic! Why the devil came you between us? I was hurt under your arm.
    Rom. I thought all for the best.   109
    Mer. Help me into some house, Benvolio,

Or I shall faint. A plague o' both your
    houses!
They have made worms' meat of me: I have
    it,
And soundly too: your houses!
            [*Exeunt Mercutio and Benvolio.*
    Rom. This gentleman, the prince's near
        ally,   114
My very friend, hath got his mortal hurt
In my behalf; my reputation stain'd
With Tybalt's slander,—Tybalt, that an
    hour
Hath been my kinsman! O sweet Juliet,
Thy beauty hath made me effeminate
And in my temper soften'd valour's steel! 120

Re-enter Benvolio.

    Ben. O Romeo, Romeo, brave Mercutio's
        dead!
That gallant spirit hath aspired the clouds,
Which too untimely here did scorn the earth.
    Rom. This day's black fate on more days
        doth depend;
This but begins the woe others must end.
    Ben. Here comes the furious Tybalt back
        again.
    Rom. Alive, in triumph! and Mercutio
        slain!
Away to heaven, respective lenity,
And fire-eyed fury be my conduct now!

Re-enter Tybalt.

Now, Tybalt, take the villain back again, 130
That late thou gavest me; for Mercutio's soul
Is but a little way above our heads,
Staying for thine to keep him company:
Either thou, or I, or both, must go with him.
    Tyb. Thou, wretched boy, that didst con-
        sort him here,
Shalt with him hence.
    Rom.   This shall determine that.
                    [*They fight; Tybalt falls.*
    Ben. Romeo, away, be gone!
The citizens are up, and Tybalt slain.
Stand not amazed: the prince will doom thee
    death,
If thou art taken: hence, be gone, away! 140
    Rom. O, I am fortune's fool!
    Ben.   Why dost thou stay?
                            [*Exit Romeo.*

---

77. **Alla stoccata,** Italian, "with the thrust"; i.e., the
fencing master wins the victory. 78. **rat-catcher,** an
allusion to Tybalt as king of cats (see II, iv, 19). 83.
dry-beat, beat soundly. 84. **pilcher,** scabbard.
88. **passado,** forward thrust; used derisively. 94. **sped,**
done for. 102. **grave man.** Mercutio thus makes puns
with his last breath. 106. **by the book of arithmetic,**
merely by theory. Back of the whole scene lies a current
controversy between the old broad-sword style of fencing
and the new French style of rapier fencing.

114. **ally,** kinsman. 115. **very,** true. 128. **respective lenity,** considerate gentleness. 129. **conduct,**
guide. 139. **doom,** adjudge. 141. **fortune's fool.**
At this crucial moment in the play Romeo again alludes
to destiny.

Enter Citizens, &c.

First Cit. Which way ran he that kill'd Mercutio?
Tybalt, that murderer, which way ran he?
Ben. There lies that Tybalt.
First Cit.　　　　Up, sir, go with me;
I charge thee in the prince's name, obey.

Enter Prince, *attended;* Montague, Capulet, *their* Wives, *and others.*

Prin. Where are the vile beginners of this fray?
Ben. O noble prince, I can discover all
The unlucky manage of this fatal brawl:
There lies the man, slain by young Romeo,
That slew thy kinsman, brave Mercutio. 150
La. Cap. Tybalt, my cousin! O my brother's child!
O prince! O cousin! husband! O, the blood is spilt
Of my dear kinsman! Prince, as thou art true,
For blood of ours, shed blood of Montague.
O cousin, cousin!
Prin. Benvolio, who began this bloody fray?
Ben. Tybalt, here slain, whom Romeo's hand did slay;
Romeo that spoke him fair, bade him bethink
How nice the quarrel was, and urged withal
Your high displeasure: all this uttered　160
With gentle breath, calm look, knees humbly bow'd,
Could not take truce with the unruly spleen
Of Tybalt deaf to peace, but that he tilts
With piercing steel at bold Mercutio's breast,
Who, all as hot, turns deadly point to point,
And, with a martial scorn, with one hand beats
Cold death aside, and with the other sends
It back to Tybalt, whose dexterity
Retorts it: Romeo he cries aloud,
'Hold, friends! friends, part!' and, swifter than his tongue,　170
His agile arm beats down their fatal points,
And 'twixt them rushes; underneath whose arm
An envious thrust from Tybalt hit the life
Of stout Mercutio, and then Tybalt fled;
But by and by comes back to Romeo,

Who had but newly entertain'd revenge,
And to 't they go like lightning, for, ere I
Could draw to part them, was stout Tybalt slain,
And, as he fell, did Romeo turn and fly.
This is the truth, or let Benvolio die.　180
La. Cap. He is a kinsman to the Montague;
Affection makes him false; he speaks not true:
Some twenty of them fought in this black strife,
And all those twenty could but kill one life.
I beg for justice, which thou, prince, must give;
Romeo slew Tybalt, Romeo must not live.
Prin. Romeo slew him, he slew Mercutio;
Who now the price of his dear blood doth owe?
Mon. Not Romeo, prince, he was Mercutio's friend;
His fault concludes but what the law should end,　190
The life of Tybalt.
Prin.　　　　And for that offence
Immediately we do exile him hence:
I have an interest in your hate's proceeding,
My blood for your rude brawls doth lie a-bleeding;
But I'll amerce you with so strong a fine
That you shall all repent the loss of mine:
I will be deaf to pleading and excuses;
Nor tears nor prayers shall purchase out abuses:
Therefore use none: let Romeo hence in haste,
Else, when he's found, that hour is his last.
Bear hence this body and attend our will: 201
Mercy but murders, pardoning those that kill.　　　　[*Exeunt.*

Scene II. *Capulet's orchard.*

Enter Juliet.

Jul. Gallop apace, you fiery-footed steeds,
Towards Phœbus' lodging: such a waggoner
As Phaethon would whip you to the west,
And bring in cloudy night immediately.
Spread thy close curtain, love-performing night,　5

148. **manage,** management.　159. **nice,** trivial.
162. **take truce,** make peace.　**unruly spleen,** ungovernable rage.　163. **tilts,** strikes.　169. **Retorts,** throws back upon his adversary.

195. **amerce,** punish by fine.
Scene ii. 3. **Phaethon,** son of Helios, who was allowed to assume the reins of the sun for a day; not being able to restrain the steeds, he had to be slain by the thunderbolt of Jupiter in order that the universe might not be destroyed.

That runaways' eyes may wink, and Romeo
Leap to these arms, untalk'd of and unseen.
Lovers can see to do their amorous rites
By their own beauties; or, if love be blind,
It best agrees with night. Come, civil night,10
Thou sober-suited matron, all in black,
And learn me how to lose a winning match,
Play'd for a pair of stainless maidenhoods:
Hood my unmann'd blood, bating in my
  cheeks,
With thy black mantle; till strange love,
  grown bold,
Think true love acted simple modesty.
Come, night; come, Romeo; come, thou day
  in night;
For thou wilt lie upon the wings of night
Whiter than new snow on a raven's back.
Come, gentle night, come, loving, black-
  brow'd night,   20
Give me my Romeo; and, when he shall die,
Take him and cut him out in little stars,
And he will make the face of heaven so fine
That all the world will be in love with night
And pay no worship to the garish sun.
O, I have bought the mansion of a love,
But not possess'd it, and, though I am sold,
Not yet enjoy'd: so tedious is this day
As is the night before some festival
To an impatient child that hath new robes 30
And may not wear them. O, here comes my
  nurse,
And she brings news; and every tongue that
  speaks
But Romeo's name speaks heavenly elo-
  quence.

Enter Nurse, *with cords.*

Now, nurse, what news? What hast thou
  there? the cords
That Romeo bid thee fetch?
  Nurse.   Ay, ay, the cords.
                                   [*Throws them down.*
Jul. Ay me! what news? why dost thou
  wring thy hands?
Nurse. Ay, well-a-day! he's dead, he's
  dead, he's dead!
We are undone, lady, we are undone!
Alack the day! he's gone, he's kill'd, he's
  dead!

6. **runaways' eyes**, a famous crux of which there is
no satisfactory explanation. The allusion to Phaethon
(l. 3) may here be repeated. 10. **civil**, well-ordered.
14. **Hood**, cover; term in falconry. The hawk's eyes
were covered so that it would not bate or beat the wings.
unmann'd, another term in falconry meaning "untamed."

Jul. Can heaven be so envious?
  Nurse.   Romeo can,   40
Though heaven cannot: O Romeo, Romeo!
Who ever would have thought it? Romeo!
Jul. What devil art thou, that dost tor-
  ment me thus?
This torture should be roar'd in dismal hell.
Hath Romeo slain himself? say thou but 'I,'
And that bare vowel 'I' shall poison more
Than the death-darting eye of cockatrice:
I am not I, if there be such an I;
Or those eyes shut, that make thee answer
  'I.'
If he be slain, say 'I'; or if not, no: 50
Brief sounds determine of my weal or woe.
  Nurse. I saw the wound, I saw it with
    mine eyes,—
God save the mark!—here on his manly
  breast:
A piteous corse, a bloody piteous corse;
Pale, pale as ashes, all bedaub'd in blood,
All in gore-blood; I swounded at the sight.
  Jul. O, break, my heart! poor bankrupt,
    break at once!
To prison, eyes, ne'er look on liberty!
Vile earth, to earth resign; end motion here;
And thou and Romeo press one heavy bier! 60
  Nurse. O Tybalt, Tybalt, the best friend
    I had!
O courteous Tybalt! honest gentleman!
That ever I should live to see thee dead!
  Jul. What storm is this that blows so
    contrary?
Is Romeo slaughter'd, and is Tybalt dead?
My dear-loved cousin, and my dearer lord?
Then, dreadful trumpet, sound the general
  doom!
For who is living, if those two are gone?
  Nurse. Tybalt is gone, and Romeo ban-
    ished;
Romeo that kill'd him, he is banished.   70
  Jul. O God! did Romeo's hand shed Ty-
    balt's blood?
  Nurse. It did, it did; alas the day, it did!
  Jul. O serpent heart, hid with a flowering
    face!
Did ever dragon keep so fair a cave?
Beautiful tyrant! fiend angelical!
Dove-feather'd raven! wolvish-ravening
  lamb!
Despised substance of divinest show!

45. **'I,'** ay, yes. 47. **cockatrice**, basilisk, a fabulous
serpent which could kill by its look. 53. **God save the
mark**, God forbid; a familiar oath originally intended
to avert ill omen. 56. **gore-blood**, clotted blood.

Just opposite to what thou justly seem'st,
A damned saint, an honourable villain!
O nature, what hadst thou to do in hell,   80
When thou didst bower the spirit of a fiend
In mortal paradise of such sweet flesh?
Was ever book containing such vile matter
So fairly bound? O, that deceit should dwell
In such a gorgeous palace!

   Nurse.   There's no trust,
No faith, no honesty in men; all perjured,
All forsworn, all naught, all dissemblers.
Ah, where's my man? give me some aqua
   vitæ:
These griefs, these woes, these sorrows make
   me old.
Shame come to Romeo!

   Jul.   Blister'd be thy tongue   90
For such a wish! he was not born to shame:
Upon his brow shame is ashamed to sit;
For 'tis a throne where honour may be
   crown'd
Sole monarch of the universal earth.
O, what a beast was I to chide at him!

   Nurse. Will you speak well of him that
   kill'd your cousin?

   Jul. Shall I speak ill of him that is my
   husband?
Ah, poor my lord, what tongue shall smooth
   thy name,
When I, thy three-hours wife, have mangled
   it?
But, wherefore, villain, didst thou kill my
   cousin?   100
That villain cousin would have kill'd my
   husband:
Back, foolish tears, back to your native
   spring;
Your tributary drops belong to woe,
Which you, mistaking, offer up to joy.
My husband lives, that Tybalt would have
   slain;
And Tybalt's dead, that would have slain
   my husband:
All this is comfort; wherefore weep I then?
Some word there was, worser than Tybalt's
   death,
That murder'd me: I would forget it fain;
But, O, it presses to my memory,   110
Like damned guilty deeds to sinners' minds:
'Tybalt is dead, and Romeo—banished;'
That 'banished,' that one word 'banished,'
Hath slain ten thousand Tybalts. Tybalt's
   death

Was woe enough, if it had ended there:
Or, if sour woe delights in fellowship
And needly will be rank'd with other griefs,
Why follow'd not, when she said 'Tybalt's
   dead,'
Thy father, or thy mother, nay, or both,
Which modern lamentation might have
   moved?   120
But with a rearward following Tybalt's
   death,
'Romeo is banished,' to speak that word,
Is father, mother, Tybalt, Romeo, Juliet,
All slain, all dead. 'Romeo is banished!'
There is no end, no limit, measure, bound,
In that word's death; no words can that woe
   sound.
Where is my father, and my mother, nurse?

   Nurse. Weeping and wailing over Tybalt's
   corse:
Will you go to them? I will bring you thither.

   Jul. Wash they his wounds with tears:
   mine shall be spent,   130
When theirs are dry, for Romeo's banish-
   ment.
Take up those cords: poor ropes, you are be-
   guiled,
Both you and I; for Romeo is exiled:
He made you for a highway to my bed;
But I, a maid, die maiden-widowed.
Come, cords, come, nurse; I'll to my wed-
   ding-bed;
And death, not Romeo, take my maiden-
   head!

   Nurse. Hie to your chamber: I'll find
   Romeo
To comfort you: I wot well where he is.
Hark ye, your Romeo will be here at night:140
I'll to him; he is hid at Laurence' cell.

   Jul. O, find him! give this ring to my true
   knight,
And bid him come to take his last farewell.
                        [Exeunt.

       SCENE III.   *Friar Laurence's cell.*

         Enter FRIAR LAURENCE.

   Fri. L. Romeo, come forth; come forth,
   thou fearful man:
Affliction is enamour'd of thy parts,
And thou art wedded to calamity.

---

81. **bower**, give lodging to. 87. **naught**, worthless.

117. **needly**, of necessity. 120. **modern**, ordinary. 121.
rearward, rear guard.
 Scene iii. 1. **fearful**, full of fear.

Enter Romeo.

Rom. Father, what news? what is the prince's doom?
What sorrow craves acquaintance at my hand,
That I yet know not?
Fri. L.   Too familiar
Is my dear son with such sour company:
I bring thee tidings of the prince's doom.
Rom. What less than dooms-day is the prince's doom?
Fri. L. A gentler judgement vanish'd from his lips,   10
Not body's death, but body's banishment.
Rom. Ha, banishment! be merciful, say 'death;'
For exile hath more terror in his look,
Much more than death: do not say 'banishment.'
Fri. L. Hence from Verona art thou banished:
Be patient, for the world is broad and wide.
Rom. There is no world without Verona walls,
But purgatory, torture, hell itself.
Hence-banished is banish'd from the world,
And world's exile is death: then banished,   20
Is death mis-term'd; calling death banishment,
Thou cutt'st my head off with a golden axe,
And smilest upon the stroke that murders me.
Fri. L. O deadly sin! O rude unthankfulness!
Thy fault our law calls death; but the kind prince,
Taking thy part, hath rush'd aside the law,
And turn'd that black word death to banishment:
This is dear mercy, and thou seest it not.
Rom. 'Tis torture, and not mercy: heaven is here,
Where Juliet lives; and every cat and dog   30
And little mouse, every unworthy thing,
Live here in heaven and may look on her;
But Romeo may not: more validity,
More honourable state, more courtship lives
In carrion-flies than Romeo: they may seize
On the white wonder of dear Juliet's hand
And steal immortal blessing from her lips,
Who, even in pure and vestal modesty,

Still blush, as thinking their own kisses sin;
But Romeo may not; he is banished: 40
Flies may do this, but I from this must fly:
They are free men, but I am banished.
And say'st thou yet that exile is not death?
Hadst thou no poison mix'd, no sharp-ground knife,
No sudden mean of death, though ne'er so mean,
But 'banished' to kill me?—'banished'?
O friar, the damned use that word in hell;
Howlings attend it: how hast thou the heart,
Being a divine, a ghostly confessor,
A sin-absolver, and my friend profess'd,   50
To mangle me with that word 'banished'?
Fri. L. Thou fond mad man, hear me but speak a word.
Rom. O, thou wilt speak again of banishment.
Fri. L. I'll give thee armour to keep off that word;
Adversity's sweet milk, philosophy,
To comfort thee, though thou art banished.
Rom. Yet 'banished'? Hang up philosophy!
Unless philosophy can make a Juliet,
Displant a town, reverse a prince's doom,
It helps not, it prevails not: talk no more.   60
Fri. L. O, then I see that madmen have no ears.
Rom. How should they, when that wise men have no eyes?
Fri. L. Let me dispute with thee of thy estate.
Rom. Thou canst not speak of that thou dost not feel:
Wert thou as young as I, Juliet thy love,
An hour but married, Tybalt murdered,
Doting like me and like me banished,
Then mightst thou speak, then mightst thou tear thy hair,
And fall upon the ground, as I do now,
Taking the measure of an unmade grave.   70
          [*Knocking within.*
Fri. L. Arise; one knocks; good Romeo, hide thyself.
Rom. Not I; unless the breath of heart-sick groans,
Mist-like, infold me from the search of eyes.
          [*Knocking.*
Fri. L. Hark, how they knock! Who's there? Romeo, arise;

---

10. **vanish'd**, issued.   26. **rush'd**, thrust (aside).
28. **dear**, gentle, loving.   33. **validity**, value.   34. **courtship**, both courtliness and wooing.

45. **mean . . . mean**, means . . . base.   63. **estate**, situation.

Thou wilt be taken. Stay awhile! Stand up;
       [*Knocking.*
Run to my study. By and by! God's will,
What simpleness is this! I come, I come!
       [*Knocking.*
Who knocks so hard? whence come you?
 what's your will?
 Nurse. [*Within*] Let me come in, and you
 shall know my errand;
I come from Lady Juliet.
 Fri. L.   Welcome, then. 80

   Enter Nurse.

 Nurse. O holy friar, O, tell me, holy friar,
Where is my lady's lord, where's Romeo?
 Fri. L. There on the ground, with his own
 tears made drunk.
 Nurse. O, he is even in my mistress' case,
Just in her case! O woful sympathy!
Piteous predicament! Even so lies she,
Blubbering and weeping, weeping and blub-
 bering.
Stand up, stand up; stand, an you be a man:
For Juliet's sake, for her sake, rise and stand;
Why should you fall into so deep an O? 90
 Rom. Nurse!
 Nurse. Ah sir! ah sir! Well, death's the
 end of all.
 Rom. Spakest thou of Juliet? how is it
 with her?
Doth she not think me an old murderer,
Now I have stain'd the childhood of our joy
With blood removed but little from her own?
Where is she? and how doth she? and what
 says
My conceal'd lady to our cancell'd love?
 Nurse. O, she says nothing, sir, but weeps
 and weeps;
And now falls on her bed; and then starts
 up, 100
And Tybalt calls; and then on Romeo cries,
And then down falls again.
 Rom.   As if that name,
Shot from the deadly level of a gun,
Did murder her; as that name's cursed hand
Murder'd her kinsman. O, tell me, friar, tell
 me,
In what vile part of this anatomy
Doth my name lodge? tell me that I may
 sack
The hateful mansion. [*Drawing his sword.*
 Fri. L.   Hold thy desperate hand:
Art thou a man? thy form cries out thou art:

94. **old** (colloquial), real, actual. 103. **level**, aim.
107. **sack**, destroy.

Thy tears are womanish; thy wild acts denote
The unreasonable fury of a beast: 111
Unseemly woman in a seeming man!
Or ill-beseeming beast in seeming both!
Thou hast amazed me: by my holy order,
I thought thy disposition better temper'd.
Hast thou slain Tybalt? wilt thou slay thy-
 self?
And slay thy lady too that lives in thee,
By doing damned hate upon thyself?
Why rail'st thou on thy birth, the heaven,
 and earth?
Since birth, and heaven, and earth, all three
 do meet 120
In thee at once; which thou at once wouldst
 lose.
Fie, fie, thou shamest thy shape, thy love,
 thy wit;
Which, like a usurer, abound'st in all,
And usest none in that true use indeed
Which should bedeck thy shape, thy love,
 thy wit:
Thy noble shape is but a form of wax,
Digressing from the valour of a man;
Thy dear love sworn but hollow perjury,
Killing that love which thou hast vow'd to
 cherish;
Thy wit, that ornament to shape and love,130
Mis-shapen in the conduct of them both,
Like powder in a skilless soldier's flask,
Is set a-fire by thine own ignorance,
And thou dismember'd with thine own de-
 fence.
What, rouse thee, man! thy Juliet is alive,
For whose dear sake thou wast but lately
 dead;
There art thou happy: Tybalt would kill
 thee,
But thou slew'st Tybalt; there art thou hap-
 py too:
The law that threaten'd death becomes thy
 friend
And turns it to exile; there art thou happy:140
A pack of blessings lights upon thy back;
Happiness courts thee in her best array;
But, like a misbehaved and sullen wench,
Thou pout'st upon thy fortune and thy
 love:
Take heed, take heed, for such die miser-
 able.
Go, get thee to thy love, as was decreed,
Ascend her chamber, hence and comfort her:
But look thou stay not till the watch be set,
For then thou canst not pass to Mantua;
Where thou shalt live, till we can find a time

To blaze your marriage, reconcile your
friends,　　　　　　　　　　　　　151
Beg pardon of the prince, and call thee back
With twenty hundred thousand times more
joy
Than thou went'st forth in lamentation.
Go before, nurse: commend me to thy lady;
And bid her hasten all the house to bed,
Which heavy sorrow makes them apt unto:
Romeo is coming.

　　Nurse. O Lord, I could have stay'd here
all the night
To hear good counsel: O, what learning is! 160
My lord, I'll tell my lady you will come.

　　Rom. Do so, and bid my sweet prepare to
chide.

　　Nurse. Here, sir, a ring she bid me give
you, sir:
Hie you, make haste, for it grows very late.
　　　　　　　　　　　　　　　[*Exit.*

　　Rom. How well my comfort is revived by
this!

　　Fri. L. Go hence; good night; and here
stands all your state:
Either be gone before the watch be set,
Or by the break of day disguised from hence:
Sojourn in Mantua; I'll find out your man,
And he shall signify from time to time　170
Every good hap to you that chances here:
Give me thy hand; 'tis late: farewell; good
night.

　　Rom. But that a joy past joy calls out on
me,
It were a grief, so brief to part with thee:
Farewell.　　　　　　　　　　　[*Exeunt.*

SCENE IV. *A room in Capulet's house.*

Enter CAPULET, LADY CAPULET, *and* PARIS.

　　Cap. Things have fall'n out, sir, so un-
luckily,
That we have had no time to move our
daughter:
Look you, she loved her kinsman Tybalt
dearly,
And so did I:—Well, we were born to die.
'Tis very late, she'll not come down to-night:
I promise you, but for your company,
I would have been a-bed an hour ago.

　　Par. These times of woe afford no time to
woo.

Madam, good night: commend me to your
daughter.

　　La. Cap. I will, and know her mind early
to-morrow;　　　　　　　　　　　　10
To-night she is mew'd up to her heaviness.

　　Cap. Sir Paris, I will make a desperate
tender
Of my child's love: I think she will be ruled
In all respects by me; nay, more, I doubt it
not.
Wife, go you to her ere you go to bed;
Acquaint her here of my son Paris' love;
And bid her, mark you me, on Wednesday
next—
But, soft! what day is this?

　　Par. 　　　　　　　　Monday, my lord.

　　Cap. Monday! ha, ha! Well, Wednesday
is too soon,
O' Thursday let it be: o' Thursday, tell her,
She shall be married to this noble earl.　21
Will you be ready? do you like this haste?
We'll keep no great ado,—a friend or two;
For, hark you, Tybalt being slain so late,
It may be thought we held him carelessly,
Being our kinsman, if we revel much:
Therefore we'll have some half a dozen
friends,
And there an end. But what say you to
Thursday?

　　Par. My lord, I would that Thursday
were to-morrow.

　　Cap. Well, get you gone: o' Thursday be
it, then.　　　　　　　　　　　　30
Go you to Juliet ere you go to bed,
Prepare her, wife, against this wedding-day.
Farewell, my lord. Light to my chamber,
ho!
Afore me! it is so very very late,
That we may call it early by and by.
Good night.　　　　　　　　　　[*Exeunt*

SCENE V. *Capulet's orchard.*

Enter ROMEO *and* JULIET *above, at the
window.*

　　Jul. Wilt thou be gone? it is not yet near
day:
It was the nightingale, and not the lark,
That pierced the fearful hollow of thine ear;
Nightly she sings on yond pomegranate-tree:
Believe me, love, it was the nightingale.　5

---

151. **blaze,** publish, divulge.　157. **apt,** ready,
inclined.　166. **here stands all your state,** your
fortune depends on what follows.
Scene iv. 2. **move,** urge.

11. **mew'd,** cooped.　12. **desperate tender,** rash
offer.　25. **held,** regarded.　34. **Afore me,** by my life.

Rom. It was the lark, the herald of the
morn,
No nightingale: look, love, what envious
streaks
Do lace the severing clouds in yonder east:
Night's candles are burnt out, and jocund
day
Stands tiptoe on the misty mountain tops. 10
I must be gone and live, or stay and die.

Jul. Yond light is not day-light, I know
it, I:
It is some meteor that the sun exhales,
To be to thee this night a torch-bearer,
And light thee on thy way to Mantua:
Therefore stay yet; thou need'st not to be
gone.

Rom. Let me be ta'en, let me be put to
death;
I am content, so thou wilt have it so.
I'll say yon grey is not the morning's eye,
'Tis but the pale reflex of Cynthia's brow; 20
Nor that is not the lark, whose notes do beat
The vaulty heaven so high above our heads:
I have more care to stay than will to go:
Come, death, and welcome! Juliet wills it
so.
How is 't, my soul? let's talk; it is not day.

Jul. It is, it is: hie hence, be gone, away!
It is the lark that sings so out of tune,
Straining harsh discords and unpleasing
sharps.
Some say the lark makes sweet division;
This doth not so, for she divideth us: 30
Some say the lark and loathed toad change
eyes;
O, now I would they had changed voices too!
Since arm from arm that voice doth us
affray,
Hunting thee hence with hunt's-up to the
day.
O, now be gone; more light and light it grows.

Rom. More light and light; more dark and
dark our woes!

Enter Nurse, *to the chamber.*

Nurse. Madam!
Jul. Nurse?
Nurse. Your lady mother is coming to
your chamber:
The day is broke; be wary, look about. [*Exit.*

Jul. Then, window, let day in, and let life
out.   41

Rom. Farewell, farewell! one kiss, and
I'll descend.   [*He goeth down.*

Jul. Art thou gone so? love, lord, ay,
husband, friend!
I must hear from thee every day in the
hour,
For in a minute there are many days:
O, by this count I shall be much in years
Ere I again behold my Romeo!

Rom.   Farewell!
I will omit no opportunity
That may convey my greetings, love, to thee.

Jul. O, think'st thou we shall ever meet
again?   51

Rom. I doubt it not; and all these woes
shall serve
For sweet discourses in our time to come.

Jul. O God, I have an ill-divining soul!
Methinks I see thee, now thou art below,
As one dead in the bottom of a tomb:
Either my eyesight fails, or thou look'st pale.

Rom. And trust me, love, in my eye so
do you:
Dry sorrow drinks our blood. Adieu, adieu!
[*Exit.*

Jul. O fortune, fortune! all men call thee
fickle: 60
If thou art fickle, what dost thou with him
That is renown'd for faith? Be fickle, for-
tune;
For then, I hope, thou wilt not keep him
long,
But send him back.

La. Cap. [*Within*] Ho, daughter! are you
up?   65

Jul. Who is 't that calls? is it my lady
mother?
Is she not down so late, or up so early?
What unaccustom'd cause procures her
hither?

Enter Lady Capulet.

La. Cap. Why, how now, Juliet!
Jul.   Madam, I am not well.
La. Cap. Evermore weeping for your cou-
sin's death?   70
What, wilt thou wash him from his grave
with tears?
An if thou couldst, thou couldst not make
him live;

---

8. **lace,** stripe. 20. **Cynthia's,** the moon's. 28.
sharps, high notes. 29. **division,** melody. 31. **change
eyes,** an allusion to a popular saying that the toad
and the lark had changed eyes, since the lark has ugly
eyes and the toad beautiful ones. 34. **hunt's-up,** a
song or tune to awaken huntsmen.

59. **Dry sorrow.** The heat of the body in sorrow and
despair was thought to descend into the bowels and dry
up the blood. 67. **down,** in bed. 68. **procures,** induces
to come.

Therefore, have done: some grief shows much
   of love;
But much of grief shows still some want of
   wit.
   Jul. Yet let me weep for such a feeling
   loss.
   La. Cap. So shall you feel the loss, but not
   the friend
Which you weep for.
   Jul.   Feeling so the loss,
I cannot choose but ever weep the friend.
   La. Cap. Well, girl, thou weep'st not so
   much for his death,
As that the villain lives which slaughter'd
   him.
   Jul. What villain, madam?
   La. Cap.   That same villain, Romeo. 81
   Jul. [*Aside*] Villain and he be many miles
   asunder.—
God pardon him! I do, with all my heart;
And yet no man like he doth grieve my
   heart.
   La. Cap. That is, because the traitor mur-
   derer lives.
   Jul. Ay, madam, from the reach of these
   my hands:
Would none but I might venge my cousin's
   death!
   La. Cap. We will have vengeance for it,
   fear thou not:
Then weep no more. I'll send to one in
   Mantua,
Where that same banish'd runagate doth
   live,   90
Shall give him such an unaccustom'd dram,
That he shall soon keep Tybalt company:
And then, I hope, thou wilt be satisfied.
   Jul. Indeed, I never shall be satisfied
With Romeo, till I behold him—dead—
Is my poor heart so for a kinsman vex'd:
Madam, if you could find out but a man
To bear a poison, I would temper it;
That Romeo should, upon receipt thereof, 99
Soon sleep in quiet. O, how my heart ab-
   hors
To hear him named, and cannot come to him,
To wreak the love I bore my cousin
Upon his body that hath slaughter'd him!
   La. Cap. Find thou the means, and I'll
   find such a man.
But now I'll tell thee joyful tidings, girl.

   Jul. And joy comes well in such a needy
   time:
What are they, I beseech your ladyship?
   La. Cap. Well, well, thou hast a careful
   father, child;
One who, to put thee from thy heaviness,
Hath sorted out a sudden day of joy,   110
That thou expect'st not nor I look'd not for.
   Jul. Madam, in happy time, what day is
   that?
   La. Cap. Marry, my child, early next
   Thursday morn,
The gallant, young and noble gentleman,
The County Paris, at Saint Peter's Church,
Shall happily make thee there a joyful bride.
   Jul. Now, by Saint Peter's Church and
   Peter too,
He shall not make me there a joyful bride.
I wonder at this haste; that I must wed
Ere he, that should be husband, comes to
   woo.   126
I pray you, tell my lord and father, madam,
I will not marry yet; and, when I do, I
   swear,
It shall be Romeo, whom you know I hate,
Rather than Paris. These are news indeed!
   La. Cap. Here comes your father; tell him
   so yourself,
And see how he will take it at your hands.

         Enter CAPULET *and* Nurse.

   Cap. When the sun sets, the air doth
   drizzle dew;
But for the sunset of my brother's son
It rains downright.
How now! a conduit, girl? what, still in tears?
Evermore showering? In one little body 131
Thou counterfeit'st a bark, a sea, a wind;
For still thy eyes, which I may call the sea,
Do ebb and flow with tears; the bark thy
   body is,
Sailing in this salt flood; the winds, thy
   sighs;
Who, raging with thy tears, and they with
   them,
Without a sudden calm, will overset
Thy tempest-tossed body. How now, wife!
Have you deliver'd to her our decree?
   La. Cap. Ay, sir; but she will none, she
   gives you thanks.   140
I would the fool were married to her grave!

---

84. **like**, so much as. 95. **dead.** This word is placed
between the clauses so that it can be understood either
with what precedes or what follows it. 98. **temper**,
used equivocally, meaning "to mix" or "to alloy."

112. **in happy time**, a vague expression like "by the
way." 130. **conduit**, water-pipe. 140. **will none**, refuses it.

Cap. Soft! take me with you, take me with you, wife.

How! will she none? doth she not give us thanks?

Is she not proud? doth she not count her blest,

Unworthy as she is, that we have wrought

So worthy a gentleman to be her bride-groom?

Jul. Not proud, you have; but thankful, that you have:

Proud can I never be of what I hate;

But thankful even for hate, that is meant love.

Cap. How now, how now, chop-logic! What is this?   150

'Proud,' and 'I thank you,' and 'I thank you not;'

And yet 'not proud:' mistress minion, you,

Thank me no thankings, nor proud me no prouds,

But fettle your fine joints 'gainst Thursday next,

To go with Paris to Saint Peter's Church,

Or I will drag thee on a hurdle thither.

Out, you green-sickness carrion! out, you baggage!

You tallow-face!

La. Cap.   Fie, fie! what, are you mad?

Jul. Good father, I beseech you on my knees,

Hear me with patience but to speak a word.

Cap. Hang thee, young baggage! dis-obedient wretch!   161

I tell thee what: get thee to church o' Thurs-day,

Or never after look me in the face:

Speak not, reply not, do not answer me;

My fingers itch. Wife, we scarce thought us blest

That God had lent us but this only child;

But now I see this one is one too much,

And that we have a curse in having her:

Out on her, hilding!

Nurse.   God in heaven bless her!

You are to blame, my lord, to rate her so.   170

Cap. And why, my lady wisdom? hold your tongue,

Good prudence; smatter with your gossips, go.

Nurse. I speak no treason.

Cap.   O, God ye god-den.

Nurse. May not one speak?

Cap.   Peace, you mumbling fool!

Utter your gravity o'er a gossip's bowl;

For here we need it not.

La. Cap.   You are too hot.

Cap. †God's bread! it makes me mad:

†Day, night, hour, tide, time, work, play,

Alone, in company, still my care hath been

To have her match'd: and having now pro-vided   180

A gentleman of noble parentage,

Of fair demesnes, youthful, and nobly train'd,

Stuff'd, as they say, with honourable parts,

Proportion'd as one's thought would wish a man;

And then to have a wretched puling fool,

A whining mammet, in her fortune's tender,

To answer 'I'll not wed; I cannot love,

I am too young; I pray you, pardon me.'

But, an you will not wed, I'll pardon you:

Graze where you will, you shall not house with me: 190

Look to 't, think on 't, I do not use to jest.

Thursday is near; lay hand on heart, advise:

An you be mine, I'll give you to my friend;

An you be not, hang, beg, starve, die in the streets,

For, by my soul, I'll ne'er acknowledge thee,

Nor what is mine shall never do thee good:

Trust to 't, bethink you; I'll not be forsworn.

[*Exit.*

Jul. Is there no pity sitting in the clouds,

That sees into the bottom of my grief?

O, sweet my mother, cast me not away!   200

Delay this marriage for a month, a week;

Or, if you do not, make the bridal bed

In that dim monument where Tybalt lies.

La. Cap. Talk not to me, for I'll not speak a word:

Do as thou wilt, for I have done with thee.

[*Exit.*

Jul. O God!—O nurse, how shall this be prevented?

My husband is on earth, my faith in heaven;

How shall that faith return again to earth,

142. **take me with you,** let me understand you. 145. **wrought,** procured. 150. **chop-logic,** a shallow and sophistical arguer. 152. **minion,** favored person; here used contemptuously. 154. **fettle,** make ready. 156. **hurdle,** a conveyance for criminals. 157. **green-sickness,** an anæmic ailment of young women; it suggests Juliet's paleness. 169. **hilding,** good-for-nothing. 170. **rate,** berate, scold.

172. **smatter,** chatter. 175. **gravity,** wisdom; used contemptuously. 177. **God's bread,** an oath by the sacrament. 182. **demesnes,** estates. 186. **mammet,** doll. **fortune's tender,** offer of good fortune. 207. **my faith in heaven.** Juliet refers to her marriage vows.

Unless that husband send it me from heaven
By leaving earth? comfort me, counsel me.
Alack, alack, that heaven should practise
    stratagems   211
Upon so soft a subject as myself!
What say'st thou? hast thou not a word of
    joy?
Some comfort, nurse.
    Nurse.   Faith, here it is.
Romeo is banish'd; and all the world to
    nothing,
That he dares ne'er come back to challenge
    you;
Or, if he do, it needs must be by stealth.
Then, since the case so stands as now it
    doth,
I think it best you married with the county.
O, he's a lovely gentleman!   220
Romeo's a dishclout to him: an eagle, mad-
    am,
Hath not so green, so quick, so fair an eye
As Paris hath. Beshrew my very heart,
I think you are happy in this second match,
For it excels your first: or if it did not,
Your first is dead; or 'twere as good he
    were,
As living here and you no use of him.
    Jul. Speakest thou from thy heart?
    Nurse.   And from my soul too;
Or else beshrew them both.
    Jul.   Amen!
    Nurse.   What?
    Jul. Well, thou hast comforted me mar-
    vellous much.   230
Go in; and tell my lady I am gone,
Having displeased my father, to Laurence'
    cell,
To make confession and to be absolved.
    Nurse. Marry, I will; and this is wisely
    done.   [*Exit.*
    Jul. Ancient damnation! O most wicked
    fiend!
Is it more sin to wish me thus forsworn,
Or to dispraise my lord with that same
    tongue
Which she hath praised him with above
    compare
So many thousand times? Go, counsellor;
Thou and my bosom henceforth shall be
    twain.   240
I'll to the friar, to know his remedy:
If all else fail, myself have power to die.[*Exit.*

---

   211. stratagems, dreadful deeds. **222. green.** Note
that green was an admired color for eyes.

ACT IV.

SCENE I. *Friar Laurence's cell.*

Enter FRIAR LAURENCE *and* PARIS.

    Fri. L. On Thursday, sir? the time is very
    short.
    Par. My father Capulet will have it so;
And I am nothing slow to slack his haste.
    Fri. L. You say you do not know the
    lady's mind:
Uneven is the course, I like it not.
    Par. Immoderately she weeps for Ty-
    balt's death,
And therefore have I little talk'd of love;
For Venus smiles not in a house of tears.
Now, sir, her father counts it dangerous
That she doth give her sorrow so much
    sway,   10
And in his wisdom hastes our marriage,
To stop the inundation of her tears;
Which, too much minded by herself alone,
May be put from her by society:
Now do you know the reason of this haste.
    Fri. L. [*Aside*] I would I knew not why
    it should be slow'd.
Look, sir, here comes the lady towards my
    cell.

Enter JULIET.

    Par. Happily met, my lady and my wife!
    Jul. That may be, sir, when I may be a
    wife.
    Par. That may be must be, love, on
    Thursday next.   20
    Jul. What must be shall be.
    Fri. L.   That's a certain text.
    Par. Come you to make confession to
    this father?
    Jul. To answer that, I should confess to
    you.
    Par. Do not deny to him that you love
    me.
    Jul. I will confess to you that I love him.
    Par. So will ye, I am sure, that you love
    me.
    Jul. If I do so, it will be of more price,
Being spoke behind your back, than to your
    face.
    Par. Poor soul, thy face is much abused
    with tears.
    Jul. The tears have got small victory by
    that;   30
For it was bad enough before their spite.

---

   5. Uneven, not straightforward.

Par. Thou wrong'st it, more than tears,
with that report.

Jul. That is no slander, sir, which is a
truth;
And what I spake, I spake it to my face.

Par. Thy face is mine, and thou hast
slander'd it.

Jul. It may be so, for it is not mine own.
Are you at leisure, holy father, now;
Or shall I come to you at evening mass?

Fri. L. My leisure serves me, pensive
daughter, now.
My lord, we must entreat the time alone. 40

Par. God shield I should disturb de-
votion!
Juliet, on Thursday early will I rouse ye:
Till then, adieu; and keep this holy kiss. [*Exit.*

Jul. O, shut the door! and when thou hast
done so,
Come weep with me; past hope, past cure,
past help!

Fri. L. Ah, Juliet, I already know thy
grief;
It strains me past the compass of my wits:
I hear thou must, and nothing may pro-
rogue it,
On Thursday next be married to this county.

Jul. Tell me not, friar, that thou hear'st
of this,　　　　　　　　　　50
Unless thou tell me how I may prevent it:
If, in thy wisdom, thou canst give no help,
Do thou but call my resolution wise,
And with this knife I'll help it presently.
God join'd my heart and Romeo's, thou our
hands;
And ere this hand, by thee to Romeo seal'd,
Shall be the label to another deed,
Or my true heart with treacherous revolt
Turn to another, this shall slay them both:
Therefore, out of thy long-experienced
time,　　　　　　　　　　60
Give me some present counsel, or, behold,
'Twixt my extremes and me this bloody knife
Shall play the umpire, arbitrating that
Which the commission of thy years and art
Could to no issue of true honour bring.
Be not so long to speak; I long to die,
If what thou speak'st speak not of remedy.

Fri. L. Hold, daughter: I do spy a kind
of hope,
Which craves as desperate an execution

As that is desperate which we would prevent.
If, rather than to marry County Paris,　71
Thou hast the strength of will to slay thyself,
Then is it likely thou wilt undertake
A thing like death to chide away this shame,
That copest with death himself to scape
from it;
And, if thou darest, I'll give thee remedy.

Jul. O, bid me leap, rather than marry
Paris,
From off the battlements of yonder tower;
Or walk in thievish ways; or bid me lurk
Where serpents are; chain me with roaring
bears;　　　　　　　　　　80
Or shut me nightly in a charnel-house,
O'er-cover'd quite with dead men's rattling
bones,
With reeky shanks and yellow chapless
skulls;
Or bid me go into a new-made grave
And hide me with a dead man in his shroud;
Things that, to hear them told, have made
me tremble;
And I will do it without fear or doubt,
To live an unstain'd wife to my sweet love.

Fri. L. Hold, then; go home, be merry,
give consent
To marry Paris: Wednesday is to-morrow: 90
To-morrow night look that thou lie alone;
Let not thy nurse lie with thee in thy
chamber:
Take thou this vial, being then in bed,
And this distilled liquor drink thou off;
When presently through all thy veins shall
run
A cold and drowsy humour, for no pulse
Shall keep his native progress, but surcease:
No warmth, no breath, shall testify thou
livest;
The roses in thy lips and cheeks shall fade
To paly ashes, thy eyes' windows fall,　100
Like death, when he shuts up the day of life;
Each part, deprived of supple government,
Shall, stiff and stark and cold, appear like
death:
And in this borrow'd likeness of shrunk
death
Thou shalt continue two and forty hours,
And then awake as from a pleasant sleep.
Now, when the bridegroom in the morning
comes

---

40. **entreat**, ask to have.　41. **shield**, prevent
(that).　57. **label**, a strip attached to a deed to carry the
seal.　62. **extremes**, extreme difficulties.　64. **commission**, authority.

83. **reeky**, malodorous.　**chapless**, without the lower
jaw.　96. **humour**, a morbid fluid supposed to pass
through the body as the effect of the drug.　97. **surcease**,
cessation.

To rouse thee from thy bed, there art thou
    dead:
Then, as the manner of our country is,
In thy best robes uncover'd on the bier   110
Thou shalt be borne to that same ancient
    vault
Where all the kindred of the Capulets lie.
In the mean time, against thou shalt awake,
Shall Romeo by my letters know our drift,
And hither shall he come: and he and I
Will watch thy waking, and that very night
Shall Romeo bear thee hence to Mantua.
And this shall free thee from this present
    shame;
If no inconstant toy, nor womanish fear,
Abate thy valour in the acting it.   120
    Jul. Give me, give me! O, tell not me of
      fear!
    Fri. L. Hold; get you gone, be strong and
      prosperous
In this resolve: I'll send a friar with speed
To Mantua, with my letters to thy lord.
    Jul. Love give me strength! and strength
      shall help afford.
Farewell, dear father!   [*Exeunt.*

    Scene II. *Hall in Capulet's house.*

Enter Capulet, Lady Capulet, Nurse, *and*
    two Servingmen.

    Cap. So many guests invite as here are
      writ.   [*Exit First Servant.*
Sirrah, go hire me twenty cunning cooks.
    Sec. Serv. You shall have none ill, sir; for
I'll try if they can lick their fingers.
    Cap. How canst thou try them so?
    Sec. Serv. Marry, sir, 'tis an ill cook that
cannot lick his own fingers: therefore he that
cannot lick his fingers goes not with me.
    Cap. Go, be gone.   [*Exit Sec. Servant.*
We shall be much unfurnish'd for this time.   10
What, is my daughter gone to Friar Laurence?
    Nurse. Ay, forsooth.
    Cap. Well, he may chance to do some
      good on her:
A peevish self-will'd harlotry it is.
    Nurse. See where she comes from shrift
      with merry look.

      Enter Juliet.

    Cap. How now, my headstrong! where
have you been gadding?

    Jul. Where I have learn'd me to repent
      the sin
Of disobedient opposition
To you and your behests, and am enjoin'd
By holy Laurence to fall prostrate here,   20
And beg your pardon: pardon, I beseech you!
Henceforward I am ever ruled by you.
    Cap. Send for the county; go tell him of
      this:
I'll have this knot knit up to-morrow morn-
      ing.
    Jul. I met the youthful lord at Laurence'
      cell;
And gave him what becomed love I might,
Not stepping o'er the bounds of modesty.
    Cap. Why, I am glad on 't; this is well:
      stand up:
This is as 't should be. Let me see the county;
Ay, marry, go, I say, and fetch him hither.   30
Now, afore God! this reverend holy friar,
All our whole city is much bound to him.
    Jul. Nurse, will you go with me into my
      closet,
To help me sort such needful ornaments
As you think fit to furnish me to-morrow?
    La. Cap. No, not till Thursday; there is
      time enough.
    Cap. Go, nurse, go with her: we'll to
      church to-morrow. [*Exeunt Juliet and*
                   Nurse.
    La. Cap. We shall be short in our pro-
      vision:
'Tis now near night.
    Cap.   Tush, I will stir about,
And all things shall be well, I warrant thee,
      wife: 40
Go thou to Juliet, help to deck up her;
I'll not to bed to-night; let me alone;
I'll play the housewife for this once. What,
    ho!
They are all forth. Well, I will walk myself
To County Paris, to prepare him up
Against to-morrow: my heart is wondrous
    light,
Since this same wayward girl is so reclaim'd.
                        [*Exeunt.*

    Scene III. *Juliet's chamber.*

      Enter Juliet *and* Nurse.

    Jul. Ay, those attires are best: but, gentle
      nurse,
I pray thee, leave me to myself to-night;

---

119. **toy,** idle fancy.
Scene ii. 14. **peevish,** silly. **harlotry,** hussy.

26. **becomed,** befitting.   33. **closet,** private room

For I have need of many orisons
To move the heavens to smile upon my state,
Which, well thou know'st, is cross and full
    of sin.

Enter LADY CAPULET.

La. Cap. What, are you busy, ho? need
    you my help?
Jul. No, madam; we have cull'd such
    necessaries
As are behoveful for our state to-morrow:
So please you, let me now be left alone,
And let the nurse this night sit up with you;
For, I am sure, you have your hands full
    all,
In this so sudden business.
La. Cap.   Good night:
Get thee to bed, and rest; for thou hast need.
              [*Exeunt Lady Capulet and Nurse.*
Jul. Farewell! God knows when we shall
    meet again.
I have a faint cold fear thrills through my
    veins,
That almost freezes up the heat of life:
I'll call them back again to comfort me:
Nurse! What should she do here?
My dismal scene I needs must act alone.
Come, vial.   20
What if this mixture do not work at all?
Shall I be married then to-morrow morning?
No, no: this shall forbid it: lie thou there.
              [*Laying down her dagger.*
What if it be a poison, which the friar
Subtly hath minister'd to have me dead,
Lest in this marriage he should be dis-
    honour'd,
Because he married me before to Romeo?
I fear it is: and yet, methinks, it should not,
For he hath still been tried a holy man.
How if, when I am laid into the tomb,   30
I wake before the time that Romeo
Come to redeem me? there's a fearful point!
Shall I not, then, be stifled in the vault,
To whose foul mouth no healthsome air
    breathes in,
And there die strangled ere my Romeo
    comes?
Or, if I live, is it not very like,
The horrible conceit of death and night,
Together with the terror of the place,—

As in a vault, an ancient receptacle,
Where, for these many hundred years, the
    bones   40
Of all my buried ancestors are pack'd:
Where bloody Tybalt, yet but green in earth,
Lies festering in his shroud; where, as they
    say,
At some hours in the night spirits resort;—
Alack, alack, is it not like that I,
So early waking, what with loathsome smells,
And shrieks like mandrakes' torn out of the
    earth,
That living mortals, hearing them, run
    mad:—
O, if I wake, shall I not be distraught,
Environed with all these hideous fears?   50
And madly play with my forefathers' joints?
And pluck the mangled Tybalt from his
    shroud?
And, in this rage, with some great kinsman's
    bone,
As with a club, dash out my desperate
    brains?
O, look! methinks I see my cousin's ghost
Seeking out Romeo, that did spit his body
Upon a rapier's point: stay, Tybalt, stay!
Romeo, I come! this do I drink to thee.
    [*She falls upon her bed, within the curtains.*

SCENE IV. *Hall in Capulet's house.*

Enter LADY CAPULET *and* Nurse.

La. Cap. Hold, take these keys, and fetch
    more spices, nurse.
Nurse. They call for dates and quinces in
    the pastry.

Enter CAPULET.

Cap. Come, stir, stir, stir! the second
    cock hath crow'd,
The curfew-bell hath rung, 'tis three o'clock:
Look to the baked meats, good Angelica:
Spare not for cost.
Nurse.   Go, you cot-quean, go,
Get you to bed; faith, you'll be sick to-
    morrow
For this night's watching.

---

3. **orisons,** prayers.   5. **cross,** contrary.   8. **behoveful,** needful.   **state,** station, dignity.   25. **minister'd,** administered (something healing or the reverse).
29. **tried,** proved.

39. **As,** namely.   47. **mandrakes'.** Mandragora or
mandrake was a narcotic plant, the root of which resembled the human form; it was fabled to utter a shriek
when torn from the ground.
Scene iv.   2. **pastry,** room in which pastry was made.
4. **curfew-bell,** apparently rung at other times than at
curfew.   5. **baked meats,** pies, pastry.   6. **cot-quean,**
a man who acts the housewife.   8. **watching,** waking.

Cap. No, not a whit: what! I have watch'd ere now
All night for lesser cause, and ne'er been sick.
    La. Cap. Ay, you have been a mouse-hunt in your time;   11
But I will watch you from such watching now. [*Exeunt Lady Capulet and Nurse.*
    Cap. A jealous-hood, a jealous-hood!

Enter three or four Servingmen, *with spits, logs, and baskets.*

                                    Now, fellow,
What's there?
    First Serv. Things for the cook, sir; but I know not what.
    Cap. Make haste, make haste. [*Exit First Serv.*] Sirrah, fetch drier logs:
Call Peter, he will show thee where they are.
    Sec. Serv. I have a head, sir, that will find out logs,
And never trouble Peter for the matter. [*Exit*
    Cap. Mass, and well said; a merry whore-son, ha!
Thou shalt be logger-head. Good faith, 'tis day: 20
The county will be here with music straight,
For so he said he would: I hear him near.
                                    [*Music within.*
Nurse! Wife! What, ho! What, nurse, I say!

Re-enter Nurse.

Go waken Juliet, go and trim her up;
I'll go and chat with Paris: hie, make haste,
Make haste; the bridegroom he is come already:
Make haste, I say.   [*Exeunt.*

SCENE V.   *Juliet's chamber.*

Enter Nurse.

    Nurse. Mistress! what, mistress! Juliet! fast, I warrant her, she:
Why, lamb! why, lady! fie, you slug-a-bed!
Why, love, I say! madam! sweet-heart! why, bride!
What, not a word? you take your penny-worths now;
Sleep for a week; for the next night, I warrant,

The County Paris hath set up his rest,
That you shall rest but little. God forgive me,
Marry, and amen, how sound is she asleep!
I must needs wake her. Madam, madam, madam!
Ay, let the county take you in your bed;   10
He'll fright you up, i' faith. Will it not be?
                            [*Undraws the curtains.*
What, dress'd! and in your clothes! and down again!
I must needs wake you: Lady! lady! lady!
Alas, alas! Help, help! my lady's dead!
O, well-a-day, that ever I was born!
Some aqua vitæ, ho! My lord! my lady!

Enter LADY CAPULET.

    La. Cap. What noise is here?
    Nurse.   O lamentable day!
    La. Cap. What is the matter?
    Nurse.   Look, look! O heavy day!
    La. Cap. O me, O me! My child, my only life,
Revive, look up, or I will die with thee!   20
Help, help! Call help.

Enter CAPULET.

    Cap. For shame, bring Juliet forth; her lord is come.
    Nurse. She's dead, deceased, she's dead; alack the day!
    La. Cap. Alack the day, she's dead, she's dead, she's dead!
    Cap. Ha! let me see her: out, alas! she's cold;
Her blood is settled, and her joints are stiff;
Life and these lips have long been separated:
Death lies on her like an untimely frost
Upon the sweetest flower of all the field.
    Nurse. O lamentable day!
    La. Cap.   O woful time!   30
    Cap. Death, that hath ta'en her hence to make me wail,
Ties up my tongue, and will not let me speak.

Enter FRIAR LAURENCE *and* PARIS, *with* Musicians.

    Fri. L. Come, is the bride ready to go to church?
    Cap. Ready to go, but never to return.
O son! the night before thy wedding-day

---

11. **mouse-hunt**, hunter of women. 13. **jealous-hood**, jealousy. 19. **Mass**, by the Mass. 20. **logger-head**, blockhead.
    Scene v. 1. **fast**, fast asleep. 4. **pennyworths**, little bits.

6. **set up his rest**, a phrase from the game of *primero* meaning to complete your hand and wager on it; hence, to be resolved. 26. **settled**, probably, congealed.

Hath Death lain with thy wife. There she
      lies,
Flower as she was, deflowered by him.
Death is my son-in-law, Death is my heir;
My daughter he hath wedded: I will die,
And leave him all; life, living, all is Death's.
    Par. Have I thought long to see this morn-
      ing's face,   41
And doth it give me such a sight as this?
    La. Cap. Accursed, unhappy, wretched,
      hateful day!
Most miserable hour that e'er time saw
In lasting labour of his pilgrimage!
But one, poor one, one poor and loving
      child,
But one thing to rejoice and solace in,
And cruel death hath catch'd it from my
      sight!
    Nurse. O woe! O woful, woful, woful day!
Most lamentable day, most woful day,   50
That ever, ever, I did yet behold!
O day! O day! O day! O hateful day!
Never was seen so black a day as this:
O woful day, O woful day!
    Par. Beguiled, divorced, wronged, spited,
      slain!
Most detestable death, by thee beguiled,
By cruel cruel thee quite overthrown!
O love! O life! not life, but love in death!
    Cap. Despised, distressed, hated, mar-
      tyr'd, kill'd!
Uncomfortable time, why camest thou now
To murder, murder our solemnity?   61
O child! O child! my soul, and not my
      child!
Dead art thou! Alack! my child is dead;
And with my child my joys are buried.
    Fri. L. Peace, ho, for shame! confusion's
      cure lives not
In these confusions. Heaven and yourself
Had part in this fair maid; now heaven
      hath all,
And all the better is it for the maid:
Your part in her you could not keep from
      death,
But heaven keeps his part in eternal life.   70
The most you sought was her promotion;
For 'twas your heaven she should be ad-
      vanced:
And weep ye now, seeing she is advanced
Above the clouds, as high as heaven itself?
O, in this love, you love your child so ill,

That you run mad, seeing that she is well:
She's not well married that lives married
      long;
But she's best married that dies married
      young.
Dry up your tears, and stick your rose-
      mary
On this fair corse; and, as the custom is,   80
In all her best array bear her to church:
For though fond nature bids us all la-
      ment,
Yet nature's tears are reason's merriment.
    Cap. All things that we ordained festival,
Turn from their office to black funeral;
Our instruments to melancholy bells,
Our wedding cheer to a sad burial feast,
Our solemn hymns to sullen dirges change,
Our bridal flowers serve for a buried corse,
And all things change them to the contrary. 90
    Fri. L. Sir, go you in; and, madam, go
      with him;
And go, Sir Paris; every one prepare
To follow this fair corse unto her grave:
The heavens do lour upon you for some ill;
Move them no more by crossing their high
      will.
                    [*Exeunt Capulet, Lady Capulet,
                              Paris, and Friar.*
    First Mus. Faith, we may put up our
pipes, and be gone.
    Nurse. Honest good fellows, ah, put up,
      put up;
For, well you know, this is a pitiful case. [*Exit.*
    First Mus. Ay, by my troth, the case may
be amended.   101

Enter PETER.

    Pet. Musicians, O, musicians, 'Heart's
ease, Heart's ease:' O, an you will have me
live, play 'Heart's ease.'
    First Mus. Why 'Heart's ease'?
    Pet. O, musicians, because my heart
itself plays 'My heart is full of woe:' O, play
me some merry dump, to comfort me.   108
    First Mus. Not a dump we; 'tis no time
to play now.

---

41. **thought long**, looked forward to. 61. **solemnity**, festivity. 65. **confusion's**, destruction's.

79. **rosemary**, symbol of immortality and enduring
love; therefore used at both funerals and weddings.
83. **Yet . . . merriment.** Nature is here used as the
opposite of reason. 101. **amended**, bettered. *Stage
Direction:* **Enter Peter.** Q₂ has *Enter Will Kemp.* This
well-known comic actor was a member of Shakespeare's
company and evidently played this part. His name was
written in probably by the prompter; hence one argues
that Q₂ was set up from a play-house copy. 102.
'Heart's ease,' popular tune, as also 'My heart is full
of woe,' line 107. 108. **dump**, mournful tune.

Pet. You will not, then?

First Mus. No.

Pet. I will then give it you soundly.

First Mus. What will you give us?

Pet. No money, on my faith, but the gleek; I will give you the minstrel.   116

First Mus. Then will I give you the serving-creature.

Pet. Then will I lay the serving-creature's dagger on your pate. I will carry no crotchets: I'll re you, I'll fa you; do you note me?   121

First Mus. An you re us and fa us, you note us.

Sec. Mus. Pray you, put up your dagger, and put out your wit.

Pet. Then have at you with my wit! I will dry-beat you with an iron wit, and put up my iron dagger. Answer me like men:
   'When griping grief the heart doth wound,
     And doleful dumps the mind oppress,
Then music with her silver sound'—   130
why 'silver sound'? why 'music with her silver sound'? What say you, Simon Catling?

First Mus. Marry, sir, because silver hath a sweet sound.

Pet. Pretty! What say you, Hugh Rebeck?

Sec. Mus. I say 'silver sound,' because musicians sound for silver.

Pet. Pretty too! What say you, James Soundpost?   139

Third Mus. Faith, I know not what to say.

Pet. O, I cry you mercy; you are the singer: I will say for you. It is 'music with her silver sound,' because musicians have no gold for sounding: 143
   'Then music with her silver sound
   With speedy help doth lend redress.'
                     [*Exit.*

First Mus. What a pestilent knave is this same!

Sec. Mus. Hang him, Jack! Come, we'll in here; tarry for the mourners, and stay dinner.   [*Exeunt.*

---

115. **gleek**, jest, gibe. 120. **carry**, endure. **crotchets**, meaning both "quarter notes" and "whims." 122. **note**, set to music; used punningly. 124. **put out**, exert. 128-130. **When . . . sound.** This is a part of a song by Richard Edwards preserved in the *Paradise of Daintie Devices* (1576). 132. **Catling.** A catling was a small lute string made of catgut. 135. **Rebeck.** A rebeck was a fiddle with three strings. 139. **Soundpost.** A soundpost is the pillar or peg which supports the body of a stringed instrument. 143. **sounding**, playing music.

ACT V.

SCENE I. *Mantua. A street.*

Enter ROMEO.

Rom. If I may trust the flattering truth of sleep,
My dreams presage some joyful news at hand:
My bosom's lord sits lightly in his throne;
And all this day an unaccustom'd spirit
Lifts me above the ground with cheerful thoughts.
I dreamt my lady came and found me dead—
Strange dream, that gives a dead man leave to think!—
And breathed such life with kisses in my lips,
That I revived, and was an emperor.
Ah me! how sweet is love itself possess'd,   10
When but love's shadows are so rich in joy!

Enter BALTHASAR, *booted.*

News from Verona!—How now, Balthasar!
Dost thou not bring me letters from the friar?
How doth my lady? Is my father well?
How fares my Juliet? that I ask again;
For nothing can be ill, if she be well.

Bal. Then she is well, and nothing can be ill:
Her body sleeps in Capels' monument,
And her immortal part with angels lives.
I saw her laid low in her kindred's vault,   20
And presently took post to tell it you:
O, pardon me for bringing these ill news,
Since you did leave it for my office, sir.

Rom. Is it even so? then I defy you, stars!
Thou know'st my lodging: get me ink and paper,
And hire post-horses; I will hence to-night.

Bal. I do beseech you, sir, have patience:
Your looks are pale and wild, and do import
Some misadventure.

Rom.   Tush, thou art deceived:
Leave me, and do the thing I bid thee do.   30
Hast thou no letters to me from the friar?

Bal. No, my good lord.

Rom.   No matter: get thee gone,

---

1. **flattering**, illusive. 2. **presage some joyful news.** The premonition here is ironical. 3. **bosom's lord**, heart. 11. **shadows**, phantoms. 21. **took post.** started with post horses. 24. **then I defy you, stars.** The fatalism of this utterance is in keeping with the other references to destiny in the play.

And hire those horses; I'll be with thee
straight. [*Exit Balthasar.*
Well, Juliet, I will lie with thee to-night.
Let's see for means: O mischief, thou art
swift
To enter in the thoughts of desperate men!
I do remember an apothecary,—
And hereabouts he dwells,—which late I
noted
In tatter'd weeds, with overwhelming brows,
Culling of simples; meagre were his looks, 40
Sharp misery had worn him to the bones:
And in his needy shop a tortoise hung,
An alligator stuff'd, and other skins
Of ill-shaped fishes; and about his shelves
A beggarly account of empty boxes,
Green earthen pots, bladders and musty
seeds,
Remnants of packthread and old cakes of
roses,
Were thinly scatter'd, to make up a show.
Noting this penury, to myself I said
'An if a man did need a poison now, 50
Whose sale is present death in Mantua,
Here lives a caitiff wretch would sell it him.'
O, this same thought did but forerun my
need;
And this same needy man must sell it me.
As I remember, this should be the house.
Being holiday, the beggar's shop is shut.
What, ho! apothecary!

Enter Apothecary.

Ap. Who calls so loud?
Rom. Come hither, man. I see that thou
art poor:
Hold, there is forty ducats: let me have
A dram of poison, such soon-speeding gear 60
As will disperse itself through all the veins
That the life-weary taker may fall dead
And that the trunk may be discharged of
breath
As violently as hasty powder fired
Doth hurry from the fatal cannon's womb.
Ap. Such mortal drugs I have; but
Mantua's law
Is death to any he that utters them.
Rom. Art thou so bare and full of wretch-
edness,

And fear'st to die? famine is in thy cheeks,
Need and oppression starveth in thine eyes,70
Contempt and beggary hangs upon thy back;
The world is not thy friend nor the world's
law;
The world affords no law to make thee rich;
Then be not poor, but break it, and take this.
Ap. My poverty, but not my will,
consents.
Rom. I pay thy poverty, and not thy will.
Ap. Put this in any liquid thing you will,
And drink it off; and, if you had the strength
Of twenty men, it would dispatch you
straight.
Rom. There is thy gold, worse poison to
men's souls, 80
Doing more murders in this loathsome
world,
Than these poor compounds that thou
mayst not sell.
I sell thee poison; thou hast sold me none.
Farewell: buy food, and get thyself in flesh.
Come, cordial and not poison, go with me
To Juliet's grave; for there must I use thee.
[*Exeunt.*

SCENE II. *Friar Laurence's cell.*

Enter FRIAR JOHN.

Fri. J. Holy Franciscan friar! brother,
ho!

Enter FRIAR LAURENCE.

Fri. L. This same should be the voice of
Friar John.
Welcome from Mantua: what says Romeo?
Or, if his mind be writ, give me his letter.
Fri. J. Going to find a bare-foot brother
out,
One of our order, to associate me,
Here in this city visiting the sick,
And finding him, the searchers of the town,
Suspecting that we both were in a house
Where the infectious pestilence did reign, 10
Seal'd up the doors, and would not let us
forth;
So that my speed to Mantua there was
stay'd.

39. weeds, clothes. overwhelming, overhanging. 40. simples, medicinal herbs. 45. beggarly account, poor array. 47. cakes of roses, rose petals caked to be used as perfume. 52. caitiff, poor. 59. ducats, coins, usually gold, of varying value. 63. trunk, body. 67. utters, issues, gives out.

80-86. There . . . thee, a passage of general reflection but slightly connected with the action and having no special appropriateness to Romeo.
Scene ii. 6. associate, accompany. 8. searchers, officers of the pestilence. 12. stay'd, stopped.

Fri. L. Who bare my letter, then, to
  Romeo?

Fri. J. I could not send it,—here it is
  again,—
Nor get a messenger to bring it thee,
So fearful were they of infection.

Fri. L. Unhappy fortune! by my brother-
  hood,
The letter was not nice but full of charge
Of dear import, and the neglecting it
May do much danger. Friar John, go hence;
Get me an iron crow, and bring it straight 21
Unto my cell.

Fri. J. Brother, I'll go and bring it thee.
  [*Exit.*

Fri. L. Now must I to the monument
  alone;
Within this three hours will fair Juliet wake:
She will beshrew me much that Romeo
Hath had no notice of these accidents;
But I will write again to Mantua,
And keep her at my cell till Romeo come; 29
Poor living corse, closed in a dead man's
  tomb! [*Exit.*

SCENE III. *A churchyard; in it a tomb
  belonging to the Capulets.*

Enter PARIS, *and his* Page *bearing flowers
  and a torch.*

Par. Give me thy torch, boy: hence, and
  stand aloof:
Yet put it out, for I would not be seen.
Under yond yew-trees lay thee all along,
Holding thine ear close to the hollow ground;
So shall no foot upon the churchyard tread,
Being loose, unfirm, with digging up of
  graves,
But thou shalt hear it: whistle then to me,
As signal that thou hear'st something
  approach.
Give me those flowers. Do as I bid thee, go.

Page. [*Aside*] I am almost afraid to stand
  alone 10
Here in the churchyard; yet I will adventure.
  [*Retires.*

Par. Sweet flower, with flowers thy bridal
  bed I strew,—
O woe! thy canopy is dust and stones;—
Which with sweet water nightly I will dew,

Or, wanting that, with tears distill'd by
  moans:
The obsequies that I for thee will keep
Nightly shall be to strew thy grave and
  weep. [*The Page whistles.*
The boy gives warning something doth
  approach.
What cursed foot wanders this way to-night,
To cross my obsequies and true love's rite? 20
What, with a torch! muffle me, night, awhile.
  [*Retires.*

Enter ROMEO *and* BALTHASAR, *with a torch,
  mattock, &c.*

Rom. Give me that mattock and the
  wrenching iron.
Hold, take this letter; early in the morning
See thou deliver it to my lord and father.
Give me the light: upon thy life, I charge
  thee,
Whate'er thou hear'st or seest, stand all
  aloof,
And do not interrupt me in my course.
Why I descend into this bed of death,
Is partly to behold my lady's face;
But chiefly to take thence from her dead
  finger
A precious ring, a ring that I must use 31
In dear employment: therefore hence, be
  gone:
But if thou, jealous, dost return to pry
In what I further shall intend to do,
By heaven, I will tear thee joint by joint
And strew this hungry churchyard with
  thy limbs:
The time and my intents are savage-wild,
More fierce and more inexorable far
Than empty tigers or the roaring sea.

Bal. I will be gone, sir, and not trouble
  you. 40

Rom. So shalt thou show me friendship.
  Take thou that:
Live, and be prosperous: and farewell, good
  fellow.

Bal. [*Aside*] For all this same, I'll hide me
  hereabout:
His looks I fear, and his intents I doubt.
  [*Retires.*

Rom. Thou detestable maw, thou womb
  of death,
Gorged with the dearest morsel of the earth,

18. **charge**, importance. 21. **iron crow**, crowbar.
Scene iii. 3. **all along**, at full length.

21. **muffle**, hide. 33. **jealous**, suspicious. 45-48.
Thou . . . food. The words of these lines seem to echo
the wrenching of the door.

Thus I enforce thy rotten jaws to open,
And, in despite, I'll cram thee with more
    food!   [*Opens the tomb.*
  Par. This is that banish'd haughty Mon-
    tague,
That murder'd my love's cousin, with which
    grief,   50
It is supposed, the fair creature died;
And here is come to do some villanous shame
To the dead bodies: I will apprehend him.
                  [*Comes forward.*
Stop thy unhallow'd toil, vile Montague!
Can vengeance be pursued further than
    death?
Condemned villain, I do apprehend thee:
Obey, and go with me; for thou must die.
  Rom. I must indeed; and therefore came
    I hither.
Good gentle youth, tempt not a desperate
    man;
Fly hence, and leave me: think upon these
    gone;   60
Let them affright thee. I beseech thee,
    youth,
Put not another sin upon my head,
By urging me to fury: O, be gone!
By heaven, I love thee better than myself;
For I come hither arm'd against myself:
Stay not, be gone; live, and hereafter say,
A madman's mercy bade thee run away.
  Par. I do defy thy conjurations,
And apprehend thee for a felon here.   69
  Rom. Wilt thou provoke me? then have
    at thee, boy!   [*They fight.*
  Page. O Lord, they fight! I will go call the
    watch.   [*Exit.*
  Par. O, I am slain! [*Falls.*] If thou be
    merciful,
Open the tomb, lay me with Juliet. [*Dies.*
  Rom. In faith, I will. Let me peruse this
    face.
Mercutio's kinsman, noble County Paris!
What said my man, when my betossed soul
Did not attend him as we rode? I think
He told me Paris should have married Juliet:
Said he not so? or did I dream it so?
Or am I mad, hearing him talk of Juliet,   80
To think it was so? O, give me thy hand,
One writ with me in sour misfortune's book!
I'll bury thee in a triumphant grave;
A grave? O, no! a lantern, slaughter'd youth,

For here lies Juliet, and her beauty makes
This vault a feasting presence full of light.
Death, lie thou there, by a dead man interr'd.
          [*Laying Paris in the tomb.*
How oft when men are at the point of
    death
Have they been merry! which their keepers
    call
A lightning before death: O, how may I   90
Call this a lightning? O my love! my wife!
Death, that hath suck'd the honey of thy
    breath,
Hath had no power yet upon thy beauty:
Thou art not conquer'd; beauty's ensign
    yet
Is crimson in thy lips and in thy cheeks,
And death's pale flag is not advanced there.
Tybalt, liest thou there in thy bloody sheet?
O, what more favour can I do to thee,
Than with that hand that cut thy youth in
    twain
To sunder his that was thine enemy?   100
Forgive me, cousin! Ah, dear Juliet,
Why art thou yet so fair? shall I believe
That unsubstantial death is amorous,
And that the lean abhorred monster keeps
Thee here in dark to be his paramour?
For fear of that, I still will stay with thee;
And never from this palace of dim night
Depart again: here, here will I remain
With worms that are thy chamber-maids; O,
    here
Will I set up my everlasting rest,   110
And shake the yoke of inauspicious stars
From this world-wearied flesh. Eyes, look
    your last!
Arms, take your last embrace! and, lips, O
    you
The doors of breath, seal with a righteous
    kiss
A dateless bargain to engrossing death!
Come, bitter conduct, come, unsavoury
    guide!
Thou desperate pilot, now at once run on
The dashing rocks thy sea-sick weary bark!
Here's to my love! [*Drinks.*] O true apothe-
    cary!
Thy drugs are quick. Thus with a kiss I die.
                    [*Dies.*

---

68. **conjurations**, solemn appeals, which seem perhaps like incantations.   74. **peruse**, scrutinize.   84.
lantern, a turret full of windows.   86. **presence**, presence-chamber.   90. **lightning**,
a shedding of light; also, a revival of the spirits.   110.
set up my everlasting rest. See IV, v. 6. The meaning is "make my final determination," with allusion
also to the idea of repose.   115. **dateless**, everlasting.
engrossing, monopolizing.

Enter, at the other end of the churchyard,
FRIAR LAURENCE, *with a lantern, crow,*
and spade.

Fri. L. Saint Francis be my speed! how
    oft to-night   121
Have my old feet stumbled at graves! Who's
    there?
Bal. Here's one, a friend, and one that
    knows you well.
Fri. L. Bliss be upon you! Tell me, good
    my friend,
What torch is yond, that vainly lends his
    light
To grubs and eyeless skulls? as I discern,
It burneth in the Capels' monument.
Bal. It doth so, holy sir; and there's my
    master,
One that you love.
Fri. L.   Who is it?
Bal.   Romeo.
Fri. L. How long hath he been there?
Bal.   Full half an hour. 130
Fri. L. Go with me to the vault.
Bal.   I dare not, sir:
My master knows not but I am gone hence;
And fearfully did menace me with death,
If I did stay to look on his intents.
Fri. L. Stay, then; I'll go alone. Fear
    comes upon me:
O, much I fear some ill unlucky thing.
Bal. As I did sleep under this yew-tree
    here,
I dreamt my master and another fought,
And that my master slew him.
Fri. L.   Romeo! [*Advances.*
Alack, alack, what blood is this, which stains
The stony entrance of this sepulchre?   141
What mean these masterless and gory swords
To lie discolour'd by this place of peace?
    [*Enters the tomb.*
Romeo! O, pale! Who else? what, Paris
    too?
And steep'd in blood? Ah, what an unkind
    hour
Is guilty of this lamentable chance!
The lady stirs.   [*Juliet wakes.*
Jul. O comfortable friar! where is my
    lord?
I do remember well where I should be,
And there I am. Where is my Romeo?   150
    [*Noise within.*

Fri. L. I hear some noise. Lady, come
    from that nest
Of death, contagion, and unnatural sleep:
A greater power than we can contradict
Hath thwarted our intents. Come, come
    away.
Thy husband in thy bosom there lies dead;
And Paris too. Come, I'll dispose of thee
Among a sisterhood of holy nuns:
Stay not to question, for the watch is com-
    ing;
Come, go, good Juliet [*Noise again*], I dare
    no longer stay.
Jul. Go, get thee hence, for I will not
    away.   [*Exit Fri. L.*
What's here? a cup, closed in my true love's
    hand?   161
Poison, I see, hath been his timeless end:
O churl! drunk all, and left no friendly drop
To help me after? I will kiss thy lips;
Haply some poison yet doth hang on them,
To make me die with a restorative.
    [*Kisses him.*
Thy lips are warm.
First Watch. [*Within*] Lead, boy: which
    way?
Jul. Yea, noise? then I'll be brief. O
    happy dagger! [*Snatching Romeo's dagger.*
This is thy sheath [*Stabs herself*]; there rust,
    and let me die.   170
    [*Falls on Romeo's body, and dies.*

Enter Watch, *with the* Page *of* PARIS.

Page. This is the place; there, where the
    torch doth burn.
First Watch. The ground is bloody; search
    about the churchyard:
Go, some of you, whoe'er you find attach.
Pitiful sight! here lies the county slain;
And Juliet bleeding, warm, and newly dead,
Who here hath lain these two days buried.
Go, tell the prince: run to the Capulets:
Raise up the Montagues: some others search:
We see the ground whereon these woes do lie;
But the true ground of all these piteous woes
We cannot without circumstance descry.   181

Re-enter some of the Watch, *with* BALTHASAR.

Sec. Watch. Here's Romeo's man; we
    found him in the churchyard.
First Watch. Hold him in safety, till the
    prince come hither.

---

121. **speed**, protector and assistant. 122. **stumbled
at graves**, a bad omen. 148. **comfortable**, comforting.

162. **timeless**, everlasting, or untimely. 165. **Haply**,
perhaps. 173. **attach**, arrest.

Re-enter others of the Watch, *with* Friar
Laurence.

Third Watch. Here is a friar, that trembles, sighs, and weeps:
We took this mattock and this spade from
him,
As he was coming from this churchyard side.
First Watch. A great suspicion: stay the
friar too.

Enter the Prince *and* Attendants.

Prince. What misadventure is so early up,
That calls our person from our morning's
rest?

Enter Capulet, Lady Capulet, *and others.*

Cap. What should it be, that they so
shriek abroad?   190
La. Cap. The people in the street cry
Romeo,
Some Juliet, and some Paris; and all run,
With open outcry, toward our monument.
Prince. What fear is this which startles
in our ears?
First Watch. Sovereign, here lies the
County Paris slain;
And Romeo dead; and Juliet, dead before,
Warm and new kill'd.
Prince. Search, seek, and know how this
foul murder comes.
First Watch. Here is a friar, and slaugh-
ter'd Romeo's man;
With instruments upon them, fit to open 200
These dead men's tombs.
Cap. O heavens! O wife, look how our
daughter bleeds!
This dagger hath mista'en,—for, lo, his house
Is empty on the back of Montague,—
And it mis-sheathed in my daughter's bosom!
La. Cap. O me! this sight of death is as
a bell,
That warns my old age to a sepulchre.

Enter Montague *and others.*

Prince. Come, Montague; for thou art
early up,
To see thy son and heir more early down.
Mon. Alas, my liege, my wife is dead to-
night;   210
Grief of my son's exile hath stopp'd her
breath:

What further woe conspires against mine
age?
Prince. Look, and thou shalt see.
Mon. O thou untaught! what manners
is in this,
To press before thy father to a grave?
Prince. Seal up the mouth of outrage for
a while,
Till we can clear these ambiguities,
And know their spring, their head, their true
descent;
And then will I be general of your woes,
And lead you even to death: meantime for-
bear,   220
And let mischance be slave to patience.
Bring forth the parties of suspicion.
Fri. L. I am the greatest, able to do least,
Yet most suspected, as the time and place
Doth make against me, of this direful
murder:
And here I stand, both to impeach and purge
Myself condemned and myself excused.
Prince. Then say at once what thou dost
know in this.
Fri. L. I will be brief, for my short date
of breath
Is not so long as is a tedious tale.   230
Romeo, there dead, was husband to that
Juliet;
And she, there dead, that Romeo's faithful
wife:
I married them; and their stol'n marriage-
day
Was Tybalt's dooms-day, whose untimely
death
Banish'd the new-made bridegroom from
this city,
For whom, and not for Tybalt, Juliet pined.
You, to remove that siege of grief from her,
Betroth'd and would have married her
perforce
To County Paris: then comes she to me,
And, with wild looks, bid me devise some
mean   240
To rid her from this second marriage,
Or in my cell there would she kill herself.
Then gave I her, so tutor'd by my art,
A sleeping potion; which so took effect
As I intended, for it wrought on her
The form of death: meantime I writ to
Romeo,
That he should hither come as this dire night,

203. **house**, scabbard.

216. **outrage**, outcry.   226. **purge**, purify, cleanse.
247. **as this**, this very.

To help to take her from her borrow'd grave,
Being the time the potion's force should
   cease.
But he which bore my letter, Friar John, 250
Was stay'd by accident, and yesternight
Return'd my letter back. Then all alone
At the prefixed hour of her waking,
Came I to take her from her kindred's vault;
Meaning to keep her closely at my cell,
Till I conveniently could send to Romeo:
But when I came, some minute ere the time
Of her awaking, here untimely lay
The noble Paris and true Romeo dead.
She wakes; and I entreated her come forth, 260
And bear this work of heaven with patience:
But then a noise did scare me from the tomb;
And she, too desperate, would not go with
   me,
But, as it seems, did violence on herself.
All this I know; and to the marriage
Her nurse is privy: and, if aught in this
Miscarried by my fault, let my old life
Be sacrificed, some hour before his time,
Unto the rigour of severest law.
   Prince. We still have known thee for a
   holy man.   270
Where's Romeo's man? what can he say in
   this?
   Bal. I brought my master news of Juliet's
   death;
And then in post he came from Mantua
To this same place, to this same monument.
This letter he early bid me give his father,
And threaten'd me with death, going in the
   vault,
If I departed not and left him there.
   Prince. Give me the letter; I will look on
   it.
Where is the county's page, that raised the
   watch?
Sirrah, what made your master in this place?
   Page. He came with flowers to strew his
   lady's grave;   281

And bid me stand aloof, and so I did:
Anon comes one with light to ope the tomb;
And by and by my master drew on him;
And then I ran away to call the watch.
   Prince. This letter doth make good the
   friar's words,
Their course of love, the tidings of her
   death:
And here he writes that he did buy a poison
Of a poor 'pothecary, and therewithal   289
Came to this vault to die, and lie with Juli-
   et.
Where be these enemies? Capulet! Mon-
   tague!
See, what a scourge is laid upon your hate,
That heaven finds means to kill your joys
   with love.
And I for winking at your discords too
Have lost a brace of kinsmen: all are
   punish'd.
   Cap. O brother Montague, give me thy
   hand:
This is my daughter's jointure, for no more
Can I demand.
   Mon.   But I can give thee more:
For I will raise her statue in pure gold;
That while Verona by that name is known, 300
There shall no figure at such rate be set
As that of true and faithful Juliet.
   Cap. As rich shall Romeo's by his lady's
   lie;
Poor sacrifices of our enmity!
   Prince. A glooming peace this morning
   with it brings;
The sun, for sorrow, will not show his
   head:
Go hence, to have more talk of these sad
   things;
Some shall be pardon'd, and some pun-
   ished:
For never was a story of more woe
Than this of Juliet and her Romeo.   310
                        [*Exeunt.*

253. **prefixed**, agreed upon previously. 255. **closely**,
secretly. 273. **post**, haste. 280. **made**, was doing.

297. **jointure**, marriage portion. 301. **rate**, value.

THE PERIOD OF COMEDIES AND HISTORIES

I. SHAKESPEARE'S LIFE AND TIMES, 1595-1600

Shakespeare had achieved a reputation as a poet by the year 1594, possibly the greatest reputation he achieved during his lifetime, by the publication of *Venus and Adonis* and *The Rape of Lucrece*, and possibly also by the circulation in manuscript of the *Sonnets*. Anonymous verses prefixed to the poem *Willobie his Avisa* (1594) give us the earliest tribute to Shakespeare as a poet:

Though *Collatine* haue deerely bought,
To high renowne, a lasting life,
And found, that most in vaine haue sought,
To haue a *Faire* and *Constant* wife,
  Yet *Tarquyne* pluckt his glistering grape,
  And *Shake-speare*, paints poor *Lucrece* rape.

Some unnecessary doubt has always been attached to a more significant tribute from the hand of Edmund Spenser in *Colin Clout's Come Home Again*, written in 1594, wherein Spakespeare appears as Aetion, "though last, not least," in the list of contemporary poets:

A gentler shepheard may no where be found:
Whose Muse, full of high thoughts inuention,
Doth like himselfe Heroically sound.

When one considers that the writing of plays was not regarded by Shakespeare himself, or by others of his time, as literary work in a true sense, it is somewhat surprising that Shakespeare's work as a dramatist was acknowledged as generously as it was during the period from 1594 to 1600. In the six or seven literary allusions to Shakespeare during the period, the poems are, however, obviously regarded as of more significance than the plays. To know the story of Shakespeare's life we should consider these references.

Of them the most important as a document, if not as a tribute, is the passage in

Palladis Tamia (1598) by Francis Meres already quoted (see p. 41), in which Meres declares that the English tongue has been enriched by Sir Philip Sidney, Spenser, Daniel, Drayton, Warner, Shakespeare, Marlowe, and Chapman, even as the Greek tongue was enriched by Homer, Hesiod, and others, and the Latin tongue enriched by Virgil, Ovid, and Horace. He thinks that "the sweet witty soul of Ovid" lives in "mellifluous and honey-tongued" Shakespeare, as witnessed by his *Venus and Adonis*, his *Lucrece*, and "his sugared Sonnets among his private friends." Meres next introduces his famous comparison of Shakespeare to the Latin tragedy writer Seneca and the Latin comedy writer Plautus, declaring that Shakespeare is as excellent among the English for both tragedy and comedy as were Seneca and Plautus, respectively, for each of the two kinds, in witness whereof he cites six comedies, all extant except one which he calls "Loves Labors Wonne," and six tragedies, or rather the two tragedies, *Titus Andronicus* and *Romeo and Juliet*, and four history plays. Elsewhere in the book Meres again mentions Shakespeare in a list of the best English writers of lyric poetry, comedy, tragedy, and love poetry.

Next to this in importance perhaps is Weever's epigram *Ad Gulielmum Shakespeare* in *Epigrams in the Oldest Cut and the Newest Fashion*, published in 1599, but probably written before 1597:

Honie-tong'd *Shakespeare*, when I saw thine issue,
I swore *Apollo* got them and none other,
Their rosie-tainted features cloth'd in tissue,
Some heauen born goddesse said to be their
  mother:
Rose-cheekt *Adonis* with his amber tresses,
Faire fire-hot *Venus* charming him to loue her,

287

Chaste *Lucretia* virgine-like her dresses,
Prowd lust-stung *Tarquine* seeking still to proue
  her:
Romea Richard; more, whose names I know not,
Their sugred tongues, and power attractiue beuty
Say they are Saints, althogh that Sts they shew
  not,
For thousands vow to them subiectiue dutie:
They burn in loue thy children. *Shakespeare* het
  them,
Go, wo thy Muse more Nymphish brood beget
  them.

The last lines seem to indicate a desire on
Weever's part that Shakespeare should
write poetry rather than seek the applause
of thousands by writing plays for the
theater.

A somewhat similar allusion to those already given occurs in a poem called *A Remembrance of Some English Poets* in Richard
Barnfield's *Poems in Divers Humors* (1598):

And *Shakespeare* thou, whose hony-flowing Vaine,
(Pleasing the World) thy Praises doth obtaine.
Whose *Venus*, and whose *Lucrece* (sweete, and
  chaste)
Thy Name in fames immortall Booke haue plac't.
  Liue euer you, at least in Fame liue euer:
  Well may the Bodye dye, but Fame dies neuer.

Gabriel Harvey's marginal note (see page
115) in a copy of Speght's Chaucer, made as
early as 1598-1601, should also be mentioned.

One of the most interesting and puzzling
evidences of Shakespeare's growth in fame
comes from a trilogy by Cambridge students called the Parnassus plays, usually
dated in the years 1598-1602. The third of
the series of three dramatic satires was the
only one contemporaneously published.
The Return from Parnassus was issued in
1606 as publicly acted by the students of
St. John's College, Cambridge. The other
two parts, the first of which is known as
The Pilgrimage to Parnassus, remained in
manuscript until recent times. The Parnassus plays are made up of academic satire
against the ways of the world. At one point
in the second member of the trilogy (*2 Parnassus*, ed. W. D. Macray, 1886), Burbage and Kemp come in, boast of their
victory over Ben Jonson, and try to recruit
other poets into the service of writing plays
for them. The poets are unwilling to subject their muses to the thraldom of the
stage. The undergraduate authors are apparently impressed with the fame of Shake-

speare. Gullio, a would-be patron of the
poets, appropriates bits from Shakespeare,
and Ingenioso says,

We shall have nothing but Shakespeare and
shreds of poetry that he hath gathered at the
theatres. (ll. 1009 ff.)

And again,

Mark, Romeo and Juliet! O monstrous theft!
  (l. 1015.)

After Gullio has recited six lines from *Venus
and Adonis* as his own, Ingenioso remarks,
"Sweet Mr. Shakespeare!" (ll. 1018-1024.)
Later Gullio asks Ingenioso, an affected
courtier, to write a poem for him:

Ingen. My pen is your bounden vassal to
command. But what vein would it please you
to have them in?
Gull. Not in a vain vein (pretty, i' faith!):
make me them in two or three divers veins—in
Chaucer's, Gower's, Spenser's, and Mr. Shakespeare's. Marry, I think I shall entertain those
verses which run like these:
  Even as the sun with purple color'd face
  Had ta'en his last leave on the weeping morn,
    etc.
O sweet Mr. Shakespeare! I'le have his picture in
my study at the court. (ll. 1048 ff.)

Still later, when Ingenioso recites seven
lines in imitation of *Venus and Adonis*,
Gullio says,

No more! I am one that can judge according
to the proverb, "bovem ex unguibus." Ay,
marry, Sir, these have some life in them! Let
this duncified world esteem of Spenser and
Chaucer, I'll worship sweet Mr. Shakespeare, and
to honour him will lay his Venus and Adonis
under my pillow, as we read of one (I do not well
remember his name, but I am sure he was a king)
slept with Homer under his bed's head. (Ll. 1211-
1227.)

Shakespeare had thus become fashionable
among poetically minded young persons at
the university.

We are also enabled to infer a good many
circumstances of Shakespeare's private life
from the public records left of him for the
years 1594 to 1600. The most general of
the inferences to be drawn from these records is that he was successful and prosperous. His company at the Theater, and after
1599 at the Globe, was popular, and we may
believe in general had the better of its
rivals, the Lord Admiral's men, under
Henslowe's management at the Rose.

Whether the company is the same as the one above referred to as Lord Strange's company or not, they were certainly reconstituted about 1594 under the special influences of the family of Burbage. James Burbage, the father, was owner of the Theater; Cuthbert Burbage was a manager; and Richard Burbage became the principal actor of the troupe. The Theater operated as a sort of joint stock company of ten shares, of which the Burbages owned five and Shakespeare and four other principal actors of his company one each. Not only was Shakespeare a full-sharing actor, but he was also the principal playwright of the company.

His prosperity appears in the first record of his residence in London. The tax returns, or Subsidy Rolls, of a parliamentary subsidy granted to Queen Elizabeth for the year 1596, show Shakespeare resident in the parish of St. Helen's, Bishopsgate, near the Theater, and assessed at the respectable sum of £5. By the next year Shakespeare had evidently moved to Southwark near the Bear Garden, for the returns from Bishopsgate show his taxes delinquent. He was later located and the taxes paid. Meantime, in August 1596, his only son Hamnet was buried at Stratford. In the Public Record Office is the summary of a deed by which Shakespeare became owner by purchase of New Place in Stratford, the second largest house in the town, and a house of considerable size and importance. Shakespeare's family entered the house as residents shortly after the purchase and continued there until long after Shakespeare's death. The last of his family, his granddaughter Lady Bernard, died in 1670, and New Place was sold. Shakespeare was also interested in the purchase of land at Shottery in 1598, was listed among the chief holders of corn and malt in Stratford that same year, and sold a load of stone to the Stratford corporation in 1599.

More suggestive of Shakespeare's rapid rise in the world is his acquisition of the right to bear arms, or, in other words, his establishment in the rank and title of gentleman. The Herald's College in London preserves two drafts of a grant of arms to Shakespeare's father devised by one William Dethick and dated October 20, 1596. Although we may certainly believe that the application was put forward by William Shakespeare, John Shakespeare was still living, and the grant was drawn up in the father's name. The device for Shakespeare's coat of arms makes a somewhat easy use of the meaning of his name:

Gold on a bend sable a spear of the first, the point steeled, proper; and for his crest or cognizance a falcon, his wings displayed, argent, standing on a wreath of his colour supporting a spear—gold—steeled as aforesaid, set upon a helmet with mantels and tassels as hath been accustomed.

According to the second document, John Shakespeare, at the height of his prosperity as a Stratford burgher, had applied twenty years before to the College of Heralds in London for authority to bear arms, though the family had probably not been able to meet the expense of seeing it through until William Shakespeare had made his fortune. The grant of heraldic honors to John Shakespeare was confirmed in 1599.

Professor Leslie Hotson has recently discovered in the records of the Court of the Queen's Bench, Michaelmas term 1596, a writ against William Shakespeare, Francis Langley, and others, in which one William Wayte sought "for fear of death" to have these persons bound over to keep the peace. Among earlier entries for the same term was found a similar writ sworn out by Langley against William Gardener and William Wayte. There was evidently a quarrel between two sets of persons. Langley was owner of The Swan, and he and Shakespeare were probably associated there. Gardener was a wealthy and tyrannical justice of the peace; Wayte was his stepson. No evidence appeared as to what the quarrel was about; but, since Gardener seems to have been a meddlesome and greedy person, since he used by right of his wife (*née* Lucy) three white luces as his coat of arms, and since Wayte was a feeble character, and for other reasons, Professor Hotson believes he has found in Gardener and Wayte prototypes for Justice Shallow and his Cousin Slender. Shakespeare, he thinks, revenged himself for persecutions at the hands of Gardener by drawing portraits of them in *2 Henry IV* and *The Merry Wives of Windsor*. The latter play must, in that case, have been written soon after the autumn of 1596. Professor Hotson's interpretation of his discovery has been vigorously assailed.[1]

During this period also Shakespeare's name appeared on the title-pages of the second and third editions of *Richard II* (1598), the second edition of *Richard III* (1598), and *Love's Labour's Lost* (1598). The printer William Jaggard issued in 1599 a small volume containing twenty poems, five of which were certainly by Shakespeare. He attributed to Shakespeare the whole volume which bore the title, *The Passionate Pilgrim*. It contained four sonnets, two from the sonnet-cycle and two from the fourth act of *Love's Labour's Lost*, as well as the lyric "On a day, alack the day!" from the same play.

Contemporary drama In this particular period Shakespeare was no doubt in the contemporary view the leading dramatist. The earlier group on whose work he patterned his own were either dead or silent. The great group who were to rival him and ultimately surpass him in popular favor had not yet fairly begun. Of Jonson's earliest work little is known. An early version of *The Case is Altered* may have been written as early as 1597, but practically he becomes a great new force at the end of this period with *Every Man in his Humour* in 1598 and *Every Man out of his Humour* in 1599. He began in these plays the comedy of humors or individual eccentricities, what might be called the comedy of the personal bias. We have from George Chapman two unimportant plays of the "humors" type: *The Blind Beggar of Alexandria* in 1596 and *An Humorous Day's Mirth* in 1597. He was probably busy as a playwright during the period, but had not yet opened his characteristic vein of learning and rhetoric. Thomas Dekker was well under way, and was doing hack work for Philip Henslowe: *Old Fortunatus* and *The Shoemaker's Holiday* belong to 1599, *Patient Grissell* to 1600. He did not have it in him to rival Shakespeare or to institute anything new, though he has his own special excellences. Thomas Heywood, who has been called a "prose Shakespeare," was in a similar situation to

that of Dekker in the services of Henslowe. Heywood's early plays are lost. John Marston's short and rather acrid career as a dramatist was beginning. *Antonio and Mellida* belongs to 1599. His career as a satirist had begun with *The Metamorphosis of Pygmalion's Image* and *The Scourge of Villainy* in 1598. For the rest, there were Haughton, Munday, Chettle, Daniel, Porter, and a host of persons of whom we know only the name and one or two plays. Henry Porter's *The Two Angry Women of Abingdon*, the anonymous *Edward III* and *Captain Thomas Stukeley*, and *The Merry Devil of Edmonton* (attributed to Drayton) stand out with some special significance for the study of Shakespeare.

Contemporary non-dramatic literature Important things in non-dramatic literature were also achieved between 1594 and 1600. Four books of Richard Hooker's great work *The Laws of Ecclesiastical Polity* came out in 1594. Spenser's *Colin Clout, Astrophel, Epithalamium*, and the *Amoretti* were published in 1595; *The Faerie Queene*, Bks. IV-VI with the *Four Hymns* and *Prothalamium* in 1596. Daniel's *Civil Wars* was published in 1595. The first edition of Bacon's *Essays*, ten brief highly concentrated bundles of apothegms, appeared in 1597; Sir John Davies' noble poem *Nosce Teipsum* in 1599; Hall's *Satires* in 1597 and 1598. A large part of Chapman's translation of the *Iliad* and Joshua Sylvester's *Divine Weeks and Works* of Du Bartas were published in 1598, Fairfax's translation of Tasso's *Jerusalem Delivered* in 1600. Aleman's *Guzman de Alfarache*, a popular Spanish rogue story, appeared in Madrid in 1599. Thomas Nashe had published *The Unfortunate Traveller*, better known as "Jack Wilton," the first of the many English picaresque novels, in 1594. Finally, one likes to remember that Stow's *Survey of the Cities of London and Westminster* and the first volume of Richard Hakluyt's *Voyages* (final form) both belong to the year 1598.

During this period (1594-1600) Shakespeare probably wrote the following plays: In 1594-5, *The Taming of the Shrew* and *The Merchant of Venice;* in 1595-6, *King John* and *Richard II;* in 1596, *1 Henry IV;* in 1597, *2 Henry IV* and a revised version

---

[1] Leslie Hotson, *Shakespeare versus Shallow*, Boston, 1931; for comments see "Recent Literature of the English Renaissance," Sect. III, *Studies in Philology*, April Nos.

of *Love's Labour's Lost;* in 1598, a revised version of *Romeo and Juliet* and *Much Ado about Nothing;* in 1599, *Henry V* and *Julius Cæsar,* possibly *The Merry Wives of Windsor,* though that play may be later; in 1600, *As You Like It* and *Twelfth Night.*

It may be worth while to call attention at this time to the great series of historical plays as possibly, from the point of view of English literature as a whole, one of Shakespeare's most important achievements. England lived for years after the defeat of the Armada in a wave of patriotic fervor, so that the people demanded for their instruction and edification plays on national themes. To satisfy popular taste Shakespeare supplied them, but did not do so in a mercenary or indifferent way. The subjects were, without exception, old. Shakespeare gave them new treatment on the basis of a new and often painstaking examination of sources and on the basis of his own genius as a national poet. It will be remembered that the group of four plays beginning with *1 Henry VI* and ending with *Richard III,* which comes later in historical time, was written before the group of four plays which begins with *Richard II* and ends with *Henry V.*

Another great achievement of the period is Shakespeare's mastery of comedy. With him it is not pure comedy, not a mere matter of fun or of the antics and interplay of the rogue and the fool, since there is always

a serious element in the plot. Some worthy man or cause is in jeopardy. At this stage in his career, however, this element rarely threatens disaster so darkly as to color the whole play. Shakespeare's comedies are not yet tragi-comedies; still less are they problem-plays. If he was ever to show doubts about the moral structure of the universe, that time had not come. There is about the comedies of the middle period the freshness of English landscape and country and a realistic conception of the qualities of ordinary English life. At that time no writer knew theoretically much about the depiction of character; the doctrines of this form of art did not take shape for a long time after the year 1600. But Shakespeare, if he did not know theory, was a great and natural practitioner and filled his canvas with so many varied portraits that the art of character-drawing was implicit in his work. Petruchio and Katharina (both conventional enough in their types), Shylock and Portia, Beatrice and Benedick, Jaques and Touchstone, Viola and Malvolio are not only great pictures in and for themselves but great in the ways in which they stand in their groups; they fit in with their surroundings and belong with their dramatic companions. One can say of these comedies that they show the way in which Shakespeare looked at life.[1]

[1]For references on Shakespeare's life and times, see page 88.

II. COMEDIES OF THE SECOND PERIOD

THE MERCHANT OF VENICE

Literary relations A play apparently on the same subject as *The Merchant of Venice* is mentioned by Stephen Gosson in *The Schoole of Abuse,* published in 1579. Gosson is attacking stage plays, also poetry and music, and wishes to except two dramas from the general condemnation:

The *Iew* and *Ptoleme,* showne at the Bull, the one representing the greedinesse of worldly chusers, and bloody mindes of Usurers: The other very liuely discrybing howe seditious estates, with their owne deuises, false friendes, with their

owne swoordes, and rebellious commons in their owne snares are ouerthrowne: neither with Amorous gesture wounding the eye: nor with slouenly talke hurting the eares of the chast hearers.

It is not unreasonable to conclude that the former of these plays, which concerned a Jew, bloody-minded and usurious, and had a crucial choice as a main feature of the plot, had in it not only the bond story, or the story of Shylock and Antonio, but also the casket story, or the wooing of Portia. The original source in *Il Pecorone,* to be described later, shows the ring story already a part of the bond plot. In order to complete the story, as Shakespeare tells it, it was only necesssary that the elopement of Jessica should have been added in imitation of the episode of Abigail in *The Jew of Malta*, from which obviously were also taken suggestions for the character of Shylock. An allusion of 1580, near the time of the play referred to by Gosson, in Greene's *Mamillia*, seems also to be to the *Jew* and may give us an earlier name for the Prince of Morocco:

He which maketh choyce of bewty withou? vertue commits as much folly as *Critius* did, in choosing a golden boxe filled with rotten bones.

In the year 1579 also Gabriel Harvey signs himself in one of his letters to Spenser as "he that is faste bownde vnto the in more obligations than any marchante in Italy to any Jew there." There is also an undated popular ballad of *Gernutus* which tells the bond story without that of the lady or the caskets. This may well be pre-Shakespearean and have some connection with the old play of the *Jew*.

Anti-Semitism in London There was an outbreak of prejudice against the Jews in London in 1594, in which one is tempted to see the occasion for the production of *The Merchant of Venice*. The Jews had been banished from England in 1290 in the reign of Edward I; but there is evidence of almost continuous residence of Jews in England. A Portuguese Jewish physician, Dr. Roderigo Lopez, rising high in his profession, became Queen Elizabeth's own physician. There was also in London one Don Antonio, a pretender to the Portuguese crown, engaged in an attempt to secure aid against Philip of Spain. The Earl of Essex and the war party espoused his cause. Don Antonio had traitors among his followers who were really in the pay of King Philip, and it is generally believed that they approached Dr. Lopez with the idea of bribing him to poison Don Antonio. Later they opened negotiations with Lopez to get him to poison the Queen. Lopez entertained their base proposal, saying later that he did so in order to cheat the Spanish king out of his money and leave his royal mistress untouched. In this he was probably speaking the truth. Lopez wrote to one of Philip's agents, the letter was

intercepted, and Lopez was lodged in the Tower. When Lopez was tried for treason, he denied guilt, vacillated, confessed, and recanted his confession; but he was, nevertheless, sentenced to be hanged, drawn, and quartered. The Queen, probably doubtful of his guilt, delayed the signing of his death warrant; but anti-Semitism, easily aroused in those days, urged on the consummation of his sentence. There is a pitiful story of his attempting to address the people at his execution, of his being jeered at by the mob, and cut down alive and mutilated according to the decree. Henslowe apparently took advantage of the popular feeling to revive *The Jew of Malta* at the Rose Theater in the summer and autumn of 1594. Some critics have seen in his presentation of a new play, the "Venesyon comody," on August 25, 1594, the first appearance of *The Merchant of Venice*. This Venetian comedy may have been an anti-Semitic play, or even a version of the story of *The Merchant of Venice*, but can hardly have been Shakespeare's play, since the Lord Chamberlain's troupe was apparently no longer acting in Henslowe's theater. The following political connection, however, may have importance. The Earl of Essex, from whom Shakespeare seems to have drawn his political views, was Lopez's chief accuser and the friend and backer of Don Antonio. The man against whom Shylock plots is called Antonio, and we may believe that the excitement about this famous trial caused Shakespeare to write a play about a Jew. The writhings of poor Lopez may be reflected with characteristic Shakespearean sympathy in the psychology of Shylock.

The date Several considerations point, however, to a date slightly later than the summer of the trial itself. One of these is the fact that the play is relatively mature in style, and stylistic tests would tend to place it as late as 1596. Also a translation was published in 1596 of Sylvain's *Orator*, a book of declamations containing amongst others an argument on the part of a Jew, situated as Shylock is, that he should have his pound of flesh. Shakespeare has made use of this argument; and, if he did not encounter the book until it was published in English, which seems probable, he was writing or revising the play as late as 1596. *The Merchant of Venice* is one of the six comedies cited by Meres in his *Palladis Tamia*, 1598.

Publication The *Merchant of Venice* was entered for publication in the Stationers' Register on July 22, 1598, by James Roberts, a friend of the players, an entry probably intended to prevent piracy. It provides that the play shall not be printed without "lycence first had from the Right honorable the Lord Chamberlen." Roberts published the play in quarto form in 1600:

The most excellent Historie of the *Merchant of Venice*. VVith the extreame crueltie of *Shylocke* the Iewe towards the sayd Merchant, in cutting a iust pound of his flesh: and the obtayning of *Portia* by the choyse of three chests. *As it hath beene diuers times acted by the Lord Chamberlaine his Seruants.* Written by William Shakespeare. AT LONDON, Printed by *I. R.* for Thomas Heyes, and are to be sold in Paules Church-yard, at the signe of the Greene Dragon. 1600.

This is the first quarto, but it was long regarded as the second, because there exists another quarto edition bearing the same date. The latter is now known to have been printed, like the second quarto of *A Midsummer-Night's Dream*, by William Jaggard in 1619. The text of the First Folio seems to have been printed from the Heyes text of 1600, which text is a good one, since the copy for it apparently came from Shakespeare's own company.

The sources: the bond There are two large component parts of the plot of *The Merchant of Venice*, and the putting of them together was a stroke of genius. As we have seen, it seems probable that this was done before Shakespeare worked upon the story, although we may believe that he not only improved the juncture but developed and interpreted the stories more fully and more dramatically than before. The first of these component parts is the theme of the bond and the pound of flesh, an old widely-distributed story resting ultimately on the provisions of Roman law which allowed creditors power over the lives and limbs of their debtors. A version is found in the thirteenth-century north English epic of *Cursor Mundi*.

Il Pecorone A fully developed form of the bond story, with localization in Venice, is found in an Italian *novella* in a collection called *Il Pecorone* by Ser Giovanni Fiorentino, published in 1558, but probably written in 1378. A Venetian merchant in this story goes into debt for ten thousand ducats to a Jewish usurer on practically the same terms as those between Antonio and Shylock. His need is more real than that of Antonio, and there is no effort to make the entry into the contract plausible by presenting it as a mere jest, on the ground that the merchant will be able to meet his obligation many times over before the bond falls due. Gianotto, the Bassanio of the piece, is a careless youth who wishes to proceed a third time in his attempt to win a lady of Belmonte. The lady in *Il Pecorone* is a somewhat mercenary person who has decreed that whoever enters her harbor must woo her by remaining awake throughout a night; in case of failure, the unhappy wooer must suffer his ship and all that he owns to be confiscated. She has the habit of giving her wooers a drug, so that they always go to sleep. Gianotto has failed twice; but the third time the Belmonte lady's waiting-woman warns him against the drugged potion and he succeeds. He then forgets in his happiness his godfather, the merchant whose life has been put in pawn for his expedition. He is awakened from his strange remissness by seeing a religious procession on St. John's day, the day on which the bond was to fall due. He departs for Venice taking with him one hundred thousand ducats, but finds the bond forfeited and the Jew inexorable. The lady too sets out disguised as a young lawyer from Bologna, advertises herself as a legal specialist in Venice, and, strangely enough, is selected to judge the case. There is no paving the way of probability by the invention of the learned cousin Bellario from Padua whose acumen was to thwart Shylock; this lady is clever enough to see through the matter without counsel. The Jew, disappointed of his prey, tears his bond in a rage. That finer piece of legal ingenuity by which Shakespeare's Shylock is held for having plotted against the life of a citizen does not appear.

Usury Not only has Shakespeare made the case rest upon Shylock's criminality, but he has contrived to give the whole trial a more general significance by depicting what were conceived to be the chief racial and religious differences between Jews and

Christians. Shylock takes interest and defends the practice. His original prejudice against Antonio rests largely upon this issue, which he does not forget even while the trial is in progress. We who are used to a wide practice of interest-taking forget the legal restrictions which still in some measure hedge it about; as also that interest-taking is still, and was then to a greater degree, a frightful weapon in the hands of the lawless and mercenary. Elizabethan political thinkers saw the danger to the state in the taking of interest. They had not only their own jurisprudence but the long centuries of the past to make them fear it and regard it with horror. They were glad to find it condemned in the Bible and eagerly seized upon Aristotle's description of money as barren. It was to the men of Shakespeare's day unnatural and sinful that money should breed money, as Antonio told Shylock, and a contravention of the biblical command that man should eat bread in the sweat of his brow.

Mercy vs. justice The Christians of the day also prided themselves on mercy as the chief article of their creed. It was often none too conspicuous in their practice, but it was nevertheless an ideal and a source of pride. The Jews, to whom was assigned strict adherence to law as their fundamental principle, were consequently regarded as barren of mercy. Shakespeare permeates the trial scene with this issue between justice and mercy. Shylock is given a chance to escape from his impending doom by the exercise of this exclusively Christian virtue of mercy; he refuses to exercise it, so that his blood is upon his own head. Portia grows eloquent in her plea for mercy, in words familiar enough; but the student may forget the historical aspect of the subject and fail to understand the scene, because he gets no vision of the Elizabethan Christian preening himself on his superiority to the Jew. Perhaps even the decree by which Shylock is compelled to become a Christian was popularly regarded, not as a bit of refined cruelty, but as a super-act of mercy, since by that means his soul would be saved. There may have been those in the audience to whom this decree, to us a cruel and cynical piece of oppression, was looked upon in the way just described; but Shakespeare

was probably further along than this in his recognition of actual values, since to his characters, Gratiano and his associates, it was certainly not an act of unusual mercy, but a very good joke on Shylock. There is nothing of the mercenary lady of Belmonte left in the charming and virtuous Portia, unless one can see it in the somewhat unsympathetic discussion of the various wooers by Portia and Nerissa, and in Portia's cavalier dismissal of Morocco and Aragon:

> A gentle riddance. Draw the curtains, go,
> Let all of his complexion choose me so,

and

> Thus hath the candle singed the moth.
> O, these deliberate fools! when they do choose,
> They have the wisdom by their wit to lose.

Sources: the caskets The story of the disposal of a lady's hand by the choice among caskets of gold, silver, and lead is also widely distributed. It appears in the Greek romance of *Barlaam and Josaphat*. Chaucer's contemporary Gower used it in his *Confessio Amantis*. It appears in Boccaccio's *Decameron*. In these cases it is merely a device to test wisdom; in a story in *Gesta Romanorum* it is made a means of testing a true lover. In that version the king of Ampluy sends his daughter to marry the son of the emperor of Rome. The emperor tries out the worthiness of the lady by making her choose among three caskets: one of pure gold, studded with gems, but containing dead men's bones—inscribed, "Whoso chooseth me shall find that he deserveth." The second is of silver, filled with earth and worms and inscribed, "Whoso chooseth me shall find that his nature desireth." The third is of lead and contains precious stones; it is inscribed, "Whoso chooseth me shall find that God has disposed to him." God directs the lady's choice, and she is received as the wife of the emperor's son. This is probably the version that came upon the stage, but Shakespeare, or the author of the old play, has given it not a religious but a social and philosophic coloring. It is made the occasion for the exposition of the popular Renaissance theme of true love.[1]

[1] C. R. Baskervill, "Bassanio as an Ideal Lover," *The Manly Anniversary Studies*, Chicago, 1923, pp. 90-103.

There lies at the basis of the choice of the caskets an ancient psychology of three levels: the level of sense and appetite, the level of judgment and knowledge, and the level of understanding and will. Beasts participate with man in the exercise of the first two of these activities. The last is spiritual, so that it is only when man participates in the divine that he rises to action on that stage. Morocco, a dark, semi-barbarous warrior, admirable in his kind, knows only enough to choose by sense and outward show. Aragon "has the wisdom by his wit to lose." He judges by the power of intellect and on the basis of knowledge. Knowing his own worth, he assumes a merit on the basis of his own clear honor. In contrast to these two Bassanio adds humility to his choice. In the contemplation of the merit of the beloved he feels himself as nothing. The feeling of helplessness and self-sacrifice, a necessary part of all true love, makes him choose the leaden casket, whose inscription is made to read,

> Who chooseth me must give and hazard all he hath,

which "rather threateneth than doth promise aught." He discards sense and judgment and proceeds by pure understanding. This teaches him to be severed from self, passion, ingenuity, riches, and honors. He is thus one that rightly loves, having learned to choose by learning to love. There is indeed in the very song, "Tell me where is fancy bred," a plain indication of the nature of the choice. "Fancy" meant, when applied to choosing in love, a choice by sense and appearance. Bassanio is warned against both ingenuity and sensuality. This was to Shakespeare no doubt the principal theme of the play; Bassanio's choice comes in the middle of the third act, as if the play had been built around it.

The story of the rings As a bridge between these two stories there is a theme which unites and reinforces them both. This is the relative power and merit of love and friendship, also a frequent subject of Renaissance speculation. The bond story is made to yield a picture of the utmost that a man will do for his friend. Antonio offers his life as a ready and willing sacrifice. Over against this is the picture of perfect love. To unite these two and bring them to an issue is the function of the episode of the rings. In *Il Pecorone* this was a mere addendum to the bond story, but in the play it is made important. The bond story serves structurally to throw the friend into danger. The ring episode rounds out and completes the play by showing how the vows of the truest love must yield to the deep and human demands of friendship. How different is this play as conceived by Shakespeare from those performances in which the casket episode is slurred over and the ring episode omitted!

The elopement of Jessica The elopement of Jessica, which is relatively less important than the themes just described, serves as a sort of plot-filler, occupying gaps in the major action. It is very likely to be misconceived by readers who do not understand the background of the play. The Elizabethans did not think lightly of the stealing away of a man's daughter. Marriages were usually a matter of parental arrangement, and parental claims were fully recognized. But in this case another factor enters. Shylock the Jew is put out of the bounds of a father's rights, and it is the mystery of genius that Shakespeare should have endowed him with a father's feelings. Because he is an avaricious and malicious Jew, it is apparently thought correct enough in this play for his daughter to run away from him and to steal his gold and jewels. By becoming a Christian she saves her soul and puts herself within the pale of humanity. It is natural enough, the Elizabethans reasoned, that she should be ashamed of her father and her race. This is one of the things in the play shocking to modern taste, but we must blame Shakespeare and not Jessica. Her love for Lorenzo is made an ideal love, and there is not in the play, so far as one can see, the least hint of blame for her unnatural conduct. When she disappears from the window to gild herself with some more of Shylock's ducats, Gratiano is moved to exclaim in rapturous admiration, "Now, by my hood, a Gentile and no Jew." And Lorenzo takes up the theme (II, vi, 52-57):

> Beshrew me but I love her heartily;
> For she is wise, if I can judge of her,
> And fair she is, if that mine eyes be true,

And true she is, as she hath proved herself,
And therefore, like herself, wise, fair and true
Shall she be placed in my constant soul.

These are not merely the rhapsodies of a lover; they are the recognized virtues of the ideal Renaissance womanhood. The same idea of her super-excellence appears also elsewhere, particularly in the dialogue of the first scene of the fifth act.

Is Shylock individualized? The puzzle in Shylock's relation to his daughter and in the play as a whole arises from the fact that, in spite of all this Elizabethan tradition of Shylock as a conventional villain and in spite of the recognizable anti-Semitism of the whole picture, Shakespeare has made Shylock appeal to us on the broadest possible grounds of humanity. "Hath not a Jew eyes?" he makes Shylock say (III, i, 62-68), "hath not a Jew hands, organs, dimensions, senses, affections, passions? fed with the same food, hurt with the same weapons, subject to the same diseases, healed by the same means, warmed and cooled by the same winter and summer, as a Christian is?" Shylock appeals to us, not only as human beings, but as husbands and fathers, when he says of the ring (ll. 126-127): "It was my turquoise; I had it of Leah when I was a bachelor: I would not have given it for a wilderness of monkeys." The audience may have laughed when Shylock said that, but to the modern reader, and possibly to Shakespeare, there is an inescapable humanizing sentiment in that recollection of Shylock's courtship. He cites the insults he has suffered, and, as he leaves the stage he says (IV, i, 395-396), "I pray you, give me leave to go from hence; I am not well." It is no wonder that the play has been distorted and turned topsy-turvy by its modern interpreters.

Stage history The stage history of *The Merchant of Venice* is important, because through it has come about a change in the conception of the play. The part of Shylock was long played as that of a pure villain rendered comic by his falling into the pit he had digged for his enemy. The actor wore a red beard like Judas and had a hooked nose. The play was done over as *The Jew of Venice* in 1701 by George Granville, later Baron Lansdowne, to suit the taste of the Restoration.

In 1741 the actor Macklin restored the Shakespearean version to the stage and laid the basis for the more humane presentation of Shylock's character. Edmund Kean carried the sympathetic method still further in 1814, and in the interpretations of Macready and Sir Henry Irving we secured the now familiar conception of Shylock as the type of a persecuted martyr and avenger. The extent to which Shakespeare's text lends itself to this modern interpretation must be the concern of all readers of *The Merchant of Venice*. Certain it is that, in order to produce the effects of the modern performance, it is necessary to cut away a great deal of Shakespeare and give a different emphasis to the play as a whole.

An annotated edition of *The Merchant of Venice* is printed on pages 327-363 of this volume.

THE TAMING OF THE SHREW

The problem: sources *The Taming of the Shrew* is a well-known and successful play on the stage. It is made up of three very distinct parts and has back of it a source of more than usual value; namely, a shrew play. *The Taming of a Shrew*, a play which had apparently belonged to the repertory of the Lord Pembroke's company, is usually regarded as that source, but probably is not; it is either, as ten Brink thought, a play derived from a common original with Shakespeare's play, or, according to a recent idea, a version of Shakespeare's play taken down from oral delivery and carefully revamped.[1] The original shrew play is lost. *The Taming of a Shrew* was published in 1594, 1596, and 1607. *The Taming of the Shrew* was published in the First Folio of 1623. There is in both plays, first of all, an Induction in which a Warwickshire drunken tinker is picked up at an ale-house by a lord returned with his train from hunting, put into the best bed in the inn, clothed and waited on as if he were a great nobleman, and ultimately persuaded that he is such indeed. This is the theme of an oriental tale which appears in the *Arabian Nights* as

[1] Peter Alexander, "The Taming of a Shrew," Literary Supplement of *The Times* (London), Sept. 16, 1926, p. 614.

"The Sleeper Awakened," and has various other versions in English and other languages. To entertain his supposed lordship a band of strolling players, like those in *Hamlet*, present a comedy which has two neatly joined plots. The one, native, popular, and farcical, tells about the taming of a shrew. This part of the plot is kept alive in a popular ballad, still current, called *A Merry Geste of a Shrewd and Curst Wife lapped in Morrelles Skin*, which is known to have been in existence before 1575. In the ballad the wife-tamer beats his wife and wraps her up in a horse's skin, newly removed and salted. The main plot of *The Taming of the Shrew* has kept a farcical quality in line with this crude source. The other plot, one of the best examples in English of the Italian comedy of intrigue, tells how a youth changes places with his servant in order to woo his lady and ultimately wins his father's consent to his union by a combination of cleverness and pure accident. This plot is based on the fourth and fifth acts of Gascoigne's *Supposes* (1566), a translation of Ariosto's *Gli Suppositi*, and Shakespeare has gone directly to Gascoigne and followed his source very closely.

Date   There seems to be no way of telling when Shakespeare did this work. The play is not mentioned by Meres in 1598, although some critics have identified it with *Love's Labour's Won*, an unknown play in Meres's list. A still larger group of critics, however, as we shall see, have thought that *Love's Labour's Won* is an early version of *All's Well That Ends Well*. *The Taming of the Shrew* seems to be an early play and must therefore have been in existence in 1598. Meres's omission of it has always seemed easily accounted for, either on the ground that he was making a formal list of examples and not pretending to give a full list of Shakespeare's comedies, or, still more likely, that the confusion of the two shrew plays, which seems to have existed in people's minds until the publication of the First Folio, prevented him from knowing that Shakespeare had made a version of his own of an older play. Stylistic qualities tell one very little about the age of the play, because the style of the play is inconsistent, and because critics have seen in the minor plot such stylistic differences from

the major plot that they have almost universally assigned it to some other hand than Shakespeare's. It may be true that Shakespeare had a collaborator in *The Taming of the Shrew*; but if so, he must have worked very closely with his associate, for the union of the plots is an almost perfect piece of joinery. Of this much we can be sure: *The Taming of the Shrew* is the revision of an older play, which is not *The Taming of a Shrew*. An examination of Shakespeare's text indicates that he was revising an old play now lost, some parts of which he left standing. His revision is thoroughgoing and drastic in the major plot of Katharina and Petruchio, and he has worked over the minor plot with great care, introducing new elements into the Gremio-Hortensio-Lucentio-Tranio plot.[1] The guess that Shakespeare worked on the play about 1595 is perhaps as good as another, for it has in its favor the fact that about that time Dekker and others were writing husband-and-wife plays for the theater.[2]

The story   Christopher Sly, the Warwickshire tinker, who has been carried into the inn and treated as a nobleman, is hard to convince.

Am not I Christopher Sly, old Sly's son of Burton-heath, by birth a pedlar, by education a card-maker, by transmutation a bear-herd, and now by present profession a tinker?

The fat ale-wife of Wincot can identify him. But under the influence of music and painting and the beautiful lady, whom they have made for him out of a page, he is convinced, and signalizes his conviction by beginning to speak blank verse like a lord. After the first scene of the play he does not speak again except to say,

'Tis a very excellent piece of work, madam lady: would 'twere done!

Perhaps Shakespeare forgot him, or, as Professor Adams suggests, he may have

[1] See Florence Huber Ashton, "The Revision of the Folio Text of *The Taming of the Shrew*," *Philological Quarterly*, VI, 151-160.

[2] *The Taming of a Shrew*, edited by F. S. Boas, The Shakespeare Classics, 1908; Chambers, *The Elizabethan Stage*, III, 472-3; IV, 48-9, and *William Shakespeare*, I, 322-328; H. Dugdale Sykes, *The Authorship of "The Taming of a Shrew,"* Shakespeare Association, 1920; A. H. Tolman, "Shakespeare's Part in *The Taming of the Shrew*," in *The Views about "Hamlet,"* New York, 1906; E. P. Kuhl, "The Authorship of *The Taming of the Shrew*," *Publ. Mod. Lang. Ass'n.*, XL, 551-618.

entrusted the task of putting Sly back on the ale-house steps to the clowns to be done *ex tempore*. The scene of the play, thus introduced, is at Padua and at a country house nearby. One Baptista Minola has two daughters, Bianca, the younger, whom Lucentio, old Gremio, and Hortensio, all wish to wed, because of her sweetness; and Kate, an elder daughter, whom nobody wishes to wed, because she is a frightful shrew. Baptista does not want Kate left on his hands, and will not let Bianca marry until Kate is out of the way. Into the midst of this dilemma there comes to Padua Petruchio, rough and ready, a soldier of fortune, a man of wealth, who says frankly he is looking for a rich wife. Hortensio engages him to marry Kate, to whose temper he hasn't the least objection. He disregards her rude refusal of his offer of marriage, swears to her father that they are on the most affectionate terms and are to be married at once. She is so swept off her feet by her unruly lover and so hostile to her father and her sister that she lets the marriage proceed. Petruchio is late at his wedding; he is dressed in outlandish garments; he cuffs the parson, makes a riot in the church, and carries her off, sword in hand, to his country place, without letting her attend the marriage feast. All this he does on the pretense that he is defending her. Her wretched horse tumbles her in the mud; in pretended rage he beats his funny servant Grumio, and all his servants. Although she is famishing he throws her food away, saying that it is not fit for her to eat. He beats and drives away the tailor and the haberdasher because of imaginary faults in new hats and gowns, so that Kate gets no new apparel. Back of the major plot lies the conception of the crude old story that a wild young woman must be tamed by physical reduction like a wild young falcon; but in Petruchio the older motive of the subjection of woman is replaced by a delightful burlesque of Katharina's own unreasonable conduct. When on the way back to Padua, Kate still without food, he makes her agree that the sun is the moon (IV, v, 2-22), something happens in Kate's mind. She seems to see the joke.

> Then, God be bless'd, it is the blessed sun:
> But sun it is not, when you say it is not;
> And the moon changes even as your mind.

The minor plot proceeds with its Italianate intrigue. Lucentio gets rid of his rivals by the aid of a clever servant Tranio and, to secure parental sanction, puts a pedant in place of his father, as in *The Supposes;* but he is forgiven, as in that play, when the real father arrives. Hortensio consoles himself with a widow. In a final scene Lucentio and Hortensio twit Petruchio with the shrewishness of Kate, and he bets them a hundred crowns apiece that Kate will prove herself more obedient than their wives, and wins his bet. The play closes with a long discourse by Katharina on the duty of obeying husbands.

Stage history The disposition of the seventeenth and eighteenth centuries to lay violent hands on the text of Shakespeare, manifests itself in no case more completely than in their handling of *The Taming of the Shrew*. The Restoration actor John Lacy produced in 1667 an abominable version called *Sauny the Scott*, in which the character of chief interest is Grumio transformed into a supposedly funny Scotch servant. The Induction is gone and also the poetry of the play. For Petruchio's humors are substituted grotesque banalities. The worst part of the story is that Lacy's farce was long popular. Garrick, though saving much of Shakespeare's text, cut the Induction and the minor plot and produced *Catharine and Petruchio* (1754), which stayed on the stage until almost the end of the nineteenth century. The true version was presented by Benjamin Webster in 1837 and by Samuel Phelps at Sadler's Wells in 1856. The modern popularity of Shakespeare's play begins with Augustin Daly's revival in 1887, on which occasion John Drew and Ada Rehan appeared in the chief rôles. In England the Benson company and others have played *The Taming of the Shrew* successfully, and in this country, among others, E. H. Sothern and Julia Marlowe.

MUCH ADO ABOUT NOTHING

Publication and date In 1600 the actors seem to have become alarmed about their stock of plays, probably on account of the publication in garbled form of Shakespeare's *Henry V*. Several plays were entered in the Stationers' Register and ordered to be stayed, that is, not published without further authority. No less than four of Shakespeare's plays, however, fell into the hands of the printers, among them *Much Ado about Nothing*. The title-page of this first and only quarto edition is as follows:

Much adoe about Nothing. *As it hath been sundrie times publikely* acted by the right honourable, the Lord Chamberlaine his seruants. *Written by William Shakespeare.* LONDON. Printed by V. S. for Andrew Wise, and William Aspley. 1600.

The text of the First Folio was set up from a copy of this quarto which had, however, apparently been used in the theater as a prompter's copy, had had a few slight corrections made in it, and had been provided with more ample stage directions. From the fact that Francis Meres does not mention *Much Ado* in his list in *Palladis Tamia* the play is thought to have been written after 1598, a supposition which suits very well the style of the play; but Meres's list, as said before, cannot be used both ways. The omission of *Much Ado about Nothing* from that list is not necessarily significant. What we know about Shakespeare's manner would lead us to think that he would be writing in just such a brilliant fashion in 1598, or in 1599 when his company was occupying the newly-constructed Globe Theater. Of the many evidences of the popularity of the play, none is better than a prefatory poem by Leonard Digges to an edition of Shakespeare's poems in 1640:

Let but *Beatrice*
And *Benedicke* be seene, loe, in a trice
The Cockpit, Galleries, Boxes, all are full.

Sources and composition The main plot of *Much Ado about Nothing* is the story of two lovers estranged by malicious villainy. The hero is made to believe that his mistress is false to him by means of a wicked deceit, in which he thinks he sees another man entering her window. The story, which has many versions, seems to have come to Shakespeare from an Italian story of Matteo Bandello in a collection published at Lucca in 1554. Whether Shakespeare read it in the original or worked from an old play is a matter of

doubt. The only bit of information suggesting an old play is found in the Revels accounts of the payment to the Earl of Leicester's players in 1574 for "their matter of Panecia." Bandello's heroine is called Fenicia for Phenicia. Since there is a play *Die schöne Phœnicia* (1595?) by the German dramatist Jakob Ayrer, which tells Bandello's story, and may, like so many of the German plays of the period, be based on an English original, one concludes that this original might have served as Shakespeare's immediate source. But the whole argument is for lack of concrete data very shadowy. A similar plot is described in Ariosto's *Orlando Furioso*, translated into English by Harington in 1591, and is borrowed thence into Spenser's *Faerie Queene* (1590), which introduces the feature of a maid dressed in her mistress's clothing, as does Shakespeare's play. Bandello's story was freely rendered into French by Belleforest in his collection known as *Histoires Tragiques* (1582), but there seem to be no special resemblances to Belleforest in Shakespeare. There are in point of fact two minor plots or episodes, both apparently original with Shakespeare, which constitute the chief interest of the play—the affair of Benedick and Beatrice and the activities of Dogberry and the Watch. In Bandello there are no parts to correspond to Benedick and Beatrice, or to Dogberry. There the solution of the plot is brought about by the remorse of the villain.

Evidences of revision Critics have always pointed to inconsistencies in *Much Ado about Nothing*. Claudio is too easily persuaded of Hero's guilt, and his rejection of her at the altar is so cruel that he appears to be, and no doubt is, a badly plot-ridden character. That is, his actions do not conform to his character, but are forced upon him by the plot. Margaret, who is represented as being innocent of evil intention against her mistress, is not present at the wedding, where it is obvious she would have been in a position to clear up the charge against her mistress. Innogen, the mother of Hero, appears twice in the stage directions, but plays no part in the comedy. Recent editors of *Much Ado about Nothing*[1] have pointed out other in-

[1] Sir Arthur Quiller-Couch and John Dover Wilson, *Much Ado about Nothing*, The New Cambridge Shakespeare, 1923.

consistencies in the form of the play, which seem to them to indicate that the parts of Benedick and Beatrice have been expanded in prose, and a corresponding amount cut out from the play as Shakespeare first wrote it, which play was mainly in verse and had practically the same plot. They find indications of this in various bad junctures between the old part and the new and attribute the hurried dramaturgy observable in the main plot to the abridgement it has suffered. A motive for such an alteration would of course be found in the popularity and interest of the Benedick-Beatrice theme. One need not suppose that Benedick and Beatrice were absent from the original play but only that they have been made dominant in the new. On the basis of a revision, Innogen would be explained as an omitted part. Margaret's action would be motivated pretty much as it is in Ariosto; namely, by supposing that she had let herself be flattered by her lover into donning her mistress's apparel. Perhaps even Claudio may have come out better in a more elaborate study of his remorse. Sympathy for him is diminished by the fact that the scene of his deception is known to us only by hearsay.

Background No array of words, however, can make Claudio's part, as such, plausible and palatable to a modern audience; but it can be seen in a different and a truer way by considering the plot in the light of its times. The Italian novel dealt in sensational plots, like the rejection of an innocent maid at the altar, which suited the taste of the Renaissance. A cruelty of that kind would not be so deeply felt or seem so very unnatural if practiced on a maid unchaste or thought to be unchaste. Seeing is believing, and Claudio thought he had seen. Shakespeare goes far toward making him attractive by showing him young, handsome, brave, a lover who falls in love at first sight, and a youth deeply smitten with contrition when he sees his mistake. But why should he offer himself in the fifth act to be married off so casually, more or less as a matter of repayment, if he had been really so deeply grieved for the loss of Hero? Here again we have the opinions of the Renaissance entering the field of interpretation. We can never understand the business-like aspect which

marriage then had. There would be no particular feeling in an Elizabethan audience that Claudio should remain unmarried and forever faithful to Hero's memory. He had read his dirge and done his part and was showing a truly generous spirit in bestowing himself as a husband on, as he thought, another of Leonato's family. Then, again, what a feature is made of eavesdropping in the forced courtship of Benedick and Beatrice! Critics have actually censured Beatrice for indulging in this unladylike practice, but the manners of the times were different; eavesdropping was not regarded so seriously as it is now. In these respects and others this typical piece of Renaissance literature needs to be considered from the point of view of its own time.

Shakespeare's part *Much Ado about Nothing* gives us further insight into Shakespeare's way of depicting life, the manifestations of human character that interested or amused him, and the dramatic devices he had learned to employ with skill. His love affairs are never soft, because he was not sentimental and probably because the bright boys in his company who played women's parts could be trusted to bring out deliciously a combination of love and humor. Benedick and Beatrice in *Much Ado* continue the stage situation of Biron and Rosaline in *Love's Labour's Lost*, though their interplay is wittier and more interesting, and there is a touch of Katharina and Petruchio in the combination. In spite of her shrewish traits Beatrice has somehow the womanly qualities of Portia and something of the charm of Rosalind. Dogberry and his associates recall not only the constable Dull in *Love's Labour's Lost* but the rude mechanicals of *A Midsummer-Night's Dream*, and Dogberry's talk, with a difference, is like that of Bottom. Friar Francis, like Friar Laurence in *Romeo and Juliet*, supplies an element of staid and prudential wisdom. The grief for Hero recalls the grief for Juliet, while the bellicosity of Leonato and Antonio reminds us of old Capulet in his gown crying, "Give me my long sword, ho!"

Coleridge on Much Ado These characters, situations, and devices, traditionally the stock-in-trade of Renaissance drama and of Shakespeare himself, are made in this play to reveal the surprises of life; as when Dogberry, contrary to all reasonable estimate of probability, is made to detect the villainy of Don John, and when Beatrice discloses in one flash her womanliness, her judgment, and her ultimate faith in Benedick in the words, "Kill Claudio." Coleridge's paragraph,[1] describing the situation in this play, presents this feature of Shakespeare's greatness from another point of view:

The interest in the plot is always on account of the characters, not *vice versa*, as in almost all other writers; the plot is a mere canvas and no more. Hence arises the true justification of the same stratagem being used in regard to Benedick and Beatrice,—the vanity in each being alike. Take away from *Much Ado about Nothing* all that is not indispensable to the plot, either as having little to do with it, or, at best, like Dogberry and his comrades, forced into its service when any other less ingeniously absurd watchmen and night-constables would have answered the necessities of the action;—take away Benedick, Beatrice, Dogberry, and the reaction of the former on the character of Hero,—and what will remain? In other writers the main agent of the plot is always the prominent character; in Shakespeare it is so, or is not so, as the character is in itself calculated, or not calculated, to form the plot. Don John is the mainspring of the plot in this play; but he is merely shown and then withdrawn.

Stage history   After the establishment of the two court companies at the time of the Restoration, Thomas Killigrew of the King's company and William D'Avenant (with Thomas Betterton) of the Duke of York's company had divided between them the plays of the pre-Cromwellian repertory. *Much Ado about Nothing* and eight others of Shakespeare's plays fell to D'Avenant, who reformed them, or caused them to be reformed, according to the taste of the time. D'Avenant himself wrote *The Law against Lovers* (1662) making it up from *Much Ado about Nothing* and *Measure for Measure*. The former play was later unhappily combined with Molière's *Princesse d'Elide* by the Reverend James Miller (1737). Rich played Shakespeare's version at Covent Garden in 1739, and Garrick, in 1748 and the years following, gained for the play a popularity it has never lost. Garrick

himself was the greatest of Benedicks, and Mrs. Pritchard and Miss Pope were famous as Beatrice. The play was successful in the hands of the Kembles. Mrs. Siddons herself acted Beatrice and Mrs. Jordan was eminent in the part. Later revivals have been no less successful. The most famous of these is that of Sir Henry Irving at the Lyceum Theater in London in 1882, on which occasion Irving played Benedick with great brilliancy. Ellen Terry gave an enchanting rendition of Beatrice, and Johnston Forbes-Robertson appeared as Claudio. There have been revivals by Beerbohm Tree, Ellen Terry, the Bensons, and many others. The play so retains its humor that it is not unusual during a performance to hear audiences laugh naturally and heartily and not because they know that it is Shakespearean comedy and supposed to be amusing.

An annotated edition of *Much Ado about Nothing* is printed on pages 364-400.

THE MERRY WIVES OF WINDSOR

Account of the play   *The Merry Wives of Windsor* is here treated among the comedies, though for correct understanding it is necessary to consider it in connection with the Henry IV plays, to which it is inseparably linked by the figure of Falstaff. A tradition dating from the early years of the eighteenth century, but universally accepted, states that *The Merry Wives of Windsor* was written by the special command of Queen Elizabeth. Charles Gildon in his *Remarks on the Plays of Shakespeare* (1710) gives it in the following language:

The Fairies, in the fifth Act, make a handsome compliment to the Queen in her Palace of Windsor, who had obliged Shakespeare to write a Play of Sir John Falstaff in Love, and which I am very well assured he performed in a fortnight; a prodigious thing, when all is so well contrived, and carried out without the least confusion.

Literary critics have not agreed with Gildon in the last statement. The play shows marks of haste, confusion, and unevenness. The theory advanced by the most recent authorities is that, the tradition being true, Shakespeare, possibly with the help of others, seized upon an old comedy in the repertory of the company and thrust into it, with more or less care, Sir John Falstaff

---

[1] "Characteristics of Shakespeare's Dramas," in *Lectures upon Shakespeare and other Dramatists*, New York, 1884, pp. 62-63.

and his companions from the Henry IV plays, including Justice Shallow, who had figured popularly in *2 Henry IV*, now provided with a Cousin Slender and an attendant Welsh Parson Evans. If this is true, the old comedy must have dealt with bourgeois life, probably in London, and must have had as its basis a story of a jealous husband. Lord Strange's men had in their repertory a "Jealous Comedy," which has sometimes been thought of as an original for *The Merry Wives of Windsor*. The story of a lover detected in making love to two or three women at the same time, as Falstaff does, occurs in a number of Italian *novelle*. There is also to be found the story of the deceived husband, whose wife has her lover carried out before his eyes in a chest or a box of feathers, as Falstaff is carried out before Ford's eyes in the hamper of soiled linen. In any case the basal theme of the play is Italian, and the attempts to connect it with the Henry IV plays are not altogether successful. Justice Shallow enters with a famous charge against Falstaff of having beaten his men, killed his deer, and broken open his lodge, but the charge and the Justice fade into nothing, with other odds and ends of plots. Falstaff begins like his old self, and now and then throughout shows something like the old wit; but he is made into a dupe by a very ordinary company of burghers, he who had outdone princes and chief justices. He speaks at times in so banal a way that the editors of the New Cambridge Shakespeare suggest that there may have been in his place in the old play an affected courtier, some of whose speeches have been left for poor Sir John to utter. Mistress Quickly too is quite transformed in character, though not in speech, and has apparently lost her adherence to Sir John. In fact the play has given great dissatisfaction to the admirers of Falstaff, though it holds the stage with a deathlike grip. A well-known novelist who had seen the play at Stratford said, however, "Treated without foolish reverence in the presentation, it becomes a very good play."

Text and date   The text is a great puzzle. A quarto, possibly stolen by a member of the company, acted for a time on the stage, and finally sold to the printer Thomas Creed, was published in 1602. It is only about half as long as the text which appeared in the First Folio in 1623. The Folio text itself has undergone revision and is thought by the New Cambridge editors to have been made up for issue in the collected edition from hastily written players' parts. The quarto, therefore, supplies some omissions in the folio text and corrects some errors. The fact that Corporal Nym, a character in *Henry V* but not in the Henry IV plays, appears in *The Merry Wives*, together with some other considerations, have made most critics place the play about 1600, after the appearance of *Henry V*. Several scholars have pointed out that the Falstaff of *The Merry Wives of Windsor* was probably formerly called Sir John Oldcastle. They judge from certain minor allusions and from the fact that in the quarto verses the name Oldcastle fills the five-foot line and the name Falstaff leaves it one syllable short. Probably *Henry V*, usually regarded as fixed in 1599, is earlier than we think; but in any case the matter is a puzzle. Professor T. W. Baldwin has recently suggested the vague possibility that the Falstaff of *The Merry Wives* may originally have been the Sir John Fastolfe of *1 Henry VI*.[1]

The story   Shallow's cousin Master Slender, almost the silliest character in literature, wishes to marry Mistress Anne Page. "Seven hundred pounds, and possibilities," is "goot gifts," says Parson Evans; and her father wants her to marry Slender. Her mother wants her to marry a hot-tempered French doctor named Caius. She wishes to marry Fenton, a spendthrift youth, who "has kept company with the wild prince and Poins." Falstaff starts in

[1] H. C. Hart, *The Merry Wives of Windsor*, Arden Shakespeare (Methuen), 1904; W. W. Greg, *Shakespeare's "Merry Wives of Windsor," 1602*, Oxford, 1902; J. M. Robertson, *The Problem of "The Merry Wives,"* Shakespeare Association, 1917; A. W. Pollard and J. Dover Wilson, "The Stolne and Surreptitious Shakespearean Texts," Literary Supplement of *The Times* (London), August 7, 1919; Sir Arthur Quiller-Couch and J. Dover Wilson, *The Merry Wives of Windsor*, Cambridge University Press, 1921; T. W. Baldwin, *The Organization and Personnel of the Shakespearean Company*, p. 235; O. J. Campbell, "The Italianate Background of *The Merry Wives of Windsor*," in *Essays and Studies* (University of Michigan), Ann Arbor, 1931. See also, particularly, Leslie Hotson, *Shakespeare versus Shallow*, pp. 111-22.

to win the affections of Mrs. Ford, whose husband is very jealous, and of Mrs. Page, whose husband is not at all jealous. He writes identical love letters to each declaring that he loves her only. The women compare letters and resolve to punish him. Mrs. Ford invites Falstaff to her house. When he arrives, Mrs. Ford rushes in to say that her irate husband is coming. They put Falstaff into a clothes basket, cover him with soiled clothes, have him carried out by their men and dumped into the river Thames. He is even so stupid as to let her persuade him to visit her again. This time Ford comes indeed, and the women dress Falstaff up as the Witch of Brentford, against whom Ford has a violent antipathy, so that Falstaff gets soundly beaten with Ford's cudgel. They now let Ford into the secret; both married couples arrange a third trick to play on the fat knight. With Mistress Quickly's aid he is persuaded to come as to an assignation into the forest to Herne's enchanted oak with buck's horns on his head. There children dressed as fairies dance about him, pinch him, and burn him with their torches until he confesses his folly, and what is worse, his wickedness, in words as stupid as his actions. While the fairy business is going on, Mistress Anne, who is a clever, nice girl, weds Fenton, Slender and Caius each carrying off a page dressed in girl's clothes under the impression that he is carrying off Mistress Anne as his bride.

Stage history The Merry Wives of Windsor suffered relatively little at the hands of Restoration adapters; so that Shakespeare's play, or something like it, occupied the boards throughout the seventeenth and eighteenth centuries, though Shakespeare's actual text was probably not followed until Charles Kean's production of 1851. In the stage history of the play we have to do with that group of actors who have had the special qualities necessary to play the part of Falstaff both in The Merry Wives of Windsor and the Henry IV plays. Shakespeare may have written the part for Thomas Pope, though a late tradition assigns it to John Heminge. In any case, John Lowin was famous in the part from 1603 to 1642. Betterton succeeded as Falstaff, and James Quin (1692-1766) became

the most famous of all Falstaffs. John Henderson (1747-1785), George Frederick Cooke (1756-1811), Samuel Phelps, and J. H. Hackett have been successful in the part. In recent times The Merry Wives of Windsor has been revived by Beerbohm Tree and Ellen Terry, the Bensons, and many others in both England and America. The play has recently been presented by the Stratford-on-Avon Players.

AS YOU LIKE IT

Publication and date As You Like It is found entered in the Stationers' Register, along with Henry V, Every Man in His Humour, and Much Ado about Nothing, as a book stayed, i.e., not printed, on August 4 of some year not given; but inasmuch as Henry V and Much Ado were published in 1600, with entries a few weeks later, there seems to be no doubt that the omitted year was 1600. As You Like It was probably withheld from publication because the players were confident of being able to protect it from pirates. If so, their confidence was justified, for the play was apparently not printed until the First Folio of 1623. Attention is often called to the fact that the play is not mentioned by Meres in 1598 and that it refers in pointed terms to Marlowe's Hero and Leander, first published in 1598. Phebe exclaims as she beholds Rosalind disguised as Ganymede (III, v, 81-2):

Dead shepherd, now I find thy saw of might,
'Who ever loved that loved not at first sight?'

This is Shakespeare's only unquestioned allusion to a contemporary poet and may fairly be taken to indicate a tender recollection of Marlowe. Between these two dates then, 1598 and 1600, one would be disposed to place As You Like It. The assignment agrees well with internal evidence derived from style.

Elements of the story: Rosalynde In As You Like It Shakespeare followed a contemporary source, and followed it with great fidelity. Thomas Lodge (1558?-1625), poet, playwright, and novelist, wrote a long romance in order, he tells us in his dedication to Lord Hunsdon, to beguile the tedium of a voyage to the "Ilands of Terceras and the

Canaries"; he called his work "*Rosalynde: Euphues Golden Legacie.* Found after his death in his cell at Silexdra. Bequeathed to Philautus Sonnes, nursed up with their father in England." This was published in 1590 with a dedication as above and an Epistle to the Gentlemen Readers, in which Lodge remarks, "*If you like it*, so; and yet I will bee yours in duetie, if you be mine in favour," thus supplying a title for Shakespeare as well as a theme. Lodge's novel is a typical work of the English Renaissance, written in the courtly, heavily-mannered style of Lyly's *Euphues*, and combining, with little thought of historical consistency, elements of romance, pastoral, and native English ballad. It is also interspersed with charming lyrics. Shakespeare discarded the euphuism, probably because it was going out of fashion by the time he wrote, but took the story over bodily, making only such modifications as he saw fit in order to change it from a novel into a play. He has compressed the action into ten days, left out an interval between the quarrel of Orlando and Oliver and the wrestling bout, caused Orlando to leave his brother's place at once, introduced the sub-plot before Orlando arrives in Arden, and made other similar changes. He has omitted accounts of the death-bed of Orlando's father, of a tourney which precedes the wrestling, and of various matters connected with the quarrel between the brothers. The motive of Oliver, who is called Saladyne in the story, is made, not greed to inherit Orlando's (Rosader's) lands, but jealousy of his handsome person and his popularity. Shakespeare makes the usurping duke a brother to the banished duke, has him banish Orlando out of prejudice, and has him ultimately repent of his wickedness; whereas in the novel the twelve peers of France revolt against the usurper, slay him, and reseat on the throne the banished duke, or king as he is in Lodge's story. There is also in the novel an episode of some length in which a band of robbers carry off Celia (Alinda), who is rescued by Rosader and Saladyne. Shakespeare has kept these robbers out of his peaceful woodland. Finally, Shakespeare has added all that pertains to Jaques, Touchstone, Audrey, William, Amiens, and other minor characters.

Gamelyn Lodge himself made use of a story, not at that time printed, a Middle English poem, *The Coke's Tale of Gamelyn*, wrongly attributed to Chaucer and found in a number of manuscripts of *The Canterbury Tales*. This is a Robin Hood story, telling of a neglected younger son, who wins prizes in wrestling, quarrels with his wicked eldest brother, runs away with an old retainer, Adam Spencer, to Sherwood forest, and becomes king of the outlaws, and who, finally, has the opportunity of having his eldest brother, who was sheriff, hanged. The Robin Hood appeal of the story is still strong in the play. Shakespeare lets us feel it, not only in the songs and in the philosophy of woodland life, but also when Charles says (I, i, 120-125) of the duke Ferdinand:

They say he is already in the forest of Arden, and a many merry men with him; and there they live like the old Robin Hood of England: they say many young gentlemen flock to him every day, and fleet the time carelessly, as they did in the golden world.

It happens that the Lord Admiral's company, the chief rivals of the Lord Chamberlain's company, had had since 1598 what must have been a very popular play, *The Downfall of Robert Earl of Huntington after called Robin Hood* by Anthony Munday and its sequel, *The Death of Robert Earl of Huntington* by Munday and Henry Chettle. *As You Like It* was probably written in order to follow the fashion or even to serve as a counter-attraction. Shakespeare probably did not know *Gamelyn*, the original Robin Hood story, but in exploiting the fashion of the forest he recurred in some matters to the older form.

Pastoralism Shakespeare, while toning down the element of romance and adventure, has taken full advantage of the atmosphere of the Robin Hood plays. He has also introduced another large literary component of Lodge's novel, namely, the pastoral feature. The pastoral mode had originated in the *Idylls* of Theocritus and the Sicilian Greek poets of the third century B.C., had been carried on by Virgil, and was one of the most popular kinds of ancient literature during the Renaissance. There was a great group of Italian and neo-Latin pastoral poets, some of whom were very familiar to Elizabethan Englishmen. The best known of native pastoral works are Spenser's *Shepheardes Calender* and Sidney's *Arcadia*. There were not only pastoral poems but pastoral romances and pastoral dramas as well. Probably the life described by Theocritus as lived by the shepherds on Mount Hybla bore some semblance to actuality, but it had long since become purely an imaginary manner of existence and a style in literature, in which shepherds tending their clean white flocks spent their time in wandering through woods and fields, making love, and discoursing on the nature of true love, the essence of friendship, the relation of youth to age, and the vanity of dwelling in towns. To have courtiers and clowns retire to this Arcadia represented a variation, and to have Arcadia and the greenwood side by side was a complication of interests. Shakespeare has retained with reasonable effectiveness Lodge's pastoral minor plot about Corin and Silvius, William and Phebe, and also Lodge's device for uniting the plots by having the proud and vain Phebe fall in love with Ganymede.

A dramatized novel The parts of Lodge's story, then, which Shakespeare has retained are somewhat descriptive and static, rather than dramatic, having about them still the quality of fiction instead of drama. The thing which he got from Lodge is a tale of true love with a charming background rather than a sharply plotted comedy. What Shakespeare has done, besides his many minor changes, to render the story better suited to the stage, is to develop a central, crucial scene which displays the principal plot. That central incident is described in these terms by the Arden editor: "Two undeclared lovers meet: the lady in disguise challenges her lover to woo her as his mistress: their courtship is thus carried on in masquerade till she is assured of his affection, when she discloses herself, and all ends happily." Shakespeare has thus given in the second scene of the third act a turning-point to his comedy which is genuinely dramatic and delightfully comic.

Shakespeare's part To make of it a drama he has resorted to accessory figures. When Celia and Rosalind set out for the forest of Arden, supposed to be the forest of Ardennes in France, but really much like the forest of Arden in Warwickshire, they took with them the court fool Touchstone. Shakespeare calls him "the clownish fool," and "the roynish clown," as if he had not expected much of him, but when Touchstone gets into the forest, he becomes one of the great original creations of Shakespeare's plays. He is a court clown and therefore in a manner a courtier; he is a city man in the presence of shepherds and rustics. "In Touchstone," says Professor Herford, "Shakespeare for the first time utilized the professional court-fool as a medium of wit and humor." It was probably the situation in which the clown was placed by the accident of the plot that gave Shakespeare this opportunity, and also the presence in his company of Robert Armin, a new type of comic actor. Touchstone has in him a certain fidelity and satirical honesty which wins our sympathy. He has also more than a dash of amusing roguery, conceit, and bravado, and a vein of nonsense at once professional and spontaneous. One of the set-pieces of the play is the issue, often seriously debated, between court life and sylvan or pastoral life. Touchstone, so to speak, attacks this on the flank, for he embodies certain traits of the courtier which were never meant to be brought into the debate. The one whose profession had been folly at the court becames a philosopher in the forest.

Jaques "Were he really possessed," says Dr. Furness of Jaques, "of all the qualities attributed to him by his critics, we should behold a man both misanthropic and genial, sensual and refined, depraved and elevated, cynical and liberal, selfish and generous, and finally, as though to make him still more like Hamlet, we should see in him the clearly marked symptoms of incipient insanity." It is often pointed out that Jaques does nothing and is yet indispensable. The puzzle is somehow brought nearer to solution by looking at him historically. He appears in the midst of a period of satire, when Jonson had set a new fashion in his *Every Man in his Humour* of ridiculing the foibles, eccentricities, and vices of the world. Jonson based his work on the theory that human eccentricity is due to faulty adjustment of the four humors, or fluids, of the body, and he designated man's vagaries and peculiarities as "humors." It has been argued that Jacques is a humor character,[1] one in whom excessive melancholy is the basis of eccentricity; in fact, that he is a malcontent like Malevole in Marston's *Malcontent* and that he was suggested to Shakespeare by that character, except that Malevole is more violent and more gross. They both show the symptoms of melancholic affection described in medical treatises. Both are sleepless; both devote themselves to contemplation only; both hold a privileged position as regards freedom to speak, particularly in the presence of their superiors; both are blunt or ironically friendly to ordinary persons; both rejoice in the grotesque folly of the professional fool; both rail at the world, especially at set classes, like women, courtiers, and professional men; both are given isolated formal speeches of a general nature, and both are most at ease in soliloquy. When one observes what other characters think and say of Jaques, one finds a good deal to confirm this view; as, for example, when the First Lord tells the duke about Jaques and the deer in the first scene of the second act; when Jaques shows rudeness to Amiens in the fifth scene, and when he describes the Fool and the eminence of folly in the seventh scene of the same act. It is true that Jaques does nothing to advance the drama except to deliver his famous speech beginning "All the world's a stage" (II, vii, 139 ff.) while Orlando fetches Adam; but he is individualized and, to that degree, important. The duke charges him (II, vii, 64-9) with having been a libertine and having plucked his melancholy as the bitter fruit of his own folly, and Jaques himself would have you believe in his dialogue with Rosalind (IV, i, 10-26) that his particular brand of melancholy is derived from a too complete knowledge of the world. His belief that there is nothing to be learned from fortunate and contented humanity, exemplified in his secession at the end to the converted duke, amounts almost to a special trait of character. Malcontent, gentle malcontent though he is, he is nevertheless employed dramatically in this play. He is set off in contrast to the duke, to the lovers, and the Fool,

and is himself delightfully parodied by the Fool and casually cast aside as a critical do-nothing by Rosalind. But he adds a sauce to the dish; for, as one might say in the words of an art critic, used about Fra Angelico's paintings, "We long for a few wolves in this impeccable sheepfold."

Rosalind There are no puzzles about Rosalind; it is only a question of adequate praise. "She is wit and womanliness in equal proportions," says one critic; another calls attention to the fact that she is like Beatrice but kinder and less ironical, that she has the charm of Viola, but is more masterful, and so on. Mrs. Jameson's familiar words usually give pleasure, and they are perhaps as satisfactory as any:

Rosalind is like a compound of essences, so volatile in their nature, and so exquisitely blended, that on any attempt to analyse them, they seem to escape us. To what else shall we compare her, all-enchanting as she is?—To the silvery summer clouds, which, even while we gaze on them, shift their hues and forms, dissolving into air, and light, and rainbow showers?—To the May-morning, flush with opening blossoms and roseate dews, and 'charm of earliest birds'?—To some wild and beautiful melody, such as some shepherd boy might 'pipe to Amaryllis in the shade'?—To a mountain streamlet, now smooth as a mirror in which the skies may glass themselves, and anon leaping and sparkling in the sunshine—or rather to the very sunshine itself? for so her genial spirit touches into life and beauty whatever it shines upon!

Stage history The history of the play interests us because of a tradition, late but plausible, that Shakespeare acted the part of Adam in the early performances.[2] There are few traces of any interest in *As You Like It* during the seventeenth century, but the play suffered garbling at the hands of Charles Johnson in 1723, when he wrote *Love in a Forest*, a sort of amalgamation of *As You Like It*, *Much Ado*, *Twelfth Night*, and *A Midsummer-Night's Dream*. Shakespeare's play came back on the stage in 1740 with great James Quin as Jaques and Mrs. Pritchard as Rosalind. *As You Like It* is not one of Shakespeare's greatest stage plays. It is, nevertheless, charming and has always been popular. It has no really great male

[1] E. E. Stoll, "Hamlet, Marston and the Malcontent Type." *Modern Philology*, III, 281-303.

[2] See page 79.

part, though various actors have done well as Orlando or Jaques, but it does have a great woman's part, dashing, boyish, and humorous. Nearly all the greatest actresses have been successful as Rosalind: Mrs. Pritchard, Peg Woffington, Sarah Siddons, Mrs. Jordan, Helen Faucit, Charlotte Cushman, Adelaide Neilson, Ada Rehan, and Julia Marlowe.

An annotated edition of *As You Like It* is printed on pages 401-438 of this volume.

TWELFTH NIGHT

Date and publication *Twelfth Night* was published first in the folio of 1623, being then licensed in the Stationers' Register as a play not formerly entered. The text is a good one and may have been set up from the author's manuscript. The *Diary* of John Manningham, barrister of the Middle Temple, records a performance before his society on Candlemasday, 1602:

Feb. 2—At our feast wee had a play called 'Twelue Night, or What you Will,' much like the Commedy of Errores, or Menechmi in Plautus, but most like and neere to that in Italian called *Inganni*. A good practise in it to make the Steward beleeve his Lady widdowe was in love with him, by counterfeyting a letter as from his Lady in generall termes, telling him what shee liked best in him, and prescribing his gesture in smiling, his apparaile, &c., and then when he came to practise making him beleeue they tooke him to be mad.

Maria's statement (III, ii, 84-6) that Malvolio "does smile his face into more lines than is in the new map with the augmentation of the Indies," may indicate that the play was written after the appearance in 1599 of a map by Emerie Mollineaux, to which the description would apply. There are other indications[1] that the play appeared between 1599 and 1602, and most critics are disposed to date it in 1600 or 1601. Metrical and other evidence agrees with this date very well, particularly as the play seems to show a growth in dramatic skill. The text of the play certainly shows two strata: an early poetical one presenting the formal plot, and a later one, largely in prose, having to do with the deception of Malvolio and other special features.

Nature of the comedy In *Twelfth Night* Shakespeare continues the vein of *Much Ado about Nothing* and *As You Like It*. He has a foreign love story carrying with it a good deal of its original atmosphere. This remoteness, as of the forest of Arden, of the setting in Illyria, mellows the lights of his picture. In its outlines it is of the Renaissance in general, but in its details it is often purely English. He has thus the poetical advantages enjoyed by the writer of romance, and at the same time the brisk freedom of the realist in the treatment of the ordinary course of man's experience. It is sometimes felt that *Twelfth Night* has nothing in it so brilliant, or so moving, as have *Much Ado* and *As You Like It;* but it has about it an evenness of tone and a perfection of detail in the depiction of ordinary life which they lack, as also a richness of Renaissance culture not found in either of them.

Complexity of source *Twelfth Night* seems to gather materials from a dozen different related works and to combine them into one of the richest treatments of a popular theme of Renaissance literature. Mr. Morton Luce[2] enumerates a dozen of these works and shows reasons for believing that at least from a majority of them Shakespeare derived material. It might be thought that Shakespeare merely followed some old play now lost and had all of this material predigested for him; but such was not his practice, at least in the writing of history plays. Even when it is known that he was following a particular dramatic source, he consulted also the chronicles, frequently more than one of them, and, as we shall see, he did not follow blindly in writing *King Lear* the old play on which it is based. There does, however, exist in *Twelfth Night* a somewhat shadowy suggestion of a dramatic source. A German comedy called *Tugend und Liebestreit*, printed in 1677, has the same major theme as *Twelfth Night*. There was also acted in Germany by English players a play on the same subject in 1608, 1626, and later dates. Creizenach thinks that this lost play of the English *Komödianten* was the immediate source of *Tugend und Liebestreit* and suggests

[1] C. H. Coote, New Shakespeare Society *Transactions*, 1877-1879, pp. 88-100.

[2] *Twelfth Night*, Arden Shakespeare (Methuen), 1906, Appendix I.

that there was thus an early English comedy on the same subject as *Twelfth Night*. If such a play existed, Shakespeare may have made use of it in composing his play.[1] But on the general question Mr. Luce quotes Hunter: "Gosson says in his *Plays Confuted* (1581) that comedies in Latin, French, Italian, and Spanish had been thoroughly ransacked to furnish the playhouses in London." The original of *Twelfth Night*, whether there was an earlier English comedy on the subject or not, was an Italian or French comedy.

Indebtedness to foreign works It will be noticed that Manningham shows familiarity with an Italian comedy called *Inganni*, which might be translated "The Frauds." Hunter was led by Manningham to investigate not less than two Italian comedies called *Gl'Inganni*, one by Nicolo Secchi acted in Milan in 1547 and published at Florence in 1562, and another by Curzio Gonzaga printed in Venice in 1592, both treating the story of a sister and a brother mistaken for each other, the sister being disguised as a man. In the latter of these plays the sister takes the assumed name of "Cesare," just as Viola takes the name of "Cesario." Hunter also discovered the far more important source comedy *Gl'Ingannati*, or "The Dupes," acted in 1531 and published at Venice in a volume entitled *Il Sacrificio, Commedia de Gl'Intronati* (The Sacrifice, a Comedy of the Deafened or Amazed) in 1537. The last mentioned play was long popular, was translated into French as *Les Abusés* by Charles Estienne (Lyon, 1543), and into Latin under the name of *Lælia*,[2] for performance by students at Cambridge in 1595. The *Gl'Inganni* plays are also probably indebted to it, and also at least one Spanish play. Bandello tells the story of the indistinguishable brother and sister in his *Novelle* (1554), and Belleforest after him in 1570 in *Histoires Tragiques*. Belleforest is the basis of Barnabe Riche's *Apolonius and Silla*, which has long been regarded as one of Shakespeare's principal sources; but one should not dispense with Riche's originals. Mr. Luce points out a number of striking parallels to Bandello and Belleforest and even to a prose version in Giraldi Cinthio's *Hecatommithi* (1565), from which Shakespeare was later to draw the plot of *Othello*. In the last-mentioned is introduced the feature of shipwreck as the means of the separation of brother and sister. That Barnabe Riche was actually used, either by Shakespeare or by the author of a lost play, seems confirmed by Professor Neilson's discovery[3] that in another of Riche's stories in the same collection (*Riche, his Farewell to the Militarie Profession*, 1581), *Two Brethren and their Wives*, occurs a scene suggestive of Malvolio's imprisonment, in which a shrewish wife is cured of her humor by having it pretended that she is insane and by reciting the *Miserere* to banish the evil spirit.

Gl'Ingannati The most important of any of these sources is the basal story in *Gl'Ingannati*. Fabrizio, son of a merchant, Virginio, takes his daughter Lelia to Modena. Gherardo, a rich old man, wishes to marry her. She loves Flaminio, who has deserted her for Isabella, daughter of Gherardo. Lelia assumes male attire and becomes a page in the service of her fickle lover. She is employed by him to court Isabella, who falls in love with her as Olivia falls in love with Cesario. Lelia tricks her master by getting Isabella to reject him. The early attachment between Lelia and Flaminio is not retained by Shakespeare, unless one might find it in Viola's particular interest in Orsino (I, ii, 28-9). Viola's service to her master, in contrast to that of Celia, is loyal. Fabrizio arrives in Modena, encounters Virginio and Gherardo, who have become aware of Lelia's behavior, is mistaken for Lelia, and, being thought insane because of his strange answers, is thrown into prison. The prison turns out to be Isabella's chamber, and Fabrizio and Isabella are, like Sebastian and Olivia, quickly betrothed. The solution is like that of *Twelfth Night*, Gherardo, like Sir Andrew Aguecheek, being the only wooer unprovided with a partner. Mr. Luce points out that in the Induction to *Il Sacrificio* is found the name *Malevolti* (evil-faced), which he thinks may have suggested the name Aguecheek; and in the same play is a character with the name

---

[1] W. Creizenach, *Schauspiele der englischen Komödianten*, 1889, p. 57.
[2] G. B. Churchill and Wolfgang Keller, "Die lateinschen Universitätsdramen Englands," *Shakespeare Jahrbuch*, XXXIV, 221-325; F. S. Boas, *University Drama in the Tudor Age*, Oxford, 1914.

[3] *Atlantic Monthly*, LXXXIX, 715.

Fabio, which may have suggested *Fabian*. Among the minor characters in *Gl'Ingannati* are suggestions for Malvolio, Sir Toby, Feste, and Maria. In a phrase in the prologue, *La Notte di Beffania* (or Epiphany), is a suggestion for the name "Twelfth Night." We have here the household of the lady Olivia in *posse* at least; but no suggestion has been made for the source of the counterfeit letter by which Malvolio is deceived, and as a suggestion for Malvolio himself we have only the presence in the Italian play of a prig and a gull.[1] The name "Malvolio" means "evil desire, or ambition," and he is a humor character whose peculiarity, or "humor," it is to attempt to climb impertinently above his own station.

The stuff of the play We do not, however, account for *Twelfth Night* simply by calling attention to the marvelous skill with which these varying elements are woven together in the plot. We have in this play a study of an Elizabethan household among the nobility, servants as well as masters; its conversation, its amusements, its gossip, and its atmosphere; the hardy sea captain Antonio on the street; priests, officers, and attendants; the customs of marriage, courtship, and betrothal; drinking, jesting, and dueling. All this is English and well-nigh perfect; but there is also a large body of the material of Renaissance comedy, liable to be overlooked, which lies back of the main theme. The well-worked Italian story had been popular because it presented certain aspects of the popular theme of love. Shakespeare employed that theme and with it we know not how much of the courtly thought about love in which it was wont to be expressed. Shakespeare, who had already written Renaissance love comedies like *The Two Gentlemen of Verona* and *The Merchant of Venice*, who was a sonneteer and a writer of amatory poetry, was entirely competent without aid of an older play to enrich the theme. One can discover in *Twelfth Night*, as in *The Merchant of Venice*, Plato's threefold division of love, as of the senses, the intellect, and the understanding. In this case, the lowest kind of love would be exemplified in the silly and impossible courtship of Sir Andrew Aguecheek and the impertinent aspirations of Malvolio; the intellectual sort, in the sentimental self-indulgence of Orsino; and the genuine or honest love, in the self-sacrificing devotion of Viola, and to a less degree in the impulsive passions of Olivia and Sebastian. Many of the questions of love which engaged the courtly circles of Italy, France, and England[2] make their appearance in this play, forming a sort of substance for the dialogue. Especially is this true in the part of Orsino; as, for example, that music is the food of love (I, i, 1-8; II, iv, 1-14); that love is a torment to the lover (I, i, 9-23; I, iv, 26; II, iv, 15-6, etc.); that the man should be older than the woman he loves (II, iv, 29-32); that man loves more deeply than woman (II, iv, 94-106) and the reverse (II, iv, 33-6; II, iv, 119-121); that concealed love meets with no fruition (II, iv, 113-118); that scorn breeds love (III, i, 156-60); that love enters through the eye (I, v, 317); that true love is jealous (IV, iii, 27); and many others.

Characters That *Twelfth Night* is a comedy of true love to even a greater degree than *As You Like It* no one has called in question, and critics have found in the more difficult part of Viola a sweetness entirely comparable to that of Rosalind. Usually on the stage she is made too plaintive, and it is only now and then that an actress has been able to retain the brightness, courage, and wit of the figure, which illuminate rather than conceal her wistfulness. The singing clown Feste is also comparable to Touchstone. He is one of Shakespeare's best pictures of clownage, and the charter of freedom stated by Viola (III, i, 67-75) seems to express the conception of the possibilities of the clown's part which Shakespeare had come to hold. Feste has indeed wit "enough to play the fool." Indeed from his manipulation comes a good deal of the action of the play. Malvolio, however, offers the most perplexing problem of interpretation to be found in the play. To see Sir Henry Irving

---

[1] Professor Alwin Thaler has suggested (*Shak. Ass'n Bull.*, VII, 57-71) that Shakespeare may have found an original of Malvolio in one William Ffarington, steward to the Earl of Derby, patron of Shakespeare's company.

[2] T. F. Crane, *Italian Social Customs of the Sixteenth Century*, New Haven, 1920, chs. XIII, VIII, XI, and *passim*; Baskervill, "Bassanio as an Ideal Lover," in *The Manly Anniversary Studies*, pp. 90-103.

and other tragic actors leave the stage vowing vengeance "on the whole pack of you" was to have the impression of the whole comedy spoiled and to feel that a dangerous madman had been turned loose on the community. This certainly cannot have been Shakespeare's intention with reference to the part. Leonard Digges refers to Malvolio as a "cross-gartered gull," which no doubt expresses the Elizabethan conception. The fact that he is a responsible servant, well thought of by his mistress, who would not have had him miscarry for the half of her dowry and later thinks him notoriously abused, has caused him to be regarded as a meritorious man cruelly humiliated by a group of those who envied him. The virtues no doubt are there, and they are acknowledged; but actors have been disposed to forget that Malvolio aspired to his mistress's hand, which, far from being a natural and admirable ambition, was in the social thinking of the time a base fault. They also forget Olivia's own plain statement of what she thinks of his disposition (I, v, 97-104). In other words, Malvolio is to be regarded as getting pretty nearly what he deserves, especially when we are assured at the end of the play that he is to be both the plaintiff and the judge in his own cause.

Stage history *Twelfth Night* was evidently popular in its own day if one may judge by recorded performances at court. It seems to have escaped the re-handlings of the Restoration, and, to do the critics and play-adapters of that period justice, the play has fewer of the traditional Shakespearean faults, such as excessive sentiment and romance and the violation of the dramatic unities, than almost any other play in the canon. There is no evidence of popularity, however, until its revival at Drury Lane in 1741, with Macklin as Malvolio and Mrs. Pritchard as Viola. Since that time *Twelfth Night* has appeared on the stage with a fair degree of frequency. Like *As You Like It* it is best acted when there is an actress adequate for the chief woman's part. Charles Lamb praised the "plaintive" Viola of Mrs. Jordan. Ellen Terry, Ada Rehan, and Julia Marlowe have played the part with conspicuous success. Professor Hart suggests that the serious turn given to the part of Malvolio has been due in some measure to the fact that great tragic actors, like John Philip Kemble and Sir Henry Irving, have so often played the part.

An annotated edition of *Twelfth Night* is printed on pages 439-474 of this volume.

III. HISTORIES OF THE SECOND PERIOD

KING JOHN

History of the play Among the "tragedies" mentioned by Francis Meres in *Palladis Tamia* is *King John*, which must, therefore, have been written before 1598. The only known early publication of the play is that of the First Folio in 1623. One is consequently left to determine the date of the play mainly by internal evidence. Since it represents stylistically about the same stage of development as *Richard II*, some critics place it just before that play and some just after it; that is, about 1595. It may thus stand midway between the early group of four plays dealing with the Wars of the Roses and the later group of four plays dealing with the earlier history of the Lancastrian usurpation.

The source *King John* rests immediately upon an earlier play called *The Troublesome Raigne of John King of England*, in two parts, published in 1591, again in 1611 as written by "W. Sh.," and in 1622 as written by "W. Shakespeare." This play was thus mistaken for Shakespeare's play, or palmed off as such, and the editors of the First Folio did not enter it in the Stationers' Register as a new play, but regarded the entry of the older form as sufficient. *King John* and *The Troublesome Raigne*, however, differ very greatly. Shakespeare has condensed the two parts into one, has rewritten it throughout line for line, changed the emphasis and developed the characters. The older playwright compressed Holinshed's chronicle, invented the main features of the plot, and gave to the whole a strongly Protestant coloring with a good deal of that exaggerated patriotism which is known as chauvinism. It is full of defamation of the French and glorification of the English, and has exploited the tradition that King John was the first of the English kings to assert national independence against the papacy. This had already given his name, hardly more, to the Protestant morality play on the Antichrist theme known as *Kynge Johan* (1448?) by Bishop John Bale.

King John in history King John could not even from Holinshed be made into a hero, Protestant or otherwise, so that we are prepared for the reduction of the title rôle at Shakespeare's hands. The conception of his character, however, is left confused and imperfect. If the story of King John were truly told for the stage, his part would be that of a king who, like Richard III, murdered, or sought to murder, his nephew and rightful sovereign, and who, like Richard II and Henry VI, lost the realms in France. He is, therefore, a poor peg on which to hang patriotism. It is hard to see just how far Shakespeare went beyond the old play for his materials, but he probably read Holinshed for himself and, in this way, came to his somewhat truer realization of the significance of the facts recorded. Scenes of the despoiling of the monasteries, which appear in *The Troublesome Raigne*, do not appear in Shakespeare, and it has been thought that Shakespeare omitted them; but it is at least as probable that Shakespeare wrote something of the sort which was later excised from his play.

The story The French king and the count of Lymoges (confused with the duke of Austria) demand the English crown for Arthur, son of Geoffrey, duke of Bretagne, an elder brother of King John. Arthur's claim is good, but John has possession. John, spurred on by his shrewish mother Elinor, proceeds to France to fight for his claim. Before he sets out there arrives at his court the most striking character of the play, Philip, the Bastard Faulconbridge, son of Richard Cœur-de-Lion. He is a blunt and daring spirit who renounces his claim to the name and estate of Faulconbridge, preferring to be regarded as the base son of a great king rather than the proper son of a base man. Faulconbridge follows the court, fights for England in the field, and becomes King John's mainstay. The armies meet before Angiers, but the governor of the city will not admit either party until he learns which is the real king. The armies fight a drawn battle and again assemble before the town. Faulconbridge wishes them to join forces, reduce the town, and then fight it out; but the canny governor makes peace between the parties by suggesting a marriage between Blanche of Spain, King John's niece, and Lewis, the Dauphin of France. John gives away vast provinces and a large dower, and in return his enemies abandon the claims of Arthur. The grief of Constance, the mother of Arthur, at her son's displacement is passionate and eloquent. Shakespeare, apparently seeing through her sentimentality, shows us that she loves mainly herself and her will in the person of her son. Pandulph, the Pope's legate, enters as the peace is consummated and excommunicates John for despoiling the monasteries and refusing to permit Stephen Langton, the pope's appointee, to become archbishop of Canterbury. The French and English armies fight, the English win, and Arthur is captured. Constance goes wild with grief and subsequently dies. Arthur is turned over by King John to Hubert, whom the king bribes to blind and then murder him. The entrance of Hubert and the executioners to carry out their black purpose opens one of Shakespeare's most moving scenes of pure humanity. Arthur so begs for his eyesight that Hubert spares him, but tells the king that Arthur is dead. John's nobles revolt at his horrid butchery. Hubert then confesses that he has spared Arthur, and John sends after the nobles to placate them; but meanwhile Arthur in a desperate attempt to escape from prison has leaped down from the wall and slain himself. The nobles, still believing John guilty of Arthur's death, join the Dauphin, who, urged on by Pandulph, is now making rapid headway in a conquest of England. John basely surrenders his crown to Pandulph in token of submission, and Pandulph orders the Dauphin to withdraw. The Dauphin refuses; the English nobles return to their allegiance to John when they learn that the Dauphin intends to put them to death after he has employed them to over-

throw John. The Dauphin, though successful in battle, has to make peace when
his reinforcements and supplies are lost
by disaster at sea. The ending is mixed,
politic, and tame, but it follows the chronicle. John, being ill with a fever, takes
refuge in a monastery at Swinstead, where
he is poisoned by a monk acting as his
taster, who thus dies himself for the sake of
destroying the king. This event is not intelligible in Shakespeare, who has omitted
scenes from *The Troublesome Raigne* in
which monasteries are sacked and the
ecclesiastics satirized. Such scenes if once
present in Shakespeare's play have been
cut out. A scene in the old play shows
John surrendering in despair his crown
to Pandulph consoled only by the thought
that at a later time the cause against the
pope will be fought and won. The result
of these omissions from Shakespeare's *King
John* is to remove from the play its extreme anti-Romanism and part at least of
its evil abuse of France. Pandulph becomes
a truly impressive ecclesiastical statesman.
In Shakespeare's hands Arthur and Constance become deeply humanized, and
Faulconbridge a simple, honest, humorous,
English patriot, who, in the midst of
crookedness and intrigue, holds fast to
love of country, honest service, and bravery
in warfare. He speaks at the end of the play:

> This England never did, nor never shall,
> Lie at the proud foot of a conqueror,
> But when it first did help to wound itself.
> Now these her princes are come home again,
> Come the three corners of the world in arms,
> And we shall shock them. Nought shall make
>   us rue,
> If England to itself do rest but true.

Stage history   *King John* has not been a
                     popular play, though its
stage history is eminently respectable. It
has in it at least three good male parts,
King John, Pandulph, and Faulconbridge,
and one female part, that of Constance, of
unusual tragic appeal. It is indeed a far
better play on the stage than it is in the
closet, a situation not unusual in Elizabethan drama. There is no evidence that
the play had any unusual vogue in its own
day or was honored by revival during the
Restoration. It all but escaped the almost
inevitable adaptation of the late seventeenth
and eighteenth centuries and might have

done so completely had not Colley Cibber
seen in it an opportunity for anti-Catholic
propaganda. In 1736 he made a version
called *Papal Tyranny in the Reign of King
John.* Soon after this Shakespeare's play
was put on by Garrick, and since his time
most of the greater Shakespearean actors
and actresses have appeared in it: Macklin,
Quin (who played King John in Cibber's
version), the Kembles and their sister Sarah
Siddons (with whom Constance was a
favorite role), and Edmund Kean and his
son Charles. Miss Ellen Terry, then ten
years old, played the part of Arthur in
Charles Kean's last revival of *King John*
in 1858 and was magnificently great in
the part of Constance toward the end of
the nineteenth century in a revival in which
Irving played the part of Pandulph.

RICHARD II

Publication   On August 29, 1597, Andrew
                   Wise entered in the Stationers'
Register "The Tragedye of Richard the
Second," and in 1597 a quarto edition was
printed for him by Valentine Simmes:

> THE Tragedie of King Richard the second.
> *As it hath beene publikely acted by the right Hon-
> ourable the Lorde Chamberlaine his Seruants.*
> LONDON. Printed by Valentine Simmes for An-
> drew Wise, and are to be sold at his shop in Paules
> church yard at the signe of the Angel. 1597.

Wise was apparently on excellent terms
with the players, and the quarto text is a
good one. Two more quartos appeared in
1598 with "By William Shakespeare" added
to the title-page. A fourth quarto, issued
in 1608, adds "With new additions of the
Parliament Sceane, and the deposing of
King Richard, As it hath been lately acted
by the Kinges Majesties seruantes, at the
Globe." This quarto contained in imperfect form the famous deposition scene, and
from it the Folio text was set up, with,
however, a better version of the deposition
scene. Each quarto rests on its predecessor.

Date   The play is mentioned by Francis
            Meres in 1598 as one of Shakespeare's
six tragedies. The entry in the Stationers'
Register and the publication in 1597 form
the latest limit for dating the play. A
number of considerations point to a time
late in the year 1595. Knight showed
certain parallels between *Richard II* and

The Civil Wars, an epic poem by Samuel Daniel, four books of which were published in 1595. Resemblances also exist between that poem and *1* and *2 Henry IV*, which follow *Richard II* in the series. Both the plays and the poem dwell on the idea of the nemesis which is to follow the deposition of a rightful king. In the following particulars *Richard II* seems to be based on Daniel's *Civil Wars:* The queen, who was historically a child of eleven, is represented in both play and poem as a grown woman, and Daniel in his *Epistle Dedicatorie* in 1609 apologizes for taking this liberty as if he were responsible for it. Richard and Bolingbroke ride together into London instead of separately as in the chronicle. The hint which Bolingbroke gives to Pierce of Exton to kill the king is almost in Daniel's words. Daniel also puts into the king's mouth a speech suggestive of his last soliloquy in the play. Finally, in both the poem and the plays Hotspur is deliberately presented as much younger than he is, in order that he may be set over against Prince Hal as a rival. Both writers may have been using a source now lost, but since the resemblances are close, it seems hardly probable that they were. The year 1595 also agrees pretty well with stylistic evidences as to the date of *Richard II*. The play has a disproportionately large amount of rhyme for a date so late as 1595; but this may possibly be accounted for on the ground that rhyme, being a conscious feature of composition, may be due to reaction or to some passing literary influence. Rhyme militates against the speech-ending test and, in some measure, against feminine endings; *Richard II* is accordingly not high in either of these respects; on the other hand, it has a full number of extra syllables in the mid-line position. There is also a good deal of the rhetorical type of blank verse, many verbal conceits, puns, and epigrams, qualities which are characteristic of Shakespeare's early work; but Shakespeare puts this kind of language mainly into the mouths of Richard and of Gaunt, as if for the purpose of marking them off from other characters. Sir E. K. Chambers has recently found a piece of evidence[1] which may confirm the date 1595, or at least show that *Richard II* was possibly a

[1] *The Elizabethan Stage*, II, 194 n.

novelty in that year. In a letter dated December 9, 1595, Sir Edward Hoby invites Sir Robert Cecil to his house in Canon Row, "where, as late as shall please you, a gate for your supper shall be open, and K. Richard present himself to your view."

Other plays on the subject One has no right to say that in *Richard II* Shakespeare was not reworking an old play; but it is certain that, if he was, he proceeded as in *Richard III*, and not as in *King John*, for he resorted immediately to Holinshed, and, except for changes to agree with Daniel's *Civil Wars*, followed it with meticulous fidelity. Two minor discrepancies have, however, been thought to indicate that Shakespeare had to do with an old play. In II, i, 167-8, York refers to "the prevention of poor Bolingbroke about his marriage," which is nowhere explained in the play; and again Carlisle at the end of the play is committed to the custody of the Abbot of Westminster, whereas in the chronicle he is sent to St. Albans. Neither of these is very significant, but there is further bibliographical evidence of greater importance. The subject was evidently familiar on the stage. There are two plays preserved which deal with the reign of Richard II, in both of which, however, there is only a superficial likeness to Shakespeare's play: *The Life and Death of Jack Straw* (1593) has to do with the peasant insurrection of 1381; and *The Tragedy of Woodstock* (1591, *Sh. Jahrbuch*, xxxv) begins with Richard's marriage to his first queen Anne of Bohemia and ends with the murder of Gloucester, the point at which *Richard II* begins. Dr. Simon Forman, a quack doctor of the reign of James I, left a diary in which he made notes on various plays he had witnessed. On April 30, 1611, he saw at the Globe a play, not now preserved, which seems to have covered the whole of Richard's reign. A "booke called Perce of Extone," by Wilson, Dekker, Drayton, and Chettle is mentioned by Henslowe in March or April, 1598, when he made a part payment for the work.

Political significance The Earl of Essex, who was a friend of Shakespeare's only known patron, the Earl of Southampton, made his strange uprising against Queen Elizabeth on February 7, 1601. For this he suffered death as a traitor on the 25th of the same month. Essex must have been a hero in Shakespeare's eyes if we may judge from his allusion in the prologue to the fifth act of *Henry V* to Essex's popularity and to the happy prospects of his expedition against the Irish rebels under Tyrone. Whatever the connection between Essex and Shakespeare may have been, Essex and Southampton spent much time seeing plays and probably exaggerated the political influence of the drama. At any rate, after Essex's disgrace and two days before that set for his rebellion, apparently as a means of stirring public sentiment, Sir Gelly Meyrick, a partisan of Essex's, arranged with Shakespeare's company for the performance of a play "of the deposing and killing of King Richard II." In the testimony of Augustine Phillips, a member of Shakespeare's company, at Essex's trial it appears that the actors considered the play "to be so old and so long out of vse that they shold have small or no Company at yt"; but in consideration of "xls more then their ordynary for yt," they played the play. Whether or not this was Shakespeare's play is a matter of doubt among critics, but most of them hold that it was. The subject of Richard II was a sore one with the Queen herself. The note of a conversation with the queen by W. Lambarde, printed by Nichols, *Progresses of Queen Elizabeth* (ed. 1788), I, A-H, p. 41, says,

Her majestie fell upon the reign of King Richard II, saying, I am Richard II, know ye not that? *W. L.* Such a wicked imagination was determined and attempted by a most unkind Gent. [i.e. Essex], the most adorned creature that ever your Majestie made. *Her Majestie.* He that will forget God, will also forget his benefactors; this tragedy was played 40tie times in open streets and houses.

Since Essex did not seek the Queen's death, it is argued that *Richard II* would not suit his purposes; but it is to be pointed out that the play does show one thing in exact line with Essex's intentions. It shows the fatal effect of ill-advisers and favorites. Essex wished to rescue the Queen from her flatterers and might have indicated the necessity of so doing by depicting in the figure of her predecessor the outcome of such conduct. Both *Richard II* and Marlowe's *Edward II* present as a live

issue the thwarting of the sovereign's evil counselors. Political significance clung to *Richard II*, for when Nahum Tate adapted it as *The Sicilian Usurper* in 1681, it gave political offense; it is also recorded of Theobald's version acted in 1718 and 1738 that on the latter occasion it was regarded as an attack on Walpole's foreign policy.

Relation to Edward II The relation of *Richard II* to Marlowe's *Edward II* is more than accidental. Marlowe had done a new and significant thing in discovering a historical character who might serve as the hero of a tragic plot and thus give the chronicle play the effect of a tragedy. Perhaps also he had a political purpose in *Edward II*. Shakespeare had followed the earlier manner of Marlowe in *Richard III*; he was now to follow the later manner in *Richard II*. The subject of Richard II is so closely parallel to that of Edward II that Shakespeare must have been put to it to avoid an uninteresting repetition. Edward II and Richard II were bad kings, both deluded by favorites, both extortioners of taxes, and both persons lacking in common judgment; both were dethroned and then murdered in prison. In connection with their downfalls there came up the question of whether or not a king might in any circumstances be dethroned, since his title came from God and his blood was doubly sacred. Marlowe presented one protagonistic figure set over against a series of secondary figures. First Gaveston is Edward's favorite; then Spencer. The part of Mortimer, who heads the rebellious nobles and wins away Edward's queen, is striking but not predominant. Mortimer is, moreover, a villain, and the issue does not fall squarely on the propriety of dethronement. Edward is misused and in some respects the victim of external circumstances. The play closes with a scene of the murder of King Edward which Charles Lamb declared "moves pity and terror beyond any scene, ancient or modern, with which I am acquainted." In *Richard II* Shakespeare, either by accident or intention, introduced marked differences from Marlowe in his handling of the dethronement theme. He has in fact made dethronement the issue of the play. The judgment of critics has been warped by their habit of interpreting *Richard II* in terms of that remorse of conscience for the dethronement and murder of a king which appears in the later plays of the series, namely, in *1* and *2 Henry IV* and *Henry V;* also in the horrid significance of the event as the first cause of the civil wars of the Roses depicted in the Henry VI plays and *Richard III.* By looking at the play within its own borders, however, one sees that it is a tragedy and not a crime with which we have to do.

The dethronement theme The theme of the dethronement of kings was one in which the Renaissance took interest and found perplexity. The weight of opinion was that no degree of inefficiency or wickedness justified the rejection of God's anointed. It would be better to bear any amount of temporary oppression than to anger the Almighty by interfering with his establishment. Any recognition of the rights of the people to determine who should rule them was still to seek. Such seems to be the basis of all the plays in Shakespeare's two great series except this one, and there are some traces of it here; but, taking the play in and for itself, it must be regarded as the clearest presentation of the issue made at that time. It could not, nor could any play, expound the topic, or desire to expound it, or advocate dethronement. The democratic forms of political thought had not yet appeared in the world. This is plain from the common knowledge of the theme already abundantly made known upon the stage. A manuscript play, *The Tragedy of Woodstock,* for example, deals with the events of the fifteen years immediately preceding the opening of Shakespeare's play. There you see the wicked self-indulgence of the king, his oppression of his people, his unworthy favorites, his own pitiful dilettantism, and his murder of his excellent and loyal uncle. It is perfectly proper to read into Shakespeare's *Richard II* the reputation of that monarch when the play was written. It was not necessary for Shakespeare to depict the evils of Richard as a ruler in order to have him condemned; he needed only to remind his audience of what they already knew. Marlowe had depicted the humanity of a weak king and made his audience sympathize mainly with his hero's sufferings. Since Shakespeare has given Richard a worthy and consistent antagonist,

wronged and righteous, in Bolingbroke, the effect produced is different and the issue of royal inviolability is more squarely raised.

Richard's tragic weakness The most striking novelty in Shakespeare's tragedy is his seizing upon the weakness of King Richard's character and making it the basis of his overthrow. *Richard II* is thus in some respects the first of Shakespeare's character tragedies, though his work is here probably far less conscious and far more due to accident of subject and to the necessity of avoiding Marlowe's method, than in such tragedies as *Othello* and *Macbeth.* We feel that Richard's tragedy is one which any man of common sense might have avoided; we do not feel that the author has depicted a situation in which even a hero might have fallen; there is no threat against the human state as such. All the sources suggest weakness in Richard's character, though his peculiar weakness seems to have been Shakespeare's invention. Richard lost his kingdom and his life without adequate opposition from his adversary. His chief enemy, therefore, must have resided within his own bosom. Shakespeare conceives of him as a sentimentalist, that is, a man whose self-consciousness takes the form of dwelling not on facts but on his conception of facts. Richard enjoys picturesque situations, reputation, and the outward shows of kingship and manliness, and neglects the essence of these qualities. This makes him the butt of flattery, his own and that of others. His action is determined, not by events themselves, but by his conception of a series of rôles to be played. He enjoys the parade and ceremony attendant upon the trial of arms at Oxford; then foolishly and inconsistently stops the duel in order to draw all eyes upon himself and his power. His sentence on Bolingbroke and Mowbray is the only means by which injustice might certainly be dealt upon both combatants. He betrays his vanity in his sensitiveness about his face and his complexion, and his cruelty and anger when he is compelled for an instant to see himself as he is. The aged patriot Gaunt on his deathbed, having told Richard of his faults, is thus addressed (II, i, 115-119):

A lunatic lean-witted fool,
Presuming on an ague's privilege,
Darest with thy frozen admonition

Make pale our cheek, chasing the royal blood
With fury from his native residence.

No less to be noted are Richard's unwarranted confidence in his very name and state when he lands from Ireland, and his equally unwarranted dejection when he learns the actual situation; his base yielding to Bolingbroke when Bolingbroke had just yielded to him; his voluntary surrender of the crown for the sake of playing the dangerous rôle of a dethroned and deserted king; his repeated comparison of himself with the sun in heaven and with the Savior. Shakespeare shows us that these same personal qualities and this same histrionic gift may be used to move the hearer, when the sentimentalist is finally stranded, when his troubles become real. In fact the most admirable thing in this poetic king is that he seems finally to discover a better nature in himself, though it manifests itself fully only in the last gallant moment of his life.

Minor characters Coleridge found in the timorously loyal York an admirably drawn character. Gaunt is the champion of patriotism on the part of the subject and of righteous rule on the part of the sovereign; his great speech (II, i, 31-68) still lives in the hearts of Englishmen. Aumerle is usually condemned, for he is inconsistent, since in the first part of the play he is one of Richard's flatterers and in the latter part one of his loyal adherents, though a traitor to the established king; but one must still remember the scene of the many challenges and his "Some honest Christian trust me with a gage." The picture of Bolingbroke with his keen, impersonal intellectuality has never had the recognition it deserves, because critics interpreting his words in the light of later plays have read guile into his actions. Richard's fall was inevitable, though Shakespeare does not exculpate Bolingbroke from treason and regicide. The point to be remembered is that, taking the play as it stands, Bolingbroke cannot be regarded as merely a usurper. It is not possible to tell clearly what Shakespeare's judgment on the dethronement issue is.

Stage history The statement on the titlepage of the fourth quarto, "As it hath been lately acted by the Kinges Majesties seruantes at the Globe," points to a revival of *Richard II* early in the reign of King James I. The issue of the later quartos (Q_5 in 1615, Q_6 in 1634) indicates for the play a certain degree of popularity in the early seventeenth century. Nahum Tate adapted it as *The Sicilian Usurper* in 1681, and a modified version by Theobald was acted in 1718 and 1738. In more or less altered versions the play was acted repeatedly in the eighteenth and nineteenth centuries. The Shakespearean version has gradually returned to the stage. Macready, Edmund Kean, Charles Kean, Junius Brutus Booth, Edwin Booth, Beerbohm Tree, and others have played it in England and America; in Germany it has been still more popular and successful.

An annotated edition of *Richard II* is printed on pages 475-518 of this volume.

1 AND *2* HENRY IV

Publication An edition of *1 Henry IV* was published in quarto by P. S. for Andrew Wise in 1598 with the following title:

THE HISTORY OF HENRIE THE FOVRTH; With the battell at Shrewsburie, *betweene the King and Lord* Henry Percy, surnamed Henrie Hotspur of the North. *With the humorous conceits of Sir* Iohn Falstalffe. AT LONDON, Printed by *P. S.* for *Andrew Wise,* dwelling in Paules Churchyard, at the signe of the Angell. 1598.

It had been entered in the Stationers' Register on February 25th of that year. In 1600 there came out, also in quarto:

THE Second part of Henrie the fourth, continuing to his death, *and coronation of Henrie* the fift. With the humours of sir Iohn Fal*staffe, and swaggering* Pistoll. *As it hath been sundrie times publikely* acted by the right honourable, the Lord Chamberlaine his seruants. *Written by William Shakespeare.* LONDON. Printed by V. S. for Andrew Wise, and William Aspley. 1600.

This had been entered in the Stationers' Register on August 23, 1600. There are two issues of the second part under this date and title, the first of which omits the first scene of the third act. No less than eight quarto editions of *1 Henry IV* appeared, from the fifth of which (1613) the Folio text was set up. There was only one quarto publication of *2 Henry IV*, and a distinct text from that of the quarto is used for the Folio. The quarto texts of both parts of the play are good, and the publishers were respectable. The texts they used probably came from the playhouse.

Falstaff and Oldcastle How the plays came to be printed is a matter of interesting speculation. It was possibly from a desire to protect the plays from piracy, but it may have been in order to advertise a correction. There is evidence of a serious offense against Lord Cobham because in the first versions of these plays the famous fat knight was called Sir John Oldcastle and not Sir John Falstaff. Lord Cobham was a descendant of Sir John Oldcastle, an honorable nobleman and a Wickliffite martyr, whom the religious prejudices of the intervening time had made into a hypocrite, a wine-bibber, and a misleader of the young prince who subsequently became King Henry V. The tradition had been embodied in the source of these plays, one of the oldest of chronicle plays, preserved for us in a degenerate version known as *The Famous Victories of Henry V* (1598). The depiction had probably given no offense, or remained unnoticed, in the old play; but, when Shakespeare's play sprang into popularity, Lord Cobham's resentment was natural. Shakespeare therefore revised his play and changed the name of his comic hero to Sir John Falstaff, perhaps a modification of the name Sir John Fastolfe, a character who is made to play a coward's part in *1 Henry VI*. Scholars after Shakespeare's death called attention to the fact that he had also done historical injustice to Sir John Fastolfe, but the name was at least less offensive than that of Sir John Oldcastle. The Lord Admiral's men, the rival company to the players at the Globe, put on the stage a chronicle play in two parts intended to mete out full justice to the Lollard martyr, *The History of the Life of Sir John Oldcastle, Lord Cobham with his Martyrdom*. The important playwrights Munday, Wilson, Drayton, and Hathway were the authors, and the first part of it was published in 1600. The year seems significant, for Shakespeare not only revised his plays but made public denial of the identification of Falstaff and Oldcastle in the epilogue to *2 Henry IV*, sent to the printers that year. "For Oldcastle died a martyr, and this is not the man," he says. The revision was not so careful

that traces of the old name may not be found, not only in *1* and *2 Henry IV*, but apparently also in *The Merry Wives of Windsor*, which in that case must have been written before the early part of the year 1598. In *1 Henry IV* (I, ii, 47-8) the prince addresses Falstaff as "my old lad of the castle," and in *2 Henry IV* (I, ii, 137) the catch-name *Old.* has been left standing before one of Falstaff's speeches in the quarto edition. Various cases have also been pointed out in which the name Oldcastle completes a line of verse which has been left one syllable short by the substitution of Falstaff for Oldcastle.

The Famous Victories and the "Oldcastle" plays A great deal of light has recently been thrown on the early history of the Henry IV plays by Professor A. E. Morgan[1] and from his monograph the following facts are derived. There was at least as early as 1588 a play acted by the Queen's men on the life of King Henry V. It covered the same ground historically as is covered by *1* and *2 Henry IV* and *Henry V*. In the year of theatrical readjustments, 1594, the Queen's company, according to Henslowe, "broke & went into the contrey to play" and are never heard of in London again. Nearly all of their repertory of plays seems to have been disposed of to the printers; but part of it fell into the hands of the Lord Admiral's company, including no doubt a copy of the old Henry V play, for Henslowe records a new play (or revision) called "harey the V" acted at the Rose on November 28, 1595, and subsequently thirteen times between that date and July 15, 1596. On May 14, 1594, a printer of no standing called Thomas Creed entered in the Stationers' Register *The Famous victories of HENRYE the FFYFTH containinge the honorable battell of Agin court*. If he published the play at once, no copy has survived. He issued without further entry *The Famous Victories of Henry V* in 1598. This is not the old Henry V play, but is a corrupt and badly degenerated version of it. In other words, it is not the immediate source from which Shakespeare worked, but is derived from that source. Mr. Dover Wilson has suggested that when the Queen's company broke

[1] *Some Problems of Shakespeare's "Henry the Fourth,"* The Shakespeare Association, 1924.

up and sold their copy to some other company, they made up this one from memory to sell to the printer; it is in too bad a state for it to have been in the repertory of any of the better London companies. It may not, however, have been made up then and there from memory, but may have been acted on the road by the remnant of the Queen's company for some time and sold to Creed. In other words, it shows not merely imperfect reporting, but the wear of the road. Another copy of the old Henry V play must have come into the hands of Shakespeare or his company. Working on this he wrote first a play on Henry IV in two parts. The plays were largely in verse and in them Falstaff was known as Oldcastle. These "Oldcastle" plays were probably written in the blank verse manner of *King John* and *Richard II*. The popularity of the Oldcastle parts caused Shakespeare to expand them and enrich them in the free prose style with which we are all familiar in the Falstaff scenes. In order to find room for the new comic parts it was necessary for him to abridge the historical parts of the plays. Professor Morgan finds unmistakable evidence of this curtailment and abundant signs of the rehandling in prose of comic scenes which were formerly in verse. Imbedded in the prose of the comic scenes of *1 Henry IV* he finds some two hundred lines of verse. They are easily discovered when one gets the clue, and a number of them show that, where there now stands the dissyllable "Falstaff," there once stood the trisyllable "Oldcastle." The verse remnants are mainly found in those passages which we know from *The Famous Victories* go back to the original Henry V play. They are fewest in the freest and most typical passages of Falstaffian humor. There are few evidences of original verse in the Shallow-Silence parts of *2 Henry IV*. Those parts, therefore, belong mainly to the latest revision.

The historical plot The originals of *1* and *2 Henry IV*, as Shakespeare first wrote them, would not have been inconsiderable plays, for they probably contained the historical plots as they now stand. These plots have merely lost a certain amount of material by excision. Sir John Oldcastle in verse would have been a poor substitute for Falstaff in prose as we have him; but the serious plots have no doubt lost something of their original interest. Hotspur probably did not appear in the old Henry V play, so that Shakespeare has built a new heroic drama connected with Hotspur round about the career of the young prince. To do this he went to the second edition of Holinshed's *Chronicles of England, Scotland, and Ireland* (1587), and to Daniel's *Civil Wars*, and, although he has followed his sources with faithfulness as to fact, he has illuminated them in marvelous fashion. From Holinshed comes the main historical business of both parts: The insurrection of Harry Percy, the rebellion of York, Bardolph, Hastings, and Mowbray, the dishonest defeat of the rebels at Gaultree, and the troubles and sorrows of Henry IV. Probably from Daniel he has taken the conception of Hotspur as a youth of Prince Hal's age, the rescue of the king by the prince during the battle of Shrewsbury, the absence of the Welsh from that conflict, and the idea that Henry IV was suffering a nemesis in his conscience for his usurpation of the throne. Much of the serious plot comes also from the old Henry V play; for example, the king's trouble about his wayward son, the incident of Hal's removal of the crown and the reconciliation which follows, and finally the rejection of his wild companions after his coronation. In some cases the same theme appears in more than one source, and Shakespeare before writing seems characteristically to have gone over the whole field of his material.

Falstaff Falstaff has been regarded as a character of puzzling complexity. To what extent the twice-depicted Oldcastle, who lies back of him, may be shining inconsistently through his fat bulk nobody can tell. In any case, his earlier forms will keep us from the fallacy of thinking of him either as an actual character such as occurs in history, or as struck out at one forging from a clear-cut and definite pattern in Shakespeare's brain. Falstaff is, from the point of view of literary history, an accident, a very happy accident, which will not bear the analysis of the critics. He will afford any amount of enjoyment to readers and theater-goers; but we cannot, in the light of his origin, expect meticulous consistency, or even believe that Shakespeare, by original conception, made him inconsistent. Shakespeare we may be sure did not worry about him at all. Even the man he pictured in *The Merry Wives of Windsor* is not the same one he pictured in *1* and *2 Henry IV*. Possibly he could not have been unless his history had been equally complex. Falstaff happened into the drama from a very varied body of antecedent circumstances. He is not entirely accounted for, as one body of critics would have us believe, by considering him as a traditional stage rogue and jester, although he plays every trick known to that species; nor is he entirely accounted for as a combination of traditional rogue and gull. He is still less, however, to be accounted for by those other critics who persist in thinking of him as a man as real Sir Walter Raleigh and a character whose every word, act, experience, and thought arise by his creator's deliberate design.[1]

Stage history The Henry IV plays must both have been popular during the lifetime of their author and probably until the closing of the theaters in 1642. Although there are few known references to actual performances, *1 Henry IV* went through eight quarto editions, and no plays are more frequently alluded to.[2] After the Restoration *1 Henry IV* was soon revived, Pepys having seen the play with varying approval no less than five times. The Restoration and the eighteenth century were the Falstaff era. The men of the time were no doubt well able to appreciate the hearty English humor of the past, and among actors there was a great series of Falstaffs. Betterton played Hotspur until 1700 and then won a great reputation as an actor of Falstaff, playing the part in *1* and *2 Henry IV* and *The Merry Wives of Windsor*, as did James Quin, who has come down in stage history as one of the greatest actors in that part. Garrick played Hotspur none too success-

[1]The student should read for varying points of view on Falstaff: Schücking, Stoll (*Modern Philology*, XII, 197-240), Bradley ("The Rejection of Falstaff," in *Oxford Lectures*), Brandes, Dowden, and other critics.
[2]R. P. Cowl, *Some Echoes in Elizabethan Drama of Shakespeare's "King Henry the Fourth*," London, 1926.

fully and later succeeded better as the King in *2 Henry IV*. John Henderson was so great a Falstaff that it was thought that he rivaled Quin. John Philip Kemble played Hotspur successfully in 1802, and in 1804 he and his brother Charles played the parts of the King and the Prince in the second part. The first part was played now and then in the nineteenth century in England and America, but the second part almost never. Both parts were played by Phelps at Sadler's Wells about the middle of the nineteenth century and by the Benson company at the Stratford Memorial Theater in 1906. Among the more successful recent revivals are those by dramatic societies at several universities. Though both parts are better plays than *The Merry Wives of Windsor*, they have not a tithe of its popularity. George Bartley (1782?-1858) was probably the most famous of the Falstaffs of the nineteenth century.

Annotated editions of *1 Henry IV* and *2 Henry IV* are printed on pages 519-561, 562-609 of this volume.

HENRY V

Text The only reliable text of *Henry V* is that of the First Folio. On August 4, 1600, the play was entered in the Stationers' Register along with *As You Like It* and *Much Ado about Nothing* to be "staied." If this was intended to prevent piracy it did not in the case of *Henry V* succeed, for a corrupt version was issued that year by Thomas Millington and John Busby without stationers' license. This quarto is a wretched thing without the choruses and without many important passages including three scenes (I, i; III, i; IV, ii). It bears no evidence of having been printed from a prompt copy. It was republished in 1602 and again by Pavier in 1619 with the fictitious date of 1608, when he was projecting a collection of Shakespeare's plays. No corrected and augmented copy of the play seems to have been issued in quarto form. It has been suggested without great probability that an actor who played the part of the Governor of Harfleur made up the version for the printers, since in the midst of the disorder of other rôles his part is relatively correct. However this may be, it seems quite certain that the quarto is not based on the Folio version as we have it. The Folio version, on the other hand, seems to be a revision of some such version as that of the quarto.[1]

Date It is usually thought that *Henry V* was written between April 15 and September 28, 1599, because of an allusion in the chorus of the fifth act (ll. 29-34) to an expedition to Ireland led by the Earl of Essex. The campaign resulted in disaster, a fact which was evidently unknown when the lines were written. The play is not included in Meres's list in 1598, although *Henry IV* appears there. The promise of the epilogue to *2 Henry IV* that "our humble author will continue the story, with Sir John in it, and make you merry with fair Katharine of France," not realized as regards Sir John, is a part of the Oldcastle apology and points as we have seen to 1598, indicating that *Henry V* had not yet been written. There is also the allusion in the chorus of the first act (ll. 12-14) to "this wooden O" which seems to be the Globe Theater, thought to have been ready for occupancy in the season of 1599.[2] The choruses may, of course, be later than the rest of the play; it is possible, therefore, that they are part of a revision of the play by Shakespeare in 1599.

Sources The serious events of the story come from Holinshed's *Chronicles* (1587), which Shakespeare followed with some license, but faithfully upon the whole. Holinshed recounts the more glorious features of the conquest of France. Henry advances an outrageous, but undoubtedly sincere, claim to the crown of France and a better one to certain provinces of that kingdom anciently belonging to his family. Fearful of waging an unjust war, he consults the leading churchmen of his land, who reassure him. It is shrewdly pointed out by the ecclesiastics that by busying the king in a foreign war they might prevent the execution of a bill in parliament for confiscating

their lands. Henry quells a treason in the form of a plot against his life by three of his favorite courtiers. He invades France and captures Harfleur; advances with a small and ill-provided army towards Calais and is forced by his misfortunes to reap the harvest of glory at Agincourt; so much in regular order from Holinshed. Shakespeare then omits Henry's far more important second campaign, three years in length, and all intervening events. He closes his play with the treaty of Troyes and Henry's betrothal to the Princess Katharine. Suggestions for the episode of the tennis balls, Pistol's capture of the French soldier, and Henry's wooing of Katharine come from the old Henry V play. (See Introduction to *1* and *2 Henry IV*.) The connections with the Henry IV plays are closely made. In the first scene of the first act the churchmen talk over with approval Henry's reformation. In the third scene of the second act the Hostess gives her memorable account of the death of Falstaff. Pistol, Bardolph, the Hostess, and the Boy are brought over from *2 Henry IV*. To them is added Nym, so "humorous" a character that he seems intended to ridicule the vogue of humor characters. To the comic side Shakespeare also adds four soldiers, typical of the four British races, Fluellen, Macmorris, Captain Jamy, and Williams. In a famous comic scene he assigns to the Welshman Fluellen the dramatic function of exposing the braggart soldier Pistol.

The theme *Henry V* is essentially epic in theme. Business of council and state, war, peace negotiations, and a courtship, all occupying the hero's mind during a single scene, are narrative rather than dramatic. *Henry V* is, nevertheless, remarkable as a chronicle play in that it remains a block of history, a series of disconnected scenes, and is at the same time a unit. The unity is achieved in some measure by centering the interest upon Henry himself, particularly as a figure at the battle of Agincourt; but also by various other devices. The choruses bridge over the intervals between the main events of the play, each selected event standing out as a piece of splendid pageantry. The play, a spectacular drama, fulfills an ideal artistic law of the chronicle play. Shakespeare realized his artistic difficulties in shaping

[1]Pollard, *Folios and Quartos*, p. 81, and *Shakespeare's War with the Pirates*, Cambridge, 1920; Adams, *A Life of William Shakespeare*, pp. 518-9, 525-532; Hardin Craig, "The Relation of the First Quarto Version to the First Folio Version of Shakespeare's *Henry V*," *Philological Quarterly*, VI, 225-234; Evelyn M. Albright, "The Folio Version of *Henry V*," *Publications of the Modern Language Association*, XLIII, 722-756; Chambers, *William Shakespeare*, I, 388-396.
[2]Chambers, *The Elizabethan Stage*, II, 414-434.

his materials for the theater, and the choruses are full of apology.

Piece out our imperfections with your thoughts,

he says; and again

And so our scene must to the battle fly;
Where—O for pity!—we shall much disgrace
With four or five most vile and ragged foils,
Right ill-disposed in brawl ridiculous,
The name of Agincourt.

And yet in no history play is the difficulty of presenting a wide range of historical events so well overcome. This is in part achieved by a feature of the play appropriate to its spectacular quality, namely, its oratory. *Henry V* has not the poetical oratory of *Richard II*, nor the popular oratory of *Julius Cæsar*, but a clear and practical eloquence of its own (I, ii, 259-310; III, i, 1-34; III, vi, 148-175; IV, iii, 18-67, 90-125). Passages of pure and beautiful poetry add to the effect (II, ii, 126-144; IV, vi, 7-32), which is in no small measure due to the exalted declamatory tone of the choruses.

Henry V   It is the figure of Henry V, however, on which most pains have been lavished. To know the king in *Henry V* one must also know Prince Hal and his career as Shakespeare conceived it in *1* and *2 Henry IV*. One should also know Bolingbroke from those plays and from *Richard II*, and the politics of all the plays. Henry has learned much from his past, so that he appears in *Henry V* with certain established traits and qualities, no doubt conceived of as due to his life experience. He is prudent and conscientious (I, ii; IV, i). The duties of kingship and not its frivolities and amenities are shown in him. He is just and unflinching in the enforcement of law and discipline (II, ii; III, iii; III, vi, 113-120). He is a man of most pronounced devotion to great objects outside of himself, modest, humble, honest, religious, sympathetic with all classes of men, with a man-to-man way of regarding his fellows, which was, and is, one of the noblest traits of his race. So naturally are these traits made to grow up in the prince and king, so well are they accounted for in the course of events, that one forgets that there lies back of them the most important theme in the social and political thinking of the Renaissance, namely, the ideal prince. One thinks at once of the three great classics of the Renaissance which are still best known to the modern world: Castiglione's *Il Cortegiano* (1528), translated into English by Hoby as *The Courtier* (1561), Elyot's *The Governour* (1531), and Macchiavelli's *Prince*. No subject interested the Renaissance so much as the training and character of statesmen. In the Tudor time it was thought most necessary, most essential, to have an educated monarch and thus to uphold the standard of righteousness in public men and affairs. The ethics of the time was largely a public ethics, so that the best men of the age were saturated in the literature of the courtier, the governor, and the prince. Sidney never stirred abroad without a copy of *The Courtier* in his pocket. The most weighty of ancient classics often contributed to this interest. Plato's *Republic* and Aristotle's *Politics* are concerned with the education of the philosopher prince; Castiglione had based his work in some measure on Cicero's *De Oratore*. Henry's princely virtues, as enumerated and depicted in *Henry V*, are the recognizable and customary group, and one cannot but believe that he was deliberately conceived as the embodiment of these ideals. "Never was such a sudden scholar made. Hear him but reason on divinity, debate of commonwealth affairs, discourse of war, or any cause of policy, the Gordian knot of it he will unloose, familiar as his garter. The prince obscured his contemplation under the veil of wildness; but, no doubt, it grew like the summer grass." (See Act I, Scene i.)

Stage history   *Henry V* must certainly have been popular in its own day, if for no other reason than because it impresses us as the finest expression of Elizabethan patriotism. A funeral elegy written in honor of the contemporary actor, Richard Burbage, connects him with the part of Henry. There is no other known contemporary allusion. The play was apparently neglected until well into the eighteenth century, at least two adaptations having proved short-lived. Garrick presented Shakespeare's play at Drury Lane in 1747 and surprised the world by leaving the part of the heroic king to Barry while he himself recited the part of the Chorus. In 1761 came a characteristic revival of *Henry V* by John Rich (1682?-1761), pantomimist and theatrical manager, at Covent Garden. The play was there treated as a spectacle, which fashion has been followed. In Charles Kean's presentation at the Princess's Theater in 1850 the siege of Harfleur was staged with the utmost attention to historical accuracy, Henry's return to London was presented, not in the words of the Chorus, but as an actual royal entry, and Mrs. Kean recited the part of the Chorus costumed as Clio, the Muse of History. These features likewise appeared in Richard Mansfield's famous American production in 1900. John Philip Kemble, Edmund Kean, Charles Kean, William Macready, Samuel Phelps, and Lewis Waller have acted the part of King Henry, usually with some show of elaboration and ornament.

An annotated edition of *Henry V* is printed on page 610-656 of this volume.

IV. A TRAGEDY OF THE SECOND PERIOD

JULIUS CÆSAR

Publication and date The only early publication of *Julius Cæsar* is that of the First Folio, where it is placed among the tragedies and called *The Tragedie of Julius Cæsar*. In the table of contents it appears as *The Life and Death of Julius Cæsar*, as if it were there thought of as a history play, which in some respects it is. The text of the Folio is good. John Weever's *Mirror of Martyrs*, written as a defense of Sir John Oldcastle, probably in 1599, alludes to the play in these lines:

The many-headed multitude were drawn
By Brutus' speech that Cæsar was ambitious;
When eloquent Mark Anthony had shown
His virtues, who but Brutus then was vicious?
Man's memory with new forgets the old;
One tale is good until another's told.

Also Thomas Platter, a physician visiting London from Basel, crossed the river and saw about two o'clock in the afternoon in a "thatch-roofed building the tragedy of the first emperor Julius Cæsar" on September 21, 1599. This would point to the Globe Theater and to *Julius Cæsar* as a new play.[1] Ben Jonson's *Everyman in his Humour*, also acted in 1599, quotes *Et tu Brute!* somewhat derisively, and remarks that "reason long since is fled to animals," which seems to allude to Anthony's

O judgement! thou art fled to brutish beasts,
And men have lost their reason.
(III, ii, 109-110.)

[1]G. Binz, "Londoner Theater und Schauspiele im Jahre 1599," *Anglia*, XXII, 456; Chambers, *The Elizabethan Stage*, II, 364-6; *Thomas Platters des Jüngeren Englandfahrt im Jahre 1599*, edited by Hans Hecht, Halle, 1929.

These references indicate that the play belongs to the year 1599, or slightly earlier.

Source The men of the Renaissance were greatly interested in the figures of Roman history. Cæsar particularly caught their attention and appealed to their imaginations. They endorsed the idea of empire, and, although they probably understood and to some degree appreciated the idea of republicanism, it seemed to them an impossible dream. Probably Cæsar, Cicero, Anthony, Cleopatra, Augustus, and the whole story of the breakdown of the Roman republic and the establishment of the glorious Roman empire, were as familiar to an Elizabethan audience as they are to us, and were relatively much more important. The Elizabethan world, which as yet had not seen Cromwell and Washington, looked to antiquity for stories of political significance, events which had ideas back of them. The chief means of rendering familiar the stories of the great men of Greece and Rome was Plutarch's *Lives of the Noble Grecians and Romans*. Plutarch was a clever Greek, who lived from about 46 A.D. to 120 A.D., lectured on philosophy in Rome, and wrote forty-six parallel lives of Grecians and Romans arranged in twos for comparison, Cicero being paired with Demosthenes, Theseus with Romulus, Cæsar with Alexander, and so forth. Plutarch's purpose was not primarily historical, but moral and fictional; and his book had a good deal of the engrossing interest of fiction and far more authority, for Plutarch was a moralist and a great observer of life. His theory of biography was that a man's character is often more clearly revealed in his idle moments, his petty tastes, and off-hand conversation than in his battles and public actions and utterances. Plutarch, who was a literary artist of great skill, found in Jacques Amyot, who translated the *Lives* into French in 1559, a person able to render him appreciatively; and, in turn, in Sir Thomas North another equally good translator who, though he did not go to Plutarch's Greek, was able to put Amyot's French into racy and effective English. North's translation was issued in 1579 and must have been well known to Shakespeare, particularly since an edition was issued in 1595 from the press of his fellow-townsman Richard Field. Shakespeare, who had already used Plutarch in the composition of *A Midsummer-Night's Dream*, was always willing to let well enough alone. He therefore made use of Plutarch's gold without trying to gild it. He respected Holinshed's chronicles only, we may believe, as he respected the general truth of history as he understood it, but Holinshed was only an annalist of poor enough tradition and little art; Plutarch, on the other hand, gave him scene by scene the very texture of what he was to say. Plutarch is the main reason for the carefully detailed portraits of the persons in the play of *Julius Cæsar*, and it may be that from Plutarch Shakespeare learned much of the art of dramatic portraiture and the complexity of human motive.

Julius Cæsar and Plutarch At any rate, it is easy to point out as we go through the play how Shakespeare has repeated event after event from Plutarch's lives of Cæsar, Brutus, and Anthony; as, for example, the behavior and fate of the tribunes Flavius and Marullus; the offering of the crown to Cæsar and the reception of his refusal of it by the mob; the formation of the conspiracy with the inclusion of Ligarius and the exclusion of Cicero; Brutus's whole course of conduct with his gradual yielding to persuasion and his refusal to bind the conspirators with oaths; all the circumstances of Cæsar's debate with himself, his wife, and with Decius Brutus as to whether or not he should go to the senate-house on the fatal Ides of March; and so on throughout the play. It must not be thought that Shakespeare does not improve on Plutarch, for

Shakespeare makes the story more vividly dramatic. Consider how much more frightful the supernatural portents which precede the death of Cæsar are rendered by having the hardy Casca with his drawn sword in his hand tremble and start as he recounts them. Then again, the greatest scene in the play, that in which Anthony over the body of Cæsar incites the mob to vengeance, seems to be Shakespeare's own. One of the most interesting things in Shakespeare's version is the way in which he has caught Plutarch's delineation of Brutus and Cassius in terms of the philosophies which they held and has made these philosophies illuminate their parts as characters in the play. Brutus is a Stoic, quite the most respectable of ancient creeds, who believes in right for right's sake. We say he is an idealist. He has steeled himself against the strokes of fate and carries the medicine for his own wounds. He follows his ideals to the end, though he wrecks the conspiracy and ultimately takes his own life, for he finds ruin at last too great for stoicism. Cassius, on the other hand, is an Epicurean, not the vulgar pleasure lover whom moderns have made typical of the sect, but an Epicurean as anciently conceived, a practical man, one who faces facts and tests all things, even the ambition of Cæsar, in terms of their effects on him himself. His strength is less than that of Brutus, because his philosophy is a philosophy of pliability. Brutus is "yoke-fellow to a lamb."

Julius Cæsar Singularly enough the one respect in which Shakespeare differs most from Plutarch is in the conception of Julius Cæsar himself. Shakespeare's Cæsar is arrogant and boastful, inconsistent and petulant, vain and deaf, superstitious and self-deluding. In Plutarch he is a far nobler and more impressive character. Here then is something which obviously requires explanation. We are asked by the ordinary critics to believe that Shakespeare has given us in the portrait of Cæsar a picture of decaying power; but the matter goes deeper than this, even if we believe that Shakespeare ever worked in a way which would have caused him to invent a thing for which there was no warrant in fact. Julius Cæsar was a popular theme on the stage of the sixteenth century in Holland, Italy, France, and

England. He had acquired a perfectly well-known stage character not unlike that in Shakespeare. Cæsar had been made the hero of various Senecan tragedies, traceable from the Latin *Julius Cæsar* of Muret and its French adaptation *César* by Jacques Grévin to Sir William Alexander's *Julius Cæsar* and the anonymous *Cæsar and Pompey, or the Tragedy of Cæsar's Revenge* (1592-6).[1] Cæsar's pride and blindness, even his superstition, were in these plays the tragic weaknesses over which brooded the vengeance of the gods.

Why *Julius Cæsar*? Brutus and Cassius, and possibly Anthony, all play more important parts in *Julius Cæsar* than does Cæsar himself; why, one asks, is the play called *Julius Cæsar?* To answer this question it is necessary to point out that the theme of Julius Cæsar was usually a tragedy in two parts, the first part dealing with the overthrow of Pompey and the death of Cæsar and the second part with Cæsar's revenge. In the latter, Cæsar's spirit returns to demand vengeance and is not laid until his enemies are destroyed. It may be that *Julius Cæsar* is in some measure a combination of these two themes, but mainly a play of Cæsar's revenge. In other words, it has a Senecan background which still makes itself felt. In the light of this it will be seen that Cæsar alive is a condensed and hasty picture of a smitten tragic hero; but that the importance of Cæsar dead is fully recognized. To Anthony he is

> the noblest man
> That ever lived in the tide of times.

Brutus calls him "the foremost man of all this world," and says

> I have not known when his affections sway'd
> More than his reason.

And Cassius's last words are

> Cæsar, thou art revenged,
> Even with the sword that kill'd thee.

The play is, therefore, named for Cæsar dead, who dying becomes the most potent character in the play. The editor of the Tudor edition quotes from North's trans-lation of a *Comparison of Alexander and Cæsar:* "He lived in the person of his successor, Augustus, who . . . established a monarchy the which . . . hath continued many hundreds of years," a statement which seems to express Shakespeare's conception of Cæsar's primacy.

Stage history *Julius Cæsar*, perhaps because of its stately classical qualities, escaped mutilation by the Restoration adapters and revisers of Shakespeare,[2] though John Sheffield, first Duke of Buckingham and Normanby (1648-1721), rewrote according to the current ideas of dramatic propriety *Julius Cæsar* as two plays, *Julius Cæsar* and *Marcus Brutus.* The play as Shakespeare wrote it, dealing in moral and philosophic fashion with ideas of governing, appeals to men of affairs and statesmen. It is a play for the grave and thoughtful, and its gravity and judicial tone, its political speculation, its clearness and purity (what was called its classical quality), caused it to become a favorite with the playgoers of the Restoration and the eighteenth century. Its vigorous declamatory passages also had an appeal. Betterton created the rôle of Brutus, and the greatest actors since his time have played one or other of its five first-rate parts. Of Betterton's acting of Brutus Colley Cibber says, "When the Betterton-Brutus was provoked in his dispute with Cassius, his spirit flew only to his eye; his steady look alone supplied that terror which he disdained an intemperance in his voice should rise to." Barton Booth, James Quin, John Philip Kemble, Junius Brutus Booth, Charles Kean, and Beerbohm Tree have been distinguished as Brutus. Because of the number of important parts *Julius Cæsar* has been a great play for combinations of great actors, all-star casts. In the performance at Covent Garden in 1838 Macready acted Brutus; Phelps, Cassius; and Vandenhoff and Elton, Anthony. On the American stage Edwin Booth and Lawrence Barrett were magnificent as Brutus and Cassius.

An annotated edition of *Julius Cæsar* is printed on pages 657-694 of this volume.

---

[1]Harry Morgan Ayres, "Shakespeare's *Julius Cæsar* in the Light of Some Other Versions," *Publ. Mod. Lang. Ass'n.*, XXV, 183-227; "Cæsar's Revenge," *ibid.*, XXX, 771-787.

[2]F. W. Kilbourne, *Alterations and Adaptations of Shakespeare*, Boston, 1906; Hazelton Spencer, *Shakespeare Improved*, Cambridge, 1928.

TEXT OF NINE PLAYS
FROM THE PERIOD OF COMEDIES
AND HISTORIES

The Merchant of Venice

Much Ado about Nothing

As You Like It

Twelfth Night

King Richard II

King Henry IV, Part I

King Henry IV, Part II

King Henry V

Julius Cæsar

THE MERCHANT OF VENICE

DRAMATIS PERSONÆ

The DUKE OF VENICE.

The PRINCE OF MOROCCO,⎫ suitors to Portia.
The PRINCE OF ARRAGON,⎭

ANTONIO, a merchant of Venice.

BASSANIO, his friend, suitor likewise to Portia.

SALANIO,⎫
SALARINO,⎪ friends to Antonio and Bassanio.
GRATIANO,⎬
SALERIO,⎭

LORENZO, in love with Jessica.

SHYLOCK, a rich Jew.

TUBAL, a Jew, his friend.

LAUNCELOT GOBBO, the clown, servant to Shylock.

OLD GOBBO, father to Launcelot.

LEONARDO, servant to Bassanio.

BALTHASAR,⎫ servants to Portia.
STEPHANO,⎭

PORTIA, a rich heiress.

NERISSA, her waiting-maid.

JESSICA, daughter to Shylock.

Magnificoes of Venice, Officers of the Court of Justice, Gaoler, Servants to Portia, and other Attendants.

SCENE: *Partly at Venice, and partly at Belmont, the seat of Portia, on the Continent.*

ACT I.

SCENE I. *Venice. A street.*

Enter ANTONIO, SALARINO, *and* SALANIO.

Ant. In sooth, I know not why I am so sad:
It wearies me; you say it wearies you;
But how I caught it, found it, or came by it,
What stuff 'tis made of, whereof it is born,
I am to learn;
And such a want-wit sadness makes of me,
That I have much ado to know myself.

Salar. Your mind is tossing on the ocean;
There, where your argosies with portly sail,
Like signiors and rich burghers on the flood,
Or, as it were, the pageants of the sea, 11
Do overpeer the petty traffickers,
That curtsy to them, do them reverence,
As they fly by them with their woven wings.

Salan. Believe me, sir, had I such venture forth,
The better part of my affections would

Be with my hopes abroad. I should be still
Plucking the grass, to know where sits the wind,
Peering in maps for ports and piers and roads;
And every object that might make me fear
Misfortune to my ventures, out of doubt 21
Would make me sad.

Salar. My wind cooling my broth
Would blow me to an ague, when I thought
What harm a wind too great at sea might do.
I should not see the sandy hour-glass run,
But I should think of shallows and of flats,
And see my wealthy Andrew dock'd in sand,
Vailing her high-top lower than her ribs
To kiss her burial. Should I go to church
And see the holy edifice of stone, 30
And not bethink me straight of dangerous rocks,
Which touching but my gentle vessel's side,
Would scatter all her spices on the stream,
Enrobe the roaring waters with my silks,
And, in a word, but even now worth this,

---

5. **am to learn**, have not learned. 9. **argosies.** large merchant ships; word derived from *Ragusa*, an Italian seaport. **portly**, large and full. 12. **overpeer**, tower over. 15. **venture forth**, investment risked.

26. **flats**, sand banks. 27. **Andrew**, name of a ship. 28. **Vailing**, lowering. **high-top**, probably top-sail. 35. **this**, probably expressed by a gesture.

And now worth nothing? Shall I have the
    thought
To think on this, and shall I lack the thought
That such a thing bechanced would make me
    sad?
But tell not me; I know, Antonio
Is sad to think upon his merchandise.   40
    Ant. Believe me, no: I thank my fortune
    for it,
My ventures are not in one bottom trusted,
Nor to one place; nor is my whole estate
Upon the fortune of this present year:
Therefore my merchandise makes me not
    sad.
    Salar. Why, then you are in love.
    Ant.   Fie, fie!
    Salar. Not in love neither? Then let us
    say you are sad,
Because you are not merry: and 'twere as
    easy
For you to laugh and leap and say you are
    merry,
Because you are not sad. Now, by two-
    headed Janus,   50
Nature hath framed strange fellows in her
    time:
Some that will evermore peep through their
    eyes
And laugh like parrots at a bag-piper,
And other of such vinegar aspect
That they'll not show their teeth in way of
    smile,
Though Nestor swear the jest be laughable.

    Enter BASSANIO, LORENZO, *and* GRATIANO.

    Salan. Here comes Bassanio, your most
    noble kinsman,
Gratiano and Lorenzo. Fare ye well:
We leave you now with better company.
    Salar. I would have stay'd till I had
    made you merry,   60
If worthier friends had not prevented me.
    Ant. Your worth is very dear in my regard.
I take it, your own business calls on you
And you embrace the occasion to depart.
    Salar. Good morrow, my good lords.
    Bass. Good signiors both, when shall we
    laugh? say, when?
You grow exceeding strange: must it be so?

    Salar. We'll make our leisures to attend
    on yours. [*Exeunt Salarino and Salanio.*
    Lor. My Lord Bassanio, since you have
    found Antonio,
We two will leave you: but at dinner-time, 70
I pray you, have in mind where we must
    meet.
    Bass. I will not fail you.
    Gra. You look not well, Signior Antonio;
You have too much respect upon the world:
They lose it that do buy it with much care:
Believe me, you are marvellously changed.
    Ant. I hold the world but as the world,
    Gratiano;
A stage where every man must play a part,
And mine a sad one.
    Gra.   Let me play the fool:
With mirth and laughter let old wrinkles
    come,   80
And let my liver rather heat with wine
Than my heart cool with mortifying groans.
Why should a man, whose blood is warm
    within,
Sit like his grandsire cut in alabaster?
Sleep when he wakes and creep into the
    jaundice
By being peevish? I tell thee what, Antonio—
I love thee, and it is my love that speaks—
There are a sort of men whose visages
Do cream and mantle like a standing pond,
And do a wilful stillness entertain,   90
With purpose to be dress'd in an opinion
Of wisdom, gravity, profound conceit,
As who should say 'I am Sir Oracle,
And when I ope my lips let no dog bark!'
O my Antonio, I do know of these
That therefore only are reputed wise
For saying nothing, when, I am very sure,
If they should speak, would almost damn
    those ears
Which, hearing them, would call their
    brothers fools.
I'll tell thee more of this another time: 100
But fish not, with this melancholy bait,
For this fool gudgeon, this opinion.
Come, good Lorenzo. Fare ye well awhile:
I'll end my exhortation after dinner.

---

42. **bottom**, ship. 50. **two-headed Janus.** Janus,
Roman god of all beginnings, was represented by a
figure with two faces, one smiling and one sad. 54. **aspect**, look; accented on second syllable. 56. **Nestor**,
a character in *Iliad*, noted for gravity. 61. **prevented**,
anticipated. 64. **occasion**, opportunity. 67. **strange**,
unfriendly. **must it be so?** Must you go? or, must
you show unfriendliness?

74. **have . . . upon**, pay too much attention to.
81. **heat with wine.** Shakespeare thinks of the liver
as the seat of the passions and wine as an agency for
inflaming them. 82. **mortifying**, deadly. 85. **jaun-
dice**, regarded as arising from the effects of violent
passions. 89. **mantle**, become covered with scum.
90. **wilful stillness**, obstinate silence. 91. **opinion**,
reputation. 92. **profound conceit**, deep thought.
99. **fools.** Cf. *St. Matthew* v, 22. 102. **gudgeon**, a
fish used for bait.

Lor. Well, we will leave you then till
dinner-time:
I must be one of these same dumb wise men,
For Gratiano never lets me speak.
   Gra. Well, keep me company but two
years moe,
Thou shalt not know the sound of thine own
tongue.
   Ant. Farewell: I'll grow a talker for this
gear.   110
   Gra. Thanks, i' faith, for silence is only
commendable
In a neat's tongue dried and a maid not
vendible. [*Exeunt Gratiano and Lorenzo.*
   Ant. Is that any thing now?
   Bass. Gratiano speaks an infinite deal of
nothing, more than any man in all Venice.
His reasons are as two grains of wheat hid
in two bushels of chaff: you shall seek all day
ere you find them, and when you have them,
they are not worth the search.
   Ant. Well, tell me now what lady is the
same
To whom you swore a secret pilgrimage,   120
That you to-day promised to tell me of?
   Bass. 'Tis not unknown to you, Antonio,
How much I have disabled mine estate,
By something showing a more swelling port
Than my faint means would grant continu-
ance:
Nor do I now make moan to be abridged
From such a noble rate; but my chief care
Is to come fairly off from the great debts
Wherein my time something too prodigal
Hath left me gaged. To you, Antonio,   130
I owe the most, in money and in love,
And from your love I have a warranty
To unburden all my plots and purposes
How to get clear of all the debts I owe.
   Ant. I pray you, good Bassanio, let me
know it;
And if it stand, as you yourself still do,
Within the eye of honour, be assured,
My purse, my person, my extremest means,
Lie all unlock'd to your occasions.
   Bass. In my school-days, when I had lost
one shaft,   140
I shot his fellow of the self-same flight
The self-same way with more advised watch,
To find the other forth, and by adventuring
both

I oft found both: I urge this childhood proof,
Because what follows is pure innocence.
I owe you much, and, like a wilful youth,
That which I owe is lost; but if you please
To shoot another arrow that self way
Which you did shoot the first, I do not doubt,
As I will watch the aim, or to find both   150
Or bring your latter hazard back again
And thankfully rest debtor for the first.
   Ant. You know me well, and herein spend
but time
To wind about my love with circumstance;
And out of doubt you do me now more
wrong
In making question of my uttermost
Than if you had made waste of all I have:
Then do but say to me what I should do
That in your knowledge may by me be done,
And I am prest unto it: therefore, speak.   160
   Bass. In Belmont is a lady richly left;
And she is fair and, fairer than that word,
Of wondrous virtues: sometimes from her
eyes
I did receive fair speechless messages:
Her name is Portia, nothing undervalued
To Cato's daughter, Brutus' Portia:
Nor is the wide world ignorant of her worth,
For the four winds blow in from every coast
Renowned suitors, and her sunny locks
Hang on her temples like a golden fleece;   170
Which makes her seat of Belmont Colchos'
strand,
And many Jasons come in quest of her.
O my Antonio, had I but the means
To hold a rival place with one of them,
I have a mind presages me such thrift,
That I should questionless be fortunate!
   Ant. Thou know'st that all my fortunes
are at sea;
Neither have I money nor commodity
To raise a present sum: therefore go forth;
Try what my credit can in Venice do: 180
That shall be rack'd, even to the utter-
most,
To furnish thee to Belmont, to fair Portia.

144. proof, test drawn from experience. **145. innocence,** sometimes defined as "foolishness"; may rather
mean "ingenuousness." **153-160. You know ... speak.**
This is the first indication of the friendship theme of the
play. **154. wind about,** approach circuitously. **160.
prest,** ready. **161. richly left.** Bassanio's frank avowal
of his desire for Portia's fortune has caused him to be
blamed as a fortune-hunter by modern critics who forget
the importance of dowry in Renaissance consideration.
166. Brutus' Portia, a woman famous in ancient times
for constancy and courage; she is a character in *Julius
Cæsar.* **168. coast,** country. **172. Jasons.** This explains *golden fleece* and *Colchos' strand,* above. **175.
presages,** i.e., which presages; relative pronoun omitted.
181. rack'd, stretched.

112. neat's. *Neat* is defined as "cattle of the ox kind."
124. something, somewhat, rather. **127. rate,** style
of living. **130. gaged,** pledged. **142. advised,** careful.
143. forth, out.

Go, presently inquire, and so will I,
Where money is, and I no question make
To have it of my trust or for my sake.

[*Exeunt.*

SCENE II. *Belmont. A room in* PORTIA'S
house.

Enter PORTIA *and* NERISSA.

Por. By my troth, Nerissa, my little body
is aweary of this great world.

Ner. You would be, sweet madam, if your
miseries were in the same abundance as your
good fortunes are: and yet, for aught I see,
they are as sick that surfeit with too much as
they that starve with nothing. It is no mean
happiness therefore, to be seated in the
mean: superfluity comes sooner by white
hairs, but competency lives longer.   10

Por. Good sentences and well pronounced.

Ner. They would be better, if well followed.

Por. If to do were as easy as to know what
were good to do, chapels had been churches
and poor men's cottages princes' palaces. It
is a good divine that follows his own instructions: I can easier teach twenty what were
good to be done, than be one of the twenty to
follow mine own teaching. The brain may
devise laws for the blood, but a hot temper
leaps o'er a cold decree: such a hare is madness the youth, to skip o'er the meshes of
good counsel the cripple. But this reasoning
is not in the fashion to choose me a husband.
O me, the word 'choose!' I may neither
choose whom I would nor refuse whom I dislike; so is the will of a living daughter curbed
by the will of a dead father. Is it not hard,
Nerissa, that I cannot choose one nor re- 29
fuse none?

Ner. Your father was ever virtuous; and
holy men at their death have good inspira-
tions: therefore the lottery, that he hath
devised in these three chests of gold, silver
and lead, whereof who chooses his meaning
chooses you, will, no doubt, never be chosen
by any rightly but one who shall rightly love.
But what warmth is there in your affection

towards any of these princely suitors that
are already come?   38

Por. I pray thee, over-name them; and as
thou namest them, I will describe them; and,
according to my description, level at my
affection.

Ner. First, there is the Neapolitan prince.

Por. Ay, that's a colt indeed, for he doth
nothing but talk of his horse; and he makes
it a great appropriation to his own good
parts, that he can shoe him himself. I am
much afeard my lady his mother played
false with a smith.   48

Ner. Then there is the County Palatine.

Por. He doth nothing but frown, as who
should say 'If you will not have me, choose:'
he hears merry tales and smiles not: I fear he
will prove the weeping philosopher when he
grows old, being so full of unmannerly sadness in his youth. I had rather be married to
a death's-head with a bone in his mouth
than to either of these. God defend me from
these two!

Ner. How say you by the French lord,
Monsieur Le Bon?   59

Por. God made him, and therefore let him
pass for a man. In truth, I know it is a sin
to be a mocker: but, he! why, he hath a horse
better than the Neapolitan's, a better bad
habit of frowning than the Count Palatine;
he is every man in no man; if a throstle sing,
he falls straight a capering: he will fence with
his own shadow: if I should marry him, I
should marry twenty husbands. If he would
despise me, I would forgive him, for if he love
me to madness, I shall never requite him. 70

Ner. What say you, then, to Falconbridge, the young baron of England?

Por. You know I say nothing to him, for
he understands not me, nor I him: he hath
neither Latin, French, nor Italian, and you
will come into the court and swear that I
have a poor pennyworth in the English. He
is a proper man's picture, but, alas, who can
converse with a dumb-show? How oddly he
is suited! I think he bought his doublet
in Italy, his round hose in France, his bon-

Scene ii. **9. comes sooner by,** brings about sooner.
11. sentences, maxims. **20. blood,** thought of as a
chief agent of the passions, which in turn were regarded as
the enemies of reason. **22. meshes,** nets; allusion to
hare-hunting with nets. A *cripple* could not follow the
hare if it skipped over the net. **23. reasoning,** discourse, talk. **27-28. will . . . will,** volition . . . testament. **32. lottery,** subject of *will,* line 35. **34. his,**
i.e., the father's.

44-48. Ay . . . smith. There is a rather hard tone in
Portia's description of her suitors. The lady of the
source was, however, much more cruel. **49. County,**
count. **51. choose,** possibly, do as you please. **53.
weeping philosopher,** Heraclitus of Ephesus, who wept
at everything. **65. throstle,** thrush. **78. proper,**
good-looking. **80. suited,** dressed. **doublet,** coat.
81. hose, trousers. **bonnet,** hat. It was a common
subject of censure in Elizabethan days that Englishmen rigged themselves out in foreign clothes.

net in Germany and his behaviour every where.

Ner. What think you of the Scottish lord, his neighbour?   84

Por. That he hath a neighbourly charity in him, for he borrowed a box of the ear of the Englishman and swore he would pay him again when he was able: I think the Frenchman became his surety and sealed under   89 for another.

Ner. How like you the young German, the Duke of Saxony's nephew?

Por. Very vilely in the morning, when he is sober, and most vilely in the afternoon, when he is drunk: when he is best, he is a little worse than a man, and when he is worst, he is little better than a beast: an the worst fall that ever fell, I hope I shall make shift to go without him.

Ner. If he should offer to choose, and choose the right casket, you should refuse to perform your father's will, if you should refuse to accept him.   101

Por. Therefore, for fear of the worst, I pray thee, set a deep glass of rhenish wine on the contrary casket, for if the devil be within and that temptation without, I know he will choose it. I will do any thing, Nerissa, ere I'll be married to a sponge.

Ner. You need not fear, lady, the having any of these lords: they have acquainted me with their determinations; which is, indeed, to return to their home and to trouble you with no more suit, unless you may be won by some other sort than your father's imposition depending on the caskets.   115

Por. If I live to be as old as Sibylla, I will die as chaste as Diana, unless I be obtained by the manner of my father's will. I am glad this parcel of wooers are so reasonable, for there is not one among them but I dote on his very absence, and I pray God grant them a fair departure.

Ner. Do you not remember, lady, in your father's time, a Venetian, a scholar and a soldier, that came hither in company of the Marquis of Montferrat?

Por. Yes, yes, it was Bassanio; as I think, he was so called.

Ner. True, madam: he, of all the men that ever my foolish eyes looked upon, was the best deserving a fair lady.   131

Por. I remember him well, and I remember him worthy of thy praise.

Enter a Serving-man.

How now! what news?

Serv. The four strangers seek for you, madam, to take their leave: and there is a forerunner come from a fifth, the Prince of Morocco, who brings word the prince his master will be here to-night.   139

Por. If I could bid the fifth welcome with so good a heart as I can bid the other four farewell, I should be glad of his approach: if he have the condition of a saint and the complexion of a devil, I had rather he should shrive me than wive me. Come, Nerissa. Sirrah, go before. Whiles we shut the gates upon one wooer, another knocks at the door.   [*Exeunt.*

SCENE III. *Venice.   A public place.*

Enter BASSANIO *and* SHYLOCK.

Shy. Three thousand ducats; well.

Bass. Ay, sir, for three months.

Shy. For three months; well.

Bass. For the which, as I told you, Antonio shall be bound.

Shy. Antonio shall become bound; well.

Bass. May you stead me? will you pleasure me? shall I know your answer?

Shy. Three thousand ducats for three months and Antonio bound.   10

Bass. Your answer to that.

Shy. Antonio is a good man.

Bass. Have you heard any imputation to the contrary?

Shy. Oh, no, no, no, no: my meaning in saying he is a good man is to have you understand me that he is sufficient. Yet his means are in supposition: he hath an argosy bound

83. **Scottish.** F has *other*, apparently substituted for *Scottish* to avoid offense to King James. 89. **became . . . another,** an allusion to the age-old alliance of the French and the Scotch against the English. The Frenchman put his seal under the Scotchman's as his surety, promising to give the Englishman another box on the ear. 96. **fall,** befall. 114. **sort,** way, manner. **imposition,** conditions imposed. 116. **Sibylla,** the Cumæan Sibyl, to whom Apollo gave as many years as there were grains in her handful of sand. 119. **parcel,** party.

141. **four.** It will be noticed that Nerissa names six suitors. Hunter suggested that four was the number of suitors in the old play which Shakespeare used as a source, and that Shakespeare himself added the Englishman and the Scotchman. 143. **condition,** character. 145. **shrive** me, act as my confessor.
Scene iii. 1. **ducats,** gold or silver coins of varying value. The sum asked for has been estimated by various persons from three thousand to one hundred thousand dollars. **well,** possibly interrogative. 7. **stead,** serve. 12. **good,** solvent.

to Tripolis, another to the Indies; I understand, moreover, upon the Rialto, he hath a
third at Mexico, a fourth for England, and
other ventures he hath, squandered abroad.
But ships are but boards, sailors but men:
there be land-rats and water-rats, water-
thieves and land-thieves, I mean pirates, and
then there is the peril of waters, winds and
rocks. The man is, notwithstanding, sufficient. Three thousand ducats; I think I
may take his bond.

Bass. Be assured you may.   29

Shy. I will be assured I may; and, that I
may be assured, I will bethink me. May I
speak with Antonio?

Bass. If it please you to dine with us.

Shy. Yes, to smell pork; to eat of the habitation which your prophet the Nazarite conjured the devil into. I will buy with you, sell
with you, talk with you, walk with you, and
so following, but I will not eat with you,
drink with you, nor pray with you. What
news on the Rialto? Who is he comes
here?   40

Enter ANTONIO

Bass. This is Signior Antonio.

Shy. [*Aside*] How like a fawning publican
he looks!
I hate him for he is a Christian,
But more for that in low simplicity
He lends out money gratis and brings down
The rate of usance here with us in Venice.
If I can catch him once upon the hip,
I will feed fat the ancient grudge I bear him.
He hates our sacred nation, and he rails,
Even there where merchants most do con-
gregate,   50
On me, my bargains and my well-won thrift,
Which he calls interest. Cursed be my tribe,
If I forgive him!

Bass. Shylock, do you hear?

Shy. I am debating of my present store,
And, by the near guess of my memory,
I cannot instantly raise up the gross
Of full three thousand ducats. What of that?
Tubal, a wealthy Hebrew of my tribe,

Will furnish me. But soft! how many
months
Do you desire? [*To Ant.*] Rest you fair, good
signior;   60
Your worship was the last man in our
mouths.

Ant. Shylock, although I neither lend nor
borrow
By taking nor by giving of excess,
Yet, to supply the ripe wants of my friend,
I'll break a custom. Is he yet possess'd
How much ye would?

Shy.   Ay, ay, three thousand
ducats.

Ant. And for three months.

Shy. I had forgot; three months; you told
me so.
Well then, your bond; and let me see; but
hear you;
Methought you said you neither lend nor
borrow
Upon advantage.

Ant.   I do never use it.   71

Shy. When Jacob grazed his uncle Laban's
sheep—
This Jacob from our holy Abram was,
As his wise mother wrought in his behalf,
The third possessor; ay, he was the third—

Ant. And what of him? did he take
interest?

Shy. No, not take interest, not, as you
would say,
Directly interest: mark what Jacob did.
When Laban and himself were compromised
That all the eanlings which were streak'd
and pied   80
Should fall as Jacob's hire, the ewes, being
rank,
In the end of autumn turned to the rams,
And, when the work of generation was
Between these woolly breeders in the act,
The skilful shepherd peel'd me certain wands
And, in the doing of the deed of kind,
He stuck them up before the fulsome ewes,
Who then conceiving did in eaning time
Fall parti-colour'd lambs, and those were
Jacob's.   89
This was a way to thrive, and he was blest:
And thrift is blessing, if men steal it not.

---

19. **Rialto,** name of the largest of the Venetian islands;
here, for *exchange, bourse.* 35. **Nazarite,** Nazarine;
cf. *St. Luke,* vii, 32, 33. 42. **publican,** Roman tax-
gatherer, a term of opprobrium. 43-53. **I . . . him.**
Shylock's hatred of Antonio, as it appears in this passage,
is general. He does not allude so much to personal
insults and injuries as to the four general grounds
enumerated. 46. **usance,** usury, interest. 47. **catch
. . . hip,** figure of speech from wrestling.

65. **possess'd,** informed. 71. **upon advantage,** for
pecuniary profit. 75. **possessor,** i.e., of God's promise.
79. **compromised,** agreed; cf. *Genesis* xxx, 35. 80.
eanlings, young lambs or kids. **pied,** spotted. 85.
me, ethical dative, originally suggesting the speaker's
interest in the matter.

Ant. This was a venture, sir, that Jacob
    served for;
A thing not in his power to bring to pass,
But sway'd and fashion'd by the hand of
    heaven.
Was this inserted to make interest good?
Or is your gold and silver ewes and rams?
    Shy. I cannot tell; I make it breed as fast:
But note me, signior.
    Ant.   Mark you this, Bassanio,
The devil can cite Scripture for his purpose.
An evil soul producing holy witness   190
Is like a villain with a smiling cheek,
A goodly apple rotten at the heart:
O, what a goodly outside falsehood hath!
    Shy. Three thousand ducats; 'tis a good
    round sum.
Three months from twelve; then, let me see;
    the rate—
    Ant. Well, Shylock, shall we be beholding
    to you?
    Shy. Signior Antonio, many a time and
    oft
In the Rialto you have rated me
About my moneys and my usances: 109
Still have I borne it with a patient shrug,
For sufferance is the badge of all our tribe.
You call me misbeliever, cut-throat dog,
And spit upon my Jewish gaberdine,
And all for use of that which is mine own.
Well then, it now appears you need my help:
Go to, then; you come to me, and you say
'Shylock, we would have moneys:' you say
    so;
You, that did void your rheum upon my
    beard
And foot me as you spurn a stranger cur   119
Over your threshold: moneys is your suit.
What should I say to you? Should I not say
'Hath a dog money? is it possible
A cur can lend three thousand ducats?' Or
Shall I bend low and in a bondman's key,
With bated breath and whispering humble-
    ness,
Say this;
'Fair sir, you spit on me on Wednesday last;
You spurn'd me such a day; another time
You call'd me dog; and for these courte-
    sies
I'll lend you thus much moneys'?   130

    Ant. I am as like to call thee so again,
To spit on thee again, to spurn thee too.
If thou wilt lend this money, lend it not
As to thy friends; for when did friendship
    take
A breed for barren metal of his friend?
But lend it rather to thine enemy,
Who, if he break, thou mayst with better
    face
Exact the penalty.
    Shy.   Why, look you, how you storm!
I would be friends with you and have your
    love,
Forget the shames that you have stain'd me
    with,   140
Supply your present wants and take no doit
Of usance for my moneys, and you'll not
    hear me:
This is kind I offer.
    Bass. This were kindness.
    Shy.   This kindness will I show.
Go with me to a notary, seal me there
Your single bond; and, in a merry sport,
If you repay me not on such a day,
In such a place, such sum or sums as are
Express'd in the condition, let the forfeit
Be nominated for an equal pound   150
Of your fair flesh, to be cut off and taken
In what part of your body pleaseth me.
    Ant. Content, i' faith: I'll seal to such a
    bond
And say there is much kindness in the Jew.
    Bass. You shall not seal to such a bond
    for me:
I'll rather dwell in my necessity.
    Ant. Why, fear not, man; I will not for-
    feit it:
Within these two months, that's a month
    before
This bond expires, I do expect return   159
Of thrice three times the value of this bond.
    Shy. O father Abram, what these Chris-
    tians are,
Whose own hard dealings teaches them
    suspect
The thoughts of others! Pray you, tell me
    this;

99-103. **The devil . . . hath.** Antonio expresses
the indignation, which would have been most keenly
felt at that time, at tampering with the Scripture. 108.
rated, censured violently. 113. **gaberdine,** cape or
mantle.

135. **breed for barren metal,** an ancient argument
against interest (see *Introduction*). F has *of* instead
of *for*. 137. **Who,** from whom. **break,** fail to pay on
time. 141. **doit,** a small Dutch coin. 146. **single
bond,** bond without other security. 153-154. **Content . . . Jew.** This ready credulity of Antonio is probably to be regarded as conventional, a thing required by
the plot and not probable in daily life. Bassanio helps
the stage probability by protesting. 162. **suspect,** i.e.,
to suspect.

If he should break his day, what should I
gain
By the exaction of the forfeiture?
A pound of man's flesh taken from a man
Is not so estimable, profitable neither,
As flesh of muttons, beefs, or goats. I say,
To buy his favour, I extend this friendship:
If he will take it, so; if not, adieu;   170
And, for my love, I pray you wrong me not.
   Ant. Yes, Shylock, I will seal unto this
bond.
   Shy. Then meet me forthwith at the
notary's;
Give him direction for this merry bond,
And I will go and purse the ducats straight,
See to my house, left in the fearful guard
Of an unthrifty knave, and presently
I will be with you.
   Ant. Hie thee, gentle Jew. [*Exit Shylock.*
The Hebrew will turn Christian: he grows
kind.   180
   Bass. I like not fair terms and a villain's
mind.
   Ant. Come on: in this there can be no dis-
may;
My ships come home a month before the day.
                                                              [*Exeunt.*

ACT II.

Scene I. *Belmont. A room in* Portia's *house.*

Flourish of cornets. Enter the Prince of
Morocco *and his train;* Portia, Nerissa,
and others attending.

   Mor. Mislike me not for my complexion,
The shadow'd livery of the burnish'd sun,
To whom I am a neighbour and near bred.
Bring me the fairest creature northward
born,
Where Phœbus' fire scarce thaws the icicles,
And let us make incision for your love,
To prove whose blood is reddest, his or mine.
I tell thee, lady, this aspect of mine
Hath fear'd the valiant: by my love, I swear
The best-regarded virgins of our clime   10
Have loved it too: I would not change this
hue,
Except to steal your thoughts, my gentle
queen.
   Por. In terms of choice I am not solely led
By nice direction of a maiden's eyes;
Besides, the lottery of my destiny

Bars me the right of voluntary choosing:
But if my father had not scanted me
And hedged me by his wit, to yield myself
His wife who wins me by that means I told
you,
Yourself, renowned prince, then stood as
fair   20
As any comer I have look'd on yet
For my affection.
   Mor.   Even for that I thank you:
Therefore, I pray you, lead me to the caskets
To try my fortune. By this scimitar
That slew the Sophy and a Persian prince,
That won three fields of Sultan Solyman,
I would outstare the sternest eyes that look,
Outbrave the heart most daring on the earth,
Pluck the young sucking cubs from the
she-bear,
Yea, mock the lion when he roars for prey, 30
To win thee, lady. But, alas the while!
If Hercules and Lichas play at dice
Which is the better man, the greater throw
May turn by fortune from the weaker hand:
So is Alcides beaten by his page;
And so may I, blind fortune leading me,
Miss that which one unworthier may attain,
And die with grieving.
   Por.   You must take your chance,
And either not attempt to choose at all
Or swear before you choose, if you choose
wrong   40
Never to speak to lady afterward
In way of marriage: therefore be advised.
   Mor. Nor will not. Come, bring me unto
my chance.
   Por. First, forward to the temple: after
dinner
Your hazard shall be made.
   Mor.   Good fortune then!
To make me blest or cursed'st among men.
                                                   [*Cornets, and exeunt.*

Scene II. *Venice. A street.*

Enter Launcelot.

   Laun. Certainly my conscience will serve
me to run from this Jew my master. The
fiend is at mine elbow and tempts me saying

---

17. scanted, limited. 24. scimitar, a sword with
curved blade. 25. Sophy, Shah of Persia. 26. Solyman, a Turkish sultan ruling 1520-1566. 32. Lichas, a
page of Hercules. 35. Alcides, Hercules. 44. temple,
probably church, in order to take the oaths.
Scene ii. 3. tempts. The situation of the tempting
fiend is a familiar one in all medieval and Renaissance
literature, perhaps commonest in morality plays.

Act II. Scene i. 7. reddest. Red blood was regarded as a sign of courage. 9. fear'd, frightened.
14. nice direction, dainty guidance.

to me 'Gobbo, Launcelot Gobbo, good Launcelot,' or 'good Gobbo,' or 'good Launcelot Gobbo, use your legs, take the start, run away.' My conscience says 'No; take heed, honest Launcelot; take heed, honest Gobbo,' or, as aforesaid, 'honest Launcelot Gobbo; do not run; scorn running with thy heels.' Well, the most coura- 10 geous fiend bids me pack: 'Via!' says the fiend; 'away!' says the fiend; 'for the heavens, rouse up a brave mind,' says the fiend, 'and run.' Well, my conscience, hanging about the neck of my heart, says very wisely to me 'My honest friend Launcelot, being an honest man's son,' or rather an honest woman's son; for, indeed, my father did something smack, something grow to, he had a kind of taste; well, my conscience says 'Launcelot, budge not.' 'Budge,' says 20 the fiend. 'Budge not,' says my conscience. 'Conscience,' say I, 'you counsel well;' 'Fiend,' say I, 'you counsel well:' to be ruled by my conscience, I should stay with the Jew my master, who, God bless the mark, is a kind of devil; and, to run away from the Jew, I should be ruled by the fiend, who, saving your reverence, is the devil himself. Certainly the Jew is the very devil incarnal; and, in my conscience, my conscience is but a kind of hard conscience, to offer to counsel me to stay with the Jew. The fiend gives the more friendly counsel: I will run, fiend; my heels are at your command; I will run.

Enter Old Gobbo, *with a basket.*

Gob. Master young man, you, I pray you, which is the way to master Jew's? 35

Laun. [*Aside*] O heavens, this is my true-begotten father! who, being more than sand-blind, high-gravel blind, knows me not: I will try confusions with him.

Gob. Master young gentleman, I pray you, which is the way to master Jew's? 41

Laun. Turn up on your right hand at the next turning, but, at the next turning of all, on your left; marry, at the very next turning, turn of no hand, but turn down indirectly to the Jew's house.

Gob. By God's sonties, 'twill be a hard

way to hit. Can you tell me whether one Launcelot, that dwells with him, dwell with him or no? 49

Laun. Talk you of young Master Launcelot? [*Aside*] Mark me now; now will I raise the waters. Talk you of young Master Launcelot?

Gob. No master, sir, but a poor man's son: his father, though I say it, is an honest exceeding poor man and, God be thanked, well to live. 55

Laun. Well, let his father be what a' will, we talk of young Master Launcelot.

Gob. Your worship's friend and Launcelot, sir.

Laun. But I pray you, ergo, old man, ergo, I beseech you, talk you of young Master Launcelot? 60

Gob. Of Launcelot, an 't please your mastership.

Laun. Ergo, Master Launcelot. Talk not of Master Launcelot, father; for the young gentleman, according to Fates and Destinies and such odd sayings, the Sisters Three and such branches of learning, is indeed deceased, or, as you would say in plain terms, gone to heaven.

Gob. Marry, God forbid! the boy was the very staff of my age, my very prop. 70

Laun. Do I look like a cudgel or a hovel-post, a staff or a prop? Do you know me, father?

Gob. Alack the day, I know you not, young gentleman: but, I pray you, tell me, is my boy, God rest his soul, alive or dead?

Laun. Do you not know me, father?

Gob. Alack, sir, I am sand-blind; I know you not.

Laun. Nay, indeed, if you had your eyes, you might fail of the knowing me: it is a wise father that knows his own child. Well, old man, I will tell you news of your son: give me your blessing: truth will come to light; murder cannot be hid long; a man's son may, but at the length truth will out.

Gob. Pray you, sir, stand up: I am sure you are not Launcelot, my boy.

Laun. Pray you, let's have no more fooling about it, but give me your blessing:

11. **pack**, begone. '**Via!**' Italian, begone. 18. **something smack**, i.e., of dishonesty. **grow to**, become an integral part of; euphemism for *stealing*. 25. **God . . . mark**, an exclamation by way of apology for introducing something; literal meaning not understood. 31. **offer**, venture, presume. 37. **sand-blind**, dim-sighted. 38. **high-gravel blind**, more than sand-blind as gravel is greater than sand. 47. **sonties**, probably a corruption of *saints* or *sanctities*.

50. **Master.** The title was applied to gentle-folk only. 55. **well to live**, possibly Gobbo's corruption of *well-to-do*. 59. **ergo**, therefore (if it means anything). 66. **Sisters Three**, possibly the Muses, nine in number. Launcelot mixes everything up; his words are a satire on pretenders to classical learning. 71. **hovel-post**, support for a hovel or open shed.

I am Launcelot, your boy that was, your
son that is, your child that shall be.   91
    Gob. I cannot think you are my son.
    Laun. I know not what I shall think of
that: but I am Launcelot, the Jew's man,
and I am sure Margery your wife is my
mother.
    Gob. Her name is Margery, indeed: I'll be
sworn, if thou be Launcelot, thou art mine
own flesh and blood. Lord worshipped
might he be! what a beard hast thou got!
thou hast got more hair on thy chin than
Dobbin my fill-horse has on his tail.   101
    Laun. It should seem, then, that Dobbin's
tail grows backward: I am sure he had more
hair of his tail than I have of my face when I
last saw him.
    Gob. Lord, how art thou changed! How
dost thou and thy master agree? I have
brought him a present. How 'gree you now?
    Laun. Well, well: but, for mine own part,
as I have set up my rest to run away, so I will
not rest till I have run some ground. My
master's a very Jew: give him a present! give
him a halter: I am famished in his service;
you may tell every finger I have with my
ribs. Father, I am glad you are come: give
me your present to one Master Bassanio,
who, indeed, gives rare new liveries: if I
serve not him, I will run as far as God has
any ground. O rare fortune! here comes the
man: to him, father; for I am a Jew, if I
serve the Jew any longer.   120

Enter BASSANIO, *with* LEONARDO *and other
followers.*

    Bass. You may do so; but let it be so
hasted that supper be ready at the farthest
by five of the clock. See these letters delivered; put the liveries to making, and
desire Gratiano to come anon to my lodging.
                                  [*Exit a Servant.*
    Laun. To him, father.
    Gob. God bless your worship!
    Bass. Gramercy! wouldst thou aught with
me?
    Gob. Here's my son, sir, a poor boy,—129
    Laun. Not a poor boy, sir, but the rich
Jew's man; that would, sir, as my father
shall specify—

    Gob. He hath a great infection, sir, as one
would say, to serve,—
    Laun. Indeed, the short and the long is, I
serve the Jew, and have a desire, as my
father shall specify—
    Gob. His master and he, saving your wor-
ship's reverence, are scarce cater-cousins—139
    Laun. To be brief, the very truth is that
the Jew, having done me wrong, doth cause
me, as my father, being, I hope, an old man,
shall frutify unto you—
    Gob. I have here a dish of doves that I
would bestow upon your worship, and my
suit is—   145
    Laun. In very brief, the suit is imperti-
nent to myself, as your worship shall know by
this honest old man; and, though I say it,
though old man, yet poor man, my father.
    Bass. One speak for both. What would
you?   150
    Laun. Serve you, sir.
    Gob. That is the very defect of the matter,
sir.
    Bass. I know thee well; thou hast
        obtain'd thy suit:
Shylock thy master spoke with me this day,
And hath preferr'd thee, if it be preferment
To leave a rich Jew's service, to become
The follower of so poor a gentleman.
    Laun. The old proverb is very well parted
between my master Shylock and you, sir:
you have the grace of God, sir, and he hath
enough.   160
    Bass. Thou speak'st it well. Go, father,
        with thy son.
Take leave of thy old master and inquire
My lodging out. Give him a livery
More guarded than his fellows': see it
        done.
    Laun. Father, in. I cannot get a service,
no; I have ne'er a tongue in my head. Well,
if any man in Italy have a fairer table which
doth offer to swear upon a book, I shall have
good fortune. Go to, here's a simple line of
life: here's a small trifle of wives: alas, fifteen
wives is nothing! eleven widows and nine

---

99. **beard**, Launcelot's hair. He kneels with his back
to old Gobbo. 101. **fill-horse**, shaft-horse. 104. **of**,
in. 110. **set . . . rest**, determined; metaphor from the
card game *primero* in which a final wager is made.
112. **very**, veritable. 114. **tell**, count. 128. **Gramercy**, thanks.

132. **infection**, for *affection* or *inclination*. 139.
cater-cousins, good friends; sometimes thought to
have meant originally fourth cousins. 143. **frutify**,
certify. Launcelot's blunder is sometimes connected
with *fructify*. 146. **impertinent**, not pertaining (to).
152. **defect**, for *purport*. 158. **old proverb**: The grace
of God is better than riches; or the Scotch form:
God's grace is gear enough. 164. **guarded**, trimmed with
braided ornaments. 167. **table**, palm. 170. **trifle of
wives**. "Long and deep lines from the Mount of
Venus toward the line of life signifieth so many wives."
—Saunders, *Chiromancie* (Furness).

maids is a simple coming-in for one man: and then to 'scape drowning thrice, and to be in peril of my life with the edge of a feather-bed; here are simple scapes. Well, if Fortune be a woman, she's a good wench for this gear. Father, come; I'll take my leave of the Jew in the twinkling of an eye. [*Exeunt Launcelot and Old Gobbo.*

Bass. I pray thee, good Leonardo, think on this:
These things being bought and orderly bestow'd,
Return in haste, for I do feast to-night　180
My best-esteem'd acquaintance: hie thee, go.

Leon. My best endeavours shall be done herein.

Enter GRATIANO.

Gra. Where is your master?
Leon.　　　Yonder, sir, he walks. [*Exit.*
Gra. Signior Bassanio!
Bass. Gratiano!
Gra. I have a suit to you.
Bass.　　　You have obtain'd it.
Gra. You must not deny me: I must go with you to Belmont.
Bass. Why, then you must. But hear thee, Gratiano;
Thou art too wild, too rude and bold of voice;
Parts that become thee happily enough　191
And in such eyes as ours appear not faults;
But where thou art not known, why, there they show
Something too liberal. Pray thee, take pain
To allay with some cold drops of modesty
Thy skipping spirit, lest through thy wild behaviour
I be misconstrued in the place I go to
And lose my hopes.
Gra.　　　Signior Bassanio, hear me:
If I do not put on a sober habit,　199
Talk with respect and swear but now and then,
Wear prayer-books in my pocket, look demurely,
Nay more, while grace is saying, hood mine eyes
Thus with my hat, and sigh and say 'amen,'
Use all the observance of civility,
Like one well studied in a sad ostent
To please his grandam, never trust me more.
Bass. Well, we shall see your bearing.

Gra. Nay, but I bar to-night: you shall not gauge me
By what we do to-night.
Bass.　　　No, that were pity:
I would entreat you rather to put on　210
Your boldest suit of mirth, for we have friends
That purpose merriment. But fare you well:
I have some business.
Gra. And I must to Lorenzo and the rest:
But we will visit you at supper-time. [*Exeunt.*

SCENE III. *The same. A room in* SHYLOCK'S *house.*

Enter JESSICA *and* LAUNCELOT.

Jes. I am sorry thou wilt leave my father so:
Our house is hell, and thou, a merry devil,
Didst rob it of some taste of tediousness.
But fare thee well, there is a ducat for thee:
And, Launcelot, soon at supper shalt thou see
Lorenzo, who is thy new master's guest:
Give him this letter; do it secretly;
And so farewell: I would not have my father
See me in talk with thee.　9
Laun. Adieu! tears exhibit my tongue. Most beautiful pagan, most sweet Jew! if a Christian did not play the knave and get thee, I am much deceived. But, adieu: these foolish drops do something drown my manly spirit: adieu.
Jes. Farewell, good Launcelot.
[*Exit Launcelot.*
Alack, what heinous sin is it in me
To be ashamed to be my father's child!
But though I am a daughter to his blood,
I am not to his manners. O Lorenzo,
If thou keep promise, I shall end this strife,　20
Become a Christian and thy loving wife.
[*Exit.*

SCENE IV. *The same. A street.*

Enter GRATIANO, LORENZO, SALARINO, *and* SALANIO.

Lor. Nay, we will slink away in supper-time,
Disguise us at my lodging and return,
All in an hour.

---

194. **pain**, pains. 199. **habit**, demeanor. 205. **sad ostent**, grave appearance.

Scene iii. 10. **exhibit**, for *restrain.* 16-21. **Alack . . . wife.** There is no evidence that Shakespeare disapproved of Jessica's frank rejection of her father, her race, or her religion.

Gra. We have not made good preparation.

Salar. We have not spoke us yet of torch-
bearers.

Salan. 'Tis vile, unless it may be quaintly
order'd,
And better in my mind not undertook.

Lor. 'Tis now but four o'clock: we have
two hours
To furnish us.

Enter LAUNCELOT, *with a letter.*

Friend Launcelot, what's the news?

Laun. An it shall please you to break up
this, it shall seem to signify.　　　　　　11

Lor. I know the hand: in faith, 'tis a fair
hand;
And whiter than the paper it writ on
Is the fair hand that writ.

Gra.　　　　　　　Love-news, in faith.

Laun. By your leave, sir.

Lor. Whither goest thou?

Laun. Marry, sir, to bid my old master
the Jew to sup to-night with my new master
the Christian.

Lor. Hold here, take this: tell gentle
Jessica　　　　　　　　　　　　　　20
I will not fail her; speak it privately.
Go, gentlemen,　　　　　　　[*Exit Launcelot.*
Will you prepare you for this masque to-
night?
I am provided of a torch-bearer.

Salar. Ay, marry, I'll be gone about it
straight.

Salan. And so will I.

Lor.　　　　　　　Meet me and Gratiano
At Gratiano's lodging some hour hence.

Salar. 'Tis good we do so.
　　　　　　　　　[*Exeunt Salar. and Salan.*

Gra. Was not that letter from fair Jessica?

Lor. I must needs tell thee all. She hath
directed　　　　　　　　　　　　30
How I shall take her from her father's house,
What gold and jewels she is furnish'd with,
What page's suit she hath in readiness.
If e'er the Jew her father come to heaven,
It will be for his gentle daughter's sake:
And never dare misfortune cross her foot,
Unless she do it under this excuse,
That she is issue to a faithless Jew.
Come, go with me; peruse this as thou goest:
Fair Jessica shall be my torch-bearer.
　　　　　　　　　　　　　　[*Exeunt.*

SCENE V. *The same. Before* SHYLOCK'S *house.*

Enter SHYLOCK *and* LAUNCELOT.

Shy. Well, thou shalt see, thy eyes shall
be thy judge,
The difference of old Shylock and Bassanio:—
What, Jessica!—thou shalt not gormandise,
As thou hast done with me:—What, Jessica!—
And sleep and snore, and rend apparel out;—
Why, Jessica, I say!

Laun.　　　　　　　　Why, Jessica!

Shy. Who bids thee call? I do not bid
thee call.

Laun. Your worship was wont to tell me
that I could do nothing without bidding.

Enter JESSICA.

Jes. Call you? what is your will?　　10

Shy. I am bid forth to supper, Jessica:
There are my keys. But wherefore should I
go?
I am not bid for love; they flatter me:
But yet I'll go in hate, to feed upon
The prodigal Christian. Jessica, my girl,
Look to my house. I am right loath to go:
There is some ill a-brewing towards my rest,
For I did dream of money-bags to-night.

Laun. I beseech you, sir, go: my young
master doth expect your reproach.　　　20

Shy. So do I his.

Laun. And they have conspired together,
I will not say you shall see a masque; but if
you do, then it was not for nothing that my
nose fell a-bleeding on Black-Monday last at
six o'clock i' the morning, falling out that
year on Ash-Wednesday was four year, in the
afternoon.

Shy. What, are there masques? Hear you
me, Jessica:
Lock up my doors; and when you hear the
drum　　　　　　　　　　　　29
And the vile squealing of the wry-neck'd fife,
Clamber not you up to the casements then,
Nor thrust your head into the public street
To gaze on Christian fools with varnish'd
faces,
But stop my house's ears, I mean my case-
ments:
Let not the sound of shallow foppery enter

5. us, ethical dative.　6. 'Tis vile, it is a vulgar and
useless thing to do.　quaintly, elegantly, tastefully.
10. break up, break open.

18. to-night, last night.　20. reproach, Launcelot's
blunder for *approach.* Shylock takes it in grim humor.
25. Black-Monday, Easter Monday, so called, according to Stow, because of a cold and stormy Easter Monday when Edward III was besieging Paris.　29-37. hear
... to-night. There is a suggestion here that Shylock
distrusts Jessica.

My sober house. By Jacob's staff, I swear,
I have no mind of feasting forth to-night:
But I will go. Go you before me, sirrah;
Say I will come. 39
   Laun. I will go before, sir. Mistress, look
out at window, for all this;
     There will come a Christian by,
     Will be worth a Jewess' eye. [*Exit.*
   Shy. What says that fool of Hagar's off-
spring, ha?
   Jes. His words were 'Farewell, mistress;'
nothing else.
   Shy. The patch is kind enough, but a huge
feeder;
Snail-slow in profit, and he sleeps by day
More than the wild-cat: drones hive not with
me;
Therefore I part with him, and part with
him 49
To one that I would have him help to waste
His borrow'd purse. Well, Jessica, go in:
Perhaps I will return immediately:
Do as I bid you; shut doors after you:
Fast bind, fast find;
A proverb never stale in thrifty mind. [*Exit.*
   Jes. Farewell; and if my fortune be not
crost,
I have a father, you a daughter, lost.
                       [*Exit.*

Scene VI. *The same.*

Enter Gratiano *and* Salarino, *masqued.*

   Gra. This is the pent-house under which
Lorenzo
Desired us to make stand.
   Salar.   His hour is almost past.
   Gra. And it is marvel he out-dwells his
hour,
For lovers ever run before the clock.
   Salar. O, ten times faster Venus' pigeons
fly
To seal love's bonds new-made, than they
are wont
To keep obliged faith unforfeited!
   Gra. That ever holds: who riseth from a
feast
With that keen appetite that he sits down?
Where is the horse that doth untread again 10
His tedious measures with the unbated fire

That he did pace them first? All things that
are,
Are with more spirit chased than enjoy'd.
How like a younker or a prodigal
The scarfed bark puts from her native bay,
Hugg'd and embraced by the strumpet wind!
How like the prodigal doth she return,
With over-weather'd ribs and ragged sails,
Lean, rent and beggar'd by the strumpet
wind!
   Salar. Here comes Lorenzo: more of this
hereafter. 20

Enter Lorenzo.

   Lor. Sweet friends, your patience for my
long abode;
Not I, but my affairs, have made you wait:
When you shall please to play the thieves for
wives,
I'll watch as long for you then. Approach;
Here dwells my father Jew. Ho! who's
within?

Enter Jessica, *above, in boy's clothes.*

   Jes. Who are you? Tell me, for more cer-
tainty,
Albeit I'll swear that I do know your tongue.
   Lor. Lorenzo, and thy love.
   Jes. Lorenzo, certain, and my love indeed,
For who love I so much? And now who
knows 30
But you, Lorenzo, whether I am yours?
   Lor. Heaven and thy thoughts are witness
that thou art.
   Jes. Here, catch this casket; it is worth
the pains.
I am glad 'tis night, you do not look on me,
For I am much ashamed of my exchange:
But love is blind and lovers cannot see
The pretty follies that themselves commit;
For if they could, Cupid himself would blush
To see me thus transformed to a boy.
   Lor. Descend, for you must be my torch-
bearer. 40
   Jes. What, must I hold a candle to my
shames?
They in themselves, good sooth, are too too
light.
Why, 'tis an office of discovery, love;
And I should be obscured.
   Lor.   So are you, sweet,
Even in the lovely garnish of a boy.

---

36. **Jacob's staff.** Cf. *Genesis* xxxii, 10, and *Hebrews* xi, 21. 44. **Hagar's offspring**, explained as *Gentile* and as *servant*. 46. **patch**, fool, fellow.
   Scene vi. 1. **pent-house**, projecting roof from a house. 5. **Venus' pigeons.** Venus's chariot was drawn by doves.

14. **younker**, youth. 15. **scarfed**, decorated with flags. 43. **office of discovery**, occupation in which I shall be seen. 45. **garnish**, outfit.

But come at once;
For the close night doth play the runaway,
And we are stay'd for at Bassanio's feast.

Jes. I will make fast the doors, and gild
    myself
With some more ducats, and be with you
    straight.   [*Exit above.*   50

Gra. Now, by my hood, a Gentile and no
    Jew.

Lor. Beshrew me but I love her heartily;
For she is wise, if I can judge of her,
And fair she is, if that mine eyes be true,
And true she is, as she hath proved herself,
And therefore, like herself, wise, fair and
    true,
Shall she be placed in my constant soul.

Enter JESSICA, *below.*

What, art thou come? On, gentlemen; away!
Our masquing mates by this time for us stay.
            [*Exit with Jessica and Salarino.*

Enter ANTONIO.

Ant. Who's there?   60
Gra. Signior Antonio!
Ant. Fie, fie, Gratiano! where are all the
    rest?
'Tis nine o'clock: our friends all stay for you.
No masque to-night: the wind is come about;
Bassanio presently will go aboard:
I have sent twenty out to seek for you.

Gra. I am glad on 't: I desire no more
    delight
Than to be under sail and gone to-night.
                        [*Exeunt.*

SCENE VII. *Belmont. A room in*
PORTIA'S *house.*

Flourish of cornets. Enter PORTIA, *with the*
PRINCE OF MOROCCO, *and their trains.*

Por. Go draw aside the curtains and dis-
    cover
The several caskets to this noble prince.
Now make your choice.

Mor. The first, of gold, who this inscrip-
    tion bears,
'Who chooseth me shall gain what many men
    desire;'

The second, silver, which this promise
    carries,
'Who chooseth me shall get as much as he
    deserves;'
This third, dull lead, with warning all as
    blunt,
'Who chooseth me must give and hazard all
    he hath.'
How shall I know if I do choose the right?   10

Por. The one of them contains my picture,
    prince:
If you choose that, then I am yours with-
    al.

Mor. Some god direct my judgement! Let
    me see;
I will survey the inscriptions back again.
What says this leaden casket?
'Who chooseth me must give and hazard all
    he hath.'
Must give: for what? for lead? hazard for
    lead?
This casket threatens. Men that hazard all
Do it in hope of fair advantages: 19
A golden mind stoops not to shows of dross;
I'll then nor give nor hazard aught for lead.
What says the silver with her virgin hue?
'Who chooseth me shall get as much as he
    deserves.'
As much as he deserves! Pause there,
    Morocco,
And weigh thy value with an even hand:
If thou be'st rated by thy estimation,
Thou dost deserve enough; and yet enough
May not extend so far as to the lady:
And yet to be afeard of my deserving
Were but a weak disabling of myself.   30
As much as I deserve! Why, that's the lady:
I do in birth deserve her, and in fortunes,
In graces and in qualities of breeding;
But more than these, in love I do deserve.
What if I stray'd no further, but chose here?
Let's see once more this saying graved in
    gold;
'Who chooseth me shall gain what many men
    desire.'
Why, that's the lady; all the world desires
    her;
From the four corners of the earth they come,
To kiss this shrine, this mortal-breathing
    saint: 40
The Hyrcanian deserts and the vasty wilds

53-56. **For she . . . true.** The qualities given to
Jessica here are those of the ideal woman; this is an
indication that there is no reaction in Shakespeare's
mind against her.
Scene vii. 1. **discover,** disclose, show.

41. **Hyrcanian.** Hyrcania was the country south of
the Caspian Sea.

Of wide Arabia are as throughfares now
For princes to come view fair Portia:
The watery kingdom, whose ambitious head
Spits in the face of heaven, is no bar
To stop the foreign spirits, but they come,
As o'er a brook, to see fair Portia.
One of these three contains her heavenly
  picture.
Is 't like that lead contains her? 'Twere
  damnation
To think so base a thought: it were too gross
To rib her cerecloth in the obscure grave. 51
Or shall I think in silver she's immured,
Being ten times undervalued to tried gold?
O sinful thought! Never so rich a gem
Was set in worse than gold. They have in
  England
A coin that bears the figure of an angel
Stamped in gold, but that's insculp'd upon;
But here an angel in a golden bed
Lies all within. Deliver me the key:
Here do I choose, and thrive I as I may!   60
    Por. There, take it, prince; and if my form
    lie there,
Then I am yours.
                [He unlocks the golden casket.
    Mor.   O hell! what have we here?
A carrion Death, within whose empty eye
There is a written scroll! I'll read the writ-
  ing.
*[Reads]*All that glisters is not gold;
    Often have you heard that told:
    Many a man his life hath sold
    But my outside to behold:
    Gilded tombs do worms infold.
    Had you been as wise as bold,   70
    Young in limbs, in judgement old,
    Your answer had not been inscroll'd:
    Fare you well; your suit is cold.

    Cold, indeed; and labour lost:
Then, farewell, heat, and welcome, frost!
Portia, adieu. I have too grieved a heart
To take a tedious leave: thus losers part.
        [Exit with his train. Flourish of cornets.
    Por. A gentle riddance. Draw the cur-
    tains, go.
Let all of his complexion choose me so.
                            [Exeunt.

SCENE VIII. *Venice. A street.*

Enter SALARINO *and* SALANIO.

    Salar. Why, man, I saw Bassanio under
    sail:
With him is Gratiano gone along;
And in their ship I am sure Lorenzo is not.
    Salan. The villain Jew with outcries raised
    the duke,
Who went with him to search Bassanio's
  ship.
    Salar. He came too late, the ship was un-
    der sail:
But there the duke was given to understand
That in a gondola were seen together
Lorenzo and his amorous Jessica:
Besides, Antonio certified the duke   10
They were not with Bassanio in his ship.
    Salan. I never heard a passion so con-
    fused,
So strange, outrageous, and so variable,
As the dog Jew did utter in the streets:
'My daughter! O my ducats! O my daughter!
Fled with a Christian! O my Christian
  ducats!
Justice! the law! my ducats, and my
  daughter!
A sealed bag, two sealed bags of ducats,
Of double ducats, stolen from me by my
  daughter!
And jewels, two stones, two rich and precious
  stones,   20
Stolen by my daughter! Justice! find the girl;
She hath the stones upon her, and the
  ducats.'
    Salar. Why, all the boys in Venice follow
    him,
Crying, his stones, his daughter, and his
  ducats.
    Salan. Let good Antonio look he keep his
    day,
Or he shall pay for this.
    Salar.   Marry, well remember'd.
I reason'd with a Frenchman yesterday,
Who told me, in the narrow seas that part
The French and English, there miscarried
A vessel of our country richly fraught: 30
I thought upon Antonio when he told me;
And wish'd in silence that it were not his.

49-60. 'Twere . . . I may. Morocco decides in a burst
of enthusiasm, without thought, actuated solely by the
superficial view. 51. cerecloth, wax cloth used in
embalming. 63. carrion Death, death's-head. 65.
glisters, glitters. 70. as wise as bold. These words
betray Morocco's error.

15-17. daughter . . . ducats. Barabas in Marlowe's *The Jew of Malta* shows the same confused passion
in Act I: "O girl! O gold! O beauty! O my bliss!"
27. reason'd, talked with. 28. narrow seas, probably
the English Channel. 30. fraught, freighted.

Salan. You were best to tell Antonio what
    you hear;
Yet do not suddenly, for it may grieve him.
    Salar. A kinder gentleman treads not the
        earth.
I saw Bassanio and Antonio part:
Bassanio told him he would make some speed
Of his return: he answer'd, 'Do not so;
Slubber not business for my sake, Bassanio,
But stay the very riping of the time;   40
And for the Jew's bond which he hath of me,
Let it not enter in your mind of love:
Be merry, and employ your chiefest thoughts
To courtship and such fair ostents of love
As shall conveniently become you there:'
And even there, his eye being big with tears,
Turning his face, he put his hand behind him,
And with affection wondrous sensible
He wrung Bassanio's hand; and so they
    parted.
    Salan. I think he only loves the world for
        him.   50
I pray thee, let us go and find him out
And quicken his embraced heaviness
With some delight or other.
    Salar.   Do we so. [*Exeunt.*

Scene IX. *Belmont. A room in* Portia's
house.

Enter Nerissa *with a* Servitor.

Ner. Quick, quick, I pray thee; draw the
    curtain straight:
The Prince of Arragon hath ta'en his oath,
And comes to his election presently.

Flourish of cornets. Enter the Prince of
Arragon, Portia, *and their trains.*

Por. Behold, there stand the caskets,
    noble prince:
If you choose that wherein I am contain'd,
Straight shall our nuptial rites be solemnized:
But if you fail, without more speech, my lord,
You must be gone from hence immediately.
    Ar. I am enjoin'd by oath to observe three
        things:
First, never to unfold to any one   10
Which casket 'twas I chose; next, if I fail
Of the right casket, never in my life
To woo a maid in way of marriage:

Lastly,
If I do fail in fortune of my choice,
Immediately to leave you and be gone.
    Por. To these injunctions every one doth
        swear
That comes to hazard for my worthless self.
    Ar. And so have I address'd me. Fortune
        now
To my heart's hope! Gold; silver; and base
    lead.   20
'Who chooseth me must give and hazard all
    he hath.'
You shall look fairer, ere I give or hazard.
What says the golden chest? ha! let me see:
'Who chooseth me shall gain what many men
    desire.'
What many men desire! that 'many' may be
    meant
By the fool multitude, that choose by show,
Not learning more than the fond eye doth
    teach;
Which pries not to the interior, but, like the
    martlet,
Builds in the weather on the outward wall,
Even in the force and road of casualty.   30
I will not choose what many men desire,
Because I will not jump with common spirits
And rank me with the barbarous multitudes.
Why, then to thee, thou silver treasure-house;
Tell me once more what title thou dost bear:
'Who chooseth me shall get as much as he de-
    serves:'
And well said too; for who shall go about
To cozen fortune and be honourable
Without the stamp of merit? Let none pre-
    sume
To wear an undeserved dignity.   40
O, that estates, degrees and offices
Were not derived corruptly, and that clear
    honour
Were purchased by the merit of the wearer!
How many then should cover that stand bare!
How many be commanded that command!
How much low peasantry would then be
    glean'd
From the true seed of honour! and how much
    honour

---

18. **hazard,** may be either a verb or a noun. 19. **address'd me,** prepared myself. 27. **Not . . . teach.**
Arragon prides himself on his judgment and attempts to
determine the issue on intellectual grounds. 28. **martlet,**
martin. 30. **casualty,** mischance. 32. **jump,** agree.
38. **cozen,** cheat. 41. **degrees,** ranks. 44. **cover . . .
bare,** i.e., put on their hats. 45. **How . . . command,**
how many then should be masters that are now servants.
46. **glean'd,** culled out.

---

39. **Slubber,** to do hastily and badly. 40. **riping of
the time,** maturity.
Scene ix. 3. **election,** choice.

Pick'd from the chaff and ruin of the times
To be new-varnish'd! Well, but to my choice:
'Who chooseth me shall get as much as he de-
          serves.'   50
I will assume desert. Give me a key for
          this,
And instantly unlock my fortunes here.
          [*He opens the silver casket.*
Por. Too long a pause for that which you
          find there.
Ar. What's here? the portrait of a blink-
          ing idiot,
Presenting me a schedule! I will read it.
How much unlike art thou to Portia!
How much unlike my hopes and my deserv-
          ings!
'Who chooseth me shall have as much as he
          deserves.'
Did I deserve no more than a fool's head?
Is that my prize? are my deserts no bet-
          ter?
     Por. To offend, and judge, are distinct
          offices   61
And of opposed natures.
     Ar.   What is here?
[*Reads*] The fire seven times tried this:
          Seven times tried that judgement is,
          That did never choose amiss.
          Some there be that shadows kiss;
          Such have but a shadow's bliss:
          There be fools alive, I wis,
          Silver'd o'er; and so was this.
          Take what wife you will to bed,   70
          I will ever be your head:
          So be gone: you are sped.

          Still more fool I shall appear
          By the time I linger here:
          With one fool's head I came to woo,
          But I go away with two.
          Sweet, adieu. I'll keep my oath,
          Patiently to bear my wroth.
          [*Exeunt Arragon and train.*
Por. Thus hath the candle singed the
          moth.
O, these deliberate fools! when they do
          choose,   80
They have the wisdom by their wit to lose.

Ner. The ancient saying is no heresy,
Hanging and wiving goes by destiny.
Por. Come, draw the curtain, Nerissa.

          Enter a Servant.

Serv. Where is my lady?
Por.   Here: what would my lord?
Serv. Madam, there is alighted at your
          gate
A young Venetian, one that comes before
To signify the approaching of his lord;
From whom he bringeth sensible regreets,
To wit, besides commends and courteous
          breath,   90
Gifts of rich value. Yet I have not seen
So likely an ambassador of love:
A day in April never came so sweet,
To show how costly summer was at hand,
As this fore-spurrer comes before his lord.
Por. No more, I pray thee: I am half
          afeard
Thou wilt say anon he is some kin to thee,
Thou spend'st such high-day wit in praising
          him.
Come, come, Nerissa; for I long to see   99
Quick Cupid's post that comes so mannerly.
Ner. Bassanio, lord Love, if thy will it be!
          [*Exeunt.*

ACT III.

Scene I.   *Venice.   A street.*

          Enter Salanio *and* Salarino.

Salan. Now, what news on the Rialto?
Salar. Why, yet it lives there unchecked
that Antonio hath a ship of rich lading
wrecked on the narrow seas; the Goodwins,
I think they call the place; a very dangerous
flat and fatal, where the carcases of many a
tall ship lie buried, as they say, if my gossip
Report be an honest woman of her word.   8
Salan. I would she were as lying a gossip
in that as ever knapped ginger or made her
neighbours believe she wept for the death of
a third husband. But it is true, without any
slips of prolixity or crossing the plain highway of talk, that the good Antonio, the hon-

---

est Antonio,——O that I had a title good
enough to keep his name company!—

Salar. Come, the full stop.

Salan. Ha! what sayest thou? Why, the
end is, he hath lost a ship.

Salar. I would it might prove the end of
his losses.   21

Salan. Let me say 'amen' betimes, lest
the devil cross my prayer, for here he comes
in the likeness of a Jew.

Enter SHYLOCK.

How now, Shylock! what news among the
merchants?

Shy. You knew, none so well, none so well
as you, of my daughter's flight.

Salar. That's certain: I, for my part, knew
the tailor that made the wings she flew withal.

Salan. And Shylock, for his own part,
knew the bird was fledged; and then it is the
complexion of them all to leave the dam.   33

Shy. She is damned for it.

Salar. That's certain, if the devil may be
her judge.

Shy. My own flesh and blood to rebel!

Salan. Out upon it, old carrion! rebels it
at these years?

Shy. I say, my daughter is my flesh and
blood.   40

Salar. There is more difference between
thy flesh and hers than between jet and
ivory; more between your bloods than there
is between red wine and rhenish. But tell us,
do you hear whether Antonio have had any
loss at sea or no?   45

Shy. There I have another bad match; a
bankrupt, a prodigal, who dare scarce show
his head on the Rialto; a beggar, that was
used to come so smug upon the mart; let him
look to his bond: he was wont to call me
usurer; let him look to his bond: he was wont
to lend money for a Christian courtesy; let
him look to his bond.   52

Salar. Why, I am sure, if he forfeit, thou
wilt not take his flesh: what's that good for?

Shy. To bait fish withal: if it will feed
nothing else, it will feed my revenge. He hath
disgraced me, and hindered me half a million;
laughed at my losses, mocked at my gains,
scorned my nation, thwarted my bargains,
cooled my friends, heated mine enemies; and
what's his reason? I am a Jew. Hath not a
Jew eyes? hath not a Jew hands, organs, dimensions, senses, affections, passions? fed
with the same food, hurt with the same
weapons, subject to the same diseases, healed
by the same means, warmed and cooled by
the same winter and summer, as a Christian
is? If you prick us, do we not bleed? if you
tickle us, do we not laugh? if you poison us,
do we not die? and if you wrong us, shall we
not revenge? If we are like you in the rest,
we will resemble you in that. If a Jew wrong
a Christian, what is his humility? Revenge.
If a Christian wrong a Jew, what should his
sufferance be by Christian example? Why,
revenge. The villany you teach me, I will
execute, and it shall go hard but I will better
the instruction.   76

Enter a Servant.

Serv. Gentlemen, my master Antonio is at
his house and desires to speak with you both.

Salar. We have been up and down to seek
him.   79

Enter TUBAL.

Salan. Here comes another of the tribe: a
third cannot be matched, unless the devil
himself turn Jew.

  [Exeunt Salan., Salar., and Servant.

Shy. How now, Tubal! what news from
Genoa? hast thou found my daughter?

Tub. I often came where I did hear of her,
but cannot find her.   86

Shy. Why, there, there, there, there! a
diamond gone, cost me two thousand ducats
in Frankfort! The curse never fell upon our
nation till now; I never felt it till now: two
thousand ducats in that; and other precious,
precious jewels. I would my daughter were
dead at my foot, and the jewels in her ear!
would she were hearsed at my foot, and the
ducats in her coffin! No news of them? Why,
so: and I know not what's spent in the
search: why, thou loss upon loss! the thief
gone with so much, and so much to find the
thief; and no satisfaction, no revenge: nor no
ill luck stirring but what lights on my shoul-

---

23. **cross,** thwart. 33. **dam,** mother-bird. 46. **match,**
bargain. 56-70. **He hath . . . revenge?** The appeal
cannot but attract sympathy to Shylock. It is speeches
like this which have brought about the modern sentimental conception of the character.

72. **humility,** humiliation he must endure. 74. **sufferance,** patience, endurance. 81. **matched,** i.e., to them.
89. **Frankfort.** There was a fair at Frankfort famous
for goldsmiths' wares. 94. **hearsed,** coffined.

ders; no sighs but of my breathing; no tears but of my shedding.   101

Tub. Yes, other men have ill luck too: Antonio, as I heard in Genoa,—

Shy. What, what, what? ill luck, ill luck?

Tub. Hath an argosy cast away, coming from Tripolis.

Shy. I thank God, I thank God. Is 't true, is 't true?

Tub. I spoke with some of the sailors that escaped the wreck.   110

Shy. I thank thee, good Tubal: good news, good news! ha, ha! where? in Genoa?

Tub. Your daughter spent in Genoa, as I heard, in one night fourscore ducats.

Shy. Thou stickest a dagger in me: I shall never see my gold again: fourscore ducats at a sitting! fourscore ducats!

Tub. There came divers of Antonio's creditors in my company to Venice, that swear he cannot choose but break.   120

Shy. I am very glad of it: I'll plague him; I'll torture him: I am glad of it.

Tub. One of them showed me a ring that he had of your daughter for a monkey.

Shy. Out upon her! Thou torturest me, Tubal: it was my turquoise; I had it of Leah when I was a bachelor: I would not have given it for a wilderness of monkeys.

Tub. But Antonio is certainly undone. 129

Shy. Nay, that's true, that's very true. Go, Tubal, fee me an officer; bespeak him a fortnight before. I will have the heart of him, if he forfeit; for, were he out of Venice, I can make what merchandise I will. Go, go, Tubal, and meet me at our synagogue; go, good Tubal; at our synagogue, Tubal.

[*Exeunt.*

SCENE II. *Belmont. A room in* PORTIA'S *house.*

Enter BASSANIO, PORTIA, GRATIANO, NERISSA, *and* Attendants.

Por. I pray you, tarry: pause a day or two
Before you hazard; for, in choosing wrong,

I lose your company: therefore forbear awhile.
There's something tells me, but it is not love,
I would not lose you; and you know yourself,
Hate counsels not in such a quality.
But lest you should not understand me well,—
And yet a maiden hath no tongue but thought,—
I would detain you here some month or two
Before you venture for me. I could teach you   10
How to choose right, but I am then forsworn;
So will I never be: so may you miss me;
But if you do, you'll make me wish a sin,
That I had been forsworn. Beshrew your eyes,
They have o'erlook'd me and divided me;
One half of me is yours, the other half yours,
Mine own, I would say; but if mine, then yours,
And so all yours. O, these naughty times
Put bars between the owners and their rights!
And so, though yours, not yours. Prove it so,   20
Let fortune go to hell for it, not I.
I speak too long; but 'tis to peize the time,
To eke it and to draw it out in length,
To stay you from election.
Bass.   Let me choose;
For as I am, I live upon the rack.
Por. Upon the rack, Bassanio! then confess
What treason there is mingled with your love.
Bass. None but that ugly treason of mistrust,
Which makes me fear the enjoying of my love:
There may as well be amity and life   30
'Tween snow and fire, as treason and my love.
Por. Ay, but I fear you speak upon the rack,
Where men enforced do speak anything.
Bass. Promise me life, and I'll confess the truth.
Por. Well then, confess and live.
Bass.   'Confess' and 'love'
Had been the very sum of my confession:
O happy torment, when my torturer

126-127. **I had it . . . bachelor.** These words are given a strong coloring of sentiment and are thought to humanize Shylock because of the allusion to his wife. It must not be forgotten, however, that the torquoise was a stone of special properties, and that Shylock may have set an actual as well as a sentimental value upon it. 131. **officer,** bailiff, police sergeant. 132-134. **I will . . . will.** Shylock's desire for revenge is constantly associated with his greed of gain.

15. **o'erlook'd,** bewitched. 18. **naughty,** good for nothing, worthless. 22. **peize,** retard (by hanging on of weights). 24. **stay,** keep, detain.

Doth teach me answers for deliverance!
But let me to my fortune and the cas-
    kets.

Por. Away, then! I am lock'd in one of
    them: 40
If you do love me, you will find me out.
Nerissa and the rest, stand all aloof.
Let music sound while he doth make his
    choice;
Then, if he lose, he makes a swan-like end,
Fading in music: that the comparison
May stand more proper, my eye shall be the
    stream
And watery death-bed for him. He may win;
And what is music then? Then music is
Even as the flourish when true subjects bow
To a new-crowned monarch: such it is   50
As are those dulcet sounds in break of day
That creep into the dreaming bridegroom's
    ear
And summon him to marriage. Now he goes,
With no less presence, but with much more
    love,
Than young Alcides, when he did redeem
The virgin tribute paid by howling Troy
To the sea-monster: I stand for sacrifice;
The rest aloof are the Dardanian wives,
With bleared visages, come forth to view
The issue of the exploit. Go, Hercules!   60
Live thou, I live: with much much more
    dismay
I view the fight than thou that makest the
    fray.

Music, whilst BASSANIO *comments on the
    caskets to himself.*

SONG.

Tell me where is fancy bred,
Or in the heart or in the head?
How begot, how nourished?
        Reply, reply.
It is engender'd in the eyes,
With gazing fed; and fancy dies
In the cradle where it lies.
        Let us all ring fancy's knell: 70
        I'll begin it,—Ding, dong, bell.

All. Ding, dong, bell.

Bass. So may the outward shows be least
    themselves:
The world is still deceived with ornament.
In law, what plea so tainted and corrupt
But, being season'd with a gracious voice,
Obscures the show of evil? In religion,
What damned error, but some sober brow
Will bless it and approve it with a text,
Hiding the grossness with fair ornament?   80
There is no vice so simple but assumes
Some mark of virtue on his outward parts:
How many cowards, whose hearts are all as
    false
As stairs of sand, wear yet upon their chins
The beards of Hercules and frowning Mars,
Who, inward search'd, have livers white as
    milk;
And these assume but valour's excrement
To render them redoubted! Look on beauty,
And you shall see 'tis purchased by the
    weight;
Which therein works a miracle in nature,   90
Making them lightest that wear most of
    it:
So are those crisped snaky golden locks
Which make such wanton gambols with the
    wind,
Upon supposed fairness, often known
To be the dowry of a second head,
The skull that bred them in the sepulchre.
Thus ornament is but the guiled shore
To a most dangerous sea; the beauteous scarf
†Veiling an Indian beauty; in a word,
The seeming truth which cunning times put
    on   100
To entrap the wisest. Therefore, thou gaudy
    gold,
Hard food for Midas, I will none of thee;
Nor none of thee, thou pale and common
    drudge
'Tween man and man: but thou, thou meagre
    lead,
Which rather threatenest than dost promise
    aught,
Thy paleness moves me more than eloquence;
And here choose I: joy be the consequence!

---

44. **swan-like**, an allusion to the belief that swans sing when they come to die. 55. **Alcides**. Hercules rescued Hesione, daughter of the Trojan king, Laomedon, from a monster to which, by command of Neptune, she was about to be sacrificed. Hercules was rewarded, however, not with the lady's love, but with a famous pair of horses. 56. **howling**, lamenting. 58. **Dardanian**, Trojan. 63. **fancy**, sensuous love. The song contains a disguised warning to Bassanio not to choose by fancy. 67. **eyes**. Love entered the heart especially through the eyes.

79. **approve**, confirm. 81. **simple**, unmixed with virtue. 84. **stairs**, steps. 86. **livers**. The liver was thought to be the seat of courage; for it to be deserted by the blood would be the condition of cowardice. 87. **valour's excrement**, beard of a brave man. 92. **crisped**, curly. 97. **guiled**, treacherous. 102. **Midas**, the Phrygian king whose touch turned everything to gold. 104-106. **but thou . . . eloquence**. Bassanio rejects outward show and does not resort to reason; trusting the power of love, he follows merely intuition.

Por. [*Aside*] How all the other passions
 fleet to air,
As doubtful thoughts, and rash-embraced de-
 spair,
And shuddering fear, and green-eyed jeal-
 ousy! 110
O love,
Be moderate; allay thy ecstasy;
In measure rein thy joy; scant this excess.
I feel too much thy blessing: make it less,
For fear I surfeit.

Bass.   What find I here?
    [*Opening the leaden casket.*
Fair Portia's counterfeit! What demi-god
Hath come so near creation? Move these
 eyes?
Or whether, riding on the balls of mine,
Seem they in motion? Here are sever'd lips,
Parted with sugar breath: so sweet a bar 120
Should sunder such sweet friends. Here in
 her hairs
The painter plays the spider and hath woven
A golden mesh to entrap the hearts of men
Faster than gnats in cobwebs: but her
 eyes,—
How could he see to do them? having made
 one,
Methinks it should have power to steal both
 his
And leave itself unfurnish'd. Yet look, how
 far
The substance of my praise doth wrong this
 shadow
In underprizing it, so far this shadow
Doth limp behind the substance. Here's the
 scroll, 130
The continent and summary of my fortune.

[*Reads*] You that choose not by the view,
 Chance as fair and choose as true!
 Since this fortune falls to you,
 Be content and seek no new.
 If you be well pleased with this
 And hold your fortune for your bliss,
 Turn you where your lady is
 And claim her with a loving kiss.

A gentle scroll. Fair lady, by your leave; 140
I come by note, to give and to receive.
Like one of two contending in a prize,
That thinks he hath done well in people's
 eyes,

Hearing applause and universal shout,
Giddy in spirit, still gazing in a doubt
Whether those peals of praise be his or no;
So, thrice-fair lady, stand I, even so;
As doubtful whether what I see be true,
Until confirm'd, sign'd, ratified by you.

Por. You see me, Lord Bassanio, where I
 stand, 150
Such as I am: though for myself alone
I would not be ambitious in my wish,
To wish myself much better; yet, for you
I would be trebled twenty times myself;
A thousand times more fair, ten thousand
 times
More rich;
That only to stand high in your account,
I might in virtues, beauties, livings, friends,
Exceed account; but the full sum of me
†Is sum of something, which, to term in
 gross, 160
Is an unlesson'd girl, unschool'd, unprac-
 tised;
Happy in this, she is not yet so old
†But she may learn; happier than this,
She is not bred so dull but she can learn;
Happiest of all is that her gentle spirit
Commits itself to yours to be directed,
As from her lord, her governor, her king.
Myself and what is mine to you and yours
Is now converted: but now I was the lord
Of this fair mansion, master of my serv-
 ants,
Queen o'er myself; and even now, but now,171
This house, these servants and this same
 myself
Are yours, my lord: I give them with this
 ring;
Which when you part from, lose, or give
 away,
Let it presage the ruin of your love
And be my vantage to exclaim on you.

Bass. Madam, you have bereft me of all
 words,
Only my blood speaks to you in my veins;
And there is such confusion in my powers,
As, after some oration fairly spoke 180
By a beloved prince, there doth appear
Among the buzzing pleased multitude;
Where every something, being blent together,
Turns to a wild of nothing, save of joy,

---

116. **counterfeit**, portrait. 127. **unfurnish'd**, i.e.,
with a companion. 141. **by note**, i.e., as directed. 142.
prize, contest.

157. **account**, computation. 173. **ring**. The ring,
which is to serve as a test in the love-friendship contest,
is thus bestowed at the very acme of the love plot. 176.
vantage, opportunity, advantage. **exclaim on**, reproach.

Express'd and not express'd. But when this
    ring
Parts from this finger, then parts life from
    hence:
O, then be bold to say Bassanio's dead!
    Ner. My lord and lady, it is now our time,
That have stood by and seen our wishes
    prosper,
To cry, good joy: good joy, my lord and lady!
    Gra. My lord Bassanio and my gentle
    lady,   191
I wish you all the joy that you can wish;
For I am sure you can wish none from me:
And when your honours mean to solemnize
The bargain of your faith, I do beseech you,
Even at that time I may be married too.
    Bass. With all my heart, so thou canst get
    a wife.
    Gra. I thank your lordship, you have got
    me one.
My eyes, my lord, can look as swift as yours:
You saw the mistress, I beheld the maid;   200
You loved, I loved for intermission.
No more pertains to me, my lord, than you.
Your fortune stood upon the casket there,
And so did mine too, as the matter falls;
For wooing here until I sweat again,
And swearing till my very roof was dry
With oaths of love, at last, if promise last,
I got a promise of this fair one here
To have her love, provided that your fortune
Achieved her mistress.
    Por.   Is this true, Nerissa? 210
    Ner. Madam, it is, so you stand pleased
    withal.
    Bass. And do you, Gratiano, mean good
    faith?
    Gra. Yes, faith, my lord.
    Bass. Our feast shall be much honour'd in
your marriage.
    Gra. We'll play with them the first boy
for a thousand ducats.
    Ner. What, and stake down?
    Gra. No; we shall ne'er win at that sport,
and stake down.   220
But who comes here? Lorenzo and his
    infidel?
What, and my old Venetian friend Salerio?

Enter Lorenzo, Jessica, *and* Salerio,
    a Messenger from Venice.

    Bass. Lorenzo and Salerio, welcome
    hither;
If that the youth of my new interest here

Have power to bid you welcome. By your
    leave,
I bid my very friends and countrymen,
Sweet Portia, welcome.
    Por.   So do I, my lord:
They are entirely welcome.
    Lor. I thank your honour. For my part,
    my lord,
My purpose was not to have seen you here;
But meeting with Salerio by the way,   231
He did intreat me, past all saying nay,
To come with him along.
    Saler.   I did, my lord;
And I have reason for it. Signor Antonio
Commends him to you.
                        [*Gives Bassanio a letter.*
    Bass.   Ere I ope his letter,
I pray you, tell me how my good friend doth.
    Saler. Not sick, my lord, unless it be in
    mind;
Nor well, unless in mind: his letter there
Will show you his estate.
    Gra. Nerissa, cheer yon stranger; bid her
    welcome.   240
Your hand, Salerio: what's the news from
    Venice?
How doth that royal merchant, good
    Antonio?
I know he will be glad of our success;
We are the Jasons, we have won the fleece.
    Saler. I would you had won the fleece that
    he hath lost.
    Por. There are some shrewd contents in
    yon same paper,
That steals the colour from Bassanio's cheek:
Some dear friend dead; else nothing in the
    world
Could turn so much the constitution
Of any constant man. What, worse and
    worse!   250
With leave, Bassanio; I am half yourself,
And I must freely have the half of anything
That this same paper brings you.
    Bass.   O sweet Portia,
Here are a few of the unpleasant'st words
That ever blotted paper! Gentle lady,
When I did first impart my love to you,
I freely told you, all the wealth I had
Ran in my veins, I was a gentleman;
And then I told you true: and yet, dear lady,
Rating myself at nothing, you shall see   260

---

206. **roof**, roof of my mouth.

228. **entirely**, cordially.   235. **Commends him**,
desires to be remembered.   239. **estate**, condition.
242. **royal merchant**, merchant prince. 246. **shrewd**,
evil, vexatious. 249. **constitution**, state of mind or
body.   250. **constant**, settled, not swayed by passion.

How much I was a braggart. When I told
you
My state was nothing, I should then have
told you
That I was worse than nothing; for, indeed,
I have engaged myself to a dear friend,
Engaged my friend to his mere enemy,
To feed my means. Here is a letter, lady;
The paper as the body of my friend,
And every word in it a gaping wound,
Issuing life-blood. But is it true, Salerio?
Have all his ventures fail'd? What, not one
hit?   270
From Tripolis, from Mexico and England,
From Lisbon, Barbary and India?
And not one vessel 'scape the dreadful touch
Of merchant-marring rocks?
  Saler.   Not one, my lord.
Besides, it should appear, that if he had
The present money to discharge the Jew,
He would not take it. Never did I know
A creature, that did bear the shape of man,
So keen and greedy to confound a man:
He plies the duke at morning and at night, 280
And doth impeach the freedom of the state,
If they deny him justice: twenty merchants,
The duke himself, and the magnificoes
Of greatest port, have all persuaded with
him;
But none can drive him from the envious plea
Of forfeiture, of justice and his bond.
  Jes. When I was with him I have heard
him swear
To Tubal and to Chus, his countrymen,
That he would rather have Antonio's flesh
Than twenty times the value of the sum   290
That he did owe him: and I know, my lord,
If law, authority and power deny not,
It will go hard with poor Antonio.
  Por. Is it your dear friend that is thus in
trouble?
  Bass. The dearest friend to me, the kind-
est man,
The best-condition'd and unwearied spirit
In doing courtesies, and one in whom
The ancient Roman honour more appears
Than any that draws breath in Italy.
  Por. What sum owes he the Jew?   300
  Bass. For me three thousand ducats.
  Por.   What, no more?
Pay him six thousand, and deface the bond;
Double six thousand, and then treble that,

Before a friend of this description
Shall lose a hair through Bassanio's fault.
First go with me to church and call me wife,
And then away to Venice to your friend;
For never shall you lie by Portia's side
With an unquiet soul. You shall have gold
To pay the petty debt twenty times over: 310
When it is paid, bring your true friend along.
My maid Nerissa and myself meantime
Will live as maids and widows. Come, away!
For you shall hence upon your wedding-day:
Bid your friends welcome, show a merry
cheer:
Since you are dear bought, I will love you
dear.
But let me hear the letter of your friend. 317
  Bass. [*Reads*] Sweet Bassanio, my ships
have all miscarried, my creditors grow cruel,
my estate is very low, my bond to the Jew is
forfeit; and since in paying it, it is impossible
I should live, all debts are cleared between
you and I, if I might but see you at my death.
Notwithstanding, use your pleasure: if your
love do not persuade you to come, let not my
letter.
  Por. O love, dispatch all business, and be
gone!
  Bass. Since I have your good leave to go
away,
I will make haste: but, till I come again,
No bed shall e'er be guilty of my stay, 330
No rest be interposer 'twixt us twain.
                       [*Exeunt.*

Scene III. *Venice. A street.*

Enter Shylock, Salarino, Antonio, *and*
Gaoler.

  Shy. Gaoler, look to him: tell not me of
mercy;
This is the fool that lent out money gratis:
Gaoler, look to him.
  Ant.   Hear me yet, good Shylock.
  Shy. I'll have my bond; speak not against
my bond:
I have sworn an oath that I will have my
bond.
Thou call'dst me dog before thou hadst a
cause;
But, since I am a dog, beware my fangs:
The duke shall grant me justice. I do wonder,

---

265. mere, absolute, complete. 281. impeach, call
in question. 283. magnificoes, chief men of Venice.
285. envious, malicious.

315. cheer, face. 324-326. Notwithstanding . . .
letter. Complete self-abnegation is here thought of as
a condition of ideal friendship as well as of ideal love.

Thou naughty gaoler, that thou art so fond
To come abroad with him at his request.　　10
　　Ant. I pray thee, hear me speak.
　　Shy. I'll have my bond; I will not hear
　　　　thee speak:
I'll have my bond; and therefore speak no
　　more.
I'll not be made a soft and dull-eyed fool,
To shake the head, relent, and sigh, and yield
To Christian intercessors. Follow not;
I'll have no speaking: I will have my bond.
　　　　　　　　　　　　　　　[Exit.
　　Salar. It is the most impenetrable cur
That ever kept with men.
　　Ant.　　　　　　　Let him alone:
I'll follow him no more with bootless prayers.
He seeks my life; his reason well I know:　21
I oft deliver'd from his forfeitures
Many that have at times made moan to me;
Therefore he hates me.
　　Salar.　　　　　I am sure the duke
Will never grant this forfeiture to hold.
　　Ant. The duke cannot deny the course of
　　　　law:
For the commodity that strangers have
With us in Venice, if it be denied,
Will much impeach the justice of his state;
Since that the trade and profit of the city　30
Consisteth of all nations. Therefore, go:
These griefs and losses have so bated me,
That I shall hardly spare a pound of flesh
To-morrow to my bloody creditor.
Well, gaoler, on. Pray God, Bassanio come
To see me pay his debt, and then I care not!
　　　　　　　　　　　　　　[Exeunt.

SCENE IV. *Belmont. A room in* PORTIA'S
　　　　　　　house.

Enter PORTIA, NERISSA, LORENZO, JESSICA,
　　　　and BALTHASAR.

　　Lor. Madam, although I speak it in your
　　　　presence,
You have a noble and a true conceit
Of god-like amity; which appears most
　　strongly
In bearing thus the absence of your lord.
But if you knew to whom you show this
　　honour,
How true a gentleman you send relief,
How dear a lover of my lord your husband,

I know you would be prouder of the work
Than customary bounty can enforce you.
　　Por. I never did repent for doing good,　10
Nor shall not now: for in companions
That do converse and waste the time to-
　　gether,
Whose souls do bear an equal yoke of love,
There must be needs a like proportion
Of lineaments, of manners and of spirit;
Which makes me think that this Antonio,
Being the bosom lover of my lord,
Must needs be like my lord. If it be so,
How little is the cost I have bestow'd
In purchasing the semblance of my soul　20
From out the state of hellish misery!
This comes too near the praising of myself;
Therefore no more of it: hear other things.
Lorenzo, I commit into your hands
The husbandry and manage of my house
Until my lord's return: for mine own part,
I have toward heaven breathed a secret vow
To live in prayer and contemplation,
Only attended by Nerissa here,
Until her husband and my lord's return:　30
There is a monastery two miles off;
And there will we abide. I do desire you
Not to deny this imposition;
The which my love and some necessity
Now lays upon you.
　　Lor.　　　　　Madam, with all my heart;
I shall obey you in all fair commands.
　　Por. My people do already know my
　　　　mind,
And will acknowledge you and Jessica
In place of Lord Bassanio and myself.
And so farewell, till we shall meet again.　40
　　Lor. Fair thoughts and happy hours at-
　　　　tend on you!
　　Jes. I wish your ladyship all heart's con-
　　　　tent.
　　Por. I thank you for your wish, and am
　　　　well pleased
To wish it back on you: fare you well,
　　　　Jessica.　*[Exeunt Jessica and Lorenzo.*
Now, Balthasar,
As I have ever found thee honest-true,
So let me find thee still. Take this same
　　letter,
And use thou all the endeavour of a man
In speed to Padua: see thou render this

---

19. **kept**, dwelt.　20. **bootless**, having gained
nothing.　27. **commodity**, facilities or privileges for
trading.　32. **bated**, diminished.

9. **customary bounty**, ordinary kindness.　20. **my
soul**, Bassanio.　25. **husbandry**, care of the household.　**manage**, administration.　33. **imposition**,
charge imposed.　49. **render**, deliver.

Into my cousin's hand, Doctor Bellario;   50
And, look, what notes and garments he doth
    give thee,
Bring them, I pray thee, with imagined
    speed
Unto the tranect, to the common ferry
Which trades to Venice. Waste no time in
    words,
But get thee gone: I shall be there before
    thee.

Balth. Madam, I go with all convenient
    speed.   [*Exit.*

Por. Come on, Nerissa; I have work in
    hand
That you yet know not of: we'll see our hus-
    bands
Before they think of us.

Ner.   Shall they see us?

Por. They shall, Nerissa; but in such a
    habit,   60
That they shall think we are accomplished
With that we lack. I'll hold thee any wager,
When we are both accoutred like young men,
I'll prove the prettier fellow of the two,
And wear my dagger with the braver grace,
And speak between the change of man and
    boy
With a reed voice, and turn two mincing
    steps
Into a manly stride, and speak of frays
Like a fine bragging youth, and tell quaint
    lies,
How honourable ladies sought my love,   70
Which I denying, they fell sick and died;
I could not do withal; then I'll repent,
And wish, for all that, that I had not kill'd
    them;
And twenty of these puny lies I'll tell,
That men shall swear I have discontinued
    school
Above a twelvemonth. I have within my
    mind
A thousand raw tricks of these bragging
    Jacks,
Which I will practise.

Ner.   Why, shall we turn to men?

Por. Fie, what a question's that,
If thou wert near a lewd interpreter!   80
But come, I'll tell thee all my whole device
When I am in my coach, which stays for us

At the park gate; and therefore haste away,
For we must measure twenty miles to-day.
                    [*Exeunt.*

Scene V. *The same. A garden.*

Enter Launcelot *and* Jessica.

Laun. Yes, truly; for, look you, the sins of
the father are to be laid upon the children:
therefore, I promise ye, I fear you. I was
always plain with you, and so now I speak
my agitation of the matter: therefore be of
good cheer, for truly I think you are damned.
There is but one hope in it that can do you
any good; and that is but a kind of bastard
hope neither.

Jes. And what hope is that, I pray thee? 10

Laun. Marry, you may partly hope that
your father got you not, that you are not the
Jew's daughter.

Jes. That were a kind of bastard hope,
indeed: so the sins of my mother should be
visited upon me.

Laun. Truly then I fear you are damned
both by father and mother: thus when I shun
Scylla, your father, I fall into Charybdis,
your mother: well, you are gone both ways. 20

Jes. I shall be saved by my husband; he
hath made me a Christian.

Laun. Truly, the more to blame he: we
were Christians enow before; e'en as many as
could well live, one by another. This making
of Christians will raise the price of hogs: if we
grow all to be pork-eaters, we shall not shortly have a rasher on the coals for money.

Enter Lorenzo.

Jes. I'll tell my husband, Launcelot, what
you say: here he comes.   30

Lor. I shall grow jealous of you shortly,
Launcelot, if you thus get my wife into corners.

Jes. Nay, you need not fear us, Lorenzo:
Launcelot and I are out. He tells me flatly,
there is no mercy for me in heaven, because I
am a Jew's daughter: and he says, you are no
good member of the commonwealth, for in
converting Jews to Christians, you raise the
price of pork.   39

---

52. **imagined speed,** speed of imagination, as quick
as thought.   53. **tranect.**   Rowe conjectured *traject*
(Italian *traghetto*, ferry).   60. **habit,** dress.   61. **accomplished,** supplied.   72. **do withal,** help it.   77.
Jacks, fellows.

Scene v. 3. **fear you,** i.e., for you. 5. **agitation,** for
cogitation. 19. **Scylla . . . Charybdis,** twin dangers of
Odyssey, xii, 235, a rock and a whirlpool guarding the
straits between Italy and Sicily. 25. **one by another,**
together. 34. **are out,** have quarreled.

Lor. I shall answer that better to the commonwealth than you can the getting up of the negro's belly: the Moor is with child by you, Launcelot.

Laun. It is much that the Moor should be more than reason: but if she be less than an honest woman, she is indeed more than I took her for.

Lor. How every fool can play upon the word! I think the best grace of wit will shortly turn into silence, and discourse grow commendable in none only but parrots. Go in, sirrah; bid them prepare for dinner.

Laun. That is done, sir; they have all stomachs.

Lor. Goodly Lord, what a wit-snapper are you! then bid them prepare dinner.

Laun. That is done too, sir; only 'cover' is the word.

Lor. Will you cover then, sir?

Laun. Not so, sir, neither; I know my duty.   59

Lor. Yet more quarrelling with occasion! Wilt thou show the whole wealth of thy wit in an instant? I pray thee, understand a plain man in his plain meaning: go to thy fellows; bid them cover the table, serve in the meat, and we will come in to dinner.

Laun. For the table, sir, it shall be served in; for the meat, sir, it shall be covered; for your coming in to dinner, sir, why, let it be as humours and conceits shall govern.   [*Exit.*

Lor. O dear discretion, how his words are suited!   70
The fool hath planted in his memory
An army of good words; and I do know
A many fools, that stand in better place,
Garnish'd like him, that for a tricksy word
Defy the matter. How cheer'st thou, Jessica?
And now, good sweet, say thy opinion,
How dost thou like the Lord Bassanio's wife?

Jes. Past all expressing. It is very meet
The Lord Bassanio live an upright life;
For, having such a blessing in his lady,   80
He finds the joys of heaven here on earth;
†And if on earth he do not mean it, then
In reason he should never come to heaven.

Why, if two gods should play some heavenly match
And on the wager lay two earthly women,
And Portia one, there must be something else
Pawn'd with the other, for the poor rude world
Hath not her fellow.

Lor.   Even such a husband
Hast thou of me as she is for a wife.   89

Jes. Nay, but ask my opinion too of that.

Lor. I will anon: first, let us go to dinner.

Jes. Nay, let me praise you while I have a stomach.

Lor. No, pray thee, let it serve for table-talk;
Then, howsoe'er thou speak'st, 'mong other things
I shall digest it.

Jes.   Well, I'll set you forth. [*Exeunt.*

ACT IV.

SCENE I. *Venice. A court of justice.*

Enter the DUKE, *the* MAGNIFICOES, ANTONIO, BASSANIO, GRATIANO, SALERIO, *and others.*

Duke. What, is Antonio here?

Ant. Ready, so please your grace.

Duke. I am sorry for thee: thou art come to answer
A stony adversary, an inhuman wretch
Uncapable of pity, void and empty
From any dram of mercy.

Ant.   I have heard
Your grace hath ta'en great pains to qualify
His rigorous course; but since he stands obdurate
And that no lawful means can carry me
Out of his envy's reach, I do oppose   10
My patience to his fury, and am arm'd
To suffer, with a quietness of spirit,
The very tyranny and rage of his.

Duke. Go one, and call the Jew into the court.

Saler. He is ready at the door: he comes, my lord.

Enter SHYLOCK.

Duke. Make room, and let him stand before our face.
Shylock, the world thinks, and I think so too,

54. stomachs, appetites. 57. 'cover,' two meanings: "spread the table for the meal" and "put on your hat." 60. quarrelling with occasion, answering perversely. 70. suited, fitted to special uses. 74. Garnish'd, i.e., with words. tricksy, fantastic. 75. Defy the matter, possibly, disregard the true sense. How cheer'st thou, what cheer? 82. mean it, i.e., lead an upright life.

Act IV. Scene i. 7. qualify, moderate. 13. tyranny, cruelty.

That thou but lead'st this fashion of thy
    malice
To the last hour of act; and then 'tis thought
Thou'lt show thy mercy and remorse more
    strange   20
Than is thy strange apparent cruelty;
And where thou now exact'st the penalty,
Which is a pound of this poor merchant's
    flesh,
Thou wilt not only loose the forfeiture,
But, touch'd with human gentleness and
    love,
Forgive a moiety of the principal;
Glancing an eye of pity on his losses,
That have of late so huddled on his back,
Enow to press a royal merchant down
And pluck commiseration of his state   30
From brassy bosoms and rough hearts of
    flint,
From stubborn Turks and Tartars, never
    train'd
To offices of tender courtesy.
We all expect a gentle answer, Jew.
    Shy. I have possess'd your grace of what I
    purpose;
And by our holy Sabbath have I sworn
To have the due and forfeit of my bond:
If you deny it, let the danger light
Upon your charter and your city's freedom.
You'll ask me, why I rather choose to have   40
A weight of carrion flesh than to receive
Three thousand ducats: I'll not answer that:
But, say, it is my humour: is it answer'd?
What if my house be troubled with a rat
And I be pleased to give ten thousand ducats
To have it baned? What, are you answer'd
    yet?
Some men there are love not a gaping pig;
Some, that are mad if they behold a cat;
And others, when the bagpipe sings i' the
    nose,
Cannot contain their urine: for affection,   50
Mistress of passion, sways it to the mood
Of what it likes or loathes. Now, for your
    answer:
As there is no firm reason to be render'd,

Why he cannot abide a gaping pig;
Why he, a harmless necessary cat;
†Why he, a woollen bag-pipe; but of force
Must yield to such inevitable shame
As to offend, himself being offended;
So can I give no reason, nor I will not,
More than a lodged hate and a certain
    loathing   60
I bear Antonio, that I follow thus
A losing suit against him. Are you answer'd?
    Bass. This is no answer, thou unfeeling
    man,
To excuse the current of thy cruelty.
    Shy. I am not bound to please thee with
    my answers.
    Bass. Do all men kill the things they do
    not love?
    Shy. Hates any man the thing he would
    not kill?
    Bass. Every offence is not a hate at first.
    Shy. What, wouldst thou have a serpent
    sting thee twice?
    Ant. I pray you, think you question with
    the Jew: 70
You may as well go stand upon the beach
And bid the main flood bate his usual height;
You may as well use question with the wolf
Why he hath made the ewe bleat for the
    lamb;
You may as well forbid the mountain pines
To wag their high tops and to make no noise,
When they are fretten with the gusts of
    heaven;
You may as well do any thing most hard,
As seek to soften that—than which what's
    harder?—
His Jewish heart: therefore, I do beseech
    you,   80
Make no more offers, use no farther means,
But with all brief and plain conveniency
Let me have judgement and the Jew his
    will.
    Bass. For thy three thousand ducats here
    is six.
    Shy. If every ducat in six thousand ducats
Were in six parts and every part a ducat,
I would not draw them; I would have my
    bond.
    Duke. How shalt thou hope for mercy,
    rendering none?
    Shy. What judgement shall I dread, doing
    no wrong?

18. fashion, mere form. **19. act**, action. **20. remorse**, pity. **26. moiety**, part, portion. **29. Enow**, enough. **35. possess'd**, informed. **38. danger**, injury. **39. Upon . . . freedom.** The Venetians were celebrated for their strict adherence to law. **43. humour**, whim, caprice. **46. baned**, killed, especially by poison. **47. gaping pig**, explained as "pig roasted whole with its mouth open"; also as "bawling" or "shouting," i.e., squealing. **50. affection**, mental state or inclination. Shylock means to say that the mental state from which passion arises may originate from mere likes and dislikes.

60. lodged, settled, steadfast. **certain**, definite. **77. fretten**, fretted. **87. draw**, receive.

You have among you many a purchased
slave,　　　　　　　　　　　　　90
Which, like your asses and your dogs and
mules,
You use in abject and in slavish parts,
Because you bought them: shall I say to you,
Let them be free, marry them to your heirs?
Why sweat they under burthens? let their
beds
Be made as soft as yours and let their palates
Be season'd with such viands? You will
answer
'The slaves are ours:' so do I answer you:
The pound of flesh, which I demand of him,
Is dearly bought; 'tis mine and I will have it.
If you deny me, fie upon your law!　　101
There is no force in the decrees of Venice.
I stand for judgement: answer; shall I have
it?
　　Duke. Upon my power I may dismiss this
court,
Unless Bellario, a learned doctor,
Whom I have sent for to determine this,
Come here to-day.
　　Saler.　　My lord, here stays without
A messenger with letters from the doctor,
New come from Padua.
　　Duke. Bring us the letters; call the mes-
senger.　　　　　　　　　　　　110
　　Bass. Good cheer, Antonio! What, man,
courage yet!
The Jew shall have my flesh, blood, bones
and all,
Ere thou shalt loose for me one drop of blood.
　　Ant. I am a tainted wether of the flock,
Meetest for death: the weakest kind of fruit
Drops earliest to the ground; and so let me:
You cannot better be employ'd, Bassanio,
Than to live still and write mine epitaph.

Enter NERISSA, *dressed like a lawyer's
clerk.*

　　Duke. Came you from Padua, from
Bellario?
　　Ner. From both, my lord. Bellario greets
your grace.　　　[*Presenting a letter.*　120
　　Bass. Why dost thou whet thy knife so
earnestly?
　　Shy. To cut the forfeiture from that bank-
rupt there.

　　Gra. Not on thy sole, but on thy soul,
harsh Jew,
Thou makest thy knife keen; but no metal
can,
No, not the hangman's axe, bear half the
keenness
Of thy sharp envy. Can no prayers pierce
thee?
　　Shy. No, none that thou hast wit enough
to make.
　　Gra. O, be thou damn'd, inexecrable dog!
And for thy life let justice be accused.
Thou almost makest me waver in my faith 130
To hold opinion with Pythagoras,
That souls of animals infuse themselves
Into the trunks of men: thy currish spirit
Govern'd a wolf, who, hang'd for human
slaughter,
Even from the gallows did his fell soul fleet,
And, whilst thou lay'st in thy unhallow'd
dam,
Infused itself in thee; for thy desires
Are wolvish, bloody, starved and ravenous.
　　Shy. Till thou canst rail the seal from off
my bond,
Thou but offend'st thy lungs to speak so
loud:　　　　　　　　　　　　140
Repair thy wit, good youth, or it will fall
To cureless ruin. I stand here for law.
　　Duke. This letter from Bellario doth
commend
A young and learned doctor to our court.
Where is he?
　　Ner.　　He attendeth here hard by,
To know your answer, whether you'll admit
him.
　　Duke. With all my heart. Some three or
four of you
Go give him courteous conduct to this place.
Meantime the court shall hear Bellario's
letter.
　　Clerk. [*Reads*] Your grace shall understand
that at the receipt of your letter I am very
sick: but in the instant that your messenger
came, in loving visitation was with me a
young doctor of Rome; his name is Balthasar.
I acquainted him with the cause in controversy between the Jew and Antonio the
merchant: we turned o'er many books together: he is furnished with my opinion;
which, bettered with his own learning, the

---

92. **parts,** duties, capacities.　121. **Why . . . earnestly.** The traditional stage-business at this point is for
the actor who plays the part of Shylock to be discovered
whetting his knife on the sole of his shoe.

134. **hang'd for human slaughter,** a possible allusion to the ancient practice of trying and punishing animals for various crimes.　135. **fleet,** flit.　140. **offend 'st,**
injurest.

greatness whereof I cannot enough commend, comes with him, at my importunity, to fill up your grace's request in my stead. I beseech you, let his lack of years be no impediment to let him lack a reverend estimation; for I never knew so young a body with so old a head. I leave him to your gracious acceptance, whose trial shall better publish his commendation.

Duke. You hear the learn'd Bellario, what he writes:
And here, I take it, is the doctor come.

Enter PORTIA, *dressed like a doctor of laws.*

Give me your hand. Come you from old Bellario?

Por. I did, my lord.

Duke. You are welcome: take your place.
Are you acquainted with the difference   171
That holds this present question in the court?

Por. I am informed throughly of the cause.
Which is the merchant here, and which the Jew?

Duke. Antonio and old Shylock, both stand forth.

Por. Is your name Shylock?

Shy.   Shylock is my name.

Por. Of a strange nature is the suit you follow;
Yet in such rule that the Venetian law
Cannot impugn you as you do proceed.   179
You stand within his danger, do you not?

Ant. Ay, so he says.

Por.   Do you confess the bond?

Ant. I do.

Por.   Then must the Jew be merciful.

Shy. On what compulsion must I? tell me that.

Por. The quality of mercy is not strain'd,
It droppeth as the gentle rain from heaven
Upon the place beneath: it is twice blest;
It blesseth him that gives and him that takes:
'Tis mightiest in the mightiest: it becomes
The throned monarch better than his crown;
His sceptre shows the force of temporal power,   190
The attribute to awe and majesty,
Wherein doth sit the dread and fear of kings;
But mercy is above this sceptred sway;
It is enthroned in the hearts of kings,

It is an attribute to God himself;
And earthly power doth then show likest God's
When mercy seasons justice. Therefore, Jew,
Though justice be thy plea, consider this,
That, in the course of justice, none of us   199
Should see salvation: we do pray for mercy;
And that same prayer doth teach us all to render
The deeds of mercy. I have spoke thus much
To mitigate the justice of thy plea;
Which if thou follow, this strict court of Venice
Must needs give sentence 'gainst the merchant there.

Shy. My deeds upon my head! I crave the law,
The penalty and forfeit of my bond.

Por. Is he not able to discharge the money?

Bass. Yes, here I tender it for him in the court;   209
Yea, twice the sum: if that will not suffice,
I will be bound to pay it ten times o'er,
On forfeit of my hands, my head, my heart:
If this will not suffice, it must appear
That malice bears down truth. And I beseech you,
Wrest once the law to your authority:
To do a great right, do a little wrong,
And curb this cruel devil of his will.

Por. It must not be; there is no power in Venice
Can alter a decree established:
'Twill be recorded for a precedent,   220
And many an error by the same example
Will rush into the state: it cannot be.

Shy. A Daniel come to judgement! yea, a Daniel!
O wise young judge, how I do honour thee!

Por. I pray you, let me look upon the bond.

Shy. Here 'tis, most reverend doctor, here it is.

Por. Shylock, there's thrice thy money offer'd thee.

Shy. An oath, an oath, I have an oath in heaven:
Shall I lay perjury upon my soul?
No, not for Venice.

Por.   Why, this bond is forfeit;

---

173. **throughly,** thoroughly.   179. **impugn,** find fault with.   180. **danger,** power to harm; possibly a legal term.   184. **strain'd,** forced, constrained; in reply to Shylock's reference to compulsion.

214. **truth,** honesty (Johnson).   223. **Daniel.** In the Apocryphal book of *Susannah*, Daniel is the judge who rescues Susannah from her false accusers.

And lawfully by this the Jew may claim 231
A pound of flesh, to be by him cut off
Nearest the merchant's heart. Be merciful:
Take thrice thy money; bid me tear the
  bond.

Shy. When it is paid according to the
  tenour.

It doth appear you are a worthy judge;
You know the law, your exposition
Hath been most sound: I charge you by the
  law,
Whereof you are a well-deserving pillar,
Proceed to judgement: by my soul I swear
There is no power in the tongue of man 241
To alter me: I stay here on my bond.

Ant. Most heartily I do beseech the court
To give the judgement.

Por.   Why then, thus it is:
You must prepare your bosom for his knife.

Shy. O noble judge! O excellent young
  man!

Por. For the intent and purpose of the law
Hath full relation to the penalty,
Which here appeareth due upon the bond.

Shy. 'Tis very true: O wise and upright
  judge!   250
How much more elder art thou than thy
  looks!

Por. Therefore lay bare your bosom.

Shy.   Ay, his breast:
So says the bond: doth it not, noble judge?
'Nearest his heart:' those are the very words.

Por. It is so. Are there balance here to
  weigh
The flesh?

Shy.   I have them ready.

Por. Have by some surgeon, Shylock, on
  your charge,
To stop his wounds, lest he do bleed to death.

Shy. Is it so nominated in the bond?

Por. It is not so express'd: but what of
  that?   260
'Twere good you do so much for charity.

Shy. I cannot find it; 'tis not in the bond.

Por. You, merchant, have you any thing
  to say?

Ant. But little: I am arm'd and well pre-
  pared.
Give me your hand, Bassanio: fare you well!
Grieve not that I am fallen to this for you;
For herein Fortune shows herself more kind
Than is her custom: it is still her use

242. **stay . . . on,** take stand upon.

To let the wretched man outlive his wealth,
To view with hollow eye and wrinkled brow
An age of poverty; from which lingering pen-
  ance   271
Of such misery doth she cut me off.
Commend me to your honourable wife:
Tell her the process of Antonio's end;
Say how I loved you, speak me fair in death;
And, when the tale is told, bid her be judge
Whether Bassanio had not once a love.
Repent but you that you shall lose your
  friend,
And he repents not that he pays your debt;
For if the Jew do cut but deep enough, 280
I'll pay it presently with all my heart.

Bass. Antonio, I am married to a wife
Which is as dear to me as life itself;
But life itself, my wife, and all the world,
Are not with me esteem'd above thy life:
I would lose all, ay, sacrifice them all
Here to this devil, to deliver you.

Por. Your wife would give you little
  thanks for that,
If she were by, to hear you make the offer.

Gra. I have a wife, whom, I protest, I love:
I would she were in heaven, so she could 291
Entreat some power to change this currish
  Jew.

Ner. 'Tis well you offer it behind her back;
The wish would make else an unquiet house.

Shy. These be the Christian husbands. I
  have a daughter;
Would any of the stock of Barrabas
Had been her husband rather than a
  Christian!   [*Aside.*]
We trifle time: I pray thee, pursue sentence.

Por. A pound of that same merchant's
  flesh is thine:
The court awards it, and the law doth give it.

Shy. Most rightful judge!   301

Por. And you must cut this flesh from off
  his breast:
The law allows it, and the court awards it.

Shy. Most learned judge! A sentence!
  Come, prepare!

Por. Tarry a little; there is something else.
This bond doth give thee here no jot of blood;
The words expressly are 'a pound of flesh:'
Take then thy bond, take thou thy pound of
  flesh;
But, in the cutting it, if thou dost shed
One drop of Christian blood, thy lands and
  goods   310
Are, by the laws of Venice, confiscate

Unto the state of Venice.

Gra. O upright judge! Mark, Jew: O learned judge!

Shy. Is that the law?

Por.   Thyself shalt see the act:
For, as thou urgest justice, be assured
Thou shalt have justice, more than thou desirest.

Gra. O learned judge! Mark, Jew: a learned judge!

Shy. I take this offer, then; pay the bond thrice
And let the Christian go.

Bass.   Here is the money.

Por. Soft!   320
The Jew shall have all justice; soft! no haste:
He shall have nothing but the penalty.

Gra. O Jew! an upright judge, a learned judge!

Por. Therefore prepare thee to cut off the flesh.
Shed thou no blood, nor cut thou less nor more
But just a pound of flesh: if thou cut'st more
Or less than a just pound, be it but so much
As makes it light or heavy in the substance,
Or the division of the twentieth part
Of one poor scruple, nay, if the scale do turn
But in the estimation of a hair,   331
Thou diest and all thy goods are confiscate.

Gra. A second Daniel, a Daniel, Jew!
Now, infidel, I have you on the hip.

Por. Why doth the Jew pause? take thy forfeiture.

Shy. Give me my principal, and let me go.

Bass. I have it ready for thee; here it is.

Por. He hath refused it in the open court:
He shall have merely justice and his bond.

Gra. A Daniel, still say I, a second Daniel!
I thank thee, Jew, for teaching me that word.

Shy. Shall I not have barely my principal?

Por. Thou shalt have nothing but the forfeiture,   343
To be so taken at thy peril, Jew.

Shy. Why, then the devil give him good of it!
I'll stay no longer question.

Por.   Tarry, Jew:
The law hath yet another hold on you.

It is enacted in the laws of Venice,
If it be proved against an alien
That by direct or indirect attempts   350
He seek the life of any citizen,
The party 'gainst the which he doth contrive
Shall seize one half his goods; the other half
Comes to the privy coffer of the state;
And the offender's life lies in the mercy
Of the duke only, 'gainst all other voice.
In which predicament, I say, thou stand'st;
For it appears, by manifest proceeding,
That indirectly and directly too
Thou hast contrived against the very life 360
Of the defendant; and thou hast incurr'd
The danger formerly by me rehearsed.
Down therefore and beg mercy of the duke.

Gra. Beg that thou mayst have leave to hang thyself:
And yet, thy wealth being forfeit to the state,
Thou hast not left the value of a cord;
Therefore thou must be hang'd at the state's charge.

Duke. That thou shalt see the difference of our spirits,
I pardon thee thy life before thou ask it:
For half thy wealth, it is Antonio's;   370
The other half comes to the general state,
Which humbleness may drive unto a fine.

Por. Ay, for the state, not for Antonio.

Shy. Nay, take my life and all: pardon not that:
You take my house when you do take the prop
That doth sustain my house; you take my life
When you do take the means whereby I live.

Por. What mercy can you render him, Antonio?

Gra. A halter gratis; nothing else, for God's sake.

Ant. So please my lord the duke and all the court   380
To quit the fine for one half of his goods,
I am content; so he will let me have
The other half in use, to render it,
Upon his death, unto the gentleman
That lately stole his daughter:

---

313. **O . . . judge.** In the modern sympathetic presentations of the character of Shylock, it is usual to subordinate the part of Gratiano in this scene. 328. **substance,** mass or gross weight. 329-30. **division . . . scruple,** fraction of the twentieth of a scruple (20 grains apothecaries' weight).

372. **humbleness,** gentleness, tractability.   381. **quit,** remit. This difficult passage is variously interpreted. It seems to mean that, as the Duke has seen fit to accept a fine instead of one-half of Shylock's goods, Antonio will in his turn merely take over the other half for the benefit of Lorenzo and Jessica. 383. **use,** probably, trust.

Two things provided more, that, for this favour,
He presently become a Christian;
The other, that he do record a gift,
Here in the court, of all he dies possess'd,
Unto his son Lorenzo and his daughter. 390

Duke. He shall do this, or else I do recant
The pardon that I late pronounced here.

Por. Art thou contented, Jew? what dost thou say?

Shy. I am content.

Por.   Clerk, draw a deed of gift.

Shy. I pray you, give me leave to go from hence;
I am not well: send the deed after me,
And I will sign it.

Duke.   Get thee gone, but do it.

Gra. In christening shalt thou have two godfathers:
Had I been judge, thou shouldst have had ten more,
To bring thee to the gallows, not the font.
                              [*Exit Shylock.*

Duke. Sir, I entreat you home with me to dinner.   401

Por. I humbly do desire your grace of pardon:
I must away this night toward Padua,
And it is meet I presently set forth.

Duke. I am sorry that your leisure serves you not.
Antonio, gratify this gentleman,
For, in my mind, you are much bound to him.   [*Exeunt Duke and his train.*

Bass. Most worthy gentleman, I and my friend
Have by your wisdom been this day acquitted
Of grievous penalties; in lieu whereof,   410
Three thousand ducats, due unto the Jew,
We freely cope your courteous pains withal.

Ant. And stand indebted, over and above,
In love and service to you evermore.

Por. He is well paid that is well satisfied;
And I, delivering you, am satisfied
And therein do account myself well paid:
My mind was never yet more mercenary.
I pray you, know me when we meet again:
I wish you well, and so I take my leave.   420

Bass. Dear sir, of force I must attempt you further:
Take some remembrance of us, as a tribute,
Not as a fee: grant me two things, I pray you,
Not to deny me, and to pardon me.

Por. You press me far, and therefore I will yield.
[*To Ant.*] Give me your gloves, I'll wear them for your sake;
[*To Bass.*] And, for your love, I'll take this ring from you:
Do not draw back your hand; I'll take no more;
And you in love shall not deny me this.

Bass. This ring, good sir, alas, it is a trifle!
I will not shame myself to give you this. 431

Por. I will have nothing else but only this;
And now methinks I have a mind to it.

Bass. There's more depends on this than on the value.
The dearest ring in Venice will I give you,
And find it out by proclamation:
Only for this, I pray you, pardon me.

Por. I see, sir, you are liberal in offers:
You taught me first to beg; and now methinks
You teach me how a beggar should be answer'd.   440

Bass. Good sir, this ring was given me by my wife;
And when she put it on, she made me vow
That I should neither sell nor give nor lose it.

Por. That 'scuse serves many men to save their gifts.
An if your wife be not a mad-woman,
And know how well I have deserved the ring,
She would not hold out enemy for ever,
For giving it to me. Well, peace be with you!
                    [*Exeunt Portia and Nerissa.*

Ant. My Lord Bassanio, let him have the ring:
Let his deservings and my love withal   450
Be valued 'gainst your wife's commandment.

Bass. Go, Gratiano, run and overtake him;
Give him the ring, and bring him, if thou canst,
Unto Antonio's house: away! make haste.
                              [*Exit Gratiano.*
Come, you and I will thither presently;

---

387. **presently**, at once. **become a Christian.**
This added penalty, frequently thought of as a piece of
cynical and gratuitous cruelty, may have carried no
shock to the sensibilities of the audience, who may have
seen in it merely a chance for Shylock's salvation. 402.
of, for. 406. **gratify**, reward. 412. **cope withal**,
match with an equivalent.

426. **gloves**, a customary and relatively valuable gift
in Elizabethan times.

And in the morning early will we both
Fly toward Belmont: come, Antonio.

[*Exeunt.*

SCENE II. *The same. A street.*

Enter PORTIA *and* NERISSA.

Por. Inquire the Jew's house out, give him
this deed
And let him sign it: we'll away to-night
And be a day before our husbands home:
This deed will be well welcome to Lorenzo.

Enter GRATIANO.

Gra. Fair sir, you are well o'erta'en:
My Lord Bassanio upon more advice
Hath sent you here this ring, and doth en-
treat
Your company at dinner.
Por.   That cannot be:
His ring I do accept most thankfully:
And so, I pray you, tell him: furthermore, 10
I pray you, show my youth old Shylock's
house.
Gra. That will I do.
Ner.   Sir, I would speak with you.
[*Aside to Por.*] I'll see if I can get my hus-
band's ring,
Which I did make him swear to keep for ever.
Por. [*Aside to Ner.*] Thou mayst, I war-
rant. We shall have old swearing
That they did give the rings away to men;
But we'll outface them, and outswear them
too.
[*Aloud*] Away! make haste: thou know'st
where I will tarry.
Ner. Come, good sir, will you show me to
this house?   [*Exeunt.*

ACT V.

SCENE I. *Belmont. Avenue to* PORTIA'S
house.

Enter LORENZO *and* JESSICA.

Lor. The moon shines bright: in such a
night as this,
When the sweet wind did gently kiss the
trees
And they did make no noise, in such a night
Troilus methinks mounted the Troyan walls

And sigh'd his soul toward the Grecian tents,
Where Cressid lay that night.
Jes.   In such a night
Did Thisbe fearfully o'ertrip the dew
And saw the lion's shadow ere himself
And ran dismay'd away.
Lor.   In such a night
Stood Dido with a willow in her hand   10
Upon the wild sea banks and waft her love
To come again to Carthage.
Jes.   In such a night
Medea gather'd the enchanted herbs
That did renew old Æson.
Lor.   In such a night
Did Jessica steal from the wealthy Jew
And with an unthrift love did run from
Venice
As far as Belmont.
Jes.   In such a night
Did young Lorenzo swear he loved her well,
Stealing her soul with many vows of faith
And ne'er a true one.
Lor.   In such a night   20
Did pretty Jessica, like a little shrew,
Slander her love, and he forgave it her.
Jes. I would out-night you, did no body
come;
But, hark, I hear the footing of a man.

Enter STEPHANO.

Lor. Who comes so fast in silence of the
night?
Steph. A friend.
Lor. A friend! what friend? your name, I
pray you, friend?
Steph. Stephano is my name; and I bring
word
My mistress will before the break of day
Be here at Belmont: she doth stray about 30
By holy crosses, where she kneels and prays
For happy wedlock hours.
Lor.   Who comes with her?
Steph. None but a holy hermit and her
maid.
I pray you, is my master yet return'd?
Lor. He is not, nor we have not heard
from him.
But go we in, I pray thee, Jessica,

Scene ii. 6. more advice, second thought. 16. old,
extraordinary.
   Act V. Scene i. 4. Troilus. Cf. Chaucer, *Troilus
and Criseyde*, lines 647-79.

7. **Thisbe.** The story of Pyramus and Thisbe was
the subject of the play presented by Bottom and his
companions in *A Midsummer-Night's Dream.* 10. **willow,** symbol of forsaken love. 11. **waft,** beckoned.
13. **Medea,** allusion to the famous sorceress of Colchis
who pretended to restore youth to Æson, father of Jason,
as told by Ovid. 24. **footing,** footsteps.

And ceremoniously let us prepare
Some welcome for the mistress of the house.

Enter LAUNCELOT.

Laun. Sola, sola! wo ha, ho! sola, sola!
Lor. Who calls?   40
Laun. Sola! did you see Master Lorenzo?
Master Lorenzo, sola, sola!
Lor. Leave hollaing, man: here.
Laun. Sola! where? where?
Lor. Here.
Laun. Tell him there's a post come from
my master, with his horn full of good news:
my master will be here ere morning. [*Exit.*
Lor. Sweet soul, let's in, and there expect
their coming.
And yet no matter: why should we go in? 50
My friend Stephano, signify, I pray you,
Within the house, your mistress is at hand;
And bring your music forth into the air.
                        [*Exit Stephano.*
How sweet the moonlight sleeps upon this
    bank!
Here will we sit and let the sounds of music
Creep in our ears: soft stillness and the night
Become the touches of sweet harmony.
Sit, Jessica. Look how the floor of heaven
Is thick inlaid with patines of bright gold:
There's not the smallest orb which thou be-
    hold'st   60
But in his motion like an angel sings,
Still quiring to the young-eyed cherubins;
Such harmony is in immortal souls;
But whilst this muddy vesture of decay
Doth grossly close it in, we cannot hear it.

Enter Musicians.

Come, ho! and wake Diana with a hymn:
With sweetest touches pierce your mistress'
    ear
And draw her home with music.   [*Music.*
Jes. I am never merry when I hear sweet
    music.
Lor. The reason is, your spirits are atten-
    tive: 70

For do but note a wild and wanton herd,
Or race of youthful and unhandled colts,
Fetching mad bounds, bellowing and neigh-
    ing loud,
Which is the hot condition of their blood;
If they but hear perchance a trumpet sound,
Or any air of music touch their ears,
You shall perceive them make a mutual
    stand,
Their savage eyes turn'd to a modest gaze
By the sweet power of music: therefore the
    poet
Did feign that Orpheus drew trees, stones
    and floods;   80
Since nought so stockish, hard and full of
    rage,
But music for the time doth change his
    nature.
The man that hath no music in himself,
Nor is not moved with concord of sweet
    sounds,
Is fit for treasons, stratagems and spoils;
The motions of his spirit are dull as night
And his affections dark as Erebus:
Let no such man be trusted. Mark the music.

Enter PORTIA *and* NERISSA.

Por. That light we see is burning in my
    hall.
How far that little candle throws his beams!
So shines a good deed in a naughty world. 91
Ner. When the moon shone, we did not
    see the candle.
Por. So doth the greater glory dim the
    less:
A substitute shines brightly as a king
Until a king be by, and then his state
Empties itself, as doth an inland brook
Into the main of waters. Music! hark!
Ner. It is your music, madam, of the
    house.
Por. Nothing is good, I see, without re-
    spect:
Methinks it sounds much sweeter than by
    day.   100
Ner. Silence bestows that virtue on it,
    madam.
Por. The crow doth sing as sweetly as the
    lark
When neither is attended, and I think

---

39. **Sola**, imitation of a postman's horn. 51. **signify**, make known. 59. **patines**, thin, circular plates of metal. 60-65. **There's not . . . hear it.** The universe was thought to be made up of revolving concentric spheres each incorporating heavenly bodies and growing larger as the distance from the earth increased. Beyond the most distant planet was the sphere of the fixed stars, and beyond that the *primum mobile.* The spheres produced, as they moved, a harmony which the soul, itself by nature harmonious, might perceive were it not rendered dull by its covering of flesh. 62. **cherubins**, cherubim. 70. **spirits are attentive.** The spirits would be in motion within the body in merriment, whereas in sadness they would be drawn to the heart, and, as it were, busy listening.

72. **race, herd.** 77. **mutual**, common or simultaneous. 79. **poet**, possibly Ovid, with whom the story of Orpheus was a favorite theme. 81. **stockish**, unfeeling. 85. **spoils**, pillage. 87. **Erebus**, classical abode of darkness. 91. **naughty**, evil. 99. **respect** consideration of circumstances.

The nightingale, if she should sing by day,
When every goose is cackling, would be
thought
No better a musician than the wren.
How many things by season season'd are
To their right praise and true perfection!
Peace, ho! the moon sleeps with Endymion
And would not be awaked.   [*Music ceases.*
Lor.   That is the voice, 110
Or I am much deceived, of Portia.
Por. He knows me as the blind man knows
the cuckoo,
By the bad voice.
Lor.   Dear lady, welcome home.
Por. We have been praying for our hus-
bands' healths,
Which speed, we hope, the better for our
words.
Are they return'd?
Lor.   Madam, they are not yet;
But there is come a messenger before,
To signify their coming.
Por.   Go in, Nerissa;
Give order to my servants that they take
No note at all of our being absent hence; 120
Nor you, Lorenzo; Jessica, nor you.
                       [*A tucket sounds.*
Lor. Your husband is at hand; I hear his
trumpet:
We are no tell-tales, madam; fear you not.
Por. This night methinks is but the day-
light sick;
It looks a little paler: 'tis a day,
Such as the day is when the sun is hid.

Enter BASSANIO, ANTONIO, GRATIANO, *and
their followers.*

Bass. We should hold day with the Antip-
odes,
If you would walk in absence of the sun.
Por. Let me give light, but let me not
be light;
For a light wife doth make a heavy husband,
And never be Bassanio so for me: 131
But God sort all! You are welcome home,
my lord.
Bass. I thank you, madam. Give welcome
to my friend.
This is the man, this is Antonio,
To whom I am so infinitely bound.

Por. You should in all sense be much
bound to him,
For, as I hear, he was much bound for you.
Ant. No more than I am well acquitted of.
Por. Sir, you are very welcome to our
house:
It must appear in other ways than words, 140
Therefore I scant this breathing courtesy.
Gra. [*To Ner.*] By yonder moon I swear
you do me wrong;
In faith, I gave it to the judge's clerk:
Would he were gelt that had it, for my part,
Since you do take it, love, so much at heart.
Por. A quarrel, ho, already! what's the
matter?
Gra. About a hoop of gold, a paltry ring
That she did give me, whose posy was
For all the world like cutler's poetry
Upon a knife, 'Love me, and leave me not.'150
Ner. What talk you of the posy or the
value?
You swore to me, when I did give it you,
That you would wear it till your hour of
death
And that it should lie with you in your grave:
Though not for me, yet for your vehement
oaths,
You should have been respective and have
kept it.
Gave it a judge's clerk! no, God's my judge,
The clerk will ne'er wear hair on 's face that
had it.
Gra. He will, an if he live to be a man.
Ner. Ay, if a woman live to be a man.   160
Gra. Now, by this hand, I gave it to a
youth,
A kind of boy, a little scrubbed boy,
No higher than thyself, the judge's clerk,
A prating boy, that begg'd it as a fee:
I could not for my heart deny it him.
Por. You were to blame, I must be plain
with you,
To part so slightly with your wife's first gift;
A thing stuck on with oaths upon your finger
And so riveted with faith unto your flesh.
I gave my love a ring and made him swear 170
Never to part with it; and here he stands;
I dare be sworn for him he would not leave it
Nor pluck it from his finger, for the wealth
That the world masters. Now, in faith,
Gratiano,

---

109. **Endymion**, shepherd of Elis who, as he slept in a cave on Mount Latmos, was visited by Diana, the moon goddess; cf. line 66, above. 121. *Stage Direction:* **tucket**, flourish on a trumpet. 127. **Antipodes**, those who dwell on the opposite side of the globe. 132. **sort**, decide.

136. **sense**, sometimes explained as "reason"; it means rather "feeling" or "emotion." 141. **breathing courtesy**, courteous speaking. 148. **posy**, a motto. 150. **leave**, part with. 156. **respective**, mindful. 162. **scrubbed**, stunted. 164. **prating**, prattling.

You give your wife too unkind a cause of
   grief:
An 'twere to me, I should be mad at it.
   Bass. [*Aside*] Why, I were best to cut my
   left hand off
And swear I lost the ring defending it.
   Gra. My Lord Bassanio gave his ring
   away
Unto the judge that begg'd it and indeed   180
Deserved it too; and then the boy, his clerk,
That took some pains in writing, he begg'd
   mine;
And neither man nor master would take
   aught
But the two rings.
   Por.   What ring gave you, my lord?
Not that, I hope, which you received of me.
   Bass. If I could add a lie unto a fault,
I would deny it; but you see my finger
Hath not the ring upon it; it is gone.
   Por. Even so void is your false heart of
   truth.
By heaven, I will ne'er come in your bed   190
Until I see the ring.
   Ner.   Nor I in yours
Till I again see mine.
   Bass.   Sweet Portia,
If you did know to whom I gave the ring,
If you did know for whom I gave the ring
And would conceive for what I gave the ring
And how unwillingly I left the ring,
When nought would be accepted but the
   ring,
You would abate the strength of your dis-
   pleasure.
   Por. If you had known the virtue of the
   ring,
Or half her worthiness that gave the ring,   200
Or your own honour to contain the ring,
You would not then have parted with the
   ring.
What man is there so much unreasonable,
If you had pleased to have defended it
With any terms of zeal, wanted the modesty
To urge the thing held as a ceremony?
Nerissa teaches me what to believe:
I'll die for 't but some woman had the
   ring.
   Bass. No, by my honour, madam, by my
   soul,
No woman had it, but a civil doctor,   210

Which did refuse three thousand ducats of
   me
And begg'd the ring; the which I did deny
   him
And suffer'd him to go displeased away;
Even he that did uphold the very life
Of my dear friend. What should I say, sweet
   lady?
I was enforced to send it after him;
I was beset with shame and courtesy;
My honour would not let ingratitude
So much besmear it. Pardon me, good lady;
For, by these blessed candles of the night,   220
Had you been there, I think you would have
   begg'd
The ring of me to give the worthy doctor.
   Por. Let not that doctor e'er come near
   my house:
Since he hath got the jewel that I loved,
And that which you did swear to keep for
   me,
I will become as liberal as you;
I'll not deny him any thing I have,
No, not my body nor my husband's bed:
Know him I shall, I am well sure of it:
Lie not a night from home; watch me like
   Argus: 230
If you do not, if I be left alone,
Now, by mine honour, which is yet mine
   own,
I'll have that doctor for my bedfellow.
   Ner. And I his clerk; therefore be well
   advised
How you do leave me to mine own protec-
   tion.
   Gra. Well, do you so: let not me take him,
   then;
For if I do, I'll mar the young clerk's pen.
   Ant. I am the unhappy subject of these
   quarrels.
   Por. Sir, grieve not you; you are welcome
   notwithstanding.
   Bass. Portia, forgive me this enforced
   wrong;   240
And, in the hearing of these many friends,
I swear to thee, even by thine own fair eyes,
Wherein I see myself—
   Por.   Mark you but that!
In both my eyes he doubly sees himself;
In each eye, one: swear by your double self,
And there's an oath of credit.
   Bass.   Nay, but hear me:

---

176. **mad,** beside oneself with wrath. 201. **contain,**
retain. 206. **ceremony,** something sacred. 210. **civil
doctor,** i.e., doctor of civil law.

230. **Argus,** i.e., with a hundred eyes. 245. **double,**
deceitful.

Pardon this fault, and by my soul I swear
I never more will break an oath with thee.

Ant. I once did lend my body for his
  wealth;
Which, but for him that had your husband's
  ring, 250
Had quite miscarried: I dare be bound again,
My soul upon the forfeit, that your lord
Will never more break faith advisedly.

Por. Then you shall be his surety. Give
  him this
And bid him keep it better than the other.

Ant. Here, Lord Bassanio; swear to keep
  this ring.

Bass. By heaven, it is the same I gave the
  doctor!

Por. I had it of him: pardon me, Bassanio;
For, by this ring, the doctor lay with me. 259

Ner. And pardon me, my gentle Gratiano;
For that same scrubbed boy, the doctor's
  clerk,
In lieu of this last night did lie with me.

Gra. Why, this is like the mending of high-
  ways
In summer, where the ways are fair enough:
What, are we cuckolds ere we have deserved
  it?

Por. Speak not so grossly. You are all
  amazed:
Here is a letter; read it at your leisure;
It comes from Padua, from Bellario:
There you shall find that Portia was the
  doctor,
Nerissa there her clerk: Lorenzo here 270
Shall witness I set forth as soon as you
And even but now return'd; I have not yet
Enter'd my house. Antonio, you are wel-
  come;
And I have better news in store for you
Than you expect: unseal this letter soon;
There you shall find three of your argosies
Are richly come to harbour suddenly:
You shall not know by what strange accident
I chanced on this letter.

Ant.   I am dumb.

Bass. Were you the doctor and I knew
  you not? 280

Gra. Were you the clerk that is to make
  me cuckold?

Ner. Ay, but the clerk that never means
  to do it,
Unless he live until he be a man.

Bass. Sweet doctor, you shall be my bedfellow:
When I am absent, then lie with my wife.

Ant. Sweet lady, you have given me life
  and living;
For here I read for certain that my ships
Are safely come to road.

Por.   How now, Lorenzo!
My clerk hath some good comforts too for
  you.

Ner. Ay, and I'll give them him without a
  fee. 290
There do I give to you and Jessica,
From the rich Jew, a special deed of gift,
After his death, of all he dies possess'd of.

Lor. Fair ladies, you drop manna in the
  way
Of starved people.

Por.   It is almost morning,
And yet I am sure you are not satisfied
Of these events at full. Let us go in;
And charge us there upon inter'gatories,
And we will answer all things faithfully.

Gra. Let it be so: the first inter'gatory 300
That my Nerissa shall be sworn on is,
Whether till the next night she had rather
  stay
Or go to bed now, being two hours to day:
But were the day come, I should wish it
  dark,
That I were couching with the doctor's
  clerk.
Well, while I live I'll fear no other thing
So sore as keeping safe Nerissa's ring.

                [*Exeunt.*

---

249. **wealth.** welfare.

298. **charge . . . inter'gatories,** take oath to answer
all things truly, like persons charged with contempt in
the court of the Queen's Bench. 306. **fear,** be apprehensive about.

MUCH ADO ABOUT NOTHING

DRAMATIS PERSONÆ

Don Pedro, prince of Arragon.
Don John, his bastard brother.
Claudio, a young lord of Florence.
Benedick, a young lord of Padua.
Leonato, governor of Messina.
Antonio, his brother.
Balthasar, attendant on Don Pedro.
Conrade, }
Borachio, } followers of Don John.
Friar Francis.
Dogberry, a constable.

Verges, a headborough.
A Sexton.
A Boy.

Hero, daughter to Leonato.
Beatrice, niece to Leonato.
Margaret, } gentlewomen attending on
Ursula, } Hero.

Messengers, Watch, Attendants, &c.

Scene: *Messina*

ACT I.

Scene I. *Before* Leonato's *house.*

Enter Leonato, Hero, *and* Beatrice, *with a* Messenger.

Leon. I learn in this letter that Don Peter of Arragon comes this night to Messina.

Mess. He is very near by this: he was not three leagues off when I left him.

Leon. How many gentlemen have you lost in this action?

Mess. But few of any sort, and none of name. 7

Leon. A victory is twice itself when the achiever brings home full numbers. I find here that Don Peter hath bestowed much honour on a young Florentine called Claudio.

Mess. Much deserved on his part and equally remembered by Don Pedro: he hath borne himself beyond the promise of his age, doing, in the figure of a lamb, the feats of a lion: he hath indeed better bettered expectation than you must expect of me to tell you how.

Leon. He hath an uncle here in Messina will be very much glad of it. 19

Mess. I have already delivered him letters, and there appears much joy in him; even so

much that joy could not show itself modest enough without a badge of bitterness.

Leon. Did he break out into tears?

Mess. In great measure.

Leon. A kind overflow of kindness: there are no faces truer than those that are so washed. How much better is it to weep at joy than to joy at weeping!

Beat. I pray you, is Signior Mountanto returned from the wars or no? 31

Mess. I know none of that name, lady: there was none such in the army of any sort.

Leon. What is he that you ask for, niece?

Hero. My cousin means Signior Benedick of Padua.

Mess. O, he's returned; and as pleasant as ever he was. 38

Beat. He set up his bills here in Messina and challenged Cupid at the flight; and my uncle's fool, reading the challenge, subscribed for Cupid, and challenged him at the bird-bolt. I pray you, how many hath he killed

---

7. **sort**, rank, or kind. **name**, reputation, or noble name. 16. **bettered**, surpassed.

23. **badge**, mark of service; here, the livery of sorrow. 26. **kind**, natural. 30. **Mountanto**. *Montant* is an upright blow in fencing; the implication is that Benedick is a bravo. Beatrice's inquiry about him betrays a certain interest. 37. **pleasant**, jocular. 39. **bills**, placards, advertisements. 40-41. **challenged . . . flight**, undertook to rival Cupid as an archer. **my uncle's fool**, usually explained as a professional fool in her uncle's service; it has also been suggested that, since Beatrice herself is a jester, and *fool* is often a pet name, Beatrice is referring to herself and thus recalling an earlier flirtation with Benedick. 42. **bird-bolt**, blunt-headed arrow used for fowling.

and eaten in these wars? But how many hath he killed? for indeed I promised to eat all of his killing.

Leon. Faith, niece, you tax Signior Benedick too much; but he'll be meet with you, I doubt it not.

Mess. He hath done good service, lady, in these wars. 49

Beat. You had musty victual, and he hath help to eat it: he is a very valiant trencherman; he hath an excellent stomach.

Mess. And a good soldier too, lady.

Beat. And a good soldier to a lady: but what is he to a lord?

Mess. A lord to a lord, a man to a man; stuffed with all honourable virtues.

Beat. It is so, indeed; he is no less than a stuffed man: but for the stuffing,—well, we are all mortal. 60

Leon. You must not, sir, mistake my niece. There is a kind of merry war betwixt Signior Benedick and her: they never meet but there's a skirmish of wit between them.

Beat. Alas! he gets nothing by that. In our last conflict four of his five wits went halting off, and now is the whole man governed with one: so that if he have wit enough to keep himself warm, let him bear it for a difference between himself and his horse; for it is all the wealth that he hath left, to be known a reasonable creature. Who is his companion now? He hath every month a new sworn brother. 73

Mess. Is 't possible?

Beat. Very easily possible: he wears his faith but as the fashion of his hat; it ever changes with the next block.

Mess. I see, lady, the gentleman is not in your books. 79

Beat. No; an he were, I would burn my study. But, I pray you, who is his companion? Is there no young squarer now that will make a voyage with him to the devil?

Mess. He is most in the company of the right noble Claudio.

Beat. O Lord, he will hang upon him like a disease: he is sooner caught than the pestilence, and the taker runs presently mad. God help the noble Claudio! if he have caught the Benedick, it will cost him a thousand pound ere a' be cured. 90

Mess. I will hold friends with you, lady.

Beat. Do, good friend.

Leon. You will never run mad, niece.

Beat. No, not till a hot January.

Mess. Don Pedro is approached. 95

Enter Don Pedro, Don John, Claudio, Benedick, *and* Balthasar.

D. Pedro. Good Signior Leonato, you are come to meet your trouble: the fashion of the world is to avoid cost, and you encounter it.

Leon. Never came trouble to my house in the likeness of your grace: for trouble being gone, comfort should remain; but when you depart from me, sorrow abides and happiness takes his leave. 102

D. Pedro. You embrace your charge too willingly. I think this is your daughter.

Leon. Her mother hath many times told me so.

Bene. Were you in doubt, sir, that you asked her?

Leon. Signior Benedick, no; for then were you a child. 109

D. Pedro. You have it full, Benedick: we may guess by this what you are, being a man. Truly, the lady fathers herself. Be happy, lady; for you are like an honourable father.

Bene. If Signior Leonato be her father, she would not have his head on her shoulders for all Messina, as like him as she is.

Beat. I wonder that you will still be talking, Signior Benedick: nobody marks you.

Bene. What, my dear Lady Disdain! are you yet living? 120

Beat. Is it possible disdain should die while she hath such meet food to feed it as Signior Benedick? Courtesy itself must convert to disdain, if you come in her presence.

Bene. Then is courtesy a turncoat. But it is certain I am loved of all ladies, only you

---

47. **meet**, even, quits. 51. **valiant trencherman**, great eater. 52. **stomach**, appetite or stomach, and a disposition to accept insults. 59. **stuffed**, stuffed with food or anything, with play on preceding sense of "filled with." 66. **five wits**, not the five senses, but the five faculties: memory, imagination, judgment, fantasy, common wit. 70. **difference**, alteration in or addition to a coat of arms, to distinguish a younger or lateral branch of a family; heraldic term, used with a play on the usual sense. 71. **to be known**, i.e., in order that he may be known as. 73. **sworn brother**, brother in arms (*frater juratus*), an allusion to the ancient practice of swearing brotherhood. 76. **faith**, allegiance, or fidelity. 77. **block**, mold for shaping hats. 78-79. **in your books**, i.e., in favor with you, in your account books for credit. 82. **squarer**, quarreler.

89. **caught the Benedick**, i.e., as if he were a disease. It seems rather too meticulous to see an allusion to a disease of that name. 91. **hold friends**, keep on friendly terms. 98. **encounter**, go to meet. 103. **embrace your charge**, accept your burden. 110. **full**, i.e., full in the face, completely. 112. **fathers herself**, shows by appearance who her father is. 117. **still**, always. 123. **convert**, change itself into.

excepted: and I would I could find in my heart that I had not a hard heart; for, truly, I love none.   128

Beat. A dear happiness to women: they would else have been troubled with a pernicious suitor. I thank God and my cold blood, I am of your humour for that: I had rather hear my dog bark at a crow than a man swear he loves me.   133

Bene. God keep your ladyship still in that mind! so some gentleman or other shall 'scape a predestinate scratched face.

Beat. Scratching could not make it worse, an 'twere such a face as yours were.

Bene. Well, you are a rare parrot-teacher.

Beat. A bird of my tongue is better than a beast of yours.   141

Bene. I would my horse had the speed of your tongue, and so good a continuer. But keep your way, i' God's name; I have done.

Beat. You always end with a jade's trick: I know you of old.

D. Pedro. That is the sum of all, Leonato. Signior Claudio and Signior Benedick, my dear friend Leonato hath invited you all. I tell him we shall stay here at the least a month; and he heartily prays some occasion may detain us longer. I dare swear he is no hypocrite, but prays from his heart.   153

Leon. If you swear, my lord, you shall not be forsworn. [*To Don John*] Let me bid you welcome, my lord: being reconciled to the prince your brother, I owe you all duty.

D. John. I thank you: I am not of many words, but I thank you.

Leon. Please it your grace lead on?   160

D. Pedro. Your hand, Leonato; we will go together.

[*Exeunt all except Benedick and Claudio.*

Claud. Benedick, didst thou note the daughter of Signior Leonato?

Bene. I noted her not; but I looked on her.

Claud. Is she not a modest young lady?

Bene. Do you question me, as an honest man should do, for my simple true judgement; or would you have me speak after my custom, as being a professed tyrant to their sex?   170

Claud. No; I pray thee speak in sober judgement.

Bene. Why, i' faith, methinks she's too low for a high praise, too brown for a fair praise and too little for a great praise: only this commendation I can afford her, that were she other than she is, she were unhandsome; and being no other but as she is, I do not like her.

Claud. Thou thinkest I am in sport: I pray thee tell me truly how thou likest her. 180

Bene. Would you buy her, that you inquire after her?

Claud. Can the world buy such a jewel?

Bene. Yea, and a case to put it into. But speak you this with a sad brow? or do you play the flouting Jack, to tell us Cupid is a good hare-finder and Vulcan a rare carpenter? Come, in what key shall a man take you, to go in the song?

Claud. In mine eye she is the sweetest lady that ever I looked on.   190

Bene. I can see yet without spectacles and I see no such matter: there's her cousin, an she were not possessed with a fury, exceeds her as much in beauty as the first of May doth the last of December. But I hope you have no intent to turn husband, have you?

Claud. I would scarce trust myself, though I had sworn the contrary, if Hero would be my wife.   198

Bene. Is 't come to this? In faith, hath not the world one man but he will wear his cap with suspicion? Shall I never see a bachelor of threescore again? Go to, i' faith; an thou wilt needs thrust thy neck into a yoke, wear the print of it and sigh away Sundays. Look; Don Pedro is returned to seek you.

Re-enter DON PEDRO.

D. Pedro. What secret hath held you here, that you followed not to Leonato's?

---

128. I love none. Note Benedick's conventional boasting about his adherence to bachelorhood. 129. dear happiness, precious good luck. 131. I am . . . that, I am of the same disposition in that matter. Beatrice counters with a similar boast as to her spinsterhood. 136. predestinate, i.e., which he would have if she married him. 143. continuer, i.e., in staying power. 145. me. 141. of your tongue, taught to speak like you; it seems a poor jest. Possibly Beatrice thought a bird preferable to a beast. 143. continuer, i.e., in staying power. 145. jade's trick, ill-conditioned horse's trick of balking or of stopping suddenly, thus throwing the rider. 156. being, since you are. 165. noted, a possible pun on the meaning, "set to music."

170. tyrant, cruel or pitiless in attitude. 185. sad, serious. 186. flouting Jack, mocking rascal. 186-187. Cupid . . . carpenter, i.e., Cupid is a beater-up of game and not a real huntsman; and Vulcan, who makes Cupid's arrows, is a carpenter, not a smith; therefore he makes bird-bolts which have wooden heads (New Cambridge). 188. go in, join in. 200-201. wear . . . suspicion, i.e., be suspected of wearing his cap to hide his cuckold's horns. 204. sigh away Sundays, i.e., when, owing to the domesticity of the day, you cannot escape from your yoke-fellow (Furness).

Bene. I would your grace would constrain me to tell.

D. Pedro. I charge thee on thy allegiance.

Bene. You hear, Count Claudio: I can be secret as a dumb man; I would have you think so; but, on my allegiance, mark you this, on my allegiance. He is in love. With who? now that is your grace's part. Mark how short his answer is;—With Hero, Leonato's short daughter.

Claud. If this were so, so were it uttered.

Bene. Like the old tale, my lord: 'it is not so, nor 'twas not so, but, indeed, God forbid it should be so.'   220

Claud. If my passion change not shortly, God forbid it should be otherwise.

D. Pedro. Amen, if you love her; for the lady is very well worthy.

Claud. You speak this to fetch me in, my lord.

D. Pedro. By my troth, I speak my thought.

Claud. And, in faith, my lord, I spoke mine.

Bene. And, by my two faiths and troths, my lord, I spoke mine.

Claud. That I love her, I feel.   230

D. Pedro. That she is worthy, I know.

Bene. That I neither feel how she should be loved nor know how she should be worthy, is the opinion that fire cannot melt out of me: I will die in it at the stake.

D. Pedro. Thou wast ever an obstinate heretic in the despite of beauty.

Claud. And never could maintain his part but in the force of his will.   239

Bene. That a woman conceived me, I thank her; that she brought me up, I likewise give her most humble thanks: but that I will have a recheat winded in my forehead, or hang my bugle in an invisible baldrick, all women shall pardon me. Because I will not do them the wrong to mistrust any, I will do myself the right to trust none; and the fine

is, for the which I may go the finer, I will live a bachelor.

D. Pedro. I shall see thee, ere I die, look pale with love.   250

Bene. With anger, with sickness, or with hunger, my lord, not with love: prove that ever I lose more blood with love than I will get again with drinking, pick out mine eyes with a ballad-maker's pen and hang me up at the door of a brothel-house for the sign of blind Cupid.   256

D. Pedro. Well, if ever thou dost fall from this faith, thou wilt prove a notable argument.

Bene. If I do, hang me in a bottle like a cat and shoot at me; and he that hits me, let him be clapped on the shoulder, and called Adam.   261

D. Pedro. Well, as time shall try: 'In time the savage bull doth bear the yoke.'

Bene. The savage bull may; but if ever the sensible Benedick bear it, pluck off the bull's horns and set them in my forehead: and let me be vilely painted, and in such great letters as they write 'Here is good horse to hire,' let them signify under my sign 'Here you may see Benedick the married man.'   270

Claud. If this should ever happen, thou wouldst be horn-mad.

D. Pedro. Nay, if Cupid have not spent all his quiver in Venice, thou wilt quake for 274 this shortly.

Bene. I look for an earthquake too, then.

D. Pedro. Well, you will temporize with the hours. In the meantime, good Signior Benedick, repair to Leonato's: commend me to him and tell him I will not fail him at supper; for indeed he hath made great preparation.   280

Bene. I have almost matter enough in me for such an embassage; and so I commit you—

Claud. To the tuition of God: From my house, if I had it,—

D. Pedro. The sixth of July: Your loving friend, Benedick.

217. **If this . . . uttered,** if I had really confided such a secret to him, yet he would have blabbed it in this manner (Steevens). 218. **old tale,** an allusion to a children's tale in which these words occurred. 222. **otherwise,** i.e., than so. 225. **fetch me in,** take me in, cheat me. 237. **despite,** contempt. 239. **force of his will,** will, refusing to be guided by reason, which was the state of the heretic as defined by the Schoolmen. 242-245. **but that . . . me,** women must pardon me for refusing to have my horn placed on my head (like a cuckold), where it will need no strap to sustain it. 243. **recheat,** blast blown to recall the hounds. 244. **baldrick,** strap that supports the horn. 247. **fine,** end.

248. **go the finer,** have more to spend on fine clothes. 252. **prove that,** if you discover. 253-254. **lose . . . drinking.** According to current theory, each sigh cost the heart a drop of blood, whereas blood was replenished by wine. 258. **argument,** theme for talk or story. 259. **bottle,** wicker basket to hold the cat used as target in shooting-matches in archery. 261. **Adam,** Adam Bell, archer outlaw of the ballads. 263. **'In time . . . yoke,'** a line from Kyd's *Spanish Tragedy*, II, i, 3. 272. **horn-mad,** stark mad (from the fury of horned beasts), with allusion to cuckoldry. 274. **Venice,** noted for licentiousness. 276. **temporize . . . hours,** come to terms, or become milder, in time. 281. **matter,** wit, intelligence. 283. **tuition,** protection.

Bene. Nay, mock not, mock not. The body of your discourse is sometime guarded with fragments, and the guards are but slightly basted on neither: ere you flout old ends any further, examine your con- 291 science: and so I leave you.   [*Exit.*

Claud. My liege, your highness now may do me good.

D. Pedro. My love is thine to teach: teach it but how,
And thou shalt see how apt it is to learn
Any hard lesson that may do thee good.

Claud. Hath Leonato any son, my lord?

D. Pedro. No child but Hero; she's his only heir.
Dost thou affect her, Claudio?

Claud.   O, my lord,
When you went onward on this ended action,
I look'd upon her with a soldier's eye,   300
That liked, but had a rougher task in hand
Than to drive liking to the name of love:
But now I am return'd and that war-thoughts
Have left their places vacant, in their rooms
Come thronging soft and delicate desires,
All prompting me how fair young Hero is,
Saying, I liked her ere I went to wars.

D. Pedro. Thou wilt be like a lover presently
And tire the hearer with a book of words.
If thou dost love fair Hero, cherish it,   310
And I will break with her and with her father
And thou shalt have her. Was 't not to this end
That thou began'st to twist so fine a story?

Claud. How sweetly you do minister to love,
That know love's grief by his complexion!
But lest my liking might too sudden seem,
I would have salved it with a longer treatise.

D. Pedro. What need the bridge much broader than the flood?
The fairest grant is the necessity.
Look, what will serve is fit: 'tis once, thou lovest,   320
And I will fit thee with the remedy.
I know we shall have revelling to-night:

I will assume thy part in some disguise
And tell fair Hero I am Claudio,
And in her bosom I'll unclasp my heart
And take her hearing prisoner with the force
And strong encounter of my amorous tale;
Then after to her father will I break;
And the conclusion is, she shall be thine. 329
In practice let us put it presently.
                                   [*Exeunt.*

SCENE II. *A room in* LEONATO'S *house.*

Enter LEONATO *and* ANTONIO, *meeting.*

Leon. How now, brother! Where is my cousin, your son? hath he provided this music?

Ant. He is very busy about it. But, brother, I can tell you strange news that you yet dreamt not of.   5

Leon. Are they good?

Ant. As the event stamps them: but they have a good cover; they show well outward. The prince and Count Claudio, walking in a thick-pleached alley in mine orchard, were thus much overheard by a man of mine: the prince discovered to Claudio that he loved my niece your daughter and meant to acknowledge it this night in a dance; and if he found her accordant, he meant to take the present time by the top and instantly 16 break with you of it.

Leon. Hath the fellow any wit that told you this?

Ant. A good sharp fellow: I will send for him; and question him yourself.   20

Leon. No, no; we will hold it as a dream till it appear itself: but I will acquaint my daughter withal, that she may be the better prepared for an answer, if peradventure this be true. Go you and tell her of it. [*Enter attendants.*] Cousins, you know what you have to do. O, I cry you mercy, friend; go you with me, and I will use your skill. Good cousin, have a care this busy time.
                                   [*Exeunt.*

---

288. guarded, ornamented. 289. guards, border or trimming on a garment. 290. old ends, old tags, quotations. 298. affect, love. 311. break, open the subject. 313. twist, draw out the thread of. 315. complexion, outward appearance. 317. salved, softened. 319. fairest . . . necessity, best gift is the necessary one. 320. 'tis once, in short.

Scene ii. 2. cousin, used loosely to denote any relative more distant than brother or sister; here, nephew. 7. event, outcome. 10. thick-pleached, made with dense hedges of intertwined shrubs. in mine orchard. Boas would read *the* for *mine*, which would enable us to understand that the conversation overheard and misunderstood by the servant had been held in Leonato's orchard; otherwise one cannot reconcile the first and second scenes as to time-relation. 15. accordant, agreeing, consenting. 16. top, forelock, as we say. 17. wit, sense, intelligence. 22. till . . . itself, till it manifest itself. 27. I . . . mercy, I beg your pardon.

SCENE III. *The same.*

Enter DON JOHN *and* CONRADE.

Con. What the good-year, my lord! why are you thus out of measure sad?

D. John. There is no measure in the occasion that breeds; therefore the sadness is without limit.

Con. You should hear reason.

D. John. And when I have heard it, what blessing brings it?

Con. If not a present remedy, at least a patient sufferance.   10

D. John. I wonder that thou, being, as thou sayest thou art, born under Saturn, goest about to apply a moral medicine to a mortifying mischief. I cannot hide what I am: I must be sad when I have cause and smile at no man's jests, eat when I have stomach and wait for no man's leisure, sleep when I am drowsy and tend on no man's business, laugh when I am merry and claw no man in his humour.   19

Con. Yea, but you must not make the full show of this till you may do it without controlment. You have of late stood out against your brother, and he hath ta'en you newly into his grace; where it is impossible you should take true root but by the fair weather that you make yourself: it is needful that you frame the season for your own harvest.   27

D. John. I had rather be a canker in a hedge than a rose in his grace, and it better fits my blood to be disdained of all than to fashion a carriage to rob love from any: in this, though I cannot be said to be a flattering honest man, it must not be denied but I am a plain-dealing villain. I am trusted with a muzzle and enfranchised with a clog; therefore I have decreed not to sing in my cage. If I had my mouth, I would bite; if I had my liberty, I would do my liking: in the meantime let me be that I am and seek not to alter me.

Con. Can you make no use of your discontent?   40

D. John. I make all use of it, for I use it only.

Who comes here?

Enter BORACHIO.

What news, Borachio?

Bora. I came yonder from a great supper: the prince your brother is royally entertained by Leonato; and I can give you intelligence of an intended marriage.

D. John. Will it serve for any model to build mischief on? What is he for a fool that betroths himself to unquietness?   50

Bora. Marry, it is your brother's right hand.

D. John. Who? the most exquisite Claudio?

Bora. Even he.

D. John. A proper squire! And who, and who? which way looks he?   55

Bora. Marry, on Hero, the daughter and heir of Leonato.

D. John. A very forward March-chick! How came you to this?

Bora. Being entertained for a perfumer, as I was smoking a musty room, comes me the prince and Claudio, hand in hand, in sad conference: I whipt me behind the arras; and there heard it agreed upon that the prince should woo Hero for himself, and having obtained her, give her to Count Claudio.

D. John. Come, come, let us thither: this may prove food to my displeasure. That young start-up hath all the glory of my overthrow: if I can cross him any way, I bless myself every way. You are both sure,   71 and will assist me?

Con. To the death, my lord.

D. John. Let us to the great supper: their cheer is the greater that I am subdued. Would the cook were of my mind! Shall we go prove what's to be done?   76

Bora. We'll wait upon your lordship.

[Exeunt.

---

1. **What the good-year,** undefined expletive.
2. **out of measure,** immeasurably. 10. **sufferance,** endurance. 12. **under Saturn.** To be born under Saturn produces a morose disposition. **goest about,** endeavorest. 13. **mortifying mischief,** deadly disease. 17. **tend on,** attend to. 19. **claw,** flatter. 26. **frame,** produce. 28. **canker,** dog rose. 30. **blood,** mood, disposition; probable reference also to Don John's illegitimacy, on which his villainy rests. 31. **fashion a carriage,** counterfeit a behavior. **rob love,** i.e., in order to steal love.

54. **proper,** fine (ironical). 58. **March-chick,** overprecocious youth (like a chick hatched prematurely). 60. **entertained,** taken into service. 61. **smoking,** fumigating. 63. **arras,** tapestry, hanging. 69. **startup,** upstart. 70. **cross,** thwart, with allusion to making the sign of the cross. 71. **sure,** trustworthy. 75. **Would . . . mind,** i.e., apparently that he might poison the food.

ACT II.

SCENE I. *A hall in* LEONATO'S *house.*

Enter LEONATO, ANTONIO, HERO, BEATRICE, *and others.*

Leon. Was not Count John here at supper?

Ant. I saw him not.

Beat. How tartly that gentleman looks! I never can see him but I am heart-burned an hour after.

Hero. He is of a very melancholy disposition.

Beat. He were an excellent man that were made just in the midway between him and Benedick: the one is too like an image and says nothing, and the other too like my lady's eldest son, evermore tattling.   11

Leon. Then half Signior Benedick's tongue in Count John's mouth, and half Count John's melancholy in Signior Benedick's face,—

Beat. With a good leg and a good foot, uncle, and money enough in his purse, such a man would win any woman in the world, if a' could get her good-will.

Leon. By my troth, niece, thou wilt never get thee a husband, if thou be so shrewd of thy tongue.   21

Ant. In faith, she's too curst.

Beat. Too curst is more than curst: I shall lessen God's sending that way; for it is said, 'God sends a curst cow short horns;' but to a cow too curst he sends none.   26

Leon. So, by being too curst, God will send you no horns.

Beat. Just, if he send me no husband; for the which blessing I am at him upon my knees every morning and evening. Lord, I could not endure a husband with a beard on his face: I had rather lie in the woollen.   33

Leon. You may light on a husband that hath no beard.

Beat. What should I do with him? dress him in my apparel and make him my waiting-gentlewoman? He that hath a beard is more than a youth, and he that hath no beard is less than a man: and he that is more than a youth is not for me, and he that is less than a man, I am not for him: therefore I will even take sixpence in earnest of the bear-ward, and lead his apes into hell.   43

Leon. Well, then, go you into hell?

Beat. No, but to the gate; and there will the devil meet me, like an old cuckold, with horns on his head, and say 'Get you to heaven, Beatrice, get you to heaven; here's no place for you maids:' so deliver I up my apes, and away to Saint Peter for the heavens; he shows me where the bachelors sit, and there live we as merry as the   52 day is long.

Ant. [*To Hero*] Well, niece, I trust you will be ruled by your father.

Beat. Yes, faith; it is my cousin's duty to make curtsy and say 'Father, as it please you.' But yet for all that, cousin, let him be a handsome fellow, or else make another curtsy and say 'Father, as it please me.'

Leon. Well, niece, I hope to see you one day fitted with a husband.   61

Beat. Not till God make men of some other metal than earth. Would it not grieve a woman to be overmastered with a piece of valiant dust? to make an account of her life to a clod of wayward marl? No, uncle, I'll none: Adam's sons are my brethren; and, truly, I hold it a sin to match in my kindred.

Leon. Daughter, remember what I told you: if the prince do solicit you in that kind, you know your answer.   71

Beat. The fault will be in the music, cousin, if you be not wooed in good time: if the prince be too important, tell him there is measure in every thing and so dance out the answer. For, hear me, Hero: wooing, wedding, and repenting, is as a Scotch jig, a measure, and a cinque pace: the first suit is hot and hasty, like a Scotch jig, and full as fantastical; the wedding, mannerly-modest, as a measure, full of state and ancientry; and then comes repentance and, with his bad legs, falls into the cinque pace faster and faster, till he sink into his grave.

---

4. **heart-burned**, suffering from heartburn, affected with indigestion. 10. **my . . . son**, spoiled child. 20. **shrewd**, sharp. 22. **curst**, ill-tempered. 25. **curst**, savage, vicious. 29. **Just**, right, exactly so. 33. **lie in the woollen**, sleep between blankets.

42. **earnest**, advanced wages. 43. **bear-ward**, one who keeps and exhibits a bear. **lead . . . hell**, ancient proverb: "Such as die maids do all lead apes in hell." 50. **for the heavens**, on my way to heaven. 51. **bachelors**, unmarried persons, or possibly, unmarried women. 63. **metal**, substance. 66. **clod . . . marl**, lump of wayward earth, i.e., a man. 70. **kind**, manner. 74. **important**, urgent, importunate. 78. **measure**, a dance; here, a stately dance. **cinque pace**, lively dance, the steps of which are supposed to be based on the number five; the first five steps of the galliard (Arden ed.). 81. **ancientry**, old-fashioned style.

Leon. Cousin, you apprehend passing 84
shrewdly.

Beat. I have a good eye, uncle; I can see a
church by daylight.

Leon. The revellers are entering, brother:
make good room. [*All put on their masks.*

Enter Don Pedro, Claudio, Benedick,
Balthasar, Don John, Borachio,
Margaret, Ursula, *and others, masked.*

D. Pedro. Lady, will you walk about with
your friend? 90

Hero. So you walk softly and look sweetly
and say nothing, I am yours for the walk;
and especially when I walk away.

D. Pedro. With me in your company?

Hero. I may say so, when I please.

D. Pedro. And when please you to say so?

Hero. When I like your favour; for God
defend the lute should be like the case!

D. Pedro. My visor is Philemon's roof;
within the house is Jove. 100

Hero. Why, then, your visor should be
thatched.

D. Pedro. Speak low, if you speak love.
[*Drawing her aside.*

Balth. Well, I would you did like me.

Marg. So would not I, for your own sake;
for I have many ill qualities.

Balth. Which is one?

Marg. I say my prayers aloud.

Balth. I love you the better: the hearers
may cry, Amen. 110

Marg. God match me with a good dancer!

Balth. Amen.

Marg. And God keep him out of my sight
when the dance is done! Answer, clerk.

Balth. No more words: the clerk is
answered.

Urs. I know you well enough; you are
Signior Antonio.

Ant. At a word, I am not.

Urs. I know you by the waggling of your
head. 120

Ant. To tell you true, I counterfeit him.

Urs. You could never do him so ill-well,
unless you were the very man. Here's his

dry hand up and down: you are he, you are
he.

Ant. At a word, I am not. 125

Urs. Come, come, do you think I do not
know you by your excellent wit? can virtue
hide itself? Go to, mum, you are he: graces
will appear, and there's an end.

Beat. Will you not tell me who told you
so?

Bene. No, you shall pardon me. 131

Beat. Nor will you not tell me who you
are?

Bene. Not now.

Beat. That I was disdainful, and that I
had my good wit out of the 'Hundred Merry
Tales:'—well, this was Signior Benedick that
said so.

Bene. What's he?

Beat. I am sure you know him well
enough.

Bene. Not I, believe me.

Beat. Did he never make you laugh? 140

Bene. I pray you, what is he?

Beat. Why, he is the prince's jester: a very
dull fool; only his gift is in devising impossible slanders: none but libertines delight in
him; and the commendation is not in his wit,
but in his villany; for he both pleases men
and angers them, and then they laugh at him
and beat him. I am sure he is in the fleet: I
would he had boarded me.

Bene. When I know the gentleman, I'll
tell him what you say. 151

Beat. Do, do: he'll but break a comparison
or two on me; which, peradventure not
marked or not laughed at, strikes him into
melancholy; and then there's a partridge
wing saved, for the fool will eat no supper
that night. [*Music.*] We must follow the
leaders.

Bene. In every good thing.

Beat. Nay, if they lead to any ill, I will
leave them at the next turning. 160

[*Dance. Then exeunt all except Don
John, Borachio, and Claudio.*

---

84. apprehend, understand. passing, exceedingly.
90. friend, lover of both sexes. 97. favour, face.
99. visor, mask. Philemon's roof, an allusion to Ovid,
Metamorphoses, viii. Philemon and Baucis, his wife,
entertained Jupiter in their peasant cottage unawares
(see *thatched*, line 102). 114. clerk, so addressed because of Balthasar's *Amen* in preceding speeches. He
is giving responses like the parish clerk. 118. At a word,
in short. 122. do . . . ill-well, imitate his imperfections
so perfectly.

124. dry hand, a sign of age. up and down, all
over, exactly. 128. mum, be silent. 135. 'Hundred
Merry Tales,' a popular collection of anecdotes published by Rastell in 1526; his point is that Beatrice borrows her wit from a book of stale jests, the Joe Miller
of the day. 143. only his gift, his only talent. impossible, incredible. 148. fleet, crowd, company.
149. boarded, accosted, with a play on the usual meaning. 152. break a comparison, make a scornful simile,
inuendo. 155-157. there's . . . night, sarcastic thrust
at Benedick, whose appetite she has before referred
to. 157. leaders, i.e., of the dance.

D. John. Sure my brother is amorous on Hero and hath withdrawn her father to break with him about it. The ladies follow her and but one visor remains.

Bora. And that is Claudio: I know him by his bearing.

D. John. Are not you Signior Benedick?

Claud. You know me well; I am he.   168

D. John. Signior, you are very near my brother in his love: he is enamoured on Hero; I pray you, dissuade him from her: she is no equal for his birth: you may do the part of an honest man in it.

Claud. How know you he loves her?

D. John. I heard him swear his affection.

Bora. So did I too; and he swore he would marry her to-night.

D. John. Come, let us to the banquet.

          [*Exeunt Don John and Borachio.*

Claud. Thus answer I in name of Benedick,
But hear these ill news with the ears of
  Claudio.   180
'Tis certain so; the prince wooes for himself.
Friendship is constant in all other things
Save in the office and affairs of love:
Therefore all hearts in love use their own
  tongues;
Let every eye negotiate for itself
And trust no agent; for beauty is a witch
Against whose charms faith melteth into
  blood.
This is an accident of hourly proof,
Which I mistrusted not. Farewell, therefore,
  Hero!

          Re-enter BENEDICK.

Bene. Count Claudio?   190

Claud. Yea, the same.

Bene. Come, will you go with me?

Claud. Whither?

Bene. Even to the next willow, about your own business, county. What fashion will you wear the garland of? about your neck, like an usurer's chain? or under your arm, like a lieutenant's scarf? You must wear it one way, for the prince hath got your Hero.

Claud. I wish him joy of her.   200

Bene. Why, that's spoken like an honest drovier: so they sell bullocks. But did you think the prince would have served you thus?

Claud. I pray you, leave me.

Bene. Ho! now you strike like the blind man: 'twas the boy that stole your meat, and you'll beat the post.   207

Claud. If it will not be, I'll leave you.

          [*Exit.*

Bene. Alas, poor hurt fowl! now will he creep into sedges. But that my Lady Beatrice should know me, and not know me! The prince's fool! Ha? It may be I go under that title because I am merry. Yea, but so I am apt to do myself wrong; I am not so reputed: it is the base, though bitter, disposition of Beatrice that puts the world into her person, and so gives me out. Well, I'll be revenged as I may.

          Re-enter DON PEDRO.

D. Pedro. Now, signior, where's the count? did you see him?   219

Bene. Troth, my lord, I have played the part of Lady Fame. I found him here as melancholy as a lodge in a warren: I told him, and I think I told him true, that your grace had got the good will of this young lady; and I offered him my company to a willow-tree, either to make him a garland, as being forsaken, or to bind him up a rod, as being worthy to be whipped.

D. Pedro. To be whipped! What's his fault?

Bene. The flat transgression of a schoolboy, who, being overjoyed with finding a. birds' nest, shows it his companion,   231
and he steals it.

D. Pedro. Wilt thou make a trust a transgression? The transgression is in the stealer.

Bene. Yet it had not been amiss the rod had been made, and the garland too; for the garland he might have worn himself, and the

169. **near**, intimate with. 178. **banquet**, course of sweetmeats following the regular repast; dessert. 181. **certain**, certainly. 187. **faith . . . blood**, honor gives way to passion. 188. **accident**, occurrence. 194. **willow**, emblem of disappointed love. 197. **usurer's chain**. Costly chains were worn by persons of the moneyed class.

202. **drovier**, cattle-dealer. 205. **like the blind man**, an allusion to the romance of Lazarillo de Tormes, in which the hero steals his master's meat and revenges himself for the beating he receives by causing the blind man to jump against a stone pillar. 210. **creep into sedges**, i.e., as wounded ducks into rushes along the river. 215. **base, though bitter.** The text is hard to construe. Yale editor paraphrases: Beatrice is base, i.e., unworthy, unjust, though her words have a sting (bitterness) which base criticisms do not usually possess. 216. **puts . . . person**, identifies the world with herself. 217. **gives me out**, represents me. 220. **Troth**, by my faith. 221. **Lady Fame**, Dame Rumor. 222. **lodge in a warren**, gamekeeper's lodge in a game preserve. 227. **bind . . . rod**, tie several willow switches into a scourge. 229. **flat**, absolute, downright.

rod he might have bestowed on you, who, as I take it, have stolen his birds' nest.

D. Pedro. I will but teach them to sing, and restore them to the owner.   240

Bene. If their singing answer your saying, by my faith, you say honestly.

D. Pedro. The Lady Beatrice hath a quarrel to you: the gentleman that danced with her told her she is much wronged by you.   245

Bene. O, she misused me past the endurance of a block! an oak but with one green leaf on it would have answered her; my very visor began to assume life and scold with her. She told me, not thinking I had been myself, that I was the prince's jester, that I was duller than a great thaw; huddling jest upon jest with such impossible conveyance upon me that I stood like a man at a mark, with a whole army shooting at me. She speaks poniards, and every word stabs: if her breath were as terrible as her terminations, there were no living near her; she would   257 infect to the north star. I would not marry her, though she were endowed with all that Adam had left him before he transgressed: she would have made Hercules have turned spit, yea, and have cleft his club to make the fire too. Come, talk not of her: you shall find her the infernal Ate in good apparel. I would to God some scholar would conjure her; for certainly, while she is here, a man may live as quiet in hell as in a sanctuary; and people sin upon purpose, because they would go thither; so, indeed, all disquiet, horror and perturbation follows her.

D. Pedro. Look, here she comes.   270

Re-enter CLAUDIO, BEATRICE, HERO, *and* LEONATO.

Bene. Will your grace command me any service to the world's end? I will go on the slightest errand now to the Antipodes that you can devise to send me on; I will fetch you a toothpicker now from the furthest inch of Asia, bring you the length of Prester John's foot, fetch you a hair off the great Cham's beard, do you any embassage to the Pigmies, rather than hold three words' conference with this harpy. You have no 280 employment for me?

D. Pedro. None, but to desire your good company.

Bene. O God, sir, here's a dish I love not: I cannot endure my Lady Tongue.   [*Exit.*

D. Pedro. Come, lady, come; you have lost the heart of Signior Benedick.   286

Beat. Indeed, my lord, he lent it me awhile; and I gave him use for it, a double heart for his single one: marry, once before he won it of me with false dice, therefore your grace may well say I have lost it.   291

D. Pedro. You have put him down, lady, you have put him down.

Beat. So I would not he should do me, my lord, lest I should prove the mother of fools. I have brought Count Claudio, whom you sent me to seek.

D. Pedro. Why, how now, count! wherefore are you sad?

Claud. Not sad, my lord.   300

D. Pedro. How then? sick?

Claud. Neither, my lord.

Beat. The count is neither sad, nor sick, nor merry, nor well; but civil count, civil as an orange, and something of that jealous complexion.

D. Pedro. I' faith, lady, I think your blazon to be true; though, I'll be sworn, if he be so, his conceit is false. Here, Claudio, I have wooed in thy name, and fair Hero is won: I have broke with her father, and his good will obtained: name the day of marriage, and God give thee joy!   312

Leon. Count, take of me my daughter, and

241. **answer . . . saying,** correspond to what you say. 244. **to,** with. 246. **misused,** abused. 252. **huddling,** piling, heaping up. 253. **impossible,** extravagant, incredible. **conveyance,** trickery. 254. **man at a mark,** man who stood by the target in archery to check off the arrows. 256. **terminations,** terms, expressions. 258. **north star,** supposed the most remote of stars. 261. **Hercules . . . spit.** Omphale put Hercules to menial tasks about the house; turning the spit was the most menial of kitchen duties. 264. **Ate,** goddess of mischief or of discord. 265. **scholar . . . conjure.** Scholars were supposed to have the power to control evil spirits, which had to be addressed in Latin. 275. **toothpicker,** toothpick.

276. **Prester John's.** Prester John was a legendary Christian king of the far East. 277. **great Cham's,** of the Khan of Tartary. 279. **Pigmies,** legendary small race which beset Hercules in his sleep (*Iliad,* Bk. iii); frequently mentioned in the Renaissance. 287-291. **Indeed . . . lost it.** This seems an unquestionable allusion to an earlier flirtation between Benedick and Beatrice; such an episode might have appeared in an earlier version of the play. 288. **use,** interest. 288-289. **double, single.** The former word seems to imply that he had her heart as well as his own, with a possible pun on the meaning of "deceitful." (It was a deceitful heart that she gave him.) The latter word seems to pun on the meanings "sincere" and "unmarried." 292. **put him down,** got the better of him. 304. **civil count.** Some editors place a comma between these words. **civil, serious, grave. civil,** pun on Seville, whence oranges came. 305. **jealous complexion.** Yellow, associated with melancholy, was the accepted symbol of jealousy. 307. **blazon,** description. 308. **conceit,** conception.

with her my fortunes: his grace hath made the match, and all grace say Amen to it. 315

Beat. Speak, count, 'tis your cue.

Claud. Silence is the perfectest herald of joy: I were but little happy, if I could say how much. Lady, as you are mine, I am yours: I give away myself for you and dote upon the exchange. 320

Beat. Speak, cousin; or, if you cannot, stop his mouth with a kiss, and let not him speak neither.

D. Pedro. In faith, lady, you have a merry heart.

Beat. Yea, my lord; I thank it, poor fool, it keeps on the windy side of care. My cousin tells him in his ear that he is in her heart.

Claud. And so she doth, cousin. 329

Beat. Good Lord, for alliance! Thus goes every one to the world but I, and I am sunburnt; I may sit in a corner and cry heigh-ho for a husband!

D. Pedro. Lady Beatrice, I will get you one.

Beat. I would rather have one of your father's getting. Hath your grace ne'er a brother like you? Your father got excellent husbands, if a maid could come by them.

D. Pedro. Will you have me, lady? 339

Beat. No, my lord, unless I might have another for working-days: your grace is too costly to wear every day. But, I beseech your grace, pardon me: I was born to speak all mirth and no matter.

D. Pedro. Your silence most offends me, and to be merry best becomes you; for, out of question, you were born in a merry hour.

Beat. No, sure, my lord, my mother cried; but then there was a star danced, and under that was I born. Cousins, God give you joy!

Leon. Niece, will you look to those things I told you of? 352

Beat. I cry you mercy, uncle. By your grace's pardon.   [*Exit.*

D. Pedro. By my troth, a pleasant-spirited lady.

Leon. There's little of the melancholy element in her, my lord: she is never sad but when she sleeps, and not ever sad then; for I have heard my daughter say, she hath often dreamed of unhappiness and waked herself with laughing. 361

D. Pedro. She cannot endure to hear tell of a husband.

Leon. O, by no means: she mocks all her wooers out of suit. 365

D. Pedro. She were an excellent wife for Benedick.

Leon. O Lord, my lord, if they were but a week married, they would talk themselves mad.

D. Pedro. County Claudio, when mean you to go to church? 371

Claud. To-morrow, my lord: time goes on crutches till love have all his rites.

Leon. Not till Monday, my dear son, which is hence a just seven-night; and a time too brief, too, to have all things answer my mind.

D. Pedro. Come, you shake the head at so long a breathing: but, I warrant thee, Claudio, the time shall not go dully by us. I will in the interim undertake one of Hercules' labours; which is, to bring Signior Benedick and the Lady Beatrice into a mountain of affection the one with the other. I would fain have it a match, and I doubt not but to fashion it, if you three will but minister such assistance as I shall give 385 you direction.

Leon. My lord, I am for you, though it cost me ten nights' watchings.

Claud. And I, my lord.

D. Pedro. And you too, gentle Hero?

Hero. I will do any modest office, my lord, to help my cousin to a good husband. 391

D. Pedro. And Benedick is not the unhopefullest husband that I know. Thus far can I praise him; he is of a noble strain, of approved valour and confirmed honesty. I will teach you how to humour your cousin, that she shall fall in love with Benedick; and I, with your two helps, will so practise on Benedick that, in despite of his quick wit and his queasy stomach, he shall fall in love

---

315. **all grace**, the source of grace, God. 327. **windy**, safe, advantageous. 331. **goes . . . world**, i.e., gets married. 332. **sunburnt**, i.e., unattractive. 333. **heigh-ho . . . husband**, title of a ballad. 344. **matter**, substance, sense. 349. **star danced**, an allusion to the belief that the sun danced at Easter. 353. **cry . . . mercy**, beg your pardon (preliminary to leaving). 357. **melancholy element**, i.e., earth, associated with the humor of melancholy in the old physiology.

359. **ever.** Most editors prefer the anonymous conjecture *even*. 361. **unhappiness**, misfortune. 365. **out of suit**, out of love, with play on the legal sense of "nonsuiting." 375. **a just seven-night**, exactly a week. 376. **answer my mind**, correspond with my intention. 378. **breathing**, pause, rest. 385. **minister**, furnish, supply. 387. **am for you**, accept your proposal. 388. **watchings**, lying awake. 395. **approved**, tested. **honesty**, honor. 398. **practise on**, work on by craft. 400. **queasy stomach**, squeamish taste.

with Beatrice. If we can do this, Cupid is no longer an archer: his glory shall be ours, for we are the only love-gods. Go in with me, and I will tell you my drift.   [*Exeunt.*   403

Scene II. *The same.*

Enter Don John *and* Borachio.

D. John. It is so; the Count Claudio shall marry the daughter of Leonato.

Bora. Yea, my lord; but I can cross it.

D. John. Any bar, any cross, any impediment will be medicinable to me: I am sick in displeasure to him, and whatsoever comes athwart his affection ranges evenly with mine. How canst thou cross this marriage?

Bora. Not honestly, my lord; but so covertly that no dishonesty shall appear in me.

D. John. Show me briefly how.   11

Bora. I think I told your lordship a year since, how much I am in the favour of Margaret, the waiting gentlewoman to Hero.

D. John. I remember.

Bora. I can, at any unseasonable instant of the night, appoint her to look out at her lady's chamber-window.

D. John. What life is in that, to be the death of this marriage?   20

Bora. The poison of that lies in you to temper. Go you to the prince your brother; spare not to tell him that he hath wronged his honour in marrying the renowned Claudio—whose estimation do you mightily hold up—to a contaminated stale, such   26 a one as Hero.

D. John. What proof shall I make of that?

Bora. Proof enough to misuse the prince, to vex Claudio, to undo Hero and kill Leonato. Look you for any other issue?   30

D. John. Only to despite them, I will endeavour any thing.

Bora. Go, then; find me a meet hour to draw Don Pedro and the Count Claudio alone: tell them that you know that Hero loves me; intend a kind of zeal both to the prince and Claudio, as,—in love of your brother's honour, who hath made this match,

and his friend's reputation, who is thus like to be cozened with the semblance of a maid, —that you have discovered thus. They   40 will scarcely believe this without trial: offer them instances; which shall bear no less likelihood than to see me at her chamber-window, hear me †call Margaret Hero, hear Margaret term me Claudio; and bring them to see this the very night before the intended wedding,—for in the meantime I will so fashion the matter that Hero shall be absent,—and there shall appear such seeming truth of Hero's disloyalty that jealousy shall be called assurance and all the prep-   51 aration overthrown.

D. John. Grow this to what adverse issue it can, I will put it in practice. Be cunning in the working this, and thy fee is a thousand ducats.

Bora. Be you constant in the accusation, and my cunning shall not shame me.

D. John. I will presently go learn their day of marriage.   [*Exeunt.*

Scene III. Leonato's *orchard.*

Enter Benedick.

Bene. Boy!
Enter Boy.
Boy. Signior?

Bene. In my chamber-window lies a book: bring it hither to me in the orchard.

Boy. I am here already, sir.   5

Bene. I know that; but I would have thee hence, and here again. [*Exit Boy.*] I do much wonder that one man, seeing how much another man is a fool when he dedicates his behaviours to love, will, after he hath laughed at such shallow follies in others, become the argument of his own scorn by falling in love: and such a man is Claudio. I have known when there was no music with him but the drum and the fife; and now had he rather hear the tabor and the pipe: 15

403. **drift,** purpose.
Scene ii. 1. **shall,** is going to. 5. **medicinable,** medicinal. 6. **displeasure,** dislike. 7. **whatsoever** . . . **mine,** whatever crosses his inclination runs parallel with mine. 21. **lies in,** rests with. 22. **temper,** mix, compound. 25. **estimation,** worth. 26. **contaminated stale,** impure harlot. 28. **misuse,** abuse; deceive. 29. **vex,** afflict. 36. **intend,** pretend. 37. **as,** i.e., saying as follows. The words between the dashes are to be understood as instructions to Don John as to what he is to say.

39. **cozened,** deceived, cheated. **semblance,** semblance only, outward appearance. 40. **that you . . . thus.** New Cambridge editor suggests that this clause be placed after *as* in line 36. 42. **instances,** evidence, proof. 44-45. **hear . . . Claudio.** Many editors follow Theobald and read *Borachio* for *Claudio.* The present reading may be defended if one imagines that, by arrangement with Margaret, Borachio is playing the part of Claudio. 50. **jealousy,** suspicion. 51. **preparation,** i.e., for the marriage. 55. **ducats,** Italian coins worth about one dollar each.
Scene iii. 5. **here already,** i.e., he will be so quick as to use no time at all. 9. **behaviours,** details of behavior. 11. **argument,** subject, theme. 15. **tabor . . . pipe,** symbols of peaceful merriment.

I have known when he would have walked
ten mile a-foot to see a good armour; and
now will he lie ten nights awake, carving the
fashion of a new doublet. He was wont to
speak plain and to the purpose, like an honest man and a soldier; and now is he turned
orthography; his words are a very fan- 21
tastical banquet, just so many strange dishes.
May I be so converted and see with these
eyes? I cannot tell; I think not: I will not be
sworn but love may transform me to an oyster; but I'll take my oath on it, till he have
made an oyster of me, he shall never make
me such a fool. One woman is fair, yet I am
well; another is wise, yet I am well; another
virtuous, yet I am well; but till all graces be
in one woman, one woman shall not come
in my grace. Rich she shall be, that's certain; wise, or I'll none; virtuous, or I'll 33
never cheapen her; fair, or I'll never look on
her; mild, or come not near me; noble, or not
I for an angel; of good discourse, an excellent
musician, and her hair shall be of what colour
it please God. Ha! the prince and Monsieur
Love! I will hide me in the arbour.   38
                                    [*Withdraws.*

Enter DON PEDRO, CLAUDIO, *and*
            LEONATO.

D. Pedro. Come, shall we hear this music?
Claud. Yea, my good lord. How still the
    evening is,   40
As hush'd on purpose to grace harmony!
D. Pedro. See you where Benedick hath
    hid himself?
Claud. O, very well, my lord: the music
    ended,
We'll fit the kid-fox with a pennyworth.

Enter BALTHASAR *with Music.*

D. Pedro. Come, Balthasar, we'll hear
    that song again.
Balth. O, good my lord, tax not so bad a
    voice
To slander music any more than once.
D. Pedro. It is the witness still of ex-
    cellency
To put a strange face on his own perfection.
I pray thee, sing, and let me woo no more.
Balth. Because you talk of wooing, I will
    sing;   51
Since many a wooer doth commence his suit
To her he thinks not worthy, yet he wooes,
Yet will he swear he loves.
D. Pedro.   Now, pray thee, come;
Or, if thou wilt hold longer argument,
Do it in notes.
Balth.   Note this before my notes;
There's not a note of mine that's worth the
    noting.
D. Pedro. Why, these are very crotchets
    that he speaks;
Note, notes, forsooth, and nothing. [*Air.* 59
Bene. Now, divine air! now is his soul rav-
ished! Is it not strange that sheeps' guts
should hale souls out of men's bodies? Well,
a horn for my money, when all's done.

            The Song.

Balth. Sigh no more, ladies, sigh no more,
            Men were deceivers ever,
        One foot in sea and one on shore,
            To one thing constant never:
        Then sigh not so, but let them go,
            And be you blithe and bonny,
        Converting all your sounds of woe 70
            Into Hey nonny, nonny.

        Sing no more ditties, sing no moe,
            Of dumps so dull and heavy;
        The fraud of men was ever so,
            Since summer first was leavy:
            Then sigh not so, &c.

D. Pedro. By my troth, a good song.
Balth. And an ill singer, my lord.

---

17. **armour,** suit of armor. 18. **carving,** planning.
21. **orthography,** either abstract for concrete, or, as
Rowe and many editors have it, an error for *orthographer.*
23. **May,** can. 33. **I'll none,** I'll have none. 34.
cheapen, ask the price of, bid for. 35-36. **noble, angel.**
Each of these words involves a pun on the meaning "a
coin," a *noble* being worth 6s. 8d. and an *angel,* 10s.
37-38. **of . . . God,** i.e., of any color whatever. Some
editors see an allusion to the practice of dyeing the hair.
38. **I . . . arbour.** Note the freedom with which the
characters in this play indulge in eavesdropping; it
was probably less objectionable as a social practice in
Shakespeare's day. *Stage Direction:* F: *Enter Prince,
Leonato, Claudio, and Jacke Wilson;* Q has *Musicke* for
and Jacke Wilson. Wilson was evidently the actor who
played Balthasar. 41. **grace harmony,** do honor to
music. 44. **kid-fox.** Cass suggests an allusion to
Spenser's *Shepheardes Calender (Ecl.* v), to the story of
the kid captured by the wily fox, seeing in Benedick's
situation something both of the wily fox and the innocent kid; most editors, however, regard the word as a
blunder. **pennyworth,** i.e., his money's worth.

48-49. **It . . . perfection,** it is always a proof of
excellence that, in demeanor, it is unconscious, or unknowing, of its own perfection (Furness). 50. **woo,**
entreat. 56. **notes,** music. 58. **crotchets,** used with
play on the meanings "whim" or "fancy," and "musical
notes." 59. **Note,** knows not, pretends not to know.
nothing, with play on *noting.* It has been suggested
that this same pun is concealed in the title of the play,
where *Nothing* would suggest *noting,* or eavesdropping.
61. **sheeps' guts,** fiddle-strings.

D. Pedro. Ha, no, no, faith; thou singest well enough for a shift.   80

Bene. An he had been a dog that should have howled thus, they would have hanged him: and I pray God his bad voice bode no mischief. I had as lief have heard the night-raven, come what plague could have come after it.

D. Pedro. Yea, marry, dost thou hear, Balthasar? I pray thee, get us some excellent music; for to-morrow night we would have it at the Lady Hero's chamber-window.

Balth. The best I can, my lord.   90

D. Pedro. Do so: farewell.[*Exit Balthasar.* Come hither, Leonato. What was it you told me of to-day, that your niece Beatrice was in love with Signior Benedick?

Claud. O, ay: stalk on, stalk on; the fowl sits. I did never think that lady would have loved any man.

Leon. No, nor I neither; but most wonderful that she should so dote on Signior Benedick, whom she hath in all outward behaviours seemed ever to abhor.   101

Bene. Is't possible? Sits the wind in that corner?

Leon. By my troth, my lord, I cannot tell what to think of it but that she loves him with an enraged affection; it is past the infinite of thought.

D. Pedro. May be she doth but counterfeit.

Claud. Faith, like enough.

Leon. O God, counterfeit! There was never counterfeit of passion came so near the life of passion as she discovers it.   111

D. Pedro. Why, what effects of passion shows she?

Claud. Bait the hook well; this fish will bite.

Leon. What effects, my lord? She will sit you, you heard my daughter tell you how.

Claud. She did, indeed.

D. Pedro. How, how, I pray you? You amaze me: I would have thought her spirit had been invincible against all assaults of affection.   120

Leon. I would have sworn it had, my lord; especially against Benedick.

Bene. I should think this a gull, but that the white-bearded fellow speaks it: knavery cannot, sure, hide himself in such reverence.

Claud. He hath ta'en the infection: hold it up.

D. Pedro. Hath she made her affection known to Benedick?

Leon. No; and swears she never will: that's her torment.   130

Claud. 'Tis true, indeed; so your daughter says: 'Shall I,' says she, 'that have so oft encountered him with scorn, write to him that I love him?'

Leon. This says she now when she is beginning to write to him; for she'll be up twenty times a night, and there will she sit in her smock till she have writ a sheet of paper: my daughter tells us all.   139

Claud. Now you talk of a sheet of paper, I remember a pretty jest your daughter told us of.

Leon. O, when she had writ it and was reading it over, she found Benedick and Beatrice between the sheet?

Claud. That.   145

Leon. O, she tore the letter into a thousand halfpence; railed at herself, that she should be so immodest to write to one that she knew would flout her; 'I measure him,' says she, 'by my own spirit; for I should flout him, if he writ to me; yea, though I love him, I should.'   151

Claud. Then down upon her knees she falls, weeps, sobs, beats her heart, tears her hair, prays, curses; 'O sweet Benedick! God give me patience!'

Leon. She doth indeed; my daughter says so: and the ecstasy hath so much overborne her that my daughter is sometime afeard she will do a desperate outrage to herself: 159 it is very true.

D. Pedro. It were good that Benedick knew of it by some other, if she will not discover it.

Claud. To what end? He would make but a sport of it and torment the poor lady worse.   163

D. Pedro. An he should, it were an alms to hang him. She's an excellent sweet lady; and, out of all suspicion, she is virtuous.

80. **shift**, makeshift.   84. **night-raven**, variously identified as the owl, the night-heron, and the bittern. 86. **Yea, marry**, a continuation of Don Pedro's speech preceding Benedick's aside.   95. **stalk . . . sits**, an allusion to the practice of hunting birds by means of a stalking-horse, i.e., a horse trained to the business, or an artificial structure resembling a horse.

123. **gull**, trick, deception.   126. **hold it up**, keep up the jest.   138. **smock**, undergarment.   145. **That**, that was it.   147. **halfpence**. Halfpence were of silver and very tiny coins.   157. **ecstasy**, madness.   164. **alms**, good deed.   166. **out of**, beyond.

Claud. And she is exceeding wise.

D. Pedro. In every thing but in loving Benedick.   169

Leon. O, my lord, wisdom and blood combatting in so tender a body, we have ten proofs to one that blood hath the victory. I am sorry for her, as I have just cause, being her uncle and her guardian.   174

D. Pedro. I would she had bestowed this dotage on me: I would have daffed all other respects and made her half myself. I pray you, tell Benedick of it, and hear what a' will say.

Leon. Were it good, think you?   179

Claud. Hero thinks surely she will die; for she says she will die, if he love her not, and she will die, ere she make her love known, and she will die, if he woo her, rather than she will bate one breath of her accustomed crossness.   184

D. Pedro. She doth well: if she should make tender of her love, 'tis very possible he'll scorn it; for the man, as you know all, hath a contemptible spirit.

Claud. He is a very proper man.

D. Pedro. He hath indeed a good outward happiness.   191

Claud. Before God! and, in my mind, very wise.

D. Pedro. He doth indeed show some sparks that are like wit.

Claud. And I take him to be valiant.

D. Pedro. As Hector, I assure you: and in the managing of quarrels you may say he is wise; for either he avoids them with great discretion, or undertakes them with a most Christian-like fear.   200

Leon. If he do fear God, a' must necessarily keep peace: if he break the peace, he ought to enter into a quarrel with fear and trembling.   203

D. Pedro. And so will he do; for the man doth fear God, howsoever it seems not in him by some large jests he will make. Well, I am sorry for your niece. Shall we go seek Benedick, and tell him of her love?

Claud. Never tell him, my lord: let her wear it out with good counsel.   210

Leon. Nay, that's impossible: she may wear her heart out first.

D. Pedro. Well, we will hear further of it by your daughter: let it cool the while. I love Benedick well; and I could wish he would modestly examine himself, to see how much he is unworthy so good a lady.

Leon. My lord, will you walk? dinner is ready.

Claud. If he do not dote on her upon this, I will never trust my expectation.   220

D. Pedro. Let there be the same net spread for her; and that must your daughter and her gentlewomen carry. The sport will be, when they hold one an opinion of another's dotage, and no such matter: that's the scene that I would see, which will be merely a dumb-show. Let us send her to call him in dinner.   227

[*Exeunt Don Pedro, Claudio, and Leonato.*

Bene. [*Coming forward*] This can be no trick: the conference was sadly borne. They have the truth of this from Hero. They seem to pity the lady: it seems her affections have their full bent. Love me! why, it must   232 be requited. I hear how I am censured: they say I will bear myself proudly, if I perceive the love come from her; they say too that she will rather die than give any sign of affection. I did never think to marry: I must not seem proud: happy are they that hear their detractions and can put them to mending. They say the lady is fair; 'tis a truth, I can bear them witness; and virtuous; 'tis so, I cannot reprove it; and wise, but for   241 loving me; by my troth, it is no addition to her wit, nor no great argument of her folly, for I will be horribly in love with her. I may chance have some odd quirks and remnants of wit broken on me, because I have railed so long against marriage: but doth not the appetite alter? a man loves the meat in his youth that he cannot endure in his age. Shall quips and sentences and these paper bullets of the brain awe a man from the career of his humour? No, the world   250 must be peopled. When I said I would die a bachelor, I did not think I should live till I were married. Here comes Beatrice. By

176. daffed, put or thrust aside. 177. half myself, i.e., my wife. 188. contemptible, contemptuous. 189. proper, fine, handsome. 190. outward happiness, fortunate in his good looks. 194. wit, sense. 206. large, indelicate. 210. counsel, consultation, deliberation.

223. carry, manage, arrange. 225. no such matter, the reality is quite otherwise. 229. sadly borne, gravely conducted. 232. bent, degree of tension and endurance. 238. put . . . mending, profit by them. 241. reprove, refute. 242. addition, honor, credit. 243. argument, proof. 245. quirks, witty conceits or jokes. 249. quips, sharp or sarcastic remarks. sentences, saws, maxims. paper bullets, i.e., taken from books. 250. career of his humour, pursuit of his inclination.

this day! she's a fair lady: I do spy some
marks of love in her.

Enter BEATRICE.

Beat. Against my will I am sent to bid
you come in to dinner.

Bene. Fair Beatrice, I thank you for your
pains.

Beat. I took no more pains for those
thanks than you take pains to thank me: if
it had been painful, I would not have come.

Bene. You take pleasure then in the
message?   262

Beat. Yea, just so much as you may take
upon a knife's point and choke a daw withal.
You have no stomach, signior: fare you well.
                                        [*Exit.*

Bene. Ha! 'Against my will I am sent to
bid you come in to dinner;' there's a double
meaning in that. 'I took no more pains for
those thanks than you took pains to thank
me;' that's as much as to say, Any pains
that I take for you is as easy as thanks. If I
do not take pity of her, I am a villain; if I
do not love her, I am a Jew. I will go get her
picture.   [*Exit.*   273

ACT III.

Scene I. Leonato's *garden.*

Enter HERO, MARGARET, *and* URSULA.

Hero. Good Margaret, run thee to the
   parlour;
There shalt thou find my cousin Beatrice
Proposing with the prince and Claudio:
Whisper her ear and tell her, I and Ursula
Walk in the orchard and our whole discourse
Is all of her; say that thou overheard'st us;
And bid her steal into the pleached bower,
Where honeysuckles, ripen'd by the sun,
Forbid the sun to enter, like favourites,
Made proud by princes, that advance their
   pride   10
Against that power that bred it: there will
   she hide her,
To listen our purpose. This is thy office;
Bear thee well in it and leave us alone.

Marg. I'll make her come, I warrant you,
   presently.   [*Exit.*

Hero. Now, Ursula, when Beatrice doth
   come,
As we do trace this alley up and down,
Our talk must only be of Benedick.
When I do name him, let it be thy part
To praise him more than ever man did merit:
My talk to thee must be how Benedick   20
Is sick in love with Beatrice. Of this matter
Is little Cupid's crafty arrow made,
That only wounds by hearsay.

Enter BEATRICE, *behind.*

                              Now begin;
For look where Beatrice, like a lapwing, runs
Close by the ground, to hear our conference.

Urs. The pleasant'st angling is to see the
   fish
Cut with her golden oars the silver stream,
And greedily devour the treacherous bait:
So angle we for Beatrice; who even now
Is couched in the woodbine coverture.   30
Fear you not my part of the dialogue.

Hero. Then go we near her, that her ear
   lose nothing
Of the false sweet bait that we lay for it.
                    [*Approaching the bower.*
No, truly, Ursula, she is too disdainful;
I know her spirits are as coy and wild
As haggerds of the rock.

Urs.   But are you sure
That Benedick loves Beatrice so entirely?

Hero. So says the prince and my new-
   trothed lord.

Urs. And did they bid you tell her of it,
   madam?

Hero. They did entreat me to acquaint her
   of it;   40
But I persuaded them, if they loved Bene-
   dick,
To wish him wrestle with affection,
And never to let Beatrice know of it.

Urs. Why did you so? Doth not the gen-
   tleman
Deserve as full as fortunate a bed
As ever Beatrice shall couch upon?

Hero. O god of love! I know he doth
   deserve
As much as may be yielded to a man:
But Nature never framed a woman's heart

---

264. **choke . . . withal,** i.e., make a mouthful for a
jackdaw.
Act III. Scene i. 3. **Proposing,** conversing. 8.
honeysuckles, identified with the woodbine. 12.
purpose, discourse, conversation.

23. **only . . . hearsay,** wounds by mere report. 30.
woodbine coverture, bower, or arbor, of honeysuckle.
36. **haggerds,** untrained female hawks. 42. **affection,**
passion; here, the passion of love. 45. **as full as,**
fully as; New Cambridge (following Boas): *at full.*

Of prouder stuff than that of Beatrice;   50
Disdain and scorn ride sparkling in her eyes,
Misprising what they look on, and her wit
Values itself so highly that to her
All matter else seems weak: she cannot love,
Nor take no shape nor project of affection,
She is so self-endeared.
    Urs.   Sure, I think so;
And therefore certainly it were not good
She knew his love, lest she make sport at it.
    Hero. Why, you speak truth. I never yet
        saw man,
How wise, how noble, young, how rarely fea-
        tured,   60
But she would spell him backward: if fair-
        faced,
She would swear the gentleman should be
        her sister;
If black, why, Nature, drawing of an antique,
Made a foul blot; if tall, a lance ill-headed;
If low, an agate very vilely cut;
If speaking, why, a vane blown with all
        winds;
If silent, why, a block moved with none.
So turns she every man the wrong side out
And never gives to truth and virtue that
Which simpleness and merit purchaseth.   70
    Urs. Sure, sure, such carping is not com-
        mendable.
    Hero. No, not to be so odd and from all
        fashions
As Beatrice is, cannot be commendable:
But who dare tell her so? If I should speak,
She would mock me into air; O, she would
        laugh me
Out of myself, press me to death with wit.
Therefore let Benedick, like cover'd fire,
Consume away in sighs, waste inwardly:
It were a better death than die with mocks,
Which is as bad as die with tickling.   80
    Urs. Yet tell her of it: hear what she will
        say.
    Hero. No; rather I will go to Benedick
And counsel him to fight against his passion.
And, truly, I'll devise some honest slanders

To stain my cousin with: one doth not know
How much an ill word may empoison liking.
    Urs. O, do not do your cousin such a
        wrong.
She cannot be so much without true judge-
        ment—
Having so swift and excellent a wit
As she is prized to have—as to refuse   90
So rare a gentleman as Signior Benedick.
    Hero. He is the only man of Italy,
Always excepted my dear Claudio.
    Urs. I pray you, be not angry with me,
        madam,
Speaking my fancy: Signior Benedick,
For shape, for bearing, argument and valour,
Goes foremost in report through Italy.
    Hero. Indeed, he hath an excellent good
        name.
    Urs. His excellence did earn it, ere he had
        it.
When are you married, madam?   100
    Hero. Why, every day, to-morrow. Come,
        go in:
I'll show thee some attires, and have thy
        counsel
Which is the best to furnish me to-morrow.
    Urs. She's limed, I warrant you: we have
        caught her, madam.
    Hero. If it proves so, then loving goes by
        haps:
Some Cupid kills with arrows, some with
        traps.
                    [*Exeunt Hero and Ursula.*
    Beat. [*Coming forward.*] What fire is in
        mine ears? Can this be true?
Stand I condemn'd for pride and scorn so
        much?
Contempt, farewell! and maiden pride, adieu!
No glory lives behind the back of such. 110
And, Benedick, love on; I will requite thee,
Taming my wild heart to thy loving hand:
If thou dost love, my kindness shall incite
        thee
To bind our loves up in a holy band;
For others say thou dost deserve, and I
Believe it better than reportingly.   [*Exit.*

52. **Misprising**, undervaluing.   55. **project**, conception, idea.   56. **self-endeared**, full of self-love. 61. **spell him backward**, say the exactly contrary thing; a possible allusion to witches' prayers which were said backward.   63. **black**, dark.   **antique** (*antic*), buffoon.   65. **agate**, diminutive person; an allusion to the small figures cut in agate for rings.   70. **simpleness**, integrity, plainness.   **purchaseth**, attains deservedly. 72. **from**, different from.   78. **Consume . . . sighs**, an allusion to the belief that each sigh costs the heart a drop of blood.   84. **some honest slanders**, slanders which do not involve her virtue.

90. **prized**, estimated.   96. **argument**, power of reason.   101. **every day, to-morrow**, every day after tomorrow.   104. **limed**, caught, as a bird in bird-lime. 105. **by haps**, by chance.   107. **What . . . ears**, an allusion to the old saying that a person's ears burn when he is being discussed in his absence.   110. **No . . . such**, no good is spoken of such persons when their backs are turned.   112. **Taming . . . hand**, figure derived from the taming of the hawk by the hand of the falconer. 114. **band**, bond.   116. **better than reportingly**, on better evidence than mere report.

SCENE II. *A room in* LEONATO'S *house.*

Enter DON PEDRO, CLAUDIO, BENEDICK, *and*
LEONATO.

D. Pedro. I do but stay till your marriage
be consummate, and then go I toward
Arragon.

Claud. I'll bring you thither, my lord, if
you'll vouchsafe me.   4

D. Pedro. Nay, that would be as great a
soil in the new gloss of your marriage as to
show a child his new coat and forbid him to
wear it. I will only be bold with Benedick
for his company; for, from the crown of his
head to the sole of his foot, he is all mirth: he
hath twice or thrice cut Cupid's bow-string
and the little hangman dare not shoot at
him; he hath a heart as sound as a bell and
his tongue is the clapper, for what his heart
thinks his tongue speaks.   14

Bene. Gallants, I am not as I have been.

Leon. So say I: methinks you are sad-
der.

Claud. I hope he be in love.

D. Pedro. Hang him, truant! there's no
true drop of blood in him, to be truly touched
with love: if he be sad, he wants money.   20

Bene. I have the toothache.

D. Pedro. Draw it.

Bene. Hang it!

Claud. You must hang it first, and draw it
afterwards.

D. Pedro. What! sigh for the toothache?

Leon. Where is but a humour or a worm.

Bene. Well, every one can master a grief
but he that has it.

Claud. Yet say I, he is in love.   30

D. Pedro. There is no appearance of fancy
in him, unless it be a fancy that he hath to
strange disguises; as, to be a Dutchman to-
day, a Frenchman to-morrow, or in the
shape of two countries at once, as, a German
from the waist downward, all slops, and a
Spaniard from the hip upward, no doublet.
Unless he have a fancy to this foolery, as it
appears he hath, he is no fool for fancy, as
you would have it appear he is.

Claud. If he be not in love with some woman, there is no believing old signs: a'

brushes his hat o' mornings; what should
that bode?

D. Pedro. Hath any man seen him at the
barber's?   44

Claud. No, but the barber's man hath
been seen with him, and the old ornament
of his cheek hath already stuffed tennis-
balls.

Leon. Indeed, he looks younger than he
did, by the loss of a beard.

D. Pedro. Nay, a' rubs himself with civet:
can you smell him out by that?   51

Claud. That's as much as to say, the sweet
youth's in love.

D. Pedro. The greatest note of it is his
melancholy.

Claud. And when was he wont to wash his
face?

D. Pedro. Yea, or to paint himself? for
the which, I hear what they say of him.

Claud. Nay, but his jesting spirit; which is
now crept into a lute-string and now governed by stops.   62

D. Pedro. Indeed, that tells a heavy tale
for him: conclude, conclude he is in love.

Claud. Nay, but I know who loves him.

D. Pedro. That would I know too: I warrant, one that knows him not.

Claud. Yes, and his ill conditions; and, in
despite of all, dies for him.

D. Pedro. She shall be buried with her face
upwards.   71

Bene. Yet is this no charm for the toothache. Old signior, walk aside with me: I have
studied eight or nine wise words to speak to
you, which these hobby-horses must not
hear.   [*Exeunt Benedick and Leonato.*

D. Pedro. For my life, to break with him
about Beatrice.

Claud. 'Tis even so. Hero and Margaret
have by this played their parts with Beatrice;
and then the two bears will not bite one another when they meet.   81

Enter DON JOHN.

D. John. My lord and brother, God save
you!

3. **bring,** escort. 11. **little hangman,** playfully applied to Cupid. 27. **Where ... worm.** Toothache was
ascribed to "humors" or unhealthy secretions and to
actual worms in the teeth. 31. **fancy,** love. 36. **slops,**
loose breeches. 37. **no doublet,** in other words, "all
cloak" (Malone).

46-47. **old ... tennis-balls.** Benedick's beard has
gone to stuff tennis-balls. 50. **civet,** perfume derived
from the civet cat. 56. **wash,** i.e., with cosmetics. 62.
stops, frets on the finger board. 68. **ill conditions,**
bad qualities. 70-71. **buried ... upwards.** Suicides
were sometimes buried with their faces downwards.
Beatrice will not be responsible for her own death. 75.
hobby-horses, buffoons. 78. **Margaret,** mistake for
Ursula.

D. Pedro. Good den, brother. 83

D. John. If your leisure served, I would speak with you.

D. Pedro. In private?

D. John. If it please you: yet Count Claudio may hear; for what I would speak of concerns him.

D. Pedro. What's the matter? 90

D. John. [*To Claudio*] Means your lordship to be married to-morrow?

D. Pedro. You know he does.

D. John. I know not that, when he knows what I know.

Claud. If there be any impediment, I pray you discover it. 97

D. John. You may think I love you not: let that appear hereafter, and aim better at me by that I now will manifest. For my brother, I think he holds you well, and in dearness of heart hath help to effect your ensuing marriage;—surely suit ill spent and labour ill bestowed. 103

D. Pedro. Why, what's the matter?

D. John. I came hither to tell you; and, circumstances shortened, for she has been too long a talking of, the lady is disloyal.

Claud. Who, Hero?

D. John. Even she; Leonato's Hero, your Hero, every man's Hero. 110

Claud. Disloyal?

D. John. The word is too good to paint out her wickedness; I could say she were worse: think you of a worse title, and I will fit her to it. Wonder not till further warrant: go but with me to-night, you shall see her chamber-window entered, even the night before her wedding-day: if you love her then, to-morrow wed her; but it would better fit your honour to change your mind.

Claud. May this be so? 120

D. Pedro. I will not think it.

D. John. If you dare not trust that you see, confess not that you know: if you will follow me, I will show you enough; and when you have seen more and heard more, proceed accordingly.

Claud. If I see any thing to-night why I should not marry her to-morrow, in the con-gregation, where I should wed, there will I shame her. 128

D. Pedro. And, as I wooed for thee to obtain her, I will join with thee to disgrace her.

D. John. I will disparage her no farther till you are my witnesses: bear it coldly but till midnight, and let the issue show itself.

D. Pedro. O day untowardly turned!

Claud. O mischief strangely thwarting!

D. John. O plague right well prevented! so will you say when you have seen the sequel.

[*Exeunt.*

SCENE III. *A street.*

Enter Dogberry *and* Verges *with the* Watch.

Dog. Are you good men and true?

Verg. Yea, or else it were pity but they should suffer salvation, body and soul.

Dog. Nay, that were a punishment too good for them, if they should have any allegiance in them, being chosen for the prince's watch. 6

Verg. Well, give them their charge, neighbour Dogberry.

Dog. First, who think you the most desart-less man to be constable? 10

First Watch. Hugh Otecake, sir, or George Seacole; for they can write and read.

Dog. Come hither, neighbour Seacole. God hath blessed you with a good name: to be a well-favoured man is the gift of fortune; but to write and read comes by nature. 16

Sec. W. Both which, master constable,—

Dog. You have: I knew it would be your answer. Well, for your favour, sir, why, give God thanks, and make no boast of it; and for your writing and reading, let that appear when there is no need of such vanity. You are thought here to be the most senseless and fit man for the constable of the watch; therefore bear you the lantern. This is your charge: you shall comprehend all vagrom men; you are to bid any man stand, in the prince's name. 27

Sec. Watch. How if a' will not stand?

Dog. Why, then, take no note of him, but let him go; and presently call the rest of the watch together and thank God you are rid of a knave.

---

83. **Good den,** good evening. 90. **What's the matter?** Many editors give this speech to Claudio, a highly probable conjecture. 99. **aim better at,** judge better of. 101. **holds you well,** i.e., thinks well of you. 106. **circumstances shortened,** without unnecessary details. 107. **a talking of,** under discussion. 112. **paint out,** portray in full. 115. **till further warrant,** till further proof appears.

134. **untowardly turned,** perversely altered. *Scene iii.* 3. **salvation,** blunder for *damnation.* 7. **charge,** instructions. 9. **desartless,** for *deserving.* 19. **favour,** appearance. 23. **senseless,** for *sensible.* 25. **comprehend,** for *apprehend.* **vagrom,** vagrant.

Verg. If he will not stand when he is bidden, he is none of the prince's subjects.

Dog. True, and they are to meddle with none but the prince's subjects. You shall also make no noise in the streets; for for the the watch to babble and to talk is most tolerable and not to be endured.

Watch. We will rather sleep than talk: we know what belongs to a watch. 40

Dog. Why, you speak like an ancient and most quiet watchman; for I cannot see how sleeping should offend: only, have a care that your bills be not stolen. Well, you are to call at all the ale-houses, and bid those that are drunk get them to bed.

Watch. How if they will not?

Dog. Why, then, let them alone till they are sober: if they make you not then the better answer, you may say they are not the men you took them for. 51

Watch. Well, sir.

Dog. If you meet a thief, you may suspect him, by virtue of your office, to be no true man; and, for such kind of men, the less you meddle or make with them, why, the more is for your honesty.

Watch. If we know him to be a thief, shall we not lay hands on him?

Dog. Truly, by your office, you may; but I think they that touch pitch will be defiled: the most peaceable way for you, if you do take a thief, is to let him show himself what he is and steal out of your company.

Verg. You have been always called a merciful man, partner.

Dog. Truly, I would not hang a dog by my will, much more a man who hath any honesty in him.

Verg. If you hear a child cry in the night, you must call to the nurse and bid her still it.

Watch. How if the nurse be asleep and will not hear us?

Dog. Why, then, depart in peace, and let the child wake her with crying; for the ewe that will not hear her lamb when it baes will never answer a calf when he bleats.

Verg. 'Tis very true.

Dog. This is the end of the charge:—you, constable, are to present the prince's own person: if you meet the prince in the night, you may stay him. 81

Verg. Nay, by'r lady, that I think a' cannot.

Dog. Five shillings to one on't, with any man that knows the statues, he may stay him: marry, not without the prince be willing; for, indeed, the watch ought to offend no man; and it is an offence to stay a man against his will.

Verg. By'r lady, I think it be so. 89

Dog. Ha, ah, ha! Well, masters, good night: an there be any matter of weight chances, call up me: keep your fellows' counsels and your own; and good night. Come, neighbour.

Watch. Well, masters, we hear our charge: let us go sit here upon the church-bench till two, and then all to bed.

Dog. One word more, honest neighbours. I pray you, watch about Signior Leonato's door; for the wedding being there to-morrow, there is a great coil to-night. Adieu: be vigitant, I beseech you. 101

[*Exeunt Dogberry and Verges.*

Enter Borachio *and* Conrade.

Bora. What, Conrade!

Watch. [*Aside*] Peace! stir not.

Bora. Conrade, I say!

Con. Here, man; I am at thy elbow.

Bora. Mass, and my elbow itched; I thought there would a scab follow.

Con. I will owe thee an answer for that: and now forward with thy tale. 109

Bora. Stand thee close, then, under this pent-house, for it drizzles rain; and I will, like a true drunkard, utter all to thee.

Watch. [*Aside*] Some treason, masters: yet stand close.

Bora. Therefore know I have earned of Don John a thousand ducats.

Con. Is it possible that any villany should be so dear?

Bora. Thou shouldst rather ask if it were possible any villany should be so rich; for when rich villains have need of poor ones, poor ones may make what price they will.

Con. I wonder at it. 123

Bora. That shows thou art unconfirmed.

100. **coil**, fuss, to-do. 101. **vigitant**, for *vigilant*. 106. **Mass**, by the Mass. 107. **scab**, scurvy fellow. 111. **pent-house**, over-hanging roof. 114. **stand close**, keep concealed. 124. **unconfirmed**, inexperienced.

Thou knowest that the fashion of a doublet, or a hat, or a cloak, is nothing to a man.

Con. Yes, it is apparel.

Bora. I mean, the fashion.

Con. Yes, the fashion is the fashion. 129

Bora. Tush! I may as well say the fool's the fool. But seest thou not what a deformed thief this fashion is?

Watch. [*Aside*] I know that Deformed; a' has been a vile thief this seven year; a' goes up and down like a gentleman: I remember his name. 136

Bora. Didst thou not hear somebody?

Con. No; 'twas the vane on the house.

Bora. Seest thou not, I say, what a deformed thief this fashion is? how giddily a' turns about all the hot bloods between fourteen and five-and-thirty? sometimes fashioning them like Pharaoh's soldiers in the reechy painting, sometime like god Bel's priests in the old church-window, sometime like the shaven Hercules in the smirched worm-eaten tapestry, where his codpiece seems as massy as his club? 147

Con. All this I see; and I see that the fashion wears out more apparel than the man. But art not thou thyself giddy with the fashion too, that thou hast shifted out of thy tale into telling me of the fashion?

Bora. Not so, neither: but know that I have to-night wooed Margaret, the Lady Hero's gentlewoman, by the name of Hero: she leans me out at her mistress' chamber-window, bids me a thousand times good night,—I tell this tale vilely:—I should first tell thee how the prince, Claudio and my master, planted and placed and possessed by my master Don John, saw afar off in the orchard this amiable encounter. 161

Con. And thought they Margaret was Hero?

Bora. Two of them did, the prince and Claudio; but the devil my master knew she

was Margaret; and partly by his oaths, which first possessed them, partly by the dark night, which did deceive them, but chiefly by my villany, which did confirm any slander that Don John had made, away went Claudio enraged; swore he would meet her, as he was appointed, next morning at the temple, and there, before the whole congregation, shame her with what he saw o'er night and send her home again without a husband.

First Watch. We charge you, in the prince's name, stand!

Sec. Watch. Call up the right master constable. We have here recovered the most dangerous piece of lechery that ever was known in the commonwealth. 181

First Watch. And one Deformed is one of them: I know him; a' wears a lock.

Con. Masters, masters,—

Sec. Watch. You'll be made bring Deformed forth, I warrant you.

Con. Masters,—

First Watch. Never speak: we charge you let us obey you to go with us. 189

Bora. We are like to prove a goodly commodity, being taken up of these men's bills.

Con. A commodity in question, I warrant you. Come, we'll obey you.   [*Exeunt.*

SCENE IV. HERO's *apartment.*

Enter HERO, MARGARET, *and* URSULA.

Hero. Good Ursula, wake my cousin Beatrice, and desire her to rise.

Urs. I will, lady.

Hero. And bid her come hither.

Urs. Well.   [*Exit.*

Marg. Troth, I think your other rabato were better.

Hero. No, pray thee, good Meg, I'll wear this.

Marg. By my troth, 's not so good; and I warrant your cousin will say so. 10

Hero. My cousin's a fool, and thou art another: I'll wear none but this.

---

126. **nothing to a man,** does not make the man.
131, 133. **deformed, Deformed.** The first occurrence carries the meaning "deforming"; the second is possibly an unexplained topical allusion. 143. **Pharaoh's soldiers,** possible allusion to some picture of the Israelites passing through the Red Sea. **reechy,** dirty, filthy.
144. **god Bel's priests,** with probable allusion to the story of Bel and the Dragon, from the Apochryphal book of *Daniel,* depicted in a stained-glass window. 145. **shaven Hercules.** There is dispute among critics as to whether the reference is to Hercules disguised as a maiden in the service of Omphale, or to some picture of a shaven Hercules which had caught Shakespeare's eye.
147. **codpiece,** article of male attire indelicately conspicuous in this tapestry. 160. **possessed,** instructed, or possibly, influenced.

178. **right master constable,** comic title on the pattern of "right worshipful," etc. 179. **recovered,** for *discovered.* 183. **lock,** lock of hair hanging down on the left shoulder; the lovelock. 189. **let . . . to,** for *obey us and.* 190. **commodity,** goods acquired. 191. **taken up,** obtained on credit. **bills,** bonds given as security, and pikes. 192. **in question,** questionable, and about to be tried under the law.
Scene iv. 6. **rabato,** either a ruff or collar-band, or the wires which held it in place. 9. **troth, 's,** faith, it is.

Marg. I like the new tire within excellently, if the hair were a thought browner; and your gown's a most rare fashion, i' faith. I saw the Duchess of Milan's gown that they praise so.   16

Hero. O, that exceeds, they say.

Marg. By my troth, 's but a night-gown in respect of yours: cloth o' gold, and cuts, and laced with silver, set with pearls, down sleeves, side sleeves, and skirts, round underborne with a bluish tinsel: but for a fine, quaint, graceful and excellent fashion, yours is worth ten on 't.   23

Hero. God give me joy to wear it! for my heart is exceeding heavy.

Marg. 'Twill be heavier soon by the weight of a man.

Hero. Fie upon thee! art not ashamed? 28

Marg. Of what, lady? of speaking honourably? Is not marriage honourable in a beggar? Is not your lord honourable without marriage? I think you would have me say, 'saving your reverence, a husband:' an bad thinking do not wrest true speaking, I'll offend nobody: is there any harm in 'the heavier for a husband'? None, I think, an it be the right husband and the right wife; otherwise 'tis light, and not heavy: ask my Lady Beatrice else; here she comes.   38

Enter BEATRICE.

Hero. Good morrow, coz.

Beat. Good morrow, sweet Hero.   40

Hero. Why, how now? do you speak in the sick tune?

Beat. I am out of all other tune, methinks.

Marg. Clap's into 'Light o' love;' that goes without a burden: do you sing it, and I'll dance it.

Beat. Ye light o' love, with your heels!

then, if your husband have stables enough, you'll see he shall lack no barns.

Marg. O illegitimate construction! I scorn that with my heels.   51

Beat. 'Tis almost five o'clock, cousin; 'tis time you were ready. By my troth, I am exceeding ill: heigh-ho!

Marg. For a hawk, a horse, or a husband?

Beat. For the letter that begins them all, H.

Marg. Well, an you be not turned Turk, there's no more sailing by the star.

Beat. What means the fool, trow?

Marg. Nothing I; but God send every one their heart's desire!   61

Hero. These gloves the count sent me; they are an excellent perfume.

Beat. I am stuffed, cousin; I cannot smell.

Marg. A maid, and stuffed! there's goodly catching of cold.

Beat. O, God help me! God help me! how long have you professed apprehension?

Marg. Ever since you left it. Doth not my wit become me rarely?   70

Beat. It is not seen enough, you should wear it in your cap. By my troth, I am sick.

Marg. Get you some of this distilled Carduus Benedictus, and lay it to your heart: it is the only thing for a qualm.

Hero. There thou prickest her with a thistle.

Beat. Benedictus! why Benedictus? you have some moral in this Benedictus.   78

Marg. Moral! no, by my troth, I have no moral meaning; I meant, plain holy-thistle. You may think perchance that I think you are in love: nay, by'r lady, I am not such a fool to think what I list, nor I list not to think what I can, nor indeed I cannot think, if I would think my heart out of thinking, that you are in love or that you will be in love or that you can be in love. Yet Benedick was such another, and now is he become a man: he swore he would never marry, and yet now, in despite of his heart, he eats his meat without grudging: and how you may

13. **tire within.** headdress in the inner room, or inner trimming of hair upon the headdress. 17. **exceeds,** excels. 18. **night-gown,** dressing-gown. 19. **in respect of,** compared to. **cuts,** slashes in a garment. 20. **laced,** trimmed. 20-22. **set . . . tinsel.** R. G. White explained *down sleeves* as tight-fitting sleeves to the wrist, and *side sleeves* as secondary ornamental sleeves hanging from the shoulder. Other editors, following Capell, explain that the pearls were set down the sleeves and the skirt, and were stitched on to strips of blue tinsel to set them off, *round* implying that the pearls encircled the sleeves and skirts in a series of rings. By the other interpretation *underborne* would mean "with a lining or undergarment of tinsel." 33. **'saving . . . husband.'** Margaret pretends to beg Hero's pardon for even mentioning a husband. 34. **wrest,** misinterpret. 37. **light,** a pun on the meaning "wanton." 42. **sick tune,** tone of a sick person. 44. **'Light o' love,'** a popular song. 45. **burden,** bass accompaniment.

49. **barns,** with pun on *bairns,* children. 51. **with my heels,** explained as a proverbial expression of scorn. 56. **H,** pun on *ache,* pronounced "aitch." 57. **turned Turk,** proverbial for "changed completely." 58. **star,** pole-star. 59. **trow,** I wonder. 64. **stuffed,** afflicted with a cold. 68. **apprehension,** wit. 72. **wear . . . cap,** i.e., as a fool does his coxcomb. 73. **Carduus Benedictus,** the blessed thistle, noted for medicinal properties. 78. **moral,** hidden meaning. 83. **list,** like. 90. **eats . . . grudging,** has a normal appetite.

be converted I know not, but methinks you look with your eyes as other women do.

Beat. What pace is this that thy tongue keeps?

Marg. Not a false gallop.   94

Re-enter URSULA.

Urs. Madam, withdraw: the prince, the count, Signior Benedick, Don John, and all the gallants of the town, are come to fetch you to church.

Hero. Help to dress me, good coz, good Meg, good Ursula.   [*Exeunt.*

SCENE V. *Another room in* LEONATO's *house.*

Enter LEONATO, *with* DOGBERRY *and* VERGES.

Leon. What would you with me, honest neighbour?

Dog. Marry, sir, I would have some confidence with you that decerns you nearly.

Leon. Brief, I pray you; for you see it is a busy time with me.

Dog. Marry, this it is, sir.

Verg. Yes, in truth it is, sir.

Leon. What is it, my good friends?   9

Dog. Goodman Verges, sir, speaks a little off the matter: an old man, sir, and his wits are not so blunt as, God help, I would desire they were; but, in faith, honest as the skin between his brows.

Verg. Yes, I thank God I am as honest as any man living that is an old man and no honester than I.

Dog. Comparisons are odorous: palabras, neighbour Verges.

Leon. Neighbours, you are tedious.   20

Dog. It pleases your worship to say so, but we are the poor duke's officers; but truly, for mine own part, if I were as tedious as a king, I could find it in my heart to bestow it all of your worship.

Leon. All thy tediousness on me, ah?

Dog. Yea, an 'twere a thousand pound more than 'tis; for I hear as good exclamation on your worship as of any man in the

city; and though I be but a poor man, I am glad to hear it.   30

Verg. And so am I.

Leon. I would fain know what you have to say.

Verg. Marry, sir, our watch to-night, excepting your worship's presence, ha' ta'en a couple of as arrant knaves as any in Messina.   36

Dog. A good old man, sir; he will be talking: as they say, When the age is in, the wit is out: God help us! it is a world to see. Well said, i' faith, neighbour Verges: well, God's a good man; an two men ride of a horse, one must ride behind. An honest soul, i' faith, sir; by my troth he is, as ever broke bread; but God is to be worshipped; all men are not alike; alas, good neighbour!

Leon. Indeed, neighbour, he comes too short of you.

Dog. Gifts that God gives.

Leon. I must leave you.   48

Dog. One word, sir: our watch, sir, have indeed comprehended two aspicious persons, and we would have them this morning examined before your worship.

Leon. Take their examination yourself and bring it me: I am now in great haste, as it may appear unto you.

Dog. It shall be suffigance.

Leon. Drink some wine ere you go: fare you well.

Enter a Messenger.

Mess. My lord, they stay for you to give your daughter to her husband.   60

Leon. I'll wait upon them: I am ready.

[*Exeunt Leonato and Messenger.*

Dog. Go, good partner, go, get you to Francis Seacole; bid him bring his pen and inkhorn to the gaol: we are now to examination these men.

Verg. And we must do it wisely.   65

Dog. We will spare for no wit, I warrant you; here's that shall drive some of them to a noncome: only get the learned writer to set down our excommunication and meet me at the gaol.   [*Exeunt.*

---

94. **false gallop**, canter.
Scene v. 3. **confidence**, possibly misused for *conference*. 4. **decerns**, for *concerns*. 10. **Goodman**, title of persons under the social rank of gentleman. 13-14. **honest . . . brows**, proverbial expression of honesty, the brow being regarded as an open book. 18. **odorous**, for *odious*. **palabras**, for *pocas palabras*, few words. 22. **poor duke's officers**, for *the duke's poor officers*. 28. **exclamation**, possibly for *acclamation*.

34. **to-night**, last night. 38. **When . . . out**, adaptation of the proverb: "When ale is in, wit is out." 39. **a world**, wonderful. 40-41. **God's . . . man**, proverbial saying. 50. **aspicious**, for *suspicious*. 56. **suffigance**, for *sufficient*. 61. **wait upon**, attend. 68. **noncome**, usually taken as contraction for *non compos mentis* (not of sound mind), but perhaps intended as a substitute for *nonplus*. 69. **excommunication**, for *examination* or *communication*.

ACT IV.

Scene I. *A church.*

Enter Don Pedro, Don John, Leonato, Friar Francis, Claudio, Benedick, Hero, Beatrice, *and attendants.*

Leon. Come, Friar Francis, be brief; only to the plain form of marriage, and you shall recount their particular duties afterwards.

Friar. You come hither, my lord, to marry this lady.

Claud. No.

Leon. To be married to her: friar, you come to marry her.

Friar. Lady, you come hither to be married to this count.   10

Hero. I do.

Friar. If either of you know any inward impediment why you should not be conjoined, I charge you, on your souls, to utter it.

Claud. Know you any, Hero?

Hero. None, my lord.

Friar. Know you any, count?

Leon. I dare make his answer, none.

Claud. O, what men dare do! what men may do! what men daily do, not knowing what they do!   21

Bene. How now! interjections? Why, then, some be of laughing, as, ah, ha, he!

Claud. Stand thee by, friar. Father, by your leave:
Will you with free and unconstrained soul
Give me this maid, your daughter?

Leon. As freely, son, as God did give her me.

Claud. And what have I to give you back, whose worth
May counterpoise this rich and precious gift?

D. Pedro. Nothing, unless you render her again.   30

Claud. Sweet prince, you learn me noble thankfulness.
There, Leonato, take her back again:
Give not this rotten orange to your friend;
She's but the sign and semblance of her honour.
Behold how like a maid she blushes here!

O, what authority and show of truth
Can cunning sin cover itself withal!
Comes not that blood as modest evidence
To witness simple virtue? Would you not swear,
All you that see her, that she were a maid,   40
By these exterior shows? But she is none:
She knows the heat of a luxurious bed;
Her blush is guiltiness, not modesty.

Leon. What do you mean, my lord?

Claud.   Not to be married,
Not to knit my soul to an approved wanton.

Leon. Dear my lord, if you, in your own proof,
Have vanquish'd the resistance of her youth,
And made defeat of her virginity,—

Claud. I know what you would say: if I have known her,
You will say she did embrace me as a husband,
And so extenuate the 'forehand sin: 51
No, Leonato,
I never tempted her with word too large;
But, as a brother to his sister, show'd
Bashful sincerity and comely love.

Hero. And seem'd I ever otherwise to you?

Claud. Out on thee! Seeming! I will write against it:
You seem to me as Dian in her orb,
As chaste as is the bud ere it be blown;
But you are more intemperate in your blood
Than Venus, or those pamper'd animals   61
That rage in savage sensuality.

Hero. Is my lord well, that he doth speak so wide?

Leon. Sweet prince, why speak not you?

D. Pedro.   What should I speak?
I stand dishonour'd, that have gone about
To link my dear friend to a common stale.

Leon. Are these things spoken, or do I but dream?

D. John. Sir, they are spoken, and these things are true.

Bene. This looks not like a nuptial.

Hero.   True! O God!

Claud. Leonato, stand I here?   70
Is this the prince? is this the prince's brother?
Is this face Hero's? are our eyes our own?

---

36. **authority**, authenticity. 38. **modest evidence**, evidence of modesty. 42. **luxurious**, lascivious, lustful. 45. **approved**, convicted. 46. **in . . . proof**, in making trial of her yourself (Wright). 51. **extenuate**, excuse, lessen. **'forehand sin**, sin of anticipating (marriage). 53. **large**, gross, licentious. 58. **Dian . . . orb**, Diana, goddess of chastity, enthroned in the moon. 63. **wide**, wide of the mark. 69. **True!** a reply to Don John's speech.

22. **interjections.** Benedick seems to be reminded, by Claudio's strained manner of utterance, of interjections, and proceeds to recite a tag from the current Latin grammars, *some . . . he.* 29. **counterpoise**, balance, be equivalent to.

Leon. All this is so: but what of this, my
    lord?
Claud. Let me but move one question to
    your daughter;
And, by that fatherly and kindly power
That you have in her, bid her answer
    truly.
Leon. I charge thee do so, as thou art
    my child.
Hero. O, God defend me! how am I beset!
What kind of catechising call you this?
Claud. To make you answer truly to your
    name.   80
Hero. Is it not Hero? Who can blot that
    name
With any just reproach?
Claud.   Marry, that can Hero;
Hero itself can blot out Hero's virtue.
What man was he talk'd with you yester-
    night
Out at your window betwixt twelve and
    one?
Now, if you are a maid, answer to this.
Hero. I talk'd with no man at that hour,
    my lord.
D. Pedro. Why, then are you no maiden.
    Leonato,
I am sorry you must hear: upon mine honour,
Myself, my brother and this grieved count 90
Did see her, hear her, at that hour last night
Talk with a ruffian at her chamber-window;
Who hath indeed, most like a liberal villain,
Confess'd the vile encounters they have had
A thousand times in secret.
D. John. Fie, fie! they are not to be
    named, my lord,
Not to be spoke of;
There is not chastity enough in language
Without offence to utter them. Thus, pretty
    lady,
I am sorry for thy much misgovernment. 100
Claud. O Hero, what a Hero hadst thou
    been,
If half thy outward graces had been placed
About thy thoughts and counsels of thy
    heart!
But fare thee well, most foul, most fair!
    farewell,
Thou pure impiety and impious purity!
For thee I'll lock up all the gates of love,

And on my eyelids shall conjecture hang,
To turn all beauty into thoughts of harm,
And never shall it more be gracious.
Leon. Hath no man's dagger here a point
    for me?   110
                        [*Hero swoons.*
Beat. Why, how now, cousin! wherefore
    sink you down?
D. John. Come, let us go. These things,
    come thus to light,
Smother her spirits up.
[*Exeunt Don Pedro, Don John, and Claudio.*
Bene. How doth the lady?
Beat.   Dead, I think. Help, uncle!
Hero! why, Hero! Uncle! Signior Benedick!
    Friar!
Leon. O Fate! take not away thy heavy
    hand.
Death is the fairest cover for her shame
That may be wish'd for.
Beat.   How now, cousin Hero!
Friar. Have comfort, lady.
Leon. Dost thou look up?   120
Friar. Yea, wherefore should she not?
Leon. Wherefore! Why, doth not every
    earthly thing
Cry shame upon her? Could she here deny
The story that is printed in her blood?
Do not live, Hero; do not ope thine eyes:
For, did I think thou wouldst not quickly die,
Thought I thy spirits were stronger than thy
    shames,
Myself would, on the rearward of reproaches,
Strike at thy life. Grieved I, I had but one?
Chid I for that at frugal nature's frame? 130
O, one too much by thee! Why had I one?
Why ever wast thou lovely in my eyes?
Why had I not with charitable hand
Took up a beggar's issue at my gates,
Who smirched thus and mired with infamy,
I might have said 'No part of it is mine;
This shame derives itself from unknown
    loins'?
But mine and mine I loved and mine I
    praised
And mine that I was proud on, mine so much
That I myself was to myself not mine,   140
Valuing of her,—why, she, O, she is fallen
Into a pit of ink, that the wide sea
Hath drops too few to wash her clean again

---

74. **move**, propose. 75. **kindly**, natural, as belonging
to a father. 83. **Hero itself**, the name Hero. 93.
liberal, unrestrained. 100. **misgovernment**, evil
conduct. 105. **pure . . . purity**. Note the oxymoron,
i.e., association of words of contradictory senses.

107. **conjecture**, evil suspicion. 109. **gracious**,
attractive, graceful. 124. **blood**, blushes. 130. **frame**,
established order. 140. **That . . . mine**, she was so
much a part of me that by comparison I was not myself
(Yale). 141. **Valuing**, when establishing the value.

And salt too little which may season give
To her foul-tainted flesh!

Bene.   Sir, sir, be patient.
For my part, I am so attired in wonder,
I know not what to say.

Beat. O, on my soul, my cousin is belied!

Bene. Lady, were you her bedfellow last
    night?

Beat. No, truly not; although, until last
    night,   150
I have this twelvemonth been her bedfellow.

Leon. Confirm'd, confirm'd! O, that is
    stronger made
Which was before barr'd up with ribs of
    iron!
Would the two princes lie, and Claudio lie,
Who loved her so, that, speaking of her foul-
    ness,
Wash'd it with tears? Hence from her! let
    her die.

Friar. Hear me a little; for I have only been
Silent so long and given way unto
†This course of fortune . . .
By noting of the lady I have mark'd   160
A thousand blushing apparitions
To start into her face, a thousand innocent
    shames
In angel whiteness beat away those blushes;
And in her eye there hath appear'd a fire,
To burn the errors that these princes hold
Against her maiden truth. Call me a fool;
Trust not my reading nor my observations,
Which with experimental seal doth warrant
The tenour of my book; trust not my age,
My reverence, calling, nor divinity,   170
If this sweet lady lie not guiltless here
Under some biting error.

Leon.   Friar, it cannot be.
Thou seest that all the grace that she hath
    left
Is that she will not add to her damnation
A sin of perjury; she not denies it:
Why seek'st thou then to cover with excuse
That which appears in proper nakedness?

Friar. Lady, what man is he you are
    accused of?

Hero. They know that do accuse me; I
    know none:
If I know more of any man alive   180
Than that which maiden modesty doth war-
    rant,

Let all my sins lack mercy! O my father,
Prove you that any man with me conversed
At hours unmeet, or that I yesternight
Maintain'd the change of words with any
    creature,
Refuse me, hate me, torture me to death!

Friar. There is some strange misprision in
    the princes.

Bene. Two of them have the very bent of
    honour;
And if their wisdoms be misled in this,
The practice of it lives in John the bastard,190
Whose spirits toil in frame of villanies.

Leon. I know not. If they speak but truth
    of her,
These hands shall tear her; if they wrong her
    honour,
The proudest of them shall well hear of it.
Time hath not yet so dried this blood of mine,
Nor age so eat up my invention,
Nor fortune made such havoc of my means,
Nor my bad life reft me so much of friends,
But they shall find, awaked in such a kind,
Both strength of limb and policy of mind, 200
Ability in means and choice of friends,
To quit me of them throughly.

Friar.   Pause awhile,
And let my counsel sway you in this case.
Your daughter here the princes left for
    dead:
Let her awhile be secretly kept in,
And publish it that she is dead indeed;
Maintain a mourning ostentation
And on your family's old monument
Hang mournful epitaphs and do all rites
That appertain unto a burial.   210

Leon. What shall become of this? what
    will this do?

Friar. Marry, this well carried shall on
    her behalf
Change slander to remorse; that is some
    good:
But not for that dream I on this strange
    course,
But on this travail look for greater birth.
She dying, as it must be so maintain'd,
Upon the instant that she was accused,
Shall be lamented, pitied and excused
Of every hearer: for it so falls out   219
That what we have we prize not to the worth

144. **season**, preservative. 164-165: **a fire . . . burn,** an allusion to the burning of heretics. 168. **experimental seal,** stamp of experience. 169. **tenour . . . book,** what he has learned from reading.

187. **misprision,** mistake, misunderstanding. 188. **bent,** inclination of the mind. 190. **practice,** trickery. 191. **frame,** contriving. 196. **invention,** power of mind. 199. **kind,** manner. 202. **quit me of,** avenge me on. **throughly,** thoroughly. 205. **kept in,** confined.

Whiles we enjoy it, but being lack'd and lost,
Why, then we rack the value, then we find
The virtue that possession would not show us
Whiles it was ours. So will it fare with Claudio:
When he shall hear she died upon his words,
The idea of her life shall sweetly creep
Into his study of imagination,
And every lovely organ of her life
Shall come apparell'd in more precious habit,
More moving-delicate and full of life,   230
Into the eye and prospect of his soul,
Than when she lived indeed; then shall he mourn,
If ever love had interest in his liver,
And wish he had not so accused her,
No, though he thought his accusation true.
Let this be so, and doubt not but success
Will fashion the event in better shape
Than I can lay it down in likelihood.
But if all aim but this be levell'd false,
The supposition of the lady's death   240
Will quench the wonder of her infamy:
And if it sort not well, you may conceal her,
As best befits her wounded reputation,
In some reclusive and religious life,
Out of all eyes, tongues, minds and injuries.
  Bene. Signior Leonato, let the friar advise you:
And though you know my inwardness and love
Is very much unto the prince and Claudio,
Yet, by mine honour, I will deal in this
As secretly and justly as your soul   250
Should with your body.
  Leon.   Being that I flow in grief,
The smallest twine may lead me.
  Friar. 'Tis well consented: presently away;
For to strange sores strangely they strain the cure.
Come, lady, die to live: this wedding-day
Perhaps is but prolong'd: have patience and endure.
        [*Exeunt all but Benedick and Beatrice.*

222. **rack**, stretch or strain beyond normal extent.
225. **upon**, in consequence of.   227. **study of imagination**, musing, imaginative contemplation.   228.
every . . . life, every feature of her lovely life.   229.
habit, dress.   231. **prospect**, range of vision.   233.
liver, the supposed seat of the passion of love.   236. **success**, result, outcome.   239. **But . . . false**, if every other
aim miscarry.   242. **sort**, turn out.   245. **injuries**, insults.   247. **inwardness**, close friendship.   251. **Being
that**, seeing that, since.   **flow in**, overflow with.   254.
For . . . cure, strange diseases require strange and
desperate cures.   256. **prolong'd**, deferred, put off.

  Bene. Lady Beatrice, have you wept all this while?
  Beat. Yea, and I will weep a while longer.
  Bene. I will not desire that.
  Beat. You have no reason; I do it freely. 260
  Bene. Surely I do believe your fair cousin is wronged.
  Beat. Ah, how much might the man de-serve of me that would right her!
  Bene. Is there any way to show such friendship?
  Beat. A very even way, but no such friend.
  Bene. May a man do it?
  Beat. It is a man's office, but not yours.
  Bene. I do love nothing in the world so well as you: is not that strange?   270
  Beat. As strange as the thing I know not. It were as possible for me to say I love nothing so well as you: but believe me not; and yet I lie not; I confess nothing, nor I deny nothing. I am sorry for my cousin.
  Bene. By my sword, Beatrice, thou lovest me.
  Beat. Do not swear, and eat it.
  Bene. I will swear by it that you love me; and I will make him eat it that says I love not you.
  Beat. Will you not eat your word?   280
  Bene. With no sauce that can be devised to it. I protest I love thee.
  Beat. Why, then, God forgive me!
  Bene. What offence, sweet Beatrice?
  Beat. You have stayed me in a happy hour: I was about to protest I loved you.
  Bene. And do it with all thy heart.
  Beat. I love you with so much of my heart that none is left to protest.
  Bene. Come, bid me do any thing for thee.
  Beat. Kill Claudio.   291
  Bene. Ha! not for the wide world.
  Beat. You kill me to deny it. Farewell.
  Bene. Tarry, sweet Beatrice.
  Beat. I am gone, though I am here: there is no love in you: nay, I pray you, let me go.
  Bene. Beatrice,—
  Beat. In faith, I will go.
  Bene. We'll be friends first.
  Beat. You dare easier be friends with me than fight with mine enemy.   301
  Bene. Is Claudio thine enemy?

266. **even**, plain, straightforward.   285. **in a happy
hour**, at an appropriate moment.   291. **Kill Claudio.**
This is a famous climax both in character and plot.
295. **gone**, i.e., in spirit.

Beat. Is he not approved in the height
a villain, that hath slandered, scorned, dis-
honoured my kinswoman? O that I were a
man! What, bear her in hand until they
come to take hands; and then, with public
accusation, uncovered slander, unmitigated
rancour,—O God, that I were a man! I
would eat his heart in the market-place.

Bene. Hear me, Beatrice,—   310

Beat. Talk with a man out at a window!
A proper saying!

Bene. Nay, but, Beatrice,—

Beat. Sweet Hero! She is wronged, she is
slandered, she is undone.

Bene. Beat—   316

Beat. Princes and counties! Surely, a
princely testimony, a goodly count, Count
Comfect; a sweet gallant, surely! O that I
were a man for his sake! or that I had any
friend would be a man for my sake! But manhood is melted into courtesies, valour into
compliment, and men are only turned into
tongue, and trim ones too: he is now as
valiant as Hercules that only tells a lie
and swears it. I cannot be a man with
wishing, therefore I will die a woman with
grieving.

Bene. Tarry, good Beatrice. By this
hand, I love thee.

Beat. Use it for my love some other way
than swearing by it.   330

Bene. Think you in your soul the Count
Claudio hath wronged Hero?

Beat. Yea, as sure as I have a thought or a
soul.

Bene. Enough, I am engaged; I will challenge him. I will kiss your hand, and so I
leave you. By this hand, Claudio shall render me a dear account. As you hear of me, so
think of me. Go, comfort your cousin: I must
say she is dead: and so, farewell. [*Exeunt.*

Scene II. *A prison.*

Enter Dogberry, Verges, *and* Sexton, *in
gowns; and the* Watch, *with* Conrade
and Borachio.

Dog. Is our whole dissembly appeared?

Verg. O, a stool and a cushion for the
sexton.

Sex. Which be the malefactors?

Dog. Marry, that am I and my partner.

Verg. Nay, that's certain; we have the exhibition to examine.

Sex. But which are the offenders that are
to be examined? let them come before master
constable.

Dog. Yea, marry, let them come before
me. What is your name, friend?   11

Bora. Borachio.

Dog. Pray, write down, Borachio. Yours,
sirrah?

Con. I am a gentleman, sir, and my name
is Conrade.

Dog. Write down, master gentleman Conrade. Masters, do you serve God?

Con. } Yea, sir, we hope.   19
Bora. }

Dog. Write down, that they hope they
serve God: and write God first; for God defend but God should go before such villains!
Masters, it is proved already that you are
little better than false knaves; and it will go
near to be thought so shortly. How answer
you for yourselves?

Con. Marry, sir, we say we are none.

Dog. A marvellous witty fellow, I assure
you; but I will go about with him. Come
you hither, sirrah; a word in your ear: sir, I
say to you, it is thought you are false knaves.

Bora. Sir, I say to you we are none.   31

Dog. Well, stand aside. 'Fore God, they
are both in a tale. Have you writ down, that
they are none?

Sex. Master constable, you go not the
way to examine: you must call forth the
watch that are their accusers.

Dog. Yea, marry, that's the eftest way.
Let the watch come forth. Masters, I charge
you, in the prince's name, accuse these men.

303. **in the height**, in the extreme. 306. **bear her in
hand**, delude with false hopes. 308. **uncovered**, open,
unconcealed. 317. **counties**, counts. 318. **count**, play
on the title and the meaning, "declaration of complaint
in an indictment." **Comfect**, comfit, sweetmeat. 323.
trim, nice (used ironically). 334. **Enough . . . engaged**.
It is of course the deeper issue over Hero's wrongs which
brings Beatrice and Benedick together and not the
absurd trick which had been played on them. 336.
this hand, i.e., Beatrice's hand.
Scene ii. The stage direction here is Capell's. QF
have *Enter the Constables, Borachio and the Towne clearke
in gownes.* Throughout the scene in Q Dogberry's lines
are given to *Kemp* (spelled variously) except that the
speech beginning in line 4 is given to *Andrew*, and the one
beginning in line 69 to *Const.* Verges's speeches are
headed *Cowley* or *Couley* except that in line 53 where he is
Const. Will Kemp and Richard Cowley were actors in
Shakespeare's company. The appearance of the actors'
names in this one scene may indicate that it is an addition to the play as originally written. 1. **dissembly**,
blunder for *assembly.* 5. **exhibition**, possibly for *commission* or *examination* (to exhibit). 14. **sirrah**, title of
address used to inferiors; Conrade resents it. 24. **go
near to**, almost. 27. **witty**, clever, cunning. 28. **go
about with**, get the better of. 33. **in a tale**, in agreement. 38. **eftest**, an unexplained blunder of Dogberry's; it apparently means "most convenient."

First Watch. This man said, sir, that Don John, the prince's brother, was a villain. 42

Dog. Write down Prince John a villain. Why, this is flat perjury, to call a prince's brother villain.

Bora. Master constable,—

Dog. Pray thee, fellow, peace: I do not like thy look, I promise thee.

Sex. What heard you him say else?

Sec. Watch. Marry, that he had received a thousand ducats of Don John for accusing the Lady Hero wrongfully. 51

Dog. Flat burglary as ever was committed.

Verg. Yea, by mass, that it is.

Sex. What else, fellow?

First Watch. And that Count Claudio did mean, upon his words, to disgrace Hero before the whole assembly, and not marry her.

Dog. O villain! thou wilt be condemned into everlasting redemption for this.

Sex. What else? 60

Watch. This is all.

Sex. And this is more, masters, than you can deny. Prince John is this morning secretly stolen away; Hero was in this manner accused, in this very manner refused, and upon the grief of this suddenly died. Master constable, let these men be bound, and brought to Leonato's: I will go before and show him their examination. [*Exit.*

Dog. Come, let them be opinioned.

Verg. †Let them be in the hands— 70

Con. Off, coxcomb!

Dog. God's my life, where's the sexton? let him write down the prince's officer coxcomb. Come, bind them. Thou naughty varlet! 74

Con. Away! you are an ass, you are an ass.

Dog. Dost thou not suspect my place? dost thou not suspect my years? O that he were here to write me down an ass! But, masters, remember that I am an ass; though it be not written down, yet forget not that I am an ass. No, thou villain, thou art full of piety, as shall be proved upon thee by good witness. I am a wise fellow, and, which is more, an officer, and, which is more, a householder, and, which is more, as pretty a piece of flesh as any is in Messina, and one that knows the law, go to; and a rich fellow enough, go to;

and a fellow that hath had losses, and one that hath two gowns and every thing handsome about him. Bring him away. O that I had been writ down an ass! [*Exeunt.*

ACT V.

Scene I. *Before* Leonato's *house.*

Enter Leonato *and* Antonio.

Ant. If you go on thus, you will kill yourself;
And 'tis not wisdom thus to second grief
Against yourself.

Leon.   I pray thee, cease thy counsel,
Which falls into mine ears as profitless
As water in a sieve: give not me counsel;
Nor let no comforter delight mine ear
But such a one whose wrongs do suit with mine.
Bring me a father that so loved his child,
Whose joy of her is overwhelm'd like mine,
And bid him speak of patience; 10
Measure his woe the length and breadth of mine
And let it answer every strain for strain,
As thus for thus and such a grief for such,
In every lineament, branch, shape, and form:
If such a one will smile and stroke his beard,
†Bid sorrow wag, cry 'hem!' when he should groan,
Patch grief with proverbs, make misfortune drunk
With candle-wasters; bring him yet to me,
And I of him will gather patience.
But there is no such man: for, brother, men 20
Can counsel and speak comfort to that grief
Which they themselves not feel; but, tasting it,
Their counsel turns to passion, which before
Would give preceptial medicine to rage,
Fetter strong madness in a silken thread,
Charm ache with air and agony with words:
No, no; 'tis all men's office to speak patience
To those that wring under the load of sorrow,
But no man's virtue nor sufficiency

---

69. **opinioned**, for *pinioned*. 74. **naughty**, wicked. 76. **suspect**, for *respect*. 81. **piety**, for *impiety*. 84. **householder**, head of a house. 85. **piece of flesh**, sample of humanity.

Act V. *Scene i.* 2-3. **second . . . yourself**, encourage grief which will destroy you. 7. **suit**, agree, accord. 12. **strain**, strong impulse or motion of the mind. 18. **candle-wasters**, those who waste candles by late study; bookworms; also explained as revelers. **yet**, why then, or, yet if you do (find such a man, bring him to me). 24. **preceptial medicine**, medicine consisting of precepts. 26. **air**, mere breath. 28. **wring**, writhe. 29. **sufficiency**, ability, power.

To be so moral when he shall endure   30
The like himself. Therefore give me no
   counsel:
My griefs cry louder than advertisement.
  Ant. Therein do men from children
   nothing differ.
  Leon. I pray thee, peace. I will be flesh
   and blood;
For there was never yet philosopher
That could endure the toothache patiently,
However they have writ the style of gods
And made a push at chance and sufferance.
  Ant. Yet bend not all the harm upon your-
   self;
Make those that do offend you suffer too.   40
  Leon. There thou speak'st reason: nay, I
   will do so.
My soul doth tell me Hero is belied;
And that shall Claudio know; so shall the
   prince
And all of them that thus dishonour her.
  Ant. Here comes the prince and Claudio
   hastily.

    Enter Don Pedro *and* Claudio.

  D. Pedro. Good den, good den.
  Claud.   Good day to both of you.
  Leon. Hear you, my lords,—
  D. Pedro. We have some haste, Leonato.
  Leon. Some haste, my lord! well, fare you
   well, my lord:
Are you so hasty now? well, all is one.
  D. Pedro. Nay, do not quarrel with us,
   good old man.   50
  Ant. If he could right himself with quar-
   relling,
Some of us would lie low.
  Claud.   Who wrongs him?
  Leon. Marry, thou dost wrong me; thou
   dissembler, thou:—
Nay, never lay thy hand upon thy sword;
I fear thee not.
  Claud.   Marry, beshrew my hand,
If it should give your age such cause of fear:
In faith, my hand meant nothing to my
   sword.

30. **moral,** prone to moralizing. 32. **advertisement,**
advice, counsel. 37. **style of,** language worthy of. 38.
push, alternative form of *pish,* expressive of indignation
or contempt. **sufferance,** suffering. 49. **now,** possibly
expletive, meaning "after all that has happened," or
"after my daughter is dead." It has been thought to refer
to Don Pedro's promise to stay a month. **all is one,** it
makes no difference. 53. **thou,** used contemptuously
instead of the more polite *you.* 55. **beshrew,** curse. 57.
my hand . . . sword, I had no intention of using my
sword.

  Leon. Tush, tush, man; never fleer and
   jest at me:
I speak not like a dotard nor a fool,
As under privilege of age to brag   60
What I have done being young, or what
   would do
Were I not old. Know, Claudio, to thy head,
Thou hast so wrong'd mine innocent child
   and me
That I am forced to lay my reverence by
And, with grey hairs and bruise of many
   days,
Do challenge thee to trial of a man.
I say thou hast belied mine innocent child;
Thy slander hath gone through and through
   her heart,
And she lies buried with her ancestors;
O, in a tomb where never scandal slept,   70
Save this of hers, framed by thy villany!
  Claud. My villany?
  Leon.   Thine, Claudio; thine, I say.
  D. Pedro. You say not right, old man.
  Leon.   My lord, my lord,
I'll prove it on his body, if he dare,
Despite his nice fence and his active practice,
His May of youth and bloom of lustihood.
  Claud. Away! I will not have to do with
   you.
  Leon. Canst thou so daff me? Thou hast
   kill'd my child:
If thou kill'st me, boy, thou shalt kill a
   man.
  Ant. He shall kill two of us, and men in-
   deed: 80
But that's no matter; let him kill one first;
Win me and wear me; let him answer me.
Come, follow me, boy; come, sir boy, come,
   follow me:
Sir boy, I'll whip you from your foining
   fence;
Nay, as I am a gentleman, I will.
  Leon. Brother,—
  Ant. Content yourself. God knows I
   loved my niece;
And she is dead, slander'd to death by vil-
   lains,
That dare as well answer a man indeed
As I dare take a serpent by the tongue: 90
Boys, apes, braggarts, Jacks, milksops!
  Leon.   Brother Antony,—

58. **fleer,** sneer (with pretended humility). 62.
to thy head, to thy face. 75. **nice fence,** dexterous
swordsmanship. 76. **lustihood,** bodily vigor. 78.
daff, put off. 82. **Win . . . me,** proverbial expression.
answer me, i.e., in a duel. 84. **foining,** thrusting.

Ant. Hold you content. What, man! I
know them, yea,
And what they weigh, even to the utmost
scruple,— 93
Scambling, out-facing, fashion-monging boys,
That lie and cog and flout, deprave and slander,
Go anticly, show outward hideousness,
And speak off half a dozen dangerous words,
How they might hurt their enemies, if they
durst;
And this is all.
Leon. But, brother Antony,—
Ant. Come, 'tis no matter: 100
Do not you meddle; let me deal in this.
D. Pedro. Gentlemen both, we will not
wake your patience.
My heart is sorry for your daughter's death:
But, on my honour, she was charged with
nothing
But what was true and very full of proof.
Leon. My lord, my lord,—
D. Pedro. I will not hear you.
Leon. No? Come, brother; away! I will
be heard.
Ant. And shall, or some of us will smart
for it. [*Exeunt Leonato and Antonio.*
D. Pedro. See, see; here comes the man we
went to seek. 110

Enter BENEDICK.

Claud. Now, signior, what news?
Bene. Good day, my lord.
D. Pedro. Welcome, signior: you are almost come to part almost a fray.
Claud. We had like to have had our two
noses snapped off with two old men without
teeth.
D. Pedro. Leonato and his brother. What
thinkest thou? Had we fought, I doubt we
should have been too young for them.
Bene. In a false quarrel there is no true
valour. I came to seek you both. 121
Claud. We have been up and down to seek
thee; for we are high-proof melancholy and
would fain have it beaten away. Wilt thou
use thy wit?
Bene. It is in my scabbard: shall I draw it?
D. Pedro. Dost thou wear thy wit by
thy side? 126

Claud. Never any did so, though very
many have been beside their wit. I will bid
thee draw, as we do the minstrels; draw, to
pleasure us.
D. Pedro. As I am an honest man, he
looks pale. Art thou sick, or angry? 131
Claud. What, courage, man! What
though care killed a cat, thou hast mettle
enough in thee to kill care.
Bene. Sir, I shall meet your wit in the
career, an you charge it against me. I pray
you choose another subject.
Claud. Nay, then, give him another staff:
this last was broke cross.
D. Pedro. By this light, he changes more
and more: I think he be angry indeed. 141
Claud. If he be, he knows how to turn his
girdle.
Bene. Shall I speak a word in your ear?
Claud. God bless me from a challenge!
Bene. [*Aside to Claudio*] You are a villain;
I jest not: I will make it good how you dare,
with what you dare, and when you dare. Do
me right, or I will protest your cowardice.
You have killed a sweet lady, and her death
shall fall heavy on you. Let me hear from
you. 151
Claud. Well, I will meet you, so I may
have good cheer.
D. Pedro. What, a feast, a feast?
Claud. I' faith, I thank him; he hath bid
me to a calf's head and a capon; the which if
I do not carve most curiously, say my
knife's naught. Shall I not find a woodcock
too?
Bene. Sir, your wit ambles well; it goes
easily. 159
D. Pedro. I'll tell thee how Beatrice
praised thy wit the other day. I said, thou
hadst a fine wit: 'True,' said she, 'a fine little
one.' 'No,' said I, 'a great wit:' 'Right,' says
she, 'a great gross one.' 'Nay,' said I, 'a good
wit:' 'Just,' said she, 'it hurts nobody.'
'Nay,' said I, 'the gentleman is wise:' 'Certain,' said she, 'a wise gentleman.' 'Nay,'

128. **beside their wit**, out of their wits. 129. **draw**, draw as a bow across a fiddle. 136. **career**, short gallop at full speed (as in tourney). **charge**, level (as a weapon). 138. **staff**, spear-shaft. 139. **broke cross**, i.e., by clumsily allowing the spear to break crosswise against his opponent's shield. 142. **turn his girdle**, explained as shifting his girdle about so that he can reach his dagger; also as a reference to wrestling, since wrestlers turned the buckles of their girdles to the back before beginning. 147-148. **Do me right**, give me satisfaction. **protest**, proclaim before witnesses. 156-158. **calf's head**, capon, **woodcock**, used as types of dullness. 157. **curiously**, daintily.

94. **Scambling**, contentious. **out-facing**, swaggering. **fashion-monging**, dandified. 95. **cog**, cheat. **deprave**, detract, traduce. 96. **anticly**, fantastically. 97. **dangerous**, threatening, haughty. 102. **wake your patience**, put your patience to any test. 123. **high-proof**, to the highest degree.

said I, 'he hath the tongues:' 'That I believe,' said she, 'for he swore a thing to me
on Monday night, which he forswore on
Tuesday morning; there's a double tongue;
there's two tongues.' Thus did she, an hour
together, trans-shape thy particular virtues:
yet at last she concluded with a sigh, thou
wast the properest man in Italy.   174

Claud. For the which she wept heartily
and said she cared not.

D. Pedro. Yea, that she did; but yet, for
all that, an if she did not hate him deadly, she
would love him dearly: the old man's
daughter told us all.   180

Claud. All, all; and, moreover, God saw
him when he was hid in the garden.

D. Pedro. But when shall we set the
savage bull's horns on the sensible Benedick's
head?

Claud. Yea, and text underneath, 'Here
dwells Benedick the married man'?   186

Bene. Fare you well, boy: you know my
mind. I will leave you now to your gossip-
like humour: you break jests as braggarts do
their blades, which, God be thanked, hurt
not. My lord, for your many courtesies I
thank you: I must discontinue your company: your brother the bastard is fled from
Messina: you have among you killed a sweet
and innocent lady. For my Lord Lackbeard
there, he and I shall meet: and, till then,
peace be with him.   [*Exit.*

D. Pedro. He is in earnest.

Claud. In most profound earnest; and,
I'll warrant you, for the love of Beatrice.

D. Pedro. And hath challenged thee.   200

Claud. Most sincerely.

D. Pedro. What a pretty thing man is
when he goes in his doublet and hose and
leaves off his wit!

Claud. He is then a giant to an ape; but
then is an ape a doctor to such a man.

D. Pedro. But, soft you, let me be: pluck
up, my heart, and be sad. Did he not say,
my brother was fled?   209

Enter DOGBERRY, VERGES, *and the* Watch,
with CONRADE *and* BORACHIO.

Dog. Come you, sir: if justice cannot tame
you, she shall ne'er weigh more reasons in her
balance: nay, an you be a cursing hypocrite
once, you must be looked to.

D. Pedro. How now? two of my brother's
men bound! Borachio one!   215

Claud. Hearken after their offence, my
lord.

D. Pedro. Officers, what offence have these
men done?

Dog. Marry, sir, they have committed
false report; moreover, they have spoken
untruth; secondarily, they are slanders;
sixth and lastly, they have belied a lady;
thirdly, they have verified unjust things;
and, to conclude, they are lying knaves.   224

D. Pedro. First, I ask thee what they have
done; thirdly, I ask thee what's their offence; sixth and lastly, why they are committed; and, to conclude, what you lay to
their charge.

Claud. Rightly reasoned, and in his own
division; and, by my troth, there's one meaning well suited.   231

D. Pedro. Who have you offended, masters, that you are thus bound to your answer?
this learned constable is too cunning to be
understood: what's your offence?

Bora. Sweet prince, let me go no farther
to mine answer: do you hear me, and let this
count kill me. I have deceived even your
very eyes: what your wisdoms could not discover, these shallow fools have brought to
light; who in the night overheard me confessing to this man how Don John your
brother incensed me to slander the Lady
Hero, how you were brought into the orchard
and saw me court Margaret in Hero's garments, how you disgraced her, when you
should marry her: my villany they have
upon record; which I had rather seal with my
death than repeat over to my shame. The
lady is dead upon mine and my master's
false accusation; and, briefly, I desire
nothing but the reward of a villain.   251

D. Pedro. Runs not this speech like iron
through your blood?

---

167. **hath the tongues,** is a linguist. 172. **trans-
shape,** distort, turn the wrong side out. 174. **properest,**
finest. 189-190. **as . . . blades,** possibly, getting their
blades broken without harming themselves. 202-204.
What . . . wit! Doublet and hose formed the Elizabethan under-costume, a cloak being worn over them
on formal occasions. The Prince possibly means to suggest that man's wit is like a cloak which he can leave
off, and go about in his natural stupidity. 205-206.
He . . . man. He is superior to an ape in stature, but
an ape is superior to him in wit. 206. **doctor,** learned
man. 207. **soft you,** gently! **pluck up,** rouse thyself.

216. **Hearken after,** inquire into. 221. **slanders,** for
slanderers. 223. **verified,** for *testified to.* 231. **well
suited,** put into many different dresses (Johnson). 233.
bound, play on the meanings "pinioned" and "headed
for a destination." **answer,** trial, account. 242. **incensed,** instigated. 249. **upon,** in consequence of.

Claud. I have drunk poison whiles he utter'd it.

D. Pedro. But did my brother set thee on to this?

Bora. Yea, and paid me richly for the practice of it.

D. Pedro. He is composed and framed of treachery:
And fled he is upon this villany.

Claud. Sweet Hero! now thy image doth appear   259
In the rare semblance that I loved it first.

Dog. Come, bring away the plaintiffs: by this time our sexton hath reformed Signior Leonato of the matter: and, masters, do not forget to specify, when time and place shall serve, that I am an ass.

Verg. Here, here comes master Signior Leonato, and the sexton too.

Re-enter LEONATO *and* ANTONIO, *with the* Sexton.

Leon. Which is the villain? let me see his eyes,   269
That, when I note another man like him,
I may avoid him: which of these is he?

Bora. If you would know your wronger, look on me.

Leon. Art thou the slave that with thy breath hast kill'd
Mine innocent child?

Bora.   Yea, even I alone.

Leon. No, not so, villain; thou beliest thyself:
Here stand a pair of honourable men;
A third is fled, that had a hand in it.
I thank you, princes, for my daughter's death:
Record it with your high and worthy deeds:
'Twas bravely done, if you bethink you of it.

Claud. I know not how to pray your patience;   281
Yet I must speak. Choose your revenge yourself;
Impose me to what penance your invention
Can lay upon my sin: yet sinn'd I not
But in mistaking.

D. Pedro.   By my soul, nor I:
And yet, to satisfy this good old man,

I would bend under any heavy weight
That he'll enjoin me to.

Leon. I cannot bid you bid my daughter live;
That were impossible: but, I pray you both,
Possess the people in Messina here   291
How innocent she died; and if your love
Can labour aught in sad invention,
Hang her an epitaph upon her tomb
And sing it to her bones, sing it to-night:
To-morrow morning come you to my house,
And since you could not be my son-in-law,
Be yet my nephew: my brother hath a daughter,
Almost the copy of my child that's dead,
And she alone is heir to both of us: 300
Give her the right you should have given her cousin,
And so dies my revenge.

Claud.   O noble sir,
Your over-kindness doth wring tears from me!
I do embrace your offer; and dispose
For henceforth of poor Claudio.

Leon. To-morrow then I will expect your coming;
To-night I take my leave. This naughty man
Shall face to face be brought to Margaret,
Who I believe was pack'd in all this wrong,
Hired to it by your brother.

Bora.   No, by my soul, she was not,
Nor knew not what she did when she spoke to me,   311
But always hath been just and virtuous
In any thing that I do know by her.

Dog. Moreover, sir, which indeed is not under white and black, this plaintiff here, the offender, did call me ass: I beseech you, let it be remembered in his punishment. And also, the watch heard them talk of one Deformed: they say he wears a key in his ear and a lock hanging by it, and borrows money in God's name, the which he hath used so long and never paid that now men grow hard-hearted and will lend nothing for God's sake: pray you, examine him upon that point.

Leon. I thank thee for thy care and honest pains.

Dog. Your worship speaks like a most thankful and reverend youth; and I praise God for you.

Leon. There's for thy pains.

Dog. God save the foundation!

Leon. Go, I discharge thee of thy prisoner, and I thank thee.   330

Dog. I leave an arrant knave with your worship; which I beseech your worship to correct yourself, for the example of others. God keep your worship well; God restore you to health! I humbly give you leave to depart; and if a merry meeting may be wished, God prohibit it! Come, neighbour.   [*Exeunt Dogberry and Verges.*

Leon. Until to-morrow morning, lords, farewell.

Ant. Farewell, my lords: we look for you to-morrow.

D. Pedro. We will not fail.

Claud.   To-night I'll mourn with Hero.

Leon. [*To the Watch*] Bring you these fellows on. We'll talk with Margaret,   341
How her acquaintance grew with this lewd fellow.   [*Exeunt, severally.*

Scene II.   Leonato's *garden.*

Enter Benedick *and* Margaret, *meeting.*

Bene. Pray thee, sweet Mistress Margaret, deserve well at my hands by helping me to the speech of Beatrice.

Marg. Will you then write me a sonnet in praise of my beauty?

Bene. In so high a style, Margaret, that no man living shall come over it; for, in most comely truth, thou deservest it.

Marg. To have no man come over me! why, shall I always keep below stairs?   10

Bene. Thy wit is as quick as the greyhound's mouth; it catches.

Marg. And yours as blunt as the fencer's foils, which hit, but hurt not.

Bene. A most manly wit, Margaret; it will not hurt a woman: and so, I pray thee, call Beatrice: I give thee the bucklers.

Marg. Give us the swords; we have bucklers of our own.   19

Bene. If you use them, Margaret, you must put in the pikes with a vice; and they are dangerous weapons for maids.

Marg. Well, I will call Beatrice to you, who I think hath legs.

Bene. And therefore will come.

[*Exit Margaret.*

[*Sings*]   The god of love,
That sits above,
And knows me, and knows me,
How pitiful I deserve,—   29
I mean in singing; but in loving, Leander the good swimmer, Troilus the first employer of pandars, and a whole bookful of these quondam carpet-mongers, whose names yet run smoothly in the even road of a blank verse, why, they were never so truly turned over and over as my poor self in love. Marry, I cannot show it in rhyme; I have tried: I can find out no rhyme to 'lady' but 'baby,' an innocent rhyme; for 'scorn,' 'horn,' a hard rhyme; for 'school,' 'fool,' a babbling rhyme; very ominous endings: no, I was not born under a rhyming planet, nor I cannot woo in festival terms.   41

Enter Beatrice.

Sweet Beatrice, wouldst thou come when I called thee?

Beat. Yea, signior, and depart when you bid me.

Bene. O, stay but till then!

Beat. 'Then' is spoken; fare you well now: and yet, ere I go, let me go with that I came; which is, with knowing what hath passed between you and Claudio.

Bene. Only foul words; and thereupon I will kiss thee.   51

Beat. Foul words is but foul wind, and foul wind is but foul breath, and foul breath is noisome; therefore I will depart unkissed.

Bene. Thou hast frighted the word out of his right sense, so forcible is thy wit. But I must tell thee plainly, Claudio undergoes my challenge; and either I must shortly hear

---

328. **God . . . foundation!** formula of those who received alms at religious houses.   342. **lewd,** wicked, worthless.

Scene ii.   6. **style,** play on the critical phrase for epic grandeur, "a high *style,*" and the word *stile.*   8. **comely,** good, with allusion to Margaret's beauty.   17. **I . . . bucklers,** I acknowledge myself beaten (in repartee).

21. **pikes,** spikes in the center of a shield.   **vice,** screw.   26-29. **The god . . . deserve,** beginning of an old song by William Elderton (Ritson).   30. **Leander.** The tale of Hero and Leander (from the Greek of Musæus?) had been written in part by Marlowe and completed and published by Chapman shortly before the date of this play (1598).   31. **Troilus,** hero of the tale of Troilus and Cressida.   Both he and Leander are stock examples of faithful lovers.   32-33. **quondam carpet-mongers,** ancient carpet-knights.   38. **innocent,** silly.   41. **festival terms,** fanciful language (suitable for festivals).   56. **his,** its.

from him, or I will subscribe him a coward.
And, I pray thee now, tell me for which of
my bad parts didst thou first fall in love with
me?   61

Beat. For them all together; which maintained so politic a state of evil that they will
not admit any good part to intermingle with
them. But for which of my good parts did
you first suffer love for me?   66

Bene. Suffer love! a good epithet! I do
suffer love indeed, for I love thee against my
will.

Beat. In spite of your heart, I think; alas,
poor heart! If you spite it for my sake, I
will spite it for yours; for I will never love
that which my friend hates.

Bene. Thou and I are too wise to woo
peaceably.

Beat. It appears not in this confession:
there's not one wise man among twenty that
will praise himself.   77

Bene. An old, an old instance, Beatrice,
that lived in the time of good neighbours. If
a man do not erect in this age his own tomb
ere he dies, he shall live no longer in monument than the bell rings and the widow
weeps.

Beat. And how long is that, think you?

Bene. Question: why, an hour in clamour
and a quarter in rheum: therefore is it most
expedient for the wise, if Don Worm, his conscience, find no impediment to the contrary,
to be the trumpet of his own virtues, as I am
to myself. So much for praising myself, who,
I myself will bear witness, is praiseworthy:
and now tell me, how doth your cousin?   91

Beat. Very ill.

Bene. And how do you?

Beat. Very ill too.

Bene. Serve God, love me and mend.
There will I leave you too, for here comes
one in haste.   96

Enter URSULA.

Urs. Madam, you must come to your
uncle. Yonder's old coil at home: it is proved
my Lady Hero hath been falsely accused, the
prince and Claudio mightily abused; and

---

59. **subscribe,** formally proclaim.   63. **politic,**
prudently governed.   67. **epithet,** expression.   79.
time . . . neighbours, good old times (when one's
neighbors spoke well of one).   84. **Question,** that is
the question. **clamour,** noise (of the bell).   85. **rheum,**
tears (of the widow).   86-87. **Don . . . conscience.** The
action of the conscience was traditionally described (in
the morality plays, etc.) as the gnawing of a worm; *St.
Mark,* ix, 48.   98. **old coil,** great disturbance.   100.
abused, deceived.

Don John is the author of all, who is fled and
gone. Will you come presently?

Beat. Will you go hear this news, signior?

Bene. I will live in thy heart, die in thy
lap and be buried in thy eyes; and moreover
I will go with thee to thy uncle's.   [*Exeunt.*

SCENE III. *A church.*

Enter DON PEDRO, CLAUDIO, *and three or
four with tapers.*

Claud. Is this the monument of Leonato?

A Lord. It is, my lord.

Claud. [*Reading out of a scroll*]

> Done to death by slanderous tongues
>   Was the Hero that here lies:
> Death, in guerdon of her wrongs,
>   Gives her fame which never dies.
> So the life that died with shame
> Lives in death with glorious fame.

Hang thou there upon the tomb,
    Praising her when I am dumb.   10
Now, music, sound, and sing your solemn
    hymn.

SONG.

> Pardon, goddess of the night,
>   Those that slew thy virgin knight;
> For the which, with songs of woe,
>   Round about her tomb they go.
>   Midnight, assist our moan;
>   Help us to sigh and groan,
>   Heavily, heavily:
>   Graves, yawn and yield your dead,
>   Till death be uttered,   20
>   Heavily, heavily.

Claud. Now, unto thy bones good night!
    Yearly will I do this rite.

D. Pedro. Good morrow, masters; put
    your torches out:
The wolves have prey'd; and look, the
    gentle day,
Before the wheels of Phœbus, round about
Dapples the drowsy east with spots of
    grey.
Thanks to you all, and leave us: fare you
    well.

Claud. Good morrow, masters: each his
    several way.

D. Pedro. Come, let us hence, and put on
    other weeds;   30
And then to Leonato's we will go.

Scene iii. 5. **guerdon,** recompense.   20. **uttered,**
sent abroad, put into circulation.   25. **have prey'd,**
have ceased preying.   30. **weeds,** garments.

Claud. And Hymen now with luckier
      issue speed's
Than this for whom we render'd up this
      woe.   [*Exeunt.*

SCENE IV. *A room in* LEONATO'S *house.*

Enter LEONATO, ANTONIO, BENEDICK, BEA-
TRICE, MARGARET, URSULA, FRIAR FRAN-
CIS, *and* HERO.

Friar. Did I not tell you she was innocent?
Leon. So are the prince and Claudio, who
      accused her
Upon the error that you heard debated:
But Margaret was in some fault for this,
Although against her will, as it appears
In the true course of all the question.
    Ant. Well, I am glad that all things sort so
      well.
    Bene. And so am I, being else by faith
      enforced
To call young Claudio to a reckoning for it.
    Leon. Well, daughter, and you gentle-
      women all,   10
Withdraw into a chamber by yourselves,
And when I send for you, come hither
      mask'd.   [*Exeunt Ladies.*
The prince and Claudio promised by this
      hour
To visit me. You know your office, brother:
You must be father to your brother's
      daughter,
And give her to young Claudio.
    Ant. Which I will do with confirm'd coun-
      tenance.
    Bene. Friar, I must entreat your pains, I
      think.
    Friar. To do what, signior?
    Bene. To bind me, or undo me; one of
      them.   20
Signior Leonato, truth it is, good signior,
Your niece regards me with an eye of favour.
    Leon. That eye my daughter lent her: 'tis
      most true.
    Bene. And I do with an eye of love requite
      her.
    Leon. The sight whereof I think you had
      from me,
From Claudio and the prince: but what's
      your will?

Bene. Your answer, sir, is enigmatical:
But, for my will, my will is your good will
May stand with ours, this day to be con-
      join'd
In the state of honourable marriage: 30
In which, good friar, I shall desire your help.
    Leon. My heart is with your liking.
    Friar.   And my help.
Here comes the prince and Claudio.

Enter DON PEDRO *and* CLAUDIO, *and two or*
                  three others.

    D. Pedro. Good morrow to this fair as-
      sembly.
    Leon. Good morrow, prince; good mor-
      row, Claudio:
We here attend you. Are you yet deter-
      mined
To-day to marry with my brother's daugh-
      ter?
    Claud. I'll hold my mind, were she an
      Ethiope.
    Leon. Call her forth, brother; here's the
      friar ready.   [*Exit Antonio.*
    D. Pedro. Good morrow, Benedick. Why,
      what's the matter,   40
That you have such a February face,
So full of frost, of storm and cloudiness?
    Claud. I think he thinks upon the savage
      bull.
Tush, fear not, man; we'll tip thy horns with
      gold
And all Europa shall rejoice at thee,
As once Europa did at lusty Jove,
When he would play the noble beast in love.
    Bene. Bull Jove, sir, had an amiable low;
And some such strange bull leap'd your
      father's cow,
And got a calf in that same noble feat   50
Much like to you, for you have just his bleat.
    Claud. For this I owe you: here comes
      other reckonings.

Re-enter ANTONIO, *with the* Ladies *masked.*

Which is the lady I must seize upon?
    Ant. This same is she, and I do give you
      her.
    Claud. Why, then she's mine. Sweet, let
      me see your face.

32. **speed's**, favor or speed us.
Scene iv. 6. **question**, investigation. 7. **sort**, turn
out, eventuate. 8. **by faith**, i.e., by his promise to
Beatrice. 17. **confirm'd**, grave, unmoved. 20. **undo**,
ruin, with play on the meaning "untie" or "unbind."

43. **I think . . . bull**, a jocular reminiscence of the
conversation in I, i, 263 ff. (See also V, i, 83-84.) 45.
Europa, Europe. 46. **Europa**, a reference to the story
of Jove's infatuation for Europa, whom he approached
in the form of a white bull and bore on his back through
the sea to the island of Crete. 52. **owe you**, i.e., an
answer.

Leon. No, that you shall not, till you take her hand
Before this friar and swear to marry her.

Claud. Give me your hand: before this holy friar,
I am your husband, if you like of me.

Hero. And when I lived, I was your other wife: [*Unmasking.*   60
And when you loved, you were my other husband.

Claud. Another Hero!

Hero.   Nothing certainer:
One Hero died defiled, but I do live,
And surely as I live, I am a maid.

D. Pedro. The former Hero! Hero that is dead!

Leon. She died, my lord, but whiles her slander lived.

Friar. All this amazement can I qualify;
When after that the holy rites are ended,
I'll tell you largely of fair Hero's death:
Meantime let wonder seem familiar,   70
And to the chapel let us presently.

Bene. Soft and fair, friar. Which is Beatrice?

Beat. [*Unmasking*] I answer to that name. What is your will?

Bene. Do not you love me?

Beat.   Why, no; no more than reason.

Bene. Why, then your uncle and the prince and Claudio
Have been deceived; they swore you did.

Beat. Do not you love me?

Bene.   Troth, no; no more than reason.

Beat. Why, then my cousin Margaret and Ursula
Are much deceived; for they did swear you did.

Bene. They swore that you were almost sick for me.   80

Beat. They swore that you were well-nigh dead for me.

Bene. 'Tis no such matter. Then you do not love me?

Beat. No, truly, but in friendly recompense.

Leon. Come, cousin, I am sure you love the gentleman.

Claud. And I'll be sworn upon 't that he loves her;
For here's a paper written in his hand,
A halting sonnet of his own pure brain,
Fashion'd to Beatrice.

Hero.   And here's another
Writ in my cousin's hand, stolen from her pocket,
Containing her affection unto Benedick.   90

Bene. A miracle! here's our own hands against our hearts. Come, I will have thee; but, by this light, I take thee for pity.

Beat. I would not deny you; but, by this good day, I yield upon great persuasion; and partly to save your life, for I was told you were in a consumption.

Bene. Peace! I will stop your mouth.
            [*Kissing her.*

D. Pedro. How dost thou, Benedick, the married man?   100

Bene. I'll tell thee what, prince; a college of wit-crackers cannot flout me out of my humour. Dost thou think I care for a satire or an epigram? No: if a man will be beaten with brains, a' shall wear nothing handsome about him. In brief, since I do purpose to marry, I will think nothing to any purpose that the world can say against it; and therefore never flout at me for what I have said against it; for man is a giddy thing, and this is my conclusion. For thy part, Claudio, I did think to have beaten thee; but in that thou art like to be my kinsman, live unbruised and love my cousin.   113

Claud. I had well hoped thou wouldst have denied Beatrice, that I might have cudgelled thee out of thy single life, to make thee a double-dealer; which, out of question, thou wilt be, if my cousin do not look exceeding narrowly to thee.

Bene. Come, come, we are friends: let's have a dance ere we are married, that we may lighten our own hearts and our wives' heels.

Leon. We'll have dancing afterward.   122

Bene. First, of my word; therefore play, music. Prince, thou art sad; get thee a wife, get thee a wife: there is no staff more reverend than one tipped with horn.

Enter a Messenger.

Mess. My lord, your brother John is ta'en in flight,
And brought with armed men back to Messina.

Bene. Think not on him till to-morrow: I'll devise thee brave punishments for him. Strike up, pipers.   [*Dance. Exeunt.*

---

59. **like of,** care for.   69. **largely,** at large, in full.
70. **let . . . familiar,** restrain your wonder.   77. **Troth,** by my troth.   87. **his own pure,** purely his own.

104-105. **beaten with brains,** subjected to ridicule.
105-106. **a' shall . . . him,** i.e., so as not to attract attention.   117. **double-dealer,** a married man and also a deceiver.   123. **of,** on.

AS YOU LIKE IT

DRAMATIS PERSONÆ

DUKE, living in banishment.
FREDERICK, his brother, and usurper of his dominions.
AMIENS, } lords attending on the ban-
JAQUES, } ished duke.
LE BEAU, a courtier attending upon Frederick.
CHARLES, wrestler to Frederick.
OLIVER,
JAQUES, } sons of Sir Rowland de Boys.
ORLANDO,
ADAM, } servants to Oliver.
DENNIS,
TOUCHSTONE, a clown.
SIR OLIVER MARTEXT, a vicar.

CORIN, } shepherds.
SILVIUS,
WILLIAM, a country fellow, in love with Audrey.
A person representing Hymen.

ROSALIND, daughter to the banished duke.
CELIA, daughter to Frederick.
PHEBE, a shepherdess.
AUDREY, a country wench.
Lords, pages, and attendants, &c.

SCENE: *Oliver's house; Duke Frederick's court; and the Forest of Arden.*

ACT I.

SCENE I. *Orchard of* OLIVER'S *house.*

Enter ORLANDO *and* ADAM.

Orl. As I remember, Adam, it was upon this fashion; bequeathed me by will but poor a thousand crowns, and, as thou sayest, charged my brother, on his blessing, to breed me well: and there begins my sadness. My brother Jaques he keeps at school, and report speaks goldenly of his profit: for my part, he keeps me rustically at home, or, to speak more properly, stays me here at home unkept; for call you that keeping for a gentleman of my birth, that differs not from the stalling of an ox? His horses are bred better; for, besides that they are fair with their feeding, they are taught their manage, and to that end riders dearly hired: but I, his brother, gain nothing under him but growth; for the which his animals on his dunghills are as much bound to him as I. Besides this nothing that he so plentifully gives me, the something that nature gave me his countenance

seems to take from me: he l ts me feed with his hinds, bars me the place of a brother, and, as much as in him lies, mines my gentility with my education. This is it, Adam, that grieves me; and the spirit of my father, which I think is within me, begins to mutiny against this servitude: I will no longer endure it, though yet I know no wise remedy how to avoid it.

Adam. Yonder comes my master, your brother.

Orl. Go apart, Adam, and thou shalt hear how he will shake me up.   30

Enter OLIVER.

Oli. Now, sir! what make you here?
Orl. Nothing: I am not taught to make any thing.
Oli. What mar you then, sir?
Orl. Marry, sir, I am helping you to mar that which God made, a poor unworthy brother of yours, with idleness.
Oli. Marry, sir, be better employed, and be naught awhile.   39

2. **bequeathed,** he (Orlando's father) bequeathed.
4. **on his blessing,** on pain of losing his blessing. 6. **school,** university. 7. **profit,** progress. 14. **manage,** action or paces of a horse. 20. **countenance,** favor, patronage.

22. **hinds,** servants. **bars me,** excludes me from. 23. **mines,** undermines. 35. **Marry,** by the Virgin Mary, with possible pun on *mar.* 39. **be naught awhile,** a slight malediction; possibly, efface yourself, withdraw.

Orl. Shall I keep your hogs and eat husks with them? What prodigal portion have I spent, that I should come to such penury?

Oli. Know you where you are, sir?

Orl. O, sir, very well: here in your orchard.

Oli. Know you before whom, sir? 45

Orl. Ay, better than him I am before knows me. I know you are my eldest brother; and, in the gentle condition of blood, you should so know me. The courtesy of nations allows you my better, in that you are the first-born; but the same tradition takes not away my blood, were there twenty brothers betwixt us: I have as much of my father in me as you; albeit, I confess, your coming before me is nearer to his reverence.

Oli. What, boy! 55

Orl. Come, come, elder brother, you are too young in this.

Oli. Wilt thou lay hands on me, villain?

Orl. I am no villain; I am the youngest son of Sir Rowland de Boys; he was my father, and he is thrice a villain that says such a father begot villains. Wert thou not my brother, I would not take this hand from thy throat till this other had pulled out thy tongue for saying so: thou hast railed on thyself.

Adam. Sweet masters, be patient: for your father's remembrance, be at accord.

Oli. Let me go, I say. 68

Orl. I will not, till I please: you shall hear me. My father charged you in his will to give me good education: you have trained me like a peasant, obscuring and hiding from me all gentleman-like qualities. The spirit of my father grows strong in me, and I will no longer endure it: therefore allow me such exercises as may become a gentleman, or give me the poor allottery my father left me by testament; with that I will go buy my fortunes. 78

Oli. And what wilt thou do? beg, when that is spent? Well, sir, get you in: I will not

long be troubled with you; you shall have some part of your will: I pray you, leave me.

Orl. I will no further offend you than becomes me for my good.

Oli. Get you with him, you old dog.

Adam. Is 'old dog' my reward? Most true, I have lost my teeth in your service. God be with my old master! he would not have spoke such a word. [*Exeunt Orlando and Adam.* 89

Oli. Is it even so? begin you to grow upon me? I will physic your rankness, and yet give no thousand crowns neither. Holla, Dennis!

Enter DENNIS.

Den. Calls your worship?

Oli. Was not Charles, the duke's wrestler, here to speak with me?

Den. So please you, he is here at the door and importunes access to you.

Oli. Call him in. [*Exit Dennis.*] 'Twill be a good way; and to-morrow the wrestling is.

Enter CHARLES.

Cha. Good morrow to your worship. 100

Oli. Good Monsieur Charles, what's the new news at the new court?

Cha. There's no news at the court, sir, but the old news: that is, the old duke is banished by his younger brother the new duke; and three or four loving lords have put themselves into voluntary exile with him, whose lands and revenues enrich the new duke; therefore he gives them good leave to wander.

Oli. Can you tell if Rosalind, the duke's daughter, be banished with her father? 111

Cha. O, no; for the duke's daughter, her cousin, so loves her, being ever from their cradles bred together, that she would have followed her exile, or have died to stay behind her. She is at the court, and no less beloved of her uncle than his own daughter; and never two ladies loved as they do.

Oli. Where will the old duke live? 119

Cha. They say he is already in the forest of Arden, and a many merry men with him; and they there live like the old Robin Hood of England: they say many young gentlemen flock to him every day, and fleet the time carelessly, as they did in the golden world. 125

Oli. What, you wrestle to-morrow before the new duke?

Cha. Marry, do I, sir; and I came to acquaint you with a matter. I am given, sir, secretly to understand that your younger brother Orlando hath a disposition to come in disguised against me to try a fall. To-morrow, sir, I wrestle for my credit; and he that escapes me without some broken limb shall acquit him well. Your brother is but young and tender; and, for your love, I would be loath to foil him, as I must, for my own honour, if he come in: therefore, out of my love to you, I came hither to acquaint you withal, that either you might stay him from his intendment or brook such disgrace well as he shall run into, in that it is a thing of his own search and altogether against my will. 143

Oli. Charles, I thank thee for thy love to me, which thou shalt find I will most kindly requite. I had myself notice of my brother's purpose herein and have by underhand means laboured to dissuade him from it, but he is resolute. I'll tell thee, Charles: it is the stubbornest young fellow of France, full of ambition, an envious emulator of every man's good parts, a secret and villanous contriver against me his natural brother: therefore use thy discretion; I had as lief thou didst break his neck as his finger. And thou wert best look to 't; for if thou dost him any slight disgrace or if he do not mightily grace himself on thee, he will practise against thee by poison, entrap thee by some treacherous device and never leave thee till he hath ta'en thy life by some indirect means or other; for, I assure thee, and almost with tears I speak it, there is not one so young and so villanous this day living. I speak but brotherly of him; but should I anatomize him to thee as he is, I must blush and weep and thou must look pale and wonder. 167

Cha. I am heartily glad I came hither to you. If he come to-morrow, I'll give him his payment: if ever he go alone again, I'll never wrestle for prize more: and so God keep your worship!

Oli. Farewell, good Charles. [*Exit Charles.*]

Now will I stir this gamester: I hope I shall see an end of him; for my soul, yet I know not why, hates nothing more than he. Yet he's gentle, never schooled and yet learned, full of noble device, of all sorts enchantingly beloved, and indeed so much in the heart of the world, and especially of my own people, who best know him, that I am altogether misprised: but it shall not be so long; this wrestler shall clear all: nothing remains but that I kindle the boy thither; which now I'll go about. [*Exit.* 185

SCENE II. *Lawn before the* Duke's *palace.*

Enter Celia *and* Rosalind.

Cel. I pray thee, Rosalind, sweet my coz, be merry.

Ros. Dear Celia, I show more mirth than I am mistress of; and would you yet I were merrier? Unless you could teach me to forget a banished father, you must not learn me how to remember any extraordinary pleasure.

Cel. Herein I see thou lovest me not with the full weight that I love thee. If my uncle, thy banished father, had banished thy uncle, the duke my father, so thou hadst been still with me, I could have taught my love to take thy father for mine: so wouldst thou, if the truth of thy love to me were so righteously tempered as mine is to thee. 14

Ros. Well, I will forget the condition of my estate, to rejoice in yours.

Cel. You know my father hath no child but I, nor none is like to have: and, truly, when he dies, thou shalt be his heir, for what he hath taken away from thy father perforce, I will render thee again in affection; by mine honour, I will; and when I break that oath, let me turn monster: therefore, my sweet Rose, my dear Rose, be merry.

Ros. From henceforth I will, coz, and devise sports. Let me see; what think you of falling in love?

Cel. Marry, I prithee, do, to make sport withal: but love no man in good earnest; nor

134. shall, will inevitably. 141. intendment, purpose, intent. 147. underhand means, reasonable or quiet methods. 151. emulator, disparager. 152. contriver, plotter. 153. natural brother, brother by blood, legitimate brother. 157. grace himself on thee, distinguish himself at your expense. 158. practise, use artifice or deceit. 164. brotherly, with a reserve proper to a brother. 165. anatomize, lay open in detail, analyze; F: anathomize. 170. payment, punishment.

174. gamester, frolicsome person. 178. noble device, lofty aspiration. sorts, classes of people. enchantingly, as if by the effect of enchantment. 182. misprised, despised. 184. kindle, incite (to go). thither, i.e., to the wrestling match.
Scene ii. 1. sweet my coz, my sweet cousin. 10. so, provided that. 12-14. if the . . . thee, if the composition of your love were really as perfect as mine.

no further in sport neither than with safety of a pure blush thou mayst in honour come off again.   32

Ros. What shall be our sport, then?

Cel. Let us sit and mock the good housewife Fortune from her wheel, that her gifts may henceforth be bestowed equally.

Ros. I would we could do so, for her benefits are mightily misplaced, and the bountiful blind woman doth most mistake in her gifts to women.   39

Cel. 'Tis true; for those that she makes fair she scarce makes honest, and those that she makes honest she makes very ill-favouredly.

Ros. Nay, now thou goest from Fortune's office to Nature's: Fortune reigns in gifts of the world, not in the lineaments of Nature.

Enter TOUCHSTONE.

Cel. No? when Nature hath made a fair creature, may she not by Fortune fall into the fire? Though Nature hath given us wit to flout at Fortune, hath not Fortune sent in this fool to cut off the argument?   50

Ros. Indeed, there is Fortune too hard for Nature, when Fortune makes Nature's natural the cutter-off of Nature's wit.

Cel. Peradventure this is not Fortune's work neither, but Nature's; who perceiveth our natural wits too dull to reason of such goddesses and hath sent this natural for our whetstone; for always the dulness of the fool is the whetstone of the wits. How now, wit! whither wander you?

Touch. Mistress, you must come away to your father.   61

Cel. Were you made the messenger?

Touch. No, by mine honour, but I was bid to come for you.

Ros. Where learned you that oath, fool?

Touch. Of a certain knight that swore by his honour they were good pancakes and swore by his honour the mustard was naught: now I'll stand to it, the pancakes

were naught and the mustard was good, and yet was not the knight forsworn.   71

Cel. How prove you that, in the great heap of your knowledge?

Ros. Ay, marry, now unmuzzle your wisdom.

Touch. Stand you both forth now: stroke your chins, and swear by your beards that I am a knave.

Cel. By our beards, if we had them, thou art.   79

Touch. By my knavery, if I had it, then I were; but if you swear by that that is not, you are not forsworn: no more was this knight, swearing by his honour, for he never had any; or if he had, he had sworn it away before ever he saw those pancakes or that mustard.

Cel. Prithee, who is't that thou meanest?

Touch. One that old Frederick, your father, loves.

Cel. My father's love is enough to honour him: enough! speak no more of him; you'll be whipped for taxation one of these days. 91

Touch. The more pity, that fools may not speak wisely what wise men do foolishly.

Cel. By my troth, thou sayest true; for since the little wit that fools have was silenced, the little foolery that wise men have makes a great show. Here comes Monsieur Le Beau.

Ros. With his mouth full of news.

Cel. Which he will put on us, as pigeons feed their young.   100

Ros. Then shall we be news-crammed.

Cel. All the better; we shall be the more marketable.

Enter LE BEAU.

Bon jour, Monsieur Le Beau: what's the news?

Le Beau. Fair princess, you have lost much good sport.

Cel. Sport! of what colour?

Le Beau. What colour, madam! how shall I answer you?

Ros. As wit and fortune will.   110

Touch. Or as the Destinies decree.

Cel. Well said: that was laid on with a trowel.

Touch. Nay, if I keep not my rank,—

30-31. **safety . . . blush,** a degree of safety costing no more than an innocent blush. **come off,** escape. 34. **housewife,** hussy; an epithet of slight contempt. 42. **ill-favouredly,** ugly, ill-favored. 49. **flout,** mock, scoff at. 53. **natural,** idiot, half-wit. 59. **whither wander you,** an allusion to the expression "wandering wits." 60. **Mistress,** not a polite title to address to a princess. 62. **messenger,** possibly, police officer. Celia says in effect, "Were you sent to arrest me?" (New Cambridge). 67. **pancakes,** fritters (which might be made of meat and so require mustard).

99. **put on,** pass off upon, communicate to. 107. **colour,** kind. 112. **laid . . . trowel,** i.e., clumsily.

Ros. Thou losest thy old smell.

Le Beau. You amaze me, ladies: I would have told you of good wrestling, which you have lost the sight of.

Ros. Yet tell us the manner of the wrestling.

Le Beau. I will tell you the beginning; and, if it please your ladyships, you may see the end; for the best is yet to do; and here, where you are, they are coming to perform it.

Cel. Well, the beginning, that is dead and buried.

Le Beau. There comes an old man and his three sons,—

Cel. I could match this beginning with an old tale.

Le Beau. Three proper young men, of excellent growth and presence.   130

Ros. With bills on their necks, 'Be it known unto all men by these presents.'

Le Beau. The eldest of the three wrestled with Charles, the duke's wrestler; which Charles in a moment threw him and broke three of his ribs, that there is little hope of life in him: so he served the second, and so the third. Yonder they lie; the poor old man, their father, making such pitiful dole over them that all the beholders take his   140 part with weeping.

Ros. Alas!

Touch. But what is the sport, monsieur, that the ladies have lost?

Le Beau. Why, this that I speak of.

Touch. Thus men may grow wiser every day: it is the first time that ever I heard breaking of ribs was sport for ladies.

Cel. Or I, I promise thee.   148

Ros. But is there any else longs to see this broken music in his sides? is there yet another dotes upon rib-breaking? Shall we see this wrestling, cousin?

Le Beau. You must, if you stay here; for here is the place appointed for the wrestling, and they are ready to perform it.

Cel. Yonder, sure, they are coming: let us now stay and see it.

Flourish. Enter Duke Frederick, *Lords,* Orlando, Charles, *and* Attendants.

Duke F. Come on: since the youth will not be entreated, his own peril on his forwardness.

Ros. Is yonder the man?   160

Le Beau. Even he, madam.

Cel. Alas, he is too young! yet he looks successfully.

Duke F. How now, daughter and cousin! are you crept hither to see the wrestling?

Ros. Ay, my liege, so please you give us leave.   167

Duke F. You will take little delight in it, I can tell you; there is such odds in the man. In pity of the challenger's youth I would fain dissuade him, but he will not be entreated. Speak to him, ladies; see if you can move him.

Cel. Call him hither, good Monsieur Le Beau.

Duke F. Do so: I'll not be by.

Le Beau. Monsieur the challenger, the princesses call for you.

Orl. I attend them with all respect and duty.

Ros. Young man, have you challenged Charles the wrestler?   179

Orl. No, fair princess; he is the general challenger: I come but in, as others do, to try with him the strength of my youth.

Cel. Young gentleman, your spirits are too bold for your years. You have seen cruel proof of this man's strength: if you saw yourself with your eyes or knew yourself with your judgement, the fear of your adventure would counsel you to a more equal enterprise. We pray you, for your own sake, to embrace your own safety and give over   190 this attempt.

Ros. Do, young sir; your reputation shall not therefore be misprised: we will make it our suit to the duke that the wrestling might not go forward.

129. proper, handsome. **131. bills,** advertisements, proclamations. **132. presents,** document presented, with pun on *presence.* **139. dole,** grief, lamentation. **149. any,** anyone. **150. broken music,** possibly, broken musical instrument (as if the ribs were part of such an instrument).

159. peril on, i.e., be upon. **163. successfully,** i.e., as if he would be successful. **169. such odds in the man,** such advantage on the side of the man (i.e., the wrestler, Charles, as contrasted with the youth, Orlando). **176. princesses call,** so Theobald; F: *princess calls.* New Cambridge editors defend the F reading on the ground that Le Beau, as an adherent of the usurping duke, would recognize only one princess. **185-187. if . . . judgement,** if you saw yourself as you really are in relation to your opponent and used your judgment. Some older editors read *our* for *your* in line 186. **192. therefore,** on that account. **misprised,** despised.

Orl. I beseech you, punish me not with your hard thoughts; wherein I confess me much guilty, to deny so fair and excellent ladies any thing. But let your fair eyes and gentle wishes go with me to my trial: wherein if I be foiled, there is but one shamed that was never gracious; if killed, but one dead that is willing to be so: I shall do my friends no wrong, for I have none to lament me, the world no injury, for in it I have nothing; only in the world I fill up a place, which may be better supplied when I have made it empty.   206

Ros. The little strength that I have, I would it were with you.

Cel. And mine, to eke out hers.

Ros. Fare you well: pray heaven I be deceived in you!   210

Cel. Your heart's desires be with you!

Cha. Come, where is this young gallant that is so desirous to lie with his mother earth?

Orl. Ready, sir; but his will hath in it a more modest working.   215

Duke F. You shall try but one fall.

Cha. No, I warrant your grace, you shall not entreat him to a second, that have so mightily persuaded him from a first.   219

Orl. An you mean to mock me after, you should not have mocked me before: but come your ways.

Ros. Now Hercules be thy speed, young man!

Cel. I would I were invisible, to catch the strong fellow by the leg.   [*They wrestle.*

Ros. O excellent young man!

Cel. If I had a thunderbolt in mine eye, I can tell who should down.

                [*Shout. Charles is thrown.*

Duke F. No more, no more.

Orl. Yes, I beseech your grace: I am not yet well breathed.   230

Duke F. How dost thou, Charles?

Le Beau. He cannot speak, my lord.

Duke F. Bear him away. What is thy name, young man?

Orl. Orlando, my liege; the youngest son of Sir Rowland de Boys.

Duke F. I would thou hadst been son to some man else:

The world esteem'd thy father honourable,
But I did find him still mine enemy:
Thou shouldst have better pleased me with this deed,   239
Hadst thou descended from another house.
But fare thee well; thou art a gallant youth:
I would thou hadst told me of another father.

        [*Exeunt Duke Fred., train, and Le Beau.*

Cel. Were I my father, coz, would I do this?

Orl. I am more proud to be Sir Rowland's son,
His youngest son; and would not change that calling,
To be adopted heir to Frederick.

Ros. My father loved Sir Rowland as his soul,
And all the world was of my father's mind:
Had I before known this young man his son,
I should have given him tears unto entreaties,   250
Ere he should thus have ventured.

Cel.   Gentle cousin,
Let us go thank him and encourage him:
My father's rough and envious disposition
Sticks me at heart. Sir, you have well deserved:
If you do keep your promises in love
But justly, as you have exceeded all promise,
Your mistress shall be happy.

Ros.   Gentleman,

        [*Giving him a chain from her neck.*

Wear this for me, one out of suits with fortune,
That could give more, but that her hand lacks means.
Shall we go, coz?

Cel.   Ay. Fare you well, fair gentleman.

Orl. Can I not say, I thank you? My better parts   261
Are all thrown down, and that which here stands up
Is but a quintain, a mere lifeless block.

Ros. He calls us back: my pride fell with my fortunes;
I'll ask him what he would. Did you call, sir?
Sir, you have wrestled well and overthrown

---

200. **gracious,** looked upon with favor. 215. **working,** endeavor. 222. **come your ways,** come on. 223. **Hercules . . . speed,** may Hercules favor you. 230. **well breathed,** put into good wind.

245. **calling,** appellation, name. 249. **known,** i.e., known to be. 250. **unto,** in addition to. 254. **Sticks me at heart,** stabs me to the heart. 258. **out . . . fortune,** not wearing the livery of fortune; not in her service; or one whose suits to fortune are rejected. 263. **quintain,** wooden figure at which to tilt.

More than your enemies.

Cel.   Will you go, coz?

Ros. Have with you. Fare you well.

        [*Exeunt Rosalind and Celia.*

Orl. What passion hangs these weights
   upon my tongue?

I cannot speak to her, yet she urged conference.   270

O poor Orlando, thou art overthrown!

Or Charles or something weaker masters
   thee.

Re-enter Le Beau.

Le Beau. Good sir, I do in friendship
   counsel you

To leave this place. Albeit you have deserved

High commendation, true applause and love,

Yet such is now the duke's condition

That he misconstrues all that you have done.

The duke is humorous: what he is indeed,

More suits you to conceive than I to speak of.

  Orl. I thank you, sir: and, pray you, tell
     me this;   280

Which of the two was daughter of the duke

That here was at the wrestling?

  Le Beau. Neither his daughter, if we judge
     by manners;

But yet indeed the lesser is his daughter:

The other is daughter to the banish'd duke,

And here detain'd by her usurping uncle,

To keep his daughter company; whose loves

Are dearer than the natural bond of sisters.

But I can tell you that of late this duke

Hath ta'en displeasure 'gainst his gentle
   niece,   290

Grounded upon no other argument

But that the people praise her for her virtues

And pity her for her good father's sake;

And, on my life, his malice 'gainst the lady

Will suddenly break forth. Sir, fare you well:

Hereafter, in a better world than this,

I shall desire more love and knowledge of you.

  Orl. I rest much bounden to you: fare you
     well.   [*Exit Le Beau.*

Thus must I from the smoke into the
   smother;

From tyrant duke unto a tyrant brother: 300

But heavenly Rosalind!   [*Exit.*

SCENE III.   *A room in the palace.*

Enter Celia *and* Rosalind.

  Cel. Why, cousin! why, Rosalind! Cupid
have mercy! not a word?

  Ros. Not one to throw at a dog.

  Cel. No, thy words are too precious to be
cast away upon curs; throw some of them at
me; come, lame me with reasons.

  Ros. Then there were two cousins laid up;
when the one should be lamed with reasons
and the other mad without any.

  Cel. But is all this for your father?   10

  Ros. No, some of it is for my child's
father. O, how full of briers is this working-
day world!

  Cel. They are but burs, cousin, thrown
upon thee in holiday foolery: if we walk not
in the trodden paths, our very petticoats will
catch them.

  Ros. I could shake them off my coat: these
burs are in my heart.

  Cel. Hem them away.

  Ros. I would try, if I could cry 'hem' and
have him.   20

  Cel. Come, come, wrestle with thy affections.

  Ros. O, they take the part of a better
wrestler than myself!

  Cel. O, a good wish upon you! you will try
in time, in despite of a fall. But, turning these
jests out of service, let us talk in good earnest: is it possible, on such a sudden, you
should fall into so strong a liking with old Sir
Rowland's youngest son?   29

  Ros. The duke my father loved his father
dearly.

  Cel. Doth it therefore ensue that you
should love his son dearly? By this kind of
chase, I should hate him, for my father
hated his father dearly; yet I hate not
Orlando.

  Ros. No, faith, hate him not, for my
sake.

  Cel. Why should I not? doth he not deserve well?   37

  Ros. Let me love him for that, and do you

268. **Have with you**, come along. 273-279. **Good
. . . speak of.** Note the courtly formality of Le Beau.
276. **condition**, state of mind, disposition. 277. **misconstrues.** The F spelling *misconsters* indicates the
pronunciation. 278. **humorous**, given to whims,
capricious, self-willed. 284. **lesser**, so Spedding; F:
taller, which is inconsistent with statements elsewhere
(see I, iii, 117) that Rosalind is the taller of the two. New
Cambridge editors find in this inconsistency in the F
evidence of the revision of the play. 291. **argument**,
cause, occasion. 299. **smoke into the smother**,
frying-pan into the fire.

Scene iii.   6. **reasons**, remarks.   12. **working-day**,
trivial.   20. **cry 'hem**,' clear away with a "hem" or a
cough, with a possible play on *him*.   27. **on such a
sudden**, so suddenly.   37. **deserve well**, i.e., to be
hated.

love him because I do. Look, here comes the
duke. 41
　Cel. With his eyes full of anger.
　Enter DUKE FREDERICK, *with* Lords.
　Duke F. Mistress, dispatch you with your
safest haste
And get you from our court.
　Ros. Me, uncle?
　Duke F. You, cousin:
Within these ten days if that thou be'st
found
So near our public court as twenty miles,
Thou diest for it.
　Ros. I do beseech your grace,
Let me the knowledge of my fault bear with
me:
If with myself I hold intelligence 49
Or have acquaintance with mine own desires,
If that I do not dream or be not frantic,—
As I do trust I am not—then, dear uncle,
Never so much as in a thought unborn
Did I offend your highness.
　Duke F. Thus do all traitors:
If their purgation did consist in words,
They are as innocent as grace itself:
Let it suffice thee that I trust thee not.
　Ros. Yet your mistrust cannot make me a
traitor:
Tell me whereon the likelihood depends.
　Duke F. Thou art thy father's daughter;
there's enough. 60
　Ros. So was I when your highness took his
dukedom;
So was I when your highness banish'd him:
Treason is not inherited, my lord;
Or, if we did derive it from our friends,
What's that to me? my father was no traitor:
Then, good my liege, mistake me not so
much
To think my poverty is treacherous.
　Cel. Dear sovereign, hear me speak.
　Duke F. Ay, Celia; we stay'd her for your
sake,
Else had she with her father ranged along. 70
　Cel. I did not then entreat to have her
stay;
It was your pleasure and your own remorse:
I was too young that time to value her;
But now I know her: if she be a traitor,
Why so am I; we still have slept together,

Rose at an instant, learn'd, play'd, eat to-
gether,
And wheresoe'er we went, like Juno's swans,
Still we went coupled and inseparable.
　Duke F. She is too subtle for thee; and her
smoothness,
Her very silence and her patience 80
Speak to the people, and they pity her.
Thou art a fool: she robs thee of thy name;
And thou wilt show more bright and seem
more virtuous
When she is gone. Then open not thy lips:
Firm and irrevocable is my doom
Which I have pass'd upon her; she is ban-
ish'd.
　Cel. Pronounce that sentence then on me,
my liege:
I cannot live out of her company.
　Duke F. You are a fool. You, niece, pro-
vide yourself:
If you outstay the time, upon mine honour, 90
And in the greatness of my word, you die.
　　　　[*Exeunt Duke Frederick and Lords.*
　Cel. O my poor Rosalind, whither wilt
thou go?
Wilt thou change fathers? I will give thee
mine.
I charge thee, be not thou more grieved than
I am.
　Ros. I have more cause.
　Cel. Thou hast not, cousin;
Prithee, be cheerful: know'st thou not, the
duke
Hath banish'd me, his daughter?
　Ros. That he hath not.
　Cel. No, hath not? Rosalind lacks then
the love
Which teacheth thee that thou and I am
one:
Shall we be sunder'd? shall we part, sweet
girl?
No: let my father seek another heir. 101
Therefore devise with me how we may fly,
Whither to go and what to bear with us;
And do not seek to take your change upon
you,
To bear your griefs yourself and leave me
out;
For, by this heaven, now at our sorrows pale,
Say what thou canst, I'll go along with thee.
　Ros. Why, whither shall we go?

43. **safest haste**, speed, which is your best security.
55. **purgation**, exculpation, freeing from accusation
of guilt. 64. **friends**, relatives, kinsfolk. 72. **remorse**,
compassion. 73. **that time**, then.

77. **Juno's swans.** It has been pointed out that it
was Venus and not Juno who possessed swans. 104.
change, change of fortune.

Cel. To seek my uncle in the forest of
  Arden.

Ros. Alas, what danger will it be to us, 110
Maids as we are, to travel forth so far!
Beauty provoketh thieves sooner than gold.

Cel. I'll put myself in poor and mean at-
  tire
And with a kind of umber smirch my face;
The like do you: so shall we pass along
And never stir assailants.

Ros.   Were it not better,
Because that I am more than common tall,
That I did suit me all points like a man?
A gallant curtle-axe upon my thigh,   119
A boar-spear in my hand; and—in my heart
Lie there what hidden woman's fear there
  will—
We'll have a swashing and a martial outside,
As many other mannish cowards have
That do outface it with their semblances.

Cel. What shall I call thee when thou art
  a man?

Ros. I'll have no worse a name than Jove's
  own page;
And therefore look you call me Ganymede.
But what will you be call'd?

Cel. Something that hath a reference to
  my state;
No longer Celia, but Aliena.   130

Ros. But, cousin, what if we assay'd to
  steal
The clownish fool out of your father's court?
Would he not be a comfort to our travel?

Cel. He'll go along o'er the wide world
  with me;
Leave me alone to woo him. Let's away,
And get our jewels and our wealth together,
Devise the fittest time and safest way
To hide us from pursuit that will be made
After my flight. Now go we in content   139
To liberty and not to banishment. [*Exeunt.*

ACT II.

Scene I. *The Forest of Arden.*

Enter Duke senior, Amiens, *and two or
three* Lords, *like foresters.*

Duke S. Now, my co-mates and brothers
  in exile,

Hath not old custom made this life more
  sweet
Than that of painted pomp? Are not these
  woods
More free from peril than the envious court?
Here feel we but the penalty of Adam,
The seasons' difference, as the icy fang
And churlish chiding of the winter's wind,
Which, when it bites and blows upon my
  body,
Even till I shrink with cold, I smile and say
'This is no flattery: these are counsellors   10
That feelingly persuade me what I am.'
Sweet are the uses of adversity,
Which, like the toad, ugly and venomous,
Wears yet a precious jewel in his head;
And this our life exempt from public haunt
Finds tongues in trees, books in the running
  brooks,
Sermons in stones and good in every thing.
I would not change it.

Ami.   Happy is your grace,
That can translate the stubbornness of fortune
Into so quiet and so sweet a style.   20

Duke S. Come, shall we go and kill us
  venison?
And yet it irks me the poor dappled fools,
Being native burghers of this desert city,
Should in their own confines with forked
  heads
Have their round haunches gored.

First Lord.   Indeed, my lord,
The melancholy Jaques grieves at that,
And, in that kind, swears you do more usurp
Than doth your brother that hath banish'd
  you.
To-day my Lord of Amiens and myself
Did steal behind him as he lay along   30
Under an oak whose antique root peeps out
Upon the brook that brawls along this wood:
To the which place a poor sequester'd stag,
That from the hunter's aim had ta'en a hurt,
Did come to languish, and indeed, my lord,
The wretched animal heaved forth such
  groans
That their discharge did stretch his leathern
  coat
Almost to bursting, and the big round tears
Coursed one another down his innocent nose

---

114. umber, brown pigment used to disguise the face.
118. suit, dress. 119, curtle-axe, broad cutting sword.
122. swashing, blustering. 127. Ganymede, the name
of Jupiter's cupbearer; used also in Lodge's *Rosalynde.*
131. assay'd, tried. 139. content, contentment.

6. as, such as. 13-14. like . . . head. The idea
that the toad was venomous comes from Pliny's *Natural
History.* The jewel referred to is the toadstone, which
was thought to be in the head of the toad. 15. exempt,
cut off. 22. irks, grieves, vexes. 23. burghers, citizens. 31. antique, ancient.

In piteous chase; and thus the hairy fool,   40
Much marked of the melancholy Jaques,
Stood on the extremest verge of the swift
      brook,
Augmenting it with tears.

  Duke S.   But what said Jaques?
Did he not moralize this spectacle?

  First Lord. O, yes, into a thousand similes.
First, for his weeping into the needless
      stream;
'Poor deer,' quoth he, 'thou makest a testa-
      ment
As worldings do, giving thy sum of more
To that which had too much:' then, being
      there alone,
Left and abandon'd of his velvet friends,   50
' 'Tis right,' quoth he; 'thus misery doth part
The flux of company:' anon a careless herd,
Full of the pasture, jumps along by him
And never stays to greet him; 'Ay,' quoth
      Jaques,
'Sweep on, you fat and greasy citizens;
'Tis just the fashion: wherefore do you look
Upon that poor and broken bankrupt there?'
Thus most invectively he pierceth through
The body of the country, city, court,
Yea, and of this our life, swearing that we   60
Are mere usurpers, tyrants and what's worse,
To fright the animals and to kill them up
In their assign'd and native dwelling-place.

  Duke S. And did you leave him in this
      contemplation?

  Sec. Lord. We did, my lord, weeping and
      commenting
Upon the sobbing deer.

  Duke S.   Show me the place:
I love to cope him in these sullen fits,
For then he's full of matter.

  First Lord. I'll bring you to him straight.
                                    [*Exeunt.*

SCENE II.   *A room in the palace.*

Enter DUKE FREDERICK, *with* Lords.

  Duke F. Can it be possible that no man
      saw them?
It cannot be: some villains of my court
Are of consent and sufferance in this.

44. **moralize,** draw out the hidden meaning of. 50.
velvet, courtier-like.   Velvet was the typical dress of the
courtier; a probable allusion also to the velvet of the
deer's horn. 58. **invectively,** with denunciation. 67.
cope, meet, encounter. 68. **matter,** sense, substance.
  Scene ii. 3. **consent and sufferance,** agreement as
to course of action and permission for events to take
place without opposition; metaphor from law.

  First Lord. I cannot hear of any that did
      see her.
The ladies, her attendants of her chamber,
Saw her a-bed, and in the morning early
They found the bed untreasured of their
      mistress.

  Sec. Lord. My lord, the roynish clown, at
      whom so oft
Your grace was wont to laugh, is also miss-
      ing.
Hisperia, the princess' gentlewoman,   10
Confesses that she secretly o'erheard
Your daughter and her cousin much com-
      mend
The parts and graces of the wrestler
That did but lately foil the sinewy Charles;
And she believes, wherever they are gone,
That youth is surely in their company.

  Duke F. Send to his brother; fetch that
      gallant hither;
If he be absent, bring his brother to me;
I'll make him find him: do this suddenly,
And let not search and inquisition quail   20
To bring again these foolish runaways.
                                    [*Exeunt.*

SCENE III.   *Before* OLIVER'S *house.*

Enter ORLANDO *and* ADAM, *meeting.*

  Orl. Who's there?

  Adam. What, my young master? O my
      gentle master!
O my sweet master! O you memory
Of old Sir Rowland! why, what make you
      here?
Why are you virtuous? why do people love
      you?
And wherefore are you gentle, strong and
      valiant?
Why would you be so fond to overcome
The bonny priser of the humorous duke?
Your praise is come too swiftly home before
      you.
Know you not, master, to some kind of
      men   10
Their graces serve them but as enemies?
No more do yours: your virtues, gentle
      master,
Are sanctified and holy traitors to you.

8. **roynish,** scurvy, coarse. 17. **that gallant,** i.e.,
Orlando. 19. **suddenly,** speedily. 20. **inquisition,**
inquiry. **quail,** fail, slacken. 21. **again,** back.
  Scene iii. 3. **memory,** memorial, memento. 7. **to,**
as to. 8. **bonny priser,** big champion or prize-fighter.

O, what a world is this, when what is comely
Envenoms him that bears it!
 Orl. Why, what's the matter?
 Adam.   O unhappy youth!
Come not within these doors; within this roof
The enemy of all your graces lives:
Your brother—no, no brother; yet the son—
Yet not the son, I will not call him son   20
Of him I was about to call his father—
Hath heard your praises, and this night he
  means
To burn the lodging where you use to lie
And you within it: if he fail of that,
He will have other means to cut you off.
I overheard him and his practices.
This is no place; this house is but a butchery:
Abhor it, fear it, do not enter it.
 Orl. Why, whither, Adam, wouldst thou
  have me go?
 Adam. No matter whither, so you come
  not here.   30
 Orl. What, wouldst thou have me go and
  beg my food?
Or with a base and boisterous sword enforce
A thievish living on the common road?
This I must do, or know not what to do:
Yet this I will not do, do how I can;
I rather will subject me to the malice
Of a diverted blood and bloody brother.
 Adam. But do not so. I have five hundred
  crowns,
The thrifty hire I saved under your father,
Which I did store to be my foster-nurse   40
When service should in my old limbs lie lame
And unregarded age in corners thrown:
Take that, and He that doth the ravens feed,
Yea, providently caters for the sparrow,
Be comfort to my age! Here is the gold;
All this I give you. Let me be your servant:
Though I look old, yet I am strong and lusty;
For in my youth I never did apply
Hot and rebellious liquors in my blood,
Nor did not with unbashful forehead woo   50
The means of weakness and debility;
Therefore my age is as a lusty winter,
Frosty, but kindly: let me go with you;
I'll do the service of a younger man
In all your business and necessities.

 Orl. O good old man, how well in thee ap-
  pears
The constant service of the antique world,
When service sweat for duty, not for meed!
Thou art not for the fashion of these times,
Where none will sweat but for promotion,   60
And having that, do choke their service up
Even with the having: it is not so with thee.
But, poor old man, thou prunest a rotten
  tree,
That cannot so much as a blossom yield
In lieu of all thy pains and husbandry.
But come thy ways; we'll go along together,
And ere we have thy youthful wages spent,
We'll light upon some settled low content.
 Adam. Master, go on, and I will follow
  thee,
To the last gasp, with truth and loyalty.   70
From seventeen years till now almost four-
  score
Here lived I, but now live here no more.
At seventeen years many their fortunes seek;
But at fourscore it is too late a week:
Yet fortune cannot recompense me better
Than to die well and not my master's debtor.
            [*Exeunt.*

SCENE IV. *The Forest of Arden.*

Enter ROSALIND *for* GANYMEDE, CELIA *for*
ALIENA, *and* TOUCHSTONE.

 Ros. O Jupiter, how weary are my spirits!
 Touch. I care not for my spirits, if my legs
were not weary.
 Ros. I could find in my heart to disgrace
my man's apparel and to cry like a woman;
but I must comfort the weaker vessel, as
doublet and hose ought to show itself courageous to petticoat: therefore courage, good
Aliena!
 Cel. I pray you, bear with me; I cannot go
no further.   10
 Touch. For my part, I had rather bear
with you than bear you; yet I should bear no
cross if I did bear you, for I think you have
no money in your purse.
 Ros. Well, this is the forest of Arden.
 Touch. Ay, now am I in Arden; the more
fool I; when I was at home, I was in a better

14-15. when . . . bears it, i.e., as did the shirt of
Nessus, or the poisoned garment sent by Medea to
Creusa. 23. use, are wont. 26. practices, designs,
plots. 27. place, residence, dwelling. butchery,
slaughter-house. 37. diverted blood, kinship diverted
from the natural course. 39. thrifty, obtained by
economy. 43-44. He . . . sparrow. See *St. Luke*, xii,
22-24. 53. kindly, natural, proper.

57. service, probably, body of servants collectively.
58. meed, reward. 65. lieu of, return for. 68. low
content, lowly contented state. 74. too late a week,
too late by a good deal.
 Scene iv. 6. weaker vessel, woman. See *1 Peter*, iii,
7. 7. doublet and hose, typical male attire. 13.
cross, coin having on it a figure of a cross.

place: but travellers must be content.

Ros. Ay, be so, good Touchstone.

Enter CORIN *and* SILVIUS.

Look you, who comes here; a young man and
an old in solemn talk.   21

Cor. That is the way to make her scorn
you still.

Sil. O Corin, that thou knew'st how I do
love her!

Cor. I partly guess; for I have loved ere
now.

Sil. No, Corin, being old, thou canst not
guess,
Though in thy youth thou wast as true a lover
As ever sigh'd upon a midnight pillow:
But if thy love were ever like to mine—
As sure I think did never man love so—
How many actions most ridiculous   30
Hast thou been drawn to by thy fantasy?

Cor. Into a thousand that I have forgotten.

Sil. O, thou didst then ne'er love so
heartily!
If thou remember'st not the slightest folly
That ever love did make thee run into,
Thou hast not loved:
Or if thou hast not sat as I do now,
Wearying thy hearer in thy mistress' praise,
Thou hast not loved:
Or if thou hast not broke from company   40
Abruptly, as my passion now makes me,
Thou hast not loved.
O Phebe, Phebe, Phebe!   [*Exit.*

Ros. Alas, poor shepherd! searching of thy
wound,   44
I have by hard adventure found mine own.

Touch. And I mine. I remember, when I
was in love I broke my sword upon a stone
and bid him take that for coming a-night to
Jane Smile; and I remember the kissing of her
batlet and the cow's dugs that her pretty
chopt hands had milked; and I remember the
wooing of a peascod instead of her, from
whom I took two cods and, giving her them
again, said with weeping tears 'Wear these
for my sake.' We that are true lovers run
into strange capers; but as all is mortal in
nature, so is all nature in love mortal in
folly.   57

Ros. Thou speakest wiser than thou art
ware of.

Touch. Nay, I shall ne'er be ware of mine
own wit till I break my shins against it.   60

Ros. Jove, Jove! this shepherd's passion
Is much upon my fashion.

Touch. And mine; but it grows something
stale with me.

Cel. I pray you, one of you question yond
man
If he for gold will give us any food:
I faint almost to death.

Touch.   Holla, you clown!

Ros. Peace, fool: he's not thy kinsman.

Cor.   Who calls?

Touch. Your betters, sir.

Cor.   Else are they very wretched.

Ros. Peace, I say. Good even to you,
friend.

Cor. And to you, gentle sir, and to you all.

Ros. I prithee, shepherd, if that love or
gold   71
Can in this desert place buy entertainment,
Bring us where we may rest ourselves and
feed:
Here's a young maid with travel much op-
press'd
And faints for succour.

Cor.   Fair sir, I pity her
And wish, for her sake more than for mine
own,
My fortunes were more able to relieve her;
But I am shepherd to another man
And do not shear the fleeces that I graze:
My master is of churlish disposition   80
And little recks to find the way to heaven
By doing deeds of hospitality:
Besides, his cote, his flocks and bounds of
feed
Are now on sale, and at our sheepcote now,
By reason of his absence, there is nothing
That you will feed on; but what is, come see,
And in my voice most welcome shall you be.

Ros. What is he that shall buy his flock
and pasture?

Cor. That young swain that you saw here
but erewhile,
That little cares for buying any thing.   90

Ros. I pray thee, if it stand with honesty,

31. **fantasy**, imagination, possibly for *fancy* meaning
"love." 44. **searching**, probing. 48. **a-night**, by night.
50. **batlet**, club or bat for beating clothes in process of
washing. 51. **chopt**, chapped. 52. **peascod**, pea pod;
regarded as a lucky gift by rustic lovers. 56. **mortal**,
excessive, very great.

58. **ware**, aware. 62. **upon**, after, according to.
75. **for succour**, for want of succor. 79. **fleeces**, flock.
80. **churlish**, niggardly, miserly. 81. **recks**, heeds,
cares. 83. **cote**, shepherd's hut. **bounds of feed**,
limits within which he has the right of pasturage. 87.
in my voice, as far as my opinion goes. 89. **erewhile**,
a short time since. 91. **stand**, be consistent.

Buy thou the cottage, pasture and the
flock,
And thou shalt have to pay for it of us.
  Cel. And we will mend thy wages. I like
this place,
And willingly could waste my time in it.
  Cor. Assuredly the thing is to be sold:
Go with me: if you like upon report
The soil, the profit and this kind of life,
I will your very faithful feeder be   99
And buy it with your gold right suddenly.
                                    [*Exeunt.*

SCENE V. *The forest.*

Enter AMIENS, JAQUES, *and others.*

SONG.

  Ami. Under the greenwood tree
        Who loves to lie with me,
        And turn his merry note
        Unto the sweet bird's throat,
  Come hither, come hither, come hither:
        Here shall he see
        No enemy
  But winter and rough weather.

  Jaq. More, more, I prithee, more.
  Ami. It will make you melancholy, Monsieur Jaques.   11
  Jaq. I thank it. More, I prithee, more. I can suck melancholy out of a song, as a weasel sucks eggs. More, I prithee, more.
  Ami. My voice is ragged: I know I cannot please you.
  Jaq. I do not desire you to please me; I do desire you to sing. Come, more; another stanzo: call you 'em stanzos?
  Ami. What you will, Monsieur Jaques.   20
  Jaq. Nay, I care not for their names; they owe me nothing. Will you sing?
  Amil More at your request than to please myself.
  Jaq. Well then, if ever I thank any man, I'll thank you; but that they call compliment is like the encounter of two dog-apes, and when a man thanks me heartily, methinks I have given him a penny and he renders me the beggarly thanks. Come, sing; and you that will not, hold your tongues.   31
  Ami. Well, I'll end the song. Sirs, cover

the while; the duke will drink under this tree.
He hath been all this day to look you.
  Jaq. And I have been all this day to avoid
him. He is too disputable for my company:
I think of as many matters as he, but I give
heaven thanks and make no boast of them.
Come, warble, come.

SONG.

  Who doth ambition shun [*All together here.*
  And loves to live i' the sun,   41
  Seeking the food he eats
  And pleased with what he gets,
Come hither, come hither, come hither:
  Here shall he see
  No enemy
But winter and rough weather.

  Jaq. I'll give you a verse to this note that
I made yesterday in despite of my invention.
  Ami. And I'll sing it.   50
  Jaq. Thus it goes:—
  If it do come to pass
  That any man turn ass,
    Leaving his wealth and ease,
    A stubborn will to please,
  Ducdame, ducdame, ducdame:
    Here shall he see
    Gross fools as he,
  An if he will come to me.
  Ami. What's that 'ducdame'?   60
  Jaq. 'Tis a Greek invocation, to call fools
into a circle. I'll go sleep, if I can; if I cannot,
I'll rail against all the first-born of Egypt.
  Ami. And I'll go seek the duke: his banquet is prepared.   [*Exeunt severally.*

SCENE VI. *The forest.*

Enter ORLANDO *and* ADAM.

  Adam. Dear master, I can go no further:
O, I die for food! Here lie I down, and measure out my grave. Farewell, kind master.
  Orl. Why, how now, Adam! no greater
heart in thee? Live a little; comfort a little;

99. **feeder,** servant.
Scene v. 3. **turn,** compose (verse, a tune). 21.
names, i.e., of debts owed, signatures (to a bond). 27.
dog-apes, possibly, dog-faced baboons. 32. **cover,**
spread the cloth for a meal.

33. **the while,** inclined to dispute. Cambridge editors, Dr. John Sampson, the gypsy word *du* fortunes or prophes fortune-teller at fair cation. This also re *Egypt* intelligible, s and in the conditio and dessert after din
Scene vi. This is o verse in F which are of the play by Shak conjecture: *comfort t*

36. **disputable,** in the meantime. 56. **Ducdame,** unexplained. New following Mr. Charles Strachey and explain *ducdame* as a corruption of *á mē,* meaning "I foretell," "I tell"; therefore as the call of a gypsy, it is a "Greek" (or sharper's) invocation. aders the allusion to *the first-born of* ice the first-born duke is banished of a gypsy. 64. **banquet,** wine ner.
ne of the prose passages printed as indicative of a manuscript revision espeare. 5. **comfort,** anonymous ee.

cheer thyself a little. If this uncouth forest yield any thing savage, I will either be food for it or bring it for food to thee. Thy conceit is nearer death than thy powers. For my sake be comfortable; hold death awhile at the arm's end: I will here be with thee presently; and if I bring thee not something to eat, I will give thee leave to die: but if thou diest before I come, thou art a mocker of my labour. Well said! thou lookest cheerly, and I'll be with thee quickly. Yet thou liest in the bleak air: come, I will bear thee to some shelter; and thou shalt not die for lack of a dinner, if there live any thing in this desert. Cheerly, good Adam!   [*Exeunt.* 20

SCENE VII. *The forest.*

A table set out. Enter DUKE *senior,* AMIENS, *and* Lords *like* outlaws.

Duke S. I think he be transform'd into a beast;
For I can no where find him like a man.
    First Lord. My lord, he is but even now gone hence:
Here was he merry, hearing of a song.
    Duke S. If he, compact of jars, grow musical,
We shall have shortly discord in the spheres.
Go, seek him: tell him I would speak with him.

Enter JAQUES.

    First Lord. He saves my labour by his own approach.
    Duke S. Why, how now, monsieur! what a life is this,
That your poor friends must woo your company?   10
What, you look merrily!
    Jaq. A fool, a fool! I met a fool i' the forest,
A motley fool; a miserable world!
As I do live by food, I met a fool;
Who laid him down and bask'd him in the sun,
And rail'd on Lady Fortune in good terms,
In good set terms and yet a motley fool.

'Good morrow, fool,' quoth I. 'No, sir,' quoth he,
'Call me not fool till heaven hath sent me fortune:'
And then he drew a dial from his poke,   20
And, looking on it with lack-lustre eye,
Says very wisely, 'It is ten o'clock:
Thus we may see,' quoth he, 'how the world wags:
'Tis but an hour ago since it was nine,
And after one hour more 'twill be eleven;
And so, from hour to hour, we ripe and ripe,
And then, from hour to hour, we rot and rot;
And thereby hangs a tale.' When I did hear
The motley fool thus moral on the time,
My lungs began to crow like chanticleer,   30
That fools should be so deep-contemplative,
And I did laugh sans intermission
An hour by his dial. O noble fool!
A worthy fool! Motley 's the only wear.
    Duke S. What fool is this?
    Jaq. O worthy fool! One that hath been a courtier,
And says, if ladies be but young and fair,
They have the gift to know it: and in his brain,
Which is as dry as the remainder biscuit
After a voyage, he hath strange places cramm'd   40
With observation, the which he vents
In mangled forms. O that I were a fool!
I am ambitious for a motley coat.
    Duke S. Thou shalt have one.
    Jaq.   It is my only suit;
Provided that you weed your better judgements
Of all opinion that grows rank in them
That I am wise. I must have liberty
Withal, as large a charter as the wind,
To blow on whom I please; for so fools have;
And they that are most galled with my folly,
They most must laugh. And why, sir, must they so?   51
The 'why' is plain as way to parish church:
He that a fool doth very wisely hit
Doth very foolishly, although he smart,
Not to seem senseless of the bob: if not,
The wise man's folly is anatomized

---

6. **uncouth**, strange, wild. 8. **conceit**, imagination. 10. **comfortable**, cheerful. 19. **Cheerly**, blithely.
Scene vii. 6. **spheres**, reference to the music supposed to be produced by the revolving concentric spheres of the Ptolemaic solar system. 13. **motley**, the particolored dress of the clown.

19. '**Call . . . fortune**,' an allusion to the proverb, "Fortune favors fools." 20. **dial**, watch, or portable sundial. **poke**, pocket. 29. **moral**, moralize. 30. **crow**, laugh merrily. 34. **only wear**, only thing worth wearing. 40. **places**, topics, subjects for discourse; or possibly, texts, wise bits. 48. **large . . . wind**, i.e., to blow where it listeth. 55. **bob**, jibe, taunt.

Even by the squandering glances of the fool.
Invest me in my motley; give me leave
To speak my mind, and I will through and
    through
Cleanse the foul body of the infected world,60
If they will patiently receive my medicine.
  Duke S. Fie on thee! I can tell what thou
    wouldst do.
  Jaq. What, for a counter, would I do but
    good?
  Duke S. Most mischievous foul sin, in
    chiding sin:
For thou thyself hast been a libertine,
As sensual as the brutish sting itself;
And all the embossed sores and headed evils,
That thou with license of free foot hast
    caught,
Wouldst thou disgorge into the general
    world.
  Jaq. Why, who cries out on pride,   70
That can therein tax any private party?
Doth it not flow as hugely as the sea,
†Till that the weary very means do ebb?
What woman in the city do I name,
When that I say the city-woman bears
The cost of princes on unworthy shoulders?
Who can come in and say that I mean her,
When such a one as she such is her neigh-
    bour?
Or what is he of basest function
That says his bravery is not on my cost,   80
Thinking that I mean him, but therein suits
His folly to the mettle of my speech?
There then; how then? what then? Let me
    see wherein
My tongue hath wrong'd him: if it do him
    right,
Then he hath wrong'd himself; if he be free,
Why then my taxing like a wild-goose flies,
Unclaim'd of any man. But who comes here?

Enter ORLANDO, *with his sword drawn.*

  Orl. Forbear, and eat no more.
  Jaq.   Why, I have eat none yet.
  Orl. Nor shalt not, till necessity be served.
  Jaq. Of what kind should this cock come
    of?

  Duke S. Art thou thus bolden'd, man, by
    thy distress,   91
Or else a rude despiser of good manners,
That in civility thou seem'st so empty?
  Orl. You touch'd my vein at first: the
    thorny point
Of bare distress hath ta'en from me the show
Of smooth civility: yet am I inland bred
And know some nurture. But forbear, I say:
He dies that touches any of this fruit
Till I and my affairs are answered.
  Jaq. An you will not be answered with
    reason, I must die.   101
  Duke S. What would you have? Your
    gentleness shall force
More than your force move us to gentleness.
  Orl. I almost die for food; and let me have
    it.
  Duke S. Sit down and feed, and welcome
    to our table.
  Orl. Speak you so gently? Pardon me, I
    pray you:
I thought that all things had been savage
    here;
And therefore put I on the countenance
Of stern commandment. But whate'er you
    are
That in this desert inaccessible,   110
Under the shade of melancholy boughs,
Lose and neglect the creeping hours of time;
If ever you have look'd on better days,
If ever been where bells have knoll'd to
    church,
If ever sat at any good man's feast,
If ever from your eyelids wiped a tear
And know what 'tis to pity and be pitied,
Let gentleness my strong enforcement be:
In the which hope I blush, and hide my
    sword.
  Duke S. True is it that we have seen better
    days,   120
And have with holy bell been knoll'd to
    church
And sat at good men's feasts and wiped our
    eyes
Of drops that sacred pity hath engender'd:
And therefore sit you down in gentleness
And take upon command what help we have
That to your wanting may be minister'd.

---

57. **squandering glances,** random shots. 63.
counter, type of a thing of no intrinsic value, as a
metal disk used in counting. 66. **sting,** carnal impulse.
67. **embossed,** swollen, tumid. **evils,** diseases, mal-
adies. 73. **weary very means,** a corrupt passage.
There are many conjectures—Singer: *wearer's very means;*
Lloyd: *tributary stream;* New Cambridge: *weary very
mints,* i.e., in coining money fast enough. 75. **city-woman,**
citizen's wife. 79. **function,** office. 80. **bravery,**
splendor, finery. 84. **right,** justice. 85. **free,** innocent.

93. **civility,** politeness, code of good manners. 94.
vein, disposition, humor. 96. **inland bred,** i.e.,
civilized. 97. **nurture,** education, training. 99.
answered, satisfied. 109. **commandment,** command. 118. **my strong enforcement,** that which
strongly supports my request. 125. **upon command,**
at pleasure.

Orl. Then but forbear your food a little
while,
Whiles, like a doe, I go to find my fawn
And give it food. There is an old poor man,
Who after me hath many a weary step   130
Limp'd in pure love: till he be first sufficed,
Oppress'd with two weak evils, age and
hunger,
I will not touch a bit.
   Duke S.   Go find him out,
And we will nothing waste till you return.
   Orl. I thank ye; and be blest for your good
comfort!   [*Exit.*
   Duke S. Thou seest we are not all alone
unhappy:
This wide and universal theatre
Presents more woeful pageants than the
scene
Wherein we play in.
   Jaq.   All the world's a stage,
And all the men and women merely players:
They have their exits and their entrances; 141
And one man in his time plays many parts,
His acts being seven ages. At first the infant,
Mewling and puking in the nurse's arms.
And then the whining school-boy, with his
satchel
And shining morning face, creeping like snail
Unwillingly to school. And then the lover,
Sighing like furnace, with a woeful ballad
Made to his mistress' eyebrow. Then a sol-
dier,
Full of strange oaths and bearded like the
pard,   150
Jealous in honour, sudden and quick in
quarrel,
Seeking the bubble reputation
Even in the cannon's mouth. And then the
justice,
In fair round belly with good capon lined,
With eyes severe and beard of formal cut,
Full of wise saws and modern instances;
And so he plays his part. The sixth age shifts
Into the lean and slipper'd pantaloon,
With spectacles on nose and pouch on side,
His youthful hose, well saved, a world too
wide   160
For his shrunk shank; and his big manly
voice,

Turning again toward childish treble, pipes
And whistles in his sound. Last scene of all,
That ends this strange eventful history,
Is second childishness and mere oblivion,
Sans teeth, sans eyes, sans taste, sans every
thing.

   Re-enter ORLANDO, *with* ADAM.

   Duke S. Welcome. Set down your vener-
able burden
And let him feed.
   Orl. I thank you most for him.
   Adam.   So had you need:
I scarce can speak to thank you for myself.170
   Duke S. Welcome; fall to: I will not
trouble you
As yet, to question you about your fortunes.
Give us some music; and, good cousin, sing.

   SONG.

Ami. Blow, blow, thou winter wind,
         Thou art not so unkind
            As man's ingratitude;
         Thy tooth is not so keen,
         Because thou art not seen,
            Although thy breath be rude.
Heigh-ho! sing, heigh-ho! unto the green
   holly: 180
Most friendship is feigning, most loving mere
   folly:
         Then, heigh-ho, the holly!
            This life is most jolly.

         Freeze, freeze, thou bitter sky,
         That dost not bite so nigh
            As benefits forgot:
         Though thou the waters warp,
         Thy sting is not so sharp
            As friend remember'd not.
Heigh-ho! sing, &c.   190

   Duke S. If that you were the good Sir
Rowland's son,
As you have whisper'd faithfully you were,
And as mine eye doth his effigies witness
Most truly limn'd and living in your face,
Be truly welcome hither: I am the duke
That loved your father: the residue of your
   fortune,
Go to my cave and tell me. Good old man,

---

132. **weak,** causing weakness. 144. **Mewling,** crying
feebly. 150. **bearded . . . pard,** having bristling mustaches like the panther's or leopard's feelers. 156.
modern, ordinary, commonplace. **instances,** anything cited in proof. 158. **pantaloon,** ridiculous,
enfeebled old man.

175. **unkind,** unnatural. 178. **Because . . . seen,**
i.e., because thou art an enemy that doth not brave us
with thy presence (Johnson). 180. **holly,** emblem of
mirth. 187. **warp,** apparently, freeze or ruffle (Onions).
193. **effigies,** likenesses, portraits. 194. **limn'd,** painted, portrayed.

Thou art right welcome as thy master is.
Support him by the arm. Give me your
  hand,
And let me all your fortunes understand. 200
[*Exeunt.*

ACT III.

Scene I. *A room in the palace.*

Enter Duke Frederick, Lords, *and* Oliver.

Duke F. Not see him since? Sir, sir, that
  cannot be:
But were I not the better part made mercy,
I should not seek an absent argument
Of my revenge, thou present. But look to
  it:
Find out thy brother, wheresoe'er he is;
Seek him with candle; bring him dead or
  living
Within this twelvemonth, or turn thou no
  more
To seek a living in our territory.
Thy lands and all things that thou dost call
  thine
Worth seizure do we seize into our hands,   10
Till thou canst quit thee by thy brother's
  mouth
Of what we think against thee.
Oli. O that your highness knew my heart
  in this!
I never loved my brother in my life.
Duke F. More villain thou. Well, push
  him out of doors;
And let my officers of such a nature
Make an extent upon his house and lands:
Do this expediently and turn him going.
[*Exeunt.*

Scene II. *The forest.*

Enter Orlando, *with a paper.*

Orl. Hang there, my verse, in witness of
  my love:
And thou, thrice-crowned queen of night,
  survey

With thy chaste eye, from thy pale sphere
  above,
  Thy huntress' name that my full life doth
    sway.
O Rosalind! these trees shall be my books
  And in their barks my thoughts I'll char-
    acter;
That every eye which in this forest looks
  Shall see thy virtue witness'd every where.
Run, run, Orlando; carve on every tree   9
The fair, the chaste and unexpressive she.
[*Exit.*
Enter Corin *and* Touchstone.

Cor. And how like you this shepherd's life,
Master Touchstone?
Touch. Truly, shepherd, in respect of itself, it is a good life; but in respect that it is a
shepherd's life, it is naught. In respect that
it is solitary, I like it very well; but in respect that it is private, it is a very vile life.
Now, in respect it is in the fields, it pleaseth
me well; but in respect it is not in the court,
it is tedious. As it is a spare life, look you, it
fits my humour well; but as there is no more
plenty in it, it goes much against my stomach.
Hast any philosophy in thee, shepherd?   23
Cor. No more but that I know the more
one sickens the worse at ease he is; and that
he that wants money, means and content is
without three good friends; that the property
of rain is to wet and fire to burn; that good
pasture makes fat sheep, and that a great
cause of the night is lack of the sun; that he
that hath learned no wit by nature nor art
may complain of good breeding or comes of a
very dull kindred.   32
Touch. Such a one is a natural philosopher. Wast ever in court, shepherd?
Cor. No, truly.
Touch. Then thou art damned.
Cor. Nay, I hope.
Touch. Truly, thou art damned, like an
ill-roasted egg all on one side.   39
Cor. For not being at court? Your reason.
Touch. Why, if thou never wast at court,
thou never sawest good manners; if thou
never sawest good manners, then thy manners must be wicked; and wickedness is sin,
and sin is damnation. Thou art in a parlous
state, shepherd.

Act III. Scene i. 2. **better**, greater. 6. **Seek . . .
candle.** See *St. Luke*, xv, 8. 11. **quit**, acquit. **mouth**,
i.e., evidence. 16. **of such a nature**, i.e., who attend to
such duties. 17. **extent**, seizure of land in execution of a
writ. 18. **expediently**, expeditiously. **turn him
going**, start him moving.
  Scene ii. 2. **thrice-crowned queen**, Diana in the
three aspects of her divinity: as Luna or Cynthia, goddess of the moon; as Diana, goddess on earth; and as
Hecate or Proserpina, goddess in the lower world.

6. **character**, inscribe. 10. **unexpressive**, inex-
pressible. **she**, mistress, love. 15. **naught**, worthless,
useless. 31. **complain . . . breeding**, i.e., of want of
good breeding. 45. **parlous**, perilous, dangerous.

Cor. Not a whit, Touchstone: those that are good manners at the court are as ridiculous in the country as the behaviour of the country is most mockable at the court. You told me you salute not at the court, but you kiss your hands: that courtesy would be uncleanly, if courtiers were shepherds.   52

Touch. Instance, briefly; come, instance.

Cor. Why, we are still handling our ewes, and their fells, you know, are greasy.

Touch. Why, do not your courtier's hands sweat? and is not the grease of a mutton as wholesome as the sweat of a man? Shallow, shallow. A better instance, I say; come.   60

Cor. Besides, our hands are hard.

Touch. Your lips will feel them the sooner. Shallow again. A more sounder instance, come.

Cor. And they are often tarred over with the surgery of our sheep; and would you have us kiss tar? The courtier's hands are perfumed with civet.

Touch. Most shallow man! thou wormsmeat, in respect of a good piece of flesh indeed! Learn of the wise, and perpend: civet is of a baser birth than tar, the very uncleanly flux of a cat. Mend the instance, shep- 71
herd.

Cor. You have too courtly a wit for me: I'll rest.

Touch. Wilt thou rest damned? God help thee, shallow man! God make incision in thee! thou art raw.   76

Cor. Sir, I am a true labourer: I earn that I eat, get that I wear, owe no man hate, envy no man's happiness, glad of other men's good, content with my harm, and the greatest of my pride is to see my ewes graze and my lambs suck.   82

Touch. That is another simple sin in you, to bring the ewes and the rams together and to offer to get your living by the copulation of cattle; to be bawd to a bell-wether, and to betray a she-lamb of a twelvemonth to a crooked-pated, old, cuckoldly ram, out of all reasonable match. If thou beest not damned for this, the devil himself will have no shepherds; I cannot see else how thou shouldst 'scape.   90

Cor. Here comes young Master Ganymede, my new mistress's brother.

Enter ROSALIND, *with a paper, reading.*

Ros. From the east to western Ind,
No jewel is like Rosalind.
Her worth, being mounted on the wind,
Through all the world bears Rosalind.
All the pictures fairest lined
Are but black to Rosalind.
Let no fair be kept in mind
But the fair of Rosalind.   100

Touch. I'll rhyme you so eight years together, dinners and suppers and sleeping-hours excepted: it is the right butter-women's rank to market.

Ros. Out, fool!

Touch. For a taste:

If a hart do lack a hind,
Let him seek out Rosalind.
If the cat will after kind,
So be sure will Rosalind.   110
Winter garments must be lined,
So must slender Rosalind.
They that reap must sheaf and bind;
Then to cart with Rosalind.
Sweetest nut hath sourest rind,
Such a nut is Rosalind.
He that sweetest rose will find
Must find love's prick and Rosa-
lind.

This is the very false gallop of verses: why do you infect yourself with them?   120

Ros. Peace, you dull fool! I found them on a tree.

Touch. Truly, the tree yields bad fruit.

Ros. I'll graff it with you, and then I shall graff it with a medlar: then it will be the earliest fruit i' the country; for you'll be rotten ere you be half ripe, and that's the right virtue of the medlar.

Touch. You have said; but whether wisely or no, let the forest judge.   130

---

49. **mockable**, deserving of ridicule. 50. **but you kiss,** without kissing. 53. **Instance,** i.e., cite an example. 55. **fells,** skin with the wool, or fleece. 68. **in respect of,** in comparison with. 69. **perpend,** reflect, consider. 75. **incision,** cutting for the purpose of letting blood. 76. **raw,** inexperienced. 77. **that,** what. 80. **harm,** ill fortune.

97. **lined,** drawn. 100. **fair,** beauty. 103. **butter-woman's rank.** The rhymes, all alike, follow each other like a line of butter-women jogging along to market; conjectural for *rank: rack,* pace of a horse. 113. **sheaf,** make into sheaves. 119. **false gallop,** canter. 120. **infect,** pollute (either morally or physically). 125. **graff,** insert a graft. **medlar,** a fruit like a small brown-skinned apple which is eaten when decayed; a pun on *meddler.* 127. **right,** true.

Enter CELIA, *with a writing.*

Ros. Peace!
Here comes my sister, reading: stand aside.

Cel. [*Reads*]

Why should this a desert be?
    For it is unpeopled? No;
Tongues I'll hang on every tree,
    That shall civil sayings show:
Some, how brief the life of man
    Runs his erring pilgrimage,
That the stretching of a span
    Buckles in his sum of age;   140
Some, of violated vows
    'Twixt the souls of friend and friend:
But upon the fairest boughs,
    Or at every sentence end,
Will I Rosalinda write,
    Teaching all that read to know
The quintessence of every sprite
    Heaven would in little show.
Therefore Heaven Nature charged
    That one body should be fill'd   150
With all graces wide-enlarged:
    Nature presently distill'd
Helen's cheek, but not her heart,
    Cleopatra's majesty,
Atalanta's better part,
    Sad Lucretia's modesty.
Thus Rosalind of many parts
    By heavenly synod was devised,
Of many faces, eyes and hearts,   159
    To have the touches dearest prized.

Heaven would that she these gifts
    should have,
And I to live and die her slave.

Ros. O most gentle pulpiter! what tedious
homily of love have you wearied your parish-
ioners withal, and never cried 'Have patience, good people'!   166

Cel. How now! back, friends! Shepherd,
go off a little. Go with him, sirrah.

Touch. Come, shepherd, let us make an
honourable retreat; though not with bag and
baggage, yet with scrip and scrippage. 171
        [*Exeunt Corin and Touchstone.*

Cel. Didst thou hear these verses?

Ros. O, yes, I heard them all, and more
too; for some of them had in them more feet
than the verses would bear.

Cel. That's no matter: the feet might bear
the verses.

Ros. Ay, but the feet were lame and could
not bear themselves without the verse and
therefore stood lamely in the verse.   180

Cel. But didst thou hear without wondering how thy name should be hanged and
carved upon these trees?

Ros. I was seven of the nine days out of
the wonder before you came; for look here
what I found on a palm-tree. I was never so
berhymed since Pythagoras' time, that I was
an Irish rat, which I can hardly remember.

Cel. Trow you who hath done this?

Ros. Is it a man?   190

Cel. And a chain, that you once wore,
about his neck. Change you colour?

Ros. I prithee, who?

Cel. O Lord, Lord! it is a hard matter for
friends to meet; but mountains may be removed with earthquakes and so encounter.

Ros. Nay, but who is it?

Cel. Is it possible?

Ros. Nay, I prithee now with most peti-
tionary vehemence, tell me who it is.   200

Cel. O wonderful, wonderful, and most
wonderful wonderful! and yet again wonderful, and after that, out of all hooping!

Ros. Good my complexion! dost thou
think, though I am caparisoned like a man, I
have a doublet and hose in my disposition?
One inch of delay more is a South-sea of discovery; I prithee, tell me who is it quickly,

136. civil sayings, maxims of civilized life. 138.
erring, wandering. 139. That, so that. 140. Buckles,
encompasses. 147. quintessence, the fifth essence or
element of the mediæval alchemists, purer even than
fire. 148. in little. In this Furness sees an allusion
to the microcosm (man); the heavenly bodies would
be composed of quintessence, which is here thought of
as the supreme quality of a person. 151. wide-
enlarged, spread through the world until they are
concentrated in Rosalind (J. C. Smith). 155. Atalanta's better part, i.e., her fleetness of foot. 156.
Sad, serious. Lucretia's. Lucretia was the Roman
lady dishonored by Tarquin, whose story Shakespeare
tells in *The Rape of Lucrece*. 160. touches, traits.
167. back, friends. Celia, reading, becomes aware of
the others; her words are addressed to Corin and
Touchstone.

170. bag and baggage. Note the pun on *baggage*,
meaning "women." 171. scrip and scrippage. New
Cambridge editors suggest that Touchstone picks up
the scrip, or writing, which Celia has been reading. 182.
should be, was said to be. 184. seven . . . wonder.
A wonder was said to last nine days. 187. Pythagoras'.
Pythagoras was a Greek philosopher credited with the
doctrine of the transmigration of souls. 188. Irish rat,
reference to a current belief that Irish enchanters could
rhyme rats to death. 189. Trow you, know you, can you
tell. 191. And a chain, i.e., and with a chain. 195-
196. friends . . . encounter, reference to the proverb,
"Friends may meet, but mountains never greet." 203.
out . . . hooping, beyond exclamations of surprise. 204.
Good my complexion! i.e., she wishes her blushes not
to betray her. 205. caparisoned, equipped (as of a
horse). 207. South-sea of discovery, probable reference to the long delays of voyages to the South Seas;
many emendations; *discovery* may mean "disclosure."

and speak apace. I would thou couldst stammer, that thou mightst pour this concealed man out of thy mouth, as wine comes out of a narrow-mouthed bottle, either too much at once, or none at all. I prithee, take the cork out of thy mouth that I may 214 drink thy tidings.

Cel. So you may put a man in your belly.

Ros. Is he of God's making? What manner of man? Is his head worth a hat, or his chin worth a beard?

Cel. Nay, he hath but a little beard. 219

Ros. Why, God will send more, if the man will be thankful: let me stay the growth of his beard, if thou delay me not the knowledge of his chin.

Cel. It is young Orlando, that tripped up the wrestler's heels and your heart both in an instant.

Ros. Nay, but the devil take mocking: speak, sad brow and true maid.

Cel. I' faith, coz, 'tis he.

Ros. Orlando?

Cel. Orlando. 230

Ros. Alas the day! what shall I do with my doublet and hose? What did he when thou sawest him? What said he? How looked he? Wherein went he? What makes he here? Did he ask for me? Where remains he? How parted he with thee? and when shalt thou see him again? Answer me in one word. 237

Cel. You must borrow me Gargantua's mouth first: 'tis a word too great for any mouth of this age's size. To say ay and no to these particulars is more than to answer in a catechism. 241

Ros. But doth he know that I am in this forest and in man's apparel? Looks he as freshly as he did the day he wrestled?

Cel. It is as easy to count atomies as to resolve the propositions of a lover; but take a taste of my finding him, and relish it with good observance. I found him under a tree, like a dropped acorn.

Ros. It may well be called Jove's tree, when it drops forth such fruit. 250

Cel. Give me audience, good madam.

Ros. Proceed.

Cel. There lay he, stretched along, like a wounded knight.

Ros. Though it be pity to see such a sight, it well becomes the ground.

Cel. Cry 'holla' to thy tongue, I prithee; it curvets unseasonably. He was furnished like a hunter. 259

Ros. O, ominous! he comes to kill my heart.

Cel. I would sing my song without a burden: thou bringest me out of tune.

Ros. Do you not know I am a woman? when I think, I must speak. Sweet, say on.

Cel. You bring me out. Soft! comes he not here? 266

Enter ORLANDO *and* JAQUES.

Ros. 'Tis he: slink by, and note him.

Jaq. I thank you for your company; but, good faith, I had as lief have been myself alone. 270

Orl. And so had I; but yet, for fashion sake, I thank you too for your society.

Jaq. God be wi' you: let's meet as little as we can.

Orl. I do desire we may be better strangers.

Jaq. I pray you, mar no more trees with writing love-songs in their barks.

Orl. I pray you, mar no moe of my verses with reading them ill-favouredly.

Jaq. Rosalind is your love's name? 280

Orl. Yes, just.

Jaq. I do not like her name.

Orl. There was no thought of pleasing you when she was christened.

Jaq. What stature is she of?

Orl. Just as high as my heart.

Jaq. You are full of pretty answers. Have you not been acquainted with goldsmiths' wives, and conned them out of rings? 289

Orl. Not so; but I answer you right painted cloth, from whence you have studied your questions.

Jaq. You have a nimble wit: I think 'twas made of Atalanta's heels. Will you sit down

---

216. **of God's making**, i.e., or his tailor's. 221. **stay**, wait for. 234. **Wherein went he**, in what clothes. 238. **Gargantua's mouth**. Gargantua is the giant in *Rabelais* who swallowed five pilgrims in a salad. 241. **catechism**, catechising. 245. **atomies**, motes. **resolve**, solve. 247. **relish**, taste, or make pleasant to the palate. 248. **observance**, attention, observation. 249. **Jove's tree**, the oak.

256. **ground**, background, with play on ordinary sense. 257. **'holla,'** stop! 258. **furnished**, equipped, dressed. 261. **burden**, undersong, bass part. 262. **bringest**, puttest. 265. **bring me out**, put me out (of my part). 269. **myself alone**, alone, by myself. 281. **just**, just so. 289. **rings**, reference to the verses inscribed in rings, posies. 290. **right**, true, perfect. **painted cloth**, canvas painted with pictures (frequently scriptural) used for hangings; here, suggestive of commonplace.

with me? and we two will rail against our mistress the world and all our misery.

Orl. I will chide no breather in the world but myself, against whom I know most faults.

Jaq. The worst fault you have is to be in love.   300

Orl. 'Tis a fault I will not change for your best virtue. I am weary of you.

Jaq. By my troth, I was seeking for a fool when I found you.

Orl. He is drowned in the brook: look but in, and you shall see him.

Jaq. There I shall see mine own figure.

Orl. Which I take to be either a fool or a cipher.

Jaq. I'll tarry no longer with you: farewell, good Signior Love.   310

Orl. I am glad of your departure: adieu, good Monsieur Melancholy. [*Exit Jaques.*

Ros. [*Aside to Celia*] I will speak to him like a saucy lackey and under that habit play the knave with him. Do you hear, forester?

Orl. Very well: what would you?

Ros. I pray you, what is 't o'clock?

Orl. You should ask me what time o' day: there's no clock in the forest.   319

Ros. Then there is no true lover in the forest; else sighing every minute and groaning every hour would detect the lazy foot of Time as well as a clock.

Orl. And why not the swift foot of Time? had not that been as proper?

Ros. By no means, sir: Time travels in divers paces with divers persons. I'll tell you who Time ambles withal, who Time trots withal, who Time gallops withal and who he stands still withal.

Orl. I prithee, who doth he trot withal? 330

Ros. Marry, he trots hard with a young maid between the contract of her marriage and the day it is solemnized: if the interim be but a se'nnight, Time's pace is so hard that it seems the length of seven year.

Orl. Who ambles Time withal?

Ros. With a priest that lacks Latin and a rich man that hath not the gout, for the one sleeps easily because he cannot study and the other lives merrily because he feels no pain, the one lacking the burden of lean and wasteful learning, the other knowing no burden of

heavy tedious penury; these Time ambles withal.

Orl. Who doth he gallop withal?

Ros. With a thief to the gallows, for though he go as softly as foot can fall, he thinks himself too soon there.   347

Orl. Who stays it still withal?

Ros. With lawyers in the vacation; for they sleep between term and term and then they perceive not how Time moves.   351

Orl. Where dwell you, pretty youth?

Ros. With this shepherdess, my sister; here in the skirts of the forest, like fringe upon a petticoat.

Orl. Are you native of this place?

Ros. As the cony that you see dwell where she is kindled.   358

Orl. Your accent is something finer than you could purchase in so removed a dwelling.

Ros. I have been told so of many: but indeed an old religious uncle of mine taught me to speak, who was in his youth an inland man; one that knew courtship too well, for there he fell in love. I have heard him read many lectures against it, and I thank God I am not a woman, to be touched with so many giddy offences as he hath generally taxed their whole sex withal.   368

Orl. Can you remember any of the principal evils that he laid to the charge of women?

Ros. There were none principal; they were all like one another as half-pence are, every one fault seeming monstrous till his fellow-fault came to match it.

Orl. I prithee, recount some of them.

Ros. No, I will not cast away my physic but on those that are sick. There is a man haunts the forest, that abuses our young plants with carving 'Rosalind' on their barks; hangs odes upon hawthorns and elegies on brambles, all, forsooth, deifying the name of Rosalind: if I could meet that fancy-monger, I would give him some good counsel, for he seems to have the quotidian of love 383 upon him.

Orl. I am he that is so love-shaked: I pray you, tell me your remedy.

---

297. **breather**, living being. 331. **hard**, probably, slow, with uneven pace. 334. **se'nnight**, week.

346. **go as softly**, walk as slowly. 357. **cony**, rabbit. 358. **kindled**, littered, brought forth young. 360. **purchase**, acquire. **removed**, remote. 361. **of**, by. 362. **religious**, i.e., member of a religious order. 364. **courtship**, play on the meaning, "knowledge of courtly manners." 372. **half-pence.** Half-pence were almost the only uniform coins in circulation. 382. **fancy-monger**, love-monger, devotee of love. 383. **quotidian**, fever recurring daily (a symptom of love); hence, *love-shaked* below.

Ros. There is none of my uncle's marks upon you: he taught me how to know a man in love; in which cage of rushes I am sure you are not prisoner.   390

Orl. What were his marks?

Ros. A lean cheek, which you have not, a blue eye and sunken, which you have not, an unquestionable spirit, which you have not, a beard neglected, which you have not; but I pardon you for that, for simply your having in beard is a younger brother's revenue: then your hose should be ungartered, your bonnet unbanded, your sleeve unbuttoned, your shoe untied and every thing about you demonstrating a careless desolation; but you are no such man; you are rather point-device in your accoutrements as loving yourself than seeming the lover of any other.   403

Orl. Fair youth, I would I could make thee believe I love.

Ros. Me believe it! you may as soon make her that you love believe it; which, I warrant, she is apter to do than to confess she does: that is one of the points in the which women still give the lie to their consciences. But, in good sooth, are you he that hangs the verses on the trees, wherein Rosalind is so admired?

Orl. I swear to thee, youth, by the white hand of Rosalind, I am that he, that unfortunate he.

Ros. But are you so much in love as your rhymes speak?

Orl. Neither rhyme nor reason can express how much.   419

Ros. Love is merely a madness, and, I tell you, deserves as well a dark house and a whip as madmen do: and the reason why they are not so punished and cured is, that the lunacy is so ordinary that the whippers are in love too. Yet I profess curing it by counsel.

Orl. Did you ever cure any so?   426

Ros. Yes, one, and in this manner. He was to imagine me his love, his mistress; and I set him every day to woo me: at which time would I, being but a moonish youth, grieve, be effeminate, changeable, longing and liking, proud, fantastical, apish, shallow, inconstant, full of tears, full of smiles, for every passion something and for no passion truly

any thing, as boys and women are for the most part cattle of this colour; would now like him, now loathe him; then entertain him, then forswear him; now weep for him, then spit at him; that I drave my suitor from his mad humour of love to a living humour   439 of madness; which was, to forswear the full stream of the world and to live in a nook merely monastic. And thus I cured him; and this way will I take upon me to wash your liver as clean as a sound sheep's heart, that there shall not be one spot of love in 't.

Orl. I would not be cured, youth.

Ros. I would cure you, if you would but call me Rosalind and come every day to my cote and woo me.

Orl. Now, by the faith of my love, I will: tell me where it is.   450

Ros. Go with me to it and I'll show it you: and by the way you shall tell me where in the forest you live. Will you go?

Orl. With all my heart, good youth.

Ros. Nay, you must call me Rosalind. Come, sister, will you go?   [*Exeunt.*

Scene III.   *The forest.*

Enter TOUCHSTONE *and* AUDREY; JAQUES *behind.*

Touch. Come apace, good Audrey: I will fetch up your goats, Audrey. And how, Audrey? am I the man yet? doth my simple feature content you?

Aud. Your features! Lord warrant us! what features?   6

Touch. I am here with thee and thy goats, as the most capricious poet, honest Ovid, was among the Goths.

Jaq. [*Aside*] O knowledge ill-inhabited, worse than Jove in a thatched house!   11

Touch. When a man's verses cannot be understood, nor a man's good wit seconded

393. **blue eye,** eye having dark circles.   394. **unquestionable,** not to be questioned.   398. **bonnet,** hat. 402. **point-device,** faultless, precise.   411. **still,** ever, always.   421. **dark . . . whip,** an allusion to the common treatment of lunatics.   430. **moonish,** changeable.

439-440. **mad . . . madness,** pass from a madness of love to a real madness; Johnson read *loving* for *living* (real, not affected).   444. **liver,** seat of the emotion of love.   447-449. **I would . . . woo me.** This introduces the central comic theme in the play, which is so slight that it might not be realized. It presents a lover making love to his mistress, she being aware of the fact, he not.
Scene iii. Stage Direction: **Audrey,** a corruption of the name Ethelreda, whence the word *tawdry,* a corruption from *St. Audrey.*   4. **feature,** shape or form of body. 5. **warrant,** assure, protect. 7, 8, 9. **goats, capricious, Goths.** Ovid (a pastoral poet; hence *goats*) was banished by Augustus to the country of the *Goths* (pun on *goats*); *capricious* is derived from Latin *capra,* she-goat.   10. **illinhabited,** ill-lodged.   11. **Jove in a thatched house,** an allusion to Ovid's *Metamorphoses,* viii, the story of Jupiter and Mercury lodging in the house of Baucis and Philemon.

with the forward child Understanding, it strikes a man more dead than a great reckoning in a little room. Truly, I would the gods had made thee poetical. 16

Aud. I do not know what 'poetical' is: is it honest in deed and word? is it a true thing?

Touch. No, truly; for the truest poetry is the most feigning; and lovers are given to poetry, and what they swear in poetry may be said as lovers they do feign.

Aud. Do you wish then that the gods had made me poetical?

Touch. I do, truly; for thou swearest to me thou art honest: now, if thou wert a poet, I might have some hope thou didst feign.

Aud. Would you not have me honest?

Touch. No, truly, unless thou wert hard-favoured; for honesty coupled to beauty is to have honey a sauce to sugar. 31

Jaq. [*Aside*] A material fool!

Aud. Well, I am not fair; and therefore I pray the gods make me honest.

Touch. Truly, and to cast away honesty upon a foul slut were to put good meat into an unclean dish.

Aud. I am not a slut, though I thank the gods I am foul. 39

Touch. Well, praised be the gods for thy foulness! sluttishness may come hereafter. But be it as it may be, I will marry thee, and to that end I have been with Sir Oliver Martext, the vicar of the next village, who hath promised to meet me in this place of the forest and to couple us.

Jaq. [*Aside*] I would fain see this meeting.

Aud. Well, the gods give us joy! 47

Touch. Amen. A man may, if he were of a fearful heart, stagger in this attempt; for here we have no temple but the wood, no assembly but horn-beasts. But what though? Courage! As horns are odious, they are necessary. It is said, 'many a man knows no end of his goods:' right; many a man has good horns, and knows no end of them. Well, that is the dowry of his wife; 'tis none of his own getting. Horns? Even so. Poor men alone?

No, no; the noblest deer hath them as huge as the rascal. Is the single man therefore blessed? No: as a walled town is more worthier than a village, so is the forehead of a married man more honourable than the bare brow of a bachelor; and by how much defence is better than no skill, by so much is a horn more precious than to want. 64 Here comes Sir Oliver.

Enter Sir Oliver Martext.

Sir Oliver Martext, you are well met: will you dispatch us here under this tree, or shall we go with you to your chapel?

Sir Oli. Is there none here to give the woman?

Touch. I will not take her on gift of any man.

Sir Oli. Truly, she must be given, or the marriage is not lawful. 71

Jaq. [*Advancing*] Proceed, proceed: I'll give her.

Touch. Good even, good Master What-ye-call't: how do you, sir? You are very well met: God 'ild you for your last company: I am very glad to see you: even a toy in hand here, sir: nay, pray be covered.

Jaq. Will you be married, motley? 79

Touch. As the ox hath his bow, sir, the horse his curb and the falcon her bells, so man hath his desires; and as pigeons bill, so wedlock would be nibbling.

Jaq. And will you, being a man of your breeding, be married under a bush like a beggar? Get you to church, and have a good priest that can tell you what marriage is: this fellow will but join you together as they join wainscot; then one of you will prove a shrunk panel and, like green timber, warp, warp. 90

Touch. [*Aside*] I am not in the mind but I were better to be married of him than of another: for he is not like to marry me well; and not being well married, it will be a good excuse for me hereafter to leave my wife.

Jaq. Go thou with me, and let me counsel thee.

Touch. Come, sweet Audrey:
We must be married, or we must live in bawdry.

15. **great . . . room**, great charge for lodging in a small room. Recent scholars see in this passage an allusion to the death of Marlowe, who was stabbed by Ingram Frysar in an inn at Deptford in a quarrel over a tavern reckoning, May 30, 1593. New Cambridge editors use the reference as a means of dating the original version of the play. 20. **feigning**, inventive, imaginative. 21. **may be said**, i.e., it may be said. 32. **material**, full of sense, or possibly, gross or carnal. 36. **foul**, ugly. 41. **foulness**, dirtiness. 43. **Sir**, usual title for a priest. 49. **stagger**, hesitate. 51. **what though?** what though it be so? 52. **necessary**, unavoidable.

58. **rascal**, deer lean and out of season. 62. **defence**, art of self-defense. 64. **than to want**, i.e., than to be without a horn. 76. **God 'ild you**, God yield you, reward you. 78. **pray be covered**, pray put on your hat. 80. **bow**, yoke. 90. **warp**, pun on the sense "go astray from the straight path" (New Cambridge). 91. **I am . . . but**, I do not know but.

Farewell, good Master Oliver: not,—   100
          O sweet Oliver,
          O brave Oliver,
     Leave me not behind thee:
but,—
          Wind away,
          Begone, I say,
     I will not to wedding with thee.
[*Exeunt Jaques, Touchstone and Audrey.*
Sir Oli. 'Tis no matter: ne'er a fantastical
knave of them all shall flout me out of my
calling.   [*Exit.*

SCENE IV. *The forest.*

Enter ROSALIND *and* CELIA.

Ros. Never talk to me; I will weep.
Cel. Do, I prithee; but yet have the grace
to consider that tears do not become a man.
Ros. But have I not cause to weep?
Cel. As good cause as one would desire;
therefore weep.
Ros. His very hair is of the dissembling
colour.
Cel. Something browner than Judas's:
marry, his kisses are Judas's own children. 10
Ros. I' faith, his hair is of a good colour.
Cel. An excellent colour: your chestnut
was ever the only colour.
Ros. And his kissing is as full of sanctity
as the touch of holy bread.
Cel. He hath bought a pair of cast lips of
Diana: a nun of winter's sisterhood kisses not
more religiously; the very ice of chastity is in
them.
Ros. But why did he swear he would come
this morning, and comes not?   21
Cel. Nay, certainly, there is no truth in
him.
Ros. Do you think so?
Cel. Yes; I think he is not a pick-purse nor
a horse-stealer, but for his verity in love, I do
think him as concave as a covered goblet or
a worm-eaten nut.
Ros. Not true in love?
Cel. Yes, when he is in; but I think he is
not in.   30

108. **fantastical knave.** Capell suggests that
Touchstone dances round the priest like a harlequin
while he sings the ballad about Oliver.
     Scene iv. 9. **browner than Judas's,** an allusion to
the traditional representation of Judas as having a red
beard. 15. **holy bread,** ordinary leavened bread which
was blessed after the Eucharist and distributed to those
who had not communed. 16. **cast,** cast off, discarded.
17. **Diana,** goddess of chastity. 26. **covered goblet,**
i.e., a goblet having a convex top and therefore more
hollow because the cover is on only when the goblet is
empty.

Ros. You have heard him swear downright he was.
Cel. 'Was' is not 'is:' besides, the oath of
a lover is no stronger than the word of a
tapster; they are both the confirmer of false
reckonings. He attends here in the forest on
the duke your father.   37
Ros. I met the duke yesterday and had
much question with him: he asked me of
what parentage I was; I told him, of as good
as he; so he laughed and let me go. But what
talk we of fathers, when there is such a man
as Orlando?   42
Cel. O, that's a brave man! he writes
brave verses, speaks brave words, swears
brave oaths and breaks them bravely, quite
traverse, athwart the heart of his lover; as a
puisny tilter, that spurs his horse but on one
side, breaks his staff like a noble goose: but
all's brave that youth mounts and folly
guides. Who comes here?

Enter CORIN.

Cor. Mistress and master, you have oft in-
     quired   50
After the shepherd that complain'd of love,
Who you saw sitting by me on the turf,
Praising the proud disdainful shepherdess
That was his mistress.
Cel.   Well, and what of him?
Cor. If you will see a pageant truly play'd,
Between the pale complexion of true love
And the red glow of scorn and proud disdain,
Go hence a little and I shall conduct you,
If you will mark it.
Ros.   O, come, let us remove:
The sight of lovers feedeth those in love. 60
Bring us to this sight, and you shall say
I'll prove a busy actor in their play. [*Exeunt.*

SCENE V. *Another part of the forest.*

Enter SILVIUS *and* PHEBE.

Sil. Sweet Phebe, do not scorn me; do not,
     Phebe;
Say that you love me not, but say not so
In bitterness. The common executioner,
Whose heart the accustom'd sight of death
     makes hard,
Falls not the axe upon the humbled neck

39. **question,** conversation. 41. **what,** why. 45.
traverse, across; with allusion to the disgrace of breaking
one's lance across the body of the adversary. 46. **puisny,**
petty, paltry (literally, junior). 56. **pale complexion.**
Sighing was believed to draw the blood from the heart.
     Scene v. 5. **Falls not,** lets not fall.

But first begs pardon: will you sterner be
†Than he that dies and lives by bloody
    drops?
Enter Rosalind, Celia, *and* Corin, *behind.*

Phe. I would not be thy executioner:
I fly thee, for I would not injure thee.
Thou tell'st me there is murder in mine eye:10
'Tis pretty, sure, and very probable,
That eyes, that are the frail'st and softest
    things,
Who shut their coward gates on atomies,
Should be call'd tyrants, butchers, mur-
    derers!
Now I do frown on thee with all my heart;
And if mine eyes can wound, now let them
    kill thee:
Now counterfeit to swoon; why now fall
    down;
Or if thou canst not, O, for shame, for
    shame,
Lie not, to say mine eyes are murderers!
Now show the wound mine eye hath made in
    thee: 20
Scratch thee but with a pin, and there re-
    mains
Some scar of it; lean but upon a rush,
The cicatrice and capable impressure
Thy palm some moment keeps; but now mine
    eyes,
Which I have darted at thee, hurt thee not,
Nor, I am sure, there is no force in eyes
That can do hurt.
Sil.   O dear Phebe,
If ever,—as that ever may be near,—
You meet in some fresh cheek the power of
    fancy,
Then shall you know the wounds invisible 30
That love's keen arrows make.
Phe.   But till that time
Come not thou near me: and when that time
    comes,
Afflict me with thy mocks, pity me not;
As till that time I shall not pity thee.
Ros. And why, I pray you? Who might be
    your mother,
That you insult, exult, and all at once,
Over the wretched? What though you have
    no beauty,—

As, by my faith, I see no more in you
Than without candle may go dark to bed—
Must you be therefore proud and pitiless?
Why, what means this? Why do you look on
    me?   41
I see no more in you than in the ordinary
Of nature's sale-work. 'Od's my little life,
I think she means to tangle my eyes too!
No, faith, proud mistress, hope not after it:
'Tis not your inky brows, your black silk
    hair,
Your bugle eyeballs, nor your cheek of
    cream,
That can entame my spirits to your worship.
You foolish shepherd, wherefore do you fol-
    low her,
Like foggy south puffing with wind and rain?
You are a thousand times a properer man 51
Than she a woman: 'tis such fools as you
That makes the world full of ill-favour'd
    children:
'Tis not her glass, but you, that flatters her;
And out of you she sees herself more
    proper
Than any of her lineaments can show her.
But, mistress, know yourself: down on your
    knees,
And thank heaven, fasting, for a good man's
    love:
For I must tell you friendly in your ear,   59
Sell when you can: you are not for all mar-
    kets:
Cry the man mercy; love him; take his offer:
Foul is most foul, being foul to be a scoff-
    er.
So take her to thee, shepherd: fare you well.
Phe. Sweet youth, I pray you, chide a
    year together:
I had rather hear you chide than this man
    woo.
Ros. He's fallen in love with your foulness
and she'll fall in love with my anger. If it be
so, as fast as she answers thee with frowning
looks, I'll sauce her with bitter words. Why
look you so upon me?   70
Phe. For no ill will I bear you.

6. **But first begs**, without first begging. 7. **Than
. . . drops**, obscure line; probable meaning: "Will you
be sterner than he (the executioner) who makes his living (lives and dies) by shedding blood?" 11. **sure**,
surely. 23. **cicatrice**, mark, impression. **capable**,
receptive, impressible. **impressure**, impression. 29.
fancy, love. 33. **mocks**, mockeries, taunts. 36. **all
at once**, i.e., all in a breath.

39. **without candle**, i.e., your beauty is not so
brilliant that it will suffice to light you to bed. 43.
sale-work, ready-made work, i.e., not of the best
quality. '**Od's**, minced form of *God's*, used in petty oaths.
47. **bugle**, tube-shaped glass bead; here, black. 48.
entame, subdue. **to your worship**, to worship you.
50. **foggy south**. South was the direction from which
came fog and rain. 51. **properer**, handsomer. 55. **out
of you**, i.e., as her mirror. 61. **Cry the man mercy**,
beg the man's pardon. 62. **foul**, two meanings of the
word played upon: Ugliness is most ugly when it is
rough and abusive.

Ros. I pray you, do not fall in love with me,
For I am falser than vows made in wine:
Besides, I like you not. If you will know my house,
'Tis at the tuft of olives here hard by.
Will you go, sister? Shepherd, ply her hard.
Come, sister. Shepherdess, look on him better,
And be not proud: though all the world could see,
None could be so abused in sight as he.
Come, to our flock.   80

[*Exeunt Rosalind, Celia and Corin.*

Phe. Dead shepherd, now I find thy saw of might,
'Who ever loved that loved not at first sight?'
Sil. Sweet Phebe,—
Phe.   Ha, what say'st thou, Silvius?
Sil. Sweet Phebe, pity me.
Phe. Why, I am sorry for thee, gentle Silvius.
Sil. Wherever sorrow is, relief would be:
If you do sorrow at my grief in love,
By giving love your sorrow and my grief
Were both extermined.
Phe. Thou hast my love: is not that neighbourly?   90
Sil. I would have you.
Phe.   Why, that were covetousness.
Silvius, the time was that I hated thee,
And yet it is not that I bear thee love;
But since that thou canst talk of love so well,
Thy company, which erst was irksome to me,
I will endure, and I'll employ thee too:
But do not look for further recompense
Than thine own gladness that thou are employ'd.
Sil. So holy and so perfect is my love,
And I in such a poverty of grace,   100
That I shall think it a most plenteous crop
To glean the broken ears after the man
That the main harvest reaps: loose now and then
A scatter'd smile, and that I'll live upon.

Phe. Know'st thou the youth that spoke to me erewhile?
Sil. Not very well, but I have met him oft;
And he hath bought the cottage and the bounds
That the old carlot once was master of.
Phe. Think not I love him, though I ask for him;
'Tis but a peevish boy; yet he talks well;   110
But what care I for words? yet words do well
When he that speaks them pleases those that hear.
It is a pretty youth: not very pretty:
But, sure, he's proud, and yet his pride becomes him:
He'll make a proper man: the best thing in him
Is his complexion; and faster than his tongue
Did make offence his eye did heal it up.
He is not very tall; yet for his years he's tall:
His leg is but so so; and yet 'tis well:
There was a pretty redness in his lip,   120
A little riper and more lusty red
Than that mix'd in his cheek; 'twas just the difference
Betwixt the constant red and mingled damask.
There be some women, Silvius, had they mark'd him
In parcels as I did, would have gone near
To fall in love with him; but, for my part,
I love him not nor hate him not; and yet
I have more cause to hate him than to love him:
For what had he to do to chide at me?
He said mine eyes were black and my hair black;   130
And, now I am remember'd, scorn'd at me:
I marvel why I answer'd not again:
But that's all one; omittance is no quittance.
I'll write to him a very taunting letter,
And thou shalt bear it: wilt thou, Silvius?
Sil. Phebe, with all my heart.
Phe.   I'll write it straight;
The matter's in my head and in my heart:
I will be bitter with him and passing short.
Go with me, Silvius.   [*Exeunt.*

81-82. **Dead . . . sight.** Line 82 is quoted from Marlowe's *Hero and Leander*, Sestiad I, 176. Marlowe died on May 30, 1593; the poem was not printed until 1598. New Cambridge editors would date the first version of the play as 1593 in part by this reference. The publication of the poem may, of course, have occasioned the quotation. 89. **extermined**, exterminated. 90. **neighbourly.** This serves to take back Phebe's preceding statement, since love was divided into conjugal love and neighborly love. 100. **poverty of grace.** Love is his divinity, and love has been ungracious to him.

107. **bounds**, i.e., bounds within which he can feed stock. 108. **carlot**, peasant, countryman. 110. **peevish**, silly, senseless. 123. **constant**, uniform. **mingled damask**, striped red and white damask, i.e., the color of the damask rose (pink or rose color). 125. **In parcels**, piecemeal, in detail. 129. **what . . . do**, what business had he. 131. **am remember'd**, remember, recollect. 136. **straight**, immediately.

ACT IV.

Scene I. *The forest.*

Enter Rosalind, Celia, *and* Jaques.

Jaq. I prithee, pretty youth, let me be better acquainted with thee.

Ros. They say you are a melancholy fellow.

Jaq. I am so; I do love it better than laughing.

Ros. Those that are in extremity of either are abominable fellows and betray themselves to every modern censure worse 7 than drunkards.

Jaq. Why, 'tis good to be sad and say nothing.

Ros. Why then, 'tis good to be a post. 9

Jaq. I have neither the scholar's melancholy, which is emulation, nor the musician's, which is fantastical, nor the courtier's, which is proud, nor the soldier's, which is ambitious, nor the lawyer's, which is politic, nor the lady's, which is nice, nor the lover's, which is all these: but it is a melancholy of mine own, compounded of many simples, extracted from many objects, and indeed the sundry contemplation of my travels, in which my often rumination wraps me in a most humorous sadness. 20

Ros. A traveller! By my faith, you have great reason to be sad: I fear you have sold your own lands to see other men's; then, to have seen much and to have nothing, is to have rich eyes and poor hands.

Jaq. Yes, I have gained my experience.

Ros. And your experience makes you sad: I had rather have a fool to make me merry than experience to make me sad; and to travel for it too!

Enter Orlando.

Orl. Good day and happiness, dear Rosalind!

Jaq. Nay, then, God be wi' you, an you talk in blank verse. *[Exit.* 32

Ros. Farewell, Monsieur Traveller: look you lisp and wear strange suits, disable all the benefits of your own country, be out of

love with your nativity and almost chide God for making you that countenance you are, or I will scarce think you have swam in a gondola. Why, how now, Orlando! where have you been all this while? You a lover! An you serve me such another trick, never come in my sight more. 41

Orl. My fair Rosalind, I come within an hour of my promise.

Ros. Break an hour's promise in love! He that will divide a minute into a thousand parts and break but a part of the thousandth part of a minute in the affairs of love, it may be said of him that Cupid hath clapped him o' the shoulder, but I'll warrant him heartwhole.

Orl. Pardon me, dear Rosalind. 50

Ros. Nay, an you be so tardy, come no more in my sight: I had as lief be wooed of a snail.

Orl. Of a snail?

Ros. Ay, of a snail; for though he comes slowly, he carries his house on his head; a better jointure, I think, than you make a woman: besides, he brings his destiny with him.

Orl. What's that? 58

Ros. Why, horns, which such as you are fain to be beholding to your wives for: but he comes armed in his fortune and prevents the slander of his wife.

Orl. Virtue is no horn-maker; and my Rosalind is virtuous.

Ros. And I am your Rosalind. 65

Cel. It pleases him to call you so; but he hath a Rosalind of a better leer than you.

Ros. Come, woo me, woo me, for now I am in a holiday humour and like enough to consent. What would you say to me now, an I were your very very Rosalind? 71

Orl. I would kiss before I spoke.

Ros. Nay, you were better speak first, and when you were gravelled for lack of matter, you might take occasion to kiss. Very good orators, when they are out, they will spit; and for lovers lacking—God warn us!—matter, the cleanliest shift is to kiss.

---

7. **modern**, ordinary. **censure**, opinion, judgment. 14. **politic**, crafty, or insincere (out of pretended sympathy for his client). 15. **nice**, fastidious. 17. **simples**, ingredients (usually herbs) of a drug. 34. **disable**, depreciate, disparage.

38. **swam in a gondola**, i.e., been in Venice. 48. **clapped . . . shoulder**, tapped on the shoulder by way of arrest. 56. **jointure**, marriage-settlement. 60. **beholding**, beholden, indebted. 61. **armed . . . fortune**, i.e., with the horns of a cuckold which it was his fate to earn. **prevents**, anticipates. 67. **leer**, complexion, countenance. 74. **gravelled**, stuck, at a standstill. 76. **out**, at a loss. 77. **warn**, for *warrant* (defend). 78. **cleanliest shift**, best way out of it.

Orl. How if the kiss be denied?

Ros. Then she puts you to entreaty, and there begins new matter. 81

Orl. Who could be out, being before his beloved mistress?

Ros. Marry, that should you, if I were your mistress, or I should think my honesty ranker than my wit.

Orl. What, of my suit?

Ros. Not out of your apparel, and yet out of your suit. Am not I your Rosalind?

Orl. I take some joy to say you are, because I would be talking of her.

Ros. Well, in her person I say I will not have you.

Orl. Then in mine own person I die. 93

Ros. No, faith, die by attorney. The poor world is almost six thousand years old, and in all this time there was not any man died in his own person, videlicet, in a love-cause. Troilus had his brains dashed out with a Grecian club; yet he did what he could to die before, and he is one of the patterns of love. Leander, he would have lived many a fair year, though Hero had turned nun, if it had not been for a hot midsummer night; for, good youth, he went but forth to wash him in the Hellespont and being taken with the cramp was drowned: and the foolish chroniclers of that age found it was 'Hero of Sestos.' But these are all lies: men have died from time to time and worms have eaten them, but not for love.

Orl. I would not have my right Rosalind of this mind, for, I protest, her frown might kill me. 110

Ros. By this hand, it will not kill a fly. But come, now I will be your Rosalind in a more coming-on disposition, and ask me what you will, I will grant it.

Orl. Then love me, Rosalind.

Ros. Yes, faith, will I, Fridays and Saturdays and all.

Orl. And wilt thou have me?

Ros. Ay, and twenty such.

Orl. What sayest thou? 120

Ros. Are you not good?

Orl. I hope so.

Ros. Why then, can one desire too much of a good thing? Come, sister, you shall be the priest and marry us. Give me your hand, Orlando. What do you say, sister?

Orl. Pray thee, marry us.

Cel. I cannot say the words.

Ros. You must begin, 'Will you, Orlando—'

Cel. Go to. Will you, Orlando, have to wife this Rosalind? 131

Orl. I will.

Ros. Ay, but when?

Orl. Why now; as fast as she can marry us.

Ros. Then you must say, 'I take thee, Rosalind, for wife.'

Orl. I take thee, Rosalind, for wife. 137

Ros. I might ask you for your commission; but I do take thee, Orlando, for my husband: there's a girl goes before the priest; and certainly a woman's thought 141 runs before her actions.

Orl. So do all thoughts; they are winged.

Ros. Now tell me how long you would have her after you have possessed her.

Orl. For ever and a day. 145

Ros. Say 'a day,' without the 'ever.' No, no, Orlando; men are April when they woo, December when they wed: maids are May when they are maids, but the sky changes when they are wives. I will be more jealous of thee than a Barbary cock-pigeon over his hen, more clamorous than a parrot against rain, more new-fangled than an ape, more giddy in my desires than a monkey: I will weep for nothing, like Diana in the fountain, and I will do that when you are disposed to be merry; I will laugh like a hyen, and 157 that when thou art inclined to sleep.

Orl. But will my Rosalind do so?

Ros. By my life, she will do as I do.

Orl. O, but she is wise. 160

Ros. Or else she could not have the wit to do this: the wiser, the waywarder: make the doors upon a woman's wit and it will out at the casement; shut that and 'twill out at the key-hole; stop that, 'twill fly with the smoke out at the chimney.

86. **ranker,** better grown. 94. **attorney,** proxy. 97. **Troilus,** hero of the story of Troilus and Cressida, pattern of faithful love. 100. **Leander,** hero of the story of Hero and Leander, who lost his life swimming the Hellespont to visit his sweetheart; also a pattern of faithful love. Both the *club* and the *cramp* are Shakespeare's inventions, 105. **chroniclers.** Hanmer read *coroners* because of the use of the word *found* in the same passage.

138. **ask . . . commission,** ask you what authority you have for taking her. 140. **goes before,** anticipates. 151. **Barbary cock-pigeon.** The epithet suggests oriental jealousy (Furness). 152. **against,** before, in expectation of. 155. **Diana in the fountain.** Diana, of course, frequently appeared as the centerpiece of fountains. Stow's *Survey of London* describes the setting up of a fountain with a Diana in green marble in the year 1596. 157. **hyen,** hyena. 162. **make,** shut.

Orl. A man that had a wife with such a wit, he might say 'Wit, whither wilt?'

Ros. Nay, you might keep that check for it till you met your wife's wit going to your neighbour's bed.   171

Orl. And what wit could wit have to excuse that?

Ros. Marry, to say she came to seek you there. You shall never take her without her answer, unless you take her without her tongue. O, that woman that cannot make her fault her husband's occasion, let her never nurse her child herself, for she will breed it like a fool!

Orl. For these two hours, Rosalind, I will leave thee.   181

Ros. Alas! dear love, I cannot lack thee two hours.

Orl. I must attend the duke at dinner: by two o'clock I will be with thee again.

Ros. Ay, go your ways, go your ways; I knew what you would prove: my friends told me as much, and I thought no less: that flattering tongue of yours won me: 'tis but one cast away, and so, come, death! Two o'clock is your hour?

Orl. Ay, sweet Rosalind.   191

Ros. By my troth, and in good earnest, and so God mend me, and by all pretty oaths that are not dangerous, if you break one jot of your promise or come one minute behind your hour, I will think you the most pathetical break-promise and the most hollow lover and the most unworthy of her you call Rosalind that may be chosen out of the gross band of the unfaithful: therefore beware my censure and keep your promise.   200

Orl. With no less religion than if thou wert indeed my Rosalind: so adieu.

Ros. Well, Time is the old justice that examines all such offenders, and let Time try: adieu.   [*Exit Orlando.*

Cel. You have simply misused our sex in your love-prate: we must have your doublet and hose plucked over your head, and show the world what the bird hath done to her own nest.

Ros. O coz, coz, coz, my pretty little coz,

that thou didst know how many fathom deep I am in love! But it cannot be sounded: my affection hath an unknown bottom, like the bay of Portugal.

Cel. Or rather, bottomless, that as fast as you pour affection in, it runs out.   217

Ros. No, that same wicked bastard of Venus that was begot of thought, conceived of spleen and born of madness, that blind rascally boy that abuses every one's eyes because his own are out, let him be judge how deep I am in love. I'll tell thee, Aliena, I cannot be out of the sight of Orlando: I'll go find a shadow and sigh till he come.

Cel. And I'll sleep.   [*Exeunt.*

SCENE II.   *The forest.*

Enter JAQUES, Lords, *and* Foresters.

Jaq. Which is he that killed the deer?

A Lord. Sir, it was I.

Jaq. Let's present him to the duke, like a Roman conqueror; and it would do well to set the deer's horns upon his head, for a branch of victory. Have you no song, forester, for this purpose?

For. Yes, sir.

Jaq. Sing it: 'tis no matter how it be in tune, so it make noise enough.   10

SONG.

For. What shall he have that kill'd the deer?
    His leather skin and horns to wear.
        Then sing him home;
        [*The rest shall bear this burden.*
    Take thou no scorn to wear the horn;
    It was a crest ere thou wast born:
        Thy father's father wore it,
        And thy father bore it:
    The horn, the horn, the lusty horn
    Is not a thing to laugh to scorn.
                                [*Exeunt.*

SCENE III.   *The forest.*

Enter ROSALIND *and* CELIA.

Ros. How say you now? Is it not past two o'clock? and here much Orlando!

---

168. **'Wit, whither wilt?'** a common Elizabethan expression meaning "Hold your tongue." Johnson saw in it an allusion to some well-known story now lost. 177. **her husband's occasion,** occasion against her husband. 196. **pathetical,** possibly, pitiable, miserable, or passion-moving. 201. **religion,** strict fidelity. 206. **simply misused,** absolutely slandered.

220. **spleen,** sudden anger or spite. 225. **shadow,** shady place.
Scene ii. The scene presents a procession of huntsmen with their kill and is full of the customs of the chase, reflecting also the heathen background of the ceremony in the decking of the chief huntsman with the hide and horns of the slain deer as a fetish. 14. **Take ... scorn,** be not ashamed.
Scene iii. 2. **and ... Orlando,** ironical; Steevens: *here's much Orlando.*

Cel. I warrant you, with pure love and troubled brain, he hath ta'en his bow and arrows and is gone forth to sleep. Look, 5 who comes here.

Enter SILVIUS.

Sil. My errand is to you, fair youth;
My gentle Phebe bid me give you this:
I know not the contents; but, as I guess
By the stern brow and waspish action
Which she did use as she was writing of it, 10
It bears an angry tenour: pardon me;
I am but as a guiltless messenger.

Ros. Patience herself would startle at this letter
And play the swaggerer; bear this, bear all:
She says I am not fair, that I lack manners;
She calls me proud, and that she could not love me,
Were man as rare as phœnix. 'Od's my will!
Her love is not the hare that I do hunt:
Why writes she so to me? Well, shepherd, well,
This is a letter of your own device. 20

Sil. No, I protest, I know not the contents:
Phebe did write it.

Ros. 　　Come, come, you are a fool
And turn'd into the extremity of love.
I saw her hand: she has a leathern hand,
A freestone-colour'd hand: I verily did think
That her old gloves were on, but 'twas her hands:
She has a huswife's hand; but that's no matter:
I say she never did invent this letter;
This is a man's invention and his hand.

Sil. Sure, it is hers. 30

Ros. Why, 'tis a boisterous and a cruel style,
A style for challengers; why, she defies me,
Like Turk to Christian: women's gentle brain
Could not drop forth such giant-rude invention,
Such Ethiope words, blacker in their effect
Than in their countenance. Will you hear the letter?

Sil. So please you, for I never heard it yet;
Yet heard too much of Phebe's cruelty.

Ros. She Phebes me: mark how the tyrant writes. 　　　　　[*Reads.*
Art thou god to shepherd turn'd, 40
That a maiden's heart hath burn'd?
Can a woman rail thus?

Sil. Call you this railing?

Ros. [*Reads*]
Why, thy godhead laid apart,
Warr'st thou with a woman's heart?
Did you ever hear such railing?
Whiles the eye of man did woo me,
That could do no vengeance to me.
Meaning me a beast.
If the scorn of your bright eyne 50
Have power to raise such love in mine,
Alack, in me what strange effect
Would they work in mild aspect!
Whiles you chid me, I did love;
How then might your prayers move!
He that brings this love to thee
Little knows this love in me:
And by him seal up thy mind;
Whether that thy youth and kind
Will the faithful offer take 60
Of me and all that I can make;
Or else by him my love deny,
And then I'll study how to die.

Sil. Call you this chiding?

Cel. Alas, poor shepherd! 65

Ros. Do you pity him? no, he deserves no pity. Wilt thou love such a woman? What, to make thee an instrument and play false strains upon thee! not to be endured! Well, go your way to her, for I see love hath made thee a tame snake, and say this to her: that if she love me, I charge her to love thee; if she will not, I will never have her unless thou entreat for her. If you be a true lover, hence, and not a word; for here comes more company. 　　　　　[*Exit Silvius.*

Enter OLIVER.

Oli. Good morrow, fair ones: pray you, if you know,
Where in the purlieus of this forest stands
A sheep-cote fenced about with olive trees?

5. **sleep**, unexpected turn; one would have expected her to say *hunt*. 17. **phœnix**, a fabulous bird of Arabia, the only one of its kind, which lived five hundred years and was reborn of its own ashes. 23. **turn'd**, brought. 25. **freestone-colour'd**, color of freestone, brown. 27. **huswife's hand**, i.e., hard with housework. 29. **invention**, conception. **hand**, handwriting, with play on the ordinary meaning. 35. **Ethiope**, blackamoor; here, black.

39. **Phebes**, i.e., treats cruelly. 48. **vengeance**, mischief, harm. 53. **aspect**, appearance of a planet; astrological term. 59. **youth and kind**, youthful nature. 68. **instrument**, tool and musical instrument. 76. **fair ones**, sometimes thought inappropriate as addressed to a boy as well as a girl, but there is nothing against such a greeting. 77. **purlieus**, tracts of land on the border of a forest.

Cel. West of this place, down in the neighbour bottom:
The rank of osiers by the murmuring stream
Left on your right hand brings you to the place.   81
But at this hour the house doth keep itself;
There's none within.
   Oli. If that an eye may profit by a tongue,
Then should I know you by description;
Such garments and such years: 'The boy is fair,
Of female favour, and bestows himself
Like a ripe sister: the woman low
And browner than her brother.' Are not you
The owner of the house I did enquire for?   90
   Cel. It is no boast, being ask'd, to say we are.
   Oli. Orlando doth commend him to you both,
And to that youth he calls his Rosalind
He sends this bloody napkin. Are you he?
   Ros. I am: what must we understand by this?
   Oli. Some of my shame; if you will know of me
What man I am, and how, and why, and where
This handkercher was stain'd.
   Cel.   I pray you, tell it.
   Oli. When last the young Orlando parted from you
He left a promise to return again   100
Within an hour, and pacing through the forest,
Chewing the food of sweet and bitter fancy,
Lo, what befel! he threw his eye aside,
And mark what object did present itself:
Under an oak, whose boughs were moss'd with age
And high top bald with dry antiquity,
A wretched ragged man, o'ergrown with hair,
Lay sleeping on his back: about his neck
A green and gilded snake had wreathed itself,
Who with her head nimble in threats approach'd   110
The opening of his mouth; but suddenly,
Seeing Orlando, it unlink'd itself,
And with indented glides did slip away
Into a bush: under which bush's shade
A lioness, with udders all drawn dry,

Lay couching, head on ground, with catlike watch,
When that the sleeping man should stir; for 'tis
The royal disposition of that beast
To prey on nothing that doth seem as dead:
This seen, Orlando did approach the man   120
And found it was his brother, his elder brother.
   Cel. O, I have heard him speak of that same brother;
And he did render him the most unnatural
That lived amongst men.
   Oli.   And well he might so do,
For well I know he was unnatural.
   Ros. But, to Orlando: did he leave him there,
Food to the suck'd and hungry lioness?
   Oli. Twice did he turn his back and purposed so;
But kindness, nobler ever than revenge,   129
And nature, stronger than his just occasion,
Made him give battle to the lioness,
Who quickly fell before him: in which hurtling
From miserable slumber I awaked.
   Cel. Are you his brother?
   Ros.   Was't you he rescued?
   Cel. Was't you that did so oft contrive to kill him?
   Oli. 'Twas I; but 'tis not I: I do not shame
To tell you what I was, since my conversion
So sweetly tastes, being the thing I am.
   Ros. But, for the bloody napkin?
   Oli.   By and by.
When from the first to last betwixt us two   140
Tears our recountments had most kindly bathed,
As how I came into that desert place:—
In brief, he led me to the gentle duke,
Who gave me fresh array and entertainment,
Committing me unto my brother's love;
Who led me instantly unto his cave,
There stripp'd himself, and here upon his arm
The lioness had torn some flesh away,
Which all this while had bled; and now he fainted

79. **neighbour bottom**, neighboring dell. 80. **rank of osiers**, row of willows. 87. **favour**, aspect, look. **bestows**, behaves. 88. **ripe sister**, mature or elder sister. 94. **napkin**, handkerchief. 113. **indented**, zigzag. 115. **udders . . . dry**, therefore fierce with hunger.

126. **to**, with regard to. 130. **just occasion**, fair chance (of revenge). 132. **hurtling**, clattering, clashing. 136. **do not shame**, am not ashamed. 139. **for**, as regards. 141. **recountments**, relation, recital. 142. **As**, as for instance.

And cried, in fainting, upon Rosalind.   150
Brief, I recover'd him, bound up his wound;
And, after some small space, being strong at
    heart,
He sent me hither, stranger as I am,
To tell this story, that you might excuse
His broken promise, and to give this napkin
Dyed in his blood unto the shepherd youth
That he in sport doth call his Rosalind.

        [Rosalind swoons.

Cel. Why, how now, Ganymede! sweet
Ganymede!
Oli. Many will swoon when they do look
on blood.   159
Cel. There is more in it. Cousin Gany-
mede!
Oli. Look, he recovers.
Ros. I would I were at home.
Cel.   We'll lead you thither.
I pray you, will you take him by the arm?
Oli. Be of good cheer, youth: you a man!
you lack a man's heart.   165
Ros. I do so, I confess it. Ah, sirrah, a
body would think this was well counter-
feited! I pray you, tell your brother how
well I counterfeited. Heigh-ho!   169
Oli. This was not counterfeit: there is too
great testimony in your complexion that it
was a passion of earnest.
Ros. Counterfeit, I assure you.
Oli. Well then, take a good heart and
counterfeit to be a man.
Ros. So I do: but, i' faith, I should have
been a woman by right.
Cel. Come, you look paler and paler: pray
you, draw homewards. Good sir, go with us.
Oli. That will I, for I must bear answer
back   180
How you excuse my brother, Rosalind.
Ros. I shall devise something: but, I pray
you, commend my counterfeiting to him.
Will you go?   *[Exeunt.*

ACT V.

Scene I. *The forest.*

Enter Touchstone *and* Audrey.

Touch. We shall find a time, Audrey; patience, gentle Audrey.

Aud. Faith, the priest was good enough,
for all the old gentleman's saying.   4
Touch. A most wicked Sir Oliver, Audrey,
a most vile Martext. But, Audrey, there is a
youth here in the forest lays claim to you.
Aud. Ay, I know who 'tis; he hath no
interest in me in the world: here comes the
man you mean.   10
Touch. It is meat and drink to me to see a
clown: by my troth, we that have good wits,
have much to answer for; we shall be flouting; we cannot hold.

Enter William.

Will. Good even, Audrey.
Aud. God ye good even, William.
Will. And good even to you, sir.
Touch. Good even, gentle friend. Cover
thy head, cover thy head; nay, prithee, be
covered. How old are you, friend?   20
Will. Five and twenty, sir.
Touch. A ripe age. Is thy name William?
Will. William, sir.
Touch. A fair name. Wast born i' the
forest here?
Will. Ay, sir, I thank God.
Touch. 'Thank God;' a good answer. Art
rich?
Will. Faith, sir, so so.
Touch. 'So so' is good, very good, very
excellent good; and yet it is not; it is but so
so. Art thou wise?   31
Will. Ay, sir, I have a pretty wit.
Touch. Why, thou sayest well. I do now
remember a saying, 'The fool doth think he is
wise, but the wise man knows himself to be a
fool.' The heathen philosopher, when he had
a desire to eat a grape, would open his lips
when he put it into his mouth; meaning
thereby that grapes were made to eat and
lips to open. You do love this maid?   40
Will. I do, sir.
Touch. Give me your hand. Art thou
learned?
Will. No, sir.   43
Touch. Then learn this of me: to have, is
to have; for it is a figure in rhetoric that
drink, being poured out of a cup into a glass,
by filling the one doth empty the other; for

---

151. **Brief**, in brief. **recover'd**, brought back to
consciousness or health. 166. **sirrah**. Onions suggests
that this is addressed to Rosalind to herself, since the
word is frequently so used in soliloquies. 172. **passion
of earnest**, real attack.

4. **old gentleman's**, interesting comment on the
age of Jaques. 12. **clown**, countryman. 13. **shall**,
must. **flouting**, scoffing, expressing contempt. 16.
God ye good even, God give you good evening. 36-40.
The heathen . . . open. New Cambridge editors eluci-
date this as a way of telling William (whose mouth is
probably gaping like a rustic's) that the grape (Audrey)
is not for his lips. 46-47. **drink . . . other**, i.e., both
Touchstone and William cannot possess Audrey.

all your writers do consent that ipse is he: now, you are not ipse, for I am he.

Will. Which he, sir?   50

Touch. He, sir, that must marry this woman. Therefore, you clown, abandon,— which is in the vulgar leave,—the society,— which in the boorish is company,—of this female,—which in the common is woman; which together is, abandon the society of this female, or, clown, thou perishest; or, to thy better understanding, diest; or, to wit, I kill thee, make thee away, translate thy life into death, thy liberty into bondage: I will deal in poison with thee, or in bastinado, or in 60 steel; I will bandy with thee in faction; I will o'errun thee with policy; I will kill thee a hundred and fifty ways: therefore tremble, and depart.

Aud. Do, good William.

Will. God rest you merry, sir. [*Exit.* 65

Enter CORIN.

Cor. Our master and mistress seeks you; come, away, away!

Touch. Trip, Audrey! trip, Audrey! I attend, I attend.   [*Exeunt.*

SCENE II. *The forest.*

Enter ORLANDO *and* OLIVER.

Orl. Is 't possible that on so little acquaintance you should like her? that but seeing you should love her? and loving woo? and, wooing, she should grant? and will you persever to enjoy her?   5

Oli. Neither call the giddiness of it in question, the poverty of her, the small acquaintance, my sudden wooing, nor her sudden consenting; but say with me, I love Aliena; say with her that she loves me; consent with both that we may enjoy each other: it shall be to your good; for my father's house and all the revenue that was old Sir Rowland's will I estate upon you, and here live and die a shepherd.   14

Orl. You have my consent. Let your wedding be to-morrow: thither will I invite the duke and all's contented followers. Go you and prepare Aliena; for look you, here comes my Rosalind.

Enter ROSALIND.

Ros. God save you, brother.   20

Oli. And you, fair sister.   [*Exit.*

Ros. O, my dear Orlando, how it grieves me to see thee wear thy heart in a scarf!

Orl. It is my arm.

Ros. I thought thy heart had been wounded with the claws of a lion.

Orl. Wounded it is, but with the eyes of a lady.

Ros. Did your brother tell you how I counterfeited to swoon when he showed me your handkercher?   30

Orl. Ay, and greater wonders than that.

Ros. O, I know where you are: nay, 'tis true: there was never any thing so sudden but the fight of two rams and Cæsar's thrasonical brag of 'I came, saw, and overcame:' for your brother and my sister no sooner met but they looked, no sooner looked but they loved, no sooner loved but they sighed, no sooner sighed but they asked one another the reason, no sooner knew the reason but they sought the remedy; and in these degrees have they made a pair of stairs to marriage which they will climb incontinent, or else be incontinent before marriage: they are in the very wrath of love and they will together; clubs cannot part them.   45

Orl. They shall be married to-morrow, and I will bid the duke to the nuptial. But, O, how bitter a thing it is to look into happiness through another man's eyes! By so much the more shall I to-morrow be at the height of heart-heaviness, by how much I shall think my brother happy in having what he wishes for.

Ros. Why then, to-morrow I cannot serve your turn for Rosalind?

Orl. I can live no longer by thinking.   55

Ros. I will weary you then no longer with idle talking. Know of me then, for now I speak to some purpose, that I know you are a gentleman of good conceit: I speak not this that you should bear a good opinion of my knowledge, insomuch I say I know you are; neither do I labour for a greater esteem than may in some little measure draw a belief

48. ipse, Latin, *he himself*. 60. bastinado, duel with cudgels. 61. bandy, contend. faction, contest, strife. 62. policy, craft, stratagems. 65. God . . . merry, common salutation at parting.

Scene ii. 4. persever. Accent is on second syllable. 13. estate, settle as an estate, bestow.

21. sister, i.e., future sister-in-law. 23. wear . . . scarf, possible allusion to Orlando's wearing his heart on his sleeve. 32. where you are, what you mean. 34. thrasonical, boastful; from Thraso, the boaster in Terence's *Eunuchus*. 41. degrees, play on the original meaning, "steps." 42. incontinent, immediately. 44. wrath, impetuosity, ardor. 59. conceit, intelligence, mental capacity. 61. insomuch, inasmuch as.

from you, to do yourself good and not to grace me. Believe then, if you please, that I can do strange things: I have, since I was three year old, conversed with a magician, most profound in his art and yet not damnable. If you do love Rosalind so near the 68 heart as your gesture cries it out, when your brother marries Aliena, shall you marry her: I know into what straits of fortune she is driven; and it is not impossible to me, if it appear not inconvenient to you, to set her before your eyes to-morrow human as she is and without any danger. 75

Orl. Speakest thou in sober meanings?

Ros. By my life, I do; which I tender dearly, though I say I am a magician. Therefore, put you in your best array; bid your friends; for if you will be married to-morrow, you shall, and to Rosalind, if you will. 81

Enter SILVIUS *and* PHEBE.

Look, here comes a lover of mine and a lover of hers.

Phe. Youth, you have done me much ungentleness,
To show the letter that I writ to you.

Ros. I care not if I have: it is my study
To seem despiteful and ungentle to you:
You are there followed by a faithful shepherd;
Look upon him, love him; he worships you.

Phe. Good shepherd, tell this youth what 'tis to love.

Sil. It is to be all made of sighs and tears;
And so am I for Phebe. 91

Phe. And I for Ganymede.

Orl. And I for Rosalind.

Ros. And I for no woman.

Sil. It is to be all made of faith and service;
And so am I for Phebe.

Phe. And I for Ganymede.

Orl. And I for Rosalind.

Ros. And I for no woman.

Sil. It is to be all made of fantasy, 100
All made of passion and all made of wishes,

All adoration, duty, and observance,
All humbleness, all patience and impatience,
†All purity, all trial, all observance;
And so am I for Phebe.

Phe. And so am I for Ganymede.

Orl. And so am I for Rosalind.

Ros. And so am I for no woman. 108

Phe. If this be so, why blame you me to love you?

Sil. If this be so, why blame you me to love you?

Orl. If this be so, why blame you me to love you?

Ros. Who do you speak to, 'Why blame you me to love you?'

Orl. To her that is not here, nor doth not hear. 117

Ros. Pray you, no more of this; 'tis like the howling of Irish wolves against the moon. [*To Sil.*] I will help you, if I can: [*To Phe.*] I would love you, if I could. To-morrow meet me all together. [*To Phe.*] I will marry you, if ever I marry woman, and I'll be married to-morrow: [*To Orl.*] I will satisfy you, if ever I satisfied man, and you shall be married to-morrow: [*To Sil.*] I will content you, if what pleases you contents you, and you shall be married to-morrow. [*To Orl.*] As you love Rosalind, meet: [*To Sil.*] as you love Phebe, meet: and as I love no woman, I'll meet. So fare you well: I have left you commands. 131

Sil. I'll not fail, if I live.

Phe. Nor I.

Orl. Nor I. [*Exeunt.*

SCENE III. *The forest.*

Enter TOUCHSTONE *and* AUDREY.

Touch. To-morrow is the joyful day, Audrey; to-morrow will we be married.

Aud. I do desire it with all my heart; and I hope it is no dishonest desire to desire to be a woman of the world. Here come two of the banished duke's pages. 6

---

64. **grace me**, get me credit. 66. **conversed**, associated. 67. **damnable**, worthy of condemnation, i.e., he was not a practicer of forbidden magic. 69. **gesture**, bearing. **cries it out**, proclaims. 74-5. **human . . . danger**, i.e., not a phantom but the real Rosalind without any of the danger generally conceived to attend the rites of incantation (Johnson). 77. **tender dearly**, value highly, a possible reference to the anti-witchcraft statutes of Elizabeth, by which witchcraft causing death was punishable by death.

102. **observance**, respect. 109. **to love**, for loving. 119. **howling . . . moon**, a probable allusion to the rebellion of the Irish rebels against Elizabeth, the Virgin Queen. 120-131. **I will . . . commands.** This comic denouement, or unknotting of the plot-complications, is unusually skillful. The audience has the flattering sense of superior understanding and at the same time has its curiosity appealed to.
Scene iii. This scene has no dramatic purpose; it serves merely as entertainment. The suggestion has been made that it is an attempt on the part of Shakespeare's theater to rival the similar attractions offered just at the time by the children at Blackfriars theater. 4. **dishonest**, immodest. 5. **woman of the world**, married woman.

Enter two Pages.

First Page. Well met, honest gentleman.

Touch. By my troth, well met. Come, sit, sit, and a song.   9

Sec. Page. We are for you: sit i' the middle.

First Page. Shall we clap into 't roundly, without hawking or spitting or saying we are hoarse, which are the only prologues to a bad voice?   14

Sec. Page. I' faith, i' faith; and both in a tune, like two gipsies on a horse.

Song.

It was a lover and his lass,
　With a hey, and a ho, and a hey nonino,
That o'er the green corn-field did pass
　In the spring time, the only pretty ring
　　time,   20
When birds do sing, hey ding a ding, ding:
Sweet lovers love the spring.

Between the acres of the rye,
　With a hey, and a ho, and a hey nonino,
These pretty country folks would lie,
　In spring time, &c.

This carol they began that hour,
　With a hey, and a ho, and a hey nonino,
How that a life was but a flower
　In spring time, &c.   30

And therefore take the present time,
　With a hey, and a ho, and a hey nonino;
For love is crowned with the prime
　In spring time, &c.

Touch. Truly, young gentlemen, though there was no great matter in the ditty, yet the note was very untuneable.

First Page. You are deceived, sir: we kept time, we lost not our time.   39

---

10. **sit i' the middle,** sit between us (in order to enter into the song). 11. **clap . . . roundly,** begin at once and with spirit. 13. **the only prologues,** only the prologues. 15. **both in a tune,** both in unison, or both keep in time. 20. **ring time,** time most apt for marriage. 23. **acres,** fields, or according to Ridgeway, grass balks dividing grainfields into strips. 27. **carol,** originally a ring-dance; hence, any kind of song at a festival. 31. **And . . . time.** This stanza stands second in F; MS. discovered by Chappell (*Popular Music of the Olden Time*, p. 204) places it at the end, where it properly belongs. 33. **prime,** spring; also, choicest quality. 36. **matter,** sense, meaning. 37. **untuneable,** discordant.

Touch. By my troth, yes; I count it but time lost to hear such a foolish song. God be wi' you; and God mend your voices! Come, Audrey.   [*Exeunt.*

Scene IV. *The forest.*

Enter Duke senior, Amiens, Jaques, Orlando, Oliver, *and* Celia.

Duke S. Dost thou believe, Orlando, that the boy
Can do all this that he hath promised?

Orl. I sometimes do believe, and sometimes do not;
†As those that fear they hope, and know they fear.

Enter Rosalind, Silvius, *and* Phebe.

Ros. Patience once more, whiles our compact is urged:
You say, if I bring in your Rosalind,
You will bestow her on Orlando here?

Duke S. That would I, had I kingdoms to give with her.

Ros. And you say, you will have her, when I bring her?

Orl. That would I, were I of all kingdoms king.   10

Ros. You say, you'll marry me, if I be willing?

Phe. That will I, should I die the hour after.

Ros. But if you do refuse to marry me,
You'll give yourself to this most faithful shepherd?

Phe. So is the bargain.

Ros. You say, that you'll have Phebe, if she will?

Sil. Though to have her and death were both one thing.

Ros. I have promised to make all this matter even.
Keep you your word, O duke, to give your daughter;
You yours, Orlando, to receive his daughter:
Keep your word, Phebe, that you'll marry me,   21
Or else refusing me, to wed this shepherd:
Keep your word, Silvius, that you'll marry her,
If she refuse me: and from hence I go,

Scene iv. 4. **they hope,** that they merely hope; many conjectures on this difficult line.

To make these doubts all even.   25

           [*Exeunt Rosalind and Celia.*

  Duke S. I do remember in this shepherd boy

Some lively touches of my daughter's favour.

  Orl. My lord, the first time that I ever saw him

Methought he was a brother to your daughter:

But, my good lord, this boy is forest-born, 30

And hath been tutor'd in the rudiments

Of many desperate studies by his uncle,

Whom he reports to be a great magician,

Obscured in the circle of this forest.

       Enter Touchstone *and* Audrey.

  Jaq. There is, sure, another flood toward, and these couples are coming to the ark. Here comes a pair of very strange beasts, which in all tongues are called fools.

  Touch. Salutation and greeting to you all!

  Jaq. Good my lord, bid him welcome: this is the motley-minded gentleman that I have so often met in the forest: he hath been a courtier, he swears.   43

  Touch. If any man doubt that, let him put me to my purgation. I have trod a measure; I have flattered a lady; I have been politic with my friend, smooth with mine enemy; I have undone three tailors; I have had four quarrels, and like to have fought one.

  Jaq. And how was that ta'en up?   50

  Touch. Faith, we met, and found the quarrel was upon the seventh cause.

  Jaq. How seventh cause? Good my lord, like this fellow.

  Duke S. I like him very well.   55

  Touch. God 'ild you, sir; I desire you of the like. I press in here, sir, amongst the rest of the country copulatives, to swear and to forswear; according as marriage binds and blood breaks: a poor virgin, sir, an ill-favoured thing, sir, but mine own; a poor humour of mine, sir, to take that that no man else will: rich honesty dwells like a miser, sir, in a poor house; as your pearl in your foul oyster.   64

  Duke S. By my faith, he is very swift and sententious.

  Touch. According to the fool's bolt, sir, and such dulcet diseases.

  Jaq. But, for the seventh cause; how did you find the quarrel on the seventh cause? 70

  Touch. Upon a lie seven times removed:— bear your body more seeming, Audrey:—as thus, sir. I did dislike the cut of a certain courtier's beard: he sent me word, if I said his beard was not cut well, he was in the mind it was: this is called the Retort Courteous. If I sent him word again 'it was not well cut,' he would send me word, he cut it to please himself: this is called the Quip Modest. If again 'it was not well cut,' he disabled my judgement: this is called the Reply Churlish. If again, 'it was not well cut,' he would answer, I spake not true: this is called the Reproof Valiant. If again 'it was not well cut,' he would say, I lied: this is called the Countercheck Quarrelsome: and so to the Lie Circumstantial and the Lie Direct.   86

  Jaq. And how oft did you say his beard was not well cut?

  Touch. I durst go no further than the Lie Circumstantial, nor he durst not give me the Lie Direct; and so we measured swords and parted.   91

  Jaq. Can you nominate in order now the degrees of the lie?

  Touch. O sir, we quarrel in print, by the book; as you have books for good manners: I will name you the degrees. The first, the Retort Courteous; the second, the Quip Modest; the third, the Reply Churlish; the fourth, the Reproof Valiant; the fifth, the Countercheck Quarrelsome; the sixth, the Lie with Circumstance; the seventh, the Lie Direct. All these you may avoid but the Lie Direct; and you may avoid that too, with an

If. I knew when seven justices could not
take up a quarrel, but when the parties were
met themselves, one of them thought but of
an If, as, 'If you said so, then I said so;'
and they shook hands and swore brothers.
Your If is the only peace-maker; much 108
virtue in If.

Jaq. Is not this a rare fellow, my lord?
he's as good at any thing and yet a fool. 110

Duke S. He uses his folly like a stalking-
horse and under the presentation of that he
shoots his wit.

Enter Hymen, Rosalind, *and* Celia.
Still Music.

Hym. Then is there mirth in heaven,
     When earthly things made even
          Atone together.
     Good duke, receive thy daughter:
     Hymen from heaven brought her,
          Yea, brought her hither,
     That thou mightst join her hand with
          his   120
     Whose heart within his bosom is.

Ros. [*To duke*] To you I give myself, for I
     am yours.
[*To Orl.*] To you I give myself, for I am
     yours.

Duke S. If there be truth in sight, you are
     my daughter.

Orl. If there be truth in sight, you are my
     Rosalind.

Phe. If sight and shape be true,
Why then, my love adieu!

Ros. I'll have no father, if you be not he:
I'll have no husband, if you be not he:
Nor ne'er wed woman, if you be not she. 130

Hym. Peace, ho! I bar confusion:
     'Tis I must make conclusion
          Of these most strange events:
     Here's eight that must take hands
     To join in Hymen's bands,
          If truth holds true contents.
     You and you no cross shall part:

You and you are heart in heart:
     You to his love must accord,
          Or have a woman to your lord: 140
     You and you are sure together,
     As the winter to foul weather.
     Whiles a wedlock-hymn we sing,
     Feed yourselves with questioning;
     That reason wonder may diminish,
     How thus we met, and these things
          finish.

SONG.

     Wedding is great Juno's crown:
          O blessed bond of board and bed!
     'Tis Hymen peoples every town;
          High wedlock then be honoured: 150
     Honour, high honour and renown,
     To Hymen, god of every town!

Duke S. O my dear niece, welcome thou
     art to me!
Even daughter, welcome, in no less degree.

Phe. I will not eat my word, now thou art
     mine;
Thy faith my fancy to thee doth combine.

Enter Jaques de Boys.

Jaq. de B. Let me have audience for a
     word or two:
I am the second son of old Sir Rowland,
That bring these tidings to this fair assem-
     bly.   159
Duke Frederick, hearing how that every day
Men of great worth resorted to this forest,
Address'd a mighty power; which were on
     foot,
In his own conduct, purposely to take
His brother here and put him to the sword:
And to the skirts of this wild wood he came;
Where meeting with an old religious man,
After some question with him, was converted
Both from his enterprise and from the world,
His crown bequeathing to his banish'd
     brother,
And all their lands restored to them again 170
That were with him exiled. This to be true,
I do engage my life.

Duke S.   Welcome, young man;

---

107. **swore brothers**, allusion to the practice of swearing brotherhood, becoming *fratres jurati*. 111. **stalking-
horse**, a real or artificial horse under cover of which the
hunter approaches his game. 112. **presentation**, semblance. *Stage Direction:* **Hymen**, god of marriage. **Still
Music**, soft music. 116. **Atone**, are at one. 125. **sight**.
Johnson wished to read *shape* to be in accord with Phebe's *sight and shape*. 136. **If . . . contents**, if truth be
true. This offers a rhyme for *events* above. The quality
of the verse in Hymen's song is so poor as to make many
editors suspect that the lines are not Shakespeare's.

139. **accord**, agree, consent. 140. **to**, for. 141. **sure**,
closely united. 147. **Juno's.** Juno was queen of gods,
presiding over wedlock. 150. **High**, solemn. 154. **Even
daughter**, i.e., my daughter equally with Rosalind.
Stage Direction: **Jaques de Boys**, second son of Sir
Rowland de Boys (mentioned in Act I, Scene i, line 6); F:
Enter Second Brother; New Cambridge editors suggest
that this character had a larger part in the original form
of the play. 162. **Address'd**, prepared. 163. **In . . .
conduct**, under his own command. 166. **religious
man**, hermit. 167. **question**, conversation.

Thou offer'st fairly to thy brothers' wedding:
To one his lands withheld, and to the other
A land itself at large, a potent dukedom.
First, in this forest let us do those ends
That here were well begun and well begot:
And after, every of this happy number
That have endured shrewd days and nights
    with us
Shall share the good of our returned fortune,
According to the measure of their states. 181
Meantime, forget this new-fall'n dignity
And fall into our rustic revelry.
Play, music! And you, brides and bride-
    grooms all,
With measure heap'd in joy, to the measures
    fall.

    Jaq. Sir, by your patience. If I heard you
    rightly,
The duke hath put on a religious life
And thrown into neglect the pompous court?

    Jaq. de B. He hath.   189

    Jaq. To him will I: out of these conver-
    tites
There is much matter to be heard and
    learn'd.
[*To duke*] You to your former honour I be-
    queath;
Your patience and your virtue well deserves
    it:
[*To Orl.*] You to a love that your true faith
    doth merit:
[*To Oli.*] You to your land and love and great
    allies:
[*To Sil.*] You to a long and well-deserved bed:
[*To Touch.*] And you to wrangling; for thy
    loving voyage
Is but for two months victuall'd. So, to your
    pleasures:

I am for other than for dancing measures.

    Duke S. Stay, Jaques, stay.   200

    Jaq. To see no pastime I: what you
    would have
I'll stay to know at your abandon'd cave.
                    [*Exit.*

    Duke S. Proceed, proceed: we will begin
    these rites,
As we do trust they'll end, in true delights.
                 [*A dance.*

EPILOGUE.

    Ros. It is not the fashion to see the lady
the epilogue; but it is no more unhandsome
than to see the lord the prologue. If it be
true that good wine needs no bush, 'tis true
that a good play needs no epilogue; yet to
good wine they do use good bushes, and good
plays prove the better by the help of good
epilogues. What a case am I in then, that
am neither a good epilogue nor cannot
insinuate with you in the behalf of a good
play! I am not furnished like a beggar, 10
therefore to beg will not become me: my way
is to conjure you; and I'll begin with the
women. I charge you, O women, for the love
you bear to men, to like as much of this play
as please you: and I charge you, O men, for
the love you bear to women—as I perceive
by your simpering, none of you hates them—
that between you and the women the play
may please. If I were a woman I would kiss
as many of you as had beards that pleased
me, complexions that liked me and breaths
that I defied not: and, I am sure, as many as
have good beards or good faces or sweet
breaths will, for my kind offer, when I make
curtsy, bid me farewell.   [*Exeunt.* 25

---

    173. **offer'st fairly**, contributest handsomely. 174.
the other, i.e., Orlando. 176. **do those ends**, accomplish those purposes. 179. **shrewd**, bad, evil. 181.
states, fortunes. 185. **measures**, stately dances; here,
dances. 186. **by your patience**, by your leave, i.e.,
let the music wait a moment. 188. **pompous**, ceremonious. 190. **convertites**, converts. 191. **matter**,
sound sense, good stuff.

    Epilogue. 2. **unhandsome**, in bad taste. 4. **good
. . . bush**, a proverb derived from the custom of displaying at the tavern door a piece of ivy or holly to denote
that wine was for sale there. 9. **insinuate**, ingratiate
myself. 10. **furnished**, dressed, equipped. 15. **as
please**, as may please. 19. **If I were a woman**.
Women's parts on the Elizabethan stage were played by
boys in female costume. 22. **defied**, disliked. 25. **bid
me farewell**, i.e., applaud me.

TWELFTH NIGHT;
OR, WHAT YOU WILL

DRAMATIS PERSONÆ

ORSINO, Duke of Illyria.
SEBASTIAN, brother to Viola.
ANTONIO, a sea captain, friend to Sebastian.
A Sea Captain, friend to Viola.
VALENTINE, ⎤ gentlemen attending on
CURIO, ⎦ the Duke.
SIR TOBY BELCH, uncle to Olivia.
SIR ANDREW AGUECHEEK.
MALVOLIO, steward to Olivia.

FABIAN, ⎤
FESTE, a Clown, ⎦ servants to Olivia.

OLIVIA.
VIOLA.
MARIA, Olivia's woman.
Lords, Priests, Sailors, Officers, Musicians, and other Attendants.

SCENE: *A city in Illyria, and the sea-coast near it.*

ACT I.

SCENE I. *The* DUKE'S *palace.*

Enter DUKE, CURIO, *and other* Lords; Musicians *attending.*

Duke. If music be the food of love, play on;
Give me excess of it, that, surfeiting,
The appetite may sicken, and so die.
That strain again! it had a dying fall:
O, it came o'er my ear like the sweet sound,
That breathes upon a bank of violets,
Stealing and giving odour! Enough; no more:
'Tis not so sweet now as it was before.
O spirit of love! how quick and fresh art thou,
That, notwithstanding thy capacity   10
Receiveth as the sea, nought enters there,
Of what validity and pitch soe'er,
But falls into abatement and low price,
Even in a minute: so full of shapes is fancy

That it alone is high fantastical.
    Cur. Will you go hunt, my lord?
    Duke.   What, Curio?
    Cur. The hart.
    Duke. Why, so I do, the noblest that I have:
O, when mine eyes did see Olivia first,
Methought she purged the air of pestilence!
That instant was I turn'd into a hart;   21
And my desires, like fell and cruel hounds,
E'er since pursue me.

Enter VALENTINE.

                     How now! what news from her?
    Val. So please my lord, I might not be admitted;
But from her handmaid do return this answer:
The element itself, till seven years' heat,
Shall not behold her face at ample view;
But, like a cloistress, she will veiled walk
And water once a day her chamber round
With eye-offending brine: all this to season 30
A brother's dead love, which she would keep fresh
And lasting in her sad remembrance.
    Duke. O, she that hath a heart of that fine frame

Title. **Twelfth Night**, the feast of the Epiphany, or the visit of the Magi. It occurred on the twelfth night after Christmas. The association of this name with "What You Will" lends some plausibility to the suggestion that the title came from the Prologue to *Gl'Ingannati*, an Italian comedy on a similar theme, which states that the story came from the brains of its authors "just as you draw your lots on Twelfth Night."
Act I. Scene i. 1-15. **If music . . . fantastical.** These opening lines reflect Orsino's sentimentality. He is swept away by a superficial passion which he parades but does not deeply feel. 1. **food of love.** See *Antony and Cleopatra* II, v, 1-2. 4. **fall,** cadence. 9. **quick,** living, active. 12. **validity,** value. **pitch,** highest point of a falcon's flight. 14. **fancy,** sensuous love.

18. **noblest . . . have,** i.e., his noblest part, his heart. 23. **pursue me,** reference to the story in Ovid of Actæon, who was transformed into a hart and killed by his own hounds. 26. **element,** sky. 30. **season,** keep fresh.

To pay this debt of love but to a brother,
How will she love, when the rich golden shaft
Hath kill'd the flock of all affections else
That live in her; when liver, brain and heart,
These sovereign thrones, are all supplied, and
    fill'd
Her sweet perfections with one self king!
Away before me to sweet beds of flowers: 40
Love-thoughts lie rich when canopied with
    bowers.   [*Exeunt.*

Scene II. *The sea-coast.*

Enter Viola, *a* Captain, *and* Sailors.

Vio. What country, friends, is this?
Cap. This is Illyria, lady.
Vio. And what should I do in Illyria?
My brother he is in Elysium.
Perchance he is not drown'd: what think you,
    sailors?
Cap. It is perchance that you yourself
    were saved.
Vio. O my poor brother! and so perchance
    may he be.
Cap. True, madam: and, to comfort you
    with chance,
Assure yourself, after our ship did split,
When you and those poor number saved with
    you   10
Hung on our driving boat, I saw your brother,
Most provident in peril, bind himself,
Courage and hope both teaching him the
    practice,
To a strong mast that lived upon the sea;
Where, like Arion on the dolphin's back,
I saw him hold acquaintance with the waves
So long as I could see.
Vio. For saying so, there's gold:
Mine own escape unfoldeth to my hope,
Whereto thy speech serves for authority, 20
The like of him. Know'st thou this country?
Cap. Ay, madam, well; for I was bred and
    born
Not three hours' travel from this very place.
Vio. Who governs here?
Cap. A noble duke, in nature as in name.
Vio. What is his name?

Cap. Orsino.
Vio. Orsino! I have heard my father
    name him:
He was a bachelor then.
Cap. And so is now, or was so very late; 30
For but a month ago I went from hence,
And then 'twas fresh in murmur,—as, you
    know,
What great ones do the less will prattle of,—
That he did seek the love of fair Olivia.
Vio. What's she?
Cap. A virtuous maid, the daughter of a
    count
That died some twelvemonth since, then
    leaving her
In the protection of his son, her brother,
Who shortly also died: for whose dear love,
They say, she hath abjured the company 40
And sight of men.
Vio.   O that I served that lady
And might not be delivered to the world,
Till I had made mine own occasion mellow,
What my estate is!
Cap.   That were hard to compass;
Because she will admit no kind of suit,
No, not the duke's.
Vio. There is a fair behaviour in thee,
    captain;
And though that nature with a beauteous
    wall
Doth oft close in pollution, yet of thee
I will believe thou hast a mind that suits 50
With this thy fair and outward character.
I prithee, and I'll pay thee bounteously,
Conceal me what I am, and be my aid
For such disguise as haply shall become
The form of my intent. I'll serve this duke:
Thou shalt present me as an eunuch to him:
It may be worth thy pains; for I can sing
And speak to him in many sorts of music
That will allow me very worth his service.
What else may hap to time I will commit; 60
Only shape thou thy silence to my wit.
Cap. Be you his eunuch, and your mute
    I'll be:
When my tongue blabs, then let mine eyes
    not see.
Vio. I thank thee: lead me on. [*Exeunt.*

---

35. **golden shaft,** i.e., of Cupid. 37. **liver, brain and heart.** In mediæval and Elizabethan psychology these organs were the seats of the passions. 39. **self,** single. *Scene ii.* 2. **Illyria,** a country along the eastern shore of the Adriatic. 4. **Elysium,** abode of the blessed. 8. **chance,** i.e., what chance may bring about. 11. **driving,** drifting. 14. **lived,** kept afloat. 15. **Arion,** a Greek poet who, when thrown into the sea by sailors, so charmed the dolphins with his lyre that they saved him. This was a favorite subject for pageants and paintings. 21. **like of him,** i.e., he, too, may be saved.

29. **bachelor.** Viola manifests a slight, possibly feminine, interest in Orsino. 32. **murmur,** gossip. 42. **delivered,** discovered, made known. 43. **mellow,** ready or convenient (to be made known). 47. **behaviour.** The word means "appearance" as well as "behavior." 53. **me,** ethical dative. 55. **form of my intent,** nature of my purpose, with suggestion of outward appearance in *form.* 59. **allow me,** cause me to be acknowledged. 61. **wit,** plan, invention.

Scene III. Olivia's *house*.

Enter Sir Toby Belch *and* Maria.

Sir To. What a plague means my niece, to take the death of her brother thus? I am sure care 's an enemy to life.

Mar. By my troth, Sir Toby, you must come in earlier o' nights: your cousin, my lady, takes great exceptions to your ill hours.

Sir. To. Why, let her except, before excepted.

Mar. Ay, but you must confine yourself within the modest limits of order.　　9

Sir To. Confine! I'll confine myself no finer than I am: these clothes are good enough to drink in; and so be these boots too: an they be not, let them hang themselves in their own straps.

Mar. That quaffing and drinking will undo you: I heard my lady talk of it yesterday; and of a foolish knight that you brought in one night here to be her wooer.

Sir To. Who, Sir Andrew Aguecheek?

Mar. Ay, he.

Sir To. He's as tall a man as any 's in Illyria.

Mar. What's that to the purpose?　　21

Sir To. Why, he has three thousand ducats a year.

Mar. Ay, but he'll have but a year in all these ducats: he's a very fool and a prodigal.

Sir To. Fie, that you'll say so! he plays o' the viol-de-gamboys, and speaks three or four languages word for word without book, and hath all the good gifts of nature.　　29

Mar. He hath indeed, almost natural: for besides that he's a fool, he's a great quarreller; and but that he hath the gift of a coward to allay the gust he hath in quarrelling, 'tis thought among the prudent he would quickly have the gift of a grave.

Sir To. By this hand, they are scoundrels and substractors that say so of him. Who are they?

Mar. They that add, moreover, he's drunk nightly in your company.　　39

Sir To. With drinking healths to my niece: I'll drink to her as long as there is a passage in my throat and drink in Illyria: he's a coward and a coystrill that will not drink to my niece till his brains turn o' the toe like a parish-top. What, wench! Castiliano vulgo! for here comes Sir Andrew Agueface.

Enter Sir Andrew Aguecheek.

Sir And. Sir Toby Belch! how now, Sir Toby Belch!

Sir To. Sweet Sir Andrew!

Sir And. Bless you, fair shrew.　　50

Mar. And you too, sir.

Sir To. Accost, Sir Andrew, accost.

Sir And. What's that?

Sir To. My niece's chambermaid.

Sir And. Good Mistress Accost, I desire better acquaintance.

Mar. My name is Mary, sir.

Sir And. Good Mistress Mary Accost,—

Sir To. You mistake, knight: 'accost' is front her, board her, woo her, assail her.　60

Sir And. By my troth, I would not undertake her in this company. Is that the meaning of 'accost'?

Mar. Fare you well, gentlemen.

Sir To. An thou let part so, Sir Andrew, would thou mightst never draw sword again.

Sir And. An you part so, mistress, I would I might never draw sword again. Fair lady, do you think you have fools in hand?

Mar. Sir, I have not you by the hand.　70

Sir And. Marry, but you shall have; and here's my hand.

Mar. Now, sir, 'thought is free:' I pray you, bring your hand to the buttery-bar and let it drink.

Sir And. Wherefore, sweet-heart? what's your metaphor?

Mar. It's dry, sir.

Sir And. Why, I think so: I am not such an ass but I can keep my hand dry. But what's your jest?　　80

Mar. A dry jest, sir.

Sir And. Are you full of them?

Mar. Ay, sir, I have them at my fingers'

---

5. **cousin.** The word covers various degrees of relationship; here, niece. 7. **except, before excepted,** legal phrase, *exceptis excipiendis,* "with the exceptions before named." Sir Toby means that enough exceptions to his behavior have already been taken. 9. **modest,** moderate. 10. **confine myself,** dress myself. 20. **tall,** bold, with a pun on literal meaning. 27. **viol-de-gamboys,** bass viol. 28. **without book,** by heart. Sir Andrew's complete ignorance of languages and lack of all accomplishments is one of the sources of Sir Toby's fun at his expense. 30. **natural,** with pun on the sense "born idiot." 33. **allay the gust,** moderate the pleasure. 37. **substractors,** for *detractors.*

43. **coystrill,** knave, base fellow. 45. **parish-top,** a large top provided by the parish to be whipped, apparently for exercise in cold weather. **Castiliano vulgo,** literally, vulgar Spaniard; possibly a slang phrase, or nonsense. 52. **Accost,** make up to. 54. **chambermaid,** lady's maid. 73. **'thought is free,'** reply to *do you think,* above. 74-5. **bring . . . drink,** said to be a proverbial phrase meaning to ask at once for a kiss and a present (Kenrick, quoted by Luce). 77. **dry,** i.e., a sign of age and debility. 81. **dry,** dull. 83. **fingers' ends.** Sir Andrew is holding her by the hand.

ends: marry, now I let go your hand, I am
barren.   [*Exit.*   84

Sir To. O knight, thou lackest a cup of
canary: when did I see thee so put down?

Sir And. Never in your life, I think; unless you see canary put me down. Methinks
sometimes I have no more wit than a Christian or an ordinary man has: but I am a
great eater of beef and I believe that does
harm to my wit.   91

Sir To. No question.

Sir And. An I thought that, I'ld forswear
it. I'll ride home to-morrow, Sir Toby.

Sir To. Pourquoi, my dear knight?

Sir And. What is 'pourquoi'? do or not do?
I would I had bestowed that time in the
tongues that I have in fencing, dancing and
bear-baiting: O, had I but followed the arts!

Sir To. Then hadst thou had an excellent
head of hair.   101

Sir And. Why, would that have mended
my hair?

Sir To. Past question; for thou seest it will
not curl by nature.

Sir And. But it becomes me well enough,
does't not?

Sir To. Excellent; it hangs like flax on a
distaff; and I hope to see a housewife take
thee between her legs and spin it off.   110

Sir And. Faith, I'll home to-morrow, Sir
Toby: your niece will not be seen; or if she
be, it's four to one she'll none of me: the
count himself here hard by woos her.

Sir To. She'll none o' the count: she'll not
match above her degree, neither in estate,
years, nor wit; I have heard her swear 't.
Tut, there's life in 't, man.

Sir And. I'll stay a month longer. I am a
fellow o' the strangest mind i' the world; I
delight in masques and revels sometimes altogether.   121

Sir To. Art thou good at these kickshawses, knight?

Sir And. As any man in Illyria, whatsoever he be, under the degree of my betters;
and yet I will not compare with an old man.

Sir To. What is thy excellence in a galliard, knight?

Sir And. Faith, I can cut a caper.

Sir To. And I can cut the mutton to 't. 130

Sir And. And I think I have the back-
trick simply as strong as any man in Illyria.

Sir To. Wherefore are these things hid?
wherefore have these gifts a curtain before
'em? are they like to take dust, like Mistress
Mall's picture? why dost thou not go to
church in a galliard and come home in a
coranto? My very walk should be a jig; I
would not so much as make water but in a
sink-a-pace. What dost thou mean? Is
it a world to hide virtues in? I did think,
by the excellent constitution of thy leg, it
was formed under the star of a galliard.

Sir And. Ay, 'tis strong, and it does indifferent well in a flame-coloured stock.
Shall we set about some revels?

Sir To. What shall we do else? were we
not born under Taurus?   147

Sir And. Taurus! That's sides and heart.

Sir To. No, sir; it is legs and thighs. Let
me see thee caper: ha! higher: ha, ha! excellent!   [*Exeunt.*

SCENE IV. *The* DUKE'S *palace.*

Enter VALENTINE, *and* VIOLA *in man's attire.*

Val. If the duke continue these favours towards you, Cesario, you are like to be much
advanced: he hath known you but three
days, and already you are no stranger.

Vio. You either fear his humour or my
negligence, that you call in question the continuance of his love: is he inconstant, sir, in
his favours?

Val. No, believe me.

Vio. I thank you. Here comes the count.

Enter DUKE, CURIO, *and* Attendants.

Duke. Who saw Cesario, ho?   10

Vio. On your attendance, my lord; here.

Duke. Stand you a while aloof. Cesario,
Thou know'st no less but all; I have unclasp'd
To thee the book even of my secret soul:

---

86. **canary,** sack, a wine from the Canary Islands.
90. **beef,** traditional cause of dull wits. The English
were frequently twitted on account of the coarseness
and quantity of their food and the dullness of their wit.
95. **Pourquoi,** why. 98. **tongues,** languages and
tongs (used for curling hair). 99. **arts.** Cf. *nature,*
below. 122. **kickshawses,** corruption of the French
words *quelque chose;* delicacies, fancy dishes. 126. **old
man,** a puzzling reference. Furness suggests that Sir
Andrew wishes to express deference to age.

129. **cut a caper.** Sir Andrew uses the phrase in the
ordinary sense. Sir Toby makes a pun referring to
caper sauce. 131. **back-trick,** some figure in the galliard;
apparently, dancing backward. 135. **Mistress Mall's
picture.** It has been suggested (1) that this refers to
Moll Cutpurse or some other notorious female criminal;
(2) that it is Maria's picture; (3) that it is a picture of no
particular person. 138. **coranto,** lively dance. 140.
sink-a-pace, French, *cinque-pace,* a dance. 143. **under the star,** i.e. a star favorable to dancing. Men's
destinies and characters were thought to be controlled
by the stars. 145. **stock,** stocking. 147, 148. **Taurus,**
the constellation. Sir Andrew is mistaken, since Leo
governed *sides and hearts* in medical astrology.
Scene iv. 12. **you,** addressed to the attendants.

Therefore, good youth, address thy gait unto
  her;
Be not denied access, stand at her doors,
And tell them, there thy fixed foot shall grow
Till thou have audience.
  Vio.   Sure, my noble lord,
If she be so abandon'd to her sorrow
As it is spoke, she never will admit me.   20
  Duke. Be clamorous and leap all civil
    bounds
Rather than make unprofited return.
  Vio. Say I do speak with her, my lord,
    what then?
  Duke. O, then unfold the passion of my
    love,
Surprise her with discourse of my dear faith:
It shall become thee well to act my woes;
She will attend it better in thy youth
Than in a nuncio's of more grave aspect.
  Vio. I think not so, my lord.
  Duke.   Dear lad, believe it;
For they shall yet belie thy happy years,   30
That say thou art a man: Diana's lip
Is not more smooth and rubious; thy small
    pipe
Is as the maiden's organ, shrill and sound,
And all is semblative a woman's part.
I know thy constellation is right apt
For this affair. Some four or five attend him;
All, if you will; for I myself am best
When least in company. Prosper well in this,
And thou shalt live as freely as thy lord,
To call his fortunes thine.
  Vio.   I'll do my best   40
To woo your lady: [*Aside*] yet, a barful strife!
Whoe'er I woo, myself would be his wife.
                                    [*Exeunt.*

SCENE V. *Olivia's house.*

Enter MARIA *and* CLOWN.

  Mar. Nay, either tell me where thou hast
been, or I will not open my lips so wide as a
bristle may enter in way of thy excuse: my
lady will hang thee for thy absence.
  Clo. Let her hang me: he that is well

hanged in this world needs to fear no colours.
  Mar. Make that good.
  Clo. He shall see none to fear.
  Mar. A good lenten answer: I can tell thee
where that saying was born, of 'I fear no
colours.'   10
  Clo. Where, good Mistress Mary?
  Mar. In the wars; and that may you be
bold to say in your foolery.
  Clo. Well, God give them wisdom that
have it; and those that are fools, let them
use their talents.
  Mar. Yet you will be hanged for being so
long absent; or to be turned away, is not that
as good as a hanging to you?   19
  Clo. Many a good hanging prevents a bad
marriage; and, for turning away, let summer
bear it out.
  Mar. You are resolute, then?
  Clo. Not so, neither; but I am resolved on
two points.   25
  Mar. That if one break, the other will
hold; or, if both break, your gaskins fall.
  Clo. Apt, in good faith; very apt. Well, go
thy way; if Sir Toby would leave drinking,
thou wert as witty a piece of Eve's flesh as
any in Illyria.   31
  Mar. Peace, you rogue, no more o' that.
Here comes my lady: make your excuse
wisely, you were best.   [*Exit.*
  Clo. Wit, an't be thy will, put me into
good fooling! Those wits, that think they
have thee, do very oft prove fools; and I, that
am sure I lack thee, may pass for a wise man:
for what says Quinapalus? 'Better a witty
fool than a foolish wit.'   40

Enter Lady OLIVIA *with* MALVOLIO.

God bless thee, lady!
  Oli. Take the fool away.
  Clo. Do you not hear, fellows? Take
away the lady.
  Oli. Go to, you're a dry fool; I'll no more
of you: besides, you grow dishonest.   46
  Clo. Two faults, madonna, that drink and
good counsel will amend: for give the dry fool
drink, then is the fool not dry: bid the dishonest man mend himself; if he mend, he is
no longer dishonest; if he cannot let the

---

15. **address thy gait,** go. 21. **civil bounds,** bounds of
civility. 25. **dear,** concerning one intimately. 28.
nuncio's, messenger's. 30. **yet,** i.e., for a long time
to come. 34. **semblative,** resembling, like. 41-42. **yet
. . . wife.** Such asides as this have an important part
in Shakespeare's dramatic exposition, since there are
people in the audience who cannot understand by process of inference what a situation is; they need to be told.
41. **barful,** full of impediments.
  Scene v. Stage Direction: **Clown,** the technical word
for those who played comic parts in the theater. *Fool*
is more commonly used in the text to denote the jester
or domestic fool.

6. **fear no colours,** fear no enemies, with pun on *colors*
and *collars* (halters). 8. **lenten,** meager, scanty (like
lenten fare). 27. **gaskins,** hose, breeches, held up by
laces or *points;* hence Maria's quibble. 29. **Sir Toby.**
The Clown hints at a match between Maria and Sir
Toby. 39. **Quinapalus,** apparently an invented authority. 45. **dry,** dull. 46. **dishonest,** probably, ill-
behaved.

botcher mend him. Any thing that's mended is but patched: virtue that transgresses is but patched with sin; and sin that amends is but patched with virtue. If that this simple syllogism will serve, so; if it will not, what remedy? As there is no true cuckold but calamity, so beauty's a flower. The lady bade take away the fool; therefore, I say again, take her away.

Oli. Sir, I bade them take away you.   60

Clo. Misprision in the highest degree! Lady, cucullus non facit monachum; that's as much to say as I wear not motley in my brain. Good madonna, give me leave to prove you a fool.

Oli. Can you do it?

Clo. Dexteriously, good madonna.

Oli. Make your proof.

Clo. I must catechize you for it, madonna: good my mouse of virtue, answer me.

Oli. Well, sir, for want of other idleness, I'll bide your proof.   71

Clo. Good madonna, why mournest thou?

Oli. Good fool, for my brother's death.

Clo. I think his soul is in hell, madonna.

Oli. I know his soul is in heaven, fool.

Clo. The more fool, madonna, to mourn for your brother's soul being in heaven. Take away the fool, gentlemen.

Oli. What think you of this fool, Malvolio? doth he not mend?   80

Mal. Yes, and shall do till the pangs of death shake him: infirmity, that decays the wise, doth ever make the better fool.

Clo. God send you, sir, a speedy infirmity, for the better increasing your folly! Sir Toby will be sworn that I am no fox; but he will not pass his word for two pence that you are no fool.

Oli. How say you to that, Malvolio?   88

Mal. I marvel your ladyship takes delight in such a barren rascal: I saw him put down the other day with an ordinary fool that has no more brain than a stone. Look you now, he's out of his guard already; unless you laugh and minister occasion to him, he is gagged. I protest, I take these wise men, that crow so at these set kind of fools, no better than the fools' zanies.   96

Oli. O, you are sick of self-love, Malvolio, and taste with a distempered appetite. To be generous, guiltless and of free disposition, is to take those things for bird-bolts that you deem cannon-bullets: there is no slander in an allowed fool, though he do nothing but rail; nor no railing in a known discreet man, though he do nothing but reprove.   104

Clo. Now Mercury endue thee with leasing, for thou speakest well of fools!

Re-enter MARIA.

Mar. Madam, there is at the gate a young gentleman much desires to speak with you.

Oli. From the Count Orsino, is it?

Mar. I know not, madam: 'tis a fair young man, and well attended.   111

Oli. Who of my people hold him in delay?

Mar. Sir Toby, madam, your kinsman.

Oli. Fetch him off, I pray you; he speaks nothing but madman: fie on him! [*Exit Maria.*] Go you, Malvolio: if it be a suit from the count, I am sick, or not at home; what you will, to dismiss it. [*Exit Malvolio.*] Now you see, sir, how your fooling grows old, and people dislike it.   119

Clo. Thou hast spoke for us, madonna, as if thy eldest son should be a fool; whose skull Jove cram with brains! for,—here he comes, —one of thy kin has a most weak pia mater.

Enter SIR TOBY.

Oli. By mine honour, half drunk. What is he at the gate, cousin?

Sir To. A gentleman.

Oli. A gentleman! what gentleman?

Sir To. 'Tis a gentleman here—a plague o' these pickle-herring! How now, sot!

Clo. Good Sir Toby!   130

Oli. Cousin, cousin, how have you come so early by this lethargy?

Sir To. Lechery! I defy lechery. There's one at the gate.

Oli. Ay, marry, what is he?

Sir. To. Let him be the devil, an he will, I care not: give me faith, say I. Well, it's all one.   [*Exit.*

Oli. What's a drunken man like, fool?

Clo. Like a drowned man, a fool and a

---

52. **botcher,** mender of old clothes and shoes. 61. **Misprision,** mistake, misunderstanding, with suggestion of the legal use meaning "contempt," the arrest or imprisonment of the wrong person. 62. **cucullus . . . monachum,** the cowl does not make the monk. 63. **motley,** the many-colored garment of jesters. 69. **mouse of virtue,** term of endearment. 70. **idleness,** pastime. This and Olivia's patience at the Clown's gibe about her mourning indicate that she grows weary of her self-imposed seclusion. 91. **ordinary fool,** probably a fool from the street not regularly attached to a household. 96. **zanies,** fools' subordinates or imitators.

97. **sick of self-love.** This shows Olivia's recognition of Malvolio's self-conceit. 100. **bird-bolts,** blunt arrows for shooting small birds. 102. **allowed,** licensed. 105. **Mercury,** god of lying and thievery. **leasing,** lying. 115. **madman,** i.e., the words of madness. 123. **pia mater,** soft inner lining of the brain. 128. **here.** Sir Toby hiccoughs at this point and tries to conceal his condition. 137. **give me faith.** Sir Toby relies on faith, not works.

mad man: one draught above heat makes him a fool; the second mads him; and a third drowns him.   141

Oli. Go thou and seek the crowner, and let him sit o' my coz; for he's in the third degree of drink, he's drowned: go, look after him.

Clo. He is but mad yet, madonna; and the fool shall look to the madman.   [*Exit.*

Re-enter MALVOLIO.

Mal. Madam, yond young fellow swears he will speak with you. I told him you were sick; he takes on him to understand so much, and therefore comes to speak with you. I told him you were asleep; he seems to have a foreknowledge of that too, and therefore comes to speak with you. What is to be said to him, lady? he's fortified against any denial.

Oli. Tell him he shall not speak with me.

Mal. Has been told so; and he says, he'll stand at your door like a sheriff's post, and be the supporter to a bench, but he'll speak with you.

Oli. What kind o' man is he?

Mal. Why, of mankind.   160

Oli. What manner of man?

Mal. Of very ill manner; he'll speak with you, will you or no.

Oli. Of what personage and years is he?

Mal. Not yet old enough for a man, nor young enough for a boy; as a squash is before 'tis a peascod, or a codling when 'tis almost an apple: 'tis with him in standing water, between boy and man. He is very well-favoured and he speaks very shrewishly; one would think his mother's milk were scarce out of him.   171

Oli. Let him approach: call in my gentle-woman.

Mal. Gentlewoman, my lady calls. [*Exit.*

Re-enter MARIA.

Oli. Give me my veil: come, throw it o'er my face.
We'll once more hear Orsino's embassy.

Enter VIOLA, *and* Attendants.

Vio. The honourable lady of the house, which is she?

Oli. Speak to me; I shall answer for her. Your will?   180

Vio. Most radiant, exquisite and un-matchable beauty,—I pray you, tell me if this be the lady of the house, for I never saw her: I would be loath to cast away my speech, for besides that it is excellently well penned, I have taken great pains to con it. Good beauties, let me sustain no scorn; I am very comptible, even to the least sinister usage.

Oli. Whence came you, sir?   189

Vio. I can say little more than I have studied, and that question's out of my part. Good gentle one, give me modest assurance if you be the lady of the house, that I may proceed in my speech.

Oli. Are you a comedian?

Vio. No, my profound heart: and yet, by the very fangs of malice I swear, I am not that I play. Are you the lady of the house?

Oli. If I do not usurp myself, I am.   198

Vio. Most certain, if you are she, you do usurp yourself; for what is yours to bestow is not yours to reserve. But this is from my commission: I will on with my speech in your praise, and then show you the heart of my message.

Oli. Come to what is important in 't: I for-give you the praise.

Vio. Alas, I took great pains to study it, and 'tis poetical.   207

Oli. It is the more like to be feigned: I pray you, keep it in. I heard you were saucy at my gates, and allowed your approach rather to wonder at you than to hear you. If you be not mad, be gone; if you have reason, be brief: 'tis not that time of moon with me to make one in so skipping a dialogue.

Mar. Will you hoist sail, sir? here lies your way.

Vio. No, good swabber; I am to hull here a little longer. Some mollification for your giant, sweet lady. Tell me your mind: I am a messenger.   220

Oli. Sure, you have some hideous matter to deliver, when the courtesy of it is so fearful. Speak your office.

Vio. It alone concerns your ear. I bring no overture of war, no taxation of homage:

---

140. **above heat,** above the point at which the body grows warm with drinking. 142. **crowner,** coroner. 157. **sheriff's post,** post before the sheriff's door on which proclamations and notices were fixed. 165-171. **Not yet . . . him.** Malvolio speaks nowhere else in this vein. 166. **squash,** unripe pea pod. 167. **peascod,** pea pod. **codling,** unripe apple. 170. **shrewishly,** sharply; possibly, like a woman.

181. **Most . . . beauty.** This line is a part of Viola's prepared speech. The same style peeps out in a few places further on. 186. **con,** learn by heart. 188. **comptible,** susceptible, sensitive. 201. **from,** outside of. 213. **moon,** as affecting lunatics. 214. **skipping,** flighty, frivolous. 217. **swabber,** one who washes the decks; a nautical retort to *hoist* sail (l. 215). 218-19. **Some . . . giant,** pray pacify your giant; alluding ironically to Maria's small size. 222. **courtesy,** ceremonious introduction. 223. **office,** commission. 225. **taxation,** demand for the payment of.

I hold the olive in my hand; my words are
as full of peace as matter.

Oli. Yet you began rudely. What are you?
what would you?   229

Vio. The rudeness that hath appeared in
me have I learned from my entertainment.
What I am, and what I would, are as secret
as maidenhead; to your ears, divinity, to any
other's, profanation.

Oli. Give us the place alone; we will hear
this divinity. [*Exeunt Maria and Attendants.*
Now, sir, what is your text?

Vio. Most sweet lady,—

Oli. A comfortable doctrine, and much
may be said of it. Where lies your text? 240

Vio. In Orsino's bosom.

Oli. In his bosom! In what chapter of his
bosom?

Vio. To answer by the method, in the first
of his heart.   245

Oli. O, I have read it: it is heresy. Have
you no more to say?

Vio. Good madam, let me see your
face.

Oli. Have you any commission from your
lord to negotiate with my face? You are now
out of your text: but we will draw the curtain
and show you the picture. Look you, sir,
such a one I was this present: is 't not well
done?   [*Unveiling.*

Vio. Excellently done, if God did all.

Oli. 'Tis in grain, sir; 'twill endure wind
and weather.   256

Vio. 'Tis beauty truly blent, whose red
and white
Nature's own sweet and cunning hand laid
on:
Lady, you are the cruell'st she alive,
If you will lead these graces to the grave 260
And leave the world no copy.

Oli. O, sir, I will not be so hard-hearted; I
will give out divers schedules of my beauty:
it shall be inventoried, and every particle and
utensil labelled to my will: as, item, two lips,
indifferent red; item, two grey eyes, with lids
to them; item, one neck, one chin, and so
forth. Were you sent hither to praise me?

Vio. I see you what you are, you are too
proud;

But, if you were the devil, you are fair. 270
My lord and master loves you: O, such love
Could be but recompensed, though you were
crown'd
The nonpareil of beauty!

Oli.   How does he love me?

Vio. With adorations, fertile tears,
With groans that thunder love, with sighs of
fire.

Oli. Your lord does know my mind; I can-
not love him:
Yet I suppose him virtuous, know him noble,
Of great estate, of fresh and stainless youth;
In voices well divulged, free, learn'd and
valiant;   279
And in dimension and the shape of nature
A gracious person: but yet I cannot love him;
He might have took his answer long ago.

Vio. If I did love you in my master's
flame,
With such a suffering, such a deadly life,
In your denial I would find no sense;
I would not understand it.

Oli.   Why, what would you?

Vio. Make me a willow cabin at your
gate,
And call upon my soul within the house;
Write loyal cantons of contemned love
And sing them loud even in the dead of night;
Halloo your name to the reverberate hills
And make the babbling gossip of the air 292
Cry out 'Olivia!' O, you should not rest
Between the elements of air and earth,
But you should pity me!

Oli.   You might do much.
What is your parentage?

Vio. Above my fortunes, yet my state is
well:
I am a gentleman.

Oli.   Get you to your lord; 298
I cannot love him: let him send no more;
Unless, perchance, you come to me again,
To tell me how he takes it. Fare you well:
I thank you for your pains: spend this for
me.

Vio. I am no fee'd post, lady; keep your
purse:
My master, not myself, lacks recompense.
Love make his heart of flint that you shall
love;

---

239. **comfortable**, comforting. 244. **method**, i.e.,
your method. 253. **this present**, just now, presently.
Since it was customary to hang curtains in front of pictures, Olivia in unveiling speaks as if she were displaying
a picture of herself. 255. **in grain**, fast dyed. 263.
schedules, inventories. 265. **labelled**, added as a
codicil.

274. **fertile**, copious. 283. **flame**, passion. 284.
deadly, death-doomed. 287. **willow cabin**, arbor.
288. **my soul**, i.e., Olivia. 289. **cantons**, songs.
292. **babbling . . . air**, echo. 303. **fee'd post**, hired
messenger. 305. **his**, the man's.

And let your fervour, like my master's, be
Placed in contempt! Farewell, fair cruelty.
　　　　　　　　　　　　　　　　[*Exit.*
　Oli. 'What is your parentage?'
'Above my fortunes, yet my state is well:
I am a gentleman.' I'll be sworn thou art;
Thy tongue, thy face, thy limbs, actions and
　　spirit, 311
Do give thee five-fold blazon: not too fast:
　soft, soft!
Unless the master were the man. How
　now!
Even so quickly may one catch the plague?
Methinks I feel this youth's perfections
With an invisible and subtle stealth
To creep in at mine eyes. Well, let it be.
What ho, Malvolio!

Re-enter MALVOLIO.

　Mal.　　　　Here, madam, at your service.
　Oli. Run after that same peevish mes-
senger,
The county's man: he left this ring behind
　him, 320
Would I or not: tell him I'll none of it.
Desire him not to flatter with his lord,
Nor hold him up with hopes; I am not for
　him:
If that the youth will come this way to-
　morrow,
I'll give him reasons for 't: hie thee, Malvolio.
　Mal. Madam, I will. 　　　　[*Exit.*
　Oli. I do I know not what, and fear to find
Mine eye too great a flatterer for my
　mind.
Fate, show thy force: ourselves we do not
　owe;
What is decreed must be, and be this so.
　　　　　　　　　　　　　　　　Exit.

ACT II.

SCENE I. *The sea-coast.*

Enter ANTONIO *and* SEBASTIAN.

　Ant. Will you stay no longer? nor will you
not that I go with you?
　Seb. By your patience, no. My stars shine
darkly over me: the malignancy of my fate
might perhaps distemper yours; therefore I

shall crave of you your leave that I may bear
my evils alone: it were a bad recompense for
your love, to lay any of them on you.
　Ant. Let me yet know of you whither you
are bound. 10
　Seb. No, sooth, sir: my determinate voyage is mere extravagancy. But I perceive in
you so excellent a touch of modesty, that you
will not extort from me what I am willing to
keep in; therefore it charges me in manners
the rather to express myself. You must
know of me then, Antonio, my name is
Sebastian, which I called Roderigo. My
father was that Sebastian of Messaline,
whom I know you have heard of. He left
behind him myself and a sister, both born
in an hour: if the heavens had been pleased,
would we had so ended! but you, sir, altered
that; for some hour before you took me from
the breach of the sea was my sister
drowned. 24
　Ant. Alas the day!
　Seb. A lady, sir, though it was said she
much resembled me, was yet of many
accounted beautiful: but, though I could not
with such estimable wonder overfar believe
that, yet thus far I will boldly publish her;
she bore a mind that envy could not but call
fair. She is drowned already, sir, with salt
water, though I seem to drown her remembrance again with more. 33
　Ant. Pardon me, sir, your bad entertainment.
　Seb. O good Antonio, forgive me your
trouble.
　Ant. If you will not murder me for my
love, let me be your servant. 37
　Seb. If you will not undo what you have
done, that is, kill him whom you have recovered, desire it not. Fare ye well at once:
my bosom is full of kindness, and I am yet so
near the manners of my mother, that upon
the least occasion more mine eyes will tell
tales of me. I am bound to the Count
Orsino's court: farewell. 　　　　[*Exit.*
　Ant. The gentleness of all the gods go
　　with thee!
I have many enemies in Orsino's court,
Else would I very shortly see thee there.

---

310. **thou,** suggestive of tenderness. She has used
your before (l. 308). 312. **blazon,** heraldic description.
317. **eyes.** Love was thought to enter through the eye.
Act II. Scene i. 4. **malignancy,** malevolence (of
the stars). 5. **distemper,** disorder, disturb.

12. **extravagancy,** aimless wandering. 15. **it charges
me,** I am bound. 16. **express,** reveal. 19. **Messaline,**
possibly, Mytilene; otherwise unidentified. 21. **an,** one.
29. **estimable wonder,** admiring judgment. 34.
entertainment, reception. 41. **kindness,** tenderness.
42. **manners . . . mother,** womanish qualities.

But, come what may, I do adore thee so, 48
That danger shall seem sport, and I will go.
[*Exit.*

SCENE II. *A street.*

Enter VIOLA, MALVOLIO *following.*

Mal. Were not you even now with the
Countess Olivia?

Vio. Even now, sir; on a moderate pace I
have since arrived but hither.

Mal. She returns this ring to you, sir: you
might have saved me my pains, to have taken
it away yourself. She adds, moreover, that
you should put your lord into a desperate
assurance she will none of him: and one thing
more, that you be never so hardy to come
again in his affairs, unless it be to report
your lord's taking of this. Receive it so. 12

Vio. She took the ring of me: I'll none of
it.

Mal. Come, sir, you peevishly threw it to
her; and her will is, it should be so returned:
if it be worth stooping for, there it lies in
your eye; if not, be it his that finds it. [*Exit.*

Vio. I left no ring with her: what means
this lady?
Fortune forbid my outside have not charm'd
her!
She made good view of me; indeed, so much,
That sure methought her eyes had lost her
tongue, 21
For she did speak in starts distractedly.
She loves me, sure; the cunning of her passion
Invites me in this churlish messenger.
None of my lord's ring! why, he sent her
none.
I am the man: if it be so, as 'tis,
Poor lady, she were better love a dream.
Disguise, I see, thou art a wickedness,
Wherein the pregnant enemy does much.
How easy is it for the proper-false 30
In women's waxen hearts to set their forms!
Alas, our frailty is the cause, not we!
For such as we are made of, such we be.
How will this fadge? my master loves her
dearly;
And I, poor monster, fond as much on him;

And she, mistaken, seems to dote on me.
What will become of this? As I am man,
My state is desperate for my master's love;
As I am woman,—now alas the day!—
What thriftless sighs shall poor Olivia
breathe!
O time! thou must untangle this, not I; 41
It is too hard a knot for me to untie!
[*Exit.*

SCENE III. OLIVIA'S *house.*

Enter SIR TOBY *and* SIR ANDREW.

Sir To. Approach, Sir Andrew: not to be
abed after midnight is to be up betimes; and
'diluculo surgere,' thou know'st,—

Sir And. Nay, by my troth, I know not:
but I know, to be up late is to be up late.

Sir To. A false conclusion: I hate it as an
unfilled can. To be up after midnight and to
go to bed then, is early: so that to go to bed
after midnight is to go to bed betimes. Does
not our life consist of the four elements? 10

Sir And. Faith, so they say; but I think it
rather consists of eating and drinking.

Sir To. Thou'rt a scholar; let us therefore
eat and drink. Marian, I say! a stoup of wine!

Enter CLOWN.

Sir And. Here comes the fool, i' faith.

Clo. How now, my hearts! did you never
see the picture of 'we three'?

Sir To. Welcome, ass. Now let's have a
catch. 18

Sir And. By my troth, the fool has an excellent breast. I had rather than forty shillings I had such a leg, and so sweet a breath to
sing, as the fool has. In sooth, thou wast in
very gracious fooling last night, when thou
spokest of Pigrogromitus, of the Vapians
passing the equinoctial of Queubus: 'twas
very good, i' faith. I sent thee sixpence for
thy leman: hadst it? 26

Clo. I did impeticos thy gratillity; for

Scene ii. 8. **desperate**, without hope. 10. **hardy**,
audacious. 13. **She . . . it.** Viola tells a quick and
friendly lie to shield Olivia. 21. **lost**, caused her to lose.
29. **pregnant**, quick, resourceful; possibly alluding to
Satan. 30. **proper-false**, handsome and deceitful.
31. **set their forms**, stamp their images. 34. **fadge**,
fit (as an explanation). 35. **monster**, i.e., being both
man and woman.

Scene iii. 3. **'diluculo surgere'** (*saluberrimum est*),
to rise early is most healthful; a sentence from Lilly's
Latin Grammar. 10. **four elements**, air, fire, earth, and
water. 13. **Thou'rt a scholar.** Sir Toby is making fun
of him. 14. **stoup**, drinking vessel. 17. **picture of 'we
three,'** picture of two asses inscribed "we three," the
spectator being the third. 18. **catch**, a song so arranged
that the second singer takes up the first line just as the
first singer is beginning the second line, and so on. 21.
leg, probably, obeisance made by drawing back one
leg and bending the other. 24-25. **Pigrogromitus . . .
Queubus**, mock erudition. 26. **leman**, sweetheart.
27. **impeticos thy gratillity**, suggests "impetticoat thy
gratuity."

Malvolio's nose is no whipstock: my lady
has a white hand, and the Myrmidons are
no bottle-ale houses.

Sir And. Excellent! why, this is the best
fooling, when all is done. Now, a song. 31

Sir To. Come on; there is sixpence for
you: let's have a song.

Sir And. There's a testril of me too: if one
knight give a—

Clo. Would you have a love-song, or a
song of good life?

Sir To. A love-song, a love-song.

Sir And. Ay, ay: I care not for good life.

Clo. [*Sings*]

O mistress mine, where are you roam-
　　ing? 40
O, stay and hear; your true love's com-
　　ing,
　　That can sing both high and low:
Trip no further, pretty sweeting;
Journeys end in lovers meeting,
　　Every wise man's son doth know.

Sir And. Excellent good, i' faith.

Sir To. Good, good.

Clo. [*Sings*]

What is love? 'tis not hereafter;
Present mirth hath present laughter;
　　What's to come is still unsure: 50
In delay there lies no plenty;
Then come kiss me, sweet and twenty,
　　Youth's a stuff will not endure.

Sir And. A mellifluous voice, as I am true
knight.

Sir To. A contagious breath.

Sir And. Very sweet and contagious, i'
faith. 57

Sir To. To hear by the nose, it is dulcet in
contagion. But shall we make the welkin
dance indeed? shall we rouse the night-owl
in a catch that will draw three souls out of
one weaver? shall we do that? 62

Sir And. An you love me, let's do 't: I am
dog at a catch.

Clo. By'r lady, sir, and some dogs will
catch well.

Sir And. Most certain. Let our catch be,
'Thou knave.'

Clo. 'Hold thy peace, thou knave,' knight?
I shall be constrained in 't to call thee knave,
knight. 70

Sir And. 'Tis not the first time I have constrained one to call me knave. Begin, fool: it
begins 'Hold thy peace.'

Clo. I shall never begin if I hold my peace.

Sir And. Good, i' faith. Come, begin.

　　　　　　　　　　　　　[*Catch sung.*

Enter MARIA.

Mar. What a caterwauling do you keep
here! If my lady have not called up her
steward Malvolio and bid him turn you out
of doors, never trust me. 79

Sir To. My lady's a Cataian, we are politicians, Malvolio's a Peg-a-Ramsey, and 'Three
merry men be we.' Am not I consanguine-
ous? am I not of her blood? Tillyvally.
Lady! [*Sings*] 'There dwelt a man in Babylon, lady, lady!'

Clo. Beshrew me, the knight's in admirable fooling.

Sir And. Ay, he does well enough if he be
disposed, and so do I too: he does it with a
better grace, but I do it more natural.

Sir To. [*Sings*] 'O, the twelfth day of
December,'— 91

Mar. For the love o' God, peace!

Enter MALVOLIO.

Mal. My masters, are you mad? or what
are you? Have you no wit, manners, nor
honesty, but to gabble like tinkers at this
time of night? Do ye make an alehouse of
my lady's house, that ye squeak out your
coziers' catches without any mitigation or
remorse of voice? Is there no respect of
place, persons, nor time in you?

---

28. **whipstock,** whip-handle. It may suggest Malvolio's habit of prying into matters which he has no
authority to punish. 29. **Myrmidons,** followers of
Achilles; here, perhaps, a tavern of high grade. **bottle-
ale,** used contemptuously of taverns because they sold
low-class drink. 34. **testril,** a coin worth six pence.
37. **good life,** respectability. 40. **O mistress mine.**
This song is found in several Elizabethan song-books,
but is nevertheless thought by some authorities to be
Shakespeare's. 43. **sweeting,** sweet one. 52. **sweet
and twenty,** possibly meant originally "twenty times
as sweet," *twenty* being used as an intensive. 59. **welkin
dance,** drink till the sky seems to turn round (Johnson).
61-62. **draw . . . weaver,** usually explained as a reference
to psalm-singing weavers, Protestant refugees from
Belgium. There is a reference also to the Renaissance
conception of the soul which was held to be three-fold,
the vegetal, the sensible, and the intellectual soul.

64. **dog at,** clever at. 80. **Cataian,** explained as
Chinese, i.e., from Cathay, suggested by *caterwauling.*
politicians, schemers, intriguers. 81. **Peg-a-Ramsey,**
common name of a tune, evidently of low character.
83. **Tillyvally,** a term of contempt, possibly from a
song. 84. **'There . . . lady,'** first line of a ballad having
the refrain "Lady, lady." Sir Toby's use of the word,
above, suggested the song. 89. **natural,** unconsciously
suggesting idiocy. 90-91. **'O . . . December.'** Professor Kittredge suggests that this is the ballad of *Mussel-
burgh Field* in Child's *English and Scottish Popular Ballads,* IV, 507.

Sir To. We did keep time, sir, in our catches. Sneck up! 101

Mal. Sir Toby, I must be round with you. My lady bade me tell you, that, though she harbours you as her kinsman, she's nothing allied to your disorders. If you can separate yourself and your misdemeanours, you are welcome to the house; if not, an it would please you to take leave of her, she is very willing to bid you farewell.

Sir To. 'Farewell, dear heart, since I must needs be gone.' 110

Mar. Nay, good Sir Toby.

Clo. 'His eyes do show his days are almost done.'

Mal. Is 't even so?

Sir To. 'But I will never die.'

Clo. Sir Toby, there you lie.

Mal. This is much credit to you.

Sir To. 'Shall I bid him go?'

Clo. 'What an if you do?'

Sir To. 'Shall I bid him go, and spare not?'

Clo. 'O no, no, no, no, you dare not.' 121

Sir To. Out o' tune, sir: ye lie. Art any more than a steward? Dost thou think, because thou art virtuous, there shall be no more cakes and ale?

Clo. Yes, by Saint Anne, and ginger shall be hot i' the mouth too.

Sir To. Thou'rt i' the right. Go, sir, rub your chain with crums. A stoup of wine, Maria! 129

Mal. Mistress Mary, if you prized my lady's favour at any thing more than contempt, you would not give means for this uncivil rule: she shall know of it, by this hand. [*Exit.*

Mar. Go shake your ears.

Sir And. 'Twere as good a deed as to drink when a man's a-hungry, to challenge him the field, and then to break promise with him and make a fool of him.

Sir To. Do 't, knight: I'll write thee a challenge; or I'll deliver thy indignation to him by word of mouth. 141

Mar. Sweet Sir Toby, be patient for tonight: since the youth of the count's was

to-day with my lady, she is much out of quiet. For Monsieur Malvolio, let me alone with him: if I do not gull him into a nayword, and make him a common recreation, do not think I have wit enough to lie straight in my bed: I know I can do it.

Sir To. Possess us, possess us; tell us something of him. 150

Mar. Marry, sir, sometimes he is a kind of puritan.

Sir And. O, if I thought that, I 'ld beat him like a dog!

Sir To. What, for being a puritan? thy exquisite reason, dear knight?

Sir And. I have no exquisite reason for 't, but I have reason good enough. 158

Mar. The devil a puritan that he is, or any thing constantly, but a time-pleaser; an affectioned ass, that cons state without book and utters it by great swarths: the best persuaded of himself, so crammed, as he thinks, with excellencies, that it is his grounds of faith that all that look on him love him; and on that vice in him will my revenge find notable cause to work. 166

Sir To. What wilt thou do?

Mar. I will drop in his way some obscure epistles of love; wherein, by the colour of his beard, the shape of his leg, the manner of his gait, the expressure of his eye, forehead, and complexion, he shall find himself most feelingly personated. I can write very like my lady your niece: on a forgotten matter we can hardly make distinction of our hands.

Sir To. Excellent! I smell a device.

Sir And. I have 't in my nose too.

Sir To. He shall think, by the letters that thou wilt drop, that they come from my niece, and that she's in love with him. 180

Mar. My purpose is, indeed, a horse of that colour.

Sir And. And your horse now would make him an ass.

Mar. Ass, I doubt not.

Sir And. O, 'twill be admirable!

Mar. Sport royal, I warrant you: I know my physic will work with him. I will plant

101. **Sneck up!** go hang! 102. **round,** frank, outspoken. 104. **nothing,** not at all. 109. **'Farewell** . . . **gone,'** from the ballad, *Corydon's Farewell to Phyllis.* 125. **cakes and ale,** reveling (proverbial). 126. **Saint Anne,** invoked because of her care for material welfare. 128-129. **Go . . . crums,** i.e., scour your steward's chain with crumbs; attend to your own business. 132. **give means,** i.e., by supplying drink. 133. **rule,** conduct.

146. **nayword,** byword. 147. **recreation,** laughingstock. 152. **puritan.** It was Sir Andrew's humor to hate Puritans. Shakespeare makes Maria say below that Malvolio is not a Puritan but a time-pleaser and an affected ass. It is therefore misleading to say that there is here any satire against Puritans in the figure of Malvolio. 160. **affectioned,** affected. 161. **cons** . . . **book,** learns the phrases of high society by heart. 162. **best persuaded,** has the best opinion. 171. **expressure,** expression. 173. **personated,** described.

you two, and let the fool make a third, where he shall find the letter: observe his construction of it. For this night, to bed, and dream on the event. Farewell. 　　　　　[*Exit.* 192

Sir To. Good night, Penthesilea.

Sir And. Before me, she's a good wench.

Sir To. She's a beagle, true-bred, and one that adores me: what o' that?

Sir And. I was adored once too.

Sir To. Let's to bed, knight. Thou hadst need send for more money.

Sir And. If I cannot recover your niece, I am a foul way out. 　　　　　　　　201

Sir To. Send for money, knight: if thou hast her not i' the end, call me cut.

Sir And. If I do not, never trust me, take it how you will.

Sir To. Come, come, I'll go burn some sack; 'tis too late to go to bed now: come, knight; come, knight. 　　　　　　[*Exeunt.*

Scene IV. *The* Duke's *Palace.*

Enter Duke, Viola, Curio, *and others.*

Duke. Give me some music. Now, good
　　morrow, friends.
Now, good Cesario, but that piece of song,
That old and antique song we heard last
　　night:
Methought it did relieve my passion much,
More than light airs and recollected terms
Of these most brisk and giddy-paced times:
Come, but one verse.

Cur. He is not here, so please your lordship, that should sing it.

Duke. Who was it? 　　　　　　　　10

Cur. Feste, the jester, my lord; a fool that the lady Olivia's father took much delight in. He is about the house.

Duke. Seek him out, and play the tune the
　　while. 　　　[*Exit Curio. Music plays.*
Come hither, boy: if ever thou shalt love,
In the sweet pangs of it remember me;
For such as I am all true lovers are,
Unstaid and skittish in all motions else,
Save in the constant image of the creature

That is beloved. How dost thou like this
　　tune?

Vio. It gives a very echo to the seat 　21
Where Love is throned.

Duke. Thou dost speak masterly:
My life upon 't, young though thou art,
　　thine eye
Hath stay'd upon some favour that it loves:
Hath it not, boy?

Vio. 　　　　A little, by your favour.

Duke. What kind of woman is 't?

Vio. 　　　　　　Of your complexion.

Duke. She is not worth thee, then. What
　　years, i' faith?

Vio. About your years, my lord.

Duke. Too old, by heaven: let still the
　　woman take 　　　　　　　　30
An elder than herself; so wears she to him,
So sways she level in her husband's heart:
For, boy, however we do praise ourselves,
Our fancies are more giddy and unfirm,
More longing, wavering, sooner lost and
　　worn,
Than women's are.

Vio. 　　　　I think it well, my lord.

Duke. Then let thy love be younger than
　　thyself,
Or thy affection cannot hold the bent;
For women are as roses, whose fair flower
Being once display'd, doth fall that very
　　hour. 　　　　　　　　　　40

Vio. And so they are: alas, that they are
　　so;
To die, even when they to perfection grow!

Re-enter Curio *and* Clown.

Duke. O, fellow, come, the song we had
　　last night.
Mark it, Cesario, it is old and plain;
The spinsters and the knitters in the sun
And the free maids that weave their thread
　　with bones
Do use to chant it: it is silly sooth,

---

193. **Penthesilea**, queen of the Amazons; another ironical allusion to Maria's stature. 195. **beagle**, small hound; possibly also alluding to Maria's size. 200. **recover**, win. 201. **foul way out**, explained as "out of pocket" and as "off the track." 203. **cut**, a horse with a docked tail. 206. **sack**, Canary wine.
Scene iv. 3. **antique**, quaint. 5. **recollected terms**, artificial expressions. 18. **motions**, inward promptings or impulses.

21. **seat**, i.e., the heart. 25. **stay'd . . . favour,** rested upon some face. 27. **complexion,** external appearance. 30-40. **Too old . . . hour.** A somewhat absurd use has been made of this passage to prove that Shakespeare, who was younger than his wife, is expressing a personal opinion. The idea is, of course, a commonplace in Renaissance love literature. 31. **wears she,** adapts herself. 32. **sways she level,** rules steadily; or possibly the figure is drawn from scales evenly balanced. 33. **praise,** appraise. 34. **fancies,** amorous inclinations. 38. **bent,** degree of tension (as in archery). 45. **spinsters,** those who spin. 46. **free, carefree.** **bones,** bobbins with which bone-lace was made. 47. **silly sooth,** simple truth.

And dallies with the innocence of love,
Like the old age.
  Clo. Are you ready, sir?   50
  Duke. Ay; prithee, sing.   [*Music.*

                    SONG.

  Clo. Come away, come away, death,
      And in sad cypress let me be laid;
    Fly away, fly away, breath;
      I am slain by a fair cruel maid.
    My shroud of white, stuck all with yew,
      O, prepare it!
    My part of death, no one so true
          Did share it.

    Not a flower, not a flower sweet,   60
      On my black coffin let there be strown;
    Not a friend, not a friend greet
      My poor corpse, where my bones shall
          be thrown:
    A thousand thousand sighs to save,
        Lay me, O, where
    Sad true lover never find my grave,
          To weep there!

  Duke. There's for thy pains.
  Clo. No pains, sir; I take pleasure in
singing, sir.   70
  Duke. I'll pay thy pleasure then.
  Clo. Truly, sir, and pleasure will be paid,
one time or another.
  Duke. Give me now leave to leave thee.
  Clo. Now, the melancholy god protect
thee; and the tailor make thy doublet of
changeable taffeta, for thy mind is a very
opal. I would have men of such constancy
put to sea, that their business might be every
thing and their intent every where; for that's
it that always makes a good voyage of
nothing. Farewell.   [*Exit.*
  Duke. Let all the rest give place.
            [*Curio and Attendants retire.*
                  Once more, Cesario,   82
Get thee to yond same sovereign cruelty:
Tell her, my love, more noble than the world,
Prizes not quantity of dirty lands;
The parts that fortune hath bestow'd upon
    her,
Tell her, I hold as giddily as fortune;

But 'tis that miracle and queen of gems
That nature pranks her in attracts my soul.
  Vio. But if she cannot love you, sir?   90
  Duke. I cannot be so answer'd.
  Vio.   Sooth, but you must.
Say that some lady, as perhaps there is,
Hath for your love as great a pang of heart
As you have for Olivia: you cannot love her;
You tell her so; must she not then be an-
    swer'd?
  Duke. There is no woman's sides
Can bide the beating of so strong a passion
As love doth give my heart; no woman's
    heart
So big, to hold so much; they lack retention.
Alas, their love may be call'd appetite,   100
No motion of the liver, but the palate,
That suffer surfeit, cloyment and revolt;
But mine is all as hungry as the sea,
And can digest as much: make no compare
Between that love a woman can bear me
And that I owe Olivia.
  Vio.   Ay, but I know—
  Duke. What dost thou know?
  Vio. Too well what love women to men
      may owe:
In faith, they are as true of heart as we.
My father had a daughter loved a man,   110
As it might be, perhaps, were I a woman,
I should your lordship.
  Duke.   And what's her history?
  Vio. A blank, my lord. She never told
      her love,
But let concealment, like a worm i' the bud,
Feed on her damask cheek: she pined in
      thought,
And with a green and yellow melancholy
She sat like patience on a monument,
Smiling at grief. Was not this love indeed?
We men may say more, swear more: but in-
    deed
Our shows are more than will; for still we
    prove   120
Much in our vows, but little in our love.

49. old age, old times. 53. cypress, interpreted as meaning coffin of cypress wood, or bier strewn with sprigs of cypress. 58-59. My part . . . it, no one died for love so true to love as I (Luce). 75. melancholy god, Saturn, if the Clown has any god in mind. 76. doublet, close-fitting body garment with or without sleeves. 77. taffeta, silk. 80-81. for . . . nothing, possibly ironical, meaning that such changeable enterprise will make a good voyage come to nothing. 86. parts, gifts, as wealth or rank. 87. giddily, carelessly, insecurely.

89. pranks, adorns. 96-106. There is . . . Olivia. The Duke has just said in lines 33-36 that men are more inconstant than women. 99. retention, constancy, power of retaining. 101. liver . . . palate. The distinction seems to be that real love is a passion of the liver, whereas fancy (light love) is born in the eye and nourished in the palate. 102. That suffer, that suffers. That is sometimes thought to refer back to their (l.100). cloyment, satiety to the point of losing appetite. revolt, sickness, revulsion. 113. blank, i.e., her history is a blank. 115. damask, red like the damask rose. 116. green and yellow. "Green denoted hopefulness and yellow jealousy; so that a green and yellow melancholy was a melancholy in which there was jealousy, yet hope. This accords exactly with the state of mind of Viola" (Hunter).

Duke. But died thy sister of her love, my
   boy?
Vio. I am all the daughters of my father's
   house,
And all the brothers too: and yet I know not.
Sir, shall I to this lady?
   Duke.   Ay, that's the theme.
To her in haste; give her this jewel; say,
My love can give no place, bide no denay.
                         [Exeunt.

SCENE V. OLIVIA's *garden.*

Enter SIR TOBY, SIR ANDREW, *and* FABIAN.

Sir To. Come thy ways, Signior Fabian.
Fab. Nay, I'll come: if I lose a scruple of
this sport, let me be boiled to death with
melancholy.
Sir To. Wouldst thou not be glad to have
the niggardly rascally sheep-biter come by
some notable shame?
Fab. I would exult, man: you know, he
brought me out o' favour with my lady
about a bear-baiting here.   10
Sir To. To anger him we'll have the bear
again; and we will fool him black and blue:
shall we not, Sir Andrew?
Sir And. An we do not, it is pity of our
lives.
Sir To. Here comes the little villain.

Enter MARIA.

How now, my metal of India!   17
Mar. Get ye all three into the box-tree:
Malvolio's coming down this walk: he has
been yonder i' the sun practising behaviour
to his own shadow this half hour: observe
him, for the love of mockery; for I know this
letter will make a contemplative idiot of him.
Close, in the name of jesting! Lie thou there
[*throws down a letter*]; for here comes the
trout that must be caught with tickling. 26
                         [Exit.

Enter MALVOLIO.

Mal. 'Tis but fortune; all is fortune.
Maria once told me she did affect me: and I
have heard herself come thus near, that,

should she fancy, it should be one of my com-
plexion. Besides, she uses me with a more
exalted respect than any one else that fol-
lows her. What should I think on 't?   33
Sir To. Here's an overweening rogue!
Fab. O, peace! Contemplation makes a
rare turkey-cock of him: how he jets under
his advanced plumes!
Sir And. 'Slight, I could so beat the rogue!
Sir To. Peace, I say.
Mal. To be Count Malvolio!   40
Sir To. Ah, rogue!
Sir And. Pistol him, pistol him.
Sir To. Peace, peace!
Mal. There is example for 't; the lady of
the Strachy married the yeoman of the ward-
robe.
Sir And. Fie on him, Jezebel!
Fab. O, peace! now he's deeply in: look
how imagination blows him.
Mal. Having been three months married
to her, sitting in my state,—   50
Sir To. O, for a stone-bow, to hit him in
the eye!
Mal. Calling my officers about me, in
my branched velvet gown; having come
from a daybed, where I have left Olivia
sleeping,—
Sir To. Fire and brimstone!
Fab. O, peace, peace!   57
Mal. And then to have the humour of
state; and after a demure travel of regard,
telling them I know my place as I would
they should do theirs, to ask for my kinsman
Toby,—   61
Sir To. Bolts and shackles!
Fab. O peace, peace, peace! now, now.
Mal. Seven of my people, with an obedient start, make out for him: I frown the
while; and perchance wind up my watch, or
play with my—some rich jewel. Toby approaches; courtesies there to me—
Sir To. Shall this fellow live?
Fab. Though our silence be drawn from
us with cars, yet peace.   71

---

127. **denay,** denial.
   Scene v. 3. **boiled to death.** Melancholy being a
settled passion, the spirits descended to the intestines,
carrying with them their boiling heat. 6. **sheep-biter,**
sheep-killing dog. 17. **metal,** gold, probably with pun
on *mettle,* spirit. 23. **contemplative,** i.e., from con-
templating himself. 26. **tickling,** groping gently with
the hands—a method of fishing. 28. **she,** i.e., Olivia.

30. **fancy,** fall in love. 36. **jets,** struts. 44. **lady of
the Strachy,** apparently a lady who had married below
her station; no satisfactory explanation. 46. **Jezebel,**
a blunder of Sir Andrew, unless, as has been suggested, we
should read *her* for *him* in this line. 48. **blows,** puffs up.
50. **state,** chair of state. 51. **stone-bow,** cross-bow
for shooting stones. 54. **branched,** adorned with a
figured pattern suggesting branches. 55. **daybed,** sofa,
couch. 58. **humour of state,** idiosyncrasies allowed
to persons of rank. 59. **demure . . . regard,** grave
survey of the company. 61. **Toby,** i.e., not *Sir* Toby.
66. **wind up my watch,** an impressive act in those
days. 71. **cars,** used like "team of horses."

Mal. I extend my hand to him thus,
quenching my familiar smile with an austere
regard of control,—   74

Sir To. And does not Toby take you a
blow o' the lips then?

Mal. Saying, 'Cousin Toby, my fortunes
having cast me on your niece give me this
prerogative of speech,'—

Sir To. What, what?   80

Mal. 'You must amend your drunkenness.'

Sir To. Out, scab!

Fab. Nay, patience, or we break the
sinews of our plot.

Mal. 'Besides, you waste the treasure of
your time with a foolish knight,'—

Sir And. That's me, I warrant you.

Mal. 'One Sir Andrew,'—

Sir And. I knew 'twas I; for many do call
me fool.   90

Mal. What employment have we here?
                              [*Taking up the letter.*

Fab. Now is the woodcock near the gin.

Sir To. O, peace! and the spirit of humours intimate reading aloud to him!

Mal. By my life, this is my lady's hand:
these be her very C's, her U's and her T's;
and thus makes she her great P's. It is, in
contempt of question, her hand.

Sir And. Her C's, her U's and her T's:
why that?   100

Mal. [*Reads*] 'To the unknown beloved,
this, and my good wishes:'—her very phrases!
By your leave, wax. Soft! and the impressure her Lucrece, with which she uses to seal:
'tis my lady. To whom should this be?

Fab. This wins him, liver and all.

Mal. [*Reads*]

   Jove knows I love:
       But who?
   Lips, do not move;
       No man must know.   110

'No man must know.' What follows? the
numbers altered! 'No man must know:' if
this should be thee, Malvolio?

Sir To. Marry, hang thee, brock!

Mal. [*Reads*]

   I may command where I adore;
       But silence, like a Lucrece knife,

With bloodless stroke my heart doth
gore:
   M, O, A, I, doth sway my life.

Fab. A fustian riddle!

Sir To. Excellent wench, say I.   120

Mal. 'M, O, A, I, doth sway my life.'
Nay, but first, let me see, let me see, let
me see.

Fab. What dish o' poison has she dressed
him!

Sir To. And with what wing the staniel
checks at it!   125

Mal. 'I may command where I adore.'
Why, she may command me: I serve her; she
is my lady. Why, this is evident to any
formal capacity; there is no obstruction in
this: and the end,—what should that alpha-
betical position portend? If I could make
that resemble something in me,—Softly!
M, O, A, I,—

Sir To. O, ay, make up that: he is now
at a cold scent.   134

Fab. Sowter will cry upon 't for all this,
though it be as rank as a fox.

Mal. M,—Malvolio; M,—why, that begins my name.

Fab. Did not I say he would work it out?
the cur is excellent at faults.   140

Mal. M,—but then there is no consonancy in the sequel; that suffers under probation: A should follow, but O does.

Fab. And O shall end, I hope.

Sir To. Ay, or I'll cudgel him, and make
him cry O!

Mal. And then I comes behind.

Fab. Ay, an you had any eye behind you,
you might see more detraction at your heels
than fortunes before you.   150

Mal. M, O, A, I; this simulation is not as
the former: and yet, to crush this a little, it
would bow to me, for every one of these
letters are in my name. Soft! here follows
prose.

[*Reads*] 'If this fall into thy hand, revolve.

In my stars I am above thee; but be not
afraid of greatness: some are born great, some
achieve greatness and some have greatness
thrust upon 'em. Thy Fates open their
hands; let thy blood and spirit embrace
them; and, to inure thyself to what thou art
like to be, cast thy humble slough and appear fresh. Be opposite with a kinsman,
surly with servants; let thy tongue tang arguments of state; put thyself into the trick of
singularity: she thus advises thee that sighs
for thee. Remember who commended thy
yellow stockings, and wished to see thee ever
cross-gartered: I say, remember. Go to,
thou art made, if thou desirest to be so; if
not, let me see thee a steward still, the fellow
of servants, and not worthy to touch Fortune's fingers. Farewell. She that would
alter services with thee,　　　　　　172
　　　The Fortunate-Unhappy.'

Daylight and champain discovers not more:
this is open. I will be proud, I will read
politic authors, I will baffle Sir Toby, I will
wash off gross acquaintance, I will be point-
devise the very man. I do not now fool myself, to let imagination jade me; for every
reason excites to this, that my lady loves me.
She did commend my yellow stockings of
late, she did praise my leg being cross-
gartered; and in this she manifests herself to
my love, and with a kind of injunction drives
me to these habits of her liking. I thank my
stars I am happy. I will be strange, stout,
in yellow stockings, and cross-gartered, even
with the swiftness of putting on. Jove and
my stars be praised! Here is yet a postscript.
[*Reads*] 'Thou canst not choose but know who I
am. If thou entertainest my love, let it appear in thy smiling; thy smiles become thee
well; therefore in my presence still smile,
dear my sweet, I prithee.'　　　　　193

Jove, I thank thee: I will smile; I will do
everything that thou wilt have me. [*Exit.*

Fab. I will not give my part of this sport
for a pension of thousands to be paid from
the Sophy.

Sir To. I could marry this wench for this
device.　　　　　200

Sir And. So could I too.

Sir To. And ask no other dowry with her
but such another jest.

Sir And. Nor I neither.

Fab. Here comes my noble gull-catcher.

　　　　　Re-enter Maria.

Sir To. Wilt thou set thy foot o' my
neck?

Sir And. Or o'mine either?

Sir To. Shall I play my freedom at tray-
trip, and become thy bond-slave?

Sir And. I' faith, or I either?　　　210

Sir To. Why, thou hast put him in such a
dream, that when the image of it leaves him
he must run mad.

Mar. Nay, but say true; does it work
upon him?

Sir To. Like aqua-vitæ with a midwife.

Mar. If you will then see the fruits of the
sport, mark his first approach before my
lady: he will come to her in yellow stockings,
and 'tis a colour she abhors, and cross-
gartered, a fashion she detests; and he will
smile upon her, which will now be so unsuit-
able to her disposition, being addicted to a
melancholy as she is, that it cannot but turn
him into a notable contempt. If you will
see it, follow me.　　　　　225

Sir To. To the gates of Tartar, thou most
excellent devil of wit!

Sir And. I'll make one too.　　　[*Exeunt.*

ACT III.

Scene I.　Olivia's *garden.*

Enter Viola, *and* Clown *with a tabor.*

Vio. Save thee, friend, and thy music:
dost thou live by thy tabor?

Clo. No, sir, I live by the church.

Vio. Art thou a churchman?

Clo. No such matter, sir: I do live by the
church; for I do live at my house, and my
house doth stand by the church.

Vio. So thou mayst say, the king lies by a

---

156. **stars**, fortunes.　159. **blood and spirit**, i.e.,
as the agents of passion.　161. **slough**, skin of a snake.
162. **opposite**, contradictory.　163. **tang**, sound loud
with.　164. **trick of singularity**, eccentricity of manner.
167. **cross-gartered**, wearing garters above and below
the knee so as to cross behind it (Onions).　174. **champain**, open country.　175. **open**, obvious.　176. **politic**,
dealing with state affairs.　177. **point-devise**, extremely precise.　179. **jade**, trick.　185. **strange**, odd
and distant.　**stout**, haughty.　198. **Sophy**, Shah of
Persia.

208. **tray-trip**, a game with dice, success in which
depended on throwing a three.　216. **aqua-vitæ**, ardent spirits.　226. **Tartar**, the infernal regions.
Act III. Scene i. 2. **tabor**, drum used by clowns and
jesters.　8. **lies by**, i.e., resides near.

beggar, if a beggar dwell near him; or, the church stands by thy tabor, if thy tabor stand by the church. 11

Clo. You have said, sir. To see this age! A sentence is but a cheveril glove to a good wit: how quickly the wrong side may be turned outward!

Vio. Nay, that's certain; they that dally nicely with words may quickly make them wanton.

Clo. I would, therefore, my sister had had no name, sir. 20

Vio. Why, man?

Clo. Why, sir, her name's a word; and to dally with that word might make my sister wanton. But indeed words are very rascals since bonds disgraced them.

Vio. Thy reason, man?

Clo. Troth, sir, I can yield you none without words; and words are grown so false, I am loath to prove reason with them.

Vio. I warrant thou art a merry fellow and carest for nothing. 31

Clo. Not so, sir, I do care for something; but in my conscience, sir, I do not care for you: if that be to care for nothing, sir, I would it would make you invisible.

Vio. Art not thou the Lady Olivia's fool?

Clo. No, indeed, sir; the Lady Olivia has no folly: she will keep no fool, sir, till she be married; and fools are as like husbands as pilchards are to herrings; the husband 's the bigger: I am indeed not her fool, but her corrupter of words.

Vio. I saw thee late at the Count Orsino's.

Clo. Foolery, sir, does walk about the orb like the sun, it shines every where. I would be sorry, sir, but the fool should be as oft with your master as with my mistress: I think I saw your wisdom there. 47

Vio. Nay, an thou pass upon me, I'll no more with thee. Hold, there's expenses for thee.

Clo. Now Jove, in his next commodity of hair, send thee a beard! 51

Vio. By my troth, I'll tell thee, I am almost sick for one; [*Aside*] though I would not have it grow on my chin. Is thy lady within?

Clo. Would not a pair of these have bred, sir?

Vio. Yes, being kept together and put to use. 57

Clo. I would play Lord Pandarus of Phrygia, sir, to bring a Cressida to this Troilus. 59

Vio. I understand you, sir; 'tis well begged.

Clo. The matter, I hope, is not great, sir, begging but a beggar: Cressida was a beggar. My lady is within, sir. I will construe to them whence you come; who you are and what you would are out of my welkin, I might say 'element,' but the word is overworn.   [*Exit*.

Vio. This fellow is wise enough to play the fool;
And to do that well craves a kind of wit:
He must observe their mood on whom he jests,
The quality of persons, and the time, 70
And, like the haggard, check at every feather
That comes before his eye. This is a practice
As full of labour as a wise man's art:
For folly that he wisely shows is fit;
But wise men, folly-fall'n, quite taint their wit.

Enter SIR TOBY *and* SIR ANDREW.

Sir To. Save you, gentleman.

Vio. And you, sir.

Sir And. Dieu vous garde, monsieur.

Vio. Et vous aussi; votre serviteur.

Sir And. I hope, sir, you are; and I am yours. 81

Sir To. Will you encounter the house? my niece is desirous you should enter, if your trade be to her.

Vio. I am bound to your niece, sir; I mean, she is the list of my voyage.

Sir To. Taste your legs, sir; put them to motion.

Vio. My legs do better understand me, sir, than I understand what you mean by bidding me taste my legs. 91

---

13. **cheveril,** kid skin. 25. **bonds disgraced them,** i.e., were needed to make them good. 40. **pilchards,** fish resembling herring. 48. **pass upon me,** make jokes at my expense. 50. **commodity,** supply. 55. **pair of these,** two coins like the one he had just received.

58. **Pandarus,** the go-between in the story of Troilus and Cressida; uncle to Cressida. 62. **begging . . . Cressida,** a reference to Henryson's *Testament of Cresseid* in which the heroine becomes a leper and a beggar. The Clown desires another coin to be the mate of the one he has, as Cressida, the beggar, was mate to Troilus. 65. **welkin,** sky; here used with play upon *element,* one of whose meanings was "sky." 67-75. **This fellow . . . wit.** Note the comment on fools as a class. 71. **haggard,** untrained hawk. 75. **taint their wit,** lose their reputation for wisdom. 78. **Dieu . . . monsieur,** God keep you, sir. 79. **Et . . . serviteur,** and you, too; I am your servant. 82. **encounter,** high-sounding word to express "enter." 86. **list,** border (of cloth); hence, limit, goal. 87. **Taste,** try.

Sir To. I mean, to go, sir, to enter.

Vio. I will answer you with gait and entrance. But we are prevented.

Enter OLIVIA *and* MARIA.

Most excellent accomplished lady, the heavens rain odours on you!

Sir And. That youth's a rare courtier: 'Rain odours;' well.

Vio. My matter hath no voice, lady, but to your own most pregnant and vouchsafed ear.   100

Sir And. 'Odours,' 'pregnant' and 'vouchsafed:' I'll get 'em all three all ready.

Oli. Let the garden door be shut, and leave me to my hearing. [*Exeunt Sir Toby, Sir Andrew, and Maria.*] Give me your hand, sir.

Vio. My duty, madam, and most humble service.

Oli. What is your name?

Vio. Cesario is your servant's name, fair princess.

Oli. My servant, sir! 'Twas never merry world   109

Since lowly feigning was call'd compliment:
You're servant to the Count Orsino, youth.

Vio. And he is yours, and his must needs be yours:

Your servant's servant is your servant, madam.

Oli. For him, I think not on him: for his thoughts,

Would they were blanks, rather than fill'd with me!

Vio. Madam, I come to whet your gentle thoughts

On his behalf.

Oli.   O, by your leave, I pray you,

I bade you never speak again of him:
But, would you undertake another suit,
I had rather hear you to solicit that   120
Than music from the spheres.

Vio.   Dear lady,—

Oli. Give me leave, beseech you. I did send,

After the last enchantment you did here,
A ring in chase of you: so did I abuse
Myself, my servant and, I fear me, you:
Under your hard construction must I sit,

To force that on you, in a shameful cunning,
Which you knew none of yours: what might you think?   128

Have you not set mine honour at the stake
And baited it with all the unmuzzled thoughts

That tyrannous heart can think? To one of your receiving

Enough is shown: a cypress, not a bosom,
Hideth my heart. So, let me hear you speak.

Vio. I pity you.

Oli.   That's a degree to love.

Vio. No, not a grize; for 'tis a vulgar proof,

That very oft we pity enemies.

Oli. Why, then, methinks 'tis time to smile again.

O world, how apt the poor are to be proud!
If one should be a prey, how much the better
To fall before the lion than the wolf!   140

[*Clock strikes.*

The clock upbraids me with the waste of time.

Be not afraid, good youth, I will not have you:

And yet, when wit and youth is come to harvest,

Your wife is like to reap a proper man:
There lies your way, due west.

Vio. Then westward-ho! Grace and good disposition

Attend your ladyship!
You'll nothing, madam, to my lord by me?

Oli. Stay:

I prithee, tell me what thou think'st of me.

Vio. That you do think you are not what you are.   151

Oli. If I think so, I think the same of you.

Vio. Then think you right: I am not what I am.

Oli. I would you were as I would have you be!

Vio. Would it be better, madam, than I am?

I wish it might, for now I am your fool.

---

127. **To force,** for forcing. 129. **stake.** The figure of speech is from bear-baiting. 131. **receiving,** capacity, intelligence. 132. **cypress,** described as a thin gauze-like material, mostly black in color. 135. **grize,** step corresponding to *degree* in the preceding line. **vulgar proof,** common experience. 144. **proper,** handsome. 146. **westward-ho,** the cry of Thames watermen to attract western-bound passengers. 151. **That you . . . are,** that you think you are in love with a man, and you are mistaken (Luce). 152. **If I . . . you,** if I think I lower myself, I think the same of you, i.e., that you are a nobleman in disguise. 156. **now . . . fool.** You are making a fool of me, but implying, also, I am making a fool of you.

---

100. **pregnant,** ready. 110. **lowly feigning,** pretending to be of low degree. 121. **music from the spheres,** reference to the belief that the heavenly bodies were fixed in hollow concentric spheres which revolved one about the other producing a harmony too exquisite to be heard by human ears.

Oli. O, what a deal of scorn looks beauti-
ful
In the contempt and anger of his lip!
A murderous guilt shows not itself more soon
Than love that would seem hid: love's night
    is noon.   160
Cesario, by the roses of the spring,
By maidhood, honour, truth and every
    thing,
I love thee so, that, maugre all thy pride,
Nor wit nor reason can my passion hide.
Do not extort thy reasons from this clause,
For that I woo, thou therefore hast no cause;
But rather reason thus with reason fetter,
Love sought is good, but given unsought is
    better.
    Vio. By innocence I swear, and by my
    youth,
I have one heart, one bosom and one truth,
And that no woman has; nor never none   171
Shall mistress be of it, save I alone.
And so adieu, good madam: never more
Will I my master's tears to you deplore.
    Oli. Yet come again; for thou perhaps
    mayst move
That heart, which now abhors, to like his
    love.   [*Exeunt.*

Scene II. Olivia's *house.*

Enter Sir Toby, Sir Andrew, *and* Fabian

    Sir And. No, faith, I'll not stay a jot
longer.
    Sir To. Thy reason, dear venom, give thy
reason.
    Fab. You must needs yield your reason,
Sir Andrew.
    Sir And. Marry, I saw your niece do more
favours to the count's serving-man than ever
she bestowed upon me; I saw't i' the orchard.
    Sir To. Did she see thee the while, old
boy? tell me that.   10
    Sir And. As plain as I see you now.
    Fab. This was a great argument of love in
her toward you.
    Sir And. 'Slight, will you make an ass o'
me?
    Fab. I will prove it legitimate, sir, upon
the oaths of judgement and reason.
    Sir To. And they have been grand-jury-
men since before Noah was a sailor.   18

    Fab. She did show favour to the youth in
your sight only to exasperate you, to awake
your dormouse valour, to put fire in your
heart, and brimstone in your liver. You
should then have accosted her; and with
some excellent jests, fire-new from the mint,
you should have banged the youth into
dumbness. This was looked for at your
hand, and this was balked: the double gilt
of this opportunity you let time wash off, and
you are now sailed into the north of my
lady's opinion; where you will hang like
an icicle on a Dutchman's beard, unless you
do redeem it by some laudable attempt either
of valour or policy.   31
    Sir And. An 't be any way, it must be with
valour; for policy I hate: I had as lief be a
Brownist as a politician.
    Sir To. Why, then, build me thy fortunes
upon the basis of valour. Challenge me the
count's youth to fight with him; hurt him in
eleven places: my niece shall take note of it;
and assure thyself, there is no love-broker in
the world can more prevail in man's commendation with woman than report of
valour.
    Fab. There is no way but this, Sir Andrew.
    Sir And. Will either of you bear me a
challenge to him?   44
    Sir To. Go, write it in a martial hand; be
curst and brief; it is no matter how witty, so
it be eloquent and full of invention: taunt
him with the license of ink: if thou thou'st
him some thrice, it shall not be amiss; and
as many lies as will lie in thy sheet of paper,
although the sheet were big enough for the
bed of Ware in England, set 'em down: go,
about it. Let there be gall enough in thy
ink, though thou write with a goose-pen, no
matter: about it.   54
    Sir And. Where shall I find you?
    Sir To. We'll call thee at the cubiculo:
go.   [*Exit Sir Andrew.*
    Fab. This is a dear manakin to you, Sir
Toby.

    21. dormouse valour. The dormouse was proverbi-
ally sleepy. **27. double gilt,** twice plated; quibble on
guilt. **28. north,** i.e., out of the warmth and sunshine
of her favor. **31. valour or policy,** frequently associated as the qualities of a nobleman; *policy* means
"discretion." **34. Brownist,** early name of the Inde-
pendents, from the name of the founder, Robert Brown
(1582). **politician,** intriguer. **39. love-broker,** one
who acts as an agent between lovers. **46. curst,** ill-
tempered. **48. thou'st.** *Thou* was used only between
friends or to inferiors. **51. bed of Ware,** a famous bed-
stead capable of holding twelve persons, said to have
been at the Stag Inn in Ware in Hertfordshire. **56.
cubiculo,** Italian or Latin for *lodging.*

    163. maugre, in spite of.
    Scene ii. **8. orchard,** garden. **14. 'Slight,** oath, by
God's light.

Sir To. I have been dear to him, lad, some two thousand strong, or so.

Fab. We shall have a rare letter from him: but you'll not deliver 't?   61

Sir To. Never trust me, then; and by all means stir on the youth to an answer. I think oxen and wainropes cannot hale them together. For Andrew, if he were opened, and you find so much blood in his liver as will clog the foot of a flea, I'll eat the rest of the anatomy.

Fab. And his opposite, the youth, bears in his visage no great presage of cruelty.

Enter MARIA.

Sir To. Look, where the youngest wren of nine comes.   71

Mar. If you desire the spleen, and will laugh yourselves into stitches, follow me. Yond gull Malvolio is turned heathen, a very renegado; for there is no Christian, that means to be saved by believing rightly, can ever believe such impossible passages of grossness. He's in yellow stockings.

Sir To. And cross-gartered?   79

Mar. Most villanously; like a pedant that keeps a school i' the church. I have dogged him, like his murderer. He does obey every point of the letter that I dropped to betray him: he does smile his face into more lines than is in the new map with the augmentation of the Indies: you have not seen such a thing as 'tis. I can hardly forbear hurling things at him. I know my lady will strike him: if she do, he'll smile and take 't for a great favour.

Sir To. Come, bring us, bring us where he is.   [*Exeunt.*

SCENE III. *A street.*

Enter SEBASTIAN *and* ANTONIO.

Seb. I would not by my will have troubled you;

But, since you make your pleasure of your pains,

I will no further chide you.

   Ant. I could not stay behind you: my desire,

More sharp than filed steel, did spur me forth;

And not all love to see you, though so much

As might have drawn one to a longer voyage,

But jealousy what might befall your travel,

Being skilless in these parts; which to a stranger,

Unguided and unfriended, often prove   10

Rough and unhospitable: my willing love,

The rather by these arguments of fear,

Set forth in your pursuit.

   Seb.   My kind Antonio,

I can no other answer make but thanks,

†And thanks; and ever......oft good turns

Are shuffled off with such uncurrent pay:

But, were my worth as is my conscience firm,

You should find better dealing. What's to do?

Shall we go see the reliques of this town?

   Ant. To-morrow, sir: best first go see your lodging.   20

   Seb. I am not weary, and 'tis long to night:

I pray you, let us satisfy our eyes

With the memorials and the things of fame

That do renown this city.

   Ant.   Would you'ld pardon me;

I do not without danger walk these streets:

Once, in a sea-fight, 'gainst the count his galleys

I did some service; of such note indeed,

That were I ta'en here it would scarce be answer'd.

   Seb. Belike you slew great number of his people.

   Ant. The offence is not of such a bloody nature;   30

Albeit the quality of the time and quarrel

Might well have given us bloody argument.

It might have since been answer'd in repaying

What we took from them; which, for traffic's sake,

Most of our city did: only myself stood out;

For which, if I be lapsed in this place,

I shall pay dear.

---

64. **wainropes**, cart-ropes. 71. **nine**. Wrens have many young birds which are all small; presumably the last hatched would be smallest. 72. **spleen**, great laughter, since the spleen was the source of the passion of loud laughter. 75. **renegado**, Spanish, *renegado*, deserter. 77. **passages of grossness**, grossly foolish tricks. 80. **pedant**, schoolmaster. 85. **new map**. This is regarded as a reference to a map published in the 1599 edition of Hakluyt's *Voyages*, which showed more of the East Indies than had ever been mapped before. The reference is used in dating the play.

6. **not all love**, not altogether love. 8. **jealousy**, anxiety. 9. **skilless**, ignorant, unacquainted with. 15. **And thanks**, etc. This corrupt line is usually made to read, *And thanks and ever thanks. Too oft*, etc. 17. **worth**, wealth. 19. **reliques**, antiquities. 26. **count his**, count's. 28. **answer'd**, defended. 36. **lapsed**, probably, caught.

Seb.   Do not then walk too open.

Ant. It doth not fit me. Hold, sir, here's
    my purse.

In the south suburbs, at the Elephant,

Is best to lodge: I will bespeak our diet, 40

Whiles you beguile the time and feed your
    knowledge

With viewing of the town: there shall you
    have me.

Seb. Why I your purse?

Ant. Haply your eye shall light upon
    some toy

You have desire to purchase; and your store,

I think, is not for idle markets, sir.

Seb. I'll be your purse-bearer and leave
    you

For an hour.

Ant. To the Elephant.

Seb.   I do remember. [*Exeunt.*

SCENE IV. *Olivia's garden.*

Enter OLIVIA *and* MARIA.

Oli. I have sent after him: he says he'll
    come;

How shall I feast him? what bestow of him?

For youth is bought more oft than begg'd or
    borrow'd.

I speak too loud.

Where is Malvolio? he is sad and civil,

And suits well for a servant with my for-
    tunes:

Where is Malvolio?   7

Mar. He's coming, madam; but in very
strange manner. He is, sure, possessed,
madam.

Oli. Why, what's the matter? does he
rave?   10

Mar. No, madam, he does nothing but
smile: your ladyship were best to have some
guard about you, if he come; for, sure, the
man is tainted in 's wits.

Oli. Go call him hither. [*Exit Maria.*] I
    am as mad as he,

If sad and merry madness equal be.

Re-enter MARIA, *with* MALVOLIO.

How now, Malvolio!

Mal. Sweet lady, ho, ho.

Oli. Smilest thou?

I sent for thee upon a sad occasion.   20

Mal. Sad, lady! I could be sad: this does
make some obstruction in the blood, this
cross-gartering; but what of that? if it please
the eye of one, it is with me as the very true
sonnet is, 'Please one, and please all.'

Oli. Why, how dost thou, man? what is
the matter with thee?

Mal. Not black in my mind, though
yellow in my legs. It did come to his hands,
and commands shall be executed: I think
we do know the sweet Roman hand.   31

Oli. Wilt thou go to bed, Malvolio?

Mal. To bed! ay, sweet-heart, and I'll
come to thee.

Oli. God comfort thee! Why dost thou
smile so and kiss thy hand so oft?

Mar. How do you, Malvolio?

Mal. At your request! yes; nightingales
answer daws.

Mar. Why appear you with this ridiculous
boldness before my lady?   41

Mal. 'Be not afraid of greatness:' 'twas
well writ.

Oli. What meanest thou by that, Malvolio?

Mal. 'Some are born great,'—

Oli. Ha!

Mal. 'Some achieve greatness,'—

Oli. What sayest thou?

Mal. 'And some have greatness thrust
upon them.'   50

Oli. Heaven restore thee!

Mal. 'Remember who commended thy
yellow stockings,'—

Oli. Thy yellow stockings!

Mal. 'And wished to see thee cross-
gartered.'

Oli. Cross-gartered!

Mal. 'Go to, thou art made, if thou
desirest to be so;'—

Oli. Am I made?   59

Mal. 'If not, let me see thee a servant still.'

Oli. Why, this is very midsummer madness.

Enter Servant.

Ser. Madam, the young gentleman of the
Count Orsino's is returned: I could hardly

---

39. **Elephant,** name of an inn. 40. **diet,** dinner,
food. 46. **idle markets,** unnecessary purchases.
Scene iv. 1. **he . . . come,** i.e., suppose he says, etc.
9. **possessed,** i.e., with an evil spirit.

25. **sonnet,** song, ballad. 'Please . . . all,' the refrain
of a ballad. 28. **black . . . yellow,** possible reference
to a ballad (Collier). 33. **sweet-heart . . . thee,**
possible reference to a ballad (W. J. Craig). 38. **nightingales answer daws,** i.e., I may answer you. 61.
midsummer madness, a proverbial phrase; the midsummer moon was supposed to cause madness.

entreat him back: he attends your ladyship's pleasure.

Oli. I'll come to him. [*Exit Servant.*] Good Maria, let this fellow be looked to. Where's my cousin Toby? Let some of my people have a special care of him: I would not have him miscarry for the half of my dowry.   [*Exeunt Olivia and Maria.*   70

Mal. O, ho! do you come near me now? no worse man than Sir Toby to look to me! This concurs directly with the letter: she sends him on purpose, that I may appear stubborn to him; for she incites me to that in the letter. 'Cast thy humble slough,' says she; 'be opposite with a kinsman, surly with servants; let thy tongue tang with arguments of state; put thyself into the trick of singularity;' and consequently sets down the manner how; as, a sad face, a reverend 80 carriage, a slow tongue, in the habit of some sir of note, and so forth. I have limed her; but it is Jove's doing, and Jove make me thankful! And when she went away now, 'Let this fellow be looked to:' fellow! not Malvolio, nor after my degree, but fellow. Why, every thing adheres together, that no dram of a scruple, no scruple of a scruple, no obstacle, no incredulous or unsafe circumstance—What can be said? Nothing that can be can come between me and the full prospect of my hopes. Well, Jove, not I, is the doer of this, and he is to be thanked. 92

Re-enter Maria, *with* Sir Toby *and* Fabian.

Sir To. Which way is he, in the name of sanctity? If all the devils of hell be drawn in little, and Legion himself possessed him, yet I'll speak to him.

Fab. Here he is, here he is. How is 't with you, sir? how is 't with you, man?

Mal. Go off; I discard you: let me enjoy my private: go off.   100

Mar. Lo, how hollow the fiend speaks within him! did not I tell you? Sir Toby, my lady prays you to have a care of him.

Mal. Ah, ha! does she so?

Sir To. Go to, go to; peace, peace; we must deal gently with him: let me alone.

How do you, Malvolio? how is 't with you? What, man! defy the devil: consider, he's an enemy to mankind.

Mal. Do you know what you say?   110

Mar. La you, an you speak ill of the devil, how he takes it at heart! Pray God, he be not bewitched!

Fab. Carry his water to the wise woman.

Mar. Marry, and it shall be done to-morrow morning, if I live. My lady would not lose him for more than I'll say.

Mal. How now, mistress!

Mar. O Lord!   119

Sir To. Prithee, hold thy peace; this is not the way: do you not see you move him? let me alone with him.

Fab. No way but gentleness; gently, gently: the fiend is rough, and will not be roughly used.   124

Sir To. Why, how now, my bawcock! how dost thou, chuck?

Mal. Sir!

Sir To. Ay, Biddy, come with me. What, man! 'tis not for gravity to play at cherry-pit with Satan: hang him, foul collier!   130

Mar. Get him to say his prayers, good Sir Toby, get him to pray.

Mal. My prayers, minx!

Mar. No, I warrant you, he will not hear of godliness.

Mal. Go, hang yourselves all! you are idle shallow things: I am not of your element: you shall know more hereafter.   [*Exit.*

Sir To. Is 't possible?   139

Fab. If this were played upon a stage now, I could condemn it as an improbable fiction.

Sir To. His very genius hath taken the infection of the device, man.

Mar. Nay, pursue him now, lest the device take air and taint.

Fab. Why, we shall make him mad indeed.

Mar. The house will be the quieter.   147

Sir To. Come, we'll have him in a dark room and bound. My niece is already in the belief that he's mad: we may carry it thus, for our pleasure and his penance, till our very pastime, tired out of breath, prompt us to have mercy on him: at which time we will bring the device to the bar and crown thee for a finder of madmen. But see, but see.

---

69. **miscarry**, come to harm.   71. **come near**, understand.   79. **consequently**, thereafter.   82. **limed**, caught like a bird with bird-lime.   86. **fellow**. Malvolio takes the original meaning, companion; Olivia had used it in its degenerated sense.   88. **incredulous**, incredible. 94-5. **in little**, in miniature.   95. **Legion**, evil spirits mentioned in Scripture; *St. Mark*, v, 9.   100. **private**, privacy.

121. **move**, make angry, exasperate.   125. **bawcock**, French, *beau-coq*, fine fellow.   126. **chuck**, a form of *chick*, term of endearment.   129. **cherry-pit**, a children's game consisting of throwing cherry-stones into a hole.   130. **collier**, Satan.   142. **genius**, soul, spirit.   145. **take air**, become known.   **taint**, spoil.   154. **bar**, court.

Enter SIR ANDREW.

Fab. More matter for a May morning.

Sir And. Here's the challenge, read it: I warrant there's vinegar and pepper in 't.

Fab. Is 't so saucy?   159

Sir And. Ay, is 't, I warrant him: do but read.

Sir To. Give me. [*Reads*] 'Youth, whatsoever thou art, thou art but a scurvy fellow.'

Fab. Good, and valiant.

Sir To. [*Reads*] 'Wonder not, nor admire not in thy mind, why I do call thee so, for I will show thee no reason for 't.'

Fab. A good note; that keeps you from the blow of the law.   169

Sir To. [*Reads*] 'Thou comest to the lady Olivia, and in my sight she uses thee kindly: but thou liest in thy throat; that is not the matter I challenge thee for.'

Fab. Very brief, and to exceeding good sense—less.

Sir To. [*Reads*] 'I will waylay thee going home; where if it be thy chance to kill me,'—

Fab. Good.

Sir To. [*Reads*] 'Thou killest me like a rogue and a villain.'   180

Fab. Still you keep o' the windy side of the law: good.

Sir To. [*Reads*] 'Fare thee well; and God have mercy upon one of our souls! He may have mercy upon mine; but my hope is better, and so look to thyself. Thy friend, as thou usest him, and thy sworn enemy,
ANDREW AGUECHEEK.'
If this letter move him not, his legs cannot: I'll give 't him.   189

Mar. You may have very fit occasion for 't: he is now in some commerce with my lady, and will by and by depart.

Sir To. Go, Sir Andrew; scout me for him at the corner of the orchard like a bum-baily: so soon as ever thou seest him, draw; and, as thou drawest, swear horrible; for it comes to pass off that a terrible oath, with a swaggering accent sharply twanged off, gives manhood more approbation than ever proof itself would have earned him. Away!   200

Sir And. Nay, let me alone for swearing.
[*Exit.*

Sir To. Now will not I deliver his letter: for the behaviour of the young gentleman gives him out to be of good capacity and breeding; his employment between his lord and my niece confirms no less: therefore this letter, being so excellently ignorant, will breed no terror in the youth: he will find it comes from a clodpole. But, sir, I will deliver his challenge by word of mouth; set upon Aguecheek a notable report of valour; and drive the gentleman, as I know his youth will aptly receive it, into a most hideous opinion of his rage, skill, fury and impetuosity. This will so fright them both that they will kill one another by the look, like cockatrices.   215

Re-enter OLIVIA, *with* VIOLA.

Fab. Here he comes with your niece: give them way till he take leave, and presently after him.

Sir To. I will meditate the while upon some horrid message for a challenge.   220
[*Exeunt Sir Toby, Fabian, and Maria.*

Oli. I have said too much unto a heart of stone
And laid mine honour too unchary out:
There's something in me that reproves my fault;
But such a headstrong potent fault it is,
That it but mocks reproof.

Vio. With the same 'haviour that your passion bears
Goes on my master's grief.

Oli. Here, wear this jewel for me, 'tis my picture;
Refuse it not; it hath no tongue to vex you;
And I beseech you come again to-morrow. 230
What shall you ask of me that I'll deny,
That honour saved may upon asking give?

Vio. Nothing but this; your true love for my master.

Oli. How with mine honour may I give him that
Which I have given to you?

Vio.   I will acquit you.

Oli. Well, come again to-morrow: fare thee well:
A fiend like thee might bear my soul to hell.
[*Exit.*

156. **May**, reference to the many Mayings and holidays in May. 168. **note**, observation, remark. 181. **windy**, to windward; so that the law may get no scent of you. 191. **commerce**, conversation, intercourse. 194. **bumbaily**, minor sheriff's officer. 199. **approbation**, reputation (for courage). **proof**, trial.

209. **clodpole**, blockhead. 215. **cockatrices**, basilisks, fabulous serpents reputed to be able to kill by a mere look. 228. **jewel**, used of any piece of jewelry.

Re-enter SIR TOBY *and* FABIAN.

Sir To. Gentleman, God save thee.

Vio. And you, sir.   239

Sir To. That defence thou hast, betake thee to 't: of what nature the wrongs are thou hast done him, I know not; but thy intercepter, full of despite, bloody as the hunter, attends thee at the orchard-end: dismount thy tuck, be yare in thy preparation, for thy assailant is quick, skilful and deadly.

Vio. You mistake, sir; I am sure no man hath any quarrel to me: my remembrance is very free and clear from any image of offence done to any man.   250

Sir To. You'll find it otherwise, I assure you: therefore, if you hold your life at any price, betake you to your guard; for your opposite hath in him what youth, strength, skill and wrath can furnish man withal.

Vio. I pray you, sir, what is he?   256

Sir To. He is knight, dubbed with unhatched rapier and on carpet consideration; but he is a devil in private brawl: souls and bodies hath he divorced three; and his incensement at this moment is so implacable, that satisfaction can be none but by pangs of death and sepulchre. Hob, nob, is his word; give 't or take 't.   263

Vio. I will return again into the house and desire some conduct of the lady. I am no fighter. I have heard of some kind of men that put quarrels purposely on others, to taste their valour: belike this is a man of that quirk.   268

Sir To. Sir, no, his indignation derives itself out of a very competent injury: therefore, get you on and give him his desire. Back you shall not to the house, unless you undertake that with me which with as much safety you might answer him: therefore, on, or strip your sword stark naked; for meddle you must, that's certain, or forswear to wear iron about you.   276

Vio. This is as uncivil as strange. I beseech you, do me this courteous office, as to know of the knight what my offence to him is: it is something of my negligence, nothing of my purpose.

Sir To. I will do so. Signior Fabian, stay you by this gentleman till my return.

[*Exit.*

Vio. Pray you, sir, do you know of this matter?

Fab. I know the knight is incensed against you, even to a mortal arbitrament; but nothing of the circumstance more.

Vio. I beseech you, what manner of man is he?   289

Fab. Nothing of that wonderful promise, to read him by his form, as you are like to find him in the proof of his valour. He is, indeed, sir, the most skilful, bloody and fatal opposite that you could possibly have found in any part of Illyria. Will you walk towards him? I will make your peace 296 with him if I can.

Vio. I shall be much bound to you for 't: I am one that had rather go with sir priest than sir knight: I care not who knows so much of my mettle.   [*Exeunt.* 300

Re-enter SIR TOBY, *with* SIR ANDREW.

Sir To. Why, man, he's a very devil; I have not seen such a firago. I had a pass with him, rapier, scabbard and all, and he gives me the stuck in with such a mortal motion, that it is inevitable; and on the answer, he pays you as surely as your feet hit the ground they step on. They say he has been fencer to the Sophy.   307

Sir And. Pox on 't, I'll not meddle with him.

Sir To. Ay, but he will not now be pacified: Fabian can scarce hold him yonder.

Sir And. Plague on 't, an I thought he had been valiant and so cunning in fence, I'ld have seen him damned ere I'ld have challenged him. Let him let the matter slip, and I'll give him my horse, grey Capilet. 315

Sir To. I'll make the motion: stand here, make a good show on 't: this shall end without the perdition of souls. [*Aside*] Marry, I'll ride your horse as well as I ride you. 319

Re-enter FABIAN *and* VIOLA.

[*To Fab.*] I have his horse to take up the

---

242. **intercepter**, i.e., he who lies in wait. 243. **despite**, spite, malice. 244-5. **dismount thy tuck**, draw thy sword. 245. **yare**, ready, nimble. 257. **unhatched**, for *unhacked*. 258. **carpet consideration**, i.e., he is a carpet knight, not a warrior. 263. **Hob, nob**, originally, have or have not; here, hit or miss. 265. **conduct**, escort. 268. **quirk**, peculiar humor. 273. **that**, i.e., to give satisfaction. 275. **meddle**, engage in conflict.

286. **mortal arbitrement**, trial to the death. 294. **opposite**, antagonist. 299. **sir**, commonly used as the title of priests as well as knights. 302. **firago**, thought to be an intentional corruption of *virago*. 304. **stuck in**, stoccado, a thrust in fencing. **mortal**, deadly. 315. **Capilet**, evidently derived from *capel*, a nag. 316. **motion**, proposal. 320. **take up**, make up.

quarrel: I have persuaded him the youth's a
devil.   321
Fab. He is as horribly conceited of him;
and pants and looks pale, as if a bear were at
his heels.
Sir To. [*To Vio.*] There's no remedy, sir;
he will fight with you for's oath sake: marry,
he hath better bethought him of his quarrel,
and he finds that now scarce to be worth
talking of: therefore draw, for the supportance of his vow; he protests he will not hurt
you.   330
Vio. [*Aside*] Pray God defend me! A
little thing would make me tell them how
much I lack of a man.
Fab. Give ground, if you see him furious.
Sir To. Come, Sir Andrew, there's no remedy; the gentleman will, for his honour's
sake, have one bout with you; he cannot by
the duello avoid it: but he has promised me,
as he is a gentleman and a soldier, he will
not hurt you. Come on; to't.   340
Sir And. Pray God, he keep his oath!
Vio. I do assure you, 'tis against my will.
                                   [*They draw.*

Enter ANTONIO.

Ant. Put up your sword. If this young
    gentleman
Have done offence, I take the fault on me:
If you offend him, I for him defy you.
Sir To. You, sir! why, what are you?
Ant. One, sir, that for his love dares yet
    do more   347
Than you have heard him brag to you he will.
Sir To. Nay, if you be an undertaker, I
am for you.   [*They draw.*

Enter Officers.

Fab. O good Sir Toby, hold! here come
the officers.
Sir To. I'll be with you anon.
Vio. Pray, sir, put your sword up, if you
please.
Sir And. Marry, will I, sir; and, for that I
promised you, I'll be as good as my word: he
will bear you easily and reins well.
First Off. This is the man; do thy office.
Sec. Off. Antonio, I arrest thee at the suit
of Count Orsino.   361

Ant. You do mistake me, sir.
First Off. No, sir, no jot; I know your
    favour well,
Though now you have no sea-cap on your
    head.
Take him away: he knows I know him well.
Ant. I must obey. [*To Vio.*] This comes
    with seeking you:
But there's no remedy; I shall answer it.
What will you do, now my necessity
Makes me to ask you for my purse? It
    grieves me
Much more for what I cannot do for you   370
Than what befalls myself. You stand
    amazed;
But be of comfort.
Sec. Off. Come, sir, away.
Ant. I must entreat of you some of that
    money.
Vio. What money, sir?
For the fair kindness you have show'd me
    here,
And, part, being prompted by your present
    trouble,
Out of my lean and low ability
I'll lend you something: my having is not
    much;
I'll make division of my present with you: 380
Hold, there's half my coffer.
Ant.   Will you deny me now?
Is't possible that my deserts to you
Can lack persuasion? Do not tempt my
    misery,
Lest that it make me so unsound a man
As to upbraid you with those kindnesses
That I have done for you.
Vio.   I know of none;
Nor know I you by voice or any feature:
I hate ingratitude more in a man
Than lying, vainness, babbling, drunken-
    ness,   389
Or any taint of vice whose strong corruption
Inhabits our frail blood.
Ant.   O heavens themselves!
Sec. Off. Come, sir, I pray you, go.
Ant. Let me speak a little. This youth
    that you see here
I snatch'd one half out of the jaws of death,
Relieved him with such sanctity of love,
And to his image, which methought did
    promise   396

---

322. **is as horribly conceited**, has as horrible a conception. 338. **duello**, duelling code. 349. **undertaker**,
one who takes upon himself a task or business; here,
suggests meddling.

363. **favour**, face. 377. **part**, partly. 380. **present**,
present store. 381. **coffer**, purse. 389. **vainness**,
boastfulness. 396. **image**, what he appeared to be.

Most venerable worth, did I devotion.

First Off. What's that to us? The time goes by: away!

Ant. But O how vile an idol proves this god!

Thou hast, Sebastian, done good feature shame.

In nature there's no blemish but the mind;401

None can be call'd deform'd but the unkind:

Virtue is beauty, but the beauteous evil

Are empty trunks o'erflourish'd by the devil.

First Off. The man grows mad: away with him! Come, come, sir.

Ant. Lead me on.   [*Exit with Officers.*

Vio. Methinks his words do from such passion fly,

That he believes himself: so do not I.

Prove true, imagination, O, prove true,   409

That I, dear brother, be now ta'en for you!

Sir To. Come hither, knight; come hither, Fabian: we'll whisper o'er a couplet or two of most sage saws.

Vio. He named Sebastian: I my brother know

Yet living in my glass; even such and so

In favour was my brother, and he went

Still in this fashion, colour, ornament,

For him I imitate: O, if it prove,

Tempests are kind and salt waves fresh in love.   [*Exit.*   419

Sir To. A very dishonest paltry boy, and more a coward than a hare: his dishonesty appears in leaving his friend here in necessity and denying him; and for his cowardship, ask Fabian.

Fab. A coward, a most devout coward, religious in it.   426

Sir And. 'Slid, I'll after him again and beat him.

Sir To. Do; cuff him soundly, but never draw thy sword.

Sir And. An I do not,—   [*Exit.*

Fab. Come, let's see the event.   431

Sir To. I dare lay any money 'twill be nothing yet.   [*Exeunt.*

ACT IV.

Scene I. *Before* Olivia's *house.*

Enter Sebastian *and* Clown.

Clo. Will you make me believe that I am not sent for you?

Seb. Go to, go to, thou art a foolish fellow: Let me be clear of thee.

Clo. Well held out, i' faith! No, I do not know you; nor I am not sent to you by my lady, to bid you come speak with her; nor your name is not Master Cesario; nor this is not my nose neither. Nothing that is so is so.

Seb. I prithee, vent thy folly somewhere else: Thou know'st not me.   11

Clo. Vent my folly! he has heard that word of some great man and now applies it to a fool. Vent my folly! I am afraid this great lubber, the world, will prove a cockney. I prithee now, ungird thy strangeness and tell me what I shall vent to my lady: shall I vent to her that thou art coming?

Seb. I prithee, foolish Greek, depart from me: There's money for thee: if you tarry longer, I shall give worse payment.   21

Clo. By my troth, thou hast an open hand. These wise men that give fools money get themselves a good report—after fourteen years' purchase.

Enter Sir Andrew, Sir Toby, *and* Fabian.

Sir And. Now, sir, have I met you again? there's for you.

Seb. Why, there's for thee, and there, and there.

Are all the people mad?   29

Sir To. Hold, sir, or I'll throw your dagger o'er the house.

Clo. This will I tell my lady straight: I would not be in some of your coats for two pence.   [*Exit.*

Sir To. Come on, sir; hold.

Sir And. Nay, let him alone: I'll go another way to work with him; I'll have an action of battery against him, if there be any law in Illyria: though I struck him first, yet it's no matter for that.

---

397. **venerable,** worthy of honor (no reference to age). 400-404. **Thou hast . . . devil.** It was a widespread belief in the Renaissance that the outward and inward parts of man correspond in quality. 400. **feature,** external appearance. 402. **unkind,** not having natural affection. 404. **o'erflourish'd,** covered with ornamental carvings. 408. **so do not I,** may mean "I do not believe him" or "I do not believe myself" (in the hope that has arisen in me). 410. **That I . . . you.** This is the first move in the direction of the solution of the plot. 418. **prove,** prove true. 421. **dishonesty,** dishonorable character. 427. **'Slid,** oath, "by God's (eye-) lid."

15. **cockney,** effeminate or foppish fellow. 19. **Greek,** jester. 24. **fourteen years' purchase,** reference to the valuation of land at the price of twelve years' rental. The fool adds two years.

Seb. Let go thy hand.   40
Sir To. Come, sir, I will not let you go.
Come, my young soldier, put up your iron:
you are well fleshed; come on.
Seb. I will be free from thee. What
wouldst thou now?
If thou darest tempt me further, draw thy
sword.   45
Sir To. What, what? Nay, then I must
have an ounce or two of this malapert blood
from you.

Enter OLIVIA.

Oli. Hold, Toby; on thy life I charge thee,
hold!
Sir To. Madam!   50
Oli. Will it be ever thus? Ungracious
wretch,
Fit for the mountains and the barbarous
caves,
Where manners ne'er were preach'd! out of
my sight!
Be not offended, dear Cesario.
Rudesby, be gone!
[*Exeunt Sir Toby, Sir Andrew, and Fabian.*
I prithee, gentle friend,
Let thy fair wisdom, not thy passion, sway
In this uncivil and unjust extent
Against thy peace. Go with me to my
house,
And hear thou there how many fruitless
pranks
This ruffian hath botch'd up, that thou
thereby   60
Mayst smile at this: thou shalt not choose
but go:
Do not deny. Beshrew his soul for me,
He started one poor heart of mine in
thee.
Seb. What relish is in this? how runs the
stream?
Or I am mad, or else this is a dream:
Let fancy still my sense in Lethe steep;
If it be thus to dream, still let me sleep!
Oli. Nay, come, I prithee; would thou'ldst
be ruled by me!
Seb. Madam, I will.
Oli. O, say so, and so be!   [*Exeunt.*

SCENE II. OLIVIA'S *house.*

Enter MARIA *and* CLOWN.

Mar. Nay, I prithee, put on this gown and
this beard; make him believe thou art Sir
Topas the curate: do it quickly; I'll call
Sir Toby the whilst.   [*Exit.*
Clo. Well, I'll put it on, and I will dissemble myself in 't; and I would I were the
first that ever dissembled in such a gown. I
am not tall enough to become the function
well, nor lean enough to be thought a good
student; but to be said an honest man and
a good housekeeper goes as fairly as to say
a careful man and a great scholar. The competitors enter.   12

Enter SIR TOBY *and* MARIA.

Sir To. Jove bless thee, master Parson.
Clo. Bonos dies, Sir Toby: for, as the old
hermit of Prague, that never saw pen and
ink, very wittily said to a niece of King
Gorboduc, 'That that is is;' so I, being
master Parson, am master Parson; for, what
is 'that' but 'that,' and 'is' but 'is'?
Sir To. To him, Sir Topas.   20
Clo. What, ho, I say! peace in this prison!
Sir To. The knave counterfeits well; a
good knave.
Mal. [*Within*] Who calls there?
Clo. Sir Topas the curate, who comes to
visit Malvolio the lunatic.
Mal. Sir Topas, Sir Topas, good Sir
Topas, go to my lady.
Clo. Out, hyperbolical fiend! how vexest
thou this man! talkest thou nothing but   30
of ladies?
Sir To. Well said, master Parson.
Mal. Sir Topas, never was man thus
wronged: good Sir Topas, do not think I am
mad: they have laid me here in hideous
darkness.
Clo. Fie, thou dishonest Satan! I call
thee by the most modest terms; for I am
one of those gentle ones that will use the
devil himself with courtesy: sayest thou
that house is dark?

---

43. **fleshed**, initiated in bloodshed; reference to the
practice of giving to a hawk or hound a part of the kill to
incite it to eagerness in the chase. 47. **malapert**, saucy,
impudent. 55. **Rudesby**, ruffian. 57. **extent**, attack.
60. **botch'd up**, clumsily contrived. 63. **heart**, with
play on *hart*. 66. **Lethe**, forgetfulness.

4. **the whilst**, in the meantime. 5. **dissemble**,
disguise. 9. **said**, called. 10. **housekeeper**, good
liver, hospitable person. 15. **hermit of Prague**,
usually thought to refer to Jerome of Prague, but the
allusion is obscure. 16. **niece of King Gorboduc.**
Gorboduc was an ancient British king; his niece is apparently an invention of the Clown's. 29. **hyperbolical**,
possibly for *diabolical*.

Mal. As hell, Sir Topas.   39

Clo. Why, it hath bay windows transparent as barricadoes, and the clearstores toward the south north are as lustrous as ebony; and yet complainest thou of obstruction?

Mal. I am not mad, Sir Topas: I say to you, this house is dark.

Clo. Madman, thou errest: I say, there is no darkness but ignorance; in which thou art more puzzled than the Egyptians in   48
their fog.

Mal. I say, this house is as dark as ignorance, though ignorance were as dark as hell; and I say, there was never man thus abused. I am no more mad than you are: make the trial of it in any constant question.

Clo. What is the opinion of Pythagoras concerning wild fowl?   55

Mal. That the soul of our grandam might haply inhabit a bird.

Clo. What thinkest thou of his opinion?

Mal. I think nobly of the soul, and no way approve his opinion.   60

Clo. Fare thee well. Remain thou still in darkness: thou shalt hold the opinion of Pythagoras ere I will allow of thy wits, and fear to kill a woodcock, lest thou dispossess the soul of thy grandam. Fare thee well.

Mal. Sir Topas, Sir Topas!

Sir To. My most exquisite Sir Topas!

Clo. Nay, I am for all waters.

Mar. Thou mightst have done this without thy beard and gown: he sees thee   70
not.

Sir To. To him in thine own voice, and bring me word how thou findest him: I would we were well rid of this knavery. If he may be conveniently delivered, I would he were, for I am now so far in offence with my niece that I cannot pursue with any safety this sport to the upshot. Come by and by to my chamber.   [*Exeunt Sir Toby and Maria.*

Clo. [*Singing*] 'Hey, Robin, jolly Robin,
    Tell me how thy lady does.'

Mal. Fool!   80

Clo. 'My lady is unkind, perdy.'

Mal. Fool!

Clo. 'Alas, why is she so?'

Mal. Fool, I say!

Clo. 'She loves another'—Who calls, ha?

Mal. Good fool, as ever thou wilt deserve well at my hand, help me to a candle, and pen, ink and paper: as I am a gentleman, I will live to be thankful to thee for 't.

Clo. Master Malvolio?   90

Mal. Ay, good fool.

Clo. Alas, sir, how fell you besides your five wits?

Mal. Fool, there was never man so notoriously abused: I am as well in my wits, fool, as thou art.

Clo. But as well? then you are mad indeed, if you be no better in your wits than a fool.

Mal. They have here propertied me; keep me in darkness, send ministers to me, asses, and do all they can to face me   101
out of my wits.

Clo. Advise you what you say; the minister is here. Malvolio, Malvolio, thy wits the heavens restore! endeavour thyself to sleep, and leave thy vain bibble babble.

Mal. Sir Topas!

Clo. Maintain no words with him, good fellow. Who, I, sir? not I, sir. God be wi' you, good Sir Topas. Marry, amen. I will, sir, I will.

Mal. Fool, fool, fool, I say!   110

Clo. Alas, sir, be patient. What say you, sir? I am shent for speaking to you.

Mal. Good fool, help me to some light and some paper: I tell thee, I am as well in my wits as any man in Illyria.

Clo. Well-a-day that you were, sir!

Mal. By this hand, I am. Good fool, some ink, paper and light; and convey what I will set down to my lady: it shall advantage thee more than ever the bearing of letter did.

Clo. I will help you to 't. But tell me true, are you not mad indeed? or do you but counterfeit?   123

Mal. Believe me, I am not; I tell thee true.

Clo. Nay, I'll ne'er believe a madman till

---

41. **clearstores,** upper walls of a building containing windows by which it is lighted. 48. **Egyptians . . . fog.** See *Exodus* x, 21, 22. 53. **constant question,** consistent discussion. 54-55. **Pythagoras . . . wild fowl,** an opening for the discussion of transmigration of souls, a doctrine held by Pythagoras. 64. **woodcock,** type of stupidity because easily caught. 68. **for all waters,** i.e., able to sail in all waters. 73. **knavery,** practical joke. 78-85. '**Hey, Robin . . . another**', fragments of an old song.

92. **besides,** out of. 92-3. **five wits,** intellectual faculties given as common wit, imagination, fantasy, judgment, and memory. 94-5. **notoriously abused,** shamefully mistreated. 99. **propertied,** explained as "treated me as property and thrown me into the lumber-room"; may mean "have chosen to endow me with madness." 102. **Advise you,** take care. The Clown here again impersonates Sir Topas. 112. **shent,** scolded, rebuked. 116. **Well-a-day,** alas, would that.

I see his brains. I will fetch you light and paper and ink.

Mal. Fool, I'll requite it in the highest degree: I prithee, be gone.

Clo. [*Singing*] I am gone, sir,   130
            And anon, sir,
        I'll be with you again,
            In a trice,
            Like to the old Vice,
            Your need to sustain;

        Who, with dagger of lath,
        In his rage and his wrath,
            Cries, ah, ha! to the devil:
        Like a mad lad,
        Pare thy nails, dad;   149
            †Adieu, good man devil.   [*Exit.*

SCENE III. OLIVIA'S *garden.*

Enter SEBASTIAN.

Seb. This is the air; that is the glorious sun;
This pearl she gave me, I do feel 't and see 't;
And though 'tis wonder that enwraps me thus,
Yet 'tis not madness. Where's Antonio, then?
I could not find him at the Elephant:
Yet there he was; and there I found this credit,
That he did range the town to seek me out.
His counsel now might do me golden service;
For though my soul disputes well with my sense,
That this may be some error, but no madness,   10
Yet doth this accident and flood of fortune
So far exceed all instance, all discourse,
That I am ready to distrust mine eyes
And wrangle with my reason that persuades me
To any other trust but that I am mad
Or else the lady's mad; yet, if 'twere so,
She could not sway her house, command her followers,
Take and give back affairs and their dispatch
With such a smooth, discreet and stable bearing

134. **Vice**, the buffoon of moralities and interludes; derived from *Vitia*, the minor devils or sins associated with the chief devil. 136. **dagger of lath**, symbol of the Vice, who was apparently notorious for using it for paring his nails; cf. *Henry V*, IV, iv, 75-77.
Scene iii. 12. **instance**, precedent, example. **discourse**, reason. 15. **trust**, belief. 18. **Take and give back**, undertake and discharge.

As I perceive she does: there's something in't   20
That is deceiveable. But here the lady comes.

Enter OLIVIA *and* Priest.

Oli. Blame not this haste of mine. If you mean well,
Now go with me and with this holy man
Into the chantry by: there, before him,
And underneath that consecrated roof,
Plight me the full assurance of your faith;
That my most jealous and too doubtful soul
May live at peace. He shall conceal it
Whiles you are willing it shall come to note,
What time we will our celebration keep   30
According to my birth. What do you say?
Seb. I'll follow this good man, and go with you;
And, having sworn truth, ever will be true.
Oli. Then lead the way, good father; and heavens so shine,
That they may fairly note this act of mine!
                    [*Exeunt.*

ACT V.

SCENE I. *Before* OLIVIA'S *house.*

Enter CLOWN *and* FABIAN.

Fab. Now, as thou lovest me, let me see his letter.

Clo. Good Master Fabian, grant me another request.

Fab. Any thing.

Clo. Do not desire to see this letter.

Fab. This is, to give a dog, and in recompense desire my dog again.

Enter DUKE, VIOLA, CURIO, *and* Lords.

Duke. Belong you to the Lady Olivia, friends?   9

Clo. Ay, sir; we are some of her trappings.

Duke. I know thee well: how dost thou, my good fellow?

Clo. Truly, sir, the better for my foes and the worse for my friends.

Duke. Just the contrary; the better for thy friends.

Clo. No, sir, the worse.

Duke. How can that be?   19

21. **deceiveable**, deceptive. 24. **chantry**, chapel privately endowed. 27. **jealous**, anxious. 29. **Whiles**, until. **come to note**, become known.
Act V. Scene i. 1. **his**, i.e., Malvolio's.

Clo. Marry, sir, they praise me and make an ass of me; now my foes tell me plainly I am an ass: so that by my foes, sir, I profit in the knowledge of myself, and by my friends I am abused: so that, conclusions to be as kisses, if your four negatives make your two affirmatives, why then, the worse for my friends and the better for my foes. 26

Duke. Why, this is excellent.

Clo. By my troth, sir, no; though it please you to be one of my friends.

Duke. Thou shalt not be the worse for me: there's gold. 31

Clo. But that it would be double-dealing, sir, I would you could make it another.

Duke. O, you give me ill counsel.

Clo. Put your grace in your pocket, sir, for this once, and let your flesh and blood obey it.

Duke. Well, I will be so much a sinner, to be a double-dealer: there's another. 38

Clo. Primo, secundo, tertio, is a good play; and the old saying is, the third pays for all: the triplex, sir, is a good tripping measure; or the bells of Saint Bennet, sir, may put you in mind; one, two, three.

Duke. You can fool no more money out of me at this throw: if you will let your lady know I am here to speak with her, and bring her along with you, it may awake my bounty further. 47

Clo. Marry, sir, lullaby to your bounty till I come again. I go, sir; but I would not have you to think that my desire of having is the sin of covetousness: but, as you say, sir, let your bounty take a nap, I will awake it anon. [*Exit.*

Vio. Here comes the man, sir, that did rescue me.

Enter ANTONIO *and* Officers.

Duke. That face of his I do remember well;

Yet, when I saw it last, it was besmear'd
As black as Vulcan in the smoke of war:

A bawbling vessel was he captain of,
For shallow draught and bulk unprizable;
With which such scathful grapple did he make
With the most noble bottom of our fleet, 60
That very envy and the tongue of loss
Cried fame and honour on him. What's the matter?

First Off. Orsino, this is that Antonio
That took the Phœnix and her fraught from Candy;
And this is he that did the Tiger board,
When your young nephew Titus lost his leg:
Here in the streets, desperate of shame and state,
In private brabble did we apprehend him.

Vio. He did me kindness, sir, drew on my side;
But in conclusion put strange speech upon me:
I know not what 'twas but distraction. 71

Duke. Notable pirate! thou salt-water thief!
What foolish boldness brought thee to their mercies,
Whom thou, in terms so bloody and so dear,
Hast made thine enemies?

Ant.   Orsino, noble sir,
Be pleased that I shake off these names you give me:
Antonio never yet was thief or pirate,
Though I confess, on base and ground enough,
Orsino's enemy. A witchcraft drew me hither:
That most ingrateful boy there by your side,
From the rude sea's enraged and foamy mouth 81
Did I redeem; a wreck past hope he was:
His life I gave him and did thereto add
My love, without retention or restraint,
All his in dedication; for his sake
Did I expose myself, pure for his love,
Into the danger of this adverse town;
Drew to defend him when he was beset:
Where being apprehended, his false cunning,
Not meaning to partake with me in danger, 90
Taught him to face me out of his acquaintance,

23-24. **conclusions . . . kisses.** The Clown has only two negatives which would make but one affirmative; he needs two affirmatives and can get them if conclusions arise like kisses, there being two pairs of lips in each kiss. 29. **friends**, probably, flatterers. The Duke gives a coin to show that he is sincere. The Clown would ask for two except for seeming to be a *double-dealer*, i.e., insincere in his turn. 35. **grace**, apparently a play on *grace* meaning "favor of God," and the title, "Your *Grace*." 39-40. **Primo, secundo, tertio . . . all**, probably dicing terms. 41. **triplex**, triple time in music. 42. **Saint Bennet**, church of St. Benedict; reference to the sound of the church bell, which may have been embodied in a rhyme. 45. **throw**, i.e., of dice. 48. **lullaby**, suggested by *awake*, above.

57. **bawbling**, insignificant. 58. **unprizable**, of value too slight to be estimated. 59. **scathful**, destructive. 64. **fraught**, cargo. **Candy**, Candia, Crete. 67. **desperate . . . state**, reckless of disgrace and position. 68. **brabble**, brawl. 71. **distraction**, madness. 86. **pure**, entirely. 87. **Into**, unto. **adverse**, hostile. 91. **face me out of**, exclude me impudently from.

And grew a twenty years removed thing
While one would wink; denied me mine own
    purse,
Which I had recommended to his use
Not half an hour before.
    Viol.   How can this be?
    Duke. When came he to this town?
    Ant. To-day, my lord; and for three
    months before,
No interim, not a minute's vacancy,
Both day and night did we keep company.

       Enter OLIVIA *and* Attendants.

    Duke. Here comes the countess: now
    heaven walks on earth.   100
But for thee, fellow; fellow, thy words are
    madness:
Three months this youth hath tended upon
    me;
But more of that anon. Take him aside.
    Oli. What would my lord, but that he
    may not have,
Wherein Olivia may seem serviceable?
Cesario, you do not keep promise with me.
    Vio. Madam!
    Duke. Gracious Olivia,—
    Oli. What do you say, Cesario? Good my
    lord,—
    Vio. My lord would speak; my duty
    hushes me.   110
    Oli. If it be aught to the old tune, my lord,
It is as fat and fulsome to mine ear
As howling after music.
    Duke.   Still so cruel?
    Oli. Still so constant, lord.
    Duke. What, to perverseness? you uncivil
    lady,
To whose ingrate and unauspicious altars
My soul the faithfull'st offerings hath
    breathed out
That e'er devotion tender'd! What shall I do?
    Oli. Even what it please my lord, that
    shall become him.
    Duke. Why should I not, had I the heart
    to do it,   120
Like to the Egyptian thief at point of death,

Kill what I love?—a savage jealousy
That sometime savours nobly. But hear me
    this:
Since you to non-regardance cast my faith,
And that I partly know the instrument
That screws me from my true place in your
    favour,
Live you the marble-breasted tyrant still;
But this your minion, whom I know you love,
And whom, by heaven I swear, I tender
    dearly,
Him will I tear out of that cruel eye,   130
Where he sits crowned in his master's spite.
Come, boy, with me; my thoughts are ripe in
    mischief:
I'll sacrifice the lamb that I do love,
To spite a raven's heart within a dove.
    Vio. And I, most jocund, apt and will-
    ingly,
To do you rest, a thousand deaths would die.
    Oli. Where goes Cesario?
    Vio.   After him I love
More than I love these eyes, more than my
    life,
More, by all mores, than e'er I shall love
    wife.
If I do feign, you witnesses above   140
Punish my life for tainting of my love!
    Oli. Ay me, detested! how am I beguiled!
    Vio. Who does beguile you? who does do
    you wrong?
    Oli. Hast thou forgot thyself? is it so long?
Call forth the holy father.
    Duke.   Come, away!
    Oli. Whither, my lord? Cesario, husband,
    stay.
    Duke. Husband!
    Oli.   Ay, husband: can he that deny?
    Duke. Her husband, sirrah!
    Vio.   No, my lord, not I.
    Oli. Alas, it is the baseness of thy fear
That makes thee strangle thy propriety: 150
Fear not, Cesario; take thy fortunes up;
Be that thou know'st thou art, and then thou
    art
As great as that thou fear'st.

           Enter Priest.

            O, welcome, father!
Father, I charge thee, by thy reverence,

---

94. **recommended**, consigned, committed.   102.
Three months. This statement is inconsistent with
the hint found in I, iv, 3; it seems reasonable, however,
in this connection.   112. **fat and fulsome**, nauseating.
121. **Egyptian thief**, allusion to the story of Theagenes
and Chariclea in the *Ethiopica*, a Greek romance by
Heliodorus. The robber chief, Thyamis of Memphis,
having captured Chariclea and fallen in love with her,
was attacked by a larger band of robbers; threatened with
death, he attempted to slay her first.

123. **savours nobly**, is not without nobility.   128.
minion, darling.   136. **do you rest**, give you ease.
142. **detested**, detestable (one).   150. **strangle thy
propriety**, disavow thyself.

Here to unfold, though lately we intended
To keep in darkness what occasion now
Reveals before 'tis ripe, what thou dost know
Hath newly pass'd between this youth and
  me.

Priest. A contract of eternal bond of love,
Confirm'd by mutual joinder of your hands,
Attested by the holy close of lips,   161
Strengthen'd by interchangement of your
  rings;
And all the ceremony of this compact
Seal'd in my function, by my testimony:
Since when, my watch hath told me, toward
  my grave
I have travell'd but two hours.

Duke. O thou dissembling cub! what
  wilt thou be
When time hath sow'd a grizzle on thy case?
Or will not else thy craft so quickly grow,
That thine own trip shall be thine over-
  throw?
Farewell, and take her; but direct thy feet 171
Where thou and I henceforth may never
  meet.

Vio. My Lord, I do protest—
Oli.   O, do not swear!
Hold little faith, though thou hast too much
  fear.

Enter Sir Andrew.

Sir And. For the love of God, a surgeon!
Send one presently to Sir Toby.

Oli. What's the matter?

Sir And. He has broke my head across
and has given Sir Toby a bloody coxcomb
too: for the love of God, your help! I had
rather than forty pound I were at home.   181

Oli. Who has done this, Sir Andrew?

Sir. And. The count's gentleman, one
Cesario: we took him for a coward, but he's
the very devil incardinate.

Duke. My gentleman, Cesario?

Sir And. 'Od's lifelings, here he is! You
broke my head for nothing; and that that I
did, I was set on to do't by Sir Toby.

Vio. Why do you speak to me? I never
  hurt you: 190
You drew your sword upon me without
  cause;

But I bespake you fair, and hurt you not.

Sir And. If a bloody coxcomb be a hurt,
you have hurt me: I think you set nothing by
a bloody coxcomb.   195

Enter Sir Toby and Clown.

Here comes Sir Toby halting: you shall hear
more: but if he had not been in drink, he
would have tickled you othergates than he
did.

Duke. How now, gentleman! how is't
with you?   200

Sir To. That's all one: has hurt me, and
there's the end on't. Sot, didst see Dick surgeon, sot?

Clo. O, he's drunk, Sir Toby, an hour
agone; his eyes were set at eight i' the
morning.

Sir To. Then he's a rogue, †and a passy
measures panyn: I hate a drunken rogue.

Oli. Away with him! Who hath made this
havoc with them?

Sir And. I'll help you, Sir Toby, because
we'll be dressed together.   211

Sir To. Will you help? an ass-head and a
coxcomb and a knave, a thin-faced knave, a
gull!

Oli. Get him to bed, and let his hurt be
look'd to. [*Exeunt Clown, Fabian, Sir Toby,*
                                and Sir Andrew.

Enter Sebastian.

Seb. I am sorry, madam, I have hurt your
  kinsman;
But, had it been the brother of my blood,
I must have done no less with wit and safety.
You throw a strange regard upon me, and by
  that
I do perceive it hath offended you: 220
Pardon me, sweet one, even for the vows
We made each other but so late ago.

Duke. One face, one voice, one habit, and
  two persons,
A natural perspective, that is and is not!

Seb. Antonio, O my dear Antonio!
How have the hours rack'd and tortured me,
Since I have lost thee!

---

160. **joinder**, joining. 168. **grizzle**, gray hair. **case**, skin, or possibly, body as containing the soul. 170. **trip**, probably from the trip in wrestling; here, dissembling. 174. **little**, i.e., a little. 179. **coxcomb**, fool's cap with the crest of a cock; here, head. 185. **incardinate**, blunder for *incarnate*. 187. **'Od's lifelings**, from the oath "By God's life."

196. **halting**, limping. 198. **othergates**, otherwise. 205. **set**, fixed, closed with drink. 206-207. **passy measures panyn**; so F. Malone and others read *passy measures pavin*, which they explain as connected with Italian, *passo e mezzo* (slow moving) and *pavana* (a grave and stately dance). It may thus be connected with Sir Toby's impatience to have his wounds dressed. 218. **with wit and safety**, my wits looking out for my safety. 219. **strange regard**, look of estrangement. 224. **perspective**, any optical device or illusion.

Ant. Sebastian are you?

Seb.   Fear'st thou that, Antonio?

Ant. How have you made division of
     yourself?
An apple, cleft in two, is not more twin   230
Than these two creatures. Which is Sebas-
     tian?

Oli. Most wonderful!

Seb. Do I stand there? I never had a
     brother;
Nor can there be that deity in my nature,
Of here and every where. I had a sister,
Whom the blind waves and surges have de-
     vour'd.
Of charity, what kin are you to me?
What countryman? what name? what paren-
     tage?

Vio. Of Messaline: Sebastian was my
     father;
Such a Sebastian was my brother too,   240
So went he suited to his watery tomb:
If spirits can assume both form and suit
You come to fright us.

Seb.   A spirit I am indeed;
But am in that dimension grossly clad
Which from the womb I did participate.
Were you a woman, as the rest goes even,
I should my tears let fall upon your cheek,
And say 'Thrice-welcome, drowned Viola!'

Vio. My father had a mole upon his brow.

Seb. And so had mine.   250

Vio. And died that day when Viola from
     her birth
Had number'd thirteen years.

Seb. O, that record is lively in my soul!
He finished indeed his mortal act
That day that made my sister thirteen years.

Vio. If nothing lets to make us happy both
But this my masculine usurp'd attire,
Do not embrace me till each circumstance
Of place, time, fortune, do cohere and jump
That I am Viola: which to confirm,   260
I'll bring you to a captain in this town,
Where lie my maiden weeds; by whose gen-
     tle help
I was preserved to serve this noble count.
All the occurrence of my fortune since
Hath been between this lady and this lord.

Seb. [*To Olivia*] So comes it, lady, you
     have been mistook:

But nature to her bias drew in that.
You would have been contracted to a maid;
Nor are you therein, by my life, deceived,
You are betroth'd both to a maid and man.

Duke. Be not amazed; right noble is his
     blood.   271
If this be so, as yet the glass seems true,
I shall have share in this most happy wreck.
[*To Viola*] Boy, thou hast said to me a thou-
     sand times
Thou never shouldst love woman like to me.

Vio. And all those sayings will I over-
     swear;
And all those swearings keep as true in soul
As doth that orbed continent the fire
That severs day from night.

Duke.   Give me thy hand;
And let me see thee in thy woman's weeds. 280

Vio. The captain that did bring me first on
     shore
Hath my maid's garments: he upon some
     action
Is now in durance, at Malvolio's suit,
A gentleman, and follower of my lady's.

Oli. He shall enlarge him: fetch Malvolio
     hither:
And yet, alas, now I remember me,
They say, poor gentleman, he's much dis-
     tract.

Re-enter CLOWN *with a letter, and* FABIAN.

A most extracting frenzy of mine own
From my remembrance clearly banish'd his.
How does he, sirrah?   290

Clo. Truly, madam, he holds Belzebub at
the staves's end as well as a man in his case
may do: has here writ a letter to you; I
should have given 't you to-day morning, but
as a madman's epistles are no gospels, so it
skills not much when they are delivered.

Oli. Open 't, and read it.

Clo. Look then to be well edified when the
fool delivers the madman. [*Reads*] 'By the
Lord, madam,'—   300

Oli. How now! art thou mad?

Clo. No, madam, I do but read madness:
an your ladyship will have it as it ought to
be, you must allow Vox.

---

228. **Fear'st,** doubt'st. 235. **here and every where,**
omnipresence. 241. **suited,** dressed. 244. **dimension,**
body or bodily shape. **grossly clad,** i.e., in flesh. 245.
participate, share in common with others. 246. **as . . .
even,** since everything else agrees. 253. **record,** recollection. 256. **lets,** hinders. 259. **jump,** coincide, fit
exactly.

267. **nature . . . that,** nature was true to her bent in
that. 272. **glass,** i.e., *the natural perspective* of line 224.
276. **over-swear,** swear again. 278. **orbed continent,**
apparently, the celestial firmament which contains,
with other bodies, the sun, a fire which severs day from
night. 283. **durance,** prison, captivity. 288. **extracting,** possibly, *distracting.* 295. **epistles . . . gospels,**
an allusion to readings in the church service. 296. **skills,**
matters. 304. **Vox,** voice; allusion unknown.

Oli. Prithee, read i' thy right wits. 305

Clo. So I do, madonna; but to read his right wits is to read thus: therefore perpend, my princess, and give ear.

Oli. Read it you, sirrah.   [*To Fabian.*

Fab. [*Reads*] 'By the Lord, madam, you wrong me, and the world shall know it: though you have put me into darkness and given your drunken cousin rule over me, yet have I the benefit of my senses as well as your ladyship. I have your own letter that induced me to the semblance I put on; with the which I doubt not but to do myself much right, or you much shame. Think of me as you please. I leave my duty a little unthought of and speak out of my injury.

THE MADLY-USED MALVOLIO.'

Oli. Did he write this?   320

Clo. Ay, madam.

Duke. This savours not much of distraction.

Oli. See him deliver'd, Fabian; bring him hither.   [*Exit Fabian.*

My lord, so please you, these things further thought on,

To think me as well a sister as a wife,

One day shall crown the alliance on 't, so please you,

Here at my house and at my proper cost.

Duke. Madam, I am most apt to embrace your offer.

[*To Viola*] Your master quits you; and for your service done him,

So much against the mettle of your sex, 330

So far beneath your soft and tender breeding,

And since you call'd me master for so long,

Here is my hand: you shall from this time be

Your master's mistress.

Oli.   A sister! you are she.

Re-enter FABIAN, *with* MALVOLIO.

Duke. Is this the madman?

Oli.   Ay, my lord, this same.

How now, Malvolio!

Mal.   Madam, you have done me wrong,

Notorious wrong.

Oli.   Have I, Malvolio? no.

Mal. Lady, you have. Pray you, peruse that letter.

You must not now deny it is your hand: 339

Write from it, if you can, in hand or phrase;

Or say 'tis not your seal, not your invention:

You can say none of this: well, grant it then

And tell me, in the modesty of honour,

Why you have given me such clear lights of favour,

Bade me come smiling and cross-garter'd to you,

To put on yellow stockings and to frown

Upon Sir Toby and the lighter people;

And, acting this in an obedient hope,

Why have you suffer'd me to be imprison'd,

Kept in a dark house, visited by the priest,350

And made the most notorious geck and gull

That e'er invention play'd on? tell me why.

Oli. Alas, Malvolio, this is not my writing,

Though, I confess, much like the character:

But out of question 'tis Maria's hand.

And now I do bethink me, it was she

First told me thou wast mad; then camest in smiling,

And in such forms which here were presupposed

Upon thee in the letter. Prithee, be content:

This practice hath most shrewdly pass'd upon thee;   360

But when we know the grounds and authors of it,

Thou shalt be both the plaintiff and the judge

Of thine own cause.

Fab.   Good madam, hear me speak,

And let no quarrel nor no brawl to come

Taint the condition of this present hour,

Which I have wonder'd at. In hope it shall not,

Most freely I confess, myself and Toby

Set this device against Malvolio here,

Upon some stubborn and uncourteous parts

We had conceived against him: Maria writ

The letter at Sir Toby's great importance; 371

In recompense whereof he hath married her.

How with a sportful malice it was follow'd,

May rather pluck on laughter than revenge;

If that the injuries be justly weigh'd

That have on both sides pass'd.

Oli. Alas, poor fool, how have they baffled thee!

Clo. Why, 'some are born great, some achieve greatness, and some have greatness thrown upon them.' I was one, sir, in this interlude; one Sir Topas, sir; but that's all one. 'By the Lord, fool, I am not mad.' But do you remember? 'Madam, why laugh you at such a barren rascal? an you smile not, he's gagged:' and thus the whirligig of time brings in his revenges.

Mal. I'll be revenged on the whole pack of you.   [*Exit.*

Oli. He hath been most notoriously abused.

Duke. Pursue him, and entreat him to a peace:

He hath not told us of the captain yet: 390

When that is known and golden time convents,

A solemn combination shall be made

Of our dear souls. Meantime, sweet sister,

We will not part from hence. Cesario, come;

For so you shall be, while you are a man;

---

387. **I'll . . . you.** The reading of this line is by many modern actors so passionate and revengeful as to spoil the effect of the comedy; this cannot have been Shakespeare's intention. Olivia (lines 359-363) has declared that Malvolio shall judge his own cause; Fabian (lines 374-376) has said that the offense was so much on both sides that it is a matter for laughter rather than revenge; and the Duke would have them follow Malvolio to entreat peace. Malvolio's wrongs are not, therefore, regarded as irreparable. 391. **convents**, suits; the word elsewhere means "summons."

But when in other habits you are seen,

Orsino's mistress and his fancy's queen.

          [*Exeunt all, except Clown.*

Clo. [*Sings*]

When that I was and a little tiny boy,

    With hey, ho, the wind and the rain,

A foolish thing was but a toy,   400

    For the rain it raineth every day.

But when I came to man's estate,

    With hey, ho, &c.

'Gainst knaves and thieves men shut their gate,

    For the rain, &c.

But when I came, alas! to wive,

    With hey, ho, &c.

By swaggering could I never thrive,

    For the rain, &c.

But when I came unto my beds,   410

    With hey, ho, &c.

With toss-pots still had drunken heads,

    For the rain, &c.

A great while ago the world begun,

    With hey, ho, &c.

But that's all one, our play is done,

    And we'll strive to please you every day.   [*Exit.*

---

412. **toss-pots**, drunkards.

THE TRAGEDY OF
KING RICHARD II

DRAMATIS PERSONÆ

KING RICHARD the Second.

JOHN OF GAUNT, Duke of Lancaster,

EDMUND OF LANGLEY, Duke of York,

} uncles to the King.

HENRY, surnamed BOLINGBROKE, Duke of Hereford, son to John of Gaunt; afterwards KING HENRY IV.

DUKE OF AUMERLE, son to the Duke of York.

THOMAS MOWBRAY, Duke of Norfolk.

DUKE OF SURREY.

EARL OF SALISBURY.

LORD BERKELEY.

BUSHY,
BAGOT, } servants to King Richard.
GREEN,

EARL OF NORTHUMBERLAND.

HENRY PERCY, surnamed Hotspur, his son.

LORD ROSS.

LORD WILLOUGHBY.

LORD FITZWATER.

Bishop of Carlisle.

Abbot of Westminster.

Lord Marshal.

SIR STEPHEN SCROOP.

SIR PIERCE of Exton.

Captain of a band of Welshmen.

QUEEN to King Richard.

DUCHESS OF YORK.

DUCHESS OF GLOUCESTER.

Lady attending on the Queen.

Lords, Heralds, Officers, Soldiers, two Gardeners, Keeper, Messenger, Groom, and other Attendants.

SCENE: *England and Wales.*

ACT I.

SCENE I. *London.* KING RICHARD'S *palace.*

Enter KING RICHARD, JOHN OF GAUNT, *with other* Nobles *and* Attendants.

K. Rich. Old John of Gaunt, time-honour'd Lancaster,
Hast thou, according to thy oath and band,
Brought hither Henry Hereford thy bold son,
Here to make good the boisterous late appeal,
Which then our leisure would not let us hear,
Against the Duke of Norfolk, Thomas Mowbray?
Gaunt. I have, my liege.
K. Rich. Tell me, moreover, hast thou sounded him,
If he appeal the duke on ancient malice;
Or worthily, as a good subject should,   10
On some known ground of treachery in him?

Act I. Scene i. Stage Direction: **London.** Holinshed places this scene at Windsor; he is followed by many editors. 1. **Old John of Gaunt**, born in 1340 at Ghent; hence the surname *Gaunt.* At this time, April 29, 1398, he was only fifty-eight, although Shakespeare represents him as being very old. 2. **band,** bond. *Band* and *bond* are etymologically the same word; *band* was formerly used in both senses. 4. **appeal,** accusation, formal challenge or impeachment which the accuser was obliged to maintain in combat.

Gaunt. As near as I could sift him on that argument,
On some apparent danger seen in him
Aim'd at your highness, no inveterate malice.
K. Rich. Then call them to our presence; face to face,
And frowning brow to brow, ourselves will hear
The accuser and the accused freely speak:
High-stomach'd are they both, and full of ire,
In rage deaf as the sea, hasty as fire.

Enter BOLINGBROKE *and* MOWBRAY.

Boling. Many years of happy days befal 20
My gracious sovereign, my most loving liege!
Mow. Each day still better other's happiness;
Until the heavens, envying earth's good hap,
Add an immortal title to your crown!
K. Rich. We thank you both: yet one but flatters us,
As well appeareth by the cause you come;
Namely, to appeal each other of high treason.

12. **sift,** discover true motives by questioning. **argument,** theme, subject. 18. **High-stomach'd,** haughty, having an appetite for combat. 22. **other's,** the other's, of the next. 23. **hap,** fortune.

Cousin of Hereford, what dost thou object
Against the Duke of Norfolk, Thomas Mow-
    bray?
    Boling. First, heaven be the record to my
    speech!   30
In the devotion of a subject's love,
Tendering the precious safety of my prince,
And free from other misbegotten hate,
Come I appellant to this princely presence.
Now, Thomas Mowbray, do I turn to thee,
And mark my greeting well; for what I speak
My body shall make good upon this earth,
Or my divine soul answer it in heaven.
Thou art a traitor and a miscreant,
Too good to be so and too bad to live,   40
Since the more fair and crystal is the sky,
The uglier seem the clouds that in it fly.
Once more, the more to aggravate the note,
With a foul traitor's name stuff I thy throat;
And wish, so please my sovereign, ere I move,
What my tongue speaks my right drawn
    sword may prove.
    Mow. Let not my cold words here accuse
    my zeal:
'Tis not the trial of a woman's war,
The bitter clamour of two eager tongues,
Can arbitrate this cause betwixt us twain;50
The blood is hot that must be cool'd for this:
Yet can I not of such tame patience boast
As to be hush'd and nought at all to say:
First, the fair reverence of your highness
    curbs me
From giving reins and spurs to my free speech;
Which else would post until it had return'd
These terms of treason doubled down his
    throat.
Setting aside his high blood's royalty,
And let him be no kinsman to my liege,
I do defy him, and I spit at him;   60
Call him a slanderous coward and a villain:
Which to maintain I would allow him odds,
And meet him, were I tied to run afoot
Even to the frozen ridges of the Alps,
Or any other ground inhabitable,
Where ever Englishman durst set his foot.
Mean time let this defend my loyalty,
By all my hopes, most falsely doth he lie.
    Boling. Pale trembling coward, there I
    throw my gage,

Disclaiming here the kindred of the king, 70
And lay aside my high blood's royalty,
Which fear, not reverence, makes thee to
    except.
If guilty dread have left thee so much strength
As to take up mine honour's pawn, then stoop:
By that and all the rites of knighthood else,
Will I make good against thee, arm to arm,
What I have spoke, or thou canst worse
    devise.
    Mow. I take it up; and by that sword I
    swear,
Which gently laid my knighthood on my
    shoulder,
I'll answer thee in any fair degree,   80
Or chivalrous design of knightly trial:
And when I mount, alive may I not light,
If I be traitor or unjustly fight!
    K. Rich. What doth our cousin lay to
    Mowbray's charge?
It must be great that can inherit us
So much as of a thought of ill in him.
    Boling. Look, what I speak, my life shall
    prove it true;
That Mowbray hath received eight thousand
    nobles
In name of lendings for your highness' soldiers,
The which he hath detain'd for lewd employ-
    ments,   90
Like a false traitor and injurious villain.
Besides I say and will in battle prove,
Or here or elsewhere to the furthest verge
That ever was survey'd by English eye,
That all the treasons for these eighteen years
Complotted and contrived in this land
Fetch from false Mowbray their first head and
    spring.
Further I say and further will maintain
Upon his bad life to make all this good,
That he did plot the Duke of Gloucester's
    death,   100
Suggest his soon-believing adversaries,
And consequently, like a traitor coward,
Sluiced out his innocent soul through streams
    of blood:

28-9. **object Against**, charge criminally against. 32.
Tendering, holding dear. 34. **appellant**, accuser.
Onions construes this as an adjective meaning "accusing
or impeaching another of treason." 43. **note**, reproach.
46. **right drawn**, justly or rightly drawn. 47. **accuse
my zeal**, accuse me of wanting zeal. 49. **eager**, sharp,
biting. 58. **Setting . . . royalty**, disregarding Bolingbroke's royal blood. 65. **inhabitable**, uninhabitable.
69. **gage**, a gauntlet as a sign of the pledge to combat.

74. **pawn**, i.e., his gage. 85. **inherit**, put in possession of. 88. **nobles**, gold coins worth twenty groats
or 6s. 8d. 89. **lendings**, money advanced to soldiers
when the regular pay cannot be given (Onions). 90.
lewd, vile, base. 97. **head and spring**, synonymous
words meaning "origin." 100. **Duke of Gloucester's
death**. Thomas of Woodstock, Duke of Gloucester,
sixth (or seventh) son of Edward III and brother of
John of Gaunt, was murdered at Calais in September,
1397. To avenge his death is Bolingbroke's real motive.
The other charges are merely trumped up, and Mowbray
brushes them away in an instant (lines 124-132); Gloucester's murder is an underlying motive throughout
the earlier part of the play. 101. **Suggest**, prompt,
incite. 102. **consequently**, successively in time (not
inferential).

Which blood, like sacrificing Abel's, cries,
Even from the tongueless caverns of the earth,
To me for justice and rough chastisement;
And, by the glorious worth of my descent,
This arm shall do it, or this life be spent.
    K. Rich. How high a pitch his resolution
      soars!
Thomas of Norfolk, what say'st thou to this?
    Mow. O, let my sovereign turn away his
      face   111
And bid his ears a little while be deaf,
Till I have told this slander of his blood,
How God and good men hate so foul a liar.
    K. Rich. Mowbray, impartial are our eyes
      and ears:
Were he my brother, nay, my kingdom's heir,
As he is but my father's brother's son,
Now, by my sceptre's awe, I make a vow,
Such neighbour nearness to our sacred blood
Should nothing privilege him, nor partialize
The unstooping firmness of my upright soul:
He is our subject, Mowbray; so art thou:
Free speech and fearless I to thee allow. 123
    Mow. Then, Bolingbroke, as low as to thy
      heart,
Through the false passage of thy throat, thou
    liest.
Three parts of that receipt I had for Calais
Disbursed I duly to his highness' soldiers;
The other part reserved I by consent,
For that my sovereign liege was in my debt
Upon remainder of a dear account,   130
Since last I went to France to fetch his queen:
Now swallow down that lie. For Gloucester's
    death,
I slew him not; but to my own disgrace
Neglected my sworn duty in that case.
For you, my noble Lord of Lancaster,
The honourable father to my foe,
Once did I lay an ambush for your life,
A trespass that doth vex my grieved soul;
But ere I last received the sacrament
I did confess it, and exactly begg'd   140
Your grace's pardon, and I hope I had it.
This is my fault: as for the rest appeal'd,
It issues from the rancour of a villain,
A recreant and most degenerate traitor:
Which in myself I boldly will defend;

And interchangeably hurl down my gage
Upon this overweening traitor's foot,
To prove myself a loyal gentleman
Even in the best blood chamber'd in his
    bosom.
In haste whereof, most heartily I pray   150
Your highness to assign our trial day.
    K. Rich. Wrath-kindled gentlemen, be
      ruled by me;
Let's purge this choler without letting blood:
This we prescribe, though no physician;
Deep malice makes too deep incision;
Forget, forgive; conclude and be agreed;
Our doctors say this is no month to bleed.
Good uncle, let this end where it begun;
We'll calm the Duke of Norfolk, you your
    son.
    Gaunt. To be a make-peace shall become
      my age: 160
Throw down, my son, the Duke of Norfolk's
    gage.
    K. Rich. And, Norfolk, throw down his.
    Gaunt.   When, Harry, when?
Obedience bids I should not bid again.
    K. Rich. Norfolk, throw down, we bid;
      there is no boot.
    Mow. Myself I throw, dread sovereign, at
      thy foot.
My life thou shalt command, but not my
    shame:
The one my duty owes; but my fair name,
Despite of death that lives upon my grave,
To dark dishonour's use thou shalt not have.
I am disgraced, impeach'd and baffled here,
Pierced to the soul with slander's venom'd
    spear,   171
The which no balm can cure but his heart-
    blood
Which breathed this poison.
    K. Rich.   Rage must be withstood:
Give me his gage: lions make leopards tame.
    Mow. Yea, but not change his spots: take
      but my shame,
And I resign my gage. My dear dear lord,
The purest treasure mortal times afford
Is spotless reputation: that away,

---

105. **tongueless,** resonant but without articulate speech. 109. **pitch,** height; a term in falconry denoting the highest point of a falcon's flight before it stoops upon its prey. 113. **slander of,** disgrace or reproach to. 126. **receipt,** thing received. 130. **dear,** coming home to one intimately, for good or ill. 132-134. **For . . . case.** Mowbray's excuse is at the king's expense; he vaguely hints at the king's connivance. In Holinshed he ignores the charge. 140. **exactly,** explicitly, formally. 144. **recreant,** one untrue to his knightly honor.

153. **choler,** excess of the humor, choler, anger. **letting blood,** used with a quibble on the sense of "mortal combat." 156. **conclude,** come to a final agreement. 157. **no month to bleed.** Spring and autumn were regarded as the proper times to bleed patients. Ff have *time*; Q1 has *month.* 160. **make-peace,** peacemaker. 164. **boot,** help, avail. 170. **impeach'd,** called into question, discredited. **baffled,** disgraced, as of a recreant knight. A part of the punishment of coward knights was hanging by the heels, which is the original meaning of the word. 174. **leopards.** Malone called attention to the fact, questioned by the Clarendon Press editors, that the Norfolk crest was a golden leopard.

Men are but gilded loam or painted clay.
A jewel in a ten-times-barr'd-up chest   180
Is a bold spirit in a loyal breast.
Mine honour is my life; both grow in one;
Take honour from me, and my life is done:
Then, dear my liege, mine honour let me try;
In that I live and for that will I die.

   K. Rich. Cousin, throw up your gage; do
     you begin.

   Boling. O, God defend my soul from such
     deep sin!
Shall I seem crest-fall'n in my father's sight?
Or with pale beggar-fear impeach my height
Before this out-dared dastard? Ere my
     tongue   190
Shall wound my honour with such feeble
     wrong,
Or sound so base a parle, my teeth shall tear
The slavish motive of recanting fear,
And spit it bleeding in his high disgrace,
Where shame doth harbour, even in Mow-
     bray's face.   [*Exit Gaunt.*

   K. Rich. We were not born to sue, but to
     command;
Which since we cannot do to make you
     friends,
Be ready, as your lives shall answer it,
At Coventry, upon Saint Lambert's day: 199
There shall your swords and lances arbitrate
The swelling difference of your settled hate:
Since we can not atone you, we shall see
Justice design the victor's chivalry.
Lord marshal, command our officers at arms
Be ready to direct these home alarms.
                       [*Exeunt.*

SCENE II. *The* DUKE OF LANCASTER'S *palace.*

Enter JOHN OF GAUNT *with the* DUCHESS OF
              GLOUCESTER.

   Gaunt. Alas, the part I had in Wood-
     stock's blood
Doth more solicit me than your exclaims,
To stir against the butchers of his life!
But since correction lieth in those hands
Which made the fault that we cannot cor-
     rect,
Put we our quarrel to the will of heaven;

Who, when they see the hours ripe on earth,
Will rain hot vengeance on offenders' heads.

   Duch. Finds brotherhood in thee no
     sharper spur?
Hath love in thy old blood no living fire? 10
Edward's seven sons, whereof thyself art one,
Were as seven vials of his sacred blood,
Or seven fair branches springing from one
     root:
Some of those seven are dried by nature's
     course,
Some of those branches by the Destinies cut;
But Thomas, my dear lord, my life, my
     Gloucester,
One vial full of Edward's sacred blood,
One flourishing branch of his most royal root,
Is crack'd, and all the precious liquor spilt,
Is hack'd down, and his summer leaves all
     faded,   20
By envy's hand and murder's bloody axe.
Ah, Gaunt, his blood was thine! that bed,
     that womb,
That metal, that self mould, that fashion'd
     thee
Made him a man; and though thou livest and
     breathest,
Yet art thou slain in him: thou dost consent
In some large measure to thy father's death,
In that thou seest thy wretched brother die,
Who was the model of thy father's life.
Call it not patience, Gaunt; it is despair:
In suffering thus thy brother to be slaugh-
     ter'd,   30
Thou showest the naked pathway to thy
     life,
Teaching stern murder how to butcher thee:
That which in mean men we intitle patience
Is pale cold cowardice in noble breasts.
What shall I say? to safeguard thine own life,
The best way is to venge my Gloucester's
     death.

   Gaunt. God's is the quarrel; for God's sub-
     stitute,
His deputy anointed in His sight,
Hath caused his death: the which if wrong-
     fully,
Let heaven revenge; for I may never lift   40
An angry arm against His minister.

   Duch. Where then, alas, may I complain
     myself?

   Gaunt. To God, the widow's champion
     and defence.

---

189. **beggar-fear**, a beggar's fear. **height**, high
position. 190. **out-dared**, dared down, cowed. 192.
parle, overtures of peace, parley. 193. **motive**,
instrument. 199. **Saint Lambert's day**, September
17. 203. **design**, point out.
   Scene ii. 2. **exclaims**, exclamations. 4. **those
hands**, i.e., Richard's, whom he charges with responsibility for Gloucester's death. Gaunt is more explicit in
lines 37-41.

9. **Finds . . . spur.** The Duchess's argument of
kinship develops into that of self-defense in lines 30 ff.
23. **self mould**, selfsame mold. 36. **venge**, avenge.

Duch. Why, then, I will. Farewell, old
  Gaunt.
Thou goest to Coventry, there to behold
Our cousin Hereford and fell Mowbray fight:
O, sit my husband's wrongs on Hereford's
  spear,
That it may enter butcher Mowbray's
  breast!
Or, if misfortune miss the first career,
Be Mowbray's sins so heavy in his bosom, 50
That they may break his foaming courser's
  back,
And throw the rider headlong in the lists,
A caitiff recreant to my cousin Hereford!
Farewell, old Gaunt: thy sometimes brother's
  wife
With her companion grief must end her life.
  Gaunt. Sister, farewell; I must to Coventry:
As much good stay with thee as go with me!
  Duch. Yet one word more: grief boundeth
  where it falls,
Not with the empty hollowness, but weight:
I take my leave before I have begun, 60
For sorrow ends not when it seemeth done.
Commend me to thy brother, Edmund York.
Lo, this is all:—nay, yet depart not so;
Though this be all, do not so quickly go;
I shall remember more. Bid him—ah,
  what?—
With all good speed at Plashy visit me.
Alack, and what shall good old York there see
But empty lodgings and unfurnish'd walls,
Unpeopled offices, untrodden stones?
And what hear there for welcome but my
  groans? 70
Therefore commend me; let him not come
  there,
To seek out sorrow that dwells every where.
Desolate, desolate, will I hence and die:
The last leave of thee takes my weeping eye.
  [*Exeunt.*

SCENE III. *The lists at Coventry*

Enter the Lord Marshal *and the* DUKE OF
  AUMERLE.

  Mar. My Lord Aumerle, is Harry Hereford arm'd?

47. *O, sit . . . spear.* The Duchess regards Bolingbroke as the family champion, as he seems to have regarded himself (I, i, 106). 49. *career,* the charge of
the horse in the tourney or combat. 53. *caitiff,* cowardly. 62. *Edmund York,* Edmund of Langley, fifth son
of Edward III. 66. *Plashy,* Gloucester's seat in Essex.
68. *unfurnish'd,* bare. 73. *will I hence.* The adverb of place is used here, as frequently in Shakespeare,
without the verb of motion.
Scene iii. The events of this scene took place historically on September 16, 1398.

Aum. Yea, at all points; and longs to
  enter in.
  Mar. The Duke of Norfolk, sprightfully
  and bold,
Stays but the summons of the appellant's
  trumpet.
  Aum. Why, then, the champions are prepared, and stay
For nothing but his majesty's approach.

The trumpets sound, and the KING *enters
with his nobles,* GAUNT, BUSHY, BAGOT,
GREEN, *and others. When they are set,
enter* MOWBRAY *in arms, defendant, with
a* Herald.

  K. Rich. Marshal, demand of yonder
  champion
The cause of his arrival here in arms:
Ask him his name and orderly proceed
To swear him in the justice of his cause. 10
  Mar. In God's name and the king's, say
  who thou art
And why thou comest thus knightly clad in
  arms,
Against what man thou comest, and what
  thy quarrel:
Speak truly, on thy knighthood and thy
  oath;
As so defend thee heaven and thy valour!
  Mow. My name is Thomas Mowbray,
  Duke of Norfolk;
Who hither come engaged by my oath—
Which God defend a knight should violate!—
Both to defend my loyalty and truth
To God, my king and my succeeding issue, 20
Against the Duke of Hereford that appeals
  me;
And, by the grace of God and this mine arm,
To prove him, in defending of myself,
A traitor to my God, my king, and me:
And as I truly fight, defend me heaven!

The trumpets sound. Enter BOLINGBROKE,
appellant, in armour, with a Herald.

  K. Rich. Marshal, ask yonder knight in
  arms,
Both who he is and why he cometh hither
Thus plated in habiliments of war,
And formally, according to our law,

3. *sprightfully,* with high spirit. 7-10. *Marshal
. . . cause.* One finds here, as elsewhere in Richard's
public behavior, an illustration of what Coleridge calls
his "attention to decorum and high feeling of kingly
dignity." 18. *defend,* forbid. 28. *plated,* clothed in
armor.

Depose him in the justice of his cause. 30
  Mar. What is thy name? and wherefore
    comest thou hither,
Before King Richard in his royal lists?
Against whom comest thou? and what's thy
    quarrel?
Speak like a true knight, so defend thee
    heaven!
  Boling. Harry of Hereford, Lancaster and
    Derby
Am I; who ready here do stand in arms,
To prove, by God's grace and my body's
    valour,
In lists, on Thomas Mowbray, Duke of
    Norfolk,
That he is a traitor, foul and dangerous,
To God of heaven, King Richard and to
    me;
And as I truly fight, defend me heaven! 41
  Mar. On pain of death, no person be so
    bold
Or daring-hardy as to touch the lists,
Except the marshal and such officers
Appointed to direct these fair designs.
  Boling. Lord marshal, let me kiss my
    sovereign's hand,
And bow my knee before his majesty:
For Mowbray and myself are like two men
That vow a long and weary pilgrimage;
Then let us take a ceremonious leave 50
And loving farewell of our several friends.
  Mar. The appellant in all duty greets
    your highness,
And craves to kiss your hand and take his
    leave.
  K. Rich. We will descend and fold him in
    our arms.
Cousin of Hereford, as thy cause is right,
So be thy fortune in this royal fight!
Farewell, my blood; which if to-day thou
    shed,
Lament we may, but not revenge thee dead.
  Boling. O, let no noble eye profane a tear
For me, if I be gored with Mowbray's spear:
As confident as is the falcon's flight 61
Against a bird, do I with Mowbray fight.
My loving lord, I take my leave of you;
Of you, my noble cousin, Lord Aumerle;
Not sick, although I have to do with death,
But lusty, young, and cheerly drawing
    breath.

Lo, as at English feasts, so I regreet
The daintiest last, to make the end most
    sweet:
O thou, the earthly author of my blood,
Whose youthful spirit, in me regenerate, 70
Doth with a twofold vigour lift me up
To reach at victory above my head,
Add proof unto mine armour with thy
    prayers;
And with thy blessings steel my lance's point,
That it may enter Mowbray's waxen coat,
And furbish new the name of John a Gaunt,
Even in the lusty haviour of his son.
  Gaunt. God in thy good cause make thee
    prosperous!
Be swift like lightning in the execution;
And let thy blows, doubly redoubled, 80
Fall like amazing thunder on the casque
Of thy adverse pernicious enemy:
Rouse up thy youthful blood, be valiant and
    live.
  Boling. Mine innocency and Saint George
    to thrive!
  Mow. However God or fortune cast my
    lot,
There lives or dies, true to King Richard's
    throne,
A loyal, just and upright gentleman:
Never did captive with a freer heart
Cast off his chains of bondage and embrace
His golden uncontroll'd enfranchisement, 90
More than my dancing soul doth celebrate
This feast of battle with mine adversary.
Most mighty liege, and my companion peers,
Take from my mouth the wish of happy
    years:
As gentle and as jocund as to jest
Go I to fight: truth hath a quiet breast.
  K. Rich. Farewell, my lord: securely I
    espy
Virtue with valour couched in thine eye.
Order the trial, marshal, and begin.
  Mar. Harry of Hereford, Lancaster and
    Derby, 100
Receive thy lance; and God defend the
    right!
  Boling. Strong as a tower in hope, I cry
    amen.
  Mar. Go bear this lance to Thomas, Duke
    of Norfolk.

---

30. **Depose**, put under oath. 43. **daring-hardy**, daringly bold. 49. **pilgrimage**. Bolingbroke's figure carries a suggestion of future events of which he is unconscious. 59. **profane**, be profaned by.

67. **regreet**, greet, salute. 70. **regenerate**, born anew. 73. **proof**, resisting power of armor. 75. **waxen**, penetrable, soft. 77. **haviour**, behavior, deportment. 81. **amazing**, confusing, bewildering. **casque**, helmet. 95. **jest**, take part in a play or pastime.

First Her. Harry of Hereford, Lancaster
  and Derby,
Stands here for God, his sovereign and him-
  self,
On pain to be found false and recreant,
To prove the Duke of Norfolk, Thomas
  Mowbray,
A traitor to his God, his king and him;
And dares him to set forward to the fight.
  Sec. Her. Here standeth Thomas Mow-
  bray, Duke of Norfolk,   110
On pain to be found false and recreant,
Both to defend himself and to approve
Henry of Hereford, Lancaster, and Derby,
To God, his sovereign and to him disloyal;
Courageously and with a free desire
Attending but the signal to begin.
  Mar. Sound, trumpets; and set forward,
  combatants.   [*A charge sounded.*
Stay, the king hath thrown his warder
  down.
  K. Rich. Let them lay by their helmets
  and their spears,
And both return back to their chairs
  again: 120
Withdraw with us: and let the trumpets
  sound
While we return these dukes what we decree.
                                [*A long flourish.*
Draw near,
And list what with our council we have done.
For that our kingdom's earth should not be
  soil'd
With that dear blood which it hath fostered;
And for our eyes do hate the dire aspect
Of civil wounds plough'd up with neigh-
  bours' sword;
And for we think the eagle-winged pride
Of sky-aspiring and ambitious thoughts, 130
With rival-hating envy, set on you
To wake our peace, which in our country's
  cradle
Draws the sweet infant breath of gentle
  sleep;

Which so roused up with boisterous untuned
  drums,
With harsh-resounding trumpets' dreadful
  bray,
And grating shock of wrathful iron arms,
Might from our quiet confines fright fair
  peace
And make us wade even in our kindred's
  blood;
Therefore, we banish you our territories:
You, cousin Hereford, upon pain of life, 140
Till twice five summers have enrich'd our
  fields
Shall not regreet our fair dominions,
But tread the stranger paths of banishment.
  Boling. Your will be done: this must my
  comfort be,
That sun that warms you here shall shine on
  me;
And those his golden beams to you here lent
Shall point on me and gild my banishment.
  K. Rich. Norfolk, for thee remains a
  heavier doom,
Which I with some unwillingness pronounce:
The sly slow hours shall not determinate 150
The dateless limit of thy dear exile;
The hopeless word of 'never to return'
Breathe I against thee, upon pain of life.
  Mow. A heavy sentence, my most sov-
  ereign liege,
And all unlook'd for from your highness'
  mouth:
A dearer merit, not so deep a maim
As to be cast forth in the common air,
Have I deserved at your highness' hands.
The language I have learn'd these forty
  years,
My native English, now I must forego: 160
And now my tongue's use is to me no more
Than an unstringed viol or a harp,
Or like a cunning instrument cased up,
Or, being open, put into his hands
That knows no touch to tune the harmony:
Within my mouth you have engaol'd my
  tongue,
Doubly portcullis'd with my teeth and lips;
And dull unfeeling barren ignorance
Is made my gaoler to attend on me.

---

106. recreant, unfaithful to duty or pledge. **118.
Stay . . . down.** Shakespeare fails to disclose Richard's
motive here. According to Froissart, several noblemen
of the king's party warned him not to let the combat
proceed because the people were aroused on Bolingbroke's behalf. The victory of either knight would be
perilous to the king's own safety. It is characteristic of
Richard's love of display that he should have let the
ceremonies proceed to the very last possible moment.
warder, staff or truncheon borne by the king when presiding over a trial by combat. **122. While,** until. **125-
143. For that . . . banishment.** The king's speech
is confused, perhaps intentionally, perhaps because it is
insincere.

134-137. Which . . . peace. Syntactically the antecedent of *which* is *peace*, line 132. Both the syntax and
the metaphor have gone astray. Note the figurative
representation of *peace*, lines 132-133. **139. we . . .
territories.** Richard shows what Gardiner calls the
"unwise cunning of a madman" and takes the one
course which would be sure to work injustice to both men.

I am too old to fawn upon a nurse,   170
Too far in years to be a pupil now:
What is thy sentence then but speechless
    death,
Which robs my tongue from breathing native
    breath?
    K. Rich. It boots thee not to be compas-
    sionate:
After our sentence plaining comes too late.
    Mow. Then thus I turn me from my
    country's light,
To dwell in solemn shades of endless night.
    K. Rich. Return again, and take an oath
    with thee.
Lay on our royal sword your banish'd hands;
Swear by the duty that you owe to God—180
Our part therein we banish with yourselves—
To keep the oath that we administer:
You never shall, so help you truth and God!
Embrace each other's love in banishment;
Nor never look upon each other's face;
Nor never write, regreet, nor reconcile
This louring tempest of your home-bred hate;
Nor never by advised purpose meet
To plot, contrive, or complot any ill
'Gainst us, our state, our subjects, or our
    land.   190
    Boling. I swear.
    Mow. And I, to keep all this.
    Boling. Norfolk, so far as to mine enemy:—
By this time, had the king permitted us,
One of our souls had wander'd in the air,
Banish'd this frail sepulchre of our flesh,
As now our flesh is banish'd from this land:
Confess thy treasons ere thou fly the realm;
Since thou hast far to go, bear not along
The clogging burthen of a guilty soul.   200
    Mow. No, Bolingbroke: if ever I were
    traitor,
My name be blotted from the book of life,
And I from heaven banish'd as from hence!
But what thou art, God, thou, and I do know;
And all too soon, I fear, the king shall rue.
Farewell, my liege. Now no way can I
    stray;
Save back to England, all the world's my
    way.   [*Exit.*
    K. Rich. Uncle, even in the glasses of
    thine eyes
I see thy grieved heart: thy sad aspect

Hath from the number of his banish'd years
Pluck'd four away. [*To Boling.*] Six frozen
    winters spent,   211
Return with welcome home from banishment.
    Boling. How long a time lies in one little
    word!
Four lagging winters and four wanton springs
End in a word: such is the breath of kings.
    Gaunt. I thank my liege, that in regard
    of me
He shortens four years of my son's exile:
But little vantage shall I reap thereby;
For, ere the six years that he hath to spend
Can change their moons and bring their
    times about,   220
My oil-dried lamp and time-bewasted light
Shall be extinct with age and endless night;
My inch of taper will be burnt and done,
And blindfold death not let me see my son.
    K. Rich. Why, uncle, thou hast many
    years to live.
    Gaunt. But not a minute, king, that thou
    canst give:
Shorten my days thou canst with sullen
    sorrow,
And pluck nights from me, but not lend a
    morrow;
Thou canst help time to furrow me with age,
But stop no wrinkle in his pilgrimage;   230
Thy word is current with him for my death,
But dead, thy kingdom cannot buy my
    breath.
    K. Rich. Thy son is banish'd upon good
    advice,
Whereto thy tongue a party-verdict gave:
Why at our justice seem'st thou then to lour?
    Gaunt. Things sweet to taste prove in
    digestion sour.
You urged me as a judge; but I had rather
You would have bid me argue like a father.
O, had it been a stranger, not my child,
To smooth his fault I should have been more
    mild: 240
A partial slander sought I to avoid,
And in the sentence my own life destroy'd.

204-205. **But what . . . rue.** The prophetic irony
of this speech exposes Richard's blunder in banishing so
faithful and efficient a servant. The historical Richard
probably meant to recall Mowbray and make Bolingbroke's exile permanent; but such an intention is not
implied in this play. 208. **glasses,** mirrors.

210. **banish'd years,** years of banishment. *Banish'd*
is not a past participle, but an adjective. 211. **Pluck'd
four away.** According to Holinshed the amelioration of
Bolingbroke's sentence took place later, at Eltham,
when the king was taking leave of Bolingbroke. Dramatically, it serves to show how Richard is imposed
upon by the stronger personalities of Gaunt and Bolingbroke. 213-215. **How . . . word.** Coleridge adds
after these lines the comment, "Admirable anticipation!"
214. **wanton,** luxuriant. 230. **But . . . pilgrimage,**
efface no wrinkle that comes with time. 231. **current,**
i.e., as good as current coin. 234. **a party-verdict,** one
person's share in a joint verdict. 241. **partial slander,**
accusation of partiality. Cf. line 210.

Alas, I look'd when some of you should say,
I was too strict to make mine own away;
But you gave leave to my unwilling tongue
Against my will to do myself this wrong.

K. Rich. Cousin, farewell; and, uncle, bid
him so:
Six years we banish him, and he shall go.
[*Flourish. Exeunt King Richard and train.*

Aum. Cousin, farewell: what presence
must not know,
From where you do remain let paper show.250

Mar. My lord, no leave take I; for I will
ride,
As far as land will let me, by your side.

Gaunt. O, to what purpose dost thou
hoard thy words,
That thou return'st no greeting to thy
friends?

Boling. I have too few to take my leave of
you,
When the tongue's office should be prodigal
To breathe the abundant dolour of the heart.

Gaunt. Thy grief is but thy absence for a
time.

Boling. Joy absent, grief is present for
that time.

Gaunt. What is six winters? they are
quickly gone.   260

Boling. To men in joy; but grief makes
one hour ten.

Gaunt. Call it a travel that thou takest for
pleasure.

Boling. My heart will sigh when I miscall
it so,
Which finds it an inforced pilgrimage.

Gaunt. The sullen passage of thy weary
steps
Esteem as foil wherein thou art to set
The precious jewel of thy home return.

Boling. Nay, rather, every tedious stride
I make
Will but remember me what a deal of world
I wander from the jewels that I love   270
Must I not serve a long apprenticehood
To foreign passages, and in the end,
Having my freedom, boast of nothing else
But that I was a journeyman to grief?

Gaunt. All places that the eye of heaven
visits

Are to a wise man ports and happy havens.
Teach thy necessity to reason thus;
There is no virtue like necessity.
Think not the king did banish thee,
But thou the king. Woe doth the heavier sit,
Where it perceives it is but faintly borne. 281
Go, say I sent thee forth to purchase honour
And not the king exiled thee; or suppose
Devouring pestilence hangs in our air
And thou art flying to a fresher clime:
Look, what thy soul holds dear, imagine it
To lie that way thou go'st, not whence thou
comest:
Suppose the singing birds musicians,
The grass whereon thou tread'st the presence
strew'd,
The flowers fair ladies, and thy steps no more
Than a delightful measure or a dance;   291
For gnarling sorrow hath less power to bite
The man that mocks at it and sets it light.

Boling. O, who can hold a fire in his hand
By thinking on the frosty Caucasus?
Or cloy the hungry edge of appetite
By bare imagination of a feast?
Or wallow naked in December snow
By thinking on fantastic summer's heat?
O, no! the apprehension of the good   300
Gives but the greater feeling to the worse:
Fell sorrow's tooth doth never rankle more
Than when he bites, but lanceth not the sore.

Gaunt. Come, come, my son, I'll bring
thee on thy way:
Had I thy youth and cause, I would not stay.

Boling. Then, England's ground, farewell; sweet soil, adieu;
My mother, and my nurse, that bears me
yet!
Where'er I wander, boast of this I can,
Though banish'd, yet a trueborn Englishman.   [*Exeunt.*

SCENE IV. *The court.*

Enter the KING, *with* BAGOT *and* GREEN *at
one door; and the* DUKE OF AUMERLE *at
another.*

K. Rich. We did observe. Cousin Aumerle,
How far brought you high Hereford on his
way?

243. **look'd,** looked for, expected. 244. **too strict
to make,** i.e., in making; a gerundive use of the infinitive, common in Shakespeare. 249. **presence,** the
presence-chamber at court. 266. **foil,** metal surface used
in setting gems to show off their luster; hence, that
which sets something off to advantage. 272. **passages,**
wanderings. 274. **journeyman,** laborer hired by the
day; at the end of such service would come the settlement
in his trade.

289. **presence,** i.e., the royal presence-chamber strewn
with rushes. 291. **measure,** stately dance. 292.
gnarling, snarling, growling. 299. **fantastic,** imaginary. 300. **apprehension,** idea, product of mere
imagination. 302-303. **Fell . . . sore,** i.e., doth never
poison more than when it irritates the sore instead of
lancing to cure it. **rankle,** cause to fester, i.e., produce
irritation by poison.

Aum. I brought high Hereford, if you call him so,
But to the next highway, and there I left him.
K. Rich. And say, what store of parting tears were shed?
Aum. Faith, none for me; except the northeast wind,
Which then blew bitterly against our faces,
Awaked the sleeping rheum, and so by chance
Did grace our hollow parting with a tear.
K. Rich. What said our cousin when you parted with him?   10
Aum. 'Farewell:'
And, for my heart disdained that my tongue
Should so profane the word, that taught me craft
To counterfeit oppression of such grief
That words seem'd buried in my sorrow's grave.
Marry, would the word 'farewell' have lengthen'd hours
And added years to his short banishment,
He should have had a volume of farewells;
But since it would not, he had none of me.
K. Rich. He is our cousin, cousin; but 'tis doubt,   20
When time shall call him home from banishment,
Whether our kinsman come to see his friends,
Ourself and Bushy, Bagot here and Green
Observed his courtship to the common people;
How he did seem to dive into their hearts
With humble and familiar courtesy,
What reverence he did throw away on slaves,
Wooing poor craftsmen with the craft of smiles
And patient underbearing of his fortune,
As 'twere to banish their affects with him.   30
Off goes his bonnet to an oyster-wench;
A brace of draymen bid God speed him well
And had the tribute of his supple knee,
With 'Thanks, my countrymen, my loving friends;'
As were our England in reversion his,
And he our subjects' next degree in hope.

Green. Well, he is gone; and with him go these thoughts.
Now for the rebels which stand out in Ireland,
Expedient manage must be made, my liege,
Ere further leisure yield them further means   40
For their advantage and your highness' loss.
K. Rich. We will ourself in person to this war:
And, for our coffers, with too great a court
And liberal largess, are grown somewhat light,
We are inforced to farm our royal realm;
The revenue whereof shall furnish us
For our affairs in hand: if that come short,
Our substitutes at home shall have blank charters;
Whereto, when they shall know what men are rich,
They shall subscribe them for large sums of gold   50
And send them after to supply our wants;
For we will make for Ireland presently.

Enter BUSHY.

Bushy, what news?
Bushy. Old John of Gaunt is grievous sick, my lord,
Suddenly taken; and hath sent post haste
To entreat your majesty to visit him.
K. Rich. Where lies he?
Bushy. At Ely House.
K. Rich. Now put it, God, in the physician's mind
To help him to his grave immediately!   60
The lining of his coffers shall make coats
To deck our soldiers for these Irish wars.
Come, gentlemen, let's all go visit him.
Pray God we may make haste, and come too late!
All. Amen.   [*Exeunt.*

---

8. **rheum,** tears. **12-13. for . . . word.** This clause is the antecedent of *that.* Aumerle says that he simulated grief, pretending to be overcome by it, in order to avoid saying "Farewell" to Bolingbroke. 16. **Marry,** an oath, originally "by Mary." 20. **doubt,** doubtful. 24. **his courtship to the common people.** Compare Bolingbroke's own account, *1 Henry IV,* III, ii, 46 ff. 29. **underbearing,** bearing, enduring. 30. **affects,** affections. 35. **reversion,** right of future possession.

37. **go,** let go. 38. **rebels . . . in Ireland.** Many of the colonies planted by Henry II in the "English Pale" had thrown off their allegiance and were in rebellion. 39. **Expedient manage,** expeditious management. 43. **too great a court.** Holinshed says that Richard "kept the greatest port, and maintained the most plentiful house that euer any king in England did either before his time or since." 45. **farm,** to let the right of collecting taxes, for a present cash payment, to the highest bidder. 48. **blank charters,** ready-drawn obligations, blank spaces being left for the names of the parties and the sums they were to provide. 50. **subscribe them,** they shall here write their names under. 58. **Ely House,** palace of the Bishop of Ely in Holborn.

ACT II.

Scene I. *Ely House.*

Enter John of Gaunt *sick, with the* Duke of York, *&c.*

Gaunt. Will the king come, that I may
    breathe my last
In wholesome counsel to his unstaid youth?
    York. Vex not yourself, nor strive not
        with your breath;
For all in vain comes counsel to his ear.
    Gaunt. O, but they say the tongues of
        dying men
Enforce attention like deep harmony:
Where words are scarce, they are seldom
    spent in vain,
For they breathe truth that breathe their
    words in pain.
He that no more must say is listen'd more
    Than they whom youth and ease have
        taught to glose;   10
More are men's ends mark'd than their lives
    before:
    The setting sun, and music at the close,
As the last taste of sweets, is sweetest last,
Writ in remembrance more than things long
    past:
Though Richard my life's counsel would not
    hear,
My death's sad tale may yet undeaf his
    ear.
    York. No; it is stopp'd with other flatter-
        ing sounds,
As praises, of whose taste the wise are
    fond,
Lascivious metres, to whose venom sound
The open ear of youth doth always listen;   20
Report of fashions in proud Italy,
Whose manners still our tardy apish nation
Limps after in base imitation.
Where doth the world thrust forth a
    vanity—

So it be new, there's no respect how vile—
That is not quickly buzz'd into his ears?
Then all too late comes counsel to be heard,
Where will doth mutiny with wit's regard.
Direct not him whose way himself will
    choose:
'Tis breath thou lack'st, and that breath
    wilt thou lose.   30
    Gaunt. Methinks I am a prophet new in-
        spired
And thus expiring do foretell of him:
His rash fierce blaze of riot cannot last,
For violent fires soon burn out themselves;
Small showers last long, but sudden storms
    are short;
He tires betimes that spurs too fast betimes;
With eager feeding food doth choke the
    feeder:
Light vanity, insatiate cormorant,
Consuming means, soon preys upon itself.
This royal throne of kings, this scepter'd isle,
This earth of majesty, this seat of Mars,   41
This other Eden, demi-paradise,
This fortress built by Nature for herself
Against infection and the hand of war,
This happy breed of men, this little world,
This precious stone set in the silver sea,
Which serves it in the office of a wall
Or as a moat defensive to a house,
Against the envy of less happier lands,
This blessed plot, this earth, this realm, this
    England,   50
This nurse, this teeming womb of royal
    kings,
Fear'd by their breed and famous by their
    birth,
Renowned for their deeds as far from home,
For Christian service and true chivalry,
As is the sepulchre in stubborn Jewry
Of the world's ransom, blessed Mary's Son,
This land of such dear souls, this dear dear
    land,
Dear for her reputation through the world,
Is now leased out, I die pronouncing it,
Like to a tenement or pelting farm: 60
England, bound in with the triumphant
    sea,
Whose rocky shore beats back the envious
    siege

Act II. Scene i. There are serious difficulties in the matter of real and dramatic time in this scene and the one which precedes it. We can suppose the lapse of only an hour or two between the scenes. In the earlier scene Bolingbroke has just departed on his exile. In II, i, 277 ff. he has been to France and is on his way back; besides, we are told (II, i, 167-168) that Richard has "prevented" him about his marriage. **2. unstaid,** thoughtless, rash. **5-16. O, but . . . ear.** The rhyming measures here and elsewhere characterize Gaunt's exalted manner of speech. **9. listen'd,** listened to. **10. glose,** flatter, deceive in speech. **12. close,** harmonious chords at the end of a piece of music. **16. undeaf,** make capable of hearing. **19. venom,** pernicious, poisonous. **21. proud Italy.** Ascham, Lyly, and other sixteenth-century writers complain of the growing influence of Italian luxury.

26. buzz'd, whispered; used contemptuously. **28. with wit's regard,** against the consideration due to reason. **38. cormorant,** glutton. **40-55. This royal . . . Jewry.** These lines, except line 50, were published in *England's Parnassus* (1600) and attributed to M. Dr. (Michael Drayton). **44. infection,** pollution; possibly, plague. **55. Jewry,** Judea. **60. pelting,** paltry.

Of watery Neptune, is now bound in with
  shame,
With inky blots and rotten parchment
  bonds:
That England, that was wont to conquer
  others,
Hath made a shameful conquest of itself.
Ah, would the scandal vanish with my life,
How happy then were my ensuing death!

Enter King Richard *and* Queen, Aumerle,
  Bushy, Green, Bagot, Ross, *and* Willoughby.

York. The king is come: deal mildly with
  his youth;
For young hot colts being raged do rage the
  more.   70
Queen. How fares our noble uncle, Lan-
  caster?
K. Rich. What comfort, man? how is 't
  with aged Gaunt?
Gaunt. O, how that name befits my com-
  position!
Old Gaunt indeed, and gaunt in being old:
Within me grief hath kept a tedious fast;
And who abstains from meat that is not
  gaunt?
For sleeping England long time have I
  watch'd;
Watching breeds leanness, leanness is all
  gaunt:
The pleasure that some fathers feed upon,
Is my strict fast; I mean, my children's
  looks;   80
And therein fasting, hast thou made me
  gaunt:
Gaunt am I for the grave, gaunt as a grave,
Whose hollow womb inherits nought but
  bones.
K. Rich. Can sick men play so nicely with
  their names?
Gaunt. No, misery makes sport to mock
  itself:
Since thou dost seek to kill my name in
  me,
I mock my name, great king, to flatter thee.
K. Rich. Should dying men flatter with
  those that live?

Gaunt. No, no, men living flatter those
  that die.
K. Rich. Thou, now a-dying, say'st thou
  flatterest me.   90
Gaunt. O, no! thou diest, though I the
  sicker be.
K. Rich. I am in health, I breathe, and see
  thee ill.
Gaunt. Now He that made me knows I see
  thee ill;
Ill in myself to see, and in thee seeing ill.
Thy death-bed is no lesser than thy land
Wherein thou liest in reputation sick;
And thou, too careless patient as thou art,
Commit'st thy anointed body to the cure
Of those physicians that first wounded thee:
A thousand flatterers sit within thy crown,100
Whose compass is no bigger than thy head;
And yet, incaged in so small a verge,
The waste is no whit lesser than thy land.
O, had thy grandsire with a prophet's eye
Seen how his son's son should destroy his
  sons,
From forth thy reach he would have laid thy
  shame,
Deposing thee before thou wert possess'd,
Which art possess'd now to depose thyself.
Why, cousin, wert thou regent of the world,
It were a shame to let this land by lease;   110
But for thy world enjoying but this land,
Is it not more than shame to shame it so?
Landlord of England art thou now, not king:
Thy state of law is bondslave to the law;
And thou—
K. Rich.   A lunatic lean-witted fool,
Presuming on an ague's privilege,
Darest with thy frozen admonition
Make pale our cheek, chasing the royal blood
With fury from his native residence.
Now, by my seat's right royal majesty,   120
Wert thou not brother to great Edward's
  son,
This tongue that runs so roundly in thy head
Should run thy head from thy unreverent
  shoulders.
  Gaunt. O, spare me not, my brother Ed-
  ward's son,

---

70. **raged,** enraged. 73. **composition,** constitution.
83. **inherits,** possesses. 84. **Can . . . names?** Coleridge answers: "Yes! on a deathbed there is a feeling
which may make all things appear but as puns and equiv-
ocations. And a passion there is that carries off its own
excess by plays on words as naturally, and therefore, as
appropriately to drama, as by gesticulation, looks, or
tones." **nicely,** delicately, fantastically.

102. **verge,** circle, ring; technically, "the compass
about the king's court which extended for twelve miles."
103. **waste,** a legal use meaning "destruction of houses,
woods, lands, etc., done by a tenant to the prejudice of
the heir" (Onions). 108. **possess'd,** seized with madness. 114. **state of law,** legal status as a king. 118.
Make pale our cheek. Richard's physical sensitiveness, which caused him to turn pale readily (see III, i,
75; III, iii, 67), is recorded by Froissart and other
chroniclers. 122. **roundly,** unceremoniously.

For that I was his father Edward's son;
That blood already, like the pelican,
Hast thou tapp'd out and drunkenly ca-
    roused:
My brother Gloucester, plain well-meaning
    soul,
Whom fair befal in heaven 'mongst happy
    souls!
May be a precedent and witness good   130
That thou respect'st not spilling Edward's
    blood:
Join with the present sickness that I have;
And thy unkindness be like crooked age,
To crop at once a too long wither'd flower.
Live in thy shame, but die not shame with
    thee!
These words hereafter thy tormentors be!
Convey me to my bed, then to my grave:
Love they to live that love and honour have.
          [Exit, borne off by his Attendants.
  K. Rich. And let them die that age and
    sullens have;
For both hast thou, and both become the
    grave.   140
  York. I do beseech your majesty, impute
    his words
To wayward sickliness and age in him:
He loves you, on my life, and holds you dear
As Harry Duke of Hereford, were he here.
  K. Rich. Right, you say true: as Here-
    ford's love, so his;
As theirs, so mine; and all be as it is.

          Enter NORTHUMBERLAND.

  North. My liege, old Gaunt commends
    him to your majesty.
  K. Rich. What says he?
  North.   Nay, nothing; all is said:
His tongue is now a stringless instrument;
Words, life and all, old Lancaster hath spent.
  York. Be York the next that must be
    bankrupt so!   151
Though death be poor, it ends a mortal woe.
  K. Rich. The ripest fruit first falls, and so
    doth he;
His time is spent, our pilgrimage must be.
So much for that. Now for our Irish wars:
We must supplant those rough rug-headed
    kerns,

Which live like venom where no venom else
But only they have privilege to live.
And for these great affairs do ask some
    charge,
Towards our assistance we do seize to us 160
The plate, coin, revenues and moveables,
Whereof our uncle Gaunt did stand pos-
    sess'd.
  York. How long shall I be patient? ah,
    how long
Shall tender duty make me suffer wrong?
Not Gloucester's death, nor Hereford's ban-
    ishment,
Not Gaunt's rebukes, nor England's private
    wrongs,
Nor the prevention of poor Bolingbroke
About his marriage, nor my own disgrace,
Have ever made me sour my patient cheek,
Or bend one wrinkle on my sovereign's face.
I am the last of noble Edward's sons,   171
Of whom thy father, Prince of Wales, was
    first:
In war was never lion raged more fierce,
In peace was never gentle lamb more mild,
Than was that young and princely gentle-
    man.
His face thou hast, for even so look'd he,
Accomplish'd with the number of thy hours;
But when he frown'd, it was against the
    French
And not against his friends; his noble hand
Did win what he did spend and spent not
    that   180
Which his triumphant father's hand had won;
His hands were guilty of no kindred blood,
But bloody with the enemies of his kin.
O Richard! York is too far gone with grief,
Or else he never would compare between.
  K. Rich. Why, uncle, what's the matter?
  York.   O my liege,
Pardon me, if you please; if not, I, pleased
Not to be pardon'd, am content withal.
Seek you to seize and gripe into your hands
The royalties and rights of banish'd Here-
    ford?   190
Is not Gaunt dead, and doth not Hereford
    live?

126. pelican, allusion to the belief that the pelican
fed its young on its own blood. 139. sullens, morose-
ness, sullenness. 144. As Harry Duke of Hereford,
i.e., as he holds Harry, etc. Richard purposely misin-
terprets the ambiguous speech of York. 156. rug-
headed, rough-haired. kerns, Irish foot-soldiers.

157. no venom else, allusion to the freedom of
Ireland from reptiles, traditionally ascribed to St.
Patrick. 163. How . . . patient? Although York's
reproof is quite as severe as Gaunt's, it does not anger
the king, since he is not planning to injure York as he
is Gaunt. 166. Gaunt's rebukes, i.e., the rebuke
given to Gaunt. 173. raged, may equal enraged, as in
line 70, or we may understand a relative omitted after
lion. 177. Accomplish'd, equipped. 185. compare
between, draw comparisons. 190. royalties, privileges
belonging to a member of the royal house.

Was not Gaunt just, and is not Harry true?
Did not the one deserve to have an heir?
Is not his heir a well-deserving son?
Take Hereford's rights away, and take from
    Time
His charters and his customary rights;
Let not to-morrow then ensue to-day;
Be not thyself; for how art thou a king
But by fair sequence and succession?
Now, afore God—God forbid I say true!—200
If you do wrongfully seize Hereford's rights,
Call in the letters patents that he hath
By his attorneys-general to sue
His livery, and deny his offer'd homage,
You pluck a thousand dangers on your head,
You lose a thousand well-disposed hearts
And prick my tender patience to those
    thoughts
Which honour and allegiance cannot think.
    K. Rich. Think what you will, we seize
      into our hands
His plate, his goods, his money and his lands.
    York. I'll not be by the while: my liege,
      farewell: 211
What will ensue hereof, there's none can tell;
But by bad courses may be understood
That their events can never fall out good.
                       [Exit.
    K. Rich. Go, Bushy, to the Earl of Wilt-
    shire straight:
Bid him repair to us to Ely House
To see this business. To-morrow next
We will for Ireland; and 'tis time, I trow:
And we create, in absence of ourself,
Our uncle York lord governor of England; 220
For he is just and always loved us well.
Come on, our queen: to-morrow must we
    part;
Be merry, for our time of stay is short.
          [Flourish. Exeunt King, Queen,
              Aumerle, Bushy, Green,
                    and Bagot.
    North. Well, lords, the Duke of Lancaster
    is dead.
    Ross. And living too; for now his son is
    duke.
    Willo. Barely in title, not in revenues.

    North. Richly in both, if justice had her
    right.
    Ross. My heart is great; but it must break
    with silence,
Ere 't be disburden'd with a liberal tongue.
    North. Nay, speak thy mind; and let him
    ne'er speak more   230
That speaks thy words again to do thee
    harm!
    Willo. Tends that thou wouldst speak to
    the Duke of Hereford?
If it be so, out with it boldly, man;
Quick is mine ear to hear of good towards
    him.
    Ross. No good at all that I can do for him:
Unless you call it good to pity him,
Bereft and gelded of his patrimony.
    North. Now, afore God, 'tis shame such
    wrongs are borne
In him, a royal prince, and many moe
Of noble blood in this declining land.   240
The king is not himself, but basely led
By flatterers; and what they will inform,
Merely in hate, 'gainst any of us all,
That will the king severely prosecute
'Gainst us, our lives, our children, and our
    heirs.
    Ross. The commons hath he pill'd with
    grievous taxes,
†And quite lost their hearts: the nobles hath
    he fined
For ancient quarrels, and quite lost their
    hearts.
    Willo. And daily new exactions are
    devised,
As blanks, benevolences, and I wot not
    what:
But what, o' God's name, doth become of
    this?   251
    North. Wars have not wasted it, for
    warr'd he hath not,
But basely yielded upon compromise
That which his noble ancestors achieved
    with blows:
More hath he spent in peace than they in
    wars.
    Ross. The Earl of Wiltshire hath the
    realm in farm.

---

197. **ensue**, follow upon. 202. **Call . . . patents.**
This occurred some six weeks after Gaunt's death.
letters patents, letters addressed by a sovereign to the
patentee granting him some dignity, office, or privilege.
203. **attorneys-general,** deputies, legal substitutes.
220. **York lord governor.** It is the acme of Richard's
tragic blindness that he should appoint to the regency
a man whose loyalty was already strained to the break-
ing-point.

227. **if . . . right.** This conversation marks the
beginning of the counterplot. 242. **inform,** charge
against (used technically). 246. **pill'd,** plundered,
robbed. 247. **And . . . fined.** This line is defective in
meter, and is probably corrupt; Pope omitted *quite.* 250.
blanks, *cartes blanches,* referred to in I, iv, 48. 253.
basely yielded, allusion to Richard's unpopular foreign
policy of peace with France.

Willo. The king's grown bankrupt, like a broken man.

North. Reproach and dissolution hangeth over him.

Ross. He hath not money for these Irish wars,
His burthenous taxations notwithstanding,
But by the robbing of the banish'd duke. 261

North. His noble kinsman: most degenerate king!
But, lords, we hear this fearful tempest sing,
Yet seek no shelter to avoid the storm;
We see the wind sit sore upon our sails,
And yet we strike not, but securely perish.

Ross. We see the very wreck that we must suffer;
And unavoided is the danger now,
For suffering so the causes of our wreck.

North. Not so; even through the hollow eyes of death 270
I spy life peering; but I dare not say
How near the tidings of our comfort is.

Willo. Nay, let us share thy thoughts, as thou dost ours.

Ross. Be confident to speak, Northumberland:
We three are but thyself; and, speaking so,
Thy words are but as thoughts; therefore, be bold.

North. Then thus: I have from Port le Blanc, a bay
In Brittany, received intelligence
That Harry Duke of Hereford, Rainold Lord Cobham,
† 280
That late broke from the Duke of Exeter,
His brother, Archbishop late of Canterbury,
Sir Thomas Erpingham, Sir John Ramston,
Sir John Norbery, Sir Robert Waterton and Francis Quoint,
All these well furnish'd by the Duke of Bretagne
With eight tall ships, three thousand men of war,
Are making hither with all due expedience

And shortly mean to touch our northern shore:
Perhaps they had ere this, but that they stay
The first departing of the king for Ireland. 290
If then we shall shake off our slavish yoke,
Imp out our drooping country's broken wing,
Redeem from broking pawn the blemish'd crown,
Wipe off the dust that hides our sceptre's gilt
And make high majesty look like itself,
Away with me in post to Ravenspurgh;
But if you faint, as fearing to do so,
Stay and be secret, and myself will go.

Ross. To horse, to horse! urge doubts to them that fear.

Willo. Hold out my horse, and I will first be there.   [*Exeunt.* 300

SCENE II. *Windsor Castle.*

Enter QUEEN, BUSHY, *and* BAGOT.

Bushy. Madam, your majesty is too much sad:
You promised, when you parted with the king,
To lay aside life-harming heaviness
And entertain a cheerful disposition.

Queen. To please the king I did; to please myself
I cannot do it; yet I know no cause
Why I should welcome such a guest as grief,
Save bidding farewell to so sweet a guest
As my sweet Richard: yet again, methinks,
Some unborn sorrow, ripe in fortune's womb,
Is coming towards me, and my inward soul 11
With nothing trembles: at some thing it grieves,
More than with parting from my lord the king.

Bushy. Each substance of a grief hath twenty shadows,
Which shows like grief itself, but is not so;
For sorrow's eye, glazed with blinding tears,
Divides one thing entire to many objects;

---

266. **strike**, furl (of sails). **securely**, heedlessly, carelessly. 268. **unavoided**, unavoidable. 280. The break indicated here may be due to an omission of a line by the printer. Holinshed records that "the earle of Arundels sonne, named Thomas, which was kept in the duke of Exeters house, escaped out of the realme . . . and went to his vncle Thomas Arundell late archbishop of Canturburie." Malone supplying this detail from Holinshed inserts here the line, "The son of Richard Earl of Arundel." This puts the text into accord with Holinshed, since it is this Thomas and not Lord Cobham who escaped from the Duke of Exeter. 286. **tall**, large, stout. 287. **expedience**, expedition, swiftness.

292 **Imp out**, piece out; a term from falconry meaning to attach new feathers to a disabled wing of a bird. 293. **broking pawn**, the security held by a broker; used scornfully. 294. **gilt**, gold. 296. **Away . . . Ravenspurgh.** The Earl of Northumberland, head of the powerful family of the Percys, is the leader among the nobles in the rebellion against Richard; see V, i, 55 ff. *Ravenspurgh* was a busy seaport in Yorkshire on the Humber, destroyed since by the sea.
Scene ii. 9. **my sweet Richard.** "The amiable part of Richard's character is brought full upon us by his queen's few words" (Coleridge).

Like perspectives, which rightly gazed upon
Show nothing but confusion, eyed awry
Distinguish form: so your sweet majesty,   20
Looking awry upon your lord's departure,
Find shapes of grief, more than himself, to
wail;
Which, look'd on as it is, is nought but
shadows
Of what it is not. Then, thrice-gracious
queen,
More than your lord's departure weep not:
more's not seen;
Or if it be, 'tis with false sorrow's eye,
Which for things true weeps things imag-
inary.
   Queen. It may be so; but yet my inward
soul
Persuades me it is otherwise: howe'er it be,
I cannot but be sad; so heavy sad   30
As, though on thinking on no thought I
think,
Makes me with heavy nothing faint and
shrink.
   Bushy. 'Tis nothing but conceit, my
gracious lady.
   Queen. 'Tis nothing less: conceit is still
derived
From some forefather grief; mine is not so,
For nothing hath begot my something
grief;
Or something hath the nothing that I grieve:
'Tis in reversion that I do possess;
But what it is, that is not yet known; what
I cannot name; 'tis nameless woe, I wot.   40

Enter GREEN.

   Green. God save your majesty! and well
met, gentlemen:
I hope the king is not yet shipp'd for Ireland.
   Queen. Why hopest thou so? 'tis better
hope he is;
For his designs crave haste, his haste good
hope:
Then wherefore dost thou hope he is not
shipp'd?

Green. That he, our hope, might have
retired his power,
And driven into despair an enemy's hope,
Who strongly hath set footing in this land:
The banish'd Bolingbroke repeals himself,
And with uplifted arms is safe arrived   50
At Ravenspurgh.
   Queen.   Now God in heaven forbid!
   Green. Ah, madam, 'tis too true: and that
is worse,
The Lord Northumberland, his son young
Henry Percy,
The Lords of Ross, Beaumond, and Wil-
loughby,
With all their powerful friends, are fled to
him.
   Bushy. Why have you not proclaim'd
Northumberland
And all the rest revolted faction traitors?
   Green. We have: whereupon the Earl of
Worcester
Hath broke his staff, resign'd his steward-
ship,
And all the household servants fled with him
To Bolingbroke.   61
   Queen. So, Green, thou art the midwife to
my woe,
And Bolingbroke my sorrow's dismal heir:
Now hath my soul brought forth her prodigy,
And I, a gasping new-deliver'd mother,
Have woe to woe, sorrow to sorrow join'd.
   Bushy. Despair not, madam.
   Queen.   Who shall hinder me?
I will despair, and be at enmity
With cozening hope: he is a flatterer,
A parasite, a keeper back of death,   70
Who gently would dissolve the bands of life,
Which false hope lingers in extremity.

Enter YORK.

   Green. Here comes the Duke of York.
   Queen. With signs of war about his aged
neck:
O, full of careful business are his looks!
Uncle, for God's sake, speak comfortable
words.
   York. Should I do so, I should belie my
thoughts:

---

18. **perspectives**, pictures or figures made to appear
distorted or confused except when seen from a special
point of view. **rightly**, directly, straight. 20. **Distinguish form**, make the form distinct. 31. **As . . .
think**, as though in thinking I fix my thoughts on
nothing. 34. **'Tis nothing less**, i.e., it is anything but
that. **conceit**, conception, fancy. 36-38. **For nothing
. . . possess.** As in line 12, the Queen's play on the
antithesis between *something* and *nothing* is rather
confusing. She says: Either *nothing* caused her real
grief, or else there is *something* in this unknown subject
of her grief. The cause of the grief can only be revealed
in the future (*in reversion*).

59. **broke his staff**, i.e., in token of the resignation
of his office of Lord High Steward. Thomas Percy, Earl
of Worcester, brother of the Earl of Northumberland,
provokes the rebellion of the Percys in *1* and *2 Henry IV*.
64. **prodigy**, monstrous birth. 69. **cozening**, cheating.
72. **lingers**, causes to linger. 74. **signs of war**. York
is in armor. 76. **comfortable**, affording comfort.

Comfort's in heaven; and we are on the earth,
Where nothing lives but crosses, cares and grief.
Your husband, he is gone to save far off, 80
Whilst others come to make him lose at home:
Here am I left to underprop his land,
Who, weak with age, cannot support my-self:
Now comes the sick hour that his surfeit made;
Now shall he try his friends that flatter'd him.

Enter a Servant.

Serv. My lord, your son was gone before I came.
York. He was? Why, so! go all which way it will!
The nobles they are fled, the commons they are cold,
And will, I fear, revolt on Hereford's side.
Sirrah, get thee to Plashy, to my sister Gloucester; 90
Bid her send me presently a thousand pound:
Hold, take my ring.
Serv. My lord, I had forgot to tell your lordship,
To-day, as I came by, I called there;
But I shall grieve you to report the rest.
York. What is 't, knave?
Serv. An hour before I came, the duchess died.
York. God for his mercy! what a tide of woes
Comes rushing on this woeful land at once!
I know not what to do: I would to God, 100
So my untruth had not provoked him to it,
The king had cut off my head with my brother's.
What, are there no posts dispatch'd for Ireland?
How shall we do for money for these wars?
Come, sister,—cousin, I would say,—pray, pardon me.
Go, fellow, get thee home, provide some carts
And bring away the armour that is there.
[Exit Servant.

Gentlemen, will you go muster men?
If I know how or which way to order these affairs
Thus thrust disorderly into my hands, 110
Never believe me. Both are my kinsmen:
The one is my sovereign, whom both my oath
And duty bids defend; the other again
Is my kinsman, whom the king hath wrong'd,
Whom conscience and my kindred bids to right.
Well, somewhat we must do. Come, cousin, I'll
Dispose of you.
Gentlemen, go, muster up your men,
And meet me presently at Berkeley.
I should to Plashy too; 120
But time will not permit: all is uneven,
And every thing is left at six and seven.
[Exeunt York and Queen.
Bushy. The wind sits fair for news to go to Ireland,
But none returns. For us to levy power
Proportionable to the enemy
Is all unpossible.
Green. Besides, our nearness to the king in love
Is near the hate of those love not the king.
Bagot. And that's the wavering com-mons: for their love 129
Lies in their purses, and whoso empties them
By so much fills their hearts with deadly hate.
Bushy. Wherein the king stands generally condemn'd.
Bagot. If judgement lie in them, then so do we,
Because we ever have been near the king.
Green. Well, I will for refuge straight to Bristol castle:
The Earl of Wiltshire is already there.
Bushy. Thither will I with you; for little office
The hateful commons will perform for us,
Except like curs to tear us all to pieces.
Will you go along with us? 140
Bagot. No; I will to Ireland to his majesty.
Farewell: if heart's presages be not vain,
We three here part that ne'er shall meet again.

---

86. **your son**, the Duke of Aumerle, who had accom-panied Richard to Ireland. 90. **Sirrah**, form used in addressing inferiors. 96. **knave**, familiar term in addressing servants (without evil significance). 97. **the duchess died**. The death of the Duchess of Gloucester is anticipated by several months (in order to add to York's embarrassment).

122. **at six and seven**, at sixes and sevens, in confu-sion. 125. **Proportionable**, proportionate.

Bushy. That's as York thrives to beat back Bolingbroke.

Green. Alas, poor duke! the task he under-takes
Is numbering sands and drinking oceans dry:
Where one on his side fights, thousands will fly.
Farewell at once, for once, for all, and ever.

Bushy. Well, we may meet again.

Bagot.   I fear me, never.
                                    [*Exeunt.*

SCENE III. *Wilds in Gloucestershire.*

Enter BOLINGBROKE *and* NORTHUMBERLAND,
with Forces.

Boling. How far is it, my lord, to Berkeley now?

North. Believe me, noble lord,
I am a stranger here in Gloucestershire:
These high wild hills and rough uneven ways
Draws out our miles, and makes them wearisome;
And yet your fair discourse hath been as sugar,
Making the hard way sweet and delectable.
But I bethink me what a weary way
From Ravenspurgh to Cotswold will be found
In Ross and Willoughby, wanting your com-pany,   10
Which, I protest, hath very much beguiled
The tediousness and process of my travel:
But theirs is sweetened with the hope to have
The present benefit which I possess;
And hope to joy is little less in joy
Than hope enjoy'd: by this the weary lords
Shall make their way seem short, as mine hath done
By sight of what I have, your noble com-pany.

Boling. Of much less value is my com-pany
Than your good words. But who comes here?   20

Enter HENRY PERCY.

North. It is my son, young Harry Percy,

Sent from my brother Worcester, whenceso-ever.
Harry, how fares your uncle?

Percy. I had thought, my lord, to have learn'd his health of you.

North. Why, is he not with the queen?

Percy. No, my good lord; he hath forsook the court,
Broken his staff of office and dispersed
The household of the king.

North.   What was his reason?
He was not so resolved when last we spake together.

Percy. Because your lordship was pro-claimed traitor.   30
But he, my lord, is gone to Ravenspurgh,
To offer service to the Duke of Hereford,
And sent me over by Berkeley, to dis-cover
What power the Duke of York had levied there;
Then with directions to repair to Ravens-purgh.

North. Have you forgot the Duke of Here-ford, boy?

Percy. No, my good lord, for that is not forgot
Which ne'er I did remember: to my know-ledge,
I never in my life did look on him.

North. Then learn to know him now; this is the duke.   40

Percy. My gracious lord, I tender you my service,
Such as it is, being tender, raw and young;
Which elder days shall ripen and confirm
To more approved service and desert.

Boling. I thank thee, gentle Percy; and be sure
I count myself in nothing else so happy
As in a soul remembering my good friends;
And, as my fortune ripens with thy love,
It shall be still thy true love's recom-pense:
My heart this covenant makes, my hand thus seals it.   50

North. How far is it to Berkeley? and what stir
Keeps good old York there with his men of war?

Scene iii. 9. **Cotswold,** hilly district in Gloucester-shire. 12. **tediousness and process,** tedious process. 15. **joy,** enjoy.

22. **whencesoever,** from wherever. 42. **raw and young.** Henry Percy, called "Hotspur," was born in 1364; Prince Hal in 1388. Shakespeare represents them as of the same age. 45-49. **I thank thee . . . recom-pense.** Cf. *I Henry IV*, I, iii, 251 ff., where Hotspur bitterly recalls this speech.

Percy. There stands the castle, by yon
   tuft of trees,
Mann'd with three hundred men, as I have
   heard;
And in it are the Lords of York, Berkeley,
   and Seymour;
None else of name and noble estimate.

Enter Ross *and* Willoughby.

North. Here come the Lords of Ross and
   Willoughby,
Bloody with spurring, fiery-red with haste.
   Boling. Welcome, my lords. I wot your
      love pursues
A banish'd traitor: all my treasury   60
Is yet but unfelt thanks, which more enrich'd
Shall be your love and labour's recompense.
   Ross. Your presence makes us rich, most
      noble lord.
   Willo. And far surmounts our labour to
      attain it.
   Boling. Evermore thanks, the exchequer
      of the poor;
Which, till my infant fortune comes to
   years,
Stands for my bounty. But who comes here?

Enter Berkeley.

North. It is my Lord of Berkeley, as I
   guess.
   Berk. My Lord of Hereford, my message
      is to you.
   Boling. My lord, my answer is—to Lan-
      caster;   70
And I am come to seek that name in Eng-
   land;
And I must find that title in your tongue,
Before I make reply to aught you say.
   Berk. Mistake me not, my lord; 'tis not
      my meaning
To raze one title of your honour out:
To you, my lord, I come, what lord you will,
From the most gracious regent of this land,
The Duke of York, to know what pricks you
   on
To take advantage of the absent time
And fright our native peace with self-born
   arms.   80

Enter York *attended.*

   Boling. I shall not need transport my
      words by you;
Here comes his grace in person.
                My noble uncle! [*Kneels.*
   York. Show me thy humble heart, and not
      thy knee,
Whose duty is deceivable and false.
   Boling. My gracious uncle—
   York.   Tut, tut!
Grace me no grace, nor uncle me no uncle:
I am no traitor's uncle; and that word
   'grace'
In an ungracious mouth is but profane.
Why have those banish'd and forbidden
   legs
Dared once to touch a dust of England's
   ground?   91
But then more 'why?' why have they dared
   to march
So many miles upon her peaceful bosom,
Frighting her pale-faced villages with war
And ostentation of despised arms?
Comest thou because the anointed king is
   hence?
Why, foolish boy, the king is left behind,
And in my loyal bosom lies his power.
Were I but now the lord of such hot youth
As when brave Gaunt, thy father, and my-
   self   100
Rescued the Black Prince, that young Mars
   of men,
From forth the ranks of many thousand
   French,
O, then how quickly should this arm of
   mine,
Now prisoner to the palsy, chastise thee
And minister correction to thy fault!
   Boling. My gracious uncle, let me know
      my fault:
On what condition stands it and wherein?
   York. Even in condition of the worst
      degree,
In gross rebellion and detested treason:
Thou art a banish'd man, and here art come
Before the expiration of thy time,   111
In braving arms against thy sovereign.
   Boling. As I was banish'd, I was banish'd
      Hereford;

61. **unfelt**, impalpable, not perceived. 70. **Lancaster.** Bolingbroke will enter into no negotiations
unless his proper title is given him. 79. **the absent
time**, the time of absence. 80. **native**, entitled (i.e.,
to peace) by birth, rightful. **self-born**, indigenous,
home-sprung (Clark and Wright); some editors read
self-borne, i.e., borne for himself, not for the king.

84. **deceivable**, deceptive. 87. **Grace me no grace.**
York, as he begins, intends to do his duty by the king;
later he is won over by Bolingbroke. 91. **dust**, a
particle of dust. 92. **more 'why,'** more questions to
ask. 107. **condition**, character, quality.

But as I come, I come for Lancaster.
And, noble uncle, I beseech your grace
Look on my wrongs with an indifferent
eye:
You are my father, for methinks in you
I see old Gaunt alive; O, then, my father,
Will you permit that I shall stand con-
demn'd
A wandering vagabond; my rights and royal-
ties   120
Pluck'd from my arms perforce and given
away
To upstart unthrifts? Wherefore was I born?
If that my cousin king be King of England,
It must be granted I am Duke of Lancaster.
You have a son, Aumerle, my noble cousin;
Had you first died, and he been thus trod
down,
He should have found his uncle Gaunt a
father,
To rouse his wrongs and chase them to the
bay.
I am denied to sue my livery here,
And yet my letters-patents give me leave: 130
My father's goods are all distrain'd and sold,
And these and all are all amiss employ'd.
What would you have me do? I am a sub-
ject,
And I challenge law: attorneys are denied
me;
And therefore personally I lay my claim
To my inheritance of free descent.
    North. The noble duke hath been too
much abused.
    Ross. It stands your grace upon to do
him right.
    Willo. Base men by his endowments are
made great.
    York. My lords of England, let me tell
you this: 140
I have had feeling of my cousin's wrongs
And labour'd all I could to do him right;
But in this kind to come, in braving arms,
Be his own carver and cut out his way,
To find out right with wrong, it may not be;
And you that do abet him in this kind
Cherish rebellion and are rebels all.

    North. The noble duke hath sworn his
coming is
But for his own; and for the right of that
We all have strongly sworn to give him aid;
And let him ne'er see joy that breaks that
oath!   151
    York. Well, well, I see the issue of these
arms:
I cannot mend it, I must needs confess,
Because my power is weak and all ill left:
But if I could, by Him that gave me life,
I would attach you all and make you stoop
Unto the sovereign mercy of the king;
But since I cannot, be it known to you
I do remain as neuter. So, fare you well;
Unless you please to enter in the castle   160
And there repose you for this night.
    Boling. An offer, uncle, that we will ac-
cept:
But we must win your grace to go with us
To Bristol castle, which they say is held
By Bushy, Bagot and their complices,
The caterpillars of the commonwealth,
Which I have sworn to weed and pluck away.
    York. It may be I will go with you: but
yet I'll pause;
For I am loath to break our country's laws.
Nor friends nor foes, to me welcome you are:
Things past redress are now with me past
care.   171
                                                              [*Exeunt.*

Scene IV.   *A camp in Wales.*

Enter Salisbury *and a* Welsh Captain.

    Cap. My Lord of Salisbury, we have
stay'd ten days,
And hardly kept our countrymen together,
And yet we hear no tidings from the king;
Therefore we will disperse ourselves: fare-
well.
    Sal. Stay yet another day, thou trusty
Welshman:
The king reposeth all his confidence in thee.
    Cap. 'Tis thought the king is dead; we
will not stay.
The bay-trees in our country are all wither'd

---

114. **I come for Lancaster**, i.e., in the character of Lancaster. Compare *2 Henry IV*, IV, v, 184-186.
116. **indifferent**, impartial. 122. **unthrifts**, spend-thrifts, prodigals. 128. **to the bay**, to the extremity where the hunted animal turns on its pursuers. 129. **sue my livery**, sue for legal delivery of my freehold as heir.
131. **distrain'd**, seized by legal process. 134. **chal-lenge**, claim. 136. **free**, noble, honorable. 138. **stands . . . upon**, is incumbent upon. 143. **kind**, manner.

154. **ill left**, left with inadequate means. 156. **attach**, arrest. 159. **neuter**. Neutrality on York's part is hostility to Richard; but he is practically Boling-broke's prisoner. See line 164. 165. **Bagot**. He had gone to Ireland, not to Bristol; see II, ii, 141. **complices**, accomplices.
Scene iv. 8. **bay-trees**. "In this yeare . . . old baie trees withered, and afterwards . . . grew greene againe; a strange sight, and supposed to import some vnknowne euent" (Holinshed; in second edition, 1586, only).

And meteors fright the fixed stars of heaven;
The pale-faced moon looks bloody on the
    earth   10
And lean-look'd prophets whisper fearful
    change;
Rich men look sad and ruffians dance and
    leap,
The one in fear to lose what they enjoy,
The other to enjoy by rage and war:
These signs forerun the death or fall of
    kings.
Farewell: our countrymen are gone and fled,
As well assured Richard their king is dead.
                           [*Exit.*
  Sal. Ah, Richard, with the eyes of heavy
    mind
I see thy glory like a shooting star
Fall to the base earth from the firmament. 20
Thy sun sets weeping in the lowly west,
Witnessing storms to come, woe and unrest:
Thy friends are fled to wait upon thy foes,
And crossly to thy good all fortune goes.
                           [*Exit.*

ACT III.

Scene I. *Bristol. Before the castle.*

Enter Bolingbroke, York, Northumberland, Ross, Percy, Willoughby, *with*
Bushy *and* Green, *prisoners.*

  Boling. Bring forth these men.
Bushy and Green, I will not vex your souls—
Since presently your souls must part your
    bodies—
With too much urging your pernicious lives,
For 'twere no charity; yet, to wash your
    blood
From off my hands, here in the view of men
I will unfold some causes of your deaths.
You have misled a prince, a royal king,
A happy gentleman in blood and lineaments,
By you unhappied and disfigured clean: 10
You have in manner with your sinful hours
Made a divorce betwixt his queen and him,
Broke the possession of a royal bed
And stain'd the beauty of a fair queen's
    cheeks

With tears drawn from her eyes by your foul
    wrongs.
Myself, a prince by fortune of my birth,
Near to the king in blood, and near in love
Till you did make him misinterpret me,
Have stoop'd my neck under your in-
    juries,
And sigh'd my English breath in foreign
    clouds,   20
Eating the bitter bread of banishment;
Whilst you have fed upon my signories,
Dispark'd my parks and fell'd my forest
    woods,
From my own windows torn my household
    coat,
Razed out my imprese, leaving me no sign,
Save men's opinions and my living blood,
To show the world I am a gentleman.
This and much more, much more than twice
    all this,
Condemns you to the death. See them de-
    liver'd over
To execution and the hand of death.   30
  Bushy. More welcome is the stroke of
    death to me
Than Bolingbroke to England. Lords, fare-
    well.
  Green. My comfort is that heaven will
    take our souls
And plague injustice with the pains of hell.
  Boling. My Lord Northumberland, see
    them dispatch'd.
      [*Exeunt Northumberland and others,*
                 with the prisoners.
Uncle, you say the queen is at your house;
For God's sake, fairly let her be entreated:
Tell her I send to her my kind commends;
Take special care my greetings be deliv-
    er'd.
  York. A gentleman of mine I have dis-
    patch'd   40
With letters of your love to her at large.
  Boling. Thanks, gentle uncle. Come,
    lords, away,
To fight with Glendower and his com-
    plices:
Awhile to work, and after holiday.
                         [*Exeunt.*

---

11. lean-look'd, lean-looking. **24. crossly,** adversely.
Act III. Scene i. **4. urging,** emphasizing as reasons
(for your executions). **9. happy,** fortunate. **10. unhappied,** made wretched, ruined. **clean,** completely.
12. Made a divorce. There is no basis for this charge;
but see V, i, 71 ff. It may have been suggested by the
situation in Marlowe's *Edward II.* **14. fair queen's.**
Queen Isabella, daughter of Charles VI of France, was
only eleven years old at this time.

22. signories, lordships, estates. **23. Dispark'd,**
destroyed the enclosures and thrown the parks open. **24.
my household coat,** coat of arms, frequently emblaz-
oned on stained or painted windows. **25. imprese,**
device, emblematic design. **37. entreated,** treated.
43. Glendower. Owen Glendower was not at this time
in arms against Bolingbroke; perhaps Bolingbroke thinks
he is the Welsh commander (see preceding scene).

Scene II. *The coast of Wales. A castle in view.*

Drums: flourish and colours. Enter King Richard, *the* Bishop of Carlisle, Aumerle, *and Soldiers.*

K. Rich. Barkloughly castle call they this at hand?

Aum. Yea, my lord. How brooks your grace the air,
After your late tossing on the breaking seas?

K. Rich. Needs must I like it well: I weep for joy
To stand upon my kingdom once again.
Dear earth, I do salute thee with my hand,
Though rebels wound thee with their horses' hoofs:
As a long-parted mother with her child
Plays fondly with her tears and smiles in meeting,
So, weeping, smiling, greet I thee, my earth,
And do thee favours with my royal hands. 11
Feed not thy sovereign's foe, my gentle earth,
Nor with thy sweets comfort his ravenous sense;
But let thy spiders, that suck up thy venom,
And heavy-gaited toads lie in their way,
Doing annoyance to the treacherous feet
Which with usurping steps do trample thee:
Yield stinging nettles to mine enemies;
And when they from thy bosom pluck a flower,
Guard it, I pray thee, with a lurking adder 20
Whose double tongue may with a mortal touch
Throw death upon thy sovereign's enemies.
Mock not my senseless conjuration, lords:
This earth shall have a feeling and these stones
Prove armed soldiers, ere her native king
Shall falter under foul rebellion's arms.

Car. Fear not, my lord: that Power that made you king
Hath power to keep you king in spite of all.
The means that heaven yields must be embraced,

And not neglected; else, if heaven would, 30
And we will not, heaven's offer we refuse,
The proffer'd means of succour and redress.

Aum. He means, my lord, that we are too remiss;
Whilst Bolingbroke, through our security,
Grows strong and great in substance and in power.

K. Rich. Discomfortable cousin! know'st thou not
That when the searching eye of heaven is hid,
Behind the globe, that lights the lower world,
Then thieves and robbers range abroad unseen
In murders and in outrage, boldly here; 40
But when from under this terrestrial ball
He fires the proud tops of the eastern pines
And darts his light through every guilty hole,
Then murders, treasons and detested sins,
The cloak of night being pluck'd from off their backs,
Stand bare and naked, trembling at themselves?
So when this thief, this traitor, Bolingbroke,
Who all this while hath revell'd in the night
Whilst we were wandering with the antipodes,
Shall see us rising in our throne, the east, 50
His treasons will sit blushing in his face,
Not able to endure the sight of day,
But self-affrighted tremble at his sin.
Not all the water in the rough rude sea
Can wash the balm off from an anointed king;
The breath of worldly men cannot depose
The deputy elected by the Lord:
For every man that Bolingbroke hath press'd
To lift shrewd steel against our golden crown,
God for his Richard hath in heavenly pay 60
A glorious angel: then, if angels fight,
Weak men must fall, for heaven still guards the right.

Enter Salisbury.

Welcome, my lord: how far off lies your power?

---

1. **Barkloughly**, probably Harlech, a castle in Wales between Caernarvon and Aberystwyth. 2. **brooks**, likes, enjoys. 4. **I weep for joy.** "Shakespeare has carefully shown in him an intense love of his country, well knowing how that feeling would, in pure historic drama, redeem him in the hearts of the audience" (Coleridge). 21. **double**, forked. 23. **senseless conjuration**, adjuration of senseless things. 25. **native**, entitled (to the crown) by birth, rightful.

33. **He means . . . remiss.** The stern, practical bishop has attempted to bring Richard back to reality; Richard hardly understands; Aumerle interprets in this line. 34. **security**, confidence, heedlessness. 38. **that lights the lower world.** This clause modifies *eye of heaven.* 55. **balm**, consecrated oil used in anointing a king. 58. **press'd**, impressed, forced into the ranks. 59. **shrewd**, evil, destructive.

Sal. Nor near nor farther off, my gracious
lord,
Than this weak arm: discomfort guides my
tongue
And bids me speak of nothing but despair.
One day too late, I fear me, noble lord,
Hath clouded all thy happy days on earth:
O, call back yesterday, bid time return,
And thou shalt have twelve thousand fight-
ing men!   70
To-day, to-day, unhappy day, too late,
O'erthrows thy joys, friends, fortune and
thy state:
For all the Welshmen, hearing thou wert
dead,
Are gone to Bolingbroke, dispersed and fled.
Aum. Comfort, my liege: why looks your
grace so pale?
K. Rich. But now the blood of twenty
thousand men
Did triumph in my face, and they are fled;
And, till so much blood thither come again,
Have I not reason to look pale and dead?
All souls that will be safe fly from my side, 80
For time hath set a blot upon my pride.
Aum. Comfort, my liege; remember who
you are.
K. Rich. I had forgot myself: am I not
king?
Awake, thou coward majesty! thou sleepest.
Is not the king's name twenty thousand
names?
Arm, arm, my name! a puny subject strikes
At thy great glory. Look not to the ground,
Ye favourites of a king: are we not high?
High be our thoughts: I know my uncle
York
Hath power enough to serve our turn. But
who comes here?   90

Enter SCROOP.

Scroop. More health and happiness betide
my liege
Than can my care-tuned tongue deliver him!
K. Rich. Mine ear is open and my heart
prepared:
The worst is worldly loss thou canst unfold.
Say, is my kingdom lost? why, 'twas my care;
And what loss is it to be rid of care?

Strives Bolingbroke to be as great as we?
Greater he shall not be; if he serve God,
We'll serve Him too and be his fellow so: 99
Revolt our subjects? that we cannot mend;
They break their faith to God as well as us:
Cry woe, destruction, ruin and decay;
The worst is death, and death will have his
day.
Scroop. Glad am I that your highness is
so arm'd
To bear the tidings of calamity.
Like an unseasonable stormy day,
Which makes the silver rivers drown their
shores,
As if the world were all dissolved to tears,
So high above his limits swells the rage
Of Bolingbroke, covering your fearful land
With hard bright steel and hearts harder
than steel.   111
White-beards have arm'd their thin and hair-
less scalps
Against thy majesty; boys, with women's
voices,
Strive to speak big and clap their female
joints
In stiff unwieldy arms against thy crown:
Thy very beadsmen learn to bend their bows
Of double-fatal yew against thy state;
Yea, distaff-women manage rusty bills
Against thy seat: both young and old rebel,
And all goes worse than I have power to tell.
K. Rich. Too well, too well thou tell'st a
tale so ill.   121
Where is the Earl of Wiltshire? where is
Bagot?
What is become of Bushy? where is Green?
That they have let the dangerous enemy
Measure our confines with such peaceful
steps?
If we prevail, their heads shall pay for it:
I warrant they have made peace with
Bolingbroke.
Scroop. Peace have they made with him
indeed, my lord.
K. Rich. O villains, vipers, damn'd with-
out redemption!

112. **thin**, thin-haired (Schmidt); possibly, shrunken
to thinness. 114. **clap**, set briskly. **female**, weak and
delicate like a woman, implying their youth. 116.
beadsmen, almsmen whose duty it was to pray for the
king. 117. **double-fatal**, doubly fatal (since the wood
of the yew was used for bows and the berry as poison).
118. **manage**, wield, handle (a weapon). **bills**,
weapons used by infantry; a **bill** was a long-handled ax
with hook-shaped blade and spearhead. 122. **Bagot**.
Bagot's name seems inadvertently mentioned here.
The king speaks, line 132, of *three Judases;* Aumerle
does not ask about Bagot in line 141.

64. **near**, nearer. 65. **discomfort**, discouragement.
76. **twenty thousand men**. Holinshed puts Salisbury's force at forty thousand. 76-81. **But now . . .
pride**. Note that Richard's highly emotional speech is
in the form of a sestet.

Dogs, easily won to fawn on any man!   130
Snakes, in my heart-blood warm'd, that
    sting my heart!
Three Judases, each one thrice worse than
    Judas!
Would they make peace? terrible hell make
    war
Upon their spotted souls for this offence!
    Scroop. Sweet love, I see, changing his
        property,
Turns to the sourest and most deadly hate:
Again uncurse their souls; their peace is
    made
With heads, and not with hands: those whom
    you curse
Have felt the worst of death's destroying
    wound
And lie full low, graved in the hollow
    ground.   140
    Aum. Is Bushy, Green, and the Earl of
        Wiltshire dead?
    Scroop. Ay, all of them at Bristol lost
        their heads.
    Aum. Where is the duke my father with
        his power?
    K. Rich. No matter where; of comfort no
        man speak:
Let's talk of graves, of worms and epitaphs;
Make dust our paper and with rainy eyes
Write sorrow on the bosom of the earth,
Let's choose executors and talk of wills:
And yet not so, for what can we bequeath
Save our deposed bodies to the ground?   150
Our lands, our lives and all are Boling-
    broke's,
And nothing can we call our own but death
And that small model of the barren earth
Which serves as paste and cover to our bones.
For God's sake, let us sit upon the ground
And tell sad stories of the death of kings:
How some have been deposed; some slain in
    war;
Some haunted by the ghosts they have
    deposed;
Some poison'd by their wives; some sleeping
    kill'd;
All murder'd: for within the hollow crown   160
That rounds the mortal temples of a king
Keeps Death his court and there the antic
    sits,

Scoffing his state and grinning at his pomp,
Allowing him a breath, a little scene,
To monarchize, be fear'd and kill with looks,
Infusing him with self and vain conceit,
As if this flesh which walls about our life
Were brass impregnable, and humour'd thus
Comes at the last and with a little pin
Bores through his castle wall, and farewell
    king!   170
Cover your heads and mock not flesh and
    blood
With solemn reverence: throw away respect,
Tradition, form and ceremonious duty,
For you have but mistook me all this while:
†I live with bread like you, feel want,
Taste grief, need friends: subjected thus,
How can you say to me, I am a king?
    Car. My lord, wise men ne'er sit and wail
        their woes,
But presently prevent the ways to wail.
To fear the foe, since fear oppresseth
    strength,   180
Gives in your weakness strength unto your
    foe,
And so your follies fight against yourself.
Fear, and be slain; no worse can come to
    fight:
And fight and die is death destroying death;
Where fearing dying pays death servile
    breath.
    Aum. My father hath a power; inquire of
        him,
And learn to make a body of a limb.
    K. Rich. Thou chidest me well: proud
        Bolingbroke, I come
To change blows with thee for our day of
    doom.
This ague fit of fear is over-blown;   190
An easy task it is to win our own.
Say, Scroop, where lies our uncle with his
    power?
Speak sweetly, man, although thy looks be
    sour.
    Scroop. Men judge by the complexion of
        the sky
The state and inclination of the day:
So may you by my dull and heavy eye,
My tongue hath but a heavier tale to say.

---

153. **model**, may refer to Richard's own mortal body,
or to the grave mound. 162. **Death.** Douce called
attention to a print in the *Imagines Mortis* of a king sitting on a throne, sword in hand, surrounded by courtiers,
with a grinning skeleton arising from his crown. **antic**,
grotesque figure.

163. **Scoffing**, scoffing at. 164. **breath**, breathing-
space, moment. 166. **self and vain conceit**, selfish
and vain conceit. 168. **humour'd**, having satisfied his
humor or whim (referring to Death); sometimes defined
as "humored" or "indulged" (referring to the king). 176.
subjected, made subject to grief, want, etc. 183-185.
Fear . . . breath. To die fighting is to triumph over
death; to fear death is to become its slave.

I play the torturer, by small and small!
To lengthen out the worst that must be
    spoken: 199
Your uncle York is join'd with Bolingbroke,
And all your northern castles yielded up,
And all your southern gentlemen in arms
Upon his party.
    K. Rich.   Thou hast said enough.
Beshrew thee, cousin, which didst lead me
    forth.   [*To Aumerle.*
Of that sweet way I was in to despair!
What say you now? what comfort have we
    now?
By heaven, I'll hate him everlastingly
That bids me be of comfort any more.
Go to Flint castle: there I'll pine away;
A king, woe's slave, shall kingly woe obey.   210
That power I have, discharge; and let them
    go
To ear the land that hath some hope to grow,
For I have none: let no man speak again
To alter this, for counsel is but vain.
    Aum.   My liege, one word.
    K. Rich.   He does me double wrong
That wounds me with the flatteries of his
    tongue.
Discharge my followers: let them hence
    away,
From Richard's night to Bolingbroke's fair
    day.   [*Exeunt.*

SCENE III. *Wales. Before Flint castle.*

Enter, with drum and colours, BOLINGBROKE,
    YORK, NORTHUMBERLAND, Attendants,
    and forces.

    Boling.   So that by this intelligence we
    learn
The Welshmen are dispersed, and Salisbury
Is gone to meet the king, who lately landed
With some few private friends upon this
    coast.
    North.   The news is very fair and good, my
    lord:
Richard not far from hence hath hid his head.

    York.   It would beseem the Lord North-
    umberland
To say 'King Richard:' alack the heavy
    day
When such a sacred king should hide his
    head.
    North.   Your grace mistakes; only to be
    brief,   10
Left I his title out.
    York.   The time hath been,
Would you have been so brief with him, he
    would
Have been so brief with you, to shorten you,
For taking so the head, your whole head's
    length.
    Boling.   Mistake not, uncle, further than
    you should.
    York.   Take not, good cousin, further
    than you should,
Lest you mistake the heavens are o'er our
    heads.
    Boling.   I know it, uncle, and oppose not
    myself
Against their will. But who comes here?

    Enter PERCY.

Welcome, Harry: what, will not this castle
    yield?   20
    Percy.   The castle royally is mann'd, my
    lord,
Against thy entrance.
    Boling.   Royally!
Why, it contains no king?
    Percy.   Yes, my good lord,
It doth contain a king; King Richard lies
Within the limits of yon lime and stone:
And with him are the Lord Aumerle, Lord
    Salisbury,
Sir Stephen Scroop, besides a clergyman
Of holy reverence; who, I cannot learn.
    North.   O, belike it is the Bishop of Car-
    lisle.   30
    Boling.   Noble lords,
Go to the rude ribs of that ancient castle;
Through brazen trumpet send the breath of
    parley
Into his ruin'd ears, and thus deliver:
Henry Bolingbroke

---

198. by small and small, little by little.   204.
Beshrew thee, a mild curse. 211. That . . . discharge.
When Richard finds that he must fight for his kingship,
he prefers to relinquish it and assume the rôle of the
dethroned monarch; but see III, iii, 129-130. 212. ear,
plow. grow, produce fruit.
    Scene iii. 6. Richard . . . head. The plot here
diverges from Holinshed. Richard fled to Conway
Castle, where he found Salisbury. To this place, then,
Bolingbroke dispatched Northumberland, who induced Richard to a conference, assuring him that
Bolingbroke came merely to demand his rights and
advising that a parliament should be called to

restore order to the kingdom. On their riding forth
from Conway, Northumberland led Richard into an ambush, by which means Richard was taken to Flint
Castle as a prisoner. Later he was taken to Chester and
to London. The divergence in plot may be accounted
for by a marginal note in Holinshed which reads: "K.
Richard stealeth awaie from his armie, and taketh the
castell of Flint."

On both his knees doth kiss King Richard's
  hand
And sends allegiance and true faith of heart
To his most royal person, hither come
Even at his feet to lay my arms and power,
Provided that my banishment repeal'd   40
And lands restored again be freely granted:
If not, I'll use the advantage of my power
And lay the summer's dust with showers of
  blood
Rain'd from the wounds of slaughter'd
  Englishmen:
The which, how far off from the mind of
  Bolingbroke
It is, such crimson tempest should bedrench
The fresh green lap of fair King Richard's
  land,
My stooping duty tenderly shall show.
Go, signify as much, while here we march
Upon the grassy carpet of this plain.   50
Let's march without the noise of threatening
  drum,
That from this castle's tatter'd battlements
Our fair appointments may be well perused.
Methinks King Richard and myself should
  meet
With no less terror than the elements
Of fire and water, when their thundering
  shock
At meeting tears the cloudy cheeks of
  heaven.
Be he the fire, I'll be the yielding water:
The rage be his, whilst on the earth I rain
My waters; on the earth, and not on him.   60
March on, and mark King Richard how he
  looks.

*Parle without, and answer within. Then a
flourish. Enter on the walls,* KING RICHARD,
the BISHOP OF CARLISLE, AUMERLE,
SCROOP, *and* SALISBURY.

See, see, King Richard doth himself appear,
As doth the blushing discontented sun
From out the fiery portal of the east,
When he perceives the envious clouds are
  bent
To dim his glory and to stain the track
Of his bright passage to the occident.
    York. Yet looks he like a king: behold,
      his eye,

61. *Stage Direction:* **Parle,** overtures of peace, parley.
62-67. **See . . . occident,** assigned by Dyce to Percy, by
Warburton and Hanmer to York; but Bolingbroke is
everywhere sensitive to Richard's personal charm. See
IV, i, 304; V, vi, 40.

As bright as is the eagle's, lightens forth
Controlling majesty: alack, alack, for woe, 70
That any harm should stain so fair a show!
    K. Rich. We are amazed; and thus long
      have we stood
To watch the fearful bending of thy knee,
                                [*To North.*
Because we thought ourself thy lawful king:
And if we be, how dare thy joints forget
To pay their awful duty to our presence?
If we be not, show us the hand of God
That hath dismiss'd us from our steward-
  ship;
For well we know, no hand of blood and
  bone
Can gripe the sacred handle of our sceptre, 80
Unless he do profane, steal, or usurp.
And though you think that all, as you have
  done,
Have torn their souls by turning them from
  us,
And we are barren and bereft of friends;
Yet know, my master, God omnipotent,
Is mustering in his clouds on our behalf
Armies of pestilence; and they shall strike
Your children yet unborn and unbegot,
That lift your vassal hands against my head
And threat the glory of my precious crown. 90
Tell Bolingbroke—for yond methinks he
  stands—
That every stride he makes upon my land
Is dangerous treason: he is come to open
The purple testament of bleeding war;
But ere the crown he looks for live in peace,
Ten thousand bloody crowns of mothers'
  sons
Shall ill become the flower of England's face,
Change the complexion of her maid-pale
  peace
To scarlet indignation and bedew
Her pastures' grass with faithful English
  blood.   100
    North. The king of heaven forbid our lord
      the king
Should so with civil and uncivil arms

81. **profane,** commit sacrilege. 83. **torn their souls,**
injured their souls by treason to the king. 93-94. **open
The purple testament,** begin to carry out a bequest of
blood to England. Blood was often said to be purple.
97. **flower of England's face,** the blooming face of England. Cf. Daniel, *Civil Wars,* I, 118: "Th' vngodly
bloodshed that . . . did marre the flowre of thy chiefe
pride . . ." The abundance of Richard's metaphors is
startling. Blood, which disfigures war and also the heads
of ten thousand Englishmen, stains purple the will or
testament, makes the face of England scarlet with indignation, and bedews the grass of the pastures. 102. **civil,**
used in civil strife. **uncivil,** barbarous, violent.

Be rush'd upon! Thy thrice noble cousin
Harry Bolingbroke doth humbly kiss thy
hand;
And by the honourable tomb he swears,
That stands upon your royal grandsire's
bones,
And by the royalties of both your bloods,
Currents that spring from one most gracious
head,
And by the buried hand of warlike Gaunt,
And by the worth and honour of himself, 110
Comprising all that may be sworn or said,
His coming hither hath no further scope
Than for his lineal royalties and to beg
Enfranchisement immediate on his knees:
Which on thy royal party granted once,
His glittering arms he will commend to rust,
His barbed steeds to stables, and his heart
To faithful service of your majesty.
This swears he, as he is a prince, is just;
And, as I am a gentleman, I credit him. 120
    K. Rich. Northumberland, say thus the
    king returns:
His noble cousin is right welcome hither;
And all the number of his fair demands
Shall be accomplish'd without contradic-
tion:
With all the gracious utterance thou hast
Speak to his gentle hearing kind commends.
We do debase ourselves, cousin, do we not,
                    [*To Aumerle.*
To look so poorly and to speak so fair?
Shall we call back Northumberland, and
send
Defiance to the traitor, and so die? 130
    Aum. No, good my lord; let's fight with
    gentle words
Till time lend friends and friends their help-
ful swords.
    K. Rich. O God, O God! that e'er this
    tongue of mine,
That laid the sentence of dread banishment
On yon proud man, should take it off again
With words of sooth! O that I were as great
As is my grief, or lesser than my name!
Or that I could forget what I have been,
Or not remember what I must be now!
Swell'st thou, proud heart? I'll give thee
    scope to beat, 140
Since foes have scope to beat both thee and
me.

    Aum. Northumberland comes back from
    Bolingbroke.
    K. Rich. What must the king do now?
    must he submit?
The king shall do it: must he be deposed?
The king shall be contented: must he lose
The name of king? o' God's name, let it
    go:
I'll give my jewels for a set of beads,
My gorgeous palace for a hermitage,
My gay apparel for an almsman's gown,
My figured goblets for a dish of wood, 150
My sceptre for a palmer's walking-staff,
My subjects for a pair of carved saints
And my large kingdom for a little grave,
A little little grave, an obscure grave;
Or I'll be buried in the king's highway,
Some way of common trade, where subjects'
    feet
May hourly trample on their sovereign's
    head;
For on my heart they tread now whilst I
    live;
And buried once, why not upon my head?
Aumerle, thou weep'st, my tender-hearted
    cousin! 160
We'll make foul weather with despised tears;
Our sighs and they shall lodge the summer
    corn,
And make a dearth in this revolting land.
Or shall we play the wantons with our woes,
And make some pretty match with shedding
    tears?
As thus, to drop them still upon one place,
Till they have fretted us a pair of graves
Within the earth; and, therein laid,—there
    lies
Two kinsmen digg'd their graves with weep-
ing eyes.
Would not this ill do well? Well, well, I see
I talk but idly, and you laugh at me. 171
Most mighty prince, my Lord Northumber-
land,
What says King Bolingbroke? will his ma-
jesty
Give Richard leave to live till Richard die?
You make a leg, and Bolingbroke says ay.
    North. My lord, in the base court he doth
    attend

---

114. **Enfranchisement**, restoration to the rights of a
freeman. 116. **commend**, give over. 117. **barbed**,
armed. 136. **sooth**, cajolery, flattery.

143. **What must the king**, etc. The king characteristically throws away his advantage; Bolingbroke would
have had to put his forces at the king's command or incur
the responsibility of seizing him. 162. **lodge**, beat down.
167. **fretted**, eaten away, worn. 175. **make a leg**,
assent by making an obeisance or courtesy. 176. **base
court**, outer or lower court of a castle.

To speak with you; may it please you to
   come down.
   K. Rich. Down, down I come; like glister-
   ing Phaethon,
Wanting the manage of unruly jades.
In the base court? Base court, where kings
   grow base,   180
To come at traitors' calls and do them grace.
In the base court? Come down? Down,
   court! down, king!
For night-owls shriek where mounting larks
   should sing.   [*Exeunt from above.*
   Boling. What says his majesty?
   North.   Sorrow and grief of heart
Makes him speak fondly, like a frantic man:
Yet he is come.

   Enter KING RICHARD *and his attendants*
         below.

   Boling. Stand all apart,
And show fair duty to his majesty.
                [*He kneels down.*
My gracious lord,—
   K. Rich. Fair cousin, you debase your
   princely knee   190
To make the base earth proud with kissing
   it:
Me rather had my heart might feel your
   love
Than my unpleased eye see your courtesy.
Up, cousin, up; your heart is up, I know,
Thus high at least, although your knee be
   low.
   Boling. My gracious lord, I come but for
   mine own.
   K. Rich. Your own is yours, and I am
   yours, and all.
   Boling. So far be mine, my most re-
   doubted lord,
As my true service shall deserve your love.
   K. Rich. Well you deserve: they well de-
   serve to have,   200
That know the strong'st and surest way to
   get.
Uncle, give me your hands: nay, dry your
   eyes;
Tears show their love, but want their
   remedies.

Cousin, I am too young to be your father,
Though you are old enough to be my heir.
What you will have, I'll give, and willing too;
For do we must what force will have us do.
Set on towards London, cousin, is it so?
   Boling. Yea, my good lord.
   K. Rich.   Then I must not say no.
               [*Flourish. Exeunt.*

SCENE IV. *Langley. The* DUKE OF YORK'S
         garden.

   Enter the QUEEN *and two* Ladies.

   Queen. What sport shall we devise here in
   this garden,
To drive away the heavy thought of care?
   Lady. Madam we'll play at bowls.
   Queen. 'Twill make me think the world is
   full of rubs,
And that my fortune runs against the bias.
   Lady. Madam, we'll dance.
   Queen. My legs can keep no measure in
   delight,
When my poor heart no measure keeps in
   grief:
Therefore, no dancing, girl; some other sport.
   Lady. Madam, we'll tell tales.   10
   Queen. Of sorrow or of joy?
   Lady.   Of either, madam.
   Queen. Of neither, girl:
For if of joy, being altogether wanting,
It doth remember me the more of sorrow;
Or if of grief, being altogether had,
It adds more sorrow to my want of joy:
For what I have I need not to repeat;
And what I want it boots not to complain.
   Lady. Madam, I'll sing.
   Queen.   'Tis well that thou hast cause;
But thou shouldst please me better, wouldst
   thou weep.   20
   Lady. I could weep, madam, would it do
   you good.
   Queen. And I could sing, would weeping
   do me good,
And never borrow any tear of thee.

   Enter a Gardener, *and two* Servants.

But stay, here come the gardeners:

---

178. **glistering,** glistening. **Phaethon,** son of
Apollo, who, unable to control the horses of the sun, was
hurled from the chariot by Jupiter. 179. **manage,**
measures of control (of horses). **jades,** worthless horses.
192. **Me rather had,** a construction resulting from a
combination of "me were liefer" and "I had rather."
203. **Tears . . . remedies,** tears show love, but offer
no remedies.

204. **too . . . father.** Bolingbroke was born in 1367,
and Richard a few months later in 1368.
Scene iv. 4. **rubs,** in bowling, deflections of a running
bowl from its course. 5. **bias,** term in bowling applied
to the form of the bowl, the oblique line in which it runs,
and the kind of impetus given to cause it to run obliquely.
14. **remember,** remind. 18. **boots,** helps, avails.

Let's step into the shadow of these trees.
My wretchedness unto a row of pins,
They'll talk of state; for every one doth so
Against a change; woe is forerun with woe.
[Queen and Ladies retire.

Gard. Go, bind thou up yon dangling
apricocks,
Which, like unruly children, make their sire
Stoop with oppression of their prodigal
weight: 31
Give some supportance to the bending twigs.
Go thou, and like an executioner,
Cut off the heads of too fast growing sprays
That look too lofty in our commonwealth:
All must be even in our government.
You thus employ'd, I will go root away
The noisome weeds, which without profit
suck
The soil's fertility from wholesome flowers.

Serv. Why should we in the compass of a
pale   40
Keep law and form and due proportion,
Showing, as in a model, our firm estate,
When our sea-walled garden, the whole
land,
Is full of weeds, her fairest flowers choked
up,
Her fruit-trees all unpruned, her hedges
ruin'd,
Her knots disorder'd and her wholesome
herbs
Swarming with caterpillars?

Gard.   Hold thy peace:
He that hath suffer'd this disorder'd spring
Hath now himself met with the fall of leaf:
The weeds which his broad-spreading leaves
did shelter,   50
That seem'd in eating him to hold him up,
Are pluck'd up root and all by Bolingbroke,
I mean the Earl of Wiltshire, Bushy, Green.

Serv. What, are they dead?

Gard.   They are; and Bolingbroke
Hath seized the wasteful king. O, what pity
is it
That he had not so trimm'd and dress'd his
land
As we this garden! We at time of year
Do wound the bark, the skin of our fruit-
trees,
Lest, being over-proud in sap and blood,
With too much riches it confound itself: 60

Had he done so to great and growing men,
They might have lived to bear and he to
taste
Their fruits of duty: superfluous branches
We lop away, that bearing boughs may live:
Had he done so, himself had borne the crown,
Which waste of idle hours hath quite thrown
down.

Serv. What, think you then the king shall
be deposed?

Gard. Depress'd he is already, and
deposed
'Tis doubt he will be: letters came last night
To a dear friend of the good Duke of York's,
That tell black tidings.   71

Queen. O, I am press'd to death through
want of speaking!   *[Coming forward.*
Thou, old Adam's likeness, set to dress this
garden,
How dares thy harsh rude tongue sound this
unpleasing news?
What Eve, what serpent, hath suggested
thee
To make a second fall of cursed man?
Why dost thou say King Richard is deposed?
Darest thou, thou little better thing than
earth,
Divine his downfal? Say, where, when, and
how,
Camest thou by this ill tidings? speak, thou
wretch.   80

Gard. Pardon me, madam: little joy
have I
To breathe this news; yet what I say is true.
King Richard, he is in the mighty hold
Of Bolingbroke: their fortunes both are
weigh'd:
In your lord's scale is nothing but himself,
And some few vanities that make him light;
But in the balance of great Bolingbroke,
Besides himself, are all the English peers,
And with that odds he weighs King Richard
down.
Post you to London, and you will find it so; 90
I speak no more than every one doth know.

Queen. Nimble mischance, that art so light
of foot,
Doth not thy embassage belong to me,
And am I last that knows it? O, thou think'st
To serve me last, that I may longest keep

---

28. **Against**, just before. 29. **apricocks**, apricots.
40. **pale**, enclosure. 42. **model**, image, likeness. 46.
knots, laid-out garden plots. 60. **confound**, destroy,
undo.

69. **doubt**, doubtful. 72. **press'd to death**, allusion
to the *peine forte et dure*, inflicted by pressure of heavy
weights upon the chests of indicted persons who refused
to plead. 79. **Divine**, foretell prophetically. 93. **embassage**, message.

Thy sorrow in my breast. Come, ladies, go,
To meet at London London's king in woe.
What, was I born to this, that my sad look
Should grace the triumph of great Boling-
    broke?
Gardener, for telling me these news of woe,100
Pray God the plants thou graft'st may never
    grow.   [*Exeunt Queen and Ladies.*
    Gard. Poor queen! so that thy state might
    be no worse,
I would my skill were subject to thy curse.
Here did she fall a tear; here in this place
I'll set a bank of rue, sour herb of grace:
Rue, even for ruth, here shortly shall be
    seen,
In the remembrance of a weeping queen.
                          [*Exeunt.*

ACT IV.

Scene I. *Westminster Hall.*

Enter, as to the Parliament, Bolingbroke,
Aumerle, Northumberland, Percy,
Fitzwater, Surrey, *the* Bishop of Carlisle, *the* Abbot of Westminster, *and
another* Lord, Herald, Officers, *and* Bagot.

  Boling. Call forth Bagot.
Now, Bagot, freely speak thy mind;
What thou dost know of noble Gloucester's
    death,
Who wrought it with the king, and who
    perform'd
The bloody office of his timeless end.
  Bagot. Then set before my face the Lord
    Aumerle.
  Boling. Cousin, stand forth, and look upon
    that man.
  Bagot. My Lord Aumerle, I know your
    daring tongue
Scorns to unsay what once it hath deliver'd.
In that dead time when Gloucester's death
    was plotted,   10
I heard you say, 'Is not my arm of length,
That reacheth from the restful English court
As far as Calais, to mine uncle's head?'
Amongst much other talk, that very time,

I heard you say that you had rather refuse
The offer of an hundred thousand crowns
Than Bolingbroke's return to England;
Adding withal, how blest this land would be
In this your cousin's death.
  Aum.   Princes and noble lords,
What answer shall I make to this base
    man?
Shall I so much dishonour my fair stars,   21
On equal terms to give him chastisement?
Either I must, or have mine honour soil'd
With the attainder of his slanderous lips.
There is my gage, the manual seal of death,
That marks thee out for hell: I say, thou
    liest,
And will maintain what thou hast said is
    false
In thy heart-blood, though being all too
    base
To stain the temper of my knightly sword.
  Boling. Bagot, forbear; thou shalt not
    take it up.   30
  Aum. Excepting one, I would he were the
    best
In all this presence that hath moved me so.
  Fitz. If that thy valour stand on sym-
    pathy,
There is my gage, Aumerle, in gage to thine:
By that fair sun which shows me where thou
    stand'st,
I heard thee say, and vauntingly thou spak-
    est it,
That thou wert cause of noble Gloucester's
    death.
If thou deny'st it twenty times, thou liest;
And I will turn thy falsehood to thy heart,
Where it was forged, with my rapier's point.
  Aum. Thou darest not, coward, live to see
    that day.   41
  Fitz. Now, by my soul, I would it were
    this hour.
  Aum. Fitzwater, thou art damn'd to hell
    for this.
  Percy. Aumerle, thou liest; his honour is
    as true
In this appeal as thou art all unjust;
And that thou art so, there I throw my gage,
To prove it on thee to the extremest point
Of mortal breathing: seize it, if thou darest.
  Aum. An if I do not, may my hands rot off

105. rue, "herb of grace," a plant symbolical of repentance, ruth, or sorrow for another's misery.
    Act IV. Scene i. Stage Direction: **Westminster Hall.**
It had just been rebuilt by King Richard's orders. 1.
Call forth Bagot. Bolingbroke lends dignity to his usurpation by thus bringing forward at once the issue which
drove him to revolt. 5. **timeless,** untimely. 10. **dead,**
deathlike. 14. **that very time.** This seems to be a
mistake; Gloucester's death occurred before Bolingbroke
left England.

    21. **stars,** i.e., his sphere or fortune. 24. **attainder,**
dishonoring accusation. 25. **manual seal of death,**
death warrant. 33. **sympathy,** correspondence, or
equality, of blood or rank.

And never brandish more revengeful steel 50
Over the glittering helmet of my foe!
  Another Lord. I task the earth to the like,
    forsworn Aumerle;
And spur thee on with full as many lies
As may be holloa'd in thy treacherous ear
From sun to sun: there is my honour's pawn;
Engage it to the trial, if thou darest.
  Aum. Who sets me else? by heaven, I'll
    throw at all:
I have a thousand spirits in one breast,
To answer twenty thousand such as you.
  Surrey. My Lord Fitzwater, I do remem-
    ber well   60
The very time Aumerle and you did talk.
  Fitz. 'Tis very true: you were in presence
    then;
And you can witness with me this is true.
  Surrey. As false, by heaven, as heaven it-
    self is true.
  Fitz. Surrey, thou liest.
  Surrey.   Dishonourable boy!
That lie shall lie so heavy on my sword,
That it shall render vengeance and revenge
Till thou the lie-giver and that lie do lie
In earth as quiet as thy father's skull:
In proof whereof, there is my honour's pawn;
Engage it to the trial, if thou darest.   71
  Fitz. How fondly dost thou spur a forward
    horse!
If I dare eat, or drink, or breathe, or live,
I dare meet Surrey in a wilderness,
And spit upon him, whilst I say he lies,
And lies, and lies: there is my bond of faith,
To tie thee to my strong correction.
As I intend to thrive in this new world,
Aumerle is guilty of my true appeal:
Besides, I heard the banish'd Norfolk say 80
That thou, Aumerle, didst send two of thy
    men
To execute the noble duke at Calais.
  Aum. Some honest Christian trust me
    with a gage,
That Norfolk lies: here do I throw down this,
If he may be repeal'd, to try his honour.

  Boling. These differences shall all rest
    under gage
Till Norfolk be repeal'd: repeal'd he shall be,
And, though mine enemy, restored again
To all his lands and signories: when he's
    return'd,
Against Aumerle we will enforce his trial. 90
  Car. That honourable day shall ne'er be
    seen.
Many a time hath banish'd Norfolk fought
For Jesu Christ in glorious Christian field,
Streaming the ensign of the Christian cross
Against black pagans, Turks, and Saracens;
And toil'd with works of war, retired himself
To Italy; and there at Venice gave
His body to that pleasant country's earth,
And his pure soul unto his captain Christ, 99
Under whose colours he had fought so long.
  Boling. Why, bishop, is Norfolk dead?
  Car. As surely as I live, my lord.
  Boling. Sweet peace conduct his sweet
    soul to the bosom
Of good old Abraham! Lords appellants,
Your differences shall all rest under gage
Till we assign you to your days of trial.

        Enter YORK, *attended.*

  York. Great Duke of Lancaster, I come to
    thee
From plume-pluck'd Richard; who with will-
    ing soul
Adopts thee heir, and his high sceptre yields
To the possession of thy royal hand: 110
Ascend his throne, descending now from him;
And long live Henry, fourth of that name!
  Boling. In God's name, I'll ascend the
    regal throne.
  Car. Marry, God forbid!
Worst in this royal presence may I speak,
Yet best beseeming me to speak the truth.
Would God that any in this noble presence

91-100. **That . . . long.** "This year (1399) Thomas Mowbraie, Duke of Norffolke, died in exile at Venice" (Holinshed). "Norffolk . . . died at Venice in his return from Jerusalem" (Stow, *Annals*). 94. **Streaming,** causing to stream. 96. **toil'd,** wearied. 104. **good old Abraham.** See *St. Luke,* xvi, 22. Note Bolingbroke's exultation in dismissing the subject of the murder of Gloucester; it has served his purpose. Aumerle is left with the suspicion of guilt upon him, but he is not brought to trial. **Lords appellants,** lords who appear as formal accusers. 108. **plume-pluck'd,** humbled. 113. **In . . . throne.** Shakespeare gives no ground for Henry's claim; in Holinshed he claims the throne as descended from Henry III according to a false tradition that his ancestor, Edward Crouchback, was older than his brother Edward I, but was set aside on account of physical deformity. 114. **Marry, God forbid,** etc. Carlisle's speech, according to Holinshed, from whom it is largely taken, was made on October 22, three weeks before the deposition.

52. **task the earth,** charge the earth with the task of bearing my gage. 53. **full as many lies,** giving the lie as many times. 56. **Engage,** take up (a pledge). 57. **sets,** challenges to a game (properly, by laying down stakes). 60. **Surrey,** Richard's nephew, who with Aumerle represents the Yorkist faction. 67. **vengeance and revenge,** possibly tautological, meaning "furious revenge." 72. **fondly,** foolishly. 80. **Besides, I heard,** etc. John Hall, a groom of Mowbray's at Calais, confessed on October 18, 1399, that he and two servants sent, Mowbray told him, by Aumerle, murdered Gloucester. 65. **repeal'd,** recalled from exile.

Were enough noble to be upright judge
Of noble Richard! then true noblesse would
Learn him forbearance from so foul a wrong.
What subject can give sentence on his king?
And who sits here that is not Richard's sub-
ject?   122
Thieves are not judged but they are by to
hear,
Although apparent guilt be seen in them;
And shall the figure of God's majesty,
His captain, steward, deputy-elect,
Anointed, crowned, planted many years,
Be judged by subject and inferior breath,
And he himself not present? O, forfend it,
God,
That in a Christian climate souls refined   130
Should show so heinous, black, obscene a
deed!
I speak to subjects, and a subject speaks,
Stirr'd up by God, thus boldly for his king.
My Lord of Hereford here, whom you call
king,
Is a foul traitor to proud Hereford's king:
And if you crown him, let me prophesy:
The blood of English shall manure the
ground,
And future ages groan for this foul act;
Peace shall go sleep with Turks and infidels,
And in this seat of peace tumultuous wars 140
Shall kin with kin and kind with kind
confound;
Disorder, horror, fear and mutiny
Shall here inhabit, and this land be call'd
The field of Golgotha and dead men's skulls.
O, if you raise this house against this house,
It will the woefullest division prove
That ever fell upon this cursed earth.
Prevent it, resist it, let it not be so,
Lest child, child's children, cry against you
'woe!'
North. Well have you argued, sir; and, for
your pains,   150
Of capital treason we arrest you here.
My Lord of Westminster, be it your charge
To keep him safely till his day of trial.
May it please you, lords, to grant the com-
mons' suit.

Boling. Fetch hither Richard, that in com-
mon view
He may surrender; so we shall proceed
Without suspicion.
York.   I will be his conduct. [*Exit.*
Boling. Lords, you that here are under our
arrest,
Procure your sureties for your days of an-
swer.
Little are we beholding to your love,   160
And little look'd for at your helping hands.

Re-enter YORK, *with* RICHARD, *and* Officers
bearing the regalia.

K. Rich. Alack, why am I sent for to a
king,
Before I have shook off the regal thoughts
Wherewith I reign'd? I hardly yet have
learn'd
To insinuate, flatter, bow, and bend my
limbs:
Give sorrow leave awhile to tutor me
To this submission. Yet I well remember
The favours of these men: were they not
mine?
Did they not sometime cry, 'all hail!' to me?
So Judas did to Christ: but he, in twelve, 170
Found truth in all but one; I, in twelve
thousand, none.
God save the king! Will no man say amen?
Am I both priest and clerk? well then, amen.
God save the king! although I be not he;
And yet, amen, if heaven do think him me.
To do what service am I sent for hither?
York. To do that office of thine own good
will
Which tired majesty did make thee offer,
The resignation of thy state and crown
To Henry Bolingbroke.   180
K. Rich. Give me the crown. Here, cous-
in, seize the crown;
Here, cousin;
On this side my hand, and on that side yours.
Now is this golden crown like a deep well
That owes two buckets, filling one another,

---

119. **noblesse**, noble birth, nobleness. 131. **obscene**, odious, repulsive. 141. **kin**, relationship (of family). **kind**, relationship (of race and nation). 152. **My . . . charge.** Carlisle was committed to the Abbey of St. Albans and some months later transferred to the Abbey of Westminster. 154. **commons' suit**, probable reference to a demand that Bolingbroke ascend the throne. No such suit is known, though Holinshed says that the commons favored him.

156-157. **we . . . suspicion.** The deposition scene is without historical basis. Richard signed, perhaps under compulsion, an act of abdication, but before witnesses in the Tower. Daniel (*Civil Wars*) gives an elaborate description of the scene. 160-161. **Little . . . hands.** These lines seem to be an aside. **beholding**, obliged, indebted. 165. **insinuate**, wheedle, ingratiate one's self. 168. **favours**, countenances. 176. **To . . . hither.** Observe the two levels of Richard's speech; when he is not under stress of emotion, has no part to play, he speaks with unusual flatness. See lines 181, 203, 222; and V, v, 5. 185. **owes**, owns.

The emptier ever dancing in the air,
The other down, unseen and full of water:
That bucket down and full of tears am I,
Drinking my griefs, whilst you mount up on
    high.
    Boling. I thought you had been willing to
    resign.   190
    K. Rich. My crown I am; but still my
    griefs are mine:
You may my glories and my state depose,
But not my griefs; still am I king of those.
    Boling. Part of your cares you give me
    with your crown.
    K. Rich. Your cares set up do not pluck
    my cares down.
My care is loss of care, by old care done;
Your care is gain of care, by new care won:
The cares I give I have, though given away;
They tend the crown, yet still with me they
    stay.
    Boling. Are you contented to resign the
    crown?   200
    K. Rich. Ay, no; no, ay; for I must
    nothing be;
Therefore no no, for I resign to thee.
Now mark me, how I will undo myself:
I give this heavy weight from off my head
And this unwieldy sceptre from my hand,
The pride of kingly sway from out my heart;
With mine own tears I wash away my balm,
With mine own hands I give away my
    crown,
With mine own tongue deny my sacred state,
With mine own breath release all duty's
    rites: 210
All pomp and majesty I do forswear;
My manors, rents, revenues I forego;
My acts, decrees, and statutes I deny:
God pardon all oaths that are broke to me!
God keep all vows unbroke that swear to
    thee!
Make me, that nothing have, with nothing
    grieved,
And thou with all pleased, that hast all
    achieved!
Long mayst thou live in Richard's seat to sit,
And soon lie Richard in an earthy pit!   219
God save King Harry, unking'd Richard says,

And send him many years of sunshine days!
What more remains?
    North. No more, but that you read
These accusations and these grievous crimes
Committed by your person and your follow-
    ers
Against the state and profit of this land;
That, by confessing them, the souls of men
May deem that you are worthily deposed.
    K. Rich. Must I do so? and must I ravel
    out
My weaved-up folly? Gentle Northumber-
    land,
If thy offences were upon record,   230
Would it not shame thee in so fair a troop
To read a lecture of them? If thou wouldst,
There shouldst thou find one heinous article,
Containing the deposing of a king
And cracking the strong warrant of an
    oath,
Mark'd with a blot, damn'd in the book of
    heaven:
Nay, all of you that stand and look upon,
Whilst that my wretchedness doth bait
    myself,
Though some of you with Pilate wash your
    hands
Showing an outward pity; yet you Pilates   240
Have here deliver'd me to my sour cross,
And water cannot wash away your sin.
    North. My lord, dispatch; read o'er these
    articles.
    K. Rich. Mine eyes are full of tears, I can-
    not see:
And yet salt water blinds them not so much
But they can see a sort of traitors here.
Nay, if I turn mine eyes upon myself,
I find myself a traitor with the rest;
For I have given here my soul's consent
To undeck the pompous body of a king;   250
Made glory base and sovereignty a slave,
Proud majesty a subject, state a peasant.
    North. My lord,—
    K. Rich. No lord of thine, thou haught in-
    sulting man,
Nor no man's lord; I have no name, no title,
No, not that name was given me at the font,

---

195. **cares.** Three meanings of *care* are involved in the word play which follows: *care* in the sense of responsibility; in the sense of duty or task; in the sense of grief. 201-202. **Ay,** i.e., I. But *I* =nothing; therefore *Ay* =I=no. 204-221. **I give . . . days.** The speech follows with some faithfulness the formula of abdication, as recorded in the Rolls of Parliament. 212. **manors**, estates.

225. **state,** settled order. 232-233. **wouldst . . . shouldst.** In modern usage these words would be reversed. 239. **wash your hands.** See *St. Matthew* xxvii, 24. Richard persistently compares himself with Christ; see also III, ii, 24, 61; IV, i, 170. 254. **haught**, haughty, proud. 255. **I have no name**, an allusion to a story, circulated by the Lancastrian party, that Richard was not the son of the Black Prince, but of a canon of Bordeaux.

But 'tis usurp'd: alack the heavy day,
That I have worn so many winters out,
And know not now what name to call myself!
O that I were a mockery king of snow,   260
Standing before the sun of Bolingbroke,
To melt myself away in water-drops!
Good king, great king, and yet not greatly
      good,
An if my word be sterling yet in England,
Let it command a mirror hither straight,
That it may show me what a face I have,
Since it is bankrupt of his majesty.
    Boling. Go some of you and fetch a look-
      ing-glass.   [*Exit an attendant.*
    North. Read o'er this paper while the
      glass doth come.
    K. Rich. Fiend, thou torment'st me ere I
      come to hell!   270
    Boling. Urge it no more, my Lord North-
      umberland.
    North. The commons will not then be
      satisfied.
    K. Rich. They shall be satisfied: I'll read
      enough,
When I do see the very book indeed
Where all my sins are writ, and that's myself.

              Re-enter Attendant, *with a glass.*

Give me the glass, and therein will I read.
No deeper wrinkles yet? hath sorrow struck
So many blows upon this face of mine,
And made no deeper wounds? O flattering
      glass,
Like to my followers in prosperity,   280
Thou dost beguile me! Was this face the face
That every day under his household roof
Did keep ten thousand men? was this the face
That, like the sun, did make beholders wink?
Was this the face that faced so many follies,
And was at last out-faced by Bolingbroke?
A brittle glory shineth in this face:
As brittle as the glory is the face;
              [*Dashes the glass against the ground.*
For there it is, crack'd in a hundred shivers.
Mark, silent king, the moral of this sport,   290
How soon my sorrow hath destroy'd my face.
    Boling. The shadow of your sorrow hath
      destroy'd

The shadow of your face.
    K. Rich. Say that again.
The shadow of my sorrow! ha! let's see:
'Tis very true, my grief lies all within;
And these external manners of laments
Are merely shadows to the unseen grief
That swells with silence in the tortured soul;
There lies the substance: and I thank thee,
      king,
For thy great bounty, that not only givest 300
Me cause to wail but teachest me the way
How to lament the cause. I'll beg one boon,
And then be gone and trouble you no more.
Shall I obtain it?
    Boling.   Name it, fair cousin.
    K. Rich. 'Fair cousin'? I am greater than
      a king:
For when I was a king, my flatterers
Were then but subjects; being now a subject,
I have a king here to my flatterer.
Being so great, I have no need to beg.
    Boling. Yet ask.   310
    K. Rich. And shall I have?
    Boling. You shall.
    K. Rich. Then give me leave to go.
    Boling. Whither?
    K. Rich. Whither you will, so I were from
      your sights.
    Boling. Go, some of you convey him to the
      Tower.
    K. Rich. O, good! convey? conveyers are
      you all,
That rise thus nimbly by a true king's fall.
              [*Exeunt King Richard, some Lords,
                              and a Guard.*
    Boling. On Wednesday next we solemnly
      set down
Our coronation: lords, prepare yourselves. 320
[*Exeunt all except the Bishop of Carlisle, the
              Abbot of Westminster, and Aumerle.*
    Abbot. A woeful pageant have we here be-
      held.
    Car. The woe's to come; the children yet
      unborn
Shall feel this day as sharp to them as
      thorn.
    Aum. You holy clergymen, is there no
      plot
To rid the realm of this pernicious blot?
    Abbot. My lord,
Before I freely speak my mind herein,

260. **mockery,** counterfeit. 271. **Urge it no more.**
Herford points this out as "another touch which brings
out Bolingbroke's absence of personal rancor toward
Richard. He aims at power and is stern or clement as
policy, not passion, determines." 292-293. **The shadow
. . . face.** Your sentimental show of sorrow has destroyed your image in the glass. Note in the lines following, first, Richard's generous appreciation of a fine
phrase, and, secondly, the readiness with which he turns
aside its practical application to himself.

308. **to my flatterer,** as, or in the capacity of, my
flatterer. 313. **Then . . . go.** Richard throws away his
last small chance to make terms for himself. 316. **convey,** escort. 317. **convey,** steal, with a play upon the
normal sense of the word.

You shall not only take the sacrament
To bury mine intents, but also to effect
Whatever I shall happen to devise.   330
I see your brows are full of discontent,
Your hearts of sorrow and your eyes of
    tears:
Come home with me to supper; and I'll lay
A plot shall show us all a merry day.

                        [*Exeunt.*

ACT V.

Scene I.   *London.   A street leading to the
        Tower.*

        Enter Queen *and* Ladies.

    Queen. This way the king will come; this
        is the way
To Julius Cæsar's ill-erected tower,
To whose flint bosom my condemned lord
Is doom'd a prisoner by proud Bolingbroke:
Here let us rest, if this rebellious earth
Have any resting for her true king's queen.

        Enter Richard *and* Guard.

But soft, but see, or rather do not see,
My fair rose wither: yet look up, behold,
That you in pity may dissolve to dew,
And wash him fresh again with true-love
    tears.   10
Ah, thou, the model where old Troy did
    stand,
Thou map of honour, thou King Richard's
    tomb,
And not King Richard; thou most beauteous
    inn,
Why should hard-favour'd grief be lodged in
    thee,
When triumph is become an alehouse guest?
    K. Rich. Join not with grief, fair woman,
        do not so,
To make my end too sudden: learn, good
    soul,

To think our former state a happy dream;
From which awaked, the truth of what we
    are
Shows us but this: I am sworn brother, sweet,
To grim Necessity, and he and I   21
Will keep a league till death. Hie thee to
    France
And cloister thee in some religious house:
Our holy lives must win a new world's crown,
Which our profane hours here have stricken
    down.
    Queen. What, is my Richard both in shape
        and mind
Transform'd and weaken'd? hath Boling-
    broke deposed
Thine intellect? hath he been in thy heart?
The lion dying thrusteth forth his paw,
And wounds the earth, if nothing else, with
    rage   30
To be o'erpower'd; and wilt thou, pupil-like,
Take thy correction mildly, kiss the rod,
And fawn on rage with base humility,
Which art a lion and a king of beasts?
    K. Rich. A king of beasts, indeed; if aught
        but beasts,
I had been still a happy king of men.
Good sometime queen, prepare thee hence
    for France:
Think I am dead and that even here thou
    takest,
As from my death-bed, thy last living leave.
In winter's tedious nights sit by the fire 40
With good old folks and let them tell thee
    tales
Of woeful ages long ago betid;
And ere thou bid good night, to quit their
    griefs,
Tell thou the lamentable tale of me
And send the hearers weeping to their beds:
For why, the senseless brands will sympathize
The heavy accent of thy moving tongue
And in compassion weep the fire out;
And some will mourn in ashes, some coal-
    black,
For the deposing of a rightful king.   50

        Enter Northumberland *and* others.

    North. My lord, the mind of Bolingbroke
        is changed;
You must to Pomfret, not unto the Tower.

Act V.   Scene i.   1. This . . . come. There is no
historical authority for this interview between Richard
and the Queen; they did not meet again after Richard
left for Ireland.   In Daniel, *Civil Wars*, II, 89-94, the
Queen visits him in prison, and there is a striking parallel to Daniel in the passage (II, 66 ff.) where she
watches the king ride into the city.   2. Julius Cæsar's.
The Tower, ascribed by tradition to Julius Cæsar, was
built by the Conqueror to hold the city in subordination.
ill-erected, erected for evil ends, or under evil auspices.
8. My fair rose. Hotspur calls Richard "that sweet
lovely rose," *1 Henry IV*, I, iii, 175.   11. thou . . .
stand, thou ruined majesty that resemblest the desolate waste where Troy once stood (Malone).   12. map
of honour, i.e., the mere outline.   13. inn, mansion,
abode (with some sense, however, of its more common
meaning).

20. sworn brother, allusion to the *fratres jurati* of
chivalry.   24. new world's, heaven's.   42. betid,
past.   43. quit their griefs, make return for their
tragic tales.   52. Pomfret, Pontefract in Yorkshire,
twenty-two miles from York.

And, madam, there is order ta'en for you;
With all swift speed you must away to France.

K. Rich. Northumberland, thou ladder
wherewithal
The mounting Bolingbroke ascends my
throne,
The time shall not be many hours of age
More than it is ere foul sin gathering head
Shall break into corruption: thou shalt think,
Though he divide the realm and give thee
half,   60
It is too little, helping him to all;
And he shall think that thou, which know'st
the way
To plant unrightful kings, wilt know again,
Being ne'er so little urged, another way
To pluck him headlong from the usurped
throne.
The love of wicked men converts to fear;
That fear to hate, and hate turns one or both
To worthy danger and deserved death.

North. My guilt be on my head, and there
an end.
Take leave and part; for you must part forthwith.   70

K. Rich. Doubly divorced! Bad men, you
violate
A twofold marriage, 'twixt my crown and me,
And then betwixt me and my married wife.
Let me unkiss the oath 'twixt thee and me;
And yet not so, for with a kiss 'twas made.
Part us, Northumberland; I towards the
north,
Where shivering cold and sickness pines the
clime;
My wife to France: from whence, set forth in
pomp,
She came adorned hither like sweet May,
Sent back like Hallowmas or short'st of day.

Queen. And must we be divided? must we
part?   81

K. Rich. Ay, hand from hand, my love,
and heart from heart.

Queen. Banish us both and send the king
with me.

North. That were some love but little
policy.

Queen. Then whither he goes, thither let
me go.

K. Rich. So two, together weeping, make
one woe.
Weep thou for me in France, I for thee here;
Better far off than near, be ne'er the near.
Go, count thy way with sighs; I mine with
groans.

Queen. So longest way shall have the
longest moans.   90

K. Rich. Twice for one step I'll groan, the
way being short,
And piece the way out with a heavy heart.
Come, come, in wooing sorrow let's be brief,
Since, wedding it, there is such length in
grief:
One kiss shall stop our mouths, and dumbly
part;
Thus give I mine, and thus take I thy heart.

Queen. Give me mine own again; 'twere
no good part
To take on me to keep and kill thy heart.
So, now I have mine own again, be gone,
That I may strive to kill it with a groan.   100

K. Rich. We make woe wanton with this
fond delay:
Once more, adieu; the rest let sorrow say.

[*Exeunt.*

SCENE II. *The* DUKE OF YORK'S *palace.*

Enter YORK *and his* DUCHESS.

Duch. My lord, you told me you would
tell the rest,
When weeping made you break the story off,
Of our two cousins coming into London.

York. Where did I leave?

Duch.   At that sad stop, my lord,
Where rude misgovern'd hands from windows' tops
Threw dust and rubbish on King Richard's
head.

York. Then, as I said, the duke, great
Bolingbroke,
Mounted upon a hot and fiery steed
Which his aspiring rider seem'd to know,
With slow but stately pace kept on his
course,   10
Whilst all tongues cried 'God save thee,
Bolingbroke!'

53. **order ta'en**, arrangements made. 55. **Northumberland, thou ladder**, etc. Henry recalls this
speech, quoting lines 55 and 56 in altered form, in *2
Henry IV*, III, i, 70. 59. **corruption**, putrid matter,
pus. 66. **converts**, changes to, turns to. 74. **unkiss**, annul with a kiss (regarded as the seal of a
ceremonial bond). 77. **pines**, afflicts, distresses. 80.
Hallowmas, All Saints' Day (November 1); regarded as
the beginning of winter; ten days later in the old calendar
than it is now.

88. **Better . . . near**, better be far off than near and
yet be unable to meet. The second *near* is the old short
comparative form for "nearer."
Scene ii. 4. **leave**, leave off.

You would have thought the very windows
    spake,
So many greedy looks of young and old
Through casements darted their desiring
    eyes
Upon his visage, and that all the walls
With painted imagery had said at once
'Jesu preserve thee! welcome, Bolingbroke!'
Whilst he, from the one side to the other
    turning,
Bareheaded, lower than his proud steed's
    neck,
Bespake them thus: 'I thank you, country-
    men:'
And thus still doing, thus he pass'd along. 21
  Duch. Alack, poor Richard! where rode he
    the whilst?
  York. As in a theatre, the eyes of men,
After a well-graced actor leaves the stage,
Are idly bent on him that enters next,
Thinking his prattle to be tedious;
Even so, or with much more contempt, men's
    eyes
Did scowl on gentle Richard; no man cried
    'God save him!'
No joyful tongue gave him his welcome
    home:
But dust was thrown upon his sacred head; 30
Which with such gentle sorrow he shook
    off,
His face still combating with tears and
    smiles,
The badges of his grief and patience,
That had not God, for some strong purpose,
    steel'd
The hearts of men, they must perforce have
    melted
And barbarism itself have pitied him.
But heaven hath a hand in these events,
To whose high will we bound our calm
    contents.
To Bolingbroke are we sworn subjects now,
Whose state and honour I for aye allow. 40
  Duch. Here comes my son Aumerle
  York.   Aumerle that was;
But that is lost for being Richard's friend,
And, madam, you must call him Rutland
    now:
I am in parliament pledge for his truth
And lasting fealty to the new made king.

                  Enter AUMERLE.

  Duch. Welcome, my son: who are the
    violets now
That strew the green lap of the new come
    spring?
  Aum. Madam, I know not, nor I greatly
    care not:
God knows I had as lief be none as one.
  York. Well, bear you well in this new
    spring of time,   50
Lest you be cropp'd before you come to
    prime.
What news from Oxford? hold those justs
    and triumphs?
  Aum. For aught I know, my lord, they do.
  York. You will be there, I know.
  Aum. If God prevent not, I purpose so.
  York. What seal is that, that hangs with-
    out thy bosom?
Yea, look'st thou pale? let me see the writ-
    ing.
  Aum. My lord, 'tis nothing.
  York.   No matter, then, who see it:
I will be satisfied; let me see the writing.
  Aum. I do beseech your grace to pardon
    me: 60
It is a matter of small consequence,
Which for some reasons I would not have
    seen.
  York. Which for some reasons, sir, I mean
    to see.
I fear, I fear,—
  Duch.   What should you fear?
'Tis nothing but some bond, that he is
    enter'd into
For gay apparel 'gainst the triumph day.
  York. Bound to himself! what doth he
    with a bond
That he is bound to? Wife, thou art a fool.
Boy, let me see the writing.
  Aum. I do beseech you, pardon me; I may
    not show it.   70
  York. I will be satisfied; let me see it, I say.
  [*He plucks it out of his bosom and reads it.*
Treason! foul treason! Villain! traitor! slave!
  Duch. What is the matter, my lord?
  York. Ho! who is within there?

                Enter a Servant.

                   Saddle my horse.
God for his mercy, what treachery is here!

---

20. **Bespake,** spoke to.   25. **idly,** indifferently.   40.
allow, acknowledge.   41. **Aumerle, that was.** Aumerle, with others of Richard's party, lost all titles and
honors conferred upon him by King Richard.

46-47. **who are . . . spring?** Who are the favorites
of the new king?

Duch. Why, what is it, my lord?

York. Give me my boots, I say; saddle my
horse.   [*Exit Servant.*

Now, by mine honour, by my life, by my
troth,

I will appeach the villain.

Duch.   What is the matter?

York. Peace, foolish woman.   80

Duch. I will not peace. What is the
matter, Aumerle?

Aum. Good mother, be content; it is no
more

Than my poor life must answer.

Duch.   Thy life answer!

York. Bring me my boots: I will unto the
king.

Re-enter Servant *with boots.*

Duch. Strike him, Aumerle. Poor boy,
thou art amazed.

Hence, villain! never more come in my sight.

York. Give me my boots, I say.

Duch. Why, York, what wilt thou do?

Wilt thou not hide the trespass of thine own?

Have we more sons? or are we like to have? 90

Is not my teeming date drunk up with time?

And wilt thou pluck my fair son from mine
age,

And rob me of a happy mother's name?

Is he not like thee? is he not thine own?

York. Thou fond mad woman,

Wilt thou conceal this dark conspiracy?

A dozen of them here have ta'en. the sacrament,

And interchangeably set down their hands,

To kill the king at Oxford.

Duch.   He shall be none;

We'll keep him here: then what is that to
him?   100

York. Away, fond woman! were he twenty
times my son,

I would appeach him.

Duch.   Hadst thou groan'd for him

As I have done, thou wouldst be more pitiful.

But now I know thy mind; thou dost suspect

That I have been disloyal to thy bed,

And that he is a bastard, not thy son:

Sweet York, sweet husband, be not of that
mind:

He is as like thee as a man may be,

Not like to me, or any of my kin,

And yet I love him.

York.   Make way, unruly woman! 110
                                        [*Exit.*

Duch. After, Aumerle! mount thee upon
his horse;

Spur post, and get before him to the king,

And beg thy pardon ere he do accuse thee.

I'll not be long behind; though I be old,

I doubt not but to ride as fast as York:

And never will I rise up from the ground

Till Bolingbroke have pardon'd thee. Away,
be gone!   [*Exeunt.*

SCENE III. *A royal palace.*

Enter BOLINGBROKE, PERCY, *and other* Lords.

Boling. Can no man tell me of my unthrifty son?

'Tis full three months since I did see him last:

If any plague hang over us, 'tis he.

I would to God, my lords, he might be found:

Inquire at London, 'mongst the taverns
there,

For there, they say, he daily doth frequent,

With unrestrained loose companions,

Even such, they say, as stand in narrow
lanes,

And beat our watch, and rob our passengers;

Which he, young wanton and effeminate boy,

Takes on the point of honour to support   11

So dissolute a crew.

Percy. My lord, some two days since I saw
the prince,

And told him of those triumphs held at
Oxford.

Boling. And what said the gallant?

111. **his horse.** In Holinshed York is under way
before Aumerle starts upon his own horse.
Scene iii. 1. **my unthrifty son.** Prince Henry was
twelve years old at this time. Shakespeare has in mind
the traditions of Prince Hal's wayward youth followed
in the later plays of the series. 6. **frequent,** be there
as a matter of habit. 9. **passengers,** passers-by, way-
farers. 10-12. **Which . . . So dissolute a crew.** This
passage will not construe in strict syntax, *which* and
crew both standing as objects of *support.* 10. **wanton,**
spoilt or pampered person. **effeminate,** licentious (?)
13. **I saw the prince.** This is the first bringing together of Hotspur and Prince Hal. Bolingbroke's feelings may be further understood from *1 Henry IV*, I,
i, 78-90; and the tavern view of the matter from the
same play, II, iv, 114-121.

78. **troth,** faith, allegiance. 79. **appeach,** impeach.
80. **Peace,** keep silent. 85. **Strike him,** i.e., strike the
servant. **amazed,** confused, bewildered. 90. **Have we
more sons?** Historically this Duchess of York was the
Duke's second wife and was not Aumerle's mother. 91.
teeming date, period of child-bearing. 97-99. **A dozen
. . . Oxford.** "Hervpon was an indenture sextipartite
made, sealed with their seales, and signed with their
hands, in the which each stood bound to other, to do
their whole indeuor for the accomplishing of their purposed exploit" (Holinshed). 99. **none,** not one of them.

Percy. His answer was, he would unto
  the stews,
And from the common'st creature pluck a
  glove,
And wear it as a favour; and with that
He would unhorse the lustiest challenger.
  Boling. As dissolute as desperate; yet
  through both   20
I see some sparks of better hope, which elder
  years
May happily bring forth. But who comes
  here?

Enter AUMERLE.

Aum. Where is the king?
  Boling. What means our cousin, that he
  stares and looks
So wildly?
  Aum. God save your grace! I do beseech
  your majesty,
To have some conference with your grace
  alone.
  Boling. Withdraw yourselves, and leave
  us here alone.
                    [*Exeunt Percy and Lords.*
What is the matter with our cousin now?
  Aum. For ever may my knees grow to the
  earth,   30
My tongue cleave to my roof within my
  mouth,
Unless a pardon ere I rise or speak.
  Boling. Intended or committed was this
  fault?
If on the first, how heinous e'er it be,
To win thy after-love I pardon thee.
  Aum. Then give me leave that I may turn
  the key,
That no man enter till my tale be done.
  Boling. Have thy desire.
  York. [*Within*] My liege, beware; look to
  thyself;
Thou hast a traitor in thy presence there. 40
  Boling. Villain, I'll make thee safe.
                              [*Drawing.*
  Aum. Stay thy revengeful hand; thou
  hast no cause to fear.
  York. [*Within*] Open the door, secure, fool-
  hardy king:
Shall I for love speak treason to thy face?
Open the door, or I will break it open.

Enter YORK.

Boling. What is the matter, uncle? speak;
Recover breath; tell us how near is danger,
That we may arm us to encounter it.
  York. Peruse this writing here, and thou
  shalt know
The treason that my haste forbids me show.
  Aum. Remember, as thou read'st, thy
  promise pass'd: 51
I do repent me; read not my name there;
My heart is not confederate with my hand.
  York. It was, villain, ere thy hand did set
  it down.
I tore it from the traitor's bosom, king;
Fear, and not love, begets his penitence:
Forget to pity him, lest thy pity prove
A serpent that will sting thee to the heart.
  Boling. O heinous, strong and bold con-
  spiracy!
O loyal father of a treacherous son!   60
Thou sheer, immaculate and silver foun-
  tain,
From whence this stream through muddy
  passages
Hath held his current and defiled himself!
Thy overflow of good converts to bad,
And thy abundant goodness shall excuse
This deadly blot in thy digressing son.
  York. So shall my virtue be his vice's
  bawd;
And he shall spend mine honour with his
  shame,
As thriftless sons their scraping fathers'
  gold.
Mine honour lives when his dishonour dies, 70
Or my shamed life in his dishonour lies:
Thou kill'st me in his life; giving him breath,
The traitor lives, the true man's put to
  death.
  Duch. [*Within*] What ho, my liege! for
  God's sake, let me in.
  Boling. What shrill-voiced suppliant makes
  this eager cry?
  Duch. A woman, and thy aunt, great king;
  'tis I.
Speak with me, pity me, open the door:
A beggar begs that never begg'd before.
  Boling. Our scene is alter'd from a serious
  thing,

---

16. **stews,** houses of ill fame. 22. **happily,** haply;
possibly, combining also the modern sense of the word.
43. **secure,** unsuspecting, heedless. 44. **speak . . .
face,** i.e., by calling him *secure* and *foolhardy.*

58. **serpent,** allusion to the fable of the *Countryman
and the Viper.* See also III, ii, 131. 61-66. **Thou . . .
son.** Chambers quotes a parallel passage from Lyly's
Euphues (Arbor ed., page 191): "As the water that
springeth from the fountain's head," etc. 61. **sheer,**
clear, pure. 66. **digressing,** transgressing.

And now changed to 'The Beggar and the
King.'   80
My dangerous cousin, let your mother in:
I know she is come to pray for your foul
    sin.
  York. If thou do pardon, whosoever pray,
More sins for this forgiveness prosper may.
This fester'd joint cut off, the rest rest sound;
This let alone will all the rest confound.

Enter DUCHESS.

  Duch. O king, believe not this hard-
    hearted man!
Love loving not itself none other can.
  York. Thou frantic woman, what dost
    thou make here?
Shall thy old dugs once more a traitor rear?90
  Duch. Sweet York, be patient. Hear me,
    gentle liege.   [*Kneels.*
  Boling. Rise up, good aunt.
  Duch.   Not yet, I thee beseech:
For ever will I walk upon my knees,
And never see day that the happy sees,
Till thou give joy; until thou bid me joy,
By pardoning Rutland, my transgressing
    boy.
  Aum. Unto my mother's prayers I bend
    my knee.
  York. Against them both my true joints
    bended be.
Ill mayst thou thrive, if thou grant any
    grace!
  Duch. Pleads he in earnest? look upon his
    face;   100
His eyes do drop no tears, his prayers are in
    jest;
His words come from his mouth, ours from
    our breast:
He prays but faintly and would be denied;
We pray with heart and soul and all beside:
His weary joints would gladly rise, I know;
Our knees shall kneel till to the ground they
    grow:
His prayers are full of false hypocrisy;
Ours of true zeal and deep integrity.
Our prayers do out-pray his; then let them
    have   109

That mercy which true prayer ought to have.
  Boling. Good aunt, stand up.
  Duch.   Nay, do not say, 'stand up;'
Say 'pardon' first, and afterwards 'stand
    up.'
An if I were thy nurse, thy tongue to teach,
'Pardon' should be the first word of thy
    speech.
I never long'd to hear a word till now;
Say 'pardon,' king; let pity teach thee how:
The word is short, but not so short as sweet;
No word like 'pardon' for kings' mouths so
    meet.
  York. Speak it in French, king; say 'par-
    donne moi.'
  Duch. Dost thou teach pardon pardon to
    destroy?   120
Ah, my sour husband, my hard-hearted lord,
That set'st the word itself against the word!
Speak 'pardon' as 'tis current in our land;
The chopping French we do not understand.
Thine eye begins to speak; set thy tongue
    there;
Or in thy piteous heart plant thou thine ear;
That hearing how our plaints and prayers do
    pierce,
Pity may move thee 'pardon' to rehearse.
  Boling. Good aunt, stand up.
  Duch.   I do not sue to stand;
Pardon is all the suit I have in hand.   130
  Boling. I pardon him, as God shall pardon
    me.
  Duch. O happy vantage of a kneeling
    knee!
Yet am I sick for fear: speak it again;
Twice saying 'pardon' doth not pardon
    twain,
But makes one pardon strong.
  Boling.   With all my heart
I pardon him.
  Duch.   A god on earth thou art.
  Boling. But for our trusty brother-in-law
    and the abbot,
With all the rest of that consorted crew,
Destruction straight shall dog them at the
    heels.
Good uncle, help to order several powers 140
To Oxford, or where'er these traitors are:

---

80. 'The Beggar and the King,' one of the many
allusions in Shakespeare to the ballad of *King Cophetua
and the Beggar Maid*; see *Love's Labour's Lost*, I, ii, 114
ff.; *Romeo and Juliet*, II, i, 14; *2 Henry IV*, V, iii, 106.
81. My dangerous cousin, another example of Bolingbroke's sarcastic humor used so freely above in his interviews with Richard. 88. Love . . . can. He who does
not love his own kin can love no one else, not even the
king. 103. denied, refused.

119. 'pardonne moi,' excuse me (affectedly polite
refusal).   124. chopping, jerky, shifting suddenly;
possibly, changing (the sense of words).   130. suit,
petition (with play upon the term as used at cards).   137.
our trusty brother-in-law, i.e., John, Earl of Huntingdon, who had married Bolingbroke's sister Elizabeth.
138. consorted, confederate.

They shall not live within this world, I swear,
But I will have them, if I once know where.
Uncle, farewell: and, cousin too, adieu:
Your mother well hath pray'd, and prove you
    true.
    Duch. Come, my old son: I pray God
make thee new.   [*Exeunt.*

SCENE IV. *The same.*

Enter EXTON *and* Servant.

Exton. Didst thou not mark the king, what
    words he spake,
'Have I no friend will rid me of this living
    fear?'
Was it not so?
    Ser.   These were his very words.
    Exton. 'Have I no friend?' quoth he: he
spake it twice,
And urged it twice together, did he not?
    Serv. He did.
    Exton. And speaking it, he wistly look'd
on me;
As who should say, 'I would thou wert the
    man
That would divorce this terror from my
    heart;'
Meaning the king at Pomfret. Come, let's
    go: 10
I am the king's friend, and will rid his foe.
                                        [*Exeunt.*

SCENE V. *Pomfret castle.*

Enter KING RICHARD.

K. Rich. I have been studying how I may
    compare
This prison where I live unto the world:
And for because the world is populous
And here is not a creature but myself,
I cannot do it; yet I'll hammer it out.
My brain I'll prove the female to my soul,

My soul the father; and these two beget
A generation of still-breeding thoughts,
And these same thoughts people this little
    world,
In humours like the people of this world,   10
For no thought is contented. The better
    sort,
As thoughts of things divine, are intermix'd
With scruples and do set the word itself
Against the word:
As thus, 'Come, little ones,' and then again,
'It is as hard to come as for a camel
To thread the postern of a small needle's
    eye.'
Thoughts tending to ambition, they do plot
Unlikely wonders; how these vain weak nails
May tear a passage through the flinty ribs 20
Of this hard world, my ragged prison walls,
And, for they cannot, die in their own pride.
Thoughts tending to content flatter them-
    selves
That they are not the first of fortune's slaves,
Nor shall not be the last; like silly beggars
Who sitting in the stocks refuge their shame,
That many have and others must sit there;
And in this thought they find a kind of
    ease,
Bearing their own misfortunes on the back
Of such as have before endured the like.   30
Thus play I in one person many people,
And none contented: sometimes am I king;
Then treasons make me wish myself a
    beggar,
And so I am: then crushing penury
Persuades me I was better when a king;
Then am I king'd again: and by and by
Think that I am unking'd by Bolingbroke,
And straight am nothing: but whate'er I be,
Nor I nor any man that but man is
With nothing shall be pleased, till he be
    eased   40
With being nothing. Music do I hear?
                                        [*Music.*
Ha, ha! keep time: how sour sweet music
    is,
When time is broke and no proportion kept!
So is it in the music of men's lives.
And here have I the daintiness of ear
To check time broke in a disorder'd string;
But for the concord of my state and time
Had not an ear to hear my true time broke.

---

145. **prove you true.** Aumerle, as Duke of York, died
leading the van at Agincourt.
    Scene iv. 7. **And speaking it,** etc. Cf. Daniel's *Civil
Wars,* II, 57:

"And wisht that some would so his life esteeme,
As *ridde* him of these *feares* wherein he stood:
And there-with eyes a knight, that then was by,
Who soone could learne his lesson by his eye."

    Scene v. 1. **I have been studying,** etc. Daniel (III,
64-69) presents Richard soliloquizing, "Conferring cap-
tiue-Crownes with freedome poore," somewhat in the
spirit of this passage. 5. **I'll hammer it out.** Richard
has an artist's determination to express his idea.

10. **humours,** moods or eccentricities natural to
people's temperaments. 21. **ragged,** rugged. 26.
refuge, comfort. 46. **check,** reprove.

I wasted time, and now doth time waste me;
For now hath time made me his numbering
     clock: 50
My thoughts are minutes; and with sighs
     they jar
Their watches on unto mine eyes, the out-
     ward watch,
Whereto my finger, like a dial's point,
Is pointing still, in cleansing them from
     tears.
Now sir, the sound that tells what hour it is
Are clamorous groans, which strike upon my
     heart,
Which is the bell: so sighs and tears and
     groans
Show minutes, times, and hours: but my
     time
Runs posting on in Bolingbroke's proud joy,
While I stand fooling here, his Jack o' the
     clock.   60
This music mads me; let it sound no more;
For though it have holp madmen to their
     wits,
In me it seems it will make wise men mad.
Yet blessing on his heart that gives it me!
For 'tis a sign of love; and love to Richard
Is a strange brooch in this all-hating world.

     Enter a Groom *of the Stable.*

   Groom. Hail, royal prince!
   K. Rich.   Thanks, noble peer;
The cheapest of us is ten groats too dear.
What art thou? and how comest thou hither,
Where no man never comes but that sad dog
That brings me food to make misfortune live?
   Groom. I was a poor groom of thy stable,
     king,   72
When thou wert king; who, travelling to-
     wards York,
With much ado at length have gotten leave
To look upon my sometimes royal master's
     face.

O, how it yearn'd my heart when I beheld
In London streets, that coronation-day,
When Bolingbroke rode on roan Barbary,
That horse that thou so often hast bestrid,
That horse that I so carefully have dress'd! 80
   K. Rich. Rode he on Barbary? Tell me,
     gentle friend,
How went he under him?
   Groom. So proudly as if he disdain'd the
     ground.
   K. Rich. So proud that Bolingbroke was
     on his back!
That jade hath eat bread from my royal
     hand;
This hand hath made him proud with clap-
     ping him.
Would he not stumble? would he not fall
     down,
Since pride must have a fall, and break the
     neck
Of that proud man that did usurp his back?
Forgiveness, horse! why do I rail on thee,   90
Since thou, created to be awed by man,
Wast born to bear? I was not made a
     horse;
And yet I bear a burthen like an ass,
Spur-gall'd and tired by jauncing Boling-
     broke.

     Enter Keeper, *with a dish.*

   Keep. Fellow, give place; here is no longer
     stay.
   K. Rich. If thou love me, 'tis time thou
     wert away.
   Groom. What my tongue dares not, that
     my heart shall say.   [*Exit.*
   Keep. My lord, will't please you to fall
     to?
   K. Rich. Taste of it first, as thou art wont
     to do.   99
   Keep. My lord, I dare not: Sir Pierce of
Exton, who lately came from the king, com-
mands the contrary.
   K. Rich. The devil take Henry of Lan-
caster and thee!
Patience is stale, and I am weary of it.
               [*Beats the keeper.*
   Keep. Help, help, help!

---

50. **numbering clock.** Henley explains thus: " . . . his sighs correspond to the jarring of the pendulum, which, at the same time that it watches or numbers the seconds, marks also their progress in minutes on the dial or outward watch, to which the king compares his eyes; and their want of figures is supplied by a succession of tears, or, to use the expression of Milton, minute-drops; his finger, by as regularly wiping these tears away performs the office of the dial point; his clamorous groans are the sounds that tell the hour." 51. **jar,** tick. 60. **Jack o' the clock,** a figure which struck the ball on a clock. 62. **holp madmen to their wits,** probable allusion to the story of the cure of Saul by David. 66. **brooch,** ornament (worn in a man's hat). 68. **ten groats too dear.** There is a pun on *royal* and *noble* in the preceding lines. Though a royal (10s.) is worth 10 groats (ten times 4d.) more than a noble (6s. 8d.) is, a noble itself is 10 groats too high a price for either Richard or the Groom.

76. **yearn'd,** vexed, grieved. 78. **roan Barbary.** Boswell Stone suggests that the story of "roan Barbary" may come from an account repeated in Froissart of a grey-hound, Mathe, which forsook his old master, Richard, and followed Bolingbroke. 94. **gall'd,** annoyed; literally, made sore by rubbing. **jauncing,** making prance up and down (of a horse); here, hard-riding.

Enter Exton *and* Servants, *armed.*

K. Rich. How now! what means death in
this rude assault?
Villain, thy own hand yields thy death's
instrument.
[*Snatching an axe from a Servant and
killing him.*
Go thou, and fill another room in hell.
[*He kills another. Then Exton strikes him
down.*
That hand shall burn in never-quenching fire
That staggers thus my person. Exton, thy
fierce hand   110
Hath with the king's blood stain'd the king's
own land.
Mount, mount, my soul! thy seat is up on
high;
Whilst my gross flesh sinks downward, here
to die.   [*Dies.*
Exton. As full of valour as of royal blood:
Both have I spill'd; O would the deed were
good!
For now the devil, that told me I did well,
Says that this deed is chronicled in hell.
This dead king to the living king I'll bear:
Take hence the rest, and give them burial
here.   [*Exeunt.*

SCENE VI. *Windsor castle.*

Flourish. Enter Bolingbroke, York, *with
other* Lords, *and* Attendants.

Boling. Kind uncle York, the latest news
we hear
Is that the rebels have consumed with fire
Our town of Cicester in Gloucestershire;
But whether they be ta'en or slain we hear not.

Enter Northumberland.

Welcome, my lord: what is the news?
North. First, to thy sacred state wish I all
happiness.
The next news is, I have to London sent
The heads of Oxford, Salisbury, Blunt, and
Kent:

The manner of their taking may appear
At large discoursed in this paper here.   10
Boling. We thank thee, gentle Percy, for
thy pains;
And to thy worth will add right worthy
gains.

Enter Fitzwater.

Fitz. My lord, I have from Oxford sent to
London
The heads of Brocas and Sir Bernet Seely,
Two of the dangerous consorted traitors
That sought at Oxford thy dire overthrow.
Boling. Thy pains, Fitzwater, shall not be
forgot;
Right noble is thy merit, well I wot.

Enter Percy, *and the* Bishop of Carlisle.

Percy. The grand conspirator, Abbot of
Westminster,
With clog of conscience and sour melancholy
Hath yielded up his body to the grave;   21
But here is Carlisle living, to abide
Thy kingly doom and sentence of his pride.
Boling. Carlisle, this is your doom:
Choose out some secret place, some reverend
room,
More than thou hast, and with it joy thy life;
So as thou livest in peace, die free from strife:
For though mine enemy thou hast ever been,
High sparks of honour in thee have I seen.

Enter Exton, *with persons bearing a coffin.*

Exton. Great king, within this coffin I
present   30
Thy buried fear: herein all breathless lies
The mightiest of thy greatest enemies,
Richard of Bordeaux, by me hither brought.
Boling. Exton, I thank thee not; for thou
hast wrought
A deed of slander with thy fatal hand
Upon my head and all this famous land.
Exton. From your own mouth, my lord,
did I this deed.
Boling. They love not poison that do
poison need,
Nor do I thee: though I did wish him dead,
I hate the murderer, love him murdered.   40
The guilt of conscience take thou for thy
labour,

---

108. **room**, a particular place assigned to a person.
115. **O . . . good!** "It is said, that sir Piers of Exton,
after he had thus slaine him, wept right bitterlie, as one
stricken with the pricke of a giltie conscience, for mur-
thering him, whome he had so long time obeied as king"
(Holinshed).
Scene vi. 8. **Oxford.** No such name occurs in Holinshed; the F reads *Spencer.* Shakespeare antedates the
death of Richard, since the conspiracy was put down
before his death.

15. **consorted**, confederate. 26. **joy**, enjoy. 34.
Exton, I thank thee not. There is no mention of
Henry's repudiation of Exton in any of the *Chronicles.*
Daniel, *Civil Wars*, III, 79, has a vague parallel.

But neither my good word nor princely
    favour:
With Cain go wander thorough shades of
    night,
And never show thy head by day nor light.
Lords, I protest, my soul is full of woe,
That blood should sprinkle me to make me
    grow:
Come, mourn with me for that I do la-
    ment,
And put on sullen black incontinent:

48. incontinent, immediately.

I'll make a voyage to the Holy Land,
To wash this blood off from my guilty hand:
March sadly after; grace my mournings
    here;   51
In weeping after this untimely bier. [*Exeunt.*

49-50. **I'll make . . . hand.** Henry never fulfilled
his vow, though he had it always in mind; see *1 Henry
IV*, I, i, 19 ff.; *2 Henry IV*, III, i, 108; IV, iv, 3; v, 210 ff.
and 233 ff. 52. **In . . . bier.** Richard died probably in
January 1400; he was buried at Pomfret; his body was
then carried to London, displayed in Cheapside and St.
Paul's on March 12, 1400, and buried in an obscure
grave at Langley. Through the piety of Henry V, his
body was placed in the tomb in Westminster Abbey
which Richard himself had built for his first queen,
Anne of Bohemia.

THE FIRST PART OF
KING HENRY THE FOURTH

DRAMATIS PERSONÆ

KING HENRY the Fourth.
HENRY, Prince of Wales, \
JOHN of Lancaster, / sons to the King.
EARL OF WESTMORELAND.
SIR WALTER BLUNT.
THOMAS PERCY, Earl of Worcester.
HENRY PERCY, Earl of Northumberland.
HENRY PERCY, surnamed HOTSPUR, his son.
EDMUND MORTIMER, Earl of March.
RICHARD SCROOP, Archbishop of York.
ARCHIBALD, Earl of Douglas.
OWEN GLENDOWER.
SIR RICHARD VERNON.
SIR JOHN FALSTAFF.
SIR MICHAEL, a friend to the Archbishop of York.

POINS.
GADSHILL.
PETO.
BARDOLPH.

LADY PERCY, wife to Hotspur, and sister to Mortimer.
LADY MORTIMER, daughter to Glendower, and wife to Mortimer.
MISTRESS QUICKLY, hostess of a tavern in Eastcheap.

Lords, Officers, Sheriff, Vintner, Chamberlain, Drawers, two Carriers, Travellers, and Attendants.

SCENE: *England.*

ACT I.

SCENE I. *London. The palace.*

Enter KING HENRY, LORD JOHN OF LANCASTER, *the* EARL OF WESTMORELAND, SIR WALTER BLUNT, *and others.*

King. So shaken as we are, so wan with care,
Find we a time for frighted peace to pant,
And breathe short-winded accents of new broils
To be commenced in strands afar remote.
†No more the thirsty entrance of this soil
Shall daub her lips with her own children's blood;
No more shall trenching war channel her fields,
Nor bruise her flowerets with the armed hoofs
Of hostile paces: those opposed eyes,
Which, like the meteors of a troubled heaven,
All of one nature, of one substance bred,   11

Did lately meet in the intestine shock
And furious close of civil butchery
Shall now, in mutual well-beseeming ranks,
March all one way and be no more opposed
Against acquaintance, kindred and allies:
The edge of war, like an ill-sheathed knife,
No more shall cut his master.   Therefore, friends,
As far as to the sepulchre of Christ,
Whose soldier now, under whose blessed cross
We are impressed and engaged to fight,   21
Forthwith a power of English shall we levy;
Whose arms were moulded in their mothers' womb
To chase these pagans in those holy fields
Over whose acres walk'd those blessed feet
Which fourteen hundred years ago were nail'd
For our advantage on the bitter cross.
But this our purpose now is twelve month old,

5. **entrance,** i.e., mouth. 9. **opposed,** hostile (of enemies).

13. **close,** encounter.   19. **As far as to.** There is an idea of motion in the word *levy,* line 22.   27. **advantage,** interest.   28. **twelve month,** a year; used collectively.

And bootless 'tis to tell you we will go:
Therefore we meet not now. Then let me
hear   30
Of you, my gentle cousin Westmoreland,
What yesternight our council did decree
In forwarding this dear expedience.
    West. My liege, this haste was hot in
question,
And many limits of the charge set down
But yesternight: when all athwart there
came
A post from Wales loaden with heavy news;
Whose worst was, that the noble Mortimer,
Leading the men of Herefordshire to fight
Against the irregular and wild Glendower, 40
Was by the rude hands of that Welshman
taken,
A thousand of his people butchered;
Upon whose dead corpse there was such
misuse,
Such beastly shameless transformation,
By those Welshwomen done as may not be
Without much shame retold or spoken of.
    King. It seems then that the tidings of
this broil
Brake off our business for the Holy Land.
    West. This match'd with other did, my
gracious lord;
For more uneven and unwelcome news   50
Came from the north and thus it did import:
On Holy-rood day, the gallant Hotspur there,
Young Harry Percy and brave Archibald,
That ever-valiant and approved Scot,
At Holmedon met,
Where they did spend a sad and bloody
hour;
As by discharge of their artillery,
And shape of likelihood, the news was
told;
For he that brought them, in the very heat
And pride of their contention did take horse,
Uncertain of the issue any way.   61
    King. Here is a dear, a true industrious
friend,
Sir Walter Blunt, new lighted from his horse,
Stain'd with the variation of each soil

Betwixt that Holmedon and this seat of ours;
And he hath brought us smooth and welcome
news.
The Earl of Douglas is discomfited:
Ten thousand bold Scots, two and twenty
knights,
Balk'd in their own blood did Sir Walter see
On Holmedon's plains. Of prisoners, Hot-
spur took   70
Mordake the Earl of Fife, and eldest son
To beaten Douglas; and the Earl of Athol,
Of Murray, Angus, and Menteith:
And is not this an honourable spoil?
A gallant prize? ha, cousin, is it not?
    West. In faith,
It is a conquest for a prince to boast of.
    King. Yea, there thou makest me sad and
makest me sin
In envy that my Lord Northumberland
Should be the father to so blest a son,   80
A son who is the theme of honour's tongue;
Amongst a grove, the very straightest plant;
Who is sweet Fortune's minion and her pride:
Whilst I, by looking on the praise of him,
See riot and dishonour stain the brow
Of my young Harry. O that it could be
proved
That some night-tripping fairy had ex-
changed
In cradle-clothes our children where they lay,
And call'd mine Percy, his Plantagenet!
Then would I have his Harry, and he mine. 90
But let him from my thoughts. What think
you, coz,
Of this young Percy's pride? the prisoners,
Which he in this adventure hath surprised,
To his own use he keeps; and sends me word,
I shall have none but Mordake Earl of Fife.
    West. This is his uncle's teaching: this is
Worcester,
Malevolent to you in all aspects;
Which makes him prune himself, and bristle
up
The crest of youth against your dignity.
    King. But I have sent for him to answer
this;   100

---

31. **Of,** from. 33. **dear expedience,** urgent expedition. 34. **hot in question,** being hotly debated. 35.
limits of the charge, military arrangements; possibly,
estimates of expense. 36. **athwart,** frustrating, interrupting. 38. **worst,** i.e., worst news. 40. **irregular,**
lawless. 43-46. **upon . . . spoken of.** Holinshed also
says that the outrages are unmentionable. 49. **This . . .
other,** this piece of news matched with another. 50.
uneven, embarrassing. 55. **Holmedon,** Humbleton,
a town in Northumberland. 57. **by,** i.e., judging from.
64. **the variation of each,** every kind of.

66. **smooth,** flattering, pleasant. 69. **Balk'd,** heaped
up in balks or ridges. 71. **Mordake.** This Murdoch,
Earl of Fife, was the son of the Regent of Scotland.
Shakespeare follows the text of Holinshed in which a
comma was omitted after the word *governour:* "Mordacke
earl of Fife, son to the governour Archembald earl
Dowglas." 83. **minion,** favorite, darling. 95. **none
but Mordake.** Since the prisoner in question was of
royal blood, being grandson to Robert II, Hotspur could
not claim him as his prisoner. 97. **Malevolent, aspects,**
astrological terms. 98. **prune,** preen (as a bird its
feathers).

And for this cause awhile we must neglect
Our holy purpose to Jerusalem.
Cousin, on Wednesday next our council we
Will hold at Windsor; so inform the lords:
But come yourself with speed to us again;
For more is to be said and to be done
Than out of anger can be uttered.

West. I will, my liege.   *[Exeunt.*

SCENE II. *London. An apartment of the
Prince's.*

Enter the PRINCE OF WALES *and* FALSTAFF.

Fal. Now, Hal, what time of day is it, lad?
Prince. Thou art so fat-witted, with
drinking of old sack and unbuttoning thee
after supper and sleeping upon benches after
noon, that thou hast forgotten to demand
that truly which thou wouldst truly know.
What a devil hast thou to do with the time
of the day? Unless hours were cups of sack
and minutes capons and clocks the tongues
of bawds and dials the signs of leaping-
houses and the blessed sun himself a fair hot
wench in flame-coloured taffeta, I see no
reason why thou shouldst be so superfluous
to demand the time of the day.   13
Fal. Indeed, you come near me now, Hal;
for we that take purses go by the noon and
the seven stars, and not by Phœbus, he, 'that
wandering knight so fair.' And, I prithee,
sweet wag, when thou art king, as, God save
thy grace,—majesty I should say, for grace
thou wilt have none,—   20
Prince. What, none?
Fal. No, by my troth, not so much as will
serve to be prologue to an egg and butter.
Prince. Well, how then? come, roundly,
roundly.
Fal. Marry, then, sweet wag, when thou
art king, let not us that are squires of the
night's body be called thieves of the day's
beauty: let us be Diana's foresters, gentlemen of the shade, minions of the moon; and
let men say we be men of good government,
being governed, as the sea is, by our noble
and chaste mistress the moon, under whose
countenance we steal.   33
Prince. Thou sayest well, and it holds
well too; for the fortune of us that are the
moon's men doth ebb and flow like the sea,
being governed, as the sea is, by the moon.
As, for proof, now: a purse of gold most
resolutely snatched on Monday night and
most dissolutely spent on Tuesday morning;
got with swearing 'Lay by' and spent with
crying 'Bring in;' now in as low an ebb as
the foot of the ladder and by and by in as
high a flow as the ridge of the gallows.   43
Fal. By the Lord, thou sayest true, lad.
And is not my hostess of the tavern a most
sweet wench?
Prince. As the honey of Hybla, my old lad
of the castle. And is not a buff jerkin a most
sweet robe of durance?   49
Fal. How now, how now, mad wag! what,
in thy quips and thy quiddities? what a
plague have I to do with a buff jerkin?
Prince. Why, what a pox have I to do
with my hostess of the tavern?
Fal. Well, thou hast called her to a reckoning many a time and oft.
Prince. Did I ever call for thee to pay thy
part?
Fal. No; I'll give thee thy due, thou hast
paid all there.   60
Prince. Yea, and elsewhere, so far as my
coin would stretch; and where it would not,
I have used my credit.
Fal. Yea, and so used it that, were it not
here apparent that thou art heir apparent—
But, I prithee, sweet wag, shall there be
gallows standing in England when thou art
king? and resolution thus fobbed as it is
with the rusty curb of old father antic the
law? Do not thou, when thou art king,   70
hang a thief.
Prince. No; thou shalt.
Fal. Shall I? O rare! By the Lord, I'll
be a brave judge.
Prince. Thou judgest false already: I

Scene ii. 3. **sack,** sherry, sweet Spanish wine. 14.
come near me now. Prince Hal's speech has been full
of extravagant abuse; Falstaff parries by taking it in a
sense of his own. 16. **the seven stars,** the Pleiades.
17-18. **'that . . . fair,'** a line from some ballad. 23.
prologue, punning allusion to grace before meat. 24.
roundly, out with it. It is a wit combat. 27-29. **squires
. . . beauty.** Note the euphuistic balance. Falstaff
talks in the style of a courtier.

40. **'Lay by,'** a cry of highwaymen, like "Hands up!"
41. **'Bring in,'** i.e., the orders in the tavern. 47. **Hybla,**
a mountain region in Sicily near Syracuse, famed for
honey. 48. **old lad of the castle,** a pun on the name,
Sir John Oldcastle, borne by Falstaff in the earlier versions of the Henry IV plays. **buff jerkin,** a leather
jacket worn by officers of the law; a *robe of durance* in
two senses, since *durance* means "imprisonment" and
"durability." 51. **quips,** jests. **quiddities,** subtleties
of speech. 68. **fobbed,** cheated. 69. **antic,** the buffoon
of the old plays.

mean, thou shalt have the hanging of the thieves and so become a rare hangman.

Fal. Well, Hal, well; and in some sort it jumps with my humour as well as waiting in the court, I can tell you.

Prince. For obtaining of suits? 80

Fal. Yea, for obtaining of suits, whereof the hangman hath no lean wardrobe. 'Sblood, I am as melancholy as a gib cat or a lugged bear.

Prince. Or an old lion, or a lover's lute.

Fal. Yea, or the drone of a Lincolnshire bagpipe.

Prince. What sayest thou to a hare, or the melancholy of Moor-ditch? 88

Fal. Thou hast the most unsavoury similes and art indeed the most comparative, rascalliest, sweet young prince. But, Hal, I prithee, trouble me no more with vanity. I would to God thou and I knew where a commodity of good names were to be bought. An old lord of the council rated me the other day in the street about you, sir, but I marked him not; and yet he talked very wisely, but I regarded him not; and yet he talked wisely, and in the street too.

Prince. Thou didst well; for wisdom cries out in the streets, and no man regards 100 it.

Fal. O, thou hast damnable iteration and art indeed able to corrupt a saint. Thou hast done much harm upon me, Hal; God forgive thee for it! Before I knew thee, Hal, I knew nothing; and now am I, if a man should speak truly, little better than one of the wicked. I must give over this life, and I will give it over: by the Lord, an I do not, I am a villain: I'll be damned for never a king's son in Christendom. 109

Prince. Where shall we take a purse tomorrow, Jack?

Fal. 'Zounds, where thou wilt, lad; I'll make one; an I do not, call me villain and baffle me. 113

Prince. I see a good amendment of life in thee; from praying to purse-taking.

Fal. Why, Hal, 'tis my vocation, Hal; 'tis no sin for a man to labour in his vocation. 117

Enter POINS.

Poins! Now shall we know if Gadshill have set a match. O, if men were to be saved by merit, what hole in hell were hot enough for him? This is the most omnipotent villain that ever cried 'Stand' to a true man.

Prince. Good morrow, Ned.

Poins. Good morrow, sweet Hal. What says Monsieur Remorse? what says Sir John Sack and Sugar? Jack! how agrees the devil and thee about thy soul, that thou soldest him on Good-Friday last for a cup of Madeira and a cold capon's leg? 129

Prince. Sir John stands to his word, the devil shall have his bargain; for he was never yet a breaker of proverbs: he will give the devil his due.

Poins. Then art thou damned for keeping thy word with the devil.

Prince. Else he had been damned for cozening the devil. 137

Poins. But, my lads, my lads, to-morrow morning, by four o'clock, early at Gadshill! there are pilgrims going to Canterbury with rich offerings, and traders riding to London with fat purses: I have vizards for you all; you have horses for yourselves: Gadshill lies to-night in Rochester: I have bespoke supper to-morrow night in Eastcheap: we may do it as secure as sleep. If you will go, I will stuff your purses full of crowns; if you will not, tarry at home and be hanged.

Fal. Hear ye, Yedward; if I tarry at home and go not, I'll hang you for going. 150

Poins. You will, chops?

Fal. Hal, wilt thou make one?

Prince. Who, I rob? I a thief? not I, by my faith.

Fal. There's neither honesty, manhood, nor good fellowship in thee, nor thou camest not of the blood royal, if thou darest not stand for ten shillings.

Prince. Well then, once in my days I'll be a madcap. 160

Fal. Why, that's well said.

---

78. **waiting in the court**, in a double sense, as a courtier and a judge. 80. **suits**, suits at court and suits of clothes. 82. **'Sblood**, an oath. 83. **gib cat**, tom cat. **lugged bear**, bear dragged by a rope. 88. **Moor-ditch**, a foul ditch draining Moorfields. 99. **wisdom cries out**, etc., an allusion to *Proverbs* i, 20-24. 103. **much harm upon me**. Oldcastle was traditionally a religious hypocrite and a Lollard, or follower of John Wyclif; Falstaff retains his faculty for insincere repentance. 112. **'Zounds**, an oath, "God's wounds." 113. **baffle**, hang up by the heels as a recreant knight.

116. **vocation**, a cant term for religious conversion. 118. **Gadshill**, an old name appearing in *The Famous Victories*, apparently from a hill southeast of London, notorious for highway robberies. 119. **set a match**, arranged a robbery. In the old play Gadshill is called a "setter." 142. **vizards**, masks. 149. **Yedward**, Edward; a colloquialism. 151. **chops**, apparently alluding to Falstaff's fat jaws.

Prince. Well, come what will, I'll tarry at home.

Fal. By the Lord, I'll be a traitor then, when thou art king.

Prince. I care not.

Poins. Sir John, I prithee, leave the prince and me alone: I will lay him down such reasons for this adventure that he shall go. 169

Fal. Well, God give thee the spirit of persuasion and him the ears of profiting, that what thou speakest may move and what he hears may be believed, that the true prince may, for recreation sake, prove a false thief; for the poor abuses of the time want countenance. Farewell: you shall find me in Eastcheap.

Prince. Farewell, thou latter spring! farewell, All-hallown summer! [*Exit Falstaff.* 178

Poins. Now, my good sweet honey lord, ride with us to-morrow: I have a jest to execute that I cannot manage alone. Falstaff, Bardolph, Peto and Gadshill shall rob those men that we have already waylaid; yourself and I will not be there; and when they have the booty, if you and I do not rob them, cut this head off from my shoulders.

Prince. How shall we part with them in setting forth? 188

Poins. Why, we will set forth before or after them, and appoint them a place of meeting, wherein it is at our pleasure to fail, and then will they adventure upon the exploit themselves; which they shall have no sooner achieved, but we'll set upon them.

Prince. Yea, but 'tis like that they will know us by our horses, by our habits and by every other appointment, to be ourselves.

Poins. Tut! our horses they shall not see; I'll tie them in the wood; our vizards we will change after we leave them: and, sirrah, I have cases of buckram for the nonce, to immask our noted outward garments. 202

Prince. Yea, but I doubt they will be too hard for us.

Poins. Well, for two of them, I know them to be as true-bred cowards as ever turned back; and for the third, if he fight longer than he sees reason, I'll forswear arms. The virtue of this jest will be, the incomprehensible lies that this same fat rogue will tell us when we meet at supper: how thirty, at least, he fought with; what wards, what blows, what extremities he endured; and in the reproof of this lies the jest. 213

Prince. Well, I'll go with thee: provide us all things necessary and meet me to-morrow night in Eastcheap; there I'll sup. Farewell.

Poins. Farewell, my lord. [*Exit.*

Prince. I know you all, and will awhile uphold
The unyoked humour of your idleness:
Yet herein will I imitate the sun, 220
Who doth permit the base contagious clouds
To smother up his beauty from the world,
That, when he please again to be himself,
Being wanted, he may be more wonder'd at,
By breaking through the foul and ugly mists
Of vapours that did seem to strangle him.
If all the year were playing holidays,
To sport would be as tedious as to work;
But when they seldom come, they wish'd for come,
And nothing pleaseth but rare accidents. 230
So, when this loose behaviour I throw off
And pay the debt I never promised,
By how much better than my word I am,
By so much shall I falsify men's hopes;
And like bright metal on a sullen ground,
My reformation, glittering o'er my fault,
Shall show more goodly and attract more eyes
Than that which hath no foil to set it off.
I'll so offend, to make offence a skill; 239
Redeeming time when men think least I will.
[*Exit.*

SCENE III. *London. The palace.*

Enter the King, Northumberland, Worcester, Hotspur, Sir Walter Blunt, *with others.*

King. My blood hath been too cold and temperate,

170, 171. **spirit of persuasion, ears of profiting.** cant phrases of religious connotation. 178. **All-hallown summer.** Falstaff's summer (his youth) has lasted to All Saints' day, November 1st. 201. **cases,** suits. **for the nonce,** for the occasion. 202. **noted,** known.

208. **incomprehensible lies.** This passage serves dramatically as a preparation for the great fourth scene of the second act. 218-240. **I know . . . will.** This soliloquy is often misinterpreted. Some consider Prince Hal as a prig; others say that he, like his father, is a schemer, or that he makes a lame attempt to convince himself that he is justifiable. In point of fact, the author is merely talking to his audience and telling them his plans for his hero. Here, as is often the case in soliloquies, the speaker's character should not be judged by inferences from what he says; only the face value of the dramatist's words should be accepted.

Unapt to stir at these indignities,
And you have found me; for accordingly
You tread upon my patience: but be sure
I will from henceforth rather be myself,
Mighty and to be fear'd, than my condition;
Which hath been smooth as oil, soft as
    young down,
And therefore lost that title of respect
Which the proud soul ne'er pays but to the
    proud.
    Wor. Our house, my sovereign liege, little
    deserves   10
The scourge of greatness to be used on it;
And that same greatness too which our own
    hands
Have holp to make so portly.
    North. My lord,—
    King. Worcester, get thee gone; for I do
    see
Danger and disobedience in thine eye:
O, sir, your presence is too bold and per-
    emptory,
And majesty might never yet endure
The moody frontier of a servant brow.
You have good leave to leave us: when we
    need   20
Your use and counsel, we shall send for you.
                                        [*Exit Wor.*
You were about to speak.   [*To North.*
    North.   Yea, my good lord.
Those prisoners in your highness' name de-
    manded,
Which Harry Percy here at Holmedon took,
Were, as he says, not with such strength
    denied
As is deliver'd to your majesty:
Either envy, therefore, or misprision
Is guilty of this fault and not my son.
    Hot. My liege, I did deny no prisoners.
But I remember, when the fight was done, 30
When I was dry with rage and extreme toil,
Breathless and faint, leaning upon my sword,
Came there a certain lord, neat, and trimly
    dress'd,

Fresh as a bridegroom; and his chin new
    reap'd
Show'd like a stubble-land at harvest-home;
He was perfumed like a milliner;
And 'twixt his finger and his thumb he
    held
A pouncet-box, which ever and anon
He gave his nose and took't away again;
Who therewith angry, when it next came
    there,   40
Took it in snuff; and still he smiled and
    talk'd,
And as the soldiers bore dead bodies by,
He call'd them untaught knaves, unman-
    nerly,
To bring a slovenly unhandsome corse
Betwixt the wind and his nobility.
With many holiday and lady terms
He question'd me; amongst the rest, de-
    manded
My prisoners in your majesty's behalf.
I then, all smarting with my wounds being
    cold,
To be so pester'd with a popinjay,   50
Out of my grief and my impatience,
Answer'd neglectingly I know not what,
He should, or he should not; for he made me
    mad
To see him shine so brisk and smell so
    sweet
And talk so like a waiting-gentlewoman
Of guns and drums and wounds,—God save
    the mark!—
And telling me the sovereign'st thing on
    earth
Was parmaceti for an inward bruise;
And that it was great pity, so it was,
This villanous salt-petre should be digg'd 60
Out of the bowels of the harmless earth,
Which many a good tall fellow had destroy'd
So cowardly; and but for these vile guns,
He would himself have been a soldier.
This bald unjointed chat of his, my lord,
I answer'd indirectly, as I said;
And I beseech you, let not his report
Come current for an accusation
Betwixt my love and your high majesty.
    Blunt. The circumstance consider'd, good
    my lord,   70

---

3. **found me**, i.e., found me so. 6. **condition**, disposition. 13. **portly**, prosperous, with a suggestion of
over-prosperity. 14. **My lord.** Northumberland is
apparently about to protest against Worcester's impertinence; he is Worcester's brother and the head of
the house of Percy, but he would not remind the king
so obviously that they have seated him on his throne.
19. **moody**, passionate, angry. **frontier**, outwork or
fortification; here with play on the word *front* or *brow*.
27. **misprision**, misunderstanding. 29-69. **My liege
. . . majesty.** Hotspur's speech, containing the famous
description of the fop, is humorous, appealing, and not
unfriendly. One must always feel that the stubborn
directness of King Henry, reminiscent of the same quality
in the Bolingbroke of *Richard II*, is most unfortunate.

35. **harvest-home**, end of harvest, fields being neat
and bare. 36. **milliner**, man dealing in fancy articles.
38. **pouncet-box**, perfume box with perforated lid.
46. **lady**, ladylike. 50. **popinjay**, parrot. 56. **God
save the mark!** Probably originally a formula to avert
evil omen; here, an expression of impatience. 58. **parmaceti**, spermaceti, sperm from the whale.

Whate'er Lord Harry Percy then had said
To such a person and in such a place,
At such a time, with all the rest retold,
May reasonably die and never rise
To do him wrong or any way impeach
What then he said, so he unsay it now.

King. Why, yet he doth deny his prison-
ers,
But with proviso and exception,
That we at our own charge shall ransom
straight
His brother-in-law, the foolish Mortimer; 80
Who, on my soul, hath wilfully betray'd
The lives of those that he did lead to fight
Against that great magician, damn'd Glen-
dower,
Whose daughter, as we hear, the Earl of
March
Hath lately married. Shall our coffers, then,
Be emptied to redeem a traitor home?
Shall we buy treason? and indent with fears,
When they have lost and forfeited them-
selves?
No, on the barren mountains let him starve;
For I shall never hold that man my friend 90
Whose tongue shall ask me for one penny
cost
To ransom home revolted Mortimer.

Hot. Revolted Mortimer!
He never did fall off, my sovereign liege,
But by the chance of war: to prove that
true
Needs no more but one tongue for all those
wounds,
Those mouthed wounds, which valiantly he
took,
When on the gentle Severn's sedgy bank,
In single opposition, hand to hand,
He did confound the best part of an hour 100
In changing hardiment with great Glen-
dower:
Three times they breathed and three times
did they drink,
Upon agreement, of swift Severn's flood,
Who then, affrighted with their bloody looks,
Ran fearfully among the trembling reeds,
And hid his crisp head in the hollow bank
Bloodstained with these valiant combatants.
Never did base and rotten policy

Colour her working with such deadly wounds;
Nor never could the noble Mortimer 110
Receive so many, and all willingly:
Then let not him be slander'd with revolt.

King. Thou dost belie him, Percy, thou
dost belie him;
He never did encounter with Glendower:
I tell thee,
He durst as well have met the devil alone
As Owen Glendower for an enemy.
Art thou not ashamed? But, sirrah, hence-
forth
Let me not hear you speak of Mortimer:
Send me your prisoners with the speediest
means 120
Or you shall hear in such a kind from me
As will displease you. My Lord Northum-
berland,
We license your departure with your son.
Send us your prisoners, or you will hear of it.

[Exeunt King Henry, Blunt, and train.

Hot. An if the devil come and roar for
them,
I will not send them: I will after straight
And tell him so; for I will ease my heart,
Albeit I make a hazard of my head.

North. What, drunk with choler? stay
and pause awhile:
Here comes your uncle.

Re-enter Worcester.

Hot.   Speak of Mortimer! 130
'Zounds, I will speak of him; and let my
soul
Want mercy, if I do not join with him:
Yea, on his part I'll empty all these veins,
And shed my dear blood drop by drop in
the dust,
But I will lift the down-trod Mortimer
As high in the air as this unthankful king,
As this ingrate and canker'd Bolingbroke.

North. Brother, the king hath made your
nephew mad.

Wor. Who struck this heat up after I was
gone?

Hot. He will, forsooth, have all my
prisoners; 140
And when I urged the ransom once again

Of my wife's brother, then his cheek look'd
   pale,
And on my face he turn'd an eye of death,
Trembling even at the name of Mortimer.
 Wor. I cannot blame him: was not he
   proclaim'd
By Richard that dead is the next of blood?
 North. He was; I heard the proclamation:
And then it was when the unhappy king,—
Whose wrongs in us God pardon!—did set
   forth
Upon his Irish expedition;   150
From whence he intercepted did return
To be deposed and shortly murdered.
 Wor. And for whose death we in the
   world's wide mouth
Live scandalized and foully spoken of.
 Hot. But, soft, I pray you; did King
   Richard then
Proclaim my brother Edmund Mortimer
Heir to the crown?
 North.   He did; myself did hear it.
 Hot. Nay, then I cannot blame his cousin
   king,
That wish'd him on the barren mountains
   starve.
But shall it be, that you, that set the crown
Upon the head of this forgetful man   161
And for his sake wear the detested blot
Of murderous subornation, shall it be,
That you a world of curses undergo,
Being the agents, or base second means,
The cords, the ladder, or the hangman
   rather?
O, pardon me that I descend so low,
To show the line and the predicament
Wherein you range under this subtle king;
Shall it for shame be spoken in these days, 170
Or fill up chronicles in time to come,
That men of your nobility and power
Did gage them both in an unjust behalf,
As both of you—God pardon it!—have done,
To put down Richard, that sweet lovely
   rose,
And plant this thorn, this canker, Boling-
   broke?
And shall it in more shame be further
   spoken,
That you are fool'd, discarded and shook off

By him for whom these shames ye under-
   went?   179
No; yet time serves wherein you may redeem
Your banish'd honours and restore your-
   selves
Into the good thoughts of the world again,
Revenge the jeering and disdain'd contempt
Of this proud king, who studies day and night
To answer all the debt he owes to you
Even with the bloody payment of your
   deaths:
Therefore, I say,—
 Wor.   Peace, cousin, say no more:
And now I will unclasp a secret book,
And to your quick-conceiving discontents
I'll read you matter deep and dangerous, 190
As full of peril and adventurous spirit
As to o'er-walk a current roaring loud
On the unsteadfast footing of a spear.
 Hot. If he fall in, good night! or sink or
   swim:
Send danger from the east unto the west,
So honour cross it from the north to south,
And let them grapple: O, the blood more
   stirs
To rouse a lion than to start a hare!
 North. Imagination of some great exploit
Drives him beyond the bounds of patience.
 Hot. By heaven, methinks it were an easy
   leap,   201
To pluck bright honour from the pale-faced
   moon,
Or dive into the bottom of the deep,
Where fathom-line could never touch the
   ground,
And pluck up drowned honour by the locks;
So he that doth redeem her thence might
   wear
Without corrival all her dignities:
But out upon this half-faced fellowship!
 Wor. He apprehends a world of figures
   here,   209
But not the form of what he should attend.
Good cousin, give me audience for a while.
 Hot. I cry you mercy.
 Wor.   Those same noble Scots
That are your prisoners,—

145-152. **I cannot . . . murdered.** These lines and
the dialogue as a whole serve to connect this play with
Richard II and to make clear the political situation back
of the revolt.   163. **subornation,** oath-breaking,
treason. 164. **a world of curses.** Treason against
the king was treason against God and carried with it
actual sin. 176. **canker,** canker-rose, dog-rose.

183. **disdain'd,** disdainful. 199. **Imagination . . .
exploit.** It will be noticed that Northumberland thinks
of Hotspur as beside himself, insane; and so, according
to the theory of passions which prevailed at the time, he
was. The line quoted gives the theory of the effect of a
fixed idea, which lies back of the madness of Lear and
Othello. 207. **corrival,** rival, competitor. 208. **half-
faced,** half-hearted. Shakespeare represents Hotspur
as actuated by chivalry exaggerated to the point of
madness.

Hot.   I'll keep them all;
By God, he shall not have a Scot of them;
No, if a Scot would save his soul, he shall not:
I'll keep them, by this hand.
Wor.   You start away
And lend no ear unto my purposes.
Those prisoners you shall keep.
Hot.   Nay, I will; that's flat:
He said he would not ransom Mortimer;
Forbad my tongue to speak of Mortimer;   220
But I will find him when he lies asleep,
And in his ear I'll holla 'Mortimer!'
Nay,
I'll have a starling shall be taught to speak
Nothing but 'Mortimer,' and give it him,
To keep his anger still in motion.
Wor. Hear you, cousin; a word.
Hot. All studies here I solemnly defy,
Save how to gall and pinch this Bolingbroke:
And that same sword-and-buckler Prince of Wales,   230
But that I think his father loves him not
And would be glad he met with some mischance,
I would have him poison'd with a pot of ale.
Wor. Farewell, kinsman: I'll talk to you
When you are better temper'd to attend.
North. Why, what a wasp-stung and impatient fool
Art thou to break into this woman's mood,
Tying thine ear to no tongue but thine own!
Hot. Why, look you, I am whipp'd and scourged with rods,
Nettled and stung with pismires, when I hear
Of this vile politician, Bolingbroke.   241
In Richard's time,—what do you call the place?—
A plague upon it, it is in Gloucestershire;
'Twas where the madcap duke his uncle kept,
His uncle York; where I first bow'd my knee
Unto this king of smiles, this Bolingbroke,—
'Sblood!—
When you and he came back from Ravenspurgh.
North. At Berkley castle.
Hot. You say true: 250
Why, what a candy deal of courtesy

This fawning greyhound then did proffer me!
Look, 'when his infant fortune came to age,'
And 'gentle Harry Percy,' and 'kind cousin;'
O, the devil take such cozeners! God forgive me!
Good uncle, tell your tale; I have done.
Wor. Nay, if you have not, to it again;
We will stay your leisure.
Hot.   I have done, i' faith.
Wor. Then once more to your Scottish prisoners.
Deliver them up without their ransom straight,   260
And make the Douglas' son your only mean
For powers in Scotland; which, for divers reasons
Which I shall send you written, be assured,
Will easily be granted. You, my lord,
                    [*To Northumberland.*
Your son in Scotland being thus employ'd,
Shall secretly into the bosom creep
Of that same noble prelate, well beloved,
The archbishop.
Hot. Of York, is it not?
Wor. True; who bears hard   270
His brother's death at Bristol, the Lord Scroop.
I speak not this in estimation,
As what I think might be, but what I know
Is ruminated, plotted and set down,
And only stays but to behold the face
Of that occasion that shall bring it on.
Hot. I smell it: upon my life, it will do well.
North. Before the game is afoot, thou still let'st slip.
Hot. Why, it cannot choose but be a noble plot:
And then the power of Scotland and of York,
To join with Mortimer, ha?
Wor.   And so they shall.   281
Hot. In faith, it is exceedingly well aim'd.
Wor. And 'tis no little reason bids us speed,
To save our heads by raising of a head;
For, bear ourselves as even as we can,
The king will always think him in our debt,
And think we think ourselves unsatisfied,
Till he hath found a time to pay us home:
And see already how he doth begin
To make us strangers to his looks of love.   290

226. **in motion**, i.e., he will not allow the spirits of anger to settle or be diverted. 233. **poison'd**. This has been called malicious; it is only part of Hotspur's madness. 235. **better . . . attend**. This scene is the beginning of Hotspur's inability to listen to others. 240. **pismires**, ants. 241. **politician**, deceitful schemer. 251. **candy**, sugared, flattering.

255. **cozeners**, cheats, with pun on *cousins*. 261. **mean**, i.e., means of procuring. 272. **estimation**, guesswork. 284. **head**, i.e., head of rebellion, armed force.

Hot. He does, he does: we'll be revenged
    on him.
Wor. Cousin, farewell: no further go in
    this
Than I by letters shall direct your course.
When time is ripe, which will be suddenly,
I'll steal to Glendower and Lord Mortimer;
Where you and Douglas and our powers at
    once,
As I will fashion it, shall happily meet,
To bear our fortunes in our own strong arms,
Which now we hold at much uncertainty.
North. Farewell, good brother: we shall
    thrive, I trust.   300
Hot. Uncle, adieu: O, let the hours be
    short
Till fields and blows and groans applaud our
    sport!   [*Exeunt.*

ACT II.

Scene I. *Rochester. An inn yard.*

Enter a Carrier *with a lantern in his hand.*

First Car. Heigh-ho! an if be not four by
the day, I'll be hanged: Charles' wain is over
the new chimney, and yet our horse not
packed. What, ostler!
Ost. [*Within*] Anon, anon.   5
First Car. I prithee, Tom, beat Cut's
saddle, put a few flocks in the point; poor
jade, is wrung in the withers out of all cess.

Enter another Carrier.

Sec. Car. Peas and beans are as dank here
as a dog, and that is the next way to give
poor jades the bots: this house is turned up-
side down since Robin Ostler died.   12
First Car. Poor fellow, never joyed since
the price of oats rose; it was the death of
him.
Sec. Car. I think this be the most villanous
house in all London road for fleas: I am stung
like a tench.
First Car. Like a tench! by the mass, there

is ne'er a king christen could be better bit
than I have been since the first cock.   20
Sec. Car. Why, they will allow us ne'er a
jordan, and then we leak in your chimney;
and your chamber-lie breeds fleas like a
loach.
First Car. What, ostler! come away and
be hanged! come away.
Sec. Car. I have a gammon of bacon and
two razes of ginger, to be delivered as far as
Charing-cross.   28
First Car. God's body! the turkeys in my
pannier are quite starved. What, ostler! A
plague on thee! hast thou never an eye in thy
head? canst not hear? An 'twere not as good
deed as drink, to break the pate on thee, I am
a very villain. Come, and be hanged! hast
no faith in thee?

Enter Gadshill.

Gads. Good morrow, carriers. What's
o'clock?
First Car. I think it be two o'clock.
Gads. I prithee, lend me thy lantern, to
see my gelding in the stable.
First Car. Nay, by God, soft; I know a
trick worth two of that, i' faith.   41
Gads. I pray thee, lend me thine.
Sec. Car. Ay, when? canst tell? Lend me
thy lantern, quoth he? marry, I'll see thee
hanged first.
Gads. Sirrah carrier, what time do you
mean to come to London?
Sec. Car. Time enough to go to bed with
a candle, I warrant thee. Come, neighbour
Mugs, we'll call up the gentlemen: they will
along with company, for they have great
charge.   [*Exeunt Carriers.*
Gads. What, ho! chamberlain!   52
Cham. [*Within*] At hand, quoth pick-purse.
Gads. That's even as fair as—at hand,
quoth the chamberlain; for thou variest no
more from picking of purses than giving
direction doth from labouring; thou layest
the plot how.

Enter Chamberlain.

Cham. Good morrow, Master Gadshill. It
holds current that I told you yesternight:

Act II. Scene i. *Stage Direction:* **Carrier,** one whose
trade was conveying goods, usually by pack horses. This
scene of commonplace realism is original prose and, it is
thought, remained unmodified in the revision. 1. **by
the day,** by the sun. 2. **Charles' wain,** the constellation of the Great Bear. 3. **horse,** horses. 6. **Cut's
saddle,** packsaddle of the horse named *Cut,* meaning
"bob-tailed." 7. **flocks,** locks of wool. **point,** i.e., of
the saddle. 8. **cess,** measure, estimate. 10. **next,**
nearest, quickest. 11. **bots,** a disease of horses. 17.
tench, a kind of fish; probably an allusion to an ancient
belief that the spots on certain fishes were due to flea
bites.

19. **christen,** in christendom. 26. **gammon,** side.
27. **razes,** roots. 30. **pannier,** basket. 43. **Ay, when?
canst tell?** Don't you wish I would? 53. **At hand,
quoth pick-purse,** slang expression for "Coming immediately." Gadshill's reply shows the chamberlain's
alliance with the robbers. 60. **holds current,** holds
true.

there's a franklin in the wild of Kent hath brought three hundred marks with him in gold: I heard him tell it to one of his company last night at supper; a kind of auditor; one that hath abundance of charge too, God knows what. They are up already, and call for eggs and butter: they will away presently.

Gads. Sirrah, if they meet not with Saint Nicholas' clerks, I'll give thee this neck. 69

Cham. No, I'll none of it: I pray thee, keep that for the hangman; for I know thou worshippest Saint Nicholas as truly as a man of falsehood may.

Gads. What talkest thou to me of the hangman? if I hang, I'll make a fat pair of gallows; for if I hang, old Sir John hangs with me, and thou knowest he is no starveling. Tut! there are other Trojans that thou dreamest not of, the which for sport sake are content to do the profession some grace; that would, if matters should be looked into, for their own credit sake, make all whole. I am joined with no foot land-rakers, no long-staff sixpenny strikers, none of these mad mustachio purple-hued malt-worms; 83 but with nobility and tranquillity, burgomasters and great oneyers, such as can hold in, such as will strike sooner than speak, and speak sooner than drink, and drink sooner than pray: and yet, 'zounds, I lie; for they pray continually to their saint, the commonwealth; or rather, not pray to her, but prey on her, for they ride up and down on her and make her their boots. 91

Cham. What, the commonwealth their boots? will she hold out water in foul way?

Gads. She will, she will; justice hath liquored her. We steal as in a castle, cocksure; we have the receipt of fern-seed, we walk invisible.

Cham. Nay, by my faith, I think you are more beholding to the night than to fern-seed for your walking invisible.

Gads. Give me thy hand: thou shalt have a share in our purchase, as I am a true man. 101

Cham. Nay, rather let me have it, as you are a false thief.

Gads. Go to; 'homo' is a common name to all men. Bid the ostler bring my gelding out of the stable. Farewell, you muddy knave. [*Exeunt.*

SCENE II. *The highway, near Gadshill.*

Enter PRINCE HENRY *and* POINS.

Poins. Come, shelter, shelter: I have removed Falstaff's horse, and he frets like a gummed velvet.

Prince. Stand close.

Enter FALSTAFF.

Fal. Poins! Poins, and be hanged! Poins!

Prince. Peace, ye fat-kidneyed rascal! what a brawling dost thou keep!

Fal. Where's Poins, Hal?

Prince. He is walked up to the top of the hill: I'll go seek him. 9

Fal. I am accursed to rob in that thief's company: the rascal hath removed my horse, and tied him I know not where. If I travel but four foot by the squier further afoot, I shall break my wind. Well, I doubt not but to die a fair death for all this, if I 'scape hanging for killing that rogue. I have forsworn his company hourly any time this two and twenty years, and yet I am bewitched with the rogue's company. If the rascal have not given me medicines to make me love him, I'll be hanged; it could not be else; I have drunk medicines. Poins! Hal! a plague upon you both! Bardolph! Peto! I'll starve ere I'll rob a foot further. An 'twere not as good a deed as drink, to turn true man and to leave these rogues, I am the veriest varlet that ever chewed with a tooth. Eight yards of uneven ground is threescore and ten miles

---

61. **franklin**, a farmer owning his own land. **wild of Kent**, weald (wooded region) of Kent. 62. **marks**, coins of the value in that day of 13s. 6d. 65. **charge**, tavern bill. 68. **Saint Nicholas' clerks**, highwaymen. St. Nicholas was vulgarly supposed the patron of thieves. 77. **Trojans**, slang for *thieves*. 81. **foot land-rakers**, footpads. 82. **long-staff sixpenny strikers**, robbers with long staves who would knock down their victims for sixpence. 83. **mustachio purple-hued malt-worms**, common drunkards with mustaches stained with drink. 85. **oneyers**, many conjectures; possibly, a coinage from *ones* with pun on *owner* (White). 91. **boots**, booty, with pun on *boots*. 95. **liquored**, made waterproof by oiling, and made drunk. 96. **of fern-seed**, i.e., of becoming invisible, since fern-seed was popularly supposed to render its possessor invisible.

101. **purchase**, gettings, plunder. 104. **'homo,'** apparently a definition from the Latin grammar, meaning here, "Don't call names." The scene would suggest to sober-minded people the danger in a situation in which robbery would have royal patronage. *Scene ii.* 2. **frets**, chafes, with pun on another meaning of the word applying to velvet with the nap awry. 13. **squier**, square, measure. 20. **medicines**, ridiculous allusion to love potions. 25. **turn true man**, turn honest man; possibly, turn informer.

afoot with me; and the stony-hearted villains know it well enough: a plague upon it when thieves cannot be true one to another! [*They whistle.*] Whew! A plague upon you all! Give me my horse, you rogues; give me my horse, and be hanged!

Prince. Peace, ye fat-guts! lie down; lay thine ear close to the ground and list if thou canst hear the tread of travellers.

Fal. Have you any levers to lift me up again, being down? 'Sblood, I'll not bear mine own flesh so far afoot again for all the coin in thy father's exchequer. What a plague mean ye to colt me thus?   40

Prince. Thou liest; thou art not colted, thou art uncolted.

Fal. I prithee, good Prince Hal, help me to my horse, good king's son.

Prince. Out, ye rogue! shall I be your ostler?   45

Fal. Go hang thyself in thine own heir-apparent garters! If I be ta'en, I'll peach for this. An I have not ballads made on you all and sung to filthy tunes, let a cup of sack be my poison: when a jest is so forward, and afoot too! I hate it.

     Enter GADSHILL, BARDOLPH *and* PETO *with him.*

Gads. Stand.

Fal. So I do, against my will.   52

Poins. O, 'tis our setter: I know his voice. Bardolph, what news?

Bard. Case ye, case ye; on with your vizards: there's money of the king's coming down the hill; 'tis going to the king's exchequer.

Fal. You lie, ye rogue; 'tis going to the king's tavern.

Gads. There's enough to make us all.   60

Fal. To be hanged.

Prince. Sirs, you four shall front them in the narrow lane; Ned Poins and I will walk lower: if they 'scape from your encounter, then they light on us.

Peto. How many be there of them?

Gads. Some eight or ten.

Fal. 'Zounds, will they not rob us?

Prince. What, a coward, Sir John Paunch?

Fal. Indeed, I am not John of Gaunt, your grandfather; but yet no coward, Hal. 71

Prince. Well, we leave that to the proof.

Poins. Sirrah Jack, thy horse stands behind the hedge: when thou needest him, there thou shalt find him. Farewell, and stand fast.

Fal. Now cannot I strike him, if I should be hanged.

Prince. Ned, where are our disguises?

Poins. Here, hard by: stand close.

     [*Exeunt Prince and Poins.*

Fal. Now, my masters, happy man be his dole, say I: every man to his business.   81

     Enter the Travellers.

First Trav. Come, neighbour: the boy shall lead our horses down the hill; we'll walk afoot awhile, and ease our legs.

Thieves. Stand!

Travellers. Jesus bless us!

Fal. Strike; down with them; cut the villains' throats: ah! whoreson caterpillars! bacon-fed knaves! they hate us youth: down with them; fleece them.   90

Travellers. O, we are undone, both we and ours for ever!

Fal. Hang ye, gorbellied knaves, are ye undone? No, ye fat chuffs; I would your store were here! On, bacons, on! What, ye knaves! young men must live. You are grand-jurors, are ye? we'll jure ye, 'faith.

     [*Here they rob them and bind them. Exeunt.*

     Re-enter PRINCE HENRY *and* POINS.

Prince. The thieves have bound the true men. Now could thou and I rob the thieves and go merrily to London, it would be argument for a week, laughter for a month and a good jest for ever.

Poins. Stand close; I hear them coming.

     Enter the Thieves again.

Fal. Come, my masters, let us share, and then to horse before day. An the Prince and Poins be not two arrant cowards, there's no equity stirring: there's no more valour in that Poins than in a wild-duck.

Prince. Your money!

Poins. Villains!   110

---

40. **colt**, cheat. 47. **garters**, an allusion to a proverbial expression about hanging oneself in one's garters, with a pun on the Order of the Garter. 53. **setter**, arranger of the robbery. 55. **Case ye**, put on your disguises.

80. **happy man be his dole**, may happiness be his portion! 88. **caterpillars**, those who thrive off the commonwealth. 93 **gorbellied**, big-bellied. 94. **chuffs**, churls, rich but miserly. 95. **bacons**, swine. 107. **equity**, justice; variously interpreted.

[*As they are sharing, the Prince and
Poins set upon them; they all run
away; and Falstaff, after a blow
or two, runs away too, leaving the
booty behind them.*]

Prince. Got with much ease. Now merrily
　to horse:
The thieves are all scatter'd and possess'd
　with fear
So strongly that they dare not meet each
　other;　　　　　　　　　　　　　　113
Each takes his fellow for an officer.
Away, good Ned. Falstaff sweats to death,
And lards the lean earth as he walks along:
Were 't not for laughing, I should pity him.
　Poins. How the rogue roar'd! [*Exeunt.*

Scene III. *Warkworth castle.*

Enter HOTSPUR, *solus, reading a letter.*

Hot. 'But, for mine own part, my lord, I
could be well contented to be there, in respect
of the love I bear your house.' He could be
contented: why is he not, then? In respect of
the love he bears our house: he shows in this,
he loves his own barn better than he loves
our house. Let me see some more. 'The
purpose you undertake is dangerous;'—why,
that's certain: 'tis dangerous to take a cold,
to sleep, to drink; but I tell you, my lord
fool, out of this nettle, danger, we pluck this
flower, safety. 'The purpose you undertake
is dangerous; the friends you have named uncertain; the time itself unsorted; and your
whole plot too light for the counterpoise of
so great an opposition.' Say you so, say you
so? I say unto you again, you are a shallow
cowardly hind, and you lie. What a lack-
brain is this! By the Lord, our plot is a good
plot as ever was laid; our friends true and
constant: a good plot, good friends, and full
of expectation; an excellent plot, very good
friends. What a frosty-spirited rogue is this!
Why, my lord of York commends the plot
and the general course of the action.
'Zounds, an I were now by this rascal, I could
brain him with his lady's fan. Is there not
my father, my uncle and myself? lord Edmund Mortimer, my lord of York and Owen
Glendower? is there not besides the Douglas?

have I not all their letters to meet me in
arms by the ninth of the next month? and
are they not some of them set forward already? What a pagan rascal is this! an infidel! Ha! you shall see now in very sincerity
of fear and cold heart, will he to the king and
lay open all our proceedings. O, I could
divide myself and go to buffets, for moving
such a dish of skim milk with so honourable
an action! Hang him! let him tell the king:
we are prepared. I will set forward to-night.

Enter LADY PERCY.

How now, Kate! I must leave you within
　these two hours.
　Lady. O, my good lord, why are you thus
　alone?　　　　　　　　　　　　　　40
For what offence have I this fortnight been
A banish'd woman from my Harry's bed?
Tell me, sweet lord, what is 't that takes from
　thee
Thy stomach, pleasure and thy golden sleep?
Why dost thou bend thine eyes upon the
　earth,
And start so often when thou sit'st alone?
Why hast thou lost the fresh blood in thy
　cheeks;
And given my treasures and my rights of
　thee
To thick-eyed musing and cursed melan-
　choly?
In thy faint slumbers I by thee have watch'd,
And heard thee murmur tales of iron wars; 51
Speak terms of manage to thy bounding
　steed;
Cry 'Courage! to the field!' And thou hast
　talk'd
Of sallies and retires, of trenches, tents,
Of palisadoes, frontiers, parapets,
Of basilisks, of cannon, culverin,
Of prisoners' ransom and of soldiers slain,
And all the currents of a heady fight.
The spirit within thee hath been so at war
And thus hath so bestirr'd thee in thy sleep, 60
That beads of sweat have stood upon thy
　brow,
Like bubbles in a late-disturbed stream;
And in thy face strange motions have ap-
　pear'd,

116. lards the lean earth, an allusion to the practice
on the part of butchers of inserting fat into lean meat.
Sweat was not distinguished from fat.

52. manage, control, training (of horses). 56.
basilisks, large cannon called so from the fabulous
monster which could slay with its glance. culverin,
long cannon. 58. currents, occurrences. 61-67. beads
. . . not. The physiological aspects of violent passion
recorded here are in line with the psychology of the time.

Such as we see when men restrain their
    breath
On some great sudden hest. O, what por-
    tents are these?
Some heavy business hath my lord in hand,
And I must know it, else he loves me not.
    Hot. What, ho!

Enter Servant.

            Is Gilliams with the packet gone?
Serv. He is, my lord, an hour ago.
Hot. Hath Butler brought those horses
    from the sheriff?   70
Serv. One horse, my lord, he brought even
    now.
Hot. What horse? a roan, a crop-ear, is it
    not?
Serv. It is, my lord.
Hot.   That roan shall be my throne.
Well, I will back him straight: O esper-
    ance!
Bid Butler lead him forth into the park.
                                [*Exit Servant.*
Lady. But hear you, my lord.
Hot. What say'st thou, my lady?
Lady. What is it carries you away?
Hot. Why, my horse, my love, my horse.
Lady. Out, you mad-headed ape!   80
A weasel hath not such a deal of spleen
As you are toss'd with.   In faith,
I'll know your business, Harry, that I will.
I fear my brother Mortimer doth stir
About his title, and hath sent for you
To line his enterprize: but if you go,—
    Hot. So far afoot, I shall be weary, love.
Lady. Come, come, you paraquito, answer
    me
Directly unto this question that I ask:
In faith, I'll break thy little finger, Harry,   90
An if thou wilt not tell me all things true.
    Hot. Away,
Away, you trifler! Love! I love thee not,
I care not for thee, Kate: this is no world
To play with mammets and to tilt with
    lips:
We must have bloody noses and crack'd
    crowns,
And pass them current too. God's me, my
    horse!

What say'st thou, Kate? what would'st thou
    have with me?
    Lady. Do you not love me? do you not,
    indeed?   99
Well, do not then; for since you love me not,
I will not love myself. Do you not love me?
Nay, tell me if you speak in jest or no.
    Hot. Come, wilt thou see me ride?
And when I am o' horseback, I will swear
I love thee infinitely. But hark you, Kate:
I must not have you henceforth question me
Whither I go, nor reason whereabout:
Whither I must, I must; and, to conclude,
This evening must I leave you, gentle Kate.
I know you wise, but yet no farther wise   110
Than Harry Percy's wife: constant you are,
But yet a woman: and for secrecy,
No lady closer; for I well believe
Thou wilt not utter what thou dost not know;
And so far will I trust thee, gentle Kate.
    Lady. How! so far?
    Hot. Not an inch further.   But hark you,
    Kate:
Whither I go, thither shall you go too;
To-day will I set forth, to-morrow you.   119
Will this content you, Kate?
    Lady.   It must of force.
                                [*Exeunt.*

SCENE IV. *The Boar's-Head Tavern,
    Eastcheap.*

Enter the PRINCE, *and* POINS.

Prince. Ned, prithee, come out of that fat
room, and lend me thy hand to laugh a little.
Poins. Where hast been, Hal?
Prince. With three or four loggerheads
amongst three or four score hogsheads. I have
sounded the very base-string of humility. Sirrah, I am sworn brother to a leash of drawers;
and can call them all by their christen names,
as Tom, Dick, and Francis. They take it
already upon their salvation, that though I be
but Prince of Wales, yet I am the king of
courtesy; and tell me flatly I am no proud
Jack, like Falstaff, but a Corinthian, a lad of
mettle, a good boy, by the Lord, so they call

74. **esperance**, hope; the motto of the Percy family.
81. **spleen**, hot-headedness, contrariness.   88. **paraquito**, little parrot; term of endearment.   90. **break
thy little finger.** She probably squeezes his folded
little finger.   95. **mammets**, dolls; or else breasts.
96. **crowns**, obvious pun on the coin called a *crown*.

120. **It must of force.** Some critics have unnecessarily seen in this interview evidence of cruelty on Hotspur's part and lack of marital confidence.
    Scene iv. 1. **fat**, vat.   4. **loggerheads**, blockheads.
7. **sworn brother**, allusion to the practice of becoming
fratres jurati.   **leash of drawers**, i.e., three waiters (like
three greyhounds).   13. **Corinthian**, gay fellow, with
suggestion of profligacy.

me, and when I am king of England, I shall
command all the good lads in Eastcheap.
They call drinking deep, dyeing scarlet; and
when you breathe in your watering, they cry
'hem!' and bid you play it off. To conclude,
I am so good a proficient in one quarter of an
hour, that I can drink with any tinker in his
own language during my life. I tell thee, Ned,
thou hast lost much honour, that thou wert
not with me in this action. But, sweet Ned,—
to sweeten which name of Ned, I give thee
this pennyworth of sugar, clapped even now
into my hand by an under-skinker, one that
never spake other English in his life than
'Eight shillings and sixpence,' and 'You are
welcome,' with this shrill addition, 'Anon,
anon, sir! Score a pint of bastard in the Half-
moon,' or so. But, Ned, to drive away the
time till Falstaff come, I prithee, do thou
stand in some by-room, while I question my
puny drawer to what end he gave me the
sugar; and do thou never leave calling
'Francis,' that his tale to me may be nothing
but 'Anon.' Step aside, and I'll show thee a
precedent.

Poins. Francis!
Prince. Thou art perfect.   39
Poins. Francis!

                                          [*Exit Poins.*

Enter FRANCIS.

Fran. Anon, anon, sir. Look down into
the Pomgarnet, Ralph.
Prince. Come hither, Francis.
Fran. My lord?
Prince. How long hast thou to serve,
Francis?
Fran. Forsooth, five years, and as much
as to—
Poins. [*Within*] Francis!
Fran. Anon, anon, sir.   49
Prince. Five year! by'r lady, a long lease
for the clinking of pewter. But, Francis,
darest thou be so valiant as to play the
coward with thy indenture and show it a fair
pair of heels and run from it?

Fran. O Lord, sir, I'll be sworn upon all
the books in England, I could find in my heart.
Poins. [*Within*] Francis!
Fran. Anon, sir.
Prince. How old art thou, Francis?
Fran. Let me see—about Michaelmas
next I shall be—   61
Poins. [*Within*] Francis!
Fran. Anon, sir. Pray stay a little, my
lord.
Prince. Nay, but hark you, Francis: for
the sugar thou gavest me, 'twas a penny-
worth, was't not?
Fran. O Lord, I would it had been two!
Prince. I will give thee for it a thousand
pound: ask me when thou wilt, and thou
shalt have it.   70
Poins. [*Within*] Francis!
Fran. Anon, anon.
Prince. Anon, Francis? No, Francis; but
to-morrow, Francis; or Francis, o' Thursday;
or indeed, Francis, when thou wilt. But,
Francis!
Fran. My lord?
Prince. Wilt thou rob this leathern jerkin,
crystal-button, not-pated, agate-ring, puke-
stocking, caddis-garter, smooth-tongue, Span-
ish-pouch,—   80
Fran. O Lord, sir, who do you mean?
Prince. Why, then, your brown bastard is
your only drink; for look you, Francis, your
white canvas doublet will sully: in Barbary,
sir, it cannot come to so much.
Fran. What, sir?
Poins. [*Within*] Francis!
Prince. Away, you rogue! dost thou not
hear them call?   89
[*Here they both call him; the drawer stands
amazed, not knowing which way to go.*

Enter Vintner.

Vint. What, standest thou still, and
hearest such a calling? Look to the guests
within. [*Exit Francis.*] My lord, old Sir John,
with half-a-dozen more, are at the door: shall
I let them in?
Prince. Let them alone awhile, and then
open the door. [*Exit Vintner.*]   Poins!

18. **watering**, drinking. **20-1. tinker ... language.**
Tinker's language was cant or jargon, and tinkers were
proverbial drinkers. **26. under-skinker**, under-tapster.
31. bastard, sweet Spanish wine. **Half-moon**, name
of a room in the inn. **35. puny**, in the ordinary sense
with a pun on the original *puisné*, younger son, applied
to the second drawer. **37. precedent**, example. The
spectacle of the young prince disporting himself among
drawers may have been delightful to the popular mind,
but the scene has lost much of its humor.

78. **not-pated**, crop-haired. **puke-stocking**, dark
colored stocking. 79. **caddis-garter**, worsted garter.
Since garters were worn in sight, they needed to be of
better stuff than common worsted. The prince's epithets
seem to apply to the vintner, the boy's master. 82-85.
Why ... much. The prince talks complete nonsense
in order to bewilder Francis.

Re-enter POINS.

Poins. Anon, anon, sir.

Prince. Sirrah, Falstaff and the rest of the thieves are at the door: shall we be merry? 99

Poins. As merry as crickets, my lad. But hark ye; what cunning match have you made with this jest of the drawer? come, what's the issue?

Prince. I am now of all humours that have showed themselves humours since the old days of goodman Adam to the pupil age of this present twelve o'clock at midnight.

Re-enter FRANCIS.

What's o'clock, Francis?

Fran. Anon, anon, sir.   [*Exit.* 109

Prince. That ever this fellow should have fewer words than a parrot, and yet the son of a woman! His industry is up-stairs and down-stairs; his eloquence the parcel of a reckoning. I am not yet of Percy's mind, the Hotspur of the north; he that kills me some six or seven dozen of Scots at a breakfast, washes his hands, and says to his wife 'Fie upon this quiet life! I want work.' 'O my sweet Harry,' says she, 'how many hast thou killed to-day?' 'Give my roan horse a drench,' says he; and answers 'Some fourteen,' an hour after; 'a trifle, a trifle.' I prithee, call in Falstaff: I'll play Percy, and that damned brawn shall play Dame Mortimer his wife. 'Rivo!' says the drunkard. Call in ribs, call in tallow.   125

Enter FALSTAFF, GADSHILL, BARDOLPH, *and* PETO; FRANCIS *following with wine.*

Poins. Welcome, Jack: where hast thou been?

Fal. A plague of all cowards, I say, and a vengeance too! marry, and amen! Give me a cup of sack, boy. Ere I lead this life long, I'll sew nether stocks and mend them and foot them too. A plague of all cowards! Give me a cup of sack, rogue. Is there no virtue extant?
            [*He drinks.*

Prince. Didst thou never see Titan kiss a dish of butter? pitiful-hearted Titan, that melted at the sweet tale of the sun's! if thou didst, then behold that compound.   136

Fal. You rogue, here's lime in this sack too: there is nothing but roguery to be found in villanous man: yet a coward is worse than a cup of sack with lime in it. A villanous coward! Go thy ways, old Jack; die when thou wilt, if manhood, good manhood, be not forgot upon the face of the earth, then am I a shotten herring. There live not three good men unhanged in England; and one of them is fat and grows old: God help the while! a bad world, I say. I would I were a weaver; I could sing psalms or any thing. A plague of all cowards, I say still.

Prince. How now, wool-sack! what mutter you?   149

Fal. A king's son! If I do not beat thee out of thy kingdom with a dagger of lath, and drive all thy subjects afore thee like a flock of wild-geese, I'll never wear hair on my face more. You Prince of Wales!

Prince. Why, you whoreson round man, what's the matter?

Fal. Are not you a coward? answer me to that: and Poins there?

Poins. 'Zounds, ye fat paunch, and ye call me coward, by the Lord, I'll stab thee.   160

Fal. I call thee coward! I'll see thee damned ere I call thee coward: but I would give a thousand pound I could run as fast as thou canst. You are straight enough in the shoulders, you care not who sees your back: call you that backing of your friends? A plague upon such backing! give me them that will face me. Give me a cup of sack: I am a rogue, if I drunk to-day.

Prince. O villain! thy lips are scarce wiped since thou drunkest last.   171

Fal. All's one for that. [*He drinks.*] A plague of all cowards, still say I.

Prince. What's the matter?

Fal. What's the matter! there be four of us here have ta'en a thousand pound this day morning.

Prince. Where is it, Jack? where is it?

Fal. Where is it! taken from us it is: a hundred upon poor four of us.   180

104. **humours**, whims, caprices. Shakespeare apparently would suggest complete gayety and freedom from care. 106. **goodman**, a sort of familiar title. **pupil age**, i.e., the day is young. 113. **parcel**, item. 124. 'Rivo!' an interjection of doubtful meaning; certainly bacchanalian. 130. **nether stocks**, stockings. 134. **pitiful-hearted Titan.** Theobald suggested *butter* for *Titan*, which still seems the best way to explain this apparently contradictory passage.

137. **lime in this sack**, i.e., used as a preservative. 143. **shotten herring**, a herring that has cast its roe and is worthless. 147. **weaver**, allusion to psalm-singing Protestants from Flanders, mainly weavers. 151. **dagger of lath.** The Vice in the interludes was so armed, as no doubt other clowns were. 161-163. **I call . . . canst.** This is a typical example of Falstaff's method of turning aside an issue and at the same time maintaining his point

Prince. What, a hundred, man?   181
Fal. I am a rogue, if I were not at half-sword with a dozen of them two hours together. I have 'scaped by miracle. I am eight times thrust through the doublet, four through the hose; my buckler cut through and through; my sword hacked like a hand-saw—ecce signum! I never dealt better since I was a man: all would not do. A plague of all cowards! Let them speak: if they speak more or less than truth, they are villains and the sons of darkness.   191
Prince. Speak, sirs; how was it?
Gads. We four set upon some dozen—
Fal. Sixteen at least, my lord.
Gads. And bound them.
Peto. No, no, they were not bound.
Fal. You rogue, they were bound, every man of them; or I am a Jew else, an Ebrew Jew.
Gads. As we were sharing, some six or seven fresh men set upon us—   200
Fal. And unbound the rest, and then come in the other.
Prince. What, fought you with them all?
Fal. All! I know not what you call all; but if I fought not with fifty of them, I am a bunch of radish: if there were not two or three and fifty upon poor old Jack, then am I no two-legged creature.
Prince. Pray God you have not murdered some of them.   210
Fal. Nay, that's past praying for: I have peppered two of them; two I am sure I have paid, two rogues in buckram suits. I tell thee what, Hal, if I tell thee a lie, spit in my face, call me horse. Thou knowest my old ward; here I lay, and thus I bore my point. Four rogues in buckram let drive at me—
Prince. What, four? thou saidst but two even now.
Fal. Four, Hal; I told thee four.   220
Poins. Ay, ay, he said four.
Fal. These four came all a-front, and mainly thrust at me. I made me no more ado but took all their seven points in my target, thus.
Prince. Seven? why, there were but four even now.
Fal. In buckram?
Poins. Ay, four, in buckram suits.

Fal. Seven, by these hilts, or I am a villain else.   230
Prince. Prithee, let him alone; we shall have more anon.
Fal. Dost thou hear me, Hal?
Prince. Ay, and mark thee too, Jack.
Fal. Do so, for it is worth the listening to. These nine in buckram that I told thee of—
Prince. So, two more already.
Fal. Their points being broken,—
Poins. Down fell their hose.   239
Fal. Began to give me ground: but I followed me close, came in foot and hand; and with a thought seven of the eleven I paid.
Prince. O monstrous! eleven buckram men grown out of two!
Fal. But, as the devil would have it, three misbegotten knaves in Kendal green came at my back and let drive at me; for it was so dark, Hal, that thou couldst not see thy hand.
Prince. These lies are like their father that begets them; gross as a mountain, open, palpable. Why, thou clay-brained guts, thou knotty-pated fool, thou whoreson, obscene, greasy tallow-catch,—
Fal. What, art thou mad? art thou mad? is not the truth the truth?
Prince. Why, how couldst thou know these men in Kendal green, when it was so dark thou couldst not see thy hand? come, tell us your reason: what sayest thou to this?   259
Poins. Come, your reason, Jack, your reason.
Fal. What, upon compulsion? 'Zounds, an I were at the strappado, or all the racks in the world, I would not tell you on compulsion. Give you a reason on compulsion! if reasons were as plentiful as blackberries, I would give no man a reason upon compulsion, I.   266
Prince. I'll be no longer guilty of this sin; this sanguine coward, this bed-presser, this horseback-breaker, this huge hill of flesh,—
Fal. 'Sblood, you starveling, you elf-skin, you dried neat's tongue, you bull's pizzle, you

238. **points.** Falstaff uses *points* to mean "swords"; Poins's reply introduces a pun on the same word meaning the "laces" by which the hose were attached to the doublet and so supported. 240. **followed me,** a sort of reflexive or middle voice. 246. **Kendal green,** green cloth worn by foresters. 253. **tallow-catch,** explained as "tallow-tub," and as "tallow-keech," a roll of fat delivered by the butcher to the tallow chandler. It has been pointed out that such breathless strings of epithets of abuse are characteristic of Latin comedy. 264. **reasons . . . blackberries.** Falstaff not only avoids the issue, but also turns it into a jest by punning on the word *raisins,* which was pronounced nearly like *reasons.*

182. **half-sword,** fighting at close quarters. 187. **ecce signum,** behold the proof; familiar words from the Mass. 213. **buckram,** coarse linen cloth stiffened. 215. **ward,** guard in fencing. 223. **mainly,** powerfully.

stock-fish! O for breath to utter what is like thee! you tailor's-yard, you sheath, you bow-case, you vile standing-tuck,—   274

Prince. Well, breathe awhile, and then to it again: and when thou hast tired thyself in base comparisons, hear me speak but this.

Poins. Mark, Jack.

Prince. We two saw you four set on four and bound them, and were masters of their wealth. Mark now, how a plain tale shall put you down. Then did we two set on you four; and, with a word, out-faced you from your prize, and have it; yea, and can show it you here in the house: and, Falstaff, you carried your guts away as nimbly, with as quick dexterity, and roared for mercy and still run and roared, as ever I heard bull-calf. What a slave art thou, to hack thy sword as thou hast done, and then say it was in fight! What trick, what device, what starting-hole, canst thou now find out to hide thee from this open and apparent shame?   293

Poins. Come, let's hear, Jack; what trick hast thou now?

Fal. By the Lord, I knew ye as well as he that made ye. Why, hear you, my masters: was it for me to kill the heir-apparent? should I turn upon the true prince? why, thou knowest I am as valiant as Hercules: but beware instinct; the lion will not touch the true prince. Instinct is a great matter; I was now a coward on instinct. I shall think the better of myself and thee during my life; I for a valiant lion, and thou for a true prince. But, by the Lord, lads, I am glad you have the money. Hostess, clap to the doors: watch to-night, pray to-morrow. Gallants, lads, boys, hearts of gold, all the titles of good fellowship come to you! What, shall we be merry? shall we have a play extempore?

Prince. Content; and the argument shall be thy running away.   311

Fal. Ah, no more of that, Hal, an thou lovest me!

Enter Hostess.

Host. O Jesu, my lord the prince!

Prince. How now, my lady the hostess! what sayest thou to me?

Host. Marry, my lord, there is a nobleman of the court at door would speak with you: he says he comes from your father.   319

Prince. Give him as much as will make him a royal man, and send him back again to my mother.

Fal. What manner of man is he?

Host. An old man.

Fal. What doth gravity out of his bed at midnight? Shall I give him his answer?

Prince. Prithee, do, Jack.

Fal. 'Faith, and I'll send him packing.

                    [*Exit.*

Prince. Now, sirs: by'r lady, you fought fair; so did you, Peto; so did you, Bardolph: you are lions too, you ran away upon instinct, you will not touch the true prince; no, fie!   332

Bard. 'Faith, I ran when I saw others run.

Prince. 'Faith, tell me now in earnest, how came Falstaff's sword so hacked?

Peto. Why, he hacked it with his dagger, and said he would swear truth out of England but he would make you believe it was done in fight, and persuaded us to do the   339 like.

Bard. Yea, and to tickle our noses with spear-grass to make them bleed, and then to beslubber our garments with it and swear it was the blood of true men. I did that I did not this seven year before, I blushed to hear his monstrous devices.   344

Prince. O villain, thou stolest a cup of sack eighteen years ago, and wert taken with the manner, and ever since thou hast blushed extempore. Thou hadst fire and sword on thy side, and yet thou rannest away: what instinct hadst thou for it?   350

Bard. My lord, do you see these meteors? do you behold these exhalations?

Prince. I do.

Bard. What think you they portend?

Prince. Hot livers and cold purses.

Bard. Choler, my lord, if rightly taken.

Prince. No, if rightly taken, halter.

Re-enter FALSTAFF.

Here comes lean Jack, here comes barebone. How now, my sweet creature of bom-

272. **stock-fish**, dried cod. 274. **standing-tuck**, rapier standing on end. 283. **out-faced**, frightened. 291. **starting-hole**, point of shelter (like a rabbit's hole). The most famous of all Falstaff's evasions follows.

321. **royal.** The man is a noble (6s. 8d.); give him 3s. 4d. and he will be a *royal* (10s.) man. 348. **fire . . . side.** Bardolph is drunken, and his flaming face is continually harped upon. 355. **Hot . . . purses,** livers made hot by drink, and purses made empty by spending. 357. **halter.** The pun is on *collar* pronounced like *choler*. 359. **bombast**, cotton padding.

bast! How long is't ago, Jack, since thou sawest thine own knee? 361

Fal. My own knee! when I was about thy years, Hal, I was not an eagle's talon in the waist; I could have crept into any alderman's thumb-ring: a plague of sighing and grief! it blows a man up like a bladder. There's villanous news abroad: here was Sir John Bracy from your father; you must to the court in the morning. That same mad fellow of the north, Percy, and he of Wales, that gave Amamon the bastinado and made Lucifer cuckold and swore the devil his true liegeman upon the cross of a Welsh hook— what a plague call you him? 373

Poins. O, Glendower.

Fal. Owen, Owen, the same; and his son-in-law Mortimer, and old Northumberland, and that sprightly Scot of Scots, Douglas, that runs o' horseback up a hill perpendicular,—

Prince. He that rides at high speed and with his pistol kills a sparrow flying. 380

Fal. You have hit it.

Prince. So did he never the sparrow.

Fal. Well, that rascal hath good mettle in him; he will not run.

Prince. Why, what a rascal art thou then, to praise him so for running!

Fal. O' horseback, ye cuckoo; but afoot he will not budge a foot.

Prince. Yes, Jack, upon instinct. 389

Fal. I grant ye, upon instinct. Well, he is there too, and one Mordake, and a thousand blue-caps more: Worcester is stolen away to-night; thy father's beard is turned white with the news: you may buy land now as cheap as stinking mackerel.

Prince. Why, then, it is like, if there come a hot June and this civil buffeting hold, we shall buy maidenheads as they buy hob-nails, by the hundreds. 399

Fal. By the mass, lad, thou sayest true; it is like we shall have good trading that way. But tell me, Hal, art not thou horrible afeard? thou being heir-apparent, could the world pick thee out three such enemies again as that fiend Douglas, that spirit Percy, and that devil Glendower? Art thou not horri-

bly afraid? doth not thy blood thrill at it?

Prince. Not a whit, i' faith; I lack some of thy instinct. 409

Fal. Well, thou wilt be horribly chid to-morrow when thou comest to thy father: if thou love me, practise an answer.

Prince. Do thou stand for my father, and examine me upon the particulars of my life.

Fal. Shall I? content: this chair shall be my state, this dagger my sceptre, and this cushion my crown. 417

Prince. Thy state is taken for a joined-stool, thy golden sceptre for a leaden dagger, and thy precious rich crown for a pitiful bald crown!

Fal. Well, an the fire of grace be not quite out of thee, now shalt thou be moved. Give me a cup of sack to make my eyes look red, that it may be thought I have wept; for I must speak in passion, and I will do it in King Cambyses' vein. 426

Prince. Well, here is my leg.

Fal. And here is my speech. Stand aside, nobility.

Host. O Jesu, this is excellent sport, i' faith!

Fal. Weep not, sweet queen; for trickling tears are vain.

Host. O, the father, how he holds his countenance! 433

Fal. For God's sake, lords, convey my tristful queen;
For tears do stop the flood-gates of her eyes.

Host. O Jesu, he doth it as like one of these harlotry players as ever I see! 437

Fal. Peace, good pint-pot; peace, good tickle-brain. Harry, I do not only marvel where thou spendest thy time, but also how thou art accompanied: for though the camo-mile, the more it is trodden on the faster it grows, yet youth, the more it is wasted the sooner it wears. That thou art my son, I have partly thy mother's word, partly my own opinion, but chiefly a villanous trick of thine eye and a foolish hanging of thy nether lip, that doth warrant me. If then thou be

---

370. **Amamon**, name of a demon. **bastinado**, cudgel, or a beating with a cudgel. 372. **cross of a Welsh hook**, cross formed by the ax-head and the shaft in the Welsh halberd. 374. **O**, possibly an abbreviation of *Owen*. 380. **pistol**. There were of course no pistols in the time of King Henry's reign. 392. **blue-caps**, Scottish soldiers.

416. **state**, chair of state. 418. **joined-stool**, a stool made by a joiner; hence, of rough workmanship. 426. **King Cambyses' vein**, allusion to Thomas Preston's bombastic tragedy *Cambises*, still preserved. 427. **leg**, bow. 434. **tristful**, sorrowing. 437. **harlotry**, vagabond. 439. **tickle-brain**, strong drink. 441. **camo-mile**. This parodies an actual passage in Lyly's *Euphues* and exaggerates the balance and alliteration of the style.

son to me, here lies the point; why, being son
to me, art thou so pointed at? Shall the 449
blessed sun of heaven prove a micher and eat
blackberries? a question not to be asked.
Shall the son of England prove a thief and
take purses? a question to be asked. There
is a thing, Harry, which thou hast often
heard of and it is known to many in our land
by the name of pitch: this pitch, as ancient
writers do report, doth defile; so doth the
company thou keepest: for, Harry, now I do
not speak to thee in drink but in tears, not in
pleasure but in passion, not in words only,
but in woes also: and yet there is a virtuous
man whom I have often noted in thy company, but I know not his name.   461

Prince. What manner of man, an it like
your majesty?

Fal. A goodly portly man, i' faith, and a
corpulent; of a cheerful look, a pleasing eye
and a most noble carriage; and, as I think, his
age some fifty, or, by'r lady, inclining to three
score; and now I remember me, his name is
Falstaff: if that man should be lewdly given,
he deceiveth me; for, Harry, I see virtue in
his looks. If then the tree may be known by
the fruit, as the fruit by the tree, then, per-
emptorily I speak it, there is virtue in that
Falstaff: him keep with, the rest banish.
And tell me now, thou naughty varlet, tell
me, where hast thou been this month?

Prince. Dost thou speak like a king? Do
thou stand for me, and I'll play my father.

Fal. Depose me? if thou dost it half so
gravely, so majestically, both in word and
matter, hang me up by the heels for a rabbit-
sucker or a poulter's hare.   481

Prince. Well, here I am set.

Fal. And here I stand: judge, my masters.

Prince. Now, Harry, whence come you?

Fal. My noble lord, from Eastcheap.

Prince. The complaints I hear of thee are
grievous.

Fal. 'Sblood, my lord, they are false: nay,
I'll tickle ye for a young prince, i' faith.   489

Prince. Swearest thou, ungracious boy?
henceforth ne'er look on me. Thou art violently carried away from grace: there is a
devil haunts thee in the likeness of an old fat

man, a tun of man is thy companion. Why
dost thou converse with that trunk of humours, that bolting-hutch of beastliness,
that swollen parcel of dropsies, that huge
bombard of sack, that stuffed cloak-bag of
guts, that roasted Manningtree ox with 498
the pudding in his belly, that reverend vice,
that grey iniquity, that father ruffian, that
vanity in years? Wherein is he good, but to
taste sack and drink it? wherein neat and
cleanly, but to carve a capon and eat it?
wherein cunning, but in craft? wherein
crafty, but in villany? wherein villanous, but
in all things? wherein worthy, but in nothing?

Fal. I would your grace would take me
with you: whom means your grace?

Prince. That villanous abominable misleader of youth, Falstaff, that old white-
bearded Satan.

Fal. My lord, the man I know.   510

Prince. I know thou dost.

Fal. But to say I know more harm in him
than in myself, were to say more than I
know. That he is old, the more the pity, his
white hairs do witness it; but that he is,
saving your reverence, a whoremaster, that I
utterly deny. If sack and sugar be a fault,
God help the wicked! if to be old and merry
be a sin, then many an old host that I know
is damned: if to be fat is to be hated, then
Pharaoh's lean kine are to be loved. No,
my good lord; banish Peto, banish Bardolph,
banish Poins: but for sweet Jack Falstaff,
kind Jack Falstaff, true Jack Falstaff,
valiant Jack Falstaff, and therefore more
valiant, being, as he is, old Jack Falstaff,
banish not him thy Harry's company, banish
not him thy Harry's company: banish plump
Jack, and banish all the world.   527

Prince. I do, I will.   [*A knocking heard.*
[*Exeunt Hostess, Francis, and Bardolph.*

Re-enter Bardolph, *running.*

Bard. O, my lord, my lord! the sheriff
with a most monstrous watch is at the door.

Fal. Out, ye rogue! Play out the play: I
have much to say in the behalf of that
Falstaff.

450. **micher**, truant. 456-457. **pitch . . . defile**, an
allusion to the familiar proverb from *Ecclesiasticus*, xiii, 1,
about the defilement of touching pitch. This proverb
appears also in Lyly's *Euphues*. 480. **rabbit-sucker**,
sucking rabbit. 481. **poulter's**, poulterer's.

495. **bolting-hutch**, bin for bolted meal. 497.
bombard, leathern drinking vessel. 498. **Manningtree ox.** Manningtree, a town in Essex, had noted
fairs where, no doubt, oxen were roasted whole. 499-500.
vice . . . iniquity. These terms suggest another feature
of Manningtree, which was the acting of morality plays;
the word *vanity* also suggests a character in such plays.
521. **Pharaoh's lean kine.** See *Genesis*, xli, 3-4.

Re-enter the Hostess.

Host. O Jesu, my lord, my lord!

Prince. Heigh, heigh! the devil rides upon a fiddlestick: what's the matter?   535

Host. The sheriff and all the watch are at the door: they are come to search the house. Shall I let them in?

Fal. Dost thou hear, Hal? never call a true piece of gold a counterfeit: thou art essentially mad, without seeming so.   541

Prince. And thou a natural coward, without instinct.

Fal. I deny your major: if you will deny the sheriff, so; if not, let him enter: if I become not a cart as well as another man, a plague on my bringing up! I hope I shall as soon be strangled with a halter as another.

Prince. Go, hide thee behind the arras: the rest walk up above. Now, my masters, for a true face and good conscience.   551

Fal. Both which I have had: but their date is out, and therefore I'll hide me.

Prince. Call in the sheriff.

[*Exeunt all except the Prince and Peto.*

Enter Sheriff *and the* Carrier.

Now, master sheriff, what is your will with me?

Sher. First, pardon me, my lord. A hue and cry

Hath follow'd certain men unto this house.

Prince. What men?

Sher. One of them is well known, my gracious lord,

A gross fat man.

Car.   As fat as butter.   560

Prince. The man, I do assure you, is not here;

For I myself at this time have employ'd him.

And, sheriff, I will engage my word to thee

That I will, by to-morrow dinner-time,

Send him to answer thee, or any man,

For any thing he shall be charged withal:

And so let me entreat you leave the house.

Sher. I will, my lord. There are two gentlemen

Have in this robbery lost three hundred marks.

Prince. It may be so: if he have robb'd these men,   570

He shall be answerable; and so farewell.

Sher. Good night, my noble lord.

Prince. I think it is good morrow, is it not?

Sher. Indeed, my lord, I think it be two o'clock.   [*Exeunt Sheriff and Carrier.*

Prince. This oily rascal is known as well as Paul's. Go, call him forth.

Peto. Falstaff!—Fast asleep behind the arras, and snorting like a horse.   578

Prince. Hark, how hard he fetches breath. Search his pockets. [*He searcheth his pockets, and findeth certain papers.*] What hast thou found?

Peto. Nothing but papers, my lord.

Prince. Let's see what they be: read them.

Peto. [*Reads*]

Item, A capon, . . .	2s. 2d.
Item, Sauce, . . .	4d.
Item, Sack, two gallons, .	5s. 8d.
Item, Anchovies and sack after supper, . . .	2s. 6d.
Item, Bread, . . .	ob. 590

Prince. O monstrous! but one half-penny-worth of bread to this intolerable deal of sack! What there is else, keep close; we'll read it at more advantage: there let him sleep till day. I'll to the court in the morning. We must all to the wars, and thy place shall be honourable. I'll procure this fat rogue a charge of foot; and I know his death will be a march of twelve-score. The money shall be paid back again with advantage. Be with me betimes in the morning; and so, good morrow, Peto.   601

Peto. Good morrow, good my lord.   [*Exeunt.*

ACT III.

SCENE I. *Bangor. The Archdeacon's house.*

Enter Hotspur, Worcester, Mortimer, *and* Glendower.

Mort. These promises are fair, the parties sure,

And our induction full of prosperous hope.

---

534. the devil . . . fiddlestick, proverbial; here, an exclamation. 544. major, i.e., major premise. Falstaff denies that he is a natural coward; he does not deny that he is affected by instinct. 546. cart, hangman's cart, tumbril. 556. hue and cry, pursuit of criminals by horn and halloo; technical term.

576. Paul's, St. Paul's Cathedral, a familiar landmark. 590. ob., abbreviation for *obolus* (Greek coin) meaning "halfpenny." 597. charge of foot, command of infantry. 598. twelve-score, i.e., yards; a distance familiar from its use in archery. 599. advantage, interest. *Act III. Scene i.* 2. induction, beginning.

Hot. Lord Mortimer, and cousin Glen-
dower,
Will you sit down?
And uncle Worcester: a plague upon it!
I have forgot the map.
 Glend.   No, here it is.
Sit, cousin Percy; sit, good cousin Hotspur,
For by that name as oft as Lancaster
Doth speak of you, his cheek looks pale and
 with
A rising sigh he wisheth you in heaven. 10
 Hot. And you in hell, as oft as he hears
Owen Glendower spoke of.
 Glend. I cannot blame him: at my nativity
The front of heaven was full of fiery shapes,
Of burning cressets; and at my birth
The frame and huge foundation of the earth
Shaked like a coward.
 Hot. Why, so it would have done at the
same season, if your mother's cat had but
kittened, though yourself had never been
born. 20
 Glend. I say the earth did shake when I
was born.
 Hot. And I say the earth was not of my
 mind,
If you suppose as fearing you it shook.
 Glend. The heavens were all on fire, the
 earth did tremble.
 Hot. O, then the earth shook to see the
 heavens on fire,
And not in fear of your nativity.
Diseased nature oftentimes breaks forth
In strange eruptions; oft the teeming earth
Is with a kind of colic pinch'd and vex'd
By the imprisoning of unruly wind 30
Within her womb· which, for enlargement
 striving,
Shakes the old beldam earth and topples down
Steeples and moss-grown towers. At your
 birth
Our grandam earth, having this distempera-
 ture,
In passion shook.

Glend.   Cousin, of many men
I do not bear these crossings. Give me leave
To tell you once again that at my birth
The front of heaven was full of fiery shapes,
The goats ran from the mountains, and the
 herds
Were strangely clamorous to the frighted
 fields. 40
These signs have mark'd me extraordinary;
And all the courses of my life do show
I am not in the roll of common men.
Where is he living, clipp'd in with the sea
That chides the banks of England, Scotland,
 Wales,
Which calls me pupil, or hath read to me?
And bring him out that is but woman's son
Can trace me in the tedious ways of art
And hold me pace in deep experiments.
 Hot. I think there's no man speaks better
Welsh. I'll to dinner. 51
 Mort. Peace, cousin Percy; you will make
 him mad.
 Glend. I can call spirits from the vasty deep.
 Hot. Why, so can I, or so can any man;
But will they come when you do call for
 them?
 Glend. Why, I can teach you, cousin, to
 command
The devil.
 Hot. And I can teach thee, coz, to shame
 the devil
By telling truth: tell truth and shame the
 devil.
If thou have power to raise him, bring him
 hither, 60
And I'll be sworn I have power to shame
 him hence.
O, while you live, tell truth and shame the
 devil!
 Mort. Come, come, no more of this un-
 profitable chat.
 Glend. Three times hath Henry Boling-
 broke made head
Against my power; thrice from the banks of
 Wye
And sandy-bottom'd Severn have I sent him
Bootless home and weather-beaten back.
 Hot. Home without boots, and in foul
 weather too!
How 'scapes he agues, in the devil's name?
 Glend. Come, here's the map: shall we
 divide our right 70

---

6. map. The spectacle of rebels sitting down with a
map to divide England into parts would have been duly
shocking to the patriotic audience. There was such a
conference, but later and not among these leaders. **8.
Lancaster,** King Henry IV, formerly duke of Lancaster.
13. at my nativity. Holinshed recounts the happening
of portents at Glendower's birth; Shakespeare has
developed his vanity and strange rapt quality. He
seems to have believed in Glendower's powers in spite
of making him ridiculous. **22-23. And . . . shook.**
Hotspur ridicules Glendower and does not hesitate to
affront him, although Glendower is his ally. **27-35.
Diseased . . . shook.** These lines give the currently
accepted scientific explanation of earthquakes.

44. clipp'd in, embraced. **48. trace,** follow, keep
pace.

According to our threefold order ta'en?

Mort. The archdeacon hath divided it
Into three limits very equally:
England, from Trent and Severn hitherto,
By south and east is to my part assign'd:
All westward, Wales beyond the Severn
　　shore,
And all the fertile land within that bound,
To Owen Glendower: and, dear coz, to you
The remnant northward, lying off from
　　Trent.
And our indentures tripartite are drawn;　80
Which being sealed interchangeably,
A business that this night may execute,
To-morrow, cousin Percy, you and I
And my good Lord of Worcester will set forth
To meet your father and the Scottish power,
As is appointed us, at Shrewsbury.
My father Glendower is not ready yet,
Nor shall we need his help these fourteen
　　days.
Within that space you may have drawn to-
　　gether
Your tenants, friends and neighbouring
　　gentlemen.　90

Glend. A shorter time shall send me to
　　you, lords:
And in my conduct shall your ladies come;
From whom you now must steal and take no
　　leave,
For there will be a world of water shed
Upon the parting of your wives and you.

Hot. Methinks my moiety, north from
　　Burton here,
In quantity equals not one of yours:
See how this river comes me cranking in,
And cuts me from the best of all my land
A huge half-moon, a monstrous cantle out.100
I'll have the current in this place damm'd up;
And here the smug and silver Trent shall run
In a new channel, fair and evenly;
It shall not wind with such a deep indent,
To rob me of so rich a bottom here.

Glend. Not wind? it shall, it must; you see
　　it doth.

Mort. Yea, but
Mark how he bears his course, and runs me up
With like advantage on the other side;

Gelding the opposed continent as much　110
As on the other side it takes from you.

Wor. Yea, but a little charge will trench
　　him here
And on this north side win this cape of land;
And then he runs straight and even.

Hot. I'll have it so: a little charge will do
　　it.

Glend. I'll not have it alter'd.

Hot.　　　　　　　　　　Will not you?

Glend. No, nor you shall not.

Hot.　　　　　　Who shall say me nay?

Glend. Why, that will I.

Hot. Let me not understand you, then;
speak it in Welsh.　120

Glend. I can speak English, lord, as well as
　　you;
For I was train'd up in the English court;
Where, being but young, I framed to the harp
Many an English ditty lovely well
And gave the tongue a helpful ornament,
A virtue that was never seen in you.

Hot. Marry,
And I am glad of it with all my heart:
I had rather be a kitten and cry mew
Than one of these same metre ballad-
　　mongers;　130
I had rather hear a brazen canstick turn'd,
Or a dry wheel grate on the axle-tree;
And that would set my teeth nothing on
　　edge,
Nothing so much as mincing poetry:
'Tis like the forced gait of a shuffling nag.

Glend. Come, you shall have Trent turn'd.

Hot. I do not care: I'll give thrice so much
　　land
To any well-deserving friend;
But in the way of bargain, mark ye me,
I'll cavil on the ninth part of a hair.　140
Are the indentures drawn? shall we be gone?

Glend. The moon shines fair; you may
　　away by night:
I'll haste the writer and withal
Break with your wives of your departure
　　hence:
I am afraid my daughter will run mad,
So much she doteth on her Mortimer.
　　　　　　　　　　　　　　　　[Exit.

72. **archdeacon**, an official of an Episcopal diocese.
The divisions of the Kingdom are really very ancient;
they appear in Geoffrey of Monmouth's *Chronicle*, and
are those into which King Lear divided his kingdom.
87. **father**, father-in-law. 96. **moiety**, share; usually
one-half. 98. **comes me cranking in**, comes bending
in on my share; *me* is an ethical dative. 100. **cantle**,
piece.

122-126. **For I . . . you.** Glendower had indeed been
bred in the English court; he shows a characteristic
Welsh pride in being a poet, and Hotspur an equally characteristic scorn of the fine arts. 131. **canstick**, candle-
stick. 139-140. **But . . . hair.** Hotspur here describes
his splenetic humor. He was generous, but his generosity could never be the result of justice or reason. 143.
writer, the scrivener who would be drawing the indentures. 144. **Break with**, communicate with.

Mort. Fie, cousin Percy! how you cross my
  father!

Hot. I cannot choose: sometime he angers
  me
With telling me of the moldwarp and the ant,
Of the dreamer Merlin and his prophecies, 150
And of a dragon and a finless fish,
A clip-wing'd griffin and a moulten raven,
A couching lion and a ramping cat,
And such a deal of skimble-skamble stuff
As puts me from my faith. I tell you what;
He held me last night at least nine hours
In reckoning up the several devils' names
That were his lackeys: I cried 'hum,' and
  'well, go to,'
But mark'd him not a word. O, he is as
  tedious
As a tired horse, a railing wife;   160
Worse than a smoky house: I had rather live
With cheese and garlic in a windmill, far,
Than feed on cates and have him talk to me
In any summer-house in Christendom.

Mort. In faith, he is a worthy gentleman,
Exceedingly well read, and profited
In strange concealments, valiant as a lion
And wondrous affable and as bountiful
As mines of India. Shall I tell you, cousin?
He holds your temper in a high respect 170
And curbs himself even of his natural scope
When you come 'cross his humour; faith, he
  does:
I warrant you, that man is not alive
Might so have tempted him as you have done,
Without the taste of danger and reproof:
But do not use it oft, let me entreat you.

Wor. In faith, my lord, you are too wilful-
  blame;
And since your coming hither have done
  enough
To put him quite beside his patience.
You must needs learn, lord, to amend this
  fault: 180
Though sometimes it show greatness, cour-
  age, blood,—
And that's the dearest grace it renders you,—

Yet oftentimes it doth present harsh rage,
Defect of manners, want of government,
Pride, haughtiness, opinion and disdain:
The least of which haunting a nobleman
Loseth men's hearts and leaves behind a
  stain
Upon the beauty of all parts besides,
Beguiling them of commendation.

Hot. Well, I am school'd: good manners
  be your speed!   190
Here come our wives, and let us take our
  leave.

Re-enter GLENDOWER *with the ladies.*

Mort. This is the deadly spite that angers
  me;
My wife can speak no English, I no Welsh.

Glend. My daughter weeps: she will not
  part with you;
She'll be a soldier too, she'll to the wars.

Mort. Good father, tell her that she and
  my aunt Percy
Shall follow in your conduct speedily.
[*Glendower speaks to her in Welsh, and she
        answers him in the same.*
Glend. She is desperate here; a peevish
self-will'd harlotry, one that no persuasion
can do good upon. [*The lady speaks in Welsh.*
Mort. I understand thy looks: that pretty
  Welsh   201
Which thou pour'st down from these swell-
  ing heavens
I am too perfect in; and, but for shame,
In such a parley should I answer thee.
          [*The lady speaks again in Welsh.*
I understand thy kisses and thou mine,
And that's a feeling disputation:
But I will never be a truant, love,
Till I have learn'd thy language; for thy
  tongue
Makes Welsh as sweet as ditties highly
  penn'd,
Sung by a fair queen in a summer's bower, 210
With ravishing division, to her lute.

Glend. Nay, if you melt, then will she run
  mad. [*The lady speaks again in Welsh.*
Mort. O, I am ignorance itself in this!

Glend. She bids you on the wanton rushes
  lay you down
And rest your gentle head upon her lap,

---

149. **moldwarp**, mole. Holinshed tells us that the
division was arranged because of a prophecy which
represented King Henry as the mole and the others as
the dragon, the lion, and the wolf, who should divide
the land among them. 150. **Merlin**, the traditional
bard and prophet of the Welsh. 152. **griffin**, a fabulous
beast. 153. **ramping**, rampant, advancing on its hind
legs. 154. **skimble-skamble**, confused and foolish.
177-189. **In faith . . . commendation.** Worcester's
reproof expresses an ideal of noble courtesy and is important in the understanding of the situation. 177. **wil-
ful-blame**, wilfully guilty.

198. **peevish**, obstinate. 199. **harlotry**, silly wench.
206. **disputation**, conversation. 211. **division**, variation (in music). 214. **wanton**, soft, luxurious.

And she will sing the song that pleaseth you
And on your eyelids crown the god of
sleep,
Charming your blood with pleasing heavi-
ness,
Making such difference 'twixt wake and
sleep
As is the difference betwixt day and night 220
The hour before the heavenly-harness'd
team
Begins his golden progress in the east.

Mort. With all my heart I'll sit and hear
her sing:
By that time will our book, I think, be
drawn.

Glend. Do so;
And those musicians that shall play to you
Hang in the air a thousand leagues from
hence,
And straight they shall be here: sit, and
attend.

Hot. Come, Kate, thou art perfect in lying
down: come, quick, quick, that I may lay my
head in thy lap.   231

Lady P. Go, ye giddy goose. [*Music plays.*

Hot. Now I perceive the devil under-
stands Welsh;
And 'tis no marvel he is so humorous.
By'r lady, he is a good musician.

Lady P. Then should you be nothing but
musical, for you are altogether governed by
humours. Lie still, ye thief, and hear the lady
sing in Welsh.

Hot. I had rather hear Lady, my brach,
howl in Irish.   241

Lady P. Wouldst thou have thy head
broken?

Hot. No.

Lady P. Then be still.

Hot. Neither; 'tis a woman's fault.

Lady P. Now God help thee!

Hot. To the Welsh lady's bed.

Lady P. What's that?

Hot. Peace! she sings.

[*Here the lady sings a Welsh song.*

Hot. Come, Kate, I'll have your song too.

Lady P. Not mine, in good sooth.   251

Hot. Not yours, in good sooth! Heart! you
swear like a comfit-maker's wife. 'Not you,

in good sooth,' and 'as true as I live,' and
'as God shall mend me,' and 'as sure as day,'
And givest such sarcenet surety for thy
oaths,
As if thou never walk'st further than Fins-
bury.
Swear me, Kate, like a lady as thou art,
A good mouth-filling oath, and leave 'in
sooth,'
And such protest of pepper-gingerbread, 260
To velvet-guards and Sunday-citizens.
Come, sing.

Lady P. I will not sing.

Hot. 'Tis the next way to turn tailor, or be
red-breast teacher. An the indentures be
drawn, I'll away within these two hours;
and so, come in when ye will.   [*Exit.*

Glend. Come, come, Lord Mortimer; you
are as slow
As hot Lord Percy is on fire to go.
By this our book is drawn; we'll but seal, 270
And then to horse immediately.

Mort.   With all my heart. [*Exeunt.*

SCENE II. *London. The palace.*

Enter the KING, PRINCE OF WALES,
and others.

King. Lords, give us leave; the Prince of
Wales and I
Must have some private conference: but be
near at hand,
For we shall presently have need of you.
[*Exeunt Lords.*
I know not whether God will have it so,
For some displeasing service I have done,
That, in his secret doom, out of my blood
He'll breed revengement and a scourge for
me;
But thou dost in thy passages of life
Make me believe that thou art only mark'd
For the hot vengeance and the rod of heaven
To punish my mistreadings. Tell me else, 11
Could such inordinate and low desires,
Such poor, such bare, such lewd, such mean
attempts,
Such barren pleasures, rude society,
As thou art match'd withal and grafted to,
Accompany the greatness of thy blood

---

224. **book**, document, indentures. 234. **humorous**,
capricious. 238. **humours**, affectations or dominant
characteristics. 240. **brach**, bitch-hound. 252. **you
swear . . . wife.** Hotspur prefers more violent oaths in
accordance with the fashion of the time, when even the
Queen herself swore vigorously. 253. **comfit-maker's**,
confectioner's.

256. **sarcenet**, soft, from the silken material known as
sarcenet. 257. **Finsbury**, an archery-ground outside
Moorgate, resorted to by citizens. 261. **velvet-guards**,
wearers of velvet trimmings. 264. **turn tailor.** Tailors
were noted for singing. 270. **seal**, set their seals to.
Scene ii. 1. **give us leave**, leave us.

And hold their level with thy princely heart?
   Prince. So please your majesty, I would I
    could
Quit all offences with as clear excuse
As well as I am doubtless I can purge   20
Myself of many I am charged withal:
Yet such extenuation let me beg,
As, in reproof of many tales devised,
Which oft the ear of greatness needs must
   hear,
By smiling pick-thanks and base newsmon-
   gers,
I may, for some things true, wherein my
   youth
Hath faulty wander'd and irregular,
Find pardon on my true submission.
   King. God pardon thee! yet let me won-
   der, Harry,
At thy affections, which do hold a wing   30
Quite from the flight of all thy ancestors.
Thy place in council thou hast rudely lost,
Which by thy younger brother is supplied,
And art almost an alien to the hearts
Of all the court and princes of my blood:
The hope and expectation of thy time
Is ruin'd, and the soul of every man
Prophetically doth forethink thy fall.
Had I so lavish of my presence been,
So common-hackney'd in the eyes of men,   40
So stale and cheap to vulgar company,
Opinion, that did help me to the crown,
Had still kept loyal to possession
And left me in reputeless banishment,
A fellow of no mark nor likelihood.
By being seldom seen, I could not stir
But like a comet I was wonder'd at;
That men would tell their children 'This is
   he;'
Others would say 'Where, which is Boling-
   broke?'
And then I stole all courtesy from heaven,   50
And dress'd myself in such humility
That I did pluck allegiance from men's
   hearts,
Loud shouts and salutations from their
   mouths,
Even in the presence of the crowned king.
Thus did I keep my person fresh and new;
My presence, like a robe pontifical,
Ne'er seen but wonder'd at: and so my state,

Seldom but sumptuous, showed like a feast
And won by rareness such solemnity.
The skipping king, he ambled up and down 60
With shallow jesters and rash bavin wits,
Soon kindled and soon burnt; carded his
   state,
Mingled his royalty with capering fools,
Had his great name profaned with their
   scorns
And gave his countenance, against his name,
To laugh at gibing boys and stand the push
Of every beardless vain comparative,
Grew a companion to the common streets,
Enfeoff'd himself to popularity;
That, being daily swallow'd by men's eyes, 70
They surfeited with honey and began
To loathe the taste of sweetness, whereof a
   little
More than a little is by much too much.
So when he had occasion to be seen,
He was but as the cuckoo is in June,
Heard, not regarded; seen, but with such
   eyes
As, sick and blunted with community,
Afford no extraordinary gaze,
Such as is bent on sun-like majesty
When it shines seldom in admiring eyes;   80
But rather drowsed and hung their eyelids
   down,
Slept in his face and render'd such aspect
As cloudy men use to their adversaries,
Being with his presence glutted, gorged and
   full.
And in that very line, Harry, standest thou;
For thou hast lost thy princely privilege
With vile participation: not an eye
But is a-weary of thy common sight,
Save mine, which hath desired to see thee
   more;
Which now doth that I would not have it do,
Make blind itself with foolish tenderness.   91
   Prince. I shall hereafter, my thrice gra-
   cious lord,
Be more myself.
   King.   For all the world
As thou art to this hour was Richard then
When I from France set foot at Ravens-
   purgh,

60. **skipping,** flighty. 61. **bavin,** brushwood, soon
burnt out. 62. **carded,** debased; a term applied to the
adulteration of drinks. 65. **name,** i.e., dignity. 66.
stand the push, undergo the attack. 67. **comparative,** rival (in wit). 69. **Enfeoff'd,** gave himself up to.
The king is expressing the current view of royal dignity
and policy with reference to the populace. 77. **community,** commonness. 87. **vile participation,** base
association or companionship.

19. **Quit,** clear myself of. 25. **pick-thanks,** flatterers. 30. **affections,** tastes, mental tendencies. 43. **to
possession,** i.e., to Richard II's sovereignty. 50. **stole
. . . heaven.** He assumed a bearing of the utmost
graciousness.

And even as I was then is Percy now.
Now, by my sceptre and my soul to boot,
He hath more worthy interest to the state
Than thou the shadow of succession;
For of no right, nor colour like to right,   100
He doth fill fields with harness in the realm,
Turns head against the lion's armed jaws,
And, being no more in debt to years than
  thou,
Leads ancient lords and reverend bishops on
To bloody battles and to bruising arms.
What never-dying honour hath he got
Against renowned Douglas! whose high
  deeds,
Whose hot incursions and great name in arms
Holds from all soldiers chief majority
And military title capital   110
Through all the kingdoms that acknowledge
  Christ:
Thrice hath this Hotspur, Mars in swathling
  clothes,
This infant warrior, in his enterprizes
Discomfited great Douglas, ta'en him once,
Enlarged him and made a friend of him,
To fill the mouth of deep defiance up
And shake the peace and safety of our
  throne.
And what say you to this? Percy, Northum-
  berland,
The Archbishop's grace of York, Douglas,
  Mortimer,
Capitulate against us and are up.   120
But wherefore do I tell these news to thee?
Why, Harry, do I tell thee of my foes,
Which art my near'st and dearest enemy?
Thou that art like enough, through vassal
  fear,
Base inclination and the start of spleen,
To fight against me under Percy's pay,
To dog his heels and curtsy at his frowns,
To show how much thou art degenerate.
  Prince. Do not think so; you shall not
  find it so:
And God forgive them that so much have
  sway'd   130
Your majesty's good thoughts away from
  me!

98. **interest,** claim.   99. **shadow of succession.**
Hal's claim is a shadow compared to the real services
toward gaining the crown which Hotspur has rendered.
101. **harness,** armor.   109. **majority,** pre-eminence.
110. **capital,** chief.   112. **swathling,** swaddling.   115.
Enlarged, set free.   120. **Capitulate,** form a league.
124. **vassal,** slavish.   125. **start of spleen,** sudden
fit of ill-temper.   129-59. **Do not . . . vow.** Note the
testimony as to the soundness of Hal's character in the
way he bears the cruel reproaches of his father.

I will redeem all this on Percy's head
And in the closing of some glorious day
Be bold to tell you that I am your son;
When I will wear a garment all of blood
And stain my favours in a bloody mask,
Which, wash'd away, shall scour my shame
  with it:
And that shall be the day, whene'er it lights,
That this same child of honour and renown,
This gallant Hotspur, this all-praised knight,
And your unthought-of Harry chance to
  meet.   141
For every honour sitting on his helm,
Would they were multitudes, and on my
  head
My shames redoubled! for the time will
  come,
That I shall make this northern youth ex-
  change
His glorious deeds for my indignities.
Percy is but my factor, good my lord,
To engross up glorious deeds on my behalf;
And I will call him to so strict account,
That he shall render every glory up,   150
Yea, even the slightest worship of his time,
Or I will tear the reckoning from his heart.
This, in the name of God, I promise here:
The which if He be pleased I shall perform,
I do beseech your majesty may salve
The long-grown wounds of my intemper-
  ance:
If not, the end of life cancels all bands;
And I will die a hundred thousand deaths
Ere break the smallest parcel of this vow.
  King. A hundred thousand rebels die in
  this: 160
Thou shalt have charge and sovereign trust
  herein.

Enter BLUNT.

How now, good Blunt? thy looks are full of
  speed.
  Blunt. So hath the business that I come
  to speak of.
Lord Mortimer of Scotland hath sent word
That Douglas and the English rebels met
The eleventh of this month at Shrewsbury:
A mighty and a fearful head they are,
If promises be kept on every hand,
As ever offer'd foul play in a state.
  King. The Earl of Westmoreland set forth
  to-day;   170
With him my son, Lord John of Lancaster;

136. **favours,** features.

For this advertisement is five days old:
On Wednesday next, Harry, you shall set
   forward;
On Thursday we ourselves will march: our
   meeting
Is Bridgenorth: and, Harry, you shall march
Through Gloucestershire; by which account,
Our business valued, some twelve days
   hence
Our general forces at Bridgenorth shall meet.
Our hands are full of business: let's away;
Advantage feeds him fat, while men delay. 180
                         [*Exeunt.*

SCENE III. *Eastcheap. The Boar's-Head*
               Tavern.

Enter FALSTAFF *and* BARDOLPH.

Fal. Bardolph, am I not fallen away vilely
since this last action? do I not bate? do I not
dwindle? Why, my skin hangs about me like
an old lady's loose gown; I am withered like
an old apple-john. Well, I'll repent, and
that suddenly, while I am in some liking; I
shall be out of heart shortly, and then I shall
have no strength to repent. An I have not
forgotten what the inside of a church is made
of, I am a peppercorn, a brewer's horse: the
inside of a church! Company, villanous company, hath been the spoil of me.   12

Bard. Sir John, you are so fretful, you cannot live long.

Fal. Why, there is it: come sing me a bawdy song; make me merry. I was as virtuously
given as a gentleman need to be; virtuous
enough; swore little; diced not above seven
times a week; went to a bawdy-house not
above once in a quarter—of an hour; paid
money that I borrowed, three or four times;
lived well and in good compass: and now I
live out of all order, out of all compass.   23

Bard. Why, you are so fat, Sir John, that
you must needs be out of all compass, out of
all reasonable compass, Sir John.

Fal. Do thou amend thy face, and I'll
amend my life: thou art our admiral, thou
bearest the lantern in the poop, but 'tis in
the nose of thee; thou art the Knight of the
Burning Lamp.   30

Bard. Why, Sir John, my face does you
no harm.

Fal. No, I'll be sworn; I make as good use
of it as many a man doth of a Death's-head
or a memento mori: I never see thy face but
I think upon hell-fire and Dives that lived in
purple; for there he is in his robes, burning,
burning. If thou wert any way given to virtue, I would swear by thy face; my oath
should be 'By this fire, that's God's angel:'
but thou art altogether given over; and wert
indeed, but for the light in thy face, the son
of utter darkness. When thou rannest up
Gadshill in the night to catch my horse, if I
did not think thou hadst been an ignis
fatuus or a ball of wildfire, there's no purchase in money. O, thou art a perpetual
triumph, an everlasting bonfire-light! Thou
hast saved me a thousand marks in links
and torches, walking with thee in the night
betwixt tavern and tavern: but the sack that
thou hast drunk me would have bought me
lights as good cheap at the dearest chandler's in Europe. I have maintained that
salamander of yours with fire any time this
two and thirty years; God reward me for it!

Bard. 'Sblood, I would my face were in
your belly!

Fal. God-a-mercy! so should I be sure to
be heart-burned.

Enter HOSTESS.

How now, Dame Partlet the hen! have you
inquired yet who picked my pocket?   61

Host. Why, Sir John, what do you think,
Sir John? do you think I keep thieves in my
house? I have searched, I have inquired, so
has my husband, man by man, boy by boy,
servant by servant: the tithe of a hair was
never lost in my house before.

Fal. Ye lie, hostess: Bardolph was shaved
and lost many a hair; and I'll be sworn my
pocket was picked. Go to, you are a woman,
go.

Host. Who, I? no; I defy thee: God's light,
I was never called so in mine own house
before.

172. **advertisement**, tidings, news. 180. **Advantage . . . fat**, opportunity feeds itself fat.
  Scene iii. 2. **bate**, fall off, grow thin. 5. **apple-john**, a kind of apple still in perfect condition even when shriveled and withered. 6. **liking**, (good) bodily condition. 10. **peppercorn**, grain of pepper. **brewer's horse**, a contemptuous epithet. 22. **good compass**, reasonable limits. 25. **compass**, girth, circumference. 28. **admiral**, flagship.

35. **memento mori**, reminder of death, such as skull and crossbones. 36. **Dives**, the rich man referred to in *St. Luke*, xvi, 19-31. 39. **'By . . . angel,'** allusion to *Psalms*, civ, 4, and *Hebrews*, i, 7. 44-5. **ignis fatuus**, will-o'-the-wisp. 48. **links**, torches. 51. **good cheap**, cheap. 53. **salamander**, a fabled monster able to live in fire. 60. **Partlet**, traditional name of a hen.

Fal. Go to, I know you well enough.

Host. No, Sir John; you do not know me, Sir John. I know you, Sir John: you owe me money, Sir John; and now you pick a quarrel to beguile me of it: I bought you a dozen of shirts to your back.

Fal. Dowlas, filthy dowlas: I have given them away to bakers' wives, and they have made bolters of them.   81

Host. Now, as I am a true woman, holland of eight shillings an ell. You owe money here besides, Sir John, for your diet and by-drinkings, and money lent you, four and twenty pound.

Fal. He had his part of it; let him pay.

Host. He? alas, he is poor; he hath nothing.   88

Fal. How! poor? look upon his face; what call you rich? let them coin his nose, let them coin his cheeks: I'll not pay a denier. What, will you make a younker of me? shall I not take mine ease in mine inn but I shall have my pocket picked? I have lost a seal-ring of my grandfather's worth forty mark.

Host. O Jesu, I have heard the prince tell him, I know not how oft, that that ring was copper!

Fal. How! the prince is a Jack, a sneak-cup: 'sblood, an he were here, I would cudgel him like a dog, if he would say so.   101

Enter the PRINCE *and* PETO, *marching, and* FALSTAFF *meets them playing on his truncheon like a fife.*

How now, lad! is the wind in that door, i' faith? must we all march?

Bard. Yea, two and two, Newgate fashion.

Host. My lord, I pray you, hear me.

Prince. What sayest thou, Mistress Quickly? How doth thy husband? I love him well; he is an honest man.

Host. Good my lord, hear me.

Fal. Prithee, let her alone, and list to me.

Prince. What sayest thou, Jack?   111

Fal. The other night I fell asleep here behind the arras and had my pocket picked:

this house is turned bawdy-house; they pick pockets.

Prince. What didst thou lose, Jack?

Fal. Wilt thou believe me, Hal? three or four bonds of forty pound a-piece, and a seal-ring of my grandfather's.

Prince. A trifle, some eight-penny matter.   119

Host. So I told him, my lord; and I said I heard your grace say so: and, my lord, he speaks most vilely of you, like a foul-mouthed man as he is; and said he would cudgel you.

Prince. What! he did not?

Host. There's neither faith, truth, nor womanhood in me else.

Fal. There's no more faith in thee than in a stewed prune; nor no more truth in thee than in a drawn fox; and for womanhood, Maid Marian may be the deputy's wife of the ward to thee. Go, you thing, go.   131

Host. Say, what thing! what thing?

Fal. What thing? why, a thing to thank God on.

Host. I am no thing to thank God on, I would thou shouldst know it; I am an honest man's wife: and, setting thy knighthood aside, thou art a knave to call me so.

Fal. Setting thy womanhood aside, thou art a beast to say otherwise.   140

Host. Say, what beast, thou knave, thou?

Fal. What beast! why, an otter.

Prince. An otter, Sir John! why an otter?

Fal. Why, she's neither fish nor flesh; a man knows not where to have her.

Host. Thou art an unjust man in saying so: thou or any man knows where to have me, thou knave, thou!

Prince. Thou sayest true, hostess; and he slanders thee most grossly.   150

Host. So he doth you, my lord; and said this other day you ought him a thousand pound.

Prince. Sirrah, do I owe you a thousand pound?

Fal. A thousand pound, Hal! a million: thy love is worth a million: thou owest me thy love.

Host. Nay, my lord, he called you Jack, and said he would cudgel you.

Fal. Did I, Bardolph?   160

Bard. Indeed, Sir John, you said so.

79. dowlas, a coarse kind of linen. 81. bolters, cloths for sifting meal. 82. holland, fine linen. 83. ell, a measure of a yard and a quarter. 91. denier, one-twelfth of a sou; type of very small coin. 92. younker, youth, greenhorn. 99. sneak-cup. Nares defines this as "one who shirks his liquor"; Johnson modifies to *sneak-up*, meaning "a sneak." 104. Newgate, famous city prison in London.

129. drawn fox, fox driven from cover and wily in getting back. 152. ought, owed.

Fal. Yea, if he said my ring was copper.

Prince. I say 'tis copper: darest thou be as good as thy word now?

Fal. Why, Hal, thou knowest, as thou art but man, I dare: but as thou art prince, I fear thee as I fear the roaring of the lion's whelp.

Prince. And why not as the lion?

Fal. The king himself is to be feared as the lion: dost thou think I'll fear thee as I fear thy father? nay, an I do, I pray God my girdle break. 171

Prince. O, if it should, how would thy guts fall about thy knees! But, sirrah, there's no room for faith, truth, nor honesty in this bosom of thine; it is all filled up with guts and midriff. Charge an honest woman with picking thy pocket! why, thou whoreson, impudent, embossed rascal, if there were anything in thy pocket but tavern-reckonings, memorandums of bawdy-houses, and one poor penny-worth of sugar-candy to make thee long-winded, if thy pocket were enriched with any other injuries but these, I am a villain: and yet you will stand to it; you will not pocket up wrong: art thou 184 not ashamed?

Fal. Dost thou hear, Hal? thou knowest in the state of innocency Adam fell; and what should poor Jack Falstaff do in the days of villany? Thou seest I have more flesh than another man, and therefore more frailty. You confess then, you picked my pocket? 190

Prince. It appears so by the story.

Fal. Hostess, I forgive thee: go, make ready breakfast; love thy husband, look to thy servants, cherish thy guests: thou shalt find me tractable to any honest reason: thou seest I am pacified still. Nay, prithee, be gone. [*Exit Hostess.*] Now, Hal, to the news at court: for the robbery, lad, how is that answered?

Prince. O, my sweet beef, I must still be good angel to thee: the money is paid back again. 200

Fal. O, I do not like that paying back; 'tis a double labour.

Prince. I am good friends with my father and may do any thing.

Fal. Rob me the exchequer the first thing thou doest, and do it with unwashed hands too.

Bard. Do, my lord.

Prince. I have procured thee, Jack, a charge of foot. 209

Fal. I would it had been of horse. Where shall I find one that can steal well? O for a fine thief, of the age of two and twenty or thereabouts! I am heinously unprovided. Well, God be thanked for these rebels, they offend none but the virtuous: I laud them, I praise them.

Prince. Bardolph!

Bard. My lord? 217

Prince. Go bear this letter to Lord John of Lancaster, to my brother John; this to my Lord of Westmoreland. [*Exit Bardolph.*] Go, Peto, to horse, to horse; for thou and I have thirty miles to ride yet ere dinner time. [*Exit Peto.*] Jack, meet me to-morrow in the Temple hall at two o'clock in the afternoon.

There shalt thou know thy charge; and there receive 225
Money and order for their furniture.
The land is burning; Percy stands on high;
And either we or they must lower lie. [*Exit.*

Fal. Rare words! brave world! Hostess, my breakfast, come! 229
O, I could wish this tavern were my drum!
[*Exit.*

ACT IV.

SCENE I. *The rebel camp near Shrewsbury.*

Enter HOTSPUR, WORCESTER, *and* DOUGLAS.

Hot. Well said, my noble Scot: if speaking truth
In this fine age were not thought flattery,
Such attribution should the Douglas have,
As not a soldier of this season's stamp
Should go so general current through the world.
By God, I cannot flatter; I do defy
The tongues of soothers; but a braver place
In my heart's love hath no man than yourself:

---

177. **embossed,** swollen (with fat). 182. **injuries,** used by the prince in allusion to the pocketing of injuries, i.e., failing to resent them. 192. **Hostess, I forgive thee.** This most comic line is an indication of Falstaff's mastery.

206. **with unwashed hands,** at once. 226. **furniture,** equipment, provision. 230. **drum.** Possibly Falstaff means to say that he could wish that he might recruit his soldiers by means of this tavern.
Act IV. Scene i. 3. **attribution,** praise. 4-5. **stamp . . . current,** a figure of speech derived from coining. 6. **defy,** reject, despise. 7. **soothers,** flatterers.

Nay, task me to my word; approve me, lord.

Doug. Thou art the king of honour:　10
No man so potent breathes upon the ground
But I will beard him.

Hot.　　　　　Do so, and 'tis well.

Enter a Messenger *with letters.*

What letters hast thou there?—I can but
　thank you.

Mess. These letters come from your father.

Hot. Letters from him! why comes he not
　himself?

Mess. He cannot come, my lord; he is
　grievous sick.

Hot. 'Zounds! how has he the leisure to be
　sick
In such a justling time? Who leads his
　power?
Under whose government come they along?

Mess. His letters bear his mind, not I, my
　lord.　20

Wor. I prithee, tell me, doth he keep his
　bed?

Mess. He did, my lord, four days ere I set
　forth;
And at the time of my departure thence
He was much fear'd by his physicians.

Wor. I would the state of time had first
　been whole
Ere he by sickness had been visited:
His health was never better worth than now.

Hot. Sick now! droop now! this sickness
　doth infect
The very life-blood of our enterprise;
'Tis catching hither, even to our camp.　30
†He writes me here, that inward sickness—
And that his friends by deputation could
　not
So soon be drawn, nor did he think it meet
To lay so dangerous and dear a trust
On any soul removed but on his own.
Yet doth he give us bold advertisement,
That with our small conjunction we should
　on,
To see how fortune is disposed to us;
For, as he writes, there is no quailing now,
Because the king is certainly possess'd　40
Of all our purposes. What say you to it?

Wor. Your father's sickness is a maim to
　us.

Hot. A perilous gash, a very limb lopp'd
　off:
And yet, in faith, it is not; his present want
Seems more than we shall find it: were it good
To set the exact wealth of all our states
All at one cast? to set so rich a main
On the nice hazard of one doubtful hour?
It were not good; †for therein should we
　read
The very bottom and the soul of hope,　50
The very list, the very utmost bound
Of all our fortunes.

Doug.　　　　　'Faith, and so we should;
Where now remains a sweet reversion:
†We may boldly spend upon the hope of
　what
Is to come in:
A comfort of retirement lives in this.

Hot. A rendezvous, a home to fly unto,
If that the devil and mischance look big
Upon the maidenhead of our affairs.

Wor. But yet I would your father had
　been here.　60
The quality and hair of our attempt
Brooks no division: it will be thought
By some, that know not why he is away,
That wisdom, loyalty and mere dislike
Of our proceedings kept the earl from hence:
And think how such an apprehension
May turn the tide of fearful faction
And breed a kind of question in our cause;
For well you know we of the offering side
Must keep aloof from strict arbitrement,　70
And stop all sight-holes, every loop from
　whence
The eye of reason may pry in upon us:
This absence of your father's draws a cur-
　tain,
That shows the ignorant a kind of fear
Before not dreamt of.

Hot.　　　　　You strain too far.
I rather of his absence make this use:
It lends a lustre and more great opinion,
A larger dare to our great enterprise,
Than if the earl were here; for men must
　think,
If we without his help can make a head　80
To push against a kingdom, with his help

---

9. **task . . . word**, challenge me to make good my word. **approve**, test. 18. **justling**, jostling, busy. 36. **advertisement**, counsel, advice. 37. **conjunction**, joint force, with allusion to the conjunction of planets.

44. **want**, i.e., the lack of him. 47. **cast**, throw of the dice. **main**, number called by the caster before the dice are thrown. 48. **nice**, critical, precarious. 51. **list**, limit. 53. **reversion**, part of an estate yet to be inherited; hope of future profit. 61. **hair**, kind, nature. 67. **fearful**, timorous. 69. **offering side**, side which attacks. 70. **arbitrement**, just inquiry or investigation.

We shall o'erturn it topsy-turvy down.
Yet all goes well, yet all our joints are whole.

Doug. As heart can think: there is not
such a word
Spoke of in Scotland as this term of fear.

Enter SIR RICHARD VERNON.

Hot. My cousin Vernon! welcome, by my
soul.

Ver. Pray God my news be worth a wel-
come, lord.
The Earl of Westmoreland, seven thousand
strong,
Is marching hitherwards; with him Prince
John.

Hot. No harm: what more?

Ver.   And further, I have learn'd, 90
The king himself in person is set forth,
Or hitherwards intended speedily,
With strong and mighty preparation.

Hot. He shall be welcome too. Where is
his son,
The nimble-footed madcap Prince of Wales,
And his comrades, that daff'd the world
aside,
And bid it pass?

Ver.   All furnish'd, all in arms;
†All plumed like estridges that with the
wind
Baited like eagles having lately bathed;
Glittering in golden coats, like images; 100
As full of spirit as the month of May,
And gorgeous as the sun at midsummer;
Wanton as youthful goats, wild as young
bulls.
I saw young Harry, with his beaver on,
His cuisses on his thighs, gallantly arm'd,
Rise from the ground like feather'd Mer-
cury,
And vaulted with such ease into his seat,
As if an angel dropp'd down from the
clouds,
To turn and wind a fiery Pegasus
And witch the world with noble horseman-
ship.   110

Hot. No more, no more: worse than the
sun in March,

96. **daff'd**, put aside with a gesture. 97. **furnish'd**,
equipped. 98. **like estridges**, a reference to ostrich
plumes on crests. 99. **Baited.** Most editors prefer
bated, meaning "beating the wings impatiently." 100.
images. Images (of saints, etc.) were dressed in splendid
robes for holidays. 104. **beaver,** visor (of helmet).
105. **cuisses,** armor for the thighs. 109. **wind a fiery
Pegasus,** turn or wheel like the winged horse of Greek
mythology. 110. **witch,** bewitch. 111-112. **worse . . .
agues.** Your praise causes me worse pain than the
agues of March.

This praise doth nourish agues. Let them
come;
They come like sacrifices in their trim,
And to the fire-eyed maid of smoky war
All hot and bleeding will we offer them:
The mailed Mars shall on his altar sit
Up to the ears in blood. I am on fire
To hear this rich reprisal is so nigh
And yet not ours. Come, let me taste my
horse,
Who is to bear me like a thunderbolt 120
Against the bosom of the Prince of Wales:
Harry to Harry shall, hot horse to horse,
Meet and ne'er part till one drop down a
corse.
O that Glendower were come!

Ver.   There is more news:
I learn'd in Worcester, as I rode along,
He cannot draw his power this fourteen days.

Doug. That's the worst tidings that I hear
of yet.

Wor. Ay, by my faith, that bears a frosty
sound.

Hot. What may the king's whole battle
reach unto?

Ver. To thirty thousand.

Hot.   Forty let it be: 130
My father and Glendower being both away,
The powers of us may serve so great a day.
Come, let us take a muster speedily:
Doomsday is near; die all, die merrily.

Doug. Talk not of dying: I am out of fear
Of death or death's hand for this one-half
year.   [*Exeunt.*

SCENE II. *A public road near Coventry.*

Enter FALSTAFF *and* BARDOLPH.

Fal. Bardolph, get thee before to Coventry; fill me a bottle of sack: our soldiers shall
march through; we'll to Sutton Co'fil' to-
night.

Bard. Will you give me money, captain?

Fal. Lay out, lay out.

Bard. This bottle makes an angel.

Fal. An if it do, take it for thy labour; and
if it make twenty, take them all; I'll answer
the coinage. Bid my lieutenant Peto meet
me at town's end.   10

Bard. I will, captain: farewell.   [*Exit.*

113. **trim,** fine apparel, trappings. 118. **reprisal,**
prize.
Scene ii. 3. **Sutton Co'fil'**, Sutton Coldfield in Warwickshire near Coventry. 6. **makes an angel,** i.e., that
I have spent. *angel,* coin worth ten shillings.

Fal. If I be not ashamed of my soldiers, I am a soused gurnet. I have misused the king's press damnably. I have got, in exchange of a hundred and fifty soldiers, three hundred and odd pounds. I press me none but good householders, yeomen's sons; inquire me out contracted bachelors, such as had been asked twice on the banns; such a commodity of warm slaves, as had as lieve hear the devil as a drum; such as fear the report of a caliver worse than a struck fowl or a hurt wild-duck. I pressed me none but such toasts-and-butter, with hearts in their bellies no bigger than pins' heads, and they have bought out their services; and now my whole charge consists of ancients, corporals, lieutenants, gentlemen of companies, slaves as ragged as Lazarus in the painted cloth, where the glutton's dogs licked his sores; and such as indeed were never soldiers, but discarded unjust serving-men, younger sons to younger brothers, revolted tapsters and ostlers trade-fallen, the cankers of a calm world and a long peace, ten times more dishonourable ragged than an old faced ancient: and such have I, to fill up the rooms of them that have bought out their services, that you would think that I had a hundred and fifty tattered prodigals lately come from swine-keeping, from eating draff and husks. A mad fellow met me on the way and told me I had unloaded all the gibbets and pressed the dead bodies. No eye hath seen such scarecrows. I'll not march through Coventry with them, that's flat: nay, and the villains march wide betwixt the legs, as if they had gyves on; for indeed I had the most of them out of prison. There's but a shirt and a half in all my company; and the half shirt is two napkins tacked together and thrown over the shoulders like a herald's coat without sleeves; and the shirt, to say the truth, stolen from my host at Saint Alban's, or the red-nose innkeeper of

Daventry. But that's all one; they'll find linen enough on every hedge.   52

Enter the Prince *and* Westmoreland.

Prince. How now, blown Jack! how now, quilt!

Fal. What, Hal! how now, mad wag! what a devil dost thou in Warwickshire? My good Lord of Westmoreland, I cry you mercy: I thought your honour had already been at Shrewsbury.   59

West. Faith, Sir John, 'tis more than time that I were there, and you too; but my powers are there already. The king, I can tell you, looks for us all: we must away all night.

Fal. Tut, never fear me: I am as vigilant as a cat to steal cream.

Prince. I think, to steal cream indeed, for thy theft hath already made thee butter. But tell me, Jack, whose fellows are these that come after?

Fal. Mine, Hal, mine.   69

Prince. I did never see such pitiful rascals.

Fal. Tut, tut; good enough to toss; food for powder, food for powder; they'll fill a pit as well as better: tush, man, mortal men, mortal men.

West. Ay, but, Sir John, methinks they are exceeding poor and bare, too beggarly.

Fal. 'Faith, for their poverty, I know not where they had that; and for their bareness, I am sure they never learned that of me.

Prince. No, I'll be sworn; unless you call three fingers on the ribs bare. But, sirrah, make haste: Percy is already in the field.   81

Fal. What, is the king encamped?

West. He is, Sir John: I fear we shall stay too long.

Fal. Well.
To the latter end of a fray and the beginning
    of a feast
Fits a dull fighter and a keen guest. [*Exeunt.*

Scene III. *The rebel camp near Shrewsbury.*

Enter Hotspur, Worcester, Douglas, *and*
    Vernon.

Hot. We'll fight with him to-night.

Wor.   It may not be.

---

13. **soused gurnet**, a kind of fish pickled; opprobrious. 14. **king's press**, royal warrant for the impressment of troops. 16. **yeoman's**, small freeholder's. 17. **contracted**, engaged to be married. 21. **caliver**, musket or harquebus. **struck**, wounded. 26. **ancients**, standard bearers. 28. **painted cloth**, hangings for a room; in this case painted with the story of Lazarus, *St. Luke*, xvi, 20. 32. **cankers**, worms which destroy leaves and buds; used figuratively. 34. **old faced ancient**, defined as an old standard mended with new cloth, or as a standard presenting an old aspect. Cambridge reads *old feaz'd*, meaning "frayed." 37. **prodigals**. See *St. Luke*, xv, 15-16. 39. **draff**, hog-wash. 44. **gyves**, fetters. 50-1. **St. Alban's . . . Daventry**, towns on the road from London to Coventry.

53. **blown**, swollen, inflated. 57. **cry you mercy**, beg your pardon. 71. **toss**, i.e., on a pike.

Doug. You give him then advantage.

Ver. 　　　　　　　　Not a whit.

Hot. Why say you so? looks he not for
　supply?

Ver. So do we.

Hot. 　　His is certain, ours is doubtful.

Wor. Good cousin, be advised; stir not
　to-night.

Ver. Do not, my lord.

Doug. 　　　You do not counsel well:
You speak it out of fear and cold heart.

Ver. Do me no slander, Douglas: by my
　life,
And I dare well maintain it with my life,
If well-respected honour bid me on,　　10
I hold as little counsel with weak fear
As you, my lord, or any Scot that this day
　lives:
Let it be seen to-morrow in the battle
Which of us fears.

Doug. 　　　Yea, or to-night.

Ver. 　　　　　　　　　Content.

Hot. To-night, say I.

Ver. Come, come, it may not be. I won-
　der much,
Being men of such great leading as you are,
That you foresee not what impediments
Drag back our expedition: certain horse
Of my cousin Vernon's are not yet come
　up:
Your uncle Worcester's horse came but to-
　day;　　　　　　　　　　　　　21
And now their pride and mettle is asleep,
Their courage with hard labour tame and
　dull,
That not a horse is half the half of him-
　self.

Hot. So are the horses of the enemy
In general, journey-bated and brought low:
The better part of ours are full of rest.

Wor. The number of the king exceedeth
　ours:
For God's sake, cousin, stay till all come in.
　　　　　　[*The trumpet sounds a parley.*

Enter SIR WALTER BLUNT.

Blunt. I come with gracious offers from
　the king,　　　　　　　　　　30
If you vouchsafe me hearing and respect.

Hot. Welcome, Sir Walter Blunt; and
　would to God

You were of our determination!
Some of us love you well; and even those
　some
Envy your great deservings and good name,
Because you are not of our quality,
But stand against us like an enemy.

Blunt. And God defend but still I should
　stand so,
So long as out of limit and true rule
You stand against anointed majesty.　　40
But to my charge. The king hath sent to
　know
The nature of your griefs, and whereupon
You conjure from the breast of civil peace
Such bold hostility, teaching his duteous
　land
Audacious cruelty. If that the king
Have any way your good deserts forgot,
Which he confesseth to be manifold,
He bids you name your griefs; and with all
　speed
You shall have your desires with interest
And pardon absolute for yourself and these 50
Herein misled by your suggestion.

Hot. The king is kind; and well we know
　the king
Knows at what time to promise, when to
　pay.
My father and my uncle and myself
Did give him that same royalty he wears;
And when he was not six and twenty strong,
Sick in the world's regard, wretched and low,
A poor unminded outlaw sneaking home,
My father gave him welcome to the shore;
And when he heard him swear and vow to
　God　　　　　　　　　　　　60
He came but to be Duke of Lancaster,
To sue his livery and beg his peace,
With tears of innocency and terms of zeal,
My father, in kind heart and pity moved,
Swore him assistance and perform'd it too.
Now when the lords and barons of the realm
Perceived Northumberland did lean to him,
The more and less came in with cap and knee;
Met him in boroughs, cities, villages,
Attended him on bridges, stood in lanes,　70
Laid gifts before him, proffer'd him their
　oaths,
Gave him their heirs, as pages follow'd him
Even at the heels in golden multitudes.

---

10. **well-respected**, well weighed or considered.
26. **journey-bated**, tired from the journey.　31. **respect**, heed, attention.

36. **quality**, party, side.　38. **defend**, forbid.　51.
suggestion, prompting to evil.　62. **sue his livery**,
sue as an heir come of age for the delivery of his lands
held by the crown.　68. **more and less**, persons of all
ranks.

He presently, as greatness knows itself,
Steps me a little higher than his vow
Made to my father, while his blood was poor,
Upon the naked shore at Ravenspurgh;
And now, forsooth, takes on him to re-
    form
Some certain edicts and some strait decrees
That lie too heavy on the commonwealth, 80
Cries out upon abuses, seems to weep
Over his country's wrongs; and by this face,
This seeming brow of justice, did he win
The hearts of all that he did angle for;
Proceeded further; cut me off the heads
Of all the favourites that the absent king
In deputation left behind him here,
When he was personal in the Irish war.
    Blunt. Tut, I came not to hear this.
    Hot.   Then to the point.
In short time after, he deposed the king; 90
Soon after that, deprived him of his life;
And in the neck of that, task'd the whole
    state;
To make that worse, suffer'd his kinsman
    March,
Who is, if every owner were well placed,
Indeed his king, to be engaged in Wales,
There without ransom to lie forfeited;
Disgraced me in my happy victories,
Sought to entrap me by intelligence;
Rated mine uncle from the council-board;
In rage dismiss'd my father from the court;
Broke oath on oath, committed wrong on
    wrong, 101
And in conclusion drove us to seek out
This head of safety; and withal to pry
Into his title, the which we find
Too indirect for long continuance.
    Blunt. Shall I return this answer to the
    king?
    Hot. Not so, Sir Walter: we'll withdraw
    awhile.
Go to the king; and let there be impawn'd
Some surety for a safe return again,
And in the morning early shall my uncle 110
Bring him our purposes: and so farewell.
    Blunt. I would you would accept of grace
    and love.
    Hot. And may be so we shall.
    Blunt.   Pray God you do.
                                    [*Exeunt.*

SCENE IV. *York. The* ARCHBISHOP'S
    palace.

Enter the ARCHBISHOP OF YORK *and*
    SIR MICHAEL.

    Arch. Hie, good Sir Michael; bear this
    sealed brief
With winged haste to the lord marshal;
This to my cousin Scroop, and all the rest
To whom they are directed. If you knew
How much they do import, you would make
    haste.
    Sir M. My good lord,
I guess their tenour.
    Arch.   Like enough you do.
To-morrow, good Sir Michael, is a day
Wherein the fortune of ten thousand men
Must bide the touch; for, sir, at Shrews-
    bury,
As I am truly given to understand, 11
The king with mighty and quick-raised
    power
Meets with Lord Harry: and, I fear, Sir
    Michael,
What with the sickness of Northumber-
    land,
Whose power was in the first proportion,
And what with Owen Glendower's absence
    thence,
Who with them was a rated sinew too
And comes not in, o'er-ruled by prophecies,
I fear the power of Percy is too weak
To wage an instant trial with the king. 20
    Sir M. Why, my good lord, you need not
    fear;
There is Douglas and Lord Mortimer.
    Arch. No, Mortimer is not there.
    Sir M. But there is Mordake, Vernon,
    Lord Harry Percy,
And there is my Lord of Worcester and a
    head
Of gallant warriors, noble gentlemen.
    Arch. And so there is: but yet the king
    hath drawn
The special head of all the land together:
The Prince of Wales, Lord John of Lan-
    caster,
The noble Westmoreland and warlike Blunt;
And many moe corrivals and dear men 31
Of estimation and command in arms.

---

88. **personal**, in person. 92. **task'd**, laid taxes
upon. 95. **engaged**, in pawn, held captive. 98. **intelligence**, secret information, i.e., from spies. 99. **Rated**,
berated, drove away by scolding. 103. **head of safety**,
armed force for their protection.

1. **brief**, letter, dispatch. 10. **bide the touch**,
put to the test (like gold). 17. **rated sinew**, main
strength or support reckoned upon. 31. **moe corrivals**,
more partners in the enterprise. 32. **estimation**,
reputation, importance.

Sir M. Doubt not, my lord, they shall be
well opposed.

Arch. I hope no less, yet needful 'tis to
fear;

And, to prevent the worst, Sir Michael,
speed:

For if Lord Percy thrive not, ere the king

Dismiss his power, he means to visit us,

For he hath heard of our confederacy,

And 'tis but wisdom to make strong against
him: 39

Therefore make haste. I must go write again

To other friends; and so farewell, Sir
Michael.   [*Exeunt.*

ACT V.

SCENE I. *The* KING'S *camp near Shrewsbury.*

Enter the KING, PRINCE OF WALES, LORD
JOHN OF LANCASTER, EARL OF WEST-
MORELAND, SIR WALTER BLUNT, *and*
FALSTAFF.

King. How bloodily the sun begins to peer
Above yon busky hill! the day looks pale
At his distemperature.

Prince.   The southern wind
Doth play the trumpet to his purposes,
And by his hollow whistling in the leaves
Foretells a tempest and a blustering day.

King. Then with the losers let it sym-
pathise,
For nothing can seem foul to those that win.
                    [*The trumpet sounds.*

Enter WORCESTER *and* VERNON.

How now, my Lord of Worcester! 'tis not
well   9
That you and I should meet upon such terms
As now we meet. You have deceived our
trust,
And made us doff our easy robes of peace,
To crush our old limbs in ungentle steel:
This is not well, my lord, this is not well.
What say you to it? will you again un-
knit
This churlish knot of all-abhorred war?
And move in that obedient orb again
Where you did give a fair and natural light,
And be no more an exhaled meteor,

A prodigy of fear and a portent   20
Of broached mischief to the unborn times?
Wor. Hear me, my liege:
For mine own part, I could be well content
To entertain the lag-end of my life
With quiet hours; for I do protest,
I have not sought the day of this dislike.
King. You have not sought it! how
comes it, then?
Fal. Rebellion lay in his way, and he
found it.
Prince. Peace, chewet, peace!
Wor. It pleased your majesty to turn your
looks   30
Of favour from myself and all our house;
And yet I must remember you, my lord,
We were the first and dearest of your friends.
For you my staff of office did I break
In Richard's time; and posted day and night
To meet you on the way, and kiss your
hand,
When yet you were in place and in account
Nothing so strong and fortunate as I.
It was myself, my brother and his son,
That brought you home and boldly did out-
dare   40
The dangers of the time. You swore to us,
And you did swear that oath at Doncaster,
That you did nothing purpose 'gainst the
state;
Nor claim no further than your new-fall'n
right,
The seat of Gaunt, dukedom of Lancaster:
To this we swore our aid. But in short
space
It rain'd down fortune showering on your
head;
And such a flood of greatness fell on you,
What with our help, what with the absent
king,
What with the injuries of a wanton time,   50
The seeming sufferances that you had borne,
And the contrarious winds that held the
king
So long in his unlucky Irish wars
That all in England did repute him dead:
And from this swarm of fair advantages
You took occasion to be quickly woo'd
To gripe the general sway into your hand;
Forgot your oath to us at Doncaster;
And being fed by us you used us so

Act V. Scene i. 2. **busky**, bosky, bushy. 3. **distemperature**, ill-humor, or possibly, inclemency. 17.
orb, orbit, sphere of action. 19. **exhaled**, drawn forth
or engendered by the sun.

21. **broached**, already begun. 29. **chewet**, chough,
jackdaw. 50. **wanton**, capricious, disordered. 51.
sufferances, suffering, distress.

As that ungentle gull, the cuckoo's bird, 60
Useth the sparrow; did oppress our nest;
Grew by our feeding to so great a bulk
That even our love durst not come near your sight
For fear of swallowing; but with nimble wing
We were enforced, for safety sake, to fly
Out of your sight and raise this present head;
Whereby we stand opposed by such means
As you yourself have forged against yourself
By unkind usage, dangerous countenance,
And violation of all faith and troth 70
Sworn to us in your younger enterprise.

King. These things indeed you have articulate,
Proclaim'd at market-crosses, read in churches,
To face the garment of rebellion
With some fine colour that may please the eye
Of fickle changelings and poor discontents,
Which gape and rub the elbow at the news
Of hurlyburly innovation:
And never yet did insurrection want
Such water-colours to impaint his cause; 80
Nor moody beggars, starving for a time
Of pellmell havoc and confusion.

Prince. In both your armies there is many a soul
Shall pay full dearly for this encounter,
If once they join in trial. Tell your nephew,
The Prince of Wales doth join with all the world
In praise of Henry Percy: by my hopes,
This present enterprise set off his head,
I do not think a braver gentleman,
More active-valiant or more valiant-young,90
More daring or more bold, is now alive
To grace this latter age with noble deeds.
For my part, I may speak it to my shame,
I have a truant been to chivalry;
And so I hear he doth account me too;
Yet this before my father's majesty—
I am content that he shall take the odds
Of his great name and estimation,
And will, to save the blood on either side,
Try fortune with him in a single fight. 100

King. And, Prince of Wales, so dare we venture thee,

Albeit considerations infinite
Do make against it. No, good Worcester, no,
We love our people well; even those we love
That are misled upon your cousin's part;
And, will they take the offer of our grace,
Both he and they and you, yea, every man
Shall be my friend again and I'll be his:
So tell your cousin, and bring me word
What he will do: but if he will not yield, 110
Rebuke and dread correction wait on us
And they shall do their office. So, be gone;
We will not now be troubled with reply:
We offer fair; take it advisedly.

[Exeunt Worcester and Vernon.

Prince. It will not be accepted, on my life:
The Douglas and the Hotspur both together
Are confident against the world in arms.

King. Hence, therefore, every leader to his charge;
For, on their answer, will we set on them:
And God befriend us, as our cause is just! 120

*[Exeunt all but the Prince of Wales and
Falstaff.*

Fal. Hal, if thou see me down in the battle
and bestride me, so; 'tis a point of friendship.

Prince. Nothing but a colossus can do
thee that friendship. Say thy prayers, and
farewell.

Fal. I would 'twere bed-time, Hal, and
all well.

Prince. Why, thou owest God a death.
[Exit.

Fal. 'Tis not due yet; I would be loath to
pay him before his day. What need I be so
forward with him that calls not on me? Well,
'tis no matter; honour pricks me on. Yea,
but how if honour prick me off when I come
on? how then? Can honour set to a leg? no:
or an arm? no: or take away the grief of a
wound? no. Honour hath no skill in surgery,
then? no. What is honour? a word. What is
in that word honour? what is that honour?
air. A trim reckoning! Who hath it? he that
died o' Wednesday. Doth he feel it? no.
Doth he hear it? no. 'Tis insensible, then?
Yea, to the dead. But will it not live with

---

the living? no. Why? detraction will not
suffer it. Therefore I'll none of it. Honour is
a mere scutcheon: and so ends my catechism.   [*Exit.* 144

SCENE II. *The rebel camp.*

Enter WORCESTER *and* VERNON.

Wor. O, no, my nephew must not know,
        Sir Richard,
The liberal and kind offer of the king.
  Ver. 'Twere best he did.
  Wor.   Then are we all undone.
It is not possible, it cannot be,
The king should keep his word in loving us;
He will suspect us still and find a time
To punish this offence in other faults:
Suspicion all our lives shall be stuck full of
        eyes;
For treason is but trusted like the fox,
Who, ne'er so tame, so cherish'd and lock'd
        up,   10
Will have a wild trick of his ancestors.
Look how we can, or sad or merrily,
Interpretation will misquote our looks,
And we shall feed like oxen at a stall,
The better cherish'd, still the nearer death.
My nephew's trespass may be well forgot;
It hath the excuse of youth and heat of
        blood,
And an adopted name of privilege,
A hare-brain'd Hotspur, govern'd by a
        spleen:
All his offences live upon my head   20
And on his father's; we did train him on,
And, his corruption being ta'en from us,
We, as the spring of all, shall pay for all.
Therefore, good cousin, let not Harry know,
In any case, the offer of the king.
  Ver. Deliver what you will; I'll say 'tis so.
Here comes your cousin.

Enter HOTSPUR *and* DOUGLAS.

Hot. My uncle is return'd:
Deliver up my Lord of Westmoreland.
Uncle, what news?   30
  Wor. The king will bid you battle pres-
ently.
  Doug. Defy him by the Lord of Westmore-
land.

Hot. Lord Douglas, go you and tell him
        so.
  Doug. Marry, and shall, and very will-
ingly.   [*Exit.*
  Wor. There is no seeming mercy in the
        king.
  Hot. Did you beg any? God forbid!
  Wor. I told him gently of our grievances,
Of his oath-breaking; which he mended thus,
By now forswearing that he is forsworn:
He calls us rebels, traitors; and will scourge 40
With haughty arms this hateful name in us.

Re-enter DOUGLAS.

Doug. Arm, gentlemen; to arms! for I
        have thrown
A brave defiance in King Henry's teeth,
And Westmoreland, that was engaged, did
        bear it;
Which cannot choose but bring him quickly
        on.
  Wor. The Prince of Wales stepp'd forth
        before the king,
And, nephew, challenged you to single fight.
  Hot. O, would the quarrel lay upon our
        heads,
And that no man might draw short breath
        to-day
But I and Harry Monmouth! Tell me, tell
        me,
How show'd his tasking? seem'd it in con-
        tempt?   51
  Ver. No, by my soul; I never in my life
Did hear a challenge urged more modestly,
Unless a brother should a brother dare
To gentle exercise and proof of arms.
He gave you all the duties of a man;
Trimm'd up your praises with a princely
        tongue,
Spoke your deservings like a chronicle,
Making you ever better than his praise
By still dispraising praise valued with you; 60
And, which became him like a prince indeed,
He made a blushing cital of himself;
And chid his truant youth with such a grace
As if he master'd there a double spirit
Of teaching and of learning instantly.
There did he pause: but let me tell the world,
If he outlive the envy of this day,

---

143. **scutcheon**, emblem or hatchment carried in
funerals. It was the lowest form of symbol, having no
pennon or other insignia.
  Scene ii. 18. **adopted name of privilege.** The
meaning is that Hotspur has taken a nickname, "hotspur," to justify his rashness.

51. **tasking,** challenge. 52-69. **I never . . . wantonness.** This praise in the mouth of Hal's enemies is
hardly in character, but is conventionally introduced
to inform the audience. 56. **duties,** reverence, respect.
62. **cital,** impeachment.

England did never owe so sweet a hope,
So much misconstrued in his wantonness.

Hot. Cousin, I think thou art enamoured 70
On his follies: never did I hear
Of any prince so wild a libertine.
But be he as he will, yet once ere night
I will embrace him with a soldier's arm,
That he shall shrink under my courtesy.
Arm, arm with speed: and, fellows, soldiers, friends,
Better consider what you have to do
Than I, that have not well the gift of tongue,
Can lift your blood up with persuasion.

Enter a Messenger.

Mess. My lord, here are letters for you. 80
Hot. I cannot read them now.
O gentlemen, the time of life is short!
To spend that shortness basely were too long,
If life did ride upon a dial's point,
Still ending at the arrival of an hour.
An if we live, we live to tread on kings;
If die, brave death, when princes die with us!
Now, for our consciences, the arms are fair,
When the intent of bearing them is just.

Enter another Messenger.

Mess. My lord, prepare; the king comes
　　on apace. 90
Hot. I thank him, that he cuts me from my
　　tale,
For I profess not talking; only this—
Let each man do his best: and here draw I
A sword, whose temper I intend to stain
With the best blood that I can meet withal
In the adventure of this perilous day.
Now, Esperance! Percy! and set on.
Sound all the lofty instruments of war,
And by that music let us all embrace;
For, heaven to earth, some of us never shall
A second time do such a courtesy. 101

　　[*The trumpets sound. They embrace, and
　　　　　　　　　　　　　　　　　exeunt.*

SCENE III. *Plain between the camps.*

The KING *enters with his power. Alarum to
the battle. Then enter* DOUGLAS *and* SIR
WALTER BLUNT.

Blunt. What is thy name, that in the
　　battle thus
Thou crossest me? what honour dost thou seek

Upon my head?
Doug. Know then, my name is Douglas;
And I do haunt thee in the battle thus
Because some tell me that thou art a king.
Blunt. They tell thee true.
Doug. The Lord of Stafford dear to-day
　　hath bought
Thy likeness, for instead of thee, King Harry,
This sword hath ended him: so shall it thee,
Unless thou yield thee as my prisoner. 10
Blunt. I was not born a yielder, thou
　　proud Scot;
And thou shalt find a king that will revenge
Lord Stafford's death. [*They fight. Douglas
　　　　　　　　　　　　　　kills Blunt.*

Enter HOTSPUR.

Hot. O Douglas, hadst thou fought at
　　Holmedon thus,
I never had triumph'd upon a Scot.
Doug. All's done, all's won; here breath-
　　less lies the king.
Hot. Where?
Doug. Here.
Hot. This, Douglas? no: I know this face
　　full well:
A gallant knight he was, his name was
　　Blunt;
Semblably furnish'd like the king himself. 21
Doug. A fool go with thy soul, whither it
　　goes!
A borrow'd title hast thou bought too dear:
Why didst thou tell me that thou wert a
　　king?
Hot. The king hath many marching in his
　　coats.
Doug. Now, by my sword, I will kill all his
　　coats;
I'll murder all his wardrobe, piece by piece,
Until I meet the king.
Hot.　　　　　　　Up, and away!
Our soldiers stand full fairly for the day. 29
　　　　　　　　　　　　　　　　　[*Exeunt.*

Alarum. Enter FALSTAFF, *solus.*

Fal. Though I could 'scape shot-free at
London, I fear the shot here; here's no scoring but upon the pate. Soft! who are you?
Sir Walter Blunt: there's honour for you!
here's no vanity! I am as hot as molten lead,
and as heavy too: God keep lead out of me!
I need no more weight than mine own

---

68. **owe**, own. 84. **dial's point**, hand of watch or clock.

21. **Semblably furnish'd**, similarly accoutered. 30. **shot-free**, scot-free, without paying. 31. **scoring**, marking up of charges (often on the inn door).

bowels. I have led my ragamuffins where they are peppered: there's not three of my hundred and fifty left alive; and they are for the town's end, to beg during life. But who comes here?   40

Enter the PRINCE.

Prince. What, stand'st thou idle here?
    lend me thy sword:
Many a nobleman lies stark and stiff
Under the hoofs of vaunting enemies,
Whose deaths are yet unrevenged: I prithee,
    lend me thy sword.

Fal. O Hal, I prithee, give me leave to breathe awhile. Turk Gregory never did such deeds in arms as I have done this day. I have paid Percy, I have made him sure.

Prince. He is, indeed; and living to kill thee. I prithee, lend me thy sword.   50

Fal. Nay, before God, Hal, if Percy be alive, thou get'st not my sword; but take my pistol, if thou wilt.

Prince. Give it me: what, is it in the case?

Fal. Ay, Hal; 'tis hot, 'tis hot; there's that will sack a city. [*The Prince draws it out, and finds it to be a bottle of sack.*

Prince. What, is it a time to jest and dally now? [*He throws the bottle at him. Exit.* 58

Fal. Well, if Percy be alive, I'll pierce him. If he do come in my way, so: if he do not, if I come in his willingly, let him make a carbonado of me. I like not such grinning honour as Sir Walter hath: give me life: which if I can save, so; if not, honour comes unlooked for, and there's an end.   [*Exit.*

SCENE IV. *Another part of the field.*

Alarum. Excursions. Enter the KING, *the* PRINCE, LORD JOHN OF LANCASTER, *and* EARL OF WESTMORELAND.

King. I prithee,
Harry, withdraw thyself; thou bleed'st too
    much.
Lord John of Lancaster, go you with him.

Lan. Not I, my lord, unless I did bleed too.

Prince. I beseech your majesty, make up,
Lest your retirement do amaze your friends.

King. I will do so.
My Lord of Westmoreland, lead him to his
    tent.

West. Come, my lord, I'll lead you to your
    tent.

Prince. Lead me, my lord? I do not need
    your help: 10
And God forbid a shallow scratch should
    drive
The Prince of Wales from such a field as this,
Where stain'd nobility lies trodden on,
And rebels' arms triumph in massacres!

Lan. We breathe too long: come, cousin
    Westmoreland,
Our duty this way lies; for God's sake, come.
    [*Exeunt Prince John and Westmoreland.*

Prince. By God, thou hast deceived me,
    Lancaster;
I did not think thee lord of such a spirit:
Before, I loved thee as a brother, John;
But now, I do respect thee as my soul.   20

King. I saw him hold Lord Percy at the
    point
With lustier maintenance than I did look for
Of such an ungrown warrior.

Prince.   O, this boy
Lends mettle to us all!   [*Exit.*

Enter DOUGLAS.

Doug. Another king! they grow like
    Hydra's heads:
I am the Douglas, fatal to all those
That wear those colours on them: what art
    thou,
That counterfeit'st the person of a king?

King. The king himself; who, Douglas,
    grieves at heart
So many of his shadows thou hast met   30
And not the very king. I have two boys
Seek Percy and thyself about the field:
But, seeing thou fall'st on me so luckily,
I will assay thee: so, defend thyself.

Doug. I fear thou art another counterfeit;
And yet, in faith, thou bear'st thee like a
    king:
But mine I am sure thou art, whoe'er thou
    be,
And thus I win thee. [*They fight; the King being in danger, re-enter Prince of Wales.*

Prince. Hold up thy head, vile Scot, or
    thou art like

---

46. **Turk Gregory**, a sort of combined allusion to the famous pope Gregory the Great and to the Grand Turk. 59. **Percy . . . pierce.** Current pronunciation probably rendered the pun more obvious than it is now. 62. **carbonado**, meat scored across for broiling.
Scene iv. 5. **make up**, go forward. 6. **amaze**, alarm.

22. **maintenance**, bearing, demeanor. 25. **Hydra's heads**, allusion to the Lernean Hydra, whose heads grew again as fast as they were cut off.

Never to hold it up again! the spirits   40
Of valiant Shirley, Stafford, Blunt, are in my
      arms:
It is the Prince of Wales that threatens thee;
Who never promiseth but he means to pay.
                    [*They fight: Douglas flies.*
Cheerly, my lord: how fares your grace?
Sir Nicholas Gawsey hath for succour sent,
And so hath Clifton: I'll to Clifton straight.
  King. Stay, and breathe awhile:
Thou hast redeem'd thy lost opinion,
And show'd thou makest some tender of my
      life,
In this fair rescue thou hast brought to me. 50
  Prince. O God! they did me too much in-
      jury
That ever said I hearken'd for your death.
If it were so, I might have let alone
The insulting hand of Douglas over you,
Which would have been as speedy in your
      end
As all the poisonous potions in the world
And saved the treacherous labour of your
      son.
  King. Make up to Clifton: I'll to Sir
Nicholas Gawsey.   [*Exit.*

                Enter HOTSPUR.

  Hot. If I mistake not, thou art Harry
      Monmouth.
  Prince. Thou speak'st as if I would deny
      my name.   60
  Hot. My name is Harry Percy.
  Prince.   Why, then I see
A very valiant rebel of the name.
I am the Prince of Wales; and think not,
      Percy,
To share with me in glory any more:
Two stars keep not their motion in one
      sphere;
Nor can one England brook a double reign,
Of Harry Percy and the Prince of Wales.
  Hot. Nor shall it, Harry; for the hour is
      come
To end the one of us; and would to God
Thy name in arms were now as great as mine!
  Prince. I'll make it greater ere I part
      from thee;   71
And all the budding honours on thy crest
I'll crop, to make a garland for my head.

  Hot. I can no longer brook thy vanities.
                    [*They fight.*

                Enter FALSTAFF.

  Fal. Well said, Hal! to it, Hal! Nay, you
shall find no boy's play here, I can tell you.

Re-enter DOUGLAS; *he fights with* FALSTAFF,
who falls down as if he were dead, and exit
DOUGLAS. HOTSPUR *is wounded, and falls.*

  Hot. O, Harry, thou hast robb'd me of my
      youth!
I better brook the loss of brittle life
Than those proud titles thou hast won of
      me;
They wound my thoughts worse than thy
      sword my flesh: 80
But thought's the slave of life, and life time's
      fool;
And time, that takes survey of all the world,
Must have a stop. O, I could prophesy,
But that the earthy and cold hand of death
Lies on my tongue: no, Percy, thou art dust,
And food for—   [*Dies.*
  Prince. For worms, brave Percy: fare
      thee well, great heart!
Ill-weaved ambition, how much art thou
      shrunk!
When that this body did contain a spirit,
A kingdom for it was too small a bound; 90
But now two paces of the vilest earth
Is room enough: this earth that bears thee
      dead
Bears not alive so stout a gentleman.
If thou wert sensible of courtesy,
I should not make so dear a show of zeal:
But let my favours hide thy mangled face;
And, even in thy behalf, I'll thank myself
For doing these fair rites of tenderness.
Adieu, and take thy praise with thee to
      heaven!
Thy ignominy sleep with thee in the grave,100
But not remember'd in thy epitaph!
                [*He spieth Falstaff on the ground.*
What, old acquaintance! could not all this
      flesh
Keep in a little life? Poor Jack, farewell!
I could have better spared a better man:
O, I should have a heavy miss of thee,
If I were much in love with vanity!

---

49. **makest some tender,** hast some care for. 52.
hearken'd, listened (as for welcome intelligence). 65.
Two stars . . . sphere, proverbial allusion to the fact
that each planet has its own orbit.

81-83. **But . . . stop.** Thought ends with life, and
life is ended by time; and time, though it serve as the
measure for the world, must itself come to an end. 95.
dear, affectionate. 96. **favours,** knots of ribbon.

Death hath not struck so fat a deer to-day,
Though many dearer, in this bloody fray.
Embowell'd will I see thee by and by:
Till then in blood by noble Percy lie. [*Exit.*110

Fal. [*Rising up*] Embowelled! if thou em-
bowel me to-day, I'll give you leave to powder me and eat me too to-morrow. 'Sblood,
'twas time to counterfeit, or that hot termagant Scot had paid me scot and lot too.
Counterfeit? I lie, I am no counterfeit: to
die, is to be a counterfeit; for he is but the
counterfeit of a man who hath not the life of
a man: but to counterfeit dying, when a man
thereby liveth, is to be no counterfeit, but
the true and perfect image of life indeed.
The better part of valour is discretion; in the
which better part I have saved my life.
'Zounds, I am afraid of this gunpowder
Percy, though he be dead: how, if he should
counterfeit too and rise? by my faith, I am
afraid he would prove the better counterfeit.
Therefore I'll make him sure; yea, and I'll
swear I killed him. Why may not he rise as
well as I? Nothing confutes me but eyes,
and nobody sees me. Therefore, sirrah
[*stabbing him*], with a new wound in your
thigh, come you along with me.   132
        [*Takes up Hotspur on his back.*

Re-enter the PRINCE OF WALES *and* LORD
        JOHN OF LANCASTER.

Prince. Come, brother John; full bravely
        hast thou flesh'd
Thy maiden sword.
Lan.   But, soft! whom have we here?
Did you not tell me this fat man was dead?
Prince. I did; I saw him dead,
Breathless and bleeding on the ground. Art
        thou alive?
Or is it fantasy that plays upon our eyesight?
I prithee, speak; we will not trust our eyes
Without our ears: thou art not what thou
        seem'st.   140
Fal. No, that's certain; I am not a double
man: but if I be not Jack Falstaff, then am I
a Jack. There is Percy [*throwing the body

down*]: if your father will do me any honour,
so; if not, let him kill the next Percy himself.
I look to be either earl or duke, I can assure
you.

Prince. Why, Percy I killed myself and
        saw thee dead.

Fal. Didst thou? Lord, Lord, how this
world is given to lying! I grant you I was
down and out of breath; and so was he: but
we rose both at an instant and fought a long
hour by Shrewsbury clock. If I may be
believed, so; if not, let them that should
reward valour bear the sin upon their own
heads. I'll take it upon my death, I gave
him this wound in the thigh: if the man were
alive and would deny it, 'zounds, I would
make him eat a piece of my sword.

Lan. This is the strangest tale that ever I
        heard.

Prince. This is the strangest fellow,
        brother John.
Come, bring your luggage nobly on your
        back:
For my part, if a lie may do thee grace,   161
I'll gild it with the happiest terms I have.
        [*A retreat is sounded.*
The trumpet sounds retreat; the day is ours.
Come, brother, let us to the highest of the
        field,
To see what friends are living, who are dead.
        [*Exeunt Prince of Wales and Lancaster.*
Fal. I'll follow, as they say, for reward.
He that rewards me, God reward him! If I
do grow great, I'll grow less; for I'll purge,
and leave sack, and live cleanly as a noble-
man should do.   [*Exit.*

SCENE V. *Another part of the field.*

The trumpets sound. Enter the KING, PRINCE
OF WALES, LORD JOHN OF LANCASTER,
EARL OF WESTMORELAND, *with* WOR-
CESTER *and* VERNON *prisoners.*

King. Thus ever did rebellion find rebuke.
Ill-spirited Worcester! did not we send grace,
Pardon and terms of love to all of you?
And wouldst thou turn our offers contrary?
Misuse the tenour of thy kinsman's trust?
Three knights upon our party slain to-day,
A noble earl and many a creature else

---

109. **Embowell'd,** disembowelled, i.e., for burial.
112. **powder,** salt. 114. **termagant,** violent; derived
from the name of a heathen god of the Saracens in the
miracle play of St. Nicholas. 115. **scot and lot,** used
figuratively to denote complete payment. 132. *Stage
Direction:* **Takes up,** etc. Bodies of slain persons had
to be removed from the stage in the Elizabethan theater.
This is a famous case of Shakespeare's skill in having the
duty performed naturally. 138. **fantasy,** imagination
or delusion. Note that the Prince seems to show real
fear at what he thinks is Falstaff's ghost.

167-170. **If I do . . . should do.** Note the recurrence of Falstaff's repentance. It is part of the ancient
conception of Falstaff as a hypocritical Lollard.

Had been alive this hour,
If like a Christian thou hadst truly borne
Betwixt our armies true intelligence.   10
   Wor. What I have done my safety urged
    me to;
And I embrace this fortune patiently,
Since not to be avoided it falls on me.
   King. Bear Worcester to the death and
    Vernon too:
Other offenders we will pause upon.
                  [Exeunt Worcester and Vernon,
                            guarded.
How goes the field?
   Prince. The noble Scot, Lord Douglas,
    when he saw
The fortune of the day quite turn'd from
    him,
The noble Percy slain, and all his men
Upon the foot of fear, fled with the rest;   20
And falling from a hill, he was so bruised
That the pursuers took him. At my tent
The Douglas is; and I beseech your grace
I may dispose of him.
   King.   With all my heart.
   Prince. Then, brother John of Lancaster,
    to you
This honourable bounty shall belong:

20. **upon the foot of fear**, in flight.

Go to the Douglas, and deliver him
Up to his pleasure, ransomless and free:
His valour shown upon our crests to-day
Hath taught us how to cherish such high
    deeds   30
Even in the bosom of our adversaries.
   Lan. I thank your grace for this high
    courtesy,
Which I shall give away immediately.
   King. Then this remains, that we divide
    our power.
You, son John, and my cousin Westmore-
    land
Towards York shall bend you with your
    dearest speed,
To meet Northumberland and the prelate
    Scroop,
Who, as we hear, are busily in arms:
Myself and you, son Harry, will towards
    Wales,
To fight with Glendower and the Earl of
    March.   40
Rebellion in this land shall lose his sway,
Meeting the check of such another day:
And since this business so fair is done,
Let us not leave till all our own be won.
                            [Exeunt.

36. **dearest**, heartfelt, most earnest.

THE SECOND PART OF
KING HENRY THE FOURTH

DRAMATIS PERSONÆ

RUMOUR, the Presenter.
KING HENRY the Fourth.
HENRY, PRINCE OF WALES, afterwards King Henry V.,
THOMAS, DUKE OF CLARENCE, } his sons.
PRINCE JOHN OF LANCASTER,
PRINCE HUMPHREY OF GLOUCESTER
EARL OF WARWICK.
EARL OF WESTMORELAND.
EARL OF SURREY.
GOWER.
HARCOURT.
BLUNT.
Lord Chief-Justice of the King's Bench.
A Servant of the Chief-Justice.
EARL OF NORTHUMBERLAND.
SCROOP, Archbishop of York.
LORD MOWBRAY.
LORD HASTINGS.
LORD BARDOLPH.
SIR JOHN COLEVILE.
TRAVERS and MORTON, retainers of Northumberland.

SIR JOHN FALSTAFF.
His Page.
BARDOLPH.
PISTOL.
POINS.
PETO.
SHALLOW, } country justices.
SILENCE,
DAVY, Servant to Shallow.
MOULDY, SHADOW, WART, FEEBLE, and BULLCALF, recruits.
FANG and SNARE, sheriff's officers.

LADY NORTHUMBERLAND.
LADY PERCY.
MISTRESS QUICKLY, hostess of a tavern in Eastcheap.
DOLL TEARSHEET.

Lords and Attendants; Porter, Drawers, Beadles, Grooms, &c.
A Dancer, speaker of the epilogue.

SCENE: *England.*

INDUCTION.

Warkworth. Before the castle.

Enter Rumour, *painted full of tongues.*

Rum. Open your ears; for which of you will stop
The vent of hearing when loud Rumour speaks?
I, from the orient to the drooping west,
Making the wind my post-horse, still unfold
The acts commenced on this ball of earth:
Upon my tongues continual slanders ride,
The which in every language I pronounce,
Stuffing the ears of men with false reports.
I speak of peace, while covert enmity
Under the smile of safety wounds the world:
And who but Rumour, who but only I,   11
Make fearful musters and prepared defence,
Whiles the big year, swoln with some other grief,
Is thought with child by the stern tyrant war,
And no such matter? Rumour is a pipe
Blown by surmises, jealousies, conjectures,
And of so easy and so plain a stop
That the blunt monster with uncounted heads,
The still-discordant wavering multitude,
Can play upon it. But what need I thus   20

The Second Part of King Henry IV. The play is supposed to open immediately after the battle of Shrewsbury, in which Henry Percy, or Hotspur, and the Scottish Earl of Douglas have been overthrown. We are concerned first of all with the news of the battle.
Induction. Stage Direction: Rumour . . . tongues.
Rumor wears a symbolic costume. Virgil describes her as full of eyes, ears, and tongues (Æneid, iv, 174).

17. stop, hole in wind instruments.   18. blunt, stupid, dull-witted.

My well-known body to anatomize
Among my household? Why is Rumour here?
I run before King Harry's victory;
Who in a bloody field by Shrewsbury
Hath beaten down young Hotspur and his
    troops,
Quenching the flame of bold rebellion
Even with the rebels' blood. But what
    mean I
To speak so true at first? my office is
To noise abroad that Harry Monmouth fell
Under the wrath of noble Hotspur's sword, 30
And that the king before the Douglas' rage
Stoop'd his anointed head as low as death.
This have I rumour'd through the peasant
    towns
Between that royal field of Shrewsbury
And this worm-eaten hold of ragged stone,
Where Hotspur's father, old Northumber-
    land,
Lies crafty-sick: the posts come tiring on,
And not a man of them brings other news
Than they have learn'd of me: from Ru-
    mour's tongues
They bring smooth comforts false, worse
    than true wrongs.   [*Exit.* 40

ACT I.

Scene I. *The same.*

Enter Lord Bardolph.

L. Bard. Who keeps the gate here, ho?

The Porter *opens the gate.*

            Where is the earl?
Port. What shall I say you are?
L. Bard.   Tell thou the earl
That the Lord Bardolph doth attend him
    here.
Port. His lordship is walk'd forth into the
    orchard:
Please it your honour, knock but at the gate,
And he himself will answer.

Enter Northumberland.

L. Bard.   Here comes the earl.
                    [*Exit Porter.*
North. What news, Lord Bardolph? every
    minute now
Should be the father of some stratagem:

The times are wild; contention, like a horse
Full of high feeding, madly hath broke
    loose   10
And bears down all before him.
    L. Bard.   Noble earl,
I bring you certain news from Shrewsbury.
    North. Good, an God will!
    L. Bard.   As good as heart can wish:
The king is almost wounded to the death;
And, in the fortune of my lord your son,
Prince Harry slain outright; and both the
    Blunts
Kill'd by the hand of Douglas; young Prince
    John
And Westmoreland and Stafford fled the
    field;
And Harry Monmouth's brawn, the hulk
    Sir John,
Is prisoner to your son: O, such a day,   20
So fought, so follow'd and so fairly won,
Came not till now to dignify the times,
Since Cæsar's fortunes!
    North.   How is this derived?
Saw you the field? came you from Shrews-
    bury?
    L. Bard. I spake with one, my lord, that
    came from thence,
A gentleman well bred and of good name,
That freely render'd me these news for
    true.
    North. Here comes my servant Travers,
    whom I sent
On Tuesday last to listen after news.

Enter Travers.

L. Bard. My lord, I over-rode him on the
    way;   30
And he is furnish'd with no certainties
More than he haply may retail from me.
    North. Now, Travers, what good tidings
    comes with you?
    Tra. My lord, Sir John Umfrevile turn'd
    me back
With joyful tidings; and, being better
    horsed,
Out-rode me. After him came spurring hard
A gentleman, almost forspent with speed,
That stopp'd by me to breathe his bloodied
    horse.
He ask'd the way to Chester; and of him
I did demand what news from Shrewsbury:40

---

21. **anatomize**, lay open minutely, explain. 33.
peasant, rural, or provincial. 35. **hold**, stronghold.
37. **crafty-sick**, feigning sickness.
    Act I. Scene i. 2. **What**, etc., of what name and
station. 8. **stratagem**, deed of violence.

15. **in the fortune of**, by the good fortune of. 19.
brawn, fleshy part of the body; an allusion to Falstaff's
fatness. 21. **follow'd**, carried through. 37. **forspent**,
exhausted. 38. **bloodied**, i.e., with spurring.

He told me that rebellion had bad luck
And that young Harry Percy's spur was cold.
With that, he gave his able horse the head,
And bending forward struck his armed heels
Against the panting sides of his poor jade
Up to the rowel-head, and starting so
He seem'd in running to devour the way,
Staying no longer question.

　　North.　　　　　　　Ha! Again:
Said he young Harry Percy's spur was cold?
Of Hotspur Coldspur? that rebellion　　50
Had met ill luck?

　　L. Bard.　　My lord, I'll tell you what;
If my young lord your son have not the day,
Upon mine honour, for a silken point
I'll give my barony: never talk of it.

　　North. Why should that gentleman that
　　rode by Travers
Give then such instances of loss?

　　L. Bard.　　　　　　Who, he?
He was some hilding fellow that had stolen
The horse he rode on, and, upon my life,
Spoke at a venture. Look, here comes more
　　news.

Enter MORTON.

　　North. Yea, this man's brow, like to a
　　title-leaf,　　60
Foretells the nature of a tragic volume:
So looks the strand whereon the imperious
　　flood
Hath left a witness'd usurpation.
Say, Morton, didst thou come from Shrews-
　　bury?

　　Mor. I ran from Shrewsbury, my noble
　　lord;
Where hateful death put on his ugliest mask
To fright our party.

　　North.　　How doth my son and brother?
Thou tremblest; and the whiteness in thy
　　cheek
Is apter than thy tongue to tell thy errand.
Even such a man, so faint, so spiritless,　70
So dull, so dead in look, so woe-begone,
Drew Priam's curtain in the dead of night,
And would have told him half his Troy was
　　burnt;
But Priam found the fire ere he his tongue,
And I my Percy's death ere thou report'st it.

This thou wouldst say, 'Your son did thus
　　and thus;
Your brother thus: so fought the noble
　　Douglas:'
Stopping my greedy ear with their bold
　　deeds:
But in the end, to stop my ear indeed,
Thou hast a sigh to blow away this praise,　80
Ending with 'Brother, son, and all are
　　dead.'

　　Mor. Douglas is living, and your brother,
　　yet;
But, for my lord your son,—

　　North.　　　　　Why, he is dead.
See what a ready tongue suspicion hath!
He that but fears the thing he would not
　　know
Hath by instinct knowledge from others'
　　eyes
That what he fear'd is chanced. Yet speak,
　　Morton;
Tell thou an earl his divination lies,
And I will take it as a sweet disgrace
And make thee rich for doing me such
　　wrong.　90

　　Mor. You are too great to be by me
　　gainsaid:
Your spirit is too true, your fears too cer-
　　tain.

　　North. Yet, for all this, say not that
　　Percy's dead.
I see a strange confession in thine eye:
Thou shakest thy head and hold'st it fear or
　　sin
To speak a truth. If he be slain, say so;
The tongue offends not that reports his
　　death:
And he doth sin that doth belie the dead,
Not he which says the dead is not alive.
Yet the first bringer of unwelcome news　100
Hath but a losing office, and his tongue
Sounds ever after as a sullen bell,
Remember'd tolling a departing friend.

　　L. Bard. I cannot think, my lord, your son
　　is dead.

　　Mor. I am sorry I should force you to
　　believe
That which I would to God I had not seen;
But these mine eyes saw him in bloody state,
Rendering faint quittance, wearied and out-
　　breathed,

---

45. **jade**, tired horse. 46. **rowel-head**, the end of the spur, in which the barbed wheel turns. 53. **point**, lace for fastening hose to doublet. 57. **hilding**, good-for-nothing. 63. **witness'd usurpation**, evidence of its ravages. 72. **Priam's.** Priam was the king of Troy.

91. **gainsaid**, contradicted. 95. **fear**, cause of fear. 103. **tolling**, ringing the passing bell for. 108. **quittance**, requital, i.e., resistance.

To Harry Monmouth; whose swift wrath
    beat down
The never-daunted Percy to the earth,   110
From whence with life he never more sprung
    up.
In few, his death, whose spirit lent a fire
Even to the dullest peasant in his camp,
Being bruited once, took fire and heat away
From the best-temper'd courage in his
    troops;
For from his metal was his party steel'd;
Which once in him abated, all the rest
Turn'd on themselves, like dull and heavy
    lead:
And as the thing that's heavy in itself,
Upon enforcement flies with greatest speed,
So did our men, heavy in Hotspur's loss, 121
Lend to this weight such lightness with their
    fear
That arrows fled not swifter toward their aim
Than did our soldiers, aiming at their safety,
Fly from the field. Then was that noble
    Worcester
Too soon ta'en prisoner; and that furious
    Scot,
The bloody Douglas, whose well-labouring
    sword
Had three times slain the appearance of the
    king,
'Gan vail his stomach and did grace the
    shame
Of those that turn'd their backs, and in his
    flight,   130
Stumbling in fear, was took. The sum of all
Is that the king hath won, and hath sent out
A speedy power to encounter you, my lord,
Under the conduct of young Lancaster
And Westmoreland. This is the news at full.
    North. For this I shall have time enough
    to mourn.
In poison there is physic; and these news,
Having been well, that would have made me
    sick,
Being sick, have in some measure made me
    well:
And as the wretch, whose fever-weaken'd
    joints,
Like strengthless hinges, buckle under
    life,   141

Impatient of his fit, breaks like a fire
Out of his keeper's arms, even so my limbs,
Weaken'd with grief, being now enraged with
    grief,
Are thrice themselves. Hence, therefore,
    thou nice crutch!
A scaly gauntlet now with joints of steel
Must glove this hand: and hence, thou sickly
    quoif!
Thou art a guard too wanton for the head
Which princes, flesh'd with conquest, aim
    to hit.
Now bind my brows with iron; and approach
The ragged'st hour that time and spite dare
    bring   151
To frown upon the enraged Northumber-
    land!
Let heaven kiss earth! now let not Nature's
    hand
Keep the wild flood confined! let order die!
And let this world no longer be a stage
To feed contention in a lingering act;
But let one spirit of the first-born Cain
Reign in all bosoms, that, each heart being
    set
On bloody courses, the rude scene may end,
And darkness be the burier of the dead! 160
    Tra. This strained passion doth you
    wrong, my lord.
    L. Bard. Sweet earl, divorce not wisdom
    from your honour.
    Mor. The lives of all your loving com-
    plices
Lean on your health; the which, if you give
    o'er
To stormy passion, must perforce decay.
You cast the event of war, my noble lord,
And summ'd the account of chance, before
    you said
'Let us make head.' It was your presur-
    mise,
That, in the dole of blows, your son might
    drop:
You knew he walk'd o'er perils, on an edge,
More likely to fall in than to get o'er; 171
You were advised his flesh was capable
Of wounds and scars and that his forward
    spirit

---

112. **In few,** in few words. 114. **bruited,** noised
abroad, reported. 116. **metal,** courage, temperament.
120. **enforcement,** compulsion. 128. **appearance,** i.e.,
warriors dressed like the king. 129. **'Gan vail,** began to
abate or lower (his courage). 141. **buckle,** bend (under
stress).

144. **grief . . . grief,** hardship . . . sorrow. 145. **nice,**
delicate, not able to withstand. 147. **quoif,** close-
fitting cap. 148. **wanton,** effeminate. 149. **flesh'd,**
inflamed by foretaste of success. 161. **strained,** excessive. 163. **complices,** allies, confederates. 166.
cast, calculated. 168. **make head,** muster forces (for
rebellion). 169. **dole,** dealing, or distribution. 172. **advised,** aware. **capable,** accessible to, liable to.

Would lift him where most trade of danger
    ranged:
Yet did you say 'Go forth;' and none of this,
Though strongly apprehended, could restrain
The stiff-borne action: what hath then be-
    fallen,
Or what hath this bold enterprise brought
    forth,
More than that being which was like to be?
    L. Bard. We all that are engaged to this
    loss   180
Knew that we ventured on such dangerous
    seas
That if we wrought out life 'twas ten to one;
And yet we ventured, for the gain proposed
Choked the respect of likely peril fear'd;
And since we are o'erset, venture again.
Come, we will all put forth, body and goods.
    Mor. 'Tis more than time: and, my most
    noble lord,
I hear for certain, and do speak the truth,
The gentle Archbishop of York is up
With well-appointed powers: he is a man 190
Who with a double surety binds his followers.
My lord your son had only but the corpse,
But shadows and the shows of men, to fight;
For that same word, rebellion, did divide
The action of their bodies from their souls;
And they did fight with queasiness, con-
    strain'd,
As men drink potions, that their weapons
    only
Seem'd on our side; but, for their spirits and
    souls,
This word, rebellion, it had froze them up,
As fish are in a pond. But now the bishop 200
Turns insurrection to religion:
Supposed sincere and holy in his thoughts,
He's followed both with body and with mind;
And doth enlarge his rising with the blood
Of fair King Richard, scraped from Pomfret
    stones;
Derives from heaven his quarrel and his
    cause;
Tells them he doth bestride a bleeding land,
Gasping for life under great Bolingbroke;
And more and less do flock to follow him.

North. I knew of this before; but, to speak
    truth,   210
This present grief had wiped it from my
    mind.
Go in with me; and counsel every man
The aptest way for safety and revenge:
Get posts and letters, and make friends with
    speed:
Never so few, and never yet more need.
                            [*Exeunt.*

SCENE II. *London. A street.*

Enter FALSTAFF, *with his* Page *bearing his sword and buckler.*

    Fal. Sirrah, you giant, what says the doctor to my water?
    Page. He said, sir, the water itself was a good healthy water; but, for the party that owed it, he might have more diseases than he knew for.
    Fal. Men of all sorts take a pride to gird at me: the brain of this foolish-compounded clay, man, is not able to invent any thing that tends to laughter, more than I invent or is invented on me: I am not only witty in myself, but the cause that wit is in other men. I do here walk before thee like a sow that hath overwhelmed all her litter but one. If the prince put thee into my service for any other reason than to set me off, why then I have no judgement. Thou 17 whoreson mandrake, thou art fitter to be worn in my cap than to wait at my heels. I was never manned with an agate till now: but I will inset you neither in gold nor silver, but in vile apparel, and send you back again to your master, for a jewel,—the juvenal, the prince your master, whose chin is not yet fledged. I will sooner have a beard grow in the palm of my hand than he shall get one on his cheek; and yet he will not stick to say his face is a face-royal: God may finish it when he will, 'tis not a hair amiss yet: he may keep it still at a face-royal, for a barber shall never earn sixpence out of it; and yet he'll be crowing as if he had writ man ever since his father was a bachelor. He may

174. **trade**, passing to and fro as over a path. 177. **stiff-borne**, obstinately carried out. 180. **engaged to,** involved in. 184. **Choked the respect of,** prevented (us) from considering. 192. **corpse,** used as plural here, referring to living bodies. 193. **fight,** to use for fighting. 204. **enlarge,** enhance the merit of his insurrection (Hunter); widen the limits or scope (Onions). 205. **Pomfret.** Richard was murdered at Pomfret Castle. 208. **Bolingbroke,** King Henry IV. 209. **more and less,** all classes.

Scene ii. 7. **gird,** banter, attack with words. 8. **foolish-compounded,** composed of folly. 11-13. **I am . . . men,** a masterly comment on Falstaff. 18. **mandrake,** a poisonous plant whose root was supposed to resemble the human figure. 20. **agate,** small figure cut in agate for jewelry. 21. **inset,** set. 23. **juvenal,** youth. 28. **face-royal** face of the king on the *royal,* a coin, with pun (l. 30) on *royal face.*

keep his own grace, but he's almost out of mine, I can assure him. What said Master Dombledon about the satin for my short cloak and my slops?

Page. He said, sir, you should procure him better assurance than Bardolph: he would not take his band and yours; he liked not the security. 39

Fal. Let him be damned, like the glutton! pray God his tongue be hotter! A whoreson Achitophel! a rascally yea-forsooth knave! to bear a gentleman in hand, and then stand upon security! The whoreson smooth-pates do now wear nothing but high shoes, and bunches of keys at their girdles; and if a man is through with them in honest taking up, then they must stand upon security. I had as lief they would put ratsbane in my mouth as offer to stop it with security. I looked a' should have sent me two and twenty yards of satin, as I am a true knight, and he sends me security. Well, he may sleep in security; for he hath the horn of abundance, and the lightness of his wife shines through it: and yet cannot he see, though he have his own lanthorn to light him. Where's Bardolph? 55

Page. He's gone into Smithfield to buy your worship a horse.

Fal. I bought him in Paul's, and he'll buy me a horse in Smithfield: an I could get me but a wife in the stews, I were manned, horsed, and wived. 61

Enter the Lord Chief-Justice *and* Servant.

Page. Sir, here comes the nobleman that committed the prince for striking him about Bardolph.

Fal. Wait close; I will not see him.

Ch. Just. What's he that goes there?

Serv. Falstaff, an't please your lordship.

Ch. Just. He that was in question for the robbery? 69

Serv. He, my lord: but he hath since done good service at Shrewsbury; and, as I hear,

is now going with some charge to the Lord John of Lancaster.

Ch. Just. What, to York? Call him back again.

Serv. Sir John Falstaff!

Fal. Boy, tell him I am deaf.

Page. You must speak louder; my master is deaf. 79

Ch. Just. I am sure he is, to the hearing of any thing good. Go, pluck him by the elbow; I must speak with him.

Serv. Sir John!

Fal. What! a young knave, and begging! Is there not wars? is there not employment? doth not the king lack subjects? do not the rebels need soldiers? Though it be a shame to be on any side but one, it is worse shame to beg than to be on the worst side, were it worse than the name of rebellion can tell how to make it. 90

Serv. You mistake me, sir.

Fal. Why, sir, did I say you were an honest man? setting my knighthood and my soldiership aside, I had lied in my throat, if I had said so.

Serv. I pray you, sir, then set your knight-hood and your soldiership aside; and give me leave to tell you, you lie in your throat, if you say I am any other than an honest man.

Fal. I give thee leave to tell me so! I lay aside that which grows to me! If thou get-test any leave of me, hang me; if thou takest leave, thou wert better be hanged. You hunt counter: hence! avaunt! 103

Serv. Sir, my lord would speak with you.

Ch. Just. Sir John Falstaff, a word with you.

Fal. My good lord! God give your lord-ship good time of day. I am glad to see your lordship abroad: I heard say your lordship was sick: I hope your lordship goes abroad by advice. Your lordship, though not clean past your youth, hath yet some smack of age in you, some relish of the saltness of time; and I most humbly beseech your lord-ship to have a reverent care of your health.

Ch. Just. Sir John, I sent for you before your expedition to Shrewsbury. 116

Fal. An't please your lordship, I hear his majesty is returned with some discomfort from Wales.

---

36. **slops,** loose breeches. 40. **glutton,** a reference to the parable of Dives (*St. Luke*, xvi, 19-31). 42. **Achito-phel,** counselor of Absalom (*2 Samuel*, xv-xvii). **yea-forsooth,** contemptuous allusion to polite oaths. 43. **bear . . . in hand,** delude with false hopes. 44. **smooth-pates,** allusion to the short hair of tradesmen. 47. **tak-ing up,** obtaining on credit. 54. **horn,** an allusion to the cuckold's horn, as also in *lanthorn* below. 56. **Smith-field,** famous then as now as a livestock market. 58. **Paul's,** St. Paul's Cathedral, resort of serving-men seek-ing employment. 60. **stews,** houses of ill fame. 68. **in question,** under judicial examination. 70. **done good service.** This passage is cited by those who insist that Falstaff was a man of courage.

100. **grows to,** is an integral part of. 103. **hunt counter,** a hunting term meaning "run backward on the trail." 111. **smack of age,** the savor of age. 118. **discomfort,** grief of mind.

Ch. Just. I talk not of his majesty: you would not come when I sent for you.   121

Fal. And I hear, moreover, his highness is fallen into this same whoreson apoplexy.

Ch. Just. Well, God mend him! I pray you, let me speak with you.

Fal. This apoplexy is, as I take it, a kind of lethargy, an't please your lordship; a kind of sleeping in the blood, a whoreson tingling.

Ch. Just. What tell you me of it? be it as it is.   130

Fal. It hath it original from much grief, from study and perturbation of the brain: I have read the cause of his effects in Galen: it is a kind of deafness.

Ch. Just. I think you are fallen into the disease; for you hear not what I say to you.

Fal. Very well, my lord, very well: rather, an't please you, it is the disease of not listening, the malady of not marking, that I am troubled withal.   140

Ch. Just. To punish you by the heels would amend the attention of your ears; and I care not if I do become your physician.

Fal. I am as poor as Job, my lord, but not so patient: your lordship may minister the potion of imprisonment to me in respect of poverty; but how should I be your patient to follow your prescriptions, the wise may make some dram of a scruple, or indeed a scruple itself.

Ch. Just. I sent for you, when there were matters against you for your life, to come speak with me.   153

Fal. As I was then advised by my learned counsel in the laws of this land-service, I did not come.

Ch. Just. Well, the truth is, Sir John, you live in great infamy.

Fal. He that buckles him in my belt cannot live in less.

Ch. Just. Your means are very slender, and your waste is great.   160

Fal. I would it were otherwise; I would my means were greater, and my waist slenderer.

Ch. Just. You have misled the youthful prince.

Fal. The young prince hath misled me: I am the fellow with the great belly, and he my dog.

Ch. Just. Well, I am loath to gall a new-healed wound: your day's service at Shrewsbury hath a little gilded over your night's exploit on Gad's-hill: you may thank the unquiet time for your quiet o'er-posting that action.   171

Fal. My lord?

Ch. Just. But since all is well, keep it so: wake not a sleeping wolf.

Fal. To wake a wolf is as bad as to smell a fox.

Ch. Just. What! you are as a candle, the better part burnt out.

Fal. A wassail candle, my lord, all tallow: if I did say of wax, my growth would approve the truth.   181

Ch. Just. There is not a white hair on your face but should have his effect of gravity.

Fal. His effect of gravy, gravy, gravy.

Ch. Just. You follow the young prince up and down, like his ill angel.   186

Fal. Not so, my lord; your ill angel is light; but I hope he that looks upon me will take me without weighing: and yet, in some respects, I grant, I cannot go: I cannot tell. Virtue is of so little regard in these costermonger times that true valour is turned bearherd: pregnancy is made a tapster, and hath his quick wit wasted in giving reckonings: all the other gifts appertinent to man, as the malice of this age shapes them, are not worth a gooseberry. You that are old consider not the capacities of us that are young; you do measure the heat of our livers with the bitterness of your galls: and we that are in the vaward of our youth, I must confess, 200 are wags too.

Ch. Just. Do you set down your name in the scroll of youth, that are written down old

---

123. **apoplexy**, paralysis. 131. **it original**, its origin. 133. **Galen**, the famous Greek authority on medicine. 141. **punish . . . heels**, punish in the stocks. 148-49. **dram of a scruple**, small portion of doubt, with puns on *dram* and *scruple* as weights. 154-156. **As I . . . come.** Falstaff means to say that his counsel, learned in the laws of military service, has advised him that while he was so engaged he was not liable to arrest.

170. **o'er-posting**, escaping the consequences of. 175. **smell a fox**, suspect something, smell a mouse. 179. **wassail candle**, candle lighted up at a feast. 183. **his effect**, i.e., its effect as the outward sign of gravity. Falstaff pretends to hear the word as *gravy*, the pronunciation of which would be much closer to *gravity* than now. 186. **ill angel**, an evil attendant spirit. Falstaff quibbles on the other sense of the word meaning "a clipped angel," a coin worth 6s. 8d., current at 10s. 190. **cannot go**, i.e., walk, with pun on the meaning "pass current." 191. **Virtue**, valor. **costermonger**, commercial; used contemptuously. 192. **pregnancy**, quickness (of wit). 194. **appertinent**, belonging to, becoming to. 198-199. **heat . . . galls.** The liver was the source of vegetative spirits and active in youth; the gall was the seat of melancholy and prevalent in age. 200. **vaward**, vanguard, early part.

with all the characters of age? Have you not a moist eye? a dry hand? a yellow cheek? a white beard? a decreasing leg? an increasing belly? is not your voice broken? your wind short? your chin double? your wit single? and every part about you blasted with antiquity? and will you yet call yourself young? Fie, fie, fie, Sir John!   209

Fal. My lord, I was born about three of the clock in the afternoon, with a white head and something a round belly. For my voice, I have lost it with halloing and singing of anthems. To approve my youth further, I will not: the truth is, I am only old in judgement and understanding; and he that will caper with me for a thousand marks, let him lend me the money, and have at him! For the box of the ear that the prince gave you, he gave it like a rude prince, and you took it like a sensible lord. I have checked him for it, and the young lion repents; marry, not in ashes and sackcloth, but in new silk and old sack.   223

Ch. Just. Well, God send the prince a better companion!

Fal. God send the companion a better prince! I cannot rid my hands of him.

Ch. Just. Well, the king hath severed you and Prince Harry: I hear you are going with Lord John of Lancaster against the Archbishop and the Earl of Northumberland.   230

Fal. Yea; I thank your pretty sweet wit for it. But look you pray, all you that kiss my lady Peace at home, that our armies join not in a hot day; for, by the Lord, I take but two shirts out with me, and I mean not to sweat extraordinarily: if it be a hot day, and I brandish any thing but a bottle, I would I might never spit white again. There is not a dangerous action can peep out his head but I am thrust upon it: well, I cannot last ever: but it was alway yet the trick of our English nation, if they have a good thing, to make it too common. If ye will needs say I am an old man, you should give me rest. I would to God my name were not so terrible to the enemy as it is: I were better to be eaten to

death with a rust than to be scoured to nothing with perpetual motion.

Ch. Just. Well, be honest, be honest; and God bless your expedition!

Fal. Will your lordship lend me a thousand pound to furnish me forth?   251

Ch. Just. Not a penny, not a penny; you are too impatient to bear crosses. Fare you well: commend me to my cousin Westmoreland. [*Exeunt Chief-Justice and Servant.*

Fal. If I do, fillip me with a three-man beetle. A man can no more separate age and covetousness than a' can part young limbs and lechery: but the gout galls the one, and the pox pinches the other; and so both the degrees prevent my curses. Boy!   260

Page. Sir?

Fal. What money is in my purse?

Page. Seven groats and two pence.

Fal. I can get no remedy against this consumption of the purse: borrowing only lingers and lingers it out, but the disease is incurable. Go bear this letter to my Lord of Lancaster; this to the prince; this to the Earl of Westmoreland; and this to old Mistress Ursula, whom I have weekly sworn to marry since I perceived the first white hair on my chin. About it: you know where to find me. [*Exit Page.*] A pox of this gout! or, a gout of this pox! for the one or the other plays the rogue with my great toe. 'Tis no matter if I do halt; I have the wars for my colour, and my pension shall seem the more reasonable. A good wit will make use of any thing: I will turn diseases to commodity.   [*Exit.*

SCENE III.   *York.   The* ARCHBISHOP'S
palace.

Enter the ARCHBISHOP, *the* LORDS HASTINGS,
MOWBRAY, *and* BARDOLPH.

Arch. Thus have you heard our cause and
    know our means;
And, my most noble friends, I pray you all,
Speak plainly your opinions of our hopes:
And first, lord marshal, what say you to it?

Mowb. I well allow the occasion of our
    arms;
But gladly would be better satisfied

---

206. **single,** weak, with play on *double,* strong. 212. **something a,** a somewhat. 214. **approve,** prove. 217. **marks,** coins worth 13s. 4d. 218. **have at him,** let him come. 219. **box of the ear.** This event of the striking of the Chief Justice by the young prince is important in *The Famous Victories*; Shakespeare does not depict the scene. 221. **checked,** rebuked. 223. **sack,** sherry wine, with pun on *sackcloth.* 238. **spit white.** Spitting white is a sign of thirst.

253. **crosses,** quibble on bearing affliction and receiving money; money was often marked with a figure of the cross. 255. **fillip . . . beetle,** tap me with a mallet wielded by three men. 263. **groats,** four pence. 277. **colour,** reasonable excuse. 279. **commodity,** profit.

How in our means we should advance our-
  selves
To look with forehead bold and big enough
Upon the power and puissance of the king.
   Hast. Our present musters grow upon the
      file   10
To five and twenty thousand men of choice;
And our supplies live largely in the hope
Of great Northumberland, whose bosom
  burns
With an incensed fire of injuries.
   L. Bard. The question then, Lord Hast-
      ings, standeth thus;
Whether our present five and twenty thous-
      and
May hold up head without Northumberland?
   Hast. With him, we may.
   L. Bard.   Yea, marry, there's the point:
But if without him we be thought too feeble,
My judgement is, we should not step too far
Till we had his assistance by the hand;   21
For in a theme so bloody-faced as this
Conjecture, expectation, and surmise
Of aids incertain should not be admitted.
   Arch. 'Tis very true, Lord Bardolph; for
      indeed
It was young Hotspur's case at Shrewsbury.
   L. Bard. It was, my lord; who lined him-
      self with hope,
Eating the air on promise of supply,
Flattering himself in project of a power
Much smaller than the smallest of his
      thoughts: 30
And so, with great imagination
Proper to madmen, led his powers to death
And winking leap'd into destruction.
   Hast. But, by your leave, it never yet did
      hurt
To lay down likelihoods and forms of hope.
   L. Bard. †Yes, if this present quality of
      war,
Indeed the instant action: a cause on foot
Lives so in hope as in an early spring

We see the appearing buds; which to prove
      fruit,
Hope gives not so much warrant as despair 40
That frosts will bite them. When we mean
      to build,
We first survey the plot, then draw the
      model;
And when we see the figure of the house,
Then must we rate the cost of the erection;
Which if we find outweighs ability,
What do we then but draw anew the model
In fewer offices, or at last desist
To build at all? Much more, in this great
      work,
Which is almost to pluck a kingdom down
And set another up, should we survey   50
The plot of situation and the model,
Consent upon a sure foundation,
Question surveyors, know our own estate,
How able such a work to undergo,
To weigh against his opposite; or else
We fortify the paper and in figures,
Using the names of men instead of men:
Like one that draws the model of a house
Beyond his power to build it; who, half
      through,
Gives o'er and leaves his part-created cost 60
A naked subject to the weeping clouds
And waste for churlish winter's tyranny.
   Hast. Grant that our hopes, yet likely of
      fair birth,
Should be still-born, and that we now pos-
      sess'd
The utmost man of expectation,
I think we are a body strong enough,
Even as we are, to equal with the king.
   L. Bard. What, is the king but five and
      twenty thousand?
   Hast. To us no more; nay, not so much,
      Lord Bardolph.
For his divisions, as the times do brawl,   70
Are in three heads: one power against the
      French,
And one against Glendower; perforce a third
Must take up us: so is the unfirm king
In three divided; and his coffers sound
With hollow poverty and emptiness.
   Arch. That he should draw his several
      strengths together
And come against us in full puissance,

---

7. **in**, with.   22. **theme**, business.   27. **lined**,
strengthened.   29. **project . . . power**, anticipation of
an armed force.   33. **winking**, with eyes shut.   35.
forms of hope, shapes that hope assumes.   36–41. **Yes
. . . them.** These lines have been variously interpreted.
The following interpretation is from the Yale Shakespeare: Lord Hastings has just been remonstrating with
Lord Bardolph for his pessimism, saying that hope never
injured any cause. Lord Bardolph replies: "Yes, it
does—if, for example, this present business of war (indeed this very action now contemplated, this cause that
is now on foot), lives merely on such desperate hopes as
buds which appear too early in the spring; for hope gives
less warrant that these buds will become fruit than despair gives that the frosts will destroy them." If we read
Yes, if, in line 36 as *Yet is*, and understand *which* as the
subject of *Lives*, in line 38, we obtain a fair sense.

47. **offices**, apartments devoted to household business.
55. **opposite**, opponent.   60. **part-created cost**,
partly finished splendor.   67. **equal with**, cope on equal
terms with.   73. **take up**, encounter, oppose.   76.
several strengths, various armies.

Need not be dreaded.

Hast.　　　　　If he should do so,
He leaves his back unarm'd, the French and
　　Welsh
Baying him at the heels: never fear that.　80
L. Bard. Who is it like should lead his
　forces hither?
Hast. The Duke of Lancaster and West-
　moreland;
Against the Welsh, himself and Harry Mon-
　mouth:
But who is substituted 'gainst the French,
I have no certain notice.
Arch.　　　　　Let us on,
And publish the occasion of our arms.
The commonwealth is sick of their own
　choice;
Their over-greedy love hath surfeited:
An habitation giddy and unsure
Hath he that buildeth on the vulgar heart.　90
O thou fond many, with what loud applause
Didst thou beat heaven with blessing Boling-
　broke,
Before he was what thou wouldst have him
　be!
And being now trimm'd in thine own desires,
Thou, beastly feeder, art so full of him,
That thou provokest thyself to cast him up.
So, so, thou common dog, didst thou dis-
　gorge
Thy glutton bosom of the royal Richard;
And now thou wouldst eat thy dead vomit
　up,
And howl'st to find it. What trust is in these
　times?　　　　　　　　　　　　　　100
They that, when Richard lived, would have
　him die,
Are now become enamour'd on his grave:
Thou, that threw'st dust upon his goodly
　head
When through proud London he came sigh-
　ing on
After the admired heels of Bolingbroke,
Criest now 'O earth, yield us that king again,
And take thou this!' O thoughts of men
　accursed!
Past and to come seems best; things present
　worst.
Mowb. Shall we go draw our numbers and
　set on?
Hast. We are time's subjects, and time
　bids be gone.　　　　　[*Exeunt.*　110

ACT II.

Scene I.　*London.　A street.*

*Enter Hostess, FANG and his Boy with her,
　and SNARE following.*

Host. Master Fang, have you entered the
action?
Fang. It is entered.
Host. Where's your yeoman? Is't a lusty
yeoman? will a' stand to't?
Fang. Sirrah, where's Snare?
Host. O Lord, ay! good Master Snare.
Snare. Here, here.
Fang. Snare, we must arrest Sir John Falstaff.
Host. Yea, good Master Snare; I have
entered him and all.　　　　　　　　　11
Snare. It may chance cost some of us our
lives, for he will stab.
Host. Alas the day! take heed of him; he
stabbed me in mine own house, and that
most beastly: in good faith, he cares not what
mischief he does, if his weapon be out: he
will foin like any devil; he will spare neither
man, woman, nor child.
Fang. If I can close with him, I care not
for his thrust.　　　　　　　　　　　21
Host. No, nor I neither: I'll be at your
elbow.
Fang. An I but fist him once; an a' come
but within my vice,—
Host. I am undone by his going; I warrant you, he's an infinitive thing upon my
score. Good Master Fang, hold him sure:
good Master Snare, let him not 'scape. A'
comes continuantly to Pie-corner—saving
your manhoods—to buy a saddle; and he is
indited to dinner to the Lubber's-head in
Lumbert street, to Master Smooth's the
silkman: I pray ye, since my exion is entered
and my case so openly known to the world,
let him be brought in to his answer. A
hundred mark is a long one for a poor lone
woman to bear: and I have borne, and borne,
and borne, and have been fubbed off, and
fubbed off, and fubbed off, from this day

---

4. **yeoman**, sheriff's officer.　11. **entered**, brought action against in court.　18. **foin**, thrust in fencing. 23. **fist**, i.e., seize.　24. **vice**, grip.　25. **going**, i.e., without paying.　26. **infinitive**, for *infinite*, endless. 29. **continuantly**, for *incontinently*, immediately.　31. **indited**, for *invited*.　**Lubber's-head**, blunder for *Libbard's-head* (Leopard's-head Inn).　32. **Lumbert**, for *Lombard*.　33. **exion**, action, lawsuit.　35. **A hundred . . . one.** The mark was 13s. 4d; possible puns on the *hundred mark* as a distance, and on *one* and *ow'n* (owing). 37. **fubbed off**, for *fobbed off*, i.e., put off with excuses.

to that day, that it is a shame to be thought
on. There is no honesty in such dealing;
unless a woman should be made an ass and
a beast, to bear every knave's wrong. 41
Yonder he comes; and that arrant malmsey-
nose knave, Bardolph, with him. Do your
offices, do your offices: Master Fang and
Master Snare, do me, do me, do me your
offices.

Enter FALSTAFF, Page, *and* BARDOLPH.

Fal. How now! whose mare's dead? what's
the matter?

Fang. Sir John, I arrest you at the suit of
Mistress Quickly.   49

Fal. Away, varlets! Draw, Bardolph: cut
me off the villain's head: throw the quean in
the channel.

Host. Throw me in the channel! I'll
throw thee in the channel. Wilt thou? wilt
thou? thou bastardly rogue! Murder,
murder! Ah, thou honey-suckle villain! wilt
thou kill God's officers and the king's?
Ah, thou honey-seed rogue! thou art a
honey-seed, a man-queller, and a woman-
queller.

Fal. Keep them off, Bardolph.   60

Fang. A rescue! a rescue!

Host. Good people, bring a rescue or two.
Thou wo't, wo't thou? thou wo't, wo't ta?
do, do, thou rogue! do, thou hemp-seed!

Fal. Away, you scullion! you rampallian!
you fustilarian! I'll tickle your catastrophe.

Enter the LORD CHIEF-JUSTICE, *and his
men.*

Ch. Just. What is the matter? keep the
peace here, ho!

Host. Good my lord, be good to me. I
beseech you, stand to me.   70

Ch. Just. How now, Sir John! what are
   you brawling here?
Doth this become your place, your time and
   business?
You should have been well on your way to
   York.
Stand from him, fellow: wherefore hang'st
   upon him?

Host. O my most worshipful lord, an't
please your grace, I am a poor widow of
Eastcheap, and he is arrested at my suit.

Ch. Just. For what sum?   78

Host. It is more than for some, my lord;
it is for all, all I have. He hath eaten me out
of house and home; he hath put all my substance into that fat belly of his: but I will
have some of it out again, or I will ride thee
o' nights like the mare.

Fal. I think I am as like to ride the mare,
if I have any vantage of ground to get up.

Ch. Just. How comes this, Sir John? Fie!
what man of good temper would endure
this tempest of exclamation? Are you not
ashamed to enforce a poor widow to so rough
a course to come by her own?   90

Fal. What is the gross sum that I owe
thee?

Host. Marry, if thou wert an honest man,
thyself and the money too. Thou didst swear
to me upon a parcel-gilt goblet, sitting in my
Dolphin-chamber, at the round table, by a
sea-coal fire, upon Wednesday in Wheeson
week, when the prince broke thy head for
liking his father to a singing-man of Windsor,
thou didst swear to me then, as I was washing
thy wound, to marry me and make me my
lady thy wife. Canst thou deny it? Did not
goodwife Keech, the butcher's wife, come in
then and call me gossip Quickly? coming in
to borrow a mess of vinegar; telling us she
had a good dish of prawns; whereby thou
didst desire to eat some; whereby I told thee
they were ill for a green wound? And didst
thou not, when she was gone down stairs,
desire me to be no more so familiarity with
such poor people; saying that ere long they
should call me madam? And didst thou not
kiss me and bid me fetch thee thirty shillings? I put thee now to thy book-oath:
deny it, if thou canst.   112

Fal. My lord, this is a poor mad soul; and
she says up and down the town that her
eldest son is like you: she hath been in good
case, and the truth is, poverty hath distracted her. But for these foolish officers, I
beseech you I may have redress against
them.

42. **malmsey-nose**, red-nosed. 51. **quean**, jade,
hussy. 52. **channel**, street gutter. 56. **honey-suckle**,
for *homicidal*. 58. **honey-seed**, for *homicide*. 59. **man-
queller**, murderer. 63. **wo't thou**? wilt thou? 64.
hemp-seed, a possible allusion to the hangman's rope;
hempseed was commonly associated with invisibility.
65. **scullion**, a term of abuse. **rampallian**, ruffian;
usually applied to men. 66. **fustilarian,** a comic formation on the word *fustilugs*, a fat, frowsy woman (Onions).

84. **mare**, nightmare. 94. **parcel-gilt**, partly gilt.
95. **Dolphin-chamber**, one of the fanciful names for
chambers in inns. 96. **sea-coal**, bituminous coal,
brought by the sea. **Wheeson**, Whitsun. 97. **liking**,
likening. 101. **goodwife**, title of married women;
Keech means "a lump of tallow." 102. **gossip**, familiar
term applied to a female friend. 104. **mess of vinegar**,
enough vinegar for one meal. 115. **in good case**, well-
to-do.

Ch. Just. Sir John, Sir John, I am well acquainted with your manner of wrenching the true cause the false way. It is not a confident brow, nor the throng of words that come with such more than impudent sauciness from you, can thrust me from a level consideration: you have, as it appears to me, practised upon the easy-yielding spirit of this woman, and made her serve your uses both in purse and in person.

Host. Yea, in truth, my lord.

Ch. Just. Pray thee, peace. Pay her the debt you owe her, and unpay the villany you have done her: the one you may do with sterling money, and the other with current repentance.   132

Fal. My lord, I will not undergo this sneap without reply. You call honourable boldness impudent sauciness: if a man will make courtesy and say nothing, he is virtuous: no, my lord, my humble duty remembered, I will not be your suitor. I say to you, I do desire deliverance from these officers, being upon hasty employment in the king's affairs.   140

Ch. Just. You speak as having power to do wrong: but answer in the effect of your reputation, and satisfy the poor woman.

Fal. Come hither, hostess.

Enter GOWER.

Ch. Just. Now, Master Gower, what news?

Gow. The king, my lord, and Harry Prince of Wales
Are near at hand: the rest the paper tells.

Fal. As I am a gentleman.

Host. Faith, you said so before.

Fal. As I am a gentleman. Come, no more words of it.   151

Host. By this heavenly ground I tread on, I must be fain to pawn both my plate and the tapestry of my dining-chambers.

Fal. Glasses, glasses, is the only drinking: and for thy walls, a pretty slight drollery, or the story of the Prodigal, or the German hunting in water-work, is worth a thousand of these bed-hangings and these fly-bitten tapestries. Let it be ten pound, if thou canst. Come, and 'twere not for thy

humours, there's not a better wench in England. Go, wash thy face, and draw the action. Come, thou must not be in this humour with me; dost not know me? come, come, I know thou wast set on to this. 165

Host. Pray thee, Sir John, let it be but twenty nobles: i' faith, I am loath to pawn my plate, so God save me, la!

Fal. Let it alone; I'll make other shift: you'll be a fool still.   170

Host. Well, you shall have it, though I pawn my gown. I hope you'll come to supper. You'll pay me all together?

Fal. Will I live? [*To Bardolph*] Go, with her, with her; hook on, hook on.

Host. Will you have Doll Tearsheet meet you at supper?

Fal. No more words; let's have her.

[*Exeunt Hostess, Bardolph, Officers, and Boy.*

Ch. Just. I have heard better news.

Fal. What's the news, my lord?   180

Ch. Just. Where lay the king last night?

Gow. At Basingstoke, my lord.

Fal. I hope, my lord, all's well: what is the news, my lord?

Ch. Just. Come all his forces back?

Gow. No; fifteen hundred foot, five hundred horse,
Are march'd up to my lord of Lancaster,
Against Northumberland and the Archbishop.

Fal. Comes the king back from Wales, my noble lord?

Ch. Just. You shall have letters of me presently: 190
Come, go along with me, good Master Gower.

Fal. My lord!

Ch. Just. What's the matter?

Fal. Master Gower, shall I entreat you with me to dinner?

Gow. I must wait upon my good lord here; I thank you, good Sir John.

Ch. Just. Sir John, you loiter here too long, being you are to take soldiers up in counties as you go.   200

Fal. Will you sup with me, Master Gower?

Ch. Just. What foolish master taught you these manners, Sir John?

Fal. Master Gower, if they become me

---

132. **current repentance,** genuine repentance; allusion to current coin. 134. **sneap,** reproof, snub. 142. **effect of,** manner becoming. 155. **Glasses . . . drinking.** It is a question of selling her cups of silver and pewter and using glasses for serving drinks. 156. **drollery,** comic picture. 158. **water-work,** water color, i.e., a picture of a German hunting scene.

162. **draw,** withdraw. 167. **nobles,** coins current at 6s. 8d. 175. **hook on,** follow her. 182. **Basingstoke,** a town in Hampshire fifty miles from London. 199. **being . . . up,** seeing that you are to levy soldiers

not, he was a fool that taught them me. This is the right fencing grace, my lord; tap for tap, and so part fair.   207

Ch. Just. Now the Lord lighten thee! thou art a great fool.   [*Exeunt.*

Scene II. *London. Another street.*

Enter Prince Henry *and* Poins.

Prince. Before God, I am exceeding weary.

Poins. Is't come to that? I had thought weariness durst not have attached one of so high blood.

Prince. Faith, it does me; though it discolours the complexion of my greatness to acknowledge it. Doth it not show vilely in me to desire small beer?

Poins. Why, a prince should not be so loosely studied as to remember so weak a composition.   9

Prince. Belike then my appetite was not princely got; for, by my troth, I do now remember the poor creature, small beer. But, indeed, these humble considerations make me out of love with my greatness. What a disgrace is it to me to remember thy name! or to know thy face to-morrow! or to take note how many pair of silk stockings thou hast, viz. these, and those that were thy peach-coloured ones! or to bear the inventory of thy shirts, as, one for superfluity, and another for use! But that the tennis-court-keeper knows better than I; for it is a low ebb of linen with thee when thou keepest not racket there; as thou hast not done a great while, because the rest of thy low countries have made a shift to eat up thy holland: and God knows, whether those that bawl out the ruins of thy linen shall inherit his kingdom: but the midwives say the children are not in the fault; whereupon the world increases, and kindreds are mightily strengthened.   30

Poins. How ill it follows, after you have laboured so hard, you should talk so idly! Tell me, how many good young princes would

do so, their fathers being so sick as yours at this time is?

Prince. Shall I tell thee one thing, Poins?

Poins. Yes, faith; and let it be an excellent good thing.

Prince. It shall serve among wits of no higher breeding than thine.

Poins. Go to; I stand the push of your one thing that you will tell.   41

Prince. Marry, I tell thee, it is not meet that I should be sad, now my father is sick: albeit I could tell to thee, as to one it pleases me, for fault of a better, to call my friend, I could be sad, and sad indeed too.

Poins. Very hardly upon such a subject.

Prince. By this hand, thou thinkest me as far in the devil's book as thou and Falstaff for obduracy and persistency: let the end try the man. But I tell thee, my heart bleeds inwardly that my father is so sick: and keeping such vile company as thou art hath in reason taken from me all ostentation of sorrow.

Poins. The reason?

Prince. What wouldst thou think of me, if I should weep?

Poins. I would think thee a most princely hypocrite.   59

Prince. It would be every man's thought; and thou art a blessed fellow to think as every man thinks: never a man's thought in the world keeps the road-way better than thine: every man would think me an hypocrite indeed. And what accites your most worshipful thought to think so?

Poins. Why, because you have been so lewd and so much engraffed to Falstaff.   67

Prince. And to thee.

Poins. By this light, I am well spoke on; I can hear it with mine own ears: the worst that they can say of me is that I am a second brother and that I am a proper fellow of my hands; and those two things, I confess, I cannot help. By the mass, here comes Bardolph.

Enter Bardolph *and* Page.

Prince. And the boy that I gave Falstaff: a' had him from me Christian; and look, if the fat villain have not transformed him ape.

---

207. **tap for tap**, tit for tat. 208. **lighten**, enlighten; with side reference to Falstaff's weight.
Scene ii. 3. **attached**, seized; an allusion to arrest by bill of attachment. 7. **small beer**, weak kind of beer. 9. **studied**, versed, inclined. 10. **Belike**, I suppose. 25. **holland**, a kind of linen; pun on *Holland* as a low country. 26. **bawl out**, bawl in swaddling clothes made out of Poins's old shirts (Herford).

40. **push**, attack, onset. 42. **Marry**, current oath; corruption of *Mary*. 49. **devil's book**, devil's favor, or devil's debt. 65. **accites**, excites. 67. **engraffed**, closely attached to. 71. **a second brother**, as a second brother he would have no inheritance. 72-3. **proper . . . hands**, capital fellow in using my hands (for stealing?).

Bard. God save your grace!

Prince. And yours, most noble Bardolph!

Bard. Come, you virtuous ass, you bashful fool, must you be blushing? wherefore blush you now? What a maidenly man-at-arms are you become! Is't such a matter to get a pottle-pot's maidenhead?   83

Page. A' calls me e'en now, my lord, through a red lattice, and I could discern no part of his face from the window: at last I spied his eyes, and methought he had made two holes in the ale-wife's new petticoat and so peeped through.

Prince. Has not the boy profited?   90

Bard. Away, you whoreson upright rabbit, away!

Page. Away, you rascally Althæa's dream, away!

Prince. Instruct us, boy; what dream, boy?

Page. Marry, my lord, Althæa dreamed she was delivered of a fire-brand; and therefore I call him her dream.

Prince. A crown's worth of good interpretation: there 'tis, boy.   100

Poins. O, that this good blossom could be kept from cankers! Well, there is sixpence to preserve thee.

Bard. An you do not make him hanged among you, the gallows shall have wrong.

Prince. And how doth thy master, Bardolph?

Bard. Well, my lord. He heard of your grace's coming to town: there's a letter for you.

Poins. Delivered with good respect. And how doth the martlemas, your master?   110

Bard. In bodily health, sir.

Poins. Marry, the immortal part needs a physician; but that moves not him: though that be sick, it dies not.

Prince. I do allow this wen to be as familiar with me as my dog; and he holds his place; for look you how he writes.   117

Poins. [*Reads*] 'John Falstaff, knight,'—

every man must know that, as oft as he has occasion to name himself: even like those that are kin to the king; for they never prick their finger but they say, 'There's some of the king's blood spilt.' 'How comes that?' says he, that takes upon him not to conceive. The answer is as ready as a borrower's cap, 'I am the king's poor cousin, sir.'   126

Prince. Nay, they will be kin to us, or they will fetch it from Japhet. But to the letter:

Poins. [*Reads*] 'Sir John Falstaff, knight, to the son of the king, nearest his father, Harry Prince of Wales, greeting.' Why, this is a certificate.

Prince. Peace!   133

Poins. [*Reads*] 'I will imitate the honourable Romans in brevity:' he sure means brevity in breath, short-winded. 'I commend me to thee, I commend thee, and I leave thee. Be not too familiar with Poins; for he misuses thy favours so much, that he swears thou art to marry his sister Nell. Repent at idle times as thou mayest; and so, farewell.   141

'Thine, by yea and no, which is as much
    as to say, as thou usest him, JACK
    FALSTAFF with my familiars, JOHN
    with my brothers and sisters, and
    SIR JOHN with all Europe.'
My lord, I'll steep this letter in sack and make him eat it.

Prince. That's to make him eat twenty of his words. But do you use me thus, Ned? must I marry your sister?   151

Poins. God send the wench no worse fortune! But I never said so.

Prince. Well, thus we play the fools with the time, and the spirits of the wise sit in clouds and mock us. Is your master here in London?

Bard. Yea, my lord.

Prince. Where sups he? doth the old boar feed in the old frank?   160

Bard. At the old place, my lord, in East-cheap.

Prince. What company?

Page. Ephesians, my lord, of the old church.

83. pottle-pot's, two-quart tankard's. 93. Althæa's dream. Althæa dreamed that her new-born son would live only so long as a brand on the fire lasted. The Page (ll. 96-97) relates Hecuba's dream. 99. crown's worth, five shillings. 102. cankers, worms which destroy buds and leaves. 103. to preserve thee, allusion to the cross on the sixpence. 110. martlemas, Martinmas (November 11); probably short for *Martinmas beef.* Beeves were regularly slaughtered and salted at that season. 118. Poins. [Reads]. From this point Q and F assign the reading of the letter to the Prince, which is correct; the change to Poins is due to Hanmer.

128. Japhet, one of the sons of Noah (*Genesis*, x, 2-5). 135. Romans. Warburton suggested *Roman* as an allusion to Cæsar's "I came, I saw, I conquered." 160. frank, sty, pen. 164. Ephesians, cant term for good fellows. old church, allusion to the ancient and authoritative church at Ephesus.

Prince. Sup any women with him?

Page. None, my lord, but old Mistress Quickly and Mistress Doll Tearsheet.

Prince. What pagan may that be?

Page. A proper gentlewoman, sir, and a kinswoman of my master's.   170

Prince. Even such kin as the parish heifers are to the town bull. Shall we steal upon them, Ned, at supper?

Poins. I am your shadow, my lord; I'll follow you.

Prince. Sirrah, you boy, and Bardolph, no word to your master that I am yet come to town: there's for your silence.

Bard. I have no tongue, sir.   179

Page. And for mine, sir, I will govern it.

Prince. Fare you well; go. [*Exeunt Bardolph and Page.*] This Doll Tearsheet should be some road.

Poins. I warrant you, as common as the way between Saint Alban's and London.

Prince. How might we see Falstaff bestow himself to-night in his true colours, and not ourselves be seen?

Poins. Put on two leathern jerkins and aprons, and wait upon him at his table as drawers.   191

Prince. From a God to a bull? a heavy descension! it was Jove's case. From a prince to a prentice? a low transformation! that shall be mine; for in every thing the purpose must weigh with the folly. Follow me, Ned.   [*Exeunt.*

Scene III. *Warkworth. Before the castle.*

Enter Northumberland, Lady Northumberland, *and* Lady Percy.

North. I pray thee, loving wife, and gentle daughter,
Give even way unto my rough affairs:
Put not you on the visage of the times
And be like them to Percy troublesome.

Lady N. I have given over, I will speak no more:
Do what you will; your wisdom be your guide.

North. Alas, sweet wife, my honour is at pawn;

And, but my going, nothing can redeem it.

Lady P. O yet, for God's sake, go not to these wars!
The time was, father, that you broke your word,   10
When you were more endear'd to it than now;
When your own Percy, when my heart's dear Harry,
Threw many a northward look to see his father
Bring up his powers; but he did long in vain.
Who then persuaded you to stay at home?
There were two honours lost, yours and your son's.
For yours, the God of heaven brighten it!
For his, it stuck upon him as the sun
In the grey vault of heaven, and by his light
Did all the chivalry of England move   20
To do brave acts: he was indeed the glass
Wherein the noble youth did dress themselves:
He had no legs that practised not his gait;
And speaking thick, which nature made his blemish,
Became the accents of the valiant;
For those that could speak low and tardily
Would turn their own perfection to abuse,
To seem like him: so that in speech, in gait,
In diet, in affections of delight,
In military rules, humours of blood,   30
He was the mark and glass, copy and book,
That fashion'd others. And him, O wondrous him!
O miracle of men! him did you leave,
Second to none, unseconded by you,
To look upon the hideous god of war
In disadvantage; to abide a field
Where nothing but the sound of Hotspur's name
Did seem defensible: so you left him.
Never, O never, do his ghost the wrong
To hold your honour more precise and nice   40
With others than with him! let them alone:
The marshal and the archbishop are strong:
Had my sweet Harry had but half their numbers,
To-day might I, hanging on Hotspur's neck,
Have talk'd of Monmouth's grave.

---

168. **pagan**, courtesan; a cant name.   186. **bestow**, behave.   192. **heavy descension**, grievous descent. 193. **Jove's case**, an allusion to Jupiter, who for love of Europa transformed himself into a bull.   196. **weigh with**, counterbalance.

11. **endear'd**, pledged.   19. **grey**, used to describe the dull or cold light of a cloudy day.   20. **chivalry**, men-at-arms.   24. **thick.** Most authorities define as "quickly" or "fast;" it probably refers to stammering. 30. **humours of blood**, fancies, whims.   38. **defensible**, able to make defense.

North.   Beshrew your heart,
Fair daughter, you do draw my spirits from
    me
With new lamenting ancient oversights.
But I must go and meet with danger there,
Or it will seek me in another place
And find me worse provided.
Lady N.   O, fly to Scotland,   50
Till that the nobles and the armed commons
Have of their puissance made a little taste.
Lady P. If they get ground and vantage of
    the king,
Then join you with them, like a rib of steel,
To make strength stronger; but, for all our
    loves,
First let them try themselves. So did your
    son;
He was so suffer'd: so came I a widow;
And never shall have length of life enough
To rain upon remembrance with mine eyes,
That it may grow and sprout as high as
    heaven,   60
For recordation to my noble husband.
North. Come, come, go in with me. 'Tis
    with my mind
As with the tide swell'd up unto his height,
That makes a still-stand, running neither
    way:
Fain would I go to meet the archbishop,
But many thousand reasons hold me back.
I will resolve for Scotland: there am I,
Till time and vantage crave my company.
                                        [*Exeunt.*

SCENE IV. *London. The Boar's-head Tavern
        in Eastcheap.*

Enter two Drawers.

First Draw. What the devil hast thou
brought there? apple-johns? thou knowest
Sir John cannot endure an apple-john.
Sec. Draw. Mass, thou sayest true. The
prince once set a dish of apple-johns before
him, and told him there were five more Sir
Johns, and, putting off his hat, said 'I will
now take my leave of these six dry, round,
old, withered knights.' It angered him to
the heart: but he hath forgot that.   10
First Draw. Why, then, cover, and set
them down: and see if thou canst find out

Sneak's noise; Mistress Tearsheet would fain
hear some music. Dispatch: the room where
they supped is too hot; they'll come in
straight.
Sec. Draw. Sirrah, here will be the prince
and Master Poins anon; and they will put
on two of our jerkins and aprons; and Sir
John must not know of it: Bardolph hath
brought word.   20
First Draw. By the mass, here will be old
Utis: it will be an excellent stratagem.
Sec. Draw. I'll see if I can find out Sneak.
                                        [*Exit.*

Enter Hostess *and* DOLL TEARSHEET.

Host. I' faith, sweetheart, methinks now
you are in an excellent good temperality:
your pulsidge beats as extraordinarily as
heart would desire; and your color, I warrant
you, is as red as any rose, in good truth, la!
But, i' faith, you have drunk too much
canaries; and that's a marvelous searching
wine, and it perfumes the blood ere one can
say 'What's this?' How do you now?   32
Dol. Better than I was: hem!
Host. Why, that's well said; a good heart's
worth gold. Lo, here comes Sir John.

Enter FALSTAFF.

Fal. [*Singing*] 'When Arthur first in court'
—Empty the jordan. [*Exit First Drawer.*]—
[*Singing*] 'And was a worthy king.' How
now, Mistress Doll!
Host. Sick of a calm; yea, good faith.   40
Fal. So is all her sect; an they be once in a
calm, they are sick.
Dol. You muddy rascal, is that all the
comfort you give me?
Fal. You make fat rascals, Mistress Doll.
Dol. I make them! gluttony and diseases
make them; I make them not.
Fal. If the cook help to make the glut-
tony, you help to make the diseases, Doll:
we catch of you, Doll, we catch of you; grant
that, my poor virtue, grant that.   51
Dol. Yea, joy, our chains and our jewels.
Fal. 'Your brooches, pearls, and ouches:'

---

57. **came**, became. 61. **recordation**, remembrance.
64. **still-stand**, standstill. 68. **vantage**, opportunity.
    Scene iv. 2. **apple-john**, a kind of apple said to
keep two years and to be in perfect condition when
shriveled and withered.

13. **Sneak's noise**, band of musicians. 21. **old Utis**,
rare fun. *Utas* was the term of eight days or the eighth
day after a feast; hence, a period of merry-making. 25.
temperality, for *temper*, or *temperature*. 26. **pulsidge**,
for *pulse*. **extraordinarily**, for *ordinarily*. 30. **canaries**, light sweet wine from the Canary islands. 40.
calm, probably pun on *qualm*. 45. **fat rascals**. A *rascal* was a lean deer; used here with pun on *rascal* meaning
"good-for-nothing." 53. **ouches**, gems, or jewels.
The line is from a ballad.

for to serve bravely is to come halting off, you
know: to come off the breach with his pike
bent bravely, and to surgery bravely; to
venture upon the charged chambers
bravely,—

Dol. Hang yourself, you muddy conger,
hang yourself!   59

Host. By my troth, this is the old fashion;
you two never meet but you fall to some discord: you are both, i' good truth, as rheumatic as two dry toasts: you cannot one bear
with another's confirmities. What the good-
year! one must bear, and that must be you:
you are the weaker vessel, as they say, the
emptier vessel.   66

Dol. Can a weak empty vessel bear such a
huge full hogshead? there's a whole merchant's venture of Bourdeaux stuff in him;
you have not seen a hulk better stuffed in
the hold. Come, I'll be friends with thee,
Jack: thou art going to the wars; and
whether I shall ever see thee again or no,
there is nobody cares.

Re-enter First Drawer.

First Draw. Sir, Ancient Pistol's below,
and would speak with you.

Dol. Hang him, swaggering rascal! let him
not come hither: it is the foul-mouthed'st
rogue in England.   78

Host. If he swagger, let him not come here:
no, by my faith; I must live among my
neighbours; I'll no swaggerers: I am in good
name and fame with the very best: shut the
door; there comes no swaggerers here: I have
not lived all this while, to have swaggering
now: shut the door, I pray you.

Fal. Dost thou hear, hostess?

Host. Pray ye, pacify yourself, Sir John:
there comes no swaggerers here.

Fal. Dost thou hear? it is mine ancient. 89

Host. Tilly-fally, Sir John, ne'er tell me:
your ancient swaggerer comes not in my
doors. I was before Master Tisick, the
debuty, t' other day; and, as he said to me,
'twas no longer ago than Wednesday last,
'I' good faith, neighbour Quickly,' says he;

Master Dumbe, our minister was by then;
'neighbour Quickly,' says he, 'receive those
that are civil; for,' said he, 'you are in an ill
name:' now a' said so, I can tell whereupon;
'for,' says he, 'you are an honest woman, and
well thought on; therefore take heed what
guests you receive: receive,' says he, 'no
swaggering companions.' There comes none
here: you would bless you to hear what he
said: no, I'll no swaggerers.   104

Fal. He's no swaggerer, hostess; a tame
cheater, i' faith; you may stroke him as
gently as a puppy greyhound: he'll not swagger with a Barbary hen, if her feathers turn
back in any show of resistance. Call him up,
drawer.   [*Exit* First Drawer. 109

Host. Cheater, call you him? I will bar no
honest man my house, nor no cheater: but I
do not love swaggering, by my troth; I am
the worse, when one says swagger: feel,
masters, how I shake; look you, I warrant
you.

Dol. So you do, hostess.

Host. Do I? yea, in very truth, do I, an
'twere an aspen leaf: I cannot abide swaggerers.

Enter PISTOL, BARDOLPH, *and* Page.

Pist. God save you, Sir John!   119

Fal. Welcome, Ancient Pistol. Here,
Pistol, I charge you with a cup of sack: do
you discharge upon mine hostess.

Pist. I will discharge upon her, Sir John,
with two bullets.

Fal. She is pistol-proof, sir; you shall
hardly offend her.

Host. Come, I'll drink no proofs nor no
bullets: I'll drink no more than will do me
good, for no man's pleasure, I.

Pist. Then to you, Mistress Dorothy; I
will charge you.   131

Dol. Charge me! I scorn you, scurvy companion. What! you poor, base, rascally,
cheating, lack-linen mate! Away, you
mouldy rogue, away! I am meat for your
master.

Pist. I know you, Mistress Dorothy.   136

Dol. Away, you cut-purse rascal! you

---

58. **conger,** conger-eel; applied abusively. 62. **rheumatic.** This is a misused term; she probably meant to
say *choleric.* 64. **confirmities,** for *infirmities.* **What
. . . year!** expletive; no special meaning. 69. **Bourdeaux
stuff,** wine. 74. **Ancient,** ensign, standard bearer; a
common military title. 79. **swagger,** bluster. 90.
Tilly-fally, expression of contempt. 92. **Tisick** suggests an elderly citizen with a cough. 93. **debuty,**
deputy of the ward; a grave citizen charged with the
good conduct of his ward.

96. **Master Dumbe.** Ministers who could not
preach were said to be dumb. 105. **tame cheater,** one
who won at gaming by cheating; probably acted also as
decoy. The Cambridge editors suggest *chetah,* the
hunting leopard. 108. **Barbary hen,** guinea hen. 110.
Cheater, rogue, as above; Mistress Quickly understands
the word as *escheator,* an officer of the king's exchequer.
131. **charge,** pledge, drink to. 132. **companion,**
fellow; term of contempt.

filthy bung, away! by this wine, I'll thrust my knife in your mouldy chaps, an you play the saucy cuttle with me. Away, you bottle-ale rascal! you basket-hilt stale juggler, you! Since when, I pray you, sir? God's light, with two points on your shoulder? much! 143

Pist. God let me not live, but I will murder your ruff for this.

Fal. No more, Pistol; I would not have you go off here: discharge yourself of our company, Pistol.

Host. No, good Captain Pistol; not here, sweet captain. 150

Dol. Captain! thou abominable damned cheater, art thou not ashamed to be called captain? An captains were of my mind, they would truncheon you out, for taking their names upon you before you have earned them. You a captain! you slave, for what? for tearing a poor whore's ruff in a bawdy-house? He a captain! hang him, rogue! he lives upon mouldy stewed prunes and dried cakes. A captain! God's light, these villains will make the word as odious as the word 'occupy;' which was an excellent good word before it was ill sorted: therefore captains had need look to't. 162

Bard. Pray thee, go down, good ancient.

Fal. Hark thee hither, Mistress Doll.

Pist. Not I: I tell thee what, Corporal Bardolph, I could tear her: I'll be revenged of her.

Page. Pray thee, go down.

Pist. I'll see her damned first; to Pluto's damned lake, by this hand, to the infernal deep, with Erebus and tortures vile also. Hold hook and line, say I. Down, down, dogs! down, faitors! Have we not Hiren 173 here?

Host. Good Captain Peesel, be quiet; 'tis very late, i' faith: I beseek you now, aggravate your choler.

Pist. These be good humours, indeed!

Shall pack-horses
And hollow pamper'd jades of Asia,
Which cannot go but thirty mile a-day,
Compare with Cæsars, and with Cannibals,
And Trojan Greeks? nay, rather damn them
with 181
King Cerberus; and let the welkin roar.
Shall we fall foul for toys?

Host. By my troth, captain, these are very bitter words.

Bard. Be gone, good ancient: this will grow to a brawl anon.

Pist. Die men like dogs! give crowns like pins! Have we not Hiren here? 189

Host. O' my word, captain, there's none such here. What the good-year! do you think I would deny her? For God's sake, be quiet.

Pist. Then feed, and be fat, my fair Calipolis. 193
Come, give 's some sack.
'Si fortune me tormente, sperato me contento.'
Fear we broadsides? no, let the fiend give fire:
Give me some sack: and, sweetheart, lie thou there.
                    [*Laying down his sword.*
Come we to full points here; and are etceteras nothing?

Fal. Pistol, I would be quiet. 199

Pist. Sweet knight, I kiss thy neif: what! we have seen the seven stars.

Dol. For God's sake, thrust him down stairs: I cannot endure such a fustian rascal.

Pist. Thrust him down stairs! know we not Galloway nags?

Fal. Quoit him down, Bardolph, like a shove-groat shilling: nay, an a' do nothing but speak nothing, a' shall be nothing here.

Bard. Come, get you down stairs.

Pist. What! shall we have incision? shall we imbrue? [*Snatching up his sword.* 210

---

138. **bung,** pickpocket. 140. **cuttle,** cutthroat or cutpurse. 141. **basket-hilt,** sword hilt with protector for the hand; evidently a term of contempt, possibly suggesting a sword trickster or a braggart swordsman. 142. **God's light,** by God's light. 143. **points,** tags for securing armor. **much,** ironical for *not much,* or *no.* 145. **ruff,** large frilled collar. 154. **truncheon,** staff carried by captains. 169-173. **I'll see . . . here.** This is the first of the characteristic ranting speeches of this famous character. His allusions are to old plays in the heroic drama; it is his "humor" to allude to them. 173. **faitors,** impostors, cheats; doubtful meaning here. **Hiren,** an allusion to a lost play by Peele, *Turkish Mahomet and the Fair Greek. Hiren* is Irene. 175. **beseek,** beseech. **aggravate,** blunder for *moderate.* 177. **humours,** freaks of conduct; current slang.

177-179. **Shall . . . a-day,** misquotation from Marlowe's *Second Part of Tamburlaine,* IV, iv, 1-2. 183. **toys,** trifles. 193. **Then . . . Calipolis,** burlesque of a line in Peele's *Battle of Alcazar.* 195. **'Si . . . contento,'** if fortune torments me, hope contents me. It is not clear what language Pistol is speaking, Italian or Spanish. The Cambridge editors think he is reading the motto on his sword. Such a saying was widely current. 198. **full points,** full stop. 200. **neif,** fist. 201. **seven stars,** Pleiades. 203. **fustian,** nonsensical. 205. **Galloway nags,** an inferior breed of horses. 206. **Quoit,** throw. 207. **shove-groat shilling,** an Edward VI shilling used in shove-groat, a game in which the coins were shoved toward a mark. 208. **speak nothing,** talk nonsense. **be nothing here,** be gone from here. 210. **incision,** bloodshed. **imbrue,** shed blood.

Then death rock me asleep, abridge my dole-
ful days!   211
Why, then, let grievous, ghastly, gaping
wounds
Untwine the Sisters Three! Come, Atropos,
I say!

Host. Here's goodly stuff toward!

Fal. Give me my rapier, boy.

Dol. I pray thee, Jack, I pray thee, do not
draw.

Fal. Get you down stairs.

         [*Drawing, and driving Pistol out.*

Host. Here's a goodly tumult! I'll forswear keeping house, afore I'll be in these
tirrits and frights. So; murder, I warrant
now. Alas, alas! put up your naked weapons, put up your naked weapons.   223

         [*Exeunt Pistol and Bardolph.*

Dol. I pray thee, Jack, be quiet; the rascal's gone. Ah, you whoreson little valiant
villain, you!

Host. Are you not hurt i' the groin? methought a' made a shrewd thrust at your
belly.

Re-enter BARDOLPH.

Fal. Have you turned him out o' doors?

Bard. Yea, sir. The rascal's drunk: you
have hurt him, sir, i' the shoulder.   231

Fal. A rascal! to brave me!

Dol. Ah, you sweet little rogue, you!
Alas, poor ape, how thou sweatest! come, let
me wipe thy face; come on, you whoreson
chops: ah, rogue! i' faith, I love thee: thou
art as valorous as Hector of Troy, worth five
of Agamemnon, and ten times better than
the Nine Worthies: ah, villain!

Fal. A rascally slave! I will toss the rogue
in a blanket.   241

Dol. Do, an thou darest for thy heart: an
thou dost, I'll canvass thee between a pair of
sheets.

Enter Music.

Page. The music is come, sir.

Fal. Let them play. Play, sirs. Sit on my

knee, Doll. A rascal bragging slave! the
rogue fled from me like quicksilver.   248

Dol. I' faith, and thou followedst him like
a church. Thou whoreson little tidy Bartholomew boar-pig, when wilt thou leave
fighting o' days and foining o' nights, and begin to patch up thine old body for heaven?

Enter, behind, PRINCE HENRY *and* POINS,
disguised.

Fal. Peace, good Doll! do not speak like
a death's-head; do not bid me remember
mine end.

Dol. Sirrah, what humour's the prince of?

Fal. A good shallow young fellow: a'
would have made a good pantler, a' would
ha' chipped bread well.

Dol. They say Poins has a good wit.   260

Fal. He a good wit? hang him, baboon!
his wit's as thick as Tewksbury mustard;
there's no more conceit in him than is in a
mallet.

Dol. Why does the prince love him so,
then?   264

Fal. Because their legs are both of a big-
ness, and a' plays at quoits well, and eats
conger and fennel, and drinks off candles'
ends for flap-dragons, and rides the wild-
mare with the boys, and jumps upon joined-
stools, and swears with a good grace, and
wears his boots very smooth, like unto the
sign of the leg, and breeds no bate with telling of discreet stories; and such other gambol
faculties a' has, that show a weak mind and
an able body, for the which the prince admits him: for the prince himself is such
another; the weight of a hair will turn the
scales between their avoirdupois.   277

Prince. Would not this nave of a wheel
have his ears cut off?

Poins. Let's beat him before his whore.

Prince. Look, whether the withered elder
hath not his poll clawed like a parrot.

Poins. Is it not strange that desire should
so many years outlive performance?

Fal. Kiss me, Doll.

---

211. **death . . . asleep**, quotation from a current poem
about Anne Boleyn. 213. **Sisters Three**, allusion to
the three fates, Clotho, Lachesis, and Atropos. *Atropos* severed the thread of life. 214. **toward**, about to
happen. 221. **tirrits**, possibly *terrors*. 232. **brave**,
defy. 236. **chops**, fat jaws. 237. **Hector of Troy**,
leader of the Trojans; the type of valor. 238. **Agamemnon**, leader of the Greeks at Troy. 239. **Nine Worthies**,
traditional group of the nine greatest men; usually three
Christians, three pagans, and three Jews; e.g., Arthur,
Charlemagne, Godfrey of Boulogne; Hector, Alexander,
Julius Cæsar; Joshua, David, Judas Maccabæus.

250. **Bartholomew boar-pig**, allusion to roast pig at
Bartholomew fair. 258. **pantler**, servant in charge of a
pantry. 262. **Tewksbury mustard.** Tewksbury was
famous for mustard. 263. **conceit**, wit. 267. **fennel**,
yellow-flowered herb used in pickles and sauces. 268.
flap-dragons, raisins snatched out of burning spirits
and swallowed in the game of snapdragon. **wild-
mare**, see-saw. 269. **joined-stools**, stools made by
joiners. 271. **breeds no bate**, causes no strife. 272.
gambol, sportive. 278. **nave**, hub; reference to Falstaff's rotundity.

Prince. Saturn and Venus this year in conjunction! what says the almanac to that?

Poins. And, look, whether the fiery Trigon, his man, be not lisping to his master's old tables, his note-book, his coun- 290 sel-keeper.

Fal. Thou dost give me flattering busses.

Dol. By my troth, I kiss thee with a most constant heart.

Fal. I am old, I am old.

Dol. I love thee better than I love e'er a scurvy young boy of them all.

Fal. What stuff wilt have a kirtle of? I shall receive money o' Thursday: shalt have a cap to-morrow. A merry song, come: it grows late; we'll to bed. Thou'lt forget me when I am gone. 300

Dol. By my troth, thou'lt set me a-weeping, and thou sayest so: prove that ever I dress myself handsome till thy return: well, hearken at the end.

Fal. Some sack, Francis.

Prince.⎫
Poins. ⎬ Anon, anon, sir. [*Coming forward.*

Fal. Ha! a bastard son of the king's? And art not thou Poins his brother?

Prince. Why, thou globe of sinful continents, what a life dost thou lead! 310

Fal. A better than thou: I am a gentleman; thou art a drawer.

Prince. Very true, sir; and I come to draw you out by the ears.

Host. O, the Lord preserve thy good grace! by my troth, welcome to London. Now, the Lord bless that sweet face of thine! O Jesu, are you come from Wales?

Fal. Thou whoreson mad compound of majesty, by this light flesh and corrupt blood, thou art welcome. 321

Dol. How, you fat fool! I scorn you.

Poins. My lord, he will drive you out of your revenge and turn all to a merriment, if you take not the heat.

Prince. You whoreson candle-mine, you, how vilely did you speak of me even now before this honest, virtuous, civil gentlewoman!

Host. God's blessing of your good heart! and so she is, by my troth. 330

Fal. Didst thou hear me?

Prince. Yea, and you knew me, as you did when you ran away by Gad's-hill: you knew I was at your back, and spoke it on purpose to try my patience.

Fal. No, no, no; not so; I did not think thou wast within hearing.

Prince. I shall drive you then to confess the wilful abuse; and then I know how to handle you.

Fal. No abuse, Hal, o' mine honour; no abuse. 340

Prince. Not to dispraise me, and call me pantler and bread-chipper and I know not what?

Fal. No abuse, Hal.

Poins. No abuse?

Fal. No abuse, Ned, i' the world; honest Ned, none. I dispraised him before the wicked, that the wicked might not fall in love with him; in which doing, I have done the part of a careful friend and a true subject, and thy father is to give me thanks for it. No abuse, Hal: none, Ned, none: no, faith, boys, none. 351

Prince. See now, whether pure fear and entire cowardice doth not make thee wrong this virtuous gentlewoman to close with us. Is she of the wicked? is thine hostess here of the wicked? or is thy boy of the wicked? or honest Bardolph, whose zeal burns in his nose, of the wicked? 358

Poins. Answer, thou dead elm, answer.

Fal. The fiend hath pricked down Bardolph irrecoverable; and his face is Lucifer's privy-kitchen, where he doth nothing but roast malt-worms. For the boy, there is a good angel about him; but the devil outbids him too.

Prince. For the women?

Fal. For one of them, she is in hell already, and burns poor souls. For the other, I owe her money; and whether she be damned for that, I know not.

Host. No, I warrant you. 369

Fal. No, I think thou art not; I think thou art quit for that. Marry, there is another indictment upon thee, for suffering flesh to be eaten in thy house, contrary to the law; for the which I think thou wilt howl.

Host. All victuallers do so: what's a joint of mutton or two in a whole Lent?

Prince. You, gentlewoman,—

Dol. What says your grace?

Fal. His grace says that which his flesh rebels against.   [*Knocking within.*   380

Host. Who knocks so loud at door? Look to the door there, Francis.

Enter PETO.

Prince. Peto, how now! what news?

Peto. The king your father is at Westminster;

And there are twenty weak and wearied posts

Come from the north: and, as I came along,

I met and overtook a dozen captains,

Bare-headed, sweating, knocking at the taverns,

And asking every one for Sir John Falstaff.

Prince. By heaven, Poins, I feel me much to blame,   390

So idly to profane the precious time,

When tempest of commotion, like the south

Borne with black vapour, doth begin to melt

And drop upon our bare unarmed heads.

Give me my sword and cloak. Falstaff, good night.

[*Exeunt Prince Henry, Poins, Peto, and Bardolph.*

Fal. Now comes in the sweetest morsel of the night, and we must hence and leave it unpicked. [*Knocking within.*] More knocking at the door!

Re-enter BARDOLPH.

How now! what's the matter?   400

Bard. You must away to court, sir, presently;

A dozen captains stay at door for you.

Fal. [*To the Page*] Pay the musicians, sirrah. Farewell, hostess; farewell, Doll. You see, my good wenches, how men of merit are sought after: the undeserver may sleep, when the man of action is called on. Farewell, good wenches: if I be not sent away post, I will see you again ere I go.

Dol. I cannot speak; if my heart be not ready to burst,—well, sweet Jack, have a care of thyself.

Fal. Farewell, farewell. [*Exeunt Falstaff and Bardolph.*

Host. Well, fare thee well: I have known thee these twenty nine years, come peascod-time; but an honester and truer-hearted man,—well, fare thee well.

Bard. [*Within*] Mistress Tearsheet!

Host. What's the matter?

Bard. [*Within*] Bid Mistress Tearsheet come to my master.   419

Host. O, run, Doll, run; run, good Doll: come. [*She comes blubbered.*] Yea, will you come, Doll?   [*Exeunt.*

ACT III.

SCENE I. *Westminster. The palace.*

Enter the KING *in his nightgown, with a* Page.

King. Go call the Earls of Surrey and of Warwick;

But, ere they come, bid them o'er-read these letters,

And well consider of them: make good speed.

[*Exit Page.*

How many thousand of my poorest subjects

Are at this hour asleep! O sleep, O gentle sleep,

Nature's soft nurse, how have I frighted thee,

That thou no more wilt weigh my eyelids down

And steep my senses in forgetfulness?

Why rather, sleep, liest thou in smoky cribs,

Upon uneasy pallets stretching thee   10

And hush'd with buzzing night-flies to thy slumber,

Than in the perfumed chambers of the great,

Under the canopies of costly state,

And lull'd with sound of sweetest melody?

O thou dull god, why liest thou with the vile

In loathsome beds, and leavest thou the kingly couch

A watch-case or a common 'larum-bell?

Wilt thou upon the high and giddy mast

Seal up the ship-boy's eyes, and rock his brains

---

421. *Stage Direction:* **blubbered**, disfigured with weeping.

Act III. Scene i. Stage Direction: **nightgown**, dressing-gown. 5-31. O sleep . . . crown. This is one of the better known passages of the play, having a beauty independent of its appropriateness in the mouth of the weary king. 9. cribs, hovels. 15. dull, drowsy. vile, i.e., in rank. 17. watch-case, sentry-box.

---

372. **flesh to be eaten,** allusion to enactments to prevent the sale of meat in Lent. 379. **grace,** used quibblingly on the meanings "royal grace" and "heavenly grace." 392. **south,** southwind, regarded as a breeder of tempests. 393. **Borne with,** laden with.

In cradle of the rude imperious surge   20
And in the visitation of the winds,
Who take the ruffian billows by the top,
Curling their monstrous heads and hanging
    them
With deafening clamour in the slippery
    clouds,
That, with the hurly, death itself awakes?
Canst thou, O partial sleep, give thy repose
To the wet sea-boy in an hour so rude,
And in the calmest and most stillest night,
With all appliances and means to boot,
Deny it to a king? Then happy low, lie
    down!   30
Uneasy lies the head that wears a crown.

Enter Warwick *and* Surrey.

War. Many good morrows to your maj-
    esty!
King. Is it good morrow, lords?
War. 'Tis one o'clock, and past.
King. Why, then, good morrow to you all,
    my lords.
Have you read o'er the letters that I sent
    you?
War. We have, my liege.
King. Then you perceive the body of our
    kingdom
How foul it is; what rank diseases grow,
And with what danger, near the heart of it. 40
War. It is but as a body yet distemper'd;
Which to his former strength may be re-
    stored
With good advice and little medicine:
My Lord Northumberland will soon be
    cool'd.
King. O God! that one might read the
    book of fate,
And see the revolution of the times
Make mountains level, and the continent,
Weary of solid firmness, melt itself
Into the sea! and, other times, to see
The beachy girdle of the ocean   50
Too wide for Neptune's hips; how chances
    mock,
And changes fill the cup of alteration
With divers liquors! O, if this were seen,
The happiest youth, viewing his progress
    through,
What perils past, what crosses to ensue,

Would shut the book, and sit him down and
    die.
    'Tis not ten years gone
Since Richard and Northumberland, great
    friends,
Did feast together, and in two years after
Were they at wars: it is but eight years since
This Percy was the man nearest my soul,   61
Who like a brother toil'd in my affairs
And laid his love and life under my foot,
Yea, for my sake, even to the eyes of
    Richard
Gave him defiance. But which of you was
    by—
You, cousin Nevil, as I may remember—
                              [*To Warwick.*
When Richard, with his eye brimful of tears,
Then check'd and rated by Northumber-
    land,
Did speak these words, now proved a proph-
    ecy?   69
'Northumberland, thou ladder by the which
My cousin Bolingbroke ascends my throne;'
Though then, God knows, I had no such in-
    tent
But that necessity so bow'd the state
That I and greatness were compell'd to kiss:
'The time shall come,' thus did he follow it,
'The time will come, that foul sin, gathering
    head,
Shall break into corruption:' so went on,
Foretelling this same time's condition
And the division of our amity.
War. There is a history in all men's lives,
Figuring the nature of the times deceased; 81
The which observed, a man may prophesy,
With a near aim, of the main chance of
    things
As yet not come to life, which in their seeds
And weak beginnings lie intreasured.
Such things become the hatch and brood of
    time;
And by the necessary form of this
King Richard might create a perfect guess
That great Northumberland, then false to
    him,
Would of that seed grow to a greater false-
    ness;   90
Which should not find a ground to root upon,
Unless on you.

---

24. **slippery**, i.e., giving the waves nothing to hold by.
25. **hurly**, tumult. 28. **most stillest**, double superlative, as often. 30. **low**, humble. 39. **foul**, infected.
47. **continent**, dry land.

56. **shut the book**, expression of despair. He would
shut the book of his future. 64. **to the eyes**, to the face.
67. **Richard**. See *Richard II*, V, i, 55 ff. 81. **Figuring**,
symbolizing. 85. **intreasured**, in store. 87. **necessary
form**, logical necessity.

King.   Are these things then necessities?

Then let us meet them like necessities:
And that same word even now cries out on
us:
They say the bishop and Northumberland
Are fifty thousand strong.

War.   It cannot be, my lord;
Rumour doth double, like the voice and
echo,
The numbers of the fear'd. Please it your
grace
To go to bed. Upon my soul, my lord,
The powers that you already have sent forth
Shall bring this prize in very easily.   101
To comfort you the more, I have received
A certain instance that Glendower is dead.
Your majesty hath been this fortnight ill,
And these unseason'd hours perforce must
add
Unto your sickness.

King.   I will take your counsel:
And were these inward wars once out of
hand,
We would, dear lords, unto the Holy Land.
                                        [*Exeunt.*

SCENE II. *Gloucestershire. Before* JUSTICE
SHALLOW'S *house.*

Enter SHALLOW *and* SILENCE, *meeting;*
MOULDY, SHADOW, WART, FEEBLE, BULL-
CALF, *a Servant or two with them.*

Shal. Come on, come on, come on, sir;
give me your hand, sir, give me your hand,
sir: an early stirrer, by the rood! And how
doth my good cousin Silence?

Sil. Good morrow, good cousin Shallow.

Shal. And how doth my cousin, your bedfellow? and your fairest daughter and mine,
my god-daughter Ellen?

Sil. Alas, a black ousel, cousin Shallow!   9

Shal. By yea and nay, sir, I dare say my
cousin William is become a good scholar: he
is at Oxford still, is he not?

Sil. Indeed, sir, to my cost.

Shal. A' must, then, to the inns o' court
shortly. I was once of Clement's Inn, where
I think they will talk of mad Shallow yet.

Sil. You were called 'lusty Shallow' then,
cousin.   18

Shal. By the mass, I was called any thing;
and I would have done any thing indeed too,
and roundly too. There was I, and little John
Doit of Staffordshire, and black George
Barnes, and Francis Pickbone, and Will
Squele, a Cotswold man; you had not four such
swinge-bucklers in all the inns o' court again:
and I may say to you, we knew where the
bona-robas were and had the best of them
all at commandment. Then was Jack Falstaff, now Sir John, a boy, and page to
Thomas Mowbray, Duke of Norfolk.

Sil. This Sir John, cousin, that comes
hither anon about soldiers?   31

Shal. The same Sir John, the very same.
I see him break Skogan's head at the court-
gate, when a' was a crack not thus high: and
the very same day did I fight with one Sampson Stockfish, a fruiterer, behind Gray's Inn.
Jesu, Jesu, the mad days that I have spent!
and to see how many of my old acquaintance
are dead!

Sil. We shall all follow, cousin.   39

Shal. Certain, 'tis certain; very sure, very
sure: death, as the Psalmist saith, is certain
to all; all shall die. How a good yoke of bullocks at Stamford fair?

Sil. By my troth, I was not there.

Shal. Death is certain. Is old Double of
your town living yet?

Sil. Dead, sir.   47

Shal. Jesu, Jesu, dead! a' drew a good
bow; and dead! a' shot a fine shoot: John a
Gaunt loved him well, and betted much
money on his head. Dead! a' would have
clapped i' the clout at twelve score; and
carried you a forehand shaft a fourteen and
fourteen and a half, that it would have done
a man's heart good to see. How a score of
ewes now?

Sil. Thereafter as they be: a score of good
ewes may be worth ten pounds.

---

103. **certain instance**, sure evidence, proof. 105.
unseason'd, unseasonable.
  Scene ii. 1. **Come on.** In Shallow's repetitions there
is a suggestion of fussiness and possibly old age. 3. **rood**,
cross. 9. **ousel**, blackbird. 15. **Clement's Inn**, one
of the inns of court, or colleges of law.

17. **lusty**, merry. 21. **roundly**, thoroughly. 24.
Cotswold, Cotswold Hills; a region famous for athletic
sports. 25. **swinge-bucklers**, roysterers, swash-buck-
lers. 27. **bona-robas**, showily dressed wantons. 29.
page to Thomas Mowbray. Both Sir John Oldcastle (Falstaff's original) and Sir John Fastolfe (for
whom Falstaff was renamed) were pages to the Duke of
Norfolk, who figures in the play *Richard II.* 33.
Skogan. There was a court-jester to Edward IV whose
name was John Skogan, and a jest-book known as
"Skogan's Jests." 34. **crack**, pert little boy. 42. **How**,
how much. 52. **clapped i' the clout**, hit the bull's-
eye. **twelve score**, i.e., yards. 53. **forehand shaft**,
arrow used for shooting straight before one.

Shal. And is old Double dead?

Sil. Here come two of Sir John Falstaff's
men, as I think.   60

Enter BARDOLPH *and one with him.*

Bard. Good morrow, honest gentlemen: I
beseech you, which is Justice Shallow?

Shal. I am Robert Shallow, sir; a poor
esquire of this county, and one of the king's
justices of the peace: what is your good pleasure with me?

Bard. My captain, sir, commends him to
you; my captain, Sir John Falstaff, a tall
gentleman, by heaven, and a most gallant
leader.   68

Shal. He greets me well, sir. I knew him
a good backsword man. How doth the good
knight? may I ask how my lady his wife doth?

Bard. Sir, pardon; a soldier is better accommodated than with a wife.

Shal. It is well said, in faith, sir; and it is
well said indeed too. Better accommodated!
it is good; yea, indeed, is it: good phrases are
surely, and ever were, very commendable.
Accommodated! it comes of 'accommodo:'
very good; a good phrase.   79

Bard. Pardon me, sir; I have heard the
word. Phrase call you it? by this good day, I
know not the phrase; but I will maintain the
word with my sword to be a soldier-like
word, and a word of exceeding good command, by heaven. Accommodated; that is,
when a man is, as they say, accommodated;
or when a man is, being, whereby a' may be
thought to be accommodated; which is an
excellent thing.

Shal. It is very just.   89

Enter FALSTAFF.

Look, here comes good Sir John. Give me
your good hand, give me your worship's good
hand: by my troth, you like well and bear
your years very well: welcome, good Sir John.

Fal. I am glad to see you well, good Master Robert Shallow: Master Surecard, as I
think?

Shal. No, Sir John; it is my cousin Silence,
in commission with me.

Fal. Good Master Silence, it well befits
you should be of the peace.

Sil. Your good worship is welcome.   100

Fal. Fie! this is hot weather, gentlemen.
Have you provided me here half a dozen
sufficient men?

Shal. Marry, have we, sir. Will you sit?

Fal. Let me see them, I beseech you.

Shal. Where's the roll? where's the roll?
where's the roll? Let me see, let me see, let
me see. So, so, so, so, so, so, so: yea, marry,
sir: Ralph Mouldy! Let them appear as I
call; let them do so, let them do so. Let me
see; where is Mouldy?   111

Moul. Here, an't please you.

Shal. What think you, Sir John? a good-
limbed fellow; young, strong, and of good
friends.

Fal. Is thy name Mouldy?

Moul. Yea, an't please you.

Fal. 'Tis the more time thou wert used.

Shal. Ha, ha, ha! most excellent, i' faith!
things that are mouldy lack use: very singular good! in faith, well said, Sir John, very
well said.   120

Fal. Prick him.

Moul. I was pricked well enough before,
an you could have let me alone: my old dame
will be undone now for one to do her husbandry and her drudgery: you need not to
have pricked me; there are other men fitter
to go out than I.

Fal. Go to: peace, Mouldy; you shall go.
Mouldy, it is time you were spent.

Moul. Spent!   129

Shal. Peace, fellow, peace; stand aside:
know you where you are? For the other, Sir
John: let me see: Simon Shadow!

Fal. Yea, marry, let me have him to sit
under: he's like to be a cold soldier.

Shal. Where's Shadow?

Shad. Here, sir.

Fal. Shadow, whose son art thou?

Shad. My mother's son, sir.

Fal. Thy mother's son! like enough, and
thy father's shadow: so the son of the female
is the shadow of the male: it is often so, indeed; but much of the father's substance!

Shal. Do you like him, Sir John?   143

Fal. Shadow will serve for summer; prick
him, for we have a number of shadows to fill
up the muster-book.

---

70. **backsword man,** single-stick fencer. 72. **accommodated,** furnished, equipped; a bit of fine language
on Bardolph's part. 92. **like well,** are in good condition.
95. **Surecard,** boon companion. 99. **of the peace,** i.e.,
a magistrate; reference to the name *Silence.*

103. **sufficient,** fit for service. 122. **pricked,**
dressed; with quibble on the meaning, "marked, or
designated, for service." 144-46. **Shadow . . . muster-
book,** an allusion to the practice of employing false
muster-lists and drawing pay for imaginary soldiers.

Shal. Thomas Wart!

Fal. Where's he?

Wart. Here, sir.

Fal. Is thy name Wart? 150

Wart. Yea, sir.

Fal. Thou art a very ragged wart.

Shal. Shall I prick him down, Sir John?

Fal. It were superfluous; for his apparel is built upon his back and the whole frame stands upon pins: prick him no more.

Shal. Ha, ha, ha! you can do it, sir; you can do it: I commend you well. Francis Feeble!

Fee. Here, sir.

Fal. What trade art thou, Feeble? 160

Fee. A woman's tailor, sir.

Shal. Shall I prick him, sir?

Fal. You may: but if he had been a man's tailor, he'ld ha' pricked you. Wilt thou make as many holes in an enemy's battle as thou hast done in a woman's petticoat? 166

Fee. I will do my good will, sir: you can have no more.

Fal. Well said, good woman's tailor! well said, courageous Feeble! thou wilt be as valiant as the wrathful dove or most magnanimous mouse. Prick the woman's tailor: well, Master Shallow; deep, Master Shallow.

Fee. I would Wart might have gone, sir.

Fal. I would thou wert a man's tailor, that thou mightst mend him and make him fit to go. I cannot put him to a private soldier that is the leader of so many thousands: let that suffice, most forcible Feeble.

Fee. It shall suffice, sir. 180

Fal. I am bound to thee, reverend Feeble. Who is next?

Shal. Peter Bullcalf o' the green!

Fal. Yea, marry, let's see Bullcalf.

Bull. Here, sir.

Fal. 'Fore God, a likely fellow! Come, prick me Bullcalf till he roar again.

Bull. O Lord! good my lord captain,—

Fal. What, dost thou roar before thou art pricked? 190

Bull. O Lord, sir! I am a diseased man.

Fal. What disease hast thou?

Bull. A whoreson cold, sir, a cough, sir, which I caught with ringing in the king's affairs upon his coronation-day, sir.

Fal. Come, thou shalt go to the wars in a gown; we will have away thy cold; and I will

take such order that thy friends shall ring for thee. Is here all? 199

Shal. Here is two more called than your number; you must have but four here, sir: and so, I pray you, go in with me to dinner.

Fal. Come, I will go drink with you, but I cannot tarry dinner. I am glad to see you, by my troth, Master Shallow.

Shal. O, Sir John, do you remember since we lay all night in the windmill in Saint George's field?

Fal. No more of that, good Master Shallow, no more of that.

Shal. Ha! 'twas a merry night. And is Jane Nightwork alive? 211

Fal. She lives, Master Shallow.

Shal. She never could away with me.

Fal. Never, never; she would always say she could not abide Master Shallow.

Shal. By the mass, I could anger her to the heart. She was then a bona-roba. Doth she hold her own well?

Fal. Old, old, Master Shallow. 219

Shal. Nay, she must be old; she cannot choose but be old; certain she's old; and had Robin Nightwork by old Nightwork before I came to Clement's Inn.

Sil. That's fifty five years ago.

Shal. Ha, cousin Silence, that thou hadst seen that that this knight and I have seen! Ha, Sir John, said I well?

Fal. We have heard the chimes at midnight, Master Shallow. 229

Shal. That we have, that we have, that we have; in faith, Sir John, we have: our watchword was 'Hem boys!' Come, let's to dinner; come, let's to dinner: Jesus, the days that we have seen! Come, come.

[*Exeunt Falstaff and the Justices.*

Bull. Good Master Corporate Bardolph, stand my friend; and here's four Harry ten shillings in French crowns for you. In very truth, sir, I had as lief be hanged, sir, as go: and yet, for mine own part, sir, I do not care; but rather, because I am unwilling, and, for mine own part, have a desire to stay with my friends; else, sir, I did not care, for mine own part, so much.

Bard. Go to; stand aside.

165. **battle**, army. 177. **to**, in the character of. 178. **thousands**, i.e., of vermin.

207. **Saint George's field**, open space between Lambeth and Southwark; a muster-ground. 213. **away with**, get on with. 235. **Corporate**, for *corporal*. 236. **Harry ten shillings**, i.e., coined in the reign of Henry VII; current at half the face value. The reference is anachronistic.

Moul. And, good master corporal captain, for my old dame's sake, stand my friend: she has nobody to do any thing about her when I am gone; and she is old, and cannot help herself: you shall have forty, sir.

Bard. Go to; stand aside.   249

Fee. By my troth, I care not; a man can die but once: we owe God a death: I'll ne'er bear a base mind: an't be my destiny, so; an't be not, so: no man is too good to serve's prince; and let it go which way it will, he that dies this year is quit for the next.

Bard. Well said; thou'rt a good fellow.

Fee. Faith, I'll bear no base mind.

Re-enter FALSTAFF *and the* Justices.

Fal. Come, sir, which men shall I have?

Shal. Four of which you please.

Bard. Sir, a word with you: I have three pound to free Mouldy and Bullcalf.   261

Fal. Go to; well.

Shal. Come, Sir John, which four will you have?

Fal. Do you choose for me.

Shal. Marry, then, Mouldy, Bullcalf, Feeble and Shadow.

Fal. Mouldy and Bullcalf: for you, Mouldy, stay at home till you are past service: and for your part, Bullcalf, grow till you come unto it: I will none of you.   271

Shal. Sir John, Sir John, do not yourself wrong: they are your likeliest men, and I would have you served with the best.

Fal. Will you tell me, Master Shallow, how to choose a man? Care I for the limb, the thewes, the stature, bulk, and big assemblance of a man! Give me the spirit, Master Shallow. Here's Wart; you see what a ragged appearance it is: a' shall charge you and discharge you with the motion of a   280 pewterer's hammer, come off and on swifter than he that gibbets on the brewer's bucket. And this same half-faced fellow, Shadow; give me this man: he presents no mark to the enemy; the foeman may with as great aim level at the edge of a penknife. And for a retreat; how swiftly will this Feeble the woman's tailor run off! O, give me the spare

men, and spare me the great ones. Put me a caliver into Wart's hand, Bardolph.   290

Bard. Hold, Wart, traverse; thus, thus, thus.

Fal. Come, manage me your caliver. So; very well: go to: very good, exceeding good. O, give me always a little, lean, old, chapt, bald shot. Well said, i' faith, Wart; thou'rt a good scab: hold, there's a tester for thee.

Shal. He is not his craft's master; he doth not do it right. I remember at Mile-end Green, when I lay at Clement's Inn,—I was then Sir Dagonet in Arthur's show,—there was a little quiver fellow, and a' would manage you his piece thus; and a' would about and about, and come you in and come you in: 'rah, tah, tah,' would a' say; 'bounce' would a' say; and away again would a' go, and again would a' come: I shall ne'er see such a   306 fellow.

Fal. These fellows will do well, Master Shallow. God keep you, Master Silence: I will not use many words with you. Fare you well, gentlemen both: I thank you: I must a dozen mile to-night. Bardolph, give the soldiers coats.

Shal. Sir John, the Lord bless you! God prosper your affairs! God send us peace! At your return visit our house; let our old acquaintance be renewed: peradventure I will with ye to the court.

Fal. 'Fore God, I would you would, Master Shallow.

Shal. Go to; I have spoke at a word. God keep you.   320

Fal. Fare you well, gentle gentlemen. [*Exeunt Justices.*] On, Bardolph; lead the men away. [*Exeunt Bardolph, Recruits, &c.*] As I return, I will fetch off these justices: I do see the bottom of Justice Shallow. Lord, Lord, how subject we old men are to this vice of lying! This same starved justice hath done nothing but prate to me of the wildness of his youth, and the feats he hath done

248. **forty,** i.e., shillings. 255. **quit,** exempt, clear. 277. **assemblance,** appearance. 280-81. **charge, discharge, come off and on,** terms in the drilling of troops. 282. **gibbets on,** hangs as on a gibbet; a reference to the skill of brewer's men in swinging buckets upon the gibbet or yoke which they wore on their shoulders.

290. **caliver,** light musket or harquebus. 291. **traverse,** march. 295. **shot,** marksman. 296. **scab,** scurvy fellow. **tester,** sixpence. 298-300. **I remember . . . show.** There was held annually at Mile-end Green an exhibition of archery called Arthur's show; in this show Shallow played the part of Sir Dagonet, King Arthur's fool. 301. **quiver,** nimble. 304. **'bounce,'** bang! 319. **at a word,** briefly and sincerely. 324. **fetch off,** get the better of. 325. **see . . . Shallow.** The character of Shallow, which became immediately popular on the London stage, afforded not only the opportunity of laughing at a stupid and pompous country justice, but of presenting the ancient spectacle of the fool being fleeced by the rogue.

about Turnbull Street; and every third word a lie, duer paid to the hearer than the Turk's tribute. I do remember him at Clement's 331 Inn like a man made after supper of a cheese-paring: when a' was naked, he was, for all the world, like a forked radish, with a head fantastically carved upon it with a knife: a' was so forlorn, that his dimensions to any thick sight were invincible: a' was the very genius of famine; yet lecherous as a monkey, and the whores called him mandrake: a' came ever in the rearward of the fashion, and sung those tunes to the overscutched hus-wives that he heard the carmen whistle, and sware they were his fancies or his good- 342 nights. And now is this Vice's dagger be-come a squire, and talks as familiarly of John a Gaunt as if he had been sworn brother to him; and I'll be sworn a' ne'er saw him but once in the Tilt-yard; and then he burst his head for crowding among the marshal's men. I saw it, and told John a Gaunt he beat his own name; for you might have thrust him and all his apparel into an eel-skin; the case of a treble hautboy was a mansion for him, a court: and now has he land and beefs. Well, I'll be acquainted with him, if I return; and it shall go hard but I will make him a phi-losopher's two stones to me: if the young dace be a bait for the old pike, I see no reason in the law of nature but I may snap at him. Let time shape, and there an 358 end.   [*Exit.*

ACT IV.

SCENE I. *Yorkshire. Gaultree Forest.*

Enter the ARCHBISHOP OF YORK, MOWBRAY, HASTINGS, *and others.*

Arch. What is this forest call'd?
Hast. 'Tis Gaultree Forest, an 't shall please your grace.

329. **Turnbull Street,** a street in Clerkenwell, ill reputed. 330. **Turk's tribute.** Much of Christendom was paying tribute to the sultan of Turkey. 336. **forlorn,** meager, thin. 339. **mandrake,** root of a plant, the white mandrake, said to resemble the body of a man; said also to be an emblem of incontinence. 340. **overscutched huswives,** outworn prostitutes. 342. **fancies ... good-nights,** love songs, of which he claims authorship. 343. **Vice's dagger.** The Vice, or comic character of the morality plays, was armed with a wooden dagger. 351. **hautboy,** oboe. 355. **philosopher's two stones,** i.e., yield twice as much as the philosopher's stone, which would produce boundless wealth. 356. **young dace ... old pike.** The fish dace, or luce, was the food of the pike; this passage has been thought to allude to Shakespeare's animosity for Sir Thomas Lucy of Charlecote. See pp. 83, 84, 289.
Act IV. Scene i. 2. **Gaultree Forest,** ancient forest of Galtres, north of York.

Arch. Here stand, my lords; and send dis-coverers forth
To know the numbers of our enemies.
Hast. We have sent forth already.
Arch.   'Tis well done.
My friends and brethren in these great affairs,
I must acquaint you that I have received
New-dated letters from Northumberland;
Their cold intent, tenour and substance, thus:
Here doth he wish his person, with such powers   10
As might hold sortance with his quality,
The which he could not levy; whereupon
He is retired, to ripe his growing fortunes,
To Scotland: and concludes in hearty prayers
That your attempts may overlive the hazard
And fearful meeting of their opposite.
Mowb. Thus do the hopes we have in him touch ground
And dash themselves to pieces.

Enter a Messenger.

Hast.   Now, what news?
Mess. West of this forest, scarcely off a mile,
In goodly form comes on the enemy;   20
And, by the ground they hide, I judge their number
Upon or near the rate of thirty thousand.
Mowb. The just proportion that we gave them out.
Let us sway on and face them in the field.
Arch. What well-appointed leader fronts us here?

Enter WESTMORELAND.

Mowb. I think it is my Lord of West-moreland.
West. Health and fair greeting from our general,
The prince, Lord John and Duke of Lan-caster.
Arch. Say on, my Lord of Westmoreland, in peace:
What doth concern your coming?
West.   Then, my lord,   30
Unto your grace do I in chief address
The substance of my speech. If that re-bellion
Came like itself, in base and abject routs,
Led on by bloody youth, guarded with rags,

11. **hold sortance,** accord. 15. **overlive,** outlive. 23. **just proportion,** exact size. 24. **sway on,** move on. 34. **bloody,** passionate. **guarded,** adorned, trimmed.

And countenanced by boys and beggary,
I say, if damn'd commotion so appear'd,
In his true, native and most proper shape,
You, reverend father, and these noble lords
Had not been here, to dress the ugly form
Of base and bloody insurrection 40
With your fair honours. You, lord arch-
  bishop,
Whose see is by a civil peace maintain'd,
Whose beard the silver hand of peace hath
  touch'd,
Whose learning and good letters peace hath
  tutor'd,
Whose white investments figure innocence,
The dove and very blessed spirit of peace,
Wherefore do you so ill translate yourself
Out of the speech of peace that bears such
  grace,
Into the harsh and boisterous tongue of war;
Turning your books to †graves, your ink to
  blood, 50
Your pens to lances and your tongue divine
To a loud trumpet and a point of war?
  Arch. Wherefore do I this? so the question
  stands.
Briefly to this end: we are all diseased,
And with our surfeiting and wanton hours
Have brought ourselves into a burning
  fever,
And we must bleed for it; of which disease
Our late king, Richard, being infected, died.
But, my most noble Lord of Westmoreland,
I take not on me here as a physician, 60
Nor do I as an enemy to peace
Troop in the throngs of military men;
But rather show awhile like fearful war,
To diet rank minds sick of happiness
And purge the obstructions which begin to
  stop
Our very veins of life. Hear me more
  plainly.
I have in equal balance justly weigh'd
What wrongs our arms may do, what wrongs
  we suffer,
And find our griefs heavier than our offences.
We see which way the stream of time doth
  run, 70
And are enforced from our most quiet there
By the rough torrent of occasion;
And have the summary of all our griefs,

When time shall serve, to show in articles;
Which long ere this we offer'd to the king,
And might by no suit gain our audience:
When we are wrong'd and would unfold our
  griefs,
We are denied access unto his person
Even by those men that most have done us
  wrong.
The dangers of the days but newly gone, 80
Whose memory is written on the earth
With yet appearing blood, and the examples
Of every minute's instance, present now,
Hath put us in these ill-beseeming arms,
Not to break peace or any branch of it,
But to establish here a peace indeed,
Concurring both in name and quality.
  West. When ever yet was your appeal de-
  nied?
Wherein have you been galled by the king?
What peer hath been suborn'd to grate on
  you, 90
That you should seal this lawless bloody
  book
Of forged rebellion with a seal divine
And consecrate commotion's bitter edge?
  Arch. †My brother general, the common-
  wealth,
To brother born an household cruelty,
I make my quarrel in particular.
  West. There is no need of any such re-
  dress;
Or if there were, it not belongs to you.
  Mowb. Why not to him in part, and to us
  all
That feel the bruises of the days before, 100
And suffer the condition of these times
To lay a heavy and unequal hand
Upon our honours?
  West.   O, my good Lord Mowbray,
Construe the times to their necessities,
And you shall say indeed, it is the time,
And not the king, that doth you injuries.
Yet for your part, it not appears to me
Either from the king or in the present time
That you should have an inch of any ground
To build a grief on: were you not restored 110
To all the Duke of Norfolk's signories,
Your noble and right well remember'd
  father's?

Mowb. What thing, in honour, had my
    father lost,
That need to be revived and breathed in me?
The king that loved him, as the state stood
    then,
Was force perforce compell'd to banish him:
And then that Henry Bolingbroke and he,
Being mounted and both roused in their
    seats,
Their neighing coursers daring of the spur,
Their armed staves in charge, their beavers
    down,   120
Their eyes of fire sparkling through sights of
    steel
And the loud trumpet blowing them to-
    gether,
Then, then, when there was nothing could
    have stay'd
My father from the breast of Bolingbroke,
O, when the king did throw his warder
    down,
His own life hung upon the staff he threw;
Then threw he down himself and all their
    lives
That by indictment and by dint of sword
Have since miscarried under Bolingbroke.
    West. You speak, Lord Mowbray, now
    you know not what.   130
The Earl of Hereford was reputed then
In England the most valiant gentleman:
Who knows on whom fortune would then
    have smiled?
But if your father had been victor there,
He ne'er had borne it out of Coventry:
For all the country in a general voice
Cried hate upon him; and all their prayers
    and love
Were set on Hereford, whom they doted on
And bless'd and graced indeed, more than
    the king.
But this is mere digression from my purpose.
Here come I from our princely general   141
To know your griefs; to tell you from his
    grace
That he will give you audience; and wherein
It shall appear that your demands are just,
You shall enjoy them, every thing set off
That might so much as think you enemies.

Mowb. But he hath forced us to compel
    this offer;
And it proceeds from policy, not love.
    West. Mowbray, you overween to take it
    so;
This offer comes from mercy, not from fear:
For, lo! within a ken our army lies,   151
Upon mine honour, all too confident
To give admittance to a thought of fear.
Our battle is more full of names than yours,
Our men more perfect in the use of arms,
Our armour all as strong, our cause the best;
Then reason will our hearts should be as
    good:
Say you not then our offer is compell'd.
    Mowb. Well, by my will we shall admit no
    parley.
    West. That argues but the shame of your
    offence: 160
A rotten case abides no handling.
    Hast. Hath the Prince John a full com-
    mission,
In very ample virtue of his father,
To hear and absolutely to determine
Of what conditions we shall stand upon?
    West. That is intended in the general's
    name:
I muse you make so slight a question.
    Arch. Then take, my Lord of Westmore-
    land, this schedule,
For this contains our general grievances:
Each several article herein redress'd,   170
All members of our cause, both here and
    hence,
That are insinew'd to this action,
Acquitted by a true substantial form
And present execution of our wills
To us and to our purposes confined,
We come within our awful banks again
And knit our powers to the arm of peace.
    West. This will I show the general. Please
    you, lords,
In sight of both our battles we may meet;
And either end in peace, which God so
    frame!   180
Or to the place of difference call the swords
Which must decide it.
    Arch.   My lord, we will do so.
                          [*Exit West.*

---

116. **force perforce**, by violent constraint.   117 ff.
These lines give the subject of the play *Richard II.*   120.
armed staves, lances. **in charge**, in rest for the
charge. **beavers**, movable fronts of helmets. 121.
sights of steel, visors, eye-holes of the helmet. 125.
warder, staff of command. 131. **Earl of Hereford**,
title of King Henry IV in the earlier part of the play of
Richard II. 145. **set off**, put out of consideration.

149. **overween**, are arrogant or presumptuous. 151.
ken, seeing distance. 154. **names**, noble names. 163.
virtue, authority. 166. **intended**, understood, implied.
167. **muse**, wonder. **slight**, trivial. 172. **insinew'd**,
joined as by strong sinews. 176. **awful banks**, banks
or bounds of respect.

Mowb. There is a thing within my bosom tells me
That no conditions of our peace can stand.
　Hast. Fear you not that: if we can make our peace
Upon such large terms and so absolute
As our conditions shall consist upon,
Our peace shall stand as firm as rocky mountains.
　Mowb. Yea, but our valuation shall be such
That every slight and false-derived cause, 190
Yea, every idle, nice and wanton reason
Shall to the king taste of this action;
That, were our royal faiths martyrs in love,
We shall be winnow'd with so rough a wind
That even our corn shall seem as light as chaff
And good from bad find no partition.
　Arch. No, no, my lord. Note this; the king is weary
Of dainty and such picking grievances:
For he hath found to end one doubt by death
Revives two greater in the heirs of life, 200
And therefore will he wipe his tables clean
And keep no tell-tale to his memory
That may repeat and history his loss
To new remembrance; for full well he knows
He cannot so precisely weed this land
As his misdoubts present occasion:
His foes are so enrooted with his friends
That, plucking to unfix an enemy,
He doth unfasten so and shake a friend:
So that this land, like an offensive wife 210
That hath enraged him on to offer strokes,
As he is striking, holds his infant up
And hangs resolved correction in the arm
That was uprear'd to execution.
　Hast. Besides, the king hath wasted all his rods
On late offenders, that he now doth lack
The very instruments of chastisement:
So that his power, like to a fangless lion,
May offer, but not hold.
　Arch.　　　　　　'Tis very true:

And therefore be assured, my good lord marshal, 220
If we do now make our atonement well,
Our peace will, like a broken limb united,
Grow stronger for the breaking.
　Mowb.　　　　　　Be it so.
Here is return'd my Lord of Westmoreland.

Re-enter WESTMORELAND.

　West. The prince is here at hand: pleaseth your lordship
To meet his grace just distance 'tween our armies.
　Mowb. Your grace of York, in God's name, then, set forward.
　Arch. Before, and greet his grace: my lord, we come.　　　[*Exeunt.*

SCENE II. *Another part of the forest.*

Enter, from one side, MOWBRAY, *attended; afterwards the* ARCHBISHOP, HASTINGS, *and others: from the other side,* PRINCE JOHN OF LANCASTER, *and* WESTMORELAND; *Officers, and others with them.*

　Lan. You are well encounter'd here, my cousin Mowbray:
Good day to you, gentle lord archbishop;
And so to you, Lord Hastings, and to all.
My Lord of York, it better show'd with you
When that your flock, assembled by the bell,
Encircled you to hear with reverence
Your exposition on the holy text
Than now to see you here an iron man,
Cheering a rout of rebels with your drum, 9
Turning the word to sword and life to death.
That man that sits within a monarch's heart,
And ripens in the sunshine of his favour,
Would he abuse the countenance of the king,
Alack, what mischiefs might he set abroach
In shadow of such greatness! With you, lord bishop,
It is even so. Who hath not heard it spoken
How deep you were within the books of God?
To us the speaker in his parliament;
To us the imagined voice of God himself;
The very opener and intelligencer 20
Between the grace, the sanctities of heaven

189. **valuation**, what we are valued at. 193. **royal faiths**, allegiance to the king. He means: "were our integrity unimpeachable and our devotion to the throne that of martyrs." 198. **dainty**, over-particular. **picking**, fastidious. 203. **history**, record, chronicle. 206. **misdoubts**, suspicions. 210-214. **like . . . execution.** The figure is mixed by being partly simile and partly metaphor; the meaning is, however, clear. 210. **offensive wife**, wife having provoked her husband to offer blows. 213. **hangs resolved correction**, stops the punishment which had been determined upon. 216. **late**, other recent. 219. **May . . . hold**, offer violence, but not hold out in the purpose of carrying it out.

225. **pleaseth**, may it please. 226. **just**, exact. 228. **Before**, i.e., go before.
Scene ii. 8. **iron man**, warrior clad in armor. 14. **set abroach**, set on foot, begin. 17. **within the books**, in the good graces. 18. **speaker**, allusion to the speaker of the Parliament, who acted as the voice or interpreter of the house. 20. **opener**, revealer. **intelligencer**, interpreter, secret agent.

And our dull workings. O, who shall believe
But you misuse the reverence of your place,
Employ the countenance and grace of heaven,
As a false favourite doth his prince's name,
In deeds dishonourable? You have ta'en up,
Under the counterfeited zeal of God,
The subjects of his substitute, my father,
And both against the peace of heaven and
    him
Have here up-swarm'd them.
    Arch.   Good my Lord of Lancaster, 30
I am not here against your father's peace;
But, as I told my Lord of Westmoreland,
The time misorder'd doth, in common
    sense,
Crowd us and crush us to this monstrous
    form,
To hold our safety up. I sent your grace
The parcels and particulars of our grief,
The which hath been with scorn shoved
    from the court,
Whereon this Hydra son of war is born;
Whose dangerous eyes may well be charm'd
    asleep
With grant of our most just and right
    desires,   40
And true obedience, of this madness cured,
Stoop tamely to the foot of majesty.
    Mowb. If not, we ready are to try our
    fortunes
To the last man.
    Hast.   And though we here fall down,
We have supplies to second our attempt:
If they miscarry, theirs shall second them;
And so success of mischief shall be born
And heir from heir shall hold this quarrel up
Whiles England shall have generation.
    Lan. You are too shallow, Hastings, much
    too shallow,   50
To sound the bottom of the after-times.
    West. Pleaseth your grace to answer them
    directly
How far forth you do like their articles.
    Lan. I like them all, and do allow them
    well,

And swear here, by the honour of my blood,
My father's purposes have been mistook,
And some about him have too lavishly
Wrested his meaning and authority.
My lord, these griefs shall be with speed
    redress'd;
Upon my soul, they shall. If this may please
    you,   60
Discharge your powers unto their several
    counties,
As we will ours: and here between the armies
Let's drink together friendly and embrace,
That all their eyes may bear those tokens
    home
Of our restored love and amity.
    Arch. I take your princely word for these
    redresses.
    Lan. I give it you, and will maintain my
    word:
And thereupon I drink unto your grace.
    Hast. Go, captain, and deliver to the
    army
This news of peace: let them have pay, and
    part: 70
I know it will well please them. Hie thee,
    captain.   [*Exit Officer.*
    Arch. To you, my noble Lord of West-
    moreland.
    West. I pledge your grace; and, if you
    knew what pains
I have bestow'd to breed this present peace,
You would drink freely: but my love to ye
Shall show itself more openly hereafter.
    Arch. I do not doubt you.
    West.   I am glad of it.
Health to my lord and gentle cousin, Mow-
    bray.
    Mowb. You wish me health in very happy
    season;
For I am, on the sudden, something ill.   80
    Arch. Against ill chances men are ever
    merry;
But heaviness foreruns the good event.
    West. Therefore be merry, coz; since
    sudden sorrow
Serves to say thus, 'some good thing comes
    to-morrow.'
    Arch. Believe me, I am passing light in
    spirit.
    Mowb. So much the worse, if your own
    rule be true.   [*Shouts within.*

22. **dull workings**, stupid endeavors. 27. **zeal**.
Herford suggests a play on *seal*. 28. **substitute**. deputy.
Note the current theory of the position and function of
the king. In this speech the Prince gives a preliminary
justification of the breach of faith with the rebels, whom
he regarded as outside the pale of rectitude. 33. **time
misorder'd**, disorders of the time. 36. **parcels**, items,
parts. 38. **Hydra**. The Lernæan hydra was a fabulous
monster with several heads; when one was cut off, others
grew in its place. 42. **Stoop tamely**, yield, submit; a
metaphor from falconry. 45. **supplies**, forces in reserve. 47. **success**, succession. 49. **generation**, issue,
offspring. 54. **allow**, approve, sanction.

70. **part**, depart. 81. **Against**, when about to face.
85. **passing**, exceedingly.

Lan. The word of peace is render'd: hark, how they shout!

Mowb. This had been cheerful after victory.

Arch. A peace is of the nature of a conquest;

For then both parties nobly are subdued,   90
And neither party loser.

Lan.   Go, my lord,
And let our army be discharged too.
                        [*Exit Westmoreland.*

And, good my lord, so please you, let our trains

March by us, that we may peruse the men
We should have coped withal.

Arch.   Go, good Lord Hastings,
And, ere they be dismiss'd, let them march by.   [*Exit Hastings.*

Lan. I trust, lords, we shall lie to-night together.

Re-enter WESTMORELAND.

Now cousin, wherefore stands our army still?

West. The leaders, having charge from you to stand,

Will not go off until they hear you speak.   100

Lan. They know their duties.

Re-enter HASTINGS.

Hast. My lord, our army is dispersed already:

Like youthful steers unyoked, they take their courses

East, west, north, south; or, like a school broke up,

Each hurries toward his home and sporting-place.

West. Good tidings, my Lord Hastings; for the which

I do arrest thee, traitor, of high treason:

And you, lord archbishop, and you, lord Mowbray,

Of capital treason I attach you both.

Mowb. Is this proceeding just and honourable?

West. Is your assembly so?   111

Arch. Will you thus break your faith?

Lan.   I pawn'd thee none:

I promised you redress of these same grievances

Whereof you did complain; which, by mine honour,

I will perform with a most Christian care.

But for you, rebels, look to taste the due

Meet for rebellion and such acts as yours.

Most shallowly did you these arms commence,

Fondly brought here and foolishly sent hence.

Strike up our drums, pursue the scatter'd stray: 120

God, and not we, hath safely fought to-day.

Some guard these traitors to the block of death,

Treason's true bed and yielder up of breath.
                        [*Exeunt.*

SCENE III. *Another part of the forest.*

Alarum. Excursions. Enter FALSTAFF *and* COLEVILE, *meeting.*

Fal. What's your name, sir? of what condition are you, and of what place, I pray?

Cole. I am a knight, sir; and my name is Colevile of the dale.

Fal. Well, then, Colevile is your name, a knight is your degree, and your place the dale: Colevile shall be still your name, a traitor your degree, and the dungeon your place, a place deep enough; so shall you be still Colevile of the dale.   10

Cole. Are not you Sir John Falstaff?

Fal. As good a man as he, sir, whoe'er I am. Do ye yield, sir? or shall I sweat for you? If I do sweat, they are the drops of thy lovers, and they weep for thy death: therefore rouse up fear and trembling, and do observance to my mercy.

Cole. I think you are Sir John Falstaff, and in that thought yield me.   19

Fal. I have a whole school of tongues in this belly of mine, and not a tongue of them all speaks any other word but my name. An I had but a belly of any indifferency, I were simply the most active fellow in Europe: my womb, my womb, my womb, undoes me. Here comes our general.   26

---

94. **peruse,** survey. 95. **coped withal,** encountered, fought with. 109. **capital,** punishable by death. 112-123. **I pawn'd . . . breath.** Prince John's perfidy seems nowhere censured by Shakespeare; this possibly finds its explanation in the way in which the theory of the time regarded rebels. To modern ears the Prince's words seem false indeed. 112. **pawn'd,** pledged.

118. **shallowly,** without adequate cause. 120. **stray,** stragglers.

Scene iii. 2. **condition,** rank. 14. **drops,** tears. 17. **observance,** reverence, homage. 23. **indifferency,** moderate size. 25. **womb,** belly.

Enter PRINCE JOHN OF LANCASTER, WEST-
MORELAND, BLUNT, *and others.*

Lan. The heat is past; follow no further
　now:
Call in the powers, good cousin Westmore-
　land.　　　　　　　　　　[*Exit Westmoreland.*
Now, Falstaff, where have you been all this
　while?
When every thing is ended, then you come: 30
These tardy tricks of yours will, on my life,
One time or other break some gallows' back.

Fal. I would be sorry, my lord, but it
should be thus: I never knew yet but rebuke
and check was the reward of valour. Do
you think me a swallow, an arrow, or a
bullet? have I, in my poor and old motion,
the expedition of thought? I have speeded
hither with the very extremest inch of
possibility; I have foundered nine score and
odd posts: and here, travel-tainted as I am,
have, in my pure and immaculate valour,
taken Sir John Colevile of the dale, a most
furious knight and valorous enemy. But
what of that? he saw me, and yielded; that
I may justly say, with the hook-nosed fellow
of Rome, 'I came, saw, and overcame.'　　47

Lan. It was more of his courtesy than
your deserving.

Fal. I know not: here is he, and here
I yield him: and I beseech your grace, let it
be booked with the rest of this day's deeds;
or, by the Lord, I will have it in a particular
ballad else, with mine own picture on the
top on't, Colevile kissing my foot: to the
which course if I be enforced, if you do not
all show like gilt two-pences to me, and I in
the clear sky of fame o'ershine you as much
as the full moon doth the cinders of the element, which show like pins' heads to her,
believe not the word of the noble: therefore
let me have right, and let desert mount.　 61

Lan. Thine's too heavy to mount.

Fal. Let it shine, then.

Lan. Thine's too thick to shine.

Fal. Let it do something, my good lord,
that may do me good, and call it what you
will.

Lan. Is thy name Colevile?

Cole. It is, my lord.

Lan. A famous rebel art thou, Colevile. 69

Fal. And a famous true subject took him.

Cole. I am, my lord, but as my betters are
That led me hither: had they been ruled by
　me,
You should have won them dearer than you
　have.

Fal. I know not how they sold themselves:
but thou, like a kind fellow, gavest thyself
away gratis; and I thank thee for thee.

Re-enter WESTMORELAND.

Lan. Now, have you left pursuit?

West. Retreat is made and execution
　stay'd.

Lan. Send Colevile with his confederates
To York, to present execution:　　　　　80
Blunt, lead him hence; and see you guard
　him sure.
　　[*Exeunt Blunt and others with Colevile.*
And now dispatch we toward the court, my
　lords:
I hear the king my father is sore sick:
Our news shall go before us to his majesty,
Which, cousin, you shall bear to comfort
　him,
And we with sober speed will follow you.

Fal. My lord, I beseech you, give me leave
　to go
Through Gloucestershire: and, when you
　come to court,
Stand my good lord, pray, in your good
　report.

Lan. Fare you well, Falstaff: I, in my
　condition,　　　　　　　　　　　　90
Shall better speak of you than you deserve.
　　　　　　　　[*Exeunt all but Falstaff.*

Fal. I would you had but the wit: 'twere
better than your dukedom. Good faith, this
same young sober-blooded boy doth not love
me; nor a man cannot make him laugh; but
that's no marvel, he drinks no wine. There's
never none of these demure boys come to any
proof; for thin drink doth so over-cool their
blood, and making many fish-meals, that
they fall into a kind of male green-sickness;
and then, when they marry, they get

---

27. **heat,** pursuit, race.　38. **expedition,** speed.
41. **posts,** post-horses.　46. **hook-nosed fellow of
Rome,** Julius Cæsar.　53. **particular ballad,** allusion
to the practice of having broadside ballads written and
published.　58. **cinders of the element,** stars.　64.
thick, dim.

82. **dispatch we,** let us hasten.　92-135. **I would ...
to sack.** This famous speech on the virtue of sack
will be found to embody the current physiological conception of the action and virtue of wine in the human
system. There is back of it, however, the idea that
Falstaff is too excessive in his own practice to be a
proper proponent of the cause.　97. **come to any proof,**
turn out well.　100. **green-sickness,** a kind of anæmia
affecting young women.

wenches: they are generally fools and cowards; which some of us should be too, but for inflammation. A good sherris-sack hath a 103 two-fold operation in it. It ascends me into the brain; dries me there all the foolish and dull and crudy vapours which environ it; makes it apprehensive, quick, forgetive, full of nimble fiery and delectable shapes; which, delivered o'er to the voice, the tongue, which is the birth, becomes excellent wit. The second property of your excellent sherris is, the warming of the blood; which, before cold and settled, left the liver white and pale, which is the badge of pusillanimity and cowardice; but the sherris warms it and makes it course from the inwards to the parts extreme: it illumineth the face, which as a beacon gives warning to all the rest of this little kingdom, man, to arm; and then the vital commoners and inland petty spirits muster me all to their captain, the heart, 120 who, great and puffed up with this retinue, doth any deed of courage; and this valour comes of sherris. So that skill in the weapon is nothing without sack, for that sets it a-work; and learning a mere hoard of gold kept by a devil, till sack commences it and sets it in act and use. Hereof comes it that Prince Harry is valiant; for the cold blood he did naturally inherit of his father, he hath, like lean, sterile and bare land, manured, husbanded and tilled with excellent endeavour of drinking good and good store of fertile sherris, that he is become very hot and valiant. If I had a thousand sons, the first humane principle I would teach them should be, to forswear thin potations and to addict themselves to sack. 135

Enter BARDOLPH.

How now, Bardolph?

Bard. The army is discharged all and gone.

Fal. Let them go. I'll through Gloucestershire; and there will I visit Master Robert Shallow, esquire: I have him already tempering between my finger and my thumb,

and shortly will I seal with him. Come away.   [*Exeunt.*

SCENE IV. *Westminster. The Jerusalem Chamber.*

Enter the KING, *the* PRINCES THOMAS OF CLARENCE *and* HUMPHREY OF GLOUCESTER, WARWICK, *and others.*

King. Now, lords, if God doth give successful end
To this debate that bleedeth at our doors,
We will our youth lead on to higher fields
And draw no swords but what are sanctified.
Our navy is address'd, our power collected,
Our substitutes in absence well invested,
And every thing lies level to our wish:
Only, we want a little personal strength;
And pause us, till these rebels, now afoot,
Come underneath the yoke of government. 10
War. Both which we doubt not but your majesty
Shall soon enjoy.
King.   Humphrey, my son of Gloucester,
Where is the prince your brother?
Glou. I think he's gone to hunt, my lord, at Windsor.
King. And how accompanied?
Glou.   I do not know, my lord.
King. Is not his brother, Thomas of Clarence, with him?
Glou. No, my good lord; he is in presence here.
Clar. What would my lord and father?
King. Nothing but well to thee, Thomas of Clarence.
How chance thou art not with the prince thy brother?   20
He loves thee, and thou dost neglect him, Thomas;
Thou hast a better place in his affection
Than all thy brothers: cherish it, my boy,
And noble offices thou mayst effect
Of mediation, after I am dead,
Between his greatness and thy other brethren:
Therefore omit him not; blunt not his love,
Nor lose the good advantage of his grace
By seeming cold or careless of his will;

---

103. **inflammation**, excitement with liquor. **sherris-sack**, kind of wine imported from Spain. 106. **crudy**, defined as "thick"; wet and cold vapors were conducive to dullness. 107. **apprehensive**, quick to perceive. **forgetive**, seems to mean "inventive"; it has been connected with *forge*. 118. **little kingdom**, microcosm. Man was thought of as a microcosm corresponding in parts and qualities to the universe, or macrocosm. 140. **tempering**, softening (like a piece of wax).

Scene iv. 3. **higher fields**. He will lead them on a crusade. 5. **address'd**, ready, prepared. 6. **substitutes**, deputies. **invested**, i.e., with power. 7. **level**, conformable.

For he is gracious, if he be observed:　　30
He hath a tear for pity and a hand
Open as day for melting charity:
Yet notwithstanding, being incensed, he's
　　flint,
As humorous as winter and as sudden
As flaws congealed in the spring of day.
His temper, therefore, must be well observed:
Chide him for faults, and do it reverently,
When you perceive his blood inclined to
　　mirth;
But, being moody, give him line and scope,
Till that his passions, like a whale on ground,
Confound themselves with working. Learn
　　this, Thomas,　　41
And thou shalt prove a shelter to thy friends,
A hoop of gold to bind thy brothers in,
That the united vessel of their blood,
Mingled with venom of suggestion—
As, force perforce, the age will pour it in—
Shall never leak, though it do work as strong
As aconitum or rash gunpowder.
　　Clar. I shall observe him with all care and
　　love.
　　King. Why art thou not at Windsor with
　　him, Thomas?　　50
　　Clar. He is not there to-day; he dines in
　　London.
　　King. And how accompanied? canst thou
　　tell that?
　　Clar. With Poins, and other his continual
　　followers.
　　King. Most subject is the fattest soil to
　　weeds;
And he, the noble image of my youth,
Is overspread with them: therefore my grief
Stretches itself beyond the hour of death:
The blood weeps from my heart when I do
　　shape
In forms imaginary the unguided days
And rotten times that you shall look upon　　60
When I am sleeping with my ancestors.
For when his headstrong riot hath no curb,

When rage and hot blood are his counsellors,
When means and lavish manners meet to-
　　gether,
O, with what wings shall his affections fly
Towards fronting peril and opposed decay!
　　War. My gracious lord, you look beyond
　　him quite:
The prince but studies his companions
Like a strange tongue, wherein, to gain the
　　language,
'Tis needful that the most immodest word
Be look'd upon and learn'd; which once
　　attain'd,　　71
Your highness knows, comes to no further
　　use
But to be known and hated. So, like gross
　　terms,
The prince will in the perfectness of time
Cast off his followers; and their memory
Shall as a pattern or a measure live,
By which his grace must mete the lives of
　　others,
Turning past evils to advantages.
　　King. 'Tis seldom when the bee doth leave
　　her comb
In the dead carrion.

Enter WESTMORELAND.

　　Who's here? Westmoreland?　　80
　　West. Health to my sovereign, and new
　　happiness
Added to that that I am to deliver!
Prince John your son doth kiss your grace's
　　hand:
Mowbray, the Bishop Scroop, Hastings and
　　all
Are brought to the correction of your law;
There is not now a rebel's sword unsheathed,
But Peace puts forth her olive every where.
The manner how this action hath been borne
Here at more leisure may your highness read,
With every course in his particular.　　90
　　King. O Westmoreland, thou art a sum-
　　mer bird,
Which ever in the haunch of winter sings
The lifting up of day.

Enter HARCOURT.

　　Look, here's more news.

---

30. **observed,** paid proper respect. 32. **melting,** tearful. 33. **flint,** i.e., in emitting fire. 34. **humorous,** unpredictable in action. 35. **flaws,** defined as "snow" (Onions), or as "blades of ice seen at the edge of water on winter mornings" (Yale). **spring of day,** early morning. 36. **temper,** disposition, mood. 39. **moody,** angry. **line,** full play, scope. 40. **whale on ground.** Holinshed tells of a whale cast up on the coast of Kent in July, 1573, which, beating itself about in the sand, perished. 41. **Confound,** exhaust, consume. 44. **united . . . blood,** i.e., the king. 45. **suggestion,** incitement to wrong-doing. 47. **never leak,** an allusion to the belief that aconitum, or wolf's bane, was so powerful in its action that it could make its way through the strongest vessel. 58. **weeps from my heart,** an allusion to the belief that each sigh cost the heart a drop of blood.

64. **lavish,** unrestrained, licentious. 66. **fronting . . . decay,** danger and ruin which confront him. 67. **look beyond,** misjudge. 77. **mete,** measure. 79-80. **leave . . . carrion,** an expression of the belief that the Prince will not forsake his evil company. 90. **course,** proceeding. **his particular,** its detail. 92. **haunch,** latter end. 93. **lifting up,** dawn.

Har. From enemies heaven keep your majesty;
And, when they stand against you, may they fall
As those that I am come to tell you of!
The Earl Northumberland and the Lord Bardolph,
With a great power of English and of Scots,
Are by the sheriff of Yorkshire overthrown:
The manner and true order of the fight   100
This packet, please it you, contains at large.
     King. And wherefore should these good news make me sick?
Will Fortune never come with both hands full,
But write her fair words still in foulest letters?
She either gives a stomach and no food;
Such are the poor, in health; or else a feast
And takes away the stomach; such are the rich,
That have abundance and enjoy it not.
I should rejoice now at this happy news;
And now my sight fails, and my brain is giddy: 110
O me! come near me; now I am much ill.
     Glou. Comfort, your majesty!
     Clar.   O my royal father!
     West. My sovereign lord, cheer up yourself, look up.
     War. Be patient, princes; you do know, these fits
Are with his highness very ordinary.
Stand from him, give him air; he'll straight be well.
     Clar. No, no, he cannot long hold out these pangs:
The incessant care and labour of his mind
Hath wrought the mure that should confine it in
So thin that life looks through and will break out.   120
     Glou. The people fear me; for they do observe
Unfather'd heirs and loathly births of nature:
The seasons change their manners, as the year
Had found some months asleep and leap'd them over.

Clar. The river hath thrice flow'd, no ebb between;
And the old folk, time's doting chronicles,
Say it did so a little time before
That our great-grandsire, Edward, sick'd and died.
     War. Speak lower, princes, for the king recovers.
     Glou. This apoplexy will certain be his end.   130
     King. I pray you, take me up, and bear me hence
Into some other chamber: softly, pray.
                                   [*Exeunt.*

SCENE V. *Another chamber.*

The KING *lying on a bed:* CLARENCE, GLOUCESTER, WARWICK, *and others in attendance.*

     King. Let there be no noise made, my gentle friends;
Unless some dull and favourable hand
Will whisper music to my weary spirit.
     War. Call for the music in the other room.
     King. Set me the crown upon my pillow here.
     Clar. His eye is hollow, and he changes much.
     War. Less noise, less noise!

Enter PRINCE HENRY.

     Prince. Who saw the Duke of Clarence?
     Clar. I am here, brother, full of heaviness.
     Prince. How now! rain within doors, and none abroad!
How doth the king?   10
     Glou. Exceeding ill.
     Prince.   Heard he the good news yet!
Tell it him.
     Glou. He alter'd much upon the hearing it.
     Prince. If he be sick with joy, he'll recover without physic.
     War. Not so much noise, my lords: sweet prince, speak low;
The king your father is disposed to sleep.
     Clar. Let us withdraw into the other room.
     War. Will't please your grace to go along with us?

95. **stand against**, oppose in arms. 99. **sheriff of Yorkshire**, identified as Thomas de Rokeby. 119. **wrought the mure**, built the wall. 121. **fear**, frighten. 122. **Unfather'd**, supernaturally generated.

125. **The river . . . between.** This event is recorded by Holinshed as having happened on October 12, 1411. There are many cases in which Shakespeare follows Holinshed in recording portents in nature.
Scene v. 2. **dull**, soft, soothing. 3. **music**. The medical practice of the time attributed healing power to music. 6. **changes**, changes color, turns pale.

Prince. No; I will sit and watch here by
  the king. [*Exeunt all but the Prince.*   20
Why doth the crown lie there upon his
  pillow,
Being so troublesome a bedfellow?
O polish'd perturbation! golden care!
That keep'st the ports of slumber open wide
To many a watchful night! sleep with it now!
Yet not so sound and half so deeply sweet
As he whose brow with homely biggen
  bound
Snores out the watch of night. O majesty!
When thou dost pinch thy bearer, thou dost
  sit
Like a rich armour worn in heat of day,   30
That scalds with safety. By his gates of
  breath
There lies a downy feather which stirs not:
Did he suspire, that light and weightless
  down
Perforce must move. My gracious lord! my
  father!
This sleep is sound indeed; this is a sleep
That from this golden rigol hath divorced
So many English kings. Thy due from me
Is tears and heavy sorrows of the blood,
Which nature, love, and filial tenderness,
Shall, O dear father, pay thee plenteously: 40
My due from thee is this imperial crown,
Which, as immediate from thy place and
  blood,
Derives itself to me. Lo, here it sits,
Which God shall guard: and put the world's
  whole strength
Into one giant arm, it shall not force
This lineal honour from me: this from thee
Will I to mine leave, as 'tis left to me.
                                        [*Exit.*
  King. Warwick! Gloucester! Clarence!

Re-enter WARWICK, GLOUCESTER, CLARENCE,
                and the rest.

  Clar. Doth the king call?
  War. What would your majesty? How
  fares your grace?   50
  King. Why did you leave me here alone,
  my lords?

  Clar. We left the prince my brother here,
  my liege,
Who undertook to sit and watch by you.
  King. The Prince of Wales! Where is he?
  let me see him:
He is not here.
  War. This door is open; he is gone this
  way.
  Glou. He came not through the chamber
  where we stay'd.
  King. Where is the crown? who took it
  from my pillow?
  War. When we withdrew, my liege, we
  left it here.
  King. The prince hath ta'en it hence: go,
  seek him out.   60
Is he so hasty that he doth suppose
My sleep my death?
Find him, my Lord of Warwick; chide him
  hither.   [*Exit Warwick.*
This part of his conjoins with my disease,
And helps to end me. See, sons, what things
  you are!
How quickly nature falls into revolt
When gold becomes her object!
For this the foolish over-careful fathers
Have broke their sleep with thoughts, their
  brains with care,
Their bones with industry;   70
For this they have engross'd and piled up
The canker'd heaps of strange-achieved gold;
For this they have been thoughtful to invest
Their sons with arts and martial exercises:
When, like the bee, culling from every
  flower
The virtuous sweets,
Our thighs pack'd with wax, our mouths with
  honey,
We bring it to the hive, and, like the bees,
Are murdered for our pains. This bitter taste
Yield his engrossments to the ending father.

Re-enter WARWICK.

Now, where is he that will not stay so long   81
Till his friend sickness hath determined me?
  War. My lord, I found the prince in the
  next room,
Washing with kindly tears his gentle cheeks,

---

23. **perturbation**, agitation by the passions; here
used to mean the cause of agitation. 24. **ports**, gates.
25. **watchful**, wakeful. **sleep with it**, i.e., if you can.
27. **biggen**, nightcap. 28. **watch of night**, period of
night. 31. **scalds**, burns (while providing safety). 33.
suspire, breathe. 36. **rigol**, circle, crown. 38. **blood**,
usually taken as meaning the source of tears and sorrows; probably, parenthood, blood-kinship. 42. **immediate**, passing in direct succession.

64. **part**, act, action; or rôle (?) **conjoins**, unites,
joins. 69. **thoughts**, cares. 71. **engross'd**, amassed.
72. **canker'd**, corroded, tarnished. **strange-achieved**,
gained in strange ways. 79. **Are . . . pains**. It is the
drones, not the worker-bees, that are murdered. 80.
engrossments, stored-up treasures. 82. **determined**,
ended, put an end to. 84. **kindly**, natural.

With such a deep demeanour in great sorrow
That tyranny, which never quaff'd but blood,
Would, by beholding him, have wash'd his
    knife
With gentle eye-drops. He is coming hither.
  King. But wherefore did he take away
    the crown?

Re-enter PRINCE HENRY.

Lo, where he comes. Come hither to me,
    Harry.   90
Depart the chamber, leave us here alone.
            [*Exeunt Warwick and the rest.*
  Prince. I never thought to hear you speak
    again.
  King. Thy wish was father, Harry, to
    that thought:
I stay too long by thee, I weary thee.
Dost thou so hunger for mine empty chair
That thou wilt needs invest thee with my
    honours
Before thy hour be ripe? O foolish youth!
Thou seek'st the greatness that will over-
    whelm thee.
Stay but a little; for my cloud of dignity
Is held from falling with so weak a wind 100
That it will quickly drop: my day is dim.
Thou hast stolen that which after some few
    hours
Were thine without offence; and at my death
Thou hast seal'd up my expectation:
Thy life did manifest thou lovedst me not,
And thou wilt have me die assured of it.
Thou hidest a thousand daggers in thy
    thoughts,
Which thou hast whetted on thy stony heart,
To stab at half an hour of my life.
What! canst thou not forbear me half an
    hour?   110
Then get thee gone and dig my grave thy-
    self,
And bid the merry bells ring to thine ear
That thou art crowned, not that I am dead.
Let all the tears that should bedew my
    hearse
Be drops of balm to sanctify thy head:
Only compound me with forgotten dust;
Give that which gave thee life unto the
    worms.
Pluck down my officers, break my decrees;
For now a time is come to mock at form:

Harry the Fifth is crown'd: up, vanity!   120
Down, royal state! all you sage counsellors,
    hence!
And to the English court assemble now,
From every region, apes of idleness!
Now, neighbour confines, purge you of your
    scum:
Have you a ruffian that will swear, drink,
    dance,
Revel the night, rob, murder, and commit
The oldest sins the newest kind of ways?
Be happy, he will trouble you no more;
England shall double gild his treble guilt, 129
England shall give him office, honour, might;
For the fifth Harry from curb'd license
    plucks
The muzzle of restraint, and the wild dog
Shall flesh his tooth on every innocent.
O my poor kingdom, sick with civil blows!
When that my care could not withhold thy
    riots,
What wilt thou do when riot is thy care?
O, thou wilt be a wilderness again,
Peopled with wolves, thy old inhabitants!
  Prince. O, pardon me, my liege! but for
    my tears,
The moist impediments unto my speech,   140
I had forestall'd this dear and deep rebuke
Ere you with grief had spoke and I had
    heard
The course of it so far. There is your crown;
And He that wears the crown immortally
Long guard it yours! If I affect it more
Than as your honour and as your renown,
Let me no more from this obedience rise,
Which my most inward true and duteous
    spirit
Teacheth, this prostrate and exterior bend-
    ing.
God witness with me, when I here came in,150
And found no course of breath within your
    majesty,
How cold it struck my heart! If I do feign,
O, let me in my present wildness die
And never live to show the incredulous
    world
The noble change that I have purposed!
Coming to look on you, thinking you dead,
And dead almost, my liege, to think you
    were,

---

104. **seal'd up**, confirmed fully. 110. **forbear**, spare.
115. **balm**, consecrated oil used in anointing the king
at his coronation. 119. **form**, laws, orderly usages.

120. **vanity**, folly. 124. **neighbour confines**, territories of neighboring countries. 136. **care**, special study.
141. **dear and deep**, heartfelt and severe. 144. **immortally**, eternally. 145. **affect**, love, be fond of. 147.
obedience, obeisance. 148. **inward**, sincere.

I spake unto this crown as having sense,
And thus upbraided it: 'The care on thee
　　depending
Hath fed upon the body of my father;　　160
Therefore, thou best of gold art worst of
　　gold:
Other, less fine in carat, is more precious,
Preserving life in medicine potable;
But thou, most fine, most honour'd, most
　　renown'd,
Hath eat thy bearer up.' Thus, my most
　　royal liege,
Accusing it, I put it on my head,
To try with it, as with an enemy
That had before my face murder'd my
　　father,
The quarrel of a true inheritor.
But if it did infect my blood with joy,　　170
Or swell my thoughts to any strain of pride;
If any rebel or vain spirit of mine
Did with the least affection of a welcome
Give entertainment to the might of it,
Let God for ever keep it from my head
And make me as the poorest vassal is
That doth with awe and terror kneel to it!
　　King. O my son,
God put it in thy mind to take it hence,
That thou mightst win the more thy father's
　　love,　　180
Pleading so wisely in excuse of it!
Come hither, Harry, sit thou by my bed;
And hear, I think, the very latest counsel
That ever I shall breathe. God knows, my
　　son,
By what by-paths and indirect crook'd ways
I met this crown; and I myself know well
How troublesome it sat upon my head.
To thee it shall descend with better quiet,
Better opinion, better confirmation;
For all the soil of the achievement goes　　190
With me into the earth. It seem'd in me
But as an honour snatch'd with boisterous
　　hand,
And I had many living to upbraid
My gain of it by their assistances;
Which daily grew to quarrel and to blood-
　　shed,

Wounding supposed peace: all these bold
　　fears
Thou see'st with peril I have answered;
For all my reign hath been but as a scene
Acting that argument: and now my death
Changes the mode; for what in me was pur-
　　chased,　　200
Falls upon thee in a more fairer sort;
So thou the garland wear'st successively.
Yet, though thou stand'st more sure than I
　　could do,
Thou art not firm enough, since griefs are
　　green;
And all my friends, which thou must make
　　thy friends,
Have but their stings and teeth newly ta'en
　　out;
By whose fell working I was first advanced
And by whose power I well might lodge a
　　fear
To be again displaced: which to avoid,
I cut them off; and had a purpose now,　　210
To lead out many to the Holy Land,
Lest rest and lying still might make them
　　look
Too near unto my state. Therefore, my
　　Harry,
Be it thy course to busy giddy minds
With foreign quarrels; that action, hence
　　borne out,
May waste the memory of the former days.
More would I, but my lungs are wasted so
That strength of speech is utterly denied me.
How I came by the crown, O God forgive;
And grant it may with thee in true peace
　　live!　　220
　　Prince. My gracious liege,
You won it, wore it, kept it, gave it me;
Then plain and right must my possession be:
Which I with more than with a common pain
'Gainst all the world will rightfully maintain.

Enter LORD JOHN OF LANCASTER.

　　King. Look, look, here comes my John of
　　Lancaster.
　　Lan. Health, peace, and happiness to my
　　royal father!

---

162. **carat**, standard of fineness in gold. **precious**, double meaning suggesting, besides the usual sense, the idea of curing. 163. **medicine potable**, potable gold, an elixir, thought from Galen's time to possess magical power to cure. 169. **inheritor**, owner. 171. **strain**, height of emotion. 172. **vain**, vainglorious. 173. **affection**, inclination of mind. 188. **quiet**, by some defined as "conscience"; more probably, peace and acquiescence. 189. **opinion**, public opinion, reputation.

200. **mode**, key in which music is written; here suggestive of *mood*, state of mind. **purchased**, acquired by doubtful means. 201. **sort**, manner, way. 202. **successively**, by right of succession. 204. **green**, fresh. 207. **fell working**, evil effort. 214-216. **Be it . . . days**. The idea expressed in these lines was a commonly held political doctrine of the time. 215. **hence**, in other lands. 216. **waste**, efface, obliterate.

King. Thou bring'st me happiness and peace, son John;
But health, alack, with youthful wings is flown
From this bare wither'd trunk: upon thy sight 230
My worldly business makes a period.
Where is my Lord of Warwick?
Prince. My Lord of Warwick!

Re-enter WARWICK, *and others.*

King. Doth any name particular belong
Unto the lodging where I first did swoon?
War. 'Tis call'd Jerusalem, my noble lord.
King. Laud be to God! even there my life must end.
It hath been prophesied to me many years,
I should not die but in Jerusalem;
Which vainly I supposed the Holy Land: 239
But bear me to that chamber; there I'll lie;
In that Jerusalem shall Harry die.

[*Exeunt.*

ACT V.

SCENE I. *Gloucestershire.* SHALLOW'S *house.*

Enter SHALLOW, FALSTAFF, BARDOLPH, *and* Page.

Shal. By cock and pie, sir, you shall not away to-night. What, Davy, I say!
Fal. You must excuse me, Master Robert Shallow.
Shal. I will not excuse you; you shall not be excused; excuses shall not be admitted; there is no excuse shall serve; you shall not be excused. Why, Davy!

Enter DAVY.

Davy. Here, sir. 9
Shal. Davy, Davy, Davy, Davy, let me see, Davy; let me see, Davy; let me see: yea, marry, William cook, bid him come hither. Sir John, you shall not be excused.
Davy. Marry, sir, thus; those precepts cannot be served: and, again, sir, shall we sow the headland with wheat?
Shal. With red wheat, Davy. But for William cook: are there no young pigeons?
Davy. Yes, sir. Here is now the smith's note for shoeing and plough-irons. 20
Shal. Let it be cast and paid. Sir John, you shall not be excused.
Davy. Now, sir, a new link to the bucket must needs be had: and, sir, do you mean to stop any of William's wages, about the sack he lost the other day at Hinckley fair?
Shal. A' shall answer it. Some pigeons, Davy, a couple of short-legged hens, a joint of mutton, and any pretty little tiny kickshaws, tell William cook. 30
Davy. Doth the man of war stay all night, sir?
Shal. Yea, Davy. I will use him well: a friend i' the court is better than a penny in purse. Use his men well, Davy; for they are arrant knaves, and will backbite.
Davy. No worse than they are backbitten, sir; for they have marvellous foul linen.
Shal. Well conceited, Davy: about thy business, Davy. 40
Davy. I beseech you, sir, to countenance William Visor of Woncot against Clement Perkes of the hill.
Shal. There is many complaints, Davy, against that Visor: that Visor is an arrant knave, on my knowledge.
Davy. I grant your worship that he is a knave, sir; but yet, God forbid, sir, but a knave should have some countenance at his friend's request. An honest man, sir, is able to speak for himself, when a knave is not. I have served your worship truly, sir, this eight years; and if I cannot once or twice in a quarter bear out a knave against an honest man, I have but a very little credit with your worship. The knave is mine honest friend, sir; therefore, I beseech your worship, let him be countenanced. 57
Shal. Go to; I say he shall have no wrong. Look about, Davy. [*Exit Davy.*] Where are

231. **makes a period,** comes to an end, rounds out a whole (as a sentence ends). 234. **lodging,** apartment. 235. **Jerusalem,** a chamber adjoining the southwest tower of Westminster Abbey, so called perhaps from tapestries hung there which depicted matters connected with Jerusalem. This chamber was the traditional place of the king's death, and its occurrence there was regarded as the fulfillment of the prophecy referred to.
Act V. Scene i. 1. **cock and pie,** a trivial oath. 2. **What,** an exclamation of impatience. 14. **precepts,** writs requiring something to be done.

15. **served,** executed, fulfilled. 16. **headland,** strip of plowed land at the end of furrows; Q: *hade land,* which might mean "high land." 26. **Hinckley,** market town in Leicestershire. 27. **answer,** pay for. 29. **kickshaws,** fancy dishes; from French *quelque chose.* 39. **Well conceited,** ingeniously punned. 41. **countenance,** favor. 42-3. **Visor, Perkes.** Madden identified these names in Gloucestershire records. It is therefore thought that Shakespeare must have had intimate knowledge of Gloucestershire. 53. **bear out,** testify in favor of. 59. **Look about,** look sharp, be on the alert.

you, Sir John? Come, come, come, off with your boots. Give me your hand, Master Bardolph.

Bard. I am glad to see your worship.

Shal. I thank thee with all my heart, kind Master Bardolph: and welcome, my tall fellow [*to the Page*]. Come, Sir John.   66

Fal. I'll follow you, good Master Robert Shallow. [*Exit Shallow.*] Bardolph, look to our horses. [*Exeunt Bardolph and Page.*] If I were sawed into quantities, I should make four dozen of such bearded hermit's staves as Master Shallow. It is a wonderful thing to see the semblable coherence of his men's spirits and his: they, by observing of him, do bear themselves like foolish justices; he, by conversing with them, is turned into a justice-like serving-man: their spirits are so married in conjunction with the participation of society that they flock together in consent, like so many wild-geese. If I had   79 a suit to Master Shallow, I would humour his men with the imputation of being near their master: if to his men, I would curry with Master Shallow that no man could better command his servants. It is certain that either wise bearing or ignorant carriage is caught, as men take diseases, one of another: therefore let men take heed of their company. I will devise matter enough out of this Shallow to keep Prince Harry in continual laughter the wearing out of six fashions, which is four terms, or two actions, and a' shall laugh without intervallums. O, it is much that a lie with a slight oath and a jest with a sad brow will do with a fellow that never had the ache in his shoulders! O, you shall see him laugh till his face be like a wet cloak ill laid up!   95

Shal. [*Within*] Sir John!

Fal. I come Master Shallow; I come, Master Shallow.   [*Exit.*

SCENE II. *Westminster. The palace.*

Enter WARWICK *and the* LORD CHIEF-
JUSTICE, *meeting.*

War. How now, my lord chief-justice! whither away?

Ch. Just. How doth the king?

War. Exceeding well; his cares are now all ended.

Ch. Just. I hope, not dead.

War.   He's walk'd the way of nature;
And to our purposes he lives no more.

Ch. Just. I would his majesty had call'd me with him:
The service that I truly did his life
Hath left me open to all injuries.

War. Indeed I think the young king loves you not.

Ch. Just. I know he doth not, and do arm myself   10
To welcome the condition of the time,
Which cannot look more hideously upon me
Than I have drawn it in my fantasy.

Enter LANCASTER, CLARENCE, GLOUCESTER,
WESTMORELAND, *and others.*

War. Here come the heavy issue of dead Harry:
O that the living Harry had the temper
Of him, the worst of these three gentlemen!
How many nobles then should hold their places,
That must strike sail to spirits of vile sort!

Ch. Just. O God, I fear all will be overturn'd!

Lan. Good morrow, cousin Warwick, good morrow.   20

Glou. } Good morrow, cousin.
Clar. }

Lan. We meet like men that had forgot to speak.

War. We do remember; but our argument
Is all too heavy to admit much talk.

Lan. Well, peace be with him that hath made us heavy!

Ch. Just. Peace be with us, lest we be heavier!

Glou. O, good my lord, you have lost a friend indeed;
And I dare swear you borrow not that face
Of seeming sorrow, it is sure your own.

Lan. Though no man be assured what grace to find,   30
You stand in coldest expectation:
I am the sorrier; would 'twere otherwise.

Clar. Well, you must now speak Sir John Falstaff fair;

Which swims against your stream of quality.
  Ch. Just. Sweet princes, what I did, I did in honour,
Led by the impartial conduct of my soul;
And never shall you see that I will beg
A ragged and forestall'd remission.
If truth and upright innocency fail me,
I'll to the king my master that is dead,   40
And tell him who hath sent me after him.
  War. Here comes the prince.

Enter KING HENRY *the Fifth, attended.*

  Ch. Just. Good morrow; and God save your majesty!
  King. This new and gorgeous garment, majesty,
Sits not so easy on me as you think.
Brothers, you mix your sadness with some fear:
This is the English, not the Turkish court;
Not Amurath an Amurath succeeds,
But Harry Harry. Yet be sad, good brothers,
For, by my faith, it very well becomes you: 50
Sorrow so royally in you appears
That I will deeply put the fashion on
And wear it in my heart: why then, be sad;
But entertain no more of it, good brothers,
Than a joint burden laid upon us all.
For me, by heaven, I bid you be assured,
I'll be your father and your brother too;
Let me but bear your love, I'll bear your cares:
Yet weep that Harry's dead; and so will I;
But Harry lives, that shall convert those tears   60
By number into hours of happiness.
  Princes. We hope no other from your majesty.
  King. You all look strangely on me: and you most;
You are, I think, assured I love you not.
  Ch. Just. I am assured, if I be measured rightly,
Your majesty hath no just cause to hate me.
  King. No!
How might a prince of my great hopes forget
So great indignities you laid upon me?
What! rate, rebuke, and roughly send to prison   70

The immediate heir of England! Was this easy?
May this be wash'd in Lethe, and forgotten?
  Ch. Just. I then did use the person of your father;
The image of his power lay then in me:
And, in the administration of his law,
Whiles I was busy for the commonwealth,
Your highness pleased to forget my place,
The majesty and power of law and justice,
The image of the king whom I presented,
And struck me in my very seat of judgement;
Whereon, as an offender to your father,   81
I gave bold way to my authority
And did commit you. If the deed were ill,
Be you contented, wearing now the garland,
To have a son set your decrees at nought,
To pluck down justice from your awful bench,
To trip the course of law and blunt the sword
That guards the peace and safety of your person;
Nay, more, to spurn at your most royal image
And mock your workings in a second body.   90
Question your royal thoughts, make the case yours;
Be now the father and propose a son,
Hear your own dignity so much profaned,
See your most dreadful laws so loosely slighted,
Behold yourself so by a son disdain'd;
And then imagine me taking your part
And in your power soft silencing your son:
After this cold considerance, sentence me;
And, as you are a king, speak in your state
What I have done that misbecame my place,
My person, or my liege's sovereignty.   101
  King. You are right, justice, and you weigh this well;
Therefore still bear the balance and the sword;
And I do wish your honours may increase,
Till you do live to see a son of mine
Offend you and obey you, as I did.
So shall I live to speak my father's words:

---

34. **swims . . . quality**, goes against the current of your honor. 38. **A ragged . . . remission**, a half-hearted (*beggarly*) pardon, which is sure to be refused, or whose effect is gone before it is granted. 48. **Amurath**, one of the few contemporary allusions in the play. The Turkish sultan Amurath IV succeeded his father in 1596; he called his brothers to a feast and had them strangled. 62. **no other**, nothing else.

71. **immediate heir**, next heir in succession. **easy**, of small importance. 72. **wash'd in Lethe**, forgotten; an allusion to the river of forgetfulness in Hades. 73-121. **I then . . . directions**. This episode, derived from Sir Thomas Elyot's *Governour*, figured largely in all the accounts of the reformation of Prince Hal, including *The Famous Victories*. 73. **use the person**, make use of my prerogative as personal representative. 79. **image**, counterpart. **presented**, impersonated. 83. **commit**, i.e., to prison. 86. **awful**, commanding awe. 90. **second body**, representative. 92. **propose**, imagine, suppose. 97. **soft**, gently. 98. **cold considerance**, calm reflection. 99. **state**, condition or capacity as king. 103. **balance, sword**, emblems of justice.

'Happy am I, that have a man so bold,
That dares do justice on my proper son;
And not less happy, having such a son,   110
That would deliver up his greatness so
Into the hands of justice.' You did commit
    me:
For which, I do commit into your hand
The unstained sword that you have used to
    bear;
With this remembrance, that you use the
    same
With the like bold, just and impartial spirit
As you have done 'gainst me. There is my
    hand.
You shall be as a father to my youth:
My voice shall sound as you do prompt mine
    ear,
And I will stoop and humble my intents 120
To your well-practised wise directions.
And, princes all, believe me, I beseech you:
My father is gone wild into his grave,
For in his tomb lie my affections;
And with his spirit sadly I survive,
To mock the expectation of the world,
To frustrate prophecies and to raze out
Rotten opinion, who hath writ me down
After my seeming. The tide of blood in me
Hath proudly flow'd in vanity till now: 130
Now doth it turn and ebb back to the sea,
Where it shall mingle with the state of
    floods
And flow henceforth in formal majesty.
Now call we our high court of parliament:
And let us choose such limbs of noble counsel,
That the great body of our state may go
In equal rank with the best govern'd nation;
That war, or peace, or both at once, may be
As things acquainted and familiar to us;
In which you, father, shall have foremost
    hand.
Our coronation done, we will accite,   141
As I before remember'd, all our state:
And, God consigning to my good intents,
No prince nor peer shall have just cause to
    say,
God shorten Harry's happy life one day!
    [Exeunt.

SCENE III.   *Gloucestershire.*   SHALLOW'S
    orchard.

Enter FALSTAFF, SHALLOW, SILENCE, DAVY,
    BARDOLPH, *and the* Page.

Shal. Nay, you shall see my orchard,
where, in an arbour, we will eat a last year's
pippin of my own graffing, with a dish of
caraways, and so forth: come, cousin Silence:
and then to bed.

Fal. 'Fore God, you have here a goodly
dwelling and a rich.

Shal. Barren, barren, barren; beggars all,
beggars all, Sir John: marry, good air.
Spread, Davy; spread, Davy: well said,
Davy.   10

Fal. This Davy serves you for good uses;
he is your serving-man and your husband.

Shal. A good varlet, a good varlet, a very
good varlet, Sir John: by the mass, I have
drunk too much sack at supper: a good
varlet. Now sit down, now sit down: come,
cousin.

Sil. Ah, sirrah! quoth-a, we shall
Do nothing but eat, and make good cheer,
    [*Singing.*
And praise God for the merry year;
When flesh is cheap and females dear,   20
And lusty lads roam here and there
        So merrily,
And ever among so merrily.

Fal. There's a merry heart! Good Master
Silence, I'll give you a health for that
anon.

Shal. Give Master Bardolph some wine,
Davy.   27

Davy. Sweet sir, sit; I'll be with you anon;
most sweet sir, sit. Master page, good master
page, sit. Proface! What you want in meat,
we'll have in drink: but you must bear; the
heart's all.   [*Exit.*

Shal. Be merry, Master Bardolph; and,
my little soldier there, be merry.

Sil. Be merry, be merry, my wife has all;
    [*Singing.*
For women are shrews, both short and tall:

115. remembrance, reminder, admonition. 123-24.
My . . . affections. He means that, since his own
wildness has disappeared with his father's death, that
wildness is buried along with his father. 127. raze
out, erase. 129. After my seeming, according to
what I seemed. 132. state of floods, majesty of ocean.
135. limbs, members. 137. equal rank, step by step.
141. accite, summon. 142. remember'd, mentioned.
state, governing body of nobles. 143. consigning to,
sanctioning.

3. graffing, grafting. 4. caraways, sweetmeats
containing caraway seeds. 9. Spread, spread the cloth.
said, done. 12. husband, manager of the household.
13. varlet, servant; normally used in a bad sense, but
here affectionately. 17. sirrah, address to subordinates;
here addressed by the singer to himself. quoth-a, said
he (the singer). 23. ever among, all the while. 30.
Proface, formula of welcome to a meal, meaning "May
it do you good." 30-31. What . . . drink, a proverbial
saying. want, lack. 31. bear, be forbearing, excuse
the deficiencies of the entertainment.

'Tis merry in hall when beards wag all,
And welcome merry Shrove-tide.
Be merry, be merry.

Fal. I did not think Master Silence had
been a man of this mettle.   41

Sil. Who, I? I have been merry twice
and once ere now.

Re-enter Davy

Davy. There's a dish of leather-coats for
you.   [*To Bardolph.*

Shal. Davy!

Davy. Your worship! I'll be with you
straight [*to Bardolph*]. A cup of wine, sir?

Sil. A cup of wine that's brisk and fine,
[*Singing.*
And drink unto the leman mine;
And a merry heart lives long-a. 50

Fal. Well said, Master Silence.

Sil. An we shall be merry, now comes in
the sweet o' the night.

Fal. Health and long life to you, Master
Silence.

Sil. Fill the cup, and let it come; [*Singing.*
I'll pledge you a mile to the bottom.

Shal. Honest Bardolph, welcome: if thou
wantest any thing, and wilt not call, beshrew
thy heart. Welcome, my little tiny thief [*to
the Page*], and welcome indeed too. I'll
drink to Master Bardolph, and to all the
cavaleros about London.   63

Davy. I hope to see London once ere I die.

Bard. An I might see you there, Davy,—

Shal. By the mass, you'll crack a quart together, ha! will you not, Master Bardolph?

Bard. Yea, sir, in a pottle-pot.

Shal. By God's liggens, I thank thee: the
knave will stick by thee, I can assure thee
that. A' will not out; he is true bred.   71

Bard. And I'll stick by him, sir.

Shal. Why, there spoke a king. Lack nothing: be merry. [*Knocking within.*] Look
who's at door there, ho! who knocks?
[*Exit Davy.*

Fal. Why, now you have done me right.
[*To Silence, seeing him take off a bumper.*

Sil.   Do me right,   [*Singing.*

And dub me knight:
Samingo.

Is't not so?   80

Fal. 'Tis so.

Sil. Is't so? Why then, say an old man
can do somewhat.

Re-enter Davy.

Davy. An't please your worship, there's
one Pistol come from the court with news.

Fal. From the court! let him come in.

Enter Pistol.

How now, Pistol!

Pist. Sir John, God save you!   88

Fal. What wind blew you hither, Pistol?

Pist. Not the ill wind which blows no
man to good. Sweet knight, thou art now
one of the greatest men in this realm.

Sil. By'r lady, I think a' be, but goodman
Puff of Barson.

Pist. Puff!
Puff in thy teeth, most recreant coward base!
Sir John, I am thy Pistol and thy friend,
And helter-skelter have I rode to thee,
And tidings do I bring and lucky joys   99
And golden times and happy news of price.

Fal. I pray thee now, deliver them like a
man of this world.

Pist. A foutre for the world and worldlings base!
I speak of Africa and golden joys.

Fal. O base Assyrian knight, what is thy
news?
Let King Cophetua know the truth thereof.

Sil. And Robin Hood, Scarlet, and John.
[*Singing.*

Pist. Shall dunghill curs confront the
Helicons?
And shall good news be baffled?
Then, Pistol, lay thy head in Furies' lap. 110

Shal. Honest gentleman, I know not your
breeding.

37. **'Tis . . . all**, an old English proverb. 38. **Shrove-
tide**, the day before Ash-Wednesday; a season of merry-
making. 42. **twice and once**, adverbial expression denoting something like "now and again." 44. **leather-
coats**, russet apples. 48. **brisk**, agreeably sharp to the
taste. **fine**, clear. 49. **leman**, sweetheart. 57. **mile**,
i.e., if it were a mile. 63. **cavaleros**, cavaliers. 69.
liggens, an original oath of Shallow's. 71. **will not out**,
will not fail you. 77. **Do me right**, pledge me.

78-79. **dub . . . Samingo**, fragment of a drinking song,
with an allusion to the selection of one to be dubbed
knight in the drinking bout; *Samingo* is a refrain; it appears also as "San Domingo." 83. **somewhat**, something. 93. **but**, except. **goodman Puff of Barson**,
an allusion to some fat man not known. 102. **man of
this world**, ordinary man. 103. **foutre**, a contemptuous expression. 104. **Africa**, fabled for wealth. 106.
Cophetua. King Cophetua married a beggar maid
according to the popular ballad, *King Cophetua and the
Beggar-Maid*. 107. **And . . . John**, a scrap from the
ballad, *Robin Hood and the Pinner of Wakefield*. 108.
Helicons. Helicon was the abode of the Muses; Pistol
resents the intrusion of Robin Hood. 109. **baffled**,
treated with contumely. 112. **breeding**, parentage,
rank.

Pist. Why then, lament therefore.

Shal. Give me pardon, sir: if, sir, you come with news from the court, I take it there's but two ways, either to utter them, or to conceal them. I am, sir, under the king, in some authority.   118

Pist. Under which king, Besonian? speak, or die.

Shal. Under King Harry.

Pist.   Harry the Fourth? or Fifth?

Shal. Harry the Fourth.

Pist.   A foutre for thine office!   121
Sir John, thy tender lambkin now is king;
Harry the Fifth's the man. I speak the
    truth:
When Pistol lies, do this; and fig me, like
The bragging Spaniard.

Fal. What, is the old king dead?

Pist. As nail in door: the things I speak are just.

Fal. Away, Bardolph! saddle my horse.
Master Robert Shallow, choose what office
thou wilt in the land, 'tis thine. Pistol, I
will double-charge thee with dignities.   131

Bard. O joyful day!
I would not take a knighthood for my
    fortune.

Pist. What! I do bring good news.

Fal. Carry Master Silence to bed. Master
Shallow, my Lord Shallow,—be what thou
wilt; I am fortune's steward—get on thy
boots: we'll ride all night. O sweet Pistol!
Away, Bardolph! [*Exit Bard.*] Come, Pistol,
utter more to me; and withal devise something to do thyself good. Boot, boot,
Master Shallow: I know the young king is
sick for me. Let us take any man's horses;
the laws of England are at my commandment. Blessed are they that have been
my friends; and woe to my lord chief-
justice!   145

Pist. Let vultures vile seize on his lungs
    also!
'Where is the life that late I led?' say they:
Why, here it is; welcome these pleasant
    days!   [*Exeunt.*

Scene IV. *London. A street.*

Enter Beadles, *dragging in* Hostess
Quickly *and* Doll Tearsheet.

Host. No, thou arrant knave; I would to
God that I might die, that I might have thee
hanged: thou hast drawn my shoulder out
of joint.

First Bead. The constables have delivered
her over to me; and she shall have whipping-
cheer enough, I warrant her: there hath been
a man or two lately killed about her.   7

Dol. Nut-hook, nut-hook, you lie. Come
on; I'll tell thee what, thou damned tripe-
visaged rascal, an the child I now go with do
miscarry, thou wert better thou hadst struck
thy mother, thou paper-faced villain.

Host. O the Lord, that Sir John were
come! he would make this a bloody day to
somebody. But I pray God the fruit of her
womb miscarry!

First Bead. If it do, you shall have a dozen
of cushions again; you have but eleven now.
Come, I charge you both go with me; for the
man is dead that you and Pistol beat
amongst you.   19

Dol. I'll tell you what, you thin man in a
censer, I will have you as soundly swinged
for this,—you blue-bottle rogue, you filthy
famished correctioner, if you be not swinged,
I'll forswear half-kirtles.

First Bead. Come, come, you she knight-
errant, come.

Host. O God, that right should thus overcome might! Well, of sufferance comes
ease.

Dol. Come, you rogue, come; bring me to
a justice.   30

Host. Ay, come, you starved blood-hound.

Dol. Goodman death, goodman bones!

Host. Thou atomy, thou!

Dol. Come, you thin thing; come, you
rascal.

First Bead. Very well.   [*Exeunt.*

119. **Besonian,** beggar; probably a low, beggarly
soldier. Shallow is thus designated because of his
assertion of authority. 124. **do this.** Pistol makes
a vulgar gesture, said to consist in thrusting the thumb
between the first and middle finger; in any case, to make
such gesture was called *to fig.* 142-145. **Let us . . .
chief-justice.** Those who take seriously the danger
to the realm from Falstaff before his rejection stress
this passage. 147. '**Where . . . led?**' fragment of a
ballad.

3. **shoulder out of joint,** a reference to the rough
methods of arrest in vogue. 5. **whipping-cheer,**
banquet of lashes with a whip. 7. **about her,** in her company. 8. **Nut-hook,** hook for pulling down branches in
nutting; here, a constable. 9-12. **tripe-visaged . . .
paper-faced,** allusions to the sallow complexion of the
first Beadle. 20. **thin . . . censer,** probable allusion to
the figure of a man embossed on the lid of the censer,
or perfume pan. 22. **blue-bottle,** an allusion to the
beadle's blue coat. 23. **correctioner,** one who administered correction. 24. **half-kirtle,** probably, a
short petticoat which was attached to a jacket, the two
together forming a kirtle. 28. **sufferance,** suffering.
33. **atomy,** skeleton.

Scene V. *A public place near Westminster Abbey.*

Enter two Grooms, *strewing rushes.*

First Groom. More rushes, more rushes.
Sec. Groom. The trumpets have sounded twice.
First Groom. 'Twill be two o'clock ere they come from the coronation: dispatch, dispatch. [*Exeunt.*

Enter Falstaff, Shallow, Pistol, Bardolph, *and* Page.

Fal. Stand here by me, Master Robert Shallow; I will make the king do you grace: I will leer upon him as a' comes by; and do but mark the countenance that he will give me.
Pist. God bless thy lungs, good knight. 9
Fal. Come here, Pistol; stand behind me. O, if I had had time to have made new liveries, I would have bestowed the thousand pound I borrowed of you. But 'tis no matter; this poor show doth better: this doth infer the zeal I had to see him.
Shal. It doth so.
Fal. It shows my earnestness of affection,—
Shal. It doth so.
Fal. My devotion,—
Shal. It doth, it doth, it doth. 20
Fal. As it were, to ride day and night; and not to deliberate, not to remember, not to have patience to shift me,—
Shal. It is best, certain.
Fal. But to stand stained with travel, and sweating with desire to see him; thinking of nothing else, putting all affairs else in oblivion, as if there were nothing else to be done but to see him. 29
Pist. 'Tis 'semper idem,' for 'obsque hoc nihil est:' 'tis all in every part.
Shal. 'Tis so, indeed.
Pist. My knight, I will inflame thy noble liver,
And make thee rage.
Thy Doll, and Helen of thy noble thoughts,
Is in base durance and contagious prison;
Haled thither

By most mechanical and dirty hand:
Rouse up revenge from ebon den with fell Alecto's snake,
For Doll is in. Pistol speaks nought but truth. 40
Fal. I will deliver her.
[*Shouts within, and the trumpets sound.*
Pist. There roar'd the sea, and trumpet-clangor sounds.

Enter the King *and his train, the* Lord Chief-Justice *among them.*

Fal. God save thy grace, King Hal! my royal Hal!
Pist. The heavens thee guard and keep, most royal imp of fame!
Fal. God save thee, my sweet boy!
King. My lord chief-justice, speak to that vain man.
Ch. Just. Have you your wits? know you what 'tis you speak?
Fal. My king! my Jove! I speak to thee, my heart! 50
King. I know thee not, old man: fall to thy prayers;
How ill white hairs become a fool and jester!
I have long dream'd of such a kind of man,
So surfeit-swell'd, so old and so profane;
But, being awaked, I do despise my dream.
Make less thy body hence, and more thy grace;
Leave gormandizing; know the grave doth gape
For thee thrice wider than for other men.
Reply not to me with a fool-born jest:
Presume not that I am the thing I was; 60
For God doth know, so shall the world perceive,
That I have turn'd away my former self;
So will I those that kept me company.
When thou dost hear I am as I have been,
Approach me, and thou shalt be as thou wast,
The tutor and the feeder of my riots:
Till then, I banish thee, on pain of death,
As I have done the rest of my misleaders,

7. **leer,** smile. 12. **bestowed,** spent. 23. **shift me,** change my apparel. 30-31. **'semper . . . est,'** always the same, for without this there is nothing. Pistol mistranslates nonsensically. 36. **durance,** imprisonment. **contagious,** pestilential, pernicious.

38. **mechanical,** pertaining to a mechanical occupation, base 39. **Rouse . . . snake.** This seems to be rant from the various plays which called for vengeance. Alecto was one of the Furies, who were depicted with snakes twined in their hair. 40. **in,** i.e., in Bridewell, a prison for prostitutes. 56. **hence,** henceforth. 59. **Reply . . . jest.** The king girds at Falstaff on the old subject of his size and sees perhaps a reply kindling in Falstaff's eye. One wonders in vain what the colossal jester would have said.

Not to come near our person by ten mile.
For competence of life I will allow you,   70
That lack of means enforce you not to evil:
And, as we hear you do reform yourselves,
We will, according to your strengths and
    qualities,
Give you advancement. Be it your charge,
    my lord,
To see perform'd the tenour of our word.
Set on.   [*Exeunt King, &c.*
Fal. Master Shallow, I owe you a thou-
sand pound.
Shal. Yea, marry, Sir John; which I be-
seech you to let me have home with me.   80
Fal. That can hardly be, Master Shallow.
Do not you grieve at this; I shall be sent for
in private to him: look you, he must seem
thus to the world: fear not your advance-
ments; I will be the man yet that shall make
you great.
Shal. I cannot well perceive how, unless
you should give me your doublet and stuff
me out with straw. I beseech you, good Sir
John, let me have five hundred of my thousand.   90
Fal. Sir, I will be as good as my word:
this that you heard was but a colour.
Shal. A colour that I fear you will die in,
Sir John.
Fal. Fear no colours: go with me to dinner: come, Lieutenant Pistol; come, Bardolph: I shall be sent for soon at night.

Re-enter Prince John, *the* Lord Chief-
    Justice; Officers *with them.*

Ch. Just. Go, carry Sir John Falstaff to
    the Fleet:
Take all his company along with him.
Fal. My lord, my lord,—
Ch. Just. I cannot now speak: I will hear
    you soon.   100
Take them away.
Pist. Si fortuna me tormenta, spero con-
    tenta.   [*Exeunt all but Prince John and
        the Chief-Justice.*
Lan. I like this fair proceeding of the
    king's:
He hath intent his wonted followers
Shall all be very well provided for;

But all are banish'd till their conversations
Appear more wise and modest to the world.
Ch. Just. And so they are.
Lan. The king hath call'd his parliament,
    my lord.
Ch. Just. He hath.   110
Lan. I will lay odds that, ere this year
    expire,
We bear our civil swords and native fire
As far as France: I heard a bird so sing,
Whose music, to my thinking, pleased the
    king.
Come, will you hence?   [*Exeunt.*

EPILOGUE.

Spoken by a Dancer.

First my fear; then my courtesy; last my
speech. My fear is, your displeasure; my
courtesy, my duty; and my speech, to beg
your pardons. If you look for a good speech
now, you undo me: for what I have to say is
of mine own making; and what indeed I
should say will, I doubt, prove mine own
marring. But to the purpose, and so to the
venture. Be it known to you, as it is very
well, I was lately here in the end of a displeasing play, to pray your patience for it
and to promise you a better. I meant indeed to pay you with this; which, if like an
ill venture it come unluckily home, I break,
and you, my gentle creditors, lose. Here
I promised you I would be and here I commit my body to your mercies: bate me some
and I will pay you some and, as most debtors
do, promise you infinitely.   18
If my tongue cannot entreat you to acquit
me, will you command me to use my legs?
and yet that were but light payment, to
dance out of your debt. But a good conscience will make any possible satisfaction,
and so would I. All the gentlewomen here
have forgiven me: if the gentlemen will not,
then the gentlemen do not agree with the
gentlewomen, which was never seen before
in such an assembly.   27

One word more, I beseech you. If you be not too much cloyed with fat meat, our humble author will continue the story, with Sir John in it, and make you merry with fair Katharine of France: where, for any thing I know, Falstaff shall die of a sweat, unless already a' be killed with your hard opinions; for Oldcastle died a martyr, and this is not the man. My tongue is weary; when my legs are too, I will bid you good night: and so kneel down before you; but, indeed, to pray for the queen.   38

28. **One word more.** If, as seems probable, there was an epilogue written to be spoken by a dancer in the play in its first Shakespearean form (where Falstaff was called Oldcastle), this last paragraph was added at the time of revision. 31. **Sir John in it.** Shakespeare evidently intended to introduce Falstaff into a play on Henry V and, subsequent to the writing of this Epilogue, gave up the intention. Coleridge suggested that Falstaff had no place in the new world of glorious enthusiasm and patriotic fervor which opened with the coronation of King Henry. In any case, this promise in the Epilogue is very hard to reconcile with a theory of the very early composition of *Henry V*. It is not ordinarily thought that the revision from Oldcastle to Falstaff was made very long before the publication of the Q of *1 Henry IV* (1598), and yet a quarto version of *Henry V*, printed in 1600, depicts the death of Falstaff before the opening of the French campaign. 34. **Oldcastle died a martyr.** It is supposed with good reason, since there was an extensive controversy, that the Lord Cobham of the day resented the caricature of his ancestor, Sir John Oldcastle, Lollard martyr under Henry V (1417), and that this epilogue, together with the change of the name to *Falstaff*, was intended to placate him. 38. **pray for the queen**, a customary way to end plays.

THE LIFE OF
KING HENRY THE FIFTH

DRAMATIS PERSONÆ

KING HENRY the Fifth.
DUKE OF GLOUCESTER, } brothers to the
DUKE OF BEDFORD, } King.
DUKE OF EXETER, uncle to the King.
DUKE OF YORK, cousin to the King.
EARLS OF SALISBURY, WESTMORELAND,
    and WARWICK.
ARCHBISHOP OF CANTERBURY.
BISHOP OF ELY.
EARL OF CAMBRIDGE.
LORD SCROOP.
SIR THOMAS GREY.
SIR THOMAS ERPINGHAM, GOWER, FLU-
    ELLEN, MACMORRIS, JAMY, officers
    in King Henry's army.
BATES, COURT, WILLIAMS, soldiers in the
    same.
PISTOL, NYM, BARDOLPH.
Boy.
A Herald.
CHARLES the Sixth, King of France.

LEWIS, the Dauphin.
DUKES OF BURGUNDY, ORLEANS, and
    BOURBON.
The Constable of France.
RAMBURES and GRANDPRÉ, French
    Lords.
Governor of Harfleur.
MONTJOY, a French Herald.
Ambassadors to the King of England.

ISABEL, Queen of France.
KATHARINE, daughter to Charles and
    Isabel.
ALICE, a lady attending on her.
Hostess of a tavern in Eastcheap, form-
    erly Mistress Quickly, and now
    married to Pistol.

Lords, Ladies, Officers, Soldiers, Citizens,
    Messengers, and Attendants.
               Chorus.

SCENE: *England; afterwards France.*

PROLOGUE.

Enter Chorus.

Chor. O for a Muse of fire, that would
    ascend
The brightest heaven of invention,
A kingdom for a stage, princes to act
And monarchs to behold the swelling scene!
Then should the warlike Harry, like himself,
Assume the port of Mars; and at his heels,
Leash'd in like hounds, should famine,
    sword and fire
Crouch for employment. But pardon, gentles
    all,
The flat unraised spirits that have dared
On this unworthy scaffold to bring forth   10

So great an object: can this cockpit hold
The vasty fields of France? or may we cram
Within this wooden O the very casques
That did affright the air at Agincourt?
O, pardon! since a crooked figure may
Attest in little place a million;
And let us, ciphers to this great accompt,
On your imaginary forces work.
Suppose within the girdle of these walls
Are now confined two mighty monarchies, 20
Whose high upreared and abutting fronts
The perilous narrow ocean parts asunder:
Piece out our imperfections with your
    thoughts;
Into a thousand parts divide one man,
And make imaginary puissance;

Prologue. **Chorus.** It will be noticed that the Chorus carries part of the action in *Henry V* and that Shakespeare uses it to win the sympathy of the audience for his theatrical limitations. 6. **port,** bearing. 7. **famine, sword and fire.** According to Holinshed, Henry told the people of Rouen that Bellona, the goddess of battle, had three hand-maidens attendant upon her called "blood, fire, and famine." 10. **scaffold,** stage.

11. **cockpit.** Elizabethan theaters were used for cock-fighting. One of them was called the *Cockpit.* 13. **O,** refers to a round theater such as the Globe. **casques,** helmets. 16. **Attest,** stand for. 17. **accompt,** account. 18. **imaginary forces,** forces of imagination. Shakespeare recognizes here the part the audience must have in the play. 22. **narrow ocean,** the English channel.

Think, when we talk of horses, that you see
    them
Printing their proud hoofs i' the receiving
    earth;
For 'tis your thoughts that now must deck
    our kings,
Carry them here and there; jumping o'er
    times,
Turning the accomplishment of many years
Into an hour-glass: for the which supply, 31
Admit me Chorus to this history;
Who prologue-like your humble patience
    pray,
Gently to hear, kindly to judge, our play.
                           [*Exit.*

ACT I.

SCENE I. *London.* *An ante-chamber in the*
      KING'S *palace.*

Enter the ARCHBISHOP OF CANTERBURY, *and*
    the BISHOP OF ELY.

  Cant. My lord, I'll tell you; that self bill
    is urged,
Which in the eleventh year of the last king's
    reign
Was like, and had indeed against us pass'd,
But that the scambling and unquiet time
Did push it out of farther question.
  Ely. But how, my lord, shall we resist it
    now?
  Cant. It must be thought on. If it pass
    against us,
We lose the better half of our possession:
For all the temporal lands which men de-
    vout
By testament have given to the church 10
Would they strip from us; being valued thus:
As much as would maintain, to the king's
    honour,
Full fifteen earls and fifteen hundred knights,
Six thousand and two hundred good esquires;
And, to relief of lazars and weak age,
Of indigent faint souls past corporal toil,
A hundred almshouses right well supplied;
And to the coffers of the king beside,
A thousand pounds by the year: thus runs
    the bill.
  Ely. This would drink deep.
  Cant.   'Twould drink the cup and all.
  Ely. But what prevention?   21

  Cant. The king is full of grace and fair
    regard.
  Ely. And a true lover of the holy church.
  Cant. The courses of his youth promised
    it not.
The breath no sooner left his father's body,
But that his wildness, mortified in him,
Seem'd to die too; yea, at that very moment
Consideration, like an angel, came
And whipp'd the offending Adam out of him,
Leaving his body as a paradise,   30
To envelope and contain celestial spirits.
Never was such a sudden scholar made;
Never came reformation in a flood,
With such a heady currance, scouring faults;
Nor never Hydra-headed wilfulness
So soon did lose his seat and all at once
As in this king.
  Ely.   We are blessed in the change.
  Cant. Hear him but reason in divinity,
And all-admiring with an inward wish
You would desire the king were made a
    prelate: 40
Hear him debate of commonwealth affairs,
You would say it hath been all in all his
    study:
List his discourse of war, and you shall hear
A fearful battle render'd you in music:
Turn him to any cause of policy,
The Gordian knot of it he will unloose,
Familiar as his garter: that, when he speaks,
The air, a charter'd libertine, is still,
And the mute wonder lurketh in men's ears,
To steal his sweet and honey'd sentences; 50
So that the art and practic part of life
Must be the mistress to this theoric:
Which is a wonder how his grace should
    glean it,
Since his addiction was to courses vain,
His companies unletter'd, rude and shallow,
His hours fill'd up with riots, banquets,
    sports,
And never noted in him any study,
Any retirement, any sequestration

---

29. **offending Adam,** original sin. Henry's offenses
have been driven out of him as Adam was driven out of
Paradise. 34. **heady currance,** headlong current. 35.
Hydra-headed, an allusion to the Lernean Hydra overcome by Hercules. 38–47. **Hear . . . garter.** These
lines enumerate the principal subjects of princely education. Note that policy (statecraft) as well as war held
a recognized place. 46. **Gordian knot,** an allusion to
the knot of Gordius, of which it was foretold that whoever should untie it should rule Asia. Alexander solved
the problem by cutting the knot. 47. **Familiar,** familiarly. **that,** so that. 48. **charter'd libertine,** one
privileged to lead a dissolute life. 51. **practic,** practical.
52. **theoric,** theory. 55. **companies,** companions.
57. **noted,** denoted.

---

31. **supply,** service.
Act I. *Scene* i. 1. **self,** same. 4. **scambling,** unsettled. 15. **lazars,** lepers.

From open haunts and popularity.

Ely. The strawberry grows underneath
the nettle   60
And wholesome berries thrive and ripen best
Neighbour'd by fruit of baser quality:
And so the prince obscured his contemplation
Under the veil of wildness; which, no doubt,
Grew like the summer grass, fastest by night,
Unseen, yet crescive in his faculty.

Cant. It must be so; for miracles are
ceased;
And therefore we must needs admit the means
How things are perfected.

Ely.   But, my good lord,
How now for mitigation of this bill   70
Urged by the commons? Doth his majesty
Incline to it, or no?

Cant.   He seems indifferent,
Or rather swaying more upon our part
Than cherishing the exhibiters against us;
For I have made an offer to his majesty,
Upon our spiritual convocation
And in regard of causes now in hand,
Which I have open'd to his grace at large
As touching France, to give a greater sum
Than ever at one time the clergy yet   80
Did to his predecessors part withal.

Ely. How did this offer seem received, my
lord?

Cant. With good acceptance of his maj-
esty;
Save that there was not time enough to hear,
As I perceived his grace would fain have
done,
The severals and unhidden passages
Of his true titles to some certain dukedoms
And generally to the crown and seat of
France
Derived from Edward, his great-grandfather.

Ely. What was the impediment that broke
this off?   90

Cant. The French ambassador upon that
instant
Craved audience; and the hour, I think, is
come
To give him hearing: is it four o'clock?

Ely. It is.

Cant. Then go we in, to know his embassy;
Which I could with a ready guess declare,

Before the Frenchman speak a word of it.

Ely. I'll wait upon you, and I long to
hear it.   [*Exeunt.*

SCENE II. *The same. The Presence chamber.*

Enter KING HENRY, GLOUCESTER, BEDFORD,
EXETER, WARWICK, WESTMORELAND, *and*
Attendants.

K. Hen. Where is my gracious Lord of
Canterbury?

Exe. Not here in presence.

K. Hen.   Send for him, good uncle.

West. Shall we call in the ambassador, my
liege?

K. Hen. Not yet, my cousin: we would be
resolved,
Before we hear him, of some things of weight
That task our thoughts, concerning us and
France.

Enter the ARCHBISHOP OF CANTERBURY, *and
the* BISHOP OF ELY.

Cant. God and his angels guard your
sacred throne
And make you long become it!

K. Hen.   Sure, we thank you.
My learned lord, we pray you to proceed
And justly and religiously unfold   10
Why the law Salique that they have in
France
Or should, or should not, bar us in our claim:
And God forbid, my dear and faithful lord,
That you should fashion, wrest, or bow your
reading,
Or nicely charge your understanding soul
With opening titles miscreate, whose right
Suits not in native colours with the truth;
For God doth know how many now in health
Shall drop their blood in approbation
Of what your reverence shall incite us to.   20
Therefore take heed how you impawn our
person,
How you awake our sleeping sword of war:
We charge you, in the name of God, take
heed;

---

59. **popularity**, intercourse with low society. 63.
obscured, concealed. 66. **crescive**, tending to grow.
74. **exhibiters**, those who introduce bills in Parliament.
79. **to give a greater sum.** An underlying motive of
the churchmen in urging on the French war is here disclosed. 86. **severals**, particulars. **unhidden passages**,
plain facts.

Scene ii. 4. **cousin**, a term applied to various relatives and apparently applied by kings merely as a term of
address. 8-32. **Sure . . . baptism.** Shakespeare wishes
to indicate in this scene the extreme uprightness of his
hero. 11. **law Salique.** Shakespeare brings in what
Neilson calls "a show of expert advice," in order that
Henry may go to the war with a clear conscience. 15.
nicely, strictly. 16. **opening**, examining. **miscreate**,
improperly framed. 21. **impawn**, pledge.

For never two such kingdoms did contend
Without much fall of blood; whose guiltless
    drops
Are every one a woe, a sore complaint
'Gainst him whose wrongs give edge unto
    the swords
That make such waste in brief mortality.
Under this conjuration speak, my lord;
For we will hear, note and believe in heart
That what you speak is in your conscience
    wash'd   31
As pure as sin with baptism.
    Cant. Then hear me, gracious sovereign,
    and you peers,
That owe yourselves, your lives and services
To this imperial throne. There is no bar
To make against your highness' claim to
    France
But this, which they produce from Phara-
    mond,
'In terram Salicam mulieres ne succedant:'
'No woman shall succeed in Salique land:'
Which Salique land the French unjustly glose
To be the realm of France, and Phara-
    mond
The founder of this law and female bar.   42
Yet their own authors faithfully affirm
That the land Salique is in Germany,
Between the floods of Sala and of Elbe;
Where Charles the Great, having subdued
    the Saxons,
There left behind and settled certain French;
Who, holding in disdain the German women
For some dishonest manners of their life,
Establish'd then this law; to wit, no female
Should be inheritrix in Salique land: 51
Which Salique, as I said, 'twixt Elbe and
    Sala,
Is at this day in Germany call'd Meisen.
Then doth it well appear the Salique law
Was not devised for the realm of France;
Nor did the French possess the Salique land
Until four hundred one and twenty years
After defunction of King Pharamond,
Idly supposed the founder of this law;
Who died within the year of our redemption
Four hundred twenty-six; and Charles the
    Great   61
Subdued the Saxons, and did seat the French
Beyond the river Sala, in the year
Eight hundred five. Besides, their writers
    say,

King Pepin, which deposed Childeric,
Did, as their general, being descended
Of Blithild, which was daughter to King
    Clothair,
Make claim and title to the crown of France.
Hugh Capet also, who usurp'd the crown 69
Of Charles the duke of Lorraine, sole heir male
Of the true line and stock of Charles the
    Great,
To find his title with some shows of truth,
Though, in pure truth, it was corrupt and
    naught,
Convey'd himself as heir to the Lady Lin-
    gare,
Daughter to Charlemain, who was the son
To Lewis the emperor, and Lewis the son
Of Charles the Great. Also King Lewis the
    Tenth,
Who was sole heir to the usurper Capet,
Could not keep quiet in his conscience,
Wearing the crown of France, till satisfied
That fair Queen Isabel, his grandmother, 81
Was lineal of the Lady Ermengare,
Daughter to Charles the foresaid duke of
    Lorraine:
By the which marriage the line of Charles the
    Great
Was re-united to the crown of France.
So that, as clear as is the summer's sun,
King Pepin's title and Hugh Capet's claim,
King Lewis his satisfaction, all appear
To hold in right and title of the female:
So do the kings of France unto this day; 90
Howbeit they would hold up this Salique law
To bar your highness claiming from the fe-
    male,
And rather choose to hide them in a net
Than amply to imbar their crooked titles
Usurp'd from you and your progenitors.
    K. Hen. May I with right and conscience
    make this claim?
    Cant. The sin upon my head, dread sov-
    ereign!
For in the book of Numbers is it writ,
When the man dies, let the inheritance 99
Descend unto the daughter. Gracious lord,
Stand for your own; unwind your bloody
    flag;

66. **heir general,** heir to the whole kingdom. 72.
find, to provide or trace out. 75. **Charlemain,** Charles
the Bald. 82. **lineal of,** descended from. 88. **Lewis
his,** Lewis's. 93. **net,** possibly expressive of something
easily seen through; also explained as "a tangle of con-
tradictions." 94. **imbar,** secure; sometimes defined as
"exclude." 98. **Numbers.** See *Numbers,* xxvii, 8.

40. **glose,** explain. 58. **defunction,** death. 61.
Charles the Great, Charlemagne.

Look back into your mighty ancestors:
Go, my dread lord, to your great-grandsire's
    tomb,
From whom you claim; invoke his warlike
    spirit,
And your great-uncle's, Edward the Black
    Prince,
Who on the French ground play'd a tragedy,
Making defeat on the full power of France,
Whiles his most mighty father on a hill
Stood smiling to behold his lion's whelp
Forage in blood of French nobility.   110
O noble English, that could entertain
With half their forces the full pride of France
And let another half stand laughing by,
All out of work and cold for action!

Ely. Awake remembrance of these valiant
    dead
And with your puissant arm renew their
    feats:
You are their heir; you sit upon their throne;
The blood and courage that renowned them
Runs in your veins; and my thrice-puissant
    liege
Is in the very May-morn of his youth,   120
Ripe for exploits and mighty enterprises.

Exe. Your brother kings and monarchs of
    the earth
Do all expect that you should rouse yourself,
As did the former lions of your blood.

West. They know your grace hath cause
    and means and might;
So hath your highness; never king of Eng-
    land
Had nobles richer and more loyal subjects,
Whose hearts have left their bodies here in
    England
And lie pavilion'd in the fields of France.

Cant. O, let their bodies follow, my dear
    liege,   130
With blood and sword and fire to win your
    right;
In aid whereof we of the spiritualty
Will raise your highness such a mighty sum
As never did the clergy at one time
Bring in to any of your ancestors.

K. Hen. We must not only arm to invade
    the French,
But lay down our proportions to defend

Against the Scot, who will make road upon us
With all advantages.

Cant. They of those marches, gracious
    sovereign,   140
Shall be a wall sufficient to defend
Our inland from the pilfering borderers.

K. Hen. We do not mean the coursing
    snatchers only,
But fear the main intendment of the Scot,
Who hath been still a giddy neighbour to us;
For you shall read that my great-grandfather
Never went with his forces into France
But that the Scot on his unfurnish'd kingdom
Came pouring, like the tide into a breach,
With ample and brim fulness of his force, 150
Galling the gleaned land with hot assays,
Girding with grievous siege castles and towns;
That England, being empty of defence,
Hath shook and trembled at the ill neigh-
    bourhood.

Cant. She hath been then more fear'd than
    harm'd, my liege;
For hear her but exampled by herself:
When all her chivalry hath been in France
And she a mourning widow of her nobles,
She hath herself not only well defended
But taken and impounded as a stray   160
The King of Scots; whom she did send to
    France,
To fill King Edward's fame with prisoner
    kings
And make her chronicle as rich with praise
As is the ooze and bottom of the sea
With sunken wreck and sumless treasuries.

West. But there's a saying very old and
    true,
          'If that you will France win,
          Then with Scotland first begin:'
For once the eagle England being in prey,
To her unguarded nest the weasel Scot   170
Comes sneaking and so sucks her princely
    eggs,
Playing the mouse in absence of the cat,
To tear and havoc more than she can eat.

Exe. It follows then the cat must stay at
    home:
Yet that is but a crush'd necessity,
Since we have locks to safeguard necessaries,

---

108. **his most mighty father.** Holinshed gives the
story of Edward III's watching the battle of Crecy (1346)
as recounted in the text. 114. **cold for action,** cold for
want of action. 137. **lay down our proportions,** set
down the proper numbers.

140. **marches,** borders. 143. **coursing snatchers,**
mounted raiders. 144. **intendment,** plan. 151.
gleaned, stripped (of defenders). **assays,** assaults.
155. **fear'd,** frightened. 160. **impounded as a stray.**
David Bruce was captured and imprisoned in 1346
while Edward III was in France. 173. **havoc,** the
signal for slaughter; here, destroy. 175. **crush'd,** forced.

And pretty traps to catch the petty thieves.
While that the armed hand doth fight abroad,
The advised head defends itself at home;
For government, though high and low and
　　lower,　　　　　　　　　　　　　　180
Put into parts, doth keep in one consent,
Congreeing in a full and natural close,
Like music.
　　Cant.　　Therefore doth heaven divide
The state of man in divers functions,
Setting endeavour in continual motion;
To which is fixed, as an aim or butt,
Obedience: for so work the honey-bees,
Creatures that by a rule in nature teach
The act of order to a peopled kingdom.
They have a king and officers of sorts;　190
Where some, like magistrates, correct at
　　home,
Others, like merchants, venture trade abroad,
Others, like soldiers, armed in their stings,
Make boot upon the summer's velvet buds,
Which pillage they with merry march bring
　　home
To the tent-royal of their emperor;
Who, busied in his majesty, surveys
The singing masons building roofs of gold,
The civil citizens kneading up the honey,
The poor mechanic porters crowding in　200
Their heavy burdens at his narrow gate,
The sad-eyed justice, with his surly hum,
Delivering o'er to executors pale
The lazy yawning drone. I this infer,
That many things, having full reference
To one consent, may work contrariously:
As many arrows, loosed several ways,
Come to one mark; as many ways meet in
　　one town;
As many fresh streams meet in one salt sea;
As many lines close in the dial's centre;　210
So may a thousand actions, once afoot,
End in one purpose, and be all well borne
Without defeat. Therefore to France, my
　　liege.
Divide your happy England into four;
Whereof take you one quarter into France,
And you withal shall make all Gallia shake.
If we, with thrice such powers left at home,
Cannot defend our own doors from the dog,

Let us be worried and our nation lose
The name of hardiness and policy.　　220
　　K. Hen.　Call in the messengers sent from
　　　　the Dauphin.　[*Exeunt some Attendants.*
Now are we well resolved; and, by God's help,
And yours, the noble sinews of our power,
France being ours, we'll bend it to our awe,
Or break it all to pieces: or there we'll sit,
Ruling in large and ample empery
O'er France and all her almost kingly duke-
　　doms,
Or lay these bones in an unworthy urn,
Tombless, with no remembrance over them:
Either our history shall with full mouth　230
Speak freely of our acts, or else our grave,
Like Turkish mute, shall have a tongueless
　　mouth,
Not worshipp'd with a waxen epitaph.

　　　　　　Enter Ambassadors *of France.*

Now are we well prepared to know the pleas-
　　ure
Of our fair cousin Dauphin; for we hear
Your greeting is from him, not from the king.
　　First Amb.　May 't please your majesty to
　　　　give us leave
Freely to render what we have in charge;
Or shall we sparingly show you far off
The Dauphin's meaning and our embassy?240
　　K. Hen.　We are no tyrant, but a Christian
　　　　king;
Unto whose grace our passion is as subject
As are our wretches fetter'd in our prisons:
Therefore with frank and with uncurbed
　　plainness
Tell us the Dauphin's mind.
　　First Amb.　　　　　Thus, then, in few.
Your highness, lately sending into France,
Did claim some certain dukedoms, in the
　　right
Of your great predecessor, King Edward the
　　Third.
In answer of which claim, the prince our
　　master
Says that you savour too much of your youth,
And bids you be advised there's nought in
　　France　　　　　　　　　　　　251
That can be with a nimble galliard won;

182. **Congreeing,** agreeing together. **close,** cadence.
184-204. **The state of man . . . drone.** This elaborate
comparison of human society to a hive of bees is a familiar
Renaissance theme. It expresses the current political
theory of the naturalness of rank and class and the
necessity of order. 194. **boot,** booty. 202. **sad-eyed,**
grave-eyed. 203. **executors,** executioners. 216. **Gallia,**
Latin name for France.

220. **hardiness and policy,** bravery and statesman-
ship, the two highest virtues of a king. 221. **Dauphin,**
heir apparent to the French throne. 226. **empery,**
dominion. 233. **waxen epitaph,** allusion to the custom
of affixing epitaphs to tombs. It is explained that the
epitaph was stuck on with wax. 252. **galliard,** a lively
dance.

You cannot revel into dukedoms there.
He therefore sends you, meeter for your
  spirit,
This tun of treasure; and, in lieu of this,
Desires you let the dukedoms that you claim
Hear no more of you. This the Dauphin
  speaks.
  K. Hen. What treasure, uncle?
  Exe.   Tennis-balls, my liege.
  K. Hen. We are glad the Dauphin is so
  pleasant with us;
His present and your pains we thank you for:
When we have match'd our rackets to these
  balls,   261
We will, in France, by God's grace, play a set
Shall strike his father's crown into the hazard.
Tell him he hath made a match with such a
  wrangler
That all the courts of France will be disturb'd
With chaces. And we understand him well,
How he comes o'er us with our wilder days,
Not measuring what use we made of them.
We never valued this poor seat of England;
And therefore, living hence, did give ourself
To barbarous license; as 'tis ever common
That men are merriest when they are from
  home.   272
But tell the Dauphin I will keep my state,
Be like a king and show my sail of greatness
When I do rouse me in my throne of France:
For that I have laid by my majesty
And plodded like a man for working-days,
But I will rise there with so full a glory
That I will dazzle all the eyes of France,   279
Yea, strike the Dauphin blind to look on us.
And tell the pleasant prince this mock of his
Hath turn'd his balls to gun-stones; and his
  soul
Shall stand sore charged for the wasteful
  vengeance
That shall fly with them: for many a thous-
  and widows
Shall this his mock mock out of their dear
  husbands;
Mock mothers from their sons, mock castles
  down;
And some are yet ungotten and unborn

That shall have cause to curse the Dauphin's
  scorn.
But this lies all within the will of God,
To whom I do appeal; and in whose name
Tell you the Dauphin I am coming on,   291
To venge me as I may and to put forth
My rightful hand in a well-hallow'd cause.
So get you hence in peace; and tell the
  Dauphin
His jest will savour but of shallow wit,
When thousands weep more than did laugh
  at it.
Convey them with safe conduct. Fare you
  well.   [*Exeunt Ambassadors.*
  Exe. This was a merry message.
  K. Hen. We hope to make the sender
  blush at it.   299
Therefore, my lords, omit no happy hour
That may give furtherance to our expedition;
For we have now no thought in us but France,
Save those to God, that run before our busi-
  ness.
Therefore let our proportions for these wars
Be soon collected and all things thought upon
That may with reasonable swiftness add
More feathers to our wings; for, God before,
We'll chide this Dauphin at his father's door.
Therefore let every man now task his thought,
That this fair action may on foot be brought.
                          [*Exeunt. Flourish.*

ACT II.

PROLOGUE.

Flourish.   Enter Chorus.

  Chor. Now all the youth of England are on
  fire,
And silken dalliance in the wardrobe lies:
Now thrive the armourers, and honour's
  thought
Reigns solely in the breast of every man:
They sell the pasture now to buy the horse,
Following the mirror of all Christian kings,
With winged heels, as English Mercuries.
For now sits Expectation in the air,
And hides a sword from hilts unto the point
With crowns imperial, crowns and coronets,
Promised to Harry and his followers.   11
The French, advised by good intelligence
Of this most dreadful preparation,
Shake in their fear and with pale policy

---

255. **tun**, a cask. Holinshed speaks of "a barrel of Paris
balls." 263. **hazard**, in tennis, the side of the court into
which the ball is served. 264. **wrangler**, stubborn
adversary. 266. **chaces.** A *chace* is the second bound
of a ball which the opponent fails to return; obvious
pun on *chase*. 267. **comes o'er**, taunts. 269-280.
We never . . . on us. The king speaks ironically
to the disadvantage of England, suggesting that his
mind is fixed on France. 269. **seat**, throne. 270.
living hence, not frequenting the royal court. 282.
gun-stones, cannon balls.

304. **proportions**, levies.

Seek to divert the English purposes.
O England! model to thy inward greatness,
Like little body with a mighty heart,
What mightst thou do, that honour would
    thee do,
Were all thy children kind and natural!
But see thy fault! France hath in thee found
    out   20
A nest of hollow bosoms, which he fills
With treacherous crowns; and three cor-
    rupted men,
One, Richard Earl of Cambridge, and the
    second,
Henry Lord Scroop of Masham, and the third,
Sir Thomas Grey, knight, of Northumber-
    land,
Have, for the gilt of France,—O guilt in-
    deed!—
Confirm'd conspiracy with fearful France;
And by their hands this grace of kings must
    die,
If hell and treason hold their promises,
Ere he take ship for France, and in South-
    ampton.   30
Linger your patience on; †and we'll digest
The abuse of distance; force a play:
The sum is paid; the traitors are agreed;
The king is set from London; and the scene
Is now transported, gentles, to Southamp-
    ton;
There is the playhouse now, there must you
    sit:
And thence to France shall we convey you
    safe,
And bring you back, charming the narrow
    seas
To give you gentle pass; for, if we may,
We'll not offend one stomach with our play.
But, till the king come forth, and not till
    then,   41
Unto Southampton do we shift our scene.
                                        [*Exit.*

SCENE I. *London. A street.*

Enter Corporal NYM *and* Lieutenant
BARDOLPH

Bard. Well met, Corporal Nym.
Nym. Good morrow, Lieutenant Bardolph.

Bard. What, are Ancient Pistol and you
friends yet?   4
Nym. For my part, I care not: I say little;
but when time shall serve, there shall be
smiles; but that shall be as it may. I dare
not fight; but I will wink and hold out mine
iron: it is a simple one; but what though? it
will toast cheese, and it will endure cold as
another man's sword will: and there's an end.
Bard. I will bestow a breakfast to make
you friends; and we'll be all three sworn
brothers to France: let it be so, good Corporal Nym.   14
Nym. Faith, I will live so long as I may,
that's the certain of it; and when I cannot
live any longer, I will do as I may: that is
my rest, that is the rendezvous of it.
Bard. It is certain, corporal, that he is
married to Nell Quickly: and certainly she
did you wrong; for you were troth-plight to
her.   21
Nym. I cannot tell: things must be as they
may: men may sleep, and they may have
their throats about them at that time; and
some say knives have edges. It must be as
it may: though patience be a tired mare, yet
she will plod. There must be conclusions.
Well, I cannot tell.

Enter PISTOL *and* Hostess.

Bard. Here comes Ancient Pistol and his
wife: good corporal, be patient here. How
now, mine host Pistol!   30
Pist. Base tike, call'st thou me host?
Now, by this hand, I swear, I scorn the term;
Nor shall my Nell keep lodgers.
Host. No, by my troth, not long; for we
cannot lodge and board a dozen or fourteen
gentlewomen that live honestly by the prick
of their needles, but it will be thought we
keep a bawdy house straight. [*Nym and
Pistol draw.*] O well a day, Lady, if he be not
drawn now! we shall see wilful adultery and
murder committed.   40
Bard. Good lieutenant! good corporal!
offer nothing here.

3. **Ancient**, ensign. 7. **smiles**. Nym is ordinarily
regarded as a humor character, i.e., a character presenting one special peculiarity or disposition. It may
be, however, that he is a travesty of the humor characters on the current stage. It is his "humor" to use
words in completely contrary senses; for example, he
describes the actions of a coward as a means of suggesting
his own bravery. 8. **wink**, shut his eyes. 13. **sworn
brothers**, a comical allusion to *fratres jurati*. 14. **to
France**, i.e., as we go to France. 18. **rendezvous**,
one of Nym's absurd words. 31. **tike**, cur. 38. **Lady**,
an oath by the Virgin Mary.

18. **would**, would have. 19. **kind**, having the good
qualities of nature well developed. 22. **crowns**, crown
pieces. 26. **gilt**, gold. 31-32. **digest The abuse of
distance**, overcome the difficulties of representing distance. 32. **force a play**, make a play in spite of difficulties. 41-42. **But . . . scene**. The meaning is that
the scene will be shifted to Southampton, but not until
the king comes forth.

Nym. Pish!   43

Pist. Pish for thee, Iceland dog! thou
prick-ear'd cur of Iceland!

Host. Good Corporal Nym, show thy
valour, and put up your sword.

Nym. Will you shog off? I would have
you solus.

Pist. 'Solus,' egregious dog? O viper vile!
The 'solus' in thy most mervailous face;   50
The 'solus' in thy teeth, and in thy throat,
And in thy hateful lungs, yea, in thy maw,
perdy,
And, which is worse, within thy nasty mouth!
I do retort the 'solus' in thy bowels;
For I can take, and Pistol's cock is up,
And flashing fire will follow.   56

Nym. I am not Barbason; you cannot conjure me. I have an humour to knock you
indifferently well. If you grow foul with me,
Pistol, I will scour you with my rapier, as I
may, in fair terms: if you would walk off, I
would prick your guts a little, in good terms,
as I may: and that's the humour of it.

Pist. O braggart vile and damned furious
wight!
The grave doth gape, and doting death is
near;
Therefore exhale.   66

Bard. Hear me, hear me what I say: he
that strikes the first stroke, I'll run him up
to the hilts, as I am a soldier.

                                   [*Draws.*

Pist. An oath of mickle might; and fury
shall abate.   70
Give me thy fist, thy fore-foot to me give:
Thy spirits are most tall.

Nym. I will cut thy throat, one time or
other, in fair terms: that is the humour of it.

Pist. 'Couple a gorge!'
That is the word. I thee defy again.
O hound of Crete, think'st thou my spouse
to get?
No; to the spital go,
And from the powdering-tub of infamy   79

Fetch forth the lazar kite of Cressid's kind,
Doll Tearsheet she by name, and her espouse:
I have, and I will hold, the quondam Quickly
For the only she; and—pauca, there's
enough.
Go to.

Enter the Boy.

Boy. Mine host Pistol, you must come to
my master, and you, hostess: he is very sick,
and would to bed. Good Bardolph, put thy
face between his sheets, and do the office of a
warming-pan. Faith, he's very ill.

Bard. Away, you rogue!   90

Host. By my troth, he'll yield the crow a
pudding one of these days. The king has
killed his heart. Good husband, come home
presently.   [*Exeunt Hostess and Boy.*

Bard. Come, shall I make you two
friends? We must to France together: why
the devil should we keep knives to cut one
another's throats?

Pist. Let floods o'erswell, and fiends for
food howl on!

Nym. You'll pay me the eight shillings I
won of you at betting?

Pist. Base is the slave that pays.   100

Nym. That now I will have: that's the
humour of it.

Pist. As manhood shall compound: push
home.   [*They draw.*

Bard. By this sword, he that makes the
first thrust, I'll kill him; by this sword, I will.

Pist. Sword is an oath, and oaths must
have their course.

Bard. Corporal Nym, an thou wilt be
friends, be friends: an thou wilt not, why,
then, be enemies with me too. Prithee, put
up.

Nym. I shall have my eight shillings I won
of you at betting?   111

Pist. A noble shalt thou have, and present
pay;
And liquor likewise will I give to thee,
And friendship shall combine, and brother-
hood:
I'll live by Nym, and Nym shall live by me;
Is not this just? for I shall sutler be   116

---

44. **Iceland dog.** Pistol's humor is to use extravagant epithets (this being one), tags from current plays,
and scraps of foreign languages. 47. **shog,** slang or
cant for *move.* 50. **mervailous,** apparently, *marvelous.*
52. **perdy,** par Dieu. 55. **take,** explained as "take
fire"; more probably, bewitch. 57. **Barbason,** apparently the name of a fiend, though no such name is known.
Pistol's rant suggests to Nym the words of a conjuror.
66. **exhale,** draw (sword). 70. **mickle might,** great
power. 75. **'Couple a gorge!'** *coupe la gorge,* cut the
throat. 77. **hound of Crete,** parallel to *Iceland dog*
(l. 44). 79. **powdering-tub,** tub used for salting beef;
here, alluding to a method of curing a disease.

80. **lazar,** leprous. **kite,** a term of opprobrium.
Cressid's kind. Cressida was proverbial as a courtesan.
She is represented in Robert Henryson's *Testament of
Cresseid* as being rejected by Diomede and infected with
leprosy. 83. **pauca,** in brief. 88. **face.** Bardolph's
face was fiery with drinking. 103. **compound,** settle
(a difference). 112. **noble,** a gold coin. 116. **sutler,**
seller of liquor and provisions to the soldiers.

Unto the camp, and profits will accrue.
Give me thy hand.

Nym.   I shall have my noble?
Pist. In cash most justly paid.   120
Nym. Well, then, that's the humour of 't.

Re-enter Hostess.

Host. As ever you came of women, come
in quickly to Sir John. Ah, poor heart! he
is so shaked of a burning quotidian tertian,
that it is most lamentable to behold. Sweet
men, come to him.

Nym. The king hath run bad humours on
the knight; that's the even of it.

Pist. Nym, thou hast spoke the right;
His heart is fracted and corroborate.   130

Nym. The king is a good king: but it
must be as it may; he passes some humours
and careers.

Pist. Let us condole the knight; for, lamb-
kins, we will live.

Scene II. *Southampton. A council-chamber.*

Enter Exeter, Bedford, *and*
Westmoreland.

Bed. 'Fore God, his grace is bold, to trust
these traitors.

Exe. They shall be apprehended by and by.
West. How smooth and even they do bear
themselves!
As if allegiance in their bosoms sat,
Crowned with faith and constant loyalty.

Bed. The king hath note of all that they
intend,
By interception which they dream not of.

Exe. Nay, but the man that was his bed-
fellow,
Whom he hath dull'd and cloy'd with gra-
cious favours,
That he should, for a foreign purse, so sell   10
His sovereign's life to death and treachery.

Trumpets sound. Enter King Henry,
Scroop, Cambridge, Grey, *and* Attendants.

K. Hen. Now sits the wind fair, and we
will aboard.

My Lord of Cambridge, and my kind Lord
of Masham,
And you, my gentle knight, give me your
thoughts:
Think you not that the powers we bear with
us
Will cut their passage through the force of
France,
Doing the execution and the act
For which we have in head assembled them?

Scroop. No doubt, my liege, if each man
do his best.

K. Hen. I doubt not that; since we are
well persuaded   20
We carry not a heart with us from hence
That grows not in a fair consent with ours,
Nor leave not one behind that doth not wish
Success and conquest to attend on us.

Cam. Never was monarch better fear'd
and loved
Than is your majesty: there's not, I think, a
subject
That sits in heart-grief and uneasiness
Under the sweet shade of your government.

Grey. True: those that were your father's
enemies
Have steep'd their galls in honey and do
serve you   30
With hearts create of duty and of zeal.

K. Hen. We therefore have great cause of
thankfulness;
And shall forget the office of our hand,
Sooner than quittance of desert and merit
According to the weight and worthiness.

Scroop. So service shall with steeled
sinews toil,
And labour shall refresh itself with hope,
To do your grace incessant services.

K. Hen. We judge no less. Uncle of
Exeter,
Enlarge the man committed yesterday,   40
That rail'd against our person: we consider
It was excess of wine that set him on;
And on his more advice we pardon him.

Scroop. That's mercy, but too much
security:
Let him be punish'd, sovereign, lest example
Breed, by his sufferance, more of such a
kind.

K. Hen. O, let us yet be merciful.

---

124. **quotidian tertian.** Mistress Quickly confuses
terms; a *quotidian* fever was one that came daily; a
tertian fever, one that came every three days.   130.
fracted and corroborate. Like the others, Pistol
believes Falstaff's heart is broken by the king's rejection
of him. *Corroborate* (strengthened) may be used for *corrupted*.   132-3. **he . . . careers,** he indulges in some
humors and pranks. *Career* means the dashing back and
forward of a horse at full speed.

18. **head,** armed force.   43. **more advice,** thinking
better of it.   47. **let us yet be merciful.** The device
of having traitors convict themselves from their own
mouths is obvious.

Cam. So may your highness, and yet
    punish too.
Grey. Sir,
You show great mercy, if you give him
    life,
After the taste of much correction.   51
    K. Hen. Alas, your too much love and
    care of me
Are heavy orisons 'gainst this poor wretch!
If little faults, proceeding on distemper,
Shall not be wink'd at, how shall we stretch
    our eye
When capital crimes, chew'd, swallow'd and
    digested,
Appear before us? We'll yet enlarge that
    man,
Though Cambridge, Scroop and Grey, in
    their dear care
And tender preservation of our person,
Would have him punish'd. And now to our
    French causes: 60
Who are the late commissioners?
    Cam. I one, my lord:
Your highness bade me ask for it to-day.
    Scroop. So did you me, my liege.
    Grey. And I, my royal sovereign.
    K. Hen. Then, Richard Earl of Cam-
    bridge, there is yours;
There yours, Lord Scroop of Masham; and,
    sir knight,
Grey of Northumberland, this same is yours:
Read them; and know, I know your worthi-
    ness.
My Lord of Westmoreland, and uncle
    Exeter,   70
We will aboard to night. Why, how now,
    gentlemen!
What see you in those papers that you lose
So much complexion? Look ye, how they
    change!
Their cheeks are paper. Why, what read you
    there,
That hath so cowarded and chased your
    blood
Out of appearance?
    Cam.   I do confess my fault;
And do submit me to your highness' mercy.
    Grey. }
    Scroop. } To which we all appeal.
    K. Hen. The mercy that was quick in us
    but late,

By your own counsel is suppress'd and
    kill'd: 80
You must not dare, for shame, to talk of
    mercy;
For your own reasons turn into your bosoms,
As dogs upon their masters, worrying you.
See you, my princes and my noble peers,
These English monsters! My Lord of Cam-
    bridge here,
You know how apt our love was to accord
To furnish him with all appertinents
Belonging to his honour; and this man
Hath, for a few light crowns, lightly con-
    spired,
And sworn unto the practices of France,   90
To kill us here in Hampton: to the which
This knight, no less for bounty bound to us
Than Cambridge is, hath likewise sworn.
    But, O,
What shall I say to thee, Lord Scroop? thou
    cruel,
Ingrateful, savage and inhuman creature!
Thou that didst bear the key of all my
    counsels,
That knew'st the very bottom of my soul,
That almost mightst have coin'd me into
    gold,
Wouldst thou have practised on me for thy
    use!
May it be possible, that foreign hire   100
Could out of thee extract one spark of evil
That might annoy my finger? 'tis so strange,
That, though the truth of it stands off as
    gross
As black and white, my eye will scarcely see
    it.
Treason and murder ever kept together,
As two yoke-devils sworn to either's purpose,
Working so grossly in a natural cause,
That admiration did not hoop at them:
But thou, 'gainst all proportion, didst bring
    in
Wonder to wait on treason and on murder:110
And whatsoever cunning fiend it was
That wrought upon thee so preposterously
Hath got the voice in hell for excellence:
All other devils that suggest by treasons
Do botch and bungle up damnation
With patches, colours, and with forms being
    fetch'd
From glistering semblances of piety;

---

53. **orisons**, prayers. 54. **distemper**, drunkenness.
55. **stretch our eye**, wink at, seem not to see. 61. **late**,
newly appointed. 63. **it**, i.e., my commission. 79.
quick, alive.

87. **appertinents**, things appertaining (to). 102.
annoy, injure. 108. **admiration**, wonder. **hoop**,
shout with astonishment. 117. **glistering**, shining.

But he that temper'd thee bade thee stand
   up,
Gave thee no instance why thou shouldst do
   treason,
Unless to dub thee with the name of traitor.
If that same demon that hath gull'd thee
   thus   121
Should with his lion gait walk the whole
   world,
He might return to vasty Tartar back,
And tell the legions 'I can never win
A soul so easy as that Englishman's.'
O, how hast thou with jealousy infected
The sweetness of affiance! Show men dutiful?
Why, so didst thou: seem they grave and
   learned?
Why, so didst thou: come they of noble
   family?
Why, so didst thou: seem they religious?   130
Why, so didst thou: or are they spare in
   diet,
Free from gross passion or of mirth or anger,
Constant in spirit, not swerving with the
   blood,
Garnish'd and deck'd in modest complement,
Not working with the eye without the ear,
And but in purged judgement trusting
   neither?
Such and so finely bolted didst thou seem:
And thus thy fall hath left a kind of blot,
To mark the full-fraught man and best in-
   dued
With some suspicion. I will weep for thee; 140
For this revolt of thine, methinks, is like
Another fall of man. Their faults are open:
Arrest them to the answer of the law;
And God acquit them of their practices!
   Exe. I arrest thee of high treason, by the
name of Richard Earl of Cambridge.
   I arrest thee of high treason, by the name
of Henry Lord Scroop of Masham.
   I arrest thee of high treason, by the name
of Thomas Grey, knight, of Northumber-
land.   150
   Scroop. Our purposes God justly hath
discover'd;
And I repent my fault more than my death;
Which I beseech your highness to forgive,
Although my body pay the price of it.

   Cam. For me, the gold of France did not
   seduce;
Although I did admit it as a motive
The sooner to effect what I intended:
But God be thanked for prevention;
Which I in sufferance heartily will rejoice,
Beseeching God and you to pardon me.   160
   Grey. Never did faithful subject more re-
joice
At the discovery of most dangerous treason
Than I do at this hour joy o'er myself,
Prevented from a damned enterprise:
My fault, but not my body, pardon,
   sovereign.
   K. Hen. God quit you in his mercy! Hear
   your sentence.
You have conspired against our royal person,
Join'd with an enemy proclaim'd and from
   his coffers
Received the golden earnest of our death;
Wherein you would have sold your king to
   slaughter,   170
His princes and his peers to servitude,
His subjects to oppression and contempt
And his whole kingdom into desolation.
Touching our person seek we no revenge;
But we our kingdom's safety must so tender,
Whose ruin you have sought, that to her laws
We do deliver you. Get you therefore
   hence,
Poor miserable wretches, to your death:
The taste whereof, God of his mercy give 179
You patience to endure, and true repent-
   ance
Of all your dear offences! Bear them hence.
     [*Exeunt Cambridge, Scroop and Grey,
              guarded.*
Now, lords, for France; the enterprise where-
   of
Shall be to you, as us, like glorious.
We doubt not of a fair and lucky war,
Since God so graciously hath brought to light
This dangerous treason lurking in our way
To hinder our beginnings. We doubt not now
But every rub is smoothed on our way.
Then forth, dear countrymen: let us deliver
Our puissance into the hand of God,   190
Putting it straight in expedition.
Cheerly to sea; the signs of war advance:
No king of England, if not king of France.
                 [*Exeunt.*

118-142. **But he . . . fall of man.** The theory of
villainy reflected in this passage seems to indicate a
belief, found elsewhere in Shakespeare, in the possibility
of complete and gratuitous wickedness. 118. **temper'd**,
molded. 123. **Tartar**, for *Tartarus*, hell. 137. **bolted**,
sifted (like flour).

175. **our kingdom's safety.** The king's position
with reference to himself and his kingdom is that of the
traditional ideal prince. **tender**, care for. 181. **dear**,
grievous. 188. **rub**, obstacle; a term from bowls.

SCENE III. *London. Before a tavern.*

Enter PISTOL, Hostess, NYM, BARDOLPH,
and Boy.

Host. Prithee, honey-sweet husband, let
me bring thee to Staines.

Pist. No; for my manly heart doth yearn.
Bardolph, be blithe: Nym, rouse thy vaunt-
ing veins:
Boy, bristle thy courage up; for Falstaff he
is dead,
And we must yearn therefore.

Bard. Would I were with him, where-
some'er he is, either in heaven or in hell!   8

Host. Nay, sure, he's not in hell: he's in
Arthur's bosom, if ever man went to Arthur's
bosom. A' made a finer end and went away
an it had been any christom child; a' parted
even just between twelve and one, even at
the turning o' the tide: for after I saw him
fumble with the sheets and play with flowers
and smile upon his fingers' ends, I knew there
was but one way; for his nose was as sharp
as a pen, and a' babbled of green fields.
'How now, Sir John!' quoth I: 'what, man!
be o' good cheer.' So a' cried out, 'God, God,
God!' three or four times. Now I, to comfort him, bid him a' should not think of God;
I hoped there was no need to trouble himself
with any such thoughts yet. So a' bade me
lay more clothes on his feet: I put my hand
into the bed and felt them, and they were as
cold as any stone; then I felt to his knees,
and they were as cold as any stone, and so
upward and upward, and all was as cold
as any stone.

Nym. They say he cried out of sack.

Host. Ay, that a' did.   30

Bard. And of women.

Host. Nay, that a' did not.

Boy. Yes, that a' did; and said they were
devils incarnate.

Host. A' could never abide carnation;
'twas a colour he never liked.

Boy. A' said once, the devil would have
him about women.

Host. A' did in some sort, indeed, handle
women; but then he was rheumatic, and
talked of the whore of Babylon.   41

Boy. Do you not remember, a' saw a flea
stick upon Bardolph's nose, and a' said it
was a black soul burning in hell-fire?

Bard. Well, the fuel is gone that maintained that fire: that's all the riches I got
in his service.

Nym. Shall we shog? the king will be gone
from Southampton.

Pist. Come, let's away. My love, give
me thy lips.
Look to my chattels and my movables: 50
Let senses rule; the word is 'Pitch and Pay:'
Trust none;
For oaths are straws, men's faiths are wafer-
cakes,
And hold-fast is the only dog, my duck:
Therefore, Caveto be thy counsellor.
Go, clear thy crystals. Yoke-fellows in
arms,
Let us to France; like horse-leeches, my
boys,
To suck, to suck, the very blood to suck!

Boy. And that's but unwholesome food,
they say.   60

Pist. Touch her soft mouth, and march.

Bard. Farewell, hostess.   [*Kissing her.*

Nym. I cannot kiss, that is the humour of
it; but, adieu.

Pist. Let housewifery appear: keep close,
I thee command.

Host. Farewell; adieu.   [*Exeunt.*

SCENE IV. *France. The* KING'S *palace.*

Flourish. Enter the FRENCH KING, *the* DAU-
PHIN, *the* DUKES OF BERRI *and* BRETAGNE,
the CONSTABLE, *and others.*

Fr. King. Thus comes the English with
full power upon us;
And more than carefully it us concerns

---

2. **Staines,** first stage on the road to Southampton.
7-8. **Would . . . hell!** Bardolph pays what would seem
to be an ultimate tribute to good fellowship. 9-28. **Nay,
sure . . . stone.** Mistress Quickly is here reciting a
series of traditional signs of death. 10. **Arthur's
bosom.** Mistress Quickly probably meant *Abraham's
bosom,* mentioned in the parable of Lazarus. 11. **A',**
he. 12. **an,** as if. **christom.** The reference is to
chrism, the consecrated oil used at baptism, or to *chrisom,*
a white robe put upon the child in token of innocence;
it is probably the latter, since, if the child died, the
chrisom was used as a shroud. 18. **a' babbled of
green fields.** This line contains Theobald's famous
emendation. F has *and a Table of greene fields.* Falstaff
would seem to have been reciting the twenty-third psalm.
29. **of,** against.

44. **black soul burning in hell-fire,** a reminiscence
of the play of Doomsday in the mystery plays. 51.
senses, possibly, common sense. **'Pitch and Pay,'** proverbial for "cash payment"; supposed to be derived from
a rule at Cloth-Hall in London, that, when a bale of
cloth was deposited (*pitched*), a penny must be paid.
54. **hold-fast.** Cf. the proverb, "Brag is a good dog,
but hold-fast is a better." 55. **Caveto,** be cautious;
Latin imperative of *caveo.* 56. **clear thy crystals,**
wipe thine eyes. 65. **keep close,** don't gad about.

To answer royally in our defences.
Therefore the Dukes of Berri and of Bre-
tagne,
Of Brabant and of Orleans, shall make forth,
And you, Prince Dauphin, with all swift dis-
patch,
To line and new repair our towns of war
With men of courage and with means de-
fendant;
For England his approaches makes as fierce
As waters to the sucking of a gulf.   10
It fits us then to be as provident
As fear may teach us out of late examples
Left by the fatal and neglected English
Upon our fields.
  Dau.   My most redoubted father,
It is most meet we arm us 'gainst the foe;
For peace itself should not so dull a kingdom,
Though war nor no known quarrel were in
question,
But that defences, musters, preparations,
Should be maintain'd, assembled and col-
lected,
As were a war in expectation.   20
Therefore, I say 'tis meet we all go forth
To view the sick and feeble parts of France:
And let us do it with no show of fear;
No, with no more than if we heard that
England
Were busied with a Whitsun morris-dance:
For, my good liege, she is so idly king'd,
Her sceptre so fantastically borne
By a vain, giddy, shallow, humorous youth,
That fear attends her not.
  Con.   O peace, Prince Dauphin!
You are too much mistaken in this king: 30
Question your grace the late ambassadors,
With what great state he heard their em-
bassy,
How well supplied with noble counsellors,
How modest in exception, and withal
How terrible in constant resolution,
And you shall find his vanities forespent
Were but the outside of the Roman Brutus,
Covering discretion with a coat of folly;
As gardeners do with ordure hide those
roots
That shall first spring and be most delicate.40
  Dau. Well, 'tis not so, my lord high con-
stable;

But though we think it so, it is no matter:
In cases of defence 'tis best to weigh
The enemy more mighty than he seems:
So the proportions of defence are fill'd;
Which of a weak and niggardly projection
Doth, like a miser, spoil his coat with scant-
ing
A little cloth.
  Fr. King.   Think we King Harry strong;
And, princes, look you strongly arm to meet
him.
The kindred of him hath been flesh'd upon
us;   50
And he is bred out of that bloody strain
That haunted us in our familiar paths:
Witness our too much memorable shame
When Cressy battle fatally was struck,
And all our princes captived by the hand
Of that black name, Edward, Black Prince of
Wales;
Whiles that his mountain sire, on mountain
standing,
Up in the air, crown'd with the golden sun,
Saw his heroical seed, and smiled to see him,
Mangle the work of nature and deface   60
The patterns that by God and by French
fathers
Had twenty years been made. This is a stem
Of that victorious stock; and let us fear
The native mightiness and fate of him.

        Enter a Messenger.

  Mess. Ambassadors from Harry King of
England
Do crave admittance to your majesty.
  Fr. King. We'll give them present audi-
ence.
Go, and bring them.
        [*Exeunt Messenger and certain Lords.*
You see this chase is hotly follow'd, friends.
  Dau. Turn head, and stop pursuit; for
coward dogs
Most spend their mouths when what they
seem to threaten   70
Runs far before them. Good my sovereign,
Take up the English short, and let them
know

---

25. **Whitsun morris-dance**, a dance performed on various holidays by persons in fancy costumes. 28. **humorous**, capricious. 34. **exception**, making objections. 36. **forespent**, past. 37. **Brutus**. The elder Brutus pretended insanity in order to overthrow the Tarquins.

46. **Which . . . projection**, i.e., defense is futile if calculated on a niggardly scale. 48-64. **Think we . . . him.** This is a passage of exaggerated patriotism on Shakespeare's part, the tendency of which is to belittle the enemy. It is inconceivable that the French should talk so. There is much of this chauvinism in *Henry V*. 50. **flesh'd**, initiated in bloodshed. Hawks and hounds when rewarded with part of the kill were said to be fleshed. 64. **fate**, what he is destined to do. 67. **present**, immediate. 70. **spend their mouths**, bay.

Of what a monarchy you are the head:
Self-love, my liege, is not so vile a sin
As self-neglecting.

Re-enter Lords, *with* Exeter *and train.*

Fr. King.   From our brother England?
Exe. From him; and thus he greets your
    majesty.
He wills you, in the name of God Almighty,
That you divest yourself, and lay apart
The borrow'd glories that by gift of heaven,
By law of nature and of nations, 'long   80
To him and to his heirs; namely, the crown
And all wide-stretched honours that pertain
By custom and the ordinance of times
Unto the crown of France. That you may
    know
'Tis no sinister nor no awkward claim,
Pick'd from the worm-holes of long-vanish'd
    days,
Nor from the dust of old oblivion raked,
He sends you this most memorable line,
In every branch truly demonstrative;
Willing you overlook this pedigree: 90
And when you find him evenly derived
From his most famed of famous ancestors,
Edward the Third, he bids you then resign
Your crown and kingdom, indirectly held
From him the native and true challenger.
Fr. King. Or else what follows?
Exe. Bloody constraint; for if you hide the
    crown
Even in your hearts, there will he rake
    for it:
Therefore in fierce tempest is he coming,
In thunder and in earthquake, like a Jove, 100
That, if requiring fail, he will compel;
And bids you, in the bowels of the Lord,
Deliver up the crown, and to take mercy
On the poor souls for whom this hungry war
Opens his vasty jaws; and on your head
Turning the widows' tears, the orphans'
    cries,
The dead men's blood, the pining maidens'
    groans,
For husbands, fathers and betrothed lovers,
That shall be swallow'd in this controversy.
This is his claim, his threatening, and my
    message;   110

Unless the Dauphin be in presence here,
To whom expressly I bring greeting too.
   Fr. King. For us, we will consider of this
    further:
To-morrow shall you bear our full intent
Back to our brother England.
   Dau.   For the Dauphin,
I stand here for him: what to him from
    England?
   Exe. Scorn and defiance; slight regard,
    contempt,
And any thing that may not misbecome
The mighty sender, doth he prize you at.
Thus says my king; an if your father's
    highness   120
Do not, in grant of all demands at large,
Sweeten the bitter mock you sent his maj-
    esty,
He'll call you to so hot an answer of it,
That caves and womby vaultages of France
Shall chide your trespass and return your
    mock
In second accent of his ordnance.
   Dau. Say, if my father render fair re-
    turn,
It is against my will; for I desire
Nothing but odds with England: to that end,
As matching to his youth and vanity,   130
I did present him with the Paris balls.
   Exe. He'll make your Paris Louvre shake
    for it,
Were it the mistress-court of mighty Europe:
And, be assured, you'll find a difference,
As we his subjects have in wonder found,
Between the promise of his greener days
And these he masters now: now he weighs
    time
Even to the utmost grain: that you shall
    read
In your own losses, if he stay in France.
   Fr. King. To-morrow shall you know our
    mind at full.   140
   Exe. Dispatch us with all speed, lest that
    our king
Come here himself to question our delay;
For he is footed in this land already.
   Fr. King. You shall be soon dispatch'd
    with fair conditions:
A night is but small breath and little pause
To answer matters of this consequence.
                  [Flourish. Exeunt.

---

80. law of nature and of nations. This seems to be
a reference to the current theory that international law
is derived from the law of nature. **'long,** belong. **88.
line,** pedigree. **91. evenly,** directly. **102. bowels,**
mercy. Cf. *Philippians,* i, 8.

124. womby vaultages, deep caverns. **131. Paris
balls,** tennis balls. **132. Louvre,** the French royal
palace. **136. greener,** younger, cruder.

ACT III.

PROLOGUE.

Enter Chorus.

Chor. Thus with imagined wing our swift scene flies
In motion of no less celerity
Than that of thought. Suppose that you have seen
The well-appointed king at Hampton pier
Embark his royalty; and his brave fleet
With silken streamers the young Phœbus fanning:
Play with your fancies, and in them behold
Upon the hempen tackle ship-boys climbing;
Hear the shrill whistle which doth order give
To sounds confused; behold the threaden sails,   10
Borne with the invisible and creeping wind,
Draw the huge bottoms through the furrow'd sea,
Breasting the lofty surge: O, do but think
You stand upon the rivage and behold
A city on the inconstant billows dancing;
For so appears this fleet majestical,
Holding due course to Harfleur. Follow, follow:
Grapple your minds to sternage of this navy,
And leave your England, as dead midnight still,
Guarded with grandsires, babies and old women,   20
Either past or not arrived to pith and puissance;
For who is he, whose chin is but enrich'd
With one appearing hair, that will not follow
These cull'd and choice-drawn cavaliers to France?
Work, work your thoughts, and therein see a siege;
Behold the ordnance on their carriages,
With fatal mouths gaping on girded Harfleur.
Suppose the ambassador from the French comes back;
Tells Harry that the king doth offer him
Katharine his daughter, and with her, to dowry,   30
Some petty and unprofitable dukedoms.
The offer likes not: and the nimble gunner
With linstock now the devilish cannon touches, [*Alarum, and chambers go off.*
And down goes all before them. Still be kind,
And eke out our performance with your mind.   [*Exit.*

SCENE I. *France. Before Harfleur.*

Alarum. Enter King Henry, Exeter, Bedford, Gloucester, *and* Soldiers, *with scaling-ladders.*

K. Hen. Once more unto the breach, dear friends, once more;
Or close the wall up with our English dead.
In peace there's nothing so becomes a man
As modest stillness and humility:
But when the blast of war blows in our ears,
Then imitate the action of the tiger;
Stiffen the sinews, summon up the blood,
Disguise fair nature with hard-favour'd rage;
Then lend the eye a terrible aspect;
Let it pry through the portage of the head   10
Like the brass cannon; let the brow o'erwhelm it
As fearfully as doth a galled rock
O'erhang and jutty his confounded base,
Swill'd with the wild and wasteful ocean.
Now set the teeth and stretch the nostril wide,
Hold hard the breath and bend up every spirit
To his full height. On, on, you noblest English,
Whose blood is fet from fathers of war-proof!
Fathers that, like so many Alexanders,
Have in these parts from morn till even fought   20
And sheathed their swords for lack of argument:
Dishonour not your mothers; now attest
That those whom you call'd fathers did beget you.
Be copy now to men of grosser blood,
And teach them how to war. And you, good yeomen,
Whose limbs were made in England, show us here

33. linstock, staff holding a gunner's match. *Stage Direction:* chambers, small cannon.
   Scene i. 6-17. Then imitate . . . height. This passage indicates Shakespeare's theory of the operations of the passions. Everywhere he entertains the idea that the spiritual depends upon the physical state. 10. portage, porthole. 11. o'erwhelm, project over. 12. galled, washed away, undermined. 13. jutty, overhang. 14. Swill'd, washed. 18. fet, fetched. war-proof, proved in war.

1. imagined wing, wings of imagination. 14. rivage, banks. 18. to sternage, astern. 32. likes, pleases.

The mettle of your pasture; let us swear
That you are worth your breeding; which I
   doubt not;
For there is none of you so mean and base,
That hath not noble lustre in your eyes.   30
I see you stand like greyhounds in the slips,
Straining upon the start. The game's afoot:
Follow your spirit, and upon this charge
Cry 'God for Harry, England, and Saint
   George!'
   [*Exeunt. Alarum, and chambers go off.*

Scene II. *The same.*

Enter NYM, BARDOLPH, PISTOL, *and* Boy.

Bard. On, on, on, on, on! to the breach, to
the breach!
Nym. Pray thee, corporal, stay: the
knocks are too hot; and, for mine own part, I
have not a case of lives: the humour of it is
too hot, that is the very plain-song of it.
Pist. The plain-song is most just; for
  humours do abound:
Knocks go and come; God's vassals drop and
  die;
    And sword and shield,
    In bloody field,
Doth win immortal fame.   10
Boy. Would I were in an alehouse in
London! I would give all my fame for a pot
of ale and safety.
Pist. And I:
  If wishes would prevail with me,
  My purpose should not fail with me,
  But thither would I hie.
Boy. As duly, but not as truly,
  As bird doth sing on bough.   20

Enter FLUELLEN.

Flu. Up to the breach, you dogs! avaunt,
you cullions!   [*Driving them forward.*
Pist. Be merciful, great duke, to men of
mould.
Abate thy rage, abate thy manly rage,
Abate thy rage, great duke!
Good bawcock, bate thy rage; use lenity,
  sweet chuck!

Nym. These be good humours! your
honour wins bad humours.   28
   [*Exeunt all but Boy.*
Boy. As young as I am, I have observed
these three swashers. I am boy to them all
three: but all they three, though they would
serve me, could not be man to me; for indeed
three such antics do not amount to a man.
For Bardolph, he is white-livered and red-
faced; by the means whereof a' faces it out,
but fights not. For Pistol, he hath a killing
tongue and a quiet sword; by the means
whereof a' breaks words, and keeps whole
weapons. For Nym, he hath heard that men
of few words are the best men; and therefore
he scorns to say his prayers, lest a' should
be thought a coward: but his few bad words
are matched with as few good deeds; for a'
never broke any man's head but his own, 43
and that was against a post when he was
drunk. They will steal any thing, and call it
purchase. Bardolph stole a lute-case, bore it
twelve leagues, and sold it for three half-
pence. Nym and Bardolph are sworn
brothers in filching, and in Calais they stole
a fire-shovel: I knew by that piece of service
the men would carry coals. They would have
me as familiar with men's pockets as their
gloves or their handkerchers: which makes
much against my manhood, if I should take
from another's pocket to put into mine; for it
is plain pocketing up of wrongs. I must
leave them, and seek some better service:
their villany goes against my weak stomach,
and therefore I must cast it up.   57
   [*Exit.*

Re-enter FLUELLEN, GOWER *following.*

Gow. Captain Fluellen, you must come
presently to the mines; the Duke of Gloucester would speak with you.   60
Flu. To the mines! tell you the duke, it
is not so good to come to the mines; for,
look you, the mines is not according to the
disciplines of the war: the concavities of it
is not sufficient; for, look you, th' athversary,

---

27. **mettle of your pasture**, quality of your breeding (literally, "feeding"). 31. **slips**, leashes.

Scene ii. 5. **case**, set. 6. **plain-song**, air without any variations. Nym probably means "that is the truth of the matter." 22. **cullions**, rascals. 23. **men of mould**, mere mortals. 26. **bawcock**, French, *beau coq,* fine fellow. **chuck**, a term of endearment.

30. **swashers**, swashbucklers. 33. **antics**, grotesque figures. 34. **white-livered**, cowardly. In extreme fear the blood was thought to sink below the liver, leaving it bloodless. 45. **purchase**, thieves' cant for "stolen goods." 50. **carry coals**, proverbial expression for submitting to insult or degradation. 54. **pocketing up of**, putting up with. 64. **disciplines of the war.** It is Fluellen's humor to discuss the science of warfare, about which there were many books from Greek and Roman times down to the Renaissance.

you may discuss unto the duke, look you, is digt himself four yard under the countermines: by Cheshu, I think a' will plow up all, if there is not better directions.   68

Gow. The Duke of Gloucester, to whom the order of the siege is given, is altogether directed by an Irishman, a very valiant gentleman, i' faith.

Flu. It is Captain Macmorris, is it not?

Gow. I think it be.   73

Flu. By Cheshu, he is an ass, as in the world: I will verify as much in his beard: he has no more directions in the true disciplines of the wars, look you, of the Roman disciplines, than is a puppy-dog.

Enter MACMORRIS and Captain JAMY.

Gow. Here a' comes; and the Scots captain, Captain Jamy, with him.   80

Flu. Captain Jamy is a marvellous falorous gentleman, that is certain; and of great expedition and knowledge in th' aunchient wars, upon my particular knowledge of his directions: by Cheshu, he will maintain his argument as well as any military man in the world, in the disciplines of the pristine wars of the Romans.

Jamy. I say gud-day, Captain Fluellen.

Flu. God-den to your worship, good Captain James.   90

Gow. How now, Captain Macmorris! have you quit the mines? have the pioners given o'er?

Mac. By Chrish, la! tish ill done: the work ish give over, the trompet sound the retreat. By my hand, I swear, and my father's soul, the work ish ill done; it ish give over: I would have blowed up the town, so Chrish save me, la! in an hour: O, tish ill done, tish ill done; by my hand, tish ill done!   99

Flu. Captain Macmorris, I beseech you now, will you voutsafe me, look you, a few disputations with you, as partly touching or concerning the disciplines of the war, the Roman wars, in the way of argument, look you, and friendly communication; partly to satisfy my opinion, and partly for the satisfaction, look you, of my mind, as touching the direction of the military discipline; that is the point.   108

Jamy. It sall be vary gud, gud feith, gud captains bath: and I sall quit you with gud leve, as I may pick occasion; that sall I, marry.   111

Mac. It is no time to discourse, so Chrish save me: the day is hot, and the weather, and the wars, and the king, and the dukes: it is no time to discourse. The town is beseeched, and the trumpet call us to the breach; and we talk, and, be Chrish, do nothing: 'tis shame for us all: so God sa' me, 'tis shame to stand still; it is shame, by my hand: and there is throats to be cut, and works to be done; and there ish nothing done, so Chrish sa' me, la!   121

Jamy. By the mess, ere theise eyes of mine take themselves to slomber, ay'll de gud service, or ay'll lig i' the grund for it; ay, or go to death; and ay'll pay 't as valorously as I may, that sall I suerly do, that is the breff and the long. Marry, I wad full fain hear some question 'tween you tway.

Flu. Captain Macmorris, I think, look you, under your correction, there is not many of your nation—   131

Mac. Of my nation! What ish my nation? Ish a villain, and a bastard, and a knave, and a rascal—What ish my nation? Who talks of my nation?

Flu. Look you, if you take the matter otherwise than is meant, Captain Macmorris, peradventure I shall think you do not use me with that affability as in discretion you ought to use me, look you; being as good a man as yourself, both in the disciplines of war, and in the derivation of my birth, and in other particularities.   142

Mac. I do not know you so good a man as myself: so Chrish save me, I will cut off your head.

Gow. Gentlemen both, you will mistake each other.

Jamy. A! that's a foul fault.

[*A parley sounded.*

Gow. The town sounds a parley.   149

Flu. Captain Macmorris, when there is more better opportunity to be required,

---

65. **discuss**, explain. 67. **Cheshu**, an attempt to represent Fluellen's broken English. This is in general better done than that of Jamy, the Scotchman, and much better than the Irish dialect of Macmorris, which is hardly recognizable. Shakespeare probably knew the Welsh well, the Scotch to some degree, and the Irish very slightly. 74. **as**, as great as is. 89. **God-den**, good evening. 92. **pioners**, pioneers, engineering troops.

110. **quit**, requite. 116. **beseeched**, for *besieged*. 122. **mess**, Mass. 124. **lig**, lie. 127. **breff**, short. 132-135 **What . . . nation.** Macmorris is ready to fight even at the mention of his country.

look you, I will be so bold as to tell you I
know the disciplines of war; and there is an
end.   [*Exeunt.*

SCENE III. *The same. Before the gates.*

The Governor *and some* Citizens *on the walls;
the English forces below. Enter* KING
HENRY *and his train.*

K. Hen. How yet resolves the governor of
     the town?
This is the latest parle we will admit:
Therefore to our best mercy give yourselves;
Or like to men proud of destruction
Defy us to our worst: for, as I am a soldier,
A name that in my thoughts becomes me
     best,
If I begin the battery once again,
I will not leave the half-achieved Harfleur
Till in her ashes she lie buried.
The gates of mercy shall be all shut up,   10
And the flesh'd soldier, rough and hard of
     heart,
In liberty of bloody hand shall range
With conscience wide as hell, mowing like
     grass
Your fresh-fair virgins and your flowering
     infants.
What is it then to me, if impious war,
Array'd in flames like to the prince of fiends,
Do, with his smirch'd complexion, all fell
     feats
Enlink'd to waste and desolation?
What is 't to me, when you yourselves are
     cause,
If your pure maidens fall into the hand   20
Of hot and forcing violation?
What rein can hold licentious wickedness
When down the hill he holds his fierce career?
We may as bootless spend our vain command
Upon the enraged soldiers in their spoil
As send precepts to the leviathan
To come ashore. Therefore, you men of
     Harfleur,
Take pity of your town and of your people,
Whiles yet my soldiers are in my command;
Whiles yet the cool and temperate wind of
     grace   30
O'erblows the filthy and contagious clouds
Of heady murder, spoil and villany.

If not, why, in a moment look to see
The blind and bloody soldier with foul hand
Defile the locks of your shrill-shrieking
     daughters;
Your fathers taken by the silver beards,
And their most reverend heads dash'd to the
     walls,
Your naked infants spitted upon pikes,
Whiles the mad mothers with their howls
     confused
Do break the clouds, as did the wives of
     Jewry   40
At Herod's bloody-hunting slaughtermen.
What say you? will you yield, and this avoid,
Or, guilty in defence, be thus destroy'd?
     Gov. Our expectation hath this day an
     end:
The Dauphin, whom of succours we entreat-
     ed,
Returns us that his powers are yet not ready
To raise so great a siege. Therefore, great
     king,
We yield our town and lives to thy soft
     mercy.
Enter our gates; dispose of us and ours;
For we no longer are defensible.   50
     K. Hen. Open your gates. Come, uncle
     Exeter,
Go you and enter Harfleur; there remain,
And fortify it strongly 'gainst the French:
Use mercy to them all. For us, dear uncle,
The winter coming on and sickness growing
Upon our soldiers, we will retire to Calais.
To-night in Harfleur will we be your guest;
To-morrow for the march are we addrest.
     [*Flourish. The king and his train enter
                                   the town.*

SCENE IV. *The* FRENCH KING'S *palace.*

Enter KATHARINE *and* ALICE.

Kath. Alice, tu as été en Angleterre, et tu
parles bien le langage.
     Alice. Un peu, madame.

Scene iii. 2. **parle**, parley. 11. **flesh'd**, hardened by
bloodshed. 17. **fell**, savage. 26. **precepts**, summons.
leviathan, whale. 31. **O'erblows**, blows away. Contagion was thought to reside in clouds and mists. 32.
heady, headlong.

50. **defensible**, able to defend ourselves. 58. **addrest**, prepared.
           SCENE IV, TRANSLATION.
     Kath. Alice, you have been in England and speak the
language well.
     Alice. A little, my lady.
     Kath. I pray you, teach me; I have to learn to speak
it. What do you call *la main* in English?
     Alice. *La main?* it is called de hand.
     Kath. De hand. And *les doigts?*
     Alice. *Les doigts?* Dear me, I forget *les doigts.* I think
that they are called de fingres; yes, de fingres.
     Kath. *La main*, de hand; *les doigts*, de fingres. I think
that I am a clever scholar; I have learned two English
words in no time. What do you call *les ongles?*

Kath. Je te prie, m'enseignez; il faut que j'apprenne à parler. Comment appelez-vous la main en Anglois?

Alice. La main? elle est appelée de hand.

Kath. De hand. Et les doigts?

Alice. Les doigts? ma foi, j'oublie les doigts; mais je me souviendrai. Les doigts? je pense qu'ils sont appelés de fingres; oui, de fingres.

Kath. La main, de hand; les doigts, de fingres. Je pense que je suis le bon écolier; j'ai gagné deux mots d'Anglois vîtement. Comment appelez-vous les ongles?

Alice. Les ongles? nous les appelons de nails.

Kath. De nails. Écoutez; dites-moi, si je parle bien: de hand, de fingres, et de nails.

Alice. C'est bien dit, madame; il est fort bon Anglois. 20

Kath. Dites-moi l'Anglois pour le bras.

Alice. De arm, madame.

Kath. Et le coude?

Alice. De elbow.

Kath. De elbow. Je m'en fais la répétition de tous les mots que vous m'avez appris dès à présent.

Alice. Il est trop difficile, madame, comme je pense.

Kath. Excusez-moi, Alice; écoutez: de hand, de fingres, de nails, de arma, de bilbow.

Alice. De elbow, madame. 32

Kath. O Seigneur Dieu, je m'en oublie! de elbow. Comment appelez-vous le col?

Alice. De neck, madame.

Kath. De nick. Et le menton?

Alice. De chin.

Kath. De sin. Le col, de nick; le menton, de sin. 39

Alice. Oui. Sauf votre honneur, en vérite, vous prononcez les mots aussi droit que les natifs d'Angleterre.

Kath. Je ne doute point d'apprendre, par la grace de Dieu, et en peu de temps.

Alice. N'avez vous pas déjà oublié ce que je vous ai enseigné?

Kath. Non, je reciterai à vous promptement: de hand, de fingres, de mails,—

Alice. De nails, madame.

Kath. De nails, de arm, de ilbow.

Alice. Sauf votre honneur, de elbow. 50

Kath. Ainsi dis-je; de elbow, de nick, et de sin. Comment appelez-vous le pied et la robe?

Alice. De foot, madame; et de coun.

Kath. De foot et de coun! O Seigneur Dieu! ce sont mots de son mauvais, corruptible, gros, et impudique, et non pour les dames d'honneur d'user: je ne voudrais prononcer ces mots devant les seigneurs de France pour tout le monde. Foh! le foot et le coun! Néanmoins, je réciterai une autre fois ma leçon ensemble: de hand, de fingres, de nails, de arm, de elbow, de nick, de sin, de foot, de coun.

Alice. Excellent, madame!

Kath. C'est assez pour une fois: allons-nous à dîner. [*Exeunt.*

Alice. *Les ongles?* We call them de nails.

Kath. De nails. Listen; tell me whether or not I speak correctly: de hand, de fingres, and de nails.

Alice. That is correct, my lady; it is very good English.

Kath. Tell me the English for *le bras*.

Alice. De arm, my lady.

Kath. And *le coude?*

Alice. De elbow.

Kath. De elbow. I am going to repeat all the words you have taught me so far.

Alice. It is too hard, my lady, I fear.

Kath. Pardon me, Alice; listen: de hand, de fingres, de nails, de arma, de bilbow.

Alice. De elbow, my lady.

Kath. O Lord, I can't remember! de elbow. What do you call *le col?*

Alice. De neck, my lady.

Kath. De nick. And *le menton?*

Alice. De chin.

Kath. De sin. *Le col,* de nick; *le menton,* de sin.

Alice. Yes. On my word, really you pronounce the words just as English people themselves do.

Kath. I have no doubt that I shall learn, with God's help, in a very short time.

Alice. Have you not already forgotten what I have taught you?

Kath. No, I shall recite to you at once: de hand, de fingres, de mails—

Alice. De nails, my lady.

Kath. De nails, de arm, de ilbow.

Alice. By your leave, de elbow.

Kath. That's what I said; de elbow, de nick, and de sin. What do you call *le pied* and *la robe?*

Alice. De foot, my lady; and de coun.

Kath. De foot and de coun! O Lord! those are naughty words, wicked, coarse, and immodest, and are not fit to be used by nice ladies; I wouldn't say those words before French gentlemen for the whole world. Bah! le foot and le coun! Nevertheless, I shall recite my whole lesson once more: de hand, de fingres, de nails, de arm, de elbow, de nick, de sin, de foot, de coun.

Alice. Excellent, my lady.

Kath. That's enough for one time; let's go to dinner.

SCENE V.　*The same.*

Enter the KING OF FRANCE, *the* DAUPHIN, *the* DUKE OF BOURBON, *the* CONSTABLE OF FRANCE, *and others.*

Fr. King. 'Tis certain he hath pass'd the river Somme.

Con. And if he be not fought withal, my lord,
Let us not live in France; let us quit all
And give our vineyards to a barbarous people.

Dau. O Dieu vivant! shall a few sprays
  of us,
The emptying of our fathers' luxury,
Our scions, put in wild and savage stock,
Spirt up so suddenly into the clouds,
And overlook their grafters?
  Bour. Normans, but bastard Normans,
    Norman bastards!   10
Mort de ma vie! if they march along
Unfought withal, but I will sell my duke-
  dom,
To buy a slobbery and a dirty farm
In that nook-shotten isle of Albion.
  Con. Dieu de batailles! where have they
    this mettle?
Is not their climate foggy, raw and dull,
On whom, as in despite, the sun looks pale,
Killing their fruit with frowns? Can sodden
  water,
A drench for sur-rein'd jades, their barley-
  broth,   19
Decoct their cold blood to such valiant heat?
And shall our quick blood, spirited with
  wine,
Seem frosty? O, for honour of our land,
Let us not hang like roping icicles
Upon our houses' thatch, whiles a more
  frosty people
Sweat drops of gallant youth in our rich
  fields!
Poor we may call them in their native lords.
  Dau. By faith and honour,
Our madams mock at us, and plainly say
Our mettle is bred out and they will give
Their bodies to the lust of English youth   30
To new-store France with bastard warriors.
  Bour. They bid us to the English dancing-
    schools,
And teach lavoltas high and swift corantos;
Saying our grace is only in our heels,
And that we are most lofty runaways.
  Fr. King. Where is Montjoy the herald?
    speed him hence:
Let him greet England with our sharp
  defiance.
Up, princes! and, with spirit of honour edged
More sharper than your swords, hie to the
  field: 39

Charles Delabreth, high constable of France;
You Dukes of Orleans, Bourbon, and of
  Berri,
Alençon, Brabant, Bar, and Burgundy;
Jaques Chatillon, Rambures, Vaudemont,
Beaumont, Grandpré, Roussi, and Faucon-
  berg,
Foix, Lestrale, Bouciqualt, and Charolois;
High dukes, great princes, barons, lords and
  knights,
For your great seats now quit you of great
  shames.
Bar Harry England, that sweeps through our
  land
With pennons painted in the blood of Har-
  fleur: 49
Rush on his host, as doth the melted snow
Upon the valleys, whose low vassal seat
The Alps doth spit and void his rheum upon:
Go down upon him, you have power enough,
And in a captive chariot into Rouen
Bring him our prisoner
  Con.   This becomes the great.
Sorry am I his numbers are so few,
His soldiers sick and famish'd in their march,
For I am sure, when he shall see our army,
He'll drop his heart into the sink of fear
And for achievement offer us his ransom. 60
  Fr. King. Therefore, lord constable, haste
    on Montjoy,
And let him say to England that we send
To know what willing ransom he will give.
Prince Dauphin, you shall stay with us in
  Rouen.
  Dau. Not so, I do beseech your majesty.
  Fr. King. Be patient, for you shall remain
    with us.
Now forth, lord constable and princes all,
And quickly bring us word of England's fall.
                                    [*Exeunt.*

SCENE VI. *The English camp in Picardy.*

Enter GOWER *and* FLUELLEN, *meeting.*

  Gow. How now, Captain Fluellen! come
you from the bridge?
  Flu. I assure you, there is very excellent
services committed at the bridge.
  Gow. Is the Duke of Exeter safe?
  Flu. The Duke of Exeter is as magnani-

---

5. **sprays**, branches. 6. **luxury**, lust. 9. **overlook**,
rise above. **grafters**, trees from which scions are taken.
14. **nook-shotten**, full of nooks and angles. 18. **sodden**, boiled. 19. **sur-rein'd jades**, overridden horses.
barley-broth, beer. 20. **Decoct**, warm up. 23. **roping**, hanging down like a rope. 33. **lavoltas** . . .
corantos, fashionable dances. 36. **Montjoy**, title of
the chief herald of France. Shakespeare apparently
took it for a name.

52. **void his rheum**, spit.
Scene vi. 2. **bridge.** According to Holinshed, the
French were beaten in their attempt to break down the
bridge over the Ternois.

mous as Agamemnon; and a man that I love
and honour with my soul, and my heart, and
my duty, and my life, and my living, and
my uttermost power: he is not—God be
praised and blessed!—any hurt in the world;
but keeps the bridge most valiantly, with
excellent discipline. There is an aunchient
lieutenant there at the pridge, I think in my
very conscience he is as valiant a man as
Mark Antony; and he is a man of no estimation in the world; but I did see him do as
gallant service.

Gow. What do you call him?

Flu. He is called Aunchient Pistol.

Gow. I know him not.   20

Enter PISTOL.

Flu. Here is the man.

Pist. Captain, I thee beseech to do me
favours:
The Duke of Exeter doth love thee well.

Flu. Ay, I praise God; and I have merited
some love at his hands.

Pist. Bardolph, a soldier, firm and sound
of heart,
And of buxom valour, hath, by cruel fate,
And giddy Fortune's furious fickle wheel,
That goddess blind,   29
That stands upon the rolling restless stone—

Flu. By your patience, Aunchient Pistol.
Fortune is painted blind, with a muffler afore
her eyes, to signify to you that Fortune is
blind; and she is painted also with a wheel,
to signify to you, which is the moral of it,
that she is turning, and inconstant, and
mutability, and variation: and her foot,
look you, is fixed upon a spherical stone,
which rolls, and rolls, and rolls: in good
truth, the poet makes a most excellent description if it: Fortune is an excellent moral.

Pist. Fortune is Bardolph's foe, and
frowns on him;   41
For he hath stolen a pax, and hanged must
a' be:
A damned death!
Let gallows gape for dog; let man go free
And let not hemp his wind-pipe suffocate:
But Exeter hath given the doom of death
For pax of little price.

13. **aunchient lieutenant.** Fluellen, who is at this
time impressed with Pistol, gives him two titles.   27.
buxom, lively.   42. **pax.** Holinshed describes the object
stolen as a *pyx,* the vessel containing the consecrated
host. Shakespeare may have changed this into *pax,* a
plate stamped with a picture of Christ, since the offense
would be less shocking.

Therefore, go speak; the duke will hear thy
voice;
And let not Bardolph's vital thread be cut
With edge of penny cord and vile reproach: 50
Speak, captain, for his life, and I will thee
requite.

Flu. Aunchient Pistol, I do partly understand your meaning.

Pist. Why then, rejoice therefore.

Flu. Certainly, aunchient, it is not a
thing to rejoice at: for if, look you, he were
my brother, I would desire the duke to use
his good pleasure, and put him to execution;
for discipline ought to be used.

Pist. Die and be damn'd! and figo for
thy friendship!   60

Flu. It is well.

Pist. The fig of Spain!   [*Exit.*

Flu. Very good.

Gow. Why, this is an arrant counterfeit
rascal; I remember him now; a bawd, a cutpurse.

Flu. I'll assure you, a' uttered as prave
words at the pridge as you shall see in a summer's day. But it is very well; what he has
spoke to me, that is well, I warrant you,
when time is serve.   69

Gow. Why, 'tis a gull, a fool, a rogue,
that now and then goes to the wars, to grace
himself at his return into London under the
form of a soldier. And such fellows are
perfect in the great commanders' names:
and they will learn you by rote where services were done; at such and such a sconce,
at such a breach, at such a convoy; who
came off bravely, who was shot, who disgraced, what terms the enemy stood on; and
this they con perfectly in the phrase of war,
which they trick up with new-tuned oaths:
and what a beard of the general's cut and a
horrid suit of the camp will do among foaming bottles and ale-washed wits, is wonderful
to be thought on. But you must learn to
know such slanders of the age, or else you
may be marvellously mistook.

Flu. I tell you what, Captain Gower; I do
perceive he is not the man that he would
gladly make show to the world he is: if I find
a hole in his coat, I will tell him my mind.
[*Drum heard.*] Hark you, the king is coming,
and I must speak with him from the pridge.91

60. **figo,** fig.   70. **gull,** dupe.   76. **sconce,** a fort.

Drum and colours. Enter KING HENRY,
     GLOUCESTER, *and* Soldiers.

God pless your majesty!
     K. Hen. How now, Fluellen! camest thou
     from the bridge?
Flu. Ay, so please your majesty. The
Duke of Exeter has very gallantly maintained the pridge: the French is gone off, look
you; and there is gallant and most prave
passages; marry, th' athversary was have
possession of the pridge; but he is enforced
to retire, and the Duke of Exeter is master
of the pridge: I can tell your majesty, the
duke is a prave man.   101
     K. Hen. What men have you lost,
Fluellen?
Flu. The perdition of th' athversary hath
been very great, reasonable great: marry, for
my part, I think the duke hath lost never a
man, but one that is like to be executed for
robbing a church, one Bardolph, if your
majesty know the man: his face is all bubukles, and whelks, and knobs, and flames o'
fire: and his lips blows at his nose, and it is
like a coal of fire, sometimes plue and sometimes red; but his nose is executed, and his
fire's out.
     K. Hen. We would have all such offenders
so cut off: and we give express charge, that in
our marches through the country, there be
nothing compelled from the villages, nothing
taken but paid for, none of the French upbraided or abused in disdainful language; for
when lenity and cruelty play for a kingdom,
the gentler gamester is the soonest winner.120

     Tucket. Enter MONTJOY.

Mont. You know me by my habit.
     K. Hen. Well then I know thee: what shall
     I know of thee?
Mont. My master's mind.
     K. Hen. Unfold it.
Mont. Thus says my king: Say thou to
Harry of England: Though we seemed dead,
we did but sleep: advantage is a better soldier than rashness. Tell him we could have
rebuked him at Harfleur, but that we
thought not good to bruise an injury till it
were full ripe: now we speak upon our cue,
and our voice is imperial: England shall
repent his folly, see his weakness, and admire our sufferance. Bid him therefore consider of his ransom; which must proportion
the losses we have borne, the subjects we
have lost, the disgrace we have digested;
which in weight to re-answer, his pettiness
would bow under. For our losses, his ex- 137
chequer is too poor; for the effusion of our
blood, the muster of his kingdom too faint
a number; and for our disgrace, his own
person, kneeling at our feet, but a weak and
worthless satisfaction. To this add defiance:
and tell him, for conclusion, he hath betrayed
his followers, whose condemnation is pronounced. So far my king and master; so
much my office.   145
     K. Hen. What is thy name? I know thy
     quality.
Mont. Montjoy.
     K. Hen. Thou dost thy office fairly.
     Turn thee back,
And tell thy king I do not seek him now;
But could be willing to march on to Calais 150
Without impeachment: for, to say the sooth,
Though 'tis no wisdom to confess so much
Unto an enemy of craft and vantage,
My people are with sickness much enfeebled,
My numbers lessen'd, and those few I have
Almost no better than so many French;
Who when they were in health, I tell thee,
     herald,
I thought upon one pair of English legs
Did march three Frenchmen. Yet, forgive
     me, God,
That I do brag thus! This your air of
     France   160
Hath blown that vice in me; I must repent.
Go therefore, tell thy master here I am;
My ransom is this frail and worthless trunk,
My army but a weak and sickly guard;
Yet, God before, tell him we will come on,
Though France himself and such another
     neighbour
Stand in our way. There's for thy labour,
     Montjoy.
Go, bid thy master well advise himself:
If we may pass, we will; if we be hinder'd,
We shall your tawny ground with your red
     blood   170
Discolour: and so, Montjoy, fare you well.

---

103. **perdition**, losses.   108. **bubukles.** Fluellen
confuses *bubo* and *carbuncle*.   109. **whelks**, boils.   110-
111. **and his lips . . . fire.** This is the last of the many
jokes about Bardolph's fiery face.   120. *Stage Direction:*
Tucket, trumpet signal.   121. **habit**, tabard, herald's
coat.

136. **re-answer**, be an equivalent for.   146. **quality**,
profession.   151. **impeachment**, hindrance.   153.
vantage, favorable situation.

The sum of all our answer is but this:
We would not seek a battle, as we are;
Nor, as we are, we say we will not shun it:
So tell your master.

Mont. I shall deliver so. Thanks to your
highness.　　　　　　　　　　　*[Exit.*

Glou. I hope they will not come upon us
now.

K. Hen. We are in God's hand, brother,
not in theirs.

March to the bridge; it now draws toward
night:

Beyond the river we'll encamp ourselves,　180
And on to-morrow bid them march away.
　　　　　　　　　　　　　[Exeunt.

SCENE VII. *The French camp, near Agincourt.*

Enter the CONSTABLE OF FRANCE, *the* LORD
RAMBURES, ORLEANS, DAUPHIN, *with
others.*

Con. Tut! I have the best armour of the
world. Would it were day!

Orl. You have an excellent armour; but
let my horse have his due.

Con. It is the best horse of Europe.

Orl. Will it never be morning?

Dau. My Lord of Orleans, and my lord
high constable, you talk of horse and
armour?

Orl. You are as well provided of both as
any prince in the world.　　　　　　　10

Dau. What a long night is this! I will
not change my horse with any that treads
but on four pasterns. Ça, ha! he bounds
from the earth, as if his entrails were hairs;
le cheval volant, the Pegasus, chez les
narines de feu! When I bestride him, I soar,
I am a hawk: he trots the air; the earth sings
when he touches it; the basest horn of his
hoof is more musical than the pipe of
Hermes.

Orl. He's of the colour of the nutmeg.　20

Dau. And of the heat of the ginger. It is
a beast for Perseus: he is pure air and fire;
and the dull elements of earth and water
never appear in him, but only in patient
stillness while his rider mounts him: he is
indeed a horse; and all other jades you may
call beasts.

Con. Indeed, my lord, it is a most absolute and excellent horse.

Dau. It is the prince of palfreys; his neigh
is like the bidding of a monarch and his countenance enforces homage.　　　　　　31

Orl. No more, cousin.

Dau. Nay, the man hath no wit that cannot, from the rising of the lark to the lodging
of the lamb, vary deserved praise on my pal-
frey: it is a theme as fluent as the sea: turn
the sands into eloquent tongues, and my
horse is argument for them all: 'tis a subject
for a sovereign to reason on, and for a sovereign's sovereign to ride on; and for the
world, familiar to us and unknown, to lay
apart their particular functions and wonder
at him. I once writ a sonnet in his praise and
began thus: 'Wonder of nature,'—

Orl. I have heard a sonnet begin so to
one's mistress.

Dau. Then did they imitate that which I
composed to my courser, for my horse is my
mistress.

Orl. Your mistress bears well.　　　　48

Dau. Me well; which is the prescript
praise and perfection of a good and particular mistress.

Con. Nay, for methought yesterday your
mistress shrewdly shook your back.　　52

Dau. So perhaps did yours.

Con. Mine was not bridled.

Dau. O then belike she was old and
gentle; and you rode, like a kern of Ireland,
your French hose off, and in your strait
strossers.　　　　　　　　　　　57

Con. You have good judgement in horse-
manship.

Dau. Be warned by me, then: they that
ride so and ride not warily, fall into foul
bogs. I had rather have my horse to my
mistress.

Con. I had as lief have my mistress a
jade.

Dau. I tell thee, constable, my mistress
wears his own hair.

Con. I could make as true a boast as
that, if I had a sow to my mistress.

Dau. 'Le chien est retourné à son propre
vomissement, et la truie lavée au bourbier:'
thou makest use of any thing.　　　　70

Scene vii. **14. hairs,** used as stuffing for tennis balls.
15-16. le cheval . . . feu, the flying horse, Pegasus, with
nostrils breathing fire. **19. pipe of Hermes.** Hermes
charmed Argus to sleep with playing on his pipe.

34. lodging, lying down.　**49. prescript,** regular.
50. particular, one's own.　**52. shrewdly,** viciously.
56. kern, foot soldier.　**57. strossers,** trousers. French
hose were wide.　**68-69. 'Le chien . . . bourbier.'** Cf.
2 Peter, ii, 22.

Con. Yet do I not use my horse for my mistress, or any such proverb so little kin to the purpose.

Ram. My lord constable, the armour that I saw in your tent to-night, are those stars or suns upon it?

Con. Stars, my lord.

Dau. Some of them will fall to-morrow, I hope.

Con. And yet my sky shall not want.

Dau. That may be, for you bear a many superfluously, and 'twere more honour some were away.   81

Con. Even as your horse bears your praises; who would trot as well, were some of your brags dismounted.

Dau. Would I were able to load him with his desert! Will it never be day? I will trot to-morrow a mile, and my way shall be paved with English faces.   88

Con. I will not say so, for fear I should be faced out of my way: but I would it were morning; for I would fain be about the ears of the English.

Ram. Who will go to hazard with me for twenty prisoners?

Con. You must first go yourself to hazard, ere you have them.

Dau. 'Tis midnight; I'll go arm myself.
                                      [*Exit.*

Orl. The Dauphin longs for morning.

Ram. He longs to eat the English.

Con. I think he will eat all he kills.   100

Orl. By the white hand of my lady, he's a gallant prince.

Con. Swear by her foot, that she may tread out the oath.

Orl. He is simply the most active gentleman of France.

Con. Doing is activity; and he will still be doing.

Orl. He never did harm, that I heard of.

Con. Nor will do none to-morrow: he will keep that good name still.   111

Orl. I know him to be valiant.

Con. I was told that by one that knows him better than you.

Orl. What's he?

Con. Marry, he told me so himself; and he said he cared not who knew it.

Orl. He needs not; it is no hidden virtue in him.   119

Con. By my faith, sir, but it is; never any body saw it but his lackey: 'tis a hooded valour; and when it appears, it will bate.

Orl. Ill will never said well.   123

Con. I will cap that proverb with 'There is flattery in friendship.'

Orl. And I will take up that with 'Give the devil his due.'

Con. Well placed: there stands your friend for the devil: have at the very eye of that proverb with 'A pox of the devil.'   130

Orl. You are the better at proverbs, by how much 'A fool's bolt is soon shot.'

Con. You have shot over.

Orl. 'Tis not the first time you were overshot.

Enter a Messenger.

Mess. My lord high constable, the English lie within fifteen hundred paces of your tents.

Con. Who hath measured the ground?

Mess. The Lord Grandpré.

Con. A valiant and most expert gentleman. Would it were day! Alas, poor Harry of England! he longs not for the dawning as we do.   141

Orl. What a wretched and peevish fellow is this king of England, to mope with his fat-brained followers so far out of his knowledge!

Con. If the English had any apprehension, they would run away.

Orl. That they lack; for if their heads had any intellectual armour, they could never wear such heavy head-pieces.   149

Ram. That island of England breeds very valiant creatures; their mastiffs are of unmatchable courage.

Orl. Foolish curs, that run winking into the mouth of a Russian bear and have their heads crushed like rotten apples! You may as well say, that's a valiant flea that dare eat his breakfast on the lip of a lion.   157

Con. Just, just; and the men do sympathize with the mastiffs in robustious and rough coming on, leaving their wits with their wives: and then give them great meals of beef and iron and steel, they will eat like wolves and fight like devils.   163

90. **faced out of my way,** put to shame. 93. **go to hazard,** bet.

121. **hooded valour.** The hawk was kept hooded to prevent it from beating its wings (baiting); here the implication is that the prince will prepare for flight. 123-127. **Ill will . . . his due,** an example of the game of proverb capping. 142. **peevish,** foolish. 145. **apprehension,** as used by the constable it means "sense" and "sense of danger." Orleans takes it to mean "sense" or "perception" only. 153. **winking,** with eyes shut.

Orl. Ay, but these English are shrewdly out of beef.

Con. Then shall we find to-morrow they have only stomachs to eat and none to fight. Now is it time to arm: come, shall we about it?

Orl. It is now two o'clock: but, let me see, by ten

We shall have each a hundred Englishmen.

[*Exeunt.*

ACT IV.
PROLOGUE.

Enter Chorus.

Chor. Now entertain conjecture of a time
When creeping murmur and the poring dark
Fills the wide vessel of the universe.
From camp to camp through the foul womb
of night
The hum of either army stilly sounds,
That the fix'd sentinels almost receive
The secret whispers of each other's watch:
Fire answers fire, and through their paly
flames
Each battle sees the other's umber'd face;
Steed threatens steed, in high and boastful
neighs   10
Piercing the night's dull ear; and from the
tents
The armourers, accomplishing the knights,
With busy hammers closing rivets up,
Give dreadful note of preparation:
The country cocks do crow, the clocks do
toll,
And the third hour of drowsy morning name.
Proud of their numbers and secure in soul,
The confident and over-lusty French
Do the low-rated English play at dice;
And chide the cripple tardy-gaited night   20
Who, like a foul and ugly witch, doth limp
So tediously away. The poor condemned
English,
Like sacrifices, by their watchful fires
Sit patiently and inly ruminate
The morning's danger, and their gesture sad
Investing lank-lean cheeks and war-worn
coats

Presenteth them unto the gazing moon
So many horrid ghosts. O now, who will be-
hold
The royal captain of this ruin'd band
Walking from watch to watch, from tent to
tent,   30
Let him cry 'Praise and glory on his head!'
For forth he goes and visits all his host,
Bids them good morrow with a modest smile
And calls them brothers, friends and coun-
trymen.
Upon his royal face there is no note
How dread an army hath enrounded him;
Nor doth he dedicate one jot of colour
Unto the weary and all-watched night,
But freshly looks and over-bears attaint
With cheerful semblance and sweet majesty;
That every wretch, pining and pale before,
Beholding him, plucks comfort from his
looks: 42
A largess universal like the sun
His liberal eye doth give to every one,
Thawing cold fear, that mean and gentle all
Behold, as may unworthiness define,
A little touch of Harry in the night.
And so our scene must to the battle fly;
Where—O for pity!—we shall much disgrace
With four or five most vile and ragged foils,
Right ill-disposed in brawl ridiculous,   51
The name of Agincourt. Yet sit and see,
Minding true things by what their mockeries
be.   [*Exit.*

SCENE I. *The English camp at Agincourt.*

Enter KING HENRY, BEDFORD, *and*
GLOUCESTER.

K. Hen. Gloucester, 'tis true that we are
in great danger;
The greater therefore should our courage be.
Good morrow, brother Bedford. God Al-
mighty!
There is some soul of goodness in things evil,
Would men observingly distil it out.
For our bad neighbour makes us early stir-
rers,
Which is both healthful and good husbandry:
Besides, they are our outward consciences,

164. shrewdly, cursedly.
Act IV. Prologue. 2. poring, straining the eyes to see. 9. umber'd, shadowed, possibly by firelight. 12. accomplishing, equipping. 13. rivets. Parts of the armor might be riveted together even after it had been donned. 18. over-lusty, merry. 22. The poor condemned English. Shakespeare has somewhat exaggerated the wretchedness of the English in order to exalt the courage of his hero. 25. gesture, bearing.

36. enrounded, surrounded. 38. all-watched, worn out with watching. 39. over-bears attaint, overcomes the effects of weariness and depression. 45. mean and gentle, those of high and those of low birth. 49-53. we shall . . . be. This is a rather famous apology for the inadequacy of Shakespeare's stage. 53. Minding, forming a conception of.
Scene i. 8. they, may refer to *things evil*, above, or to the French.

And preachers to us all, admonishing
That we should dress us fairly for our end.
Thus may we gather honey from the weed,
And make a moral of the devil himself.   12

Enter ERPINGHAM.

Good morrow, old Sir Thomas Erpingham:
A good soft pillow for that good white head
Were better than a churlish turf of France.
   Erp. Not so, my liege: this lodging likes
    me better,
Since I may say 'Now lie I like a king.'
   K. Hen. 'Tis good for men to love their
    present pains
Upon example; so the spirit is eased:
And when the mind is quicken'd, out of
    doubt,   20
The organs, though defunct and dead before,
Break up their drowsy grave and newly
    move,
With casted slough and fresh legerity.
Lend me thy cloak, Sir Thomas. Brothers
    both,
Commend me to the princes in our camp;
Do my good morrow to them, and anon
Desire them all to my pavilion.
   Glou. We shall, my liege.
   Erp. Shall I attend your grace?
   K. Hen.   No, my good knight,
Go with my brothers to my lords of England:
I and my bosom must debate a while,   31
And then I would no other company.
   Erp. The Lord in heaven bless thee, noble
    Harry!
                [Exeunt all but King.
   K. Hen. God-a-mercy, old heart! thou
    speak'st cheerfully.

Enter PISTOL.

   Pist. Qui va là?
   K. Hen. A friend.
   Pist. Discuss unto me; art thou officer?
Or art thou base, common and popular?
   K. Hen. I am a gentleman of a company.
   Pist. Trail'st thou the puissant pike?   40
   K. Hen. Even so. What are you?
   Pist. As good a gentleman as the emperor.
   K. Hen. Then you are a better than the
    king.

   Pist. The king's a bawcock, and a heart of
    gold,
A lad of life, an imp of fame;   45
Of parents good, of fist most valiant:
I kiss his dirty shoe, and from heart-string
I love the lovely bully. What is thy name?
   K. Hen. Harry le Roy.
   Pist. Le Roy! a Cornish name: art thou
of Cornish crew?   50
   K. Hen. No, I am a Welshman.
   Pist. Know'st thou Fluellen?
   K. Hen. Yes.
   Pist. Tell him, I'll knock his leek about
    his pate
Upon Saint Davy's day.
   K. Hen. Do not you wear your dagger in
your cap that day, lest he knock that about
yours.
   Pist. Art thou his friend?
   K. Hen. And his kinsman too.
   Pist. The figo for thee, then!   60
   K. Hen. I thank you: God be with you!
   Pist. My name is Pistol call'd.   *[Exit.*
   K. Hen. It sorts well with your fierceness.

Enter FLUELLEN and GOWER.

   Gow. Captain Fluellen!
   Flu. So! in the name of Jesu Christ, speak
lower. It is the greatest admiration in the
universal world, when the true and aunchient
prerogatifes and laws of the wars is not kept:
if you would take the pains but to examine
the wars of Pompey the Great, you shall find,
I warrant you, that there is no tiddle taddle
nor pibble pabble in Pompey's camp; I warrant you, you shall find the ceremonies of
the wars, and the cares of it, and the forms
of it, and the sobriety of it, and the modesty
of it, to be otherwise.
   Gow. Why, the enemy is loud; you hear
him all night.
   Flu. If the enemy is an ass and a fool and
a prating coxcomb, is it meet, think you,
that we should also, look you, be an ass and
a fool and a prating coxcomb? in your own
conscience, now?   81
   Gow. I will speak lower.

---

10. **dress,** prepare. 19. **Upon example,** as an
example. 23. **slough,** skin of a snake. **legerity,**
nimbleness. 35. **Qui va là?** Who goes there? 38. **popular,** of low birth. 40. **Trail'st . . . pike?** Are you in
the infantry? The pike was a long weapon which, in the
pike-exercise, was grasped below the head, the foot
being allowed to trail on the ground.

45. **imp,** child. 51. **Welshman.** Henry was born at
Monmouth on the border of Wales; it seems to have been
thought of as a Welsh city. 54-55. **leek . . . Saint
Davy's day.** On St. David's day, March 1, the leek
was worn in memory of a Welsh victory over the Saxons,
since St. David, their leader, had commanded his followers to wear leeks in their caps on that occasion. The
leek is therefore a patriotic emblem. 81. **conscience,**
inmost thought.

Flu. I pray you and beseech you that you will.   [*Exeunt Gower and Fluellen.*

K. Hen. Though it appear a little out of fashion,

There is much care and valour in this Welshman.

Enter three soldiers, JOHN BATES, ALEXANDER COURT, *and* MICHAEL WILLIAMS.

Court. Brother John Bates, is not that the morning which breaks yonder?

Bates. I think it be: but we have no great cause to desire the approach of day.   90

Will. We see yonder the beginning of the day, but I think we shall never see the end of it. Who goes there?

K. Hen. A friend.

Will. Under what captain serve you?

K. Hen. Under Sir Thomas Erpingham.

Will. A good old commander and a most kind gentleman: I pray you, what thinks he of our estate?

K. Hen. Even as men wrecked upon a sand, that look to be washed off the next tide.   101

Bates. He hath not told his thought to the king?

K. Hen. No; nor it is not meet he should. For, though I speak to you, I think the king is but a man, as I am: the violet smells to him as it doth to me; the element shows to him as it doth to me; all his senses have but human conditions: his ceremonies laid by, in his nakedness he appears but a man; and though his affections are higher mounted than ours, yet, when they stoop, they stoop with the like wing. Therefore when he sees reason of fears, as we do, his fears, out of doubt, be of the same relish as ours are: yet, in reason, no man should possess him with any appearance of fear, lest he, by showing it, should dishearten his army.   117

Bates. He may show what outward courage he will; but I believe, as cold a night as 'tis, he could wish himself in Thames up to the neck; and so I would he were, and I by him, at all adventures, so we were quit here.

K. Hen. By my troth, I will speak my conscience of the king: I think he would not wish himself any where but where he is.

Bates. Then I would he were here alone; so should he be sure to be ransomed, and a many poor men's lives saved.   128

K. Hen. I dare say you love him not so ill, to wish him here alone, howsoever you speak this to feel other men's minds: methinks I could not die any where so contented as in the king's company; his cause being just and his quarrel honourable.

Will. That's more than we know.

Bates. Ay, or more than we should seek after; for we know enough, if we know we are the king's subjects: if his cause be wrong, our obedience to the king wipes the crime of it out of us.   139

Will. But if the cause be not good, the king himself hath a heavy reckoning to make, when all those legs and arms and heads, chopped off in a battle, shall join together at the latter day and cry all 'We died at such a place;' some swearing, some crying for a surgeon, some upon their wives left poor behind them, some upon the debts they owe, some upon their children rawly left. I am afeard there are few die well that die in a battle; for how can they charitably dispose of any thing, when blood is their argument? Now, if these men do not die well, it will be a black matter for the king that led them to it; whom to disobey were against all proportion of subjection.   153

K. Hen. So, if a son that is by his father sent about merchandise do sinfully miscarry upon the sea, the imputation of his wickedness, by your rule, should be imposed upon his father that sent him: or if a servant, under his master's command transporting a sum of money, be assailed by robbers and die in many irreconciled iniquities, you may call the business of the master the author of the servant's damnation: but this is not so: the king is not bound to answer the particular endings of his soldiers, the father of his son, nor the master of his servant; for they purpose not their death, when they purpose their services. Besides, there is no king, be his cause never so spotless, if it come to the arbitrement of swords, can try it out with all

---

107. **element**, sky. **shows**, looks. 112. **stoop**, swoop down.

147. **rawly**, without provision. 153. **proportion of subjection**, proper duty of a subject. 154-196. **So, if . . . prepare.** The king's speech presents the customary case made out for those responsible for war. Battle becomes God's instrument for punishing the guilty. Such speculations are not infrequent in the literature of the time. Henry continues his discourse on the responsibilities and cares of kingship in lines 247-301. 155. **sinfully miscarry**, die in their sins.

unspotted soldiers: some peradventure have on them the guilt of premeditated and contrived murder; some, of beguiling virgins with the broken seals of perjury; some, making the wars their bulwark, that have before gored the gentle bosom of peace with pillage and robbery. Now, if these men have 175 defeated the law and outrun native punishment, though they can outstrip men, they have no wings to fly from God: war is his beadle, war is his vengeance; so that here men are punished for before-breach of the king's laws in now the king's quarrel: where they feared the death, they have borne life away; and where they would be safe, they perish: then if they die unprovided, no more is the king guilty of their damnation than he was before guilty of those impieties for the which they are now visited. Every subject's duty is the king's; but every subject's soul is his own. Therefore should every soldier in the wars do as every sick man in his bed, wash every mote out of his conscience: and dying so, death is to him advantage; or not dying, the time was blessedly lost wherein such preparation was gained: and in him that escapes, it were not sin to think that, making God so free an offer, He let him outlive that day to see His greatness and to teach others how they should prepare. 196

Will. 'Tis certain, every man that dies ill, the ill upon his own head, the king is not to answer it. 199

Bates. I do not desire he should answer for me; and yet I determine to fight lustily for him.

K. Hen. I myself heard the king say he would not be ransomed.

Will. Ay, he said so, to make us fight cheerfully: but when our throats are cut, he may be ransomed, and we ne'er the wiser.

K. Hen. If I live to see it, I will never trust his word after. 208

Will. You pay him then. That's a perilous shot out of an elder-gun, that a poor and a private displeasure can do against a monarch! you may as well go about to turn the sun to ice with fanning in his face with a peacock's feather. You'll never trust his word after! come, 'tis a foolish saying.

K. Hen. Your reproof is something too round: I should be angry with you, if the time were convenient.

Will. Let it be a quarrel between us, if you live. 220

K. Hen. I embrace it.

Will. How shall I know thee again?

K. Hen. Give me any gage of thine, and I will wear it in my bonnet: then, if ever thou darest acknowledge it, I will make it my quarrel.

Will. Here's my glove: give me another of thine.

K. Hen. There. 228

Will. This will I also wear in my cap: if ever thou come to me and say, after tomorrow, 'This is my glove,' by this hand, I will take thee a box on the ear.

K. Hen. If ever I live to see it, I will challenge it.

Will. Thou darest as well be hanged.

K. Hen. Well, I will do it, though I take thee in the king's company.

Will. Keep thy word: fare thee well.

Bates. Be friends, you English fools, be friends: we have French quarrels enow, if you could tell how to reckon. 241

K. Hen. Indeed, the French may lay twenty French crowns to one, they will beat us; for they bear them on their shoulders: but it is no English treason to cut French crowns, and to-morrow the king himself will be a clipper.   [*Exeunt Soldiers.*

Upon the king! let us our lives, our souls,
Our debts, our careful wives,
Our children and our sins lay on the king!
We must bear all. O hard condition,   250
Twin-born with greatness, subject to the breath
Of every fool, whose sense no more can feel
But his own wringing! What infinite heart's-ease
Must kings neglect, that private men enjoy!
And what have kings, that privates have not too,
Save ceremony, save general ceremony?
And what art thou, thou idol ceremony?
What kind of god art thou, that suffer'st more
Of mortal griefs than do thy worshippers?

---

173. **bulwark,** refuge. 176. **native,** at home. 183. **unprovided,** unprepared. 210. **elder-gun,** popgun made from a hollowed branch of elder.

217. **round,** direct, brusque. 245. **crowns,** double pun on *crown* meaning "coin" and *crown* meaning "head." 246. **clipper,** one who mutilates coins by clipping the edges. 253. **wringing,** suffering.

What are thy rents? what are thy comings
    in?   260
O ceremony, show me but thy worth!
What is thy soul of adoration?
Art thou aught else but place, degree and
    form,
Creating awe and fear in other men?
Wherein thou art less happy being fear'd
Than they in fearing.
What drink'st thou oft, instead of homage
    sweet,
But poison'd flattery? O, be sick, great
    greatness,
And bid thy ceremony give thee cure!
Think'st thou the fiery fever will go out   270
With titles blown from adulation?
Will it give place to flexure and low bend-
    ing?
Canst thou, when thou command'st the
    beggar's knee,
Command the health of it? No, thou proud
    dream,
That play'st so subtly with a king's repose;
I am a king that find thee, and I know
'Tis not the balm, the sceptre and the ball,
The sword, the mace, the crown imperial,
The intertissued robe of gold and pearl,
The farced title running 'fore the king,   280
The throne he sits on, nor the tide of pomp
That beats upon the high shore of this world,
No, not all these, thrice-gorgeous ceremony,
Not all these, laid in bed majestical,
Can sleep so soundly as the wretched slave,
Who with a body fill'd and vacant mind
Gets him to rest, cramm'd with distressful
    bread;
Never sees horrid night, the child of hell,
But, like a lackey, from the rise to set
Sweats in the eye of Phœbus and all night   290
Sleeps in Elysium; next day after dawn
Doth rise and help Hyperion to his horse,
And follows so the ever-running year,
With profitable labour, to his grave:
And, but for ceremony, such a wretch,
Winding up days with toil and nights with
    sleep,
Had the fore-hand and vantage of a king.
The slave, a member of the country's peace,
Enjoys it; but in gross brain little wots

What watch the king keeps to maintain the
    peace,   300
Whose hours the peasant best advantages.

Re-enter ERPINGHAM.

  Erp. My lord, your nobles, jealous of your
    absence,
Seek through your camp to find you.
  K. Hen.   Good old knight,
Collect them all together at my tent:
I'll be before thee.
  Erp.   I shall do 't, my lord. [*Exit.*
  K. Hen. O God of battles! steel my
    soldiers' hearts;
Possess them not with fear; take from them
    now
The sense of reckoning, if the opposed num-
    bers
Pluck their hearts from them. Not to-day,
    O Lord,
O, not to-day, think not upon the fault   310
My father made in compassing the crown!
I Richard's body have interred new;
And on it have bestow'd more contrite tears
Than from it issued forced drops of blood:
Five hundred poor I have in yearly pay,
Who twice a-day their wither'd hands hold up
Toward heaven, to pardon blood; and I have
    built
Two chantries, where the sad and solemn
    priests
Sing still for Richard's soul. More will I do;
Though all that I can do is nothing worth, 320
Since that my penitence comes after all,
Imploring pardon.

Re-enter GLOUCESTER.

  Glou. My liege!
  K. Hen. My brother Gloucester's voice?
    Ay;
I know thy errand, I will go with thee:
The day, my friends and all things stay for
    me.   [*Exeunt.*

SCENE II. *The French camp.*

Enter the DAUPHIN, ORLEANS, RAMBURES,
    and others.

  Orl. The sun doth gild our armour; up,
    my lords!

---

262. **soul of adoration**, essence of the adoration
(paid thee). 271. **blown**, breathed. 276. **find**, find
out. 280. **farced**, stuffed with pompous phrases. 287.
distressful, earned by hard work. 291. **Elysium**, the
abode of the blessed. 292. **Hyperion**, the sun-god.
The peasant is up before the sun. 298. **member**,
sharer. 299. **wots**, knows.

301. **advantages**, derives advantage from. 302.
jealous of, apprehensive because of. 306-322. **O God
. . . pardon.** This passage contains the principal evidence of Shakespeare's presentation of his hero as a religious man. The fault the king refers to is the
deposition and murder of Richard II, a theme which
runs through all the plays of this series.

Dau. Montez à cheval! My horse! varlet!
  laquais! ha!
Orl. O brave spirit!
Dau. Via! les eaux et la terre.
Orl. Rien puis? l'air et le feu.
Dau. Ciel, cousin Orleans.

     Enter CONSTABLE.

Now, my lord constable!
  Con. Hark, how our steeds for present
    service neigh!
  Dau. Mount them, and make incision in
    their hides,   9
That their hot blood may spin in English eyes,
And dout them with superfluous courage, ha!
  Ram. What, will you have them weep our
    horses' blood?
How shall we, then, behold their natural tears?

     Enter Messenger.

  Mess. The English are embattled, you
    French peers.
  Con. To horse, you gallant princes!
    straight to horse!
Do but behold yon poor and starved band,
And your fair show shall suck away their
  souls,
Leaving them but the shales and husks of
  men.
There is not work enough for all our hands;
Scarce blood enough in all their sickly veins 20
To give each naked curtle-axe a stain,
That our French gallants shall to-day draw
  out,
And sheathe for lack of sport: let us but blow
  on them,
The vapour of our valour will o'erturn them.
'Tis positive 'gainst all exceptions, lords,
That our superfluous lackeys and our peas-
  ants,
Who in unnecessary action swarm
About our squares of battle, were enow
To purge this field of such a hilding foe,
Though we upon this mountain's basis by 30
Took stand for idle speculation:
But that our honours must not. What's to
  say?
A very little little let us do,

And all is done. Then let the trumpets sound
The tucket sonance and the note to mount;
For our approach shall so much dare the field
That England shall couch down in fear and
  yield.

     Enter GRANDPRÉ.

  Grand. Why do you stay so long, my lords
    of France?
Yon island carrions, desperate of their bones,
Ill-favouredly become the morning field: 40
Their ragged curtains poorly are let loose,
And our air shakes them passing scornfully:
Big Mars seems bankrupt in their beggar'd
  host
And faintly through a rusty beaver peeps:
The horsemen sit like fixed candlesticks,
With torch-staves in their hand; and their
  poor jades
Lob down their heads, dropping the hides
  and hips,
The gum down-roping from their pale-dead
  eyes,
And in their pale dull mouths the gimmal bit
Lies foul with chew'd grass, still and motion-
  less;   50
And their executors, the knavish crows,
Fly o'er them, all impatient for their hour.
Description cannot suit itself in words
To demonstrate the life of such a battle
In life so lifeless as it shows itself.
  Con. They have said their prayers, and
    they stay for death.
  Dau. Shall we go send them dinners and
    fresh suits
And give their fasting horses provender,
And after fight with them?
  Con. I stay but for my guidon: to the field!
I will the banner from a trumpet take,   61
And use it for my haste. Come, come, away!
The sun is high, and we outwear the day.
                       [Exeunt.

    SCENE III.   *The English camp.*

Enter GLOUCESTER, BEDFORD, EXETER, ER-
PINGHAM, *with all his host:* SALISBURY
and WESTMORELAND.

  Glou. Where is the king?

Bed. The king himself is rode to view their
battle.

West. Of fighting men they have full three
score thousand.

Exe. There's five to one; besides, they all
are fresh.

Sal. God's arm strike with us! 'tis a
fearful odds.

God be wi' you, princes all; I'll to my charge:
If we no more meet till we meet in heaven,
Then, joyfully, my noble Lord of Bedford,
My dear Lord Gloucester, and my good Lord
Exeter,
And my kind kinsman, warriors all, adieu!

Bed. Farewell, good Salisbury; and good
luck go with thee!   11

Exe. Farewell, kind lord; fight valiantly
to-day:
And yet I do thee wrong to mind thee of it,
For thou art framed of the firm truth of
valour.   *[Exit Salisbury.*

Bed. He is as full of valour as of kindness;
Princely in both.

Enter the KING.

West.   O that we now had here
But one ten thousand of those men in
England
That do no work to-day!

K. Hen.   What's he that wishes so?
My cousin Westmoreland? No, my fair
cousin:
If we are mark'd to die, we are enow   20
To do our country loss; and if to live,
The fewer men, the greater share of honour.
God's will! I pray thee, wish not one man
more.
By Jove, I am not covetous for gold,
Nor care I who doth feed upon my cost;
It yearns me not if men my garments wear;
Such outward things dwell not in my desires:
But if it be a sin to covet honour,
I am the most offending soul alive.
No, faith, my coz, wish not a man from
England: 30
God's peace! I would not lose so great an
honour
As one man more, methinks, would share
from me
For the best hope I have. O, do not wish
one more!

Rather proclaim it, Westmoreland, through
my host,
That he which hath no stomach to this fight,
Let him depart; his passport shall be made
And crowns for convoy put into his purse:
We would not die in that man's company
That fears his fellowship to die with us.
This day is call'd the feast of Crispian.   40
He that outlives this day, and comes safe
home,
Will stand a tip-toe when this day is named,
And rouse him at the name of Crispian.
He that shall live this day, and see old age,
Will yearly on the vigil feast his neighbours,
And say 'To-morrow is Saint Crispian:'
Then will he strip his sleeve and show his
scars,
And say 'These wounds I had on Crispin's
day.'
Old men forget; yet all shall be forgot,
But he'll remember with advantages   50
What feats he did that day: then shall our
names,
Familiar in his mouth as household words,
Harry the king, Bedford and Exeter,
Warwick and Talbot, Salisbury and Glou-
cester,
Be in their flowing cups freshly remember'd.
This story shall the good man teach his son;
And Crispin Crispian shall ne'er go by,
From this day to the ending of the world,
But we in it shall be remembered;   59
We few, we happy few, we band of brothers;
For he to-day that sheds his blood with me
Shall be my brother; be he ne'er so vile,
This day shall gentle his condition:
And gentlemen in England now a-bed
Shall think themselves accursed they were
not here,
And hold their manhoods cheap whiles any
speaks
That fought with us upon Saint Crispin's
day.

Re-enter SALISBURY.

Sal. My sovereign lord, bestow yourself
with speed:
The French are bravely in their battles set,
And will with all expedience charge on us.

37. **crowns for convoy,** travel pay. 39. **That fears
. . . us,** that is afraid to risk his life in our company.
40. **Crispian.** Crispinus and Crispianus were martyrs
in France in the fourth century; they were shoemakers by
13. **mind,** remind. 18-67. **What's . . . day.** Henry's   trade and became the patron saints of that craft. 45.
famous speech contrasts strongly in its dignity and   **vigil,** evening before a feast day. 50. **advantages,**
manliness with the boastful frivolity of the French.   additions of his own. 63. **gentle,** raise to the rank of
26. **yearns,** grieves.   gentleman. 70. **expedience,** speed.

K. Hen. All things are ready, if our minds
be so. 71

West. Perish the man whose mind is backward now!

K. Hen. Thou dost not wish more help
from England, coz?

West. God's will! my liege, would you and
I alone,
Without more help, could fight this royal
battle!

K. Hen. Why, now thou hast unwish'd
five thousand men;
Which likes me better than to wish us one.
You know your places: God be with you
all!

Tucket. Enter MONTJOY.

Mont. Once more I come to know of thee,
King Harry, 79
If for thy ransom thou wilt now compound,
Before thy most assured overthrow:
For certainly thou art so near the gulf,
Thou needs must be englutted. Besides, in
mercy,
The constable desires thee thou wilt mind
Thy followers of repentance; that their souls
May make a peaceful and a sweet retire
From off these fields, where, wretches, their
poor bodies
Must lie and fester.

K. Hen. Who hath sent thee now?

Mont. The Constable of France.

K. Hen. I pray thee, bear my former
answer back: 90
Bid them achieve me and then sell my bones.
Good God! why should they mock poor
fellows thus?
The man that once did sell the lion's skin
While the beast lived, was killed with hunt-
ing him.
A many of our bodies shall no doubt
Find native graves; upon the which, I trust,
Shall witness live in brass of this day's work:
And those that leave their valiant bones in
France,
Dying like men, though buried in your dung-
hills,
They shall be famed; for there the sun shall
greet them, 100
And draw their honours reeking up to
heaven,
Leaving their earthly parts to choke your
clime,

The smell whereof shall breed a plague in
France.
Mark then abounding valour in our English,
That being dead, like to the bullet's grazing,
Break out into a second course of mischief,
Killing in relapse of mortality.
Let me speak proudly: tell the constable
We are but warriors for the working-day;
Our gayness and our gilt are all besmirch'd
With rainy marching in the painful field; 111
There's not a piece of feather in our host—
Good argument, I hope, we will not fly—
And time hath worn us into slovenry:
But, by the mass, our hearts are in the trim;
And my poor soldiers tell me, yet ere night
They'll be in fresher robes, or they will pluck
The gay new coats o'er the French soldiers'
heads
And turn them out of service. If they do
this,—
As, if God please, they shall,—my ransom
then 120
Will soon be levied. Herald, save thou thy
labour;
Come thou no more for ransom, gentle
herald:
They shall have none, I swear, but these my
joints;
Which if they have as I will leave 'em them,
Shall yield them little, tell the constable.

Mont. I shall, King Harry. And so fare
thee well:
Thou never shalt hear herald any more. [_Exit._

K. Hen. I fear thou'lt once more come
again for ransom.

Enter YORK.

York. My lord, most humbly on my knee
I beg
The leading of the vaward. 130

K. Hen. Take it, brave York. Now,
soldiers, march away:
And how thou pleasest, God, dispose the
day! [_Exeunt._

SCENE IV. _The field of battle._

Alarum. Excursions. Enter PISTOL, _French
Soldier, and_ BOY.

Pist. Yield, cur!

---

83. **englutted**, swallowed up. 96. **native**, in their
own land.

105. **grazing**, glancing off. 107. **Killing . . . mortality**, killing (their foes) as they fall back (decompose)
into their elements. 130. **vaward**, vanguard.
Scene iv. The battle has, so to speak, been fought in
anticipation. This is the only bit of actual conflict. If it
has any dramatic value, it may suggest the greatness of
a victory in which the cowardly Pistol might make so
easy a capture.

Fr. Sol. Je pense que vous êtes gentil-homme de bonne qualité.

Pist. Qualtitie calmie custure me! Art thou a gentleman? what is thy name? discuss.

Fr. Sol. O Seigneur Dieu!

Pist. O, Signieur Dew should be a gentle-man:

Perpend my words, O Signieur Dew, and mark;

O Signieur Dew, thou diest on point of fox,

Except, O signieur, thou do give to me 10
Egregious ransom.

Fr. Sol. O, prenez miséricorde! ayez pitié de moi!

Pist. Moy shall not serve; I will have forty moys;

Or I will fetch thy rim out at thy throat 15
In drops of crimson blood.

Fr. Sol. Est-il impossible d'échapper la force de ton bras?

Pist. Brass, cur!

Thou damned and luxurious mountain goat,
Offer'st me brass? 21

Fr. Sol. O pardonnez moi!

Pist. Say'st thou me so? is that a ton of moys?

Come hither, boy: ask me this slave in French

What is his name.

Boy. Écoutez: comment êtes-vous appelé?

Fr. Sol. Monsieur le Fer.

Boy. He says his name is Master Fer.

Pist. Master Fer! I'll fer him, and firk him, and ferret him: discuss the same in French unto him. 31

Boy. I do not know the French for fer, and ferret, and firk.

Pist. Bid him prepare; for I will cut his throat.

Fr. Sol. Que dit-il, monsieur?

Boy. Il me commande de vous dire que vous faites vous prêt; car ce soldat ici est disposé tout à cette heure de couper votre gorge.

Pist. Owy, cuppele gorge, permafoy.

Peasant, unless thou give me crowns, brave crowns; 40

Or mangled shalt thou be by this my sword.

Fr. Sol. O, je vous supplie, pour l'amour de Dieu, me pardonner! Je suis gentil-homme de bonne maison: gardez ma vie, et je vous donnerai deux cents écus.

Pist. What are his words?

Boy. He prays you to save his life: he is a gentleman of a good house; and for his ransom he will give you two hundred crowns.

Pist. Tell him my fury shall abate, and I
The crowns will take. 51

Fr. Sol. Petit monsieur, que dit-il?

Boy. Encore qu'il est contre son jurement de pardonner aucun prisonnier, néanmoins, pour les écus que vous l'avez promis, il est content de vous donner la liberté, le franchisement.

Fr. Sol. Sur mes genoux je vous donne mille remercîmens; et je m'estime heureux que je suis tombé entre les mains d'un chevalier, je pense, le plus brave, vaillant, et très distingué seigneur d'Angleterre. 61

Pist. Expound unto me, boy.

Boy. He gives you, upon his knees, a thousand thanks; and he esteems himself happy that he hath fallen into the hands of one, as he thinks, the most brave, valorous, and thrice-worthy signieur of England.

Pist. As I suck blood, I will some mercy show.

Follow me! 69

Boy. Suivez-vous le grand capitaine. [*Exeunt Pistol, and French Soldier.*] I did never know so full a voice issue from so empty a heart: but the saying is true, 'The empty vessel makes the greatest sound.' Bardolph and Nym had ten times more valour than this roaring devil i' the old play, that every one may pare his nails with a wooden dagger; and they are both hanged; and so would

---

2-3. **Je . . . qualité,** I think that you are a gentleman of high rank. Most of Pistol's replies are nonsense. 4. **calmie custure me.** These words are perhaps derived from the refrain of a popular song, supposed to be Irish, "Calen o custure me" (Young maiden, my treasure). 8. **Perpend,** attend to, consider. 9. **fox,** sword. 12-13. **O . . . moi!** Oh, have mercy! have pity on me! 14. **Moy.** Pistol, not understanding the French, imagines that a coin is referred to. 15. **rim,** midriff, diaphragm. 17-18. **Est-il . . . bras?** Is there no way to escape the strength of your arm? 26. **Écoutez . . . appelé?** Listen: what is your name? 29. **firk,** trounce. 30. **ferret,** probably, worry like a ferret. 35-38. **Que . . . gorge,** What does he say, sir? *Boy:* He bids me tell you that you must prepare yourself, because this soldier intends to cut your throat immediately.

42-45. **O, . . . écus,** Oh, I pray you, for the love of God, to pardon me. I am a gentleman of a good house; preserve my life, and I shall give you two hundred crowns. 52-56. **Petit . . . franchisement.** What does he say, little sir? *Boy:* I tell you again that it is against his oath to pardon any prisoner; nevertheless for the sake of the crowns you have promised, he is willing to give you your liberty, your freedom. 57-61. **Sur . . . d'Angleterre,** On my knees I give you a thousand thanks; and I consider myself happy that I have fallen into the hands of a knight, as I think, the bravest, most valiant and distinguished gentleman in England. 70. **Suivez-vous . . . capitaine,** Follow the great captain. 76. **old play,** an allusion probably to moralities or interludes rather than the mystery plays. The Vice is traditionally associated with the wooden dagger; this passage would indicate that he had long nails.

this be, if he durst steal any thing adventurously. I must stay with the lackeys, with the luggage of our camp: the French might have a good prey of us, if he knew of it; for there is none to guard it but boys.   [*Exit*.

SCENE V. *Another part of the field*.

Enter CONSTABLE, ORLEANS, BOURBON, DAUPHIN, *and* RAMBURES.

Con. O diable!

Orl. O seigneur ! le jour est perdu, tout est perdu!

Dau. Mort de ma vie! all is confounded, all!
Reproach and everlasting shame
Sits mocking in our plumes. O méchante fortune!
Do not run away.   [*A short alarum*.

Con.   Why, all our ranks are broke.

Dau. O perdurable shame! let's stab ourselves.
Be these the wretches that we play'd at dice for?

Orl. Is this the king we sent to for his ransom?

Bour. Shame and eternal shame, nothing but shame!   10
Let us die in honour: once more back again;
And he that will not follow Bourbon now,
Let him go hence, and with his cap in hand,
Like a base pandar, hold the chamber-door
Whilst by a slave, no gentler than my dog,
His fairest daughter is contaminated.

Con. Disorder, that hath spoil'd us, friend us now!
Let us on heaps go offer up our lives.

Orl. We are enow yet living in the field
To smother up the English in our throngs, 20
If any order might be thought upon.

Bour. The devil take order now! I'll to the throng:
Let life be short; else shame will be too long.
          [*Exeunt*.

SCENE VI. *Another part of the field*.

Alarums. Enter KING HENRY *and forces,*
EXETER, *and others*.

K. Hen. Well have we done, thrice valiant countrymen:

Scene v. 2. O . . . perdu, O sir, the day is lost, all is lost. 7. perdurable, everlasting.

But all's not done; yet keep the French the field.

Exe. The Duke of York commends him to your majesty.

K. Hen. Lives he, good uncle? thrice within this hour
I saw him down; thrice up again, and fighting;
From helmet to the spur all blood he was.

Exe. In which array, brave soldier, doth he lie,
Larding the plain; and by his bloody side,
Yoke-fellow to his honour-owing wounds,
The noble Earl of Suffolk also lies.   10
Suffolk first died: and York, all haggled over,
Comes to him, where in gore he lay insteep'd,
And takes him by the beard; kisses the gashes
That bloodily did yawn upon his face;
And cries aloud 'Tarry, dear cousin Suffolk!
My soul shall thine keep company to heaven:
Tarry, sweet soul, for mine, then fly abreast,
As in this glorious and well-foughten field
We kept together in our chivalry!'
Upon these words I came and cheer'd him up: 20
He smiled me in the face, raught me his hand,
And, with a feeble gripe, says 'Dear my lord,
Commend my service to my sovereign.'
So did he turn and over Suffolk's neck
He threw his wounded arm and kiss'd his lips;
And so espoused to death, with blood he seal'd
A testament of noble-ending love.
The pretty and sweet manner of it forced
Those waters from me which I would have stopp'd;
But I had not so much of man in me,   30
And all my mother came into mine eyes
And gave me up to tears.

K. Hen.   I blame you not;
For, hearing this, I must perforce compound
With mistful eyes, or they will issue too.
          [*Alarum*.
But, hark! what new alarum is this same?
The French have reinforced their scatter'd men:
Then every soldier kill his prisoners:
Give the word through.   [*Exeunt*.

9. honour-owing, honor-owning, honorable. 21. raught, past tense of reach. 31. mother, the tenderer part of me. 37. kill his prisoners. This follows Holinshed, who says that Henry, alarmed by the outcry of the lackeys and boys of the camp, feared a new attack and ordered the prisoners killed as a means of precaution. Gower, scene vii, 9-10, attributes the king's action to revenge.

SCENE VII. *Another part of the field.*

Enter FLUELLEN *and* GOWER.

Flu. Kill the poys and the luggage! 'tis expressly against the law of arms: 'tis as arrant a piece of knavery, mark you now, as can be offer't; in your conscience, now, is it not?

Gow. 'Tis certain there's not a boy left alive; and the cowardly rascals that ran from the battle ha' done this slaughter: besides, they have burned and carried away all that was in the king's tent; wherefore the king, most worthily, hath caused every soldier to cut his prisoner's throat. O, 'tis a gallant king!   11

Flu. Ay, he was porn at Monmouth, Captain Gower. What call you the town's name where Alexander the Pig was born?

Gow. Alexander the Great.

Flu. Why, I pray you, is not pig great? the pig, or the great, or the mighty, or the huge, or the magnanimous, are all one reckonings, save the phrase is a little variations.

Gow. I think Alexander the Great was born in Macedon: his father was called Philip of Macedon, as I take it.   22

Flu. I think it is in Macedon where Alexander is porn. I tell you, captain, if you look in the maps of the 'orld, I warrant you sall find, in the comparisons between Macedon and Monmouth, that the situations, look you, is both alike. There is a river in Macedon; and there is also moreover a river at Monmouth: it is called Wye at Monmouth; but it is out of my prains what is the name of the other river; but 'tis all one, 'tis alike as my fingers is to my fingers, and there is salmons in both. If you mark Alexander's life well, Harry of Monmouth's life is come after it indifferent well; for there is figures in all things. Alexander, God knows, and you know, in his rages, and his furies, and his wraths, and his cholers, and his moods, and his displeasures, and his indignations, and also being a little intoxicates in his prains, did, in his ales and his angers, look you, kill his best friend, Cleitus.   41

Gow. Our king is not like him in that: he never killed any of his friends.

Flu. It is not well done, mark you now, to take the tales out of my mouth, ere it is made and finished. I speak but in the figures and comparisons of it: as Alexander killed his friend Cleitus, being in his ales and his cups; so also Harry Monmouth, being in his right wits and his good judgements, turned away the fat knight with the great-belly doublet: he was full of jests, and gipes, and knaveries, and mocks; I have forgot his name.   53

Gow. Sir John Falstaff.

Flu. That is he: I'll tell you there is good men porn at Monmouth.

Gow. Here comes his majesty.

Alarum. Enter KING HENRY, *and forces;* WARWICK, GLOUCESTER, EXETER, *and others.*

K. Hen. I was not angry since I came to France
Until this instant. Take a trumpet, herald;
Ride thou unto the horsemen on yon hill: 60
If they will fight with us, bid them come down,
Or void the field; they do offend our sight:
If they'll do neither, we will come to them,
And make them skirr away, as swift as stones
Enforced from the old Assyrian slings:
Besides, we'll cut the throats of those we have,
And not a man of them that we shall take
Shall taste our mercy. Go and tell them so.

Enter MONTJOY.

Exe. Here comes the herald of the French, my liege.

Glo. His eyes are humbler than they used to be.   70

K. Hen. How now! what means this, herald? know'st thou not
That I have fined these bones of mine for ransom?
Comest thou again for ransom?

Mont.   No, great king:
I come to thee for charitable license,
That we may wander o'er this bloody field
To look our dead, and then to bury them;
To sort our nobles from our common men.
For many of our princes—woe the while!—

---

35. **figures,** probably, analogies, points of comparison. 41. **Cleitus,** one of the generals of Alexander the Great.

51. **great-belly doublet,** a long waistcoat then in style. 54. **Sir John Falstaff,** the last allusion to the fat knight. One cannot escape the impression that in Shakespeare's thought the rejection of Falstaff was a matter of some importance. 62. **void,** leave. 64. **skirr,** scurry. 65. **Enforced,** discharged. 72. **fined,** agreed to pay as a fine or ransom.

Lie drown'd and soak'd in mercenary blood;
So do our vulgar drench their peasant limbs
In blood of princes; and their wounded
   steeds   81
Fret fetlock deep in gore and with wild rage
Yerk out their armed heels at their dead
   masters,
Killing them twice. O, give us leave, great
   king,
To view the field in safety and dispose
Of their dead bodies!

   K. Hen.   I tell thee truly, herald,
I know not if the day be ours or no;
For yet a many of your horsemen peer
And gallop o'er the field.

   Mont.   The day is yours.

   K. Hen. Praised be God, and not our
   strength, for it!   90
What is this castle call'd that stands hard by?

   Mont. They call it Agincourt.

   K. Hen. Then call we this the field of
   Agincourt,
Fought on the day of Crispin Crispianus.

   Flu. Your grandfather of famous memory,
an't please your majesty, and your great-
uncle Edward the Plack Prince of Wales, as
I have read in the chronicles, fought a most
prave pattle here in France.

   K. Hen. They did, Fluellen.   100

   Flu. Your majesty says very true; if your
majesties is remembered of it, the Welshmen
did good service in a garden where leeks did
grow, wearing leeks in their Monmouth caps;
which, your majesty know, to this hour is an
honourable badge of the service; and I do
believe your majesty takes no scorn to wear
the leek upon Saint Tavy's day.

   K. Hen. I wear it for a memorable honour;
For I am Welsh, you know, good countryman.   110

   Flu. All the water in Wye cannot wash
your majesty's Welsh plood out of your
pody, I can tell you that: God pless it and
preserve it, as long as it pleases his grace,
and his majesty too!

   K. Hen. Thanks, good my countryman.

   Flu. By Jeshu, I am your majesty's
countryman, I care not who know it; I will
confess it to all the 'orld: I need not to be
ashamed of your majesty, praised be God, so
long as your majesty is an honest man.   120

   K. Hen. God keep me so! Our heralds go
   with him:
Bring me just notice of the numbers dead
On both our parts. Call yonder fellow hither.
       [*Points to Williams. Exeunt Heralds
                          with Montjoy.*

   Exe. Soldier, you must come to the king.

   K. Hen. Soldier, why wearest thou that
glove in thy cap?

   Will. An 't please your majesty, 'tis the
gage of one that I should fight withal, if he
be alive.

   K. Hen. An Englishman?   129

   Will. An 't please your majesty, a rascal
that swaggered with me last night; who, if
alive and ever dare to challenge this glove,
I have sworn to take him a box o' th' ear: or
if I can see my glove in his cap, which he
swore, as he was a soldier, he would wear if
alive, I will strike it out soundly.

   K. Hen. What think you, Captain Fluellen? is it fit this soldier keep his oath?

   Flu. He is a craven and a villain else, an 't
please your majesty, in my conscience.   140

   K. Hen. It may be his enemy is a gentleman of great sort, quite from the answer
of his degree.

   Flu. Though he be as good a gentleman
as the devil is, as Lucifer and Belzebub himself, it is necessary, look your grace, that he
keep his vow and his oath: if he be perjured,
see you now, his reputation is as arrant a
villain and a Jacksauce, as ever his black shoe
trod upon God's ground and his earth, in my
conscience, la!   150

   K. Hen. Then keep thy vow, sirrah,
when thou meetest the fellow.

   Will. So I will, my liege, as I live.

   K. Hen. Who servest thou under?

   Will. Under Captain Gower, my liege.

   Flu. Gower is a good captain, and is good
knowledge and literatured in the wars.

   K. Hen. Call him hither to me, soldier.

   Will. I will, my liege.   [*Exit.* 159

   K. Hen. Here, Fluellen, wear thou this
favour for me and stick it in thy cap: when
Alençon and myself were down together, I
plucked this glove from his helm: if any man
challenge this, he is a friend to Alençon, and

---

79. **mercenary**, of mercenary soldiers. 83. **Yerk,**
kick. 88. **peer,** appear

148. **Jacksauce,** saucy knave. 161-166. **when . . .**
love. This rather crude jest of the king's, contrived at
such a solemn moment, is an example of Shakespeare's
mixture of the serious and the comic, the ground of much
adverse criticism by Continental writers.

an enemy to our person; if thou encounter any such, apprehend him, an thou dost me love.

Flu. Your grace doo's me as great honours as can be desired in the hearts of his subjects: I would fain see the man, that has but two legs, that shall find himself aggriefed at this glove; that is all; but I would fain see it once, an please God of his grace that I might see.

K. Hen. Knowest thou Gower?

Flu. He is my dear friend, an please you.

K. Hen. Pray thee, go seek him, and bring him to my tent.

Flu. I will fetch him.   [*Exit.*

K. Hen. My Lord of Warwick, and my brother Gloucester,
Follow Fluellen closely at the heels:
The glove which I have given him for a favour
May haply purchase him a box o' th' ear; 181
It is the soldier's; I by bargain should
Wear it myself. Follow, good cousin Warwick:
If that the soldier strike him, as I judge
By his blunt bearing he will keep his word,
Some sudden mischief may arise of it;
For I do know Fluellen valiant
And, touch'd with choler, hot as gunpowder,
And quickly will return an injury: 189
Follow, and see there be no harm between them.
Go you with me, uncle of Exeter. [*Exeunt.*

SCENE VIII. *Before* KING HENRY'S *pavilion.*

Enter GOWER *and* WILLIAMS.

Will. I warrant it is to knight you, captain.

Enter FLUELLEN.

Flu. God's will and his pleasure, captain, I beseech you now, come apace to the king: there is more good toward you peradventure than is in your knowledge to dream of.

Will. Sir, know you this glove?

Flu. Know the glove! I know the glove is a glove.

Will. I know this; and thus I challenge it.
                              [*Strikes him.*

188. **choler,** anger.

Flu. 'Sblood! an arrant traitor as any is in the universal world, or in France, or in England!   11

Gow. How now, sir! you villain!

Will. Do you think I'll be forsworn?

Flu. Stand away, Captain Gower; I will give treason his payment into plows, I warrant you.

Will. I am no traitor.

Flu. That's a lie in thy throat. I charge you in his majesty's name, apprehend him: he's a friend of the Duke Alençon's.   19

Enter WARWICK *and* GLOUCESTER.

War. How now, how now! what's the matter?

Flu. My Lord of Warwick, here is—praised be God for it!—a most contagious treason come to light, look you, as you shall desire in a summer's day. Here is his majesty.

Enter KING HENRY *and* EXETER.

K. Hen. How now! what's the matter?

Flu. My liege, here is a villain and a traitor, that, look your grace, has struck the glove which your majesty is take out of the helmet of Alençon.   28

Will. My liege, this was my glove; here is the fellow of it; and he that I gave it to in change promised to wear it in his cap: I promised to strike him, if he did: I met this man with my glove in his cap, and I have been as good as my word.

Flu. Your majesty hear now, saving your majesty's manhood, what an arrant, rascally, beggarly, lousy knave it is: I hope your majesty is pear me testimony and witness, and will avouchment, that this is the glove of Alençon, that your majesty is give me; in your conscience, now.   40

K. Hen. Give me thy glove, soldier: look, here is the fellow of it.
'Twas I, indeed, thou promised'st to strike;
And thou hast given me most bitter terms.

Flu. And please your majesty, let his neck answer for it, if there is any martial law in the world.

K. Hen. How canst thou make me satisfaction?

Will. All offences, my lord, come from the heart: never came any from mine that might offend your majesty.   51

K. Hen. It was ourself thou didst abuse.

Will. Your majesty came not like yourself: you appeared to me but as a common man; witness the night, your garments, your lowliness; and what your highness suffered under that shape, I beseech you take it for your own fault and not mine: for had you been as I took you for, I made no offence; therefore, I beseech your highness, pardon me.   60

K. Hen. Here, uncle Exeter, fill this glove with crowns,
And give it to this fellow. Keep it, fellow;
And wear it for an honour in thy cap
Till I do challenge it. Give him the crowns:
And, captain, you must needs be friends with him.

Flu. By this day and this light, the fellow has mettle enough in his belly. Hold, there is twelve pence for you; and I pray you to serve God, and keep you out of prawls, and prabbles, and quarrels, and dissensions, and, I warrant you, it is the better for you.   71

Will. I will none of your money.

Flu. It is with a good will; I can tell you, it will serve you to mend your shoes: come, wherefore should you be so pashful? your shoes is not so good: 'tis a good silling, I warrant you, or I will change it.

Enter an English Herald.

K. Hen. Now, herald, are the dead number'd?

Her. Here is the number of the slaughter'd French.

K. Hen. What prisoners of good sort are taken, uncle?   80

Exe. Charles Duke of Orleans, nephew to the king;
John Duke of Bourbon, and Lord Bouciqualt:
Of other lords and barons, knights and squires,
Full fifteen hundred, besides common men.

K. Hen. This note doth tell me of ten thousand French
That in the field lie slain: of princes, in this number,
And nobles bearing banners, there lie dead

One hundred twenty-six: added to these,
Of knights, esquires, and gallant gentlemen,
Eight thousand and four hundred; of the which,   90
Five hundred were but yesterday dubb'd knights:
So that, in these ten thousand they have lost,
There are but sixteen hundred mercenaries;
The rest are princes, barons, lords, knights, squires,
And gentlemen of blood and quality.
The names of those their nobles that lie dead:
Charles Delabreth, high constable of France;
Jacques of Chatillon, admiral of France;
The master of the cross-bows, Lord Rambures;
Great Master of France, the brave Sir Guichard Dolphin,   100
John Duke of Alençon, Anthony Duke of Brabant,
The brother to the Duke of Burgundy,
And Edward Duke of Bar: of lusty earls,
Grandpré and Roussi, Fauconberg and Foix,
Beaumont and Marle, Vaudemont and Lestrale.
Here was a royal fellowship of death!
Where is the number of our English dead?
                [*Herald shews him another paper.*
Edward the Duke of York, the Earl of Suffolk,
Sir Richard Ketly, Davy Gam, esquire:
None else of name; and of all other men   110
But five and twenty. O God, thy arm was here;
And not to us, but to thy arm alone,
Ascribe we all! When, without stratagem,
But in plain shock and even play of battle,
Was ever known so great and little loss
On one part and on the other? Take it, God,
For it is none but thine!

Exe.   'Tis wonderful!

K. Hen. Come, go we in procession to the village:
And be it death proclaimed through our host
To boast of this or take that praise from God
Which is his only.   121

Flu. Is it not lawful, an please your majesty, to tell how many is killed?

K. Hen. Yes, captain; but with this acknowledgement,
That God fought for us.

53-60. **Your . . . pardon me.** The situation is saved
by these manly words of the common soldier. 85-117.
This note . . . thine. The catalogue of the slain is
straight from Holinshed. Neilson calls attention to
the return of the act to the high level of the king's piety.

110. **name**, rank, importance.

Flu. Yes, my conscience, he did us great good.

K. Hen. Do we all holy rites;
Let there be sung 'Non nobis' and 'Te Deum;'
The dead with charity enclosed in clay:
And then to Calais; and to England then; 130
Where ne'er from France arrived more happy men.   [*Exeunt.*

ACT V.

PROLOGUE.

Enter Chorus.

Chor. Vouchsafe to those that have not read the story,
That I may prompt them: and of such as have,
I humbly pray them to admit the excuse
Of time, of numbers and due course of things,
Which cannot in their huge and proper life
Be here presented. Now we bear the king
Toward Calais: grant him there; there seen,
Heave him away upon your winged thoughts
Athwart the sea. Behold, the English beach
Pales in the flood with men, with wives and boys, 10
Whose shouts and claps out-voice the deep-mouth'd sea,
Which like a mighty whiffler 'fore the king
Seems to prepare his way: so let him land,
And solemnly see him set on to London.
So swift a pace hath thought that even now
You may imagine him upon Blackheath;
Where that his lords desire him to have borne
His bruised helmet and his bended sword
Before him through the city: he forbids it,
Being free from vainness and self-glorious pride; 20
Giving full trophy, signal and ostent
Quite from himself to God. But now behold,
In the quick forge and working-house of thought,
How London doth pour out her citizens!

The mayor and all his brethren in best sort,
Like to the senators of the antique Rome,
With the plebeians swarming at their heels,
Go forth and fetch their conquering Cæsar in:
As by a lower but loving likelihood,
Were now the general of our gracious empress, 30
As in good time he may, from Ireland coming,
Bringing rebellion broached on his sword,
How many would the peaceful city quit,
To welcome him! much more, and much more cause,
Did they this Harry. Now in London place him;
As yet the lamentation of the French
Invites the King of England's stay at home;
The emperor's coming in behalf of France,
To order peace between them; and omit
All the occurrences, whatever chanced, 40
Till Harry's back-return again to France:
There must we bring him; and myself have play'd
The interim, by remembering you 'tis past.
Then brook abridgement, and your eyes advance,
After your thoughts, straight back again to France.   [*Exit.*

SCENE I. *France. The English camp.*

Enter FLUELLEN *and* GOWER.

Gow. Nay, that's right; but why wear you your leek to-day? Saint Davy's day is past.

Flu. There is occasions and causes why and wherefore in all things: I will tell you, asse my friend, Captain Gower: the rascally, scauld, beggarly, lousy, pragging knave, Pistol, which you and yourself and all the world know to be no petter than a fellow, look you now, of no merits, he is come to me and prings me pread and salt yesterday, look you, and bid me eat my leek: it was in a place where I could not breed no contention with him; but I will be so bold as to wear it in my cap till I see him once again,

Act V. Between Acts IV and V there is historically an interval of about five years during which Henry made a second campaign in France and brought the French to terms in the Treaty of Troyes.
Stage Direction: **Chorus.** In modern presentations of the play, notably in that of Mansfield, the return to London described in this prologue is made the basis for great spectacular display. 10. **Pales,** impales, surrounds. 12. **whiffler,** an usher heading the procession to clear the way. 21. **signal,** token (of victory). **ostent,** external show.

29-35. **As by ... him,** one of the few unquestionable allusions by Shakespeare to contemporary events. The Earl of Essex had left London on his Irish expedition on March 27, 1599; he returned unsuccessful and under a cloud on September 28 of the same year. These lines, therefore, must have been written between the dates mentioned. 32. **broached,** transfixed, spitted. 38. **emperor's.** The emperor of Germany, Sigismund, came to England in behalf of France in May, 1416.
Scene i. 6. **scauld,** scurvy.

and then I will tell him a little piece of my desires.

Enter PISTOL.

Gow. Why, here he comes, swelling like a turkey-cock.

Flu. 'Tis no matter for his swellings nor his turkey-cocks. God pless you, Aunchient Pistol! you scurvy, lousy knave, God pless you!

Pist. Ha! art thou bedlam? dost thou thirst, base Trojan,   20
To have me fold up Parca's fatal web?
Hence! I am qualmish at the smell of leek.

Flu. I peseech you heartily, scurvy, lousy knave, at my desires, and my requests, and my petitions, to eat, look you, this leek: because, look you, you do not love it, nor your affections and your appetites and your disgestions doo's not agree with it, I would desire you to eat it.   28

Pist. Not for Cadwallader and all his goats.

Flu. There is one goat for you. [*Strikes him.*] Will you be so good, scauld knave, as eat it?   31

Pist. Base Trojan, thou shalt die.

Flu. You say very true, scauld knave, when God's will is: I will desire you to live in the mean time, and eat your victuals: come, there is sauce for it. [*Strikes him.*] You called me yesterday mountain-squire; but I will make you to-day a squire of low degree. I pray you, fall to: if you can mock a leek, you can eat a leek.

Gow. Enough, captain: you have astonished him.   41

Flu. I say, I will make him eat some part of my leek, or I will peat his pate four days. Bite, I pray you; it is good for your green wound and your ploody coxcomb.

Pist. Must I bite?

Flu. Yes, certainly, and out of doubt and out of question too, and ambiguities.

Pist. By this leek, I will most horribly revenge: I eat and eat, I swear—   50

Flu. Eat, I pray you: will you have some more sauce to your leek? there is not enough leek to swear by.

Pist. Quiet thy cudgel; thou dost see I eat.

Flu. Much good do you, scauld knave, heartily. Nay, pray you, throw none away; the skin is good for your broken coxcomb. When you take occasions to see leeks hereafter, I pray you, mock at 'em; that is all.

Pist. Good.   60

Flu. Ay, leeks is good: hold you, there is a groat to heal your pate.

Pist. Me a groat!

Flu. Yes, verily and in truth, you shall take it; or I have another leek in my pocket, which you shall eat.

Pist. I take thy groat in earnest of revenge.

Flu. If I owe you any thing, I will pay you in cudgels: you shall be a woodmonger, and buy nothing of me but cudgels. God b' wi' you, and keep you, and heal your pate.
                                                [*Exit.*

Pist. All hell shall stir for this.   71

Gow. Go, go; you are a counterfeit cowardly knave. Will you mock at an ancient tradition, begun upon an honourable respect, and worn as a memorable trophy of predeceased valour and dare not avouch in your deeds any of your words? I have seen you gleeking and galling at this gentleman twice or thrice. You thought, because he could not speak English in the native garb, he could not therefore handle an English cudgel: you find it otherwise; and henceforth let a Welsh correction teach you a good English condition. Fare ye well.   [*Exit.* 84

Pist. Doth Fortune play the huswife with me now?
News have I, that my Nell is dead i' the spital
Of malady of France;
And there my rendezvous is quite cut off.
Old I do wax; and from my weary limbs
Honour is cudgelled. Well, bawd I'll turn,   90
And something lean to cutpurse of quick hand.
To England will I steal, and there I'll steal:
And patches will I get unto these cudgell'd scars,

20. bedlam, crazy. Trojan, dissolute fellow; a current term of contempt. 21. Parca's. The fates, or Parcæ, spun the web of life. 29. Cadwallader, last king of the Welsh. Pistol makes the customary taunt that the Welsh were goatherds. 37. mountain-squire, an allusion to the mountainous surface of Wales. 38. squire of low degree, the name of an old romance. 40. astonished, terrified.

62. groat, a coin worth four pence. 75. respect, consideration, reason. 78. gleeking and galling, gibing and scoffing. 85. huswife, hussy. 86. Nell, F: *Doll;* text follows Capell on the ground that Mistress Quickly's name was Nell. spital, hospital.

And swear I got them in the Gallia wars. 94
[*Exit.*

SCENE II. *France. A royal palace.*

Enter, at one door, KING HENRY, EXETER,
BEDFORD, GLOUCESTER, WARWICK, WEST-
MORELAND, *and other* Lords; *at another, the*
FRENCH KING, QUEEN ISABEL, *the* PRIN-
CESS KATHARINE, ALICE *and other* Ladies;
the DUKE OF BURGUNDY, *and his train.*

K. Hen. Peace to this meeting, wherefore
we are met!
Unto our brother France, and to our sister,
Health and fair time of day; joy and good
wishes
To our most fair and princely cousin Katha-
rine;
And, as a branch and member of this royalty,
By whom this great assembly is contrived,
We do salute you, Duke of Burgundy;
And, princes French, and peers, health to
you all!
Fr. King. Right joyous are we to behold
your face,
Most worthy brother England; fairly met: 10
So are you, princes English, every one.
Q. Isa. So happy be the issue, brother
England,
Of this good day and of this gracious meet-
ing,
As we are now glad to behold your eyes;
Your eyes, which hitherto have borne in
them
Against the French, that met them in their
bent,
The fatal balls of murdering basilisks:
The venom of such looks, we fairly hope,
Have lost their quality, and that this day 19
Shall change all griefs and quarrels into
love.
K. Hen. To cry amen to that, thus we
appear.
Q. Isa. You English princes all, I do salute
you.

94. **And swear . . . wars.** Here one places Johnson's
famous note: "The comic scenes of The History of Henry
the Fourth and Fifth are now at an end, and all the
comic personages are now dismissed. Falstaff and Mrs.
Quickly are dead; Nym and Bardolph are hanged;
Gadshill was lost immediately after the robbery; Poins
and Peto have vanished since, one knows not how; and
Pistol is now beaten into obscurity. I believe every
reader regrets their departure."
Scene ii. 1. **wherefore,** an account of which (the
peace). 16. **bent,** gaze. 17. **basilisks.** The basilisk
was a fabulous monster which killed with its gaze; also,
a large cannon. Note that *balls* is probably a pun on
eyeballs.

Bur. My duty to you both, on equal love,
Great Kings of France and England! That I
have labour'd,
With all my wits, my pains and strong
endeavours,
To bring your most imperial majesties
Unto this bar and royal interview,
Your mightiness on both parts best can wit-
ness.
Since then my office hath so far prevail'd
That, face to face and royal eye to eye, 30
You have congreeted, let it not disgrace me,
If I demand, before this royal view,
What rub or what impediment there is,
Why that the naked, poor and mangled
Peace,
Dear nurse of arts, plenties and joyful births,
Should not in this best garden of the world
Our fertile France, put up her lovely visage?
Alas, she hath from France too long been
chased,
And all her husbandry doth lie on heaps,
Corrupting in it own fertility. 40
Her vine, the merry cheerer of the heart,
Unpruned dies; her hedges even-pleach'd,
Like prisoners wildly over-grown with hair,
Put forth disorder'd twigs; her fallow leas
The darnel, hemlock and rank fumitory
Doth root upon, while that the coulter rusts
That should deracinate such savagery;
The even mead, that erst brought sweetly
forth
The freckled cowslip, burnet and green
clover,
Wanting the scythe, all uncorrected, rank, 50
Conceives by idleness and nothing teems
But hateful docks, rough thistles, kecksies,
burs,
Losing both beauty and utility.
And as our vineyards, fallows, meads and
hedges,
Defective in their natures, grow to wildness,
Even so our houses and ourselves and
children
Have lost, or do not learn for want of time,
The sciences that should become our coun-
try;
But grow like savages,—as soldiers will

27. **bar,** court. 31. **congreeted,** greeted each other.
33. **rub,** obstacle. 40. **it,** its. 42. **even-pleach'd,**
smoothly intertwined. 44. **fallow,** uncultivated. **leas,**
meadows. 45. **darnel,** a weed. **fumitory,** a weed with
a bitter taste. 47. **deracinate,** root out. 48. **erst,**
formerly. 49. **burnet,** an herb. 51. **teems,** grows.
52. **kecksies,** dry-stemmed plants, possibly dried
hemlock stalks. 54. **fallows,** land plowed and left lying.

That nothing do but meditate on blood,— 60
To swearing and stern looks, defused attire
And every thing that seems unnatural.
Which to reduce into our former favour
You are assembled: and my speech entreats
That I may know the let, why gentle Peace
Should not expel these inconveniences
And bless us with her former qualities.

K. Hen. If, Duke of Burgundy, you would
the peace,
Whose want gives growth to the imperfec-
tions
Which you have cited, you must buy that
peace   70
With full accord to all our just demands;
Whose tenours and particular effects
You have enscheduled briefly in your hands.

Bur. The king hath heard them; to the
which as yet
There is no answer made.

K. Hen.   Well then the peace,
Which you before so urged, lies in his answer.

Fr. King. I have but with a cursory eye
O'erglanced the articles: pleaseth your grace
To appoint some of your council presently
To sit with us once more, with better heed 80
To re-survey them, we will suddenly
Pass our accept and peremptory answer.

K. Hen. Brother, we shall. Go, uncle
Exeter,
And brother Clarence, and you, brother
Gloucester,
Warwick and Huntingdon, go with the king;
And take with you free power to ratify,
Augment, or alter, as your wisdoms best
Shall see advantageable for our dignity,
Any thing in or out of our demands,
And we'll consign thereto. Will you, fair
sister,   90
Go with the princes, or stay here with
us?

Q. Isa. Our gracious brother, I will go
with them:
Haply a woman's voice may do some good,
When articles too nicely urged be stood on.

K. Hen. Yet leave our cousin Katharine
here with us:

She is our capital demand, comprised
Within the fore-rank of our articles.

Q. Isa. She hath good leave.

          [*Exeunt all except Henry, Katharine,
                              and Alice.*

K. Hen.   Fair Katharine, and most fair,
Will you vouchsafe to teach a soldier terms
Such as will enter at a lady's ear   100
And plead his love-suit to her gentle heart?

Kath. Your majesty shall mock at me; I
cannot speak your England.

K. Hen. O fair Katharine, if you will love
me soundly with your French heart, I will be
glad to hear you confess it brokenly with
your English tongue. Do you like me,
Kate?

Kath. Pardonnez-moi, I cannot tell vat is
'like me.'

K. Hen. An angel is like you, Kate, and
you are like an angel.   111

Kath. Que dit-il? que je suis semblable à
les anges?

Alice. Oui, vraiment, sauf votre grace,
ainsi dit-il.

K. Hen. I said so, dear Katharine; and I
must not blush to affirm it.

Kath. O bon Dieu! les langues des hommes
sont pleines de tromperies.

K. Hen. What says she, fair one? that the
tongues of men are full of deceits?   121

Alice. Oui, dat de tongues of de mans is be
full of deceits: dat is de princess.

K. Hen. The princess is the better Eng-
lishwoman. I' faith, Kate, my wooing is fit
for thy understanding: I am glad thou canst
speak no better English; for, if thou couldst,
thou wouldst find me such a plain king that
thou wouldst think I had sold my farm to
buy my crown. I know no ways to mince it in
love, but directly to say 'I love you:' then if
you urge me farther than to say 'do you in
faith?' I wear out my suit. Give me your
answer; i' faith, do: and so clap hands and a
bargain: how say you, lady?   134

Kath. Sauf votre honneur, me understand
vell.

K. Hen. Marry, if you would put me to
verses or to dance for your sake, Kate, why
you undid me: for the one, I have neither
words nor measure, and for the other, I have
no strength in measure, yet a reasonable

---

61. **defused**, disordered.   63. **favour**, appearance.
65. **let**, hindrance.   72. **Whose . . . effects**, whose
general purport and specific details.   73. **enscheduled**,
drawn up in writing.   77. **cursorary**, cursory, hasty.
81. **suddenly**, speedily.   90. **consign**, agree, subscribe.
94. **nicely**, with insistence on detail.   **stood on**, insisted
on.

112-115. **Que . . . dit-il**, What does he say? That I
am like the angels?   *Alice:* Yes truly, save your grace,
he says so.   133. **clap**, clasp.

measure in strength. If I could win a lady at leap-frog, or by vaulting into my saddle 142 with my armour on my back, under the correction of bragging be it spoken, I should quickly leap into a wife. Or if I might buffet for my love, or bound my horse for her favours, I could lay on like a butcher and sit like a jack-an-apes, never off. But, before God, Kate, I cannot look greenly nor gasp out my eloquence, nor I have no cunning in protestation; only downright oaths, which I never use till urged, nor never break for urging. If thou canst love a fellow of this temper, Kate, whose face is not worth sun-burning, that never looks in his glass for love of any thing he sees there, let thine eye be thy cook. I speak to thee plain soldier: if thou canst love me for this, take me; if not, to say to thee that I shall die, is true; but for thy love, be the Lord, no; yet I love thee too. And while thou livest, dear Kate, take 160 a fellow of plain and uncoined constancy; for he perforce must do thee right, because he hath not the gift to woo in other places: for these fellows of infinite tongue, that can rhyme themselves into ladies' favours, they do always reason themselves out again. What! a speaker is but a prater; a rhyme is but a ballad. A good leg will fall; a straight back will stoop; a black beard will turn white; a curled pate will grow bald; a fair face will wither; a full eye will wax hollow: but a good heart, Kate, is the sun and the moon; or rather the sun and not the moon; for it shines bright and never changes, but keeps his course truly. If thou would have such a one, take me; and take me, take a soldier; take a soldier, take a king. And what sayest thou then to my love? speak, my fair, and fairly, I pray thee.

Kath. Is it possible dat I sould love de enemy of France?　　　　　　　　　179

K. Hen. No; it is not possible you should love the enemy of France, Kate: but, in loving me, you should love the friend of France; for I love France so well that I will not part with a village of it; I will have it all mine; and, Kate, when France is mine and I am yours, then yours is France and you are mine.

Kath. I cannot tell vat is dat.

K. Hen. No, Kate? I will tell thee in French; which I am sure will hang upon my tongue like a new-married wife about her husband's neck, hardly to be shook off. Je quand sur le possession de France, et 192 quand vous avez le possession de moi,— let me see, what then? Saint Denis be my speed! —donc votre est France et vous êtes mienne. It is as easy for me, Kate, to conquer the kingdom as to speak so much more French: I shall never move thee in French, unless it be to laugh at me.

Kath. Sauf votre honneur, le François que vous parlez, il est meilleur que l' Anglois lequel je parle.　　　　　　　201

K. Hen. No, faith, is't not, Kate: but thy speaking of my tongue, and I thine, most truly-falsely, must needs be granted to be much at one. But, Kate, dost thou under-stand thus much English, canst thou love me?

Kath. I cannot tell.　　　　　　　207

K. Hen. Can any of your neighbours tell, Kate? I'll ask them. Come, I know thou lovest me: and at night, when you come into your closet, you'll question this gentlewoman about me; and I know, Kate, you will to her dispraise those parts in me that you love with your heart: but, good Kate, mock me mercifully; the rather, gentle princess, be-cause I love thee cruelly. If ever thou beest mine, Kate, as I have a saving faith within me tells me thou shalt, I get thee with scambling, and thou must therefore needs prove a good soldier-breeder: shall not thou and I, between Saint Denis and Saint George, compound a boy, half French, half English, that shall go to Constantinople and take the Turk by the beard? shall we not? what sayest thou, my fair flower-de-luce?　　　　　　　　　　　224

Kath. I do not know dat.

K. Hen. No; 'tis hereafter to know, but now to promise: do but now promise, Kate, you will endeavour for your French part of such a boy; and for my English moiety take the word of a king and a bachelor. How

---

145. **buffet**, box. 146. **bound**, make prance. 148. **jack-an-apes**, monkey. 156. **cook.** Probably the meaning is that she must dress him with fine qualities as a cook dresses meat. 161. **uncoined**, not coined for circulation; therefore, fixed, steady. 167. **fall**, shrink.

192-195. **Je quand . . . mienne,** When I have posses-sion of France, and you have possession of me . . . then France is yours and you are mine. 194. **Saint Denis,** patron saint of France. 199-201. **Sauf . . . parle,** Save your honor, the French that you speak is better than the English that I speak. 218. **scambling,** scrambling, struggling. 224. **flower-de-luce,** fleur-de-lis, the em-blem of France. 229. **moiety;** part.

answer you, la plus belle Katharine du
monde, mon très cher et devin déesse?

Kath. Your majestee ave fausse French
enough to deceive de most sage demoiselle
dat is en France.   235

K. Hen. Now, fie upon my false French!
By mine honour, in true English, I love thee,
Kate: by which honour I dare not swear thou
lovest me; yet my blood begins to flatter me
that thou dost, notwithstanding the poor
and untempering effect of my visage. Now,
beshrew my father's ambition! he was thinking of civil wars when he got me: therefore
was I created with a stubborn outside, with
an aspect of iron, that, when I come to woo
ladies, I fright them. But, in faith, Kate, the
elder I wax, the better I shall appear: my
comfort is, that old age, that ill layer up of
beauty, can do no more spoil upon my face:
thou hast me, if thou hast me, at the worst;
and thou shalt wear me, if thou wear me,
better and better: and therefore tell me, most
fair Katharine, will you have me? Put off
your maiden blushes; avouch the thoughts of
your heart with the looks of an empress; take
me by the hand, and say 'Harry of England,
I am thine:' which word thou shalt no sooner
bless mine ear withal, but I will tell thee
aloud 'England is thine, Ireland is thine,
France is thine, and Henry Plantagenet is
thine;' who, though I speak it before his face,
if he be not fellow with the best king, thou
shalt find the best king of good fellows.
Come, your answer in broken music; for thy
voice is music and thy English broken; therefore, queen of all, Katharine, break thy mind
to me in broken English; wilt thou   265
have me?

Kath. Dat is as it sall please de roi mon
père.

K. Hen. Nay, it will please him well, Kate;
it shall please him, Kate.

Kath. Den it sall also content me.   270

K. Hen. Upon that I kiss your hand, and
I call you my queen.

Kath. Laissez, mon seigneur, laissez,
laissez: ma foi, je ne veux point que vous
abaissiez votre grandeur en baisant la main

d'une de votre seigneurie indigne serviteur;
excusez-moi, je vous supplie, mon très-
puissant seigneur.

K. Hen. Then I will kiss your lips, Kate.

Kath. Les dames et demoiselles pour être
baisées devant leur noces, il n'est pas la
coutume de France.   281

K. Hen. Madam my interpreter, what
says she?

Alice. Dat it is not be de fashion pour les
ladies of France,—I cannot tell vat is baiser
en Anglish.

K. Hen. To kiss.   287

Alice. Your majesty entendre bettre que
moi.

K. Hen. It is not the fashion for the maids
in France to kiss before they are married,
would she say?

Alice. Oui, vraiment.   292

K. Hen. O Kate, nice customs curtsy to
great kings. Dear Kate, you and I cannot be
confined within the weak list of a country's
fashion: we are the makers of manners, Kate;
and the liberty that follows our places stops
the mouth of all find-faults; as I will do
yours, for upholding the nice fashion of your
country in denying me a kiss: therefore,
patiently and yielding. [*Kissing her.*] You
have witchcraft in your lips, Kate: there is
more eloquence in a sugar touch of them than
in the tongues of the French council; and
they should sooner persuade Harry of
England than a general petition of monarchs.
Here comes your father.   306

Re-enter the FRENCH KING *and his* QUEEN,
BURGUNDY, *and other* Lords.

Bur. God save your majesty! my royal
cousin, teach you our princess English?

K. Hen. I would have her learn, my fair
cousin, how perfectly I love her; and that is
good English.

Bur. Is she not apt?

K. Hen. Our tongue is rough, coz, and my
condition is not smooth; so that, having
neither the voice nor the heart of flattery
about me, I cannot so conjure up the spirit
of love in her, that he will appear in his true
likeness.   317

231-232. **la plus . . . déesse**, the most beautiful
Katharine in the world, my very dear and divine goddess.
241. **untempering**, unwinsome. 262. **broken music**,
music in parts for different instruments. 273-277.
Laissez . . . seigneur. Don't, my lord, don't, don't; by
my faith, I do not wish you to lower your greatness by
kissing the hand of your unworthy servant; excuse me,
I beg you, my most powerful lord.

279-281. **Les dames . . . France**, It is not customary
in France for ladies and young girls to be kissed before
their marriage. 288. **Your . . . moi**, Your majesty
understands better than I. 292. **Oui, vraiment**, Yes,
truly. 293. **nice**, overscrupulous.

Bur. Pardon the frankness of my mirth, if I answer you for that. If you would conjure in her, you must make a circle; if conjure up love in her in his true likeness, he must appear naked and blind. Can you blame her then, being a maid yet rosed over with the virgin crimson of modesty, if she deny the appearance of a naked blind boy in her naked seeing self? It were, my lord, a hard condition for a maid to consign to.

K. Hen. Yet they do wink and yield, as love is blind and enforces.

Bur. They are then excused, my lord, when they see not what they do.   330

K. Hen. Then, good my lord, teach your cousin to consent winking.

Bur. I will wink on her to consent, my lord, if you will teach her to know my meaning: for maids, well summered and warm kept, are like flies at Bartholomew-tide, blind, though they have their eyes; and then they will endure handling, which before would not abide looking on.   338

K. Hen. This moral ties me over to time and a hot summer; and so I shall catch the fly, your cousin, in the latter end and she must be blind too.

Bur. As love is, my lord, before it loves.

K. Hen. It is so: and you may, some of you, thank love for my blindness, who cannot see many a fair French city for one fair French maid that stands in my way.

Fr. King. Yes, my lord, you see them perspectively, the cities turned into a maid; for they are all girdled with maiden walls that war hath never entered.   350

K. Hen. Shall Kate be my wife?

Fr. King. So please you.

K. Hen. I am content; so the maiden cities you talk of may wait on her: so the maid that stood in the way for my wish shall show me the way to my will.

Fr. King. We have consented to all terms of reason.

K. Hen. Is't so, my lords of England?

West. The king hath granted every article: His daughter first, and then in sequel all,   361 According to their firm proposed natures.

Exe. Only he hath not yet subscribed this: Where your majesty demands, that the King of France, having any occasion to write for matter of grant, shall name your highness in this form and with this addition, in French, Notre très-cher fils Henri, Roi d'Angleterre, Héritier de France; and thus in Latin, Præclarissimus filius noster Henricus, Rex 370 Angliæ, et Hæres Franciæ.

Fr. King. Nor this I have not, brother, so denied, But your request shall make me let it pass.

K. Hen. I pray you then, in love and dear alliance, Let that one article rank with the rest; And thereupon give me your daughter.

Fr. King. Take her, fair son, and from her blood raise up Issue to me; that the contending kingdoms Of France and England, whose very shores look pale With envy of each other's happiness, May cease their hatred, and this dear conjunction   380 Plant neighbourhood and Christian-like accord In their sweet bosoms, that never war advance His bleeding sword 'twixt England and fair France.

All. Amen!

K. Hen. Now, welcome, Kate: and bear me witness all, That here I kiss her as my sovereign queen.
          [*Flourish.*

Q. Isa. God, the best maker of all marriages, Combine your hearts in one, your realms in one! As man and wife, being two, are one in love, So be there 'twixt your kingdoms such a spousal,   390 That never may ill office, or fell jealousy, Which troubles oft the bed of blessed marriage, Thrust in between the paction of these kingdoms, To make divorce of their incorporate league; That English may as French, French Englishmen, Receive each other. God speak this Amen!

All. Amen!

326. consign, agree. 336. Bartholomew-tide, St. Bartholomew's Day, August 24. 347. perspectively, distorted by a perspective glass.

368. fils, son. 369. Héritier, heir. Præclarissimus, most renowned. Shakespeare repeats an error in Holinshed for præcarissimus, i.e., most dear. 393. paction, alliance, compact.

K. Hen. Prepare we for our marriage: on
  which day,
My Lord of Burgundy, we'll take your oath,
And all the peers', for surety of our leagues.
Then shall I swear to Kate, and you to me;
And may our oaths well kept and prosperous
  be! [*Sennet. Exeunt.* 402

EPILOGUE.

Enter Chorus.

Chor. Thus far, with rough and all-unable
  pen,
Our bending author hath pursued the
  story,
In little room confining mighty men,
  Mangling by starts the full course of their
  glory.

402. *Stage Direction:* **Sennet,** set of notes played on
a trumpet.
  Epilogue. 2. **bending,** i.e., under the weight of his
task.

Small time, but in that small most greatly
  lived
  This star of England: Fortune made his
  sword;
By which the world's best garden he
  achieved,
  And of it left his son imperial lord.
Henry the Sixth, in infant bands crown'd
  King
  Of France and England, did this king suc-
  ceed;   10
Whose state so many had the managing,
  That they lost France and made his Eng-
  land bleed:
Which oft our stage hath shown; and, for
  their sake,
In your fair minds let this acceptance take.
                                        [*Exit.*

13. **Which . . . shown,** a reference to the three parts
of *King Henry VI,* which were written probably about
1591-2 and may have been revived about the time that
Henry V was on the stage. The older play show some
evidence of late revision.

JULIUS CÆSAR

DRAMATIS PERSONÆ

JULIUS CÆSAR.

OCTAVIUS CÆSAR,
MARCUS ANTONIUS, } triumvirs after the death of Julius Cæsar.
M. ÆMILIUS LEPIDUS,

CICERO,
PUBLIUS, } senators.
POPILIUS LENA,

MARCUS BRUTUS,
CASSIUS,
CASCA,
TREBONIUS, } conspirators against Julius Cæsar.
LIGARIUS,
DECIUS BRUTUS,
METELLUS CIMBER,
CINNA,

FLAVIUS and MARULLUS, tribunes.

ARTEMIDORUS of Cnidos, a teacher of Rhetoric.

A Soothsayer.

CINNA, a poet.   Another Poet.

LUCILIUS,
TITINIUS,
MESSALA, } friends to Brutus and Cassius.
Young CATO,
VOLUMNIUS,

VARRO,
CLITUS,
CLAUDIUS, } servants to Brutus.
STRATO,
LUCIUS,
DARDANIUS,

PINDARUS, servant to Cassius.

CALPURNIA, wife to Cæsar.
PORTIA, wife to Brutus.

Senators, Citizens, Guards, Attendants, &c.

SCENE: *Rome: the neighbourhood of Sardis: the neighbourhood of Philippi.*

ACT I.

SCENE I. *Rome. A street.*

Enter FLAVIUS, MARULLUS, *and certain* Commoners.

Flav. Hence! home, you idle creatures, get you home:
Is this a holiday? what! know you not,
Being mechanical, you ought not walk
Upon a labouring day without the sign
Of your profession? Speak, what trade art thou?

First Com. Why, sir, a carpenter.

Mar. Where is thy leather apron and thy rule?
What dost thou with thy best apparel on?
You, sir, what trade are you?   9

Sec. Com. Truly, sir, in respect of a fine workman, I am but, as you would say, a cobbler.

Mar. But what trade art thou? answer me directly.

Sec. Com. A trade, sir, that, I hope, I may use with a safe conscience; which is, indeed, sir, a mender of bad soles.

Mar. What trade, thou knave? thou naughty knave, what trade?

Sec. Com. Nay, I beseech you, sir, be not out with me: yet, if you be out, sir, I can mend you.

Mar. What meanest thou by that? mend me, thou saucy fellow!   21

Sec. Com. Why, sir, cobble you.

Flav. Thou art a cobbler, art thou?

Sec. Com. Truly, sir, all that I live by is with the awl: I meddle with no tradesman's matters, nor women's matters, but with awl. I am, indeed, sir, a surgeon to old shoes; when they are in great danger, I recover

3. **mechanical**, of the class of mechanics or artisans.
4. **sign**, garb and implements.

16. **naughty**, worthless. 18. **out**, i.e., of temper. 26. **with awl**, F: *withal*, without punctuation after the word. There is thus a pun on the word *withal* meaning "nevertheless."

them. As proper men as ever trod upon neat's
leather have gone upon my handiwork.   30
    Flav. But wherefore art not in thy shop
to-day?
Why dost thou lead these men about the
    streets?
    Sec. Com. Truly, sir, to wear out their
shoes, to get myself into more work. But,
indeed, sir, we make holiday, to see Cæsar
and to rejoice in his triumph.
    Mar. Wherefore rejoice? What conquest
    brings he home?
What tributaries follow him to Rome,
To grace in captive bonds his chariot-wheels?
You blocks, you stones, you worse than
    senseless things!   40
O you hard hearts, you cruel men of Rome,
Knew you not Pompey? Many a time and oft
Have you climb'd up to walls and battle-
    ments,
To towers and windows, yea, to chimney-
    tops,
Your infants in your arms, and there have sat
The live-long day, with patient expectation,
To see great Pompey pass the streets of
    Rome:
And when you saw his chariot but appear,
Have you not made an universal shout,
That Tiber trembled underneath her banks,
To hear the replication of your sounds   51
Made in her concave shores?
And do you now put on your best attire?
And do you now cull out a holiday?
And do you now strew flowers in his way
That comes in triumph over Pompey's blood?
Be gone!
Run to your houses, fall upon your knees,
Pray to the gods to intermit the plague
That needs must light on this ingratitude. 60
    Flav. Go, go, good countrymen, and, for
    this fault,
Assemble all the poor men of your sort;

Draw them to Tiber banks, and weep your
    tears
Into the channel, till the lowest stream
Do kiss the most exalted shores of all.
            [Exeunt all the Commoners.
See, whether their basest metal be not moved;
They vanish tongue-tied in their guiltiness.
Go you down that way towards the Capitol;
This way will I: disrobe the images,   69
If you do find them deck'd with ceremonies.
    Mar. May we do so?
You know it is the feast of Lupercal.
    Flav. It is no matter; let no images
Be hung with Cæsar's trophies. I'll about,
And drive away the vulgar from the streets:
So do you too, where you perceive them thick.
These growing feathers pluck'd from
    Cæsar's wing
Will make him fly an ordinary pitch,
Who else would soar above the view of
    men   79
And keep us all in servile fearfulness.
            [Exeunt.

    Scene II. *A public place.*

Flourish. Enter Cæsar; Antony, *for the
course;* Calpurnia, Portia, Decius,
Cicero, Brutus, Cassius, *and* Casca;
*a great crowd following, among them a
Soothsayer.*

    Cæs. Calpurnia!
    Casca.   Peace, ho! Cæsar speaks.
    Cæs.   Calpurnia!
    Cal. Here, my lord.
    Cæs. Stand you directly in Antonius' way,
When he doth run his course. Antonius!
    Ant. Cæsar, my lord?
    Cæs. Forget not, in your speed, Antonius,
To touch Calpurnia; for our elders say,
The barren, touched in this holy chase,
Shake off their sterile curse.
    Ant.   I shall remember:
When Cæsar says 'do this,' it is perform'd. 10
    Cæs. Set on; and leave no ceremony out.
                  [Flourish.

---

    29. proper, handsome. **neat's.** *Neat* means "cattle
of the ox kind." **36. triumph.** Cæsar had just overthrown the sons of Pompey in Spain at the battle of
Munda (March 17, 45 B.C.). He is celebrating his
triumph, which is resented because it is over Romans and
not foreign enemies (cf. line 56, below). The triumph is
disguised by the celebration of the feast of the Lupercalia.
42. Pompey. Cæsar had overthrown the great soldier,
Pompey, at the battle of Pharsalia in 48 B.C., and Pompey
had been murdered in Egypt. This story was itself the
subject of various tragedies. In the dramatic treatment
of the whole theme the tragedy of Pompey had been a
first part, and the tragedy of Cæsar a second part. In
this lies the reason for the name of this play. **50. her.**
The Roman custom was to speak of Father Tiber, but the
English feeling for rivers as feminine here prevails. **51.**
replication, echo.

    69. images, statues. **70. ceremonies,** ceremonial
trappings. **72. Lupercal,** a feast of purification in honor
of Pan celebrated from ancient times in Rome on February 15th of each year. The celebrants, called *Luperci,*
raced around the Palatine Hill and the circus carrying
thongs of goat-skin called *februa* (whence *February*). With
these they struck those who came in their way. Women
so lashed were cured of barrenness; hence Cæsar's wish
that Antony would strike Calpurnia (I, ii, 6-8).
    Scene ii. **9. sterile curse,** curse of sterility.

Sooth. Cæsar!

Cæs. Ha! who calls?

Casca. Bid every noise be still: peace yet again!

Cæs. Who is it in the press that calls on me?

I hear a tongue, shriller than all the music,

Cry 'Cæsar!' Speak; Cæsar is turn'd to hear.

Sooth. Beware the ides of March.

Cæs.   What man is that?

Bru. A soothsayer bids you beware the ides of March.

Cæs. Set him before me; let me see his face.   20

Cas. Fellow, come from the throng; look upon Cæsar.

Cæs. What say'st thou to me now? speak once again.

Sooth. Beware the ides of March.

Cæs. He is a dreamer; let us leave him: pass.   [*Sennet. Exeunt all except Brutus and Cassius.*

Cas. Will you go see the order of the course?

Bru. Not I.

Cas. I pray you, do.

Bru. I am not gamesome: I do lack some part

Of that quick spirit that is in Antony.

Let me not hinder, Cassius, your desires;   30

I'll leave you.

Cas. Brutus, I do observe you now of late:

I have not from your eyes that gentleness

And show of love as I was wont to have:

You bear too stubborn and too strange a hand

Over your friend that loves you.

Bru.   Cassius,

Be not deceived: if I have veil'd my look,

I turn the trouble of my countenance

Merely upon myself.   Vexed I am

Of late with passions of some difference,   40

Conceptions only proper to myself,

Which give some soil perhaps to my behaviours;

But let not therefore my good friends be grieved—

Among which number, Cassius, be you one—

Nor construe any further my neglect,

Than that poor Brutus, with himself at war,

Forgets the shows of love to other men.

Cas. Then, Brutus, I have much mistook your passion;

By means whereof this breast of mine hath buried

Thoughts of great value, worthy cogitations.

Tell me, good Brutus, can you see your face?   51

Bru. No, Cassius; for the eye sees not itself,

But by reflection, by some other things.

Cas. 'Tis just:

And it is very much lamented, Brutus,

That you have no such mirrors as will turn

Your hidden worthiness into your eye,

That you might see your shadow.   I have heard,

Where many of the best respect in Rome,

Except immortal Cæsar, speaking of Brutus   60

And groaning underneath this age's yoke,

Have wish'd that noble Brutus had his eyes.

Bru. Into what dangers would you lead me, Cassius,

That you would have me seek into myself

For that which is not in me?

Cas. Therefore, good Brutus, be prepared to hear:

And since you know you cannot see yourself

So well as by reflection, I, your glass,

Will modestly discover to yourself

That of yourself which you yet know not of.   70

And be not jealous on me, gentle Brutus;

Were I a common laugher, or did use

To stale with ordinary oaths my love

To every new protester; if you know

That I do fawn on men and hug them hard

And after scandal them, or if you know

That I profess myself in banqueting

To all the rout, then hold me dangerous.

                              [*Flourish, and shout.*

Bru. What means this shouting? I do fear, the people

Choose Cæsar for their king.

Cas.   Ay, do you fear it?   80

17. **Cæsar.** Cæsar's referring to himself in the third person suggests a royal habit. It was, however, his custom in his *Commentaries.* 18. **ides of March,** March 15. 24. *Stage Direction:* **Sennet,** set of notes played on a trumpet. 25. **order of the course,** performance of the race. 28. **gamesome,** fond of sports. 29. **quick,** lively. 35. **stubborn,** rough. 40. **of some difference,** conflicting. 41. **only proper,** peculiar, relating merely. 42. **give . . . to,** sully.

49. **By means whereof,** i.e., by which mistake. 71. **jealous on,** suspicious of. 73. **stale,** render stale. 74. **protester,** i.e., one who protests friendship. 76. **scandal,** slander. 77. **profess myself,** make declarations of friendship.

Then must I think you would not have it so.
Bru. I would not, Cassius; yet I love him
    well.
But wherefore do you hold me here so long?
What is it that you would impart to me?
If it be aught toward the general good,
Set honour in one eye and death i' the other,
And I will look on both indifferently:
For let the gods so speed me as I love
The name of honour more than I fear death.
Cas. I know that virtue to be in you,
    Brutus,   90
As well as I do know your outward favour.
Well, honour is the subject of my story.
I cannot tell what you and other men
Think of this life; but, for my single self,
I had as lief not be as live to be
In awe of such a thing as I myself.
I was born free as Cæsar; so were you:
We both have fed as well, and we can both
Endure the winter's cold as well as he:
For once, upon a raw and gusty day,   100
The troubled Tiber chafing with her shores,
Cæsar said to me 'Darest thou, Cassius, now
Leap in with me into this angry flood,
And swim to yonder point?' Upon the word,
Accoutred as I was, I plunged in
And bade him follow; so indeed he did.
The torrent roar'd, and we did buffet it
With lusty sinews, throwing it aside
And stemming it with hearts of controversy;
But ere we could arrive the point proposed,
Cæsar cried 'Help me, Cassius, or I sink!' 111
I, as Æneas, our great ancestor,
Did from the flames of Troy upon his
    shoulder
The old Anchises bear, so from the waves of
    Tiber
Did I the tired Cæsar. And this man
Is now become a god, and Cassius is
A wretched creature and must bend his body,
If Cæsar carelessly but nod on him.
He had a fever when he was in Spain,
And when the fit was on him, I did mark   120
How he did shake: 'tis true, this god did
    shake:
His coward lips did from their colour fly,
And that same eye whose bend doth awe the
    world

Did lose his lustre: I did hear him groan:
Ay, and that tongue of his that bade the
    Romans
Mark him and write his speeches in their
    books,
Alas, it cried 'Give me some drink, Titinius,'
As a sick girl. Ye gods, it doth amaze me
A man of such a feeble temper should
So get the start of the majestic world   130
And bear the palm alone. [*Shout. Flourish.*
Bru. Another general shout!
I do believe that these applauses are
For some new honours that are heap'd on
    Cæsar.
Cas. Why, man, he doth bestride the
    narrow world
Like a Colossus, and we petty men
Walk under his huge legs and peep about
To find ourselves dishonourable graves.
Men at some time are masters of their fates:
The fault, dear Brutus, is not in our stars,140
But in ourselves, that we are underlings.
Brutus and Cæsar: what should be in that
    'Cæsar'?
Why should that name be sounded more than
    yours?
Write them together, yours is as fair a name;
Sound them, it doth become the mouth as
    well;
Weigh them, it is as heavy; conjure with 'em,
Brutus will start a spirit as soon as Cæsar.
Now, in the names of all the gods at once,
Upon what meat doth this our Cæsar feed,
That he is grown so great? Age, thou art
    shamed!   150
Rome, thou hast lost the breed of noble
    bloods!
When went there by an age, since the great
    flood,
But it was famed with more than with one
    man?
When could they say till now, that talk'd of
    Rome,
That her wide walls encompass'd but one
    man?
Now is it Rome indeed and room enough,
When there is in it but one only man.
O, you and I have heard our fathers say,

---

82. **I love him well.** It is necessary to remember
this idea, placed so early and so emphatically, in order to
understand Shakespeare's conception of the deed that
Brutus was to do. Friendship had a high place in
Elizabethan thought. 87. **indifferently,** impartially.
109. **hearts of controversy,** competing courage. 123.
bend, glance.

124. **his,** its. 136. **Colossus,** the gigantic statue
which stood astride the entrance to the harbor of Rhodes.
155. **walls,** so Rowe. Many editions follow F and read
walks, explained as a reference to the famous paved ways
of the Romans. The Arden editor offers an explanation
of *walks* as tracts of garden, park, or forest, adding that
ancient Rome was almost entirely surrounded by a
"green girdle of gardens and pleasure grounds."

There was a Brutus once that would have
 brook'd
The eternal devil to keep his state in Rome 160
As easily as a king.

 Bru. That you do love me, I am nothing
  jealous;
What you would work me to, I have some
 aim:
How I have thought of this and of these
 times,
I shall recount hereafter; for this present,
I would not, so with love I might entreat you,
Be any further moved. What you have said
I will consider; what you have to say
I will with patience hear, and find a time
Both meet to hear and answer such high
 things.   170
Till then, my noble friend, chew upon this:
Brutus had rather be a villager
Than to repute himself a son of Rome
Under these hard conditions as this time
Is like to lay upon us.

 Cas. I am glad that my weak words
Have struck but thus much show of fire from
 Brutus.

 Bru. The games are done and Cæsar is
  returning.

 Cas. As they pass by, pluck Casca by the
  sleeve;
And he will, after his sour fashion, tell you 180
What hath proceeded worthy note to-day.

  Re-enter CÆSAR *and his Train.*

 Bru. I will do so. But, look you, Cassius,
The angry spot doth glow on Caesar's brow,
And all the rest look like a chidden train:
Calpurnia's cheek is pale; and Cicero
Looks with such ferret and such fiery eyes
As we have seen him in the Capitol,
Being cross'd in conference by some senators.

 Cas. Casca will tell us what the matter is.

 Cæs. Antonius!   190

 Ant. Cæsar?

 Cæs. Let me have men about me that are
  fat;
Sleek-headed men and such as sleep o'nights:
Yond Cassius has a lean and hungry look;
He thinks too much: such men are dangerous.

 Ant. Fear him not, Cæsar; he's not
  dangerous;

He is a noble Roman and well given.

 Cæs. Would he were fatter! But I fear
  him not:
Yet if my name were liable to fear,
I do not know the man I should avoid 200
So soon as that spare Cassius. He reads
 much;
He is a great observer and he looks
Quite through the deeds of men; he loves no
 plays,
As thou dost, Antony; he hears no music;
Seldom he smiles, and smiles in such a sort
As if he mock'd himself and scorn'd his spirit
That could be moved to smile at any thing.
Such men as he be never at heart's ease
Whiles they behold a greater than them-
 selves,
And therefore are they very dangerous. 210
I rather tell thee what is to be fear'd
Than what I fear; for always I am Cæsar.
Come on my right hand, for this ear is deaf,
And tell me truly what thou think'st of him.

  [*Sennet. Exeunt Cæsar and all his
         Train, but Casca.*

 Casca. You pull'd me by the cloak; would
  you speak with me?

 Bru. Ay, Casca; tell us what hath chanced
  to-day,
That Cæsar looks so sad.

 Casca. Why, you were with him, were you
  not?

 Bru. I should not then ask Casca what
  had chanced.   219

 Casca. Why, there was a crown offered
him: and being offered him, he put it by with
the back of his hand, thus; and then the
people fell a-shouting.

 Bru. What was the second noise for?

 Casca. Why, for that too.

 Cas. They shouted thrice: what was the
  last cry for?

 Casca. Why, for that too.

 Bru. Was the crown offered him thrice?

 Casca. Ay, marry, was 't, and he put it by
thrice, every time gentler than other, and
at every putting-by mine honest neighbours
shouted.   231

 Cas. Who offered him the crown?

 Casca. Why, Antony.

 Bru. Tell us the manner of it, gentle Casca.

 Casca. I can as well be hanged as tell the

---

159. **Brutus**, Lucius Junius Brutus, who expelled the Tarquins and founded the Roman Republic (509 B.C.). 163. **aim**, inkling. 186. **ferret**, ferret-like, i.e., small and red.

197. **given**, disposed. 204. **hears no music**, regarded as a sign of a morose and treacherous character. 228. **marry**, originally an oath, "by the Virgin Mary."

manner of it: it was mere foolery; I did 235
not mark it. I saw Mark Antony offer him a
crown;—yet 'twas not a crown neither, 'twas
one of these coronets;—and, as I told you, he
put it by once: but, for all that, to my thinking, he would fain have had it. Then he offered it to him again; then he put it by again:
but, to my thinking, he was very loath to lay
his fingers off it. And then he offered it the
third time; he put it the third time by: and
still as he refused it, the rabblement hooted
and clapped their chopped hands and threw
up their sweaty night-caps and uttered such
a deal of stinking breath because Cæsar refused the crown that it had almost choked
Cæsar; for he swounded and fell down at it:
and for mine own part, I durst not laugh, for
fear of opening my lips and receiving the bad
air. 252

Cas. But, soft, I pray you: what, did
Cæsar swound?

Casca. He fell down in the market-place,
and foamed at mouth, and was speechless.

Bru. 'Tis very like: he hath the falling
sickness.

Cas. No, Cæsar hath it not; but you and I
And honest Casca, we have the falling sickness. 258

Casca. I know not what you mean by that;
but, I am sure, Cæsar fell down. If the tag-
rag people did not clap him and hiss him,
according as he pleased and displeased them,
as they use to do the players in the theatre,
I am no true man.

Bru. What said he when he came unto
himself? 264

Casca. Marry, before he fell down, when
he perceived the common herd was glad he
refused the crown, he plucked me ope his
doublet and offered them his throat to cut.
An I had been a man of any occupation, if I
would not have taken him at a word, I would
I might go to hell among the rogues. And so
he fell. When he came to himself again, he
said, If he had done or said any thing amiss,
he desired their worships to think it was his
infirmity. Three or four wenches, where I
stood, cried 'Alas, good soul!' and forgave
him with all their hearts: but there's no heed

to be taken of them; if Cæsar had stabbed
their mothers, they would have done no
less.

Bru. And after that, he came, thus sad,
away?

Casca. Ay. 280

Cas. Did Cicero say any thing?

Casca. Ay, he spoke Greek.

Cas. To what effect?

Casca. Nay, an I tell you that, I'll ne'er
look you i' the face again: but those that
understood him smiled at one another and
shook their heads; but, for mine own part, it
was Greek to me. I could tell you more news
too: Marullus and Flavius, for pulling scarfs
off Cæsar's images, are put to silence. Fare
you well. There was more foolery yet, if I
could remember it. 291

Cas. Will you sup with me to-night, Casca?

Casca. No, I am promised forth.

Cas. Will you dine with me to-morrow?

Casca. Ay, if I be alive and your mind
hold and your dinner worth the eating.

Cas. Good: I will expect you.

Casca. Do so. Farewell, both. [*Exit.*

Bru. What a blunt fellow is this grown
to be!
He was quick mettle when he went to school.

Cas. So is he now in execution 301
Of any bold or noble enterprise,
However he puts on this tardy form.
This rudeness is a sauce to his good wit,
Which gives men stomach to digest his words
With better appetite.

Bru. And so it is. For this time I will
leave you:
To-morrow, if you please to speak with me,
I will come home to you; or, if you will, 309
Come home to me, and I will wait for you.

Cas. I will do so: till then, think of the
world. [*Exit Brutus.*
Well, Brutus, thou art noble; yet, I see,
Thy honourable metal may be wrought
From that it is disposed: therefore it is meet
That noble minds keep ever with their likes;

287. **Greek to me.** This famous phrase arose from
Casca's old Roman dislike for foreign culture. 288.
scarfs, fillets. 290. **put to silence,** probably,
dismissed from office and banished. 293. **promised
forth,** engaged to dine out. 300. **quick mettle,** lively
spirit. 303. **However,** however much. **tardy form,**
sluggishness. 312-326. **Well . . . endure.** It cannot be
that Shakespeare thought of Cassius as a base man, yet
the rôle he plays here is the villain's rôle in many plays.
There may be an underlying acceptance of the world-
wide belief that the assassination of Cæsar was one of
the calamities of history, and the agent of such a catastrophe might well be thought a villain.

238. **coronets,** chaplets, garlands. 246. **chopped,**
chapped. 247. **night-caps,** scornful allusion to the
pileus, a cap worn by the populace. Patricians went
bareheaded. 249. **swounded,** fainted. 256. **falling-
sickness,** epilepsy. 267. **me,** ethical dative. **ope,**
open. 268. **doublet,** Elizabethan jacket. 269. **occupation,** handicraft.

For who so firm that cannot be seduced?
Cæsar doth bear me hard; but he loves
   Brutus:
If I were Brutus now and he were Cassius,
He should not humour me. I will this night,
In several hands, in at his windows throw,
As if they came from several citizens,   321
Writings all tending to the great opinion
That Rome holds of his name; wherein ob-
   scurely
Cæsar's ambition shall be glanced at:
And after this let Cæsar seat him sure;
For we will shake him, or worse days endure.
                          [*Exit*.

Scene III. *The same. A street.*

*Thunder and lightning. Enter, from opposite
sides,* Casca, *with his sword drawn, and*
Cicero.

  Cic. Good even, Casca: brought you
   Cæsar home?
Why are you breathless? and why stare you
   so?
  Casca. Are not you moved, when all the
   sway of earth
Shakes like a thing unfirm? O Cicero,
I have seen tempests, when the scolding
   winds
Have rived the knotty oaks, and I have
   seen
The ambitious ocean swell and rage and
   foam,
To be exalted with the threatening clouds:
But never till to-night, never till now,
Did I go through a tempest dropping fire. 10
Either there is a civil strife in heaven,
Or else the world, too saucy with the gods,
Incenses them to send destruction.
  Cic. Why, saw you any thing more won-
   derful?
  Casca. A common slave—you know him
   well by sight—
Held up his left hand, which did flame and
   burn
Like twenty torches join'd, and yet his hand,
Not sensible of fire, remain'd unscorch'd.
Besides—I ha' not since put up my sword—
Against the Capitol I met a lion, 20
Who glared upon me, and went surly by,

Without annoying me: and there were drawn
Upon a heap a hundred ghastly women,
Transformed with their fear; who swore they
   saw
Men all in fire walk up and down the streets.
And yesterday the bird of night did sit
Even at noon-day upon the market-place,
Hooting and shrieking. When these prod-
   igies
Do so conjointly meet, let not men say
'These are their reasons; they are natural'; 30
For, I believe, they are portentous things
Unto the climate that they point upon.
  Cic. Indeed, it is a strange-disposed time:
But men may construe things after their
   fashion,
Clean from the purpose of the things them-
   selves.
Comes Cæsar to the Capitol to-morrow?
  Casca. He doth; for he did bid Antonius
Send word to you he would be there to-
   morrow.
  Cic. Good night then, Casca: this dis-
   turbed sky
Is not to walk in.
  Casca.   Farewell, Cicero. [*Exit Cicero.* 40

Enter Cassius.

  Cas. Who's there?
  Casca.   A Roman.
  Cas.   Casca, by your voice.
  Casca. Your ear is good. Cassius, what
   night is this!
  Cas. A very pleasing night to honest men.
  Casca. Who ever knew the heavens
   menace so?
  Cas. Those that have known the earth so
   full of faults.
For my part, I have walk'd about the streets,
Submitting me unto the perilous night,
And, thus unbraced, Casca, as you see,
Have bared my bosom to the thunder-stone;
And when the cross blue lightning seem'd to
   open 50
The breast of heaven, I did present myself
Even in the aim and very flash of it.
  Casca. But wherefore did you so much
   tempt the heavens?

---

317. **bear me hard**, dislike me.
Scene iii. 1. **brought**, escorted. 3. **sway**, probably,
weight. 18. **Not sensible of fire**, i.e., not feeling it.

22-23. **drawn Upon a heap**, huddled together.
ghastly, pallid. 26. **bird of night**, owl, a bird of evil
omen. 28. **prodigies**, portents. 32. **climate**, region.
35. **Clean . . . purpose**, contrary to the import or
meaning. 42. **what night**, what a night. 48. **unbraced**, with doublet unfastened. 49. **thunder-stone.**
Thunderbolts were supposed to be composed of solid
bodies.

It is the part of men to fear and tremble,
When the most mighty gods by tokens send
Such dreadful heralds to astonish us.
    Cas. You are dull, Casca, and those
        sparks of life
That should be in a Roman you do want,
Or else you use not. You look pale and gaze
And put on fear and cast yourself in wonder,
To see the strange impatience of the heavens:
But if you would consider the true cause 62
Why all these fires, why all these gliding
        ghosts,
Why birds and beasts from quality and kind,
Why old men fool and children calculate,
Why all these things change from their
        ordinance
Their natures and preformed faculties
To monstrous quality,—why, you shall find
That heaven hath infused them with these
        spirits,
To make them instruments of fear and warn-
        ing   70
Unto some monstrous state.
Now could I, Casca, name to thee a man
Most like this dreadful night,
That thunders, lightens, opens graves, and
        roars
As doth the lion in the Capitol,
A man no mightier than thyself or me
In personal action, yet prodigious grown
And fearful, as these strange eruptions are.
    Casca. 'Tis Cæsar that you mean; is it
        not, Cassius?
    Cas. Let it be who it is: for Romans now 80
Have thews and limbs like to their ancestors;
But, woe the while! our fathers' minds are
        dead,
And we are govern'd with our mothers'
        spirits;
Our yoke and sufferance show us womanish.
    Casca. Indeed, they say the senators to-
        morrow
Mean to establish Cæsar as a king;
And he shall wear his crown by sea and land,
In every place, save here in Italy.
    Cas. I know where I will wear this dagger
       then;
Cassius from bondage will deliver Cassius: 90

Therein, ye gods, you make the weak most
       strong;
Therein, ye gods, you tyrants do defeat:
Nor stony tower, nor walls of beaten brass,
Nor airless dungeon, nor strong links of iron,
Can be retentive to the strength of spirit;
But life, being weary of these worldly bars,
Never lacks power to dismiss itself.
If I know this, know all the world besides,
That part of tyranny that I do bear
I can shake off at pleasure. [*Thunder still.*
    Casca.   So can I: 100
So every bondman in his own hand bears
The power to cancel his captivity.
    Cas. And why should Cæsar be a tyrant
       then?
Poor man! I know he would not be a wolf,
But that he sees the Romans are but sheep:
He were no lion, were not Romans hinds.
Those that with haste will make a mighty fire
Begin it with weak straws: what trash is
       Rome,
What rubbish and what offal, when it serves
For the base matter to illuminate   110
So vile a thing as Cæsar! But, O grief,
Where hast thou led me? I perhaps speak
       this
Before a willing bondman; then I know
My answer must be made. But I am arm'd,
And dangers are to me indifferent.
    Casca. You speak to Casca, and to such
       a man
That is no fleering tell-tale. Hold, my hand:
Be factious for redress of all these griefs,
And I will set this foot of mine as far
As who goes farthest.
    Cas.   There's a bargain made. 120
Now know you, Casca, I have moved already
Some certain of the noblest-minded Romans
To undergo with me an enterprise
Of honourable-dangerous consequence;
And I do know, by this, they stay for me
In Pompey's porch: for now, this fearful
       night,
There is no stir or walking in the streets;
And the complexion of the element
In favour's like the work we have in hand,
Most bloody, fiery, and most terrible.   130

---

60. **put on**, show signs of. 65. **fool**, so Grant White;
F: *Fooles*, retained by many editors, the line being
punctuated with commas after *men* and *fools*. In that
case we should understand *old men* as meaning "dotards."
calculate, prophesy. 66. **ordinance**, ordinary character and nature. 78. **fearful**, fear-inspiring. 84. **yoke
and sufferance**, patience under the yoke.

106. **hinds**, females of the red deer; also, servants,
rustics. 117. **fleering**, mocking, sneering. 118. **factious**, active as a partisan. 123. **undergo**, undertake.
126. **Pompey's porch**, a magnificent colonnade built
by Pompey in 55 B.C., and attached to his great open
theater. The recesses along the sides were convenient
for such meetings. 128. **complexion of the element**,
aspect of the sky.

Casca. Stand close awhile, for here comes
one in haste.

Cas. 'Tis Cinna; I do know him by his
gait;
He is a friend.

Enter Cinna.

Cinna, where haste you so?

Cin. To find out you. Who's that? Metellus Cimber?

Cas. No, it is Casca; one incorporate

To our attempts. Am I not stay'd for, Cinna?

Cin. I am glad on't. What a fearful night
is this!
There's two or three of us have seen strange
sights.

Cas. Am I not stay'd for? tell me.

Cin.   Yes, you are.

O Cassius, if you could   140
But win the noble Brutus to our party—

Cas. Be you content: good Cinna, take
this paper,
And look you lay it in the prætor's chair,
Where Brutus may but find it; and throw
this
In at his window; set this up with wax
Upon old Brutus' statue: all this done,
Repair to Pompey's porch, where you shall
find us.
Is Decius Brutus and Trebonius there?

Cin. All but Metellus Cimber; and he's
gone   149
To seek you at your house. Well, I will hie,
And so bestow these papers as you bade me.

Cas. That done, repair to Pompey's
theatre.   [*Exit Cinna.*

Come, Casca, you and I will yet ere day
See Brutus at his house: three parts of him
Is ours already, and the man entire
Upon the next encounter yields him ours.

Casca. O, he sits high in all the people's
hearts:
And that which would appear offence in us,
His countenance, like richest alchemy,
Will change to virtue and to worthiness.   160

Cas. Him and his worth and our great
need of him

You have right well conceited. Let us go,
For it is after midnight; and ere day
We will awake him and be sure of him.
                                    [*Exeunt.*

ACT II.

Scene I. *Rome. Brutus's orchard.*

Enter Brutus.

Bru. What, Lucius, ho!
I cannot, by the progress of the stars,
Give guess how near to day. Lucius, I say!
I would it were my fault to sleep so soundly.
When, Lucius, when? awake, I say! what,
Lucius!

Enter Lucius.

Luc. Call'd you, my lord?

Bru. Give me a taper in my study,
Lucius:
When it is lighted, come and call me here.

Luc. I will, my lord.   [*Exit.*

Bru. It must be by his death: and for my
part,   10
I know no personal cause to spurn at him,
But for the general. He would be crown'd:
How that might change his nature, there's
the question.
It is the bright day that brings forth the
adder;
And that craves wary walking. Crown
him?—that;—
And then, I grant, we put a sting in him,
That at his will he may do danger with.
The abuse of greatness is, when it disjoins
Remorse from power: and, to speak truth of
Cæsar,
I have not known when his affections sway'd
More than his reason. But 'tis a common
proof,   21
That lowliness is young ambition's ladder,
Whereto the climber-upward turns his face;
But when he once attains the upmost round,
He then unto the ladder turns his back,
Looks in the clouds, scorning the base
degrees
By which he did ascend. So Cæsar may.

---

135. **incorporate**, admitted as a member. 143. **prætor's chair**, official seat of the prætor, a Roman magistrate ranking next below the consul. Brutus was prætor.
146. **old Brutus.** Brutus was reputed to be a descendant of Lucius Junius Brutus. 159. **alchemy**,
chemistry, the chief object of which was the transmutation of metals.

162. **conceited**, conceived, grasped.
Act II. Scene i. 12. **general**, i.e., for the sake of the
general welfare. 15-27. **Crown . . . ascend.** This is a
condensed statement of Brutus's motive. By *affections*
(line 20) he means "passions," but it need not be understood that he means to compliment Cæsar; rather, he
means to say that Cæsar has those cold-blooded qualities
which will make him disregard pity (*remorse*, l. 19) when
he is in power.

Then, lest he may, prevent. And, since the
　　quarrel
Will bear no colour for the thing he is,
Fashion it thus; that what he is, augmented,
Would run to these and these extremities: 31
And therefore think him as a serpent's egg
Which, hatch'd, would, as his kind, grow
　　mischievous,
And kill him in the shell.

Re-enter Lucius.

　　Luc. The taper burneth in your closet, sir.
Searching the window for a flint, I found
This paper, thus seal'd up; and, I am sure,
It did not lie there when I went to bed.
　　　　　　　　　　[*Gives him the letter.*
　　Bru. Get you to bed again; it is not day.
Is not to-morrow, boy, the ides of March? 40
　　Luc. I know not, sir.
　　Bru. Look in the calendar, and bring me
　　word.
　　Luc. I will, sir.　　　　　　　　[*Exit.*
　　Bru. The exhalations whizzing in the air
Give so much light that I may read by them.
　　　　　　　　　[*Opens the letter and reads.*
'Brutus, thou sleep'st: awake, and see thy-
　　self.
Shall Rome, &c. Speak, strike, redress!
Brutus, thou sleep'st: awake!'
Such instigations have been often dropp'd
Where I have took them up.　　　　　　50
'Shall Rome, &c.' Thus must I piece it out:
Shall Rome stand under one man's awe?
　　What, Rome?
My ancestors did from the streets of Rome
The Tarquin drive, when he was call'd a
　　king.
'Speak, strike, redress!' Am I entreated
To speak and strike? O Rome, I make thee
　　promise;
If the redress will follow, thou receivest
Thy full petition at the hand of Brutus!

Re-enter Lucius.

　　Luc. Sir, March is wasted fourteen days.
　　　　　　　　　　　[*Knocking within.*
　　Bru. 'Tis good. Go to the gate; some-
　　body knocks.　　　　　　[*Exit Lucius.* 60
Since Cassius first did whet me against
　　Cæsar,
I have not slept.

Between the acting of a dreadful thing
And the first motion, all the interim is
Like a phantasma, or a hideous dream:
The Genius and the mortal instruments
Are then in council; and the state of man,
Like to a little kingdom, suffers then
The nature of an insurrection.

Re-enter Lucius.

　　Luc. Sir, 'tis your brother Cassius at the
　　door,　　　　　　　　　　　　　　70
Who doth desire to see you.
　　Bru.　　　　　　　　Is he alone?
　　Luc. No, sir, there are moe with him.
　　Bru.　　　　　　　Do you know them?
　　Luc. No, sir; their hats are pluck'd about
　　their ears,
And half their faces buried in their cloaks,
That by no means I may discover them
By any mark of favour.
　　Bru.　　　　　Let 'em enter. [*Exit Lucius.*
They are the faction. O conspiracy,
Shamest thou to show thy dangerous brow
　　by night,
When evils are most free? O, then by day
Where wilt thou find a cavern dark enough 80
To mask thy monstrous visage? Seek none,
　　conspiracy;
Hide it in smiles and affability:
For if thou path, thy native semblance on,
Not Erebus itself were dim enough
To hide thee from prevention.

Enter the conspirators, Cassius, Casca,
　　Decius, Cinna, Metellus Cimber, *and*
　　Trebonius.

　　Cas. I think we are too bold upon your
　　rest:
Good morrow, Brutus; do we trouble you?
　　Bru. I have been up this hour, awake all
　　night.
Know I these men that come along with you?
　　Cas. Yes, every man of them, and no man
　　here　　　　　　　　　　　　　　90
But honours you; and every one doth wish
You had but that opinion of yourself

63-69. Between ... insurrection. This is one of
the most perfect expressions in Shakespeare of the
psychology of warring emotions, hesitation, and inward
conflict. The *Genius* is used to signify the soul; the
mortal instruments are the spirits, which are the agents of
reason and the will. **67. state of man,** familiar desig-
nation of man as a microcosm. **70. brother.** Cassius
had married the sister of Brutus. **76. favour,** countenance, appearance. **77. faction,** party of conspirators.
83. path, proceed. **84. Erebus,** the region of darkness
between earth and Hades.

29. colour, pretext or justification. **36. flint,** i.e.,
with which to strike a light. **44. exhalations,** meteors.

Which every noble Roman bears of you.
This is Trebonius.

Bru.   He is welcome hither.

Cas. This, Decius Brutus.

Bru.   He is welcome too.

Cas. This, Casca; this, Cinna; and this,
Metellus Cimber.

Bru. They are all welcome.
What watchful cares do interpose themselves
Betwixt your eyes and night?

Cas. Shall I entreat a word?   100

[*Brutus and Cassius whisper.*]

Dec. Here lies the east: doth not the day
break here?

Casca. No.

Cin. O, pardon, sir, it doth; and yon gray
lines
That fret the clouds are messengers of day.

Casca. You shall confess that you are
both deceived.
Here, as I point my sword, the sun arises,
Which is a great way growing on the south,
Weighing the youthful season of the year.
Some two months hence up higher toward
the north
He first presents his fire; and the high east 110
Stands, as the Capitol, directly here.

Bru. Give me your hands all over, one by
one.

Cas. And let us swear our resolution.

Bru. No, not an oath: if not the face of
men,
The sufferance of our souls, the time's
abuse,—
If these be motives weak, break off betimes,
And every man hence to his idle bed;
So let high-sighted tyranny range on,
Till every man drop by lottery. But if these,
As I am sure they do, bear fire enough   120
To kindle cowards and to steel with valour
The melting spirits of women, then, country-
men,
What need we any spur but our own cause,
To prick us to redress? what other bond
Than secret Romans, that have spoke the
word,
And will not palter? and what other oath
Than honesty to honesty engaged,

That this shall be, or we will fall for it?
Swear priests and cowards and men cautel-
ous,   129
Old feeble carrions and such suffering souls
That welcome wrongs; unto bad causes swear
Such creatures as men doubt; but do not
stain
The even virtue of our enterprise,
Nor the insuppressive mettle of our spirits,
To think that or our cause or our perform-
ance
Did need an oath; when every drop of blood
That every Roman bears, and nobly bears,
Is guilty of a several bastardy,
If he do break the smallest particle
Of any promise that hath pass'd from him.140

Cas. But what of Cicero? shall we sound
him?
I think he will stand very strong with us.

Casca. Let us not leave him out.

Cin.   No, by no means.

Met. O, let us have him, for his silver hairs
Will purchase us a good opinion
And buy men's voices to commend our deeds:
It shall be said, his judgement ruled our
hands;
Our youths and wildness shall no whit ap-
pear,
But all be buried in his gravity.

Bru. O, name him not: let us not break
with him;   150
For he will never follow any thing
That other men begin.

Cas.   Then leave him out.

Casca. Indeed he is not fit.

Dec. Shall no man else be touch'd but only
Cæsar?

Cas. Decius, well urged: I think it is not
meet,
Mark Antony, so well beloved of Cæsar,
Should outlive Cæsar: we shall find of him
A shrewd contriver; and, you know, his
means,
If he improve them, may well stretch so far
As to annoy us all: which to prevent,   160
Let Antony and Cæsar fall together.

Bru. Our course will seem too bloody,
Caius Cassius,

104. **fret**, mark with interlacing lines. 107. **growing
on**, toward. 114. **not an oath.** Brutus is thus refusing a genuine means of security in view of the importance
of oaths to conspirators and the penalties which befell
those who broke them. 115. **sufferance**, state of suffering. 118. **high-sighted**, haughty. 125. **secret**, conspiring. 126. **palter**, use trickery.

129. **cautelous**, deceitful. 130. **suffering**, long-
suffering. 134. **insuppressive**, not to be suppressed.
138. **several bastardy**, individual act dishonoring its
origin. 150. **break with**, tell to, confide in. 153. **fit.**
Plutarch tells us that they feared he lacked courage and
thought him too old; he was sixty-three. 158. **shrewd**,
malicious. 160. **annoy**, injure.

To cut the head off and then hack the limbs,
Like wrath in death and envy afterwards;
For Antony is but a limb of Cæsar:
Let us be sacrificers, but not butchers, Caius.
We all stand up against the spirit of Cæsar;
And in the spirit of men there is no blood:
O, that we then could come by Cæsar's
    spirit,
And not dismember Cæsar! But, alas,   170
Cæsar must bleed for it! And, gentle friends,
Let's kill him boldly, but not wrathfully;
Let's carve him as a dish fit for the gods,
Not hew him as a carcass fit for hounds:
And let our hearts, as subtle masters do,
Stir up their servants to an act of rage,
And after seem to chide 'em. This shall
    make
Our purpose necessary and not envious:
Which so appearing to the common eyes,
We shall be call'd purgers, not murderers. 180
And for Mark Antony, think not of him;
For he can do no more than Cæsar's arm
When Cæsar's head is off.
  Cas.   Yet I fear him;
For in the ingrafted love he bears to Cæsar—
  Bru. Alas, good Cassius, do not think of
    him:
If he love Cæsar, all that he can do
Is to himself, take thought and die for
    Cæsar:
And that were much he should; for he is
    given
To sports, to wildness and much company.
  Treb. There is no fear in him; let him
    not die;   190
For he will live, and laugh at this hereafter.
                 [*Clock strikes.*
  Bru. Peace! count the clock.
  Cas.   The clock hath stricken three.
  Treb. 'Tis time to part.
  Cas.   But it is doubtful yet,
Whether Cæsar will come forth to-day, or
    no;
For he is superstitious grown of late,
Quite from the main opinion he held once
Of fantasy, of dreams and ceremonies:
It may be, these apparent prodigies,
The unaccustom'd terror of this night,
And the persuasion of his augurers,   200
May hold him from the Capitol to-day.

  Dec. Never fear that: if he be so resolved,
I can o'ersway him; for he loves to hear
That unicorns may be betray'd with trees,
And bears with glasses, elephants with holes,
Lions with toils and men with flatterers;
But when I tell him he hates flatterers,
He says he does, being then most flattered.
Let me work;
For I can give his humour the true bent,   210
And I will bring him to the Capitol.
  Cas. Nay, we will all of us be there to fetch
    him.
  Bru. By the eighth hour: is that the utter-
    most?
  Cin. Be that the uttermost, and fail not
    then.
  Met. Caius Ligarius doth bear Cæsar hard,
Who rated him for speaking well of Pompey:
I wonder none of you have thought of him.
  Bru. Now, good Metellus, go along by
    him:
He loves me well, and I have given him rea-
    sons;
Send him but hither, and I'll fashion him. 220
  Cas. The morning comes upon 's: we'll
    leave you, Brutus.
And, friends, disperse yourselves; but all re-
    member
What you have said, and show yourselves
    true Romans.
  Bru. Good gentlemen, look fresh and
    merrily;
Let not our looks put on our purposes,
But bear it as our Roman actors do,
With untired spirits and formal constancy:
And so good morrow to you every one.
             [*Exeunt all but Brutus.*
Boy! Lucius! Fast asleep? It is no matter;
Enjoy the honey-heavy dew of slumber: 230
Thou hast no figures nor no fantasies,
Which busy care draws in the brains of men;
Therefore thou sleep'st so sound.

          Enter PORTIA.

  Por.   Brutus, my lord!
  Bru. Portia, what mean you? wherefore
    rise you now?

---

164. **envy**, malice. 187. **take thought**, despond.
188. **much he should**, a good deal for him to do. 192.
clock. Striking clocks were invented in the Middle Ages.
196. **main**, probably, prevailing or general rather than
strong. 198. **apparent**, plain, manifest.

204. **unicorns . . . betray'd**, i.e., by having the
unicorn imprison himself by driving his horn into a tree
as he charged at the hunter. 205. **glasses**, mirrors.
There was a myth to the effect that bears could be
dazzled and tamed by means of mirrors. **holes**, pitfalls.
206. **toils**, nets, snares. 210. **bent**, inclination of the
mind. 216. **rated**, scolded, chided. 218. **by him**,
by way of his house. 227. **formal constancy**, steadfast manner.

It is not for your health thus to commit
Your weak condition to the raw cold morn-
    ing.
  Por. Nor for yours neither. You've un-
    gently, Brutus,
Stole from my bed: and yesternight, at sup-
    per,
You suddenly arose, and walk'd about,   239
Musing and sighing, with your arms across,
And when I ask'd you what the matter was,
You stared upon me with ungentle looks;
I urged you further; then you scratch'd your
    head,
And too impatiently stamp'd with your foot;
Yet I insisted, yet you answer'd not,
But, with an angry wafture of your hand,
Gave sign for me to leave you: so I did;
Fearing to strengthen that impatience
Which seem'd too much enkindled, and
    withal
Hoping it was but an effect of humour,   250
Which sometime hath his hour with every
    man.
It will not let you eat, nor talk, nor sleep,
And could it work so much upon your shape
As it hath much prevail'd on your condi-
    tion,
I should not know you, Brutus. Dear my
    lord,
Make me acquainted with your cause of
    grief.
  Bru. I am not well in health, and that is
    all.
  Por. Brutus is wise, and, were he not in
    health,
He would embrace the means to come by it.
  Bru. Why, so I do. Good Portia, go to
    bed.   260
  Por. Is Brutus sick? and is it physical
To walk unbraced and suck up the humours
Of the dank morning? What, is Brutus sick,
And will he steal out of his wholesome bed,
To dare the vile contagion of the night
And tempt the rheumy and unpurged air
To add unto his sickness? No, my Brutus;
You have some sick offence within your
    mind,
Which, by the right and virtue of my place,
I ought to know of: and, upon my knees,   270

I charm you, by my once-commended
    beauty,
By all your vows of love and that great vow
Which did incorporate and make us one,
That you unfold to me, yourself, your half,
Why you are heavy, and what men to-night
Have had resort to you: for here have been
Some six or seven, who did hide their faces
Even from darkness.
  Bru.   Kneel not, gentle Portia.
  Por. I should not need, if you were gentle
    Brutus.
Within the bond of marriage, tell me,
    Brutus,   280
Is it excepted I should know no secrets
That appertain to you? Am I yourself
But, as it were, in sort or limitation,
To keep with you at meals, comfort your
    bed,
And talk to you sometimes? Dwell I but in
    the suburbs
Of your good pleasure? If it be no more,
Portia is Brutus' harlot, not his wife.
  Bru. You are my true and honourable
    wife,
As dear to me as are the ruddy drops
That visit my sad heart.   290
  Por. If this were true, then should I know
    this secret.
I grant I am a woman; but withal
A woman that Lord Brutus took to wife:
I grant I am a woman; but withal
A woman well-reputed, Cato's daughter.
Think you I am no stronger than my sex,
Being so father'd and so husbanded?
Tell me your counsels, I will not disclose 'em:
I have made strong proof of my constancy,
Giving myself a voluntary wound   300
Here, in the thigh: can I bear that with
    patience,
And not my husband's secrets?
  Bru.   O ye gods,
Render me worthy of this noble wife!
                         [*Knocking within.*
Hark, hark! one knocks: Portia, go in awhile;
And by and by thy bosom shall partake
The secrets of my heart.
All my engagements I will construe to thee,
All the charactery of my sad brows:

---

246. **wafture**, act of waving. **250. humour**, effect
of humor, i.e., a result of a disordered proportion among
the four humors of the body. **253-254. shape . . .
condition**, i.e., outward appearance . . . inner state of
mind. **266. rheumy**, i.e., causing colds, or possibly,
rheumatism. **unpurged**, not purified (by the sun).

271. **charm**, entreat. **295. Cato's daughter**. Portia
was the daughter of Cato the Younger. **300. voluntary
wound**. Plutarch recounts of Portia that in order to
give proof of her sincerity she gave herself a great gash
in the thigh with a little razor. **308. All the charactery
of**, all that is written on.

Leave me with haste. [*Exit Portia.*] Lucius, who's that knocks?

Re-enter Lucius *with* Ligarius.

Luc. Here is a sick man that would speak with you. 310

Bru. Caius Ligarius, that Metellus spake of.
Boy, stand aside. Caius Ligarius! how?

Lig. Vouchsafe good morrow from a feeble tongue.

Bru. O, what a time have you chose out, brave Caius,
To wear a kerchief! Would you were not sick!

Lig. I am not sick, if Brutus have in hand
Any exploit worthy the name of honour.

Bru. Such an exploit have I in hand, Ligarius,
Had you a healthful ear to hear of it.

Lig. By all the gods that Romans bow before, 320
I here discard my sickness! Soul of Rome!
Brave son, derived from honourable loins!
Thou, like an exorcist, hast conjured up
My mortified spirit. Now bid me run,
And I will strive with things impossible;
Yea, get the better of them. What's to do?

Bru. A piece of work that will make sick men whole.

Lig. But are not some whole that we must make sick?

Bru. That must we also. What it is, my Caius,
I shall unfold to thee, as we are going 330
To whom it must be done.

Lig. Set on your foot,
And with a heart new-fired I follow you,
To do I know not what: but it sufficeth
That Brutus leads me on.

Bru. Follow me, then. [*Exeunt*

Scene II. *Cæsar's house.*

Thunder and lightning. Enter Cæsar, *in his night-gown.*

Cæs. Nor heaven nor earth have been at peace to-night:
Thrice hath Calpurnia in her sleep cried out,

'Help, ho! they murder Cæsar!' Who's within?

Enter a Servant.

Serv. My lord?

Cæs. Go bid the priests do present sacrifice
And bring me their opinions of success.

Serv. I will, my lord. [*Exit.*

Enter Calpurnia.

Cal. What mean you, Cæsar? think you to walk forth?
You shall not stir out of your house to-day.

Cæs. Cæsar shall forth: the things that threaten'd me 10
Ne'er look'd but on my back; when they shall see
The face of Cæsar, they are vanished.

Cal. Cæsar, I never stood on ceremonies,
Yet now they fright me. There is one within,
Besides the things that we have heard and seen,
Recounts most horrid sights seen by the watch.
A lioness hath whelped in the streets;
And graves have yawn'd, and yielded up their dead;
Fierce fiery warriors fought upon the clouds,
In ranks and squadrons and right form of war, 20
Which drizzled blood upon the Capitol;
The noise of battle hurtled in the air,
Horses did neigh, and dying men did groan,
And ghosts did shriek and squeal about the streets.
O Cæsar! these things are beyond all use,
And I do fear them.

Cæs. What can be avoided
Whose end is purposed by the mighty gods?
Yet Cæsar shall go forth; for these predictions
Are to the world in general as to Cæsar.

Cal. When beggars die, there are no comets seen; 30
The heavens themselves blaze forth the death of princes.

---

309. **who's,** who is it. 313. **Vouchsafe,** deign to accept. 315. **kerchief,** headdress; *to wear a kerchief* meant "to be ill." 323. **exorcist,** conjurer. 324. **mortified,** deadened.
Scene ii. Stage Direction: **night-gown,** dressing gown.

6. **success,** the issue. 13. **stood on ceremonies,** attached importance to omens. 17-24. **A lioness . . . streets.** Similar enumerations of portents are made in I, iii, in *Hamlet* I, i, and elsewhere. These portents are very ancient and seem to be connected with the Fifteen Signs of Judgment appearing frequently in medieval literature. Most of the omens here mentioned are from Plutarch. 22. **hurtled,** clashed (of weapons). 25. **use,** custom.

Cæs. Cowards die many times before
their deaths;
The valiant never taste of death but once.
Of all the wonders that I yet have heard,
It seems to me most strange that men
should fear;
Seeing that death, a necessary end,
Will come when it will come.

Re-enter Servant.

What say the augurers?
Serv. They would not have you to stir
forth to-day.
Plucking the entrails of an offering forth,
They could not find a heart within the beast.
Cæs. The gods do this in shame of
cowardice: 41
Cæsar should be a beast without a heart,
If he should stay at home to-day for fear.
No, Cæsar shall not: danger knows full well
That Cæsar is more dangerous than he:
We are two lions litter'd in one day,
And I the elder and more terrible:
And Cæsar shall go forth.
Cal.   Alas, my lord,
Your wisdom is consumed in confidence.
Do not go forth to-day: call it my fear   50
That keeps you in the house, and not your
own.
We'll send Mark Antony to the senate-
house;
And he shall say you are not well to-day:
Let me, upon my knee, prevail in this.
Cæs. Mark Antony shall say I am not
well;
And, for thy humour, I will stay at home.

Enter DECIUS.

Here's Decius Brutus, he shall tell them so.
Dec. Cæsar, all hail! good morrow, worthy
Cæsar:
I come to fetch you to the senate-house.
Cæs. And you are come in very happy
time,   60
To bear my greeting to the senators
And tell them that I will not come to-day:
Cannot, is false, and that I dare not, falser:
I will not come to-day: tell them so, Decius.
Cal. Say he is sick.
Cæs.   Shall Cæsar send a lie?
Have I in conquest stretch'd mine arm so
far,
To be afeard to tell graybeards the truth?
Decius, go tell them Cæsar will not come.

Dec. Most mighty Cæsar, let me know
some cause,
Lest I be laugh'd at when I tell them so.   70
Cæs. The cause is in my will: I will not
come;
That is enough to satisfy the senate.
But for your private satisfaction,
Because I love you, I will let you know:
Calpurnia here, my wife, stays me at home:
She dreamt to-night she saw my statua,
Which, like a fountain with an hundred
spouts,
Did run pure blood; and many lusty Romans
Came smiling, and did bathe their hands in
it:
And these does she apply for warnings, and
portents,   80
And evils imminent; and on her knee
Hath begg'd that I will stay at home to-day.
Dec. This dream is all amiss interpreted;
It was a vision fair and fortunate:
Your statue spouting blood in many pipes,
In which so many smiling Romans bathed,
Signifies that from you great Rome shall
suck
Reviving blood, and that great men shall
press
For tinctures, stains, relics and cognizance.
This by Calpurnia's dream is signified.   90
Cæs. And this way have you well ex-
pounded it.
Dec. I have, when you have heard what
I can say:
And know it now: the senate have concluded
To give this day a crown to mighty Cæsar.
If you shall send them word you will not
come,
Their minds may change. Besides, it were a
mock
Apt to be render'd, for some one to say
'Break up the senate till another time,
When Cæsar's wife shall meet with better
dreams.'
If Cæsar hide himself, shall they not whisper
'Lo, Cæsar is afraid'?   101
Pardon me, Cæsar; for my dear dear love
To your proceeding bids me tell you this;
And reason to my love is liable.

76. **to-night**, last night. **statua**, statue. 89. **tinctures**, explained as alluding to the practice of dipping
handkerchiefs in the blood of martyrs, or as healing
medicines. **stains**, patches of color or "assimilable
traces (tinges) of Cæsar's qualities" (Mason). **relics**,
remembrances, sacred mementos. **cognizance**, heraldic
emblems. 96. **mock**, jibe. 103. **proceeding**, career.
104. **liable**, under the sway of.

Cæs. How foolish do your fears seem
    now, Calpurnia!
I am ashamed I did yield to them.
Give me my robe, for I will go.

Enter Publius, Brutus, Ligarius, Metel-
    lus, Casca, Trebonius, *and* Cinna.

And look where Publius is come to fetch me.
    Pub. Good morrow, Cæsar.
    Cæs.   Welcome, Publius.
What, Brutus, are you stirr'd so early too?110
Good morrow, Casca. Caius Ligarius,
Cæsar was ne'er so much your enemy
As that same ague which has made you lean.
What is't o'clock?
    Bru.   Cæsar, 'tis strucken eight.
    Cæs. I thank you for your pains and
    courtesy.

Enter Antony.

See! Antony, that revels long o' nights,
Is notwithstanding up. Good morrow,
    Antony.
    Ant. So to most noble Cæsar.
    Cæs.   Bid them prepare within:
I am to blame to be thus waited for.
Now, Cinna: now, Metellus: what, Tre-
    bonius!   120
I have an hour's talk in store for you;
Remember that you call on me to-day:
Be near me, that I may remember you.
    Treb. Cæsar, I will: [*Aside*] and so near
    will I be,
That your best friends shall wish I had been
    further.
    Cæs. Good friends, go in, and taste some
    wine with me;
And we, like friends, will straightway go to-
    gether.
    Bru. [*Aside*] That every like is not the
    same, O Cæsar,
The heart of Brutus yearns to think upon!
                      [*Exeunt.*

Scene III. *A street near the Capitol.*

Enter Artemidorus, *reading a paper.*

    Art. 'Cæsar, beware of Brutus; take heed
of Cassius; come not near Casca; have an eye
to Cinna; trust not Trebonius; mark well Metellus Cimber: Decius Brutus loves thee not:
thou hast wronged Caius Ligarius. There is
but one mind in all these men, and it is bent

against Cæsar. If thou beest not immortal,
look about you: security gives way to con-
spiracy. The mighty gods defend thee! Thy
lover,
                     'Artemidorus.'
Here will I stand till Cæsar pass along,   11
And as a suitor will I give him this.
My heart laments that virtue cannot live
Out of the teeth of emulation.
If thou read this, O Cæsar, thou mayst live;
If not, the Fates with traitors do contrive.
                          [*Exit.*

Scene IV. *Another part of the same street,*
before the house of Brutus.

Enter Portia *and* Lucius.

    Por. I prithee, boy, run to the senate-
    house;
Stay not to answer me, but get thee gone:
Why dost thou stay?
    Luc.   To know my errand, madam.
    Por. I would have had thee there, and
    here again,
Ere I can tell thee what thou shouldst do
    there.
O constancy, be strong upon my side,
Set a huge mountain 'tween my heart and
    tongue!
I have a man's mind, but a woman's might.
How hard it is for women to keep counsel!
Art thou here yet?
    Luc.   Madam, what should I do?
Run to the Capitol, and nothing else?   11
And so return to you, and nothing else?
    Por. Yes, bring me word, boy, if thy lord
    look well,
For he went sickly forth: and take good note
What Cæsar doth, what suitors press to him.
Hark, boy! what noise is that?
    Luc. I hear none, madam.
    Por.   Prithee, listen well;
I heard a bustling rumour, like a fray,
And the wind brings it from the Capitol.
    Luc. Sooth, madam, I hear nothing.   20

Enter the Soothsayer.

    Por. Come hither, fellow: which way hast
    thou been?
    Sooth. At mine own house, good lady.
    Por. What is't o'clock?

---

8. security, want of caution. **10. lover,** friend.
14. emulation, grudge against the superiority of others.

Sooth.   About the ninth hour, lady.

Por. Is Cæsar yet gone to the Capitol?

Sooth. Madam, not yet: I go to take my stand,

To see him pass on to the Capitol.

Por. Thou hast some suit to Cæsar, hast thou not?

Sooth. That I have, lady: if it will please Cæsar

To be so good to Cæsar as to hear me,

I shall beseech him to befriend himself.   30

Por. Why, know'st thou any harm's intended towards him?

Sooth. None that I know will be, much that I fear may chance.

Good morrow to you. Here the street is narrow:

The throng that follows Cæsar at the heels,

Of senators, of prætors, common suitors,

Will crowd a feeble man almost to death:

I'll get me to a place more void, and there

Speak to great Cæsar as he comes along.

                              [*Exit.*

Por. I must go in. Ay me, how weak a thing

The heart of woman is! O Brutus,   40

The heavens speed thee in thine enterprise!

Sure, the boy heard me: Brutus hath a suit

That Cæsar will not grant. O, I grow faint.

Run, Lucius, and commend me to my lord;

Say I am merry: come to me again,

And bring me word what he doth say to thee.

                              [*Exeunt severally.*

ACT III.

SCENE I. *Rome. Before the Capitol; the Senate sitting above.*

A crowd of people; among them ARTEMI-DORUS *and the* SOOTHSAYER. *Flourish. Enter* CÆSAR, BRUTUS, CASSIUS, CASCA, DECIUS, METELLUS, TREBONIUS, CINNA, ANTONY, LEPIDUS, POPILIUS, PUBLIUS, *and others.*

Cæs. [*To the Soothsayer*] The ides of March are come.

Sooth. Ay, Cæsar; but not gone.

Art. Hail, Cæsar! read this schedule.

Dec. Trebonius doth desire you to o'er-read,

At your best leisure, this his humble suit.

Art. O Cæsar, read mine first; for mine's a suit

That touches Cæsar nearer: read it, great Cæsar.

Cæsar. What touches us ourself shall be last served.

Art. Delay not, Cæsar; read it instantly.

Cæs. What, is the fellow mad?

Pub.   Sirrah, give place.   10

Cas. What, urge you your petitions in the street?

Come to the Capitol.

CÆSAR *goes up to the Senate-House, the rest following.*

Pop. I wish your enterprise to-day may thrive.

Cas. What enterprise, Popilius?

Pop.   Fare you well.

                              [*Advances to Cæsar.*

Bru. What said Popilius Lena?

Cas. He wish'd to-day our enterprise might thrive.

I fear our purpose is discovered.

Bru. Look, how he makes to Cæsar: mark him.

Cas. Casca, be sudden, for we fear prevention.

Brutus, what shall be done? If this be known,   20

Cassius or Cæsar never shall turn back,

For I will slay myself.

Bru.   Cassius, be constant:

Popilius Lena speaks not of our purposes;

For, look, he smiles, and Cæsar doth not change.

Cas. Trebonius knows his time; for, look you, Brutus,

He draws Mark Antony out of the way.

                              [*Exeunt Antony and Trebonius.*

Dec. Where is Metellus Cimber? Let him go,

And presently prefer his suit to Cæsar.

Bru. He is address'd: press near and second him.

Cin. Casca, you are the first that rears your hand.   30

---

37. **void**, empty.
Act III. *Scene i. Stage Direction:* **Capitol.** The scene is not located in F, but is indicated by the text. Shakespeare implies (line 12) that Cæsar was assassinated in the Capitol, but it is clear from Plutarch that it was in the portico of Pompey's theater, where the Senate was sitting. 3. **schedule**, written scroll.

8. **What . . . served.** Cæsar's pride is admirable but is made the source of his downfall. That he does not read the paper is usually regarded as an element of fate in the tragedy, but the idea just expressed is more truly Shakespearean. 29. **address'd**, ready.

Cæs. Are we all ready? What is now amiss
That Cæsar and his senate must redress?

Met. Most high, most mighty, and most
　puissant Cæsar,
Metellus Cimber throws before thy seat
An humble heart,—　　　　　　　　[*Kneeling.*

Cæs. 　　　　　I must prevent thee, Cimber.
These couchings and these lowly courtesies
Might fire the blood of ordinary men,
And turn pre-ordinance and first decree
Into the law of children. Be not fond,
To think that Cæsar bears such rebel blood　40
That will be thaw'd from the true quality
With that which melteth fools; I mean,
　sweet words,
Low-crooked court'sies and base spaniel-
　fawning.
Thy brother by decree is banished:
If thou dost bend and pray and fawn for
　him,
I spurn thee like a cur out of my way.
Know, Cæsar doth not wrong, nor without
　cause
Will he be satisfied.

Met. Is there no voice more worthy than
　my own,　　　　　　　　　　　49
To sound more sweetly in great Cæsar's ear
For the repealing of my banish'd brother?

Bru. I kiss thy hand, but not in flattery,
　Cæsar;
Desiring thee that Publius Cimber may
Have an immediate freedom of repeal.

Cæs. What, Brutus!

Cas. 　　　　Pardon, Cæsar; Cæsar, pardon:
As low as to thy foot doth Cassius fall,
To beg enfranchisement for Publius Cimber.

Cæs. I could be well moved, if I were as
　you;
If I could pray to move, prayers would move
　me:
But I am constant as the northern star,　60
Of whose true-fix'd and resting quality
There is no fellow in the firmament.
The skies are painted with unnumber'd
　sparks,
They are all fire and every one doth shine,
But there's but one in all doth hold his place:
So in the world; 'tis furnish'd well with men,

And men are flesh and blood, and apprehen-
　sive;
Yet in the number I do know but one
That unassailable holds on his rank,
Unshaked of motion: and that I am he,　70
Let me a little show it, even in this;
That I was constant Cimber should be
　banish'd,
And constant do remain to keep him so.

Cin. O Cæsar,—

Cæs. 　　　　　　Hence! wilt thou lift up
　Olympus?

Dec. Great Cæsar,—

Cæs. 　　　Doth not Brutus bootless kneel?

Casca. Speak, hands, for me!
[*Casca first, then the other Conspirators and
　　　　　Marcus Brutus stab Cæsar.*

Cæs. Et tu, Brute! Then fall, Cæsar!
　　　　　　　　　　　　　　　[*Dies.*

Cin. Liberty! Freedom! Tyranny is dead!
Run hence, proclaim, cry it about the streets.

Cas. Some to the common pulpits, and cry
　out　　　　　　　　　　　　　80
'Liberty, freedom, and enfranchisement!'

Bru. People and senators, be not af-
　frighted;
Fly not; stand still: ambition's debt is paid.

Casca. Go to the pulpit, Brutus.

Dec. 　　　　　　　And Cassius too.

Bru. Where's Publius?

Cin. Here, quite confounded with this
　mutiny.

Met. Stand fast together, lest some friend
　of Cæsar's
Should chance—

Bru. Talk not of standing. Publius, good
　cheer;
There is no harm intended to your person,　90
Nor to no Roman else: so tell them, Publius.

Cas. And leave us, Publius; lest that the
　people,
Rushing on us, should do your age some
　mischief.

Bru. Do so: and let no man abide this
　deed,
But we the doers.

　　　　　Re-enter Trebonius.

Cas. 　　　　　　Where is Antony?

---

39. **fond**, foolish. 41. **thaw'd from the true quality.** The idea is that the cool brain governed by reason
might be visited by various intruding spirits (carrying
with them heat) and so thawed. 47-48. **Know . . . satisfied.** Ben Jonson ridicules these lines in his *Discoveries*,
where he says, "Cæsar did never wrong but with just
cause." Such may have been the original text or its
reading on the stage, but the F reading is intelligible.

67. **apprehensive**, sensitive, i.e., quick to perceive or
learn. 69. **rank**, place in line or file, position. 70.
motion, inward impulse as the result of sense (sensation). 77. **Et tu, Brute!** These words, the exact origin
of which is not known, are so striking in their condensed significance that they have maintained their Latin
form unchanged. 80. **common pulpits**, public rostra.

Tre. Fled to his house amazed:
Men, wives and children stare, **cry out and
    run**
As it were doomsday.
    Bru.   Fates, we will know your pleas-
    ures:
That we shall die, we know; 'tis but the time
And drawing days out, that men stand upon.
    Cas. Why, he that cuts off twenty years of
    life   101
Cuts off so many years of fearing death.
    Bru. Grant that, and then is death a
    benefit:
So are we Cæsar's friends, that have abridged
His time of fearing death. Stoop, Romans,
    stoop,
And let us bathe our hands in Cæsar's blood
Up to the elbows, and besmear our swords:
Then walk we forth, even to the market-
    place,
And, waving our red weapons o'er our heads,
Let's all cry, 'Peace, freedom and liberty!' 110
    Cas. Stoop, then, and wash. How many
    ages hence
Shall this our lofty scene be acted over
In states unborn and accents yet unknown!
    Bru. How many times shall Cæsar bleed
    in sport,
That now on Pompey's basis lies along
No worthier than the dust!
    Cas.   So oft as that shall be,
So often shall the knot of us be call'd
The men that gave their country liberty.
    Dec. What, shall we forth?
    Cas.   Ay, every man away:
Brutus shall lead; and we will grace his heels
With the most boldest and best hearts of
    Rome.   121

Enter a Servant.

    Bru. Soft! who comes here? A friend of
    Antony's.
    Serv. Thus, Brutus, did my master bid me
    kneel;
Thus did Mark Antony bid me fall down;
And, being prostrate, thus he bade me say:
Brutus is noble, wise, valiant, and honest;
Cæsar was mighty, bold, royal, and loving:
Say I love Brutus, and I honour him;

Say I fear'd Cæsar, honour'd him and loved
    him.
If Brutus will vouchsafe that Antony   30
May safely come to him, and be resolved
How Cæsar hath deserved to lie in death,
Mark Antony shall not love Cæsar dead
So well as Brutus living; but will follow
The fortunes and affairs of noble Brutus
Thorough the hazards of this untrod state
With all true faith. So says my master
    Antony.
    Bru. Thy master is a wise and valiant
    Roman;
I never thought him worse.
Tell him, so please him come unto this place,
He shall be satisfied; and, by my honour,   141
Depart untouch'd.
    Serv.   I'll fetch him presently. [*Exit.*
    Bru. I know that we shall have him well
    to friend.
    Cas. I wish we may: but yet have I a
    mind
That fears him much; and my misgiving
    still
Falls shrewdly to the purpose.
    Bru. But here comes Antony.

Re-enter ANTONY.

              Welcome, Mark Antony.
    Ant. O mighty Cæsar! dost thou lie so
    low?
Are all thy conquests, glories, triumphs,
    spoils,
Shrunk to this little measure? Fare thee
    well.   150
I know not, gentlemen, what you intend,
Who else must be let blood, who else is rank:
If I myself, there is no hour so fit
As Cæsar's death's hour, nor no instrument
Of half that worth as those your swords,
    made rich
With the most noble blood of all this world.
I do beseech ye, if you bear me hard,
Now, whilst your purpled hands do reek and
    smoke,
Fulfil your pleasure. Live a thousand years,
I shall not find myself so apt to die: 160
No place will please me so, no mean of death,
As here by Cæsar, and by you cut off,
The choice and master spirits of this age.

97. **wives**, women. 100. **drawing days out**, pro-
longing their lives. **stand upon**, lay emphasis upon.
115. **Pompey's basis**, pedestal of Pompey's statue.
118. **liberty**. Shakespeare here exploits the glory of
tyrannicide, so much so that the play in its political
aspect may be said to turn on that issue.

131. **resolved**, convinced. 136. **Thorough**, throughout. 143. **to friend**, for a friend. 146. **Falls . . . precisely**, hits the mark precisely. 152. **let blood**, bled.
rank, plethoric or full-blooded. 157. **bear . . . hard**,
bear ill-will to. 160. **apt**, ready, prepared.

Bru. O Antony, beg not your death of us.
Though now we must appear bloody and
      cruel,
As, by our hands and this our present act,
You see we do, yet see you but our hands
And this the bleeding business they have
      done:
Our hearts you see not; they are pitiful;
And pity to the general wrong of Rome— 170
As fire drives out fire, so pity pity—
Hath done this deed on Cæsar. For your
      part,
To you our swords have leaden points, Mark
      Antony:
†Our arms, in strength of malice, and our
      hearts
Of brothers' temper, do receive you in
With all kind love, good thoughts, and rever-
      ence.
      Cas. Your voice shall be as strong as any
      man's
In the disposing of new dignities.
      Bru. Only be patient till we have appeased
The multitude, beside themselves with fear,
And then we will deliver you the cause,   181
Why I, that did love Cæsar when I struck
      him,
Have thus proceeded.
      Ant.   I doubt not of your wisdom.
Let each man render me his bloody hand:
First, Marcus Brutus, will I shake with you;
Next, Caius Cassius, do I take your hand;
Now, Decius Brutus, yours; now yours,
      Metellus;
Yours, Cinna; and, my valiant Casca, yours;
Though last, not least in love, yours, good
      Trebonius.
Gentlemen all,—alas, what shall I say?   190
My credit now stands on such slippery
      ground,
That one of two bad ways you must conceit
      me,
Either a coward or a flatterer.
That I did love thee, Cæsar, O, 'tis true:
If then thy spirit look upon us now,
Shall it not grieve thee dearer than thy
      death,
To see thy Antony making his peace,
Shaking the bloody fingers of thy foes,
Most noble! in the presence of thy corse?
Had I as many eyes as thou hast wounds, 200

Weeping as fast as they stream forth thy
      blood,
It would become me better than to close
In terms of friendship with thine enemies.
Pardon me, Julius! Here wast thou bay'd,
      brave hart;
Here didst thou fall; and here thy hunters
      stand,
Sign'd in thy spoil, and crimson'd in thy
      lethe.
O world, thou wast the forest to this hart;
And this, indeed, O world, the heart of thee.
How like a deer, strucken by many princes,
Dost thou here lie!   210
      Cas. Mark Antony,—
      Ant.   Pardon me, Caius Cassius:
The enemies of Cæsar shall say this;
Then, in a friend, it is cold modesty.
      Cas. I blame you not for praising Cæsar
      so;
But what compact mean you to have with
      us?
Will you be prick'd in number of our friends;
Or shall we on, and not depend on you?
      Ant. Therefore I took your hands, but
      was, indeed,
Sway'd from the point, by looking down on
      Cæsar.
Friends am I with you all and love you all, 220
Upon this hope, that you shall give me
      reasons
Why and wherein Cæsar was dangerous.
      Bru. Or else were this a savage spectacle:
Our reasons are so full of good regard
That were you, Antony, the son of Cæsar,
You should be satisfied.
      Ant.   That's all I seek:
And am moreover suitor that I may
Produce his body to the market-place;
And in the pulpit, as becomes a friend,
Speak in the order of his funeral.   230
      Bru. You shall, Mark Antony.
      Cas.   Brutus, a word with you.
[*Aside to Bru.*] You know not what you do:
      do not consent
That Antony speak in his funeral:

177-178. **Your . . . dignities.** Cassius better understands Antony's motives when he offers him a voice in
distributing the offices.

204. **bay'd,** brought to bay. **hart,** stag, with pun
on **heart.** 206. **Sign'd in,** marked with the signs of.
lethe, death. 207-210. **O world . . . lie.** Shakespeare
seems to have meant to depict real grief and indignation
in Antony. 213. **modesty,** moderation. 216. **prick'd
in,** set down, marked off on a list. 224. **regard,** possibly,
design, intention. 230. **order,** course. 232. **You
know not what you do.** Plutarch calls attention to
this as the second error which Brutus committed; the
first was that he failed to have Antony killed as well as
Cæsar.

Know you how much the people may be
    moved
By that which he will utter?
   Bru.   By your pardon;
I will myself into the pulpit first,
And show the reason of our Cæsar's death:
What Antony shall speak, I will protest
He speaks by leave and by permission,
And that we are contented Cæsar shall   240
Have all true rites and lawful ceremonies.
It shall advantage more than do us wrong.
   Cas. I know not what may fall; I like it
    not.
   Bru.   Mark Antony, here, take you
    Cæsar's body.
You shall not in your funeral speech blame
    us,
But speak all good you can devise of Cæsar,
And say you do 't by our permission;
Else shall you not have any hand at all
About his funeral: and you shall speak
In the same pulpit whereto I am going,   250
After my speech is ended.
   Ant.   Be it so;
I do desire no more.
   Bru.   Prepare the body then, and follow
    us.   *[Exeunt all but Antony.*
   Ant. O, pardon me, thou bleeding piece of
    earth,
That I am meek and gentle with these
    butchers!
Thou art the ruins of the noblest man
That ever lived in the tide of times.
Woe to the hand that shed this costly blood!
Over thy wounds now do I prophesy,—
Which, like dumb mouths, do ope their ruby
    lips,   260
To beg the voice and utterance of my
    tongue—
A curse shall light upon the †limbs of men;
Domestic fury and fierce civil strife
Shall cumber all the parts of Italy;
Blood and destruction shall be so in use
And dreadful objects so familiar
That mothers shall but smile when they be-
    hold
Their infants quarter'd with the hands of
    war;
All pity choked with custom of fell deeds:
And Cæsar's spirit, ranging for revenge,   270
With Ate by his side come hot from hell,

Shall in these confines with a monarch's
    voice
Cry 'Havoc,' and let slip the dogs of war
That this foul deed shall smell above the
    earth
With carrion men, groaning for burial.

         Enter a Servant.

You serve Octavius Cæsar, do you not?
   Serv. I do, Mark Antony.
   Ant. Cæsar did write for him to come to
    Rome.
   Serv. He did receive his letters, and is
    coming;
And bid me say to you by word of mouth—
O Cæsar!—   *[Seeing the body.*   280
   Ant. Thy heart is big, get thee apart and
    weep.
Passion, I see, is catching; for mine eyes,
Seeing those beads of sorrow stand in thine,
Began to water. Is thy master coming?
   Serv. He lies to-night within seven leagues
    of Rome.
   Ant. Post back with speed, and tell him
    what hath chanced:
Here is a mourning Rome, a dangerous
    Rome,
No Rome of safety for Octavius yet;   289
Hie hence, and tell him so. Yet, stay awhile;
Thou shalt not back till I have borne this
    corse
Into the market-place: there shall I try,
In my oration, how the people take
The cruel issue of these bloody men;
According to the which, thou shalt discourse
To young Octavius of the state of things.
Lend me your hand.   *[Exeunt with Cæsar's*
                         body.

        Scene II. *The Forum.*

Enter Brutus *and* Cassius, *and a throng
    of* Citizens.

   Citizens. We will be satisfied; let us be
    satisfied.
   Bru. Then follow me, and give me audi-
    ence, friends,
Cassius, go you into the other street,
And part the numbers.
Those that will hear me speak, let 'em stay
    here;

---

238. **protest**, announce. 268. **quarter'd**, slaughtered.
271. **Ate**, goddess of revenge.

273. '**Havoc**,' the signal for sack, pillage, and slaughter.
274. **That**, so that. 294. **issue**, deed.
Scene ii. 4. **part**, divide.

Those that will follow Cassius, go with him;
And public reasons shall be rendered
Of Cæsar's death.

First Cit.   I will hear Brutus speak.

Sec. Cit. I will hear Cassius; and compare
      their reasons,
When severally we hear them rendered.   10

      [*Exit Cassius, with some of the Citizens.
            Brutus goes into the
                  pulpit.*

      Third Cit. The noble Brutus is ascended:
      silence!

Bru. Be patient till the last.

Romans, countrymen, and lovers! hear me
for my cause, and be silent, that you may
hear: believe me for mine honour, and have
respect to mine honour, that you may believe: censure me in your wisdom, and awake
your senses, that you may the better judge.
If there be any in this assembly, any dear
friend of Cæsar's, to him I say, that Brutus'
love to Cæsar was no less than his. If then
that friend demand why Brutus rose against
Cæsar this is my answer:—Not that I loved
Cæsar less, but that I loved Rome more.
Had you rather Cæsar were living and die all
slaves, than that Cæsar were dead, to live all
free men? As Cæsar loved me, I weep for
him; as he was fortunate, I rejoice at it; as he
was valiant, I honour him: but, as he was
ambitious, I slew him. There is tears for his
love; joy for his fortune; honour for his
valour; and death for his ambition. Who is
here so base that would be a bondman? If
any, speak; for him have I offended. Who is
here so rude that would not be a Roman? If
any, speak; for him have I offended. Who is
here so vile that will not love his country? If
any, speak; for him have I offended. I pause
for a reply.   37

      All. None, Brutus, none.

Bru. Then none have I offended. I have
done no more to Cæsar than you shall do to
Brutus. The question of his death is enrolled
in the Capitol; his glory not extenuated,
wherein he was worthy, nor his offences enforced, for which he suffered death.   44

---

10. **severally**, individually. 12-37. **Be . . . reply.**
The speech of Brutus is in careful sententious prose. It
is Shakespeare's attempt to reproduce in style what
Plutarch means when he says, "He counterfeited that
brief compendious manner of speech of the Lacedæmon-
ians." In content the speech is original with Shakespeare.
33. **rude**, barbarous. 41. **question of**, judicial inquiry
into. 42. **extenuated**, minimized. 43. **enforced**, enlarged upon.

      Enter ANTONY *and others, with*
            CÆSAR'S *body.*

Here comes his body, mourned by Mark Antony: who, though he had no hand in his
death, shall receive the benefit of his dying, a
place in the commonwealth; as which of you
shall not? With this I depart,—that, as I
slew my best lover for the good of Rome, I
have the same dagger for myself, when it
shall please my country to need my death.

      All. Live, Brutus! live, live!   53

First Cit. Bring him with triumph home
      unto his house.

Sec. Cit. Give him a statue with his an-
      cestors.

Third Cit. Let him be Cæsar.

Fourth Cit.   Cæsar's better parts
Shall be crown'd in Brutus.

First Cit.   We'll bring him to his house
With shouts and clamours.

Bru.   My countrymen,—

Sec. Cit. Peace, silence! Brutus speaks.

First Cit.   Peace, ho!

Bru. Good countrymen, let me depart
      alone,
And, for my sake, stay here with Antony: 61
Do grace to Cæsar's corpse, and grace his
      speech
Tending to Cæsar's glories; which Mark An-
      tony,
By our permission, is allow'd to make.
I do entreat you, not a man depart,
Save I alone, till Antony have spoke.   [*Exit.*

First Cit. Stay, ho! and let us hear Mark
      Antony.

Third Cit. Let him go up into the public
      chair;
We'll hear him. Noble Antony, go up.   69

Ant. For Brutus' sake, I am beholding to
      you.   [*Goes into the pulpit.*

Fourth Cit. What does he say of Brutus?

Third Cit.   He says, for Brutus' sake,
He finds himself beholding to us all.

Fourth Cit. 'Twere best he speak no harm
      of Brutus here.

First Cit. This Cæsar was a tyrant.

Third Cit.   Nay, that's certain:
We are blest that Rome is rid of him.

Sec. Cit. Peace! let us hear what Antony
      can say.

Ant. You gentle Romans,—

Citizens.   Peace, ho! let us hear
      him.

Ant. Friends, Romans, countrymen, lend
  me your ears;
I come to bury Cæsar, not to praise him.
The evil that men do lives after them;   80
The good is oft interred with their bones;
So let it be with Cæsar. The noble Brutus
Hath told you Cæsar was ambitious:
If it were so, it was a grievous fault,
And grievously hath Cæsar answer'd it.
Here, under leave of Brutus and the rest—
For Brutus is an honourable man;
So are they all, all honourable men—
Come I to speak in Cæsar's funeral.
He was my friend, faithful and just to me:
But Brutus says he was ambitious;   91
And Brutus is an honourable man.
He hath brought many captives home to
  Rome,
Whose ransoms did the general coffers fill:
Did this in Cæsar seem ambitious?
When that the poor have cried, Cæsar hath
  wept:
Ambition should be made of sterner stuff:
Yet Brutus says he was ambitious;
And Brutus is an honourable man.
You all did see that on the Lupercal   100
I thrice presented him a kingly crown,
Which he did thrice refuse: was this ambi-
  tion?
Yet Brutus says he was ambitious;
And, sure, he is an honourable man.
I speak not to disprove what Brutus spoke,
But here I am to speak what I do know.
You all did love him once, not without
  cause:
What cause withholds you then, to mourn for
  him?
O judgement! thou art fled to brutish beasts,
And men have lost their reason. Bear with
  me;   110
My heart is in the coffin there with Cæsar,
And I must pause till it come back to me.

  First Cit. Methinks there is much reason
  in his sayings.

  Sec. Cit. If thou consider rightly of the
  matter,

Cæsar has had great wrong.
  Third Cit.   Has he, masters?
I fear there will a worse come in his place.
  Fourth Cit. Mark'd ye his words? He
  would not take the crown;
Therefore 'tis certain he was not ambitious.
  First Cit. If it be found so, some will dear
  abide it.
  Sec. Cit. Poor soul! his eyes are red as fire
  with weeping.   120
  Third Cit. There's not a nobler man in
  Rome than Antony.
  Fourth Cit. Now mark him, he begins
  again to speak.
  Ant. But yesterday the word of Cæsar
  might
Have stood against the world; now lies he
  there,
And none so poor to do him reverence.
O masters, if I were disposed to stir
Your hearts and minds to mutiny and rage,
I should do Brutus wrong, and Cassius
  wrong,
Who, you all know, are honourable men:
I will not do them wrong; I rather choose 130
To wrong the dead, to wrong myself and
  you,
Than I will wrong such honourable men.
But here's a parchment with the seal of
  Cæsar;
I found it in his closet, 'tis his will:
Let but the commons hear this testament—
Which, pardon me, I do not mean to read—
And they would go and kiss dead Cæsar's
  wounds
And dip their napkins in his sacred blood,
Yea, beg a hair of him for memory,
And, dying, mention it within their wills, 140
Bequeathing it as a rich legacy
Unto their issue.
  Fourth Cit. We'll hear the will: read it,
  Mark Antony.
  All. The will, the will! we will hear
  Cæsar's will.
  Ant. Have patience, gentle friends, I must
  not read it;
It is not meet you know how Cæsar loved
  you.
You are not wood, you are not stones, but
  men;
And, being men, hearing the will of Cæsar,
It will inflame you, it will make you mad:

  78-257. Friends . . . such another. Plutarch gives
a brief description of Antony's oration and its effect,
telling how Antony moved the audience and displayed
to them Cæsar's bloody garments. Appian tells of an
image of Cæsar in wax with three and twenty wounds;
and Dio furnishes hints for Antony's praise of Cæsar's
liberality and Cæsar's betrayal by his friends. The oration is sometimes thought to illustrate the "Asiatic" style
as opposed to the "Greek" style used by Brutus. 85.
answer'd, atoned for. 93. captives. It has been
estimated that Cæsar and Pompey sold a million captives
into slavery.

138. napkins, handkerchiefs.

'Tis good you know not that you are his
    heirs;   150
For, if you should, O, what would come of it!
  Fourth Cit. Read the will; we'll hear it,
    Antony;
You shall read us the will, Cæsar's will.
  Ant. Will you be patient? will you stay
    awhile?
I have o'ershot myself to tell you of it:
I fear I wrong the honourable men
Whose daggers have stabb'd Cæsar; I do
    fear it.
  Fourth Cit. They were traitors: honour-
    able men!
  All. The will! the testament!
  Sec. Cit. They were villains, murderers:
    the will! read the will.   160
  Ant. You will compel me, then, to read the
    will?
Then make a ring about the corpse of
    Cæsar,
And let me show you him that made the will.
Shall I descend? and will you give me leave?
  Several Cit. Come down.
  Sec. Cit. Descend.
  Third Cit. You shall have leave.
               [*Antony comes down.*
  Fourth Cit. A ring; stand round.
  First Cit. Stand from the hearse, stand
    from the body.
  Sec. Cit. Room for Antony, most noble
    Antony.   170
  Ant. Nay, press not so upon me; stand
    far off.
  Several Cit. Stand back; room; bear back.
  Ant. If you have tears, prepare to shed
    them now.
You all do know this mantle: I remember
The first time ever Cæsar put it on;
'Twas on a summer's evening, in his tent,
That day he overcame the Nervii:
Look, in this place ran Cassius' dagger
    through:
See what a rent the envious Casca made:
Through this the well-beloved Brutus
    stabb'd;   180
And as he pluck'd his cursed steel away,
Mark how the blood of Cæsar follow'd it,
As rushing out of doors, to be resolved
If Brutus so unkindly knock'd, or no;
For Brutus, as you know, was Cæsar's angel:

Judge, O you gods, how dearly Cæsar loved
    him!
This was the most unkindest cut of all;
For when the noble Cæsar saw him stab,
Ingratitude, more strong than traitors' arms,
Quite vanquish'd him: then burst his mighty
    heart;   190
And, in his mantle muffling up his face,
Even at the base of Pompey's statua,
Which all the while ran blood, great Cæsar
    fell.
O, what a fall was there, my countrymen!
Then I, and you, and all of us fell down,
Whilst bloody treason flourish'd over us.
O, now you weep; and, I perceive, you feel
The dint of pity: these are gracious drops.
Kind souls, what, weep you when you but
    behold
Our Cæsar's vesture wounded? Look you
    here,   200
Here is himself, marr'd, as you see, with
    traitors.
  First Cit. O piteous spectacle!
  Sec. Cit. O noble Cæsar!
  Third Cit. O woful day!
  Fourth Cit. O traitors, villains!
  First Cit. O most bloody sight!
  Sec. Cit. We will be revenged.
  All. Revenge! About! Seek! **Burn! Fire!**
Kill! Slay! Let not a traitor live!
  Ant. Stay, countrymen.   210
  First Cit. Peace there! hear the noble
    Antony.
  Sec. Cit. We'll hear him, we'll follow him,
    we'll die with him.
  Ant. Good friends, sweet friends, let me
    not stir you up
To such a sudden flood of mutiny.
They that have done this deed are honour-
    able:
What private griefs they have, alas, I know
    not,
That made them do it: they are wise and
    honourable,
And will, no doubt, with reasons answer you.
I come not, friends, to steal away your
    hearts: 220
I am no orator, as Brutus is;
But, as you know me all, a plain blunt man,
That love my friend; and that they know full
    well

169. **hearse,** bier.   177. **Nervii,** the Belgian tribe
whose defeat is described in Cæsar's *Gallic War,* II,
xv-xxvii.   183. **resolved,** convinced.   185. **angel,**
guardian spirit.

187. **most unkindest,** the most familiar of Shakespeare's double superlatives.   191. **muffling up.** This
detail showing the dignity of Cæsar's death appears in
almost every version of the story from ancient times
on.

That gave me public leave to speak of him:
For I have neither wit, nor words, nor worth,
Action, nor utterance, nor the power of
  speech,
To stir men's blood: I only speak right on;
I tell you that which you yourselves do know;
Show you sweet Cæsar's wounds, poor poor
  dumb mouths,
And bid them speak for me: but were I
  Brutus,   230
And Brutus Antony, there were an Antony
Would ruffle up your spirits and put a tongue
In every wound of Cæsar that should move
The stones of Rome to rise and mutiny.
  All. We'll mutiny.
  First Cit. We'll burn the house of Brutus.
  Third Cit. Away, then! come, seek the
  conspirators.
  Ant. Yet hear me, countrymen; yet hear
  me speak.
  All. Peace, ho! Hear Antony. Most noble
  Antony!
  Ant. Why, friends, you go to do you
  know not what: 240
Wherein hath Cæsar thus deserved your
  loves?
Alas, you know not: I must tell you, then:
You have forgot the will I told you of.
  All. Most true. The will! Let's stay and
  hear the will.
  Ant. Here is the will, and under Cæsar's
  seal.
To every Roman citizen he gives,
To every several man, seventy five drach-
  mas.
  Sec. Cit. Most noble Cæsar! We'll re-
  venge his death.
  Third Cit. O royal Cæsar!
  Ant. Hear me with patience.   250
  All. Peace, ho!
  Ant. Moreover, he hath left you all his
  walks,
His private arbours and new-planted or-
  chards,
On this side Tiber; he hath left them you,
And to your heirs for ever, common pleas-
  ures,
To walk abroad, and recreate yourselves.

Here was a Cæsar! when comes such another?
  First Cit. Never, never. Come, away, a-
  way!
We'll burn his body in the holy place,
And with the brands fire the traitors' houses.
Take up the body.   261
  Sec. Cit. Go fetch fire.
  Third Cit. Pluck down benches.
  Fourth Cit. Pluck down forms, windows,
  any thing. [*Exeunt Citizens with the body.*
  Ant. Now let it work. Mischief, thou art
  afoot,
Take thou what course thou wilt!

Enter a Servant.

                    How now, fellow!
  Serv. Sir, Octavius is already come to
  Rome.
  Ant. Where is he?
  Serv. He and Lepidus are at Cæsar's
  house.
  Ant. And thither will I straight to visit
  him: 270
He comes upon a wish. Fortune is merry,
And in this mood will give us any thing.
  Serv. I heard him say, Brutus and Cassius
Are rid like madmen through the gates of
  Rome.
  Ant. Belike they had some notice of the
  people,
How I had moved them. Bring me to
  Octavius.   [*Exeunt.*

SCENE III. *A street.*

Enter CINNA *the poet.*

  Cin. I dreamt to-night that I did feast
  with Cæsar,
And things unluckily charge my fantasy:
I have no will to wander forth of doors,
Yet something leads me forth.

Enter Citizens.

  First Cit. What is your name?
  Sec. Cit. Whither are you going?
  Third Cit. Where do you dwell?
  Fourth Cit. Are you a married man or a
  bachelor?
  Sec. Cit. Answer every man directly. 10
  First Cit. Ay, and briefly.
  Fourth Cit. Ay, and wisely.
  Third Cit. Ay, and truly, you were best.

225. **wit**, understanding, intelligence. 226. **Action**,
gesture. 243. **will**. Antony's holding back the mob
serves to increase their impatience. His action might be
compared to the bending and careful aiming of a great
bow. 247. **drachmas**, Greek coins of small denomi-
nation probably equivalent to the Roman denarius (a
silver coin worth about twenty cents). It is variously
estimated that Cæsar's gift would amount to from ten
to one hundred dollars for each citizen. 255. **pleasures**,
pleasure gardens (in which).

264. **forms**, benches. 275. **Belike**, likely enough.
Scene iii. 2. **fantasy**, imagination.

Cin. What is my name? Whither am I going? Where do I dwell? Am I a married man or a bachelor? Then, to answer every man directly and briefly, wisely and truly: wisely I say, I am a bachelor.

Sec. Cit. That's as much as to say, they are fools that marry: you'll bear me a bang for that, I fear. Proceed; directly. 21

Cin. Directly, I am going to Cæsar's funeral.

First Cit. As a friend or an enemy?

Cin. As a friend.

Sec. Cit. That matter is answered directly.

Fourth Cit. For your dwelling—briefly.

Cin. Briefly, I dwell by the Capitol.

Third Cit. Your name, sir, truly.

Cin. Truly, my name is Cinna.

First Cit. Tear him to pieces; he's a conspirator. 31

Cin. I am Cinna the poet, I am Cinna the poet.

Fourth Cit. Tear him for his bad verses, tear him for his bad verses.

Cin. I am not Cinna the conspirator.

Fourth Cit. It is no matter, his name's Cinna; pluck but his name out of his heart, and turn him going. 39

Third Cit. Tear him, tear him! Come, brands, ho! fire-brands: to Brutus', to Cassius'; burn all: some to Decius' house, and some to Casca's; some to Ligarius': away, go! [*Exeunt.*

ACT IV.

Scene I. *A house in Rome.*

ANTONY, OCTAVIUS, *and* LEPIDUS, *seated at a table.*

Ant. These many, then, shall die; their names are prick'd.

Oct. Your brother too must die; consent you, Lepidus?

Lep. I do consent,—

Oct. 　　　　　　　Prick him down, Antony.

Lep. Upon condition Publius shall not live,

Who is your sister's son, Mark Antony.

Ant. He shall not live; look, with a spot I damn him.

But, Lepidus, go you to Cæsar's house;
Fetch the will hither, and we shall determine
How to cut off some charge in legacies.

Lep. What, shall I find you here? 10

Oct. Or here, or at the Capitol.

[*Exit Lepidus.*

Ant. This is a slight unmeritable man,
Meet to be sent on errands: is it fit,
The three-fold world divided, he should stand
One of the three to share it?

Oct. 　　　　　　　So you thought him,
And took his voice who should be prick'd to die,
In our black sentence and proscription.

Ant. Octavius, I have seen more days than you:
And though we lay these honours on this man, 19
To ease ourselves of divers slanderous loads,
He shall but bear them as the ass bears gold,
To groan and sweat under the business,
Either led or driven, as we point the way;
And having brought our treasure where we will,
Then take we down his load, and turn him off,
Like to the empty ass, to shake his ears,
And graze in commons.

Oct. 　　　　　　　You may do your will;
But he's a tried and valiant soldier.

Ant. So is my horse, Octavius; and for that
I do appoint him store of provender: 30
It is a creature that I teach to fight,
To wind, to stop, to run directly on,
His corporal motion govern'd by my spirit.
And, in some taste, is Lepidus but so;
He must be taught and train'd and bid go forth;
A barren-spirited fellow; one that feeds
On abjects, orts and imitations,
Which, out of use and staled by other men,
Begin his fashion: do not talk of him,
But as a property. And now, Octavius, 40
Listen great things:—Brutus and Cassius

8-9. **Fetch . . . legacies**, i.e., by killing off some of the legatees. 14. **three-fold**, signifying either division into three parts or as made up of Europe, Asia, and Africa. 27. **commons**, common land. 32. **wind**, turn (horse trainer's term). 37. **On . . . imitations**, F: *On Objects, Arts, and Imitations.* In this reading *objects* would be explained as "objects of interest," *arts* as "works of art." In the text: **abjects**, things to be cast away; **orts**, fragments, refuse bits. 38. **staled**, made common or cheap. 39. **fashion**, newest fashion.

Act IV. Scene i. 1. **prick'd**, indicated by a mark; appropriate to the use of the stylus on waxen tablets. 6. **spot**, puncture with a stylus.

Are levying powers: we must straight make
    head:
Therefore let our alliance be combined,
†Our best friends made, our means stretch'd;
And let us presently go sit in council,
How covert matters may be best disclosed,
And open perils surest answered.
    Oct. Let us do so: for we are at the stake,
And bay'd about with many enemies;
And some that smile have in their hearts, I
    fear,   50
Millions of mischiefs.   [*Exeunt.*

SCENE II. *Camp near Sardis. Before*
Brutus's tent.

Drum. Enter BRUTUS, LUCILIUS, LUCIUS,
    and Soldiers; TITINIUS *and* PINDARUS
    meeting them.

    Bru. Stand, ho!
    Lucil. Give the word, ho! and stand.
    Bru. What now, Lucilius! is Cassius near?
    Lucil. He is at hand; and Pindarus is come
To do you salutation from his master.
    Bru. He greets me well. Your master,
    Pindarus,
In his own change, or by ill officers,
Hath given me some worthy cause to wish
Things done, undone: but, if he be at hand,
I shall be satisfied.
    Pin.   I do not doubt   10
But that my noble master will appear
Such as he is, full of regard and honour.
    Bru. He is not doubted. A word, Lucilius;
How he received you, let me be resolved.
    Lucil. With courtesy and with respect
    enough;
But not with such familiar instances,
Nor with such free and friendly conference,
As he hath used of old.
    Bru.   Thou hast described
A hot friend cooling: ever note, Lucilius,
When love begins to sicken and decay,   20
It useth an enforced ceremony.
There are no tricks in plain and simple faith;
But hollow men, like horses hot at hand,
Make gallant show and promise of their
    mettle;

But when they should endure the bloody
    spur,
They fall their crests, and, like deceitful
    jades,
Sink in the trial. Comes his army on?
    Lucil. They mean this night in Sardis to
    be quarter'd;
The greater part, the horse in general,
Are come with Cassius.
    Bru.   Hark! he is arrived.   30
        [*Low march within.*
March gently on to meet him.

    Enter CASSIUS *and his powers.*

    Cas. Stand, ho!
    Bru. Stand, ho! Speak the word along.
    First Sol. Stand!
    Sec. Sol. Stand!
    Third Sol. Stand!
    Cas. Most noble brother, you have done
    me wrong.
    Bru. Judge me, you gods! wrong I mine
    enemies?
And, if not so, how should I wrong a brother?
    Cas. Brutus, this sober form of yours
    hides wrongs;   40
And when you do them—
    Bru.   Cassius, be content;
Speak your griefs softly: I do know you well.
Before the eyes of both our armies here,
Which should perceive nothing but love from
    us,
Let us not wrangle: bid them move away;
Then in my tent, Cassius, enlarge your
    griefs,
And I will give you audience.
    Cas.   Pindarus,
Bid our commanders lead their charges off
A little from this ground.
    Bru. Lucilius, do you the like; and let no
    man   50
Come to our tent till we have done our con-
    ference.
Let Lucius and Titinius guard our door.
        [*Exeunt.*

SCENE III. *Brutus's tent.*

Enter BRUTUS *and* CASSIUS.

    Cas. That you have wrong'd me doth ap-
    pear in this:

---

42. **make head**, assemble forces. 44. **made**,
secured. 47. **answered**, met, faced. 48. **at the stake**,
a figure from bear-baiting.
    Scene ii. 7. **change**, i.e., in his feelings. 12. **regard**
and honour, honorable regard. 16. **familiar instances**,
instances of familiarity. 23. **hollow**, insincere. **hot at**
hand, restless when held in.

26. **fall**, lower. **jades**, worthless horses.

You have condemn'd and noted Lucius Pella
For taking bribes here of the Sardians;
Wherein my letters, praying on his side,
Because I knew the man, were slighted off.
   Bru. You wrong'd yourself to write in such a case.
   Cas. In such a time as this it is not meet
That every nice offence should bear his comment.
   Bru. Let me tell you, Cassius, you yourself
Are much condemn'd to have an itching palm;   10
To sell and mart your offices for gold
To undeservers.
   Cas.   I an itching palm!
You know that you are Brutus that speak this,
Or, by the gods, this speech were else your last.
   Bru. The name of Cassius honours this corruption,
And chastisement doth therefore hide his head.
   Cas. Chastisement!
   Bru. Remember March, the ides of March remember:
Did not great Julius bleed for justice' sake?
What villain touch'd his body, that did stab,   20
And not for justice? What, shall one of us,
That struck the foremost man of all this world
But for supporting robbers, shall we now
Contaminate our fingers with base bribes,
And sell the mighty space of our large honours
For so much trash as may be grasped thus?
I had rather be a dog, and bay the moon,
Than such a Roman.
   Cas.   Brutus, bay not me;
I'll not endure it: you forget yourself,
To hedge me in; I am a soldier, I,   30
Older in practice, abler than yourself
To make conditions.
   Bru.   Go to; you are not, Cassius.

---

2. **noted**, marked for disgrace. **Lucius Pella**, a Roman prætor in Sardis; detail from Plutarch. 4. **on his side**, in his behalf. 5. **slighted off**, put slightingly aside. 8. **nice**, trivial. **bear his comment**, be made the object of scrutiny. *his* equals *its.* 10. **to have**, for having. **itching**, covetous. 11. **mart**, market. 15. **corruption**, dishonesty in public office. 26. **trash.** It is a part of Brutus's stoic philosophy to despise money. 27. **bay**, bark at. 28. **bay.** It has the suggestion here of the meaning "bring me not to bay." 32. **make conditions**, i.e., deal with his subordinates mentioned above.

   Cas. I am.
   Bru. I say you are not.
   Cas. Urge me no more, I shall forget myself;
Have mind upon your health, tempt me no farther.
   Bru. Away, slight man!
   Cas. Is't possible?
   Bru.   Hear me, for I will speak.
Must I give way and room to your rash choler?
Shall I be frighted when a madman stares?   40
   Cas. O ye gods, ye gods! must I endure all this?
   Bru. All this! ay, more: fret till your proud heart break;
Go show your slaves how choleric you are,
And make your bondmen tremble. Must I budge?
Must I observe you? must I stand and crouch
Under your testy humour? By the gods,
You shall digest the venom of your spleen,
Though it do split you; for, from this day forth,
I'll use you for my mirth, yea, for my laughter,
When you are waspish.
   Cas.   Is it come to this?   50
   Bru. You say you are a better soldier:
Let it appear so; make your vaunting true,
And it shall please me well: for mine own part,
I shall be glad to learn of noble men.
   Cas. You wrong me every way; you wrong me, Brutus;
I said, an elder soldier, not a better:
Did I say 'better'?
   Bru.   If you did, I care not.
   Cas. When Cæsar lived, he durst not thus have moved me.
   Bru. Peace, peace! you durst not so have tempted him.
   Cas. I durst not!   60
   Bru. No.
   Cas. What, durst not tempt him!
   Bru.   For your life you durst not.
   Cas. Do not presume too much upon my love;
I may do that I shall be sorry for.
   Bru. You have done that you should be sorry for.
There is no terror, Cassius, in your threats,

---

45. **observe**, pay reverence to.

For I am arm'd so strong in honesty
That they pass by me as the idle wind,
Which I respect not. I did send to you
For certain sums of gold, which you denied
　　me:　　　　　　　　　　　　　　　70
For I can raise no money by vile means:
By heaven, I had rather coin my heart,
And drop my blood for drachmas, than to
　　wring
From the hard hands of peasants their vile
　　trash
By any indirection: I did send
To you for gold to pay my legions,
Which you denied me: was that done like
　　Cassius?
Should I have answer'd Caius Cassius so?
When Marcus Brutus grows so covetous,
To lock such rascal counters from his friends,
Be ready, gods, with all your thunderbolts; 81
Dash him to pieces!
　Cas.　　　　　　I denied you not.
　Bru. You did.
　Cas. I did not: he was but a fool that
　　brought
My answer back. Brutus hath rived my
　　heart:
A friend should bear his friend's infirmities,
But Brutus makes mine greater than they
　　are.
　Bru. I do not, till you practise them on me.
　Cas. You love me not.
　Bru.　　　　　I do not like your faults.
　Cas. A friendly eye could never see such
　　faults.　　　　　　　　　　　　90
　Bru. A flatterer's would not, though they
　　do appear
As huge as high Olympus.
　Cas. Come, Antony, and young Octavius,
　　come,
Revenge yourselves alone on Cassius,
For Cassius is aweary of the world;
Hated by one he loves; braved by his
　　brother;
Check'd like a bondman; all his faults ob-
　　served,
Set in a note-book, learn'd, and conn'd by
　　rote,
To cast into my teeth. O, I could weep
My spirit from mine eyes! There is my
　　dagger,　　　　　　　　　　　100

And here my naked breast; within, a heart
Dearer than Plutus' mine, richer than gold:
If that thou be'st a Roman, take it forth;
I, that denied thee gold, will give my heart:
Strike, as thou didst at Cæsar; for, I know,
When thou didst hate him worst, thou
　　lovedst him better
Than ever thou lovedst Cassius.
　Bru.　　　　　Sheathe your dagger:
Be angry when you will, it shall have
　　scope;
Do what you will, dishonour shall be humour.
O Cassius, you are yoked with a lamb　110
That carries anger as the flint bears fire;
Who, much enforced, shows a hasty spark,
And straight is cold again.
　Cas.　　　　　Hath Cassius lived
To be but mirth and laughter to his Brutus,
When grief, and blood ill-temper'd, vexeth
　　him?
　Bru. When I spoke that, I was ill-tem-
　　per'd too.
　Cas. Do you confess so much? Give me
　　your hand.
　Bru. And my heart too.
　Cas.　　　　　O Brutus!
　Bru.　　　　　What's the matter?
　Cas. Have not you love enough to bear
　　with me,
When that rash humour which my mother
　　gave me　　　　　　　　　　　120
Makes me forgetful?
　Bru. Yes, Cassius; and, from henceforth,
When you are over-earnest with your Brutus,
He'll think your mother chides, and leave
　　you so.
　Poet. [*Within*] Let me go in to see the
　　generals;
There is some grudge between 'em, 'tis not
　　meet
They be alone.
　Lucil. [*Within*] You shall not come to
　　them.
　Poet. [*Within*] Nothing but death shall
　　stay me.

Enter Poet, *followed by* Lucilius, Titinius,
　　　　　　and Lucius.

　Cas. How now! what's the matter?
　Poet. For shame, you generals! what do
　　you mean?　　　　　　　　　　130

---

71. **vile means**, may allude to Cassius's extortions
of money from the Rhodians; mentioned by Plutarch.
75. **indirection**, irregular or unjust means. 80. **rascal
counters**, worthless pelf. 85. **rived**, cleft. 97.
Check'd, reproved.

102. **Plutus'**. Plutus was the god of riches. 109.
humour, caprice. 115. **ill-temper'd**, i.e., with
humors.

Love, and be friends, as two such men
should be;
For I have seen more years, I'm sure, than
ye.
   Cas. Ha, ha! how vilely doth this cynic
rhyme!
   Bru. Get you hence, sirrah; saucy fellow,
hence!
   Cas. Bear with him, Brutus; 'tis his
fashion.
   Bru. I'll know his humour, when he knows
his time:
What should the wars do with these jigging
fools?
Companion, hence!
   Cas.   Away, away, be gone!
                        [Exit Poet.
   Bru. Lucilius and Titinius, bid the com-
manders
Prepare to lodge their companies to-night. 140
   Cas. And come yourselves, and bring Mes-
sala with you
Immediately to us.
          [Exeunt Lucilius and Titinius.
   Bru. Lucius, a bowl of wine! *[Exit Lucius.*
   Cas. I did not think you could have been
so angry.
   Bru. O Cassius, I am sick of many griefs.
   Cas. Of your philosophy you make no use,
If you give place to accidental evils.
   Bru. No man bears sorrow better. Portia
is dead.
   Cas. Ha! Portia!
   Bru. She is dead.
   Cas. How 'scaped I killing when I cross'd
you so?   150
O insupportable and touching loss!
Upon what sickness?
   Bru.   Impatient of my absence,
And grief that young Octavius with Mark
Antony
Have made themselves so strong:—for with
her death
That tidings came;—with this she fell dis-
tract,
And, her attendants absent, swallow'd fire.
   Cas. And died so?
   Bru.   Even so.
   Cas.   O ye immortal gods!

Re-enter LUCIUS, *with wine and taper.*

   Bru. Speak no more of her. Give me a
bowl of wine.
In this I bury all unkindness, Cassius.
   Cas. My heart is thirsty for that noble
pledge.   160
Fill, Lucius, till the wine o'erswell the
cup;
I cannot drink too much of Brutus' love.
   Bru. Come in, Titinius!   *[Exit Lucius.*

Re-enter TITINIUS, *with* MESSALA.

               Welcome, good Messala.
Now sit we close about this taper here,
And call in question our necessities.
   Cas. Portia, art thou gone?
   Bru.   No more, I pray you.
Messala, I have here received letters,
That young Octavius and Mark Antony
Come down upon us with a mighty power,
Bending their expedition toward Philippi. 170
   Mes. Myself have letters of the selfsame
tenour.
   Bru. With what addition?
   Mes. That by proscription and bills of
outlawry,
Octavius, Antony, and Lepidus,
Have put to death an hundred senators.
   Bru. Therein our letters do not well
agree;
Mine speak of seventy senators that died
By their proscriptions, Cicero being one.
   Cas. Cicero one!
   Mes.   Cicero is dead,
And by that order of proscription.   180
Had you your letters from your wife, my
lord?
   Bru. No, Messala.
   Mes. Nor nothing in your letters writ of
her?
   Bru. Nothing, Messala.
   Mes.   That, methinks, is strange.
   Bru. Why ask you? hear you aught of her
in yours?
   Mes. No, my lord.
   Bru. Now, as you are a Roman, tell me
true.
   Mes. Then like a Roman bear the truth
I tell:

---

133. **cynic,** rude fellow. 136. **humour,** whim.
time, proper time. 138. **Companion,** fellow. 146.
accidental, incidental. 156. **swallow'd fire.** Plutarch:
"Portia . . . took hot burning coals and cast them in her
mouth, and kept her mouth so close that she choked
herself."

165. **call in question,** examine into. 184. **Nothing,
Messala.** It is not clear why Brutus withholds his
knowledge of Portia's death. It may be a detail indicative of his stoical habit of suppressing grief. It can hardly
be that he is hoping to have the report contradicted.

For certain she is dead, and by strange manner.

Bru. Why, farewell, Portia. We must die,
Messala: 190
With meditating that she must die once,
I have the patience to endure it now.

Mes. Even so great men great losses
should endure.

Cas. I have as much of this in art as you,
But yet my nature could not bear it so.

Bru. Well, to our work alive. What do
you think
Of marching to Philippi presently?

Cas. I do not think it good.

Bru.   Your reason?

Cas.   This it is:
'Tis better that the enemy seek us:
So shall he waste his means, weary his sol-
diers,   200
Doing himself offence; whilst we, lying still,
Are full of rest, defence, and nimbleness.

Bru. Good reasons must, of force, give
place to better.
The people 'twixt Philippi and this ground
Do stand but in a forced affection;
For they have grudged us contribution:
The enemy, marching along by them,
By them shall make a fuller number up,
Come on refresh'd, new-added, and en-
couraged;
From which advantage shall we cut him
off,   210
If at Philippi we do face him there,
These people at our back.

Cas.   Hear me, good brother.

Bru. Under your pardon. You must note
beside,
That we have tried the utmost of our friends,
Our legions are brim-full, our cause is ripe:
The enemy increaseth every day;
We, at the height, are ready to decline.
There is a tide in the affairs of men,
Which, taken at the flood, leads on to for-
tune;
Omitted, all the voyage of their life   220
Is bound in shallows and in miseries.
On such a full sea are we now afloat;
And we must take the current when it serves,
Or lose our ventures.

Cas.   Then, with your will, go on;

We'll along ourselves, and meet them at
Philippi.

Bru. The deep of night is crept upon our
talk,
And nature must obey necessity;
Which we will niggard with a little rest.
There is no more to say?

Cas.   No more. Good night:
Early to-morrow will we rise, and hence. 230

Bru. Lucius! [*Enter Lucius.*] My gown.
[*Exit Lucius.*] Farewell, good Messala:
Good night, Titinius. Noble, noble Cassius,
Good night, and good repose.

Cas.   O my dear brother!
This was an ill beginning of the night:
Never come such division 'tween our souls!
Let it not, Brutus.

Bru.   Every thing is well.

Cas. Good night, my lord.

Bru.   Good night, good brother.

Tit. Mes. Good night, Lord Brutus.

Bru.   Farewell, every one.
[*Exeunt all but Brutus.*

Re-enter LUCIUS, *with the gown.*

Give me the gown. Where is thy instrument?

Luc. Here in the tent.

Bru.   What, thou speak'st drowsily?
Poor knave, I blame thee not; thou art
o'er-watch'd.   241
Call Claudius and some other of my men;
I'll have them sleep on cushions in my tent.

Luc. Varro and Claudius!

Enter VARRO *and* CLAUDIUS.

Var. Calls my lord?

Bru. I pray you, sirs, lie in my tent and
sleep;
It may be I shall raise you by and by
On business to my brother Cassius.

Var. So please you, we will stand and
watch your pleasure.

Bru. I will not have it so: lie down, good
sirs;   250
It may be I shall otherwise bethink me.
Look, Lucius, here's the book I sought for so;
I put it in the pocket of my gown.
[*Var. and Clau. lie down.*

Luc. I was sure your lordship did not give
it me.

---

191. **once,** at some time. 194. **art,** acquired faculty.
196. **alive,** concerning us as living. 209. **new-added,**
newly increased. 224. **ventures,** investments (of enterprises at sea).

228. **niggard,** treat in a niggardly fashion. 231.
gown, dressing gown. 239. **instrument,** lute. 241.
knave, boy. **o'er-watch'd,** exhausted for lack of rest.

Bru. Bear with me, good boy, I am much
 forgetful.
Canst thou hold up thy heavy eyes awhile,
And touch thy instrument a strain or two?
 Luc. Ay, my lord, an't please you.
 Bru.   It does, my boy:
I trouble thee too much, but thou art willing.
 Luc. It is my duty, sir.   260
 Bru. I should not urge thy duty past thy
 might;
I know young bloods look for a time of rest.
 Luc. I have slept, my lord, already.
 Bru. It was well done; and thou shalt
 sleep again;
I will not hold thee long: if I do live,
I will be good to thee. [*Music, and a song.*
This is a sleepy tune. O murderous slumber,
Lay'st thou thy leaden mace upon my boy,
That plays thee music? Gentle knave, good
 night;
I will not do thee so much wrong to wake
 thee: 270
If thou dost nod, thou break'st thy instru-
 ment;
I'll take it from thee; and, good boy, good
 night.
Let me see, let me see; is not the leaf turn'd
 down
Where I left reading? Here it is, I think.

   Enter the Ghost of CÆSAR.

How ill this taper burns! Ha! who comes
 here?
I think it is the weakness of mine eyes
That shapes this monstrous apparition.
It comes upon me. Art thou any thing?
Art thou some god, some angel, or some
 devil,
That makest my blood cold and my hair to
 stare?   280
Speak to me what thou art.
 Ghost. Thy evil spirit, Brutus.
 Bru. Why comest thou?
 Ghost. To tell thee thou shalt see me at
 Philippi.
 Bru. Well; then I shall see thee again?
 Ghost. Ay, at Philippi.
 Bru. Why, I will see thee at Philippi,
 then.   [*Exit Ghost.*

Now I have taken heart thou vanishest:
Ill spirit, I would hold more talk with thee.
Boy, Lucius! Varro! Claudius! Sirs, awake!
Claudius!   291
 Luc. The strings, my lord, are false.
 Bru. He thinks he still is at his instru-
 ment.
Lucius, awake!
 Luc. My lord?
 Bru. Didst thou dream, Lucius, that
 thou so criedst out?
 Luc. My lord, I do not know that I did
 cry.
 Bru. Yes, that thou didst: didst thou see
 any thing?
 Luc. Nothing, my lord.
 Bru. Sleep again, Lucius. Sirrah Clau-
 dius!   300
[*To Var.*] Fellow thou, awake!
 Var. My lord?
 Clau. My lord?
 Bru. Why did you so cry out, sirs, in your
 sleep?
 Var. Clau. Did we, my lord?
 Bru.   Ay: saw you any thing?
 Var. No, my lord, I saw nothing.
 Clau.   Nor I, my lord.
 Bru. Go and commend me to my brother
 Cassius;
Bid him set on his powers betimes before,
And we will follow.
 Var. Clau.   It shall be done, my lord. 309
        [*Exeunt.*

ACT V.

SCENE I. *The plains of Philippi.*

Enter OCTAVIUS, ANTONY, *and their* army.

 Oct. Now, Antony, our hopes are an-
 swered:
You said the enemy would not come down,
But keep the hills and upper regions;
It proves not so: their battles are at hand;
They mean to warn us at Philippi here,
Answering before we do demand of them.
 Ant. Tut, I am in their bosoms, and I
 know
Wherefore they do it: they could be content
To visit other places; and come down
With fearful bravery, thinking by this face 10

---

258. **an't,** if it. 267. **murderous,** producing the
likeness of death. 268. **mace,** staff, club. 275. **How
. . . burns.** It is a part of the machinery of apparitions
that lights burn low and blue. 280. **stare,** stand on end.
287. **Why . . . then.** In view of superstitious terror,
greater in Shakespeare's day than ours, this line presents
an example of marvelous courage.

Act V. Scene i. 4. **battles,** troops in battle array.
5. **warn,** summon. 7. **bosoms,** secret councils. 10.
fearful bravery, cowardly bravado. **face,** pretense.

To fasten in our thoughts that they have
 courage;
But 'tis not so.

Enter a Messenger.

Mess.   Prepare you, generals:
The enemy comes on in gallant show;
Their bloody sign of battle is hung out,
And something to be done immediately.
 Ant. Octavius, lead your battle softly on,
Upon the left hand of the even field.
 Oct. Upon the right hand I; keep thou the
 left.
 Ant. Why do you cross me in this exigent?
 Oct. I do not cross you; but I will do so. 20
    [*March.*

Drum. Enter BRUTUS, CASSIUS, *and their*
Army; LUCILIUS, TITINIUS, MESSALA, *and*
others.

 Bru. They stand, and would have parley.
 Cas. Stand fast, Titinius: we must out
 and talk.
 Oct. Mark Antony, shall we give sign of
 battle?
 Ant. No, Cæsar, we will answer on their
 charge.
Make forth; the generals would have some
 words.
 Oct. Stir not until the signal.
 Bru. Words before blows: is it so, country-
 men?
 Oct. Not that we love words better, as you
 do.
 Bru. Good words are better than bad
 strokes, Octavius.
 Ant. In your bad strokes, Brutus, you
 give good words: 30
Witness the hole you made in Cæsar's heart,
Crying 'Long live! hail, Cæsar!'
 Cas.   Antony,
The posture of your blows are yet unknown;
But for your words, they rob the Hybla
 bees,
And leave them honeyless.
 Ant.   Not stingless too.
 Bru. O, yes, and soundless too;

For you have stol'n their buzzing, Antony,
And very wisely threat before you sting.
 Ant. Villains, you did not so, when your
 vile daggers
Hack'd one another in the sides of Cæsar: 40
You show'd your teeth like apes, and fawn'd
 like hounds,
And bow'd like bondmen, kissing Cæsar's
 feet;
Whilst damned Casca, like a cur, behind
Struck Cæsar on the neck. O you flatterers!
 Cas. Flatterers! Now, Brutus, thank
 yourself:
This tongue had not offended so to-day,
If Cassius might have ruled.
 Oct. Come, come, the cause: if arguing
 make us sweat,
The proof of it will turn to redder drops.
Look;   50
I draw a sword against conspirators;
When think you that the sword goes up again?
Never, till Cæsar's three and thirty wounds
Be well avenged; or till another Cæsar
Have added slaughter to the sword of trai-
 tors.
 Bru. Cæsar, thou canst not die by traitors'
 hands,
Unless thou bring'st them with thee.
 Oct.   So I hope;
I was not born to die on Brutus' sword.
 Bru. O, if thou wert the noblest of thy
 strain,
Young man, thou couldst not die more
 honourable.   60
 Cas. A peevish schoolboy, worthless of
 such honour,
Join'd with a masker and a reveller!
 Ant. Old Cassius still!
 Oct.   Come, Antony, away!
Defiance, traitors, hurl we in your teeth:
If you dare fight to-day, come to the field;
If not, when you have stomachs.
    [*Exeunt Octavius, Antony, and their*
                                army.
 Cas. Why, now, blow wind, swell billow
 and swim bark!
The storm is up, and all is on the hazard.
 Bru. Ho, Lucilius! hark, a word with you.
 Lucil.   [*Standing forth*] My lord?
    [*Brutus and Lucilius converse apart.*
 Cas. Messala!

---

14. **bloody sign of battle.** Plutarch describes this
as an "arming scarlet coat." 17. **even,** probably,
evenly divided rather than level. 19. **exigent,** emergency. 20. **I will do so,** i.e., as I said. 21. **parley,**
conference. Dramatists have to fight many of their
battles in words. This battle takes the form of a peculiarly unbecoming verbal row. 24. **answer on their**
charge, attack when they attack. 34. **Hybla,** a mountain near Syracuse, famous in pastoral poetry.

41. **show'd your teeth,** i.e., in smiles. 48. **cause,**
issue at stake. 61. **peevish,** childish. 66. **stomachs,**
courage.

Mes. [*Standing forth*] What says my general?　　　　　　　　　　　　　70

Cas. Messala,
This is my birth-day; as this very day
Was Cassius born. Give me thy hand, Messala:
Be thou my witness that against my will
As Pompey was, am I compell'd to set
Upon one battle all our liberties.
You know that I held Epicurus strong
And his opinion: now I change my mind,
And partly credit things that do presage,
Coming from Sardis, on our former ensign　80
Two mighty eagles fell, and there they perch'd,
Gorging and feeding from our soldiers' hands;
Who to Philippi here consorted us:
This morning are they fled away and gone;
And in their steads do ravens, crows and kites,
Fly o'er our heads and downward look on us,
As we were sickly prey: their shadows seem
A canopy most fatal, under which
Our army lies, ready to give up the ghost.

Mes. Believe not so.

Cas. 　　　　　I but believe it partly;　90
For I am fresh of spirit and resolved
To meet all perils very constantly.

Bru. Even so, Lucilius.

Cas. 　　　　　Now, most noble Brutus,
The gods to-day stand friendly, that we may,
Lovers in peace, lead on our days to age!
But since the affairs of men rest still incertain,
Let's reason with the worst that may befall.
If we do lose this battle, then is this
The very last time we shall speak together:
What are you then determined to do?　　100

Bru. Even by the rule of that philosophy
By which I did blame Cato for the death
Which he did give himself, I know not how,
But I do find it cowardly and vile,
For fear of what might fall, so to prevent
The time of life: arming myself with patience
To stay the providence of some high powers
That govern us below.

Cas. 　　　　　Then, if we lose this battle,
You are contented to be led in triumph
Thorough the streets of Rome?　　　　110

Bru. No, Cassius, no: think not, thou noble Roman,
That ever Brutus will go bound to Rome;
He bears too great a mind. But this same day
Must end that work the ides of March begun;
And whether we shall meet again I know not.
Therefore our everlasting farewell take:
For ever, and for ever, farewell, Cassius!
If we do meet again, why, we shall smile;
If not, why then, this parting was well made.

Cas. For ever, and for ever, farewell, Brutus!　　　　　　　　　　　　120
If we do meet again, we'll smile indeed;
If not, 'tis true this parting was well made.

Bru. Why, then, lead on. O, that a man might know
The end of this day's business ere it come!
But it sufficeth that the day will end,
And then the end is known. Come, ho! away!　　　　　　　　　　　[*Exeunt.*

SCENE II. *The same. The field of battle.*

Alarum. Enter BRUTUS *and* MESSALA.

Bru. Ride, ride, Messala, ride, and give these bills
Unto the legions on the other side.
　　　　　　　　　　　　[*Loud alarum.*
Let them set on at once; for I perceive
But cold demeanour in Octavius' wing,
And sudden push gives them the overthrow.
Ride, ride, Messala: let them all come down.
　　　　　　　　　　　　[*Exeunt.*

SCENE III. *Another part of the field.*

Alarums. Enter CASSIUS *and* TITINIUS.

Cas. O, look, Titinius, look, the villains fly!
Myself have to mine own turn'd enemy:
This ensign here of mine was turning back;
I slew the coward, and did take it from him.

Tit. O Cassius, Brutus gave the word too early;
Who, having some advantage on Octavius,
Took it too eagerly: his soldiers fell to spoil,

---

72. **as**, redundant particle. 75. **Pompey**. The reference is to Pharsalia, and the sentence is closely repeated from Plutarch. 77. **Epicurus**, a Grecian philosopher who lived from 341 to 270 B.C. His philosophy aimed at making the best of life. 79. **presage**, foretell events. The incident of the eagles is from Plutarch. 83. **consorted**, accompanied. 93. **Even so, Lucilius.** Brutus thus ends his private conversation with Lucilius. 102. **Cato**, Cato the Younger, Brutus's father-in-law. The justifiability of his destruction of himself was long a subject of debate. 105. **prevent**, anticipate. 106. **time**, term. 107. **stay**, await.

Scene ii. 1. **bills**, orders. 2. **side**, wing. 4. **cold demeanour**, signs of faint-heartedness.
Scene iii. 3. **ensign**, bearer of the standard.

Whilst we by Antony are all enclosed.

Enter PINDARUS.

Pin. Fly further off, my lord, fly further off;

Mark Antony is in your tents, my lord: 10

Fly, therefore, noble Cassius, fly far off.

Cas. This hill is far enough. Look, look, Titinius;

Are those my tents where I perceive the fire?

Tit. They are, my lord.

Cas.　　　　Titinius, if thou lovest me,

Mount thou my horse, and hide thy spurs in him,

Till he have brought thee up to yonder troops,

And here again; that I may rest assured

Whether yon troops are friend or enemy.

Tit. I will be here again, even with a thought. [*Exit.*

Cas. Go, Pindarus, get higher on that hill;

My sight was ever thick; regard Titinius, 21

And tell me what thou notest about the field. [*Pindarus ascends the hill.*

This day I breathed first: time is come round,

And where I did begin, there shall I end;

My life is run his compass. Sirrah, what news?

Pin.[*Above*] O my lord!

Cas. What news?

Pin. [*Above*] Titinius is enclosed round about

With horsemen, that make to him on the spur;

Yet he spurs on. Now they are almost on him. 30

Now, Titinius! Now some light. O, he lights too.

He's ta'en. [*Shout.*] And, hark! they shout for joy.

Cas. Come down, behold no more.

O, coward that I am, to live so long,

To see my best friend ta'en before my face!

PINDARUS *descends.*

Come hither, sirrah:

In Parthia did I take thee prisoner;

And then I swore thee, saving of thy life,

That whatsoever I did bid thee do,

Thou shouldst attempt it. Come now, keep thine oath; 40

Now be a freeman: and with this good sword,

That ran through Cæsar's bowels, search this bosom.

Stand not to answer: here, take thou the hilts;

And, when my face is cover'd, as 'tis now,

Guide thou the sword. [*Pindarus stabs him.*]

Cæsar, thou art revenged,

Even with the sword that kill'd thee. [*Dies.*

Pin. So, I am free; yet would not so have been,

Durst I have done my will. O Cassius,

Far from this country Pindarus shall run,

Where never Roman shall take note of him. 50

[*Exit.*

Re-enter TITINIUS *with* MESSALA.

Mes. It is but change, Titinius; for Octavius

Is overthrown by noble Brutus' power,

As Cassius' legions are by Antony.

Tit. These tidings will well comfort Cassius.

Mes. Where did you leave him?

Tit.　　　　All disconsolate,

With Pindarus his bondman, on this hill.

Mes. Is not that he that lies upon the ground?

Tit. He lies not like the living. O my heart!

Mes. Is not that he?

Tit.　　　　No, this was he, Messala,

But Cassius is no more. O setting sun, 60

As in thy red rays thou dost sink to night,

So in his red blood Cassius' day is set;

The sun of Rome is set! Our day is gone;

Clouds, dews, and dangers come; our deeds are done!

Mistrust of my success hath done this deed.

Mes. Mistrust of good success hath done this deed.

O hateful error, melancholy's child,

Why dost thou show to the apt thoughts of men

The things that are not? O error, soon conceived,

Thou never comest unto a happy birth, 70

But kill'st the mother that engender'd thee!

21. **thick**, imperfect, dim. 31. **lights**, alights. 37. **Parthia**, allusion to the campaign of Crassus in Parthia, 53 B.C., in which Plutarch states that Cassius had captured Pindarus. 38. **swore thee**, made thee swear.

49. **Pindarus shall run**. Plutarch states that Pindarus was never seen again. 51. **change**, exchange. 65. **Mistrust**, i.e., on Cassius's part. 68. **apt**, liable to be impressed.

Tit. What, Pindarus! where art thou, Pindarus?

Mes. Seek him, Titinius, whilst I go to meet
The noble Brutus, thrusting this report
Into his ears; I may say, thrusting it;
For piercing steel and darts envenomed
Shall be as welcome to the ears of Brutus
As tidings of this sight.

Tit.   Hie you, Messala,
And I will seek for Pindarus the while.   79
                              [*Exit Messala.*
Why didst thou send me forth, brave
    Cassius?
Did I not meet thy friends? and did not they
Put on my brows this wreath of victory,
And bid me give it thee? Didst thou not hear
    their shouts?
Alas, thou hast misconstrued every thing!
But, hold thee, take this garland on thy
    brow;
Thy Brutus bid me give it thee, and I
Will do his bidding. Brutus, come apace,
And see how I regarded Caius Cassius.
By your leave, gods:—this is a Roman's part:
Come, Cassius' sword, and find Titinius'
    heart.   [*Kills himself.*

Alarum. Re-enter MESSALA, *with* BRUTUS,
young CATO, STRATO, VOLUMNIUS, *and*
LUCILIUS.

Bru. Where, where, Messala, doth his
    body lie?   91
Mes. Lo, yonder, and Titinius mourning
    it.
Bru. Titinius' face is upward.
Cato.   He is slain.
Bru. O Julius Cæsar, thou art mighty yet!
Thy spirit walks abroad, and turns our
    swords
In our own proper entrails.   [*Low alarums.*
Cato.   Brave Titinius!
Look, whether he have not crown'd dead
    Cassius!
Bru. Are yet two Romans living such as
    these?
The last of all the Romans, fare thee well!
It is impossible that ever Rome   100
Should breed thy fellow. Friends, I owe
    more tears
To this dead man than you shall see me pay.
I shall find time, Cassius, I shall find time.

101. **fellow**, equal.

Come, therefore, and to Thasos send his
    body:
His funerals shall not be in our camp,
Lest it discomfort us. Lucilius, come;
And come, young Cato; let us to the field.
Labeo and Flavius, set our battles on:
'Tis three o'clock; and, Romans, yet ere
    night   109
We shall try fortune in a second fight.
                              [*Exeunt.*

SCENE IV. *Another part of the field.*

Alarum. Enter fighting, Soldiers *of both
armies; then* BRUTUS, *young* CATO, LU-
CILIUS, *and others.*

Bru. Yet, countrymen, O, yet hold up
    your heads!
Cato. What bastard doth not? Who will
    go with me?
I will proclaim my name about the field:
I am the son of Marcus Cato, ho!
A foe to tyrants, and my country's friend;
I am the son of Marcus Cato, ho!
Bru. And I am Brutus, Marcus Brutus, I;
Brutus, my country's friend; know me for
    Brutus!
                              [*Exit.*
Lucil. O young and noble Cato, art thou
    down?   9
Why, now thou diest as bravely as Titinius;
And mayst be honour'd, being Cato's son.
First Sold. Yield, or thou diest.
Lucil.   Only I yield to die:
There is so much that thou wilt kill me
    straight;
                              [*Offering money.*
Kill Brutus, and be honour'd in his death.
First Sold. We must not. A noble prisoner!
Sec. Sold. Room, ho! Tell Antony, Brutus
    is ta'en.
First Sold. I'll tell the news. Here comes
    the general.

Enter ANTONY.

Brutus is ta'en, Brutus is ta'en, my lord.
Ant. Where is he?

104. **Thasos**, an island off the coast of Thrace. 106.
discomfort, discourage. 110. **second fight.** The
second battle was, in point of fact, twenty days later.
Scene iv. 7-8. **And I . . . Brutus.** This speech is
unassigned in F. It is sometimes assigned to Lucilius,
who, in lines 12-14 below, pretends to be Brutus as an act
of devotion to his master. 9. **Cato**, a son of Marcus
Cato whose death is recounted by Plutarch.

Lucil. Safe, Antony; Brutus is safe enough:
I dare assure thee that no enemy　　　　21
Shall ever take alive the noble Brutus:
The gods defend him from so great a shame!
When you do find him, or alive or dead,
He will be found like Brutus, like himself.
　Ant. This is not Brutus, friend; but, I
　　assure you,
A prize no less in worth: keep this man safe;
Give him all kindness: I had rather have
Such men my friends than enemies. Go on,
And see whether Brutus be alive or dead;　30
And bring us word unto Octavius' tent
How every thing is chanced.
　　　　　　　　　　　　[Exeunt.

SCENE V. *Another part of the field.*

Enter BRUTUS, DARDANIUS, CLITUS, STRATO,
　　　and VOLUMNIUS.

　Bru. Come, poor remains of friends, rest
　　on this rock.
　Cli. Statilius show'd the torch-light, but,
　　my lord,
He came not back: he is or ta'en or slain.
　Bru. Sit thee down, Clitus: slaying is the
　　word;
It is a deed in fashion. Hark thee, Clitus.
　　　　　　　　　　　　　[Whispers.
　Cli. What, I, my lord? No, not for all the
　　world.
　Bru. Peace then! no words.
　Cli.　　　　　I'll rather kill myself.
　Bru. Hark thee, Dardanius. *[Whispers.*
　Dar.　　　　Shall I do such a deed?
　Cli. O Dardanius!
　Dar. O Clitus!　　　　　　　　　　10
　Cli. What ill request did Brutus make to
　　thee?
　Dar. To kill him, Clitus. Look, he medi-
　　tates.
　Cli. Now is that noble vessel full of grief,
That it runs over even at his eyes.
　Bru. Come hither, good Volumnius; list a
　　word.
　Vol. What says my lord?
　Bru.　　　　Why, this, Volumnius:
The ghost of Cæsar hath appear'd to me
Two several times by night; at Sardis once,
And, this last night, here in Philippi fields:
I know my hour is come.
　Vol.　　　　Not so, my lord.　20
　Bru. Nay, I am sure it is, Volumnius.

Thou seest the world, Volumnius, how it
　goes;
Our enemies have beat us to the pit:
　　　　　　　　　　　　[Low alarums.
It is more worthy to leap in ourselves,
Than tarry till they push us. Good Volum-
　nius,
Thou know'st that we two went to school
　together:
Even for that our love of old, I prithee,
Hold thou my sword-hilts, whilst I run on
　it.
　Vol. That's not an office for a friend, my
　　lord.
　　　　　　　　　　　　[Alarum still.
　Cli. Fly, fly, my lord; there is no tarrying
　　here.　　　　　　　　　　　　30
　Bru. Farewell to you; and you; and you,
　　Volumnius.
Strato, thou hast been all this while asleep;
Farewell to thee too, Strato. Countrymen,
My heart doth joy that yet in all my life
I found no man but he was true to me.
I shall have glory by this losing day
More than Octavius and Mark Antony
By this vile conquest shall attain unto.
So fare you well at once; for Brutus' tongue
Hath almost ended his life's history:　　40
Night hangs upon mine eyes; my bones
　would rest,
That have but labour'd to attain this hour.
　　　[Alarum. Cry within, 'Fly, fly, fly!'
　Cli. Fly, my lord, fly.
　Bru.　　　　Hence! I will follow.
　　　　　　[Exeunt Clitus, Dardanius, and
　　　　　　　　　　　　　　Volumnius.
I prithee, Strato, stay thou by thy lord:
Thou art a fellow of a good respect;
Thy life hath had some smatch of honour
　in it:
Hold then my sword, and turn away thy
　face,
While I do run upon it. Wilt thou, Strato?
　Stra. Give me your hand first. Fare you
　　well, my lord.
　Bru. Farewell, good Strato. *[Runs on his
　　sword.]* Caesar, now be still:　　50
I kill'd not thee with half so good a will.
　　　　　　　　　　　　　　[Dies.

23. **pit**, the last ditch (proverbial). 33-35. **Country-**
men . . . me. These almost mystical words of Brutus,
partly explained in the lines which follow as referring
to his fame, have a much wider and deeper import. It
is the case of a great leader, defeated, overthrown, and
rejected, and yet forever triumphant in the ideals he
has held. 46. **smatch**, smack, flavor.

Alarum. Retreat. Enter Octavius, Antony, Messala, Lucilius, *and the army.*

Oct. What man is that?

Mes. My master's man. Strato, where is thy master?

Stra. Free from the bondage you are in, Messala:

The conquerors can but make a fire of him;

For Brutus only overcame h:mself,

And no man else hath honour by his death.

Lucil. So Brutus should be found. I thank thee, Brutus,

That thou hast proved Lucilius' saying true.

Oct. All that served Brutus, I will entertain them. 60

Fellow, wilt thou bestow thy time with me?

Stra. Ay, if Messala will prefer me to you.

Oct. Do so, good Messala.

Mes. How died my master, Strato?

Stra. I held the sword, and he did run on it.

Mes. Octavius, then take him to follow thee,

That did the latest service to my master.

60. **entertain**, receive in service. 62. **prefer** recommend.

Ant. This was the noblest Roman of them all:

All the conspirators save only he

Did that they did in envy of great Cæsar· 70

He only, in a general honest thought

And common good to all, made one of them.

His life was gentle, and the elements

So mix'd in him that Nature might stand up

And say to all the world 'This was a man!'

Oct. According to his virtue let us use him,

With all respect and rites of burial.

Within my tent his bones to-night shall lie,

Most like a soldier, order'd honourably.

So call the field to rest; and let's away, 80

To part the glories of this happy day.

[*Exeunt.*

68-75. **This . . . man.** This famous eulogy is based upon a statement by Plutarch that Antony cast his embroidered cloak over Brutus's body and paid the cost of Brutus's burial, and upon Plutarch's statement in his summary of the character of Brutus that even Brutus's enemies confessed that he had had no other intent but to restore the ancient institutions of Rome. 73. **gentle,** a favorite word with Shakespeare meaning "true," "cultured," "affable"; it was often applied to Shakespeare himself by his contemporaries. **elements.** Man as a microcosm was made up of earth, air, fire, and water, whose qualities were mingled in Brutus in due proportions. 80. **field,** army in the field. 81. **part.** share.

THE PERIOD OF THE TRAGEDIES

I. SHAKESPEARE'S LIFE AND TIMES, 1601-1608

Shakespeare and the theater When the Globe, the most famous of the London public playhouses, was built in 1599, one-half interest in the property was assigned to the brothers Cuthbert and Richard Burbage; the other half to five actors, Shakespeare, Kemp, Pope, Phillips, and Heminge. Kemp left the company in 1600 and in 1602 was with the Earl of Worcester's men. His place as leading comic actor was taken by Robert Armin, a man of some culture and the author of a book on comedy; so that there was a change in the nature of the comic parts introduced into Shakespeare's plays. The parts of Dogberry, Launcelot Gobbo, and Bottom had been written to suit Kemp's talent for old-fashioned clownage; but for Armin Shakespeare invented such refinements in the art as are represented by Touchstone, Feste, Lavache in *All's Well that Ends Well,* and the Fool in *King Lear.* There were other changes in the composition of the company, which are reflected in Shakespeare's adaptation of his parts to the histrionic talent at his disposal, and further changes too in the ownership of the shares, so that the value of Shakespeare's proportional share of the Globe Theater varied from time to time.

From the year 1599 to 1602 there occurred the War of the Theaters, a theatrical struggle, begun by Ben Jonson and carried on by means of satirical dramas. In *Everyman out of his Humour* (1599) Jonson ridiculed Marston, Daniel and others, who, he says in the *Conversations with Drummond,* had for three years "provoked him with their petulant styles on every stage." More immediately he had taken offense at *The Scourge of Villainy* (1598), a verse satire in which Marston directly satirized Jonson under the name of Torquatus. The Children of the Chapel Royal, who occupied the

theater which Burbage had built in Blackfriars, and the Children of Paul's, who probably acted in their own singing school in St. Paul's churchyard, assumed extraordinary importance. They had at their command the pens of Jonson himself, as well as of Chapman and others who catered to the current popular taste for social satire. On the other side was Marston, and apparently Shakespeare, although it is impossible to determine exactly what part Shakespeare took in the affair. If he wrote anything directly applicable, it has been lost or destroyed. The tone of the famous passage in *Hamlet* (II, ii, 328-379) is kindly and remonstrant rather than otherwise. He does not apparently think it well that professionals should be driven off the London stage and compelled to take the road because of the quarrels among playwrights and actors and the sudden infatuation on the part of the public for the boy actors. A passage in the second part of *The Return from Parnassus* (Dec. 1601?) seems to indicate that Shakespeare had worsted Jonson in satirical encounter.[1] In one scene (IV, v) Kemp and Burbage are represented as coming to Cambridge to recruit actors from among the students:

Kempe. Few of the university pen plays well. They smell too much of that writer, Ovid, and that writer, Metamorphosis, and talk much of Proserpina and Jupiter. Why, here's our fellow Shakespeare puts them all down; ay, and Ben Jonson too. O that Ben Jonson is a pestilent fellow: he brought up Horace giving the poets a pill, but our fellow Shakespeare hath given him a purge that made him bewray his credit.

Burbage. It is a shrewd fellow indeed. . . .

Whatever may have been the outcome of the War of the Theaters, and it is not likely to have been important, the Lord Chamber-

[1] See Chambers, *William Shakespeare,* I, 71-72, for further references.

lain's company throughout the later years of Queen Elizabeth's reign maintained its lead in the dramatic profession, so that Shakespeare and his colleagues became the King's Servants in 1603. That they were so adopted within ten days after the King's arrival in London is witnessed by a document of instructions, preserved at the Public Record Office, from the King to his Keeper of the Privy Seal. It is dated May 17, 1603, and endorsed "The Players' Privilege." Shakespeare, Burbage, Phillips, Heminge, Condell, Sly, Armin, and Cowley are mentioned by name; and with them Lawrence Fletcher, an actor who had played before the King and the Scottish court in 1599 and 1601. They are given the usual privileges of exercising their art anywhere within the kingdom and are henceforth to be known as the King's company. As the King's servants, the principal members of the troupe were also appointed to the honorary rank of Grooms of the Royal Chamber. We therefore find them duly recorded in the Accounts of the Master of the Wardrobe on March 15, 1604, as recipients of the customary grants of red cloth, so that they, dressed in the royal livery, might take part in the approaching coronation procession of the King. The same men are mentioned in these grants as in the Players' Privilege. Shakespeare's name stands second in the former document and first in the latter. In a somewhat similar manner the King's players, as grooms of the Royal Chamber, were called in attendance on the Spanish ambassador at Somerset House in August, 1604. For the end of that year and the beginning of the next the Revels Accounts have an unusually ample entry of plays performed at Whitehall. In the entry Shakespeare's plays predominate. They include *Othello*, *The Merry Wives of Windsor*, *Measure for Measure*, the "Play of Errors," *Love's Labour's Lost*, *Henry V*, and *The Merchant of Venice*. Three of these are marked in a column headed "The poets which made the plays" with the name *Shaxberd*. Final *e* in the Elizabethan handwriting is easily mistaken for final *d*, so that the entry as given is either a misreading of the present entry or a miswriting of some earlier notes in which the word had been written "Shaxbere" or "Shaxpere." The authen-

ticity of this entry is often called in question, since some scholars regard it as a forgery; but the grounds for regarding it as a forgery are hardly adequate, and its general appropriateness and consistency make it entirely worthy of credence.

In the will of Shakespeare's fellow actor and member of the King's company, Augustine Phillips, probated May 4, 1605, there is a bequest of "a thirty shillings piece of gold" to "my fellow, William Shakespeare," with other similar bequests to Condell, Beeston, Fletcher, and other members of the troupe.

Biographical Meantime during the period there are a number of records concerned with Shakespeare as a man of property. On May 1, 1602, John and William Combe conveyed to Shakespeare one hundred seven acres of land in the parish of Old Stratford. It is notable that the deed was delivered to Shakespeare's brother Gilbert and not to the poet, who was probably at that time occupied in London. On September 28th of the same year Shakespeare acquired title in copyhold (a form of tenure limited by the superior claims of a lord of the manor) of a cottage and land opposite New Place in Stratford, "one cottage and one garden by estimation a quarter of an acre." There are also records of a somewhat complicated speculation into which Shakespeare entered in 1605. He purchased an interest in the tithes of Stratford and adjacent villages from one Ralph Huband for the considerable sum of four hundred and twenty pounds. This is an instance of the strange fiduciary customs of Shakespeare's times. The collection of money originally levied for the support of the church under a tithe law had become a private and negotiable right belonging to certain persons who had contracted for such taxes by the payment of a fixed sum, and who reimbursed themselves and derived a profit by the collection of as much as they could of the total amount due under the law. Huband seems to have owned one-half interest in certain kinds of tithes in certain villages, which half, or "moiety," Shakespeare bought. Probably between January and March, 1609, there was issued, as appears from the Stratford Corporation Records, a complaint by Shakespeare and others to the Lord Chancellor of England reciting the full history of the leasing of the Stratford tithes and praying that certain other tithe-holders be required to come into the High Court of Chancery and make answer to the complaints alleged, namely, that they have not paid their proportional part of an annual rental of £27 13s. 4d. on the whole property in the tithes to one Henry Barker. Barker had thus the right to recover possession from the three dozen and more other tithe-holders. In bringing this suit Shakespeare acted the part of a public-spirited citizen and brought a much muddled business association into a state of order.[1]

The Stratford Burial Register shows the death of Shakespeare's father in 1601, of his brother Edmund in 1607, and of his mother in 1608. The Stratford Marriage Register and the Stratford Baptismal Register contribute respectively records of the marriage of Shakespeare's daughter Susanna to Dr. John Hall and the baptism in Trinity Church of Elizabeth, daughter to John Hall, and Shakespeare's first grandchild.

Literary allusions   Literary allusions to Shakespeare had by this time become fairly frequent. For example, Anthony Scoloker in the epistle prefatory to *Diaphantus, or the Passions of Love* (1604) says,

It should be like the never-too-well-read Arcadia . . . or to come home to the vulgar's element like Friendly Shakespeare's tragedies, where the comedian rides when the tragedian stands on tip-toe: 'faith it should please all, like Prince Hamlet.

The great antiquarian William Camden includes Shakespeare's name among important modern poets in his casual list in *Remains* (1605):

These may suffice for some poetical descriptions of our ancient poets; if I would come to our time, what a world could I present to you out of Sir Philip Sidney, Ed. Spencer, Samuel Daniel, Hugh Holland, Ben. Jonson, Th. Campion, Mich. Drayton, George Chapman, John Marston, William Shakespeare, and other most pregnant wits of these our times, whom succeeding ages may justly admire.

[1]Tucker Brooke, "Shakespeare's Moiety of the Stratford Tithes," *Modern Language Notes*, XL, 462-9.

The plays also come in for a share of allusions, the greatest stir being created by the Henry IV plays. Falstaff and Justice Shallow had established their popularity. The Prologue to *Sir John Oldcastle* (1599) exclaimed indignantly:

It is no pamper'd glutton we present,
Nor aged counselor to youthful sin,
But one whose virtue shone above the rest,
A valiant martyr and a virtuous peer.

A letter (1600) from Sir Charles Percy, detained in the country, to a friend in London says, "If I stay here long in this fashion, at my return I think you will find me so dull that I shall be taken for Justice Silence or Justice Shallow. . . . [The news you send me] though perhaps they will not exempt me from the opinion of a Justice Shallow in London, yet, I assure you, they will make me pass for a very sufficient gentleman in Gloucestershire." Again the postscript to a letter from the Countess of Southampton to her husband, dated the 8th of July, possibly 1599, shows a quaint reflection of the popularity of *2 Henry IV*:

All the news I can send you that I think will make you merry is that I read in a letter from London that Sir John Falstaff is by his mistress, Dame Pintpot, made father of a goodly miller's thumb, a boy that's all head and very little body; but this is a secret.

Also from the second part of *The Return from Parnassus*, in which the actor Burbage is represented as trying out for the stage a student called Philomusus, comes the following bit of dialogue:

Burbage. I like your face and the proportion of your body for Richard the Third. I pray you, Mr. Philomusus, let me see you act a little of it.
Philomusus. "Now is the winter of our discontent
Made glorious summer by the sun of York."
Burbage. Very well, I assure you!

One of the really curious references is found in the notes of a certain Captain Keeling, commander of the East India Company's ship *Dragon*, off Sierra Leone, in the years 1607 and 1608:

September 5. I sent the interpreter, according to his desire, aboard the *Hector*, where he broke fast and after came aboard me, where we gave the tragedy of *Hamlet*.

September 30. Captain Hawkins dined with me, where my companions acted *King Richard the Second.*

March 31. I invited Captain Hawkins to a fish dinner, and had *Hamlet* acted aboard me; which I permit to keep my people from idleness and unlawful games or sleep.

Other drama of the period A second great outburst of dramatic activity occurred after 1600. Shakespeare bridges a gap between Marlowe and Jonson and himself participates in the new movement. Indeed the first decade of the seventeenth century in England is a period conspicuous in the world's literature for what was accomplished in the drama. There have been preserved from that time perhaps fifty plays which have some claim to be considered interesting or important. A new set of dramatists, most of whom had already learned the art of playwriting, were at work, animated by a new spirit and encouraged as never before by noble and royal favor. There were relatively few new subjects, but there was an extraordinary intensification in the treatment of old themes. The English drama, coming at the end of the period of the European Renaissance, had taken over a group of subjects, a set of literary themes, and a psychology and ethics, personal and social, which it continued to exploit. The whole period covered was not a long one. We have many single dramatists who worked almost all the way through the Elizabethan and Jacobean drama, in close connection with each other and with the same public before them. What the drama of Kyd, Marlowe, and Greene was at the beginning, such the drama in some sense remained until the end, with, of course, changes in emphasis, further discoveries of dramatic ideas, and a constant development in power.

In the earliest period we saw the adoption by Shakespeare in *A Comedy of Errors* of the clear lines of structure in both plot and character of Italianate Latin comedy. This continues in the second period in Shakespeare's *Twelfth Night,* and in the third period, in Jonson's *Volpone* and *The Alchemist,* and Chapman's *All Fools.* There is likewise a renewed interest in the theme of revenge, begun by Thomas Kyd in *The Spanish Tragedy* and no doubt always in use by dramatists after that. It becomes the

tragedy of blood and intrigue, as exemplified in Marston's *Antonio's Revenge* (1599), Shakespeare's *Hamlet,* Chettle's *Hoffman, or The Revenge of a Father* (1602?), *The Revenger's Tragedy* (1606-7?), attributed to Cyril Tourneur, Webster's *The White Devil* (possibly before 1610), and others. Death was the only known ending for a tragedy, and we have it, gruesome and inevitable, not only in the tragedy of intrigue but especially exploited in murder plays. *Arden of Feversham* is reflected in *A Yorkshire Tragedy,* sometimes attributed to Shakespeare, and in *Macbeth* itself. Domestic drama, finding its roots in such plays as *Wily Beguiled* (1596?), *The Two Angry Women of Abingdon* (before 1598) by Henry Porter, and *The Merry Devil of Edmonton* (1603?), takes on great vitality in Thomas Heywood's *A Woman Killed with Kindness* (1603), Thomas Dekker's *The Honest Whore* (1604), Shakespeare's *Othello* and *King Lear,* and is a feature of many of the tragedies of blood and intrigue. The dramatists saw potentialities for disaster in the maladjustment of the social relationships of the sexes, in conjugal unfaithfulness, marital jealousy, avarice as a motive in marriage, the profligacy of men, and the unchastity of women. Woman begins to come into the center of dramatic interest, where she remained in the decade following 1610, begins to be regarded in the ways characteristic of a disillusioned and degenerate society; that is, as the unfortunate victim of man's lust and greed, as a martyr in the cause of hapless love, or as the embodiment of unchastity. The older romance goes on as pastoralism, or as adventure, which latter we see in Heywood's *Fortune by Land and Sea* (1603?), a sort of chronicle play, and his *Fair Maid of the West* (1603?). It is against these, and, we may believe, many far worse plays, that Beaumont directs his satire in *The Knight of the Burning Pestle* (1607). To this romantic impulse belongs *Pericles* (1607-8), a play to whose influence much importance must be attached. The ransacking of classical literature continued with unabated zeal, not only for satiric method and the reinforcement of opinion, but for subjects, as for example, in Heywood's *The Rape of Lucrece* (1608), Webster's *Appius and Virginia* (1608?), Jonson's *Sejanus* (1603) and Shakespeare's *Coriolanus* and *Antony and Cleopatra*. But no classification based on subject-matter or theme really classifies, for every possible combination seems to occur; so that we are driven back in our study to a consideration of individual dramatists.

Individual dramatists Of newer developments after 1600 there seem to be two of greatest importance. One is the adoption of a realistic, often satiric, point of view. Dekker, Heywood, Jonson, Rowley, and Middleton are the realists of the period. They fall into two definite groups. Jonson became the exponent of satire and criticism. He not only learned the method and practiced it with the utmost skill but taught others to practice it. He achieves in his comedies from *Everyman in his Humour* (1598) to *Bartholomew Fair* (1614) a genuine greatness in pure comedy, cool, objective, Aristophanic, and executed with the maturity of touch that characterizes the great veterans of literature like John Dryden. There is nothing Jonson cannot do well, lyric, tragic, comic, or expository. Very different is the realism of Dekker. He came to his knowledge of the world by a hard road. So obscure, so disorganized, so wretched was his life that we know neither the date of his birth nor of his death. We know only that his life was largely wasted. Lamb's words, "He had poetry enough for anything" are trite, but almost universally admitted to be true. We catch a glimpse of him as Henslowe's hack in 1598, but that very year the curious Meres mentions him as eminent for tragedy. Always in debt and often in prison, he acquired a wide knowledge of the seamy side of life and a vast pity for it, an appreciation of the sweetness, even the dignity, of simple and lowly life, and a talent for exquisite simple expression in prose, rhyme, and blank verse. *The Shoemaker's Holiday* (1599), *The Honest Whore*, particularly the second part (1605?), *Westward Ho* (1604) and *Northward Ho* (1605) (in both of which he collaborated with Webster), and other plays give expression to his qualities. Middleton combines something of the objectivity of Jonson with the intimacy of Dekker in such plays as *Michaelmas Term*, *A Trick to Catch the Old One*, and *A Mad World, my Masters*, all of which were probably written between 1604 and 1606.

The other new feature of the period is a growing use of psychology. As stated in the general introduction to this volume, the dramatists and other writers of the end of the sixteenth and the beginning of the seventeenth centuries became suddenly, almost morbidly, aware of the implications of ancient psychology with reference to man's earthly life. They saw him in an unstable position not from fate or external force only, but from his liability to be overcome by the passions of his own soul. Reason and the passions were at war, and for the passions to dominate might mean madness, ecstasy, tragic error, and disaster; or folly, eccentricity, and incongruous maladjustment. The mixture within the man of the four humors—blood, phlegm, choler, and bile—determined temperament. An overabundance of one humor made the individual too sanguine, too phlegmatic, too choleric, or too melancholy. He thus became the creature of a ruling passion. The segregation of these qualities in their combinations and their varied effects gave Jonson and his followers the basis for the portrayal of types and the occasion for satire. In tragedy it was not a matter of temperament but of the indulgence of a passion such as anger, revenge, jealousy, ambition, avarice, or lust. *Coriolanus* is a study of pride, *Hamlet* (in part at least) of melancholy, *Macbeth* of ambition, *Othello* of jealousy, and so on. The psychological interest which appears in Shakespeare during this his greatest period appears also in his contemporaries.

Non-dramatic literature In 1600 appeared *England's Helicon*, a notable poetical miscellany containing the best pastoral and lyrical poetry of the age of Spenser, and in 1602 *A Poetical Rhapsody* (issued by Francis and Walter Davison), another poetical miscellany containing poems by Thomas Campion and others of the great lyrical group (many of the authors even now utterly unknown) who were writing at that time. Campion's *A Booke of Ayres* had been published in 1601, and in 1602 he published his brilliant *Observations in the Art of English Poesy*. In this essay he attacks the use of rhyme. Perhaps the same year appeared Samuel Daniel's *Defence of Ryme*, an adequate reply to Campion. These two critical treatises mark the termination of a long war on the subject of versification. In 1603 appeared John Florio's translation of Montaigne's *Essays*, a book of great influence on Shakespeare.[1] Bacon's *Advancement of Learning*, his first important philosophic work and one of the great classics of the age, appeared in 1605. In that year also came out Camden's *Remains*. The seventh edition of his Latin work *Britannia* was prepared in 1607 and translated into English by Philemon Holland with Camden's assistance in 1610. It is one of the great monuments of English antiquity and history. In 1608 Bishop Joseph Hall published his *Characters of Vertues and Vices*, the first to appear in English of the series of character sketches after the manner of the Greek writer Theophrastus. Non-dramatic literature was relatively inferior to dramatic literature.

Shakespeare's work   From 1601 to 1608 Shakespeare wrote the following plays. Few of the dates can be given with certainty: 1601, *All's Well that Ends Well* (?*Love's Labour's Won*, 1590) and *Troilus and Cressida* (possibly later revised); 1602-3, *Hamlet* (final version); 1603-4, *Measure for Measure;* 1604, *Othello;* 1605, *Timon of Athens* (not completed?) and *King Lear;* 1606, *Macbeth* and *Antony and Cleopatra;* 1607, *Pericles;* 1608, *Coriolanus*.

What circumstances may there have been in Shakespeare's private life or in the complexion of his thought which might have caused him to turn his great powers during the years from 1603 to 1607 to the production of tragedy? So far as we can see he was extremely prosperous and successful. His bereavements were natural and inevitable, and the worst one, the death of his only son, was some years behind him. It is certain that he read Montaigne's *Essays*, published in the translation of John Florio in 1603. They deepened his thinking, no doubt, but they did not necessarily give to his thought a despairing cast. Essex, who may have been his political leader, had met his death in 1602; Southampton, who was certainly at an earlier time his friend and patron, had been released from prison and was enjoying the favor of the new king. All that can be said is that Shakespeare came, in the course of

his life's experience, to a deeper, more comprehensive, and ultimately less secure view of man's destiny, and chose to devote his talent to the displaying of this philosophy in tragedies on the stage. It does not sufficiently account for Shakespeare's work to say that tragedy became the fashion of the London stage. Such a thing may have started him in the vein; no doubt it did; but his depiction of man in relation to the tragic possibilities of existence is too momentous to be regarded merely as a fashion of the stage. In the eye of Shakespearean tragedy man is unstable, unassured, and unassurable.

If it were only a question of the tragedies, one might say that Shakespeare deliberately turned his artist's mind toward the terrible, and was himself relatively unaffected; but we have also to do with three mirthless comedies which Dowden rightly described as serious, dark, and ironical. In *All's Well that Ends Well* he revamped, with no great care, enthusiasm, or consistency, an old Renaissance comedy, of somewhat the same nature as *The Two Gentlemen of Verona*. *All's Well that Ends Well* was possibly originally called *Love's Labour's Won*, the play mentioned by Meres, which Shakespeare probably had written in the early nineties. *Measure for Measure* he wrote about 1604 on the basis of *Promos and Cassandra*, a drama by George Whetstone, and an Italian tale by Giraldi Cinthio. *Troilus and Cressida* comes somewhere between 1599 and 1609. The three plays present a world in which sex relations are awry. No one of them is without disillusion, dark irony, and wistful melancholy. Illicit love sets the action going or twists it from its natural course. In *All's Well* virtue wins a decided victory; in *Measure for Measure* it fights a drawn battle; in *Troilus and Cressida* it suffers defeat. Because of the nature of these comedies and their appearance in the period of profound tragedies, Dowden described Shakespeare's work from 1600 to 1607 as written *de profundis* or "out of the depths." *All's Well that Ends Well, Troilus and Cressida,* and *Measure for Measure* are certainly suggestive of the pessimism of *Hamlet, Macbeth,* and *King Lear*. As we sketch the comedies it will be seen that, to some extent at least, *All's Well that Ends*

---

[1] G. C. Taylor, *Shakespeare's Debt to Montaigne*, Cambridge, 1925; J. M. Robertson, *Montaigne and Shakespeare*, London, 1897.

Well and *Measure for Measure* have in them a faith in womanly purity equal to that which appears in *Othello* and *King Lear*. What makes them seem out of harmony is the fact that, with situations which call for tragedy as loudly as anything in the tragedies mentioned, we are nevertheless provided with happy endings. With reference to *Troilus and Cressida* one can only say that, insofar as it is a love story, it is more bitter in its conception of womanly faithlessness than is any tragedy.[1]

[1]For references on Shakespeare's life and times see page 88.

II. COMEDIES OF THE THIRD PERIOD

ALL'S WELL THAT ENDS WELL

Date and source
All's Well that Ends Well was published first in the folio edition of 1623. We are, moreover, reasonably certain that there had been no earlier edition of the play, because it is one of those mentioned in the Stationers' Register on November 8, 1623, as not previously entered for publication. There is no certain external evidence about the play until this entry. From the fact that *Love's Labour's Won* is listed by Francis Meres in *Palladis Tamia* as one of Shakespeare's comedies there has, however, arisen a fascinating problem in connection with *All's Well that Ends Well*. It would appear from Meres's list that there existed in 1598 a Shakespearean comedy now lost. Its title suggests that it may have been a companion piece to *Love's Labour's Lost* and for that reason probably an early comedy. The play, however, may have been preserved but preserved under a different name. Attempts have, accordingly, been made to prove that *All's Well that Ends Well* is *Love's Labour's Won* revised and renamed. In favor of this is the fact that the old name would suit the theme of *All's Well that Ends Well* and its source, which is one of the stories in Boccaccio's *Decameron*. The story belongs to the third day in that work, on which were told tales of lovers who had overcome apparently insuperable obstacles, such as that overcome by Helena in the plot of *All's Well that Ends Well*. There is even a passage in the play which seems to allude to the earlier title. Helena says to Bertram (V, iii, 314-315):

> This is done:
> Will you be mine, now you are doubly won?

Internal evidence, moreover, gives overwhelming proof that *All's Well that Ends Well* was written at two different times. A large part of the principal story appears in rhymed couplets. There are letters in sonnet-form, lyrical dialogue, puns and conceits. All of these things are regarded as characteristic of Shakespeare's early style. Interspersed with these rhetorical parts are passages of blank verse closely compacted in thought and free with reference to the limits of the line; in other words, in Shakespeare's later style. Because of the unmistakable presence of these two styles most critics have assigned the original composition to about 1590-2 and the revision to about 1602-3. Resemblances in spirit and tone as well as in sentiment and style to *Hamlet* and *Measure for Measure* have caused the selection of the latter date. It is, however, only fair to say that important scholars have insisted that *Love's Labour's Won* is to be identified with *Much Ado about Nothing*, or with *The Taming of the Shrew*, and that the two styles of *All's Well* should both be dated much later; that is, the original composition about 1598-1600 and the revision about 1607.

The story
The scene of *All's Well that Ends Well*, like its source in Boccaccio, is laid in France and in Tuscany. The heroine is Helena, orphan daughter of a distinguished physician, Gerard of Narbonne. After her father's death Helena has been taken into the household of the Countess of Roussillon, a wise and charming old woman. Helena has fallen in love with the handsome Bertram, son to the Countess. Her love is of course hopeless because of differences in birth and fortune between her and Bertram. She loves "a bright, par-

ticular star" and "hopes to wed it." It is her doctrine that

> Our remedies oft in ourselves do lie,
> Which we ascribe to heaven.

Her opportunity comes in the illness of the King of France. His incurable "fistula" has baffled all physicians. Helena with a recipe of her father's sets out to the French court, whither Bertram has already gone, to heal the king and thus elevate herself to a station sufficiently noble for her to wed Bertram. She is aided in her enterprise with the advice and sympathy of the Countess and of Lafeu, an old nobleman, a friend of the Countess, and a frank and kindly person. With Bertram is Parolles, a boaster and a coward, whom in the revision of the play Shakespeare has made somewhat responsible for Bertram's misdeeds. Shakespeare perhaps felt that the burden laid by the plot on Bertram was too great for him to bear, if he is to hold any part of our sympathies, unless some excuse for his action was provided. Helena succeeds in healing the French king and as a reward is ennobled and given the privilege of choosing a husband from among the lords in attendance at the king's court. She promptly chooses Bertram. Bertram has been anxious to get away from home into the great world. Helena is revolting to him as part of the life of which he has grown tired. He refuses to marry her, but for fear of the king's displeasure finally accepts her as his wife. He behaves very badly in the matter, concealing from her the blow which he intends to strike. Under the influence of Parolles he runs away to the Italian wars, leaving for Helena a letter in which he declares that he will not live with her as a husband until she can obtain a certain ring from his finger—which will be never. During his soldiering in Italy the cowardice of Parolles is exposed, so that even Bertram must recognize it. Helena appears in Italy and by means of the clever intrigue of the source in Boccaccio succeeds in carrying out the hard and humiliating terms of Bertram's letter. All the parties return again to Roussillon, the plot is revealed, Bertram is convinced (put in jeopardy of his life, indeed, for his falsity), and accepts Helena, saying to the king:

> If she, my liege, can make me know this clearly,
> I'll love her dearly, ever, ever dearly.

History of the play *All's Well that Ends Well* has never been popular on the stage and obviously could not be. It has been revived rarely except on those occasions when, for the sake of paying homage to the master dramatist, all of the plays in the canon have been put on the stage. Its literary life, however, is not inconsiderable. Helena is universally admired, Coleridge referring to her as "Shakespeare's loveliest creation." The domestic atmosphere of the household of the Countess of Roussillon, the Countess herself, the kindly cynical old Lafeu, the grateful king, the vulgar bitter Fool, even the braggart Parolles, all serve to keep alive a badly mixed-up and patched-up play.

TROILUS AND CRESSIDA

Date and publication An entry in the Stationers' Register for February 7, 1603, gives an approximate date for *Troilus and Cressida*. A publisher named James Roberts entered his copy to print, "when he hath got sufficient authority for it, the book of Troilus and Cressida as it is acted by Lord Chamberlain's men." One does not know why he lacked authority. Perhaps he was acting in behalf of the players and in order to prevent the piracy of the play. It was re-entered to R. Bonian and H. Walley on January 28, 1609, and printed that year. It seems almost certain that the printing was unauthorized, for the title-page appears in two somewhat inconsistent forms. The texts are in all particulars exactly the same, but what appears to be the earlier has this title:

THE Historie of Troylus *and* Cresseida. *As it was acted by the Kings Maiesties seruants at the Globe. Written by* William Shakespeare. LONDON. Imprinted by *G. Eld* for *R. Bonian* and *H. Walley*, and are to be sold at the spred Eagle in Paules Church-yeard, ouer against the great North doore. 1609.

The second issue substitutes for the first part of the title the following:

The Famous Historie of Troylus *and* Cresseid. *Excellently expressing the beginning of their loues, with the conceited wooing of* Pandarus *Prince of* Licia.

This second issue has a thing unique among Shakespearean quartos, namely, a preface or epistle to the reader beginning, "A Neuer writer, to a neuer reader. Newes." It declares that the play is "neuer stal'd with the Stage, neuer clapper-clawd with the palmes of the vulgar." It also declares that the play is published against "the grand possessors wills." The new title-page and the epistle seem to be designed to evade the consequences of publishing a play to which the publishers had no proper title.

Troilus and Cressida stands in the First Folio between the "Histories" and the "Tragedies" and is not listed in the table of contents, possibly because the editors were in doubt as to its classification. The subject was an extremely familiar one in sixteenth century drama and literature. A comedy called *Troilus and Pandarus* was performed at court in 1515, and there are records of other plays on the subject. Henslowe's *Diary* for 1599 shows that Dekker and Chettle were preparing for Henslowe a play to be called *Troylles and Cresseda* (Henslowe's spelling), though when it was finished it was called *Agamemnon*. This can hardly have been the play referred to in *Histriomastix* (a play written by Marston in 1599 apparently on the basis of a still older play), for this reference seems to connect Shakespeare with the subject of Troilus and Cressida before the end of the century:

> *Troy.*—Come, Cressida, my cresset light,
> Thy face doth shine both day and night,
> Behold, behold thy garter blue
> Thy knight his valiant elbow wears,
> That when he *shakes* his furious *speare*,
> The foe, in shivering fearful sort,
> May lay him down in death to snort.

Our present version of the play may not be Shakespeare's first version, but a rewriting to remove from it the traces of the controversy connected with the War of the Theaters.

The prologue to the play, as given in the folio version, alludes unmistakably to Jonson's *Poetaster*, which appeared in the summer of 1601. In the light of this and of the first entry in the Stationers' Register one concludes the play in its final form was probably written about 1601-2. The play comes from the period of the end of the war between the regular companies and the children's companies but is not a part of that controversy, though possibly the earlier version, referred to in *Histriomastix*, was. Fleay's attempt to connect it with that quarrel by identifying Jonson with Ajax and Marston with Thersites is not regarded by Shakespeare scholars as successful, but has points in its favor. When the Folio was printed the text used was a different one from that of the quarto of 1609, probably the playhouse manuscript in possession of the King's company.

No play in Shakespeare has perhaps been more misunderstood than has *Troilus and Cressida*. Critics have been perplexed by it, and it has had no stage career, although the performance by Cambridge students in 1922 indicated that the play has decided dramatic value and charm. Dowden was so uncertain as to the significance of *Troilus and Cressida* that he declined to discuss it in the first edition of *Shakespeare, his Mind and Art*. Later, in the preface to the third edition, he wrote, "I now believe this strange and difficult play was a last attempt to continue comedy, made when Shakespeare had ceased to be able to smile genially and when he must be either ironical or taking a deep, passionate, and tragical view of life." "It is," he says, "the comedy of disillusion." From a point of view which insists on interpreting Shakespeare's plays as reflections of his private life and of his attitude toward the world, this is no doubt inescapable. In other words, if one must believe that when Shakespeare wrote tragedy he felt tragically about the world as it affected him and his fellow human beings, then *Troilus and Cressida* could have arisen only from an embittered mind.[1]

Sources The tale of Troilus and his love Cressida is the proverbial case of the fickle woman who deserts a faithful lover. It came originally as an offshoot of the tale of Troy,[2] not as told by Homer in the *Iliad*, but as invented by Benoit de Ste.-Maure in *Le Roman de Troie* in the twelfth

[1]See W. W. Lawrence, *Shakespeare's Problem Comedies*, New York, 1931.
[2]See J. S. P. Tatlock (*Publ. Mod. Lang. Ass'n.*, XXX, 672-770), W. W. Lawrence (*Shakespearean Studies*, Columbia Univ., New York, 1916, pp. 187-211), H. E. Rollins (*Publ. Mod. Lang. Ass'n.*, XXXII, 383-429), P. Alexander (4 *Library*, IX. 267-86).

century and amplified into a long poem *Il Filostrato* by Boccaccio before the middle of the fourteenth century, and by Chaucer in *Troilus and Creseyde* later in the same century. Chaucer told the story sympathetically; his Creseyde is something more than a faithless woman. But Chaucer's treatment is only one of many and by no means the most influential of the group. Shakespeare seems to have done in this case what he also did in the characterization of Julius Cæsar and of Cleopatra. He interpreted his character according to the current tradition and not according to his source. He probably took his material largely from *Troilus and Creseyde*, but he followed Chaucer in substance, not at all in spirit. This mediæval love story he retold with a frankness and cynicism no greater than the events justify and no more realistically than it had been told before. He placed it against a background of the siege of Troy, and here again he is baffling and unsatisfactory to modern taste. We draw our conceptions of the Trojan War from Homer. Shakespeare probably knew some part of Chapman's translation of the *Iliad* and made some use of it, particularly in the characterization of Thersites; but what he really followed in both event and sympathy was the mediæval romance of Troy. He followed Raoul le Fevre's *Recueil des Histoires de Troye*, as translated and published by Caxton, and probably also Lydgate's *Troy Book*, translated from Guido delle Colonne's *Historia Trojana*. These romances do not present the fall of Troy as merely the result of a war of antiquity. They render it personal and immediate. They sympathize with the Trojans. The English, the Italians, the French, and even the Scandinavians—all imitating the Romans—regarded the Trojans as their ancestors and conceived of the Greeks as crafty, cowardly, and brutal enemies. Hence it is easy to see that Shakespeare and his audience sided with the Trojans. Shakespeare serves the Greeks much better than the tradition warranted. Thersites is a "deformed and scurrilous Greek," Ajax a stupid bully, Achilles a selfish coward, and Menelaus a somewhat ignoble figure. But, on the other hand, Agamemnon is a sagacious and dignified commander of troops, Nestor a sage, and Ulysses one of Shakespeare's real triumphs in the creation of manly character. Ulysses is so statesmanlike, so shrewd, so wise, and withal so kindly that he suggests one of the statesman for whom Elizabeth's reign celebrated. Among the Trojans, who are as a whole much more admirable, Hector is a truly noble figure, offsetting Ulysses on the Greek side; and Troilus, a model of love and courage, suggests Romeo. The play presents a wealth of Renaissance learning.

The story Troilus loves Cressida with a deep and unselfish love. He wins her through the despicable services of her uncle Pandarus, not however, until she has displayed the arts of the coquette in order to inflame his love. This tale of illicit love is set over against the love of Paris for Helen, the stolen wife of the Greek Menelaus. As the play opens the Greeks are torn by dissension, so that they cannot succeed in capturing Troy. Achilles is enraged at Agamemnon, the Greek general, and is sulking in his tent in company with his beloved Patroclus, as in the *Iliad*. Ulysses tries with all his wisdom and eloquence to make peace between them and heal the breach. The issue of the play arises when Hector, the principal warrior among the Trojans, challenges some Grecian to single combat. The Greeks select Ajax as their representative in the hope of arousing Achilles to action by appealing to his jealousy of Ajax; it is in vain. The Trojan leaders debate on the propriety of returning Helen to her former husband and thus ending the war. Hector wishes to do this, but Troilus stands out against it; so that in spite of the warnings of their sister Cassandra, a prophetess whose fate it is to have her prophecies disregarded, Hector gives in to Troilus and Paris and the war goes on. Calchas, the father of Cressida, a Trojan renegade to the Greeks, who has left his daughter behind him in Troy, provides for an exchange of prisoners, so that he may regain his daughter Cressida by exchanging her for the Trojan Antenor. Diomedes has charge of the exchange. Cressida parts from Troilus with renewed oaths of everlasting love and accompanies Diomedes. When she arrives in the Greek camp, she kisses the Greeks all round, except Ulysses, who sees her for what she is. Diomedes, breaking through the thin veneer of her coquetry, takes Cressida for his mistress. Then occur feastings between Greeks and

Trojans in the Greek camp. Ulysses accompanies Troilus to Calchas's tent where Troilus overhears Cressida's carryings on with Diomedes. Troilus returns to Troy disillusioned and bitter. On the next morning Hector slays Patroclus, who was wearing the armor of Achilles. At this Achilles goes to battle. He does not, however, meet Hector in fair fight, but surrounds him with the Myrmidons and murders him; then he ties his body to the tail of his horse and drags it about the walls of Troy. The play ends with a curse delivered by Troilus against Pandarus, the go-between. On the basis of this sorry tale critics have been led to believe that Shakespeare was satirizing the heroes of antiquity pricked on thereto by his jealousy of Chapman the translator of Homer; but the idea is absurd. Shakespeare has merely put on the stage the mediæval Troy story, and has elevated rather than debased the tale in so doing.

Stage history Dryden rewrote Shakespeare's *Troilus and Cressida* in 1679 under the title *Troilus and Cressida; or, Truth Found too Late*. He took great pains to adapt the play to the refined tastes of his age, and, although one resents his tampering with the work of his betters, his version is not without merit, for Dryden was an excellent workman. In it Cressida is true to Troilus, encourages Diomedes only in order to assist her father to escape from the Greek camp, and, when reproached by Troilus for infidelity, slays herself. *Troilus and Cressida* has almost no further stage history.

MEASURE FOR MEASURE

Date King James VI of Scotland arrived in London on May 7, 1603, to succeed Queen Elizabeth on the throne of England. Plays had been inhibited at the Queen's death on March 24th, but were allowed again on May 9th. On May 19th the Lord Chamberlain's Company was licensed as the King's Company and placed under royal patronage. About this time the plague began raging in the city, and on May 26th the theaters were closed. Shakespeare's company then traveled in the country. Also because of the plague, King James remained absent from the city, staying first at Wilton and then at Hampton Court, thus delaying his royal entry into London until March 15, 1604. On that occasion the leading members of the King's Company, as Grooms of the Royal Chamber, received liveries and took part in the ceremony. When the theaters opened on April 9, 1604, Shakespeare's company had probably its first great opportunity to win the new king's favor. A Revels Office account, the authenticity of which has long been debated but is now usually admitted, has been preserved which gives a list of plays presented before and after Christmas of that year. "John Heminges one of his Majesties players" was paid for plays performed by the King's Company. They included "Mesure for Mesur by Shaxberd."

If *Measure for Measure* was not written for this occasion, it must at least have been very extensively revised. In Act I, scene i, ll. 67-72 is a possible allusion to King James's well advertised modesty, for the Duke remarks that though he loves the people, he does not "like to stage me to their eyes." Malone saw in the use of the word "sweat" (I, ii, 84) an allusion to the recent plague. And Pompey's speech at the beginning of Act IV, scene iii, seems to refer to the recently proclaimed "statute of stabbing." Parts of the play at least and its general temper and style associate it with *Othello*. Everything seems to point to 1604 as the date of composition. *Measure for Measure* appeared in print for the first time in the Folio of 1623, and like *All's Well that Ends Well* was one of the plays entered in the Stationer's Register as never having been printed or licensed. The play is very uneven and mixed in style, almost as much so as *All's Well that Ends Well*, and one is tempted to see in it, not a new composition, but a hasty revision.

Source In the matter of sources Shakespeare seems to have taken his characteristic pains. It used to be said that *Measure for Measure* rests solely on a play called *Promos and Cassandra* by George Whetstone (1578), but more recent and more careful studies seem to indicate that Shakespeare in writing *Measure for Measure* consulted not only Whetstone's play but Whetstone's translation in prose of the same narrative from Giraldi Cinthio's *Hecatommithi*, the story in the *Hecatommithi* itself, and even *Epitia*, a Latin play by Giraldi.

The story The scene is laid in Vienna and is so marked in the Folio. That city is suffering greatly from lawlessness, particularly sexual vice. The Duke who is the governor of the city apparently despairs of enforcing the laws himself. He, therefore, turns over the government of the city to a deputy, one Angelo, a severe moralist with a great reputation for uprightness, but with at least one breach of promise in his own past. It is sometimes thought on inadequate grounds that the Duke gave up his government in order to expose the professional reformer and to indicate that reforming a city by a cruel exaction of penalties is not a proper thing. The Duke goes away on a pretended journey and presently returns disguised as a friar to correct the injuries done by his pious substitute.

The story of the play, widely known over Europe for at least two centuries, arises out of Angelo's rigid enforcement of a law which makes it a capital offense to beget an illegitimate child. Claudio has offended with his sweetheart Juliet. His chaste and beautiful sister Isabella goes to Angelo to plead for her brother's life. Angelo, who prides himself on being above all temptation, makes to Isabella the base proposal that he will spare Claudio's life if she will yield to his lust. She scorns him, then visits her brother in prison feeling sure that Claudio will die rather than see her sacrifice her honor. This gives occasion for one of Shakespeare's famous scenes, albeit a somewhat pessimistic one. At first Claudio declares he will "encounter darkness as a bride" and hug it in his arms; but later he sees it differently and makes his cringing, eloquent speech:

> Ay, but to die, and go we know not where;
> To lie in cold obstruction and to rot.

He desires Isabella to yield, but she bids him perish in his ignominy. At this point the Duke, who knows what has happened, begins to operate the machine, and the consistency of the major plot suffers. He arranges to have Isabella pretend to consent to Angelo's proposal, but substitutes for her Mariana, a former betrothed of Angelo, rejected by him because she had lost her fortune. Angelo thus consummates his marriage with Mariana. It helps this bad plot to remember

that a betrothal had the validity of a marriage, but nothing can save the plot from its ingrained unpleasantness. Angelo decrees, in spite of his apparent victory, that Claudio shall die. But before the execution can be achieved, the Duke reveals himself, resumes his authority, and proceeds to set everything to rights. Claudio is forgiven and marries Juliet. Angelo formally weds Mariana. Isabella and the Duke are betrothed. The immoral people in the underplot, whom Claudio's imprisonment has brought into the story, are also all forgiven.

As Shakespeare first wrote the play he seems to have followed the story as told by Whetstone in *Promos and Cassandra* with greater fidelity than appears in the present version. Those parts of the plot which differ most from Whetstone bear the marks of being additions and changes. According to Whetstone Cassandra (Isabella) yields to the evil proposal of Promos (Angelo), who even then condemns her brother to death. The brother escapes from prison through the mercy of his jailer, the king (Duke) returns, exposes Promos, condemns him to marry the wronged Cassandra and to suffer death. Cassandra then pleads for his life and he is spared. There is nothing in Whetstone's play which corresponds to Mariana and her relation to Angelo. This is the very part which appears on textual grounds to have been introduced into the play after it was first written. Moreover, it is perfectly plain that in the use of the device of the unrecognized wife Shakespeare was borrowing from his own play of *All's Well that Ends Well*, where a similar ruse is resorted to in Helena's behalf. There are verbal parallels between *Measure for Measure* and *All's Well* that confirm this. The effect of the introduction of the Mariana episode is to ameliorate the plot; for bad as the story is in *Measure for Measure*, it is worse in *Promos and Cassandra*.[1]

Measure for Measure is a poor play from the points of view of structure, subjectmatter, dramatic consistency, and the characterization of minor figures. On the other hand, it contains some of Shakespeare's finest dramatic poetry. Isabella is one of

[1]See R. H. Wilson, "The Mariana Plot of *Measure for Measure*," *Philological Quarterly*, IX, 341-50.

Shakespeare's greatest women. Angelo too is extremely well done, and the Duke, although often misunderstood because of an anachronistic interpretation, becomes, if seen with the eyes of Shakespeare's age, a character of poise and wisdom.

Stage history *Measure for Measure* in spite of its touches of beauty remains one of Shakespeare's worst plays. Its badness, however, has not prevented it from having great popularity on the stage.

It was acted, often in modified form, in the late seventeenth century, and was extremely popular with the great Shakespearean actors of the eighteenth and early nineteenth centuries. Colley Cibber, Garrick, Mrs. Siddons, Miss O'Neill, John Philip Kemble, and Macready, all appeared in it. Miss Neilson revived it in London and New York in 1876 and 1880 respectively, and there are those still living who have seen one or more of Madame Modjeska's revivals.

III. TRAGEDIES OF THE THIRD PERIOD

HAMLET

Editions The first edition of *Hamlet*, a quarto, has the following title-page:

THE Tragicall Historie of HAMLET *Prince of Denmarke*. By William Shake-speare. As it hath beene diuerse times acted by his Highnesse seruants in the Cittie of London: as also in the two Vniuersities of Cambridge and Oxford, and elsewhere. At London printed for N. L. and Iohn Trundell. 1603.

The second quarto has this title-page:

THE Tragicall Historie of HAMLET, *Prince of Denmarke*. By William Shakespeare. Newly imprinted and enlarged to almost as much againe as it was, according to the true and perfect Coppie. AT LONDON, Printed by I. R. for N. L. and are to be sold at his shoppe vnder Saint Dunstons Chu ch in Fleet-street. 1604.

"N. L." is Nicholas Ling and "I. R." is James Roberts. On July 26, 1602, Roberts had entered in the Stationers' Register "A Booke called the Revenge of Hamlett Prince of Denmarke as yt was latelie Acted by the Lord Chamberlayne his servantes." Roberts's name is not mentioned on the title-page of the first quarto, and the book, which seems to have been Ling's property, was assigned from his estate in 1607 to John Smethwick. Either Ling forestalled Roberts in the issue of the first quarto and they subsequently made terms with each other in the issue of the second, Ling as printer and Roberts as publisher, or they were partners in both enterprises. Roberts had a good position in the trade and was apparently a

friend of the players, since he enjoyed the privilege of printing the players' bills. He did not, however, print Q_1. Less is known about Ling, whose record is not good. Q_1 has all the marks of being "stolne and surreptitious," and Ling probably had the whip-hand over Roberts in the issue of this play. An additional part of Q_2 was issued with a change of date to 1605. John Smethwick printed a third edition (Q_4) in 1611, and later an undated quarto from which a series of no less than four others was issued before the end of the seventeenth century. There was never a second issue of Q_1. The Folio prints what is regarded as a distinct text from the quartos. Though it resembles the second quarto, it is evidently a playhouse copy possibly abridged for acting; at any rate, it contains eighty-five lines not in Q_2 and omits 218 lines which are in Q_2.

Date Before considering the question of date it is necessary to consider the nature of Q_1. The earliest known copy of it was discovered by Sir Henry Bunbury in 1823. It was first regarded as an imperfect reproduction of an earlier version of the text as we have it in Q_2 and the First Folio. Later, following Collier in 1843, it came to be regarded as a badly botched version of the true text taken down in the theater by a shorthand writer and made ready for the press by that person or by an indifferent poet employed to revise it. This is still the view of notable scholars.[1] Of recent years,

[1] W. Creizenach, "Hamletfragen," *Shakespeare Jahrbuch*, XLII, 76-85; B. A. P. Van Dam, *The Text of Shakespeare's "Hamlet,"* London, 1924.

however, the first view has been more and more positively stated and argued for.[1] Mr. Robertson believes that certain passages in Q1 are actually borrowed from an old play of Hamlet by Thomas Kyd. Mr. Dover Wilson, anticipated in part by Professor Henry David Gray, has put forward the hypothesis that Shakespeare made a revision of Kyd's play in 1591-2, with a brief transcript for the road in 1593. He has also offered the suggestion, now widely accepted, that in the piracy of Q1 we have to do not with a stenographer-pirate, but with an actor-pirate, some dishonest member of Shakespeare's company who had been earlier the purveyor to the printer of other bad quartos. Mr. Wilson thinks he has discovered traces of the pirate in the fact that the rôles which he played are used as the starting-point for the reconstruction of the play, his parts being more correctly given and the scenes in which he appeared being best remembered. According to this theory the pirate played in succession the parts of Marcellus, Voltimand, a Player, second Gravedigger, Churlish Priest, and English Ambassador. Professor Hubbard and Professor Stoll give reasons to show that Shakespeare wrote the tragedy twice and that Q1 is, therefore, a corruption of his first draft. These reasons are independent of the theory of how Q1 came into existence. Professor Hubbard investigates the readings of the text of Q1 in their relation to the readings of other quartos and the folios and shows the independence and authenticity of that version. Professor Stoll finds positive evidence of a plot revision of the original of Q1 in the direction of compactness and increase of dramatic interest; in the shifting of the "Get thee to a nunnery" scene, together with the "To be or not to be" soliloquy which

precedes it (III, i, 56-196), from the second act to the third; in the absence from Q1 of Hamlet's soliloquy (IV, iv, 32-66), "How all occassions do inform against me," and of the passage (III, iv, 202-210) about "hoisting the enginer with his own petar"; in the changes in the interview with his mother by which she is less involved in Hamlet's plot for revenge; and in other matters.

Q1 and Q2 *Hamlet* is not mentioned by Meres in 1598, and, since it was always a famous play, it probably would have been if Shakespeare had written his version by that time. The play in both quartos contains an allusion to the child actors and the War of the Theaters (II, ii, 340-379). This allusion could not have been made before 1598 when the Children of the Chapel Royal began to act at Blackfriars and probably points to 1599-1601, when they had become serious rivals of the adult companies and forced them to leave London for the provinces. A reference to *Hamlet* in Harvey's *Marginalia* was probably made between 1598 and 1601; and we have the entry of the play in the Stationers' Register in 1602. The original of Q1 may, therefore, date from 1598-1601, Q2 from 1603-4, unless of course Q1 is to be regarded merely as a pirated version of Q2. It is also important to note that there was a revival of the "tragedy of blood" during these years. Henslowe's company revived *The Spanish Tragedy* in 1597, and in 1601 and 1602 Henslowe paid Ben Jonson for "adicyons" to that play. Marston wrote revenge plays for the Children of Paul's, Chettle and others for Henslowe's company, and it is natural enough to suppose that Shakespeare may have been called upon to recast the famous old revenge play of Hamlet for his company.

The old Hamlet There are unmistakable traces of an early revenge play called *Hamlet*. It is alluded to by Thomas Nashe in his *Epistle to the Gentlemen Students of Both Universities*, prefixed to Greene's *Menaphon* (1589), and was acted at Newington Butts on June 9, 1594, while the Lord Admiral's and the Lord Chamberlain's companies were acting there under Henslowe's management. In Thomas Lodge's pamphlet *Wits miserie, and the Worlds madnesse, discovering the Devils incarnate of this Age* (1596), one of his evil spirits, "Hate-

[1]Adams, *Life of William Shakespeare*, pp. 520-1; F. S. Boas, *The Works of Thomas Kyd*, London, 1901, Introduction; F. G. Hubbard, *The First Quarto Edition of Shakespeare's "Hamlet,"* Madison, 1920, and "The Readings of the First Quarto of *Hamlet*," *Publication of the Modern Language Association*, xxxviii, 792-822; Pollard, *Shakespeare's Fight with the Pirates*; J. M. Robertson, *The Problem of "Hamlet*," London, 1919; E. E. Stoll, *Hamlet: An Historical and Comparative Study*, Minneapolis, 1919; J. D. Wilson, "The Copy for *Hamlet*, 1603," and "The *Hamlet* Transcript, 1593," *The Library*, July and October, 1918; Henry David Gray, "The First Quarto of *Hamlet*," *Modern Language Review*, x, 171-180, "Thomas Kyd and the First Quarto of *Hamlet*," *Publ. Mod. Lang. Ass'n*, xlii, 721-735, and "Reconstruction of a Lost Play," *Philological Quarterly*, VII, 254-274.

Virtue, a foul lubber," "looks as pale as the visard of the Ghost, which cried so miserably at the theator, *Hamlet reuenge*." "My name's Hamlet reuenge," exclaims a character in Dekker's *Satiromastix* (1602), as if the phrase was a sort of catch-word. The passage in Nashe's *Epistle* has been made to yield a suggestion as to the authorship of the old play. Nashe, like Greene in *A Groatsworth of Wit*, is criticizing the actors and certain dramatists who write for them:

... I will turne backe to my first text of Studies of delight, and talke a little in friendship with a few of our triuiall translators. It is a common practise now a dayes amongst a sort of shifting companions, that runne through euery Art and thriue by none, to leaue the trade of *Nouerint*, whereto they were borne, and busie themselues with the endeuours of Art, that could scarcely Latinize their neck verse if they should haue neede; yet English *Seneca* read by Candlelight yeelds many good sentences, as *Blood is a begger*, and so forth; and if you intreate him faire in a frostie morning, hee will affoord you whole Hamlets, I should say handfulls of Tragicall speeches. But O griefe! *Tempus edax rerum*, whats that will last alwayes? The Sea exhaled by droppes will in continuance bee drie, and *Seneca*, let blood line by line and page by page, at length must needes die to our Stage; which makes his famished followers to imitate the Kidde in *Æsop*, who, enamoured with the Foxes newfangles, forsooke all hopes of life to leape into a newe occupation; and these men, renouncing all possibilities of credite or estimation, to intermeddle with Italian Translations: Wherein how poorely they haue plodded, (as those that are neither prouenzall men, nor are able to distinguish of Articles,) let all indifferent Gentlemen who haue trauelled in that tongue discerne by their twopennie Pamphlets. And no maruell though their home borne mediocritie bee such in this matter; for what can bee hoped of those that thrust *Elisium* into hell, and haue not learned, so long as they haue liued in the Spheres, the iust measure of the Horizon without an hexameter? Sufficeth them to bodge vp a blanke verse with ifs and ands, and otherwhile for recreation after their Candlestuffe, hauing starched their beards most curiously, to make a Peripateticall path into the inner parts of the Citie, and spend two or three howers in turning ouer French *Doudie*, where they attract more infection in one minute, then they can do eloquence all daies of their life, by conuersing with any Authors of like argument.

Many of the allusions in this peculiar passage have never been explained; but it does point to a play of *Hamlet* in the Senecan style, done by a person who was born to the trade of noverint, or scrivener, who occupied himself in translations, was evidently not a university man, but ground out his work like a hack writer by candlelight. Thomas Kyd fulfills these conditions. He was the most Senecan of Elizabethan dramatists; he translated at least two works from the French; his father was a scrivener; and his name seems to be glanced at in the allusion to the "Kidde in Æsop." Moreover, his only absolutely authentic original play, *The Spanish Tragedy*, bears in its theme and its devices the very closest resemblance to *Hamlet*. Malone denied the authorship of the old *Hamlet* to Shakespeare, and Fleay attributed the play to Kyd. Since that time many critics have written on the question, and Fleay's attribution, particularly in the light of this obscure passage, is pretty generally accepted.[1]

Fratricide Punished   Is it possible to ascertain more nearly the nature of the old *Hamlet*? Among the many English plays which entered Germany in the period from 1590 to 1600 is one called *Hamlet* which was acted at Dresden by a company of English actors under John Green in 1626. What seems to be a late modernized version of it (1710) is preserved under the name *Der bestrafte Brudermord*, or *Fratricide Punished*. It tells the Hamlet story pretty much as we know it, but with certain characteristics which connect it with the pre-Shakespearean period, such as an explanatory prologue, spoken by Alecto, in the manner of Seneca and of Kyd in *The Spanish Tragedy*. The character Polonius is called Corambis in Q_1, and in *Fratricide Punished* the court chamberlain is called Corambus. So far as the story can be made out in its degenerated form, it is closer to the first quarto than to the second and is all the way through more primitive in its appeal than either. Because this play is regarded by many scholars as certainly based on the old *Hamlet*, probably by Kyd,

[1]Fleay, *Biographical Chronicle of the English Drama*, s. v. Kyd, ii, 26; G. Sarrazin, *Thomas Kyd und Sein Kreis*, Berlin, 1892; Boas, *Works of Thomas Kyd*; Robertson, *The Problem of "Hamlet"*; Chambers, *The Elizabethan Stage*, III, 397, IV, 234. But see McKerrow, *The Works of Thomas Nashe*, London, 1904-1910, III, 311, IV, 444, and Chambers, *William Shakespeare*, I, 422-423.

it seems worth while to summarize its contents. We know from other sources that the old play had in it a ghost demanding revenge, a scene on a "frostie morning" like that on the battlements of Elsinore, and that it was Senecan. In the German play, as also probably in the old *Hamlet*, there is the secret murder and adultery betrayed to the son by the return of the wronged man's ghost; the feigned madness, treated comically; delay and self-reproach; attempts by the court chamberlain, the lady with eavesdroppers, and the hero's mother to discover the cause of Hamlet's madness; the play-within-the-play; the sparing of the king while at prayer in order to slay his soul as well as his body; the unintentional slaying of the court chamberlain; the voyage to England; Ophelia's madness; the fencing bout with poisoned foils and the poisoned drink; and the final combination of vengeance and death in the last scene.

Saxo and Belleforest It is proper enough to believe in any case that the old play had thus much plot development, for back of it there lies a source from remote antiquity already highly developed. There was a Hamlet-saga alluded to in Scandanavian literature at least as early as the tenth century. Indeed there is a great body of critical writing devoted to Hamlet as the story appeared long before the sixteenth century.[1] Saxo Grammaticus wrote between 1180 and 1208 his *Historia Danica*. In this, like Geoffrey of Monmouth in England, he gathered up legends and traditions and made them into a connected history. In his third and fourth books he gives us the history of Amlethus, or Hamlet. Horwendil, the father of Hamlet, is murdered by his brother Fengo, who marries Horwendil's wife Gerutha. Hamlet pretends to be foolish in order to secure revenge, but his folly is the mask of an almost superhuman cunning. A woman is put in his way in order that he may betray his true state of mind through love of her, but he is too shrewd to give himself away. He has an interview with his mother, also

[1] I. Gollancz, *The Sources of "Hamlet,"* London, 1926; Josef Schick, *Corpus Hamleticum*, Berlin, 1912; Kemp Malone, *The Literary History of "Hamlet,"* Heidelberg, 1923; Oliver Elton, "On Saxo's Hamlet," Appendix to *The First Nine Books of the Danish History of Saxo Grammaticus*, London, 1894.

planned to make him betray himself, and during the interview kills an eavesdropper who is covered with a quilt. Fengo sends Hamlet to England bearing a letter to the English king by the terms of which Hamlet is to be put to death. He has with him two companions. He alters the letter, inserting their names, and they suffer death in his stead. He returns to Denmark, sets fire to the hall, slays his uncle and all his courtiers, makes a speech to the people, and ascends the throne. The story has a long sequel, which does not appear in the play. Hamlet returns to England, marries two different wives, and by the second of them is betrayed to death. There is no Laertes, no Fortinbras, no duel, no ghost, no play-within-a-play. Thomas Kyd could have invented these things, for they were all well within the range of his technique. Hamlet is an heroic figure in Saxo, who saw in him a marvelous combination of wit and bravery. Saxo probably reinforced the story from that of Lucius Junius Brutus in Roman legendary history; but it is notable that Hamlet was interesting to Saxo for his wit and his bravery and to this very day, these qualities do much to explain the popularity of the character. Saxo's story was freely translated into French by Belleforest and included in his *Histoires Tragiques* (1570), a book which Shakespeare must have known. Those who have doubted Shakespeare's ability to read French have thought that Shakespeare worked solely from an old play, or used an English translation of Belleforest's story. Such a translation was issued in 1608 by Thomas Pavier with the title *The Hystorie of Hamblet*, but that publication draws certain details from the play and seems rather to have been occasioned by its popularity than to have been its source.

Summary It is hazardous to express opinions on questions on which there is such fundamental disagreement as on those of the date and sources of *Hamlet*, and any opinion here given must be understood as subject to doubts. It might, however, be helpful to the student to say that the author believes (1) that Thomas Kyd about 1589 wrote a play, now lost, on the Hamlet story as told by Belleforest, (2) that Kyd's play survives in a degenerated form in the German *Der bestrafte Bruder-mord*, (3) that Q_1 is a badly garbled stage version of Shakespeare's first play on the subject, which he probably wrote about 1598-1601, and (4) that Q_2 is his final revision, made in 1603-4.

Difficulties of the story We have seen that the old play had a reputation for noise and fury and that the story was crude and savage. Of it Shakespeare has made the subtlest and most refined of all his works. The bloodshed is still there. Fortinbras exclaims about the slaughter at the end,

> Such a sight as this
> Becomes the field, but here shows much amiss.

Hamlet's deeds are full of the old ferocity, although there is always a slight shock connected with having it pointed out. He treats Ophelia as if she were the decoy for an ambush of murderous villains, although to us she is palpably innocent. He refrains from killing the king at his prayers, because he is not content with killing his body, but wishes that

> his soul may be as damn'd and black
> As hell, whereto it goes.

He stabs Polonius with the frank but rather cruel explanation,

> Thou wretched, rash, intruding fool, farewell!
> I took thee for thy better.

He sends Rosencrantz and Guildenstern to their death in England with no compunction; and he shows a lion's courage in the last act in carrying through his revenge and in wresting as he dies the cup from the hand of Horatio:

> Give me the cup; let go; by heaven, I'll have't.

But how different is the total impression made by this character and this play from that of the source! This difference of impression constitutes the problem of *Hamlet* criticism. It was characteristic of Shakespeare that, when he wrote a revenge play, he should write it in an original way; for, although he followed the fashion of his time, he did not follow it in the way of common men. There were difficulties in the story when he undertook it, which the refinements he wrought in it rather increased than les-

sened. To have had the king surrounded by an armed guard, so that access to his person was impossible without finesse, would have made Hamlet's pretense of insanity plausible. It was so in Saxo and Belleforest and we may believe also in some measure in Kyd, since guards are mentioned in *Fratricide Punished*, but it apparently did not suit Shakespeare to write a tragedy in which the tragic obstacles were physical. Thus Hamlet's delay is unmotivated, since when the ghost appears and its mandate is accepted, there is no obstacle to serve as an excuse for delay. Shakespeare has also subordinated the revenge motive, as if he could not have his ghost crying out, "Blood is a beggar" and "Hamlet, revenge." And, although we may admit readily with Mr. Corbin that the Elizabethan audience was capable of regarding madness as comic and did have it so presented before them, possibly to some extent in the old *Hamlet*, we cannot but think that Shakespeare has put also this idea into the background.[1]

Romantic interpretation It is the convention of revenge tragedies that the hero often reminds himself of his duty to the dead, or is reminded of it by somebody else. Sometimes the jealous ghost reappears to urge the hero on in his task. *Hamlet* has this feature in a no more marked way, however, than has *The Spanish Tragedy* and other plays of the type. Hamlet is presented as a solitary figure who often reminds himself in his soliloquies of his duty; once the ghost comes back to remind him. Hamlet even soundly abuses himself for his delay; but, as Professor Stoll points out, it is largely a matter of reminding himself and spurring himself on and is not a matter of self-distrust, as if he doubted his ability to carry out the filial task of killing his father's murderer; two of Hamlet's emphatic soliloquies result in his starting off with new vim (II, ii, 575-634; IV, iv, 32-66) toward his goal, the one culminating in the play by which he detects the king's guilt, and the other in his escape from the trap to slay him in England and ultimately in the execution of revenge. No critic seems to have noticed that there was anything wrong

[1] John Corbin, *The Elizabethan Hamlet*, London, 1895.

with Hamlet's will, his power to act, until the period of the Romantic movement; then by reconceiving the situation and by making the most of his self-reproaches, the critics gave us a new Hamlet. What they did was to forget that Hamlet was a character in a play and that the play was to go on for five acts. They made of him a man in the ordinary world with a task before him which he lacked the ability to carry out. This romantic conception has led to a sort of criticism which many men have rejoiced in. They have given Hamlet a psychology which would account for him if they were in his place. On this assumption critics have written eloquently and enriched the world with new thoughts on the nature of voluntary action. They have found motives for Hamlet's inaction and for his actions which Shakespeare never dreamed of, made of Hamlet a type of whole races, and have found a Hamlet in every human soul. There is no objection to this if one only knows what one is doing; but no one can surpass the original consistency of Shakespeare's Danish prince. There are, however, great modern names on the side of romantic interpretation. Goethe found the play representative of "the effects of a great action laid upon a soul unfit for the performance of it—an oak tree planted in a costly jar." Coleridge saw in Hamlet "an overbalance in the contemplative faculty, one who vacillates from sensibility, and procrastinates from thought, and loses the power of action in the energy of resolve." Some critics now offer criticisms more objective; but in general the world has taken Hamlet to its heart and made of him its representative both in vacillation and in ultimate nobility. Nor would one say that they are altogether wrong; but it is they and not Shakespeare who have conceived the tale in this way.

Hamlet's resolution   When Shakespeare's characters make up their minds, it is surprising how vigorously they act. They do not always have a plan. In fact his villains, like Iago and Richard III, are purely opportunist, merely taking advantage of what turns up. Hamlet, after his soliloquy in the fourth act, shows a quiet steadiness and determination which does not desert him. It is as if the occasion of his delay were past, as, to be sure, with the

approach of the fifth act, it is. It is only frankness to say, however, that Shakespeare has softened the outline of the revenge plot without meaning to destroy the essential heroism of his avenger. He has made him melancholy and has recognized that like all tragic heroes he is under a malignant star. That is probably the correct interpretation of his lines from which Goethe starts:

> The time is out of joint: O cursed spite,
> That ever I was born to set it right!

One must also feel the softening of mood which comes from contemplative richness and makes the play forever suggestive of the deepest human passion and the broadest human wisdom.

Stage history   The anonymous *A Funeral Elegy on the Death of the famous Actor, Richard Burbage* connects him with the parts of Hamlet, Othello, and King Lear. This is borne out by other traditions, and there is no doubt that Burbage was the first great Hamlet. Nicholas Rowe, Shakespeare's first editor, states (1709) that "the top of his [Shakespeare's] performance was the Ghost in his own *Hamlet.*" After the Restoration *Hamlet* fell into excellent hands. Thomas Betterton appeared in the play in D'Avenant's (the Duke of York's) company at the new theater in Lincoln's Inn Fields on August 24, 1661, and thenceforward for many years helped by his greatness as an actor to secure the vogue of *Hamlet* through the succeeding centuries and to save the play from mutilation. "I never," says Colley Cibber, "heard a line in tragedy come from Betterton, wherein my judgment, my ear, and my imagination were not fully satisfied." It is said that Betterton was instructed in playing the part of Hamlet by D'Avenant, who remembered the playing of Joseph Taylor, an actor in Shakespeare's company before the closing of the theaters in 1642. There is thus a continuity in theatrical tradition in the acting of *Hamlet.* David Garrick was famous as Hamlet, though his version was rather badly garbled in the fifth act. Readers of *Tom Jones* will remember the visit of Jones and Partridge to the playhouse (Bk. XVI, ch. v) and Partridge's contempt for the naturalness of Garrick: "I am sure, if I had seen a ghost, I should have looked in the very same manner and done just as he did." John Philip Kemble continued the Garrick tradition into the nineteenth century, when there occurred a famous rivalry between him and his younger contemporary Edmund Kean, Kemble acting the part with evenness of tone and dignity of bearing and Kean anticipating the passionate eccentricity with which we are familiar on the modern stage. Macready and Phelps, both well-known in the part of Hamlet, continued the older tradition, while Booth and Irving followed the methods of Kean. Forbes-Robertson's *Hamlet* was a combination of the two styles; it had beauty and dignity and, at the same time, naturalness and wit. Kean, Irving (with Ellen Terry as Ophelia), and Forbes-Robertson all made tours to America, and the great American Hamlet, Edwin Booth, played successfully in Europe. After about 1900 Mr. E. H. Sothern (later with Miss Julia Marlowe as Ophelia) played *Hamlet* frequently in America, as did Mr. Robert Mantell. *Hamlet* stays on the stage. It is possibly in its own appeal the greatest of stage plays, and to act the part of Hamlet successfully has been, and is, the goal of tragic actors. The playing of *Hamlet* with the actors wearing modern clothes was an interesting novelty of the season 1925-6 in London and New York, there being almost general testimony to the effect that the play lost little or none of its charm when so presented.

An annotated edition of *Hamlet* is printed on pages 735-794 of this volume.

OTHELLO

Publication A quarto edition of *Othello* came out in 1622, the year before the issue of the play among "the Tragedies" in the First Folio. It bore the following title-page:

THE Tragœdy of Othello, The Moore of Venice. *As it hath beene diuerse times acted at the* Globe, and at the Black Friers, by *his Maiesties Seruants. Written by* VVilliam Shakespeare. *LONDON,* Printed by *N. O.* for *Thomas Walkley,* and are to be sold at his shop, at the Eagle and Child, in Brittans Bursse. 1622.

Walkley, who had entered the play in the Stationers' Register on October 6, 1621, supplies a short preface, "The Stationer to the Reader," which contains nothing of interest except that "the Authors name is sufficient to vent his worke." The quarto is a good text, probably a playhouse copy, but was not followed by the Folio editors, whose version is about 160 lines longer. The quarto is usually regarded as having been cut from it for acting, but in point of fact, the Folio is a revision of the quarto and is the later, longer text of the two. A second quarto (1630) was printed from the first and a third (1655) from the second.

Date *Othello* is dated with a good deal of unanimity in the year 1604. Malone stated that it was acted that year. He had evidently seen an entry in the account books of the Revels Office, printed later by Peter Cunningham (1842), but subsequently long regarded as a forgery, since the leaf containing the entry had been torn out of its proper place. It was left for Mr. Ernest Law, who subjected the entry to careful tests and to the opinions of handwriting experts, to prove it genuine and to clear the name of the unfortunate Cunningham from the charge of forgery.[1] The entry in question is a curious one, showing payments to the King's Majesty's players on Hallowmas Day (November 1), 1604, for "a play in the Banketinge house att Whitehall called The Moore of Venis." On the Sunday following was presented *The Merry Wives of Windsor;* on St. Stephen's day, *Measure for Measure;* on Innocent's night, "The plaie of Errors," the last two mentioned being attributed to "Shaxberd." General considerations of style and technique would lead one to think that *Othello* must have been a new play at that time. The first quarto seems to reflect the early stage of the play in its retention in the text of oaths which, in accordance with the statute of 1606 against the use of the name of God profanely in plays, have been carefully expunged from the folio text. Almost no other considerations affecting the question of date have ever been urged.

Source *Othello* is one of the very few plays of Shakespeare for which no dramatic source is known or suspected. He seems to have worked directly from a novel in a popular collection of Giraldi

[1] *Some Supposed Shakespeare Forgeries,* London, 1911; *More about Shakespeare Forgeries,* London, 1913. But see S. A. Tannenbaum, *Shakespeare Forgeries in the Revels Accounts,* New York, 1928.

Cinthio's *Hecatommithi* (1565).[1] No translation of this story is known to have been made into English, so that Shakespeare must have worked from the Italian, or from the French translation of 1584. If in *Julius Cæsar* and elsewhere Shakespeare showed a disposition to be faithful to good sources, he here at least shows an equal disposition to change bad ones. Such a transmutation of base metal into gold as he effects in Giraldi's tale is hardly to be found in the study of literary history. In Giraldi's version we find in the service of Venice a warlike Moor who has married, in spite of the opposition of her relatives, a lovely Venetian lady named Disdemona. She had fallen in love with him not from erring fancy but for his noble qualities. They lived together in Venice happily until the Moor was sent to military command at Cyprus. Disdemona insisted on accompanying him; he took also his ensign, an intriguing scoundrel, very handsome, a boaster, and a coward. The ensign fell in love with Disdemona, who rejected his advances because of her love for her husband. The ensign's love was turned to hatred so that he formed a plot to ruin her by accusing her of infidelity to her husband. A captain in Othello's command was the object of the ensign's malignity. This captain soon afterwards struck and wounded a sentry and was discharged from his command. Disdemona interceded for him, a fact that gave the ensign a chance to further his plot. He aroused the Moor to jealous fury by having him see, but not overhear, a conversation with the captain, which the Moor wrongly supposed was about the captain's relations with Disdemona, and finally confirmed the Moor's suspicions by showing in the possession of a lady connected with the captain a handkerchief of special beauty which the ensign had caused to be stolen from Disdemona and had left on the captain's bed. The instrument for this theft was the ensign's own child, and almost the most striking scene in the tale is the picture of Disdemona fondling the child as it steals away the handkerchief.

At the Moor's request the ensign promised to kill the captain, wounded him, and then joined the Moor in Disdemona's chamber where they beat her to death "with a stocking filled with sand." The Moor diverted suspicion from himself by pulling down the ceiling of the room and giving it out that the lady had been killed by a falling beam. He was, however, so filled with remorse that he turned on the ensign, degraded him, and drove him out of his service. The ensign revealed the crime to the captain, who made it known to the Venetian senate. The Moor was arrested, tortured, tried, and banished, and later was slain by Disdemona's relatives. Later also, and for another cause, the ensign was put to the torture and died from the effects. No names are used except that of Disdemona. Steevens suggested that the name of Othello comes from Reynold's *God's Revenge against Adultery*, where there is mention of "Othello, an old German soldier." Giraldi's story is thought to be connected with a certain Venetian nobleman, Christopher Moro, commandant in Cyprus, who returned to Venice in 1508 after having lost his wife. The tale was at any rate thought of as practically contemporary, and the play retains from its source a realistic manner and atmosphere not elsewhere found in Shakespeare's tragedies. Professor Parrott makes the interesting suggestion that Othello reflects the vogue of the domestic tragedy, pointing out that Heywood's *A Woman Killed with Kindness* belongs to the year 1603.[2] As Shakespeare first wrote *Othello* he apparently followed Giraldi's story in providing Cassio (Giraldi's Captain) with both a wife and a mistress. Later he decided on what are sufficiently obvious grounds to dispense with the wife as unnecessary or in the way and proceeded to obliterate the part. Some of it he gave to Bianca, but not every trace of the first version is removed from the play; as, for example, Iago's otherwise inexplicable verse about Cassio (I, i, 21):

A fellow almost damn'd in a fair wife

and Bianca's words, possibly originally written for Cassio's wife (V, i, 122-3):

[1]For other suggestions as to sources see A. H. Krappe, "The Source of *Othello*, Act III, sc. ii, ll. 157-161," *Modern Language Review*, XIII, 44-45, and Lillian Winstanley "*Othello*" as the Tragedy of Italy, London, 1924.

[2]T. M. Parrott, *Othello*, Tudor Shakespeare, Introduction.

I am no strumpet; but of life as honest
As you that thus abuse me.

The first quarto shows bibliographical evidences of this revision in interruption of meter and in mislining of verse.

The plot The plot of *Othello* is thus an intrigue of a conventional character; that is, it depends for its acceptance by the audience on the granting of belief by them that such a thing might occur. Professor Stoll has argued that the issue in *Othello* rests on the convention of "the calumniator believed,"[1] and has argued strongly against the widely current views of those who would find in Othello, when he falls a victim to Iago's treachery, a rational psychology in the modern sense, whether this is done by supposing that in spite of Othello's statement that he was "not easily jealous," he had a predisposition to jealousy, or that he was blinded by passion; or indeed that Othello was intended to be so stupid as to be taken in by Iago, if we are to suppose him to be at the same time a wise statesman, an experienced soldier, and a master among men. Shakespeare obviously presents the figure of a noble, simple, sensible, efficient man suddenly assailed and overthrown by the base passion of jealousy, and depicts, as almost nowhere else in literature, the power and pathos of such a figure. He asks his audience to believe, moreover, as in all conscience it must be believed of such a man, that he was not prone to jealousy. Against Othello he pits a character especially conceived to win our artistic belief that he might delude Othello even in such a matter as the treason of his wife and his best friend. Of course an Othello in real life—we have here to do not with real life but with a play—would be, by his very character and experience, particularly likely to have been loyal and just to his wife and his best friend, to have come to an understanding with his precious wife and heard her story if any such suspicion arose, and since he was a man of arms, to have had it out with Cassio sword to sword. Iago is represented as a man of perfect reputation; not even his own wife knows his concealed diabolical nature. The whole play rings with the words, "honest

[1] E. E. Stoll, *Othello: an Historical and Comparative Study*, Minneapolis, 1915.

Iago." If we go to life, instead of remaining within the ample and sufficient confines of art, we have to think it unlikely, to say the least, that such a man could have such a reputation, that he could so easily take in his dupe Roderigo, much less his shrewd wife Emilia, or his manly and experienced commander. Shakespeare has said, with the sensationalism of his time, "This marvelous, this unusual, this difficult thing you shall see done," and we must as readers and students simply grant him, let us say once more, "that willing suspension of disbelief for the moment which constitutes poetic faith." He compels us to do this willy-nilly when we see the play. The fact is that Othello, though not easily jealous or at all likely to be made jealous by the means employed, is furiously jealous. Desdemona and Cassio remain silent under the exigencies of the plot when it would have been altogether more natural for them to speak. Emilia, although she knows her husband has the handkerchief, fails to say anything about it even when she sees that its loss is occasioning trouble to her beloved mistress. These are defects in the story, if you will, but they are not necessarily defects in the play; they are the hard terms of the bond. It may certainly be said that, partly because of the close limits of his task, as well as by the nature of his rather sordid story of domestic intrigue, Shakespeare has gone further here in refined dramatic skill, in poetry of inexhaustible truth and beauty, and in the expression of the depths of human passion, than perhaps in any other play.

Workmanship On the stage Shakespeare's play asks no favors of anybody. *Othello* is even true to the psychology of the passions as Shakespeare knew it. Shakespeare was not a psychologist, but it reinforces his plausibility to observe that in his conception the passions were savage instincts in every human soul, and no character was proof against them. He knew that men of tragic possibilities are prone to passion. It is Hamlet who says to Horatio (III, ii, 76-9):

Give me that man
That is not passion's slave, and I will wear him
In my heart's core, ay, in my heart of heart,
As I do thee.

The passions were a chief source of danger, for they might seize upon a man and shove reason from its seat. The maddening Lear cries out for patience; Iago bids Othello be patient at the very moment when the suggestion of a loss of self-control will hasten that loss. When the irascible passions get control, excess, fury, and madness result. Iago, after his words about "trifles light as air," even gives away his psychological method when he says (III, iii, 325-9):

The Moor already changes with my poison:
Dangerous conceits are, in their natures, poisons,
Which at the first are scarce found to distaste,
But with a little act upon the blood,
Burn like the mines of sulphur.

These "dangerous conceits," images of Desdemona's wickedness and Othello's disgrace, are the means by which Iago keeps Othello's passions all agog, and prevents the better, reasonable nature of the Moor from assuming its control. By these means Othello's conduct and situation are made plausible, so that the great first conception of Othello remains throughout, however much it may be shaken. It appears in his grief: "O, Iago, the pity of it, Iago!" And again in his moving reminiscences (III, iii, 348-54):

Farewell the tranquil mind! farewell content!
Farewell the plumed troop, and the big wars,
That make ambition virtue! O, farewell!
Farewell the neighing steed, and the shrill trump,
The spirit-stirring drum, the ear-piercing fife,
The royal banner, and all quality,
Pride, pomp and circumstance of glorious war!

It asserts itself again gloriously at the end of the play in the hero's full awareness of the nature of his deed and in his death. His soldiership goes with him even in his fury, in the form of a blunt and immediate habit of acting on his resolution. In fact Shakespeare never forgets the fundamental conception of his character.

Iago On Iago, the instrument of Othello's ruin, Shakespeare has lavished a wealth of dramatic skill. Iago's subtlety and cleverness are such as to lead many critics to think that Othello's actions are completely accounted for by the supreme diabolism of his adversary. That this is sufficient for the stage no one who has seen a great Iago can ever seriously call in question; as for example, "the plausible cunning and indescribable malignity of Edwin Booth" in the character of Iago. To what extent Shakespeare regarded Iago as a demon in human form, having no motive and needing none, since he had chosen evil as his good, has long been in debate. The Renaissance could conceive, better than we, of complete human depravity. It thought of historical characters, like Richard III and Cesare Borgia, as all bad. This doctrine was derived wrongly from Machiavelli's *Prince*. Machiavelli himself became the symbol of such human diabolism.[1] Iago has the outlook and the main traits of the Machiavel, though certainly he is more individualized than Richard III and Edmund in *Lear*. Nevertheless, Iago has personal motives which he expresses more than once, and it is doubtful if their force has been realized since Coleridge's phrase about "the motive hunting of a motiveless malignity" became current. Iago is a soldier of the mercenary type familiar to the Renaissance. He has learned his soldiership in the field and has all of the hatred of the theoretical soldier which those so trained often acquire; he has also the professional soldier's belief in the ultimate justice of promotion by seniority, "old gradation," as he calls it. He has worked hard, or at least has kept his service record unspotted, in order that he may achieve promotion, and it has been denied him on what to him are contemptible and infuriating terms. He has even tried the use of influence to secure advancement (I, i, 8-17):

Three great ones of the city,
In personal suit to make me his lieutenant,
Off-capp'd to him: and, by the faith of man,
I know my price, I am worth no worse a place:
But he, as loving his own pride and purposes,
Evades them, with a bombast circumstance
Horribly stuff'd with epithets of war;
And, in conclusion,
Nonsuits my mediators; for, 'Certes,' says he,
'I have already chose my officer.'

Iago shows all the way through complete presence of mind and self-control, as if he had been conceived of as having undergone the most rigorous military discipline.

[1] E. S. Meyer, *Machiavelli and the Elizabethan Drama*, Weimar, 1897.

These traits fit in with his opportunism, his pride of intellect, and his skill; he does not plan far ahead, but lives, soldier-like, from task to task and from day to day. As for the rumors of relations between Othello and Emilia, which he himself does not believe and yet determines to avenge, his words seem to imply that "mere suspicion in that kind," since it touches a man's reputation abroad, must be treated as if it were the truth. Iago is a man very tender of his reputation. Professor Parrott thus states this view:

This motive has a twofold aspect: on the one hand his dominating sense of superiority to his fellows, on the other his craving to demonstrate this superiority by making them his puppets. Regarded in this light, Iago's motives appear perfectly adequate to account for his inception of the plot. Wounded pride and lust of power are not commonly regarded as weak impulses to action. It must be remembered, moreover, that Iago enters upon this intrigue without realizing its full and fatal consequences. There is not a hint that he originally contemplated the double murder of Cassio and Desdemona. Apparently all that he anticipated was such action on the part of Othello as should secure his own immediate ends. . . . Too much has been written on the superhuman intellect of Iago. It is plain, I think, to any one who regards the play as a whole, that Iago, with all his gifts, was a limited and unimaginative intelligence. As a soldier he must have been a brilliant tactician, but a wretched strategist.[1]

Stage history Few Shakespearean plays have more brilliant stage histories than *Othello*. The effectiveness of the style of the tragedy, its almost unique reliance on the art of the actor, and the fact that it has two great parts set over against each other as protagonist and antagonist are the elements of its greatness as a stage play. Othello was Burbage's part, and he was succeeded in the rôle in Shakespeare's company by Field. Joseph Taylor played Iago. There are an unusual number of performances of *Othello* recorded in the years preceding the closing of the theaters in 1642, and the play was one of the first revived after the Restoration. Pepys, the diarist, saw it with Burt in the title rôle at the Cockpit on October 11, 1660. Malone states that Desdemona was the first of Shakespeare's female parts

[1]*Othello*, Tudor Shakespeare, Introduction, pp. xviii-xix.

to be played by a woman. Betterton was splendid as Othello, and, singularly enough, James Quin, the famous Falstaff, was popular in the part. Garrick was relatively unsuccessful as Othello, and one thinks that he should have essayed the rôle of Iago instead. In 1785 Mrs. Siddons played Desdemona to her brother John Philip Kemble's Othello at Drury Lane Theater in London. Edmund Kean was apparently transcendent as Othello, and his praises ring through all the criticism of the time. Two occasions in his acting of the part may be worth mentioning. When he visited America in 1826 he played Othello opposite the Iago of the brilliant young actor Edwin Forrest, later himself famous as Othello. Three weeks before Kean's death he broke down in mortal illness on the stage while playing Othello with his son Charles Kean as Iago. Several great occasions in the playing of *Othello* are connected with the career of Edwin Booth, who played both Othello and Iago supremely well and was able to alternate the two parts. In 1881 Booth and Irving, with Ellen Terry as Desdemona, played an engagement at the Lyceum Theater in London and frequently exchanged the two principal parts. In 1886 Booth played Iago at the Academy of Music in New York to the Othello of the illustrious Italian actor Salvini. Tree, Forbes-Robertson, and William Faversham have revived *Othello* during the present century.

An annotated edition of *Othello* is printed on pages 795-844 of this volume.

KING LEAR

Publication On November 26, 1607, there was properly entered in the Stationers' Register by Nathaniel Butter and John Busby *A Booke called Master William Shakespeare his historye of Kinge Lear, as yt was played before the Kinges maiestie at Whitehall vppon Sainct Stephens night at Christmas Last, by his maieties servantes playinge vsually at the Globe on the Banksyde.* The next year was issued Q₁, with the title-page:

M. William Shak-speare: *HIS* True Chronicle Historie of the life and death of King LEAR and his three Daughters. *With the vnfortunate life of* Edgar, *sonne* and heire to the Earle of Gloster, and his sullen and assumed humor of TOM of

Bedlam: *As it was played before the Kings Maiestie at Whitehall vpon S.* Stephans *night in Christmas Hollidayes.* By his Maiesties Seruants playing vsually at the Gloabe on the Bancke-side. *LONDON,* Printed for *Nathaniel Butter,* and are to be sold at his shop in *Pauls* Church-yard at the signe of the Pide Bull neere St. *Austins* Gate. 1608.

How Butter and Busby, who were not very reputable printers, were able to make this apparently authorized issue is not clear. They seem to have printed from a copy which was particularly illegible. Some of the sheets were corrected after others had been printed off, so that it follows that in different copies of the same edition there are both corrected and uncorrected sheets. Mr. Pollard thinks that the text of the play in the First Folio was set up from a copy of this quarto with, however, the correction from a manuscript of certain sheets which were present in the playhouse quarto in the uncorrected form.[1] It is usually thought, however, that the Folio editors discarded the quarto in favor of an independent manuscript text in their own possession, since their text omits about three hundred lines contained in the quarto and adds over a hundred not found in the quarto. The correct explanation of the relation of the quarto and the Folio versions is probably this: Shakespeare's manuscript, having been revised by him and thereby rendered somewhat illegible, was copied. The revised manuscript got into the hands of the printers and was issued as the quarto. The clean copy stayed in the playhouse, underwent further alteration, and became ultimately the text of the play in the Folio. There exists another quarto also dated 1608, but really printed in 1619 by Pavier when he was intending to issue a collection of Shakespeare's plays; for some reason, not fully known, he gave this and the quartos of several other plays fictitious dates.

Date   The entry quoted from the Stationers' Register shows that *King Lear* was written before December 26, St. Stephen's day, 1606. The publication of Harsnet's *Declaration of Popish Impostures* in 1603 fixes a date earlier than which it could not have been written, since from that book Shakespeare drew the names of Edgar's fiends and other slight matters. One cir-

cumstance may fix the date still more closely by giving an indication of the time when his tragedy began to make a stir as a popular play. An anonymous play, *The True Chronicle History of King Leir, and his three daughters, Gonorill, Ragan, and Cordella,* was fished up, entered in the Stationers' Register, and published in 1605. It had already been entered in the Stationers' Register in 1594, but apparently not published. The entry of 1605 (May 8) speaks of the book as "the Tragicall historie of king Leir, etc." The play is not a tragedy and the way it is described, as well as the fact of its publication, may very well be due to the reputation of Shakespeare's play. The year 1605 is thus indicated as the year when Shakespeare's play was staged. *King Lear* is in Shakespeare's late, highly condensed style, so that internal evidence would also place it in the very middle of his tragical period.

Sources   For his sources Shakespeare went not only to *King Leir,* based on Holinshed, but to Holinshed himself, to *The Mirror for Magistrates,* to the *Faerie Queene,* and possibly to Warner's *Albion's England.* The plot of Gloucester and his sons, which stands as a parallel to the Lear story, he found in Sidney's *Arcadia.*[2] At the basis of the main story lies a folk tale about a love test set by a father for his three daughters, the youngest of whom replies too frankly to suit the jealous father, is disinherited, but turns out finally to be the only daughter whose filial piety was sincere. Geoffrey of Monmouth had placed this story in *Historia Regum Britonum,* written about 1135, and it had become, in poems and chronicles, a regular part of the history of **England.** Mr. Perrett shows that Shakespeare consulted Geoffrey himself; but when the full list of sources including Geoffrey is considered, one has little enough of *King Lear* as we know it.[3] The *Arcadia* is, however, a rich and varied work, which served as an important source of ideas as well as events. The story of King Lear did not originally have a tragic ending, since by the intervention of the French king Lear was restored to his throne and reigned

---

[1] *Folios and Quartos,* p. 53.

[2] Wilfred Perrett, *The Story of King Lear,* Berlin, 1904.
[3] Madeleine Doran, "Elements in the Composition of *King Lear,*" *Studies in Philology,* XXX, 34-58.

until his death. Cordelia's end was tragic, but her misfortune did not come until after the death of Lear when she was dethroned and murdered by her wicked nephews. In the original story Lear does not give his whole kingdom away, but retains part of it. He is not so much overthrown by his daughters as by his sons-in-law, who rebel against him to get his kingdom. He goes to France for aid and gets it. There is no trace in the *Arcadia* of the nefarious intrigue between Edmund and the daughters of Lear, nor of the repentance of the wicked brother; so that these matters are also original with Shakespeare. A happy ending was restored to the play during the Restoration by Nahum Tate and long held the modern stage. Of this change Charles Lamb said:

A happy ending!—as if the living martyrdom that Lear has gone through, the flaying of his feelings alive, did not make a fair dismissal from the stage of life the only decorous thing for him.

Political backgrounds Critics have found in Shakespeare's changes and additions justification and enrichment of the theme; but so to accept the masterpiece is not the full story, and it detracts nothing from Shakespeare's art to discover whence his thoughts, feelings, and moral judgments may in some measure have come. Miss Winstanley has published a series of studies in which she attempts to show that *Hamlet, Macbeth,* and *King Lear* reflect immediately the matters of most absorbing political interest to Englishmen in the early years of the reign of James I.[1] Without accepting her entire list of multifarious parallels between the three tragedies and state papers, Huguenot memoirs, accounts of the Gunpowder Plot, and histories, memorials, and letters of Mary Queen of Scots, with accounts of current French politics and the massacre of St. Bartholomew, or without accepting her general conclusion that Shakespeare meant his tragedies as vast allegories of political import,

one may nevertheless admit that she has opened up a background of plot, intrigue, fear, murder, and violence which undoubtedly did occupy the minds of the men of this time, and that this background is one which Shakespeare in his great tragedies reflected. She thinks that Lear was meant to typify both Darnley, the father of James I, and Coligny, the victim of Catharine de Medici; that the daughters represent Queen Mary; that Oswald is Rizzio, and that Edmund stands for Bothwell. These parallels in violence, if not in event, reveal an insight into royal intrigue and crime, into the state of a kingdom such as that of Scotland or France at such a period, and, particularly, into the world-scheme according to which Shakespeare and the men of his time saw order grow out of, or lapse back into, chaos.

Ethical interpretation Nature in Renaissance thinking is power, growth, generation. Left alone, it is chaos; combed, subdued, and directed by man's law and God's law, it is civilization and order. A crime against nature is the most heinous of all crimes. Consider the following statement of the doctrine in Wilson's *Arte of Rhetorique* and its applicability to *King Lear:*[2]

. . . the wisdome of Princes, and the feare of Gods threate, which was vttered by his worde, forced men by a lawe, both to allowe things confirmed by nature, and to beare with old custome, or els they should not onely suffer in body temporall punishment, but also lose their soules for euer. Nature is a right that phantasie hath not framed, but God hath graffed and giuen man power thereunto, whereof these are deriued:

Religion, and acknowledging of God.
Naturall loue to our children, and other.
Thankfulnesse to all men.
Stoutnesse, both to withstand and reuenge.
Reuerence to the superior.
Assured and constaunt trueth in things.

When Lear gives over the sovereignty of his kingdom to the wicked, chaos comes again. The voice of the Fool, no less than the voice of the wise Kent, a practical voice, rings out through the earlier part of the play to make clear this situation. Point by point the play presents, to the accompaniment of wars and the rebellion of subjects, evidences

[1]Lillian Winstanley, *Hamlet and the Scottish Succession,* Cambridge, 1921; *Macbeth, King Lear, and Contemporary History,* Cambridge, 1922. See also various writings on the political use of the stage: Richard Simpson, New Sh. Soc. 1874, pp. 371 ff., 396 ff.; T. S. Graves, *Modern Philology,* IX, 545 ff.; XIV, 525 ff.; *Anglia,* XXXVIII, 137 ff.; R. W. Bond, edition of Lyly's works; Feuillerat, *John Lyly,* London, 1910; Edith Rickert, *Modern Philology,* XXI, 53-87, 133-154.

[2] *Wilson's Arte of Rhetorique,* edited by G. H. Mair, Oxford, 1909, p. 32.

of the violation of natural fundamentals: the sympathetic agony of nature, portents, extremes in cruelty, beggary, and insanity. The cruelty and tyranny of Regan and Goneril and the wickedness of Edmund violate "the naturall loue to our children, and other." Edmund, himself under "the plague of custom" because of his illegitimacy, declares that nature (that is, chaotic nature) is his goddess: "Now, gods, stand up for bastards!" (I, ii, 1-22). The royal state of the king, the embodiment of authority and honor, is lost, and the loyal service of Kent is rejected in favor of the base flattery of Oswald (II, ii); thus is the "reuerence to the superior" put to naught. As to thankfulness to all men, Lear has "given all," and ingratitude, the "marble-hearted fiend," has established itself in the family and the kingdom. Kent and Cordelia, who stand for "assured and constaunt trueth in things," are banished and disgraced. Even "stoutnesse, both to withstand and reuenge," is not forgotten in the conduct of Edgar and the kindliness of Lear (II, iv, 275-81).

> You see me here, you gods, a poor old man,
> As full of grief as age; wretched in both!
> If it be you that stir these daughters' hearts
> Against their father, fool me not so much
> To bear it tamely; touch me with noble anger,
> And let not women's weapons, water-drops,
> Stain my man's cheeks!

Finally, "religion, and acknowledging of God" are not forgotten in the moral system of this play. Lear is a pagan, close to nature, so that the stars and the gods are never off his lips. The faith of the good men of the play is a religious faith, though pagan, like that of Albany when he hears of the death of Cornwall (IV, ii, 78-81):

> This shows you are above,
> You justicers, that these our nether crimes
> So speedily can venge!

Edmund, on the other hand, scorning the heavenly influence of the stars, is obviously an infidel (I, ii, 128-145). King Lear, then, pictures, in the tragedy of a king, who is also kingship, and of a father, who is also fatherhood, the return to chaos in a kingdom and a royal family, the ruin of the centers and, therefore, of the whole body politic. This is the ultimate idea of evil in the philosophy of the Renaissance.

Stage history King Lear, possibly the greatest of Shakespeare's tragedies, has not been completely fortunate in its stage history. It is naturally supposed that the part of Lear was written for Richard Burbage. There are few, if any, traces of performance before the closing of the theaters in 1642; but the play must have been well known, for it was quickly revived after the Restoration, Betterton probably playing in Shakespeare's version. This was, however, completely superseded by Nahum Tate's adaptation (1681), which held the stage until 1838, when Macready restored the original. Garrick restored part of Shakespeare's text in the place of Tate's lines, and Kean restored Shakespeare's tragic ending; but Betterton, Garrick, Spranger Barry, Kemble, and Kean himself retained either all or part of Tate's alterations. Tate gave the tragedy a happy ending with the idea that the stage should show truth and virtue always triumphant. He banished the Fool as too indecorous for tragedy and constructed a love plot between Edgar and Cordelia resulting in their bethrothal. Lear was restored to all of his kingdom except Albany's share. When one thinks of the play in this form one wonders at the triumphs of the great tragic actors. Betterton and Garrick were famous in the part of Lear. When Kean was praised for his brilliancy in Othello, he said, "The London audience have no notion of what I can do until they see me over the dead body of Cordelia." Kean, it will be remembered, restored the tragic ending. There were also some great Lears in the nineteenth century, Samuel Phelps, John McCullough, Edwin Forrest, Edwin Booth, and Sir Henry Irving (1892). In more recent times it has been impossible to see the play except in the excellent work of Mr. Robert Mantell.

An annotated edition of King Lear is printed on pages 845-897 of this volume.

MACBETH

Publication and text Macbeth is one of the greatest of Shakespeare's plays, and, at the same time, a play for which we have one of the worst texts. Its first printing in the folio of 1623 offers a text which is thought to have been cut down for stage presentation and contaminated with the work of another man. Doubts have been expressed as to the authenticity of various passages. These doubts have reduced themselves to certainty in the case of the scene containing the long speech of Hecate and the song (III, v), a similar later speech and song (IV, i, 39-43), and the speech of the first witch in the same scene (125-132). These lines are different in style and not in harmony with Shakespeare's conception of the witches as it appears elsewhere in the play. They closely resemble the style of certain passages of Thomas Middleton's *The Witch*, dating probably after 1613; moreover, the two songs, "Come away, come away" and "Black spirits, and white," are found in Middleton's play. The Restoration adaptation of *Macbeth*, probably by Sir William D'Avenant, gives the songs in full as in *The Witch*. It is generally believed that Middleton, who was younger than Shakespeare and also wrote for the King's Company, was engaged on the occasion of some revival of *Macbeth* to adapt the play to a somewhat different form of dramatic entertainment, one in which there would be songs and dances by witches. Possibly to make room for ballet features, the precious dramatic craftsmanship of Shakespeare was cut away; so that certain passages of the text are hopelessly corrupt and obscure, certain matters of the plot are inconsistent, and the story of Macbeth's reign is told more barely and scantily than one would believe possible in the author who had just written *King Lear*.

Date Dr. Simon Forman, a quack and astrologer, had the interesting habit of visiting the theater and noting down the plots of plays which he saw "for common Pollicie"; that is, for what he might learn from them. He saw *Macbeth* on the second of April, 1610, at the Globe and gives a rather full but not very accurate summary of the plot. This cannot, however, have been the first performance. *The Puritan, or The Widow of Watling Street*, published in 1607, contains a line suggestive of Banquo's ghost: "Instead of a jester we'll have a ghost in a white sheet sit at the upper end of the table"; and the play for several reasons seems to belong to the year 1606. *Macbeth* is filled to overflowing with matters which would be agreeable to King James. Oldys, the antiquary, records a tradition

that the king wrote Shakespeare a letter. It possibly commanded him to write this play, which develops the king's royal descent from Fleance the son of Banquo, and thus from all the line of British kings back to Brute. The play also stresses the king's divine right as indicated by his possession of the royal touch to cure the king's evil, a power reasserted by James in 1605 (IV, iii, 140-159). James had been proclaimed "King of Great Britain, France, and Ireland," on October 24, 1604, and was for the next few years anxious to carry out the complete union of England and Scotland as Great Britain; hence the "twofold balls and treble sceptres" of the show of kings (IV, i, 112-121). The Porter's "farmer, that hanged himself on the expectation of plenty," (II, iii, 5) has been thought to reflect the not unusual agricultural situation of the season of 1606, when, though crops were good, prices were low; and his other allusion to the "equivocator, that could swear in both scales against either scale," has been taken pretty generally as referring to the trial of Garnet in March, 1606, for complicity in the Gunpowder Plot, which had been discovered in November, 1605. The most peculiar bit of evidence, however, is that of an entertainment presented before the king during a progress to Oxford. At the gates of St. John's College three youths, representing nymphs or sybils, or as we should say from the play, witches, prophesied the reign of Banquo's descendants and delivered orations in Latin and English. The king, as descendant of Banquo, may have been so well pleased with this testimonial to the acceptance of him as the extender of the Arthurian empire to the entire island of Britain in accordance with supernatural prophecy, that he may have desired to see the subject treated more at large. Sir E. K. Chambers suggests that *Macbeth* was produced on the occasion of the visit of the king of Denmark to England in July, 1606.[1]

Source There can be no doubt that the subject of the triumph of Banquo's offspring was recognized as one of the greatest interest to the King and to those Englishmen who were loyal to the Scottish succession, as most Englishmen were. Especially in *Macbeth* there was foreshadowed the

[1] Edition of *Macbeth*, Arden Shakespeare (Heath).

triumph of Protestantism and insular independence, since the play carried as a story the theme of the escape and survival of the royal seed when it was beset by murder, usurpation, and tyranny. For the material of this story Shakespeare went to Holinshed's *Chronicles;* in the first instance to the account of the reigns of Duncan and Macbeth, in the second, to the chronicle of King Duff. From the latter he borrowed the story of how Donwald, a man whom King Duff never suspected, murdered King Duff in the castle of Forres. Having, with the aid of his wife, drugged the two chamberlains who lay with the king, Donwald, although he greatly abhorred the deed and did it only at the instigation of his wife, induced four of his servants to cut the king's throat. When morning came, he slew the chamberlains and cleared himself of the crime by his power and authority, though not without being suspected by certain noblemen because of his over-diligence. There were great portents in the kingdom that year both of sun and moon; certain horses in Lothian ate their own flesh; and a "sparhauke" was strangled by an owl. Thirdly, from the chronicle of King Kenneth, who had murdered Malcolm Duff, is drawn the idea of a voice, which Kenneth heard as he lay in his bed at night, warning him of the sure detection of his crime, so that he was filled with dread and passed the night without any sleep. Finally, from the chronicle of King Edward the Confessor comes the account of how that saintly monarch cured the king's evil by his touch, and the story of Siward's invasion of Scotland in which he overthrew Macbeth. The chronicle of King Macbeth contains within it the story of Macduff. These Scottish chronicles were for Shakespeare a brilliant and spirited source, far better than the chronicles of English kings which he had used earlier in his career. Holinshed's compilation had drawn on the Latin of Hector Boece (1527), and to him probably is to be attributed the vividness of the narratives. Boece had drawn from Fordun, a historian of the fourteenth century.

Shakespeare's additions What then were the features which Shakespeare added to the rather detailed account he had pieced together from Holinshed? It will be observed that he treats the chronicles with great freedom, combining as he does the reigns of two different kings. Besides this great transposition Shakespeare's most important changes are the increase in importance of the part played by Lady Macbeth, the development, even beyond the superstitious chroniclers, of the supernatural element, and the addition of particular detail. Miss Winstanley argues, from an elaborate and not always convincing series of parallel passages from contemporary documents, that the play was particularly designed to please King James not only in the matter of its emphasis upon his descent from the prophetically established royal line, evident in the vision of kings and in the power of touch for the king's evil, but also in the matter of the inheritance by King James of the united crowns of England and Scotland. She shows that the murder of Darnley, the king's father, was compared by contemporary historians to the murder of King Duff. She points out numerous parallels between the murder of Duncan and the murder of Darnley and cites contemporary charges against Bothwell as being in league with the witches. She draws also reinforcing detail from contemporary accounts of the massacre of St. Bartholomew, where she compares the reluctance and remorse of Charles IX with these qualities in Macbeth, and the wicked zeal of Catharine, the queen mother, in instigating him to perpetrate the slaughter with the wicked ardor of Lady Macbeth. She finds again in Coligny a parallel for Duncan. Miss Winstanley's theory is here presented because it reveals a background of contemporary significance.

The witches Belief in witchcraft was widespread and general in the sixteenth century. King James himself was a firm believer in witchcraft and was an authority on the subject to the extent that when Reginald Scot wrote *The Discovery of Witchcraft* (1584) against the belief in witches, King James considered Scot's opinions "damnable," and wrote his *Demonologie* (1597) to confute them. It is also said that he ordered all copies of Scot's book to be burned. Scot gives a good deal of detail about sorcery, and it is usually thought that Shakespeare drew on his book for the witchlore in *Macbeth.* He knew Harsnet's *Declaration of Egregious Popish Impostures* (1603), as is shown by *King Lear.* It has long been thought with very good reason that some of the witchlore in *Macbeth* comes from accounts of various Scottish witch-trials published about 1590. Scotch witches had the power of prophecy through their master spirits and were guilty of the practices described in *Macbeth*. They raised storms, beset vessels at sea, danced ceremonial dances in threes, made witch-broth quite like that in *Macbeth*, and, particularly, sailed the sea in sieves. They were serious and dangerous creatures, and often deluded the unsuspecting by telling them partial truths. The "wierd sisters," although they are made up externally like the witches of vulgar superstition, are thought of by Holinshed as "goddesses of destiny, . . . nymphs, or feiries," who had the knowledge of prophecy. In Shakespeare they are, however, of the evil one, and not impartial like fates or norns. It is still a question to what extent Shakespeare meant that the free will of Macbeth was interfered with by "supernatural soliciting."

Holinshed's chronicle of King Macbeth has incorporated two very ancient pieces of folklore, namely, the story of the moving forest and the one of the man not born of woman. Shakespeare's use of them is exactly the same as that of Holinshed, for we are told there that Macbeth "by this prophecie put all fear out of his heart."

The greatness of *Macbeth* We may well believe that the violent events and temper of the time contribute to *Macbeth* as to *King Lear*. This is at least true in the contribution of a background in the minds of serious people, a background of pulsating interest in the questions of religion, state, royalty, and patriotism appealed to by the plays. After all, this would be only another evidence of the greatness of both plays. *Macbeth* is the play, more perhaps than any other, in which Shakespeare has been thought to challenge comparison with Æschylus. His plot is bare, free from disturbing episodes, and perfectly unified from a dramatic standpoint, having also what Sir E. K. Chambers calls "unity of the philosophic idea." The two great personages are both cast in noble mould, both consistently conceived and perfectly adjusted the one to the other. Macbeth is man yielding to temptation and plunging deeper and deeper into sin. Lady Macbeth is

woman in the nature of her ambitions (as far as one can see, largely for her husband and for social position), in her sense of the importance of tangible things and of bearing and deportment, and in her methods with her husband. Both are in a large way typical. Perhaps Macbeth, as conceived of by Elizabethan audiences, would be more immediately condemned as a villain than he is by us. Ambition to them was fundamentally a sin, and the idea of surrendering one's soul to the devil was more immediately horrible. The persons of a king and of a guest had about them an especial sanctity, and Macbeth murders his king who is also his guest. Well may he speak of

> mine eternal jewel
> Given to the common enemy of man. . . .

When Macbeth expresses the wish that

> this blow
> Might be the be-all and the end-all here,
> But here, upon this bank and shoal of time,
> We'ld jump the life to come,

he seems to place every hope upon the earthly life and to sacrifice every noble ideal and every manly virtue to a wicked ambition; but, in so doing, he does not rid himself of the fear of human justice. The element of earthly fear in his composition is large. He seems rather to be preyed upon throughout by dread of punishment, by horrible dreams, startings, and agonies, than moved by any spiritualized remorse or repentance. *Macbeth* thus becomes a drama of fear, horror, and the most perturbing passions. Elizabethan psychology understood that these perturbations must be controlled if there were to be efficient and successful actions. Lady Macbeth is better able to dominate her feelings, so that her breakdown comes only when the load has grown too heavy for her body and her will to bear. The passions were localized in Elizabethan psychology, as indeed their manifestations are, in the members of the body—in hair, hands, limbs—so that one recalls the modern theory of the emotions as arising from physical states when one hears Lady Macbeth's fiery admonitions to her husband; she fully understands that emotional control depends on bodily quiescence (III, iv, 63-67):

O, these flaws and starts,
Impostors to true fear, would well become
A woman's story at a winter's fire,
Authorized by her grandam.   Shame itself!
Why do you make such faces?

Stage history   *Macbeth*, as we have seen,
had suffered some corruption
before its publication in the First Folio of
1623, a corruption which introduced into it
an element of light opera—songs and a ballet
of witches. What had begun thus early was
carried yet further after the Restoration.
D'Avenant wrote more songs for *Macbeth*
and modified much of its condensed and
weighty English into something commonplace and flat. Betterton appeared in D'Avenant's version at the theater in Lincoln's Inn
Fields, where Pepys saw the play three times
and commended it ominously for "variety."
In 1672 Matthew Locke (1630?-1677) composed witch music for D'Avenant's version.
It is certainly an ironical exposure of the
shallowness of Restoration dramatic criticism that this most pure, somber, and perfect
of Shakespeare's tragedies should have been
thus deformed, and one learns from it how
little weight is to be attached to critical prat-
ings about decorum and dramatic propriety.
Garrick gave himself great credit for restoring Shakespeare's play to the stage, but in
point of fact he did not completely restore
it. He retained the witch songs and by
writing a dying speech for Macbeth kept
himself on the stage until the end. He was,
however, famous as Macbeth, and one hears
that in the dagger scene he was especially
impressive and that in the murder scene his
face "grew whiter and whiter." Mrs.
Pritchard was his Lady Macbeth. Macklin
is remembered for having costumed himself
and his fellows in Highland garb instead of
the military uniforms with tie-wigs then
customary. The Kembles achieved great
success in *Macbeth*. John Philip Kemble
was Macbeth; Charles Kemble, Macduff;
and their sister, Mrs. Siddons, Lady Macbeth. Kemble had no actor enter as the
ghost of Banquo in the banquet scene, but
made of it a ghost of the mind of Macbeth;
in this he was followed by Macready, Booth,
and Irving. Lady Macbeth was the most
famous part of the most famous of Shakespearean actresses, Mrs. Siddons. Reynolds

painted her as "The Tragic Muse," and Galt
speaks of the "low deep accent of apprehension, or of conscious conspiracy which she
sustained throughout [the part of Lady
Macbeth], especially as it influenced the
utterance of her Medean invocation to the

spirits
That tend on mortal thought,

and still more in the subsequent scene, where
she chastises with her valour the hesitation
of Macbeth." Edmund Kean dispensed
with the clap-trap of the witches and followed Shakespeare's conception of them as
spirits of malign power and dignity. Macbeth was Macready's greatest rôle, and he
was possibly the greatest of Macbeths. He
was supported by Helen Faucit in the character of Lady Macbeth. Samuel Phelps
restored (1847) Shakespeare's text. Irving
played *Macbeth* first in 1875, and in 1896 in
partnership with Ellen Terry brought the
play to America. He conceived Macbeth
as a remorseless villain, a conception which
gave room for Miss Terry's sympathetic
interpretation of Lady Macbeth. Revivals
of the play have been frequent in later years.
Those of Beerbohm Tree, Mrs. Patrick
Campbell, Violet Vanbrugh, Charlotte Cushman, Madame Modjeska, and Sothern and
Marlowe have been noteworthy. *Macbeth*
has been popular on the German stage and
even on those of France and Italy.

An annotated edition of *Macbeth* is
printed on pages 898-934 of this volume.

ANTONY AND CLEOPATRA

Publication   There is a difference of opinion
and date   as to whether *Antony and Cleopatra* belongs to 1606 or 1607,
but practically no doubt that it belongs to
one or the other year. It represents, along
with *Timon of Athens* and *Coriolanus*, a
return to Plutarch for source material, and is
usually considered the earliest of these three
plays. It was entered in the Register of the
Stationers' Company along with *Pericles* on
May 20, 1608, by Edward Blount. No issue
of the texts followed these entries, which
were possibly intended to forestall illegal
publication. If so, the entry was not successful in the case of *Pericles*, since a bad quarto

of that play came out with a different publisher in 1609. *Antony and Cleopatra* did not appear in print until the publication of the First Folio in 1623, when it was relicensed as if it had never been entered before. The best piece of evidence for 1606 or 1607 comes from its relation to Samuel Daniel's tragedy *Cleopatra*. This was first published in 1594 and is a drama on the classical model. It is made up largely of soliloquy and of long speeches and is moralistic and reflective in tone. It tells the story of Cleopatra after the death of Antony, and Shakespeare seems to have known the play. On the other hand, Daniel, who had the reputation of borrowing from others, seems to have remodeled his play under the influence of Shakespeare's *Antony and Cleopatra*, publishing it as "newly altered" in 1607. In the new version he uses dialogue more freely than in the old and makes a greater use than he had before of some of the characters who appear in Shakespeare's play. There are even a few rather striking parallels to *Antony and Cleopatra* in the verse of the new play.[1] Also Barnabe Barnes's *The Divils Charter*, acted early in 1607, contains what seems to be a parody of the death scene of Cleopatra where she applies the asp to her breast. *Macbeth*, on which Shakespeare was at work at about the same time, shows some familiarity (III, i, 54-7) with the life of Antony in Plutarch.

Sources Shakespeare must have known Daniel's *Cleopatra* and the Countess of Pembroke's *Antonius, a Tragedie*, which had been Daniel's model for his first version. Perhaps he was acquainted with other plays now lost, for the subject was well known on the stage. The Countess of Pembroke's play is a translation of Robert Garnier's *Marc Antoine*. Étienne Jodelle had written *Cléopâtre Captive* in the middle of the sixteenth century. Other French, English, and German plays on Cleopatra are known. Back of the Renaissance there lies a large body of Cleopatra literature, for Antony and Cleopatra had taken their place among the world's famous lovers. This is important to remember in considering Shakespeare's use of Plutarch. Although he went

to the life of Antony in Plutarch's *Lives of the Noble Grecians and Romans*, and followed it very closely as regards the Cleopatra of the final act, he did not get from it his initial conception of this character.

Cleopatra Plutarch blames Antony for falling victim to infatuation and throwing away the world for love of Cleopatra. He is mainly interested in the downfall of the great Roman and its significance in politics, history, and morals. He dwells on the magnificence of Cleopatra, tells about her gifts of gold and silver, the sumptuousness of her household, the splendor of her feasts, how eight wild boars were roasted whole in the kitchen of Antony, and so on. Cleopatra is beautiful, flattering, charming; but she is also great. She ruled a kingdom unaided; she was cultured; she knew many languages; and, characteristically, Plutarch tells a good deal about her humor and describes the sports and amusements of Antony and Cleopatra in Alexandria. Now, when we come to Shakespeare we find him with a different conception. To him the Cleopatra of the first three acts is fickle, vain, mercenary, unscrupulous, and the living embodiment of sensuality. This is easily illustrated from the second, third, and fifth scenes of the first act, and all through, at least as far as the thirteenth scene of the third act. But when we pass that point we have to do with a different character. She seems suddenly to possess womanly fidelity, is steadfast and resolute, and, being left to occupy the stage alone in the last act, advances to an heroic death. Professor Schücking[2] has argued that Shakespeare has not been consistent in the portraiture of the character, for he started out with one conception and ended with another, knowing, no doubt, that on the stage the inconsistency would not be apparent. Professor Schücking insists that, if Shakespeare had thought of the character of the first three acts as the same as that of the last two, some evidence of that better nature would have been revealed earlier. It is impossible, he thinks, that any woman of the character of the first Cleopatra could have manifested the qualities of the later one. There is this to be said in favor of his contention. The play

---

[1] R. H. Case, *The Tragedy of Antony and Cleopatra*, Arden Shakespeare (Methuen), Introduction.

[2] *Character Problems in Shakespeare's Plays*, pp. 119 ff.

was evidently hastily written. It is not worked down to the fine point of connection that marks *Macbeth* and *Coriolanus*. It lacks general plan. After the middle of the play, Shakespeare more or less puts Plutarch on the stage. There is a multitude of short scenes which reproduce the source almost literally, so that the play is comparatively confused in its dramaturgy. It is often spoken of as a chronicle play in form and is said to lack, except in its great figures, the quality of tragedy. Shakespeare had two conflicting ideas to present, the one derived from the popular conception of Cleopatra as the mistress of sensual love and the other the Plutarchan story of the woman who loved Antony so well that she followed him to the shades of death. It may be that in the earlier part of the play, which is dramatically so much more carefully done, he was following the first of these ideas, and that in the later part he was plunging hurriedly through the second. The question to be decided is whether Shakespeare gives us anything to show that he meant Cleopatra to be so profoundly moved by the misfortunes of Antony that her nature was changed. There is no clear marking of the probability of such a conversion, and it is very unlike Shakespeare to leave such a matter obscure. There is, however, a clear and powerful marking of the moment of the change. It is the scene of Antony's rage when he thinks wrongly that Cleopatra has withdrawn her fleet from the battle and has caused his defeat. She feels the scourge of his tongue when he says (III, xiii, 116-122),

I found you as a morsel cold upon
Dead Cæsar's trencher; nay, you were a fragment
Of Cneius Pompey's; besides what hotter hours,
Unregister'd in vulgar fame, you have
Luxuriously pick'd out: for, I am sure,
Though you can guess what temperance should be,
You know not what it is.

Under his reproaches she is perfectly meek. "O, is't come to this?" "I must stay his time." "Not know me yet?" These are her replies, and from that moment she has her new nobility. Many critics find in her holding back part of her treasure, in her blandishments of Octavius, and in her false message to Antony that she was dead, a basis for the belief that she was still the old

Cleopatra, anxious at any cost to save her life, even willing to secure another lover in the crafty Octavius; but to construe it so is to read things into the text that are not there. Plutarch makes it perfectly clear that Cleopatra had resolved to die: "Cleopatra finely deceiveth Octavius Cæsar, as though she desired to live."

Stage history *Antony and Cleopatra* has not been frequently played on the stage or, as a whole, successfully. Dryden's *All for Love, or the World Lost* (1678) differs from other Restoration treatments of Shakespeare. It is not so much an adaptation of *Antony and Cleopatra* as an independent dramatization of the same subject on Dryden's lines. He took great pains with it and was proud of the result. He wrote in blank verse, observed the unities of time, place, and action with some fidelity, and achieved a far superior unity, if unity be considered narrowly; but, on the other hand, what he gained in the narrow field he lost in the broad one. *Antony and Cleopatra* is a drama of a world empire, with Antony bestriding it like a colossus, and all its variation reflected in the "infinite variety" of Cleopatra. In Dryden's version Antony chiefly suffers, becoming a "bankrupt of honor and fortune." Clownage, thought to be too strong an element in Enobarbus, is banished with him. Cleopatra is tamed. This version, which is, in spite of what has been said, a truly noble work, superseded *Antony and Cleopatra* on the stage for many years. Garrick tried unsuccessfully to revive Shakespeare's version in 1758. Macready likewise failed in 1833. The performance of Samuel Phelps in 1849 was the first modern success in the performance of Shakespeare's play. He played Antony to crowded houses throughout the season. Isabella Dallas Glyn (1823-1889), a tragic actress of stately bearing and excellent elocution, was his Cleopatra; she again appeared in this part at Drury Lane Theater in 1873. Since the middle of the nineteenth century there have been all-told perhaps a dozen revivals of *Antony and Cleopatra* in England and America. The most successful was that of Beerbohm Tree (1906-7) at His Majesty's Theater in London, on which occasion Tree played Antony, Miss Constance Collier, Cleopatra, and Basil Gill, Octavius. Other notable performances are those of Kyrle Bellew and Mrs. Potter in New York in 1889, Charles Coghlan and Mrs. Langtry in London in 1890, and Sothern and Marlowe in 1910.

An annotated edition of *Antony and Cleopatra* is printed on pages 935-987 of this volume.

CORIOLANUS

Publication and date *Coriolanus* was first published in a rather difficult text in the First Folio of 1623, the textual difficulties being rendered greater by the closely packed, obscure, late style in which the play is composed. There is very little external evidence to assist in dating *Coriolanus*. One is rather sorry for this deficiency in contemporary comment, because one would like to know how a play of such pronounced political import as this impressed a Jacobean audience. Because the style of the play has so many features of Shakespeare's late style, many editors have placed it in 1608-1610, but such dating is unsure. One might concede that *Coriolanus* is later than *Antony and Cleopatra*, but one would naturally believe that it arose out of the same return to Plutarch which produced the latter play. A renewed interest in Roman history seems also reflected in *Appius and Virginia*, a play written about 1608 for the Queen's players by Webster and possibly Heywood. The dating of that play, however, is so vague that nothing can be told about it. Sir E. K. Chambers has suggested that *Coriolanus* may have been written in 1606 or 1608.

Source and theme *Coriolanus* is a carefully wrought work, contrasting in this respect with *Antony and Cleopatra*, to which, however, it is greatly inferior in variety of interest and pure poetry. *Coriolanus* has a story to tell and a definite theme to develop, so that it is one of the plays in which we may be quite certain of Shakespeare's meaning. It depicts the struggles between the plebeians and the patricians of old Rome and comes directly out of Plutarch, who had himself conceived the character of Coriolanus in terms not greatly other than those in which Shakespeare conceived it. Coriolanus is a noble patrician and a great warrior bred from his cradle by his mother Volumnia to fight, to be proud, and to despise the plebeians. In him aristocratic pride is the finest virtue; but it turns out that his strength becomes his weakness, and the selfishness of his pride is his ruin. He saves his country and earns every honor that it can bestow upon him; but when he sues according to the law for the consulship and goes through the form of election by the plebeians, displaying reluctantly his multitudinous wounds, he behaves with such pride and bitterness that he defeats his own ends. He has consented to seek the consulship to gratify his mother's ambitions; but the pride that she taught him places him at the mercy of the rabble and their demagogues, so that he is banished from Rome with the greatest and most cruel injustice and ingratitude. In this situation Coriolanus puts his wrongs and their vengeance above the welfare of his country and joins the enemies of Rome, so that Rome is at the mercy of his martial prowess. Then it is that his mother, conceived of as a noble Roman matron, teaches him the lesson she should have taught before. She induces him to renounce his private revenge, spare his country, and, consequently, give himself up to death at the hands of the Volscians, whom he has betrayed. Thus a lesson of ultimate patriotism is taught, a lesson which must have been gratifying to the monarchic minds of King James's court and may have been applicable, for all we know, to the stories of men in that age.

Plutarch The story in the most faithful detail Shakespeare draws from Plutarch, and yet not without significant changes and not without all of the intercalary matters which are necessary to render a historical episode visible upon the stage and comprehensible to the commonplace intelligences of an audience in a theater. Plutarch's three uprisings of the plebeians are condensed into one. Shakespeare makes the banishment of Coriolanus not the result of his opposition to the plebeian demand for free corn, but immediately the result of the prejudice arising out of his proud behavior when he sought election to the consulship; it is thus a meaner, narrower, more ungrateful thing which he suffers in Shakespeare than in Plutarch. Shakespeare omits irrelevant incidents and the customary Roman portents which attend the banishment of Coriolanus, who is thus made more definitely and personally responsible. Shakespeare invents the byplay of the action, such as the orations and the dialogues in the streets between groups of citizens and officers. In Plutarch it is Valeria, a Roman matron, friend of the wife of Coriolanus, who takes the lead in the salvation of her country and induces the mother, wife, and children of Coriolanus to beg him to desist; by a stroke of rare genius Shakespeare has put the whole burden upon Volumnia, the mother of Coriolanus. It is she who induces her son to sacrifice himself for the country he was about to destroy. Finally, Shakespeare has created Menenius Agrippa. This humorous person, as one of the pleasantest of the aged patricians, is made by Plutarch to deliver a short speech to the plebeians in defense of the senate, in which he tells them the notable tale of the rebellion of the members of man's body against the belly. Shakespeare has developed Menenius into a friend of Coriolanus and the mouthpiece of common sense and reasonable compromise. Many of Plutarch's actual words are transferred to Shakespeare's play, transformed from noble prose to nobler verse.[1] The marvelously realistic sixth scene of the fourth act is based on the following passages:

Now on the other side, the city of Rome was in marvelous uproar and discord, the nobility against the commonality, and chiefly for Martius' condemnation and banishment.

There was one that had delivered a bondman of his that had offended him into the hands of other slaves and bondmen, and had commended them to whip him up and down the market-place, and afterwards to kill him: and they had him in execution, whipping him cruelly, they did so martyr the poor wretch, that, for the cruel smart and pain he felt, he turned and writhed his body in strange and pitiful sort. The procession by chance came by even at the same time, and many that followed it were heartily moved and offended

[1] C. F. Tucker Brooke, *Shakespeare's Plutarch*, Oxford, 1909.

with the sight, saying: that this was no good sight to behold, nor meet to meet in procession-time.

The first of these passages gives us the discontent of the citizens (IV, vi, 139-146):

Citizens. Faith, we hear fearful news.
First Cit. For mine own part,
When I said, banish him, I said, 'twas pity.
Second Cit. And so did I.
Third Cit. And so did I; and, to say the truth, so did very many of us: that we did, we did for the best; and though we willingly consented to his banishment, yet it was against our will.

The second passage probably suggested the whipping of the slave (IV, vi, 37-47):

Æd. Worthy tribunes,
There is a slave, whom we have put in prison,
Reports, the Volsces with two several powers
Are enter'd in the Roman territories,
And with the deepest malice of the war
Destroy what lies before 'em.
Men. 'Tis Aufidius,
Who, hearing of our Marcius' banishment,
Thrusts forth his horns again into the world;
Which were enshell'd when Marcius stood for Rome,
And durst not once peep out.
Sic. Come, what talk you
Of Marcius?
Bru. Go see this rumourer whipp'd.

Coriolanus According to Plutarch Coriolanus was a loud-voiced warrior and of an enraptured valor. "For he was even such another, as Cato would have a soldier and a captain to be, not only terrible and fierce to lay about him, but to make an enemy afeard with the sound of his voice, and the grimness of his countenance"; and going to battle "oft holding up his hands to heaven, he besought the gods to be gracious and favorable unto him, that he might come in time to the battle, and in a good hour to hazard his life in defense of his countrymen." Blown with battle and covered with wounds, he refused to leave the field, but "began afresh to chase those that fled, until such time as the army of the enemies was utterly overthrown, and numbers of them slain and taken prisoners." He was likewise unselfish and magnanimous, refusing special share in the spoil and asking only that his humble friend and host among the Corioli should be spared. But one is also given to understand that his opinions were the stiff opinions of an aristocrat. He insisted that indulgence of the plebeians encouraged them to disobedience and bred civil confusion and anarchy; and when he put forward his political opinions, he did not do so dispassionately, but in a manner of speaking, bold, rough, and unpleasant. Plutarch knew his faults:

For he was a man too full of passion and choler, and too much given over to self-will and opinion, as one of a high mind and great courage, that lack the gravity and affability that is gotten with judgment of learning and reason, which only is to be looked for in a governor of State: and that remembered not how wilfulness is the thing of the world, which a governor of a commonwealth, for pleasing, should shun, being that which Plato called solitariness; as in the end, all men that are wilfully given to self-opinion and obstinate mind, and who will never yield to other's reasons but to their own, remain without company, and forsaken of all men. For a man that will live in the world must needs have patience, which lusty bloods make but a mock at.

And so he "spitteth out anger from the most weak and passioned part of the heart, much like the matter of an imposthume."

Menenius Coriolanus not only wrongs himself; he is also deeply wronged. Shakespeare had this double aspect to bring out, and he invented for his purpose the shrewd, good-natured old patrician Menenius, who was both friendly to Coriolanus and well aware of the political crookedness and the personal spite of the demagogues Sicinius and Brutus (II, i, 1-106). Menenius knew the fickleness and cowardice of the mob, the weakness of the senate, the very truth of the whole matter. Perhaps he casts away his dignity as a useless thing. His voice is often cynical, but he yields and compromises, persuades and cajoles. He regards Coriolanus as his son; he checks him, bids him be silent, reasons with him, apologizes for him, praises him, and loves him. On the whole he rises to something very like nobility; witness the bitterness of his words after the failure of his mission to Coriolanus:

I neither care for the world nor your general: for such things as you, I can scarce think there's any, ye're so slight. He that hath a will to die by himself fears it not from another: let your

general do his worst. For you, be that you are, long; and your misery increase with your age! I say to you, as I was said to, Away!
(V, ii, 108-114.)

He stands out, as a sort of Prince Hohenstiel-Schwangau, one of those who endeavor, in the midst of ignorance, selfishness, and animosity, to carry on the world's business.

Volumnia All of the subordinate characters serve in some degree to mirror forth the personality of Coriolanus, but perhaps the most triumphant depiction in the play is of the relation of mother and son. Coriolanus's noble Roman traits are completely the result of his mother's teaching (I, iii, 6-17):

When yet he was but tender-bodied and the only son of my womb, when youth with comeliness plucked all gaze his way, when for a day of kings' entreaties a mother should not sell him an hour from her beholding, I, considering how honour would become such a person, that it was no better than picture-like to hang by the wall, if renown made it not stir, was pleased to let him seek danger where he was like to find fame. To a cruel war I sent him; from whence he returned, his brows bound with oak.

He is, as it were, groomed to run a course for fame. His own prowess and glory are paramount, and the shrewd remark of the first Citizen (I, i, 37-41) foretells the fatal error:

Though soft-conscienced men can be content to say it was for his country, he did it to please his mother, and to be partly proud; which he is, even to the altitude of his virtue.

In the third act when Volumnia tries to teach her son to be a politician, it is too late; there is now no room in his character for compromise and servility. He promises her that he will conduct himself wisely and graciously at his trial; but he can no more save himself by policy from banishment or the Tarpeian rock in Rome than he could save himself from the swords of the Antiates by policy in the field. Volumnia by her great speeches in the fifth act has to teach him, at the cost of his life, the lesson of self-sacrifice for the sake of his native land.

Aufidius The nature of Coriolanus is again mirrored forth in the mind of his great adversary Tullus Aufidius, also a man who prized personal glory above everything, even above honor. To give him a victory over Coriolanus is like a shout of triumph in behalf of guile, so that in this matter Shakespeare has done a peculiar thing. It is Aufidius who speaks a funeral elegy over Coriolanus at the end. His case is parallel to that of the crafty Octavius who, at the end of *Antony and Cleopatra*, is impersonal enough to give Antony his meed of praise. We have here at the end of the fourth act, in the words of the practical man Aufidius, a profound analysis of Coriolanus and his fate (IV, vii, 35-55):

First he was
A noble servant to them; but he could not
Carry his honours even: whether 'twas pride,
Which out of daily fortune ever taints
The happy man; whether defect of judgement,
To fail in the disposing of those chances
Which he was lord of; or whether nature,
Not to be other than one thing, not moving
From the casque to the cushion, but commanding
        peace
Even with the same austerity and garb
As he controll'd the war; but one of these—
As he hath spices of them all, not all,
For I dare so far free him—made him fear'd,
So hated, and so banish'd: but he has a merit,
To choke it in the utterance. So our virtues
Lie in the interpretation of the time:
And power, unto itself most commendable,
Hath not a tomb so evident as a chair
To extol what it hath done.
One fire drives out one fire; one nail, one nail;
Rights by rights falter, strengths by strengths do
        fail.

Shakespeare seems here to tell us very plainly that virtue is a relative matter, that honor will not "live with the living," and that "to have done is to hang quite out of fashion, like a rusty mail, in monumental mockery." It may even come about in this world that, as in the case of Coriolanus, a man's chief merit may become a contributory weakness to produce his fall. This is a well-known feature of Shakespeare's tragic thought. "In almost all [of Shakespeare's tragic heroes]" says Bradley, "we observe a marked one-sidedness, a predisposition in some particular direction; a total incapacity, in certain circumstances, of resisting the force which draws in this direction. . . . In the circumstances where we see the hero

placed, his tragic trait, which is also his greatness, is fatal to him."[1]

Stage history The glorious stage days of Coriolanus (as a theme) were before England and America were democratized and when enlightened opinion still regarded the gulf between the noble and the common man as unbridgeable. Specifically, Coriolanus was a theme dear to the hearts of Restoration royalists and eighteenth century Tories. It cannot be said, however, that Shakespeare's treatment of the theme in his tragedy of *Coriolanus* fared very well at their hands. The adapter of *King Lear*, Nahum Tate, conscious of the applicability of the patrician-plebeian issue to the party strifes of his own day, produced (1782) a version of *Coriolanus*, which he called *The Ingratitude of a Commonwealth, or the Fall of Caius Martius Coriolanus*. For some reason, not entirely clear, Tate chooses to accumulate horrors. Virgilia commits suicide, Menenius is murdered, Aufidius is slain, and Volumnia goes insane. John Dennis, a critic who admired Shakespeare with many reservations, rewrote *Coriolanus* as *The Invasion of his Country or the Fatal Resentment* (1719). The poet Thomson wrote on strictly classical lines a *Coriolanus* acted after his death in 1749. Thomson's tragedy was combined with Shakespeare's *Coriolanus* to form the acting version of John Philip Kemble. In it Mrs. Siddons played Volumnia. Kemble had saved enough of Shakespeare to make himself greatly celebrated as Coriolanus, and with that part he closed his career in 1817. Edmund Kean appeared in Shakespeare's version in 1820. His realistic style was gaining ground against the rhetorical stateliness of Kemble; but *Coriolanus* is not a play which will stand realism, and Kean was a failure in it. In 1819 Macready began his career as Coriolanus. He had the voice and person for the part, and he saw in the character of Coriolanus the faults as well as the merits of the patrician. Macready and his American contemporary, Edwin Forrest, who in some respects resembled him, were the last great actors in the rôle of Coriolanus. A disaster in the illustrious career of Irving was the failure of his sump-

[1] *Shakespearean Tragedy*, pp. 20-21.

tuous revival of *Coriolanus* in 1901. The naturalistic stage customs of our day are against the play.

TIMON OF ATHENS

Authorship and publication A play belonging to this period, most obscure in its history, is *Timon of Athens*. It has been recognized for nearly a century that in this play we have a work for which Shakespeare is only partly responsible; but whether Shakespeare revised the incomplete work of another man, or whether another man revised the incomplete work of Shakespeare, critics have by no means been able to agree upon. The most recent hypothesis and, all told, the most plausible, is that of Professor T. M. Parrott.[1] He sees in *Timon of Athens* a play which Shakespeare began shortly after he had completed *King Lear*. The reason for this belief is that the style of the unquestioned portions is of about the same degree of maturity and complexity as that of *King Lear*, and not so far advanced as *Macbeth* and *Antony and Cleopatra*. Having outlined the main features of the play as we have it by writing up those parts which his inspiration invited him to write, Shakespeare laid it aside for *Macbeth* and more attractive tasks, and never completed it. After his death in 1616 and after the actor Field joined the King's Company in the same year, Chapman, a friend of Field's, was employed to complete Shakespeare's play. This he did loosely and less dramatically than Shakespeare would have done it and at too great a length. This draft by Chapman was cut down and prepared for the stage, possibly by Field. We can thus account for the hand of Shakespeare, the hand of Chapman, also fairly recognizable, and the hand of a hasty and inferior reviser who cut down the Chapman parts and filled in poorly some gaps which Chapman had left unfilled. The play was first published in the folio of 1623.

Story and source *Timon of Athens* is at best not dramatically effective. It lives because of the figure of Timon the Misanthrope, a few striking scenes, and

many great speeches. Shakespeare found the story in Plutarch's *Life of Antony*. He may also have amplified it by reference to the dialogue *Timon the Misanthrope* by the Greek satirist Lucian, since a number of places recall Lucian's words. There is also an old play on Timon which Shakespeare may have known. He was no doubt caught by the figure of Timon; for, as Professor Parrott suggests, Timon in his disillusionment resembles Lear. Timon of Athens was a historical character of the age of Pericles in Greece, a nobleman who squandered his fortune on friends and flatterers. In the play he is completely generous. However, complete and indiscriminate generosity is folly. Timon gets into debt; his lands are sold; his flatterers forsake him. The senate refuses to help him, although he has at an earlier time saved the state from its enemies. This circumstance in the play, however, is introduced artistically too late. Misanthropy rises in Timon's heart, and before he forsakes Athens he invites his false friends to a banquet. The feast is served in covered dishes, and when the covers are removed it is found that the dishes contain only water. Timon denounces his guests and throws the water over them. He then forsakes Athens for a cave in the woods. Meantime Alcibiades, Timon's friend, also misused by the senate and banished, raises an army to attack his native city. Timon, while digging for roots in the woods to serve as food, finds gold. He is visited by Alcibiades with his army and his mistresses. He lavishes gold on them in the hope and belief that it will ruin them and other men, for he hates all men. The news of his wealth brings his flatterers again on his trail, and to them he gives gold with the same dark purpose. When the senators, now made fearful by the invasion of Alcibiades, come to beg Timon to succor Athens, they get curses for their pains. They succeed, however, in making terms with Alcibiades by promising to punish his and Timon's enemies. This strangely static plot then comes to a close with the description of Timon's tomb on the seashore by a soldier who has found it, and by the reading of Timon's epitaph.

Timon of Athens, in spite of its fragmentary and imperfect form, shows clearly that

[1] *The Problem of "Timon of Athens,"* The Shakespeare Association, 1923.

it is conceived of in the Shakespearean way. It again presents the contrast between the man of action and the man of thought and feeling, as in Bolingbroke and Richard II, Fortinbras and Hamlet, Octavius and Antony. Alcibiades, unattractive person though he is, is a man of action. When he is banished and misused by his countrymen, he does not retreat to the wilderness to live on roots and rail at the folly and ingratitude of men. He raises an army and threatens Athens with fire and sword, so that the Senate sues for peace. His action recalls that of Coriolanus. Indeed, *Timon of Athens, Coriolanus*, and *Antony and Cleopatra* all have much in common and may be said to constitute a separate group of tragedies in spirit half way between the passionate naturalism of *Hamlet, Othello*, and *King Lear* and the calm indifferentism of *Cymbeline* and *The Tempest*, to which group *Macbeth* is transitional. The Plutarchan plays are more convinced in their pessimism about human nature than the earlier plays of the same period and more certain that the rulers of the earth put appetite before duty, that the populace is a mere rabble, and that men of sense and virtue, like Enobarbus and Menenius Agrippa, speak only to deaf ears. Passion and reason are still at war, but passion has grown old, violent, and sordid, and reason has become selfish and cold-blooded.

Stage history The stage history of Shakespeare's *Timon of Athens* is almost a blank. It has been played but rarely, and, so far as can be ascertained, always in a modified version. The play had some attention during the seventeenth and eighteenth centuries in Thomas Shadwell's adaptation (1678). It was acted at Drury Lane Theater in 1816 in what may have been an abridged form of the original.

TEXT OF FIVE PLAYS FROM THE PERIOD OF THE TRAGEDIES

Hamlet

Othello

King Lear

Macbeth

Antony and Cleopatra

HAMLET, PRINCE OF DENMARK

DRAMATIS PERSONÆ

CLAUDIUS, king of Denmark.
HAMLET, son to the late, and nephew to the present king.
POLONIUS, lord chamberlain.
HORATIO, friend to Hamlet.
LAERTES, son to Polonius.
VOLTIMAND,
CORNELIUS,
ROSENCRANTZ, } courtiers.
GUILDENSTERN,
OSRIC,
A Gentleman,
A Priest.
MARCELLUS, } officers.
BERNARDO,

FRANCISCO, a soldier.
REYNALDO, servant to Polonius.
Players.
Two Clowns, grave-diggers.
FORTINBRAS, prince of Norway.
A Captain.
English Ambassadors.

GERTRUDE, queen of Denmark, and mother to Hamlet.
OPHELIA, daughter to Polonius.

Lords, Ladies, Officers, Soldiers, Sailors, Messengers, and other Attendants.
Ghost of Hamlet's Father.

SCENE: *Denmark.*

ACT I.

SCENE I. *Elsinore. A platform before the castle.*

FRANCISCO *at his post. Enter to him*
BERNARDO.

Ber. Who's there?
Fran. Nay, answer me: stand, and unfold yourself.
Ber. Long live the king!
Fran. Bernardo?
Ber. He.
Fran. You come most carefully upon your hour.
Ber. 'Tis now struck twelve; get thee to bed, Francisco.
Fran. For this relief much thanks: 'tis bitter cold,
And I am sick at heart.
Ber. Have you had quiet guard?

Fran. Not a mouse stirring. 10
Ber. Well, good night.
If you do meet Horatio and Marcellus,
The rivals of my watch, bid them make haste.
Fran. I think I hear them. Stand, ho!
Who's there?

Enter HORATIO *and* MARCELLUS.

Hor. Friends to this ground.
Mar. And liegemen to the Dane.
Fran. Give you good night.
Mar. O, farewell, honest soldier:
Who hath relieved you?
Fran. Bernardo has my place.
Give you good night. [*Exit.*
Mar. Holla! Bernardo!
Ber. Say,
What, is Horatio there?
Hor. A piece of him.
Ber. Welcome, Horatio: welcome, good
Marcellus. 20
Mar. What, has this thing appear'd again to-night?

Act. I. Scene i. Stage Direction: **platform**, a level space on the battlements of the royal castle at Elsinore, a Danish seaport; now Helsingör. **2. me.** This is emphatic, since Francisco is the sentry. **3. Long live the king,** evidently the password, though Horatio and Marcellus use a different one in line 15.

18. **Give you,** God give you. 19. **piece of him,** a casual answer implying flippancy.

Ber. I have seen nothing.

Mar. Horatio says 'tis but our fantasy,
And will not let belief take hold of him
Touching this dreaded sight, twice seen of
us:
Therefore I have entreated him along
With us to watch the minutes of this night;
That if again this apparition come,
He may approve our eyes and speak to it.

Hor. Tush, tush, 'twill not appear.

Ber.   Sit down awhile;   30
And let us once again assail your ears,
That are so fortified against our story
What we have two nights seen.

Hor.   Well, sit we down,
And let us hear Bernardo speak of this.

Ber. Last night of all,
When yond same star that's westward from
the pole
Had made his course to illume that part of
heaven
Where now it burns, Marcellus and myself,
The bell then beating one,—

Enter Ghost.

Mar. Peace, break thee off; look, where
it comes again!   40

Ber. In the same figure, like the king
that's dead.

Mar. Thou art a scholar; speak to it,
Horatio.

Ber. Looks it not like the king? mark it,
Horatio.

Hor. Most like: it harrows me with fear
and wonder.

Ber. It would be spoke to.

Mar.   Question it, Horatio.

Hor. What art thou that usurp'st this
time of night,
Together with that fair and warlike form
In which the majesty of buried Denmark
Did sometimes march? by heaven I charge
thee, speak!

Mar. It is offended.

Ber.   See, it stalks away!   50

Hor. Stay! speak, speak! I charge thee,
speak!   [*Exit Ghost.*

Mar. 'Tis gone, and will not answer.

Ber. How now, Horatio! you tremble and
look pale:
Is not this something more than fantasy?
What think you on 't?

Hor. Before my God, I might not this
believe
Without the sensible and true avouch
Of mine own eyes.

Mar.   Is it not like the king?

Hor. As thou art to thyself:
Such was the very armour he had on   60
When he the ambitious Norway combated;
So frown'd he once, when, in an angry parle,
He smote the sledded Polacks on the ice.
'Tis strange.

Mar. Thus twice before, and jump at this
dead hour,
With martial stalk hath he gone by our watch.

Hor. In what particular thought to work
I know not;
But in the gross and scope of my opinion,
This bodes some strange eruption to our state.

Mar. Good now, sit down, and tell me, he
that knows,   70
Why this same strict and most observant
watch
So nightly toils the subject of the land,
And why such daily cast of brazen cannon,
And foreign mart for implements of war;
Why such impress of shipwrights, whose
sore task
Does not divide the Sunday from the week;
What might be toward, that this sweaty
haste
Doth make the night joint-labourer with the
day:
Who is 't that can inform me?

Hor.   That can I;
At least, the whisper goes so. Our last king, 80
Whose image even but now appear'd to us,
Was, as you know, by Fortinbras of Norway,
Thereto prick'd on by a most emulate pride,
Dared to the combat; in which our valiant
Hamlet—

29. **approve**, corroborate, justify.   36. **yond same star**, probably part of the constellation of the Great Bear, since this was used to tell time by.   42. **scholar**. Exorcisms were performed in Latin, which Horatio as an educated man would be able to speak.   44. **harrows**, lacerates the feelings.   45. **It would . . . to.** A ghost could not speak until spoken to.   **Question**, speak to. 49. **sometimes**, formerly.

57. **sensible**, invoking the use of the senses.   62. **angry parle**, parley or conference ending in a fight. 63. **smote**, defeated.   **sledded Polacks**, Polanders using sledges.   The Earl of Rochester (1761) explained *sleaded* (Q₁F) or *sledded* (Q₂) as "loaded with lead" and *pollax* (Q₁-₂F) as "pole-ax," the idea being that the elder Hamlet dashed his pole-ax against the ice while engaged in a parley; this is upheld by Schmidt and others.   68. **gross and scope**, general drift   70. **Good now**, an expression denoting entreaty or expostulation. 72. **toils**, causes or makes to toil.   **subject**, people, subjects. 73. **cast**, casting, founding.   74. **mart**, buying and selling, traffic.   75. **impress**, impressment.   77. **toward**, imminent, about to happen.   83. **prick'd on**, incited. **emulate**, ambitious.

For so this side of our known world esteem'd
　　him—
Did slay this Fortinbras; who, by a seal'd
　　compact,
Well ratified by law and heraldry,
Did forfeit, with his life, all those his lands
Which he stood seized of, to the conqueror:
Against the which, a moiety competent　90
Was gaged by our king; which had return'd
To the inheritance of Fortinbras,
Had he been vanquisher; as, by the same
　　covenant,
And carriage of the article design'd,
His fell to Hamlet. Now, sir, young Fortin-
　　bras,
Of unimproved mettle hot and full,
Hath in the skirts of Norway here and there
Shark'd up a list of lawless resolutes,
For food and diet, to some enterprise
That hath a stomach in 't; which is no
　　other—　　　　　　　　　　　　　100
As it doth well appear unto our state—
But to recover of us, by strong hand
And terms compulsatory, those foresaid lands
So by his father lost: and this, I take it,
Is the main motive of our preparations,
The source of this our watch and the chief
　　head
Of this post-haste and romage in the land.
　　Ber. I think it be no other but e'en so:
Well may it sort that this portentous figure
Comes armed through our watch; so like the
　　king　　　　　　　　　　　　　　110
That was and is the question of these wars.
　　Hor. A mote it is to trouble the mind's eye.
In the most high and palmy state of Rome,
A little ere the mightiest Julius fell,
The graves stood tenantless and the sheeted
　　dead
Did squeak and gibber in the Roman streets:
†As stars with trains of fire and dews of
　　blood,
Disasters in the sun; and the moist star

Upon whose influence Neptune's empire
　　stands
Was sick almost to doomsday with eclipse:120
And even the like precurse of fierce events,
As harbingers preceding still the fates
And prologue to the omen coming on,
Have heaven and earth together demonstrated
Unto our climatures and countrymen.—
But soft, behold! lo, where it comes again!

　　　　　　　Re-enter Ghost.

I'll cross it, though it blast me. Stay, illusion!
If thou hast any sound, or use of voice,
Speak to me:
If there be any good thing to be done,　130
That may to thee do ease and grace to me,
Speak to me:　　　　　　　　[*Cock crows.*
If thou art privy to thy country's fate,
Which, happily, foreknowing may avoid,
O, speak!
Or if thou hast uphoarded in thy life
Extorted treasure in the womb of earth,
For which, they say, you spirits oft walk in
　　death,
Speak of it: stay, and speak! Stop it, Marcel-
　　lus.
　　Mar. Shall I strike at it with my par-
　　tisan?　　　　　　　　　　　　140
　　Hor. Do, if it will not stand.
　　Ber.　　　　　　　　　　'Tis here!
　　Hor.　　　　　　　　　　　'Tis here!
　　Mar. 'Tis gone!　　　　[*Exit Ghost.*
We do it wrong, being so majestical,
To offer it the show of violence;
For it is, as the air, invulnerable,
And our vain blows malicious mockery.
　　Ber. It was about to speak, when the cock
　　crew.
　　Hor. And then it started like a guilty
　　thing
Upon a fearful summons. I have heard,
The cock, that is the trumpet to the morn,
Doth with his lofty and shrill-sounding
　　throat　　　　　　　　　　　　151
Awake the god of day; and, at his warning,
Whether in sea or fire, in earth or air,

87. **law and heraldry**, civil law and also the courts
of chivalry. 89. **seized**, possessed. 90. **moiety competent**, adequate or sufficient portion. 93. **covenant.**
The Q2 reading, *comart*, has been interpreted by some
editors as meaning "joint bargain." 94. **carriage**,
import, bearing. 96. **unimproved**, not turned to
account. **hot and full**, full of fight. 98. **Shark'd up**,
got together in haphazard fashion. **resolutes**, desper-
adoes. 99. **food and diet**, no pay but their keep. 100.
stomach, opportunity for courage, with quibble on
literal meaning. 107. **romage**, bustle, commotion.
113. **palmy state**, triumphant sovereignty. 117. **As
. . . blood.** This abrupt transition suggests that matter
is possibly omitted between lines 116 and 117. **stars
. . . fire**, i.e., comets. 118. **Disasters**, unfavorable
aspects. **moist star**, the moon. governing tides.

119. **Neptune's empire**, the sea. 120. **sick . . .
doomsday.** See *St. Matthew*, xxiv, 20; *Revelation*, vi, 12.
121. **precurse**, heralding. 123. **prologue**, introduction.
127. **cross**, meet, face; thus bringing down the evil
influence on the person who crosses it. 131. **grace**,
honor. 133-139. **If thou . . . it.** Horatio recites the
traditional reasons why ghosts might walk. 134. **happily**, haply. 140. **partisan**, long-handled spear with a
blade having lateral projections. 147. **cock crew.** According to traditional ghost lore spirits returned to their
confines at cock-crow.

The extravagant and erring spirit hies
To his confine: and of the truth herein
This present object made probation.

Mar. It faded on the crowing of the cock.
Some say that ever 'gainst that season comes
Wherein our Saviour's birth is celebrated,
The bird of dawning singeth all night long:
And then, they say, no spirit dare stir abroad;
The nights are wholesome; then no planets
   strike,   162
No fairy takes, nor witch hath power to
   charm,
So hallow'd and so gracious is the time.

Hor. So have I heard and do in part be-
   lieve it.
But, look, the morn, in russet mantle clad,
Walks o'er the dew of yon high eastward
   hill:
Break we our watch up; and by my advice,
Let us impart what we have seen to-night
Unto young Hamlet; for, upon my life,   170
This spirit, dumb to us, will speak to him.
Do you consent we shall acquaint him with
   it,
As needful in our loves, fitting our duty?

Mar. Let's do 't, I pray; and I this morning know
Where we shall find him most conveniently.
                        [Exeunt.

SCENE II. *A room of state in the castle.*

Enter the KING, QUEEN, HAMLET, POLONIUS,
   LAERTES, VOLTIMAND, CORNELIUS, Lords,
   and Attendants.

King. Though yet of Hamlet our dear
   brother's death
The memory be green, and that it us befitted
To bear our hearts in grief and our whole
   kingdom
To be contracted in one brow of woe,
Yet so far hath discretion fought with nature
That we with wisest sorrow think on him,
Together with remembrance of ourselves.
Therefore our sometime sister, now our queen,
The imperial jointress to this warlike state,
Have we, as 'twere with a defeated joy,— 10

With an auspicious and a dropping eye,
With mirth in funeral and with dirge in
   marriage,
In equal scale weighing delight and dole,—
Taken to wife: nor have we herein barr'd
Your better wisdoms, which have freely gone
With this affair along. For all, our thanks.
Now follows, that you know, young Fortin-
   bras,
Holding a weak supposal of our worth,
Or thinking by our late dear brother's death
Our state to be disjoint and out of frame, 20
Colleagued with the dream of his advantage,
He hath not fail'd to pester us with message,
Importing the surrender of those lands
Lost by his father, with all bonds of law,
To our most valiant brother. So much for
   him.
Now for ourself and for this time of meeting:
Thus much the business is: we have here writ
To Norway, uncle of young Fortinbras,—
Who, impotent and bed-rid, scarcely hears
Of this his nephew's purpose,—to suppress 30
His further gait herein; in that the levies,
The lists and full proportions, are all made
Out of his subject: and we here dispatch
You, good Cornelius, and you, Voltimand,
For bearers of this greeting to old Norway;
Giving to you no further personal power
To business with the king, more than the
   scope
Of these delated articles allow.
Farewell, and let your haste commend your
   duty.

Cor. In that and all things will we show
Vol. our duty.   40

King. We doubt it nothing: heartily fare-
   well. *[Exeunt Voltimand and Cornelius.*
And now, Laertes, what's the news with you?
You told us of some suit; what is 't, Laertes?
You cannot speak of reason to the Dane,
And lose your voice: what wouldst thou beg,
   Laertes,
That shall not be my offer, not thy asking?
The head is not more native to the heart,
The hand more instrumental to the mouth,

---

154. **extravagant and erring,** wandering. Both
words mean the same thing. 155. **confine,** place of confinement. 156. **probation,** proof, trial. 162. **planets
strike.** Planets were regarded as malignant and might
strike travelers by night. 163. **takes,** bewitches, takes
evil effect. 164. **gracious,** full of goodness.
   Scene ii. 9. **jointress,** dowager, widow who holds an
estate settled on her to be enjoyed after her husband's
death. 10. **defeated,** ruined.

17. **that,** that which. 18. **weak supposal,** low
estimate. 20. **disjoint,** distracted, out of joint. **frame,**
order. 21. **Colleagued,** added to. **dream . . . advantage,** visionary hope of success. 23. **Importing,** pur-
porting, pertaining to. 31. **gait,** proceeding. 32.
proportions, estimate of forces or supplies for war;
hence, forces or supplies (col-
lectively). 38. **delated,** expressly stated. 44. **the
Dane,** Danish king. 45. **lose your voice,** speak in vain.
47. **native,** closely connected, related. 48. **instrumental,** serviceable.

Than is the throne of Denmark to thy father.
What wouldst thou have, Laertes?

Laer.　　　　　　　My dread lord, 50
Your leave and favour to return to France;
From whence though willingly I came to Denmark,
To show my duty in your coronation,
Yet now, I must confess, that duty done,
My thoughts and wishes bend again toward France
And bow them to your gracious leave and pardon.

King. Have you your father's leave? What says Polonius?

Pol. He hath, my lord, wrung from me my slow leave
By laboursome petition, and at last
Upon his will I seal'd my hard consent: 60
I do beseech you, give him leave to go.

King. Take thy fair hour, Laertes; time be thine,
And thy best graces spend it at thy will!
But now, my cousin Hamlet, and my son,—

Ham. [*Aside*] A little more than kin, and less than kind.

King. How is it that the clouds still hang on you?

Ham. Not so, my lord; I am too much i' the sun.

Queen. Good Hamlet, cast thy nighted colour off,
And let thine eye look like a friend on Denmark.
Do not for ever with thy vailed lids 70
Seek for thy noble father in the dust:
Thou know'st 'tis common; all that lives must die,
Passing through nature to eternity.

Ham. Ay, madam, it is common.

Queen.　　　　　　　If it be,
Why seems it so particular with thee?

Ham. Seems, madam! nay, it is; I know not 'seems.'
'Tis not alone my inky cloak, good mother,

Nor customary suits of solemn black,
Nor windy suspiration of forced breath,
No, nor the fruitful river in the eye, 80
Nor the dejected 'haviour of the visage,
Together with all forms, moods, shapes of grief,
That can denote me truly: these indeed seem,
For they are actions that a man might play:
But I have that within which passeth show;
These but the trappings and the suits of woe.

King. 'Tis sweet and commendable in your nature, Hamlet,
To give these mourning duties to your father:
But, you must know, your father lost a father;
That father lost, lost his, and the survivor bound 90
In filial obligation for some term
To do obsequious sorrow: but to persever
In obstinate condolement is a course
Of impious stubbornness; 'tis unmanly grief;
It shows a will most incorrect to heaven,
A heart unfortified, a mind impatient,
An understanding simple and unschool'd:
For what we know must be and is as common
As any the most vulgar thing to sense,
Why should we in our peevish opposition 100
Take it to heart? Fie! 'tis a fault to heaven,
A fault against the dead, a fault to nature,
To reason most absurd; whose common theme
Is death of fathers, and who still hath cried,
From the first corse till he that died to-day,
'This must be so.' We pray you, throw to earth
This unprevailing woe, and think of us
As of a father: for let the world take note,
You are the most immediate to our throne;
And with no less nobility of love 110
Than that which dearest father bears his son,
Do I impart toward you. For your intent
In going back to school in Wittenberg,
It is most retrograde to our desire:
And we beseech you, bend you to remain

---

56. **leave and pardon**, permission to depart. 62. **Take . . . hour**, enjoy the privileges of youth. 65. **A little . . . kind**, my relation to you has become more than kinship warrants; it has also become unnatural. 67. **I am . . . sun.** The senses seem to be: I am too much out of doors, I am too much in the sun of your grace (ironical), I am too much of a son to you. Johnson suggested an allusion to the proverb, "Out of heaven's blessing into the warm sun," i.e., Hamlet is out of house and home in being deprived of the kingship. 70. **vailed**, downcast. 74. **Ay . . . common**, it is common, but it hurts nevertheless; possibly a reference to the commonplace quality of the Queen's remark.

78. **customary suits**, suits prescribed by custom for mourning. 79. **windy suspiration**, heavy sighing. **forced breath**, i.e., by the distress of the heart. 92. **obsequious**, dutiful. 93. **condolement**, sorrowing. 95. **incorrect**, untrained, uncorrected. 99. **vulgar thing**, common experience. 107. **unprevailing**, unavailing. 109. **most immediate**, next in succession. 110. **nobility**, high degree. 112. **impart**. The object is apparently *love* (l. 110). 113. **Wittenberg**, famous German university founded in 1502. 114. **retrograde**, contrary. 115. **bend you**, incline yourself; imperative.

Here, in the cheer and comfort of our eye,
Our chiefest courtier, cousin, and our son.
  Queen. Let not thy mother lose her prayers, Hamlet:
I pray thee, stay with us; go not to Wittenberg.
  Ham. I shall in all my best obey you, madam.   120
  King. Why, 'tis a loving and a fair reply:
Be as ourself in Denmark. Madam, come;
This gentle and unforced accord of Hamlet
Sits smiling to my heart: in grace whereof,
No jocund health that Denmark drinks to-day,
But the great cannon to the clouds shall tell,
And the king's rouse the heavens shall bruit again,
Re-speaking earthly thunder. Come away.
                        [*Exeunt all but Hamlet.*
  Ham. O, that this too too solid flesh would melt,
Thaw and resolve itself into a dew!   130
Or that the Everlasting had not fix'd
His canon 'gainst self-slaughter! O God! God!
How weary, stale, flat and unprofitable,
Seem to me all the uses of this world!
Fie on 't! ah fie! 'tis an unweeded garden,
That grows to seed; things rank and gross in nature
Possess it merely. That it should come to this!
But two months dead: nay, not so much, not two:
So excellent a king; that was, to this,   139
Hyperion to a satyr; so loving to my mother
That he might not beteem the winds of heaven
Visit her face too roughly. Heaven and earth!
Must I remember? why, she would hang on him,
As if increase of appetite had grown
By what it fed on: and yet, within a month—
Let me not think on 't—Frailty, thy name is woman!—
A little month, or ere those shoes were old
With which she follow'd my poor father's body,

Like Niobe, all tears:—why she, even she—
O God! a beast, that wants discourse of reason,   150
Would have mourn'd longer—married with my uncle,
My father's brother, but no more like my father
Than I to Hercules: within a month:
Ere yet the salt of most unrighteous tears
Had left the flushing in her galled eyes,
She married. O, most wicked speed, to post
With such dexterity to incestuous sheets!
It is not nor it cannot come to good:
But break, my heart; for I must hold my tongue.

Enter HORATIO, MARCELLUS, *and* BERNARDO.

  Hor. Hail to your lordship!
  Ham.   I am glad to see you well: 160
Horatio,—or I do forget myself.
  Hor. The same, my lord, and your poor servant ever.
  Ham. Sir, my good friend; I'll change that name with you:
And what make you from Wittenberg, Horatio?
Marcellus?
  Mar. My good lord—
  Ham. I am very glad to see you. Good even, sir.
But what, in faith, make you from Wittenberg?
  Hor. A truant disposition, good my lord.
  Ham. I would not hear your enemy say so,   170
Nor shall you do mine ear that violence
To make it truster of your own report
Against yourself: I know you are no truant.
But what is your affair in Elsinore?
We'll teach you to drink deep ere you depart.
  Hor. My lord, I came to see your father's funeral.
  Ham. I pray thee, do not mock me, fellow-student;
I think it was to see my mother's wedding.

---

117. **cousin,** usual term of courtesy of a king to his nobles. · 127. **rouse,** draft of liquor. **bruit again,** echo. 137. **merely,** completely, entirely. 140. **Hyperion,** god of the sun in the older régime of ancient gods; here, probably Apollo. 141. **beteem,** allow.

149. **Niobe,** Tantalus's daughter, who boasted that she had more sons and daughters than Leto; for this Apollo and Artemis slew her children. She was turned by Zeus into a stone on Mt. Sipylus. 150. **discourse of reason,** process or faculty of reason. 156. **post,** hasten. 157. **dexterity,** facility. 163. **I'll . . . you,** I'll be your servant, you shall be my friend (Johnson); also explained as "I'll exchange the name of friend with you."

Hor. Indeed, my lord, it follow'd hard upon.

Ham. Thrift, thrift, Horatio! the funeral baked meats   180
Did coldly furnish forth the marriage tables.
Would I had met my dearest foe in heaven
Or ever I had seen that day, Horatio!
My father!—methinks I see my father.

Hor. Where, my lord?

Ham.   In my mind's eye, Horatio.

Hor. I saw him once; he was a goodly king.

Ham. He was a man, take him for all in all,
I shall not look upon his like again.

Hor. My lord, I think I saw him yester-night.

Ham. Saw? who?   190

Hor. My lord, the king your father.

Ham.   The king my father!

Hor. Season your admiration for a while
With an attent ear, till I may deliver,
Upon the witness of these gentlemen,
This marvel to you.

Ham.   For God's love, let me hear.

Hor. Two nights together had these gentlemen,
Marcellus and Bernardo, on their watch,
In the dead vast and middle of the night,
Been thus encounter'd. A figure like your father,
Armed at point exactly, cap-a-pe,   200
Appears before them, and with solemn march
Goes slow and stately by them: thrice he walk'd
By their oppress'd and fear-surprised eyes,
Within his truncheon's length; whilst they, distill'd
Almost to jelly with the act of fear,
Stand dumb and speak not to him. This to me
In dreadful secrecy impart they did;
And I with them the third night kept the watch:
Where, as they had deliver'd, both in time,
Form of the thing, each word made true and good,   210

The apparition comes: I knew your father;
These hands are not more like.

Ham.   But where was this?

Mar. My lord, upon the platform where we watch'd.

Ham. Did you not speak to it?

Hor.   My lord, I did;
But answer made it none: yet once me-thought
It lifted up it head and did address
Itself to motion, like as it would speak;
But even then the morning cock crew loud,
And at the sound it shrunk in haste away,
And vanish'd from our sight.

Ham.   'Tis very strange.   220

Hor. As I do live, my honour'd lord, 'tis true;
And we did think it writ down in our duty
To let you know of it.

Ham. Indeed, indeed, sirs, but this troubles me.
Hold you the watch to-night?

Mar.}
Ber. }   We do, my lord.

Ham. Arm'd, say you?

Mar.}
Ber. }   Arm'd, my lord.

Ham. From top to toe?

Mar.}
Ber. }   My lord, from head to foot.

Ham. Then saw you not his face?

Hor. O, yes, my lord; he wore his beaver up.   230

Ham. What, look'd he frowningly?

Hor. A countenance more in sorrow than in anger.

Ham. Pale or red?

Hor. Nay, very pale.

Ham.   And fix'd his eyes upon you?

Hor. Most constantly.

Ham.   I would I had been there.

Hor. It would have much amazed you.

Ham. Very like, very like. Stay'd it long?

Hor. While one with moderate haste might tell a hundred.

Mar.}
Ber. }   Longer, longer.

Hor. Not when I saw't.

Ham.   His beard was grizzled,—no? 240

Hor. It was, as I have seen it in his life,
A sable silver'd.

---

179. **hard**, close. 180. **baked meats**, meat pies.
182. **dearest**, direst. The adjective *dear* in Shakespeare has two different origins: O.E. dēore, "beloved," and O.E. dēor, "fierce." *Dearest* is the superlative of the second.
192. **Season your admiration**, restrain your astonishment. 200. **cap-a-pe**, from head to foot. 203. **oppress'd**, distressed. 204. **truncheon**, officer's staff.
distill'd, softened, weakened. 205. **act**, action.

216. **it**, its. 230. **beaver**, visor on the helmet. 242. **sable**, black color.

Ham.   I will watch to-night;
Perchance 'twill walk again.
   Hor.   I warrant it will.
   Ham. If it assume my noble father's person,
I'll speak to it, though hell itself should gape
And bid me hold my peace. I pray you all,
If you have hitherto conceal'd this sight,
Let it be tenable in your silence still;
And whatsoever else shall hap to-night,
Give it an understanding, but no tongue: 250
I will requite your loves. So, fare you well:
Upon the platform, 'twixt eleven and twelve,
I'll visit you.
   All.   Our duty to your honour.
   Ham. Your loves, as mine to you: farewell.
                   · [*Exeunt all but Hamlet.*
My father's spirit in arms! all is not well;
I doubt some foul play: would the night
   were come!
Till then sit still, my soul: foul deeds will
   rise,
Though all the earth o'erwhelm them, to
   men's eyes.   [*Exit.*

Scene III. *A room in Polonius' house.*

Enter Laertes *and* Ophelia

   Laer. My necessaries are embark'd: farewell:
And, sister, as the winds give benefit
And convoy is assistant, do not sleep,
But let me hear from you.
   Oph.   Do you doubt that?
   Laer. For Hamlet and the trifling of his
   favour,
Hold it a fashion and a toy in blood,
A violet in the youth of primy nature,
Forward, not permanent, sweet, not lasting,
The perfume and suppliance of a minute;
No more.
   Oph. No more but so?
   Laer.   Think it no more: 10
For nature, crescent, does not grow alone
In thews and bulk, but, as this temple waxes,
The inward service of the mind and soul

Grows wide withal. Perhaps he loves you
   now,
And now no soil nor cautel doth besmirch
The virtue of his will: but you must fear,
His greatness weigh'd, his will is not his
   own;
For he himself is subject to his birth:
He may not, as unvalued persons do,
Carve for himself; for on his choice depends 20
The safety and health of this whole state;
And therefore must his choice be circum-
   scribed
Unto the voice and yielding of that body
Whereof he is the head. Then if he says he
   loves you,
It fits your wisdom so far to believe it
As he in his particular act and place
May give his saying deed; which is no further
Than the main voice of Denmark goes
   withal.
Then weigh what loss your honour may sus-
   tain,
If with too credent ear you list his songs, 30
Or lose your heart, or your chaste treasure
   open
To his unmaster'd importunity.
Fear it, Ophelia, fear it, my dear sister,
And keep you in the rear of your affection,
Out of the shot and danger of desire.
The chariest maid is prodigal enough,
If she unmask her beauty to the moon:
Virtue itself 'scapes not calumnious strokes:
The canker galls the infants of the spring,
Too oft before their buttons be disclosed, 40
And in the morn and liquid dew of youth
Contagious blastments are most imminent.
Be wary then; best safety lies in fear:
Youth to itself rebels, though none else near.
   Oph. I shall the effect of this good lesson
   keep,
As watchman to my heart. But, good my
   brother,
Do not, as some ungracious pastors do,
Show me the steep and thorny way to
   heaven;
Whiles, like a puff'd and reckless libertine,

Scene iii. 3. **convoy is assistant**, means of conveyance are at hand. 6. **fashion**, custom, prevailing usage. **toy in blood**, passing amorous fancy. 7. **primy**, in its prime. 8. **Forward**, precocious. 9. **suppliance of a minute**, diversion to fill up a minute. 10. **so**. Q₂F place a period after this word. The punctuation concerns the extent to which Ophelia is obedient to Laertes's suggestion. 11. **crescent**, growing, waxing. 12. **thews**, bodily strength. **temple**, body.

14. **withal**, also. 15. **soil**, blemish. **cautel**, crafty device. 16. **virtue . . . will**, good intentions. 19. **unvalued**, of no value (as to rank). 23. **voice and yielding**, support, approval. 27. **deed**, effect. 32. **unmaster'd**, unrestrained. 36. **chariest**, most scrupulously modest. 39. **The canker . . . spring**, the canker-worm destroys the young plants of spring. 40. **buttons**, buds. **disclosed**, opened. 41. **liquid dew**, i.e., time when dew is fresh. 42. **blastments**, blights. 47. **ungracious**, graceless. 49. **puff'd**, bloated.

Himself the primrose path of dalliance
　　treads,　　　　　　　　　　　　　　50
And recks not his own rede.
　　Laer.　　　　　　O, fear me not.
I stay too long: but here my father comes.

　　　　　Enter POLONIUS.

A double blessing is a double grace;
Occasion smiles upon a second leave.
　　Pol. Yet here, Laertes! aboard, aboard,
　　for shame!
The wind sits in the shoulder of your sail,
And you are stay'd for. There; my blessing
　　with thee!
And these few precepts in thy memory
See thou character. Give thy thoughts no
　　tongue,
Nor any unproportion'd thought his act.　60
Be thou familiar, but by no means vulgar.
Those friends thou hast, and their adoption
　　tried,
Grapple them to thy soul with hoops of steel;
But do not dull thy palm with entertainment
Of each new-hatch'd, unfledged comrade.
　　Beware
Of entrance to a quarrel, but being in,
Bear 't that the opposed may beware of thee.
Give every man thy ear, but few thy voice;
Take each man's censure, but reserve thy
　　judgement.
Costly thy habit as thy purse can buy,　70
But not express'd in fancy; rich, not gaudy;
For the apparel oft proclaims the man,
And they in France of the best rank and
　　station
†Are of a most select and generous chief in
　　that.
Neither a borrower nor a lender be;
For loan oft loses both itself and friend,
And borrowing dulls the edge of husbandry.
This above all: to thine own self be true,
And it must follow, as the night the day,
Thou canst not then be false to any man.　80

---

51. **recks**, heeds. **rede**, counsel.　53. **double**, i.e.,
Laertes has already bade his father good-by.　54. **Occasion**, opportunity.　58. **precepts.** Many parallels have
been found to the series of maxims which follows, one of
the closest being that in Lyly's *Euphues.*　59. **character**,
inscribe; accent on second syllable.　60. **unproportion'd**, inordinate.　61. **familiar**, friendly. **vulgar**,
common.　64. **dull thy palm**, make thyself less sensitive to true hospitality.　65. **unfledged**, immature.
69. **censure**, opinion.　71. **express'd in fancy**, fantastical in design.　74. **Are of . . . that.** Onions defines
chief as "in chief," "mainly," "principally." Rowe and
Delius omit *of* and place a comma after *generous.* Collier
changes *chief* to *choice. Chief* is usually taken as a substantive meaning "head," "eminence."　77. **husbandry**,
thrift.

Farewell: my blessing season this in thee!
　　Laer. Most humbly do I take my leave,
　　my lord.
　　Pol. The time invites you; go; your serv-
　　ants tend.
　　Laer. Farewell, Ophelia; and remember
　　well
What I have said to you.
　　Oph.　　　　　　'Tis in my memory lock'd,
And you yourself shall keep the key of it.
　　Laer. Farewell.　　　　　　　　　[*Exit.*
　　Pol. What is 't, Ophelia, he hath said to
　　you?
　　Oph. So please you, something touching
　　the Lord Hamlet.
　　Pol. Marry, well bethought:　　　　90
'Tis told me, he hath very oft of late
Given private time to you; and you your-
　　self
Have of your audience been most free and
　　bounteous:
If it be so, as so 't is put on me,
And that in way of caution, I must tell
　　you,
You do not understand yourself so clearly
As it behoves my daughter and your honour.
What is between you? give me up the truth.
　　Oph. He hath, my lord, of late made many
　　tenders
Of his affection to me.　　　　　　　100
　　Pol. Affection! pooh! you speak like a
　　green girl,
Unsifted in such perilous circumstance.
Do you believe his tenders, as you call them?
　　Oph. I do not know, my lord, what I
　　should think.
　　Pol. Marry, I'll teach you: think yourself
　　a baby;
That you have ta'en these tenders for true
　　pay,
Which are not sterling. Tender yourself
　　more dearly;
Or—not to crack the wind of the poor phrase,
Running it thus—you'll tender me a fool.
　　Oph. My lord, he hath importuned me
　　with love　　　　　　　　　　　　110
In honourable fashion.
　　Pol. Ay, fashion you may call it; go to, go
　　to.

---

81. **season**, mature.　94. **put on**, impressed on.　99,
103. **tenders**, offers.　102. **Unsifted**, untried.　106.
tenders, promises to pay.　107. **sterling**, legal currency. **Tender**, hold.　108. **crack the wind**, i.e., run
it until it is broken-winded.　109. **tender . . . fool**, show
me a fool (for a daughter).　112. **fashion**, mere form,
pretense. **go to**, common phrase of reproach.

Oph. And hath given countenance to his speech, my lord,
With almost all the holy vows of heaven.

Pol. Ay, springes to catch woodcocks. I do know,
When the blood burns, how prodigal the soul
Lends the tongue vows: these blazes, daughter,
Giving more light than heat, extinct in both,
Even in their promise, as it is a-making, 119
You must not take for fire. From this time
Be somewhat scanter of your maiden presence;
Set your entreatments at a higher rate
Than a command to parley. For Lord Hamlet,
Believe so much in him, that he is young,
And with a larger tether may he walk
Than may be given you: in few, Ophelia,
Do not believe his vows; for they are brokers,
Not of that dye which their investments show,
But mere implorators of unholy suits,
Breathing like sanctified and pious bawds, 130
The better to beguile. This is for all:
I would not, in plain terms, from this time forth,
Have you so slander any moment leisure,
As to give words or talk with the Lord Hamlet.
Look to 't, I charge you: come your ways.

Oph. I shall obey, my lord.   [*Exeunt.*

Scene IV. *The platform.*

Enter Hamlet, Horatio, *and* Marcellus.

Ham. The air bites shrewdly; it is very cold.

Hor. It is a nipping and an eager air.

Ham. What hour now?

Hor.   I think it lacks of twelve.

Mar. No, it is struck.

Hor. Indeed? I heard it not: then it draws near the season

Wherein the spirit held his wont to walk.

[*A flourish of trumpets, and ordnance shot off, within.*

What does this mean, my lord?

Ham. The king doth wake to-night and takes his rouse,
Keeps wassail, and the swaggering up-spring reels;
And, as he drains his draughts of Rhenish down,   10
The kettle-drum and trumpet thus bray out
The triumph of his pledge.

Hor.   Is it a custom?

Ham. Ay, marry, is 't:
But to my mind, though I am native here
And to the manner born, it is a custom
More honour'd in the breach than the observance.
This heavy-headed revel east and west
Makes us traduced and tax'd of other nations:
They clepe us drunkards, and with swinish phrase
Soil our addition; and indeed it takes   20
From our achievements, though perform'd at height,
The pith and marrow of our attribute.
So, oft it chances in particular men,
That for some vicious mole of nature in them,
As, in their birth—wherein they are not guilty,
Since nature cannot choose his origin—
By the o'ergrowth of some complexion,
Oft breaking down the pales and forts of reason,
Or by some habit that too much o'er-leavens
The form of plausive manners, that these men,   30
Carrying, I say, the stamp of one defect,
Being nature's livery, or fortune's star,—

---

113. **countenance,** credit, support. 115. **springes,** snares. **woodcocks,** birds easily caught; type of stupidity. 122. **entreatments,** conversations, interviews. 123. **command to parley,** mere invitation to talk. 124. **so . . . him,** this much concerning him. 126. **in few,** briefly. 127. **brokers,** go-betweens, procurers. 128. **dye,** color or sort. **investments,** clothes. 129. **implorators for,** solicitors of. 130. **Breathing,** speaking. **bawds,** so Theobald. Many editors follow the Q₂F reading, *bond,* which would mean "agreements." 133. **slander,** bring disgrace or reproach upon.
Scene iv. 1. **it . . . cold.** The question mark which follows this in F would indicate that Hamlet has just come upon the platform.

8. **wake,** stay awake, hold revel. **rouse,** carouse, drinking-bout. 9. **wassail,** carousal. **up-spring,** last and wildest dance at German merrymakings (Elze). **reels,** reels through. 10. **Rhenish,** Rhine wine. 12. **triumph . . . pledge,** his glorious achievement as a drinker. 15. **to . . . born,** destined by birth to be subject to the custom in question (Onions). 17-38. **This . . . scandal.** The omission of this passage from F may be due to deference to the queen of James I, who was a Danish princess. 18. **tax'd of,** censured by. 19. **clepe,** call. **with swinish phrase,** by calling us swine. 20. **addition,** title. 22. **attribute,** reputation. 24. **mole of nature,** natural blemish in one's constitution. 27. **complexion,** particular combination of humors forming a temperament. 28. **pales,** palings (as of a fortification). 29. **o'er-leavens,** makes too light. 30. **plausive,** pleasing. 32. **nature's livery,** endowment from nature. **fortune's star,** the position in which one is placed by fortune; a reference to astrology. The two phrases are aspects of the same thing.

Their virtues else—be they as pure as grace,
As infinite as man may undergo—
Shall in the general censure take corruption
From that particular fault: the dram of †eale
Doth all the noble substance †of a doubt
To his own scandal.
　　Hor.　　　　　Look, my lord, it comes!

Enter Ghost.

　　Ham. Angels and ministers of grace defend us!
Be thou a spirit of health or goblin damn'd, 40
Bring with thee airs from heaven or blasts from hell,
Be thy intents wicked or charitable,
Thou comest in such a questionable shape
That I will speak to thee: I'll call thee Hamlet,
King, father, royal Dane: O, answer me!
Let me not burst in ignorance; but tell
Why thy canonized bones, hearsed in death,
Have burst their cerements; why the sepulchre,
Wherein we saw thee quietly inurn'd,
Hath oped his ponderous and marble jaws, 50
To cast thee up again. What may this mean,
That thou, dead corse, again in complete steel
Revisit'st thus the glimpses of the moon,
Making night hideous; and we fools of nature
So horridly to shake our disposition
With thoughts beyond the reaches of our souls?
Say, why is this? wherefore? what should we do?　　　　　[*Ghost beckons Hamlet.*
　　Hor. It beckons you to go away with it,
As if it some impartment did desire
To you alone.
　　Mar.　　　　Look, with what courteous action　　　　　60
It waves you to a more removed ground:
But do not go with it.

　　Hor.　　　　　No, by no means.
　　Ham. It will not speak; then I will follow it.
　　Hor. Do not, my lord.
　　Ham.　　　Why, what should be the fear?
I do not set my life at a pin's fee;
And for my soul, what can it do to that,
Being a thing immortal as itself?
It waves me forth again: I'll follow it.
　　Hor. What if it tempt you toward the flood, my lord,
Or to the dreadful summit of the cliff　　70
That beetles o'er his base into the sea,
And there assume some other horrible form,
Which might deprive your sovereignty of reason
And draw you into madness? think of it:
The very place puts toys of desperation,
Without more motive, into every brain
That looks so many fathoms to the sea
And hears it roar beneath.
　　Ham.　　　　　It waves me still.
Go on; I'll follow thee.
　　Mar. You shall not go, my lord.
　　Ham.　　　　Hold off your hands.　　80
　　Hor. Be ruled; you shall not go.
　　Ham.　　　　My fate cries out,
And makes each petty artery in this body
As hardy as the Nemean lion's nerve.
Still am I call'd. Unhand me, gentlemen.
By heaven, I'll make a ghost of him that lets me!
I say, away! Go on; I'll follow thee.
　　　　　　　[*Exeunt Ghost and Hamlet.*
　　Hor. He waxes desperate with imagination.
　　Mar. Let's follow; 'tis not fit thus to obey him.
　　Hor. Have after. To what issue will this come?
　　Mar. Something is rotten in the state of Denmark.　　　　　90
　　Hor. Heaven will direct it.
　　Mar.　　　Nay, let's follow him. [*Exeunt.*

34. **undergo**, bear the weight of. 36-38. **the dram . . . scandal**, a famous crux; *dram of eale* has had various interpretations, the preferred one being probably, "a dram of evil." The following emendations of *of a doubt* have been offered: (1) *oft adoubt* or *adout* (often erase or "do out"), (2) *antidote* (counteract). Dowden suggests that *scandal* may be a verb to be read with *Doth*, giving the general interpretation, "Out of a mere doubt or suspicion the dram of evil degrades in reputation all the noble substance to its own [substance]." 39. **ministers of grace**, messengers of God. 43. **questionable**, inviting question or conversation. 47. **canonized**, buried according to the canon of the church. **hearsed**, coffined. 48. **cerements**, grave-clothes. 53. **glimpses of the moon**, the earth by night. 54. **fools of nature**, persons limited in intelligence by nature. 59. **impartment**, communication. 61. **removed**, remote.

71. **beetles o'er**, overhangs threateningly. 73. **deprive . . . reason**, take away the sovereignty of your reason. It was thought that evil spirits would sometimes assume the form of departed spirits in order to work madness in a human creature. 75. **toys of desperation**, freakish notions of suicide. 83. **Nemean lion's**. The Nemean lion was one of the monsters slain by Hercules. **nerve**, sinew, tendon. The point is that the arteries which were carrying the spirits out into the body were functioning and were as stiff and hard as the sinews of the lion. 85. **lets**, hinders. 89. **issue**, outcome. 91. **it**, i.e., the outcome.

Scene V. *Another part of the platform.*

Enter Ghost *and* Hamlet.

Ham. Where wilt thou lead me? speak;
   I'll go no further.
Ghost. Mark me.
Ham.   I will.
Ghost.   My hour is almost come,
When I to sulphurous and tormenting flames
Must render up myself.
Ham.   Alas, poor ghost!
Ghost. Pity me not, but lend thy serious
   hearing
To what I shall unfold.
Ham.   Speak; I am bound to hear.
Ghost. So art thou to revenge, when thou
   shalt hear.
Ham. What?
Ghost. I am thy father's spirit,
Doom'd for a certain term to walk the night,
And for the day confined to fast in fires,   11
Till the foul crimes done in my days of
   nature
Are burnt and purged away. But that I am
   forbid
To tell the secrets of my prison-house,
I could a tale unfold whose lightest word
Would harrow up thy soul, freeze thy young
   blood,
Make thy two eyes, like stars, start from
   their spheres,
Thy knotted and combined locks to part
And each particular hair to stand an end,
Like quills upon the fretful porpentine: 20
But this eternal blazon must not be
To ears of flesh and blood. List, list, O,
   list!
If thou didst ever thy dear father love—
Ham. O God!
Ghost. Revenge his foul and most un-
   natural murder.
Ham. Murder!
Ghost. Murder most foul, as in the best
   it is;
But this most foul, strange and unnatural.
Ham. Haste me to know't, that I, with
   wings as swift
As meditation or the thoughts of love,   30

May sweep to my revenge.
Ghost.   I find thee apt;
And duller shouldst thou be than the fat
   weed
That roots itself in ease on Lethe wharf,
Wouldst thou not stir in this. Now, Ham-
   let, hear:
'Tis given out that, sleeping in my orchard,
A serpent stung me; so the whole ear of
   Denmark
Is by a forged process of my death
Rankly abused: but know, thou noble youth,
The serpent that did sting thy father's life
Now wears his crown.
Ham.   O my prophetic soul!   40
My uncle!
Ghost. Ay, that incestuous, that adult-
   erate beast,
With witchcraft of his wit, with traitorous
   gifts,—
O wicked wit and gifts, that have the power
So to seduce!—won to his shameful lust
The will of my most seeming-virtuous queen:
O Hamlet, what a falling-off was there!
From me, whose love was of that dignity
That it went hand in hand even with the vow
I made to her in marriage, and to decline   50
Upon a wretch whose natural gifts were poor
To those of mine!
But virtue, as it never will be moved,
Though lewdness court it in a shape of
   heaven,
So lust, though to a radiant angel link'd,
Will sate itself in a celestial bed,
And prey on garbage.
But, soft! methinks I scent the morning
   air;
Brief let me be. Sleeping within my orchard,
My custom always of the afternoon,   60
Upon my secure hour thy uncle stole,
With juice of cursed hebenon in a vial,
And in the porches of my ears did pour
The leperous distilment; whose effect
Holds such an enmity with blood of man
That swift as quicksilver it courses through
The natural gates and alleys of the body,
And with a sudden vigour it doth posset

---

11. **fast,** probably, do without food. It has been sometimes taken in the sense of doing general penance. 17. **spheres,** orbits. 18. **knotted,** perhaps, intricately arranged (Onions). **combined,** tied, bound. 20. **porpentine,** porcupine. 21. **eternal blazon,** promulgation or proclamation of eternity, revelation of the hereafter. 25. **unnatural,** i.e., pertaining to fratricide.

32. **fat weed.** Many suggestions have been offered as to the particular plant intended, including asphodel; probably, a general figure for plants growing along rotting wharves and piles. 33. **Lethe wharf,** bank of the river of forgetfulness in Hades. 37. **process,** official narrative. 42. **adulterate,** adulterous. 61. **secure,** confident, unsuspicious. 62. **hebenon,** generally supposed to mean henbane. Elze conjectured *hemlock;* Nicholson, *ebenus* meaning "yew." 64. **leperous,** causing leprosy. 68. **posset,** coagulate, curdle.

And curd, like eager droppings into milk,
The thin and wholesome blood: so did it
　　mine;　　　　　　　　　　　　　　70
And a most instant tetter bark'd about,
Most lazar-like, with vile and loathsome
　　crust,
All my smooth body.
Thus was I, sleeping, by a brother's hand
Of life, of crown, of queen, at once dis-
　　patch'd:
Cut off even in the blossoms of my sin,
Unhousel'd, disappointed, unaneled,
No reckoning made, but sent to my account
With all my imperfections on my head:
O, horrible! O, horrible! most horrible!　80
If thou hast nature in thee, bear it not;
Let not the royal bed of Denmark be
A couch for luxury and damned incest.
But, howsoever thou pursuest this act,
Taint not thy mind, nor let thy soul contrive
Against thy mother aught: leave her to
　　heaven
And to those thorns that in her bosom lodge,
To prick and sting her. Fare thee well at
　　once!
The glow-worm shows the matin to be near,
And 'gins to pale his uneffectual fire:　　90
Adieu, adieu! Hamlet, remember me. [Exit.
　　Ham. O all you host of heaven! O earth!
　　　what else?
And shall I couple hell? O, fie! Hold, hold,
　　my heart;
And you, my sinews, grow not instant old,
But bear me stiffly up. Remember thee!
Ay, thou poor ghost, while memory holds
　　a seat
In this distracted globe. Remember thee!
Yea, from the table of my memory
I'll wipe away all trivial fond records,
All saws of books, all forms, all pressures
　　past,　　　　　　　　　　　　　　100
That youth and observation copied there;
And thy commandment all alone shall live
Within the book and volume of my brain,
Unmix'd with baser matter: yes, by heaven!

69. eager, sour, acid. 72. lazar-like, leper-like. 75.
dispatch'd, suddenly bereft. 77. Unhousel'd, without
having received the sacrament. disappointed, unready,
without equipment for the last journey. unaneled,
without having received extreme unction. 80. O . . .
horrible! Many editors give this line to Hamlet;
Garrick and Sir Henry Irving spoke it in that part. 83.
luxury, lechery. 85. Taint . . . mind, probably, deprave not thy character, do nothing except in the pursuit
of a natural revenge. 89. matin, morning. 90. uneffectual fire, cold light. 93. couple, add. 97. distracted globe, confused head. 98. table, literally,
writing tablet. 100. pressures, impressions stamped.

O most pernicious woman!
O villain, villain, smiling, damned villain!
My tables,—meet it is I set it down,
That one may smile, and smile, and be a
　　villain;
At least I'm sure it may be so in Denmark:
　　　　　　　　　　　　　　　　[Writing.
So, uncle, there you are. Now to my word;
It is 'Adieu, adieu! remember me.'　　　111
I have sworn 't.
　　Mar.⎫ [Within] My lord, my lord,—
　　Hor. ⎭
　　Mar. [Within] Lord Hamlet,—
　　Hor. 　　　　[Within] Heaven secure him!
　　Ham. So be it!
　　Hor. [Within] Hillo, ho, ho, my lord!
　　Ham. Hillo, ho, ho, boy! come, bird,
　　come.

　　　　Enter HORATIO and MARCELLUS.

　　Mar. How is 't, my noble lord?
　　Hor. 　　　　　What news, my lord?
　　Ham. O, wonderful!
　　Hor. 　　　　　　Good my lord, tell it.
　　Ham. No; you'll reveal it.
　　Hor. Not I, my lord, by heaven.
　　Mar. 　　　　　　Nor I, my lord. 120
　　Ham. How say you, then; would heart of
　　　man once think it?
But you'll be secret?
　　Hor.⎫
　　Mar.⎭　　　　　Ay, by heaven, my lord.
　　Ham. There's ne'er a villain dwelling in
　　　all Denmark
But he's an arrant knave.
　　Hor. There needs no ghost, my lord,
　　　come from the grave
To tell us this.
　　Ham. 　　Why, right; you are i' the right;
And so, without more circumstance at all,
I hold it fit that we shake hands and part:
You, as your business and desire shall point
　　you;
For every man has business and desire, 130
Such as it is; and for mine own poor part,
Look you, I'll go pray.
　　Hor. These are but wild and whirling
　　　words, my lord.
　　Ham. I'm sorry they offend you, heartily;
Yes, 'faith, heartily.
　　Hor. 　　　　There's no offence, my lord.

110. word, watchword. 115. Hillo, ho, ho, a falconer's call to a hawk in air. 124. arrant, thorough-
going. 127. more circumstance, further beating about
the bush.

Ham. Yes, by Saint Patrick, but there is, Horatio,
And much offence too. Touching this vision here,
It is an honest ghost, that let me tell you:
For your desire to know what is between us,
O'ermaster't as you may. And now, good friends, 140
As you are friends, scholars and soldiers,
Give me one poor request.

Hor. What is't, my lord? we will.

Ham. Never make known what you have seen to-night.

Hor. \
Mar. } My lord, we will not.

Ham.   Nay, but swear't.

Hor.   In faith,
My lord, not I.

Mar.   Nor I, my lord, in faith.

Ham. Upon my sword.

Mar.   We have sworn, my lord, already.

Ham. Indeed, upon my sword, indeed.

Ghost. [*Beneath*] Swear.

Ham. Ah, ha, boy! say'st thou so? art thou there, truepenny? 150
Come on—you hear this fellow in the cellarage—
Consent to swear.

Hor.   Propose the oath, my lord.

Ham. Never to speak of this that you have seen,
Swear by my sword.

Ghost. [*Beneath*] Swear.

Ham. Hic et ubique? then we'll shift our ground.
Come hither, gentlemen,
And lay your hands again upon my sword:
Never to speak of this that you have heard,
Swear by my sword. 160

Ghost. [*Beneath*] Swear.

Ham. Well said, old mole! canst work i' the earth so fast?
A worthy pioner! Once more remove, good friends.

Hor. O day and night, but this is wondrous strange!

Ham. And therefore as a stranger give it welcome.
There are more things in heaven and earth, Horatio,
Than are dreamt of in your philosophy.
But come;
Here, as before, never, so help you mercy,
How strange or odd soe'er I bear myself, 170
As I perchance hereafter shall think meet
To put an antic disposition on,
That you, at such times seeing me, never shall,
With arms encumber'd thus, or this head-shake,
Or by pronouncing of some doubtful phrase,
As 'Well, well, we know,' or 'We could, an if we would,'
Or 'If we list to speak,' or 'There be, an if they might,'
Or such ambiguous giving out, to note
That you know aught of me: this not to do,
So grace and mercy at your most need help you, 180
Swear.

Ghost. [*Beneath*] Swear.

Ham. Rest, rest, perturbed spirit! [*They swear*]. So, gentlemen,
With all my love I do commend me to you:
And what so poor a man as Hamlet is
May do, to express his love and friending to you,
God willing, shall not lack. Let us go in together;
And still your fingers on your lips, I pray.
The time is out of joint: O cursed spite,
That ever I was born to set it right! 190
Nay, come, let's go together. [*Exeunt.*

ACT II.

SCENE I. *A room in Polonius' house.*

Enter POLONIUS *and* REYNALDO.

Pol. Give him this money and these notes, Reynaldo.

Rey. I will, my lord.

Pol. You shall do marvellous wisely, good Reynaldo,
Before you visit him, to make inquire
Of his behaviour.

Rey.   My lord, I did intend it.

---

136. **Saint Patrick**, a possible reference to St. Patrick as keeper of Purgatory and patron saint of all blunders and confusion. 138. **honest**, i.e., a real ghost and not an evil spirit. 147. **sword**, i.e., the hilt in the form of a cross. 150. **truepenny**, good old boy, or the like. 156. **Hic et ubique?** here and everywhere? 163. **pioner,** digger, miner.

172. **antic**, fantastic. 174. **encumber'd**, folded or entwined. 178. **giving out**, profession of knowledge. **to note**, to give a sign. 186. **friending**, friendliness.

Pol. Marry, well said; very well said. Look you, sir,
Inquire me first what Danskers are in Paris;
And how, and who, what means, and where they keep,
What company, at what expense; and finding
By this encompassment and drift of question   10
That they do know my son, come you more nearer
Than your particular demands will touch it:
Take you, as 'twere, some distant knowledge of him;
As thus, 'I know his father and his friends,
And in part him:' do you mark this, Reynaldo?
Rey. Ay, very well, my lord.
Pol. 'And in part him; but' you may say 'not well:
But, if 't be he I mean, he's very wild;
Addicted so and so:' and there put on him
What forgeries you please; marry, none so rank   20
As may dishonour him; take heed of that;
But, sir, such wanton, wild and usual slips
As are companions noted and most known
To youth and liberty.
Rey.   As gaming, my lord.
Pol. Ay, or drinking, fencing, swearing, quarrelling,
Drabbing: you may go so far.
Rey. My lord, that would dishonour him.
Pol. 'Faith, no; as you may season it in the charge.
You must not put another scandal on him,
That he is open to incontinency;   30
That's not my meaning: but breathe his faults so quaintly
That they may seem the taints of liberty,
The flash and outbreak of a fiery mind,

A savageness in unreclaimed blood,
Of general assault.
Rey.   But, my good lord,—
Pol. Wherefore should you do this?
Rey.   Ay, my lord,
I would know that.
Pol.   Marry, sir, here's my drift;
And, I believe, it is a fetch of wit:
You laying these slight sullies on my son,
As 'twere a thing a little soil'd i' the working,
Mark you,   41
Your party in converse, him you would sound,
Having ever seen in the prenominate crimes
The youth you breathe of guilty, be assured
He closes with you in this consequence;
'Good sir,' or so, or 'friend,' or 'gentleman,'
According to the phrase or the addition
Of man and country.
Rey.   Very good, my lord.
Pol. And then, sir, does he this—he does
—what was I about to say? By the mass, I was about to say something: where did I leave?   51
Rey. At 'closes in the consequence,' at 'friend or so,' and 'gentleman.'
Pol. At 'closes in the consequence,' ay, marry;
He closes thus: 'I know the gentleman;
I saw him yesterday, or t'other day,
Or then, or then; with such, or such; and, as you say,
There was a' gaming; there o'ertook in 's rouse;
There falling out at tennis:' or perchance,
'I saw him enter such a house of sale,'   60
Videlicet, a brothel, or so forth.
See you now;
Your bait of falsehood takes this carp of truth:
And thus do we of wisdom and of reach,
With windlasses and with assays of bias,
By indirections find directions out:

---

7. **me**, i.e., for me; ethical dative. **Danskers**, inhabitants of Dantzig; here, mistakenly used to mean "Danes." 8. **keep**, live. 10. **encompassment**, roundabout talking; **drift**, gradual approach or course. 11-12. **come . . . it**, leave questioning and come nearer by throwing out a bait of imperfect knowledge (Arden). 13. **Take**, assume, pretend. 19. **put on**, impute to. 20. **forgeries**, invented tales. **rank**, excessive. 22. **wanton**, sportive, unrestrained. 25. **fencing**, indicative of the ill-repute of professional fencers and fencing schools in Elizabethan times. 26. **Drabbing**, associating with immoral women. 30. **incontinency**, habitual loose behavior. Malone's interpretation would make this habitual incontinency the *scandal* described; Hudson would read *open to* as *open of*, meaning "open in his practice of." 31. **quaintly**, delicately, ingeniously. 32. **taints of liberty**, blemishes due to freedom.

34. **unreclaimed**, untamed. 35. **general assault**, tendency that assails all untrained youth. 38. **fetch of wit**, clever trick. The F reading, *fetch of warrant*, would mean "a warranted device." 43. **ever**, at any time. **prenominate**, before-mentioned. 45. **closes . . . consequence**, agrees with you in this conclusion. 47. **addition**, title. 49-51. **And then . . . leave**. Malone's arrangement of Q2F as prose is probably correct, since Polonius is represented as letting his mind wander in confusion. 58. **o'ertook in 's rouse**, overcome by drink. 61. **Videlicet**, namely. 64. **reach**, capacity, ability. 65. **windlasses**, i.e., circuitous paths. **assays of bias**, attempts that resemble the course of the bowl, which, being weighted on one side, has a curving motion. 66. **indirections**, devious courses. **directions**, straight courses, i.e., the truth.

So by my former lecture and advice,
Shall you my son. You have me, have you
 not?
Rey. My lord, I have.
Pol.   God be wi' you; fare you well.
Rey. Good my lord!   70
Pol. Observe his inclination in yourself.
Rey. I shall, my lord.
Pol. And let him ply his music.
Rey.   Well, my lord.
Pol. Farewell!

                              [*Exit Reynaldo.*

                 Enter OPHELIA.

        How now, Ophelia! what's the matter?
Oph. O, my lord, my lord, I have been so
 affrighted!
Pol. With what, i' the name of God?
Oph. My lord, as I was sewing in my
 closet,
Lord Hamlet, with his doublet all unbraced,
No hat upon his head; his stockings foul'd,
Ungarter'd, and down-gyved to his ancle;   80
Pale as his shirt; his knees knocking each
 other;
And with a look so piteous in purport
As if he had been loosed out of hell
To speak of horrors,—he comes before me.
Pol. Mad for thy love?
Oph.   My lord, I do not know;
But truly, I do fear it.
Pol.   What said he?
Oph. He took me by the wrist and held me
 hard;
Then goes he to the length of all his arm;
And, with his other hand thus o'er his brow,
He falls to such perusal of my face   90
As he would draw it. Long stay'd he so;
At last, a little shaking of mine arm
And thrice his head thus waving up and
 down,
He raised a sigh so piteous and profound
As it did seem to shatter all his bulk
And end his being: that done, he lets me go:
And, with his head over his shoulder turn'd,
He seem'd to find his way without his eyes;
For out o' doors he went without their helps,
And, to the last, bended their light on me. 100

Pol. Come, go with me: I will go seek the
 king.
This is the very ecstasy of love,
Whose violent property fordoes itself
And leads the will to desperate undertakings
As oft as any passion under heaven
That does afflict our natures. I am sorry.
What, have you given him any hard words of
 late?
Oph. No, my good lord, but, as you did
 command,
I did repel his letters and denied
His access to me.
Pol.   That hath made him mad. 110
I am sorry that with better heed and judge-
 ment
I had not quoted him: I fear'd he did but
 trifle,
And meant to wreck thee; but, beshrew my
 jealousy!
By heaven, it is as proper to our age
To cast beyond ourselves in our opinions
As it is common for the younger sort
To lack discretion. Come, go we to the king:
This must be known; which, being kept close,
 might move
More grief to hide than hate to utter love.

                              [*Exeunt.*

        SCENE II. *A room in the castle.*

Enter KING, QUEEN, ROSENCRANTZ, GUILD-
    ENSTERN, *and* Attendants.

King. Welcome, dear Rosencrantz and
 Guildenstern!
Moreover that we much did long to see you,
The need we have to use you did provoke
Our hasty sending. Something have you
 heard
Of Hamlet's transformation; so call it,
Sith nor the exterior nor the inward man
Resembles that it was. What it should be,
More than his father's death, that thus hath
 put him
So much from the understanding of himself,
I cannot dream of: I entreat you both,   10
That, being of so young days brought up
 with him,

---

67. **lecture,** admonition. 71. **Observe . . . yourself,**
"in your own person, not by spies" (Johnson), or "conform your own conduct to his inclination" (Clarendon
Press); or "test him by studying yourself." 73. **ply his
music,** probably to be taken literally. 77. **closet,**
private chamber. 78. **doublet,** close-fitting coat. **unbraced,** unfastened. 80. **down-gyved,** fallen to the
ankles (like gyves or fetters). 95. **bulk,** body.

102. **ecstasy,** the kind of madness arising from the
dominance of a passion such as love. 103. **property,**
nature. **fordoes,** destroys. 113. **beshrew my jealousy,**
curse my suspicion. 115. **cast beyond,** overshoot,
miscalculate. 118-119. **might . . . love,** i.e., I might
cause more grief to others by hiding the knowledge of
Hamlet's love to Ophelia than hatred to me and mine by
telling of it.
Scene ii. 11. **of . . . days,** from such early youth.

And sith so neighbour'd to his youth and
   haviour,
That you vouchsafe your rest here in our
   court
Some little time: so by your companies
To draw him on to pleasures, and to gather,
So much as from occasion you may glean,
Whether aught, to us unknown, afflicts him
   thus,
That, open'd, lies within our remedy.
   Queen. Good gentlemen, he hath much
   talk'd of you;
And sure I am two men there are not living 20
To whom he more adheres. If it will please
   you
To show us so much gentry and good will
As to expend your time with us awhile,
For the supply and profit of our hope,
Your visitation shall receive such thanks
As fits a king's remembrance.
   Ros.   Both your majesties
Might, by the sovereign power you have of us,
Put your dread pleasures more into command
Than to entreaty.
   Guil.   But we both obey,
And here give up ourselves, in the full bent 30
To lay our service freely at your feet,
To be commanded.
   King. Thanks, Rosencrantz and gentle
   Guildenstern.
   Queen. Thanks, Guildenstern and gentle
   Rosencrantz:
And I beseech you instantly to visit
My too much changed son. Go, some of you,
And bring these gentlemen where Hamlet is.
   Guil. Heavens make our presence and our
   practices
Pleasant and helpful to him!
   Queen.   Ay, amen!
   [*Exeunt Rosencrantz, Guildenstern, and
              some Attendants.*

       Enter POLONIUS.

   Pol. The ambassadors from Norway, my
   good lord,   40
Are joyfully return'd.
   King. Thou still hast been the father of
   good news.
   Pol. Have I, my lord? I assure my good
   liege,

I hold my duty, as I hold my soul,
Both to my God and to my gracious king:
And I do think, or else this brain of mine
Hunts not the trail of policy so sure
As it hath used to do, that I have found
The very cause of Hamlet's lunacy.
   King. O, speak of that; that do I long to
   hear.   50
   Pol. Give first admittance to the ambas-
   sadors;
My news shall be the fruit to that great feast.
   King. Thyself do grace to them, and
   bring them in.   [*Exit Polonius.*
He tells me, my dear Gertrude, he hath
   found
The head and source of all your son's dis-
   temper.
   Queen. I doubt it is no other but the main;
His father's death, and our o'erhasty mar-
   riage.
   King. Well, we shall sift him.

   Re-enter POLONIUS, *with* VOLTIMAND *and*
               CORNELIUS.

             Welcome, my good friends!
Say, Voltimand, what from our brother Nor-
   way?
   Volt. Most fair return of greetings and
   desires.   60
Upon our first, he sent out to suppress
His nephew's levies; which to him appear'd
To be a preparation 'gainst the Polack;
But, better look'd into, he truly found
It was against your highness: whereat grieved,
That so his sickness, age and impotence
Was falsely borne in hand, sends out arrests
On Fortinbras; which he, in brief, obeys;
Receives rebuke from Norway, and in fine
Makes vow before his uncle never more   70
To give the assay of arms against your
   majesty.
Whereon old Norway, overcome with joy,
Gives him three thousand crowns in annual
   fee,
And his commission to employ those soldiers,
So levied as before, against the Polack:
With an entreaty, herein further shown,
                [*Giving a paper.*
That it might please you to give quiet pass
Through your dominions for this enterprise,

---

13. **vouchsafe your rest**, please to stay. 22. **gentry**, courtesy. 24. **supply and profit**, aid and successful outcome. 30. **in . . . bent**, to the utmost degree of our mental capacity.

47. **policy**, conduct of public affairs. 56. **main**, chief point, principal concern. 67. **borne in hand**, deluded. 69. **in fine**, finally. 71. **assay**, assault, trial (of arms).

On such regards of safety and allowance
As therein are set down.
  King.   It likes us well;   80
And at our more consider'd time we'll read,
Answer, and think upon this business.
Meantime we thank you for your well-took
  labour:
Go to your rest; at night we'll feast together:
Most welcome home!
          [Exeunt Voltimand and Cornelius.
  Pol.   This business is well ended.
My liege, and madam, to expostulate
What majesty should be, what duty is,
Why day is day, night night, and time is
  time,
Were nothing but to waste night, day and
  time.
Therefore, since brevity is the soul of wit, 90
And tediousness the limbs and outward
  flourishes,
I will be brief: your noble son is mad:
Mad call I it; for, to define true madness,
What is 't but to be nothing else but mad?
But let that go.
  Queen.   More matter, with less art.
  Pol. Madam, I swear I use no art at all.
That he is mad, 'tis true: 'tis true 'tis pity;
And pity 'tis 'tis true: a foolish figure;
But farewell it, for I will use no art.
Mad let us grant him, then: and now re-
  mains
That we find out the cause of this effect, 101
Or rather say, the cause of this defect,
For this effect defective comes by cause:
Thus it remains, and the remainder thus.
Perpend.
I have a daughter—have while she is mine—
Who, in her duty and obedience, mark,
Hath given me this: now gather, and surmise.
                      [Reads.
'To the celestial and my soul's idol, the most
beautified Ophelia,'—   110
That's an ill phrase, a vile phrase; 'beautified'
is a vile phrase: but you shall hear. Thus:
                      [Reads.
'In her excellent white bosom, these, &c.'
  Queen. Came this from Hamlet to her?
  Pol. Good madam, stay awhile; I will be
  faithful.   *[Reads.*

'Doubt thou the stars are fire;
  Doubt that the sun doth move;
Doubt truth to be a liar;
  But never doubt I love.   119
'O dear Ophelia, I am ill at these numbers;
I have not art to reckon my groans: but that
I love thee best, O most best, believe it.
Adieu.
      'Thine evermore, most dear lady,
        whilst this machine is to him,
                      Hamlet.'
This, in obedience, hath my daughter shown
  me,
And more above, hath his solicitings,
As they fell out by time, by means and place,
All given to mine ear.
  King.   But how hath she
Received his love?
  Pol.   What do you think of me?
  King. As of a man faithful and honour-
  able.
  Pol. I would fain prove so. But what
  might you think,   131
When I had seen this hot love on the wing—
As I perceived it, I must tell you that,
Before my daughter told me—what might
  you,
Or my dear majesty your queen here, think,
If I had play'd the desk or table-book,
Or given my heart a winking, mute and dumb,
Or look'd upon this love with idle sight;
What might you think? No, I went round to
  work,
And my young mistress thus I did bespeak:
'Lord Hamlet is a prince, out of thy star; 141
This must not be:' and then I prescripts gave
  her,
That she should lock herself from his resort,
Admit no messengers, receive no tokens.
Which done, she took the fruits of my advice;
And he, repulsed—a short tale to make—
Fell into a sadness, then into a fast,
Thence to a watch, thence into a weakness,
Thence to a lightness, and, by this declension,
Into the madness wherein now he raves, 150

---

79. **safety and allowance**, pledges of safety to the country and terms of permission for the troops to pass. 81. **consider'd**, suitable for deliberation. 90. **wit**, sound sense or judgment. 91. **flourishes**, ostentatious embellishments. 98. **figure**, figure of speech. 105. **Perpend**, consider.

120. **ill at . . . numbers**, unskilled at writing verses. 121. **reckon**, number metrically, scan (Yale). 124. **machine**, bodily frame. 126. **more above**, moreover. 127. **fell out**, occurred. **means**, opportunities (of access). 136. **play'd . . . table-book**, i.e., remained shut up, concealed his information. 137. **given . . . winking**, given my heart a signal to keep silent. 139. **round**, roundly, straightforwardly. 140. **bespeak**, address. 141. **out . . . star**, above thee in position; thy fortune does not include so high a destiny. 148. **watch**, state of sleeplessness. 149. **lightness**, light-headedness. **declension**, decline, deterioration.

And all we mourn for.

King.　　　　　　　Do you think 'tis this?

Queen. It may be, very likely.

Pol. Hath there been such a time—I'd
fain know that—
That I have positively said "Tis so,'
When it proved otherwise?

King.　　　　　　Not that I know.

Pol. [*Pointing to his head and shoulder*]
　　　Take this from this, if this be other-
　　　wise:
If circumstances lead me, I will find
Where truth is hid, though it were hid indeed
Within the centre.

King.　　　　How may we try it further?

Pol. You know, sometimes he walks four
　　　hours together　　　　　　　　160
Here in the lobby.

Queen.　　　　　So he does indeed.

Pol. At such a time I'll loose my daughter
　　　to him:
Be you and I behind an arras then;
Mark the encounter: if he love her not
And be not from his reason fall'n thereon,
Let me be no assistant for a state,
But keep a farm and carters.

King.　　　　　　　We will try it.

Queen. But, look, where sadly the poor
　　　wretch comes reading.

Pol. Away, I do beseech you, both away:
I'll board him presently.

　　　　[*Exeunt King, Queen, and Attendants.*

　　　　　Enter HAMLET, *reading.*

　　　　　　O, give me leave:　170
How does my good Lord Hamlet?

Ham. Well, God-a-mercy.

Pol. Do you know me, my lord?

Ham. Excellent well; you are a fishmonger.

Pol. Not I, my lord.

Ham. Then I would you were so honest a
man.

Pol. Honest, my lord!

Ham. Ay, sir; to be honest, as this world
goes, is to be one man picked out of ten
thousand.

Pol. That's very true, my lord.　　　180

Ham. For if the sun breed maggots in a

dead dog, being a god kissing carrion,—Have
you a daughter?

Pol. I have, my lord.

Ham. Let her not walk i' the sun: conception is a blessing: but not as your daughter
may conceive. Friend, look to 't.

Pol. [*Aside*] How say you by that? Still
harping on my daughter: yet he knew me not
at first; he said I was a fishmonger: he is far
gone, far gone: and truly in my youth I suffered much extremity for love; very near
this. I'll speak to him again. What do you
read, my lord?

Ham. Words, words, words.

Pol. What is the matter, my lord?　195

Ham. Between who?

Pol. I mean, the matter that you read, my
lord.

Ham. Slanders, sir: for the satirical rogue
says here that old men have grey beards, that
their faces are wrinkled, their eyes purging
thick amber and plum-tree gum and that
they have a plentiful lack of wit, together
with most weak hams: all which, sir, though
I most powerfully and potently believe, yet I
hold it not honesty to have it thus set down,
for yourself, sir, should be old as I am, if like
a crab you could go backward.

Pol. [*Aside*] Though this be madness, yet
there is method in 't. Will you walk out of
the air, my lord?

Ham. Into my grave.　　　　　　210

Pol. Indeed, that is out o' the air. [*Aside*]
How pregnant sometimes his replies are! a
happiness that often madness hits on, which
reason and sanity could not so prosperously
be delivered of. I will leave him, and suddenly contrive the means of meeting between
him and my daughter.—My honourable lord,
I will most humbly take my leave of you.

Ham. You cannot, sir, take from me any
thing that I will more willingly part withal:

---

159. **centre,** middle point of the earth. 163. **arras,**
hanging tapestry. 164. **encounter,** style or manner
of address, behavior. 170. **board,** accost. 174. **fishmonger,** an opprobrious expression possibly meaning
"bawd," "procurer."

182. **god kissing carrion,** the sun-god shining on a
dead body. The Q₂F reading, *good kissing carrion,* some
editors explain as "carrion fit for kissing by the sun."
Hamlet is supposed to be reading the matter from the
book he is carrying. 185. **i' the sun,** in the sunshine of
princely favors (Chambers). **conception,** quibble on
understanding and *pregnancy.* 188. **by,** concerning.
195. **matter,** substance. 196. **Between who?** Hamlet
deliberately takes *matter* as meaning "basis of dispute";
modern usage demands *whom* instead of *who.* 198. **satirical rogue.** Warburton saw an allusion to the tenth
satire of Juvenal. In point of fact there were dozens of
books in circulation in Shakespeare's time which contained such descriptions of old age, but we need not assume that Shakespeare supposed Hamlet to be carrying
any particular book. 200. **purging,** discharging. 205.
honesty, decency. 213. **happiness,** felicity of expression. 214. **prosperously,** successfully. 220. **withal,**
with.

except my life, except my life, except my life.

Pol. Fare you well, my lord.

Ham. These tedious old fools!

Enter ROSENCRANTZ *and* GUILDEN-
STERN.

Pol. You go to seek the Lord Hamlet; there he is.

Ros. [*To Polonius*] God save you, sir!
                                    [*Exit Polonius.*

Guil. My honoured lord!

Ros. My most dear lord!

Ham. My excellent good friends! How dost thou, Guildenstern? Ah, Rosencrantz! Good lads, how do ye both?   230

Ros. As the indifferent children of the earth.

Guil. Happy, in that we are not over-happy;

On fortune's cap we are not the very button.

Ham. Nor the soles of her shoe?

Ros. Neither, my lord.

Ham. Then you live about her waist, or in the middle of her favours?

Guil. 'Faith, her privates we.

Ham. In the secret parts of fortune? O, most true; she is a strumpet. What's the news?   240

Ros. None, my lord, but that the world's grown honest.

Ham. Then is doomsday near: but your news is not true. Let me question more in particular: what have you, my good friends, deserved at the hands of fortune, that she sends you to prison hither?

Guil. Prison, my lord!

Ham. Denmark's a prison.

Ros. Then is the world one.   250

Ham. A goodly one; in which there are many confines, wards and dungeons, Denmark being one o' the worst.

Ros. We think not so, my lord.

Ham. Why, then, 'tis none to you; for there is nothing either good or bad, but thinking makes it so: to me it is a prison.

Ros. Why then, your ambition makes it one; 'tis too narrow for your mind.   259

Ham. O God, I could be bounded in a nut-shell and count myself a king of infinite space, were it not that I have bad dreams.

Guil. Which dreams indeed are ambition, for the very substance of the ambitious is merely the shadow of a dream.

Ham. A dream itself is but a shadow.

Ros. Truly, and I hold ambition of so airy and light a quality that it is but a shadow's shadow.   268

Ham. Then are our beggars bodies, and our monarchs and outstretched heroes the beggars' shadows. Shall we to the court? for, by my fay, I cannot reason.

Ros. }
Guil. } We'll wait upon you.

Ham. No such matter: I will not sort you with the rest of my servants, for, to speak to you like an honest man, I am most dreadfully attended. But, in the beaten way of friendship, what make you at Elsinore?

Ros. To visit you, my lord; no other occasion.   279

Ham. Beggar that I am, I am even poor in thanks; but I thank you: and sure, dear friends, my thanks are too dear a halfpenny. Were you not sent for? Is it your own inclining? Is it a free visitation? Come, deal justly with me: come, come; nay, speak.

Guil. What should we say, my lord?

Ham. Why, any thing, but to the purpose. You were sent for; and there is a kind of confession in your looks which your modesties have not craft enough to colour: I know the good king and queen have sent for you.   291

Ros. To what end, my lord?

Ham. That you must teach me. But let me conjure you, by the rights of our fellowship, by the consonancy of our youth, by the obligation of our ever-preserved love, and by what more dear a better proposer could charge you withal, be even and direct with me, whether you were sent for, or no?

Ros. [*Aside to Guil.*] What say you?   300

Ham. [*Aside*] Nay, then, I have an eye of you.—If you love me, hold not off.

Guil. My lord, we were sent for.

Ham. I will tell you why; so shall my anticipation prevent your discovery, and   305

---

231. **indifferent**, ordinary. 252. **confines**, places of confinement.

264. **very . . . ambitious**, that seemingly most substantial thing which the ambitious pursue (Hudson). 272. **fay, faith. reason**, argue. 273. **wait upon**, accompany. 274. **sort**, class. 276. **dreadfully attended**, poorly provided with servants. 277. **in the . . . friendship**, as a matter of course among friends. 278. **what make you**, what are you doing. 282. **a**, i.e., at a. 284. **free**, voluntary. 294. **conjure**, adjure. 295. **consonancy of our youth**, the fact that we are of the same age. 297. **better proposer**, one more skillful in finding proposals. 305. **prevent your discovery**, forestall your disclosure.

your secrecy to the king and queen moult no feather. I have of late—but wherefore I know not—lost all my mirth, forgone all custom of exercises; and indeed it goes so heavily with my disposition that this goodly frame, the earth, seems to me a sterile promontory, this most excellent canopy, the air, look you, this brave o'erhanging firmament, this majestical roof fretted with golden fire, why, it appears no other thing to me than a foul and pestilent congregation of vapours. What a piece of work is a man! how noble in reason! how infinite in faculty! in form and moving how express and admirable! in action how like an angel! in apprehension how like a god! the beauty of the world! the paragon of animals! And yet, to me, what is this quintessence of dust? man delights not me: no, nor woman neither, though by your smiling 323 you seem to say so.

Ros. My lord, there was no such stuff in my thoughts.

Ham. Why did you laugh then, when I said 'man delights not me'? 327

Ros. To think, my lord, if you delight not in man, what lenten entertainment the players shall receive from you: we coted them on the way; and hither are they coming, to offer you service. 331

Ham. He that plays the king shall be welcome; his majesty shall have tribute of me; the adventurous knight shall use his foil and target; the lover shall not sigh gratis; the humorous man shall end his part in peace; the clown shall make those laugh whose lungs are tickle o' the sere; and the lady shall say her mind freely, or the blank verse shall halt for 't. What players are they? 340

Ros. Even those you were wont to take delight in, the tragedians of the city.

Ham. How chances it they travel? their residence, both in reputation and profit, was better both ways. 345

Ros. I think their inhibition comes by the means of the late innovation.

Ham. Do they hold the same estimation they did when I was in the city? are they so followed? 350

Ros. No, indeed, are they not.

Ham. How comes it? do they grow rusty?

Ros. Nay, their endeavour keeps in the wonted pace: but there is, sir, an aery of children, little eyases, that cry out on the top of question, and are most tyrannically clapped for 't: these are now the fashion, and so berattle the common stages—so they call them—that many wearing rapiers are afraid of goose-quills and dare scarce come 360 thither.

Ham. What, are they children? who maintains 'em? how are they escoted? Will they pursue the quality no longer than they can sing? will they not say afterwards, if they should grow themselves to common players —as it is most like, if their means are no better—their writers do them wrong, to make them exclaim against their own succession? 368

Ros. 'Faith, there has been much to do on both sides; and the nation holds it no sin to tarre them to controversy: there was, for a while, no money bid for argument, unless the poet and the player went to cuffs in the question.

Ham. Is 't possible? 374

Guil. O, there has been much throwing about of brains.

Ham. Do the boys carry it away?

Ros. Ay, that they do, my lord; Hercules and his load too. 379

Ham. It is not very strange; for mine uncle

313. **fretted**, adorned. 317. **faculty**, capacity. 318. **express**, well-framed (?) exact (?) 319. **apprehension**, understanding. 321. **quintessence**, the fifth essence of ancient philosophy, supposed to be the substance of the heavenly bodies and to be latent in all things. 329. **lenten**, meager. 330. **coted**, overtook and passed beyond. 334. **foil and target**, sword and shield. 336. **humorous man**, actor who takes the part of the humor characters. 338. **tickle o' the sere**, easy on the trigger. 338-340. **the lady . . . for't**, the lady (fond of talking) shall have opportunity to talk, blank verse or no blank verse. 344. **residence**, remaining in one place. 346. **inhibition**, formal prohibition (from acting plays in the city or, possibly, at court). 347. **innovation**. The

allusion is either to the introduction into plays of satire on persons or to the introduction of the Children of the Revels into Blackfriars Theater (January, 1603). The actors have been forced to take to the road by two things—some "inhibition" and the rivalry of the children. 352-379. **How . . . load too**. The passage (omitted from Qq) is the famous one dealing with the war of the theaters (1599-1602), namely, the rivalry between the children's companies and the adult actors. 354. **aery**, nest. 355. **eyases**, young hawks. 355-356. **cry . . . question**, speak in a high key dominating conversation (Clarendon Press). clamor forth the height of controversy (Dowden). It is also suggested that there is reference to decrying the leaders of the dramatic profession. 356. **tyrannically**, outrageously. 358. **berattle**, fill with din. **common stages**, public theaters. 359. **many wearing rapiers**, many men of fashion, who were afraid to patronize the common players for fear of being satirized by the poets who wrote for the children. 360. **goose-quills**, i.e., satire. 362. **escoted**, maintained. 363-364. **no longer . . . sing**, i.e., until their voices change. 365. **common**, regular. 368. **exclaim against**, run down, detract. **succession**, future careers. 371. **tarre**, set on (as dogs). 372. **argument**, probably, plot for a play. 373. **question**, controversy. 377. **carry it away**, win the day. 378-379. **Hercules . . . load**, regarded as an allusion to the sign of the Globe Theater, which was Hercules bearing the world on his shoulder.

is king of Denmark, and those that would make mows at him while my father lived, give twenty, forty, fifty, an hundred ducats a-piece for his picture in little. 'Sblood, there is something in this more than natural, if philosophy could find it out. 385

[*Flourish of trumpets within.*

Guil. There are the players.

Ham. Gentlemen, you are welcome to Elsinore. Your hands, come then: the appurtenance of welcome is fashion and ceremony: let me comply with you in this garb, lest my extent to the players, which, I tell you, must show fairly outward, should more appear like entertainment than yours. You are welcome: but my uncle-father and aunt-mother are deceived. 394

Guil. In what, my dear lord?

Ham. I am but mad north-north-west: when the wind is southerly I know a hawk from a handsaw.

Re-enter POLONIUS.

Pol. Well be with you, gentlemen!

Ham. Hark you, Guildenstern; and you too: at each ear a hearer: that great baby you see there is not yet out of his swaddling-clouts. 401

Ros. Happily he's the second time come to them; for they say an old man is twice a child.

Ham. I will prophesy he comes to tell me of the players; mark it. You say right, sir: o' Monday morning; 'twas so indeed.

Pol. My lord, I have news to tell you.

Ham. My lord, I have news to tell you. When Roscius was an actor in Rome,— 410

Pol. The actors are come hither, my lord.

Ham. Buz, buz!

Pol. Upon mine honour,—

Ham. Then came each actor on his ass,—

Pol. The best actors in the world, either for tragedy, comedy, history, pastoral, pas-toral-comical, historical-pastoral, tragical-historical, tragical - comical - historical - pas-toral, scene individable, or poem unlimited: Seneca cannot be too heavy, nor Plautus too light. For the law of writ and the liberty, these are the only men. 421

Ham. O Jephthah, judge of Israel, what a treasure hadst thou!

Pol. What a treasure had he, my lord?

Ham. Why,

'One fair daughter, and no more,
The which he loved passing well.'

Pol. [*Aside*] Still on my daughter.

Ham. Am I not i' the right, old Jephthah?

Pol. If you call me Jephthah, my lord, I have a daughter that I love passing well. 431

Ham. Nay, that follows not.

Pol. What follows, then, my lord?

Ham. Why,

'As by lot, God wot,'

and then, you know,

'It came to pass, as most like it was,'—

the first row of the pious chanson will show you more; for look, where my abridgement comes. 439

Enter four or five Players.

You are welcome, masters; welcome, all. I am glad to see thee well. Welcome, good friends. O, my old friend! thy face is valanced since I saw thee last: comest thou to beard me in Denmark? What, my young lady and mistress! By'r lady, your ladyship is nearer to heaven than when I saw you last, by the altitude of a chopine. Pray God, your voice, like a piece of uncurrent gold, be not cracked within the ring. Masters, you are all welcome. We'll e'en to 't like French falconers, fly at any thing we see: we'll have a speech straight: come, give us a taste of your quality; come, a passionate speech. 452

382. **ducats,** gold coins worth 9s. 4d. 383. **in little,** in miniature. 390. **comply,** observe the formalities of courtesy. **garb,** manner. 391. **extent,** showing of kindness. 396. **I am . . . north-north-west,** I am only partly mad, i.e., in only one point of the compass. 397. **handsaw.** Hanmer's proposed reading *hernshaw* would mean "heron"; *handsaw* may be an early corruption of *hernshaw.* Another view regards *hawk* as the variant of *hack,* a tool of the pickax type, and *handsaw* as a saw operated by hand. 401. **swaddling-clouts,** cloths in which to wrap a newborn baby. 402. **Happily,** haply, by chance. 407. **o' Monday morning,** said to mislead Polonius. 410. **Roscius,** a famous Roman actor. 412. **Buz, buz,** according to Blackstone, an interjection used at Oxford to denote stale news. 414. **Then . . . ass,** probably a quotation, not identified.

418. **scene individable,** a play observing the unity of place. **poem unlimited,** a play disregarding the unities of time and place. 419. **Seneca,** writer of Latin tragedies, model of early Elizabethan writers of tragedy. **Plautus,** writer of Latin comedy. 420. **law . . . liberty,** obligation to be faithful to the text of written plays and freedom to improvise (Hudson); pieces written according to rules and without rules, i.e., "classical" and "romantic" dramas (Chambers). 422. **Jephthah . . . Israel.** A popular ballad of *Jephthah's Daughter* has been preserved in several forms. 437. **like,** probable. 438. **row,** possibly, stanza. **pious chanson,** scriptural ballad. 439. **abridgement comes,** opportunity comes for cutting short the conversation. 442. **valanced,** fringed (with a beard). 447. **chopine,** kind of shoe raised by the thickness of the heel, worn in Italy, particularly at Venice. 448. **uncurrent,** not passable as lawful coinage. 449. **cracked within the ring.** In the centers of coins were rings enclosing the sovereign's head; if the coin was cracked within this ring, it was unfit for currency. 451. **straight,** at once.

First Play. What speech, my lord?

Ham. I heard thee speak me a speech once, but it was never acted; or, if it was, not above once; for the play, I remember, pleased not the million; 'twas caviare to the general: but it was—as I received it, and others, whose judgements in such matters cried in the top of mine—an excellent play, well digested in the scenes, set down with as much modesty as cunning. I remember, 461 one said there were no sallets in the lines to make the matter savoury, nor no matter in the phrase that might indict the author of affectation; but called it an honest method, as wholesome as sweet, and by very much more handsome than fine. One speech in it I chiefly loved: 'twas Æneas' tale to Dido; and thereabout of it especially, where he speaks of Priam's slaughter: if it live in your memory, begin at this line: let me see, let me see—   471

'The rugged Pyrrhus, like the Hyrcanian
        beast,'—

it is not so:—it begins with Pyrrhus:—

'The rugged Pyrrhus, he whose sable arms,
Black as his purpose, did the night re-
        semble
When he lay couched in the ominous horse,
Hath now this dread and black complexion
        smear'd
With heraldry more dismal; head to foot
Now is he total gules; horridly trick'd
With blood of fathers, mothers, daughters,
        sons,   480
Baked and impasted with the parching
        streets,
That lend a tyrannous and damned light
To their lord's murder: roasted in wrath
        and fire,
And thus o'er-sized with coagulate gore,
With eyes like carbuncles, the hellish
        Pyrrhus

Old grandsire Priam seeks.'
So, proceed you.

Pol. 'Fore God, my lord, well spoken, with good accent and good discretion.

First Play.   'Anon he finds him
Striking too short at Greeks; his antique
        sword,   491
Rebellious to his arm, lies where it falls,
Repugnant to command: unequal match'd,
Pyrrhus at Priam drives; in rage strikes
        wide;
But with the whiff and wind of his fell
        sword
The unnerved father falls. Then senseless
        Ilium,
Seeming to feel this blow, with flaming
        top
Stoops to his base, and with a hideous
        crash
Takes prisoner Pyrrhus' ear: for, lo! his
        sword,
Which was declining on the milky head 500
Of reverend Priam, seem'd i' the air to
        stick:
So, as a painted tyrant, Pyrrhus stood,
And like a neutral to his will and matter,
Did nothing.
But, as we often see, against some storm,
A silence in the heavens, the rack stand
        still,
The bold winds speechless and the orb
        below
As hush as death, anon the dreadful
        thunder
Doth rend the region, so, after Pyrrhus'
        pause,   509
Aroused vengeance sets him new a-work;
And never did the Cyclops' hammers
        fall
On Mars's armour forged for proof eterne
With less remorse than Pyrrhus' bleeding
        sword
Now falls on Priam.
Out, out, thou strumpet, Fortune! All
        you gods,
In general synod, take away her pow-
        er;
Break all the spokes and fellies from her
        wheel,

457. **caviare to the general**, not relished by the multitude (like caviare). 459. **cried in the top of**, spoke with greater authority than. 460. **digested**, arranged. 461. **modesty**, moderation. **cunning**, skill. 462. **sallets**, salads; here, spicy improprieties. 464. **indict**, convict. 466-467. **as wholesome . . . fine**. Its beauty was not that of elaborate ornament, but that of order and proportion (Chambers). 468. **Æneas' tale to Dido.** The lines recited by the player are imitated from Marlowe and Nashe's *Dido Queen of Carthage* (II, i, 214 ff.). They are written in such a way that the conventionality of the play within a play is raised above that of ordinary drama. 472. **Pyrrhus**, a Greek hero in the Trojan war. **Hyrcanian beast**, the tiger; see Virgil, *Æneid*, IV, 266. 476. **ominous horse**, Trojan horse. 479. **gules**, red; a heraldic term. **trick'd**, spotted, smeared. 481. **impasted**, made into a paste. 484. **o'er-sized**, covered as with size or glue.

493. **Repugnant**, offering resistance. 496. **Then senseless Ilium**, insensible Troy. 502. **painted tyrant**, tyrant in a picture. 503. **matter**, task. 505. **against**, before. 506. **rack**, mass of clouds. 509. **region**, sky. 512. **proof eterne**, eternal resistance to assault. 516. **synod**, assembly. 517 **fellies**, pieces of wood forming the rim of a wheel.

And bowl the round nave down the hill of
    heaven,
As low as to the fiends!'
Pol. This is too long.   520
Ham. It shall be to the barber's, with
your beard. Prithee, say on: he's for a jig or
a tale of bawdry, or he sleeps: say on: come
to Hecuba.   523
First Play. 'But who, O, who had seen
the mobled queen—'
Ham. 'The mobled queen?'
Pol. That's good; 'mobled queen' is good.
First Play. 'Run barefoot up and down,
    threatening the flames
With bisson rheum; a clout upon that
    head
Where late the diadem stood, and for a
    robe,   530
About her lank and all o'er-teemed loins,
A blanket, in the alarm of fear caught
    up;
Who this had seen, with tongue in venom
    steep'd,
'Gainst Fortune's state would treason
    have pronounced:
But if the gods themselves did see her then
When she saw Pyrrhus make malicious
    sport
In mincing with his sword her husband's
    limbs,
The instant burst of clamour that she
    made,
Unless things mortal move them not at
    all,
Would have made milch the burning eyes
    of heaven,   540
And passion in the gods.'
Pol. Look, whether he has not turned his
colour and has tears in 's eyes. Pray you, no
more.
Ham. 'Tis well; I'll have thee speak out
the rest soon. Good my lord, will you see the
players well bestowed? Do you hear, let
them be well used; for they are the abstract
and brief chronicles of the time: after your
death you were better have a bad epitaph
than their ill report while you live.   551

Pol. My lord, I will use them according
to their desert.
Ham. God's bodykins, man, much better:
use every man after his desert, and who
should 'scape whipping? Use them after
your own honour and dignity: the less they
deserve, the more merit is in your bounty.
Take them in.
Pol. Come, sirs.   559
Ham. Follow him, friends: we'll hear a
play to-morrow. [*Exit Polonius with all the
Players but the First.*] Dost thou hear me,
old friend; can you play the Murder of
Gonzago?
First Play. Ay, my lord.
Ham. We'll ha 't to-morrow night. You
could, for a need, study a speech of some
dozen or sixteen lines, which I would set
down and insert in 't, could you not?
First Play. Ay, my lord.   569
Ham. Very well. Follow that lord; and
look you mock him not. [*Exit First Player.*]
My good friends, I'll leave you till night:
you are welcome to Elsinore.
Ros. Good my lord!
Ham. Ay, so, God be wi' ye; [*Exeunt
Rosencrantz and Guildenstern.*] Now I am
    alone.   575
O, what a rogue and peasant slave am I!
Is it not monstrous that this player here,
But in a fiction, in a dream of passion,
Could force his soul so to his own conceit
That from her working all his visage wann'd,
Tears in his eyes, distraction in 's aspect,
A broken voice, and his whole function suit-
    ing   582
With forms to his conceit? and all for noth-
    ing!
For Hecuba!
What's Hecuba to him, or he to Hecuba,
That he should weep for her? What would
    he do,
Had he the motive and the cue for passion
That I have? He would drown the stage
    with tears
And cleave the general ear with horrid
    speech,   589
Make mad the guilty and appal the free,

---

518. **nave**, hub. 522. **jig**, comic performance given
at the end or in an interval of a play. 523. **bawdry**,
indecency. **Hecuba**, wife of Priam, king of Troy.
525. **mobled**, muffled. 529. **bisson rheum**, blinding
tears. **clout**, piece of cloth. 531. **o'er-teemed**, worn
out with bearing children. 534. **state**, power, majesty.
pronounced, proclaimed. 540. **milch**, moist with
tears. 542. **turned**, changed. 548. **abstract**, summary account.

554. **bodykins**, diminutive form of the oath, "by
God's body." 567. **dozen or sixteen lines.** Critics have
amused themselves by trying to locate Hamlet's lines.
Lucianus's speech, III, ii, 266, ff., is the best guess. 576.
peasant, base. 579. **conceit**, imagination. 580.
wann'd, grew pale. 582-583. **his . . . conceit**, his
whole being responded with forms to suit his thought.
590. **free**, free from guilt, innocent.

Confound the ignorant, and amaze indeed
The very faculties of eyes and ears.
Yet I,
A dull and muddy-mettled rascal, peak,
Like John-a-dreams, unpregnant of my
    cause,
And can say nothing; no, not for a king,
Upon whose property and most dear life
A damn'd defeat was made. Am I a coward?
Who calls me villain? breaks my pate across?
Plucks off my beard, and blows it in my face?
Tweaks me by the nose? gives me the lie i'
    the throat,   601
As deep as to the lungs? who does me this?
Ha!
'Swounds, I should take it: for it cannot be
But I am pigeon-liver'd and lack gall
To make oppression bitter, or ere this
I should have fatted all the region kites
With this slave's offal: bloody, bawdy villain!
Remorseless, treacherous, lecherous, kind-
    less villain!
O, vengeance!   610
Why, what an ass am I! This is most brave,
That I, the son of a dear father murder'd,
Prompted to my revenge by heaven and hell,
Must, like a whore, unpack my heart with
    words,
And fall a-cursing, like a very drab,
A scullion!
Fie upon 't! foh! About, my brain! I have
    heard
That guilty creatures sitting at a play
Have by the very cunning of the scene
Been struck so to the soul that presently   620
They have proclaim'd their malefactions;
For murder, though it have no tongue, will
    speak
With most miraculous organ. I'll have
    these players
Play something like the murder of my father
Before mine uncle: I'll observe his looks;
I'll tent him to the quick: if he but blench,
I know my course. The spirit that I have
    seen

May be the devil: and the devil hath power
To assume a pleasing shape; yea, and per-
    haps
Out of my weakness and my melancholy, 630
As he is very potent with such spirits,
Abuses me to damn me: I'll have grounds
More relative than this: the play's the
    thing
Wherein I'll catch the conscience of the
    king.   [*Exit.*

ACT III.

Scene I. *A room in the castle.*

Enter King, Queen, Polonius, Ophelia,
Rosencrantz, *and* Guildenstern.

King. And can you, by no drift of circum-
    stance,
Get from him why he puts on this con-
    fusion,
Grating so harshly all his days of quiet
With turbulent and dangerous lunacy?
Ros. He does confess he feels himself dis-
    tracted;
But from what cause he will by no means
    speak.
Guil. Nor do we find him forward to be
    sounded,
But, with a crafty madness, keeps aloof,
When we would bring him on to some con-
    fession
Of his true state.
Queen.   Did he receive you well? 10
Ros. Most like a gentleman.
Guil. But with much forcing of his dis-
    position.
Ros. Niggard of question; but, of our
    demands,
Most free in his reply.
Queen.   Did you assay him
To any pastime?
Ros. Madam, it so fell out, that certain
    players
We o'er-raught on the way: of these we told
    him;
And there did seem in him a kind of joy

---

594. **muddy-mettled**, dull-spirited. **peak**, mope,
pine. 595. **John-a-dreams**, an expression occurring
elsewhere in Elizabethan literature to indicate a dreamer.
unpregnant of, not quickened by. 597. **property**,
proprietorship (of crown and life). 598. **defeat**, destruction. 605. **pigeon-liver'd**. The pigeon was supposed to secrete no gall; if Hamlet, so he says, had had
gall, he would have felt the bitterness of oppression, and
avenged it. 607. **region kites**, kites of the air. 609.
kindless, unnatural. 615. **drab**, prostitute. 616.
scullion, kitchen servant. 617. **About**, about it, or
turn thou right about. 626. **tent**, probe. **blench**,
quail, flinch.

628. **May be the devil.** Hamlet's suspicion is
properly grounded in the belief of the time. 631. **spirits**,
humors. 633. **relative**, closely related, definite. **this**,
i.e., the ghost's story.
Act III. Scene i. 1. **drift of circumstance**, roundabout methods. 7. **forward**, willing. 12. **forcing of
his disposition**, i.e., against his will. 13. **Niggard of
question**, sparing of conversation. 14. **assay**, challenge. 17. **o'er-raught**, overtook.

To hear of it: they are about the court,
And, as I think, they have already order 20
This night to play before him.

Pol.   'Tis most true:
And he beseech'd me to entreat your
    majesties
To hear and see the matter.

King. With all my heart; and it doth
    much content me
To hear him so inclined.
Good gentlemen, give him a further edge,
And drive his purpose on to these delights.

Ros. We shall, my lord.
            [*Exeunt Rosencrantz and
                        Guildenstern.*

King.   Sweet Gertrude, leave us too;
For we have closely sent for Hamlet hither,
That he, as 'twere by accident, may here 30
Affront Ophelia:
Her father and myself, lawful espials,
Will so bestow ourselves that, seeing, un-
    seen,
We may of their encounter frankly judge,
And gather by him, as he is behaved,
If 't be the affliction of his love or no
That thus he suffers for.

Queen.   I shall obey you.
And for your part, Ophelia, I do wish
That your good beauties be the happy cause
Of Hamlet's wildness: so shall I hope your
    virtues   40
Will bring him to his wonted way again,
To both your honours.

Oph.   Madam, I wish it may.
                        [*Exit Queen.*

Pol. Ophelia, walk you here. Gracious,
    so please you,
We will bestow ourselves. [*To Ophelia*] Read
    on this book;
That show of such an exercise may colour
Your loneliness. We are oft to blame in
    this,—
'Tis too much proved—that with devotion's
    visage
And pious action we do sugar o'er
The devil himself.

King. [*Aside*] O, 'tis too true!
How smart a lash that speech doth give my
    conscience!   50
The harlot's cheek, beautied with plastering
    art,

26. **edge**, incitement. 29. **closely**, secretly. 31.
Affront, confront. 32. **lawful espials**, legitimate spies.
40. **wildness**, madness. 43. **Gracious**, your grace
(addressed to the king). 45. **exercise**, act of devotion.

Is not more ugly to the thing that helps it
Than is my deed to my most painted word:
O heavy burthen!

Pol. I hear him coming: let's withdraw,
    my lord. [*Exeunt King and Polonius.*

Enter Hamlet.

Ham. To be, or not to be: that is the
    question:
Whether 'tis nobler in the mind to suffer
The slings and arrows of outrageous fortune,
Or to take arms against a sea of troubles,
And by opposing end them? To die: to
    sleep;   60
No more; and by a sleep to say we end
The heart-ache and the thousand natural
    shocks
That flesh is heir to, 'tis a consummation
Devoutly to be wish'd. To die, to sleep;
To sleep: perchance to dream: ay, there's
    the rub;
For in that sleep of death what dreams may
    come
When we have shuffled off this mortal coil,
Must give us pause: there's the respect
That makes calamity of so long life;
For who would bear the whips and scorns of
    time,   70
The oppressor's wrong, the proud man's
    contumely,
The pangs of despised love, the law's delay,
The insolence of office and the spurns
That patient merit of the unworthy takes,
When he himself might his quietus make
With a bare bodkin? who would fardels bear,
To grunt and sweat under a weary life,
But that the dread of something after death,
The undiscover'd country from whose bourn
No traveller returns, puzzles the will   80
And makes us rather bear those ills we
    have
Than fly to others that we know not of?

52. **to**, compared to. **thing**, i.e., the cosmetic. 54.
O heavy burthen! The king's sudden repentance
serves to convince the audience of his guilt. It is to be
noted also that the current theory of psychology provided for sudden changes such as this by the ready
movement of spirits to the heart. 59. **sea**. The mixed
metaphor of this speech has often been commented on;
Theobald's emendation *siege* has sometimes been spoken
on the stage. 65. **rub**, obstacle (in the game of bowls).
67. **shuffled**, sloughed, cast. **coil**, usually means
"turmoil"; here, possibly "body" (conceived of as wound
about the soul like rope); *clay*, *soil*, *veil*, have been
suggested as emendations. 69. **of . . . life**, so long lived.
70. **time**, the world. 72. **despised**, rejected. 73.
office, office-holders. **spurns**, insults. 75. **quietus**,
acquittance; here, death. 76. **bare bodkin**, mere dagger; *bare* is sometimes understood as "unsheathed."
fardels, burdens. 79. **bourn**, boundary.

Thus conscience does make cowards of us all;
And thus the native hue of resolution
Is sicklied o'er with the pale cast of thought,
And enterprises of great pitch and moment
With this regard their currents turn awry,
And lose the name of action.—Soft you
   now!
The fair Ophelia! Nymph, in thy orisons
Be all my sins remember'd.

Oph.   Good my lord, 90
How does your honour for this many a day?

Ham. I humbly thank you; well, well,
   well.

Oph. My lord, I have remembrances of
   yours,
That I have longed long to re-deliver;
I pray you, now receive them.

Ham.   No, not I;
I never gave you aught.

Oph. My honour'd lord, you know right
   well you did;
And, with them, words of so sweet breath
   composed
As made the things more rich: their perfume
   lost,
Take these again; for to the noble mind 100
Rich gifts wax poor when givers prove un-
   kind.
There, my lord.

Ham. Ha, ha! are you honest?

Oph. My lord?

Ham. Are you fair?

Oph. What means your lordship?

Ham. That if you be honest and fair,
your honesty should admit no discourse to
your beauty.

Oph. Could beauty, my lord, have better
commerce than with honesty?   110

Ham. Ay, truly; for the power of beauty
will sooner transform honesty from what it is
to a bawd than the force of honesty can
translate beauty into his likeness: this was
sometime a paradox, but now the time gives
it proof. I did love you once.

Oph. Indeed, my lord, you made me believe so.

Ham. You should not have believed me;
for virtue cannot so inoculate our old stock
but we shall relish of it: I loved 120
you not.

Oph. I was the more deceived.

Ham. Get thee to a nunnery: why wouldst
thou be a breeder of sinners? I am myself
indifferent honest; but yet I could accuse
me of such things that it were better
my mother had not borne me: I am very
proud, revengeful, ambitious, with more
offences at my beck than I have thoughts
to put them in, imagination to give them
shape, or time to act them in. What should
such fellows as I do crawling between earth
and heaven? We are arrant knaves, all;
believe none of us. Go thy ways to a nunnery. Where's your father?   133

Oph. At home, my lord.

Ham. Let the doors be shut upon him,
that he may play the fool no where but in's
own house. Farewell.

Oph. O, help him, you sweet heavens!

Ham. If thou dost marry, I'll give thee
this plague for thy dowry: be thou as chaste
as ice, as pure as snow, thou shalt not escape
calumny. Get thee to a nunnery, go: farewell. Or, if thou wilt needs marry, marry a
fool; for wise men know well enough what
monsters you make of them. To a nunnery,
go, and quickly too. Farewell.   146

Oph. O heavenly powers, restore him!

Ham. I have heard of your paintings too,
well enough; God has given you one face,
and you make yourselves another: you jig,
you amble, and you lisp, and nick-name
God's creatures, and make your wantonness
your ignorance. Go to, I'll no more on 't; it
hath made me mad. I say, we will have no
more marriages: those that are married
already, all but one, shall live; the rest shall
keep as they are. To a nunnery, go. [*Exit.*

Oph. O, what a noble mind is here o'erthrown!   158

---

83. **conscience**, probably, inhibition by the faculty
of reason restraining the will from doing wrong. 84.
native hue, natural color; metaphor derived from the
color of the face. 85. **sicklied o'er**, given a sickly tinge.
cast, shade of color. 86. **pitch**, height; metaphor from
falconry. **moment**, importance. 87. **regard**, respect,
consideration. **currents**, courses. 89. **orisons**, prayers.
103. **honest**, sincere, truthful. 105. **fair**, honorable,
just. 107. **honest and fair**, chaste and beautiful. 108.
your honesty, your chastity. **discourse to**, familiar
intercourse with. 110. **commerce**, intercourse. 115.
the time, the present age.

119. **inoculate**, graft (metaphorical). 120. **but . . .
it**, i.e., that we do not still have about us a taste of the
old stock. 128. **beck**, command. 133. **Where's your
father?** A piece of apparently quite old stage business
has Polonius stick his head out from behind the arras
before this question, so that Hamlet sees him. Ophelia's
lie thus convinces him of her falsity. From this point,
Hamlet apparently feigns madness more violently. 145.
monsters, an allusion to the horns of the cuckold. 148.
your, indefinite use. 150. **jig**, move with jerky motion; probable allusion to the *jig*, or song and dance, of
the current stage. 152-153. **make . . . ignorance**, i.e.,
excuse your wantonness on the ground of your ignorance.
156. **one**, i.e., the king.

The courtier's, soldier's, scholar's, eye,
  tongue, sword;
The expectancy and rose of the fair state, 160
The glass of fashion and the mould of form,
The observed of all observers, quite, quite
  down!
And I, of ladies most deject and wretched,
That suck'd the honey of his music vows,
Now see that noble and most sovereign
  reason,
Like sweet bells jangled, out of tune and
  harsh;
That unmatch'd form and feature of blown
  youth
Blasted with ecstasy: O, woe is me,
To have seen what I have seen, see what I
  see!

Re-enter KING *and* POLONIUS.

King. Love! his affections do not that
  way tend;   170
Nor what he spake, though it lack'd form a
  little,
Was not like madness. There's something in
  his soul,
O'er which his melancholy sits on brood;
And I do doubt the hatch and the disclose
Will be some danger: which for to prevent,
I have in quick determination
Thus set it down: he shall with speed to
  England,
For the demand of our neglected tribute:
Haply the seas and countries different
With variable objects shall expel   180
This something-settled matter in his heart,
Whereon his brains still beating puts him
  thus
From fashion of himself. What think you
  on 't?
Pol. It shall do well: but yet do I believe
The origin and commencement of his grief
Sprung from neglected love. How now,
  Ophelia!
You need not tell us what Lord Hamlet said;
We heard it all. My lord, do as you please;
But, if you hold it fit, after the play
Let his queen mother all alone entreat him 190

To show his grief: let her be round with him;
And I'll be placed, so please you, in the ear
Of all their conference. If she find him
  not,
To England send him, or confine him where
Your wisdom best shall think.
  King.   It shall be so:
Madness in great ones must not unwatch'd
  go.   [*Exeunt.*

SCENE II.   *A hall in the castle.*

Enter HAMLET *and* Players.

Ham. Speak the speech, I pray you, as I
pronounced it to you, trippingly on the
tongue: but if you mouth it, as many of
your players do, I had as lief the town-crier
spoke my lines. Nor do not saw the air too
much with your hand, thus, but use all gently; for in the very torrent, tempest, and, as
I may say, the whirlwind of passion, you
must acquire and beget a temperance that
may give it smoothness. O, it offends me 9
to the soul to hear a robustious periwig-
pated fellow tear a passion to tatters, to
very rags, to split the ears of the groundlings,
who for the most part are capable of nothing
but inexplicable dumb-shows and noise: I
would have such a fellow whipped for o'er-
doing Termagant; it out-herods Herod:
pray you, avoid it.
First Play. I warrant your honour.   17
Ham. Be not too tame neither, but let
your own discretion be your tutor: suit the
action to the word, the word to the action;
with this special observance, that you o'er-
step not the modesty of nature: for any
thing so overdone is from the purpose of playing, whose end, both at the first and now,
was and is, to hold, as 't were, the mirror
up to nature; to show virtue her own
feature, scorn her own image, and the very
age and body of the time his form and pres-

---

193. **find him**, find him out.
Scene ii. 4. **your**, indefinite use. 10. **robustious**, violent, boisterous. **periwig-pated**, wearing a wig. 12. **groundlings**, those who stood in the yard of the theater. 13. **capable of**, susceptible of being influenced by. 14. **inexplicable**, of no significance worth explaining. 16. **Termagant**, a god of the Saracens; a character in the St. Nicholas play, where one of his worshipers, leaving him in charge of goods, returns to find them stolen; whereupon he beats the god (or idol), which howls vociferously. **Herod**, Herod of Jewry; a character in *The Slaughter of the Innocents* and other mystery plays. The part was played with great noise and fury. 26. **very age**, actual generation. 27. **pressure**, stamp, impressed character.

160. **expectancy**, source of hope. 162. **observed . . . observers**, courted by all courtiers. 167. **feature**, whole shape of the body. **blown**, blooming. 168. **ecstasy**, madness. 174. **disclose**, disclosure or revelation (by chipping of the shell). 180. **variable**, various. 182. **Whereon . . . beating.** The Elizabethan theory of the ill effects of the fixed idea is the same as that of current psychiatry. 183. **From . . . himself**, out of his natural manner.

sure. Now this overdone, or come tardy 28
off, though it make the unskilful laugh,
cannot but make the judicious grieve; the
censure of the which one must in your allowance o'erweigh a whole theatre of others.
O, there be players that I have seen play,
and heard others praise, and that highly,
not to speak it profanely, that, neither
having the accent of Christians nor the gait
of Christian, pagan, nor man, have so strut-
ted and bellowed that I have thought some
of nature's journeymen had made men and
not made them well, they imitated hu- 39
manity so abominably.

First Play. I hope we have reformed that
indifferently with us, sir. 41

Ham. O, reform it altogether. And let
those that play your clowns speak no more
than is set down for them; for there be of
them that will themselves laugh, to set on
some quantity of barren spectators to laugh
too; though, in the mean time, some necessary question of the play be then to be considered: that's villanous, and shows a most
pitiful ambition in the fool that uses it.
Go, make you ready. 　*[Exeunt Players.* 50

Enter POLONIUS, ROSENCRANTZ, *and* GUILD-
ENSTERN.

How now, my lord! will the king hear this
piece of work?

Pol. And the queen too, and that presently.

Ham. Bid the players make haste. [*Exit
Polonius.*] Will you two help to hasten
them?

Ros.
Guil. } We will, my lord.

　[Exeunt Rosencrantz and Guildenstern.
Ham. What ho! Horatio!

Enter HORATIO.

Hor. Here, sweet lord, at your service.

Ham. Horatio, thou art e'en as just a
man

As e'er my conversation coped withal. 60

Hor. O, my dear lord,—

Ham. 　　　　Nay, do not think I flatter;
For what advancement may I hope from
thee
That no revenue hast but thy good spirits,
To feed and clothe thee? Why should the
poor be flatter'd?
No, let the candied tongue lick absurd pomp,
And crook the pregnant hinges of the knee
Where thrift may follow fawning. Dost
thou hear?
Since my dear soul was mistress of her
choice
And could of men distinguish, her election
Hath seal'd thee for herself; for thou hast
been 70
As one, in suffering all, that suffers nothing,
A man that fortune's buffets and rewards
Hast ta'en with equal thanks: and blest are
those
Whose blood and judgement are so well
commingled,
That they are not a pipe for fortune's finger
To sound what stop she please. Give me
that man
That is not passion's slave, and I will wear
him
In my heart's core, ay, in my heart of heart,
As I do thee.—Something too much of this.—
There is a play to-night before the king; 80
One scene of it comes near the circum-
stance
Which I have told thee of my father's death:
I prithee, when thou seest that act afoot,
Even with the very comment of thy soul
Observe mine uncle: if his occulted guilt
Do not itself unkennel in one speech,
It is a damned ghost that we have seen,
And my imaginations are as foul
As Vulcan's stithy. Give him heedful note;
For I mine eyes will rivet to his face, 90
And after we will both our judgements join
In censure of his seeming.

Hor. 　　　　　　Well, my lord:

If he steal aught the whilst this play is play-
ing,
And 'scape detecting, I will pay the theft.
Ham. They are coming to the play; I
must be idle:
Get you a place.

Danish march. A flourish. Enter KING,
QUEEN, POLONIUS, OPHELIA, ROSEN-
CRANTZ, GUILDENSTERN, *and others.*

King. How fares our cousin Hamlet?
Ham. Excellent, i' faith; of the chame-
leon's dish: I eat the air, promise-crammed:
you cannot feed capons so.   100
King. I have nothing with this answer,
Hamlet; these words are not mine.
Ham. No, nor mine now. [*To Polonius*]
My lord, you played once i' the university,
you say?
Pol. That did I, my lord; and was ac-
counted a good actor.
Ham. What did you enact?
Pol. I did enact Julius Cæsar: I was killed
i' the Capitol; Brutus killed me.
Ham. It was a brute part of him to kill
so capital a calf there.   Be the players
ready?   111
Ros. Ay, my lord; they stay upon your
patience.
Queen. Come hither, my dear Hamlet,
sit by me.
Ham. No, good mother, here's metal
more attractive.
Pol. [*To the King*] O, ho! do you mark
that?
Ham. Lady, shall I lie in your lap?
            [*Lying down at Ophelia's feet.*
Oph. No, my lord.   120
Ham. I mean, my head upon your lap?
Oph. Ay, my lord.
Ham. Do you think I meant country
matters?
Oph. I think nothing, my lord.
Ham. That's a fair thought to lie between
maids' legs.
Oph. What is, my lord?
Ham. Nothing.
Oph. You are merry, my lord.
Ham. Who, I?   130
Oph. Ay, my lord.

Ham. O God, your only jig-maker. What
should a man do but be merry? for, look
you, how cheerfully my mother looks, and
my father died within these two hours.
Oph. Nay, 'tis twice two months, my
lord.   136
Ham. So long? Nay then, let the devil
wear black, for I'll have a suit of sables. O
heavens! die two months ago, and not forgotten yet? Then there's hope a great
man's memory may outlive his life half a year:
but, by'r lady, he must build churches, then;
or else shall he suffer not thinking on, with
the hobby-horse, whose epitaph is 'For,
O, for, O, the hobby-horse is forgot.'   145

Hautboys play. The dumb-show enters.

Enter a King *and a* Queen *very lovingly; the*
Queen *embracing him, and he her. She
kneels, and makes show of protestation unto
him. He takes her up, and declines his
head upon her neck: lays him down upon
a bank of flowers: she, seeing him asleep,
leaves him. Anon comes in a fellow, takes off
his crown, kisses it, and pours poison in
the* King's *ears, and exit. The* Queen *returns; finds the* King *dead, and makes
passionate action. The* Poisoner, *with some
two or three* Mutes, *comes in again, seeming
to lament with her. The dead body is carried
away. The* Poisoner *wooes the* Queen *with
gifts: she seems loath and unwilling awhile,
but in the end accepts his love.   [Exeunt.*
Oph. What means this, my lord?
Ham. Marry, this is miching mallecho;
it means mischief.
Oph. Belike this show imports the argument of the play.   150

Enter Prologue.

Ham. We shall know by this fellow: the
players cannot keep counsel; they'll tell all.
Oph. Will he tell us what this show
meant?
Ham. Ay, or any show that you'll show
him: be not you ashamed to show, he'll not
shame to tell you what it means.

---

95. **idle**, crazy, or not attending to anything serious.
98. **chameleon's dish.** Chameleons were supposed
to feed on air. 101. **have . . . with**, make nothing of.
102. **are not mine**, mean nothing to me.

132. **your only**, only your. **jig-maker**, composer of
jigs (song and dance). 138. **suit of sables**, garments
trimmed with the fur of the sable, with a quibble on *sable*
meaning "black." 143. **suffer . . . on**, undergo oblivion. 144-145. 'For . . . forgot,' verse of a song occurring also in *Love's Labour's Lost*, III, i, 30. The hobby-
horse was a character in the Morris Dance. 145. *Stage
Direction:* **Hautboys**, wooden double-reed instruments
of high pitch. 147. **miching mallecho**, sneaking mischief; the latter word is supposed to be Spanish *malhecho.*

Oph. You are naught, you are naught:
I'll mark the play.

   Pro. For us, and for our tragedy,
Here stooping to your clemency,160
We beg your hearing patiently.

                       [*Exit.*

   Ham. Is this a prologue, or the posy of a
ring?

   Oph. 'Tis brief, my lord.

   Ham. As woman's love.

     Enter two Players, King *and* Queen.

   P. King. Full thirty times hath Phœbus'
cart gone round
Neptune's salt wash and Tellus' orbed
ground,
And thirty dozen moons with borrow'd
sheen
About the world have times twelve thirties
been,
Since love our hearts and Hymen did our
hands
Unite commutual in most sacred bands. 170

   P. Queen. So many journeys may the sun
and moon
Make us again count o'er ere love be done!
But, woe is me, you are so sick of late,
So far from cheer and from your former state,
That I distrust you. Yet, though I distrust,
Discomfort you, my lord, it nothing must:
For women's fear and love holds quantity;
In neither aught, or in extremity.
Now, what my love is, proof hath made you
know;
And as my love is sized, my fear is so: 180
Where love is great, the littlest doubts are
fear;
Where little fears grow great, great love
grows there.

   P. King. 'Faith, I must leave thee, love,
and shortly too;
My operant powers their functions leave to
do:
And thou shalt live in this fair world behind,
Honour'd, beloved; and haply one as kind
For husband shalt thou—

   P. Queen   O, confound the rest!

Such love must needs be treason in my
   breast:
In second husband let me be accurst!   189
None wed the second but who kill'd the first.

   Ham. [*Aside*] Wormwood, wormwood.

   P. Queen. The instances that second mar-
   riage move
Are base respects of thrift, but none of love:
A second time I kill my husband dead,
When second husband kisses me in bed.

   P. King. I do believe you think what now
   you speak;
But what we do determine oft we break.
Purpose is but the slave to memory,
Of violent birth, but poor validity:
Which now, like fruit unripe, sticks on the
   tree;   200
But fall, unshaken, when they mellow be.
Most necessary 'tis that we forget
To pay ourselves what to ourselves is debt:
What to ourselves in passion we propose,
The passion ending, doth the purpose lose.
The violence of either grief or joy
Their own enactures with themselves de-
   stroy:
Where joy most revels, grief doth most
   lament;
Grief joys, joy grieves, on slender accident.
This world is not for aye, nor 'tis not
   strange   210
That even our loves should with our fortunes
   change;
For 'tis a question left us yet to prove,
Whether love lead fortune, or else fortune
   love.
The great man down, you mark his favourite
   flies;
The poor advanced makes friends of en-
   emies.
And hitherto doth love on fortune tend;
For who not needs shall never lack a friend,
And who in want a hollow friend doth try,
Directly seasons him his enemy.
But, orderly to end where I begun,   220
Our wills and fates do so contrary run
That our devices still are overthrown;
Our thoughts are ours, their ends none of
   our own:
So think thou wilt no second husband wed;
But die thy thoughts when thy first lord is
   dead.

---

157. **naught**, improper, bad. 160. **stooping**, bowing.
162. **posy**, motto. 166. **salt wash**, the sea. **Tellus'**.
Tellus was a goddess personifying the earth (*orbed
ground*). 167. **borrow'd**, i.e., reflected. 169. **Hymen**,
god of matrimony. 170. **commutual**, intensely mutual.
175. **distrust**, am anxious about. 177. **holds quantity**,
keeps proportion between. 184. **operant**, active.
leave, cease. 187. **confound**, strike dumb.

192. **instances**, inducements, motives. 193. **respects
of thrift**, considerations of interest. 207. **enactures**,
fulfillments. 210. **aye**, ever. 218. **who**, whoever. 219.
seasons, matures, ripens. 223. **ends**, results.

P. Queen. Nor earth to me give food, nor
   heaven light!
Sport and repose lock from me day and
   night!
To desperation turn my trust and hope!
An anchor's cheer in prison be my scope! 229
Each opposite that blanks the face of joy
Meet what I would have well and it destroy!
Both here and hence pursue me lasting
   strife,
If, once a widow, ever I be wife!
  Ham. If she should break it now!
  P. King. 'Tis deeply sworn. Sweet, leave
me here awhile;
My spirits grow dull, and fain I would be-
  guile
The tedious day with sleep.   [*Sleeps.*
  P. Queen.   Sleep rock thy brain;
And never come mischance between us
  twain!   [*Exit.*
  Ham. Madam, how like you this play?
  Queen. The lady doth protest too much,
methinks.   240
  Ham. O, but she'll keep her word.
  King. Have you heard the argument? Is
there no offence in 't?
  Ham. No, no, they do but jest, poison in
jest; no offence i' the world.
  King. What do you call the play?   246
  Ham. The Mouse-trap. Marry, how?
Tropically. This play is the image of a
murder done in Vienna: Gonzago is the
duke's name; his wife, Baptista: you shall
see anon; 't is a knavish piece of work: but
what o' that? your majesty and we that
have free souls, it touches us not: let the
galled jade wince, our withers are unwrung.

Enter LUCIANUS.

This is one Lucianus, nephew to the king.
  Oph. You are as good as a chorus, 255
my lord.
  Ham. I could interpret between you and
your love, if I could see the puppets dallying.

Oph. You are keen, my lord, you are keen.
  Ham. It would cost you a groaning to
take off my edge.   260
  Oph. Still better, and worse.
  Ham. So you must take your husbands.
Begin, murderer; pox, leave thy damnable
faces, and begin. Come: 'the croaking raven
doth bellow for revenge.'
  Luc. Thoughts black, hands apt, drugs
    fit, and time agreeing;
Confederate season, else no creature see-
    ing;
Thou mixture rank, of midnight weeds
    collected,
With Hecate's ban thrice blasted, thrice
    infected,
Thy natural magic and dire property, 270
On wholesome life usurp immediately.
  [*Pours the poison into the sleeper's ears.*
  Ham. He poisons him i' the garden for 's
estate. His name's Gonzago: the story is
extant, and writ in choice Italian: you shall
see anon how the murderer gets the love of
Gonzago's wife.
  Oph. The king rises.
  Ham. What, frighted with false fire!
  Queen. How fares my lord?
  Pol. Give o'er the play.
  King. Give me some light: away!   280
  All. Lights, lights, lights!
  [*Exeunt all but Hamlet and Horatio.*

  Ham. Why, let the stricken deer go weep,
    The hart ungalled play;
    For some must watch, while some
      must sleep:
    So runs the world away.
Would not this, sir, and a forest of feathers—
if the rest of my fortunes turn Turk with
me—with two Provincial roses on my razed
shoes, get me a fellowship in a cry of players,
sir?

261. **Still . . . worse,** more keen, less decorous
(Caldecott). 263. **pox,** an imprecation. 264-265. **'the
croaking . . . revenge,'** possibly reminiscent of the *True
Tragedie of Richard the Third:* "The screeking raven sits
croaking for revenge. Whole herds of beasts come
bellowing for revenge." 267. **Confederate,** conspiring
(to assist the murderer). 269. **Hecate,** the goddess of
witchcraft. **ban,** curse. 277. **false fire,** fireworks, or a
blank discharge. 282-285. **Why . . . away,** probably
from an old ballad, with allusion to the popular belief
that a wounded deer retires to weep and die. Cf. *As
You Like It,* II, i, 66. 286. **this,** i.e., the play. **feathers,**
allusion to the plumes which Elizabethan actors were
fond of wearing. 287. **turn Turk with,** go back on.
288. **two Provincial roses,** rosettes of ribbon like the
roses of Provins near Paris, or else the roses of Provence.
razed, cut, slashed (by way of ornament). 289. **fellowship . . . players,** partnership in a theatrical company. **cry,** pack (as of hounds).

229. **An anchor's,** an anchorite's. **cheer,** fare; sometimes printed as *chair.* 230. **opposite,** adversary. **blanks,**
causes to *blanche* or grow pale. 248. **Tropically,** figuratively. The Q1 reading, *trapically,* suggests a pun on
trap in *Mouse-trap* (l. 247). **image,** representation.
249. **Gonzago.** In 1538 Luigi Gonzago murdered the
Duke of Urbano by pouring poisoned lotion in his ears.
253. **galled jade,** horse whose hide is rubbed with
saddle or harness. **withers,** the part between the horse's
shoulder-blades. **unwrung,** not wrung or twisted.
255. **chorus.** In many Elizabethan plays the action
was explained by an actor known as the "chorus"; at a
puppet show the actor who explained the action was
known as an "interpreter," as indicated by the lines following.

Hor. Half a share.   290
Ham. A whole one, I.
    For thou dost know, O Damon dear,
    This realm dismantled was
    Of Jove himself; and now reigns here
    A very, very—pajock.
Hor. You might have rhymed.
Ham. O good Horatio, I'll take the ghost's word for a thousand pound. Didst perceive?
Hor. Very well, my lord.
Ham. Upon the talk of the poisoning?
Hor. I did very well note him.   301
Ham. Ah, ha! Come, some music! come, the recorders!
    For if the king like not the comedy,
    Why then, belike, he likes it not, perdy.
Come, some music!

Re-enter ROSENCRANTZ *and* GUILDENSTERN.

Guil. Good my lord, vouchsafe me a word with you.
Ham. Sir, a whole history.
Guil. The king, sir,—   310
Ham. Ay, sir, what of him?
Guil. Is in his retirement marvellous distempered.
Ham. With drink, sir?
Guil. No, my lord, rather with choler.
Ham. Your wisdom should show itself more richer to signify this to his doctor; for, for me to put him to his purgation would perhaps plunge him into far more choler.319
Guil. Good my lord, put your discourse into some frame and start not so wildly from my affair.
Ham. I am tame, sir: pronounce.
Guil. The queen, your mother, in most great affliction of spirit, hath sent me to you.
Ham. You are welcome.   325
Guil. Nay, good my lord, this courtesy is not of the right breed. If it shall please you to make me a wholesome answer, I will do

your mother's commandment: if not, your pardon and my return shall be the end of my business.
Ham. Sir, I cannot.   331
Guil. What, my lord?
Ham. Make you a wholesome answer; my wit's diseased: but, sir, such answer as I can make, you shall command; or, rather, as you say, my mother: therefore no more, but to the matter: my mother, you say,—
Ros. Then thus she says; your behaviour hath struck her into amazement and ad-   339
miration.
Ham. O wonderful son, that can so astonish a mother! But is there no sequel at the heels of this mother's admiration? Impart.
Ros. She desires to speak with you in her closet, ere you go to bed.
Ham. We shall obey, were she ten times our mother. Have you any further trade with us?
Ros. My lord, you once did love me.
Ham. So I do still, by these pickers and stealers.   349
Ros. Good my lord, what is your cause of distemper? you do, surely, bar the door upon your own liberty, if you deny your griefs to your friend.
Ham. Sir, I lack advancement.
Ros. How can that be, when you have the voice of the king himself for your succession in Denmark?
Ham. Ay, sir, but 'While the grass grows,' —the proverb is something musty.   359

Re-enter Players *with recorders.*

O, the recorders! let me see one. To withdraw with you:—why do you go about to recover the wind of me, as if you would drive me into a toil?
Guil. O, my lord, if my duty be too bold, my love is too unmannerly.   364
Ham. I do not well understand that. Will you play upon this pipe?
Guil. My lord, I cannot.
Ham. I pray you.

---

290. **Half a share,** allusion to the custom in dramatic companies of dividing the ownership into a number of shares among the householders. 292-295. **For thou dost . . . very,** probably from an old ballad having to do with Damon and Pythias. 293. **dismantled,** tripped, divested. 295. **pajock,** peacock (a bird with a bad reputation). Skeat suggested that the word was *patchock,* diminutive of *patch,* clown. 303. **recorders,** wind-instruments of the flute kind. 305. **perdy,** corruption of *par dieu.* 315. **choler,** bilious disorder, with quibble on the sense "anger." 321. **frame,** order. 328. **wholesome,** sensible.

337. **matter,** matter in hand.   339. **admiration,** wonder. 348. **pickers and stealers,** hands, so-called from the catechism, "to keep my hands from picking and stealing." 356. **voice,** support. 358. **'While . . . grows,'** The rest of the proverb is "the silly horse starves." Hamlet may be destroyed while he is waiting for the succession to the kingdom (Malone). 360. **withdraw,** speak in private. 361. **recover the wind,** get to the windward side. 362. **toil,** snare. 363-364. **if . . . unmannerly,** if I am using an unmannerly boldness, it is my love which occasions it.

Guil. Believe me, I cannot.

Ham. I do beseech you. 370

Guil. I know no touch of it, my lord.

Ham. 'Tis as easy as lying: govern these ventages with your fingers and thumb, give it breath with your mouth, and it will discourse most eloquent music. Look you, these are the stops.

Guil. But these cannot I command to any utterance of harmony; I have not the skill. 378

Ham. Why, look you now, how unworthy a thing you make of me! You would play upon me; you would seem to know my stops; you would pluck out the heart of my mystery; you would sound me from my lowest note to the top of my compass: and there is much music, excellent voice, in this little organ; yet cannot you make it speak. 'Sblood, do you think I am easier to be played on than a pipe? Call me what instrument you will, though you can fret me, 388 yet you cannot play upon me.

Enter Polonius.

God bless you, sir!

Pol. My lord, the queen would speak with you, and presently.

Ham. Do you see yonder cloud that's almost in shape of a camel?

Pol. By the mass, and 'tis like a camel, indeed.

Ham. Methinks it is like a weasel.

Pol. It is backed like a weasel.

Ham. Or like a whale?

Pol. Very like a whale. 399

Ham. Then I will come to my mother by and by. They fool me to the top of my bent. I will come by and by.

Pol. I will say so.

Ham. By and by is easily said.

[*Exit Polonius.*

Leave me, friends.

[*Exeunt all but Hamlet.*

'Tis now the very witching time of night,
When churchyards yawn and hell itself breathes out

Contagion to this world: now could I drink hot blood,
And do such bitter business as the day
Would quake to look on. Soft! now to my mother. 410
O heart, lose not thy nature; let not ever
The soul of Nero enter this firm bosom:
Let me be cruel, not unnatural:
I will speak daggers to her, but use none;
My tongue and soul in this be hypocrites;
How in my words soever she be shent,
To give them seals never, my soul, consent!

[*Exit.*

Scene III. *A room in the castle.*

Enter King, Rosencrantz, *and* Guildenstern.

King. I like him not, nor stands it safe with us
To let his madness range. Therefore prepare you;
I your commission will forthwith dispatch,
And he to England shall along with you:
The terms of our estate may not endure
Hazard so near us as doth hourly grow
Out of his lunacies.

Guil. We will ourselves provide:
Most holy and religious fear it is
To keep those many many bodies safe
That live and feed upon your majesty. 10

Ros. The single and peculiar life is bound,
With all the strength and armour of the mind,
To keep itself from noyance; but much more
That spirit upon whose weal depend and rest
The lives of many. The cease of majesty
Dies not alone; but, like a gulf, doth draw
What's near it with it: it is a massy wheel,
Fix'd on the summit of the highest mount,
To whose huge spokes ten thousand lesser things
Are mortised and adjoin'd; which, when it falls, 20
Each small annexment, petty consequence,
Attends the boisterous ruin. Never alone

---

373. **ventages**, stops of the recorders. 384. **compass**, range of voice. 385. **organ**, musical instrument, i.e., the pipe. 388. **fret**, quibble on meaning "irritate" and the piece of wood, gut, or metal which regulates the fingering. 401. **top of my bent**, limit of endurance, i.e., extent to which a bow may be bent. 402. **by and by**, immediately. 406. **witching time**, i.e., time when spells are cast.

412. **Nero**, murderer of his mother, Agrippina. 416. **shent**, rebuked. 417. **give them seals**, confirm with deeds.
Scene iii. 3. **dispatch**, prepare. 5. **terms**, condition, circumstances. **estate**, state. 8. **fear**, caution. 11. **single and peculiar**, individual and private. 13. **noyance**, harm. 16. **gulf**, whirlpool.

Did the king sigh, but with a general groan.

King. Arm you, I pray you, to this speedy
voyage;
For we will fetters put upon this fear,
Which now goes too free-footed.

Ros.⎱
Guil.⎰   We will haste us.

[*Exeunt Rosencrantz and Guildenstern.*

Enter POLONIUS.

Pol. My lord, he's going to his mother's
closet:
Behind the arras I'll convey myself,
To hear the process; I'll warrant she'll tax
him home: 29
And, as you said, and wisely was it said,
'Tis meet that some more audience than a
mother,
Since nature makes them partial, should
o'erhear
The speech, of vantage. Fare you well, my
liege:
I'll call upon you ere you go to bed,
And tell you what I know.

King.   Thanks, dear my lord.
[*Exit Polonius.*

O, my offence is rank, it smells to heaven;
It hath the primal eldest curse upon 't,
A brother's murder. Pray can I not,
Though inclination be as sharp as will:
My stronger guilt defeats my strong in-
tent;   40
And, like a man to double business bound,
I stand in pause where I shall first begin,
And both neglect. What if this cursed hand
Were thicker than itself with brother's blood,
Is there not rain enough in the sweet heavens
To wash it white as snow? Whereto serves
mercy
But to confront the visage of offence?
And what's in prayer but this two-fold
force,
To be forestalled ere we come to fall,   49
Or pardon'd being down? Then I'll look up;
My fault is past. But, O, what form of pray-
er
Can serve my turn? 'Forgive me my foul
murder'?

That cannot be: since I am still possess'd
Of those effects for which I did the murder,
My crown, mine own ambition and my
queen.
May one be pardon'd and retain the offence?
In the corrupted currents of this world
Offence's gilded hand may shove by justice,
And oft 'tis seen the wicked prize itself
Buys out the law: but 'tis not so above;   60
There is no shuffling, there the action lies
In his true nature; and we ourselves com-
pell'd,
Even to the teeth and forehead of our
faults,
To give in evidence. What then? what
rests?
Try what repentance can: what can it not?
Yet what can it when one can not repent?
O wretched state! O bosom black as death!
O limed soul, that, struggling to be free,
Art more engaged! Help, angels! Make
assay!
Bow, stubborn knees; and, heart with strings
of steel,   70
Be soft as sinews of the new-born babe!
All may be well.   [*Retires and kneels.*

Enter HAMLET.

Ham. Now might I do it pat, now he is
praying;
And now I'll do 't. And so he goes to
heaven;
And so am I revenged. That would be
scann'd:
A villain kills my father; and for that,
I, his sole son, do this same villain send
To heaven.
O, this is hire and salary, not revenge.
He took my father grossly, full of bread;   80
With all his crimes broad blown, as flush as
May;

---

55. **ambition**, i.e., realization of ambition.   56.
offence, benefit accruing from offense.   57. **currents**,
courses.   58. **gilded hand**, hand offering gold as a
bribe.   59. **wicked prize**, prize won by wickedness.   61.
shuffling, escape by trickery.   **lies**, is sustainable.   63.
teeth and forehead, very face.   64. **rests**, remains.
68. **limed**, caught as with bird lime.   69. **assay**, trial.
73-95. **Now might . . . goes.** This may be described as
the crucial passage in the interpretation of Hamlet's
character.   One school of critics, following Coleridge, has
held that Hamlet fails to kill the king because of weakness of will; this group regards what he says as merely
so many excuses for not doing his duty.   A more recent
and undoubtedly a sounder group take Hamlet's reasons
literally, saying that, like other heroes of revenge tragedies, he wishes to make his vengeance equivalent and
complete.   75. **would be scann'd**, needs to be looked
into.   80. **full of bread**, allusion to *Ezekiel*, xvi, 49.
81. **broad blown** in full bloom.   **flush**, lusty.

---

24. **Arm**, prepare.   28. **arras**, screen of tapestry
placed around the walls of household apartments.
convey, implication of secrecy; *convey* was often used
to mean "steal."   29. **process**, interview.   **tax him
home**, reprove him severely.   33. **of vantage**, from a
point of vantage.   39. **sharp as will**, i.e., his desire is
as strong as his determination.   47. **confront**, oppose
directly.   49. **forestalled**, prevented.

And how his audit stands who knows save
heaven?
But in our circumstance and course of
thought,
'Tis heavy with him: and am I then re-
venged,
To take him in the purging of his soul,
When he is fit and season'd for his pass-
age?
No!
Up, sword; and know thou a more horrid
hent:
When he is drunk asleep, or in his rage,
Or in the incentuous pleasure of his bed; 90
At gaming, swearing, or about some act
That has no relish of salvation in 't;
Then trip him, that his heels may kick at
heaven,
And that his soul may be as damn'd and
black
As hell, whereto it goes. My mother stays:
This physic but prolongs thy sickly days.
                                        [*Exit.*
King. [*Rising*] My words fly up, my
thoughts remain below:
Words without thoughts never to heaven go.
                                        [*Exit.*

SCENE IV. *The Queen's closet.*

Enter QUEEN *and* POLONIUS.

Pol. He will come straight. Look you
lay home to him:
Tell him his pranks have been too broad to
bear with,
And that your grace hath screen'd and stood
between
Much heat and him. I'll sconce me even
here.
Pray you, be round with him.
Ham. [*Within*] Mother, mother, mother!
Queen.   I'll warrant you,
Fear me not: withdraw, I hear him coming.
              [*Polonius hides behind the arras.*

Enter HAMLET.

Ham. Now, mother, what's the matter?

83. **in . . . course,** as we see it in our mortal situation.
86. **fit . . . passage,** i.e., reconciled to heaven by forgiveness of his sins. 88. **hent,** seizing; or, more probably, occasion of seizure. 89. **drunk asleep,** in a
drunken sleep. **rage,** sexual passion. 96. **physic,**
purging (by prayer).
    Scene iv. 1. **lay home,** talk plainly. 2. **broad,** un-
restrained. 4. **Much heat,** i.e., the king's anger.
sconce, hide.

Queen. Hamlet, thou hast thy father
much offended.
Ham. Mother, you have my father much
offended.   10
Queen. Come, come, you answer with an
idle tongue.
Ham. Go, go, you question with a wicked
tongue.
Queen. Why, how now, Hamlet!
Ham.   What's the matter now?
Queen. Have you forgot me?
Ham.   No, by the rood, not so:
You are the queen, your husband's brother's
wife;
And—would it were not so!—you are my
mother.
Queen. Nay, then, I'll set those to you
that can speak.
Ham. Come, come, and sit you down; you
shall not budge;
You go not till I set you up a glass
Where you may see the inmost part of you. 20
Queen. What wilt thou do? thou wilt
not murder me?
Help, help, ho!
Pol. [*Behind*] What, ho! help, help, help!
Ham. [*Drawing*] How now! a rat? Dead,
for a ducat, dead!
              [*Makes a pass through the arras.*
Pol. [*Behind*] O, I am slain!
                              [*Falls and dies.*
Queen. O me, what hast thou done?
Ham.   Nay, I know not:
Is it the king?
Queen. O, what a rash and bloody deed is
this!
Ham. A bloody deed! almost as bad, good
mother,
As kill a king, and marry with his brother.
Queen. As kill a king!
Ham.   Ay, lady, 'twas my word. 30
[*Lifts up the arras and discovers Polonius.*
Thou wretched, rash, intruding fool, farewell!
I took thee for thy better: take thy fortune;
Thou find'st to be too busy is some danger.
Leave wringing of your hands: peace! sit you
down,
And let me wring your heart; for so I shall,
If it be made of penetrable stuff,
If damned custom have not brass'd it so

9-10. **thy father . . . my father,** i.e., Claudius . . .
the elder Hamlet. 14. **rood,** cross. 26. **Is it the king?**
The fact that Hamlet thinks he is stabbing the king is
an indication that he does not lack will to carry out his
revenge. 37. **brass'd,** brazoned, hardened.

That it be proof and bulwark against sense.

Queen. What have I done, that thou
　darest wag thy tongue
In noise so rude against me?

Ham. 　　　　Such an act 　40
That blurs the grace and blush of modesty,
Calls virtue hypocrite, takes off the rose
From the fair forehead of an innocent love
And sets a blister there, makes marriage-
　vows
As false as dicers' oaths: O, such a deed
As from the body of contraction plucks
The very soul, and sweet religion makes
A rhapsody of words: heaven's face doth
　glow;
Yea, this solidity and compound mass,
With tristful visage, as against the doom,50
Is thought-sick at the act.

Queen. 　　　　　Ay me, what act,
That roars so loud, and thunders in the
　index?

Ham. Look here, upon this picture, and
　on this.
The counterfeit presentment of two brothers.
See, what a grace was seated on this brow;
Hyperion's curls; the front of Jove himself;
An eye like Mars, to threaten and com-
　mand;
A station like the herald Mercury
New-lighted on a heaven-kissing hill;
A combination and a form indeed, 　　60
Where every god did seem to set his seal,
To give the world assurance of a man:
This was your husband. Look you now,
　what follows:
Here is your husband; like a mildew'd ear,
Blasting his wholesome brother. Have you
　eyes?
Could you on this fair mountain leave to
　feed,
And batten on this moor? Ha! have you
　eyes?
You cannot call it love; for at your age
The hey-day in the blood is tame, it's
　humble,

And waits upon the judgement: and what
　judgement 　　70
Would step from this to this? Sense, sure,
　you have,
Else could you not have motion; but sure,
　that sense
Is apoplex'd; for madness would not err,
Nor sense to ecstasy was ne'er so thrall'd
But it reserved some quantity of choice,
To serve in such a difference. What devil
　was 't
That thus hath cozen'd you at hoodman-
　blind?
Eyes without feeling, feeling without sight,
Ears without hands or eyes, smelling sans all,
Or but a sickly part of one true sense 　80
Could not so mope.
O shame! where is thy blush? Rebellious
　hell,
If thou canst mutine in a matron's bones,
To flaming youth let virtue be as wax,
And melt in her own fire: proclaim no shame
When the compulsive ardour gives the
　charge,
Since frost itself as actively doth burn
And reason pandars will.

Queen. 　　　　O Hamlet, speak no more:
Thou turn'st mine eyes into my very soul;
And there I see such black and grained spots
As will not leave their tint.

Ham. 　　　　　Nay, but to live 91
In the rank sweat of an enseamed bed,
Stew'd in corruption, honeying and making
　love
Over the nasty sty,—

Queen. 　　　O, speak to me no more;
These words, like daggers, enter in mine ears;
No more, sweet Hamlet!

Ham. 　　　　A murderer and a villain;
A slave that is not twentieth part the tithe
Of your precedent lord; a vice of kings;

---

38. **proof**, armor. **sense**, feeling. 44. **sets a blister**,
brands as a harlot. 46. **contraction**, betrothal. 48.
rhapsody, string. 49. **this . . . mass**, the earth itself. 50. **tristful**, sad. **doom**, Last Judgment. 51.
thought-sick, sick with anxiety. 52. **index**, prelude
or preface. 54. **counterfeit presentment**, portrayed
representation; on the stage the portraits are sometimes
presented as miniatures, sometimes as pictures on the
wall. 56. **Hyperion**, the sun-god. **front**, forehead.
58. **station**, manner of standing. 62. **assurance**,
pledge, guarantee. 64. **mildew'd ear**. See *Genesis*, xli,
5-7. 67. **batten**, grow fat. **moor**, barren upland.
69. **hey-day**, state of excitement.

71-72. **Sense . . . motion.** Sense and motion are
functions of the middle or sensible soul, the possession of
sense being the basis of motion. 73. **apoplex'd**, par-
alyzed. Mental derangement was thus of three sorts:
apoplexy, ecstasy, and diabolic possession. 74. **thrall'd**,
enslaved. 75. **quantity of choice**, fragment of the
power to choose. 76. **difference**, disagreement. 77.
cozen'd, tricked, cheated. **hoodman-blind**, blind-
man's buff. 79. **sans**, without. 81. **mope**, be in a
depressed, spiritless state, act aimlessly. 83. **mutine**,
mutiny, rebel. 86. **charge**, order, command. 88.
reason pandars will. The normal and proper situation
was one in which reason guided the will in the direction
of good; here, reason is perverted and leads in the direction of evil. 90. **grained**, dyed in grain. 92. **enseamed**, loaded with grease, greased. 98. **precedent
lord**, i.e., the elder Hamlet. **vice of kings**, buffoon of
kings; a reference to the *Vice*, or clown, of the morality
plays and interludes.

A cutpurse of the empire and the rule,
That from a shelf the precious diadem stole, 100
And put it in his pocket!
Queen. No more!
Ham. A king of shreds and patches,—

Enter Ghost.

Save me, and hover o'er me with your wings,
You heavenly guards! What would your
gracious figure?
Queen. Alas, he's mad!
Ham. Do you not come your tardy son to
chide,
That, lapsed in time and passion, lets go
by
The important acting of your dread com-
mand?
O, say!
Ghost. Do not forget: this visitation 110
Is but to whet thy almost blunted purpose.
But, look, amazement on thy mother sits:
O, step between her and her fighting soul:
Conceit in weakest bodies strongest works:
Speak to her, Hamlet.
Ham. How is it with you, lady?
Queen. Alas, how is 't with you,
That you do bend your eye on vacancy
And with the incorporal air do hold dis-
course?
Forth at your eyes your spirits wildly
peep;
And, as the sleeping soldiers in the alarm, 120
Your bedded hair, like life in excrements,
Start up, and stand an end. O gentle son,
Upon the heat and flame of thy distemper
Sprinkle cool patience. Whereon do you
look?
Ham. On him, on him! Look you, how
pale he glares!
His form and cause conjoin'd, preaching to
stones,
Would make them capable. Do not look
upon me;
Lest with this piteous action you convert
My stern effects: then what I have to do 129

Will want true colour; tears perchance for
blood.
Queen. To whom do you speak this?
Ham. Do you see nothing there?
Queen. Nothing at all; yet all that is I see.
Ham. Nor did you nothing hear?
Queen. No, nothing but ourselves.
Ham. Why, look you there! look, how it
steals away!
My father, in his habit as he lived!
Look, where he goes, even now, out at the
portal! [*Exit Ghost.*
Queen. This is the very coinage of your
brain:
This bodiless creation ecstasy
Is very cunning in.
Ham. Ecstasy! 139
My pulse, as yours, doth temperately keep
time,
And makes as healthful music: it is not mad-
ness
That I have utter'd: bring me to the test,
And I the matter will re-word, which mad-
ness
Would gambol from. Mother, for love of
grace,
Lay not that flattering unction to your soul,
That not your trespass, but my madness
speaks:
It will but skin and film the ulcerous place,
Whiles rank corruption, mining all within,
Infects unseen. Confess yourself to heaven;
Repent what's past; avoid what is to come; 150
And do not spread the compost on the
weeds,
To make them ranker. Forgive me this my
virtue;
For in the fatness of these pursy times
Virtue itself of vice must pardon beg,
Yea, curb and woo for leave to do him good.
Queen. O Hamlet, thou hast cleft my
heart in twain.
Ham. O, throw away the worser part of it,
And live the purer with the other half.
Good night: but go not to mine uncle's bed;
Assume a virtue, if you have it not. 160

---

102. **shreds and patches**, i.e., motley, the traditional costume of the Vice. 107. **lapsed . . . passion**, having suffered time to slip and passion to cool (Johnson); also explained as "engrossed in casual events and lapsed into mere fruitless passion, so that he no longer entertains a rational purpose." 108. **important**, urgent. 112. **amazement**, frenzy, distraction. 114. **Conceit**, imagination. 118. **incorporal**, immaterial. 121. **bedded**, laid in smooth layers. **excrements.** The hair was considered an excrement or voided part of the body. 122. **an**, on. 126. **conjoin'd**, united. 127. **capable**, susceptible. 128-129. **convert . . . effects**, divert me from my stern duty. For *effects* Singer conjectures *affects* (affections of the mind).

130. **want true colour**, lack good reason so that (with a play on the normal sense of *colour*) I shall shed tears instead of blood. 138. **ecstasy**, madness arising from the predominance of a passion. 143. **re-word**, repeat in words. 144. **gambol**, skip away. 145. **unction**, ointment used medicinally or as a rite; suggestion that forgiveness for sin may not be so easily achieved. 148. **mining**, working under the surface. 150. **what is to come**, i.e., the sins of the future. 151. **compost**, manure. 152. **this my virtue**, this virtue of mine, i.e., in reproving you. 153. **fatness**, grossness. **pursy**, short-winded, corpulent. 155. **curb**, bow, bend the knee.

That monster, custom, who all sense doth
　　eat,
Of habits devil, is angel yet in this,
That to the use of actions fair and good
He likewise gives a frock or livery,
That aptly is put on. Refrain to-night,
And that shall lend a kind of easiness
To the next abstinence: the next more easy;
For use almost can change the stamp of
　　nature,
†And either . . . the devil, or throw him out
With wondrous potency. Once more, good
　　night:　　　　　　　　　　　　　170
And when you are desirous to be bless'd,
I'll blessing beg of you. For this same lord,
　　　　　　　　　　　[*Pointing to Polonius.*
I do repent: but heaven hath pleased it so,
To punish me with this and this with me,
That I must be their scourge and minister.
I will bestow him, and will answer well
The death I gave him. So, again, good
　　night.
I must be cruel, only to be kind:
Thus bad begins and worse remains behind.
One word more, good lady.
　　Queen.　　　　　　What shall I do?　　180
　　Ham. Not this, by no means, that I bid
　　you do:
Let the bloat king tempt you again to bed;
Pinch wanton on your cheek; call you his
　　mouse;
And let him, for a pair of reechy kisses,
Or paddling in your neck with his damn'd
　　fingers,
Make you to ravel all this matter out,
That I essentially am not in madness,
But mad in craft. 'Twere good you let him
　　know;
For who, that's but a queen, fair, sober,
　　wise,
Would from a paddock, from a bat, a gib,190
Such dear concernings hide? who would do
　　so?
No, in despite of sense and secrecy,
Unpeg the basket on the house's top,
Let the birds fly, and, like the famous ape,

To try conclusions, in the basket creep,
And break your own neck down.
　　Queen. Be thou assured, if words be made
　　of breath,
And breath of life, I have no life to breathe
What thou hast said to me.
　　Ham. I must to England; you know that?
　　Queen.　　　　　　　　　　　Alack, 200
I had forgot: 'tis so concluded on.
　　Ham. There's letters seal'd: and my two
　　schoolfellows,
Whom I will trust as I will adders fang'd,
They bear the mandate; they must sweep
　　my way,
And marshal me to knavery. Let it work;
For 'tis the sport to have the enginer
Hoist with his own petar: and 't shall go
　　hard
But I will delve one yard below their mines,
And blow them at the moon: O, 'tis most
　　sweet,
When in one line two crafts directly meet. 210
This man shall set me packing:
I'll lug the guts into the neighbour room.
Mother, good night. Indeed this counsellor
Is now most still, most secret and most
　　grave,
Who was in life a foolish prating knave.
Come, sir, to draw toward an end with
　　you.
Good night, mother.
　　　　　[*Exeunt severally; Hamlet dragging
　　　　　　　　　　　　　　　in Polonius.*

ACT IV.

Scene I.　*A room in the castle.*

Enter King, Queen, Rosencrantz, *and*
　　Guildenstern.

　　King. There's matter in these sighs, these
　　profound heaves:
You must translate: 'tis fit we understand
　　them.
Where is your son?
　　Queen. Bestow this place on us a little
　　while.
　　　　　[*Exeunt Rosencrantz and Guildenstern.*

161. **sense**, feeling, sensibility.　163. **use**, habitual
practice.　171. **be bless'd**, become blessed, i.e., repentant.　176. **answer**, account for.　182. **bloat**,
bloated.　184. **reechy**, dirty, filthy.　187. **essentially**,
in my essential nature.　190. **paddock**, toad.　**gib**,
tomcat.　191. **dear concernings**, important affairs.
194. **the famous ape**. A letter from Sir John Suckling
seems to supply other details of the story, otherwise not
identified: "It is the story of the jackanapes and the
partridges; thou starest after a beauty till it be lost to
thee, then let'st out another, and starest after that till
it is gone too."

195. **conclusions**, experiments.　204. **sweep my
way**, clear my path.　206. **enginer**, constructor of
military works, or possibly, artilleryman.　207. **Hoist**,
blown up. **petar**, defined as a small engine of war used
to blow in a door or make a breach, and as a case filled
with explosive materials.　210. **two crafts**, two acts
of guile, with quibble on the sense of "two ships."　211.
set me packing, set me to making schemes, and set
me to lugging (him), and, possibly, send me off in a hurry.
216. **draw**, come, with quibble on literal sense.

Ah, mine own lord, what have I seen to-
night!

King. What, Gertrude? How does
Hamlet?

Queen. Mad as the sea and wind, when
both contend
Which is the mightier: in his lawless fit,
Behind the arras hearing something stir,
Whips out his rapier, cries, 'A rat, a rat!' 10
And, in this brainish apprehension, kills
The unseen good old man.

King.   O heavy deed!
It had been so with us, had we been there:
His liberty is full of threats to all;
To you yourself, to us, to every one.
Alas, how shall this bloody deed be answer'd?
It will be laid to us, whose providence
Should have kept short, restrain'd and out of
haunt,
This mad young man: but so much was our
love,
We would not understand what was most fit;
But, like the owner of a foul disease, 21
To keep it from divulging, let it feed
Even on the pith of life. Where is he gone?

Queen. To draw apart the body he hath
kill'd:
O'er whom his very madness, like some ore
Among a mineral of metals base,
Shows itself pure; he weeps for what is done.

King. O Gertrude, come away!
The sun no sooner shall the mountains touch,
But we will ship him hence: and this vile
deed
We must, with all our majesty and skill, 31
Both countenance and excuse. Ho, Guilden-
stern!

Re-enter ROSENCRANTZ *and* GUILDENSTERN.

Friends both, go join you with some further
aid:
Hamlet in madness hath Polonius slain,
And from his mother's closet hath he dragg'd
him:
Go seek him out; speak fair, and bring the
body
Into the chapel. I pray you, haste in this.
      [Exeunt Rosencrantz and Guildenstern.
Come, Gertrude, we'll call up our wisest
friends;

And let them know, both what we mean to
do,
†And what's untimely done.............. 40
Whose whisper o'er the world's diameter,
As level as the cannon to his blank,
Transports his poison'd shot, may miss our
name,
And hit the woundless air. O, come away!
My soul is full of discord and dismay.
                      [Exeunt.

SCENE II.   *Another room in the castle.*

Enter HAMLET.

Ham. Safely stowed.

Ros. }
Guil. } *[Within]* Hamlet! Lord Hamlet!

Ham. But soft, what noise? who calls on
Hamlet? O, here they come.

Enter ROSENCRANTZ *and* GUILDERSTERN.

Ros. What have you done, my lord, with
the dead body?

Ham. Compounded it with dust, whereto
'tis kin.

Ros. Tell us where 'tis, that we may take
it thence
And bear it to the chapel.

Ham. Do not believe it.

Ros. Believe what? 10

Ham. That I can keep your counsel and
not mine own. Besides, to be demanded of
a sponge! what replication should be made
by the son of a king?

Ros. Take you me for a sponge, my lord?

Ham. Ay, sir, that soaks up the king's
countenance, his rewards, his authorities.
But such officers do the king best service in
the end: he keeps them, like an ape, in the
corner of his jaw; first mouthed, to be last
swallowed: when he needs what you have
gleaned, it is but squeezing you, and, sponge,
you shall be dry again. 23

Ros. I understand you not, my lord.

Ham. I am glad of it: a knavish speech
sleeps in a foolish ear.

Ros. My lord, you must tell us where the
body is, and go with us to the king.

<hr>

11. **brainish,** headstrong, passionate. **apprehension,** conception, imagination. 17. **providence,** foresight. 18. **short.** i.e., on a short tether. **out of haunt,**
secluded. 22. **divulging,** becoming evident. 26. **mineral,** mine. 36. **fair,** civilly.

41. **diameter,** extent from side to side. 42. **level,**
straight. **blank,** white spot in the center of a target.
44. **woundless,** invulnerable.
Scene ii. 11. **keep your counsel.** Hamlet is aware
of their treachery but says nothing about it. 12. **demanded of,** questioned by. 13. **replication,** reply.
17. **countenance,** patronage, favor. **authorities,**
authoritative backing.

Ham. The body is with the king, but the king is not with the body. The king is a thing—

Guil. A thing, my lord!   31

Ham. Of nothing: bring me to him. Hide fox, and all after.   [*Exeunt.*

SCENE III. *Another room in the castle.*

Enter KING, *attended.*

King. I have sent to seek him, and to find the body.

How dangerous is it that this man goes loose!

Yet must not we put the strong law on him:

He's loved of the distracted multitude,

Who like not in their judgement, but their eyes;

And where 'tis so, the offender's scourge is weigh'd,

But never the offence. To bear all smooth and even,

This sudden sending him away must seem

Deliberate pause: diseases desperate grown

By desperate appliance are relieved,   10

Or not at all.

Enter ROSENCRANTZ.

How now! what hath befall'n?

Ros. Where the dead body is bestow'd, my lord,

We cannot get from him.

King.   But where is he?

Ros. Without, my lord; guarded, to know your pleasure.

King. Bring him before us.

Ros. Ho, Guildenstern! bring in my lord.

Enter HAMLET *and* GUILDENSTERN.

King. Now, Hamlet, where's Polonius?

Ham. At supper.

King. At supper! where?   19

Ham. Not where he eats, but where he is eaten: a certain convocation of politic worms

are e'en at him. Your worm is your only emperor for diet: we fat all creatures else to fat us, and we fat ourselves for maggots: your fat king and your lean beggar is but variable service, two dishes, but to one table: that's the end.   26

King. Alas, alas!

Ham. A man may fish with the worm that hath eat of a king, and eat of the fish that hath fed of that worm.   30

King. What dost thou mean by this?

Ham. Nothing but to show you how a king may go a progress through the guts of a beggar.

King. Where is Polonius?

Ham. In heaven; send thither to see: if your messenger find him not there, seek him i' the other place yourself. But indeed, if you find him not within this month, you shall nose him as you go up the stairs into the lobby.

King. Go seek him there.   40

[*To some Attendants.*

Ham. He will stay till you come.

[*Exeunt Attendants.*

King. Hamlet, this deed, for thine especial safety,—

Which we do tender, as we dearly grieve

For that which thou hast done,—must send thee hence

With fiery quickness: therefore prepare thyself;

The bark is ready, and the wind at help,

The associates tend, and everything is bent

For England.

Ham.   For England!

King.   Ay, Hamlet.

Ham.   Good.

King. So is it, if thou knew'st our purposes.

Ham. I see a cherub that sees them. But, come; for England! Farewell, dear mother.

King. Thy loving father, Hamlet.   52

Ham. My mother: father and mother is man and wife; man and wife is one flesh; and so, my mother. Come, for England!

[*Exit.*

King. Follow him at foot; tempt him with speed aboard;

Delay it not; I'll have him hence to-night:

Away! for every thing is seal'd and done

29-30. **The body . . . body.** There are many interpretations; possibly, "The body lies in death with the king, my father; but my father walks disembodied" (Dowden); or "Claudius has the bodily possession of kingship, but kingliness, or justice of inheritance, is not with him." Yale editor explains, "The King is still alive (i.e., with *his* body), but he is not with the dead body (i.e., Polonius)." 32-33. **Hide . . , after,** an old signal cry in the game of hide-and-seek.

Scene iii. 4. **distracted,** i.e., without power of forming logical judgments. 6. **scourge,** punishment. **weigh'd,** taken into consideration. 9. **Deliberate pause,** considered action. 21. **convocation . . . worms,** allusion to the Diet of Worms (1521). **politic,** crafty.

25. **variable service,** a variety of dishes. 33. **progress,** royal journey of state. 43. **tender,** regard, hold dear. 50. **cherub.** Cherubim are angels of knowledge (Dowden). 56. **at foot,** close behind, at heel.

That else leans on the affair: pray you,
make haste.
        [*Exeunt Rosencrantz and Guildenstern.*
And, England, if my love thou hold'st at
    aught—   60
As my great power thereof may give thee
    sense,
Since yet thy cicatrice looks raw and red
After the Danish sword, and thy free awe
Pays homage to us—thou mayst not coldly
    set
Our sovereign process; which imports at full,
By letters congruing to that effect,
The present death of Hamlet. Do it,
    England;
For like the hectic in my blood he rages,
And thou must cure me: till I know 'tis done,
Howe'er my haps, my joys were ne'er
    begun.   [*Exit.* 70

Scene IV.   *A plain in Denmark.*

Enter Fortinbras, *a* Captain, *and* Soldiers,
marching.

  For. Go, captain, from me greet the
    Danish king;
Tell him that, by his license, Fortinbras
Craves the conveyance of a promised march
Over his kingdom. You know the rendez-
    vous.
If that his majesty would aught with us,
We shall express our duty in his eye;
And let him know so.
  Cap.   I will do 't, my lord.
  For. Go softly on.
        [*Exeunt Fortinbras and Soldiers.*

Enter Hamlet, Rosencrantz, Guildenstern, *and others.*

  Ham. Good sir, whose powers are these?
  Cap. They are of Norway, sir.   10
  Ham. How purposed, sir, I pray you?
  Cap. Against some part of Poland.
  Ham. Who commands them, sir?
  Cap. The nephew to old Norway, Fortin-
    bras.
  Ham. Goes it against the main of Poland,
    sir,

Or for some frontier?
  Cap. Truly to speak, and with no addi-
    tion,
We go to gain a little patch of ground
That hath in it no profit but the name.
To pay five ducats, five, I would not farm
    it;   20
Nor will it yield to Norway or the Pole
A ranker rate, should it be sold in fee.
  Ham. Why, then the Polack never will
    defend it.
  Cap. Yes, it is already garrison'd.
  Ham. Two thousand souls and twenty
    thousand ducats
Will not debate the question of this straw:
This is the imposthume of much wealth and
    peace,
That inward breaks, and shows no cause
    without
Why the man dies. I humbly thank you, sir.
  Cap. God be wi' you, sir.   [*Exit.*
  Ros.   Will 't please you go, my lord? 30
  Ham. I'll be with you straight. Go a
    little before. [*Exeunt all except Hamlet.*
How all occasions do inform against me,
And spur my dull revenge! What is a man,
If his chief good and market of his time
Be but to sleep and feed? a beast, no more.
Sure, he that made us with such large dis-
    course,
Looking before and after, gave us not
That capability and god-like reason
To fust in us unused. Now, whether it be
Bestial oblivion, or some craven scruple 40
Of thinking too precisely on the event,
A thought which, quarter'd, hath but one
    part wisdom
And ever three parts coward, I do not know
Why yet I live to say 'This thing's to do;'
Sith I have cause and will and strength and
    means
To do 't. Examples gross as earth exhort
    me:
Witness this army of such mass and charge
Led by a delicate and tender prince,
Whose spirit with divine ambition puff'd
Makes mouths at the invisible event, 50

    63. **free awe**, awe still felt, but no longer enforced by
arms. 65. **process**, formal command, mandate. 68.
hectic, fever. 70. **haps**, fortunes.
    Scene iv. 2. **license**, leave. 3. **conveyance**, escort,
convoy. 6. **in his eye**, in his presence. 8. **softly**,
slowly. 15. **main**, country itself.

    17. **addition**, amplification. 20. **farm it**, take a
lease of it. 22. **ranker**, greater, higher. **fee**, fee simple.
26. **debate . . . straw**, settle this trifling matter. 27.
imposthume, purulent abscess or swelling. 32.
occasions, incidents, events. **inform against**, show
up, betray (i.e., his tardiness). 34. **market of his time**,
the best use he makes of his time, or, that for which he
sells his time (Johnson). 36. **discourse**, "discourse of
reason," i.e., process or faculty of reasoning. 39. **fust**,
grow moldy. 41. **event**, outcome. 45. **Sith**, since.

Exposing what is mortal and unsure
To all that fortune, death and danger dare,
Even for an egg-shell. Rightly to be great
Is not to stir without great argument,
But greatly to find quarrel in a straw
When honour's at the stake. How stand I
    then,
That have a father kill'd, a mother stain'd,
Excitements of my reason and my blood,
And let all sleep? while, to my shame, I see
The imminent death of twenty thousand
    men,
That, for a fantasy and trick of fame,   61
Go to their graves like beds, fight for a
    plot
Whereon the numbers cannot try the cause,
Which is not tomb enough and continent
To hide the slain? O, from this time forth,
My thoughts be bloody, or be nothing worth!
    [*Exit*.

SCENE V. *Elsinore. A room in the castle*.

Enter QUEEN, HORATIO, *and a* Gentleman.

Queen. I will not speak with her.
Gent. She is importunate, indeed distract:
Her mood will needs be pitied.
Queen.   What would she have?
Gent. She speaks much of her father;
    says she hears
There's tricks i' the world; and hems, and
    beats her heart;
Spurns enviously at straws; speaks things in
    doubt,
That carry but half sense: her speech is
    nothing,
Yet the unshaped use of it doth move
The hearers to collection; they aim at it,
And botch the words up fit to their own
    thoughts;   10
Which, as her winks, and nods, and gestures
    yield them,
Indeed would make one think there might be
    thought,
Though nothing sure, yet much unhappily.

Hor. 'Twere good she were spoken with:
    for she may strew
Dangerous conjectures in ill-breeding minds.
Queen. Let her come in.   [*Exit Horatio*.
To my sick soul, as sin's true nature is,
Each toy seems prologue to some great
    amiss:
So full of artless jealousy is guilt,
It spills itself in fearing to be spilt.   20

Re-enter HORATIO, *with* OPHELIA.

Oph. Where is the beauteous majesty of
    Denmark?
Queen. How now, Ophelia!
Oph. [*Sings*] How should I your true love
    know
        From another one?
    By his cockle hat and staff,
        And his sandal shoon.
Queen. Alas, sweet lady, what imports
    this song?
Oph. Say you? may, pray you, mark.
[*Sings*]   He is dead and gone, lady,
        He is dead and gone;   30
    At his head a grass-green turf,
        At his heels a stone.
Queen. Nay, but, Ophelia,—
Oph. Pray you, mark
[*Sings*] White his shroud as the mountain
    snow,—

Enter KING.

Queen. Alas, look here, my lord.
Oph. [*Sings*] Larded with sweet flowers;
    Which bewept to the grave did go
        With true-love showers.
King. How do you, pretty lady?   40
Oph. Well, God 'ild you! They say the
owl was a baker's daughter. Lord, we know
what we are, but know not what we may be.
God be at your table!
King. Conceit upon her father.
Oph. Pray you, let's have no words of
this; but when they ask you what it means,
say you this:

---

54. **argument**, cause. 58. **Excitements of**, incentives to. **blood**, passion. 61. **trick**, toy, trifle. 62. **plot**, i.e., of ground. 64. **continent**, that which contains.
Scene v. 5. **tricks**, deceptions. **heart**, i.e., breast. 6. **Spurns . . . straws**, kicks spitefully at small objects in her path. **in doubt**, in hesitation or perplexity. 8. **unshaped**, unformed, artless. 9. **collection**, inference. **aim**, guess. 10. **botch**, patch. 11. **yield**, deliver, bring forth (her words). 13. **nothing**, not at all. **much unhappily**, expressive of much unhappiness.

15. **ill-breeding minds**, minds bent on mischief. 18. **toy**, trifle. **great amiss**, calamity, disaster. 19-20. **So full . . . spilt**, guilt is so full of suspicion that it unskillfully betrays itself in fearing to be betrayed (Onions). 25. **cockle hat**, hat with cockle shell stuck in it as a sign that the wearer had been a pilgrim to the shrine of St. James of Compostella. The pilgrim's garb was a conventional disguise for lovers. 26. **shoon**, shoes. 37. **Larded**, decorated, garnished. 41. **God 'ild**, God yield or reward. 42. **owl**, reference to a monkish legend that a baker's daughter was turned into an owl for refusing bread to the Savior; quoted by Douce. 45. **Conceit**, imagination.

[*Sings*] To-morrow is Saint Valentine's day,
    All in the morning betime,
  And I a maid at your window,   50
    To be your Valentine.
Then up he rose, and donn'd his
    clothes,
  And dupp'd the chamber-door;
Let in the maid, that out a maid
    Never departed more.

King. Pretty Ophelia!

Oph. Indeed, la, without an oath, I'll
make an end on 't:

[*Sings*] By Gis and by Saint Charity,
    Alack, and fie for shame!   60
Young men will do 't, if they come
    to 't;
  By cock, they are to blame.
Quoth she, before you tumbled me,
    You promised me to wed.
So would I ha' done, by yonder sun,
    An thou hadst not come to my bed.

King. How long hath she been thus?

Oph. I hope all will be well. We must be
patient: but I cannot choose but weep, to
think they should lay him i' the cold ground.
My brother shall know of it: and so I thank
you for your good counsel. Come, my
coach! Good night, ladies; good night,
sweet ladies; good night, good night.   74
                     [*Exit.*

King. Follow her close; give her good
watch, I pray you.
                     [*Exit Horatio.*
O, this is the poison of deep grief; it
    springs
All from her father's death. O Gertrude,
    Gertrude,
When sorrows come, they come not single
    spies,
But in battalions. First, her father slain:
Next, your son gone; and he most violent
    author   80
Of his own just remove: the people muddied,
Thick and unwholesome in their thoughts
    and whispers,
For good Polonius' death; and we have done
    but greenly,
In hugger-mugger to inter him: poor
    Ophelia

Divided from herself and her fair judge-
    ment,
Without the which we are pictures, or mere
    beasts:
Last, and as much containing as all these,
Her brother is in secret come from France;
Feeds on his wonder, keeps himself in
    clouds,
And wants not buzzers to infect his ear   90
With pestilent speeches of his father's death;
Wherein necessity, of matter beggar'd,
Will nothing stick our person to arraign
In ear and ear. O my dear Gertrude, this,
Like to a murdering-piece, in many places
Gives me superfluous death. [*A noise within.*

Queen.   Alack, what noise is this?

King. Where are my Switzers? Let them
guard the door.

        Enter another Gentleman.

What is the matter?

Gent.   Save yourself, my lord:
The ocean, overpeering of his list,
Eats not the flats with more impetuous
    haste
Than young Laertes, in a riotous head, 101
O'erbears your officers. The rabble call him
    lord;
And, as the world were now but to begin,
Antiquity forgot, custom not known,
The ratifiers and props of every word,
They cry 'Choose we: Laertes shall be king:'
Caps, hands, and tongues, applaud it to the
    clouds:
'Laertes shall be king, Laertes king!'

Queen. How cheerfully on the false trail
    they cry!   109
O, this is counter, you false Danish dogs!

King. The doors are broke.
                     [*Noise within.*

  Enter LAERTES, *armed;* DANES *following.*

Laer. Where is this king? Sirs, stand you
    all without.

Danes. No, let 's come in.

Laer.   I pray you, give me leave.

---

51. **Valentine.** This song alludes to the belief that the first girl seen by a man on the morning of this day was his valentine or true-love (Halliwell). 53. **dupp'd**, opened. 59. **Gis**, Jesus. 62. **cock**, perversion of *God* in oaths. 83. **greenly**, foolishly. 84. **hugger-mugger**, secret haste.

89. **in clouds**, invisible. 90. **buzzers**, gossipers. 93. **nothing stick**, not hesitate. 94. **In ear and ear**, in everybody's ears. 95. **murdering-piece**, small cannon or mortar; suggestion of numerous missiles fired. 97. **Switzers**, Swiss guards, mercenaries. 99. **overpeering**, overflowing. **list**, boundary. 101. **head**, armed force. 105. **word**, probably, title or custom; *ward, weal,* and *work* have been suggested as emendations. 110. **counter**, a hunting term meaning following the trail in a direction opposite to that which the game has taken.

Danes. We will, we will.

[*They retire without the door.*

Laer. I thank you: keep the door. O
thou vile king,

Give me my father!

Queen.   Calmly, good Laertes.

Laer. That drop of blood that's calm proclaims me bastard,

Cries cuckold to my father, brands the harlot

Even here, between the chaste unsmirched
brow

Of my true mother.

King.   What is the cause, Laertes,

That thy rebellion looks so giant-like?   121

Let him go, Gertrude; do not fear our person:

There's such divinity doth hedge a king,

That treason can but peep to what it would,

Acts little of his will. Tell me, Laertes,

Why thou art thus incensed. Let him go,
Gertrude.

Speak, man.

Laer. Where is my father?

King.   Dead.

Queen.   But not by him.

King. Let him demand his fill.

Laer. How came he dead? I'll not be
juggled with: 130

To hell, allegiance! vows, to the blackest
devil!

Conscience and grace, to the profoundest
pit!

I dare damnation. To this point I stand,

That both the worlds I give to negligence,

Let come what comes; only I'll be revenged

Most throughly for my father.

King.   Who shall stay you?

Laer. My will, not all the world:

And for my means, I'll husband them so well,

They shall go far with little.

King.   Good Laertes,

If you desire to know the certainty   140

Of your dear father's death, is 't writ in your
revenge,

That, swoopstake, you will draw both friend
and foe,

Winner and loser?

Laer. None but his enemies.

King.   Will you know them then?

Laer. To his good friends thus wide I'll
ope my arms;

And like the kind life-rendering pelican,

Repast them with my blood.

King.   Why, now you speak

Like a good child and a true gentleman.

That I am guiltless of your father's death,

And am most sensibly in grief for it,   150

It shall as level to your judgement pierce

As day does to your eye.

Danes. [*Within*] Let her come in.

Laer. How now! what noise is that?

Re-enter OPHELIA.

O heat, dry up my brains! tears seven times
salt,

Burn out the sense and virtue of mine eye!

By heaven, thy madness shall be paid with
weight,

Till our scale turn the beam. O rose of May!

Dear maid, kind sister, sweet Ophelia!

O heavens! is 't possible, a young maid's
wits

Should be as mortal as an old man's life?   160

Nature is fine in love, and where 'tis fine,

It sends some precious instance of itself

After the thing it loves.

Oph. [*Sings*]

They bore him barefaced on the bier;

Hey non nonny, nonny, hey nonny;

And in his grave rain'd many a tear:—

Fare you well, my dove!

Laer. Hadst thou thy wits, and didst persuade revenge,

It could not move thus.

Oph. [*Sings*] You must sing a-down a-
down,

An you call him a-down-a.   171

O, how the wheel becomes it! It is the false
steward, that stole his master's daughter.

Laer. This nothing 's more than matter.

Oph. There's rosemary, that's for remembrance; pray, love, remember: and there is
pansies, that 's for thoughts.

Laer. A document in madness, thoughts
and remembrance fitted.   179

---

122. **fear**, fear for. 124. **peep**, look. **would**, wishes
to do. 132. **grace**, favor of God. His breach of allegiance would be a sin. 134. **give to negligence**. He
despises both the here and the hereafter. 137. **My will**.
He will not be stopped except by his own will. 142.
swoopstake, literally, drawing the whole stake at once,
i.e., indiscriminately.

146. **pelican**, reference to the belief that the pelican
feeds its young with its own blood. 147. **Repast**, feed.
150. **sensibly**, feelingly. 154. **heat**, probably the heat
generated by the passion of grief. 172. **wheel**, spinning
wheel as accompaniment to the song (Onions); refrain
(Steevens). **false steward**. The story is unknown.
175. **rosemary**, used as a symbol of remembrance both
at weddings and at funerals. 177. **pansies**, emblems of
love and courtship. Cf. French *pensées*. 178. **document**, piece of instruction or lesson.

Oph. There's fennel for you, and colum-
bines: there's rue for you; and here's some
for me: we may call it herb-grace o' Sundays:
O, you must wear your rue with a difference.
There's a daisy: I would give you some violets, but they withered all when my father
died: they say he made a good end,— 186
[*Sings*] For bonny sweet Robin is all my
joy.

Laer. Thought and affliction, passion, hell
itself,
She turns to favour and to prettiness.

Oph. [*Sings*] And will he not come again? 190
　　And will he not come again?
　　　　No, no, he is dead:
　　　　Go to thy death-bed:
　　He never will come again.

　　His beard was as white as snow,
　　All flaxen was his poll:
　　　　He is gone, he is gone,
　　　　And we cast away moan:
　　God ha' mercy on his soul!
And of all Christian souls, I pray God. God
be wi' ye. 　　　　　　　　　 [*Exit.*

Laer. Do you see this, O God? 201

King. Laertes, I must commune with your
grief,
Or you deny me right. Go but apart,
Make choice of whom your wisest friends you
will,
And they shall hear and judge 'twixt you and
me:
If by direct or by collateral hand
They find us touch'd, we will our kingdom
give,
Our crown, our life, and all that we call ours,
To you in satisfaction; but if not, 209
Be you content to lend your patience to us,
And we shall jointly labour with your soul
To give it due content.

Laer. 　　　　　Let this be so;

180. **fennel**, emblem of flattery. **columbine**, emblem of unchastity (?) or ingratitude (?) 181. **rue**, emblem of repentance. It was usually mingled with holy
water and then known as *herb of grace*. Ophelia is probably playing on the two meanings of *rue*, "repentant"
and "even for ruth (pity)"; the former signification is
for the Queen, the latter for herself. 183. **difference**,
an heraldic term for the distinction in the coats of arms
of different branches of the same family. 184. **daisy**,
emblem of dissembling, faithlessness. **violets**, emblems of faithfulness. 187. **For . . . joy**, probably
a line from a Robin Hood ballad. 188. **Thought**, melancholy thought. **passion**, sorrowful emotion, or possibly,
suffering. 189. **favour**, attraction, charm. 190. **And
. . . again?** This song appeared in the song-books as
"The Merry Milkmaids" or "The Milkmaids' Dumps."
196. **poll**, head. 198. **cast away**, shipwrecked. 203.
right, my rights. 206. **collateral**, indirect. 207.
touch'd, implicated.

His means of death, his obscure funeral—
No trophy, sword, nor hatchment o'er his
bones,
No noble rite nor formal ostentation—
Cry to be heard, as 'twere from heaven to
earth,
That I must call 't in question.

King. 　　　　　　　So you shall;
And where the offence is let the great axe fall.
I pray you, go with me. 　　　　　[*Exeunt.*

SCENE VI. 　*Another room in the castle.*

Enter HORATIO *and a* Servant.

Hor. What are they that would speak
with me?

Serv. Sailors, sir: they say they have letters for you.

Hor. Let them come in. 　[*Exit Servant.*
I do not know from what part of the world
I should be greeted, if not from lord Hamlet.

Enter Sailors.

First Sail. God bless you, sir.

Hor. Let him bless thee too.

First Sail. He shall, sir, an 't please him.
There's a letter for you, sir; it comes from the
ambassador that was bound for England; if
your name be Horatio, as I am let to know
it is. 　　　　　　　　　　　　　　　11

Hor. [*Reads*] 'Horatio, when thou shalt
have overlooked this, give these fellows some
means to the king: they have letters for him.
Ere we were two days old at sea, a pirate of
very warlike appointment gave us chase.
Finding ourselves too slow of sail, we put on
a compelled valour, and in the grapple I
boarded them: on the instant they got clear
of our ship; so I alone became their prisoner.
They have dealt with me like thieves of 21
mercy: but they knew what they did; I am to
do a good turn for them. Let the king have
the letters I have sent; and repair thou to me
with as much speed as thou wouldst fly
death. I have words to speak in thine ear
will make thee dumb; yet are they much too
light for the bore of the matter. These good
fellows will bring thee where I am. Rozen-
crantz and Guildenstern hold their course for

214. **hatchment**, tablet displaying the armorial
bearings of a deceased person.
Scene vi. 14. **means**, means of access. 21. **thieves of
mercy**, merciful thieves. 27. **bore**, caliber, importance.

England: of them I have much to tell thee.
Farewell.   30
   'He that thou knowest thine, HAMLET.'
Come, I will make you way for these your
  letters;
And do't the speedier, that you may direct
  me
To him from whom you brought them.
          [*Exeunt.*

SCENE VII. *Another room in the castle.*

Enter KING *and Laertes.*

King. Now must your conscience my ac-
  quittance seal,
And you must put me in your heart for friend,
Sith you have heard, and with a knowing ear,
That he which hath your noble father slain
Pursued my life.
Laer.   It well appears: but tell me
Why you proceeded not against these feats,
So crimeful and so capital in nature,
As by your safety, wisdom, all things else,
You mainly were stirr'd up.
King.   O, for two special reasons;
Which may to you, perhaps, seem much un-
  sinew'd,   10
But yet to me they are strong. The queen
  his mother
Lives almost by his looks; and for myself—
My virtue or my plague, be it either which—
She's so conjunctive to my life and soul,
That, as the star moves not but in his sphere,
I could not but by her. The other motive,
Why to a public count I might not go,
Is the great love the general gender bear him;
Who, dipping all his faults in their affection,
Would, like the spring that turneth wood to
  stone,   20
Convert his gyves to graces; so that my ar-
  rows,
Too slightly timber'd for so loud a wind,
Would have reverted to my bow again,

And not where I had aim'd them.
Laer. And so have I a noble father lost;
A sister driven into desperate terms,
Whose worth, if praises may go back again,
Stood challenger on mount of all the age
For her perfections: but my revenge will come.
King. Break not your sleeps for that: you
  must not think   30
That we are made of stuff so flat and dull
That we can let our beard be shook with
  danger
And think it pastime. You shortly shall hear
  more:
I loved your father, and we love ourself;
And that, I hope, will teach you to imagine—

Enter a Messenger.

How now! what news?
Mess.   Letters, my lord, from Hamlet:
This to your majesty; this to the queen.
King. From Hamlet! who brought them?
Mess. Sailors, my lord, they say; I saw
  them not:
They were given me by Claudio; he re-
  ceived them   40
Of him that brought them.
King.   Laertes, you shall hear them.
Leave us.   [*Exit Messenger.*
[*Reads*] 'High and mighty, You shall
know I am set naked on your kingdom. To-
morrow shall I beg leave to see your kingly
eyes: when I shall, first asking your pardon
thereunto, recount the occasion of my sud-
den and more strange return.
          'HAMLET.'
What should this mean? Are all the rest
  come back?   50
Or is it some abuse, and no such thing?
Laer. Know you the hand?
King. 'Tis Hamlet's character. 'Naked!'
And in a postscript here, he says 'alone.'
Can you advise me?
Laer. I'm lost in it, my lord. But let him
  come;
It warms the very sickness in my heart,
That I shall live and tell him to his teeth,
'Thus didst thou.'
King.   If it be so, Laertes—

Scene vii. **1. conscience,** knowledge that this is true.
5. Pursued, sought. **7. capital,** punishable by death.
9. mainly, greatly, very much. **10. unsinew'd,** weak.
14. conjunctive, conformable (the next line suggesting
planetary conjunction). **15. sphere,** the hollow sphere
in which, according to Ptolemaic astronomy, the planets
were supposed to move. **17. count,** account, reckoning.
18. general gender, common people. **20. spring,**
i.e., one heavily charged with lime. **21. gyves,** fetters;
here, faults, or possibly, punishments inflicted (on him).
22. slightly timber'd, light. **loud,** strong. For *loud
a wind* Jennens would retain the Q₂ reading, *loved Arm'd,*
explaining, "one so loved and armed with the affections
of the people"; for *so loud a wind* Elze suggests *solid arms*
to agree with his reading *grieves* (for *gyves*) in line 21.

26. terms, state, condition. **27. go back,** i.e., to
Ophelia's former virtues. **28. on mount,** set up on
high (Onions), mounted (on horseback). **of all the age,**
qualifies *challenger* and not *mount*. **37. to the queen.**
One hears no more of the letter to the queen. **40.
Claudio.** This character does not appear in the play.
44. naked, unprovided (with retinue). **51. abuse,**
deception. **53. character,** handwriting.

As how should it be so? how otherwise?—
Will you be ruled by me?
    Laer.   Ay, my lord;   60
So you will not o'errule me to a peace.
    King. To thine own peace. If he be now
        return'd,
As checking at his voyage, and that he means
No more to undertake it, I will work him
To an exploit, now ripe in my device,
Under the which he shall not choose but fall:
And for his death no wind of blame shall
        breathe,
But even his mother shall uncharge the
        practice
And call it accident.
    Laer.   My lord, I will be ruled;
The rather, if you could devise it so   70
That I might be the organ.
    King.   It falls right.
You have been talk'd of since your travel
        much,
And that in Hamlet's hearing, for a quality
Wherein, they say, you shine: your sum of
        parts
Did not together pluck such envy from him
As did that one, and that, in my regard,
Of the unworthiest siege.
    Laer.   What part is that, my lord?
    King. A very riband in the cap of youth,
Yet needful too; for youth no less becomes
The light and careless livery that it wears   80
Than settled age his sables and his weeds,
Importing health and graveness. Two
        months since,
Here was a gentleman of Normandy:—
I've seen myself, and served against, the
        French,
And they can well on horseback: but this
        gallant
Had witchcraft in 't; he grew unto his seat;
And to such wondrous doing brought his
        horse,
As had he been incorpsed and demi-natured
With the brave beast: so far he topp'd my
        thought,

That I, in forgery of shapes and tricks,   90
Come short of what he did.
    Laer.   A Norman was 't?
    King. A Norman.
    Laer. Upon my life, Lamond.
    King.   The very same.
    Laer. I know him well: he is the brooch
        indeed
And gem of all the nation.
    King. He made confession of you,
And gave you such a masterly report
For art and exercise in your defence
And for your rapier most especial,
That he cried out, 'twould be a sight indeed,
If one could match you: the scrimers of their
        nation,   101
He swore, had neither motion, guard, nor
        eye,
If you opposed them. Sir, this report of his
Did Hamlet so envenom with his envy
That he could nothing do but wish and beg
Your sudden coming o'er, to play with him.
Now, out of this,—
    Laer.   What out of this, my lord?
    King. Laertes, was your father dear to
        you?
Or are you like the painting of a sorrow,
A face without a heart?
    Laer.   Why ask you this?   110
    King. Not that I think you did not love
        your father;
But that I know love is begun by time;
And that I see, in passages of proof,
Time qualifies the spark and fire of it.
There lives within the very flame of love
A kind of wick or snuff that will abate it;
And nothing is at a like goodness still;
For goodness, growing to a plurisy,
Dies in his own too much: that we would do,
We should do when we would; for this
        'would' changes   120
And hath abatements and delays as many
As there are tongues, are hands, are acci-
        dents;
And then this 'should' is like a spendthrift
        sigh,

59. **As . . . otherwise**, how can this (Hamlet's return) be true? (yet) how otherwise than true (since we have the evidence of his letter)? Some editors read *How should it not be so*, etc., making the words refer to Laertes's desire to meet with Hamlet. 63. **checking at**, used in falconry of a bird leaving the quarry to fly at a chance bird. 68. **uncharge the practice**, not object to the stratagem. 71. **organ**, agent, instrument. 77. **siege**, rank. 81. **sables**, rich garments. **weeds**, clothing. 82. **health**, welfare, prosperity. 85. **can well**, are skilled. 88. **incorpsed and demi-natured**, of one body and nearly of one nature (like the centaur). 89. **topp'd**, surpassed.

90. **forgery**, invention. 93. **Lamond**. This refers possibly to Pietro Monte, instructor to Louis XII's master of the horse (Hudson). 96. **confession**, report. 98. **art and exercise**, skillful exercise. **defence**, science of defense in sword practice. 101. **scrimers**, fencers. 106. **play**, fence. 113. **passages of proof**, proved instances. 117. **still**, ever. 118. **plurisy**, excess, plethora. 119. **in his own too much**, of its own excess. 121. **abatements**, diminutions. 122. **accidents**, occurrences, incidents. 123. **spendthrift**, an allusion to the belief that each sigh cost the heart a drop of blood.

That hurts by easing. But, to the quick o'
  the ulcer:—
Hamlet comes back: what would you under-
  take,
To show yourself your father's son in deed
More than in words?
  Laer.   To cut his throat i' the church.
  King. No place, indeed, should murder
    sanctuarize;
Revenge should have no bounds. But, good
  Laertes,
Will you do this, keep close within your
  chamber.   130
Hamlet return'd shall know you are come
  home:
We'll put on those shall praise your excel-
  lence
And set a double varnish on the fame
The Frenchman gave you, bring you in fine
  together
And wager on your heads: he, being remiss,
Most generous and free from all contriving,
Will not peruse the foils; so that, with
  ease,
Or with a little shuffling, you may choose
A sword unbated, and in a pass of practice
Requite him for your father.
  Laer.   I will do 't: 140
And, for that purpose, I'll anoint my sword.
I bought an unction of a mountebank,
So mortal that, but dip a knife in it,
Where it draws blood no cataplasm so rare,
Collected from all simples that have virtue
Under the moon, can save the thing from
  death
That is but scratch'd withal: I'll touch my
  point
With this contagion, that, if I gall him
  slightly,
It may be death.
  King.   Let's further think of this;
Weigh what convenience both of time and
  means   150
May fit us to our shape: if this should fail,
And that our drift look through our bad per-
  formance,

'Twere better not assay'd: therefore this
  project
Should have a back or second, that might
  hold,
If this should blast in proof. Soft! let me see:
We'll make a solemn wager on your cun-
  nings:
I ha 't:
When in your motion you are hot and dry—
As make your bouts more violent to that
  end—
And that he calls for drink, I'll have pre-
  pared him   160
A chalice for the nonce, whereon but sipping,
If he by chance escape your venom'd stuck,
Our purpose may hold there.

Enter QUEEN.

                    How now, sweet queen!
  Queen. One woe doth tread upon an-
    other's heel,
So fast they follow: your sister's drown'd,
  Laertes.
  Laer. Drown'd! O, where?
  Queen. There is a willow grows aslant a
    brook,
That shows his hoar leaves in the glassy
  stream;
There with fantastic garlands did she come
Of crow-flowers, nettles, daisies, and long
  purples   170
That liberal shepherds give a grosser name,
But our cold maids do dead men's fingers
  call them:
There, on the pendent boughs her coronet
  weeds
Clambering to hang, an envious sliver broke;
When down her weedy trophies and herself
Fell in the weeping brook. Her clothes
  spread wide;
And, mermaid-like, awhile they bore her up:
Which time she chanted snatches of old
  tunes;
As one incapable of her own distress,
Or like a creature native and indued   180

124. **quick o' the ulcer**, heart of the difficulty. 128. **sanctuarize**, protect from punishment; allusion to the right of sanctuary with which certain religious places were invested. 139. **unbated**, not blunted, having no button. **pass of practice**, treacherous thrust. 142. **mountebank**, quack-doctor. 144. **cataplasm**, plaster or poultice. 145. **simples**, herbs. 146. **Under the moon**, i.e., when collected by moonlight to add to their medicinal value. 148. **gall**, graze, wound. 151. **shape**, part we propose to act. 152. **drift . . . performance**, intention be disclosed by our bungling.

155. **blast in proof**, burst in the test (like a cannon). 156. **cunnings**, skills. The F reading, *commings*, is explained by Caldecott and Knight as "bouts at fence." 161. **chalice**, cup. **for the nonce**, for the occasion. 162. **stuck**, thrust (from *stoccado*). 167. **willow**, for its significance of forsaken love. 168. **hoar**, white (i.e., on the underside). 170. **crow-flowers**, buttercups. **long purples**, early purple orchis. 171. **liberal**, prob-ably, free-spoken. 173. **coronet**, garlanded, made into a chaplet. 174. **sliver**, branch. 175. **weedy**, i.e., of plants. 179. **incapable**, lacking capacity to apprehend. 180. **indued**, endowed with qualities fitting her for living in water.

Unto that element: but long it could not be
Till that her garments, heavy with their
      drink,
Pull'd the poor wretch from her melodious
      lay
To muddy death.
   Laer.   Alas, then, she is drown'd?
   Queen. Drown'd, drown'd.
   Laer. Too much of water hast thou, poor
      Ophelia,
And therefore I forbid my tears: but yet
It is our trick; nature her custom holds,
Let shame say what it will: when these are
      gone,
The woman will be out. Adieu, my lord: 190
I have a speech of fire, that fain would blaze,
But that this folly douts it.   [*Exit.*
   King.   Let's follow, Gertrude:
How much I had to do to calm his rage!
Now fear I this will give it start again;
Therefore let's follow.   [*Exeunt.*

ACT V.

SCENE I. *A churchyard.*

Enter two Clowns, *with spades, &c.*

   First Clo. Is she to be buried in Christian
burial that wilfully seeks her own salvation?
   Sec. Clo. I tell thee she is; and therefore
make her grave straight: the crowner hath
sat on her, and finds it Christian burial.
   First Clo. How can that be, unless she
drowned herself in her own defence?
   Sec. Clo. Why, 'tis found so.   8
   First Clo. It must be 'se offendendo;' it
cannot be else. For here lies the point:
if I drown myself wittingly, it argues an
act: and an act hath three branches; it is,
to act, to do, and to perform: argal, she
drowned herself wittingly.   14
   Sec. Clo. Nay, but hear you, goodman
delver,—

   First Clo. Give me leave. Here lies the
water; good: here stands the man; good: if
the man go to this water, and drown himself,
it is, will he, nill he, he goes,—mark you
that; but if the water come to him and drown
him, he drowns not himself: argal, he that
is not guilty of his own death shortens not
his own life.
   Sec. Clo. But is this law?   23
   First Clo. Ay, marry, is 't; crowner's quest
law.
   Sec. Clo. Will you ha' the truth on 't? If
this had not been a gentlewoman, she should
have been buried out o' Christian burial. 28
   First Clo. Why, there thou say'st: and the
more pity that great folk should have
countenance in this world to drown or hang
themselves, more than their even Christian.
Come, my spade. There is no ancient
gentlemen but gardeners, ditchers, and
grave-makers: they hold up Adam's profession.
   Sec. Clo. Was he a gentleman?
   First Clo. A' was the first that ever bore
arms.
   Sec. Clo. Why, he had none.   39
   First Clo. What, art a heathen? How
dost thou understand the Scripture? The
Scripture says 'Adam digged:' could he dig
without arms? I'll put another question to
thee: if thou answerest me not to the purpose, confess thyself—   44
   Sec. Clo. Go to.
   First Clo. What is he that builds stronger
than either the mason, the shipwright, or
the carpenter?
   Sec. Clo. The gallows-maker; for that
frame outlives a thousand tenants.   50
   First Clo. I like thy wit well, in good faith:
the gallows does well; but how does it well?
it does well to those that do ill: now thou
dost ill to say the gallows is built stronger
than the church: argal, the gallows may do
well to thee. To 't again, come.
   Sec. Clo. 'Who builds stronger than a
mason, a shipwright, or a carpenter?'
   First Clo. Ay, tell me that, and unyoke.
   Sec. Clo. Marry, now I can tell.   60

186-187. **Too . . . tears,** an illustration of the fact
that puns were not inappropriate in any circumstances
in Shakespeare's time. 188. **trick,** way. 189-190.
when . . . out, when my tears are all shed, the woman
in me will be satisfied. 192. **douts,** does out, ex-
tinguishes.
   Act V. Scene i. Stage Direction: **Clowns.** The word
clown was used to denote peasants as well as humorous
characters; here applied to the rustic type of clowns. 4.
straight, straightway, immediately; Johnson interprets
"from east to west in a direct line, parallel with the
church." **crowner,** coroner. 9. '**se offendendo,**' for
se defendendo, term used in verdicts of justifiable homicide. 11. **wittingly,** intentionally. 12. **three branches,**
parody of legal phraseology. 13. **argal,** corruption of
ergo, therefore. 15. **delver,** digger.

24. **quest,** inquest. 29. **there thou say'st,** that's
right. 31. **countenance,** privilege. 32. **even,** fellow.
35. **hold up,** maintain, continue. 44. **confess thyself,**
"and be hanged" completes the proverb. 45. **Go to,**
perhaps, "begin," or some other form of concession. 59.
unyoke, after this great effort you may unharness the
team of your wits (Dowden).

First Clo. To 't.

Sec. Clo. Mass, I cannot tell.

Enter Hamlet *and* Horatio, *at a distance.*

First Clo. Cudgel thy brains no more about it, for your dull ass will not mend his pace with beating; and, when you are asked this question next, say 'a grave-maker:' the houses that he makes last till doomsday. Go, get thee to †Yaughan: fetch me a stoup of liquor.   [*Exit Sec. Clown.*

[*He digs, and sings.*

In youth, when I did love, did love,
    Methought it was very sweet,   70
To contract, O, the time, for, ah, my
        behove,
    O, methought, there was nothing meet.

Ham. Has this fellow no feeling of his business, that he sings at grave-making?

Hor. Custom hath made it in him a property of easiness.

Ham. 'Tis e'en so: the hand of little employment hath the daintier sense.

First Clo. [*Sings*]
    But age, with his stealing steps,
        Hath claw'd me in his clutch,   80
    And hath shipped me intil the land,
        As if I had never been such.

[*Throws up a skull.*

Ham. That skull had a tongue in it, and could sing once: how the knave jowls it to the ground, as if it were Cain's jaw-bone, that did the first murder! It might be the pate of a politician, which this ass now o'er-reaches; one that would circumvent God, might it not?

Hor. It might, my lord.   89

Ham. Or of a courtier; which could say 'Good morrow, sweet lord! How dost thou, good lord?' This might be my lord such-a-one, that praised my lord such-a-one's horse, when he meant to beg it; might it not?

Hor. Ay, my lord.   95

Ham. Why, e'en so: and now my Lady Worm's; chapless, and knocked about the mazzard with a sexton's spade: here's fine revolution, an we had the trick to see 't. Did these bones cost no more the breeding, but to play at loggats with 'em? mine ache to think on 't.   101

First Clo. [*Sings*]
    A pick-axe, and a spade, a spade,
        For and a shrouding sheet:
    O, a pit of clay for to be made
        For such a guest is meet.

[*Throws up another skull.*

Ham. There's another: why may not that be the skull of a lawyer? Where be his quiddities now, his quillets, his cases, his tenures, and his tricks? why does he suffer this rude knave now to knock him about the sconce with a dirty shovel, and will not tell him of his action of battery? Hum! This fellow   112 might be in 's time a great buyer of land, with his statutes, his recognizances, his fines, his double vouchers, his recoveries: is this the fine of his fines, and the recovery of his recoveries, to have his fine pate full of fine dirt? will his vouchers vouch him no more of his purchases, and double ones too, than the length and breadth of a pair of indentures? The very conveyances of his lands will hardly lie in this box; and must the inheritor   121 himself have no more, ha?

Hor. Not a jot more, my lord.

Ham. Is not parchment made of sheep-skins?   123

Hor. Ay, my lord, and of calf-skins too.

Ham. They are sheep and calves which seek out assurance in that. I will speak to this fellow. Whose grave's this, sirrah?

First Clo. Mine, sir.

[*Sings*] O, a pit of clay for to be made
        For such a guest is meet.   130

---

62. **Mass,** by the Mass. 68. **Yaughan,** probably a London tavern-keeper; many emendations. **stoup,** two-quart measure. 69. **In . . . love.** This and the two following stanzas, with nonsensical variations, are from a poem attributed to Lord Vaux and printed in *Tottel's Miscellany* (1557). The *O* and *ah* are possibly grunts of the digger or (Clarendon Press) represent drawling notes. 71. **behove,** benefit. 76. **property of easiness,** a peculiarity that now is easy. 84. **jowls,** dashes. 85. **Cain's jaw-bone,** allusion to the old tradition that Cain slew Abel with the jaw-bone of an ass. 87. **politician,** schemer, plotter. **o'er-reaches,** quibble on the literal sense and the sense "circumvent"; the F reading, *o'er Offices*, Onions defines as "lords it over by virtue of his office."

97. **chapless,** having no lower jaw. 98. **mazzard,** head. 100. **loggats,** a game in which six sticks are thrown to lie as near as possible to a stake fixed in the ground, or block of wood on a floor. 103. **For and,** and moreover. 107. **quiddities,** subtleties, quibbles. 108. **quillets,** verbal niceties, subtle distinctions. **tenures,** the holding of a piece of property or office or the conditions or period of such holding. 110. **sconce,** head. 114. **statutes, recognizances,** legal terms connected with the transfer of land. 115. **vouchers,** persons called on to warrant a tenant's title. **recoveries,** process for transfer of entailed estate. 116. **fine.** The four uses of this word are as follows: (1) end, (2) legal process, (3) elegant, (4) small. 119. **indentures,** conveyances or contracts. 121. **inheritor,** possessor, owner. 124. **calf-skins,** parchments. 126. **assurance in that,** safety in legal parchments.

Ham. I think it be thine, indeed; for thou liest in 't.

First Clo. You lie out on 't, sir, and therefore it is not yours: for my part, I do not lie in 't, and yet it is mine.

Ham. Thou dost lie in 't, to be in 't and say it is thine: 'tis for the dead, not for the quick; therefore thou liest.

First Clo. 'Tis a quick lie, sir; 'twill away again, from me to you.   140

Ham. What man dost thou dig it for?

First Clo. For no man, sir.

Ham. What woman, then?

First Clo. For none, neither.

Ham. Who is to be buried in 't?

First Clo. One that was a woman, sir; but, rest her soul, she's dead.   147

Ham. How absolute the knave is! we must speak by the card, or equivocation will undo us. By the Lord, Horatio, these three years I have taken note of it; the age is grown so picked that the toe of the peasant comes so near the heel of the courtier, he galls his kibe. How long hast thou been a grave-maker?

First Clo. Of all the days i' the year, I came to 't that day that our last king Hamlet overcame Fortinbras.   157

Ham. How long is that since?

First Clo. Cannot you tell that? every fool can tell that: it was the very day that young Hamlet was born; he that is mad, and sent into England.

Ham. Ay, marry, why was he sent into England?

First Clo. Why, because he was mad: he shall recover his wits there; or, if he do not, it's no great matter there.

Ham. Why?

First Clo. 'Twill not be seen in him there; there the men are as mad as he.   170

Ham. How came he mad?

First Clo. Very strangely, they say.

Ham. How strangely?

First Clo. Faith, e'en with losing his wits.

Ham. Upon what ground?

First Clo. Why, here in Denmark: I have been sexton here, man and boy, thirty years.

Ham. How long will a man lie i' the earth ere he rot?   179

First Clo. I' faith, if he be not rotten before he die—as we have many pocky corses now-a-days, that will scarce hold the laying in—he will last you some eight year or nine year: a tanner will last you nine year.   184

Ham. Why he more than another?

First Clo. Why, sir, his hide is so tanned with his trade, that he will keep out water a great while; and your water is a sore decayer of your whoreson dead body. Here's a skull now; this skull has lain in the earth three and twenty years.   191

Ham. Whose was it?

First Clo. A whoreson mad fellow's it was: whose do you think it was?

Ham. Nay, I know not.

First Clo. A pestilence on him for a mad rogue! a' poured a flagon of Rhenish on my head once. This same skull, sir, was Yorick's skull, the king's jester.

Ham. This?   200

First Clo. E'en that.

Ham. Let me see. [*Takes the skull.*] Alas, poor Yorick! I knew him, Horatio: a fellow of infinite jest, of most excellent fancy: he hath borne me on his back a thousand times; and now, how abhorred in my imagination it is! my gorge rises at it. Here hung those lips that I have kissed I know not how oft. Where be your gibes now? your gambols? your songs? your flashes of merriment, that were wont to set the table on a roar? Not one now, to mock your own grinning? quite chapfallen? Now get you to my lady's chamber, and tell her, let her paint an inch thick, to this favour she must come; make her laugh at that. Prithee, Horatio, tell me one thing.

Hor. What's that, my lord?

Ham. Dost thou think Alexander looked o' this fashion i' the earth?

Hor. E'en so.   220

Ham. And smelt so? pah!

[*Puts down the skull.*

Hor. E'en so, my lord.

Ham. To what base uses we may return, Horatio! Why may not imagination trace the noble dust of Alexander, till he find it stopping a bung-hole?   226

Hor. 'Twere to consider too curiously, to consider so.

Ham. No, faith, not a jot; but to follow

---

139. **quick**, alive. 148. **absolute**, positive, decided. 149. **by the card**, with precision, i.e., by the mariner's card on which the points of the compass were marked. **equivocation**, ambiguity in the use of terms. 150. **three years.** Dowden suspected an allusion to the poor law of 1601. 152. **picked**, refined, fastidious. 153. **kibe**, chilblain. 177. **thirty years.** This statement with that in line 160 shows Hamlet's age to be thirty years.

181. **pocky**, rotten, diseased. 189. **whoreson**, an intensive of little meaning. 198. **Yorick.** Nicholson regarded the reference as a compliment to Kemp's great predecessor, the clown Will Tarleton. 215. **favour**, countenance, face. 227. **curiously**, minutely.

him thither with modesty enough, and likelihood to lead it: as thus: Alexander died, Alexander was buried, Alexander returneth into dust; the dust is earth; of earth we make loam; and why of that loam, whereto he was converted, might they not stop a beer-barrel?

Imperious Cæsar, dead and turn'd to clay,
Might stop a hole to keep the wind away:
O, that that earth, which kept the world in awe,   238
Should patch a wall to expel the winter's flaw!

But soft! but soft! aside: here comes the king,

Enter Priests, *&c. in procession; the Corpse of* Ophelia, Laertes *and* Mourners, *following;* King, Queen, *their trains, &c.*

The queen, the courtiers: who is this they follow?   241
And with such maimed rites? This doth betoken
The corse they follow did with desperate hand
Fordo it own life: 'twas of some estate.
Couch we awhile, and mark.
                    [*Retiring with* Horatio.
Laer. What ceremony else?
Ham.   That is Laertes,
A very noble youth: mark.
Laer. What ceremony else?
First Priest. Her obsequies have been as far enlarged
As we have warranty: her death was doubtful;
And, but that great command o'ersways the order,   251
She should in ground unsanctified have lodged
Till the last trumpet; for charitable prayers,
Shards, flints and pebbles should be thrown on her:
Yet here she is allow'd her virgin crants,
Her maiden strewments and the bringing home
Of bell and burial.
Laer. Must there no more be done?

---

230. **modesty**, moderation, freedom from exaggeration. 234. **loam**, clay paste for brickmaking. 236. **Imperious**, imperial. 239. **flaw**, gust of wind. 244. **Fordo**, destroy. **it**, its. 245. **Couch**, hide, lurk. 249. **enlarged**, extended, referring to the fact that suicides are not given full burial rites. 250. **doubtful**, suspicious. 254. **Shards**, broken bits of pottery. 255. **crants**, garlands customarily hung upon the biers of unmarried women. 256. **strewments**, traditional strewing of flowers. 256-257. **bringing . . . burial**, strictly, the bridal procession from church; applied to a maid's funeral.

First Priest.   No more be done:
We should profane the service of the dead
To sing a requiem and such rest to her   260
As to peace-parted souls.
Laer.   Lay her i' the earth:
And from her fair and unpolluted flesh
May violets spring! I tell thee, churlish priest,
A ministering angel shall my sister be,
When thou liest howling.
Ham.   What, the fair Ophelia!
Queen. Sweets to the sweet: farewell!
                    [*Scattering flowers.*
I hoped thou shouldst have been my Hamlet's wife;
I thought thy bride-bed to have deck'd, sweet maid,
And not have strew'd thy grave.
Laer.   O, treble woe
Fall ten times treble on that cursed head,   270
Whose wicked deed thy most ingenious sense
Deprived thee of! Hold off the earth awhile,
Till I have caught her once more in mine arms: [*Leaps into the grave.*
Now pile your dust upon the quick and dead,
Till of this flat a mountain you have made,
To o'ertop old Pelion, or the skyish head
Of blue Olympus.
Ham. [*Advancing*]   What is he whose grief
Bears such an emphasis? whose phrase of sorrow
Conjures the wandering stars, and makes them stand
Like wonder-wounded hearers? This is I,   280
Hamlet the Dane.   [*Leaps into the grave.*
Laer.   The devil take thy soul!
                    [*Grappling with him.*
Ham. Thou pray'st not well.
I prithee, take thy fingers from my throat;
For, though I am not splenitive and rash,
Yet have I something in me dangerous,
Which let thy wiseness fear: hold off thy hand.
King. Pluck them asunder.
Queen.   Hamlet, Hamlet!
All. Gentlemen,—
Hor.   Good my lord, be quiet.
                    [*The Attendants part them, and they come out of the grave.*

---

261. **peace-parted**, allusion to the text, "Lord, now lettest thou thy servant depart in peace." 265. **howling**, i.e., in hell. 271. **ingenious sense**, probably, reason (as the most ingenious of the senses). 276. **Pelion**. Olympus, Pelion, and Ossa are mountains in the north of Thessaly. 279. **wandering stars**, planets. 284. **splenitive**, quick-tempered.

Ham. Why, I will fight with him upon this theme
Until my eyelids will no longer wag.   290
Queen. O my son, what theme?
Ham. I loved Ophelia: forty thousand brothers
Could not, with all their quantity of love,
Make up my sum. What wilt thou do for her?
King. O, he is mad, Laertes.
Queen. For love of God, forbear him.
Ham. 'Swounds, show me what thou'lt do:
Woo't weep? woo't fight? woo't fast? woo't tear thyself?
Woo't drink up eisel? eat a crocodile?
I'll do't. Dost thou come here to whine? 300
To outface me with leaping in her grave?
Be buried quick with her, and so will I:
And, if thou prate of mountains, let them throw
Millions of acres on us, till our ground,
Singeing his pate against the burning zone,
Make Ossa like a wart! Nay, an thou'lt mouth,
I'll rant as well as thou.
Queen.   This is mere madness:
And thus awhile the fit will work on him;
Anon, as patient as the female dove,
When that her golden couplets are disclosed,
His silence will sit drooping.
Ham.   Hear you, sir;   311
What is the reason that you use me thus?
I loved you ever: but it is no matter;
Let Hercules himself do what he may,
The cat will mew and dog will have his day.
                                        [*Exit.*
King. I pray you, good Horatio, wait upon him.   [*Exit Horatio.*
[*To Laertes*] Strengthen your patience in our last night's speech;
We'll put the matter to the present push.
Good Gertrude, set some watch over your son.
This grave shall have a living monument: 320

An hour of quiet shortly shall we see;
Till then, in patience our proceeding be.
                                        [*Exeunt.*

Scene II.   *A hall in the castle.*

Enter Hamlet *and* Horatio.

Ham. So much for this, sir: now shall you see the other;
You do remember all the circumstance?
Hor. Remember it, my lord!
Ham. Sir, in my heart there was a kind of fighting,
That would not let me sleep: methought I lay
Worse than the mutines in the bilboes. Rashly,
And praised be rashness for it, let us know,
Our indiscretion sometimes serves us well,
When our deep plots do pall: and that should teach us
There's a divinity that shapes our ends,   10
Rough-hew them how we will,—
Hor.   That is most certain.
Ham. Up from my cabin,
My sea-gown scarf'd about me, in the dark
Groped I to find out them; had my desire,
Finger'd their packet, and in fine withdrew
To mine own room again; making so bold,
My fears forgetting manners, to unseal
Their grand commission; where I found, Horatio,—
O royal knavery!—an exact command,   19
Larded with many several sorts of reasons
Importing Denmark's health and England's too,
With, ho! such bugs and goblins in my life,
That, on the supervise, no leisure bated,
No, not to stay the grinding of the axe,
My head should be struck off.
Hor.   Is't possible?
Ham. Here's the commission: read it at more leisure.
But wilt thou hear me how I did proceed?

---

290. **wag**, move (not used ludicrously). 293. **quantity.** Dowden suggests that the word is used in a deprecatory sense (little bits, fragments). 296. **forbear**, leave alone. 297. **'Swounds**, oath, "God's wounds." 298. **Woo't**, wilt thou. 299. **eisel**, vinegar. Some editors have taken this to be the name of a river, such as the Yssel, the Weissel, and the Nile. 310. **golden couplets.** The pigeon lays two eggs; the young when hatched are covered with golden down (Dowden). 317. **in**, by recalling. 318. **present push**, immediate test. 320. **living**, lasting; also refers (for Laertes's benefit) to the plot against Hamlet.

Scene ii. 6. **mutines**, mutineers. **bilboes**, shackles. *Rashly* goes with line 12. 9. **pall**, fail. 11. **Rough-hew**, shape roughly. Dowden suggests that it may mean "bungle." 13. **sea-gown**, "a sea-gown, or a coarse, high-collered, and short-sleeved gowne, reaching down to the mid-leg, and used most by seamen and saylors" (Cotgrave, quoted by Singer). 15. **Finger'd**, pilfered, filched. 20. **Larded**, interspersed. 22. **such . . . life**, such imaginary dangers if I were allowed to live, or such exaggeration of the actual facts of my life. **bugs**, bugbears. 23. **supervise**, perusal. **leisure bated**, delay allowed.

Hor. I beseech you.

Ham. Being thus be-netted round with
villanies,—
Ere I could make a prologue to my brains,30
They had begun the play—I sat me down,
Devised a new commission, wrote it fair:
I once did hold it, as our statists do,
A baseness to write fair and labour'd much
How to forget that learning, but, sir, now
It did me yeoman's service: wilt thou
know
The effect of what I wrote?

Hor.   Ay, good my lord.

Ham. An earnest conjuration from the
king,
As England was his faithful tributary,
As love between them like the palm might
flourish,   40
As peace should still her wheaten garland
wear
And stand a comma 'tween their amities,
And many such-like 'As'es of great charge,
That, on the view and knowing of these
contents,
Without debatement further, more or less,
He should the bearers put to sudden death,
Not shriving-time allow'd.

Hor.   How was this seal'd?

Ham. Why, even in that was heaven or-
dinant.
I had my father's signet in my purse,   49
Which was the model of that Danish seal;
Folded the writ up in form of the other,
Subscribed it, gave 't the impression, placed
it safely,
The changeling never known. Now, the next
day
Was our sea-fight; and what to this was
sequent
Thou know'st already.

Hor. So Guildenstern and Rosencrantz go
to 't.

Ham. Why, man, they did make love to
this employment;
They are not near my conscience; their
defeat

Does by their own insinuation grow: 59
'Tis dangerous when the baser nature comes
Between the pass and fell incensed points
Of mighty opposites.

Hor.   Why, what a king is this!

Ham. Does it not, thinks't thee, stand
me now upon—
He that hath kill'd my king and whored my
mother,
Popp'd in between the election and my
hopes,
Thrown out his angle for my proper life,
And with such cozenage—is 't not perfect
conscience,
To quit him with this arm? and is 't not to be
damn'd,
To let this canker of our nature come
In further evil?   70

Hor. It must be shortly known to him
from England
What is the issue of the business there.

Ham. It will be short: the interim is mine;
And a man's life's no more than to say 'One.'
But I am very sorry, good Horatio,
That to Laertes I forgot myself;
For, by the image of my cause, I see
The portraiture of his: I'll court his favours:
But, sure, the bravery of his grief did put me
Into a towering passion.

Hor.   Peace! who comes here? 80

Enter Osric.

Osr. Your lordship is right welcome back
to Denmark.

Ham. I humbly thank you, sir. Dost
know this water-fly?

Hor. No, my good lord.   85

Ham. Thy state is the more gracious; for
'tis a vice to know him. He hath much land,
and fertile: let a beast be lord of beasts, and
his crib shall stand at the king's mess: 'tis a
chough; but, as I say, spacious in the possession of dirt.   90

Osr. Sweet lord, if your lordship were at
leisure, I should impart a thing to you from
his majesty.

30-31. prologue . . . play, i.e., before I could begin
to think, my mind had made its decision. 33. statists,
statesmen. 34. fair, in a clear hand. 36. yeoman's,
i.e., faithful. 41. wheaten garland, symbol of peace.
42. comma, smallest break or separation (Gollancz).
Here amity begins and amity ends the period, and peace
stands between like a dependent clause (Dowden). 43.
'As'es, probably the "whereases" of a formal document,
with play on the word ass. charge, import, and burden.
47. shriving-time, time for absolution. 48. ordinant,
directing. 54. sequent, subsequent. 58. defeat,
destruction.

59. insinuation, interference. 61. pass, thrust.
fell incensed, fiercely angered. 63. stand, become
incumbent. 65. election. The Danish throne was
filled by election. 66. angle, fish-hook. proper, own.
67. cozenage, trickery. 68. quit, pay off. 69. canker,
ulcer, or possibly the worm which destroys buds and
leaves. 79. bravery, bravado. 84. water-fly, vain or
busily idle person. 89. his crib . . . mess, he shall eat
at the king's table, i.e., be one of the group of persons
(usually four) constituting a mess at a banquet. 90.
chough, probably, chattering jackdaw; also explained
as chuff, provincial boor or churl.

Ham. I will receive it, sir, with all dili-gence of spirit. Put your bonnet to his right use; 'tis for the head.

Osr. I thank your lordship, it is very hot.

Ham. No, believe me, 'tis very cold; the wind is northerly.   99

Osr. It is indifferent cold, my lord, in-deed.

Ham. But yet methinks it is very sultry and hot for my complexion.

Osr. Exceedingly, my lord; it is very sultry,—as 'twere,—I cannot tell how. But, my lord, his majesty bade me signify to you that he has laid a great wager on your head: sir, this is the matter,—

Ham. I beseech you, remember—   108

[*Hamlet moves him to put on his hat.*

Osr. Nay, good my lord; for mine ease, in good faith. Sir, here is newly come to court Laertes; believe me, an absolute gentleman, full of most excellent differences, of very soft society and great showing: indeed, to speak feelingly of him, he is the card or calendar of gentry, for you shall find in him the continent of what part a gentleman would see.   116

Ham. Sir, his definement suffers no perdi-tion in you; though, I know, to divide him inventorially would dizzy the arithmetic of memory, †and yet but yaw neither, in re-spect of his quick sail. But, in the verity of ex-tolment, I take him to be a soul of great article; and his infusion of such dearth and rareness, as, to make true diction of him, his semblable is his mirror; and who else would trace him, his umbrage, nothing more.   126

Osr. Your lordship speaks most infallibly of him.

Ham. The concernancy, sir? why do we wrap the gentleman in our more rawer breath?

Osr. Sir?   130

Hor. Is't not possible to understand in another tongue? You will do't, sir, really.

Ham. What imports the nomination of this gentleman?

Osr. Of Laertes?

Hor. His purse is empty already; all's golden words are spent.

Ham. Of him, sir.

Ors. I know you are not ignorant—   139

Ham. I would you did, sir; yet, in faith, if you did, it would not much approve me. Well, sir?

Osr. You are not ignorant of what ex-cellence Laertes is—

Ham. I dare not confess that, lest I should compare with him in excellence; but, to know a man well, were to know himself.

Osr. I mean, sir, for his weapon; but in the imputation laid on him by them, in his meed he's unfellowed.   150

Ham. What's his weapon?

Osr. Rapier and dagger.

Ham. That's two of his weapons: but, well.

Osr. The king, sir, hath wagered with him six Barbary horses: against the which he has imponed, as I take it, six French rapiers and poniards, with their assigns, as girdle, hangers, and so: three of the carriages, in faith, are very dear to fancy, very responsive to the hilts, most delicate carriages, 160 and of very liberal conceit.

Ham. What call you the carriages?

Hor. I knew you must be edified by the margent ere you had done.

Osr. The carriages, sir, are the hang-ers.

Ham. The phrase would be more german to the matter, if we could carry cannon by our sides: I would it might be hangers till then. But, on: six Barbary horses against six French swords, their assigns, and three liberal-conceited carriages; that's the French bet against the Danish. Why is this 'im-poned,' as you call it?   171

Osr. The king, sir, hath laid, that in a

---

100. **indifferent**, somewhat. 108. **remember**, i.e., remember thy courtesy; conventional phrase for "Be covered." 109. **mine ease**, conventional reply declining the invitation of "Remember thy courtesy." 112. **differ-ences**, peculiarities. **soft**, gentle. 113. **showing**, dis-tinguished appearance. 114. **feelingly**, with just per-ception. **card**, chart, map. 115. **gentry**, good-breed-ing. **continent**, sum and substance. 117. **define-ment**, definition. **perdition**, loss, diminution. 118. **divide him inventorially**, i.e., enumerate his graces. 120. **yaw**, to move unsteadily (of a ship). Dowden's note: To enumerate in detail the perfections of Laertes would bewilder the computations of memory, yet for all that—in spite of the calculations—the enumeration would stagger to and fro (and so fall behind) in compari-son with Laertes's quick sailing (or, possibly, considering *its* quick sail, which ought to steady the ship). 122. **article**, moment or importance. 123. **infusion**, in-fused temperament, character imparted by nature. **dearth and rareness**, rarity. 124. **semblable**, like, match. 125. **trace**, follow. 126. **umbrage**, shadow. 128. **concernancy**, import. 129. **breath**, speech.

131-132. **Is't . . . tongue?** probably, can you not understand your jargon when somebody else uses it? 133. **nomination**, naming. 141. **approve**, commend. 146-147. **but . . . himself**, but to know a man as ex-cellent were to know Laertes. 149. **imputation**, reputa-tion. 150. **meed**, merit. 155-156. **he has imponed**, he has wagered. 158. **hangers**, straps on the sword-belt from which the sword hung. 159. **dear . . . fancy**, fancifully made. **responsive**, probably, well-balanced; corresponding closely (Onions). 160. **delicate**, i.e., in workmanship. **liberal conceit**, elaborate design. 163. **margent**, margin of a book, place for explanatory notes. 165. **german**, germain, appropriate.

dozen passes between yourself and him, he shall not exceed you three hits: he hath laid on twelve for nine; and it would come to immediate trial, if your lordship would vouchsafe the answer.

Ham. How if I answer 'no'?

Osr. I mean, my lord, the opposition of your person in trial. 179

Ham. Sir, I will walk here in the hall: if it please his majesty, 't is the breathing time of day with me; let the foils be brought, the gentleman willing, and the king hold his purpose, I will win for him an I can; if not, I will gain nothing but my shame and the odd hits. 185

Osr. Shall I re-deliver you e'en so?

Ham. To this effect, sir; after what flourish your nature will.

Osr. I commend my duty to your lordship.

Ham. Yours, yours. [*Exit Osric.*] He does well to commend it himself; there are no tongues else for 's turn.

Hor. This lapwing runs away with the shell on his head. 194

Ham. He did comply with his dug, before he sucked it. Thus has he—and many more of the same breed that I know the drossy age dotes on—only got the tune of the time and outward habit of encounter; a kind of yesty collection, which carries them through and through the most †fond and winnowed opinions; and do but blow them to their trial, 202 the bubbles are out.

Enter a Lord.

Lord. My lord, his majesty commended him to you by young Osric, who brings back to him, that you attend him in the hall: he sends to know if your pleasure hold to play with Laertes, or that you will take longer time.

Ham. I am constant to my purposes; they follow the king's pleasure: if his fitness speaks, mine is ready; now or whensoever, provided I be so able as now. 211

Lord. The king and queen and all are coming down.

Ham. In happy time.

Lord. The queen desires you to use some gentle entertainment to Laertes before you fall to play.

Ham. She well instructs me. [*Exit Lord.*

Hor. You will lose this wager, my lord. 219

Ham. I do not think so; since he went into France, I have been in continual practice; I shall win at the odds. But thou wouldst not think how ill all's here about my heart: but it is no matter.

Hor. Nay, good my lord,— 224

Ham. It is but foolery; but it is such a kind of gain-giving, as would perhaps trouble a woman.

Hor. If your mind dislike any thing, obey it: I will forestal their repair hither, and say you are not fit. 229

Ham. Not a whit, we defy augury: there's a special providence in the fall of a sparrow. If it be now, 'tis not to come; if it be not to come, it will be now; if it be not now, yet it will come: the readiness is all: since no man has aught of what he leaves, what is 't to leave betimes? Let be. 235

Enter KING, QUEEN, LAERTES, Lords, OSRIC, *and* Attendants *with foils, &c.*

King. Come, Hamlet, come, and take this hand from me.

[*The King puts Laertes' hand into Hamlet's.*

Ham. Give me your pardon, sir: I've done you wrong;
But pardon 't, as you are a gentleman.
This presence knows,
And you must needs have heard, how I am punish'd 240
With sore distraction. What I have done,
That might your nature, honour and exception
Roughly awake, I here proclaim was madness.
Was 't Hamlet wrong'd Laertes? Never Hamlet:
If Hamlet from himself be ta'en away,
And when he's not himself does wrong Laertes,
Then Hamlet does it not, Hamlet denies it.
Who does it, then? His madness: if 't be so,

Hamlet is of the faction that is wrong'd;
His madness is poor Hamlet's enemy.   250
Sir, in this audience,
Let my disclaiming from a purposed evil
Free me so far in your most generous
     thoughts,
That I have shot mine arrow o'er the house,
And hurt my brother.
     Laer. ·   I am satisfied in nature,
Whose motive, in this case, should stir me
     most
To my revenge: but in my terms of honour
I stand aloof; and will no reconcilement,
Till by some elder masters, of known honour,
I have a voice and precedent of peace,   260
To keep my name ungored. But till that
     time,
I do receive your offer'd love like love,
And will not wrong it.
     Ham.   I embrace it freely;
And will this brother's wager frankly play.
Give us the foils. Come on.
     Laer.   Come, one for me.
     Ham. I'll be your foil, Laertes: in mine
     ignorance
Your skill shall, like a star i' the darkest
     night,
Stick fiery off indeed.
     Laer.   You mock me, sir.
     Ham. No, by this hand.
     King. Give them the foils, young Osric.
     Cousin Hamlet,   270
You know the wager?
     Ham.   Very well, my lord;
Your grace hath laid the odds o' the weaker
     side.
     King. I do not fear it; I have seen you
     both:
But since he is better'd, we have therefore
     odds.
     Laer. This is too heavy, let me see an-
     other.
     Ham. This likes me well. These foils have
     all a length?   [*They prepare to play.*
     Osr. Ay, my good lord.
     King. Set me the stoups of wine upon
     that table.

If Hamlet give the first or second hit,
Or quit in answer of the third exchange, 280
Let all the battlements their ordnance fire;
The king shall drink to Hamlet's better
     breath;
And in the cup an union shall he throw,
Richer than that which four successive kings
In Denmark's crown have worn. Give me
     the cups;
And let the kettle to the trumpet speak,
The trumpet to the cannoneer without,
The cannons to the heavens, the heavens to
     earth,
'Now the king drinks to Hamlet.' Come,
     begin:
And you, the judges, bear a wary eye.   290
     Ham. Come on, sir.
     Laer.   Come, my lord. [*They play.*
     Ham.   One.
     Laer.   No.
     Ham.   Judgement.
     Osr. A hit, a very palpable hit.
     Laer.   Well; again.
     King. Stay; give me drink. Hamlet, this
     pearl is thine;
Here's to thy health.
         [*Trumpets sound, and cannon shot off*
                        within.
               Give him the cup.
     Ham. I'll play this bout first; set it by
     awhile.
Come. [*They play.*] Another hit; what say
     you?
     Laer. A touch, a touch, I do confess.
     King. Our son shall win.
     Queen.   He's fat, and scant of breath.
Here, Hamlet, take my napkin, rub thy
     brows: 299
The queen carouses to thy fortune, Hamlet.
     Ham. Good madam!
     King.   Gertrude, do not drink.
     Queen. I will, my lord; I pray you, pardon
     me.
     King. [*Aside*] It is the poison'd cup: it is
     too late.
     Ham. I dare not drink yet, madam; by
     and by.
     Queen. Come, let me wipe thy face.

---

255. **brother.** With reference to the F reading, *mother,* Dowden calls attention to Gertrude's request to "use some gentle entertainment" to Laertes. **nature,** i.e., he is personally satisfied, but his honor must be satisfied by the rules of the code of honor. 260. **voice,** authoritative pronouncement. 266. **foil,** quibble on the two senses, "background which sets something off," and "blunted rapier for fencing." 268. **Stick fiery off,** stand out brilliantly.

283. **union,** pearl. 286. **kettle,** kettledrum. 293. **pearl,** i.e., the poison. 298. **fat.** There is a tradition that *fat* describes Richard Burbage, the original Hamlet, known to have been corpulent. Many editors define it as "soft, out of training." It has been recently suggested that *fat* means "sweaty." Emendations *faint* and *hot* have been proposed. 300. **carouses,** drinks a toast.

Laer. My lord, I'll hit him now.

King.　　　　　　　I do not think't.

Laer. [*Aside*] And yet 'tis almost 'gainst
　　my conscience.

Ham. Come, for the third, Laertes: you
　　but dally;

I pray you, pass with your best violence;

I am afeard you make a wanton of me.　310

Laer. Say you so? come on. [*They play.*

Osr. Nothing, neither way.

Laer. Have at you now!

[*Laertes wounds Hamlet; then, in scuffling, they change rapiers, and Hamlet
wounds Laertes.*

King.　　　Part them; they are incensed.

Ham. Nay, come, again. [*The Queen falls.*

Osr.　　　Look to the queen there, ho!

Hor. They bleed on both sides. How is it,
　　my lord?

Osr. How is't, Laertes?

Laer. Why, as a woodcock to mine own
　　springe, Osric;

I am justly kill'd with mine own treachery.

Ham. How does the queen?

King.　　　She swounds to see them bleed.

Queen. No, no, the drink, the drink,—O
　　my dear Hamlet,—　　　　　　320

The drink, the drink! I am poison'd. [*Dies.*

Ham. O villany! Ho! let the door be
　　lock'd:

Treachery! Seek it out.

Laer. It is here, Hamlet: Hamlet, thou
　　art slain;

No medicine in the world can do thee good;

In thee there is not half an hour of life;

The treacherous instrument is in thy hand,

Unbated and envenom'd: the foul practice

Hath turn'd itself on me; lo, here I lie,　329

Never to rise again: thy mother's poison'd:

I can no more: the king, the king's to blame.

Ham. The point envenom'd too!

Then, venom, to thy work. [*Stabs the King.*

All. Treason! treason!

King. O, yet defend me, friends; I am but
　　hurt.

Ham. Here, thou incestuous, murderous,
　　damned Dane,

Drink off this potion. Is thy union here?

Follow my mother.　　　　[*King dies.*

Laer.　　　　　He is justly served;

It is a poison temper'd by himself.

Exchange forgiveness with me, noble Ham-
　　let:

Mine and my father's death come not upon
　　thee,　　　　　　　　　341

Nor thine on me!　　　　　[*Dies.*

Ham. Heaven make thee free of it! I
　　follow thee.

I am dead, Horatio. Wretched queen,
　　adieu!

You that look pale and tremble at this
　　chance,

That are but mutes or audience to this act,

Had I but time—as this fell sergeant, death,

Is strict in his arrest—O, I could tell you—

But let it be. Horatio, I am dead;

Thou livest; report me and my cause aright

To the unsatisfied.

Hor.　　　　　Never believe it:　351

I am more an antique Roman than a Dane:

Here's yet some liquor left.

Ham.　　　　　As thou'rt a man,

Give me the cup: let go; by heaven, I'll
　　have't.

O good Horatio, what a wounded name,

Things standing thus unknown, shall live
　　behind me!

If thou didst ever hold me in thy heart,

Absent thee from felicity awhile,

And in this harsh world draw thy breath in
　　pain,

To tell my story. [*March afar off, and shot
　　within.*

　　　　　　What warlike noise is this?

Osr. Young Fortinbras, with conquest
　　come from Poland,　　　　　361

To the ambassadors of England gives

This warlike volley.

Ham.　　　　　O, I die, Horatio;

The potent poison quite o'er-crows my
　　spirit:

I cannot live to hear the news from England;

But I do prophesy the election lights

---

310. **wanton**, spoiled child. 313. *Stage Direction:*
in scuffling, they change rapiers. Occurs in F and
indicates that at the Globe Theater the exchange was
played as a chance occurrence and was not, as Friesen
suggests, a part of the regular tactics of fence. Actors
have adopted various methods of exchanging rapiers.
Sir Johnston Forbes-Robertson's way was very convincing. He got scratched, grew suspicious, disarmed
Laertes, and forced the exchange. 314. **ho!** supposed
by Staunton to be a signal to stop the combat. 317.
woodcock, as type of stupidity or as decoy. **springe**,
trap, snare. 319. **swounds**, swoons. 328. **unbated**,
not blunted with a button. **practice**, plot, stratagem.

---

339. **temper'd**, mixed. 346. **mutes**, performers in a
play who speak no words. 347. **sergeant**, sheriff's
officer. Chambers takes the word to mean the officer who
enforces a judgment of a tribunal or the commands of a
person in authority. 352. **Roman**. It was the Roman
custom to follow masters in death (Yale). 364. **o'er-
crows**, triumphs over.

On Fortinbras: he has my dying voice;
So tell him, with the occurrents, more and
    less,
Which have solicited. The rest is silence.
                                    [*Dies.*

Hor. Now cracks a noble heart. Good
    night, sweet prince;   370
And flights of angels sing thee to thy rest!
Why does the drum come hither?
                            [*March within.*

Enter FORTINBRAS, *the* English Ambassa-
    dors, *and others.*

Fort. Where is this sight?
Hor.   What is it ye would see?
If aught of woe or wonder, cease your search.
Fort. This quarry cries on havoc. O
    proud death,
What feast is toward in thine eternal cell,
That thou so many princes at a shot
So bloodily hast struck?
First Amb.   The sight is dismal;
And our affairs from England come too late:
The ears are senseless that should give us
    hearing,   380
To tell him his commandment is fulfill'd,
That Rosencrantz and Guildenstern are
    dead:
Where should we have our thanks?
Hor.   Not from his mouth,
Had it the ability of life to thank you:
He never gave commandment for their
    death.
But since, so jump upon this bloody
    question,
You from the Polack wars, and you from
    England,
Are here arrived, give order that these
    bodies
High on a stage be placed to the view;   389

And let me speak to the yet unknowing
    world
How these things came about: so shall you
    hear
Of carnal, bloody, and unnatural acts,
Of accidental judgements, casual slaughters,
Of deaths put on by cunning and forced
    cause,
And, in this upshot, purposes mistook
Fall'n on the inventors' heads: all this can I
Truly deliver.
Fort.   Let us haste to hear it,
And call the noblest to the audience.
For me, with sorrow I embrace my fortune:
I have some rights of memory in this king-
    dom,   400
Which now to claim my vantage doth invite
    me.
Hor. Of that I shall have also cause to
    speak,
And from his mouth whose voice will draw
    on more:
But let this same be presently perform'd,
Even while men's minds are wild; lest more
    mischance,
On plots and errors, happen.
Fort.   Let four captains
Bear Hamlet, like a soldier, to the stage;
For he was likely, had he been put on,
To have proved most royally: and, for his
    passage,
The soldiers' music and the rites of war   410
Speak loudly for him.
Take up the bodies: such a sight as this
Becomes the field, but here shows much
    amiss.
Go, bid the soldiers shoot.
        [*A dead march. Exeunt, bearing off the
        dead bodies; after which a peal of ord-
        nance is shot off.*

---

368. **occurrents**, events, incidents. 369. **solicited**,
moved, urged. 375. **quarry**, heap of dead. **cries on
havoc**, calls for merciless slaughter. 376. **toward**, in
preparation. **eternal**, used to express extreme abhorrence. 383. **his mouth**, i.e., the king's. 386. **jump**,
immediately following. **question**, dispute. 389.
stage, platform.

392-396. **Of carnal . . . heads.** The words bear detailed reference to the tragic issues of the play. 400. **of
memory**, traditional, remembered. 403. **draw on
more**, lead more to speak. 406. **On**, on account of,
or possibly, on top of, in addition to. 409. **passage**,
death. 413. **field**, i.e., of battle.

OTHELLO
THE MOOR OF VENICE

DRAMATIS PERSONÆ

DUKE OF VENICE.

BRABANTIO, a senator.

Other Senators.

GRATIANO, brother to Brabantio.

LODOVICO, kinsman to Brabantio.

OTHELLO, a noble Moor in the service of the Venetian state.

CASSIO, his lieutenant.

IAGO, his ancient.

RODERIGO, a Venetian gentleman.

MONTANO, Othello's predecessor in the government of Cyprus.

Clown, servant to Othello.

DESDEMONA, daughter to Brabantio and wife to Othello.

EMILIA, wife to Iago.

BIANCA, mistress to Cassio.

Sailor, Messenger, Herald, Officers, Gentlemen, Musicians, and Attendants.

SCENE: *Venice: a Sea-port in Cyprus.*

ACT I

SCENE I. *Venice. A street.*

Enter RODERIGO *and* IAGO

Rod. Tush! never tell me; I take it much unkindly
That thou, Iago, who hast had my purse
As if the strings were thine, shouldst know of this.

Iago. 'Sblood, but you will not hear me:
If ever I did dream of such a matter,
Abhor me.

Rod. Thou told'st me thou didst hold him in thy hate.

Iago. Despise me, if I do not. Three great ones of the city,
In personal suit to make me his lieutenant,
Off-capp'd to him: and, by the faith of man,
I know my price, I am worth no worse a place: 11
But he, as loving his own pride and purposes,
Evades them, with a bombast circumstance
Horribly stuff'd with epithets of war;
And, in conclusion,

Nonsuits my mediators; for, 'Certes,' says he,
'I have already chose my officer.'
And what was he?
Forsooth, a great arithmetician,
One Michael Cassio, a Florentine,   20
†A fellow almost damn'd in a fair wife;
That never set a squadron in the field,
Nor the division of a battle knows
More than a spinster; unless the bookish theoric,
Wherein the toged consuls can propose
As masterly as he: mere prattle, without practice,
Is all his soldiership. But he, sir, had the election:
And I, of whom his eyes had seen the proof
At Rhodes, at Cyprus and on other grounds
Christian and heathen, must be be-lee'd and calm'd   30
By debitor and creditor: this counter-caster,
He, in good time, must his lieutenant be,

4. **'Sblood,** an oath, "by God's blood." 8. **great ones of the city.** Iago means to indicate his importance in the community; this is suggested also by his use of the word *worth* in line 11.

19. **arithmetician,** a man whose military knowledge was merely theoretical, based on books of tactics. 21. **A . . . wife.** This line is usually regarded as an error on Shakespeare's part, since Cassio has no wife; *wife* is sometimes taken to mean "woman." Possibly in Shakespeare's first version of the play Cassio had a wife as he did in the source. 23. **division.** disposition of a battle line. 24. **theoric.** theory. 25. **toged.** wearing the toga. **propose.** discuss. 29. **Rhodes, Cyprus.** islands in the Mediterranean south of Asia Minor, long subject to contention between the Venetians and the Turks. 31. **counter-caster,** contemptuous term for an arithmetician. 32. **in good time.** forsooth.

And I—God bless the mark!—his Moor-
  ship's ancient.
  Rod. By heaven, I rather would have been
    his hangman.
  Iago. Why, there's no remedy; 'tis the
    curse of service,
Preferment goes by letter and affection,
And not by old gradation, where each second
Stood heir to the first. Now, sir, be judge
  yourself,
Whether I in any just term am affined
To love the Moor.
  Rod.   I would not follow him then. 40
  Iago. O, sir, content you;
I follow him to serve my turn upon him:
We cannot all be masters, nor all masters
Cannot be truly follow'd. You shall mark
Many a duteous and knee-crooking knave,
That, doting on his own obsequious bondage,
Wears out his time, much like his master's
  ass,
For nought but provender, and when he's
  old, cashier'd:
Whip me such honest knaves. Others there
  are
Who, trimm'd in forms and visages of duty,
Keep yet their hearts attending on them-
  selves,   51
And, throwing but shows of service on their
  lords,
Do well thrive by them and when they have
  lined their coats
Do themselves homage: these fellows have
  some soul;
And such a one do I profess myself. For, sir,
It is as sure as you are Roderigo,
Were I the Moor, I would not be Iago:
In following him, I follow but myself;
Heaven is my judge, not I for love and duty,
But seeming so, for my peculiar end: 60
For when my outward action doth demon-
  strate
The native act and figure of my heart
In compliment extern, 'tis not long after
But I will wear my heart upon my sleeve
For daws to peck at: I am not what I am.
  Rod. What a full fortune does the thick-
    lips owe,

If he can carry 't thus!
  Iago.   Call up her father,
Rouse him: make after him, poison his de-
  light,
Proclaim him in the streets; incense her
  kinsmen,
And, though he in a fertile climate dwell, 70
Plague him with flies: though that his joy be
  joy,
Yet throw such changes of vexation on 't,
As it may lose some colour.
  Rod. Here is her father's house; I'll
    call aloud.
  Iago. Do, with like timorous accent and
    dire yell
As when, by night and negligence, the fire
Is spied in populous cities.
  Rod. What, ho, Brabantio! Signior Bra-
    bantio, ho!
  Iago. Awake! what, ho, Brabantio!
    thieves! thieves! thieves!
Look to your house, your daughter and your
  bags!   80
Thieves! thieves!

    BRABANTIO *appears above, at a window.*

  Bra. What is the reason of this terrible
    summons?
What is the matter there?
  Rod. Signior, is all your family within?
  Iago. Are your doors lock'd?
  Bra.   Why, wherefore ask you this?
  Iago. 'Zounds, sir, you're robb'd; for
    shame, put on your gown;
Your heart is burst, you have lost half your
  soul;
Even now, now, very now, an old black ram
Is tupping your white ewe. Arise, arise;
Awake the snorting citizens with the bell, 90
Or else the devil will make a grandsire of
  you:
Arise, I say.
  Bra. What, have you lost your wits?
  Rod. Most reverend signior, do you know
    my voice?
  Bra. Not I: what are you?
  Rod. My name is Roderigo.
  Bra.   The worser welcome:
I have charged thee not to haunt about my
  doors:
In honest plainness thou hast heard me say
My daughter is not for thee; and now, in
  madness,

33. God bless the mark! anciently, a pious interjection to avert evil omens. **ancient,** standard bearer,
ensign. **37. old gradation,** seniority. Iago here expresses a characteristic prejudice of professional soldiers.
39. affined, bound. **41-55. O, sir ... myself.** These
lines are an expression of Iago's ethics. **57. Were ...
Iago,** Were I in the position of the Moor, I should not
feel as Iago feels. **63. compliment extern,** outward
civility. **66. thick-lips,** probably, African.

75. timorous, used ironically. **90. snorting,** snoring.

Being full of supper and distempering
    draughts,
Upon malicious bravery, dost thou come 100
To start my quiet.
  Rod. Sir, sir, sir,—
  Bra.   But thou must needs be sure
My spirit and my place have in them power
To make this bitter to thee.
  Rod.   Patience, good sir.
  Bra. What tell'st thou me of robbing?
    this is Venice;
My house is not a grange.
  Rod.   Most grave Brabantio,
In simple and pure soul I come to you.
  Iago. 'Zounds, sir, you are one of those
that will not serve God, if the devil bid you.
Because we come to do you service and you
think we are ruffians, you'll have your 110
daughter covered with a Barbary horse;
you'll have your nephews neigh to you; you'll
have coursers for cousins and gennets for
germans.
  Bra. What profane wretch art thou?
  Iago. I am one, sir, that comes to tell you
your daughter and the Moor are now making
the beast with two backs.
  Bra. Thou art a villain.
  Iago.   You are—a senator.
  Bra. This thou shalt answer; I know thee,
    Roderigo.   120
  Rod. Sir, I will answer any thing. But, I
    beseech you,
If 't be your pleasure and most wise consent,
As partly I find it is, that your fair daughter,
At this odd-even and dull watch o' the night,
Transported, with no worse nor better guard
But with a knave of common hire, a gon-
    dolier,
To the gross clasps of a lascivious Moor,—
If this be known to you and your allowance,
We then have done you bold and saucy
    wrongs;   129
But if you know not this, my manners tell me
We have your wrong rebuke. Do not believe
That, from the sense of all civility,
I thus would play and trifle with your rev-
    erence:
Your daughter, if you have not given her
    leave,
I say again, hath made a gross revolt;
Tying her duty, beauty, wit and fortunes

In an extravagant and wheeling stranger
Of here and every where. Straight satisfy
    yourself:
If she be in her chamber or your house,
Let loose on me the justice of the state   140
For thus deluding you.
  Bra.   Strike on the tinder, ho!
Give me a taper! call up all my people!
This accident is not unlike my dream:
Belief of it oppresses me already.
Light, I say! light!   [*Exit above.*
  Iago.   Farewell; for I must leave you:
It seems not meet, nor wholesome to my
    place,
To be produced—as, if I stay, I shall—
Against the Moor: for, I do know, the state,
However this may gall him with some check,
Cannot with safety cast him, for he's em-
    bark'd
With such loud reason to the Cyprus wars,151
Which even now stand in act, that, for their
    souls,
Another of his fathom they have none,
To lead their business: in which regard,
Though I do hate him as I do hell-pains,
Yet, for necessity of present life,
I must show out a flag and sign of love,
Which is indeed but sign. That you shall
    surely find him,   158
Lead to the Sagittary the raised search;
And there will I be with him. So, farewell.
                                    [*Exit.*

Enter, below, Brabantio, *and* Servants *with
    torches.*

  Bra. It is too true an evil: gone she is;
And what's to come of my despised time
Is nought but bitterness. Now, Roderigo,
Where didst thou see her? O unhappy girl!
With the Moor, say'st thou? Who would be
    a father!
How didst thou know 'twas she? O, she
    deceives me
Past thought! What said she to you? Get
    more tapers:
Raise all my kindred. Are they married,
    think you?
  Rod. Truly, I think they are.
  Bra. O heaven! How got she out? O
    treason of the blood!   170

---

100. **bravery,** defiance, bravado. 101. **start,** startle. 106. **grange,** farmhouse. 112. **nephews,** grandsons. 113. **gennets,** small Spanish horses. 114. **germans,** near relatives. 124. **odd-even,** about midnight. 128. **allowance,** permission. 132. **from,** contrary to.

137. **extravagant,** wandering. **wheeling,** wandering, vagabond. 141. **tinder,** charred linen kept in a metal box, and ignited by a spark from flint and steel. 143. **accident,** occurrence, event. 150. **cast,** dismiss. 159. **Sagittary,** probably an inn.

Fathers, from hence trust not your daughters' minds

By what you see them act. Is there not
charms

By which the property of youth and maidhood

May be abused? Have you not read, Roderigo,

Of some such thing?

Rod.   Yes, sir, I have indeed.

Bra. Call up my brother. O, would you
had her!

Some one way, some another. Do you know
Where we may apprehend her and the Moor?

Rod. I think I can discover him, if you
please

To get good guard and go along with me.   180

Bra. Pray you, lead on. At every house
I'll call;

I may command at most. Get weapons, ho!
And raise some special officers of night.
On, good Roderigo: I'll deserve your pains.

                              [*Exeunt.*

SCENE II. *Another street.*

Enter OTHELLO, IAGO, *and* Attendants
with torches.

Iago. Though in the trade of war I have
slain men,

Yet do I hold it very stuff o' the conscience
To do no contrived murder: I lack iniquity
Sometimes to do me service: nine or ten
times

I had thought to have yerk'd him here under
the ribs.

Oth. 'Tis better as it is.

Iago.   Nay, but he prated,
And spoke such scurvy and provoking terms
Against your honour

That, with the little godliness I have,
I did full hard forbear him. But, I pray you,
sir,   10

Are you fast married? Be assured of this,
That the magnifico is much beloved,
And hath in his effect a voice potential
As double as the duke's: he will divorce you;
Or put upon you what restraint and griev-
ance

The law, with all his might to enforce it on,
Will give him cable.

Oth.   Let him do his spite;
My services which I have done the signiory
Shall out-tongue his complaints. 'Tis yet
to know,—

Which, when I know that boasting is an
honour,   20

I shall promulgate—I fetch my life and
being

From men of royal siege, and my demerits
May speak unbonneted to as proud a fortune
As this that I have reach'd: for know, Iago,
But that I love the gentle Desdemona,
I would not my unhoused free condition
Put into circumscription and confine
For the sea's worth. But, look! what lights
come yond?

Iago. Those are the raised father and his
friends:

You were best go in.

Oth.   Not I; I must be found: 30
My parts, my title and my perfect soul
Shall manifest me rightly. Is it they?

Iago. By Janus, I think no.

Enter CASSIO, *and certain* Officers *with*
torches.

Oth. The servants of the duke, and my
lieutenant.

The goodness of the night upon you, friends!
What is the news?

Cas. The duke does greet you, general,
And he requires your haste-post-haste
appearance,

Even on the instant.

Oth.   What is the matter, think you?

Cas. Something from Cyprus, as I may
divine:

It is a business of some heat: the galleys   40
Have sent a dozen sequent messengers
This very night at one another's heels,
And many of the consuls, raised and met,
Are at the duke's already: you have been
hotly call'd for;

When, being not at your lodging to be
found,

The senate hath sent about three several
quests

To search you out.

Oth.　　　　　'Tis well I am found by you.
I will but spend a word here in the house,
And go with you.　　　　　　　　[*Exit.*

Cas.　　　　　Ancient, what makes he here?

Iago. 'Faith, he to-night hath boarded a
　　　land carack:　　　　　　　　　　50
If it prove lawful prize, he's made for ever.

Cas. I do not understand.

Iago.　　　　　　　　He's married.

Cas.　　　　　　　　To who?

　　　　　Re-enter OTHELLO.

Iago. Marry, to—Come, captain, will you
　　　go?

Oth.　　　　　　　Have with you.

Cas. Here comes another troop to seek for
　　　you.

Iago. It is Brabantio. General, be ad-
　　　vised;
He comes to bad intent.

Enter BRABANTIO, RODERIGO, *and* Officers
　　　with torches and weapons.

Oth.　　　　　Holla! stand there!

Rod. Signior, it is the Moor.

Bra.　　　　　Down with him, thief!
　　　　　　　[*They draw on both sides.*

Iago. You, Roderigo! come, sir, I am for
　　　you.

Oth. Keep up your bright swords, for the
　　　dew will rust them.
Good signior, you shall more command with
　　　years　　　　　　　　　　　　60
Than with your weapons.

Bra. O thou foul thief, where hast thou
　　　stow'd my daughter?
Damn'd as thou art, thou hast enchanted
　　　her;
For I'll refer me to all things of sense,
If she in chains of magic were not bound,
Whether a maid so tender, fair and happy,
So opposite to marriage that she shunn'd
The wealthy curled darlings of our nation,
Would ever have, to incur a general mock, 69
Run from her guardage to the sooty bosom
Of such a thing as thou, to fear, not to de-
　　　light.
Judge me the world, if 'tis not gross in sense

That thou hast practised on her with foul
　　　charms,
Abused her delicate youth with drugs or
　　　minerals
That weaken motion: I'll have't disputed on;
'Tis probable and palpable to thinking.
I therefore apprehend and do attach thee
For an abuser of the world, a practiser
Of arts inhibited and out of warrant.
Lay hold upon him: if he do resist,　　　80
Subdue him at his peril.

Oth.　　　　　Hold your hands,
Both you of my inclining, and the rest:
Were it my cue to fight, I should have known
　　　it
Without a prompter. Where will you that I
　　　go
To answer this your charge?

Bra.　　　　　To prison, till fit time
Of law and course of direct session
Call thee to answer.

Oth.　　　　　What if I do obey?
How may the duke be therewith satisfied,
Whose messengers are here about my side,
Upon some present business of the state　90
To bring me to him?

First Off. 'Tis true, most worthy signior;
The duke's in council, and your noble self,
I am sure, is sent for.

Bra.　　　　　How! the duke in council!
In this time of the night! Bring him away:
Mine's not an idle cause: the duke himself,
Or any of my brothers of the state,
Cannot but feel this wrong as 'twere their
　　　own;
For if such actions may have passage free,
Bond-slaves and pagans shall our statesmen
　　　be.　　　　　　　　　　[*Exeunt.*

　　SCENE III. *A council-chamber.*

The DUKE *and* Senators *sitting at a table;*
　　　　　Officers *attending.*

Duke. There is no composition in these
　　　news
That gives them credit.

---

50. **carack**, large merchant ship. 59. **Keep . . .
them.** In most stage versions of *Othello* the hero enters
for the first time at this point; it is a brilliant stage
entrance. 64. **of sense**, possessing mental faculties.
70. **guardage**, guardianship. 71. **fear**, frighten. 72.
gross in sense, easily discernible in apprehension
or perception.

74. **minerals**, medicine, poison. 75. **weaken motion**,
lessen the power of movement; since inward promptings
of all sorts were dependent on sense. Brabantio therefore
thinks that Desdemona's unnatural conduct is due to
drugs. **disputed on**, argued in court by professional
counsel. 78. **abuser of the world**, corrupter of society.
79. **inhibited**, prohibited. 82. **inclining**, following,
party. 86. **course of direct session**, regular legal
proceedings. 99. **Bond-slaves and pagans**, contemptuous references to Othello's past history.
Scene iii. 1. **composition**, consistency.

First Sen.   Indeed, they are dis-
    proportion'd;
My letters say a hundred and seven galleys.
Duke. And mine, a hundred and forty.
Sec. Sen.   And mine, two hundred:
But though they jump not on a just ac-
    count,—
As in these cases, where the aim reports,
'Tis oft with difference—yet do they all
    confirm
A Turkish fleet, and bearing up to Cyprus.
Duke. Nay, it is possible enough to judge-
    ment:
I do not so secure me in the error,   10
But the main article I do approve
In fearful sense.
Sailor. [*Within*] What, ho! what, ho!
    what, ho!
First Off. A messenger from the galleys.

                Enter a Sailor.

Duke.   Now, what's the business?
Sail. The Turkish preparation makes for
    Rhodes;
So was I bid report here to the state
By Signior Angelo.
Duke. How say you by this change?
First Sen.   This cannot be,
By no assay of reason: 'tis a pageant,
To keep us in false gaze. When we con-
    sider
The importancy of Cyprus to the Turk,   20
And let ourselves again but understand,
That as it more concerns the Turk than
    Rhodes,
So may he with more facile question bear it,
For that it stands not in such warlike brace,
But altogether lacks the abilities
That Rhodes is dress'd in: if we make
    thought of this,
We must not think the Turk is so unskil-
    ful
To leave that latest which concerns him
    first,
Neglecting an attempt of ease and gain,
To wake and wage a danger profitless.   30
Duke. Nay, in all confidence, he's not for
    Rhodes.
First Off. Here is more news.

                Enter a Messenger.

Mess. The Ottomites, reverend and gra-
    cious,
Steering with due course towards the isle of
    Rhodes,
Have there injointed them with an after
    fleet.
First Sen. Ay, so I thought. How many,
    as you guess?
Mess. Of thirty sail: and now they do re-
    stem
Their backward course, bearing with frank
    appearance
Their purposes toward Cyprus.   Signior
    Montano,
Your trusty and most valiant servitor,   40
With his free duty recommends you thus,
And prays you to believe him.
Duke. 'Tis certain, then, for Cyprus.
Marcus Luccicos, is not he in town?
First Sen. He's now in Florence.
Duke. Write from us to him; post-post-
    haste dispatch.
First Sen. Here comes Brabantio and the
    valiant Moor.

    Enter Brabantio, Othello, Iago,
        Roderigo, *and* Officers.

Duke. Valiant Othello, we must straight
    employ you
Against the general enemy Ottoman.
[*To Brabantio*] I did not see you; welcome,
    gentle signior;   50
We lack'd your counsel and your help to-
    night.
Bra. So did I yours.   Good your grace,
    pardon me;
Neither my place nor aught I heard of busi-
    ness
Hath raised me from my bed, nor doth the
    general care
Take hold on me, for my particular grief
Is of so flood-gate and o'erbearing nature
That it engluts and swallows other sor-
    rows
And it is still itself.
Duke.   Why, what's the matter?
Bra. My daughter! O, my daughter!
Duke and Sen.   Dead?
Bra.   Ay, to me;
She is abused, stol'n from me, and corrupted

By spells and medicines bought of mounte-
   banks;   61
For nature so preposterously to err,
Being not deficient, blind, or lame of sense,
Sans witchcraft could not.
   Duke. Whoe'er he be that in this foul
   proceeding
Hath thus beguiled your daughter of herself
And you of her, the bloody book of law
You shall yourself read in the bitter letter
After your own sense, yea, though our
   proper son
Stood in your action.
   Bra.   Humbly I thank your grace. 70
Here is the man, this Moor, whom now, it
   seems,
Your special mandate for the state-affairs
Hath hither brought.
   Duke and Sen. We are very sorry for 't.
   Duke [*To Othello*] What, in your own part,
   can you say to this?
   Bra. Nothing, but this is so.
   Oth. Most potent, grave, and reverend
   signiors,
My very noble and approved good masters,
That I have ta'en away this old man's
   daughter,
It is most true; true, I have married her:
The very head and front of my offending 80
Hath this extent, no more. Rude am I in
   my speech,
And little bless'd with the soft phrase of
   peace;
For since these arms of mine had seven years'
   pith,
Till now some nine moons wasted, they have
   used
Their dearest action in the tented field,
And little of this great world can I speak,
More than pertains to feats of broil and
   battle,
And therefore little shall I grace my cause
In speaking for myself. Yet, by your gra-
   cious patience,
I will a round unvarnish'd tale deliver   90
Of my whole course of love; what drugs,
   what charms,
What conjuration and what mighty magic,
For such proceeding I am charged withal,
I won his daughter.

   Bra.   A maiden never bold;
Of spirit so still and quiet, that her motion
Blush'd at herself; and she, in spite of nature,
Of years, of country, credit, every thing,
To fall in love with what she fear'd to look
   on!
It is a judgement maim'd and most imperfect
That will confess perfection so could err 100
Against all rules of nature, and must be
   driven
To find out practices of cunning hell,
Why this should be. I therefore vouch
   again
That with some mixtures powerful o'er the
   blood,
Or with some dram conjured to this effect,
He wrought upon her.
   Duke.   To vouch this, is no proof,
Without more wider and more overt test
Than these thin habits and poor likelihoods
Of modern seeming do prefer against him.
   First Sen. But, Othello, speak: 110
Did you by indirect and forced courses
Subdue and poison this young maid's affec-
   tions?
Or came it by request and such fair question
As soul to soul affordeth?
   Oth.   I do beseech you,
Send for the lady to the Sagittary,
And let her speak of me before her father:
If you do find me foul in her report,
The trust, the office I do hold of you,
Not only take away, but let your sentence
Even fall upon my life.
   Duke.   Fetch Desdemona hither. 120
   Oth. Ancient, conduct them; you best
   know the place.
              [*Exeunt Iago and Attendants.*
And, till she come, as truly as to heaven
I do confess the vices of my blood,
So justly to your grave ears I'll present
How I did thrive in this fair lady's love,
And she in mine.
   Duke. Say it, Othello.
   Oth. Her father loved me; oft invited me;
Still question'd me the story of my life,
From year to year, the battles, sieges, for-
   tunes,
That I have pass'd.   131

---

64. **Sans**, without. 69. **proper**, own. 70. **Stood . . .
action**, was under your accusation. 83. **pith**, strength,
vigor. 85. **dearest**, most grievously felt (Schmidt).
89. **patience**, sufferance, permission. 90. **round**,
straightforward.

95-96. **motion . . . herself**, inward impulses blushed
at themselves. 103. **vouch**, assert. 111-112. **Did . . .
affections**. The possibility of such enchantment is
accepted by the court; it would be as readily accepted
by an Elizabethan audience. The English Parliament
of the year 1604 denounced by law the employment of
magic to secure love. 129. **Still**, continually.

I ran it through, even from my boyish days,
To the very moment that he bade me tell it;
Wherein I spake of most disastrous chances,
Of moving accidents by flood and field,
Of hair-breadth scapes i' the imminent deadly breach,
Of being taken by the insolent foe
And sold to slavery, of my redemption thence
And portance in my travels' history:
Wherein of antres vast and deserts idle, 140
Rough quarries, rocks and hills whose heads touch heaven,
It was my hint to speak,—such was the process;
And of the Cannibals that each other eat,
The Anthropophagi and men whose heads
Do grow beneath their shoulders. This to hear
Would Desdemona seriously incline:
But still the house-affairs would draw her thence:
Which ever as she could with haste dispatch,
She'ld come again, and with a greedy ear
Devour up my discourse: which I observing,
Took once a pliant hour, and found good means 151
To draw from her a prayer of earnest heart
That I would all my pilgrimage dilate,
Whereof by parcels she had something heard,
But not intentively: I did consent,
And often did beguile her of her tears,
When I did speak of some distressful stroke
That my youth suffer'd. My story being done,
She gave me for my pains a world of sighs:
She swore, in faith, 'twas strange, 'twas passing strange, 160
'Twas pitiful, 'twas wondrous pitiful:
She wish'd she had not heard it, yet she wish'd
That heaven had made her such a man: she thank'd me,
And bade me, if I had a friend that loved her,
I should but teach him how to tell my story,
And that would woo her. Upon this hint I spake:
She loved me for the dangers I had pass'd,
And I loved her that she did pity them.
This only is the witchcraft I have used:
Here comes the lady; let her witness it. 170

Enter Desdemona, Iago, *and* Attendants.

Duke. I think this tale would win my daughter too.
Good Brabantio,
Take up this mangled matter at the best:
Men do their broken weapons rather use
Than their bare hands.
    Bra.   I pray you, hear her speak:
If she confess that she was half the wooer,
Destruction on my head, if my bad blame
Light on the man! Come hither, gentle mistress:
Do you perceive in all this noble company
Where most you owe obedience?
    Des.   My noble father,180
I do perceive here a divided duty:
To you I am bound for life and education;
My life and education both do learn me
How to respect you; you are the lord of duty;
I am hitherto your daughter: but here's my husband,
And so much duty as my mother show'd
To you, preferring you before her father,
So much I challenge that I may profess
Due to the Moor my lord.
    Bra.   God be wi' you! I have done.
Please it your grace, on to the state-affairs:
I had rather to adopt a child than get it. 191
Come hither, Moor:
I here do give thee that with all my heart
Which, but thou hast already, with all my heart
I would keep from thee. For your sake, jewel,
I am glad at soul I have no other child;
For thy escape would teach me tyranny,
To hang clogs on them. I have done, my lord.
    Duke. Let me speak like yourself, and lay a sentence,
Which, as a grise or step, may help these lovers 200
Into your favour.

---

136. **imminent**, i.e., impending parts when a gap has been made in a fortification. 139. **portance**, conduct. 140. **antres**, caverns. **idle**, barren, unprofitable. 142. **hint**, occasion. 143. **eat**, ate. 144. **Anthropophagi**, man-eaters, a term from Pliny's *Natural History*. **whose . . . shoulders.** Tales of tribes of headless men appear in Pliny and in the voyages of travelers, such as Raleigh's *Discovery of Guiana*. 153. **dilate**, relate in detail. 155. **intentively**, attentively. 163. **her**, i.e., for her.

190. **on to**, i.e., proceed with. 195. **For your sake**, on your account. 199. **like yourself**, i.e., in a like strain of resignation. 200. **grise**, step.

When remedies are past, the griefs are ended
By seeing the worst, which late on hopes
    depended.
To mourn a mischief that is past and gone
Is the next way to draw new mischief on.
What cannot be preserved when fortune
    takes,
Patience her injury a mockery makes.
The robb'd that smiles steals something
    from the thief;
He robs himself that spends a bootless grief.
   Bra. So let the Turk of Cyprus us beguile;
We lose it not, so long as we can smile. 211
He bears the sentence well that nothing bears
But the free comfort which from thence he
    hears,
But he bears both the sentence and the
    sorrow
That, to pay grief, must of poor patience
    borrow.
These sentences, to sugar, or to gall,
Being strong on both sides, are equivocal:
But words are words; I never yet did hear
That the bruised heart was pierced through
    the ear.
I humbly beseech you, proceed to the affairs
    of state.   220
   Duke. The Turk with a most mighty
preparation makes for Cyprus. Othello, the
fortitude of the place is best known to you;
and though we have there a substitute of
most allowed sufficiency, yet opinion, a
sovereign mistress of effects, throws a more
safer voice on you: you must therefore be
content to slubber the gloss of your new
fortunes with this more stubborn and bois-
terous expedition.   229
   Oth. The tyrant custom, most grave
    senators,
Hath made the flinty and steel couch of war
My thrice-driven bed of down: I do agnize
A natural and prompt alacrity
I find in hardness, and do undertake
These present wars against the Ottomites.
Most humbly therefore bending to your
    state,
I crave fit disposition for my wife,
Due reference of place and exhibition,

With such accommodation and besort
As levels with her breeding.
   Duke.   If you please, 240
Be 't at her father's.
   Bra.   I'll not have it so.
   Oth. Nor I.
   Des.   Nor I; I would not there reside,
To put my father in impatient thoughts
By being in his eye. Most gracious duke,
To my unfolding lend your prosperous ear;
And let me find a charter in your voice,
To assist my simpleness.
   Duke. What would you, Desdemona?
   Des. That I did love the Moor to live with
    him,   249
My downright violence and storm of fortunes
May trumpet to the world: my heart's
    subdued
Even to the very quality of my lord:
I saw Othello's visage in his mind,
And to his honours and his valiant parts
Did I my soul and fortunes consecrate.
So that, dear lords, if I be left behind,
A moth of peace, and he go to the war,
The rites for which I love him are bereft me,
And I a heavy interim shall support
By his dear absence. Let me go with him.260
   Oth. Let her have your voices.
Vouch with me, heaven, I therefore beg it
    not,
To please the palate of my appetite,
Nor to comply with heat—the young affects
In me defunct—and proper satisfaction,
But to be free and bounteous to her mind:
And heaven defend your good souls, that you
    think
I will your serious and great business scant
For she is with me: no, when light-wing'd
    toys
Of feather'd Cupid seel with wanton dullness
My speculative and officed instruments, 271
That my disports corrupt and taint my
    business,
Let housewives make a skillet of my helm,
And all indign and base adversities
Make head against my estimation!

202-220. **When . . . state.** The sententious matter
in this passage is cast into rhyme, as not infrequently in
Shakespeare. 205. **next,** nearest. 213. **comfort,** i.e.,
the consolation that it may be borne with patience. 223.
fortitude, strength. 225. **allowed,** acknowledged.
opinion, public opinion, reputation. 228. **slubber,**
soil, sully. 232. **thrice-driven,** thrice sifted. **agnize,**
confess. 234. **hardness,** hardship.

238. **exhibition,** allowance. 239. **besort,** suitable
company. 245. **prosperous,** propitious. 246. **charter,**
privilege. 247. **simpleness,** simplicity. 252. **quality,**
nature. 258. **rites.** Some editors read *rights.* 260.
dear, deeply felt. 264. **affects,** inclinations, desires.
270. **seel,** in falconry, to make blind by sewing up the
eyes of the hawk in training. 271. **speculative,** having
ability to see. **officed,** official, active. 272. **That,** so
that. **disports,** pastime. **taint,** impair. 273. **skillet,**
defined as "a small kettle"; usually means "a frying
pan of the older style." 274. **indign,** unworthy,
shameful.

Duke. Be it as you shall privately deter-
mine,
Either for her stay or going: the affair cries
haste,
And speed must answer it.
　First Sen. You must away to-night.
　Oth.　　　　　　　With all my heart.
　Duke. At nine i' the morning here we'll
meet again.　　　　　　　　　　　280
Othello, leave some officer behind,
And he shall our commission bring to you;
With such things else of quality and respect
As doth import you.
　Oth.　So please your grace, my ancient;
A man he is of honesty and trust:
To his conveyance I assign my wife,
With what else needful your good grace shall
think
To be sent after me.
　Duke.　　　　Let it be so.
Good night to every one. [*To Brab.*] And,
noble signior,
If virtue no delighted beauty lack,　　290
Your son-in-law is far more fair than black.
　First Sen. Adieu, brave Moor; use Desde-
mona well.
　Bra. Look to her, Moor, if thou hast eyes
to see:
She has deceived her father, and may thee.
　　[*Exeunt Duke, Senators, Officers, &c.*
　Oth. My life upon her faith! Honest Iago,
My Desdemona must I leave to thee:
I prithee, let thy wife attend on her;
And bring them after in the best advantage.
Come, Desdemona; I have but an hour
Of love, of worldly matters and direction, 300
To spend with thee: we must obey the time.
　　[*Exeunt Othello and Desdemona.*
　Rod. Iago,—
　Iago. What say'st thou, noble heart?
　Rod. What will I do, thinkest thou?
　Iago. Why, go to bed, and sleep.
　Rod. I will incontinently drown myself.
　Iago. If thou dost, I shall never love thee
after. Why, thou silly gentleman!
　Rod. It is silliness to live when to live is
torment; and then have we a prescription to
die when death is our physician.　　311

Iago. O villanous! I have looked upon the
world for four times seven years; and since I
could distinguish betwixt a benefit and an
injury, I never found man that knew how to
love himself. Ere I would say, I would
drown myself for the love of a guinea-hen,
I would change my humanity with a baboon.
　Rod. What should I do? I confess it is my
shame to be so fond; but it is not in my
virtue to amend it.　　　　　　　　321
　Iago. Virtue! a fig! 'tis in ourselves that
we are thus or thus. Our bodies are our
gardens, to the which our wills are gardeners;
so that if we will plant nettles, or sow lettuce,
set hyssop and weed up thyme, supply it
with one gender of herbs, or distract it with
many, either to have it sterile with idleness,
or manured with industry, why, the power
and corrigible authority of this lies in our
wills. If the balance of our lives had not one
scale of reason to poise another of sensuality,
the blood and baseness of our natures would
conduct us to most preposterous conclusions:
but we have reason to cool our raging motions, our carnal stings, our unbitted lusts,
whereof I take this that you call love 336
to be a sect or scion.
　Rod. It cannot be.
　Iago. It is merely a lust of the blood and a
permission of the will. Come, be a man.
Drown thyself! drown cats and blind puppies. I have professed me thy friend and I
confess me knit to thy deserving with cables
of perdurable toughness; I could never better
stead thee than now. Put money in thy
purse; follow thou the wars; defeat thy favour with an usurped beard; I say, put
money in thy purse. It cannot be that
Desdemona should long continue her love to
the Moor,—put money in thy purse,—nor
he his to her: it was a violent commencement,
and thou shalt see an answerable sequestration:—put but money in thy purse.
These Moors are changeable in their wills:—
fill thy purse with money:—the food that to

313. **four times seven.** Clarke expresses surprise
that Iago should be so young and so versed in worldly
ways. Twenty-eight was, however, a maturer age in
Shakespeare's time. 322. **Virtue! a fig!** This passage
states the ethics, the infidelity, of selfishness. 325.
hyssop, an herb of the mint family. 327. **gender**, kind.
328. **idleness**, want of cultivation. 334-335. **reason
. . . motions.** Iago understands the warfare between
reason and sensuality, but his ethics are totally inverted;
reason works in him not good, as it should according to
natural law, but evil, which he has chosen for his good.
337. **sect**, cutting. 344. **perdurable**, very durable.
346. **defeat thy favour**, disguise thy face. 351. **answerable sequestration**, a separation corresponding.

275. **estimation**, reputation. 283. **of quality**, pertaining to your rank. 284. **import**, concern. 290.
delighted, delightful. 293-294. **Look to her, Moor,**
etc., a tragic premonition delivered casually. 295.
Honest Iago, an evidence of Iago's carefully built reputation. 298. **in the best advantage**, at the most
favorable opportunity. 306. **incontinently**, immediately.

him now is as luscious as locusts, shall be to him shortly as bitter as coloquintida. She must change for youth: when she is sated with his body, she will find the error of her choice: she must have change, she must: therefore put money in thy purse. If thou wilt needs damn thyself, do it a more delicate way than drowning. Make all the money thou canst: if sanctimony and a frail vow betwixt an erring barbarian and a super-subtle Venetian be not too hard for my wits and all the tribe of hell, thou shalt enjoy her; therefore make money. A pox of drowning thyself! it is clean out of the way: seek thou rather to be hanged in compassing thy joy than to be drowned and go without her.

Rod. Wilt thou be fast to my hopes, if I depend on the issue? 370

Iago. Thou art sure of me:—go, make money:—I have told thee often, and I re-tell thee again and again, I hate the Moor: my cause is hearted; thine hath no less reason. Let us be conjunctive in our revenge against him; if thou canst cuckold him, thou dost thyself a pleasure, me a sport. There are many events in the womb of time which will be delivered. Traverse! go, provide thy money. We will have more of this to-morrow. Adieu.

Rod. Where shall we meet i' the morning?

Iago. At my lodging.

Rod. I'll be with thee betimes.

Iago. Go to; farewell. Do you hear, Roderigo?

Rod. What say you?

Iago. No more of drowning, do you hear?

Rod. I am changed: I'll go sell all my land. [*Exit.*

Iago. Thus do I ever make my fool my purse;
For I mine own gain'd knowledge should profane, 390
If I would time expend with such a snipe,
But for my sport and profit. I hate the Moor;

And it is thought abroad, that 'twixt my sheets
He has done my office: I know not if't be true;
But I, for mere suspicion in that kind,
Will do as if for surety. He holds me well;
The better shall my purpose work on him.
Cassio's a proper man: let me see now:
To get his place and to plume up my will
In double knavery—How, how?—Let's see:—
After some time, to abuse Othello's ear 401
That he is too familiar with his wife.
He hath a person and a smooth dispose
To be suspected, framed to make women false.
The Moor is of a free and open nature,
That thinks men honest that but seem to be so,
And will as tenderly be led by the nose
As asses are.
I have 't. It is engender'd. Hell and night
Must bring this monstrous birth to the world's light. [*Exit.*

ACT II.

Scene I. *A Sea-port in Cyprus. An open place near the quay.*

Enter Montano *and two* Gentlemen.

Mon. What from the cape can you discern at sea?

First Gent. Nothing at all: it is a high-wrought flood;
I cannot, 'twixt the heaven and the main,
Descry a sail.

Mon. Methinks the wind hath spoke aloud at land;
A fuller blast ne'er shook our battlements:
If it hath ruffian'd so upon the sea,
What ribs of oak, when mountains melt on them,
Can hold the mortise? What shall we hear of this?

Sec. Gent. A segregation of the Turkish fleet: 10

---

354. **locusts**, of doubtful meaning; defined as fruit of the carob tree (*Matthew*, iii, 4), as honeysuckle, and as lollipops or sugar-sticks. 355. **coloquintida**, colocynth or bitter apple. 362. **erring**, wandering, vagabond. 374. **hearted**, fixed in the heart. 375. **conjunctive**, united. 379. **Traverse!** go (military term). 391. **snipe**, gull, fool. 392–410. **I hate . . . light.** This is the passage about which Coleridge used his famous phrase, "the motive-hunting of a motiveless malignity." It is to be doubted, however, if Shakespeare thought of Iago's villainy as completely gratuitous. He here recites two motives of supreme potency with Iago: his professional displacement, and the fact that he has been made the subject of scandal because of Othello; reputation was to him of supreme importance.

398. **proper**, handsome. 399. **plume up**, glorify. 402. **he**, i.e., Cassio. 403. **dispose**, external manner. 405–408. **The Moor . . . are.** This tribute to Othello, and other such speeches, must be regarded as a dramatic convention intended to give information to the audience. No villain would talk so in real life. 409. **Hell and night**. Note Iago's allegiance to the devil.

Act II. Scene i. 7. **ruffian'd**, raged. 9. **mortise**, the socket hollowed out in fitting timbers. 10. **segregation**, dispersion.

For do but stand upon the foaming shore,
The chidden billow seems to pelt the
  clouds;
The wind-shaked surge, with high and mon-
  strous mane,
Seems to cast water on the burning bear,
And quench the guards of the ever-fixed
  pole:
I never did like molestation view
On the enchafed flood.
    Mon.   If that the Turkish fleet
Be not enshelter'd and embay'd, they are
  drown'd;
It is impossible they bear it out.   19

        Enter a third Gentleman.

    Third Gent. News, lads! our wars are
  done.
The desperate tempest hath so bang'd the
  Turks,
That their designment halts: a noble ship of
  Venice
Hath seen a grievous wreck and sufferance
On most part of their fleet.
    Mon. How! is this true?
    Third Gent.   The ship is here put in,
A Veronesa; Michael Cassio,
Lieutenant to the warlike Moor Othello,
Is come on shore: the Moor himself at sea,
And is in full commission here for Cyprus.
    Mon. I am glad on 't; 'tis a worthy gov-
  ernor.
    Third Gent. But this same Cassio, though
  he speak of comfort   31
Touching the Turkish loss, yet he looks
  sadly,
And prays the Moor be safe; for they were
  parted
With foul and violent tempest.
    Mon.   Pray heavens he be;
For I have served him, and the man com-
  mands
Like a full soldier. Let's to the seaside, ho!
As well to see the vessel that's come in
As to throw out our eyes for brave Othello,
Even till we make the main and the aerial
  blue
An indistinct regard.
    Third Gent.   Come, let's do so;   40

For every minute is expectancy
Of more arrivance.

        Enter Cassio.

    Cas. Thanks, you the valiant of this
  warlike isle,
That so approve the Moor! O, let the
  heavens
Give him defence against the elements,
For I have lost him on a dangerous sea.
    Mon. Is he well shipp'd?
    Cas. His bark is stoutly timber'd, and his
  pilot
Of very expert and approved allowance;
Therefore my hopes, not surfeited to death, 50
Stand in bold cure.
        [*A cry within* 'A sail, a sail, a sail!'

        Enter a fourth Gentleman.

    Cas. What noise?
    Fourth Gent. The town is empty; on the
  brow o' the sea
Stand ranks of people, and they cry 'A sail!'
    Cas. My hopes do shape him for the gov-
  ernor.   [*Guns heard.*
    Sec. Gent. They do discharge their shot
  of courtesy:
Our friends at least.
    Cas.   I pray you, sir, go forth,
And give us truth who 'tis that is arrived.
    Sec. Gent. I shall.   [*Exit.*
    Mon. But, good lieutenant, is your gen-
  eral wived?   60
    Cas. Most fortunately: he hath achieved
  a maid
That paragons description and wild fame;
One that excels the quirks of blazoning pens,
And in the essential vesture of creation
Does tire the ingener.

       Re-enter second Gentleman.

            How now! who has put in?
    Sec. Gent. 'Tis one Iago, ancient to the
  general.
    Cas. Has had most favourable and happy
  speed:
Tempests themselves, high seas and howling
  winds,

---

14. **bear**, a constellation. 15. **quench the guards**,
overwhelm the guards of the pole, i.e., the constellation
of Boötes. 17. **enchafed**, angry. 22. **designment**,
enterprise. 23. **sufferance**, disaster. 36. **full**, perfect.
39-40. **make . . . regard**, cause the blue of the sea and
the air to grow indistinct in our view.

42. **arrivance**, arrival. 49. **allowance**, reputation.
62. **paragons**, surpasses. 63. **quirks**, witty conceits.
blazoning, setting forth honorably in words. 64. **vesture of creation**, "the real qualities with which creation
has invested her" (Johnson). 65. **ingener**, inventor.

The gutter'd rocks and congregated sands,—
Traitors ensteep'd to clog the guiltless
    keel,—
As having sense of beauty, do omit   71
Their mortal natures, letting go safely by
The divine Desdemona.
  Mon.   What is she?
  Cas. She that I spake of, our great cap-
    tain's captain,
Left in the conduct of the bold Iago,
Whose footing here anticipates our thoughts
A se'nnight's speed. Great Jove, Othello
    guard,
And swell his sail with thine own powerful
    breath,
That he may bless this bay with his tall
    ship,
Make love's quick pants in Desdemona's
    arms,
Give renew'd fire to our extinced spirits, 81
And bring all Cyprus comfort!

Enter DESDEMONA, EMILIA, IAGO,
    RODERIGO, *and* Attendants.

                            O, behold,
The riches of the ship is come on shore!
Ye men of Cyprus, let her have your knees.
Hail to thee, lady! and the grace of heaven,
Before, behind thee and on every hand,
Enwheel thee round!
  Des.   I thank you, valiant Cassio.
What tidings can you tell me of my lord?
  Cas. He is not yet arrived: nor know I
    aught
But that he's well and will be shortly here.
  Des. O, but I fear—How lost you com-
    pany?   91
  Cas. The great contention of the sea and
    skies
Parted our fellowship—But, hark! a sail.
        [*Within* 'A sail, a sail!' *Guns heard.*
  Sec. Gent. They give their greeting to the
    citadel:
This likewise is a friend.
  Cas.   See for the news.
                            [*Exit Gentleman.*
Good ancient, you are welcome. [*To Emilia*]
    Welcome, mistress:
Let it not gall your patience, good Iago,
That I extend my manners; 'tis my breeding
That gives me this bold show of courtesy. 100
                            [*Kissing her.*

  Iago. Sir, would she give you so much of
    her lips
As of her tongue she oft bestows on me,
You'ld have enough.
  Des.   Alas, she has no speech.
  Iago. In faith, too much;
I find it still, when I have list to sleep:
Marry, before your ladyship, I grant,
She puts her tongue a little in her heart,
And chides with thinking.
  Emil. You have little cause to say so.
  Iago. Come on, come on; you are pictures
    out of doors,   110
Bells in your parlours, wild-cats in your
    kitchens,
Saints in your injuries, devils being offended,
Players in your housewifery, and housewives
    in your beds.
  Des. O, fie upon thee, slanderer!
  Iago. Nay, it is true, or else I am a Turk:
You rise to play and go to bed to work.
  Emil. You shall not write my praise.
  Iago.   No, let me not.
  Des. What wouldst thou write of me, if
    thou shouldst praise me?
  Iago. O gentle lady, do not put me to 't;
For I am nothing, if not critical.   120
  Des. Come on, assay. There's one gone
    to the harbour?
  Iago. Ay, madam.
  Des. I am not merry; but I do beguile
The thing I am, by seeming otherwise.
Come, how wouldst thou praise me?
  Iago. I am about it; but indeed my in-
    vention
Comes from my pate as birdlime does from
    frize;
It plucks out brains and all: but my Muse
    labours,
And thus she is deliver'd.
If she be fair and wise, fairness and wit, 130
The one's for use, the other useth it.
  Des. Well praised! How if she be black
    and witty?
  Iago. If she be black, and thereto have a
    wit,
She'll find a white that shall her blackness
    fit.
  Des. Worse and worse.

---

69. **gutter'd**, jagged, trenched. 70. **ensteep'd**,
lying under water. 77. **se'nnight's**, week's.

105. **list**, desire, inclination. 113. **housewives**,
huzzies. 120. **critical**, censorious. 127. **birdlime**,
sticky substance smeared on twigs to catch small birds.
frize, coarse woolen cloth. 130-161. **If she . . . beer.**
This is an illustration of the familiar game of wit-combat
as practiced in Shakespeare's time. 134. **white**, a fair
person, with word-play on *wight*.

Emil. How if fair and foolish?

Iago. She never yet was foolish that was fair;

For even her folly help'd her to an heir.

Des. These are old fond paradoxes to make fools laugh i' the alehouse. What miserable praise hast thou for her that's foul and foolish?

Iago. There's none so foul and foolish thereunto,

But does foul pranks which fair and wise ones do. 143

Des. O heavy ignorance! thou praisest the worst best. But what praise couldst thou bestow on a deserving woman indeed, one that, in the authority of her merit, did justly put on the vouch of very malice itself?

Iago. She that was ever fair and never proud,

Had tongue at will and yet was never loud,

Never lack'd gold and yet went never gay, 151

Fled from her wish and yet said 'Now I may,'

She that being anger'd, her revenge being nigh,

Bade her wrong stay and her displeasure fly,

She that in wisdom never was so frail

To change the cod's head for the salmon's tail,

She that could think and ne'er disclose her mind,

See suitors following and not look behind,

She was a wight, if ever such wight were,—

Des. To do what? 160

Iago. To suckle fools and chronicle small beer.

Des. O most lame and impotent conclusion! Do not learn of him, Emilia, though he be thy husband. How say you, Cassio? is he not a most profane and liberal counsellor?

Cas. He speaks home, madam: you may relish him more in the soldier than in the scholar.

Iago. [*Aside*] He takes her by the palm: ay, well said, whisper: with as little a web as this will I ensnare as great a fly as Cassio. Ay, smile upon her, do; I will gyve thee in thine own courtship. You say true; 'tis so, indeed: if such tricks as these strip you out

of your lieutenantry, it had been better you had not kissed your three fingers so oft, which now again you are most apt to play the sir in. Very good; well kissed! an excellent courtesy! 'tis so, indeed. Yet again your fingers to your lips? would they were clyster-pipes for your sake! [*Trumpet within.*] The Moor! I know his trumpet. 180

Cas. 'Tis truly so.

Des. Let's meet him and receive him.

Cas. Lo, where he comes!

Enter OTHELLO *and* Attendants.

Oth. O my fair warrior!

Des.　　　　　　　　My dear Othello!

Oth. It gives me wonder great as my content

To see you here before me. O my soul's joy!

If after every tempest come such calms,

May the winds blow till they have waken'd death!

And let the labouring bark climb hills of seas

Olympus-high and duck again as low 190

As hell's from heaven! If it were now to die,

'Twere now to be most happy; for, I fear,

My soul hath her content so absolute

That not another comfort like to this

Succeeds in unknown fate.

Des.　　　　　　　The heavens forbid

But that our loves and comforts should increase,

Even as our days do grow!

Oth.　　　　　　Amen to that, sweet powers!

I cannot speak enough of this content;

It stops me here; it is too much of joy: 199

And this, and this, the greatest discords be

　　　　　　　　　　　　[*Kissing her.*

That e'er our hearts shall make!

Iago. [*Aside*] O, you are well tuned now!

But I'll set down the pegs that make this music,

As honest as I am.

Oth.　　　　　Come, let us to the castle.

News, friends; our wars are done, the Turks are drown'd.

How does my old acquaintance of this isle?

Honey, you shall be well desired in Cyprus;

I have found great love amongst them. O my sweet,

---

148. **put on the vouch**, challenge the testimony. 156. **To change . . . tail**, to exchange a delicacy for mere refuse. 161. **chronicle small beer**, keep petty household accounts. 165. **liberal**, free, wanton. 166. **speaks home**, i.e., without reserve. 171. **gyve**, fetter, shackle. 172. **courtship**, courtesy.

175. **kissed your three fingers.** He kisses his own hand as a token of reverence. 176. **the sir**, i.e., the fine gentleman. 179. **clyster-pipes**, tubes used for injections. 203. **set down the pegs**, lower the pitch of the strings (of a musical instrument).

I prattle out of fashion, and I dote
In mine own comforts. I prithee, good
    Iago,
Go to the bay and disembark my coffers:
Bring thou the master to the citadel; · 211
He is a good one, and his worthiness
Does challenge much respect. Come, Desde-
    mona,
Once more, well met at Cyprus.

[*Exeunt Othello, Desdemona, and Attendants.*

Iago. Do thou meet me presently at the
harbour. Come hither. If thou be'st valiant,—as, they say, base men being in love
have then a nobility in their natures more
than is native to them,—list me. The lieutenant tonight watches on the court of
guard:—first, I must tell thee this—Desdemona is directly in love with him.   221

Rod. With him! why, 'tis not possible.

Iago. Lay thy finger thus, and let thy soul
be instructed. Mark me with what violence
she first loved the Moor, but for bragging and
telling her fantastical lies: and will she love
him still for prating? let not thy discreet
heart think it. Her eye must be fed; and
what delight shall she have to look on the
devil? When the blood is made dull with the
act of sport, there should be, again to inflame
it and to give satiety a fresh appetite, loveli-
ness in favour, sympathy in years, manners
and beauties; all which the Moor is defective
in: now, for want of these required conven-
iences, her delicate tenderness will find itself
abused, begin to heave the gorge, disrelish
and abhor the Moor; very nature will 236
instruct her in it and compel her to some
second choice. Now, sir, this granted,—as it
is a most pregnant and unforced position—
who stands so eminent in the degree of this
fortune as Cassio does? a knave very voluble;
no further conscionable than in putting on
the mere form of civil and humane seeming,
for the better compassing of his salt and most
hidden loose affection? why, none; why,
none: a slipper and subtle knave, a finder of
occasions, that has an eye can stamp and
counterfeit advantages, though true advantage never present itself; a devilish knave.
Besides, the knave is handsome, young, and
hath all those requisites in him that folly and

green minds look after: a pestilent complete
knave; and the woman hath found him already.   253

Rod. I cannot believe that in her; she's
full of most blessed condition.

Iago. Blessed fig's-end! the wine she
drinks is made of grapes: if she had been
blessed, she would never have loved the
Moor. Blessed pudding! Didst thou not see
her paddle with the palm of his hand? didst
not mark that?

Rod. Yes, that I did; but that was but
courtesy.   262

Iago. Lechery, by this hand; an index and
obscure prologue to the history of lust and
foul thoughts. They met so near with their
lips that their breaths embraced together.
Villanous thoughts, Roderigo! when these
mutualities so marshal the way, hard at hand
comes the master and main exercise, the incorporate conclusion, Pish! But, sir, be you
ruled by me: I have brought you from Venice. Watch you to-night; for the command,
I'll lay 't upon you. Cassio knows you not.
I'll not be far from you: do you find some
occasion to anger Cassio, either by speaking
too loud, or tainting his discipline; or from
what other course you please, which the time
shall more favourably minister.   277

Rod. Well.

Iago. Sir, he is rash and very sudden in
choler, and haply may strike at you: provoke
him, that he may; for even out of that will I
cause these of Cyprus to mutiny; whose
qualification shall come into no true taste
again but by the displanting of Cassio. So
shall you have a shorter journey to your desires by the means I shall then have to prefer
them; and the impediment most profitably
removed, without the which there were no
expectation of our prosperity.

Rod. I will do this, if I can bring it to any
opportunity.   290

Iago. I warrant thee. Meet me by and by
at the citadel: I must fetch his necessaries
ashore. Farewell.

Rod. Adieu.   [*Exit.*

Iago. That Cassio loves her, I do well be-
    lieve it;
That she loves him, 'tis apt and of great
    credit:

---

219. **court of guard**, guard house. 231. **favour**, personal appearance. 239. **pregnant**, obvious. 242. **conscionable**, conscientious. 244. **salt**, licentious. 246. **slipper**, slippery. 248. **advantages**, opportunities, produced like coins in minting.

255. **condition**, mental disposition, character. 275. **tainting**, disparaging. 283. **qualification**, condition. 291. **by and by**, immediately. 296. **apt**, natural. **credit**, credibility.

The Moor, howbeit that I endure him not,
Is of a constant, loving, noble nature,
And I dare think he'll prove to Desdemona
A most dear husband. Now, I do love her
    too;   300
Not out of absolute lust, though peradventure
I stand accountant for as great a sin,
But partly led to diet my revenge,
For that I do suspect the lusty Moor
Hath leap'd into my seat; the thought whereof
Doth, like a poisonous mineral, gnaw my inwards;
And nothing can or shall content my soul
Till I am even'd with him, wife for wife,
Or failing so, yet that I put the Moor
At least into a jealousy so strong   310
That judgement cannot cure. Which thing
    to do,
If this poor trash of Venice, whom I trash
For his quick hunting, stand the putting on,
I'll have our Michael Cassio on the hip,
Abuse him to the Moor in the rank garb—
For I fear Cassio with my night-cap too—
Make the Moor thank me, love me and
    reward me,
For making him egregiously an ass
And practising upon his peace and quiet 319
Even to madness. 'Tis here, but yet confused:
Knavery's plain face is never seen till used.
                                          [*Exit.*

SCENE II. *A street.*

Enter a Herald *with a proclamation;* People
                following.

Her. It is Othello's pleasure, our noble
and valiant general, that, upon certain tidings now arrived, importing the mere perdition of the Turkish fleet, every man put himself into triumph; some to dance, some to
make bonfires, each man to what sport and
revels his addiction leads him: for, besides
these beneficial news, it is the celebration of
his nuptial. So much was his pleasure should
be proclaimed. All offices are open, and
there is full liberty of feasting from this

present hour of five till the bell have told
eleven. Heaven bless the isle of Cyprus and
our noble general Othello!   [*Exeunt.*

SCENE III. *A hall in the castle.*

Enter OTHELLO, DESDEMONA, CASSIO, *and*
                Attendants.

Oth. Good Michael, look you to the guard
    to-night:
Let's teach ourselves that honourable stop,
Not to outsport discretion.
    Cas. Iago hath direction what to do;
But, notwithstanding, with my personal eye
Will I look to 't.
    Oth.   Iago is most honest.
Michael, good night: to-morrow with your
    earliest
Let me have speech with you. [*To Desdemona*] Come, my dear love,
The purchase made, the fruits are to ensue;
That profit's yet to come 'tween me and
    you.   10
Good night.
        [*Exeunt Othello, Desdemona, and
                        Attendants.*

Enter IAGO.

    Cas. Welcome, Iago; we must to the
watch.
    Iago. Not this hour, lieutenant; 'tis not
yet ten o' the clock. Our general cast us thus
early for the love of his Desdemona; who let
us not therefore blame: he hath not yet made
wanton the night with her; and she is sport
for Jove.
    Cas. She's a most exquisite lady.
    Iago. And, I'll warrant her, full of game.
    Cas. Indeed, she's a most fresh and delicate creature.   21
    Iago. What an eye she has! methinks it
sounds a parley of provocation.
    Cas. An inviting eye; and yet methinks
right modest.
    Iago. And when she speaks, is it not an
alarum to love?
    Cas. She is indeed perfection.
    Iago. Well, happiness to their sheets!
Come, lieutenant, I have a stoup of wine;

---

312. **trash . . . trash,** worthless thing . . . hold in
check. The second use of the word is as a hunting term.
313. **putting on,** incitement to quarrel. 314. **on the
hip,** at an advantage (wrestling term).
Scene ii. 3. **mere,** utter, absolute. 10. **offices,**
rooms where food and drink were kept.

Scene iii. 2. **stop,** restraint. 14. **cast,** dismissed.
30. **stoup,** measure of liquor, two quarts.

and here without are a brace of Cyprus gallants that would fain have a measure to the health of black Othello.

Cas. Not to-night, good Iago: I have very poor and unhappy brains for drinking: I could well wish courtesy would invent some other custom of entertainment.

Iago. O, they are our friends; but one cup: I'll drink for you.   39

Cas. I have drunk but one cup to-night, and that was craftily qualified too, and, behold, what innovation it makes here: I am unfortunate in the infirmity, and dare not task my weakness with any more.

Iago. What, man! 'tis a night of revels: the gallants desire it.

Cas. Where are they?

Iago. Here at the door; I pray you, call them in.

Cas. I'll do 't; but it dislikes me. [*Exit.*

Iago. If I can fasten but one cup upon him,
With that which he hath drunk to-night already,   51
He'll be as full of quarrel and offence
As my young mistress' dog. Now, my sick fool Roderigo,
Whom love hath turn'd almost the wrong side out,
To Desdemona hath to-night caroused
Potations pottle-deep; and he's to watch:
Three lads of Cyprus, noble swelling spirits,
That hold their honours in a wary distance,
The very elements of this warlike isle,
Have I to-night fluster'd with flowing cups,60
And they watch too. Now, 'mongst this flock of drunkards,
Am I to put our Cassio in some action
That may offend the isle.—But here they come:
If consequence do but approve my dream,
My boat sails freely, both with wind and stream.

Re-enter CASSIO; *with him* MONTANO *and* Gentlemen; *Servants following with wine.*

Cas. 'Fore God, they have given me a rouse already.

Mon. Good faith, a little one; not past a pint, as I am a soldier.

Iago. Some wine, ho!   70
[*Sings*] And let me the canakin clink, clink;
And let me the canakin clink:
A soldier's a man;
A life's but a span;
Why, then, let a soldier drink.
Some wine, boys!

Cas. 'Fore God, an excellent song.

Iago. I learned it in England, where, indeed, they are most potent in potting: your Dane, your German, and your swag-bellied Hollander—Drink, ho!—are nothing to your English.   81

Cas. Is your Englishman so expert in his drinking?

Iago. Why, he drinks you, with facility, your Dane dead drunk; he sweats not to overthrow your Almain; he gives your Hollander a vomit, ere the next pottle can be filled.

Cas. To the health of our general!

Mon. I am for it, lieutenant; and I'll do you justice.   90

Iago. O sweet England!
King Stephen was a worthy peer,
His breeches cost him but a crown;
He held them sixpence all too dear,
With that he call'd the tailor lown.
He was a wight of high renown,
And thou art but of low degree:
'Tis pride that pulls the country down;
Then take thine auld cloak about thee.
Some wine, ho!   100

Cas. Why, this is a more exquisite song than the other.

Iago. Will you hear 't again?

Cas. No; for I hold him to be unworthy of his place that does those things. Well, God's above all; and there be souls must be saved, and there be souls must not be saved.

Iago. It's true, good lieutenant.

Cas. For mine own part,—no offence to the general, nor any man of quality,—I hope to be saved.   111

Iago. And so do I too, lieutenant.

Cas. Ay, but, by your leave, not before me; the lieutenant is to be saved before the

35-37. **I could . . . entertainment.** This sentence expresses the current opinion that it was polite and proper to drink socially. 41. **craftily qualified,** slyly diluted, i.e., by Cassio himself. 42. **innovation,** disturbance. 56. **pottle-deep,** to the bottom of the tankard. 58. **hold . . . distance,** i.e., are extremely sensitive of their honor. 61. **watch,** are members of the guard. 64. **approve,** confirm. 67. **rouse,** full draft of liquor.

71. **canakin,** small drinking vessel. 86. **Almain,** German. 89. **I'll . . . justice,** i.e., drink as much as you. 92-99. **King . . . thee,** a version of a popular ballad, found also in the *Percy Folio.* 95. **lown,** lout, loon. 110. **quality,** rank, position.

ancient. Let's have no more of this; let's to
our affairs.— Forgive us our sins!—Gentlemen, let's look to our business. Do not
think, gentlemen, I am drunk: this is my
ancient; this is my right hand, and this is my
left: I am not drunk now; I can stand well
enough, and speak well enough.   120
All. Excellent well.
Cas. Why, very well then; you must not
think then that I am drunk.   [*Exit.*
Mon. To the platform, masters; come,
let's set the watch.
Iago. You see this fellow that is gone
before;
He is a soldier fit to stand by Cæsar
And give direction: and do but see his vice;
'Tis to his virtue a just equinox,
The one as long as the other: 'tis pity of him.
I fear the trust Othello puts him in,   131
On some odd time of his infirmity,
Will shake this island.
Mon.   But is he often thus?
Iago. 'Tis evermore the prologue to his
sleep:
He'll watch the horologe a double set,
If drink rock not his cradle.
Mon.   It were well
The general were put in mind of it.
Perhaps he sees it not; or his good nature
Prizes the virtue that appears in Cassio, 139
And looks not on his evils: is not this true?

Enter Roderigo.

Iago. [*Aside to him*] How now, Roderigo!
I pray you, after the lieutenant; go.
                              [*Exit Roderigo.*
Mon. And 'tis great pity that the noble
Moor
Should hazard such a place as his own
second
With one of an ingraft infirmity:
It were an honest action to say
So to the Moor.
Iago.   Not I, for this fair island:
I do love Cassio well; and would do much
To cure him of this evil—But, hark! what
noise?   [*Cry within:* 'Help! help!']

Re-enter Cassio, *driving in* Roderigo.

Cas. You rogue! you rascal!

Mon.   What's the matter, lieutenant?
Cas. A knave teach me my duty!   151
I'll beat the knave into a twiggen bottle.
Rod. Beat me!
Cas.   Dost thou prate, rogue?
                              [*Striking Roderigo.*
Mon.   Nay, good lieutenant;
                              [*Staying him.*
I pray you, sir, hold your hand.
Cas.   Let me go, sir,
Or I'll knock you o'er the mazzard.
Mon.   Come, come, you're drunk.
Cas. Drunk!   [*They fight.*
Iago. [*Aside to Roderigo*] Away, I say; go
out, and cry a mutiny. [*Exit Roderigo.*
Nay, good lieutenant,—alas, gentlemen;—
Help, ho!—Lieutenant,—sir,—Montano,—
sir;—   159
Help, masters!—Here's a goodly watch in-
deed!   [*Bell rings.*
Who's that which rings the bell?—Diablo,
ho!
The town will rise: God's will, lieutenant,
hold!
You will be shamed for ever.

Re-enter Othello *and* Attendants.

Oth.   What is the matter here?
Mon. 'Zounds, I bleed still; I am hurt to
the death.   [*Faints.*
Oth. Hold, for your lives!
Iago. Hold, ho! Lieutenant,—sir,—Mon-
tano,—gentlemen,—
Have you forgot all sense of place and
duty?
Hold! the general speaks to you; hold, hold,
for shame!
Oth. Why, how now, ho! from whence
ariseth this?
Are we turn'd Turks, and to ourselves do
that
Which heaven hath forbid the Ottomites?171
For Christian shame, put by this barbarous
brawl:
He that stirs next to carve for his own rage
Holds his soul light; he dies upon his motion.
Silence that dreadful bell: it frights the isle
From her propriety. What is the matter,
masters?
Honest Iago, that look'st dead with grieving,

---

129. **equinox**, equal length of days and nights; used
figuratively to mean "counterpart." 135. **horologe**,
clock. **double set**, twice around. 145. **ingraft**,
ingrafted, inveterate.

152. **twiggen**, covered with woven twigs. 155.
mazzard, head. 161. **Diablo**, the Devil; a scrap of
Spanish. 170. **turn'd Turks**, changed completely for
the worse; proverbial. 173. **carve for**, indulge. 176.
propriety, proper state or condition.

Speak, who began this? on thy love, I charge
　　thee.

Iago. I do not know: friends all but now,
　　even now, 　　　　　　　　　　179
In quarter, and in terms like bride and
　　groom
Devesting them for bed; and then, but
　　now—
As if some planet had unwitted men—
Swords out, and tilting one at other's breast,
In opposition bloody. I cannot speak
Any beginning to this peevish odds;
And would in action glorious I had lost
Those legs that brought me to a part of it!

Oth. How comes it, Michael, you are thus
　　forgot?

Cas. I pray you, pardon me; I cannot
　　speak.

Oth. Worthy Montano, you were wont be
　　civil; 　　　　　　　　　　　190
The gravity and stillness of your youth
The world hath noted, and your name is
　　great
In mouths of wisest censure: what's the
　　matter,
That you unlace your reputation thus
And spend your rich opinion for the name
Of a night-brawler? give me answer to it.

Mon. Worthy Othello, I am hurt to dan-
　　ger:
Your officer, Iago, can inform you,—
While I spare speech, which something now
　　offends me,—
Of all that I do know: nor know I aught 200
By me that's said or done amiss this night;
Unless self-charity be sometimes a vice,
And to defend ourselves it be a sin
When violence assails us.

Oth. 　　　　　　　Now, by heaven,
My blood begins my safer guides to rule;
And passion, having my best judgement
　　collied,
Assays to lead the way: if I once stir,
Or do but lift this arm, the best of you
Shall sink in my rebuke. Give me to know
How this foul rout began, who set it on; 210
And he that is approved in this offence,
Though he had twinn'd with me, both at a
　　birth,

Shall lose me. What! in a town of war,
Yet wild, the people's hearts brimful of fear,
To manage private and domestic quarrel,
In night, and on the court and guard of
　　safety!
'Tis monstrous. Iago, who began 't?

Mon. If partially affined, or leagued in
　　office,
Thou dost deliver more or less than truth,
Thou art no soldier.

Iago. 　　　　Touch me not so near: 220
I had rather have this tongue cut from my
　　mouth
Than it should do offence to Michael Cassio;
Yet, I persuade myself, to speak the truth
Shall nothing wrong him. Thus it is, gen-
　　eral.
Montano and myself being in speech,
There comes a fellow crying out for help;
And Cassio following him with determined
　　sword,
To execute upon him. Sir, this gentleman
Steps in to Cassio, and entreats his pause:
Myself the crying fellow did pursue, 　230
Lest by his clamour—as it so fell out—
The town might fall in fright: he, swift of
　　foot,
Outran my purpose; and I return'd the
　　rather
For that I heard the clink and fall of swords,
And Cassio high in oath; which till to-night
I ne'er might say before. When I came
　　back—
For this was brief—I found them close to-
　　gether,
At blow and thrust; even as again they were
When you yourself did part them.
More of this matter cannot I report: 　240
But men are men; the best sometimes forget:
Though Cassio did some little wrong to him,
As men in rage strike those that wish them
　　best,
Yet surely Cassio, I believe, received
From him that fled some strange indignity,
Which patience could not pass.

Oth. 　　　　　　I know, Iago,
Thy honesty and love doth mince this mat-
　　ter,
Making it light to Cassio. Cassio, I love
　　thee;
But never more be officer of mine.

---

180. **In quarter,** on terms. 185. **peevish odds,**
childish quarrel. 193. **censure,** judgment. 194.
unlace, degrade. 205-207. **My blood . . . way.** This
is the first indication of Othello's psychology; he is a
man whose judgment may be overthrown by his passion.
206. **collied,** darkened. 207. **Assays,** attempts. 211.
approved in, found guilty of.

216. **court and guard,** spot and guarding place i.e.,
the main guardhouse. 218. **affined,** bound by a tie.
228. **execute,** give effect to (his anger).

Re-enter DESDEMONA, *attended.*

Look, if my gentle love be not raised up! 250
I'll make thee an example.

Des.   What's the matter?

Oth. All's well now, sweeting; come away
to bed.

Sir, for your hurts, myself will be your surgeon:

Lead him off. [*To Montano, who is led off.*
Iago, look with care about the town,
And silence those whom this vile brawl dis-
tracted.
Come, Desdemona: 'tis the soldiers' life
To have their balmy slumbers waked with
strife. [*Exeunt all but Iago and Cassio.*

Iago. What, are you hurt, lieutenant?

Cas. Ay, past all surgery.   260

Iago. Marry, heaven forbid!

Cas. Reputation, reputation, reputation!
O, I have lost my reputation! I have lost the
immortal part of myself, and what remains is
bestial. My reputation, Iago, my rep-   265
utation!

Iago. As I am an honest man, I thought
you had received some bodily wound; there
is more sense in that than in reputation.
Reputation is an idle and most false imposition; oft got without merit, and lost without
deserving: you have lost no reputation at all,
unless you repute yourself such a loser.
What, man! there are ways to recover the
general again: you are but now cast in his
mood, a punishment more in policy than in
malice; even so as one would beat his offence-
less dog to affright an imperious lion: sue to
him again, and he's yours.   277

Cas. I will rather sue to be despised than
to deceive so good a commander with so
slight, so drunken, and so indiscreet an officer.
Drunk? and speak parrot? and squabble?
swagger? swear? and discourse fustian with
one's own shadow? O thou invisible spirit
of wine, if thou hast no name to be known
by, let us call thee devil!

Iago. What was he that you followed with
your sword? What had he done to you?

Cass. I know not.

Iago. Is't possible?   288

Cas. I remember a mass of things, but
nothing distinctly; a quarrel, but nothing
wherefore. O God, that men should put an

enemy in their mouths to steal away their
brains! that we should, with joy, pleasance,
revel and applause, transform ourselves into
beasts!

Iago. Why, but you are now well enough:
how came you thus recovered?

Cas. It hath pleased the devil drunkenness to give place to the devil wrath: one
unperfectness shows me another, to make
me frankly despise myself.   300

Iago. Come, you are too severe a moraler:
as the time, the place, and the condition of
this country stands, I could heartily wish
this had not befallen; but, since it is as it is,
mend it for your own good.

Cas. I will ask him for my place again; he
shall tell me I am a drunkard! Had I as
many mouths as Hydra, such an answer
would stop them all. To be now a sensible
man, by and by a fool, and presently a beast!
O strange! Every inordinate cup is unblessed
and the ingredient is a devil.   312

Iago. Come, come, good wine is a good
familiar creature, if it be well used: exclaim
no more against it. And, good lieutenant, I
think you think I love you.

Cas. I have well approved it, sir. I
drunk!   317

Iago. You or any man living may be
drunk at a time, man. I'll tell you what you
shall do. Our general's wife is now the general: I may say so in this respect, for that he
hath devoted and given up himself to the
contemplation, mark, and denotement of
her parts and graces: confess yourself freely
to her; importune her help to put you in your
place again: she is of so free, so kind, so apt,
so blessed a disposition, she holds it a vice in
her goodness not to do more than she is re-
quested: this broken joint between you and
her husband entreat her to splinter; and, my
fortunes against any lay worth naming, this
crack of your love shall grow stronger   331
than it was before.

Cas. You advise me well.

Iago. I protest, in the sincerity of love
and honest kindness.

Cas. I think it freely; and betimes in the
morning I will beseech the virtuous Desde-

---

268. **sense**, sensibility. 281. **speak parrot**, talk
nonsense; *discourse fustian*, below, has the same meaning.

299. **unperfectness**, imperfection. 308. **Hydra**, the
Lernæan Hydra, a monster with many heads, slain by
Hercules as the second of his twelve labors. 311. **unblessed**, accursed. 317. **approved**, proved. 323.
denotement, observation. 329. **splinter**, bind with
splints. 330. **lay**, stake, wager.

mona to undertake for me: I am desperate
of my fortunes if they check me here.

Iago. You are in the right. Good night,
lieutenant; I must to the watch.   340

Cas. Good night, honest Iago.   [*Exit.*

Iago. And what's he then that says I play
the villain?
When this advice is free I give and honest,
Probal to thinking and indeed the course
To win the Moor again? For 'tis most easy
The inclining Desdemona to subdue
In any honest suit: she's framed as fruitful
As the free elements. And then for her
To win the Moor—were 't to renounce his
baptism,
All seals and symbols of redeemed sin,   350
His soul is so enfetter'd to her love,
That she may make, unmake, do what she
list,
Even as her appetite shall play the god
With his weak function. How am I then a
villain
To counsel Cassio to this parallel course,
Directly to his good? Divinity of hell!
When devils will the blackest sins put on,
They do suggest at first with heavenly
shows,
As I do now: for whiles this honest fool
Plies Desdemona to repair his fortunes   360
And she for him pleads strongly to the Moor,
I'll pour this pestilence into his ear,
That she repeals him for her body's lust;
And by how much she strives to do him
good,
She shall undo her credit with the Moor.
So will I turn her virtue into pitch,
And out of her own goodness make the net
That shall enmesh them all.

Re-enter Roderigo.

              How now, Roderigo!   368

Rod. I do follow here in the chase, not like
a hound that hunts, but one that fills up the
cry. My money is almost spent; I have been
to-night exceedingly well cudgelled; and I
think the issue will be, I shall have so much
experience for my pains, and so, with no
money at all and a little more wit, return
again to Venice.

---

344. **Probal**, probable.   346. **inclining**, favorably
disposed.   355. **parallel**, probably, corresponding to his
best interest.   356. **Divinity of hell!** This is another
significant alignment of Iago with the powers of evil.
358. **suggest**, tempt.   363. **repeals him**, i.e., attempts
to get him restored.   371. **cry**, pack.

Iago. How poor are they that have not
patience!
What wound did ever heal but by degrees?
Thou know'st we work by wit, and not by
witchcraft;
And wit depends on dilatory time.
Does't not go well? Cassio hath beaten thee,
And thou, by that small hurt, hast cashier'd
Cassio: 381
Though other things grow fair against the
sun,
Yet fruits that blossom first will first be ripe:
Content thyself awhile. By the mass, 'tis
morning;
Pleasure and action make the hours seem
short.
Retire thee; go where thou art billeted:
Away, I say; thou shalt know more hereafter:
Nay, get thee gone. [*Exit Roderigo.*] Two
things are to be done:
My wife must move for Cassio to her mis-
tress;
I'll set her on;   390
Myself the while to draw the Moor apart,
And bring him jump when he may Cassio
find
Soliciting his wife: ay, that's the way:
Dull not device by coldness and delay. [*Exit.*

ACT III

Scene I. *Before the castle.*

Enter Cassio *and some* Musicians.

Cas. Masters, play here; I will content
your pains;
Something that's brief; and bid 'Good morrow, general.'   [*Music.*

Enter Clown.

Clo. Why, masters, have your instruments
been in Naples, that they speak i' the nose
thus?

First Mus. How, sir, how!

Clo. Are these, I pray you, wind-instruments?

First Mus. Ay, marry, are they, sir.

Clo. O, thereby hangs a tail.

First Mus. Whereby hangs a tale, sir?   9

Clo. Marry, sir, by many a wind-instru-

---

392. **jump**, precisely.
Act III. Scene i. 1. **content**, reward.   4. **speak i'
the nose**, i.e., like Neapolitans, who spoke a nasal
dialect.

ment that I know. But, masters, here's
money for you: and the general so likes your
music, that he desires you, for love's sake, to
make no more noise with it.

First Mus. Well, sir, we will not.

Clo. If you have any music that may not
be heard, to 't again: but, as they say, to hear
music the general does not greatly care.

First Mus. We have none such, sir.

Clo. Then put up your pipes in your bag,
for I'll away: go; vanish into air; away!   21

                                    [*Exeunt Musicians.*

Cas. Dost thou hear, my honest friend?

Clo. No, I hear not your honest friend; I
hear you.

Cas. Prithee, keep up thy quillets. There's
a poor piece of gold for thee: if the gentlewoman that attends the general's wife be
stirring, tell her there's one Cassio entreats
her a little favour of speech: wilt thou do
this?

Clo. She is stirring, sir: if she will stir
hither, I shall seem to notify unto her.   31

Cas. Do, good my friend.   [*Exit Clown.*

Enter IAGO.

                              In happy time, Iago.

Iago. You have not been a-bed, then?

Cas. Why, no; the day had broke
Before we parted. I have made bold, Iago,
To send in to your wife: my suit to her
Is, that she will to virtuous Desdemona
Procure me some access.

Iago.   I'll send her to you presently;
And I'll devise a mean to draw the Moor
Out of the way, that your converse and busi-
ness
May be more free.   41

Cas. I humbly thank you for 't. [*Exit Iago.*
                    I never knew
A Florentine more kind and honest.

Enter EMILIA.

Emil. Good morrow, good lieutenant: I
am sorry
For your displeasure; but all will sure be well.
The general and his wife are talking of it;
And she speaks for you stoutly: the Moor
replies,
That he you hurt is of great fame in Cyprus

And great affinity and that in wholesome
wisdom
He might not but refuse you, but he protests
he loves you   50
And needs no other suitor but his likings
To take the safest occasion by the front
To bring you in again.

Cas.   Yet, I beseech you,
If you think fit, or that it may be done,
Give me advantage of some brief discourse
With Desdemona alone.

Emil.   Pray you, come in:
I will bestow you where you shall have time
To speak your bosom freely.

Cas. I am much bound to you. [*Exeunt.*

SCENE II. *A room in the castle.*

Enter OTHELLO, IAGO, *and* Gentlemen.

Oth. These letters give, Iago, to the pilot;
And by him do my duties to the senate:
That done, I will be walking on the works;
Repair there to me.

Iago.   Well, my good lord, I'll do 't.

Oth. This fortification, gentlemen, shall
we see 't?

Gent. We'll wait upon your lordship.

                                    [*Exeunt.*

SCENE III. *The garden of the castle.*

Enter DESDEMONA, CASSIO, *and* EMILIA.

Des. Be thou assured, good Cassio, I will
do
All my abilities in thy behalf.

Emil. Good madam, do: I warrant it
grieves my husband,
As if the case were his.

Des. O, that's an honest fellow. Do not
doubt, Cassio,
But I will have my lord and you again
As friendly as you were.

Cas.   Bounteous madam,
Whatever shall become of Michael Cassio,
He's never any thing but your true serv-
ant.

Des. I know 't; I thank you. You do love
my lord: 10
You have known him long; and be you well
assured
He shall in strangeness stand no further off

---

25. **quillets**, quibbles.   31. **seem to**, a current
colloquialism having no particular meaning. 43. **Florentine**, i.e., even a Florentine; Iago was a Venetian,
Cassio a Florentine.

49. **affinity**, kindred, family connection.   52. **by
the front**, i.e., by the forelock.
    Scene iii. 12. **strangeness**, distant behavior.

Than in a politic distance.

Cas.   Ay, but, lady,
That policy may either last so long,
Or feed upon such nice and waterish diet,
Or breed itself so out of circumstance,
That, I being absent and my place supplied,
My general will forget my love and service.

Des. Do not doubt that; before Emilia
here
I give thee warrant of thy place: assure
thee,
If I do vow a friendship, I'll perform it   21
To the last article: my lord shall never rest;
I'll watch him tame and talk him out of
patience;
His bed shall seem a school, his board a shrift;
I'll intermingle every thing he does
With Cassio's suit: therefore be merry,
Cassio;
For thy solicitor shall rather die
Than give thy cause away.

Emil. Madam, here comes my lord.

Cas. Madam, I'll take my leave.   30

Des. Why, stay, and hear me speak.

Cas. Madam, not now: I am very ill at
ease,
Unfit for mine own purposes.

Des. Well, do your discretion.

                                 [*Exit Cassio.*

Enter OTHELLO *and* IAGO.

Iago. Ha! I like not that.

Oth.   What dost thou say?

Iago. Nothing, my lord: or if—I know not
what.

Oth. Was not that Cassio parted from my
wife?

Iago. Cassio, my lord! No, sure, I cannot
think it,
That he would steal away so guilty-like,
Seeing you coming.

Oth.   I do believe 'twas he.   40

Des. How now, my lord!
I have been talking with a suitor here,
A man that languishes in your displeasure.

Oth. Who is 't you mean?

Des. Why, your lieutenant, Cassio. Good
my lord,
If I have any grace or power to move you,
His present reconciliation take;
For if he be not one that truly loves you,

That errs in ignorance and not in cunning,
I have no judgement in an honest face: 50
I prithee, call him back.

Oth.   Went he hence now?

Des. Ay, sooth; so humbled
That he hath left part of his grief with me,
To suffer with him. Good love, call him
back.

Oth. Not now, sweet Desdemona; some
other time.

Des. But shall 't be shortly?

Oth.   The sooner, sweet, for you.

Des. Shall 't be to-night at supper?

Oth.   No, not to-night.

Des. To-morrow dinner, then?

Oth.   I shall not dine at home;
I meet the captains at the citadel.

Des. Why, then, to-morrow night; or
Tuesday morn;   60
On Tuesday noon, or night; on Wednesday
morn:
I prithee, name the time, but let it not
Exceed three days: in faith, he's penitent;
And yet his trespass, in our common
reason—
Save that, they say, the wars must make
examples
Out of their best—is not almost a fault
To incur a private check. When shall he
come?
Tell me, Othello: I wonder in my soul,
What you would ask me, that I should deny,
Or stand so mammering on. What! Michael
Cassio,   70
That came a-wooing with you, and so many
a time,
When I have spoke of you dispraisingly,
Hath ta'en your part; to have so much to do
To bring him in! Trust me, I could do
much,—

Oth. Prithee, no more: let him come when
he will;
I will deny thee nothing.

Des.   Why, this is not a boon;
'Tis as I should entreat you wear your
gloves,
Or feed on nourishing dishes, or keep you
warm,
Or sue to you to do a peculiar profit
To your own person: nay, when I have a
suit   80
Wherein I mean to touch your love indeed,

---

16. **breed . . . circumstance**, increase itself so on
account of accidents. 23. **watch him tame**, tame him
by keeping him from sleeping (a term from falconry).
24. **shrift**, confession. 28. **away**, up.

70. **mammering on**, wavering; originally, *stammer-ing.*

It shall be full of poise and difficult weight
And fearful to be granted.

Oth.　　　　　　　I will deny thee nothing:
Whereon, I do beseech thee, grant me this,
To leave me but a little to myself.

Des. Shall I deny you? no: farewell, my lord.

Oth. Farewell, my Desdemona: I'll come to thee straight.

Des. Emilia, come. Be as your fancies teach you:
Whate'er you be, I am obedient.

　　　　　　　[*Exeunt Desdemona and Emilia.*

Oth. Excellent wretch! Perdition catch my soul,　　　　　　　　　　　　　90
But I do love thee! and when I love thee not,
Chaos is come again.

Iago. My noble lord,—

Oth.　　　　What dost thou say, Iago?

Iago. Did Michael Cassio, when you woo'd my lady,
Know of your love?

Oth. He did, from first to last: why dost thou ask?

Iago. But for a satisfaction of my thought;
No further harm.

Oth.　　　　Why of thy thought, Iago?

Iago. I did not think he had been acquainted with her.

Oth. O, yes; and went between us very oft.

Iago. Indeed!　　　　　　　　　　　101

Oth. Indeed! ay, indeed: discern'st thou aught in that?
Is he not honest?

Iago.　　　　　　Honest, my lord!

Oth.　　　　·　Honest! ay, honest.

Iago. My lord, for aught I know.

Oth. What dost thou think?

Iago.　　　　　Think, my lord!

Oth.　　　　　　　Think, my lord!
By heaven, he echoes me,
As if there were some monster in his thought
Too hideous to be shown. Thou dost mean something:
I heard thee say even now, thou likedst not that,　　　　　　　　　　　109
When Cassio left my wife: what didst not like?
And when I told thee he was of my counsel
In my whole course of wooing, thou criedst
'Indeed!'

And didst contract and purse thy brow together,
As if thou then hadst shut up in thy brain
Some horrible conceit: if thou dost love me,
Show me thy thought.

Iago. My lord, you know I love you.

Oth.　　　　　I think thou dost;
And, for I know thou'rt full of love and honesty,
And weigh'st thy words before thou givest them breath,
Therefore these stops of thine fright me the more:　　　　　　　　　　　120
For such things in a false disloyal knave
Are tricks of custom, but in a man that's just
They are close delations, working from the heart
That passion cannot rule.

Iago.　　　　　　For Michael Cassio,
I dare be sworn I think that he is honest.

Oth. I think so too.

Iago.　　　　Men should be what they seem;
Or those that be not, would they might seem none!

Oth. Certain, men should be what they seem.

Iago. Why, then, I think Cassio's an honest man.

Oth. Nay, yet there's more in this:　　130
I prithee, speak to me as to thy thinkings,
As thou dost ruminate, and give thy worst of thoughts
The worst of words.

Iago.　　　　　Good my lord, pardon me:
Though I am bound to every act of duty,
I am not bound to that all slaves are free to.
Utter my thoughts? Why, say they are vile and false;
As where's that palace whereinto foul things
Sometimes intrude not? who has a breast so pure,
But some uncleanly apprehensions
Keep leets and law-days and in session sit 140
With meditations lawful?

Oth. Thou dost conspire against thy friend, Iago,
If thou but think'st him wrong'd and makest his ear
A stranger to thy thoughts.

Iago.　　　　　I do beseech you—

---

82. **poise**, weight, heaviness. 90. **wretch**, term of affectionate endearment with a connotation of pity.

115. **conceit**, idea, thought. 123. **close delations**, secret or involuntary accusations. 140. **Keep leets**, hold courts. **law-days**, court-days.

Though I perchance am vicious in my guess,
As, I confess, it is my nature's plague
To spy into abuses, and oft my jealousy
Shapes faults that are not—that your
    wisdom yet,
From one that so imperfectly conceits,
Would take no notice, nor build yourself a
    trouble   150
Out of his scattering and unsure observance.
It were not for your quiet nor your good,
Nor for my manhood, honesty, or wisdom,
To let you know my thoughts.
    Oth.   What dost thou mean?
    Iago. Good name in man and woman, dear
    my lord,
Is the immediate jewel of their souls:
Who steals my purse steals trash; 'tis some-
    thing, nothing;
'Twas mine, 'tis his, and has been slave to
    thousands;
But he that filches from me my good name
Robs me of that which not enriches him   160
And makes me poor indeed.
    Oth. By heaven, I'll know thy thoughts.
    Iago. You cannot, if my heart were in
    your hand;
Nor shall not, whilst 'tis in my custody.
    Oth. Ha!
    Iago. O, beware, my lord, of jealousy;
It is the green-eyed monster which doth
    mock
The meat it feeds on: that cuckold lives in
    bliss
Who, certain of his fate, loves not his
    wronger;
But, O, what damned minutes tells he o'er
Who dotes, yet doubts, suspects, yet strongly
    loves!   170
    Oth. O misery!
    Iago. Poor and content is rich and rich
    enough,
But riches fineless is as poor as winter
To him that ever fears he shall be poor.
Good heaven, the souls of all my tribe defend
From jealousy!
    Oth.   Why, why is this?
Think'st thou I'ld make a life of jealousy,
To follow still the changes of the moon
With fresh suspicions? No; to be once in
    doubt
Is once to be resolved: exchange me for a
    goat,

When I shall turn the business of my soul 181
To such exsufflicate and blown surmises,
Matching thy inference. 'Tis not to make
    me jealous
To say my wife is fair, feeds well, loves com-
    pany,
Is free of speech, sings, plays and dances well;
Where virtue is, these are more virtuous:
Nor from mine own weak merits will I draw
The smallest fear or doubt of her revolt;
For she had eyes, and chose me. No, Iago;
I'll see before I doubt; when I doubt, prove;
And on the proof, there is no more but this,—
Away at once with love or jealousy!
    Iago. I am glad of it; for now I shall have
    reason
To show the love and duty that I bear you
With franker spirit: therefore, as I am bound,
Receive it from me. I speak not yet of proof.
Look to your wife; observe her well with
    Cassio;
Wear your eye thus, not jealous nor secure:
I would not have your free and noble nature,
Out of self-bounty, be abused; look to 't: 200
I know our country disposition well;
In Venice they do let heaven see the pranks
They dare not show their husbands; their
    best conscience
Is not to leave 't undone, but keep 't un-
    known.
    Oth. Dost thou say so?
    Iago. She did deceive her father, marry-
    ing you;
And when she seem'd to shake and fear your
    looks,
She loved them most.
    Oth.   And so she did.
    Iago.   Why, go to then;
She that, so young, could give out such a
    seeming,
To seel her father's eyes up close as oak— 210
He thought 'twas witchcraft—but I am
    much to blame;
I humbly do beseech you of your pardon
For too much loving you.
    Oth.   I am bound to thee for ever.
    Iago. I see this hath a little dash'd your
    spirits.
    Oth. Not a jot, not a jot.

---

145. **vicious**, wrong. 147. **jealousy**, suspicion of
evil. 149. **conceits**, judges. 173. **fineless**, boundless.

182. **exsufflicate and blown**, unsubstantial and
inflated. 198. **secure**, free from uneasiness. 200. **self-
bounty**, inherent or natural goodness. 201. **our
country disposition**, the disposition (toward wickedness) of our native country. 209. **seeming**, false appearance. 210. **seel**, blind (a term from falconry).

Iago.   I' faith, I fear it has.
I hope you will consider what is spoke
Comes from my love. But I do see you're
    moved:
I am to pray you not to strain my speech
To grosser issues nor to larger reach
Than to suspicion.   220
    Oth. I will not.
    Iago.   Should you do so, my lord,
My speech should fall into such vile success
As my thoughts aim not at. Cassio's my
    worthy friend—
My lord, I see you're moved.
    Oth.   No, not much moved:
I do not think but Desdemona's honest.
    Iago. Long live she so! and long live you
    to think so!
    Oth. And yet, how nature erring from
    itself,—
    Iago. Ay, there's the point: as—to be
    bold with you—
Not to affect many proposed matches
Of her own clime, complexion, and degree, 230
Whereto we see in all things nature tends—
Foh! one may smell in such a will most
    rank,
Foul disproportion, thoughts unnatural.
But pardon me; I do not in position
Distinctly speak of her; though I may fear
Her will, recoiling to her better judgement,
May fall to match you with her country
    forms
And happily repent.
    Oth.   Farewell, farewell:
If more thou dost perceive, let me know
    more;
Set on thy wife to observe: leave me, Iago. 240
    Iago. [*Going*] My lord, I take my leave.
    Oth. Why did I marry? This honest
    creature doubtless
Sees and knows more, much more, than he
    unfolds.
    Iago. [*Returning*] My Lord, I would I
    might entreat your honour
To scan this thing no further; leave it to
    time:
Though it be fit that Cassio have his place,
For, sure, he fills it up with great ability,
Yet, if you please to hold him off awhile,

You shall by that perceive him and his
    means: 249
Note, if your lady strain his entertainment
With any strong or vehement importunity;
Much will be seen in that. In the mean
    time,
Let me be thought too busy in my fears—
As worthy cause I have to fear I am—
And hold her free, I do beseech your honour.
    Oth. Fear not my government.
    Iago. I once more take my leave. [*Exit.*
    Oth. This fellow's of exceeding honesty,
And knows all qualities, with a learned spirit,
Of human dealings. If I do prove her hag-
    gard,
Though that her jesses were my dear heart-
    strings,   261
I'ld whistle her off and let her down the
    wind,
To prey at fortune. Haply, for I am black
And have not those soft parts of conversation
That chamberers have, or for I am declined
Into the vale of years,—yet that's not
    much—
She's gone. I am abused; and my relief
Must be to loathe her. O curse of marriage,
That we can call these delicate creatures ours,
And not their appetites! I had rather be a
    toad,   270
And live upon the vapour of a dungeon,
Than keep a corner in the thing I love
For others' uses. Yet, 'tis the plague of
    great ones;
Prerogatived are they less than the base;
'Tis destiny unshunnable, like death:
Even then this forked plague is fated to us
When we do quicken. Desdemona comes:

    Re-enter DESDEMONA *and* EMILIA.

If she be false, O, then heaven mocks itself!
I'll not believe 't.
    Des.   How now, my dear Othello!
Your dinner, and the generous islanders 280
By you invited, do attend your presence.
    Oth. I am to blame.
    Des.   Why do you speak so faintly?
Are you not well?

222. **success**, consequences. 232. **will**, sensuality.
233. **disproportion**, abnormality. 234. **position**, formal assertion. 236. **recoiling to**, falling back upon, or
recoiling against. 237. **fall to**, apply (herself) to.
country forms, probably, after the manner of her
country. 238. **happily**, perhaps. **repent**, i.e., of her
marriage.

250. **strain his entertainment**, urge his reinstate-
ment. 255. **hold her free**, regard her as innocent. 256.
government, self-control. 260. **haggard**, wild, in-
tractable; a haggard was a wild female hawk caught when
in her adult plumage. 261. **jesses**, straps fastened
around the legs of a trained hawk. 263. **at fortune**, at
random. 264. **conversation**, social intercourse. 265.
chamberers, gallants. 274. **Prerogatived**, privileged.
276. **forked**, an allusion to the horns of the cuckold.
277. **quicken**, receive life. 280. **generous**, noble.

Oth. I have a pain upon my forehead here.

Des. 'Faith, that's with watching; 'twill away again:
Let me but bind it hard, within this hour
It will be well.

Oth.　　　　Your napkin is too little:

[*He puts the handkerchief from him; and it drops.*

Let it alone. Come, I'll go in with you.

Des. I am very sorry that you are not well.

[*Exeunt Othello and Desdemona.*

Emil. I am glad I have found this napkin:
This was her first remembrance from the Moor: 　291
My wayward husband hath a hundred times
Woo'd me to steal it; but she so loves the token,
For he conjured her she should ever keep it,
That she reserves it evermore about her
To kiss and talk to. I'll have the work ta'en out,
And give 't Iago: what he will do with it
Heaven knows, not I;
I nothing but to please his fantasy.

Re-enter IAGO.

Iago. How now! what do you here alone?

Emil. Do not you chide; I have a thing for you. 　301

Iago. A thing for me? it is a common thing—

Emil. Ha!

Iago. To have a foolish wife.

Emil. O, is that all? What will you give me now
For that same handkerchief?

Iago.　　　　What handkerchief?

Emil. What handkerchief!
Why, that the Moor first gave to Desdemona;
That which so often you did bid me steal.

Iago. Hast stol'n it from her? 　310

Emil. No, 'faith; she let it drop by negligence,
And, to the advantage, I, being here, took 't up.
Look, here it is.

Iago.　　　　A good wench; give it me.

Emil. What will you do with 't, that you have been so earnest
To have me filch it?

Iago. [*Snatching it*] Why, what's that to you?

Emil. If it be not for some purpose of import,
Give 't me again: poor lady, she'll run mad
When she shall lack it.

Iago. Be not acknown on 't; I have use for it.
Go, leave me.　　　　[*Exit Emilia.* 　320
I will in Cassio's lodging lose this napkin,
And let him find it. Trifles light as air
Are to the jealous confirmations strong
As proofs of holy writ: this may do something.
The Moor already changes with my poison:
Dangerous conceits are, in their natures, poisons,
Which at the first are scarce found to distaste,
But with a little act upon the blood,
Burn like the mines of sulphur. I did say so:
Look, where he comes!

Re-enter OTHELLO.

　　　　Not poppy, nor mandragora, 　330
Nor all the drowsy syrups of the world,
Shall ever medicine thee to that sweet sleep
Which thou owedst yesterday.

Oth.　　　　Ha! ha! false to me?

Iago. Why, how now, general! no more of that.

Oth. Avaunt! be gone! thou hast set me on the rack:
I swear 'tis better to be much abused
Than but to know 't a little.

Iago.　　　　How now, my lord!

Oth. What sense had I of her stol'n hours of lust?
I saw 't not, thought it not, it harm'd not me:
I slept the next night well, was free and merry;
I found not Cassio's kisses on her lips: 　341
He that is robb'd, not wanting what is stol'n,
Let him not know 't, and he's not robb'd at all.

Iago. I am sorry to hear this.

Oth. I had been happy, if the general camp,

---

287. **napkin**, handkerchief. 293. **to steal it.** Pilfering was so customary in Shakespeare's time that Queen Elizabeth's suite would despoil the noblemen who entertained her on her progresses. 296. **work ta'en out**, embroidery copied. 312. **to the advantage**, opportunely.

319. **Be not acknown on 't**, do not confess knowledge of it. 326. **conceits**, ideas, thoughts. 328. **act**, action, working. 333 **owedst**, ownedst.

Pioners and all, had tasted her sweet body,
So I had nothing known. O, now, for ever
Farewell the tranquil mind! farewell content!
Farewell the plumed troop, and the big wars,
That make ambition virtue! O, farewell! 350
Farewell the neighing steed, and the shrill
    trump,
The spirit-stirring drum, the ear-piercing
    fife,
The royal banner, and all quality,
Pride, pomp and circumstance of glorious
    war!
And, O you mortal engines, whose rude
    throats
The immortal Jove's dread clamours coun-
    terfeit,
Farewell! Othello's occupation's gone!
    Iago. Is 't possible, my lord?
    Oth. Villain, be sure thou prove my love
    a whore,
Be sure of it; give me the ocular proof; 360
Or, by the worth of man's eternal soul,
Thou hadst been better have been born
    a dog
Than answer my waked wrath!
    Iago.   Is 't come to this?
    Oth. Make me to see 't; or, at the least, so
    prove it,
That the probation bear no hinge nor loop
To hang a doubt on; or woe upon thy life!
    Iago. My noble lord,—
    Oth. If thou dost slander her and torture
    me,
Never pray more; abandon all remorse;
On horror's head horrors accumulate; 370
Do deeds to make heaven weep, all earth
    amazed;
For nothing canst thou to damnation add
Greater than that.
    Iago.   O grace! O heaven forgive me!
Are you a man? have you a soul or sense?
God be wi' you; take mine office. O wretched
    fool,
That livest to make thine honesty a vice!
O monstrous world! Take note, take note, O
    world,
To be direct and honest is not safe.
I thank you for this profit; and from hence
I'll love no friend, sith love breeds such
    offence.   380
    Oth. Nay, stay: thou shouldst be honest.

    Iago. I should be wise, for honesty's a
    fool
And loses that it works for.
    Oth.   By the world,
I think my wife be honest and think she is
    not;
I think that thou art just and think thou art
    not.
I'll have some proof. Her name, that was as
    fresh
As Dian's visage, is now begrimed and black
As mine own face. If there be cords, or
    knives,
Poison, or fire, or suffocating streams,
I'll not endure it. Would I were satisfied!
    Iago. I see, sir, you are eaten up with
    passion: 391
I do repent me that I put it to you.
You would be satisfied?
    Oth.   Would! nay, I will.
    Iago. And may: but, how? how satisfied,
    my lord?
Would you, the supervisor, grossly gape on—
Behold her topp'd?
    Oth.   Death and damnation! O!
    Iago. It were a tedious difficulty, I think,
To bring them to that prospect: damn them
    then,
If ever mortal eyes do see them bolster
More than their own! What then? how then?
What shall I say? Where's satisfaction? 401
It is impossible you should see this,
Were they as prime as goats, as hot as
    monkeys,
As salt as wolves in pride, and fools as
    gross
As ignorance made drunk. But yet, I say,
If imputation and strong circumstances,
Which lead directly to the door of truth,
Will give you satisfaction, you may have 't.
    Oth. Give me a living reason she's dis-
    loyal.
    Iago. I do not like the office: 410
But, sith I am enter'd in this cause so far,
Prick'd to 't by foolish honesty and love,
I will go on. I lay with Cassio lately;
And, being troubled with a raging tooth,
I could not sleep.
There are a kind of men so loose of soul,
That in their sleeps will mutter their affairs:
One of this kind is Cassio:

---

346. **Pioners**, pioneers or sappers, a low grade of
soldiers. 354. **circumstance**, attendant fact; here,
formal display. 355. **mortal engines**, i.e., cannon.
369. **remorse**, pity, compassion. 380. **sith**, since.

404. **salt**, wanton, sensual. 406. **imputation**, i.e.,
opinion founded on strong circumstantial evidence
(Schmidt).

In sleep I heard him say 'Sweet Desdemona,
Let us be wary, let us hide our loves;' 420
And then, sir, would he gripe and wring my
hand,
Cry 'O sweet creature!' and then kiss me
hard,
As if he pluck'd up kisses by the roots
That grew upon my lips: then laid his leg
Over my thigh, and sigh'd, and kiss'd; and
then
Cried 'Cursed fate that gave thee to the
Moor!'

Oth. O monstrous! monstrous!

Iago. Nay, this was but his dream.

Oth. But this denoted a foregone conclusion:

'Tis a shrewd doubt, though it be but a
dream.

Iago. And this may help to thicken other
proofs 430
That do demonstrate thinly.

Oth. I'll tear her all to pieces.

Iago. Nay, but be wise: yet we see nothing done;
She may be honest yet. Tell me but this,
Have you not sometimes seen a handkerchief
Spotted with strawberries in your wife's
hand?

Oth. I gave her such a one; 'twas my first
gift.

Iago. I know not that: but such a hand-
kerchief—
I am sure it was your wife's—did I to-day
See Cassio wipe his beard with.

Oth. If it be that,—

Iago. If it be that, or any that was hers, 440
It speaks against her with the other proofs.

Oth. O, that the slave had forty thousand
lives!
One is too poor, too weak for my revenge.
Now do I see 'tis true. Look here, Iago;
All my fond love thus do I blow to heaven.
'Tis gone.
Arise, black vengeance, from thy hollow cell!
Yield up, O love, thy crown and hearted
throne
To tyrannous hate! Swell, bosom, with thy
fraught,
For 'tis of aspics' tongues!

Iago. Yet be content. 450

Oth. O, blood, blood, blood!

Iago. Patience, I say; your mind perhaps
may change.

Oth. Never, Iago. Like to the Pontic sea,
Whose icy current and compulsive course
Ne'er feels retiring ebb, but keeps due on
To the Propontic and the Hellespont,
Even so my bloody thoughts, with violent
pace,
Shall ne'er look back, ne'er ebb to humble
love,
Till that a capable and wide revenge
Swallow them up. Now, by yond marble
heaven, 460
[*Kneels*] In the due reverence of a sacred vow
I here engage my words.

Iago. Do not rise yet.

[*Kneels*] Witness, you ever-burning lights
above,
You elements that clip us round about,
Witness that here Iago doth give up
The execution of his wit, hands, heart,
To wrong'd Othello's service! Let him com-
mand,
And to obey shall be in me remorse,
What bloody business ever. [*They rise.*

Oth. I greet thy love,
Not with vain thanks, but with acceptance
bounteous, 470
And will upon the instant put thee to 't:
Within these three days let me hear thee say
That Cassio's not alive.

Iago. My friend is dead; 'tis done at your
request:
But let her live.

Oth. Damn her, lewd minx! O, damn her!
Come, go with me apart; I will withdraw,
To furnish me with some swift means of
death
For the fair devil. Now art thou my lieu-
tenant.

Iago. I am your own for ever. [*Exeunt.*

SCENE IV. *Before the castle.*

Enter DESDEMONA, EMILIA, *and* Clown.

Des. Do you know, sirrah, where Lieutenant Cassio lies?

453-456. **Pontic . . . Propontic . . . Hellespont.**
Steevens refers to Holland's *Pliny*, bk. II, ch. 97 (1601):
"And the sea Pontus euermore floweth and runneth out
into Propontic, but the sea neuer retireth backe againe
within Pontus [the Black Sea]." 459. **capable**, comprehensive. 460. **marble**, i.e., gleaming like marble.
464. **clip**, surround, embrace. 466. **execution**, exercise.
468. **remorse**, conscience, solemn obligation.

428. **foregone conclusion**, previous trial or experience (not used in our sense). 448. **hearted**, fixed
in the heart. 449. **fraught**, freight, burden. 450.
aspics', venomous serpents'.

Clo. I dare not say he lies any where.

Des. Why, man?

Clo. He's a soldier, and for one to say a soldier lies, is stabbing.

Des. Go to: where lodges he?

Clo. To tell you where he lodges, is to tell you where I lie.

Des. Can any thing be made of this?   10

Clo. I know not where he lodges, and for me to devise a lodging and say he lies here or he lies there, were to lie in mine own throat.

Des. Can you inquire him out, and be edified by report?

Clo. I will catechize the world for him; that is, make questions, and by them answer.

Des. Seek him, bid him come hither: tell him I have moved my lord on his behalf, and hope all will be well.   20

Clo. To do this is within the compass of man's wit; and therefore I will attempt the doing it.   [*Exit.*

Des. Where should I lose that handkerchief, Emilia?

Emil. I know not, madam.

Des. Believe me, I had rather have lost
  my purse
Full of crusadoes: and, but my noble Moor
Is true of mind and made of no such base-
  ness
As jealous creatures are, it were enough
To put him to ill thinking.

Emil.   Is he not jealous?

Des. Who, he? I think the sun where he
  was born   30
Drew all such humours from him.

Emil.   Look, where he comes.

Des. I will not leave him now till Cassio
Be call'd to him.

Enter OTHELLO.

          How is 't with you, my lord?

Oth. Well, my good lady. [*Aside*] O, hardness to dissemble!—
How do you, Desdemona?

Des.   Well, my good lord.

Oth. Give me your hand: this hand is
  moist, my lady.

Des. It yet hath felt no age nor known no
  sorrow.

Oth. This argues fruitfulness and liberal
  heart:

Hot, hot, and moist: this hand of yours re-
  quires   39
A sequester from liberty, fasting and prayer,
Much castigation, exercise devout;
For here's a young and sweating devil
  here,
That commonly rebels. 'Tis a good hand,
A frank one.

Des.   You may, indeed, say so;
For 'twas that hand that gave away my
  heart.

Oth. A liberal hand: the hearts of old gave
  hands;
But our new heraldry is hands, not hearts.

Des. I cannot speak of this. Come now,
  your promise.

Oth. What promise, chuck?

Des. I have sent to bid Cassio come speak
  with you.   50

Oth. I have a salt and sorry rheum offends
  me;
Lend me thy handkerchief.

Des.   Here, my lord.

Oth. That which I gave you.

Des.   I have it not about me.

Oth. Not?

Des.   No, indeed, my lord.

Oth.   That is a fault.
That handkerchief
Did an Egyptian to my mother give;
She was a charmer, and could almost read
The thoughts of people: she told her, while
  she kept it,
'Twould make her amiable and subdue my
  father
Entirely to her love, but if she lost it   60
Or made a gift of it, my father's eye
Should hold her loathed and his spirits
  should hunt
After new fancies: she, dying, gave it me;
And bid me, when my fate would have me
  wive,
To give it her. I did so: and take heed on 't;
Make it a darling like your precious eye;
To lose 't or give 't away were such perdi-
  tion
As nothing else could match.

Des.   Is 't possible?

40. **sequester**, separation, sequestration.   47. **new
. . . hearts.** This is thought by Warburton and some
later critics to allude to the creation of a new order of
baronets by King James I in 1611, the arms for which
were a hand gules on a field argent.   More probably,
however, it is a current expression referring to marriages
in which there is a joining of hands without the giving
of hearts.   51. **sorry rheum**, painful tears.   56. **Egyptian**, gypsy.

26. **crusadoes**, Portuguese gold coins.   31. **humours**, bodily fluids which, according to early physiology, produced moods and mental dispositions.

Oth. 'Tis true: there's magic in the web of it:
A sibyl, that had number'd in the world 70
The sun to course two hundred compasses,
In her prophetic fury sew'd the work;
The worms were hallow'd that did breed the silk;
And it was dyed in mummy which the skilful
Conserved of maidens' hearts.

    Des.   Indeed! is 't true?

    Oth. Most veritable; therefore look to 't well.

    Des. Then would to God that I had never seen 't!

    Oth. Ha! wherefore?

    Des. Why do you speak so startingly and rash?

    Oth. Is 't lost? is 't gone? speak, is it out o' the way? 80

    Des. Heaven bless us!

    Oth. Say you?

    Des. It is not lost; but what an if it were?

    Oth. How!

    Des. I say, it is not lost.

    Oth.   Fetch 't, let me see 't.

    Des. Why, so I can, sir, but I will not now.
This is a trick to put me from my suit:
Pray you, let Cassio be received again.

    Oth. Fetch me the handkerchief: my mind misgives.

    Des. Come, come; 90
You'll never meet a more sufficient man.

    Oth. The handkerchief!

    Des.   I pray, talk me of Cassio.

    Oth. The handkerchief!

    Des.   A man that all his time
Hath founded his good fortunes on your love,
Shared dangers with you,—

    Oth. The handkerchief!

    Des. In sooth, you are to blame.

    Oth. Away!   [*Exit.*

    Emil. Is not this man jealous?

    Des. I ne'er saw this before. 100
Sure, there's some wonder in this handkerchief:
I am most unhappy in the loss of it.

    Emil. 'Tis not a year or two shows us a man:

They are all but stomachs, and we all but food;
They eat us hungerly, and when they are full,
They belch us. Look you, Cassio and my husband!

    Enter Cassio *and* Iago.

    Iago. There is no other way; 'tis she must do 't:
And, lo, the happiness! go, and importune her.

    Des. How now, good Cassio! what's the news with you?

    Cas. Madam, my former suit: I do beseech you 110
That by your virtuous means I may again
Exist, and be a member of his love
Whom I with all the office of my heart
Entirely honour: I would not be delay'd.
If my offence be of such mortal kind
That nor my service past, nor present sorrows,
Nor purposed merit in futurity,
Can ransom me into his love again,
But to know so must be my benefit;
So shall I clothe me in a forced content, 120
And shut myself up in some other course,
To fortune's alms.

    Des.   Alas, thrice-gentle Cassio!
My advocation is not now in tune;
My lord is not my lord; nor should I know him,
Were he in favour as in humour alter'd.
So help me every spirit sanctified,
As I have spoken for you all my best
And stood within the blank of his displeasure
For my free speech! you must awhile be patient:
What I can do I will; and more I will 130
Than for myself I dare: let that suffice you.

    Iago. Is my lord angry?

    Emil.   He went hence but now,
And certainly in strange unquietness.

    Iago. Can he be angry? I have seen the cannon,
When it hath blown his ranks into the air,
And, like the devil, from his very arm
Puff'd his own brother:—and can he be angry?

---

70. **had number'd . . . compasses.** "We say, I counted the clock to strike four; so she numbered the sun to course, to run two hundred compasses, two hundred annual circuits" (Johnson). 74. **mummy,** medicinal or magical preparation from the flesh of mummified bodies. 75. **Conserved of,** preserved out of.

119. **to know . . . benefit,** to know that my case is hopeless will end my vain endeavor. 123. **advocation,** advocacy. 128. **blank,** white spot in the center of a target; here, range.

Something of moment then: I will go meet
him:
There's matter in't indeed, if he be angry.139
Des. I prithee, do so. [*Exit Iago*.
Something, sure, of state,
Either from Venice, or some unhatch'd prac-
tice
Made demonstrable here in Cyprus to him,
Hath puddled his clear spirit; and in such
cases
Men's natures wrangle with inferior things,
Though great ones are their object. 'Tis
even so;
For let our finger ache, and it indues
Our other healthful members even to that
sense
Of pain: nay, we must think men are not
gods,
Nor of them look for such observances
As fit the bridal. Beshrew me much, Emilia,
I was, unhandsome warrior as I am,   151
Arraigning his unkindness with my soul;
But now I find I had suborn'd the wit-
ness,
And he's indicted falsely.
    Emil. Pray heaven it be state-matters,
as you think,
And no conception nor no jealous toy
Concerning you.
    Des. Alas the day! I never gave him
cause.
    Emil. But jealous souls will not be an-
swer'd so;
They are not ever jealous for the cause, 160
But jealous for they are jealous: 'tis a mon-
ster
Begot upon itself, born on itself.
    Des. Heaven keep that monster from
Othello's mind!
    Emil. Lady, amen.
    Des. I will go seek him. Cassio, walk here
about:
If I do find him fit, I'll move your suit
And seek to effect it to my uttermost.
    Cas. I humbly thank your ladyship.
            [*Exeunt Desdemona and Emilia*.

Enter BIANCA.

    Bian. Save you, friend Cassio!
    Cas.   What make you from home?
How is it with you, my most fair Bianca?170

I' faith, sweet love, I was coming to your
house.
    Bian. And I was going to your lodging,
Cassio.
What, keep a week away? seven days and
nights?
Eight score eight hours? and lovers' absent
hours,
More tedious than the dial eight score
times?
O weary reckoning!
    Cas.   Pardon me, Bianca:
I have this while with leaden thoughts been
press'd;
But I shall, in a more continuate time,
Strike off this score of absence. Sweet
Bianca,
    [*Giving her Desdemona's handkerchief*.
Take me this work out.
    Bian.   O Cassio, whence came this?180
This is some token from a newer friend:
To the felt absence now I feel a cause:
Is 't come to this? Well, well.
    Cas.   Go to, woman!
Throw your vile guesses in the devil's
teeth,
From whence you have them. You are
jealous now
That this is from some mistress, some remem-
brance:
No, in good troth, Bianca.
    Bian.   Why, whose is it?
    Cas. I know not, sweet: I found it in my
chamber.
I like the work well: ere it be demanded—
As like enough it will—I'ld have it copied:190
Take it, and do 't; and leave me for this time.
    Bian. Leave you! wherefore?
    Cas. I do attend here on the general;
And think it no addition, nor my wish,
To have him see me woman'd.
    Bian.   Why, I pray you?
    Cas. Not that I love you not.
    Bian.   But that you do not love me.
I pray you, bring me on the way a little,
And say if I shall see you soon at night.
    Cas. 'Tis but a little way that I can bring
you;
For I attend here: but I'll see you soon. 200
    Bian. 'Tis very good; I must be circum-
stanced.   [*Exeunt*.

---

143. **puddled**, sullied the purity of. 146. **indues**,
brings to the same condition. 151. **unhandsome**,
unfair. 156. **conception**, mere fancy.

178. **continuate**, uninterrupted. Q: *conuenient*. 180.
Take . . . out, i.e., copy this embroidery for me. 194.
addition, honor. 201. **circumstanced**, governed by
circumstances.

ACT IV.

Scene I. *Cyprus. Before the castle.*

Enter Othello *and* Iago.

Iago. Will you think so?
Oth.   Think so, Iago!
Iago.   What,
To kiss in private?
Oth.   An unauthorized kiss.
Iago. Or to be naked with her friend in
    bed
An hour or more, not meaning any harm?
Oth. Naked in bed, Iago, and not mean
    harm!
It is hypocrisy against the devil:
They that mean virtuously, and yet do so,
The devil their virtue tempts, and they
    tempt heaven.
Iago. So they do nothing, 'tis a venial
    slip:
But if I give my wife a handkerchief,—   10
Oth. What then?
Iago. Why, then, 'tis hers, my lord; and,
    being hers,
She may, I think, bestow 't on any man.
Oth. She is protectress of her honour too:
May she give that?
Iago. Her honour is an essence that's not
    seen;
They have it very oft that have it not:
But, for the handkerchief,—
Oth. By heaven, I would most gladly have
    forgot it.
Thou said'st—O, it comes o'er my memory,
As doth the raven o'er the infected house,21
Boding to all—he had my handkerchief.
Iago. Ay, what of that?
Oth.   That's not so good now.
Iago.   What,
If I had said I had seen him do you wrong?
Or heard him say,—as knaves be such
    abroad,
Who having, by their own importunate
    suit,
Or voluntary dotage of some mistress,
Convinced or supplied them, cannot choose
But they must blab—

Oth.   Hath he said any thing?
Iago. He hath, my lord; but be you well
    assured,   30
No more than he'll unswear.
Oth.   What hath he said?
Iago. 'Faith, that he did—I know not
    what he did.
Oth. What? what?
Iago. Lie—
Oth.   With her?
Iago.   With her, on her; what you
    will.
Oth. Lie with her! lie on her! We say lie
on her, when they belie her. Lie with her!
that's fulsome.—Handkerchief—confessions
—handkerchief!—To confess, and be hanged
for his labour;—first, to be hanged, and then
to confess.—I tremble at it. Nature would
not invest herself in such shadowing passion
without some instruction. It is not words
that shake me thus. Pish! Noses, ears, and
lips. — Is 't possible? — Confess — handkerchief!—O devil!   [*Falls in a trance.*

Iago. Work on,
My medicine, work! Thus credulous fools
    are caught;
And many worthy and chaste dames even
    thus,
All guiltless, meet reproach. What, ho! my
    lord!
My lord, I say! Othello!

Enter Cassio.

                    How now, Cassio!
Cas. What's the matter?   50
Iago. My lord is fall'n into an epilepsy:
This is his second fit; he had one yesterday.
Cas. Rub him about the temples.
Iago.   No, forbear:
The lethargy must have his quiet course:
If not, he foams at mouth and by and by
Breaks out to savage madness. Look, he
    stirs:
Do you withdraw yourself a little while,
He will recover straight: when he is gone,
I would on great occasion speak with you.
                              [*Exit Cassio.*
How is it, general? have you not hurt your
    head?   60
Oth. Dost thou mock me?

---

1. **Will you think so?** It will be noticed that Iago
has made enormous progress in his attack on the peace
of mind of Othello in the interval between acts; Othello
has become utterly credulous. 21. **raven . . . house,**
allusion to the belief that the raven hovered over a house
of sickness or infection. 28. **Convinced or supplied,**
i.e., mistresses gained by importunity and those who
doted voluntarily.

40-42. **Nature . . . instruction,** i.e., my jealousy
cannot be merely the result of natural imagination, but
must have some foundation in fact. 54. **lethargy,**
unconscious condition.

Iago.   I mock you! no, by heaven.
Would you would bear your fortune like a
     man!
  Oth. A horned man's a monster and a
     beast.
  Iago. There's many a beast then in a
     populous city,
And many a civil monster.
  Oth. Did he confess it?
  Iago.   Good sir, be a man;
Think every bearded fellow that's but yoked
May draw with you: there's millions now
     alive
That nightly lie in those unproper beds
Which they dare swear peculiar: your case is
     better.   70
O, 'tis the spite of hell, the fiend's arch-mock,
To lip a wanton in a secure couch,
And to suppose her chaste! No, let me
     know;
And knowing what I am, I know what she
     shall be.
  Oth. O, thou art wise; 'tis certain.
  Iago.   Stand you awhile apart;
Confine yourself but in a patient list.
Whilst you were here o'erwhelmed with your
     grief—
A passion most unsuiting such a man—
Cassio came hither: I shifted him away,
And laid good 'scuse upon your ecstasy,   80
Bade him anon return and here speak with
     me;
The which he promised. Do but encave
     yourself,
And mark the fleers, the gibes, and notable
     scorns,
That dwell in every region of his face;
For I will make him tell the tale anew,
Where, how, how oft, how long ago, and
     when
He hath, and is again to cope your wife:
I say, but mark his gesture. Marry, pa-
     tience;
Or I shall say you are all in all in spleen,
And nothing of a man.
  Oth.   Dost thou hear, Iago?   90
I will be found most cunning in my patience;
But—dost thou hear?—most bloody.
  Iago.   That's not amiss;

But yet keep time in all. Will you withdraw?
                              [*Othello retires.*
Now will I question Cassio of Bianca,
A housewife that by selling her desires
Buys herself bread and clothes: it is a crea-
     ture
That dotes on Cassio; as 'tis the strumpet's
     plague
To beguile many and be beguiled by one:
He, when he hears of her, cannot refrain
From the excess of laughter. Here he comes:

             Re-enter CASSIO.

As he shall smile, Othello shall go mad;   101
And his unbookish jealousy must construe
Poor Cassio's smiles, gestures and light be-
     haviour,
Quite in the wrong. How do you now, lieu-
     tenant?
  Cas. The worser that you give me the ad-
     dition
Whose want even kills me.
  Iago. Ply Desdemona well, and you are
     sure on 't.
[*Speaking lower*] Now, if this suit lay in
     Bianca's power,
How quickly should you speed!
  Cas.   Alas, poor caitiff!
  Oth. Look, how he laughs already!   110
  Iago. I never knew woman love man so.
  Cas. Alas, poor rogue! I think, i' faith,
     she loves me.
  Oth. Now he denies it faintly, and laughs
     it out.
  Iago. Do you hear, Cassio?
  Oth.   Now he importunes him
To tell it o'er: go to; well said, well said.
  Iago. She gives it out that you shall marry
     her:
Do you intend it?
  Cas. Ha, ha, ha!   120
  Oth. Do you triumph, Roman? do you
     triumph?
  Cas. I marry her! what? a customer! Pri-
     thee, bear some charity to my wit; do not
     think it so unwholesome. Ha, ha, ha!
  Oth. So, so, so, so: they laugh that win.
  Iago. 'Faith, the cry goes that you shall
     marry her.

65. **civil,** i.e., in civilized society. 69. **unproper,**
not belonging exclusively to an individual. The meaning
"improper" is post-Shakespearean. 70. **peculiar,**
private, one's own. 76. **patient list,** within the bounds
of patience. 80. **ecstasy,** swoon. 82. **encave,** conceal.
83. **fleers,** sneers. 89. **spleen,** i.e., overcome by angry
passion.

93. **keep time,** use judgment and order. Iago here
seems to betray a little uneasiness with reference to the
forces he has awakened. 102. **unbookish,** ignorant.
105. **addition,** title. 121. **Roman.** The epithet arises
from the association of the Romans with the idea of
triumph. 122. **customer,** prostitute.

Cas. Prithee, say true.

Iago. I am a very villain else.

Oth. Have you scored me? Well. 130

Cas. This is the monkey's own giving out: she is persuaded I will marry her, out of her own love and flattery, not out of my promise.

Oth. Iago beckons me; now he begins the story.

Cas. She was here even now; she haunts me in every place. I was the other day talking on the sea-bank with certain Venetians; and thither comes the bauble, and, by this hand, she falls me thus about my neck—140

Oth. Crying, 'O dear Cassio!' as it were: his gesture imports it.

Cas. So hangs, and lolls, and weeps upon me; so hales, and pulls me: ha, ha, ha!

Oth. Now he tells how she plucked him to my chamber. O, I see that nose of yours, but not that dog I shall throw it to.

Cas. Well, I must leave her company.

Iago. Before me! look, where she comes.

Cas. 'Tis such another fitchew! marry, a perfumed one. 151

Enter BIANCA.

What do you mean by this haunting of me?

Bian. Let the devil and his dam haunt you! What did you mean by that same handkerchief you gave me even now? I was a fine fool to take it. I must take out the work?—A likely piece of work, that you should find it in your chamber, and not know who left it there! This is some minx's token, and I must take out the work? There; give it your hobby-horse: wheresoever you had it, I'll take out no work on 't. 161

Cas. How now, my sweet Bianca! how now! how now!

Oth. By heaven, that should be my handkerchief!

Bian. An you'll come to supper to-night, you may; an you will not, come when you are next prepared for. [*Exit.*

Iago. After her, after her.

Cas. 'Faith, I must; she'll rail in the street else. 171

Iago. Will you sup there?

Cas. 'Faith, I intend so.

Iago. Well, I may chance to see you; for I would very fain speak with you.

Cas. Prithee, come; will you?

Iago. Go to; say no more. [*Exit Cassio.*

Oth. [*Advancing*] How shall I murder him, Iago?

Iago. Did you perceive how he laughed at his vice? 181

Oth. O Iago!

Iago. And did you see the handkerchief?

Oth. Was that mine?

Iago. Yours, by this hand: and to see how he prizes the foolish woman your wife! she gave it him, and he hath given it his whore.

Oth. I would have him nine years a-killing. A fine woman! a fair woman! a sweet woman!

Iago. Nay, you must forget that. 190

Oth. Ay, let her rot, and perish, and be damned to-night; for she shall not live: no, my heart is turned to stone; I strike it, and it hurts my hand. O, the world hath not a sweeter creature: she might lie by an emperor's side and command him tasks.

Iago. Nay, that's not your way. 197

Oth. Hang her! I do but say what she is: so delicate with her needle: an admirable musician: O! she will sing the savageness out of a bear: of so high and plenteous wit and invention:— 201

Iago. She's the worse for all this.

Oth. O, a thousand thousand times: and then, of so gentle a condition!

Iago. Ay, too gentle.

Oth. Nay, that's certain: but yet the pity of it, Iago! O Iago, the pity of it, Iago!

Iago. If you are so fond over her iniquity, give her patent to offend; for, if it touch not you, it comes near nobody. 210

Oth. I will chop her into messes: cuckold me!

Iago. O, 'tis foul in her.

Oth. With mine officer!

Iago. That's fouler.

Oth. Get me some poison, Iago; this night: I'll not expostulate with her, lest her body and beauty unprovide my mind again: this night, Iago. 219

Iago. Do it not with poison, strangle her in her bed, even the bed she hath contaminated.

---

130. **scored me**, made up my reckoning, or branded me. 139. **bauble**, foolish person, trifler. 149. **Before me!** on my soul! 150. **fitchew**, polecat. 160. **hobby-horse**, lover; used contemptuously.

197. **your way**, i.e., the way you should think of her. 209. **patent**, license. 211. **messes**, dishes of food. 218. **unprovide**, weaken, unfit.

Oth. Good, good: the justice of it pleases: very good.

Iago. And for Cassio, let me be his undertaker: you shall hear more by midnight.

Oth. Excellent good. [*A trumpet within.*]
  What trumpet is that same?

Iago. Something from Venice, sure. 'tis Lodovico
Come from the duke: and, see, your wife is with him.

Enter LODOVICO, DESDEMONA, *and*
Attendants.

Lod. Save you, worthy general!

Oth.   With all my heart, sir.

Lod. The duke and senators of Venice greet you.   [*Gives him a letter.*

Oth. I kiss the instrument of their pleasures.   [*Opens the letter, and reads.*

Des. And what's the news, good cousin Lodovico?

Iago. I am very glad to see you, signior; Welcome to Cyprus.

Lod. I thank you. How does Lieutenant Cassio?

Iago. Lives, sir.

Des. Cousin, there's fall'n between him and my lord
An unkind breach: but you shall make all well.

Oth. Are you sure of that?

Des. My lord?

Oth. [*Reads*] 'This fail you not to do, as you will—'   240

Lod. He did not call; he's busy in the paper.
Is there division 'twixt my lord and Cassio?

Des. A most unhappy one: I would do much
To atone them, for the love I bear to Cassio.

Oth. Fire and brimstone!

Des.   My lord?

Oth.   Are you wise?

Des. What, is he angry?

Lod.   May be the letter moved him;
For, as I think, they do command him home,
Deputing Cassio in his government.

Des. Trust me, I am glad on 't.

Oth.   Indeed!

Des.   My lord?

Oth. I am glad to see you mad.

Des.   Why, sweet Othello,—

Oth. [*Striking her*] Devil!   251

Des. I have not deserved this.

Lod. My lord, this would not be believed in Venice,
Though I should swear I saw 't: 'tis very much:
Make her amends; she weeps.

Oth.   O devil, devil!
If that the earth could teem with woman's tears,
Each drop she falls would prove a crocodile.
Out of my sight!

Des. I will not stay to offend you. [*Going.*

Lod. Truly, an obedient lady:
I do beseech your lordship, call her back.   260

Oth. Mistress!

Des.   My lord?

Oth.   What would you with her, sir?

Lod. Who, I, my lord?

Oth. Ay; you did wish that I would make her turn:
Sir, she can turn, and turn, and yet go on,
And turn again; and she can weep, sir, weep;
And she's obedient, as you say, obedient,
Very obedient. Proceed you in your tears.
Concerning this, sir,—O well-painted passion!—
I am commanded home. Get you away;
I'll send for you anon. Sir, I obey the mandate,   270
And will return to Venice. Hence, avaunt!
                                        [*Exit Desdemona.*
Cassio shall have my place. And, sir, to-night,
I do entreat that we may sup together:
You are welcome, sir, to Cyprus.—Goats and monkeys!   [*Exit.*

Lod. Is this the noble Moor whom our full senate
Call all in all sufficient? Is this the nature
Whom passion could not shake? whose solid virtue
The shot of accident, nor dart of chance,
Could neither graze nor pierce?

Iago.   He is much changed.

Lod. Are his wits safe? is he not light of brain?   280

Iago. He's that he is: I may not breathe my censure

---

224. **undertaker,** i.e., let me settle with him.   248. **government,** office.

257. **prove a crocodile,** i.e., by weeping crocodile tears; the crocodile had the habit of shedding copious and feigned tears over the body of the man he was eating.   268. **well-painted passion,** well simulated emotion.

What he might be: if what he might he is not,
I would to heaven he were!
　　Lod.　　　　　　What, strike his wife!
　Iago. 'Faith, that was not so well; yet
　　would I knew
That stroke would prove the worst!
　　Lod.　　　　　　　　　Is it his use?
Or did the letters work upon his blood,
And new-create this fault?
　Iago.　　　　　　Alas, alas!
It is not honesty in me to speak
What I have seen and known. You shall
　　observe him,
And his own courses will denote him so　290
That I may save my speech: do but go
　　after,
And mark how he continues.
　Lod. I am sorry that I am deceived in
　　him.　　　　　　　　　　*[Exeunt.*

SCENE II.　*A room in the castle.*

Enter OTHELLO *and* EMILIA.

　Oth. You have seen nothing then?
　Emil. Nor ever heard, nor ever did sus-
　　pect.
　Oth. Yes, you have seen Cassio and she
　　together.
　Emil. But then I saw no harm, and then
　　I heard
Each syllable that breath made up between
　　them.
　Oth. What, did they never whisper?
　Emil.　　　　　　　Never, my lord.
　Oth. Nor send you out o' the way?
　Emil. Never.
　Oth. To fetch her fan, her gloves, her
　　mask, nor nothing?
　Emil. Never, my lord.　　　　　　10
　Oth. That's strange.
　Emil. I durst, my lord, to wager she is
　　honest,
Lay down my soul at stake: if you think
　　other,
Remove your thought; it doth abuse your
　　bosom.
If any wretch have put this in your head,
Let heaven requite it with the serpent's
　　curse!
For, if she be not honest, chaste, and true,
There's no man happy; the purest of their
　　wives

Is foul as slander.
　Oth.　　　　　　Bid her come hither: go.
　　　　　　　　　　　　　　　　[Exit Emilia.
She says enough; yet she's a simple bawd 20
That cannot say as much.　This is a subtle
　　whore,
A closet lock and key of villanous secrets:
And yet she'll kneel and pray; I have seen
　　her do 't.

Enter DESDEMONA *with* EMILIA.

　Des. My lord, what is your will?
　Oth.　　　　　Pray, chuck, come hither.
　Des. What is your pleasure?
　Oth.　　　　　　Let me see your eyes;
Look in my face.
　Des.　　　　What horrible fancy's this?
　Oth. [*To Emilia*] Some of your function,
　　mistress;
Leave procreants alone and shut the door;
Cough, or cry 'hem', if any body come:
Your mystery, your mystery: nay, dispatch.
　　　　　　　　　　　　　　　[Exit Emilia.
　Des. Upon my knees, what doth your
　　speech import?　　　　　　　　　　31
I understand a fury in your words,
But not the words.
　Oth. Why, what art thou?
　Des.　　　Your wife, my lord; your true
And loyal wife.
　Oth.　　　Come, swear it, damn thyself;
Lest, being like one of heaven, the devils
　　themselves
Should fear to seize thee: therefore be double
　　damn'd:
Swear thou art honest.
　Des.　　　Heaven doth truly know it.
　Oth. Heaven truly knows that thou art
　　false as hell.
　Des. To whom, my lord? with whom? how
　　am I false?　　　　　　　　　　40
　Oth. O Desdemona! away! away! away!
　Des. Alas the heavy day!　Why do you
　　weep?
Am I the motive of these tears, my lord?
If haply you my father do suspect
An instrument of this your calling back,
Lay not your blame on me: if you have lost
　　him,

22. **closet lock and key,** complete storeroom. 27.
function, profession. 30. **mystery,** trade, occupation.
41. **O . . . away.** Othello's rejection of testimony in the
form of the assurance he would most like to receive is
often regarded as an example of the dramatic convention of the "calumniator believed."

Scene ii.　16. serpent's curse. Cf. *Genesis*, iii, 14.

Why, I have lost him too.

Oth.   Had it pleased heaven
To try me with affliction; had they rain'd
All kinds of sores and shames on my bare
   head,
Steep'd me in poverty to the very lips,   50
Given to captivity me and my utmost hopes,
I should have found in some place of my soul
A drop of patience: but, alas, to make me
A fixed figure for the time of scorn
To point his slow unmoving finger at!
Yet could I bear that too; well, very well:
But there, where I have garner'd up my
   heart,
Where either I must live, or bear no life;
The fountain from the which my current
   runs,
Or else dries up; to be discarded thence!   60
Or keep it as a cistern for foul toads
To knot and gender in! Turn thy complex-
   ion there,
Patience, thou young and rose-lipp'd cheru-
   bin,—
Ay, there, look grim as hell!
   Des. I hope my noble lord esteems me
      honest.
   Oth. O, ay; as summer flies are in the
      shambles,
That quicken even with blowing. O thou
   weed,
Who art so lovely fair and smell'st so sweet
That the sense aches at thee, would thou
   hadst ne'er been born!
   Des. Alas, what ignorant sin have I com-
      mitted?   70
   Oth. Was this fair paper, this most goodly
      book,
Made to write 'whore' upon? What com-
   mitted!
Committed! O thou public commoner!
I should make very forges of my cheeks,
That would to cinders burn up modesty,
Did I but speak thy deeds. What committed!
Heaven stops the nose at it and the moon
   winks,
The bawdy wind that kisses all it meets

Is hush'd within the hollow mine of earth,
And will not hear it. What committed!   80
Impudent strumpet!
   Des.   By heaven, you do me wrong.
   Oth. Are not you a strumpet?
   Des.   No, as I am a Christian:
If to preserve this vessel for my lord
From any other foul unlawful touch
Be not to be a strumpet, I am none.
   Oth. What, not a whore?
   Des.   No, as I shall be saved.
   Oth. Is 't possible?
   Des. O, heaven forgive us!
   Oth.   I cry you mercy, then:
I took you for that cunning whore of Venice
That married with Othello. [*Raising his voice*]
      You, mistress,   90
That have the office opposite to Saint Peter,
And keep the gate of hell!

                Re-enter EMILIA.

                       You, you, ay, you!
We have done our course; there's money for
   your pains:
I pray you, turn the key and keep our
   counsel.   [*Exit.*
   Emil. Alas, what does this gentleman con-
      ceive?
How do you, madam? how do you, my good
   lady?
   Des. 'Faith, half asleep.
   Emil. Good madam, what's the matter
      with my lord?
   Des. With who?
   Emil. Why, with my lord, madam.   100
   Des. Who is thy lord?
   Emil.   He that is yours, sweet lady.
   Des. I have none: do not talk to me,
      Emilia;
I cannot weep; nor answer have I none,
But what should go by water. Prithee, to-
   night
Lay on my bed my wedding sheets: remem-
   ber;
And call thy husband hither.
   Emil.   Here's a change indeed! [*Exit.*
   Des. 'Tis meet I should be used so, very
      meet.
How have I been behaved, that he might
   stick
The small'st opinion on my least misuse?

48. **they,** heavenly powers. 54-55. **A fixed figure . . .
finger at!** Othello possibly thinks of himself as a man
set in a pillory at whom the scornful world points in
mockery. There seems to be a comparison with the
sundial, whose gnomon, or indicator, becomes the finger
of scornful time. For *unmoving* some editors adopt the
F reading, *and moving.* 62. **gender,** engender. **Turn
thy complexion,** grow pale. "At such an object do
thou, patience, thyself change color; at this do thou,
even thou, rosy cherub as thou art, look grim as hell"
(Johnson). 73. **commoner,** prostitute.

83. **vessel,** body; *1 Thessalonians,* iv, 4. 104. **go by
water,** be expressed by tears. 109. **opinion,** censure.
misuse, evil conduct.

Re-enter Emilia *with* Iago.

Iago. What is your pleasure, madam?
　How is 't with you?　　　　　　　110
Des. I cannot tell. Those that do teach
　young babes
Do it with gentle means and easy tasks:
He might have chid me so; for, in good
　faith,
I am a child to chiding.
　Iago.　　　　　What's the matter, lady?
Emil. Alas, Iago, my lord hath so be-
　whored her,
Thrown such despite and heavy terms upon
　her,
As true hearts cannot bear.
　Des. Am I that name, Iago?
　Iago.　　　　What name, fair lady?
Des. Such as she says my lord did say I
　was.
Emil. He call'd her whore: a beggar in his
　drink　　　　　　　　　　　120
Could not have laid such terms upon his
　callet.
　Iago. Why did he so?
　Des. I do not know; I am sure I am none
　such.
Iago. Do not weep, do not weep. Alas the
　day!
Emil. Hath she forsook so many noble
　matches,
Her father and her country and her
　friends,
To be call'd whore? would it not make one
　weep?
Des. It is my wretched fortune.
　Iago.　　　　　Beshrew him for 't!
How comes this trick upon him?
　Des.　　　　　Nay, heaven doth know.
Emil. I will be hang'd, if some eternal
　villain,　　　　　　　　　　130
Some busy and insinuating rogue,
Some cogging, cozening slave, to get some
　office,
Have not devised this slander; I'll be hang'd
　else.
　Iago. Fie, there is no such man; it is im-
　possible.
Des. If any such there be, heaven pardon
　him!
Emil. A halter pardon him! and hell gnaw
　his bones!

Why should he call her whore? who keeps her
　company?
What place? what time? what form? what
　likelihood?
The Moor's abused by some most villanous
　knave,
Some base notorious knave, some scurvy
　fellow.
O heaven, that such companions thou'ldst
　unfold,　　　　　　　　　　141
And put in every honest hand a whip
To lash the rascals naked through the world
Even from the east to the west!
　Iago.　　　　　Speak within door.
Emil. O, fie upon them! Some such
　squire he was
That turn'd your wit the seamy side without,
And made you to suspect me with the Moor.
　Iago. You are a fool; go to.
　Des.　　　　　O good Iago,
What shall I do to win my lord again?
Good friend, go to him; for, by this light of
　heaven,　　　　　　　　　　150
I know not how I lost him. Here I kneel:
If e'er my will did trespass 'gainst his love,
Either in discourse of thought or actual deed,
Or that mine eyes, mine ears, or any sense,
Delighted them in any other form;
Or that I do not yet, and ever did,
And ever will—though he do shake me off
To beggarly divorcement—love him dearly,
Comfort forswear me! Unkindness may do
　much;　　　　　　　　　　159
And his unkindness may defeat my life,
But never taint my love. I cannot say
　'whore:'
It doth abhor me now I speak the word;
To do the act that might the addition
　earn
Not the world's mass of vanity could make
　me.
　Iago. I pray you, be content; 'tis but his
　humour:
The business of the state does him offence,
And he does chide with you.
　Des. If 'twere no other,—
　Iago.　　　　　'Tis but so, I warrant.
　　　　　　　　　　[Trumpets within.
Hark, how these instruments summon to
　supper!
The messengers of Venice stay the meat: 170

---

116. **despite**, contempt, scorn. 119. **says.** F: *said.*
121. **callet**, lewd woman. 132. **cogging**, deceiving.
cozening, cheating.

141. **companions**, fellows; used contemptuously.
144. **Speak within door**, do not speak so loud. 153.
discourse, range. 160. **defeat**, destroy. 170. **stay
the meat**, are waiting for supper.

Go in, and weep not; all things shall be
well.

[*Exeunt Desdemona and Emilia.*

Enter RODERIGO.

How now, Roderigo!

Rod. I do not find that thou dealest justly
with me.

Iago. What in the contrary?   175

Rod. Every day thou daffest me with some
device, Iago; and rather, as it seems to me
now, keepest from me all conveniency than
suppliest me with the least advantage of
hope. I will indeed no longer endure it,
nor am I yet persuaded to put up in peace
what already I have foolishly suffered.

Iago. Will you hear me, Roderigo?

Rod. 'Faith, I have heard too much, for
your words and performances are no kin
together.

Iago. You charge me most unjustly. 186

Rod. With nought but truth. I have
wasted myself out of my means. The jewels
you have had from me to deliver to Desdemona would half have corrupted a votarist:
you have told me she hath received them and
returned me expectations and comforts of
sudden respect and acquaintance, but   192
I find none.

Iago. Well; go to; very well.

Rod. Very well! go to! I cannot go to,
man; nor 'tis not very well: nay, I think it
is scurvy, and begin to find myself fopped
in it.

Iago. Very well.

Rod. I tell you 'tis not very well. I will
make myself known to Desdemona: if she
will return me my jewels, I will give over
my suit and repent my unlawful solicitation;
if not, assure yourself I will seek satisfaction
of you.

Iago. You have said now.   204

Rod. Ay, and said nothing but what I
protest intendment of doing.

Iago. Why, now I see there's mettle in
thee, and even from this instant do build on
thee a better opinion than ever before. Give
me thy hand, Roderigo: thou hast taken
against me a most just exception; but yet,

I protest, I have dealt most directly in thy
affair.

Rod. It hath not appeared.   213

Iago. I grant indeed it hath not appeared,
and your suspicion is not without wit and
judgement. But, Roderigo, if thou hast
that in thee indeed, which I have greater
reason to believe now than ever, I mean
purpose, courage and valour, this night
show it: if thou the next night following
enjoy not Desdemona, take me from this
world with treachery and devise en-   221
gines for my life.

Rod. Well, what is it? is it within reason
and compass?

Iago. Sir, there is especial commission
come from Venice to depute Cassio in Othello's place.

Rod. Is that true? why, then Othello and
Desdemona return again to Venice.   228

Iago. O, no; he goes into Mauritania and
takes away with him the fair Desdemona,
unless his abode be lingered here by some
accident: wherein none can be so determinate
as the removing of Cassio.

Rod. How do you mean, removing of
him?

Iago. Why, by making him uncapable
of Othello's place; knocking out his
brains.

Rod. And that you would have me to
do?   237

Iago. Ay, if you dare do yourself a profit
and a right. He sups to-night with a harlotry, and thither will I go to him: he knows
not yet of his honourable fortune. If you
will watch his going thence, which I will
fashion to fall out between twelve and one,
you may take him at your pleasure: I will
be near to second your attempt, and he shall
fall between us. Come, stand not amazed
at it, but go along with me; I will show you
such a necessity in his death that you shall
think yourself bound to put it on him. It is
now high supper-time, and the night grows
to waste: about it.   250

Rod. I will hear further reason for this.

Iago. And you shall be satisfied.

[*Exeunt.*

---

176. **daffest me**, putst me off with an excuse. 178.
conveniency, advantage, opportunity. 181. **put up**,
submit to. 192. **respect**, notice, attention. 197.
fopped, fooled, duped. 204. **You . . . now**, well said,
quite right (Schmidt). 206. **intendment**, purpose,
intention.

221. **engines**, defined as "instruments of torture,"
and as "devices of plots" (against my life). 229. **Mauritania**, Roman name of northwest Africa, supposed
land of the Moors. 232. **determinate**, decisive. 239.
harlotry, courtesan. 249. **high supper-time**, defined
as "high time for supper"; *high* probably means "quite."

SCENE III. *Another room in the castle.*

Enter OTHELLO, LODOVICO, DESDEMONA,
   EMILIA, *and* Attendants.

Lod. I do beseech you, sir, trouble yourself
   no further.

Oth. O, pardon me; 'twill do me good to
   walk.

Lod. Madam, good night; I humbly thank
   your ladyship.

Des. Your honour is most welcome.

Oth.   Will you walk, sir?

O,—Desdemona,—

Des. My lord?

Oth. Get you to bed on the instant; I will
   be returned forthwith: dismiss your attendant there: look it be done.

Des. I will, my lord.   10

[*Exeunt Othello, Lodovico, and Attendants.*

Emil. How goes it now? he looks gentler
   than he did.

Des. He says he will return incontinent:
He hath commanded me to go to bed,
And bade me to dismiss you.

Emil.   Dismiss me!

Des. It was his bidding; therefore, good
   Emilia,
Give me my nightly wearing, and adieu:
We must not now displease him.

Emil. I would you had never seen him!

Des. So would not I: my love doth so
   approve him,
That even his stubbornness, his checks, his
   frowns,—   20
Prithee, unpin me,—have grace and favour
   in them.

Emil. I have laid those sheets you bade
   me on the bed.

Des. All's one. Good faith, how foolish are
   our minds!
If I do die before thee, prithee, shroud
   me
In one of those same sheets.

Emil.   Come, come, you talk.

Des. My mother had a maid call'd
   Barbara:
She was in love, and he she loved proved
   mad
And did forsake her: she had a song of
   'willow;'
An old thing 'twas, but it express'd her
   fortune,

And she died singing it: that song to-
   night   30
Will not go from my mind; I have much to
   do,
But to go hang my head all at one side,
And sing it like poor Barbara. Prithee, dispatch.

Emil. Shall I go fetch your night-gown?

Des.   No, unpin me here.
This Lodovico is a proper man.

Emil. A very handsome man.

Des. He speaks well.

Emil. I know a lady in Venice would have
walked barefoot to Palestine for a touch of
his nether lip.   40

Des. [*Singing*] The poor soul sat sighing
   by a sycamore tree,
   Sing all a green willow;
Her hand on her bosom, her head on her
   knee,
   Sing willow, willow, willow:
The fresh streams ran by her, and mur-
   mur'd her moans;
   Sing willow, willow, willow;
Her salt tears fell from her, and soften'd
   the stones;—

Lay by these:—

[*Singing*] Sing willow, willow, willow;
Prithee, hie thee; he'll come anon:—   50

[*Singing*] Sing all a green willow must be my
   garland.

Let nobody blame him; his scorn I approve,—

Nay, that's not next.—Hark! who is 't that
   knocks?

Emil. It's the wind.

Des. [*Singing*] I call'd my love false love;
   but what said he then?
   Sing willow, willow, willow:
If I court moe women, you'll couch with
   moe men.—

So, get thee gone; good night. Mine eyes
   do itch;
Doth that bode weeping?

Emil.   'Tis neither here nor there.

Des. I have heard it said so. O, these
   men, these men!   60
Dost thou in conscience think,—tell me,
   Emilia,—

---

32. **But to**, not to.   34. **night-gown**, dressing-gown.
41-57. **The poor soul**, etc. Desdemona's song is a
popular ballad apparently well-known in Shakespeare's
time. In the versions preserved the forsaken lover is a
man. Shakespeare has changed it to apply to Desdemona, and has made it personal by introducing the
pathetic little sketch of Barbara, her mother's maid.

12. **incontinent**, immediately.   20. **stubbornness**,
roughness, harshness.

That there be women do abuse their hus-
    bands
In such gross kind?
    Emil.   There be some such, no
    question.
    Des. Wouldst thou do such a deed for all
    the world?
    Emil. Why, would not you?
    Des.   No, by this heavenly light!
    Emil. Nor I neither by this heavenly
light; I might do 't as well i' the dark.
    Des. Wouldst thou do such a deed for all
    the world?
    Emil. The world's a huge thing: it is a
    great price
For a small vice.   69
    Des. In troth, I think thou wouldst
    not.
    Emil. In troth, I think I should; and un-
do 't when I had done. Marry, I would not
do such a thing for a joint-ring, nor for
measures of lawn, nor for gowns, petticoats,
nor caps, nor any petty exhibition; but, for
the whole world,—why, who would not make
her husband a cuckold to make him a monarch? I should venture purgatory for 't.
    Des. Beshrew me, if I would do such a
    wrong
For the whole world.   79
    Emil. Why, the wrong is but a wrong i'
the world; and having the world for your
labour, 'tis a wrong in your own world, and
you might quickly make it right.
    Des. I do not think there is any such
    woman.
    Emil. Yes, a dozen; and as many to the
vantage as would store the world they played
for.
But I do think it is their husbands' faults
If wives do fall: say that they slack their
    duties,
And pour our treasures into foreign laps,
Or else break out in peevish jealousies, 90
Throwing restraint upon us; or say they
    strike us,
Or scant our former having in despite;
Why, we have galls, and though we have
    some grace,
Yet have we some revenge. Let husbands
    know

Their wives have sense like them: they see
    and smell
And have their palates both for sweet and
    sour,
As husbands have. What is it that they do
When they change us for others? Is it
    sport?
I think it is: and doth affection breed it?
I think it doth: is 't frailty that thus errs? 100
It is so too: and have not we affections,
Desires for sport, and frailty, as men have?
Then let them use us well: else let them
    know,
The ills we do, their ills instruct us so.
    Des. Good night, good night: heaven me
    such uses send,
Not to pick bad from bad, but by bad mend!
                        [*Exeunt.*

ACT V.

Scene I. *Cyprus.* *A street.*

Enter Iago *and* Roderigo.

    Iago. Here, stand behind this bulk;
    straight will he come:
Wear thy good rapier bare, and put it home:
Quick, quick; fear nothing; I'll be at thy
    elbow:
It makes us, or it mars us; think on that,
And fix most firm thy resolution.
    Rod. Be near at hand; I may miscarry in 't.
    Iago. Here, at thy hand: be bold, and
    take thy stand.   [*Retires.*
    Rod. I have no great devotion to the deed;
And yet he hath given me satisfying rea-
    sons:
'Tis but a man gone. Forth, my sword: he
    dies.   10
    Iago. I have rubb'd this young quat
    almost to the sense,
And he grows angry. Now, whether he kill
    Cassio,
Or Cassio him, or each do kill the other,
Every way makes my gain: live Roderigo,
He calls me to a restitution large
Of gold and jewels that I bobb'd from him,
As gifts to Desdemona;
It must not be: if Cassio do remain,
He hath a daily beauty in his life

---

    73. **joint-ring,** a ring made in separable halves as a
lover's token. 75. **exhibition,** gift, present. 85-86. **to
the vantage,** in addition, to boot. 92. **having,** allowance (of money). 93. **galls,** are capable of resenting
injury and insult. **grace,** i.e., to forgive.

    99. **affection,** inclination, bent of mind.
    Act V. Scene i. 1. **bulk,** framework projecting from
the front of a shop. 11. **quat,** pimple, pustule; used
contemptuously. **to the sense,** to the quick. 16.
bobb'd, filched cunningly.

That makes me ugly; and, besides, the Moor
May unfold me to him; there stand I in much peril: 21
No, he must die. But so: I hear him coming.

Enter Cassio.

Rod. I know his gait, 'tis he.—Villain' thou diest!   [*Makes a pass at Cassio·*
Cas. That thrust had been mine enemy indeed,
But that my coat is better than thou know'st:
I will make proof of thine.
                    [*Draws, and wounds Roderigo.*
Rod.   O, I am slain!
[*Iago from behind wounds Cassio in the leg, and exit.*
Cas. I am maim'd for ever. Help, ho! murder! murder!   [*Falls.*

Enter Othello.

Oth. The voice of Cassio: Iago keeps his word.
Rod. O, villain that I am!
Oth.   It is even so.
Cas. O, help, ho! light! a surgeon!   30
Oth. 'Tis he:—O brave Iago, honest and just,
That hast such noble sense of thy friend's wrong!
Thou teachest me. Minion, your dear lies dead,
And your unblest fate hies: strumpet, I come.
Forth of my heart those charms, thine eyes, are blotted;
Thy bed, lust-stain'd, shall with lust's blood be spotted.   [*Exit.*

Enter Lodovico *and* Gratiano.

Cas. What, ho! no watch? no passage? murder! murder!
Gra. 'Tis some mischance; the cry is very direful.
Cas. O, help!
Lod. Hark!   40
Rod. O wretched villain!
Lod. Two or three groan: it is a heavy night:

These may be counterfeits: let's think 't unsafe
To come in to the cry without more help.
Rod. Nobody come? then shall I bleed to death.
Lod. Hark!

Re-enter Iago, *with a light.*

Gra. Here's one comes in his shirt, with light and weapons.
Iago. Who's there? whose noise is this that cries on murder?
Lod. We do not know.
Iago.   Did not you hear a cry?
Cas. Here, here! for heaven's sake, help me!
Iago.   What's the matter?   50
Gra. This is Othello's ancient, as I take it.
Lod. The same indeed; a very valiant fellow.
Iago. What are you here that cry so grievously?
Cas. Iago? O, I am spoil'd, undone by villains!
Give me some help.
Iago. O me, lieutenant! what villains have done this?
Cas. I think that one of them is hereabout,
And cannot make away.
Iago.   O treacherous villains!
What are you there? come in, and give some help.   [*To Lodovico and Gratiano.*
Rod. O, help me here!   60
Cas. That's one of them.
Iago.   O murderous slave! O villain!
                    [*Stabs Roderigo.*
Rod. O damn'd Iago! O inhuman dog!
Iago. Kill men i' the dark!—Where be these bloody thieves?—
How silent is this town!—Ho! murder! murder!—
What may you be? are you of good or evil?
Lod. As you shall prove us, praise us.
Iago. Signior Lodovico?
Lod. He, sir.
Iago. I cry you mercy. Here's Cassio hurt by villains.
Gra. Cassio!   70
Iago. How is 't, brother!
Cas. My leg is cut in two.
Iago.   Marry, heaven forbid!
Light, gentlemen: I'll bind it with my shirt.

21. **unfold**, reveal, betray. 25. **coat**, coat of mail.
33. **Minion**, hussy, jade. 37. **passage**, people passing.
42. **heavy**, thick, cloudy.

48. **cries on**, cries out. 65. **What**, who.

Enter BIANCA.

Bian. What is the matter, ho? who is 't
that cried?

Iago. Who is 't that cried?

Bian. O my dear Cassio! my sweet Cassio!
O Cassio, Cassio, Cassio!

Iago. O notable strumpet! Cassio, may
you suspect
Who they should be that have thus mangled
you?

Cas. No.   80

Gra. I am sorry to find you thus: I have
been to seek you.

Iago. Lend me a garter. So. O, for a
chair,
To bear him easily hence!

Bian. Alas, he faints! O Cassio, Cassio,
Cassio!

Iago. Gentlemen all, I do suspect this
trash
To be a party in this injury.
Patience awhile, good Cassio. Come, come;
Lend me a light. Know we this face or no?
Alas, my friend and my dear countryman
Roderigo! no:—yes, sure:—O heaven! Rod-
erigo.   90

Gra. What, of Venice?

Iago. Even he, sir: did you know him?

Gra.   Know him! ay.

Iago. Signior Gratiano? I cry you gentle
pardon;
These bloody accidents must excuse my
manners,
That so neglected you.

Gra.   I am glad to see you.

Iago. How do you, Cassio? O, a chair, a
chair!

Gra. Roderigo!

Iago. He, he, 'tis he. [*A chair brought in.*]
O, that's well said; the chair.
Some good man bear him carefully from
hence;
I'll fetch the general's surgeon. [*To Bianca*]
For you, mistress,   100
Save you your labour. He that lies slain
here, Cassio,
Was my dear friend: what malice was be-
tween you?

Cas. None in the world; nor do I know
the man.

Iago. [*To Bian.*] What, look you pale? O,
bear him out o' the air.

[*Cassio and Roderigo are borne off.*

Stay you, good gentlemen. Look you pale,
mistress?
Do you perceive the gastness of her eye?
Nay, if you stare, we shall hear more anon.
Behold her well; I pray you, look upon
her:
Do you see, gentlemen? nay, guiltiness will
speak,
Though tongues were out of use.   110

Enter EMILIA.

Emil. 'Las, what's the matter? what's the
matter, husband?

Iago. Cassio hath here been set on in the
dark
By Roderigo and fellows that are scaped:
He's almost slain, and Roderigo dead.

Emil. Alas, good gentleman! alas, good
Cassio!

Iago. This is the fruit of whoring. Prithee,
Emilia,
Go know of Cassio where he supp'd to-night.
[*To Bianca*] What, do you shake at that?

Bian. He supp'd at my house; but I therefore shake not.

Iago. O, did he so? I charge you, go with
me.   120

Emil. Fie, fie upon thee, strumpet!

Bian. I am no strumpet; but of life as
honest
As you that thus abuse me.

Emil.   As I! foh! fie upon thee!

Iago. Kind gentlemen, let's go see poor
Cassio dress'd.
Come, mistress, you must tell 's another tale.
Emilia, run you to the citadel,
And tell my lord and lady what hath happ'd.
Will you go on? I pray. [*Aside*] This is the
night
That either makes me or fordoes me quite.

[*Exeunt.*

SCENE II. *A bedchamber in the castle:* DES-
DEMONA *in bed asleep; a light burning.*

Enter OTHELLO.

Oth. It is the cause, it is the cause, my
soul,—

---

106. **gastness,** terror, ghastliness.   129. **fordoes,**
undoes, ruins.   Iago's uneasiness is again apparent in
this scene.
Scene ii.   1. **It is the cause.**   If Othello's words are
taken quite generally to mean that he defends his act on
the grounds of pure justice, one must suppose a shift in
the sense after the first line, for *it* in line 2 seems to
refer to Desdemona's supposed unchastity. The passage
has caused much perplexity.

---

82. **chair,** sedan chair.   85. **trash,** worthless thing,
ie.., Bianca.

Let me not name it to you, you chaste
    stars!—
It is the cause. Yet I'll not shed her blood;
Nor scar that whiter skin of hers than snow,
And smooth as monumental alabaster.
Yet she must die, else she'll betray more
    men.
Put out the light, and then put out the light:
If I quench thee, thou flaming minister,
I can again thy former light restore,
Should I repent me: but once put out thy
    light,   10
Thou cunning'st pattern of excelling nature,
I know not where is that Promethean heat
That can thy light relume. When I have
    pluck'd the rose,
I cannot give it vital growth again,
It must needs wither: I'll smell it on the tree.
          [*Kissing her.*
Ah, balmy breath, that dost almost persuade
Justice to break her sword! One more, one
    more.
Be thus when thou art dead, and I will kill
    thee,
And love thee after. One more, and this the
    last:
So sweet was ne'er so fatal. I must weep, 20
But they are cruel tears: this sorrow's
    heavenly;
It strikes where it doth love. She wakes.
  Des. Who's there? Othello?
  Oth.   Ay, Desdemona.
  Des. Will you come to bed, my lord?
  Oth. Have you pray'd to-night, Des-
    demona?
  Des.   Ay, my lord.
  Oth. If you bethink yourself of any crime
Unreconciled as yet to heaven and grace,
Solicit for it straight.
  Des. Alas, my lord, what do you mean by
    that?
  Oth. Well, do it, and be brief; I will
    walk by: 30
I would not kill thy unprepared spirit;
No; heaven forfend! I would not kill thy
    soul.
  Des. Talk you of killing?
  Oth.   Ay, I do.
  Des.   Then heaven
Have mercy on me!
  Oth.   Amen, with all my heart!

  Des. If you say so, I hope you will not
    kill me.
  Oth. Hum!
  Des. And yet I fear you; for you are fatal
    then
When your eyes roll so: why I should fear
    I know not,
Since guiltiness I know not; but yet I feel
    I fear.
  Oth. Think on thy sins.
  Des.   They are loves I bear to you. 40
  Oth. Ay, and for that thou diest.
  Des. That death's unnatural that kills for
    loving.
Alas, why gnaw you so your nether lip?
Some bloody passion shakes your very
    frame:
These are portents; but yet I hope, I hope,
They do not point on me.
  Oth.   Peace, and be still!
  Des. I will so. What's the matter?
  Oth. That handkerchief which I so loved
    and gave thee
Thou gavest to Cassio.
  Des.   No, by my life and soul!
Send for the man, and ask him.
  Oth.   Sweet soul, take heed, 50
Take heed of perjury; thou art on thy death-
    bed.
  Des. Ay, but not yet to die.
  Oth.   Yes, presently:
Therefore confess thee freely of thy sin;
For to deny each article with oath
Cannot remove nor choke the strong con-
    ception
That I do groan withal. Thou art to die.
  Des. Then Lord have mercy on me!
  Oth.   I say, amen.
  Des. And have you mercy too! I never did
Offend you in my life; never loved Cassio
But with such general warranty of heaven 60
As I might love; I never gave him token.
  Oth. By heaven, I saw my handkerchief
    in 's hand.
O perjured woman! thou dost stone my heart,
And makest me call what I intend to do
A murder, which I thought a sacrifice:
I saw the handkerchief.
  Des.   He found it then;
I never gave it him: send for him hither;
Let him confess a truth.
  Oth.   He hath confess'd.

---

12. **Promethean heat,** divine fire; allusion to the
theft of fire from heaven by Prometheus. 13. **relume,**
rekindle. 21. **this . . . heavenly,** this tenderness, with
which I lament the punishment which justice compels me
to inflict, is a holy passion (Johnson).

55. **conception,** plan, intention. 63. **stone,** turn to
stone, harden; Othello means that he will be tempted to
kill her in sheer anger because of her perjury.

Des. What, my lord?

Oth. That he hath used thee.

Des.   How? unlawfully?

Oth.   Ay.   70

Des. He will not say so.

Oth.   No, his mouth is stopp'd;
Honest Iago hath ta'en order for 't.

Des. O! my fear interprets: what, is he
   dead?

Oth. Had all his hairs been lives, my great
   revenge
Had stomach for them all.

Des. Alas! he is betray'd and I undone.

Oth. Out, strumpet! weep'st thou for him
   to my face?

Des. O, banish me, my lord, but kill me not!

Oth. Down, strumpet!

Des. Kill me to-morrow: let me live to-
   night!   80

Oth. Nay, if you strive,—

Des. But half an hour!

Oth.   Being done, there is no pause.

Des. But while I say one prayer!

Oth.   It is too late.   [*He stifles her.*

Emil. [*Within*] My lord, my lord! what,
   ho! my lord, my lord!

Oth. What noise is this? Not dead? not
   yet quite dead?
I that am cruel am yet merciful;
I would not have thee linger in thy pain:
So, so.

Emil. [*Within*] What, ho! my lord, my
   lord!

Oth.   Who's there?

Emil. [*Within*] O, good my lord, I would
   speak a word with you!   90

Oth. Yes: 'tis Emilia. By and by. She's
   dead.
'Tis like she comes to speak of Cassio's
   death.—
The noise was here. Ha! no more moving?
Still as the grave. Shall she come in? were 't
   good?—
I think she stirs again:—no. What's best
   to do?
If she come in, she'll sure speak to my wife:
My wife! my wife! what wife? I have no
   wife.

O, insupportable! O heavy hour!
Methinks it should be now a huge eclipse
Of sun and moon, and that the affrighted
   globe
Should yawn at alteration.

Emil. [*Within*] I do beseech you   101
That I may speak with you, O, good my
   lord!

Oth. I had forgot thee: O, come in,
   Emilia:
Soft; by and by. Let me the curtains draw.
Where art thou?   [*Unlocks the door.*

Enter EMILIA.

         What's the matter with thee now?

Emil. O, my good lord, yonder's foul murders done!

Oth. What, now?

Emil. But now, my lord.

Oth. It is the very error of the moon;
She comes more nearer earth than she was
   wont,
And makes men mad.   111

Emil. Cassio, my lord, hath kill'd a
   young Venetian
Call'd Roderigo.

Oth.   Roderigo kill'd!
And Cassio kill'd!

Emil.   No, Cassio is not kill'd.

Oth. Not Cassio kill'd! then murder's out
   of tune,
And sweet revenge grows harsh.

Des. O, falsely, falsely murder'd!

Emil.   Alas, what cry is that?

Oth. That! what?

Emil. Out, and alas! that was my lady's
   voice.   119
Help! help, ho! help! O lady, speak again!
Sweet Desdemona! O sweet mistress, speak!

Des. A guiltless death I die.

Emil. O, who hath done this deed?

Des. Nobody; I myself. Farewell:
Commend me to my kind lord: O, farewell!   [*Dies.*

Oth. Why, how should she be murder'd?

Emil.   Alas, who knows?

Oth. You heard her say herself, it was
   not I.

Emil. She said so: I must needs report the
   truth.

72. **ta'en order**, taken measures. 75. **stomach**,
appetite. 82. **Being . . . pause**, i.e., when the execution
of the deed has once begun, there is no stopping. 88.
So, so. "The stage tradition, dating apparently from
the time of Garrick, is for Othello to stab Desdemona.
There is, however, no necessity for assuming such an
action, and it is more likely that he renews his attempt
to smother her" (Parrott).

101. **yawn**, gape in amazement, i.e., there would be
an earthquake, since according to Pliny, earthquakes
often happen during eclipses. **at alteration**, at the
change. 109. **error**, aberration, irregularity.

Oth. She's, like a liar, gone to burning
hell:
'Twas I that kill'd her.

    Emil.   O, the more angel she, 130
And you the blacker devil!

    Oth. She turn'd to folly, and she was a
whore.

    Emil. Thou dost belie her, and thou art a
devil.

    Oth. She was false as water.

    Emil.   Thou art rash as fire, to say
That she was false: O, she was heavenly true!

    Oth. Cassio did top her; ask thy husband
else.
O, I were damn'd beneath all depth in hell,
But that I did proceed upon just grounds
To this extremity. Thy husband knew it all.

    Emil. My husband!   140

    Oth. Thy husband.

    Emil. That she was false to wedlock?

    Oth. Ay, with Cassio. Nay, had she been
true,
If heaven would make me such another
world
Of one entire and perfect chrysolite,
I'ld not have sold her for it.

    Emil. My husband!

    Oth.   Ay, 'twas he that told me first:
An honest man he is, and hates the slime
That sticks on filthy deeds.

    Emil.   My husband!

    Oth. What needs this iteration, woman?
I say thy husband.   150

    Emil. O mistress, villany hath made
mocks with love!
My husband say that she was false!

    Oth.   He, woman;
I say thy husband: dost understand the
word?
My friend, thy husband, honest, honest Iago.

    Emil. If he say so, may his pernicious soul
Rot half a grain a day! he lies to the heart:
She was too fond of her most filthy bargain.

    Oth. Ha!

    Emil. Do thy worst:
This deed of thine is no more worthy
heaven   160
Than thou wast worthy her.

    Oth.   Peace, you were best.

    Emil. Thou hast not half that power to do
me harm

As I have to be hurt. O gull! O dolt!
As ignorant as dirt! thou has done a
deed—
I care not for thy sword; I'll make thee
known,
Though I lost twenty lives.—Help! help, ho!
help!
The Moor hath kill'd my mistress! Murder!
murder!

    Enter MONTANO, GRATIANO, IAGO,
        and others.

    Mon. What is the matter? How now,
general!

    Emil. O, are you come, Iago? you have
done well,
That men must lay their murders on your
neck.

    Gra. What is the matter?   171

    Emil. Disprove this villain, if thou be'st a
man:
He says thou told'st him that his wife was
false:
I know thou didst not, thou'rt not such a
villain:
Speak, for my heart is full.

    Iago. I told him what I thought, and told
no more
Than what he found himself was apt and
true.

    Emil. But did you ever tell him she was
false?

    Iago. I did.

    Emil. You told a lie; an odious, damned
lie;   180
Upon my soul, a lie, a wicked lie.
She false with Cassio!—did you say with
Cassio?

    Iago. With Cassio, mistress. Go to, charm
your tongue.

    Emil. I will not charm my tongue; I am
bound to speak:
My mistress here lies murder'd in her bed,—

    All. O heavens forfend!

    Emil. And your reports have set the
murder on.

    Oth. Nay, stare not, masters: it is true, in-
deed.

    Gra. 'Tis a strange truth.

    Mon. O monstrous act!

    Emil.   Villany, villany, villany! 190
I think upon 't, I think: I smell 't: O villany!—

---

132. **folly,** unchastity. 145. **chrysolite,** the golden
stone; a name given to various precious stones of green
color. 151. **made mocks with,** derided, made sport of.

163. **to be hurt,** i.e., to endure hurting. 177. **apt,**
natural, likely. 183. **charm,** keep silent.

I thought so then:—I'll kill myself for grief:—
O villany, villany!

Iago. What, are you mad? I charge you, get you home.

Emil. Good gentlemen, let me have leave to speak:
'Tis proper I obey him, but not now.
Perchance, Iago, I will ne'er go home.

Oth. O! O! O!   [*He falls on the bed.*

Emil. Nay, lay thee down and roar;
For thou hast kill'd the sweetest innocent
That e'er did lift up eye.

Oth. [*Rising*] O, she was foul!   200
I scarce did know you, uncle: there lies your niece,
Whose breath, indeed, these hands have newly stopp'd:
I know this act shows horrible and grim.

Gra. Poor Desdemona! I am glad thy father's dead:
Thy match was mortal to him, and pure grief
Shore his old thread in twain: did he live now,
This sight would make him do a desperate turn,
Yea, curse his better angel from his side,
And fall to reprobation.

Oth. 'Tis pitiful; but yet Iago knows   210
That she with Cassio hath the act of shame
A thousand times committed; Cassio confess'd it:
And she did gratify his amorous works
With that recognizance and pledge of love
Which I first gave her; I saw it in his hand:
It was a handkerchief, an antique token
My father gave my mother.

Emil. O heaven! O heavenly powers!

Iago. Come, hold your peace.

Emil. 'Twill out, 'twill out: I peace!
No, I will speak as liberal as the north: 220
Let heaven and men and devils, let them all,
All, all, cry shame against me, yet I'll speak.

Iago. Be wise, and get you home.

Emil.   I will not.
          [*Iago offers to stab Emilia.*
Gra.   Fie!

Your sword upon a woman?

Emil. O thou dull Moor! that handkerchief thou speak'st of
I found by fortune and did give my husband;
For often, with a solemn earnestness,
More than indeed belong'd to such a trifle,
He begg'd of me to steal it.

Iago.   Villanous whore!

Emil. She give it Cassio! no, alas! I found it,   230
And I did give 't my husband.

Iago.   Filth, thou liest!

Emil. By heaven, I do not, I do not, gentlemen.
O murderous coxcomb! what should such a fool
Do with so good a woman?

Oth.   Are there no stones in heaven
But what serve for the thunder?—Precious villain!
          [*He runs at Iago: Iago, from behind, stabs
                    Emilia, and exit.*

Gra. The woman falls; sure, he hath kill'd his wife.

Emil. Ay, ay: O, lay me by my mistress' side.

Gra. He's gone, but his wife's kill'd.

Mon. 'Tis a notorious villain. Take you this weapon,
Which I have here recover'd from the Moor:
Come, guard the door without; let him not pass,   241
But kill him rather. I'll after that same villain,
For 'tis a damned slave.
          [*Exeunt Montano and Gratiano.*

Oth.   I am not valiant neither,
But every puny whipster gets my sword:
But why should honour outlive honesty?
Let it go all.

Emil. What did thy song bode, lady?
Hark, canst thou hear me? I will play the swan,
And die in music. [*Singing*] Willow, willow, willow.—
Moor, she was chaste; she loved thee, cruel Moor;
So come my soul to bliss, as I speak true;   250

192. **then,** i.e., at some earlier time, probably IV, ii, 130-144, when she suspected the machinations of *some eternal villain:* she did not, however, suspect Iago until this moment. 206. **Shore,** cut. 209. **reprobation,** damnation, rejection by God. 214. **recognizance,** token. 217. **My . . . mother.** This statement is not consistent with that in III, iv, 56, though perhaps not utterly irreconcilable. 220. **liberal as the north,** freely as the north wind.

226. **fortune,** chance. 233. **coxcomb,** fool; addressed to Othello. 234. **stones in heaven,** thunderbolts. It was supposed that real stones fell with the thunder and caused the damage. 244. **whipster,** contemptible fellow. 245. **honour outlive honesty.** Othello realizes that he has done a shameful deed; he asks why his reputation for valor should endure.

So speaking as I think, I die, I die. [*Dies.*
  Oth. I have another weapon in this
    chamber;
It is a sword of Spain, the ice-brook's
    temper:—
O, here it is. Uncle, I must come forth.
  Gra. [*Within*] If thou attempt it, it will
    cost thee dear:
Thou hast no weapon, and perforce must
    suffer.
  Oth. Look in upon me then and speak
    with me,
Or, naked as I am, I will assault thee.

Re-enter GRATIANO.

  Gra. What is the matter?
  Oth.   Behold, I have a weapon;
A better never did itself sustain   260
Upon a soldier's thigh: I have seen the day,
That, with this little arm and this good
    sword,
I have made my way through more impedi-
    ments
Than twenty times your stop: but, O vain
    boast!
Who can control his fate? 'tis not so now.
Be not afraid, though you do see me
    weapon'd;
Here is my journey's end, here is my butt,
And very sea-mark of my utmost sail.
Do you go back dismay'd? 'tis a lost fear;
Man but a rush against Othello's breast, 270
And he retires. Where should Othello go?
Now, how dost thou look now? O ill-starr'd
    wench!
Pale as thy smock! when we shall meet at
    compt,
This look of thine will hurl my soul from
    heaven,
And fiends will snatch at it. Cold, cold, my
    girl!
Even like thy chastity. O cursed slave!
Whip me, ye devils,
From the possession of this heavenly sight!
Blow me about in winds! roast me in sulphur!
Wash me in steep-down gulfs of liquid fire!280
O Desdemona! Desdemona! dead!
Oh! Oh! Oh!

Enter LODOVICO, MONTANO, CASSIO *carried
in a chair, and* Officers *with* IAGO, *prisoner.*

  Lod. Where is this rash and most un-
    fortunate man?
  Oth. That's he that was Othello: here I
    am.
  Lod. Where is that viper? bring the villain
    forth.
  Oth. I look down towards his feet; but
    that's a fable.
If that thou be'st a devil, I cannot kill thee.
                     [*Wounds Iago.*
  Lod. Wrench his sword from him.
  Iago.   I bleed, sir; but not kill'd.
  Oth. I am not sorry neither: I'ld have thee
    live;
For, in my sense, 'tis happiness to die.   290
  Lod. O thou Othello, that wert once so
    good,
Fall'n in the practice of a damned slave,
What shall be said to thee?
  Oth.   Why, any thing:
An honourable murderer, if you will;
For nought I did in hate, but all in honour.
  Lod. This wretch hath part confess'd his
    villany:
Did you and he consent in Cassio's death?
  Oth. Ay.
  Cas. Dear general, I never gave you
    cause.
  Oth. I do believe it, and I ask you par-
    don.
Will you, I pray, demand that demi-devil 301
Why he hath thus ensnared my soul and
    body?
  Iago. Demand me nothing: what you
    know, you know:
From this time forth I never will speak word.
  Lod. What, not to pray?
  Gra.   Torments will ope your lips.
  Oth. Well, thou dost best.
  Lod. Sir, you shall understand what hath
    befall'n,
Which, as I think, you know not. Here is a
    letter
Found in the pocket of the slain Roderigo;
And here another: the one of them imports310
The death of Cassio to be undertook
By Roderigo.
  Oth. O villain!

---

253. **ice-brook's temper**, usually defined as "tempered in ice-cold water." F has *Ice brookes*, Q, *Isebrookes*;
Onions notes that *Isebrooke* is the Elizabethan form for
Innsbruck, once noted for fine steel. 258. **naked**, unarmed. 264. **your stop**, what you can stop. 267. **butt**,
mark for archery, goal, limit. 268. **sea-mark**, beacon.
270. **Man**, provide, as in manning a gun. 273. **smock**,
inner garment. **compt**, account, judgment day.

286. **towards his feet**, i.e., to see if they were cloven
like a devil's. 304. **From . . . word.** Iago has all the
way through the self-command of a soldier; his refusal
to speak is characteristic.

Cas.   Most heathenish and most gross!
Lod. Now here's another discontented
    paper,
Found in his pocket too; and this, it seems,
Roderigo meant to have sent this damned
    villain;
But that belike Iago in the interim
Came in and satisfied him.
    Oth.   O the pernicious caitiff!
How came you, Cassio, by that handkerchief
That was my wife's?
    Cas.   I found it in my chamber: 320
And he himself confess'd but even now
That there he dropp'd it for a special purpose
Which wrought to his desire.
    Oth.   O fool! fool! fool!
Cas. There is besides in Roderigo's letter,
How he upbraids Iago, that he made him
Brave me upon the watch; whereon it came
That I was cast: and even but now he spake,
After long seeming dead, Iago hurt him,
Iago set him on.
    Lod. You must forsake this room, and
        go with us: 330
Your power and your command is taken off,
And Cassio rules in Cyprus.   For this slave,
If there be any cunning cruelty
That can torment him much and hold him
    long,
It shall be his.   You shall close prisoner rest,
Till that the nature of your fault be known
To the Venetian state.   Come, bring him
    away.
    Oth. Soft you; a word or two before you go.
I have done the state some service, and they
    know 't.   339
No more of that.   I pray you, in your letters,
When you shall these unlucky deeds relate,
Speak of me as I am; nothing extenuate,
Nor set down aught in malice: then must
    you speak
Of one that loved not wisely but too well;
Of one not easily jealous, but being wrought

Perplex'd in the extreme; of one whose hand,
Like the base Indian, threw a pearl away
Richer than all his tribe; of one whose
    subdued eyes,
Albeit unused to the melting mood,
Drop tears as fast as the Arabian trees   350
Their medicinal gum.   Set you down this;
And say besides, that in Aleppo once,
Where a malignant and a turban'd Turk
Beat a Venetian and traduced the state,
I took by the throat the circumcised dog,
And smote him, thus.   [*Stabs himself.*
    Lod. O bloody period!
    Gra.   All that's spoke is marr'd.
    Oth. I kiss'd thee ere I kill'd thee: no way
        but this;
Killing myself, to die upon a kiss.
              [*Falls on the bed, and dies.*
    Cas. This did I fear, but thought he had
        no weapon;   360
For he was great of heart.
    Lod.   [*To Iago*] O Spartan dog,
More fell than anguish, hunger, or the sea!
Look on the tragic loading of this bed;
This is thy work: the object poisons sight;
Let it be hid.   Gratiano, keep the house,
And seize upon the fortunes of the Moor,
For they succeed on you.   To you, lord
    governor,
Remains the censure of this hellish villain;
The time, the place, the torture: O, enforce
    it!
Myself will straight aboard; and to the state
This heavy act with heavy heart relate.   371
              [*Exeunt.*

346. Perplex'd, confounded, distracted.   **347. Indian,** so Q and F 2-3-4; F1: *Iudean,* which has been defended by some editors as an allusion to Herod, who
slew Mariamne in a fit of jealousy, or as an allusion to
Judas Iscariot, the betrayer of Christ.   Coleridge thought
that Othello compares himself to a rude Indian—American savage.   If *Indian* is correct, there may be back of
the reading some story which we do not know.   **350-351.
tears . . . gum.**   Back of the comparison of tears to
Arabian gums lies Pliny's description of the aromatic
wealth of Arabia.   **352. Aleppo,** a Turkish city where
the Venetians had special trading privileges.   It is
stated that it was immediate death for a Christian to
strike a Turk in Aleppo; Othello risked his life for the
honor of Venice.   **357. period,** termination, conclusion.
361. Spartan dog.   Spartan dogs were noted for their
savagery.

314. **discontented,** expressing dissatisfaction.   318.
caitiff, wretch.   **331. taken off,** taken away.   342.
extenuate, diminish, depreciate; the idea is contrasted
with the thought of *malice* in the following line.

KING LEAR

DRAMATIS PERSONÆ

LEAR, king of Britain.
KING OF FRANCE.
DUKE OF BURGUNDY.
DUKE OF CORNWALL.
DUKE OF ALBANY.
EARL OF KENT.
EARL OF GLOUCESTER.
EDGAR, son to Gloucester.
EDMUND, bastard son to Gloucester.
CURAN, a courtier.
Old Man, tenant to Gloucester.
Doctor.
Fool.

OSWALD, steward to Goneril.
A Captain employed by Edmund.
Gentleman attendant on Cordelia.
A Herald.
Servants to Cornwall.

GONERIL,
REGAN, } daughters to Lear.
CORDELIA,

Knights of Lear's train, Captains, Messengers, Soldiers, and Attendants.

SCENE: *Britain.*

ACT I.

SCENE I. *King Lear's palace.*

Enter KENT, GLOUCESTER, *and* EDMUND.

Kent. I thought the king had more affected the Duke of Albany than Cornwall.

Glou. It did always seem so to us: but now, in the division of the kingdom, it appears not which of the dukes he values most; for equalities are so weighed, that curiosity in neither can make choice of either's moiety. 7

Kent. Is not this your son, my lord?

Glou. His breeding, sir, hath been at my charge: I have so often blushed to acknowledge him, that now I am brazed to it. 11

Kent. I cannot conceive you.

Glou. Sir, this young fellow's mother could: whereupon she grew round-wombed, and had, indeed, sir, a son for her cradle ere she had a husband for her bed. Do you smell a fault?

Kent. I cannot wish the fault undone, the issue of it being so proper. 18

Glou. But I have, sir, a son by order of law, some year elder than this, who yet is no dearer in my account: though this knave came something saucily into the world before he was sent for, yet was his mother fair; there was good sport at his making, and the whoreson must be acknowledged. Do you know this noble gentleman, Edmund?

Edm. No, my lord.

Glou. My lord of Kent: remember him hereafter as my honourable friend.

Edm. My services to your lordship.

Kent. I must love you, and sue to know you better. 31

Edm. Sir, I shall study deserving.

Glou. He hath been out nine years, and away he shall again. The king is coming.

Sennet. Enter KING LEAR, CORNWALL, ALBANY, GONERIL, REGAN, CORDELIA, *and* Attendants.

Lear. Attend the lords of France and Burgundy, Gloucester. 35

Glou. I shall, my liege.

[*Exeunt Gloucester and Edmund.*

---

1. **affected,** loved. 5. **equalities,** equivalences (in the lands assigned). 6. **curiosity,** nicety, close scrutiny. 7. **moiety,** share, portion. 11. **brazed,** hardened. 18. **proper,** handsome.

22. **something,** somewhat. 33. **out,** abroad. 34. *Stage Direction:* **Sennet,** a set of notes played on a trumpet to accompany a procession.

Lear. Meantime we shall express our
    darker purpose.
Give me the map there. Know that we
    have divided
In three our kingdom: and 'tis our fast in-
    tent
To shake all cares and business from our
    age;   40
Conferring them on younger strengths,
    while we
Unburthen'd crawl toward death. Our son
    of Cornwall,
And you, our no less loving son of Albany,
We have this hour a constant will to publish
Our daughters' several dowers, that future
    strife
May be prevented now. The princes,
    France and Burgundy,
Great rivals in our youngest daughter's love,
Long in our court have made their amorous
    sojourn,
And here are to be answer'd. Tell me, my
    daughters,—
Since now we will divest us, both of rule,   50
Interest of territory, cares of state,—
Which of you shall we say doth love us
    most?
That we our largest bounty may extend
Where nature doth with merit challenge.
    Goneril,
Our eldest-born, speak first.
  Gon. Sir, I love you more than words can
    wield the matter;
Dearer than eye-sight, space, and liberty;
Beyond what can be valued, rich or rare;
No less than life, with grace, health, beauty,
    honour;
As much as child e'er loved, or father found;
A love that makes breath poor, and speech
    unable;   61
Beyond all manner of so much I love you.
  Cor. [*Aside*] What shall Cordelia do?
    Love, and be silent.
  Lear. Of all these bounds, even from this
    line to this,
With shadowy forests and with champains
    rich'd,
With plenteous rivers and wide-skirted
    meads,

We make thee lady: to thine and Albany's
    issue
Be this perpetual. What says our second
    daughter,
Our dearest Regan, wife to Cornwall? Speak.
  Reg. Sir, I am made   70
Of the self-same metal that my sister is,
And prize me at her worth. In my true
    heart
I find she names my very deed of love;
Only she comes too short: that I profess
Myself an enemy to all other joys,
Which the most precious square of sense
    possesses;
And find I am alone felicitate
In your dear highness' love.
  Cor.   [*Aside*] Then poor Cordelia!
And yet not so; since, I am sure, my love's
More richer than my tongue.   80
  Lear. To thee and thine hereditary ever
Remain this ample third of our fair kingdom;
No less in space, validity, and pleasure,
Than that conferr'd on Goneril. Now, our
    joy,
Although the last, not least; to whose young
    love
The vines of France and milk of Burgundy
Strive to be interess'd; what can you say to
    draw
A third more opulent than your sisters?
    Speak.
  Cor. Nothing, my lord.
  Lear. Nothing!   90
  Cor. Nothing.
  Lear. Nothing will come of nothing: speak
    again.
  Cor. Unhappy that I am, I cannot heave
My heart into my mouth: I love your
    majesty
According to my bond; nor more nor less.
  Lear. How, how, Cordelia! mend your
    speech a little,
Lest it may mar your fortunes.
  Cor.   Good my lord,
You have begot me, bred me, loved me: I
Return those duties back as are right fit,
Obey you, love you, and most honour you.100

---

39. **fast intent**, firm intention. 44. **constant**, fixed.
54. **Where . . . challenge**, where both natural affection
and merit claim it as due. 56. **wield the matter**, avail
in expressing. 64. **bounds**. The division of Lear's
kingdom seems to be a traditional one; it appears also
in *1 Henry IV*, III, i, 70 ff. 65. **shadowy**, shady.
champains, plains.

73. **deed of love**, love in very deed. 74. **that**, in
that. 76. **square of sense**, reference to the psychological diagram of the mental powers in the form of a
square whose sides are sense, appetite, motion, and
judgment. 77. **felicitate**, made happy. 83. **validity**,
value. 87. **to be interess'd**, to a right in. 88. **A third
more opulent**. Lear probably refers to the crown
which he intends for Cordelia, since the parts of the
kingdom are declared equal. 95. **bond**, duty, obligation.

Why have my sisters husbands, if they say
They love you all? Haply, when I shall wed,
That lord whose hand must take my plight
    shall carry
Half my love with him, half my care and
    duty:
Sure, I shall never marry like my sisters,
To love my father all.
    Lear. But goes thy heart with this?
    Cor.   Ay, good my lord.
    Lear. So young, and so untender?
    Cor. So young, my lord, and true.
    Lear. Let it be so; thy truth, then, be thy
    dower.   110
For, by the sacred radiance of the sun,
The mysteries of Hecate, and the night;
By all the operation of the orbs
From whom we do exist, and cease to be;
Here I disclaim all my paternal care,
Propinquity and property of blood,
And as a stranger to my heart and me
Hold thee, from this, for ever. The barbar-
    ous Scythian,
Or he that makes his generation messes
To gorge his appetite, shall to my bosom 120
Be as well neighbour'd, pitied, and relieved,
As thou my sometime daughter.
    Kent.   Good my liege,—
    Lear. Peace, Kent!
Come not between the dragon and his wrath.
I loved her most, and thought to set my rest
On her kind nursery. Hence, and avoid my
    sight!
So be my grave my peace, as here I give
Her father's heart from her! Call France;
    who stirs?
Call Burgundy. Cornwall and Albany,
With my two daughters' dowers digest this
    third: 130
Let pride, which she calls plainness, marry
    her.
I do invest you jointly with my power,
Pre-eminence, and all the large effects
That troop with majesty. Ourself, by
    monthly course,
With reservation of an hundred knights,
By you to be sustain'd, shall our abode
Make with you by due turns. Only we still
    retain

The name, and all the additions to a king;
The sway, revenue, execution of the rest,
Beloved sons, be yours: which to confirm, 140
This coronet part betwixt you.
                     [Giving the crown.
    Kent.   Royal Lear,
Whom I have ever honour'd as my king,
Loved as my father, as my master fol-
    low'd,
As my great patron thought on in my
    prayers,—
    Lear. The bow is bent and drawn, make
    from the shaft.
    Kent. Let it fall rather, though the fork
    invade
The region of my heart: be Kent unman-
    nerly,
When Lear is mad. What wilt thou do, old
    man?
Think'st thou that duty shall have dread to
    speak,
When power to flattery bows? To plainness
    honour's bound,   150
When majesty stoops to folly. Reverse thy
    doom;
And, in thy best consideration, check
This hideous rashness: answer my life my
    judgement,
Thy youngest daughter does not love thee
    least;
Nor are those empty-hearted whose low
    sound
Reverbs no hollowness.
    Lear.   Kent, on thy life, no more.
    Kent. My life I never held but as a pawn
To wage against thy enemies; nor fear to
    lose it,
Thy safety being the motive.
    Lear.   Out of my sight!
    Kent. See better, Lear; and let me still
    remain   160
The true blank of thine eye.
    Lear. Now, by Apollo,—
    Kent.   Now, by Apollo, king,
Thou swear'st thy gods in vain.
    Lear.   O, vassal! miscreant!
                  [Laying his hand on his sword.

---

103. **plight**, pledge. 112. **Hecate**, goddess of witchcraft. 118. **this**, this time forth. **Scythian**, typical
of barbarity from the time of Herodotus. 119. **generation**, children. 125. **set my rest**, repose myself; a
phrase from a game of cards, meaning "to stake all."
126. **nursery**, nursing. 130. **digest**, divide. 133.
effects, outward shows.

138. **additions**, titles, marks of distinction. 141.
coronet, i.e., the crown intended for Cordelia. 145.
make from, get out of the way of. 146. **fall**, fly, go.
fork, barbed head of an arrow. 150-151. **To . . . folly.**
Allegiance demands frankness when kingship stoops to
folly. 153. **answer my life**, let my life answer. 157.
pawn, stake, wager. 158. **wage**, hazard, wager. 161.
blank, white center of the target. 162. **by Apollo**.
The play of *King Lear* is rather carefully pagan in all of
its externals.

Alb. ⎫
Corn. ⎭ Dear sir, forbear.

Kent. Do;
Kill thy physician, and the fee bestow
Upon thy foul disease. Revoke thy doom;
Or, whilst I can vent clamour from my
    throat,
I'll tell thee thou dost evil.
    Lear.   Hear me, recreant!
On thine allegiance, hear me!   170
Since thou hast sought to make us break our
    vow,
Which we durst never yet, and with strain'd
    pride
To come between our sentence and our
    power,
Which nor our nature nor our place can bear,
Our potency made good, take thy reward.
Five days we do allot thee, for provision
To shield thee from diseases of the world;
And on the sixth to turn thy hated back
Upon our kingdom: if, on the tenth day
    following,   179
Thy banish'd trunk be found in our
    dominions,
The moment is thy death. Away! by Jupiter,
This shall not be revoked.
    Kent. Fare thee well, king: sith thus thou
    wilt appear,
Freedom lives hence, and banishment is here.
[*To Cordelia*] The gods to their dear shelter
    take thee, maid,
That justly think'st, and hast most rightly
    said!
[*To Regan and Goneril*] And your large
    speeches may your deeds approve,
That good effects may spring from words of
    love.
Thus Kent, O princes, bids you all adieu;
He'll shape his old course in a country new.
                           [*Exit.*

    Flourish. Re-enter GLOUCESTER, *with*
FRANCE, BURGUNDY, *and* Attendants.

    Glou. Here's France and Burgundy, my
    noble lord.   191
    Lear. My lord of Burgundy,
We first address towards you, who with this
    king
Hath rivall'd for our daughter: what, in the
    least,

Will you require in present dower with her,
Or cease your quest of love?
    Bur.   Most royal majesty,
I crave no more than what your highness
    offer'd,
Nor will you tender less.
    Lear.   Right noble Burgundy,
When she was dear to us, we did hold her so;
But now her price is fall'n. Sir, there she
    stands: 200
If aught within that little seeming sub-
    stance,
Or all of it, with our displeasure pieced,
And nothing more, may fitly like your grace,
She's there, and she is yours.
    Bur.   I know no answer.
    Lear. Will you, with those infirmities she
    owes,
Unfriended, new-adopted to our hate,
Dower'd with our curse, and stranger'd with
    our oath,
Take her, or leave her?
    Bur.   Pardon me, royal sir;
Election makes not up on such conditions.
    Lear. Then leave her, sir; for, by the
    power that made me,   210
I tell you all her wealth. [*To France*] For
    you, great king,
I would not from your love make such a
    stray,
To match you where I hate; therefore be-
    seech you
To avert your liking a more worthier way
Than on a wretch whom nature is ashamed
Almost to acknowledge hers.
    France.   This is most strange,
That she, that even but now was your best
    object,
The argument of your praise, balm of your
    age,
Most best, most dearest, should in this trice
    of time   219
Commit a thing so monstrous, to dismantle
So many folds of favour. Sure, her offence
Must be of such unnatural degree,
That monsters it, or your fore-vouch'd
    affection
Fall'n into taint: which to believe of her,

---

172. **strain'd**, excessive. 175. **Our potency made
good**, our authority being maintained. 177. **diseases**,
troubles, discomforts. 183. **sith**, since. 193. **address**,
address ourself.

201. **seeming**, probably, specious, insincere; taken
also with *little* to mean "seemingly small." 202. **pieced**,
added. 203. **like**, please. 205. **owes**, owns, possesses.
207. **stranger'd**, estranged. 209. **Election . . . up**,
choice comes to no decision. 212. **make such a stray**,
stray so far. 218. **argument**, subject. 223. **monsters**, makes monstrous. **fore-vouch'd**, hitherto affirmed. 224. **taint**, decay.

Must be a faith that reason without miracle
Could never plant in me.
   Cor.   I yet beseech your majesty,—
If for I want that glib and oily art,
To speak and purpose not; since what I well
   intend,
I'll do't before I speak,—that you make
   known   229
It is no vicious blot, murder, or foulness,
No unchaste action, or dishonour'd step,
That hath deprived me of your grace and
   favour;
But even for want of that for which I am
   richer,
A still-soliciting eye, and such a tongue
As I am glad I have not, though not to have
   it
Hath lost me in your liking.
   Lear.   Better thou
Hadst not been born than not to have
   pleased me better.
   France. Is it but this,—a tardiness in
   nature
Which often leaves the history unspoke 239
That it intends to do? My lord of Bur-
   gundy,
What say you to the lady? Love's not love
When it is mingled with regards that stand
Aloof from the entire point. Will you have
   her?
She is herself a dowry.
   Bur.   Royal Lear,
Give but that portion which yourself pro-
   posed,
And here I take Cordelia by the hand,
Duchess of Burgundy.
   Lear. Nothing: I have sworn; I am firm.
   Bur. I am sorry, then, you have so lost a
   father
That you must lose a husband.
   Cor.   Peace be with Burgundy!
Since that respects of fortune are his love, 251
I shall not be his wife.
   France. Fairest Cordelia, that art most
   rich, being poor;
Most choice, forsaken; and most loved, de-
   spised!
Thee and thy virtues here I seize upon:
Be it lawful I take up what's cast away.
Gods, gods! 'tis strange that from their
   cold'st neglect
My love should kindle to inflamed respect.

Thy dowerless daughter, king, thrown to
   my chance,
Is queen of us, of ours, and our fair France:
Not all the dukes of waterish Burgundy 261
Can buy this unprized precious maid of me.
Bid them farewell, Cordelia, though unkind:
Thou losest here, a better where to find.
   Lear. Thou hast her, France: let her be
   thine; for we
Have no such daughter, nor shall ever see
That face of hers again. Therefore be gone
Without our grace, our love, our benison.
Come, noble Burgundy.
                 [Flourish. Exeunt all but France,
                    Goneril, Regan, and Cordelia.
   France. Bid farewell to your sisters. 270
   Cor. The jewels of our father, with wash'd
   eyes
Cordelia leaves you: I know you what you
   are;
And like a sister am most loath to call
Your faults as they are named. Use well our
   father:
To your professed bosoms I commit him:
But yet, alas, stood I within his grace,
I would prefer him to a better place.
So, farewell to you both.
   Reg. Prescribe not us our duties.
   Gon.   Let your study 27*
Be to content your lord, who hath received
   you
At fortune's alms. You have obedience
   scanted,
And well are worth the want that you have
   wanted.
   Cor. Time shall unfold what plaited
   cunning hides:
Who cover faults, at last shame them derides.
Well may you prosper!
   France.   Come, my fair Cordelia.
              [Exeunt France and Cordelia.
   Gon. Sister, it is not a little I have to say
of what most nearly appertains to us both.
I think our father will hence to-night.
   Reg. That's most certain, and with you;
next month with us. 290
   Gon. You see how full of changes his age
is; the observation we have made of it hath

---

261. **waterish**, well-watered (with rivers); used contemptuously, water being the symbol of fickleness.
262. **unprized**, not appreciated, or priceless. 264.
here ... where, used as nouns. 275. **professed**, i.e.,
full of professions (avowals). 281. **At**, i.e., priced at.
282. **well ... wanted**, well deserve the lack of affection
which you yourself have shown ; *want* may, however,
refer to her dowry. 283. **plaited**, folded, insincere.

---

234. **still-soliciting**, ever-begging. 242. **regards**,
considerations. 251. **respects**, considerations, motives.

not been little: he always loved our sister
most; and with what poor judgement he
hath now cast her off appears too grossly.

Reg. 'Tis the infirmity of his age: yet he
hath ever but slenderly known himself.   297

Gon. The best and soundest of his time
hath been but rash; then must we look to
receive from his age, not alone the imperfections of long-engraffed condition, but
therewithal the unruly waywardness that
infirm and choleric years bring with them.

Reg. Such unconstant starts are we like to
have from him as this of Kent's banishment.

Gon. There is further compliment of leave-
taking between France and him. Pray you,
let's hit together: if our father carry authority with such dispositions as he bears, this last
surrender of his will but offend us.   310

Reg. We shall further think on't.

Gon. We must do something, and i' the
heat.   [*Exeunt.*

SCENE II. *The Earl of Gloucester's castle.*

Enter EDMUND, *with a letter.*

Edm. Thou, nature, art my goddess; to
thy law
My services are bound. Wherefore should I
Stand in the plague of custom, and permit
The curiosity of nations to deprive me,
For that I am some twelve or fourteen moon-
shines
Lag of a brother? Why bastard? wherefore
base?
When my dimensions are as well compact,
My mind as generous, and my shape as true,
As honest madam's issue? Why brand they
us
With base? with baseness? bastardy? base,
base?   10
Who, in the lusty stealth of nature, take
More composition and fierce quality

295. **grossly**, obviously. 298. **time**, lifetime. 301.
long-engraffed condition, long-implanted habit.
Goneril's case against Lear, which seems in this explanatory scene to be Shakespeare's, is (1) that "he hath ever
but slenderly known himself" (self-knowledge was a
Renaissance ideal), (2) that he has the infirmity of old
age, and (3) that he is habituated to self-indulgence.
308. **hit**, agree. 310. **offend**, harm, injure. 312. **i'
the heat**, i.e., while the iron is hot.
    Scene ii. 1. **nature**, natural force; also, course of life
undisciplined by culture. 3. **plague**, vexatious injustice. Warburton suggested *plage* meaning "place,"
"boundary." 4. **curiosity**, nicety, fastidiousness. 5.
moonshines, months. 6. **Lag of**, later than. 7.
dimensions, bodily parts or proportions. **compact**,
knit together.

Than doth, within a dull, stale, tired bed,
Go to the creating a whole tribe of fops,
Got 'tween asleep and wake? Well, then,
Legitimate Edgar, I must have your land:
Our father's love is to the bastard Ed-
mund
As to the legitimate: fine word,—legiti-
mate!
Well, my legitimate, if this letter speed,   19
And my invention thrive, Edmund the base
Shall top the legitimate. I grow; I prosper:
Now, gods, stand up for bastards!

Enter GLOUCESTER.

Glou. Kent banish'd thus! and France in
choler parted!
And the king gone to-night! subscribed his
power!
Confined to exhibition! All this done
Upon the gad! Edmund, how now! what
news?

Edm. So please your lordship, none.
                     [*Putting up the letter.*

Glou. Why so earnestly seek you to put up
that letter?

Edm. I know no news, my lord.

Glou. What paper were you reading?   30

Edm. Nothing, my lord.

Glou. No? What needed, then, that terrible dispatch of it into your pocket? the
quality of nothing hath not such need to hide
itself. Let's see: come, if it be nothing, I
shall not need spectacles.

Edm. I beseech you, sir, pardon me: it is
a letter from my brother, that I have not all
o'er-read; and for so much as I have perused,
I find it not fit for your o'er-looking.   40

Glou. Give me the letter, sir.

Edm. I shall offend, either to detain or
give it. The contents, as in part I understand them, are to blame.

Glou. Let's see, let's see.

Edm. I hope, for my brother's justification, he wrote this but as an essay or   47
taste of my virtue.

Glou. [*Reads*] 'This policy and reverence
of age makes the world bitter to the best of
our times; keeps our fortunes from us till our
oldness cannot relish them. I begin to find
an idle and fond bondage in the oppression

24. **subscribed**, surrendered. 25. **exhibition**, allowance. 26. **Upon the gad!** suddenly, as if pricked by a
gad. 32. **terrible**, terrified. 47. **essay**, assay, trial.
48. **policy and reverence of**, i.e., policy of reverencing.

of aged tyranny; who sways, not as it hath power, but as it is suffered. Come to me, that of this I may speak more. If our father would sleep till I waked him, you should enjoy half his revenue for ever, and live the beloved of your brother,

EDGAR.'

Hum—conspiracy!—'Sleep till I waked him, —you should enjoy half his revenue,'—My son Edgar! Had he a hand to write this? a heart and brain to breed it in?—When came this to you? who brought it? 62

Edm. It was not brought me, my lord; there's the cunning of it; I found it thrown in at the casement of my closet.

Glou. You know the character to be your brother's?

Edm. If the matter were good, my lord, I durst swear it were his; but, in respect of that, I would fain think it were not. 70

Glou. It is his.

Edm. It is his hand, my lord; but I hope his heart is not in the contents.

Glou. Hath he never heretofore sounded you in this business?

Edm. Never, my lord: but I have heard him oft maintain it to be fit, that, sons at perfect age, and fathers declining, the father should be as ward to the son, and the son manage his revenue. 79

Glou. O villain, villain! His very opinion in the letter! Abhorred villain! Unnatural, detested, brutish villain! worse than brutish! Go, sirrah, seek him; I'll apprehend him: abominable villain! Where is he?

Edm. I do not well know, my lord. If it shall please you to suspend your indignation against my brother till you can derive from him better testimony of his intent, you shall run a certain course; where, if you violently proceed against him, mistaking his purpose, it would make a great gap in your own honour, and shake in pieces the heart of his obedience. I dare pawn down my life for him, that he hath wrote this to feel my affection to your honour, and to no further pretence of danger. 95

Glou. Think you so?

Edm. If your honour judge it meet, I will place you where you shall hear us confer of this, and by an auricular assurance have your

satisfaction; and that without any further delay than this very evening. 101

Glou. He cannot be such a monster—

Edm. Nor is not, sure.

Glou. To his father, that so tenderly and entirely loves him. Heaven and earth! Edmund, seek him out; wind me into him, I pray you: frame the business after your own wisdom. I would unstate myself, to be in a due resolution.

Edm. I will seek him, sir, presently; convey the business as I shall find means, and acquaint you withal. 111

Glou. These late eclipses in the sun and moon portend no good to us: though the wisdom of nature can reason it thus and thus, yet nature finds itself scourged by the sequent effects: love cools, friendship falls off, brothers divide: in cities, mutinies; in countries, discord; in palaces, treason; and the bond cracked 'twixt son and father. This villain of mine comes under the prediction; there's son against father: the king falls from bias of nature; there's father against child. We have seen the best of our time: machinations, hollowness, treachery, and all ruinous disorders, follow us disquietly to our graves. Find out this villain, Edmund; it shall lose thee nothing; do it carefully. And the noble and true-hearted Kent banished! his offence, honesty! 'Tis strange. 127

[*Exit.*

Edm. This is the excellent foppery of the world, that, when we are sick in fortune,— often the surfeit of our own behaviour,—we make guilty of our disasters the sun, the moon, and the stars: as if we were villains by necessity; fools by heavenly compulsion; knaves, thieves, and treachers, by spherical predominance; drunkards, liars, and adulterers, by an enforced obedience of planetary influence; and all that we are evil in, by a divine thrusting on: an admirable evasion

---

65. **closet**, private room. 77. **declining**, becoming feeble. 82. **detested**, detestable. 89. **where**, whereas. 95. **pretence**, intention, purpose.

106. **wind me into him**, insinuate yourself into his confidence; *me* is an ethical dative. 108. **unstate myself**, give up my position and dignity. **due resolution**, actual certainty. 109. **convey**, manage with secrecy. 112-127. **These . . . strange.** The fact that there were eclipses of the sun and moon in the autumn of 1605 has been regarded as an indication of the date of the play; also the references to discord, mutinies, and treason have been thought to refer to the Gunpowder Plot (Nov. 5, 1605). 114. **wisdom of nature**, natural science. 115. **sequent**, consequent, following. 122. **bias**, curve of a ball in bowling; here, tendency. 128. **foppery**, foolishness. 131. **disasters**, unfavorable aspects. 134. **treachers**, traitors. **spherical predominance**, ascendancy of planets. Edmund's denial of planetary influence must be set down as a sort of religious infidelity.

of whoremaster man, to lay his goatish disposition to the charge of a star! My father
compounded with my mother under the
dragon's tail; and my nativity was under
Ursa major; so that it follows, I am rough
and lecherous. Tut, I should have been that
I am, had the maidenliest star in the firmament twinkled on my bastardizing. Edgar—

Enter EDGAR.

and pat he comes like the catastrophe of the
old comedy: my cue is villanous melancholy, with a sigh like Tom o' Bedlam. O,
these eclipses do portend these divisions!
fa, sol, la, mi.

Edg. How now, brother Edmund! what
serious contemplation are you in?   151
Edm. I am thinking, brother, of a prediction I read this other day, what should follow
these eclipses.

Edg. Do you busy yourself about that?
Edm. I promise you, the effects he writes
of succeed unhappily; as of unnaturalness
between the child and the parent; death,
dearth, dissolutions of ancient amities; divisions in state, menaces and maledictions
against king and nobles; needless diffidences,
banishment of friends, dissipation of cohorts,
nuptial breaches, and I know not what.   163
Edg. How long have you been a sectary
astronomical?

Edm. Come, come; when saw you my
father last?

Edg. Why, the night gone by.
Edm. Spake you with him?
Edg. Ay, two hours together.   170
Edm. Parted you in good terms? Found
you no displeasure in him by word or coun-
tenance?

Edg. None at all.
Edm. Bethink yourself wherein you may
have offended him: and at my entreaty forbear his presence till some little time hath
qualified the heat of his displeasure; which
at this instant so rageth in him, that with
the mischief of your person it would scarcely
allay.   179
Edg. Some villain hath done me wrong.

---

148. **Tom o' Bedlam.** See II, iii, 14, below. 157.
succeed, come to pass. 161. **diffidences,** distrust of
others. 162. **dissipation of cohorts,** breaking up of
military organizations; probably corrupt; *disputation* or
dissention of consorts has been suggested. 164. **sectary
astronomical,** student of astronomy. 178. **mischief
of,** harm to. 179. **allay,** be allayed.

Edm. That's my fear. I pray you, have a
continent forbearance till the speed of his rage
goes slower; and, as I say, retire with me to
my lodging, from whence I will fitly bring
you to hear my lord speak: pray ye, go;
there's my key: if you do stir abroad, go
armed.

Edg. Armed, brother!
Edm. Brother, I advise you to the best; go
armed: I am no honest man if there be any
good meaning towards you: I have told you
what I have seen and heard; but faintly,
nothing like the image and horror of it: pray
you, away.

Edg. Shall I hear from you anon?
Edm. I do serve you in this business.
                              [*Exit Edgar.*
A credulous father! and a brother noble,
Whose nature is so far from doing harms,
That he suspects none; on whose foolish
  honesty
My practices ride easy! I see the business.
Let me, if not by birth, have lands by wit: 199
All with me's meet that I can fashion fit.
                              [*Exit.*

SCENE III.   *The Duke of Albany's palace.*

Enter GONERIL, *and* OSWALD, *her steward.*

Gon. Did my father strike my gentleman
  for chiding of his fool?
Osw. Yes, madam.
Gon. By day and night he wrongs me;
  every hour
He flashes into one gross crime or other,
That sets us all at odds: I'll not endure it:
His knights grow riotous, and himself up-
  braids us
On every trifle. When he returns from
  hunting,
I will not speak with him; say I am sick:
If you come slack of former services,   9
You shall do well; the fault of it I'll an-
  swer.
Osw. He's coming, madam; I hear him.
                              [*Horns within.*
Gon. Put on what weary negligence you
  please,
You and your fellows; I'ld have it come to
  question:
If he dislike it, let him to our sister,

---

182. **continent,** restraining. 198. **practices,** plots.

Whose mind and mine, I know, in that are
    one,
Not to be over-ruled.   Idle old man,
That still would manage those authorities
That he hath given away! Now, by my life,
Old fools are babes again; and must be used
With checks as flatteries,—when they are
    seen abused.   20
Remember what I tell you.
    Osw.   Well, madam.
    Gon. And let his knights have colder looks
    among you;
What grows of it, no matter; advise your
    fellows so:
I would breed from hence occasions, and I
    shall
That I may speak: I'll write straight to my
    sister,
To hold my very course.   Prepare for dinner.
                                        [*Exeunt.*

SCENE IV. *A hall in the same.*

Enter KENT, *disguised.*

    Kent. If but as well I other accents
    borrow,
That can my speech defuse, my good intent
May carry through itself to that full issue
For which I razed my likeness. Now,
    banish'd Kent,
If thou canst serve where thou dost stand
    condemn'd,
So may it come, thy master, whom thou
    lovest,
Shall find thee full of labours.

Horns within.   Enter LEAR, Knights,
    and Attendants.

    Lear. Let me not stay a jot for dinner; go
get it ready. [*Exit an Attendant.*] How now!
what art thou?   10
    Kent. A man, sir.
    Lear. What dost thou profess? what
wouldst thou with us?
    Kent. I do profess to be no less than I
seem; to serve him truly that will put me in

trust; to love him that is honest; to converse
with him that is wise, and says little; to fear
judgement; to fight when I cannot choose;
and to eat no fish.
    Lear. What art thou?
    Kent. A very honest-hearted fellow, and
as poor as the king.   21
    Lear. If thou be as poor for a subject as he
is for a king, thou art poor enough. What
wouldst thou?
    Kent. Service.
    Lear. Who wouldst thou serve?
    Kent. You.
    Lear. Dost thou know me, fellow?
    Kent. No, sir; but you have that in your
countenance which I would fain call master.
    Lear. What's that?   31
    Kent. Authority.
    Lear. What services canst thou do?
    Kent. I can keep honest counsel, ride, run,
mar a curious tale in telling it, and deliver a
plain message bluntly: that which ordinary
men are fit for, I am qualified in; and the best
of me is diligence.
    Lear. How old art thou?   39
    Kent. Not so young, sir, to love a woman
for singing, nor so old to dote on her for any
thing: I have years on my back forty eight.
    Lear. Follow me; thou shalt serve me: if I
like thee no worse after dinner, I will not
part from thee yet. Dinner, ho, dinner!
Where's my knave? my fool? Go you, and
call my fool hither.   [*Exit an Attendant.*

Enter OSWALD.

You, you, sirrah, where's my daughter?
    Osw. So please you,—   [*Exit.*
    Lear. What says the fellow there? Call
the clotpoll back. [*Exit a Knight.*] Where's
my fool, ho? I think the world's asleep. 52

Re-enter Knight.

How now! where's that mongrel?
    Knight. He says, my lord, your daughter
is not well.
    Lear. Why came not the slave back to me
when I called him?
    Knight. Sir, he answered me in the
roundest manner, he would not.   58

16. **Idle,** foolish, silly. 20. **With . . . abused.** The
line, probably corrupt, yields a sort of meaning if one
understands *as* to mean "as well as," *they* to refer to *Old
fools,* and *abused* to mean "deceived" or "misguided."
24. **breed from hence occasions.** One sees in Goneril
greater initiative than in Regan.
    Scene iv. 2. **defuse,** confuse; hence, disguise. 4.
razed, erased. 12. **What . . . profess?** what is thy
profession?

16. **converse,** associate. 18. **eat no fish.** Warburton's explanation is usually followed: Roman Catholics,
who observed the custom of eating fish on Fridays, were
thought of as enemies of the government. 35. **curious,**
complicated, intricate. 51. **clotpoll,** blockhead. 58.
roundest, plainest.

Lear. He would not! 60

Knight. My lord, I know not what the matter is; but, to my judgement, your highness is not entertained with that ceremonious affection as you were wont; there's a great abatement of kindness appears as well in the general dependants as in the duke himself also and your daughter.

Lear. Ha! sayest thou so?

Knight. I beseech you, pardon me, my lord, if I be mistaken; for my duty cannot be silent when I think your highness wronged. 71

Lear. Thou but rememberest me of mine own conception: I have perceived a most faint neglect of late; which I have rather blamed as mine own jealous curiosity than as a very pretence and purpose of unkindness: I will look further into 't. But where's my fool? I have not seen him this two days.

Knight. Since my young lady's going into France, sir, the fool hath much pined away. 80

Lear. No more of that; I have noted it well. Go you, and tell my daughter I would speak with her. [*Exit an Attendant.*] Go you, call hither my fool. [*Exit an Attendant.*

Re-enter OSWALD.

O, you sir, you, come you hither, sir: who am I, sir?

Osw. My lady's father.

Lear. 'My lady's father'! my lord's knave: you whoreson dog! you slave! you cur!

Osw. I am none of these, my lord; I beseech your pardon. 91

Lear. Do you bandy looks with me, you rascal? [*Striking him.*

Osw. I'll not be struck, my lord.

Kent. Nor tripped neither, you base football player.

[*Tripping up his heels.*

Lear. I thank thee, fellow; thou servest me, and I'll love thee.

Kent. Come, sir, arise, away! I'll teach you differences: away, away! If you will measure your lubber's length again, tarry: but away! go to; have you wisdom? so. 102

[*Pushes Oswald out.*

Lear. Now, my friendly knave, I thank thee: there's earnest of thy service.

[*Giving Kent money.*

Enter Fool.

Fool. Let me hire him too: here's my coxcomb. [*Offering Kent his cap.*

Lear. How now, my pretty knave! how dost thou?

Fool. Sirrah, you were best take my coxcomb.

Kent. Why, fool? 110

Fool. Why, for taking one's part that's out of favour: nay, an thou canst not smile as the wind sits, thou'lt catch cold shortly: there, take my coxcomb: why, this fellow has banished two on 's daughters, and did the third a blessing against his will; if thou follow him, thou must needs wear my coxcomb. How now, nuncle! Would I had two coxcombs and two daughters!

Lear. Why, my boy? 119

Fool. If I gave them all my living, I'ld keep my coxcombs myself. There's mine; beg another of thy daughters.

Lear. Take heed, sirrah; the whip.

Fool. Truth's a dog must to kennel; he must be whipped out, when Lady the brach may stand by the fire and stink.

Lear. A pestilent gall to me!

Fool. Sirrah, I'll teach thee a speech.

Lear. Do.

Fool. Mark it, nuncle: 130
Have more than thou showest,
Speak less than thou knowest,
Lend less than thou owest,
Ride more than thou goest,
Learn more than thou trowest,
Set less than thou throwest;
Leave thy drink and thy whore,
And keep in-a-door,
And thou shalt have more
Than two tens to a score. 140

Kent. This is nothing, fool.

Fool. Then 'tis like the breath of an unfee'd lawyer; you gave me nothing for 't. Can you make no use of nothing, nuncle?

72. **rememberest**, remindest. 74. **faint**, slight, or indifferent, half-hearted. 75. **jealous curiosity**, overscrupulous regard for his own dignity. 76. **pretence**, intention, purpose. 92. **bandy**, strike a ball to and fro, as in tennis; here figurative, give and take. 95. **football player.** Football was a rough, dangerous, public sport without organization or officials, and under statutory ban; it was played in the streets by the worst element of the population.

109. **coxcomb**, fool's cap. 117. **nuncle**, contraction of *mine uncle*, customary address of the licensed fool to his superior. 120. **living**, property. 125. **brach**, a female hound. 131. **showest**, seemest to have. 133. **owest**, possessest. 134. **goest**, i.e., on foot. 135. **trowest**, believest. 136. **Set . . . throwest**, stake less at dice than you have a chance to throw, i.e., don't bet all you can. 138. **in-a-door**, at home.

Lear. Why, no, boy; nothing can be made out of nothing.

Fool. [*To Kent*] Prithee, tell him, so much the rent of his land comes to: he will not believe a fool.

Lear. A bitter fool!   150

Fool. Dost thou know the difference, my boy, between a bitter fool and a sweet fool?

Lear. No, lad; teach me.

Fool. That lord that counsell'd thee

> To give away thy land,
> Come place him here by me,
> Do thou for him stand:
> The sweet and bitter fool
> Will presently appear;
> The one in motley here,   160
> The other found out there.

Lear. Dost thou call me fool, boy?

Fool. All thy other titles thou hast given away; that thou wast born with.

Kent. This is not altogether fool, my lord.

Fool. No, faith, lords and great men will not let me; if I had a monopoly out, they would have part on't: and ladies too, they will not let me have all fool to myself; they'll be snatching. Give me an egg, nuncle, and I'll give thee two crowns.   171

Lear. What two crowns shall they be?

Fool. Why, after I have cut the egg i' the middle, and eat up the meat, the two crowns of the egg. When thou clovest thy crown i' the middle, and gavest away both parts, thou borest thy ass on thy back o'er the dirt: thou hadst little wit in thy bald crown, when thou gavest thy golden one away. If I speak like myself in this, let him be whipped that first finds it so.   180

[*Singing*] Fools had ne'er less wit in a year;
> For wise men are grown foppish,
> They know not how their wits to wear,
> Their manners are so apish.

Lear. When were you wont to be so full of songs, sirrah?

Fool. I have used it, nuncle, ever since thou madest thy daughters thy mother: for when thou gavest them the rod, and put'st down thine own breeches,   190

[*Singing*] Then they for sudden joy did weep,
> And I for sorrow sung,
> That such a king should play bo-peep,
> And go the fools among.

Prithee, nuncle, keep a schoolmaster that can teach thy fool to lie: I would fain learn to lie.

Lear. An you lie, sirrah, we'll have you whipped.   198

Fool. I marvel what kin thou and thy daughters are: they'll have me whipped for speaking true, thou'lt have me whipped for lying; and sometimes I am whipped for holding my peace. I had rather be any kind o' thing than a fool: and yet I would not be thee, nuncle; thou hast pared thy wit o' both sides, and left nothing i' the middle: here comes one o' the parings.

Enter GONERIL.

Lear. How now, daughter! what makes that frontlet on? Methinks you are too much of late i' the frown.   209

Fool. Thou wast a pretty fellow when thou hadst no need to care for her frowning; now thou art an O without a figure; I am better than thou art now; I am a fool, thou art nothing. [*To Gon.*] Yes, forsooth, I will hold my tongue; so your face bids me, though you say nothing. Mum, mum,
> He that keeps nor crust nor crum,
> Weary of all, shall want some.

[*Pointing to Lear*] That's a shealed peascod.

Gon. Not only, sir, this your all-licensed fool,
But other of your insolent retinue   221
Do hourly carp and quarrel; breaking forth
In rank and not-to-be-endured riots. Sir,
I had thought, by making this well known unto you,
To have found a safe redress; but now grow fearful,
By what yourself too late have spoke and done,
That you protect this course, and put it on
By your allowance; which if you should, the fault

154. **That lord.** A lord, Skálliger, in the old play of *King Leir* is apparently referred to; no such advice is given Lear in this play. 160. **motley**, the parti-colored dress of the fool. 167. **monopoly.** This allusion would be well understood, since the granting of monopolies by King James was a current abuse. **out**, taken out, granted. 182. **foppish**, foolish. 187. **used it**, been in the habit of doing it.

191-194. **Then . . . among.** These lines, and probably others below, are no doubt taken from old songs. 208. **frontlet**, a band worn on the forehead; here, frowning visage. 212. **O without a figure**, cipher of no value unless joined to a figure. 219. **shealed peascod**, shelled pea pod. 221. **other**, others. 227. **put it on**, encourage it. 228. **allowance**, approval.

Would not 'scape censure, nor the redresses
    sleep,
Which, in the tender of a wholesome weal, 230
Might in their working do you that offence,
Which else were shame, that then necessity
Will call discreet proceeding.

Fool. For, you know, nuncle,
The hedge-sparrow fed the cuckoo so
    long,
That it had it head bit off by it young.
So, out went the candle, and we were left
    darkling.

Lear. Are you our daughter?

Gon. Come, sir,
I would you would make use of that good
    wisdom,   240
Whereof I know you are fraught; and put
    away
These dispositions, that of late transform
    you
From what you rightly are.

Fool. May not an ass know when the cart
draws the horse? Whoop, Jug! I love thee.

Lear. Doth any here know me? This is
not Lear:
Doth Lear walk thus? speak thus? Where
    are his eyes?
Either his notion weakens, his discernings
Are lethargied—Ha! waking? 'tis not so.
Who is it that can tell me who I am? 250

Fool. Lear's shadow.

Lear. I would learn that; for, by the
marks of sovereignty, knowledge, and reason,
I should be false persuaded I had daughters.

Fool. Which they will make an obedient
father.

Lear. Your name, fair gentlewoman?

Gon. This admiration, sir, is much o' the
    savour
Of other your new pranks. I do beseech you
To understand my purposes aright: 260
As you are old and reverend, you should be
    wise.
Here do you keep a hundred knights and
    squires;
Men so disorder'd, so debosh'd and bold,

That this our court, infected with their
    manners,
Shows like a riotous inn: epicurism and
    lust
Make it more like a tavern or a brothel
Than a graced palace. The shame itself
    doth speak
For instant remedy: be then desired
By her, that else will take the thing she
    begs,
A little to disquantity your train;   270
And the remainder, that shall still depend,
To be such men as may besort your age,
And know themselves and you.

Lear.   Darkness and devils!
Saddle my horses; call my train together.
Degenerate bastard! I'll not trouble thee:
Yet have I left a daughter.

Gon. You strike my people; and your dis-
    order'd rabble
Make servants of their betters.

Enter ALBANY.

Lear. Woe, that too late repents,—
                            [*To Alb.*]
   O, sir, are you come?
Is it your will? Speak, sir. Prepare my
    horses.
Ingratitude, thou marble-hearted fiend, 281
More hideous when thou show'st thee in a
    child
Than the sea-monster!

Alb.   Pray, sir, be patient.

Lear. [*To Gon.*] Detested kite! thou liest:
My train are men of choice and rarest parts,
That all particulars of duty know,
And in the most exact regard support
The worships of their name. O most small
    fault,
How ugly didst thou in Cordelia show!
That, like an engine, wrench'd my frame of
    nature   290
From the fix'd place; drew from my heart all
    love,
And added to the gall. O Lear, Lear, Lear!
Beat at this gate, that let thy folly in,
                   [*Striking his head.*

---

229. **nor the redresses sleep,** punishment for the
riotous conduct of Lear's attendants will be inflicted.
230. **tender . . . weal,** preservation of the peace of the
state. 232-233. **necessity . . . proceeding,** i.e., everyone will justify her because of the necessity of the action.
236. **it.** The second and third *its* are possessives. 237.
darkling, in the dark. 241. **fraught,** filled. 245.
Whoop, Jug! I love thee, regarded as a quotation from
an old song; used by the Fool to cover up his impertinence. *Jug,* probably, Joan. 248. **notion,** intellectual
power. 255. **Which,** whom. 263. **debosh'd,** de-
bauched.

265. **epicurism,** luxury. 267. **graced,** honorable.
270. **disquantity,** diminish. 271. **depend,** be dependants. 272. **besort,** befit. 283. **sea-monster,** possible
allusion to the hippopotamus reputed in Egyptian
mythology to be a monster of ingratitude; the whale has
also been suggested. W. J. Craig suggests that no
particular monster is meant, but that the allusion is to
the monsters of classical mythology slain by Hercules
and Perseus. 287. **in . . . regard,** with extreme care.
288. **worships,** honors. 290. **engine.** the rack.

And thy dear judgement out! Go, go, my
  people.
  Alb. My lord, I am guiltless, as I am
  ignorant
Of what hath moved you.
  Lear.   It may be so, my lord.
Hear, nature, hear; dear goddess, hear!
Suspend thy purpose, if thou didst intend
To make this creature fruitful!
Into her womb convey sterility!   300
Dry up in her the organs of increase;
And from her derogate body never spring
A babe to honour her! If she must teem,
Create her child of spleen; that it may live,
And be a thwart disnatured torment to her!
Let it stamp wrinkles in her brow of youth;
With cadent tears fret channels in her cheeks;
Turn all her mother's pains and benefits
To laughter and contempt; that she may feel
How sharper than a serpent's tooth it is 310
To have a thankless child! Away, away!
                                          {*Exit.*
  Alb. Now, gods that we adore, whereof
  comes this?
  Gon. Never afflict yourself to know the
  cause;
But let his disposition have that scope
That dotage gives it.

Re-enter Lear.

  Lear. What, fifty of my followers at a clap!
Within a fortnight!
  Alb.   What's the matter, sir?
  Lear. I'll tell thee: [*To Gon.*] Life and
  death! I am ashamed
That thou hast power to shame my manhood
  thus;
That these hot tears, which break from me
  perforce,   320
Should make thee worth them. Blasts and
  fogs upon thee!
The untented woundings of a father's curse
Pierce every sense about thee! Old fond
  eyes,
Beweep this cause again, I'll pluck ye out,
And cast you, with the waters that you lose,
To temper clay. Yea, is it come to this?
Let it be so: yet have I left a daughter,
Who, I am sure, is kind and comfortable:

When she shall hear this of thee, with her
  nails
She'll flay thy wolvish visage. Thou shalt
  find
That I'll resume the shape which thou dost
  think   331
I have cast off for ever: thou shalt, I warrant
  thee.
        [*Exeunt Lear, Kent, and Attendants.*
  Gon. Do you mark that, my lord?
  Alb. I cannot be so partial, Goneril,
To the great love I bear you,—
  Gon. Pray you, content. What, Oswald,
  ho!
[*To the Fool*] You, sir, more knave than fool,
  after your master.
  Fool. Nuncle Lear, nuncle Lear, tarry and
take the fool with thee.
        A fox, when one has caught her,   340
        And such a daughter,
        Should sure to the slaughter,
        If my cap would buy a halter:
        So the fool follows after.   [*Exit.*
  Gon. This man hath had good counsel:—a
  hundred knights!
'Tis politic and safe to let him keep
At point a hundred knights: yes, that, on
  every dream,
Each buzz, each fancy, each complaint, dis-
  like,
He may enguard his dotage with their
  powers,   349
And hold our lives in mercy. Oswald, I say!
  Alb. Well, you may fear too far.
  Gon.   Safer than trust too far:
Let me still take away the harms I fear,
Not fear still to be taken: I know his heart.
What he hath utter'd I have writ my sister:
If she sustain him and his hundred knights,
When I have show'd the unfitness,—

Re-enter Oswald.

                          How now, Oswald!
What, have you writ that letter to my sister?
  Osw. Yes, madam.
  Gon. Take you some company, and away
  to horse:
Inform her full of my particular fear;   360
And thereto add such reasons of your own
As may compact it more. Get you gone;
And hasten your return. [*Exit Oswald.*] No,
  no, my lord,

---

294. **dear**, precious, valued. 297. **nature . . . dear
goddess.** This is the first of Lear's terrible curses. 302.
derogate, debased. 305. **thwart**, contrary. **disnatured**, without natural affection. 307. **cadent**,
falling. 322. **untented**, not cleansed with lint, and
therefore liable to fester. 328. **comfortable**, willing to
comfort.

347. **At point**, under arms. 348. **buzz**, idle rumor.
349. **enguard**, surround with a guard. 353. **taken**,
overtaken (by the *harms*). 362. **compact**, confirm.

This milky gentleness and course of yours
Though I condemn not, yet, under pardon,
You are much more attask'd for want of
    wisdom
Than praised for harmful mildness.

Alb. How far your eyes may pierce I
    cannot tell:
Striving to better, oft we mar what's well.

Gon. Nay, then—   370
Alb. Well, well; the event.   [*Exeunt.*

SCENE V. *Court before the same.*

Enter LEAR, KENT, *and* Fool.

Lear. Go you before to Gloucester with
these letters. Acquaint my daughter no
further with any thing you know than comes
from her demand out of the letter. If your
diligence be not speedy, I shall be there afore
you.

Kent. I will not sleep, my lord, till I have
delivered your letter.   [*Exit.*

Fool. If a man's brains were in's heels,
were't not in danger of kibes?

Lear. Ay, boy.   10

Fool. Then, I prithee, be merry; thy wit
shall ne'er go slip-shod.

Lear. Ha, ha, ha!

Fool. Shalt see thy other daughter will use
thee kindly; for though she's as like this as a
crab's like an apple, yet I can tell what I can
tell.

Lear. Why, what canst thou tell, my
boy?

Fool. She will taste as like this as a crab
does to a crab. Thou canst tell why one's
nose stands i' the middle on's face?   20

Lear. No.

Fool. Why, to keep one's eyes of either
side's nose; that what a man cannot smell
out, he may spy into.

Lear. I did her wrong—

Fool. Canst tell how an oyster makes his
shell?

Lear. No.

Fool. Nor I neither; but I can tell why a
snail has a house.   30

Lear. Why?

Fool. Why, to put his head in; not to give
it away to his daughters, and leave his horns
without a case.

Lear. I will forget my nature. So kind a
father! Be my horses ready?

Fool. Thy asses are gone about 'em. The
reason why the seven stars are no more than
seven is a pretty reason.

Lear. Because they are not eight?   40

Fool. Yes, indeed: thou wouldst make a
good fool.

Lear. To take't again perforce! Monster
ingratitude!

Fool. If thou wert my fool, nuncle, I'ld
have thee beaten for being old before thy
time.

Lear. How's that?

Fool. Thou shouldst not have been old till
thou hadst been wise.

Lear. O, let me not be mad, not mad,
    sweet heaven!   50
Keep me in temper: I would not be mad!

Enter Gentleman.

How now! are the horses ready?

Gent. Ready, my lord.

Lear. Come, boy.

Fool. She that's a maid now, and laughs at
    my departure,
Shall not be a maid long, unless things be cut
    shorter.   [*Exeunt.*

ACT II.

SCENE I. *The Earl of Gloucester's castle.*

Enter EDMUND, *and* CURAN *meets him.*

Edm. Save thee, Curan.

Cur. And you, sir. I have been with your
father, and given him notice that the Duke
of Cornwall and Regan his duchess will be
here with him this night.

Edm. How comes that?

Cur. Nay, I know not. You have heard
of the news abroad; I mean the whispered

---

364. **This . . . yours,** the cowardly weakness of your
course. 366. **attask'd,** taken to task, blamed. 371.
the event, time will show.
    Scene v. 9. **kibes,** chilblains, or ulcerated sores on
the heels. 12. **slip-shod,** in slippers. There are no
brains, thinks the Fool, in Lear's heels when they are
on their way to visit Regan. 15. **kindly,** double sense:
according to filial nature and according to her own
nature. 16. **a crab's . . . apple,** seems proverbial for
"a crab-apple's an apple." 25. **her,** Lear again thinks
of Cordelia.

38. **seven stars,** the Pleiades. 50. **let . . . mad.** Lear
thus marks his first symptom of coming madness. It
will be noted that he thinks of madness as the loss of the
even balance of spirits, i.e., temper, and as the forgetting
of his nature.
    Act II. Scene i. 1. **Save thee,** i.e., God save thee.

ones, for they are yet but ear-kissing arguments?

Edm. Not I: pray you, what are they?　10

Cur. Have you heard of no likely wars toward, 'twixt the Dukes of Cornwall and Albany?

Edm. Not a word.

Cur. You may do, then, in time. Fare you well, sir.　　　　　　　　[*Exit.*

Edm. The duke be here to-night? The better! best!

This weaves itself perforce into my business.

My father hath set guard to take my brother;

And I have one thing, of a queasy question,

Which I must act: briefness and fortune, work!　20

Brother, a word; descend: brother, I say!

Enter EDGAR.

My father watches: O sir, fly this place;

Intelligence is given where you are hid;

You have now the good advantage of the night:

Have you not spoken 'gainst the Duke of Cornwall?

He's coming hither; now, i' the night, i' the haste,

And Regan with him: have you nothing said

Upon his party 'gainst the Duke of Albany?

Advise yourself.

Edg.　　　I am sure on 't, not a word.

Edm. I hear my father coming: pardon me;　30

In cunning I must draw my sword upon you:

Draw; seem to defend yourself; now quit you well.

Yield: come before my father. Light, ho, here!

Fly, brother. Torches, torches! So, farewell.

　　　　　　　　　　　　[*Exit Edgar.*

Some blood drawn on me would beget opinion　　　　　　　[*Wounds his arm.*

Of my more fierce endeavour: I have seen drunkards

Do more than this in sport. Father, father!

Stop, stop! No help?

Enter GLOUCESTER, *and* Servants *with torches.*

Glou. Now, Edmund, where's the villain?

Edm. Here stood he in the dark, his sharp sword out,　40

Mumbling of wicked charms, conjuring the moon

To stand auspicious mistress,—

Glou.　　　　　　　But where is he?

Edm. Look, sir, I bleed.

Glou.　　　Where is the villain, Edmund?

Edm. Fled this way, sir. When by no means he could—

Glou. Pursue him, ho! Go after. [*Exeunt some Servants.*] By no means what?

Edm. Persuade me to the murder of your lordship;

But that I told him, the revenging gods

'Gainst parricides did all their thunders bend;

Spoke, with how manifold and strong a bond

The child was bound to the father; sir, in fine,

Seeing how loathly opposite I stood　51

To his unnatural purpose, in fell motion,

With his prepared sword, he charges home

My unprovided body, lanced mine arm:

But when he saw my best alarum'd spirits,

Bold in the quarrel's right, roused to the encounter,

Or whether gasted by the noise I made,

Full suddenly he fled.

Glou.　　　　　　Let him fly far:

Not in this land shall he remain uncaught;

And found—dispatch. The noble duke my master,　60

My worthy arch and patron, comes tonight:

By his authority I will proclaim it,

That he which finds him shall deserve our thanks,

Bringing the murderous coward to the stake;

He that conceals him, death.

Edm. When I dissuaded him from his intent,

And found him pight to do it, with curst speech

I threaten'd to discover him: he replied,

---

9. **ear-kissing**, lightly whispered. 19. **queasy question**, hazardous, or ticklish, nature. 20. **briefness**, promptitude. 28. **Upon his party**, possibly, on his (i.e., Cornwall's) side. This would be confusing; Edmund is credited with making it so in order to frighten Edgar. It may mean, "Have you said nothing about the party Cornwall is forming against Albany?" 29. **Advise yourself**, probably, recollect. 31. **cunning**, pretense. 32. **quit you**, acquit yourself. 35. **beget**, create (for me).

'Thou unpossessing bastard! dost thou think,
If I would stand against thee, would the reposal
Of any trust, virtue, or worth in thee   71
Make thy words faith'd? No: what I should deny,—
As this I would; ay, though thou didst produce
My very character,—I'ld turn it all
To thy suggestion, plot, and damned practice:
And thou must make a dullard of the world,
If they not thought the profits of my death
Were very pregnant and potential spurs
To make thee seek it.'
    Glou.   Strong and fasten'd villain!
Would he deny his letter? I never got him. 80
                                 [*Tucket within.*
Hark, the duke's trumpets! I know not why he comes.
All ports I'll bar; the villain shall not 'scape;
The duke must grant me that: besides, his picture
I will send far and near, that all the kingdom
May have due note of him; and of my land,
Loyal and natural boy, I'll work the means
To make thee capable.

Enter Cornwall, Regan, *and* Attendants.

    Corn. How now, my noble friend! since I came hither,
Which I can call but now, I have heard strange news.
    Reg. If it be true, all vengeance comes too short   90
Which can pursue the offender. How dost, my lord?
    Glou. O, madam, my old heart is crack'd, is crack'd!
    Reg. What, did my father's godson seek your life?
He whom my father named? your Edgar?
    Glou. O, lady, lady, shame would have it hid!
    Reg. Was he not companion with the riotous knights
That tend upon my father?
    Glou. I know not, madam: 'tis too bad, too bad.

    Edm. Yes, madam, he was of that consort.
    Reg. No marvel, then, though he were ill affected: 100
'Tis they have put him on the old man's death,
To have the expense and waste of his revenues.
I have this present evening from my sister
Been well inform'd of them; and with such cautions,
That if they come to sojourn at my house,
I'll not be there.
    Corn.   Nor I, assure thee, Regan.
Edmund, I hear that you have shown your father
A child-like office.
    Edm.   'Twas my duty, sir.
    Glou. He did bewray his practice; and received
This hurt you see, striving to apprehend him.   110
    Corn. Is he pursued?
    Glou.   Ay, my good lord.
    Corn. If he be taken, he shall never more
Be fear'd of doing harm: make your own purpose,
How in my strength you please. For you, Edmund,
Whose virtue and obedience doth this instant
So much commend itself, you shall be ours:
Natures of such deep trust we shall much need;
You we first seize on.
    Edm.   I shall serve you, sir,
Truly, however else.
    Glou.   For him I thank your grace.
    Corn. You know not why we came to visit you,—   120
    Reg. Thus out of season, threading dark-eyed night:
Occasions, noble Gloucester, of some poise,
Wherein we must have use of your advice:
Our father he hath writ, so hath our sister,
Of differences, which I least thought it fit
To answer from our home; the several messengers
From hence attend dispatch. Our good old friend,
Lay comforts to your bosom; and bestow

---

69. **unpossessing**, unable to inherit, beggarly. 70. **I would**, I should. **reposal**, placing. 72. **faith'd**, believed. 75. **suggestion**, evil suggestion. **practice**, evil contrivance. 76. **make . . . world**, think the world an idiot. 77. **If . . . thought**, if they had not thought. 78. **pregnant**, obvious. 79. **Strong and fasten'd**, obdurate and confirmed. 82. **ports**, gates. 86. **natural**, having natural feeling. 87. **capable**, able to inherit.

99. **consort**, set, company. 101. **put . . . on**, incited him to. 109. **bewray**, disclose. 114. **in my strength**, by my power and authority. **For**, as for. 121. **threading**, passing through (as thread through the eye of a needle). 122. **poise**, weight, importance. 125. **differences**, quarrels. **which**, the letter. 127. **attend dispatch**, wait to be dispatched.

Your needful counsel to our business,
Which craves the instant use.

Glou. I serve you, madam: 130
Your graces are right welcome. [*Exeunt.*

Scene II. *Before Gloucester's castle.*

Enter Kent *and* Oswald, *severally.*

Osw. Good dawning to thee, friend: art of
this house?

Kent. Ay.

Osw. Where may we set our horses?

Kent. I' the mire.

Osw. Prithee, if thou lovest me, tell me.

Kent. I love thee not.

Osw. Why, then, I care not for thee.

Kent. If I had thee in Lipsbury pinfold, I
would make thee care for me. 10

Osw. Why dost thou use me thus? I know
thee not.

Kent. Fellow, I know thee.

Osw. What dost thou know me for?

Kent. A knave; a rascal; an eater of broken
meats; a base, proud, shallow, beggarly,
three-suited, hundred-pound, filthy, worsted-
stocking knave; a lily-livered, action-taking
knave, a whoreson, glass-gazing, super-
serviceable, finical rogue; one-trunk-in- 20
heriting slave; one that wouldst be a bawd,
in way of good service, and art nothing but
the composition of a knave, beggar, coward,
pandar, and the son and heir of a mongrel
bitch: one whom I will beat into clamorous
whining, if thou deniest the least syllable of
thy addition.

Osw. Why, what a monstrous fellow art
thou, thus to rail on one that is neither known
of thee nor knows thee! 29

Kent. What a brazen-faced varlet art
thou, to deny thou knowest me! Is it two
days ago since I tripped up thy heels, and
beat thee before the king? Draw, you
rogue: for, though it be night, yet the moon

shines; I'll make a sop o' the moonshine of
you: draw, you whoreson cullionly barber-
monger, draw. [*Drawing his sword.*

Osw. Away! I have nothing to do 37
with thee.

Kent. Draw, you rascal: you come with
letters against the king; and take vanity the
puppet's part against the royalty of her
father: draw, you rogue, or I'll so carbonado
your shanks: draw, you rascal; come your
ways.

Osw. Help, ho! murder! help!

Kent. Strike, you slave; stand, rogue,
stand; you neat slave, strike. [*Beating him.*

Osw. Help, ho! murder! murder! 46

Enter Edmund, *with his rapier drawn,*
Cornwall, Regan, Gloucester,
and Servants.

Edm. How now! What's the matter?

Kent. With you, goodman boy, an you
please: come, I'll flesh ye: come on, young
master.

Glou. Weapons! arms! What's the matter
here? 51

Corn. Keep peace, upon your lives;
He dies that strikes again. What is the
  matter?

Reg. The messengers from our sister and
the king.

Corn. What is your difference? speak.

Osw. I am scarce in breath, my lord.

Kent. No marvel, you have so bestirred
your valour. You cowardly rascal, nature
disclaims in thee: a tailor made thee. 60

Corn. Thou art a strange fellow: a tailor
make a man?

Kent. Ay, a tailor, sir: a stone-cutter or a
painter could not have made him so ill,
though he had been but two hours at the
trade.

Corn. Speak yet, how grew your quarrel?

Osw. This ancient ruffian, sir, whose life I
have spared at suit of his gray beard,— 68

Kent. Thou whoreson zed! thou unnecessary letter! My lord, if you will give me

Scene ii. 9. **Lipsbury pinfold.** This phrase is unexplained. *Pinfold* means "pound for stray animals."
Critics have tried to see in it an allusion to the prize-
ring; Nares supposes the allusion may be to the teeth
within the pinfold of the lips. 17. **three-suited,**
probable allusion to three suits a year allowed to servants.
hundred-pound, possible allusion to the minimum
property-qualification for the status of gentleman; sometimes seen as a reference to James I's wholesale creation
of knights. **worsted-stocking,** too poor and menial
to wear silk stockings. 18. **action-taking,** settling
quarrels by resort to law instead of arms, cowardly. 19.
glass-gazing, fond of looking in the mirror. **super-
serviceable,** officious. 20. **finical,** excessively particular, probably, in dress. **one-trunk-inheriting,** possessing effects sufficient for one trunk only. 26. **addition,** descriptive title.

35. **sop o' the moonshine,** supposed punning allusion
to a dish called "eggs in moonshine." 36. **cullionly
barber-monger,** base frequenter of barber-shops, fop.
39-40. **vanity the puppet's part.** Vanity was a character
in the morality plays. 41. **carbonado,** cut you crosswise like meat for broiling. 45. **neat,** foppish. 47.
matter. Kent takes the secondary meaning, "cause
for quarrel." 48. **goodman boy,** contemptuously. 49.
flesh, initiate in bloodshed. 60. **disclaims in,** disowns.
69. **zed,** the letter Z, a Greek character; in the spelling
of English words, known but unnecessary, and often
not included in dictionaries.

leave, I will tread this unbolted villain into
mortar, and daub the walls of a jakes with
him. Spare my gray beard, you wagtail?

Corn. Peace, sirrah!   74

You beastly knave, know you no reverence?

Kent. Yes, sir; but anger hath a privilege.

Corn. Why art thou angry?

Kent. That such a slave as this should
wear a sword,

Who wears no honesty. Such smiling rogues
as these,

Like rats, oft bite the holy cords a-twain   80

Which are too intrinse t' unloose; smooth
every passion

That in the natures of their lords rebel;

Bring oil to fire, snow to their colder moods;

Renege, affirm, and turn their halcyon
beaks

With every gale and vary of their masters,

Knowing nought, like dogs, but following.

A plague upon your epileptic visage!

Smile you my speeches, as I were a fool?

Goose, if I had you upon Sarum plain,

I'ld drive ye cackling home to Camelot.   90

Corn. What, art thou mad, old fellow?

Glou. How fell you out? say that.

Kent. No contraries hold more antipathy
Than I and such a knave.

Corn. Why dost thou call him knave?
What's his offence?

Kent. His countenance likes me not.

Corn. No more, perchance, does mine, nor
his, nor hers.

Kent. Sir, 'tis my occupation to be plain:
I have seen better faces in my time

Than stands on any shoulder that I see 100

Before me at this instant.

Corn.   This is some fellow,

Who, having been praised for bluntness, doth
affect

A saucy roughness, and constrains the garb

Quite from his nature: he cannot flatter, he,

An honest mind and plain, he must speak
truth!

An they will take it, so; if not, he's plain.

These kind of knaves I know, which in this
plainness

Harbour more craft and more corrupter ends

Than twenty silly ducking observants

That stretch their duties nicely.   110

Kent. Sir, in good sooth, in sincere verity,

Under the allowance of your great aspect,

Whose influence, like the wreath of radiant fire

On flickering Phœbus' front,—

Corn.   What mean'st by this?

Kent. To go out of my dialect, which you
discommend so much. I know, sir, I am no
flatterer: he that beguiled you in a plain accent was a plain knave; which for my part I
will not be, though I should win your displeasure to entreat me to 't.   120

Corn. What was the offence you gave him?

Osw. I never gave him any:

It pleased the king his master very late

To strike at me, upon his misconstruction;

When he, conjunct, and flattering his displeasure,

Tripp'd me behind; being down, insulted,
rail'd,

And put upon him such a deal of man,

That worthied him, got praises of the king

For him attempting who was self-subdued;

And, in the fleshment of this dread exploit, 130

Drew on me here again.

Kent.   None of these rogues and
cowards

But Ajax is their fool.

Corn.   Fetch forth the stocks!

You stubborn ancient knave, you reverend
braggart,

We'll teach you—

Kent.   Sir, I am too old to learn:

Call not your stocks for me: I serve the king;

On whose employment I was sent to you:

You shall do small respect, show too bold
malice

Against the grace and person of my master,

Stocking his messenger.

Corn. Fetch forth the stocks! As I have
  life and honour,   140
There shall he sit till noon.

Reg. Till noon! till night, my lord; and all
  night too.

Kent. Why, madam, if I were your
  father's dog,
You should not use me so.

Reg.   Sir, being his knave, I will.

Corn. This is a fellow of the self-same
  colour
Our sister speaks of. Come, bring away the
  stocks!   *[Stocks brought out.*

Glou. Let me beseech your grace not to
  do so:
His fault is much, and the good king his
  master
Will check him for't: your purposed low cor-
  rection   149
Is such as basest and contemned'st wretches
For pilferings and most common trespasses
Are punish'd with: the king must take it ill,
That he's so slightly valued in his messenger,
Should have him thus restrain'd.

Corn.   I'll answer that.

Reg. My sister may receive it much more
  worse,
To have her gentleman abused, assaulted,
For following her affairs. Put in his legs.
                              [Kent is put in the stocks.
Come, my good lord, away.
            [Exeunt all but Gloucester and Kent.

Glou. I am sorry for thee, friend; 'tis the
  duke's pleasure,
Whose disposition, all the world well knows,
Will not be rubb'd nor stopp'd: I'll entreat
  for thee.   161

Kent. Pray, do not, sir: I have watched
  and travell'd hard;
Some time I shall sleep out, the rest I'll
  whistle.
A good man's fortune may grow out at heels:
Give you good morrow!

Glou. The duke's to blame in this; 'twill
  be ill taken   *[Exit.*

Kent. Good king, that must approve the
  common saw,
Thou out of heaven's benediction comest

To the warm sun!
Approach, thou beacon to this under globe,
That by thy comfortable beams I may   171
Peruse this letter! Nothing almost sees
  miracles
But misery: I know 'tis from Cordelia,
Who hath most fortunately been inform'd
Of my obscured course; and shall find time
†From this enormous state, seeking to give
Losses their remedies. All weary and o'er-
  watch'd,
Take vantage, heavy eyes, not to behold
This shameful lodging.   179
Fortune, good night: smile once more; turn
  thy wheel!   *[Sleeps.*

Scene III. *A wood.*

Enter Edgar.

Edg. I heard myself proclaim'd;
And by the happy hollow of a tree
Escaped the hunt. No port is free; no
  place,
That guard, and most unusual vigilance,
Does not attend my taking. Whiles I may
  'scape,
I will preserve myself: and am bethought
To take the basest and most poorest shape
That ever penury, in contempt of man,
Brought near to beast: my face I'll grime
  with filth;
Blanket my loins; elf all my hair in knots;   10
And with presented nakedness out-face
The winds and persecutions of the sky.
The country gives me proof and precedent
Of Bedlam beggars, who, with roaring voices,
Strike in their numb'd and mortified bare
  arms
Pins, wooden pricks, nails, sprigs of rosemary;
And with this horrible object, from low
  farms,
Poor pelting villages, sheep-cotes, and mills,
Sometime with lunatic bans, sometime with
  prayers,

171. **comfortable**, useful. 175-177. **and . . . reme-dies**, an obscure passage. Daniel's conjecture of *she'll* for *shall* makes a sort of sense. 177. **o'er-watch'd**, exhausted with watching.
Scene iii. 3. **port**, means of exit. 5. **attend**, watch, wait for. 6. **am bethought**, it has occurred to me. 10. **elf**, tangle into elf-locks. 14. **Bedlam beggars**, called also "Tom o' Bedlams" and "Abraham men"; they were lunatic patients of Bethlehem Hospital turned out to beg for their bread. Dekker in the *Bellman of London*, 1608, gives a description of their characteristics which closely parallels the one in the text. 15. **mortified**, numbed, insensible. 16. **wooden pricks**, skewers. 17. **object**, appearance. **low**, lowly. 18. **pelting**, paltry, petty. 19. **bans**, curses.

145. **colour**, kind, complexion. 149. **check**, reprove, rebuke. 161. **rubb'd**, hindered, obstructed; term from bowls. 162. **watched**, gone without sleep. 163. **sleep out**, sleep through. 165. **Give you**, i.e., God give you. 167. **approve**, prove true. **saw**, proverb: "To run out of God's blessing into the warm sun," meaning "to go from better to worse."

Enforce their charity. Poor Turlygod! poor
    Tom!   20
That's something yet: Edgar I nothing am.
                                          [*Exit.*

Scene IV. *Before Gloucester's castle. Kent
                    in the stocks.*

        Enter Lear, Fool, *and* Gentleman.

    Lear. 'Tis strange that they should so
        depart from home,
And not send back my messenger.
    Gent.   As I learn'd,
The night before there was no purpose in
        them
Of this remove.
    Kent.   Hail to thee, noble master!
    Lear. Ha!
Makest thou this shame thy pastime?
    Kent.   No, my lord.
    Fool. Ha, ha! he wears cruel garters.
Horses are tied by the heads, dogs and bears
by the neck, monkeys by the loins, and men
by the legs: when a man's over-lusty at legs,
then he wears wooden nether-stocks.   11
    Lear. What's he that hath so much thy
        place mistook
To set thee here?
    Kent.   It is both he and she;
Your son and daughter.
    Lear. No.
    Kent. Yes.
    Lear. No, I say.
    Kent. I say, yea.
    Lear. No, no, they would not.
    Kent. Yes, they have.   20
    Lear. By Jupiter, I swear, no.
    Kent. By Juno, I swear, ay.
    Lear.   They durst not do 't;
They could not, would not do 't; 'tis worse
        than murder,
To do upon respect such violent outrage:
Resolve me, with all modest haste, which
        way
Thou mightst deserve, or they impose, this
        usage,
Coming from us.

    Kent.   My lord, when at their home
I did commend your highness' letters to
        them,
Ere I was risen from the place that show'd
My duty kneeling, came there a reeking
        post,
Stew'd in his haste, half breathless, panting
        forth   31
From Goneril his mistress salutations;
Deliver'd letters, spite of intermission,
Which presently they read: on whose con-
        tents,
They summon'd up their meiny, straight
        took horse;
Commanded me to follow, and attend
The leisure of their answer; gave me cold
        looks:
And meeting here the other messenger,
Whose welcome, I perceived, had poison'd
        mine,—
Being the very fellow that of late   40
Display'd so saucily against your high-
        ness,—
Having more man than wit about me, drew:
He raised the house with loud and coward
        cries.
Your son and daughter found this trespass
        worth
The shame which here it suffers.
    Fool. Winter's not gone yet, if the wild-
geese fly that way.
                Fathers that wear rags
                    Do make their children blind;
                But fathers that bear bags   50
                    Shall see their children kind.
                Fortune, that arrant whore,
                    Ne'er turns the key to the poor.
But, for all this, thou shalt have as many
dolours for thy daughters as thou canst tell in
a year.
    Lear. O, how this mother swells up toward
        my heart!
Hysterica passio, down, thou climbing
        sorrow,
Thy element's below! Where is this daughter?
    Kent. With the earl, sir, here within.
    Lear.   Follow me not;
Stay here.   [*Exit.* 60

---

20. **Turlygod,** meaning unknown; Warburton proposed *Turlipin,* the name of an order of mad beggars in
France. 21. **nothing,** probably, not at all, in no respect.
    Scene iv. 4. **remove,** change of residence (of royalty).
7. **cruel,** Q: *crewell,* a double meaning: (1) "unkind," (2)
"crewel," a thin yarn of which garters were made. 11.
nether-stocks, stockings. 24. **upon respect,** deliberately. 25. **Resolve,** inform. **modest,** becoming, fit.

28. **commend,** deliver, commit. 33. **spite of intermission,** in spite of interrupting me. 35. **meiny,**
household. 41. **Display'd,** behaved ostentatiously. 42.
drew, i.e., my sword. 55. **dolours,** griefs, with pun on
dollars. 55. **tell,** count. 56-57. **mother, Hysterica
passio,** a disease, apparently called by both these names,
accompanied by a sense of strangulation. Lear mistakes
the epigastric discomfort of extreme grief for the disease.

Gent. Made you no more offence but what
you speak of?

Kent. None.
How chance the king comes with so small a
      train?

Fool. An thou hadst been set i' the stocks
for that question, thou hadst well deserved
it.

Kent. Why, fool?

Fool. We'll set thee to school to an ant, to
teach thee there's no labouring i' the winter.
All that follow their noses are led by their
eyes but blind men; and there's not a nose
among twenty but can smell him that's
stinking. Let go thy hold when a great
wheel runs down a hill, lest it break thy neck
with following it; but the great one that goes
up the hill, let him draw thee after. When
a wise man gives thee better counsel, give
me mine again: I would have none but
knaves follow it, since a fool gives it.

      That sir which serves and seeks for gain,
        And follows but for form,   80
      Will pack when it begins to rain,
        And leave thee in the storm.
      But I will tarry; the fool will stay,
        And let the wise man fly:
      The knave turns fool that runs away;
        The fool no knave, perdy.

Kent. Where learned you this, fool?

Fool. Not i' the stocks, fool.

Re-enter LEAR, *with* GLOUCESTER.

Lear. Deny to speak with me? They are
      sick? they are weary?
They have travell'd all the night? Mere
      fetches;   90
The images of revolt and flying off.
Fetch me a better answer.

Glou.   My dear lord,
You know the fiery quality of the duke;
How unremoveable and fix'd he is
In his own course.

Lear. Vengeance! plague! death! con-
      fusion!
Fiery? what quality? Why, Gloucester, Glou-
      cester,
I'ld speak with the Duke of Cornwall and his
      wife.

Glou. Well, my good lord, I have inform'd
      them so.

Lear. Inform'd them! Dost thou under-
      stand me, man?   100

Glou. Ay, my good lord.

Lear. The king would speak with Corn-
      wall; the dear father
Would with his daughter speak, commands
      her service:
Are they inform'd of this? My breath and
      blood!
Fiery? the fiery duke? Tell the hot duke
      that—
No, but not yet: may be he is not well:
Infirmity doth still neglect all office
Whereto our health is bound; we are not
      ourselves
When nature, being oppress'd, commands
      the mind
To suffer with the body: I'll forbear;   110
And am fall'n out with my more headier will,
To take the indisposed and sickly fit
For the sound man. Death on my state!
      wherefore   [*Looking on Kent.*
Should he sit here? This act persuades me
That this remotion of the duke and her
Is practice only. Give me my servant forth.
Go tell the duke and 's wife I'ld speak with
      them,
Now, presently: bid them come forth and
      hear me,
Or at their chamber-door I'll beat the drum
Till it cry sleep to death.   120

Glou. I would have all well betwixt you.
                                      [*Exit.*

Lear. O me, my heart, my rising heart!
      but, down!

Fool. Cry to it, nuncle, as the cockney did
to the eels when she put 'em i' the paste alive;
she knapped 'em o' the coxcombs with a
stick, and cried 'Down, wantons, down!'
'Twas her brother that, in pure kindness to
his horse, buttered his hay.

Enter CORNWALL, REGAN, GLOUCESTER, *and*
                    Servants.

Lear. Good morrow to you both.

64. **chance**, chances it. 79. **sir**, great person. 81.
pack, take himself off. 89. **Deny**, refuse. 90. **fetches**,
pretexts, dodges. 91. **images**, signs. **flying off**,
desertion. 93. **quality**, disposition.

111-112. **am . . . take**, am wrong because of my more
impetuous will in taking. 115. **remotion**, removal.
116. **practice**, artifice. 120. **cry sleep to death**, i.e.,
put an end to sleep. 123. **cockney**, a word of disputed
origin and meaning. It is said to have meant a pampered, affected woman, a spoiled child, a milksop; the
passage here suggests the meaning "cook." 125. **knapped 'em**, Q: *rapt um;* Steevens preferred the Q reading
because *knap* means properly "to break asunder."
coxcombs, heads.

Corn.   Hail to your grace!
                                    [*Kent is set at liberty.*
Reg. I am glad to see your highness. 130
Lear. Regan, I think you are; I know
    what reason
I have to think so: if thou shouldst not be
    glad,
I would divorce me from thy mother's
    tomb,
Sepulchring an adultress. [*To Kent*] O, are
    you free?
Some other time for that.   Beloved Regan,
Thy sister's naught: O Regan, she hath
    tied
Sharp-tooth'd unkindness, like a vulture,
    here: [*Points to his heart.*
I can scarce speak to thee; thou'lt not
    believe
With how depraved a quality—O Regan!
Reg. I pray you, sir, take patience: I have
    hope   140
You less know how to value her desert
Than she to scant her duty.
    Lear.   Say, how is that?
Reg. I cannot think my sister in the least
Would fail her obligation: if, sir, perchance
She have restrain'd the riots of your fol-
    lowers,
'Tis on such ground, and to such wholesome
    end,
As clears her from all blame.
    Lear. My curses on her!
    Reg.   O, sir, you are old;
Nature in you stands on the very verge 149
Of her confine: you should be ruled and led
By some discretion, that discerns your state
Better than you yourself. Therefore, I pray
    you,
That to our sister you do make return;
Say you have wrong'd her, sir.
    Lear.   Ask her forgiveness?
Do you but mark how this becomes the
    house:
'Dear daughter, I confess that I am old;
                                    [*Kneeling.*
Age is unnecessary: on my knees I beg
That you'll vouchsafe me raiment, bed, and
    food.'
Reg. Good sir, no more; these are un-
    sightly tricks:

Return you to my sister.
    Lear.   [*Rising*] Never, Regan: 160
She hath abated me of half my train;
Look'd black upon me; struck me with her
    tongue,
Most serpent-like, upon the very heart:
All the stored vengeances of heaven fall
On her ingrateful top! Strike her young
    bones,
You taking airs, with lameness!
    Corn.   Fie, sir, fie!
Lear. You nimble lightnings, dart your
    blinding flames
Into her scornful eyes! Infect her beauty,
You fen-suck'd fogs, drawn by the powerful
    sun,
To fall and blast her pride!   170
    Reg. O the blest gods! so will you wish on
    me,
When the rash mood is on.
    Lear. No, Regan, thou shalt never have
    my curse:
Thy tender-hefted nature shall not give
Thee o'er to harshness: her eyes are fierce;
    but thine
Do comfort and not burn. 'Tis not in thee
To grudge my pleasures, to cut off my
    train,
To bandy hasty words, to scant my sizes,
And in conclusion to oppose the bolt
Against my coming in: thou better know'st
The offices of nature, bond of childhood, 181
Effects of courtesy, dues of gratitude;
Thy half o' the kingdom hast thou not for-
    got,
Wherein I thee endow'd.
    Reg.   Good sir, to the purpose.
    Lear. Who put my man i' the stocks?
                                    [*Tucket within.*
    Corn.   What trumpet's that?
    Reg. I know 't, my sister's: this approves
    her letter,
That she would soon be here.

Enter OSWALD.

                                    Is your lady come?

---

139. **quality**, character. 140-142. **I have . . . duty.**
The passage does not construe literally; the sense is
plain. 150. **confine**, assigned boundary. 151. **discretion**, discreet person. 155. **how . . . house**, how
this would be suitable to our position.

161. **abated . . . of**, diminished from, deprived of.
165. **ingrateful top**, ungrateful head. **young bones**,
i.e., unborn child. 166. **taking**, blasting, infecting.
169. **fen-suck'd.** It was supposed that the sun sucked
up poisons from fens or marshes. 170. **fall**, cause to
fall. 174. **tender-hefted**, set in a tender delicate
frame (Wright); gentle. 178. **sizes**, allowances. 180-
183. **thou . . . forgot.** Note that Lear enumerates
what are ethically the pillars of society. 186. **approves**,
confirms.

Lear. This is a slave, whose easy-borrow'd pride
Dwells in the fickle grace of her he follows.
Out, varlet, from my sight!
Corn.   What means your grace?
Lear. Who stock'd my servant? Regan, I have good hope   191
Thou didst not know on't. Who comes here?
O heavens,

Enter GONERIL.

If you do love old men, if your sweet sway
Allow obedience, if yourselves are old,
Make it your cause; send down, and take my part!
[*To Gon.*] Art not ashamed to look upon this beard?
O Regan, wilt thou take her by the hand?
Gon. Why not by the hand, sir? How have I offended?
All's not offence that indiscretion finds
And dotage terms so.
Lear.   O sides, you are too tough;
Will you yet hold? How came my man i' the stocks?   201
Corn. I set him there, sir: but his own disorders
Deserved much less advancement.
Lear.   You! did you?
Reg. I pray you, father, being weak, seem so.
If, till the expiration of your month,
You will return and sojourn with my sister,
Dismissing half your train, come then to me:
I am now from home, and out of that provision
Which shall be needful for your entertainment.
Lear. Return to her, and fifty men dismiss'd?   210
No, rather I abjure all roofs, and choose
To wage against the enmity o' the air;
To be a comrade with the wolf and owl,—
Necessity's sharp pinch! Return with her?
Why, the hot-blooded France, that dowerless took

Our youngest born, I could as well be brought
To knee his throne, and, squire-like, pension beg
To keep base life afoot. Return with her?
Persuade me rather to be slave and sumpter
To this detested groom. [*Pointing at Oswald.*
Gon.   At your choice, sir.
Lear. I prithee, daughter, do not make me mad: 221
I will not trouble thee, my child; farewell:
We'll no more meet, no more see one another:
But yet thou art my flesh, my blood, my daughter;
Or rather a disease that's in my flesh,
Which I must needs call mine: thou art a boil,
A plague-sore, an embossed carbuncle,
In my corrupted blood. But I'll not chide thee;
Let shame come when it will, I do not call it:
I do not bid the thunder-bearer shoot,   230
Nor tell tales of thee to high-judging Jove:
Mend when thou canst; be better at thy leisure:
I can be patient; I can stay with Regan,
I and my hundred knights.
Reg.   Not altogether so:
I look'd not for you yet, nor am provided
For your fit welcome. Give ear, sir, to my sister;
For those that mingle reason with your passion
Must be content to think you old, and so—
But she knows what she does.
Lear.   Is this well spoken?
Reg. I dare avouch it, sir: what, fifty followers?   240
Is it not well? What should you need of more?
Yea, or so many, sith that both charge and danger
Speak 'gainst so great a number? How, in one house,
Should many people, under two commands,
Hold amity? 'Tis hard; almost impossible.
Gon. Why might not you, my lord, receive attendance

From those that she calls servants or from
  mine?
  Reg. Why not, my lord? If then they
    chanced to slack you,
We could control them. If you will come to
  me,—
For now I spy a danger,—I entreat you 250
To bring but five and twenty: to no more
Will I give place or notice.
  Lear. I gave you all—
  Reg.   And in good time you gave it.
  Lear. Made you my guardians, my de-
    positaries;
But kept a reservation to be follow'd
With such a number. What, must I come to
  you
With five and twenty, Regan? said you so?
  Reg. And speak 't again, my lord; no
    more with me.
  Lear. Those wicked creatures yet do look
    well-favour'd,
When others are more wicked; not being
    the worst   260
Stands in some rank of praise. [*To Gon.*]
    I'll go with thee:
Thy fifty yet doth double five-and-twenty,
And thou art twice her love.
  Gon.   Hear me, my lord:
What need you five and twenty, ten, or five,
To follow in a house where twice so many
Have a command to tend you?
  Reg.   What need one?
  Lear. O, reason not the need: our basest
    beggars
Are in the poorest thing superfluous:
Allow not nature more than nature needs,
Man's life's as cheap as beast's: thou art a
    lady;   270
If only to go warm were gorgeous,
Why, nature needs not what thou gorgeous
    wear'st,
Which scarcely keeps thee warm. But, for
    true need,—
You heavens, give me that patience, patience
    I need!

You see me here, you gods, a poor old
    man,
As full of grief as age; wretched in both!
If it be you that stir these daughters' hearts
Against their father, fool me not so much
To bear it tamely; touch me with noble
    anger,
And let not women's weapons, water-drops,
Stain my man's cheeks! No, you unnatural
    hags,   281
I will have such revenges on you both,
That all the world shall—I will do such
    things,—
What they are, yet I know not; but they
    shall be
The terrors of the earth. You think I'll
    weep;
No, I'll not weep:
I have full cause of weeping; but this heart
Shall break into a hundred thousand flaws,
Or ere I'll weep. O fool, I shall go mad!
    [*Exeunt Lear, Gloucester, Kent, and Fool.
                        Storm and tempest.*
  Corn. Let us withdraw; 'twill be a storm.
  Reg. This house is little: the old man and
    his people   291
Cannot be well bestow'd.
  Gon. 'Tis his own blame; hath put himself
    from rest,
And must needs taste his folly.
  Reg. For his particular, I'll receive him
    gladly,
But not one follower.
  Gon.   So am I purposed.
Where is my lord of Gloucester?
  Corn. Follow'd the old man forth: he is
    return'd.

Re-enter GLOUCESTER.

  Glou. The king is in high rage.
  Corn.   Whither is he going?
  Glou. He calls to horse; but will I know
    not whither.   300
  Corn. 'Tis best to give him way; he leads
    himself.
  Gon. My lord, entreat him by no means
    to stay.

---

248. **slack**, be careless in their attendance on. 252.
notice, countenance. 254. **my guardians.** Lear
understands his contract to be that the daughters were
guardians, or stewardesses, of his realm under him.
259-260. **Those . . . wicked.** Bad as Goneril is, there
is a more exquisite quality of cruelty in Regan. 266. **tend**,
wait on. **What need one?** Lear's answer (ll. 267 ff.)
is in some respects an expression of the underlying theme
of the story: Why *reason*, i.e., discuss, the *need*, since it
is not a question of need? It is a spiritual, not a temporal,
matter which is involved. 274. **patience**. Patience
seems to have been a term for the counterbalance which
reason might set up against the passions.

279. **noble anger.** One cannot understand either
the character of Lear or the significance of his story
without a sound conception of righteous indignation as
a noble virtue; with it is connected the ethical propriety
of revenge. 285. **terrors of the earth.** Note the
artistic effect of vague suggestion at this moment of
extreme tension. 288. **flaws**, shivers, splinters. 292.
bestow'd, lodged. 293. **blame**, fault. 295. **For his
particular**, as for him individually.

Glou. Alack, the night comes on, and the
　　bleak winds
Do sorely ruffle; for many miles about
There's scarce a bush.
　　Reg.　　　　O, sir, to wilful men,
The injuries that they themselves procure
Must be their schoolmasters. Shut up your
　　doors:
He is attended with a desperate train;
And what they may incense him to, being
　　apt　　　　　　　　　　　　　　　309
To have his ear abused, wisdom bids fear.
　　Corn. Shut up your doors, my lord; 'tis a
　　wild night:
My Regan counsels well: come out o' the
　　storm.　　　　　　　　　　　[*Exeunt.*

ACT III.

Scene I. *A heath.*

Storm still.　Enter Kent *and a* Gentleman,
meeting.

　　Kent. Who's there, besides foul weather?
　　Gent. One minded like the weather, most
　　unquietly.
　　Kent. I know you. Where's the king?
　　Gent. Contending with the fretful ele-
　　ment;
Bids the wind blow the earth into the sea,
Or swell the curled waters 'bove the main,
That things might change or cease; tears his
　　white hair,
Which the impetuous blasts, with eyeless
　　rage,
Catch in their fury, and make nothing of;
Strives in his little world of man to out-
　　scorn　　　　　　　　　　　　　10
The to-and-fro-conflicting wind and rain.
This night, wherein the cub-drawn bear
　　would couch,
The lion and the belly-pinched wolf
Keep their fur dry, unbonneted he runs,
And bids what will take all.
　　Kent.　　　　But who is with him?
　　Gent. None but the fool; who labours to
　　out-jest

His heart-struck injuries.
　　Kent.　　　　Sir, I do know you;
And dare, upon the warrant of my note,
Commend a dear thing to you. There is
　　division,
Although as yet the face of it be cover'd　20
With mutual cunning, 'twixt Albany and
　　Cornwall;
Who have—as who have not, that their great
　　stars
Throned and set high?—servants, who seem
　　no less,
Which are to France the spies and specula-
　　tions
Intelligent of our state; what hath been seen,
Either in snuffs and packings of the dukes,
Or the hard rein which both of them have
　　borne
Against the old kind king; or something
　　deeper,
Whereof perchance these are but furnishings;
But, true it is, from France there comes a
　　power　　　　　　　　　　　　30
Into this scatter'd kingdom; who already,
Wise in our negligence, have secret feet
In some of our best ports, and are at point
To show their open banner. Now to you:
If on my credit you dare build so far
To make your speed to Dover, you shall find
Some that will thank you, making just report
Of how unnatural and bemadding sorrow
The king hath cause to plain.
I am a gentleman of blood and breeding;　40
And, from some knowledge and assurance,
　　offer
This office to you.
　　Gent. I will talk further with you.
　　Kent.　　　　　　　No, do not.
For confirmation that I am much more
Than my out-wall, open this purse, and take
What it contains. If you shall see Cordelia,—
As fear not but you shall,—show her this
　　.ring;
And she will tell you who your fellow is
That yet you do not know. Fie on this storm!
I will go seek the king.　　　　　　50
　　Gent. Give me your hand: have you no
　　more to say?

---

304. **ruffle**, bluster. 308. **desperate train**, body
of desperate followers. 309. **incense him to**, incite
him to undertake.
　Act III. Scene i. 4. **element**, air. 6. **main**, main-
land. 10. **little world of man**, the microcosm; allusion to the theory that man is an epitome of the macrocosm, or universe, and moves in accordance with its
laws and influences. 12. **cub-drawn**, famished, with
udders sucked dry. **couch**, lie close.

18. **upon . . . note**, on the strength of what I know.
19. **Commend**, entrust. **dear**, important, momentous.
24. **speculations**, scouts, spies. Johnson conjectured
speculators. 26. **snuffs**, quarrels. **packings**, plots.
29. **furnishings**, outward shows. 31. **scatter'd**,
divided. 33. **at point**, ready. 38. **bemadding**, distracting. 39. **plain**, complain of. 45. **out-wall**,
exterior. 48. **fellow**, companion.

Kent. Few words, but, to effect, more than
　all yet;
That, when we have found the king,—in
　which your pain
That way, I'll this,—he that first lights on
　him
Holla the other.　　　　　[*Exeunt severally.*

SCENE II. *Another part of the heath. Storm
　　　　　　　　　still.*

Enter LEAR *and* Fool.

Lear. Blow, winds, and crack your cheeks!
　rage! blow!
You cataracts and hurricanoes, spout
Till you have drench'd our steeples, drown'd
　the cocks!
You sulphurous and thought-executing fires,
Vaunt-couriers to oak-cleaving thunderbolts,
Singe my white head! And thou, all-shaking
　thunder,
Smite flat the thick rotundity o' the world!
Crack nature's moulds, all germens spill at
　once,
That make ingrateful man!　　　　　9

Fool. O nuncle, court holy-water in a dry
house is better than this rain-water out o'
door. Good nuncle, in, and ask thy daughters' blessing: here's a night pities neither
wise man nor fool.

Lear. Rumble thy bellyful! Spit, fire!
spout, rain!
Nor rain, wind, thunder, fire, are my daugh-
　ters:
I tax not you, you elements, with unkindness;
I never gave you kingdom, call'd you chil-
　dren,
You owe me no subscription: then let fall
Your horrible pleasure; here I stand, your
　slave,
A poor, infirm, weak, and despised old man:
But yet I call you servile ministers,　　21
That have with two pernicious daughters
　join'd
Your high engender'd battles 'gainst a head
So old and white as this. O! O! 'tis foul!

Fool. He that has a house to put 's head
in has a good head-piece.
　　The cod-piece that will house
　　　Before the head has any,
　　The head and he shall louse;
　　　So beggars marry many.　　　30
　　The man that makes his toe
　　　What he his heart should make
　　Shall of a corn cry woe,
　　　And turn his sleep to wake.
For there was never yet fair woman but she
made mouths in a glass.

Lear. No, I will be the pattern of all
　patience;
I will say nothing.

Enter KENT.

Kent. Who's there?
Fool. Marry, here's grace and a cod-piece;
that's a wise man and a fool.　　　41

Kent. Alas, sir, are you here? things that
　love night
Love not such nights as these; the wrathful
　skies
Gallow the very wanderers of the dark,
And make them keep their caves: since I was
　man,
Such sheets of fire, such bursts of horrid
　thunder,
Such groans of roaring wind and rain, I
　never
Remember to have heard: man's nature can-
　not carry
The affliction nor the fear.

Lear.　　　　　　Let the great gods, 49
That keep this dreadful pother o'er our
　heads,
Find out their enemies now. Tremble, thou
　wretch,
That hast within thee undivulged crimes,
Unwhipp'd of justice: hide thee, thou bloody
　hand;
Thou perjured, and thou simular man of
　virtue
That art incestuous: caitiff, to pieces shake,

52. to effect, to the purpose. 53-54. your pain
That way, laborious quest (take you) that way.
　Scene ii. 2. hurricanoes, waterspouts. 3. cocks,
weathercocks. 4. thought-executing, probably, acting with the quickness of thought. 5. Vaunt-couriers,
forerunners. 8. germens, germs, seeds. spill, destroy. 10. court holy-water, flattery. 18. subscription, allegiance. 23. high engender'd battles, battalions levied in the heavens.

27-34. The cod-piece . . . wake. A man who prefers
a mean member in place of a vital one shall suffer enduring
pain where others would suffer merely a twinge. Lear
had preferred Regan and Goneril to Cordelia (Furness).
40. cod-piece, the front part of the close-fitting hose
worn by men; here applied by the fool to himself. 44.
Gallow, frighten, terrify. 48. carry, bear, endure. 49.
Let the great gods, etc. This is an expression of Lear's
faith in the power of the gods, or, as we should say, God;
it is the symbol of the retention of his sanity. When he
loses his reason he loses also his faith in divinity. 50.
pother, turmoil. 54. simular man, pretender.

That under covert and convenient seeming
Hast practised on man's life: close pent-up
    guilts,
Rive your concealing continents, and cry
These dreadful summoners grace. I am a
    man
More sinn'd against than sinning.

Kent.   Alack, bare-headed!   60
Gracious my lord, hard by here is a hovel;
Some friendship will it lend you 'gainst the
    tempest:
Repose you there; while I to this hard
    house —
More harder than the stones whereof 'tis
    raised;
Which even but now, demanding after you,
Denied me to come in—return, and force
Their scanted courtesy.

Lear.   My wits begin to turn.
Come on, my boy: how dost, my boy? art
    cold?
I am cold myself. Where is this straw, my
    fellow?
The art of our necessities is strange,   70
That can make vile things precious. Come,
    your hovel.
Poor fool and knave, I have one part in my
    heart
That's sorry yet for thee.

Fool. [*Singing*] He that has and a little tiny
    wit,—
    With hey, ho, the wind and the rain,—
Must make content with his fortunes fit,
    For the rain it raineth every day.

Lear. True, my good boy. Come, bring us
    to this hovel.   [*Exeunt Lear and Kent.*

Fool. This is a brave night to cool a
    courtezan.
I'll speak a prophecy ere I go: 80
    When priests are more in word than mat-
        ter;
    When brewers mar their malt with water;
    When nobles are their tailors' tutors;

    No heretics burn'd, but wenches' suitors;
    When every case in law is right;
    No squire in debt, nor no poor knight;
    When slanders do not live in tongues;
    Nor cutpurses come not to throngs;
    When usurers tell their gold i' the field;
    And bawds and whores do churches build;
    Then shall the realm of Albion   91
    Come to great confusion:
    Then comes the time, who lives to see 't,
    That going shall be used with feet.
This prophecy Merlin shall make; for I live
    before his time.   [*Exit.*

SCENE III. *Gloucester's castle.*

Enter GLOUCESTER *and* EDMUND.

Glou. Alack, alack, Edmund, I like not
this unnatural dealing. When I desired their
leave that I might pity him, they took from
me the use of mine own house; charged me,
on pain of their perpetual displeasure,
neither to speak of him, entreat for him, nor
any way sustain him.

Edm. Most savage and unnatural!   7

Glou. Go to; say you nothing. There's a
division betwixt the dukes; and a worse
matter than that: I have received a letter
this night; 'tis dangerous to be spoken; I
have locked the letter in my closet: these
injuries the king now bears will be revenged
home; there's part of a power already footed:
we must incline to the king. I will seek him,
and privily relieve him: go you and maintain
talk with the duke, that my charity be not
of him perceived: if he ask for me, I am ill,
and gone to bed. Though I die for it, as no
less is threatened me, the king my old master
must be relieved. There is some strange
thing toward, Edmund; pray you, be careful.   [*Exit.* 21

Edm. This courtesy, forbid thee, shall the
    duke
Instantly know; and of that letter too:
This seems a fair deserving, and must draw
    me
That which my father loses; no less than all:
The younger rises when the old doth fall.
    [*Exit.*

---

56. **seeming,** hypocrisy. 57. **practised on,** plotted
against. 58. **continents,** that which encloses. **cry
. . . grace,** pray for mercy at the hands of the officers
of divine justice. A **summoner** was the police officer
of an ecclesiastical court. 60. **More sinn'd against
than sinning.** This famous phrase is a perfect indication that Lear is still sane. 63. **hard,** cruel. 65. **Which,**
i.e., the owners of the house. **demanding,** I inquiring.
66. **Denied,** refused to let me. 67. **My wits begin to
turn,** a premonition followed by an expression of more
than Lear's normal sanity, since it is his first reflection of
sympathy for others. 80-95. **I'll . . . time.** Omitted
in Q and usually regarded as an interpolation in the text
of F. Merlin was a magician of King Arthur's court; a
prophecy of Merlin, somewhat like these lines, is found
in Holinshed and other places.

Scene iii. 14. **home,** fully. **footed,** landed. 22.
courtesy, forbid thee, i.e., this kindness to Lear you
were forbidden to show. 24. **fair deserving,** meritorious
action.

SCENE IV. *The heath. Before a hovel.*

Enter LEAR, KENT, *and* Fool.

Kent. Here is the place, my lord; good my
    lord, enter:
The tyranny of the open night's too rough
For nature to endure.   [*Storm still.*
    Lear.   Let me alone.
    Kent. Good my lord, enter here.
    Lear.   Wilt break my heart?
    Kent. I had rather break mine own. Good
    my lord, enter.
    Lear. Thou think'st 'tis much that this
    contentious storm
Invades us to the skin: so 'tis to thee;
But where the greater malady is fix'd,
The lesser is scarce felt. Thou 'ldst shun a
    bear;
But if thy flight lay toward the raging sea, 10
Thou 'ldst meet the bear i' the mouth. When
    the mind's free,
The body's delicate: the tempest in my mind
Doth from my senses take all feeling else
Save what beats there. Filial ingratitude!
Is it not as this mouth should tear this
    hand
For lifting food to't? But I will punish
    home:
No, I will weep no more. In such a night
To shut me out! Pour on; I will endure.
In such a night as this! O Regan, Goneril!
Your old kind father, whose frank heart gave
    all,—   20
O, that way madness lies; let me shun that;
No more of that.
    Kent.   Good my lord, enter here.
    Lear. Prithee, go in thyself; seek thine
    own ease:
This tempest will not give me leave to ponder
On things would hurt me more. But I'll go
    in.
[*To the Fool*] In, boy; go first. You houseless
    poverty,—
Nay, get thee in. I'll pray, and then I'll
    sleep.   [*Fool goes in.*
Poor naked wretches, wheresoe'er you are,
That bide the pelting of this pitiless storm,

How shall your houseless heads and unfed
    sides,   30
Your loop'd and window'd raggedness, de-
    fend you
From seasons such as these? O, I have ta'en
Too little care of this! Take physic, pomp;
Expose thyself to feel what wretches feel,
That thou mayst shake the superflux to
    them,
And show the heavens more just.
    Edg. [*Within*] Fathom and half, fathom
and half! Poor Tom!
             [*The Fool runs out from the hovel.*
    Fool. Come not in here, nuncle, here's a
spirit. Help me, help me!   40
    Kent. Give me thy hand. Who's there?
    Fool. A spirit, a spirit: he says his name's
poor Tom.
    Kent. What art thou that dost grumble
there i' the straw? Come forth.

Enter EDGAR *disguised as a madman.*

    Edg. Away! the foul fiend follows me!
Through the sharp hawthorn blows the cold
    wind.
Hum! go to thy cold bed, and warm thee.
    Lear. Hast thou given all to thy two
    daughters?
And art thou come to this?   50
    Edg. Who gives any thing to poor Tom?
whom the foul fiend hath led through fire and
through flame, through ford and whirlpool,
o'er bog and quagmire; that hath laid knives
under his pillow, and halters in his pew; set
ratsbane by his porridge; made him proud of
heart, to ride on a bay trotting-horse over
four-inched bridges, to course his own
shadow for a traitor. Bless thy five wits! 59
Tom's a-cold,—O, do de, do de, do de. Bless
thee from whirlwinds, star-blasting, and
taking! Do poor Tom some charity, whom
the foul fiend vexes: there could I have him
now,—and there,—and there again, and
there.   [*Storm still.*
    Lear. What, have his daughters brought
    him to this pass?   65

---

8. greater malady. There was a familiar belief that
one passion might drive out or allay another. **15. as,**
as if. **28-36. Poor naked wretches,** etc. Lear's error
has been a violation of that law of nature which is
called justice. His sufferings have brought him round
to a complete recognition and expression of general
distributive justice. This quality, we may suppose, was
in his nature, but his obstinacy and self-conceit had
stifled it. **29. bide,** endure.

31. loop'd and window'd, full of openings like
windows and loopholes. **35. superflux,** superfluity, a
word suggestive of the ethics of ownership in society.
49-50. Hast . . . this. Lear can interpret only in terms
of his own great sorrow; the passage illustrates obsession
and is still sound psychologically, or psychiatrically.
59. five wits, the five mental faculties: common wit,
imagination, fantasy, judgment, memory. **61. star-
blasting,** blighting by influence of the stars. **62. taking,** bewitching.

Couldst thou save nothing? Didst thou give
    them all?

Fool. Nay, he reserved a blanket, else we
had been all shamed.

Lear. Now, all the plagues that in the pen-
    dulous air
Hang faded o'er men's faults light on thy
    daughters!   70

Kent. He hath no daughters, sir.

Lear. Death, traitor! nothing could have
    subdued nature
To such a lowness but his unkind daughters.
Is it the fashion, that discarded fathers
Should have thus little mercy on their flesh?
Judicious punishment! 'twas this flesh begot
Those pelican daughters.

Edg. Pillicock sat on Pillicock-hill:
Halloo, halloo, loo, loo!

Fool. This cold night will turn us all to
fools and madmen.   81

Edg. Take heed o' the foul fiend: obey thy
parents; keep thy word justly; swear not;
commit not with man's sworn spouse; set
not thy sweet heart on proud array. Tom's
a-cold.

Lear. What hast thou been?   86

Edg. A serving-man, proud in heart and
mind; that curled my hair; wore gloves in my
cap; served the lust of my mistress' heart,
and did the act of darkness with her; swore
as many oaths as I spake words, and broke
them in the sweet face of heaven: one that
slept in the contriving of lust, and waked to
do it: wine loved I deeply, dice dearly; and in
woman out-paramoured the Turk: false of
heart, light of ear, bloody of hand; hog in
sloth, fox in stealth, wolf in greediness, dog in
madness, lion in prey. Let not the creaking
of shoes nor the rustling of silks betray thy
poor heart to woman: keep thy foot out of
brothels, thy hand out of plackets, thy pen
from lenders' books, and defy the foul
fiend.   101
Still through the hawthorn blows the cold
    wind:
Says suum, mun, ha, no, nonny.
Dolphin my boy, my boy, sessa! let him
    trot by.   [*Storm still.*

Lear. Why, thou wert better in thy grave
than to answer with thy uncovered body this
extremity of the skies. Is man no more than
this? Consider him well. Thou owest the
worm no silk, the beast no hide, the sheep no
wool, the cat no perfume. Ha! here's three
on 's are sophisticated! Thou art the thing
itself: unaccommodated man is no more but
such a poor, bare, forked animal as thou art.
Off, off, you lendings! come, unbutton here.
                          [*Tearing off his clothes.*

Fool. Prithee, nuncle, be contented; 'tis a
naughty night to swim in. Now a little fire in
a wild field were like an old lecher's heart;
a small spark, all the rest on 's body cold.
Look, here comes a walking fire.   119

Enter GLOUCESTER, *with a torch.*

Edg. This is the foul fiend Flibbertigibbet:
he begins at curfew, and walks till the first
cock; he gives the web and the pin, squints
the eye, and makes the hare-lip; mildews the
white wheat, and hurts the poor creature of
earth.
S. Withold footed thrice the old;
He met the night-mare, and her nine-fold;
    Bid her alight,
    And her troth plight,
And, aroint thee, witch, aroint thee!

Kent. How fares your grace?   130

Lear. What's he?

Kent. Who's there? What is 't you seek?

Glou. What are you there? Your names?

Edg. Poor Tom; that eats the swimming
frog, the toad, the tadpole, the wall-newt and
the water; that in the fury of his heart, when
the foul fiend rages, eats cow-dung for sallets;
swallows the old rat and the ditch-dog; drinks
the green mantle of the standing pool; who is
whipped from tithing to tithing, and stock-

punished, and imprisoned; who hath had
three suits to his back, six shirts to his body,
horse to ride, and weapon to wear;   143
    But mice and rats, and such small deer,
    Have been Tom's food for seven long year.
Beware my follower. Peace, Smulkin; peace,
    thou fiend!

    Glou. What, hath your grace no better
    company?

    Edg. The prince of darkness is a gentle-
man:
Modo he's call'd, and Mahu.

    Glou. Our flesh and blood is grown so vile,
    my lord,   150
That it doth hate what gets it.

    Edg. Poor Tom's a-cold.

    Glou. Go in with me: my duty cannot
    suffer
To obey in all your daughters' hard com-
    mands:
Though their injunction be to bar my doors,
And let this tyrannous night take hold upon
    you,
Yet have I ventured to come seek you out,
And bring you where both fire and food is
    ready.

    Lear. First let me talk with this phi-
    losopher.
What is the cause of thunder?   160

    Kent. Good my lord, take his offer; go
    into the house.

    Lear. I'll talk a word with this same
    learned Theban.
What is your study?

    Edg. How to prevent the fiend, and to kill
    vermin.

    Lear. Let me ask you one word in private.

    Kent. Importune him once more to go,
    my lord;
His wits begin to unsettle.

    Glou. Canst thou blame him? [*Storm still.*
His daughters seek his death; ah, that good
    Kent!
He said it would be thus, poor banish'd man!
Thou say'st the king grows mad; I'll tell thee,
    friend,   170
I am almost mad myself: I had a son,
Now outlaw'd from my blood; he sought
    my life,
But lately, very late: I loved him, friend:

No father his son dearer: truth to tell thee,
The grief hath crazed my wits. What a
    night's this!
I do beseech your grace,—

    Lear.   O, cry you mercy, sir.
Noble philosopher, your company.

    Edg. Tom's a-cold.

    Glou. In, fellow, there, into the hovel:
    keep thee warm.

    Lear. Come, let's in all.

    Kent.   This way, my lord.

    Lear.   With him;
I will keep still with my philosopher.   181

    Kent. Good my lord, soothe him; let him
    take the fellow.

    Glou. Take him you on.

    Kent. Sirrah, come on; go along with us.

    Lear. Come, good Athenian.

    Glou. No words, no words: hush.

    Edg. Child Rowland to the dark tower
    came,
    His word was still,—Fie, foh, and fum,
    I smell the blood of a British man.
                         [*Exeunt.*

Scene V. *Gloucester's castle.*

Enter Cornwall *and* Edmund.

    Corn. I will have my revenge ere I depart
his house.

    Edm. How, my lord, I may be censured,
that nature thus gives way to loyalty, something fears me to think of.

    Corn. I now perceive, it was not alto-
gether your brother's evil disposition made
him seek his death; but a provoking merit,
set a-work by a reproveable badness in
himself.   9

    Edm. How malicious is my fortune, that I
must repent to be just! This is the letter he
spoke of, which approves him an intelligent
party to the advantages of France. O
heavens! that this treason were not, or not
I the detector!

    Corn. Go with me to the duchess.

    Edm. If the matter of this paper be
certain, you have mighty business in hand.

---

144. **deer,** probably, animals generally. 146. **Smulkin,** another name occurring in Harsnet. 149. **Modo
. . . Mahu,** two superior fiends in Harsnet. 162. **learned
Theban,** possibly a current phrase to indicate a philosopher. 164. **prevent,** probably, forestall, anticipate.

182. **soothe,** humor, indulge. 187. **Child Rowland,**
etc., fragments of the ballad *Child Rowland and Burd
Ellen.* The theme of Browning's *Childe Rowland to the
Dark Tower Came* is derived from these lines.
Scene v. 4-5. **something fears me,** somewhat fright-
ens me. 8. **provoking merit,** etc., i.e., a forward-
looking merit (in Edgar) incited by the badness of
Gloucester. 12. **approves him,** proves him to be.
intelligent, aware (in the legal sense).

Corn. True or false, it hath made thee earl of Gloucester. Seek out where thy father is, that he may be ready for our apprehension. 20

Edm. [*Aside*] If I find him comforting the king, it will stuff his suspicion more fully.—I will persevere in my course of loyalty, though the conflict be sore between that and my blood.

Corn. I will lay trust upon thee; and thou shalt find a dearer father in my love. [*Exeunt.*

SCENE VI. *A chamber in a farmhouse adjoining the castle.*

Enter GLOUCESTER, LEAR, KENT, Fool, *and* EDGAR.

Glou. Here is better than the open air; take it thankfully. I will piece out the comfort with what addition I can: I will not be long from you.

Kent. All the power of his wits have given way to his impatience: the gods reward your kindness! [*Exit Gloucester.* 6

Edg. Frateretto calls me; and tells me Nero is an angler in the lake of darkness. Pray, innocent, and beware the foul fiend.

Fool. Prithee, nuncle, tell me whether a madman be a gentleman or a yeoman? 11

Lear. A king, a king!

Fool. No, he's a yeoman that has a gentleman to his son; for he's a mad yeoman that sees his son a gentleman before him.

Lear. To have a thousand with red burning spits
Come hissing in upon 'em,—

Edg. The foul fiend bites my back.

Fool. He's mad that trusts in the tameness of a wolf, a horse's health, a boy's love, or a whore's oath. 21

Lear. It shall be done; I will arraign them straight.
[*To Edgar*] Come, sit thou here, most learned justicer;
[*To the Fool*] Thou, sapient sir, sit here. Now, you she foxes!

Edg. Look, where he stands and glares!

Wantest thou eyes at trial, madam?
Come o'er the bourn, Bessy, to me,—

Fool. Her boat hath a leak,
And she must not speak 29
Why she dares not come over to thee.

Edg. The foul fiend haunts poor Tom in the voice of a nightingale. Hopdance cries in Tom's belly for two white herring. Croak not, black angel; I have no food for thee.

Kent. How do you, sir? Stand you not so amazed:
Will you lie down and rest upon the cushions?

Lear. I'll see their trial first. Bring in the evidence.
[*To Edgar*] Thou robed man of justice, take thy place;
[*To the Fool*] And thou, his yoke-fellow of equity,
Bench by his side: [*To Kent*] you are o' the commission, 40
Sit you too.

Edg. Let us deal justly.
Sleepest or wakest thou, jolly shepherd?
Thy sheep be in the corn;
And for one blast of thy minikin mouth,
Thy sheep shall take no harm.
Pur! the cat is gray.

Lear. Arraign her first; 'tis Goneril. I here take my oath before this honourable assembly, she kicked the poor king her father.

Fool. Come hither, mistress. Is your name Goneril? 52

Lear. She cannot deny it.

Fool. Cry you mercy, I took you for a joint-stool.

Lear. And here's another, whose warp'd looks proclaim
What store her heart is made on. Stop her there!
Arms, arms, sword, fire! Corruption in the place!
False justicer, why hast thou let her 'scape?

26. **Wantest . . . trial,** meaning doubtful. Possibly Edgar alludes to the staring fiend. 27. **Come . . . me,** first line of a ballad by William Birche (1558). 32. **Hopdance,** a fiend. 33. **white herring,** fresh herring or pickled herring; at any rate, not a red herring. **Croak,** make a rumbling sound in the stomach to denote hunger. 37. **evidence,** witnesses. 39. **yoke-fellow,** partner. 40. **Bench,** sit on the judgment-seat. **o' the commission,** a justice of peace. 45. **minikin,** pretty, dainty. 47. **Pur!** Perhaps for the sound of a cat, or the name of a demon, or both. There is a fiend in Harsnet named Purre. 55. **joint-stool,** a folding stool, or a stool made by a joiner. The expression has a proverbial meaning not understood on which the Fool is punning in his reference to the stool Lear has placed before them to represent Goneril.

24. **blood,** nature.
Scene vi. 7. **Frateretto,** another of the fiends from Harsnet. 8. **Nero is an angler,** pointed out as an allusion to *Rabelais,* ii, 30, where Nero is described as a fiddler and Trajan as an angler. 9. **innocent,** simpleton, fool. 15. **gentleman before him.** It has been often pointed out that this passage has a strange applicability to Shakespeare himself, since he had seen to it that his father, John Shakespeare, was granted arms by the College of Heralds in 1599. 23. **justicer,** judge.

Edg. Bless thy five wits!   60

Kent. O pity! Sir, where is the patience now,

That you so oft have boasted to retain?

Edg. [*Aside*] My tears begin to take his part so much,

They'll mar my counterfeiting

Lear. The little dogs and all,

Tray, Blanch, and Sweet-heart, see, they bark at me.

Edg. Tom will throw his head at them. Avaunt, you curs!

Be thy mouth or black or white,

Tooth that poisons if it bite;   70

Mastiff, greyhound, mongrel grim,

Hound or spaniel, brach or lym,

Or bobtail tike or trundle-tail,

Tom will make them weep and wail:

For, with throwing thus my head,

Dogs leap the hatch, and all are fled.

Do de, de, de. Sessa! Come, march to wakes and fairs and market-towns. Poor Tom, thy horn is dry.   79

Lear. Then let them anatomize Regan; see what breeds about her heart. Is there any cause in nature that makes these hard hearts? [*To Edgar*] You, sir, I entertain for one of my hundred; only I do not like the fashion of your garments: you will say they are Persian attire; but let them be changed.

Kent. Now, good my lord, lie here and rest awhile.

Lear. Make no noise, make no noise; draw the curtains: so, so, so. We'll go to supper i' the morning. So, so, so.   91

Fool. And I'll go to bed at noon.

Re-enter GLOUCESTER.

Glou. Come hither, friend: where is the king my master?

Kent. Here, sir; but trouble him not, his wits are gone.

Glou. Good friend, I prithee, take him in thy arms;

I have o'erheard a plot of death upon him:

There is a litter ready; lay him in 't,

And drive towards Dover, friend, where thou shalt meet

Both welcome and protection. Take up thy master: 99

If thou shouldst dally half an hour, his life,

With thine, and all that offer to defend him,

Stand in assured loss: take up, take up;

And follow me, that will to some provision

Give thee quick conduct.

Kent.   Oppressed nature sleeps:

This rest might yet have balm'd thy broken sinews,

Which, if convenience will not allow,

Stand in hard cure. [*To the Fool*] Come, help to bear thy master;

Thou must not stay behind.

Glou.   Come, come, away.

       [*Exeunt all but Edgar.*

Edg. When we our betters see bearing our woes,

We scarcely think our miseries our foes.   110

Who alone suffers suffers most i' the mind,

Leaving free things and happy shows behind:

But then the mind much sufferance doth o'erskip,

When grief hath mates, and bearing fellowship.

How light and portable my pain seems now,

When that which makes me bend makes the king bow,

He childed as I father'd! Tom, away!

Mark the high noises; and thyself bewray,

When false opinion, whose wrong thought defiles thee,

In thy just proof, repeals and reconciles thee.

What will hap more to-night, safe 'scape the king!   121

Lurk, lurk.   [*Exit.*

SCENE VII. *Gloucester's castle.*

Enter CORNWALL, REGAN, GONERIL, EDMUND, *and* Servants.

Corn. Post speedily to my lord your husband; show him this letter: the army of France is landed. Seek out the villain Gloucester.   [*Exeunt some of the Servants.*

---

63. **Edg. [Aside]**. Edgar's counterfeiting has been so perfect that this is needed to remind the audience that it is counterfeit. 72. **lym**, lymmer, a species of bloodhound which runs by scent. 73. **tike**, small dog, cur. **trundle-tail**, curly tail. 76. **hatch**, lower half of a divided door. 83. **entertain**, engage. 86. **Persian attire**, rich, gorgeous attire (ironical). 96. **upon**, against

102. **Stand in assured loss**, will assuredly be lost. 105. **balm'd**, cured, healed. 109-122. **When . . . lurk**. These lines do not appear in F. Their genuineness is sometimes questioned, but such general comment for the enlightenment of the audience is not unusual. 113. **sufferance**, suffering. 114. **bearing**, tribulation. 115. **portable**, endurable. 117. **He . . . father'd**, he has found the same cruelty in his children which I found in my father. 118. **bewray**, betray, reveal. 120. **repeals**, recalls, restores. 121. **What . . . king!** whatever else happens, may the king escape!

Reg. Hang him instantly.

Gon. Pluck out his eyes.

Corn. Leave him to my displeasure. Edmund, keep you our sister company: the revenges we are bound to take upon your traitorous father are not fit for your beholding. Advise the duke, where you are going, to a most festinate preparation: we are 10 bound to the like. Our posts shall be swift and intelligent betwixt us. Farewell, dear sister: farewell, my lord of Gloucester.

Enter OSWALD.

How now! where's the king?　　　　　14

Osw. My lord of Gloucester hath convey'd him hence:
Some five or six and thirty of his knights,
Hot questrists after him, met him at gate;
Who, with some other of the lords dependants,
Are gone with him towards Dover; where they boast　　　　　19
To have well-armed friends.

Corn.　　　　Get horses for your mistress.

Gon. Farewell, sweet lord, and sister.

Corn. Edmund, farewell.

[*Exeunt Goneril, Edmund, and Oswald.*
　　　　Go seek the traitor Gloucester,
Pinion him like a thief, bring him before us.
[*Exeunt other Servants.*
Though well we may not pass upon his life
Without the form of justice, yet our power
Shall do a courtesy to our wrath, which men
May blame, but not control. Who's there? the traitor?

Enter GLOUCESTER, *brought in by two or three.*

Reg. Ingrateful fox! 'tis he.

Corn. Bind fast his corky arms.

Glou. What mean your graces? Good my friends, consider　　　　　30
You are my guests: do me no foul play, friends.

Corn. Bind him, I say.

[*Servants bind him.*

Reg.　　　　Hard, hard. O filthy traitor!

Glou. Unmerciful lady as you are, I'm none.

Corn. To this chair bind him. Villain,
thou shalt find—　　　[*Regan plucks his beard.*

Glou. By the kind gods, 'tis most ignobly done
To pluck me by the beard.

Reg. So white, and such a traitor!

Glou.　　　　　　　　Naughty lady,
These hairs, which thou dost ravish from my chin,
Will quicken, and accuse thee: I am your host:
With robbers' hands my hospitable favours
You should not ruffle thus. What will you do?

Corn. Come, sir, what letters had you late from France?　　　　　42

Reg. Be simple answerer, for we know the truth.

Corn. And what confederacy have you with the traitors
Late footed in the kingdom?

Reg. To whose hands have you sent the lunatic king?
Speak.

Glou. I have a letter guessingly set down,
Which came from one that's of a neutral heart,
And not from one opposed.

Corn.　　　　　　Cunning.

Reg.　　　　　　　　And false.

Corn. Where hast thou sent the king?　50

Glou. To Dover.

Reg. Wherefore to Dover? Wast thou not charged at peril—

Corn. Wherefore to Dover? Let him first answer that.

Glou. I am tied to the stake, and I must stand the course.

Reg. Wherefore to Dover, sir?

Glou. Because I would not see thy cruel nails
Pluck out his poor old eyes; nor thy fierce sister
In his anointed flesh stick boarish fangs.
The sea, with such a storm as his bare head
In hell-black night endured, would have buoy'd up,　　　　　60
And quench'd the stelled fires:

9-10. **Advise . . . to,** i.e., advise him to make. 10. **festinate,** hasty. 11. **bound,** ready. 12. **intelligent,** serviceable in bearing intelligence. 13. **my . . . Gloucester,** i.e., Edmund. In line 15 the reference is to Gloucester himself. 17. **questrists,** searchers. 24. **pass upon,** pass sentence upon. 29. **corky,** withered with age.

39. **quicken,** come to life. 40. **hospitable favours.** Gloucester appeals to the sacredness of hospitality; the meaning is "the features of me, your host." 43. **simple answerer,** straightforward answerer. F has *simple answer'd,* i.e., straightforward in your answers. 54. **tied to the stake,** like a bear to be baited with dogs. 60. **buoy'd,** lifted itself. 61. **stelled,** fixed; sometimes defined as "starry."

Yet, poor old heart, he holp the heavens to
  rain.
If wolves had at thy gate howl'd that stern
  time,
Thou shouldst have said 'Good porter, turn
  the key,'
All cruels else subscribed: but I shall see
The winged vengeance overtake such
  children.

  Corn. See 't shalt thou never. Fellows,
  hold the chair.
Upon these eyes of thine I'll set my foot.
  Glou. He that will think to live till he be
  old,
Give me some help! O cruel! O you gods! 70
  Reg. One side will mock another; the
  other too.
  Corn. If you see vengeance —
  First Serv.   Hold your hand,
  my lord:
I have served you ever since I was a child;
But better service have I never done you
Than now to bid you hold.
  Reg.   How now, you dog!
  First Serv. If you did wear a beard upon
  your chin,
I'd shake it on this quarrel. What do you
  mean?
  Corn. My villain! [*They draw and fight.*
  First Serv. Nay, then, come on, and take
  the chance of anger.
  Reg. Give me thy sword. A peasant stand
  up thus!   80
    [*Takes a sword, and runs at him behind.*
  First serv. O, I am slain! My lord, you
  have one eye left
To see some mischief on him. O!
                    [*Dies.*
  Corn. Lest it see more, prevent it. Out,
  vile jelly!
Where is thy lustre now?
  Glou. All dark and comfortless. Where's
  my son Edmund?
Edmund, enkindle all the sparks of nature,
To quit this horrid act.
  Reg.   Out, treacherous villain!
Thou call'st on him that hates thee: it was he

That made the overture of thy treasons to
  us;
Who is too good to pity thee.   90
  Glou. O my follies! then Edgar was abused.
Kind gods, forgive me that, and prosper
  him!
  Reg. Go thrust him out at gates, and let
  him smell
His way to Dover. [*Exit one with Glouces-
  ter.*] How is 't, my lord? how look
  you?
  Corn. I have received a hurt: follow me,
  lady.
Turn out that eyeless villain; throw this
  slave
Upon the dunghill. Regan, I bleed apace:
Untimely comes this hurt: give me your arm.
                    [*Exit Cornwall, led by Regan.*
  Sec. Serv. I'll never care what wickedness
  I do,
If this man come to good.
  Third Serv.   If she live long, 100
And in the end meet the old course of
  death,
Women will all turn monsters.
  Sec. Serv. Let's follow the old earl, and get
  the Bedlam
To lead him where he would: his roguish
  madness
Allows itself to any thing.
  Third Serv. Go thou: I'll fetch some flax
  and whites of eggs
To apply to his bleeding face. Now, heaven
  help him!   [*Exeunt severally.*

ACT IV.

Scene I. *The heath.*

Enter Edgar.

  Edg. Yet better thus, and known to be
  contemn'd,
Than still contemn'd and flatter'd. To be
  worst,
The lowest and most dejected thing of
  fortune,
Stands still in esperance, lives not in fear:

62. **holp,** helped. 63. **stern,** so F; Q: *heard that
dearn.* Many editors follow Capell, *howl'd that dearn,* in
which *dearn* means "dire," "dreary." 65. **All . . . subscribed,** all their usual cruelties condoned or forgiven;
so Q; F: *subscribe,* which may mean "All other cruel
creatures show forgiveness except you." 66. **winged
vengeance.** Note Gloucester's faith in the rectitude of
the gods; note also that in this speech he twice suggests
ironically his own fate. 78. **villain,** servant, bondman.
87. **quit,** repay, revenge.

89. **overture,** disclosure. 98. **Untimely,** inoppor-
tunely. 101. **old,** customary, natural. 103. **Bedlam,**
Bedlamite, lunatic.
  Act IV. Scene i. 3. **dejected . . . of,** debased or
humbled by. 4. **esperance,** hope.

The lamentable change is from the best;
The worst returns to laughter. Welcome,
then,
Thou unsubstantial air that I embrace!
The wretch that thou hast blown unto the
worst
Owes nothing to thy blasts. But who comes
here?

Enter GLOUCESTER, *led by an* Old Man.

My father, poorly led? World, world, O
world!
But that thy strange mutations make us
hate thee,   11
Life would not yield to age.

  Old Man. O, my good lord, I have been
your tenant, and your father's tenant, these
fourscore years.

  Glou. Away, get thee away; good friend,
be gone:
Thy comforts can do me no good at all;
Thee they may hurt.

  Old Man. Alack, sir, you cannot see your
way.

  Glou. I have no way, and therefore want
no eyes;   20
I stumbled when I saw: full oft 'tis seen,
Our means secure us, and our mere defects
Prove our commodities. O dear son Edgar,
The food of thy abused father's wrath!
Might I but live to see thee in my touch,
I'ld say I had eyes again!

  Old Man.   How now! Who's there?

  Edg. [*Aside*] O gods! Who is't can say 'I
am at the worst'?
I am worse than e'er I was.

  Old Man.   'Tis poor mad Tom.

  Edg. [*Aside*] And worse I may be yet: the
worst is not
So long as we can say 'This is the worst.' 30

  Old Man. Fellow, where goest?

  Glou.   Is it a beggar-man?

  Old Man. Madman and beggar too.

  Glou. He has some reason, else he could
not beg.
I' the last night's storm I such a fellow saw;
Which made me think a man a worm: my
son
Came then into my mind; and yet my mind
Was then scarce friends with him: I have
heard more since.

As flies to wanton boys, are we to the gods,
They kill us for their sport.

  Edg. [*Aside*] How should this be?   39
Bad is the trade that must play fool to sorrow,
Angering itself and others.—Bless thee,
master!

  Glou. Is that the naked fellow?

  Old Man.   Ay, my lord.

  Glou. Then, prithee, get thee gone: if, for
my sake,
Thou wilt o'ertake us, hence a mile or twain,
I' the way toward Dover, do it for ancient
love;
And bring some covering for this naked soul,
Who I'll entreat to lead me.

  Old Man.   Alack, sir, he is mad.

  Glou. 'Tis the times' plague, when mad-
men lead the blind.
Do as I bid thee, or rather do thy pleasure;
Above the rest, be gone.   50

  Old Man. I'll bring him the best 'parel
that I have,
Come on't what will.   [*Exit.*

  Glou. Sirrah, naked fellow,—

  Edg. Poor Tom's a-cold. [*Aside*] I cannot daub it further.

  Glou. Come hither, fellow.

  Edg. [*Aside*] And yet I must.—Bless thy
sweet eyes, they bleed.   56

  Glou. Know'st thou the way to Dover?

  Edg. Both stile and gate, horse-way and
foot-path. Poor Tom hath been scared out of
his good wits: bless thee, good man's son,
from the foul fiend! five fiends have been in
poor Tom at once; of lust, as Obidicut;
Hobbididance, prince of dumbness; Mahu, of
stealing; Modo, of murder; Flibbertigibbet,
of mopping and mowing, who since possesses
chambermaids and waiting-women. So,
bless thee, master!

  Glou. Here, take this purse, thou whom
the heavens' plagues
Have humbled to all strokes: that I am
wretched
Makes thee the happier: heavens, deal so
still!
Let the superfluous and lust-dieted man, 70

11. **mutations,** changes, variations. 22. **Our means
secure us,** our resources make us over-confident. 23.
commodities. benefits.

38-39. **As . . . sport.** This is a clear statement of
Gloucester's loss of faith, which he signalizes (l. 76) by
forming a plan to commit suicide. 51. **'parel,** apparel.
54. **daub it further,** keep up the disguise. 62-64.
Obidicut . . . Flibbertigibbet, fiends borrowed, as
before, from Harsnet. 65. **mopping and mowing,**
making grimaces and mouths. 70. **superfluous,** having a superfluity. **lust-dieted,** probably, feeding
luxuriously.

That slaves your ordinance, that will not see
Because he doth not feel, feel your power
  quickly; 72
So distribution should undo excess,
And each man have enough. Dost thou
  know Dover?
  Edg. Ay, master.
  Glou. There is a cliff, whose high and
  bending head
Looks fearfully in the confined deep:
Bring me but to the very brim of it,
And I'll repair the misery thou dost bear
With something rich about me: from that
  place
I shall no leading need.
  Edg.   Give me thy arm: 81
Poor Tom shall lead thee.   [*Exeunt.*

SCENE II. *Before the Duke of Albany's
  palace.*

Enter GONERIL *and* EDMUND.

  Gon. Welcome, my lord: I marvel our mild
  husband
Not met us on the way.

Enter OSWALD.

                    Now, where's your master?
  Osw. Madam, within; but never man so
  changed.
I told him of the army that was landed;
He smiled at it: I told him you were coming;
His answer was 'The worse:' of Gloucester's
  treachery,
And of the loyal service of his son,
When I inform'd him, then he call'd me sot,
And told me I had turn'd the wrong side out:
What most he should dislike seems pleasant
  to him; 10
What like, offensive.
  Gon. [*To Edm.*] Then shall you go no
  further.
It is the cowish terror of his spirit,
That dares not undertake: he'll not feel
  wrongs
Which tie him to an answer. Our wishes on
  the way

May prove effects. Back, Edmund, to my
  brother;
Hasten his musters and conduct his powers:
I must change arms at home, and give the
  distaff
Into my husband's hands. This trusty ser-
  vant
Shall pass between us: ere long you are like
  to hear,
If you dare venture in your own behalf, 20
A mistress's command. Wear this; spare
  speech;   [*Giving a favour.*
Decline your head: this kiss, if it durst speak,
Would stretch thy spirits up into the air:
Conceive, and fare thee well.
  Edm. Yours in the ranks of death.
  Gon.   My most dear Gloucester!
                    [*Exit Edmund.*
O, the difference of man and man!
To thee a woman's services are due:
My fool usurps my body.
  Osw.   Madam, here comes my lord.
                    [*Exit.*
Enter ALBANY.

  Gon. I have been worth the whistle.
  Alb.   O Goneril!
You are not worth the dust which the rude
  wind 30
Blows in your face. I fear your disposition:
That nature, which contemns it origin,
Cannot be border'd certain in itself;
She that herself will sliver and disbranch
From her material sap, perforce must wither
And come to deadly use.
  Gon. No more; the text is foolish.
  Alb. Wisdom and goodness to the vile
  seem vile:
Filths savour but themselves. What have
  you done?
Tigers, not daughters, what have you per-
  form'd?
A father, and a gracious aged man, 41
Whose reverence even the head-lugg'd bear
  would lick,
Most barbarous, most degenerate! have you
  madded.

71. **slaves your ordinance**, i.e., makes the laws of
heaven his slaves. 73. **distribution**, the principle of
distributive justice in ethics.
  Scene ii. 1. **mild**, used ironically. 8. **sot**, fool. 9.
turn'd the wrong side out, put a wrong interpretation
on the matter. 12. **cowish**, cowardly. 13-14. **he'll
. . . answer**, i.e., in his cowardice he will ignore injuries
he ought to resent. 14. **Our . . . way**, my wishes expressed to you on the way.

15. **prove effects**, come to pass. 17. **arms, distaff**,
i.e., she must turn warrior and give into Albany's hands
the *arms*, or insignia, of housewifery. 24. **Conceive**,
understand, take my meaning. 29. **whistle**. She alludes to the proverb: "It is a poor dog that is not worth
the whistling," meaning that she considers herself
worthy of his attendance. 31. **fear**, fear for. 32. **it**,
its. 33. **border'd**, kept within bounds. 34. **sliver**,
tear off. 35. **material sap**, nourishing substance. 39.
savour but, care only for. 42. **head-lugg'd**, dragged
by the head and infuriated. 43. **madded**, driven mad.

Could my good brother suffer you to do it?
A man, a prince, by him so benefited!
If that the heavens do not their visible spirits
Send quickly down to tame these vile
　　offences,
It will come,
Humanity must perforce prey on itself,
Like monsters of the deep.
　　Gon.　　　　　　　Milk-liver'd man! 50
That bear'st a cheek for blows, a head for
　　wrongs:
Who hast not in thy brows an eye discerning
Thine honour from thy suffering; that not
　　know'st
Fools do those villains pity who are punish'd
Ere they have done their mischief. Where's
　　thy drum?
France spreads his banners in our noiseless
　　land,
With plumed helm thy state begins to threat;
Whiles thou, a moral fool, sit'st still, and
　　criest
'Alack, why does he so?'
　　Alb.　　　　　　　See thyself, devil!
Proper deformity seems not in the fiend 60
So horrid as in woman.
　　Gon.　　　　　　　O vain fool!
　　Alb. Thou changed and self-cover'd thing,
　　for shame,
Be-monster not thy feature. Were 't my fit-
　　ness
To let these hands obey my blood,
They are apt enough to dislocate and tear
Thy flesh and bones: howe'er thou art a fiend,
A woman's shape doth shield thee.
　　Gon. Marry, your manhood now—

　　　　　　Enter a Messenger.

　　Alb. What news?
　　Mess. O, my good lord, the Duke of Corn-
　　wall's dead;　　　　　　　　　　　70
Slain by his servant, going to put out
The other eye of Gloucester.
　　Alb.　　　　　　Gloucester's eyes!
　　Mess. A servant that he bred, thrill'd with
　　remorse,
Opposed against the act, bending his sword

To his great master; who, thereat enraged,
Flew on him, and amongst them fell'd him
　　dead;
But not without that harmful stroke, which
　　since
Hath pluck'd him after.
　　Alb.　　　　　This shows you are above,
You justicers, that these our nether crimes
So speedily can venge! But, O poor Glou-
　　cester!
Lost he his other eye?
　　Mess.　　　　　Both, both, my lord. 81
This letter, madam, craves a speedy answer;
'Tis from your sister.
　　Gon. [*Aside*] One way I like this well;
But being widow, and my Gloucester with
　　her,
May all the building in my fancy pluck
Upon my hateful life: another way,
The news is not so tart.—I'll read, and
　　answer.　　　　　　　　　　[*Exit.*
　　Alb. Where was his son when they did
　　take his eyes?
　　Mess. Come with my lady hither.
　　Alb.　　　　　　He is not here.　90
　　Mess. No, my good lord; I met him back
　　again.
　　Alb. Knows he the wickedness?
　　Mess. Ay, my good lord; 'twas he in-
　　form'd against him;
And quit the house on purpose, that their
　　punishment
Might have the freer course.
　　Alb.　　　　　Gloucester, I live
To thank thee for the love thou show'dst the
　　king,
And to revenge thine eyes. Come hither,
　　friend:
Tell me what more thou know'st. [*Exeunt.*

Scene III.　*The French camp near Dover.*

　　　　Enter Kent *and a* Gentleman.

　　Kent. Why the King of France is so
suddenly gone back know you the reason?
　　Gent. Something he left imperfect in the
state, which since his coming forth is thought
of; which imports to the kingdom so much
fear and danger, that his personal return was
most required and necessary.

47. offences, offenders. 50. Milk-liver'd, cowardly.
56. noiseless, peaceful, having none of the bustle of war.
58. moral, moralizing. 60. Proper, i.e., the deformity
appropriate to the fiend. 62. self-cover'd, having the
true self concealed. 63. Be-monster . . . . feature, do
not, being fiend, take on the outward form of woman.
my fitness, suitable for me. 64. blood, passion. 66.
howe'er, although. 68. now. Some copies of Q have
mew, as an exclamation of disgust. 73. remorse, pity.
74-75. bending . . . To, directing his sword against.

78-79. This . . . justicers, premonition of ultimate
justice. 88. tart, painful, grievous. 91. back, going
back.
　　Scene iii. 5. imports, portends.

Kent. Who hath he left behind him general?

Gent. The Marshal of France, Monsieur La Far. 10

Kent. Did your letters pierce the queen to any demonstration of grief?

Gent. Ay, sir; she took them, read them in my presence;
And now and then an ample tear trill'd down
Her delicate cheek: it seem'd she was a queen
Over her passion; who, most rebel-like,
Sought to be king o'er her.

Kent.   O, then it moved her.

Gent. Not to a rage: patience and sorrow strove
Who should express her goodliest. You have seen
Sunshine and rain at once: her smiles and tears 20
†Were like a better way: those happy smilets,
That play'd on her ripe lip, seem'd not to know
What guests were in her eyes; which parted thence,
As pearls from diamonds dropp'd. In brief,
Sorrow would be a rarity most beloved,
If all could so become it.

Kent.   Made she no verbal question?

Gent. 'Faith, once or twice she heaved the name of 'father'
Pantingly forth, as if it press'd her heart;
Cried 'Sisters! sisters! Shame of ladies! sisters!
Kent! father! sisters! What, i' the storm? i' the night? 30
Let pity not be believed!' There she shook
The holy water from her heavenly eyes,
And clamour moisten'd: then away she started
To deal with grief alone.

Kent.   It is the stars,
The stars above us, govern our conditions;
Else one self mate and mate could not beget
Such different issues. You spoke not with her since?

Gent. No.

Kent. Was this before the king return'd?

Gent.   No, since.

Kent. Well, sir, the poor distressed Lear's i' the town; 40
Who sometime, in his better tune, remembers
What we are come about, and by no means
Will yield to see his daughter.

Gent.   Why, good sir?

Kent. A sovereign shame so elbows him: his own unkindness,
That stripp'd her from his benediction, turn'd her
To foreign casualties, gave her dear rights
To his dog-hearted daughters, these things sting
His mind so venomously, that burning shame
Detains him from Cordelia.

Gent.   Alack, poor gentleman!

Kent. Of Albany's and Cornwall's powers you heard not? 50

Gent. 'Tis so, they are afoot.

Kent. Well, sir, I'll bring you to our master Lear,
And leave you to attend him: some dear cause
Will in concealment wrap me up awhile;
When I am known aright, you shall not grieve
Lending me this acquaintance. I pray you, go
Along with me.   [*Exeunt.*

SCENE IV. *The same. A tent.*

Enter, with drum and colours, CORDELIA, Doctor, *and* Soldiers.

Cor. Alack, 'tis he: why, he was met even now
As mad as the vex'd sea; singing aloud;
Crown'd with rank fumiter and furrow-weeds,
With bur-docks, hemlock, nettles, cuckoo-flowers,
Darnel, and all the idle weeds that grow
In our sustaining corn. A century send forth;

41. **sometime**, sometimes. **better tune**, saner moments. 44. **elbows**, thrusts away, or possibly, stands at his elbow. 45. **turn'd**, expelled.
Scene iv. 3. **rank**, coarsely luxuriant. **fumiter**, the weed *earth-smoke*. **furrow-weeds**, weeds growing in the furrows of plowed land. 4. **bur-docks**, Q: *hor-docks*. Some editors follow Collier: *hoar-docks*, i.e., white-leaved. **cuckoo-flowers**, possibly, cowslips. 5. **Darnel**, a weed of the grass kind. The plants mentioned in this passage are probably selected because of their bitter and poisonous quality. 6. **sustaining**, giving sustenance. **century**, usually interpreted as a troup of 100 men, as in the Roman army; also taken to mean "sentry" or "scout."

14. **trill'd**, trickled. 21. **like a better way**, possibly, better than this. **smilets**, smiles. 22. **ripe**, probably, red (W. J. Craig). 27. **heaved**, breathed out. 34. **It is the stars.** One of the many expressions in the play of the inscrutability of Providence. 35. **conditions**, characters, temperaments. 36. **and mate**, Q: *and make*, meaning "marital partner."

Search every acre in the high-grown field,
And bring him to our eye. [*Exit an Officer.*]
    What can man's wisdom
In the restoring his bereaved sense?
He that helps him take all my outward
    worth.   10
  Doct. There is means, madam:
Our foster-nurse of nature is repose,
The which he lacks; that to provoke in
    him,
Are many simples operative, whose power
Will close the eye of anguish.
  Cor.   All blest secrets,
All you unpublish'd virtues of the earth,
Spring with my tears! be aidant and re-
    mediate   •
In the good man's distress! Seek, seek for
    him;
Lest his ungovern'd rage dissolve the life
That wants the means to lead it.

Enter a Messenger.

  Mess.   News, madam;   20
The British powers are marching hitherward.
  Cor. 'Tis known before; our preparation
    stands
In expectation of them. O dear father,
It is thy business that I go about;
Therefore great France
My mourning and important tears hath
    pitied.
No blown ambition doth our arms incite,
But love, dear love, and our aged father's
    right:
Soon may I hear and see him!   [*Exeunt.*

Scene V. *Gloucester's castle.*

Enter REGAN *and* OSWALD.

  Reg. But are my brother's powers set
    forth?
  Osw.   Ay, madam.
  Reg. Himself in person there?
  Osw.   Madam, with much ado:
Your sister is the better soldier.
  Reg. Lord Edmund spake not with your
    lord at home?
  Osw. No, madam.

  Reg. What might import my sister's letter
    to him?
  Osw. I know not, lady.
  Reg. 'Faith, he is posted hence on serious
    matter.
It was great ignorance, Gloucester's eyes
    being out,
To let him live: where he arrives he moves 10
All hearts against us: Edmund, I think, is
    gone,
In pity of his misery, to dispatch
His nighted life; moreover, to descry
The strength o' the enemy.
  Osw. I must needs after him, madam, with
    my letter.
  Reg. Our troops set forth to-morrow: stay
    with us;
The ways are dangerous.
  Osw.   I may not, madam:
My lady charged my duty in this business.
  Reg. Why should she write to Edmund?
    Might not you
Transport her purposes by word? Belike, 20
Something—I know not what: I'll love thee
    much,
Let me unseal the letter.
  Osw.   Madam, I had rather—
  Reg. I know your lady does not love her
    husband;
I am sure of that: and at her late being here
She gave strange œillades and most speaking
    looks
To noble Edmund. I know you are of her
    bosom.
  Osw. I, madam?
  Reg. I speak in understanding; you are, I
    know't:
Therefore I do advise you, take this note:
My lord is dead; Edmund and I have talk'd;
And more convenient is he for my hand   31
Than for your lady's: you may gather more.
If you do find him, pray you, give him this;
And when your mistress hears thus much
    from you,
I pray, desire her call her wisdom to her.
So, fare you well.
If you do chance to hear of that blind traitor,
Preferment falls on him that cuts him off.

8. can, knows. wisdom, science. 9. bereaved, snatched away. 14. simples, medicinal plants. operative, effective. 17. aidant and remediate, helpful and remedial. 26. important, importunate. 27. blown, puffed up with pride.

6. import, to bear as its purport, to express (Onions). 11-14. Edmund . . . enemy. Note the irony which reveals Edmund's real reason as it states his pretended one. 20. word, word of mouth. Belike, it may be. 25. œillades, amorous glances. 26. of her bosom, in her confidence. 29. take this note, take note of this. 30. have talk'd, are affianced to one another (W. J. Craig).

Osw. Would I could meet him, madam! I
        should show
What party I do follow.
Reg.   Fare thee well. [*Exeunt.*   40

SCENE VI. *Fields near Dover.*

Enter GLOUCESTER, *and* EDGAR *dressed like
            a peasant.*

Glou. When shall we come to the top of
        that same hill?
Edg. You do climb up it now: look, how
        we labour.
Glou. Methinks the ground is even.
Edg.   Horrible steep.
Hark, do you hear the sea?
Glou.   No, truly.
Edg. Why, then, your other senses grow
        imperfect
By your eyes' anguish.
Glou.   So may it be, indeed:
Methinks thy voice is alter'd; and thou
        speak'st
In better phrase and matter than thou didst.
Edg. You're much deceived: in nothing
        am I changed
But in my garments.
Glou. Methinks you're better spoken.   10
Edg. Come on, sir; here's the place: stand
        still.   How fearful
And dizzy 'tis, to cast one's eyes so low!
The crows and choughs that wing the mid-
        way air
Show scarce so gross as beetles: half way
        down
Hangs one that gathers samphire, dreadful
        trade!
Methinks he seems no bigger than his head:
The fishermen, that walk upon the beach,
Appear like mice; and yond tall anchoring
        bark,
Diminish'd to her cock; her cock, a buoy
Almost too small for sight: the murmuring
        surge,   20
That on the unnumber'd idle pebbles chafes,
Cannot be heard so high.   I'll look no more;
Lest my brain turn, and the deficient sight
Topple down headlong.

Glou.   Set me where you stand.
Edg. Give me your hand: you are now
        within a foot
Of the extreme verge: for all beneath the
        moon
Would I not leap upright.
Glou.   Let go my hand.
Here, friend, 's another purse; in it a jewel
Well worth a poor man's taking: fairies and
        gods
Prosper it with thee! Go thou farther off; 30
Bid me farewell, and let me hear thee going.
Edg. Now fare you well, good sir.
Glou.   With all my heart.
Edg. Why I do trifle thus with his despair
Is done to cure it.
Glou. [*Kneeling*] O you mighty gods!
This world I do renounce, and, in your sights,
Shake patiently my great affiction off:
If I could bear it longer, and not fall
To quarrel with your great opposeless wills,
My snuff and loathed part of nature should
Burn itself out.   If Edgar live, O, bless him!
Now, fellow, fare thee well. [*He falls forward.*
Edg.   Gone, sir: farewell.   42
And yet I know not how conceit may rob
The treasury of life, when life itself
Yields to the theft: had he been where he
        thought,
By this, had thought been past.   Alive or
        dead?
Ho, you sir! friend! Hear you, sir! speak!
Thus might he pass indeed: yet he revives.
What are you, sir?
Glou.   Away, and let me die.
Edg. Hadst thou been aught but gossa-
        mer, feathers, air,
So many fathom down precipitating,   50
Thou 'dst shiver'd like an egg: but thou dost
        breathe;
Hast heavy substance; bleed'st not; speak'st;
        art sound.
Ten masts at each make not the altitude
Which thou hast perpendicularly fell:
Thy life's a miracle. Speak yet again.
Glou. But have I fall'n, or no?
Edg. From the dread summit of this
        chalky bourn.

Scene vi. **11-24. here's . . . headlong.** This famous
passage might almost be taken to symbolize the want
of scenery on Shakespeare's own stage; his atmosphere
had to be in large measure the creation of his poetry.
13. choughs, jackdaws. **15. samphire,** an herb
called sea-fennel and the herb of St. Pierre, used for
pickles. **19. cock,** cock-boat. **21. unnumber'd,**
innumerable.

33-80. Why I do . . . patient thoughts. This
passage has important moral and theological import.
Its plain teaching is against suicide; in that, as in other
matters, the play is Christian in spite of its pagan setting;
see lines 75-77. **38. opposeless,** irresistible. **39. snuff,**
useless residue; the metaphor is taken from the smoking
wick of a candle. **42. conceit,** imagination. **47. pass,**
die. **53. at each,** end to end. **57. bourn,** limit,
boundary.

Look up a-height; the shrill-gorged lark so far
Cannot be seen or heard: do but look up.

Glou. Alack, I have no eyes.   60
Is wretchedness deprived that benefit,
To end itself by death? 'Twas yet some
  comfort,
When misery could beguile the tyrant's rage,
And frustrate his proud will.

Edg.   Give me your arm:
Up: so. How is 't? Feel you your legs? You
  stand.

Glou. Too well, too well.

Edg.   This is above all strangeness.
Upon the crown o' the cliff, what thing was
  that
Which parted from you?

Glou.   A poor unfortunate beggar.

Edg. As I stood here below, methought his
  eyes
Were two full moons; he had a thousand
  noses,   70
Horns whelk'd and waved like the enridged
  sea:
It was some fiend; therefore, thou happy
  father,
Think that the clearest gods, who make them
  honours
Of men's impossibilities, have preserved thee.

Glou. I do remember now: henceforth I'll
  bear
Affliction till it do cry out itself
'Enough, enough,' and die. That thing you
  speak of,
I took it for a man; often 'twould say
'The fiend, the fiend:' he led me to that
  place.

Edg. Bear free and patient thoughts. But
  who comes here?   80

Enter LEAR, *fantastically dressed with wild
  flowers.*

The safer sense will ne'er accommodate
His master thus.

Lear. No, they cannot touch me for coining;
I am the king himself.

Edg. O thou side-piercing sight!   85

Lear. Nature's above art in that respect.
There's your press-money. That fellow

handles his bow like a crow-keeper: draw me
a clothier's yard. Look, look, a mouse!
Peace, peace; this piece of toasted cheese will
do't. There's my gauntlet; I'll prove it on a
giant. Bring up the brown bills. O, well
flown, bird! i' the clout, i' the clout: hewgh!
Give the word.

Edg. Sweet marjoram.

Lear. Pass.

Glou. I know that voice.   96

Lear. Ha! Goneril, with a white beard!
They flattered me like a dog; and told me I
had white hairs in my beard ere the black
ones were there. To say 'ay' and 'no' to
every thing that I said!—'Ay' and 'no' too
was no good divinity. When the rain came
to wet me once, and the wind to make me
chatter; when the thunder would not peace
at my bidding; there I found 'em, there I
smelt 'em out. Go to, they are not men o'
their words: they told me I was every thing;
'tis a lie, I am not ague-proof.   107

Glou. The trick of that voice I do well remember:
Is 't not the king?

Lear.   Ay, every inch a king:
When I do stare, see how the subject quakes.
I pardon that man's life. What was thy
  cause?
Adultery?
Thou shalt not die: die for adultery! No:
The wren goes to 't, and the small gilded
  fly
Does lecher in my sight.
Let copulation thrive; for Gloucester's bas-
  tard son
Was kinder to his father than my daughters
Got 'tween the lawful sheets.
To 't, luxury, pell-mell! for I lack soldiers.
Behold yond simpering dame,   120
Whose face between her forks presages snow;
That minces virtue, and does shake the head
To hear of pleasure's name;

---

58. **a-height**, on high. **shrill-gorged**, shrill-throated. 71. **whelk'd**, explained as "twisted"; also as "swollen, as with whelks or knobs." **enridged**, furrowed. 73. **clearest**, most righteous. 74. **men's impossibilities**, things impossible to men. 80. **free**, probably, free from fear. 81. **safer**, saner. **accommodate**, furnish, equip. 83. **touch**, arrest, prosecute. 87. **press-money**, bonus given soldiers when they were pressed into service.

88. **crow-keeper**, scarecrow; or possibly, crow-frightener. 89. **clothier's yard**, arrow the length of a cloth yard. 92. **brown bills**, soldiers carrying pikes, or the pikes themselves. **well flown, bird!** Lear may think he is hawking, or he may be speaking of the flight of an arrow. 93. **clout**, target. **word**, password. 98-107. **They flattered . . . ague-proof.** This strangely sane passage echoes one of the themes of the play, namely, the wickedness of flattery. 104. **peace**, hold its peace. 108. **trick**, peculiar characteristic. 109. **Ay, every inch a king.** Gloucester's words bring Lear back to the recollection of his kingly state, and he begins to speak in blank verse, irregular to correspond to his wandering sanity. The whole passage is full of the deepest social pessimism. It is the reflection in Lear's crazed mind of the chaos, domestic and political, wrought in the state by wickedness in high places. 119. **luxury**, lust.

The fitchew, nor the soiled horse, goes to't
With a more riotous appetite.   125
Down from the waist they are Centaurs,
Though women all above:
But to the girdle do the gods inherit,
Beneath is all the fiends';
There's hell, there's darkness, there's the sul-
    phurous pit,   130
Burning, scalding, stench, consumption; fie,
fie, fie! pah, pah! Give me an ounce of civet,
good apothecary, to sweeten my imagination:
there's money for thee.

Glou. O, let me kiss that hand!

Lear. Let me wipe it first; it smells of
mortality.

Glou. O ruin'd piece of nature! This great
world   137
Shall so wear out to nought. Dost thou
know me?

Lear. I remember thine eyes well enough.
Dost thou squiny at me? No, do thy worst,
blind Cupid; I'll not love. Read thou this
challenge; mark but the penning of it.   142

Glou. Were all the letters suns, I could not
see one.

Edg. I would not take this from report;
it is,
And my heart breaks at it.

Lear. Read.

Glou. What, with the case of eyes?   147

Lear. O, ho, are you there with me? No
eyes in your head, nor no money in your
purse? Your eyes are in a heavy case, your
purse in a light: yet you see how this world
goes.

Glou. I see it feelingly.   152

Lear. What, art mad? A man may see
how this world goes with no eyes. Look with
thine ears: see how yond justice rails upon
yond simple thief. Hark, in thine ear: change
places; and, handy-dandy, which is the
justice, which is the thief? Thou hast seen
a farmer's dog bark at a beggar?

Glou. Ay, sir.   160

Lear. And the creature run from the cur?
There thou mightst behold the great image

of authority: a dog's obeyed in office.
Thou rascal beadle, hold thy bloody hand!
Why dost thou lash that whore? Strip thine
    own back;
Thou hotly lust'st to use her in that kind
For which thou whipp'st her. The usurer
    hangs the cozener.
Through tatter'd clothes small vices do
    appear;
Robes and furr'd gowns hide all. Plate sin
    with gold,   169
And the strong lance of justice hurtless breaks;
Arm it in rags, a pigmy's straw does pierce it.
None does offend, none, I say, none; I'll able
    'em:
Take that of me, my friend, who have the
    power
To seal the accuser's lips. Get thee glass
    eyes;
And, like a scurvy politician, seem
To see the things thou dost not. Now, now,
    now, now:
Pull off my boots: harder, harder: so.

Edg. O, matter and impertinency mix'd!
Reason in madness!

Lear. If thou wilt weep my fortunes, take
    my eyes.   180
I know thee well enough; thy name is Glou-
cester:
Thou must be patient; we came crying
hither:
Thou know'st, the first time that we smell
    the air,
We wawl and cry. I will preach to thee:
    mark.

Glou. Alack, alack the day!

Lear. When we are born, we cry that we
    are come
To this great stage of fools: this' a good
    block;
It were a delicate stratagem, to shoe
A troop of horse with felt: I'll put't in proof;
And when I have stol'n upon these sons-in-
    law,   190
Then, kill, kill, kill, kill, kill, kill!

Enter a Gentleman, *with* Attendants.

Gent. O, here he is: lay hand upon him.
    Sir,
Your most dear daughter—

Lear. No rescue? What, a prisoner? I am
even

---

124. **fitchew,** polecat. **soiled horse,** horse turned
out to grass. 126. **Centaurs,** fabulous monsters, half
man, half horse. 128. **But,** only. **inherit,** possess.
137. **piece,** masterpiece. 140. **squiny,** squint, look
askance. 147. **case,** mere sockets. 148. **are . . . me?**
is that what you refer to? 157. **handy-dandy,** take
your choice of hands, as in a well-known child's game.
161-171. **And the . . . pierce it.** Into these ravings
should be read the conception of a state resting upon
authority solely, and this state fallen into ruin because
the holders of this divinely constituted authority are
themselves corrupt.

167. **cozener,** cheater. 172. **able,** give warrant to.
175. **politician,** trickster. 187. **this',** this is. **block,**
probably, hat, from the form on which it was molded.

The natural fool of fortune. Use me well;
You shall have ransom. Let me have
　surgeons;
I am cut to the brains.
　Gent.　　　　You shall have any thing.
　Lear. No seconds? all myself?
Why, this would make a man a man of salt,
To use his eyes for garden water-pots,　200
Ay, and laying autumn's dust.
　Gent.　　　　　　Good sir,—
　Lear. I will die bravely, like a bride-
　groom. What!
I will be jovial: come, come; I am a king,
My masters, know you that.
　Gent. You are a royal one, and we obey
　you.
　Lear. Then there's life in 't. Nay, if you
get it, you shall get it with running. Sa, sa,
sa, sa.　　　[*Exit running; Attendants follow.*
　Gent. A sight most pitiful in the meanest
　wretch,
Past speaking of in a king! Thou hast one
　daughter,
Who redeems nature from the general curse
Which twain have brought her to.　211
　Edg. Hail, gentle sir.
　Gent.　　Sir, speed you: what's your will?
　Edg. Do you hear aught, sir, of a battle
　toward?
　Gent. Most sure and vulgar: every one
　hears that,
Which can distinguish sound.
　Edg.　　　　　But, by your favour,
How near's the other army?
　Gent. Near and on speedy foot; the main
　descry
Stands on the hourly thought.
　Edg.　　　　I thank you, sir: that's all.
　Gent. Though that the queen on special
　cause is here,
Her army is moved on.
　Edg.　　　　　I thank you, sir.　220
　　　　　　　　　　　　[*Exit Gent.*
　Glou. You ever-gentle gods, take my
　breath from me;
Let not my worser spirit tempt me again
To die before you please!
　Edg.　　　　　Well pray you, father.
　Glou. Now, good sir, what are you?
　Edg. A most poor man, made tame to for-
　tune's blows;

Who, by the art of known and feeling
　sorrows,
Am pregnant to good pity. Give me your
　hand,
I'll lead you to some biding.
　Glou.　　　　　　Hearty thanks:
The bounty and the benison of heaven
To boot, and boot!

　　　　　　　Enter OSWALD.

　Osw.　　A proclaim'd prize! Most happy!
That eyeless head of thine was first framed
　flesh　231
To raise my fortunes. Thou old unhappy
　traitor,
Briefly thyself remember: the sword is out
That must destroy thee.
　Glou.　　　　　Now let thy friendly hand
Put strength enough to 't.
　　　　　　　　　　　　[*Edgar interposes.*
　Osw.　　　　Wherefore, bold peasant,
Darest thou support a publish'd traitor?
　Hence;
Lest that the infection of his fortune take
Like hold on thee. Let go his arm.
　Edg. Chill not let go, zir, without vurther
'casion.　240
　Osw. Let go, slave, or thou diest!
　Edg. Good gentleman, go your gait, and
let poor volk pass. An chud ha' bin zwag-
gered out of my life, 'twould not ha' bin zo
long as 'tis by a vortnight. Nay, come not
near th' old man; keep out, che vor ye, or
ise try whether your costard or my ballow
be the harder: chill be plain with you.
　Osw. Out, dunghill!
　Edg. Chill pick your teeth, zir: come; no
matter vor your foins.　251
　　　　[*They fight, and Edgar knocks him down.*
　Osw. Slave, thou hast slain me: villain,
take my purse;
If ever thou wilt thrive, bury my body;
And give the letters which thou find'st about
　me
To Edmund earl of Gloucester; seek him out
Upon the British party: O, untimely death!
　　　　　　　　　　　　　　　　　　[*Dies.*

199. **man of salt**, of salt tears.　212. **speed you**,
God speed you.　213. **toward**, impending.　214. **vulgar**, in every one's mouth, generally known.　215.
Which, who.　217-218. **the main . . . thought**, the
full view of the main body is expected every hour.

226. **feeling**, heart-felt, deep.　227. **pregnant**, disposed, inclined.　228. **biding**, abiding place.　230. **To
boot, and boot!** i.e., in addition (to my thanks), I wish
you the bounty of heaven.　233. **thyself remember**,
confess thy sins.　239. **Chill**, I will. Edgar adopts a
dialect, apparently of the south country.　242. **go your
gait**, go your own way.　243. **An chud**, if I could.　246.
che vor ye, I warn you.　247. **ise**, I shall. **costard**, an
apple, slang for *head*. **ballow**, cudgel.　249. **dunghill**,
person of the lowest extraction.　251. **foins**, thrusts in
fencing.

Edg. I know thee well: a serviceable villain;
As duteous to the vices of thy mistress
As badness would desire.

    Glou.   What, is he dead?

    Edg. Sit you down, father; rest you.   260
Let's see these pockets: the letters that he speaks of
May be my friends. He's dead; I am only sorry
He had no other death's-man. Let us see:
Leave, gentle wax; and, manners, blame us not:
To know our enemies' minds, we'ld rip their hearts;
Their papers, is more lawful.   266

    [*Reads*] 'Let our reciprocal vows be remembered. You have many opportunities to cut him off: if your will want not, time and place will be fruitfully offered. There is nothing done, if he return the conqueror: then am I the prisoner, and his bed my gaol; from the loathed warmth whereof deliver me, and supply the place for your labour.

    'Your—wife, so I would say—
             'Affectionate servant,
                     'GONERIL.'

O undistinguish'd space of woman's will!
A plot upon her virtuous husband's life;
And the exchange my brother! Here, in the sands,
                        280
Thee I'll rake up, the post unsanctified
Of murderous lechers: and in the mature time
With this ungracious paper strike the sight
Of the death-practised duke: for him 'tis well
That of thy death and business I can tell.

    Glou. The king is mad: how stiff is my vile sense,
That I stand up, and have ingenious feeling
Of my huge sorrows! Better I were distract:
So should my thoughts be sever'd from my griefs,
And woes by wrong imaginations lose   290
The knowledge of themselves.

    Edg.   Give me your hand:
                     [*Drum afar off.*

Far off, methinks, I hear the beaten drum:
Come, father, I'll bestow you with a friend.
                     [*Exeunt.*

SCENE VII.   *A tent in the French camp.*
LEAR *on a bed asleep, soft music playing;*
Gentleman, and others attending.

    Enter CORDELIA, KENT, *and* Doctor.

    Cor. O thou good Kent, how shall I live and work,
To match thy goodness? My life will be too short,
And every measure fail me.

    Kent. To be acknowledged, madam, is o'er-paid.
All my reports go with the modest truth;
Nor more nor clipp'd, but so.

    Cor.   Be better suited:
These weeds are memories of those worser hours:
I prithee, put them off.

    Kent.   Pardon me, dear madam;
Yet to be known shortens my made intent: 9
My boon I make it, that you know me not
Till time and I think meet.

    Cor. Then be't so, my good lord. [*To the Doctor*] How does the king?

    Doct. Madam, sleeps still.

    Cor. O you kind gods,
Cure this great breach in his abused nature!
The untuned and jarring senses, O, wind up
Of this child-changed father!

    Doct.   So please your majesty
That we may wake the king: he hath slept long.

    Cor. Be govern'd by your knowledge, and proceed
I' the sway of your own will. Is he array'd?

    Gent. Ay, madam; in the heaviness of his sleep   21
We put fresh garments on him.

    Doct. Be by, good madam, when we do awake him;
I doubt not of his temperance.

    Cor.   Very well.

    Doct. Please you, draw near. Louder the music there!

Cor. O my dear father! Restoration hang
Thy medicine on my lips; and let this kiss
Repair those violent harms that my two
    sisters
Have in thy reverence made!
    Kent.   Kind and dear princess!
    Cor. Had you not been their father, these
    white flakes   30
Had challenged pity of them. Was this a
    face
To be opposed against the warring winds?
To stand against the deep dread-bolted
    thunder?
In the most terrible and nimble stroke
Of quick, cross lightning? to watch—poor
    perdu!—
With this thin helm? Mine enemy's dog,
Though he had bit me, should have stood
    that night
Against my fire; and wast thou fain, poor
    father,
To hovel thee with swine, and rogues for-
    lorn,
In short and musty straw? Alack, alack! 40
'Tis wonder that thy life and wits at once
Had not concluded all. He wakes; speak to
    him.
    Doct. Madam, do you; 'tis fittest.
    Cor. How does my royal lord? How fares
    your majesty?
    Lear. You do me wrong to take me out o'
    the grave:
Thou art a soul in bliss; but I am bound
Upon a wheel of fire, that mine own tears
Do scald like molten lead.
    Cor.   Sir, do you know me?
    Lear. You are a spirit, I know: when did
    you die?
    Cor. Still, still, far wide!   50
    Doct. He's scarce awake: let him alone
    awhile.
    Lear. Where have I been? Where am I?
    Fair daylight?
I am mightily abused. I should e'en die with
    pity,
To see another thus. I know not what to say.
I will not swear these are my hands: let's see;
I feel this pin prick. Would I were assured
Of my condition!
    Cor.   O, look upon me, sir,

And hold your hands in benediction o'er me:
No, sir, you must not kneel.
    Lear.   Pray, do not mock me:
I am a very foolish fond old man,   60
Fourscore and upward, not an hour more nor
    less;
And, to deal plainly,
I fear I am not in my perfect mind.
Methinks I should know you, and know this
    man;
Yet I am doubtful: for I am mainly ignorant
What place this is; and all the skill I have
Remembers not these garments; nor I know
    not
Where I did lodge last night. Do not laugh
    at me;
For, as I am a man, I think this lady
To be my child Cordelia.
    Cor.   And so I am, I am.   70
    Lear. Be your tears wet? yes, 'faith. I
    pray, weep not:
If you have poison for me, I will drink it.
I know you do not love me; for your sisters
Have, as I do remember, done me wrong:
You have some cause, they have not.
    Cor.   No cause, no cause.
    Lear. Am I in France?
    Kent.   In your own kingdom, sir.
    Lear. Do not abuse me.
    Doct. Be comforted, good madam: the
    great rage,
You see, is kill'd in him: and yet it is danger
To make him even o'er the time he has lost. 80
Desire him to go in; trouble him no more
Till further settling.
    Cor. Will 't please your highness walk?
    Lear.   You must bear with me:
Pray you now, forget and forgive: I am old
    and foolish.
    [*Exeunt all but Kent and Gentleman.*
    Gent. Holds it true, sir, that the Duke of
Cornwall was so slain?
    Kent. Most certain, sir.
    Gent. Who is conductor of his people?
    Kent. As 'tis said, the bastard son of
Gloucester.   90
    Gent. They say Edgar, his banished son,
is with the Earl of Kent in Germany.

---

33. **dread-bolted**, furnished with the dreadful thunderstone. 35. **perdu**, soldier placed in a position of peculiar danger. 42. **concluded all**, come to an end all together.

65. **mainly**, perfectly. 73-75. **I know . . . not.** This pathetic passage is not merely the strugglings of Lear's mind back to recognition; it is also a momentary restoration of the bargain-and-sale ethics which characterized the partition of his kingdom. 80. **even o'er**, give an account of, go over in his mind. 82. **settling**, composing of his mind.

Kent. Report is changeable. 'Tis time to
look about; the powers of the kingdom ap-
proach apace.   95
Gent. The arbitrement is like to be bloody.
Fare you well, sir.   [*Exit.*
   Kent. My point and period will be
     throughly wrought,
Or well or ill, as this day's battle's fought. 99
                         [*Exit.*

ACT V.

SCENE I. *The British camp, near Dover.*

Enter, with drum and colours, EDMUND,
REGAN, Gentlemen, *and* Soldiers.

   Edm. Know of the duke if his last purpose
hold,
Or whether since he is advised by aught
To change the course: he's full of alteration
And self-reproving: bring his constant
     pleasure. [*To a Gentleman, who goes out.*
   Reg. Our sister's man is certainly mis-
carried.
   Edm. 'Tis to be doubted, madam.
   Reg.   Now, sweet lord,
You know the goodness I intend upon you:
Tell me — but truly — but then speak the
     truth,
Do you not love my sister?
   Edm.   In honour'd love.
   Reg. But have you never found my broth-
er's way   10
To the forfended place?
   Edm.   That thought abuses you.
   Reg. I am doubtful that you have been
     conjunct
And bosom'd with her, as far as we call hers.
   Edm. No, by mine honour, madam.
   Reg. I never shall endure her: dear my lord,
Be not familiar with her.
   Edm.   Fear me not:
She and the duke her husband!

Enter, with drum and colours, ALBANY,
GONERIL, *and* Soldiers.

   Gon. [*Aside*] I had rather lose the battle
than that sister
Should loosen him and me.

   Alb. Our very loving sister, well be-met. 20
Sir, this I hear; the king is come to his
     daughter,
With others whom the rigour of our state
Forced to cry out. Where I could not be
     honest,
I never yet was valiant: for this business,
It toucheth us, as France invades our land,
Not bolds the king, with others, whom, I
     fear,
Most just and heavy causes make oppose.
   Edm. Sir, you speak nobly.
   Reg.   Why is this reason'd?
   Gon. Combine together 'gainst the enemy;
For these domestic and particular broils   30
Are not the question here.
   Alb.   Let's then determine
With the ancient of war on our proceedings.
   Edm. I shall attend you presently at your
tent.
   Reg. Sister, you'll go with us?
   Gon. No.
   Reg. 'Tis most convenient; pray you, go
     with us.
   Gon. [*Aside*] O, ho, I know the riddle.—
I will go.

As they are going out, enter EDGAR *disguised.*

   Edg. If e'er your grace had speech with
     man so poor,
Hear me one word.
   Alb.   I'll overtake you. Speak.
           [*Exeunt all but Albany and Edgar.*
   Edg. Before you fight the battle, ope this
     letter.   40
If you have victory, let the trumpet sound
For him that brought it: wretched though I
     seem,
I can produce a champion that will prove
What is avouched there. If you miscarry,
Your business of the world hath so an end,
And machination ceases. Fortune love you!
   Alb. Stay till I have read the letter.
   Edg.   I was forbid it.
When time shall serve, let but the herald
     cry,
And I'll appear again.
   Alb. Why, fare thee well: I will o'erlook
     thy paper.   [*Exit Edgar.*   50

---

96. **arbitrement**, decision by arms. 98. **period**, end aimed at.

Act V. Scene i. 4. **constant pleasure**, settled decision. 5. **miscarried**, lost, perished. 9. **honour'd**, honorable. 11. **forfended**, forbidden. 12. **doubtful**, afraid. **conjunct**, joined. 13. **bosom'd with her**, in her confidence; suggesting also her embraces.

26. **Not . . . others**, not because France encourages the king and others. 27. **heavy causes**, weighty reasons. **make oppose**, compel to fight (against us). 32. **ancient of war**, veteran soldiers. 36. **convenient**, proper, befitting. 44. **avouched**, formally asserted. **miscarry**, perish, come to destruction. 50. **o'erlook**, peruse.

Re-enter EDMUND.

Edm. The enemy's in view; draw up your
　powers.
Here is the guess of their true strength and
　forces
By diligent discovery; but your haste
Is now urged on you.
　Alb.　　　　We will greet the time. [*Exit.*
　Edm. To both these sisters have I sworn
　my love;
Each jealous of the other, as the stung
Are of the adder. Which of them shall I
　take?
Both? one? or neither? Neither can be
　enjoy'd,
If both remain alive: to take the widow
Exasperates, makes mad her sister Goneril;
And hardly shall I carry out my side,　61
Her husband being alive. Now then we'll
　use
His countenance for the battle; which being
　done,
Let her who would be rid of him devise
His speedy taking off. As for the mercy
Which he intends to Lear and to Cordelia,
The battle done, and they within our power,
Shall never see his pardon; for my state
Stands on me to defend, not to debate.　69
　　　　　　　　　　　　　　　　[*Exit.*

SCENE II. *A field between the two camps.*

*Alarum within. Enter, with drum and
colours,* LEAR, CORDELIA, *and* Soldiers,
over the stage; and exeunt.

Enter EDGAR *and* GLOUCESTER.

　Edg. Here, father, take the shadow of
　this tree
For your good host; pray that the right may
　thrive:
If ever I return to you again,
I'll bring you comfort.
　Glou.　　　　Grace go with you, sir!
　　　　　　　　　　　　　　　[*Exit Edgar.*

Alarum and retreat within. Re-enter EDGAR.

　Edg. Away, old man; give me thy hand;
　away!

King Lear hath lost, he and his daughter
　ta'en:
Give me thy hand; come on.
　Glou. No farther, sir; a man may rot even
　here.
　Edg. What, in ill thoughts again? Men
　must endure
Their going hence, even as their coming
　hither:　　　　　　　　　　　　　　　10
Ripeness is all: come on.
　Glou.　　　　And that's true too. [*Exeunt.*

SCENE III. *The British camp near Dover.*

Enter, in conquest, with drum and colours,
　EDMUND; LEAR *and* CORDELIA, *prisoners;*
　Captain, Soldiers, &c.

　Edm. Some officers take them away: good
　guard,
Until their greater pleasures first be known
That are to censure them.
　Cor.　　　　We are not the first
Who, with best meaning, have incurr'd the
　worst.
For thee, oppressed king, am I cast down;
Myself could else out-frown false fortune's
　frown.
Shall we not see these daughters and these
　sisters?
　Lear. No, no, no, no! Come, let's away
　to prison:
We two alone will sing like birds i' the cage:
When thou dost ask me blessing, I'll kneel
　down,　　　　　　　　　　　　　　　10
And ask of thee forgiveness: so we'll live,
And pray, and sing, and tell old tales, and
　laugh
At gilded butterflies, and hear poor rogues
Talk of court news; and we'll talk with them
　too,
Who loses and who wins; who's in, who's out;
And take upon's the mystery of things,
As if we were God's spies: and we'll wear out,
In a wall'd prison, packs and sects of great
　ones,
That ebb and flow by the moon.
　Edm.　　　　　　Take them away.

---

53. **discovery,** reconnoitering. 54. **greet the time,**
face the situation. 56. **jealous,** suspicious. 61. **carry
out my side,** win my game; possibly a figure from cards.
68-69. **my state . . . debate,** my position depends upon
maintenance by force, not on debate.

9-11. **Men . . . all,** a stern utterance of the doctrine
of fortitude, repeatedly applied to poor Gloucester. It
must be said, however, that fortitude is the crowning
quality of Edgar's character. 11. **Ripeness,** readiness.
　Scene iii. 3. **censure,** pass sentence on. 13. **gilded
butterflies,** courtiers. 17. **wear out,** forget, efface from
memory. 18. **packs,** combinations, confederacies.
sects, parties.

Lear. Upon such sacrifices, my Cordelia, 20
The gods themselves throw incense. Have I
    caught thee?
He that parts us shall bring a brand from
    heaven,
And fire us hence like foxes. Wipe thine
    eyes;
The good-years shall devour them, flesh and
    fell,
Ere they shall make us weep: we'll see 'em
    starve first.
Come. [*Exeunt Lear and Cordelia, guarded.*
    Edm. Come hither, captain; hark.
Take thou this note [*giving a paper*]; go
    follow them to prison:
One step I have advanced thee; if thou dost
As this instructs thee, thou dost make thy
    way
To noble fortunes: know thou this, that men
Are as the time is: to be tender-minded 31
Does not become a sword: thy great em-
    ployment
Will not bear question; either say thou'lt
    do 't,
Or thrive by other means.
    Capt.   I'll do 't, my lord.
    Edm. About it; and write happy when
    thou hast done.
Mark, I say, instantly; and carry it so
As I have set it down.
    Capt. I cannot draw a cart, nor eat dried
    oats;
If it be man's work, I'll do it.   [*Exit.*

Flourish.   *Enter* ALBANY, GONERIL, REGAN,
    another Captain, *and* Soldiers.

    Alb. Sir, you have shown to-day your
    valiant strain,   40
And fortune led you well: you have the
    captives
That were the opposites of this day's strife:
We do require them of you, so to use them
As we shall find their merits and our safety
May equally determine.
    Edm.   Sir, I thought it fit
To send the old and miserable king
To some retention and appointed guard;
Whose age has charms in it, whose title
    more,

To pluck the common bosom on his side,
And turn our impress'd lances in our eyes   50
Which do command them. With him I sent
    the queen;
My reason all the same; and they are ready
To-morrow, or at further space, to appear
Where you shall hold your session. At this
    time
We sweat and bleed: the friend hath lost his
    friend;
And the best quarrels, in the heat, are cursed
By those that feel their sharpness:
The question of Cordelia and her father
Requires a fitter place.
    Alb.   Sir, by your patience,
I hold you but a subject of this war,   60
Not as a brother.
    Reg.   That's as we list to grace him.
Methinks our pleasure might have been de-
    manded,
Ere you had spoke so far. He led our
    powers;
Bore the commission of my place and person;
The which immediacy may well stand up,
And call itself your brother.
    Gon.   Not so hot:
In his own grace he doth exalt himself,
More than in your addition.
    Reg.   In my rights,
By me invested, he compeers the best.
    Gon. That were the most, if he should
    husband you.   70
    Reg. Jesters do oft prove prophets.
    Gon.   Holla, holla!
That eye that told you so look'd but a-
    squint.
    Reg. Lady, I am not well; else I should
    answer
From a full-flowing stomach. General,
Take thou my soldiers, prisoners, patrimony;
Dispose of them, of me; the walls are thine:
Witness the world, that I create thee here
My lord and master.
    Gon.   Mean you to enjoy him?
    Alb. The let-alone lies not in your good
    will.
    Edm. Nor in thine, lord.

---

23. **fire . . . foxes**, i.e., as foxes are driven out of their holes by fire and smoke. 24. **good-years**, apparently a general word for evil; thought sometimes to be the name of a disease. **flesh and fell**, flesh and skin. 33. **bear question**, be argued about. 35. **write happy**, call yourself happy. 36. **carry**, enact. 47. **retention**, custody.

49. **common bosom**, the affection of the mob. 50. **impress'd lances**, weapons of troops impressed into service. 58. **question**, cause. 61. **list**, please. 64. **commission**, warrant as representative. 65. **immediacy**, next in authority, or nearness of his being my agent. 69. **compeers**, is equal with. 72. **That eye . . . a-squint**, reference to a proverb: Love being jealous makes a good eye look asquint. 74. **full-flowing stomach**, full tide of angry rejoinder. 76. **the walls are thine**, probably a phrase signifying complete surrender; many conjectures.

Alb.   Half-blooded fellow, yes.   80
Reg. [*To Edmund*] Let the drum strike,
  and prove my title thine.
Alb. Stay yet; hear reason. Edmund, I
  arrest thee
On capital treason; and, in thine attaint,
This gilded serpent [*pointing to Gon.*]. For
  your claim, fair sister,
I bar it in the interest of my wife;
'Tis she is sub-contracted to this lord,
And I, her husband, contradict your bans.
If you will marry, make your loves to me,
My lady is bespoke.
Gon.   An interlude!
Alb. Thou art arm'd, Gloucester: let the
  trumpet sound: 90
If none appear to prove upon thy head
Thy heinous, manifest, and many treasons,
There is my pledge [*throwing down a glove*];
  I'll prove it on thy heart,
Ere I taste bread, thou art in nothing less
Than I have here proclaim'd thee.
Reg.   Sick, O, sick!
Gon. [*Aside*] If not, I'll ne'er trust
  medicine.
Edm. There's my exchange [*throwing
  down a glove*]: what in the world he is
That names me traitor, villain-like he lies:
Call by thy trumpet: he that dares approach,
On him, on you, who not? I will maintain 100
My truth and honour firmly.
Alb. A herald, ho!
Edm.   A herald, ho, a herald!
Alb. Trust to thy single virtue; for thy
  soldiers,
All levied in my name, have in my name
Took their discharge.
Reg.   My sickness grows upon me.
Alb. She is not well; convey her to my
  tent.   [*Exit Regan, led.*

Enter a Herald.

Come hither, herald,—Let the trumpet
  sound,—
And read out this.   108
Capt. Sound, trumpet! [*A trumpet sounds.*
Her. [*Reads*] 'If any man of quality or
degree within the lists of the army will main-
tain upon Edmund, supposed Earl of
Gloucester, that he is a manifold traitor, let

him appear by the third sound of the trump-
et: he is bold in his defence.'
Edm. Sound!   [*First trumpet.*
Her. Again!   [*Second trumpet.*
Her. Again!   [*Third trumpet.*
                        [*Trumpet answers within.*

Enter EDGAR, *at the third sound, armed,
        with a trumpet before him.*

Alb. Ask him his purposes, why he
  appears
Upon this call o' the trumpet.
Her.   What are you?
Your name, your quality? and why you
  answer   120
This present summons?
Edg.   Know, my name is lost;
By treason's tooth bare-gnawn and canker-
  bit:
Yet am I noble as the adversary
I come to cope.
Alb.   Which is that adversary?
Edg. What's he that speaks for Edmund
  Earl of Gloucester?
Edm. Himself: what say'st thou to him?
Edg.   Draw thy sword,
That, if my speech offend a noble heart,
Thy arm may do thee justice: here is mine.
Behold, it is the privilege of mine honours,
My oath, and my profession: I protest,   130
Maugre thy strength, youth, place, and
  eminence,
Despite thy victor sword and fire-new
  fortune,
Thy valour and thy heart, thou art a traitor;
False to thy gods, thy brother, and thy
  father;
Conspirant 'gainst this high-illustrious
  prince;
And, from the extremest upward of thy head
To the descent and dust below thy foot,
A most toad-spotted traitor. Say thou 'No,'
This sword, this arm, and my best spirits,
  are bent
To prove upon thy heart, whereto I speak, 140
Thou liest.
Edm. In wisdom I should ask thy name;
But, since thy outside looks so fair and
  warlike,

And that thy tongue some say of breeding
   breathes,
What safe and nicely I might well delay
By rule of knighthood, I disdain and spurn:
Back do I toss these treasons to thy head;
With the hell-hated lie o'erwhelm thy heart;
Which, for they yet glance by and scarcely
   bruise,
This sword of mine shall give them instant
   way,
Where they shall rest for ever. Trumpets,
   speak!   150
   [*Alarums. They fight. Edmund falls.*
   Alb. Save him, save him!
   Gon.   This is practice, Gloucester:
By the law of arms thou wast not bound to
   answer
An unknown opposite; thou art not van-
   quish'd,
But cozen'd and beguiled.
   Alb.   Shut your mouth, dame,
Or with this paper shall I stop it. Hold, sir;
Thou worse than any name, read thine own
   evil:
No tearing, lady; I perceive you know it.
             [*Gives the letter to Edmund.*
   Gon. Say, if I do, the laws are mine, not
   thine:
Who can arraign me for't?
   Alb.   Most monstrous! oh!
Know'st thou this paper?
   Gon.   Ask me not what I know. [*Exit.*
   Alb. Go after her: she's desperate; govern
   her.   161
   Edm. What you have charged me with,
   that have I done;
And more, much more; the time will bring it
   out:
'Tis past, and so am I. But what art thou
That hast this fortune on me? If thou'rt
   noble,
I do forgive thee.
   Edg.   Let's exchange charity.
I am no less in blood than thou art, Edmund;
If more, the more thou hast wrong'd me.
My name is Edgar, and thy father's son.
The gods are just, and of our pleasant vices
Make instruments to plague us: 171
The dark and vicious place where thee he got
Cost him his eyes.

   Edm.   Thou hast spoken right, 'tis
   true;
The wheel is come full circle; I am here.
   Alb. Methought thy very gait did pro-
   phesy
A royal nobleness: I must embrace thee:
Let sorrow split my heart, if ever I
Did hate thee or thy father!
   Edg.   Worthy prince, I know't.
   Alb. Where have you hid yourself?
How have you known the miseries of your
   father?   180
   Edg. By nursing them, my lord. List a
   brief tale;
And when 'tis told, O, that my heart would
   burst!
The bloody proclamation to escape,
That follow'd me so near,—O, our lives'
   sweetness!
That we the pain of death would hourly die
Rather than die at once!—taught me to shift
Into a madman's rags; to assume a sem-
   blance
That very dogs disdain'd: and in this habit
Met I my father with his bleeding rings,
Their precious stones new lost; became his
   guide,   190
Led him, begg'd for him, saved him from
   despair;
Never,—O fault!—reveal'd myself unto him,
Until some half-hour past, when I was arm'd:
Not sure, though hoping, of this good
   success,
I ask'd his blessing, and from first to last
Told him my pilgrimage: but his flaw'd
   heart,
Alack, too weak the conflict to support!
'Twixt two extremes of passion, joy and
   grief,
Burst smilingly.
   Edm. This speech of yours hath moved
   me,
And shall perchance do good: but speak you
   on;   200
You look as you had something more to say.
   Alb. If there be more, more woeful, hold it
   in;
For I am almost ready to dissolve,
Hearing of this.
   Edg.   This would have seem'd a
   period

---

143. **say,** flavor, indication; possibly for *assay*, proof.
146. **head,** i.e., to thy teeth. 147. **hell-hated,** hated
as hell is hated. 161. **govern,** restrain. 165. **fortune,**
victory, success.

174. **wheel,** wheel of fortune. 189. **rings,** sockets.
192. **fault,** mistake. 194. **success,** result of an action.
196. **flaw'd,** cracked, damaged by a flaw.

To such as love not sorrow; but another,
To amplify too much, would make much
    more,
And top extremity.
Whilst I was big in clamour came there in a
    man,
Who, having seen me in my worst estate,
Shunn'd my abhorr'd society; but then,
    finding   210
Who 'twas that so endured, with his strong
    arms
He fasten'd on my neck, and bellow'd out
As he'ld burst heaven; threw him on my
    father;
Told the most piteous tale of Lear and him
That ever ear received: which in recounting
His grief grew puissant, and the strings of life
Began to crack: twice then the trumpets
    sounded,
And there I left him tranced.
    Alb.   But who was this?
    Edg. Kent, sir, the banish'd Kent; who in
        disguise
Follow'd his enemy king, and did him
    service   220
Improper for a slave.

Enter a Gentleman, *with a bloody knife.*

    Gent. Help, help, O, help!
    Edg.   What kind of help?
    Alb.   Speak, man.
    Edg. What means that bloody knife?
    Gent.   'Tis hot, it smokes;
It came even from the heart of—O, she's
    dead!
    Alb. Who dead? speak, man.
    Gent. Your lady, sir, your lady: and her
        sister
By her is poisoned; she hath confess'd it.
    Edm. I was contracted to them both: all
        three
Now marry in an instant.
    Edg.   Here comes Kent.
    Alb. Produce their bodies, be they alive
        or dead: 230
This judgement of the heavens, that makes
    us tremble,
Touches us not with pity. [*Exit Gentleman.*

Enter KENT.

O, is this he?

218. **tranced,** entranced, senseless.

The time will not allow the compliment
Which very manners urges.
    Kent.   I am come
To bid my king and master aye good night:
Is he not here?
    Alb.   Great thing of us forgot!
Speak, Edmund, where's the king? and
    where's Cordelia?
See'st thou this object, Kent?
        [*The bodies of Goneril and Regan are
                                    brought in.*
    Kent. Alack, why thus?
    Edm.   Yet Edmund was beloved:
The one the other poison'd for my sake, 240
And after slew herself.
    Alb. Even so.   Cover their faces.
    Edm. I pant for life: some good I mean
    to do,
Despite of mine own nature.   Quickly send,
Be brief in it, to the castle; for my writ
Is on the life of Lear and on Cordelia:
Nay, send in time.
    Alb.   Run, run, O, run!
    Edg. To who, my lord?   Who hath the
        office? send
Thy token of reprieve.
    Edm. Well thought on: take my sword, 250
Give it the captain.
    Alb. Haste thee, for thy life. [*Exit Edgar.*
    Edm. He hath commission from thy wife
        and me
To hang Cordelia in the prison, and
To lay the blame upon her own despair,
That she fordid herself.
    Alb. The gods defend her! Bear him hence
        awhile.   [*Edmund is borne off.*

Re-enter LEAR, *with* CORDELIA *dead in his
arms;* EDGAR, Captain, *and others following.*

    Lear. Howl, howl, howl, howl!   O, you
    are men of stones:
Had I your tongues and eyes, I'ld use them
    so
That heaven's vault should crack.   She's
    gone for ever!
I know when one is dead, and when one
    lives;   260
She's dead as earth.   Lend me a looking-
    glass;

236. **forgot,** forgotten. There is an improbability in
this forgetfulness. 243-244. **some good . . . nature.**
It is made clear to us in the first act that Edmund, born
outside the pale of social organization, is adverse and
hostile to the laws of gods and men; he repents and is
therefore not an inhuman monster; note the implication
of line 239. 255. **fordid,** destroyed.

If that her breath will mist or stain the stone,
Why, then she lives.

Kent. Is this the promised end?

Edg. Or image of that horror?

Alb. Fall, and cease!

Lear. This feather stirs; she lives! if it be so,
It is a chance which does redeem all sorrows
That ever I have felt.

Kent. [*Kneeling*] O my good master!

Lear. Prithee, away.

Edg. 'Tis noble Kent, your friend.

Lear. A plague upon you, murderers, traitors all!
I might have saved her; now she's gone for ever! 270
Cordelia, Cordelia! stay a little. Ha!
What is't thou say'st? Her voice was ever soft,
Gentle, and low, an excellent thing in woman.
I kill'd the slave that was a-hanging thee.

Capt. 'Tis true, my lords, he did.

Lear. Did I not, fellow?
I have seen the day, with my good biting falchion
I would have made them skip: I am old now,
And these same crosses spoil me. Who are you?
Mine eyes are not o' the best: I'll tell you straight.

Kent. If fortune brag of two she loved and hated, 280
One of them we behold.

Lear. This is a dull sight. Are you not Kent?

Kent. The same,
Your servant Kent. Where is your servant Caius?

Lear. He's a good fellow, I can tell you that;
He'll strike, and quickly too: he's dead and rotten.

Kent. No, my good lord; I am the very man,—

Lear. I'll see that straight.

Kent. That, from your first of difference and decay,

Have follow'd your sad steps.

Lear. You are welcome hither.

Kent. Nor no man else: all's cheerless, dark, and deadly. 290
Your eldest daughters have fordone themselves,
And desperately are dead.

Lear. Ay, so I think.

Alb. He knows not what he says: and vain it is
That we present us to him.

Edg. Very bootless.

Enter a Captain.

Capt. Edmund is dead, my lord.

Alb. That's but a trifle here.
You lords and noble friends, know our intent.
What comfort to this great decay may come
Shall be applied: for us, we will resign,
During the life of this old majesty,
To him our absolute power: [*To Edgar and Kent*] you, to your rights; 300
With boot, and such addition as your honours
Have more than merited. All friends shall taste
The wages of their virtue, and all foes
The cup of their deservings. O, see, see!

Lear. And my poor fool is hang'd! No, no, no life!
Why should a dog, a horse, a rat, have life,
And thou no breath at all? Thou'lt come no more,
Never, never, never, never, never!
Pray you, undo this button: thank you, sir.
Do you see this? Look on her, look, her lips, 310
Look there, look there! [*Dies.*

Edg. He faints! My lord, my lord!

Kent. Break, heart; I prithee, break!

Edg. Look up, my lord.

Kent. Vex not his ghost: O, let him pass! he hates him much
That would upon the rack of this tough world
Stretch him out longer.

---

262. **mist**, becloud. **stone**, crystal (of which the mirror is made). 263. **end**, Last Judgment. 264. **Fall, and cease!** possibly, let the heavens fall and all things cease. 276. **falchion**, sword; properly, a sword curved at the point with the edge on the convex side. 288. **first of difference**, beginning of your change of fortune for the worst.

292. **desperately**, in despair. 305. **my poor fool**, i.e., Cordelia. It has sometimes been wrongly thought that this refers to the Fool, but *fool*, as here used, is a term of endearment. 313-315. **he hates . . . longer.** These words of Kent's seem a complete rejoinder to those amiable critics of the eighteenth century who took delight in Tate's version, in which Cordelia was permitted to come back to life, and Lear was restored to his throne.

Edg.   He is gone, indeed.
Kent. The wonder is, he hath endured so
    long:
He but usurp'd his life.
    Alb. Bear them from hence. Our present
    business
Is general woe. [*To Kent and Edgar*] Friends
    of my soul, you twain
Rule in this realm, and the gored state
    sustain.   320

Kent. I have a journey, sir, shortly to go;
My master calls me, I must not say no.
    Alb. The weight of this sad time we must
    obey;
Speak what we reel, not what we ought to
    say.
The oldest hath borne most: we that are
    young
Shall never see so much, nor live so long.
                    [*Exeunt, with a dead march.*

MACBETH

DRAMATIS PERSONÆ

DUNCAN, king of Scotland.
MALCOLM, } his sons.
DONALBAIN,
MACBETH, } generals of the king's army.
BANQUO,
MACDUFF,
LENNOX,
ROSS, } noblemen of Scotland.
MENTEITH,
ANGUS,
CAITHNESS,
FLEANCE, son to Banquo.
SIWARD, Earl of Northumberland, general of the English forces.
Young SIWARD, his son.
SEYTON, an officer attending on Macbeth.
Boy, son to Macduff.

An English Doctor.
A Scotch Doctor.
A Soldier.
A Porter.
An Old Man.

LADY MACBETH.
LADY MACDUFF.
Gentlewoman attending on Lady Macbeth.

HECATE.
Three Witches.
Apparitions.

Lords, Gentlemen, Officers, Soldiers, Murderers, Attendants, and Messengers.

SCENE: *Scotland: England.*

ACT I.

SCENE I. *A desert place.*

Thunder and lightning. Enter three Witches.

First Witch. When shall we three meet again
In thunder, lightning, or in rain?
Sec. Witch. When the hurlyburly's done,
When the battle's lost and won.
Third Witch. That will be ere the set of sun.
First Witch. Where the place?
Sec. Witch. Upon the heath.
Third Witch. There to meet with Macbeth.

Act I. Scene i. Many critics have praised this scene. Coleridge declares that it strikes the keynote of the whole drama, the guilt and evil which hangs like a pall over the play. Mr. Henry Cuningham, on the other hand, holds that it is a later addition by an inferior hand, since it gives a cheap and vulgar conception of the "weird sisters." "Paddock" and "Graymalkin," he thinks, are borrowed from IV, i, and "Fair is foul, and foul is fair" is an echo of the opening remark of Macbeth in I, iii, 38, the true and original beginning of the play. Lines 1–7 are certainly open to no objection. 3. **hurlyburly's,** tumult's.

First Witch. I come, Graymalkin!
Sec. Witch. Paddock calls.
Third Witch. Anon. 10
All. Fair is foul, and foul is fair:
Hover through the fog and filthy air.
[Exeunt.

SCENE II. *A camp near Forres.*

Alarum within. Enter DUNCAN, MALCOLM, DONALBAIN, LENNOX, *with* Attendants, *meeting a bleeding* Sergeant.

Dun. What bloody man is that? He can report,
As seemeth by his plight, of the revolt
The newest state.
Mal. This is the sergeant

8. **Graymalkin,** gray cat, name of the witch's familiar spirit. 9. **Paddock,** toad; also, a familiar. 10. **Anon,** at once.
Scene ii. This scene Mr. Cuningham would also reject because of inconsistencies noted below and because of inferiority and roughness of style.
Stage Direction: **Alarum,** noise of battle.

After wife's death honour honour his grief heart wish Peerless human [handwritten marginalia]

Who like a good and hardy soldier fought
'Gainst my captivity. Hail, brave friend!
Say to the king the knowledge of the broil
As thou didst leave it.

    Ser.   Doubtful it stood;
As two spent swimmers, that do cling
    together
And choke their art. The merciless Macdon-
    wald—
Worthy to be a rebel, for to that   10
The multiplying villanies of nature
Do swarm upon him—from the western isles
Of kerns and gallowglasses is supplied;
And fortune, on his damned quarrel smiling,
Show'd like a rebel's whore: but all's too
    weak:
For brave Macbeth—well he deserves that
    name—
Disdaining fortune, with his brandish'd steel,
Which smoked with bloody execution,
Like valour's minion carved out his passage
Till he faced the slave;   20
†Which ne'er shook hands, nor bade farewell
    to him,
Till he unseam'd him from the nave to the
    chaps,
And fix'd his head upon our battlements.

    Dun. O valiant cousin! worthy gentle-
    man!

    Ser. As whence the sun 'gins his reflection
Shipwrecking storms and direful thunders
    break,
So from that spring whence comfort seem'd
    to come
Discomfort swells. Mark, king of Scotland,
    mark:
No sooner justice had with valour arm'd
Compell'd these skipping kerns to trust their
    heels,   30
But the Norweyan lord surveying vantage,
With furbish'd arms and new supplies of
    men
Began a fresh assault.

    Dun.   Dismay'd not this
Our captains, Macbeth and Banquo?

    Ser.   Yes;
As sparrows eagles, or the hare the lion.
If I say sooth, I must report they were

As cannons overcharged with double cracks,
    so they
Doubly redoubled strokes upon the foe:
Except they meant to bathe in reeking
    wounds,
Or memorize another Golgotha,   40
I cannot tell.
But I am faint, my gashes cry for help.

    Dun. So well thy words become thee as
    thy wounds;
They smack of honour both. Go get him
    surgeons.   [*Exit Sergeant, attended.*
Who comes here?

             Enter Ross.

    Mal.   The worthy thane of Ross.

    Len. What a haste looks through his eyes!
    So should he look
That seems to speak things strange.

    Ross.   God save the king!

    Dun. Whence camest thou, worthy thane?

    Ross.   From Fife, great king;
Where the Norweyan banners flout the sky
And fan our people cold. Norway himself,   50
With terrible numbers,
Assisted by that most disloyal traitor
The thane of Cawdor, began a dismal
    conflict;
Till that Bellona's bridegroom, lapp'd in
    proof,
Confronted him with self-comparisons,
Point against point rebellious, arm 'gainst
    arm,
Curbing his lavish spirit: and, to conclude,
The victory fell on us.

    Dun.   Great happiness!

    Ross.   That now
Sweno, the Norways' king, craves com-
    position;
Nor would we deign him burial of his men   60
Till he disbursed at Saint Colme's inch
Ten thousand dollars to our general use.

    Dun. No more that thane of Cawdor shall
    deceive

---

6. **broil**, battle. 8. **spent**, tired out. 9. **choke their art**, render their skill useless. 10. **to that**, in addition to. 13. **kerns**, light-armed Irish foot-soldiers. **gallowglasses**, retainers of Irish chiefs, armed with axes. 19. **minion**, favorite, darling. 21. **Which**, who, i.e., Macbeth. 22. **nave**, navel. **chaps**, jaws. 26. **break**, supplied by Pope. 28. **Mark**, listen, take heed. 31. **surveying vantage**, perceiving a good opportunity.

37. **cracks**, discharges of cannon. 40. **memorize**, make memorable or famous. **Golgotha**, "place of a skull," where the Savior was crucified (*St. Mark*, xv, 22). 45. **thane**, Scottish title of honor, roughly equivalent to *earl*. 47. **seems to speak**, probably, is about to speak. 49. **flout**, mock, insult. 53. **dismal**, disastrous, calamitous. 54. **Bellona's bridegroom**, i.e., Macbeth. Bellona was the Roman goddess of war. **proof**, impenetrable armor. 55. **self-comparisons**, comparisons between their two selves. 57. **lavish**, insolent, unrestrained. 59. **Norways'**, Norwegians'. **composition**, agreement, treaty of peace. 61. **Saint Colme's inch**, Inchcolm, the Isle of St. Columba in the Firth of Forth. 62. **general**, public.

Others see a greatness in Man. [handwritten marginalia]

Our bosom interest: go pronounce his present death,
And with his former title greet Macbeth.

Ross. I'll see it done.

Dun. What he hath lost noble Macbeth
hath won.   [*Exeunt.*

SCENE. III.   *A heath near Forres.*

Thunder. Enter the three Witches.

First Witch. Where hast thou been, sister?

Sec. Witch. Killing swine.

Third Witch. Sister, where thou?

First Witch. A sailor's wife had chestnuts
in her lap,
And munch'd, and munch'd, and munch'd:—
'Give me,' quoth I:
'Aroint thee, witch!' the rump-fed ronyon
cries.
Her husband's to Aleppo gone, master o' the
Tiger:
But in a sieve I'll thither sail,
And, like a rat without a tail,
I'll do, I'll do, and I'll do.   10

Sec. Witch. I'll give thee a wind.

First Witch. Thou'rt kind.

Third Witch. And I another.

First Witch. I myself have all the other,
And the very ports they blow,
All the quarters that they know
I' the shipman's card.
I will drain him dry as hay:
Sleep shall neither night nor day
Hang upon his pent-house lid;   20
He shall live a man forbid:
Weary se'nnights nine times nine
Shall he dwindle, peak and pine:
Though his bark cannot be lost,
Yet it shall be tempest-tost.
Look what I have.

Sec. Witch. Show me, show me.

First Witch. Here I have a pilot's thumb,
Wreck'd as homeward he did come.
              [*Drum within.*

---

64. **bosom**, close and affectionate.
Scene iii. 5. **munch'd**, chewed with closed lips. 6. **Aroint thee**, avaunt, begone. **rump-fed**, probably, fed on refuse. **ronyon**, mangy creature; a term of contempt. 7. **Tiger**, a ship's name. 8. **in a sieve**. Sailing in sieves was one of the things confessed by the witches in the Scottish witchcraft trials. 9. **without a tail**. A familiar or a transformed witch could be recognized by some bodily defect. 15. **blow**, blow upon. 17. **shipman's card**, compass card, or a chart. 20. **penthouse lid**, eyelid. 21. **forbid**, accursed. 22. **se'nnights**, weeks.

Third Witch. A drum, a drum!   30
Macbeth doth come.

All. The weird sisters, hand in hand,
Posters of the sea and land,
Thus do go about, about:
Thrice to thine and thrice to mine
And thrice again, to make up nine.
Peace! the charm's wound up.

Enter MACBETH *and* BANQUO.

Macb. So foul and fair a day I have not
seen.

Ban. How far is't call'd to Forres? What
are these
So wither'd and so wild in their attire,   40
That look not like the inhabitants o' the
earth,
And yet are on't? Live you? or are you
aught
That man may question? You seem to
understand me,
By each at once her choppy finger laying
Upon her skinny lips: you should be women,
And yet your beards forbid me to interpret
That you are so.

Macb.   Speak, if you can: what are you?

First Witch. All hail, Macbeth! hail to
thee, thane of Glamis!

Sec. Witch. All hail, Macbeth! hail to thee,
thane of Cawdor!

Third Witch. All hail, Macbeth, that
shalt be king hereafter!   50

Ban. Good sir, why do you start, and
seem to fear
Things that do sound so fair? I' the name
of truth,
Are ye fantastical, or that indeed
Which outwardly ye show? My noble
partner
You greet with present grace and great prediction
Of noble having and of royal hope,
That he seems rapt withal: to me you speak
not.
If you can look into the seeds of time,
And say which grain will grow and which
will not,
Speak then to me, who neither beg nor fear 60
Your favours nor your hate.

First Witch. Hail!

---

32. **weird**, connected with fate. 33. **Posters of**, travelers over. 53. **fantastical**, a prey to fantasy or imagination. 54. **show**, appear. 56. **having**, estate, possessions.

Sec. Witch. Hail!

Third Witch. Hail!

First Witch. Lesser than Macbeth, and greater.

Sec. Witch. Not so happy, yet much happier.

Third Witch. Thou shalt get kings, though thou be none:

So all hail, Macbeth and Banquo!

First Witch. Banquo and Macbeth, all hail!

Macb. Stay, you imperfect speakers, tell me more: 70

By Sinel's death I know I am thane of Glamis;

But how of Cawdor? the thane of Cawdor lives,

A prosperous gentleman; and to be king

Stands not within the prospect of belief,

No more than to be Cawdor. Say from whence

You owe this strange intelligence? or why

Upon this blasted heath you stop our way

With such prophetic greeting? Speak, I charge you.   [*Witches vanish.*

Ban. The earth hath bubbles, as the water has,

And these are of them. Whither are they vanish'd?   80

Macb. Into the air; and what seem'd corporal melted

As breath into the wind. Would they had stay'd!

Ban. Were such things here as we do speak about?

Or have we eaten on the insane root

That takes the reason prisoner?

Macb. Your children shall be kings.

Ban.   You shall be king.

Macb. And thane of Cawdor too: went it not so?

Ban. To the selfsame tune and words. Who's here?

Enter Ross *and* Angus.

Ross. The king hath happily received, Macbeth,

The news of thy success; and when he reads

Thy personal venture in the rebels' fight,   91

His wonders and his praises do contend

Which should be thine or his: silenced with that,

In viewing o'er the rest o' the selfsame day,

He finds thee in the stout Norweyan ranks,

Nothing afeard of what thyself didst make,

Strange images of death. As thick as hail

Came post with post; and every one did bear

Thy praises in his kingdom's great defence,

And pour'd them down before him.

Ang.   We are sent   100

To give thee from our royal master thanks;

Only to herald thee into his sight,

Not pay thee.

Ross. And, for an earnest of a greater honour,

He bade me, from him, call thee thane of Cawdor:

In which addition, hail, most worthy thane!

For it is thine.

Ban.   What, can the devil speak true?

Macb. The thane of Cawdor lives: why do you dress me

In borrow'd robes?

Ang.   Who was the thane lives yet;

But under heavy judgement bears that life 110

Which he deserves to lose. Whether he was combined

With those of Norway, or did line the rebel

With hidden help and vantage, or that with both

He labour'd in his country's wreck, I know not;

But treasons capital, confess'd and proved,

Have overthrown him.

Macb. [*Aside*] Glamis, and thane of Cawdor!

The greatest is behind. [*To Ross and Angus*] Thanks for your pains.

[*To Ban.*] Do you not hope your children shall be kings,

When those that gave the thane of Cawdor to me

Promised no less to them?

Ban.   That trusted home   120

Might yet enkindle you unto the crown,
Besides the thane of Cawdor. But 'tis
    strange:
And oftentimes, to win us to our harm,
The instruments of darkness tell us truths,
Win us with honest trifles, to betray's
In deepest consequence.
Cousins, a word, I pray you.

    Macb.   [*Aside*] Two truths are told,
As happy prologues to the swelling act
Of the imperial theme.—I thank you, gen-
    tlemen.
[*Aside*] This supernatural soliciting   130
Cannot be ill, cannot be good: if ill,
Why hath it given me earnest of success,
Commencing in a truth? I am thane of
    Cawdor:
If good, why do I yield to that suggestion
Whose horrid image doth unfix my hair
And make my seated heart knock at my
    ribs,
Against the use of nature? Present fears
Are less than horrible imaginings:
My thought, whose murder yet is but fan-
    tastical,
Shakes so my single state of man that func-
    tion   140
Is smother'd in surmise, and nothing is
But what is not.

    Ban.   Look, how our partner's rapt.

    Macb. [*Aside*] If chance will have me
    king, why, chance may crown me,
Without my stir.

    Ban.   New honours come upon him,
Like our strange garments, cleave not to
    their mould
But with the aid of use.

    Macb.   [*Aside*] Come what come may,
Time and the hour runs through the rough-
    est day.

    Ban. Worthy Macbeth, we stay upon
    your leisure.

    Macb. Give me your favour: my dull
    brain was wrought

---

126. **deepest consequence**, matters of the greatest
importance. 129. **imperial theme**, theme of empire.
130. **supernatural soliciting**, temptation by supernatural beings. 134. **suggestion**, temptation. Macbeth
is imaginative, and, therefore, ambitious; it is on the
imaginative side of his nature that he is assailed. 135.
unfix my hair, make it stand on end. 140. **single
state of man**, whole being; an obvious allusion to the
doctrine of the microcosm, according to which the being
of man is a counterpart of the macrocosm, or universe.
140-142. **function . . . not**, power of action is lost in
speculation and only unreal imaginings have (for me)
any reality. 144. **stir**, bestirring (myself). **come**, i.e.,
which have come. 145. **strange**, new. 149. **favour**,
pardon.

With things forgotten. Kind gentlemen,
    your pains   150
Are register'd where every day I turn
The leaf to read them. Let us toward the
    king.
Think upon what hath chanced, and, at
    more time,
The interim having weigh'd it, let us speak
Our free hearts each to other.

    Ban.   Very gladly.

    Macb. Till then, enough. Come, friends.
                               [*Exeunt.*

      Scene IV. *Forres. The palace.*

Flourish. Enter Duncan, Malcolm, Donal-
    bain, Lennox, *and* Attendants.

    Dun. Is execution done on Cawdor? Are
    not
Those in commission yet return'd?

    Mal.   My liege,
They are not yet come back. But I have spoke
With one that saw him die: who did report
That very frankly he confess'd his treasons,
Implor'd your highness' pardon and set forth
A deep repentance: nothing in his life
Became him like the leaving it; he died
As one that had been studied in his death
To throw away the dearest thing he owed,   10
As 'twere a careless trifle.

    Dun.   There's no art
To find the mind's construction in the face:
He was a gentleman on whom I built
An absolute trust.

Enter Macbeth, Banquo, Ross, *and* Angus.

                  O worthiest cousin!
The sin of my ingratitude even now
Was heavy on me: thou art so far before
That swiftest wing of recompense is slow
To overtake thee. Would thou hadst less de-
    served,
That the proportion both of thanks and pay-
    ment
Might have been mine! only I have left to
    say,   20
More is thy due than more than all can pay.

    Macb. The service and the loyalty I owe,

---

153. **at more time**, at a time of greater leisure. 155.
Our free hearts, our hearts freely.
  Scene iv. 2. **commission**, those having warrant to
see to the execution of Cawdor. 11. **careless**, uncared
for. 22-27. **The service . . . honour.** One need not
consider this speech devoid of sincerity. Macbeth has
indeed plotted to murder the king, but has resolved to
leave the issue to chance; his words have a loyal sound.

In doing it, pays itself. Your highness' part
Is to receive our duties; and our duties
Are to your throne and state children and
    servants,
Which do but what they should, by doing
    every thing
Safe toward your love and honour.
    Dun.   Welcome hither:
I have begun to plant thee, and will labour
To make thee full of growing. Noble Ban-
    quo,
That hast no less deserved, nor must be
    known   30
No less to have done so, let me infold thee
And hold thee to my heart.
    Ban.   There if I grow,
The harvest is your own.
    Dun.   My plenteous joys,
Wanton in fulness, seek to hide themselves
In drops of sorrow. Sons, kinsmen, thanes,
And you whose places are the nearest,
    know
We will establish our estate upon
Our eldest, Malcolm, whom we name here-
    after
The Prince of Cumberland; which honour
    must
Not unaccompanied invest him only,   40
But signs of nobleness, like stars, shall shine
On all deservers. From hence to Inverness,
And bind us further to you.
    Macb. The rest is labour, which is not
    used for you:
I'll be myself the harbinger and make joyful
The hearing of my wife with your approach;
So humbly take my leave.
    Dun.   My worthy Cawdor!
    Macb. [*Aside*] The Prince of Cumberland!
    that is a step
On which I must fall down, or else o'erleap,
For in my way it lies. Stars, hide your fires;
Let not light see my black and deep desires:
The eye wink at the hand; yet let that be, 52
Which the eye fears, when it is done, to see.
                                        [*Exit.*

27. **Safe toward**, securely directed toward. 37. **establish our estate**, fix the succession of our state. 42. **Inverness**, the seat of Macbeth's castle. 45. **harbinger**, forerunner, messenger. 50. **in my way it lies**. Prince of Cumberland was the title of the heir apparent to Duncan's throne. The monarchy was not hereditary, and Macbeth had a right to believe that he himself might be chosen as Duncan's successor; he here states the issue as to whether or not he will interfere with the course of circumstance. 52. **eye wink at the hand**. Professor Fairchild discovers in this an allusion to an emblem in Alciatus which pictures an eye set in a hand to symbolize attention to one's deeds.

    Dun. True, worthy Banquo; he is full so
    valiant,
And in his commendations I am fed;
It is a banquet to me. Let's after him,
Whose care is gone before to bid us welcome:
It is a peerless kinsman. [*Flourish. Exeunt.*

SCENE V. *Inverness. Macbeth's castle.*

Enter LADY MACBETH, *reading a letter.*

    Lady M. 'They met me in the day of
success; and I have learned by the perfectest
report, they have more in them than mortal
knowledge. When I burned in desire to question them further, they made themselves air,
into which they vanished. Whiles I stood
rapt in the wonder of it, came missives from
the king, who all-hailed me "Thane of Cawdor"; by which title, before, these weird sisters saluted me, and referred me to the coming on of time, with "Hail, king that shalt
be!" This have I thought good to deliver
thee, my dearest partner of greatness, that
thou mightst not lose the dues of rejoicing, by
being ignorant of what greatness is promised
thee. Lay it to thy heart, and farewell.'
Glamis thou art, and Cawdor; and shalt be
What thou art promised: yet do I fear thy
    nature;
It is too full o' the milk of human kindness
To catch the nearest way: thou wouldst be
    great;
Art not without ambition, but without   20
The illness should attend it: what thou
    wouldst highly,
That wouldst thou holily; wouldst not play
    false,
And yet wouldst wrongly win: thou 'ldst
    have, great Glamis,
That which cries 'Thus thou must do, if thou
    have it;
And that which rather thou dost fear to do
Than wishest should be undone.' Hie thee
    hither,
That I may pour my spirits in thine ear;
And chastise with the valour of my tongue
All that impedes thee from the golden round,

    Scene v. 7. **missives**, messengers. 18. **milk of human kindness**, gentleness of human nature. Macbeth is Duncan's *peerless kinsman* (I, iv, 58), and this is another testimony to the uprightness of his character when the play begins. 21. **illness**, evil. 24-26. **That which . . . undone**. Many editors end the quotation after *it*, which refers to the crown. A meaning for the passage can be had by understanding *that which* in line 25 as meaning "that's what." 29. **golden round**, the crown.

Which fate and metaphysical aid doth seem
To have thee crown'd withal.

Enter a Messenger.

What is your tidings? 31
Mess. The king comes here to-night.
Lady M.   Thou'rt mad to say it:
Is not thy master with him? who, were't so,
Would have inform'd for preparation.
Mess. So please you, it is true: our thane
   is coming:
One of my fellows had the speed of him,
Who, almost dead for breath, had scarcely
   more
Than would make up his message.
Lady M.   Give him tending;
He brings great news.   [*Exit Messenger.*
            The raven himself is hoarse
That croaks the fatal entrance of Duncan 40
Under my battlements. Come, you spirits
That tend on mortal thoughts, unsex me
   here,
And fill me from the crown to the toe top-full
Of direst cruelty! make thick my blood;
Stop up the access and passage to remorse,
That no compunctious visitings of nature
Shake my fell purpose, nor keep peace be-
   tween
The effect and it! Come to my woman's
   breasts,
And take my milk for gall, you murdering
   ministers,
Wherever in your sightless substances 50
You wait on nature's mischief! Come, thick
   night,
And pall thee in the dunnest smoke of hell,
That my keen knife see not the wound it
   makes,
Nor heaven peep through the blanket of the
   dark,
To cry 'Hold, hold!'

Enter MACBETH.

Great Glamis! worthy Cawdor!
Greater than both, by the all-hail hereafter!

Thy letters have transported me beyond
This ignorant present, and I feel now
The future in the instant.
Macb.   My dearest love, 59
Duncan comes here to-night.
Lady M.   And when goes hence?
Macb. To-morrow, as he purposes.
Lady M.   O, never
Shall sun that morrow see!
Your face, my thane, is as a book where
   men
May read strange matters. To beguile the
   time,
Look like the time; bear welcome in your
   eye,
Your hand, your tongue: look like the inno-
   cent flower,
But be the serpent under't. He that's com-
   ing
Must be provided for: and you shall put
This night's great business into my dis-
   patch;
Which shall to all our nights and days to
   come 70
Give solely sovereign sway and master-
   dom.
Macb. We will speak further.
Lady M.   Only look up clear;
To alter favour ever is to fear:
Leave all the rest to me.   [*Exeunt.*

SCENE VI. *Before Macbeth's castle.*

Hautboys and torches. Enter DUNCAN, MAL-
   COLM, DONALBAIN, BANQUO, LENNOX,
   MACDUFF, ROSS, ANGUS, *and* Attendants.

Dun. This castle hath a pleasant seat; the
   air
Nimbly and sweetly recommends itself
Unto our gentle senses.
Ban.   This guest of summer,
The temple-haunting martlet, does approve,
By his loved mansionry, that the heaven's
   breath
Smells wooingly here: no jutty, frieze,
Buttress, nor coign of vantage, but this bird
Hath made his pendent bed and procreant
   cradle:

---

30. **metaphysical,** supernatural. 36. **had the speed of,** outstripped. 42. **tend on . . . thoughts,** are the instruments of deadly or murderous thoughts. The spirits conveying various passions were the tools of thought. 44-45. **make . . . remorse.** By making the blood thick it would be less able to flow out in generous passions and thus awaken remorse or pity. 46. **compunctious . . . nature,** natural feelings of pity and conscience. 49. **murdering ministers,** evil angels. 50. **sightless,** invisible. 52. **pall,** envelope. **dunnest,** darkest.

72. **clear,** serenely. 73. **To alter . . . fear,** to change the aspect of one's face is always to feel fear.
Scene vi. 3. **gentle senses,** a case of transferred epithet. It is the air which seems gentle to the senses. 6. **jutty,** projection of wall or building. 7. **coign of vantage,** convenient corner, i.e., for nesting.

Where they most breed and haunt, I have
  observed,
The air is delicate.

Enter LADY MACBETH.

Dun. See, see, our honour'd hostess! 10
The love that follows us sometime is our
  trouble,
Which still we thank as love. Herein I teach
  you
How you shall bid God 'ild us for your
  pains,
And thank us for your trouble.

Lady M.   All our service
In every point twice done and then done
  double
Were poor and single business to contend
Against those honours deep and broad
  wherewith
Your majesty loads our house: for those of
  old,
And the late dignities heap'd up to them,
We rest your hermits.

Dun.   Where's the thane of
  Cawdor?
We coursed him at the heels, and had a pur-
  pose   21
To be his purveyor: but he rides well;
And his great love, sharp as his spur, hath
  holp him
To his home before us. Fair and noble
  hostess,
We are your guest to-night.

Lady M.   Your servants ever
Have theirs, themselves and what is theirs,
  in compt,
To make their audit at your highness' pleas-
  ure,
Still to return your own.

Dun.   Give me your hand;
Conduct me to mine host: we love him
  highly,   29
And shall continue our graces towards
  him.
By your leave, hostess.   [*Exeunt.*

10. **delicate**, delicious. 11. **follows**, attends. **some-time**, sometimes. 13. **God 'ild us**, God reward us, i.e., thank us. Duncan means that, since he is there because he loves them they should thank him even for the trouble he causes them. 16. **single**, small, inconsiderable. **contend Against**, vie with. 20. **rest**, remain. **her-mits**, i.e., those who will pray for you like hermits or beadsmen. 22. **purveyor**, an officer sent ahead of the king to provide for his entertainment; here, forerunner. 23. **holp**, helped. 26. **in compt**, under obligation (to serve the king).

SCENE VII. *Macbeth's castle.*

Hautboys and torches. Enter a Sewer, *and
divers* Servants *with dishes and service, and
pass over the stage. Then enter* MACBETH.

Macb. If it were done when 'tis done, then
  'twere well
It were done quickly: if the assassination
Could trammel up the consequence, and
  catch
With his surcease success; that but this blow
Might be the be-all and the end-all here,
But here, upon this bank and shoal of time,
We'ld jump the life to come. But in these
  cases
We still have judgement here; that we but
  teach
Bloody instructions, which, being taught, re-
  turn
To plague the inventor: this even-handed
  justice   10
Commends the ingredients of our poison'd
  chalice
To our own lips. He's here in double trust;
First, as I am his kinsman and his subject,
Strong both against the deed; then, as his
  host,
Who should against his murderer shut the
  door,
Not bear the knife myself. Besides, this
  Duncan
Hath borne his faculties so meek, hath
  been
So clear in his great office, that his virtues
Will plead like angels, trumpet-tongued,
  against
The deep damnation of his taking-off;   20
And pity, like a naked new-born babe,
Striding the blast, or heaven's cherubim,
  horsed
Upon the sightless couriers of the air,
Shall blow the horrid deed in every eye,
That tears shall drown the wind. I have no
  spur
To prick the sides of my intent, but only
Vaulting ambition, which o'erleaps itself
And falls on the other.

Scene vii. Stage Direction: **Hautboys**, wooden double-reed musical instruments. **Sewer**, chief servant who di-rected the placing of dishes on the table; or, according to an earlier sense, the servant whose duty it was to act as taster and guard against poison. 3. **trammel up**, entangle in a net, prevent. 4. **surcease**, cessation. 17. **faculties**, prerogatives. 20. **taking-off**, murder. Macbeth is perfectly conscious of the nature of his sin. 28. **other**, i.e., the other side of my intent.

Enter LADY MACBETH.

How now! what news?

Lady M. He has almost supp'd: why have you left the chamber?

Macb. Hath he ask'd for me?

Lady M.   Know you not he has? 30

Macb. We will proceed no further in this business:

He hath honour'd me of late; and I have bought

Golden opinions from all sorts of people,

Which would be worn now in their newest gloss,

Not cast aside so soon.

Lady M.   Was the hope drunk

Wherein you dress'd yourself? hath it slept since?

And wakes it now, to look so green and pale

At what it did so freely? From this time

Such I account thy love. Art thou afeard

To be the same in thine own act and valour

As thou art in desire? Wouldst thou have that   41

Which thou esteem'st the ornament of life,

And live a coward in thine own esteem,

Letting 'I dare not' wait upon 'I would,'

Like the poor cat i' the adage?

Macb.   Prithee, peace:

I dare do all that may become a man;

Who dares do more is none.

Lady M.   What beast was't, then,

That made you break this enterprise to me?

When you durst do it, then you were a man;

And, to be more than what you were, you would   50

Be so much more the man. Nor time nor place

Did then adhere, and yet you would make both:

They have made themselves, and that their fitness now

Does unmake you. I have given suck, and know

How tender 'tis to love the babe that milks me:

I would, while it was smiling in my face,

Have pluck'd my nipple from his boneless gums,

And dash'd the brains out, had I so sworn as you

Have done to this.

Macb.   If we should fail?

Lady M.   We fail!

But screw your courage to the sticking-place,   60

And we'll not fail. When Duncan is asleep—

Whereto the rather shall his day's hard journey

Soundly invite him—his two chamberlains

Will I with wine and wassail so convince

That memory, the warder of the brain,

Shall be a fume, and the receipt of reason

A limbeck only: when in swinish sleep

Their drenched natures lie as in a death,

What cannot you and I perform upon

The unguarded Duncan? what not put upon

His spongy officers, who shall bear the guilt

Of our great quell?

Macb.   Bring forth men-children only; 72

For thy undaunted mettle should compose

Nothing but males. Will it not be received,

When we have mark'd with blood those sleepy two

Of his own chamber and used their very daggers,

That they have done't?

Lady M.   Who dares receive it other,

As we shall make our griefs and clamour roar

Upon his death?

Macb.   I am settled, and bend up

Each corporal agent to this terrible feat. 80

Away, and mock the time with fairest show:

False face must hide what the false heart doth know.   [*Exeunt.*

---

45. **adage**, "The cate would eate fyshe, and would not wet her feete" (Heywood). **47-51. beast . . . man**, if you are a man, it must have been a beast that prompted you to *break* (disclose) this enterprise to me; if it is unmanly to do the deed, it was unmanly to suggest it. Note that it was Macbeth who had suggested the murder. A well-known teacher of Shakespeare identifies Lady Macbeth's method as the universal feminine method of persuading men: (1) You do not love me (l. 39). (2) You are afraid (ll. 39-45). (3) If I were a man, I would do it (ll. 56-58). Surely one must also add: (4) You said you would do it (ll. 58-59). 52. **adhere**, agree, suit.

60. **sticking-place**, probably a metaphor from the tightening of the strings of a musical instrument. 64. **wassail**, carousal, drink. **convince**, overpower. 65-67. **warder of the brain . . . limbeck only.** The brain was divided into three ventricles, imagination in front, memory at the back, and between them the seat of reason. The fumes of wine would deaden memory and judgment. **limbeck**, alembic, still. 70. **put upon**, attribute to. 71. **spongy**, drunken. 72. **quell**, murder. 74. **received**, as truth. 77. **other**, otherwise. 79. **settled**, determined. **bend up . . . feat.** The language all the way through the passage about the deed is not primarily figurative, but drawn from current psychology. A stiffly maintained head of passion is necessary for action. "To alter favour ever is to fear" (I, v, 73); hence, the bodily agents must be immovable, the blood thick, and the passage to remorse closed.

ACT II.

Scene I. *Court of Macbeth's castle.*

Enter Banquo, *and* Fleance *bearing a torch before him.*

Ban. How goes the night, boy?

Fle. The moon is down; I have not heard the clock.

Ban. And she goes down at twelve.

Fle.   I take 't, 'tis later, sir.

Ban. Hold, take my sword. There's husbandry in heaven;
Their candles are all out. Take thee that too.
A heavy summons lies like lead upon me,
And yet I would not sleep: merciful powers,
Restrain in me the cursed thoughts that nature
Gives way to in repose!

Enter Macbeth, *and a* Servant *with a torch.*

                              Give me my sword.
Who's there?   10

Macb. A friend.

Ban. What, sir, not yet at rest? The king's a-bed:
He hath been in unusual pleasure, and
Sent forth great largess to your offices.
This diamond he greets your wife withal,
By the name of most kind hostess; and shut up
In measureless content.

Macb.   Being unprepared,
Our will became the servant to defect;
Which else should free have wrought.

Ban.   All's well.
I dreamt last night of the three weird sisters:
To you they have show'd some truth.

Macb.   I think not of them:
Yet, when we can entreat an hour to serve,
We would spend it in some words upon that business,   23
If you would grant the time.

Ban.   At your kind'st leisure.

Macb. If you shall cleave to my consent, when 'tis,
It shall make honour for you.

Ban.   So I lose none
In seeking to augment it, but still keep

My bosom franchised and allegiance clear,
I shall be counsell'd.

Macb.   Good repose the while!

Ban. Thanks, sir: the like to you!   30
                       [*Exeunt Banquo and Fleance.*

Macb. Go bid thy mistress, when my drink is ready,
She strike upon the bell. Get thee to bed.
                              [*Exit Servant.*
Is this a dagger which I see before me,
The handle toward my hand? Come, let me clutch thee.
I have thee not, and yet I see thee still.
Art thou not, fatal vision, sensible
To feeling as to sight? or art thou but
A dagger of the mind, a false creation,
Proceeding from the heat-oppressed brain?
I see thee yet, in form as palpable   40
As this which now I draw.
Thou marshall'st me the way that I was going;
And such an instrument I was to use.
Mine eyes are made the fools o' the other senses,
Or else worth all the rest; I see thee still,
And on thy blade and dudgeon gouts of blood,
Which was not so before. There's no such thing:
It is the bloody business which informs
Thus to mine eyes. Now o'er the one half-world
Nature seems dead, and wicked dreams abuse   50
The curtain'd sleep; witchcraft celebrates
Pale Hecate's offerings, and wither'd murder,
Alarum'd by his sentinel, the wolf,
Whose howl's his watch, thus with his stealthy pace,
With Tarquin's ravishing strides, towards his design
Moves like a ghost. Thou sure and firm-set earth,
Hear not my steps, which way they walk, for fear
Thy very stones prate of my whereabout,
And take the present horror from the time,
Which now suits with it. Whiles I threat, he lives: 60

---

4. **husbandry**, economy. 14. **offices**, servants' quarters. Some editors read *officers*. 25. **If you . . . 'tis.** If you give me your support when the fulfillment occurs.

28. **franchised**, free (from guilt). **clear**, unstained. 36. **sensible**, tangible, perceptible. 46. **dudgeon**, hilt of a dagger. **gouts**, drops. 48. **informs**, takes form or shape. 52. **Hecate's.** Hecate was the goddess of witchcraft.

Words to the heat of deeds too cold breath
gives.
[*A bell rings.*
I go, and it is done; the bell invites me.
Hear it not, Duncan; for it is a knell
That summons thee to heaven or to hell.
[*Exit.*

Scene II. *The same.*

Enter Lady Macbeth.

Lady M. That which hath made them
drunk hath made me bold;
What hath quench'd them hath given me
fire. Hark! Peace!
It was the owl that shriek'd, the fatal bell-
man,
Which gives the stern'st good-night. He is
about it:
The doors are open; and the surfeited grooms
Do mock their charge with snores: I have
drugg'd their possets,
That death and nature do contend about
them,
Whether they live or die.
Macb. [*Within*] Who's there? what, ho!
Lady M. Alack, I am afraid they have
awaked,   10
And 'tis not done. The attempt and not the
deed
Confounds us. Hark! I laid their daggers
ready;
He could not miss 'em. Had he not resem-
bled
My father as he slept, I had done 't.

Enter Macbeth.

My husband!
Macb. I have done the deed. Didst thou
not hear a noise?
Lady M. I heard the owl scream and the
crickets cry.
Did not you speak?
Macb.   When?
Lady M.   Now.
Macb.   As I descended?
Lady M. Ay.

Macb. Hark!
Who lies i' the second chamber?
Lady M.   Donalbain.   20
Macb. This is a sorry sight.
[*Looking on his hands.*
Lady M. A foolish thought, to say a
sorry sight.
Macb. There's one did laugh in 's sleep,
and one cried 'Murder!'
That they did wake each other: I stood and
heard them:
But they did say their prayers, and address'd
them
Again to sleep.
Lady M. There are two lodged together.
Macb. One cried 'God bless us!' and 'A-
men' the other;
As they had seen me with these hangman's
hands.
Listening their fear, I could not say 'Amen,'
When they did say 'God bless us!'
Lady M. Consider it not so deeply.   30
Macb. But wherefore could not I pro-
nounce 'Amen'?
I had most need of blessing, and 'Amen'
Stuck in my throat.
Lady M.   These deeds must not be
thought
After these ways; so, it will make us mad.
Macb. Methought I heard a voice cry
'Sleep no more!
Macbeth does murder sleep,' the innocent
sleep,
Sleep that knits up the ravell'd sleave of
care,
The death of each day's life, sore labour's
bath,
Balm of hurt minds, great nature's second
course,
Chief nourisher in life's feast,—
Lady M.   What do you mean?
Macb. Still it cried 'Sleep no more!' to all
the house: 41
'Glamis hath murder'd sleep, and therefore
Cawdor
Shall sleep no more; Macbeth shall sleep no
more.'

Scene ii. 1. **bold.** Lady Macbeth has deliberately
taken wine to bolster up her courage; this is denied by
some critics. 5. **grooms,** servants. 6. **possets,** hot
milk poured on ale or wine and spiced, a bedtime drink
common at the time. 12. **Confounds,** ruins. 13-14.
Had he . . . done 't. This, one of the few personal
touches in the part of Lady Macbeth, prepares us for
the terrible effect her crime was yet to have upon her.

21. **sorry,** wretched. 25. **address'd them,** settled
themselves. 26. **two,** possibly, Malcolm and Donalbain
thus half-awakened by their father's murder. 29.
Listening, listening to. 34. **it will make us mad.**
This idea of the effect of obsession on sanity is firmly
fixed in Shakespeare's psychology. 37. **ravell'd sleave,**
tangled unwrought silk. 39. **second course.** Ordinary
feasts had two courses; only the more elaborate ones had
three; hence, the second course was the *chief nourisher*
and the conclusion of the feast.

Lady M. Who was it that thus cried?
Why, worthy thane,
You do unbend your noble strength, to think
So brainsickly of things. Go get some water,
And wash this filthy witness from your hand.
Why did you bring these daggers from the
place?
They must lie there: go carry them; and
smear
The sleepy grooms with blood.
   Macb.   I'll go no more: 50
I am afraid to think what I have done;
Look on't again I dare not.
   Lady M.   Infirm of purpose!
Give me the daggers: the sleeping and the
dead
Are but as pictures: 'tis the eye of childhood
That fears a painted devil. If he do bleed,
I'll gild the faces of the grooms withal;
For it must seem their guilt.
               [Exit. Knocking within.
   Macb.   Whence is that knocking?
How is't with me, when every noise appals
me?
What hands are here? ha! they pluck out
mine eyes.
Will all great Neptune's ocean wash this
blood
Clean from my hand? No, this my hand
will rather   61
The multitudinous seas incarnadine,
Making the green one red.

        Re-enter Lady Macbeth.

Lady M. My hands are of your colour;
but I shame
To wear a heart so white. *[Knocking within.]*
I hear a knocking
At the south entry: retire we to our cham-
ber:
A little water clears us of this deed:
How easy is it, then! Your constancy
Hath left you unattended. *[Knocking within.]*
Hark! more knocking.
Get on your nightgown, lest occasion call us,
And show us to be watchers. Be not lost 71
So poorly in your thoughts.

Macb. To know my deed, 'twere best not
know myself.   *[Knocking within.*
Wake Duncan with thy knocking! I would
thou couldst!   *[Exeunt.*

      Scene III. *The same.*

   Knocking within. Enter a Porter.

   Porter. Here's a knocking indeed! If a
man were porter of hell-gate, he should have
old turning the key. *[Knocking within.]*
Knock, knock, knock! Who's there, i' the
name of Beelzebub? Here's a farmer, that
hanged himself on the expectation of plenty:
come in time; have napkins enow about you;
here you'll sweat for 't. *[Knocking within.]*
Knock, knock! Who's there, in the other
devil's name? Faith, here's an equivocator,
that could swear in both the scales against
either scale; who committed treason enough
for God's sake, yet could not equivocate to
heaven: O, come in, equivocator. *[Knocking
within.]* Knock, knock, knock! Who's there?
Faith, here's an English tailor come hither,
for stealing out of a French hose: come in,
tailor; here you may roast your goose. *[Knock-
ing within.]* Knock, knock; never at quiet!
What are you? But this place is too cold for
hell. I'll devil-porter it no further: I had
thought to have let in some of all professions
that go the primrose way to the everlasting
bonfire. *[Knocking within.]* Anon, anon! I
pray you, remember the porter.
                  [Opens the gate.

    Enter Macduff *and* Lennox.

   Macd. Was it so late, friend, ere you went
to bed,
That you do lie so late?

---

46. **brainsickly**, insanely, madly. 56-57. **gild . . .
guilt.** The pun would be more obvious to Shakespeare's
audience than to us, for gold was ordinarily thought of
as red. 62. **incarnadine**, make red. 63. **one red,**
one all-pervading red. F has *Making the Greene one, Red,*
which some editors have followed. 64. **shame**, am
ashamed. 68-69. **Your constancy . . . unattended,**
your firmness has deserted you. 70. **nightgown,**
dressing gown. 72. **poorly**, dejectedly.

73. **To know . . . deed.** It were better to be lost in
my thoughts than to have consciousness of my deed.
   Scene iii. 2. **porter of hell-gate.** The game the
porter plays with himself is based on the mystery play
of *Harrowing of Hell,* in which Christ knocks at the
gate of Hell, supplied, we may believe, with a humorous porter. 3. **old,** colloquial use, as in "a high old
time." 5-6. **Here's a farmer . . . plenty.** This is
thought to allude to the conditions of the year 1606
when there were abundant harvests and low prices. 7.
come in time, you have come in good time. **napkins,**
handkerchiefs, i.e., to wipe off the sweat. 10. **equivocator.** This is regarded as an allusion to the trial of
the Jesuit Henry Garnet for treason in the spring of 1606,
and to the doctrine of equivocation said to have been
presented in his defense; according to this doctrine a lie
was not a lie if the utterer had in his mind a different
meaning in which the utterance was true. 17. **French
hose,** very narrow breeches and therefore hard for the
tailor to steal cloth from when he made them. 18.
goose, tailor's smoothing iron.

Port. 'Faith, sir, we were carousing till the second cock: and drink, sir, is a great provoker of three things.

Macd. What three things does drink especially provoke?   30

Port. Marry, sir, nose-painting, sleep, and urine. Lechery, sir, it provokes, and unprovokes; it provokes the desire, but it takes away the performance: therefore, much drink may be said to be an equivocator with lechery: it makes him, and it mars him; it sets him on, and it takes him off; it persuades him, and disheartens him; makes him stand to, and not stand to; in conclusion, equivocates him in a sleep, and, giving him the lie, leaves him.   40

Macd. I believe drink gave thee the lie last night.

Port. That it did, sir, i' the very throat on me: but I requited him for his lie; and, I think, being too strong for him, though he took up my legs sometime, yet I made a shift to cast him.

Macd. Is thy master stirring?

Enter MACBETH.

Our knocking has awaked him; here he comes.

Len. Good morrow, noble sir.

Macb.   Good morrow, both.

Macd. Is the king stirring, worthy thane?

Macb.   Not yet.

Macd. He did command me to call timely on him: 51

I have almost slipp'd the hour.

Macb.   I'll bring you to him.

Macd. I know this is a joyful trouble to you;

But yet 'tis one.

Macb. The labour we delight in physics pain.

This is the door.

Macd.   I'll make so bold to call,

For 'tis my limited service.   [*Exit.*

Len. Goes the king hence to-day?

Macb.   He does: he did appoint so.

Len. The night has been unruly: where we lay,

Our chimneys were blown down; and, as they say,   60

Lamentings heard i' the air; strange screams of death,

And prophesying with accents terrible

Of dire combustion and confused events

New hatch'd to the woeful time: the obscure bird

Clamour'd the livelong night: some say, the earth

Was feverous and did shake.

Macb.   'Twas a rough night.

Len. My young remembrance cannot parallel

A fellow to it.

Re-enter MACDUFF.

Macd. O horror, horror, horror! Tongue nor heart

Cannot conceive nor name thee!

Macb. }
Len. }   What's the matter?

Macd. Confusion now hath made his masterpiece!   71

Most sacrilegious murder hath broke ope

The Lord's anointed temple, and stole thence

The life o' the building!

Macb.   What is 't you say? the life?

Len. Mean you his majesty?

Macd. Approach the chamber, and destroy your sight

With a new Gorgon: do not bid me speak;

See, and then speak yourselves.

                    [*Exeunt Macbeth and Lennox.*

                                        Awake, awake!

Ring the alarum-bell. Murder and treason!

Banquo and Donalbain! Malcolm! awake! 80

Shake off this downy sleep, death's counterfeit,

And look on death itself! up, up, and see

The great doom's image! Malcolm! Banquo!

As from your graves rise up, and walk like sprites,

To countenance this horror! Ring the bell.

                                        [*Bell rings.*

Enter LADY MACBETH.

Lady M. What's the business,

That such a hideous trumpet calls to parley

The sleepers of the house? speak, speak!

---

27. **cock,** cockcrow. 51. **timely,** betimes, early. 52. **slipp'd,** let slip. 55. **physics,** cures. 57. **limited,** appointed.

64. **obscure bird,** owl, the bird of darkness. 71. **Confusion,** destruction. 73. **The Lord's anointed temple,** allusion to the king as God's anointed representative. 77. **Gorgon,** allusion to the monsters of Greek mythology whose look turned the beholders to stone. 85. **countenance,** be in keeping with.

Macd.   O gentle lady,
'Tis not for you to hear what I can speak:
The repetition, in a woman's ear,   90
Would murder as it fell.

Enter Banquo.

                                    O Banquo, Banquo,
Our royal master's murder'd!
   Lady M.   Woe, alas!
What, in our house?
   Ban.   Too cruel any where.
Dear Duff, I prithee, contradict thyself,
And say it is not so.

Re-enter Macbeth *and* Lennox, *with* Ross.

   Macb. Had I but died an hour before this
chance,
I had lived a blessed time; for, from this
instant,
There's nothing serious in mortality:
All is but toys: renown and grace is dead;
The wine of life is drawn, and the mere lees
Is left this vault to brag of.   101

Enter Malcolm *and* Donalbain.

   Don. What is amiss?
   Macb.   You are, and do not know't:
The spring, the head, the fountain of your
blood
Is stopp'd; the very source of it is stopp'd.
   Macd. Your royal father's murdered.
   Mal.   O, by whom?
   Len. Those of his chamber, as it seem'd,
had done't:
Their hands and faces were all badged with
blood;
So were their daggers, which unwiped we
found
Upon their pillows:
They stared, and were distracted; no man's
life   110
Was to be trusted with them.
   Macb. O, yet I do repent me of my fury,
That I did kill them.
   Macd.   Wherefore did you so?
   Macb. Who can be wise, amazed, temper-
ate and furious,
Loyal and neutral, in a moment? No man:
The expedition of my violent love
Outrun the pauser, reason. Here lay Dun-
can,

His silver skin laced with his golden blood;
And his gash'd stabs look'd like a breach in
nature
For ruin's wasteful entrance: there, the mur-
derers,   120
Steep'd in the colours of their trade, their
daggers
Unmannerly breech'd with gore: who could
refrain,
That had a heart to love, and in that heart
Courage to make's love known?
   Lady M.   Help me hence, ho!
   Macd. Look to the lady.
   Mal. [*Aside to Don.*] Why do we hold our
tongues,
That most may claim this argument for ours?
   Don. [*Aside to Mal.*] What should be
spoken here, where our fate,
Hid in an auger-hole, may rush, and seize us?
Let's away;
Our tears are not yet brew'd.
   Mal. [*Aside to Don.*] Nor our strong sorrow
Upon the foot of motion.
   Ban.   Look to the lady: 131
                        [*Lady Macbeth is carried out.*
And when we have our naked frailties hid,
That suffer in exposure, let us meet,
And question this most bloody piece of work,
To know it further. Fears and scruples
   shake us:
In the great hand of God I stand; and thence
Against the undivulged pretence I fight
Of treasonous malice.
   Macd.   And so do I.
   All.   So all.
   Macb. Let's briefly put on manly readi-
ness,
And meet i' the hall together.
   All.   Well contented.
[*Exeunt all but Malcolm and Donalbain.*
   Mal. What will you do? Let's not consort
   with them: 141
To show an unfelt sorrow is an office
Which the false man does easy. I'll to Eng-
land.

122. **breech'd**, covered to the hilts with gore (as with
breeches). 124. **Help me hence, ho!** This timely
fainting of Lady Macbeth is usually taken as pretense
done in order to make a diversion in behalf of her
husband, but it need not be so understood. 126. **argument**, theme, subject. 128. **in an auger-hole**, in
some obscure place. 136-138. **and thence . . . malice.**
With God's help I will fight against the as-yet-unknown
purpose which prompted this treason. If Banquo here
suspects Macbeth, nothing comes of it, for when we next
see him he is a loyal servant to the new king. 139.
manly readiness, men's clothing, or armor. 143. **easy**,
easily.

98. **mortality,** mortal life. 107. **badged,** marked as
with a badge or emblem. 116. **expedition,** haste.

Don. To Ireland, I; our separated fortune
Shall keep us both the safer: where we are,
There's daggers in men's smiles: the near in
　blood,
The nearer bloody.

　Mal.　　This murderous shaft that's shot
Hath not yet lighted, and our safest way
Is to avoid the aim. Therefore, to horse;
And let us not be dainty of leave-taking, 150
But shift away: there's warrant in that
　theft
Which steals itself, when there's no mercy
　left.　　　　　　　　　　　[*Exeunt.*

SCENE IV. *Outside Macbeth's castle.*

Enter ROSS *and an* old Man.

Old M. Threescore and ten I can remem-
　ber well:
Within the volume of which time I have
　seen
Hours dreadful and things strange; but this
　sore night
Hath trifled former knowings.

　Ross.　　　　　Ah, good father,
Thou seest, the heavens, as troubled with
　man's act,
Threaten his bloody stage: by the clock, 'tis
　day,
And yet dark night strangles the travelling
　lamp:
Is 't night's predominance, or the day's
　shame,
That darkness does the face of earth entomb,
When living light should kiss it?

　Old M.　　　　'Tis unnatural,　10
Even like the deed that's done. On Tuesday
　last,
A falcon, towering in her pride of place,
Was by a mousing owl hawk'd at and
　kill'd.

　Ross. And Duncan's horses—a thing
　　most strange and certain—
Beauteous and swift, the minions of their
　race,
Turn'd wild in nature, broke their stalls,
　flung out,

Contending 'gainst obedience, as they would
　make
War with mankind.

　Old M.　　　'Tis said they eat each other.

　Ross. They did so, to the amazement of
　　mine eyes
That look'd upon 't. Here comes the good
　　Macduff.　　　　　　　　　　20

Enter MACDUFF.

How goes the world, sir, now?

　Macd.　　　　Why, see you not?

　Ross. Is 't known who did this more than
　　bloody deed?

　Macd. Those that Macbeth hath slain.

　Ross.　　　　　Alas, the day!
What good could they pretend?

　Macd.　　　　They were suborn'd:
Malcolm and Donalbain, the king's two
　sons,
Are stol'n away and fled; which puts upon
　them
Suspicion of the deed.

　Ross.　　　　　'Gainst nature still!
Thriftless ambition, that wilt ravin up
Thine own life's means! Then 'tis most
　like
The sovereignty will fall upon Macbeth. 30

　Macd. He is already named, and gone to
　　Scone
To be invested.

　Ross.　　Where is Duncan's body?

　Macd. Carried to Colmekill,
The sacred storehouse of his predecessors,
And guardian of their bones.

　Ross.　　　　Will you to Scone?

　Macd. No, cousin, I'll to Fife.

　Ross.　　　　Well, I will thither.

　Macd. Well, may you see things well done
　　there: adieu!
Lest our old robes sit easier than our new!

　Ross. Farewell, father.

　Old M. God's benison go with you; and
　　with those　　　　　　　　　40
That would make good of bad, and friends
　of foes!　　　　　　　　　[*Exeunt.*

---

146. **near**, nearer, i.e., the nearer in relationship the greater the danger of being murdered. 148. **lighted**, descended. 151. **shift**, steal.
　Scene iv. 4. **trifled . . . knowings**, made trivial all former knowledge. 8. **predominance**, ascendancy, superior influence (of a heavenly body). 12. **towering**, soaring (term in falconry). **place**, pitch, highest point in the falcon's flight. 14. **horses**, pronounced as one syllable, indicating the old form of the plural then in common use.

24. **pretend**, intend, design. **suborn'd**, procured to do an evil action. 28. **ravin up**, devour ravenously. 31. **Scone**, ancient royal city of Scotland near Perth. The stone of Scone, on which Jacob rested his head at Bethel, was carried to England by Edward I. It has ever since formed a part of the coronation chair of English kings in Westminster Abbey. 33. **Colmekill**, Icolmkill, i.e., Cell of St. Columba, the barren islet of Iona in the Western Islands, a sacred spot where the kings were buried; here called a *storehouse*. 40. **benison**, blessing.

ACT III.

Scene I. *Forres. The palace.*

Enter Banquo.

Ban. Thou hast it now: king, Cawdor,
   Glamis, all,
As the weird women promised, and, I fear,
Thou play'dst most foully for 't: yet it was
   said
It should not stand in thy posterity,
But that myself should be the root and father
Of many kings. If there come truth from
   them—
As upon thee, Macbeth, their speeches
   shine—
Why, by the verities on thee made good,
May they not be my oracles as well,   9
And set me up in hope? But hush! no more.

Sennet sounded. Enter Macbeth, *as king,*
   Lady Macbeth, *as queen,* Lennox, Ross,
   Lords, Ladies, *and* Attendants.

Macb. Here's our chief guest.
Lady M.   If he had been forgotten,
It had been as a gap in our great feast,
And all-thing unbecoming.
Macb. To-night we hold a solemn supper,
   sir,
And I'll request your presence.
Ban.   Let your highness
Command upon me; to the which my duties
Are with a most indissoluble tie
For ever knit.
Macb. Ride you this afternoon?
Ban. Ay, my good lord.   20
Macb. We should have else desired your
   good advice,
Which still hath been both grave and pros-
   perous,
In this day's council; but we'll take to-mor-
   row.
Is 't far you ride?
Ban. As far, my lord, as will fill up the
   time
'Twixt this and supper: go not my horse the
   better,
I must become a borrower of the night
For a dark hour or twain.

Macb.   Fail not our feast.
Ban. My lord, I will not.
Macb. We hear, our bloody cousins are
   bestow'd   30
In England and in Ireland, not confess-
   ing
Their cruel parricide, filling their hearers
With strange invention: but of that to-
   morrow,
When therewithal we shall have cause of
   state
Craving us jointly. Hie you to horse: adieu,
Till you return at night. Goes Fleance with
   you?
Ban. Ay, my good lord: our time does call
   upon 's.
Macb. I wish your horses swift and sure
   of foot;
And so I do commend you to their backs.
Farewell.   [*Exit Banquo.* 40
Let every man be master of his time
Till seven at night: to make society
The sweeter welcome, we will keep ourself
Till supper-time alone: while then, God be
   with you!
   [*Exeunt all but Macbeth, and an attendant.*
Sirrah, a word with you: attend those men
Our pleasure?
Atten. They are, my lord, without the
   palace gate.
Macb. Bring them before us.
                                [*Exit Attendant.*
              To be thus is nothing;
But to be safely thus.—Our fears in Ban-
   quo
Stick deep; and in his royalty of nature   50
Reigns that which would be fear'd: 'tis much
   he dares;
And, to that dauntless temper of his mind,
He hath a wisdom that doth guide his valour
To act in safety. There is none but he
Whose being I do fear: and, under him,
My Genius is rebuked; as, it is said,
Mark Antony's was by Cæsar. He chid the
   sisters
When first they put the name of king upon
   me,

7. shine, are brilliantly manifest. 10. *Stage Direction:* Sennet, a set of notes played on a trumpet to
denote the approach of a procession. 13. all-thing,
in every way. 14. solemn, ceremonious.

30. bestow'd, lodged. 34. cause of state, questions
of state. 44. while, till. 45. Sirrah, used in addressing
inferiors. 48-49. To be . . . thus. This is explained in
several ways, of which the following is perhaps correct:
"To be thus (i.e., on the throne) is nothing unless we are
safely on the throne." 52-54. to that . . . safety.
Macbeth here attributes to Banquo the perfect virtue of
courage. 56. My Genius. This passage is a borrowing
from Plutarch's *Life of Antony;* Antony's good angel or
genius was abashed, it is said, before that of Octavius.

And bade them speak to him: then prophet-
like
They hail'd him father to a line of kings: 60
Upon my head they placed a fruitless crown,
And put a barren sceptre in my gripe,
Thence to be wrench'd with an unlineal
hand,
No son of mine succeeding. If 't be so,
For Banquo's issue have I filed my mind;
For them the gracious Duncan have I mur-
der'd;
Put rancours in the vessel of my peace
Only for them; and mine eternal jewel
Given to the common enemy of man,
To make them kings, the seed of Banquo
kings!   70
Rather than so, come fate into the list,
And champion me to the utterance! Who's
there?

Re-enter Attendant, *with two* Murderers.

Now go to the door, and stay there till we
call.   [*Exit Attendant.*
Was it not yesterday we spoke together?
    First Mur. It was, so please your high-
ness.
    Macb.   Well then, now
Have you consider'd of my speeches? Know
That it was he in the times past which held
you
So under fortune, which you thought had
been
Our innocent self: this I made good to you
In our last conference, pass'd in probation
with you,   80
How you were borne in hand, how cross'd,
the instruments,
Who wrought with them, and all things else
that might
To half a soul and to a notion crazed
Say 'Thus did Banquo.'
    First Mur.   You made it known to us.
    Macb. I did so, and went further, which
is now
Our point of second meeting. Do you find
Your patience so predominant in your
nature

That you can let this go? Are you so gos-
pell'd
To pray for this good man and for his issue,
Whose heavy hand hath bow'd you to the
grave
And beggar'd yours for ever?
    First Mur.   We are men, my liege. 91
    Macb. Ay, in the catalogue ye go for
men;
As hounds and greyhounds, mongrels, span-
iels, curs,
Shoughs, water-rugs and demi-wolves are
clept
All by the name of dogs: the valued file
Distinguishes the swift, the slow, the subtle,
The housekeeper, the hunter, every one
According to the gift which bounteous
nature
Hath in him closed, whereby he does receive
Particular addition, from the bill   100
That writes them all alike: and so of men.
Now, if you have a station in the file,
Not i' the worst rank of manhood, say 't;
And I will put that business in your bosoms,
Whose execution takes your enemy off,
Grapples you to the heart and love of us,
Who wear our health but sickly in his life,
Which in his death were perfect.
    Sec. Mur.   I am one, my liege,
Whom the vile blows and buffets of the
world
Have so incensed that I am reckless what 110
I do to spite the world.
    First Mur.   And I another
So weary with disasters, tugg'd with fortune,
That I would set my life on any chance,
To mend it, or be rid on 't.
    Macb.   Both of you
Know Banquo was your enemy.
    Both Mur.   True, my lord.
    Macb. So is he mine; and in such bloody
distance,
That every minute of his being thrusts
Against my near'st of life: and though I
could
With barefaced power sweep him from my
sight

62. **gripe**, grasp.   65. **filed**, defiled.   68-69. **mine
eternal . . . man.** Macbeth had understood his bargain when he professed a willingness to *jump the life to
come* (I, vii, 7); he here acknowledges it.   71. **list**,
lists, place of combat.   72. **champion me**, fight with
me in single combat.   **to the utterance**, to the last
extremity; French *à l'outrance.*   80. **probation**, proof,
i.e., in detail.   81. **borne in hand**, deceived (by false
promises).   83. **notion**, mind.

88. **gospell'd**, imbued with the gospel spirit.   94.
Shoughs, a kind of shaggy dog, called also *shocks.*
water-rugs, rough water dogs (?) **demi-wolves**, apparently a cross-breed with the wolf.   **clept**, called.
95. **valued file**, list classified according to value.   97.
housekeeper, watch-dog.   100. **Particular . . . bill**,
particular qualification apart from the catalogue.   112.
tugg'd with, pulled about by (as in wrestling).   It is
plain that these are not professional murderers, but
desperate men.   116. **distance**, hostility.   118. **near'st
of life**, most vital interests.

And bid my will avouch it, yet I must not, 120
For certain friends that are both his and
   mine,
Whose loves I may not drop, but wail his fall
Who I myself struck down; and thence it is,
That I to your assistance do make love,
Masking the business from the common eye
For sundry weighty reasons.

Sec. Mur.   We shall, my lord,
Perform what you command us.

First Mur.   Though our lives—

Macb. Your spirits shine through you.
   Within this hour at most
I will advise you where to plant yourselves;
Acquaint you with the perfect spy o' the
   time,   130
The moment on 't; for 't must be done to-
   night,
And something from the palace; always
   thought
That I require a clearness: and with him—
To leave no rubs nor botches in the work—
Fleance his son, that keeps him company,
Whose absence is no less material to me
Than is his father's, must embrace the fate
Of that dark hour. Resolve yourselves apart:
I'll come to you anon.

Both Mur.   We are resolved, my lord.

Macb. I'll call upon you straight: abide
   within.   [*Exeunt Murderers.* 140
It is concluded. Banquo, thy soul's flight,
If it find heaven, must find it out to-night.
                              [*Exit.*

SCENE II. *The palace.*

Enter LADY MACBETH *and a* Servant.

Lady M. Is Banquo gone from court?

Serv. Ay, madam, but returns again to-
   night.

Lady M. Say to the king, I would attend
   his leisure
For a few words.

Serv.   Madam, I will.   [*Exit.*

Lady M.   Nought's had, all's spent,
Where our desire is got without content:

'Tis safer to be that which we destroy
Than by destruction dwell in doubtful joy.

Enter MACBETH.

How now, my lord! why do you keep alone,
Of sorriest fancies your companions making,
Using those thoughts which should indeed
   have died   10
With them they think on? Things without all
   remedy
Should be without regard: what's done is
   done.

Macb. We have scotch'd the snake, not
   kill'd it:
She'll close and be herself, whilst our poor
   malice
Remains in danger of her former tooth.
But let the frame of things disjoint, both the
   worlds suffer,
Ere we will eat our meal in fear and sleep
In the affliction of these terrible dreams
That shake us nightly: better be with the
   dead,
Whom we, to gain our peace, have sent to
   peace,   20
Than on the torture of the mind to lie
In restless ecstasy. Duncan is in his grave;
After life's fitful fever he sleeps well;
Treason has done his worst: nor steel, nor
   poison,
Malice domestic, foreign levy, nothing,
Can touch him further.

Lady M.   Come on;
Gentle my lord, sleek o'er your rugged looks;
Be bright and jovial among your guests to-
   night.

Macb. So shall I, love; and so, I pray, be
   you:
Let your remembrance apply to Banquo; 30
Present him eminence, both with eye and
   tongue:
†Unsafe the while, that we
Must lave our honours in these flattering
   streams,
And make our faces vizards to our hearts,
Disguising what they are.

---

120. **avouch,** warrant, i.e., destroy him as an act of royal will. 128. **Your spirits . . . you,** i.e., the spirits of hatred and revenge rise into their faces. 130. **perfect spy o' the time,** knowledge or espial of the exact time; many conjectures. 132. **something,** somewhat, some distance. **thought,** being borne in mind. 133. **clearness,** freedom from suspicion. 134. **rubs,** obstacles (on the bowling-green), impediments. 138. **Resolve yourselves,** make up your minds.

13. **scotch'd,** cut, gashed. 14. **close,** be united, heal. 16. **frame of things,** universe. **both the worlds suffer,** heaven and earth perish. 22. **ecstasy,** state of being beside oneself in frenzy, passion, or madness. 27. **sleek o'er,** smooth. 31. **Present him eminence,** distinguish him with favor. Macbeth has apparently not confided his plot to his wife, yet it is hard to see why he gives her these directions. 32-33. **Unsafe . . . streams,** we are unsafe so long as we have to keep our dignities unsullied by means of flattery. The text is probably corrupt. 34. **vizards,** masks.

Lady M.   You must leave this.
Macb. O, full of scorpions is my mind,
    dear wife!
Thou know'st that Banquo, and his Fleance,
    lives.
Lady M. But in them nature's copy's not
    eterne.
Macb. There's comfort yet; they are
    assailable;
Then be thou jocund: ere the bat hath flown
His cloister'd flight, ere to black Hecate's
    summons   41
The shard-borne beetle with his drowsy
    hums
Hath rung night's yawning peal, there shall
    be done
A deed of dreadful note.
Lady M.   What's to be done?
Macb. Be innocent of the knowledge,
    dearest chuck,
Till thou applaud the deed. Come, seeling
    night,
Scarf up the tender eye of pitiful day;
And with thy bloody and invisible hand
Cancel and tear to pieces that great bond
Which keeps me pale! Light thickens; and
    the crow   50
Makes wing to the rooky wood:
Good things of day begin to droop and
    drowse;
Whiles night's black agents to their preys do
    rouse.
Thou marvell'st at my words: but hold thee
    still:
Things bad begun make strong themselves
    by ill.
So, prithee, go with me.   [*Exeunt.*

SCENE III. *A park near the palace.*

Enter three Murderers.

First Mur. But who did bid thee join with
    us?
Third Mur.   Macbeth.
Sec. Mur. He needs not our mistrust,
    since he delivers

Our offices and what we have to do
To the direction just.
First Mur.   Then stand with us.
The west yet glimmers with some streaks of
    day:
Now spurs the lated traveller apace
To gain the timely inn; and near approaches
The subject of our watch.
Third Mur.   Hark! I hear horses.
Ban. [*Within*] Give us a light there, ho!
Sec. Mur.   Then 'tis he: the rest
That are within the note of expectation   10
Already are i' the court.
First Mur.   His horses go about.
Third Mur. Almost a mile: but he does
    usually,
So all men do, from hence to the palace gate
Make it their walk.
Sec. Mur.   A light, a light!

Enter BANQUO, *and* FLEANCE *with a torch.*

Third Mur.   'Tis he.
First Mur. Stand to 't.
Ban. It will be rain to-night.
First Mur.   Let it come down.
                    [*They set upon Banquo.*
Ban. O, treachery! Fly, good Fleance,
    fly, fly, fly!
Thou mayst revenge. O slave!
                    [*Dies. Fleance escapes*
Third Mur. Who did strike out the light?
First Mur.   Was 't not the way?
Third Mur. There's but one down; the
    son is fled.
Sec. Mur.   We have lost   20
Best half of our affair.
First Mur. Well, let's away, and say how
    much is done.   [*Exeunt.*

SCENE IV. *The same. Hall in the palace.*

A banquet prepared. Enter MACBETH, LADY
MACBETH, ROSS, LENNOX, Lords, *and* Attendants.

Macb. You know your own degrees; sit
    down: at first
And last the hearty welcome.
Lords.   Thanks to your majesty.

38. **nature's copy**, lease of life (i.e., by copyhold);
possibly, man. **eterne**, perpetual. 42. **shard-borne**,
borne on shards, or horny wing-cases. 43. **yawning**,
drowsy. 44. **note**, significance. 45. **chuck**, term of
endearment. 46. **seeling**, eye-closing. Night is pictured here as a falconer sewing up the eyes of day lest
it should struggle against the deed that is to be done
(Parrott). 47. **Scarf up**, blindfold. 49. **bond**, Banquo's lease of life. 51. **rooky**, full of rooks.
    Scene iii. 2-3. **He needs . . . Our offices**, we need
not mistrust him, since he reports upon our business.

4. **To**, according to. **just**, exactly. That is, they
know he comes from Macbeth; it has been thought by
certain ingenious critics that the Third Murderer is
Macbeth. 6. **lated**, belated. 10. **note of expectation**,
list of those expected.
    Scene iv. 1. **degrees**, ranks. 1-2. **at first And last**,
from the beginning to the end (of the feast).

Macb. Ourself will mingle with society,
And play the humble host.
Our hostess keeps her state, but in best time
We will require her welcome.

Lady M. Pronounce it for me, sir, to all
our friends;
For my heart speaks they are welcome.

First Murderer *appears at the door.*

Macb. See, they encounter thee with their
hearts' thanks.   9
Both sides are even: here I'll sit i' the midst:
Be large in mirth; anon we'll drink a meas-
ure
The table round. [*Approaching the door.*]
There's blood upon thy face.

Mur. 'Tis Banquo's then.

Macb. 'Tis better thee without than he
within.
Is he dispatch'd?

Mur. My lord, his throat is cut; that I did
for him.

Macb. Thou art the best o' the cut-throats:
yet he's good
That did the like for Fleance: if thou didst it,
Thou art the nonpareil.

Mur.   Most royal sir,
Fleance is 'scaped.   20

Macb. Then comes my fit again: I had
else been perfect,
Whole as the marble, founded as the rock,
As broad and general as the casing air:
But now I am cabin'd, cribb'd, confined,
bound in
To saucy doubts and fears. But Banquo's
safe?

Mur. Ay, my good lord: safe in a ditch he
bides,
With twenty trenched gashes on his head;
The least a death to nature.

Macb.   Thanks for that.
There the grown serpent lies; the worm that's
fled
Hath nature that in time will venom breed, 30
No teeth for the present. Get thee gone: to-
morrow
We'll hear, ourselves, again. [*Exit Murderer.*

5. **state**, canopied chair of state. 6. **require**, request.
11. **large**, unrestrained. 14. **'Tis better . . . within.**
It is better for it to be on the outside of thee than on the
inside of him; sometimes explained as "better that his
blood should be on thy face than he in this room."
20. **Fleance is 'scaped.** If *Macbeth* is regarded as a
tragedy of fate, this must be taken as marking its turning-point. 23. **casing**, enveloping. 24-25. **bound in
To**, confined along with. 25. **saucy**, sharp (Koppel);
impudent (Schmidt). 26. **bides**, lies. 29. **worm**,
small serpent. 32. **hear, ourselves**, talk it over.

Lady M.   My royal lord,
You do not give the cheer: the feast is sold
That is not often vouch'd, while 'tis a-
making,
'Tis given with welcome: to feed were best at
home;
From thence the sauce to meat is ceremony;
Meeting were bare without it.

Macb.   Sweet remembrancer!
Now, good digestion wait on appetite,
And health on both!

Len.   May 't please your highness sit.
[*The Ghost of Banquo enters, and sits in
Macbeth's place.*

Macb. Here had we now our country's
honour roof'd,   40
Were the graced person of our Banquo pres-
ent;
Who may I rather challenge for unkindness
Than pity for mischance!

Ross.   His absence, sir,
Lays blame upon his promise. Please 't your
highness
To grace us with your royal company.

Macb. The table's full.

Len.   Here is a place reserved, sir.

Macb. Where?

Len. Here, my good lord. What is 't that
moves your highness?

Macb. Which of you have done this?

Lords.   What, my good lord?

Macb. Thou canst not say I did it: never
shake   50
Thy gory locks at me.

Ross. Gentlemen rise; his highness is not
well.

Lady M. Sit, worthy friends: my lord is
often thus,
And hath been from his youth: pray you,
keep seat;
The fit is momentary; upon a thought
He will again be well: if much you note him,
You shall offend him and extend his passion:
Feed, and regard him not. Are you a man?

Macb. Ay, and a bold one, that dare look
on that
Which might appal the devil.

Lady M.   O proper stuff!   60
This is the very painting of your fear:
This is the air-drawn dagger which, you said,

34. **vouch'd**, assurance given that it is not sold like
a meal at an inn. 40. **roof'd**, under one roof. 41.
graced, gracious. 42. **Who may I**, whom I hope I
may. 55. **upon a thought**, in a moment. 57. **extend**,
prolong. 60. **O proper stuff!** O veritable nonsense!

Led you to Duncan. O, these flaws and
    starts,
Impostors to true fear, would well become
A woman's story at a winter's fire,
Authorized by her grandam. Shame itself!
Why do you make such faces? When all's
    done,
You look but on a stool.

    Macb. Prithee, see there! behold! look! lo!
    how say you?
Why, what care I? If thou canst nod, speak
    too.   70
If charnel-houses and our graves must send
Those that we bury back, our monuments
Shall be the maws of kites. [*Ghost vanishes.*

    Lady M. What, quite unmann'd in folly?

    Macb. If I stand here, I saw him.

    Lady M.   Fie, for shame!

    Macb. Blood hath been shed ere now, i'
    the olden time,
Ere humane statue purged the gentle weal;
Ay, and since too, murders have been per-
    form'd
Too terrible for the ear: the time has been,
That, when the brains were out, the man
    would die,
And there an end; but now they rise again, 80
With twenty mortal murders on their
    crowns,
And push us from our stools: this is more
    strange
Than such a murder is.

    Lady M.   My worthy lord,
Your noble friends do lack you.

    Macb.   I do forget.
Do not muse at me, my most worthy friends;
I have a strange infirmity, which is nothing
To those that know me. Come, love and
    health to all;
Then I'll sit down. Give me some wine; fill
    full.
I drink to the general joy o' the whole
    table,
And to our dear friend Banquo, whom we
    miss;   90
Would he were here! to all, and him, we
    thirst,
And all to all.

    Lords.   Our duties, and the pledge.

Re-enter Ghost.

    Macb. Avaunt! and quit my sight! let the
    earth hide thee!
Thy bones are marrowless, thy blood is cold;
Thou hast no speculation in those eyes
Which thou dost glare with!

    Lady M.   Think of this, good peers,
But as a thing of custom: 'tis no other;
Only it spoils the pleasure of the time.

    Macb. What man dare, I dare: 99
Approach thou like the rugged Russian bear,
The arm'd rhinoceros, or the Hyrcan tiger;
Take any shape but that, and my firm nerves
Shall never tremble: or be alive again,
And dare me to the desert with thy sword;
†If trembling I inhabit then, protest me
The baby of a girl. Hence, horrible shadow!
Unreal mockery, hence! [*Ghost vanishes.*
              Why, so: being gone,
I am a man again. Pray you, sit still.

    Lady M. You have displaced the mirth,
    broke the good meeting,
With most admired disorder.

    Macb.   Can such things be, 110
And overcome us like a summer's cloud,
Without our special wonder? You make me
    strange
Even to the disposition that I owe,
When now I think you can behold such
    sights,
And keep the natural ruby of your cheeks,
When mine is blanch'd with fear.

    Ross.   What sights, my lord?

    Lady M. I pray you, speak not; he grows
    worse and worse;
Question enrages him. At once, good night:
Stand not upon the order of your going,
But go at once.

    Len.   Good night; and better health 120
Attend his majesty!

    Lady M.   A kind good night to all!
[*Exeunt all but Macbeth and Lady M.*

---

63. **flaws,** outbursts of passion. 64. **to,** compared
with. 73. **maws,** stomachs. If the body were devoured
by kites, the ghost could not rise. 76. **humane.** This
spelling carried both meanings: "appertaining to mankind" and "befitting man." **purged . . . weal,** cleansed
the commonwealth of violence and made it gentle. 81.
mortal murders, deadly wounds. 84. **lack,** miss.
85. **muse,** wonder, marvel. 91. **thirst,** desire to drink.
92. **all to all,** all good wishes to all.

93. **Avaunt!** Note the recoil to the courage of desperation, which Macbeth was to show again in the last
moment of his life. 95. **speculation,** light of living
intellect; also defined as "power of sight." 100-101. **bear
. . . tiger.** Bears of Russia and tigers of Hyrcania
were types of ferocity. **arm'd,** sheathed in armor. 105.
If trembling . . . then, if then I tremble (i.e., put on
trembling as a garment). Some editors prefer the
reading due to Pope and Steevens: "If trembling I
inhabit thee." 106. **baby of a girl,** (puny) infant of an
immature mother; some editors prefer "girl's doll."
109. **displaced,** banished. 110. **admired,** amazing,
wondered at. 119. **Stand . . . order,** do not wait for
the ceremonies.

Macb. It will have blood; they say, blood
    will have blood:
Stones have been known to move and trees to
    speak;
Augurs and understood relations have
By magot-pies and choughs and rooks
    brought forth
The secret'st man of blood. What is the
    night?
Lady M. Almost at odds with morning,
    which is which.
Macb. How say'st thou, that Macduff
    denies his person
At our great bidding?
    Lady M.   Did you send to him, sir?
Macb. I hear it by the way; but I will
    send: 130
There's not a one of them but in his house
I keep a servant fee'd. I will to-morrow,
And betimes I will, to the weird sisters:
More shall they speak; for now I am bent to
    know,
By the worst means, the worst. For mine
    own good,
All causes shall give way: I am in blood
Stepp'd in so far that, should I wade no
    more,
Returning were as tedious as go o'er:
Strange things I have in head, that will to
    hand;
Which must be acted ere they may be
    scann'd.
Lady M. You lack the season of all na-
    tures, sleep.   141
Macb. Come, we'll to sleep. My strange
    and self-abuse
Is the initiate fear that wants hard use:
We are yet but young in deed.   [*Exeunt.*

SCENE V. *A Heath.*

Thunder. Enter the three Witches,
        meeting HECATE.

First Witch. Why, how now, Hecate! you
    look angerly.

Hec. Have I not reason, beldams as you
    are,
Saucy and overbold? How did you dare
To trade and traffic with Macbeth
In riddles and affairs of death;
And I, the mistress of your charms,
The close contriver of all harms,
Was never call'd to bear my part,
Or show the glory of our art?
And, which is worse, all you have done   10
Hath been but for a wayward son,
Spiteful and wrathful, who, as others do,
Loves for his own ends, not for you.
But make amends now: get you gone,
And at the pit of Acheron
Meet me i' the morning: thither he
Will come to know his destiny:
Your vessels and your spells provide,
Your charms and every thing beside.
I am for the air; this night I'll spend   20
Unto a dismal and a fatal end:
Great business must be wrought ere noon;
Upon the corner of the moon
There hangs a vaporous drop profound;
I'll catch it ere it come to ground:
And that distill'd by magic sleights
Shall raise such artificial sprites
As by the strength of their illusion
Shall draw him on to his confusion:
He shall spurn fate, scorn death, and bear   30
His hopes 'bove wisdom, grace and fear:
And you all know, security
Is mortals' chiefest enemy.

    [*Music and a song within:* 'Come away,
                        come away,' &c.
Hark! I am call'd; my little spirit, see,
Sits in a foggy cloud, and stays for me.
                                        [*Exit.*
First Witch. Come, let's make haste; she'll
    soon be back again.   [*Exeunt.*

SCENE VI. *Forres. The palace.*

Enter LENNOX *and another* Lord.

Len. My former speeches have but hit
    your thoughts,
Which can interpret further: only, I say,
Things have been strangely borne. The
    gracious Duncan

123. **Stones**, thought to be an allusion to rocking-stones. 124. **Augurs**, probably, auguries. **understood relations**, secret mystical connections. 125. **magot-pies**, magpies. 141. **season**, seasoning, relish. 142. **self-abuse**, self-delusion. 143. **initiate**, of the beginner. **use**, experience. Macbeth will accustom himself to crime and thus grow indifferent and bold. His new theory is already signalized by his trembling defiance of Banquo's ghost, his independence of Lady Macbeth, and his half-formed plot against Macduff.
    Scene v. Practically all critics agree that this scene is

not by Shakespeare. 7. **close**, secret. 15. **Acheron**, a river of hell. 24. **profound**, ready to drop (?) of deep significance (?) 27. **artificial**, produced by magical arts. 32. **security**, confidence, over-confidence.

Was pitied of Macbeth: marry, he was dead:
And the right-valiant Banquo walk'd too
    late;
Whom, you may say, if 't please you, Fleance
    kill'd,
For Fleance fled: men must not walk too late.
Who cannot want the thought how mon-
    strous
It was for Malcolm and for Donalbain
To kill their gracious father? damned fact! 10
How it did grieve Macbeth! did he not
    straight
In pious rage the two delinquents tear,
That were the slaves of drink and thralls of
    sleep?
Was not that nobly done? Ay, and wisely
    too;
For 'twould have anger'd any heart alive
To hear the men deny 't. So that, I say,
He has borne all things well: and I do think
That had he Duncan's sons under his key—
As, an't please heaven, he shall not—they
    should find
What 'twere to kill a father; so should
    Fleance.   20
But, peace! for from broad words and
    'cause he fail'd
His presence at the tyrant's feast, I hear
Macduff lives in disgrace: sir, can you tell
Where he bestows himself?
    Lord.   The son of Duncan,
From whom this tyrant holds the due of
    birth,
Lives in the English court, and is received
Of the most pious Edward with such grace
That the malevolence of fortune nothing
Takes from his high respect: thither Mac-
    duff
Is gone to pray the holy king, upon his aid 30
To wake Northumberland and warlike
    Siward:
That, by the help of these—with Him above
To ratify the work—we may again
Give to our tables meat, sleep to our nights,
Free from our feasts and banquets bloody
    knives,
Do faithful homage and receive free honours:
All which we pine for now: and this report
Hath so exasperate the king that he

Prepares for some attempt of war.
    Len.   Sent he to Macduff?
    Lord. He did: and with an absolute 'Sir,
    not I,'   40
The cloudy messenger turns me his back,
And hums, as who should say 'You'll rue the
    time
That clogs me with this answer.'
    Len.   And that well might
Advise him to a caution, to hold what dis-
    tance
His wisdom can provide. Some holy angel
Fly to the court of England and unfold
His message ere he come, that a swift bless-
    ing
May soon return to this our suffering country
Under a hand accursed!
    Lord.   I'll send my prayers with him.
                [*Exeunt.*

ACT IV.

SCENE I. *A cavern. In the middle, a boiling
cauldron.*

Thunder. Enter the three Witches.

First Witch. Thrice the brinded cat hath
    mew'd.
Sec. Witch. Thrice and once the hedge-pig
    whined.
Third Witch. Harpier cries 'Tis time, 'tis
    time.
First Witch. Round about the cauldron
    go;
In the poison'd entrails throw.
†Toad, that under cold stone
Days and nights has thirty one
Swelter'd venom sleeping got,
Boil thou first i' the charmed pot.
    All. Double, double toil and trouble;   10
Fire burn, and cauldron bubble.
    Sec. Witch. Fillet of a fenny snake,
In the cauldron boil and bake;
Eye of newt and toe of frog,
Wool of bat and tongue of dog,
Adder's fork and blind-worm's sting,
Lizard's leg and howlet's wing,

8. **want the thought,** help thinking. 13. **thralls,**
slaves. 19. **an't,** if it. 21. **from,** on account of.
broad, open, plain. 22. **tyrant's,** usurper's. 27.
Edward, Edward the Confessor. 30. **upon his aid,**
in aid of Malcolm. 35. **Free . . . feasts,** free our feasts
from. 36. **free,** freely bestowed, or the honors pertaining to freemen.

40. **absolute,** curt, peremptory. 41. **cloudy,** sullen.
48. **suffering country Under,** country suffering under.
    Act IV. Scene i. 1. **brinded,** marked with streaks
(as by fire), brindled. 2. **hedge-pig,** hedge-hog. 3.
Harpier, form doubtful, probably intended for *harpy.*
6. **cold,** two syllables. 8. **venom.** The toad was commonly thought to be venomous. 16. **fork,** forked
tongue. **blind-worm,** a harmless kind of snake called
also *slow worm.* 17. **howlet's,** owl's.

For a charm of powerful trouble,
Like a hell-broth boil and bubble.
　　All. Double, double toil and trouble; 20
Fire burn and cauldron bubble.
　　Third Witch. Scale of dragon, tooth of
　　　wolf,
Witches' mummy, maw and gulf
Of the ravin'd salt-sea shark,
Root of hemlock digg'd i' the dark,
Liver of blaspheming Jew,
Gall of goat, and slips of yew
Sliver'd in the moon's eclipse,
Nose of Turk and Tartar's lips,
Finger of birth-strangled babe   30
Ditch-deliver'd by a drab,
Make the gruel thick and slab:
Add thereto a tiger's chaudron,
For the ingredients of our cauldron.
　　All. Double, double toil and trouble;
Fire burn and cauldron bubble.
　　Sec. Witch. Cool it with a baboon's blood,
Then the charm is firm and good.

　　Enter HECATE *to the other three Witches.*

　　Hec. O, well done! I commend your
　　　pains;
And every one shall share i' the gains: 40
And now about the cauldron sing,
Like elves and fairies in a ring,
Enchanting all that you put in.
　　[*Music and a song:* 'Black spirits,' &c.
　　　　　　　　　　　　[*Hecate retires.*
　　Sec. Witch. By the pricking of my thumbs,
Something wicked this way comes.
　　　　　Open, locks,
　　　　　Whoever knocks!

　　Enter MACBETH.

　　Macb. How now, you secret, black, and
　　　midnight hags!
What is 't you do?
　　All.　　　　　　A deed without a name.
　　Macb. I conjure you, by that which you
　　　profess,   50
Howe'er you come to know it, answer me:
Though you untie the winds and let them
　　fight
Against the churches; though the yesty
　　waves

Confound and swallow navigation up;
Though bladed corn be lodged and trees
　　blown down;
Though castles topple on their warders'
　　heads;
Though palaces and pyramids do slope
Their heads to their foundations; though the
　　treasure
Of nature's germens tumble all together,
Even till destruction sicken; answer me 60
To what I ask you.
　　First Witch.　　　Speak.
　　Sec. Witch.　　　　　　Demand.
　　Third Witch.　　　　　　　　We'll answer.
　　First Witch. Say, if thou'dst rather hear it
　　　from our mouths,
Or from our masters?
　　Macb.　　　　　　Call 'em; let me see 'em.
　　First Witch. Pour in sow's blood, that
　　　hath eaten
Her nine farrow; grease that's sweaten
From the murderer's gibbet throw
Into the flame.
　　All.　　　　　Come, high or low;
Thyself and office deftly show!

　　Thunder. First Apparition: *an armed Head.*

　　Macb. Tell me, thou unknown power,—
　　First Witch.　　　He knows thy thought:
Hear his speech, but say thou nought.   70
　　First App. Macbeth! Macbeth! Macbeth!
　　　beware Macduff;
Beware the thane of Fife. Dismiss me.
　　Enough.　　　　　　　　[*Descends.*
　　Macb. Whate'er thou art, for thy good
　　　caution, thanks;
Thou hast harp'd my fear aright: but one
　　word more,—
　　First Witch. He will not be commanded:
　　here's another,
More potent than the first.

　　Thunder. Second Apparition: *a bloody Child.*

　　Sec. App. Macbeth! Macbeth! Macbeth!
　　Macb. Had I three ears, I'ld hear thee.
　　Sec. App. Be bloody, bold, and resolute;
　　　laugh to scorn

---

23. **gulf,** gullet. 24. **ravin'd,** ravenous. 28. **Sliver'd,** broken off (as a branch). 32. **slab,** viscous, thick. 33. **chaudron,** entrails. 39-43. **O, well . . . in.** These lines are universally regarded as non-Shakespearean. 53. **yesty,** foamy.

55. **bladed,** in the blade, still green. **corn,** general name for wheat and other grains. **lodged,** thrown down, laid. 59. **nature's germens,** seeds or elements, from which nature operates. 60. **sicken,** be surfeited. 65. **nine farrow,** litter of nine. 68. *Stage Direction:* **armed Head.** This symbolizes the head of Macbeth cut off by Macduff and presented by him to Malcolm. 74. **harp'd,** hit, touched. 76. *Stage Direction:* **bloody Child.** This symbolizes Macduff (see V, viii, 15-16).

The power of man, for none of woman born 80
Shall harm Macbeth.   [*Descends.*

Macb. Then live, Macduff: what need I
     fear of thee?
But yet I'll make assurance double sure,
And take a bond of fate: thou shalt not live;
That I may tell pale-hearted fear it lies,
And sleep in spite of thunder.

*Thunder: Third Apparition: a Child crowned,
     with a tree in his hand.*

                              What is this
That rises like the issue of a king,
And wears upon his baby-brow the round
And top of sovereignty?
     All.   Listen, but speak not to't.
     Third App. Be lion-mettled, proud; and
          take no care   90
Who chafes, who frets, or where conspirers
     are:
Macbeth shall never vanquish'd be until
Great Birnam wood to high Dunsinane hill
Shall come against him.   [*Descends.*
     Macb.   That will never be:
Who can impress the forest, bid the tree
Unfix his earth-bound root? Sweet bode-
     ments! good!
Rebellion's head, rise never till the wood
Of Birnam rise, and our high-placed Macbeth
Shall live the lease of nature, pay his breath
To time and mortal custom. Yet my heart
Throbs to know one thing: tell me, if your
     art   101
Can tell so much: shall Banquo's issue ever
Reign in this kingdom?
     All.   Seek to know no more.
     Macb. I will be satisfied: deny me this,
And an eternal curse fall on you! Let me
     know.
Why sinks that cauldron? and what noise is
     this?   [*Hautboys.*
     First Witch. Show!
     Sec. Witch. Show!
     Third Witch. Show!
     All. Show his eyes, and grieve his heart;
Come like shadows, so depart!   111

---

*A show of Eight Kings, the last with a glass
     in his hand; Banquo's Ghost following.*

     Macb. Thou art too like the spirit of
          Banquo; down!
Thy crown does sear mine eye-balls. And
     thy hair,
Thou other gold-bound brow, is like the first.
A third is like the former. Filthy hags!
Why do you show me this? A fourth! Start,
     eyes!
What, will the line stretch out to the crack of
     doom?
Another yet! A seventh! I'll see no more:
And yet the eighth appears, who bears a glass
Which shows me many more; and some I
     see   120
That two-fold balls and treble sceptres carry:
Horrible sight! Now, I see, 'tis true;
For the blood-bolter'd Banquo smiles upon
     me,
And points at them for his. [*Apparitions
     vanish.*] What, is this so?
     First Witch. Ay, sir, all this is so: but
          why
Stands Macbeth thus amazedly?
Come, sisters, cheer we up his sprites,
And show the best of our delights:
I'll charm the air to give a sound,
While you perform your antic round;   130
That this great king may kindly say,
Our duties did his welcome pay.

     [*Music. The Witches dance, and then
          vanish, with Hecate.*

     Macb. Where are they? Gone? Let this
          pernicious hour
Stand aye accursed in the calendar!
Come in, without there!

                    Enter LENNOX.

     Len.   What's your grace's will?
     Macb. Saw you the weird sisters?
     Len.   No, my lord.
     Macb. Came they not by you?
     Len.   No, indeed, my lord.

---

83. **double**, doubly. 86. **Stage Direction: Child . . .
hand.** This third apparition symbolizes Malcolm, the
royal child. 88-89. **round . . . sovereignty**, seems to
allude to the shape of a crown as made up of a lower
round and a top part, and also to the rounding out and
culmination in sovereignty. 93. **Birnam, Dunsinane.**
Birnam is a hill near Dunkeld, twelve miles from Dunsinane, which is seven miles from Perth. 95. **impress**,
like soldiers. 96. **bodements**, prophecies. 99. **lease
of nature**, natural period. 106. **noise**, music.

112. **Thou . . . Banquo.** This would be the first in
the succession of Scottish kings down to James I, therefore Fleance, whose coronation was the thing most
dreaded by Macbeth. 117. **crack of doom**, possibly,
thunder announcing Doomsday. 121. **two-fold balls**,
a probable reference to the double coronation of James
at Westminster and Scone, as king of England and
Scotland. **treble sceptres**, almost certainly refers to
James's assumed title of King of Great Britain, France,
and Ireland. 123. **blood-bolter'd**, having his hair
matted with blood. 125-135. **Ay, sir . . . there.** These
lines are also held to be spurious. 130. **antic round**,
grotesque dance in a circle.

Macb. Infected be the air whereon they
    ride;
And damn'd all those that trust them! I did
    hear
The galloping of horse: who was't came by?
    Len. 'Tis two or three, my lord, that
    bring you word   141
Macduff is fled to England.
    Macb.   Fled to England!
    Len. Ay, my good lord.
    Macb. Time, thou anticipatest my dread
    exploits:
The flighty purpose never is o'ertook
Unless the deed go with it: from this mo-
    ment
The very firstlings of my heart shall be
The firstlings of my hand. And even now,
To crown my thoughts with acts, be it
    thought and done:
The castle of Macduff I will surprise;   150
Seize upon Fife; give to the edge o' the sword
His wife, his babes, and all unfortunate
    souls
That trace him in his line. No boasting like a
    fool:
This deed I'll do before this purpose cool.
But no more sights!—Where are these
    gentlemen?
Come, bring me where they are.   [*Exeunt.*

Scene II. *Fife. Macduff's castle.*

Enter Lady Macduff, *her* Son, *and* Ross.

    L. Macd. What had he done, to make him
    fly the land?
    Ross. You must have patience, madam.
    L. Macd.   He had none:
His flight was madness: when our actions do
    not,
Our fears do make us traitors.
    Ross.   You know not
Whether it was his wisdom or his fear.
    L. Macd. Wisdom! to leave his wife, to
    leave his babes,
His mansion and his titles in a place
From whence himself does fly? He loves us
    not;
He wants the natural touch: for the poor
    wren,
The most diminutive of birds, will fight,   10

Her young ones in her nest, against the
    owl.
All is the fear and nothing is the love;
As little is the wisdom, where the flight
So runs against all reason.
    Ross.   My dearest coz,
I pray you, school yourself: but for your
    husband,
He is noble, wise, judicious, and best knows
The fits o' the season. I dare not speak
    much further;
But cruel are the times, when we are traitors
And do not know ourselves, when we hold
    rumour
From what we fear, yet know not what we
    fear,   20
But float upon a wild and violent sea
Each way and move. I take my leave of
    you:
Shall not be long but I'll be here again:
Things at the worst will cease, or else climb
    upward
To what they were before. My pretty cousin,
Blessing upon you!
    L. Macd. Father'd he is, and yet he's
    fatherless.
    Ross. I am so much a fool, should I stay
    longer,
It would be my disgrace and your discom-
    fort:
I take my leave at once.   [*Exit.*
    L. Macd. Sirrah, your father's dead: 30
And what will you do now? How will you
    live?
    Son. As birds do, mother.
    L. Macd.   What, with worms and flies?
    Son. With what I get, I mean; and so do
    they.
    L. Macd. Poor bird! thou'ldst never fear
    the net nor lime,
The pitfall nor the gin.
    Son. Why should I, mother? Poor birds
    they are not set for.
My father is not dead, for all your saying.
    L. Macd. Yes, he is dead: how wilt thou
    do for a father?
    Son. Nay, how will you do for a husband?
    L. Macd. Why, I can buy me twenty at
    any market.   40

145. **flighty**, fleeting. 153. **trace**, follow.
Scene ii. 2. **He had none.** Patience was the virtue
by which the faculties were controlled; hence, *His flight
was madness* (l. 3). 7. **titles**, possessions. 9. **touch**, affection, feeling.

17. **fits o' the season**, violent disorders of the time.
19. **know ourselves**, know ourselves (or possibly, each
other) to be traitors. Owing to Macbeth's system of
espionage even good men have grown suspicious of each
other. 19. **hold**, accept, believe. 23. **Shall**, it shall.
34. **lime**, bird-lime. 35. **gin**, snare. 36. **they**, the
snares.

Son. Then you'll buy 'em to sell again.

L. Macd. Thou speak'st with all thy wit;
and yet, i' faith,
With wit enough for thee.

Son. Was my father a traitor, mother?

L. Macd. Ay, that he was.

Son. What is a traitor?

L. Macd. Why, one that swears and lies.

Son. And be all traitors that do so?

L. Macd. Every one that does so is a
traitor, and must be hanged.   50

Son. And must they all be hanged that
swear and lie?

L. Macd. Every one.

Son. Who must hang them?

L. Macd. Why, the honest men.

Son. Then the liars and swearers are fools,
for there are liars and swearers enow to beat
the honest men and hang up them.

L. Macd. Now, God help thee, poor
monkey! But how wilt thou do for a father?

Son. If he were dead, you'ld weep for
him: if you would not, it were a good sign
that I should quickly have a new father.   63

L. Macd. Poor prattler, how thou talk'st!

Enter a Messenger.

Mess. Bless you, fair dame! I am not to
you known,
Though in your state of honour I am perfect.
I doubt some danger does approach you
nearly;
If you will take a homely man's advice,
Be not found here; hence, with your little
ones.
To fright you thus, methinks, I am too
savage;   70
To do worse to you were fell cruelty,
Which is too nigh your person. Heaven pre-
serve you!
I dare abide no longer.   [*Exit.*

L. Macd. Whither should I fly?
I have done no harm. But I remember now
I am in this earthly world; where to do harm
Is often laudable, to do good sometime
Accounted dangerous folly: why then, alas,
Do I put up that womanly defence,
To say I have done no harm?

Enter Murderers.

What are these faces?

First Mur. Where is your husband?   80

L. Macd. I hope, in no place so unsanctified
Whert such as thou mayst find him.

First Mur.   He's a traitor.

Son. Thou liest, thou shag-hair'd villain!

First Mur.   What, you egg!
[*Stabbing him.*
Young fry of treachery!

Son.   He has kill'd me, mother:
Run away, I pray you!   [*Dies.*
[*Exit Lady Macduff, crying* 'Murder!'
Exeunt Murderers, following her.

SCENE III. *England. Before the King's
palace.*

Enter MALCOLM *and* MACDUFF.

Mal. Let us seek out some desolate shade,
and there
Weep our sad bosoms empty.

Macd.   Let us rather
Hold fast the mortal sword, and like good
men
Bestride our down-fall'n birthdom: each new
morn
New widows howl, new orphans cry, new
sorrows
Strike heaven on the face, that it resounds
As if it felt with Scotland and yell'd out
Like syllable of dolour.

Mal.   What I believe I'll wail,
What know believe, and what I can re-
dress,
As I shall find the time to friend, I will.   10
What you have spoke, it may be so per-
chance.
This tyrant, whose sole name blisters our
tongues,
Was once thought honest: you have loved
him well;
He hath not touch'd you yet. I am young;
but something
You may deserve of him through me, and
wisdom

47. **swears and lies,** swears allegiance and breaks his oath. 61-63. **If he . . . father.** This is an example of Shakespeare's treatment of children. The child has a precocity appropriate only to grown people, and yet his ideas are offered in a childish way. There was no knowledge of the psychology of childhood in Shake-speare's day. 66. **in . . . honour,** with your honorable rank. **perfect,** perfectly acquainted.

83. **egg,** used contemptuously of the young. 84. **fry,** swarm of young fishes; contemptuously used. *Scene iii.* 2. **Weep . . . empty.** Up to line 117 Malcolm suspects Macduff of being an emissary of Macbeth sent thither to ensnare him; he is testing out Macduff. 4. **Bestride,** stand over in defense. **birth-dom,** fatherland. 10. **to friend,** for my friend. 12. **sole,** mere.

To offer up a weak poor innocent lamb
To appease an angry god.
   Macd. I am not treacherous.
   Mal.   But Macbeth is.
A good and virtuous nature may recoil
In an imperial charge. But I shall crave
   your pardon;   20
That which you are my thoughts cannot
   transpose:
Angels are bright still, though the brightest
   fell:
Though all things foul would wear the brows
   of grace,
Yet grace must still look so.
   Macd.   I have lost my hopes.
   Mal. Perchance even there where I did
   find my doubts.
Why in that rawness left you wife and child,
Those precious motives, those strong knots
   of love,
Without leave-taking? I pray you,
Let not my jealousies be your dishonours,
But mine own safeties. You may be rightly
   just,   30
Whatever I shall think.
   Macd.   Bleed, bleed, poor country!
Great tyranny! lay thou thy basis sure,
For goodness dare not check thee: wear thou
   thy wrongs;
The title is affeer'd! Fare thee well, lord:
I would not be the villain that thou think'st
For the whole space that's in the tyrant's
   grasp,
And the rich East to boot.
   Mal.   Be not offended:
I speak not as in absolute fear of you.
I think our country sinks beneath the yoke;
It weeps, it bleeds; and each new day a gash
Is added to her wounds: I think withal   41
There would be hands uplifted in my right;
And here from gracious England have I offer
Of goodly thousands: but, for all this,
When I shall tread upon the tyrant's head,
Or wear it on my sword, yet my poor country
Shall have more vices than it had before,
More suffer and more sundry ways than ever,
By him that shall succeed.
   Macd.   What should he be?
   Mal. It is myself I mean: in whom I know
All the particulars of vice so grafted   51

That, when they shall be open'd, black Mac-
   beth
Will seem as pure as snow, and the poor
   state
Esteem him as a lamb, being compared
With my confineless harms.
   Macd.   Not in the legions
Of horrid hell can come a devil more damn'd
In evils to top Macbeth.
   Mal.   I grant him bloody,
Luxurious, avaricious, false, deceitful,
Sudden, malicious, smacking of every sin
That has a name: but there's no bottom,
   none,
In my voluptuousness: your wives, your
   daughters,   61
Your matrons and your maids, could not
   fill up
The cistern of my lust, and my desire
All continent impediments would o'erbear
That did oppose my will: better Macbeth
Than such an one to reign.
   Macd.   Boundless intemperance
In nature is a tyranny; it hath been
The untimely emptying of the happy throne
And fall of many kings. But fear not yet
To take upon you what is yours: you may 70
Convey your pleasures in a spacious plenty,
And yet seem cold, the time you may so
   hoodwink.
We have willing dames enough; there cannot
   be
That vulture in you, to devour so many
As will to greatness dedicate themselves,
Finding it so inclined.
   Mal.   With this there grows
In my most ill-composed affection such
A stanchless avarice that, were I king,
I should cut off the nobles for their lands,
Desire his jewels and this other's house: 80
And my more-having would be as a sauce
To make me hunger more; that I should
   forge
Quarrels unjust against the good and loyal,
Destroying them for wealth.
   Macd.   This avarice
Sticks deeper, grows with more pernicious
   root

19. recoil, fall away, degenerate. **20. imperial
charge**, royal command. **24. so**, like grace. **26. rawness**, haste, unpreparedness. **34. affeer'd**, confirmed,
certified. **43. England**, king of England. **48. sundry**,
various. **49. What**, who.

52. open'd, unfolded (like buds). **55. my confineless harms**, the boundless injuries I shall inflict.
58. Luxurious, lustful. **59. Sudden**, violent, passionate. **64. continent**, restraining. **67. tyranny**, usurpation. **69. yet**, nevertheless. **71. Convey**, manage with
secrecy. **72. the time . . . hoodwink**, you may so
deceive the age. **77. ill-composed affection**, evil
disposition. **78. stanchless**, insatiable.

Than summer-seeming lust, and it hath been
The sword of our slain kings: yet do not fear;
Scotland hath foisons to fill up your will,
Of your mere own: all these are portable,
With other graces weigh'd.   90

   Mal. But I have none: the king-becoming
     graces,
As justice, verity, temperance, stableness,
Bounty, perseverance, mercy, lowliness,
Devotion, patience, courage, fortitude,
I have no relish of them, but abound
In the division of each several crime,
Acting it many ways. Nay, had I power, I
     should
Pour the sweet milk of concord into hell,
Uproar the universal peace, confound
All unity on earth.

   Macd.   O Scotland, Scotland! 100

   Mal. If such a one be fit to govern, speak:
I am as I have spoken.

   Macd.   Fit to govern!
No, not to live. O nation miserable,
With an untitled tyrant bloody-scepter'd,
When shalt thou see thy wholesome days
     again,
Since that the truest issue of thy throne
By his own interdiction stands accursed,
And does blaspheme his breed? Thy royal
     father
Was a most sainted king: the queen that bore
     thee,
Oftener upon her knees than on her feet, 110
Died every day she lived. Fare thee well!
These evils thou repeat'st upon thyself
Have banish'd me from Scotland. O my
     breast,
Thy hope ends here!

   Mal.   Macduff, this noble passion,
Child of integrity, hath from my soul
Wiped the black scruples, reconciled my
     thoughts
To thy good truth and honour. Devilish
     Macbeth
By many of these trains hath sought to win
     me
Into his power, and modest wisdom plucks
     me

From over-credulous haste: but God above
Deal between thee and me! for even now 121
I put myself to thy direction, and
Unspeak mine own detraction, here abjure
The taints and blames I laid upon myself,
For strangers to my nature. I am yet
Unknown to woman, never was forsworn,
Scarcely have coveted what was mine own,
At no time broke my faith, would not betray
The devil to his fellow, and delight
No less in truth than life: my first false
     speaking   130
Was this upon myself: what I am truly,
Is thine and my poor country's to command:
Whither indeed, before thy here-approach,
Old Siward, with ten thousand warlike
     men,
Already at a point, was setting forth.
Now we'll together; and the chance of good-
     ness
Be like our warranted quarrel! Why are you
     silent?

   Macd. Such welcome and unwelcome
     things at once
'Tis hard to reconcile.

Enter a Doctor.

   Mal. Well; more anon.—Comes the king
     forth, I pray you?   140

   Doct. Ay, sir; there are a crew of wretched
     souls
That stay his cure: their malady convinces
The great assay of art; but at his touch—
Such sanctity hath heaven given his hand—
They presently amend.

   Mal.   I thank you, doctor. [*Exit Doctor.*

   Macd. What's the disease he means?

   Mal.   'Tis call'd the evil:
A most miraculous work in this good king;
Which often, since my here-remain in Eng-
     land,
I have seen him do. How he solicits heaven,
Himself best knows: but strangely-visited
     people,   150
All swoln and ulcerous, pitiful to the eye,
The mere despair of surgery, he cures,
Hanging a golden stamp about their necks,

---

86. **summer-seeming**, passing away with youth,
transitory. 88. **foisons**, resources. 89. **your mere
own**, what is absolutely your own. **portable**, bearable.
90. **With**, against. 91. **king-becoming graces.** The
list which follows is a typical enumeration of the princely
virtues of the Renaissance. 95. **relish of**, flavor or
trace of. 104. **untitled**, lacking rightful title. 107.
interdiction, authoritative exclusion. 108. **blaspheme**,
slander, defame. 111. **Died . . . lived**, lived a life of
daily mortification (Delius). 118. **trains**, plots, artifices.

126. **forsworn**, perjured. 135. **at a point**, ready,
prepared. 136. **chance of goodness**, chance of success.
141. **crew**, company. 142. **convinces**, conquers. 143.
assay of art, efforts of medical skill. 146. **evil**, disease,
i.e., scrofula. The passage is an obvious compliment to
James I, who claimed the miraculous power of the royal
touch. 150. **strangely-visited**, afflicted by strange
diseases. 153. **stamp**, coin (hung around the necks of
the persons touched).

Put on with holy prayers: and 'tis spoken,
To the succeeding royalty he leaves
The healing benediction. With this strange
   virtue,
He hath a heavenly gift of prophecy,
And sundry blessings hang about his throne,
That speak him full of grace.

Enter Ross.

Macd.   See, who comes here?
Mal. My countryman; but yet I know
   him not.   160
Macd. My ever-gentle cousin, welcome
   hither.
Mal. I know him now. Good God, be-
   times remove
The means that makes us strangers!
Ross.   Sir, amen.
Macd. Stands Scotland where it did?
Ross.   Alas, poor country!
Almost afraid to know itself. It cannot
Be call'd our mother, but our grave; where
   nothing,
But who knows nothing, is once seen to
   smile;
Where sighs and groans and shrieks that
   rend the air
Are made, not mark'd; where violent sorrow
   seems
A modern ecstasy: the dead man's knell 170
Is there scarce ask'd for who; and good men's
   lives
Expire before the flowers in their caps,
Dying or ere they sicken.
Macd.   O, relation
Too nice, and yet too true!
Mal.   What's the newest grief?
Ross. That of an hour's age doth hiss the
   speaker:
Each minute teems a new one.
Macd.   How does my wife?
Ross. Why, well.
Macd.   And all my children?
Ross.   Well too.
Macd. The tyrant has not batter'd at
   their peace?
Ross. No; they were well at peace when
   I did leave 'em.
Macd. Be not a niggard of your speech:
   how goes 't?   180

Ross. When I came hither to transport
   the tidings,
Which I have heavily borne, there ran a
   rumour
Of many worthy fellows that were out;
Which was to my belief witness'd the rather,
For that I saw the tyrant's power a-foot:
Now is the time of help; your eye in Scotland
Would create soldiers, make our women
   fight,
To doff their dire distresses.
Mal.   Be 't their comfort
We are coming thither: gracious England
   hath
Lent us good Siward and ten thousand men;
An older and a better soldier none   191
That Christendom gives out.
Ross.   Would I could answer
This comfort with the like! But I have words
That would be howl'd out in the desert air,
Where hearing should not latch them.
Macd.   What concern they?
The general cause? or is it a fee-grief
Due to some single breast?
Ross.   No mind that's honest
But in it shares some woe; though the main
   part
Pertains to you alone.
Macd.   If it be mine,
Keep it not from me, quickly let me have it.
Ross. Let not your ears despise my tongue
   for ever,   201
Which shall possess them with the heaviest
   sound
That ever yet they heard.
Macd.   Hum! I guess at it.
Ross. Your castle is surprised; your wife
   and babes
Savagely slaughter'd: to relate the manner,
Were, on the quarry of these murder'd deer,
To add the death of you.
Mal.   Merciful heaven!
What, man! ne'er pull your hat upon your
   brows;
Give sorrow words: the grief that does not
   speak
Whispers the o'er-fraught heart and bids it
   break.   210

182. **heavily,** sadly. 183. **out,** in arms. 188. **doff,**
put off, get rid of. 189. **England,** the king of England.
192. **gives out,** tells of, proclaims. 195. **latch,** catch
the sound of. 196. **fee-grief,** a grief with an individual
owner. 202. **possess,** fill, put in possession of. 206.
quarry, heap of slaughtered deer at a hunt. 209-210.
the grief . . . break. The conception of the broken
heart is to be taken literally. 210. **Whispers,** whispers
to. **o'er-fraught,** overburdened.

166. **nothing,** nobody. 167. **once,** ever. 170.
modern ecstasy, commonplace excitement. 174. **nice,**
fastidious, particular. 175. **hiss,** cause to be hissed.
176. **teems,** teems with. 177. **children,** three syllables.

Macd. My children too?

Ross.   Wife, children, servants, all
That could be found.

Macd.   And I must be from thence!
My wife kill'd too?

Ross.   I have said.

Mal.   Be comforted:
Let's make us medicines of our great revenge,
To cure this deadly grief.

Macd. He has no children. All my pretty
    ones?
Did you say all? O hell-kite! All?
What, all my pretty chickens and their dam
At one fell swoop?

Mal. Dispute it like a man.

Macd.   I shall do so; 220
But I must also feel it as a man:
I cannot but remember such things were,
That were most precious to me. Did heaven
    look on,
And would not take their part? Sinful
    Macduff,
They were all struck for thee! naught that I
    am,
Not for their own demerits, but for mine,
Fell slaughter on their souls. Heaven rest
    them now!

Mal. Be this the whetstone of your sword:
    let grief
Convert to anger; blunt not the heart, en-
    rage it.

Macd. O, I could play the woman with
    mine eyes   230
And braggart with my tongue! But, gentle
    heavens,
Cut short all intermission; front to front
Bring thou this fiend of Scotland and myself;
Within my sword's length set him; if he
    'scape,
Heaven forgive him too!

Mal.   This tune goes manly.
Come, go we to the king; our power is ready;
Our lack is nothing but our leave: Macbeth
Is ripe for shaking, and the powers above
Put on their instruments. Receive what
    cheer you may: 239

The night is long that never finds the day.
                                    [*Exeunt.*

ACT V.

SCENE I. *Dunsinane. Ante-room in the
                        castle.*

Enter a Doctor of Physic *and a*
        Waiting-Gentlewoman.

Doct. I have two nights watched with
you, but can perceive no truth in your report. When was it she last walked?

Gent. Since his majesty went into the
field, I have seen her rise from her bed,
throw her nightgown upon her, unlock her
closet, take forth paper, fold it, write upon 't,
read it, afterwards seal it, and again return
to bed; yet all this while in a most fast
sleep.   9

Doct. A great perturbation in nature, to
receive at once the benefit of sleep, and do
the effects of watching! In this slumbery
agitation, besides her walking and other
actual performances, what, at any time,
have you heard her say?

Gent. That, sir, which I will not report
after her.

Doct. You may to me: and 'tis most meet
you should.

Gent. Neither to you nor any one, having
no witness to confirm my speech.   21

Enter LADY MACBETH, *with a taper.*

Lo you, here she comes! This is her very
guise; and, upon my life, fast asleep. Observe her; stand close.

Doct. How came she by that light?

Gent. Why, it stood by her: she has light
by her continually; 'tis her command.

Doct. You see, her eyes are open.

Gent. Ay, but their sense is shut.

Doct. What is it she does now? Look, how
she rubs her hands.   31

Gent. It is an accustomed action with her,
to seem thus washing her hands: I have
known her continue in this a quarter of an
hour.

Lady M. Yet here's a spot.

Doct. Hark! she speaks: I will set down

214. **Let's make . . . revenge.** This line expresses
the current thought about revenge, not sanctioned by
Christianity, but bearing a sort of sanction from the
philosophy of Seneca and other ancients. 216. **He has
no children**, a notable example of Shakespeare's penetrative and constructive imagination. 220. **Dispute**,
fight on the issue; not "reason upon it." 229. **Convert**,
change. 232. **intermission**, delay. 237. **Our lack . . .
leave**, we need not only to take our leave, or possibly, we
need only permission to depart. 239. **Put on their
instruments**, set us on as their instruments.

Act V. Scene i. 12. **effects of watching**, deeds
characteristic of waking. 24. **close**, concealed. 29.
sense is shut, Rowe's emendation of F, *sense are shut*,
which is evidently the correct text, *sense* being taken
as a plural.

what comes from her, to satisfy my remembrance the more strongly.   38

Lady M. Out, damned spot! out, I say!—
One: two: why, then 'tis time to do 't.—Hell
is murky!—Fie, my lord, fie! a soldier, and
afeard? What need we fear who knows it,
when none can call our power to account?—
Yet who would have thought the old man to
have had so much blood in him.

Doct. Do you mark that?

Lady M. The thane of Fife had a wife:
where is she now?—What, will these hands
ne'er be clean?—No more o' that, my lord, no
more o' that: you mar all with this starting.   50

Doct. Go to, go to; you have known what
you should not.

Gent. She has spoke what she should not,
I am sure of that: heaven knows what she
has known.

Lady M. Here's the smell of the blood
still: all the perfumes of Arabia will not
sweeten this little hand. Oh, oh, oh!

Doct. What a sigh is there! The heart is
sorely charged.   60

Gent. I would not have such a heart in my
bosom for the dignity of the whole body.

Doct. Well, well, well,—

Gent. Pray God it be, sir.

Doct. This disease is beyond my practice:
yet I have known those which have walked
in their sleep who have died holily in their
beds.

Lady M. Wash your hands, put on your
nightgown; look not so pale.—I tell you yet
again, Banquo's buried; he cannot come out
on 's grave.   71

Doct. Even so?

Lady M. To bed, to bed! there's knocking
at the gate: come, come, come, come, give me
your hand. What's done cannot be undone.
—To bed, to bed, to bed!   [*Exit.*

Doct. Will she go now to bed?

Gent. Directly.

Doct. Foul whisperings are abroad: un-
natural deeds
Do breed unnatural troubles: infected minds
To their deaf pillows will discharge their
secrets: 81
More needs she the divine than the physi-
cian.
God, God forgive us all! Look after her;

Remove from her the means of all annoyance,
And still keep eyes upon her. So, good
night:
My mind she has mated, and amazed my
sight.
I think, but dare not speak.

Gent.   Good night, good doctor.
                              [*Exeunt.*

SCENE II. *The country near Dunsinane.*

Drum and colours. Enter MENTEITH, CAITH-
NESS, ANGUS, LENNOX, *and* Soldiers.

Ment. The English power is near, led on
by Malcolm,
His uncle Siward and the good Macduff:
Revenges burn in them; for their dear causes
Would to the bleeding and the grim alarm
Excite the mortified man.

Ang.   Near Birnam wood
Shall we well meet them; that way are they
coming.

Caith. Who knows if Donalbain be with
his brother?

Len. For certain, sir, he is not: I have
a file
Of all the gentry: there is Siward's son,
And many unrough youths that even now 10
Protest their first of manhood.

Ment.   What does the tyrant?

Caith. Great Dunsinane he strongly forti-
fies:
Some say he's mad: others that lesser hate
him
Do call it valiant fury: but, for certain,
He cannot buckle his distemper'd cause
Within the belt of rule.

Ang.   Now does he feel
His secret murders sticking on his hands;
Now minutely revolts upbraid his faith-
breach;
Those he commands move only in com-
mand,
Nothing in love: now does he feel his title 20
Hang loose about him, like a giant's robe
Upon a dwarfish thief.

Ment.   Who then shall blame

---

84. **annoyance,** i.e., harming herself. 86. **mated,**
bewildered, stupefied.
Scene ii. 3. **dear,** deeply felt (personal). 4. **alarm,**
call to battle. 5. **mortified,** dead. 8. **file,** list, roster.
10. **unrough,** beardless. 11. **Protest,** assert publicly.
18. **minutely,** happening every minute.

60. **sorely charged,** heavily burdened with passions.
71. **on's,** of his.

His pester'd senses to recoil and start,
When all that is within him does condemn
Itself for being there?
    Caith.   Well, march we on,
To give obedience where 'tis truly owed:
Meet we the medicine of the sickly weal,
And with him pour we in our country's purge
Each drop of us.
    Len.   Or so much as it needs,
To dew the sovereign flower and drown the
    weeds.   30
Make we our march towards Birnam.
                        [*Exeunt, marching.*

SCENE III.   *Dunsinane. A room in the
castle.*

Enter MACBETH, *Doctor, and* Attendants.

    Macb. Bring me no more reports; let them
    fly all:
Till Birnam wood remove to Dunsinane,
I cannot taint with fear. What's the boy
    Malcolm?
Was he not born of woman? The spirits that
    know
All mortal consequences have pronounced me
    thus:
'Fear not, Macbeth; no man that's born of
    woman
Shall e'er have power upon thee.' Then fly,
    false thanes,
And mingle with the English epicures:
The mind I sway by and the heart I bear
Shall never sag with doubt nor shake with
    fear.

Enter a Servant.

The devil damn thee black, thou cream-faced
    loon!   11
Where got'st thou that goose look?
    Serv. There is ten thousand—
    Macb.   Geese, villain?
    Serv.   Soldiers, sir.
    Macb. Go, prick thy face, and over-red
    thy fear,

Thou lily-liver'd boy. What soldiers, patch?
Death of thy soul! those linen cheeks of
    thine
Are counsellors to fear. What soldiers, whey-
    face?
    Serv. The English force, so please you.
    Macb. Take thy face hence. [*Exit Servant.*
                Seyton!—I am sick at heart,
When I behold—Seyton, I say!—This push
Will cheer me ever, or disseat me now.   21
I have lived long enough: my way of life
Is fall'n into the sear, the yellow leaf;
And that which should accompany old age,
As honour, love, obedience, troops of friends,
I must not look to have; but, in their stead,
Curses, not loud but deep, mouth-honour,
    breath,
Which th poor heart would fain deny, and
    dare not.
Seyton!

Enter SEYTON.

    Sey. What is your gracious pleasure?
    Macb.   What news more?   30
    Sey. All is confirm'd, my lord, which was
    reported.
    Macb. I'll fight till from my bones my
    flesh be hack'd.
Give me my armour.
    Sey.   'Tis not needed yet.
    Macb. I'll put it on.
Send out moe horses; skirr the country
    round;
Hang those that talk of fear. Give me mine
    armour.
How does your patient, doctor?
    Doct.   Not so sick, my lord,
As she is troubled with thick-coming fancies,
That keep her from her rest.
    Macb.   Cure her of that.
Canst thou not minister to a mind diseased, 40
Pluck from the memory a rooted sorrow,
Raze out the written troubles of the brain
And with some sweet oblivious antidote
Cleanse the stuff'd bosom of that perilous
    stuff
Which weighs upon the heart?
    Doct.   Therein the patient
Must minister to himself.

---

    23. pester'd, troubled, embarrassed. **recoil**, fall
away, degenerate. **27. medicine**, i.e., Malcolm. **30.
dew**, bedew.
    Scene iii. **1. them**, the thanes. **3. taint**, become
imbued with (an undesirable quality). **5. mortal
consequences**, what befalls man. Cuningham prefers
either *consequents* or (following Singer) *consequence*,
both of which are metrically better than the text. **8.
epicures**, luxury-loving persons. Holinshed refers to
the introduction of luxurious habits of living by the
English into Scotland. **9. sway by**, am directed or
swayed by. **11. loon**, stupid fellow. **14. over-red**, over-
den over. The servant's blood has all retired into his
lower abdomen on account of his fear, so that he is very
pale and there is no blood in his liver, where his courage
should have resided—hence, *lily-liver'd* (l. 15).

    15. patch, domestic fool; here used contemptuously. **17
counsellors to fear**, i.e., they suggest fear in conformity with the psychological doctrine elsewhere put forward
in the play; e.g., in I, v, 73. **20. push**, crisis, onset. **35.
moe**, more. **skirr**, scour. **43. oblivious**, causing forgetfulness.

Macb. Throw physic to the dogs; I'll
    none of it.

Come, put mine armour on; give me my
    staff.

Seyton, send out. Doctor, the thanes fly
    from me.

Come, sir, dispatch. If thou couldst, doctor,
    cast   50

The water of my land, find her disease,

And purge it to a sound and pristine health,

I would applaud thee to the very echo,

That should applaud again.—Pull 't off, I
    say.—

What rhubarb, senna, or what purgative
    drug,

Would scour these English hence? Hear'st
    thou of them?

    Doct. Ay, my good lord; your royal prep-
    aration

Makes us hear something.

    Macb.   Bring it after me.

I will not be afraid of death and bane,

Till Birnam forest come to Dunsinane.   60

    Doct. [*Aside*] Were I from Dunsinane
    away and clear,

Profit again should hardly draw me here.

                       [*Exeunt.*

Scene IV. *Country near Birnam wood.*

Drum and colours. Enter Malcolm, *old*
Siward *and his* Son, Macduff, Menteith, Caithness, Angus, Lennox, Ross,
and Soldiers, *marching.*

    Mal. Cousins, I hope the days are near at
    hand

That chambers will be safe.

    Ment.   We doubt it nothing.

    Siw. What wood is this before us?

    Ment.   The wood of Birnam.

    Mal. Let every soldier hew him down a
    bough

And bear 't before him: thereby shall we
    shadow

The numbers of our host and make discovery

Err in report of us.

    Soldiers.   It shall be done.

    Siw. We learn no other but the confident
    tyrant

Keeps still in Dunsinane, and will endure

Our setting down before 't.

    Mal.   'Tis his main hope: 10

For where there is advantage to be given,

Both more and less have given him the
    revolt,

And none serve with him but constrained
    things

Whose hearts are absent too.

    Macd.   Let our just censures

Attend the true event, and put we on

Industrious soldiership.

    Siw.   The time approaches

That will with due decision make us know

What we shall say we have and what we owe.

Thoughts speculative their unsure hopes
    relate,

But certain issue strokes must arbitrate: 20

Towards which advance the war.

                   [*Exeunt, marching.*

Scene V. *Dunsinane. Within the castle.*

Enter Macbeth, Seyton, *and* Soldiers, *with
drum and colours.*

    Macb. Hang out our banners on the out-
    ward walls:

The cry is still 'They come:' our castle's
    strength

Will laugh a siege to scorn: here let them lie

Till famine and the ague eat them up:

Were they not forced with those that should
    be ours,

We might have met them dareful, beard to
    beard,

And beat them backward home.

              [*A cry of women within*

              What is that noise?

    Sey. It is the cry of women, my good lord.

                       [*Exit.*

    Macb. I have almost forgot the taste of
    fears:

The time has been, my senses would have
    cool'd   10

To hear a night-shriek; and my fell of hair

Would at a dismal treatise rouse and stir

As life were in 't: I have supp'd full with
    horrors;

Direness, familiar to my slaughterous
   thoughts,
Cannot once start me.

Re-enter SEYTON.

               Wherefore was that cry?
  Sey. The queen, my lord, is dead.
  Macb. She should have died hereafter;
There would have been a time for such a
   word.
To-morrow, and to-morrow, and to-morrow,
Creeps in this petty pace from day to day   20
To the last syllable of recorded time,
And all our yesterdays have lighted fools
The way to dusty death. Out, out, brief
   candle!
Life's but a walking shadow, a poor player
That struts and frets his hour upon the stage
And then is heard no more: it is a tale
Told by an idiot, full of sound and fury,
Signifying nothing.

Enter a Messenger.

Thou comest to use thy tongue; thy story
   quickly.
  Mess. Gracious my lord,   30
I should report that which I say I saw,
But know not how to do it.
  Macb.   Well, say, sir.
  Mess. As I did stand my watch upon the
   hill,
I look'd toward Birnam, and anon, me-
   thought,
The wood began to move.
  Macb.   Liar and slave!
  Mess. Let me endure your wrath, if 't be
   not so:
Within this three mile may you see it com-
   ing;
I say, a moving grove.
  Macb.   If thou speak'st false,
Upon the next tree shalt thou hang alive,
Till famine cling thee: if thy speech be sooth,
I care not if thou dost for me as much.   41
I pull in resolution, and begin

To doubt the equivocation of the fiend
That lies like truth: 'Fear not, till Birnam
   wood
Do come to Dunsinane:' and now a wood
Comes toward Dunsinane. Arm, arm, and
   out!
If this which he avouches does appear,
There is nor flying hence nor tarrying here.
I 'gin to be aweary of the sun,
And wish the estate o' the world were now
   undone.   50
Ring the alarum-bell! Blow, wind! come,
   wrack!
At least we'll die with harness on our back.
                       [Exeunt.

Scene VI. *Dunsinane. Before the castle*

Drum and colours. Enter MALCOLM, *old*
SIWARD, MACDUFF, *and their* Army, *with
boughs.*

  Mal. Now near enough: your leavy
   screens throw down,
And show like those you are. You, worthy
   uncle,
Shall, with my cousin, your right-noble son,
Lead our first battle: worthy Macduff and
   we
Shall take upon's what else remains to do,
According to our order.
  Siw.   Fare you well.
Do we but find the tyrant's power to-night,
Let us be beaten, if we cannot fight.
  Macd. Make all our trumpets speak; give
   them all breath,   9
Those clamorous harbingers of blood and
   death.   *[Exeunt.*

Scene VII. *Another part of the field.*

Alarums. Enter MACBETH.

  Macb. They have tied me to a stake; I
   cannot fly,
But, bear-like, I must fight the course.
   What's he
That was not born of woman? Such a one
Am I to fear, or none.

14. slaughterous thoughts, thoughts of murder.
17. She should . . . hereafter. Her death should
have been deferred to some more peaceful hour (Johnson); or, she would have died some day. An old suggestion, never accepted by the critics, would punctuate
as follows: *She should have died. Hereafter there,* etc. **18.
such a word,** i.e., as death. **19-28. To-morrow . . .
nothing.** The first sentence is not easy to construe,
but the whole passage is clear. **40. cling,** cause to
shrivel up. **sooth,** truth. **42. pull in,** explained as
"check," "restrain." Johnson conjectured *pall,* grow
stale, fail—a preferable reading.

51. wrack, ruin.
Scene vi. **4. battle,** main body of an armed force.
Scene vii. **2. bear-like . . . course.** This is a simile
from the sport of bear-baiting, in which the bear was
tied to a stake and dogs were set upon him; the *course*
was a bout or round.

Enter young SIWARD.

Yo. Siw. What is thy name?
Macb.   Thou'lt be afraid to hear it.
Yo. Siw. No; though thou call'st thyself a
hotter name
Than any is in hell.
Macb.   My name's Macbeth.
Yo. Siw. The devil himself could not pro-
nounce a title
More hateful to mine ear.
Macb.   No, nor more fearful.
Yo. Siw. Thou liest, abhorred tyrant;
with my sword   10
I'll prove the lie thou speak'st.
          [*They fight and young Siward is slain.*
Macb.   Thou wast born of woman.
But swords I smile at, weapons laugh to
scorn,
Brandish'd by man that's of a woman born.
                                        [*Exit.*

Alarums. Enter MACDUFF.

Macd. That way the noise is. Tyrant,
show thy face!
If thou be'st slain and with no stroke of mine,
My wife and children's ghosts will haunt me
still.
I cannot strike at wretched kerns, whose
arms
Are hired to bear their staves: either thou,
Macbeth,
Or else my sword with an unbatter'd edge
I sheathe again undeeded. There thou
shouldst be;   20
By this great clatter, one of greatest note
Seems bruited. Let me find him, fortune!
And more I beg not.
                              [*Exit. Alarums.*

Enter MALCOLM *and old* SIWARD.

Siw. This way, my lord; the castle's
gently render'd:
The tyrant's people on both sides do fight;
The noble thanes do bravely in the war;
The day almost itself professes yours,
And little is to do.
Mal.   We have met with foes
That strike beside us.
Siw.   Enter, sir, the castle.   29
                              [*Exeunt. Alarums.*

17. **kerns,** properly, Irish foot-soldiers; here applied
contemptuously to the rank and file.   22. **bruited,**
noised abroad, announced.

SCENE VIII. *Another part of the field.*

Enter MACBETH.

Macb. Why should I play the Roman fool,
and die
On mine own sword? whiles I see lives, the
gashes
Do better upon them.

Enter MACDUFF.

Macd.   Turn, hell-hound, turn!
Macb. Of all men else I have avoided
thee:
But get thee back; my soul is too much
charged
With blood of thine already.
Macd.   I have no words:
My voice is in my sword: thou bloodier
villain
Than terms can give thee out! [*They fight.*
Macb.   Thou losest labour:
As easy mayst thou the intrenchant air
With thy keen sword impress as make me
bleed: 10
Let fall thy blade on vulnerable crests;
I bear a charmed life, which must not yield
To one of woman born.
Macd.   Despair thy charm;
And let the angel whom thou still hast served
Tell thee, Macduff was from his mother's
womb
Untimely ripp'd.
Macb.   Accursed be that tongue that tells
me so,
For it hath cow'd my better part of man!
And be these juggling fiends no more be-
lieved,
That palter with us in a double sense;   20
That keep the word of promise to our ear,
And break it to our hope. I'll not fight with
thee.
Macd. Then yield thee, coward,
And live to be the show and gaze o' the
time:
We'll have thee, as our rarer monsters are,

1. **Roman fool.** Shakespeare had staged deep arguments from Plutarch on the propriety of suicide when
he wrote *Julius Cæsar*, and was probably now reading
on the same issue in the *Life of Antony*. He here seems
to give voice to the northern temper. Macbeth is a
man in whom the impulse to live is overmastering. 9.
intrenchant, invulnerable, indivisible.   14. **angel,**
evil angel, Macbeth's genius.   18. **cow'd . . . man,**
subdued my soul, or spirit, or mind. Macbeth's invul-
nerability was, in some measure, his belief in his in-
vulnerability.

Painted upon a pole, and underwrit,
'Here may you see the tyrant.'

Macb.   I will not yield,
To kiss the ground before young Malcolm's
      feet,
And to be baited with the rabble's curse.   29
Though Birnam wood be come to Dunsinane,
And thou opposed, being of no woman
      born,
Yet I will try the last. Before my body
I throw my warlike shield. Lay on, Macduff,
And damn'd be him that first cries 'Hold,
      enough!' [*Exeunt, fighting. Alarums.*

*Retreat. Flourish. Enter, with drum and
colours,* MALCOLM, *old* SIWARD, ROSS, *the
other* Thanes, *and* Soldiers.

Mal. I would the friends we miss were
      safe arrived.

Siw. Some must go off: and yet, by these
      I see,
So great a day as this is cheaply bought.

Mal. Macduff is missing, and your noble
      son.

Ross. Your son, my lord, has paid a sol-
      dier's debt:
He only lived but till he was a man;   40
The which no sooner had his prowess con-
      firm'd
In the unshrinking station where he fought,
But like a man he died.

Siw.   Then he is dead?

Ross. Ay, and brought off the field: your
      cause of sorrow
Must not be measured by his worth, for then
It hath no end.

Siw.   Had he his hurts before?

Ross. Ay, on the front.

26. **Painted upon a pole,** i.e., painted on a board suspended on a pole. 30-34. **Though . . . enough.** Macbeth's recoil to courage would be explained in the psychology of the time as the setting up in him of a new impulse of passion. His repugnance to submission drives out his craven fear. 34. *Stage Direction:* **Exeunt, fighting.** F has *Enter fighting and Macbeth slain,* which is inconsistent with the stage direction after line 53. It may, however, indicate that at some early performances Macbeth was slain on the stage. 42. **unshrinking station,** post from which he did not shrink.

Siw.   Why then, God's soldier be he!
Had I as many sons as I have hairs,
I would not wish them to a fairer death:
And so, his knell is knoll'd.

Mal.   He's worth more sorrow,   50
And that I'll spend for him.

Siw.   He's worth no more:
They say he parted well, and paid his score:
And so, God be with him! Here comes newer
      comfort.

Re-enter MACDUFF, *with* MACBETH'S *head.*

Macd. Hail, king! for so thou art: behold,
      where stands
The usurper's cursed head: the time is free:
I see thee compass'd with thy kingdom's
      pearl,
That speak my salutation in their minds;
Whose voices I desire aloud with mine:
Hail, King of Scotland!

All.   Hail, King of Scotland! [*Flourish.*

Mal. We shall not spend a large expense
      of time   60
Before we reckon with your several loves,
And make us even with you. My thanes and
      kinsmen,
Henceforth be earls, the first that ever Scot-
      land
In such an honour named. What's more to
      do,
Which would be planted newly with the time,
As calling home our exiled friends abroad
That fled the snares of watchful tyranny;
Producing forth the cruel ministers
Of this dead butcher and his fiend-like queen,
Who, as 'tis thought, by self and violent
      hands   70
Took off her life; this, and what needful else
That calls upon us, by the grace of Grace,
We will perform in measure, time and place:
So, thanks to all at once and to each one,
Whom we invite to see us crown'd at Scone.
      [*Flourish. Exeunt.*

52. **parted,** died. 56. **thy kingdom's pearl,** the flower of thy kingdom. 63. **Henceforth be earls,** a detail from Holinshed. *Earl* was an English title. 70. **self and violent,** her own violent.

ANTONY AND CLEOPATRA

DRAMATIS PERSONÆ

MARK ANTONY,
OCTAVIUS CÆSAR, } triumvirs.
M. ÆMILIUS LEPIDUS,
SEXTUS POMPEIUS.

DOMITIUS ENOBARBUS,
VENTIDIUS,
EROS,
SCARUS, } friends to Antony.
DERCETAS,
DEMETRIUS,
PHILO,

MECÆNAS,
AGRIPPA,
DOLABELLA,
PROCULEIUS, } friends to Cæsar.
THYREUS,
GALLUS,

MENAS,
MENECRATES, } friends to Pompey.
VARRIUS,

TAURUS, lieutenant-general to Cæsar.
CANIDIUS, lieutenant-general to Antony.
SILIUS, an officer in Ventidius's army.
EUPHRONIUS, an ambassador from Antony to Cæsar.

ALEXAS,
MARDIAN, a Eunuch, } attendants on
SELEUCUS, } Cleopatra.
DIOMEDES,
A Soothsayer.
A Clown.

CLEOPATRA, queen of Egypt.
OCTAVIA, sister to Cæsar and wife to Antony.
CHARMIAN, } attendants on Cleopatra.
IRAS,

Officers, Soldiers, Messengers, and other Attendants.

SCENE: *In several parts of the Roman empire.*

ACT I.

SCENE I. *Alexandria. A room in Cleopatra's palace.*

Enter DEMETRIUS and PHILO.

Phi. Nay, but this dotage of our general's
O'erflows the measure: those his goodly eyes,
That o'er the files and musters of the war
Have glow'd like plated Mars, now bend, now turn,
The office and devotion of their view
Upon a tawny front: his captain's heart,
Which in the scuffles of great fights hath burst
The buckles on his breast, reneges all temper,

And is become the bellows and the fan
To cool a gipsy's lust.

Flourish. Enter ANTONY, CLEOPATRA, *her Ladies, the Train, with Eunuchs fanning her.*

Look, where they come: 10
Take but good note, and you shall see in him
The triple pillar of the world transform'd
Into a strumpet's fool: behold and see.

Cleo. If it be love indeed, tell me how much.

Ant. There's beggary in the love that can be reckon'd.

Cleo. I'll set a bourn how far to be beloved.

---

4. **plated**, clothed in armor.   5. **office**, service.
6. **tawny**, yellowish brown.   **front**, face; with play on the meaning "foremost line of battle."   8. **reneges**, renounces.   **temper**, self-restraint.

10. **gipsy's**, suggests that Cleopatra was an Egyptian, and also used as an opprobrious epithet.   12. **triple**, third; allusion to the Triumvirate composed of Antony, Lepidus, and Octavius Cæsar.   16. **bourn**, boundary

Ant. Then must thou needs find out new
heaven, new earth.

Enter an Attendant.

Att. News, my good lord, from Rome.
Ant.   Grates me: the sum.
Cleo. Nay, hear them, Antony:
Fulvia perchance is angry; or, who knows 20
If the scarce-bearded Cæsar have not sent
His powerful mandate to you, 'Do this, or
this;
Take in that kingdom, and enfranchise that;
Perform 't, or else we damn thee.'
Ant.   How, my love!
Cleo. Perchance! nay, and most like:
You must not stay here longer, your dis-
mission
Is come from Cæsar; therefore hear it,
Antony.
Where's Fulvia's process? Cæsar's I would
say? both?
Call in the messengers. As I am Egypt's
queen,
Thou blushest, Antony; and that blood of
thine   30
Is Cæsar's homager: else so thy cheek pays
shame
When shrill-tongued Fulvia scolds. The mes-
sengers!
Ant. Let Rome in Tiber melt, and the
wide arch
Of the ranged empire fall! Here is my space.
Kingdoms are clay: our dungy earth alike
Feeds beast as man: the nobleness of life
Is to do thus; when such a mutual pair
                     [*Embracing.*
And such a twain can do 't, in which I bind,
On pain of punishment, the world to weet
We stand up peerless.
Cleo.   Excellent falsehood! 40
Why did he marry Fulvia, and not love her?
I'll seem the fool I am not; Antony
Will be himself.
Ant.   But stirr'd by Cleopatra.
Now, for the love of Love and her soft hours,
Let's not confound the time with conference
harsh:

There's not a minute of our lives should
stretch
Without some pleasure now. What sport to-
night?
Cleo. Hear the ambassadors.
Ant.   Fie, wrangling queen!
Whom every thing becomes, to chide, to
laugh,
To weep; whose every passion fully strives
To make itself, in thee, fair and admired! 51
No messenger, but thine; and all alone
To-night we'll wander through the streets
and note
The qualities of people. Come, my queen;
Last night you did desire it: speak not to us.
       [*Exeunt Ant. and Cleo. with their train.*
Dem. Is Cæsar with Antonius prized so
slight?
Phi. Sir, sometimes, when he is not
Antony,
He comes too short of that great property
Which still should go with Antony.
Dem.   I am full sorry
That he approves the common liar, who   60
Thus speaks of him at Rome: but I will
hope
Of better deeds to-morrow. Rest you happy!
                       [*Exeunt.*

SCENE II.   *The same.   Another room.*

Enter CHARMIAN, IRAS, ALEXAS, *and a*
Soothsayer.

Char. Lord Alexas, sweet Alexas, most
any thing Alexas, almost most absolute
Alexas, where's the soothsayer that you
praised so to the queen? O, that I knew this
husband, which, you say, must charge his
horns with garlands!
Alex. Soothsayer!
Sooth. Your will?
Char. Is this the man? Is 't you, sir, that
know things?
Sooth. In nature's infinite book of secrecy
A little I can read.
Alex.   Show him your hand.   10

Enter ENOBARBUS.

Eno. Bring in the banquet quickly; wine
enough
Cleopatra's health to drink.

18. **Grates me**, it vexes me. **the sum**, i.e., be brief.
20. **Fulvia**, Antony's wife, of whom Cleopatra is jealous.
23. **Take in**, conquer. **enfranchise**, set free. 26.
dismission, dismissal. 28. **process**, summons. 31.
homager, vassal. 34. **ranged**, ordered, or possibly,
extended. 37. **mutual**, exchanging equal love. 39.
weet, wit, know. 43. **stirr'd**, moved, excited. The
meaning depends somewhat on lines 40-42, which
Johnson thought were spoken as an aside.

54. **qualities**, characteristics. 60. **approves**, cor-
roborates.
Scene ii. 11. **banquet**, dessert.

Char. Good sir, give me good fortune.

Sooth. I make not, but foresee.

Char. Pray, then, foresee me one.

Sooth. You shall be yet far fairer than you
are.

Char. He means in flesh.

Iras. No, you shall paint when you are
old.

Char. Wrinkles forbid!

Alex. Vex not his prescience; be attentive.

Char. Hush! 21

Sooth. You shall be more beloving than
beloved.

Char. I had rather heat my liver with
drinking.

Alex. Nay, hear him.

Char. Good now, some excellent fortune!
Let me be married to three kings in a fore-
noon, and widow them all: let me have a
child at fifty, to whom Herod of Jewry may
do homage: find me to marry me with Octavius Cæsar, and companion me with my 30
mistress.

Sooth. You shall outlive the lady whom
you serve.

Char. O excellent! I love long life better
than figs.

Sooth. You have seen and proved a fairer
former fortune
Than that which is to approach.

Char. Then belike my children shall have
no names: prithee, how many boys and
wenches must I have?

Sooth. If every of your wishes had a womb,
And fertile every wish, a million. 39

Char. Out, fool! I forgive thee for a
witch.

Alex. You think none but your sheets are
privy to your wishes.

Char. Nay, come, tell Iras hers.

Alex. We'll know all our fortunes.

Eno. Mine, and most of our fortunes, to-
night, shall be—drunk to bed.

Iras. There's a palm presages chastity, if
nothing else.

Char. E'en as the o'erflowing Nilus pre-
sageth famine. 50

Iras. Go, you wild bedfellow, you cannot
soothsay.

Char. Nay, if an oily palm be not a fruitful
prognostication, I cannot scratch mine ear.
Prithee, tell her but a worky-day fortune.

Sooth. Your fortunes are alike.

Iras. But how, but how? give me particulars.

Sooth. I have said.

Iras. Am I not an inch of fortune better
than she?

Char. Well, if you were but an inch of fortune better than I, where would you choose
it?

Iras. Not in my husband's nose. 63

Char. Our worser thoughts heavens mend!
Alexas,—come, his fortune, his fortune! O,
let him marry a woman that cannot go, sweet
Isis, I beseech thee! and let her die too, and
give him a worse! and let worse follow worse,
till the worst of all follow him laughing to his
grave, fifty-fold a cuckold! Good Isis, hear
me this prayer, though thou deny me a matter of more weight; good Isis, I beseech thee!

Iras. Amen. Dear goddess, hear that
prayer of the people! for, as it is a heart-
breaking to see a handsome man loose-wived,
so it is a deadly sorrow to behold a foul knave
uncuckolded: therefore, dear Isis, keep decorum, and fortune him accordingly!

Char. Amen. 79

Alex. Lo, now, if it lay in their hands to
make me a cuckold, they would make themselves whores, but they'ld do't!

Eno. Hush! here comes Antony.

Char. Not he; the queen.

Enter CLEOPATRA.

Cleo. Saw you my lord?

Eno. No, lady.

Cleo. Was he not here?

Char. No, madam. 85

Cleo. He was disposed to mirth; but on
the sudden
A Roman thought hath struck him. Enobarbus!

Eno. Madam?

23. **with drinking**, with wine rather than love. 28.
Herod of Jewry, the pattern of a blustering tyrant, so
presented in the mystery plays. She would like such a
son. 29. **find me**, by examining my hand. 32. **better
than figs**, probably a proverbial expression, although
no citations are forthcoming. Malone saw in this an
allusion to the asp in the basket of figs in Act V. Many
commentators interpret the soothsayer's words in terms
of the outcome of the play. 38. **every of**, every one of.
40. **I forgive . . . witch**, probably, I forgive thee because thou art a wizard; possibly, I have no opinion of
your powers as a soothsayer.

53. **oily palm**, sweaty or moist palm; indication of a
wanton disposition. 55. **worky-day**, ordinary. 67.
Isis, Egyptian goddess of earth and fertility. 87.
Roman thought. Schmidt explains as "a thought of
Rome"; possibly to be explained as "a thought of duty
and virtue."

Cleo. Seek him, and bring him hither.
Where's Alexas?

Alex. Here, at your service. My lord approaches.   90

Cleo. We will not look upon him: go with us.   [*Exeunt.*

Enter ANTONY *with a* Messenger *and*
Attendants.

Mess. Fulvia thy wife first came into the field.

Ant. Against my brother Lucius?

Mess. Ay:
But soon that war had end, and the time's state
Made friends of them, jointing their force
'gainst Cæsar;
Whose better issue in the war, from Italy,
Upon the first encounter, drave them.

Ant.   Well, what worst?

Mess. The nature of bad news infects the teller.

Ant. When it concerns the fool or coward.
On: 100
Things that are past are done with me. 'Tis thus;
Who tells me true, though in his tale lie death,
I hear him as he flatter'd.

Mess.   Labienus—
This is stiff news—hath, with his Parthian force,
Extended Asia from Euphrates;
His conquering banner shook from Syria
To Lydia and to Ionia;
Whilst—

Ant.   Antony, thou wouldst say,—

Mess.   O, my lord!

Ant. Speak to me home, mince not the general tongue:
Name Cleopatra as she is call'd in Rome;   110
Rail thou in Fulvia's phrase; and taunt my faults
With such full license as both truth and malice
Have power to utter. O, then we bring forth weeds,
When our quick minds lie still; and our ills told us

Is as our earing. Fare thee well awhile.

Mess. At your noble pleasure.   [*Exit.*

Ant. From Sicyon, ho, the news! Speak there!

First Att. The man from Sicyon,—is there such an one?

Sec. Att. He stays upon your will.

Ant.   Let him appear.
These strong Egyptian fetters I must break,
Or lose myself in dotage.

Enter another Messenger.

What are you?   121

Sec. Mess. Fulvia thy wife is dead.

Ant.   Where died she?

Sec. Mess. In Sicyon:
Her length of sickness, with what else more serious
Importeth thee to know, this bears.
[*Gives a letter.*

Ant.   Forbear me.
[*Exit Sec. Messenger.*
There's a great spirit gone! Thus did I desire it:
What our contempt doth often hurl from us,
We wish it ours again; the present pleasure,
By revolution lowering, does become
The opposite of itself: she's good, being gone;
The hand could pluck her back that shoved her on.   131
I must from this enchanting queen break off:
Ten thousand harms, more than the ills I know,
My idleness doth hatch. How now! Enobarbus!

Re-enter ENOBARBUS.

Eno. What's your pleasure, sir?

Ant. I must with haste from hence.

Eno. Why, then, we kill all our women:
we see how mortal an unkindness is to them;
if they suffer our departure, death's the word.

Ant. I must be gone.   140

Eno. Under a compelling occasion, let
women die: it were pity to cast them away
for nothing; though, between them and a
great cause, they should be esteemed nothing. Cleopatra, catching but the least noise
of this, dies instantly; I have seen her die

96. jointing, uniting. 103. Labienus, emissary of
Brutus and Cassius to Orodes, king of Parthia; after
Philippi he became the commander of the Parthian
forces. 105. Extended, seized upon; legal phrase.
Euphrates, accented on first syllable. 109. general
tongue, common report. 111. Fulvia's phrase.
Plutarch says she was of a "peevish, crooked, and
troublesome nature." 114-115. our ills . . . earing,
telling us our faults improves us as plowing improves
land run to weeds. 117. Sicyon, ancient city of Greece.
125. Forbear me, leave me. 129. By revolution
lowering, growing worse by the revolution of time.
131. could, would be willing to.

twenty times upon far poorer moment: I do
think there is mettle in death, which commits some loving act upon her, she hath such
a celerity in dying.   149

Ant. She is cunning past man's thought.

Eno. Alack, sir, no; her passions are made
of nothing but the finest part of pure love: we
cannot call her winds and waters sighs and
tears; they are greater storms and tempests
than almanacs can report: this cannot be
cunning in her; if it be, she makes a shower
of rain as well as Jove.

Ant. Would I had never seen her!   158

Eno. O, sir, you had then left unseen a
wonderful piece of work; which not to have
been blest withal would have discredited
your travel.

Ant. Fulvia is dead.

Eno. Sir?

Ant. Fulvia is dead.

Eno. Fulvia!

Ant. Dead.   166

Eno. Why, sir, give the gods a thankful
sacrifice. When it pleaseth their deities to
take the wife of a man from him, it shows to
man the tailors of the earth; comforting
therein, that when old robes are worn out,
there are members to make new. If there
were no more women but Fulvia, then had
you indeed a cut, and the case to be lamented: this grief is crowned with consolation; your old smock brings forth a new
petticoat: and indeed the tears live in an
onion that should water this sorrow.   177

Ant. The business she hath broached in
    the state
Cannot endure my absence.

Eno. And the business you have broached
here cannot be without you; especially that
of Cleopatra's, which wholly depends on
your abode.   182

Ant. No more light answers. Let our
    officers
Have notice what we purpose. I shall break
The cause of our expedience to the queen,
And get her leave to part. For not alone
The death of Fulvia, with more urgent
    touches,

Do strongly speak to us; but the letters too
Of many our contriving friends in Rome
Petition us at home: Sextus Pompeius   190
Hath given the dare to Cæsar, and com-
    mands
The empire of the sea: our slippery people,
Whose love is never link'd to the deserver
Till his deserts are past, begin to throw
Pompey the Great and all his dignities
Upon his son; who, high in name and power,
Higher than both in blood and life, stands up
For the main soldier: whose quality, going
    on,
The sides o' the world may danger: much is
    breeding,   199
Which, like the courser's hair, hath yet but
    life,
And not a serpent's poison. Say, our pleas-
    ure,
To such whose place is under us, requires
Our quick remove from hence.

Eno. I shall do't.   [*Exeunt.*

SCENE III. *The same. Another room.*

Enter CLEOPATRA, CHARMIAN, IRAS, *and*
            ALEXAS.

Cleo. Where is he?

Char.   I did not see him since.

Cleo. See where he is, who's with him,
    what he does:
I did not send you: if you find him sad,
Say I am dancing; if in mirth, report
That I am sudden sick: quick, and return.
                              [*Exit Alexas.*

Char. Madam, methinks, if you did love
    him dearly,
You do not hold the method to enforce
The like from him.

Cleo.   What should I do, I do not?

Char. In each thing give him way, cross
    him in nothing.

Cleo. Thou teachest like a fool; the way to
    lose him.   10

Char. Tempt him not so too far; I wish,
    forbear:

146. upon . . . moment, for less important reasons.
150. cunning, clever in dissembling. 169-172. it shows
. . . new. Many explanations of this obscure passage;
Johnson's is as good as any: "It shows man the tailors of
the earth comforting him in this . . . that the deities have
made other women to take her place." *Members* may,
however, mean "persons." 175. smock, woman's inner
garment. 182. abode, staying. 185. expedience,
expedition, or haste. 187. urgent touches, pressing
feelings or motives.

189. Of . . . friends, many friends working in our
interest. 190. Petition us at home, i.e., to come home.
Sextus Pompeius, son of Pompey the Great and now
leader of the party opposed to Cæsar. 194-196. throw
. . . Upon, bestow . . . upon. 197. blood and life,
mettle and vitality. 198. main, principal. quality,
nature and condition, or possibly, soldiership. 199.
sides, frame. danger, endanger. 200. like . . . hair,
allusion to the popular belief that a horsehair put into
water will turn to a snake.
Scene iii. 8. like, same.

In time we hate that which we often fear.
But here comes Antony.

Enter ANTONY.

Cleo.   I am sick and sullen.
Ant. I am sorry to give breathing to my
    purpose,—
Cleo. Help me away, dear Charmian; I
    shall fall:
It cannot be thus long, the sides of nature
Will not sustain it.
Ant.   Now, my dearest queen,—
Cleo. Pray you, stand farther from me.
Ant.   What's the matter?
Cleo. I know, by that same eye, there's
    some good news.   19
What says the married woman? You may
    go:
Would she had never given you leave to
    come!
Let her not say 'tis I that keep you here:
I have no power upon you; hers you are.
Ant. The gods best know,—
Cleo.   O, never was there queen
So mightily betray'd! yet at the first
I saw the treasons planted.
Ant.   Cleopatra,—
Cleo. Why should I think you can be
    mine and true,
Though you in swearing shake the thronèd
    gods,
Who have been false to Fulvia? Riotous
    madness,
To be entangled with those mouth-made
    vows,
Which break themselves in swearing!
Ant.   Most sweet queen,—   31
Cleo. Nay, pray you, seek no colour for
    your going,
But bid farewell, and go: when you sued
    staying,
Then was the time for words: no going then;
Eternity was in our lips and eyes,
Bliss in our brows' bent; none our parts so
    poor,
But was a race of heaven: they are so still,
Or thou, the greatest soldier of the world,
Art turn'd the greatest liar.

Ant.   How now, lady!
Cleo. I would I had thy inches; thou
    shouldst know   40
There were a heart in Egypt.
Ant.   Hear me, queen:
The strong necessity of time commands
Our services awhile; but my full heart
Remains in use with you. Our Italy
Shines o'er with civil swords: Sextus Pom-
    peius
Makes his approaches to the port of Rome:
Equality of two domestic powers
Breed scrupulous faction: the hated, grown
    to strength,
Are newly grown to love: the condemn'd
    Pompey,
Rich in his father's honour, creeps apace   50
Into the hearts of such as have not thrived
Upon the present state, whose numbers
    threaten;
And quietness, grown sick of rest, would
    purge
By any desperate change: my more particu-
    lar,
And that which most with you should safe
    my going,
Is Fulvia's death.
Cleo. Though age from folly could not
    give me freedom,
It does from childishness: can Fulvia die?
Ant. She's dead, my queen:
Look here, and at thy sovereign leisure read 60
The garboils she awaked; at the last, best:
See when and where she died.
Cleo.   O most false love!
Where be the sacred vials thou shouldst fill
With sorrowful water? Now I see, I see,
In Fulvia's death, how mine received shall
    be.
Ant. Quarrel no more, but be prepared to
    know
The purposes I bear; which are, or cease,
As you shall give the advice. By the fire
That quickens Nilus' slime, I go from hence
Thy soldier, servant; making peace or war 70
As thou affect'st.
Cleo.   Cut my lace, Charmian, come;
But let it be: I am quickly ill, and well,

---

14. **breathing**, utterance. 16. **sides of nature**, i.e., her body cannot contain her swelling heart, and she will die. Enobarbus has already borne testimony to her use of this device. 20. **married woman**, i.e., Fulvia. 26. **planted**, probably in the gardener's sense. 37. **race of heaven**, of heavenly origin; defined also as "smack or flavor of heaven."

44. **in use**, i.e., in usufruct, for use. 48. **scrupulous**, cautious, or carping. **faction**, dissension, party strife. 53. **purge**, be restored to activity (as by medicinal purgation). 54. **particular**, personal affair. 55. **safe**, make safe. 61. **garboils**, disturbances, commotions. 63. **sacred vials**, alluding to the supposed custom of the Romans of putting bottles filled with tears in the graves of the departed.

So Antony loves.

Ant.   My precious queen, forbear;
And give true evidence to his love, which
     stands
An honourable trial.

Cleo.   So Fulvia told me.
I prithee, turn aside and weep for her;
Then bid adieu to me, and say the tears
Belong to Egypt: good now, play one scene
Of excellent dissembling; and let it look
Like perfect honour.

Ant.   You'll heat my blood: no more. 80

Cleo. You can do better yet; but this is
     meetly.

Ant. Now, by my sword,—

Cleo.   And target. Still he mends;
But this is not the best. Look, prithee,
     Charmian,
How this Herculean Roman does become
The carriage of his chafe.

Ant. I'll leave you, lady.

Cleo.   Courteous lord, one word.
Sir, you and I must part, but that's not
     it:
Sir, you and I have loved, but there's not it;
That you know well: something it is I
     would,—
O, my oblivion is a very Antony,   90
And I am all forgotten.

Ant.   But that your royalty
Holds idleness your subject, I should take
     you
For idleness itself.

Cleo.   'Tis sweating labour
To bear such idleness so near the heart
As Cleopatra this. But, sir, forgive me;
Since my becomings kill me, when they do
     not
Eye well to you: your honour calls you hence;
Therefore be deaf to my unpitied folly,
And all the gods go with you! upon your
     sword
Sit laurel victory! and smooth success   100
Be strew'd before your feet!

Ant.   Let us go. Come;
Our separation so abides, and flies,

That thou, residing here, go'st yet with me,
And I, hence fleeting, here remain with thee.
Away!   [*Exeunt.*

SCENE IV. *Rome. Cæsar's house.*

Enter OCTAVIUS CÆSAR, *reading a letter,*
     LEPIDUS, *and their* Train.

Cæs. You may see, Lepidus, and hence-
     forth know,
It is not Cæsar's natural vice to hate
Our great competitor: from Alexandria
This is the news: he fishes, drinks, and
     wastes
The lamps of night in revel; is not more man-
     like
Than Cleopatra; nor the queen of Ptolemy
More womanly than he; hardly gave audi-
     ence, or
Vouchsafed to think he had partners: you
     shall find there
A man who is the abstract of all faults
That all men follow.

Lep.   I must not think there are   10
Evils enow to darken all his goodness:
His faults in him seem as the spots of heaven,
More fiery by night's blackness; hereditary,
Rather than purchased; what he cannot
     change,
Than what he chooses.

Cæs. You are too indulgent. Let us grant,
     it is not
Amiss to tumble on the bed of Ptolemy;
To give a kingdom for a mirth; to sit
And keep the turn of tippling with a slave;
To reel the streets at noon, and stand the
     buffet   20
With knaves that smell of sweat: say this
     becomes him,—
As his composure must be rare indeed
Whom these things cannot blemish,—yet
     must Antony
No way excuse his soils, when we do bear
So great weight in his lightness. If he fill'd
His vacancy with his voluptuousness,
Full surfeits, and the dryness of his bones,
Call on him for't: but to confound such time,

---

73. **So,** if only. 74. **evidence,** testimony, i.e., by
her behavior. 78. **Egypt,** the Queen of Egypt. 81.
meetly, fairly good. 82. **target,** shield. 84. **Herculean.** Antony claimed descent from Anton, son of Hercules. 84-85. **does . . . chafe,** lends grace to his angry
deportment. 90-91. **my oblivion . . . forgotten,** my
forgetful memory is like Antony, and, like him, has
forgotten my power over it. 91-92. **your royalty . . .
subject,** if you did not consciously employ trifling
(banter) to serve your royal purposes. 97. **Eye,** appear
to the eye.

Scene iv. 3. **competitor,** associate. 6. **Ptolemy,** allusion to Cleopatra's husband, her brother, whom she
was supposed to have poisoned. 9. **abstract,** epitome.
14. **purchased,** acquired. 20. **reel,** stagger along. 22.
composure, composition, temperament. 24. **soils,**
blemishes. 25. **lightness,** levity, with play on literal
meaning. 25-28. **If he . . . for't,** if he filled his idle
hours with voluptuousness, gluttony, and the ruin of
his health, let him pay for it. 28. **confound,** waste.

That drums him from his sport, and speaks
  as loud
As his own state and ours,—'tis to be chid 30
As we rate boys, who, being mature in know-
  ledge,
Pawn their experience to their present
  pleasure,
And so rebel to judgement.

Enter a Messenger.

Lep.   Here's more news.
  Mess. Thy biddings have been done; and
    every hour,
Most noble Cæsar, shalt thou have report
How 'tis abroad. Pompey is strong at sea;
And it appears he is beloved of those
That only have fear'd Cæsar: to the ports
The discontents repair, and men's reports 39
Give him much wrong'd.
  Cæs.   I should have known no less.
It hath been taught us from the primal state,
That he which is was wish'd until he were;
And the ebb'd man, ne'er loved till ne'er
  worth love,
Comes dear'd by being lack'd. This common
  body,
Like to a vagabond flag upon the stream,
Goes to and back, lackeying the varying tide,
To rot itself with motion.
  Mess.   Cæsar, I bring thee word,
Menecrates and Menas, famous pirates,
Make the sea serve them, which they ear
  and wound
With keels of every kind: many hot inroads 50
They make in Italy; the borders maritime
Lack blood to think on 't, and flush youth
  revolt:
No vessel can peep forth, but 'tis as soon
Taken as seen; for Pompey's name strikes
  more
Than could his war resisted.
  Cæs.   Antony,
Leave thy lascivious wassails. When thou
  once
Wast beaten from Modena, where thou
  slew'st
Hirtius and Pansa, consuls, at thy heel

Did famine follow; whom thou fought'st
  against,
Though daintily brought up, with patience
  more   60
Than savages could suffer: thou didst drink
The stale of horses, and the gilded puddle
Which beasts would cough at: thy palate
  then did deign
The roughest berry on the rudest hedge;
Yea, like the stag, when snow the pasture
  sheets,
The barks of trees thou browsed'st; on the
  Alps
It is reported thou didst eat strange flesh,
Which some did die to look on: and all
  this—
It wounds thine honour that I speak it now—
Was borne so like a soldier, that thy cheek 70
So much as lank'd not.
  Lep.   'Tis pity of him.
  Cæs. Let his shames quickly
Drive him to Rome: 'tis time we twain
Did show ourselves i' the field; and to that
  end
Assemble we immediate council: Pompey
Thrives in our idleness.
  Lep.   To-morrow, Cæsar,
I shall be furnish'd to inform you rightly
Both what by sea and land I can be able
To front this present time.
  Cæs.   Till which encounter,
It is my business too. Farewell.   80
  Lep. Farewell, my lord: what you shall
    know meantime
Of stirs abroad, I shall beseech you, sir,
To let me be partaker.
  Cæs.   Doubt not, sir;
I knew it for my bond.   [*Exeunt.*

SCENE V. *Alexandria. Cleopatra's palace.*

Enter CLEOPATRA, CHARMIAN, IRAS, *and*
    MARDIAN.

  Cleo. Charmian!
  Char. Madam?
  Cleo. Ha, ha!
Give me to drink mandragora.
  Char.   Why, madam?
  Cleo. That I might sleep out this great
    gap of time

My Antony is away.

Char.　　　　You think of him too much.

Cleo. O, 'tis treason!

Char.　　　　　Madam, I trust, not so.

Cleo. Thou, eunuch Mardian!

Mar.　　What's your highness' pleasure?

Cleo. Not now to hear thee sing; I take no
　pleasure
In aught an eunuch has: 'tis well for thee, 10
That, being unseminar'd, thy freer thoughts
May not fly forth of Egypt. Hast thou affec-
　tions?

Mar. Yes, gracious madam.

Cleo. Indeed!

Mar. Not in deed, madam; for I can do
　nothing
But what indeed is honest to be done:
Yet have I fierce affections, and think
What Venus did with Mars.

Cleo.　　　　　O Charmian,
Where think'st thou he is now? Stands he,
　or sits he?
Or does he walk? or is he on his horse?　　20
O happy horse, to bear the weight of Antony!
Do bravely, horse! for wot'st thou whom
　thou movest?
The demi-Atlas of this earth, the arm
And burgonet of men. He's speaking now,
Or murmuring 'Where's my serpent of old
　Nile?'
For so he calls me: now I feed myself
With most delicious poison. Think on me,
That am with Phœbus' amorous pinches
　black,
And wrinkled deep in time? Broad-fronted
　Cæsar,
When thou wast here above the ground, I
　was　　30
A morsel for a monarch: and great Pompey
Would stand and make his eyes grow in my
　brow;
There would he anchor his aspect and die
With looking on his life.

Enter ALEXAS.

Alex.　　　　Sovereign of Egypt, hail!

Cleo. How much unlike art thou Mark
　Antony!
Yet, coming from him, that great medicine
　hath

With his tinct gilded thee.
How goes it with my brave Mark Antony?

Alex. Last thing he did, dear queen,
He kiss'd,—the last of many doubled kis-
　ses,—　　　　　　　　　　　　　　40
This orient pearl. His speech sticks in my
　heart.

Cleo. Mine ear must pluck it thence.

Alex.　　　　　'Good friend,' quoth he,
'Say, the firm Roman to great Egypt sends
This treasure of an oyster; at whose foot,
To mend the petty present, I will piece
Her opulent throne with kingdoms; all the
　east,
Say thou, shall call her mistress.' So he
　nodded,
†And soberly did mount an arm-gaunt steed,
Who neigh'd so high, that what I would
　have spoke
Was beastly dumb'd by him.

Cleo.　　　　What, was he sad or merry? 50

Alex. Like to the time o' the year between
　the extremes
Of hot and cold, he was nor sad nor merry.

Cleo. O well-divided disposition! Note
　him,
Note him, good Charmian, 'tis the man; but
　note him:
He was not sad, for he would shine on those
That make their looks by his; he was not
　merry,
Which seem'd to tell them his remembrance
　lay
In Egypt with his joy; but between both:
O heavenly mingle! Be'st thou sad or merry,
The violence of either thee becomes,　　60
So does it no man else. Met'st thou my
　posts?

Alex. Ay, madam, twenty several mes-
　sengers:
Why do you send so thick?

Cleo.　　　　Who's born that day
When I forget to send to Antony,
Shall die a beggar. Ink and paper, Char-
　mian.
Welcome, my good Alexas. Did I, Char-
　mian,
Ever love Cæsar so?

Char.　　　　　O that brave Cæsar!

Cleo. Be choked with such another em-
　phasis!

---

11. **unseminar'd**, deprived of virility.　22. **wot'st,**
knowest.　23. **demi-Atlas.** She disregards Lepidus
as a triumvir.　24. **burgonet,** light casque or steel cap.
29. **Cæsar,** Julius Cæsar.　33. **aspect,** look, glance.
36. **medicine,** drug, elixir; possibly, physician.

37. **tinct,** color.　48. **arm-gaunt,** gaunt from bearing
arms in warlike service, or with gaunt limbs; many
emendations.　50. **dumb'd,** silenced.　62. **several,**
separate.

Say, the brave Antony.
 Char.   The valiant Cæsar!
 Cleo. By Isis, I will give thee bloody
  teeth,   70
If thou with Cæsar paragon again
My man of men.
 Char. By your most gracious pardon,
I sing but after you.
 Cleo.   My salad days,
When I was green in judgement: cold in
  blood,
To say as I said then! But, come, away;
Get me ink and paper:
He shall have every day a several greeting,
Or I'll unpeople Egypt.   [*Exeunt.*

ACT II.

Scene I. *Messina. Pompey's house.*

Enter Pompey, Menecrates, *and* Menas,
 in warlike manner.

 Pom. If the great gods be just, they shall
  assist
The deeds of justest men.
 Mene.   Know, worthy Pompey,
That what they do delay, they not deny.
 Pom. Whiles we are suitors to their
  throne, decays
The thing we sue for.
 Mene. We, ignorant of ourselves,
Beg often our own harms, which the wise
  powers
Deny us for our good; so find we profit
By losing of our prayers.
 Pom.   I shall do well:
The people love me, and the sea is mine;
My powers are crescent, and my auguring
  hope
Says it will come to the full. Mark Antony 11
In Egypt sits at dinner, and will make
No wars without doors: Cæsar gets money
  where
He loses hearts: Lepidus flatters both,
Of both is flatter'd; but he neither loves,
Nor either cares for him.

 Men.   Cæsar and Lepidus
Are in the field: a mighty strength they
  carry.
 Pom. Where have you this? 'tis false.
 Men.   From Silvius, sir.
 Pom. He dreams: I know they are in
  Rome together,
Looking for Antony. But all the charms of
  love,   20
Salt Cleopatra, soften thy waned lip!
Let witchcraft join with beauty, lust with
  both!
Tie up the libertine in a field of feasts,
Keep his brain fuming; Epicurean cooks
Sharpen with cloyless sauce his appetite;
That sleep and feeding may prorogue his
  honour
Even till a Lethe'd dulness!

Enter Varrius.

        How now, Varrius!
 Var. This is most certain that I shall de-
  liver:
Mark Antony is every hour in Rome
Expected: since he went from Egypt 'tis 30
A space for further travel.
 Pom. I could have given less matter
A better ear. Menas, I did not think
This amorous surfeiter would have donn'd
  his helm
For such a petty war: his soldiership
Is twice the other twain: but let us rear
The higher our opinion, that our stirring
Can from the lap of Egypt's widow pluck
The ne'er-lust-wearied Antony.
 Men.   I cannot hope
Cæsar and Antony shall well greet together:
His wife that's dead did trespasses to Cæsar;
His brother warr'd upon him; although, I
  think,   41
Not moved by Antony.
 Pom.   I know not, Menas,
How lesser enmities may give way to greater.
Were't not that we stand up against them
  all,
'Twere pregnant they should square between
  themselves;

---

71. **paragon**, compare on equal terms. 73-75. **My salad . . . then!** The F punctuation puts a comma after *judgement* instead of a colon. This is correct from the simple fact that hot and dry, not cold and wet (*green*), represent the elementary condition of judgment. She means to say that she spoke as she did then because she was in her salad days, when her judgment was green and her blood cold.
Act II. Scene i. 10. **crescent**, on the increase. **auguring**, prophesying.

21. **Salt**, wanton. **waned**, faded, withered. 23. **Tie up . . . feasts**, probably, as an animal might be staked out in a rich pasture. 25. **cloyless**, which will not satiate. 26. **prorogue**, defer the operation of. 27. **Lethe'd**, oblivious. 31. **space**, time enough. 36. **opinion**, of ourselves. 37. **Egypt's widow**, Cleopatra, widow of the young king Ptolemy. 41. **His brother**, Lucius Antonius. **warr'd**; so F₂; F: *wan'd*. 45. **pregnant**, very probable. **square**, quarrel, or fight.

For they have entertained cause enough
To draw their swords: but how the fear of us
May cement their divisions and bind up
The petty difference, we yet not know.
Be't as our gods will have 't! It only stands
Our lives upon to use our strongest hands. 51
Come, Menas.　　　　　　　　　*[Exeunt.*

SCENE II. *Rome. The house of Lepidus.*

Enter ENOBARBUS *and* LEPIDUS.

Lep. Good Enobarbus, 'tis a worthy deed,
And shall become you well, to entreat your
　　captain
To soft and gentle speech.
　　Eno.　　　　　I shall entreat him
To answer like himself: if Cæsar move him,
Let Antony look over Cæsar's head
And speak as loud as Mars. By Jupiter,
Were I the wearer of Antonius' beard,
I would not shave 't to-day.
　　Lep.　　　　　　'Tis not a time
For private stomaching.
　　Eno.　　　　　Every time　　　9
Serves for the matter that is then born in 't.
　　Lep. But small to greater matters must
　　give way.
　　Eno. Not if the small come first.
　　Lep.　　　　Your speech is passion:
But, pray you, stir no embers up. Here
　　comes
The noble Antony.

Enter ANTONY *and* VENTIDIUS.

　　Eno.　　　　And yonder, Cæsar.

Enter CÆSAR, MECÆNAS, *and* AGRIPPA.

　　Ant. If we compose well here, to Parthia:
Hark, Ventidius.
　　Cæs.　　　　I do not know,
Mecænas; ask Agrippa.
　　Lep.　　　　　Noble friends,
That which combined us was most great,
　　and let not
A leaner action rend us. What's amiss,
May it be gently heard: when we debate　20
Our trivial difference loud, we do commit

Murder in healing wounds: then, noble part-
　　ners,
The rather, for I earnestly beseech,
Touch you the sourest points with sweetest
　　terms,
Nor curstness grow to the matter.
　　Ant.　　　　　　'Tis spoken well.
Were we before our armies, and to fight,
I should do thus.　　　　　　*[Flourish.*
　　Cæs. Welcome to Rome.
　　Ant.　　　　　　Thank you.
　　Cæs.　　　　　　　　　Sit.
　　Ant.　　　　　　　　Sit, sir.
　　Cæs.　　　　　　　　Nay, then.
　　Ant. I learn, you take things ill which are
　　not so,
Or being, concern you not.
　　Cæs.　　　　　I must be laugh'd at, 30
If, or for nothing or a little, I
Should say myself offended, and with you
Chiefly i' the world; more laugh'd at, that I
　　should
Once name you derogately, when to sound
　　your name
It not concern'd me.
　　Ant.　　　My being in Egypt, Cæsar,
What was't to you?
　　Cæs. No more than my residing here at
　　Rome
Might be to you in Egypt: yet, if you there
Did practise on my state, your being in
　　Egypt
Might be my question.
　　Ant.　　　How intend you, practised? 40
　　Cæs. You may be pleased to catch at mine
　　intent
By what did here befal me. Your wife and
　　brother
Made wars upon me; and their contestation
Was theme for you, you were the word of war.
　　Ant. You do mistake your business; my
　　brother never
Did urge me in his act: I did inquire it;
And have my learning from some true re-
　　ports,
That drew their swords with you. Did he
　　not rather
Discredit my authority with yours;

50-51. It . . . upon, it solely and vitally concerns our
lives.
　Scene ii. 8. I would not shave 't. Since plucking
the beard was a symbolic act for starting a fight, this
means that, if he were Antony, he would not avoid a contest. 9. stomaching, giving way to resentment. 15.
compose, come to an agreement. to Parthia, I shall
go to Parthia.

25. curstness, ill-humor. grow to, be added to (the
real business). 34. derogately, disparagingly. 39.
practise on, plot or intrigue against. 40. question,
business. 44. theme for you, had you for theme, or
supplied you with a ground for your intrigues (Cuningham). 46. urge me . . . act, claim that he was fighting
in my behalf. inquire, inquire into.

And make the wars alike against my
　　stomach,　　　　　　　　　　　　50
Having alike your cause? Of this my letters
Before did satisfy you. If you'll patch a
　　quarrel,
As matter whole you have not to make it
　　with,
It must not be with this.

　　Cæs.　　　　　　　　You praise yourself
By laying defects of judgement to me; but
You patch'd up your excuses.

　　Ant.　　　　　　　　　Not so, not so;
I know you could not lack, I am certain on 't,
Very necessity of this thought, that I,
Your partner in the cause 'gainst which he
　　fought,
Could not with graceful eyes attend those
　　wars
Which fronted mine own peace. As for my
　　wife,　　　　　　　　　　　　　61
I would you had her spirit in such another:
The third o' the world is yours; which with a
　　snaffle
You may pace easy, but not such a wife.

　　Eno. Would we had all such wives, that
the men might go to wars with the women!

　　Ant. So much uncurbable, her garboils,
　　Cæsar,
Made out of her impatience, which not
　　wanted
Shrewdness of policy too, I grieving grant
Did you too much disquiet: for that you must
But say, I could not help it.

　　Cæs.　　　　　　　I wrote to you　　71
When rioting in Alexandria; you
Did pocket up my letters, and with taunts
Did gibe my missive out of audience.

　　Ant.　　　　　　　　　　　　Sir,
He fell upon me ere admitted: then
Three kings I had newly feasted, and did
　　want
Of what I was i' the morning: but next day
I told him of myself; which was as much
As to have ask'd him pardon. Let this fellow
Be nothing of our strife; if we contend,　　80
Out of our question wipe him.

　　Cæs.　　　　　　　You have broken
The article of your oath; which you shall
　　never

Have tongue to charge me with.

　　Lep.　　　　　　　　　Soft, Cæsar!

　　Ant.　　　　　　　　　　　　No,
Lepidus, let him speak:
The honour is sacred which he talks on now,
Supposing that I lack'd it. But, on, Cæsar;
The article of my oath.

　　Cæs. To lend me arms and aid when I
　　required them;
The which you both denied.

　　Ant.　　　　　　　Neglected, rather;
And then when poison'd hours had bound me
　　up　　　　　　　　　　　　　　90
From mine own knowledge. As nearly as I
　　may,
I'll play the penitent to you: but mine
　　honesty
Shall not make poor my greatness, nor my
　　power
Work without it. Truth is, that Fulvia,
To have me out of Egypt, made wars here;
For which myself, the ignorant motive, do
So far ask pardon as befits mine honour
To stoop in such a case.

　　Lep.　　　　　　　　'Tis noble spoken.

　　Mec. If it might please you, to enforce no
　　further
The griefs between ye: to forget them quite
Were to remember that the present need　　101
Speaks to atone you.

　　Lep.　　　　　Worthily spoken, Mecænas.

　　Eno. Or, if you borrow one another's love
for the instant, you may, when you hear no
more words of Pompey, return it again: you
shall have time to wrangle in when you have
nothing else to do.

　　Ant. Thou art a soldier only: speak no
　　more.

　　Eno. That truth should be silent I had
almost forgot.　　　　　　　　　　　110

　　Ant. You wrong this presence; therefore
speak no more.

　　Eno. Go to, then; your considerate stone.

　　Cæs. I do not much dislike the matter, but
The manner of his speech: for 't cannot be
We shall remain in friendship, our conditions
So differing in their acts. Yet, if I knew
What hoop should hold us stanch, from edge
　　to edge
O' the world I would pursue it.

　　Agr.　　　　　Give me leave, Cæsar,—

50. **stomach**, inclination. 51. **Having . . . cause**, I
having the same cause of resentment that you had. 52.
patch a quarrel, make a quarrel out of shreds and
patches, since you have no real ground. 60. **graceful
eyes attend**, regard favorably. 63-4. **which . . . wife**,
which you may put through its paces easily with a
snaffle-bit, but you cannot so control such a wife. 67.
garboils, brawls. 74. **missive**, messenger.

93-94. **my power . . . it.** He seems to mean that he
will not exert his power unless his greatness (*honour*) is
recognized as intact. 112. **your . . . stone**, I shall continue to reflect, but be as silent as a stone.

Cæs. Speak, Agrippa.

Agr. Thou hast a sister by the mother's side,　　　120
Admired Octavia: great Mark Antony
Is now a widower.

Cæs.　　　　Say not so, Agrippa:
If Cleopatra heard you, your reproof
Were well deserved of rashness.

Ant. I am not married, Cæsar: let me
hear Agrippa further speak.

Agr. To hold you in perpetual amity,
To make you brothers, and to knit your hearts
With an unslipping knot, take Antony
Octavia to his wife; whose beauty claims　130
No worse a husband than the best of men;
Whose virtue and whose general graces speak
That which none else can utter. By this marriage,
All little jealousies, which now seem great,
And all great fears, which now import their dangers,
Would then be nothing: truths would be tales,
Where now half tales be truths: her love to both
Would, each to other and all loves to both,
Draw after her. Pardon what I have spoke;
For 'tis a studied, not a present thought,　140
By duty ruminated.

Ant.　　　　Will Cæsar speak?

Cæs. Not till he hears how Antony is touch'd
With what is spoke already.

Ant.　　　　What power is in Agrippa,
If I would say, 'Agrippa, be it so,'
To make this good?

Cæs.　　　　The power of Cæsar, and
His power unto Octavia.

Ant.　　　　May I never
To this good purpose, that so fairly shows,
Dream of impediment! Let me have thy hand:
Further this act of grace; and from this hour
The heart of brothers govern in our loves　150
And sway our great designs!

Cæs.　　　　There is my hand.
A sister I bequeath you, whom no brother
Did ever love so dearly: let her live
To join our kingdoms and our hearts; and never

Fly off our loves again!

Lep.　　　　Happily, amen!

Ant. I did not think to draw my sword
'gainst Pompey;
For he hath laid strange courtesies and great
Of late upon me: I must thank him only,
Lest my remembrance suffer ill report;
At heel of that, defy him.

Lep.　　　　Time calls upon 's:
Of us must Pompey presently be sought,　161
Or else he seeks out us.

Ant.　　　　Where lies he?

Cæs. About the mount Misenum.

Ant. What is his strength by land?

Cæs. Great and increasing: but by sea
He is an absolute master.

Ant.　　　　So is the fame.
Would we had spoke together! Haste we for it:
Yet, ere we put ourselves in arms, dispatch we
The business we have talk'd of.

Cæs.　　　　With most gladness;
And do invite you to my sister's view,　170
Whither straight I'll lead you.

Ant.　　　　Let us, Lepidus,
Not lack your company.

Lep.　　　　Noble Antony,
Not sickness should detain me.

　　　[*Flourish. Exeunt Cæsar, Antony, and
　　　　　　　　　　　　　　Lepidus.*

Mec. Welcome from Egypt, sir.

Eno. Half the heart of Cæsar, worthy
Mecænas! My honourable friend, Agrippa!

Agr. Good Enobarbus!

Mec. We have cause to be glad that matters are so well digested. You stayed well by 't in Egypt.　　　180

Eno. Ay, sir; we did sleep day out of countenance, and made the night light with drinking.

Mec. Eight wild-boars roasted whole at a breakfast, and but twelve persons there; is this true?

Eno. This was but as a fly by an eagle: we had much more monstrous matter of feast, which worthily deserved noting.

Mec. She's a most triumphant lady, if report be square to her.　　　190

Eno. When she first met Mark Antony,

---

121. **Octavia**, full sister, not half-sister, of Octavius. 135. **import**, carry with them. 146. **unto**. over.

155. **Fly off . . . again**, desert each other again. 160. **At heel of**, immediately after. 166. **fame**, rumor, report. 170. **my sister's view**, to see my sister. 182. **light**, giddy and frivolous, with pun on the commoner meaning. 190. **square**, just.

she pursed up his heart, upon the river of
Cydnus.

Agr. There she appeared indeed; or my
reporter devised well for her.

Eno. I will tell you.
The barge she sat in, like a burnish'd throne,
Burn'd on the water: the poop was beaten
    gold;
Purple the sails, and so perfumed that
The winds were love-sick with them; the
    oars were silver,
Which to the tune of flutes kept stroke, and
    made   200
The water which they beat to follow faster,
As amorous of their strokes. For her own
    person,
It beggar'd all description: she did lie
In her pavilion—cloth-of-gold of tissue—
O'er-picturing that Venus where we see
The fancy outwork nature: on each side her
Stood pretty dimpled boys, like smiling
    Cupids,
With divers-colour'd fans, whose wind did
    seem
To glow the delicate cheeks which they did
    cool,
And what they undid did.

Agr.   O, rare for Antony! 210

Eno. Her gentlewomen, like the Nereides,
So many mermaids, tended her i' the eyes,
And made their bends adornings: at the
    helm
A seeming mermaid steers: the silken tackle
Swell with the touches of those flower-soft
    hands,
That yarely frame the office. From the barge
A strange invisible perfume hits the sense
Of the adjacent wharfs. The city cast
Her people out upon her; and Antony, 219
Enthroned i' the market-place, did sit alone,
Whistling to the air; which, but for vacancy,
Had gone to gaze on Cleopatra too
And made a gap in nature.

Agr.   Rare Egyptian!

Eno. Upon her landing, Antony sent to
    her,

Invited her to supper: she replied,
It should be better he became her guest;
Which she entreated: our courteous Antony,
Whom ne'er the word of 'No' woman heard
    speak,
Being barber'd ten times o'er, goes to the
    feast,
And for his ordinary pays his heart   230
For what his eyes eat only.

Agr.   Royal wench!
She made great Cæsar lay his sword to bed:
He plough'd her, and she cropp'd.

Eno.   I saw her once
Hop forty paces through the public street;
And having lost her breath, she spoke, and
    panted,
That she did make defect perfection,
And, breathless, power breathe forth.

Mec. Now Antony must leave her utterly.

Eno. Never; he will not:
Age cannot wither her, nor custom stale 240
Her infinite variety: other women cloy
The appetites they feed; but she makes
    hungry
Where most she satisfies: for vilest things
Become themselves in her; that the holy
    priests
Bless her when she is riggish.

Mec. If beauty, wisdom, modesty, can
    settle
The heart of Antony, Octavia is
A blessed lottery to him.

Agr.   Let us go.
Good Enobarbus, make yourself my guest 249
Whilst you abide here.

Eno. Humbly, sir, I thank you. [*Exeunt.*

SCENE III. *The same. Cæsar's house.*

Enter ANTONY, CÆSAR, OCTAVIA *between*
them, and Attendants.

Ant. The world and my great office will
    sometimes
Divide me from your bosom.

Octa.   All which time
Before the gods my knee shall bow my
    prayers
To them for you.

Ant.   Good night, sir. My Octavia,

192. **upon . . . Cydnus,** upon the banks of, or more
probably, on the river of Cydnus, by the spectacle described below. 204. **cloth-of-gold of tissue,** cloth
made of gold thread and silk woven together (Onions);
very obscure. Possibly there should be a comma after
gold. 205. **that Venus,** usually thought to refer to the
Venus Anadyomene of Apelles. 209. **glow,** cause to
glow. 212. **tended her i' the eyes,** waited in her
sight. 213. **made . . . adornings,** possibly, added to
their beauty by their obeisances; many interpretations.
216. **yarely,** nimbly, briskly. 218. **wharfs,** banks.

230. **ordinary,** meal, supper. 232. **Cæsar,** Julius
Cæsar, by whom Cleopatra had a son named Cæsarion.
245. **riggish,** wanton. 248. **lottery,** prize..

Read not my blemishes in the world's report:
I have not kept my square; but that to come
Shall be all done by the rule. Good night,
  dear lady.
Good night, sir.
    Cæs. Good night.
                  [Exeunt Cæsar and Octavia.

       Enter Soothsayer.

    Ant. Now, sirrah; you do wish yourself in
  Egypt?   10
    Sooth. Would I had never come from
  thence, nor you
Thither!
    Ant. If you can, your reason?
    Sooth.   I see it in
My motion, have it not in my tongue: but
  yet
Hie you to Egypt again.
    Ant.   Say to me,
Whose fortunes shall rise higher, Cæsar's or
  mine?
    Sooth. Cæsar's.
Therefore, O Antony, stay not by his side:
Thy demon, that's thy spirit which keeps
  thee, is
Noble, courageous, high, unmatchable,   20
Where Cæsar's is not; but, near him, thy
  angel
Becomes a fear, as being o'erpower'd: there-
  fore
Make space enough between you.
    Ant.   Speak this no more.
    Sooth. To none but thee; no more, but
  when to thee.
If thou dost play with him at any game,
Thou art sure to lose; and, of that natural
  luck,
He beats thee 'gainst the odds: thy lustre
  thickens,
When he shines by: I say again, thy spirit
Is all afraid to govern thee near him;
But, he away, 'tis noble.
    Ant.   Get thee gone: 30

Say to Ventidius I would speak with him:
                  [Exit Soothsayer.
He shall to Parthia. Be it art or hap,
He hath spoken true: the very dice obey
  him;
And in our sports my better cunning faints
Under his chance: if we draw lots, he speeds;
His cocks do win the battle still of mine,
When it is all to nought; and his quails ever
Beat mine, inhoop'd, at odds. I will to
  Egypt:
And though I make this marriage for my
  peace,
I' the east my pleasure lies.

       Enter Ventidius.

              O, come, Ventidius,   40
You must to Parthia: your commission's
  ready;
Follow me, and receive 't.   *[Exeunt.*

      Scene IV. *The same. A street.*

Enter Lepidus, Mecænas, *and* Agrippa.

    Lep. Trouble yourselves no further: pray
  you, hasten
Your generals after.
    Agr.   Sir, Mark Antony
Will e'en but kiss Octavia, and we'll follow.
    Lep. Till I shall see you in your soldier's
  dress,
Which will become you both, farewell.
    Mec.   We shall,
As I conceive the journey, be at the Mount
Before you, Lepidus.
    Lep.   Your way is shorter;
My purposes do draw me much about:
You'll win two days upon me.
    Mec. }
                    Sir, good success!
    Agr. }
    Lep. Farewell.   *[Exeunt.* 10

    Scene V. *Alexandria. Cleopatra's palace.*

    Enter Cleopatra, Charmian, Iras, *and*
               Alexas.

    Cleo. Give me some music; music, moody
  food

---

6. **kept my square,** kept within his duty. Shakespeare means Antony to be what is called good-hearted;
Antony is probably truly repentant, but unstable.
13-14. **in My motion,** probably refers to the motions of his spirits; might be rendered as "instinctively."
19. **demon,** guardian spirit, in accordance with the
doctrine that each of us is attended by a special angel, or
by two angels, a good and a bad. Macbeth declares his
genius is rebuked by that of Banquo as "Mark Antony's
was by Cæsar" (*Macbeth*, III, i, 54-57). This play and
Macbeth were probably written about the same time.
27. **thickens,** grows dim. 30. **he away, 'tis,** Pope's
emendation of F, *he alway 'tis.*

32. **hap,** accident, chance. 34. **cunning,** skill. 35.
chance, luck. **speeds,** wins. 38. **inhoop'd.** The birds
were inclosed in hoops to make them fight. **I will to
Egypt.** Antony makes a gambler's decision.
Scene iv. 6. **the Mount,** Mount Misenum.

Of us that trade in love.

Attend.   The music, ho!

Enter MARDIAN *the Eunuch.*

Cleo. Let it alone; let's to billiards: come,
    Charmian.

Char. My arm is sore; best play with
    Mardian.

Cleo. As well a woman with an eunuch
    play'd
As with a woman. Come, you'll play with
    me, sir?

Mar. As well as I can, madam.

Cleo. And when good will is show'd,
    though 't come too short,
The actor may plead pardon. I'll none now:
Give me mine angle; we'll to the river: there,
My music playing far off, I will betray   11
Tawny-finn'd fishes; my bended hook shall
    pierce
Their slimy jaws; and, as I draw them up,
I'll think them every one an Antony,
And say 'Ah, ha! you're caught.'

Char.   'Twas merry when
You wager'd on your angling; when your
    diver
Did hang a salt-fish on his hook, which he
With fervency drew up.

Cleo.   That time,—O times!—
I laugh'd him out of patience; and that night
I laugh'd him into patience: and next morn,
Ere the ninth hour, I drunk him to his bed;
Then put my tires and mantles on him,
    whilst   22
I wore his sword Philippan.

Enter a Messenger.

                        O, from Italy!
Ram thou thy fruitful tidings in mine ears,
That long time have been barren.

Mess.   Madam, madam,—

Cleo. Antonius dead!—If thou say so,
    villain,
Thou kill'st thy mistress: but well and free,
If thou so yield him, there is gold, and here
My bluest veins to kiss; a hand that kings
Have lipp'd, and trembled kissing.   30

Mess. First, madam, he is well.

Cleo.   Why, there's more gold.
But, sirrah, mark, we use
To say the dead are well: bring it to that,
The gold I give thee will I melt and pour
Down thy ill-uttering throat.

Mess. Good madam, hear me.

Cleo.   Well, go to, I will;
But there's no goodness in thy face: if
    Antony
Be free and healthful,—so tart a favour
To trumpet such good tidings! If not well,
Thou shouldst come like a Fury crown'd
    with snakes,   40
Not like a formal man.

Mess.   Will 't please you hear me?

Cleo. I have a mind to strike thee ere thou
    speak'st:
Yet, if thou say Antony lives, is well,
Or friends with Cæsar, or not captive to him,
I'll set thee in a shower of gold, and hail
Rich pearls upon thee.

Mess.   Madam, he's well.

Cleo.   Well said.

Mess. And friends with Cæsar.

Cleo.   Thou 'rt an honest man.

Mess. Cæsar and he are greater friends
    than ever.

Cleo. Make thee a fortune from me.

Mess.   But yet, madam,—

Cleo. I do not like 'But yet,' it does allay
The good precedence; fie upon 'But yet'!   51
'But yet' is as a gaoler to bring forth
Some monstrous malefactor. Prithee, friend,
Pour out the pack of matter to mine ear,
The good and bad together: he's friends with
    Cæsar;
In state of health thou say'st; and thou
    say'st free.

Mess. Free, madam! no; I made no such
    report:
He's bound unto Octavia.

Cleo.   For what good turn?

Mess. For the best turn i' the bed.

Cleo.   I am pale, Charmian.

Mess. Madam, he's married to Octavia.   60

Cleo. The most infectious pestilence upon
    thee!   [*Strikes him down.*

Mess. Good madam, patience.

Cleo.   What say you? Hence,
                        [*Strikes him again.*

3. **billiards.** There were no billiards in those days.
10. **angle,** rod and line. 17. **salt-fish . . . hook,** an
incident recorded in Plutarch; an ancient jest. 22.
tires, probably, headdresses, though it may be general
for "attire." 23. **Philippan,** apparently named for the
victory of Philippi.

32. **use,** are accustomed. 38. **tart a favour,** sour a
visage. 41. **formal man,** ordinary man, or in form of
man. 51. **good precedence,** the good news which
preceded it.

Horrible villain! or I'll spurn thine eyes
Like balls before me; I'll unhair thy head:
　　　　　[*She hales him up and down.*
Thou shalt be whipp'd with wire, and stew'd
　　in brine,
Smarting in lingering pickle.

Mess.　　　　　Gracious madam,
I that do bring the news made not the match.

Cleo. Say 'tis not so, a province I will
　　give thee,
And make thy fortunes proud: the blow thou
　　hadst
Shall make thy peace for moving me to rage;
And I will boot thee with what gift beside 71
Thy modesty can beg.

Mess.　　　　　He's married, madam.

Cleo. Rogue, thou hast lived too long.
　　　　　[*Draws a knife.*

Mess.　　　　　Nay, then I'll run.
What mean you, madam? I have made no
　　fault.　　　　　[*Exit.*

Char. Good madam, keep yourself within
　　yourself:
The man is innocent.

Cleo. Some innocents 'scape not the
　　thunderbolt.
Melt Egypt into Nile! and kindly creatures
Turn all to serpents! Call the slave again: 79
Though I am mad, I will not bite him: call.

Char. He is afeard to come.

Cleo.　　　　　I will not hurt him.
　　　　　[*Exit Charmian.*
These hands do lack nobility, that they strike
A meaner than myself; since I myself
Have given myself the cause.

Re-enter CHARMIAN *and* Messenger.

　　　　　Come hither, sir.
Though it be honest, it is never good
To bring bad news: give to a gracious message
An host of tongues: but let ill tidings tell
Themselves when they be felt.

Mess.　　　　　I have done my duty.

Cleo. Is he married?
I cannot hate thee worser than I do,　　90
If thou again say 'Yes.'

Mess.　　　　　He's married, madam.

Cleo. The gods confound thee! dost thou
　　hold there still?

Mess. Should I lie, madam?

Cleo.　　　　　O, I would thou didst,
So half my Egypt were submerged and made
A cistern for scaled snakes! Go, get thee
　　hence:
Hadst thou Narcissus in thy face, to me
Thou wouldst appear most ugly. He is
　　married?

Mess. I crave your highness' pardon.

Cleo.　　　　　He is married?

Mess. Take no offence that I would not
　　offend you:
To punish me for what you make me do　100
Seems much unequal: he's married to
　　Octavia.

Cleo. O, that his fault should make a
　　knave of thee,
That art not what thou'rt sure of! Get thee
　　hence:
The merchandise which thou hast brought
　　from Rome
Are all too dear for me: lie they upon thy
　　hand,
And be undone by 'em! [*Exit Messenger.*

Char.　　　　　Good your highness, patience.

Cleo. In praising Antony, I have dis-
　　praised Cæsar.

Char. Many times, madam.

Cleo.　　　　　I am paid for't now.
Lead me from hence;
I faint: O Iras, Charmian! 'tis no matter.　110
Go to the fellow, good Alexas; bid him
Report the feature of Octavia, her years,
Her inclination, let him not leave out
The colour of her hair: bring me word quick-
　　ly.　　　　　[*Exit Alexas.*
Let him for ever go:—let him not—Char-
　　mian,
Though he be painted one way like a Gorgon,
The other way's a Mars. Bid you Alexas
　　　　　[*To Mardian.*
Bring me word how tall she is. Pity me,
　　Charmian,
But do not speak to me. Lead me to my
　　chamber.　　　　　[*Exeunt.*

---

96. **Narcissus**, a pattern of beauty. 101. **unequal**, unjust. 103. **That art . . . of!** Many interpretations and conjectures; Cuningham: that art not thyself the thing of which thou art so hatefully positive; Gollancz: that art not the evil thing of which thou art so certain. Cuningham suggests *act* for *art*, which would indicate that Cleopatra had in mind the censure of Antony, which appears again in line 107. 112. **feature**, shape or form of body. 113. **inclination**, disposition. 116-117. **Though he . . . Mars.** This alludes to a type of picture known as a perspective, which shows different objects when looked at from different points of view.

71. **boot thee with**, give thee into the bargain. 77. **Some . . . thunderbolt.** The gods usually do not smite the innocent (see *King Lear*, III, ii, 49-59). 83-84. **since . . . cause**, since I myself (in striking an inferior) am the real offender who has deserved the blows.

SCENE VI. *Near Misenum.*

Flourish. Enter POMPEY *and* MENAS *at one side, with drum and trumpet: at another,* CÆSAR, ANTONY, LEPIDUS, ENOBARBUS, MECÆNAS, *with* Soldiers *marching.*

Pom. Your hostages I have, so have you mine;
And we shall talk before we fight.
Cæs.   Most meet
That first we come to words; and therefore have we
Our written purposes before us sent;
Which, if thou hast consider'd, let us know
If 'twill tie up thy discontented sword,
And carry back to Sicily much tall youth
That else must perish here.
Pom.   To you all three,
The senators alone of this great world,
Chief factors for the gods, I do not know   10
Wherefore my father should revengers want,
Having a son and friends; since Julius Cæsar,
Who at Philippi the good Brutus ghosted,
There saw you labouring for him. What was't
That moved pale Cassius to conspire; and what
Made the all-honour'd, honest Roman, Brutus,
With the arm'd rest, courtiers of beauteous freedom,
To drench the Capitol; but that they would
Have one man but a man? And that is it   19
Hath made me rig my navy; at whose burthen
The anger'd ocean foams; with which I meant
To scourge the ingratitude that despiteful Rome
Cast on my noble father.
Cæs.   Take your time.
Ant. Thou canst not fear us, Pompey, with thy sails;
We'll speak with thee at sea: at land, thou know'st
How much we do o'er-count thee.
Pom.   At land, indeed,
Thou dost o'er-count me of my father's house:

But, since the cuckoo builds not for himself,
Remain in't as thou mayst.
Lep.   Be pleased to tell us—
For this is from the present—how you take   30
The offers we have sent you.
Cæs.   There's the point.
Ant. Which do not be entreated to, but weigh
What it is worth embraced.
Cæs.   And what may follow,
To try a larger fortune.
Pom.   You have made me offer
Of Sicily, Sardinia; and I must
Rid all the sea of pirates; then, to send
Measures of wheat to Rome; this 'greed upon,
To part with unhack'd edges, and bear back
Our targes undinted.
Cæs. Ant. Lep. That's our offer.
Pom.   Know, then,   40
I came before you here a man prepared
To take this offer: but Mark Antony
Put me to some impatience: though I lose
The praise of it by telling, you must know,
When Cæsar and your brother were at blows,
Your mother came to Sicily and did find
Her welcome friendly.
Ant.   I have heard it, Pompey;
And am well studied for a liberal thanks
Which I do owe you.
Pom.   Let me have your hand:
I did not think, sir, to have met you here.   50
Ant. The beds i' the east are soft; and thanks to you,
That call'd me timelier than my purpose hither;
For I have gain'd by't.
Cæs.   Since I saw you last,
There is a change upon you.
Pom.   Well, I know not
What counts harsh fortune casts upon my face;
But in my bosom shall she never come,
To make my heart her vassal.
Lep.   Well met here.
Pom. I hope so, Lepidus. Thus we are agreed:
I crave our composition may be written,
And seal'd between us.
Cæs.   That's the next to do.   60

---

7. **tall,** sturdy. 13. **ghosted,** haunted. 24. **fear,** cause to fear. 27. **Thou dost . . . house.** Plutarch informs us that Antony bought the elder Pompey's house at auction and later refused to pay for it; *o'er-count* has possibly the suggestion of cheating.

30. **from the present,** away from the business. 38. **edges,** swords. 39. **targes,** shields. 48. **well studied,** well prepared by thinking. 52. **timelier,** earlier. 55. **What counts . . . face.** The figure is from casting accounts or reckonings. 59. **composition,** agreement.

Pom. We'll feast each other ere we part;
and let's
Draw lots who shall begin.
Ant.   That will I, Pompey.
Pom. No, Antony, take the lot: but, first
Or last, your fine Egyptian cookery
Shall have the fame. I have heard that
Julius Cæsar
Grew fat with feasting there.
Ant.   You have heard much.
Pom. I have fair meanings, sir.
Ant.   And fair words to them.
Pom. Then so much have I heard:
And I have heard, Apollodorus carried—
Eno. No more of that: he did so.
Pom.   What, I pray you? 70
Eno. A certain queen to Cæsar in a mat-
tress.
Pom. I know thee now: how farest thou,
soldier?
Eno.   Well;
And well am like to do; for, I perceive,
Four feasts are toward.
Pom.   Let me shake thy hand;
I never hated thee: I have seen thee fight,
When I have envied thy behaviour.
Eno.   Sir,
I never loved you much; but I ha' praised ye,
When you have well deserved ten times as
much
As I have said you did.
Pom.   Enjoy thy plainness, 80
It nothing ill becomes thee.
Aboard my galley I invite you all:
Will you lead, lords?
Cæs. Ant. Lep. Show us the way, sir.
Pom.   Come.

        [*Exeunt all but Menas and Enobarbus.*
Men. [*Aside*] Thy father, Pompey, would
ne'er have made this treaty.—You and I
have known, sir.
Eno. At sea, I think.
Men. We have, sir.
Eno. You have done well by water.
Men. And you by land. 90
Eno. I will praise any man that will praise
me; though it cannot be denied what I have
done by land.
Men. Nor what I have done by water.

Eno. Yes, something you can deny for
your own safety: you have been a great thief
by sea.
Men. And you by land.
Eno. There I deny my land service. But
give me your hand, Menas: if our eyes had
authority, here they might take two thieves
kissing. 101
Men. All men's faces are true, whatsom-
e'er their hands are.
Eno. But there is never a fair woman has
a true face.
Men. No slander; they steal hearts.
Eno. We came hither to fight with you.
Men. For my part, I am sorry it is turned
to a drinking. Pompey doth this day laugh
away his fortune. 110
Eno. If he do, sure, he cannot weep 't back
again.
Men. You've said, sir. We looked not for
Mark Antony here: pray you, is he married
to Cleopatra?
Eno. Cæsar's sister is called Octavia.
Men. True, sir; she was the wife of Caius
Marcellus.
Eno. But she is now the wife of Marcus
Antonius.
Men. Pray ye, sir? 120
Eno. 'Tis true.
Men. Then is Cæsar and he for ever knit
together.
Eno. If I were bound to divine of this
unity, I would not prophesy so.
Men. I think the policy of that purpose
made more in the marriage than the love of
the parties.
Eno. I think so too. But you shall find,
the band that seems to tie their friendship
together will be the very strangler of their
amity: Octavia is of a holy, cold, and still
conversation. 131
Men. Who would not have his wife so?
Eno. Not he that himself is not so; which
is Mark Antony. He will to his Egyptian
dish again: then shall the sighs of Octavia
blow the fire up in Cæsar; and, as I said before, that which is the strength of their
amity shall prove the immediate author of
their variance. Antony will use his affection
where it is: he married but his occasion here.

69-71. **Apollodorus . . . mattress.** This alludes to a
tale told by Plutarch according to which Cleopatra had
herself done up in a mattress and carried secretly on the
shoulders of Apollodorus into a castle to meet Julius
Cæsar. 74. **toward**, about to occur. 86. **known,**
known each other.

120. **Pray ye**, are you in earnest? 124. **divine of**,
prophesy about. 129. **strangler**, destroyer. Later
folios have *stranger*, which Rowe changed to *estranger*.
131. **conversation**, behavior, manner of life. 140.
occasion, according to his personal interests.

Men. And thus it may be. Come, sir, will you aboard? I have a health for you.

Eno. I shall take it, sir: we have used our throats in Egypt.

Men. Come, let's away.   [*Exeunt.*

Scene VII. *On board Pompey's galley, off Misenum.*

Music plays. Enter two or three Servants *with a banquet.*

First Serv. Here they'll be, man. Some o' their plants are ill-rooted already; the least wind i' the world will blow them down.

Sec. Serv. Lepidus is high-coloured.

First Serv. They have made him drink alms-drink.

Sec. Serv. As they pinch one another by the disposition, he cries out 'No more;' reconciles them to his entreaty, and himself to the drink.

First Serv. But it raises the greater war between him and his discretion.   11

Sec. Serv. Why, this it is to have a name in great men's fellowship: I had as lief have a reed that will do me no service as a partisan I could not heave.

First Serv. To be called into a huge sphere, and not to be seen to move in 't, are the holes where eyes should be, which pitifully disaster the cheeks.

A sennet sounded. Enter Cæsar, Antony, Lepidus, Pompey, Agrippa, Mecænas, Enobarbus, Menas, *with other captains.*

Ant. [*To Cæsar*] Thus do they, sir: they take the flow o' the Nile   20
By certain scales i' the pyramid; they know,
By the height, the lowness, or the mean, if dearth
Or foison follow: the higher Nilus swells,

The more it promises: as it ebbs, the seedsman
Upon the slime and ooze scatters his grain,
And shortly comes to harvest.

Lep. You've strange serpents there.

Ant. Ay, Lepidus.

Lep. Your serpent of Egypt is bred now of your mud by the operation of your sun: so is your crocodile.   31

Ant. They are so.

Pom. Sit,—and some wine! A health to Lepidus!

Lep. I am not so well as I should be, but I'll ne'er out.

Eno. Not till you have slept; I fear me you'll be in till then.

Lep. Nay, certainly, I have heard the Ptolemies' pyramises are very goodly things; without contradiction, I have heard that.   41

Men. [*Aside to Pom.*] Pompey, a word.

Pom.   [*Aside to Men.*] Say in mine ear: what is 't?

Men. [*Aside to Pom.*] Forsake thy seat, I do beseech thee, captain,
And hear me speak a word.

Pom. [*Aside to Men.*] Forbear me till anon.
This wine for Lepidus!

Lep. What manner o' thing is your crocodile?

Ant. It is shaped, sir, like itself; and it is as broad as it hath breadth: it is just so high as it is, and moves with it own organs: it lives by that which nourisheth it; and the elements once out of it, it transmigrates.   51

Lep. What colour is it of?

Ant. Of it own colour too.

Lep. 'Tis a strange serpent.

Ant. 'Tis so. And the tears of it are wet.

Cæs. Will this description satisfy him?

Ant. With the health that Pompey gives him, else he is a very epicure.

Pom. [*Aside to Men.*] Go hang, sir, hang! Tell me of that? away!
Do as I bid you. Where's this cup I call'd for?

Men. [*Aside to Pom.*] If for the sake of merit thou wilt hear me,   61

Scene vii. *Stage Direction:* **banquet,** a course of the feast, probably, dessert. 2. **plants,** soles of the feet, with pun on usual sense. 6. **alms-drink.** Malone thought this meant his share and the others' too; more probably, the leavings, ordinarily saved for alms-people, besides his own share; Cuningham suggests "drinks taken as a work of charity, i.e., to further the reconciliation." 7. **pinch . . . disposition,** chafe one another, fall to bickering. Lepidus stops them but has to join them in fresh bumpers of drink. 14. **partisan,** long-bladed spear having one or more cutting edges, used by infantry. 18. **disaster,** disfigure; an astrological term following *sphere,* two lines above. 23. **foison,** plenty.

29. **Your,** colloquial use; not readily translatable. 36. **I'll ne'er out,** I'll never refuse a toast. 38. **in,** in for it; also, in drink. 40. **pyramises,** pyramids. 49. **it own,** its own, i.e., at its dissolution; the word *elements* may, however, mean "vital elements." 55. **tears,** allusion to the ancient belief that the crocodile wept over its victim before devouring it.

Rise from thy stool.

Pom. [*Aside to Men.*] I think thou'rt mad. The matter?   [*Rises, and walks aside.*

Men. I have ever held my cap off to thy fortunes.

Pom. Thou hast served me with much faith. What's else to say? Be jolly, lords.

Ant.   These quick-sands, Lepidus, Keep off them, for you sink.

Men. Wilt thou be lord of all the world?

Pom.   What say'st thou?

Men. Wilt thou be lord of the whole world? That's twice.

Pom. How should that be?

Men.   But entertain it, And, though thou think me poor, I am the man Will give thee all the world.

Pom.   Hast thou drunk well?   71

Men. No, Pompey, I have kept me from the cup. Thou art, if thou darest be, the earthly Jove: Whate'er the ocean pales, or sky inclips, Is thine, if thou wilt ha 't.

Pom.   Show me which way.

Men. These three world-sharers, these competitors, Are in thy vessel: let me cut the cable; And, when we are put off, fall to their throats: All there is thine.

Pom.   Ah, this thou shouldst have done, And not have spoke on 't! In me 'tis villany; In thee 't had been good service. Thou must know,   81 'Tis not my profit that does lead mine honour; Mine honour, it. Repent that e'er thy tongue Hath so betray'd thine act: being done unknown, I should have found it afterwards well done; But must condemn it now. Desist, and drink.

Men. [*Aside*] For this, I'll never follow thy pall'd fortunes more. Who seeks, and will not take when once 'tis offer'd, Shall never find it more.

Pom.   This health to Lepidus!   90

Ant. Bear him ashore. I'll pledge it for him, Pompey.

Eno. Here's to thee, Menas!

Men.   Enobarbus, welcome!

Pom. Fill till the cup be hid.

Eno. There's a strong fellow, Menas.
[*Pointing to the Attendant who carries off Lepidus.*

Men. Why?

Eno. A' bears the third part of the world, man; see'st not?

Men. The third part, then, is drunk: would it were all, That it might go on wheels!

Eno. Drink thou; increase the reels.   100

Men. Come.

Pom. This is not yet an Alexandrian feast.

Ant. It ripens towards it. Strike the vessels, ho! Here is to Cæsar!

Cæs.   I could well forbear 't. It's monstrous labour, when I wash my brain, And it grows fouler.

Ant.   Be a child o' the time.

Cæs. Possess it, I'll make answer: But I had rather fast from all four days Than drink so much in one.

Eno. Ha, my brave emperor!
[*To Antony.*
Shall we dance now the Egyptian Bacchanals, And celebrate our drink?

Pom.   Let's ha 't, good soldier.   111

Ant. Come, let's all take hands, Till that the conquering wine hath steep'd our sense In soft and delicate Lethe.

Eno.   All take hands. Make battery to our ears with the loud music: That while I'll place you: then the boy shall sing; The holding every man shall bear as loud As his strong sides can volley.
[*Music plays. Enobarbus places them hand in hand.*

THE SONG

Come, thou monarch of the vine,   120
Plumpy Bacchus with pink eyne!
In thy fats our cares be drown'd,

99. **go on wheels**, go fast or easily; proverbial. 100. **increase the reels**, increase the reeling and whirling of drunkenness. Steevens conjectured, *And grease the wheels*. 103. **Strike the vessels**, tap the casks; also explained as "clash your drinking vessels together." 105. **wash my brain**, drink copiously. 106. **And it grows.** F has *grow*, with which reading *And* would mean "if." 107. **Possess it**, have your way. 114. **Lethe**, forgetfulness. 117. **holding**, refrain, burden. 121. **pink eyne**, winking, half-shut eyes. 122. **fats**, vats, vessels.

63. **held my cap off**, been a faithful servant. 65. **quick-sands.** Lepidus probably collapses at this point. 74. **pales**, impales, fences in. **inclips**, embraces. 88. **pall'd**, decayed, waning.

With thy grapes our hairs be crown'd:
Cup us, till the world go round,
Cup us, till the world go round!

Cæs. What would you more? Pompey,
good night. Good brother,
Let me request you off: our graver business
Frowns at this levity. Gentle lords, let's
part;
You see we have burnt our cheeks: strong
Enobarb
Is weaker than the wine; and mine own
tongue
Splits what it speaks: the wild disguise hath
almost 131
Antick'd us all. What needs more words?
Good night.
Good Antony, your hand.
Pom. I'll try you on the shore.
Ant. And shall, sir: give 's your hand.
Pom. O Antony,
You have my father's house,—But, what?
we are friends.
Come, down into the boat.
Eno. Take heed you fall not.
[*Exeunt all but Enobarbus and Menas.*
Menas, I'll not on shore.
Men. No, to my cabin.
These drums! these trumpets, flutes! what!
Let Neptune hear we bid a loud farewell
To these great fellows: sound and be hang'd,
sound out! [*Sound a flourish, with drums.*
Eno. Ho! says a'. There's my cap. 141
Men. Ho! Noble captain, come. [*Exeunt.*

ACT III.

SCENE I. *A plain in Syria.*

Enter VENTIDIUS *as it were in triumph, with*
SILIUS, *and other* Romans, Officers, *and*
Soldiers; *the dead body of* PACORUS *borne
before him.*

Ven. Now, darting Parthia, art thou
struck; and now
Pleased fortune does of Marcus Crassus'
death

---

131. **disguise,** drunkenness. 132. **Antick'd,** made
like buffoons.
Act III. Scene i. 1. **darting Parthia,** Orodes, king
of Parthia. The Parthians were famous for archery and
for the Parthian dart which they discharged as they fled.
Pacorus was the son of Orodes. 2. **Marcus Crassus'
death.** Crassus, member of the first triumvirate with
Pompey and Julius Cæsar, was overthrown and treacher-
ously murdered by Orodes in B.C. 53.

Make me revenger. Bear the king's son's
body
Before our army. Thy Pacorus, Orodes,
Pays this for Marcus Crassus.
Sil. Noble Ventidius,
Whilst yet with Parthian blood thy sword is
warm,
The fugitive Parthians follow; spur through
Media,
Mesopotamia, and the shelters whither
The routed fly: so thy grand captain Antony
Shall set thee on triumphant chariots and 10
Put garlands on thy head.
Ven. O Silius, Silius,
I have done enough; a lower place, note well,
May make too great an act: for learn this,
Silius;
Better to leave undone, than by our deed
Acquire too high a fame when him we serve 's
away.
Cæsar and Antony have ever won
More in their officer than person: Sossius,
One of my place in Syria, his lieutenant,
For quick accumulation of renown,
Which he achieved by the minute, lost his
favour. 20
Who does i' the wars more than his captain
can
Becomes his captain's captain: and ambition,
The soldier's virtue, rather makes choice of
loss,
Than gain which darkens him.
I could do more to do Antonius good,
But 'twould offend him; and in his offence
Should my performance perish.
Sil. Thou hast, Ventidius, that
Without the which a soldier, and his sword,
Grants scarce distinction. Thou wilt write
to Antony?
Ven. I'll humbly signify what in his
name, 30
That magical word of war, we have effected;
How, with his banners and his well-paid
ranks,
The ne'er-yet-beaten horse of Parthia
We have jaded out o' the field.
Sil. Where is he now?
Ven. He purposeth to Athens: whither,
with what haste

---

12. **lower place,** i.e., one of lower rank. 20. **lost his
favour.** No authority has been discovered for this
somewhat improbable charge against Antony. 24.
darkens him, deprives him of luster or renown. 29.
Grants scarce distinction, can scarcely be distinguished. 34. **jaded,** driven exhausted, beaten.

The weight we must convey with 's will permit,
We shall appear before him. On, there; pass
along!   [*Exeunt.*

SCENE II. *Rome. An ante-chamber in
Cæsar's house.*

Enter AGRIPPA *at one door,* ENOBARBUS
at another.

Agr. What, are the brothers parted?
Eno. They have dispatch'd with Pompey,
he is gone;
The other three are sealing. Octavia weeps
To part from Rome; Cæsar is sad; and
Lepidus,
Since Pompey's feast, as Menas says, is
troubled
With the green sickness.
Agr.   'Tis a noble Lepidus.
Eno. A very fine one: O, how he loves
Cæsar!
Agr. Nay, but how dearly he adores Mark
Antony!
Eno. Cæsar? Why, he's the Jupiter of
men.
Agr. What's Antony? The god of Jupiter.
Eno. Spake you of Cæsar? How! the non-
pareil!   11
Agr. O Antony! O thou Arabian bird!
Eno. Would you praise Cæsar, say
'Cæsar:' go no further.
Agr. Indeed, he plied them both with ex-
cellent praises.
Eno. But he loves Cæsar best; yet he loves
Antony:
Ho! hearts, tongues, figures, scribes, bards,
poets, cannot
Think, speak, cast, write, sing, number, ho!
His love to Antony. But as for Cæsar,
Kneel down, kneel down, and wonder.
Agr.   Both he loves.
Eno. They are his shards, and he their
beetle. [*Trumpets within.*] So;   20
This is to horse. Adieu, noble Agrippa.

Agr. Good fortune, worthy soldier; and
farewell.

Enter CÆSAR, ANTONY, LEPIDUS, *and*
OCTAVIA.

Ant. No further, sir.
Cæs. You take from me a great part of
myself;
Use me well in 't. Sister, prove such a wife
As my thoughts make thee, and as my
farthest band
Shall pass on thy approof. Most noble
Antony,
Let not the piece of virtue, which is set
Betwixt us as the cement of our love,
To keep it builded, be the ram to batter 30
The fortress of it; for better might we
Have loved without this mean, if on both
parts
This be not cherish'd.
Ant.   Make me not offended
In your distrust.
Cæs.   I have said.
Ant.   You shall not find,
Though you be therein curious, the least cause
For what you seem to fear: so, the gods keep
you,
And make the hearts of Romans serve your
ends!
We will here part.
Cæs. Farewell, my dearest sister, fare thee
well:
The elements be kind to thee, and make   40
Thy spirits all of comfort! fare thee well.
Oct. My noble brother!
Ant. The April's in her eyes: it is love's
spring,
And these the showers to bring it on. Be
cheerful.
Oct. Sir, look well to my husband's
house; and—
Cæs.   What,
Octavia?
Oct. I'll tell you in your ear.
Ant. Her tongue will not obey her heart,
nor can
Her heart inform her tongue,—the swan's
down-feather,

36. with 's, with us.
  Scene ii. 2. dispatch'd, concluded the business. 3.
sealing, bringing matters to a conclusion. 6. green
sickness, a kind of anæmia supposed to affect young
women; used ironically, Lee thinks, with reference to the
love (?) Lepidus bore to Cæsar and Antony. 11. nonpareil, one having no equal. 12. Arabian bird, the
fabled phœnix, which arose fresh from its ashes and of
which there was only one. 17. cast, calculate. number,
write verses. 20. shards, wings (by means of which
the dull Lepidus might rise from earth).

26-27. as my . . . approof, such as my utmost bond
shall be justified on what thou shalt prove to be. 28.
piece, masterpiece. 32. mean, means. 35. curious,
particular, extremely careful. 48. swan's down-
feather. The figure seems to refer to a condition of
inertia due to conflicting passions; it may have some
reference to Octavia's affections divided between husband and brother.

That stands upon the swell at full of tide,
And neither way inclines.   50

Eno. [*Aside to Agr.*] Will Cæsar weep?

Agr.   [*Aside to Eno.*] He has a cloud
in 's face.

Eno. [*Aside to Agr.*] He were the worse
for that, were he a horse;
So is he, being a man.

Agr. [*Aside to Eno.*] Why, Enobarbus,
When Antony found Julius Cæsar dead,
He cried almost to roaring; and he wept
When at Philippi he found Brutus slain.

Eno. [*Aside to Agr.*] That year, indeed, he
was troubled with a rheum;
What willingly he did confound he wail'd,
Believe 't, till I wept too.

Cæs.   No, sweet Octavia,
You shall hear from me still; the time shall
not   60
Out-go my thinking on you.

Ant.   Come, sir, come;
I'll wrestle with you in my strength of love:
Look, here I have you; thus I let you go,
And give you to the gods.

Cæs.   Adieu; be happy!

Lep. Let all the number of the stars give
light
To thy fair way!

Cæs. Farewell, farewell! [*Kisses Octavia.*

Ant.   Farewell!

[*Trumpets sound. Exeunt.*

Scene III. *Alexandria. Cleopatra's
palace.*

Enter Cleopatra, Charmian, Iras,
and Alexas.

Cleo. Where is the fellow?

Alex.   Half afeard to come.

Cleo. Go to, go to.

Enter the Messenger *as before.*

Come hither, sir.

Alex.   Good majesty,
Herod of Jewry dare not look upon you
But when you are well pleased.

Cleo.   That Herod's head
I'll have: but how, when Antony is gone

Through whom I might command it? Come
thou near.

Mess. Most gracious majesty,—

Cleo. Didst thou behold Octavia?

Mess. Ay, dread queen.

Cleo. Where?   10

Mess. Madam, in Rome;
I look'd her in the face, and saw her led
Between her brother and Mark Antony.

Cleo. Is she as tall as me?

Mess.   She is not, madam.

Cleo. Didst hear her speak? is she shrill-
tongued or low?

Mess. Madam, I heard her speak; she is
low-voiced.

Cleo. That's not so good: he cannot like
her long.

Char. Like her! O Isis! 'tis impossible.

Cleo. I think so, Charmian: dull of tongue,
and dwarfish!
What majesty is in her gait? Remember,   20
If e'er thou look'dst on majesty.

Mess.   She creeps:
Her motion and her station are as one;
She shows a body rather than a life,
A statue than a breather.

Cleo.   Is this certain?

Mess. Or I have no observance.

Char.   Three in Egypt
Cannot make better note.

Cleo.   He's very knowing;
I do perceive 't: there's nothing in her yet:
The fellow has good judgement.

Char.   Excellent.

Cleo. Guess at her years, I prithee.

Mess.   Madam,
She was a widow,—

Cleo.   Widow! Charmian, hark.   30

Mess. And I do think she's thirty.

Cleo. Bear'st thou her face in mind? is 't
long or round?

Mess. Round even to faultiness.

Cleo. For the most part, too, they are
foolish that are so.
Her hair, what colour?

Mess. Brown, madam: and her forehead
As low as she would wish it.

Cleo.   There's gold for thee.
Thou must not take my former sharpness ill:

---

51. **cloud in 's face**, phrase applied to some marking
in a horse's face which was regarded as a blemish. 57.
rheum, running at the eyes; used of any discharge of
mucous from the head. 58. **confound**, destroy. **wail'd**,
bewailed. 61. **Out-go**, outstrip; the phrase is also interpreted as "I shall think of you while life lasts."

22. **station**, manner of standing. 24. **breather**,
living being. 25. **observance**, ability to observe. 32.
face . . . round. Physiognomy taught that very round
faces denoted silliness. 37. **As low . . . it.** Low foreheads were attributes of ugliness. **as she would wish
it**, as could be (cant phrase).

I will employ thee back again; I find thee
Most fit for business: go make thee ready; 40
Our letters are prepared.　[*Exit Messenger.*
　　Char.　　　　　　A proper man.
　　Cleo. Indeed, he is so: I repent me much
That so I harried him. Why, methinks, by
　　him,
This creature 's no such thing.
　　Char.　　　　　　Nothing, madam.
　　Cleo. The man hath seen some majesty,
　　and should know.
　　Char. Hath he seen majesty? Isis else
　　defend,
And serving you so long!
　　Cleo. I have one thing more to ask him
　　yet, good Charmian:
But 'tis no matter; thou shalt bring him to
　　me　　　　　　　　　　　　　　49
Where I will write. All may be well enough.
　　Char. I warrant you, madam. [*Exeunt.*

SCENE IV.　*Athens.　A room in Antony's
house.*

Enter ANTONY *and* OCTAVIA.

　　Ant. Nay, nay, Octavia, not only that,—
That were excusable, that, and thousands
　　more
Of semblable import,—but he hath waged
New wars 'gainst Pompey; made his will, and
　　read it
To public ear:
Spoke scantly of me: when perforce he could
　　not
But pay me terms of honour, cold and sickly
He vented them; most narrow measure lent
　　me:
When the best hint was given him, he not
　　took 't,
Or did it from his teeth.
　　Oct.　　　　　O my good lord, 10
Believe not all; or, if you must believe,
Stomach not all. A more unhappy lady,
If this division chance, ne'er stood between,
Praying for both parts:
The good gods will mock me presently,

When I shall pray, 'O, bless my lord and
　　husband!'
Undo that prayer, by crying out as loud,
'O, bless my brother!' Husband win, win
　　brother,
Prays, and destroys the prayer; no midway
'Twixt these extremes at all.
　　Ant.　　　　　Gentle Octavia, 20
Let your best love draw to that point, which
　　seeks
Best to preserve it: if I lose mine honour,
I lose myself: better I were not yours
Than yours so branchless. But, as you re-
　　quested,
Yourself shall go between 's: the mean time,
　　lady,
I'll raise the preparation of a war
Shall stain your brother: make your soonest
　　haste;
So your desires are yours.
　　Oct.　　　　　　Thanks to my lord.
The Jove of power make me most weak, most
　　weak,
Your reconciler! Wars 'twixt you twain
　　would be　　　　　　　　　　　　30
As if the world should cleave, and that slain
　　men
Should solder up the rift.
　　Ant. When it appears to you where this
　　begins,
Turn your displeasure that way; for our
　　faults
Can never be so equal, that your love
Can equally move with them. Provide
　　your going;
Choose your own company, and command
　　what cost
Your heart has mind to.　　　　[*Exeunt.*

SCENE V.　*The same.　Another room.*

Enter ENOBARBUS *and* EROS, *meeting.*

　　Eno. How now, friend Eros!
　　Eros. There's strange news come, sir.
　　Eno. What, man?
　　Eros. Cæsar and Lepidus have made
wars upon Pompey.
　　Eno. This is old: what is the success? 6
　　Eros. Cæsar, having made use of him in
the wars 'gainst Pompey, presently denied

him rivality; would not let him partake in
the glory of the action: and not resting here,
accuses him of letters he had formerly wrote
to Pompey; upon his own appeal, seizes him:
so the poor third is up, till death enlarge his
confine.   13

    Eno. Then, world, thou hast a pair of
      chaps, no more;
And throw between them all the food thou
    hast,
They'll grind the one the other. Where's
    Antony?

    Eros. He's walking in the garden—thus;
    and spurns
The rush that lies before him; cried, 'Fool
    Lepidus!'
And threats the throat of that his officer   19
That murder'd Pompey.

    Eno.   Our great navy's rigg'd.

    Eros. For Italy and Cæsar. More, Domi-
tius;
My lord desires you presently: my news
I might have told hereafter.

    Enos.   'Twill be naught:
But let it be. Bring me to Antony.

    Eros. Come, sir.   [*Exeunt.*

SCENE VI. *Rome. Cæsar's house.*

Enter CÆSAR, AGRIPPA, *and* MECÆNAS.

    Cæs. Contemning Rome, he has done all
    this, and more,
In Alexandria: here's the manner of 't:
I' the market-place, on a tribunal silver'd,
Cleopatra and himself in chairs of gold
Were publicly enthroned: at the feet sat
Cæsarion, whom they call my father's son,
And all the unlawful issue that their lust
Since then hath made between them. Unto
    her
He gave the stablishment of Egypt; made
    her
Of lower Syria, Cyprus, Lydia,   10
Absolute queen.

---

    9. **rivality,** rights of a partner. 12. **his own appeal,**
Cæsar's own accusation. 13. **up,** shut up (in prison).
14. **pair of chaps,** two jaws (destined to grind each
other). **no more.** The meaning is "no more than one
pair." 20. **Pompey.** Pompey met defeat in Sicily,
escaped thence to the East with designs against Antony,
and is supposed to have been murdered by Antony's
orders; here Antony blames his officer.
    Scene vi. 3. **tribunal,** seat of eminence. 9. **stablish-**
ment, settled possession. The first 19 lines of this scene
reflect the point of view of imperial Rome, with which
Plutarch is strongly in sympathy, namely, the impiety
of the establishment of independent kingdoms on Roman
soil.

    Mec.   This in the public eye?

    Cæs. I' the common show-place, where
    they exercise.
His sons he there proclaim'd the kings of
    kings:
Great Media, Parthia, and Armenia,
He gave to Alexander; to Ptolemy he assign'd
Syria, Cilicia, and Phœnicia: she
In the habiliments of the goddess Isis
That day appear'd; and oft before gave
    audience,
As 'tis reported, so.

    Mec.   Let Rome be thus
Inform'd.

    Agr. Who, queasy with his insolence   20
Already, will their good thoughts call from
    him.

    Cæs. The people know it; and have now
    received
His accusations.

    Agr.   Who does he accuse?

    Cæs. Cæsar: and that, having in Sicily
Sextus Pompeius spoil'd, we had not rated
    him
His part o' the isle: then does he say, he lent
    me
Some shipping unrestored: lastly, he frets
That Lepidus of the triumvirate
Should be deposed; and, being, that we de-
    tain
All his revenue.

    Agr.   Sir, this should be answer'd. 30

    Cæs. 'Tis done already, and the messenger
    gone.
I have told him, Lepidus was grown too
    cruel;
That he his high authority abused,
And did deserve his change: for what I have
    conquer'd,
I grant him part; but then, in his Armenia,
And other of his conquer'd kingdoms, I
Demand the like.

    Mec.   He'll never yield to that.

    Cæs. Nor must not then be yielded to in
    this.

Enter OCTAVIA *with her train.*

    Oct. Hail, Cæsar, and my lord! hail, most
    dear Cæsar!

    Cæs. That ever I should call thee cast-
    away!

    Oct. You have not call'd me so, nor have
    you cause.   41

---

    20. **queasy,** disgusted, i.e., the Roman people. 25.
rated, allotted.

Cæs. Why have you stol'n upon us thus?
  You come not
Like Cæsar's sister: the wife of Antony
Should have an army for an usher, and
The neighs of horse to tell of her approach
Long ere she did appear; the trees by the
  way
Should have borne men; and expectation
  fainted,
Longing for what it had not; nay, the dust
Should have ascended to the roof of heaven,
Raised by your populous troops: but you are
  come   50
A market-maid to Rome; and have pre-
  vented
The ostentation of our love, which, left un-
  shown,
Is often left unloved: we should have met
  you
By sea and land; supplying every stage
With an augmented greeting.
  Oct.   Good my lord,
To come thus was I not constrain'd, but
  did it
On my free will. My lord, Mark Antony,
Hearing that you prepared for war, ac-
  quainted
My grieved ear withal; whereon, I begg'd
His pardon for return.
  Cæs.   Which soon he granted,   60
Being an obstruct 'tween his lust and him.
  Oct. Do not say so, my lord.
  Cæs.   I have eyes upon him,
And his affairs come to me on the wind.
Where is he now?
  Oct.   My lord, in Athens.
  Cæs. No, my most wronged sister; Cleo-
  patra
Hath nodded him to her. He hath given his
  empire
Up to a whore; who now are levying
The kings o' the earth for war: he hath as-
  sembled
Bocchus, the king of Libya; Archelaus,
Of Cappadocia; Philadelphos, king   70
Of Paphlagonia; the Thracian king, Adallas;
King Malchus of Arabia; King of Pont;
Herod of Jewry; Mithridates, king
Of Comagene; Polemon and Amyntas,
The kings of Mede and Lycaonia,

With a more larger list of sceptres.
  Oct.   Ay me, most wretched,
That have my heart parted betwixt two
  friends
That do afflict each other!
  Cæs.   Welcome hither:
Your letters did withhold our breaking forth;
Till we perceived, both how you were wrong
  led,   80
And we in negligent danger. Cheer your
  heart:
Be you not troubled with the time, which
  drives
O'er your content these strong necessities;
But let determined things to destiny
Hold unbewail'd their way. Welcome to
  Rome;
Nothing more dear to me. You are abused
Beyond the mark of thought: and the high
  gods,
To do you justice, make them ministers
Of us and those that love you. Best of
  comfort;
And ever welcome to us.
  Agr.   Welcome, lady.   90
  Mec. Welcome, dear madam.
Each heart in Rome does love and pity you:
Only the adulterous Antony, most large
In his abominations, turns you off;
And gives his potent regiment to a trull,
That noises it against us.
  Oct.   Is it so, sir?
  Cæs. Most certain. Sister, welcome: pray
  you,
Be ever known to patience: my dear'st sister!
                                        [*Exeunt.*

Scene VII. *Near Actium. Antony's camp.*

  Enter Cleopatra *and* Enobarbus.

  Cleo. I will be even with thee, doubt it
  not.
  Eno. But why, why, why?
  Cleo. Thou hast forspoke my being in
  these wars,
And say'st it is not fit.
  Eno.   Well, is it, is it?

---

50. **populous,** numerous. 52. **ostentation,** public
display. 61. **obstruct,** impediment. 69-76. **Bocchus
. . . sceptres.** The list of powers is from Plutarch and
is somewhat confused, as here, in North's translation.
Libya is here correctly given; in line 10 Shakespeare
followed North in writing *Lydia.*

81. **negligent danger,** danger neglected, or danger
through negligence. 88. **make them.** This is Capell's
emendation of F *makes his,* which can be perfectly well
construed, since *makes* may have a plural subject, and
his may mean "its" and refer to *justice.* 89. **Best of comfort,** i.e., may you have, etc. 93. **large,** free, unrestrained. 95. **regiment,** government, rule. **trull,**
worthless woman or prostitute. 96. **noises it,** is
clamorous.
Scene vii. 3. **forspoke,** spoken against.

Cleo. If not denounced against us, why
    should not we
Be there in person?
    Eno. [*Aside*] Well, I could reply:
If we should serve with horse and mares to-
    gether,
The horse were merely lost; the mares would
    bear
A soldier and his horse.
    Cleo.   What is 't you say?   10
    Eno. Your presence needs must puzzle
    Antony;
Take from his heart, take from his brain,
    from 's time,
What should not then be spared. He is
    already
Traduced for levity; and 'tis said in Rome
That Photinus an eunuch and your maids
Manage this war.
    Cleo.   Sink Rome, and their
    tongues rot
That speak against us! A charge we bear i'
    the war,
And, as the president of my kingdom, will
Appear there for a man. Speak not against
    it;
I will not stay behind.
    Eno.   Nay, I have done.   20
Here comes the emperor.

      Enter ANTONY *and* CANIDIUS.

    Ant.   Is it not strange, Canidius,
That from Tarentum and Brundusium
He could so quickly cut the Ionian sea,
And take in Toryne? You have heard on 't,
    sweet?
    Cleo. Celerity is never more admired
Than by the negligent.
    Ant.   A good rebuke,
Which might have well becomed the best of
    men,
To taunt at slackness. Canidius, we
Will fight with him by sea.
    Cleo.   By sea! what else?

Can. Why will my lord do so?
    Ant.   For that he dares us to 't.
    Eno. So hath my lord dared him to single
    fight.   31
    Can. Ay, and to wage this battle at Phar-
    salia,
Where Cæsar fought with Pompey: but these
    offers,
Which serve not for his vantage, he shakes
    off;
And so should you.
    Eno.   Your ships are not well mann'd;
Your mariners are muleters, reapers, people
Ingross'd by swift impress; in Cæsar's fleet
Are those that often have 'gainst Pompey
    fought:
Their ships are yare; yours, heavy: no dis-
    grace
Shall fall you for refusing him at sea,   40
Being prepared for land.
    Ant.   By sea, by sea.
    Eno. Most worthy sir, you therein throw
    away
The absolute soldiership you have by land;
Distract your army, which doth most consist
Of war-mark'd footmen; leave unexecuted
Your own renowned knowledge; quite forego
The way which promises assurance; and
Give up yourself merely to chance and
    hazard,
From firm security.
    Ant.   I'll fight at sea.   49
    Cleo. I have sixty sails, Cæsar none better.
    Ant. Our overplus of shipping will we
    burn;
And, with the rest full-mann'd, from the head
    of Actium
Beat the approaching Cæsar. But if we fail,
We then can do 't at land.

      Enter a Messenger.

                    Thy business?
    Mess. The news is true, my lord; he is
    descried;
Cæsar has taken Toryne.
    Ant. Can he be there in person? 'tis im-
    possible;
Strange that his power should be. Canidius,
Our nineteen legions thou shalt hold by land,
And our twelve thousand horse. We'll to
    our ship:

5-6. **If not . . . person.** Cuningham suggests that
this means "even if the war were not declared against
me (which it is)," etc. This is better than the more
obvious meaning, since historically the war was declared
against Cleopatra and not Antony. 9. **merely,** utterly.
15. **That . . . maids.** So F, without punctuation.
Shakespeare uses *an eunuch* to describe Mardian,
not Photinus. 17. **A charge . . . war.** Plutarch states
that Cleopatra wished to go to the war to prevent
Antony from being reconciled to Octavia; she bribed
Canidius to argue for her, so that Antony consented.
Plutarch says it was predestined that the government of
all the world should fall into Octavius Cæsar's hands.

36. **muleters,** F: *Militers*; F₂: *Muliters*. *Militers*
may mean "soldiers." 37. **Ingross'd,** collected. **impress,** impressment. 39. **yare,** easily managed.

Away, my Thetis!

Enter a Soldier.

            How now, worthy soldier! 61
Sold. O noble emperor, do not fight by
  sea;
Trust not to rotten planks: do you misdoubt
This sword and these my wounds? Let the
  Egyptians
And the Phœnicians go a-ducking: we
Have used to conquer, standing on the earth,
And fighting foot to foot.
Ant.   Well, well; away!
[*Exeunt Antony, Cleopatra, and Enobarbus.*
Sold. By Hercules, I think I am 'i the right.
Can. Soldier, thou art: but his whole
  action grows
Not in the power on 't: so our leader 's led, 70
And we are women's men.
Sold.   You keep by land
The legions and the horse whole, do you not?
Can. Marcus Octavius, Marcus Justeius,
Publicola, and Cælius, are for sea:
But we keep whole by land. This speed of
  Cæsar's
Carries beyond belief.
Sold.   While he was yet in Rome,
His power went out in such distractions as
Beguiled all spies.
Can.   Who's his lieutenant, hear you?
Sold. They say, one Taurus.
Can.   Well I know the man.

Enter a Messenger.

Mess. The emperor calls Canidius.   80
Can. With news the time's with labour,
  and throes forth,
Each minute, some.   [*Exeunt.*

SCENE VIII. *A plain near Actium.*

Enter CÆSAR, *and* TAURUS, *with his army,
marching.*

Cæs. Taurus!

Taur. My lord?
Cæs. Strike not by land; keep whole: pro-
  voke not battle,
Till we have done at sea. Do not exceed 4
The prescript of this scroll: our fortune lies
Upon this jump.   [*Exeunt.*

SCENE IX. *Another part of the plain.*

Enter ANTONY *and* ENOBARBUS.

Ant. Set we our squadrons on yond side o'
  the hill,
In eye of Cæsar's battle; from which place
We may the number of the ships behold,
And so proceed accordingly.   [*Exeunt.*

SCENE X. *Another part of the plain.*

CANIDIUS *marcheth with his land army one
way over the stage; and* TAURUS, *the lieutenant of* CÆSAR, *the other way. After
their going in, is heard the noise of a sea-
fight.*

Alarum. Enter ENOBARBUS.

Eno. Naught, naught, all naught! I can
  behold no longer:
The Antoniad, the Egyptian admiral,
With all their sixty, fly and turn the rudder:
To see 't mine eyes are blasted.

Enter SCARUS.

Scar.   Gods and goddesses,
All the whole synod of them!
Eno.   What's thy passion?
Scar. The greater cantle of the world is
  lost
With very ignorance; we have kiss'd away
Kingdoms and provinces.
Eno.   How appears the fight?
Scar. On our side like the token'd pesti-
  lence,
Where death is sure. Yon ribaudred nag of
  Egypt,—   10

61. **Thetis**, sea goddess. 63. **misdoubt**, mistrust.
69-70. **his whole . . . on 't**, usually taken to mean
"his whole action proceeds not from the source of its
possible power." Johnson interpreted, with some propriety, "his whole conduct becomes ungoverned by the
right, or by reason." Canidius shows, like the others,
a soldier's disgust with Antony's infatuation, and is less
definitely a traitor than in Plutarch. 76. **Carries beyond**, surpasses (like an arrow in archery). 77. **distractions**, detachments. 81. **throes**, puts in agony.
Gollancz suggests that the F reading, *throwes forth*, may
mean "brings forth."

5. **prescript**, direction. 6. **jump**, hazard.
Scene ix. 2. **battle**, army.
Scene x. 2. **Antoniad**, the name of Cleopatra's
admiral or chief galley of her fleet. 5. **synod**, assembly
of the gods. 6. **cantle**, corner; hence, piece or part.
9. **token'd pestilence** Certain red spots appeared on
the bodies of the plague-smitten, which were, according
to Steevens, called "God's tokens," i.e., of death. Shakespeare had many ways of fighting battles on the stage;
all had to be more or less indirect. In this one two old
soldiers on the hill give their report. 10. **ribaudred
nag**, wanton jade (abusive); many conjectures.

Whom leprosy o'ertake!—i' the midst o' the
  fight,
When vantage like a pair of twins appear'd,
Both as the same, or rather ours the elder,
The breese upon her, like a cow in June,
Hoists sails and flies.
  Eno.   That I beheld:
Mine eyes did sicken at the sight, and could
  not
Endure a further view.
  Scar.   She once being loof'd,
The noble ruin of her magic, Antony,
Claps on his sea-wing, and, like a doting
  mallard,   20
Leaving the fight in height, flies after her:
I never saw an action of such shame;
Experience, manhood, honour, ne'er before
Did violate so itself.
  Eno.   Alack, alack!

  Enter CANIDIUS.

  Can. Our fortune on the sea is out of
  breath,
And sinks most lamentably. Had our general
Been what he knew himself, it had gone well:
O, he has given example for our flight,
Most grossly, by his own!
  Eno.   Ay, are you thereabouts?
Why, then, good night indeed.   30
  Can. Toward Peloponnesus are they fled.
  Scar. 'Tis easy to 't; and there I will
  attend
What further comes.
  Can.   To Cæsar will I render
My legions and my horse: six kings already
Show me the way of yielding.
  Eno.   I'll yet follow
The wounded chance of Antony, though my
  reason
Sits in the wind against me.   [*Exeunt.*

  SCENE XI. *Alexandria. Cleopatra's
          palace.*

  Enter ANTONY *with* Attendants.

  Ant. Hark! the land bids me tread no
  more upon 't;
It is ashamed to bear me! Friends, come
  hither.

I am so lated in the world, that I
Have lost my way forever: I have a ship
Laden with gold; take that, divide it; fly,
And make your peace with Cæsar.
  All.   Fly! not we.
  Ant. I have fled myself; and have in-
  structed cowards
To run and show their shoulders. Friends,
  be gone;
I have myself resolved upon a course
Which has no need of you; be gone: 10
My treasure's in the harbour, take it. O,
I follow'd that I blush to look upon:
My very hairs do mutiny; for the white
Reprove the brown for rashness, and they
  them
For fear and doting. Friends, be gone: you
  shall
Have letters from me to some friends that
  will
Sweep your way for you. Pray you, look not
  sad,
Nor make replies of loathness: take the hint
Which my despair proclaims; let that be left
Which leaves itself: to the sea-side straight-
  way:
I will possess you of that ship and treasure. 21
Leave me, I pray, a little: pray you now:
Nay, do so; for, indeed, I have lost com-
  mand,
Therefore I pray you: I'll see you by and by.
                              [*Sits down.*

  Enter CLEOPATRA *led by* CHARMIAN *and*
          IRAS; EROS *following.*

  Eros. Nay, gentle madam, to him, com-
  fort him.
  Iras. Do, most dear queen.
  Char. Do! why: what else?
  Cleo. Let me sit down. O Juno!
  Ant. No, no, no, no, no.
  Eros. See you here, sir?   30
  Ant. O fie, fie, fie!
  Char. Madam!
  Iras. Madam, O good empress!
  Eros. Sir, sir,—
  Ant. Yes, my lord, yes; he at Philippi
  kept

---

13. **elder,** more advanced. 14. **breese,** gadfly. 18.
loof'd, luffed, brought close to the wind. 20. **mallard,**
drake. 29. **thereabouts,** of that opinion. 32. **to 't,**
to get to it. 33. **render,** surrender. 36. **wounded
chance,** broken fortunes. 37. **Sits . . . against,** is in
opposition to.

3. **lated,** belated, benighted. 8. **show their shoulders,** common expression for "show their backs." 18.
loathness, unwillingness. 23. **lost command.** Johnson rightly interpreted this as "lost command of his
emotion"; the usual interpretation is "lost command of
his troops." 35. **my lord,** sometimes thought to be
addressed to an imaginary interlocutor or, in bitterness,
to Cæsar; probably it is to Eros (ironically). **he,** i.e.,
Octavius, to whom Plutarch attributes poor soldiership
at Philippi.

His sword e'en like a dancer; while I struck
The lean and wrinkled Cassius; and 'twas I
That the mad Brutus ended: he alone
Dealt on lieutenantry, and no practice had
In the brave squares of war: yet now—No
    matter.   40
  Cleo. Ah, stand by.
  Eros. The queen, my lord, the queen.
  Iras. Go to him, madam, speak to him:
He is unqualitied with very shame.
  Cleo. Well then, sustain me: O!
  Enos. Most noble sir, arise; the queen ap-
    proaches;
Her head's declined, and death will seize her,
  but
Your comfort makes the rescue.
  Ant. I have offended reputation,
A most unnoble swerving.
  Eros.   Sir, the queen. 50
  Ant. O, whither hast thou led me, Egypt?
  See,
How I convey my shame out of thine eyes
By looking back what I have left behind
'Stroy'd in dishonour.
  Cleo.   O my lord, my lord,
Forgive my fearful sails! I little thought
You would have follow'd.
  Ant.   Egypt, thou knew'st too well
My heart was to thy rudder tied by the
  strings,
And thou shouldst tow me after: o'er my
  spirit
Thy full supremacy thou knew'st, and that
Thy beck might from the bidding of the
  gods
Command me.
  Cleo.   O, my pardon!
  Ant.   Now I must 61
To the young man send humble treaties,
  dodge
And palter in the shifts of lowness; who
With half the bulk o' the world play'd as I
  pleased,
Making and marring fortunes. You did
  know
How much you were my conqueror; and
  that

My sword, made weak by my affection,
  would
Obey it on all cause.
  Cleo.   Pardon, pardon!
  Ant. Fall not a tear, I say; one of them
  rates
All that is won and lost: give me a kiss; 70
Even this repays me. We sent our school-
  master;
Is he come back? Love, I am full of lead.
Some wine, within there, and our viands!
  Fortune knows
We scorn her most when most she offers
  blows.   *[Exeunt.*

SCENE XII. *Egypt. Cæsar's camp.*

Enter CÆSAR, DOLABELLA, THYREUS, *with
others.*

  Cæs. Let him appear that's come from
  Antony.
Know you him?
  Dol.   Cæsar, 'tis his schoolmaster:
An argument that he is pluck'd, when hither
He sends so poor a pinion of his wing,
Which had superfluous kings for messengers
Not many moons gone by.

Enter EUPHRONIUS, *ambassador from
Antony.*

  Cæs.   Approach, and speak.
  Euph. Such as I am, I come from Antony:
I was of late as petty to his ends
As is the morn-dew on the myrtle-leaf
To his grand sea.
  Cæs.   Be 't so: declare thine office. 10
  Euph. Lord of his fortunes he salutes
  thee, and
Requires to live in Egypt: which not granted,
He lessens his requests; and to thee sues
To let him breathe between the heavens and
  earth,
A private man in Athens: this for him.
Next, Cleopatra does confess thy greatness;
Submits her to thy might; and of thee craves
The circle of the Ptolemies for her heirs,
Now hazarded to thy grace.
  Cæs.   For Antony,

---

36. **sword . . . dancer**, seems to allude to swords
worn for ornament only, as by dancers. 39. **Dealt on
lieutenantry**, let his subordinates do the fighting. 40.
squares, squadrons. 44. **unqualitied**, not himself.
51-54. **See . . . dishonour**, see how I withdraw my
disgrace from your presence and reflect on the ruin of
my fortunes and honor. 57. **by the strings**, heart-
strings. In judging Antony's conduct and repentance
we must remember that Shakespeare viewed his act as
that of a man utterly infatuated and one whose reason
was unhinged. 62. **treaties**, propositions for settlement.
63. **palter**, use trickery.

69. **Fall**, cause to fall. **rates**, is worth. 71. **schoolmaster**, Euphronius, tutor to his children by Cleopatra.
Scene xii. 3. **argument**, proof. 8-10. **as petty . . .
sea**, as insignificant compared to his great ends as is the
dewdrop on the myrtle leaf compared to the grand sea;
several interpretations. 12. **Requires**, asks. 18.
circle, crown.

I have no ears to his request. The queen 20
Of audience nor desire shall fail, so she
From Egypt drive her all-disgraced friend,
Or take his life there: this if she perform,
She shall not sue unheard. So to them both.
    Euph. Fortune pursue thee!
    Cæs.   Bring him through the bands.
                        [*Exit Euphronius.*
[*To Thyreus*] To try thy eloquence, now 'tis
    time: dispatch;
From Antony win Cleopatra: promise,
And in our name, what she requires; add
    more,
From thine invention, offers: women are not
In their best fortunes strong; but want will
    perjure   30
The ne'er-touch'd vestal: try thy cunning,
    Thyreus;
Make thine own edict for thy pains, which
    we
Will answer as a law.
    Thyr.   Cæsar, I go.
    Cæs. Observe how Antony becomes his
    flaw,
And what thou think'st his very action
    speaks
In every power that moves.
    Thyr.   Cæsar, I shall. [*Exeunt.*

SCENE XIII. *Alexandria. Cleopatra's
                palace.*

Enter CLEOPATRA, ENOBARBUS, CHARMIAN,
            and IRAS.

    Cleo. What shall we do, Enobarbus?
    Eno.   Think, and die.
    Cleo. Is Antony or we in fault for this?
    Eno. Antony only, that would make his
    will
Lord of his reason. What though you fled
From that great face of war, whose several
    ranges
Frighted each other? why should he follow?
The itch of his affection should not then
Have nick'd his captainship; at such a point,

When half to half the world opposed, he
    being
The meered question: 'twas a shame no
    less
Than was his loss, to course your flying
    flags,   11
And leave his navy gazing.
    Cleo.   Prithee, peace.

Enter ANTONY *with* EUPHRONIUS, *the
                Ambassador.*

    Ant. Is that his answer?
    Euph. Ay, my lord.
    Ant. The queen shall then have courtesy,
    so she
Will yield us up.
    Euph.   He says so.
    Ant.   Let her know 't.
To the boy Cæsar send this grizzled head,
And he will fill thy wishes to the brim
With principalities.
    Cleo.   That head, my lord?
    Ant. To him again: tell him he wears the
    rose   20
Of youth upon him; from which the world
    should note
Something particular: his coin, ships, legions,
May be a coward's; whose ministers would
    prevail
Under the service of a child as soon
As i' the command of Cæsar: I dare him
    therefore
To lay his gay comparisons apart,
And answer me declined, sword against
    sword,
Ourselves alone. I'll write it: follow me.
                [*Exeunt Antony and Euphronius.*
    Eno. [*Aside*] Yes, like enough, high-
    battled Cæsar will
Unstate his happiness, and be staged to the
    show,   30
Against a sworder! I see men's judgements
    are
A parcel of their fortunes; and things out-
    ward
Do draw the inward quality after them,

---

32. **Make . . . pains,** decree thine own reward. 34.
becomes his flaw, bears his misfortune and disgrace.
36. **power that moves,** faculty or passion that manifests
itself.

Scene xiii. 1. **Think, and die,** take thought on our
situation, and die. 3-4. **his will . . . reason.** Since
will might operate against *reason*, they were often
thought of as opposing forces. 5. **ranges,** ranks, lines
(of ships). 8. **nick'd,** cut short (from being nicked), or
(from gaming) got the better of, since a *nick* was a winning throw in games of chance (Cuningham).

10. **meered question,** sole ground of quarrel (if
we suppose the word is coined from *mere*). Many conjectures, including Johnson: *mooted;* Cuningham: *moved* (or
meued); Rowe: *meer.* 11. **course,** pursue (as in hunting).
15. **so,** if. 26. **gay comparisons,** the wealth and
splendor just mentioned (to be compared to Antony's
poverty). 27. **declined,** in fortune. 29. **high-battled,**
provided with noble armies. 30. **Unstate,** strip of
dignity. **staged,** exhibited publicly. 31. **sworder,**
gladiator. 32. **parcel of,** of a piece with (Steevens).

To suffer all alike. That he should dream,
Knowing all measures, the full Cæsar will
Answer his emptiness! Cæsar, thou hast sub-
dued
His judgement too.

Enter an Attendant.

Att.   A messenger from Cæsar.
Cleo. What, no more ceremony? See, my
women!
Against the blown rose may they stop their
nose
That kneel'd unto the buds. Admit him, sir.
                              [*Exit Attendant.*
Eno. [*Aside*] Mine honesty and I begin to
square.   41
The loyalty well held to fools does make
Our faith mere folly: yet he that can endure
To follow with allegiance a fall'n lord
Does conquer him that did his master con-
quer,
And earns a place i' the story.

Enter THYREUS.

Cleo.   Cæsar's will?
Thyr. Hear it apart.
Cleo.   None but friends: say boldly.
Thyr. So, haply, are they friends to
Antony.
Eno. He needs as many, sir, as Cæsar
has;
Or needs not us. If Cæsar please, our master
Will leap to be his friend: for us, you know 51
Whose he is we are, and that is, Cæsar's.
Thyr.   So.
Thus then, thou most renown'd: Cæsar en-
treats,
Not to consider in what case thou stand'st,
Further than he is Cæsar.
Cleo.   Go on: right royal.
Thyr. He knows that you embrace not
Antony
As you did love, but as you fear'd him.
Cleo.   O!
Thyr. The scars upon your honour, there-
fore, he
Does pity, as constrained blemishes,
Not as deserved.
Cleo.   He is a god, and knows 60
What is most right: mine honour was not
yielded,
But conquer'd merely.

41. **square**, quarrel. 55. **Cæsar**, a noble person.

Eno.   [*Aside*] To be sure of that,
I will ask Antony. Sir, sir, thou art so leaky,
That we must leave thee to thy sinking, for
Thy dearest quit thee.   [*Exit.*
Thyr.   Shall I say to Cæsar
What you require of him? for he partly begs
To be desired to give. It much would please
him,
That of his fortunes you should make a staff
To lean upon: but it would warm his spirits,
To hear from me you had left Antony,   70
†And put yourself under his shrowd,
The universal landlord.
Cleo.   What's your name?
Thyr. My name is Thyreus.
Cleo.   Most kind messenger,
Say to great Cæsar this: in deputation
I kiss his conquering hand: tell him, I am
prompt
To lay my crown at 's feet, and there to kneel:
Tell him, from his all-obeying breath I hear
The doom of Egypt.
Thyr.   'Tis your noblest course.
Wisdom and fortune combating together,
If that the former dare but what it can,   80
No chance may shake it. Give me grace to
lay
My duty on your hand.
Cleo.   Your Cæsar's father oft,
When he hath mused of taking kingdoms in,
Bestow'd his lips on that unworthy place,
As it rain'd kisses.

Re-enter ANTONY *and* ENOBARBUS.

Ant.   Favours, by Jove that thunders!
What art thou, fellow?
Thyr.   One that but performs
The bidding of the fullest man, and worthiest
To have command obey'd.
Eno.   [*Aside*] You will be whipp'd.
Ant. Approach, there! Ah, you kite!
Now, gods and devils!
Authority melts from me: of late, when I
cried 'Ho!'   90
Like boys unto a muss, kings would start
forth,
And cry 'Your will?' Have you no ears? I am
Antony yet.

71. **shrowd**, shelter, protection. 74. **Say . . . deputation.** Punctuation of the text follows Theobald in
putting a larger stop after *this*; F has a comma at the
end of the line, where we should put a colon, which gives
a better sense. *deputation*, by deputy. 77. **all-obeying**,
obeyed by all. 81. **grace** to all, the honor. 87. **fullest**, most
complete in all respects. 89. **kite**, Cleopatra (?) 91.
muss, scramble,

Enter Attendants.

      Take hence this Jack, and whip him.
  Eno. [*Aside*] 'Tis better playing with a
lion's whelp
Than with an old one dying.
  Ant.   Moon and stars!
Whip him. Were 't twenty of the greatest
    tributaries
That do acknowledge Cæsar, should I find
    them
So saucy with the hand of she here,—what's
    her name,   98
Since she was Cleopatra? Whip him, fellows,
Till, like a boy, you see him cringe his face,
And whine aloud for mercy: take him hence.
  Thyr. Mark Antony!
  Ant.   Tug him away: being whipp'd,
Bring him again: this Jack of Cæsar's shall
Bear us an errand to him.
             [*Exeunt Attendants with Thyreus.*
You were half blasted ere I knew you: ha!
Have I my pillow left unpress'd in Rome,
Forborne the getting of a lawful race,
And by a gem of women, to be abused
By one that looks on feeders?
  Cleo.   Good my lord,—
  Ant. You have been a boggler ever: 110
But when we in our viciousness grow hard—
O misery on 't!—the wise gods seel our
    eyes;
In our own filth drop our clear judgements;
    make us
Adore our errors; laugh at 's, while we strut
To our confusion.
  Cleo.   O, is 't come to this?
  Ant. I found you as a morsel cold upon
Dead Cæsar's trencher; nay, you were a
    fragment
Of Cneius Pompey's; besides what hotter
    hours,
Unregister'd in vulgar fame, you have
Luxuriously pick'd out: for, I am sure,   120
Though you can guess what temperance
    should be,
You know not what it is.
  Cleo.   Wherefore is this?
  Ant. To let a fellow that will take rewards
And say 'God quit you!' be familiar with

My playfellow, your hand; this kingly seal
And plighter of high hearts! O, that I were
Upon the hill of Basan, to outroar
The horned herd! for I have savage cause;
And to proclaim it civilly, were like
A halter'd neck which does the hangman
    thank
For being yare about him.

Re-enter Attendants *with* THYREUS.

               Is he whipp'd?   131
  First Att. Soundly, my lord.
  Ant.   Cried he? and begg'd a' pardon?
  First Att. He did ask favour.
  Ant. If that thy father live, let him repent
Thou wast not made his daughter; and be
    thou sorry
To follow Cæsar in his triumph, since
Thou hast been whipp'd for following him:
    henceforth
The white hand of a lady fever thee,
Shake thou to look on 't. Get thee back to
    Cæsar,   139
Tell him thy entertainment: look, thou say
He makes me angry with him; for he seems
Proud and disdainful, harping on what I
    am,
Not what he knew I was: he makes me
    angry;
And at this time most easy 'tis to do 't,
When my good stars, that were my former
    guides,
Have empty left their orbs, and shot their
    fires
Into the abysm of hell. If he mislike
My speech and what is done, tell him he has
Hipparchus, my enfranched bondman, whom
He may at pleasure whip, or hang, or
    torture,
As he shall like, to quit me: urge it thou: 151
Hence with thy stripes, begone!
                   [*Exit Thyreus.*
  Cleo. Have you done yet?
  Ant.   Alack, our terrene moon
Is now eclipsed; and it portends alone
The fall of Antony!
  Cleo.   I must stay his time.

93. **Jack**, contemptuous epithet. 100. **cringe**, transitive use. 109. **feeders**, servants. 110. **boggler**, waverer; often used of shying horses. 112. **seel**, blind; a term in falconry for closing the eyes of wild hawks by sewing the eyelids together. 120. **Luxuriously**, lustfully. 121. **temperance**, probably, chastity.

127. **hill of Basan**, allusion to *Psalms*, lxviii, 15, and xxii, 12; apparently to the Prayer Book version. 131. **yare**, ready, quick. 138. **fever**, put thee in a fever (imperative). 146. **orbs**, spheres. 149. **Hipparchus**. According to Plutarch the man was a deserter. **enfranched**, enfranchised. 153. **terrene**, earthly, i.e., Cleopatra eclipsed like the moon.

Ant. To flatter Cæsar, would you mingle
　　eyes
With one that ties his points?
　　Cleo.　　　　　　Not know me yet?
Ant. Cold-hearted toward me?
　　Cleo.　　　　　　Ah, dear, if I be so,
From my cold heart let heaven engender
　　hail,
And poison it in the source; and the first
　　stone　　　　　　　　　　　　　160
Drop in my neck: as it determines, so
Dissolve my life! The next Cæsarion smite!
Till by degrees the memory of my womb,
Together with my brave Egyptians all,
By the discandying of this pelleted storm,
Lie graveless, till the flies and gnats of Nile
Have buried them for prey!
　　Ant.　　　　　I am satisfied.
Cæsar sits down in Alexandria; where
I will oppose his fate. Our force by land
Hath nobly held; our sever'd navy too　170
Have knit again, and fleet, threatening most
　　sea-like.
Where hast thou been, my heart? Dost thou
　　hear, lady?
If from the field I shall return once more
To kiss these lips, I will appear in blood;
I and my sword will earn our chronicle:
There's hope in 't yet.
　　Cleo. That's my brave lord!
　　Ant. I will be treble-sinew'd, hearted,
　　breathed,
And fight maliciously: for when mine hours
Were nice and lucky, men did ransom lives 180
Of me for jests; but now I'll set my teeth,
And send to darkness all that stop me. Come,
Let's have one other gaudy night: call to
　　me
All my sad captains; fill our bowls once more;
Let's mock the midnight bell.
　　Cleo.　　　　It is my birth-day:
I had thought to have held it poor; but, since
　　my lord
Is Antony again, I will be Cleopatra.
　　Ant. We will yet do well.
　　Cleo. Call all his noble captains to my
　　lord.

Ant. Do so, we'll speak to them; and to-
　　night I'll force　　　　　　　190
The wine peep through their scars. Come
　　on, my queen;
There's sap in 't yet. The next time I do
　　fight,
I'll make death love me; for I will contend
Even with his pestilent scythe.
　　　　　　　　[*Exeunt all but Enobarbus.*
　　Eno. Now he'll outstare the lightning.
　　To be furious,
Is to be frighted out of fear; and in that
　　mood
The dove will peck the estridge; and I see
　　still,
A diminution in our captain's brain
Restores his heart: when valour preys on
　　reason,
It eats the sword it fights with. I will seek 200
Some way to leave him.　　　　　[*Exit.*

ACT IV.

SCENE I. *Before Alexandria. Cæsar's camp.*

Enter CÆSAR, AGRIPPA, *and* MECÆNAS, *with
　　his army;* CÆSAR *reading a letter.*

　　Cæs. He calls me boy; and chides, as he
　　had power
To beat me out of Egypt; my messenger
He hath whipp'd with rods; dares me to
　　personal combat,
Cæsar to Antony: let the old ruffian know
I have many other ways to die; meantime
Laugh at his challenge.
　　Mec.　　　　　Cæsar must think,
When one so great begins to rage, he's
　　hunted
Even to falling. Give him no breath, but
　　now
Make boot of his distraction: never anger
Made good guard for itself.
　　Cæs.　　　　Let our best heads 10
Know, that to-morrow the last of many
　　battles
We mean to fight: within our files there are,

<hr>

157. **points,** laces by which articles of clothing were
secured.　161. **determines,** comes to an end.　165.
pelleted, falling in pellets.　171. **fleet,** float.　180.
nice, dainty, effeminate.　183. **gaudy,** festive.　185.
birth-day. Plutarch notes that Cleopatra, to clear
herself cf suspicion, made at this juncture more of Antony
than she ever had, and that the celebration of her birth-
day was part of her program.

195-200. **Now he'll . . . with.** Enobarbus is Shakespeare's mouthpiece; hence, this soliloquy is significant.
Enobarbus analyzes for us Antony's psychological and
ethical state and does so in Aristotelian terms. Note the
two aphorisms, *To be furious,* etc., and *when valour preys,*
etc.　Antony's recoil to valor is factitious and lacks the
balance or steadying power of reason.
　Act IV. Scene i. 9. **Make boot,** take advantage.

Of those that served Mark Antony but late,
Enough to fetch him in. See it done: 14
And feast the army; we have store to do 't,
And they have earn'd the waste. Poor
    Antony!   [*Exeunt.*

SCENE II. *Alexandria. Cleopatra's palace.*

Enter ANTONY, CLEOPATRA, ENOBARBUS,
CHARMIAN, IRAS, ALEXAS, *with others.*

Ant. He will not fight with me, Domitius.
Eno.   No.
Ant. Why should he not?
Eno. He thinks, being twenty times of
    better fortune,
He is twenty men to one.
Ant.   To-morrow, soldier,
By sea and land I'll fight: or I will live,
Or bathe my dying honour in the blood
Shall make it live again. Woo 't thou fight
    well?
Eno. I'll strike, and cry 'Take all.'
Ant.   Well said; come on.
Call forth my household servants: let's to-
    night
Be bounteous at our meal.

    Enter three or four Servitors.

    Give me thy hand, 10
Thou hast been rightly honest;—so hast
    thou;—
Thou,—and thou,—and thou:—you have
    served me well,
And kings have been your fellows.
Cleo. [*Aside to Eno.*] What means this?
Eno. [*Aside to Cleo.*] 'Tis one of those odd
    tricks which sorrow shoots
Out of the mind.
Ant.   And thou art honest too.
I wish I could be made so many men,
And all of you clapp'd up together in
An Antony, that I might do you service
So good as you have done.
All.   The gods forbid!
Ant. Well, my good fellows, wait on me
    to-night: 20
Scant not my cups; and make as much of me
As when mine empire was your fellow too,
And suffer'd my command.

14. **fetch him in**, capture him.
Scene ii. 7. **Woo't**, wilt. 8. **'Take all,'** apparently
a gaming phrase meaning "If you beat me you get everything."

Cleo. [*Aside to Eno.*] What does he mean?
Eno. [*Aside to Cleo.*] To make his followers
    weep.
Ant.   Tend me to-night;
May be it is the period of your duty:
Haply you shall not see me more; or if,
A mangled shadow: perchance to-morrow
You'll serve another master. I look on you
As one that takes his leave. Mine honest
    friends,
I turn you not away; but, like a master   30
Married to your good service, stay till death:
Tend me to-night two hours, I ask no more,
And the gods yield you for 't!
Eno.   What mean you, sir,
To give them this discomfort? Look, they
    weep;
And I, an ass, am onion-eyed: for shame,
Transform us not to women.
Ant.   Ho, ho, ho!
Now the witch take me, if I meant it thus!
Grace grow where those drops fall! My
    hearty friends,
You take me in too dolorous a sense;
For I spake to you for your comfort; did
    desire you   40
To burn this night with torches: know, my
    hearts,
I hope well of to-morrow; and will lead you
Where rather I'll expect victorious life
Than death and honour. Let's to supper,
    come,
And drown consideration.   [*Exeunt.*

SCENE III. *The same. Before the palace.*

Enter two Soldiers *to their guard.*

First Sold. Brother, good night: to-mor-
    row is the day.
Sec. Sold. It will determine one way: fare
    you well.
Heard you of nothing strange about the
    streets?
First Sold. Nothing. What news?
Sec. Sold. Belike 'tis but a rumour. Good
    night to you.
First Sold. Well, sir, good night.

    Enter two other Soldiers.

Sec. Sold. Soldiers, have careful watch.

33. **yield**, reward.

Third Sold. And you. Good night, good
night.

[*They place themselves in every corner of
the stage.*

Fourth Sold. Here we: and if to-morrow
Our navy thrive, I have an absolute hope 10
Our landmen will stand up.

Third Sold.   'Tis a brave army,
And full of purpose.

[*Music of the hautboys as under the stage.*

Fourth Sold. Peace! what noise?

First Sold.   List, list!

Sec. Sold. Hark!

First Sold.   Music i' the air.

Third Sold.   Under the earth. 13

Fourth Sold. It signs well, does it not?

Third Sold.   No.

First Sold.   Peace, I say!
What should this mean?

Sec. Sold. 'Tis the god Hercules, whom
Antony loved,
Now leaves him.

First Sold. Walk; let's see if other watchmen
Do hear what we do.

          [*They advance to another post.*

Sec. Sold.   How now, masters.

All.   [*Speaking together*] How now!
How now! do you hear this?

First Sold.   Ay; is't not strange? 20

Third Sold. Do you hear, masters? do you
hear?

First Sold. Follow the noise so far as we
have quarter;
Let's see how it will give off.

All.   Content. 'Tis strange. [*Exeunt.*

SCENE IV. *The same. A room in the palace.*

Enter ANTONY *and* CLEOPATRA, CHARMIAN,
and others attending.

Ant. Eros! mine armour, Eros!

Cleo.   Sleep a little.

Ant. No, my chuck. Eros, come; mine
armour, Eros!

Enter EROS *with armour.*

Come, good fellow, put mine iron on:
If fortune be not ours to-day, it is
Because we brave her: come.

Cleo.   Nay, I'll help too.
What's this for?

Ant.   Ah, let be, let be! thou art
The armourer of my heart: false, false; this,
this.

Cleo. Sooth, la, I'll help: thus it must be.

Ant.   Well, well;
We shall thrive now. Seest thou, my good
fellow?
Go put on thy defences.

Eros.   Briefly, sir.   10

Cleo. Is not this buckled well?

Ant.   Rarely, rarely:
He that unbuckles this, till we do please
To daff 't for our repose, shall hear a storm.
Thou fumblest, Eros; and my queen's a
squire
More tight at this than thou: dispatch. O
love,
That thou couldst see my wars to-day, and
knew'st
The royal occupation! thou shouldst see
A workman in 't.

Enter an armed Soldier.

          Good morrow to thee; welcome:
Thou look'st like him that knows a warlike
charge:
To business that we love we rise betime,   20
And go to't with delight.

Sold.   A thousand, sir,
Early though 't be, have on their riveted
trim,
And at the port expect you.

          [*Shout. Trumpets flourish.*

Enter Captains *and* Soldiers.

Capt. The morn is fair. Good morrow,
general.

All. Good morrow, general.

Ant.   'Tis well blown, lads:
This morning, like the spirit of a youth

13. **Music . . . earth.** This strange bit is from Plutarch, who, however, makes the music the symbol of the
departure of the god of Antony's "singular devotion,"
namely Bacchus. Shakespeare tells us that it is the god
Hercules, whom Antony claimed as his ancestor and
whom he imitated. 14. **signs well,** is a good sign. 23.
give off, cease, end. **Content,** all right, agreed.
Scene iv. 2. **chuck,** term of endearment.

5. **brave,** defy. 7. **armourer,** armor-bearer; i.e., she
provides armor to steel his heart. **false,** wrong. 13.
daff't, doff it, take it off. 15. **tight,** deft, skillful. 20.
betime, betimes. 23. **port,** gate. 25. **well blown,**
probably refers to the flourish of trumpets above, but
has been thought to refer to the blossoming or breaking
forth of the morning.

That means to be of note, begins betimes.
So, so; come, give me that: this way; well
    said.
Fare thee well, dame, whate'er becomes of
    me:
This is a soldier's kiss: rebukeable [*Kisses her.* 30
And worthy shameful check it were, to stand
On more mechanic compliment; I'll leave
    thee
Now, like a man of steel. You that will
    fight,
Follow me close; I'll bring you to 't. Adieu.
    [*Exeunt Antony, Eros, Captains, and*
                      Soldiers.
  Char. Please you, retire to your cham-
    ber.
  Cleo.   Lead me.
He goes forth gallantly. That he and Cæsar
    might
Determine this great war in single fight!
Then, Antony,—but now—Well, on.
                         [*Exeunt.*

Scene V. *Alexandria. Antony's camp.*

Trumpets sound. Enter Antony *and* Eros;
  a Soldier *meeting them.*

  Sold. The gods make this a happy day to
    Antony!
  Ant. Would thou and those thy scars had
    once prevail'd
To make me fight at land!
  Sold.   Hadst thou done so,
The kings that have revolted, and the sol-
    dier
That has this morning left thee, would have
    still
Follow'd thy heels.
  Ant.   Who's gone this morning?
  Sold.   Who!
One ever near thee: call for Enobarbus,
He shall not hear thee; or from Cæsar's
    camp
Say 'I am none of thine.'
  Ant.   What say'st thou?
  Sold.   Sir,
He is with Cæsar.
  Eros.   Sir, his chests and treasure 10
He has not with him.
  Ant.   Is he gone?

  Sold.   Most certain.
  Ant. Go, Eros, send his treasure after; do
    it;
Detain no jot, I charge thee: write to him—
I will subscribe—gentle adieus and greet-
    ings;
Say that I wish he never find more cause
To change a master. O, my fortunes have
Corrupted honest men! Dispatch.—Eno-
    barbus!   [*Exeunt.*

Scene VI. *Alexandria. Cæsar's camp.*

Flourish. Enter Cæsar, Agrippa, *with*
    Enobarbus, *and others.*

  Cæs. Go forth, Agrippa, and begin the
    fight:
Our will is Antony be took alive;
Make it so known.
  Agr. Cæsar, I shall.   [*Exit.*
  Cæs. The time of universal peace is near:
Prove this a prosperous day, the three-
    nook'd world
Shall bear the olive freely.

Enter a Messenger.

  Mess.   Antony
Is come into the field.
  Cæs.   Go charge Agrippa
Plant those that have revolted in the van,
That Antony may seem to spend his fury 10
Upon himself. [*Exeunt all but Enobarbus.*
  Eno. Alexas did revolt; and went to
    Jewry on
Affairs of Antony; there did persuade
Great Herod to incline himself to Cæsar,
And leave his master Antony: for this pains
Cæsar hath hang'd him. Canidius and the
    rest
That fell away have entertainment, but
No honourable trust. I have done ill;
Of which I do accuse myself so sorely,
That I will joy no more.

Enter a Soldier *of* Cæsar's.

  Sold.   Enobarbus, Antony 20

---

31. **check**, censure. **stand On**, be particular about,
insist on. 32. **mechanic**, vulgar.

14. **subscribe**, sign.
  Scene vi. 5. **The time . . . near.** This is Plutarch's
theme and the justification of imperial Rome; it was
handed down as a political and historical belief to the
Renaissance. Shakespeare no doubt shared it. 6. **three-
nook'd**, three cornered; thought to refer to the division
of power among the triumvirs, and also to the main
regions of the Roman world, East, West, and Africa.
17. **entertainment**, employment.

Hath after thee sent all thy treasure, with
His bounty overplus: the messenger
Came on my guard; and at thy tent is now
Unloading of his mules.
　Eno.　　　　　　　I give it you.
　Sold. Mock not, Enobarbus.
I tell you true: best you safed the bringer
Out of the host; I must attend mine office,
Or would have done 't myself. Your emperor
Continues still a Jove.　　　　　[*Exit.*
　Eno. I am alone the villain of the earth, 30
And feel I am so most. O Antony,
Thou mine of bounty, how wouldst thou
　　have paid
My better service, when my turpitude
Thou dost so crown with gold! This blows
　　my heart:
If swift thought break it not, a swifter mean
Shall outstrike thought: but thought will
　　do 't, I feel.
I fight against thee! No: I will go seek
Some ditch wherein to die; the foul'st best
　　fits
My latter part of life.　　　　[*Exit.* 39

SCENE VII. *Field of battle between the camps.*

Alarum. Drums and trumpets. Enter
AGRIPPA *and others.*

　Agr. Retire, we have engaged ourselves
　　too far:
Cæsar himself has work, and our oppression
Exceeds what we expected.　　[*Exeunt.*

Alarums. Enter ANTONY, *and* SCARUS
wounded.

　Scar. O my brave emperor, this is fought
　　indeed!
Had we done so at first, we had droven them
　　home
With clouts about their heads.
　Ant.　　　　　Thou bleed'st apace.
　Scar. I had a wound here that was like a
　　T,
But now 'tis made an H.

　Ant.　　　　　They do retire.
　Scar. We'll beat 'em into bench-holes: I
　　have yet
Room for six scotches more.　　　　10

Enter EROS.

　Eros. They are beaten, sir; and our ad-
　　vantage serves
For a fair victory.
　Scar.　　　　Let us score their backs,
And snatch 'em up, as we take hares, behind:
'Tis sport to maul a runner.
　Ant.　　　　　I will reward thee
Once for thy spritely comfort, and ten-fold
For thy good valour. Come thee on.
　Scar.　　　　I'll halt after. [*Exeunt.*

SCENE VIII. *Under the walls of Alexandria.*

Alarum. Enter ANTONY, *in a march;*
SCARUS, *with others.*

　Ant. We have beat him to his camp: run
　　one before,
And let the queen know of our gests. To-
　　morrow,
Before the sun shall see 's, we'll spill the blood
That has to-day escaped. I thank you all;
For doughty-handed are you, and have
　　fought
Not as you served the cause, but as 't had
　　been
Each man's like mine; you have shown all
　　Hectors.
Enter the city, clip your wives, your friends,
Tell them your feats; whilst they with joy-
　　ful tears
Wash the congealment from your wounds,
　　and kiss　　　　　　　　　　　10
The honour'd gashes whole. [*To Scarus.*] Give
　　me thy hand;

Enter CLEOPATRA, *attended.*

To this great fairy I'll commend thy acts,
Make her thanks bless thee. [*To Cleo.*] O thou
　　day o' the world,
Chain mine arm'd neck; leap thou, attire and
　　all,

---

26. **best you safed,** it were best you safeguarded.
34. **blows,** causes his heart to swell with passions. 35.
mean, means; i.e., he will stab himself. 36. **thought,**
probably in the sense of sorrow. **do't,** i.e., break his
heart.
　Scene vii. 2. **oppression,** difficulty. 6. **clouts,**
bandages, or blows and knocks. **apace,** fast. 8. **H,** i.e.,
the bottom of the *T* has been cut across; some see in this
a pun on the pronunciation of *H* like modern *ache.*

10. **scotches,** cuts.
　Scene viii. 2. **gests,** deeds. 6. **as't,** as if it. 7.
shown, shown yourselves. 8. **clip,** embrace. 10. **congealment,** clotted blood. 12. **fairy,** enchantress.

Through proof of harness to my heart, and
　　there
Ride on the pants triumphing!
　　Cleo.　　　　　　　Lord of lords!
O infinite virtue, comest thou smiling from
The world's great snare uncaught?
　　Ant.　　　　　　My nightingale,
We have beat them to their beds. What, girl!
　　though grey
Do something mingle with our younger
　　brown, yet ha' we　　　　　　　　　20
A brain that nourishes our nerves, and can
Get goal for goal of youth. Behold this man;
Commend unto his lips thy favouring hand:
Kiss it, my warrior: he hath fought to-day
As if a god, in hate of mankind, had
Destroy'd in such a shape.
　　Cleo.　　　　　　I'll give thee, friend,
An armour all of gold; it was a king's.
　　Ant. He has deserved it, were it car-
　　buncled
Like holy Phœbus' car. Give me thy hand:
Through Alexandria make a jolly march;　30
Bear our hack'd targets like the men that
　　owe them:
Had our great palace the capacity
To camp this host, we all would sup together,
And drink carouses to the next day's fate,
Which promises royal peril. Trumpeters,
With brazen din blast you the city's ear;
Make mingle with our rattling tabourines;
That heaven and earth may strike their
　　sounds together,
Applauding our approach.　　　　*[Exeunt.* 39

SCENE IX. *Cæsar's camp.*

Sentinels *at their post.*

　First Sold. If we be not relieved within
　　this hour,
We must return to the court of guard: the
　　night
Is shiny; and they say we shall embattle
By the second hour i' the morn.

Sec. Sold.　　　　　　This last day was
A shrewd one to 's.

Enter ENOBARBUS.

　Eno.　　　　O, bear me witness, night,—
　Third Sold. What man is this?
　Sec. Sold.　　　Stand close, and list him.
　Eno. Be witness to me, O thou blessed
　　móon,
When men revolted shall upon record
Bear hateful memory, poor Enobarbus did
Before thy face repent!
　First Sold.　　　　　Enobarbus!
　Third Sold.　　　　　　Peace!　　10
Hark further.
　Eno. O sovereign mistress of true melan-
　　choly,
The poisonous damp of night disponge upon
　　me,
That life, a very rebel to my will,
May hang no longer on me: throw my heart
Against the flint and hardness of my fault;
Which, being dried with grief, will break to
　　powder,
And finish all foul thoughts. O Antony,
Nobler than my revolt is infamous,
Forgive me in thine own particular;　　20
But let the world rank me in register
A master-leaver and a fugitive:
O Antony! O Antony!　　　　　　*[Dies.*
　Sec. Sold.　　　Let's speak
To him.
　First Sold.　Let's hear him, for the things
　　he speaks
May concern Cæsar.
　Third Sold. Let's do so. But he sleeps.
　First Sold. Swoons rather, for so bad a
　　prayer as his
Was never yet for sleep.
　Sec. Sold.　　　Go we to him.
　Third Sold. Awake, sir, awake; speak to us.
　Sec. Sold.　　　　　Hear you, sir?　29
　First Sold. The hand of death hath raught
　　him. *[Drums afar off.]* Hark! the drums
Demurely wake the sleepers. Let us bear
　　him

15. **proof of harness**, proof-armor, tested armor.
16. **pants**, heart-beats. 17. **virtue**, valor. 20. **something**, somewhat. 21. **nerves**, sinews, tendons, i.e.,
parts of the body in which strength resides, the brain
being the source of true courage. 28. **carbuncled**, set
with carbuncles; apparently a vague recollection of
Ovid, *Metamorphoses*, ii, where the yoke of Phœbus' car
is said to be set with chrysolites (Furness). 31. **owe**,
own. 37. **mingle**, union, mingling. **tabourines**,
drums.
　Scene ix. 2. **court of guard**, guardroom. 3. **embattle**, fall in for the combat.

5. **shrewd**, ill, curst. 12. **mistress . . . melancholy**,
the moon, so addressed because of her influence in causing lunacy. 13. **disponge**, pour down. 17. **dried with
grief**. Enobarbus has passed into the condition of
despair, his spirits having descended into his bowels,
leaving his heart dry. 20. **particular**, personal capacity.
30. **raught**, reached. 31. **Demurely**, with subdued
sound (Onions).

To the court of guard; he is of note: our hour
Is fully out.
    Third Sold. Come on, then;
He may recover yet.   [*Exeunt with the body.*

SCENE X.   *Between the two camps.*

Enter ANTONY *and* SCARUS, *with their Army.*

    Ant. Their preparation is to-day by sea;
We please them not by land.
    Scar.   For both, my lord.
    Ant. I would they 'ld fight i' the fire or i'
    the air;
We 'ld fight there too. But this it is; our foot
Upon the hills adjoining to the city
Shall stay with us: order for sea is given;
†They have put forth the haven . . .
Where their appointment we may best dis-
    cover,
And look on their endeavour.   [*Exeunt.*   9

SCENE XI.   *Another part of the same.*

Enter CÆSAR, *and his Army.*

    Cæs. But being charged, we will be still by
    land,
Which, as I tak't, we shall; for his best force
Is forth to man his galleys. To the vales,
And hold our best advantage.   [*Exeunt.*

SCENE XII.   *Another part of the same.*

Enter ANTONY *and* SCARUS.

    Ant. Yet they are not join'd: where yond
    pine does stand,
I shall discover all: I'll bring thee word
Straight, how 'tis like to go.   [*Exit.*
    Scar.   Swallows have built
In Cleopatra's sails their nests: the augurers
Say they know not, they cannot tell; look
    grimly,

And dare not speak their knowledge. Antony
Is valiant, and dejected; and, by starts,
His fretted fortunes give him hope, and fear,
Of what he has, and has not.
        [*Alarum afar off, as at a sea-fight.*

Re-enter ANTONY.

    Ant.   All is lost;   10
This foul Egyptian hath betrayed me:
My fleet hath yielded to the foe; and yonder
They cast their caps up and carouse together
Like friends long lost. Triple-turn'd whore! 'tis thou
Hath sold me to this novice; and my heart
Makes only wars on thee. Bid them all
    fly;
For when I am revenged upon my charm,
I have done all. Bid them all fly; begone.
                   [*Exit Scarus.*
O sun, thy uprise shall I see no more:
Fortune and Antony part here; even here
Do we shake hands. All come to this? The
    hearts   20
That spaniel'd me at heels, to whom I gave
Their wishes, do discandy, melt their sweets
On blossoming Cæsar; and this pine is
    bark'd,
That overtopp'd them all. Betray'd I am:
O this false soul of Egypt! this grave charm,—
Whose eye beck'd forth my wars, and call'd
    them home;
Whose bosom was my crownet, my chief
    end,—
Like a right gipsy, hath, at fast and loose,
Beguilded me to the very heart of loss.
What, Eros, Eros!

Enter CLEOPATRA.

           Ah, thou spell! Avaunt!   30
    Cleo. Why is my lord enraged against his
    love?
    Ant. Vanish, or I shall give thee thy
    deserving,
And blemish Cæsar's triumph. Let him take
    thee,
And hoist thee up to the shouting plebeians:

    Scene x. **6-8. order . . . Where.** Line 7 is probably incomplete; but if *order . . . haven* is treated as parenthetical, *Where* (whither) may be taken to refer to *hills* (l. 5) and the passage construed. **7. forth,** forth from.
    Scene xi. **1. But being,** unless we are.
    Scene xii. **3-5. Swallows . . . tell.** This gives a slight indication of how Shakespeare used his source. The swallows are mentioned in connection with Actium. It is said by Plutarch in that place that swallows built under the poop of Cleopatra's galley and that others came and drove them away; it is interpreted as an evil

omen. But this allusion Shakespeare took not from the text, but from the marginal note. The note says, "An ill signe, foreshewed by swallowes breding in Cleopatraes shippe." **13. Triple-turn'd,** three times faithless. **16. charm,** charmer. **22. discandy,** melt. **25. grave charm,** destructive witchcraft. **26. beck'd,** beckoned. **27. crownet,** coronet. **28. right,** veritable. **gipsy,** double sense: Egyptian and gypsy (rogue). **fast and loose,** a cheating game the name of which is still proverbial.

Follow his chariot, like the greatest spot
Of all thy sex; most monster-like, be shown
For poor'st diminutives, for doits; and let
Patient Octavia plough thy visage up
With her prepared nails. [*Exit Cleopatra.*
　　　　　　　　　'Tis well thou'rt gone,
If it be well to live: but better 'twere　　40
Thou fell'st into my fury, for one death
Might have prevented many. Eros, ho!
The shirt of Nessus is upon me: teach me,
Alcides, thou mine ancestor, thy rage:
Let me lodge Lichas on the horns o' the
　　moon;
And with those hands, that grasp'd the
　　heaviest club,
Subdue my worthiest self. The witch shall
　　die:
To the young Roman boy she hath sold me,
　　and I fall
Under this plot; she dies for 't. Eros, ho! 49
　　　　　　　　　　　　　　　　[*Exit*

Scene XIII.　*Alexandria.　Cleopatra's palace.*

Enter CLEOPATRA, CHARMIAN, IRAS, *and* MARDIAN.

Cleo. Help me, my women! O, he is more
　　mad
Than Telamon for his shield; the boar of
　　Thessaly
Was never so emboss'd.
Char.　　　　　　　To the monument!
There lock yourself, and send him word you
　　are dead.
The soul and body rive not more in part-
　　ing
Than greatness going off.
Cleo.　　　　　　　To the monument!
Mardian, go tell him I have slain myself;
Say, that the last I spoke was 'Antony,'

---

35. **spot,** disgrace.　36. **shown,** exhibited.　37.
diminutives, undersized creatures; or, if *doits* is correct, small coins.　**doits,** Thirlby's conjecture for F
Dolts, meaning "fools."　43. **shirt of Nessus,** the famous
garment dipped in the centaur's blood, which Dejanira
used as a love-charm for Hercules, thus causing his
death.　44. **Alcides,** Hercules.　45. **Lichas,** servant of
Hercules who was cast by his raging master into the sea.
Scene xiii.　2. **Telamon,** Ajax Telamon, who after
the capture of Troy went mad and slew himself when he
was not awarded the shield and armor of Achilles.　**boar
of Thessaly,** the boar sent by Diana to ravage the fields
of Caledon, and slain by Meleager.　3. **emboss'd,** foaming at the mouth, or driven to extremity.　5. **rive,** split,
sever.

And word it, prithee, piteously: hence,
　　Mardian,　　　　　　　　　　　　9
And bring me how he takes my death. To
　　the monument!　　　　　　　[*Exeunt.*

Scene XIV.　*The same.　Another room.*

Enter ANTONY *and* EROS.

Ant. Eros, thou yet behold'st me?
Eros.　　　　　　　Ay, noble lord.
Ant. Sometime we see a cloud that's drag-
　　onish;
A vapour sometime like a bear or lion,
A tower'd citadel, a pendant rock,
A forked mountain, or blue promontory
With trees upon 't, that nod unto the
　　world,
And mock our eyes with air: thou hast seen
　　these signs;
They are black vesper's pageants.
Eros.　　　　　　　Ay, my lord.
Ant. That which is now a horse, even with
　　a thought
The rack dislimns, and makes it indistinct, 10
As water is in water.
Eros.　　　　　　　It does, my lord.
Ant. My good knave Eros, now thy cap-
　　tain is
Even such a body: here I am Antony;
Yet cannot hold this visible shape, my knave.
I made these wars for Egypt; and the
　　queen,—
Whose heart I thought I had, for she had
　　mine;
Which whilst it was mine had annex'd unto 't
A million more, now lost,—she, Eros, has
Pack'd cards with Cæsar, and false-play'd
　　my glory
Unto an enemy's triumph.　　　　　20
Nay, weep not, gentle Eros; there is left us
Ourselves to end ourselves.

Enter MARDIAN.

　　　　　　　　　O, thy vile lady!
She has robb'd me of my sword.
Mar.　　　　　　　No, Antony;

---

10. **bring me,** i.e., word.
Scene xiv.　10. **rack,** floating vapor or cloud.　**dislimns,** effaces.　12. **knave,** boy.　19. **Pack'd,** shuffled
so as to cheat.

My mistress loved thee, and her fortunes
   mingled
With thine entirely.

   Ant.   Hence, saucy eunuch; peace!
She hath betray'd me and shall die the death.

   Mar. Death of one person can be paid but
   once,
And that she has discharged: what thou
   wouldst do
Is done unto thy hand: the last she spake
Was 'Antony! most noble Antony!'   30
Then in the midst a tearing groan did break
The name of Antony; it was divided
Between her heart and lips: she render'd life,
Thy name so buried in her.

   Ant.   Dead, then?
   Mar.   Dead.

   Ant. Unarm, Eros; the long day's task is
   done,
And we must sleep. [*To Mar.*] That thou
   depart'st hence safe,
Does pay thy labour richly; go.

                    [*Exit Mardian.*
               Off, pluck off:
The seven-fold shield of Ajax cannot keep
The battery from my heart. O, cleave, my
   sides!
Heart, once be stronger than thy continent,
Crack thy frail case! Apace, Eros, apace. 41
No more a soldier: bruised pieces, go;
You have been nobly borne. From me
   awhile.   [*Exit Eros.*
I will o'ertake thee, Cleopatra, and
Weep for my pardon. So it must be, for
   now
All length is torture: since the torch is out,
Lie down, and stray no farther: now all
   labour
Mars what it does; yea, very force entangles
Itself with strength: seal then, and all is
   done.
Eros!—I come, my queen:—Eros!—Stay for
   me: 50
Where souls do couch on flowers, we'll hand
   in hand,
And with our sprightly port make the ghosts
   gaze:

Dido and her Æneas shall want troops,
And all the haunt be ours. Come, Eros,
   Eros!

Re-enter EROS.

   Eros. What would my lord?
   Ant.   Since Cleopatra died,
I have lived in such dishonour, that the
   gods
Detest my baseness. I, that with my sword
Quarter'd the world, and o'er green Nep-
   tune's back
With ships made cities, condemn myself to
   lack
The courage of a woman; less noble mind 60
Than she which by her death our Cæsar
   tells
'I am conqueror of myself.' Thou art sworn,
   Eros,
That, when the exigent should come, which
   now
Is come indeed, when I should see behind me
The inevitable prosecution of
Disgrace and horror, that, on my com-
   mand,
Thou then wouldst kill me: do't; the time is
   come:
Thou strikest not me, 'tis Cæsar thou de-
   feat'st.
Put colour in thy cheek.

   Eros.   The gods withhold me!
Shall I do that which all the Parthian darts,
Though enemy, lost aim, and could not?

   Ant.   Eros, 71
Wouldst thou be window'd in great Rome
   and see
Thy master thus with pleach'd arms, bend-
   ing down
His corrigible neck, his face subdued
To penetrative shame, whilst the wheel'd
   seat
Of fortunate Cæsar, drawn before him,
   branded
His baseness that ensued?

   Eros.   I would not see't.
   Ant. Come, then; for with a wound I must
   be cured.

---

33. **render'd**, gave up. 38. **seven-fold shield.** The
shield of Ajax was made of brass and was reinforced with
seven thicknesses of ox-hide. 39. **battery from my
heart**, ordinarily taken to mean the swelling of his
heart denoted in its beating. Cuningham thinks it
means the battery of calamity from outside. 40. **continent**, container, i.e., his sides. 46. **length**, length
of life. 49. **seal**, make an end. 51. **couch**, lie. 52.
port, bearing, behavior.

53. **Dido . . . troops**, i.e., Antony and Cleopatra will
be the most distinguished lovers there; they will out-
shine even Dido and Æneas. 60. **less noble mind**,
being a less noble-minded person. 63. **exigent**, exigency, decisive moment. 65. **prosecution**, pursuit. 68.
defeat'st, frustratest. 72. **window'd**, placed in a window to look on. 73. **pleach'd**, folded. 74. **corrigible**,
submissive to correction. 76. **branded**, rendered conspicuous as by a brand. 77. **ensued**, followed.

Draw that thy honest sword, which thou
    hast worn
Most useful for thy country.

    Eros.   O, sir, pardon me! 80
    Ant. When I did make thee free, sworest
    thou not then
To do this when I bade thee? Do it at once;
Or thy precedent services are all
But accidents unpurposed. Draw, and
    come.

    Eros. Turn from me, then, that noble
    countenance,
Wherein the worship of the whole world lies.

    Ant. Lo thee!   [*Turning from him.*
    Eros. My sword is drawn.
    Ant.   Then let it do at once
The thing why thou hast drawn it.

    Eros.   My dear master,
My captain, and my emperor, let me say, 90
Before I strike this bloody stroke, farewell.

    Ant. 'Tis said, man; and farewell.
    Eros. Farewell, great chief. Shall I strike
    now?

    Ant. Now, Eros.
    Eros. Why, there then: thus I do escape
    the sorrow
Of Antony's death.   [*Kills himself.*
    Ant.   Thrice-nobler than myself!
Thou teachest me, O valiant Eros, what
I should, and thou couldst not. My queen
    and Eros
Have by their brave instruction got upon
    me
A nobleness in record: but I will be
A bridegroom in my death, and run into 't 100
As to a lover's bed. Come, then; and, Eros,
Thy master dies thy scholar: to do thus
        [*Falling on his sword.*
I learn'd of thee. How! not dead? not dead?
The guard, ho! O, dispatch me!

Enter Dercetas *and* Guard.

    First Guard.   What's the noise?
    Ant. I have done my work ill, friends: O,
    make an end
Of what I have begun.

    Sec. Guard.   The star is fall'n.
    First Guard. And time is at his period.
    All.   Alas, and woe!

    Ant. Let him that loves me strike me
    dead.

    First Guard.   Not I.
    Sec. Guard. Nor I.
    Third Guard. Nor any one.   110
         [*Exeunt Guard.*
    Der. Thy death and fortunes bid thy fol-
    lowers fly.
This sword but shown to Cæsar, with this
    tidings,
Shall enter me with him.

Enter Diomedes.

    Dio. Where's Antony?
    Der.   There, Diomed, there.
    Dio.   Lives he?
Wilt thou not answer, man? [*Exit Dercetas.*
    Ant. Art thou there, Diomed? Draw thy
    sword, and give me
Sufficing strokes for death.

    Dio.   Most absolute lord,
My mistress Cleopatra sent me to thee.

    Ant. When did she send thee?
    Dio.   Now, my lord.
    Ant.   Where is she?
    Dio. Lock'd in her monument. She had a
    prophesying fear   120
Of what hath come to pass: for when she
    saw—
Which never shall be found—you did suspect
She had disposed with Cæsar, and that your
    rage
Would not be purged, she sent you word she
    was dead;
But, fearing since how it might work, hath
    sent
Me to proclaim the truth; and I am come,
I dread, too late.

    Ant. Too late, good Diomed: call my
    guard, I prithee.
    Dio. What, ho, the emperor's guard!
    The guard, what, ho!
Come, your lord calls!   130

Enter four. or five of the Guard *of* Antony.

    Ant. Bear me, good friends, where Cleo-
    patra bides;
'Tis the last service that I shall command
    you.

---

83. **precedent**, former. 98-99. **got upon . . . record**,
created in me an obvious and recorded nobleness; also
interpreted as "won for themselves (upon me) a noble
place in the story" (Cuningham).

113. **enter me with**, recommend me to. 123. **disposed with**, come to terms with.

First Guard. Woe, woe are we, sir, you
    may not live to wear
All your true followers out.
    All.   Most heavy day!
Ant. Nay, good my fellows, do not please
    sharp fate
To grace it with your sorrows: bid that wel-
    come
Which comes to punish us, and we punish it
Seeming to bear it lightly. Take me up:
I have led you oft: carry me now, good
    friends,
And have my thanks for all.   140
              [Exeunt, bearing Antony.

SCENE XV. *The same. A monument.*

Enter CLEOPATRA, *and her maids aloft,
with* CHARMIAN *and* IRAS.

Cleo. O Charmian, I will never go from
    hence.
Char. Be comforted, dear madam.
Cleo.   No, I will not:
All strange and terrible events are welcome,
But comforts we despise; our size of sorrow,
Proportion'd to our cause, must be as great
As that which makes it.

Enter, below, DIOMEDES.

           How now! is he dead?
Dio. His death's upon him, but not dead.
Look out o' the other side your monument;
His guard have brought him thither.

Enter, below, ANTONY, *borne by the* Guard.

Cleo.   O sun,
Burn the great sphere thou movest in! dark-
    ling stand   10
The varying shore o' the world. O Antony,
Antony, Antony! Help, Charmian, help,
    Iras, help;
Help, friends below; let's draw him hither.
Ant.   Peace!
Not Cæsar's valour hath o'erthrown Antony,
But Antony's hath triumph'd on itself.

Cleo. So it should be, that none but An-
    tony
Should conquer Antony; but woe 'tis so!
Ant. I am dying, Egypt, dying; only
I here importune death awhile, until
Of many thousand kisses the poor last   20
I lay upon thy lips.
Cleo.   I dare not, dear,—
Dear my lord, pardon,—I dare not,
Lest I be taken: not the imperious show
Of the full-fortuned Cæsar ever shall
Be brooch'd with me; if knife, drugs, ser-
    pents, have
Edge, sting, or operation, I am safe:
Your wife Octavia, with her modest eyes
And still conclusion, shall acquire no hon-
    our
Demuring upon me. But come, come, An-
    tony,—
Help me, my women,—we must draw thee
    up: 30
Assist, good friends.
Ant.   O, quick, or I am gone.
Cleo. Here's sport indeed! How heavy
    weighs my lord!
Our strength is all gone into heaviness,
That makes the weight: had I great Juno's
    power,
The strong-wing'd Mercury should fetch
    thee up,
And set thee by Jove's side. Yet come a lit-
    tle,—
Wishers were ever fools,—O, come, come,
    come;
        [They heave Antony aloft to Cleopatra.
And welcome, welcome! die where thou hast
    lived:
Quicken with kissing: had my lips that
    power,
Thus would I wear them out.
All.   A heavy sight!   40
Ant. I am dying, Egypt, dying:
Give me some wine, and let me speak a little.
Cleo. No, let me speak; and let me rail so
    high,
That the false housewife Fortune break her
    wheel,
Provoked by my offence.

---

136. **To grace,** by gracing or honoring.
Scene xv. 4. **our size of sorrow,** i.e. the size of our
sorrow. 10. **sphere.** The sun is here thought of as fixed
in a great sphere with which it revolved around the earth.
darkling, in darkness. 11. **varying shore,** varying between night and day. Presumably if the sun had burned
its sphere, earth's shore would no longer vary between
light and darkness.

23. **imperious,** imperial. 25. **brooch'd,** adorned
(as with a brooch). 28. **still conclusion,** composed
and quiet judgment. 29. **Demuring,** looking demurely, i.e., with affected modesty. 33. **heaviness,**
sadness, with play on *weight.* 44. **housewife.** The
proper form is (as in F) *Huswife,* used in a bad sense
meaning "hussy," "wanton."

Ant.   One word, sweet queen:
Of Cæsar seek your honour, with your
    safety. O!
    Cleo. They do not go together.
    Ant.   Gentle, hear me:
None about Cæsar trust but Proculeius.
    Cleo. My resolution and my hands I'll
    trust;
None about Cæsar.   50
    Ant. The miserable change now at my
    end
Lament nor sorrow at; but please your
    thoughts
In feeding them with those my former for-
    tunes
Wherein I lived, the greatest prince o' the
    world,
The noblest; and do now not basely die,
Not cowardly put off my helmet to
My countryman,—a Roman by a Roman
Valiantly vanquish'd. Now my spirit is
    going;
I can no more.
    Cleo.   Noblest of men, woo't die?
Hast thou no care of me? shall I abide   60
In this dull world, which in thy absence is
No better than a sty? O, see, my women,
    [*Antony dies.*
The crown o' the earth doth melt. My lord!
O, wither'd is the garland of the war,
The soldier's pole is fall'n: young boys and
    girls
Are level now with men; the odds is gone,
And there is nothing left remarkable
Beneath the visiting moon.   [*Faints.*
    Char.   O, quietness, lady!
    Iras. She is dead too, our sovereign.
    Char.   Lady!
    Iras.   Madam!
    Char. O madam, madam, madam!
    Iras.   Royal Egypt,   70
    Empress!
    Char. Peace, peace, Iras!
    Cleo. No more, but e'en a woman, and
    commanded
By such poor passion as the maid that milks
And does the meanest chares. It were for me
To throw my sceptre at the injurious gods;

To tell them that this world did equal theirs
Till they had stol'n our jewel. All's but
    naught;
Patience is sottish, and impatience does
Become a dog that's mad: then is it sin   80
To rush into the secret house of death,
Ere death dare come to us? How do you,
    women?
What, what! good cheer! Why, how now,
    Charmian!
My noble girls! Ah, women, women, look,
Our lamp is spent, it's out! Good sirs, take
    heart:
We'll bury him; and then, what's brave,
    what's noble,
Let's do it after the high Roman fashion,
And make death proud to take us. Come,
    away:
This case of that huge spirit now is cold:
Ah, women, women! come; we have no friend
But resolution, and the briefest end.   91
    [*Exeunt; those above bearing off
        Antony's body.*

ACT V.

SCENE I.   *Alexandria. Cæsar's camp.*

Enter CÆSAR, AGRIPPA, DOLABELLA, MECÆ-
NAS, GALLUS, PROCULEIUS, *and others, his
council of war.*

    Cæs. Go to him, Dolabella, bid him yield;
Being so frustrate, tell him he mocks
The pauses that he makes.
    Dol.   Cæsar, I shall. [*Exit*

Enter DERCETAS, *with the sword of* ANTONY.

    Cæs. Wherefore is that? and what art thou
    that darest
Appear thus to us?
    Der.   I am call'd Dercetas;
Mark Antony I served, who best was worthy
Best to be served: whilst he stood up and
    spoke,
He was my master; and I wore my life
To spend upon his haters. If thou please
To take me to thee, as I was to him   10

57. **a Roman by a Roman.** Shakespeare follows
Plutarch very closely in his account of Antony's death,
and repeats simply and admiringly the rhetoric of his
source. 65. **pole**, lodestar; also explained as "banner or
standard." 67. **remarkable**, distinguished, noteworthy.
75. **chares**, chores, drudgery.

79. **sottish**, merely stupid. 85. **Good sirs**, addressed
to the women.
Act V. Scene i. 2. **frustrate**, frustrated, baffled.
2-3. **mocks . . . makes**, makes himself ridiculous by
his delays.

I'll be to Cæsar; if thou pleasest not,
I yield thee up my life.
    Cæs.   What is 't thou say'st?
    Der. I say, O Cæsar, Antony is dead.
    Cæs. The breaking of so great a thing
    should make
A greater crack: †the round world
Should have shook lions into civil streets,
And citizens to their dens: the death of
    Antony
Is not a single doom; in the name lay
A moiety of the world.
    Der.   He is dead, Cæsar;
Not by a public minister of justice,   20
Nor by a hired knife; but that self hand,
Which writ his honour in the acts it did,
Hath, with the courage which the heart did
    lend it,
Splitted the heart. This is his sword;
I robb'd his wound of it; behold it stain'd
With his most noble blood.
    Cæs.   Look you sad, friends?
The gods rebuke me, but it is tidings
To wash the eyes of kings.
    Agr.   And strange it is,
That nature must compel us to lament
Our most persisted deeds.
    Mer.   His taints and honours 30
Waged equal with him.
    Agr.   A rarer spirit never
Did steer humanity: but you, gods, will give
    us
Some faults to make us men. Cæsar is
    touch'd.
    Mec. When such a spacious mirror's set
    before him,
He needs must see himself.
    Cæs.   O Antony!
I have follow'd thee to this; but we do lance
Diseases in our bodies: I must perforce
Have shown to thee such a declining day,
Or look on thine; we could not stall together
In the whole world: but yet let me lament, 40
With tears as sovereign as the blood of
    hearts,
That thou, my brother, my competitor
In top of all design, my mate in empire,
Friend and companion in the front of war,

The arm of mine own body, and the heart
Where mine his thoughts did kindle,—that
    our stars,
Unreconcilable, should divide
Our equalness to this. Hear me, good
    friends,—
But I will tell you at some meeter season:

Enter an Egyptian.

The business of this man looks out of him; 50
We'll hear him what he says. Whence are
    you?
    Egyp. A poor Egyptian yet. The queen
    my mistress,
Confined in all she has, her monument,
Of thy intents desires instruction,
That she preparedly may frame herself
To the way she's forced to.
    Cæs.   Bid her have good heart:
She soon shall know of us, by some of ours,
How honourable and how kindly we
Determine for her; for Cæsar cannot live
To be ungentle.   59
    Egyp. So the gods preserve thee!
                      [Exit.
    Cæs. Come hither, Proculeius. Go and
    say,
We purpose her no shame: give her what
    comforts
The quality of her passion shall require,
Lest, in her greatness, by some mortal stroke
She do defeat us; for her life in Rome
Would be eternal in our triumph: go,
And with your speediest bring us what she
    says,
And how you find of her.
    Pro.   Cæsar, I shall. *[Exit.*
    Cæs. Gallus, go you along. *[Exit Gallus.]*
    Where's Dolabella,
To second Proculeius?
    All.   Dolabella! 70
    Cæs. Let him alone, for I remember now
How he's employ'd: he shall in time be ready.
Go with me to my tent; where you shall see
How hardly I was drawn into this war;
How calm and gentle I proceeded still
In all my writings: go with me, and see
What I can show in this.   *[Exeunt.*

19. **moiety**, one-half. 27. **but it is**, if it be not. 30. **persisted**, persistently desired or pursued. 31. **Waged equal**, were equal (with him), contended equally. 32. **humanity**, human nature. 39. **stall**, dwell. 42. **competitor**, associate (probably with slight sense of rivalry). 43. **In . . . design**, in height of, i.e., in all-daring, enterprise.

49. **meeter**, more fitting. 55-56. **frame . . . to,** conform or mold to. 59. **Determine**, decide. 65. **life in Rome**, presence in Rome alive. 66. **eternal in our triumph**, would be eternally recorded in our triumph (Schmidt); may be merely intensive, i.e., would contribute in the highest degree to our triumph (Cuningham).

SCENE II. *Alexandria. A room in the monument.*

Enter CLEOPATRA, CHARMIAN, *and* IRAS.

Cleo. My desolation does begin to make
A better life. 'Tis paltry to be Cæsar;
Not being Fortune, he's but Fortune's knave,
A minister of her will: and it is great
To do that thing that ends all other deeds;
Which shackles accidents and bolts up
    change;
Which sleeps, and never palates more the
    dug,
The beggar's nurse and Cæsar's.

Enter, to the gates of the monument, PROCU-
    LEIUS, GALLUS, *and* Soldiers.

Pro. Cæsar sends greeting to the Queen of
    Egypt;
And bids thee study on what fair demands 10
Thou mean'st to have him grant thee.
Cleo.   What's thy name?
Pro. My name is Proculeius.
Cleo.   Antony
Did tell me of you, bade me trust you; but
I do not greatly care to be deceived,
That have no use for trusting. If your mas-
    ter
Would have a queen his beggar, you must
    tell him,
That majesty, to keep decorum, must
No less beg than a kingdom: if he please
To give me conquer'd Egypt for my son,
He gives me so much of mine own, as I 20
Will kneel to him with thanks.
Pro.   Be of good cheer;
You're fall'n into a princely hand, fear
    nothing:
Make your full reference freely to my lord,
Who is so full of grace, that it flows over
On all that need: let me report to him
Your sweet dependency; and you shall find
A conqueror that will pray in aid for kind-
    ness,
Where he for grace is kneel'd to.

Cleo.   Pray you, tell him
I am his fortune's vassal, and I send him
The greatness he has got. I hourly learn 30
A doctrine of obedience; and would gladly
Look him i' the face.
Pro.   This I'll report, dear lady.
Have comfort, for I know your plight is
    pitied
Of him that caused it.
Gal. You see how easily she may be sur-
    prised:

[*Here Proculeius and two of the Guard
    ascend the monument by a ladder
    placed against a window, and, having
    descended, come behind Cleopatra.
    Some of the Guard unbar and open the
    gates.*

[*To Proculeius and the Guard*] Guard her till
    Cæsar come.   [*Exit.*
Iras. Royal queen!
Char. O Cleopatra! thou art taken, queen.
Cleo. Quick, quick, good hands.
                  [*Drawing a dagger.*
Pro.   Hold, worthy lady, hold:
          [*Seizes and disarms her.*
Do not yourself such wrong, who are in this
Relieved, but not betray'd.
Cleo.   What, of death too,
That rids our dogs of languish?
Pro.   Cleopatra,
Do not abuse my master's bounty by 43
The undoing of yourself: let the world see
His nobleness well acted, which your death
Will never let come forth.
Cleo.   Where art thou, death?
Come hither, come! come, come, and take a
    queen
Worth many babes and beggars!
Pro.   O, temperance, lady!
Cleo. Sir, I will eat no meat, I'll not drink,
    sir;
If idle talk will once be necessary, 50
I'll not sleep neither: this mortal house I'll
    ruin,
Do Cæsar what he can. Know, sir, that I
Will not wait pinion'd at your master's court;

1-2. **My desolation . . . life.** Cleopatra tells what she means in the lines which follow; she contemplates a deed which will show her contempt of fortune. 3. **knave,** servant. 6. **bolts up,** fetters or locks up. 7-8. **Which sleeps . . . Cæsar's.** To commit suicide would be to render oneself independent of accident and change, i.e., to sleep and never taste more the breast that nurses both Cæsar and the beggar. 14. **care . . . deceived,** whether I am deceived or not. 20. **as,** that. 27. **pray in aid,** beg assistance; a legal term meaning "to call in the assistance of an outside person."

29-30. **I send . . . got,** I own his superiority with complete submission (Johnson). 42. **languish,** lingering disease. 44. **undoing,** destruction. 48. **temperance,** moderation. 50-51. **If idle . . . neither.** If interpreted as punctuated, Cleopatra would say that, if she once gives way to idle talk, she will not sleep. If we take the clause, *If . . . necessary,* as parenthetical, it becomes a sort of giving away of her secret determination to slay herself. 53. **pinion'd,** bound.

Nor once be chastised with the sober eye
Of dull Octavia. Shall they hoist me up
And show me to the shouting varletry
Of censuring Rome? Rather a ditch in Egypt
Be gentle grave unto me! rather on Nilus'
   mud
Lay me stark naked, and let the water-flies
Blow me into abhorring! rather make   60
My country's high pyramides my gibbet,
And hang me up in chains!
  Pro.   You do extend
These thoughts of horror further than you
   shall
Find cause in Cæsar.

      Enter DOLABELLA.

  Dol.   Proculeius,
What thou hast done thy master Cæsar
   knows,
And he hath sent for thee: for the queen,
I'll take her to my guard.
  Pro.   So, Dolabella,
It shall content me best: be gentle to her.
[*To Cleo.*] To Cæsar I will speak what you
   shall please,
If you'll employ me to him.
  Cleo.   Say, I would die.   70
      [*Exeunt Proculeius and Soldiers.*
  Dol. Most noble empress, you have heard
   of me?
  Cleo. I cannot tell.
  Dol.   Assuredly you know me.
  Cleo. No matter, sir, what I have heard or
   known.
You laugh when boys or women tell their
   dreams;
Is't not your trick?
  Dol.   I understand not, madam.
  Cleo. I dream'd there was an Emperor
   Antony:
O, such another sleep, that I might see
But such another man!
  Dol.   If it might please ye,—
  Cleo. His face was as the heavens; and
   therein stuck
A sun and moon, which kept their course, and
   lighted   80
The little O, the earth.
  Dol.   Most sovereign creature,—
  Cleo. His legs bestrid the ocean: his rear'd
   arm

Crested the world: his voice was propertied
As all the tuned spheres, and that to friends;
But when he meant to quail and shake the
   orb,
He was as rattling thunder. For his bounty,
There was no winter in 't; an autumn 'twas
That grew the more by reaping: his de-
   lights
Were dolphin-like; they show'd his back
   above
The element they lived in: in his livery   90
Walk'd crowns and crownets; realms and
   islands were
As plates dropp'd from his pocket.
  Dol.   Cleopatra!
  Cleo. Think you there was, or might be,
   such a man
As this I dream'd of?
  Dol.   Gentle madam, no.
  Cleo. You lie, up to the hearing of the
   gods.
But, if there be, or ever were, one such,
It's past the size of dreaming: nature wants
   stuff
To vie strange forms with fancy; yet, to
   imagine
An Antony, were nature's piece 'gainst fancy,
Condemning shadows quite.
  Dol.   Hear me, good madam.   100
Your loss is as yourself, great; and you bear
   it
As answering to the weight: would I might
   never
O'ertake pursued success, but I do feel,
By the rebound of yours, a grief that smites
My very heart at root.
  Cleo.   I thank you, sir.
Know you what Cæsar means to do with
   me?
  Dol. I am loath to tell you what I would
   you knew.
  Cleo. Nay, pray you, sir,—
  Dol.   Though he be honourable,—
  Cleo. He'll lead me, then, in triumph?
  Dol. Madam, he will; I know 't.   110
[*Flourish, and shout within,* 'Make way
                   there: Cæsar!'

---

83. **Crested,** formed a crest for; an allusion to raised
arms used as crests in heraldry. 83-84. **propertied . . .
friends,** endowed with qualities which, when he spoke
to friends, recalled the music of the spheres. 85. **quail,**
make quail, overawe. **orb,** world. 92. **plates,** pieces
of money. 97. **past . . . dreaming,** no dream can come
up to it. 98. **To vie . . . fancy,** to equal the strange
forms produced by fancy. 99. **piece,** masterpiece.
103 **but I do,** if I do not.

---

  56. **varletry,** rabble. 60. **abhorring,** abhorrence,
abomination.

Enter Cæsar, Gallus, Proculeius, Mecænas, Seleucus, *and others of his train.*

Cæs. Which is the Queen of Egypt?

Dol. It is the emperor, madam.

[*Cleopatra kneels.*

Cæs. Arise, you shall not kneel:
I pray you, rise; rise, Egypt.

Cleo.   Sir, the gods
Will have it thus; my master and my lord
I must obey.

Cæs.   Take to you no hard thoughts:
The record of what injuries you did us,
Though written in our flesh, we shall remem-
ber
As things but done by chance.

Cleo.   Sole sir o' the world,   120
I cannot project mine own cause so well
To make it clear; but do confess I have
Been laden with like frailties which before
Have often shamed our sex.

Cæs.   Cleopatra, know,
We will extenuate rather than enforce:
If you apply yourself to our intents,
Which towards you are most gentle, you
shall find
A benefit in this change; but if you seek
To lay on me a cruelty, by taking   129
Antony's course, you shall bereave your-
self
Of my good purposes, and put your children
To that destruction which I'll guard them
from,
If thereon you rely. I'll take my leave.

Cleo. And may, through all the world:
'tis yours; and we,
Your scutcheons and your signs of conquest,
shall
Hang in what place you please. Here, my
good lord.

Cæs. You shall advise me in all for Cleopatra.

Cleo. This is the brief of money, plate,
and jewels,
I am possess'd of: 'tis exactly valued;
Not petty things admitted. Where's Seleucus?   140

Sel. Here, madam.

Cleo. This is my treasurer: let him speak,
my lord,
Upon his peril, that I have reserved
To myself nothing. Speak the truth, Seleucus.

Sel. Madam,
I had rather seal my lips, than, to my peril,
Speak that which is not.

Cleo.   What have I kept back?

Sel. Enough to purchase what you have
made known.

Cæs. Nay, blush not Cleopatra; I approve
Your wisdom in the deed.

Cleo.   See, Cæsar! O, behold,
How pomp is follow'd! mine will now be
yours;   151
And, should we shift estates, yours would be
mine.
The ingratitude of this Seleucus does
Even make me wild: O slave, of no more
trust
Than love that's hired! What, goest thou
back? thou shalt
Go back, I warrant thee; but I'll catch thine
eyes,
Though they had wings: slave, soulless
villain, dog!
O rarely base!

Cæs.   Good queen, let us entreat you.

Cleo. O Cæsar, what a wounding shame
is this,
That thou, vouchsafing here to visit me,   160
Doing the honour of thy lordliness
To one so meek, that mine own servant
should
Parcel the sum of my disgraces by
Addition of his envy! Say, good Cæsar,
That I some lady trifles have reserved,
Immoment toys, things of such dignity
As we greet modern friends withal; and say,
Some nobler token I have kept apart
For Livia and Octavia, to induce
Their mediation; must I be unfolded   170
With one that I have bred? The gods! it
smites me
Beneath the fall I have. [*To Seleucus*
Prithee, go hence;
Or I shall show the cinders of my spirits

125. **enforce**, lay stress upon. 126. **If you** . . .
intents, if you fall in with my plans. 130. **bereave**,
deprive. 134. **And may**, may take your leave throughout the world. 135. **scutcheons**, shields showing
armorial bearings. 138. **brief**, list or schedule. 140.
Not petty things admitted, petty things omitted.

151. **mine**, my followers. 163. **Parcel**, specify or
particularize. 165. **lady**, ladylike, feminine. 167.
modern, everyday, ordinary. 169. **Livia**, Cæsar's
wife. 170-171. **unfolded With**, exposed by.

Through the ashes of my chance: wert thou
    a man,
Thou wouldst have mercy on me.
Cæs.   Forbear, Seleucus.
                [*Exit Seleucus.*
Cleo. Be it known, that we, the greatest,
    are misthought
For things that others do; and, when we fall,
We answer others' merits in our name.
Are therefore to be pitied.
Cæs.   Cleopatra,
Not what you have reserved, nor what
    acknowledged,   180
Put we i' the roll of conquest: still be 't yours,
Bestow it at your pleasure; and believe,
Cæsar's no merchant, to make prize with you
Of things that merchants sold. Therefore be
    cheer'd;
Make not your thoughts your prisons: no,
    dear queen;
For we intend so to dispose you as
Yourself shall give us counsel. Feed, and
    sleep:
Our care and pity is so much upon you,
That we remain your friend; and so, adieu.
Cleo. My master, and my lord!
Cæs.   Not so. Adieu.
    [*Flourish. Exeunt Cæsar and his train.*
Cleo. He words me, girls, he words me,
    that I should not   191
Be noble to myself: but, hark thee, Char-
    mian.   [*Whispers Charmian.*
Iras. Finish, good lady; the bright day is
    done,
And we are for the dark.
Cleo.   Hie thee again:
I have spoke already, and it is provided;
Go put it to the haste.
Char.   Madam, I will.

Re-enter DOLABELLA.

Dol. Where is the queen?
Char.   Behold, sir. [*Exit.*
Cleo.   Dolabella!
Dol. Madam, as thereto sworn by your
    command,

Which my love makes religion to obey,
I tell you this: Cæsar through Syria   200
Intends his journey; and within three days
You with your children will he send before:
Make your best use of this: I have per-
    form'd
Your pleasure and my promise.
Cleo.   Dolabella,
I shall remain your debtor.
Dol.   I your servant.
Adieu, good queen; I must attend on Cæsar.
Cleo. Farewell, and thanks.
                [*Exit Dolabella.*
      Now, Iras, what think'st thou?
Thou, an Egyptian puppet, shalt be shown
In Rome, as well as I: mechanic slaves
With greasy aprons, rules, and hammers,
    shall   210
Uplift us to the view; in their thick breaths,
Rank of gross diet, shall we be enclouded,
And forced to drink their vapour.
Iras.   The gods forbid!
Cleo. Nay, 'tis most certain, Iras: saucy
    lictors
Will catch at us, like strumpets; and scald
    rhymers
Ballad us out o' tune: the quick comedians,
Extemporally will stage us, and present
Our Alexandrian revels; Antony
Shall be brought drunken forth, and I shall
    see
Some squeaking Cleopatra boy my greatness
I' the posture of a whore.
Iras.   O the good gods! 221
Cleo. Nay, that's certain.
Iras. I'll never see 't; for, I am sure, my
    nails
Are stronger than mine eyes.
Cleo.   Why, that's the way
To fool their preparation, and to conquer
Their most absurd intents.

Re-enter CHARMIAN.

          Now, Charmian!
Show me, my women, like a queen: go fetch
My best attires: I am again for Cydnus,
To meet Mark Antony: sirrah Iras, go.

---

174. **chance**, her misfortunes, through which her
resentment will show like fire through ashes. 175. **Forbear**, withdraw. 176. **misthought**, misjudged. 178.
We answer . . . name, we are accountable in our name
for the deserts (misdeeds) of others. 186. **dispose**, dispose of. 191. **He words me.** Cleopatra sees through
Cæsar's treachery exactly as in the source, where, however, such subtlety is not meant to detract from Cæsar's
nobility. 193. **Finish**, end, die. 195. **it**, the asp.

199. **religion**, sacred duty. 208. **an Egyptian puppet**, thought to be an allusion to Elizabethan puppet-
shows, of which there were many. 214. **lictors**, minor
officials in attendance on Roman magistrates. 215.
scald, scurvy, mean. 216. **quick**, lively, sprightly. 220.
boy, allusion to the practice of having women's parts
acted by boys on the Elizabethan stage.

Now, noble Charmian, we'll dispatch indeed;
And, when thou hast done this chare, I'll
   give thee leave   231
To play till doomsday. Bring our crown and
   all.
Wherefore's this noise?
           [*Exit Iras. A noise within.*

       Enter a Guardsman.

Guard.   Here is a rural fellow
That will not be denied your highness'
   presence:
He brings you figs.
   Cleo. Let him come in. [*Exit Guardsman.*
           What poor an instrument
May do a noble deed! he brings me liberty.
My resolution's placed, and I have nothing
Of woman in me: now from head to foot
I am marble-constant; now the fleeting moon
No planet is of mine.

   Re-enter Guardsman, *with* Clown *bringing in
       a basket.*

Guard.   This is the man.   241
Cleo. Avoid, and leave him.
              [*Exit Guardsman.*
Hast thou the pretty worm of Nilus there,
That kills and pains not?
   Clown. Truly, I have him: but I would
not be the party that should desire you to
touch him, for his biting is immortal; those
that do die of it do seldom or never recover.
   Cleo. Rememberest thou any that have
   died on't?   249
   Clown. Very many, men and women too.
I heard of one of them no longer than yesterday: a very honest woman, but something
given to lie; as a woman should not do, but
in the way of honesty: how she died of the
biting of it, what pain she felt: truly, she
makes a very good report o' the worm; but he
that will believe all that they say, shall never
be saved by half that they do: but this is
most fallible, the worm's an odd worm.
   Cleo. Get thee hence; farewell.   260
   Clown. I wish you all joy of the worm.
          [*Setting down his basket.*
   Cleo. Farewell.

   Clown. You must think this, look you,
that the worm will do his kind.
   Cleo. Ay, ay; farewell.
   Clown. Look you, the worm is not to be
trusted but in the keeping of wise people; for,
indeed, there is no goodness in the worm.
   Cleo. Take thou no care; it shall be
heeded.
   Clown. Very good. Give it nothing, I
pray you, for it is not worth the feeding. 271
   Cleo. Will it eat me?
   Clown. You must not think I am so simple
but I know the devil himself will not eat a
woman: I know that a woman is a dish for the
gods, if the devil dress her not. But, truly,
these same whoreson devils do the gods great
harm in their women; for in every ten that
they make, the devils mar five.
   Cleo. Well, get thee gone; farewell.   280
   Clown. Yes, forsooth: I wish you joy o'
the worm.   [*Exit.*

   Re-enter Iras *with a robe, crown, &c.*

   Cleo. Give me my robe, put on my crown;
   I have
Immortal longings in me: now no more
The juice of Egypt's grape shall moist this
   lip:
Yare, yare, good Iras; quick. Methinks I
   hear
Antony call; I see him rouse himself
To praise my noble act; I hear him mock
The luck of Cæsar, which the gods give men
To excuse their after wrath: husband, I
   come:
Now to that name my courage prove my
   title!   291
I am fire and air; my other elements
I give to baser life. So; have you done?
Come then, and take the last warmth of my
   lips.
Farewell, kind Charmian; Iras, long farewell.
      [*Kisses them. Iras falls and dies.*
Have I the aspic in my lips? Dost fall?
If thou and nature can so gently part,
The stroke of death is as a lover's pinch,
Which hurts, and is desired. Dost thou lie
   still?

---

   231. chare, task.   **240. marble-constant,** firm as
marble. **242. Avoid,** withdraw. **243. worm,** snake.
247. immortal, blunder for *mortal.* **259. fallible,**
blunder for *infallible.*

   264. do his kind, do what its nature dictates. **284.
Immortal longings,** longings for immortality. **286.
Yare,** quick. **292. my other elements,** earth and
water. Through fire and air she will escape this baser
life and gain her immortality. **296. aspic,** asp, venomous serpent.

If thus thou vanishest, thou tell'st the world
It is not worth leave-taking. 301
  Char. Dissolve, thick cloud, and rain;
    that I may say,
The gods themselves do weep!
  Cleo.   This proves me base:
If she first meet the curled Antony,
He'll make demand of her, and spend that
    kiss
Which is my heaven to have. Come, thou
    mortal wretch,
      [*To an asp, which she applies to her
                   breast.*
With thy sharp teeth this knot intrinsicate
Of life at once untie: poor venomous fool,
Be angry, and dispatch. O, couldst thou
    speak, 309
That I might hear thee call great Cæsar ass
Unpolicied!
  Char.   O eastern star!
  Cleo.   Peace, peace!
Dost thou not see my baby at my breast,
That sucks the nurse asleep?
  Char.   O, break! O, break!
  Cleo. As sweet as balm, as soft as air, as
    gentle,—
O Antony!—Nay, I will take thee too:
      [*Applying another asp to her arm.*
What should I stay—   [*Dies.*
  Char. In this vile world? So, fare thee
    well.
Now boast thee, death, in thy possession lies
A lass unparallel'd. Downy windows, close;
And golden Phœbus never be beheld 320
Of eyes again so royal! Your crown's awry;
I'll mend it, and then play.

      Enter the Guard, *rushing in.*

  First Guard. Where is the queen?
  Char.   Speak softly, wake her not.
  First Guard. Cæsar hath sent—
  Char.   Too slow a messenger.
                [*Applies an asp.*
O, come apace, dispatch! I partly feel thee.
  First Guard. Approach, ho! All's not
    well: Cæsar's beguiled.

---

  304. curled. Probably she thinks of Antony as she
first saw him, *barber'd ten times o'er* (Cuningham). **305.
He'll make . . . kiss,** he will inquire of her concerning
me and kiss her for giving him intelligence (Johnson).
306. mortal, deadly. **wretch,** creature. **307. intrinsicate,** intricate. **311. Unpolicied,** devoid of
policy, stupid. **316. What,** why. **326. beguiled,**
cheated.

  Sec. Guard. There's Dolabella sent from
    Cæsar; call him.
  First Guard. What work is here! Char-
    mian, is this well done?
  Char. It is well done, and fitting for a
    princess
Descended of so many royal kings. 330
Ah, soldier!   [*Dies.*

      Re-enter DOLABELLA.

  Dol. How goes it here?
  Sec. Guard.   All dead.
  Dol.   Cæsar, thy thoughts
Touch their effects in this: thyself art coming
To see perform'd the dreaded act which thou
So sought'st to hinder.
    [*Within* 'A way there, a way for Cæsar!'

Re-enter CÆSAR *and all his train, marching.*

  Dol. O sir, you are too sure an augurer;
That you did fear is done.
  Cæs.   Bravest at the last,
She levell'd at our purposes, and, being royal,
Took her own way. The manner of their
    deaths? 340
I do not see them bleed.
  Dol.   Who was last with them?
  First Guard. A simple countryman, that
    brought her figs:
This was his basket.
  Cæs.   Poison'd, then.
  First Guard.   O Cæsar,
This Charmian lived but now; she stood and
    spake:
I found her trimming up the diadem
On her dead mistress; tremblingly she stood
And on the sudden dropp'd.
  Cæs.   O noble weakness!
If they had swallow'd poison, 'twould ap-
    pear
By external swelling: but she looks like sleep,
As she would catch another Antony 350
In her strong toil of grace.
  Dol.   Here, on her breast,
There is a vent of blood and something
    blown:
The like is on her arm.
  First Guard. This is an aspic's trail: and
    these fig-leaves

---

  333. Touch their effects, meet with realization.
337. augurer, foreteller of future events. **339. levell'd
at,** guessed (as one might aim a weapon). **352. something blown,** somewhat swollen.

Have slime upon them, such as the aspic
   leaves
Upon the caves of Nile.
  Cæs.   Most probable
That so she died; for her physician tells
   me
She hath pursued conclusions infinite
Of easy ways to die. Take up her bed;
And bear her women from the monument:
She shall be buried by her Antony: 361
No grave upon the earth shall clip in it

   358. **conclusions**, experiments.   362. **clip**, clasp,
hold.

A pair so famous. High events as these
Strike those that make them: and their
   story is
No less in pity than his glory which
Brought them to be lamented. Our army
   shall
In solemn show attend this funeral;
And then to Rome. Come, Dolabella, see
High order in this great solemnity. [*Exeunt.*

   363-366. **High events . . . lamented**, the very
causers of events, like the present, cannot help being
touch'd by them: and the pitifulness of them will set
them as high in fame as conquest will the person that
wrought them (Steevens).

THE PERIOD OF THE ROMANCES

I. SHAKESPEARE'S LIFE AND TIMES, 1609-1616

Shakespeare's life With reference to Shakespeare's life and work from 1609 until his death in 1616 there is to be found a good deal of information and no small amount of praise. His connections with the theater no doubt grew less and less close until he abandoned the writing of plays about 1611 or 1612 and retired to Stratford. To what extent he had continued to perform as an actor no one can tell. Perhaps he had never been supremely important in that capacity. One imagines that his stays at his pleasant home in Stratford grew longer and his sojourns in London grew shorter as time went on and that finally he was able to turn over even the writing of plays to hands more fashionable than his, to Beaumont and Fletcher, Chapman, Webster, and Ben Jonson. One could not, however, say that Shakespeare's latest work shows any noticeable diminution either in power or in spirit. He comes out of the period of gloom represented by the tragedies and the mirthless comedies (if there was such a period in his private life) and produces at least two plays which for pure and charming gayety are almost unrivaled, namely, *The Winter's Tale* and *The Tempest*; nor can it be said that either *Cymbeline* or *Pericles* is lacking in dramatic vigor and natural charm. It has been usual to speak of the last group of plays as romances, which is an appropriate term in consideration of the fact that the plays of the period have something of the adventurous quality of the Greek romance and all, except possibly *The Tempest*, have ascertainable source-connections with that widely influential form of literature.

It would, however, be better to think of the plays of the last period of Shakespeare's work, except *The Tempest*, as tragi-comedies (dramas having the elements of tragedy but without a fatal issue), since tragi-comedy was probably the form that Shakespeare was consciously producing. The Folio editors found the classification of *Cymbeline* puzzling, not knowing whether to place it among comedies or tragedies. That they chose to place it among the tragedies is an evidence of Shakespeare's success in writing tragi-comedy; but that they had no doubt as to the classification of *The Winter's Tale* and *The Tempest* indicates that those two are merely romantic comedies with more than usually threatening features. *Pericles* was a most popular play on the London stage, so that it is a pity we have so poor a version of it. In fact, it may be that *Pericles* is the original romance (leading up to tragi-comedy) of the group of plays produced by Shakespeare and by Beaumont and Fletcher. It is alluded to as a well-known play in a poem called *Pimlyco* in 1609, and it was probably a year or two old at that time. It stayed on the stage and was a popular success. Since it has the qualities later developed in the romances, or tragi-comedies, and since it was a popular play, one suspects that it may have been a determining influence on the drama. Shakespeare was at best responsible for only a part of it and possibly not a sufficient part to make the Folio editors regard it as his play; but it may, all the same, have started him and his younger colleagues, Beaumont and Fletcher, on a new tack. As for *Henry VIII* and *The Two Noble Kinsmen*, their qualities are too divergent to be associated readily with the major plays of this period.

Henry VIII was being played at the time (June 30, 1613) that the Globe Theater was burned. A letter of Thomas Lorkin to Sir Thomas Puckering recounts it as follows:

No longer since than yesterday, while Burbage his company were acting at the Globe the play of Henry VIII, and there shooting off of certain chambers in way of triumph, the fire catched and fastened upon the thatch of the house, and there burned so furiously, as it consumed the whole house, and all in less than two hours, the people having enough to do to save themselves.

The company moved to the Blackfriars Theater and after a time proceeded with the erection of the new Globe. Shakespeare was one of the proprietors and continued to derive an income from its operation; but otherwise he seems to have had no connection with it. If the manuscripts belonging to the theater were stored at the Globe at the time of the fire, some enterprising persons must have done posterity a favor by carrying them out of harm's way; the manuscripts may, of course, have been stored at the Blackfriars. The Globe was at once rebuilt.

Literary allusions The story of the last, as of other periods of Shakespeare's life, presents its quota of panegyrics on the poet. John Davies of Hereford in *The Scourge of Folly* (1611?) thus apostrophizes him:

To our English Terence, Mr. Will. Shake-speare.

Some say (good Will)—which I in sport do sing—
Had'st thou not played some kingly parts in sport,
Thou hadst been a companion for a king,
And been a king among the meaner sort.
Some others rail; but, rail as they think fit,
Thou hast no railing but a reigning wit,
And honesty thou sow'st, which they do reap,
So to increase their stock which they do keep.

The following wretched sonnet is from *Run, and a Great Cast* (1614) by Thomas Freeman:

To Master W. Shakespeare

Shakespeare, that nimble Mercury, thy brain,
Lulls many hundred Argus-eyes asleep,
So fit for all thou fashionest thy vein.
At the horse-foot fountain thou hast drunk full deep:
Virtue's or vice's theme to thee all one is.
Who loves chaste life, there's Lucrece for a teacher;
Who list read lust, there's Venus and Adonis,
True model of a most lascivious lecher.
Besides in plays thy wit winds like Meander,
Whence needy new-composers borrow more
Than Terence doth from Plautus and Menander.
But to praise thee aright I want thy store.
Then let thine own works thine own worth upraise,
And help t'adorn thee with deserved bays.

A truer picture of the actual contemporary view of Shakespeare can perhaps be had from the following excerpt from the Induction to Ben Jonson's *Bartholomew Fair:*

If there be never a servant-monster i' the Fair, who can help it, he says; nor a nest of antics? He is loath to make nature afraid in his plays, like those that beget *Tales, Tempests,* and such like drolleries—to mix his head with other men's heels.

From this it is apparent that Ben Jonson did not admire *The Tempest,* and if by "a nest of antics" and "such like drolleries" he refers, as Professor Brooke suggests, to the tricks of Autolycus and the anti-mask in *The Winter's Tale* as well, it is also apparent that he does not approve of that play. The critical vogue was with Jonson and the younger dramatists, and Shakespeare was out of style. One wonders if he quit writing for the stage for that reason. John Webster, who certainly borrowed extensively from Shakespeare both in language and technique, in the address prefixed to his *White Devil* in 1612, makes, after he has heartily praised Ben Jonson, Chapman, and Beaumont and Fletcher, a vague and patronizing reference to "the right happy and copious industry of Master Shakespeare, Master Decker, and Master Heywood."

Latest records Shakespeare purchased also at least one more piece of real estate, for what purpose it is impossible to guess, a house in Blackfriars, London, in 1613. He did not pay the full purchase price, and the mortgage deed executed for the unpaid balance furnishes one of the six absolutely unquestioned examples of his signature. John Combe, a wealthy bachelor of Stratford and Shakespeare's friend, left him a legacy of five pounds in his will, which was put into execution in July, 1614. Shakespeare was also consulted by various persons at Stratford during the popular resistance to William Combe's attempt to enclose Welcombe Common. Shakespeare was on friendly terms with Combe and at the same time had property interests involved, so that he was apparently consulted as an important and fair-minded citizen. Combe attempted to secure Shakespeare's support of his high-handed project by executing a contract under the terms of which Shakespeare's own interests would be protected. The matter is obscure, and one wishes that more light might be thrown upon it.[1]

One of the most interesting documents from the later period was discovered by Mr. C. W. Wallace in the Public Record Office in 1909. It consists of the records of a lawsuit entered into in 1612 by Stephen Belott against his father-in-law Christopher Mountjoy, a Huguenot wigmaker who lived in St. Olave's parish, Silver Street, London, in order to secure the payment of a dower promised at the time of the marriage. In this suit Shakespeare was summoned as a witness and made deposition on five interrogatories. It turns out that Shakespeare was a lodger in Mountjoy's house at the time of the marriage in 1604 and, since he states in his testimony that he had known Mountjoy for more than ten years, for some time before that. Shakespeare admits that, at the solicitation of Mountjoy's wife, he had acted as an intermediary in the arrangement of the marriage between Belott and Mountjoy's daughter. There is some apparent hesitation in his testimony, as if, though willing to do justice to the son-in-law, he had no desire to involve his former landlord.

Shakespeare's will is dated March 24, 1616, almost exactly a month before his death. Handwriting experts have decided from the imperfect character of the three signatures endorsed on each of the three pages of the will that Shakespeare was ill at the time the will was executed. They have even suggested that his hand was at the time affected with something like palsy. On the testimony of the somewhat unreliable vicar of Stratford, John Ward, one is asked to believe that Michael Drayton and Ben Jonson visited Shakespeare at New Place in the spring of 1616, and had a "merry meeting, but it seems drank too hard, for Shakespeare died of a feavour there contracted." The will disposes of all of the property of which Shakespeare is known to have died possessed, the greater share of it going to his daughter Susanna. A fair sum went to his daughter Judith, married that year to Thomas Quyny, and

legacies to various relatives and friends, ten pounds to the poor of Stratford, his sword to Mr. Thomas Combe, 28s. 8d. apiece to five Stratford friends and to his fellows John Heminge, Richard Burbage, and Henry Condell to buy them mourning rings. An interlineation contains the bequest of his "second best bed with the furniture" to his wife and is the only mention of her name in the will. It has been pointed out that her dower rights to one-third of all freehold property were not subject to bequest and that, in an age when beds were relatively much more valuable than they are now, even a second-best bed might be a proper legacy; but certainly the will shows no great solicitude for her comfort. A good deal has been made of this in the attempt to establish the truth of a conjecture that Shakespeare was not happy with his wife. But there is really in the will no ground for the supposition. New Place was to be the home of Shakespeare's favorite daughter Susanna, wife of the distinguished physician Dr. John Hall. Mrs. Shakespeare would make her home with her daughter and with her dower rights secured by law would be quite as wealthy as she would need to be. There was, moreover, a local tradition which credited her with the wish to be buried in the grave with her husband.

The date of Shakespeare's death, April 23, 1616, is inscribed on his monument, which is an elaborate structure standing in the chancel of Trinity Church. It was built by the London sculptors Garret and Nicholas Johnson before 1623. To what extent it was tampered with at a later time is not certain. The full epitaph is as follows:

Judicio Pylium, genio Socratem, arte Maronem:
Terra tegit, populus mæret, Olympus habet.

Stay, passenger, why goest thou by so fast?
Read, if thou canst, whom envious death hath placed
Within this monument: Shakespeare, with whom
Quick nature died; whose name doth deck this tomb
Far more than cost; sith all that he hath writ
Leaves living art but page to serve his wit.

Obiit anno domini 1616. Ætatis 53. Die 23 Apr.

These lines, which seem to indicate, as well as anything could, the high reputation in which Shakespeare was held as a poet at

[1]Mrs. C. C. Stopes, Shakespeare's Environment, pp. 81 ff., and 336 ff.

the time of his death, are not so well known as those inscribed over Shakespeare's grave near the north wall of the chancel. A local tradition assigns them to Shakespeare himself and implies that he wrote them "to suit the capacity of clerks and sextons," whom he wished apparently to frighten out of the idea of digging up his bones and placing them in the charnel house near which he was buried. They have been regarded both as the merest doggerel and as verse possessed of grotesque and rustic power:

> Good frend, for Jesus' sake forbeare
> To dig the dust enclosed heare;
> Bleste be the man that spares thes stones,
> And curst be he that moves my bones.

Other dramatists The outstanding feature in the history of English drama during the period from 1608 to 1616, aside from the last plays of Shakespeare, is the appearance of the famous literary partners Francis Beaumont (1584?-1616) and John Fletcher (1579-1625). Both were men of good family and both were well educated. They were intimate friends, and tradition says that they lived together on the Bankside and were both "sealed of the tribe of Ben"; that is, they were of the group of young men who frequented the Mermaid Tavern and listened to the words of wisdom of the great and dominant, if not domineering, Ben Jonson. The following quotation comes from *Master Francis Beaumont's Letter to Ben Jonson:*

> Methinks the little wit I had is lost
> Since I saw you! For wit is like a rest
> Held up at tennis, which men do best
> With the best gamesters. What things have we seen
> Done at the Mermaid! heard words that have been
> So nimble, and so full of subtle flame,
> As if that every one from whence they came
> Had meant to put his whole wit in a jest,
> And had resolved to live a fool the rest
> Of his dull life!

Although Beaumont and Fletcher were very different from each other, the qualities that each had seem to have reinforced and balanced those of the other, each mind supplying what the other lacked. Beaumont is believed to have been superior to Fletcher in constructive power and poetic imagination. To him are attributed the pictures of

innocent maidenhood which are found in the plays, the more individualized characterization, and the ability to maintain suspense. His blank verse style is less mannered than that of Fletcher and more like that of Webster and Shakespeare. Fletcher is noted for lyrical sweetness, rhetorical fluency, and a realistic grasp of commoner human traits. He is the master of dialogue and of comic inventiveness. His blank verse style verges on prose, because of his use of extra syllables at the cæsura and at the end of the line, thus giving better the effect of conversation. One attributes to Fletcher the typical parts, such as the blunt soldier and the gay young libertine. Both men are aristocratic to a point of infatuation with royalty, both romantic, both sentimental. Probably both of them are responsible for the most obvious quality of their work, their sensationalism, their use of surprise. Certainly Beaumont had a share in it, and certainly Fletcher was a master of the art of piling event on event until the last possibility of sensational surprise and sentimental emotion is exhausted. Their partnership was short-lived, for Beaumont died in 1616. Yet so vital was it that all of the many works of Fletcher subsequent to Beaumont's death, works done in collaboration with Massinger, Field, Daborne, Middleton, and others, were collected in 1647 and published under the names of Francis Beaumont and John Fletcher. Indeed they are still so known. The two authors may have been working together as early as 1606, and their partnership must have been in full swing in 1609, to which year is ordinarily assigned *Philaster*, the typical play in the new mode. *The Woman Hater* (1606?) and *The Knight of the Burning Pestle* (1607), both comedies, are regarded as substantially the work of Beaumont alone; *Philaster* (1609?), tragicomedy, *The Maid's Tragedy* (1611?), tragedy, *A King and No King* (1611), tragicomedy, *Cupid's Revenge* (1612), tragedy, *The Scornful Lady* (1613-1616), comedy of manners, are the result of collaboration between Beaumont and Fletcher; and *The Faithful Shepherdess* (1608-1609), pastoral comedy, *Bonduca* (1609-1614), tragedy, *Monsieur Thomas* (1610-1616), comedy, and *Valentinian* (1610-1614), tragedy, are the work of Fletcher alone. These are the principal plays written by the two men jointly or severally during the period we are considering.

It is, however, only with *Philaster*, and perhaps others of the earlier plays, that we have to do in connection with the dramas of Shakespeare. It has been the habit to think of Shakespeare as having been influenced in his earlier years by Marlowe and his contemporaries, of his having influenced in some measure his own contemporaries and dominated his successors. It is perfectly obvious, however, that Jonson, and probably Chapman, were more potent influences on Shakespeare's successors than was Shakespeare himself. The really surprising idea is that Shakespeare may, so to speak, have been influenced by his successors. That is, when Beaumont and Fletcher captured the public ear with *Philaster*, Shakespeare may actually have modified his dramatic form to agree with the new fashion. This idea was put forward by Professor Thorndike in 1901.[1] It is not a perfectly acceptable idea, but nevertheless has a great deal to commend it. Shakespeare did introduce masques into *Cymbeline* and *The Tempest*, if somebody else did not do it for him; there is a sensational quality in the plot of *Cymbeline* very like that of *Philaster*, a use of surprise in *The Winter's Tale*, and an increase in the element of adventure in all the latest plays quite in conformity with the new drama of Beaumont and Fletcher. But it is easy to exaggerate these resemblances. There is plenty of action in most of Shakespeare's plays, no little melodrama, and a good deal of romance and adventure. He is also fond of sentiment, which is indeed one of his greatest charms. The suggestion has been made above that Shakespeare himself may have started, not necessarily the whole movement—it would be too much to claim that—but at least so much of that movement as he himself ever participated in, with the play of *Pericles*.

During this period Middleton was still writing comedies, such as *A Chaste Maid in Cheapside* (1611), and had not yet begun his great career in serious drama in which he was to produce with Rowley *A Fair Quarrel* (1617) and *The Changeling* (1623),

and by himself *Women Beware Women* (1625-1627). Jonson further secured his fame for all time with *The Alchemist* in 1610, and produced his second stiff classical tragedy *Catiline his Conspiracy* in 1611 and his typical comedy of manners *Bartholomew Fair* in 1614. Dekker was chiefly engaged in writing pamphlets (*The Gull's Hornbook* in 1609) and in dramatic collaboration, his best dramatic work having already been done. John Webster wrote his second great tragic masterpiece *The Duchess of Malfi* in 1613 or 1614. Massinger had so far appeared only as a collaborator with Fletcher, Field, and Daborne in the production of plays for the King's Company. During this period Chapman did his greatest work. He had a genius for ethical thought, and when he was genuinely moved, and not merely inflated with learning and pedantry, was capable of great poetry. *Bussy D'Ambois* had been written in 1604. He followed this with *Charles, Duke of Byron* (1608), possibly his greatest play, *The Revenge of Bussy D'Ambois* (1610?), and *Chabot, Admiral of France* (1613?). The mass of serious thought that went into the composition of this group of tragedies makes them a worthy contribution to English drama.

Non-dramatic literature In non-dramatic literature the great monument of the time is the Authorized Version of the Bible, which appeared in 1611 after seven years' labor of the best scholars in England. The translation was a result of the Hampton Court Conference in 1604 and was made at the suggestion of King James. After the work had been done in six sections by six committees, it was subjected to a revision lasting two years by a general committee. The Authorized Version is in the best of English, written at a time when the language was in its finest literary state. A second edition of Bacon's *Essays* appeared in 1612, greatly amplified, and increased in number from ten to thirty-eight. Chapman published his complete translation of Homer's *Iliad*, twelve books in 1610 and twelve in 1611. The final edition of *The Mirror for Magistrates* was published in 1610, the complete version of Daniel's *Civil Wars* in 1609, Drayton's *Polyolbion* in 1613, works which look backward on a sixteenth century now dead.

---

[1] A. H. Thorndike, *The Influence of Beaumont and Fletcher on Shakespeare*, Worcester, Mass., 1901.

The chief poet of the period was William Browne of Tavistock (*Britannia's Pastorals* in 1613 and 1616, *The Shepheards Pipe* in 1614), a poet important neither then nor now. To 1614 belong Sir Thomas Overbury's *Characters* and Sir Walter Raleigh's *History of the World*.

Plays of the period *Cymbeline* is dated 1609-1610; *The Winter's Tale*, 1611; *The Tempest*, 1611; *Henry VIII* 1613. *Pericles*, 1607, must be listed here because of its kinship with other plays of the period. These five plays are the undisputed work of Shakespeare during this period; to them may be added without inconsistency *The Two Noble Kinsmen*, 1613, in the writing of which Shakespeare undoubtedly had a hand.

Dowden on the romances The comments of Edward Dowden in the last chapter of his book, *Shakspere, His Mind and Art*, on Shakespeare's final period—a period which Dowden himself may almost be said to have discovered—are possibly the finest ever made. "In the latest plays of Shakspere," he says, "the sympathetic reader may discern unmistakably a certain abandonment of the common joy of the world, a certain remoteness from the usual pleasures and sadnesses of life, and, at the same time, all the more, this tender bending over those who are, like children, still absorbed in their individual joys and sorrows." He goes on,

Over the beauty of youth and the love of youth there is shed, in these plays of Shakspere's final period, a clear yet tender luminousness not elsewhere to be perceived in his writings. In his earlier plays, Shakspere writes concerning young men and maidens—their loves, their mirth, their griefs—as one who is among them; who has a lively, personal interest in their concerns; who can make merry with them, treat them familiarly, and, if need be, can mock them into good sense. There is nothing in these early plays wonderful, strangely beautiful, pathetic, about youth and its joys and sorrows. In the histories and tragedies, as was to be expected, more massive, broader, or more profound objects of interest engage the poet's imagination. But in these latest plays, the beautiful pathetic light is always present. There are the sufferers, aged, experienced, tried—Queen Katharine, Prospero, Hermione. And over against these are the children, absorbed in their happy and exquisite egoism—Perdita and Miranda, Florizel and Ferdinand, and the boys of old Belarius.[1]

[1]For references on Shakespeare's life and times see page 88.

II. PLAYS OF THE FOURTH PERIOD

PERICLES PRINCE OF TYRE

Publication The first mention of *Pericles* is found in the Stationers' Register under the date May 20, 1608:

Edward Blount. Entred for his copie vnder thandes of Sir George Buck knight and Master Warden Seton A booke called the booke of Pericles prynce of Tyre.

No edition is known following on this entry. However, the next year a very bad text of the play appeared in quarto published by Henry Gossen. It was reissued the same year. Subsequently reprints came out in 1611, 1619, 1630, and 1635. The play was printed in the Third Folio in 1664 with six others which are certainly spurious. These were reprinted in the Fourth Folio, 1685, and included by Nicholas Rowe in his editions of 1709 and 1714. Alexander Pope excluded the seven plays from his edition in 1725, and no editor reintroduced any of them until Malone put *Pericles* back in the canon by including it in his edition of 1790. Since that time all editors have allowed *Pericles* a place among Shakespeare's plays.

Date and significance *Pericles* was probably written about 1607. Professor T. S. Graves discovered data, not accepted by Chambers, which indicate that the play was acted in the public theaters in the winter of 1606-7.[1] In the *Calendar of State Papers*, Venetian, he found a statement that a Venetian ambassador named Guistinian went with the French ambassador and his wife to a presentation of *Pericles*, which

[1]"On the Date and Significance of *Pericles*," *Modern Philology*, XIII, 545-566.

cost him twenty crowns. Guistinian was in London from January 5, 1606, to November 23, 1608. From the correspondence between Guistinian and the French ambassador, Boderie, and from records of the plague which show when the theaters were closed, Graves arrived at the conclusion that the date of this particular performance fell within the period above named. He found also that this Venetian Guistinian was attempting during that time to get permission to export a shipment of grain to Venice, and infers that he paid the twenty crowns for a performance of this play, which pictures Pericles as a benefactor to Tarsus in that he gave the citizens grain, in order to excite the ambition of James I to be a similar benefactor to Venice. The text of the play as we have it is so bad that the conventional stylistic tests used in dating the plays are invalid in determining its date. Other circumstances, however, corroborate the date 1606-7, the consideration of which involves a discussion of the sources.

Source and authorship   In 1607 was republished a translation by Lawrence Twine of the romance of Apollonius of Tyre, which is the source of the Pericles story. This translation was entered in the Stationers' Register in 1576, and was printed (perhaps the second edition) about 1594. That the popularity of the play prompted the reappearance of the Twine version in 1607 is in all probability the case. The story is also found in Gower's *Confessio Amantis*. The play follows Twine quite closely as to incident. The playwright, however, made use of the *Confessio Amantis*, since Gower appears throughout the play as "Chorus." Many changes have been made in the play in the names of characters. The brothel scene is somewhat refined in the play, a detail for which Shakespeare is given the credit. In 1608 another prose version by George Wilkins appeared with the title-page:

The Painfull Aduentures of *Pericles* Prince of Tyre. Being the true History of the Play of Pericles, as it was lately presented by the worthy and ancient poet Iohn Gower. At London Printed by T. P. *for* Nat: Butter, 1608.

The statement here that the novel is "a true history of the Play of Pericles" seems

adequate proof that the play is the earlier of the two. There can be no doubt that one is closely patterned after the other. The striking parallel in passages and the peculiarity of details can admit of no other possibility. On the basis of these similarities and their correspondence in style with other known work of Wilkins, the majority of critics ascribe to Wilkins the first authorship of the play and to Shakespeare the revision of it.[1] Recently the play has been assigned as a whole to Thomas Heywood, with Shakespeare recognized as only a reviser.[2]

The story   Antiochus, king of Antioch, having seduced his own daughter, is unwilling to give her in marriage to any suitor. To prevent anyone's winning her he has devised a riddle in which is a baffling allusion to the incestuous relationship. He has proclaimed that whoever is able to solve his riddle shall be given the daughter in marriage, but that whoever fails shall be put to death. As the play opens, Pericles, the young prince of Tyre, is about to make trial of his wit in explaining the riddle. He reads it and understands it at once. Refusing to admit that the riddle is solved, Antiochus temporizes with the young prince, offering him forty days' respite in which to figure out the meaning. He then contrives means to slay Pericles secretly lest his own sin be disclosed. Pericles anticipates Antiochus by escaping to Tyre. Knowing, however, that he will be pursued, he secretly departs for Tarsus with a great store of provisions. On arriving at the city he finds the people suffering from famine and generously gives them all the food which he has brought with him, thus winning their gratitude as well as that of the governor, Cleon. Word soon reaches him at Tarsus that Antiochus is still in pursuit and that he should flee elsewhere.

[1]Fleay, *Life and Work of Shakespeare*, pp. 158-9; Delius, *Shakespeare Jahrbuch*, III, 175-204; R. Boyle, *New Sh. Soc. Trans.*, 1882, pp. 313-340. For a fresher view see Harry T. Baker, "The Relation of *Pericles* to George Wilkins' Novel," *Publ. Mod. Lang. Ass'n*, XXIII, 100-118, H. Dugdale Sykes in *Sidelights on Shakespeare* (Stratford, 1919), and Chambers, *William Shakespeare*, I, 518-528.

[2]See H. D. Gray, "Heywood's *Pericles*, Revised by Shakespeare," *Publ. Mod. Lang. Ass'n*, XL, 507-529; D. L. Thomas, "On the Play *Pericles*," *Englische Studien*, XXXIX, 210-239.

Pericles takes to sea once more and is shipwrecked; he is cast destitute and alone on the shores of Pentapolis. Here by his prowess in arms and his gracious bearing as a courtier, he wins the favor of the King, Simonides, and the love of his daughter, Thaisa. Pericles marries the princess without revealing to her that he is a prince. Some months after their marriage, Pericles receives word from Tyre that Antiochus and his daughter are dead, and that he may return safely to his own country. He sets sail, taking with him Thaisa. They are beset by a storm, and in the tumult Thaisa dies in giving birth to a daughter. The sailors demand that the dead body be buried at sea. Pericles takes such care in preparing the chest in which she is placed that it is carried afloat to the coast of Ephesus. Here it is found by Cerimon, a famous physician, who opens it. He succeeds in restoring to life Thaisa, who is not dead but only in a trance. She becomes a votaress in the temple of Diana at Ephesus.

Pericles proceeds to Tarsus where he leaves his daughter, Marina, in the care of Cleon, the governor, and his wife Dionyza. With her he also leaves a nurse who had formerly attended Marina's mother. He departs for Tyre, promising to return for Marina after she is grown. The child believes that Cleon and Dionyza are her parents. After fourteen years Marina's nurse dies, and on her deathbed tells the girl of her true parentage. Dionyza, who is jealous of Marina, hires a villain to take the girl to the seaside and slay her. Before he can accomplish his crime, pirates rush in and save Marina's life, but take her prisoner. The would-be murderer reports to Dionyza that he has thrown the body of Marina into the sea, whereupon Cleon and Dionyza erect a monument and assume all the outward shows of sorrow.

Marina is taken to Mytilene where she is sold to a procuress. The girl's beauty and virtue are so appealing that she is able to preserve her chastity. She wins the admiration of Lysimachus, the governor, who redeems her from the brothel and makes it possible for her to earn an honest living.

Pericles, meanwhile, has returned to Tarsus for his daughter. He is so overwhelmed with grief at her supposed death

that he takes an oath to abjure all human contacts. Driven by winds at sea, his ships arrive at the coast of Mytilene. Lysimachus, the governor, comes out to meet him, and, finding him unapproachable, sends for Marina, whose winsomeness he is confident can break through Pericles's grief. The interview between Marina and Pericles results in recognition. Pericles is then advised in a dream to go to Ephesus. After bestowing Marina on Lysimachus in marriage, he goes to Ephesus where he finds his wife Thaisa. Pericles has become king, not only of Tyre, but of Pentapolis and Antioch also. The play ends in the rewarding of the virtuous and the punishment of the wicked.

Stage history　　The story of the play has been told thus at length because of its extraordinary popularity before the closing of the theaters in 1642. It is referred to again and again by writers, always with admiration and frequently with reference to its popularity. There is a record of its performance at court in 1619 and of its revival at the Globe Theater as late as 1631. It will be seen that the play has many of the elements of Jacobean tragicomedy and decadent romance. It abounds in sensational situations and surprises. The repulsiveness of certain parts of its theme are characteristic of the age. The early date of *Pericles*, its romantic story, and its sentimental beauty must have done much to set the style of the new drama. *Pericles* has no recent stage history. Even the Restoration yawned over it, and it was not honored with an adaptation until that of George Lillo, who presented a modified version of the last two acts at Covent Garden in 1738. Samuel Phelps revived *Pericles* at Sadler's Wells Theater in London in 1854. Since then it has rarely, if ever, made an appearance on the stage.

CYMBELINE

Publication and date　　There is no text of *Cymbeline* except that which appears in the Folio of 1623, and that is a bad one. The play is so irregular in construction and so incredible in plot that many critics, with no adequate reason, have thought it a first draft. The Vision of Posthumus (V, iv) and some other parts have been regarded as the work of another hand than Shakespeare's, and hasty composition under pressure of a ruling fashion is the hypothesis pretty generally held. A better hypothesis would regard the play as Shakespeare's experiment in a new form. On one leaf of his *Diary* Dr. Simon Forman gives, under date of April 20, 1610, a summary of the plot of *Macbeth*. On the leaf preceding he gives, with no date at all, a summary of "Cimbalin, King of England." The natural inference is that he saw *Cymbeline* a short time before he saw *Macbeth*. Other entries of plays seen are, however, dated in the year 1611, and, if Forman made these notes on the plays witnessed in one particular season, he must have made a mistake in writing down the year in which he saw *Macbeth*. In that case the date of his attendance on *Macbeth*, and presumably on *Cymbeline*, would be 1611. It does not greatly matter, for there are other reasons, partly those of style and meter, for believing that *Cymbeline* was written in 1609 or 1610.

Romantic comedy There has been worked out, as we have seen, a quite definite and plausible theory to account for a change which took place in the fashion of the London stage about the year 1608 or 1609. This is connected with the work of Beaumont and Fletcher, dramatists of the new era, who replaced the simpler and more ingenuous comedy and tragedy of Shakespeare with a drama of sensationalism and surprise. *Philaster, or Love Lies a Bleeding* (1609?) is thought to have started the fashion. It has been contended that these new dramatists influenced their master and that their methods and temper appear in Shakespeare's latest plays, particularly in *Cymbeline*. Beaumont and Fletcher went in for ingenious plots, which to the very end might turn out to be either tragic or comic, plots which placed hard sensuality and courtly vice side by side with the ideals of saintly chastity and spotless honor. They kept many features of the older drama: maidens in boys' attire, adventures by land and sea, family separations and reunions, and sentimental pastoralism. Dramatically the plays are highly finished, with fewer stiff soliloquies and asides and more dramatic depiction by dialogue and action. Chiefly, they play on the sensational and

develop the possibilities of the surprising. Their verse loses rigidity and grows conversational. Inasmuch as *Cymbeline*, though preserving much of Shakespeare's genuineness in thought, action, and manner, is, compared to some of his earlier comedies and tragedies, a dramatic hodge-podge of the Beaumont-Fletcher school, one places it about the same time as *Philaster* and sees in it resemblances to that play. There is, however, no evidence to tell us definitely which is the earlier, *Cymbeline* or *Philaster*. The late Professor Dowden was of the opinion that it is at least an open question.[1] He thought that Shakespeare had opened up a romantic vein in the work he did in *Pericles* and might well have continued his experiment in *Cymbeline* on a much more thorough-going scale. Dowden regarded it as possible that Shakespeare may himself have originated the form of tragi-comedy or romance, represented typically by *Cymbeline*, *The Winter's Tale*, and *The Tempest* and by six plays believed on good grounds to be the joint work of Beaumont and Fletcher. *Philaster* was written for the King's Company, as were Shakespeare's romances, so that the dramatists must have been closely associated. Indeed it is generally conceded that Fletcher was Shakespeare's collaborator in *Henry VIII*, *The Two Noble Kinsmen*, and, probably, in the lost play called *The History of Cardenio*.

Sources The source-problem of *Cymbeline* is complex and interesting, and inasmuch as it reveals a good deal about the structure and nature of the play, it is worth going into. In its sources *Cymbeline* connects itself with the work Shakespeare had been doing earlier in his career. The outer shell of the play is derived from Holinshed, and from that part of Holinshed from which had come *King Lear*. Cymbeline was, like Lear, one of the mythical kings of Britain. We learn from Holinshed that Cymbeline had been brought up in Rome and knighted by Cæsar and that his sons were Guiderius and Arviragus; but, according to Holinshed, it was not Cymbeline who refused to pay the Roman tribute but his successor Guiderius. Most of the details in the first scene of the

---

[1] A. H. Thorndike, *The Influence of Beaumont and Fletcher on Shakespeare; Cymbeline*, edited by Edward Dowden, Arden Shakespeare (Methuen), Introduction.

third act come also from Holinshed, and many of the names in *Cymbeline* are picked up here and there in the *Chronicles*. One incident of real importance (V, iii, 52) comes from Holinshed, namely, the prodigious exploit of Belarius, Guiderius, and Arviragus—

A narrow lane, an old man, and two boys—

which is related of a Scotsman named Haie in a battle against the Danes. *Cymbeline* has in it many references to Roman affairs, and thus connects itself also with Plutarch.

These things are, however, of small account compared to the central incident of the play, which is based on Boccaccio's version in the *Decameron* (ninth novel, second day) of a widely current story in which a man made a wager that his wife's honor would be proof against seduction. There is every reason to think that Shakespeare knew Boccaccio, with whom he could have become acquainted through the original, a French translation, or an English translation now lost; but some details he seems to have adopted from other versions of the story. These details are so widely distributed that it is impossible to tell their source with certainty. Some are paralleled in *Westward for Smelts*, a prose tale not known to have been printed before 1620. There are two early French romances which tell the tale of the wager, the *Roman de la Violette* by Gibert de Montreuil and *del Conte de Poitiers*, and also a French miracle play. German, Scandinavian, Gaelic, and English versions have also been discovered.[1]

To join the story of the British king with the Italian novel Shakespeare needed to create Imogen, the wronged lady, the daughter of the British king, and to supply the story of the stealing away of the king's sons by Belarius and the machinery by which Imogen is united to her brothers. Here too there trails behind Shakespeare a series of vague sources. An old play, *The Rare Triumphs of Love and Fortune* (1589), tells how one Hermione, brought up like Posthumus as the king's ward, marries in spite of the king's opposition the princess Fidelia and, like Posthumus, is driven from the court. Hermione also has an encounter

with Fidelia's brother Armenio, a coward and a bully suggestive of Cloten. Fidelia flees to the cave of a hermit, formerly a courtier banished unjustly like Belarius. The play also contains reference to a sleeping-powder and to apparel stolen by a servant and used for disguise. It undoubtedly resembles *Cymbeline*. The adventures of Imogen also find fairly close parallel in those of the heroine of the nursery tale of *Little Snow White*. There are indeed many suggestions of sources and parallels. The conclusion one would draw from this fact is that back of the poor text of *Cymbeline* there was originally a carefully constructed play, and that in *Cymbeline* Shakespeare has paid the most minute attention to the dramatic effects of the situation.

Interpretation We would agree that dramatically *Cymbeline* is a very different thing from *Much Ado about Nothing* and other comedies of the earlier period in which there is likewise an element of sensationalism and intrigue. *Cymbeline* exploits situation, and in order to do this it is less consistent in characterization, less plausible in plot-construction, and in general is less careful in the telling of its story. Instead of being narrated and explained as they are put on the stage, the events are acted without comment. In this respect the play no doubt marks a technical advance in the direction of the natural. The style also seems to reflect this. There are more run-on lines than ever, more light and weak endings, and all told a more conversational effect in the verse. It is not, however, greater drama but worse. One has to enjoy it in a different way. One goes to it, not for profound conviction, as one goes to *Lear*, but for dramatic thrills and surprises, for the appreciation of situations as distinguished from characters. In order that situations may be realized individuality suffers. One watches the rage, the self-sacrifice, the grief, the passion of Posthumus. He rivals Othello in passion and his cue is the same, but we do not know him as we know Othello. Cloten seems to be at least two separate kinds of fool and talks at times so rationally and so prince-like that some critics have thought that the Cymbeline plot with the part of Cloten must have been written up several years before,

[1] See W. W. Lawrence, *Shakespeare's Problem Comedies*, New York, 1931, pp. 174-233.

perhaps when Shakespeare was hunting through Holinshed on the occasion of his composition of *King Lear*. One would not sacrifice too much to this idea in the criticism of Imogen. She has been a prime favorite with the critics of Shakespeare's women, and, though one admits that she plays the standardized rôle of love-lorn maiden and that her part is conventional, even that she is idealized beyond Shakespeare's other women; yet one feels that she is somehow saved from being classed with Beaumont and Fletcher's heroines by her whimsical humor, her frankness, and her spontaneity.

The denouement Another way of stating the point of the newer criticism of *Cymbeline* is to say that Shakespeare here held his threads separate until the very end, making no prefiguring of the happy denouement. The last scene of the play has been praised as Shakespeare's greatest achievement in the untangling of complications. A score of issues are there met and a score of dangerous possibilities ended happily. This is a leading feature of his latest technique and of the technique of his later contemporaries. We saw him in *Hamlet* protracting over five acts a theme which might have been solved in one. Because there is so much to tell and so much time to pass away in plots and counterplots, his hero seems, even to himself, to hesitate unnaturally. When one declares that *The Tempest* observes the Aristotelian unities of time, place, and action, one means that in that play Shakespeare has covered in his dramatic representation only so much of his sequence of events as would have made a fifth act in his earlier plays. His writing up to his denouement in *Cymbeline* shows him leaning in the direction of the structural unity he was to achieve more completely in *The Tempest*.

Stage history Although *Cymbeline* has not in general been a popular acting drama, there are, nevertheless, glorious pages in its stage history. Sir Henry Herbert, Master of the Revels under Charles I, records (January 1, 1633) that "Cymbeline was acted at Court by the King's Players. Well liked by the King." The play suffered much from adaptations to the stage in the seventeenth and eighteenth

centuries. Indeed it is supposed that Tom D'Urfey's *The Injured Princess, or The Fatal Wager* (1682) is the worst of vile alterations. Different stage versions, all more or less wrenched away from the original, were produced in 1720, 1755, and 1759. Garrick produced the play, with what Genest calls "some most judicious changes," in 1761, and with him in 1767 and 1770 Mrs. Barry played the part of Imogen. John Philip Kemble revived the play in 1785 with Mrs. Siddons as Imogen. Macready (1818), Edmund Kean (1823), and Charles Kemble (1827) appeared in the part of Posthumus. With Macready was Helen Faucit, famous in the part of Imogen. Another celebrated Imogen was the English actress Adelaide Neilson (1877). The last great revival of *Cymbeline* was that of Irving and Ellen Terry in 1896, in which Irving played Iachimo and Miss Terry Imogen. The drama is difficult for the stage because of its complexity both in plot and style, but the playing of Imogen at least has often been met with popular enthusiasm.

An annotated edition of *Cymbeline* is printed on pages 1013-1065 of this volume.

THE WINTER'S TALE

Publication and date There is no edition of *The Winter's Tale* before that of the First Folio of 1623. In spite of the late and complicated style in which the play is written, a feature that would make the reproduction of the play difficult, the version of the Folio is a good one and there are relatively few difficulties in the text. *The Winter's Tale* is one of the latest of Shakespeare's plays, and it so happens that it can be very accurately dated. The same diary of Simon Forman, the London doctor, which gives an account of *Macbeth* shows also that Forman saw Shakespeare's *The Winter's Tale* at the Globe on May 15, 1611, and recorded a fairly accurate summary of the plot in his "Booke of Plaies." Sir Henry Herbert, Master of the Revels, allowed on August 19, 1623, to the King's players a play called "Winters Tale, formerly allowed by Sir George Buc," who had been appointed Master of the Revels in August, 1610. This would place the play between August, 1610, and the date on which Forman saw it acted. Professor Thorndike, in the work before cited, has drawn the limits still more narrowly by arguing that the dance of twelve satyrs (IV, iv) before Polixenes is imitated from Jonson's *Masque of Oberon*, which was performed at court on January 1, 1611. Every feature of the play agrees with this date (namely, between January 1, 1611, and May 15 of that year): its elliptical style, its large number of light and weak endings, and its community of spirit with the romantic comedy of those particular years.

Sources   It has been known ever since the beginning of the eighteenth century that Shakespeare went for the subject of this play to a novel called *Pandosto, the Triumph of Time* by Robert Greene, who had uttered against him nineteen years before the famous reproach contained in *A Groatsworth of Wit*. Many names are changed; in fact only the name Mopsa is left from *Pandosto* and that is reapplied. There are also striking and not always necessary changes in plot. No intermediary drama has been found, and one is tempted to believe that Shakespeare worked from memory rather than from the text. The relation between *The Winter's Tale* and *Pandosto* is very different, for example, from that which exists between *Coriolanus* and its source. The euphuism of Lyly and the elaborate and courtly pastoralism of Sidney, both of which Greene imitated, do not manifest themselves in *The Winter's Tale*. The events which take place in *Pandosto* in Sicily are transferred to Bohemia, and *vice versa*. But in no case has Shakespeare more completely made over a source, and nothing is more completely transformed than the pastoralism of Greene's novel. Shakespeare's shepherds are real people, and Greene's are the puppets of the traditional pastoral. The one thing that Shakespeare has retained from his source is the wild and romantic improbability which, as we have seen, characterized *Cymbeline*. It is at least possible that Shakespeare knew the version of the story appearing in Francis Sabie's poems, *The Fisherman's Tale* (1595) and its sequel *Flora's Fortune* (1595), in which some of the more striking differences from Greene which Shakespeare adopted are to be found.

Interpretation   *The Winter's Tale* is much like *Cymbeline* in the looseness of its plot and in its disregard of probability. Perhaps nothing in *Cymbeline* forms so powerful a binding force for the whole play as does the use of the Greek oracle in *The Winter's Tale*. In fact it may be said that through the whole play there is an atmosphere of Greek piety, which serves to explain the seclusion of Hermione, and which gives color and pathos to the abasement of Leontes. Like *Cymbeline* and *The Tempest*, *The Winter's Tale* shows a determination that all shall end well. Leontes and Othello are affected by the same passion; it may even be said that the action of Leontes is quite as violent as Othello's, though much less excusable. Shakespeare seems, however, to tell us that by repentance and by obeying a god we may escape at least a part of the consequences of the most tragic sin. The secondary title of *Pandosto* is "The Triumph of Time," which means that time and the generations may restore much that the passion of the moment has destroyed. Since it is in the power of time

To o'erthrow law and in one self-born hour
To plant and o'erwhelm custom,

there is in *The Winter's Tale* not only a unity of tone and of intention, but also in its own fashion a unity of plot; it is but another illustration of Shakespeare's ability to find unity in a wide diversity. Nowhere, for example, is there greater variety and vigor in characterization of individuals. Hermione is one of Shakespeare's most steadfast characters, standing out as an example of noble and independent womanhood. Autolycus is his most famous rogue, bringing with him the ethics and the lingo of the fraternity of rogues and vagabonds. Florizel and Perdita are a pair of lovers as charming, as simple, and as youthful as Romeo and Juliet. In Mamillius Shakespeare is sometimes said to have achieved his greatest triumph in the depiction of childhood. Most of his children are pathetic figures. Camillo and Paulina are the perfection of faithful royal servants, and their union is perhaps not wholly the gratuitous match-making with which comedies are wont to close.

The statue of Hermione The use of the device of the living statue in the denouement of *The Winter's Tale* was sufficiently common to occasion no surprise. The story of Pygmalion from Greek mythology was of course well known, and Marston's *Metamorphosis of Pygmalion's Image* (1598), an amatory poem, was popular. A statue is brought to life in Lyly's *Woman in the Moon* (1597), and the hero of the anonymous play *The Trial of Chivalry* (1600?) impersonates his own statue in order to overhear the words of his ladylove. The device of the living statue appears elsewhere in Renaissance literature. The puzzling thing is not that Shakespeare employs it, even so cleverly, but that the whole thing comes as a complete surprise. The audience has been left in ignorance of the fact that Hermione is still alive until toward the end of the play. This is not the dramatic habit of Shakespeare, who practically always takes his audience into his confidence. If one considers also the fact that Hermione's prototype in *Pandosto* actually dies, one is led to suspect that the happy restoration of Hermione may be an afterthought on Shakespeare's part, an improvement possibly introduced into the play as a revision after the play had been written. Certain bibliographical peculiarities in the parts of the text concerned lend some color to this supposition.

Stage history *The Winter's Tale* seems to have been popular in its own day. It was played at court in 1611 (?), 1613, 1624, and 1634. After this it is not heard of for a long time, for the story of *The Winter's Tale* was too rambling and the play did too great violence to the three unities to be endurable to the taste of the Restoration. In 1741 *The Winter's Tale* was revived at the theater in Goodman's Fields. Soon after this (1756) it underwent drastic alterations by Garrick and appeared as *Florizel and Perdita* (made up mainly from the last two acts), in which form it continued to be acted during the rest of the eighteenth century. John Philip Kemble played Leontes to Mrs. Siddons's Hermione in a version not greatly different from the original (1802). The indefatigable reviver of Shakespeare, Samuel Phelps, put *The Winter's Tale* on at Sadler's Wells in 1845-6,

and in 1856 Charles Kean selected it for production on the grandest possible scale. Those were the days when historical accuracy was sought at all costs, and *The Winter's Tale* was, somewhat inappropriately, given a presentation perfectly Greek to the last detail. Nothing could be further from Aeschylus than Shakespeare's version of Robert Greene's imitation of the romances of the Romanized Greeks of the third and fourth centuries A.D. Ellen Terry was Mamillius in those performances. In 1906 she played Hermione in Beerbohm Tree's revival. In 1887 the American actress Mary Anderson played the double rôle of Hermione and Perdita and won great admiration by her performance. In that production Sir Johnston Forbes-Robertson was Leontes. The Ben Greet company gave a successful performance of *The Winter's Tale* in the Elizabethan manner about 1910. Miss Matthison acted the part of Hermione.

An annotated edition of *The Winter's Tale* is printed on pages 1066-1109 of this volume.

THE TEMPEST

Date and publication *The Tempest* is dated with a good deal of certainty in the year 1610 or 1611. The play was acted at court in 1611 and in 1613, and in the composition of it Shakespeare reveals a knowledge of certain pamphlets published in 1610. On July 28, 1609, the *Sea Venture*, a ship bearing Sir Thomas Gates, Sir George Somers, and Captain Newport was cast away on the Bermudas. The fleet, of which the *Sea Venture* was the flagship, had been dispersed by a storm a few days before; it was bearing supplies and settlers to the new colonies in Virginia. The shipwrecked party spent several months in Bermuda, built two small vessels from the timbers of their wrecked ship, and proceeded to Virginia. Accounts of the adventure were subsequently published in London, where there had been much uneasiness as to the fate of the shipwrecked persons. Silvester Jourdan's account, *A Discovery of the Barmudas, otherwise called the Isle of Divels*, was published in 1610; and another by William Strachey is dated July 15, 1610, although it does not seem to have been published until 1625. The chances are that Shakespeare saw it in manuscript. It is called *A true Reportory of the Wracke and Redemption of Sir* Thomas Gates *Knight; upon, and from the Ilands of the Bermudas*. Evidences of Shakespeare's use of these works will be found in the notes. *The Tempest* was first published in the folio edition of 1623.

Sources No direct source for the main story of Shakespeare's play has been discovered. For minor passages, however, there are an unusual number of parallels, not only to Jourdan and Strachey, but to others. Gonzalo's description of the ideal commonwealth (II, i, 147-168) offers the closest resemblance yet discovered between the works of Shakespeare and the *Essays* of Montaigne. Prospero's famous speech about "this insubstantial pageant" (IV, i, 148-158) is closely paralleled in *The Tragedie of Darius* by Sir William Alexander (1603); and another speech of Prospero's (V, i, 33-50) is borrowed from Ovid's *Metamorphoses*. No less than three suggestions have been made as to Shakespeare's source for the main story of *The Tempest*, and in each case obvious resemblances exist; but the resemblances are in fundamentals of plot and not in such detail as to enable one to say that we have a source rather than a parallel version of the same original. There is a Spanish collection of stories called *Winter Nights* by Antonio de Eslava, the fourth of which tells of the adventures of King Dardano of Bulgaria and his daughter Serafina.[1] These stories were published in 1609 and 1610. There is also a play known as *The Fair Sidea* by the German playwright Jacob Ayrer, which must have been written before 1605, when Ayrer died. It may have been brought to England or an account of it given there. Finally, there are facts from Italian history late in the fifteenth and early in the sixteenth century which in names and events offer rather striking parallels to *The Tempest*. These had been recounted by William Thomas in *The Historie of Italy* in 1549. The Spanish story and the German play have the magician prince, banished

with his only daughter, who subsequently gets his enemies into his power, regains his inheritance, and effects a union between his daughter and the son of his enemy. We seem to draw nearest of all to the dramatic substance of *The Tempest*, though no nearer to Shakespeare's immediate source, in a group of plots or scenarios of the Italian *commedie dell' arte*, printed by Sgr. Neri in 1913. Four of these offer resemblances, sometimes quite close, to the adventures of the shipwrecked crew on the enchanted island.[2] What we may have to do with, although there is not a shred of evidence for it, is Shakespeare reworking an old play out of that Elizabethan storehouse of invention, the Tudor drama of the sixteenth century.

The story as Shakespeare tells it A recent critic has suggested that the play may once have presented, not the closely unified scene and action that it now presents, but a rambling plot like the other romances, covering much time and happening in several places. He finds in the repetitions in Prospero's narrative to Miranda in the second scene of the first act evidence that the matters there recounted were once acted out in full. The cutting down, he thinks, was done in order to make room for the elaborate masque which appears in the fourth act.[3] The play is after all so well constructed and so intelligible in all its parts that it is hard to call successfully in question its integrity.

Many critics have been of the opinion that *The Tempest* is Shakespeare's farewell to the stage, and that in Prospero's laying aside his mantle we have Shakespeare leaving his art and the mighty magic of his pen. When, however, one reads the large significance of the play as the delineation of ideal power and justice in the world, one is disposed to think that that of itself is a sufficient motive for its composition. Applications may be made to Shakespeare and to others, but an intention on Shakespeare's part to symbolize his own career is harder to believe in.

---

[1] Gustav Becker, "Zur Quellenfrage von Shakespeares Tempest," *Shakespeare Jahrbuch*, XLIII, 155 ff.

[2] F. Neri, *Scenari delle Maschere in Arcadia*, Citta di Castello, 1913; Chambers, *William Shakespeare*, I, 493-494.

[3] *The Tempest*, edited by Sir Arthur Quiller-Couch and J. Dover Wilson, Cambridge, 1921.

Prospero Whatever views we may adopt with reference to the personal significance of *The Tempest* to its author must not blind us to the actual greatness of the conception of Prospero. We may trust the expression of it, in honest admiration, to the pen of the late Professor Dowden in the chapter and work quoted earlier in this section:

It is not chiefly because Prospero is a great enchanter, now about to break his magic staff, to drown his book deeper than ever plummet sounded, to dismiss his airy spirits, and to return to the practical service of his Dukedom, that we identify Prospero in some measure with Shakspere himself. It is rather because the temper of Prospero, the grave harmony of his character, his self-mastery, his calm validity of will, his sensitiveness to wrong, his unfaltering justice, and, with these, a certain abandonment, a remoteness from the common joys and sorrows of the world, are characteristic of Shakspere as discovered to us in all his latest plays. Prospero is an harmonious and fully developed *will*. In the earlier play of fairy enchantments, *A Midsummer-Night's Dream*, the "human mortals" wander to and fro in a maze of error, misled by the mischievous frolic of Puck, the jester and clown of Fairy-land. But here the spirits of the elements, and Caliban, the gross genius of brute matter—needful for the service of life—are brought under subjection to the human will of Prospero.

What is more, Prospero has entered into complete possession of himself. Shakspere has shown us his quick sense of injury, his intellectual impatience, his occasional moment of keen irritability, in order that we may be more deeply aware of his abiding strength and self-possession, and that we may perceive how these have been grafted upon a temperament not impassive or unexcitable. And Prospero has reached not only the higher levels of moral attainment; he has also reached an altitude of thought from which he can survey the whole of human life, and see how small and yet how great it is. His heart is sensitive; he is profoundly touched by the joy of the children with whom, in the egoism of their love, he passes for a thing of secondary interest; he is deeply moved by the perfidy of his brother. His brain is readily set a-work, and can with difficulty be checked from eager and excessive energizing; he is subject to the access of sudden and agitating thought. But Prospero masters his own sensitiveness, emotional and intellectual:

"We are such stuff
As dreams are made on, and our little life

Is rounded with a sleep. Sir, I am vex'd;
Bear with my weakness; my old brain is troubled:
Be not disturb'd with my infirmity;
If you be pleased, retire into my cell
And there repose: a turn or two I'll walk,
To still my beating mind."

"Such stuff as dreams are made on." Nevertheless, in this little life, in this dream, Prospero will maintain his dream rights and fulfil his dream duties. In the dream, he, a Duke, will accomplish Duke's work. Having idealized everything, Shakspere has left everything real.

History of the play The spectacular quality of *The Tempest* together with its subtle suggestiveness in the field of primitive life as contrasted with civilized life has made it one of the most popular of Shakespeare's plays. It has been a favorite with poets and lovers of Shakespeare. Dryden and D'Avenant rewrote it in 1667 as *The Tempest, or the Enchanted Island*. This version pleased Samuel Pepys and suited the taste of the age, but it does frightful violence to practically everything we think worth while in Shakespeare. Since the discontinuance of Dryden and D'Avenant's impossible version, *The Tempest* has not often been seen upon the stage, and when it has, there has been a tendency, as in Sir Herbert Tree's presentation in 1904, to accompany it with a wealth of scenic magnificence. The exploitations of the operatic possibilities of *The Tempest* have tended to displace the original play. The Dryden-D'Avenant version, with its Hippolito, "one that never saw woman," and its Dorinda, "one that never saw man," and its operatic ending, had its effect on the performances of Garrick (1756), John Philip Kemble (1767, 1789), and even the performances of Macready (1821). Samuel Phelps, as Prospero, played Shakespeare's play at Sadler's Wells in 1847, and Charles Kean, in the same part, directed an elaborate revival in 1857. The play, so marvelously attractive as literature, is possibly deficient in genuine dramatic quality. If so, one can understand the universal resort to the assistance of spectacular devices by those who have staged it. Prospero's part, which has been played by the greatest of English actors, is too easy and uniform. The rôle of Miranda for some reason does not reward the efforts of the great actresses.

Strangely enough it is the part of Caliban which has attracted the attention of some of the greater actors of recent years. Sir F. R. Benson, Sir Herbert Tree, and Sir Philip Ben Greet have taken the part and displayed great ingenuity in their attempts to delineate Shakespeare's "savage and deformed slave."

An annotated edition of *The Tempest* is printed on pages 1110-1142 of this volume.

HENRY VIII

Publication and date The last of the chronicle plays appeared in print for the first time in the First Folio (1623) and there bears the title *The Famous History of the Life of King Henry the Eight*. Since the "Histories" are arranged in historical sequence according to the reigns of the monarchs for whom they are named, *Henry VIII* follows *Richard III* and is last in the group. A play on the subject of Henry VIII, which it seems overcautious to regard as other than Shakespeare's *Henry VIII*, was being acted at the Globe playhouse on June 29, 1613, when it was burned to the ground. The fire made so great a sensation that a number of accounts of it have been preserved. The following is from Sir Henry Wotton's letter to his nephew Sir Edmund Bacon, July 2, 1613:

Now, to let matters of state sleep, I will entertain you at the present with what has happened this week at the Bank's side. The King's players had a new play, called *All is True*, representing some principal pieces of the reign of Henry VIII, which was set forth with many extraordinary circumstances of pomp and majesty, even to the matting of the stage; the Knights of the Order with their Georges and garters, the Guards with their embroidered coats, and the like: sufficient in truth within a while to make greatness very familiar, if not ridiculous. Now, King Henry making a masque at the Cardinal Wolsey's house, and certain chambers being shot off at his entry, some of the paper, or other stuff, wherewith one of them was stopped, did light on the thatch, where being thought at first but an idle smoke, and their eyes more attentive to the show, it kindled inwardly, and ran round like a train, consuming within less than an hour the whole house to the very grounds. This was the fatal period of that virtuous fabric, wherein yet nothing did perish but wood and straw, and a few forsaken cloaks;

only one man had his breeches set on fire, that would perhaps have broiled him, if he had not by the benefit of a provident wit put it out with bottle ale.

The play is referred to as "new"; and, although it is called *All is True*, Wotton says significantly "representing some principal pieces of the reign of Henry VIII," which is exactly what *Henry VIII* does. That *All is True* was a secondary title for the play is sufficiently indicated by the Prologue (ll. 9, 18, 21), which reiterates the words "true" and "truth." These words were, moreover, in a certain way symbolic of Henry VIII, whose willfulness and selfishness the popular mind commuted into rugged honesty. A stage direction (I, iv, 49) seems corroborative, since it reads, "chambers discharged." A set of verses preserved in manuscript, reprinted by Halliwell-Phillipps (*Outlines*, I, 310), refers to the King and Wolsey and to the actors Burbage, Condell, and Heminge. Indeed, the play conforms completely to our expectation, is in no way inconsistent with the records of the fire, and was chosen as Shakespeare's by Heminge and Condell themselves for inclusion in the First Folio. We may, therefore, conclude that the play dates from a short time before the fire.

Source The first four acts follow with surprising fidelity Holinshed's *Chronicle of England, Scotland, and Ireland*, not only in text, which often seems a paraphrase of prose in verse, but in event and in conception of characters. Holinshed himself followed two sources and is inconsistent in conception of characters and in chronology. The play makes matters worse in these respects, besides showing evidences of haste in composition. Holinshed is based on Polydore Vergil, who hated Wolsey, in the earlier part of his account of the reign. In the later part Holinshed substitutes a brilliant and sympathetic biography of Wolsey by George Cavendish, Gentleman Usher to the Cardinal, an adherent so faithful that he followed Wolsey into disgrace and served him until his death. There are thus two conflicting conceptions of Wolsey in Holinshed, both of which reappear in the play. King Henry appears in the play in the static and conventional, albeit kingly, figure of Holinshed, that is, as "Oberon," "bluff King Hal," the exponent of truth at any cost, scholarly, and conscientious. Katharine, as reflected by Holinshed from Polydore Vergil, is deeply wronged and pathetic. Holinshed's account of the reign of Henry VIII is one of the most vivid and most unreliable of his stories of English kings. The play puts Holinshed on the stage as a set of dramatic scenes fundamentally inconsistent with each other and often unrelated. It treats them with the spirit and technique of a historical pageant: First, the fall of Buckingham, with an unfavorable view of Wolsey; secondly, the rejection of Katharine of Aragon; thirdly, the fall of Wolsey, sympathetically presented; fourthly, the rise of Cranmer and the marriage with Anne Bullen; lastly, the christening of the infant Elizabeth, with a prophetic view of her future greatness. This part (the fifth act) comes from Foxe's *Acts and Monuments*. The play has no structural or philosophic unity. Such unity as it has is the mere settling of the mind after dwelling upon a series of sensational past events, as if one should say, "God moves in a mysterious way his wonders to perform."

Authorship On purely external evidence *Henry VIII* has as good a claim to be regarded as the work of Shakespeare as many unquestioned plays in the canon; and yet scholarly opinion is almost agreed, on the basis of purely internal evidence, that Shakespeare's part in it is less than that of John Fletcher. Indeed there is one piece of testimony which connects the play with Shakespeare's name. At the time of the revival of the play after the Restoration John Downes, prompter to the Duke of York's men, records a tradition in *Roscius Anglicanus* (1708) that D'Avenant was able to instruct Betterton in the acting of Henry VIII, for "he had it from Old *Mr. Lowen*, that had his Instructions from *Mr. Shakespear* himself." Fletcher wrote blank verse with a strong mannerism. His lines are prevailingly end-stopped, and nearly half of them have double or "feminine" endings. The poet Tennyson, who was excellent in the determination of meter, told his friend James Spedding that the meter of much of *Henry VIII* was like that of Fletcher. As a result of this con-

versation Spedding made his study *Who wrote Shakespeare's Henry VIII?*[1] His results, based on his count of feminine endings and checked by his feeling for style, gave Shakespeare only Act I, sc. i and ii; Act II, sc. iii and iv (Katharine's trial); Act III, sc. ii (to the King's exit); Act V, sc. i. This determination, which was later confirmed by the metrical studies of Fleay and Furnivall, still stands. Sir Sidney Lee suggested that Fletcher may have been assisted here and there in his portion by Massinger, and Robert Boyle puts Massinger into the play to the practical exclusion of Shakespeare. It will be noted that Spedding's division gives to Fletcher the most famous passage of the play, Wolsey's farewell to Cromwell (III, ii, 204-459). Nowhere else did Fletcher write so well, and yet it is difficult to escape the conclusion that he wrote this except on the somewhat difficult hypothesis that Shakespeare here and elsewhere in the play imitated Fletcher's style.

If Shakespeare and Fletcher worked together on *Henry VIII*, what was the nature of their collaboration? Sir E. K. Chambers, although he has nowhere presented the matter in detail, seems to be of opinion that back of *Henry VIII* lies a lost play called *Buckingham*, written, so he supposes, by Shakespeare for the Earl of Sussex's men in the winter of 1592-3 and brought by Shakespeare to the Lord Chamberlain's company in 1594. His idea evidently is that, when in 1613 Shakespeare for some reason came out of his retirement at Stratford to the assistance of his fellows in London, he and Fletcher collaborated in the rewriting of this old play. Professor Schelling calls attention to the great crop of chronicle histories dealing with the immediate past which appeared at the end of the Queen's reign, such as two non-extant plays on the fall of Wolsey (1600, 1601), Rowley's vigorous *When You See Me You Know Me* (1604), and Heywood's *If You Know Not Me You Know Nobody* (1604-5), and suggests that at this time Shakespeare may have begun a play later finished by Fletcher as *Henry VIII*. Spedding, Fleay, Furni-

[1]Published in *The Gentleman's Magazine*, August, 1850, and subsequently republished in the *Transactions* of the New Shakespeare Society, 1874.

vall, and Thorndike argue for an actual division of the material to be treated and a definite collaboration. The main ground of this opinion is the obvious lateness of the Shakespearean parts.[1]

Story of the play In *Henry VIII* we see first the rivalry of Buckingham and Wolsey ending in Buckingham's condemnation for treason. He goes to his death complaining that his servants have played him false and betrayed him to the King. Meantime, the King has fallen in love with Anne Bullen, upon whom he has bestowed great gifts and whom he has created Marchioness of Pembroke. Henry next raises the famous issue as to the validity of his marriage with Katharine, who before he married her had been betrothed to his dead brother Arthur. His hypocrisy, though patent to posterity, is not exposed in the play. Katharine is tried; Wolsey opposes the divorce, which is nevertheless granted. Again, though Katharine is treated with matchless sympathy, there is no open reflection on the King as the cause of her suffering. Henry gets an inventory of Wolsey's vast wealth and seizes it as his own. Cranmer rises into Wolsey's place. The King weds Anne Bullen, who is crowned in great state. Cranmer is accused of disloyalty but escapes condemnation. Then follows the glory of the birth of Elizabeth, reported seriously and prophetically by the nobles and retold in very good comic style by the Porter and his Man. The play ends with the christening of Elizabeth. In no play are there fuller stage directions and a more obvious intention to have it staged as a historical pageant.

Stage history There seems no very close correlation in Shakespeare's plays between literary excellence and stage success. Indeed, *Henry VIII*, comparatively speaking, is not a great play. Most readers agree with Dr. Johnson's sharp criticism to the effect that "the genius of Shakespeare comes in and goes out with Katharine." *Henry VIII* has, nevertheless, a rather illustrious stage history. It

has lent itself to spectacular production, and the greatest Shakespearean actors and actresses have been engaged in playing it. During the Restoration Betterton played the King and Mrs. Betterton Katharine. Pepys liked the play so well that he saw it a second time. It was revived a dozen times or more in the eighteenth century, conspicuously, with Barton Booth as Henry, in 1727, the year of the coronation of George II. In 1788 John Philip Kemble played the King, and Mrs. Siddons was magnificent as Katharine. In a later revival (1806) Kemble played Wolsey and Mrs. Siddons again Queen Katharine. Edmund Kean and Macready also presented the play, and Charles Kean, in the rôle of Wolsey, revived it sumptuously in 1855. Irving also played Wolsey in his great production at the Lyceum Theater in 1892; Ellen Terry played Katharine, and Forbes-Robertson, Buckingham. Beerbohm Tree brought the play to New York in 1916 in honor of the tercentenary of Shakespeare's death.

THE TWO NOBLE KINSMEN

Publication and date In 1634 was entered in the Stationers' Register by John Watterson "A Tragi Comedy called the two noble kinsmen by John Fletcher and William Shakespeare." The same year appeared: *The Two Noble Kinsmen: Presented at the Black-friers by the Kings Maiesties servants, with great applause: Written by the memorable Worthies of their time; Mr. John Fletcher, and Mr. William Shakespeare, Gent.* Tho. Cotes for John Watterson.

The Two Noble Kinsmen is to be dated pretty certainly in 1613.[2]

Authorship In spite of the testimony of the title-page of the 1634 quarto, critical opinion has been much divided on the question of whether or not Shakespeare had any hand in the composition of *The Two Noble Kinsmen;* about Fletcher's hand there is no doubt. It is obvious at a glance that the play was written by two authors of very different styles; one of these styles seems to be

[1] Robert Boyle, *Henry VIII*, New Shakespeare Society *Transactions*, 1880, 1886; Chambers, *The Elizabethan Stage*, II, 95, 130, 202, 217, 219, and *William Shakespeare*, I, 495-498; F. E. Schelling, *Elizabethan Drama*, I, 287, II, 383; Lee, *Life of William Shakespeare*, pp. 268-272.

[2] Chambers, *The Elizabethan Stage*, III, 226-7; *William Shakespeare*, I, 528-532.

Fletcher's and the other compares in some respects with Shakespeare's in his latest period. The only objection to Shakespeare's part-authorship is that the parts of the play attributed to him fall far short of the quality of *Cymbeline*, *The Winter's Tale*, and *The Tempest*. On the other hand, it is hard to find any other author who could equal some of the poetry in those parts. Professor C. H. Herford has advanced the hypothesis that the Shakespearean parts are late poetical fragments pieced together by Fletcher, and, some critics add, Massinger. The subject of the authorship of the play has engaged a great deal of attention, and opinions are still very much divided.[1]

Source and history *The Two Noble Kinsmen* is based immediately on Chaucer's *The Knight's Tale*, recounting in dramatic form and in close detail the story of the rivalry of the two Theban cousins, Palamon and Arcite, for the hand of the fair Emilia—their imprisonment, their infatuation with the lady, their quarrel, their escapes from prison, their duel in the lists, the victory and death of Arcite, and the union of Palamon and Emilia.

A play called *Palæmon and Arcyte* by Richard Edwards was performed before Queen Elizabeth at Oxford in 1566, and a "Palamon and Arsett" is mentioned in Henslowe's *Diary* in 1594; but neither play could have affected *The Two Noble Kinsmen* very greatly since, as announced in its prologue, it is a new play and since it follows Chaucer with great fidelity. At the time of the Restoration, *The Two Noble Kinsmen*, having been altered by D'Avenant, was produced (1664) under the name of *The Rivals* (published in 1668), since when the stage history of the play is a complete blank. It has perhaps been performed on rare occasions on the public stage in Germany and possibly by amateurs in England and America.

[1] See edition of the play by Harold Littlehale, New Shakespeare Society, 1876, 1881; and Chambers, as in the preceding note.

III. A NOTE ON DOUBTFUL AND LOST PLAYS

The Shakespeare canon The latest editor of the Shakespeare *Apochrypha* enumerates forty-two plays, other than those included in the First Folio, which at one time or another have been ascribed to Shakespeare.[1] Thirty-six plays, some of them attributed in whole or in part to other authors, have the sanction of having been included by Heminge and Condell in the folio edition of *Shakespeare's Comedies, Histories and Tragedies* in 1623. The effect of recent intensive study of the First Folio has been to increase the respect of scholars for the work of Shakespeare's two fellow-actors and to make disagreement with them more cautious. The canon now stands pretty much as the contents of the First Folio. To the thirty-six therein contained *Pericles* has been added. Few scholars doubt that Shakespeare had a hand

[1] *The Shakespeare Apocrypha*, edited by C. F. Tucker Brooke, Oxford, 1908, 1918. See bibliography of the subject of doubtful plays in *Cambridge History of English Literature*, V, 442-4.

in *The Two Noble Kinsmen*. Recently a noteworthy attempt has been made to establish Shakespeare's authorship of certain scenes in *Sir Thomas More*. Beyond this there is nothing established or accepted with reference to any of the vast group of doubtful plays. If the list be reduced by the rejection of utterly baseless attributions, there remains a body of about fifteen plays which may be thought of without absurdity as possibly somehow touched by Shakespeare's hand.

Additions to the Third Folio A number of the doubtful plays were published with Shakespeare's name or initials on their title-pages, in some cases while he was living and in other cases after his death, and a group of seven of them was included in the second printing of the Third Folio of 1664: *Pericles Prince of Tyre, The London Prodigal, The History of Thomas Lord Cromwell, Sir John Oldcastle Lord Cobham, The Puritan or the Widow of Watling Street, The Yorkshire Tragedy, The Tragedy* of *Locrine*. Of these *Pericles* has been accepted since the time of Malone as in large part the work of Shakespeare. *The London Prodigal* was published in 1605 by Nathaniel Butter (who published *King Lear*), "As it was plaied by the Kings Maiesties seruants. By William Shakespeare". It is a very good comedy of London life, full of humors and manners, but unlike anything known to have been written by Shakespeare. *Thomas Lord Cromwell* was printed for William Jones in 1602, "As it hath beene sundrie times publikely Acted by the Right Honorable the Lord Chamberlaine his Seruants. Written by W. S." It is a poverty-stricken specimen of the biographical history play. There seem to be no grounds for attributing it to Shakespeare, since even the initials "W. S." may have been intended to designate some other author. *Sir John Oldcastle*, ascribed to Shakespeare in a quarto of 1600, is known from Henslowe's *Diary* to have been written for the Lord Admiral's company by Drayton, Hathway, Munday, and Wilson. *The Puritan*, a fair comedy of manners, was printed by G. Eld in 1607, as "Acted by the Children of Paules. Written by W. S." Professor Brooke points out certain resemblances between this play and *Eastward Ho* and suggests tentatively that Marston had a hand in it. There seems no reason to connect it with Shakespeare. *A Yorkshire Tragedy* is on better ground. Shakespeare's name appears both in the entry in the Stationers' Register and on the title-page of the quarto of 1608. In the latter place it is also stated that it was "Acted by his Maiesties Players at the Globe." So far, however, as the use of Shakespeare's name is concerned, it may well have been due to the desire of the notorious piratical publisher, Thomas Pavier, to make dishonest gain. *A Yorkshire Tragedy* is a murder play, hasty and formless, but of great intensity. The Calverly murder, which it dramatizes, had occurred in 1605, and Shakespeare's company had no doubt taken immediate advantage of the sensation to prepare and present the play. It is hard to think that Shakespeare at such a time in his career could have been employed on such a job; but, since there are prose passages in the play of profound psychological knowledge and insight and of breathless intensity, many critics have thought that they at least show the touch of his hand. *Locrine* is a tragedy of an early stiff type, like *Gorboduc* and *The Misfortunes of Arthur*; and, since it resembles the works of Robert Greene, *Selimus*(?) and *Alphonsus, King of Aragon*, Professor Brooke argues strongly that it is Greene's work and earlier than either of those mentioned. It was printed by Thomas Creed in 1595 as "Newly set foorth, overseene and corrected, By W. S." This may mean exactly what it says, and the "W. S." may be anybody whom those initials fit who had revised the play.

The Charles II group In the library of King Charles II was a volume in which three quartos were bound together and given on the outside the title "Shakespeare, Vol. I." The volume contained *Fair Em*, *Mucedorus*, and *The Merry Devil of Edmonton*. All had been printed anonymously, all were popular favorites, and the binding together and labeling may have been due to the belief that Shakespeare had written all of the most popular plays of the preceding generation, or to any other ignorant belief. *Fair Em* was printed first without date (as acted by Lord Strange's servants) and later, in 1631, for John Wright. It is a crude comedy, rather pleasant, made up of two plots loosely joined. The Miller's daughter of Manchester, the heroine, has three noble lovers, whose faiths are duly tested, and the right one selected. With this is a legend of Richard Coeur de Lion. The comedy gives a truly middle-class picture of royal and noble life. It has been attributed to Robert Greene, because it is thought to resemble *The Pinner of Wakefield*, which, in turn, is thought to resemble *Friar Bacon and Friar Bungay*. *Fair Em* belongs to about 1590. *Mucedorus* was one of the most popular plays of the age. It appeared in at least seventeen quarto editions, the third of which (1610) states that it is "Amplified with new additions, as it was acted before the Kings Maiestie at White-hall on Shrove-Sunday night. By his Highnes Seruants usually playing at the Globe." The first edition was in 1598. It is mere impertinence to attribute the original play to Shakespeare; but, since the "new additions" referred to on the title-page of the third quarto are superior to the rest of the play, they have sometimes been regarded as Shakespeare's. Robert Greene has again been regarded without sufficient warrant as original author. The text of *The Merry Devil of Edmonton*, a better play than either of the others, looks as if the play had been worn by much acting and many alterations. The suspected Revels Accounts of Peter Cunningham connect it with Shakespeare's company, as does the title-page of the first quarto, printed for Arthur Johnson in 1608. The play was again entered in the Stationers' Register to Humphrey Moseley, the bookseller, in 1653, this time with Shakespeare's name as author. *The Merry Devil of Edmonton* was a popular play and was early connected with Shakespeare's name. There is no other probability of its being his play, and but little of his having revised it; but it would do him no discredit.

Other attributions The remaining plays worthy of consideration find their connection with Shakespeare on various grounds. A play whose case is like that of *The Two Noble Kinsmen* (see page 1006), but by no means so good, is *The Birth of Merlin*. The first edition was published by Francis Kirkman in 1662. It is said on the title-page to have been "Written by William Shakespear and William Rowley." Kirkman, an unreliable person, also attributed the tragi-comedy of *The Birth of Merlin* to Shakespeare and Rowley in his catalogues. The play seems to date from the reign of King James. Recent critics, though willing to let Rowley suffer, have denied vigorously any share in the authorship of so poor and so loosely constructed a play to Shakespeare. *Arden of Feversham*, the first of the murder plays and splendidly written, was published without attribution of authorship by Edward White in 1592. Edward Jacob, a citizen of Feversham, printed the play in 1770 and attributed it to Shakespeare. His grounds for doing so were inadequate, nor have any valid grounds been found since. It is absurd to argue against the possibility, since the authorship would be as appropriate and becoming in Shakespeare as in Kyd or another. The story is of a murder done at Feversham in 1551, the account of which is embodied in Holinshed. There is no evidence so far discovered which connects it with Shakespeare or any other dramatist. *Edward III* is another anonymous play selected for Shakespeare because of its merit. It was first printed by Cuthbert Burby in 1596 and first attributed to Shakespeare in a bookseller's leaflet in 1654. The Shakespeare scholar Edward Capell edited it in 1760 and argued that it was by Shakespeare. The arguments consist mainly in appreciative criticism of the play and of the discovery that it quotes one line from the 94th sonnet: "Lilies that fester smell far worse than weeds." A number of high authorities in the nineteenth century felt sure of Shakespeare's hand at least in the first episode.

Sir Thomas More There exists in Harleian Ms. 7368 at the British Museum a play labeled "The Booke of Sir Thomas Moore." It was first edited for the Shakespeare Society by Alexander Dyce in 1844. In 1871 the Shakespeare scholars Richard Simpson and James Spedding put forward the idea that certain scenes in this play were not only the work of Shakespeare but were written in his own hand. Simpson rested his case mainly on literary evidence and the "Shakespearian flavor." The play is a biographical chronicle made up of three main episodes, or groups of scenes. The first of these describes the anti-alien riots of the "ill May-day" of 1517 and introduces Sir Thomas More, sheriff of London, in the act of pacifying the anti-alien rioters by his oratory. Since the subject was one of immediate bearing on a current issue in the London of about 1595, it was only to be expected that the authorities would not suffer it to be performed. The play shows evidence, therefore, of having been heavily cut by the censor, Edward Tilney, who bade the players leave the insurrection wholly out. The result of his censorship is the disappearance of two long passages. The play seems to have been originally written by Anthony Munday, and perhaps in anticipation of the objections of the censor another hand was employed to rewrite these scenes of the mob in a style not calculated to give offense. There are three such sheets, a total of 147 lines. They are gay, vigorous, and wise. The rioters talk in a genuinely comic way, like the mob in *Julius Cæsar*, or Cade's followers in *2 Henry VI*. Then More appears, addresses them good-naturedly, pointing out the blessings of peace and order and the godlike position of the King. In 1916 Sir E. Maunde Thompson, the paleographer, reasserted Shakespeare's authorship of these three sheets dealing with the "ill May-day" mob and attempted to prove by comparison with the handwriting of the six unquestioned signatures of Shakespeare that these sheets were indeed written in Shakespeare's hand. Since that time there has been a controversy pro and con. The play is dated by various critics from 1592 to 1601.[1]

Lost plays   A drama called *The History of Cardenio* was entered in the Stationers' Register, but apparently never printed, by Humphrey Moseley on September 9, 1653, as "by Mr. Fletcher and Shakespeare." A play *Cardenno* or *Cardenna* was twice acted before the King by Shakespeare's company in 1613, it being probably the same play as *The History of Cardenio*. There is, moreover, a puzzling later history. The theme is an episode in Cervantes's *Don Quixote* (Part I, chs. xxiii-xxxvii). In

---

[1] Sir E. Maunde Thompson, *Shakespeare's Handwriting*, London, 1916; A. W. Pollard and others, *Shakespeare's Hand in the Play of Sir Thomas More*, Cambridge, 1923; Sir E. K. Chambers, *The Elizabethan Stage*, IV, 32-4; Sir Sidney Lee, *Life of William Shakespeare*, Preface to latest edition; S. A. Tannenbaum, *The Booke of Sir Thomas Moore*, New York, 1927.

1728 Lewis Theobald, the editor of Shakespeare, published *The Double Falsehood, or the Distrest Lovers*, a play on the story of Cardenio. This was described by Theobald as "written originally by W. Shakespeare, and now revised and adapted to the stage by Mr. Theobald." Theobald claimed to have in his possession three manuscripts of the original; but none of them is now known, and many critics have suspected Theobald of having written *The Double Falsehood* himself and palmed it off as originally the work of Shakespeare. Theobald was, however, a reputable man, and his play strongly suggests Fletcher if not Shakespeare.

At the same time that Moseley entered *The History of Cardenio* in the Stationers' Register, he also entered *The Merry Devil of Edmonton*, which he ascribed to Shakespeare, "*Henry ye first*, & *Hen: the 2d* by Shakespeare, & Davenport." On June 29, 1660, he entered "*The History of King Stephen; Duke Humphrey, a Tragedy; Iphis & Iantha or a marriage without a man*, a Comedy [all four inclosed in brackets]: by Will. Shakespeare."

Among the manuscript plays burned by John Warburton's cook were "*Henry ye 1st* by Will. Shakespear & Rob. Davenport, *Duke Humphrey* [by] Will. Shakespear," and "A Play by Will. Shakespear."[2]

---

[2] W. W. Greg, "The Bakings of Betsy," *The Library*, 3rd ser., II, 225 ff.

TEXT OF THREE PLAYS
FROM THE PERIOD OF THE
ROMANCES

Cymbeline
The Winter's Tale
The Tempest

CYMBELINE

DRAMATIS PERSONÆ

CYMBELINE, king of Britain.

CLOTEN, son to the Queen by a former husband.

POSTHUMUS LEONATUS, a gentleman, husband to Imogen.

BELARIUS, a banished lord, disguised under the name of Morgan.

GUIDERIUS, } sons to Cymbeline, disguised
ARVIRAGUS, } under the names of Polydore and Cadwal, supposed sons to Morgan.

PHILARIO, friend to Posthumus, } Italians.
IACHIMO, friend to Philario, }

CAIUS LUCIUS, general of the Roman forces.

PISANIO, servant to Posthumus.

CORNELIUS, a physician.

A Roman Captain.

Two British Captains.

A Frenchman, friend to Philario.

Two Lords of Cymbeline's court.

Two Gentlemen of the same.

Two Gaolers.

Queen, wife to Cymbeline.

IMOGEN, daughter to Cymbeline by a former queen.

HELEN, a lady attending on Imogen.

Lords, Ladies, Roman Senators, Tribunes, a Soothsayer, a Dutchman, a Spaniard, Musicians, Officers, Captains, Soldiers, Messengers, and other attendants.
Apparitions.

SCENE: *Britain; Rome.*

ACT I.

SCENE I. *Britain. The garden of Cymbeline's palace.*

Enter two Gentlemen.

First Gent. You do not meet a man but frowns: our bloods
No more obey the heavens than our courtiers
Still seem as does the king.
 Sec. Gent.   But what's the matter?
First Gent. His daughter, and the heir of 's kingdom, whom
He purposed to his wife's sole son—a widow
That late he married—hath referr'd herself
Unto a poor but worthy gentleman: she's wedded;
Her husband banish'd; she imprison'd: all
Is outward sorrow; though I think the king

Be touch'd at very heart.
 Sec. Gent.   None but the king?   10
First Gent. He that hath lost her too; so is the queen,
That most desired the match; but not a courtier,
Although they wear their faces to the bent
Of the king's looks, hath a heart that is not
Glad at the thing they scowl at.
 Sec. Gent.   And why so?
First Gent. He that hath miss'd the princess is a thing
Too bad for bad report: and he that hath her—
I mean, that married her, alack, good man!
And therefore banish'd—is a creature such
As, to seek through the regions of the earth
For one his like, there would be something failing   21
In him that should compare. I do not think

So fair an outward and such stuff within
Endows a man but he.
   Sec. Gent.   You speak him far.
   First Gent. I do extend him, sir, within
    himself,   25
Crush him together rather than unfold
His measure duly.
   Sec. Gent.   What's his name and birth?
   First Gent. I cannot delve him to the root:
    his father
Was called Sicilius, who did join his honour
Against the Romans with Cassibelan,   30
But had his titles by Tenantius whom
He served with glory and admired success,
So gain'd the sur-addition Leonatus;
And had, besides this gentleman in question,
Two other sons, who in the wars o' the time
Died with their swords in hand; for which
    their father,
Then old and fond of issue, took such sorrow
That he quit being, and his gentle lady,
Big of this gentleman our theme, deceased
As he was born. The king he takes the babe
To his protection, calls him Posthumus Leo-
    natus,   41
Breeds him and makes him of his bed-
    chamber,
Puts to him all the learnings that his time
Could make him the receiver of; which he
    took,
As we do air, fast as 'twas minister'd,
And in 's spring became a harvest, lived in
    court—
Which rare it is to do—most praised, most
    loved,
A sample to the youngest, to the more ma-
    ture   48
A glass that feated them, and to the graver
A child that guided dotards; to his mis-
    tress,
For whom he now is banish'd, her own price
Proclaims how she esteem'd him and his vir-
    tue;
By her election may be truly read
What kind of man he is.

   Sec. Gent.   I honour him
Even out of your report. But, pray you, tell
    me,
Is she sole child to the king?
   First Gent.   His only child.
He had two sons: if this be worth your hear-
    ing,
Mark it: the eldest of them at three years old,
I' the swathing-clothes the other, from their
    nursery
Were stol'n, and to this hour no guess in
    knowledge   60
Which way they went.
   Sec. Gent.   How long is this ago?
   First Gent. Some twenty years.
   Sec. Gent. That a king's children should
    be so convey'd,
So slackly guarded, and the search so slow,
That could not trace them!
   First Gent.   Howsoe'er 'tis strange,
Or that the negligence may well be laugh'd
    at,
Yet is it true, sir.
   Sec. Gent.   I do well believe you.
   First Gent. We must forbear: here comes
    the gentleman,
The queen, and princess.   *[Exeunt.*

Enter the QUEEN, POSTHUMUS, *and* IMOGEN.

   Queen. No, be assured you shall not find
    me, daughter,   70
After the slander of most stepmothers,
Evil-eyed unto you: you're my prisoner, but
Your gaoler shall deliver you the keys
That lock up your restraint. For you, Post-
    humus,
So soon as I can win the offended king,
I will be known your advocate: marry, yet
The fire of rage is in him, and 'twere good
You lean'd unto his sentence with what pa-
    tience
Your wisdom may inform you.
   Post.   Please your highness,
I will from hence to-day.
   Queen.   You know the peril. 80
I'll fetch a turn about the garden, pitying
The pangs of barr'd affections, though the
    king
Hath charged you should not speak together.
                        [Exit.
   Imo.   O
Dissembling courtesy! How fine this tyrant

---

24. **speak . . . far**, go far in praising him. 25. **I do . . .**
himself, I magnify his virtues within the limits of what
he actually is. 29. **join his honour**, give his honorable
assistance. 30. **Cassibelan**, according to Holinshed,
Lud's younger brother and successor. 31. **Tenantius**,
son of King Lud and apparently regarded as Cymbeline's
predecessor. 33. **sur-addition**, additional title. 38.
quit being, left existence, died. 39. **Big**, great with
young. 40. **king he**, pleonastic subject. 41. **Posthu-**
mus, accent on second syllable. 43. **time**, age. 48.
sample, example. 49. **feated them**, constrained them
to propriety (Onions); made them *feat*, that is, graceful
or elegant (Dowden). Rowe conjectured *featur'd*.

78. **lean'd unto**, deferred to.

Can tickle where she wounds! My dearest
  husband,
I something fear my father's wrath; but
  nothing—
Always reserved my holy duty—what
His rage can do on me: you must be gone;
And I shall here abide the hourly shot
Of angry eyes, not comforted to live, 90
But that there is this jewel in the world
That I may see again.
    Post.   My queen! my mistress!
O lady, weep no more, lest I give cause
To be suspected of more tenderness
Than doth become a man. I will remain
The loyal'st husband that did e'er plight
  troth:
My residence in Rome at one Philario's,
Who to my father was a friend, to me
Known but by letter: thither write, my
  queen,
And with mine eyes I'll drink the words you
  send, 100
Though ink be made of gall.

              Re-enter QUEEN.

    Queen.   Be brief, I pray you:
If the king come, I shall incur I know not
How much of his displeasure. [*Aside*] Yet
  I'll move him
To walk this way: I never do him wrong,
But he does buy my injuries, to be friends;
Pays dear for my offences.   [*Exit.*
    Post.   Should we be taking leave
As long a term as yet we have to live,
The loathness to depart would grow. Adieu!
    Imo. Nay, stay a little:
Were you but riding forth to air yourself, 110
Such parting were too petty. Look here,
  love;
This diamond was my mother's: take it,
  heart;
But keep it till you woo another wife,
When Imogen is dead.
    Post.   How, how: another?
You gentle gods, give me but this I have,
And sear up my embracements from a next
With bonds of death! [*Putting on the ring.*]
    Remain, remain thou here

While sense can keep it on. And, sweetest,
  fairest,
As I my poor self did exchange for you,
To your so infinite loss, so in our trifles 120
I still win of you: for my sake wear this;
It is a manacle of love; I'll place it
Upon this fairest prisoner.
            [*Putting a bracelet upon her arm.*
    Imo.   O the gods!
When shall we see again?

        Enter CYMBELINE *and* Lords.

    Post.   Alack, the king!
    Cym. Thou basest thing, avoid! hence,
  from my sight!
If after this command thou fraught the court
With thy unworthiness, thou diest: away!
Thou'rt poison to my blood.
    Post.   The gods protect you!
And bless the good remainders of the court!
I am gone.   [*Exit.*
    Imo. There cannot be a pinch in death 130
More sharp than this is.
    Cym.   O disloyal thing,
That shouldst repair my youth, thou heap'st
A year's age on me.
    Imo.   I beseech you, sir,
Harm not yourself with your vexation:
I am senseless of your wrath; a touch more
  rare
Subdues all pangs, all fears.
    Cym.   Past grace? obedience?
    Imo. Past hope, and in despair; that way,
  past grace.
    Cym. That mightst have had the sole son
  of my queen!
    Imo. O blest, that I might not! I chose an
  eagle,
And did avoid a puttock.   140
    Cym. Thou took'st a beggar; wouldst have
  made my throne
A seat for baseness.
    Imo.   No; I rather added
A lustre to it.
    Cym.   O thou vile one!
    Imo.   Sir,
It is your fault that I have loved Posthumus:
You bred him as my playfellow, and he is

---

86. **something**, somewhat. **nothing**, not at all.
105. **But . . . friends**, that he does not reward me for
the injuries I have done him in order that I may be
friends with him. The statement gives an idea of the
doting quality of the king. 116. **sear up**, dry up,
blight; suggestion also of *cere*, cover with wax, as the
linen of a shroud.

124. **see**, see each other (reciprocal sense). 126.
fraught, burden. 129. **remainders**, those who remain.
135. **touch more rare**, feeling more overpowering or
exquisite. Imogen's description of her courage holds
throughout the play; love means so much to her that
she has no fear. 140. **puttock**, kite, bird of prey the
name of which was often used as a contemptuous epithet.

A man worth any woman, overbuys me
Almost the sum he pays.

Cym. What, art thou mad?

Imo. Almost, sir: heaven restore me!
Would I were
A neat-herd's daughter, and my Leonatus
Our neighbour shepherd's son!

Cym. Thou foolish thing! 150

Re-enter QUEEN.

They were again together: you have done
Not after our command. Away with her,
And pen her up.

Queen. Beseech your patience. Peace,
Dear lady daughter, peace! Sweet sovereign,
Leave us to ourselves; and make yourself
some comfort
Out of your best advice.

Cym. Nay, let her languish
A drop of blood a day; and, being aged,
Die of this folly!

[*Exeunt Cymbeline and Lords.*

Queen. Fie! you must give way.

Enter PISANIO.

Here is your servant. How now, sir! What
news?

Pis. My lord your son drew on my master.

Queen. Ha! 160
No harm, I trust, is done?

Pis. There might have been,
But that my master rather play'd than
fought
And had no help of anger: they were parted
By gentlemen at hand.

Queen. I am very glad on 't.

Imo. Your son's my father's friend; he
takes his part.
To draw upon an exile! O brave sir!
I would they were in Afric both together;
Myself by with a needle, that I might
prick
The goer-back. Why came you from your
master?

Pis. On his command: he would not suffer
me 170
To bring him to the haven; left these notes
Of what commands I should be subject to,
When 't pleased you to employ me.

Queen. This hath been
Your faithful servant: I dare lay mine honour
He will remain so.

Pis. I humbly thank your highness.

Queen. Pray, walk awhile.

Imo. About some half-hour hence,
I pray you, speak with me: you shall at
least
Go see my lord aboard: for this time leave
me. [*Exeunt.*

SCENE II. *The same. A public place.*

Enter CLOTEN *and two* LORDS.

First Lord. Sir, I would advise you to shift
a shirt; the violence of action hath made you
reek as a sacrifice: where air comes out, air
comes in: there's none abroad so wholesome
as that you vent.

Clo. If my shirt were bloody, then to shift
it. Have I hurt him?

Sec. Lord. [*Aside*] No, 'faith; not so much
as his patience. 9

First Lord. Hurt him! his body's a passable carcass, if he be not hurt: it is a throughfare for steel, if it be not hurt.

Sec. Lord. [*Aside*] His steel was in debt; it
went o' the backside the town.

Clo. The villain would not stand me.

Sec. Lord. [*Aside*] No; but he fled forward
still, toward your face.

First Lord. Stand you! You have land
enough of your own: but he added to your
having; gave you some ground. 20

Sec. Lord. [*Aside*] As many inches as you
have oceans. Puppies!

Clo. I would they had not come between
us.

Sec. Lord. [*Aside*] So would I, till you had
measured how long a fool you were upon the
ground.

Clo. And that she should love this fellow
and refuse me!

Sec. Lord. [*Aside*] If it be a sin to make a
true election, she is damned. 30

First Lord. Sir, as I told you always, her
beauty and her brain go not together: she's a
good sign, but I have seen small reflection of
her wit.

146-147. **overbuys . . . pays,** pays more for me than
I am worth by almost as much as, in giving himself,
he has given for me. 149. **neat-herd's,** cowherd's.
153. **Beseech,** I beseech. 156. **best advice,** most
mature reflection.

176. **walk,** go aside, withdraw.
Scene ii. 10. **passable,** affording free passage. 11.
throughfare, thoroughfare. 30. **election,** choice;
a theological expression. 33. **sign,** semblance, appearance.

Sec. Lord. [*Aside*] She shines not upon fools, lest the reflection should hurt her.

Clo. Come, I'll to my chamber. Would there had been some hurt done!

Sec. Lord. [*Aside*] I wish not so; unless it had been the fall of an ass, which is no great hurt.

Clo. You'll go with us?   40

First Lord. I'll attend your lordship.

Clo. Nay, come, let's go together.

Sec. Lord. Well, my lord.   [*Exeunt.*

SCENE III. *A room in Cymbeline's palace.*

Enter IMOGEN *and* PISANIO.

Imo. I would thou grew'st unto the shores o' the haven,
And question'dst every sail: if he should write,
And I not have it, 'twere a paper lost,
As offer'd mercy is. What was the last
That he spake to thee?

Pis.   It was his queen, his queen!

Imo. Then waved his handkerchief?

Pis.   And kiss'd it, madam.

Imo. Senseless linen! happier therein than I!
And that was all?

Pis.   No, madam; for so long
As he could make me with this eye or ear
Distinguish him from others, he did keep 10
The deck, with glove, or hat, or handkerchief,
Still waving, as the fits and stirs of 's mind
Could best express how slow his soul sail'd on,
How swift his ship.

Imo.   Thou shouldst have made him
As little as a crow, or less, ere left
To after-eye him.

Pis.   Madam, so I did.

Imo. I would have broke mine eye-strings; crack'd them, but
To look upon him, till the diminution
Of space had pointed him sharp as my needle,
Nay, follow'd him, till he had melted from 20
The smallness of a gnat to air, and then
Have turn'd mine eye and wept. But, good Pisanio,
When shall we hear from him?

Pis.   Be assured, madam,
With his next vantage.

Imo. I did not take my leave of him, but had
Most pretty things to say: ere I could tell him
How I would think on him at certain hours
Such thoughts and such, or I could make him swear
The shes of Italy should not betray
Mine interest and his honour, or have charged him,   30
At the sixth hour of morn, at noon, at midnight,
To encounter me with orisons, for then
I am in heaven for him; or ere I could
Give him that parting kiss which I had set
Betwixt two charming words, comes in my father
And like the tyrannous breathing of the north
Shakes all our buds from growing.

Enter a Lady.

Lady.   The queen, madam,
Desires your highness' company.

Imo. Those things I bid you do, get them dispatch'd.
I will attend the queen.

Pis.   Madam, I shall. [*Exeunt.*   40

SCENE IV. *Rome. Philario's house.*

Enter PHILARIO, IACHIMO, *a* Frenchman, *a* Dutchman, *and a* Spaniard.

Iach. Believe it, sir, I have seen him in Britain: he was then of a crescent note, expected to prove so worthy as since he hath been allowed the name of; but I could then have looked on him without the help of admiration, though the catalogue of his endowments had been tabled bv his side and I to peruse him by items.

Phi. You speak of him when he was less furnished than now he is with that which makes him both without and within.   10

Scene iii. 4. **offer'd mercy**, apparently, pardon offered, but coming too late. 15. **left**, you left off. 16. **after-eye**, look after.

24. **vantage**, opportunity. 29. **shes**, women. 32. **encounter**, meet. **orisons**, prayers. 35. **charming**, having magical potency. 36. **north**, north wind.
Scene iv. 2. **crescent note**, growing reputation or importance. 7. **tabled**, set down in a list. 10. **makes ... within**, establishes him both as regards his fortune and his character.

French. I have seen him in France: we had very many there could behold the sun with as firm eyes as he.

Iach. This matter of marrying his king's daughter, wherein he must be weighed rather by her value than his own, words him, I doubt not, a great deal from the matter.

French. And then his banishment.   18

Iach. Ay, and the approbation of those that weep this lamentable divorce under her colours are wonderfully to extend him; be it but to fortify her judgement, which else an easy battery might lay flat, for taking a beggar without less quality. But how comes it he is to sojourn with you? How creeps acquaintance?

Phi. His father and I were soldiers together; to whom I have been often bound for no less than my life. Here comes the Briton: let him be so entertained amongst you as suits, with gentlemen of your knowing, to a stranger of his quality.   30

Enter POSTHUMUS.

I beseech you all, be better known to this gentleman, whom I commend to you as a noble friend of mine: how worthy he is I will leave to appear hereafter, rather than story him in his own hearing.

French. Sir, we have known together in Orleans.

Post. Since when I have been debtor to you for courtesies, which I will be ever to pay and yet pay still.   40

French. Sir, you o'er-rate my poor kindness: I was glad I did atone my countryman and you; it had been pity you should have been put together with so mortal a purpose as then each bore, upon importance of so slight and trivial a nature.

Post. By your pardon, sir, I was then a young traveller; rather shunned to go even with what I heard than in my every action to be guided by others' experiences: but upon my mended judgement—if I offend not to say it is mended—my quarrel was not altogether slight.   51

French. 'Faith, yes, to be put to the arbitrement of swords, and by such two that would by all likelihood have confounded one the other, or have fallen both.

Iach. Can we, with manners, ask what was the difference?   56

French. Safely, I think: 'twas a contention in public, which may, without contradiction, suffer the report. It was much like an argument that fell out last night, where each of us fell in praise of our country mistresses; this gentleman at that time vouching—and upon warrant of bloody affirmation—his to be more fair, virtuous, wise, chaste, constant-qualified and less attemptable than any the rarest of our ladies in France.

Iach. That lady is not now living, or this gentleman's opinion by this worn out.

Post. She holds her virtue still and I my mind.

Iach. You must not so far prefer her 'fore ours of Italy.   71

Post. Being so far provoked as I was in France, I would abate her nothing, though I profess myself her adorer, not her friend.

Iach. As fair and as good—a kind of hand-in-hand comparison—had been something too fair and too good for any lady in Britain. If she went before others I have seen, as that diamond of yours outlustres many I have beheld, I could not but believe she excelled many: but I have not seen the most precious diamond that is, nor you the lady.

Post. I praised her as I rated her: so do I my stone.   84

Iach. What do you esteem it at?

Post. More than the world enjoys.

Iach. Either your unparagoned mistress is dead, or she's outprized by a trifle.

Post. You are mistaken: the one may be sold, or given, if there were wealth enough for the purchase, or merit for the gift: the other is not a thing for sale, and only the gift of the gods.

Iach. Which the gods have given you?   94

Post. Which, by their graces, I will keep.

Iach. You may wear her in title yours: but, you know, strange fowl light upon neighbouring ponds. Your ring may be stolen too: so your brace of unprizable esti-

16-17. words . . . matter, causes him to be described as other (and better) than he is. 20-21. under her colours, in Imogen's party, influenced by her. 21. extend him, increase his reputation. 24. without less, with less (double negative). quality, rank, position. 29. knowing, knowledge, *savoir faire*. 34. story, give an account of. 36. known together, been acquainted. 39-40. which . . . still, for which I shall be forever in debt and yet be paying always. 42. atone, set at one, reconcile. 45. importance, matter, occasion. 47. go even, accord, agree.

54. confounded, destroyed. 59. suffer the report, be reported or told. 63. bloody affirmation, affirming the truth with his blood. 65. constant-qualified, endowed with constancy. attemptable, open to attempts on their virtue. 74. friend, lover. 99. unprizable, invaluable. estimations, things highly esteemed.

mations; the one is but frail and the other casual; a cunning thief, or a that way accomplished courtier, would hazard the winning both of first and last. 102

Post. Your Italy contains none so accomplished a courtier to convince the honour of my mistress, if, in the holding or loss of that, you term her frail. I do nothing doubt you have store of thieves; notwithstanding, I fear not my ring.

Phi. Let us leave here, gentlemen. 109

Post. Sir, with all my heart. This worthy signior, I thank him, makes no stranger of me; we are familiar at first.

Iach. With five times so much conversation, I should get ground of your fair mistress, make her go back, even to the yielding, had I admittance and opportunity to friend.

Post. No, no. 117

Iach. I dare thereupon pawn the moiety of my estate to your ring; which, in my opinion, o'ervalues it something: but I make my wager rather against your confidence than her reputation: and, to bar your offence herein too, I durst attempt it against any lady in the world.

Post. You are a great deal abused in too bold a persuasion; and I doubt not you sustain what you're worthy of by your attempt.

Iach. What's that? 127

Post. A repulse: though your attempt, as you call it, deserve more; a punishment too.

Phi. Gentlemen, enough of this: it came in too suddenly; let it die as it was born, and, I pray you, be better acquainted.

Iach. Would I had put my estate and my neighbour's on the approbation of what I have spoke! 135

Post. What lady would you choose to assail?

Iach. Yours; whom in constancy you think stands so safe. I will lay you ten thousands ducats to your ring, that, commend me to the court where your lady is, with no more advantage than the opportunity of a second conference, and I will bring from thence that honour of hers which you imagine so reserved. 143

Post. I will wage against your gold, gold to it: my ring I hold dear as my finger; 'tis part of it.

Iach. You are afraid, and therein the wiser. If you buy ladies' flesh at a million a dram, you cannot preserve it from tainting: but I see you have some religion in you, that you fear.

Post. This is but a custom in your tongue; you bear a graver purpose, I hope. 151

Iach. I am the master of my speeches, and would undergo what's spoken, I swear.

Post. Will you? I shall but lend my diamond till your return: let there be covenants drawn between's: my mistress exceeds in goodness the hugeness of your unworthy thinking: I dare you to this match: here's my ring.

Phi. I will have it no lay. 159

Iach. By the gods, it is one. If I bring you no sufficient testimony that I have enjoyed the dearest bodily part of your mistress, my ten thousand ducats are yours; so is your diamond too: if I come off, and leave her in such honour as you have trust in, she your jewel, this your jewel, and my gold are yours: provided I have your commendation for my more free entertainment. 167

Post. I embrace these conditions; let us have articles betwixt us. Only, thus far you shall answer: if you make your voyage upon her and give me directly to understand you have prevailed, I am no further your enemy; she is not worth our debate: if she remain unseduced, you not making it appear otherwise, for your ill opinion and the assault you have made to her chastity you shall answer me with your sword. 176

Iach. Your hand; a covenant: we will have these things set down by lawful counsel, and straight away for Britain, lest the bargain should catch cold and starve: I will fetch my gold and have our two wagers recorded.

Post. Agreed. 182

[*Exeunt Posthumus and Iachimo.*

French. Will this hold, think you?

Phil. Signior Iachimo will not from it. Pray, let us follow 'em.

[*Exeunt.*

---

104. to, as to. convince, overcome. 105. in . . . that, on the question of holding or losing her honor. 108. fear, fear for. 109. leave, leave off, cease. 115. go back, succumb, give way. 116. to friend, as my friend. 118. moiety, half. 124-125. abused . . . persuasion, deceived by too bold an opinion. 134. approbation, attestation, confirmation. 144. wage, lay as a wager.

153. undergo, undertake to perform. 158. I dare . . . match. In partial extenuation of Posthumus's shameful wager it may be pointed out that Shakespeare's was an age of gaming and that the Italian story which he follows here brought with it an atmosphere of often brutal gallantry. 159. I . . . lay, I will not let it be a wager. 178. counsel, legal adviser. 180. starve, die of cold.

SCENE V.   *Britain.   A room in Cymbeline's palace.*

Enter QUEEN, Ladies, *and* CORNELIUS.

Queen. Whiles yet the dew's on ground, gather those flowers;
Make haste: who has the note of them?
First Lady.   I, madam.
Queen. Dispatch.   [*Exeunt Ladies.*
Now, master doctor, have you brought those drugs?
Cor. Pleaseth your highness, ay: here they are, madam: [*Presenting a small box.*
But I beseech your grace, without offence,—
My conscience bids me ask—wherefore you have
Commanded of me these most poisonous compounds,
Which are the movers of a languishing death;
But though slow, deadly?
Queen.   I wonder, doctor, 10
Thou ask'st me such a question.   Have I not been
Thy pupil long?   Hast thou not learn'd me how
To make perfumes? distil? preserve? yea, so
That our great king himself doth woo me oft
For my confections?   Having thus far pro-
ceeded,—
Unless thou think'st me devilish—is't not meet
That I did amplify my judgement in
Other conclusions?   I will try the forces
Of these thy compounds on such creatures as
We count not worth the hanging, but none human,   20
To try the vigour of them and apply
Allayments to their act, and by them gather
Their several virtues and effects.
Cor.   Your highness
Shall from this practice but make hard your heart:
Besides, the seeing these effects will be
Both noisome and infectious.
Queen.   O, content thee.

Enter PISANIO.

[*Aside*] Here comes a flattering rascal; upon him
Will I first work: he's for his master,

And enemy to my son.   How now, Pisanio!
Doctor, your service for this time is ended; 30
Take your own way.
Cor.   [*Aside*] I do suspect you, madam;
But you shall do no harm.
Queen. [*To Pisanio*] Hark thee, a word.
Cor. [*Aside*] I do not like her.   She doth think she has
Strange lingering poisons: I do know her spirit,
And will not trust one of her malice with
A drug of such damn'd nature.   Those she has
Will stupify and dull the sense awhile;
Which first, perchance, she'll prove on cats and dogs,
Then afterward up higher: but there is 40
No danger in what show of death it makes,
More than the locking-up the spirits a time,
To be more fresh, reviving.   She is fool'd
With a most false effect; and I the truer,
So to be false with her.
Queen.   No further service, doctor,
Until I send for thee.
Cor.   I humbly take my leave. [*Exit.*
Queen. Weeps she still, say'st thou?   Dost thou think in time
She will not quench and let instructions enter
Where folly now possesses?   Do thou work:
When thou shalt bring me word she loves my son,
I'll tell thee on the instant thou art then 50
As great as is thy master, greater, for
His fortunes all lie speechless and his name
Is at last gasp: return he cannot, nor
Continue where he is: to shift his being
Is to exchange one misery with another,
And every day that comes comes to decay
A day's work in him.   What shalt thou expect,
To be depender on a thing that leans,
Who cannot be new built, nor has no friends,
So much as but to prop him? [*The Queen drops the box: Pisanio takes it up.*] Thou takest up   60
Thou know'st not what; but take it for thy labour:

<hr>

33-44. **I do . . . her.** This is an occurrence of the typical aside, i.e., one which carries matter important to the plot.   Although the play is a late one, Shakespeare still retains this stage convention characteristic of his earlier plays.   41. **locking-up the spirits.**   This was the current theory of medicine with reference to potions whose effects were temporary, such as the one employed here and that in *Romeo and Juliet.*   43. **truer,** more honest.   47. **quench,** become cool.   54. **shift his being,** change his abode.   56. **decay,** destroy.   58. **leans,** is about to fall.

<hr>

2. **note,** list.   15. **confections,** compounds of drugs. 18. **conclusions,** experiments.   26. **content thee,** do not trouble thyself.

It is a thing I made, which hath the king
Five times redeem'd from death: I do not
    know
What is more cordial. Nay, I prithee, take
    it;
It is an earnest of a further good
That I mean to thee. Tell thy mistress how
The case stands with her; do't as from
    thyself.
Think what a chance thou changest on, but
    think
Thou hast thy mistress still, to boot, my son,
Who shall take notice of thee: I'll move the
    king   70
To any shape of thy preferment such
As thou'lt desire; and then myself, I chiefly,
That set thee on to this desert, am bound
To load thy merit richly. Call my women:
Think on my words.   [*Exit Pisanio.*
                  A sly and constant knave,
Not to be shaked; the agent for his master
And the remembrancer of her to hold
The hand-fast to her lord. I have given him
    that
Which, if he take, shall quite unpeople her
Of liegers for her sweet, and which she after,
Except she bend her humour, shall be
    assured   81
To taste of too.

            Re-enter PISANIO *and* Ladies.

            So, so: well done, well done:
The violets, cowslips, and the primroses,
Bear to my closet. Fare thee well, Pisanio;
Think on my words.
                    [*Exeunt Queen and Ladies.*
Pis.   And shall do:
But when to my good lord I prove untrue,
I'll choke myself: there's all I'll do for you.
                                          [*Exit.*

SCENE VI. *The same. Another room in the
                    palace.*

            Enter IMOGEN.

Imo. A father cruel, and a step-dame
    false;
A foolish suitor to a wedded lady,

That hath her husband banish'd;—O, that
    husband!
My supreme crown of grief! and those
    repeated
Vexations of it! Had I been thief-stol'n,
As my two brothers, happy! but most miser-
    able
Is the desire that's glorious: blest be those,
How mean soe'er, that have their honest
    wills,
Which seasons comfort. Who may this be?
    Fie!

            Enter PISANIO *and* IACHIMO.

Pis. Madam, a noble gentleman of
    Rome,
Comes from my lord with letters.
Iach.   Change you, madam? 11
The worthy Leonatus is in safety
And greets your highness dearly.
                              [*Presents a letter.*
Imo.   Thanks, good sir:
You're kindly welcome.
Iach. [*Aside*] All of her that is out of door
    most rich!
If she be furnish'd with a mind so rare,
She is alone the Arabian bird, and I
Have lost the wager. Boldness be my
    friend!
Arm me, audacity, from head to foot!
Or, like the Parthian, I shall flying fight; 20
Rather, directly fly.
Imo. [*Reads*] 'He is one of the noblest
note, to whose kindnesses I am most infi-
nitely tied. Reflect upon him accordingly,
as you value your trust—
                              LEONATUS.'
So far I read aloud:
But even the very middle of my heart
Is warm'd by the rest, and takes it thank-
fully.
You are as welcome, worthy sir, as I
Have words to bid you, and shall find it so
In all that I can do.
Iach.   Thanks, fairest lady. 31
What, are men mad? Hath nature given
    them eyes

---

64. **cordial**, restorative. 65. **earnest**, money paid
to secure a bargain. 76. **shaked**, shaken (in his loyalty).
77. **remembrancer of her**, one who reminds her. 78.
hand-fast, marriage contract. 79. **unpeople her**,
deprive her of the services of. 80. **liegers**, ambassadors.
81. **Except . . . humour**, unless she change her mind
(about not accepting Cloten). 84. **closet**, private
chamber.

5-6. **thief-stol'n . . . brothers.** This is one of the
few allusions in the earlier part of the play to the story of
the stolen princes with which the latter half of the play
is mainly concerned; the first allusion occurs in I, i,
57-62. 9. **seasons comfort**, gives happiness its proper
quality. 11. **Change you**, do you change color? 17.
Arabian bird, the phœnix; pattern of rarity and beauty.
20. **Parthian**, an allusion to the Parthian shot, the
Parthians being proverbial in ancient times for discharging a flight of arrows as they fled.

To see this vaulted arch, and the rich crop
Of sea and land, which can distinguish
    'twixt
The fiery orbs above and the twinn'd stones
Upon the number'd beach? and can we not
Partition make with spectacles so precious
'Twixt fair and foul?
   Imo.   What makes your admiration?
   Iach. It cannot be i' the eye, for apes and
    monkeys
'Twixt two such shes would chatter this way
    and   40
Contemn with mows the other; nor i' the
    judgement,
For idiots in this case of favour would
Be wisely definite; nor i' the appetite;
Sluttery to such neat excellence opposed
Should make desire vomit emptiness,
Not so allured to feed.
   Imo. What is the matter, trow?
   Iach.   The cloyed will,
That satiate yet unsatisfied desire, that tub
Both fill'd and running, ravening first the
    lamb
Longs after for the garbage.
   Imo.   What, dear sir,   50
Thus raps you? Are you well?
   Iach. Thanks, madam; well. [*To Pisanio*]
    Beseech you, sir, desire
My man's abode where I did leave him: he
Is strange and peevish.
   Pis.   I was going, sir,
To give him welcome.   [*Exit.*
   Imo. Continues well my lord? His health,
    beseech you?
   Iach. Well, madam.
   Imo. Is he disposed to mirth? I hope he is.
   Iach. Exceeding pleasant; none a stranger
    there
So merry and so gamesome: he is call'd   60
The Briton reveller.
   Imo.   When he was here,
He did incline to sadness, and oft-times
Not knowing why.
   Iach.   I never saw him sad.

There is a Frenchman his companion, one
An eminent monsieur, that, it seems, much
    loves
A Gallian girl at home; he furnaces
The thick sighs from him, whiles the jolly
    Briton—
Your lord, I mean—laughs from 's free lungs,
    cries 'O,
Can my sides hold, to think that man, who
    knows
By history, report, or his own proof,   70
What woman is, yea, what she cannot choose
But must be, will his free hours languish for
Assured bondage?'
   Imo.   Will my lord say so?
   Iach. Ay, madam, with his eyes in flood
    with laughter:
It is a recreation to be by
And hear him mock the Frenchman. But,
    heavens know,
Some men are much to blame.
   Imo.   Not he, I hope.
   Iach. Not he: but yet heaven's bounty to-
    wards him might
Be used more thankfully. In himself, 'tis
    much;
In you, which I account his beyond all tal-
    ents,   80
Whilst I am bound to wonder, I am bound
To pity too.
   Imo.   What do you pity, sir?
   Iach. Two creatures heartily.
   Imo.   Am I one, sir?
You look on me: what wreck discern you in
    me
Deserves your pity?
   Iach.   Lamentable! What,
To hide me from the radiant sun and solace
I' the dungeon by a snuff?
   Imo.   I pray you, sir,
Deliver with more openness your answers
To my demands. Why do you pity me?
   Iach. That others do—   90
I was about to say—enjoy your——But
It is an office of the gods to venge it,
Not mine to speak on 't.
   Imo.   You do seem to know
Something of me, or what concerns me: pray
    you,—

---

33. **crop**, harvest, produce. 35. **twinn'd**, exactly
alike. 36. **number'd**, abounding (in stones). 37.
spectacles, organs of vision. 41. **mows**, grimaces,
wry faces. 42. **in . . . favour**, in presence of a face of
such beauty. 43. **definite**, resolute. 44. **Sluttery**, the
condition of being sluttish or unclean. 45-46. **Should
. . . feed**, desire would refuse to satisfy itself and turn
away in disgust. 47. **trow**, I wonder. 48-49. **That
. . . desire, that tub . . . running**, in apposition with
will. **ravening**, devouring greedily. 51. **raps**, transports. 52-53. **desire . . . abode**, bid my servant remain.
54. **strange and peevish**, strange to the place and
foolish.

66. **Gallian**, Gallic, French. **furnaces**, gives forth
like a furnace. 70. **proof**, experience. 80. **talents**,
evil inclinations or passions, or the phrase may mean
"exceeding any sum." Dowden interprets: In his own
peculiar gifts heaven's bounty is much; in you—who are
his—heaven's bounty to him is beyond all gifts. 86.
solace, take delight. 87. **snuff**, burning candle-wick.

Since doubting things go ill often hurts more
Than to be sure they do; for certainties
Either are past remedies, or, timely know-
    ing,
The remedy then born—discover to me
What both you spur and stop.

    Iach.   Had I this cheek
To bathe my lips upon; this hand, whose
    touch,   100
Whose every touch, would force the feeler's
    soul
To the oath of loyalty; this object, which
Takes prisoner the wild motion of mine eye,
Fixing it only here; should I, damn'd then,
Slaver with lips as common as the stairs
That mount the Capitol; join gripes with
    hands
Made hard with hourly falsehood—false-
    hood, as
With labour; then by-peeping in an eye
Base and unlustrous as the smoky light
That's fed with stinking tallow; it were fit
That all the plagues of hell should at one
    time   111
Encounter such revolt.

    Imo.   My lord, I fear,
Has forgot Britian.

    Iach.   And himself. Not I,
Inclined to this intelligence, pronounce
The beggary of his change; but 'tis your
    graces
That from my mutest conscience to my
    tongue
Charms this report out.

    Imo.   Let me hear no more.

    Iach. O dearest soul! your cause doth
    strike my heart
With pity, that doth make me sick. A lady
So fair, and fasten'd to an empery,   120
Would make the great'st king double,—to be
    partner'd
With tomboys hired with that self exhibition
Which your own coffers yield! with diseased
    ventures
That play with all infirmities for gold
Which rottenness can lend nature! such
    boil'd stuff

As well might poison poison! Be revenged;
Or she that bore you was no queen, and you
Recoil from your great stock.

    Imo.   Revenged!
How should I be revenged? If this be true,—
As I have such a heart that both mine ears
Must not in haste abuse—if it be true,   131
How should I be revenged?

    Iach.   Should he make me
Live, like Diana's priest, betwixt cold sheets,
Whiles he is vaulting variable ramps,
In your despite, upon your purse? Revenge
    it.
I dedicate myself to your sweet pleasure,
More noble than that runagate to your bed,
And will continue fast to your affection,
Still close as sure.

    Imo.   What, ho, Pisanio!

    Iach. Let me my service tender on your
    lips.   140

    Imo. Away! I do condemn mine ears that
    have
So long attended thee. If thou wert hon-
    ourable,
Thou wouldst have told this tale for virtue,
    not
For such an end thou seek'st,—as base as
    strange.
Thou wrong'st a gentleman, who is as far
From thy report as thou from honour, and
Solicit'st here a lady that disdains
Thee and the devil alike. What ho, Pisanio!
The king my father shall be made acquainted
Of thy assault: if he shall think it fit,   150
A saucy stranger in his court to mart
As in a Romish stew and to expound
His beastly mind to us, he hath a court
He little cares for and a daughter who
He not respects at all. What, ho, Pisanio!

    Iach. O happy Leonatus! I may say:
The credit that thy lady hath of thee
Deserves thy trust, and thy most perfect
    goodness
Her assured credit. Blessed live you long!
A lady to the worthiest sir that ever   160
Country call'd his! and you his mistress,
    only
For the most worthiest fit! Give me your
    pardon.
I have spoke this, to know if your affiance

---

95. **doubting**, suspecting that. 98. **remedy then
born**, i.e., is then born. **discover**, reveal; imperative
mood. 99. **spur and stop**, disclose and then conceal.
108. **by-peeping**, giving sidelong glances; there is a
charge against the behavior of Posthumus. 112. **Encounter**, meet. **revolt**, inconstancy. 116. **mutest**,
most silent. 120. **empery**, empire. 121. **double**, as
having twice the power. **partner'd**, put on a level,
compelled to be partners with. 122. **tomboys**, wantons.
self, same. **exhibition**, allowance.

128. **Recoil**, fall away, degenerate. 130. **As**, for.
133. **priest**, priestess. 134. **ramps**, probably, wantons,
prostitutes. 137. **runagate**, renegade. 142. **attended**,
listened to. 151. **saucy**, insolent. **to mart**, should
bargain. 160. **sir**, man. 163. **affiance**, fidelity.

Were deeply rooted; and shall make your
　　lord,
That which he is, new o'er: and he is one
The truest manner'd; such a holy witch
That he enchants societies into him;
Half all men's hearts are his.

Imo.　　　　　　　You make amends.

Iach. He sits 'mongst men like a de-
　　scended god:
He hath a kind of honour sets him off,　　170
More than a mortal seeming. Be not angry,
Most mighty princess, that I have adven-
　　tured
To try your taking of a false report; which
　　hath
Honour'd with confirmation your great
　　judgement
In the election of a sir so rare,
Which you know cannot err: the love I bear
　　him
Made me to fan you thus, but the gods made
　　you,
Unlike all others, chaffless. Pray, your par-
　　don.

Imo. All's well, sir: take my power i' the
　　court for yours.

Iach. My humble thanks. I had almost
　　forgot　　180
To entreat your grace but in a small request,
And yet of moment too, for it concerns
Your lord; myself and other noble friends
Are partners in the business.

Imo.　　　　Pray, what is 't?

Iach. Some dozen Romans of us and your
　　lord—
The best feather of our wing—have mingled
　　sums
To buy a present for the emperor;
Which I, the factor for the rest, have done
In France: 'tis plate of rare device, and
　　jewels
Of rich and exquisite form; their values
　　great;　　190
And I am something curious, being strange,
To have them in safe stowage: may it please
　　you
To take them in protection?

Imo.　　　　　　　Willingly;
And pawn mine honour for their safety:
　　since

My lord hath interest in them, I will keep
　　them
In my bedchamber.

Iach.　　　　　　They are in a trunk,
Attended by my men: I will make bold
To send them to you, only for this night;
I must aboard to-morrow.

Imo.　　　　　　　O, no, no.

Iach. Yes, I beseech; or I shall short my
　　word　　200
By lengthening my return. From Gallia
I cross'd the seas on purpose and on promise
To see your grace.

Imo.　　　　I thank you for your pains:
But not away to-morrow!

Iach.　　　　　　O, I must, madam:
Therefore I shall beseech you, if you please
To greet your lord with writing, do 't to-
　　night:　　206
I have outstood my time; which is material
To the tender of our present.

Imo.　　　　　　I will write.
Send your trunk to me; it shall safe be
　　kept,
And truly yielded you. You're very welcome.
　　　　　　　　　　　　　　[*Exeunt.*

ACT II.

SCENE I. *Britain. Before Cymbeline's palace.*

Enter CLOTEN *and two* Lords.

Clo. Was there ever man had such luck!
when I kissed the jack, upon an up-cast to be
hit away! I had a hundred pound on 't: and
then a whoreson jackanapes must take me
up for swearing; as if I borrowed mine oaths
of him and might not spend them at my
pleasure.

First Lord. What got he by that? You
have broke his pate with your bowl.

Sec. Lord. [*Aside*] If his wit had been like
him that broke it, it would have run all
out.　　10

Clo. When a gentleman is disposed to

---

165. **new o'er,** refreshed and renewed by, made over
again by. 166. **witch,** charmer, fascinating person;
used of men as well as women. 167. **into,** unto. 177.
fan, test; figure from winnowing of grain. 178. **chaffless,**
without chaff, perfect. 191. **curious,** anxious.

196. **In my bedchamber.** The strangeness of
Iachimo's request and Imogen's compliance with it may
be better understood if one remembers that bedchambers
were storage places for treasure, and also that strangers
lodging at inns were often in fear of robbery in Shakespeare's day. 200. **short my word,** impair my promise.
207. **outstood,** outstayed. 208. **tender of our present,** offering of our gift.
Act II. Scene i. 2. **kissed the jack,** touched and lay
near the small bowl used as target in the game of bowls.
up-cast, throw in the game of bowls. 4. **take me up,**
take me to task.

swear, it is not for any standers-by to curtail his oaths, ha?

Sec. Lord. No, my lord; [*Aside*] nor crop the ears of them.

Clo. Whoreson dog! I give him satisfaction? Would he had been one of my rank!

Sec. Lord. [*Aside*] To have smelt like a fool.   18

Clo. I am not vexed more at any thing in the earth: a pox on 't! I had rather not be so noble as I am; they dare not fight with me, because of the queen my mother: every Jack-slave hath his bellyful of fighting, and I must go up and down like a cock that nobody can match.

Sec. Lord. [*Aside*] You are cock and capon too; and you crow, cock, with your comb on.

Clo. Sayest thou?

Sec. Lord. It is not fit your lordship should undertake every companion that you give offence to.   30

Clo. No, I know that: but it is fit I should commit offence to my inferiors.

Sec. Lord. Ay, it is fit for your lordship only.

Clo. Why, so I say.

First Lord. Did you hear of a stranger that's come to court to-night?

Clo. A stranger, and I not know on 't!

Sec. Lord. [*Aside*] He's a strange fellow himself, and knows it not.

First Lord. There's an Italian come; and, 'tis thought, one of Leonatus' friends.   41

Clo. Leonatus! a banished rascal; and he's another, whatsoever he be. Who told you of this stranger?

First Lord. One of your lordship's pages.

Clo. Is it fit I went to look upon him? is there no derogation in 't?

Sec. Lord. You cannot derogate, my lord.

Clo. Not easily, I think.   49

Sec. Lord. [*Aside*] You are a fool granted; therefore your issues, being foolish, do not derogate.

Clo. Come, I'll go see this Italian: what I have lost to-day at bowls I'll win to-night of him. Come, go.

Sec. Lord. I'll attend your lordship.
                 (*Exeunt Cloten and First Lord.*
That such a crafty devil as is his mother
Should yield the world this ass! a woman that
Bears all down with her brain; and this her
    son
Cannot take two from twenty, for his heart,
And leave eighteen. Alas, poor princess,   61
Thou divine Imogen, what thou endurest,
Betwixt a father by thy step-dame govern'd,
A mother hourly coining plots, a wooer
More hateful than the foul expulsion is
Of thy dear husband, than that horrid act
Of the divorce he 'ld make! The heavens
    hold firm
The walls of thy dear honour, keep unshaked
That temple, thy fair mind, that thou mayst
    stand,   69
To enjoy thy banish'd lord and this great
    land!   [*Exit.*

SCENE II. *Imogen's bedchamber in Cymbe-*
line's palace: a trunk in one corner of it.

IMOGEN *in bed, reading: a* Lady *attending.*

Imo. Who's there? my woman Helen?
Lady.   Please you, madam.
Imo. What hour is it?
Lady.   Almost midnight, madam.
Imo. I have read three hours then: mine
    eyes are weak:
Fold down the leaf where I have left: to bed:
Take not away the taper, leave it burning;
And if thou canst awake by four o' the clock,
I prithee, call me. Sleep hath seized me
    wholly.   [*Exit Lady.*
To your protection I commend me, gods.
From fairies and the tempters of the night
Guard me, beseech ye.   10
    [*Sleeps. Iachimo comes from the trunk.*
Iach. The crickets sing, and man's o'er-
    labour'd sense
Repairs itself by rest. Our Tarquin thus
Did softly press the rushes, ere he waken'd
The chastity he wounded. Cytherea,
How bravely thou becomest thy bed, fresh
    lily,
And whiter than the sheets! That I might
    touch!

---

12. **curtail**, shorten, abridge. The word is a corruption of *curtal*, formed to suggest the bobbing of a dog's tail; hence, *crop the ears* (of the *oaths*) below. 17. **rank**, social class; taken, in the aside which follows, to mean "rankness." 22. **Jack-slave**, lowborn fellow. 25. **capon**, perhaps used quibblingly for *cap on*, i.e., with fool's cap or coxcomb. 27. **Sayest thou?** what dost thou say? 29. **undertake**, engage with, give satisfaction. **companion**, fellow (contemptuous). 47. **derogation**, action unbecoming his position. 51. **issues**, deeds, actions.

Scene ii. 9. **fairies**, evil fairies. 12. **Our Tarquin**, the Roman Sextus Tarquinius in the story of Lucrece. 13. **press the rushes.** Elizabethan floors were strewn with rushes; certainly those in the days of Cymbeline and Tarquin were not. 14. **Cytherea**, Venus.

But kiss; one kiss! Rubies unparagon'd,
How dearly they do 't! 'Tis her breathing
　　that
Perfumes the chamber thus: the flame o' the
　　taper
Bows toward her, and would under-peep her
　　lids,
To see the enclosed lights, now canopied　21
Under these windows, white and azure laced
With blue of heaven's own tinct. But my
　　design,
To note the chamber: I will write all down:
Such and such pictures; there the window;
　　such
The adornment of her bed; the arras; figures,
Why, such and such; and the contents o' the
　　story.
Ah, but some natural notes about her body,
Above ten thousand meaner moveables
Would testify, to enrich mine inventory.　30
O sleep, thou ape of death, lie dull upon
　　her!
And be her sense but as a monument,
Thus in a chapel lying! Come off, come off:
　　　　　　　　　[Taking off her bracelet.
As slippery as the Gordian knot was hard!
'Tis mine; and this will witness outwardly,
As strongly as the conscience does within,
To the madding of her lord. On her left
　　breast
A mole cinque-spotted, like the crimson
　　drops
I' the bottom of a cowslip: here's a voucher,
Stronger than ever law could make: this
　　secret
Will force him think I have pick'd the lock
　　and ta'en　　　　　　　　　　　　41
The treasure of her honour. No more. To
　　what end?
Why should I write this down, that's riveted,
Screw'd to my memory? She hath been read-
　　ing late
The tale of Tereus; here the leaf's turn'd
　　down
Where Philomel gave up. I have enough:

To the trunk again, and shut the spring of
　　it.
Swift, swift, you dragons of the night, that
　　dawning
May have the raven's eye! I lodge in fear;
Though this a heavenly angel, hell is here.
　　　　　　　　　　　　[Clock strikes.
One, two, three: time, time!　　　　51
　　　[Goes into the trunk. The scene closes.

SCENE III.　An ante-chamber adjoining
　　　　　　Imogen's apartments.

Enter CLOTEN and Lords.

First Lord. Your lordship is the most
patient man in loss, the most coldest that
ever turned up ace.
Clo. It would make any man cold to lose.
First Lord. But not every man patient
after the noble temper of your lordship. You
are most hot and furious when you win.
Clo. Winning will put any man into
courage. If I could get this foolish Imogen,
I should have gold enough. It's almost
morning, is 't not?　　　　　　　　10
First Lord. Day, my lord.
Clo. I would this music would come: I
am advised to give her music o' mornings;
they say it will penetrate.

Enter Musicians.

Come on; tune: if you can penetrate her with
your fingering, so; we'll try with tongue too:
if none will do, let her remain; but I'll never
give o'er. First, a very excellent good-
conceited thing; after, a wonderful sweet
air, with admirable rich words to it: and then
let her consider.　　　　　　　　21

SONG.

Hark, hark! the lark at heaven's gate sings,
　　And Phœbus 'gins arise,
His steeds to water at those springs
　　On chaliced flowers that lies;
And winking Mary-buds begin
　　To ope their golden eyes:

---

22. **windows**, eyelids. 23. **tinct**, color. 26. **arras**, hangings of tapestry. Mason joins with the next word and reads *arras-figures*. 27. **story**, subject set forth in embroidery on the tapestry. 34. **Gordian knot**. According to prophecy whoever untied the knot binding the yoke to the pole of the chariot of Gordius, peasant king of Phrygia, should be king of all Asia. Alexander severed the knot with his sword. 37. **madding**, maddening, making mad. 38. **cinque-spotted**, with five spots. 45. **Tereus**, mythical king of Thrace, who dishonored Philomela, sister of his wife, Procne. He had Philomela's tongue cut out so that she could not tell the story, but she wove it into a tapestry.

49. **raven's eye**. The raven was supposed to wake at early dawn. 50. **this**, this is. 51. **time, time!** Iachimo remembers that Imogen is to be called at four. *Scene iii*. 2. **most coldest**, coolest, most deliberate. 4. **cold**, gloomy, dispirited. 15. **penetrate**, touch. 16. **so**, it is well. 25. **lies**, usually explained as the old northern plural in "s." 26. **winking**, having eyes shut. **Mary-buds**, buds of marigolds.

With every thing that pretty is,
  My lady sweet, arise:
    Arise, arise.   30

Clo. So, get you gone. If this penetrate, I
will consider your music the better: if it do
not, it is a vice in her ears, which horse-hairs
and calves'-guts, nor the voice of unpaved
eunuch to boot, can never amend.
                         [Exeunt Musicians.
Sec. Lord. Here comes the king.
Clo. I am glad I was up so late; for that's
the reason I was up so early: he cannot
choose but take this service I have done
fatherly.

       Enter CYMBELINE *and* QUEEN.

Good morrow to your majesty and to my
gracious mother.   41
  Cym. Attend you here the door of our
stern daughter?
Will she not forth?
  Clo. I have assailed her with music, but
she vouchsafes no notice.
  Cym. The exile of her minion is too new;
She hath not yet forgot him: some more time
Must wear the print of his remembrance out,
And then she's yours.
  Queen. You are most bound to the king,
Who lets go by no vantages that may   50
Prefer you to his daughter. Frame your-
  self
To orderly soliciting, and be friended
With aptness of the season; make denials
Increase your services; so seem as if
You were inspired to do those duties which
You tender to her; that you in all obey her,
Save when command to your dismission
  tends,
And therein you are senseless.
  Clo.   Senseless! not so.

       Enter a Messenger.

  Mess. So like you, sir, ambassadors from
  Rome;
The one is Caius Lucius.
  Cym.   A worthy fellow,   60
Albeit he comes on angry purpose now;

But that's no fault of his: we must receive
  him
According to the honour of his sender;
And towards himself, his goodness forespent
  on us,
We must extend our notice. Our dear son,
When you have given good morning to your
  mistress,
Attend the queen and us; we shall have need
To employ you towards this Roman. Come,
  our queen.   *[Exeunt all but Cloten.*
  Clo. If she be up, I'll speak with her; if
  not,
Let her lie still and dream. [*Knocks*] By your
  leave, ho!   70
I know her women are about her: what
If I do line one of their hands? 'Tis gold
Which buys admittance; oft it doth; yea,
  and makes
Diana's rangers false themselves, yield up
Their deer to the stand o' the stealer; and
  'tis gold
Which makes the true man kill'd and saves
  the thief;
Nay, sometime hangs both thief and true
  man: what
Can it not do and undo? I will make
One of her women lawyer to me, for
I yet not understand the case myself.   80
[*Knocks*] By your leave.

       Enter a Lady.

  Lady. Who's there that knocks?
  Clo.   A gentleman.
  Lady.   No more?
  Clo. Yes, and a gentlewoman's son.
  Lady.   That's more
Than some, whose tailors are as dear as
  yours,
Can justly boast of. What's your lordship's
  pleasure?
  Clo. Your lady's person: is she ready?
  Lady.   Ay,
To keep her chamber.
  Clo.   There is gold for you;
Sell me your good report.
  Lady. How! my good name? or to report
  of you

32. **consider**, reward. 33. **horse-hairs**, of the fiddle-bow. 34. **calves'-guts**, fiddle-strings. 39. **fatherly**, as a father. 51. **Prefer**, recommend. **Frame**, conform. 57. **dismission**, dismissal, rejection. 58. **senseless**, insensible (to her commands). Cloten understands the word as meaning "stupid."

64. **forespent**, previously bestowed. 72. **line**, i.e., with gold. 74. **rangers**, nymphs (vowed to chastity). **false**, verb meaning "turn false"; or, possibly, an adjective. 75. **stand**, station of huntsman waiting for game. 88. **good report**, favorable speech. The Lady understands another meaning of the expression, namely "reputation," "good name."

What I shall think is good?—The prin-
cess!   90

Enter IMOGEN.

Clo. Good morrow, fairest: sister, your
sweet hand.   [*Exit Lady.*
Imo. Good morrow, sir. You lay out too
much pains
For purchasing but trouble: the thanks I give
Is telling you that I am poor of thanks
And scarce can spare them.
Clo.   Still, I swear I love you.
Imo. If you but said so, 'twere as deep
with me:
If you swear still, your recompense is still
That I regard it not.
Clo.   This is no answer.
Imo. But that you shall not say I yield
being silent,
I would not speak. I pray you, spare me:
'faith,   100
I shall unfold equal discourtesy
To your best kindness: one of your great
knowing
Should learn, being taught, forbearance.
Clo. To leave you in your madness, 'twere
my sin:
I will not.
Imo. Fools are not mad folks.
Clo.   Do you call me fool?
Imo. As I am mad, I do:
If you'll be patient, I'll no more be mad;
That cures us both. I am much sorry, sir,
You put me to forget a lady's manners, 110
By being so verbal: and learn now, for all,
That I, which know my heart, do here pro-
nounce,
By the very truth of it, I care not for you,
And am so near the lack of charity—
To accuse myself—I hate you; which I had
rather
You felt than make 't my boast.
Clo.   You sin against
Obedience, which you owe your father. For
The contract you pretend with that base
wretch,
One bred of alms and foster'd with cold
dishes,
With scraps o' the court, it is no contract,
none: 120
And though it be allow'd in meaner parties—

Yet who than he more mean?—to knit their
souls,
On whom there is no more dependency
But brats and beggary, in self-figured knot;
Yet you are curb'd from that enlargement
by
The consequence o' the crown, and must not
soil
The precious note of it with a base slave,
A hilding for a livery, a squire's cloth,
A pantler, not so eminent.
Imo.   Profane fellow!
Wert thou the son of Jupiter and no more 130
But what thou art besides, thou wert too
base
To be his groom: thou wert dignified enough,
Even to the point of envy, if 'twere made
Comparative for your virtues, to be styled
The under-hangman of his kingdom, and
hated
For being preferr'd so well.
Clo.   The south-fog rot him!
Imo. He never can meet more mischance
than come
To be but named of thee. His meanest gar-
ment,
That ever hath but clipp'd his body, is dearer
In my respect than all the hairs above
thee,   140
Were they all made such men. How now,
Pisanio!

Enter PISANIO.

Clo. 'His garment!' Now the devil—
Imo. To Dorothy my woman hie thee pre-
sently—
Clo. 'His garment!'
Imo.   I am sprited with a fool,
Frighted, and anger'd worse: go bid my
woman
Search for a jewel that too casually
Hath left mine arm: it was thy master's:
'shrew me,
If I would lose it for a revenue
Of any king's in Europe. I do think
I saw 't this morning: confident I am   150
Last night 'twas on mine arm; I kiss'd it:
I hope it be not gone to tell my lord

---

102. **knowing**, knowledge, discernment; ironical.
111. **By . . . verbal.** If the phrase refers to Cloten, the
meaning of *verbal* is "verbose"; if to Imogen, "plain-
spoken." In either case there is a suggestion of "playing
with words." 117. **For**, as for.

124. **self-figured**, self-contracted. 125. **enlargement**, liberty. 126. **consequence**, succession. 128.
hilding, good-for-nothing fellow. **for**, fit for. **cloth**,
dress, livery. 129. **pantler**, servant who has charge of
the pantry. 134. **Comparative for**, proportioned to,
comparing with. 136. **south-fog.** The south wind was
supposed to be charged with poisonous vapors and
diseases. 139. **clipp'd**, embraced, enclosed. 144.
sprited, haunted. 147. **'shrew me**, beshrew me; a
mild imprecation.

That I kiss aught but he.
Pis.   'Twill not be lost.
Imo. I hope so: go and search.
                         [*Exit Pisanio.*
Clo.   You have abused me:
'His meanest garment!'
Imo.   Ay, I said so, sir:
If you will make 't an action, call witness to 't.
Clo. I will inform your father.
Imo.   Your mother too:
She's my good lady, and will conceive, I
     hope,
But the worst of me. So, I leave you, sir,
To the worst of discontent.   [*Exit.*
Clo.   I'll be revenged: 160
'His meanest garment!' Well.   [*Exit.*

SCENE IV. *Rome. Philario's house.*

Enter POSTHUMUS *and* PHILARIO.

Post. Fear it not, sir: I would I were so
     sure
To win the king as I am bold her honour
Will remain hers.
Phi.   What means do you make to him?
Post. Not any, but abide the change of
     time,
Quake in the present winter's state and wish
That warmer days would come: in these
     sear'd hopes,
I barely gratify your love; they failing,
I must die much your debtor.
Phi. Your very goodness and your com-
     pany
O'erpays all I can do. By this, your king 10
Hath heard of great Augustus: Caius Lucius
Will do 's commission throughly: and I think
He'll grant the tribute, send the arrearages,
Or look upon our Romans, whose remem-
     brance
Is yet fresh in their grief.
Post.   I do believe,
Statist though I am none, nor like to be,
That this will prove a war; and you shall hear
The legions now in Gallia sooner landed
In our not-fearing Britain than have tidings
Of any penny tribute paid. Our country-
     men   20

156. **action,** action at law. 158. **my good lady,**
patroness (ironical).
     Scene iv. 2. **bold,** confident. 6. **sear'd,** withered,
blighted; F: *fear'd,* frequently and properly retained,
meaning "mixed with fear." 14. **Or look,** before he
will look. 16. **Statist,** statesman.

Are men more order'd than when Julius
     Cæsar
Smiled at their lack of skill, but found their
     courage
Worthy his frowning at: their discipline,
Now mingled with their courages, will make
     known
To their approvers they are people such
That mend upon the world.

Enter IACHIMO.

Phi.   See! Iachimo!
Post. The swiftest harts have posted you
     by land;
And winds of all the corners kiss'd your sails,
To make your vessel nimble.
Phi.   Welcome, sir.
Post. I hope the briefness of your answer
     made   30
The speediness of your return.
Iach.   Your lady
Is one of the fairest that I have look'd upon.
Post. And therewithal the best; or let her
     beauty
Look through a casement to allure false
     hearts
And be false with them.
Iach.   Here are letters for you.
Post. Their tenour good, I trust.
Iach.   'Tis very like.
Phi. Was Caius Lucius in the Britain
     court
When you were there?
Iach.   He was expected then,
But not approach'd.
Post.   All is well yet.   39
Sparkles this stone as it was wont? or is 't
     not
Too dull for your good wearing?
Iach.   If I had lost it,
I should have lost the worth of it in gold.
I'll make a journey twice as far, to enjoy
A second night of such sweet shortness which
Was mine in Britain, for the ring is won.
Post. The stone's too hard to come by.
Iach.   Not a whit,
Your lady being so easy.
Post.   Make not, sir,
Your loss your sport: I hope you know that
     we
Must not continue friends.
Iach.   Good sir, we must,   49

21. **more order'd,** better disciplined and governed.
25. **approvers,** those who test (their courage).

If you keep covenant. Had I not brought
The knowledge of your mistress home, I
      grant
We were to question further: but I now
Profess myself the winner of her honour,
Together with your ring; and not the
      wronger
Of her or you, having proceeded but
By both your wills.
      Post.   If you can make 't apparent
That you have tasted her in bed, my hand
And ring is yours; if not, the foul opinion
You had of her pure honour gains or loses
Your sword or mine, or masterless leaves
      both   60
To who shall find them.
      Iach.   Sir, my circumstances,
Being so near the truth as I will make them,
Must first induce you to believe: whose
      strength
I will confirm with oath; which, I doubt not,
You'll give me leave to spare, when you shall
      find
You need it not.
      Post.   Proceed.
      Iach.   First, her bedchamber,—
Where, I confess, I slept not, but profess
Had that was well worth watching—it was
      hang'd
With tapestry of silk and silver; the story 69
Proud Cleopatra, when she met her Roman,
And Cydnus swell'd above the banks, or for
The press of boats or pride: a piece of work
So bravely done, so rich, that it did strive
In workmanship and value; which I wonder'd
Could be so rarely and exactly wrought,
Since the true life on 't was—
      Post.   This is true;
And this you might have heard of here, by
      me,
Or by some other.
      Iach.   More particulars
Must justify my knowledge.
      Post.   So they must,
Or do your honour injury.
      Iach.   The chimney   80
Is south the chamber, and the chimney-piece
Chaste Dian bathing: never saw I figures
So likely to report themselves: the cutter

Was as another nature, dumb; outwent her,
Motion and breath left out.
      Post.   This is a thing
Which you might from relation likewise
      reap,
Being, as it is, much spoke of.
      Iach.   The roof o' the chamber
With golden cherubins is fretted: her and-
      irons—
I had forgot them—were two winking Cupids
Of silver, each on one foot standing, nicely 90
Depending on their brands.
      Post.   This is her honour!
Let it be granted you have seen all this—and
      praise
Be given to your remembrance—the de-
      scription
Of what is in her chamber nothing saves
The wager you have laid.
      Iach.   Then, if you can,
                              [*Showing the bracelet.*
Be pale: I beg but leave to air this jewel;
      see!
And now 'tis up again: it must be married
To that your diamond; I'll keep them.
      Post.   Jove!
Once more let me behold it: is it that
Which I left with her?
      Iach.   Sir—I thank her—that: 100
She stripp'd it from her arm; I see her yet;
Her pretty action did outsell her gift,
And yet enrich'd it too: she gave it me, and
      said
She prized it once.
      Post.   May be she pluck'd it off
To send it me.
      Iach.   She writes so to you, doth she?
      Post. O, no, no, no! 'tis true. Here, take
      this too;   [*Gives the ring.*
It is a basilisk unto mine eye,
Kills me to look on 't. Let there be no honour
Where there is beauty; truth, where sem-
      blance; love,
Where there's another man: the vows of
      women   110
Of no more bondage be, to where they are
      made,

52. **question**, debate; here, settle matters by a duel. 61. **circumstances**, details, particulars. 68. **watching**, keeping awake for. 71. **Cydnus**, a river in Cilicia, the scene of the meeting of Antony and Cleopatra which is described in *Antony and Cleopatra*, II, ii, 191-231. 83-85. **the cutter . . . out**, the sculptor, though unable to

impart voice, was like nature; indeed surpassed her but for motion and breath. 86. **relation**, hearsay. 88. **fretted**, adorned with carved or embossed work in decorative patterns (Onions). 89. **winking**, blind. 91. **Depending**, leaning. **brands**, torches, i.e., of the Cupids. 97. **up**, put up, pocketed. 102 **outsell**, exceed in value. 107. **basilisk**, a fabulous reptile, called also cockatrice, said to be hatched by a serpent from a cock's egg and to be able to kill by its look. 111. **bond-age**, obligation.

Than they are to their virtues; which is
    nothing.
O, above measure false!
    Phi.   Have patience, sir,
And take your ring again; 'tis not yet won:
It may be probable she lost it; or
Who knows if one of her women, being cor-
    rupted,
Hath stol'n it from her?
    Post.   Very true;
And so, I hope, he came by 't. Back my
    ring:
Render to me some corporal sign about her,
More evident than this; for this was stolen.
    Iach. By Jupiter, I had it from her arm.
    Post. Hark you, he swears; by Jupiter he
    swears.   122
'Tis true:—nay, keep the ring—'tis true: I
    am sure
She would not lose it: her attendants are
All sworn and honourable:—they induced to
    steal it!
And by a stranger!—No, he hath enjoy'd
    her:
The cognizance of her incontinency
Is this: she hath bought the name of whore
    thus dearly.
There, take thy hire; and all the fiends of
    hell
Divide themselves between you!
    Phi.   Sir, be patient: 130
This is not strong enough to be believed
Of one persuaded well of—
    Post.   Never talk on 't;
She hath been colted by him.
    Iach.   If you seek
For further satisfying, under her breast—
Worthy the pressing—lies a mole, right
    proud
Of that most delicate lodging: by my life,
I kiss'd it; and it gave me present hunger
To feed again, though full. You do re-
    member
This stain upon her?
    Post.   Ay, and it doth confirm
Another stain, as big as hell can hold, 140
Were there no more but it.
    Iach.   Will you hear more?
    Post. Spare your arithmetic: never count
    the turns;
Once, and a million!
    Iach.   I'll be sworn—

127. **cognizance,** mark or token by which a thing
is recognized.

    Post.   No swearing.
If you will swear you have not done 't, you
    lie;
And I will kill thee, if thou dost deny
Thou'st made me cuckold.
    Iach.   I'll deny nothing.
    Post. O, that I had her here, to tear her
    limb-meal!
I will go there and do 't, i' the court, before
Her father. I'll do something—   [*Exit.*
    Phi.   Quite besides 149
The government of patience! You have won:
Let's follow him, and pervert the present
    wrath
He hath against himself.
    Iach.   With all my heart. [*Exeunt.*

SCENE V.   *Another room in Philario's house.*

Enter POSTHUMUS.

    Post. Is there no way for men to be but
    women
Must be half-workers? We are all bastards;
And that most venerable man which I
Did call my father, was I know not where
When I was stamp'd; some coiner with his
    tools
Made me a counterfeit: yet my mother
    seem'd
The Dian of that time: so doth my wife
The nonpareil of this. O, vengeance, ven-
    geance!
Me of my lawful pleasure she restrain'd
And pray'd me oft forbearance; did it with 10
A pudency so rosy the sweet view on 't
Might well have warm'd old Saturn; that I
    thought her
As chaste as unsunn'd snow. O, all the
    devils!
This yellow Iachimo, in an hour,—was 't
    not?—
Or less,—at first?—perchance he spoke not,
    but,
Like a full-acorn'd boar, a German one,
Cried 'O!' and mounted; found no opposi-
    tion
But what he look'd for should oppose and she
Should from encounter guard. Could I find
    out

147. **limb-meal,** limb from limb. 149. **besides,**
beyond. 151. **pervert,** turn, divert.
    Scene v. 8. **nonpareil,** one that has no equal. 11.
pudency, modesty.

The woman's part in me! For there's no
    motion   20
That tends to vice in man, but I affirm
It is the woman's part: be it lying, note it,
The woman's; flattering, hers; deceiving,
    hers;
Lust and rank thoughts, hers, hers; revenges,
    hers;
Ambitions, covetings, change of prides, dis-
    dain,
Nice longing, slanders, mutability,
All faults that may be named, nay, that hell
    knows,
Why, hers, in part or all; but rather, all;
For even to vice
They are not constant, but are changing
    still
One vice, but of a minute old, for one   31
Not half so old as that. I'll write against
    them,
Detest them, curse them: yet 'tis greater skill
In a true hate, to pray they have their will:
The very devils cannot plague them better.
                        [*Exit.*

ACT III.

SCENE I. *Britain. A hall in Cymbeline's
palace.*

Enter in state, CYMBELINE, QUEEN, CLOTEN,
and Lords *at one door, and at another,*
CAIUS LUCIUS *and* Attendants.

    Cym. Now say, what would Augustus
    Cæsar with us?
    Luc. When Julius Cæsar, whose remem-
    brance yet
Lives in men's eyes and will to ears and
    tongues
Be theme and hearing ever, was in this
    Britain
And conquer'd it, Cassibelan, thine uncle,—
Famous in Cæsar's praises, no whit less
Than in his feats deserving it—for him
And his succession granted Rome a tribute,
Yearly three thousand pounds, which by
    thee lately
Is left untender'd.
    Queen.   And, to kill the marvel, 10
Shall be so ever.

    Clo.   There be many Cæsars,
Ere such another Julius. Britain is
A world by itself; and we will nothing pay
For wearing our own noses.
    Queen.   That opportunity
Which then they had to take from 's, to
    resume
We have again. Remember, sir, my liege,
The kings your ancestors, together with
The natural bravery of your isle, which
    stands
As Neptune's park, ribbed and paled in
With rocks unscaleable and roaring waters,
With sands that will not bear your enemies'
    boats,   21
But suck them up to the topmast. A kind of
    conquest
Cæsar made here; but made not here his
    brag
Of 'Came' and 'saw' and 'overcame:' with
    shame—
The first that ever touch'd him—he was
    carried
From off our coast, twice beaten; and his
    shipping—
Poor ignorant baubles!—on our terrible seas,
Like egg-shells moved upon their surges,
    crack'd
As easily 'gainst our rocks: for joy whereof
The famed Cassibelan, who was once at
    point—   30
O giglot fortune!—to master Cæsar's sword,
Made Lud's town with rejoicing fires bright
And Britons strut with courage.
    Clo. Come, there's no more tribute to be
paid: our kingdom is stronger than it was at
that time; and, as I said, there is no moe such
Cæsars: other of them may have crook'd
noses, but to owe such straight arms, none.
    Cym. Son, let your mother end.   39
    Clo. We have yet many among us can
gripe as hard as Cassibelan: I do not say I
am one; but I have a hand. Why tribute?
why should we pay tribute? If Cæsar can
hide the sun from us with a blanket, or put
the moon in his pocket, we will pay him
tribute for light; else, sir, no more tribute,
pray you now.
    Cym. You must know,   47
Till the injurious Romans did extort

---

20. **motion**, impulse; a broad term for both mental
and physical action. 25. **change of prides**, varying
vanities (in dress, etc.). 26. **Nice**, capricious, or wanton.
32. **write against**, denounce.

27. **ignorant**, silly, unskilled. 30. **Cassibelan**. The
incident referred to is recorded of Nennius, brother of
Cassibelan, in Holinshed. 31. **giglot**, lewd, wanton.
32. **Lud's town**, London. 48. **injurious**, malicious,
or insolent.

This tribute from us, we were free: Cæsar's
  ambition,
Which swell'd so much that it did almost
  stretch   50
The sides o' the world, against all colour
  here
Did put the yoke upon 's; which to shake off
Becomes a warlike people, whom we reckon
Ourselves to be.
  Clo. and Lords. We do.
  Cym.   Say, then to Cæsar,
Our ancestor was that Mulmutius which
Ordain'd our laws, whose use the sword of
  Cæsar
Hath too much mangled; whose repair and
  franchise
Shall, by the power we hold, be our good
  deed,
Though Rome be therefore angry: Mulmu-
  tius made our laws,   59
Who was the first of Britain which did put
His brows within a golden crown and call'd
Himself a king.
  Luc.   I am sorry, Cymbeline,
That I am to pronounce Augustus Cæsar—
Cæsar, that hath more kings his servants
  than
Thyself domestic officers—thine enemy:
Receive it from me, then: war and confusion
In Cæsar's name pronounce I 'gainst thee:
  look
For fury not to be resisted. Thus defied,
I thank thee for myself.
  Cym.   Thou art welcome, Caius.
Thy Cæsar knighted me; my youth I spent
Much under him; of him I gather'd honour;
Which he to seek of me again, perforce,   72
Behoves me keep at utterance. I am perfect
That the Pannonians and Dalmatians for
Their liberties are now in arms; a precedent
Which not to read would show the Britons
  cold:
So Cæsar shall not find them.
  Luc.   Let proof speak.   77
  Clo. His majesty bids you welcome. Make
pastime with us a day or two, or longer: if

you seek us afterwards in other terms, you
shall find us in our salt-water girdle: if you
beat us out of it, it is yours; if you fall in the
adventure, our crows shall fare the better
for you; and there's an end.
  Luc. So, sir.
  Cym. I know your master's pleasure and
he mine:
All the remain is 'Welcome!' [*Exeunt.* 87

Scene II. *Another room in the palace.*

Enter Pisanio, *with a letter.*

  Pis. How! of adultery? Wherefore write
  you not
What monster's her accuser? Leonatus!
O master! what a strange infection
Is fall'n into thy ear! What false Italian,
As poisonous-tongued as handed, hath
  prevail'd
On thy too ready hearing? Disloyal! No:
She's punish'd for her truth, and undergoes,
More goddess-like than wife-like, such as-
  saults
As would take in some virtue. O my master!
Thy mind to her is now as low as were   10
Thy fortunes. How! that I should murder
  her?
Upon the love and truth and vows which I
Have made to thy command? I, her? her
  blood?
If it be so to do good service, never
Let me be counted serviceable. How look I,
That I should seem to lack humanity
So much as this fact comes to? [*Reading*]
  'Do 't: the letter
That I have sent her, by her own command
Shall give thee opportunity.' O damn'd
  paper!
Black as the ink that 's on thee! Senseless
  bauble,   20
Art thou a feodary for this act, and look'st
So virgin-like without? Lo, here she comes.
I am ignorant in what I am commanded.

Enter Imogen.

  Imo. How now, Pisanio!
  Pis. Madam, here is a letter from my
  lord.

51. **against all colour,** in opposition to all reason.
53. **whom,** which. 55. **Mulmutius.** Holinshed gives
an account of the beneficent reign of Mulmutius. 57.
franchise, free exercise. 73. **at utterance,** to the last
extremity. **I am perfect,** I am well aware. 78-84. **His
majesty ... end.** It has been pointed out that this and
other speeches by Cloten in this scene are on a higher
level of intelligence than might be expected from his usual
boorish stupidity. There may be evidence of tampering
with the text or of a change of conception, although even
the better speeches are characteristically impudent.

87. **remain,** remainder, rest.
Scene ii. 9. **take in,** cause to yield, conquer. 10.
to, compared to. 21. **feodary,** accomplice.

Imo. Who? thy lord? that is my lord, Leonatus!
O, learn'd indeed were that astronomer
That knew the stars as I his characters;
He 'ld lay the future open. You good gods,
Let what is here contain'd relish of love, 30
Of my lord's health, of his content, yet not
That we two are asunder; let that grieve him:
Some griefs are med'cinable; that is one of them,
For it doth physic love: of his content,
All but in that! Good wax, thy leave. Blest be
You bees that make these locks of counsel! Lovers
And men in dangerous bonds pray not alike:
Though forfeiters you cast in prison, yet
You clasp young Cupid's tables. Good news, gods! 39
[*Reads*] 'Justice, and your father's wrath, should he take me in his dominion, could not be so cruel to me, as you, O the dearest of creatures, would even renew me with your eyes. Take notice that I am in Cambria, at Milford-Haven: what your own love will out of this advise you, follow. So he wishes you all happiness, that remains loyal to his vow, and your, increasing in love,
LEONATUS POSTHUMUS.'
O, for a horse with wings! Hear'st thou, Pisanio? 50
He is at Milford-Haven: read, and tell me
How far 'tis thither. If one of mean affairs
May plod it in a week, why may not I
Glide thither in a day? Then, true Pisanio,—
Who long'st, like me, to see thy lord; who long'st,—
O, let me ·bate,—but not like me—yet long'st,
But in a fainter kind:—O, not like me;
For mine's beyond beyond—say, and speak thick;
Love's counsellor should fill the bores of hearing, 59
To the smothering of the sense—how far it is
To this same blessed Milford: and by the way
Tell me how Wales was made so happy as
To inherit such a haven: but first of all,

How we may steal from hence, and for the gap
That we shall make in time, from our hence-going
And our return, to excuse: but first, how get hence:
Why should excuse be born or e'er begot?
We'll talk of that hereafter. Prithee, speak,
How many score of miles may we well ride
'Twixt hour and hour?
Pis.   One score 'twixt sun and sun,
Madam, 's enough for you: [*Aside*] and too much too. 71
Imo. Why, one that rode to 's execution, man,
Could never go so slow: I have heard of riding wagers,
Where horses have been nimbler than the sands
That run i' the clock's behalf. But this is foolery:
Go bid my woman feign a sickness; say
She'll home to her father: and provide me presently
A riding-suit, no costlier than would fit
A franklin's housewife.
Pis.   Madam, you're best consider.
Imo. I see before me, man: nor here, nor here, 80
Nor what ensues, but have a fog in them,
That I cannot look through. Away, I prithee;
Do as I bid thee: there's no more to say;
Accessible is none but Milford way. [*Exeunt.*

SCENE III. *Wales: a mountainous country with a cave.*

Enter, from the cave, BELARIUS; GUIDERIUS, *and* ARVIRAGUS *following.*

Bel. A goodly day not to keep house, with such
Whose roof's as low as ours! Stoop, boys; this gate
Instructs you how to adore the heavens and bows you

---

28. **characters**, handwriting. 38. **forfeiters**, those who forfeit their bonds. 39. **tables**, tablets. The contrast is between the waxen seals on forfeited bonds and on love letters. 44. **Cambria**, Wales. 52. **mean**, ordinary. 56. **bate**, deduct from (what I have said). 58. **thick**, quickly, fast.

67. **or e'er**, before. 75. **i' the clock's behalf**, i.e., doing the service of a clock. 79. **franklin's**, yeoman's. A *franklin* was a farmer who owned his own land but was not of noble birth. **you're best**, you had better.
Scene iii. The second theme of the plot begins at this point; it proceeds with its complications, entwining itself with the major plot, and finally is solved in the great fifth scene of the fifth act. 1. **keep house**, stay at home. 3. **bows you**, makes you bow.

To a morning's holy office: the gates of
   monarchs
Are arch'd so high that giants may jet
   through
And keep their impious turbans on, without
Good morrow to the sun. Hail, thou fair
   heaven!
We house i' the rock, yet use thee not so
   hardly
As prouder livers do.
   Gui.   Hail, heaven!
   Arv.   Hail, heaven!
   Bel. Now for our mountain sport: up to
   yond hill;   10
Your legs are young; I'll tread these flats.
   Consider,
When you above perceive me like a crow,
That it is place which lessens and sets off:
And you may then revolve what tales I have
   told you
Of courts, of princes, of the tricks in war:
This service is not service, so being done,
But being so allow'd: to apprehend thus,
Draws us a profit from all things we see;
And often, to our comfort, shall we find
The sharded beetle in a safer hold   20
Than is the full-wing'd eagle. O, this life
Is nobler than attending for a check,
Richer than doing nothing for a bauble,
Prouder than rustling in unpaid-for silk:
Such gain the cap of him that makes 'em fine,
Yet keeps his book uncross'd: no life to ours.
   Gui. Out of your proof you speak: we,
   poor unfledged,
Have never wing'd from view o' the nest, nor
   know not
What air 's from home. Haply this life is best,
If quiet life be best; sweeter to you   30
That have a sharper known; well correspond-
   ing
With your stiff age: but unto us it is
A cell of ignorance; travelling a-bed;
A prison for a debtor, that not dares
To stride a limit.
   Arv.   What should we speak of

When we are old as you? when we shall
   hear
The rain and wind beat dark December, how,
In this our pinching cave, shall we discourse
The freezing hours away? We have seen
   nothing;
We are beastly, subtle as the fox for prey,   40
Like warlike as the wolf for what we eat;
Our valour is to chase what flies; our cage
We make a quire, as doth the prison'd
   bird,
And sing our bondage freely.
   Bel.   How you speak!
Did you but know the city's usuries
And felt them knowingly; the art o' the
   court,
As hard to leave as keep; whose top to climb
Is certain falling, or so slippery that
The fear's as bad as falling; the toil o' the
   war,
A pain that only seems to seek out danger   50
I' the name of fame and honour; which dies
   i' the search,
And hath as oft a slanderous epitaph
As record of fair act; nay, many times,
Doth ill deserve by doing well; what's worse,
Must court'sy at the censure:—O boys, this
   story
The world may read in me: my body's
   mark'd
With Roman swords, and my report was
   once
First with the best of note: Cymbeline loved
   me,
And when a soldier was the theme, my name
Was not far off: then was I as a tree   60
Whose boughs did bend with fruit: but in
   one night,
A storm or robbery, call it what you will,
Shook down my mellow hangings, nay, my
   leaves,
And left me bare to weather.
   Gui.   Uncertain favour!
   Bel. My fault being nothing—as I have
   told you oft—
But that two villains, whose false oaths pre-
   vail'd
Before my perfect honour, swore to Cymbe-
   line
I was confederate with the Romans: so
Follow'd my banishment, and this twenty
   years

5. **jet**, walk pompously, strut. One may recognize
in the speeches of Belarius the popular and traditional
theme of the vanity and falsity of kingly courts. 17.
allow'd, acknowledged. 20. **sharded**, covered with
shards or the sheaths of insects' wings. 22. **attending**,
doing service (at court). **check**, reproof. 25-26. **Such
. . . uncross'd**, such a one finds his tailor obsequious
without having to pay his bill. 27. **proof**, experience.
we, poor unfledged. The youths of royal blood are
represented as having born in them a taste for kingly
courts and noble deeds. 29. **air's from**, air there is
away from. 35. **stride a limit**, overpass a bound.

41. **Like**, equally. 58. **note**, distinction, importance.
63. **hangings**, hanging fruit.

This rock and these demesnes have been my
world;   70
Where I have lived at honest freedom, paid
More pious debts to heaven than in all
The fore-end of my time. But up to the
mountains!
This is not hunters' language: he that strikes
The venison first shall be the lord o' the
feast;
To him the other two shall minister;
And we will fear no poison, which attends
In place of greater state. I'll meet you in the
valleys.
            [*Exeunt Guiderius and Arviragus.*
How hard it is to hide the sparks of nature!
These boys know little they are sons to the
king;   80
Nor Cymbeline dreams that they are alive.
They think they are mine; and though
train'd up thus meanly
I' the cave wherein they bow, their thoughts
do hit
The roofs of palaces, and nature prompts
them
In simple and low things to prince it much
Beyond the trick of others. This Polydore,
The heir of Cymbeline and Britain, who
The king his father call'd Guiderius,—Jove!
When on my three-foot stool I sit and tell
The warlike feats I have done, his spirits fly
out   90
Into my story: say 'Thus mine enemy fell,
And thus I sat my foot on 's neck;' even
then
The princely blood flows in his cheek, he
sweats,
Strains his young nerves and puts himself in
posture
That acts my words. The younger brother,
Cadwal,
Once Arviragus, in as like a figure,
Strikes life into my speech and shows much
more
His own conceiving.—Hark, the game is
roused!—
O Cymbeline! heaven and my conscience
knows
Thou didst unjustly banish me: whereon, 100

At three and two years old, I stole these
babes;
Thinking to bar thee of succession, as
Thou reft'st me of my lands. Euriphile,
Thou wast their nurse; they took thee for
their mother,
And every day do honour to her grave:
Myself, Belarius, that am Morgan call'd,
They take for natural father. The game is up.
                                            [*Exit.*

SCENE IV. *Country near Milford-Haven.*

        Enter PISANIO *and* IMOGEN.

Imo. Thou told'st me, when we came
from horse, the place
Was near at hand: ne'er long'd my mother so
To see me first, as I have now. Pisanio!
man!
Where is Posthumus? What is in thy mind,
That makes thee stare thus? Wherefore
breaks that sigh
From the inward of thee? One, but painted
thus,
Would be interpreted a thing perplex'd
Beyond self-explication: put thyself
Into a haviour of less fear, ere wildness
Vanquish my staider senses. What's the
matter?   10
Why tender'st thou that paper to me, with
A look untender? If 't be summer news,
Smile to 't before; if winterly, thou need'st
But keep that countenance still. My hus-
band's hand!
That drug-damn'd Italy hath out-crafted
him,
And he's at some hard point. Speak, man:
thy tongue
May take off some extremity, which to read
Would be even mortal to me.
Pis.   Please you, read;
And you shall find me, wretched man, a
thing
The most disdain'd of fortune.   20
Imo. [*Reads*] 'Thy mistress, Pisanio, hath
played the strumpet in my bed; the testi-
monies whereof lie bleeding in me. I speak
not out of weak surmises, but from proof as
strong as my grief and as certain as I expect

---

70. **demesnes**, domains, regions.   73. **fore-end**,
earlier part.   83. **bow**, stoop in entering.   85. **prince**,
play the prince.   94. **nerves**, sinews, parts of the body
in which the chief strength lies.   99-103. **O Cymbeline
. . . lands.** Even in this late play Shakespeare resorts
to the primitive dramaturgy of his earliest days and has
a long story told in soliloquy.

103. **reft'st**, didst deprive.
Scene iv. 9. **haviour**, behavior.   15. **drug-damn'd**,
condemned for its drugs and poisons.   **out-crafted**,
excelled in craft.   17. **take off**, have recourse to, reveal.
extremity, cruelty.

my revenge. That part thou, Pisanio, must
act for me, if thy faith be not tainted with
the breach of hers. Let thine own hands
take away her life: I shall give thee opportunity at Milford-Haven. She hath my letter for the purpose: where, if thou fear to
strike and to make me certain it is done, thou
art the pandar to her dishonour and equally
to me disloyal.'   33

   Pis. What shall I need to draw my sword?   .
      the paper
Hath cut her throat already. No, 'tis slander,
Whose edge is sharper than the sword, whose
      tongue
Outvenoms all the worms of Nile, whose
      breath
Rides on the posting winds and doth belie
All corners of the world: kings, queens and
      states,
Maids, matrons, nay, the secrets of the grave
This viperous slander enters. What cheer,
      madam?   41
   Imo. False to his bed! What is it to be
      false?
To lie in watch there and to think on him?
To weep 'twixt clock and clock? if sleep
      charge nature,
To break it with a fearful dream of him
And cry myself awake? that's false to 's bed,
      is it?
   Pis. Alas, good lady!
   Imo. I false! Thy conscience witness:
      Iachimo,
Thou didst accuse him of incontinency;   49
Thou then look'dst like a villain; now me-
      thinks
Thy favour's good enough. Some jay of
      Italy
†Whose mother was her painting, hath be-
      tray'd him:
Poor I am stale, a garment out of fashion;
And, for I am richer than to hang by the
      walls,
I must be ripp'd:—to pieces with me!—O,
Men's vows are women's traitors! All good
      seeming,
By thy revolt, O husband, shall be thought

Put on for villany; not born where 't grows,
But worn a bait for ladies.
   Pis.   Good madam, hear me.
   Imo. True honest men being heard, like
      false Æneas,   60
Were in his time thought false, and Sinon's
      weeping
Did scandal many a holy tear, took pity
From most true wretchedness: so thou, Post-
      humus,
Wilt lay the leaven on all proper men;
Goodly and gallant shall be false and per-
      jured
From thy great fail. Come, fellow, be thou
      honest:
Do thou thy master's bidding: when thou
      see'st him,
A little witness my obedience: look!
I draw the sword myself: take it, and hit
The innocent mansion of my love, my heart:
Fear not; 'tis empty of all things but grief: 71
Thy master is not there, who was indeed
The riches of it: do his bidding; strike.
Thou mayst be valiant in a better cause;
But now thou seem'st a coward.
   Pis.   Hence, vile instrument!
Thou shalt not damn my hand.
   Imo.   Why, I must die;
And if I do not by thy hand, thou art
No servant of thy master's. Against self-
      slaughter
There is a prohibition so divine
That cravens my weak hand. Come, here's
      my heart.   80
Something 's afore 't. Soft, soft! we'll no
      defence;
Obedient as the scabbard. What is here?
The scriptures of the loyal Leonatus,
All turn'd to heresy? Away, away,
Corrupters of my faith! you shall no more
Be stomachers to my heart. Thus may poor
      fools
Believe false teachers: though those that are
      betray'd
Do feel the treason sharply, yet the traitor
Stands in worse case of woe.

32. **pandar,** accomplice. 37. **worms,** serpents. 38.
posting, hurrying. 39. **states,** persons of high rank.
43. **in watch,** awake. 44. **charge,** lead, burden
(figurative). 45. **fearful,** full of fear. 51. **favour,**
aspect, look. **jay,** flashy or light woman. 52. **Whose
. . . painting,** explained as "who owed her beauty to her
painted face"; i.e., a creature born and made up of the
paint pot (Dowden); also as "whose painted face was the
sum of her woman-like qualities."

60. **Æneas,** thought of as the pattern of faithless
love because of his desertion of Dido. 61. **Sinon's.**
The Greek Sinon by his guile persuaded the Trojans to
introduce within the walls of Troy the wooden horse
filled with armed men. 64. **lay the leaven on,** taint,
corrupt. **proper,** respectable, or possibly, handsome.
66. **fail,** fault, offense. 80. **cravens,** renders cowardly.
83. **scriptures,** writings. It suggests the ordinary
meaning, which is played on in what follows; also, the
letters which she has from Leonatus have been as Holy
Writ to her. 86. **stomachers,** ornamental coverings
for the breast.

And thou, Posthumus, thou that didst set up
My disobedience 'gainst the king my father
And make me put into contempt the suits   92
Of princely fellows, shalt hereafter find
It is no act of common passage, but
A strain of rareness: and I grieve myself
To think, when thou shalt be disedged by her
That now thou tirest on, how thy memory
Will then be pang'd by me.   Prithee, dis-
    patch:
The lamb entreats the butcher: where's thy
    knife?
Thou art too slow to do thy master's bidding,
When I desire it too.
    Pis.   O gracious lady,   101
Since I received command to do this business
I have not slept one wink.
    Imo.   Do't, and to bed then.
    Pis. I'll wake mine eye-balls blind first.
    Imo.   Wherefore then
Didst undertake it? Why hast thou abused
So many miles with a pretence? this place?
Mine action and thine own? our horses'
    labour?
The time inviting thee? the perturb'd court,
For my being absent? whereunto I never
Purpose return. Why hast thou gone so far,
To be unbent when thou hast ta'en thy
    stand,   111
The elected deer before thee?
    Pis.   But to win time
To lose so bad employment; in the which
I have consider'd of a course.   Good lady,
Hear me with patience.
    Imo.   Talk thy tongue weary; speak:
I have heard I am a strumpet; and mine ear,
Therein false struck, can take no greater
    wound,
Nor tent to bottom that.   But speak.
    Pis.   Then, madam,
I thought you would not back again.
    Imo.   Most like;
Bringing me here to kill me.
    Pis.   Not so, neither: 120
But if I were as wise as honest, then
My purpose would prove well.   It cannot be
But that my master is abused:
Some villain, ay, and singular in his art,

Hath done you both this cursed injury.
    Imo. Some Roman courtezan.
    Pis.   No, on my life.
I'll give but notice you are dead and send
    him
Some bloody sign of it; for 'tis commanded
I should do so: you shall be miss'd at court,
And that will well confirm it.
    Imo.   Why, good fellow, 130
What shall I do the while? where bide? how
    live?
Or in my life what comfort, when I am
Dead to my husband?
    Pis.   If you'll back to the court—
    Imo. No court, no father; nor no more ado
†With that harsh, noble, simple nothing,
That Cloten, whose love-suit hath been to
    me
As fearful as a siege.
    Pis.   If not at court,
Then not in Britain must you bide.
    Imo.   Where then?
Hath Britain all the sun that shines? Day,
    night,
Are they not but in Britain? I' the world's
    volume   140
Our Britain seems as of it, but not in't;
In a great pool a swan's nest: prithee, think
There's livers out of Britain.
    Pis.   I am most glad
You think of other place. The ambassador,
Lucius the Roman, comes to Milford-Haven
To-morrow: now, if you could wear a mind
Dark as your fortune is, and but disguise
That which, to appear itself, must not yet be
But by self-danger, you should tread a course
†Pretty and full of view; yea, haply, near 150
The residence of Posthumus; so nigh at least
That though his actions were not visible, yet
Report should render him hourly to your ear
As truly as he moves.
    Imo.   O, for such means!
Though peril to my modesty, not death on 't,
I would adventure.
    Pis.   Well, then, here's the point:
You must forget to be a woman; change
Command into obedience: fear and nice-
    ness—

---

90. **set up**, incite, encourage. 93. **fellows**, equals in
rank. 94-95. **It is . . . rareness**, that my choice of you
is no act of ordinary occurrence but a rare and high-
pitched impulse (of the heart). 96. **disedged**, surfeited.
97. **tirest on**, tearest or devourest (as a bird of prey).
98. **pang'd**, pained. 104. **wake**, remain awake, watch.
111. **unbent**, with unbent bow. 112. **elected**, chosen.
118. **Nor . . . that**, nor probe that to the bottom.

135. **With . . . nothing**. This line has puzzled commentators, and there are many emendations; but there
seems no reason not to read it straight on and regard it
as a good example of Imogen's admirable use of epithets.
147. **Dark**, obscure, mean. 148. **That which**, i.e.,
the fact that she is a woman. 150. **Pretty**, fair, advantageous. **full of view**, promising. 158. **niceness**,
coyness, reserve.

The handmaids of all women, or, more truly,
Woman it pretty self—into a waggish cour-
age;   160
Ready in gibes, quick-answer'd, saucy and
As quarrelous as the weasel; nay, you must
Forget that rarest treasure of your cheek,
Exposing it—but, O, the harder heart!
Alack, no remedy!—to the greedy touch
Of common-kissing Titan, and forget
Your laboursome and dainty trims, wherein
You made great Juno angry.
    Imo.   Nay, be brief:
I see into thy end, and am almost
A man already.
    Pis. First, make yourself but like one. 170
Fore-thinking this, I have already fit—
'Tis in my cloak-bag—doublet, hat, hose, all
That answer to them: would you in their
        serving,
And with what imitation you can borrow
From youth of such a season, 'fore noble
        Lucius
Present yourself, desire his service, tell him
Wherein you're happy,—which you'll make
        him know,
If that his head have ear in music,—doubt-
less
With joy he will embrace you, for he's
        honourable
And doubling that, most holy. Your means
        abroad,   180
You have me, rich; and I will never fail
Beginning nor supplyment.
    Imo.   Thou art all the comfort
The gods will diet me with. Prithee, away:
There's more to be consider'd; but we'll even
All that good time will give us: this attempt
I am soldier to, and will abide it with
A prince's courage. Away, I prithee.
    Pis. Well, madam, we must take a short
        farewell,
Lest, being miss'd, I be suspected of
Your carriage from the court. My noble
        mistress,   190
Here is a box; I had it from the queen:
What's in't is precious; if you are sick at sea,

Or stomach-qualm'd at land, a dram of this
Will drive away distemper. To some shade,
And fit you to your manhood. May the gods
Direct you to the best!
    Imo. Amen: I thank thee.
                            [*Exeunt, severally.*

SCENE V. *A room in Cymbeline's palace.*

Enter CYMBELINE, QUEEN, CLOTEN, LUCIUS,
        Lords, *and* Attendants.

    Cym. Thus far; and so farewell.
    Luc.   Thanks, royal sir.
My emperor hath wrote, I must from hence;
And am right sorry that I must report ye
My master's enemy.
    Cym.   Our subjects, sir,
Will not endure his yoke; and for ourself
To show less sovereignty than they, must
        needs
Appear unkinglike.
    Luc.   So, sir: I desire of you
A conduct over-land to Milford-Haven.
Madam, all joy befal your grace!
    Queen.   And you!
    Cym. My lords, you are appointed for
        that office;   10
The due of honour in no point omit.
So farewell, noble Lucius.
    Luc.   Your hand, my lord.
    Clo. Receive it friendly; but from this
        time forth
I wear it as your enemy.
    Luc.   Sir, the event
Is yet to name the winner: fare you well.
    Cym. Leave not the worthy Lucius, good
        my lords,
Till he have cross'd the Severn. Happiness!
                    [*Exeunt Lucius and Lords.*
    Queen. He goes hence frowning: but it
        honours us
That we have given him cause.
    Clo.   'Tis all the better;
Your valiant Britons have their wishes in it.
    Cym. Lucius hath wrote already to the
        emperor   21
How it goes here. It fits us therefore ripely

160. it, its. waggish, roguish. 162. quarrelous,
quarrelsome. 164. harder, too hard. 166. common-
kissing, kissing everybody and everything. Titan, god
of the sun. 167. laboursome . . . trims, elaborate
and dainty apparel. 171. Fore-thinking, foreseeing,
anticipating. fit, ready. 173. in their serving, employing them. 175. such a season, i.e., of such an age
as you will represent. 177. happy, gifted, skillful. 180.
Your means abroad, as to your means while you are
abroad. 184. even, keep even with, profit by. 186.
soldier to, enlisted to, devoted to.

194. drive away distemper. The presentation and
subsequent employment of the potion reflects a naïve
attitude toward the curative powers of drugs characteristic of the Elizabethan age.
    Scene v.   8. conduct, safe-conduct, escort. 13.
Receive, etc. In this scene, as in Act III, Scene i,
Cloten speaks with better sense than in the earlier
scenes of the play. 22. fits, befits. ripely, speedily.

Our chariots and our horsemen be in readi-
  ness:
The powers that he already hath in Gallia
Will soon be drawn to head, from whence he
  moves
His war for Britain.
Queen.   'Tis not sleepy business;
But must be look'd to speedily and strongly.
Cym. Our expectation that it would be
  thus
Hath made us forward. But, my gentle
  queen,
Where is our daughter? She hath not ap-
  pear'd   30
Before the Roman, nor to us hath tender'd
The duty of the day: she looks us like
A thing more made of malice than of duty:
We have noted it. Call her before us; for
We have been too slight in sufferance.
                              [*Exit an Attendant.*
Queen.   Royal sir,
Since the exile of Posthumus, most retired
Hath her life been; the cure whereof, my
  lord,
'Tis time must do. Beseech your majesty,
Forbear sharp speeches to her: she's a lady
So tender of rebukes that words are strokes
And strokes death to her.

                  Re-enter Attendant.

Cym.   Where is she, sir? How
Can her contempt be answer'd?
Atten.   Please you, sir,
Her chambers are all lock'd; and there's no
  answer   43
That will be given to the loudest noise we
  make.
Queen. My lord, when last I went to visit
  her,
She pray'd me to excuse her keeping close,
Whereto constrain'd by her infirmity,
She should that duty leave unpaid to you,
Which daily she was bound to proffer: this
She wish'd me to make known; but our great
  court   50
Made me to blame in memory.
Cym.   Her doors lock'd?
Not seen of late? Grant, heavens, that which
  I fear
Prove false!   [*Exit.*

Queen.   Son, I say, follow the king.
Clo. That man of hers, Pisanio, her old
  servant,
I have not seen these two days.
Queen.   Go, look after. [*Exit Cloten.*
Pisanio, thou that stand'st so for Post-
  humus!
He hath a drug of mine; I pray his absence
Proceed by swallowing that, for he believes
It is a thing most precious. But for her,
Where is she gone? Haply, despair hath
  seized her,   60
Or, wing'd with fervour of her love, she's
  flown
To her desired Posthumus: gone she is
To death or to dishonour; and my end
Can make good use of either: she being down,
I have the placing of the British crown.

                  Re-enter CLOTEN.

How now, my son!
Clo.   'Tis certain she is fled.
Go in and cheer the king: he rages; none
Dare come about him.
Queen. [*Aside*] All the better: may
This night forestall him of the coming day!
                                          [*Exit.*
Clo. I love and hate her: for she's fair and
  royal,   70
And that she hath all courtly parts more ex-
  quisite
Than lady, ladies, woman; from every one
The best she hath, and she, of all com-
  pounded,
Outsells them all; I love her therefore: but
Disdaining me and throwing favours on
The low Posthumus slanders so her judge-
  ment
That what's else rare is choked; and in that
  point
I will conclude to hate her, nay, indeed,
To be revenged upon her. For when fools 79
Shall—

                  Enter PISANIO.

Who is here? What, are you packing,
  sirrah?
Come hither: ah, you precious pandar!
  Villain,

---

25. **drawn to head,** brought together, levied. 32.
looks us, seems to us. 35. **slight in sufferance,** careless in permitting it. 50. **great court,** important
courtly business.

58. **by,** from. 69. **forestall,** deprive. 71. **that,**
because. **parts,** endowments, graces. 74. **Outsells,**
outvalues, excels. 80. **packing,** running off, or possibly,
plotting.

Where is thy lady? In a word; or else　　82
Thou art straightway with the fiends.

Pis.　　　　　　　　　O, good my lord!

Clo. Where is thy lady? or, by Jupiter,—
I will not ask again. Close villain,
I'll have this secret from thy heart, or rip
Thy heart to find it. Is she with Posthumus?
From whose so many weights of baseness cannot
A dram of worth be drawn.

Pis.　　　　　　　　　Alas, my lord,
How can she be with him? When was she miss'd?　　90
He is in Rome.

Clo.　　　Where is she, sir? Come nearer;
No further halting: satisfy me home
What is become of her.

Pis. O, my all-worthy lord!

Clo.　　　　　　　　All-worthy villain!
Discover where thy mistress is at once,
At the next word: no more of 'worthy lord!'
Speak, or thy silence on the instant is
Thy condemnation and thy death.

Pis.　　　　　　　　　Then, sir,
This paper is the history of my knowledge　99
Touching her flight.　　*[Presenting a letter.*

Clo.　　　　　　Let's see 't. I will pursue her
Even to Augustus' throne.

Pis.　　　　　*[Aside]* Or this, or perish.
She's far enough; and what he learns by this
May prove his travel, not her danger.

Clo.　　　　　　　　　Hum!

Pis. *[Aside]* I'll write to my lord she's dead. O Imogen,
Safe mayst thou wander, safe return again!

Clo. Sirrah, is this letter true?

Pis. Sir, as I think.　　　　　　107

Clo. It is Posthumus' hand; I know 't.
Sirrah, if thou wouldst not be a villain, but
do me true service, undergo those employments
wherein I should have cause to use
thee with a serious industry, that is, what
villany soe'er I bid thee do, to perform it
directly and truly, I would think thee an
honest man: thou shouldst neither want my
means for thy relief nor my voice for thy
preferment.

Pis. Well, my good lord.　　　　117

Clo. Wilt thou serve me? for since patiently
and constantly thou hast stuck to the
bare fortune of that beggar Posthumus, thou
canst not, in the course of gratitude, but be a
diligent follower of mine: wilt thou serve me?

Pis. Sir, I will.　　　　　123

Clo. Give me thy hand; here's my purse.
Hast any of thy late master's garments in thy
possession?

Pis. I have, my lord, at my lodging, the
same suit he wore when he took leave of my
lady and mistress.

Clo. The first service thou dost me, fetch
that suit hither: let it be thy first service;
go.　　　　　131

Pis. I shall, my lord.　　　　*[Exit.*

Clo. Meet thee at Milford-Haven!—I forgot
to ask him one thing; I'll remember 't
anon:—even there, thou villain Posthumus,
will I kill thee. I would these garments were
come. She said upon a time—the bitterness
of it I now belch from my heart—that she
held the very garment of Posthumus in more
respect than my noble and natural person,
together with the adornment of my qualities.
With that suit upon my back, will I ravish
her: first kill him, and in her eyes; there shall
she see my valour, which will then be a torment
to her contempt. He on the ground,
my speech of insultment ended on his dead
body, and when my lust hath dined,—which,
as I say, to vex her I will execute in the clothes
that she so praised,—to the court I'll knock
her back, foot her home again. She hath despised
me rejoicingly, and I'll be merry in　150
my revenge.

Re-enter PISANIO *with the clothes.*

Be those the garments?

Pis. Ay, my noble lord.

Clo. How long is 't since she went to
Milford-Haven?

Pis. She can scarce be there yet.

Clo. Bring this apparel to my chamber;
that is the second thing that I have commanded
thee: the third is, that thou wilt be a
voluntary mute to my design. Be but
duteous, and true preferment shall tender
itself to thee. My revenge is now at Milford:
would I had wings to follow it! Come, and
be true.　　　　　*[Exit.*

Pis. Thou bid'st me to my loss: for true
to thee

---

82. **In a word**, answer in a word.　85. **Close**, secret.
88. **whose so many**, so many of whose.　92. **home**,
completely.　95. **Discover**, reveal.

145. **insultment**, contemptuous triumph (Onions).
149. **foot**, kick.

Were to prove false, which I will never be,
To him that is most true. To Milford go,
And find not her whom thou pursuest. Flow,
    flow,
You heavenly blessings, on her! This fool's
    speed
Be cross'd with slowness; labour be his meed!
                                    [*Exit.*

SCENE VI. *Wales. Before the cave of
                Belarius.*

Enter IMOGEN, *in boy's clothes.*

Imo. I see a man's life is a tedious one:
I have tired myself, and for two nights to-
    gether
Have made the ground my bed. I should be
    sick,
But that my resolution helps me. Milford,
When from the mountain-top Pisanio show'd
    thee,
Thou wast within a ken: O Jove! I think
Foundations fly the wretched; such, I
    mean,
Where they should be relieved. Two beggars
    told me
I could not miss my way: will poor folks
    lie,
That have afflictions on them, knowing 'tis 10
A punishment or trial? Yes; no wonder,
When rich ones scarce tell true. To lapse in
    fulness
Is sorer than to lie for need, and falsehood
Is worse in kings than beggars. My dear
    lord!
Thou art one o' the false ones. Now I think
    on thee,
My hunger's gone; but even before, I was
At point to sink for food. But what is this?
Here is a path to 't: 'tis some savage hold:
I were best not call; I dare not call: yet
    famine,
Ere clean it o'erthrow náture, makes it
    valiant.
Plenty and peace breeds cowards: hardness
    ever   21
Of hardiness is mother. Ho! who's here?
If any thing that's civil, speak; if savage,

Take or lend. Ho! No answer? Then I'll
    enter.
Best draw my sword; and if mine enemy
But fear the sword like me, he'll scarcely look
    on 't.
Such a foe, good heavens! [*Exit, to the cave.*

Enter BELARIUS, GUIDERIUS, *and*
            ARVIRAGUS.

Bel. You, Polydore, have proved best
    woodman and
Are master of the feast: Cadwal and I
Will play the cook and servant; 'tis our
    match:
The sweat of industry would dry and die, 31
But for the end it works to. Come; our
    stomachs
Will make what's homely savoury: weariness
Can snore upon the flint, when resty sloth
Finds the down pillow hard. Now peace be
    here,
Poor house, that keep'st thyself!
Gui.   I am throughly weary.
Arv. I am weak with toil, yet strong in
    appetite.
Gui. There is cold meat i' the cave; we'll
    browse on that,
Whilst what we have kill'd be cook'd.
Bel. [*Looking into the cave*] Stay; come
    not in.   40
But that it eats our victuals, I should think
Here were a fairy.
Gui.   What's the matter, sir?
Bel. By Jupiter, an angel! or, if not,
An earthly paragon! Behold divineness
No elder than a boy!

Re-enter IMOGEN.

Imo. Good masters, harm me not:
Before I enter'd here, I call'd; and thought
To have begg'd or bought what I have took:
    good troth,
I have stol'n nought, nor would not, though
    I had found
Gold strew'd i' the floor. Here's money for
    my meat: 50
I would have left it on the board so soon
As I had made my meal, and parted
With prayers for the provider.
Gui.   Money, youth?

Scene vi. 6. **within a ken**, within sight. 7. **Foundations**, quibbling use, denoting fixed places and charitable institutions (Schmidt). 13. **sorer**, worse, more wicked. 16. **even**, just. 18. **hold**, stronghold, fastness. 20. **clean**, altogether. 21. **hardness**, hardship. 22. **hardiness**, hardihood, bravery.

24. **Take or lend**, take my life or give me food. Dowden explains: "Take what I have before you lend me food." 28. **woodman**, huntsman. 30. **match**, agreement, bargain. 34. **resty**, sluggish, indolent.

Arv. All gold and silver rather turn to
dirt!
As 'tis no better reckon'd, but of those
Who worship dirty gods.

Imo.   I see you're angry:
Know, if you kill me for my fault, I should
Have died had I not made it.

Bel.   Whither bound?

Imo. To Milford-Haven.

Bel. What's your name?   60

Imo. Fidele, sir. I have a kinsman who
Is bound for Italy; he embark'd at Milford;
To whom being going, almost spent with
hunger,
I am fall'n in this offence.

Bel.   Prithee, fair youth,
Think us no churls, nor measure our good
minds
By this rude place we live in. Well en-
counter'd!
'Tis almost night: you shall have better cheer
Ere you depart; and thanks to stay and
eat it.
Boys, bid him welcome.

Gui.   Were you a woman, youth,
I should woo hard but be your groom. In
honesty,   70
I bid for you as I 'ld buy.

Arv.   I 'll make 't my comfort
He is a man; I 'll love him as my brother:
And such a welcome as I 'ld give to him
After long absence, such is yours: most wel-
come!
Be sprightly, for you fall 'mongst friends.

Imo.   'Mongst friends,
If brothers. [*Aside*] Would it had been so,
that they
Had been my father's sons! then had my
prize
Been less, and so more equal ballasting
To thee, Posthumus.

Bel.   He wrings at some distress.

Gui. Would I could free 't!

Arv.   Or I, whate'er it be,   80
What pain it cost, what danger. Gods!

Bel.   Hark, boys.
[*Whispering.*

Imo. Great men,
That had a court no bigger than this cave,
That did attend themselves and had the
virtue

Which their own conscience seal'd them—
laying by
That nothing-gift of differing multitudes—
Could not out-peer these twain. Pardon
me, gods!
I 'ld change my sex to be companion with
them,
Since Leonatus's false.

Bel.   It shall be so.
Boys, we'll go dress our hunt. Fair youth,
come in: 90
Discourse is heavy, fasting; when we have
supp'd,
We'll mannerly demand thee of thy story,
So far as thou wilt speak it.

Gui.   Pray, draw near.

Arv. The night to the owl and morn to the
lark less welcome.

Imo. Thanks, sir.

Arv. I pray, draw near.   [*Exeunt.*

SCENE VII. *Rome. A public place.*

Enter two Senators *and* Tribunes.

First Sen. This is the tenour of the em-
peror's writ:
That since the common men are now in
action
'Gainst the Pannonians and Dalmatians,
And that the legions now in Gallia are
Full weak to undertake our wars against
The fall'n-off Britons, that we do incite
The gentry to this business. He creates
Lucius proconsul: and to you the tribunes,
For this immediate levy, he commends   9
His absolute commission. Long live Cæsar!

First Tri. Is Lucius general of the forces?

Sec. Sen.   Ay.

First Tri. Remaining now in Gallia?

First Sen.   With those legions
Which I have spoke of, whereunto your levy
Must be supplyant: the words of your com-
mission
Will tie you to the numbers and the time
Of their dispatch.

First Tri.   We will discharge our duty.
[*Exeunt.*

64. **in**, into. 71. **I bid . . . buy**, I bid for you as one
who would have you. 77. **prize**, value, i.e., she would
not have been heir to the throne. 79. **wrings**, writhes.

85-86. **laying . . . multitudes**, disregarding the
valueless gift of the fickle mob (as spectators). 87.
out-peer, excel. 90. **hunt**, game taken in the hunt.
Scene vii. 6. **fall'n-off**, revolted. 9. **commends**,
delivers, presents. F has *commands*, which may be
retained with the meaning, "commands to be given."
14. **supplyant**, reinforcing, auxiliary.

ACT IV.

SCENE I. *Wales: near the cave of Belarius.*

Enter CLOTEN.

Clo. I am near to the place where they should meet, if Pisanio have mapped it truly. How fit his garments serve me! Why should his mistress, who was made by him that made the tailor, not be fit too? the rather—saving reverence of the word—for 'tis said a woman's fitness comes by fits. Therein I must play the workman. I dare speak it to myself—for it is not vain-glory for a man and his glass to confer in his own chamber—I mean, the lines of my body are as well drawn as his; no less young, more strong, not beneath him in fortunes, beyond him in the advantage of the time, above him in birth, alike conversant in general services, and more remarkable in single oppositions: 15 yet this imperceiverant thing loves him in my despite. What mortality is! Posthumus, thy head, which now is growing upon thy shoulders, shall within this hour be off; thy mistress enforced; thy garments cut to pieces before thy face: and all this done, spurn her home to her father; who may haply be a little angry for my so rough usage; but my mother, having power of his testiness, shall turn all into my commendations. My horse is tied up safe: out, sword, and to a sore purpose! Fortune, put them into my hand! This is the very description of their meeting-place; and the fellow dares not deceive me.   [*Exit.*

SCENE II. *Before the cave of Belarius.*

Enter, from the cave, BELARIUS, GUIDERIUS, ARVIRAGUS, *and* IMOGEN.

Bel. [*To Imogen*] You are not well: remain here in the cave;
We'll come to you after hunting.

Arv.   [*To Imogen*] Brother, stay here:
Are we not brothers?

Imo.   So man and man should be;

But clay and clay differs in dignity,
Whose dust is both alike. I am very sick.

Gui. Go you to hunting; I'll abide with him.

Imo. So sick I am not, yet I am not well;
But not so citizen a wanton as
To seem to die ere sick: so please you, leave me;
Stick to your journal course: the breach of custom   10
Is breach of all. I am ill, but your being by me
Cannot amend me; society is no comfort
To one not sociable: I am not very sick,
Since I can reason of it. Pray you, trust me here:
I'll rob none but myself; and let me die,
Stealing so poorly.

Gui.   I love thee; I have spoke it:
How much the quantity, the weight as much,
As I do love my father.

Bel.   What! how! how!

Arv. If it be sin to say so, sir, I yoke me
In my good brother's fault: I know not why
I love this youth; and I have heard you say,
Love's reason 's without reason: the bier at door,   22
And a demand who is 't shall die, I'ld say
'My father, not this youth.'

Bel.   [*Aside*] O noble strain!
O worthiness of nature! breed of greatness!
Cowards father cowards and base things sire base:
Nature hath meal and bran, comtempt and grace.
I'm not their father; yet who this should be,
Doth miracle itself, loved before me.
'Tis the ninth hour o' the morn.

Arv.   Brother, farewell.   30

Imo. I wish ye sport.

Arv.   You health. So please you, sir.

Imo. [*Aside*] These are kind creatures.
Gods, what lies I have heard!
Our courtiers say all's savage but at court:
Experience, O, thou disprovest report!
The imperious seas breed monsters, for the dish
Poor tributary rivers as sweet fish.
I am sick still; heart-sick. Pisanio,
I'll now taste of thy drug. [*Swallows some.*

Gui.   I could not stir him:
He said he was gentle, but unfortunate;
Dishonestly afflicted, but yet honest.   40
  Arv. Thus did he answer me: yet said, hereafter
I might know more.
  Bel.   To the field, to the field!
We'll leave you for this time: go in and rest.
  Arv.   We'll not be long away.
  Bel.   Pray, be not sick,
For you must be our housewife.
  Imo.   Well or ill,
I am bound to you.
  Bel.   And shalt be ever.
          [*Exit Imogen, to the cave.*
This youth, howe'er distress'd, appears he hath had
Good ancestors.
  Arv.   How angel-like he sings!
  Gui. But his neat cookery! he cut our roots
In characters,
And sauced our broths, as Juno had been sick
And he her dieter.
  Arv.   Nobly he yokes   51
A smiling with a sigh, as if the sigh
Was that it was, for not being such a smile;
The smile mocking the sigh, that it would fly
From so divine a temple, to commix
With winds that sailors rail at.
  Gui.   I do note
That grief and patience, rooted in him both,
Mingle their spurs together.
  Arv.   Grow, patience!
And let the stinking elder, grief, untwine
His perishing root with the increasing vine! 60
  Bel. It is great morning. Come, away!—
Who's there?

          Enter CLOTEN.

  Clo. I cannot find those runagates; that villain
Hath mock'd me. I am faint.
  Bel.   'Those runagates!'
Means he not us? I partly know him: 'tis
Cloten, the son o' the queen. I fear some ambush.
I saw him not these many years, and yet

I know 'tis he. We are held as outlaws: hence!
  Gui. He is but one: you and my brother search
What companies are near: pray you, away;
Let me alone with him.
              [*Exeunt Belarius and Arviragus.*
  Clo.   Soft! What are you   70
That fly me thus? some villain mountaineers?
I have heard of such. What slave art thou?
  Gui.   A thing
More slavish did I ne'er than answering
A slave without a knock.
  Clo.   Thou art a robber,
A law-breaker, a villain: yield thee, thief.
  Gui. To who? to thee? What art thou? Have not I
An arm as big as thine? a heart as big?
Thy words, I grant, are bigger, for I wear not
My dagger in my mouth. Say what thou art,
Why I should yield to thee?
  Clo.   Thou villain base,   80
Know'st me not by my clothes?
  Gui.   No, nor thy tailor, rascal,
Who is thy grandfather: he made those clothes,
Which, as it seems, make thee.
  Clo.   Thou precious varlet,
My tailor made them not.
  Gui.   Hence, then, and thank
The man that gave them thee. Thou art some fool;
I am loath to beat thee.
  Clo.   Thou injurious thief,
Hear but my name, and tremble.
  Gui.   What's thy name?
  Clo. Cloten, thou villain.
  Gui. Cloten, thou double villain, be thy name,
I cannot tremble at it: were it Toad, or Adder, Spider,   90
'Twould move me sooner.
  Clo.   To thy further fear,
Nay, to thy mere confusion, thou shalt know
I am son to the queen.
  Gui.   I am sorry for't; not seeming
So worthy as thy birth.
  Clo.   Art not afeard?
  Gui. Those that I reverence those I fear, the wise:
At fools I laugh, not fear them.

---

39. **gentle**, of gentle blood. 49. **characters**, letters.
53. **that**, what. 58. **spurs**, roots of a tree (used of
projecting roots). 59. **elder**, elder-tree. **untwine**,
cease to twine. 61. **great morning**, broad day.

81. **Know'st . . . clothes.** Cloten is dressed as one
from the court. 86. **injurious**, malicious, insulting.
92. **mere**, utter, absolute.

Clo.   Die the death:
When I have slain thee with my proper hand,
I'll follow those that even now fled hence,
And on the gates of Lud's-town set your
    heads:
Yield, rustic mountaineer.   100

[*Exeunt, fighting.*

Re-enter BELARIUS *and* ARVIRAGUS.

Bel. No companies abroad?
Arv. None in the world: you did mistake
    him, sure.
Bel. I cannot tell: long is it since I saw
    him,
But time hath nothing blurr'd those lines of
    favour
Which then he wore; the snatches in his
    voice,
And burst of speaking, were as his: I am
    absolute
'Twas very Cloten.
Arv.   In this place we left them:
I wish my brother make good time with him,
You say he is so fell.
Bel.   Being scarce made up,
I mean, to man, he had not apprehension 110
Of roaring terrors; for the effect of judgement
Is oft the cause of fear. But, see, thy
    brother.

Re-enter GUIDERIUS, *with* CLOTEN's *head.*

Gui. This Cloten was a fool, an empty
    purse;
There was no money in 't: not Hercules
Could have knock'd out his brains, for he had
    none:
Yet I not doing this, the fool had borne
My head as I do his.
Bel.   What hast thou done?
Gui. I am perfect what: cut off one
    Cloten's head,
Son to the queen, after his own report;
Who call'd me traitor, mountaineer, and
    swore   120
With his own single hand he'ld take us in,
Displace our heads where—thank the gods!
    —they grow,
And set them on Lud's-town.

Bel.   We are all undone.
Gui. Why, worthy father, what have we
    to lose,
But that he swore to take, our lives? The
    law
Protects not us: then why should we be
    tender
To let an arrogant piece of flesh threat us,
Play judge and executioner all himself,
For we do fear the law? What company
Discover you abroad?
Bel.   No single soul   130
Can we set eye on; but in all safe reason
He must have some attendants. Though his
    humour
Was nothing but mutation, ay, and that
From one bad thing to worse; not frenzy, not
Absolute madness could so far have raved
To bring him here alone; although perhaps
It may be heard at court that such as we
Cave here, hunt here, are outlaws, and in
    time
May make some stronger head; the which he
    hearing—
As it is like him—might break out, and swear
He 'ld fetch us in; yet is 't not probable   141
To come alone, either he so undertaking,
Or they so suffering: then on good ground we
    fear,
If we do fear this body hath a tail
More perilous than the head.
Arv.   Let ordinance
Come as the gods foresay it: howsoe'er,
My brother hath done well.
Bel.   I had no mind
To hunt this day: the boy Fidele's sickness
Did make my way long forth.
Gui.   With his own sword,
Which he did wave against my throat, I
    have ta'en   150
His head from him: I'll throw 't into the
    creek
Behind our rock; and let it to the sea,
And tell the fishes he's the queen's son,
    Cloten:
That's all I reck.   [*Exit.*
Bel.   I fear 'twill be revenged:
Would, Polydore, thou hadst not done 't!
    though valour

Becomes thee well enough.

Arv.   Would I had done 't,
So the revenge alone pursued me! Polydore,
I love thee brotherly, but envy much
Thou hast robb'd me of this deed: I would
    revenges,
That possible strength might meet, would
    seek us through   160
And put us to our answer.

Bel.   Well, 'tis done:
We'll hunt no more to-day, nor seek for
    danger
Where there's no profit. I prithee, to our
    rock;
You and Fidele play the cooks: I'll stay
Till hasty Polydore return, and bring him
To dinner presently.

Arv.   Poor sick Fidele!
I'll willingly to him: to gain his colour
I'ld let a parish of such Clotens blood,
And praise myself for charity.   [*Exit.*

Bel.   O thou goddess,
Thou divine Nature, how thyself thou bla-
    zon'st   170
In these two princely boys! They are as
    gentle
As zephyrs blowing below the violet,
Not wagging his sweet head; and yet as
    rough,
Their royal blood enchafed, as the rudest
    wind,
That by the top doth take the mountain pine,
And make him stoop to the vale.   'Tis
    wonder
That an invisible instinct should frame them
To royalty unlearn'd, honour untaught,
Civility not seen from other, valour   179
That wildly grows in them, but yields a crop
As if it had been sow'd.   Yet still it's strange
What Cloten's being here to us portends,
Or what his death will bring us.

Re-enter GUIDERIUS.

Gui.   Where's my brother?
I have sent Cloten's clotpoll down the
    stream,
In embassy to his mother: his body's hostage
For his return.   [*Solemn music.*

Bel.   My ingenious instrument!

Hark, Polydore, it sounds! But what oc-
    casion
Hath Cadwal now to give it motion? Hark!

Gui. Is he at home?

Bel.   He went hence even now.

Gui. What does he mean? since death of
    my dear'st mother   190
It did not speak before. All solemn things
Should answer solemn accidents.   The
    matter?
Triumphs for nothing and lamenting toys
Is jollity for apes and grief for boys.
Is Cadwal mad?

Bel.   Look, here he comes,
And brings the dire occasion in his arms
Of what we blame him for.

Re-enter ARVIRAGUS, *with* IMOGEN, *as dead,
    bearing her in his arms.*

Arv.   The bird is dead
That we have made so much on. I had
    rather
Have skipp'd from sixteen years of age to
    sixty,
To have turn'd my leaping-time into a
    crutch,   200
Than have seen this.

Gui.   O sweetest, fairest lily!
My brother wears thee not the one half so
    well
As when thou grew'st thyself.

Bel.   O melancholy!
Who ever yet could sound thy bottom? find
The ooze, to show what coast thy sluggish
    crare
Might easiliest harbour in? Thou blessed
    thing!
Jove knows what man thou mightst have
    made; but I,
Thou diedst, a most rare boy, of melancholy.
How found you him?

Arv.   Stark, as you see:
Thus smiling, as some fly had tickled slum-
    ber,   210
Not as death's dart, being laugh'd at; his
    right cheek
Reposing on a cushion.

Gui.   Where?

Arv.   O' the floor;
His arms thus leagued: I thought he slept,
    and put

160. That . . . meet, that strength such as ours
might resist. seek us through, call us to account.
167. gain his colour, restore him to health. 168. let
. . . blood, let a parish full of such Clotens suffer death.
170. blazon'st, proclaim'st. 184. clotpoll, head.

193. toys, trifles. 198. on, of. 205. crare, skiff,
small boat; F: *care*, which may be retained as meaning
"a vessel in search of a harbor."

My clouted brogues from off my feet, whose
　rudeness
Answer'd my steps too loud.
　　Gui.　　　　　　　　　　Why, he but sleeps:
If he be gone, he'll make his grave a bed;
With female fairies will his tomb be haunted,
And worms will not come to thee.
　　Arv.　　　　　　　　　With fairest flowers
Whilst summer lasts and I live here, Fidele,
I'll sweeten thy sad grave: thou shalt not
　lack　　　　　　　　　　　　　　　　220
The flower that's like thy face, pale primrose,
　nor
The azured harebell, like thy veins, no,
　nor
The leaf of eglantine, whom not to slander,
Out-sweeten'd not thy breath: the ruddock
　would,
With charitable bill,—O bill, sore-shaming
Those rich-left heirs that let their fathers lie
Without a monument!—bring thee all this;
Yea, and furr'd moss besides, when flowers
　are none,
To winter-ground thy corse.
　　Gui.　　　　　　　　　Prithee, have done;
And do not play in wench-like words with
　that　　　　　　　　　　　　　　　　230
Which is so serious. Let us bury him,
And not protract with admiration what
Is now due debt. To the grave!
　　Arv.　　　　　　Say, where shall's lay him?
　　Gui. By good Euriphile, our mother.
　　Arv.　　　　　　　　　　Be't so:
And let us, Polydore, though now our voices
Have got the mannish crack, sing him to the
　ground,
As once our mother; use like note and words,
Save that Euriphile must be Fidele.
　　Gui. Cadwal,
I cannot sing: I'll weep, and word it with
　thee;　　　　　　　　　　　　　　　240
For notes of sorrow out of tune are worse
Than priests and fanes that lie.
　　Arv.　　　　　　　　We'll speak it, then.
　　Bel. Great griefs, I see, medicine the less;
　for Cloten
Is quite forgot. He was a queen's son, boys;
And though he came our enemy, remember
He was paid for that: though mean and
　mighty, rotting

Together, have one dust, yet reverence,
That angel of the world, doth make distinc-
　tion
Of place 'tween high and low. Our foe was
　princely;
And though you took his life, as being our
　foe,　　　　　　　　　　　　　　　250
Yet bury him as a prince.
　　Gui.　　　　　　Pray you, fetch him hither.
Thersites' body is as good as Ajax',
When neither are alive.
　　Arv.　　　　　　　　If you'll go fetch him,
We'll say our song the whilst. Brother, be-
　gin.　　　　　　　　　　　　[*Exit Belarius.*
　　Gui. Nay, Cadwal, we must lay his head
　to the east;
My father hath a reason for't.
　　Arv.　　　　　　　　　'Tis true.
　　Gui. Come on then, and remove him.
　　Arv.　　　　　　　　　So. Begin.

　　　　　　　　　SONG.

Gui. Fear no more the heat o' the sun,
　　Nor the furious winter's rages;
　Thou thy worldly task hast done,　260
　　Home art gone, and ta'en thy wages:
　Golden lads and girls all must,
　　As chimney-sweepers, come to dust.

Arv. Fear no more the frown o' the great;
　　Thou art past the tyrant's stroke;
　Care no more to clothe and eat;
　　To thee the reed is as the oak:
　The sceptre, learning, physic, must
　All follow this, and come to dust.

Gui. Fear no more the lightning-flash,　270
Arv.　Nor the all-dreaded thunder-stone;
Gui. Fear not slander, censure rash;
Arv.　Thou hast finish'd joy and moan:
Both. All lovers young, all lovers must
　　Consign to thee, and come to dust.

Gui. No exorciser harm thee!
Arv. Nor no witchcraft charm thee!
Gui. Ghost unlaid forbear thee!
Arv. Nothing ill come near thee!
Both. Quiet consummation have;　　280
　　And renowned be thy grave!

---

214. **clouted brogues**, heavy shoes studded with
nails. 224. **ruddock**, robin redbreast. 229. **winter-
ground**, cover so as to protect from frost. 230. **wench-
like**, womanish. 232. **admiration**, wonder (suggestive
of *veneration*). 242. **fanes**, temples.

252. **Thersites' . . . Ajax'.** Thersites was the base
scoffer in the *Iliad*; Ajax, a Greek hero. 271. **thunder-
stone**, thunderbolt (the supposed solid body accompanying a stroke of lightning). 276. **exorciser**, conjurer.
280. **consummation**, end, death.

Re-enter Belarius, *with the body of* Cloten.

Gui. We have done our obsequies: come,
   lay him down.

Bel. Here's a few flowers; but 'bout mid-
   night, more:
The herbs that have on them cold dew o' the
   night
Are strewings fitt'st for graves. Upon their
   faces.
You were as flowers, now wither'd: even so
These herblets shall, which we upon you
   strew.
Come on, away: apart upon our knees.
The ground that gave them first has them
   again:
Their pleasures here are past, so is their
   pain.   290
       [*Exeunt Belarius, Guiderius, and*
                   Arviragus.

Imo. [*Awaking*] Yes, sir, to Milford-
   Haven; which is the way?—
I thank you.—By yond bush?—Pray, how
   far thither?
'Ods pittikins! can it be six mile yet?—
I have gone all night. 'Faith, I'll lie down
   and sleep.
But, soft! no bedfellow!—O gods and god-
   desses!   [*Seeing the body of Cloten.*
These flowers are like the pleasures of the
   world;
This bloody man, the care on't. I hope I
   dream;
For so I thought I was a cave-keeper,
And cook to honest creatures: but 'tis not so;
'Twas but a bolt of nothing, shot at nothing,
Which the brain makes of fumes: our very
   eyes   301
Are sometimes like our judgements, blind.
   Good faith,
I tremble still with fear: but if there be
Yet left in heaven as small a drop of pity
As a wren's eye, fear'd gods, a part of it!
The dream's here still: even when I wake,
   it is
Without me, as within me; not imagined,
   felt.
A headless man! The garments of Pos-
   thumus!
I know the shape of 's leg: this is his hand;

His foot Mercurial; his Martial thigh;   310
The brawns of Hercules: but his Jovial face—
Murder in heaven?—How!—'Tis gone. Pis-
   anio,
All curses madded Hecuba gave the Greeks,
And mine to boot, be darted on thee! Thou,
Conspired with that irregulous devil, Cloten,
Hast here cut off my lord. To write and read
Be henceforth treacherous! Damn'd Pisanio
Hath with his forged letters,—damn'd
   Pisanio—
From this most bravest vessel of the world
Struck the main-top! O Posthumus! alas, 320
Where is thy head? where's that? Ay me!
   where's that?
Pisanio might have kill'd thee at the heart,
And left this head on. How should this be?
   Pisanio?
'Tis he and Cloten: malice and lucre in them
Have laid this woe here. O, 'tis pregnant,
   pregnant!
The drug he gave me, which he said was
   precious
And cordial to me, have I not found it
Murderous to the senses? That confirms it
   home:
This is Pisanio's deed, and Cloten's: O!
Give colour to my pale cheek with thy blood,
That we the horrider may seem to those   331
Which chance to find us: O, my lord, my
   lord!   [*Falls on the body.*

Enter Lucius, *a* Captain *and other* Officers,
        and a Soothsayer.

Cap. To them the legions garrison'd in
   Gallia,
After your will, have cross'd the sea, attending
You here at Milford-Haven with your ships:
They are in readiness.
Luc.   But what from Rome?
Cap. The senate hath stirr'd up the con-
   finers
And gentlemen of Italy, most willing spirits,
That promise noble service: and they come
Under the conduct of bold Iachimo,   340
Syenna's brother.
Luc.   When expect you them?
Cap. With the next benefit o' the wind.

---

287. **herblets**, small herbs, flowers. 293. **'Ods pittikins**, God's pity (diminutive oath). 298. **cave-keeper**,
one who dwells in a cave. 301. **fumes**, vapors engendered of humors which, according to current theory, rose
up into the brain and, by affecting imagination in the
forechamber of the brain, caused dreams.

310. **Mercurial**, nimble and swift like the foot of
Mercury. **Martial**, powerful for war like that of Mars.
311. **brawns**, muscles; here, arms. **Jovial**, Jove-like.
313. **madded**, maddened. **Hecuba**, wife of Priam,
king of Troy. 315. **irregulous**, lawless. 325. **pregnant**, probable in the highest degree. 333. **To**, in
addition to. 334. **After**, according to. 337. **confiners**,
borderers. 341. **Syenna's**, of the ruler of Sienna.

Luc.   This forwardness
Makes our hopes fair. Command our pres-
          ent numbers
Be muster'd; bid the captains look to 't.
          Now, sir,
What have you dream'd of late of this war's
          purpose?
    Sooth. Last night the very gods show'd
          me a vision—
I fast and pray'd for their intelligence—thus:
I saw Jove's bird, the Roman eagle, wing'd
From the spongy south to this part of the
          west,
There vanish'd in the sunbeams: which por-
          tends—   350
Unless my sins abuse my divination—
Success to the Roman host.
    Luc.   Dream often so,
And never false. Soft, ho! what trunk is here
Without his top? The ruin speaks that
          sometime
It was a worthy building. How! a page!
Or dead, or sleeping on him? But dead
          rather;
For nature doth abhor to make his bed
With the defunct, or sleep upon the dead.
Let 's see the boy's face.
    Cap.   He's alive, my lord.
    Luc. He'll then instruct us of this body.
          Young one,   360
Inform us of thy fortunes, for it seems
They crave to be demanded. Who is this
Thou makest thy bloody pillow? Or who was
          he
That, otherwise than noble nature did,
Hath alter'd that good picture? What's thy
          interest
In this sad wreck? How came it? Who is it?
What art thou?
    Imo.   I am nothing: or if not,
Nothing to be were better. This was my
          master,
A very valiant Briton and a good,
That here by mountaineers lies slain.
          Alas!   370
There is no more such masters: I may wander
From east to occident, cry out for service,
Try many, all good, serve truly, never
Find such another master.
    Luc.   'Lack, good youth!
Thou movest no less with thy complaining
          than

Thy master in bleeding: say his name, good
          friend.
    Imo. Richard du Champ. [*Aside*] If I do
          lie and do
No harm by it, though the gods hear, I hope
They'll pardon it.—Say you, sir?
    Luc.   Thy name?
    Imo.   Fidele, sir.
    Luc. Thou dost approve thyself the very
          same: 380
Thy name well fits thy faith, thy faith thy
          name.
Wilt take thy chance with me? I will not say
Thou shalt be so well master'd, but, be sure,
No less beloved. The Roman emperor's let-
          ters,
Sent by a consul to me, should not sooner
Than thine own worth prefer thee: go with
          me.
    Imo. I'll follow, sir. But first, an 't please
          the gods,
I'll hide my master from the flies, as deep
As these poor pickaxes can dig; and when
With wild wood-leaves and weeds I ha'
          strew'd his grave,   390
And on it said a century of prayers,
Such as I can, twice o'er, I'll weep and sigh;
And leaving so his service, follow you,
So please you entertain me.
    Luc.   Ay, good youth;
And rather father thee than master thee.
My friends,
The boy hath taught us manly duties: let us
Find out the prettiest daisied plot we can,
And make him with our pikes and partisans
A grave: come, arm him. Boy, he is pre-
          ferr'd   400
By thee to us, and he shall be interr'd
As soldiers can. Be cheerful; wipe thine
          eyes:
Some falls are means the happier to arise.
                                        [*Exeunt.*

SCENE III. *A room in Cymbeline's palace.*

Enter CYMBELINE, Lords, PISANIO, *and*
          Attendants.

    Cym. Again; and bring me word how 'tis
          with her.   [*Exit an Attendant.*

---

386. **prefer**, recommend. 391. **century**, hundred.
394. **entertain**, take into service. 399. **partisans**,
long-handled weapons with pointed and sharp-edged
heads; halberds. 400. **arm**, take up into the arms.

A fever with the absence of her son,
A madness, of which her life's in danger. Heavens,
How deeply you at once do touch me! Imogen,
The great part of my comfort, gone; my queen
Upon a desperate bed, and in a time
When fearful wars point at me; her son gone,
So needful for this present: it strikes me, past
The hope of comfort. But for thee, fellow,
Who needs must know of her departure and
Dost seem so ignorant, we'll enforce it from thee   11
By a sharp torture.

Pis.   Sir, my life is yours;
I humbly set it at your will; but, for my mistress,
I nothing know where she remains, why gone,
Nor when she purposes return. Beseech your highness,
Hold me your loyal servant.

First Lord.   Good my liege,
The day that she was missing he was here:
I dare be bound he's true and shall perform
All parts of his subjection loyally. For Cloten,
There wants no diligence in seeking him,   20
And will, no doubt, be found.

Cym.   The time is troublesome.
[*To Pisanio*] We'll slip you for a season; but our jealousy
Does yet depend.

First Lord. So please your majesty,
The Roman legions, all from Gallia drawn,
Are landed on your coast, with a supply
Of Roman gentlemen, by the senate sent.

Cym. Now for the counsel of my son and queen!
I am amazed with matter.

First Lord.   Good my liege,
Your preparation can affront no less
Than what you hear of: come more, for more you're ready: 30
The want is but to put those powers in motion
That long to move.

Cym.   I thank you. Let's withdraw;
And meet the time as it seeks us. We fear not

What can from Italy annoy us; but
We grieve at chances here.   Away!
                    [*Exeunt all but Pisanio.*

Pis. I heard no letter from my master since
I wrote him Imogen was slain: 'tis strange:
Nor hear I from my mistress, who did promise
To yield me often tidings; neither know I
What is betid to Cloten; but remain   40
Perplex'd in all. The heavens still must work.
Wherein I am false I am honest; not true, to be true.
These present wars shall find I love my country,
Even to the note o' the king, or I'll fall in them.
All other doubts, by time let them be clear'd:
Fortune brings in some boats that are not steer'd.   [*Exit.*

SCENE IV.   *Wales: before the cave of Belarius.*

Enter BELARIUS, GUIDERIUS, *and* ARVIRAGUS.

Gui. The noise is round about us.

Bel.   Let us from it.

Arv. What pleasure, sir, find we in life, to lock it
From action and adventure?

Gui.   Nay, what hope
Have we in hiding us? This way, the Romans
Must or for Britons slay us, or receive us
For barbarous and unnatural revolts
During their use, and slay us after.

Bel.   Sons,
We'll higher to the mountains; there secure us.
To the king's party there's no going: newness
Of Cloten's death—we being not known, not muster'd   10
Among the bands—may drive us to a render
Where we have lived, and so extort from 's that
Which we have done, whose answer would be death

Drawn on with torture.

Gui.   This is, sir, a doubt
In such a time nothing becoming you,
Nor satisfying us.

Arv.   It is not likely
That when they hear the Roman horses
    neigh,
Behold their quarter'd fires, have both their
    eyes
And ears so cloy'd importantly as now,
That they will waste their time upon our
    note,   20
To know from whence we are.

Bel.   O, I am known
Of many in the army: many years,
Though Cloten then but young, you see, not
    wore him
From my remembrance. And, besides, the
    king
Hath not deserved my service nor your
    loves;
Who find in my exile the want of breeding,
The certainty of this hard life; aye hopeless
To have the courtesy your cradle promised,
But to be still hot summer's tanlings and
The shrinking slaves of winter.

Gui.   Than be so   30
Better to cease to be. Pray, sir, to the
    army:
I and my brother are not known; yourself
So out of thought, and thereto so o'ergrown,
Cannot be question'd.

Arv.   By this sun that shines,
I'll thither: what thing is it that I never
Did see man die! scarce ever look'd on blood,
But that of coward hares, hot goats, and
    venison!
Never bestrid a horse, save one that had
A rider like myself, who ne'er wore rowel
Nor iron on his heel! I am ashamed   40
To look upon the holy sun, to have
The benefit of his blest beams, remaining
So long a poor unknown.

Gui.   By heavens, I'll go:
If you will bless me, sir, and give me leave,
I'll take the better care, but if you will not,
The hazard therefore due fall on me by
The hands of Romans!

Arv.   So say I: amen.

Bel. No reason I, since of your lives you
    set
So slight a valuation, should reserve
My crack'd one to more care. Have with
    you, boys!   50
If in your country wars you chance to die,
That is my bed too, lads, and there I'll lie:
Lead, lead. [*Aside*] The time seems long;
    their blood thinks scorn,
Till it fly out and show them princes born.
                           [*Exeunt.*

ACT V.

Scene I. *Britain. The Roman camp.*

Enter Posthumus, *with a bloody
        handkerchief.*

Post. Yea, bloody cloth, I'll keep thee,
    for I wish'd
Thou shouldst be colour'd thus. You
    married ones,
If each of you should take this course, how
    many
Must murder wives much better than them-
    selves
For wrying but a little! O Pisanio!
Every good servant does not all commands:
No bond but to do just ones. Gods! if you
Should have ta'en vengeance on my faults, I
    never
Had lived to put on this: so had you saved
The noble Imogen to repent, and struck   10
Me, wretch more worth your vengeance.
    But, alack,
You snatch some hence for little faults;
    that's love,
To have them fall no more: you some permit
†To second ills with ills, each elder worse,
And make them dread it, to the doers'
    thrift.
But Imogen is your own: do your best wills,
And make me blest to obey! I am brought
    hither
Among the Italian gentry, and to fight
Against my lady's kingdom: 'tis enough
That, Britain, I have kill'd thy mistress;
    peace!   20

18. **quarter'd fires,** regularly disposed, or simply camp fires. 20. **our note,** noting us. 26-28. **Who . . . promised,** you who find in exile want of breeding and the certain results of this hard life; yes, are even hopeless of ever finding the refinement promised you by your high birth. 29. **tanlings,** those tanned by the sun. 33. **o'ergrown,** i.e., with hair and beard. 34-35. **By this . . . thither.** This is the theme of the inevitable outcropping of princely blood.

Act V. Scene i. 5. **wrying,** swerving from the right course. 9. **put on,** incite, encourage. 12-13. **that's . . . more,** that is an act of kindness, since it makes them sin no more. 14. **elder,** thing of later date. 15. **dread . . . thrift.** Possibly this means that the guilty, by knowing of the further progress of evil, repent before committing more crimes.

I'll give no wound to thee. Therefore, good
    heavens,
Hear patiently my purpose: I'll disrobe me
Of these Italian weeds and suit myself
As does a Briton peasant: so I'll fight
Against the part I come with; so I'll die
For thee, O Imogen, even for whom my life
Is every breath a death; and thus, unknown,
Pitied nor hated, to the face of peril
Myself I'll dedicate. Let me make men
    know
More valour in me than my habits show. 30
Gods, put the strength o' the Leonati in me!
To shame the guise o' the world, I will begin
The fashion, less without and more within.
                         [Exit.

Scene II. *Field of battle between the British and Roman camps.*

Enter, from one side, Lucius, Iachimo, *and the* Roman Army: *from the other side, the* British Army; Leonatus Posthumus *following, like a poor soldier. They march over and go out. Then enter again, in skirmish,* Iachimo *and* Posthumus: *he vanquisheth and disarmeth* Iachimo, *and then leaves him.*

Iach. The heaviness and guilt within my
    bosom
Takes off my manhood: I have belied a lady,
The princess of this country, and the air
    on 't
Revengingly enfeebles me; or could this carl,
A very drudge of nature's, have subdued
    me
In my profession? Knighthoods and hon-
    ours, borne
As I wear mine, are titles but of scorn.
If that thy gentry, Britain, go before
This lout as he exceeds our lords, the odds
Is that we scarce are men and you are gods. 10
                         [Exit.

The battle continues; the Britons *fly;* Cymbeline *is taken: then enter, to his rescue,* Belarius, Guiderius, *and* Arviragus.

Bel. Stand, stand! We have the ad-
    vantage of the ground;
The lane is guarded: nothing routs us but

The villany of our fears.
Gui. ⎱
Arv. ⎰   Stand, stand, and fight!

Re-enter Posthumus, *and seconds the* Britons: *they rescue* Cymbeline, *and exeunt. Then re-enter* Lucius, *and* Iachimo, *with* Imogen.

Luc. Away, boy, from the troops, and
    save thyself;
For friends kill friends, and the disorder's
    such
As war were hoodwink'd.
Iach.   'Tis their fresh supplies.
Luc. It is a day turn'd strangely: or
    betimes
Let's re-inforce, or fly.   *[Exeunt.*

Scene III. *Another part of the field.*

Enter Posthumus *and a* British Lord.

Lord. Camest thou from where they made
    the stand?
Post.   I did:
Though you, it seems, come from the fliers.
Lord.   I did.
Post. No blame be to you, sir; for all was
    lost,
But that the heavens fought: the king
    himself
Of his wings destitute, the army broken,
And but the backs of Britons seen, all fly-
    ing
Through a strait lane; the enemy full-
    hearted,
Lolling the tongue with slaughtering, having
    work
More plentiful than tools to do't, struck
    down
Some mortally, some slightly touch'd, some
    falling   10
Merely through fear; that the strait pass was
    damm'd
With dead men hurt behind, and cowards
    living
To die with lengthen'd shame.
Lord.   Where was this lane?
Post. Close by the battle, ditch'd, and
    wall'd with turf;
Which gave advantage to an ancient soldier,
An honest one, I warrant; who deserved
So long a breeding as his white beard came to,

---

23. **weeds,** clothing.   25. **part,** party, side.   30. **habits,** garments.   32. **guise,** practice, custom.
  Scene ii.   3. **on 't,** of it.   4. **carl,** churl, peasant.   8. **go before.**excel

---

  Scene iii.   7. **strait,** narrow. **full-hearted,** full of courage and confidence.   17. **breeding,** life.

In doing this for 's country: athwart the lane,
He, with two striplings—lads more like to
  run
The country base than to commit such
  slaughter;   20
With faces fit for masks, or rather fairer
Than those for preservation cased, or
  shame,—
Made good the passage; cried to those that
  fled,
'Our Britain's harts die flying, not our men:
To darkness fleet souls that fly backwards.
  Stand;
Or we are Romans and will give you that
Like beasts which you shun beastly, and may
  save,
But to look back in frown: stand, stand.'
  These three,
Three thousand confident, in act as many—
For three performers are the file when all   30
The rest do nothing—with this word 'Stand,
  stand,'
Accommodated by the place, more charming
With their own nobleness, which could have
  turn'd
A distaff to a lance, gilded pale looks,
Part shame, part spirit renew'd; that some,
  turn'd coward
But by example—O, a sin in war,
Damn'd in the first beginners!—gan to
  look
The way that they did, and to grin like
  lions
Upon the pikes o' the hunters. Then began
A stop i' the chaser, a retire, anon   40
A rout, confusion thick; forthwith they fly
Chickens, the way which they stoop'd
  eagles; slaves,
The strides they victors made: and now our
  cowards,
Like fragments in hard voyages, became
The life o' the need: having found the back-
  door open
Of the unguarded hearts, heavens, how they
  wound!
Some slain before; some dying; some their
  friends
O'er-borne i' the former wave: ten, chased by
  one,

Are now each one the slaughter-man of
  twenty: 49
Those that would die or ere resist are grown
The mortal bugs o' the field.
  Lord.   This was strange chance:
A narrow lane, an old man, and two boys.
  Post. Nay, do not wonder at it: you are
  made
Rather to wonder at the things you hear
Than to work any. Will you rhyme upon 't,
And vent it for a mockery? Here is one:
'Two boys, an old man twice a boy, a lane,
Preserved the Britons, was the Romans'
  bane.'
  Lord. Nay, be not angry, sir.
  Post.   'Lack, to what end?
Who dares not stand his foe, I'll be his friend;
For if he'll do as he is made to do,   61
I know he'll quickly fly my friendship too.
You have put me into rhyme.
  Lord.   Farewell; you're angry.
  Post. Still going? [*Exit Lord.*] This is a
  lord! O noble misery,
To be i' the field, and ask 'what news?' of me!
To-day how many would have given their
  honours
To have saved their carcases! took heel to
  do 't,
And yet died too! I, in mine own woe
  charm'd,
Could not find death where I did hear him
  groan,
Nor feel him where he struck: being an ugly
  monster,   70
'Tis strange he hides him in fresh cups, soft
  beds,
Sweet words; or hath more ministers than
  we
That draw his knives i' the war. Well, I will
  find him:
For being now a favourer to the Briton,
No more a Briton, I have resumed again
The part I came in: fight I will no more,
But yield me to the veriest hind that shall
Once touch my shoulder. Great the slaugh-
  ter is
Here made by the Roman; great the answer
  be
Britons must take. For me, my ransom's
  death;   80

---

20. base, prisoner's base, a game in which rapid
running is the means to victory. 22. cased, covered.
shame, modesty, shyness. 28. But . . . frown, by
merely looking back in defiance. 30. file, rank (of
soldiers). 32. charming, bewitching. 34. gilded,
imparted a flush or color. 37. gan, began. 42. stoop'd,
swooped over (like eagles). 42-43. slaves . . . made,
retracing, as slaves, the steps they took as victors.
44. fragments, scraps, fragments of food.

50. or ere, rather than. 51. mortal bugs, deadly
bugbears. 52. A narrow . . . boys, a line highly condensed and most suggestive. 59. 'Lack, alack; ex
clamation expressing sorrow. 60. stand, withstand.
64. noble misery, miserable nobility. 68. charm'd,
i.e., made invulnerable. 77. hind, servant, rustic. 79.
answer, retaliation.

On either side I come to spend my breath;
Which neither here I'll keep nor bear again,
But end it by some means for Imogen.

Enter two British Captains *and* Soldiers.

First Cap. Great Jupiter be praised! Lucius is taken.
'Tis thought the old man and his sons were
    angels.
Sec. Cap. There was a fourth man, in a
    silly habit,
That gave the affront with them.
First Cap.   So 'tis reported:
But none of 'em can be found. Stand! who's
    there?
Post. A Roman,
Who had not now been drooping here, if
    seconds   90
Had answer'd him.
Sec. Cap.   Lay hands on him; a dog!
A leg of Rome shall not return to tell
What crows have peck'd them here. He
    brags his service
As if he were of note: bring him to the king.

Enter Cymbeline, Belarius, Guiderius,
Arviragus, Pisanio, Soldiers, Attendants, *and* Roman Captives. *The* Captains
present Posthumus *to* Cymbeline, *who
delivers him over to a* Gaoler: *then exeunt
omnes.*

Scene IV. *A British prison.*

Enter Posthumus *and two* Gaolers.

First Gaol. You shall not now be stol'n,
    you have locks upon you;
So graze as you find pasture.
Sec. Gaol.   Ay, or a stomach.
               [*Exeunt Gaolers.*
Post. Most welcome, bondage! for thou
    are a way,
I think, to liberty: yet am I better
Than one that's sick o' the gout; since he
    had rather
Groan so in perpetuity than be cured
By the sure physician, death, who is the key
To unbar these locks. My conscience, thou
    art fetter'd
More than my shanks and wrists: you good
    gods, give me

The penitent instrument to pick that bolt, 10
Then, free for ever! Is 't enough I am sorry?
So children temporal fathers do appease;
Gods are more full of mercy. Must I repent?
I cannot do it better than in gyves,
Desired more than constrain'd: to satisfy,
If of my freedom 'tis the main part, take
No stricter render of me than my all.
I know you are more clement than vile men,
Who of their broken debtors take a third,
A sixth, a tenth, letting them thrive again 20
On their abatement: that's not my desire:
For Imogen's dear life take mine; and though
'Tis not so dear, yet 'tis a life; you coin'd it:
'Tween man and man they weigh not every
    stamp;
Though light, take pieces for the figure's
    sake:
You rather mine, being yours: and so, great
    powers,
If you will take this audit, take this life,
And cancel these cold bonds. O Imogen!
I'll speak to thee in silence.   [*Sleeps.*

Solemn music. Enter, as in an apparition,
Sicilius Leonatus, *father to Posthumus,
an old man, attired like a warrior; leading
in his hand an ancient matron, his wife,
and mother to Posthumus, with music before
them: then, after other music, follow the two
young* Leonati, *brothers to Posthumus,
with wounds as they died in the wars. They
circle* Posthumus *round, as he lies sleeping.*

Sici. No more, thou thunder-master, show 30
    Thy spite on mortal flies:
With Mars fall out, with Juno chide,
    That thy adulteries
    Rates and revenges.
Hath my poor boy done aught but well,
    Whose face I never saw?
I died whilst in the womb he stay'd
    Attending nature's law:
Whose father then, as men report
    Thou orphans' father art,   40
Thou shouldst have been, and shielded
    him
    From this earth-vexing smart.

14. **gyves**, fetters. 15. **constrain'd**, forced upon me.
17. **stricter**, more restricted. **render**, surrender. 24.
stamp, coin. 25. **pieces**, coins. **for . . . sake**, for the
sake of the image stamped upon it. 30–122. **No more
. . . behest.** The vision, like the masque in the fourth
act of *The Tempest*, is usually thought to be by some other
hand than Shakespeare's. Certainly both compositions
are of poetic quality inferior to that of the plays in which
they stand; they would have been added (in case they are
later additions) to gratify the taste for masques in the
court of James I.

86. **silly**, simple. 90. **seconds**, supporters. 91.
answer'd him, done as he did.

Moth. Lucina lent not me her aid,
　　But took me in my throes;
　　That from me was Posthumus ript,
　　Came crying 'mongst his foes,
　　　A thing of pity!

Sici. Great nature, like his ancestry,
　　Moulded the stuff so fair,
　　That he deserved the praise o' the
　　　world,
　　As great Sicilius' heir.　　　　51

First Bro. When once he was mature for man,
　　In Britain where was he
　　That could stand up his parallel;
　　Or fruitful object be
　　In eye of Imogen, that best
　　Could deem his dignity?

Moth. With marriage wherefore was he
　　　mock'd,
　　To be exiled, and thrown
　　From Leonati seat, and cast　　60
　　From her his dearest one,
　　　Sweet Imogen?

Sici. Why did you suffer Iachimo,
　　Slight thing of Italy,
　　To taint his noblier heart and brain
　　With needless jealousy;
　　And to become the geck and scorn
　　O' th' other's villany?

Sec. Bro. For this from stiller seats we came,
　　Our parents and us twain,　　70
　　That striking in our country's cause
　　Fell bravely and were slain,
　　Our fealty and Tenantius' right
　　With honour to maintain.

First Bro. Like hardiment Posthumus hath
　　To Cymbeline perform'd:
　　Then, Jupiter, thou king of gods,
　　Why hast thou thus adjourn'd
　　The graces for his merits due,
　　Being all to dolours turn'd?　　80

Sici. Thy crystal window ope; look out;
　　No longer exercise
　　Upon a valiant race thy harsh
　　And potent injuries.

Moth. Since, Jupiter, our son is good,
　　Take off his miseries.

Sici. Peep through thy marble mansion;
　　help;

Or we poor ghosts will cry
　　To the shining synod of the rest
　　Against thy deity.　　　　　90

Both Bro. Help, Jupiter; or we appeal,
　　And from thy justice fly.

JUPITER *descends in thunder and lightning,
sitting upon an eagle: he throws a thunderbolt. The Ghosts fall on their knees.*

Jup. No more, you petty spirits of region
　　low,
Offend our hearing; hush! How dare you
　　ghosts
Accuse the thunderer, whose bolt, you know,
　　Sky-planted batters all rebelling coasts?
Poor shadows of Elysium, hence, and rest
　　Upon your never-withering banks of
　　　flowers:
Be not with mortal accidents opprest;　　99
　　No care of yours it is; you know 'tis ours.
Whom best I love I cross; to make my gift,
　　The more delay'd, delighted. Be content;
Your low-laid son our godhead will uplift:
　　His comforts thrive, his trials well are spent.
Our Jovial star reign'd at his birth, and in
　　Our temple was he married. Rise, and fade.
He shall be lord of lady Imogen,
　　And happier much by his affliction made.
This tablet lay upon his breast, wherein　109
　　Our pleasure his full fortune doth confine:
And so, away: no further with your din　111
　　Express impatience, lest you stir up mine.
　　Mount, eagle, to my palace crystalline.
　　　　　　　　　　　[*Ascends.*
Sici. He came in thunder; his celestial
　　breath
Was sulphurous to smell: the holy eagle
Stoop'd, as to foot us: his ascension is
More sweet than our blest fields: his royal
　　bird
Prunes the immortal wing and cloys his
　　beak,
As when his god is pleased.
All.　　　　　　　　Thanks, Jupiter!
Sici. The marble pavement closes, he is
　　enter'd　　　　　　　　　　120
His radiant roof. Away! and, to be blest,
Let us with care perform his great behest.
　　　　　　　　　　[*The Ghosts vanish.*

---

67. geck, dupe.　75. **hardiment**, bold exploit.　78.
adjourn'd. deferred.

89. **synod**, assembly of the gods.　102. **delighted**,
delighted in.　105. **Jovial star**, the planet Jupiter, the
happiest of all stars to be born under.　110. **confine**,
precisely state.　116. **foot**, spurn.　118. **Prunes**,
preens, arranges the feathers with the beak. **cloys**,
claws, strokes with the claw (Schmidt).

Post. [*Waking*] Sleep, thou hast been a
    grandsire, and begot
A father to me; and thou hast created
A mother and two brothers: but, O scorn!
Gone! they went hence so soon as they were
    born:
And so I am awake. Poor wretches that
    depend
On greatness' favour dream as I have done,
Wake and find nothing. But, alas, I swerve:
Many dream not to find, neither deserve, 130
And yet are steep'd in favours; so am I,
That have this golden chance and know not
    why.
What fairies haunt this ground? A book? O
    rare one!
Be not, as is our fangled world, a garment
Nobler than that it covers: let thy effects
So follow, to be most unlike our courtiers,
As good as promise. 137
[*Reads*] 'When as a lion's whelp shall, to
himself unknown, without seeking find, and
be embraced by a piece of tender air; and
when from a stately cedar shall be lopped
branches, which, being dead many years,
shall after revive, be jointed to the old stock
and freshly grow; then shall Posthumus end
his miseries, Britain be fortunate and flourish
in peace and plenty.'
'Tis still a dream, or else such stuff as mad-
    men
Tongue and brain not; either both or nothing;
Or senseless speaking or a speaking such
As sense cannot untie. Be what it is,
The action of my life is like it, which 150
I'll keep, if but for sympathy.

Re-enter Gaolers.

First Gaol. Come, sir, are you ready for
death?
Post. Over-roasted rather; ready long ago.
First Gaol. Hanging is the word, sir: if you
be ready for that, you are well cooked.
Post. So, if I prove a good repast to the
spectators, the dish pays the shot. 158
First Gaol. A heavy reckoning for you, sir.
But the comfort is, you shall be called to no
more payments, fear no more tavern-bills;
which are often the sadness of parting, as the
procuring of mirth: you come in faint for

want of meat, depart reeling with too much
drink; sorry that you have paid too much,
and sorry that you are paid too much; purse
and brain both empty; the brain the heavier
for being too light, the purse too light, being
drawn of heaviness: of this contradiction 168
you shall now be quit. O, the charity of a
penny cord! it sums up thousands in a trice:
you have no true debitor and creditor but it;
of what's past, is, and to come, the discharge:
your neck, sir, is pen, book and counters; so
the acquittance follows.
Post. I am merrier to die than thou art
to live.
First Gaol. Indeed, sir, he that sleeps
feels not the tooth-ache: but a man that were
to sleep your sleep, and a hangman to help
him to bed, I think he would change places
with his officer; for, look you, sir, you know
not which way you shall go. 182
Post. Yes, indeed do I, fellow.
First Gaol. Your death has eyes in 's head
then; I have not seen him so pictured: you
must either be directed by some that take
upon them to know, or to take upon yourself
that which I am sure you do not know, or
jump the after inquiry on your own peril: and
how you shall speed in your journey's end, I
think you'll never return to tell one. 191
Post. I tell thee, fellow, there are none
want eyes to direct them the way I am going,
but such as wink and will not use them.
First Gaol. What an infinite mock is this,
that a man should have the best use of eyes to
see the way of blindness! I am sure hanging 's
the way of winking.

Enter a Messenger.

Mess. Knock off his manacles; bring your
prisoner to the king. 200
Post. Thou bring'st good news; I am
called to be made free.
First Gaol. I'll be hang'd then.
Post. Thou shalt be then freer than a
gaoler; no bolts for the dead. 205
    [*Exeunt all but the First Gaoler.*
First Gaol. Unless a man would marry a
gallows and beget young gibbets, I never saw
one so prone. Yet, on my conscience, there
are verier knaves desire to live, for all he be a

---

125. **scorn**, mockery. 129. **swerve**, mistake, go
astray. 133. **book**, tablet or scroll. 134. **fangled**,
characterized by fopperies or gaudiness. 138. **When as**,
when. 147. **Tongue**, speak of. **brain**, understand.
149. **Be what it is**, let it be what it may. 158. **shot**,
tavern reckoning.

168. **drawn**, tapped, emptied. 171. **debitor and
creditor**, accounting book. 173. **counters**, round
pieces of metal used for calculating. 189. **jump**,
hazard. 190. **how . . . speed**, how you will succeed.
194. **wink**, shut the eyes. 208. **prone**, ready, eager.

Roman: and there be some of them too that
die against their wills; so should I, if I were
one. I would we were all of one mind, and
one mind good; O, there were desolation of
gaolers and gallowses! I speak against 214
my present profit, but my wish hath a preferment in 't.   [*Exit*.

SCENE V. *Cymbeline's tent.*

Enter CYMBELINE, BELARIUS, GUIDERIUS,
ARVIRAGUS, PISANIO, Lords, Officers, *and*
Attendants.

Cym. Stand by my side, you whom the
        gods have made
Preservers of my throne. Woe is my heart
That the poor soldier that so richly fought,
Whose rags shamed gilded arms, whose
        naked breast
Stepp'd before targes of proof, cannot be
        found:
He shall be happy that can find him, if
Our grace can make him so.
    Bel.   I never saw
Such noble fury in so poor a thing;
Such precious deeds in one that promised
        nought
But beggary and poor looks.
    Cym.   No tidings of him? 10
Pis. He hath been search'd among the
        dead and living,
But no trace of him.
    Cym.   To my grief, I am
The heir of his reward; [*To Belarius, Guider-
ius, and Arviragus*] which I will add
To you, the liver, heart and brain of Britain,
By whom I grant she lives. 'Tis now the time
To ask of whence you are. Report it.
    Bel.   Sir,
In Cambria are we born, and gentlemen:
Further to boast were neither true nor modest,
Unless I add, we are honest.
    Cym.   Bow your knees.
Arise my knights o' the battle: I create you 20
Companions to our person and will fit you
With dignities becoming your estates.

Enter CORNELIUS *and* Ladies.

There's business in these faces. Why so sadly
Greet you our victory? you look like Romans,

And not o' the court of Britain.
    Cor.   Hail, great king!
To sour your happiness, I must report
The queen is dead.
    Cym.   Who worse than a physician
Would this report become? But I consider,
By medicine life may be prolong'd, yet death
Will seize the doctor too. How ended she? 30
    Cor. With horror, madly dying, like her
        life,
Which, being cruel to the world, concluded
Most cruel to herself. What she confess'd
I will report, so please you: these her women
Can trip me, if I err; who with wet cheeks
Were present when she finish'd.
    Cym.   Prithee, say.
    Cor. First, she confess'd she never loved
        you, only
Affected greatness got by you, not you:
Married your royalty, was wife to your place;
Abhorr'd your person.
    Cym.   She alone knew this; 40
And, but she spoke it dying, I would not
Believe her lips in opening it. Proceed.
    Cor. Your daughter, whom she bore in
        hand to love
With such integrity, she did confess
Was as a scorpion to her sight; whose life,
But that her flight prevented it, she had
Ta'en off by poison.
    Cym.   O most delicate fiend!
Who is 't can read a woman? Is there more?
    Cor. More, sir, and worse. She did con-
        fess she had   49
For you a mortal mineral; which, being took,
Should by the minute feed on life and ling-
        ering
By inches waste you: in which time she pur-
        posed,
By watching, weeping, tendance, kissing, to
O'ercome you with her show, and in time,
When she had fitted you with her craft, to
        work
Her son into the adoption of the crown:
But, failing of her end by his strange ab-
        sense,
Grew shameless-desperate; open'd, in despite
Of heaven and men, her purposes; repented

214. **gallowses**, gallows, or possibly, hangmen.
Scene v. 5. **targes of proof**, shields of steel hardened
to withstand certain tests.

35. **trip**, refute, contradict. 37-40. **First . . . person.**
This is the first of the series of discoveries by which the
plot is resolved. 38. **Affected**, loved. 43. **bore in
hand**, pretended with false appearances. 47. **delicate**,
subtle, ingenious. 50. **mortal mineral**, deadly poison.
55. **fitted**, prepared. 56. **adoption**, right of an adopted
heir. 58. **shameless-desperate**, shamelessly desperate.
open'd, revealed.

The evils she hatch'd were not effected; so 60
Despairing died.
　　Cym.　　　Heard you all this, her women?
　　First Lady. We did, so please your highness.
　　Cym.　　　　　　Mine eyes
Were not in fault, for she was beautiful;
Mine ears, that heard her flattery; nor my
　　heart,
That thought her like her seeming; it had
　　been vicious
To have mistrusted her: yet, O my daughter!
That it was folly in me, thou mayst say,
And prove it in thy feeling. Heaven mend all!

Enter Lucius, Iachimo, *the* Soothsayer, *and
other* Roman Prisoners, *guarded;* Posthumus *behind, and* Imogen.

Thou comest not, Caius, now for tribute;
　　that
The Britons have razed out, though with the
　　loss　　　　　　　　　　　　　　70
Of many a bold one; whose kinsmen have
　　made suit
That their good souls may be appeased with
　　slaughter
Of you their captives, which ourself have
　　granted:
So think of your estate.
　　Luc. Consider, sir, the chance of war: the
　　day
Was yours by accident; had it gone with us,
We should not, when the blood was cool,
　　have threaten'd
Our prisoners with the sword. But since the
　　gods
Will have it thus, that nothing but our lives
May be call'd ransom, let it come: suf-
　　ficeth　　　　　　　　　　　　　80
A Roman with a Roman's heart can suffer:
Augustus lives to think on 't: and so much
For my peculiar care. This one thing only
I will entreat; my boy, a Briton born,
Let him be ransom'd: never master had
A page so kind, so duteous, diligent,
So tender over his occasions, true,
So feat, so nurse-like: let his virtue join
With my request, which I'll make bold your
　　highness
Cannot deny; he hath done no Briton
　　harm,　　　　　　　　　　　　90

Though he have served a Roman: save him,
　　sir,
And spare no blood beside.
　　Cym.　　　I have surely seen him:
His favour is familiar to me. Boy,
Thou hast look'd thyself into my grace,
†And art mine own. I know not why, where-
　　fore,
To say 'live, boy:' ne'er thank thy master;
　　live:
And ask of Cymbeline what boon thou wilt,
Fitting my bounty and thy state, I'll give it;
Yea, though thou do demand a prisoner,
The noblest ta'en.
　　Imo. I humbly thank your highness. 100
　　Luc. I do not bid thee beg my life, good
　　lad;
And yet I know thou wilt.
　　Imo.　　　No, no: alack,
There's other work in hand: I see a thing
Bitter to me as death: your life, good master,
Must shuffle for itself.
　　Luc.　　　The boy disdains me,
He leaves me, scorns me: briefly die their joys
That place them on the truth of girls and
　　boys.
Why stands he so perplex'd?
　　Cym.　　　What wouldst thou, boy?
I love thee more and more: think more and
　　more
What's best to ask. Know'st him thou
　　look'st on? speak,　　　　　　110
Wilt have him live? Is he thy kin? thy
　　friend?
　　Imo. He is a Roman; no more kin to me
Than I to your highness; who, being born
　　your vassal,
Am something nearer.
　　Cym.　　　Wherefore eyest him so?
　　Imo. I'll tell you, sir, in private, if you
　　please
To give me hearing
　　Cym.　　　Ay, with all my heart,
And lend my best attention. What's thy
　　name?
　　Imo. Fidele, sir.
　　Cym.　　Thou'rt my good youth, my page;
I'll be thy master: walk with me; speak
　　freely.
　　　　　[*Cymbeline and Imogen converse
　　　　　　　　　　　　　　　apart.*
　　Bel. Is not this boy revived from death?
　　Arv.　　　One sand another 120

70. **razed out**, erased. 83. **peculiar**, particular, individual. 87. **occasions**, particular wants or require-
ments. 88. **feat**, adroit, neat.

93. **favour**, countenance.

Not more resembles that sweet rosy lad
Who died, and was Fidele. What think
  you?
  Gui. The same dead thing alive.
  Bel. Peace, peace! see further; he eyes us
    not; forbear;
Creatures may be alike: were 't he, I am sure
He would have spoke to us.
  Gui.   But we saw him dead.
  Bel. Be silent; let's see further.
  Pis.   [*Aside*] It is my mistress:
Since she is living, let the time run on
To good or bad.
            [*Cymbeline and Imogen come forward.*
  Cym.   Come, stand thou by our side;
Make thy demand aloud. [*To Iachimo*] Sir,
  step you forth;   130
Give answer to this boy, and do it freely;
Or, by our greatness and the grace of it,
Which is our honour, bitter torture shall
Winnow the truth from falsehood. On, speak
  to him.
  Imo. My boon is, that this gentleman may
    render
Of whom he had this ring.
  Post.   [*Aside*] What's that to him?
  Cym. That diamond upon your finger, say
How came it yours?
  Iach. Thou 'lt torture me to leave un-
    spoken that
Which, to be spoke, would torture thee.
  Cym.   How! me?   140
  Iach. I am glad to be constrain'd to utter
    that
Which torments me to conceal. By villany
I got this ring: 'twas Leonatus' jewel;
Whom thou didst banish; and—which more
  may grieve thee,
As it doth me—a nobler sir ne'er lived
'Twixt sky and ground. Wilt thou hear
  more, my lord?
  Cym. All that belongs to this.
  Iach.   That paragon, thy daughter,—
For whom my heart drops blood, and my
  false spirits
Quail to remember— Give me leave; I faint.
  Cym. My daughter! what of her? Renew
    thy strength: 150
I had rather thou shouldst live while nature
  will
Than die ere I hear more: strive, man, and
  speak.
  Iach. Upon a time,—unhappy was the
    clock

That struck the hour!—it was in Rome,—ac-
  cursed
The mansion where!—'twas at a feast,—O,
  would
Our viands had been poison'd, or at least
Those which I heaved to head!—the good
  Posthumus—
What should I say? he was too good to be
Where ill men were; and was the best of
  all
Amongst the rarest of good ones,—sitting
  sadly,
Hearing us praise our loves of Italy   161
For beauty that made barren the swell'd
  boast
Of him that best could speak, for feature,
  laming
The shrine of Venus, or straight-pight
  Minerva,
Postures beyond brief nature, for condi-
  tion,
A shop of all the qualities that man
Loves woman for, besides that hook of
  wiving,
Fairness which strikes the eye—
  Cym.   I stand on fire:
Come to the matter.
  Iach.   All too soon I shall,
Unless thou wouldst grieve quickly. This
  Posthumus,   170
Most like a noble lord in love and one
That had a royal lover, took his hint;
And, not dispraising whom we praised,—
  therein
He was as calm as virtue—he began
His mistress' picture; which by his tongue
  being made,
And then a mind put in 't, either our brags
Were crack'd of kitchen-trulls, or his descrip-
  tion
Proved us unspeaking sots.
  Cym.   Nay, nay, to the purpose.
  Iach. Your daughter's chastity—there it
    begins.   179
He spake of her, as Dian had hot dreams,
And she alone were cold: whereat I, wretch,
Made scruple of his praise; and wager'd with
  him

157. **heaved to head,** raised to lips. 163. **feature,**
whole turn and cast of body (Schmidt); comeliness.
laming, making seem crippled. 164. **shrine,** image.
straight-pight, erect. 165. **Postures,** forms, attitudes. **beyond brief nature,** immortal. **condition,**
temper of mind. 166. **shop,** store. 167. **hook of
wiving,** the incentive to matrimony. 177. **crack'd of,**
boasted in praise of. **kitchen-trulls,** kitchen maids.
178. **unspeaking sots,** speechless blockheads.

Pieces of gold 'gainst this which then he
    wore
Upon his honour'd finger, to attain
In suit the place of 's bed and win this ring
By hers and mine adultery. He, true knight,
No lesser of her honour confident
Than I did truly find her, stakes this ring;
And would so, had it been a carbuncle 189
Of Phœbus' wheel, and might so safely, had it
Been all the worth of 's ' car. Away to
    Britain
Post I in this design: well may you, sir,
Remember me at court; where I was taught
Of your chaste daughter the wide difference
'Twixt amorous and villanous. Being thus
    quench'd
Of hope, not longing, mine Italian brain
'Gan in your duller Britain operate
Most vilely; for my vantage, excellent:
And, to be brief, my practice so prevail'd,
That I return'd with simular proof enough 200
To make the noble Leonatus mad,
By wounding his belief in her renown
With tokens thus, and thus; averring notes
Of chamber-hanging, pictures, this her brace-
    let,—
O cunning, how I got it!—nay, some marks
Of secret on her person, that he could not
But think her bond of chastity quite crack'd,
I having ta'en the forfeit. Whereupon—
Methinks, I see him now—
    Post. [*Advancing*] Ay, so thou dost,
Italian fiend! Ay me, most credulous fool, 210
Egregious murderer, thief, any thing
That's due to all the villains past, in being,
To come! O, give me cord, or knife, or poison,
Some upright justicer! Thou, king, send out
For torturers ingenious: it is I
That all the abhorred things o' the earth
    amend
By being worse than they. I am Posthumus,
That kill'd thy daughter:—villain-like, I
    lie—
That caused a lesser villain than myself,
A sacrilegious thief, to do 't: the temple 220
Of virtue was she; yea, and she herself.
Spit, and throw stones, cast mire upon me,
    set
The dogs o' the street to bay me: every vil-
    lain
Be call'd Posthumus Leonatus; and

Be villany less that 'twas! O Imogen!
My queen, my life, my wife! O Imogen,
Imogen, Imogen!
    Imo.   Peace, my lord; hear, hear—
    Post. Shall's have a play of this? Thou
    scornful page,
There lie thy part.   [*Striking her: she falls.*
    Pis.   O, gentlemen, help!
Mine and your mistress! O, my lord Post-
    humus! 230
You ne'er kill'd Imogen till now. Help, help!
Mine honour'd lady!
    Cym.   Does the world go round?
    Post. How come these staggers on me?
    Pis.   Wake, my mistress!
    Cym. If this be so, the gods do mean to
    strike me
To death with mortal joy.
    Pis.   How fares my mistress?
    Imo. O, get thee from my sight;
Thou gavest me poison: dangerous fellow,
    hence!
Breathe not where princes are.
    Cym.   The tune of Imogen!
    Pis. Lady,
The gods throw stones of sulphur on me, if 240
That box I gave you was not thought by me
A precious thing: I had it from the queen.
    Cym. New matter still?
    Imo.   It poison'd me.
    Cor.   O gods!
I left out one thing which the queen con-
    fess'd,
Which must approve thee honest: 'If Pisanio
Have' said she 'given his mistress that con-
    fection
Which I gave him for cordial, she is served
As I would serve a rat.'
    Cym.   What's this, Cornelius?
    Cor. The queen, sir, very oft importuned
    me
To temper poisons for her, still pretending 250
The satisfaction of her knowledge only
In killing creatures vile, as cats and dogs,
Of no esteem: I, dreading that her purpose
Was of more danger, did compound for her
A certain stuff, which, being ta'en, would
    cease
The present power of life, but in short time

189. **would so,** would have done so. 192. **Post,**
hasten. 200. **simular,** simulated, or pretended. 216-
217. **That . . . they.** The thought is that great crimes
make lesser ones look better by comparison.

229. **There lie thy part.** Shakespeare perhaps
reaches his most sensational height in this episode, when
Posthumus strikes down his unknown love. It is in the
vein of Beaumont and Fletcher. 233. **staggers,** dizzi-
ness, bewilderment. 238. **tune,** sound of voice. 246.
confection, composition of drugs.

All offices of nature should again
Do their due functions. Have you ta'en of it?

Imo. Most like I did, for I was dead.

Bel.   My boys,
There was our error.

Gui.   This is, sure, Fidele. 260

Imo. Why did you throw your wedded
      lady from you?
Think that you are upon a rock; and now
Throw me again.   [*Embracing him.*

Post.   Hang there like fruit, my soul,
Till the tree die!

Cym.   How now, my flesh, my child!
What, makest thou me a dullard in this act?
Wilt thou not speak to me?

Imo.   [*Kneeling*] Your blessing, sir.

Bel. [*To Guiderius and Arviragus*] Though
      you did love this youth, I blame ye not;
You had a motive for 't.

Cym.   My tears that fall
Prove holy water on thee! Imogen,
Thy mother's dead.

Imo.   I am sorry for 't, my lord. 270

Cym. O, she was naught; and long of her
      it was
That we meet here so strangely: but her son
Is gone, we know not how nor where.

Pis.   My lord,
Now fear is from me, I'll speak troth. Lord
      Cloten,
Upon my lady's missing, came to me
With his sword drawn; foam'd at the mouth,
      and swore,
If I discover'd not which way she was gone,
It was my instant death. By accident,
I had a feigned letter of my master's
Then in my pocket; which directed him 280
To seek her on the mountains near to Mil-
      ford;
Where, in a frenzy, in my master's garments,
Which he enforced from me, away he posts
With unchaste purpose and with oath to
      violate
My lady's honour: what became of him
I further know not.

Gui.   Let me end the story:
I slew him there.

Cym.   Marry, the gods forfend!
I would not thy good deeds should from my
      lips

Pluck a hard sentence: prithee, valiant
      youth,
Deny 't again.

Gui.   I have spoke it, and I
did it.   290

Cym. He was a prince.

Gui. A most incivil one: the wrongs he
      did me
Were nothing prince-like; for he did provoke
      me
With language that would make me spurn
      the sea,
If it could so roar to me: I cut off 's head;
And am right glad he is not standing here
To tell this tale of mine.

Cym.   I am sorry for thee:
By thine own tongue thou art condemn'd,
      and must
Endure our law: thou'rt dead.

Imo.   That headless man
I thought had been my lord.

Cym.   Bind the offender, 300
And take him from our presence.

Bel.   Stay, sir king:
This man is better than the man he slew,
As well descended as thyself; and hath
More of thee merited than a band of Clotens
Had ever scar for. [*To the Guard*] Let his
      arms alone;
They were not born for bondage.

Cym.   Why, old soldier,
Wilt thou undo the worth thou art unpaid
      for,
By tasting of our wrath? How of descent
As good as we?

Arv.   In that he spake too far.

Cym. And thou shalt die for 't.

Bel.   We will die all three: 310
But I will prove that two on 's are as good
As I have given out him. My sons, I must,
For mine own part, unfold a dangerous
      speech,
Though, haply, well for you.

Arv.   Your danger 's ours.

Gui. And our good his.

Bel.   Have at it then, by leave.
Thou hadst, great king, a subject who
Was call'd Belarius.

Cym.   What of him? he is
A banish'd traitor.

Bel.   He it is that hath

---

262. **rock,** cliff, rocky eminence. 263. *Stage Direction:*
Embracing him, added by Hanmer and making
clear a passage regarded as obscure. 271. **naught,** a
naughty thing, wicked. **long of,** owing to. 274.
roth, truth.

312. **given out,** reported. 315. **Have at it,** I'll
proceed (with my story). **by leave,** with your permission.

Assumed this age; indeed a banish'd man;
I know not how a traitor.

Cym.   Take him hence: 320
The whole world shall not save him.

Bel.   Not too hot:
First pay me for the nursing of thy sons;
And let it be confiscate all, so soon
As I have received it.

Cym.   Nursing of my sons!

Bel. I am too blunt and saucy: here's my
     knee:
Ere I arise, I will prefer my sons;
Then spare not the old father. Mighty sir,
These two young gentlemen, that call me
     father
And think they are my sons, are none of
     mine;   329
They are the issue of your loins, my liege,
And blood of your begetting.

Cym.   How! my issue!

Bel. So sure as you your father's. I, old
     Morgan,
Am that Belarius whom you sometime
     banish'd:
Your pleasure was my mere offence, my
     punishment
Itself, and all my treason; that I suffer'd
Was all the harm I did. These gentle
     princes—
For such and so they are—these twenty
     years
Have I train'd up: those arts they have as I
Could put into them; my breeding was, sir,
     as   339
Your highness knows. Their nurse, Euriph-
     ile,
Whom for the theft I wedded, stole these
     children
Upon my banishment: I moved her to 't,
Having received the punishment before,
For that which I did then: beaten for loyalty
Excited me to treason: their dear loss,
The more of you 'twas felt, the more it
     shaped
Unto my end of stealing them. But, gracious
     sir,
Here are your sons again; and I must lose
Two of the sweet'st companions in the world.
The benediction of these covering heavens 350
Fall on their heads like dew! for they are
     worthy

To inlay heaven with stars.

Cym.   Thou weep'st, and speak'st.
The service that you three have done is more
Unlike than this thou tell'st. I lost my chil-
     dren:
If these be they, I know not how to wish
A pair of worthier sons.

Bel.   Be pleased awhile.
This gentleman, whom I call Polydore,
Most worthy prince, as yours, is true Gui-
     derius:
This gentleman, my Cadwal, Arviragus, 359
Your younger princely son; he, sir, was
     lapp'd
In a most curious mantle, wrought by the
     hand
Of his queen mother, which for more pro-
     bation
I can with ease produce.

Cym.   Guiderius had
Upon his neck a mole, a sanguine star;
It was a mark of wonder.

Bel.   This is he;
Who hath upon him still that natural stamp:
It was wise nature's end in the donation,
To be his evidence now.

Cym.   O, what, am I
A mother to the birth of three? Ne'er mother
Rejoiced deliverance more. Blest pray you
     be,   370
That, after this strange starting from your
     orbs,
You may reign in them now! O Imogen,
Thou hast lost by this a kingdom.

Imo.   No, my lord;
I have got two worlds by 't. O my gentle
     brothers,
Have we thus met? O, never say hereafter
But I am truest speaker: you call'd me
     brother,
When I was but your sister; I you brothers,
When ye were so indeed.

Cym.   Did you e'er meet?

Arv. Ay, my good lord.

Gui.   And at first meeting loved;
Continued so, until we thought he died. 380

Cor. By the queen's dram she swallow'd.

Cym.   O rare instinct!
When shall I hear all through? This fierce
     abridgement
Hath to it circumstantial branches, which

Distinction should be rich in. Where? how
    lived you?
And when came you to serve our Roman
    captive?
How parted with your brothers? how first
    met them?
Why fled you from the court? and whither?
    These,
And your three motives to the battle, with
I know not how much more, should be de-
    manded;
And all the other by-dependencies,   390
From chance to chance: but nor the time nor
    place
Will serve our long inter'gatories. See,
Posthumus anchors upon Imogen,
And she, like harmless lightning, throws her
    eye
On him, her brothers, me, her master, hitting
Each object with a joy: the counterchange
Is severally in all. Let's quit this ground,
And smoke the temple with our sacrifices.
[*To Belarius*] Thou art my brother; so we'll
    hold thee ever.
    Imo. You are my father too, and did re-
    lieve me,   400
To see this gracious season.
    Cym.   All o'erjoy'd,
Save these in bonds: let them be joyful too,
For they shall taste our comfort.
    Imo.   My good master,
I will yet do you service.
    Luc.   Happy be you!
    Cym. The forlorn soldier, that so nobly
    fought,
He would have well becomed this place, and
    graced
The thankings of a king.
    Post.   I am, sir,
The soldier that did company these three
In poor beseeming; 'twas a fitment for   409
The purpose I then follow'd. That I was he,
Speak, Iachimo: I had you down and might
Have made you finish.
    Iach. [*Kneeling*] I am down again:
But now my heavy conscience sinks my knee,
As then your force did. Take that life, be-
    seech you,

Which I so often owe: but your ring first;
And here the bracelet of the truest princess
That ever swore her faith.
    Post.   Kneel not to me:
The power that I have on you is to spare you;
The malice towards you to forgive you: live,
And deal with others better.
    Cym.   Nobly doom'd!   420
We'll learn our freeness of a son-in-law;
Pardon's the word to all.
    Arv.   You holp us, sir,
As you did mean indeed to be our brother;
Joy'd are we that you are.
    Post. Your servant, princes. Good my
    lord of Rome,
Call forth your soothsayer: as I slept, me-
    thought
Great Jupiter, upon his eagle back'd,
Appear'd to me, with other spritely shows
Of mine own kindred: when I waked, I found
This label on my bosom; whose containing
Is so from sense in hardness, that I can   431
Make no collection of it: let him show
His skill in the construction.
    Luc.   Philarmonus!
    Sooth. Here, my good lord.
    Luc.   Read, and declare the meaning.
    Sooth. [*Reads*] 'When as a lion's whelp
shall, to himself unknown, without seeking
find, and be embraced by a piece of tender
air; and when from a stately cedar shall be
lopped branches, which, being dead many
years, shall after revive, be jointed to the old
stock, and freshly grow; then shall Posthu-
mus end his miseries, Britain be fortunate
and flourish in peace and plenty.'   442
Thou, Leonatus, art the lion's whelp;
The fit and apt construction of thy name,
Being Leo-natus, doth import so much.
[*To Cymbeline*] The piece of tender air, thy
    virtuous daughter,
Which we call 'mollis aer;' and 'mollis aer'
We term it 'mulier:' which 'mulier' I divine
Is this most constant wife; who, even now,
Answering the letter of the oracle,   450
Unknown to you, unsought, were clipp'd
    about
With this most tender air.

---

388. **your three motives**, the motives of you three.
390. **by-dependencies**, attendant circumstances. 391.
chance to chance, event to event. 396-397. **the counterchange . . . all**, the exchange is in all and severally
in each. 405. **forlorn**, lost, not to be found. 409.
beseeming, appearance. **fitment**, equipment. 412.
made you finish, put an end to you. 413. **sinks**,
causes to sink.

420. **doom'd**, pronounced judgment, decreed. 421.
freeness, liberality, generosity. 428. **spritely**, ghostly,
in the form of spirits. **shows**, appearances. 430. **label**,
tablet. 430-431. **whose . . . hardness**, whose meaning
is so remote from sense in its difficulty. 432. **collection
of**, inference or deduction from. 445. **Leo-natus**, one
born of the lion. 447. '**mollis aer**,' tender air; a fanciful
derivation of Latin *mulier*, woman.

Cym.   This hath some seeming.

Sooth. The lofty cedar, royal Cymbeline,
Personates thee: and thy lopp'd branches
  point
Thy two sons forth; who, by Belarius stol'n,
For many years thought dead, are now re-
  vived,
To the majestic cedar join'd, whose issue
Promises Britain peace and plenty.

Cym.   Well;
My peace we will begin. And, Caius Lucius,
Although the victor, we submit to Cæsar, 460
And to the Roman empire; promising
To pay our wonted tribute, from the which
We were dissuaded by our wicked queen;
Whom heavens, in justice, both on her and
  hers,
Have laid most heavy hand.

Sooth. The fingers of the powers above do
  tune
The harmony of this peace. The vision
Which I made known to Lucius, ere the
  stroke

Of this yet scarce-cold battle, at this instant
Is full accomplish'd; for the Roman eagle, 470
From south to west on wing soaring aloft,
Lessen'd herself, and in the beams o' the sun
So vanish'd: which foreshow'd our princely
  eagle,
The imperial Cæsar, should again unite
His favour with the radiant Cymbeline,
Which shines here in the west.

Cym.   Laud we the gods;
And let our crooked smokes climb to their
  nostrils
From our blest altars. Publish we this peace
To all our subjects. Set we forward: let
A Roman and a British ensign wave   480
Friendly together: so through Lud's-town
  march:
And in the temple of great Jupiter
Our peace we'll ratify; seal it with feasts.
Set on there! Never was a war did cease,
Ere bloody hands were wash'd, with such a
  peace.

                        [Exeunt.

---

452. **This . . . seeming,** this seems well-founded
(Gollancz).

476. **Laud,** praise.   484. **Set on there!** forward
march!

THE WINTER'S TALE

DRAMATIS PERSONÆ

LEONTES, king of Sicilia.
MAMILLIUS, young prince of Sicilia.
CAMILLO,
ANTIGONUS,
CLEOMENES, } Four Lords of Sicilia.
DION,
POLIXENES, king of Bohemia.
FLORIZEL, prince of Bohemia.
ARCHIDAMUS, a Lord of Bohemia.
Old Shepherd, reputed father of Perdita.
Clown, his son.
AUTOLYCUS, a rogue.
A Mariner.
A Gaoler.

HERMIONE, queen to Leontes.
PERDITA, daughter to Leontes and Hermione.
PAULINA, wife to Antigonus.
EMILIA, a lady attending on Hermione.

MOPSA,
DORCAS, } Shepherdesses.

Other Lords and Gentlemen, Ladies, Officers, and Servants, Shepherds, and Shepherdesses.

Time, as Chorus.

SCENE: *Sicilia, and Bohemia.*

ACT I.

SCENE I. *Antechamber in* LEONTES' *palace.*

Enter CAMILLO *and* ARCHIDAMUS.

Arch. If you shall chance, Camillo, to visit Bohemia, on the like occasion whereon my services are now on foot, you shall see, as I have said, great difference betwixt our Bohemia and your Sicilia.

Cam. I think, this coming summer, the King of Sicilia means to pay Bohemia the visitation which he justly owes him.

Arch. Wherein our entertainment shall shame us we will be justified in our loves; for indeed— 10

Cam. Beseech you,—

Arch. Verily, I speak it in the freedom of my knowledge: we cannot with such magnificence—in so rare—I know not what to say. We will give you sleepy drinks, that your senses, unintelligent of our insufficience, may, though they cannot praise us, as little accuse us.

Cam. You pay a great deal too dear for what's given freely. 19

Arch. Believe me, I speak as my understanding instructs me and as mine honesty puts it to utterance.

Cam. Sicilia cannot show himself overkind to Bohemia. They were trained together in their childhoods; and there rooted betwixt them then such an affection, which cannot choose but branch now. Since their more mature dignities and royal necessities made separation of their society, their encounters, though not personal, have been royally attorneyed with interchange of gifts, letters, loving embassies; that they have seemed to be together, though absent, shook hands, as over a vast, and embraced, as it were, from the ends of opposed winds. The heavens continue their loves! 35

Act I. Scene i. The conversation between the two noblemen serves to bring out the unruffled friendship between Leontes and Polixenes; it is, of course, full of dramatic irony.

30. **attorneyed**, carried out by deputy. 33. **vast**, boundless, desolate sea.

Arch. I think there is not in the world either malice or matter to alter it. You have an unspeakable comfort of your young prince Mamillius: it is a gentleman of the greatest promise that ever came into my note.   40

Cam. I very well agree with you in the hopes of him: it is a gallant child; one that indeed physics the subject, makes old hearts fresh: they that went on crutches ere he was born desire yet their life to see him a man.

Arch. Would they else be content to die?

Cam. Yes; if there were no other excuse why they should desire to live.

Arch. If the king had no son, they would desire to live on crutches till he had one. 50

[*Exeunt.*

SCENE II. *A room of state in the same.*

Enter LEONTES, HERMIONE, MAMILLIUS, POLIXENES, CAMILLO, *and* Attendants.

Pol. Nine changes of the watery star hath been
The shepherd's note since we have left our throne
Without a burthen: time as long again
Would be fill'd up, my brother, with our thanks;
And yet we should, for perpetuity,
Go hence in debt: and therefore, like a cipher,
Yet standing in rich place, I multiply
With one 'We thank you' many thousands moe
That go before it.

Leon.   Stay your thanks a while;
And pay them when you part.

Pol.   Sir, that's to-morrow.   10
I am question'd by my fears, of what may chance
Or breed upon our absence; that may blow
No sneaping winds at home, to make us say
'This is put forth too truly:' besides, I have stay'd
To tire your royalty.

Leon.   We are tougher, brother,
Than you can put us to't.

Pol.   No longer stay.

Leon. One seven-night longer.

Pol.   Very sooth, to-morrow.

Leon. We'll part the time between's then; and in that
I'll no gainsaying.

Pol.   Press me not, beseech you, so.
There is no tongue that moves, none, none i' the world,   20
So soon as yours could win me: so it should now,
Were there necessity in your request, although
'Twere needful I denied it. My affairs
Do even drag me homeward: which to hinder
Were in your love a whip to me; my stay
To you a charge and trouble: to save both,
Farewell, our brother.

Leon. Tongue-tied our queen? speak you.

Her. I had thought, sir, to have held my peace until
You had drawn oaths from him not to stay. You, sir,
Charge him too coldly. Tell him, you are sure   30
All in Bohemia's well; this satisfaction
The by-gone day proclaim'd: say this to him,
He's beat from his best ward.

Leon.   Well said, Hermione.

Her. To tell, he longs to see his son, were strong:
But let him say so then, and let him go;
But let him swear so, and he shall not stay,
We'll thwack him hence with distaffs.
Yet of your royal presence I'll adventure
The borrow of a week. When at Bohemia
You take my lord, I'll give him my commission   40
To let him there a month behind the gest
Prefix'd for 's parting: yet, good deed, Leontes,
I love thee not a jar o' the clock behind
What lady-she her lord. You'll stay?

Pol.   No, madam.

Her. Nay, but you will?

Pol.   I may not, verily.

Her. Verily!
You put me off with limber vows; but I,
Though you would seek to unsphere the stars with oaths,

<hr>

37. **of**, in the person of. 40. **note**, observation. 43. **physics the subject**, acts as a cordial to the people. *Scene ii.* 1. **watery star**, moon. 9. **Stay**, restrain. 13. **sneaping**, pinching with cold. 16. **Than ... to't**, than anything you can do to try us.

17. **seven-night**, common expression for *week*. 19. **I'll no gainsaying**, I will have no refusal. 25. **your love a whip**, to make your love a punishment. 39. **borrow**, borrowing. 40. **take**, charm, captivate. 41. **gest**, time allotted for a halt. 42. **good deed**, a mild oath. 43. **jar**, tick. 47. **limber**, pliant.

Should yet say 'Sir, no going.' Verily,
You shall not go: a lady's 'Verily' 's　　50
As potent as a lord's. Will you go yet?
Force me to keep you as a prisoner,
Not like a guest; so you shall pay your fees
When you depart, and save your thanks.
　　　How say you?
My prisoner? or my guest? by your dread
　　　'Verily,'
One of them you shall be.
　　Pol.　　　　　　Your guest, then, madam:
To be your prisoner should import offending;
Which is for me less easy to commit
Than you to punish.
　　Her.　　　　　　Not your gaoler, then,
But your kind hostess. Come, I'll question
　　　you
Of my lord's tricks and yours when you were
　　　boys:　　61
You were pretty lordings then?
　　Pol.　　　　　　We were, fair queen,
Two lads that thought there was no more
　　　behind
But such a day to-morrow as to-day,
And to be boy eternal.
　　Her.　　　　　　Was not my lord
The verier wag o' the two?
　　Pol. We were as twinn'd lambs that did
　　　frisk i' the sun,
And bleat the one at the other: what we
　　　changed
Was innocence for innocence; we knew not
The doctrine of ill-doing, nor dream'd　　70
That any did. Had we pursued that life,
And our weak spirits ne'er been higher
　　　rear'd
With stronger blood, we should have an-
　　　swer'd heaven
Boldly 'not guilty;' the imposition clear'd
Hereditary ours.
　　Her.　　　　　By this we gather
You have tripp'd since.
　　Pol.　　　　　O my most sacred lady!
Temptations have since then been born to 's;
　　　for
In those unfledged days was my wife a girl;
Your precious self had then not cross'd the
　　　eyes
Of my young play-fellow.
　　Her.　　　　　Grace to boot!　　80

Of this make no conclusion, lest you say
Your queen and I are devils: yet go on;
The offences we have made you do we'll
　　　answer,
If you first sinn'd with us and that with us
You did continue fault and that you slipp'd
　　　not
With any but with us.
　　Leon.　　　　　　Is he won yet?
　　Her. He'll stay, my lord.
　　Leon.　　　　At my request he would not.
Hermione, my dearest, thou never spokest
To better purpose.
　　Her.　　　　Never?
　　Leon.　　　　Never, but once.
　　Her. What! have I twice said well? when
　　　was 't before?　　90
I prithee tell me; cram 's with praise, and
　　　make 's
As fat as tame things: one good deed dying
　　　tongueless
Slaughters a thousand waiting upon that.
Our praises are our wages: you may ride 's
With one soft kiss a thousand furlongs ere
With spur we heat an acre. But to the goal:
My last good deed was to entreat his stay:
What was my first? it has an elder sister,
Or I mistake you: O, would her name were
　　　Grace!
But once before I spoke to the purpose: when?
Nay, let me have 't; I long.
　　Leon.　　　　Why, that was when　　101
Three crabbed months had sour'd themselves
　　　to death,
Ere I could make thee open thy white hand
And clap thyself my love: then didst thou
　　　utter
'I am yours for ever.'
　　Her.　　　　　　'Tis grace indeed.
Why, lo you now, I have spoke to the pur-
　　　pose twice:
The one for ever earn'd a royal husband;
The other for some while a friend.
　　Leon.　　　　　[*Aside*] Too hot, too hot!
To mingle friendship far is mingling bloods.
I have tremor cordis on me: my heart dances;
But not for joy; not joy. This entertain-
　　　ment　　111
May a free face put on, derive a liberty
From heartiness, from bounty, fertile bosom,
And well become the agent; 't may, I grant;

---

53. **fees.** Persons leaving prison were obliged to pay for their lodging whether guilty or not. 57. **import**, imply. 74-75. **imposition . . . ours**, original sin, although imposed upon us by heredity, was swept clean away (Furness). 80. **Grace to boot!** a mild oath, "favor of God be our help!"

85. **fault**, offense. 96. **heat**, traverse (as a horse driven by the spur). 104. **clap**, clasp hands, plight troth. 110. **tremor cordis**, fluttering of the heart. 112. **free**, unreserved.

But to be paddling palms and pinching
  fingers,
As now they are, and making practised
  smiles,
As in a looking-glass, and then to sigh, as
  'twere
The mort o' the deer; O, that is entertain-
  ment
My bosom likes not, nor my brows! Mamil-
  lius,
Art thou my boy?
  Mam.   Ay, my good lord.
  Leon.   I' fecks! 120
Why, that's my bawcock. What, hast
  smutch'd thy nose?
They say it is a copy out of mine. Come,
  captain,
We must be neat; not neat, but cleanly, cap-
  tain:
And yet the steer, the heifer and the calf
Are all call'd neat.—Still virginalling
Upon his palm!—How now, you wanton calf!
Art thou my calf?
  Mam.   Yes, if you will, my lord.
  Leon. Thou want'st a rough pash and the
  shoots that I have,
To be full like me: yet they say we are
Almost as like as eggs; women say so,   130
That will say any thing: but were they false
As o'er-dyed blacks, as wind, as waters, false
As dice are to be wish'd by one that fixes
No bourn 'twixt his and mine, yet were it
  true
To say this boy were like me. Come, sir page,
Look on me with your welkin eye: sweet
  villain!
Most dear'st! my collop! Can thy dam?—
  may 't be?—
Affection! thy intention stabs the centre:
Thou dost make possible things not so held,
Communicatest with dreams;—how can this
  be?—   140
With what's unreal thou coactive art,

And fellow'st nothing: then 'tis very credent
Thou mayst co-join with something; and
  thou dost,
And that beyond commission, and I find it,
And that to the infection of my brains
And hardening of my brows.
  Pol.   What means Sicilia?
  Her. He something seems unsettled.
  Pol.   How, my lord!
What cheer? how is 't with you, best brother?
  Her.   You look
As if you held a brow of much distraction:
Are you moved, my lord?
  Leon.   No, in good earnest.   150
How sometimes nature will betray its folly,
Its tenderness, and make itself a pastime
To harder bosoms! Looking on the lines
Of my boy's face, methoughts I did recoil
Twenty-three years, and saw myself un-
  breech'd,
In my green velvet coat, my dagger muzzled,
Lest it should bite its master, and so prove,
As ornaments oft do, too dangerous.
How like, methought, I then was to this
  kernel,
This squash, this gentleman. Mine honest
  friend,   160
Will you take eggs for money?
  Mam. No, my lord, I'll fight.
  Leon. You will! why, happy man be's
  dole! My brother,
Are you so fond of your young prince as we
Do seem to be of ours?
  Pol.   If at home, sir,
He's all my exercise, my mirth, my matter,
Now my sworn friend and then mine enemy,
My parasite, my soldier, statesman, all:
He makes a July's day short as December,
And with his varying childness cures in me 170
Thoughts that would thick my blood.
  Leon.   So stands this squire
Officed with me: we two will walk, my lord,
And leave you to your graver steps. Her-
  mione,
How thou lovest us, show in our brother's
  welcome;
Let what is dear in Sicily be cheap:
Next to thyself and my young rover, he's
Apparent to my heart.

118. **mort**, note sounded on a horn at the death of a deer. 120. **I' fecks**, in faith. 121. **bawcock**, French, *beau coq*, fine fellow. 123. **not . . . cleanly**. Leontes changes the word because *neat* reminds him of the cuckold's horns. 125. **virginalling**, playing on the virginals, a keyed instrument of the piano class; here, touching hands. 128. **pash**, head. **shoots**, horns; an allusion to the cuckold's horns. 132. **o'er-dyed blacks**, probably, black garments whose fabric is destroyed by dye. 134. **bourn**, boundary. 136. **welkin**, blue like the sky. 137. **collop**, piece of meat; here, a term of endearment. 138. **Affection . . . centre**, amorous affection by power goes straight to the center; a puzzling line. 139-146. **Thou . . . brows**. Affection, in the sense of amorous affection, is able to pursue its course by dreams, unrealities, mere nothings. It is then credible that when it has realities to work upon, it will have yet more power.

142. **credent**, credible. 144. **commission**, what is lawful. 154. **recoil**, go back in memory. 160. **squash**, unripe peascod. 161. **take eggs for money**, proverbial for "be imposed upon." 163. **happy . . . dole**, proverbial, "may good fortune be his lot." 170. **childness**, childishness. 171. **thick my blood**. Melancholy thoughts would thicken the blood. 172. **Officed**, placed in particular function.

Her.   If you would seek us,
We are yours i' the garden: shall's attend
    you there?
    Leon. To your own-bents dispose you:
    you'll be found,
Be you beneath the sky. [*Aside*] I am angling
    now,   180
Though you perceive me not how I give line.
Go to, go to!
How she holds up the neb, the bill to him!
And arms her with the boldness of a wife
To her allowing husband!
[*Exeunt Polixenes, Hermione, and Attendants.*
                Gone already!
Inch-thick, knee-deep, o'er head and ears a
    fork'd one!
Go, play, boy, play: thy mother plays, and I
Play too, but so disgraced a part, whose issue
Will hiss me to my grave: contempt and
    clamour
Will be my knell. Go, play, boy, play. There
    have been,   190
Or I am much deceived, cuckolds ere now;
And many a man there is, even at this pre-
    sent,
Now while I speak this, holds his wife by the
    arm,
That little thinks she has been sluiced in's
    absence
And his pond fish'd by his next neighbour, by
Sir Smile, his neighbour: nay, there's com-
    fort in't
Whiles other men have gates and those gates
    open'd,
As mine, against their will. Should all des-
    pair
That have revolted wives, the tenth of man-
    kind
Would hang themselves. Physic for't there
    is none;   200
It is a bawdy planet, that will strike
Where 'tis predominant; and 'tis powerful,
    think it,
From east, west, north and south: be it con-
    cluded,
No barricado for a belly; know't;
It will let in and out the enemy
With bag and baggage: many thousand on's

Have the disease, and feel 't not. How now,
    boy!
    Mam. I am like you, they say.
    Leon.   Why, that's some comfort.
What, Camillo there?
    Cam. Ay, my good lord.   210
    Leon. Go play, Mamillius; thou 'rt an
    honest man.   [*Exit Mamillius.*
Camillo, this great sir will yet stay longer.
    Cam. You had much ado to make his
    anchor hold:
When you cast out, it still came home.
    Leon.   Didst note it?
    Cam. He would not stay at your petitions;
    made
His business more material.
    Leon.   Didst perceive it?
[*Aside*] They're here with me already,
    whispering, rounding
'Sicilia is a so-forth:' 'tis far gone,
When I shall gust it last. How came 't,
    Camillo,
That he did stay?
    Cam.   At the good queen's entreaty. 220
    Leon. At the queen's be 't: 'good' should
    be pertinent;
But, so it is, it is not. Was this taken
By any understanding pate but thine?
For thy conceit is soaking, will draw in
More than the common blocks: not noted,
    is 't,
But of the finer natures? by some severals
Of head-piece extraordinary? lower messes
Perchance are to this business purblind? say.
    Cam. Business, my lord! I think most un-
    derstand
Bohemia stays here longer.
    Leon.   Ha!
    Cam.   Stays here longer. 230
    Leon. Ay, but why?
    Cam. To satisfy your highness and the en-
    treaties
Of our most gracious mistress.
    Leon.   Satisfy!
The entreaties of your mistress! satisfy!
Let that suffice. I have trusted thee, Cam-
    illo

178. shall's, shall we. 179. To . . . you, do with
yourselves according to the inclinations of your minds.
183. neb, beak; here, nose. 184. arms her with,
assumes. 188. issue, outcome. 201. strike, blast,
destroy by a malign influence. 202. predominant, in
the ascendant (used of a planet).

216. material, important. 217-219. They're . . .
last. Staunton pointed out that these words refer to the
king's fear of public disgrace and shame. Note *contempt
and clamour*, line 189. 217. rounding, whispering. 219.
gust, taste; here, hear of. 221. pertinent, i.e., appropriately applied. 222. so, as. taken, perceived. 224.
conceit, intelligence. soaking, very receptive. 225.
blocks, blockheads. 226. severals, individuals. 227.
lower messes, persons of a lower rank. 228. purblind,
blind.

With all the nearest things to my heart, as
    well
My chamber-councils, wherein, priest-like,
    thou
Hast cleansed my bosom, I from thee de-
    parted
Thy penitent reform'd: but we have been
Deceived in thy integrity, deceived   240
In that which seems so.

Cam.   Be it forbid, my lord!

Leon. To bide upon 't, thou art not honest,
    or,
If thou inclinest that way, thou art a coward,
Which hoxes honesty behind, restraining
From course required; or else thou must be
    counted
A servant grafted in my serious trust
And therein negligent; or else a fool
That seest a game play'd home, the rich
    stake drawn,
And takest it all for jest.

Cam.   My gracious lord,
I may be negligent, foolish and fearful; 250
In every one of these no man is free,
But that his negligence, his folly, fear,
Among the infinite doings of the world,
Sometime puts forth. In your affairs, my
    lord,
If ever I were wilful-negligent,
It was my folly; if industriously
I play'd the fool, it was my negligence,
Not weighing well the end; if ever fearful
To do a thing, where I the issue doubted,
Whereof the execution did cry out   260
Against the non-performance, 'twas a fear
Which oft infects the wisest: these, my lord,
Are such allow'd infirmities that honesty
Is never free of. But, beseech your grace,
Be plainer with me; let me know my trespass
By its own visage: if I then deny it,
'Tis none of mine.

Leon.   Ha' not you seen, Camillo,—
But that's past doubt, you have, or your
    eye-glass
Is thicker than a cuckold's horn,—or heard,—
For to a vision so apparent rumor   270
Cannot be mute,—or thought,—for cogi-
    tation
Resides not in that man that does not
    think,—

My wife is slippery? If thou wilt confess,
Or else be impudently negative,
To have nor eyes nor ears nor thought, then
    say
My wife's a hobby-horse, deserves a name
As rank as any flax-wench that puts to
Before her troth-plight: say 't and justify 't.

Cam. I would not be a stander-by to hear
My sovereign mistress clouded so, with-
    out   280
My present vengeance taken: 'shrew my
    heart,
You never spoke what did become you less
Than this; which to reiterate were sin
As deep as that, though true.

Leon.   Is whispering nothing?
Is leaning cheek to cheek? is meeting noses?
Kissing with inside lip? stopping the career
Of laughter with a sigh?—a note infallible
Of breaking honesty—horsing foot on foot?
Skulking in corners? wishing clocks more
    swift?
Hours, minutes? noon, midnight? and all
    eyes
Blind with the pin and web but theirs, theirs
    only,   291
That would unseen be wicked? is this
    nothing?
Why, then the world and all that's in 't is
    nothing;
The covering sky is nothing; Bohemia
    nothing;
My wife is nothing; nor nothing have these
    nothings,
If this be nothing.

Cam.   Good my lord, be cured
Of this diseased opinion, and betimes;
For 'tis most dangerous.

Leon.   Say it be, 'tis true.

Cam. No, no, my lord.

Leon.   It is; you lie, you lie:
I say thou liest, Camillo, and I hate thee, 300
Pronounce thee a gross lout, a mindless
    slave,
Or else a hovering temporizer, that
Canst with thine eyes at once see good and
    evil,
Inclining to them both: were my wife's
    liver
Infected as her life, she would not live
The running of one glass.

Cam.   Who does infect her?

Leon. Why, he that wears her like her
    medal, hanging

About his neck, Bohemia: who, if I

Had servants true about me, that bare eyes

To see alike mine honour as their profits, 310

Their own particular thrifts, they would do
    that

Which should undo more doing: ay, and
    thou,

His cupbearer,—whom I from meaner form

Have bench'd and rear'd to worship, who
    mayst see

Plainly as heaven sees earth and earth sees
    heaven,

How I am galled,—mightst bespice a cup,

To give mine enemy a lasting wink;

Which draught to me were cordial.

Cam.   Sir, my lord,

I could do this, and that with no rash potion,

But with a lingering dram that should not
    work

Maliciously like poison: but I cannot   321

Believe this crack to be in my dread mistress,

So sovereignly being honourable.

I have loved thee,—

Leon.   †Make that thy question,
    and go rot!

Dost think I am so muddy, so unsettled,

To appoint myself in this vexation, sully

The purity and whiteness of my sheets,

Which to preserve is sleep, which being
    spotted

Is goads, thorns, nettles, tails of wasps,

Give scandal to the blood o' the prince my
    son,

Who I do think is mine and love as mine, 331

Without ripe moving to 't? Would I do this?

Could man so blench?

Cam.   I must believe you, sir:

I do; and will fetch off Bohemia for 't;

Provided that, when he's removed, your
    highness

Will take again your queen as yours at first,

Even for your son's sake; and thereby for
    sealing

The injury of tongues in courts and king-
    doms

Known and allied to yours.

Leon.   Thou dost advise me

Even so as I mine own course have set down:

I'll give no blemish to her honour, none. 341

    Cam. My lord,

Go then; and with a countenance as clear

As friendship wears at feasts, keep with
    Bohemia

And with your queen. I am his cupbearer:

If from me he have wholesome beverage,

Account me not your servant.

Leon.   This is all:

Do 't and thou hast the one half of my heart;

Do 't not, thou split'st thine own.

Cam.   I'll do 't, my lord.

Leon. I will seem friendly, as thou hast
    advised me.   [*Exit.*   350

    Cam. O miserable lady! But, for me,

What case stand I in? I must be the poisoner

Of good Polixenes; and my ground to do 't

Is the obedience to a master, one

Who in rebellion with himself will have

All that are his so too. To do this deed,

Promotion follows. If I could find example

Of thousands that had struck anointed kings

And flourish'd after, I'ld not do 't; but since

Nor brass nor stone nor parchment bears not
    one,   360

Let villany itself forswear 't. I must

Forsake the court: to do 't, or no, is certain

To me a break-neck. Happy star reign now!

Here comes Bohemia.

Re-enter POLIXENES.

Pol.   This is strange: methinks

My favour here begins to warp. Not speak?

Good day, Camillo.

Cam.   Hail, most royal sir!

Pol. What is the news i' the court?

Cam.   None rare, my lord.

Pol. The king hath on him such a counte-
    nance

As he had lost some province and a region

Loved as he loves himself: even now I met
    him

With customary compliment; when he,   371

Wafting his eyes to the contrary and falling

A lip of much contempt, speeds from me
    and

So leaves me to consider what is breeding

That changeth thus his manners.

Cam. I dare not know, my lord.

---

311. **thrifts**, gains.   314. **bench'd**, raised to authority.   317. **lasting wink**, death.   323. **So . . . honourable**, being so supremely honorable.   326. **appoint**, equip, array.   332. **ripe**, urgent, pressing. 334. **fetch off**, make way with.

352. **case**, position.   357–361. **If I . . . forswear't.** This is a well-recognized principle of Renaissance morality.   363. **break-neck**, destruction, ruin.   365. **warp**, change, grow askew.   372. **Wafting . . . contrary**, turning in an opposite direction. **falling**, letting fall.

Pol. How! dare not! do not. Do you
    know, and dare not?
Be intelligent to me: 'tis thereabouts;
For, to yourself, what you do know, you must,
And cannot say, you dare not. Good
    Camillo,   380
Your changed complexions are to me a
    mirror
Which shows me mine changed too; for I
    must be
A party in this alteration, finding
Myself thus alter'd with 't.
    Cam.   There is a sickness
Which puts some of us in distemper, but
I cannot name the disease; and it is caught
Of you that yet are well.
    Pol.   How! caught of me!
Make me not sighted like the basilisk:
I have look'd on thousands, who have sped
    the better
By my regard, but kill'd none so. Camillo,—
As you are certainly a gentleman, thereto 391
Clerk-like experienced, which no less adorns
Our gentry than our parents' noble names,
In whose success we are gentle,—I beseech
    you,
If you know aught which does behove my
    knowledge
Thereof to be inform'd, imprison 't not
In ignorant concealment.
    Cam.   I may not answer.
    Pol. A sickness caught of me, and yet I
    well!
I must be answer'd. Dost thou hear, Cam-
    illo?
I conjure thee, by all the parts of man   400
Which honour does acknowledge, whereof
    the least
Is not this suit of mine, that thou declare
What incidency thou dost guess of harm
Is creeping toward me; how far off, how
    near;
Which way to be prevented, if to be;
If not, how best to bear it.
    Cam.   Sir, I will tell you;
Since I am charged in honour and by him
That I think honourable: therefore mark my
    counsel,
Which must be even as swiftly follow'd as
I mean to utter it, or both yourself and me 410

Cry lost, and so good night!
    Pol.   On, good Camillo.
    Cam. I am appointed him to murder you.
    Pol. By whom, Camillo?
    Cam.   By the king.
    Pol.   For what?
    Cam. He thinks, nay, with all confidence
    he swears,
As he had seen 't or been an instrument
To vice you to 't, that you have touch'd his
    queen
Forbiddenly.
    Pol.   O, then my best blood turn
To an infected jelly and my name
Be yoked with his that did betray the Best!
Turn then my freshest reputation to   420
A savour that may strike the dullest nostril
Where I arrive, and my approach be shunn'd,
Nay, hated too, worse than the great'st infec-
    tion
That e'er was heard or read!
    Cam.   Swear his thought over
By each particular star in heaven and
By all their influences, you may as well
Forbid the sea for to obey the moon
As or by oath remove or counsel shake
The fabric of his folly, whose foundation
Is piled upon his faith and will continue 430
The standing of his body.
    Pol.   How should this grow?
    Cam. I know not: but I am sure 'tis
    safer to
Avoid what's grown than question how 'tis
    born.
If therefore you dare trust my honesty,
That lies enclosed in this trunk which you
Shall bear along impawn'd, away to-night!
Your followers I will whisper to the business,
And will by twos and threes at several
    posterns
Clear them o' the city. For myself, I'll put
My fortunes to your service, which are here
By this discovery lost. Be not uncertain; 441
For, by the honour of my parents, I
Have utter'd truth: which if you seek to
    prove,
I dare not stand by; nor shall you be safer
Than one condemn'd by the king's own
    mouth, thereon

---

378. **Be . . . thereabouts**, be intelligible—it must be
something of this nature: that you know and dare not
tell (Furness). 381. **changed**, grown pale. 388. **basilisk**, a fabulous reptile whose look was thought to be
fatal. 394. **whose success**, succession from whom.

416. **vice**, impel. 419. **his . . . Best**, a reference to
Judas. 424. **Swear . . . over**, overcome his thought by
swearing. 431. **standing**, life, existence. **How . . .
grow**, How could this suspicion have arisen? 435.
trunk, body. 436. **impawn'd**, i.e., as a pledge of good
faith. 441. **discovery**, revelation, disclosure. 444.
stand by, stay to see the result.

His execution sworn.

Pol. I do believe thee:
I saw his heart in 's face. Give me thy hand:
Be pilot to me and thy places shall
Still neighbour mine. My ships are ready and
My people did expect my hence departure 450
Two days ago. This jealousy
Is for a precious creature: as she's rare,
Must it be great, and as his person's mighty,
Must it be violent, and as he does conceive
He is dishonour'd by a man which ever
Profess'd to him, why, his revenges must
In that be made more bitter. Fear o'er-
shades me:
Good expedition be my friend, and comfort
†The gracious queen, part of his theme, but
nothing
Of his ill-ta'en suspicion! Come, Camillo; 460
I will respect thee as a father if
Thou bear'st my life off hence: let us avoid.

Cam. It is in mine authority to command
The keys of all the posterns: please your
highness
To take the urgent hour. Come, sir, away.
[*Exeunt.*

ACT II.

Scene I. *A room in* Leontes' *palace.*

Enter Hermione, Mamillius, *and* Ladies.

Her. Take the boy to you: he so troubles
me,
'Tis past enduring.

First Lady. Come, my gracious lord,
Shall I be your playfellow?

Mam. No, I'll none of you.

First Lady. Why, my sweet lord?

Mam. You'll kiss me hard and speak to
me as if
I were a baby still. I love you better.

Sec. Lady. And why so, my lord?

Mam. Not for because
Your brows are blacker; yet black brows,
they say,
Become some women best, so that there be
not

Too much hair there, but in a semicircle, 10
Or a half-moon made with a pen.

Sec. Lady. Who taught you this?

Mam. I learnt it out of women's faces.
Pray now
What colour are your eyebrows?

First Lady. Blue, my lord.

Mam. Nay, that's a mock: I have seen a
lady's nose
That has been blue, but not her eyebrows.

First Lady. Hark ye;
The queen your mother rounds apace: we
shall
Present our services to a fine new prince
One of these days; and then you'ld wanton
with us,
If we would have you.

Sec. Lady. She is spread of late
Into a goodly bulk: good time encounter
her!

Her. What wisdom stirs amongst you?
Come, sir, now 21
I am for you again: pray you, sit by us,
And tell's a tale.

Mam. Merry or sad shall 't be?

Her. As merry as you will.

Mam. A sad tale's best for winter: I have
one
Of sprites and goblins.

Her. Let's have that, good sir.
Come on, sit down: come on, and do your
best
To fright me with your sprites; you're
powerful at it.

Mam. There was a man—

Her. Nay, come, sit down; then on.

Mam. Dwelt by a churchyard: I will tell
it softly; 30
Yond crickets shall not hear it.

Her. Come on, then,
And give 't me in mine ear.

Enter Leontes, *with* Antigonus, Lords,
and others.

Leon. Was he met there? his train? Camillo with him?

---

456. **Profess'd,** openly professed friendship. 458-
460. **Good . . . suspicion.** May my hasty departure
prove my best course, and bring what comfort it may
to the gracious queen, whose name cannot but be linked
with mine in the king's thoughts, but who is not yet
the fatal object of his ill-founded suspicion (Furness).
462. **avoid,** depart.

18. **wanton,** sport, play. 25. **A sad tale's best for
winter.** This may have some connection with the
title, *The Winter's Tale.* 31. **crickets,** meaning court
ladies "with their tittering and chirping laughter"
(Furnivall). Mamillius is one of Shakespeare's most
successful children, having about him some actual
childishness. Shakespeare's children are hardly more
in their language and ideas than diminutive grown
people, and yet in spite of this they create an impression
of childhood.

First Lord. Behind the tuft of pines I met
  them; never
Saw I men scour so on their way: I eyed them
Even to their ships.

Leon.   How blest am I
In my just censure, in my true opinion!
Alack, for lesser knowledge! how accursed
In being so blest! There may be in the cup
A spider steep'd, and one may drink, depart, 40
And yet partake no venom, for his knowledge
Is not infected: but if one present
The abhorr'd ingredient to his eye, make
  known
How he hath drunk, he cracks his gorge, his
  sides,
With violent hefts. I have drunk, and seen
  the spider.
Camillo was his help in this, his pandar:
There is a plot against my life, my crown;
All's true that is mistrusted: that false
  villain
Whom I employ'd was pre-employ'd by him:
He has discover'd my design, and I   50
Remain a pinch'd thing; yea, a very trick
For them to play at will. How came the
  posterns
So easily open?

First Lord.   By his great authority;
Which often hath no less prevail'd than so
On your command.

Leon.   I know 't too well.
Give me the boy: I am glad you did not nurse
  him:
Though he does bear some signs of me, yet
  you
Have too much blood in him.

Her.   What is this? sport?

Leon. Bear the boy hence; he shall not
  come about her;
Away with him! and let her sport herself 60
With that she's big with; for 'tis Polixenes
Has made thee swell thus.

Her.   But I 'ld say he had not,
And I'll be sworn you would believe my
  saying,
Howe'er you lean to the nayward.

Leon.   You, my lords,
Look on her, mark her well; be but about
To say 'she is a goodly lady,' and
The justice of your hearts will thereto add

''Tis pity she's not honest, honourable:'
Praise her but for this her without-door form,
Which on my faith deserves high speech, and
  straight   70
The shrug, the hum or ha, these petty brands
That calumny doth use—O, I am out—
That mercy does, for calumny will sear
Virtue itself: these shrugs, these hums and
  ha's,
When you have said 'she's goodly,' come
  between
Ere you can say 'she's honest:' but be 't
  known,
From him that has most cause to grieve it
  should be,
She's an adulteress.

Her.   Should a villain say so,
The most replenish'd villain in the world, 79
He were as much more villain: you, my lord,
Do but mistake.

Leon.   You have mistook, my lady,
Polixenes for Leontes: O thou thing!
Which I'll not call a creature of thy place,
Lest barbarism, making me the precedent,
Should a like language use to all degrees
And mannerly distinguishment leave out
Betwixt the prince and beggar: I have said
She's an adulteress; I have said with whom:
More, she's a traitor and Camillo is
A federary with her, and one that knows 90
What she should shame to know herself
But with her most vile principal, that she's
A bed-swerver, even as bad as those
That vulgars give bold'st titles, ay, and privy
To this their late escape.

Her.   No, by my life,
Privy to none of this. How will this grieve
  you,
When you shall come to clearer knowledge,
  that
You thus have publish'd me! Gentle my lord,
You scarce can right me throughly then to
  say
You did mistake.

Leon.   No; if I mistake   100
In those foundations which I build upon,
The centre is not big enough to bear
A school-boy's top. Away with her! to prison!
He who shall speak for her is afar off guilty
But that he speaks.

---

37. **censure**, judgment. 38. **Alack, for lesser knowledge**, would that my knowledge were less. 45. **hefts**, heavings, retchings. 51. **pinch'd**, powerless, ridiculous. 62. **I 'ld**, I need only. 64. **nayward**, disbelief.

69. **without-door**, outward. 72. **out**, wrong. 73. **does**, uses. 83. **place**, position. 86. **mannerly distinguishment**, polite distinctions. 90. **federary**, confederate, accomplice. 94. **vulgars**, common people. 102. **centre**, center of the earth. 104. **afar off**, to some degree.

Her.   There's some ill planet reigns:
I must be patient till the heavens look
With an aspect more favourable. Good my
      lords,
I am not prone to weeping, as our sex
Commonly are; the want of which vain dew
Perchance shall dry your pities: but I have 110
That honourable grief lodged here which
      burns
Worse than tears drown: beseech you all, my
      lords,
With thoughts so qualified as your charities
Shall best instruct you, measure me; and so
The king's will be perform'd!
      Leon.   Shall I be heard?
      Her. Who is't that goes with me? Be-
      seech your highness,
My women may be with me; for you see
My plight requires it. Do not weep, good
      fools;
There is no cause: when you shall know your
      mistress
Has deserved prison, then abound in tears 120
As I come out: this action I now go on
Is for my better grace. Adieu, my lord:
I never wish'd to see you sorry; now
I trust I shall. My women, come; you have
      leave.
      Leon. Go, do our bidding; hence!
            [*Exit Queen, guarded; with Ladies.*
      First Lord. Beseech your highness, call the
      queen again.
      Ant. Be certain what you do, sir, lest your
      justice
Prove violence; in the which three great ones
      suffer,
Yourself, your queen, your son.
      First Lord.   For her, my lord,
I dare my life lay down and will do't, sir, 130
Please you to accept it, that the queen is
      spotless
I' the eyes of heaven and to you; I mean,
In this which you accuse her.
      Ant.   If it prove
†She's otherwise, I'll keep my stables where
I lodge my wife; I'll go in couples with her;
Than when I feel and see her no farther trust
      her;
For every inch of woman in the world,
Ay, every dram of woman's flesh is false,

If she be.
      Leon.   Hold your peaces.
      First Lord.   Good my lord,—
      Ant. It is for you we speak, not for our-
      selves: 140
You are abused and by some putter-on
That will be damn'd for 't; would I knew the
      villain,
†I would land-damn him. Be she honour-
      flaw'd,
I have three daughters; the eldest is eleven;
The second and the third, nine, and some five;
If this prove true, they'll pay for 't: by mine
      honour,
I'll geld 'em all; fourteen they shall not see,
To bring false generations: they are co-heirs;
And I had rather glib myself than they
Should not produce fair issue.
      Leon.   Cease; no more.
You smell this business with a sense as cold 151
As is a dead man's nose: but I do see 't and
      feel 't,
As you feel doing thus; and see withal
The instruments that feel.
      Ant.   If it be so,
We need no grave to bury honesty:
There's not a grain of it the face to sweeten
Of the whole dungy earth.
      Leon.   What! lack I credit?
      First Lord. I had rather you did lack than
      I, my lord,
Upon this ground; and more it would content
      me   159
To have her honour true than your suspicion,
Be blamed for 't how you might.
      Leon.   Why, what need we
Commune with you of this, but rather follow
Our forceful instigation? Our prerogative
Calls not your counsels, but our natural
      goodness
Imparts this; which if you, or stupified
Or seeming so in skill, cannot or will not
Relish a truth like us, inform yourselves
We need no more of your advice: the matter,
The loss, the gain, the ordering on 't, is all
Properly ours.
      Ant.   And I wish, my liege,   170
You had only in your silent judgment tried it,
Without more overture.
      Leon.   How could that be?

115. **heard**, obeyed. 121. **action**, indictment. 134.
stables, usually regarded as equivalent to *kennels*; but
Moorman suggests "station"—*stabilis statio*—interpreting the passage, "I'll keep my station in the same
place where my wife is lodged." 135. **couples**, i. e., like
hounds.

141. **putter-on**, instigator. 143. **land-damn him**,
possibly, make a hell on earth for him; many conjectures.
145. **some**, about. 148. **false generations**, illegitimate
children. 149. **glib**, geld. 153. **As . . . thus**, possibly
expressed by a gesture. 159. **Upon this ground**, in
this matter. 164. **Calls**, calls for. 172. **overture**,
disclosure.

Either thou art most ignorant by age,
Or thou wert born a fool. Camillo's flight,
Added to their familiarity,
Which was as gross as ever touch'd conjec-
    ture,
That lack'd sight only, nought for approba-
    tion
But only seeing, all other circumstances
Made up to the deed, doth push on this pro-
    ceeding:
Yet, for a greater confirmation,   180
For in an act of this importance 'twere
Most piteous to be wild, I have dispatch'd in
    post
To sacred Delphos, to Apollo's temple,
Cleomenes and Dion, whom you know
Of stuff'd sufficiency: now from the oracle
They will bring all; whose spiritual counsel
    had,
Shall stop or spur me. Have I done well?
    First Lord. Well done, my lord.
    Leon. Though I am satisfied and need no
        more
Than what I know, yet shall the oracle 190
Give rest to the minds of others, such as he
Whose ignorant credulity will not
Come up to the truth. So have we thought
    it good
From our free person she should be confined,
Lest that the treachery of the two fled hence
Be left her to perform. Come, follow us;
We are to speak in public; for this business
Will raise us all.
    Ant. [*Aside*] To laughter, as I take it,
If the good truth were known.   [*Exeunt.*

SCENE II. *A prison.*

Enter PAULINA, *a* Gentleman, *and*
    Attendants.

    Paul. The keeper of the prison, call to
        him;
Let him have knowledge who I am.
                              [*Exit Gent.*
                                    Good lady,
No court in Europe is too good for thee;
What dost thou then in prison?

Re-enter Gentleman, *with the* Gaoler.

                        Now, good sir,

You know me, do you not?
    Gaol.   For a worthy lady
And one whom much I honour.
    Paul.   Pray you then,
Conduct me to the queen.
    Gaol.   I may not, madam:
To the contrary I have express command-
    ment.
    Paul. Here's ado,
To lock up honesty and honour from   10
The access of gentle visitors! Is 't lawful,
    pray you,
To see her women? any of them? Emilia?
    Gaol. So please you, madam,
To put apart these your attendants, I
Shall bring Emilia forth.
    Paul.   I pray now, call her.
Withdraw yourselves.
        [*Exeunt Gentleman and Attendants.*
    Gaol.   And, madam,
I must be present at your conference.
    Paul. Well, be 't so, prithee. [*Exit Gaoler.*
Here's such ado to make no stain a stain
As passes colouring.

Re-enter Gaoler, *with* EMILIA.

                    Dear gentlewoman,   20
How fares our gracious lady?
    Emil. As well as one so great and so
    forlorn
May hold together: on her frights and griefs,
Which never tender lady hath borne greater,
She is something before her time deliver'd.
    Paul. A boy?
    Emil.   A daughter, and a goodly babe,
Lusty and like to live: the queen receives
Much comfort in 't; says 'My poor prisoner,
I am innocent as you.'
    Paul.   I dare be sworn:
These dangerous unsafe lunes i' the king,
    beshrew them!   30
He must be told on 't, and he shall: the office
Becomes a woman best; I'll take 't upon me:
If I prove honey-mouth'd, let my tongue
    blister
And never to my red-look'd anger be
The trumpet any more. Pray you, Emilia,
Commend my best obedience to the queen:
If she dares trust me with her little babe,
I'll show 't the king and undertake to be
Her advocate to the loud'st. We do not know
How he may soften at the sight o' the child: 40

The silence often of pure innocence
Persuades when speaking fails.

   Emil.   Most worthy madam,
Your honour and your goodness is so evident
That your free undertaking cannot miss
A thriving issue: there is no lady living
So meet for this great errand.   Please your
     ladyship
To visit the next room, I'll presently
Acquaint the queen of your most noble offer;
Who but to-day hammer'd of this design,
But durst not tempt a minister of honour, 50
Lest she should be denied.

   Paul.   Tell her, Emilia,
I'll use that tongue I have: if wit flow from 't
As boldness from my bosom, let 't not be
    doubted
I shall do good.

   Emil.   Now be you blest for it!
I'll to the queen: please you, come something
    nearer.

   Gaol. Madam, if 't please the queen to send
    the babe,
I know not what I shall incur to pass it,
Having no warrant.

   Paul.   You need not fear it, sir:
This child was prisoner to the womb and is
By law and process of great nature thence 60
Freed and enfranchised, not a party to
The anger of the king nor guilty of,
If any be, the trespass of the queen.

   Gaol. I do believe it.

   Paul. Do not you fear: upon mine honour,
I will stand betwixt you and danger. [*Exeunt*

SCENE III. *A room in* LEONTES' *palace.*

Enter LEONTES, ANTIGONUS, Lords, *and*
       Servants.

   Leon. Nor night nor day no rest: it is but
    weakness
To bear the matter thus; mere weakness. If
The cause were not in being,—part o' the
    cause,
She the adulteress; for the harlot king
Is quite beyond mine arm, out of the blank
And level of my brain, plot-proof; but she

    44. **free**, generous. 49. **hammer'd of**, insisted on.
57. **pass it**, let it pass. 63. **If any be**, if there be any
guilt.
    Scene iii. 4. **harlot**, lewd. 5. **blank**, white spot
in the center of a target. 6. **level**, aim of a weapon, or
range of a missile.

I can hook to me: say that she were gone,
Given to the fire, a moiety of my rest
Might come to me again. Who's there?

   First Serv.   My lord?

   Leon. How does the boy?   9

   First Serv.   He took good rest to-night;
'Tis hoped his sickness is discharged.

   Leon. To see his nobleness!
Conceiving the dishonour of his mother,
He straight declined, droop'd, took it deeply,
Fasten'd and fix'd the shame on 't in himself,
Threw off his spirit, his appetite, his sleep,
And downright languish'd. Leave me solely:
    go,
See how he fares. [*Exit Serv.*] Fie, fie! no
    thought of him;
The very thought of my revenges that way
Recoil upon me: in himself too mighty, 20
And in his parties, his alliance; let him be
Until a time may serve: for present ven-
    geance,
Take it on her. Camillo and Polixenes
Laugh at me, make their pastime at my
    sorrow:
They should not laugh if I could reach them,
    nor
Shall she within my power.

Enter PAULINA, *with a child.*

   First Lord.   You must not enter.

   Paul. Nay, rather, good my lords, be
    second to me:
Fear you his tyrannous passion more, alas,
Than the queen's life? a gracious innocent
    soul,
More free than he is jealous.

   Ant.   That's enough. 30

   Sec. Serv. Madam, he hath not slept to-
    night; commanded
None should come at him.

   Paul.   Not so hot, good sir:
I come to bring him sleep. 'Tis such as you,
That creep like shadows by him and do sigh
At each his needless heavings, such as you
Nourish the cause of his awaking: I
Do come with words as medicinal as true,
Honest as either, to purge him of that
    humour
That presses him from sleep.

   Leon.   What noise there, ho?

   Paul. No noise, my lord; but needful con-
    ference 40

    23. **Take it**, let it be taken. 27. **be second to**, aid,
second. 30. **free**, guiltless, innocent.

About some gossips for your highness.

Leon.   How!
Away with that audacious lady! Antigonus,
I charged thee that she should not come
      about me:
I knew she would.

Ant.   I told her so, my lord,
On your displeasure's peril and on mine,
She should not visit you.

Leon.   What, canst not rule her?

Paul. From all dishonesty he can: in this,
Unless he take the course that you have done,
Commit me for committing honour, trust it,
He shall not rule me.

Ant.   La you now, you hear: 50
When she will take the rein I let her run;
But she'll not stumble.

Paul.   Good my liege, I come;
And, I beseech you, hear me, who profess
Myself your loyal servant, your physician,
Your most obedient counsellor, yet that dare
Less appear so in comforting your evils,
Than such as most seem yours: I say, I come
From your good queen.

Leon.   Good queen!

Paul.   Good queen, my lord,
Good queen; I say good queen;
And would by combat make her good, so
      were I
A man, the worst about you.

Leon.   Force her hence.   61

Paul. Let him that makes but trifles of
      his eyes
First hand me: on mine own accord I'll off;
But first I'll do my errand. The good queen,
For she is good, hath brought you forth a
      daughter;
Here 'tis; commends it to your blessing.
      [*Laying down the child.*

Leon.   Out!
A mankind witch! Hence with her, out o'
      door:
A most intelligencing bawd!

Paul.   Not so:
I am as ignorant in that as you
In so entitling me, and no less honest   70
Than you are mad; which is enough, I'll
      warrant,
As this world goes, to pass for honest.

Leon.   Traitors!
Will you not push her out? Give her the
      bastard.
Thou dotard! thou art woman-tired, un-
      roosted
By thy dame Partlet here. Take up the
      bastard;
Take't up, I say; give't to thy crone.

Paul.   For ever
Unvenerable be thy hands, if thou
Takest up the princess by that forced base-
      ness
Which he has put upon't!

Leon.   He dreads his wife.

Paul. So I would you did; then 'twere past
      all doubt   80
You'ld call your children yours.

Leon.   A nest of traitors!

Ant. I am none, by this good light.

Paul.   Nor I, nor any
But one that's here, and that's himself, for he
The sacred honour of himself, his queen's,
His hopeful son's, his babe's, betrays to
      slander,
Whose sting is sharper than the sword's; and
      will not—
For, as the case now stands, it is a curse
He cannot be compell'd to't—once remove
The root of his opinion, which is rotten
As ever oak or stone was sound.

Leon.   A callet   90
Of boundless tongue, who late hath beat her
      husband
And now baits me! This brat is none of
      mine;
It is the issue of Polixenes:
Hence with it, and together with the dam
Commit them to the fire!

Paul.   It is yours;
And, might we lay the old proverb to your
      charge,
So like you, 'tis the worse. Behold, my lords,
Although the print be little, the whole matter
And copy of the father, eye, nose, lip,
The trick of's frown, his forehead, nay, the
      valley,   100
The pretty dimples of his chin and cheek,

41. **gossips**, godfathers and godmothers. 49. **Commit**, to prison. 56-57. **comforting . . . yours**, encouraging your evil courses, than those flatterers who seem to be your most loyal servants. 67. **mankind**, masculine, violent. 68. **intelligencing**, conveying secret intelligence.

74. **woman-tired**, henpecked, from *tire* in falconry, meaning "tear." **unroosted**, driven from perch. 75. **Partlet**, name of the hen in *Reynard the Fox*, who appears as *Pertelote* in the *Nun's Priest's Tale* of Chaucer. 78. **forced baseness**, false attribution of illegitimacy. 79. **He . . . wife**, he (Antigonus) is afraid of his wife (Paulina). 90. **callet**, lewd woman. 96. **old proverb**. The sense of the proverb is given by Overbury ("Character of a Sergeant"): "The devil calls him his white son; he's so like him, that he is the worse for it."

His smiles,
The very mould and frame of hand, nail,
   finger:
And thou, good goddess Nature, which hast
   made it
So like to him that got it, if thou hast
The ordering of the mind too, 'mongst all
   colours
No yellow in't, lest she suspect, as he does,
Her children not her husband's!
   Leon.   A gross hag!
And, lozel, thou art worthy to be hang'd,
That wilt not stay her tongue.
   Ant.   Hang all the husbands   110
That cannot do that feat, you'll leave your-
   self
Hardly one subject.
   Leon.   Once more, take her hence.
   Paul. A most unworthy and unnatural
   lord
Can do no more.
   Leon.   I'll ha' thee burnt.
   Paul.   I care not:
It is an heretic that makes the fire,
Not she which burns in't. I'll not call you
   tyrant;
But this most cruel usage of your queen,
Not able to produce more accusation
Than your own weak-hinged fancy, some-
   thing savours
Of tyranny and will ignoble make you,   120
Yea, scandalous to the world.
   Leon.   On your allegiance,
Out of the chamber with her! Were I a
   tyrant,
Where were her life? she durst not call me so,
If she did know me one. Away with her!
   Paul. I pray you, do not push me; I'll be
   gone.
Look to your babe, my lord; 'tis yours: Jove
   send her
A better guiding spirit! What needs these
   hands?
You, that are thus so tender o'er his follies,
Will never do him good, not one of you.
So, so: farewell; we are gone.   [*Exit.*   130
   Leon. Thou, traitor, hast set on thy wife
   to this.
My child? away with't! Even thou, that hast
A heart so tender o'er it, take it hence
And see it instantly consumed with fire;

Even thou and none but thou. Take it up
   straight:
Within this hour bring me word 'tis done,
And by good testimony, or I'll seize thy life,
With what thou else call'st thine. If thou
   refuse
And wilt encounter with my wrath, say so;
The bastard brains with these my proper
   hands
Shall I dash out. Go, take it to the fire; 141
For thou set'st on thy wife.
   Ant.   I did not, sir:
These lords, my noble fellows, if they please,
Can clear me in't.
   Lords.   We can: my royal liege,
He is not guilty of her coming hither.
   Leon. You're liars all.
   First Lord. Beseech your highness, give us
   better credit:
We have always truly served you, and be-
   seech you
So to esteem of us, and on our knees we beg,
As recompense of our dear services   150
Past and to come, that you do change this
   purpose,
Which being so horrible, so bloody, must
Lead on to some foul issue: we all kneel.
   Leon. I am a feather for each wind that
   blows:
Shall I live on to see this bastard kneel
And call me father? better burn it now
Than curse it then. But be it; let it live.
It shall not neither. You, sir, come you
   hither;
You that have been so tenderly officious
With Lady Margery, your midwife there, 160
To save this bastard's life,—for 'tis a bas-
   tard,
So sure as this beard's grey,—what will you
   adventure
To save this brat's life?
   Ant.   Any thing, my lord,
That my ability may undergo
And nobleness impose: at least thus much:
I'll pawn the little blood which I have left
To save the innocent: any thing possible.
   Leon. It shall be possible. Swear by this
   sword
Thou wilt perform my bidding.
   Ant.   I will, my lord.
   Leon. Mark and perform it, see'st thou?
   for the fail   170

---

107. **yellow,** suggestive of jealousy. 109. **lozel,** worthless person, scoundrel. 127. **What . . . hands?** She is being pushed from the room.

164. **undergo,** undertake. 170. **fail,** failure.

Of any point in 't shall not only be
Death to thyself but to thy lewd-tongued
    wife,
Whom for this time we pardon. We enjoin
    thee,
As thou art liege-man to us, that thou carry
This female bastard hence and that thou
    bear it
To some remote and desert place quite out
Of our dominions, and that there thou leave
    it,
Without more mercy, to it own protection
And favour of the climate. As by strange
    fortune
It came to us, I do in justice charge thee, 180
On thy soul's peril and thy body's torture,
That thou commend it strangely to some
    place
Where chance may nurse or end it. Take it
    up.
    Ant. I swear to do this, though a present
    death
Had been more merciful. Come on, poor
    babe:
Some powerful spirit instruct the kites and
    ravens
To be thy nurses! Wolves and bears, they
    say,
Casting their savageness aside have done
Like offices of pity. Sir, be prosperous
In more than this deed does require! And
    blessing   190
Against this cruelty fight on thy side,
Poor thing, condemn'd to loss!
                       [Exit with the child.
    Leon.   No, I'll not rear
Another's issue.

Enter a Servant.

    Serv.   Please your highness, posts
From those you sent to the oracle are come
An hour since: Cleomenes and Dion,
Being well arrived from Delphos, are both
    landed,
Hasting to the court.
    First Lord.   So please you, sir,
    their speed
Hath been beyond account.
    Leon.   Twenty three days
They have been absent: 'tis good speed; fore-
    tells
The great Apollo suddenly will have   200

The truth of this appear. Prepare you, lords;
Summon a session, that we may arraign
Our most disloyal lady, for, as she hath
Been publicly accused, so shall she have
A just and open trial. While she lives
My heart will be a burthen to me. Leave
    me,
And think upon my bidding.   *[Exeunt.*

ACT III.

Scene I. *A sea-port in Sicilia.*

Enter Cleomenes and Dion.

    Cleo. The climate's delicate, the air most
    sweet,
Fertile the isle, the temple much surpassing
The common praise it bears.
    Dion.   I shall report,
For most it caught me, the celestial habits,
Methinks I so should term them, and the
    reverence
Of the grave wearers. O, the sacrifice!
How ceremonious, solemn and unearthly
It was i' the offering!
    Cleo.   But of all, the burst
And the ear-deafening voice o' the oracle,
Kin to Jove's thunder, so surprised my sense,
That I was nothing.
    Dion.   If the event o' the journey
Prove as successful to the queen,—O be 't
    so!—   12
As it hath been to us rare, pleasant, speedy,
The time is worth the use on 't.
    Cleo.   Great Apollo
Turn all to the best! These proclamations,
So forcing faults upon Hermione,
I little like.
    Dion.   The violent carriage of it
Will clear or end the business: when the
    oracle,
Thus by Apollo's great divine seal'd up,
Shall the contents discover, something
    rare   20
Even then will rush to knowledge. Go: fresh
    horses!
And gracious be the issue!   *[Exeunt.*

---

178. **it**, its.   182. **commend**, deliver, commit.
strangely, as a foreigner.   192. **loss**, perdition.

Act III. Scene i. 2. **isle.** Shakespeare follows
Greene's *Pandosto* in erroneously placing Delphi on an
island. 8. **burst**, utterance. 14. **worth . . . on't**,
well employed. 17. **carriage**, execution, management.
19. **divine**, here applied to a priest of the heathen religion. 21. **fresh horses.** This indicates that the scene
is laid at some point on the return journey.

SCENE II. *A court of Justice.*

Enter LEONTES, Lords, *and* Officers.

Leon. This sessions, to our great grief we
    pronounce,
Even pushes 'gainst our heart: the party
    tried
The daughter of a king, our wife, and one
Of us too much beloved. Let us be clear'd
Of being tyrannous, since we so openly
Proceed in justice, which shall have due
    course,
Even to the guilt or the purgation.
Produce the prisoner.
    Off. It is his highness' pleasure that the
    queen
Appear in person here in court. Silence! 10

Enter HERMIONE *guarded;* PAULINA *and*
Ladies *attending.*

Leon. Read the indictment.
    Off. [Reads] Hermione, queen to the worthy
Leontes, king of Sicilia, thou art here accused
and arraigned of high treason, in committing
adultery with Polixenes, king of Bohemia,
and conspiring with Camillo to take away
the life of our sovereign lord the king, thy
royal husband: the pretence whereof being
by circumstances partly laid open, thou,
Hermione, contrary to the faith and alle-
giance of a true subject, didst counsel and
aid them, for their better safety, to fly away
by night.
    Her. Since what I am to say must be but
    that
Which contradicts my accusation and
The testimony on my part no other
But what comes from myself, it shall scarce
    boot me
To say 'not guilty:' mine integrity
Being counted falsehood, shall, as I express
    it,
Be so received. But thus: if powers divine
Behold our human actions, as they do,   30
I doubt not then but innocence shall make
False accusation blush and tyranny
Tremble at patience. You, my lord, best
    know,
Who least will seem to do so, my past life
Hath been as continent, as chaste, as true,
As I am now unhappy; which is more

Than history can pattern, though devised
And play'd to take spectators. For behold
    me
A fellow of the royal bed, which owe
A moiety of the throne, a great king's
    daughter,   40
The mother to a hopeful prince, here standing
To prate and talk for life and honour 'fore
Who please to come and hear. For life, I
    prize it
As I weigh grief, which I would spare: for
    honour,
'Tis a derivative from me to mine,
And only that I stand for. I appeal
To your own conscience, sir, before Polixenes
Came to your court, how I was in your grace,
How merited to be so; since he came,
With what encounter so uncurrent I   50
Have strain'd to appear thus: if one jot
    beyond
The bond of honour, or in act or will
That way inclining, harden'd be the hearts
Of all that hear me, and my near'st of kin
Cry fie upon my grave!
    Leon.   I ne'er heard yet
That any of these bolder vices wanted
Less impudence to gainsay what they did
Than to perform it first.
    Her.   That's true enough;
Though 'tis a saying, sir, not due to me.
    Leon. You will not own it.
    Her.   †More than mistress of   60
Which comes to me in name of fault, I must
    not
At all acknowledge. For Polixenes,
With whom I am accused, I do confess
I loved him as in honour he required,
With such a kind of love as might become
A lady like me, with a love even such,
So and no other, as yourself commanded:
Which not to have done I think had been in
    me
Both disobedience and ingratitude
To you and toward your friend, whose love
    had spoke,   70
Even since it could speak, from an infant,
    freely
That it was yours. Now, for conspiracy,

---

1. **sessions**, sitting of a court of justice. **pronounce**,
declare. 7. **purgation**, clearing from the accusation.
18. **pretence**, purpose, design.

39. **owe**, own. 43–46. **For . . . for.** As for life, it
is only grief to me, and I would willingly dismiss it; as
for honor, it is transmitted by descent from me to mine,
and that only I maintain. 50–51. **With . . . thus**, (I
ask) by what behavior so improper I have exceeded
bounds so that I appear thus (in disgrace). 56. **wanted**,
lacked. 59. **due**, applicable. 60–62. **More . . . acknowledge**, I will not acknowledge that I am answerable
for more than what may be called faults; i.e., she is not
guilty of the *bolder vices* of line 56.

I know not how it tastes; though it be dish'd
For me to try how: all I know of it
Is that Camillo was an honest man;
And why he left your court, the gods them-
selves,
Wotting no more than I, are ignorant.

Leon. You knew of his departure, as you
know
What you have underta'en to do in 's absence.

Her. Sir,   80
You speak a language that I understand not:
My life stands in the level of your dreams,
Which I'll lay down.

Leon.   Your actions are my dreams;
You had a bastard by Polixenes,
And I but dream'd it. As you were past all
shame,—
Those of your fact are so—so past all truth:
Which to deny concerns more than avails;
for as
Thy brat hath been cast out, like to itself,
No father owning it,—which is, indeed,
More criminal in thee than it,—so thou   90
Shalt feel our justice, in whose easiest pas-
sage
Look for no less than death.

Her.   Sir, spare your threats:
The bug which you would fright me with I
seek.
To me can life be no commodity:
The crown and comfort of my life, your
favour,
I do give lost; for I do feel it gone,
But know not how it went. My second joy
And first-fruits of my body, from his presence
I am barr'd, like one infectious. My third
comfort,
Starr'd most unluckily, is from my breast, 100
The innocent milk in it most innocent mouth,
Haled out to murder: myself on every post
Proclaim'd a strumpet: with immodest ha-
tred
The child-bed privilege denied, which 'longs
To women of all fashion; lastly, hurried
Here to this place, i' the open air, before
I have got strength of limit. Now, my liege,
Tell me what blessings I have here alive,
That I should fear to die? Therefore pro-
ceed.

82. **in . . . dreams**, at the mercy of your hallucina-
tions. 86. **fact**, evil deed, crime. 87. **Which . . .
avails**, to deny this is more trouble than it is worth.
88. **like to itself**, as it ought to be (Furness); *left* has
been suggested as an emendation of *like*. 93. **bug**,
bogey, imaginary object of terror. 94. **commodity**,
convenience. 100. **Starr'd**, fated. 101. **it**, its. 103.
immodest, immoderate. 105. **fashion**, kinds, sorts.
107. **strength of limit**, limited strength.

But yet hear this; mistake me not; no life, 110
I prize it not a straw, but for mine hon-
our,
Which I would free, if I shall be condemn'd
Upon surmises, all proofs sleeping else
But what your jealousies awake, I tell you
'Tis rigour and not law. Your honours all,
I do refer me to the oracle:
Apollo be my judge!

First Lord.   This your request
Is altogether just: therefore bring forth,
And in Apollo's name, his oracle.

> [*Exeunt certain Officers.*

Her. The Emperor of Russia was my
father: 120
O that he were alive, and here beholding
His daughter's trial! that he did but see
The flatness of my misery, yet with eyes
Of pity, not revenge!

Re-enter Officers, *with* Cleomenes *and* Dion.

Off. You here shall swear upon this sword
of justice,
That you, Cleomenes and Dion, have
Been both at Delphos, and from thence have
brought
This seal'd-up oracle, by the hand deliver'd
Of great Apollo's priest and that since then
You have not dared to break the holy seal 130
Nor read the secrets in 't.

Cleo. Dion.   All this we swear.

Leon. Break up the seals and read.

Off. [*Reads*] Hermione is chaste; Polixenes
blameless; Camillo a true subject; Leontes a
jealous tyrant; his innocent babe truly be-
gotten; and the king shall live without an
heir, if that which is lost be not found.

Lords. Now blessed be the great Apollo!

Her.   Praised!

Leon. Hast thou read truth?

Off.   Ay, my lord; even so
As it is here set down.   140

Leon. There is no truth at all i' the oracle:
The sessions shall proceed: this is mere falsehood.

Enter Servant.

Serv. My lord the king, the king!

Leon.   What is the business?

Serv. O sir, I shall be hated to report it!

110. **no life**, i.e., I do not ask for life. 115. **rigour**,
tyranny, injustice. 120. **Emperor of Russia**. In
Pandosto it is the wife of Egistus (Polixenes) who is
daughter of the Emperor of Russia. 123. **flatness**,
absoluteness.

The prince your son, with mere conceit and
    fear
Of the queen's speed, is gone.
  Leon.   How! gone!
  Serv.   Is dead.
  Leon. Apollo's angry; and the heavens
    themselves
Do strike at my injustice. [*Hermione swoons.*]
    How now there!
  Paul. This news is mortal to the queen:
    look down
And see what death is doing.
  Leon.   Take her hence: 150
Her heart is but o'ercharged; she will re-
    cover:
I have too much believed mine own suspi-
    cion:
Beseech you, tenderly apply to her
Some remedies for life.
[*Exeunt Paulina and Ladies, with Hermione.*
                        Apollo, pardon
My great profaneness 'gainst thine oracle!
I'll reconcile me to Polixenes,
New woo my queen, recall the good Camillo,
Whom I proclaim a man of truth, of mercy;
For, being transported by my jealousies
To bloody thoughts and to revenge, I chose
Camillo for the minister to poison   161
My friend Polixenes: which had been done,
But that the good mind of Camillo tardied
My swift command, though I with death
    and with
Reward did threaten and encourage him,
Not doing't and being done: he, most hu-
    mane
And fill'd with honour, to my kingly guest
Unclasp'd my practice, quit his fortunes here,
Which you knew great, and to the hazard
Of all incertainties himself commended,   170
No richer than his honour: how he glisters
Thorough my rust! and how his piety
Does my deeds make the blacker!

Re-enter PAULINA

  Paul.   Woe the while!
O, cut my lace, lest my heart, cracking it,
Break too!

  First Lord.   What fit is this, good lady?
  Paul. What studied torments, tyrant, hast
    for me?
What wheels? racks? fires? what flaying?
    boiling?
In leads or oils? what old or newer torture
Must I receive, whose every word deserves
To taste of thy most worst? Thy tyranny 180
Together working with thy jealousies,
Fancies too weak for boys, too green and
    idle
For girls of nine, O, think what they have
    done
And then run mad indeed, stark mad! for
    all
Thy by-gone fooleries were but spices of
    it.
That thou betray'dst Polixenes, 'twas noth-
    ing;
That did but show thee, of a fool, inconstant
And damnable ingrateful: nor was't much,
That wouldst have poison'd good Camillo's
    honour,
To have him kill a king; poor trespasses, 190
More monstrous standing by: whereof I
    reckon
The casting forth to crows thy baby-daughter
To be or none or little; though a devil
Would have shed water out of fire ere done't:
Nor is't directly laid to thee, the death
Of the young prince, whose honourable
    thoughts,
Thoughts high for one so tender, cleft the
    heart
That could conceive a gross and foolish sire
Blemish'd his gracious dam: this is not, no,
Laid to thy answer: but the last,—O lords, 200
When I have said, cry 'woe!'—the queen, the
    queen,
The sweet'st, dear'st creature's dead, and
    vengeance for't
Not dropp'd down yet.
  First Lord.   The higher powers forbid!
  Paul. I say she's dead; I'll swear 't. If
    word nor oath
Prevail not, go and see: if you can bring
Tincture or lustre in her lip, her eye,
Heat outwardly or breath within, I'll serve
    you
As I would do the gods. But, O thou tyrant!
Do not repent these things, for they are
    heavier

---

145. **conceit**, imagination, deep thinking. 146.
speed, fortune, what might happen. 154. **Apollo,
pardon**. The suddenness of Leontes's conversion is
characteristic of Shakespeare's treatment of conscience,
and connects itself with the current psychological theory
of the sudden predominance of one emotion. 163.
tardied, delayed in executing. 166. **Not . . . done**,
i.e., reward if he did it, and death if he did not. 168.
Unclasp'd my practice, disclosed my conspiracy.
171. **No richer than**, with no riches except.

185. **spices**, foretastes, samples. 187. **of**, for.

Than all thy woes can stir: therefore betake
   thee   210
To nothing but despair. A thousand knees
Ten thousand years together, naked, fast-
   ing,
Upon a barren mountain, and still winter
In storm perpetual, could not move the
   gods
To look that way thou wert.
   Leon.   Go on, go on:
Thou canst not speak too much; I have de-
   served
All tongues to talk their bitterest.
   First Lord.   Say no more:
Howe'er the business goes, you have made
   fault
I' the boldness of your speech.
   Paul.   I am sorry for 't:
All faults I make, when I shall come to know
   them,   220
I do repent. Alas! I have show'd too much
The rashness of a woman: he is touch'd
To the noble heart. What's gone and what's
   past help
Should be past grief: do not receive afflic-
   tion
At my petition; I beseech you, rather
Let me be punish'd, that have minded you
Of what you should forget. Now, good my
   liege,
Sir, royal sir, forgive a foolish woman:
The love I bore your queen—lo, fool again!—
I'll speak of her no more, nor of your chil-
   dren;
I'll not remember you of my own lord,   231
Who is lost too: take your patience to you,
And I'll say nothing.
   Leon.   Thou didst speak but well
When most the truth; which I receive much
   better
Than to be pitied of thee. Prithee, bring
   me
To the dead bodies of my queen and son:
One grave shall be for both: upon them
   shall
The causes of their death appear, unto
Our shame perpetual. Once a day I'll
   visit
The chapel where they lie, and tears shed
   there   240
Shall be my recreation: so long as nature
Will bear up with this exercise, so long

I daily vow to use it. Come and lead me
Unto these sorrows.   [*Exeunt.*

SCENE III. *Bohemia. A desert country near
the sea.*

Enter ANTIGONUS *with a Child, and a*
Mariner.

   Ant. Thou art perfect then, our ship hath
   touch'd upon
The deserts of Bohemia?
   Mar.   Ay, my lord; and fear
We have landed in ill time: the skies look
   grimly
And threaten present blusters. In my con-
   science,
The heavens with that we have in hand are
   angry
And frown upon 's.
   Ant. Their sacred wills be done! Go, get
   aboard;
Look to thy bark: I'll not be long before
I call upon thee.
   Mar. Make your best haste, and go not 10
Too far i' the land: 'tis like to be loud
   weather;
Besides, this place is famous for the creatures
Of prey that keep upon 't.
   Ant.   Go thou away:
I'll follow instantly.
   Mar.   I am glad at heart
To be so rid o' the business.   [*Exit.*
   Ant.   Come, poor babe:
I have heard, but not believed, the spirits o'
   the dead
May walk again: if such thing be, thy
   mother
Appear'd to me last night, for ne'er was
   dream
So like a waking. To me comes a creature,
Sometimes her head on one side, some
   another;
I never saw a vessel of like sorrow,   21
So fill'd and so becoming: in pure white
   robes,
Like very sanctity, she did approach
My cabin where I lay; thrice bow'd before
   me,

Scene iii. **1. perfect**, certain. **2. deserts of Bohemia.** Shakespeare's famous blunder is really a
blunder in his source, which he merely repeats. **21.
vessel**, creature. **22. becoming**, apparently, imbued
with grace and fitness. The association of the word
with *fill'd* has caused Moorman to suspect that we have
here a typographical error for *beteeming*, meaning "overflowing."

225. my petition. She has bid him, in lines 210-211,
betake himself to despair. **231. remember**, remind.

And gasping to begin some speech, her eyes
Became two spouts: the fury spent, anon
Did this break from her: 'Good Antigonus,
Since fate, against thy better disposition,
Hath made thy person for the thrower-out
Of my poor babe, according to thine oath,   30
Places remote enough are in Bohemia,
There weep and leave it crying; and, for the babe
Is counted lost for ever, Perdita,
I prithee, call 't. For this ungentle business,
Put on thee by my lord, thou ne'er shalt see
Thy wife Paulina more.' And so, with shrieks,
She melted into air. Affrighted much,
I did in time collect myself and thought
This was so and no slumber. Dreams are toys:
Yet for this once, yea, superstitiously,   40
I will be squared by this. I do believe
Hermione hath suffer'd death, and that
Apollo would, this being indeed the issue
Of King Polixenes, it should here be laid,
Either for life or death, upon the earth
Of its right father. Blossom, speed thee well!
There lie, and there thy character: there these;
Which may, if fortune please, both breed thee, pretty,
And still rest thine. The storm begins: poor wretch,   49
That for thy mother's fault art thus exposed
To loss and what may follow! Weep I cannot,
But my heart bleeds; and most accursed am I
To be by oath enjoin'd to this. Farewell!
The day frowns more and more: thou'rt like to have
A lullaby too rough: I never saw
The heavens so dim by day. A savage clamour!   56
Well may I get aboard! This is the chase:
I am gone for ever. [*Exit, pursued by a bear.*

Enter a Shepherd.

Shep. I would there were no age between sixteen and three-and-twenty, or that youth would sleep out the rest; for there is nothing in the between but getting wenches with child, wronging the ancientry, stealing, fighting—Hark you now! Would any but these boiled brains of nineteen and two-and-twenty hunt this weather? They have scared away two of my best sheep, which I fear the wolf will sooner find than the master: if any where I have them, 'tis by the seaside, browsing of ivy. Good luck, an 't be thy will! what have we here? Mercy on 's, a barne; a very pretty barne! A boy or a child, I   71 wonder? A pretty one; a very pretty one: sure, some 'scape: though I am not bookish, yet I can read waiting-gentlewoman in the 'scape. This has been some stair-work, some trunk-work, some behind-door-work: they were warmer that got this than the poor thing is here. I'll take it up for pity: yet I'll tarry till my son come; he hallooed but even now. Whoa, ho, hoa!

Enter Clown.

Clo. Hilloa, loa!   80
Shep. What, art so near? If thou'lt see a thing to talk on when thou art dead and rotten, come hither. What ailest thou, man?
Clo. I have seen two such sights, by sea and by land! but I am not to say it is a sea, for it is now the sky: betwixt the firmament and it you cannot thrust a bodkin's point.
Shep. Why, boy, how is it?   88
Clo. I would you did but see how it chafes, how it rages, how it takes up the shore! but that's not to the point. O, the most piteous cry of the poor souls! sometimes to see 'em, and not to see 'em; now the ship boring the moon with her main-mast, and anon swallowed with yest and froth, as you'ld thrust a cork into a hogshead. And then for the land-service, to see how the bear tore out his shoulder-bone; how he cried to me for help and said his name was Antigonus, a nobleman. But to make an end of the ship, to see how the sea flap-dragoned it: but, first, how the poor souls roared, and the sea mocked them; and how the poor gentleman roared and the bear mocked him, both roaring louder than the sea or weather.   104
Shep. Name of mercy, when was this, boy?
Clo. Now, now: I have not winked since I

41. **squared**, directed in my course.   47. **character**, written account, the same which subsequently served to identify Perdita. **there these.** The reference is to the ornaments found by the shepherd (ll. 120-126).   48. **breed**, keep, support. **pretty**, pretty one.   49. **rest**, remain, i.e., a residue remain.   57. **This . . . chase.** Antigonus here sees the pursuing bear.   63. **ancientry**, old people.

64. **boiled brains**, hot-headed youths.   69. **ivy.** *Pandosto* has this detail, stating that the shepherd sought his sheep browsing on sea ivy.   70. **barne**, child.   71. **child**, female infant.   73. **'scape**, escapade, especially a transgression of the laws of chastity.   90. **takes up**, swallows.   95. **yest**, foam.   97. **land-service**, military service; here, doings on land; used blunderingly.   100 **flap-dragoned**, swallowed as one would a flap-drago[n] i.e., a raisin or the like snatched up out of burning bra[n] in the game of snap-dragon.

saw these sights: the men are not yet cold under water, nor the bear half dined on the gentleman: he's at it now.

Shep. Would I had been by, to have helped the old man!   111

Clo. I would you had been by the ship side, to have helped her: there your charity would have lacked footing.

Shep. Heavy matters! heavy matters! but look thee here, boy. Now bless thyself: thou mettest with things dying, I with things new-born. Here's a sight for thee; look thee, a bearing-cloth for a squire's child! look thee here; take up, take up, boy; open 't. So, let's see: it was told me I should be rich by the fairies. This is some changeling: open 't. What's within, boy?   123

Clo. You're a made old man: if the sins of your youth are forgiven you, you're well to live. Gold! all gold!

Shep. This is fairy gold, boy, and 'twill prove so: up with 't, keep it close: home, home, the next way. We are lucky, boy; and to be so still requires nothing but secrecy. Let my sheep go: come, good boy, the next way home.   131

Clo. Go you the next way with your findings. I'll go see if the bear be gone from the gentleman and how much he hath eaten: they are never curst but when they are hungry: if there be any of him left, I'll bury it.

Shep. That's a good deed. If thou mayest discern by that which is left of him what he is, fetch me to the sight of him.

Clo. Marry, will I; and you shall help to put him i' the ground.   141

Shep. 'Tis a lucky day, boy, and we'll do good deeds on 't.   [*Exeunt.*

ACT IV. SCENE I.

Enter TIME, *the* Chorus.

Time. I, that please some, try all, both joy and terror

Of good and bad, that makes and unfolds error,

Now take upon me, in the name of Time,

To use my wings. Impute it not a crime

To me or my swift passage, that I slide

O'er sixteen years and leave the growth un-tried

Of that wide gap, since it is in my power

To o'erthrow law and in one self-born hour

To plant and o'erwhelm custom. Let me pass

The same I am, ere ancient'st order was   10

Or what is now received: I witness to

The times that brought them in; so shall I do

To the freshest things now reigning and make stale

The glistering of this present, as my tale

Now seems to it. Your patience this allowing,

I turn my glass and give my scene such growing

As you had slept between: Leontes leaving,

The effects of his fond jealousies so grieving

That he shuts up himself, imagine me,

Gentle spectators, that I now may be   20

In fair Bohemia; and remember well,

I mentioned a son o' the king's, which Florizel

I now name to you; and with speed so pace

To speak of Perdita, now grown in grace

Equal with wondering: what of her ensues

I list not prophesy; but let Time's news

Be known when 'tis brought forth. A shep-herd's daughter,

And what to her adheres, which follows after,

Is the argument of Time. Of this allow,

If ever you have spent time worse ere now;   30

If never, yet that Time himself doth say

He wishes earnestly you never may.   [*Exit.*

SCENE II. *Bohemia.   The palace of* POLIXENES.

Enter POLIXENES *and* CAMILLO.

Pol. I pray thee, good Camillo, be no more importunate: 'tis a sickness denying thee any thing; a death to grant this.

Cam. It is fifteen years since I saw my country: though I have for the most part been aired abroad, I desire to lay my bones there. Besides, the penitent king, my master, hath sent for me; to whose feeling sorrows I might be some allay, or I o'erween to think so, which is another spur to my departure.   10

Pol. As thou lovest me, Camillo, wipe not out the rest of thy services by leaving me

119. **bearing-cloth**, child's christening-robe. 125. **well to live**, well to do. 135. **curst**, savage, vicious.
Act IV. Scene i. Stage Direction: **Time, the Chorus.** Herford suggests that this device is borrowed from the title, *Pandosto, or the Triumph of Time.* It may be said, however, that the triumph of time is an expression of the unifying principle of the whole comedy. 2. **makes and unfolds**, make and unfold.

6. **growth untried**, progress unknown. 8. **self-born**, self-same. 14. **glistering**, glistening, freshness. *Scene ii.* 6. **been . . . abroad**, lived in foreign lands. 9. **allay**, means of abatement. **o'erween**, am presumptuous.

now: the need I have of thee thine own goodness hath made; better not to have had thee
than thus to want thee: thou, having made
me businesses which none without thee can
sufficiently manage, must either stay to execute them thyself or take away with thee the
very services thou hast done; which if I have
not enough considered, as too much I can- 20
not, to be more thankful to thee shall be my
study, and my profit therein the heaping
friendships. Of that fatal country, Sicilia,
prithee speak no more; whose very naming
punishes me with the remembrance of that
penitent, as thou callest him, and reconciled
king, my brother; whose loss of his most
precious queen and children are even now to
be afresh lamented. Say to me, when sawest
thou the Prince Florizel, my son? Kings are
no less unhappy, their issue not being gracious, than they are in losing them when they
have approved their virtues.   32

Cam. Sir, it is three days since I saw the
prince. What his happier affairs may be, are
to me unknown: but I have missingly noted,
he is of late much retired from court and is
less frequent to his princely exercises than
formerly he hath appeared.   38

Pol. I have considered so much, Camillo,
and with some care; so far that I have eyes
under my service which look upon his removedness; from whom I have this intelligence, that he is seldom from the house of a
most homely shepherd; a man, they say,
that from very nothing, and beyond the
imagination of his neighbours, is grown into
an unspeakable estate.

Cam. I have heard, sir, of such a man,
who hath a daughter of most rare note: the
report of her is extended more than can be
thought to begin from such a cottage.   50

Pol. That's likewise part of my intelligence; but, I fear, the angle that plucks our
son thither. Thou shalt accompany us to the
place; where we will, not appearing what we
are, have some question with the shepherd;
from whose simplicity I think it not uneasy
to get the cause of my son's resort thither.
Prithee, be my present partner in this business, and lay aside the thoughts of Sicilia.

Cam. I willingly obey your command. 60

Pol. My best Camillo! We must disguise
ourselves.   [*Exeunt.*

SCENE III. *A road near the* Shepherd's *cottage.*

Enter AUTOLYCUS, *singing.*

When daffodils begin to peer,
  With heigh! the doxy over the dale,
Why, then comes in the sweet o' the year;
  For the red blood reigns in the winter's
    pale.

The white sheet bleaching on the hedge,
  With heigh! the sweet birds, O, how they
    sing!
Doth set my pugging tooth on edge;
  For a quart of ale is a dish for a king.

The lark, that tirra-lyra chants,
  With heigh! with heigh! the thrush and
    the jay,   10
Are summer songs for me and my aunts,
  While we lie tumbling in the hay.

I have served Prince Florizel and in my time
wore three-pile; but now I am out of service:

But shall I go mourn for that, my dear?
  The pale moon shines by night:
And when I wander here and there,
  I then do most go right.

If tinkers may have leave to live,
  And bear the sow-skin budget,   20
Then my account I well may give,
  And in the stocks avouch it.

My traffic is sheets; when the kite builds,
look to lesser linen. My father named me
Autolycus; who being, as I am, littered under
Mercury, was likewise a snapper-up of un-
considered trifles. With die and drab I purchased this caparison, and my revenue is the
silly cheat. Gallows and knock are too powerful on the highway: beating and hanging
are terrors to me: for the life to come, I
sleep out the thought of it. A prize! a prize! 32

Enter Clown.

Clo. Let me see: every 'leven wether tods;
every tod yields pound and odd shilling;
fifteen hundred shorn, what comes the wool
to?

---

2. **doxy**, beggar's mistress. 4. **pale**, defined as "paleness"; more probably, enclosure. 7. **pugging**, thievish.
14. **three-pile**, three-pile velvet, i.e., velvet having
very rich pile or nap. 20. **budget**, wallet. 23. **kite**.
The kite was supposed to carry off small pieces of linen
with which to construct its nest. 27-29. **With . . .
cheat**, with dice and women I got this outfit (his rags),
and the simple fool is the source of my revenue. *Cheat*
is also defined as "petty thieving." **knock**, possibly,
resistance. 33. **every . . . tods**, every eleven rams
yield a *tod*, i.e., a bulk of wool weighing twenty-eight
pounds.

---

22. **heaping**, heaping up of. 32. **approved**, proved.
35. **missingly**, regretfully or with a sense of loss. 40-41.
eyes . . . service, i.e., servants. 41. **removedness**, absence. 52. **angle**, fishing-hook.

Aut. [*Aside*] If the springe hold, the cock's mine.   37

Clo. I cannot do't without counters. Let me see; what am I to buy for our sheepshearing feast? Three pound of sugar, five pound of currants, rice,—what will this sister of mine do with rice? But my father hath made her mistress of the feast, and she lays it on. She hath made me four and twenty 43 nosegays for the shearers, three-man-songmen all, and very good ones; but they are most of them means and bases; but one puritan amongst them, and he sings psalms to hornpipes. I must have saffron to colour the warden pies; mace; dates?—none, that's out of my note; nutmegs, seven; a race or two of ginger, but that I may beg; four pound of prunes, and as many of raisins o' the sun. 52

Aut. O that ever I was born!

[*Grovelling on the ground.*

Clo. I' the name of me—

Aut. O, help me, help me! pluck but off these rags; and then, death, death!

Clo. Alack, poor soul! thou hast need of more rags to lay on thee, rather than have these off.

Aut. O sir, the loathsomeness of them offends me more than the stripes I have received, which are mighty ones and millions.61

Clo. Alas, poor man! a million of beating may come to a great matter.

Aut. I am robbed, sir, and beaten; my money and apparel ta'en from me, and these detestable things put upon me.

Clo. What, by a horseman, or a footman?

Aut. A footman, sweet sir, a footman. 68

Clo. Indeed, he should be a footman by the garments he has left with thee: if this be a horseman's coat, it hath seen very hot service. Lend me thy hand, I'll help thee: come, lend me thy hand.

Aut. O, good sir, tenderly, O!

Clo. Alas, poor soul!

Aut. O, good sir, softly, good sir! I fear, sir, my shoulder-blade is out.

Clo. How now! canst stand?

Aut. [*Picking his pocket*] Softly, dear sir;

good sir, softly. You ha' done me a charitable office.   81

Clo. Dost lack any money? I have a little money for thee.

Aut. No, good sweet sir; no, I beseech you, sir: I have a kinsman not past three quarters of a mile hence, unto whom I was going; I shall there have money, or any thing I want: offer me no money, I pray you; that kills my heart.

Clo. What manner of fellow was he that robbed you?   90

Aut. A fellow, sir, that I have known to go about with troll-my-dames: I knew him once a servant of the prince: I cannot tell, good sir, for which of his virtues it was, but he was certainly whipped out of the court.

Clo. His vices, you would say; there's no virtue whipped out of the court: they cherish it to make it stay there; and yet it will no more but abide.   99

Aut. Vices, I would say, sir. I know this man well: he hath been since an ape-bearer; then a process-server, a bailiff; then he compassed a motion of the Prodigal Son, and married a tinker's wife within a mile where my land and living lies; and, having flown over many knavish professions, he settled only in rogue: some call him Autolycus.

Clo. Out upon him! prig, for my life, prig: he haunts wakes, fairs and bear-baitings.

Aut. Very true, sir; he, sir, he; that's the rogue that put me into this apparel.   111

Clo. Not a more cowardly rogue in all Bohemia: if you had but looked big and spit at him, he'ld have run.

Aut. I must confess to you, sir, I am no fighter: I am false of heart that way; and that he knew, I warrant him.

Clo. How do you now?

Aut. Sweet sir, much better than I was; I can stand and walk: I will even take my leave of you, and pace softly towards my kinsman's.

Clo. Shall I bring thee on the way? 122

Aut. No, good-faced sir; no, sweet sir.

Clo. Then fare thee well: I must go buy spices for our sheep-shearing.

Aut. Prosper you, sweet sir! [*Exit Clown.*] Your purse is not hot enough to purchase

---

36. **springe**, snare. **cock's**, woodcock's. The woodcock was proverbially stupid. 38. **counters**, token coins used in reckoning. 44. **three-man-song-men**, singers of catches or rounds. 46. **means**, tenors. 47. **psalms to hornpipes**, psalms to merry tunes. 49. **warden**, made of the warden pear. 50. **note**. apparently, list; yet if the clown could not read, it would mean "observation" or "memory." **race**, root. 52. **o' the sun**, dried in the sun. 54. **me—**, possibly the beginning of *mercy*.

92. **troll-my-dames**, a game in which the object was to "troll" balls through arches set on a board. 99. **abide**, probably, make a temporary stay. 101. **ape-bearer**, one who carries a monkey about for exhibition. 102-103. **compassed a motion**, got possession of a puppet-show. 108. **prig**, thief.

your spice. I'll be with you at your sheep-shearing too: if I make not this cheat bring out another and the shearers prove sheep, let me be unrolled and my name put in the book of virtue! 131

[*Sings*] Jog on, jog on, the foot-path way,
　　　And merrily hent the stile-a:
　　　A merry heart goes all the day,
　　　Your sad tires in a mile-a. [*Exit*.

SCENE IV. *The* Shepherd's *cottage*.

Enter FLORIZEL *and* PERDITA.

Flo. These your unusual weeds to each part of you
Do give a life: no shepherdess, but Flora
Peering in April's front. This your sheep-shearing
Is as a meeting of the petty gods,
And you the queen on 't.
Per.　　　　Sir, my gracious lord,
To chide at your extremes it not becomes me:
O, pardon, that I name them! Your high self,
The gracious mark o' the land, you have ob-scured
With a swain's wearing, and me, poor lowly maid,
Most goddess-like prank'd up: but that our feasts 10
In every mess have folly and the feeders
Digest it with a custom, I should blush
To see you so attired, sworn, I think,
To show myself a glass.
Flo.　　　　I bless the time
When my good falcon made her flight across
Thy father's ground.
Per.　　　　Now Jove afford you cause!
To me the difference forges dread; your greatness
Hath not been used to fear. Even now I tremble
To think your father, by some accident,
Should pass this way as you did: O, the Fates!
How would he look, to see his work so noble 21

128. **cheat**, swindle, fraud. 130. **unrolled**, taken off the roll (of rogues and vagabonds). 132. **Jog on**, written to a popular tune of the day. 133. **hent**, take. *Scene iv.* 1. **weeds**, clothes. 6. **extremes**, extravagant statements. 8. **mark**, example, pattern. 12. **with a custom**, from habit. 13. **sworn**, as though you were sworn. 14. **To . . . glass**, to show me myself as in a mirror. 17. **difference**, of rank.

Vilely bound up? What would he say? Or how
Should I, in these my borrow'd flaunts, be-hold
The sternness of his presence?
Flo.　　　　Apprehend
Nothing but jollity. The gods themselves,
Humbling their deities to love, have taken
The shapes of beasts upon them: Jupiter
Became a bull, and bellow'd; the green Nep-tune
A ram, and bleated; and the fire-robed god,
Golden Apollo, a poor humble swain, 30
As I seem now. Their transformations
Were never for a piece of beauty rarer,
Nor in a way so chaste, since my desires
Run not before mine honour, nor my lusts
Burn hotter than my faith.
Per.　　　　O, but, sir,
Your resolution cannot hold, when 'tis
Opposed, as it must be, by the power of the king:
One of these two must be necessities,
Which then will speak, that you must change this purpose,
Or I my life.
Flo.　　　　Thou dearest Perdita, 40
With these forced thoughts, I prithee, darken not
The mirth o' the feast. Or I'll be thine, my fair,
Or not my father's. For I cannot be
Mine own, not any thing to any, if
I be not thine. To this I am most constant,
Though destiny say no. Be merry, gentle;
Strangle such thoughts as these with any thing
That you behold the while. Your guests are coming:
Lift up your countenance, as it were the day
Of celebration of that nuptial which 50
We two have sworn shall come.
Per.　　　　O lady Fortune,
Stand you auspicious!
Flo.　　　　See, your guests approach:
Address yourself to entertain them sprightly,
And let's be red with mirth.

Enter Shepherd, Clown, MOPSA; DORCAS, *and others, with* POLIXENES *and* CAMILLO *disguised*.

Shep. Fie, daughter! when my old wife lived, upon

22. **bound up**, like a book. 23. **flaunts**, finery. 41. **forced**, far-fetched, unnatural.

This day she was both pantler, butler, cook,
Both dame and servant; welcomed all,
    served all;
Would sing her song and dance her turn;
    now here,
At upper end o' the table, now i' the middle;
On his shoulder, and his; her face o' fire   60
With labour and the thing she took to quench
    it,
She would to each one sip. You are retired,
As if you were a feasted one and not
The hostess of the meeting: pray you, bid
These unknown friends to 's welcome; for it is
A way to make us better friends, more
    known.
Come, quench your blushes and present
    yourself
That which you are, mistress o' the feast:
    come on,
And bid us welcome to your sheep-shearing,
As your good flock shall prosper.
    Per.   [*To Pol.*] Sir, welcome: 70
It is my father's will I should take on me
The hostess-ship o' the day. [*To Cam.*] You're
    welcome, sir.
Give me those flowers there, Dorcas. Rever-
    end sirs,
For you there's rosemary and rue; these keep
Seeming and savour all the winter long:
Grace and remembrance be to you both,
And welcome to our shearing!
    Pol.   Shepherdess,—
A fair one are you—well you fit our ages
With flowers of winter.
    Per.   Sir, the year growing ancient,
Not yet on summer's death, nor on the
    birth   80
Of trembling winter, the fairest flowers o' the
    season
Are our carnations and streak'd gillyvors,
Which some call nature's bastards: of that
    kind
Our rustic garden's barren; and I care not
To get the slips of them.
    Pol.   Wherefore, gentle maiden,
Do you neglect them?
    Per.   For I have heard it said
There is an art which in their piedness
    shares
With great creating nature.
    Pol.   Say there be;

Yet nature is made better by no mean
But nature makes that mean: so, over that
    art
Which you say adds to nature, is an art   91
That nature makes. You see, sweet maid, we
    marry
A gentler scion to the wildest stock,
And make conceive a bark of baser kind
By bud of nobler race: this is an art
Which does mend nature, change it rather,
    but
The art itself is nature.
    Per.   So it is.
    Pol. Then make your garden rich in gilly-
    vors,
And do not call them bastards.
    Per.   I'll not put
The dibble in earth to set one slip of them; 100
No more than were I painted I would wish
This youth should say 'twere well and only
    therefore
Desire to breed by me. Here's flowers for
    you;
Hot lavender, mints, savory, marjoram;
The marigold, that goes to bed wi' the sun
And with him rises weeping: these are flowers
Of middle summer, and I think they are
    given
To men of middle age. You're very wel-
    come.
    Cam. I should leave grazing, were I of
    your flock,
And only live by gazing.
    Per.   Out, alas!   110
You'ld be so lean, that blasts of January
Would blow you through and through. Now,
    my fair'st friend,
I would I had some flowers o' the spring that
    might
Become your time of day; and yours, and
    yours,
That wear upon your virgin branches yet
Your maidenheads growing: O Proserpina,
For the flowers now, that frighted thou
    let'st fall
From Dis's waggon! daffodils,
That come before the swallow dares, and
    take
The winds of March with beauty; violets
    dim,

---

56. **pantler**, servant in charge of the pantry. 65.
to's, of ours. 75. **Seeming**, outward form. 82. **gillyvors**, gillyflower—a kind of carnation. 83. **nature's
bastards.** As indicated in lines 86-88, they are a result
of artificial breeding.

89. **mean**, means. 92-97. **You see . . . nature**,
ironical allusion to the union of the prince with the shepherdess. 104. **Hot**, eager, ardent; here, aromatic. 116.
Proserpina, stolen away by Pluto when, according to
Ovid, she was gathering flowers in her garden. 118.
Dis's waggon, Pluto's chariot. 119. **take**, bewitch,
fascinate.

But sweeter than the lids of Juno's eyes 121
Or Cytherea's breath; pale primroses,
That die unmarried, ere they can behold
Bright Phœbus in his strength—a malady
Most incident to maids; bold oxlips and
The crown imperial; lilies of all kinds,
The flower-de-luce being one! O, these I lack,
To make you garlands of, and my sweet
    friend,
To strew him o'er and o'er!
   Flo.   What, like a corse?
   Per. No, like a bank for love to lie and
    play on;   130
Not like a corse; or if, not to be buried,
But quick and in mine arms. Come, take
    your flowers:
Methinks I play as I have seen them do
In Whitsun pastorals: sure this robe of mine
Does change my disposition.
   Flo.   What you do
Still betters what is done. When you speak,
    sweet,
I'ld have you do it ever: when you sing,
I'ld have you buy and sell so, so give alms,
Pray so; and, for the ordering your affairs,
To sing them too: when you do dance, I wish
    you   140
A wave o' the sea, that you might ever do
Nothing but that; move still, still so,
And own no other function: each your doing,
So singular in each particular,
Crowns what you are doing in the present
    deed,
That all your acts are queens.
   Per.   O Doricles,
Your praises are too large: but that your
    youth,
And the true blood which peepeth fairly
    through 't,
Do plainly give you out an unstain'd shep-
    herd,
With wisdom I might fear, my Doricles, 150
You woo'd me the false way.
   Flo.   I think you have
As little skill to fear as I have purpose
To put you to 't. But come; our dance, I
    pray:

Your hand, my Perdita: so turtles pair,
That never mean to part.
   Per.   I'll swear for 'em.
   Pol. This is the prettiest low-born lass
    that ever
Ran on the green-sward: nothing she does or
    seems
But smacks of something greater than her-
    self,
Too noble for this place.
   Cam.   He tells her something
That makes her blood look out: good sooth,
    she is   160
The queen of curds and cream.
   Clo.   Come on, strike up!
   Dor. Mopsa must be your mistress:
    marry, garlic,
To mend her kissing with!
   Mop.   Now, in good time!
   Clo. Not a word, a word; we stand upon
    our manners.
Come, strike up!
   [*Music. Here a dance of Shepherds and*
                           Shepherdesses.
   Pol. Pray, good shepherd, what fair
    swain is this
Which dances with your daughter?
   Shep. They call him Doricles; and boasts
    himself
To have a worthy feeding: but I have it
Upon his own report and I believe it;   170
He looks like sooth. He says he loves my
    daughter:
I think so too; for never gazed the moon
Upon the water as he'll stand and read
As 'twere my daughter's eyes: and, to be
    plain,
I think there is not half a kiss to choose
Who loves another best.
   Pol.   She dances featly.
   Shep. So she does any thing; though I re-
    port it,
That should be silent: if young Doricles
Do light upon her, she shall bring him that
Which he not dreams of.   180

Enter Servant.

   Serv. O master, if you did but hear the
pedlar at the door, you would never dance
again after a tabor and pipe; no, the bagpipe
could not move you: he sings several tunes
faster than you'll tell money; he utters them

---

122. **Cytherea's**, Venus's. 123. **unmarried**, allusion
not understood. Cf. Milton's *Lycidas:* "The rathe
primrose that forsaken dies." 126. **crown imperial**,
handsome fritillary, a flower from the Levant, cultivated
in English gardens. 127. **flower-de-luce**, fleur-de-lis.
132. **quick**, alive. 134. **Whitsun pastorals**, thought
to allude to English morris dances often performed at
Whitsuntide; so also were the mystery plays. 143. **each
your doing**, each thing you do. 145. **what . . . deed**,
what you are at present doing. 152. **skill**, reason,
cause.

154. **turtles**, turtle-doves, as symbols of faithful love.
169. **feeding**, pasturage. 171. **sooth**, truth. 176.
featly, gracefully.

as he had eaten ballads and all men's ears
grew to his tunes.   186

Clo. He could never come better; he shall
come in. I love a ballad but even too well, if
it be doleful matter merrily set down, or a
very pleasant thing indeed and sung lamentably.   190

Ser. He hath songs for man or woman, of
all sizes; no milliner can so fit his customers
with gloves: he has the prettiest love-songs
for maids; so without bawdry, which is
strange; with such delicate burthens of dildos
and fadings, 'jump her and thump her;' and
where some stretch-mouthed rascal would, as
it were, mean mischief and break a foul gap
into the matter, he makes the maid to
answer 'Whoop, do me no harm, good man;'
puts him off, slights him, with 'Whoop, do
me no harm, good man.'   201

Pol. This is a brave fellow.

Clo. Believe me, thou talkest of an admirable conceited fellow. Has he any unbraided
wares?   204

Serv. He hath ribbons of all the colours i'
the rainbow; points more than all the lawyers in Bohemia can learnedly handle, though
they come to him by the gross: inkles, caddisses, cambrics, lawns: why, he sings 'em
over as they were gods or goddesses; you
would think a smock were a she-angel, he so
chants to the sleeve-hand and the work
about the square on 't.   212

Clo. Prithee bring him in; and let him
approach singing.

Per. Forewarn him that he use no scurrilous words in 's tunes.   [*Exit Servant.*

Clo. You have of these pedlars, that have
more in them than you 'ld think, sister.

Per. Ay, good brother, or go about to
think.

Enter Autolycus, *singing.*

Lawn as white as driven snow;   220
Cyprus black as e'er was crow;
Gloves as sweet as damask roses;
Masks for faces and for noses;

Bugle bracelet, necklace amber,
Perfume for a lady's chamber;
Golden quoifs and stomachers,
For my lads to give their dears:
Pins and poking-sticks of steel,
What maids lack from head to heel:
Come buy of me, come; come buy, come
buy;
Buy, lads, or else you lasses cry: 231
Come buy.

Clo. If I were not in love with Mopsa,
thou shouldst take no money of me; but being enthralled as I am, it will also be the
bondage of certain ribbons and gloves.

Mop. I was promised them against the
feast; but they come not too late now.

Dor. He hath promised you more than
that, or there be liars.   240

Mop. He hath paid you all he promised
you: may be, he has paid you more, which
will shame you to give him again.

Clo. Is there no manners left among
maids? will they wear their plackets where
they should bear their faces? Is there not
milking-time, when you are going to bed, or
kiln-hole, to whistle off these secrets, but you
must be tittle-tattling before all our guests?
'tis well they are whispering: clamour your
tongues, and not a word more.   251

Mop. I have done. Come, you promised
me a tawdry-lace and a pair of sweet gloves.

Clo. Have I not told thee how I was cozened by the way and lost all my money?

Aut. And indeed, sir, there are cozeners
abroad; therefore it behoves men to be wary.

Clo. Fear not thou, man, thou shalt lose
nothing here.

Aut. I hope so, sir; for I have about me
many parcels of charge.   261

Clo. What hast here? ballads?

Mop. Pray now, buy some: I love a ballad in print o' life, for then we are sure they
are true.

Aut. Here's one to a very doleful tune,
how a usurer's wife was brought to bed of
twenty money-bags at a burthen and how
she longed to eat adders' heads and toads
carbonadoed.   268

---

187. **better**, at a better time. 192. **milliner**, dealer
in goods from Milan; here, a dealer in women's wear.
195. **burthens**, under-songs; here, the bass of refrains.
dildos and fadings, words used as part of the refrains
of ballads. 198. **gap**, a gross parenthesis (Staunton).
203. **admirable conceited**, admirably ingenious. 204.
unbraided, unfaded. 206. **points**, laces for fastening
clothes; also, headings in an argument. 208. **inkles**,
kind of tape. **caddisses**, worsted tapes used for garters.
212. **sleeve-hand**, wrist-band. **square**, the embroidered bosom of a garment. 217. **of these pedlars**, a
sort of partitive genitive case after *have.* 221. **Cyprus**,
crêpe.

224. **Bugle bracelet**, bracelet of black gloss beads.
226. **quoifs**, close-fitting caps. 228. **poking-sticks**,
rods used for stiffening the plaits of ruffs. 248. **kiln-
hole**, fire-hole in a kiln used in making malt; evidently a
customary gossiping-place. 250. **clamour**, silence. 253.
tawdry-lace, cheap and showy lace, or neckerchief,
much worn by women in Shakespeare's time; so called
from St. Audrey's fair or because St. Audrey suffered a
tumor in the throat from wearing rich necklaces. **sweet**,
with perfume. 261. **parcels of charge**, valuable parcels. 268. **carbonadoed**, scored across and grilled.

Mop. Is it true, think you?

Aut. Very true, and but a month old. 270

Dor. Bless me from marrying a usurer!

Aut. Here's the midwife's name to 't, one Mistress Tale-porter, and five or six honest wives that were present. Why should I carry lies abroad?

Mop. Pray you now, buy it.

Clo. Come on, lay it by: and let's first see moe ballads; we'll buy the other things anon.

Aut. Here's another ballad of a fish, that appeared upon the coast on Wednesday the fourscore of April, forty thousand fathom above water, and sung this ballad against the hard hearts of maids: it was thought she was a woman and was turned into a cold fish for she would not exchange flesh with one that loved her: the ballad is very pitiful and as true.

Dor. Is it true too, think you?

Aut. Five justices' hands at it, and witnesses more than my pack will hold.

Clo. Lay it by too: another. 290

Aut. This is a merry ballad, but a very pretty one.

Mop. Let's have some merry ones.

Aut. Why, this is a passing merry one and goes to the tune of 'Two maids wooing a man:' there's scarce a maid westward but she sings it; 'tis in request, I can tell you.

Mop. We can both sing it: if thou'lt bear a part, thou shalt hear; 'tis in three parts. 299

Dor. We had the tune on 't a month ago.

Aut. I can bear my part; you must know 'tis my occupation; have at it with you.

SONG.

A. Get you hence, for I must go
    Where it fits not you to know.

 D. Whither? *M.* O, whither? *D.* Whither?

M. It becomes thy oath full well,
    Thou to me thy secrets tell.

 D. Me too, let me go thither.

M. Or thou goest to the grange or mill.

D. If to either, thou dost ill. 310

A. Neither. *D.* What, neither? *A.*
    Neither.

D. Thou hast sworn my love to be.

M. Thou hast sworn it more to me:
    Then whither goest? say, whither?

Clo. We'll have this song out anon by our-

selves: my father and the gentlemen are in sad talk, and we'll not trouble them. Come, bring away thy pack after me. Wenches, I'll buy for you both. Pedlar, let's have the first choice. Follow me, girls. 320

    [*Exit with Dorcas and Mopsa.*

Aut. And you shall pay well for 'em.

       [*Follows singing.*

 Will you buy any tape,
  Or lace for your cape,
 My dainty duck, my dear-a?
  Any silk, any thread,
  And toys for your head,
 Of the new'st and finest, finest wear-a?
 Come to the pedlar;
 Money's a medler, 329
 That doth utter all men's ware-a. [*Exit.*

Re-enter Servant.

Serv. Master, there is three carters, three shepherds, three neat-herds, three swineherds, that have made themselves all men of hair, they call themselves Saltiers, and they have a dance which the wenches say is a gallimaufry of gambols, because they are not in 't; but they themselves are o' the mind, if it be not too rough for some that know little but bowling, it will please plentifully.

Shep. Away! we'll none on 't: here has been too much homely foolery already. I know, sir, we weary you. 342

Pol. You weary those that refresh us: pray, let's see these four threes of herdsmen.

Serv. One three of them, by their own report, sir, hath danced before the king; and not the worst of the three but jumps twelve foot and a half by the squier.

Shep. Leave your prating: since these good men are pleased, let them come in; but quickly now. 351

Serv. Why, they stay at door, sir. [*Exit.*

Here a dance of twelve Satyrs.

Pol. O, father, you'll know more of that hereafter.

---

317. **sad,** serious. 330. **utter,** put on the market. 333. **men of hair,** dressed in skins. 334. **Saltiers,** for *satyrs.* 336. **gallimaufry,** medley, jumble. 339. **bowling,** a game played mainly by the aristocracy, who might find the satyr dance too rough. 346. **danced before the king.** Professor Thorndike (*Influence of Beaumont and Fletcher on Shakespeare,* pp. 32–34) argues that this masque of satyrs was borrowed from Jonson's *Masque of Oberon,* acted at Court, January 1, 1611. This play would, then, be dated after that event. 348. **squier,** foot rule.

---

279. **ballad of a fish.** Such a ballad was actually entered in the Stationers' Register in 1604.

[*To Cam.*] Is it not too far gone? 'Tis time
   to part them.
He's simple and tells much. [*To Flor.*] How
   now, fair shepherd!
Your heart is full of something that does take
Your mind from feasting. Sooth, when I was
   young
And handed love as you do, I was wont
To load my she with knacks: I would have
   ransack'd
The pedlar's silken treasury and have pour'd
   it
To her acceptance; you have let him go 361
And nothing marted with him. If your lass
Interpretation should abuse and call this
Your lack of love or bounty, you were
   straited
For a reply, at least if you make a care
Of happy holding her.

Flo.   Old sir, I know
She prizes not such trifles as these are:
The gifts she looks from me are pack'd and
   lock'd
Up in my heart; which I have given already,
But not deliver'd. O, hear me breathe my
   life 370
Before this ancient sir, who, it should seem,
Hath sometime loved! I take thy hand, this
   hand,
As soft as dove's down and as white as it,
Or Ethiopian's tooth, or the fann'd snow
   that's bolted
By the northern blasts twice o'er.

Pol.   What follows this?
How prettily the young swain seems to wash
The hand was fair before! I have put you
   out:
But to your protestation; let me hear
What you profess.

Flo.   Do, and be witness to't. 379

Pol. And this my neighbour too?

Flo.   And he, and more
Than he, and men, the earth, the heavens,
   and all:
That, were I crown'd the most imperial
   monarch,
Thereof most worthy, were I the fairest
   youth
That ever made eye swerve, had force and
   knowledge

More than was ever man's, I would not prize
   them
Without her love; for her employ them all;
Commend them and condemn them to her
   service
Or to their own perdition.

Pol.   Fairly offer'd.

Cam. This shows a sound affection.

Shep.   But, my daughter,
Say you the like to him?

Per.   I cannot speak 390
So well, nothing so well; no, nor mean better:
By the pattern of mine own thoughts I cut
   out
The purity of his.

Shep.   Take hands, a bargain!
And, friends unknown, you shall bear wit-
   ness to't:
I give my daughter to him, and will make
Her portion equal his.

Flo.   O, that must be
I' the virtue of your daughter: one being
   dead,
I shall have more than you can dream of yet;
Enough then for your wonder. But, come
   on, 399
Contract us 'fore these witnesses.

Shep.   Come, your hand;
And, daughter, yours.

Pol.   Soft, swain, awhile, beseech you;
Have you a father?

Flo.   I have: but what of him?

Pol. Knows he of this?

Flo.   He neither does nor shall.

Pol. Methinks a father
Is at the nuptial of his son a guest
That best becomes the table. Pray you once
   more,
Is not your father grown incapable
Of reasonable affairs? is he not stupid
With age and altering rheums? can he speak?
   hear? 409
Know man from man? dispute his own
   estate?
Lies he not bed-rid? and again does nothing
But what he did being childish?

Flo.   No, good sir;
He has his health and ampler strength
   indeed
Than most have of his age.

Pol.   By my white beard,
You offer him, if this be so, a wrong

---

358. **handed,** handled. 359. **knacks,** knickknacks.
362. **marted,** trafficked. 363. **Interpretation should
abuse,** should interpret wrongly. 364. **straited,** em-
barrassed. 368. **looks,** expects. 374. **bolted,** sifted.

409. **altering rheums,** weakening colds.

Something unfilial: reason my son
Should choose himself a wife, but as good
    reason
The father, all whose joy is nothing else
But fair posterity, should hold some counsel
In such a business.

Flo.   I yield all this;   420
But for some other reasons, my grave sir,
Which 'tis not fit you know, I not acquaint
My father of this business.

Pol.   Let him know 't.

Flo. He shall not.

Pol.   Prithee, let him.

Flo.   No, he must not.

Shep. Let him, my son: he shall not need
    to grieve
At knowing of thy choice.

Flo.   Come, come, he must not.
Mark our contract.

Pol.   Mark your divorce, young sir,
                 [*Discovering himself.*
Whom son I dare not call; thou art too base
To be acknowledged: thou a sceptre's heir,
That thus affect'st a sheep-hook! Thou old
    traitor,   430
I am sorry that by hanging thee I can
But shorten thy life one week. And thou,
    fresh piece
Of excellent witchcraft, who of force must
    know
The royal fool thou copest with,—

Shep.   O, my heart!

Pol. I'll have thy beauty scratch'd with
    briers, and made
More homely than thy state. For thee, fond
    boy,
If I may ever know thou dost but sigh
That thou no more shalt see this knack, as
    never
I mean thou shalt, we'll bar thee from suc-
    cession;
Not hold thee of our blood, no, not our kin,
Far than Deucalion off: mark thou my
    words: 441
Follow us to the court. Thou churl, for this
    time,
Though full of our displeasure, yet we free
    thee
From the dead blow of it. And you, enchant-
    ment,—

Worthy enough a herdsman; yea, him too,
That makes himself, but for our honour
    therein,
Unworthy thee,—if ever henceforth thou
These rural latches to his entrance open,
Or hoop his body more with thy embraces,
I will devise a death as cruel for thee   450
As thou art tender to 't.   [*Exit.*

Per.   Even here undone!
I was not much afeard; for once or twice
I was about to speak and tell him plainly,
The selfsame sun that shines upon his court
Hides not his visage from our cottage but
Looks on alike. Will 't please you, sir, be
    gone?
I told you what would come of this: beseech
    you,
Of your own state take care: this dream of
    mine,—
Being now awake, I'll queen it no inch
    farther,   459
But milk my ewes and weep.

Cam.   Why, how now, father!
Speak ere thou diest.

Shep.   I cannot speak, nor think,
Nor dare to know that which I know. O sir!
You have undone a man of fourscore three,
That thought to fill his grave in quiet, yea,
To die upon the bed my father died,
To lie close by his honest bones: but now
Some hangman must put on my shroud and
    lay me
Where no priest shovels in dust. O cursed
    wretch,
That knew'st this was the prince, and
    wouldst adventure   469
To mingle faith with him! Undone! undone!
If I might die within this hour, I have lived
To die when I desire.   [*Exit.*

Flo.   Why look you so upon me?
I am but sorry, not afeard; delay'd,
But nothing alter'd: what I was, I am;
More straining on for plucking back, not
    following
My leash unwillingly.

Cam.   Gracious my lord,
You know your father's temper: at this time
He will allow no speech, which I do guess

---

416. **reason**, it is reasonable. 434. **copest**, hast to do with. 438. **knack**, knickknack, referring to Perdita. 441. **Far**, F: *farre*, meaning "farther." **Deucalion**, the Noah of classical mythology. 444. **enchantment**, referring to Perdita.

445. **yea, him**, i.e., worthy of him. 456. **alike**, possibly, indifferently. 465. **died**, i.e., died on. 468. **Where . . . dust.** It was the duty of the priest in the burial service to cast earth on the body while saying, "Earth to earth." The shepherd's meaning is that he will be deprived of the rite of Christian burial. 475. **straining on**, i.e., like a hound on the leash; a figure from coursing.

You do not purpose to him; and as hardly
Will he endure your sight as yet, I fear: 480
Then, till the fury of his highness settle,
Come not before him.

Flo.   I not purpose it.
I think, Camillo?

Cam.   Even he, my lord.

Per. How often have I told you 'twould
be thus!
How often said, my dignity would last
But till 'twere known!

Flo.   It cannot fail but by
The violation of my faith; and then
Let nature crush the sides o' the earth to-
gether
And mar the seeds within! Lift up thy looks:
From my succession wipe me, father; I 490
Am heir to my affection.

Cam.   Be advised.

Flo. I am, and by my fancy: if my reason
Will thereto be obedient, I have reason;
If not, my senses, better pleased with mad-
ness,
Do bid it welcome.

Cam.   This is desperate, sir.

Flo. So call it: but it does fulfil my vow;
I needs must think it honesty. Camillo,
Not for Bohemia, nor the pomp that may
Be thereat glean'd, for all the sun sees or
The close earth wombs or the profound seas
hide   500
In unknown fathoms, will I break my oath
To this my fair beloved: therefore, I pray
you,
As you have ever been my father's honour'd
friend,
When he shall miss me,—as, in faith, I mean
not
To see him any more,—cast your good
counsels
Upon his passion: let myself and fortune
Tug for the time to come. This you may
know
And so deliver, I am put to sea
With her whom here I cannot hold on shore;
And most opportune to our need I have 510
A vessel rides fast by, but not prepared
For this design. What course I mean to hold
Shall nothing benefit your knowledge, nor
Concern me the reporting.

Cam.   O my lord!

I would your spirit were easier for advice,
Or stronger for your need.

Flo.   Hark, Perdita. [*Drawing her aside.*
I'll hear you by and by.

Cam.   He's irremoveable,
Resolved for flight. Now were I happy, if
His going I could frame to serve my turn,
Save him from danger, do him love and
honour,   520
Purchase the sight again of dear Sicilia
And that unhappy king, my master, whom
I so much thirst to see.

Flo.   Now, good Camillo;
I am so fraught with curious business that
I leave out ceremony.

Cam.   Sir, I think
You have heard of my poor services, i' the
love
That I have borne your father?

Flo.   Very nobly
Have you deserved: it is my father's music
To speak your deeds, not little of his care
To have them recompensed as thought on.

Cam.   Well, my lord, 530
If you may please to think I love the king
And through him what is nearest to him,
which is
Your gracious self, embrace but my direction:
If your more ponderous and settled project
May suffer alteration, on mine honour,
I'll point you where you shall have such
receiving
As shall become your highness; where you
may
Enjoy your mistress, for the whom, I see,
There's no disjunction to be made, but by—
As heavens forfend!—your ruin; marry her,
And, with my best endeavours in your ab-
sence,   541
Your discontenting father strive to qualify
And bring him up to liking.

Flo.   How, Camillo,
May this, almost a miracle, be done?
That I may call thee something more than
man
And after that trust to thee.

Cam.   Have you thought on
A place whereto you'll go?

Flo.   Not any yet:
But as the unthought-on accident is guilty

---

489. **mar the seeds**, a frequent figure in Shakespeare
for the destruction of life. 492. **fancy**, love. 513.
Shall . . . knowledge, shall not profit you to know.

524. **curious**, anxious or particular. 530. **as**, as
soon as. 542. **discontenting**, discontented, displeased.
qualify, appease, pacify. 543. **bring . . . up to**, raise
him to the pitch of. 548. **unthought-on**, unexpected.

To what we wildly do, so we profess   549
Ourselves to be the slaves of chance and flies
Of every wind that blows.
    Cam.   Then list to me:
This follows, if you will not change your
    purpose
But undergo this flight, make for Sicilia,
And there present yourself and your fair
    princess,
For so I see she must be, 'fore Leontes:
She shall be habited as it becomes
The partner of your bed. Methinks I see
Leontes opening his free arms and weeping
His welcomes forth; asks thee the son forgive-
    ness,
As 'twere i' the father's person; kisses the
    hands   560
Of your fresh princess; o'er and o'er divides
    him
'Twixt his unkindness and his kindness; the
    one
He chides to hell and bids the other grow
Faster than thought or time.
    Flo.   Worthy Camillo,
What colour for my visitation shall I
Hold up before him?
    Cam.   Sent by the king your father
To greet him and to give him comforts. Sir,
The manner of your bearing towards him,
    with
What you as from your father shall deliver,
Things known betwixt us three, I'll write
    you down: 570
The which shall point you forth at every
    sitting
What you must say; that he shall not per-
    ceive
But that you have your father's bosom there
And speak his very heart.
    Flo.   I am bound to you:
There is some sap in this.
    Cam.   A course more promising
Than a wild dedication of yourselves
To unpath'd waters, undream'd shores,
    most certain
To miseries enough; no hope to help you,
But as you shake off one to take another;
Nothing so certain as your anchors, who   580
Do their best office, if they can but stay you
Where you'll be loath to be: besides you
    know

Prosperity's the very bond of love,
Whose fresh complexion and whose heart to-
    gether
Affliction alters.
    Per.   One of these is true:
I think affliction may subdue the cheek,
But not take in the mind.
    Cam.   Yea, say you so?
There shall not at your father's house these
    seven years
Be born another such.
    Flo.   My good Camillo,
She is as forward of her breeding as   590
†She is i' the rear our birth.
    Cam.   I cannot say 'tis pity
She lacks instructions, for she seems a mis-
    tress
To most that teach.
    Per.   Your pardon, sir; for this
I'll blush you thanks.
    Flo.   My prettiest Perdita!
But O, the thorns we stand upon! Camillo,
Preserver of my father, now of me,
The medicine of our house, how shall we
    do?
We are not furnish'd like Bohemia's son,
Nor shall appear in Sicilia.
    Cam.   My lord,
Fear none of this: I think you know my
    fortunes   600
Do all lie there: it shall be so my care
To have you royally appointed as if
The scene you play were mine. For instance,
    sir,
That you may know you shall not want, one
    word.   *[They talk aside.*

Re-enter AUTOLYCUS.

    Aut. Ha, ha! what a fool Honesty is! and
Trust, his sworn brother, a very simple
gentleman! I have sold all my trumpery; not
a counterfeit stone, not a ribbon, glass,
pomander, brooch, table-book, ballad, knife,
tape, glove, shoe-tie, bracelet, horn-ring, to
keep my pack from fasting: they throng who
should buy first, as if my trinkets had been
hallowed and brought a benediction to the
buyer: by which means I saw whose purse
was best in picture; and what I saw, to my

558. **free**, generous, gracious. 561. **divides him**, probably, is divided in his speech. 565. **colour**, pretext, excuse. 571. **point you forth**, indicate to you.

586. **subdue the cheek**, i.e., with tears. 587. **take in**, overcome. 597. **medicine**, physician. 599. **appear**, i.e., as such. 603. **For instance**, as a proof. 609. **pomander**, ball composed of perfumes. **table-book**, notebook. 615. **best in picture**, i.e., to look at

good use I remembered. My clown, who 616
wants but something to be a reasonable man,
grew so in love with the wenches' song, that
he would not stir his pettitoes till he had both
tune and words; which so drew the rest of the
herd to me that all their other senses stuck in
ears: you might have pinched a placket, it
was senseless; 'twas nothing to geld a cod-
piece of a purse; I could have filed keys off
that hung in chains: no hearing, no feeling,
but my sir's song, and admiring the nothing
of it. So that in this time of lethargy I picked
and cut most of their festival purses; and
had not the old man come in with whoo-bub
against his daughter and the king's son and
scared my choughs from the chaff, I had not
left a purse alive in the whole army.

[*Camillo, Florizel, and Perdita come forward.*

Cam. Nay, but my letters, by this means
    being there
So soon as you arrive, shall clear that doubt.
Flo. And those that you'll procure from
    King Leontes—
Cam. Shall satisfy your father.
Per.   Happy be you!
All that you speak shows fair.
Cam.   Who have we here? 635
                [*Seeing Autolycus.*
We'll make an instrument of this, omit
Nothing may give us aid.
Aut. If they have overheard me now, why,
hanging.
Cam. How now, good fellow! why shakest
thou so? Fear not, man; here's no harm in-
tended to thee.
Aut. I am a poor fellow, sir.
Cam. Why, be so still; here's nobody will
steal that from thee: yet for the outside of
thy poverty we must make an exchange;
therefore discase thee instantly,— thou must
think there's a necessity in 't,—and change
garments with this gentleman: though the
pennyworth on his side be the worst, yet
hold thee, there's some boot.   650
Aut. I am a poor fellow, sir. [*Aside*] I
know ye well enough.
Cam. Nay, prithee, dispatch: the gentleman is half flayed already.

Aut. Are you in earnest, sir? [*Aside*] I
smell the trick on 't.
Flo. Dispatch, I prithee.
Aut. Indeed, I have had earnest; but I
cannot with conscience take it.
Cam. Unbuckle, unbuckle.   660
[*Florizel and Autolycus exchange garments.*
Fortunate mistress,—let my prophecy
Come home to ye!—you must retire yourself
Into some covert: take your sweetheart's hat
And pluck it o'er your brows, muffle your
    face,
Dismantle you, and, as you can, disliken
The truth of your own seeming; that you
    may—
For I do fear eyes over—to shipboard
Get undescried.
Per.   I see the play so lies
That I must bear a part.
Cam.   No remedy. 669
Have you done there?
Flo.   Should I now meet my father,
He would not call me son.
Cam.   Nay, you shall have no hat.
                [*Giving it to Perdita.*
Come, lady, come. Farewell, my friend.
Aut.   Adieu, sir.
Flo. O Perdita, what have we twain
    forgot!
Pray you, a word.
Cam. [*Aside*] What I do next, shall be to
    tell the king
Of this escape and whither they are bound;
Wherein my hope is I shall so prevail
To force him after: in whose company
I shall review Sicilia, for whose sight
I have a woman's longing.
Flo.   Fortune speed us!
Thus we set on, Camillo, to the sea-side. 681
Cam. The swifter speed the better.
        [*Exeunt Florizel, Perdita, and Camillo.*
Aut. I understand the business, I hear it:
to have an open ear, a quick eye, and a
nimble hand, is necessary for a cut-purse; a
good nose is requisite also, to smell out work
for the other senses. I see this is the time
that the unjust man doth thrive. What an
exchange had this been without boot! What
a boot is here with this exchange! Sure the
gods do this year connive at us, and we may
do any thing extempore. The prince himself

---

619. **pettitoes,** pig's feet; here, feet.   621. **stuck
in ears,** were occupied with their ears.   622. **pinched a
placket,** stolen a petticoat.   623. **geld a codpiece,**
remove from a pocket.   626. **my sir's,** the Clown's.
629. **whoo-bub,** hubbub.   631. **choughs . . . chaff,**
jackdaw's from the chaff; here, the Clown's from his
allurements.   636. **this,** i.e., Autolycus.   646. **discase,**
undress.   650. **boot,** something to boot (giving him
money).   654. **flayed,** skinned; here, undressed.

658. **earnest,** money paid as an installment to secure
a bargain.   663. **covert,** secret place.   665-666. **disliken
. . . seeming,** disguise your outward appearance.   667.
eyes over, overseeing eyes.

is about a piece of iniquity, stealing away from his father with his clog at his heels: if I thought it were a piece of honesty to acquaint the king withal, I would not do 't: I hold it the more knavery to conceal it; and therein am I constant to my profession. 698

Re-enter Clown *and* Shepherd.

Aside, aside; here is more matter for a hot brain: every lane's end, every shop, church, session, hanging, yields a careful man work.

Clo. See, see; what a man you are now! There is no other way but to tell the king she's a changeling and none of your flesh and blood.

Shep. Nay, but hear me.

Clo. Nay, but hear me.

Shep. Go to, then. 708

Clo. She being none of your flesh and blood, your flesh and blood has not offended the king; and so your flesh and blood is not to be punished by him. Show those things you found about her, those secret things, all but what she has with her: this being done, let the law go whistle: I warrant you.

Shep. I will tell the king all, every word, yea, and his son's pranks too; who, I may say, is no honest man, neither to his father nor to me, to go about to make me the king's brother-in-law. 720

Clo. Indeed, brother-in-law was the farthest off you could have been to him and then your blood had been the dearer by I know how much an ounce.

Aut. [*Aside*] Very wisely, puppies!

Shep. Well, let us to the king: there is that in this fardel will make him scratch his beard.

Aut. [*Aside*] I know not what impediment this complaint may be to the flight of my master.

Clo. Pray heartily he be at palace. 730

Aut. [*Aside*] Though I am not naturally honest, I am so sometimes by chance: let me pocket up my pedlar's excrement. [*Takes off his false beard.*] How now, rustics! whither are you bound?

Shep. To the palace, an it like your worship.

Aut. Your affairs there, what, with whom,

the condition of that fardel, the place of your dwelling, your names, your ages, of what having, breeding, and any thing that is fitting to be known, discover. 741

Clo. We are but plain fellows, sir.

Aut. A lie; you are rough and hairy. Let me have no lying: it becomes none but tradesmen, and they often give us soldiers the lie: but we pay them for it with stamped coin, not stabbing steel; therefore they do not give us the lie.

Clo. Your worship had like to have given us one, if you had not taken yourself with the manner. 751

Shep. Are you a courtier, an 't like you, sir?

Aut. Whether it like me or no, I am a courtier. Seest thou not the air of the court in these enfoldings? hath not my gait in it the measure of the court? receives not thy nose court-odour from me? reflect I not on thy baseness court-contempt? Thinkest thou, for that I insinuate, or †toaze from thee thy business, I am therefore no courtier? I am courtier cap-a-pe; and one that will either push on or pluck back thy business there: whereupon I command thee to open thy affair.

Shep. My business, sir, is to the king.

Aut. What advocate hast thou to him?

Shep. I know not, an 't like you. 766

Clo. Advocate's the court-word for a pheasant: say you have none.

Shep. None, sir; I have no pheasant, cock nor hen.

Aut. How blessed are we that are not
simple men!

Yet nature might have made me as these are, Therefore I will not disdain.

Clo. This cannot be but a great courtier.

Shep. His garments are rich, but he wears them not handsomely. 776

Clo. He seems to be the more noble in being fantastical: a great man, I'll warrant; I know by the picking on 's teeth.

Aut. The fardel there? what's i' the fardel? Wherefore that box? 781

Shep. Sir, there lies such secrets in this

---

694. **clog**, encumbrance, referring to Perdita. 699. **hot**, active, ardent. 704. **changeling**, child left by the fairies. 719. **go about**, make it his object. 727. **fardel**, bundle, burden. 733. **excrement**, hair, beard.

738. **condition**, quality. 745. **they . . . lie**, i.e., they sell it to us (Johnson). 750-751. **taken . . . manner**, taken with the thing stolen in your possession (a legal phrase); hence, caught yourself in the act. 752. **an 't . . . you**, if you please. 759. **toaze**, tear. 761. **cap-a-pe**, head to foot. 768. **pheasant**, F: *Pheazant;* Kenrick's emendation, *present,* is frequently adopted; it presupposes a blunder in words by the shepherd. 779. **picking on's teeth**, a stylish thing to do in Shakespeare's time.

fardel and box, which none must know but the king; and which he shall know within this hour, if I may come to the speech of him.

Aut. Age, thou hast lost thy labour.

Shep. Why, sir?

Aut. The king is not at the palace; he is gone aboard a new ship to purge melancholy and air himself: for, if thou beest capable of things serious, thou must know the king is full of grief.   791

Shep. So 'tis said, sir; about his son, that should have married a shepherd's daughter.

Aut. If that shepherd be not in hand-fast, let him fly: the curses he shall have, the tortures he shall feel, will break the back of man, the heart of monster.

Clo. Think you so, sir?   798

Aut. Not he alone shall suffer what wit can make heavy and vengeance bitter; but those that are germane to him, though removed fifty times, shall all come under the hangman: which though it be great pity, yet it is necessary. An old sheep-whistling rogue, a ram-tender, to offer to have his daughter come into grace! Some say he shall be stoned; but that death is too soft for him, say I: draw our throne into a sheep-cote! all deaths are too few, the sharpest too easy.

Clo. Has the old man e'er a son, sir, do you hear, an 't like you, sir?   810

Aut. He has a son, who shall be flayed alive; then 'nointed over with honey, set on the head of a wasp's nest; then stand till he be three quarters and a dram dead; then recovered again with aqua-vitæ or some other hot infusion; then, raw as he is, and in the hottest day prognostication proclaims, shall he be set against a brick-wall, the sun looking with a southward eye upon him, where he is to behold him with flies blown to death. But what talk we of these traitorly rascals, whose miseries are to be smiled at, their offences being so capital? Tell me, for you seem to be honest plain men, what you have to the king: being something gently considered, I'll bring you where he is aboard, tender your persons to his presence, whisper him in your behalfs; and if it be in man besides the king to effect your suits, here is man shall do it.   828

Clo. He seems to be of great authority: close with him, give him gold; and though authority be a stubborn bear, yet he is oft led by the nose with gold: show the inside of your purse to the outside of his hand, and no more ado. Remember 'stoned,' and 'flayed alive.'

Shep. An 't please you, sir, to undertake the business for us, here is that gold I have: I'll make it as much more and leave this young man in pawn till I bring it you.

Aut. After I have done what I promised?

Shep. Ay, sir.   840

Aut. Well, give me the moiety. Are you a party in this business?

Clo. In some sort, sir: but though my case be a pitiful one, I hope I shall not be flayed out of it.   844

Aut. O, that's the case of the shepherd's son: hang him, he'll be made an example.

Clo. Comfort, good comfort! We must to the king and show our strange sights: he must know 'tis none of your daughter nor my sister; we are gone else. Sir, I will give you as much as this old man does when the business is performed, and remain, as he says, your pawn till it be brought you.   853

Aut. I will trust you. Walk before toward the sea-side; go on the right hand: I will but look upon the hedge and follow you.

Clo. We are blest in this man, as I may say, even blest.

Shep. Let's before as he bids us: he was provided to do us good.   860

[*Exeunt Shepherd and Clown.*

Aut. If I had a mind to be honest, I see Fortune would not suffer me: she drops booties in my mouth. I am courted now with a double occasion, gold and a means to do the prince my master good; which who knows how that may turn back to my advancement? I will bring these two moles, these blind ones, aboard him: if he think it fit to shore them again and that the complaint they have to the king concerns him nothing, let him call me rogue for being so far officious; for I am proof against that title and what shame else belongs to 't. To him will I present them: there may be matter in it.   [*Exit.*

794. **hand-fast**, firm hold. 807. **our throne**, indicative of Autolycus's assumed position of courtier. 824. **being . . . considered**, if I receive a gentlemanly consideration, i.e., a bribe. 825. **tender . . . persons**, introduce you.

830. **close with him**, accept his offer. 841. **moiety**, half. 845. **case**, condition, and skin.

ACT V.

SCENE I. *A room in* LEONTES' *palace.*

Enter LEONTES, CLEOMENES, DION, PAU-
LINA, *and Servants.*

Cleo. Sir, you have done enough, and
　　have perform'd
A saint-like sorrow: no fault could you make,
Which you have not redeem'd; indeed, paid
　　down
More penitence than done trespass: at the
　　last,
Do as the heavens have done, forget your
　　evil;
With them forgive yourself.

Leon. 　　　　　Whilst I remember
Her and her virtues, I cannot forget
My blemishes in them, and so still think of
The wrong I did myself; which was so much,
That heirless it hath made my kingdom
　　and 　　　　　　　　　　　　　　10
Destroy'd the sweet'st companion that e'er
　　man
Bred his hopes out of.

Paul. 　　　　True, too true, my lord:
If, one by one, you wedded all the world,
Or from the all that are took something good,
To make a perfect woman, she you kill'd
Would be unparallel'd.

Leon. 　　　　I think so. Kill'd!
She I kill'd! I did so: but thou strikest me
Sorely, to say I did; it is as bitter
Upon thy tongue as in my thought: now,
　　good now,
Say so but seldom.

Cleo. 　　　　Not at all, good lady: 　　20
You might have spoken a thousand things
　　that would
Have done the time more benefit and graced
Your kindness better.

Paul. 　　　　You are one of those
Would have him wed again.

Dion. 　　　　　If you would not so,
You pity not the state, nor the remem-
　　brance
Of his most sovereign name; consider little
What dangers, by his highness' fail of issue,
May drop upon his kingdom and devour
Incertain lookers on. What were more holy
Than to rejoice the former queen is well? 　30
What holier than, for royalty's repair,

For present comfort and for future good,
To bless the bed of majesty again
With a sweet fellow to 't?

Paul. 　　　　There is none worthy,
Respecting her that's gone. Besides, the
　　gods
Will have fulfill'd their secret purposes;
For has not the divine Apollo said,
Is 't not the tenour of his oracle,
That King Leontes shall not have an heir
Till his lost child be found? which that it
　　shall,
Is all as monstrous to our human reason 　41
As my Antigonus to break his grave
And come again to me; who, on my life,
Did perish with the infant. 'Tis your counsel
My lord should to the heavens be contrary,
Oppose against their wills. [*To Leontes.*]
　　Care not for issue;
The crown will find an heir: great Alexander
Left his to the worthiest; so his successor
Was like to be the best.

Leon. 　　　　　Good Paulina,
Who hast the memory of Hermione, 　　50
I know, in honour, O, that ever I
Had squared me to thy counsel! then, even
　　now,
I might have look'd upon my queen's full
　　eyes,
Have taken treasure from her lips—

Paul. 　　　　　And left them
More rich for what they yielded.

Leon. 　　　　　Thou speak'st truth.
No more such wives; therefore, no wife: one
　　worse,
And better used, would make her sainted
　　spirit
Again possess her corpse, and on this stage,
Where we're offenders now, appear soul-
　　vex'd,
†And begin, 'Why to me?'

Paul. 　　　　Had she such power, 　60
She had just cause.

Leon. 　　　She had; and would incense me
To murder her I married.

Paul. 　　　　I should so.
Were I the ghost that walk'd, I 'ld bid you
　　mark
Her eye, and tell me for what dull part in 't

---

27. **fail**, failure. 29. **Incertain**, not knowing what
to think or do (Schmidt). 30. **well**, happy, at rest.

35. **Respecting**, in comparison with. 45. **should
. . . contrary.** This is the religious theme of the play; it
explains the action of Hermione in hiding herself away
and permitting Leontes to expiate his sin. 52. **squared
me**, adjusted or regulated myself. 60. **'Why to me?'**
i.e., why this offense to me?

You chose her; then I 'ld shriek, that even
     your ears
Should rift to hear me; and the words that
     follow'd
Should be 'Remember mine.'
     Leon.   Stars, stars,
And all eyes else dead coals! Fear thou no
     wife;
I'll have no wife, Paulina.
     Paul.   Will you swear
Never to marry but by my free leave?   70
     Leon. Never, Paulina; so be blest my
     spirit!
     Paul. Then, good my lords, bear witness
     to his oath.
     Cleo. You tempt him over-much.
     Paul.   Unless another,
As like Hermione as is her picture,
Affront his eye.
     Cleo.   Good madam,—
     Paul.   I have done.
Yet, if my lord will marry,—if you will, sir,
No remedy, but you will,—give me the office
To choose you a queen: she shall not be so
     young
As was your former; but she shall be such
As, walk'd your first queen's ghost, it should
     take joy   80
To see her in your arms.
     Leon.   My true Paulina,
We shall not marry till thou bid'st us.
     Paul.   That
Shall be when your first queen's again in
     breath;
Never till then.

           Enter a Gentleman.

     Gent. One that gives out himself Prince
     Florizel,
Son of Polixenes, with his princess, she
The fairest I have yet beheld, desires access
To your high presence.
     Leon.   What with him? he comes not
Like to his father's greatness: his approach,
So out of circumstance and sudden, tells us 90
'Tis not a visitation framed, but forced
By need and accident. What train?
     Gent.   But few,
And those but mean.
     Leon.   His princess, say you, with him?
     Gent. Ay, the most peerless piece of earth,
     I think,

That e'er the sun shone bright on.
     Paul.   O Hermione,
As every present time doth boast itself
Above a better gone, so must thy grave
Give way to what's seen now! Sir, you your-
     self
Have said and writ so, but your writing now
Is colder than that theme, 'She had not
     been,   100
Nor was not to be equall'd;'—thus your
     verse
Flow'd with her beauty once: 'tis shrewdly
     ebb'd,
To say you have seen a better.
     Gent.   Pardon, madam:
The one I have almost forgot,—your par-
     don,—
The other, when she has obtain'd your eye,
Will have your tongue too. This is a crea-
     ture,
Would she begin a sect, might quench the
     zeal
Of all professors else, make proselytes
Of who she but bid follow.
     Paul.   How! not women?
     Gent. Women will love her, that she is a
     woman   110
More worth than any man; men, that she is
The rarest of all women.
     Leon.   Go, Cleomenes;
Yourself, assisted with your honour'd
     friends,
Bring them to our embracement. Still, 'tis
     strange   [*Exeunt Cleomenes and others.*
He thus should steal upon us.
     Paul.   Had our prince,
Jewel of children, seen this hour, he had
     pair'd
Well with this lord: there was not full a
     month
Between their births.
     Leon. Prithee, no more; cease; thou
     know'st
He dies to me again when talk'd of: sure, 120
When I shall see this gentleman, thy speeches
Will bring me to consider that which may
Unfurnish me of reason. They are come.

     Re-enter Cleomenes *and others, with*
           Florizel *and* Perdita.

Your mother was most true to wedlock,
     prince;

---

66. **rift,** split. 75. **Affront,** confront. 90. **out of
circumstance,** without ceremony.

113. **assisted with,** accompanied by. 123. **Unfurnish,** deprive, divest.

For she did print your royal father off,
Conceiving you: were I but twenty one,
Your father's image is so hit in you,
His very air, that I should call you brother,
As I did him, and speak of something wildly
By us perform'd before.　Most dearly wel-
　come!
And your fair princess, — goddess! — O,
　alas!　　　　　　　　　　　　　　131
I lost a couple, that 'twixt heaven and earth
Might thus have stood begetting wonder as
You, gracious couple, do: and then I lost—
All mine own folly—the society,
Amity too, of your brave father, whom,
Though bearing misery, I desire my life
Once more to look on him.
　Flo.　　　　　　By his command
Have I here touch'd Sicilia and from him
Give you all greetings that a king, at
　friend,　　　　　　　　　　　　　140
Can send his brother: and, but infirmity
Which waits upon worn times hath some-
　thing seized
His wish'd ability, he had himself
The lands and waters 'twixt your throne and
　his
Measured to look upon you; whom he loves—
He bade me say so—more than all the
　sceptres
And those that bear them living.
　Leon.　　　　　　O my brother,
Good gentleman! the wrongs I have done
　thee stir
Afresh within me, and these thy offices,
So rarely kind, are as interpreters　　150
Of my behind-hand slackness.　Welcome
　hither,
As is the spring to the earth.　And hath he
　too
Exposed this paragon to the fearful usage,
At least ungentle, of the dreadful Neptune,
To greet a man not worth her pains, much
　less
The adventure of her person?
　Flo.　　　　　　Good my lord,
She came from Libya.
　Leon.　　　　Where the warlike Smalus,
That noble honour'd lord, is fear'd and
　loved?
　Flo. Most royal sir, from thence; from
　him, whose daughter

His tears proclaim'd his, parting with her:
　thence,　　　　　　　　　　　　160
A prosperous south-wind friendly, we have
　cross'd,
To execute the charge my father gave me
For visiting your highness: my best train
I have from your Sicilian shores dismiss'd;
Who for Bohemia bend, to signify
Not only my success in Libya, sir,
But my arrival and my wife's in safety
Here where we are.
　Leon.　　　　The blessed gods
Purge all infection from our air whilst you
Do climate here! You have a holy father, 170
A graceful gentleman; against whose person,
So sacred as it is, I have done sin:
For which the heavens, taking angry note,
Have left me issueless; and your father's
　blest,
As he from heaven merits it, with you
Worthy his goodness.　What might I have
　been,
Might I a son and daughter now have look'd
　on,
Such goodly things as you!

　　　　　Enter a Lord.

　Lord.　　　　　　Most noble sir,
That which I shall report will bear no credit,
Were not the proof so nigh.　Please you,
　great sir,　　　　　　　　　　180
Bohemia greets you from himself by me;
Desires you to attach his son, who has—
His dignity and duty both cast off—
Fled from his father, from his hopes, and
　with
A shepherd's daughter.
　Leon.　　　　Where's Bohemia? speak.
　Lord. Here in your city; I now came from
　him:
I speak amazedly; and it becomes
My marvel and my message.　To your court
Whiles he was hastening, in the chase, it
　seems,
Of this fair couple, meets he on the way 190
The father of this seeming lady and
Her brother, having both their country
　quitted
With this young prince.
　Flo.　　　　Camillo has betray'd me;
Whose honour and whose honesty till now

---

127. **hit,** exactly reproduced.　137. **my life,** while I live.　140. **at friend,** friendly.　142. **worn times,** old age.　149. **offices,** messages of good-will.　156. **adventure,** hazard.

170. **climate,** dwell, reside (in this clime).　171. **graceful,** full of grace, gracious.　187. **amazedly,** perplexedly.　**it,** i.e., my manner of speaking.　188. **marvel,** astonishment, wonder.

Endured all weathers.

Lord.   Lay 't so to his charge:
He's with the king your father.

Leon.   Who? Camillo?

Lord. Camillo, sir; I spake with him; who
  now
Has these poor men in question. Never saw I
Wretches so quake: they kneel, they kiss the
  earth;   199
Forswear themselves as often as they speak:
Bohemia stops his ears, and threatens them
With divers deaths in death.

Per.   O my poor father!
The heaven sets spies upon us, will not have
Our contract celebrated.

Leon.   You are married?

Flo. We are not, sir, nor are we like to be;
The stars, I see, will kiss the valleys first:
The odds for high and low 's alike.

Leon.   My lord,
Is this the daughter of a king?

Flo.   She is,
When once she is my wife.

Leon. That 'once,' I see by your good
  father's speed,   210
Will come on very slowly. I am sorry,
Most sorry, you have broken from his liking
Where you were tied in duty, and as sorry
Your choice is not so rich in worth as beauty,
That you might well enjoy her.

Flo.   Dear, look up:
Though Fortune, visible an enemy,
Should chase us with my father, power no jot
Hath she to change our loves. Beseech you,
  sir,
Remember since you owed no more to time
Than I do now: with thought of such affec-
  tions,   220
Step forth mine advocate; at your request
My father will grant precious things as trifles.

Leon. Would he do so, I 'ld beg your
  precious mistress,
Which he counts but a trifle.

Paul.   Sir, my liege,
Your eye hath too much youth in 't: not a
  month
'Fore your queen died, she was more worth
  such gazes
Than what you look on now.

Leon.   I thought of her,
Even in these looks I made. [*To Florizel.*]
  But your petition
Is yet unanswer'd. I will to your father:

Your honour not o'erthrown by your desires,
I am friend to them and you: upon which
  errand   231
I now go toward him; therefore follow me
And mark what way I make: come, good my
  lord.   [*Exeunt.*

SCENE II. *Before* LEONTES' *palace.*

Enter AUTOLYCUS *and a* Gentleman.

Aut. Beseech you, sir, were you present at
this relation?

First Gent. I was by at the opening of the
fardel, heard the old shepherd deliver the
manner how he found it: whereupon, after a
little amazedness, we were all commanded
out of the chamber; only this methought I
heard the shepherd say, he found the child.

Aut. I would most gladly know the issue
of it.   9

First Gent. I make a broken delivery of
the business; but the changes I perceived in
the king and Camillo were very notes of
admiration: they seemed almost, with staring on one another, to tear the cases of their
eyes; there was speech in their dumbness,
language in their very gesture; they looked
as they had heard of a world ransomed, or
one destroyed: a notable passion of wonder
appeared in them; but the wisest beholder,
that knew no more but seeing, could not say
if the importance were joy or sorrow; but in
the extremity of the one, it must needs be.

Enter another Gentleman.

Here comes a gentleman that haply knows
more. The news, Rogero?   23

Sec. Gent. Nothing but bonfires: the oracle
is fulfilled; the king's daughter is found: such
a deal of wonder is broken out within this
hour that ballad-makers cannot be able to
express it.

Enter a third Gentleman.

Here comes the Lady Paulina's steward: he
can deliver you more. How goes it now, sir?

---

207. **The odds . . . alike.** Fortune is the same for the
high and low. 214. **worth,** merit. 219. **since,** when.

230. **Your . . . desires,** i.e., if your honor, etc.
Scene ii. 2. **relation,** narrative, account. Shakespeare has chosen to solve the plot of the young lovers
by reporting the solution in conversation. 12-13. **notes
of admiration,** exclamations of wonder. 14-15. **cases
of their eyes,** eyelids. 19. **no . . . seeing,** nothing
except what he could see. 20. **importance,** import,
meaning. 27. **ballad-makers,** reference to the Elizabethan practice of writing ballads on notable current
events.

this news which is called true is so like an old tale, that the verity of it is in strong suspicion: has the king found his heir?   32

Third Gent. Most true, if ever truth were pregnant by circumstance: that which you hear you'll swear you see, there is such unity in the proofs. The mantle of Queen Hermione's, her jewel about the neck of it, the letters of Antigonus found with it which they know to be his character, the majesty of the creature in resemblance of the mother, the affection of nobleness which nature shows above her breeding, and many other evidences proclaim her with all certainty to be the king's daughter. Did you see the meeting of the two kings?

Sec. Gent. No.   45

Third Gent. Then have you lost a sight, which was to be seen, cannot be spoken of. There might you have beheld one joy crown another, so and in such manner that it seemed sorrow wept to take leave of them, for their joy waded in tears. There was casting up of eyes, holding up of hands, with countenance of such distraction that they were to be known by garment, not by favour. Our king, being ready to leap out of himself for joy of his found daughter, as if that joy were now become a loss, cries 'O, thy mother, thy mother!' then asks Bohemia forgiveness; then embraces his son-in-law; then again worries he his daughter with clipping her; now he thanks the old shepherd, which stands by like a weather-bitten conduit of many kings' reigns. I never heard of such another encounter, which lames report to follow it and undoes description to do it.

Sec. Gent. What, pray you, became of Antigonus, that carried hence the child?

Third Gent. Like an old tale still, which will have matter to rehearse, though credit be asleep and not an ear open. He was torn to pieces with a bear: this avouches the shepherd's son; who has not only his innocence, which seems much, to justify him, but a handkerchief and rings of his that Paulina knows.

First Gent. What became of his bark and his followers?   73

Third Gent. Wrecked the same instant of their master's death and in the view of the shepherd: so that all the instruments which aided to expose the child were even then lost when it was found. But O, the noble combat that 'twixt joy and sorrow was fought in Paulina! She had one eye declined for the loss of her husband, another elevated that the oracle was fulfilled: she lifted the princess from the earth, and so locks her in embracing, as if she would pin her to her heart that she might no more be in danger of losing.

First Gent. The dignity of this act was worth the audience of kings and princes; for by such was it acted.   88

Third Gent. One of the prettiest touches of all and that which angled for mine eyes, caught the water though not the fish, was when, at the relation of the queen's death, with the manner how she came to 't bravely confessed and lamented by the king, how attentiveness wounded his daughter; till, from one sign of dolour to another, she did, with an 'Alas,' I would fain say, bleed tears, for I am sure my heart wept blood. Who was most marble there changed colour; some swooned, all sorrowed: if all the world could have seen 't, the woe had been universal.   100

First Gent. Are they returned to the court?

Third Gent. No: the princess hearing of her mother's statue, which is in the keeping of Paulina,—a piece many years in doing and now newly performed by that rare Italian master, Julio Romano, who, had he himself eternity and could put breath into his work, would beguile Nature of her custom, so perfectly he is her ape: he so near to Hermione hath done Hermione that they say one would speak to her and stand in hope of answer: thither with all greediness of affection are they gone, and there they intend 112 to sup.

Sec. Gent. I thought she had some great matter there in hand; for she hath privately twice or thrice a day, ever since the death of Hermione, visited that removed house. Shall we thither and with our company piece the rejoicing?

First Gent. Who would be thence that has the benefit of access? every wink of an eye

---

34. **pregnant by circumstance**, made cogent by circumstantial evidence (Moorman). 40. **affection of**, natural disposition to. 52. **countenance**, bearing, demeanor. 54. **favour**, look, appearance. 59. **clipping**, embracing.

98. **marble**, hard-hearted. 106. **Julio Romano**, Italian painter and sculptor of the sixteenth century; an anachronism in this play. 108. **custom**, trade. 111. **affection**, desire. 117. **piece**, add to, augment.

some new grace will be born: our absence makes us unthrifty to our knowledge. 121 Let's along.   [*Exeunt Gentlemen.*

Aut. Now, had I not the dash of my former life in me, would preferment drop on my head. I brought the old man and his son aboard the prince; told him I heard them talk of a fardel and I know not what: but he at that time, over-fond of the shepherd's daughter, so he then took her to be, who began to be much sea-sick, and himself little better, extremity of weather continuing, this mystery remained undiscovered. But 'tis all one to me; for had I been the finder out of this secret, it would not have rel- 132 ished among my other discredits.

Enter Shepherd *and* Clown.

Here come those I have done good to against my will, and already appearing in the blossoms of their fortune.

Shep. Come, boy; I am past moe children, but thy sons and daughters will be all gentlemen born.

Clo. You are well met, sir. You denied to fight with me this other day, because I was no gentleman born. See you these clothes? say you see them not and think me still no gentleman born: you were best say these robes are not gentlemen born: give me the lie, do, and try whether I am not now a gentleman born.

Aut. I know you are now, sir, a gentleman born.

Clo. Ay, and have been so any time these four hours.

Shep. And so have I, boy.   149

Clo. So you have: but I was a gentleman born before my father; for the king's son took me by the hand, and called me brother; and then the two kings called my father brother; and then the prince my brother and the princess my sister called my father father; and so we wept, and there was the first gentleman-like tears that ever we shed.

Shep. We may live, son, to shed many more.

Clo. Ay; or else 'twere hard luck, being in so preposterous estate as we are.   159

Aut. I humbly beseech you, sir, to pardon

me all the faults I have committed to your worship and to give me your good report to the prince my master.

Shep. Prithee, son, do; for we must be gentle, now we are gentlemen.

Clo. Thou wilt amend thy life?

Aut. Ay, an it like your good worship.

Clo. Give me thy hand: I will swear to the prince thou art as honest a true fellow as any is in Bohemia.   170

Shep. You may say it, but not swear it.

Clo. Not swear it, now I am a gentleman? Let boors and franklins say it, I'll swear it.

Shep. How if it be false, son?

Clo. If it be ne'er so false, a true gentleman may swear it in the behalf of his friend: and I'll swear to the prince thou art a tall fellow of thy hands and that thou wilt not be drunk; but I know thou art no tall fellow of thy hands and that thou wilt be drunk: but I'll swear it, and I would thou wouldst be a tall fellow of thy hands.   181

Aut. I will prove so, sir, to my power.

Clo. Ay, by any means prove a tall fellow: if I do not wonder how thou darest venture to be drunk, not being a tall fellow, trust me not. Hark! the kings and the princes, our kindred, are going to see the queen's picture. Come, follow us: we'll be thy good masters.

[*Exeunt.*

SCENE III.   *A chapel in* Paulina's *house.*

Enter Leontes, Polixenes, Florizel, Perdita, Camillo, Paulina, Lords, *and* Attendants.

Leon. O grave and good Paulina, the great comfort
That I have had of thee!

Paul.   What, sovereign sir,
I did not well I meant well. All my services
You have paid home: but that you have vouchsafed,
With your crown'd brother and these your contracted
Heirs of your kingdoms, my poor house to visit,
It is a surplus of your grace, which never
My life may last to answer.

Leon.   O Paulina,
We honour you with trouble: but we came

---

121. **unthrifty to**, not likely to increase. 132. **relished**, found acceptance. 159. **preposterous**, probably blunder for *prosperous*.

173. **franklins**, farmers who owned their own land.

To see the statue of our queen: your gallery
Have we pass'd through, not without much
    content
In many singularities; but we saw not   12
That which my daughter came to look upon,
The statue of her mother.
    Paul.   As she lived peerless,
So her dead likeness, I do well believe,
Excels whatever yet you look'd upon
Or hand of man hath done; therefore I keep
    it
Lonely, apart. But here it is: prepare
To see the life as lively mock'd as ever
Still sleep mock'd death: behold, and say 'tis
    well. [*Paulina draws a curtain, and dis-*
    covers Hermione standing like a statue.
I like your silence, it the more shows off 21
Your wonder: but yet speak; first, you, my
    liege.
Comes it not something near?
    Leon.   Her natural posture!
Chide me, dear stone, that I may say in-
    deed
Thou art Hermione; or rather, thou art she
In thy not chiding, for she was as tender
As infancy and grace. But yet, Paulina,
Hermione was not so much wrinkled, noth-
    ing
So aged as this seems.
    Pol.   O, not by much.
    Paul. So much the more our carver's
    excellence;   30
Which lets go by some sixteen years and
    makes her
As she lived now.
    Leon.   As now she might have done,
So much to my good comfort, as it is
Now piercing to my soul. O, thus she stood,
Even with such life of majesty, warm life,
As now it coldly stands, when first I woo'd
    her!
I am ashamed: does not the stone rebuke me
For being more stone than it? O royal piece,
There's magic in thy majesty, which has
My evils conjured to remembrance and 40
From thy admiring daughter took the spirits,
Standing like stone with thee.
    Per.   And give me leave,
And do not say 'tis superstition, that
I kneel and then implore her blessing. Lady,
Dear queen, that ended when I but began,
Give me that hand of yours to kiss.
    Paul.   O, patience!

The statue is but newly fix'd, the colour's
Not dry.
    Cam. My lord, your sorrow was too sore
    laid on,
Which sixteen winters cannot blow away, 50
So many summers dry: scarce any joy
Did ever so long live; no sorrow
But kill'd itself much sooner.
    Pol.   Dear my brother,
Let him that was the cause of this have power
To take off so much grief from you as he
Will piece up in himself.
    Paul.   Indeed, my lord,
If I had thought the sight of my poor image
Would thus have wrought you,—for the
    stone is mine—
I 'ld not have show'd it.
    Leon.   Do not draw the curtain.
    Paul. No longer shall you gaze on 't, lest
    your fancy   60
May think anon it moves.
    Leon.   Let be, let be.
Would I were dead, but that, methinks, al-
    ready—
What was he that did make it? See, my lord,
Would you not deem it breathed? and that
    those veins
Did verily bear blood?
    Pol.   Masterly done:
The very life seems warm upon her lip.
    Leon. The fixture of her eye has motion
    in 't,
As we are mock'd with art.
    Paul.   I'll draw the curtain:
My lord's almost so far transported that
He'll think anon it lives.
    Leon.   O sweet Paulina, 70
Make me to think so twenty years together!
No settled senses of the world can match
The pleasure of that madness. Let 't alone.
    Paul. I am sorry, sir, I have thus far
    stirr'd you: but
I could afflict you farther.
    Leon.   Do, Paulina;
For this affliction has a taste as sweet
As any cordial comfort. Still, methinks,
There is an air comes from her: what fine
    chisel
Could ever yet cut breath? Let no man
    mock me,
For I will kiss her.
    Paul.   Good my lord, forbear: 80
The ruddiness upon her lip is wet;
You'll mar it if you kiss it, stain your own

---

12. **singularities**, rarities, curiosities. 28. **nothing**,
by no means. 41. **admiring**, rapt with amazement.

67. **fixture**, fixedness. stability.

With oily painting. Shall I draw the curtain?
Leon. No, not these twenty years.
Per. So long could I
Stand by, a looker on.
Paul. Either forbear,
Quit presently the chapel, or resolve you
For more amazement. If you can behold it,
I'll make the statue move indeed, descend
And take you by the hand: but then you'll
think—
Which I protest against—I am assisted 90
By wicked powers.
Leon. What you can make her do,
I am content to look on: what to speak,
I am content to hear; for 'tis as easy
To make her speak as move.
Paul. It is required
You do awake your faith. Then all stand still;
On: those that think it is unlawful business
I am about, let them depart.
Leon. Proceed:
No foot shall stir.
Paul. Music, awake her; strike! [*Music.*
'Tis time; descend; be stone no more; ap-
proach; 99
Strike all that look upon with marvel. Come,
I'll fill your grave up: stir, nay, come away,
Bequeath to death your numbness, for from
him
Dear life redeems you. You perceive she
stirs: [*Hermione comes down.*
Start not; her actions shall be holy as
You hear my spell is lawful: do not shun her
Until you see her die again; for then
You kill her double. Nay, present your hand:
When she was young you woo'd her; now in
age
Is she become the suitor?
Leon. O, she's warm!
If this be magic, let it be an art 110
Lawful as eating.
Pol. She embraces him.
Cam. She hangs about his neck:
If she pertain to life let her speak too.
Pol. Ay, and make 't manifest where she
has lived,
Or how stolen from the dead.
Paul. That she is living,
Were it but told you, should be hooted at
Like an old tale: but it appears she lives,
Though yet she speak not. Mark a little while.
Please you to interpose, fair madam: kneel
And pray your mother's blessing. Turn,
good lady; 120

96. **On,** let us proceed. 107. **double,** twice over.

Our Perdita is found.
Her. You gods, look down
And from your sacred vials pour your graces
Upon my daughter's head! Tell me, mine
own,
Where hast thou been preserved? where
lived? how found
Thy father's court? for thou shalt hear that
I,
Knowing by Paulina that the oracle
Gave hope thou wast in being, have pre-
served
Myself to see the issue.
Paul. There's time enough for that;
Lest they desire upon this push to trouble
Your joys with like relation. Go together,
You precious winners all; your exultation
Partake to every one. I, an old turtle, 132
Will wing me to some wither'd bough and
there
My mate, that's never to be found again,
Lament till I am lost.
Leon. O, peace, Paulina!
Thou shouldst a husband take by my
consent,
As I by thine a wife: this is a match,
And made between 's by vows. Thou hast
found mine;
But how, is to be question'd; for I saw her,
As I thought, dead, and have in vain said
many 140
A prayer upon her grave. I'll not seek far—
For him, I partly know his mind—to find
thee
An honourable husband. Come, Camillo,
And take her by the hand, whose worth and
honesty
Is richly noted and here justified
By us, a pair of kings. Let's from this place.
What! look upon my brother: both your
pardons,
That e'er I put between your holy looks
My ill suspicion. This is your son-in-law 149
And son unto the king, who, heavens direct-
ing,
Is troth-plight to your daughter. Good
Paulina,
Lead us from hence, where we may leisurely
Each one demand and answer to his part
Perform'd in this wide gap of time since first
We were dissever'd: hastily lead away.
[*Exeunt.*

129. **push,** emergency. 130. **like relation,** similar
narrative. 132. **Partake to,** share with, communicate.
145. **noted,** reputed. 147. **What . . . brother,** addressed to Hermione.

THE TEMPEST

DRAMATIS PERSONÆ

ALONSO, King of Naples.
SEBASTIAN, his brother.
PROSPERO, the right Duke of Milan.
ANTONIO, his brother, the usurping Duke of Milan.
FERDINAND, son to the King of Naples.
GONZALO, an honest old Counsellor.
ADRIAN,
FRANCISCO, } Lords.
CALIBAN, a savage and deformed Slave.
TRINCULO, a Jester.
STEPHANO, a drunken Butler.
Master of a Ship.

Boatswain.
Mariners.

MIRANDA, daughter to Prospero.
ARIEL, an airy Spirit.
IRIS,
CERES,
JUNO, } presented by Spirits.
Nymphs,
Reapers,

Other Spirits attending on Prospero.

SCENE—*A ship at Sea: an island.*

ACT I.

SCENE I. *On a ship at sea: a tempestuous noise of thunder and lightning heard.*

Enter a Ship-Master *and a* Boatswain.

Mast. Boatswain!
Boats. Here, master: what cheer?
Mast. Good, speak to the mariners: fall to't, yarely, or we run ourselves aground: bestir, bestir. [*Exit.*

Enter Mariners.

Boats. Heigh, my hearts! cheerly, cheerly, my hearts! yare, yare! Take in the topsail. Tend to the master's whistle. Blow, till thou burst thy wind, if room enough!

Enter ALONZO, SEBASTIAN, ANTONIO, FERDINAND, GONZALO, *and others.*

Alon. Good boatswain, have care. Where's the master? Play the men. 11
Boats. I pray now, keep below.

Ant. Where is the master, boatswain?
Boats. Do you not hear him? You mar our labour: keep your cabins: you do assist the storm.
Gon. Nay, good, be patient.
Boats. When the sea is. Hence! What cares these roarers for the name of king? To cabin: silence! trouble us not.
Gon. Good, yet remember whom thou hast aboard. 21
Boats. None that I more love than myself. You are a counsellor; if you can command these elements to silence, and work the peace of the present, we will not hand a rope more; use your authority: if you cannot, give thanks you have lived so long, and make yourself ready in your cabin for the mischance of the hour, if it so hap. Cheerly, good hearts! Out of our way, I say. [*Exit.* 29
Gon. I have great comfort from this fellow: methinks he hath no drowning mark upon him; his complexion is perfect gallows. Stand fast, good Fate, to his hanging: make

the rope of his destiny our cable, for our own doth little advantage. If he be not born to be hanged, our case is miserable. [*Exeunt.* 36

Re-enter Boatswain.

Boats. Down with the topmast! yare! lower, lower! Bring her to try with main-course. [*A cry within.*] A plague upon this howling! they are louder than the weather or our office.   40

Re-enter SEBASTIAN, ANTONIO, *and*
GONZALO.

Yet again! what do you here? Shall we give o'er and drown? Have you a mind to sink?
Seb. A pox o' your throat, you bawling, blasphemous, incharitable dog!
Boats. Work you then.
Ant. Hang, cur! hang, you whoreson, insolent noisemaker! We are less afraid to be drowned than thou art.
Gon. I'll warrant him for drowning; though the ship were no stronger than a nutshell and as leaky as an unstanched wench.   51
Boats. Lay her a-hold, a-hold! set her two courses off to sea again; lay her off.

Enter Mariners *wet.*

Mariners. All lost! to prayers, to prayers! all lost!   55
Boats. What, must our mouths be cold?
Gon. The king and prince at prayers! let's assist them,
For our case is as theirs.
Seb.   I'm out of patience.
Ant. We are merely cheated of our lives by drunkards:
This wide-chapp'd rascal — would thou mightst lie drowning   60
The washing of ten tides!
Gon.   He'll be hang'd yet,
Though every drop of water swear against it
And gape at widest to glut him.

35. **doth little advantage**, is of little benefit. 38. **Bring . . . course**, sail her close to the wind by means of the mainsail. 40. **they . . . office**, the passengers make more noise than the winds or than we do at work. 49. **warrant him for drowning**, guarantee that he will never be drowned. 52. **a-hold**, close to the wind. 53. **courses**, probably, sails; i.e., they would set her foresail as well as her mainsail. 56. **must . . . cold**, let us heat up our mouths with liquor. 59. **merely**, absolutely, entirely. 60. **wide-chapp'd**, with mouth wide open. 60-61. **lie . . . tides**. Pirates were hanged on the shore and left until three tides had come in. 63. **glut**, swallow.

[*A confused noise within:* 'Mercy on us!'—
'We split, we split!'—'Farewell my wife and children!'—
'Farewell, brother!'—'We split, we split, we split!']   65
Ant. Let's all sink with the king.
Seb. Let's take leave of him.
                                 [*Exeunt Ant. and Seb.*
Gon. Now would I give a thousand furlongs of sea for an acre of barren ground, long heath, brown furze, any thing. The wills above be done! but I would fain die a dry death.   [*Exeunt.*

SCENE II. *The island. Before* PROSPERO'S
cell.

Enter PROSPERO *and* MIRANDA.

Mir. If by your art, my dearest father, you have
Put the wild waters in this roar, allay them.
The sky, it seems, would pour down stinking pitch,
But that the sea, mounting to the welkin's cheek,
Dashes the fire out. O, I have suffer'd
With those that I saw suffer: a brave vessel,
Who had, no doubt, some noble creature in her,
Dash'd all to pieces. O, the cry did knock
Against my very heart. Poor souls, they perish'd.
Had I been any god of power, I would   10
Have sunk the sea within the earth or ere
It should the good ship so have swallow'd and
The fraughting souls within her.
Pros.   Be collected:
No more amazement: tell your piteous heart
There's no harm done.
Mir.   O, woe the day!
Pros.   No harm.
I have done nothing but in care of thee,
Of thee, my dear one, thee, my daughter, who

64. **split**, on the rocks. 69. **long heath**, defined as "open barren ground"; also as "heather." 70. **furze**, broom, or gorse (a prickly shrub); F: *firrs*, taken to mean "firs" (New Cambridge).
Scene ii. 3. **stinking pitch**, suggestion of heat. 4. **But that**, were it not that. **welkin's cheek**, cheek or side of the sky. 6. **brave**, gallant. 13. **fraughting**, forming the cargo. 14. **amazement**, astonishment, bewilderment. **piteous**, pitiful.

Art ignorant of what thou art, nought
   knowing
Of whence I am, nor that I am more better
Than Prospero, master of a full poor cell,   20
And thy no greater father.
   Mir.   More to know
Did never meddle with my thoughts.
   Pros.   'Tis time
I should inform thee farther. Lend thy hand,
And pluck my magic garment from me. So:
                       [*Lays down his mantle.*
Lie there, my art. Wipe thou thine eyes;
   have comfort.
The direful spectacle of the wreck, which
   touch'd
The very virtue of compassion in thee,
I have with such provision in mine art
So safely ordered that there is no soul—
No, not so much perdition as an hair   30
Betid to any creature in the vessel
Which thou heard'st cry, which thou saw'st
   sink. Sit down;
For thou must now know farther.
   Mir.   You have often
Begun to tell me what I am, but stopp'd
And left me to a bootless inquisition,
Concluding 'Stay: not yet.'
   Pros.   The hour 's now come;
The very minute bids thee ope thine ear;
Obey and be attentive. Canst thou remember
A time before we came unto this cell?
I do not think thou canst, for then thou wast
   not   40
Out three years old.
   Mir.   Certainly, sir, I can.
   Pros. By what? by any other house or
   person?
Of any thing the image tell me that
Hath kept with thy remembrance.
   Mir.   'Tis far off
And rather like a dream than an assurance
That my remembrance warrants. Had I not
Four or five women once that tended me?
   Pros. Thou hadst, and more, Miranda.
   But how is it
That this lives in thy mind? What seest
   thou else
In the dark backward and abysm of time?   50

If thou remember'st aught ere thou camest
   here,
How thou camest here thou mayst.
   Mir.   But that I do not.
   Pros. Twelve year since, Miranda, twelve
   year since,
Thy father was the Duke of Milan and
A prince of power.
   Mir.   Sir, are not you my father?
   Pros. Thy mother was a piece of virtue,
   and
She said thou wast my daughter; and thy
   father
Was Duke of Milan; and thou his only heir
And princess no worse issued.
   Mir.   O the heavens!
What foul play had we, that we came from
   thence?   60
Or blessed was 't we did?
   Pros.   Both, both, my girl:
By foul play, as thou say'st, were we heaved
   thence,
But blessedly holp hither.
   Mir.   O, my heart bleeds
To think o' the teen that I have turn'd you
   to,
Which is from my remembrance! Please you,
   farther.
   Pros. My brother and thy uncle, call'd
   Antonio—
I pray thee, mark me—that a brother should
Be so perfidious!—he whom next thyself
Of all the world I loved and to him put
The manage of my state; as at that time   70
Through all the signories it was the first
And Prospero the prime duke, being so
   reputed
In dignity, and for the liberal arts
Without a parallel; those being all my study,
The government I cast upon my brother
And to my state grew stranger, being trans-
   ported
And rapt in secret studies. Thy false uncle—
Does thou attend me?
   Mir.   Sir, most heedfully.
   Pros. Being once perfected how to grant
   suits,
How to deny them, who to advance and who

20. **full**, very, exceedingly. 22. **meddle**, mingle. 24. **So**, used with a gesture, meaning "good," "very well." 28. **provision**, foresight. 29. **no soul**, i.e., lost; many emendations. 30. **perdition**, loss. 35. **bootless inquisition**, profitless inquiry. 41. **Out**, fully. 45-46. **assurance . . . warrants**, certainty that my memory guarantees.

56. **piece**, masterpiece. 59. **issued**, born. 64. **teen . . . to**, trouble I have brought you into. 65. **from**, i.e., has no place in. 70. **manage**, management. 71. **signories**, states of northern Italy. 73. **liberal arts**, allusion to the learned studies of the Middle Ages. 76. **state**, position as ruler. 77. **secret studies**, magic, the occult. 79. **perfected**, informed completely.

To trash for over-topping, new created   81
The creatures that were mine, I say, or
    changed 'em,
Or else new form'd 'em; having both the key
Of officer and office, set all hearts i' the state
To what tune pleased his ear; that now he
    was
The ivy which had hid my princely trunk,
And suck'd my verdure out on 't. Thou at-
    tend'st not.
    Mir. O, good sir, I do.
    Pros.   I pray thee, mark me.
I, thus neglecting worldly ends, all dedicated
To closeness and the bettering of my mind 90
With that which, but by being so retired,
O'er-prized all popular rate, in my false
    brother
Awaked an evil nature; and my trust,
Like a good parent, did beget of him
A falsehood in its contrary as great
As my trust was; which had indeed no limit,
A confidence sans bound. He being thus
    lorded,
Not only with what my revenue yielded,
But what my power might else exact, like one
†Who having into truth, by telling of it,   100
Made such a sinner of his memory,
To credit his own lie, he did believe
He was indeed the duke; out o' the substitu-
    tion,
And executing the outward face of royalty,
With all prerogative: hence his ambition
    growing—
Dost thou hear?
    Mir.   Your tale, sir, would cure deafness.
    Pros. To have no screen between this part
    he play'd
And him he play'd it for, he needs will be
Absolute Milan. Me, poor man, my library
Was dukedom large enough: of temporal
    royalties   110
He thinks me now incapable; confederates—

81. trash, check a hound by tying a weight to its
neck. over-topping, running too far ahead of the pack.
83. key, tool for tuning stringed instruments, with suggestion of the usual meaning. 90. closeness, retirement, seclusion. 91-92. but . . . rate, except that it
was done in retirement, (would have) surpassed in value
all popular estimate. 93. Awaked. I in line 89 is the
subject. 95. in its contrary, of an opposite kind.
97. sans, without. lorded, raised to lordship. 100-102.
[W]ho . . . lie, a difficult passage; the meaning is: He had
[li]ed so long that he believed his own lies. New Cam-
[brid]ge editors read minted for into, interpreting the pas-
[sage] as a figure from coining of baser metals, so that
[into] means "counting," substitution means "the sub-
[stitutin]g of baser metals for gold," and executing . . .
[it] means "stamping the coins." 109. Absolute
[Milan,] actual duke of Milan. 110. royalties, preroga-
[tives an]d rights of a sovereign. 111. confederates,

So dry he was for sway—wi' the King of
    Naples
To give him annual tribute, do him hom-
    age,
Subject his coronet to his crown and bend
The dukedom yet unbow'd—alas, poor
    Milan!—
To most ignoble stooping.
    Mir.   O the heavens!
    Pros. Mark his condition and the event;
    then tell me
If this might be a brother.
    Mir.   I should sin
To think but nobly of my grandmother:
Good wombs have borne bad sons.
    Pros.   Now the condition. 120
This King of Naples, being an enemy
To me inveterate, hearkens my brother's
    suit;
Which was, that he, in lieu o' the premises
Of homage and I know not how much
    tribute,
Should presently extirpate me and mine
Out of the dukedom and confer fair Milan
With all the honours on my brother:
    whereon,
A treacherous army levied, one midnight
Fated to the purpose did Antonio open
The gates of Milan, and, i' the dead of dark-
    ness,
The ministers for the purpose hurried thence
Me and thy crying self.
    Mir.   Alack, for pity!
I, not remembering how I cried out then,
Will cry it o'er again: it is a hint
That wrings mine eyes to 't.
    Pros.   Hear a little further
And then I'll bring thee to the present
    business
Which now's upon's; without the which this
    story
Were most impertinent.
    Mir.   Wherefore did they not
That hour destroy us?
    Pros.   Well demanded, wench:
My tale provokes that question. Dear, they
    durst not,   140
So dear the love my people bore me, nor set
A mark so bloody on the business, but
With colours fairer painted their foul ends.

112. dry, thirsty. 117. condition, contract, covenant. event, outcome. 123. in . . . premises, in return
for the stipulations. 134. hint, occasion. 138. impertinent, irrelevant. 139. wench, used as a term of
affectionate address.

In few, they hurried us aboard a bark,
Bore us some leagues to sea; where they pre-
    pared
A rotten carcass of a boat, not rigg'd,
Nor tackle, sail, nor mast; the very rats
Instinctively have quit it: there they hoist us,
To cry to the sea that roar'd to us, to sigh
To the winds whose pity, sighing back again,
Did us but loving wrong.
    Mir.   Alack, what trouble 151
Was I then to you!
    Pros.   O, a cherubin
Thou wast that did preserve me. Thou didst
    smile,
Infused with a fortitude from heaven,
When I have deck'd the sea with drops full
    salt,
Under my burthen groan'd; which raised in
    me
An undergoing stomach, to bear up
Against what should ensue.
    Mir.   How came we ashore?
    Pros. By Providence divine.
Some food we had and some fresh water that
A noble Neapolitan, Gonzalo,   161
Out of his charity, who being then appointed
Master of this design, did give us, with
Rich garments, linens, stuffs and necessaries,
Which since have steaded much; so, of his
    gentleness,
Knowing I loved my books, he furnish'd me
From mine own library with volumes that
· I prize above my dukedom.
    Mir.   Would I might
But ever see that man!
    Pros. Now I arise: [*Resumes his mantle.*
Sit still, and hear the last of our sea-sorrow.
Here in this island we arrived; and here   171
Have I, thy schoolmaster, made thee more
    profit
Than other princesses can that have more
    time
For vainer hours and tutors not so careful.
    Mir. Heavens thank you for 't! And now,
    I pray you, sir,
For still 'tis beating in my mind, your reason
For raising this sea-storm?

    Pros.   Know thus far forth.
By accident most strange, bountiful Fortune,
Now my dear lady, hath mine enemies
Brought to this shore; and by my prescience
I find my zenith doth depend upon   181
A most auspicious star, whose influence
If now I court not but omit, my fortunes
Will ever after droop. Here cease more ques-
    tions:
Thou art inclined to sleep; 'tis a good
    dulness,
And give it way: I know thou canst not
    choose.   [*Miranda sleeps.*
Come away, servant, come. I am ready now.
Approach, my Ariel, come.

              Enter ARIEL.

    Ari. All hail, great master! grave sir,
    hail! I come   189
To answer thy best pleasure; be 't to fly,
To swim, to dive into the fire, to ride
On the curl'd clouds, to thy strong bidding
    task
Ariel and all his quality.
    Pros.   Hast thou, spirit,
Perform'd to point the tempest that I bade
    thee?
    Ari. To every article.
I boarded the king's ship; now on the beak,
Now in the waist, the deck, in every cabin,
I flamed amazement: sometime I'ld divide,
And burn in many places; on the topmast,
The yards and bowsprit, would I flame
    distinctly,   200
Then meet and join. Jove's lightnings, the
    precursors
O' the dreadful thunder-claps, more mo-
    mentary
And sight-outrunning were not; the fire and
    cracks
Of sulphurous roaring the most mighty
    Neptune
Seem to besiege and make his bold waves
    tremble,
Yea, his dread trident shake.
    Pros.   My brave spirit!
Who was so firm, so constant, that this coil

---

144. **few,** few words. 146. **boat,** F: *butt,* which should
be retained with the meaning "tub" (for boat). 151.
loving wrong, figure of speech called *oxymoron,* in
which, to emphasize a contrast, contradictory terms are
associated; the *wrong* done by sea and winds was wrought
by seeming sympathy. 152. **cherubin,** plural used as
singular; applied to an angelic woman. 155. **deck'd.**
New Cambridge editors read *eked,* increased. 156.
which, i.e., the smile. 157. **undergoing stomach,**
courage to undergo. 165. **steaded,** stood in good stead.

181. **zenith,** height of fortune; astrological term.
182. **influence,** power raining down from the heaven
upon man; astrological term. 185. **dulness,** drowsi-
187. **Come away,** come. 192. **task,** make dem
upon. 193. **quality,** profession, i.e., the cult of s
194. **point,** i.e., to the smallest detail. 196.
prow. 197. **waist,** midship. **deck,** poop-deck
stern. 200. **distinctly,** separately. 202. **mom**
instantaneous. 207. **coil,** tumult.

Would not infect his reason?

Ari.   Not a soul
But felt a fever of the mad and play'd
Some tricks of desperation. All but mari-
ners   210
Plunged in the foaming brine and quit
the vessel,
Then all afire with me: the king's son,
Ferdinand,
With hair up-staring,—then like reeds, not
hair,—
Was the first man that leap'd; cried, 'Hell
is empty,
And all the devils are here.'

Pros.   Why, that's my spirit!
But was not this nigh shore?

Ari.   Close by, my master.

Pros. But are they, Ariel, safe?

Ari.   Not a hair perish'd;
On their sustaining garments not a blem-
ish,
But fresher than before: and, as thou badest
me,
In troops I have dispersed them 'bout the
isle.   220
The king's son have I landed by himself;
Whom I left cooling of the air with sighs
In an odd angle of the isle and sitting,
His arms in this sad knot.

Pros.   Of the king's ship
The mariners say how thou hast disposed
And all the rest o' the fleet.

Ari.   Safely in harbour
Is the king's ship; in the deep nook, where
once
Thou call'dst me up at midnight to fetch
dew
From the still-vex'd Bermoothes, there she's
hid:
The mariners all under hatches stow'd;   230
Who, with a charm join'd to their suffer'd
labour,
I have left asleep: and for the rest o' the
fleet
Which I dispersed, they all have met again
And are upon the Mediterranean flote,
Bound sadly home for Naples,

Supposing that they saw the king's ship
wreck'd
And his great person perish.

Pros.   Ariel, thy charge
Exactly is performed: but there's more work.
What is the time o' the day?

Ari.   Past the mid season.

Pros. At least two glasses. The time
'twixt six and now   240
Must by us both be spent most preciously.

Ari. Is there more toil? Since thou dost
give me pains,
Let me remember thee what thou hast promised,
Which is not yet perform'd me.

Pros.   How now? moody?
What is 't thou canst demand?

Ari.   My liberty.

Pros. Before the time be out? no more!

Ari.   I prithee,
Remember I have done thee worthy service;
Told thee no lies, made thee no mistakings,
served
Without or grudge or grumblings: thou
didst promise
To bate me a full year.

Pros.   Dost thou forget   250
From what a torment I did free thee?

Ari.   No.

Pros. Thou dost, and think'st it much to
tread the ooze
Of the salt deep,
To run upon the sharp wind of the north,
To do me business in the veins o' the earth
When it is baked with frost.

Ari.   I do not, sir.

Pros. Thou liest, malignant thing! Hast
thou forgot
The foul witch Sycorax, who with age and
envy
Was grown into a hoop? hast thou forgot
her?

Ari. No, sir.

Pros.   Thou hast. Where was she born?
speak; tell me.   260

Ari. Sir, in Argier.

Pros.   O, was she so? I must
Once in a month recount what thou hast
been,

---

209. **fever of the mad**, i.e., such as madmen feel.
Some editors follow Dryden in reading *mind*. 213. **up-
staring**, standing on end. 218. **sustaining garments**,
[pro]bably, garments that sustained them in the sea. 223.
[ang]le, corner. 227. **nook**, bay. 228. **fetch dew**, for
[th]e incantation. 229. **Bermoothes**, Bermudas; a
[possi]ble reference to *A Discovery of the Barmudas* (1609),
[one of] the sources of the play. 234. **flote**, sea, or pos-
[sibly] flotilla, i.e., making for the Mediterranean flotilla
[(Cambridge).

240. **glasses**, i.e., hour-glasses. 242. **pains**, trouble,
labor. 243. **remember**, remind. 248. **mistakings**,
errors. 249. **or . . . or**, either . . . or. 250. **bate . . .
year**, remit me a year of service. Ariel, as a spirit,
longs for freedom; as a spirit, he is also incapable of
affection or gratitude as entertained by human beings.
261. **Argier**, Algiers.

Which thou forget'st. This damn'd witch
    Sycorax,
For mischiefs manifold and sorceries ter-
    rible
To enter human hearing, from Argier,
Thou know'st, was banish'd: for one thing
    she did
They would not take her life. Is not this
    true?
  Ari. Ay, sir.
  Pros. This blue-eyed hag was hither
    brought with child
And here was left by the sailors. Thou, my
    slave,   270
As thou report'st thyself, wast then her
    servant;
And, for thou wast a spirit too delicate
To act her earthy and abhorr'd commands,
Refusing her grand hests, she did confine
    thee,
By help of her more potent ministers
And in her most unmitigable rage,
Into a cloven pine; within which rift
Imprison'd thou didst painfully remain
A dozen years; within which space she died
And left thee there; where thou did'st vent
    thy groans   280
As fast as mill-wheels strike. Then was this
    island—
Save for the son that she did litter here,
A freckled whelp hag-born—not honour'd
    with
A human shape.
  Ari.   Yes, Caliban her son.
  Pros. Dull thing, I say so; he, that Cali-
    ban
Whom now I keep in service. Thou best
    know'st
What torment I did find thee in; thy groans
Did make wolves howl and penetrate the
    breasts
Of ever angry bears: it was a torment
To lay upon the damn'd, which Sycorax 290
Could not again undo: it was mine art,
When I arrived and heard thee, that made
    gape
The pine and let thee out.
  Ari.   I thank thee, master.

  Pros. If thou more murmur'st, I will rend
    an oak
And peg thee in his knotty entrails till
Thou hast howl'd away twelve winters.
  Ari.   Pardon, master;
I will be correspondent to command
And do my spiriting gently.
  Pros.   Do so, and after two days
I will discharge thee.
  Ari.   That's my noble master!
What shall I do? say what; what shall I do?
  Pros. Go make thyself like a nymph o' the
    sea: be subject   301
To no sight but thine and mine, invisible
To every eyeball else. Go take this shape
And hither come in 't: go, hence with
    diligence!   [*Exit Ariel.*
Awake, dear heart, awake! thou hast slept
    well;
Awake!
  Mir. The strangeness of your story put
Heaviness in me.
  Pros.   Shake it off. Come on;
We'll visit Caliban my slave, who never
Yields us kind answer.
  Mir.   'Tis a villain, sir,
I do not love to look on.
  Pros.   But, as 'tis, 310
We cannot miss him: he does make our fire,
Fetch in our wood and serves in offices
That profit us. What, ho! slave! Caliban!
Thou earth, thou! speak.
  Cal. [*Within*] There's wood enough with-
    in.
  Pros. Come forth, I say! there's other
    business for thee:
Come, thou tortoise! when?

     Re-enter Ariel *like a water-nymph.*

Fine apparition! My quaint Ariel,
Hark in thine ear.
  Ari.   My lord, it shall be done. [*Exit.*
  Pros. Thou poisonous slave, got by the
    devil himself
Upon thy wicked dam, come forth!   320

       Enter Caliban.

  Cal. As wicked dew as e'er my mother
    brush'd
With raven's feather from unwholesome

---

266. **one thing she did,** allusion not explained; taken by New Cambridge editors as evidence of a cut in the play. Lamb suggested that Shakespeare was thinking of the witch who saved Algiers from Charles V in 1541 by raising a storm that dispersed his fleet. 269. **blue-eyed,** usually interpreted as referring to dark circles under the eyes. Staunton suggested *blear-eyed.* 274. **hests,** commands. 283. **freckled,** spotted.

297. **correspondent,** responsive, submissive. **miss,** do without. 317. **quaint,** ingenious, c[?] 321. **wicked,** mischievous, harmful.

Drop on you both! a south-west blow on ye
And blister you all o'er!

Pros. For this, be sure, to-night thou shalt
    have cramps,
Side-stitches that shall pen thy breath up;
    urchins
Shall, for that vast of night that they may
    work,
All exercise on thee; thou shalt be pinch'd
As thick as honeycomb, each pinch more
    stinging
Than bees that made 'em.

Cal.   I must eat my dinner. 330
This island's mine, by Sycorax my mother,
Which thou takest from me. When thou
    camest first,
Thou strokedst me and madest much of me,
    wouldst give me
Water with berries in 't, and teach me how
To name the bigger light, and how the less,
That burn by day and night: and then I
    loved thee
And show'd thee all the qualities o' the isle,
The fresh springs, brine-pits, barren place
    and fertile:
Cursed be I that did so! All the charms
Of Sycorax, toads, beetles, bats, light on you!
For I am all the subjects that you have,   341
Which first was mine own king: and here you
    sty me
In this hard rock, whiles you do keep from
    me
The rest o' the island.

Pros.   Thou most lying slave,
Whom stripes may move, not kindness! I
    have used thee,
Filth as thou art, with human care, and
    lodged thee
In mine own cell, till thou didst seek to
    violate
The honour of my child.

Cal. O ho, O ho! would 't had been done!
Thou didst prevent me; I had peopled else 350
This isle with Calibans.

Pros.   Abhorred slave,
Which any print of goodness wilt not take,

Being capable of all ill! I pitied thee,
Took pains to make thee speak, taught thee
    each hour
One thing or other: when thou didst not,
    savage,
Know thine own meaning, but wouldst
    gabble like
A thing most brutish, I endow'd thy pur-
    poses
With words that made them known. But
    thy vile race,
Though thou didst learn, had that in 't which
    good natures
Could not abide to be with; therefore wast
    thou
Deservedly confined into this rock,   361
Who hadst deserved more than a prison.

Cal. You taught me language; and my
    profit on 't
Is, I know how to curse. The red plague rid
    you
For learning me your language!

Pros.   Hag-seed, hence!
Fetch us in fuel; and be quick, thou'rt best,
To answer other business. Shrug'st thou,
    malice?
If thou neglect'st or dost unwillingly
What I command, I'll rack thee with old
    cramps,
Fill all thy bones with aches, make thee
    roar   370
That beasts shall tremble at thy din.

Cal.   No, pray thee.
[*Aside*] I must obey: his art is of such power,
It would control my dam's god, Setebos,
And make a vassal of him.

Pros.   So, slave; hence! [*Exit Caliban.*

Re-enter ARIEL, *invisible, playing and
    singing;* FERDINAND *following.*

ARIEL'S *song.*

Come unto these yellow sands,
    And then take hands:
Courtsied when you have and kiss'd
    The wild waves whist,

---

323. **south-west**, i.e., wind (bringing disease). 326.
urchins, hedgehogs; here, suggesting goblins. 327.
vast, long hours. 328. **exercise**, practice, work. 334.
berries. Strachey's *Repertory*, one of the sources, says
that the Bermudas were full of thickets of "goodly
Cedar . . . the Berries whereof, our men seething, straining, and letting stand some three or foure daies, made a
kind of pleasant drinke." 338. **brine-pits**, salt springs.
342. **sty**, put in sty. 346. **human**, humane. 351-362.
Abhorred . . . prison. F assigns this speech to Miranda. This may be correct, since Prospero seems to

break in suddenly in line 365. 353. **capable of**, susceptible to. 357-358. **endow'd . . . known**, enabled you
to make known what was going on in your mind. 358.
race, natural disposition. 364. **red plague**, bubonic
plague. **rid**, destroy, with play on *red*. 365. **Hag-seed**,
hag's offspring. 370. **aches**, pronounced *aitches*. 373.
Setebos, mentioned in Eden's *History of Travel* (1577)
as a deity, or devil, of the Patagonians. 376-378. **Come
. . . kiss'd**, three motions before the dance—take
hands, courtsey, kiss (New Cambridge). 379. **whist**,
silent.

Foot it featly here and there;   380
And, sweet sprites, the burthen bear.
Burthen [*dispersedly*]. Hark, hark!
                                        Bow-wow.
      The watch-dogs bark:
                                        Bow-wow.
Ari. Hark, hark! I hear
      The strain of strutting chanticleer
      Cry, Cock-a-diddle-dow.
Fer. Where should this music be? i' the
      air or the earth?
It sounds no more: and, sure, it waits upon
Some god o' the island. Sitting on a bank,
Weeping again the king my father's wreck, 390
This music crept by me upon the waters,
Allaying both their fury and my passion
With its sweet air: thence I have follow'd it,
Or it hath drawn me rather. But 'tis gone.
No, it begins again.

ARIEL *sings.*

Full fathom five thy father lies;
      Of his bones are coral made;
Those are pearls that were his eyes:
      Nothing of him that doth fade
But doth suffer a sea-change   400
Into something rich and strange.
Sea-nymphs hourly ring his knell:
                        Burthen. Ding-dong.
Ari. Hark! now I hear them,—Ding-dong,
      bell.
Fer. The ditty does remember my
      drown'd father.
This is no mortal business, nor no sound
That the earth owes. I hear it now above
      me.
Pros. The fringed curtains of thine eye
      advance
And say what thou seest yond.
Mir.   What is 't? a spirit?
Lord, how it looks about! Believe me, sir 410
It carries a brave form. But 'tis a spirit.
Pros. No, wench; it eats and sleeps and
      hath such senses
As we have, such. This gallant which thou
      seest
Was in the wreck; and, but he's something
      stain'd
With grief that's beauty's canker, thou
      mightst call him

A goodly person: he hath lost his fellows
And strays about to find 'em.
Mir.   I might call him
A thing divine, for nothing natural
I ever saw so noble.
Pros.   [*Aside*] It goes on, I see,
As my soul prompts it. Spirit, fine spirit!
      I'll free thee   420
Within two days for this.
Fer.   Most sure, the goddess
On whom these airs attend! Vouchsafe my
      prayer
May know if you remain upon this island;
And that you will some good instruction give
How I may bear me here: my prime request,
Which I do last pronounce, is, O you wonder!
If you be maid or no?
Mir.   No wonder, sir;
But certainly a maid.
Fer.   My language! heavens!
I am the best of them that speak this speech,
Were I but where 'tis spoken.
Pros.   How? the best? 430
What wert thou, if the King of Naples heard
      thee?
Fer. A single thing, as I am now, that
      wonders
To hear thee speak of Naples. He does hear
      me;
And that he does I weep: myself am Naples,
Who with mine eyes, never since at ebb,
      beheld
The king my father wreck'd.
Mir.   Alack, for mercy!
Fer. Yes, faith, and all his lords; the Duke
      of Milan
And his brave son being twain.
Pros.   [*Aside*] The Duke of Milan
And his more braver daughter could control
      thee,
If now 'twere fit to do 't. At the first sight 440
They have changed eyes. Delicate Ariel,
I'll set thee free for this. [*To Fer.*] A word,
      good sir;
I fear you have done yourself some wrong: a
      word.
Mir. Why speaks my father so ungently?
      This
Is the third man that e'er I saw, the first

---

380. **featly**, neatly. 381. **burthen**, refrain. 392.
passion, feeling powerfully moving the mind. 405.
remember, commemorate. 415. **canker**, canker-
worm (feeding on buds and leaves).

419. **It goes on**, my charm works. 423. **remain**,
dwell. 429. **best**, i.e., in birth. 432. **single**, solitary,
with a suggestion of feebleness. 439. **control**, confute.
441. **changed eyes**, exchanged amorous glances, with
suggestion of the eye as the origin of the passion of love.
443. **done . . . wrong**, are mistaken.

That e'er I sigh'd for: pity move my father
To be inclined my way!

Fer.　　　　　　O, if a virgin,
And your affection not gone forth, I'll make
　you
The queen of Naples.

Pros.　　　　Soft, sir! one word more.
[*Aside*] They are both in either's powers; but
　this swift business　　　　　　450
I must uneasy make, lest too light winning
Make the prize light. [*To Fer.*] One word
　more; I charge thee
That thou attend me: thou dost here usurp
The name thou owest not; and hast put thy-
　self
Upon this island as a spy, to win it
From me, the lord on 't.

Fer.　　　　　No, as I am a man.

Mir. There's nothing ill can dwell in such
　a temple:
If the ill spirit have so fair a house,
Good things will strive to dwell with 't.

Pros.　　　　　　　Follow me.
Speak not you for him; he's a traitor. Come;
I'll manacle thy neck and feet together: 461
Sea-water shalt thou drink; thy food shall be
The fresh-brook muscles, wither'd roots and
　husks
Wherein the acorn cradled. Follow.

Fer.　　　　　　　　　　No;
I will resist such entertainment till
Mine enemy has more power.
　　　　　　[*Draws, and is charmed from moving.*

Mir.　　　　　　　O dear father,
Make not too rash a trial of him, for
He's gentle and not fearful.

Pros.　　　　　　What? I say,
My foot my tutor? Put thy sword up,
　traitor;
Who makest a show but darest not strike,
　thy conscience　　　　　　　470
Is so possess'd with guilt: come from thy
　ward,
For I can here disarm thee with this stick
And make thy weapon drop.

Mir.　　　　　　Beseech you, father.

Pros. Hence! hang not on my garments.

Mir.　　　　　　　Sir, have pity;

I'll be his surety.

Pros.　　　　Silence! one word more
Shall make me chide thee, if not hate thee.
　What!
An advocate for an impostor! hush!
Thou think'st there is no more such shapes
　as he,
Having seen but him and Caliban: foolish
　wench!
To the most of men this is a Caliban　480
And they to him are angels.

Mir.　　　　　　　My affections
Are then most humble; I have no ambition
To see a goodlier man.

Pros.　　　　　Come on; obey:
Thy nerves are in their infancy again
And have no vigour in them.

Fer.　　　　　　　So they are;
My spirits, as in a dream, are all bound up.
My father's loss, the weakness which I feel,
The wreck of all my friends, nor this man's
　threats,
To whom I am subdued, are but light to me,
Might I but through my prison once a day 490
Behold this maid: all corners else o' the earth
Let liberty make use of; space enough
Have I in such a prison.

Pros. [*Aside*] It works. [*To Fer.*] Come
　on.
Thou hast done well, fine Ariel! [*To Fer.*]
　Follow me.
[*To Ari.*] Hark what thou else shalt do me.

Mir.　　　　　　Be of comfort;
My father's of a better nature, sir,
Than he appears by speech: this is unwonted
Which now came from him.

Pros.　　　　　Thou shalt be as free
As mountain winds: but then exactly do
All points of my command.

Ari.　　　　　To the syllable. 500

Pros. Come, follow. Speak not for him.
　　　　　　　　　　　　[*Exeunt.*

ACT II.

SCENE I. *Another part of the island.*

Enter ALONSO, SEBASTIAN, ANTONIO, GON-
ZALO, ADRIAN, FRANCISCO, *and others.*

Gon. Beseech you, sir, be merry; you have
　cause,

---

451. **uneasy**, difficult. 451-452. **light . . . light**,
easy . . . cheap. 465. **entertainment**, treatment. 468.
gentle, well-born, high-spirited. **not fearful**, not dangerous (because incapable of treachery). 469. **foot**, subordinate. Miranda (the foot) presumes to instruct Prospero
(the head). 471. **come . . . ward.** New Cambridge
editors read comma after *come*, with the meaning, "Come,
off thy guard."

484. **nerves**, sinews. 491-492. **all . . . use of**, those
who are free may have all the rest of the world.

So have we all, of joy; for our escape
Is much beyond our loss. Our hint of woe
Is common; every day some sailor's wife,
The masters of some merchant and the
    merchant
Have just our theme of woe; but for the
    miracle,
I mean our preservation, few in millions
Can speak like us: then wisely, good sir,
    weigh
Our sorrow with our comfort.

Alon.   Prithee, peace.

Seb. He receives comfort like cold porridge.   10

Ant. The visitor will not give him o'er
so.

Seb. Look, he's winding up the watch of
his wit; by and by it will strike.

Gon. Sir,—

Seb. One: tell.

Gon. When every grief is entertain'd
    that 's offer'd,
Comes to the entertainer—

Seb. A dollar.

Gon. Dolour comes to him, indeed: you
have spoken truer than you purposed.   20

Seb. You have taken it wiselier than I
meant you should.

Gon. Therefore, my lord,—

Ant. Fie, what a spendthrift is he of his
    tongue!

Alon. I prithee, spare.

Gon. Well, I have done: but yet,—

Seb. He will be talking.

Ant. Which, of he or Adrian, for a good
wager, first begins to crow?

Seb. The old cock.   30

Ant. The cockerel.

Seb. Done. The wager?

Ant. A laughter.

Seb. A match!

Adr. Though this island seem to be
desert,—

Seb. Ha, ha, ha! So, you're paid.

Adr. Uninhabitable and almost inaccessible,—

Seb. Yet,—

Adr. Yet,—

Ant. He could not miss 't.   40

Adr. It must needs be of subtle, tender
and delicate temperance.

Ant. Temperance was a delicate wench.

Seb. Ay, and a subtle; as he most learnedly delivered.

Adr. The air breathes upon us here most
sweetly.

Seb. As if it had lungs and rotten ones.

Ant. Or as 'twere perfumed by a fen.

Gon. Here is every thing advantageous to
life.

Ant. True; save means to live.   50

Seb. Of that there's none, or little.

Gon. How lush and lusty the grass looks!
how green!

Ant. The ground indeed is tawny.

Seb. With an eye of green in 't.

Ant. He misses not much.

Seb. No; he doth but mistake the truth
totally.

Gon. But the rarity of it is,—which is
indeed almost beyond credit.

Seb. As many vouched rarities are.   60

Gon. That our garments, being, as they
were, drenched in the sea, hold notwithstanding their freshness and glosses, being
rather new-dyed than stained with salt
water.

Ant. If but one of his pockets could speak,
would it not say he lies?   66

Seb. Ay, or very falsely pocket up his
report.

Gon. Methinks our garments are now as
fresh as when we put them on first in Afric,
at the marriage of the king's fair daughter
Claribel to the King of Tunis.   71

Seb. 'Twas a sweet marriage, and we
prosper well in our return.

Adr. Tunis was never graced before with
such a paragon to their queen.

Gon. Not since widow Dido's time.

Ant. Widow! a pox o' that! How came
that widow in? widow Dido!

Seb. What if he had said 'widower Æneas'
too? Good Lord, how you take it!   80

---

40. **He . . . miss 't**, i.e., even if it is uninhabitable
and inaccessible, he could not refrain from talking about
it. 42. **temperance**, temperature. 43. **Temperance**,
a Puritan name for women, thought also to refer to
Temperance, a character in Chapman's *May Day* (1611).
54. **tawny**, dull brown. 55. **eye**, tinge. 60. **vouched**,
asserted. 65. **pockets**. Some editors suppose that
reference is made to mud in the pockets. There is, at
any rate, some peculiarity in Gonzalo's appearance; cf.
l. 30. 76. **widow Dido**, queen of Carthage deserted by
Æneas; possible topical reference to Chapman's *Widow's
Tears*, or some other play.

---

5. **merchant . . . merchant**, merchant vessel . . .
merchant. 11. **visitor**, one taking nourishment to the
sick. 15. **tell**, count (the strokes of the watch). 18.
dollar, widely circulated coin, the German *Thaler* and
the Spanish *piece of eight*. 33. **laughter**, sitting of eggs.
When Adrian (the *cockerel*) begins to speak (l. 35),
Sebastian loses the bet and pays with a *laugh* (*Ha, ha,
ha!* l. 36) for a *laughter*. 34. **A match**, a bargain;
agreed.

Adr. 'Widow Dido' said you? you make me study of that: she was of Carthage, not of Tunis.

Gon. This Tunis, sir, was Carthage.

Adr. Carthage?

Gon. I assure you, Carthage.   85

Seb. His word is more than the miraculous harp; he hath raised the wall and houses too.

Ant. What impossible matter will he make easy next?

Seb. I think he will carry this island home in his pocket and give it his son for an apple.   91

Ant. And, sowing the kernels of it in the sea, bring forth more islands.

Gon. Ay.

Ant. Why, in good time.

Gon. Sir, we were talking that our garments seem now as fresh as when we were at Tunis at the marriage of your daughter, who is now queen.

Ant. And the rarest that e'er came there.

Seb. Bate, I beseech you, widow Dido.   100

Ant. O, widow Dido! ay, widow Dido.

Gon. Is not, sir, my doublet as fresh as the first day I wore it? I mean, in a sort.

Ant. That sort was well fished for.

Gon. When I wore it at your daughter's marriage?

Alon. You cram these words into mine ears against

The stomach of my sense. Would I had never

Married my daughter there! for, coming thence,

My son is lost and, in my rate, she too,

Who is so far from Italy removed   110

I ne'er again shall see her. O thou mine heir

Of Naples and of Milan, what strange fish

Hath made his meal on thee?

Fran.   Sir, he may live:

I saw him beat the surges under him,

And ride upon their backs; he trod the water,

Whose enmity he flung aside, and breasted

The surge most swoln that met him; his bold head

'Bove the contentious waves he kept, and oar'd

Himself with his good arms in lusty stroke

To the shore, that o'er his wave-worn basis bow'd,   120

As stooping to relieve him: I not doubt

He came alive to land.

Alon.   No, no, he's gone.

Seb. Sir, you may thank yourself for this great loss,

That would not bless our Europe with your daughter,

But rather lose her to an African;

Where she at least is banish'd from your eye,

Who hath cause to wet the grief on 't.

Alon.   Prithee, peace.

Seb. You were kneel'd to and importuned otherwise

By all of us, and the fair soul herself

Weigh'd between loathness and obedience, at

Which end o' the beam should bow. We have lost your son,   131

I fear, for ever: Milan and Naples have

Moe widows in them of this business' making

Than we bring men to comfort them:

The fault's your own.

Alon.   So is the dear'st o' the loss.

Gon. My lord Sebastian,

The truth you speak doth lack some gentleness

And time to speak it in: you rub the sore,

When you should bring the plaster.

Seb.   Very well

Ant. And most chirurgeonly.   140

Gon. It is foul weather in us all, good sir,

When you are cloudy.

Seb.   Foul weather?

Ant.   Very foul.

Gon. Had I plantation of this isle, my lord,—

Ant. He 'ld sow 't with nettle-seed.

Seb.   Or docks, or mallows.

Gon. And were the king on 't, what would I do?

Seb. 'Scape being drunk for want of wine.

86. **miraculous harp**, allusion to Amphion's harp with which he raised the walls of Thebes. 95. **in good time**, vague expression of agreement or approbation. 100. **Bate**, leave out. 104. **sort**, lucky catch after much angling; probable suggestion of the age of the garment, with a play on *sort* in line 103. 107. **stomach . . . sense**, inclination of my mind. 109. **rate**, estimation. 113-122. **Sir . . . land**, Francisco's only speech. New Cambridge editors think the speech belongs to Gonzalo, and see in its assignment to Francisco a relic of an older version.

120. **basis**, foot, base. 127. **Who**, which (eye). 129-131. **the fair . . . bow**, the fair soul herself was poised uncertain between unwillingness and obedience as to which end of the scale should sink. 135. **dear'st o' the loss**, most precious of those lost (Ferdinand). 140. **chirurgeonly**, like a skilled surgeon. 141. **foul**, stormy. 143. **plantation**, colonization; subsequent play on the literal meaning.

Gon. I' the commonwealth I would by contraries

Execute all things; for no kind of traffic

Would I admit; no name of magistrate;

Letters should not be known; riches, poverty,   150

And use of service, none; contract, succession,

Bourn, bound of land, tilth, vineyard, none;

No use of metal, corn, or wine, or oil;

No occupation; all men idle, all;

And women too, but innocent and pure;

No sovereignty;—

Seb.   Yet he would be king on't.

Ant. The latter end of his commonwealth forgets the beginning.

Gon. All things in common nature should produce   159

Without sweat or endeavour: treason, felony,

Sword, pike, knife, gun, or need of any engine,

Would I not have; but nature should bring forth,

Of it own kind, all foison, all abundance,

To feed my innocent people.

Seb. No marrying 'mong his subjects?

Ant. None, man; all idle: whores and knaves.

Gon. I would with such perfection govern, sir,

To excel the golden age.

Seb.   God save his majesty!

Ant. Long live Gonzalo!

Gon.   And,—do you mark me, sir?

Alon. Prithee, no more: thou dost talk nothing to me.   171

Gon. I do well believe your highness; and did it to minister occasion to these gentlemen, who are of such sensible and nimble lungs that they always use to laugh at nothing.

Ant. 'Twas you we laughed at.

Gon. Who in this kind of merry fooling am nothing to you: so you may continue and laugh at nothing still.

Ant. What a blow was there given!   180

Seb. An it had not fallen flat-long.

Gon. You are gentlemen of brave mettle; you would lift the moon out of her sphere, if she would continue in it five weeks without changing.

Enter ARIEL, *invisible, playing solemn music.*

Seb. We would so, and then go a batfowling.

Ant. Nay, good my lord, be not angry.

Gon. No, I warrant you; I will not adventure my discretion so weakly. Will you laugh me asleep, for I am very heavy?

Ant. Go sleep, and hear us.   190

[*All sleep except Alon., Seb., and Ant.*

Alon. What, all so soon asleep! I wish mine eyes

Would, with themselves, shut up my thoughts: I find

They are inclined to do so.

Seb.   Please you, sir,

Do not omit the heavy offer of it:

It seldom visits sorrow; when it doth,

It is a comforter.

Ant.   We two, my lord,

Will guard your person while you take your rest,

And watch your safety

Alon.   Thank you. Wondrous heavy.

[*Alonso sleeps. Exit Ariel.*

Seb. What a strange drowsiness possesses them!

Ant. It is the quality o' the climate.

Seb.   Why   200

Doth it not then our eyelids sink? I find not

Myself disposed to sleep.

Ant.   Nor I; my spirits are nimble.

They fell together all, as by consent;

They dropp'd, as by a thunder-stroke. What might,

Worthy Sebastian? O, what might?—No more:—

And yet methinks I see it in thy face,

What thou shouldst be: the occasion speaks thee, and

147-156. I' the . . . sovereignty. This passage on man in his primitive state is based on Montaigne, *Essays,* I, xxx, and derived from Florio's translation (1603). 150. Letters, learning. 151. use of service, custom of employing servants. succession, holding of property by right of inheritance. 152. Bourn, boundaries. bound of land, landmarks. tilth, tillage of soil. 161. engine, instrument of warfare. 163. it, its. foison, plenty. 168. God, omitted in F in deference to the statute forbidding profanity on the stage. 174. sensive, endowed with sensibility. nimble, easily excited.

181. flat-long, with the flat of the sword. 182. mettle, temper, nature. 183. lift . . . sphere. As a planet in the old astronomy, the moon had a crystal sphere in which she moved. Gonzalo means that they would lift the moon out of her sphere if she remained steady in it. 185. bat-fowling, hunting birds at night with lantern and stick; also, gulling a simpleton. Gonzalo is the simpleton (or fowl), and Sebastian will use the moon as his lantern. 187. adventure, risk. 190. Go . . . us, let our laughing send you to sleep, or, go to sleep and hear us laugh at you. 194. omit, neglect. heavy, drowsy. 203. consent, agreement as to a course of action. 207. speaks, calls upon, proclaims (thee) king.

My strong imagination sees a crown
Dropping upon thy head.
   Seb.   What, art thou waking?
   Ant. Do you not hear me speak?
   Seb.   I do; and surely
It is a sleepy language and thou speak'st 211
Out of thy sleep. What is it thou didst say?
This is a strange repose, to be asleep
With eyes wide open; standing, speaking,
  moving,
And yet so fast asleep.
   Ant.   Noble Sebastian,
Thou let'st thy fortune sleep—die, rather;
  wink'st
Whiles thou art waking.
   Seb.   Thou dost snore distinctly;
There's meaning in thy snores.
   Ant. I am more serious than my custom:
  you
Must be so too, if heed me; which to do   220
Trebles thee o'er.
   Seb.   Well, I am standing water.
   Ant. I'll teach you how to flow.
   Seb.   Do so: to ebb
Hereditary sloth instructs me.
   Ant.   O,
If you but knew how you the purpose cherish
Whiles thus you mock it! how, in stripping
  it,
You more invest it! Ebbing men, indeed,
Most often do so near the bottom run
By their own fear or sloth.
   Seb.   Prithee, say on:
The setting of thine eye and cheek proclaim
A matter from thee, and a birth indeed 230
Which throes thee much to yield.
   Ant.   Thus, sir:
Although this lord of weak remembrance, this,
Who shall be of as little memory
When he is earth'd, hath here almost per-
  suaded,—
For he's a spirit of persuasion, only
Professes to persuade,—the king his son's
  alive,

'Tis as impossible that he's undrown'd
As he that sleeps here swims.
   Seb.   I have no hope
That he's undrown'd.
   Ant.   O, out of that 'no hope'
What great hope have you! no hope that
  way is   240
Another way so high a hope that even
Ambition cannot pierce a wink beyond,
But doubt discovery there. Will you grant
  with me
That Ferdinand is drown'd?
   Seb.   He's gone.
   Ant.   Then, tell me,
Who's the next heir of Naples?
   Seb.   Claribel.
   Ant. She that is queen of Tunis; she that
  dwells
Ten leagues beyond man's life; she that
  from Naples
Can have no note, unless the sun were post—
The man i' the moon's too slow—till new-
  born chins
Be rough and razorable; she that—from
  whom?   250
We all were sea-swallow'd, though some cast
  again,
And by that destiny to perform an act
Whereof what's past is prologue, what to
  come
In yours and my discharge.
   Seb.   What stuff is this! how say you?
'Tis true, my brother's daughter's queen of
  Tunis;
So is she heir of Naples; 'twixt which regions
There is some space.
   Ant.   A space whose every cubit
Seems to cry out, 'How shall that Claribel
Measure us back to Naples? Keep in Tunis,
And let Sebastian wake.' Say, this were
  death   260
That now hath seized them; why, they were
  no worse

216-217. **wink'st . . . waking,** keep'st thine eyes shut while awake. 217. **distinctly,** with separate and individual sounds. 221. **Trebles.** New Cambridge editors read *Troubles* in view of *standing water.* Onions defines as "makes thee three times as great." **standing water,** water which neither flows nor ebbs. 224. **purpose,** i.e., of being king. 225. **stripping it,** stripping off all pretense, revealing it. 226. **Ebbing men,** men whose fortunes ebb leaving them stranded. 229. **setting,** set expression. 230. **matter,** matter of importance. 231. **throes,** pains. 232. **this lord,** Gonzalo. **remembrance,** power of remembering. 234. **earth'd,** buried. 236. **Professes to persuade,** he was a privy councilor.

240. **that way,** i.e., in regard to Ferdinand's being saved. 242-243. **Ambition . . . there,** ambition itself cannot see any farther than that hope (of the crown) without doubting the reality of the objects it sees. Furness, following Nicholson's conjecture of *dout* (extinguish) for *doubt*, interprets, "when ambition pierces to its furthest wink there discovery ceases, and the crown is found." 247. **Ten . . . life,** it would take more than a lifetime to get there. 248. **note,** intimation. **post,** messenger. 250. **she . . . whom,** broken and difficult construction. *from whom?* probably, from whom will she learn? 251. **cast,** were disgorged, with pun on *casting* (of parts for a play). 254. **discharge,** performance, i.e., to get done. 259. **Measure us,** find (her) way. 259-260. **Keep . . . wake,** let her stay in Tunis, and let Sebastian wake (to his good fortune).

Than now they are. There be that can rule
  Naples
As well as he that sleeps; lords that can
  prate
As amply and unnecessarily
As this Gonzalo; I myself could make
A chough of as deep chat. O, that you bore
The mind that I do! what a sleep were this
For your advancement! Do you understand
  me?

  Seb.   Methinks I do.

  Ant.   And how does your content
Tender your own good fortune?

  Seb.   I remember
You did supplant your brother Prospero.

  Ant.   True: 271
And look how well my garments sit upon
  me;
Much feater than before: my brother's
  servants
Were then my fellows; now they are my men.

  Seb.   But, for your conscience?

  Ant.   Ay, sir; where lies that? if 'twere a
  kibe,
'Twould put me to my slipper: but I feel not
This deity in my bosom: twenty consciences,
That stand 'twixt me and Milan, candied
  be they
And melt ere they molest! Here lies your
  brother,   280
No better than the earth he lies upon,
If he were that which now he's like, that's
  dead;
Whom I, with this obedient steel, three
  inches of it,
Can lay to bed for ever; whiles you, doing
  thus,
To the perpetual wink for aye might put
This ancient morsel, this Sir Prudence, who
Should not upbraid our course. For all the
  rest,
They'll take suggestion as a cat laps milk;
They'll tell the clock to any business that
We say befits the hour.

  Seb.   Thy case, dear friend,   290
Shall be my precedent; as thou got'st Milan,
  'll come by Naples. Draw thy sword: one
  stroke
  ll free thee from the tribute which thou
  ayest;

And I the king shall love thee.

  Ant.   Draw together;
And when I rear my hand, do you the like,
To fall it on Gonzalo.

  Seb.   O, but one word.   [*They talk apart.*

Re-enter ARIEL, invisible.

  Ari.   My master through his art foresees
  the danger
That you, his friend, are in; and sends me
  forth—
For else his project dies—to keep them
  living.   [*Sings in Gonzalo's ear.*

  While you here do snoring lie,   300
  Open-eyed conspiracy
      His time doth take.
  If of life you keep a care,
  Shake off slumber, and beware:
      Awake, awake!

  Ant.   Then let us both be sudden.

  Gon.   Now, good angels
Preserve the king.   [*They wake.*

  Alon.   Why, how now? ho, awake! Why
  are you drawn?
Wherefore this ghastly looking?

  Gon.   What's the matter?

  Seb.   Whiles we stood here securing your
  repose,   310
Even now, we heard a hollow burst of bellowing
Like bulls, or rather lions: did 't not wake
  you?
It struck mine ear most terribly.

  Alon.   I heard nothing.

  Ant.   O, 'twas a din to fright a monster's
  ear,
To make an earthquake! sure, it was the roar
Of a whole herd of lions.

  Alon.   Heard you this, Gonzalo?

  Gon.   Upon mine honour, sir, I heard a
  humming,
And that a strange one too, which did awake
  me:
I shaked you, sir, and cried: as mine eyes
  open'd,   319
I saw their weapons drawn: there was a noise,
That's verily. 'Tis best we stand upon our
  guard,
Or that we quit this place: let's draw our
  weapons.

I . . . chat, I could teach a jackdaw to talk
269. content, desire, contentment. 270.
ovide for. 273. feater, more becomingly.
ore on the heel. 279. candied, frozen,

296. fall it, cause it to fall. 302. time, opportunity
306. sudden, swift in action. 317. humming, i.e.,
Ariel's song.

Alon. Lead off this ground; and let's make
　　further search
For my poor son.

Gon. Heavens keep him from these beasts!
For he is, sure, i' the island.

Alon. 　　　　　　　　Lead away.

Ari. Prospero my lord shall know what I
　　have done:
So, king, go safely on to seek thy son.
　　　　　　　　　　　　　　　　[*Exeunt.*

SCENE II. *Another part of the island.*

Enter CALIBAN *with a burden of wood. A
noise of thunder heard.*

Cal. All the infections that the sun sucks
　　up
From bogs, fens, flats, on Prosper fall and
　　make him
By inch-meal a disease! His spirits hear me
And yet I needs must curse. But they'll nor
　　pinch,
Fright me with urchin-shows, pitch me i' the
　　mire,
Nor lead me, like a firebrand, in the dark
Out of my way, unless he bid 'em; but
For every trifle are they set upon me;
Sometime like apes that mow and chatter at
　　me　　　　　　　　　　　　　　　　　　9
And after bite me, then like hedgehogs which
Lie tumbling in my barefoot way and mount
Their pricks at my footfall; sometime am I
All wound with adders who with cloven
　　tongues
Do hiss me into madness.

Enter TRINCULO.

　　　　　　　　　　　Lo, now, lo!
Here comes a spirit of his, and to torment
　　me
For bringing wood in slowly. I'll fall flat;
Perchance he will not mind me.　　　　　17

Trin. Here's neither bush nor shrub, to
bear off any weather at all, and another
storm brewing; I hear it sing i' the wind:
yond same black cloud, yond huge one, looks
like a foul bombard that would shed his liquor.
If it should thunder as it did before, I know
not where to hide my head: yond same cloud

cannot choose but fall by pailfuls. What
have we here? a man or a fish? dead or alive?
A fish: he smells like a fish; a very ancient
and fish-like smell; a kind of not of the newest Poor-John. A strange fish! Were I in 29
England now, as once I was, and had but
this fish painted, not a holiday fool there but
would give a piece of silver: there would this
monster make a man; any strange beast there
makes a man: when they will not give a doit
to relieve a lame beggar, they will lay out ten
to see a dead Indian. Legged like a man! and
his fins like arms! Warm o' my troth! I do
now let loose my opinion; hold it no longer:
this is no fish, but an islander, that hath
lately suffered by a thunderbolt. [*Thunder.*]
Alas, the storm is come again! my best way
is to creep under his gaberdine; there is no
other shelter hereabout: misery acquaints a
man with strange bed-fellows. I will here
shroud till the dregs of the storm be past. 43

Enter STEPHANO, *singing: a bottle in his hand.*

Ste. I shall no more to sea, to sea,
　　　Here shall I die ashore——
This is a very scurvy tune to sing at a man's
funeral: well, here's my comfort. [*Drinks.*
[*Sings.*

　　The master, the swabber, the boatswain
　　　　and I,
　　　　The gunner and his mate
　　Loved Mall, Meg and Marian and Mar-
　　　　gery,
　　　　But none of us cared for Kate; 51
　　For she had a tongue with a tang,
　　　　Would cry to a sailor, Go hang!
　　She loved not the savour of tar nor of
　　　　pitch,
　　Yet a tailor might scratch her where'er
　　　　she did itch:
　　　　Then to sea, boys, and let her go
　　　　　hang!

This is a scurvy tune too: but here's my
comfort.　　　　　　　　　　　　[*Drinks.*

Cal. Do not torment me: Oh!　　　　58

Ste. What's the matter? Have we devils
here? Do you put tricks upon 's with sav-

Scene ii. 3. **inch-meal**, little by little. 9. **mow**,
make faces. 19. **bear off**, keep off. 22. **foul bombard**,
dirty leathern bottle.

29. **Poor-John**, salted hake, type of poor fare. **fish.**
Malone cites a license issued by the Master of the
Revels (1632) "to shew a strange fish for half a yeare."
33. **make a man**, i.e., make his fortune. 34. **doit**, a
Dutch coin equivalent to half a farthing. 40. **gaberdine**, cloak, loose upper garment. 43. **shroud**, take
shelter. **dregs**, last remains.

ages and men of Ind, ha? I have not 'scaped drowning to be afeard now of your four legs; for it hath been said, As proper a man as ever went on four legs cannot make him give ground; and it shall be said so again while Stephano breathes at nostrils.

Cal. The spirit torments me; Oh!   66

Ste. This is some monster of the isle with four legs, who hath got, as I take it, an ague. Where the devil should he learn our language? I will give him some relief, if it be but for that. If I can recover him and keep him tame and get to Naples with him, he's a present for any emperor that ever trod on neat's-leather.   73

Cal. Do not torment me, prithee; I'll bring my wood home faster.

Ste. He's in his fit now and does not talk after the wisest. He shall taste of my bottle: if he have never drunk wine afore, it will go near to remove his fit. If I can recover him and keep him tame, I will not take too much for him; he shall pay for him that hath him, and that soundly.

Cal. Thou dost me yet but little hurt; thou wilt anon, I know it by thy trembling: now Prosper works upon thee.   84

Ste. Come on your ways; open your mouth; here is that which will give language to you, cat: open your mouth; this will shake your shaking, I can tell you, and that soundly: you cannot tell who's your friend: open your chaps again.   89

Trin. I should know that voice: it should be—but he is drowned; and these are devils: O defend me!

Ste. Four legs and two voices: a most delicate monster! His forward voice now is to speak well of his friend; his backward voice is to utter foul speeches and to detract. If all the wine in my bottle will recover him, I will help his ague. Come. Amen! I will pour some in thy other mouth.

Trin. Stephano!   100

Ste. Doth thy other mouth call me? Mercy, mercy! This is a devil, and no monster: I will leave him; I have no long spoon.

Trin. Stephano! If thou beest Stephano,

touch me and speak to me; for I am Trinculo —be not afeard—thy good friend Trinculo.

Ste. If thou beest Trinculo, come forth: I'll pull thee by the lesser legs: if any be Trinculo's legs, these are they. Thou art very Trinculo indeed! How camest thou to be the siege of this moon-calf? can he   111 vent Trinculos?

Trin. I took him to be killed with a thunder-stroke. But art thou not drowned, Stephano? I hope now thou art not drowned. Is the storm overblown? I hid me under the dead moon-calf's gaberdine for fear of the storm. And art thou living, Stephano? O Stephano, two Neapolitans 'scaped!

Ste. Prithee, do not turn me about; my stomach is not constant.

Cal. [*Aside*] These be fine things, an if they be not sprites.   121
That's a brave god and bears celestial liquor. I will kneel to him.

Ste. How didst thou 'scape? How camest thou hither? swear by this bottle how thou camest hither. I escaped upon a butt of sack which the sailors heaved o'erboard, by this bottle! which I made of the bark of a tree with mine own hands since I was cast ashore.

Cal. I'll swear upon that bottle to be thy true subject; for the liquor is not earthly.   130

Ste. Here; swear then how thou escapedst.

Trin. Swum ashore, man, like a duck: I can swim like a duck, I'll be sworn.

Ste. Here, kiss the book. Though thou canst swim like a duck, thou art made like a goose.

Trin. O Stephano, hast any more of this?

Ste. The whole butt, man: my cellar is in a rock by the sea-side where my wine is hid. How now, moon-calf! how does thine ague?   139

Cal. Hast thou not dropp'd from heaven?

Ste. Out o' the moon, I do assure thee: I was the man i' the moon when time was.

Cal. I have seen thee in her and I do adore thee:
My mistress show'd me thee and thy dog and thy bush.

Ste. Come, swear to that; kiss the book:

---

61. **Ind**, India, or vaguely, the East. 63. **proper**, handsome, elegant. 71. **recover**, restore. 73. **neat's-leather**, leather from the skin of an animal of the ox-kind. 80. **take too much**, ironical meaning: He will take as much as he can get. 83. **trembling**, suggestion of demonic possession. 87. **cat . . . mouth**, allusion to the proverb, "Good liquor will make a cat speak." 103. **long spoon**, allusion to the proverb, "He that sups with the devil has need of a long spoon."

111. **moon-calf**, monster, abortion (supposed to be caused by the influence of the moon). 120. **not constant**, unsteady. 126. **butt of sack**, barrel of Canary wine. 134. **kiss the book**. He gives him the bottle instead of the Bible on which to make his oath. 142. **when time was**, once upon a time. 144. **dog . . . bush**. See *A Midsummer-Night's Dream*, V, i, 136.

I will furnish it anon with new contents: swear.

Trin. By this good light, this is a very shallow monster! I afeard of him! A very weak monster! The man i' the moon! A most poor credulous monster! Well drawn, monster, in good sooth!   151

Cal. I'll show thee every fertile inch o' th' island;
And I will kiss thy foot: I prithee, be my god.

Trin. By this light, a most perfidious and drunken monster! when 's god's asleep, he'll rob his bottle.

Cal. I'll kiss thy foot; I'll swear myself thy subject.

Ste. Come on then; down, and swear.

Trin. I shall laugh myself to death at this puppy-headed monster. A most scurvy monster! I could find in my heart to beat him,—

Ste. Come, kiss.   161

Trin. But that the poor monster's in drink: an abominable monster!

Cal. I'll show thee the best springs; I'll pluck thee berries;
I'll fish for thee and get thee wood enough.
A plague upon the tyrant that I serve!
I'll bear him no more sticks, but follow thee,
Thou wondrous man.

Trin. A most ridiculous monster, to make a wonder of a poor drunkard!   170

Cal. I prithee, let me bring thee where crabs grow;
And I with my long nails will dig thee pig-nuts;
Show thee a jay's nest and instruct thee how
To snare the nimble marmoset; I'll bring thee
To clustering filberts and sometimes I'll get thee
Young scamels from the rock. Wilt thou go with me?

Ste. I prithee now, lead the way without any more talking. Trinculo, the king and all our company else being drowned, we will inherit here: here; bear my bottle: fellow Trinculo, we'll fill him by and by again.   181

Cal. [*Sings drunkenly*]
Farewell, master; farewell, farewell!

Trin. A howling monster; a drunken monster!

Cal. No more dams I'll make for fish;
     Nor fetch in firing
     At requiring;
     Nor scrape trencher, nor wash dish:
     'Ban, 'Ban, Cacaliban
     Has a new master: get a new man.
Freedom, hey-day! hey-day, freedom! freedom, hey-day, freedom!   191

Ste. O brave monster! Lead the way.
                                    [*Exeunt.*

ACT III.

Scene I. *Before* Prospero's *cell.*

Enter Ferdinand, *bearing a log.*

Fer. There be some sports are painful, and their labour
Delight in them sets off: some kinds of base-ness
Are nobly undergone and most poor matters
Point to rich ends. This my mean task
Would be as heavy to me as odious, but
The mistress which I serve quickens what's dead
And makes my labours pleasures: O, she is
Ten times more gentle than her father's crabbed,
And he's composed of harshness. I must re-move
Some thousands of these logs and pile them up,
Upon a sore injunction: my sweet mistress 11
Weeps when she sees me work, and says, such baseness
Had never like executor. I forget:
But these sweet thoughts do even refresh my labours,
†Most busy lest, when I do it.

Enter Miranda; *and* Prospero *at a distance, unseen.*

Mir.   Alas, now, pray you,
Work not so hard: I would the lightning had
Burnt up those logs that you are enjoin'd to pile!

---

150. **Well drawn.** Caliban takes a good draft of the wine. 174. **marmoset**, small monkey. 176. **scamels**, not explained. Keightley conjectured *seamels* (sea gulls), Theobald, *stannels* (kestrels); New Cambridge editors call attention to the fact that *seamews* occurs in Strachey's letter. 179. **inherit**, take possession.

187. **trencher**, trenchers, collectively (Onions). *Act III. Scene i.* 11. **sore**, grievous, severe. 15. **Most . . . lest**, unexplained; Spedding suggests *Most busiest when idlest;* New Cambridge editors suggest *busy-idlest*, employed in trifles.

Pray, set it down and rest you: when this
burns,
'Twill weep for having wearied you. My
father
Is hard at study; pray now, rest yourself; 20
He's safe for these three hours.
  Fer.   O most dear mistress,
The sun will set before I shall discharge
What I must strive to do.
  Mir.   If you'll sit down,
I'll bear your logs the while: pray, give me
that;
I'll carry it to the pile.
  Fer.   No, precious creature;
I had rather crack my sinews, break my
back,
Than you should such dishonour undergo,
While I sit lazy by.
  Mir.   It would become me
As well as it does you: and I should do it
With much more ease; for my good will is
to it, 30
And yours it is against.
  Pros.   Poor worm, thou art infected!
This visitation shows it.
  Mir.   You look wearily.
  Fer. No, noble mistress; 'tis fresh morning
with me
When you are by at night. I do beseech
you—
Chiefly that I might set it in my prayers—
What is your name?
  Mir.   Miranda.—O my father,
I have broke your hest to say so!
  Fer.   Admired Miranda!
Indeed the top of admiration! worth
What's dearest to the world! Full many a
lady
I have eyed with best regard and many a
time 40
The harmony of their tongues hath into
bondage
Brought my too diligent ear: for several
virtues
Have I liked several women; never any
With so full soul, but some defect in her
Did quarrel with the noblest grace she owed
And put it to the foil: but you, O you,
So perfect and so peerless, are created
Of every creature's best!
  Mir.   I do not know
One of my sex; no woman's face remember,

Save, from my glass, mine own; nor have I
seen 50
More that I may call men than you, good
friend,
And my dear father: how features are
abroad,
I am skilless of; but, by my modesty,
The jewel in my dower, I would not wish
Any companion in the world but you,
Nor can imagination form a shape,
Besides yourself, to like of. But I prattle
Something too wildly and my father's pre-
cepts
I therein do forget.
  Fer.   I am in my condition
A prince, Miranda; I do think, a king; 60
I would, not so!—and would no more endure
This wooden slavery than to suffer
The flesh-fly blow my mouth. Hear my soul
speak:
The very instant that I saw you, did
My heart fly to your service; there resides,
To make me slave to it; and for your sake
Am I this patient log-man.
  Mir.   Do you love me?
  Fer. O heaven, O earth, bear witness to
this sound
And crown what I profess with kind event
If I speak true! if hollowly, invert 70
What best is boded me to mischief! I
Beyond all limit of what else i' the world
Do love, prize, honour you.
  Mir.   I am a fool
To weep at what I am glad of.
  Pros.   Fair encounter
Of two most rare affections! Heavens rain
grace
On that which breeds between 'em!
  Fer.   Wherefore weep you?
  Mir. At mine unworthiness that dare not
offer
What I desire to give, and much less take
What I shall die to want. But this is trifling;
And all the more it seeks to hide itself, 80
The bigger bulk it shows. Hence, bashful
cunning!
And prompt me, plain and holy innocence!
I am your wife, if you will marry me;
If not, I'll die your maid: to be your fellow
You may deny me; but I'll be your servant,
Whether you will or no.

45. **owed**, possessed. 46. **put . . . foil**, disgraced it; a
wrestling phrase.

52. **features**, shapes or forms of body. 53. **skilless**,
ignorant. 69. **kind event**, favorable result. 70. **hollowly**, insincerely, falsely. 84. **fellow**, spouse.

Fer.   My mistress, dearest;
And I thus humble ever.
    Mir.   My husband, then?
Fer. Ay, with a heart as willing
As bondage e'er of freedom: here's my hand.
    Mir. And mine, with my heart in 't: and
        now farewell   90
Till half an hour hence.
Fer.   A thousand thousand!
            [*Exeunt Fer. and Mir. severally.*
Pros. So glad of this as they I cannot be,
Who are surprised withal; but my rejoicing
At nothing can be more. I'll to my book,
For yet ere supper-time must I perform
Much business appertaining.   [*Exit.*

SCENE II. *Another part of the island.*

Enter CALIBAN, STEPHANO, *and* TRINCULO.

Ste. Tell not me; when the butt is out, we
will drink water; not a drop before: therefore
bear up, and board 'em. Servant-monster,
drink to me.
    Trin. Servant-monster! the folly of this
island! They say there's but five upon this
isle: we are three of them; if th' other two
be brained like us, the state totters.
    Ste. Drink, servant-monster, when I bid
thee: thy eyes are almost set in thy head. 10
    Trin. Where should they be set else? he
were a brave monster indeed, if they were
set in his tail.
    Ste. My man-monster hath drown'd his
tongue in sack: for my part, the sea cannot
drown me; I swam, ere I could recover the
shore, five and thirty leagues off and on. By
this light, thou shalt be my lieutenant, monster, or my standard.   19
    Trin. Your lieutenant, if you list; he's no
standard.
    Ste. We'll not run, Monsieur Monster.
    Trin. Nor go neither; but you'll lie like
dogs and yet say nothing neither.
    Ste. Moon-calf, speak once in thy life, if
thou beest a good moon-calf.
    Cal. How does thy honour? Let me lick
        thy shoe.
I'll not serve him; he is not valiant.   27

Trin. Thou liest, most ignorant monster:
I am in case to justle a constable. Why,
thou deboshed fish, thou, was there ever
man a coward that hath drunk so much sack
as I to-day? Wilt thou tell a monstrous lie,
being but half a fish and half a monster?
    Cal. Lo, how he mocks me! wilt thou let
him, my lord?
    Trin. 'Lord' quoth he. That a monster
should be such a natural!   37
    Cal. Lo, lo, again! bite him to death, I
prithee.
    Ste. Trinculo, keep a good tongue in your
head: if you prove a mutineer,—the next
tree! The poor monster's my subject and he
shall not suffer indignity.
    Cal. I thank my noble lord. Wilt thou be
pleased to hearken once again to the suit I
made to thee?
    Ste. Marry, will I: kneel and repeat it; I
will stand, and so shall Trinculo.

Enter ARIEL, *invisible.*

    Cal. As I told thee before, I am subject to
a tyrant, a sorcerer, that by his cunning
hath cheated me of the island.   50
    Ari. Thou liest.
    Cal. Thou liest, thou jesting monkey,
thou: I would my valiant master would
destroy thee! I do not lie.
    Ste. Trinculo, if you trouble him any
more in 's tale, by this hand, I will supplant
some of your teeth.
    Trin. Why, I said nothing.
    Ste. Mum, then, and no more. Proceed.
    Cal. I say, by sorcery he got this isle; 60
From me he got it. If thy greatness will
Revenge it on him,—for I know thou darest,
But this thing dare not,—
    Ste. That's most certain.
    Cal. Thou shalt be lord of it and I'll serve
thee.
    Ste. How now shall this be compassed?
Canst thou bring me to the party?
    Cal. Yea, yea, my lord: I'll yield him thee
        asleep,
Where thou mayst knock a nail into his head.
    Ari. Thou liest; thou canst not.   70
    Cal. What a pied ninny's this! Thou
        scurvy patch!

I do beseech thy greatness, give him blows
And take his bottle from him: when that's
    gone
He shall drink nought but brine; for I'll not
    show him
Where the quick freshes are.   75

Ste. Trinculo, run into no further danger:
interrupt the monster one word further, and,
by this hand, I'll turn my mercy out o' doors
and make a stock-fish of thee.

Trin. Why, what did I? I did nothing.
I'll go farther off.   81

Ste. Didst thou not say he lied?

Ari. Thou liest.

Ste. Do I so? take thou that. [*Beats Trin.*]
As you like this, give me the lie another time.

Trin. I did not give the lie. Out o' your
wits and hearing too? A pox o' your bottle!
this can sack and drinking do. A murrain
on your monster, and the devil take your
fingers!

Cal. Ha, ha, ha!   90

Ste. Now, forward with your tale. Prithee,
stand farther off.

Cal. Beat him enough: after a little time
I'll beat him too.

Ste.   Stand farther.   Come, proceed.

Cal. Why, as I told thee, 'tis a custom
    with him,
I' th' afternoon to sleep: there thou mayst
    brain him,
Having first seized his books, or with a log
Batter his skull, or paunch him with a stake,
Or cut his wezand with thy knife. Remember
First to possess his books; for without
    them   100
He's but a sot, as I am, nor hath not
One spirit to command: they all do hate him
As rootedly as I.   Burn but his books.
He has brave utensils,—for so he calls
    them,—
Which, when he has a house, he'll deck
    withal.
And that most deeply to consider is
The beauty of his daughter; he himself
Calls her a nonpareil: I never saw a woman,
But only Sycorax my dam and she;
But she as far surpasseth Sycorax   110
As great'st does least.

Ste.   Is it so brave a lass?

Cal. Ay, lord; she will become thy bed, I
    warrant.
And bring thee forth brave brood.

Ste. Monster, I will kill this man: his
daughter and I will be king and queen,—
save our graces!—and Trinculo and thyself
shall be viceroys. Dost thou like the plot,
Trinculo?

Trin. Excellent.

Ste. Give me thy hand: I am sorry I beat
thee; but, while thou livest, keep a good
tongue in thy head.   121

Cal. Within this half hour will he be
    asleep:
Wilt thou destroy him then?

Ste.   Ay, on mine honour.

Ari. This will I tell my master.

Cal. Thou makest me merry; I am full of
    pleasure:
Let us be jocund: will you troll the catch
You taught me but while-ere?

Ste. At thy request, monster, I will do
reason, any reason. Come on, Trinculo, let
us sing.   [*Sings.*

        Flout 'em and scout 'em   130
        And scout 'em and flout 'em;
            Thought is free.

Cal. That's not the tune.
[*Ariel plays the tune on a tabor and pipe.*

Ste. What is this same?

Trin. This is the tune of our catch, played
by the picture of Nobody.

Ste. If thou beest a man, show thyself in
thy likeness: if thou beest a devil, take 't
as thou list.

Trin. O, forgive me my sins!

Ste. He that dies pays all debts: I defy
    thee.
Mercy upon us!   141

Cal. Art thou afeard?

Ste. No, monster, not I.

Cal. Be not afeard; the isle is full of
    noises,
Sounds and sweet airs, that give delight and
    hurt not.
Sometimes a thousand twangling instru-
    ments

---

75. **quick freshes**, running springs. 79. **stock-fish**, dried cod beaten before boiling. 88. **murrain**, plague. 99. **wezand**, windpipe. 101. **sot**, fool. 108. **nonpareil**, one having no equal.

126. **troll the catch**, sing the song. 127. **while-ere**, a while since. 130. **scout**, deride (Onions). New Cambridge editors emend, *cout* (befool). 133. *Stage Direction*: **tabor**, small drum. 136. **picture of Nobody**, an unexplained topical allusion. New Cambridge editors suggest a reference to the sign of "Nobody" used by John Trundle, book-seller and printer.

Will hum about mine ears, and sometime
    voices
That, if I then had waked after long sleep,
Will make me sleep again: and then, in
    dreaming,
The clouds methought would open and show
    riches   150
Ready to drop upon me, that, when I waked,
I cried to dream again.

    Ste. This will prove a brave kingdom to
me, where I shall have my music for nothing.

    Cal. When Prospero is destroyed.

    Ste. That shall be by and by: I remember
the story.

    Trin. The sound is going away; let's fol-
low it, and after do our work.

    Ste. Lead, monster; we'll follow. I would
I could see this taborer; he lays it on.   160

    Trin. Wilt come? I'll follow, Stephano.
                                          [*Exeunt.*

SCENE III. *Another part of the island.*

Enter ALONSO, SEBASTIAN, ANTONIO, GON-
ZALO, ADRIAN, FRANCISCO, *and others.*

    Gon. By 'r lakin, I can go no further, sir;
My old bones ache: here's a maze trod in-
    deed
Through forth-rights and meanders! By
    your patience,
I needs must rest me.

    Alon.   Old lord, I cannot blame thee,
Who am myself attach'd with weariness,
To the dulling of my spirits: sit down, and
    rest.
Even here I will put off my hope and keep it
No longer for my flatterer: he is drown'd
Whom thus we stray to find, and the sea
    mocks
Our frustrate search on land. Well, let him
    go.   10

    Ant. [*Aside to Seb.*] I am right glad that
    he's so out of hope.
Do not, for one repulse, forego the purpose
That you resolved to effect.

    Seb. [*Aside to Ant.*] The next advantage
Will we take throughly.

    Ant. [*Aside to Seb.*] Let it be to-night;
For, now they are oppress'd with travel,
    they

Will not, nor cannot, use such vigilance
As when they are fresh.

    Seb. [*Aside to Ant.*] I say, to-night: no
    more.   [*Solemn and strange music.*

    Alon. What harmony is this? My good
friends, hark!

    Gon. Marvellous sweet music!

Enter PROSPERO *above, invisible. Enter several
strange Shapes, bringing in a banquet; they
dance about it with gentle actions of salutation; and, inviting the King, &c. to eat,
they depart.*

    Alon. Give us kind keepers, heavens!
    What were these?   20

    Seb. A living drollery. Now I will believe
That there are unicorns, that in Arabia
There is one tree, the phoenix' throne, one
    phoenix
At this hour reigning there.

    Ant.   I'll believe both;
And what does else want credit, come to me,
And I'll be sworn 'tis true: travellers ne'er
    did lie,
Though fools at home condemn 'em.

    Gon.   If in Naples
I should report this now, would they believe
    me?
If I should say, I saw such islanders—
For, certes, these are people of the island— 30
Who, though they are of monstrous shape,
    yet, note,
Their manners are more gentle-kind than of
Our human generation you shall find
Many, nay, almost any.

    Pros.   [*Aside*] Honest lord,
Thou hast said well; for some of you there
    present
Are worse than devils.

    Alon.   I cannot too much muse
Such shapes, such gesture and such sound,
    expressing,
Although they want the use of tongue, a kind
Of excellent dumb discourse.

    Pros.   [*Aside*] Praise in departing.

    Fran. They vanish'd strangely.

    Seb.   No matter, since 40
They have left their viands behind; for we
    have stomachs.

---

    20. keepers, guardian angels. **21. drollery,** puppet-
show. **30. certes,** certainly. **36. muse,** marvel at.
39. Praise in departing, proverbial expression meaning, "Praise comes at the end." Yale editor interprets
as "Save your praise until the end of the performance."

    Scene iii. **1. By'r lakin,** by our Lady. **3. forth-
rights and meanders,** paths straight and crooked.
5. attach'd, seized.

Will 't please you taste of what is here?
Alon.   Not I.
Gon. Faith, sir, you need not fear. When
  we were boys,
Who would believe that there were moun-
  taineers
Dew-lapp'd like bulls, whose throats had
  hanging at 'em
Wallets of flesh? or that there were such men
Whose heads stood in their breasts? which
  now we find
Each putter-out of five for one will bring us
Good warrant of.
  Alon.   I will stand to and feed,
Although my last: no matter, since I feel 50
The best is past. Brother, my lord the duke,
Stand to and do as we.

Thunder and lightning. Enter ARIEL, *like a
  harpy; claps his wings upon the table; and,
  with a quaint device, the banquet vanishes.*

Ari. You are three men of sin, whom
  Destiny,
That hath to instrument this lower world
And what is in 't, the never-surfeited sea
Hath caused to belch up you; and on this
  island
Where man doth not inhabit; you 'mongst
  men
Being most unfit to live. I have made you
  mad;
And even with such-like valour men hang
  and drown
Their proper selves.
            [*Alon., Seb. &c. draw their swords.*
            You fools! I and my fellows 60
Are ministers of Fate: the elements,
Of whom your swords are temper'd, may as
  well
Wound the loud winds, or with bemock'd-at
  stabs
Kill the still-closing waters, as diminish
One dowle that's in my plume: my fellow-
  ministers
Are like invulnerable. If you could hurt,

Your swords are now too massy for your
  strengths
And will not be uplifted. But remember—
For that's my business to you—that you
  three
From Milan did supplant good Prospero; 70
Exposed unto the sea, which hath requit it,
Him and his innocent child: for which foul
  deed
The powers, delaying, not forgetting, have
Incensed the seas and shores, yea, all the
  creatures,
Against your peace. Thee of thy son, Alonso,
They have bereft; and do pronounce by me
Lingering perdition, worse than any death
Can be at once, shall step by step attend
You and your ways; whose wraths to guard
  you from—
Which here, in this most desolate isle, else
  falls
Upon your heads—is nothing but heart-
  sorrow   81
And a clear life ensuing.

*He vanishes in thunder; then, to soft music,
  enter the Shapes again, and dance, with
  mocks and mows, and carrying out the table.*

Pros. Bravely the figure of this harpy hast
  thou
Perform'd, my Ariel; a grace it had, de-
  vouring:
Of my instruction hast thou nothing bated
In what thou hadst to say: so, with good life
And observation strange, my meaner min-
  isters
Their several kinds have done. My high
  charms work
And these mine enemies are all knit up
In their distractions; they now are in my
  power;
And in these fits I leave them, while I visit 91
Young Ferdinand, whom they suppose is
  drown'd,
And his and mine loved darling. [*Exit above.*
  Gon. I' the name of something holy, sir,
  why stand you
In this strange stare?
  Alon.   O, it is monstrous, monstrous!

---

45. **Dew-lapp'd**, having a dewlap, or fold of skin
hanging from the neck, as cattle; often supposed to refer
to people afflicted with goiter. 48. **putter-out . . .
one**, one who invests money, or gambles on the risks of
travel on the condition that, if he returns safely, he is
to receive five times the amount deposited. 52. *Stage
Direction:* **harpy**, a fabulous monster with a woman's
face and vulture's body supposed to be a minister of
divine vengeance. **quaint device**, ingenious stage-
contrivance; perhaps harpies seemed to swallow the
food. 54. **to**, as. 65. **dowle**, soft fine feather. **plume**,
plumage (?) (Onions). 66. **like**, likewise, similarly.

71. **requit**, requited, avenged. 82. **clear**, unspotted,
innocent. 84. **devouring.** New Cambridge editors
conjecture *devoiring* (serving, waiting at table). 86.
so . . . life, with faithful reproduction. 87. **observation strange**, rare attention to detail. 88. **kinds**,
parts, duties.

Methought the billows spoke and told me
   of it;
The winds did sing it to me, and the thunder,
That deep and dreadful organ-pipe, pro-
   nounced
The name of Prosper: it did bass my trespass.
Therefore my son i' the ooze is bedded,
   and   100
I'll seek him deeper than e'er plummet
   sounded
And with him there lie mudded.   [*Exit.*
  Seb.   But one fiend at a time,
I'll fight their legions o'er.
  Ant.   I'll be thy second.
            [*Exeunt Seb. and Ant.*
  Gon. All three of them are desperate:
   their great guilt,
Like poison given to work a great time after,
Now 'gins to bite the spirits. I do beseech
   you
That are of suppler joints, follow them
   swiftly
And hinder them from what this ecstasy
May now provoke them to.
  Adr.   Follow, I pray you. [*Exeunt.*

ACT IV.

SCENE I. *Before* PROSPERO'S *cell.*

Enter PROSPERO, FERDINAND, *and* MIRANDA.

  Pros. If I have too austerely punish'd
   you,
Your compensation makes amends, for I
Have given you here a thrid of mine own
   life,
Or that for which I live; who once again
I tender to thy hand: all thy vexations
Were but my trials of thy love, and thou
Hast strangely stood the test: here, afore
   Heaven,
I ratify this my rich gift. O Ferdinand,
Do not smile at me that I boast her off,
For thou shalt find she will outstrip all
   praise   10
And make it halt behind her.
  Fer.   I do believe it
Against an oracle.

  Pros. Then, as my gift and thine own
   acquisition
Worthily purchased, take my daughter: but
If thou dost break her virgin-knot before
All sanctimonious ceremonies may
With full and holy rite be minister'd,
No sweet aspersion shall the heavens let fall
To make this contract grow; but barren hate,
Sour-eyed disdain and discord shall bestrew
The union of your bed with weeds so loathly
That you shall hate it both: therefore take
   heed,   22
As Hymen's lamps shall light you.
  Fer.   As I hope
For quiet days, fair issue and long life,
With such love as 'tis now, the murkiest den,
The most opportune place, the strong'st
   suggestion
Our worser genius can, shall never melt
Mine honour into lust, to take away
The edge of that day's celebration
When I shall think, or Phœbus' steeds are
   founder'd,   30
Or Night kept chain'd below.
  Pros.   Fairly spoke.
Sit then and talk with her; she is thine own.
What, Ariel! my industrious servant, Ariel!

Enter ARIEL.

  Ari. What would my potent master? here
   I am.
  Pros. Thou and thy meaner fellows your
   last service
Did worthily perform; and I must use you
In such another trick. Go bring the rabble,
O'er whom I give thee power, here to this
   place:
Incite them to quick motion; for I must
Bestow upon the eyes of this young couple 40
Some vanity of mine art: it is my promise,
And they expect it from me.
  Ari.   Presently?
  Pros. Ay, with a twink.
  Ari.   Before you can say 'come' and 'go,'
      And breathe twice and cry 'so, so,'
      Each one, tripping on his toe,
      Will be here with mop and mow.
      Do you love me, master? no?

---

99. **bass my trespass,** proclaimed my trespass like a bass note in music. 106. **bite the spirits,** i.e., conscience troubles them. 108. **ecstasy,** madness, frenzy.
  Act IV. Scene i. 3. **thrid,** defined as "thread," "narrative"; F: *third,* which is correct—the other thirds were Prospero himself and his wife. 7. **strangely,** extraordinarily.

16. **sanctimonious,** sacred. 18. **aspersion,** dew, shower. 23. **Hymen's.** Hymen was the Greek and Roman god of marriage. 27. **genius,** evil genius, or evil attendant spirit. 30. **founder'd,** broken down, made lame. 37. **rabble,** band, i.e., the *meaner fellows* of line 35. 41. **vanity,** illusion. 47. **mop and mow,** grimace and make faces.

Pros. Dearly, my delicate Ariel. Do not approach
Till thou dost hear me call.
Ari.　　　　　Well, I conceive. [*Exit.*　50
Pros. Look thou be true; do not give dalliance
Too much the rein: the strongest oaths are straw
To the fire i' the blood: be more abstemious,
Or else, good night your vow!
Fer.　　　　　　　　　I warrant you, sir;
The white cold virgin snow upon my heart
Abates the ardour of my liver.
Pros.　　　　　　　Well.
Now come, my Ariel! bring a corollary,
Rather than want a spirit: appear, and pertly!
No tongue! all eyes! be silent. [*Soft music.*

Enter Iris.

Iris. Ceres, most bounteous lady, thy rich leas　　　　　　　　　　　60
Of wheat, rye, barley, vetches, oats and pease;
Thy turfy mountains, where live nibbling sheep,
And flat meads thatch'd with stover, them to keep;
Thy banks with pioned and twilled brims,
Which spongy April at thy hest betrims,
To make cold nymphs chaste crowns; and thy broom-groves,
Whose shadow the dismissed bachelor loves,
Being lass-lorn; thy pole-clipt vineyard;
And thy sea-marge, sterile and rocky-hard,
Where thou thyself dost air;—the queen o' the sky,　　　　　　　　　　70
Whose watery arch and messenger am I,
Bids thee leave these, and with her sovereign grace,
Here on this grass-plot, in this very place,
To come and sport: her peacocks fly amain:
Approach, rich Ceres, her to entertain.

Enter Ceres.

Cer. Hail, many-colour'd messenger, that ne'er
Dost disobey the wife of Jupiter;
Who with thy saffron wings upon my flowers
Diffusest honey-drops, refreshing showers,
And with each end of thy blue bow dost crown　　　　　　　　　　80
My bosky acres and my unshrubb'd down,
Rich scarf to my proud earth; why hath thy queen
Summon'd me hither, to this short-grass'd green?
Iris. A contract of true love to celebrate;
And some donation freely to estate
On the blest lovers.
Cer.　　　　Tell me, heavenly bow,
If Venus or her son, as thou dost know,
Do now attend the queen? Since they did plot
The means that dusky Dis my daughter got,
Her and her blind boy's scandal'd company
I have forsworn.
Iris.　　　　Of her society　　　91
Be not afraid: I met her deity
Cutting the clouds towards Paphos and her son
Dove-drawn with her. Here thought they to have done
Some wanton charm upon this man and maid,
Whose vows are, that no bed-right shall be paid
Till Hymen's torch be lighted: but in vain;
Mars's hot minion is return'd again;
Her waspish-headed son has broke his arrows,
Swears he will shoot no more but play with sparrows　　　　　　　　　100
And be a boy right out.
Cer.　　　　High'st queen of state,
Great Juno, comes; I know her by her gait.

Enter Juno.

Juno. How does my bounteous sister? Go with me
To bless this twain, that they may prosperous be

---

56. **liver,** as the seat of the passions. 57. **corollary,** supernumerary. 58. **pertly,** briskly. 60-138. **Ceres . . . footing.** This is the most perfect example of the masque in Shakespeare. His authorship of it has, however, sometimes been called in question. It is a masque in honor of betrothal. For another example see the end of *A Midsummer-Night's Dream.* 63. **stover,** fodder for cattle. 64. **pioned and twilled,** unexplained; excavated(?) or trenched(?) (Onions), ridged (New Cambridge), grown over with peonies and lilies (Hanmer). 66. **broom-groves,** groves of broom(?) 68. **pole-clipt,** hedged in with poles. 71. **watery arch,** rainbow. 74. **amain,** with full force or speed.

81. **bosky,** covered with shrubs. **unshrubb'd down,** shrubless upland. 89. **Dis . . . got.** Pluto, god of the infernal regions, carried off Persephone, daughter of Ceres, to be his bride in Hades. 90. **scandal'd,** brought into disrepute; New Cambridge editors suggest *sandal'd.* 93. **Paphos,** a town in the island of Cyprus, sacred to Venus. 98. **Mars's . . . minion,** Venus, the beloved of Mars. 99. **waspish-headed,** fiery, hot-headed(?).

And honour'd in their issue.   [*They sing:*

Juno.   Honour, riches, marriage-blessing,
Long continuance, and increasing,
Hourly joys be still upon you!
Juno sings her blessings on you.

Cer.   Earth's increase, foison plenty, 110
Barns and garners never empty,
Vines with clustering bunches
    growing,
Plants with goodly burthen bowing;

Spring come to you at the farthest
In the very end of harvest!
Scarcity and want shall shun you;
Ceres' blessing so is on you.

Fer.   This is a most majestic vision, and
Harmonious charmingly.   May I be bold
To think these spirits?
Pros.   Spirits, which by mine art   120
I have from their confines call'd to enact
My present fancies.
Fer.   Let me live here ever;
So rare a wonder'd father and a wife
Makes this place Paradise.
    [*Juno and Ceres whisper, and send
        Iris on employment.*
Pros.   Sweet, now, silence!
Juno and Ceres whisper seriously;
There's something else to do: hush, and be
    mute,
Or else our spell is marr'd.
Iris.   You nymphs, call'd Naiads, of the
    windring brooks,
With your sedged crowns and ever-harmless
    looks,
Leave your crisp channels and on this green
    land   130
Answer your summons; Juno does command:
Come, temperate nymphs, and help to cele-
    brate
A contract of true love; be not too late.

Enter certain Nymphs.

You sunburnt sicklemen, of August weary,
Come hither from the furrow and be merry:
Make holiday; your rye-straw hats put on
And these fresh nymphs encounter every
    one
In country footing.

*Enter certain Reapers, properly habited: they
join with the Nymphs in a graceful dance;
towards the end whereof* Prospero *starts
suddenly, and speaks; after which, to a
strange, hollow, and confused noise, they
heavily vanish.*

Pros. [*Aside*] I had forgot that foul con-
    spiracy
Of the beast Caliban and his confederates 140
Against my life: the minute of their plot
Is almost come. [*To the Spirits.*] Well done!
    avoid; no more!
Fer.   This is strange: your father's in some
    passion
That works him strongly.
Mir.   Never till this day
Saw I him touch'd with anger so distem-
    per'd.
Pros.   You do look, my son, in a moved
    sort,
As if you were dismay'd: be cheerful, sir.
Our revels now are ended.   These our actors,
As I foretold you, were all spirits and
Are melted into air, into thin air: 150
And, like the baseless fabric of this vision,
The cloud-capp'd towers, the gorgeous
    palaces,
The solemn temples, the great globe itself,
Yea, all which it inherit, shall dissolve
And, like this insubstantial pageant faded,
Leave not a rack behind.   We are such stuff
As dreams are made on, and our little life
Is rounded with a sleep.   Sir, I am vex'd;
Bear with my weakness; my old brain is
    troubled:
Be not disturb'd with my infirmity: 160
If you be pleased, retire into my cell
And there repose: a turn or two I'll walk,
To still my beating mind.
Fer. Mir.   We wish your peace. [*Exeunt.*
Pros.   Come with a thought.   I thank thee,
    Ariel: come.

Enter Ariel.

Ari.   Thy thoughts I cleave to.   What's
    thy pleasure?
Pros.   Spirit,
We must prepare to meet with Caliban.

---

110. **foison plenty**, plentiful harvest.   123. **wonder'd**, wonder-performing.   128. **windring**, wandering(?)
or winding(?) 130. **crisp**, curled, rippled.   132. **temperate**, chaste.   138. **country footing**, country-dancing.

142. **avoid**, depart, withdraw.   144. **works**, affects.
145. **distemper'd**, vexed.   146. **sort**, state, condition.
156. **rack**, mass of cloud driven before the wind in the
upper air (Onions).   164. **with a thought**, on the instant.

Ari. Ay, my commander: when I presented Ceres,
I thought to have told thee of it, but I fear'd
Lest I might anger thee.
　Pros. Say again, where didst thou leave
　　these varlets? 170
　Ari. I told you, sir, they were red-hot
　　with drinking;
So full of valour that they smote the air
For breathing in their faces; beat the ground
For kissing of their feet; yet always bending
Towards their project. Then I beat my
　tabor;
At which, like unback'd colts, they prick'd
　their ears,
Advanced their eyelids, lifted up their noses
As they smelt music: so I charm'd their
　ears
That calf-like they my lowing follow'd
　through
Tooth'd briers, sharp furzes, pricking goss
　and thorns, 180
Which enter'd their frail shins: at last I left
　them
I' the filthy-mantled pool beyond your cell,
There dancing up to the chins, that the foul
　lake
O'erstunk their feet.
　Pros. 　　　　　This was well done, my
　　bird.
Thy shape invisible retain thou still:
The trumpery in my house, go bring it
　hither,
For stale to catch these thieves.
　Ari. 　　　　　I go, I go. [*Exit.*
　Pros. A devil, a born devil, on whose
　　nature
Nurture can never stick; on whom my
　pains,
Humanely taken, all, all lost, quite lost; 190
And as with age his body uglier grows,
So his mind cankers. I will plague them
　all,
Even to roaring.

Re-enter ARIEL, *loaden with glistering
apparel, &c.*

　　Come, hang them on this line.

PROSPERO *and* ARIEL *remain, invisible. Enter*
CALIBAN, STEPHANO, *and* TRINCULO, *all wet.*

　Cal. Pray you, tread softly, that the
　　blind mole may not
Hear a foot fall: we now are near his cell.
　Ste. Monster, your fairy, which you say
is a harmless fairy, has done little better
than played the Jack with us.
　Trin. Monster, I do smell all horse-piss;
at which my nose is in great indignation. 200
　Ste. So is mine. Do you hear, monster?
If I should take a displeasure against you,
look you,—
　Trin. Thou wert but a lost monster.
　Cal. Good my lord, give me thy favour
　　still.
Be patient, for the prize I'll bring thee to
Shall hoodwink this mischance: therefore
　speak softly.
All's hush'd as midnight yet.
　Trin. Ay, but to lose our bottles in the
　　pool,— 208
　Ste. There is not only disgrace and dishonour in that, monster, but an infinite loss.
　Trin. That's more to me than my wetting:
yet this is your harmless fairy, monster.
　Ste. I will fetch off my bottle, though I be
o'er ears for my labour.
　Cal. Prithee, my king, be quiet. See'st
　　thou here,
This is the mouth o' the cell: no noise, and
　enter.
Do that good mischief which may make this
　island
Thine own for ever, and I, thy Caliban,
For aye thy foot-licker.
　Ste. Give me thy hand. I do begin to
have bloody thoughts. 220
　Trin. O king Stephano! O peer! O worthy
Stephano! look what a wardrobe here is for
thee!
　Cal. Let it alone, thou fool; it is but trash.
　Trin. O, ho, monster! we know what belongs to a frippery. O king Stephano!
　Ste. Put off that gown, Trinculo; by this
hand, I'll have that gown.
　Trin. Thy grace shall have it.
　Cal. The dropsy drown this fool! what do
　　you mean 230

---

167. **presented**, as a character in the masque. 176.
unback'd, unbroken, unridden. 180. **goss**, gorse, a
prickly shrub. 182. **filthy-mantled**, covered with
vegetable coating, slimy. 184. **bird**, used as a term of
endearment. 187. **stale**, decoy. 193. **line**, probably,
lime-tree.

198. **played the Jack**, done a mean trick. *Jack* has
a double meaning, "knave" and "will-o'-the-wisp." 206.
hoodwink, cover up; hawking term. 226. **frippery**,
place where cast-off clothes are sold. **king Stephano**,
allusion to the old ballad beginning, "King Stephen was
a worthy peer."

To dote thus on such luggage? Let's alone
And do the murder first: if he awake,
From toe to crown he'll fill our skins with
    pinches,
Make us strange stuff.

Ste. Be you quiet, monster. Mistress
line, is not this my jerkin? Now is the jerkin
under the line: now, jerkin, you are like to
lose your hair and prove a bald jerkin.

Trin. Do, do: we steal by line and level,
an 't like your grace.   240

Ste. I thank thee for that jest; here's a
garment for 't: wit shall not go unrewarded
while I am king of this country. 'Steal by
line and level' is an excellent pass of pate;
there's another garment for 't.

Trin. Monster, come, put some lime upon
your fingers, and away with the rest.

Cal. I will have none on 't: we shall lose
    our time,
And all be turn'd to barnacles, or to apes .
With foreheads villanous low.   250

Ste. Monster, lay to your fingers: help to
bear this away where my hogshead of wine
is, or I'll turn you out of my kingdom: go to,
carry this.

Trin. And this.

Ste. Ay, and this.

*A noise of hunters heard. Enter divers
Spirits, in shape of dogs and hounds, and
hunt them about,* PROSPERO *and* ARIEL
setting them on.

Pros. Hey, Mountain, hey!

Ari. Silver! there it goes, Silver!

Pros. Fury, Fury! there, Tyrant, there!
hark! hark!

      [*Cal., Ste., and Trin. are driven out.*
Go charge my goblins that they grind their
    joints
With dry convulsions, shorten up their
    sinews   260
With aged cramps, and more pinch-spotted
    make them
Than pard or cat o' mountain.

---

231. **luggage**, impedimenta, heavy stuff to be carried.
236. **jerkin**, jacket made of leather. 237. **under the
line**, under the lime-tree, with punning allusion, probably, to the equinoctial line. 238. **lose your hair.**
The jerkin will lose all its hair when Stephano wears it.
239. **by line and level**, i.e., by means of instruments,
or, methodically, like dishonest carpenters and masons.
244. **pass of pate**, folly of wit. 246. **lime**, bird-lime.
249. **barnacles**, barnacle geese, formerly supposed to
be hatched from sea shells attached to trees and to
fall thence into the water; possibly, the ordinary meaning is intended. 260. **convulsions**, cramps. 262.
pard, panther or leopard. **cat o' mountain**, wild cat.

Ari.   Hark, they roar!

Pros. Let them be hunted soundly. At
    this hour
Lie at my mercy all mine enemies:
Shortly shall all my labours end, and thou
Shalt have the air at freedom: for a little
Follow, and do me service.   [*Exeunt.*

ACT V.

SCENE I. *Before* PROSPERO'S *cell.*

Enter PROSPERO *in his magic robes,
and* ARIEL.

Pros. Now does my project gather to a
    head:
My charms crack not; my spirits obey; and
    time
Goes upright with his carriage. How's the
    day?

Ari. On the sixth hour; at which time,
    my lord,
You said our work should cease.

Pros.   I did say so,
When first I raised the tempest. Say, my
    spirit,
How fares the king and 's followers?

Ari.   Confined together
In the same fashion as you gave in charge,
Just as you left them; all prisoners, sir,
In the line-grove which weather-fends your
    cell;   10
They cannot budge till your release. The
    king,
His brother and yours, abide all three dis-
    tracted
And the remainder mourning over them,
Brimful of sorrow and dismay; but chiefly
Him that you term'd, sir, 'The good old
    lord, Gonzalo;'
His tears run down his beard, like winter's
    drops
From eaves of reeds. Your charm so strongly
    works 'em
That if you now beheld them, your affections
Would become tender.

Pros.   Dost thou think so, spirit?

Act V. Scene i. 2. **crack**, figure not entirely clear;
possibly, since his project gathers "to a head," the
reference is to an ulcer; "the breaking of magic bands"
has been suggested. He may merely mean that his
charms do not fail. 3. **carriage**, burden. **How's the
day?** what time is it? 10. **weather-fends**, protects
from the weather. 17. **eaves of reeds**, thatch.

Ari. Mine would, sir, were I human.
Pros.   And mine shall.   20
Hast thou, which art but air, a touch, a
        feeling
Of their afflictions, and shall not myself,
One of their kind, that relish all as sharply,
Passion as they, be kindlier moved than thou
        art?
Though with their high wrongs I am struck
        to the quick,
Yet with my nobler reason 'gainst my fury
Do I take part: the rarer action is
In virtue than in vengeance: they being
        penitent,
The sole drift of my purpose doth extend
Not a frown further. Go release them, Ariel:
My charms I'll break, their senses I'll re-
        store,   31
And they shall be themselves.
        Ari.   I'll fetch them, sir. [*Exit.*
        Pros. Ye elves of hills, brooks, standing
        lakes and groves,
And ye that on the sands with printless foot
Do chase the ebbing Neptune and do fly him
When he comes back; you demi-puppets
        that
By moonshine do the green sour ringlets
        make,
Whereof the ewe not bites, and you whose
        pastime
Is to make midnight mushrooms, that re-
        joice
To hear the solemn curfew; by whose aid,
Weak masters though ye be, I have be-
        dimm'd   41
The noontide sun, call'd forth the mutinous
        winds,
And 'twixt the green sea and the azured vault
Set roaring war: to the dread rattling thun-
        der
Have I given fire and rifted Jove's stout oak
With his own bolt; the strong-based prom-
        ontory
Have I made shake and by the spurs pluck'd
        up
The pine and cedar: graves at my command

---

23. **all,** quite. 24. **Passion,** suffer. 27. **rarer,**
nobler. 33-57. **Ye elves . . . book.** This famous
passage is an embellished paraphrase of Golding's translation of Ovid's *Metamorphoses,* vii, 197-219. Critics
have often seen in Prospero's farewell to magic an ana-
logue to Shakespeare's farewell to the stage. *The Tempest* is probably his last complete play. After writing it
he retired to Stratford. 36. **demi-puppets,** elves and
fairies; literally, puppets of half-size. 37. **green sour
ringlets,** fairy rings, circles of grass produced by fungus
within the soil. 44-45. **to . . . fire,** the dread rattling
thunderbolt I have discharged.

Have waked their sleepers, oped, and let 'em
        forth
By my so potent art. But this rough magic
I here abjure, and, when I have required   51
Some heavenly music, which even now I
        do,
To work mine end upon their senses that
This airy charm is for, I'll break my staff,
Bury it certain fathoms in the earth,
And deeper than did ever plummet sound
I'll drown my book.   [*Solemn music.*

Re-enter Ariel *before: then* Alonso, *with a
        frantic gesture, attended by* Gonzalo; Se-
        bastian *and* Antonio *in like manner, at-
        tended by* Adrian *and* Francisco: *they all
        enter the circle which* Prospero *had made,
        and there stand charmed; which* Prospero
        observing, speaks:*

A solemn air and the best comforter
To an unsettled fancy cure thy brains,
Now useless, boil'd within thy skull! There
        stand,   60
For you are spell-stopp'd.
Holy Gonzalo, honourable man,
Mine eyes, even sociable to the show of thine,
Fall fellowly drops. The charm dissolves
        apace,
And as the morning steals upon the night,
Melting the darkness, so their rising senses
Begin to chase the ignorant fumes that
        mantle
Their clearer reason. O good Gonzalo,
My true preserver, and a loyal sir   69
To him thou follow'st! I will pay thy graces
Home both in word and deed. Most cruelly
Didst thou, Alonso, use me and my daughter:
Thy brother was a furtherer in the act.
Thou art pinch'd for't now, Sebastian.
        Flesh and blood,
You, brother mine, that entertain'd ambi-
        tion,
Expell'd remorse and nature; who, with Se-
        bastian,
Whose inward pinches therefore are most
        strong,
Would here have kill'd your king; I do for-
        give thee,
Unnatural though thou art. Their under-
        standing

---

60. **boil'd,** made hot with humors. 63. **sociable,**
sympathetic. **show,** appearance. 67. **ignorant fumes.**
The fumes which rose up into the brain to produce
sleep brought with them unconsciousness.

Begins to swell, and the approaching tide 80
Will shortly fill the reasonable shore
That now lies foul and muddy. Not one of them
That yet looks on me, or would know me:
　　Ariel,
Fetch me the hat and rapier in my cell:
I will discase me, and myself present
As I was sometime Milan: quickly, spirit;
Thou shalt ere long be free.

ARIEL *sings and helps to attire him.*

　　Where the bee sucks, there suck I:
　　In a cowslip's bell I lie;
　　There I couch when owls do cry.　　90
　　On the bat's back I do fly
　　After summer merrily.
　Merrily, merrily shall I live now
　Under the blossom that hangs on the
　　　bough.

　Pros. Why, that's my dainty Ariel! I
　　shall miss thee;
But yet thou shalt have freedom: so, so, so.
To the king's ship, invisible as thou art:
There shalt thou find the mariners asleep
Under the hatches; the master and the boat-
　　swain
Being awake, enforce them to this place, 100
And presently, I prithee.
　Ari. I drink the air before me, and return
Or ere your pulse twice beat.　　[*Exit.*
　Gon. All torment, trouble, wonder and
　　amazement
Inhabits here: some heavenly power guide us
Out of this fearful country!
　Pros.　　　　　Behold, sir king,
The wronged Duke of Milan, Prospero:
For more assurance that a living prince
Does now speak to thee, I embrace thy body;
And to thee and thy company I bid　　110
A hearty welcome.
　Alon.　　　Whether thou be'st he or no,
Or some enchanted trifle to abuse me,
As late I have been, I not know: thy pulse
Beats as of flesh and blood; and, since I saw
　　thee,
The affliction of my mind amends, with
　　which,
I fear, a madness held me: this must crave,

An if this be at all, a most strange story.
Thy dukedom I resign and do entreat
Thou pardon me my wrongs. But how
　　should Prospero
Be living and be here?
　Pros.　　　　　First, noble friend, 120
Let me embrace thine age, whose honour
　　cannot
Be measured or confined.
　Gon.　　　　　Whether this be
Or be not, I'll not swear.
　Pros.　　　　　You do yet taste
Some subtilties o' the isle, that will not let
　　you
Believe things certain. Welcome, my
　　friends all!
[*Aside to Seb. and Ant.*] But you, my brace of
　　lords, were I so minded,
I here could pluck his highness' frown upon
　　you
And justify you traitors: at this time
I will tell no tales.
　Seb. [*Aside*] The devil speaks in him.
　Pros.　　　　　　No.
For you, most wicked sir, whom to call
　　brother　　　　　130
Would even infect my mouth, I do forgive
Thy rankest fault; all of them; and require
My dukedom of thee, which perforce, I
　　know,
Thou must restore.
　Alon.　　　If thou be'st Prospero,
Give us particulars of thy preservation;
How thou hast met us here, who three hours
　　since
Were wreck'd upon this shore; where I have
　　lost—
How sharp the point of this remembrance
　　is!—
My dear son Ferdinand.
　Pros.　　　　　I am woe for't, sir.
　Alon. Irreparable is the loss, and patience
Says it is past her cure.
　Pros.　　　　　I rather think 141
You have not sought her help, of whose soft
　　grace
For the like loss I have her sovereign aid
And rest myself content.
　Alon.　　　You the like loss!
　Pros. As great to me as late; and, sup-
　　portable

85. **discase**, undress. 90. **couch**, to lie down as on a couch, or, more probably, lie hidden. 96. **so, so, so**, that will do very well. 112. **trifle**, trick of magic. abuse, deceive, cheat.

124. **subtilties**, illusions. 128. **justify you**, prove you to be. 139. **woe**, sorry. 145. **late**, i.e., as great to me as it is recent.

To make the dear loss, have I means much
    weaker
Than you may call to comfort you, for I
Have lost my daughter.
    Alon.   A daughter?
O heavens, that they were living both in
    Naples,
The king and queen there! that they were, I
    wish   150
Myself were mudded in that oozy bed
Where my son lies. When did you lose your
    daughter?
    Pros. In this last tempest. I perceive,
    these lords
At this encounter do so much admire
That they devour their reason and scarce
    think
Their eyes do offices of truth, their words
Are natural breath: but, howsoe'er you have
Been justled from your senses, know for cer-
    tain
That I am Prospero and that very duke
Which was thrust forth of Milan, who most
    strangely   160
Upon this shore, where you were wreck'd,
    was landed,
To be the lord on't. No more yet of this;
For 'tis a chronicle of day by day,
Not a relation for a breakfast nor
Befitting this first meeting. Welcome, sir;
This cell's my court: here have I few at-
    tendants
And subjects none abroad: pray you, look in.
My dukedom since you have given me again,
I will requite you with as good a thing;
At least bring forth a wonder, to content ye
As much as me my dukedom.   171

Here Prospero *discovers* Ferdinand *and*
    Miranda, *playing at chess.*

    Mir. Sweet lord, you play me false.
    Fer.   No, my dear'st love,
I would not for the world.
    Mir. Yes, for a score of kingdoms you
    should wrangle,
And I would call it fair play.
    Alon.   If this prove
A vision of the Island, one dear son
Shall I twice lose.

    Seb.   A most high miracle!
    Fer. Though the seas threaten, they are
    merciful;
I have cursed them without cause. [*Kneels.*
    Alon.   Now all the blessings
Of a glad father compass thee about!   180
Arise, and say how thou camest here.
    Mir.   O, wonder!
How many goodly creatures are there here!
How beauteous mankind is! O brave new
    world,
That has such people in't!
    Pros.   'Tis new to thee.
    Alon. What is this maid with whom thou
    wast at play?
Your eld'st acquaintance cannot be three
    hours:
Is she the goddess that hath sever'd us,
And brought us thus together?
    Fer.   Sir, she is mortal;
But by immortal Providence she's mine:
I chose her when I could not ask my father
For his advice, nor thought I had one. She
Is daughter to this famous Duke of Milan,
Of whom so often I have heard renown, 193
But never saw before; of whom I have
Received a second life; and second father
This lady makes him to me.
    Alon.   I am hers:
But, O, how oddly will it sound that I
Must ask my child forgiveness!
    Pros.   There, sir, stop:
Let us not burthen our remembrance with
A heaviness that's gone.
    Gon.   I have inly wept 200
Or should have spoke ere this. Look down,
    you gods,
And on this couple drop a blessed crown!
For it is you that have chalk'd forth the
    way
Which brought us hither.
    Alon.   I say, Amen, Gonzalo!
    Gon. Was Milan thrust from Milan, that
    his issue
Should become kings of Naples? O, rejoice
Beyond a common joy, and set it down
With gold on lasting pillars: In one voyage
Did Claribel her husband find at Tunis
And Ferdinand, her brother, found a wife 210
Where he himself was lost, Prospero his
    dukedom
In a poor isle and all of us ourselves

---

155. **devour**, render null, destroy.   174. **score**, double meaning: game or wager in which the score is reckoned by kingdoms, and also twenty kingdoms. **wrangle**, meaning (1) contend in a game or wager, and (2) argue or contend in words.

186. **eld'st**, earliest.   193. **renown**, report.

When no man was his own.
Alon. [*To Fer. and Mir.*] Give me your
hands:
Let grief and sorrow still embrace his heart
That doth not wish you joy!
Gon.   Be it so! Amen!

Re-enter ARIEL, *with the* Master *and* Boatswain *amazedly following.*

O, look, sir, look, sir! here is more of us:
I prophesied, if a gallows were on land,
This fellow could not drown. Now, blas-
phemy,
That swear'st grace o'erboard, not an oath
on shore?
Hast thou no mouth by land? What is the
news?   220
Boats. The best news is, that we have
safely found
Our king and company; the next, our ship—
Which, but three glasses since, we gave out
split—
Is tight and yare and bravely rigg'd as when
We first put out to sea.
Ari. [*Aside to Pros.*] Sir, all this service
Have I done since I went.
Pros. [*Aside to Ari.*] My tricksy spirit!
Alon. These are not natural events; they
strengthen
From strange to stranger. Say, how came
you hither?
Boats. If I did think, sir, I were well
awake,
I'ld strive to tell you. We were dead of
sleep,   230
And—how we know not—all clapp'd under
hatches;
Where but even now with strange and
several noises
Of roaring, shrieking, howling, jingling
chains,
And moe diversity of sounds, all horrible,
We were awaked; straightway, at liberty;
Where we, in all her trim, freshly beheld
Our royal, good and gallant ship, our master
Capering to eye her: on a trice, so please
you,
Even in a dream, were we divided from them
And were brought moping hither.
Ari. [*Aside to Pros.*] Was't well done? 240
Pros. [*Aside to Ari.*] Bravely, my diligence.
Thou shalt be free.

213. **own**, i.e., master of his senses.   224. **yare**,
ready.

Alon. This is as strange a maze as e'er
men trod;
And there is in this business more than
nature
Was ever conduct of: some oracle
Must rectify our knowledge.
Pros.   Sir, my liege,
Do not infest your mind with beating on
The strangeness of this business; at pick'd
leisure
Which shall be shortly, single I'll resolve
you,
Which to you shall seem probable, of every
These happen'd accidents; till when, be
cheerful   250
And think of each thing well. [*Aside to Ari.*]
Come hither, spirit:
Set Caliban and his companions free;
Untie the spell. [*Exit Ariel.*] How fares my
gracious sir?
There are yet missing of your company
Some few odd lads that you remember not.

Re-enter ARIEL, *driving in* CALIBAN, STE-
PHANO *and* TRINCULO, *in their stolen
apparel.*

Ste. Every man shift for all the rest,
and let no man take care for himself; for
all is but fortune. Coragio, bully-monster,
coragio!
Trin. If these be true spies which I wear
in my head, here's a goodly sight.   260
Cal. O Setebos, these be brave spirits in-
deed!
How fine my master is! I am afraid
He will chastise me.
Seb.   Ha, ha!
What things are these, my lord Antonio?
Will money buy 'em?
Ant.   Very like; one of them
Is a plain fish, and, no doubt, marketable.
Pros. Mark but the badges of these men,
my lords,
Then say if they be true. This mis-shapen
knave,
His mother was a witch, and one so strong
That could control the moon, make flows and
ebbs,   270

244. **conduct**, guide, leader. 246. **infest**, harass,
disturb. 247. **pick'd**, chosen. 248. **single**, i.e., when
we are alone together. F has no comma after *shortly*,
in which reading *single* means "unbroken," "absolute."
256. **shift**, contrive means. 258. **Coragio**, courage.
bully-monster, gallant monster. 267. **badges**, emblems of cloth or silver worn on the arms of retainers.

And deal in her command without her power.
These three have robb'd me; and this demi-
    devil—   272
For he's a bastard one—had plotted with
    them
To take my life. Two of these fellows you
Must know and own; this thing of darkness I
Acknowledge mine.
    Cal.   I shall be pinch'd to death.
    Alon. Is not this Stephano, my drunken
    butler?
    Seb. He is drunk now: where had he wine?
    Alon. And Trinculo is reeling ripe: where
    should they
Find this grand liquor that hath gilded 'em?
How camest thou in this pickle?   281
    Trin. I have been in such a pickle since I
saw you last that, I fear me, will never out of
my bones: I shall not fear fly-blowing.
    Seb. Why, how now, Stephano!
    Ste. O, touch me not; I am not Stephano,
    but a cramp.
    Pros. You'll be king o' the isle, sirrah?
    Ste. I should have been a sore one then.
    Alon. This is a strange thing as e'er I
    look'd on.   [*Pointing to Caliban.*
    Pros. He is as disproportion'd in his man-
    ners   290
As in his shape. Go, sirrah, to my cell;
Take with you your companions; as you look
To have my pardon, trim it handsomely.
    Cal. Ay, that I will; and I'll be wise here-
    after
And seek for grace. What a thrice-double
    ass
Was I, to take this drunkard for a god
And worship this dull fool!
    Pros.   Go to; away!
    Alon. Hence, and bestow your luggage
    where you found it.
    Seb. Or stole it, rather.
          [*Exeunt Cal., Ste., and Trin.*
    Pros. Sir, I invite your highness and your
    train   300
To my poor cell, where you shall take your
    rest
For this one night; which, part of it, I'll
    waste

With such discourse as, I not doubt, shall
    make it
Go quick away; the story of my life
And the particular accidents gone by
Since I came to this isle: and in the morn
I'll bring you to your ship and so to Naples,
Where I have hope to see the nuptial
Of these our dear-beloved solemnized;
And thence retire me to my Milan, where 310
Every third thought shall be my grave.
    Alon.   I long
To hear the story of your life, which must
Take the ear strangely.
    Pros.   I'll deliver all;
And promise you calm seas, auspicious gales
And sail so expeditous that shall catch
Your royal fleet far off. [*Aside to Ari.*] My
    Ariel, chick,
That is thy charge: then to the elements
Be free, and fare thou well! Please you,
    draw near.   [*Exeunt.*

EPILOGUE.

SPOKEN BY PROSPERO.

Now my charms are all o'erthrown,
And what strength I have's mine own,
Which is most faint: now, 'tis true,
I must be here confined by you,
Or sent to Naples. Let me not,
Since I have my dukedom got
And pardon'd the deceiver, dwell
In this bare island by your spell;
But release me from my bands
With the help of your good hands: 10
Gentle breath of yours my sails
Must fill, or else my project fails,
Which was to please. Now I want
Spirits to enforce, art to enchant,
And my ending is despair,
Unless I be relieved by prayer,
Which pierces so that it assaults
Mercy itself and frees all faults.
    As you from crimes would pardon'd be,
Let your indulgence set me free.   20

---

271. **deal . . . power**, wield the moon's power, either
without her authority, or beyond her influence. The
line is ambiguous. 280. **gilded**, flushed, made drunk.

305. **accidents**, occurrences, events. 313. **Take**,
take effect upon. **deliver**, declare, relate.
Epilogue. 10. **hands**, applause. 13. **want**, lack.

TEXTUAL VARIANTS[1]

THE COMEDY OF ERRORS

Act I: i. 16-18 *Nay . . . fairs;* so Cambridge and Globe editors; F *Nay more, if . . . Ephesus Be seene at any . . . Fayres; any* (l. 18) omitted by Pope and some later editors.   i. 39 *And by me;* so F; F$_{2-3-4}$ *And by me too,* followed by some editors.   i. 42 *Epidamnum;* so Pope; F *Epidamium.*   i. 55 *meaner;* so Delius (S. Walker conjecture); F *meane.*   i. 56 *burden, male twins;* F *burthen Male, twins.*   i. 61-62 *Unwilling . . . aboard;* so Pope; one line in F. *aboard* (l. 62); Cuningham conjectured *aboard and put to sea but scarce.*   i. 86 *at . . . mast;* so F; Hanmer *th' end of either mast.*   i. 88 *Was;* so F; Craig (Oxford Shakespeare), Rowe (first modern edition, 1709), New Cambridge *Were.*   i. 94 *Epidaurus;* F *Epidarus.*   i. 102 *encounter'd;* F *encountred;* similar changes hereafter not noted.   i. 103 *upon;* so Pope; F *up.*   i. 104 *helpful;* Rowe conjectured *helpless.*   i. 117 *bark;* so F$_2$; F *backe.*   i. 124 *hath . . . thee;* so F$_2$; F *haue . . . they.*   i. 152 *life;* so Globe; F *helpe.*   ii. 1 First Mer.; so Dyce; F Mer (ll. 24, 32 E. Mar.)   ii. 66 *clock;* so Pope; F *cooke.*   ii. 93 *God's;* so Hanmer; F *God.*   ii. 94 *an;* so Pope; F *and.*   ii. 96 *o'er-raught;* so Hanmer; F *ore-wrought.*

Act II: i. 11 *o' door;* so Capell; F *adore.*   i. 12 *ill;* so F$_{2-3-4}$; F *thus.*   i. 20-21 *Men . . . masters . . . Lords;* so Hanmer; F *Man . . . Master . . . Lord.*   i. 30 *where;* so F; Johnson conjectured *hare.*   i. 31 *forbear;* New Cambridge punctuates *forbear—.*   i. 39 *wouldst;* so Rowe; F *would.*   i. 45 *two;* F *too.*   i. 61 *thousand;* so F; F *hundred.*   i. 64 *home;* so Hanmer; not in F.   i. 68 *I know not thy mistress;* so F; Seymour *I know thy mistress not.*   i. 107 *alone, alone;* F *alone a loue;* New Cambridge *alone o' love.*   i. 110 *lose;* F *loose.*   i. 112 *Wear;* so Theobald; F *Where.*   ii. 3-4 *out By . . . report;* so F; Rowe *out. By report,.*   ii. 12 *didst;* so F$_2$; F *did didst.*   ii. 81 *men;* so Theobald; F *them.*   ii. 90 *jollity;* so F; Staunton and some editors *policy;* see comment in notes.   ii. 92 *sound ones;* so F$_{2-3-4}$; F *sound.*   ii. 99 *tiring;* so Pope; F *trying.*   ii. 103 *no time;* New Cambridge *e'en no time;* F *in no time.*   ii. 120 *or look'd, or touch'd;* so F; Steevens and other editors *look'd, touched.*   ii. 143 *crime;* many editors read *grime.*   ii. 148 *unstain'd;* F *distain'd,* retained by New Cambridge editors, who transpose lines 147 and 148; see comment in

THE COMEDY OF ERRORS (Con.)

notes.   ii. 158 *me?* so Rowe; F *me.*   ii. 177 *stronger;* so F$_4$; F *stranger.*   188 *offer'd;* so Capell; F *free'd.*   ii. 196 *drone;* so Theobald; F *Dromio.*   ii. 197 *I not;* so F; Theobald *not I.*   ii. 207 *laugh;* so Pope; F *laughes.*

Act III: i. 35 *many?* so F$_4$; F *many.*   i. 65 *pain;* so F; Cuningham *i' faith.*   i. 75 *you, sir;* F$_2$ *you sir;* F *your sir.*   i. 89 *her;* so Rowe; F *your.*   i. 108 *mirth;* so F; Theobald and some editors *wrath.*   ii. *Stage Direction: Luciana;* so F$_{2-3-4}$; F *Iuliana.*   i. 1 Luc; so Rowe; F *Iulia.*   ii. 4 *building;* so Theobald; F *buildings. ruinous;* so Capell; F *ruinate.*   ii. 16 *attaint;* so Rowe; F *attaine.*   ii. 20 *are;* so F$_2$; F *is.*   ii. 21 *but;* so Theobald; F *not.*   ii. 26 *wife;* so F$_2$; F *wise.*   ii. 46 *sister's;* so F; F *sister.*   ii. 49 *bed;* so F$_2$; F *bud. them;* so Capell; F *thee.*   ii. 57 *where;* so Rowe; F *when.*   ii. 66 *am;* so F; Capell *aim.*   ii. 111 *and;* so Theobald; F *is.*   ii. 150 *faith;* so F; Hanmer *flint.*

Act IV: i. 17 *her;* so Rowe; F *their.*   i. 42 *will;* F *will?*   i. 60 *whether;* F *whe'r.*   i. 98 *rope's end;* so F; Cuningham *rope's end sir.*   ii. 28 *sweet;* so F; New Cambridge *sweat.*   ii. 33 *hath him;* so F; Spedding *hath him by the heel.*   ii. 35 *fury;* so Theobald; F and some editors *Fairie.*   ii. 48 *That;* so F$_2$; F *Thus,* with period after *at* in the preceding line.   ii. 55 *hear;* so F$_2$; F *here.*   ii. 61 *Time;* so Rowe; F *I;* Malone *he.*   iii. 13 *What;* so F; New Cambridge *Where.*   iii. 35 *ship;* so F$_2$; F *ships.*   iii. 61 *you;* so F$_2$; not in F.   iii. 66 *then;* so F$_4$; F and some editors *thou.*   iv. 45 *the;* so F; Dyce and some editors *to.*   iv. 150. *Stage Direction:* F prints "Runne all out," after l. 149, and "Exeunt omnes as fast as may be, frighted." after l. 150; see comment in notes.   iv. 156 *saw;* so F; Capell and some editors *see.*

Act V: i. 12 *to me;* so F; Hudson, New Cambridge *with me.*   i. 33 *God's;* F$_{3-4}$ *Gods;* F *God.*   i. 79 *dull;* New Cambridge editors suggest *dull-footed,* which would fill up the line.   i. 86 *Have;* so F$_2$; F *Hath.*   i. 121 *death;* so F$_3$; F *depth.*   i. 124 *reverend;* so F$_3$; F *reuerent.*   i. 137 *Whom;* so F$_2$; F *Who.*   i. (after) 167 Enter a *Servant;* so Capell; F Enter a *Messenger,* and omits speech heading.   i. 175 *scissors;* F *Cizers.*   i. 183 *scorch;* so F; Warburton and some editors *scotch.*   i. 195 Æge.; F Mar. Fat. (Merchant Father).   i. 240 *A . . . wretch;* F *a needy-hollow-ey'd-sharpe-looking-wretch.*   i. 245 *all together;* so Rowe; F *altogether.*   i. 315 *lamps;* Rowe *lamp.*   i. 317 *All . . . err;* Rowe's punctuation; New Cam-

---

[1] Only the more significant variants are listed. Mere differences in spelling between the text and its original are ordinarily not recorded. In the case of *Richard III*, the variants are so chosen as to render available the readings of the First Folio.

THE COMEDY OF ERRORS (Con.)

bridge editors would read *All these hold witness as I cannot err.* i. 320 *boy;* so F; Hanmer *bay.* i. 333 *these. Which;* F *these, which.* i. 356-361 *Why . . . together.* These lines stand in F after line 345, where they probably belong. They were shifted by Capell, who has been followed by most modern editors. New Cambridge editors restore them. i. 388 *ERRORS;* not capitalized in F. *are arose;* so F; anonymous conjecture *here arose.* i. 405 *Go;* so F; Dyce *joy.* i. 406 *festivity;* so Johnson and most editors; F *Natiuitie.* i. 423-424 *Nay . . . brother;* printed as one line by Cuningham following F.

A MIDSUMMER-NIGHT'S DREAM

ACT I: i. 219 *stranger companies;* so Theobald; Q *strange companions.* ii. 25 *gallant;* so Q; F *gallantly.*

ACT II: i. 69 *steppe;* so Q; F *steep.* i. 79 *Ægle;* QF *Eagles;* Rowe *Ægle.*

ACT III: i. 206 *love's;* so Pope; QF *louers.* ii. 213 *like;* so Theobald; QF *life.* ii. 250 *prayers;* so Theobald; QF *praise.* ii. 257 *No, no; he'll;* Q *No, no: heele;* F *No, Sir.* ii. 279 *of doubt;* so QF; Pope's emendation *doubt.*

ACT IV: i. 177 *in sickness;* so Farmer; QF *a sickness.*

ACT V: i. 208 *mural;* so Pope; F *morall;* Q *Now is the Moon vsed.* i. 221 *man;* Theobald suggested *moon.* i. 227 *lion-fell;* QF *lion fell.* i. 279 *gleams;* so Knight; QF *beames.* i. 379 *behowls;* so Warburton; QF *beholds.*

THE TRAGEDY OF KING RICHARD III

ACT I: i. 13 *lute;* so F; Qq *loue.* i. 26 *spy;* so Qq; F *see.* i. 65 *tempers;* so Q₁; F, Q₂, ₅₋₈ *tempts;* Q₃₋₄ *temps.* i. 75 *was to her for his;* so Qq; F *was, for her.* i. 101-2 *What . . . me;* not in Q₁. i. 133 *prey;* so Qq; F and some editors *play.* i. 138 *Saint Paul;* so Qq; F *S. John.* i. 142 *What, is;* so Qq; F *Where is.* ii. 11 *wounds;* so F; Qq *holes.* ii. 19 *adders;* so Qq; F and some editors *Wolues, to.* ii. 25 *And . . . unhappiness;* so F; not in Qq. ii. 70 *no;* so Qq; F and some editors *nor.* ii. 76 *evils;* so Qq; F and some editors *crimes.* ii. 89 *Why . . . dead;* so Qq; F *Then say they were not slaine.* ii. 172 *lips;* so Qq; F and some editors *lip.* ii. 180 *for . . . Henry;* so F; Qq *twas I that kild your husband.* ii. 182 *stabb'd young Edward;* so F; Qq *kild King Henry.* ii. 202 *Glou.;* so Qq; omitted from F. ii. 203 *To . . . give;* so Qq; omitted from F. ii. 207 *suppliant;* so Qq; F and some editors *servant.* ii. 212 *more;* so Qq; F

KING RICHARD III (Con.)

and some editors *most.* ii. 213 *Crosby Place;* so Qq; F *Crosby House.* ii. 226 *Sirs . . . corse;* so Qq; omitted from F. ii. 234 *her hatred;* so Qq; F *my hatred.* ii. 237 *at all;* so Q₁₋₂; Q₃₋₈, F *withal.* iii. 5 *words;* so Qq; F *eyes.* iii. 17 *come the lords;* so Q₁₋₂; Q₃₋₈ *comes the Lords;* F *comes the Lord.* iii. 27 *in;* so Qq; F *on.* iii. 36 *Madam, we did;* so Qq; F *I, Madam.* iii. 41 *highest;* so Qq; F *height.* iii. 43 *are they;* so Qq; F *is it. complain;* so Q₈; Q₁₋₇, F *complaines.* iii. 47 *speak;* so Qq; F *look.* iii. 54 *Riv.;* so Qq; F *Grey.* iii. 58 *person;* so Qq; F *grace.* iii. 63 *of;* so Qq; F *on.* iii. 67 *kindred;* so Qq; F *children. brothers;* so F; Qq *brother.* iii. 68-9 *that . . . it;* so Steevens; Qq *to remove it;* F *whereby . . . to remove it.* iii. 76 *grant;* so Q₃₋₈; Q₁₋₂, F *grants. we;* so Qq; F *I.* iii. 80 *many fair;* so Qq; F *great.* iii. 90 *cause;* so Qq; F *means.* iii. 98 *yea;* so Qq; F *I;* many editors *ay.* This variation is frequent. iii. 106 *With;* so Qq; F *Of. I often;* so Qq; F *that oft I.* iii. 109 *thus taunted;* so Qq; F *so baited. baited;* so Qq; F *stormed.* iii. 111 *thee;* so Qq; F *Him.* iii. 114 *Tell . . . said;* so Qq; omitted from F. iii. 115 *avouch;* so Qq; F *avouch't.* iii. 116 *I dare . . . Tower;* so F; not in Qq. iii. 119 *slewest;* so F *killd'st.* iii. 125 *spilt;* so Qq; F *spent.* iii. 147 *lawful;* so Qq; F *soueraigne.* iii. 167-9 *Wert . . . abode;* so F; not in Qq. iii. 204 *loss;* so Qq; F *death.* iii. 231 *mother's heavy;* so Qq; F *heauie Mothers.* iii. 245 *time;* so Qq; F *day.* iii. 273 *Have done;* so Qq; F *Peace, peace.* iii. 276 *by . . . hopes;* so Qq; F *my hopes by you.* iii. 304 *Hast.;* so Qq; F *Buc.* iii. 309 *Q. Eliz.;* so Cambridge editors; Q₁₋₅ *Qu.;* Q₆₋₈ *Hast.;* F *Mar.;* Rowe *Dors.* iii. 321 *grace;* so Q₁₋₂; Q₃₋₈; F *noble grace. you . . . lords;* so Capell; Q₁₋₂ *you my noble Lo.;* Q₃₋₆ *you my noble Lord;* F *yours my gracious Lord.* iii. 323 *Madam;* so Qq; omitted from F. *will attend;* so Qq; F *wait upon.* iii. 327 *laid;* so Qq; F *cast.* iii. 329 *Hastings, Derby;* so Qq; F *Derby, Hastings.* iii. 330 *say;* so Qq; F *tell them.* iii. 333 *Vaughan;* so Qq; F *Dorset.* iii. 337 *old odd;* so Qq; F *odde old.* iii. 341 *deed;* so Qq; F *thing.* iii. 342 *First Murd.;* so Capell; Qq *Execu.;* F *Vil.* (also ll. 350, 355). iii. 350-1 *Tush! Fear not;* so Qq; F *Tut, tut.* iii. 353 *come;* so Qq; F *go.* iii. 354 *drop;* so Qq; F *fall.* iii. 355 *straight;* so F; not in Qq. iii. 356 *Go . . . lord;* so F; not in Qq. iv. *Stage Direction:* Brakenbury; so Qq; F *Keeper.* iv. 1 *Brak.;* so Qq; F *Keep.* (also in ll. 34, 42, 64, 75). In F Brackenbury enters after l. 75. iv. 3 *ugly . . . dreams;* so Qq; F *fearful dreams of ugly sights.* iv. 8 *dream . . . tell it;* so Qq; F *dream my Lord? I pray you tel me.* .iv 14 *a thousand;* so F; Qq *ten thousand. fearful;* so Qq; F *heauy.* iv. 21 *Lord, Lord;* so Qq; F *O Lord.* iv. 23 *ugly sights*

of; so Qq; F *sights of ugly.*   iv. 25 *Ten thousand;*
so Qq; F *A thousand.*   iv. 36-7 *and often . . .
ghost;* so F; not in Qq.   iv. 38 *Kept* so Qq; F
Stop'd.   iv. 39 *seek;* so Q₁₋₂; Q₃₋₈ *keepe;* F *find.*
iv. 43 *O, no;* so Qq; F *No, no.*   iv. 45 *Who;* so
Qq; F *I.*   iv. 46 *grim;* so Qq; F *sour.*   iv. 50
cried; so Qq; F *spake.*   iv. 54 *squeak'd;* so Q₂₋₈;
Q₁ *squakt;* F *shriek'd.*   iv. 57 *to your torments;*
so Qq; F *unto torment.*   iv. 59 *about;* so Qq;
omitted from F.   iv. 65 *I . . . afraid;* so Qq;
F *I am afraid methinks.*   iv. 66 *O Brakenbury;*
so Qq; F *Oh keeper, keeper.*   iv. 67 *bear;* so Qq;
F *give.*   iv. 69-72 *O God . . . children;* so F; not
in Qq.   iv. 73 *I . . . me;* so Qq; F *Keeper, I
prithee sit by me a-while.*   iv. 84 *Ho! . . . here;*
so F; not in Qq.   iv. 85 *In . . . hither;* so Qq;
F *what would'st thou fellow, and how cam'st thou
hither?*   iv. 86 First Murd.; so F; Qq Execu.
iv. 88 *Yea . . . brief;* so Q₁₋₂; Q₃₋₇, F *What, so
brief.*   iv. 89-90 *O sir . . . tedious;* so Q₁₋₂; *to*
omitted from Q₃₋₆; F *'Tis better (Sir) then to be
tedious.*   iv. 90 *Show him;* so Qq; F *let him see.*
iv. 96 *Here . . . asleep;* so Qq; F *There lies the
Duke asleepe, and there the Keyes.*   iv. 98 *my
. . . you;* so Q₁₋₂; Q₃₋₈ *my place to you;* F *to you
my charge.*   iv. 99 *Do so;* so Qq; F *you may, sir.*
iv. 100 *fare you well;* so F; not in Qq.   iv. 105
When . . . fool; so Qq; F *Why.*   iv. 106 *till the;*
so Qq; F *untill the great.*   iv. 113 *for it;* so Qq;
omitted from F.   iv. 115-7 *I . . . live;* so F; not
in Qq.   iv. 118 *Back;* so Qq; F *Ile back.*   iv. 119
tell; so Qq; F *and tell.*   iv. 120 *I pray thee;* so
Qq; F *Nay, I prythee. while;* so Qq; F *little.*
iv. 121 *my holy humour;* so Qq; F *this passionate
humour of mine.*   iv. 122 *would tell;* so Qq F
tels.   iv. 124 *'Faith;* so Qq; omitted from F.
iv. 128 *'Zounds;* so Qq; F *Come.*   iv. 134 *Let it
go;* so Qq; F *'Tis no matter. Let it go.*   iv. 137-8
it is . . . thing; so Qq; omitted from F.   iv. 145
that I; so Qq; F *that by chance I.*   iv. 146 *all;* so
Qq; omitted from F.   iv. 149 *'Zounds;* so Qq;
omitted from F.   iv. 154 *Tut;* so Qq; omitted
from F. *strong-framed;* so F; Qq *strong in fraud.*
iv. 155 *I . . . thee;* so Qq; omitted from F.
iv. 157-8 *to . . . gear;* so Qq; F *fall to work.*
iv. 160-1 *we . . . in;* so Qq; F *throw him into.*
iv. 163 *Hark . . . strike;* so Qq; F *Soft, he wakes.*
iv. 164 Sec. Murd.; so Qq; F *Here* and at ll. 170
and 174 F gives the speech to 1 Murd. Before
l. 164 F inserts 2 Murd. *Strike. first let's;* so
Qq; F *wee'l.*   iv. 172 Sec. Murd.; so Q₁₋₄; Q₅₋₈,
F First Murd.   iv. 175 *Your . . . pale;* so F;
not in Qq.   iv. 177 Both. *To;* Qq Am. *To;*
F 2 Murd. *To.*   iv. 186 *call'd . . . out;* so Qq;
F *drawne forth among.*   iv. 194-5 *to have . . .
sins;* so Qq; F *for any goodnesse.*   iv. 208-9
holy . . . To . . . Lancaster; so Qq; F *Sacrament
to fight In . . . Lancaster.*   iv. 218 *Why, sirs;*

so Qq; omitted from F.   iv. 221 *revenged;* so
Qq; F *avenged.*   iv. 222 *O . . . publicly;* so F;
not in Qq.   iv. 230 *our duty;* so F; Qq *the diuell.*
fault; so Qq; F *faults.*   iv. 240 Both.; Qq Am.;
F 1 Murd.   iv. 243 *And . . . other;* so Qq;
omitted from F.   iv. 246 First Murd.; so F;
Qq Am.   iv. 249 *Thou . . . thyself;* so Qq; F
Come, you deceiue your selfe.   iv. 250 *that . . .
thee;* so Qq F *that sends us to destroy you heere.*
iv. 254 Sec. Murd.; so Qq; F 1 Murd.   iv. 255
world's; so Qq; F *earths.*   iv. 264-75 *Relent . . .
lord;* Steevens's arrangement based on Tyrwhitt's
conjecture. Qq arrange thus: 264, 265, 270, 271,
272, 274 (omitting 266-9, 273, 275); F arranges
thus: 266, 267, 268, 269, 273, 264, 265, 270, 271,
274.   iv. 280 *grievous . . . done;* so Qq; F *grievous murder.*   iv. 287 *Now must I;* so Qq; F
Well, Ile go.   iv. 288 *take;* so Qq; F *giue.*

Act II: i. 5 *now in;* so Qq; F *more to.*   i. 6
set; so Qq; F *made.*   i. 7 *Rivers and Hastings;*
so Qq; F *Dorset and Riuers.*   i. 9 *heart;* so Qq;
F *soul.*   i. 25 *Dorset . . . marquess;* so F; not in
Qq.   i. 28 *my lord;* so Qq; omitted from F.
i. 33 *On . . . yours;* so Qq; F *upon your Grace.*
i. 39 *God;* so Qq; F *heauen.*   i. 40 *zeal;* so Qq;
F *loue.*   i. 44 *perfect;* so Qq; F *blessed.*   i. 45
here . . . duke; so Qq; *Heere comes Sir Richard
Ratcliffe, and the Duke.*   i. 49 *Brother;* so Qq;
F *Gloster.*   i. 52 *liege;* so Qq; F *lord* (many such
variations in the text; not noted hereafter).
i. 56 *unwittingly;* so Qq; F *unwillingly.*   i. 66 *Of
you . . . of you;* so Q₁₋₄; F *Of you and you, Lord
Riuers and of Dorset;* after l. 67 F adds *Of you
Lord Wooduill, and Lord Scales of you;* see comment in notes.   i. 75 *majesty;* so Qq; F *Highnesse* (many such variations in the text; not noted
hereafter).   i. 79 *noble;* so Qq; F *gentle.*   i. 81
Riv.; so Qq; F King.   i. 87 *soul;* so Qq; F *man*
i. 97 *grant;* so Qq; F *hear me.*   i. 98 *speak;* so
Qq; F *say. demand'st;* so Qq; F *requests.*   i. 103
the same; so Qq; F *that tongue.*   i. 104 *slew;* so
Qq; F *kill'd.*   i. 105 *cruel;* so Qq; F *bitter.*
i. 106 *rage;* so Qq; F *wrath.*   i. 116 *own;* so
Q₁₋₅; omitted from F. *gave;* so Qq; F *did giue.*
i. 130 *plead;* so Qq; F *beg.*   i. 138 *But . . . in;*
so Qq; F *Come Lords will you go.*   i. 140 *We
. . . grace;* so F; not in Qq.   ii. 1 Boy.; so Qq;
F Daugh.   ii. 3 *wring your hands;* so Qq; F *weepe
so oft.*   ii. 5 Girl.; so Qq; F Boy.   ii. 12 *grandam
. . . that;* so Qq; F *you conclude (my Grandam).*
ii. 15 *daily;* so Qq; F *earnest.*   ii. 16 *And . . . I;*
so F; not in Qq.   ii. 21 *provoked;* so Qq; F
prouok'd to it.   ii. 24 *hugg'd . . . arm;* so Qq;
F *pittied me.*   ii. 27 *Oh;* so Qq; F *Ah* (so frequently).   ii. 41 *now . . . wither'd;* so Qq; F
when the Roote is gone.   ii. 42 *the sap . . . gone;*
so Qq; F *that want their sap.*   ii. 46 *perpetual
rest;* so Qq F *nere-changing night.*   ii. 58 *limbs;*

KING RICHARD III (Con.)

so Qq; F *hands.*   ii. 60 *grief;* so Qq; F *moane.*
ii. 61 *plaints;* so Qq; F *woes.*   ii. 62 *Good;* so
Qq; F *Ah.*   ii. 80 *moans;* so Qq; F *Greefes.*
ii. 84-5 *These . . . so do not they;* so Qq; F *These
Babes for Clarence weepe, so do not they.*   ii. 89-
100 *Comfort . . . throne;* so F; not in Qq.   ii. 101
Madam; so Qq; F *Sister.*   ii. 103 *cure their;* so
Qq; F *help our.*   ii. 113 *mutual heavy;* so Qq;
F *heauie mutuall.*   ii. 117 *hearts;* so Qq; F
hates.   ii. 123-140 *Why . . . say I;* so F; not in
Qq.   ii. 142 *Ludlow;* so Qq; F *London* (also in l.
154).   ii. 143 *mother;* so Qq; F *Sister.*   ii. 144
weighty; so Qq; omitted from F.   ii. 145 Q. Eliz.,
Duch.; Qq Ans. *With . . . hearts;* so Qq; omitted
from F.   ii. 147 *be;* so Q₂₋₈; Q₁, F *stay. behind;*
so Qq; F *at home.*   ii. 150 *king;* so Qq; F *Prince.*
iii. 1 *Neighbour . . . met;* so Qq; F *Good morrow
Neighbour.*   iii. 3 *Hear . . . abroad;* in Qq First
Cit. speaks this, Sec. Cit. taking the second
half of the line; thereafter in Qq the citizens
trade speeches beginning at ll. 4, 8, 22, 31, 38;
text here follows F.   iii. 5 *troublous;* so Q₁;
Q₂₋₈ *trouble-some;* F *giddy.*   iii. 6 *Neighbours
. . . sir;* so F; Qq *Good morrow neighbors.*   iii. 8
Ay . . . while; so F; Qq *It doth.*   iii. 18 *No . . .
wot;* so F; Qq *no good my friend not so.*   iii. 25
now . . . nearest; so Qq; F *who shall now be.*
iii. 38 *souls;* so Qq; F *hearts. dread;* so Q₃₋₈;
Q₁₋₂ *bread;* F *fear.*   iii. 43 *Ensuing dangers;* so
Qq; F *Pursuing danger. Stage Direction:*
Enter . . . York; F Enter Arch-bishop; Qq Enter
Cardinal; see comment in notes.   iv. 1 Arch.;
so F; Qq Car. throughout the scene. *Northampton;* so Qq; F *Stony Stratford.*   iv. 2 *At
Stony-Stratford will they be;* so Qq; F *And at
Northampton do they rest.*   iv. 9 *young;* so Qq;
F *good.*   iv. 21 Arch.; Qq Car.; F Yor. *Why
. . . is;* so Qq; F *and so no doubt he is, my gracious
madam.*   ii. 26 *pretty;* so Qq; F *young.*   iv. 37
Enter a Messenger; so F; Qq Enter Dorset.
iv. 38 *Here . . . news;* so F; Qq *Here comes your
sonne, Lo: M. Dorset. What newes Lord Marquess?* (as two lines).   iv. 39 Mess.; so F; Qq
Dor. (so throughout). *unfold;* so Qq; F *report.*
iv. 45 Q. Eliz.; so Cambridge editors; Qq Car.;
F Arch.   iv. 48 *lady;* so Qq; F *lord.*   iv. 49
downfall; so Qq; F *ruin.*   iv. 53 *death;* so Qq;
F *blood.*   iv. 62-3 *blood against . . . self;* so Qq;
F *brother to brother, Blood to blood.*   iv. 65 *death;*
so Qq; F *earth.*   iv. 67 *I'll . . . you;* so Qq;
F *Stay, I will go with you.*
    ACT III: i. *Stage Direction:* Cardinal Bour-
chier; Qq Cardinall; F Lord Cardinall. Catesby;
so Capell; not in Qq, F.   i. 40 *in heaven;* so
Q₁₋₂; omitted from Q₃₋₈, F.   i. 43 *deep;* so Q₁₋₂;
omitted from Q₃₋₈, F.   i. 63 *seems;* so Q₁₋₂; Q₃₋₈,
F *think'st.*   i. 78 *general all-ending;* so Q₁; Q₂₋₈,
F *generall ending.*   i. 97 *dread;* so Q₁₋₂; Q₃₋₈,

KING RICHARD III (Con.)

F *deare.*   i. 120 *heavy;* so Q₁; Q₂₋₈, F *waightie.*
i. 141 *needs;* so Q₁; omitted from Q₂₋₈, F.   i. 167
what will; so Qq; F *will not.*   i. 172-3 *And . . .
coronation;* so F; not in Qq.   i. 184 *friend;* so
Q₁₋₅; F *lord.*   i. 190 *Place;* so Qq; F *House.*
i. 193 *man;* so Qq; omitted from F.   *do;* so Qq;
F *determine.*   i. 196 *stood;* so Qq; F *was.*   i. 198
all willingness; so Q₁; Q₂₋₈ *willingnesse;* F *all kind-
nesse.*   ii. 1 *What, ho;* so Qq; F *My Lord.*   ii. 2
at the door; so Qq; omitted from F.   ii. 3 *A
messenger;* so Qq; F *one.*   ii. 6 *thy master;* so
Qq; F *my Lord Stanley.*   ii. 8 *lordship;* so Qq;
F *selfe.*   ii. 10 *And . . . word;* so Qq; F *Then
certifies your Lordship, that this Night.*   ii. 11
to-night; so Qq; omitted from F.   ii. 16 *presently
you will;* so Qq F *you will presently.*   ii. 22
servant; F *good friend.*   ii. 25 *wanting;* so Qq;
F *without.*   ii. 26 *fond;* so Q₁₋₃; F *simple.*   ii. 34
My . . . I'll; so Qq; F *Ile goe, my Lord, and.*
ii. 52 *mine enemies;* so Qq; F *my adversaries.*
ii. 60-2 *I tell . . . elder;* so Qq; F *Well Catesby,
ere a fort-night make me older.*   ii. 81 *life;* so
Qq; F *days.*   ii. 96 *Stage Direction:* Enter a
Pursuivant; so F; Q₁ Enter Hastin. a Pursuant;
Q₂ Enter Hast. a Pursuiuant; Q₃₋₈ (after l. 105)
Enter Hastings a Pursuiuant; see comment in
notes.   ii. 98 *How now, sirrah;* so F; Qq *Well
met Hastings.*   ii. 100 *man;* so F; Qq *fellow.*
ii. 101 *I met thee;* so Qq; F *thou met'st me.*   ii. 108
fellow . . . me; so F; Qq *Hastings, hold spend thou
that.*   ii. 109 *God . . . lordship;* so Qq; F *I thanke
your Honor.*   ii. 113 After this line F has: Priest.
Ile wait upon your Lordship.   ii. 122 *'Tis;* so
Qq; F *Nay.*   iii. 1 *Come . . . prisoners;* so Qq;
omitted from F.   iii. 5 *keep;* so Qq; F *bless.*
iii. 7-8 *You . . . out;* so F; not in Qq.   iii. 14
thee up; so Qq; F *to thee.*   iii. 15 After this line
F has: *When shee exlaim'd on Hastings, then . . .
Buckingham, Then . . . Richard;* so Qq; F interchanges *Richard* and *Hastings.*   iii. 25 *And . . .
heaven;* so Qq; F *Farewell, untill we meet againe in
Heauen.*   iv. 1 *My . . . once;* so Qq; F *Now
Noble Peeres.*   iv. 4 *fitting;* so Qq; F *ready.*
iv. 6 Ely.; so F; Q₁₋₂ Riu.; Q₃₋₈ Bish. *judge;* so
F; Qq *guesse.*   iv. 10 *Who . . . lord;* so Qq;
omitted from F.   iv. 11 *But;* so Qq; omitted
from F.   iv. 13 *Nor . . . his;* so Qq; F *Or I of
his, my Lord.*   iv. 19 *my noble lords;* so Singer;
Q₁₋₂ *my noble Lo:;* Q₃₋₇ *My L.;* F *my Honorable
Lords.*   iv. 22 *Now . . . time;* so Qq; F *In happie
time.*   iv. 24 *hope;* so Qq; F *trust.*   iv. 32 *I
. . . grace;* so Qq; omitted from F.   iv. 32-3
My . . . Holborn; so Qq; F (following l. 31) *My
Lord of Ely, when I was last in Holborne.*   iv. 41
son; so Qq; F *Child. worshipful;* so Qq; F *wor-
shipfully.*   iv. 43 *you . . . follow;* so Qq; F *your
selfe a while, Ile goe with.*   iv. 45 *mine opinion;*
so Qq; F *my judgment.*   iv. 48 *protector;* so Qq;

KING RICHARD III (Con.)

F *the duke of Gloster.* iv. 50 *to-day;* so Qq; F *this morning.* iv. 54 *That can less;* so Q₈; Q₁₋₇ *That can lesser;* F *Can lesser.* iv. 57 *likelihood;* so Qq; F *livelihood.* iv. 60 *I . . . say;* so Qq; omitted from F. iv. 66 *noble;* so Qq; F *princely.* iv. 69 *this ill;* so Qq; F *their evil.* iv. 70 *See;* so Qq; F *Looke.* iv. 77 *Tellest thou me;* Qq *Telst thou me;* F *Talk'st thou to me.* iv. 84 *raze his helm;* Qq *race his helme;* F *rowse our Helmes.* iv. 85 *But . . . scorn;* so Qq; F *and I did scorne it, and disdaine.* iv. 87 *startled;* so Q₁₋₆; F *started.* iv. 91 *'twere triumphing at;* so Qq; F *too triumphing, how.* iv. 92 *How;* so Qq; F *To-day.* iv. 96 Rat.; so F; Qq Cat. *Dispatch, my lord;* so Qq; F *Come, dispatch.* iv. 98 *grace of mortal;* so Qq; F *state of worldly.* iv. 104-7 *Come . . . upon;* not in Qq. v. Scene division due to Pope. v. 37 *tell . . . the;* Qq *tell it you? the;* F *tell it, that.* v. 40 *What . . . so;* so Q; F *Had he done so.* v. 48 *you . . . lords;* so Qq; F *your good Graces.* v. 50-61 F assigns these lines to Buckingham. v. 53 *death;* so Qq; F *end.* v. 56 *we;* so Qq; F *I.* v. 64 *doubt you not;* so Qq; F *do not doubt.* v. 66 *cause;* so Q₁₋₅; F *case.* v. 68 *carping censures of the;* so Qq; F *censures of the carping.* v. 83 *lustful;* so Qq; F *raging.* v. 89 *just;* so Qq; F *true.* v. 94 *you . . . lord;* so Qq; F *my Lord, you know.* v. 95 *Fear;* so Qq; F *Doubt.* v. 103-5 *Go . . . Castle;* so F; not in Qq. v. 108 *of;* so Q₁₋₂; omitted from Q₃, F. v. 109 *At . . . have;* so Qq; F *Haue any time.* vi. 6 *brought;* so Qq; F *sent.* vi. 8 *lived Lord Hastings;* so Qq; F *Hastings liu'd.* vi. 10 *Why who's;* so Qq; F *Who is.* vi. 11 *seeth not;* so Cambridge editors; Qq *sees not;* F *cannot see.* vi. 12 *blind;* so Qq; F *bold.* vi. 14 *bad;* so Qq; F *ill.* vii. 1 *my lord;* so Qq; F *how now.* vii. 3 *and speak;* so Qq; F *say.* vii. 5-6 *his . . . France;* so F; not in Qq. vii. 25 *statuas;* so Cambridge editors; Q₁ illegible misprint; F *Statues.* vii. 26 *Gazed;* so Qq; F *Star'd.* vii. 37 *And . . . few;* so F; not in Qq. vii. 39 *loving;* so Qq; *chearefull.* vii. 43 *No . . . lord;* so Qq; omitted from F. vii. 49 *build;* so Qq; F *make.* vii. 58-9 *Here . . . he;* so Qq; F *Now Catesby, what sayes your Lord to my request.* vii. 59 *My . . . grace;* so Qq; F *He doth entreat your Grace, my Noble Lord.* vii. 65 *thy lord again;* so Qq; F *the gracious Duke.* vii. 66 *citizens;* so Qq; F *Aldermen.* vii. 67 *and matters;* so Qq; F *in matter.* vii. 70 *I'll . . . lord;* so Qq; F *Ile signifie so much vnto him straight.* vii. 72 *lolling;* so Pope; Qq, F *lulling.* *day-bed;* so Qq; F *Loue-bed.* vii. 78 *gracious;* so Qq; F *virtuous.* vii. 79 *himself;* so Qq; F *his Grace.* vii. 81 *forbid;* so Qq; F *defend.* vii. 82 *I . . . will;* so Qq; F *I feare he will: here Catesby comes againe.* vii. 83 *How . . . lord;* so Qq; F *Now Catesby, what sayes his Grace.* vii. 85 *speak with;*

KING RICHARD III (Con.)

so Qq; F *come to.* vii. 87 *My . . . fears;* so Qq; F *He feares, my Lord.* vii. 90 *I . . . him;* so Qq; F *we come to him in perfit loue.* vii. 93 *hard;* so Qq; F *much.* vii. 98-9 *And . . . man;* so F; not in Qq. vii. 105 *rather . . . you;* so Qq; F *doe beseech your Grace to.* vii. 107 *Neglect;* so Qq; F *Deferr'd.* vii. 120 *Your . . . birth;* so F; not in Qq. vii. 127 *Her . . . plants;* so Cambridge editors; F *His . . . plants;* not in Qq; vii. 129 *blind;* so Qq; F *darke.* *dark;* so Qq; F *deepe.* vii. 132 *And . . . land;* so F; not in Qq. vii. 140 *suit;* so Qq; F *cause.* vii. 141 *know not whether;* so Q₁₋₄; F *cannot tell, if.* vii. 144-53 *If . . . you;* so F; not in Qq. vii. 161 *As I had;* so Qq; F *That I would.* vii. 166 *if need were;* so Qq; F *were there need.* vii. 184 *children;* so Qq; F *sons.* vii. 187 *lustful;* so Qq; F *wanton.* vii. 188 *all his thoughts;* so Qq; F *his degree.* vii. 191 *term;* so Qq; F *call.* vii. 202 *Refuse . . . love;* so F; not in Qq. vii. 214 *whether;* so Qq; F *know, where.* vii. 219 *'zounds! I'll;* so Qq; F *we will.* vii. 220 *O . . . Buckingham;* so Qq; omitted from F. vii. 222 *Do . . . it;* so Qq; F *If you denie them, all the Land will rue it.* vii. 239 *kingly;* so Qq; F *Royall.* vii. 240 *Richard;* so Q₁₋₂; Q₃, F *King Richard.* *royal;* so Qq; F *worthie.* vii. 241 May. and Cit.; so Cambridge editors; Qq Mayor; F All. vii. 243 *please, since;* so Malone; Qq *will, since.* vii. 245 *And . . . leave;* so F; not in Qq.

Act IV: i. 2-6 *Led . . . day;* so F; not in Qq. i. 4 *princes;* so Theobald; F *Prince.* i. 11 Stage Direction: Enter Brakenbury; so Capell; Q₁₋₂ Enter Lieutenant; Q₃₋₈ Enter the Lieutenant of the Tower; F Enter the Lieutenant. i. 15 Brak.; Qq, F Lieu. (also in ll. 19, 27). i. 17 *straitly;* so Qq; F *strictly.* i. 18 *why;* so Qq; omitted from F. i. 19 *I . . . mercy;* so Qq; omitted from F. i. 22 *should keep;* so Qq; F *shall barre.* i. 37 *Despiteful . . . news;* so F; not in Qq. i. 51 *To . . . you;* so Qq; F *In your behalfe, to meet you on the way.* i. 70 *dead;* so Qq; F *deare.* i. 79 *Even . . . space;* so Qq; F *Within so small a time.* i. 82 *ever since;* so Qq; F *hitherto.* *kept;* so Qq; F *held.* i. 84 *Have I enjoy'd;* so Qq; F *Did I enjoy.* i. 85 *have . . . dreams;* so Qq; F *with his timorous Dreames was still awak'd.* i. 90 Q. Eliz.; so Cambridge editors; Q₁, F Dors.; Q₂₋₈ Qu. i. 93 *guard;* so Qq; F *tend.* i. 98-104 *Stay . . . farewell;* so Q; not in Qq. ii. 24 *breath . . . pause;* so Q₁₋₆; F *litle breath, some pawse.* ii. 26 *your grace immediately;* so Qq; F *you herein presently.* ii. 27 *bites the;* so Q₁₋₆; F *gnawes his.* ii. 36 *My lord;* so Qq; omitted from F. ii. 37 *mind;* so Qq; F *spirit.* ii. 41 *hither;* so Cambridge editors; Qq *hither presently;* F *hither, Boy.* ii. 45 *breath;* so Qq; F *breath? Well, be it so.* ii. 45 Enter

KING RICHARD III (Con.)

Stanley; so F; Qq Enter Darby. *How . . . you;* so Qq; F *How now, Lord Stanley, what's the newes?* ii. 46-8 *My . . . abides;* so Qq; F *Know, my louing Lord, the Marquesse Dorset As I heare is fled to Richmond, In the parts where he abides.* ii. 50-1 *My . . . abroad;* so Qq; F *very grieuous sicke.* ii. 54 *mean-born;* Qq *meane borne;* F *meane poore.* ii. 58 *wife;* so Qq; F *Queene.* ii. 71 *Ay, my lord;* so Cambridge editors; Qq *I my Lord;* F *Please you.* ii. 83-5 *'Tis . . . lord;* so Qq; F *I will dispatch it straight.* ii. 98 *As I remember;* so Qq; F *I doe remember me.* ii. 101 *perhaps, perhaps;* so Qq; F *perhaps.* ii. 102-19 *My . . . to-day;* so Qq; omitted from F. ii. 120 *Why . . . no;* so Qq; F *May it please you to resolue me in my suit.* ii. 121 *Tut, tut;* so Qq; omitted from F. ii. 123 *Is . . . rewards;* so Qq; F *And is it thus; repayes. true;* so Qq; F *deepe.* ii. 124 *deep;* so Qq; omitted from F. iii. 1 *deed;* so Qq; F *Act.* iii. 2 *arch act;* so Q_{1-6}; F *arch deed.* iii. 7 *kind;* so Q_{1-5}; F *milde.* iii. 9 *Lo;* so Qq; F *O. those tender;* so Q_{1-5}; F *the gentle.* iii. 22 *bring;* so Qq; F *beare.* ii. 23 *hail;* so Qq; F *health.* ii. 27 *my lord;* so Qq; omitted from F. iii. 31 *soon at;* so Q_{1-6}; F *soone, and.* iii. 35 *soon;* so Qq; F *then.* Tir. *I humbly take my leaue.* iii. 40 *Breton;* so Capell; Qq *Brittaine;* F *Britaine.* iii. 43 Enter Catesby; so Qq; F Enter Ratcliffe. iii. 44 Cate.; so Qq; F (and l. 46) Rat. iii. 51 *heard;* so Qq; F *learn'd.* iii. 56 *Come;* so Qq; F *Go.* iv. 4 *adversaries;* so Qq; F *enemies.* iv. 9 *young;* so Qq; F *poore.* iv. 17-9 *So . . . dead.* In Qq these lines follow l. 34. iv. 18 *mute and dumb;* so Qq; F *still and mute.* iv. 20-1 *Plantagenet . . . debt;* so F; not in Qq. iv. 28 *Brief . . . days;* so F; not in Qq. iv. 37 *woes;* so Qq; F *greefes.* iv. 39 *Tell . . . mine;* so Qq; omitted from F. iv. 41 *Harry;* so Cambridge editors; Qq *Richard;* F *Husband.* iv. 52-3 *That . . . souls;* F transposes these lines; not in Qq. iv. 87 *sweet;* so Qq; F *faire.* iv. 88-9 *A dream . . . flag;* so Qq; F *A dreame of what thou wast, a garish Flagge A sign of Dignity, a Breath, a Bubble.* iv. 90 *To . . . shot;* F inserts this line between the two preceding lines. iv. 93 *children;* so Qq; F *two Sonnes.* iv. 94 *to . . . cries;* so Qq; F *and kneeles, and sayes.* iv. 100-1 *For . . . sues;* F transposes these lines. iv. 102 *For . . . me;* in Qq after l. 104. iv. 105 *wheel'd;* so Qq; F *whirl'd.* iv. 120 *fairer;* so Qq; F *sweeter.* iv. 127 *their client;* so Hanmer; Q_{1-3} *your Client;* F *their Clients.* iv. 128 *intestate;* so Qq; F *intestine.* iv. 131 *not at all;* so Q_{1-6}; F *nothing els.* iv. 135 *I . . . drum;* so Qq; F *The Trumpet sounds.* iv. 141 *graven;* so Qq; F *branded.* iv. 143 *two;* so Qq; F *poore.* iv. 147 *kind Hastings;* so Qq; F *the gentle.* After this line F has: Duch. *Where is kinde Hastings?* iv. 159 *O . . . hear;* so F;

KING RICHARD III (Con.)

not in Qq. iv. 163 *anguish, pain and;* so Qq; F *torment and in.* iv. 171 *bloody, treacherous;* so Qq; F *slye, and bloody.* iv. 172 *More . . . hatred;* so F; not in Qq. iv. 177 *sight;* so Qq; F *eye.* iv. 178 *your grace;* so Qq; F *you Madam.* iv. 187 *heavy;* so Qq; F *greeuous.* iv. 211 *of royal blood;* so Qq; F *a Royall Princesse.* iv. 221-34 *You . . . bosom;* so F; not in Qq. iv. 238 *wrong'd;* so Qq; F *harm'd.* iv. 243 *No, to;* so Qq; F *Vnto. honour;* so Qq; F *Fortune.* iv. 264 *Say;* so Qq; F *Well.* iv. 267 *I, even I;* so Qq; F *Euen so. what;* so Qq; F *How. madam;* so Qq; omitted from F. iv. 276-7 *which . . . body;* so F; not in Qq. iv. 278 *dry;* so Qq; F *wipe.* iv. 279 *force;* so Qq; F *moue.* iv. 280 *story;* so Qq; F *Letter. acts;* so Qq; F *deeds.* iv. 284 *Come . . . me;* so Qq; F *You mocke me Madam.* iv. 288-342 *Say . . . years;* so F; not in Qq. iv. 323 *loan;* so Theobald; F *Loue.* iv. 355 *love;* so Qq; F *low.* iv. 359 *in . . . her;* so Qq; F *plainly to her, tell.* iv. 364-5 *Harp . . . break;* so Q_1; l. 365 omitted from Q_{2-8}. F transposes the lines. iv. 366 K. Rich.; so Qq; omitted from F. iv. 369 *holy;* so Qq; F *Lordly.* iv. 376 *Then . . . misusest;* so Qq; F *is selfe-misvs'd.* iv. 377 *God . . . God's;* so Qq; F *Heauen. Heauens.* iv. 380 *Had not been;* so Qq; F *Thou had'st not.* iv. 382 *brow;* so Qq; F *head.* iv. 385 *playfellows;* so Qq; F *Bed-fellows.* iv. 387 *What . . . now;* so F; not in Qq. iv. 391 *parents;* so Qq; F *Fathers.* iv. 394 *wither'd;* so Qq; F *barren.* iv. 396 *time misused;* so Qq; F *times ill-vs'd. o'erpast;* so Qq; F *repast.* iv. 398 *attempt;* so Qq; F *Affayres.* iv. 400 *Heaven . . . hours;* so F; not in Qq. iv. 403 *pure;* so Qq; F *deere.* iv. 407 *this . . . me;* so Qq; F *my selfe, and thee.* iv. 408 *To thee, herself;* so Qq; F *Her selfe, the Land.* iv. 412 *good;* so Qq; F *deare.* iv. 429 *And . . . mind;* so F; not in Qq. iv. 430 *and so;* so F; not in Qq. iv. 432 *How . . . news;* so F; not in Qq. iv. 443 *Fly . . . duke;* so Qq; F *Catesby, flye to the Duke.* Cat. *I will, my Lord, with all conuenient haste.* Rich. *Catesby come hither.* iv. 445 *stand'st;* so Q_{1-3}; F *stay'st. still;* so Qq; F *here.* iv. 446 *sovereign . . . mind;* so Qq; F *Liege, tell me your Highnesse pleasure.* iv. 452 *What . . . shall;* so Qq; F *What, may it please you, shall I.* iv. 456 *My . . . mind is changed;* so Qq; F *My mind is chang'd.* Enter Lord Stanley; so F; Qq Enter Darby. iv. 457 *How now;* so Qq; F *Stanley.* iv. 458 Stan.; so F; Qq Dar. (so throughout the scene). *None . . . lord;* so Cambridge editors; Qq *None good my Lord;* F *None, good my Liege.* iv. 459 *it . . . told;* so Qq; F *well may be reported.* iv. 467 *sir . . . as you guess;* so Q_{1-6}; F *as you guesse* iv. 485 *Richard;* so Qq; F *me.* iv. 492 *I . . . sir;* so Qq; F *But Ile not trust thee.* iv. 496 *hear*

KING RICHARD III (Con.)

you; so Qq; omitted from F.   iv. 497 *faith;* so Qq; F *heart.*   iv. 503 *brother there;* so Qq; F *elder Brother.*   iv. 507 *their . . . increaseth;* so Qq; F *the Rebels, and their power growes strong.*   iv. 508 *the Duke of;* so Qq; F *great.*   iv. 510 *Take . . . thou;* so Q₁₋₅; F *There, take thou that, till thou.* iv. 523 *Breton;* so Capell; Qq, F *Brittaine.*   iv. 529 *away for Brittany;* so Cambridge editors; Qq *away for Brittaine;* F *his course againe for Britaine.* iv. 536 *tidings;* so Q₁₋₅; F *Newes.*   v. Scene iv continued in Qq.   v. 2 *this most bloody;* so Qq; F *the most deadly.*   v. 13 *noble fame;* so Qq F *great name.*   v. 16 *Return . . . him;* so Qq; F *So get thee gone: commend me to thy Lord.*   v. 17 *Tell him;* so Qq; F *Withall say, that.*   v. 19 *These letters;* so Qq; F *My Letter.*

ACT V.   i. *Stage Direction:* Enter . . . led; so Cambridge editors; Qq Enter Buckingham; F Enter Buckingham with Halberds, led.   i. 2 Sher.; so F; Qq Rat. (also in l. 11).   i. 3 *Rivers, Grey;* so Qq; F *Gray & Riuers.*   i. 11 *It . . . lord;* so Qq; F *It is.*   i. 25 *is . . . head;* so Qq; F *falles heauy on my necke.*   i. 28 *sirs, convey me;* so Qq; F *leade me Officers.*   ii. 11 *Lies;* so Qq; F *Is.*   ii. 17 Oxf.; so F; Qq I Lo. *swords;* so Qq; F *men.*   ii. 18 *that bloody;* so Qq; F *this guilty.*   ii. 19 Herb.; F Her.; Qq 2 Lo. *fly;* so Qq; F *turne.*   ii. 20 Blunt.; so F; Qq 3 Lo. ii. 21 *greatest;* so Qq; F *deerest. shrink;* so Qq; F *flye.*   iii. 3 Sur.; so F; Qq Cat.   iii. 5 K. Rich; so F; not in Qq.   iii. 6 *gracious;* so Qq; F *louing.*   iii. 7 *there;* so Q₁₋₆; omitted from F iii. 9 *foe;* so Qq; F *Traitors.*   iii. 10 *utmost power;* so Q; Qq *greatest number.*   iii. 11 *battalion;* so Qq; F *Battalia.*   iii. 13 *party;* so Qq; F *Faction.* iii. 14 *my . . . Valiant;* so Qq; F *the Tent: Come Noble.*   iii. 15 *field;* so Qq; F *ground.*   iii. 21 *signal;* so Qq; F *token.*   iii. 23-6 *Give . . . strength;* so Q; Qq have these lines after l. 44. iii. 26 *strength;* so Qq; F *Power.*   iii. 27-8 *My . . . me;* so F; not in Qq.   iii. 33 *Blunt . . . go'st;* so Qq; F *(Captaine) do for me.*   iii. 40 *Good . . . him;* so Qq; F *Sweet Blunt, make some good meanes to speak with him.*   iii. 41 *scroll;* so Qq; F *Note.*   iii. 43 *And . . . to-night;* so Q; not in Qq.   iii. 44 *Good . . . gentlemen;* so F; Qq *Farewell good Blunt.*   iii. 46 *air;* so Qq; F *Dew.*   iii. 47-8 *It's supper-time . . . o'clock;* so F; Qq *It is sixe of the clocke, full supper time* (Q₃₋₈ omit *the*).   iii. 58 *Catesby;* so Qq; F *Rat-cliffe.*   iii. 59 Cate.; so Qq; F Rat.   iii. 104 *thoughts;* so Qq; F *noise.*   iii. 125 *deadly;* so Q₁; omitted from Q₂₋₈, F.   iii. 146-50 *Blood . . . sake;* so Q₃₋₈, F; Q₁₋₂ transpose with ll. 151-8. iii. 208 *'Zounds;* so Qq; omitted from F.   iii. 212-4 *O Ratcliff . . . my lord;* so Qq; omitted from F.   iii. 262 *quit;* so Pope; Qq, F *quits.* iii. 293 *out all;* so Q₁; omitted from Q₂₋₈, F.

KING RICHARD III (Con.)

iii. 304 K. Rich. [Reads]; so Capell; omitted from Qq, F.   iii. 317 *Bretons;* so Capell; Qq, F *Brit-taines.*   iii. 319 *ventures;* so Capell; Qq, F *adven-tures.*   iii. 324 *Bretagne;* so Hanmer; Qq *Brit-taine;* F *Britaine.*   iii. 325 *milk-sop;* so F; Q₁₋₅ *milkesopt.*   iii. 333 *Bretons;* Qq, F *Britaines.* v. 11 *if . . . you;* so Q₂₋₈; Q₁ *it is please you;* F (*if you please*).   v. 13 Der.; so F; not in Qq. Ferrers; so Capell; Qq, F *Ferris.*   v. 15 *becomes;* so Rowe; Qq, F *become.*

ROMEO AND JULIET

ACT I: i. 134 *That . . . alone;* so Q₁; Q₂ and F *Which then most sought, wher most might not be found: Being too many by my weary selfe.*   i. 159 *sun;* Theobald's emendation for *same* as in Qq and F.   i. 237 *put;* Q₂ and F *puts;* the verb in "s" with a plural subject occurs frequently in Shakespeare.   ii. 29 *female;* so Q₁; Q₂ and F *fennel;* see comment in notes.   ii. 88 *lovest;* Q₂ and F *loves.*   iii. 52 *its;* Qq and F *it,* which is probably correct, since the form "its" for the possessive is later.

ACT II: i. 13 *Adam;* so Upton; Qq and F *Abraham;* see comment in notes.   v. 16 *many;* Johnson's emendation *to marry* is often followed. v. 26 *jaunt;* Q₂ reads *jaunce,* followed by Cambridge editors.

ACT III: i. 124 *more;* so Q₁; Q₂ and F *mo,* the old form of the word.

ACT IV: iii. 29. After this line Q₁ has *I will not entertain so bad a thought.*   iii. 58 *Romeo . . . thee.* So Q₁; other Qq and F have *Romeo, Romeo, Romeo, heeres drinke; I drinke to thee.* v. 101 *Stage Direction;* Enter *Peter;* Q₂ Enter *Will Kemp;* see comment in notes.

ACT V: iii. 107. After this line Q₂ and F have the following reading (text of Q₂):
Depart againe, come lye thou in my arme,
Heer's to thy health, where ere thou tumblest in.
O true Apothecarie!
Thy drugs are quicke. Thus with a kisse I die.

THE MERCHANT OF VENICE

ACT I: ii. 83 *Scottish;* so Q; F *other;* see comment in notes.

ACT II: ii. 29 *incarnal;* Q₁ *incarnall;* F *incarnation.*   ii. 39 *confusions;* Q *conclusions.* v. 43 *Jewess';* so Pope; Q and F *Jewes.*

ACT III: ii. 106 *paleness;* so Q₁; Warburton, *plainness,* followed by many editors.   ii. 113 *rein;* so Q₃; Q₁ *range;* Q₂ and F *rain.*   v. 82 *mean it, then;* so Q₁; Q₂ *meane it, then meane it;* F *meane it, it is.*

ACT V: i. 148 *posy;* Q₁ and F *poesie.*

MUCH ADO ABOUT NOTHING

Act I: i. 59 *stuffing, — well;* Theobald's punctuation; QF no punctuation. i. 96 *you are;* so F; Q *are you.* i. 138 *yours;* so Q; F *your.* i. 147 *That is;* so Q; F *This is.* i. 226 *speak;* so F; Q *spoke.* i. 254 *ballad-maker's;* so Q; F *Ballet.* ii. 11 *thus much;* so Q; F *thus.* iii. 9 *at least;* so Q; F *yet.* iii. 25 *true;* so Q; omitted from F. iii. 56 *on;* so F; Q *one.*

Act II: i. 43 *bear-ward;* Collier's emendation of QF *Berrord.* i. 59 *curtsy;* Q *cursis;* F *curt-sie;* Capell *court'sy;* Stevens *courtesy.* *Father;* not in QF. i. 88 *Stage Direction: Balthasar, Don John;* QF *Balthasar, or dumbe John.* i. 100. *Jove;* so Q; F *Loue.* i. 104, 107, 109 *Balth.;* so Theobald; QF assign these speeches to Bene. i. 215 *though;* Johnson conjectured *the,* followed by many editors. i. 223 *I told;* F omits *I.* i. 224 *good will;* Q *goodwil;* F *will.* i. 227 *up;* omitted from F. i. 251 *that I;* so Q; F *and that I.* i. 284 *my Lady Tongue;* F *this Lady tongue.* i. 289 *his;* so Q; F *a.* i. 305 *that;* so Q; F *a.* i. 316 *cue;* QF *Qu.* i. 328 *her;* so Q; F *my.* i. 361 *unhappiness;* Theobald *an happiness;* Warburton and Johnson *an unhappiness.* ii. 376 *my;* omitted from F. ii. 37 *in love;* so Q; F *in a love.* ii. 45 *Claudio;* Theobald *Borachio;* see comment in notes. ii. 50 *truth;* so Q; F *truths.* ii. 56 *you;* so Q; F *thou.* iii. 38 *Stage Direction:* Enter *Don Pedro,* etc.; F has Enter Prince, Leonato, Claudio, and Jacke Wilson; Q has Musicke for and Jacke Wilson; see comment in notes. iii. 44 *kid-fox;* Warburton, *hid-fox;* Onions suggests *cub-fox.* iii. 72 *moe;* so Q; F *more.* iii. 74 *was;* so Q; F *were.* iii. 141 *us of;* so F; Q *of us.* iii. 162 *make but;* so Q; F *but make.* iii. 195 *And . . . valiant;* assigned by Q to Claudio; by F to Leonato. iii. 197 *say;* so Q; *see.* iii. 199 *most;* omitted from F. iii. 207 *seek;* so Q; F *see.* iii. 217 *unworthy so;* so Q; F *unworthy to have so.* iii. 223 *gentlewomen;* so Q; F *gentlewoman.* iii. 232 *their;* so Q; F *the.*

Act III: i. 12 *purpose;* so F; Q *propose.* i. 32 *lose;* so F₂; QF *loose.* i. 79 *better death than;* so Theobald; Q *better death, then;* F *better death, to;* F₂₋₄ *bitter death, to;* Rowe *bitter death to.* ii. 28 *can;* so Pope; QF *cannot.* ii. 34-37 *or . . . doublet;* omitted from F. ii. 39 *appear;* so Q; F *to appeare.* ii. 54-55 *The greatest . . . melancholy;* Q assigns to Benedick. ii. 61 *now . . . governed;* Boas *new crept . . . now governed,* followed by New Cambridge editors. ii. 64 *conclude, conclude;* so Q; F *conclude.* ii. 117-118 *her then, to-morrow;* so Hanmer; QF *her, then to morrow.* ii. 127 *her to-morrow, in;* so Rowe; QF *her to morrow in;* Capell *her; tomorrow, in.* ii. 133 *midnight;* so Q; F *night.* iii. 37 *to talk;* so Q; F *talk.* iii. 45 *those;* so Q; F *them.* iii. 85

MUCH ADO ABOUT NOTHING (Con.)

statues; so F; Q *statutes.* iii. 134 *year;* Q *yeere;* F *yeares.* iii. 148 *I see;* so Q; F *see.* iii. 162 *they;* so Q; F *thy.* iii. 187-189 Speech-distribution follows Theobald. QF assign *Masters . . . us* to Conrade. iv. 33 *'saving . . . husband';* no quotations marks in QF. iv. 49 *you'll see;* Q *youl see;* F *you'll looke.* v. 11 *off;* so Capell; QF *of.* v. 27 *pound;* so Q; F *times.* v. 55 *it may;* so Q; F *may.* v. 64 *examination;* so Q; F *examine.* *these;* so Q; F *those.*

Act IV: i. 77 *do so;* so Q; F *doe.* i. 88 *are you;* so Q; F *you are.* i. 97 *spoke;* so Q; F *spoken.* i. 128 *rearward;* so F₂₋₄; Q *wereward;* F *reward.* i. 135 *smirched;* so Q; F *smeered.* i. 145 *foul-tainted;* so Dyce; QF *foule tainted.* i. 154 *two;* so Q; omitted from F. i. 157-159 *Hear . . . fortune:* text is corrupt; printed as prose in QF, arranged as verse by Pope. New Cambridge editors would omit *for . . . fortune.* i. 204 *princes;* QF *princesse.* i. 230 *moving-delicate;* so Capell; QF *mouing delicate.* i. 277 *swear, and;* Q *sweare and;* F *sweare by it and.* i. 293 *deny it;* so Q; F *deny.* i. 335 *so I leave;* F omits *I.* ii. Enter *Dogberry,* etc.; so Capell; QF Enter the Constables, Borachio, and the Towne clearke (F Clerke) in gownes; see comment in notes. ii. 19-22 *Yea, sir . . . villains;* omitted from F. ii. 38 *eftest;* Theobald *deftest;* Rowe *easiest.* ii. 53 *by mass;* so Q; F *by th' masse.* ii. 70-71 *Let . . . coxcomb;* Q assigns to Couley; F to Sex.; Theobald to Conrade; Warburton gave *Let . . . hands* to the Sexton (following F) and gave *Of coxcomb* to Conrade; he also read *in bands* for *in the hands.* Capell restored Verges from Q, since Couley and Verges are the same, and emended *Of Coxcomb* to *Off, coxcomb;* Malone gave us the present text; New Cambridge editors *Let them be — in the hands.* ii. 86 *any is in;* so Q; F *any in.*

Act V: i. 6 *comforter;* so Q; F *comfort.* i. 7 *do;* so Q; F *doth.* i. 16 *Bid . . . hem;* so Capell; QF *And sorrow, wagge, crie him.* Steevens conjectured *And sorry wag, cry 'hem,'* which is probably the best offered. i. 96 *anticly;* QF *antiquely;* i. 97 *off;* so Theobald; QF *of.* i. 115 *like;* QF *likt.* i. 162 *said;* so Q; F *saies.* i. 273 *thou;* so Q; F *thou thou.* i. 325 *reverend;* so F; Q *reverent.* ii. 36 *it in rhyme;* Q *it in rime;* F *it rime.* ii. 37, 38 *rhyme, rhyme;* so Q; F *time time.* ii. 41 *nor;* so Q; F *for.* ii. 81 *monument;* so Q; F *monuments.* ii. 82 *bell rings;* so Q; F *Bels ring.* iii. 3 *Claud.;* so Capell; QF *Epitaph.* iii. 10 *dumb;* F *dombe;* Q *dead.* iii. 21 *Heavily, heavily;* so Q; F *heauenly, heauenly.* iii. 23 *rite;* so Pope; QF *right.* iii. 32 *speed's;* Thirlby's conjecture for QF *speeds.* iv. 7, 17 *Ant.* These speeches are assigned in QF to *Old.* iv. 7 *sort;* so Q; F *sorts.* iv. 33 *Here . . . Claudio;* omitted

MUCH ADO ABOUT NOTHING (Con.)

from F.   iv. 50 *And;* so Q; F *A.*   iv. 54 Ant.; so Theobald; QF Leonato.   iv. 63 *defiled;* so Q; omitted from F.   iv. 80 *that;* so Q; omitted from F.   iv. 82 *such;* so Q; omitted from F.   iv. 98 Bene.; so Theobald; QF Leon.   iv. 126 *reverend;* so Q; F *reverent.*

AS YOU LIKE IT

ACT I: i. 114 *she;* so F₃; F *he.*   ii. 3 *I;* so Rowe; not in F.   ii. 89 Cel. F assigns this speech to Rosalind. New Cambridge editor follows F. ii. 90 *him: enough!* punctuation by Hanmer; F *him enough;.*   ii. 111 *decree;* so Pope; F *decrees.* ii. 176 *princesses call;* so Theobald; F *princess calls.*   ii. 220 *An;* so Theobald; not in F.   ii. 277 *misconstrues;* F *misconsters.*   ii. 284 *lesser;* so Spedding; F *taller.*   iii. 45 *ten;* so F; anonymous conjecture, *two,* approved by Cambridge editors. iii. 59 *likelihood;* so F₂₋₄; F *likelihoods.*   iii. 99 *thou;* Capell conjectured *she.   am;* Hanmer *are.* iii. 122 *martial;* F *marshall.*

ACT II: i. 19 *I would . . . it;* assigned to Amiens in F; text follows Upton and other editors. i. 31 *antique;* F *anticke.*   i. 59 *the;* so F₂₋₄; not in F.   iii. 10 *some;* so F₂₋₄; F *seeme.*   iii. 16 Orl.; not in F.   iii. 57 *service;* Keightley *fashion;* Neil *virtue;* Lettsom *temper.*   iii. 58 *meed;* so F; F₄ *need.*   iii. 73 *seventeen;* so Rowe; F *seavente.*   iv. 1 *weary;* so Theobald; F *merry.* iv. 38 *Wearying;* F *Wearing.*   iv. 44 *thy wound;* so Rowe; F *they would.*   iv. 48 *a-night;* F *a night.*   v. 1 Ami.; so Capell; not in F.   v. 3 *turn;* Rowe *tune.*   v. 40 *All together here;* F *Song. Altogether.*   v. 51 Jaq.; so F₂; F Ami. vii. 34, 36 *A worthy fool, O worthy fool;* so F; an anonymous conjecture would exchange *A* and *O.* vii. 55 *Not to;* added by Theobald.   vii. 56 *wise man's;* F *wise-man's.*   vii. 73 *weary very means;* Singer *wearer's very means;* Lloyd *tributary streams;* New Cambridge *weary very mints.*   vii. 143 *At first;* Capell *As first;* anonymous conjecture, *Act first,* or *First.*   vii. 145 *And;* so Rowe; not in F. vii. 151 *sudden;* F places comma after this word. vii. 174 Ami.; so Johnson; not in F.   vii. 182 *Then;* so Rowe; F *Thee.*   vii. 198 *master;* F *masters.*

ACT III: ii. 22 *Hast;* so Pope; F *Has't.* ii. 111 *Winter;* so F₃; F *Wintred.*   ii. 133 *a;* so Rowe; not in F.   ii. 153 *her;* so Rowe; F *his.* ii. 163 *pulpiter;* so Spedding; F *Iupiter;* Warburton *Iuniper.*   ii. 227 *maid;* anonymous conjecture in Cambridge edition *mind.*   ii. 250 *such;* so F₂; F *the.*   ii. 257 *thy;* so Rowe; F *the.* ii. 260 *heart;* so Rowe; F *hart.*   ii. 273 *be wi';* so Capell; F *buy.*   ii. 366 *lectures;* F *lectors*

AS YOU LIKE IT (Con.)

ii. 381 *deifying;* so F ; F *defying.*   ii. 390 *are;* F *art.*   ii. 439 *living;* Johnson *loving.*   iii. 57 *Horns . . . alone?;* so Theobald; F places comma after *Horns,* no mark after *so,* colon after *alone.* iii. 98-107 *Come . . . thee;* F assigns speech to Oliver.   v. 11 *'Tis pretty, sure;* no comma in F.   v. 22 *but;* so F₂; not in F.   v. 62 *foul;* Warburton conjectured *found* for the third use of the word in this line.   v. 88 *love;* Rowe placed a comma after this word.   v. 105 *erewhile;* F *yerewhile.*   v. 127 *I;* so F₂; not in F.

ACT IV: i. 1 *be;* not in F.   i. 31 *be wi';* F *buy.*   i. 46 *thousandth;* so Rowe; F *thousand.* i. 105 *chroniclers;* F *Chronoclers;* Hanmer *coroners.* i. 138 Ros.; anonymous conjecture gives this speech to Celia; approved by Cambridge editors. ii. 2 A Lord; F Lord.   ii. 8 For.; so Rowe; F Lord.; New Cambridge editors Amiens.   iii. 7 *bid;* F *did bid.*   iii. 11 *tenour;* so Theobald; F *tenure.* iii. 88 *sister;* Lettsom *forester,* followed by New Cambridge editors.   iii. 105 *oak;* so Pope; F *old oake.*   iii. 143 *In;* F *I.*   iii. 156 *his;* F *this.*

ACT V: ii. 8 *nor her;* so Rowe; F *nor.*   ii. 29 *swoon;* so Rowe; F *sound.*   ii. 35 *overcame;* so F ; F *overcome.*   ii. 114 *Who . . . to;* so Rowe; F *Why . . . too.*   iii. 20 *In the;* so F; MS. *In. ring;* so Edinburgh MS.; F *rang.*   iii. 25 *folks would;* so F; MS. *fools did.*   iii. 29 *a life;* so F; MS. *life.*   iv. 21 *your;* so Rowe; F *you your.* iv. 84 *lied;* so Hanmer; F *lie.*   iv. 85 *so to the;* so F; F *so to.*   iv. 119 *hither;* F *hether.*   iv. 120 *her;* so F₃₋₄; F₁₋₂ *his.*   iv. 156 Stage Direction: *Jaques de Boys;* F Enter Second Brother.

TWELFTH NIGHT

ACT I: i. 11 *sea;* F has full stop after this word; the comma is Rowe's emendation.   ii. 40-41 *company And sight;* F *sight And company;* transposed by Hanmer.   iii. 144 *flame-coloured;* so Rowe; F *dam'd colour'd;* Collier *dun-coloured.* v. (after) 176 Enter *Viola;* F Enter *Violente.*

ACT II: ii. 32 *our;* so F₂ F *O.*   iv. 35 *worn;* F *worne;* Hanmer *won* (for *wonne*), probably correct.   v. 124 *staniel;* so Hanmer; F *stallion.*

ACT III: i. 75 *But . . . taint;* so Rann; F *wisemens folly falne, quite taint.*   ii. 71 *nine;* so Theobald; F *mine.*   iv. 222 *out;* so Theobald; F *on't,* followed by many editors.   iv. 389 *babbling,;* no comma in F.

ACT V: i. 117 *hath;* so Capell; F *haue.* i. 206-207 *passy measures panyn;* so F; Malone and others read *passy measures pavin;* see comment in notes.   i. 370 *against;* so F; Tyrwhitt and others *in.*

THE TRAGEDY OF KING RICHARD II

ACT I: i. 70 *the king;* so Q₁; Q₂ and F *a king.* i. 77 *spoke, or thou canst worse devise;* so Q₁; F *spoken, or thou canst devise.* i. 118 *by my;* so F; Q₁ *by.* i. 157 *month;* so Q₁; F *time.* i. 162-163 *When . . . bids;* Pope's reading of Q₁ *When, Harry? when obedience bids, Obedience bids.* i. 187 *God . . . deep;* so Q₁; F *Heaven . . . foule.* Throughout the F reads *Heaven* for *God* as in Q₁. ii. 47 *sit;* so F; Q₁ *set.* iii. 20 *and my;* so Q₁; F *and his.* iii. 76 *furbish;* so Q₁; F *furnish.* iii. 128 *civil;* some copies of Q₁ read *cruell.* iii. 129-133 *And for . . . sleep;* omitted from F. iii. 227 *sullen;* so Q₁; F *sudden.* iii. 239-242 *O, had . . . destroy'd;* omitted from F. iii. 268-293 *Nay, rather . . . light;* omitted from F. iv. 20 *cousin, cousin;* so F; Q₁ *coosens coosin.* iv. 23 *Bagot . . . Green;* so Q₅; not in Q₁₋₄. iv. 53 *Bushy, what news;* so F; Q₁ *with news,* as part of the stage direction. iv. 54 *grievous;* so Q₁; F *very.*

ACT II: i. 18 *of whose . . . fond;* Collier's conjecture for Q₁ *of whose . . . found.* i. 102 *incaged;* so F; Q₁ *inraged.* i. 113 *thou now, not;* Theobald's emendation; Q₁ *thou now not, not.* i. 254 *noble;* so Q ; omitted from F. i. 280 See comment in notes. ii. 138 *The . . . will;* Pope's rearrangement of Qq and F *Will the hateful commons.* iii. 80 *self-born;* so F₃₋₄; Qq and F₁₋₂ *self-borne.*

ACT III: ii. 29-32 *The means . . . redress;* omitted from F. ii. 30 *if;* Pope's emendation not in Qq. ii. 49 *Whilst . . . antipodes;* omitted from F. ii. 84 *coward;* so Q₁; F *sluggard.* ii. 102 *and;* so Q₁; F *Losse.* ii. 134 *offence;* so F; omitted from Q₁; line 133 ends with *hell,* the line following beginning *make war.* ii. 178 *sit . . . woes;* so Q₁; F *wail their present woes.* ii. 182 *And . . . yourself;* omitted from F. ii. 203 *party;* so Q₁; F *faction.* iii. 13 *with you;* so F; not in Q₁. iii. 62-67 *See . . . occident;* assigned by Dyce to Percy, by Warburton and Hanmer to York. iii. 119 *a prince, is just;* so F; Q₁ *princess just.* iii. 171 *laugh;* so Q₁; F *mock.* iv. 11 *joy;* so Rowe; Qq and F *grief.* iv. 22 *sing;* so Qq and F; Pope's emendation *weep.* iv. 57 *We;* Capell's emendation, not in Qq and F.

ACT IV: i. 52 *task;* so Q₁; other Qq *take;* ll. 52-59 are omitted from F. i. 154-318. The deposition scene is omitted from Q₁₋₂. That it belonged to the play originally is clear from line 318. i. 210 *duty's rites;* so Q₃₋₄; F *dutious oaths.* i. 215 *that swear;* so Q₃; F *are made.* i. 220 *Harry;* so Q₃; F *Henry.* i. 251 *and sovereignty;* so Q₃; F *a sovereignty.*

ACT V: i. 25 *stricken;* so F; Q₁ *thrown.* i. 62 *And;* Rowe's emendation; not in Qq and F. i. 84 *North.;* so F; Q₁ gives this speech to the king. ii. 52 *hold . . . triumphs;* so F; Q₁ *Do these jousts and triumphs hold?* iii. 99 *I'll . . . grace;* omitted from F. iii. 106 *shall;* so F; Q. *still.* iii. 135-136 *With . . . him;* Pope's arrangement of F and Qq *I pardon him with all my heart,* where it is written as a single line. v. 31 *person* so Q₁; F and Q₂ *prison.* v. 46 *check;* so Q ; F *hear.* vi. 8 *Oxford;* F *Spencer.* vi. 43 *thorough shades;* so Cambridge editors; Q *through shades:* Q₂₋₅ and F *through the shades.*

THE FIRST PART OF KING HENRY THE FOURTH

ACT I: i. 76-77 *In faith, It is;* QF include these words in preceding speech. ii. 182 *Bardolph, Peto;* so Theobald; QF *Haruey, Rossill.*

ACT II: ii. 54 *Bardolph;* so QF; W. J. Craig *Bard.* as speech assignment. iv. 37 *precedent;* F *president;* Q *present.* iv. 434 *tristful;* so Rowe; QF *trustful.*

ACT III: iii. 66 *tithe;* F *tight.*

ACT IV: ii. 34 *faced;* so F; Q *fazed;* Cambridge *feaz'd.*

ACT V: i. 2 *busky;* so F; Q *bulky.* ii. 3 *undone;* so F; Q *under one.*

THE SECOND PART OF KING HENRY THE FOURTH

INDUCTION: 35 *hold;* so Theobald; F *hole.* ACT I: i. 116 *metal;* F *mettle;* Q *mettal.* iii. 36-55 *Yes . . . or else;* not in Q.

ACT II: ii. 118 ff. Poins.; speech assignment due to Hanmer; F assigns reading of letter to Prince. ii. 125 *borrower's;* so Theobald; F *borrowed.*

ACT IV: i. 50 *graves;* Hanmer *glaives;* Steevens *greaves;* Vaughan *gloves.* v. 75 *culling;* Q *tolling.* v. 205 *my;* QF *thy.*

THE LIFE OF KING HENRY THE FIFTH

ACT I: ii. 243 *are;* so Q; F *is.* ACT II: iii. 3 *yearn;* F *erne.* iii. 18 *a' babbled of green fields;* so Theobald; F *and a Table of greene fields.* iv. 80 *'long;* F *longs.* ACT III: i. 34 *'God . . . George';* Nielson punctuates: *'God for Harry! England and Saint George!'* ACT IV: i. 152 *whom;* F *who.* ii. 49 *gimmal;* so Johnson; F *Iymold;* Arden (Methuen) *gimmal'd;* see comment in notes. vi. 34 *mistful;* so Theobald; F *mixtfull.* vii. 76 *look;* F *booke.*

JULIUS CÆSAR

ACT I: i. 26 *with awl;* F *withal,* not punctuated. ii. 155 *walls;* so Rowe; F *walks;* see comment in notes. iii. 65 *fool;* so Grant White; F *Fooles;* see comment in notes.

ACT IV: i. 37 *On . . . imitations;* so Staunton; F *On Objects, Arts, and Imitations;* see comment in notes. iii. 28 *bay;* so Theobald; F *baite.*

ACT V: iv. 7-8 *And I . . . Brutus;* speech unassigned in F.

HAMLET

ACT I: i. 13 *rivals;* so Q₂; Q₁ *partners.* i. 14 *ho! Who's there;* so Q₂; F *who's.* i. 21 Mar.; so Q₁F; Q₂ Hora. i. 39 *beating;* so Q₂F; Q₁ *towling.* i. 45 *Question;* so Q₁F; Q₂ *Speake to.* i. 61 *he;* omitted from F. i. 63 *sledded Polacks;* Qq *sleaded pollax;* F *sledded Pollax.* i. 65 *jump;* so Qq; F *just.* i. 66 *hath . . . by;* so Q₂F; Q₁ *he passed through.* i. 93 *covenant;* so F; Q₂ *comart.* i. 98 *lawless;* so Q₂; F *landless.* i. 103 *compulsatory;* so Q₂; F *compulsative.* i. 108-125 *I think . . . countrymen;* omitted from F. i. 132 Cock crows; Q₂ places this direction at 138; omitted from F; at 128-129 Q₂ has It spreads his armes. i. 140 *at;* omitted from Q₂. i. 150 *morn;* so Q₂; Q₁ *morning;* F *day.* i. 161 *dare stir;* so Q₂; Q₁ *dare walk;* F *can walk.* i. 166 *look, the morn;* so Q₂F; Q₁ *see the Sunne.* i. 167 *eastward hill;* so Q₂; F *Easterne Hill;* Q₁ *mountaine top.* ii. *Stage Direction:* Enter the King, etc.; so Malone; Q₂ Enter Claudius, King of Denmarke, Gertrad the Queene, Counsaile: as Polonius, and his Sonne Laertes, Hamlet, Cum Alys. Chambers suggests that *Counsaile: as Polonius* may be a printer's endeavor to make sense of Corambis (name of Polonius in Q₁) Polonius, the old name being left in the manuscript with the new. ii. 11 *an . . . a;* so Q₂; F *one . . . one.* ii. 24 *bonds;* so F; Q₂ and many editors *bands.* ii. 35 *bearers;* so Qq; F *bearing.* ii. 38 *delated;* so Q₂; F *dilated;* Q₁ *related.* ii. 49 *is . . . to;* so Q₂F; Warburton and other editors *to . . . is.* ii. 53 *To . . . coronation;* so Q₂F; Q₁ *Now that the funerall rites are all performed.* ii. 58-60 *wrung . . . consent;* omitted from F. ii. 82 *moods, shapes;* so Q₂; F *Moods, shewes.* ii. 90 *lost, lost;* so Q₂F; Q₁ *dead, lost.* i. 96 *a;* so F; Q₂ *or.* ii. 127 *heavens;* so F; Q₂ *heaven.* ii. 129 *solid;* so F; Qq *sallied.* ii. 132 *O God! God!;* so Q₂; F *O God! O God!* ii. 135 *ah fie;* so Q₂; F *Oh fie, fie.* ii. 149 *even she;* so F; not in Q₂. ii. 150 *O God!;* so Q₂; F *O Heaven.* ii. 155 *in;* so Q₂; F *of.* ii. 165 *lord — ;* so Rowe; Q₂F *lord.;* Cambridge editor *lord?* ii. 170 *hear;* so Q₂; F *have.* ii. 175 *to drink deep;* so Q₁F; Q₂ *for to drinke.* ii. 178 *see;* so Q₁F; omitted from Q₂. ii. 183 *Or ever I had;*

HAMLET (Con.)

so Q₂; F *Ere I had ever;* Q₁ *Ere ever I had.* ii. 184 *My father! —* Q₂F have comma; Q₁ *O my father, my father,;* Rowe supplied dash; Cambridge editor exclamation. ii. 198 *vast;* so Q₁; Q₂F *wast;* F₂₋₄ and many editors *waste;* Malone, Steevens, Variorum *waist.* ii. 200 *Armed at point;* so Q₂; F *Arm'd at all points.* ii. 213 *watch'd;* so F; Q₂ *watch.* ii. 222 *writ down;* Q₂F; Q₁ *right done.* ii. 224 *Indeed, indeed;* so Q₁F; Q₂ *Indeede.* ii. 231 *What, look'd he;* so Q₂F; Q₁ *How look't he,.* ii. 237 *Very like, very like;* so Q₁F; Q₂ *Very like.* ii. 240 *grizzled, — no?;* so Dyce; Q₂ *grissl'd, no.;* F *grisly? no.* ii. 243 *walk;* Q₂; F *wake.* *warrant;* so Qq; F *warrant you.* ii. 255 *in arms?;* so F; Q₂ *(in armes).* iii. 9 *perfume and;* so Q₂; omitted from F. iii. 10 *so?;* so Rowe; Q₂F and some editors *so.;* see comment in notes. iii. 12 *bulk;* so F; Q₂ *bulkes.* *this;* so Q₂; F *his.* iii. 21 *safety;* so Q₂; F and many editors *sanctity;* Theobald and Hanmer *sanity.* iii. 26 *particular act and place;* so Q₂; F *peculiar Sect and force.* iii. 59 *See;* so F; Q₂ and many editors *Look.* iii. 65 *new-hatch'd;* so Q₂; F *unhatch't.* *comrade;* so F; Qq *courage.* iii. 74 *Are of . . . that;* so Q₁; Q₂ *Or . . . generous, . . . ;* F *. . . cheff . . . ;* White omits *of a* and *chief;* Staunton reads *Of a most* and suggests *sheaf;* Malone reads *chef* (heraldic), part of the escutcheon; Steevens conjectured *Select and generous, are most choice in that;* Dowden suggests *Or of a most select, are generous chief* (chiefly) *in that.* iii. 106 *these;* so Q₂; F *his.* iii. 109 *Running;* so Collier and others; Q₂ *Wrong;* F *Roaming.* iii. 114 *almost;* so Q₂; omitted from F. iii. 117 *Lends;* so Qq; F *Gives.* iii. 120 *From this time;* so Q₂; F *For this time Daughter.* iii. 128 *that dye;* so Q₂; F *the eye.* iii. 130 *bawds;* so Theobald and others; Q₂F and many editors *bonds.* iv. 1 *it . . . cold;* so Q₂; F *is it very cold?;* see comment in notes. iv. 17-38 *This . . . scandal;* omitted from F; see comment in notes. iv. 36-38 *the dram . . . scandal;* so Q₂; famous crux; numerous emendations. iv. 42 *intents;* so Q₂; F *events.* iv. 49 *inurn'd;* so F; Qq *interr'd.* iv. 53 *Revisit'st;* so F₄; Q₂ *Revisites;* F *Revisits.* iv. 61 *waves;* so Qq; F *wafts.* iv. 75-78 *The very . . . beneath;* so Q₂; omitted from F. iv. 80 *hands;* so Q₂; F *hand.* v. 1 *Where;* so F; Qq *Whither.* v. 11 *confined to fast;* Theobald conjectured *confined fast;* Warburton *too fast in;* Heath *to lasting;* Steevens *to waste in.* v. 18 *knotted;* so Qq; F *knotty.* v. 20 *fretful;* so Q₁F; Q₂ *fearefull.* v. 22 *List, list;* so Q₂; F *list Hamlet.* v. 29 *Haste me;* so Q ; F *Hast, hast me.* v. 33 *roots;* so Qq; F and many editors *rots.* v. 43 *wit;* so Pope; Q₂F *wits.* v. 45 *to his;* so Q₂; F *to to this.* v. 56 *sate;* so F; Q₂ *sort.* v. 67 *alleys;* so Hanmer; QqF *allies.* v. 91 *Adieu, adieu! Hamlet;* so F; Q₂ and many editors *Adieu, adieu,*

HAMLET (Con.)

adieu! v. 93 *Hold, hold;* so Q₂; F *hold.* v. 95 *stiffly;* so F; Q₂ *swiftly. thee!;* Q₂ *thee.;* F *thee?* see also l. 97. v. 104 *yes;* so Q₂; F *yes, yes.* v. 114 *So be it;* assigned to Marcellus in F. v. 115 *Hillo . . . lord;* assigned to Marcellus in Q₁F. v. 122 *my lord;* so Q₁F; not in Q₂. v. 136 *Horatio;* so Qq; F *my Lord.* v. 158-160 *And lay . . . sword;* so F except for comma after *sword* and colon after *heard;* Q₂ has comma after *sword* and transposes lines 159 and 160. v. 161 *Swear;* so Q₁F; Q₂ *Swear by his sword.* v. 162 *earth;* so Qq; F *ground.* v. 167 *your;* so Qq; F *our.* v. 174 *head-shake;* so Qq; F *thus, head shake.* v. 176 *Well, well;* so Q₂; F *well.* v. 177 *they;* so Qq; F *there.* v. 178 *to note;* Theobald and some editors read *denote.*

Act II: *Stage Direction:* Enter *Polonius* and *Reynaldo;* so F; Q₂ Enter old Polonius, with his man or two. i. 4 *to make inquire;* so Q₂; F *you make inquiry.* i. 28 *no;* so F; not in Q₂. i. 49-51 *And then . . . leave;* printed as verse in Q₂F; prose by Malone; see comment in notes. i. 49 *does . . . does;* so F except question mark after *this;* Q₂ *doos a this, a doos.* i. 50 *By the mass;* so Q₂; omitted from F. i. 52-53 *At . . . gentleman;* so F, where it is written as verse; not in Q₂. i. 55 *closes thus;* so Q₂; Q₁ *closeth with him thus;* F *closes with you thus.* i. 69 *be wi' you;* Q₂ *by ye;* F *buy you.* i. 75 *O, my lord;* so Q₂; F *Alas.* i. 99 *helps;* so Q₂; Q₁F and some editors *help.* i. 101 *Come;* so Q₂; omitted from F. i. 111 *heed;* so Q₂; F *speed.* i. 114 *By heaven;* so Qq; F *It seemes.* i. 119 After this line Q₂ has *Come.* ii. 5 *call;* so Q₂; F *I call.* ii. 6 *Sith nor;* so Q₂; F *Since not.* ii. 10 *dream;* so Q₂; F *deeme.* ii. 12 *sith;* so Q₃; F *since. haviour;* so F; Q₂ *humour.* ii. 17 *Whether . . . thus;* omitted from F. ii. 29 *But we;* so Q₂; F *We.* ii. 39 *Ay;* so Q₂; omitted from F. ii. 43 *I assure;* so Q₂ F *Assure you.* ii. 45 *and;* so Q₂; F and several editors *one.* ii. 54 *my dear Gertrude;* so Q₂; F and many editors *my sweet queen, that.* ii. 57 *o'erhasty;* so F; Q₂ *hastie.* ii. 73 *three;* so Q₁F; Q₂ *threescore.* ii. 85 *well;* so Q₂; F *very well.* ii. 98 *'tis 'tis;* so Q₂; F *it is.* ii. 112-113 *hear. Thus: 'In;* punctuation follows Malone, who follows Jennens; Q₂ *heare: thus in;* F *heare these in.* ii. 113 *&c;* so Q₂; omitted from F. ii. 126 *more above;* so F; Q₂ *more about. solicitings;* so Q₂; F *soliciting.* ii. 137 *winking;* so F; Q₂ *working.* ii. 142 *prescripts;* so Q₂; F *precepts.* ii. 146 *repulsed;* so F; Q₂ *repell'd.* ii. 151 *mourn;* so Q₂; F and many editors *wail.* ii. 152 *likely;* so F; Q₂ *like.* ii. 160 *four;* Hanmer and other editors read *for.* ii. 170 Enter *Hamlet,* reading; in Q₂F Hamlet enters after l. 167. ii. 174 *Excellent;* so Q₂; F *Excellent, excellent.* ii. 182 *ogd kissing carrion;* text follows

HAMLET (Con.)

Warburton; Q₂F *good kissing carrion* retained by some editors; see comment in notes. ii. 190-191 *far gone, far gone;* so F; Q₂ *farre gone.* ii. 197 *that you read;* so Q₂; F *you meane.* ii. 203 *most;* so Q₂; omitted from F. ii. 205 *yourself;* so Q₂; F *you yourself. should be;* so F; Q₂ *shall grow.* ii. 210 *grave.;* so Q₂; F *grave?* ii. 214 *sanity;* so F; Q₂ *sanctity.* ii. 215-216 *and suddenly . . . him;* so F; not in Q₂. ii. 217-218 *My honourable . . . humbly;* so F; Q₂ *My lord, I will.* ii. 219 *sir;* so F; not in Q₂. ii. 220 *will;* so Q₂ *will not.* ii. 221 *except my life;* three times as here in Q₂; F *except my life, my life.* ii. 232-233 *over-happy; On forutne's cap we;* so F; Q₂ *ever happy on Fortune's lap, We.* ii. 244-276 *Let me . . . attended;* so F; not in Q₂; see note on I, iv. 17-38. ii. 262 *bad;* Malone reads (possibly through printer's error) *had.* ii. 280 *even;* so F; Q₂ *ever.* ii. 284 *Come;* so F; Q₂ *come, come.* ii. 300 [Aside to Guil.]; supplied first in Globe; Delius conjectured that the speech was made to Hamlet. ii. 309 *heavily;* so Q₂; *heavenly.* ii. 312 *firmament;* so Q₂; omitted from F. ii. 314 *no other . . . than;* so F; Q₂ *nothing to me but.* ii. 337-338 *the clown . . . sere;* so F; not in Q₂. ii. 352-379 *How . . . load too;* omitted from Qq; see comment in notes. ii. 381 *mows;* so F; Q₂ *mouths.* ii. 382 *fifty;* so Q₂; omitted from F. ii. 383 *'Sblood;* so Q₂; omitted from F. ii. 397 *handsaw;* Hanmer proposed *hernshaw;* see comment in notes. ii. 401 *swaddling;* so Q₂; F *swathing.* ii. 416-418 *tragedy . . . -pastoral;* Q₂ omits classes of drama after *historical-pastoral.* ii. 438 *pious chanson;* so Q₂; Q₁ *godly Ballet;* F *Pons Chanson.* ii. 449 *French;* so Q₁F; Q₂ *friendly.* ii. 449 *my lord;* so F; Q₂ *my good lord.* ii. 466-467 *as wholesome . . . fine;* so Q₂; omitted from F. ii. 467 *speech;* so Q₂; F *cheefe speech.* ii. 483 *their lord's murder;* so Q₂; F *their vilde murthers.* ii. 487 *So, proceed you;* so Q₂; omitted from F. ii. 496 *Then senseless Ilium;* so F; not in Q₂. ii. 512 *Mars's armour;* so Capell; Q₂ *Marses Armor;* F *Mars his Armours.* ii. 515 *strumpet, Fortune;* so Q₂; F *strumpet-Fortune.* ii. 527 *'mobled queen' is good;* so F; omitted from Q₂. ii. 528 *flames;* so Q₂; F *flame.* ii. 529 *upon;* so Q₂; F *about.* ii. 548 *abstract;* so Q₂; F *abstracts.* ii. 554 *bodykins;* so F; Q₂ *bodkin. much;* so Q₂; Q₁ *farre;* omitted from F. ii. 566 *a;* so Q₁F; not in Q₂. *dozen;* so Q₁F; Q₂ *dosen lines.* ii. 575 *be wi' ye;* Q₂ *buy to you;* F *buy 'ye.* ii. 579 *own;* so Q₂; F *whole.* ii. 587 *the cue for;* so F; Q₂ *that for.* ii. 603 *Ha!;* separate line by Steevens; Q₂F part of succeeding line, followed by question mark in F. ii. 604 *'Swounds;* so Q₂; F *Why.* ii. 610 *O, vengeance;* so F; not in Q₂. ii. 611 *Why.;* Q₂ *Why;* F *Who? This;* so

HAMLET (Con.)

Q₂; F *I sure this.* ii. 612 *dear father;* so Q₄; Q₂ *a deere;* F *the Deere.* ii. 617 *I;* so F; Q₂ *hum, I.* ii. 626 *he but;* so F; Q₂ *a doe.*

ACT III: i. 1 *circumstance;* so F; Q₂ *conference.* i. 19 *about;* so F; Q₂ *heere about.* i. 28 *too;* so F; Q₂ *two.* i. 32 *lawful espials;* so F; not in Q₂. i. 33 *Will;* so F; Q₂ *Wee'le.* i. 49 *too;* so Q₂; omitted from F. i. 55 *let's;* so F; not in Q₂. i. 60-61 *To die: to sleep; No;* Q₂ *To die to sleepe No;* F *To dye, to sleepe No.* i. 64-65 *To die, to sleep; To sleep;* Q₂F *To die to sleepe, To sleepe.* i. 71 *proud;* so Q₂; F *poore.* i. 72 *despised;* so Q₂; F and some editors *disprised.* i. 76 *fardels;* so Q₂; F *these Fardles.* i. 83 *of us all;* so Q₁F; not in Q₂. i. 86 *pitch;* so Q₂; F *pith.* i. 87 *awry;* so Q₂; F *away.* i. 92 *you; well, well, well;* so F; Q₂ *you well.* i. 97 *you know;* so Q₂; F *I know.* i. 99 *their perfume lost;* so Q₂; F *then perfume left.* i. 108 *your honesty;* so F; Q₂ *you;* Q₁ *beauty . . . honesty.* i. 110 *commerce;* so Q₂F; Q₁ *priuiledge.* i. 130 *earth and heaven;* so Q₂; F *heauen and Earth.* i. 136 *where;* so Q₂; F *way.* i. 142 *go;* so F; not in Q₂. i. 148 *paintings;* so Q₂; F *pratlings.* i. 149 *face;* so Q₂; F *pace.* i. 150 *yourselves;* so Q₂; F *your selfe.* jig; Qq *gig;* F *gidge. you;* so F; Q₂ *&.* i. 155 *more marriages;* so F; Q₂ *mo marriage.* i. 159 *soldier's;* F places colon after this word. i. 164 *music;* so F; Q₂ *musickt.* i. 167 *feature;* so F; Q₂ *stature.* i. 175 *for;* so Q₂; omitted from F. ii. 8 *passion;* so F; Q₂ *your passion.* ii. 10 *hear;* so Q₂; F *see.* ii. 18 First Play.; Q₂F Player. ii. 31 *the which;* so F; Q₂ *which.* ii. 33 *praise;* so Q₂; F *praysd.* ii. 36 *nor man;* so Q₂ F *or Norman.* ii. 40 *abominably;* Q₂F *abhominably;* see comment in notes. ii. 56 *We . . . lord;* so F; Q₂ Ros. *I my lord.* Exeunt, etc. F Exeunt; Q₂ Exeunt they two. ii. 67 *fawning;* so Q₂; F *faining.* ii. 70 *Hath;* so F; Q₂ *S'hath.* ii. 74 *commingled;* so F; Q₂ *comedled.* ii. 89 *heedful;* so Q₂; F *needfull.* ii. 92 *In;* so Q₂; F *To.* ii. 107 *What;* so Q₂; F *And what.* ii. 114 *dear;* so Q₂; F *good.* ii. 116 *metal;* Q₂F *mettle.* ii. 119 Lying down, etc.; Rowe's stage direction. ii. 121-122 *I mean . . . lord;* not in Q₂. ii. 135 *within these;* so Q₁; Q₂F *within's.* ii. 145 Stage Direction: and he her; omitted from F. She kneels . . . him; not in Q₂. ii. 147 *miching mallecho;* so Malone; Q₂ *munching Mallico;* F *Miching Malicho;* see comment in notes. *it;* so Q₂; F *that.* ii. 152 *counsel;* so F; not in Q₂. ii. 174 *your;* so F; Q₂ *our.* ii. 176 After this line Q₂: *For women feare too much euen as they loue.* ii. 178 *In . . . extremity;* so F; Q₂: *Eyther none, in neither ought, or in extremity.* ii. 179 *love;* so F; Q₂ *lord.* ii. 181-182 *Where . . . there;* omitted from F. ii. 191 *Wormwood, wormwood;* so F; Q₂ (on margin) *That's wormwood.*

HAMLET (Con.)

ii. 206 *either;* Q₂ *eyther;* F *other.* ii. 207 *enactures;* F *ennactors.* ii. 209 *Grief . . . grieves;* so F; Q₂ *Greefe ioy, ioy griefs.* ii. 226 *to me give;* so Q₂; F *to giue me.* ii. 228-229 *To . . . scope;* omitted from F. *An anchor's;* Q₂ *And Anchors.* ii. 233 *once a widow;* so F; Q₂ *once I be a widdow.* ii. 234 *If . . . now;* on margin in Q₂. ii. 248 *Tropically;* so Q₂; Q₁ *trapically;* see comment in notes. ii. 255 *as good as a;* so Q₂; F *a good.* ii. 262 *must take;* so Q₁; Q₂F *mistake.* ii. 263 *pox;* not in Q₂. ii. 274 *writ in;* so F; Q₂ *written in very.* ii. 277 *What . . . fire;* so F; not in Q₂. ii. 315 *rather;* so F; not in Q₂. ii. 317 *his;* so F; not in Q₂. ii. 319 *far;* so F; not in Q₂. ii. 332 *What, my lord?* F assigns to Rosencrantz. ii. 342 *Impart;* so Q₂; omitted from F. ii. 348 *So I;* so F; Q₂ *And.* ii. 351 *surely;* so Q₂; F *freely. upon;* so Q₂; F *of.* ii. 360 *recorders;* so Q₂; F *recorder. one;* so Q₂; omitted from F. ii. 373 *and thumb;* so F; Q₂ *& the umber.* ii. 375 *eloquent;* so Q₂; F *excellent.* ii. 384 *the top of;* so F; not in Q₂. ii. 386 *speak;* so Q₂; omitted from F. *'Sblood;* Q₂; F *Why,* altered because it is an oath. *I;* so Q₂; F *that I.* ii. 388-389 *though . . . me;* so Q₁; Q₂ *though you fret me not, you cannot play vpon me;* F *though you can fret me, you cannot play upon me.* ii. 393 *yonder;* so Q₂; F *that.* ii. 394 *of;* so Q₂; F *like.* ii. 395 *'tis like;* Q₂ *'tis, like;* F *it's like.* ii. 400 *I will;* so Q₂; F *will I.* ii. 409 *bitter . . . day;* so F; Q₂ *business as the bitter day.* iii. 6 *near us;* so Q₂; F *dangerous.* iii. 7 *lunacies;* so F; Q₂ *browes.* iii. 14 *weal;* so Q₂; F *spirit.* iii. 17 *it is;* so F; Q₂ *or it is.* iii. 22 *ruin;* so F; Q₂ *raine.* iii. 25 *upon;* so F; Q₂ *about.* iii. 73 *it . . . praying;* so F; Q₂ *it but now a is a praying.* iii. 77 *sole;* so Q₂; F *foule.* iii. 79 *O;* Q₂ *Why;* F *Oh. hire and salary;* so F; Q₂ *base and silly.* iii. 81 *flush;* so Q₂; F *fresh.* iii. 89 *drunk asleep;* so F; Q₂ *drunke, a sleepe.* iii. 91 *gaming, swearing;* so F; Q₂ *game a swearing.* iv. 4 *sconce;* so Hanmer; Q₂F *silent.* iv. 5-6 *with . . . mother;* so F; not in Q₂. iv. 6 *warrant;* so F; Q₂ *wait.* iv. 12 *a wicked;* so Q₂; F *an idle.* iv. 16 *And : . . you;* so Q₂ (no dashes, comma after *so*); F *But would you were not so. You.* iv. 22 *Help, help, ho!;* so F; Q₂ *Helpe how.* iv. 23 *What, ho! . . . help!;* so Q₂; F *What how helpe.* iv. 44 *makes;* so F; Q₂ *sets.* iv. 48-49 *glow; Yea;* so F; Q₂ *glowe Ore.* iv. 50 *tristful;* so F; Q₂ *heated.* iv. 51-52 *Ay . . . index;* given to Queen in F; Q₂ gives *Ay . . . act?* to Queen; *That . . . index* to Hamlet. iv. 57 *and;* so Q₂; F *or.* iv. 65 *brother;* so Q₂; F *breath.* iv. 71-76 *Sense . . . difference;* so Q₂; omitted from F. iv. 88 *And;* so Q₂; F *As. pandars;* so F; Q₂ *pardons.* iv. 89 *eyes . . . very;* so F; Q₂ *very eyes into my.* iv. 91 *not leave;* so F;

HAMLET (Conl)

Q₂ *leaue there.* iv. 129 *effects;* Singer *affects.* iv. 139 *Ecstasy!;* so F; not in Q₂. iv. 145 *that;* so Q₂; F *a.* iv. 151 *on;* so Q₂; F *or;* Caldecott suggests *o'er.* iv. 158 *live;* so F; Q₂ *leave.* iv. 161-165 *That . . . put on;* so Q₂; omitted from F. iv. 167-170 *the next . . . potency;* so Q₂; omitted from F. iv. 169 *And . . . devil;* text follows Q₂; Q₄ *And Maister the devil;* Steevens suggests *And either master the devil;* Chambers suggests "*lay, curb,* etc., or *house* or *throne* the devil"; Dowden thinks *master* may have come from the early stage and has therefore greater authority. iv. 180 *One . . . lady;* so Q₂ omitted from F. iv. 202-210 *There's . . . meet;* so Q₂; omitted from F. iv. 215 *foolish;* so Q₁F; Q₂ *most foolish.*

Act IV: i. 1-2 *There's . . . translate:;* Q₂ has comma after *sighs, heaves,* and *translate;* F has full stop after *sighs.* i. 1 *matter;* so Q₂; F *matters.* i. 4 *Bestow . . . while;* so Q₂; omitted from F. i. 7 *sea;* so Q₂; F *seas.* i. 10 *Whips . . . cries;* so Q₂; F *He whips his rapier out, and cries.* i. 22 *let;* so Q₂; F *let's.* i. 39 *And;* so Q₂; F *To.* i. 40 *And . . . done;* to fill this incomplete line Theobald suggested *for, haply, slander;* Malone *so viperous slander;* Staunton *this calumny;* Capell *so, haply, slander.* i. 41-44 *Whose . . . O;* so Q₂; omitted from F. ii. 2 *Hamlet! Lord Hamlet!* not in Q₂. ii. 3 *But soft;* so Q₂; omitted from F. ii. 19 *like an ape;* so F; Q₂ *as an Ape does nuttes;* Farmer conjectured *like an ape, an apple.* ii. 32-33 *Hide . . . after;* so F; not in Q₂. iii. 11 *Enter Rosencrantz;* so F; Q₂ *Enter Rosencraus and all the rest.* iii. 16 *Ho, Guildenstern;* so F; Q₂ *How.* my; so F; Q₂ *the.* iii. 21 *politic;* so Q₂; not in F. iii. 27-30 *Alas . . . worm;* so Q₂; omitted from F. iii. 38 *within;* so Q₂; omitted from F. iii. 42 *deed;* so Q₂; F *deed of thine.* iii. 45 *With fiery quickness;* so F; not in Q₂. iii. 50 *them;* so Q₂; F *him.* iii. 64 *set;* so Q₂F; Pope *let* (hinder); Hanmer *set by.* iii. 66 *congruing;* so Q₂; F and some editors *conjuring.* iii. 70 *joys . . . begun;* so F; Q₂ *joys will nere begin.* iv. 3 *Craves;* so Q₂; F and some editors *Claims.* iv. 8 *softly;* so Q₂; F *safely.* iv. 9-66 *Good sir . . . nothing worth;* so Q₂; omitted from F; preceding stage direction also omitted. v. *Stage Direction:* Q₂ as in text; F *Enter Queen and Horatio.* Speeches given to *Gent.* in text are given to Horatio in F (ll. 2, 4). v. 9 *aim;* F *ayme;* Q₂ *yawme.* v. 14-16 *'Twere . . . come in;* the text follows Blackstone's arrangement; Q₂ gives to Horatio; F to Queen; ll. 14-15 are continued to Gentleman by Hanmer and several editors. v. 20 *Stage Direction:* Q₂ *Enter Ophelia* (after l. 16); F *Enter Ophelia, distracted;* Q₁ *Enter Ofelia playing on a Lute, and her haire downe singing.* v. 32 *stone;* after this word Q₂

HAMLET (Con.)

inserts *O, ho!* v. 37 *Larded;* so F; Q₂ *Larded all.* v. 38 *grave;* so F; Q₂ *ground.* did; so Pope and most editors; QqF *did not.* v. 41 *God 'ild;* so Capell; Q₂ *good dild;* F *God dil'd.* v. 57 *Indeed, la;* so Johnson; Q₂ *Indeede;* F *Indeed la?* v. 73-74 *Good . . . good night;* so F substantially; Q₂ *God night, Ladies, God Night. Sweet Ladyes God night, God night.* v. 89 *Feeds on his wonder;* so Johnson; Q₂ *Feeds this wonder;* F *Keepes on his wonder.* v. 96 *Alack . . . this;* so F; not in Q₂. v. 97 *Where are;* so F; Q₂ *Attend, where is.* v. 112 *this king? Sirs;* so Q₂; F *the King, sirs?* v. 119 *brow;* so Q₂F; Furness suggested *brows.* v. 137 *world;* so F; Q₂ *worlds;* Pope *world's.* v. 141 *father's death;* so F; Q₂ *father.* is't; so Q₂; F *if.* v. 142 *swoopstake;* Q₁ *swoopstake-like;* Q₂F *soopstake.* v. 146 *pelican;* so Q₂; F *politician.* v. 150 *sensibly;* so Q₂; F *sensible.* v. 151 *pierce;* so F; Q₂ *pears;* Johnson suggested *'pear.* v. 152 *Danes . . . in;* so Capell; Q₂ has the stage direction "a noise within" opposite l. 151 and assigns *Let her come in* to Laertes; F has "A noise within. Let her come in," as if a stage direction. v. 156 *with;* so Q₂; F and some editors *by.* v. 160 *an old;* so F; Q₂ *a poore.* v. 161-163 *Nature . . . loves;* so F; not in Q₂. v. 165 *Hey . . . hey nonny;* so F; Q₂ omits. v. 166 *in;* so Q₂; F *on.* rain'd; so Q₂; F *raines.* v. 167 *Fare . . . dove;* in F italicized as if part of song; Q₂ prints in Roman. v. 170-173 *You . . . daughter;* Q₂F print whole speech in Roman type. Johnson prints *You . . . a-down-a* as a song; *You* and *an you* have been regarded by some critics as directions to two singers. v. 182 *herb-grace;* so F; Q₂ *herb of grace.* v. 183 *O, you must;* Q₁ *you must;* Q₂ *you may;* F *oh, you must.* v. 195 *was as;* so Q₂; F *as;* Johnson *was.* v. 196 *All;* so F; not in Q₂. v. 199 *God ha' mercy;* so Collier; Q₂ *God a mercy;* F *Gramercy.* v. 200 *Christian;* so F; Q₂ *Christians. I pray God;* so F; not in Q₂. v. 201 *Do . . . God;* so Capell; Q₂ *Doe you this ô God;* F *Do you see this, you gods?* v. 213 *funeral;* so F; Q₂ *burial.* v. 214 *trophy, sword;* so F; Q₂ *trophe sword;* Pope *trophy sword.* vi. 2 *Serv.;* so F; Q₂ *Gent. Sailors;* so F; Q₂ *Seafaring men.* vi. 5 *Stage Direction:* *Enter Sailors;* so Q₂; F *Enter Sailor.* vi. 6, 8 *First Sail.;* so Capell; Q₂F *Say.* vi. 22 *good;* so F; not in Q₂. vi. 24 *speed;* so Q₂; F *haste.* vi. 31 *He;* so F; Q₂ *So,* with no point before *Hamlet.* vi. 32 *make;* so Q₄; not in Q₂; F and some editors *give.* vii. 7 *crimeful;* so F; Q₂ *criminall.* vii. 8 *safety;* so F; Q₂ *safetie, gretnes.* vii. 11 *But;* so Q₂; F and some editors *And.* vii. 14 *She's so conjunctive;* so F; Q₂ *She is so conclive.* vii. 20 *Would;* so F; Q₂ *Worke.* vii. 22 *loud;* so F; Q₂ *loved Arm'd;* see comment in notes. vii. 24 *And;* so F; Q₂ *But.* had aim'd; Q₂ *have aim'd;* F *had arm'd.*

HAMLET (Con.)

vii. 27 *Whose worth;* so Q₂; F *who was.* vii. 36 *How . . . Hamlet;* so F; not in Q₂. vii. 41 *Of . . . them;* so Q₂; omitted from F. vii. 48 *and more strange;* so F; not in Q₂. vii. 49 *Hamlet;* so F; not in Q₂. vii. 51 *abuse, and;* so Q₂; F *abuse? or.* vii. 60 *Ay, my lord;* so Q₂; omitted from F. vii. 61 *So you will;* so Q₂; F *If so you'l.* vii. 63 *checking at;* so F; Q₂ *the King at.* vii. 69-82 *My lord . . . graveness;* so Q₂; omitted from F. vii. 82 *since;* so Q₂; F and some editors *hence.* vii. 89 *topp'd;* so Q₂; F *past.* vii. 99 *especial;* so Q₂; F and some editors *especially.* vii. 101-103 *you . . . this;* so Q₂; F *you, Sir, This,* omitting *the scrimers . . . oppose them.* vii. 107 *What;* so Q₂; F *Why.* vii. 115-124 *There . . . ulcer;* so Q₂; omitted from F. vii. 126 *your . . . in deed;* so F; Q₂ *indeede your fathers sonne.* vii. 143 *that, but dip;* so Q₂; F *I* [ay] *but dipt.* vii. 156 *cunnings;* so Q₂; F *commings;* see comment in notes. vii. 163 *Our . . . there;* Q₂ completes this line with *but stay, what noyse?;* retained by some editors. *How . . . queen;* so F₂; not in Q₂; F *how sweet Que ne.* vii. 167 *aslant a;* so F; Q₂ *ascaunt the.* vii. 169 *There with . . . come;* so F; Q₂ *Therewith . . . make.* vii. 172 *cold;* so F; Q₂ *cull-cola.* vii. 178 *tunes;* so Q₁F; Q₂ *lauds* (chants). vii. 180 *indued;* so F; Q₂ *indewed.* vii. 184 *she is drown'd?;* so Q₂ (with period after *drown'd*); F *is she drown'd?*

Act V: i. 2 *that;* so F; Q₂ *when she.* i. 13 *to act;* so Q₂; F *an Acte.* i. 39-43 *Why . . . arms;* so F; not in Q₂. i. 50 *frame;* so F; not in Q₂. i. 62 *Stage Direction:* Enter *Hamlet,* etc.; Q₂ places this after l. 72. i. 68 *to Yaughan;* so F; Q₂ *in, and.* i. 71 *ah;* Q₂F *a.* i. 72 *there was nothing;* so F; Q₂ *there a was nothing a.* i. 80 *claw'd;* so Q₂; F *caught.* i. 81 *intil;* so F; Q₂ *into.* i. 87 *o'er-reaches;* so Q₂; F *o're Offices;* see comment in notes. i. 92 *good;* so F; Q₂ *sweet.* i. 94 *meant;* so F; Q₂ *went.* i. 107 *of;* so Q₂; F *of of.* *quiddities;* so Q₂; F *Quiddits.* i. 108 *quillets;* so F; Q₂ *quillites.* i. 109 *rude;* so F; Q₂ *madde.* i. 115-116 *is this . . . recoveries;* so F; not in Q₂. i. 118 *double ones too;* so F; Q₂ *doubles.* i. 120 *hardly;* so F; Q₂ *scarcely.* i. 128-130 *Mine . . . meet;* so F; Q₂ (as prose) *Mine, sir, or a . . . made* (omitting *For . . . meet*). *three years;* so F; Q₂ *this seauen yeres.* i. 180 *I' faith;* so F; Q₂ *Fayth.* i. 182 *now-a-days;* so F; not in Q₂. i. 189-190 *Here's . . . in the;* so F; Q₂ *heer's a skull now hath lyen you i'th.* i. 190 *three and twenty;* so F; Q₁ *this dozen yeare;* Q₂ *23.* i. 198 *This . . . sir;* so Q₂; F repeats the words. *Yorick's;* so F; Q₂ *sir Yoricks.* i. 202 *Let me see;* so F; not in Q₂. i. 206 *now;* so Q₂; F omitted from F. i. 206-207 *in my . . . it is;* so Q₂; F *my imagination is.* i. 212 *grinning;* so Q₂; F *Ieering.* i. 213 *chamber;* so Q₁F; Q₂ *table.* i. 231 *as thus;*

HAMLET (Con.)

so F; not in Q₂. i. 236 *Imperious;* so Q₂; F *imperiall.* i. 239 *winter's;* so F; Q₂ *waters.* i. 249 First Priest.; so Capell; Q₂ Doct.; F Priest. i. 250 *warranty;* so Q₂; F *warrantis;* Dyce and other editors *warrantise.* i. 255 *crants;* so Q₂; F and many editors *Rites.* i. 260 *a;* so Q₂; F *sage;* Dyce conjectured *such.* i. 270 *treble;* so F; Q₂ *double.* i. 284 *For;* so Q₂; F *Sir. and;* so F; not in Q₂. i. 285 *something in me;* so F; Q₂ *in me something.* i. 286 *wiseness;* so F; Qq *wisdom.* *hold off;* so Q₂; F *Away.* i. 288 All. Gentlemen; so Q₂; omitted from F. Hor.; so Q₂; F Gen. i. 297 *'Swounds;* so Q₂; F *Come.* *thou'lt;* so F; Q₂ *th'owt.* i. 298 *woo't fast;* so Q₂; omitted from F. i. 299 *eisel;* text from Theobald; Q₂ *Esill;* F *Esile;* see comment in notes. i. 307 Queen.; so Q₂; F Kin. ii. 1 *shall you;* so Q₂; F and some editors *let me.* ii. 9 *deep;* so Q₂; F *deare.* *pall;* Pope and other editors read *fail.* *teach;* so F; Q₂ *learn.* ii. 17 *unseal;* so F; Q₂ *unfold.* ii. 27 *me;* so F; Q₂ *now.* ii. 29-31 *villanies . . . I;* so Dyce; Q₂ *villaines, Or . . . play, I;* F *villaines, Ere . . . Play. I.* ii. 40 *like;* so Q₂; F *as.* *might;* so Q₂; F and some editors *should.* ii. 42 *comma;* Theobald conjectured *commerce;* Hanmer *cement.* ii. 43 *'As'es;* Q₂ *as sir* with comma after *like;* F *Assis.* ii. 48 *ordinant;* so Q₂; F *ordinate.* ii. 57 *Why . . . employment;* so F; not in Q₂. ii. 58 *defeat;* so F; Q₂ *debate.* ii. 63 *thinks't;* so Walker; Q₂ *thinke;* F *thinkst.* *upon;* dash is supplied by Boswell; Q₂ has question mark; F has period. ii. 68-80 *To quit . . . here;* so F; not in Q₂. ii. 78 *court;* so Theobald; Q₂F *count,* adopted by many editors. ii. 80 *Stage Direction: Osric;* so F ; Q₂ *a Courtier;* F *young Osricke.* ii. 81 and later Osr.; so F; Q₂ Cour. ii. 91 *lordship;* so Q₂; F *friendship.* ii. 95 *Put;* so F; not in Q₂. ii. 101 *But yet;* so Q₂; omitted from F. ii. 104 *But;* so F; not in Q₂. ii. 109 *good my lord;* so Q₂; F *in good faith.* ii. 110-150 *Sir . . . unfellowed;* so Q₂; omitted from F. ii. 154 *hath wagered;* so Q₂; F *ha's wag'd.* ii. 155 *he has imponed;* so Theobald; Q₂ *hee has impaund;* F *he impon'd.* 158 *hangers;* so F; Q₂ *hanger.* ii. 162-163 *I knew . . . done;* so Q₂; omitted from F. ii. 164 *carriages;* so F; Q₂ *carriage.* 166 *cannon;* so F; Q₂ *a cannon.* ii. 167 *might;* so F; not in Q₂. ii. 170 *this 'imponed,' as;* so F; Q₂ *this all.* ii. 172 *that;* so F; Q₂ and some editors *sir, that.* ii. 174-175 *laid . . . nine;* so Q₂; F *one twelve for mine.* ii. 186 *re-deliver . . . so;* so F; Q₂ *deliver you so.* 190 *Yours . . . does;* so F; Q₂ *Yours doo's.* ii. 195 *He . . . with;* so F; Q₂ *A did sir with.* ii. 197 *breed;* so Q₂; F and some editors *beavy.* ii. 198 *and outward;* so F; Q₂ *and out of an.* ii. 201 *fond and winnowed;* so F; Q₂ *prophane and trennowed; profound and renowned* has been proposed as an emendation of Q₂.

HAMLET (Con.)

ii. 202-218 Enter a *Lord . . . instruct me;* so Q₂; omitted from F. ii. 222 *But;* so F; not in Q₂. ii. 223 *how ill all's;* so Q₂; *how all.* ii. 226 *gain-giving;* so F; Q₂ *gam-giving.* ii. 233-235 *the readiness . . . Let be;* so Caldecott; Q₂ *The readines is all, since no man of ought he leaues, knowes what ist to leaue betimes, let be;* F *The readinesse is all, since no man ha's ought of what he leaues. What is't to leaue betimes?* ii. 251 *Sir . . . audience;* so F; not in Q₂. ii. 255 *brother;* so Q₁₋₂; F *Mother.* ii. 261 *keep;* so F; not in Q₂. ii. 263 *I;* so Q₂; F *I do.* ii. 265 *Come on;* so F; not in Q₂. ii. 274 *better'd;* so F; Q₂ *better.* ii. 283 *union;* so F; Q₂ *Vnice.* ii. 286 *trumpet;* so Q₂; F *trumpets.* ii. 289 Q₂ has at this line the direction, Trumpets the while. ii. 291 *Come, my lord;* so Q₂; F *Come on sir.* ii. 297 *A touch, a touch;* so F; not in Q₂. *confess;* so F; Q₂ *confest.* ii. 299 *Here . . . napkin;* so Q₂; F *Heere's a napkin.* ii. 308 *third . . . you;* so Steevens; Q₂ *third Laertes, you doe;* F *third. Laertes, you.* ii. 310 *afeard;* so F; Q₂ *sure.* ii. 322 *Ho!;* so Theobald; Q₂ *how;* F *How?* ii. 326 *hour of;* so F; Q₂ *houres.* ii. 336 *Here;* so F; Q₂ *Heare. murderous;* so F; not in Q₂. ii. 337 *off;* so F; Q₂ *of. union;* so Q₁F; Q₂ *the Onixe.* ii. 350 *cause aright;* so Q₂; F *causes right.* ii. 355 *good;* so F; Q₂ *god;* Capell follows Q₂. ii. 356 *live;* so F; Q₂ *I leave.* ii. 371 *sing;* Warburton suggested *wing.* ii. 394 *forced cause;* so F; Q₂ *for no cause.* ii. 400 *rights;* so Q₂; F *Rites.* ii. 402 *also;* so Q₂; F *always.* ii. 403 *draw on more;* so F; Q₂ *draw no more.* ii. 409 *royally;* so F; Q₂ *royall.* ii. 410 *rites;* so F; Q₂ *right.* ii. 412 *bodies;* so Q₂; F *body.*

OTHELLO

ACT I: iii. 265 *me;* so Rann; QF *my.* iii. 271 *officed;* Q *actiue.*

ACT II: i. 105 *list;* so Q; F *leaue.* iii. 152 *twiggen;* Q *wicker.* iii. 268 *sense;* Q *offence.* iii. 323 *denotement;* so Q₂; QF *deuotement,* which is probably the correct reading.

ACT III: iii. 123 *delations;* Q *denotements,* which is close to the sense. iii. 376 *livest;* so Q; F and various editors *lou'st.*

ACT IV: ii. 54 *A fixed figure;* so Q; F *The fixed figure.* ii. 55 *slow unmoving;* so Q; F *slow, and mouing.* ii. 144 *door;* Q *dores.* ii. 176 *daffest;* F *dafts;* Q *dofftst.* iii. 105 *uses;* Q *vsage.*

ACT V: ii. 150 *iteration;* so Q; F *iterance,* probably correct. ii. 209 *reprobation;* so Q; F *reprobance.* ii. 253 *ice-brook's;* F *Ice brookes;* Q *Isebrookes;* see comment in notes. ii. 347 *Indian;* so Q and F₂₋₃₋₄; F *Iudean;* see comment in notes. ii. 351 *medicinal;* so Q; F *medicinable.*

KING LEAR

ACT I: i. 5 *equalities;* so Q; F *qualities.* i. 39 *fast;* Q *first.* i. 71 *self-same metal;* F *selfe-mettle;* Q *selfe same mettall;* Q *self-same mettal.* i. 87 *interess'd;* F *interest.* i. 167 *doom;* so Q; F *thy guift;* F *thy gift.* i. 177 *diseases;* so Q; F *disasters.* i. 242 *regards;* Q *respects.* i. 283 *plaited;* Q *pleated;* F *plighted.* i. 308 *hit;* so Q; F *sit.* ii. 3 *plague;* Warburton *plage.* ii. 24 *subscribed;* so Q; F *prescrib'd.* ii. 77 *declining;* F *declin'd.* iii. 26 *my very course;* so Q; F *my course.* iv. 2 *defuse;* Theobald *diffuse.* iv. 94 *struck;* so Q; F *strucken.* iv. 125 *Lady the brach;* Q *Lady oth'e brach;* F *the Lady Brach.* iv. 141 Kent.; so F; speech given to Lear in Q. v. 8 *brains;* so FQ; Pope and many editors read *brain.*

ACT II: i. 9 *ear-kissing;* so F; Q *eare-bussing.* i. 41 *Mumbling;* so F; Q *warbling.* i. 42 *stand;* so F; Pide Bull Q *stand's.* i. 47 *revenging;* Q *revengive.* i. 55 *when;* Staunton conjectured *whe'r* to correspond to *whether* below. i. 64 *coward;* Q *caitiff,* followed in many texts. i. 70 *would the reposal;* Q *could the reposure.* i. 78 *spurs;* F *spirits.* i. 102 *expense and waste;* Q *these — and waste of his;* some copies of Pide Bull Q *the waste and spoyle of his.* i. 109 *bewray;* Q *betray.* i. 121 *threading;* Q *threatning.* i. 125 *differences;* some copies of Pide Bull Q *defences.* ii. 1 *dawning;* Q *even.* ii. 81 *intrinse;* F *intrince;* Q *intrench.* ii. 84 *Renege;* so F₂; F *revenge;* Q *reneag.* ii. 125 *conjunct;* F *compact.* ii. 150 *condemned'st;* so Capell; Q *temnest.* ii. 163 *out;* Q *on't.* iv. 7 *cruel;* Q *crewell.* iv. 64 *train;* so F; Q *number.* iv. 86 *perdy;* F *par dieu.* iv. 125 *knapp'd 'em;* Q *rapt um.* iv. 174 *tender-hefted;* Q *tender hested.* iv. 191 *stock'd;* Q *struck.*

ACT III: i. 4 *element;* so Q; F *elements.* ii. 7 *Smite;* Q *strike.* iv. 125 *S. Withold;* F *Swithold;* Theobald *St. Withold.* iv. 126 *He met the night-mare;* so F; Q *a nellthu night more.* vi. 23 *justicer;* so Theobald; Q *iustice.* vi. 72 *lym;* so Hanmer; Q *him;* F *Hym.* vi. 109-122 *When . . . lurk;* omitted from F. vii. 43 *simple answerer;* F *simple answer'd.* vii. 60 *buoy'd;* Q *bod,* some copies *layd.* vii. 63 *stern;* so F; Q *heard that dearn;* many editors follow Capell, *howl'd that dearn.* vii. 65 *subscribed;* so Q; F *subscribe.*

ACT IV: i. 65 *mopping and mowing;* Q *Mobing, & Mohing.* ll. 61-66 omitted from F. ii. 28 *My . . . body;* so F; Q₁ *My foote . . . body* (some copies); *A foole . . . bed* (some copies); Q₂ *My foote . . . head.* ii. 68 *now;* Q *mew* (some copies). iii. 22 *seem'd;* so Pope; Q *seeme.* iii. 36 *and mate;* Q *and make.* iv. 4 *bur-docks;* Q *hor-docks;* Collier *hoar-docks.* v. 25 *œillades;* Q *aliads;* F *Eliads.* v. 40 *party;* so F; Q *Lady.* vi. 169 *Plate;* so Theobald; F *Place.* vi. 202 *bridegroom;* so Q; F *smugge bridegroom.* vi. 256 *British;* so Q; F *English.*

ACT V: iii. 83 *attaint;* F *arrest.*

MACBETH

Act I: iii. 32 *weird;* F *weyward.* iii. 97-98 *hail Came;* so Rowe; F *tale Can.* vi. 4 *martlet;* so Rowe; F *bartlet.* vi. 5 *mansionry;* so Theobald; F *mansonry;* Pope *masonry.* vi. 9 *most;* so Rowe; F *must.* vii. 6 *shoal;* so Theobald. F *schoole.* vii. 47 *do;* so Rowe; F *no.*

Act II: i. 55 *strides;* so Pope; F *sides.* i. 56 *sure;* so Capell; F *sowre.* i. 57 *which way they;* so Rowe; F *which they may.* ii. 17 *Did you not speak?* Many editors, following Hunter, give this to Macbeth; and both *When?* and *Now* to Lady Macbeth. ii. 18 *Ay;* F *I.*

Act III: ii. 13 *scotch'd;* so Theobald; F *scorch'd.* iv. 32 *hear, ourselves;* Theobald conjectured *hear 't ourselves.* iv. 78 *time;* F *times.* iv. 144 *in deed;* so Theobald; F *indeed.* vi. 19 *an't;* so Theobald; F *and 't.*

Act IV: i. 97 *Rebellion's head;* so Theobald; F *Rebellious dead.* ii. 22 *Each way and move;* many emendations: Theobald *Each way and wave;* Capell *And move each way;* Staunton *Each sway and move;* Cuningham *Each way amoved.* ii. 83 *shag-hair'd;* so Steevens; F *shagge-ear'd.* iii. 15 *deserve;* so Warburton; F *discerne.* The whole passage is difficult and has been variously emended. Cuningham suggests rearrangement of lines as follows: *Hath . . . but — Something . . . me — And . . . weak — Poor . . . god;* and would supply *'tis* after *wisdom.* iii. 99 *Uproar;* F *uprore;* Keightley *unroot.* iii. 235 *tune;* so Rowe; F *time.*

Act V: i. 29 *sense is shut;* so Rowe; F *sense are shut.* iii. 21 *cheer . . . disseat;* F *cheere . . . dis-eate;* two types of emendation: Dyce *chair* with *disseat;* others *dis-ease* (F₂ *disease*) with *cheer.* iii. 55 *senna;* so F₄; F *Cyme;* F₂₋₃ *Caeny.*

ANTONY AND CLEOPATRA

Act I: ii. 5 *charge;* so Warburton; F *change.* ii. 39 *fertile;* so Warburton; F *foretell.* ii. 65 *Alexas,—come;* Theobald's emendation of F, where *Alexas* is printed as the name of a speaker. ii. 84 *Saw;* so later Ff; F *Save.* ii. 114 *minds;* so Warburton; F *windes.* ii. 117 *Sicyon;* F *Scicion. ho;* so Dyce; F *how.* ii. 141 *a compelling occasion;* Rowe's emendation of F *a compelling an occasion.* iv. 3 *Our;* so Heath and Johnson; F *One.* iv. 24 *soils;* so Malone; F *oyles.* iv. 44 *dear'd;* so Theobald; F *fear'd.* iv. 46 *lackeying;* so Theobald; F *lacking.* iv. 56 *wassails;* so Pope; F *Vassailes.* iv. 66 *browsed'st;* so F; F *brows'd.* v. 50 *dumb'd;* so Theobald; F *dumbe.* v. 74 *judgement;* colon is Warburton's; F has comma.

Act II: i. 21 *waned;* F *wand.* ii. 7 *Antonius';* Steevens's emendation of F *Anthonio's.* ii. 163 *Misenum;* F *Misena.* ii. 243 *vilest;* F *vildest.* v. 12 *Tawny-finn'd;* so Theobald; F

ANTONY AND CLEOPATRA (Con.)

Tawny fine. vii. 106 *grows;* F *grow.* vii. 117 *bear;* so Theobald; F *beate.*

Act III: iv. 9 *took 't;* so Theobald; F *look 't.* iv. 27 *stain;* Theobald conjectured *strain.* v. 14 *world;* so Hanmer; F *would. hast;* so Hanmer; F *hadst. chaps, no more;* so Hanmer; F *chaps no more.* vi. 29 *and, being, that;* Rowe's punctuation; F has comma after *that.* vi. 72 *Malchus;* so Theobald; F *Mauchus;* North, *Manchus.* vii. 36 *muleters;* F *M.iliters;* F₂ *Muliters.* xiii. 55 *Cæsar;* F *Cæsars.* xiii. 74 *Say . . . deputation;* so Theobald; F ha: comma at end of line. *deputation;* so Theoba d; F *disputation.* xiii. 162 *smite;* so Hanmeı F *smile.* xiii. 165 *discandying;* so Theobal ¹; F *discandering.*

Act IV: iv. 3 *mine;* so Hanmer; F *thine.* iv. 13 *daff't;* F *d .ft.* v. 17 *Dispatch.—Enobarbus!* Steevens's punctuation; F *Dispatch Enobarbus.* vi. 13 *persuade;* so Rowe; F *diswade.* viii. 2 *gests;* so Warburton; F *guests.* viii. 23 *favouring;* so Theobald; F *savouring.* xii. 21 *spaniel'd;* so Hanmer; F *pannelled.* xii. 37 *doits;* so Thirlby; F *Dolts.* xv. 38 *where;* so Pope; F *when.* xv. 44 *housewife;* F *Huswife.* xv. 73 *No more, but e'en a woman;* so Capell; F *No more but in a woman.*

Act V: i. 36 *lance;* so Theobald; F *launch.* i. 59-60 *cannot . . . ungentle;* so Rowe; F *leaue to be ungentle;* Capell *Leave to be gentle.* ii. 7 *dug;* so Theobald; F *dung.* ii. 56 *varletry;* F *Varlotarie.* ii. 87 *an autumn 'twas;* Theobald's and Thirlby's conjecture for F *an Anthony it was.* ii. 96 *or;* F *nor.* ii. 104 *smites;* so Capell; F *suites.* ii. 259 *fallible;* F *falliable.* ii. 321 *awry;* so Pope; F *away.*

CYMBELINE

Act I: i. 49 *feated;* so F; Rowe *featur'd;* Johnson *feared.* iv. 50 *offend not;* so Rowe; F *offend.* iv. 80 *could not but;* so Malone; F *could not.* iv. 146 *afraid;* so Warburton and Theobald; F *a Friend.* v. 80 *liegers;* F *Leidgers.* vi. 36 *number'd;* Theobald *th' unnumber'd.*

Act II: ii. *Stage Direction: Imogen . . . attending;* F has *Enter Imogen, in her Bed, and a Lady.* iii. 48 *out;* so Rowe; F *on 't;* retained by many editors. iii. 52 *soliciting;* so Collier; F *solicity.* iii. 124 *self-figured;* Theobald *self-finger'd.* iv. 6 *sear'd;* so Tyrwhitt; F *fear'd* (see comment in notes); Elze *dear;* Hudson *sore.* iv. 37 Phi.; so Capell; F *Post.* v. 16 *a German one;* so Rowe; F *a Iarmen on.* v. 27 *named;* so F₈; F *name.*

Act III: i. 20 *rocks;* so Hanmer (Seward conjecture); F *Oakes.* ii. 80 *nor here, nor here;* Heath conjectured *nor here, nor there.* iii. 2 *Stoop;* so Hanmer; F *Sleepe.* iii. 23 *bauble;* so

CYMBELINE (Con.)

Rowe; Hanmer *bribe*, followed by many editors; F *Babe*. iv. 66 *fail*; Upton *fall*. iv. 81 *afore 't*; so Rowe; F *a-foot*. iv. 104 *I'll . . . first*; Hanmer's reading of F *I'll wake mine eye-balles first*; Rowe alters *wake* to *break*; Johnson inserts *out* after *eye-balls*. iv. 135 *With . . . nothing*; Vaughan proposed *With that harsh noble — noble simply in nothing*; Elze reads *ignoble* for *noble*; F omits *nothing*. v. 44 *loudest*; Capell *loud'st*; F *lowd*. v. 55-56 *Go . . . stand'st*; F reading except that F prints colon after *after*; Vaughan and some editors *Go, look after Pisanio thou that stands*. vi. 27 *Stage Direction*: Enter *Belarius*, etc.; F begins scene vii here. vi. 71 *I bid*; Hanmer *I'd bid*. vi. 77 *prize*; Hanmer *price*. vii. 9 *commends*; so Warburton; F *commands*; see comment in notes.

ACT IV: i. 21 *thy*; Hanmer *her*. ii. 57 *him*; so Pope; F *them*. ii. 111 *effect*; so Theobald; F *defect*; see comment in notes. ii. 112 *cause*; so F; Dowden and Vaughan *cease*. ii. 132 *humour*; so Theobald; F *Honor*. ii. 168 *parish*; Hanmer *marish* (marsh). ii. 205 *crare*; F *care*; Theobald *carrick*; see comment in notes. ii. 224 *ruddock*; F *Raddocke*. ii. 229 *winter-ground*; Elze *wind around*. iii. 40 *betid*; F *betide*.

ACT V: iii. 43 *they*; so Theobald; F *the*. v. 311 *on 's*; F *one 's*.

THE WINTER'S TALE

ACT I: i. 9 *us*; F places colon after this word; followed by many editors. ii. 44 *lady-she*; so Staunton; F *lady she*. ii. 147-148 *How . . . brother*; F gives this speech to Leontes; Hanmer and most editors assign it to Polixenes.

ACT II: i. 11 *Who taught you this*; F *Who taught 'this*, indicating that *you* was elided in pronunciation.

ACT III: ii. 172 *Thorough*; F *through*, changed by Malone for the sake of scansion.

ACT IV: iv. 160 *out*; F *on 't*; Theobald's emendation. iv. 591 *rear our birth*; F *reare 'our birth*; Rowe *rear o' her birth*, probably correct. iv. 667 *eyes over* — ; so F; some editors place the dash after *eyes*, thus making the passage easily understood. iv. 730 *at palace*; F *at 'Pallace*. iv. 768 *pheasant*; so F; Kenrick *present*; see comment in notes.

THE WINTER'S TALE (Con.)

ACT V: i. 12 *True, too true*; so Theobald; F places the first *true* at the end of the preceding speech. i. 59 *Where we're offenders now, appear*; F *stage* (*Where we offendors now appeare*). i. 75 *I have done*; assigned to preceding speaker in F; Capell's emendation. i. 94 *Ay*; F *I*. iii. 18 *Lonely*; so Hanmer; F *lovely*.

THE TEMPEST

ACT I: i. 60 *chapp'd*; F *chopt*. i. 70 *furze*; F *firrs*. ii. 146 *boat*; F *butt*. ii. 173 *princesses*; F *princesse*. ii. 200 *bowsprit*; F *bore-spritt*. ii. 211-212 *Plunged . . . me*; F punctuates with semicolon after *vessel*, no mark after *me*. ii. 351-362 *Abhorred . . . prison*; assigned to Miranda in F.

ACT II: i. 36 *So . . . paid*; assigned to Ant. in F. i. 63 *glosses*; New Cambridge *gloss*. i. 94 *Ay*; F *I*; Hudson *Ah*; New Cambridge editors suggest *Sir*. i. 125 *lose*; F *loose*, retained with reason by New Cambridge. i. 168 *God*; not in F. i. 221 *Trebles*; F *Trebbles*; New Cambridge *Troubles*. i. 299 *them*; New Cambridge following Dyce *thee*. i. 308-309 New Cambridge gives *Why . . . awake* to Gonzalo; *Why . . . matter* to Alonzo. ii. 22 *foul*; so F; Upton *full*. ii. 60 *savages*; F *salvages*. ii. 176 *scamels*; many conjectures: Keightley *seamels*; Theobald *stannels*. ii. 187 *trencher*; F *trenchering*.

ACT III: i. 15 *Most . . . lest*; Spedding suggests *Most busiest when idlest*; New Cambridge *busy-idlest*. ii. 130 *scout*; so F; New Cambridge *cout*. iii. 65 *plume*; F *plumbe*. iii. 84 *devouring*; New Cambridge editors conjecture *devoiring*. iii. 93 *and mine loved*; Rowe conjectured *my*; New Cambridge editors suggest *admired*. iii. 106 *spirits*; New Cambridge *spirit*.

ACT IV: i. 3 *thrid*; F *third*. i. 7 *strangely*; Sherwin *strongly*. i. 66 *broom-groves*; Hanmer *brown groves*. i. 96 *bed-right*; Steevens *bed-rite*. i. 106 *marriage-blessing*; so Warburton; F *marriage, blessing*. i. 110-117 *Earth's . . . you*. F assigns entire song to Juno; Theobald's correction. i. 164 *thank*; New Cambridge *think*. i. 184 *feet*; New Cambridge editors conjecture *sweat*.

ACT V: i. 39 *mushrooms*; F *mushrumps*. i. 111 *Whether*; so Rowe; F *Where*. i. 236 *her*; so Theobald; F *our*. i. 248 *shortly*; no comma in F.

INDEX

(The letter *n* following a reference indicates a footnote)

1161

And gasping to begin some speech, her eyes
Became two spouts: the fury spent, anon
Did this break from her: 'Good Antigonus,
Since fate, against thy better disposition,
Hath made thy person for the thrower-out
Of my poor babe, according to thine oath,   30
Places remote enough are in Bohemia,
There weep and leave it crying; and, for the babe
Is counted lost for ever, Perdita,
I prithee, call 't. For this ungentle business,
Put on thee by my lord, thou ne'er shalt see
Thy wife Paulina more.' And so, with shrieks,
She melted into air. Affrighted much,
I did in time collect myself and thought
This was so and no slumber. Dreams are toys:
Yet for this once, yea, superstitiously,   40
I will be squared by this. I do believe
Hermione hath suffer'd death, and that
Apollo would, this being indeed the issue
Of King Polixenes, it should here be laid,
Either for life or death, upon the earth
Of its right father. Blossom, speed thee well!
There lie, and there thy character: there these;
Which may, if fortune please, both breed thee, pretty,
And still rest thine. The storm begins: poor wretch,   49
That for thy mother's fault art thus exposed
To loss and what may follow! Weep I cannot,
But my heart bleeds; and most accursed am I
To be by oath enjoin'd to this. Farewell!
The day frowns more and more: thou'rt like to have
A lullaby too rough: I never saw
The heavens so dim by day. A savage clamour!   56
Well may I get aboard! This is the chase:
I am gone for ever. [*Exit, pursued by a bear.*

Enter a Shepherd.

Shep. I would there were no age between
sixteen and three-and-twenty, or that youth
would sleep out the rest; for there is nothing
in the between but getting wenches with
child, wronging the ancientry, stealing, fighting—Hark you now! Would any but these

boiled brains of nineteen and two-and-
twenty hunt this weather? They have
scared away two of my best sheep, which I
fear the wolf will sooner find than the master:
if any where I have them, 'tis by the seaside,
browsing of ivy. Good luck, an 't be thy will!
what have we here? Mercy on 's, a barne; a
very pretty barne! A boy or a child, I   71
wonder? A pretty one; a very pretty one:
sure, some 'scape: though I am not bookish,
yet I can read waiting-gentlewoman in the
'scape. This has been some stair-work, some
trunk-work, some behind-door-work: they
were warmer that got this than the poor
thing is here. I'll take it up for pity: yet I'll
tarry till my son come; he hallooed but even
now. Whoa, ho, hoa!

Enter Clown.

Clo. Hilloa, loa!   80
Shep. What, art so near? If thou'lt see a
thing to talk on when thou art dead and
rotten, come hither. What ailest thou, man?
Clo. I have seen two such sights, by sea
and by land! but I am not to say it is a sea,
for it is now the sky: betwixt the firmament
and it you cannot thrust a bodkin's point.
Shep. Why, boy, how is it?   88
Clo. I would you did but see how it chafes,
how it rages, how it takes up the shore! but
that's not to the point. O, the most piteous
cry of the poor souls! sometimes to see 'em,
and not to see 'em; now the ship boring the
moon with her main-mast, and anon swallowed with yest and froth, as you'ld thrust
a cork into a hogshead. And then for the
land-service, to see how the bear tore out his
shoulder-bone; how he cried to me for help
and said his name was Antigonus, a nobleman. But to make an end of the ship, to see
how the sea flap-dragoned it: but, first, how
the poor souls roared, and the sea mocked
them; and how the poor gentleman roared
and the bear mocked him, both roaring
louder than the sea or weather.   104
Shep. Name of mercy, when was this, boy?
Clo. Now, now: I have not winked since I

---

41. **squared**, directed in my course. 47. **character**, written account, the same which subsequently served to identify Perdita. **there these**. The reference is to the ornaments found by the shepherd (ll. 120-126). 48. **breed**, keep, support. **pretty**, pretty one. 49. **rest**, remain, i.e., a residue remain. 57. **This . . . chase**. Antigonus here sees the pursuing bear. 63. **ancientry**, old people.

64. **boiled brains**, hot-headed youths. 69. **ivy**. *Pandosto* has this detail, stating that the shepherd sought his sheep browsing on sea ivy. 70. **barne**, child. 71. **child**, female infant. 73. **'scape**, escapade, especially a transgression of the laws of chastity. 90. **takes up**, swallows. 95. **yest**, foam. 97. **land-service**, military service; here, doings on land; used blunderingly. 100. **flap-dragoned**, swallowed as one would a flap-drago[n] i.e., a raisin or the like snatched up out of burning bra[in] in the game of snap-dragon.

Than all thy woes can stir: therefore betake
  thee   210
To nothing but despair. A thousand knees
Ten thousand years together, naked, fast-
  ing,
Upon a barren mountain, and still winter
In storm perpetual, could not move the
  gods
To look that way thou wert.
  Leon.   Go on, go on:
Thou canst not speak too much; I have de-
  served
All tongues to talk their bitterest.
  First Lord.   Say no more:
Howe'er the business goes, you have made
  fault
I' the boldness of your speech.
  Paul.   I am sorry for 't:
All faults I make, when I shall come to know
  them,   220
I do repent. Alas! I have show'd too much
The rashness of a woman: he is touch'd
To the noble heart. What's gone and what's
  past help
Should be past grief: do not receive afflic-
  tion
At my petition; I beseech you, rather
Let me be punish'd, that have minded you
Of what you should forget. Now, good my
  liege,
Sir, royal sir, forgive a foolish woman:
The love I bore your queen—lo, fool again!—
I'll speak of her no more, nor of your chil-
  dren;
I'll not remember you of my own lord,   231
Who is lost too: take your patience to you,
And I'll say nothing.
  Leon.   Thou didst speak but well
When most the truth; which I receive much
  better
Than to be pitied of thee. Prithee, bring
  me
To the dead bodies of my queen and son:
One grave shall be for both: upon them
  shall
The causes of their death appear, unto
Our shame perpetual. Once a day I'll
  visit
The chapel where they lie, and tears shed
  there   240
Shall be my recreation: so long as nature
Will bear up with this exercise, so long

I daily vow to use it. Come and lead me
Unto these sorrows.   [*Exeunt.*

SCENE III. *Bohemia. A desert country near
                  the sea.*

Enter ANTIGONUS *with a Child, and a*
                  Mariner.

  Ant. Thou art perfect then, our ship hath
    touch'd upon
The deserts of Bohemia?
  Mar.   Ay, my lord; and fear
We have landed in ill time: the skies look
  grimly
And threaten present blusters. In my con-
  science,
The heavens with that we have in hand are
  angry
And frown upon 's.
  Ant. Their sacred wills be done! Go, get
    aboard;
Look to thy bark: I'll not be long before
I call upon thee.
  Mar. Make your best haste, and go not 10
Too far i' the land: 'tis like to be loud
  weather;
Besides, this place is famous for the creatures
Of prey that keep upon 't.
  Ant.   Go thou away:
I'll follow instantly.
  Mar.   I am glad at heart
To be so rid o' the business.   [*Exit.*
  Ant.   Come, poor babe:
I have heard, but not believed, the spirits o'
  the dead
May walk again: if such thing be, thy
  mother
Appear'd to me last night, for ne'er was
  dream
So like a waking. To me comes a creature,
Sometimes her head on one side, some
  another;
I never saw a vessel of like sorrow,   21
So fill'd and so becoming: in pure white
  robes,
Like very sanctity, she did approach
My cabin where I lay; thrice bow'd before
  me,

---

225. **my petition.** She has bid him, in lines 210-211,
betake himself to despair. 231. **remember,** remind.

Scene iii. 1. **perfect,** certain. 2. **deserts of Bohemia.** Shakespeare's famous blunder is really a
blunder in his source, which he merely repeats. 21.
vessel, creature. 22. **becoming,** apparently, imbued
with grace and fitness. The association of the word
with *fill'd* has caused Moorman to suspect that we have
here a typographical error for *beteeming*, meaning "overflowing."